MAP BOOK LEGEND

Road Classification

▬▬▬▬	LIMITED ACCESS DIVIDED HIGHWAY
▬ ▬	OTHER DIVIDED HIGHWAYS
▬▬▬▬	PRINCIPAL THROUGH ROUTES
───────	OTHER THOROUGHFARES
....	MUNICIPAL STREET

Symbol Classification

94	INTERSTATE HIGHWAYS
75	U.S. HIGHWAYS
64	STATE HIGHWAYS
25	COUNTY ROADS

Trail Designation

	State Trails	Regional Trails	Local Trails
PAVED	─────	─────	─────
UNPAVED	─ ─ ─	─ ─ ─	─ ─ ─
PLANNED 2001-2002	• • • • •	• • • • •	• • • • •
ON ROAD CONNECTIONS	── ──	── ──	── ──

Additional Features

─ ─ ─ ─	CITY/TOWNSHIP BOUNDARY
▬ ▬ ▬	COUNTY BOUNDARY
▓▓▓▓▓	ZIP CODE BOUNDARY
──────	INDEPENDENT SCHOOL DISTRICT BOUNDARY
ROSEVILLE ISD #623	INDEPENDENT SCHOOL DISTRICT NAME/NUMBER
├──┼──┤	RAILROAD DESIGNATION
4000	ADDRESS RANGES
■	POINTS OF INTEREST
⬆	SCHOOLS
55117	ZIP CODE NUMBER
P&R	PARK AND RIDES
EDINA	CITY/TOWNSHIP TEXT

1	GOLF COURSE
▮	AREA OF INTEREST
▮	PARK
▮	CEMETERY
⬭	LAKE
〰	CREEK
+	SECTION CORNERS
29	SECTION NUMBERS
T113N	TOWNSHIP NUMBERS
R27W	RANGE NUMBERS
46	EXIT RAMPS

Scale in miles for map pages:

0   1/4   1/2   1   2

1"= .64 miles   **1"= 3375 feet**

Atlas created by The Lawrence
1089-10th Avenue SE
Minneapolis, MN 55414
(612) 676-3950
2002 © Copyright The Lawrence
www.lawrencegroup.co

D1609609

METRO AREA PAGE LOCATION GUIDE

CLEAR LAKE
1 CLEARWATER
Clear Lake Twp
2
3 Becker Twp
4 Orrock Twp
ZIMMERMAN
5 Livonia Twp
Stanford Twp
6 ST FRANCIS

N S E W

Clearwater Twp
15
16 Silver Creek Twp
BECKER
17
BIG LAKE
18 Big Lake Twp
19 ELK RIVER
20 Burns Twp

Corinna Twp
29
30
MONTICELLO
31
Monticello Twp
32
33 OTSEGO
34 RAMSEY

MAPLE LAKE
43 Albion Twp
Maple Lake Twp
44
45 Buffalo Twp
46 ALBERTVILLE
47
48

57
Chatham Twp
BUFFALO
58
59
ST MICHAEL
60 HANOVER
Hassan Twp
ROGERS
61
DAYTON
62

Middleview Twp
71
Marysville Twp
72
WAVERLY
MONTROSE
Rockford Twp
73
ROCKFORD
74 GREENFIELD
CORCORAN
75
76 MAPLE GROVE

HOWARD LAKE
85
86 Woodland Twp
87 DELANO Franklin Twp
88 INDEPENDENCE
LORETTO
89 MEDINA
90 PLYMOUTH

Victor Twp
99 WINSTED
100
101 WATERTOWN
MAPLE PLAIN
102 MINNETRISTA
LONG LAKE
103 ORONO
104 WAYZATA WOODLAND

Winsted Twp
113
Hollywood Twp
114
Watertown Twp
115
MOUND
116 ST BONIFACIUS
SPRING PARK ORONO MINNETONKA BEACH TONKA BAY
117 GREENWOOD EXCELSIOR SHOREWOOD
DEEPHAVEN
118 MINNETONKA

LESTER PRAIRIE
127 Bergen Twp
NEW GERMANY
128 Camden Twp
MAYER
Waconia Twp
129 WACONIA
VICTORIA
130 Laketown Twp
CHANHASSEN
131 CHASKA
132 EDEN PRAIRIE

141 PLATO
142 NORWOOD YOUNG AMERICA
143 COLOGNE
144 Dahlgren Twp
Chaska Twp
145
146 Jackson Twp SHAKOPEE

Helen Twp
155
Young America Twp
156 HAMBURG
Benton Twp
157
158
CARVER
159 Louisville Twp
PRIOR LAKE
160

Green Isle Twp
GREEN ISLE
169
Washington Lake Twp
170
Hancock Twp
171 Faxon Twp
San Francisco Twp
172 St Lawrence Twp
JORDAN
Sand Creek Twp
173
174 Spring Lake Twp

ARLINGTON
183 Arlington Twp
184 Jessenland Twp
BELLE PLAINE
185 Blakeley Twp
186 Belle Plaine Twp
187 Helena Twp
188 Cedar Lake Twp

197
198 HENDERSON
199
200
NEW PRAGUE
201 Lanesburg Twp
202 Wheatland Twp

Kelso Twp
211 Lake Prairie Twp
Henderson Twp
212 LE SUEUR Ottawa Twp
Tyrone Twp
213 Sharon Twp
Derrynane Twp
214 Lexington Twp
HEIDELBERG
215 MONTGOMERY
216 Montgomery Twp Erin Twp

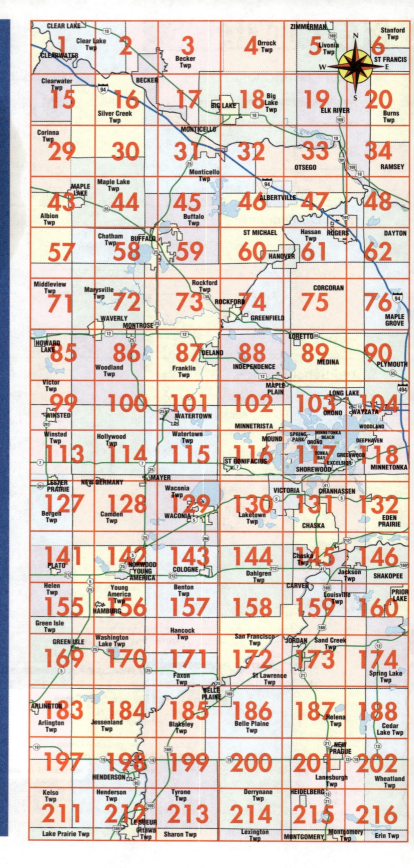

7	8	9	10	11	12	13	14
ST FRANCIS	BETHEL	Athens Twp	Oxford Twp	STACY / Lent Twp	Chisago Lake Twp / CENTER CITY / LINDSTROM	SHAFER	TAYLORS FALLS / ST CROIX FALLS
21	22	23	24	25	26	27	28
urns Twp	OAK GROVE	EAST BETHEL	Linwood Twp	Wyoming / WYOMING	CHISAGO CITY / Chisago Lake Twp	Franconia Twp	DRESSER / OSCEOLA / Osceola Twp
35	36	37	38	39	40	41	42
RAMSEY	ANDOVER		Columbus Twp	FOREST LAKE / Wyoming Twp / Forest Lake Twp	New Scandia Twp		Farmington Twp / Alden Twp
49	50	51	52	53	54	55	56
ANOKA		HAM LAKE		Forest Lake Twp		MARINE ON ST CROIX	
60	64	65	66	67	68	69	70
CHAMPLIN / BROOKLYN PARK / OSSEO	COON RAPIDS	BLAINE / CIRCLE PINES / LEXINGTON	CENTERVILLE / LINO LAKES	HUGO	May Twp	Somerset Twp / SOMERSET	Star Prairie Twp
77	78	79	80	81	82	83	84
MAPLE GROVE	SPRING LAKE PARK / FRIDLEY / NEW BRIGHTON	MOUNDS VIEW / ARDEN HILLS / SHOREVIEW	SHOREVIEW / NORTH OAKS / White Bear Twp	White Bear / White Bear Lake / DELLWOOD / MAHTOMEDI	GRANT	Stillwater Twp	Somerset Twp
91	92	93	94	95	96	97	98
BROOKLYN CENTER / CRYSTAL / PLYMOUTH / NEW HOPE / ROBBINSDALE	HILL TOP / COLUMBIA HEIGHTS / ST ANTHONY	ROSEVILLE / FALCON HEIGHTS / LAUDERDALE	VADNAIS HEIGHTS / LITTLE CANADA / MAPLEWOOD	White Bear Lake / GEM LAKE / WHITE BEAR / BIRCHWOOD VILLAGE / WILLERNIE / PINE SPRINGS / NORTH SAINT PAUL	STILLWATER / OAK PARK HEIGHTS / Baytown Twp / BAYPORT	St Joseph Twp	Richmond Twp
105	106	107	108	109	110	111	112
MEDICINE LAKE	GOLDEN VALLEY / ST LOUIS PARK	MINNEAPOLIS	SAINT PAUL	OAKDALE	LAKE ELMO / West Lakeland Twp	NORTH HUDSON / HUDSON / LAKELAND / LAKELAND SHORES	Hudson Twp / Warren Twp
119	120	121	122	123	124	125	126
HOPKINS / EDINA			LILYDALE / WEST SAINT PAUL / SOUTH SAINT PAUL / MENDOTA	LANDFALL / WOODBURY	AFTON	LAKELAND / LAKE ST CROIX BEACH / ST MARYS POINT	Troy Twp / Kinnickinnic Twp
133	134	135	136	137	138	139	140
EDEN PRAIRIE	BLOOMINGTON / RICHFIELD	INTERNATIONAL AIRPORT / MENDOTA HEIGHTS	SUNFISH LAKE / INVER GROVE HEIGHTS	NEWPORT / SAINT PAUL PARK / COTTAGE GROVE		Clifton Twp	RIVER FALLS / River Falls Twp
147	148	149	150	151	152	153	154
SHAKOPEE / PRIOR LAKE	BURNSVILLE	EAGAN		Grey Cloud Island Twp	Denmark Twp	PRESCOTT	
161	162	163	164	165	166	167	168
SAVAGE		APPLE VALLEY	ROSEMOUNT / COATES	Nininger Twp / Vermillion Twp	HASTINGS		Oak Grove Twp
175	176	177	178	179	180	181	182
Spring Lake Twp	Credit River Twp / LAKEVILLE	FARMINGTON	Empire Twp	VERMILLION / Vermillion Twp	Marshan Twp	Ravenna Twp	Diamond Bluff Twp
189	190	191	192	193	194	195	196
NEW MARKET	New Market Twp / ELKO	Eureka Twp	Castle Rock Twp	HAMPTON / NEW TRIER / Hampton Twp	Douglas Twp	MIESVILLE	Welch Twp / RED WING
203	204	205	206	207	208	209	210
Heatland Twp	Webster Twp	Greenvale Twp	Waterford Twp / Sciota Twp	RANDOLPH / Randolph Twp	CANNON FALLS	Vasa Twp	Featherstone Twp
217	218	219	220	221	222	223	224
LONSDALE / in Twp	Webster Twp / Forest Twp	Bridgewater Twp / NORTHFIELD	Northfield Twp	Stanton Twp / Warsaw Twp	Cannon Falls Twp	Leon Twp / Belle Creek Twp	Goodhue Twp

WISCONSIN

III

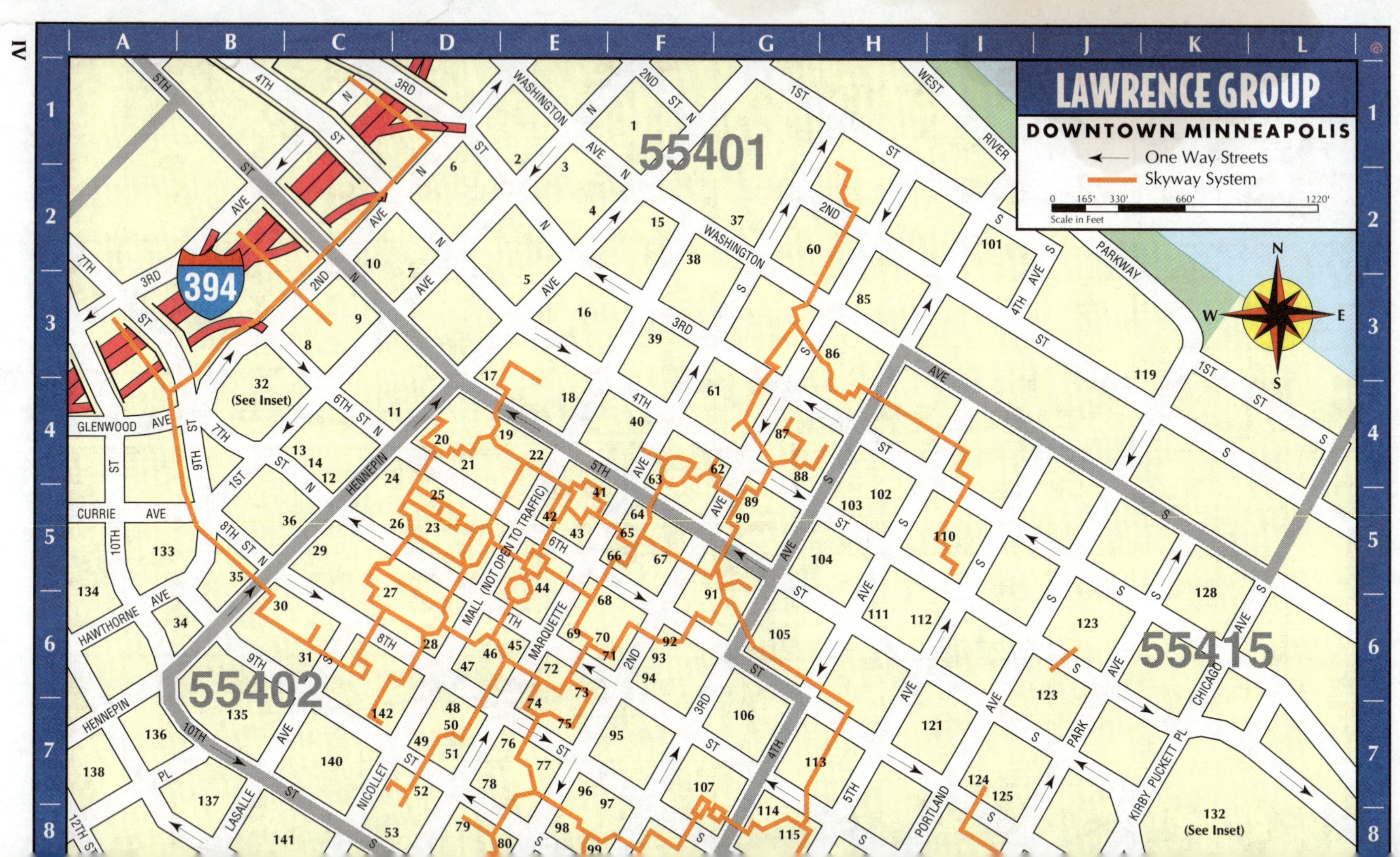
LAWRENCE GROUP
DOWNTOWN MINNEAPOLIS
One Way Streets
Skyway System
0 165' 330' 660' 1220'
Scale in Feet
N
S
E
W
55401
55402
55415
394
(NOT OPEN TO TRAFFIC)
32 (See Inset)
132 (See Inset)
WASHINGTON AVE
HENNEPIN AVE
NICOLLET MALL
MARQUETTE
WEST RIVER PARKWAY
KIRBY PUCKETT PL
CHICAGO AVE
PORTLAND AVE
PARK AVE
GLENWOOD AVE
CURRIE AVE
HAWTHORNE AVE
LASALLE
12TH ST

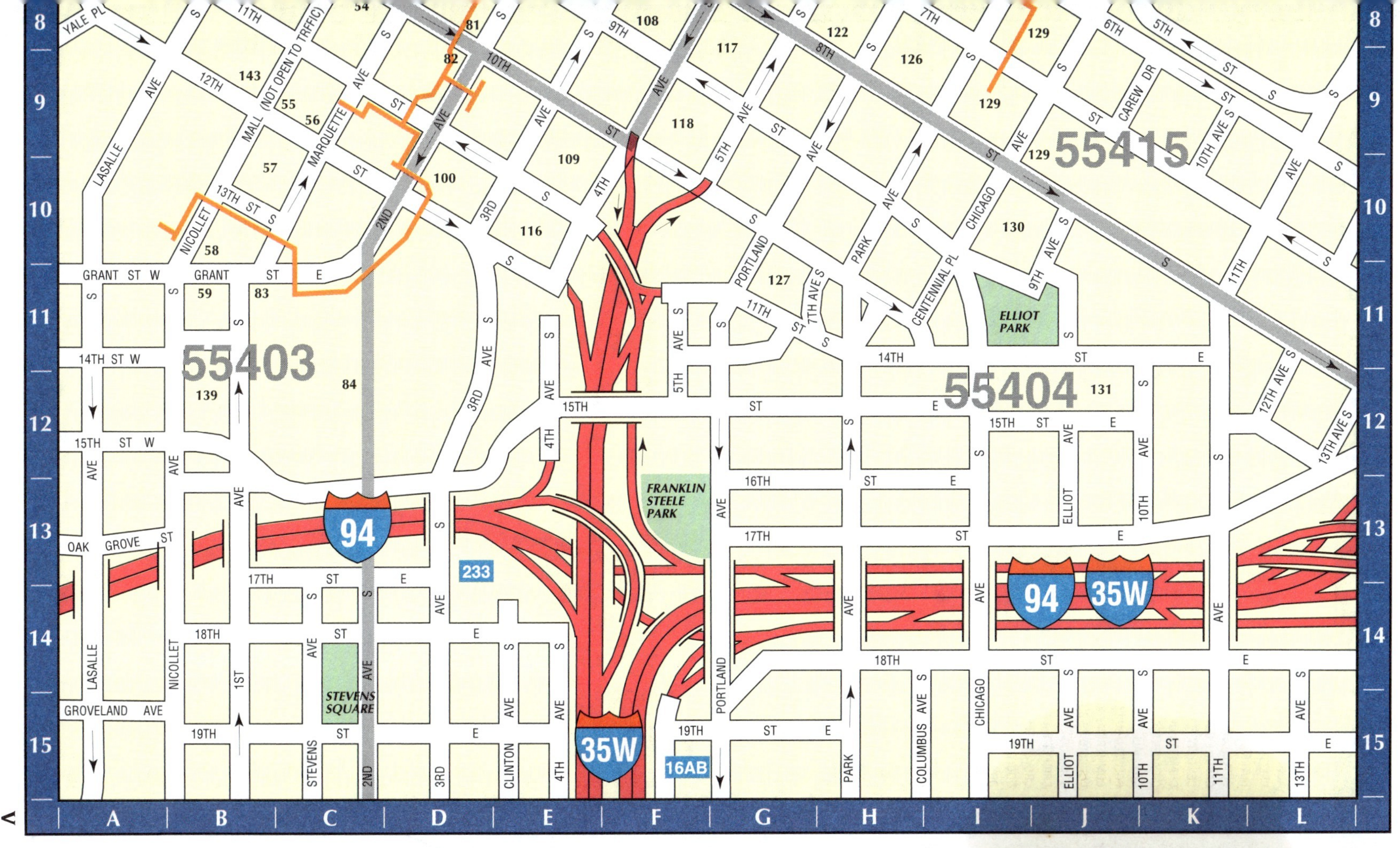
55403
55404
55415
ELLIOT PARK
FRANKLIN STEELE PARK
STEVENS SQUARE
94
35W
233
16AB
YALE PL
LASALLE AVE
NICOLLET MALL (NOT OPEN TO TRFFIC)
MARQUETTE AVE
2ND AVE
3RD AVE S
4TH AVE S
5TH AVE S
PARK AVE
PORTLAND AVE
CHICAGO AVE
7TH AVE S
9TH AVE S
10TH AVE S
11TH AVE S
12TH AVE S
13TH AVE S
ELLIOT AVE
COLUMBUS AVE S
CENTENNIAL PL
CAREW DR
GRANT ST W
GRANT ST E
14TH ST W
14TH ST E
15TH ST W
15TH ST E
16TH ST E
17TH ST E
18TH ST E
19TH ST E
OAK GROVE ST
GROVELAND AVE
1ST AVE
STEVENS AVE
CLINTON AVE
5TH ST S
6TH ST S
7TH ST S
8TH ST S
9TH ST S
10TH ST S
11TH ST S
12TH ST S
13TH ST S
11TH ST
8
9
10
11
12
13
14
15
A
B
C
D
E
F
G
H
I
J
K
L
54
55
56
57
58
59
81
82
83
84
100
108
109
116
117
118
122
126
127
129
130
131
139
143
V

DOWNTOWN MINNEAPOLIS INDEX

14. ACADEMY THEATER C-4
79. AT&T TOWER D-8
112. AUGSBURG PUBLISHING COMPANY H-6
73. BAKER BUILDING E-6
9. BUTLER NORTH BUILDING C-3
8. BUTLER SQUARE C-3
69. CARGILL BUILDING E-6
116. CENTURY PLAZA E-10
19. CHAMBER OF COMMERCE BUILDING E-4
23. CITY CENTER D-5
104. CITY HALL H-5
6. COLWELL BUILDING D-2
2. COMMERCIAL BUILDING - 4 STORY E-1
65. CONCOURSE BUILDING F-5
37. CONSECO G-2
139. CRICKET THEATER B-12
115. CROWN STERLING SUITES G-8
51. DOCTORS BUILDING D-7
50. DOWNTOWN PROFESSIONAL BUILDING D-7
127. EDEN HOUSE G-11
53. ESSEX BUILDING C-8
43. FARMERS AND MECH. BANK BUILDING E-5
103. FEDERAL COURTS BUILDING H-5
61. FEDERAL COURTS F-4
85. FEDERAL OFFICE BUILDING H-3
38. FEDERAL RESERVE BANK F-2
126. FINANCE AND COMMERCE BUILDING H-9
92. FIRST BANK BUILDING F-6
136. FIRST BAPTIST CHURCH A-7
102. FLOUR EXCHANGE BUILDING H-5
78. FOSHAY TOWER D-7
118. GETHSEMANE EPISCOPAL CHURCH F-9
110. GRAIN EXCHANGE BUILDING I-5
133. GREYHOUND BUS DEPOT A-5
1. HANSORD PONTIAC F-1
138. HARMON COURT A-7
11. HENNEPIN CENTER FOR THE ARTS D-4
105. HENNEPIN COUNTY GOVERNMENT CENTER G-6
106. HENNEPIN COUNTY GOVERNMENT CENTER G-7
125. HENNEPIN COUNTY HEALTH SERVICE BUILDING .I-7
124. HENNEPIN COUNTY JUVENILE DETENTION CENTER .I-7
129. HENNEPIN COUNTY MEDICAL CENTER J-8
111. HENNEPIN COUNTY WELFARE BUILDING H-6
82. HILTON HOTEL D-9
58. HOLIDAY INN CENTRAL B-10
132. HUBERT H HUMPHREY METRODOME K-8
46. IDS CENTER D-6
109. IDS OPERATIONS CENTER E-10
47. IDS TOWER (51 FLOORS) D-6
80. INTERNATIONAL CENTER E-8
100. IVY TOWER D-10
13. JEWELERS EXCHANGE C-4
7. KICKERNICK D-3
81. KINNARD FINANCIAL CENTER D-8
135. LASALLE BUILDING B-7
35. LINCOLN BANK BUILDING B-5
59. LORING TOWERS FOR SENIOR CITIZENS B-11
17. LUMBER EXCHANGE BUILDING D-3
113. LUTHERAN BROTHERHOOD BUILDING G-7
36. MANN THEATER C-5
40. MARQUETTE BUILDING F-4
45. MARQUETTE INN E-6
26. MARRIOTT HOTEL D-5
28. MARSHALL FIELDS D-6
3. MARTIN BUILDING E-2
98. MCCONNELL BUILDING E-8
49. MEDICAL ARTS BUILDING D-7
130. METRO MEDICAL OFFICE BUILDING I-10
107. METROPOLITAN CENTRE F-7
89. MIDLAND BANK BUILDING G-5
87. MIDLAND SQUARE G-4

48. MIDWEST PLAZA D-7
101. MILL PLACE I-2
121. MINNEAPOLIS ARMORY I-7
93. MINNEAPOLIS ATHLETIC CLUB F-6
95. MINNEAPOLIS CLUB F-7
84. MINNEAPOLIS CONVENTION CENTER C-12
39. MINNEAPOLIS PLAZA HOTEL F-3
16. MINNEAPOLIS PUBLIC LIBRARY E-3
123. MINNEAPOLIS STAR AND TRIBUNE J-6
108. MINNEGASCO ENERGY CENTER F-8
56. MN ORCHESTRA HALL C-9
74. MULTI FOODS BUILDING E-7
25. MULTI FOODS TOWER D-5
21. MURRAYS D-4
41. NATIONAL CITY BANK BUILDING E-5
15. NICOLLET HOTEL BUILDING F-2
117. NORMANDY INN G-8
131. NORTH CENTRAL BIBLE COLLEGE J-12
70. NORTHSTAR CENTER E-6
71. NORTHSTAR INN F-6
67. ONE FINANCIAL CENTER F-5
60. ONE HUNDRED WASHINGTON SQUARE G-2
63. OPUS BUILDING F-4
34. ORPHEUM THEATER B-6
75. PEAVEY BUILDING E-7
55. PEAVEY PLAZA C-9
91. PILLSBURY CENTER F-5
99. PIPER JAFFRAY TOWER E-8
20. PLYMOUTH BUILDING D-4
88. PUBLIC HEALTH CENTER G-4
90. QWEST COMMUNICATIONS BUILDING G-5
27. RADISSON HOTEL C-6
134. REGENCY PLAZA HOTEL A-5
22. RENAISSANCE SQUARE E-4
72. ROANOKE BUILDING E-6
5. SENIOR CITIZENS HI RISE APARTMENT E-3
122. SEXTON BUILDING H-8
29. SKYWAY THEATRE C-5
64. SOO-LINE BUILDING F-5
96. SAINT OLAF CATHOLIC CHURCH E-7
97. SAINT OLAF PARISH CENTER E-7
137. SAINT THOMAS UNIVERSITY B-7
30. STATE BUILDING B-6
42. SYNDICATE BUILDING E-5
140. TARGET C-7
141. TARGET PLAZA C-8
32. TARGET CENTER B-4
24. TGI FRIDAY'S D-4
66. THORP BUILDING F-5
128. THRESHER SQUARE K-5
62. TITLE INSURANCE BUILDING G-4
77. TWIN CITY FEDERAL ADDITION E-7
76. TWIN CITY FEDERAL BUILDING E-7
114. UNITED WAY BUILDING G-8
142. US BANCORP PIPER JAFFREY TOWER D-6
4. US FOOD AND DRUG ADMINISTRATION E-2
94. WCCO RADIO BUILDING F-6
54. WCCO TV C-8
86. WELLS FARGO OPERATIONS CENTER H-3
44. WELLS FARGO TOWER E-5
83. WESLEY CHURCH (METHODIST) B-11
57. WESTMINISTER CHURCH B-10
119. WHITNEY HOTEL K-3
12. WORLD THEATER C-4
10. WYMAN BUILDING C-2
18. XCEL ENERGY E-4
31. YMCA C-6
52. YOUNG QUINLAN BUILDING D-7
143. YWCA B-9

DOWNTOWN SAINT PAUL INDEX

47. ADULT DETENTION CENTER H-10
72. AGRI BANK (FARM CREDIT) J-7
97. ALLEN BUILDING L-5
95. AMERICAN CENTER BUILDING K-9
75. AMERICAN NATIONAL BANK BUILDING J-8
7. ARCHDIOCESE CHANCERY & ARCHBISHOP'S HOUSE B-8
24. ARMORY F-4
67. ART RESOURCES I-5
26. ARTS AND SCIENCES CENTER (GA HISTORY THEATER) G-6
132. ASSUMPTION CHURCH F-7
3. BEST WESTERN B-5
12. BETHESDA HOSPITAL D-1
56. BREMER TOWERS I-7
28. BUS DEPOT G-7
82. CAPITOL CENTRE BUILDING J-9
38. CAPITOL SQUARE G-5
133. CATHOLIC CHARITIES E-8
42. CATHOLIC CHARITIES I-7
23. CENTENNIAL BUILDING F-4
34. CENTRAL PARK METHODIST G-3
78. CENTRAL PARK METHODIST CHURCH I-9
8. CHILDREN'S HOSPITAL B-11
29. CHILDREN'S MUSEUM G-7
63. CITY HALL I-10
48. CITY/COUNTY CREDIT UNION H-4
65. COMMERCE BUILDING I-9
140. CROWN STERLING SUITES HOTEL I-4
126. DAYS INN O-10
66. DEGREE OF HONOR BUILDING I-9
90. EMPIRE BUILDING J-8
93. ENDICOTT BUILDING K-8
79. EXCHANGE BUILDING I-8
108. FARMERS MARKET M-6
94. FEDERAL COURT BUILDING K-8
69. FIRST BAPTIST CHURCH J-4
77. FIRST MINNESOTA BANK I-8
89. FIRST NATIONAL BANK BUILDING J-8
87. FIRST TRUST CENTER K-7
40. FITZGERALD THEATER G-7
131. GALLERY MEDICAL BUILDING F-7
130. GALLERY TOWER F-6
116. GALTIER PLAZA K-7
84. GILBERT BUILDING K-6
35. GILLETTE CHILDREN'S HOSPITAL H-3
111. GILLETTE COMPANY FACTORY M-6
21. GILLETTE HOSPITAL FOUNDATION F-2
54. GOLDEN RULE BUILDING I-6
83. HERITAGE HOUSE K-6
11. IRVINE PARK D-12
33. JAMES HILL REFERENCE LIBRARY G-10
6. JAMES J HILL HOUSE (MN HISTORICAL SOCIETY) A-9
129. KARE-TV H-9
113. KELLOGG PROFESSIONAL BUILDING N-6
80. KELLOGG SQUARE J-9
104. KTCA-TV K-8
32. LANDMARK CENTER G-9
44. LANDMARK TOWER H-9
142. LAWSON COMMONS H-9
99. LOWERTOWN BUSINESS CENTER K-5
110. LOWERTOWN COMMONS M-7
98. MARKET HOUSE L-6
68. MARKET SQUARE I-4
134. MARSHALL FIELDS BUILDING H-8
115. MCCOLL BUILDING K-7
101. MEARS PARK CENTER L-7
73. MEARS PARK PLACE J-6
1. MERIDIAN NATIONAL BANK A-2
119. MERITOR TOWER H-7
57. METRO FINANCIAL I-7
51. METRO SQUARE I-6
52. METRO STATE UNIVERSITY I-6

121. MICKEY'S DINER H-5
91. MIDWEST BUILDING J-8
76. MIDWEST FEDERAL I-8
81. MINNESOTA BUILDING I-9
55. MINNESOTA CHAMBER OF COMMERCE H-6
20. MINNESOTA CLUB F-10
53. MINNESOTA DEPARTMENT OF TOURISM I-6
50. MINNESOTA DEPARTMENT COMMERCE I-6
39. MINNESOTA DEPARTMENT OF EDUCATION G-5
41. MINNESOTA DEPARTMENT OF PUBLIC SAFETY H-5
114. MINNESOTA DEPARTMENT OF REVENUE N-11
123. MINNESOTA DEPARTMENT OF TRANSPORTATION BUILDING ...C-4
125. MINNESOTA HISTORY CENTER C-7
22. MINNESOTA JUDICIAL CENTER E-3
74. MINNESOTA MUTUAL LIFE BUILDING J-7
37. MINNESOTA PUBLIC HEALTH F-6
138. MINNESOTA PUBLIC RADIO H-7
36. MINNESOTA STATE MOTOR POOL G-3
103. MINNESOTA TELECENTER K-8
88. NALPAK BUILDING K-7
109. NORTHERN WAREHOUSE M-7
107. NORTHWESTERN BUILDING L-6
19. ORDWAY MUSIC THEATER F-9
30. ORPHEUM THEATER G-8
86. PARK SQUARE COURT K-6
92. PIONEER BUILDING J-8
61. PIONEER PRESS DISPATCH BUILDING I-9
96. POST OFFICE L-8
139. PUBLIC SAFETY ANNEX H-6
45. QWEST H-10
62. RADISSON ST. PAUL I-9
64. RAMSEY COUNTY COURTHOUSE I-10
27. RAMSEY COUNTY JUVENILE SERVICE CENTER G-7
128. RAMSEY COUNTY MORGUE F-10
46. RAMSEY COUNTY OFFICES G-11
10. RAMSEY HOUSE D-11
122. RAMSEY MEDICAL CENTER H-2
17. RIVERCENTRE E-9
49. ROSSMOR BUILDING H-5
18. ROY WILKINS AUDITORIUM F-9
15. SAINT JOSEPH'S HOSPITAL E-7
70. SAINT MARY'S CATHOLIC CHURCH K-4
5. SAINT PAUL CATHEDRAL A-8
136. SAINT PAUL CENTER H-7
105. SAINT PAUL COMMUNITY SERVICES L-8
16. SAINT PAUL COMPANIES F-9, G-8
43. SAINT PAUL HOTEL H-9
4. SAINT PAUL TECHNICAL COLLEGE A-7
25. SCIENCE MUSEUM OF MINNESOTA (OMNI THEATER) F-10
2. SEARS B-3
31. SEVENTH PLACE THEATRE G-8
13. STATE CAPITAL D-3
71. STATE EMPLOYMENT J-7
124. STATE OFFICE BUILDING C-3
85. STEVENS BUILDING K-6
58. TCF I-7
100. THE COSMOPOLITAN L-6
118. THE DEPARTMENT OF COMMERCE H-7
106. THE PARKSIDE L-6
112. TILSNER BUILDING N-6
137. TOWN COURT H-7
120. TOWN SQUARE PARK H-7
102. UNION DEPOT PLACE L-7
9. UNITED HOSPITAL B-10
14. VETERAN'S SEVICE BUILDING D-5
59. WELLS FARGO BANK I-8
60. WELLS FARGO CENTER H-8
127. WILDER BUILDING D-10
141. WORLD TRADE CENTER H-7
117. YMCA K-7

LAWRENCE GROUP

DOWNTOWN SAINT PAUL

← One Way Streets
— Skyway System

0   165'   330'   660'   1320'
Scale in Feet

55103

55102

94

35E

241B

241C

RICE PARK

VIII

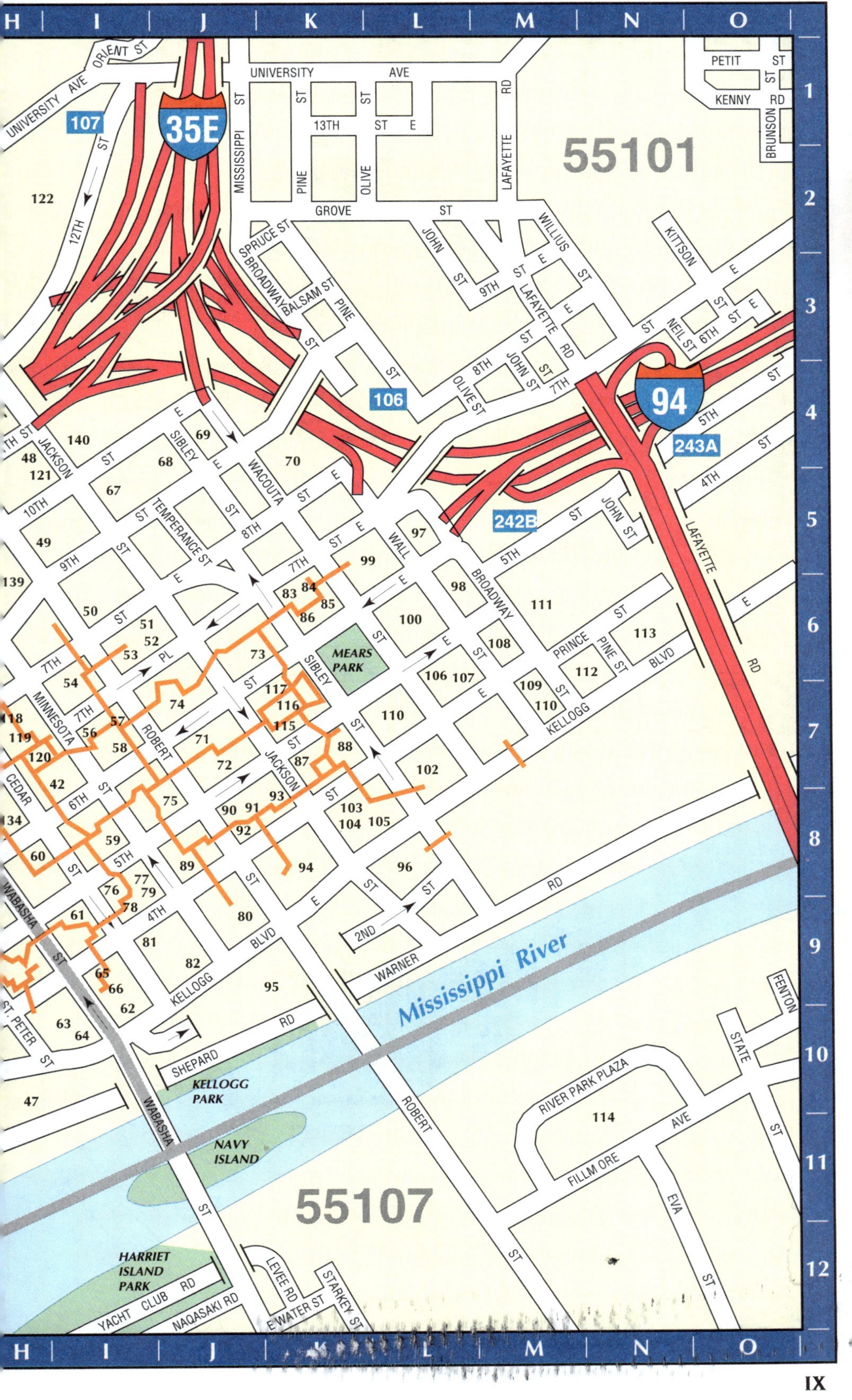
H
I
J
K
L
M
N
O
55101
55107
35E
94
107
106
242B
243A
Mississippi River
MEARS PARK
KELLOGG PARK
NAVY ISLAND
HARRIET ISLAND PARK
UNIVERSITY AVE
ORIENT ST
12TH ST
MISSISSIPPI ST
PINE ST
OLIVE ST
13TH ST E
GROVE ST
LAFAYETTE RD
PETIT ST
KENNY RD
BRUNSON ST
KITTSON ST
WILLIUS ST
JOHN ST
9TH ST E
SPRUCE ST
BROADWAY
BALSAM ST
JACKSON ST
SIBLEY ST
WACOUTA ST
WALL ST
BROADWAY
5TH ST
4TH ST
PRINCE ST
PINE ST
KELLOGG BLVD
TEMPERANCE ST
MINNESOTA ST
ROBERT ST
CEDAR ST
WABASHA ST
ST. PETER ST
SHEPARD RD
WARNER RD
2ND ST
RIVER PARK PLAZA
FILLMORE AVE
EVA ST
STATE ST
FENTON
LEVEE RD
WATER ST
STARKEY ST
YACHT CLUB RD
NAQASAKI RD
1
2
3
4
5
6
7
8
9
10
11
12

BASEBALL STADIUM
HUBERT H. HUMPHREY METRODOME

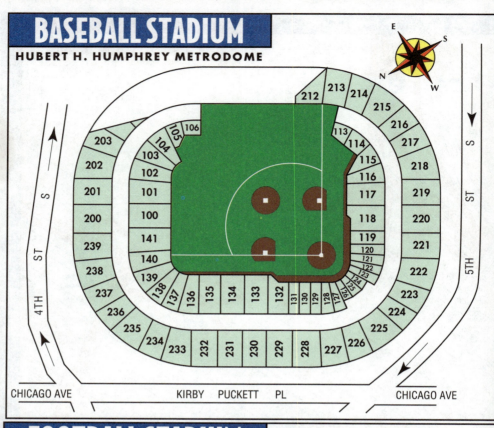

FOOTBALL STADIUM
HUBERT H. HUMPHREY METRODOME

X

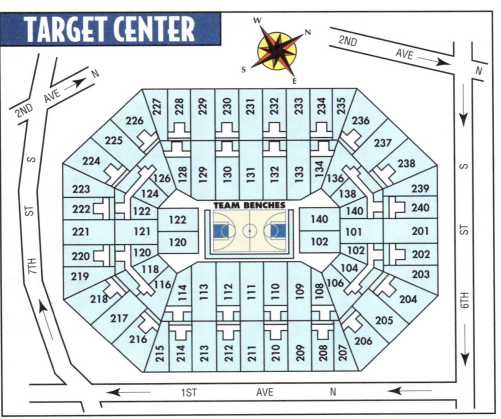

TARGET CENTER

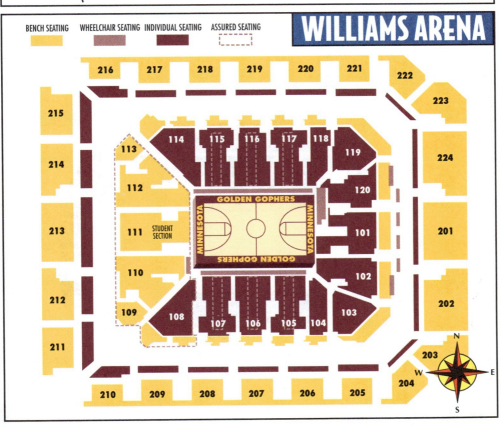

WILLIAMS ARENA

BENCH SEATING   WHEELCHAIR SEATING   INDIVIDUAL SEATING   ASSURED SEATING

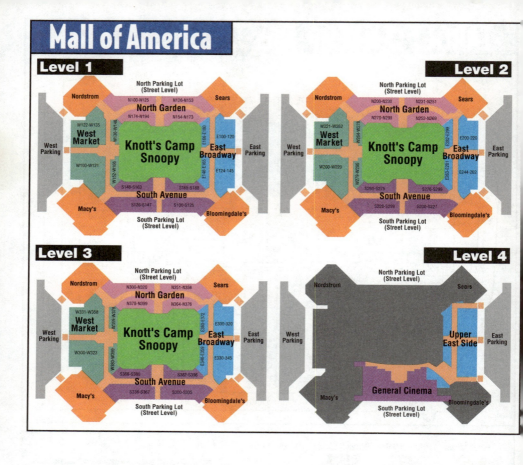

Mall of America

Level 1
Nordstrom • North Parking Lot (Street Level) • Sears
North Garden
N100-N125 | N126-N153
N174-N194 | N154-N173
West Parking
West Market
W122-W135
W100-W121
W130-W146
W152-W166
Knott's Camp Snoopy
East Broadway
E166-E180
E100-120
E124-145
East Parking
S148-S163 | S165-S188
South Avenue
Macy's
S126-S147 | S100-S125
Bloomingdale's
South Parking Lot (Street Level)

Level 2
Nordstrom • North Parking Lot (Street Level) • Sears
North Garden
N200-N230 | N231-N251
N270-N299 | N252-N269
West Parking
West Market
W221-W262
W200-W220
W223
W279-W236
Knott's Camp Snoopy
East Broadway
E282-299
E200-220
E263-281
E244-262
East Parking
S260-S275 | S276-S299
South Avenue
Macy's
S228-S299 | S200-S227
Bloomingdale's
South Parking Lot (Street Level)

Level 3
Nordstrom • North Parking Lot (Street Level) • Sears
North Garden
N300-N320 | N351-N356
N378-N399 | N364-N376
West Parking
West Market
W331-W358
W300-W323
W359-W379
W380-W399
Knott's Camp Snoopy
East Broadway
E360-E372
E300-320
E346-E359
E330-345
East Parking
S368-S380 | S382-S396
South Avenue
Macy's
S336-S367 | S300-S305
Bloomingdale's
South Parking Lot (Street Level)

Level 4
Nordstrom • North Parking Lot (Street Level) • Sears
West Parking
Upper East Side
East Parking
Macy's
General Cinema
Bloomingdale's
South Parking Lot (Street Level)

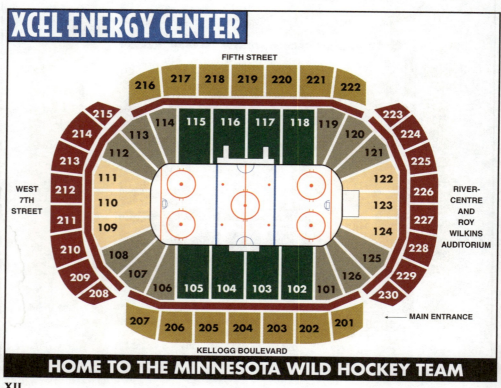

XCEL ENERGY CENTER

FIFTH STREET

216 217 218 219 220 221 222
215 114 115 116 117 118 119 223
214 113 120 224
213 112 121 225
WEST 7TH STREET 212 111 122 226 RIVER-CENTRE AND ROY WILKINS AUDITORIUM
211 110 123 227
210 109 124 228
208 108 125 229
209 107 126 230
206 106 105 104 103 102 101 201
207 206 205 204 203 202 202 201
← MAIN ENTRANCE

KELLOGG BOULEVARD

HOME TO THE MINNESOTA WILD HOCKEY TEAM

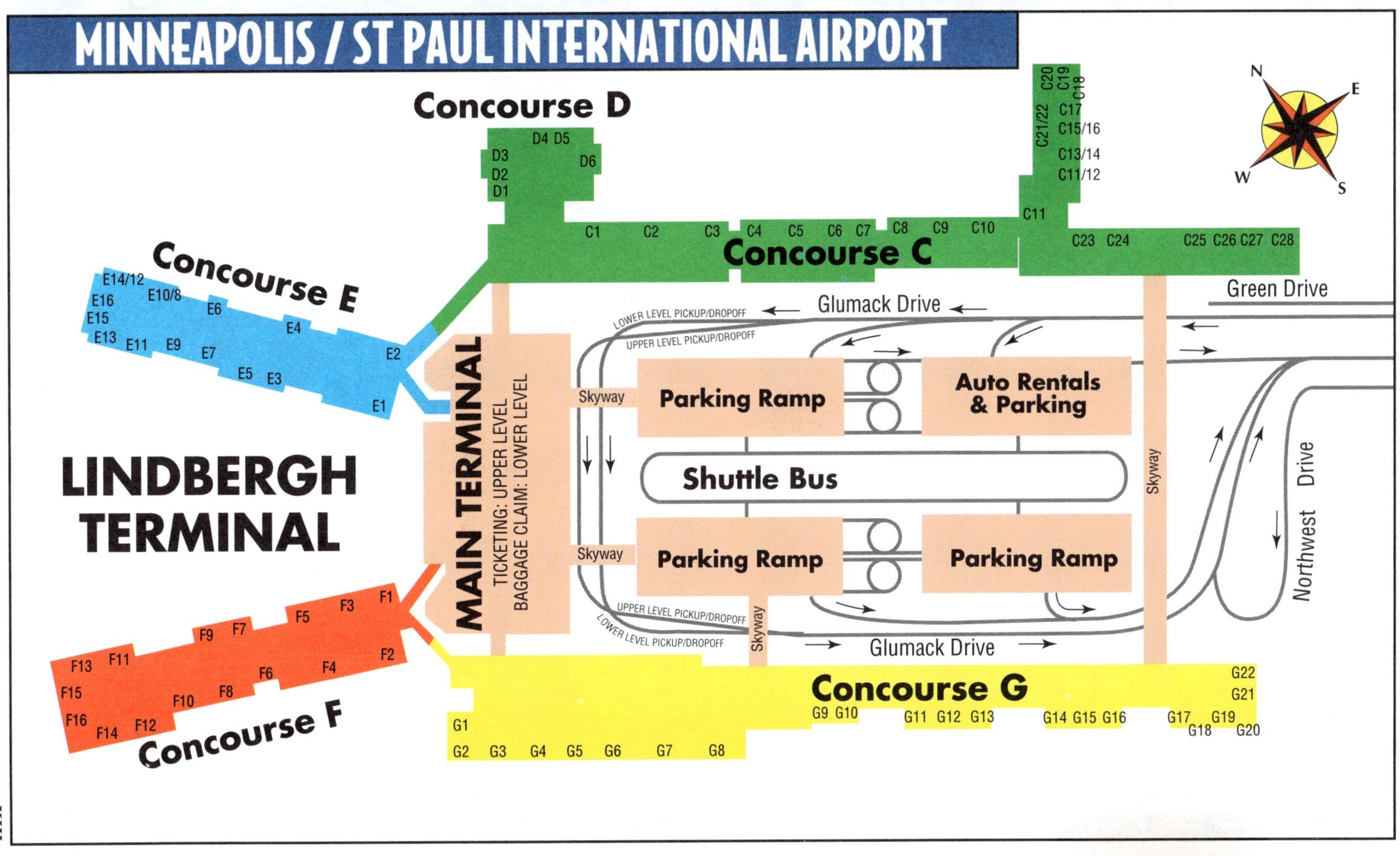

MINNEAPOLIS / ST PAUL INTERNATIONAL AIRPORT

LINDBERGH TERMINAL

MAIN TERMINAL

TICKETING: UPPER LEVEL
BAGGAGE CLAIM: LOWER LEVEL

Concourse D

Concourse C

Concourse E

Concourse F

Concourse G

Auto Rentals & Parking

Parking Ramp

Parking Ramp

Parking Ramp

Parking Ramp

Shuttle Bus

Skyway

Green Drive

Northwest Drive

Glumack Drive

UPPER LEVEL PICKUP/DROPOFF

LOWER LEVEL PICKUP/DROPOFF

XIII

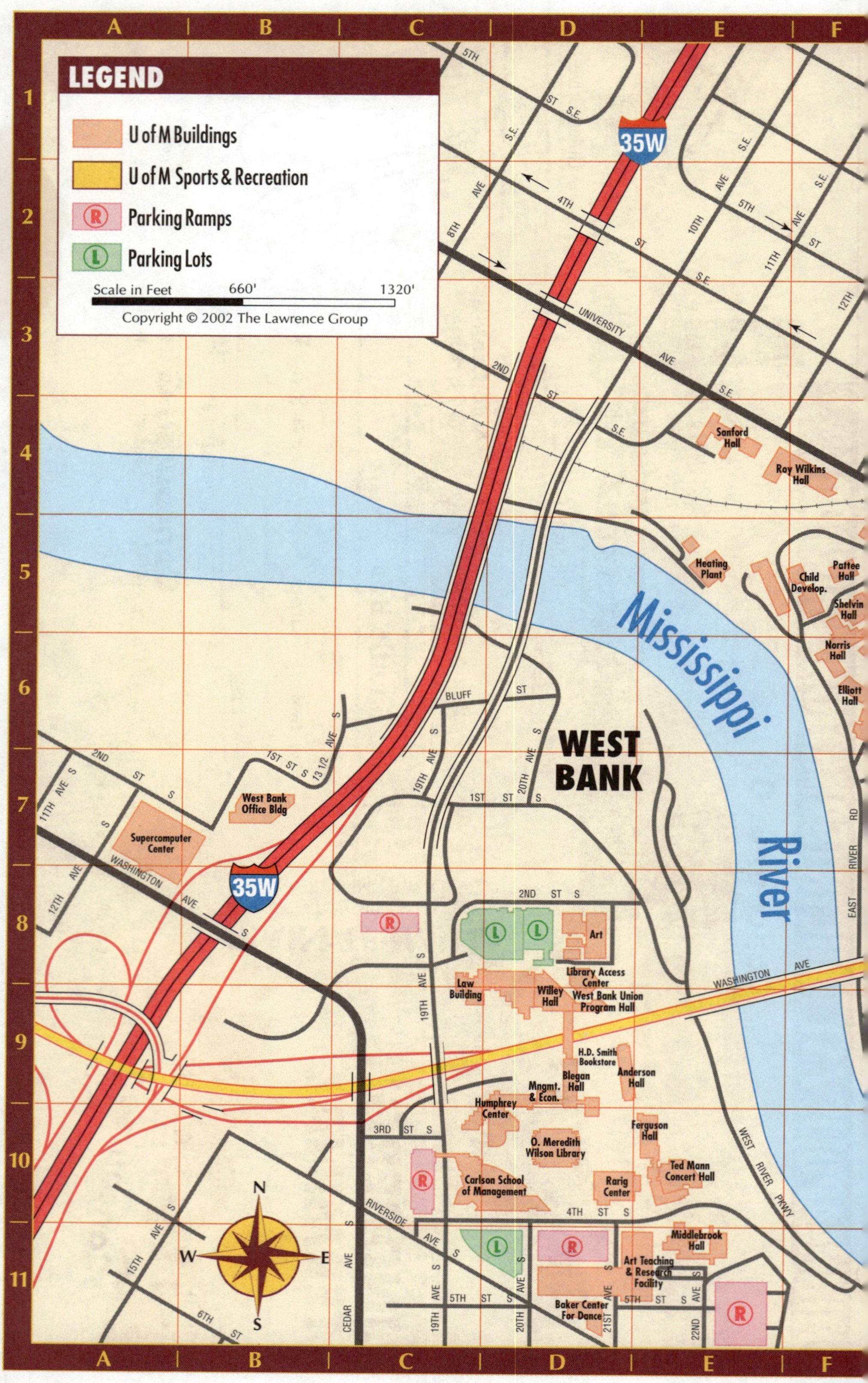
LEGEND
U of M Buildings
U of M Sports & Recreation
Parking Ramps
Parking Lots
Scale in Feet 660' 1320'
Copyright © 2002 The Lawrence Group
Mississippi River
WEST BANK
35W
Sanford Hall
Roy Wilkins Hall
Heating Plant
Child Develop.
Pattee Hall
Shelvin Hall
Norris Hall
Elliott Hall
West Bank Office Bldg
Supercomputer Center
Art
Library Access Center
Law Building
Willey Hall
West Bank Union Program Hall
H.D. Smith Bookstore
Blegan Hall
Anderson Hall
Mngmt. & Econ.
Humphrey Center
Ferguson Hall
O. Meredith Wilson Library
Ted Mann Concert Hall
Carlson School of Management
Rarig Center
Middlebrook Hall
Art Teaching & Research Facility
Baker Center For Dance
UNIVERSITY AVE S.E.
WASHINGTON AVE S
RIVERSIDE AVE S
CEDAR AVE S
WEST RIVER PKWY
EAST RIVER RD
BLUFF ST
N
S
E
W

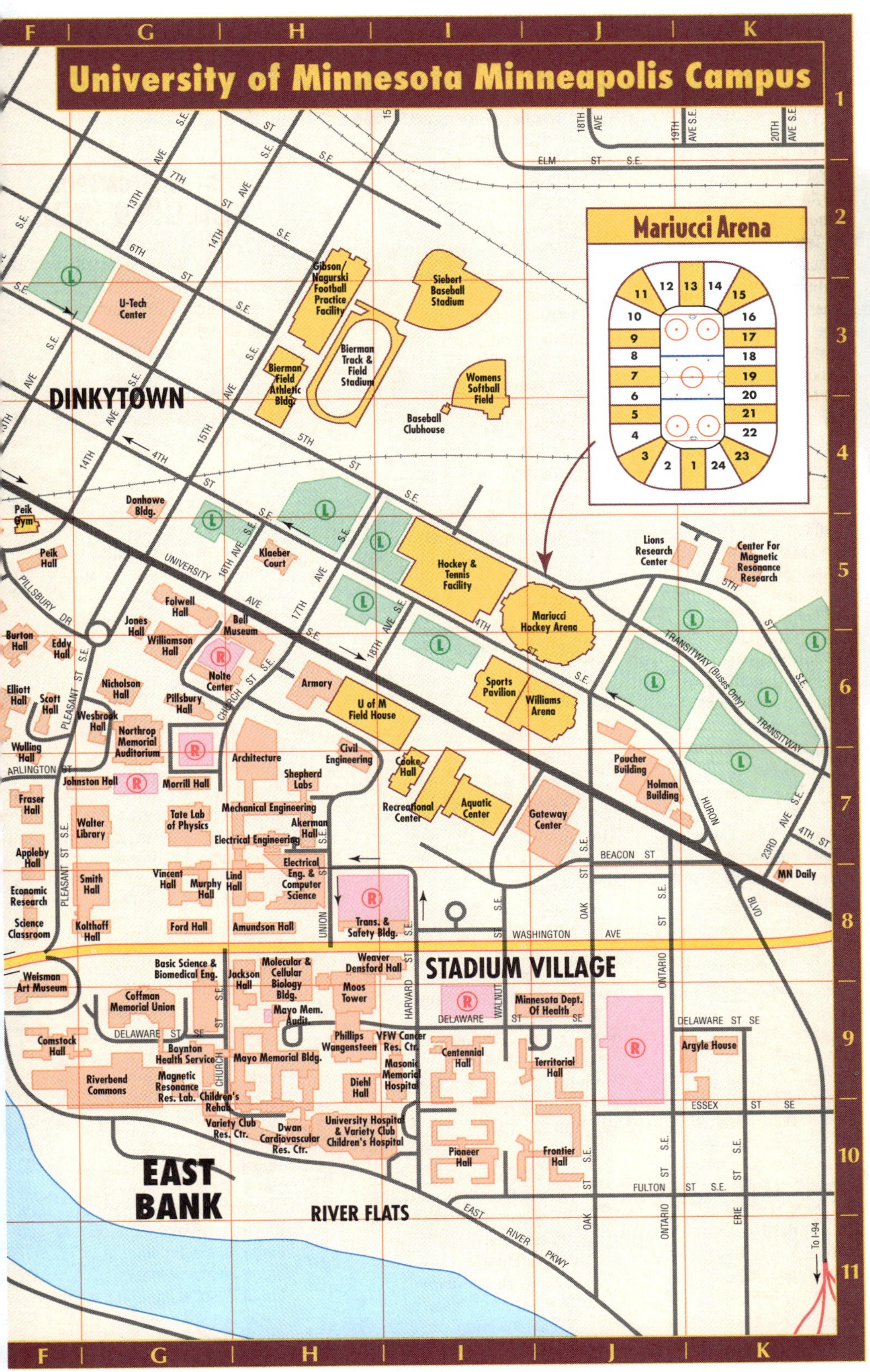

University of Minnesota Minneapolis Campus

Mariucci Arena

```
11  12  13  14  15
10              16
9               17
8               18
7               19
6               20
5               21
4               22
3   2   1  24  23
```

DINKYTOWN

U-Tech Center

Peik Gym
Peik Hall
Donhowe Bldg.
Burton Hall
Eddy Hall
Elliott Hall
Scott Hall
Wesbrook Hall
Wulling Hall
ARLINGTON ST
Johnston Hall
Fraser Hall
Walter Library
Appleby Hall
Economic Research
Science Classroom
Kolthoff Hall

Folwell Hall
Jones Hall
Williamson Hall
Nicholson Hall
Pillsbury Hall
Northrop Memorial Auditorium
Morrill Hall
Tate Lab of Physics
Mechanical Engineering
Electrical Engineering
Akerman Hall
Vincent Hall
Murphy Hall
Lind Hall
Smith Hall
Ford Hall
Amundson Hall

Klaeber Court
Bell Museum
Nolte Center
Architecture
Shepherd Labs
Electrical Eng. & Computer Science
Trans. & Safety Bldg.

Gibson Nagurski Football Practice Facility
Bierman Field Athletic Bldg.
Bierman Track & Field Stadium
Siebert Baseball Stadium
Womens Softball Field
Baseball Clubhouse

Armory
U of M Field House
Civil Engineering
Cooke Hall
Recreational Center
Aquatic Center

Hockey & Tennis Facility
Mariucci Hockey Arena
Sports Pavilion
Williams Arena

Lions Research Center
Center For Magnetic Resonance Research

Poucher Building
Holman Building
Gateway Center

BEACON ST
MN Daily

WASHINGTON   AVE

STADIUM VILLAGE

Weisman Art Museum
Comstock Hall
Riverbend Commons

Coffman Memorial Union
Basic Science & Biomedical Eng.
Jackson Hall
Molecular & Cellular Biology Bldg.
Mayo Mem. Audit.
Boynton Health Service
Magnetic Resonance Res. Lab.
Children's Rehab
Variety Club Res. Ctr.
Dwan Cardiovascular Res. Ctr.
Mayo Memorial Bldg.
Phillips Wangensteen
Diehl Hall
University Hospital & Variety Club Children's Hospital

Weaver Densford Hall
Moos Tower
VFW Cancer Res. Ctr.
Masonic Memorial Hospital

DELAWARE
Minnesota Dept. Of Health
Centennial Hall
Territorial Hall
Pioneer Hall
Frontier Hall

Argyle House
ESSEX   ST   SE
DELAWARE ST SE
FULTON   ST   SE

EAST BANK

RIVER FLATS

EAST RIVER PKWY

To I-94

XV

MINNEAPOLIS CAMPUS
BUILDING INDEX

Akerman Hall H7
Amundson Hall H8
Anderson Hall D9
Appleby Hall F7
Aquatic Center I7
Architecture H7
Argyle House K9
Armory .H6
Art Teaching & Research
  Facility D11
Art Building D8
Baker Center For Dance D11
Baseball Clubhouse I4
Basic Science & Biomedical
  Engineering G8
Bell Museum H5
Bierman Field
  Athletic Building H3
Bierman Track &
  Field Stadium H3
Blegan Hall D9
Boynton Health Service G9
Burton Hall F6
Carlson School of
  Management D10
Centennial Hall I9
Center For Magnetic Resonance
  Reasearch K5
Child Development F5
Children's Rehabilitation G9
Civil Engineering H7
Coffman Memorial Union G9
Comstock Hall F9
Cooke Hall I7
Diehl Hall H9
Donhowe Building G4
Dwan Cardiovascular
  Research Center H10
Economic Research F8
Eddy Hall F6
Electrical Engineering H7
Electrical Engineering &
  Computer Science H8
Elliott Hall F6
Ferguson Hall E10
Folwell Hall G5
Ford Hall G8
Fraser Hall F7
Frontier Hall J10
Gateway Center J7
Gibson/Nagurski Football
  Practice Facility H2
H.D. Smith Bookstore D9
Heating Plant E5
Hockey & Tennis Facilities I5
Holman Building J7
Humphrey Center D9
Jackson Hall H8
Johnston Hall G7
Jones Hall G5
Klaeber Court H5

Kolthoff Hall G8
Law Building C8
Library Access Center D8
Lind Hall H8
Lions Research Center J5
Magnetic Resonance Research
  Labratory G9
Management & Economics D9
Mariucci Hockey Arena J5
Masonic Memorial Hospital I9
Mayo Memorial Auditorium H9
Mayo Memorial Building H9
Mechanical Engineering H7
Middlebrook Hall E11
Minnesota Daily K8
Minnesota Department
  Of Health J9
Molecular & Cellular Biology H8
Moos Tower H9
Morrill Hall G7
Murphy Hall G8
Nicholson Hall G6
Nolte Center G6
Norris Hall F6
Northrop Memorial Auditorium . .G6
O. Meredith Wilson Library D10
Pattee Hall F5
Peik Gym F4
Peik Hall F5
Phillips Wangensteen H9
Pillsbury Hall G6
Pioneer Hall I10
Poucher Building J7
Rarig Center D10
Recreational Center I7
Riverbend Commons G9
Roy Wilkins Auditorium F4
Sanford Hall E4
Science Classroom F8
Scott Hall F6
Shelvin Hall F5
Shepherd Labs H7
Siebert Baseball Stadium I3
Smith Hall G8
Sports Pavilion I6
Supercomputer Center A7
Tate Lab of Physics G7
Ted Mann Concert Hall E10
Territorial Hall J9
Transportation & Safety H8
U of M Field House H6
U-Tech Center G3
University Hospital & Variety
  Club Children's Hospital H10
Variety Club Research Center . .G10
VFW Cancer Research Center I9
Vincent Hall G8
Walter Library G7
Weaver Densford Hall I8
Weisman Art Museum F8
Wesbrook Hall G6
West Bank Office Building B7
West Bank Union Program Hall . .D8

Willey Hall D9
Williams Arena J6
Williamson Hall G6
Womens Softball Field I3
Wulling Hall F6

ST PAUL CAMPUS
BUILDING INDEX

Agricultural Engineering Shops . .B7
Agricultural Pesticide Facility E3
Alderman Hall C3
Andrew Boss Lab/Meat Science . .B8
Animal Arena D8
Animal Science/Veterinary
  Medicine C7
Animal Waste Facility F4
Animal Waste Treatment Center . .F5
Bailey Hall B5
Barn C7
Barn D4
Beef Cattle Barn D5
Biological Science Center C5
Biosystems & Agricultural
  Engineering B7
Borlaug Hall C4
Building A E5
Building B E5
Building C E5
Central Library C6
Cereal Rust Lab D3
Christensen Lab C4
Classroom Office Building C6
Coffey Hall B6
Crops Research D4
Dairy Cattle C7
Dairy Cattle Teaching &
  Research Center F5
Dining Center B5
Earle Brown Continuing
  Education Center D6
Ecology Building C5
Farm & Ground Maintenance E4
Feeding Sheds D5
Food Science & Nutrition B8
Gabbert Raptor Center D7
Gortner Lab C5
Gym B3
Haecker Hall B7
Hayes Hall C4
Heating Plant C9
Hodson Hall C3
Horticulture Greenhouses D3
Isolation Buildings D8
Kaufert Laboratory B3
Large Animal Holding D7
Large Animal Teaching D7
Lewis Hospital For Companion
  Animals C7
McNeal Hall C5
Microbial & Plant Genomics D5
MMCT .D7

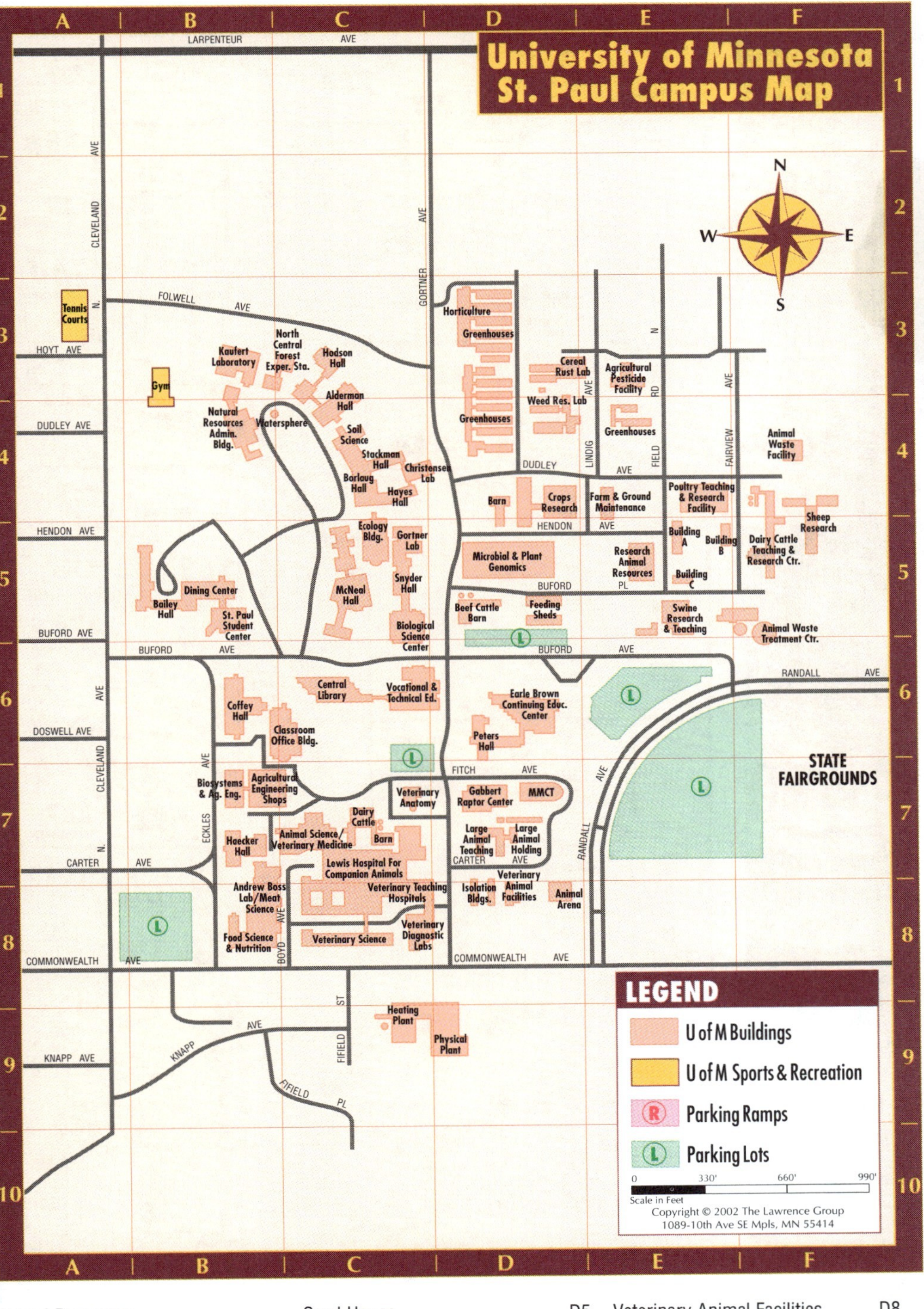

University of Minnesota
St. Paul Campus Map

LEGEND

U of M Buildings
U of M Sports & Recreation
(R) Parking Ramps
(L) Parking Lots

0   330'   660'   990'
Scale in Feet
Copyright © 2002 The Lawrence Group
1089-10th Ave SE Mpls, MN 55414

METRO MLS ZONES

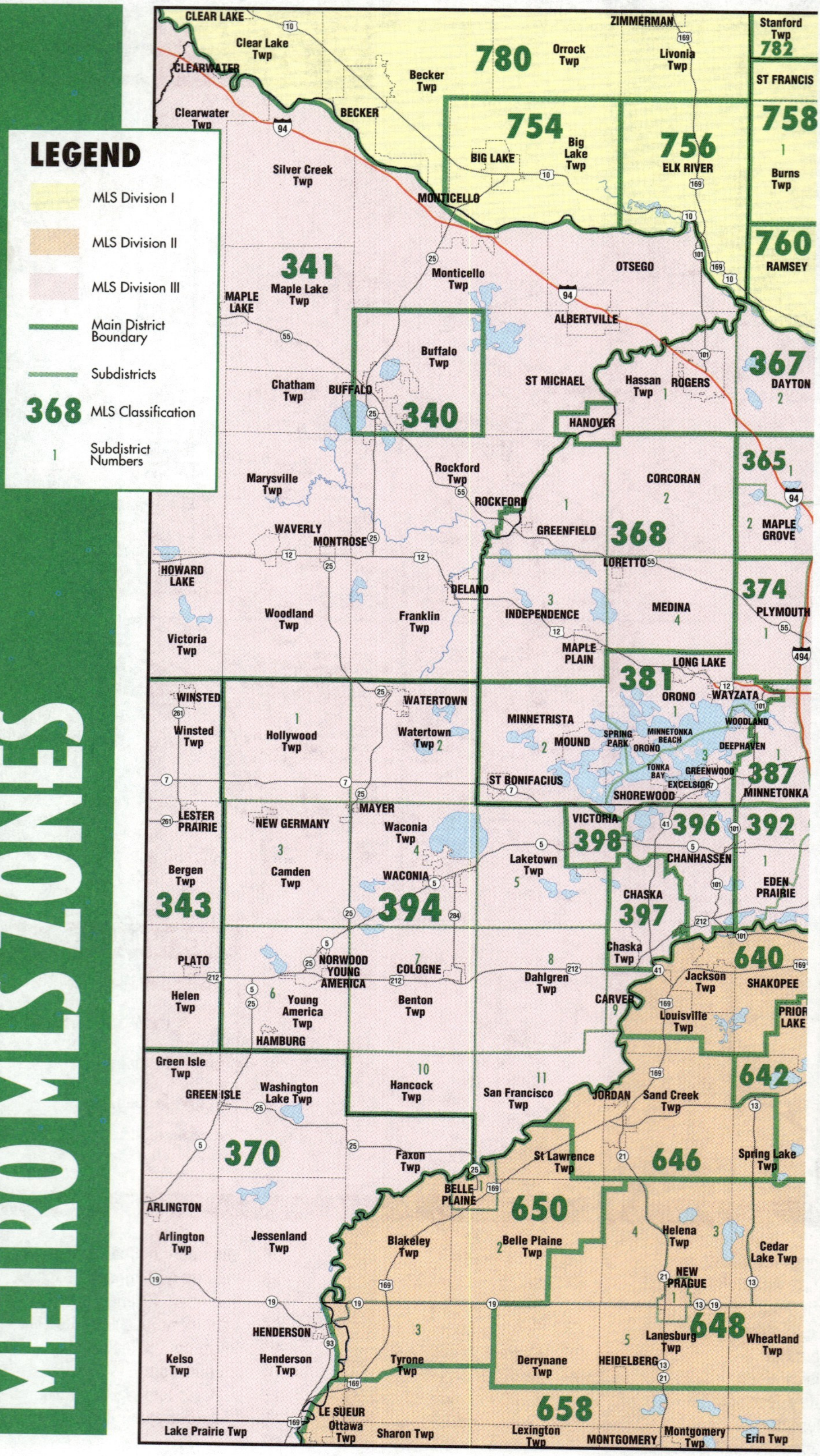

LEGEND

- MLS Division I
- MLS Division II
- MLS Division III
- Main District Boundary
- Subdistricts
- **368** MLS Classification
- 1 Subdistrict Numbers

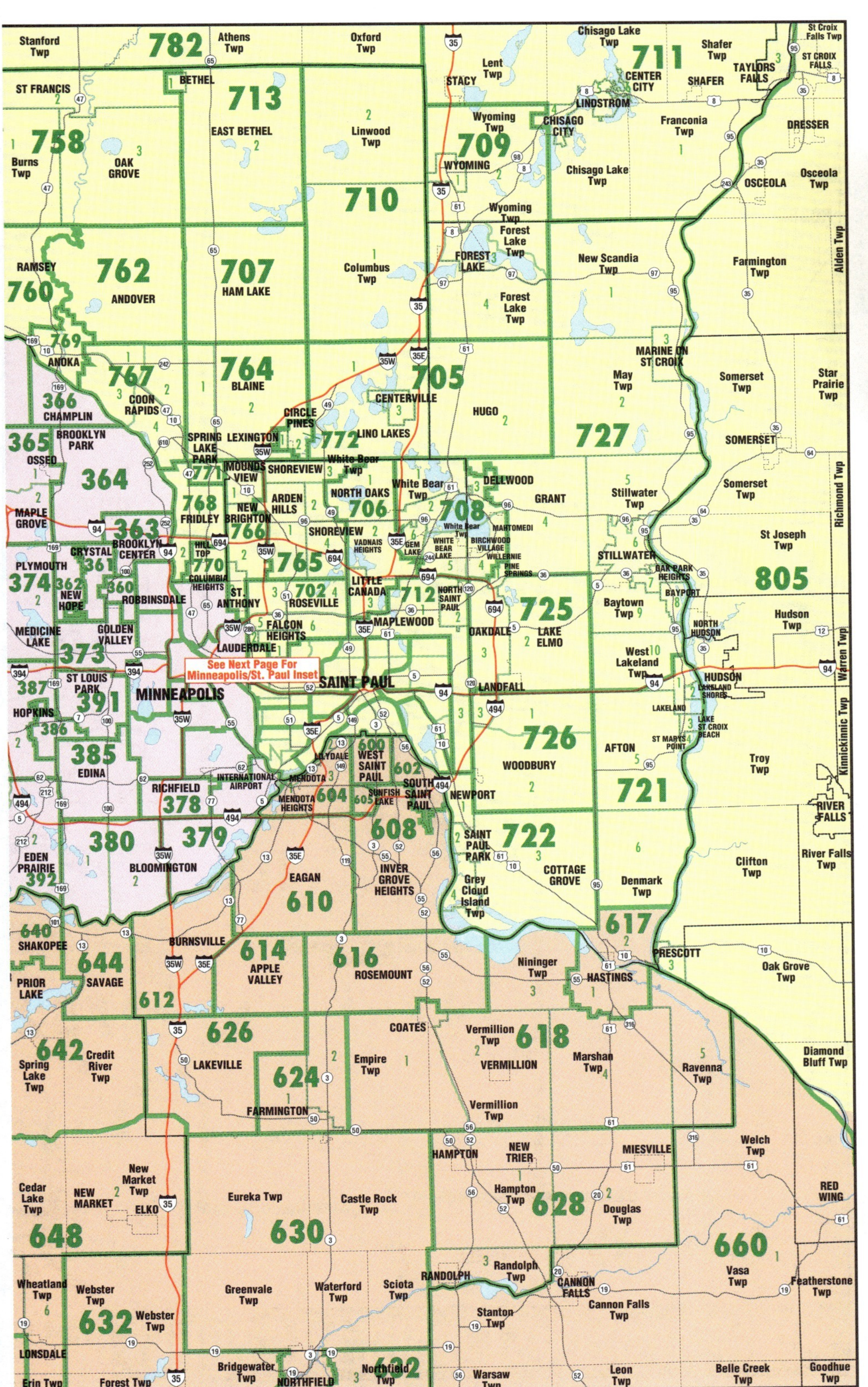

See Next Page For
Minneapolis/St. Paul Inset

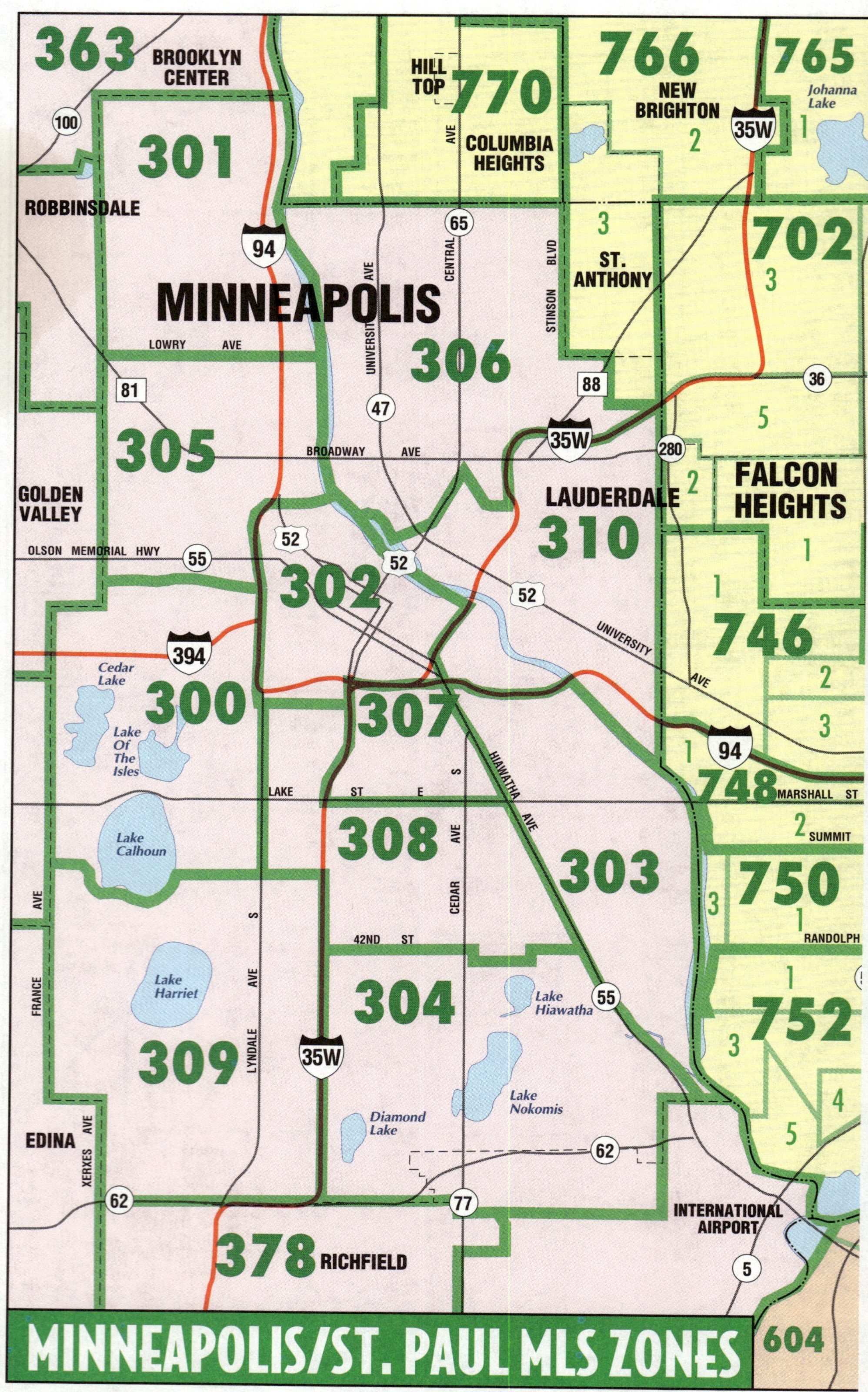

MINNEAPOLIS/ST. PAUL MLS ZONES

363 BROOKLYN CENTER

301

ROBBINSDALE

MINNEAPOLIS

305

GOLDEN VALLEY

LOWRY AVE

306

BROADWAY AVE

302

300

Cedar Lake

Lake Of The Isles

307

Lake Calhoun

308

Lake Harriet

309

304

Diamond Lake

Lake Nokomis

EDINA

378 RICHFIELD

HILL TOP 770 COLUMBIA HEIGHTS

766 NEW BRIGHTON 2

765 Johanna Lake 1

3

ST. ANTHONY

702 3

5

LAUDERDALE 310

FALCON HEIGHTS

2

1

1

746 2

3

748 1 MARSHALL ST

2 SUMMIT

303

750 3 1 RANDOLPH

Lake Hiawatha

752 3 1

5 4

INTERNATIONAL AIRPORT

604

OLSON MEMORIAL HWY

UNIVERSITY AVE

42ND ST

LAKE ST E

University AVE

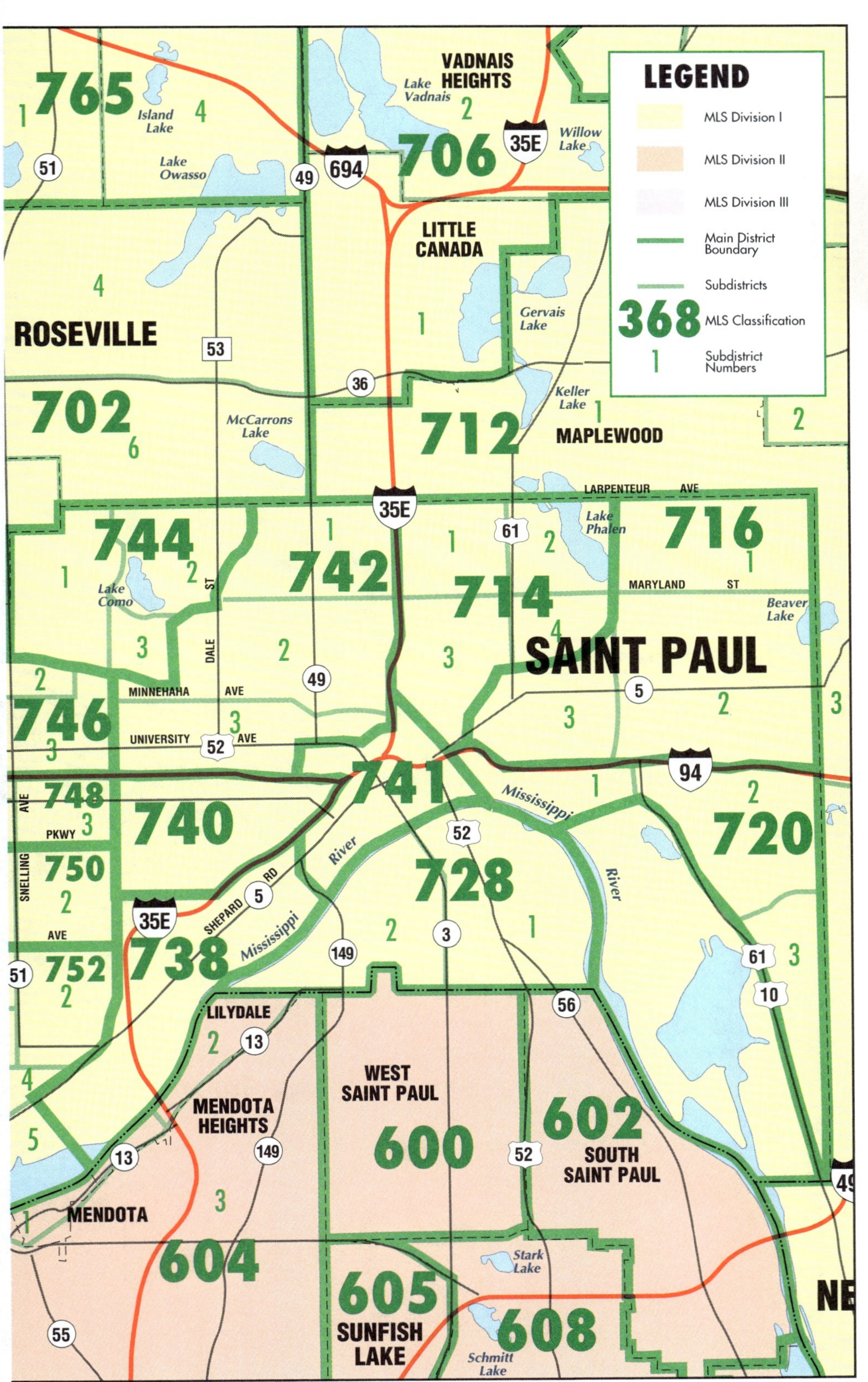

LEGEND

MLS Division I
MLS Division II
MLS Division III
Main District Boundary
Subdistricts
368 MLS Classification
1 Subdistrict Numbers

765 1 4

Island Lake
Lake Owasso
Lake Vadnais

VADNAIS HEIGHTS 2

706

35E

Willow Lake

51

49 694

LITTLE CANADA

ROSEVILLE

4

53

36

702 6

McCarrons Lake

Gervais Lake

1

Keller Lake

712

MAPLEWOOD

1 2

35E

LARPENTEUR AVE

Lake Phalen

716 1

744 1 2

Lake Como

DALE ST

742 1

61

2

MARYLAND ST

Beaver Lake

3

2

49

714 3

4

SAINT PAUL

5

3

2 3

MINNEHAHA AVE

746 3

UNIVERSITY 52 AVE

3

748 3

SNELLING AVE

PKWY

740

SHEPARD RD

5

741

Mississippi

River

52

1

94

720 2

750 2

35E

728

Mississippi River

61 3

10

AVE

752 2

738

Mississippi River

149

2 3

1

56

51

4

LILYDALE

13

MENDOTA HEIGHTS

2

13

149

WEST SAINT PAUL

600

52

602

SOUTH SAINT PAUL

49

5

MENDOTA

13

3

1

604

605

SUNFISH LAKE

Stark Lake

608

NE

55

Schmitt Lake

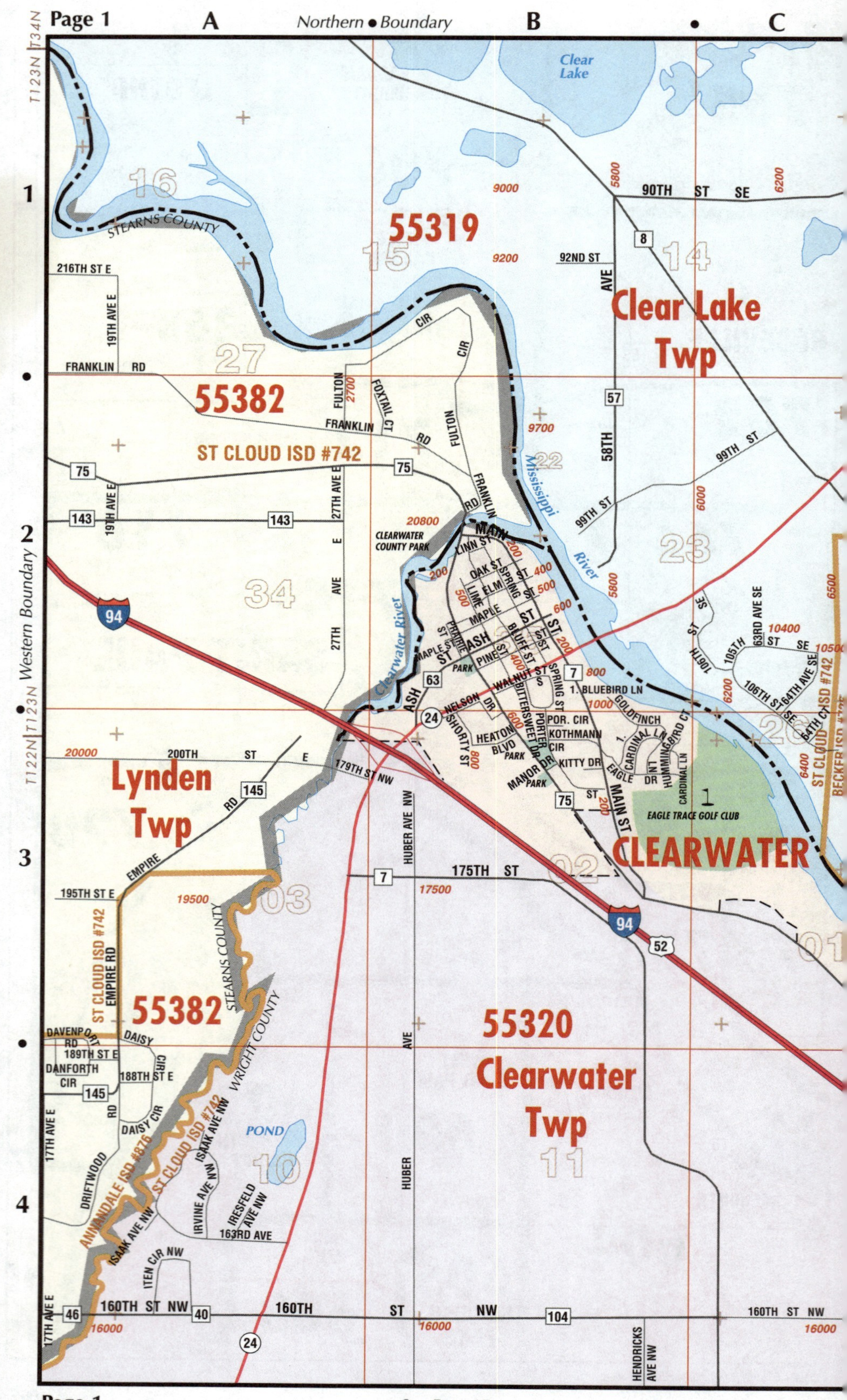

55319

Clear Lake Twp

55382

ST CLOUD ISD #742

CLEARWATER COUNTY PARK

Lynden Twp

55382

CLEARWATER

Eagle Trace Golf Club

55320

Clearwater Twp

POND

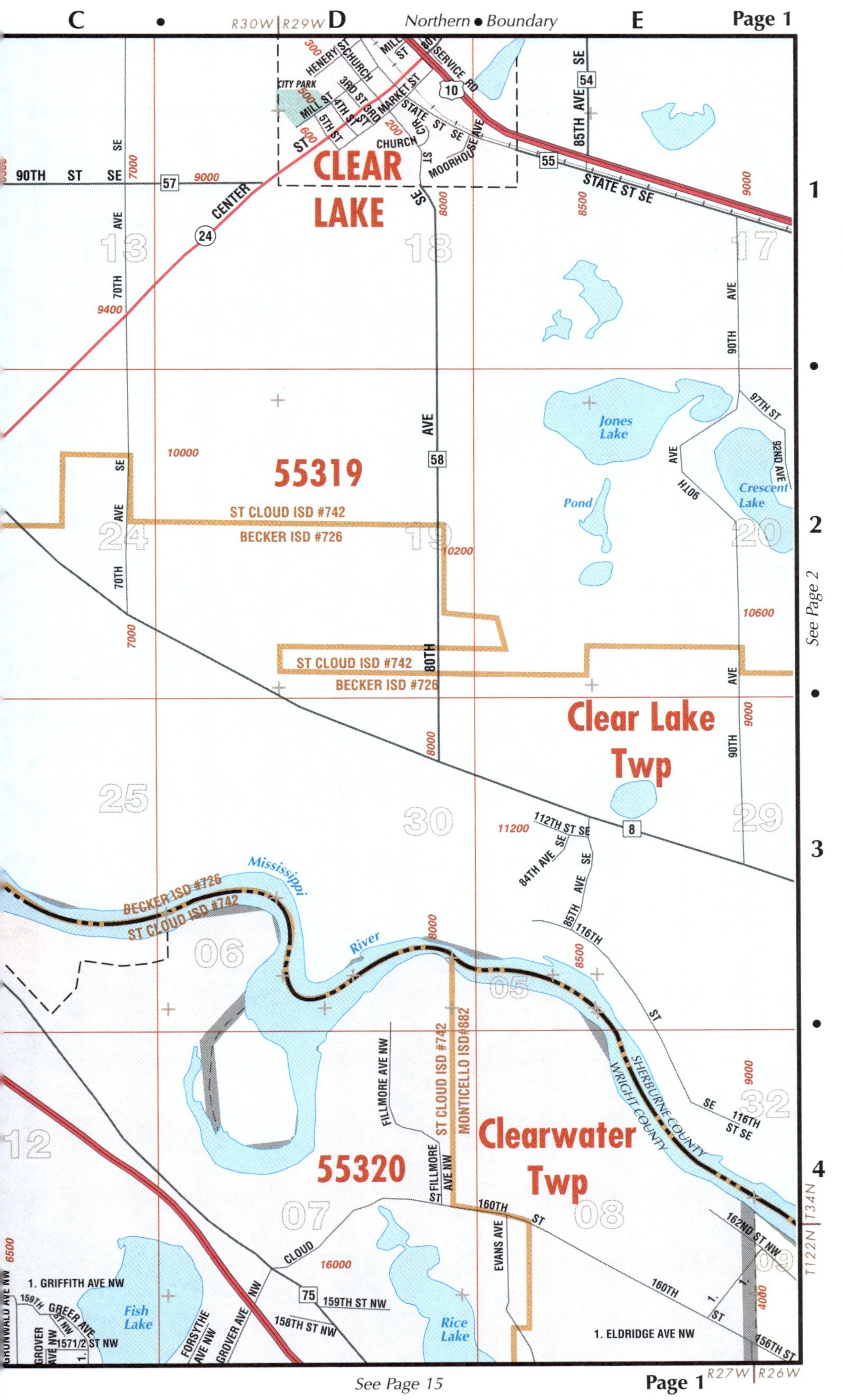

CLEAR LAKE

CITY PARK

90TH ST SE

55319

ST CLOUD ISD #742

BECKER ISD #726

ST CLOUD ISD #742

BECKER ISD #726

Jones Lake

Pond

Crescent Lake

Clear Lake Twp

Jones Lake

BECKER ISD #726

ST CLOUD ISD #742

Mississippi

River

Clearwater Twp

55320

SHERBURNE COUNTY
WRIGHT COUNTY

1. GRIFFITH AVE NW

Fish Lake

Rice Lake

1. ELDRIDGE AVE NW

See Page 2

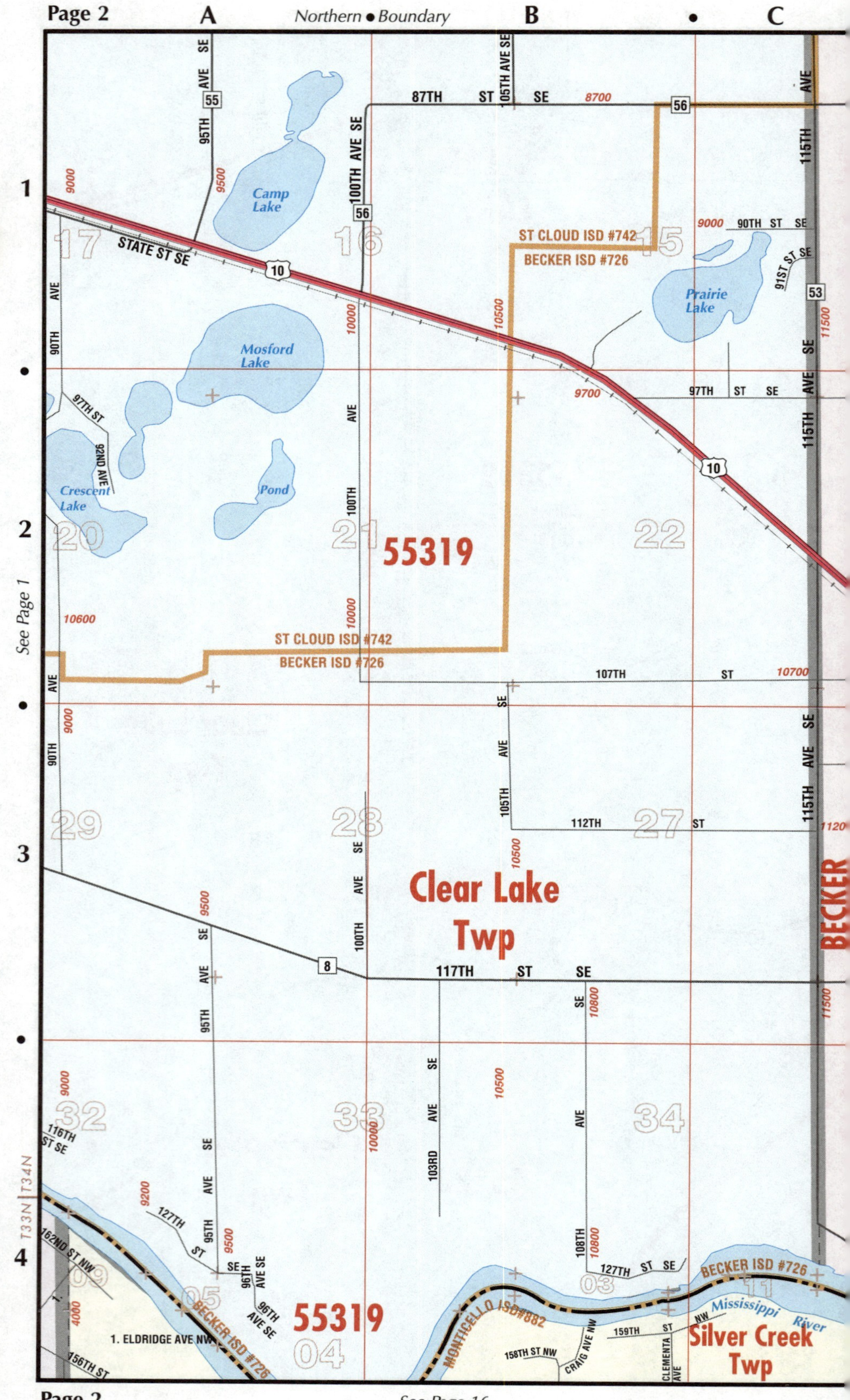

A B C

95TH AVE SE

55

105TH AVE SE

87TH   ST   SE   *8700*

56

9000

Camp
Lake

100TH AVE SE

56

17   STATE ST SE

10

9500

16

St Cloud ISD #742
BECKER ISD #726

15

9000   90TH   ST   SE

91ST ST SE

53

115TH AVE SE

11500

90TH AVE

9000

10000

10500

Mosford
Lake

Prairie
Lake

97TH ST

9700

97TH   ST   SE

10

115TH AVE SE

92ND AVE SE

100TH AVE

21

55319

22

Crescent
Lake

Pond

20

See Page 1

10600

10000

St Cloud ISD #742
BECKER ISD #726

107TH   ST   *10700*

90TH AVE

105TH AVE SE

115TH AVE SE

9000

1120

29

95TH AVE SE

9500

100TH AVE SE

28

112TH   ST

27

10500

**Clear Lake
Twp**

BECKER

8

117TH   ST   SE

11500

95TH AVE SE

100TH AVE SE

103RD AVE SE

10000

10500

108TH AVE SE

10800

32

116TH
ST SE

9000

33

34

T33N | T34N

162ND ST NW

9200

127TH   ST

95TH AVE SE

9500

96TH AVE SE

BECKER ISD #726

127TH   ST   SE

108TH AVE

10800

BECKER ISD #726

Mississippi   River

09

05

4000

55319

04

MONTICELLO ISD #882

158TH ST NW

CRAIG AVE NW

159TH   ST   NW

CLEMENTA AVE NW

03

11

**Silver Creek
Twp**

1. ELDRIDGE AVE NW

156TH ST

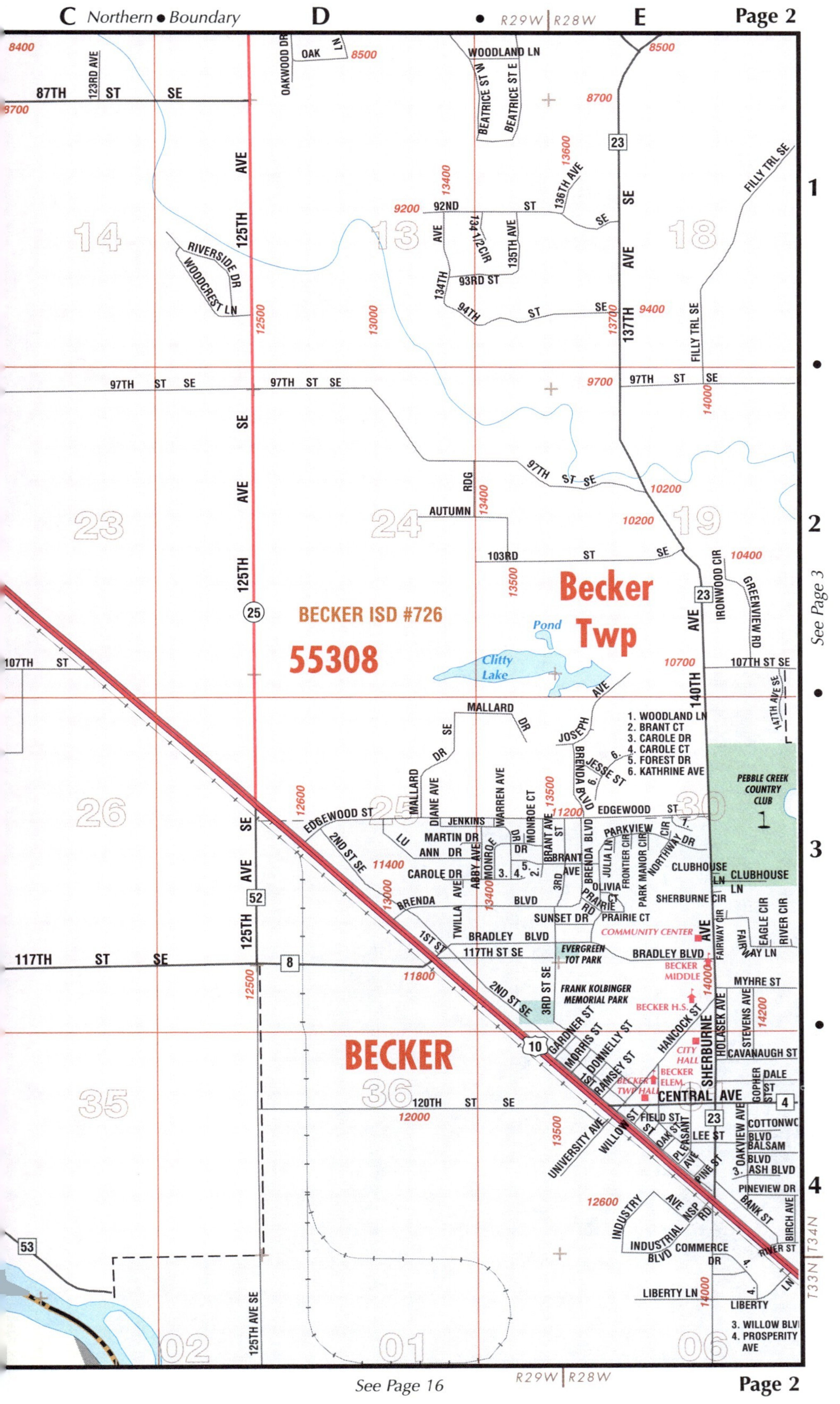

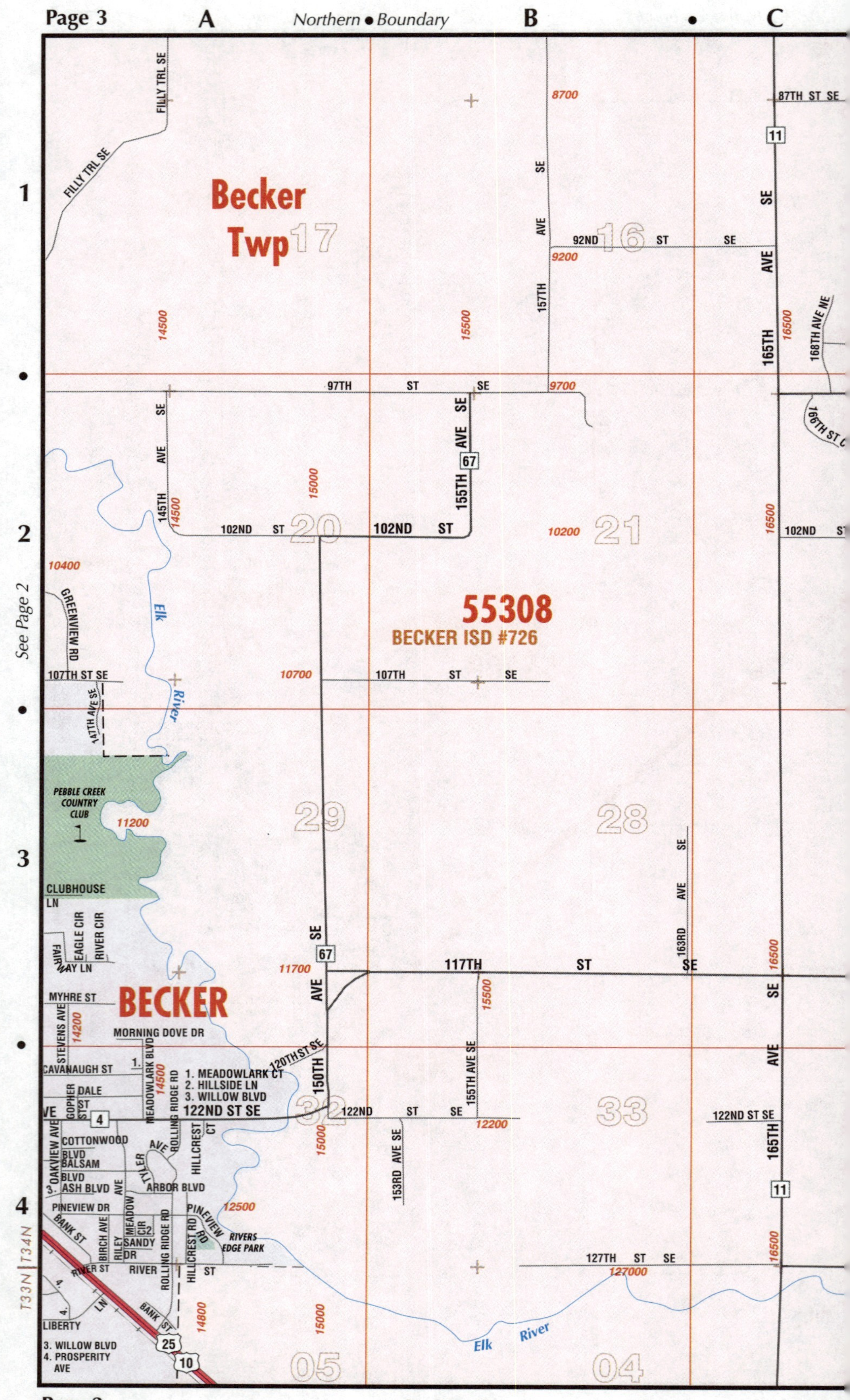

FILLY TRL SE

87TH ST SE

11

Becker
Twp 17

8700

1

92ND 16 ST SE

9200

157TH AVE SE

165TH AVE SE

168TH AVE NE

14500

15500

16500

97TH ST SE

9700

166TH ST C

10400

145TH AVE SE

14500

15000

155TH AVE SE

67

102ND ST 20 102ND ST

10200 21

165TH AVE SE

16500

102ND S

2

55308
BECKER ISD #726

GREENVIEW RD

Elk

107TH ST SE

10700

107TH ST SE

River

147TH AVE SE

PEBBLE CREEK
COUNTRY
CLUB

29

28

163RD AVE SE

11200

3

CLUBHOUSE
LN

EAGLE CIR

RIVER CIR

FAIRWAY LN

11700

67

117TH ST SE

155TH AVE SE

15500

163RD AVE SE

165TH AVE SE

16500

MYHRE ST

BECKER

STEVENS AVE

14200

MORNING DOVE DR

120TH ST SE

1. MEADOWLARK CT
2. HILLSIDE LN
3. WILLOW BLVD

CAVANAUGH ST

1.

GOPHER DALE ST

MEADOWLARK BLVD

14500

ROLLING RIDGE RD

150TH AVE SE

122ND ST 32

122ND ST SE

15000

153RD AVE SE

12200

33

122ND ST SE

165TH AVE SE

4

GOPHER ST

4

122ND ST SE

COTTONWOOD BLVD

BALSAM BLVD

OAKVIEW AVE

ASH BLVD

TYLER AVE

ARBOR BLVD

HILLCREST CT

PINEVIEW DR

12500

BIRCH AVE

RILEY ST

MEADOW CIR

SANDY DR

2.

ROLLING RIDGE RD

PINEVIEW RD

HILLCREST RD

RIVERS
EDGE PARK

BANK ST

RIVER ST

RIVER ST

LIBERTY LN

BANK ST

14800

15000

127TH ST SE

127000

16500

11

T33N T34N

25

10

3. WILLOW BLVD
4. PROSPERITY AVE

05

Elk River

04

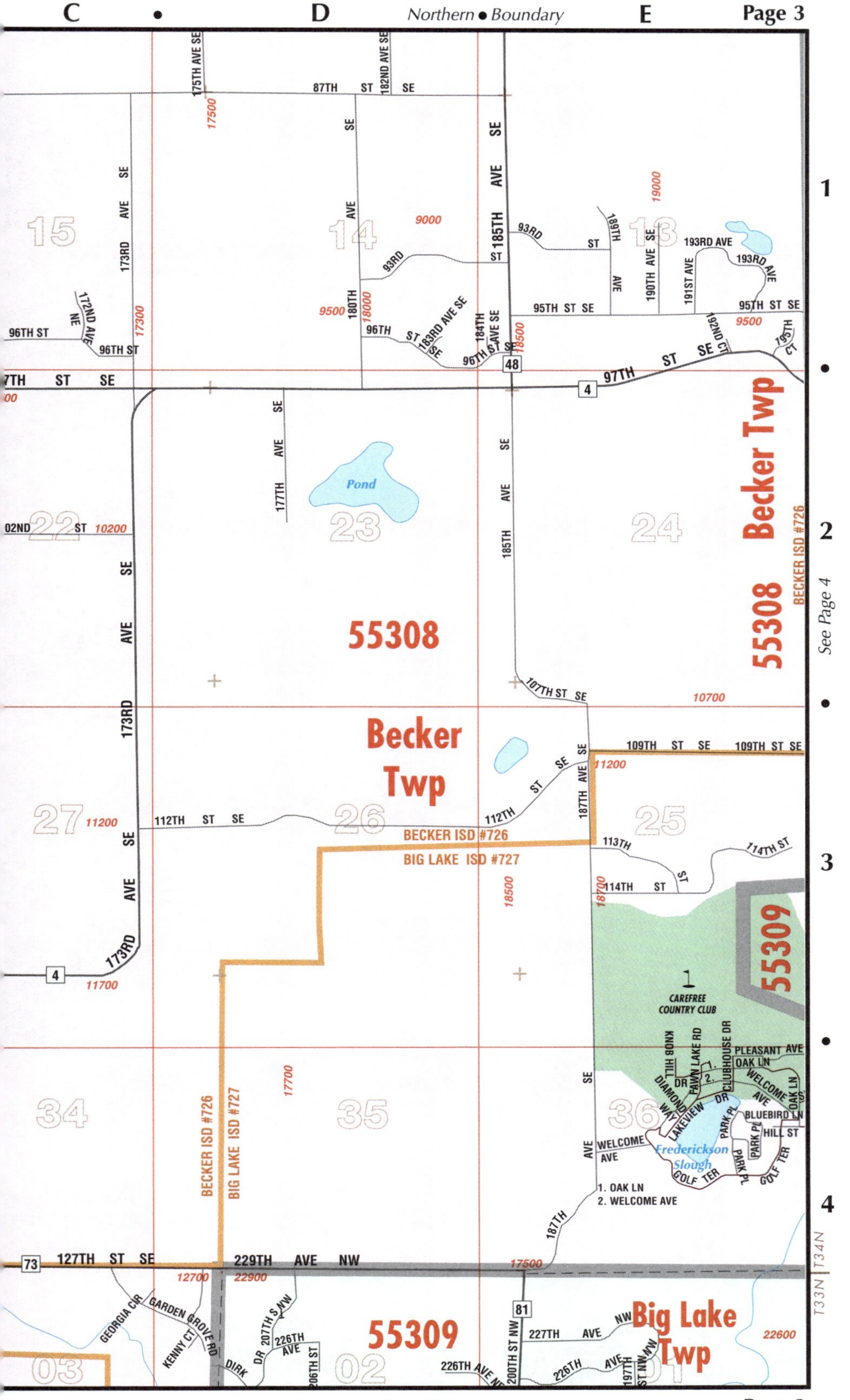

55308

Becker Twp

Becker Twp

55308

See Page 4

BECKER ISD #726

BECKER ISD #726
BIG LAKE ISD #727

55309

1
CAREFREE
COUNTRY CLUB

55309

BECKER ISD #726
BIG LAKE ISD #727

1. OAK LN
2. WELCOME AVE

Frederickson
Slough

1. OAK LN
2. WELCOME AVE

55309

Big Lake Twp

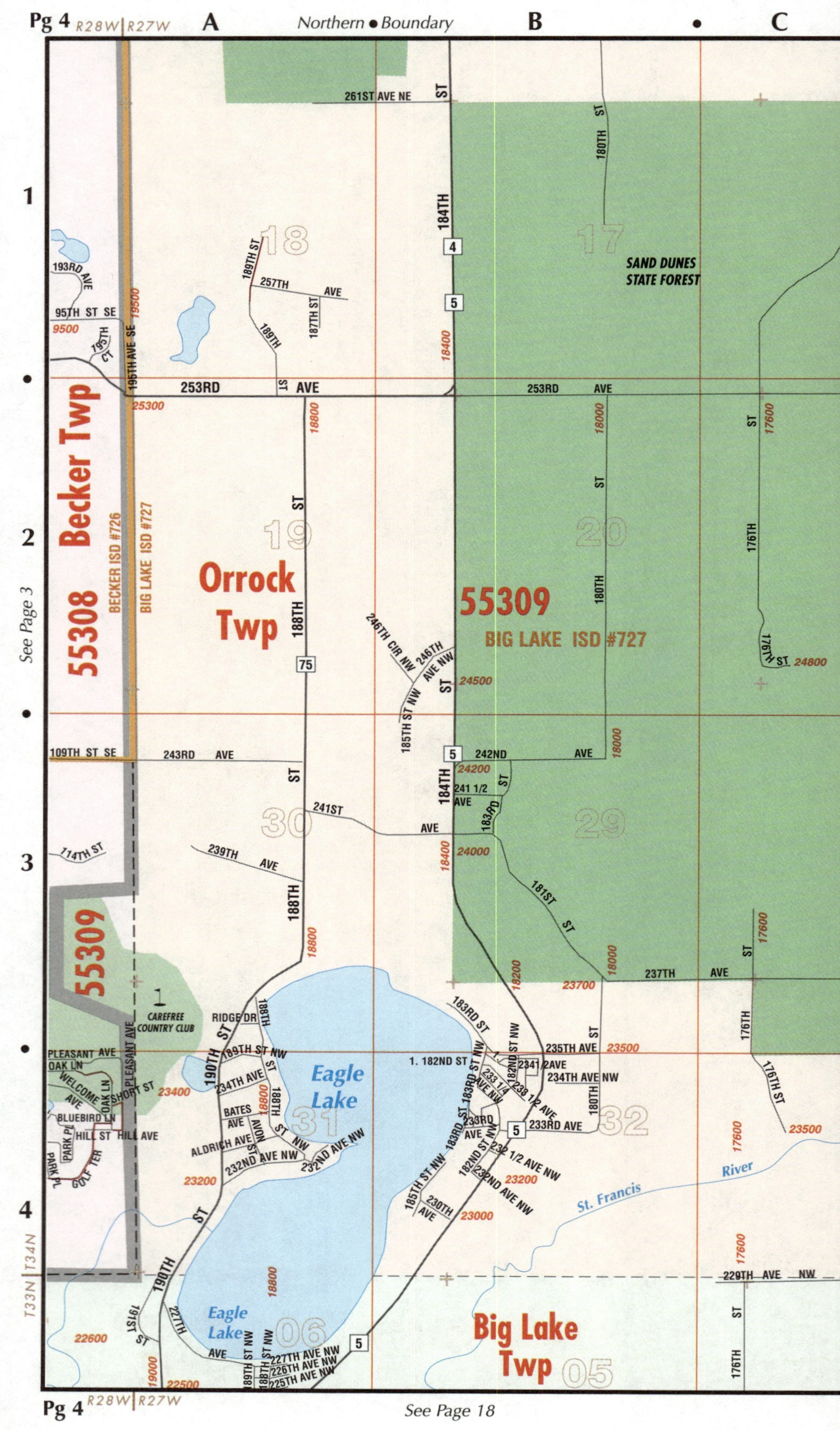

1

261ST AVE NE

SAND DUNES
STATE FOREST

ST

180TH

184TH

4

5

193RD NE

189TH ST

257TH   AVE

187TH ST

199TH

95TH ST SE

9500

195TH AVE SE

9500

195TH

18

17

176TH

ST

17600

See Page 3

Becker Twp

55308

BECKER ISD #726

BIG LAKE ISD #727

25300

253RD ST AVE

253RD   AVE

18800

**Orrock
Twp**

55309

BIG LAKE ISD #727

19

ST

188TH

75

20

180TH

ST

18000

246TH CIR NW

246TH
AVE NW
ST

24500

185TH ST NW

2

176TH ST 24800

24800

109TH ST SE

243RD   AVE

ST

188TH

241ST

AVE

5 242ND   AVE

18000

184TH 24200

241 1/2

ST

ST

18000

AVE

30

239TH   AVE

183RD

18400

24000

29

181ST ST

T14ST ST

114TH ST

55309

1

3

237TH   AVE

23700

18200

18000

176TH

ST

17600

CAREFREE
COUNTRY CLUB

RIDGE DR

188TH ST

190TH ST

183RD ST

235TH AVE 23500

182ND ST NW

234TH AVE NW

ST 176TH ST 23500

Pleasant AVE
OAK LN

PLEASANT AVE

23400

89TH ST NW

234TH AVE NW

BATES
AVE

**Eagle
Lake**

1. 182ND ST

182ND ST NW

233 1/2

232 1/2
AVE

233RD 233 1/2 AVE

180TH ST

32

WELCOME
AVE

OAK LN

SHORT ST

BLUEBIRD LN

HILL ST HILL AVE

PARK PL

GOLF TER

PARK PL

31

AVON ST

ALDRICH AVE

232ND AVE NW

232ND AVE NW

AVE

5 233RD AVE

23200

232 1/2 AVE NW

182ND ST NW

183RD ST NW

183RD ST NW

23200

River

17600

17600

St. Francis

23200

23000

23500

4

23200

185TH ST NW

230TH
AVE

232ND AVE NW

229TH AVE NW

176TH

ST

17600

T33N | T34N

**Eagle
Lake**

190TH ST

227TH

18800

06

**Big Lake
Twp** 05

22600

227TH
AVE NW

226TH AVE NW

225TH AVE NW

89TH ST NW

5

161ST ST

19000

22500

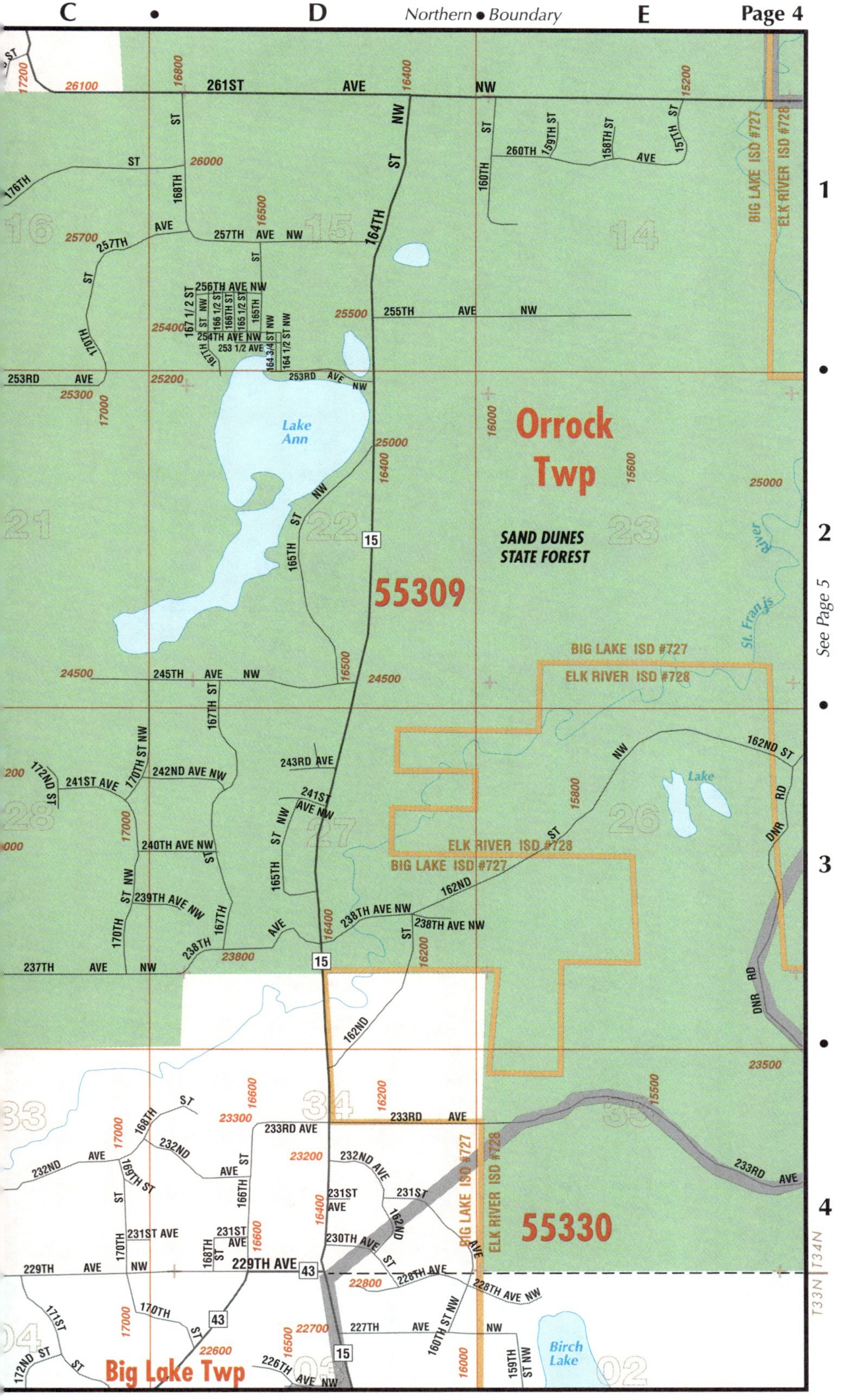

See Page 5

See Page 18

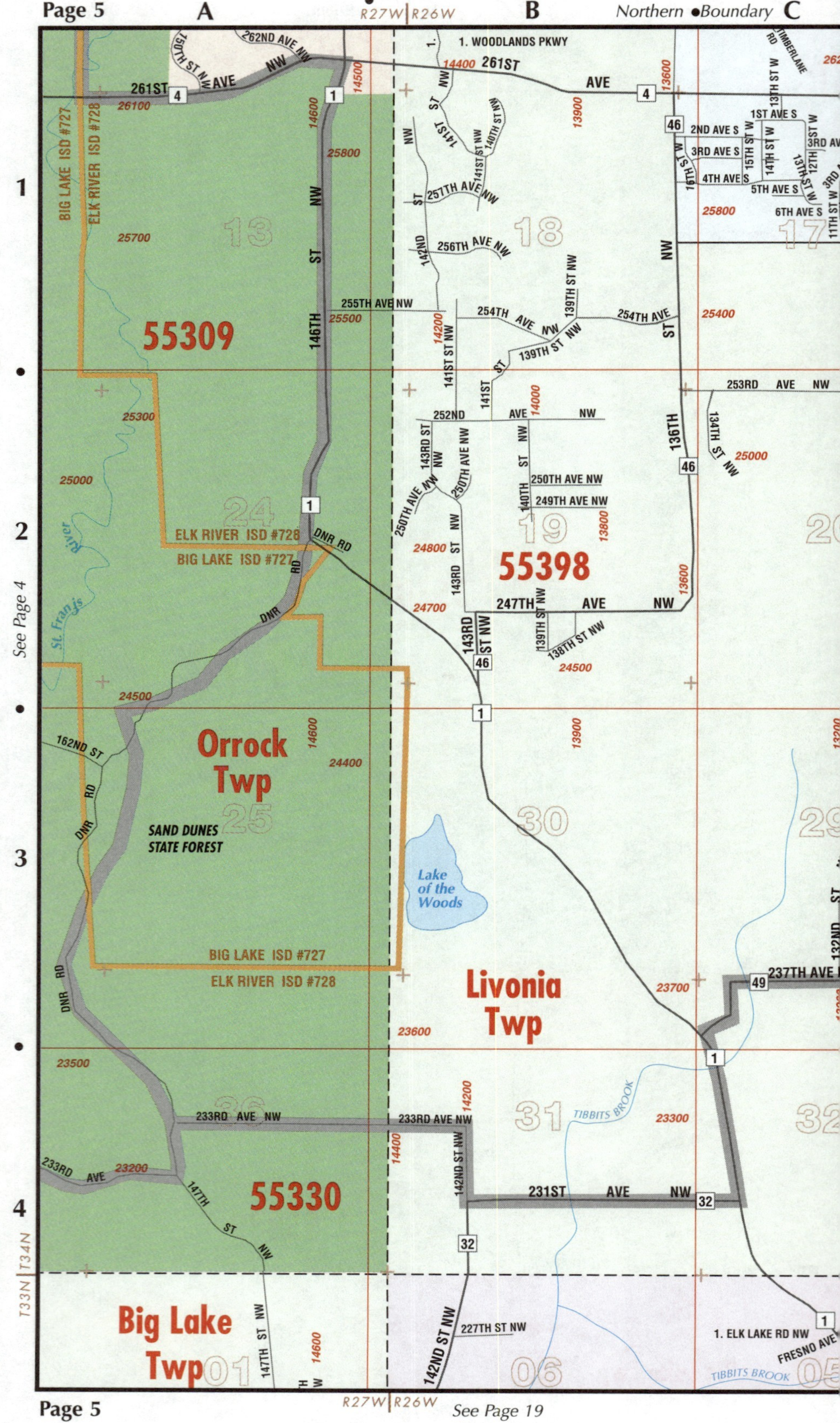

R27W | R26W

Big Lake ISD #727

ELK RIVER ISD #728

261ST   AVE
26100

262ND AVE NW

1. WOODLANDS PKWY
14400 261ST   AVE
13600

14500

55309

13

18

17

25800

25700

25800

25400

25300

253RD   AVE   NW

25000

255TH AVE NW
14200
254TH   AVE   NW   254TH   AVE
25500

256TH AVE NW

257TH AVE NW

252ND   AVE   NW
14000
251ST   AVE   NW
250TH AVE NW
249TH AVE NW

24

55398

19

20

ELK RIVER ISD #728
BIG LAKE ISD #728
DNR RD

24800

13800

24700

247TH   AVE   NW

13600

24500

1

13900

13900

162ND ST

Orrock Twp
14600
24400

25

SAND DUNES STATE FOREST

30

29

Lake of the Woods

Livonia Twp

23700

237TH AVE

49

BIG LAKE ISD #727
ELK RIVER ISD #728

23600

1

23500

233RD AVE NW

233RD AVE NW
14200

31 TIBBITS BROOK 23300

32

233RD AVE 23200
147TH ST NW

55330

26

142ND ST NW

231ST   AVE   NW

32

T33N | T34N

Big Lake Twp
01

147TH ST NW
14600

32

142ND ST NW 227TH ST NW

06

1. ELK LAKE RD NW
FRESNO AVE

TIBBITS BROOK

05

1

See Page 4

St. Francis River

DNR RD

DNR RD

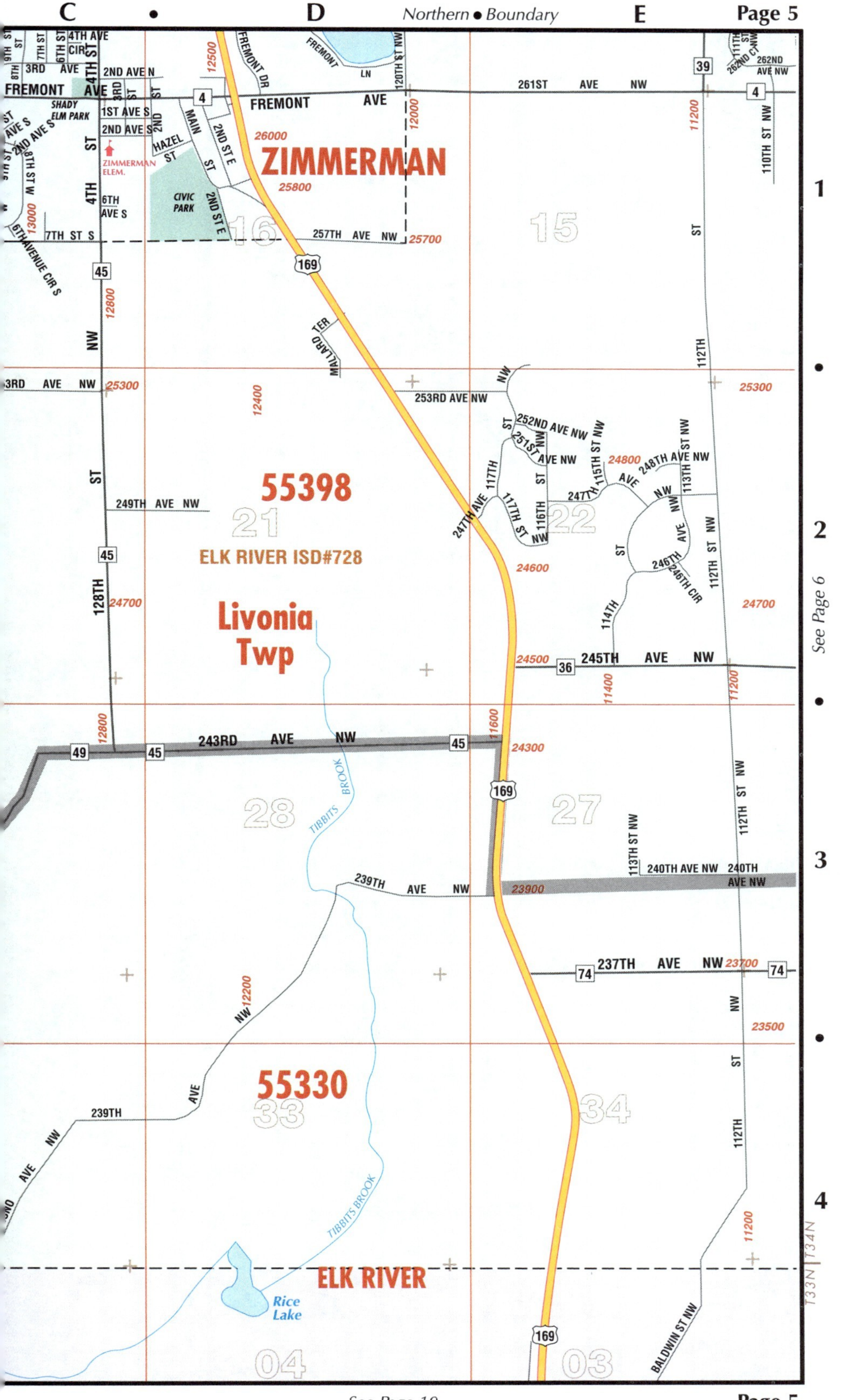

ZIMMERMAN

55398

ELK RIVER ISD#728

Livonia Twp

55330

ELK RIVER

Rice Lake

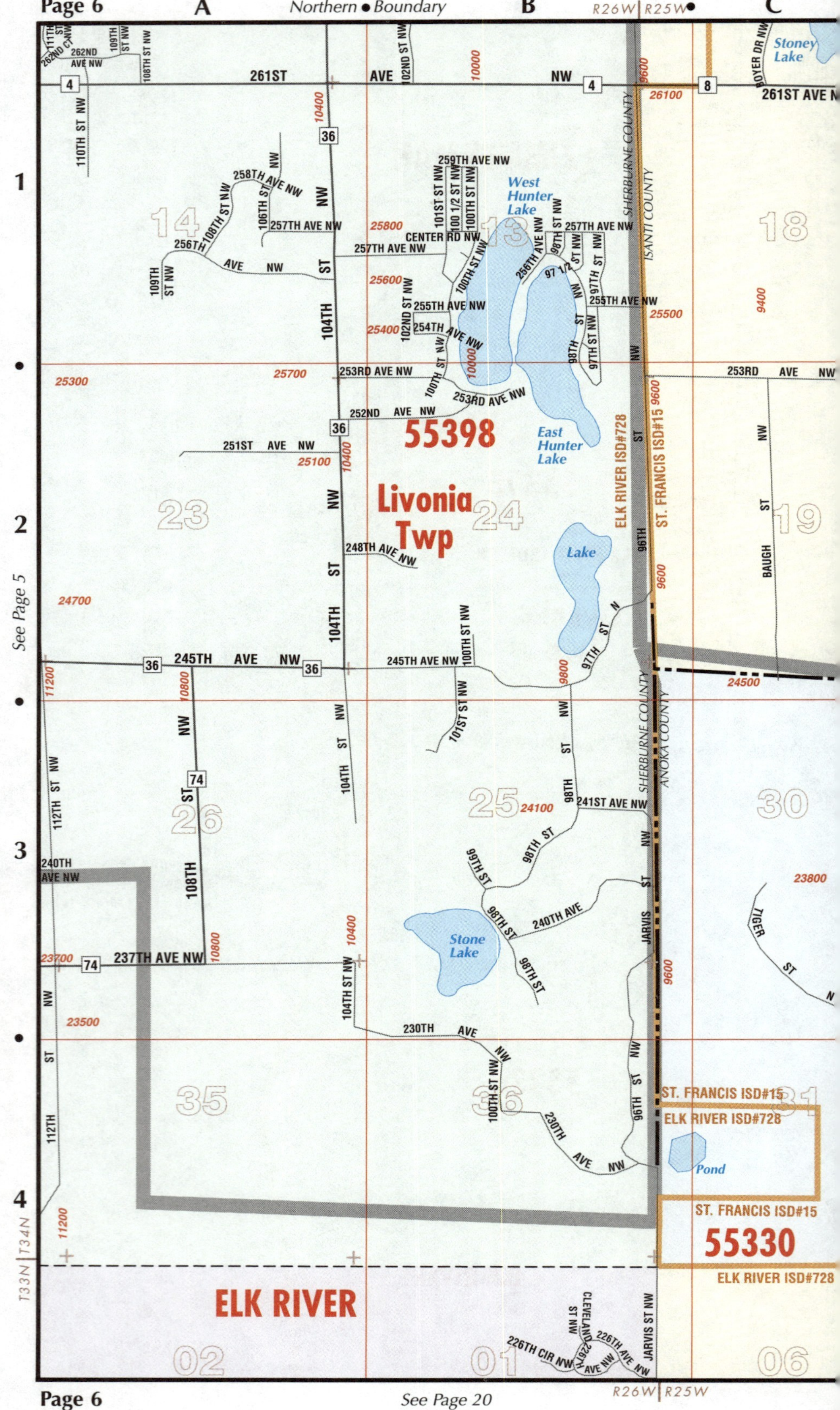

55398

Livonia Twp

ELK RIVER

55330

ST. FRANCIS ISD#15
ELK RIVER ISD#728

See Page 5

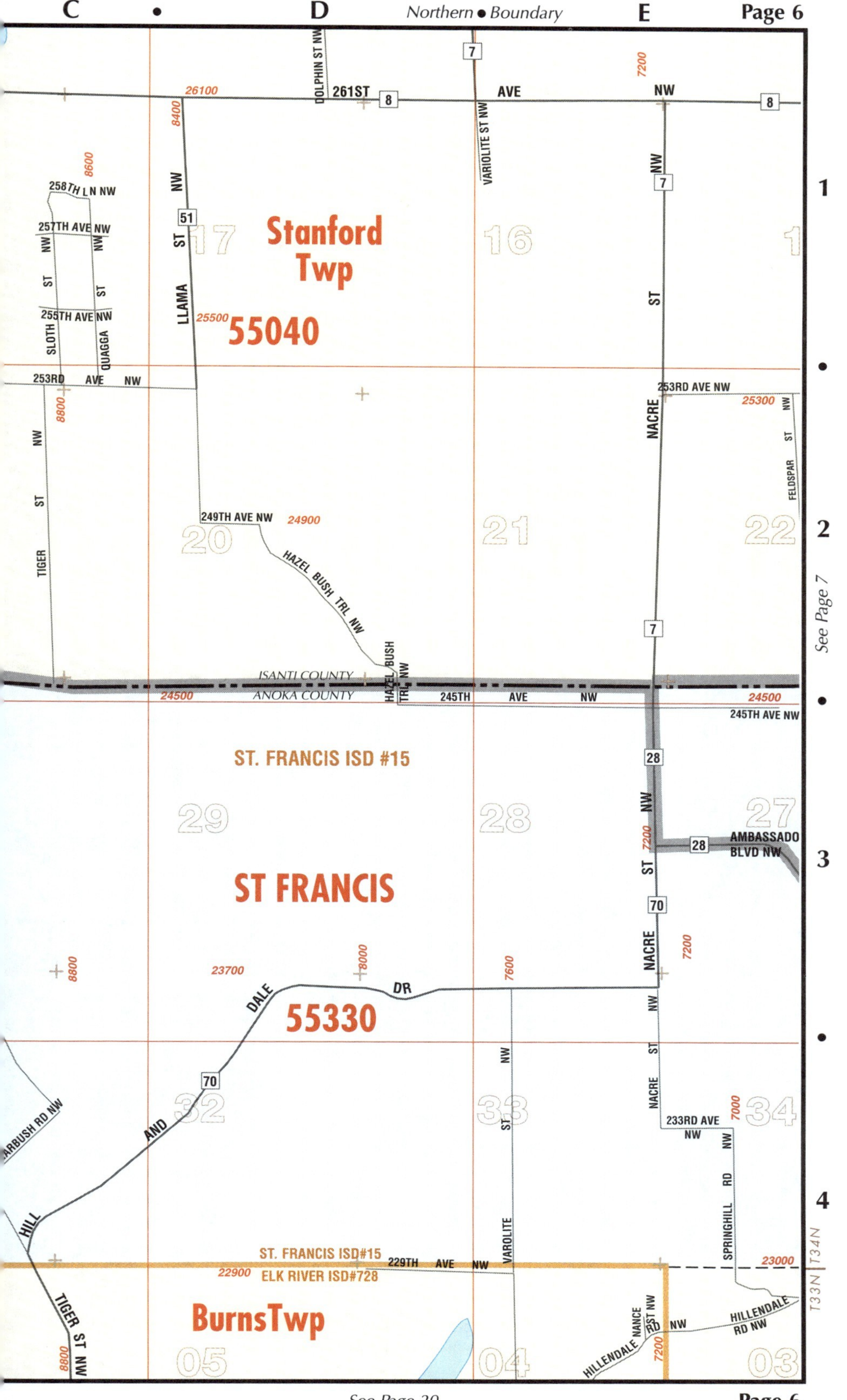

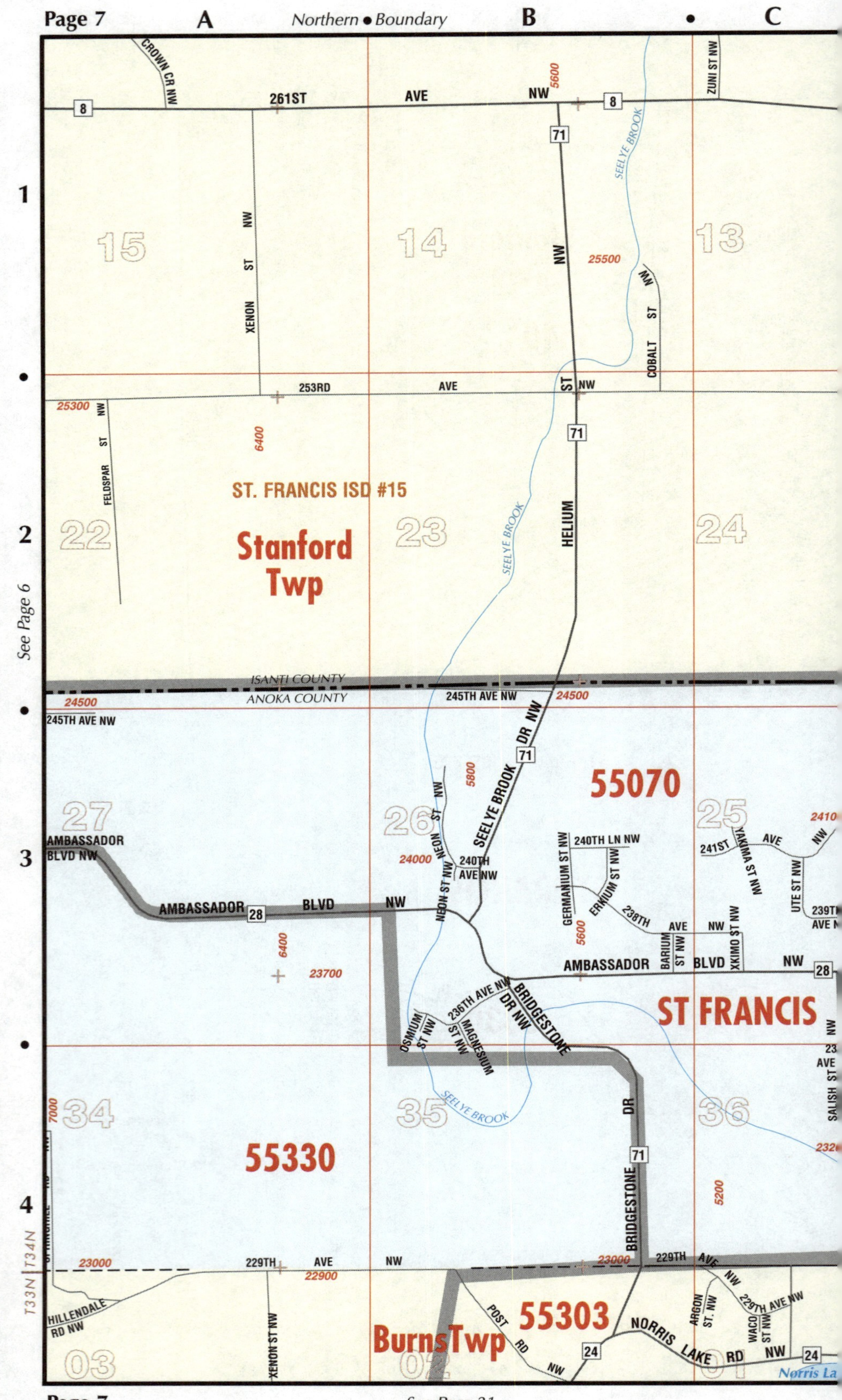

CROWN CR NW

8 261ST AVE NW 5600 8

71

ZUNI ST NW

1

15

XENON ST NW

14

SEELYE BROOK

25500

COBALT ST NW

13

253RD AVE ST NW

25300 NW

6400

71

2

FELDSPAR ST

22

ST. FRANCIS ISD #15

Stanford Twp

23

SEELYE BROOK

HELIUM

24

ISANTI COUNTY
ANOKA COUNTY

24500 245TH AVE NW 24500

245TH AVE NW

SEELYE BROOK DR NW

71

55070

3

27

Ambassador BLVD NW

AMBASSADOR 28 BLVD NW

6400

23700

26

24000

NEON ST NW NEON ST NW

5800

240TH AVE NW

5600

GERMANIUM ST NW

240TH LN NW

ERMIUM ST NW

238TH

25

241ST AVE

YAKIMA ST NW

UTE ST NW

2410

239TH AVE N

AMBASSADOR BARIUM ST NW BLVD XKIMO ST NW NW 28

ST FRANCIS

236TH AVE NW

OSMIUM ST NW

MAGNESIUM ST NW

BRIDGESTONE DR NW

SEELYE BROOK

35

BRIDGESTONE DR

71

23 AVE NW

SALISH ST NW

36

2326

4

7000

34

55330

5200

229TH AVE NW

23000

23000 229TH AVE NW

ARDEN ST NW

WACO ST NW

229TH AVE NW

T33N | T34N

22900

HILLENDALE RD NW

03

BurnsTwp

02

POST RD NW

55303

24

NORRIS LAKE RD NW

01

24

Norris La

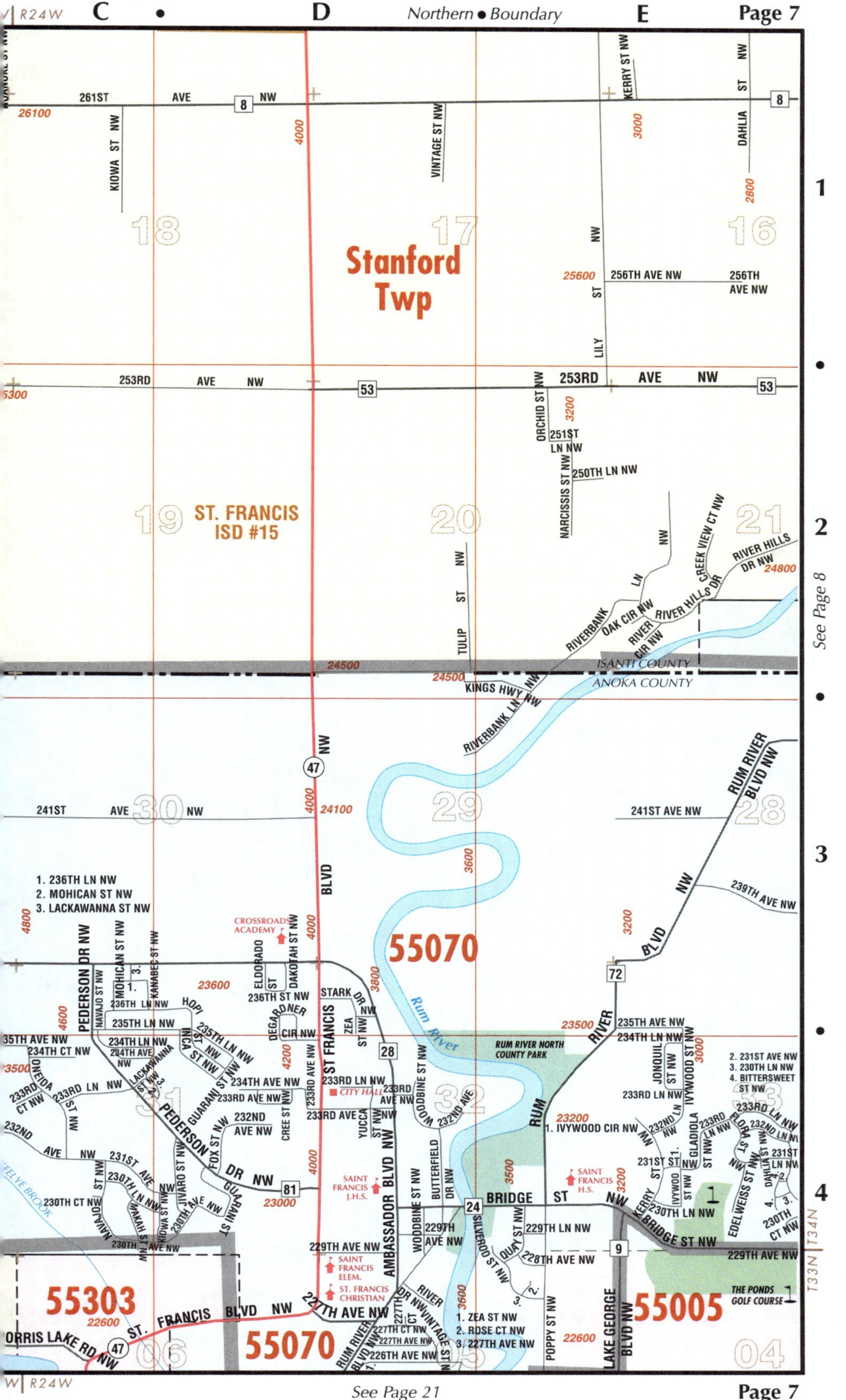

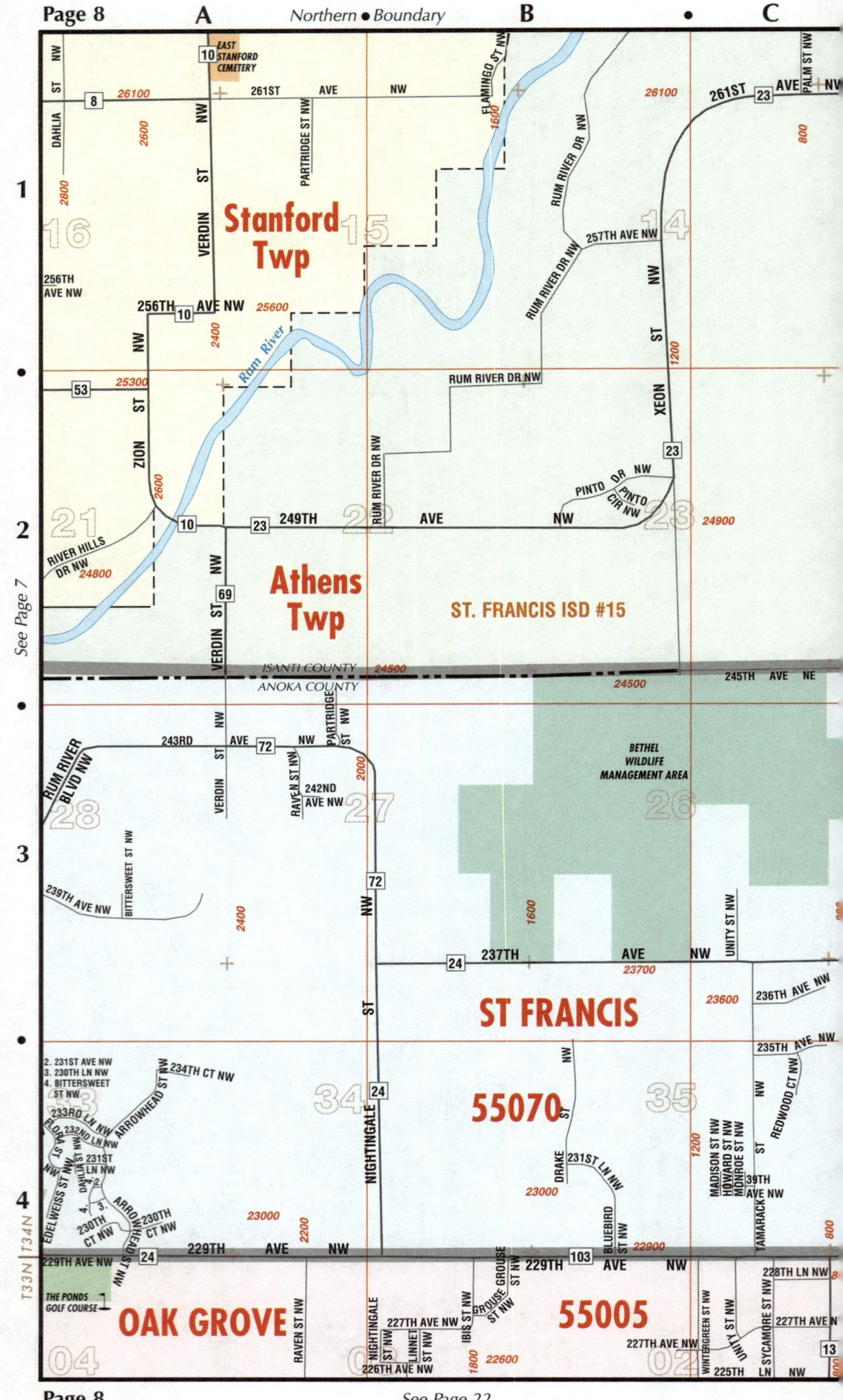

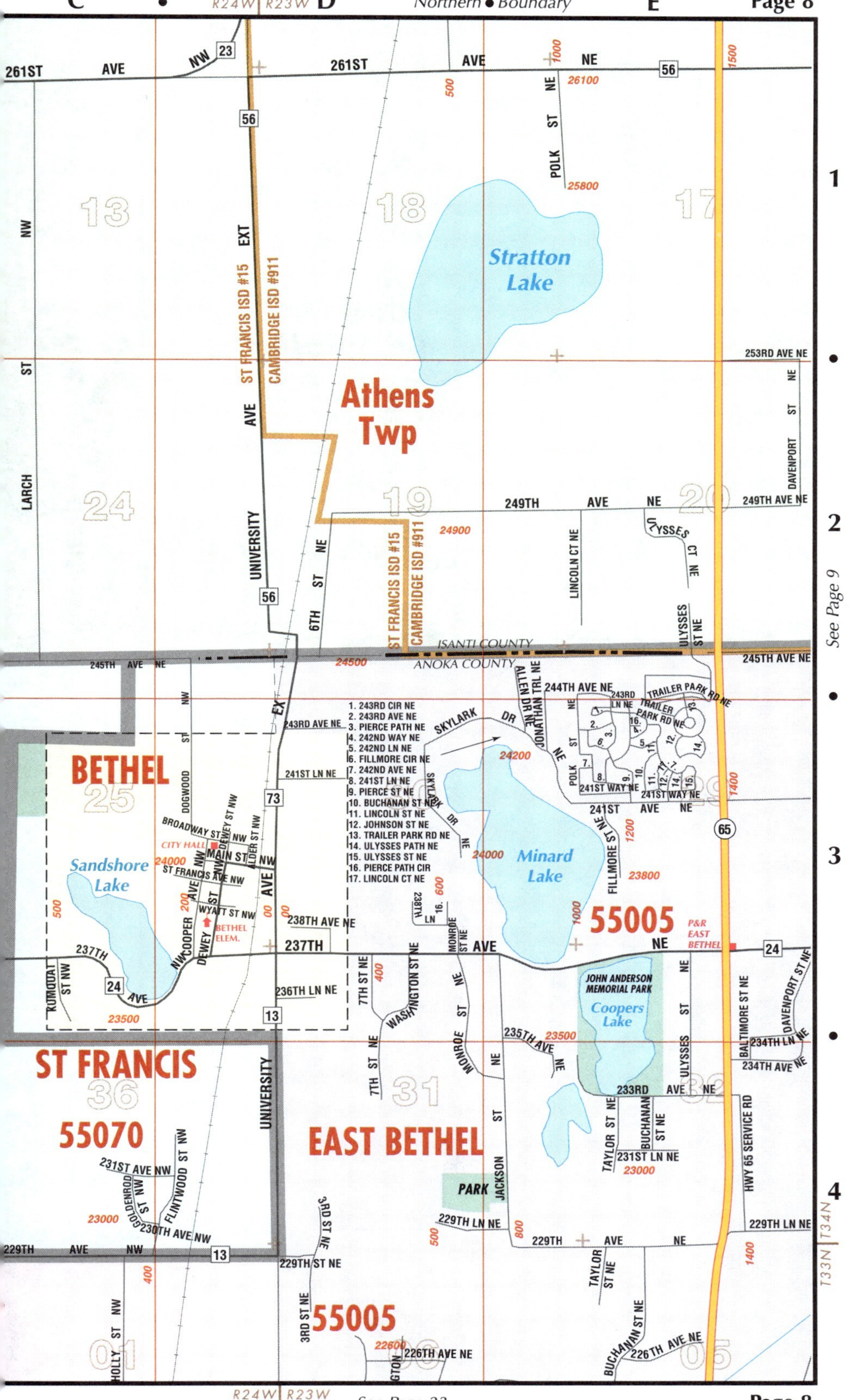

261ST AVE NW 23

261ST AVE NE 1000 26100

56

500 56

25800

POLK ST NE

13 NW 56 EXT 18 17 1

ST NW

Stratton Lake

ST FRANCIS ISD #15 EXT

CAMBRIDGE ISD #911

253RD AVE NE

Athens Twp

NE

DAVENPORT ST NE

LARCH ST

24 UNIVERSITY AVE 19 24900 249TH AVE NE 20 249TH AVE NE 2

ULYSSES CT NE

56 6TH ST NE LINCOLN CT NE ULYSSES CT NE

ULYSSES ST NE

ST FRANCIS ISD #15
CAMBRIDGE ISD #911

245TH AVE NE EX ISANTI COUNTY 24500 ANOKA COUNTY 245TH AVE NE

ST NW

243RD AVE NE 244TH AVE NE 243RD TRAILER PARK RD NE

1. 243RD CIR NE
2. 243RD AVE NE
3. PIERCE PATH NE
4. 242ND WAY NE
5. 242ND LN NE
6. FILLMORE CIR NE
7. 242ND AVE NE
8. 241ST LN NE
9. PIERCE ST NE
10. BUCHANAN ST NE
11. LINCOLN ST NE
12. JOHNSON ST NE
13. TRAILER PARK RD NE
14. ULYSSES PATH NE
15. ULYSSES ST NE
16. PIERCE PATH CIR
17. LINCOLN CT NE

BETHEL

25 DOGWOOD ST NW 241ST LN NE

73 SKYLARK DR NE 24200

BROADWAY ST NW JONATHAN TRL NE

ELDER ST NW ALLEN DR NE

POLK ST NE

241ST WAY NE 241ST WAY NE

CITY HALL MAIN ST NW 241ST AVE NE

Sandshore Lake 24000 ST FRANCIS AVE NW Minard Lake 1200

500 COOPER ST NW 200 AVE NW 00 AVE NE 24000 FILLMORE ST NE 23800

WYATT ST NW 238TH AVE NE 600 **55005** P&R EAST BETHEL

DEWEY ST NW BETHEL ELEM. 237TH SKYLARK DR NE MONROE ST NE 1000 24

237TH AVE NW 00 ST NE ULYSSES ST NE 24

KOMOCUT ST NW 24 AVE 13 236TH LN NE 287TH LN NE JOHN ANDERSON MEMORIAL PARK BALTIMORE ST NE DAVENPORT ST NE

23500 7TH ST NE WASHINGTON ST NE Coopers Lake 234TH LN NE

ST FRANCIS 235TH AVE 23500 234TH AVE NE

36 UNIVERSITY 31 7TH ST NE MONROE ST NE 233RD AVE NE 32 ULYSSES ST NE

55070 **EAST BETHEL** TAYLOR ST NE BUCHANAN ST NE HWY 65 SERVICE RD 233RD

231ST AVE NW JACKSON ST NE 231ST LN NE 23000

GOLDENROD ST NW FLINTWOOD ST NW PARK 500 800

230TH AVE NW 229TH LN NE 229TH LN NE

229TH AVE NW 13 229TH AVE NE

400 3RD ST NE TAYLOR ST NE 1400

HOLLY ST NW 229TH ST NE 3RD ST NE BUCHANAN ST NE 226TH AVE NE

04 **55005** 22600 226TH AVE NE 05

T33N | T34N

See Page 9

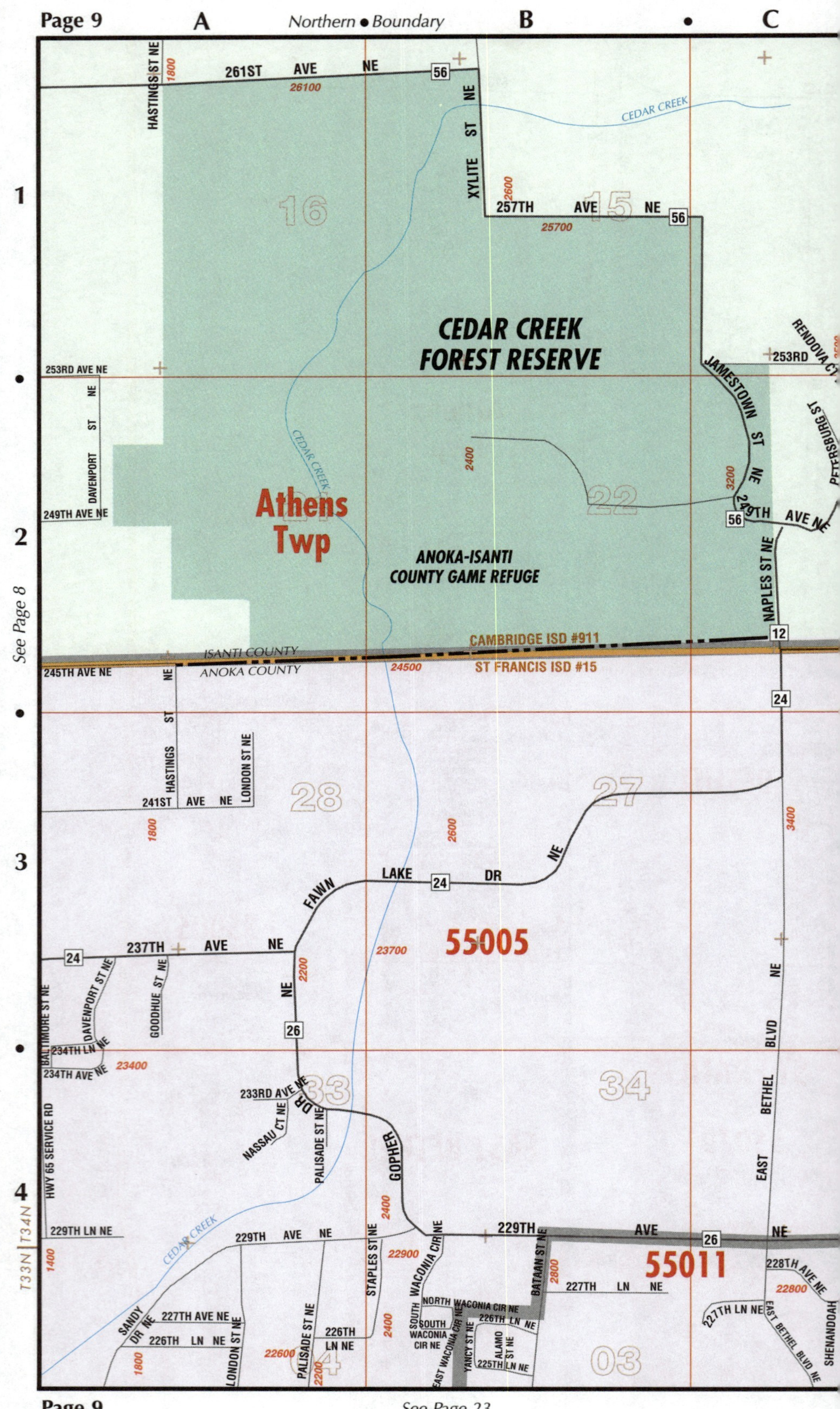

A
Northern Boundary
B
C
1
2
3
4
See Page 8
T33N T34N
261ST AVE NE
26100
HASTINGS ST NE
1800
XYLITE ST NE
CEDAR CREEK
257TH AVE NE
25700
2600
16
15
CEDAR CREEK FOREST RESERVE
253RD AVE NE
DAVENPORT ST NE
249TH AVE NE
253RD
RENDOVA CT
PETERSBURG ST
JAMESTOWN ST NE
3200
249TH AVE NE
22
2400
Athens Twp
ANOKA-ISANTI COUNTY GAME REFUGE
NAPLES ST NE
ISANTI COUNTY
ANOKA COUNTY
CAMBRIDGE ISD #911
ST FRANCIS ISD #15
24500
245TH AVE NE
HASTINGS ST NE
LONDON ST NE
241ST AVE NE
28
27
1800
2600
3400
FAWN LAKE DR NE
237TH AVE NE
23700
55005
2200
DAVENPORT ST NE
GOODHUE ST NE
BALTIMORE ST NE
234TH LN NE
234TH AVE NE
23400
233RD AVE NE
DR
33
34
NASSAU CT NE
PALISADE ST NE
GOPHER
HWY 65 SERVICE RD
EAST BETHEL BLVD NE
229TH LN NE
229TH AVE NE
2400
STAPLES ST NE
22900
WACONIA CIR NE
229TH AVE NE
BATAAN ST NE
2800
55011
228TH AVE NE
22800
227TH LN NE
227TH LN NE
CEDAR CREEK
1400
SANDY DR NE
227TH AVE NE
226TH LN NE
LONDON ST NE
1800
22600
PALISADE ST NE
2200
226TH LN NE
2400
NORTH WACONIA CIR NE
SOUTH WACONIA CIR NE
226TH LN NE
ALAMO ST NE
225TH LN NE
YANCY ST NE
EAST WACONIA CIR NE
03
EAST BETHEL BLVD NE
SHENANDOAH
56
12
24
26

See Page 23

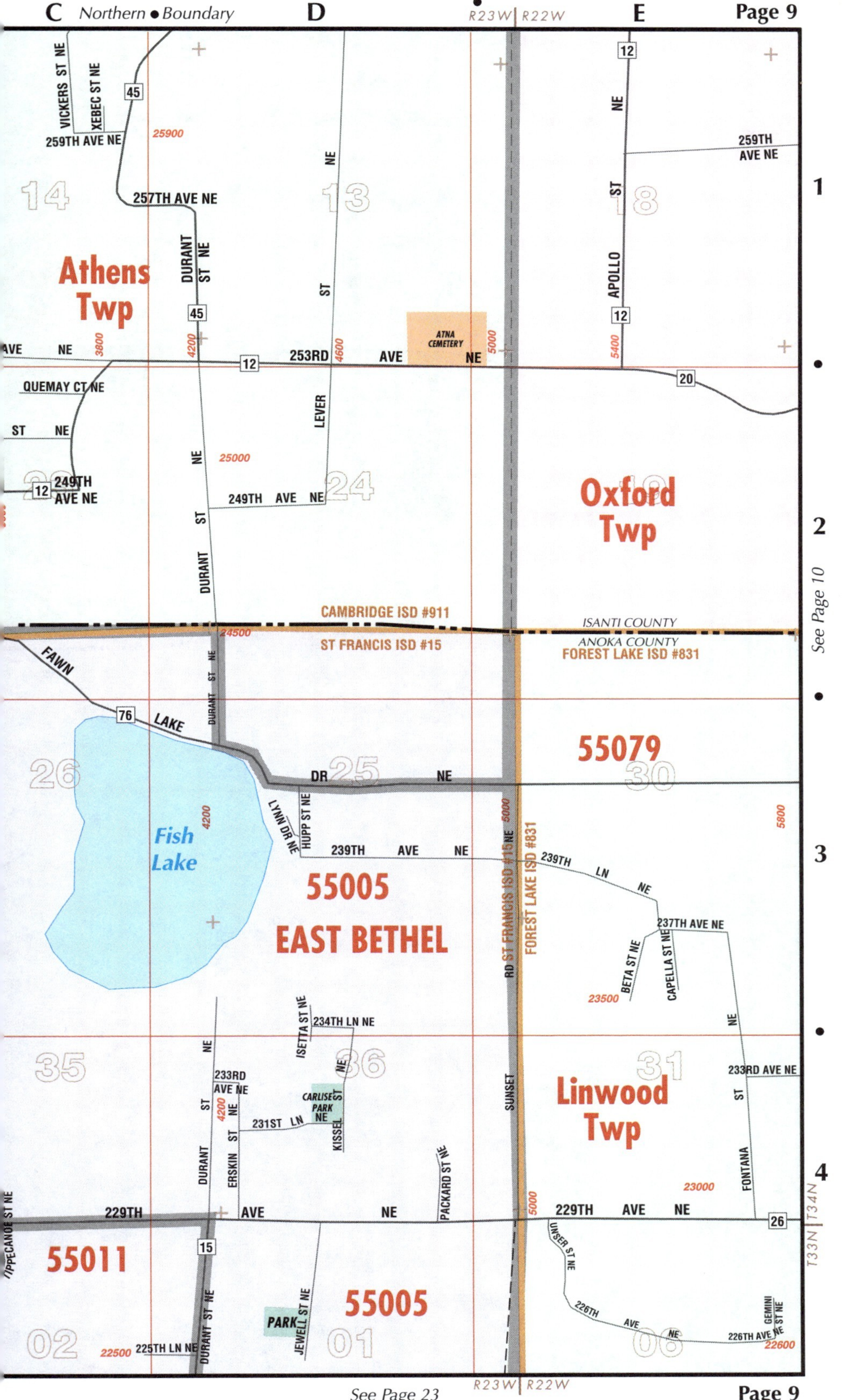

VICKERS ST NE
XEBEC ST NE
259TH AVE NE
25900
[45]

[12]
NE
ST

14

257TH AVE NE

DURANT ST NE

13

NE
ST

18
ST
NE
APOLLO

259TH
AVE NE

1

Athens
Twp

[45]

4200

4600

5000

[12]

5400

[12] 253RD AVE NE
3800

ATNA CEMETERY

[20]

QUEMAY CT NE

LEVER

ST NE

25000

NE

ST NE

Oxford
Twp

[12] 249TH
AVE NE

249TH AVE NE

DURANT ST

24

2

See Page 10

FAWN

CAMBRIDGE ISD #911

24500

ST FRANCIS ISD #15

ISANTI COUNTY
ANOKA COUNTY
FOREST LAKE ISD #831

DURANT ST NE

[76] LAKE

26

*Fish
Lake*

4200

DR **25** NE

LYNN DR NE
HUPP ST NE

239TH AVE NE

RD ST FRANCIS ISD #15 NE

6000

FOREST LAKE ISD #831

55079

30

5800

3

55005

EAST BETHEL

239TH LN NE
237TH AVE NE

BETA ST NE
CAPELLA ST NE

23500

NE

ISETTA ST NE
234TH LN NE

NE

35

ST NE

233RD
AVE NE
4200
231ST LN

**CARLISE
PARK
NE**

KISSEL

36

DURANT ST

ERSKIN ST NE

PACKARD ST NE

SUNSET

Linwood
Twp

233RD AVE NE

ST

FONTANA

31

23000

4

TIPPECANOE ST NE

229TH AVE NE

[15]

5000

229TH AVE NE

UNSER ST NE

[26]

T33N | T34N

55011

02

22500

DURANT ST NE

225TH LN NE

JEWELL ST NE

PARK ST NE

55005

01

226TH

AVE

NE

226TH AVE NE

GEMINI ST NE

22600

06

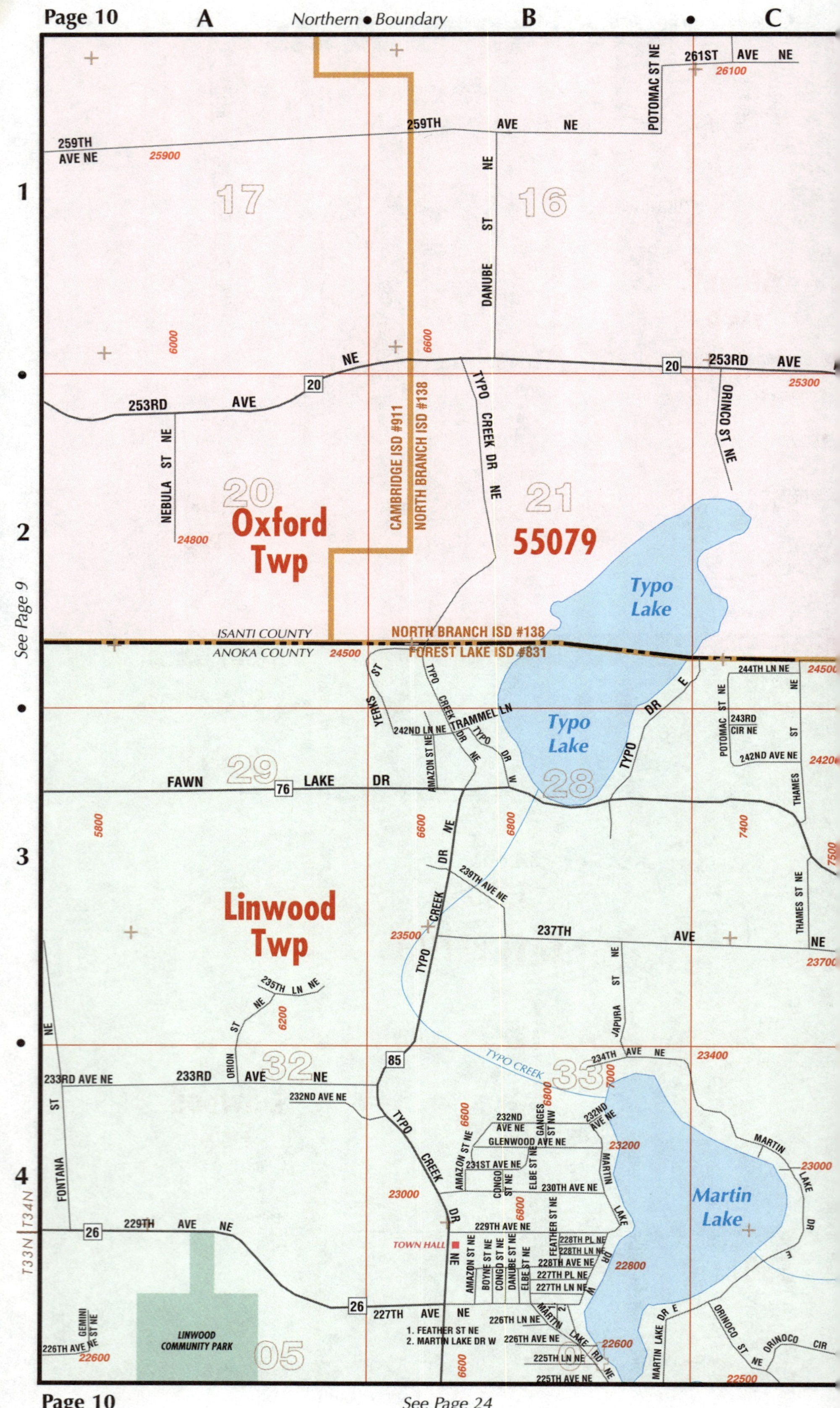

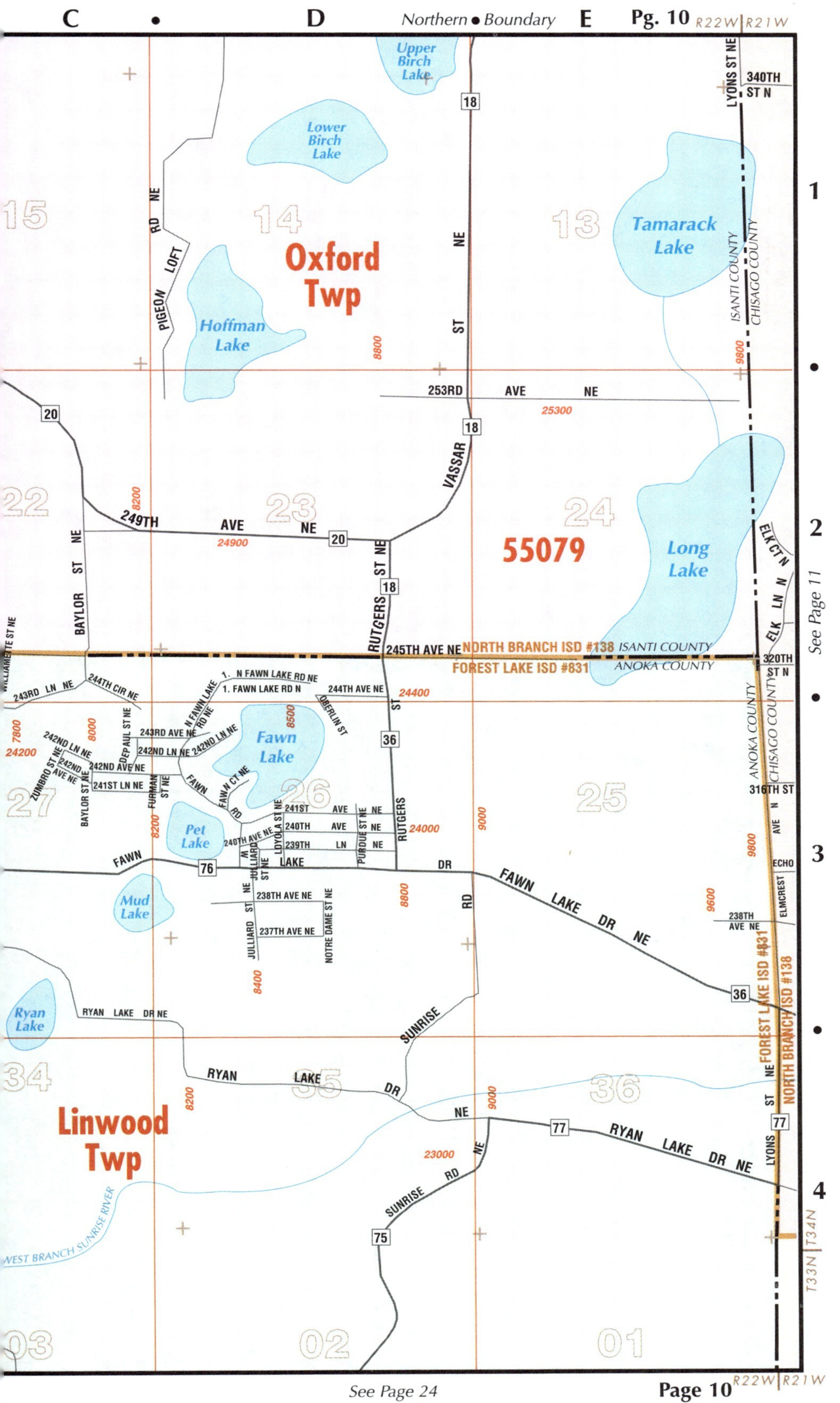

Upper Birch Lake

Lower Birch Lake

18

ST NE

15

14

Oxford Twp

PIGEON LOFT RD NE

Hoffman Lake

8800

13

Tamarack Lake

LYONS ST NE

340TH ST N

ISANTI COUNTY / CHISAGO COUNTY

9800

1

253RD AVE NE
25300

20

18

VASSAR ST NE

22

8200

249TH AVE NE
24900

BAYLOR ST NE

23

20

RUTGERS ST NE

18

24

55079

Long Lake

ELK CT N

ELK LN NE

2

See Page 11

245TH AVE NE

NORTH BRANCH ISD #138 ISANTI COUNTY
FOREST LAKE ISD #831 ANOKA COUNTY

320TH

ANOKA COUNTY / CHISAGO COUNTY

WILLAMETTE ST NE

243RD LN NE

244TH CIR NE

1. N FAWN LAKE RD NE
1. FAWN LAKE RD N

N FAWN LAKE RD NE

244TH AVE NE

AMERLIN ST

ST NE

24400

7800
8000

242ND LN NE
24200

242ND ST NE
242ND AVE NE

DEPAUL ST NE

243RD AVE NE
242ND LN NE 242ND LN NE

Fawn Lake

8500

36

316TH ST

AVE NE

27

ZUMBRO ST NE
BAYLOR ST NE
241ST LN NE

241ST AVE NE

FURMAN ST NE

FAWN CT NE

FAWN RD

26

241ST AVE NE
240TH AVE NE
239TH LN NE

PURDUE ST NE

RUTGERS

9000

25

9800

ECHO

8200

Pet Lake

240TH AVE NE

LOYOLA ST NE

24000

238TH AVE NE

3

FAWN

76

Lake

DR

FAWN LAKE DR NE

238TH AVE NE

ELMCREST

FOREST LAKE ISD #831

NORTH BRANCH ISD #138

9600

Mud Lake

JULIARD ST NE

238TH AVE NE

237TH AVE NE

NOTRE DAME ST NE

8800

SUNRISE RD

36

8400

Ryan Lake

RYAN LAKE DR NE

34

Linwood Twp

8200

RYAN LAKE DR NE

35

SUNRISE

NE

9000

36

RYAN LAKE DR NE

LYONS ST NE

77

4

23000

77

SUNRISE RD

75

T33N | T34N

03

02

01

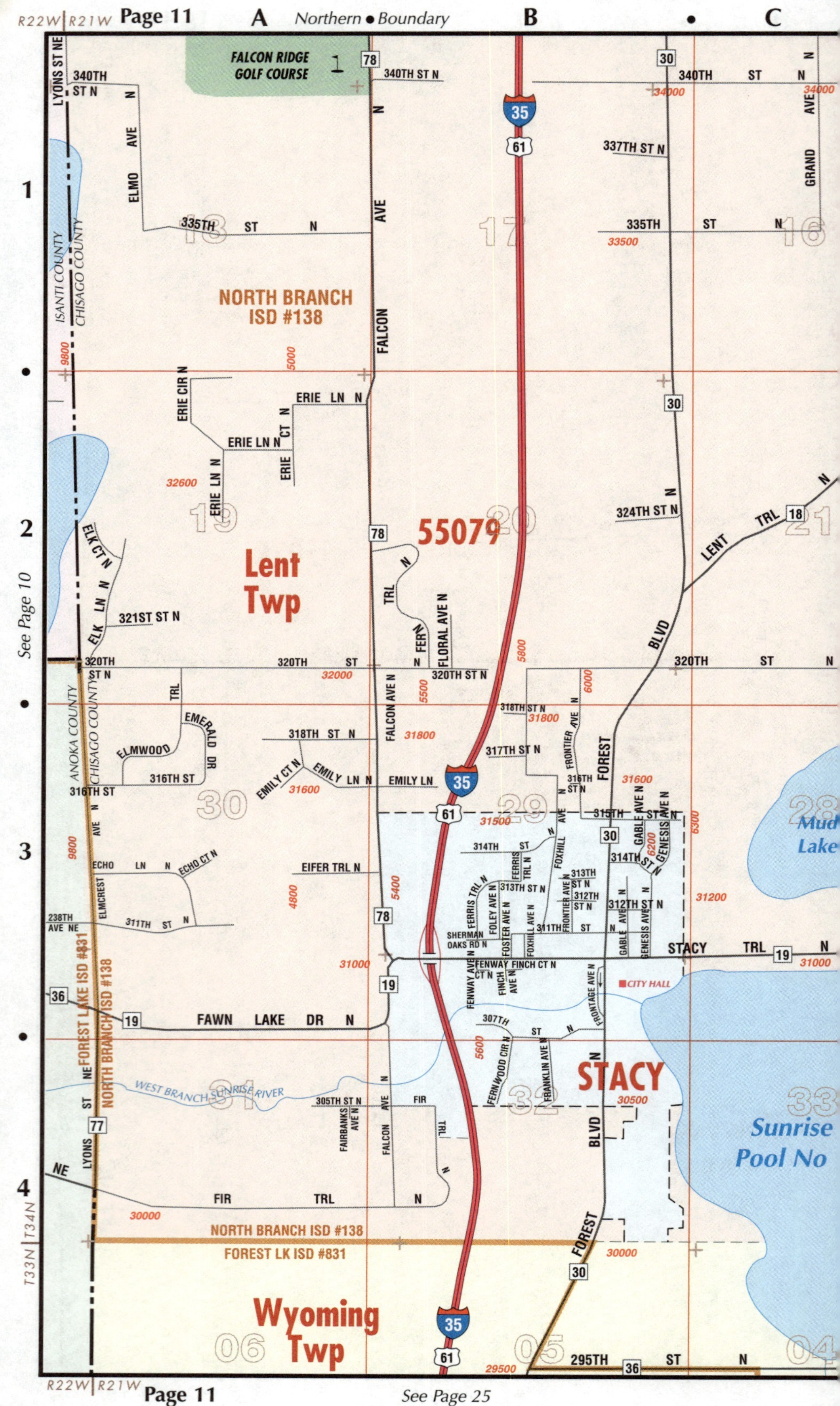

R22W R21W
Page 11
A
Northern • Boundary
B
C
1
2
3
4
See Page 10
FALCON RIDGE
GOLF COURSE
LYONS ST NE
340TH ST N
340TH ST N
340TH ST N
ELMO AVE N
335TH ST N
335TH ST N
337TH ST N
GRAND AVE N
34000
33500
ISANTI COUNTY
CHISAGO COUNTY
NORTH BRANCH
ISD #138
FALCON AVE N
ERIE CIR N
ERIE LN N
ERIE LN N
ERIE CT N
ERIE LN N
32600
9800
5000
55079
Lent
Twp
ELK CT N
ELK LN N
321ST ST N
324TH ST N
LENT TRL
FOREST BLVD
320TH ST N
320TH ST N
320TH ST N
32000
FLORAL AVE N
FERN TRL N
ANOKA COUNTY
CHISAGO COUNTY
EMERALD DR
ELMWOOD TRL
316TH ST
316TH ST
318TH ST N
EMILY CT N
EMILY LN N
EMILY LN
31800
31600
5500
5800
6000
318TH ST N
317TH ST N
FRONTIER AVE N
316TH ST N
315TH ST N
GABLE AVE N
GENESIS AVE N
31500
6300
6200
Mud
Lake
314TH ST
314TH ST N
FOXHILL AVE N
FERRIS TRL N
313TH ST N
312TH ST N
312TH ST N
311TH ST
31200
ECHO LN N
ECHO CT N
ELMCREST AVE N
EIFER TRL N
4800
5400
238TH AVE NE
311TH ST N
SHERMAN OAKS RD N
FENWAY AVE N
FENWAY FINCH CT N
FINCH AVE N
FOSTER AVE N
FOLEY AVE N
FRONTAGE AVE N
STACY TRL N
31000
31000
CITY HALL
FAWN LAKE DR N
FOREST LAKE ISD #831
NORTH BRANCH ISD #138
307TH ST N
5600
FERNWOOD CIR N
FRANKLIN AVE N
STACY
30500
WEST BRANCH SUNRISE RIVER
305TH ST N
FAIRBANKS AVE N
FALCON AVE N
FIR TRL N
LYONS ST NE
FIR TRL N
Sunrise
Pool No
30000
NORTH BRANCH ISD #138
FOREST LK ISD #831
30000
T34N
T33N
Wyoming
Twp
295TH ST N
29500
R22W R21W
Page 11
See Page 25

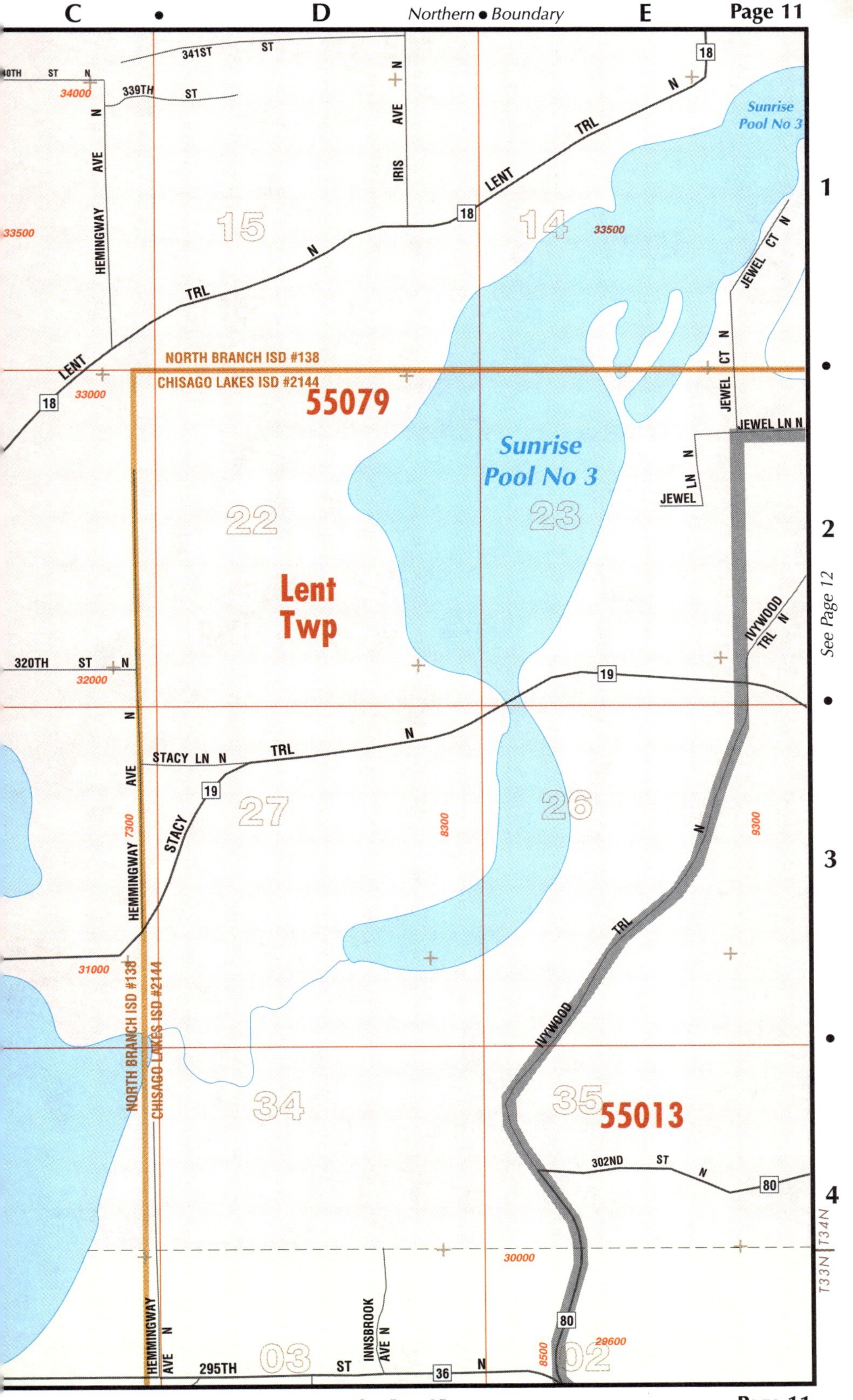

NORTH ST N
34000
341ST ST
339TH ST
Sunrise
Pool No 3
18

HEMINGWAY AVE
IRIS AVE
LENT TRL
N
N
33500
15
33500
14
TRL N
JEWEL CT N
LENT
18

1

NORTH BRANCH ISD #138
CHISAGO LAKES ISD #2144
55079
JEWEL CT N
JEWEL LN N
18 33000

22
**Sunrise
Pool No 3**
23
JEWEL LN N
JEWEL

**Lent
Twp**
IVYWOOD TRL N
See Page 12

2

320TH ST N
32000
N
19

HEMINGWAY 7900 AVE
STACY LN N
STACY
TRL
N
27
8300
26
9300
19

31000
NORTH BRANCH ISD #138
CHISAGO LAKES ISD #2144
IVYWOOD TRL N

3

34
35
55013
IVYWOOD TRL

302ND ST N
80

4

30000
T33N T34N

HEMINGWAY AVE N
295TH ST
03
INNSBROOK AVE N
36 N
8500
80
29600
02

See Page 25

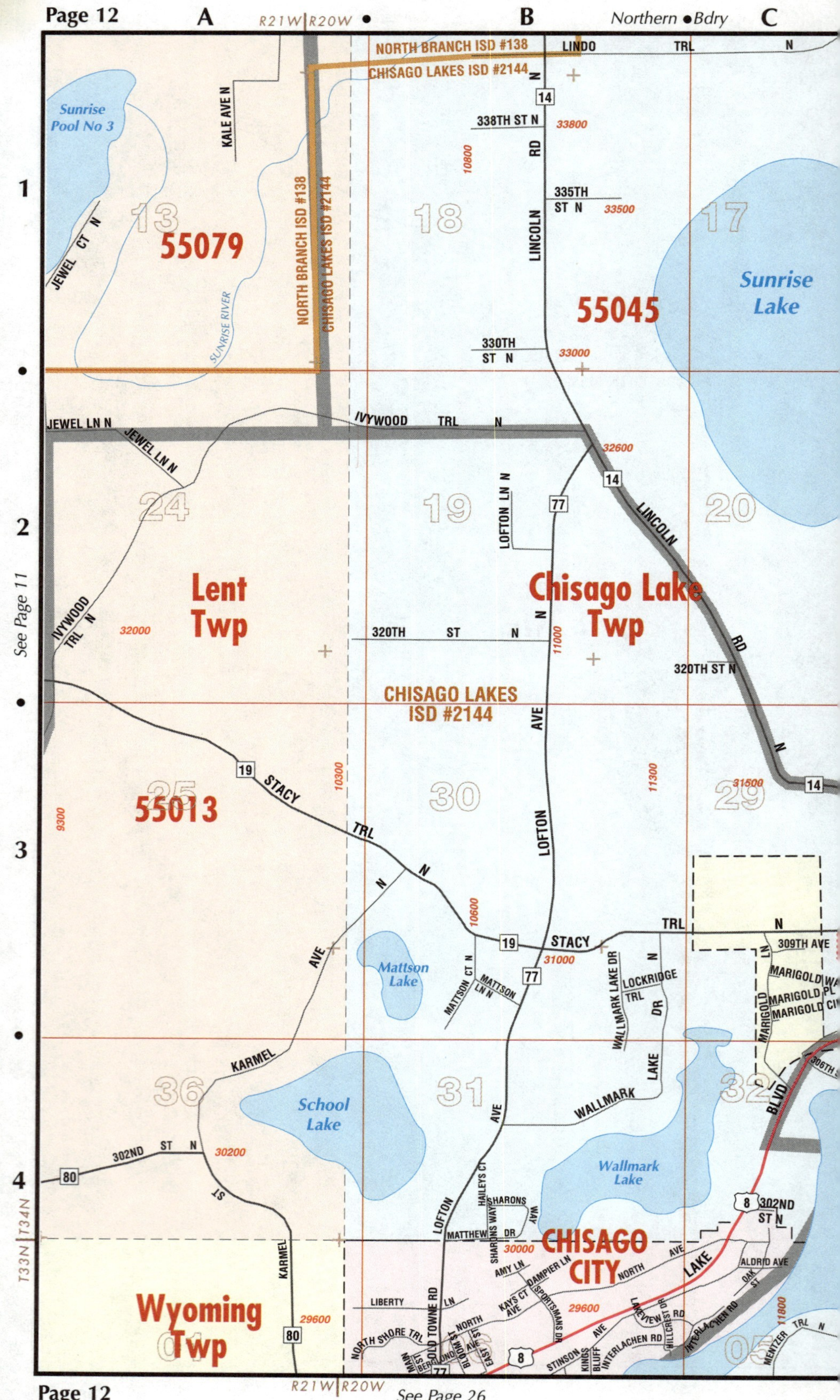

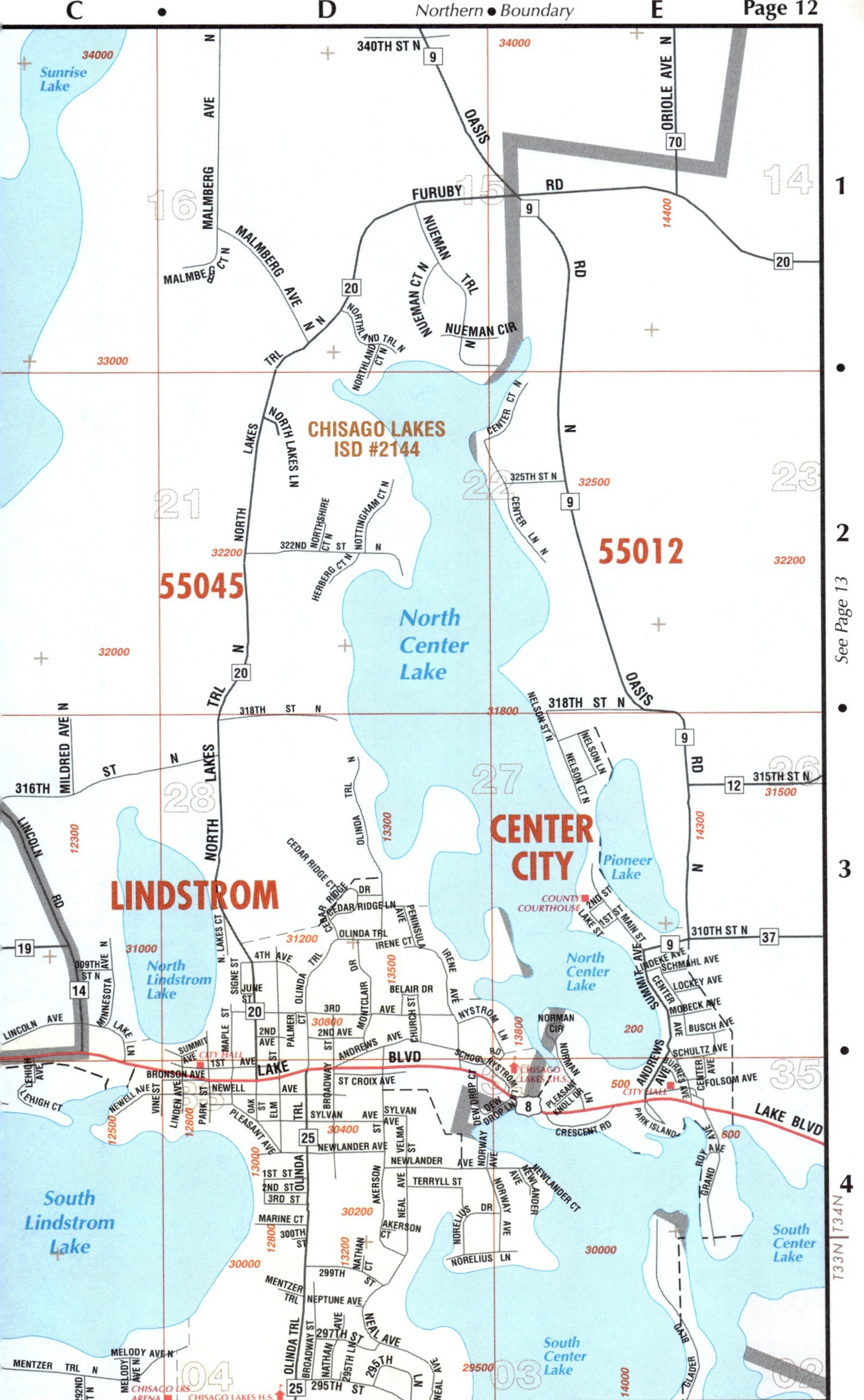

34000

Sunrise Lake

340TH ST N 9

34000

ORIOLE AVE N

70

16

MALMBERG AVE

MALMBERG CT N

MALMBERG AVE N

MALMBE AVE N

FURUBY **15** RD

9

OASIS

14

14400

20

1

33000

NORTHLAND TRL N

NORTHLAND CT N

NUEMAN CT N

NUEMAN TRL

NUEMAN CIR

20

LAKES TRL

NORTH LAKES LN

RD

RD

N

CHISAGO LAKES ISD #2144

CENTER CT N

325TH ST N

22

32500

23

32200

21

NORTH TRL N

322ND

NORTHSHIRE CT N

NOTTINGHAM CT N

HERBERG CT N

32200

CENTER LN N

9

55012

32200

55045

North Center Lake

2

32000

20

See Page 13

318TH ST N

31800

NELSON ST N

NELSON LN N

NELSON CT N

318TH ST N

OASIS

9

RD

27

316TH ST N

MILDRED AVE N

28

NORTH LAKES TRL N

OLINDA TRL N

13300

12

315TH ST N 31500

26

12300

N. LAKES CT N

CEDAR RIDGE CT N

CEDAR RIDGE DR

PENINSULA LN

Pioneer Lake

County Courthouse

2ND ST

1ST ST

MAIN ST

310TH ST N

37

3

LINCOLN RD

19

309TH ST N

14

31000

North Lindstrom Lake

SIGNE ST

4TH AVE

JUNE ST

20

PALMER ST

MAPLE ST

OLINDA TRL

3RD AVE

MONTCLAIR DR

31200

OLINDA TRL

IRENE CT

BELAIR DR

AVE

13500

IRENE AVE

NYSTROM LN

13800

NORMAN CIR

North Center Lake

200

ADEKE AVE N

SCHMAHL AVE

LOCKEY AVE

MOBECK AVE

BUSCH AVE

14300

ANDREWS AVE N

35

MINNESOTA AVE N

LAKE

SUMMIT AVE

CITY HALL

1ST

BRONSON AVE

NEWELL

PARK AVE

OAK ST

ELM ST

2ND AVE

3RD ST

ANDREWS AVE

CHURCH ST

BLVD

SCHOOL RD

NORMAN LN

CHISAGO LAKES H.S.

8

CITY HALL

500

LAKE BLVD

LINDSTROM

12500

12800

NEWELL AVE

VINE ST

LINDEN AVE

PLEASANT AVE

25

BROADWAY

ST CROIX AVE

SYLVAN AVE

SYLVAN ST

VELMA AVE

DEW DROP LN

DEW DROP LN

PLEASANT KNOLL LN

CRESCENT RD

PARK ISLAND DR

GRAND AVE N

ROY AVE

FOLSOM AVE

500

CENTER CITY

30400

13200

13000

NEWLANDER AVE

1ST ST

2ND ST

OLINDA

3RD ST

MARINE CT

300TH ST

AKERSON AVE

NEAL AVE

TERRYLL ST

NORWAY AVE

NEWLANDER AVE

NEWLANDER CT

NORELIUS DR

NORWAY AVE

30200

30000

South Lindstrom Lake

12800

13200

NATHAN CT N

AKERSON AVE

299TH ST

NORELIUS LN

30000

South Center Lake

4

T33N | T34N

MENTZER TRL

NEPTUNE AVE

297TH ST

BROADWAY ST

NATHAN AVE

295TH ST

NEAL AVE

NEAL AVE

29500

South Center Lake

14000

MENTZER TRL N

MELODY AVE N

MELODY AVE N

292ND ST N

CHISAGO LKS ARENA

OLINDA TRL N

295TH ST

25

CHISAGO LAKES H.S.

04

03

GLADER

OASIS

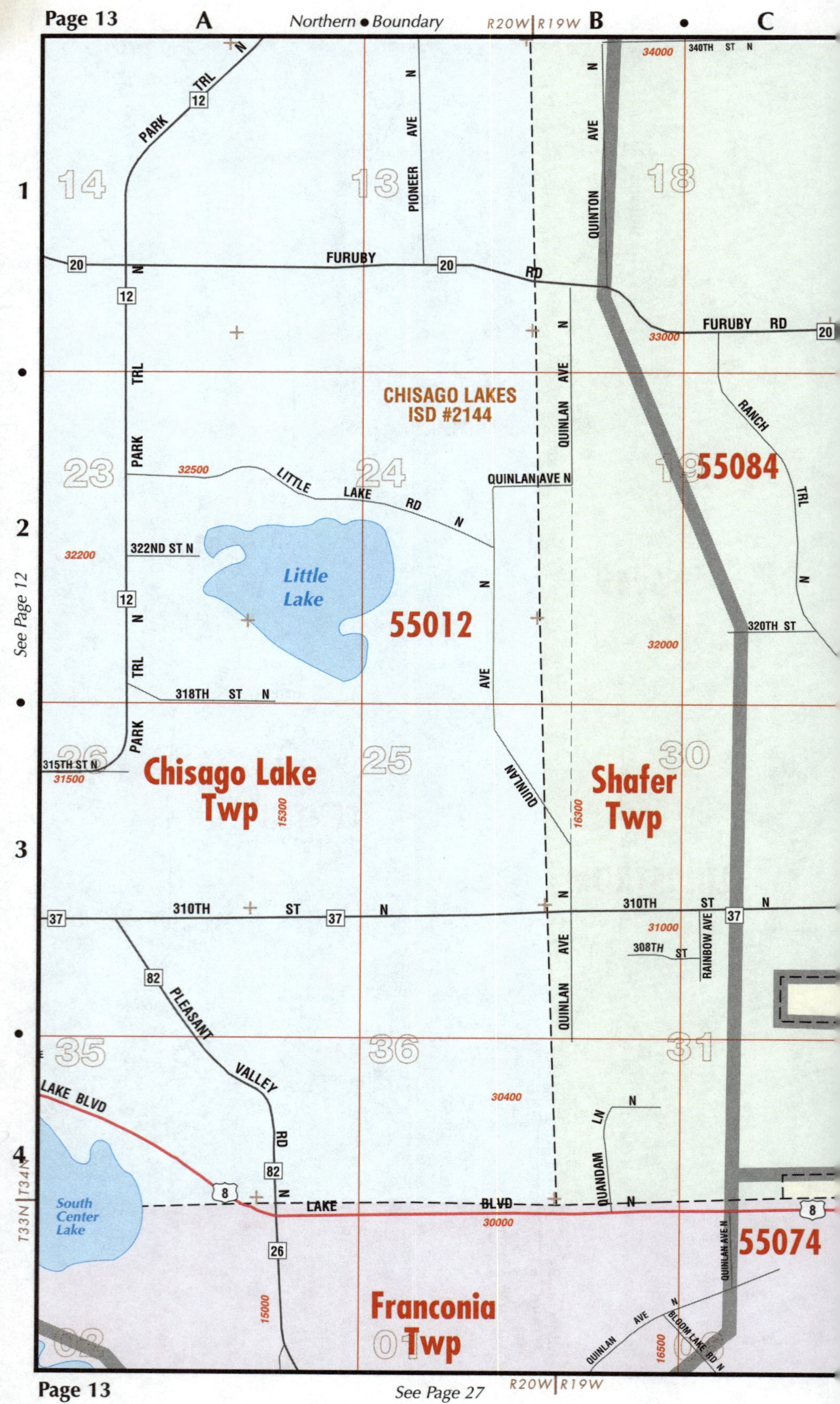

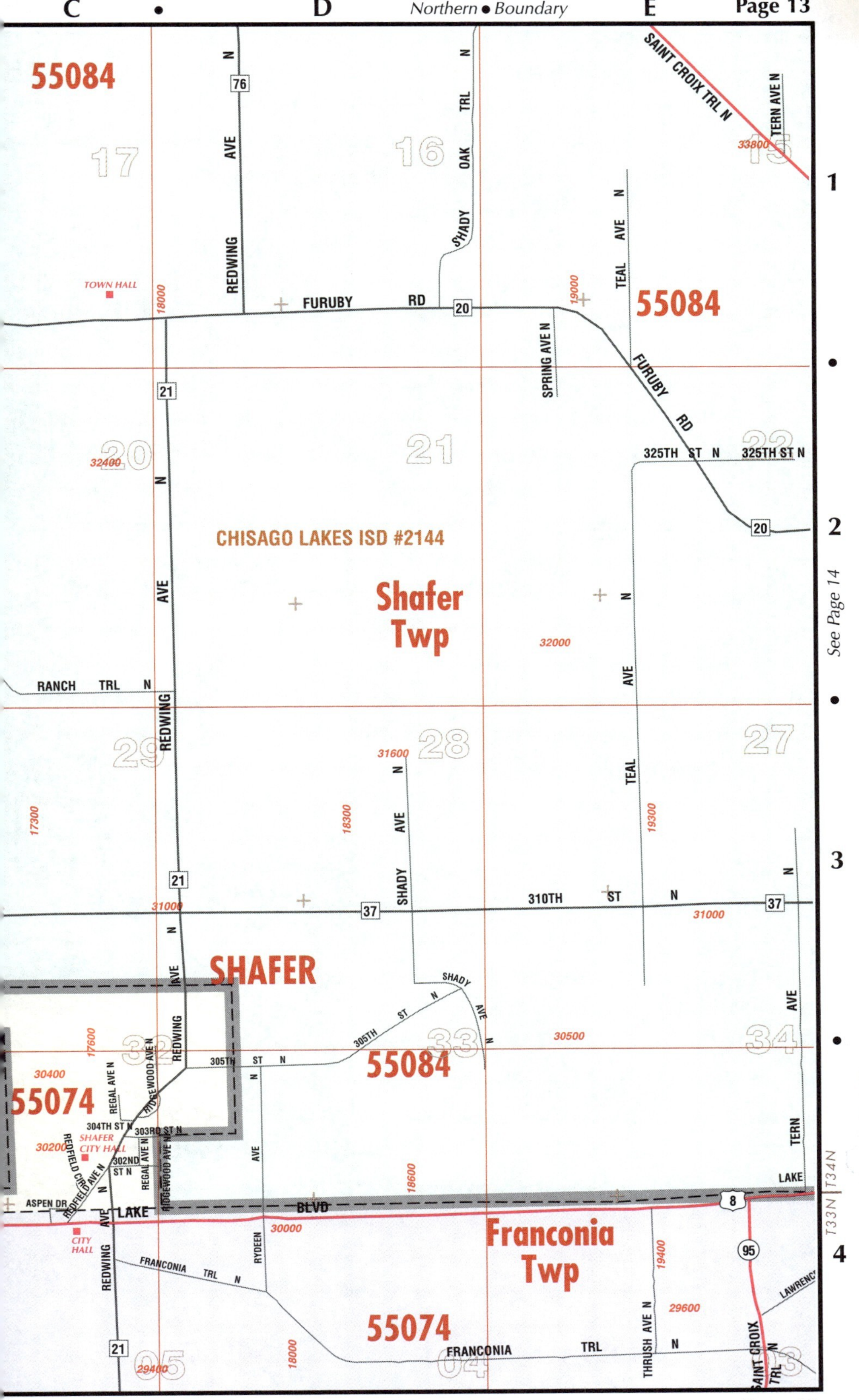

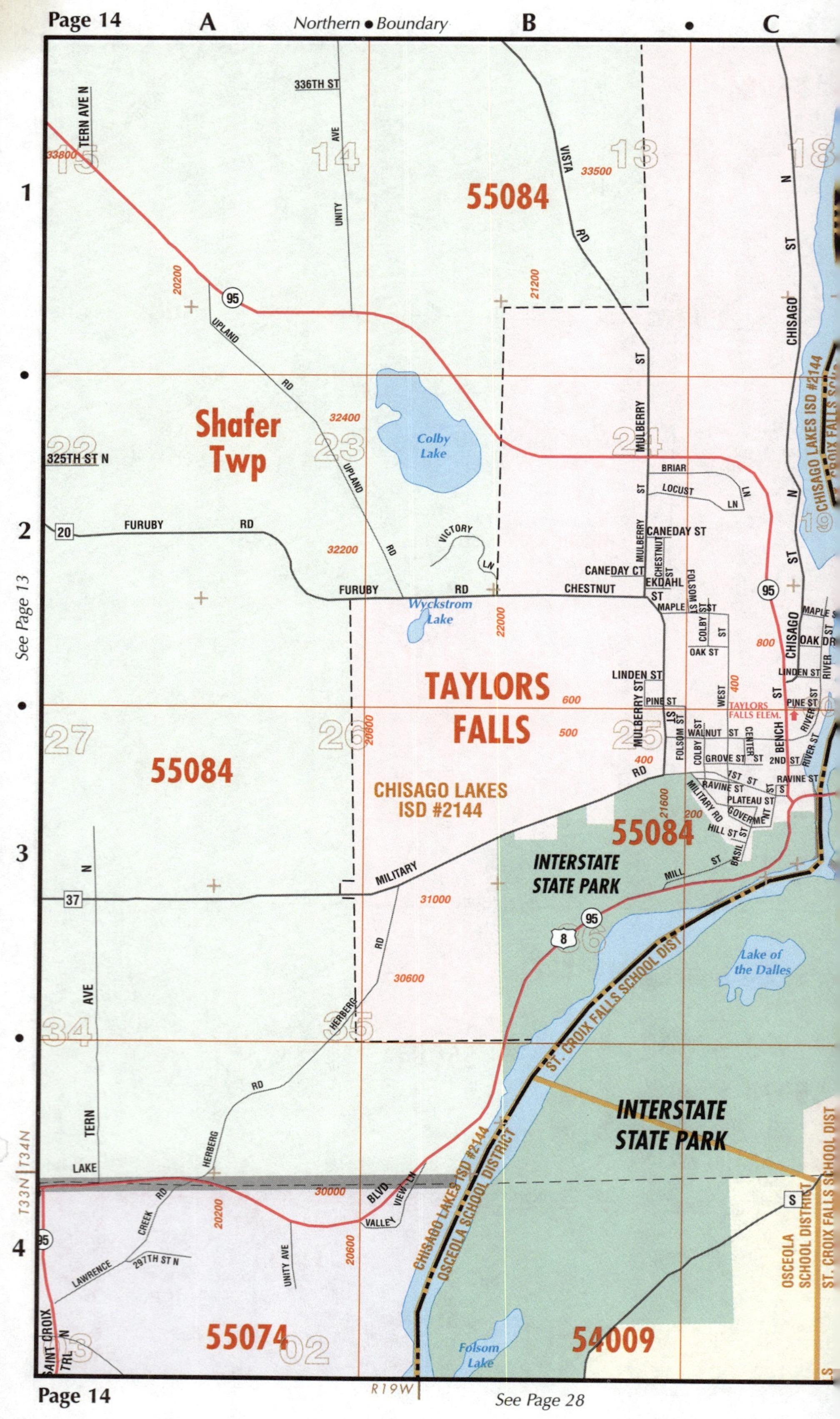

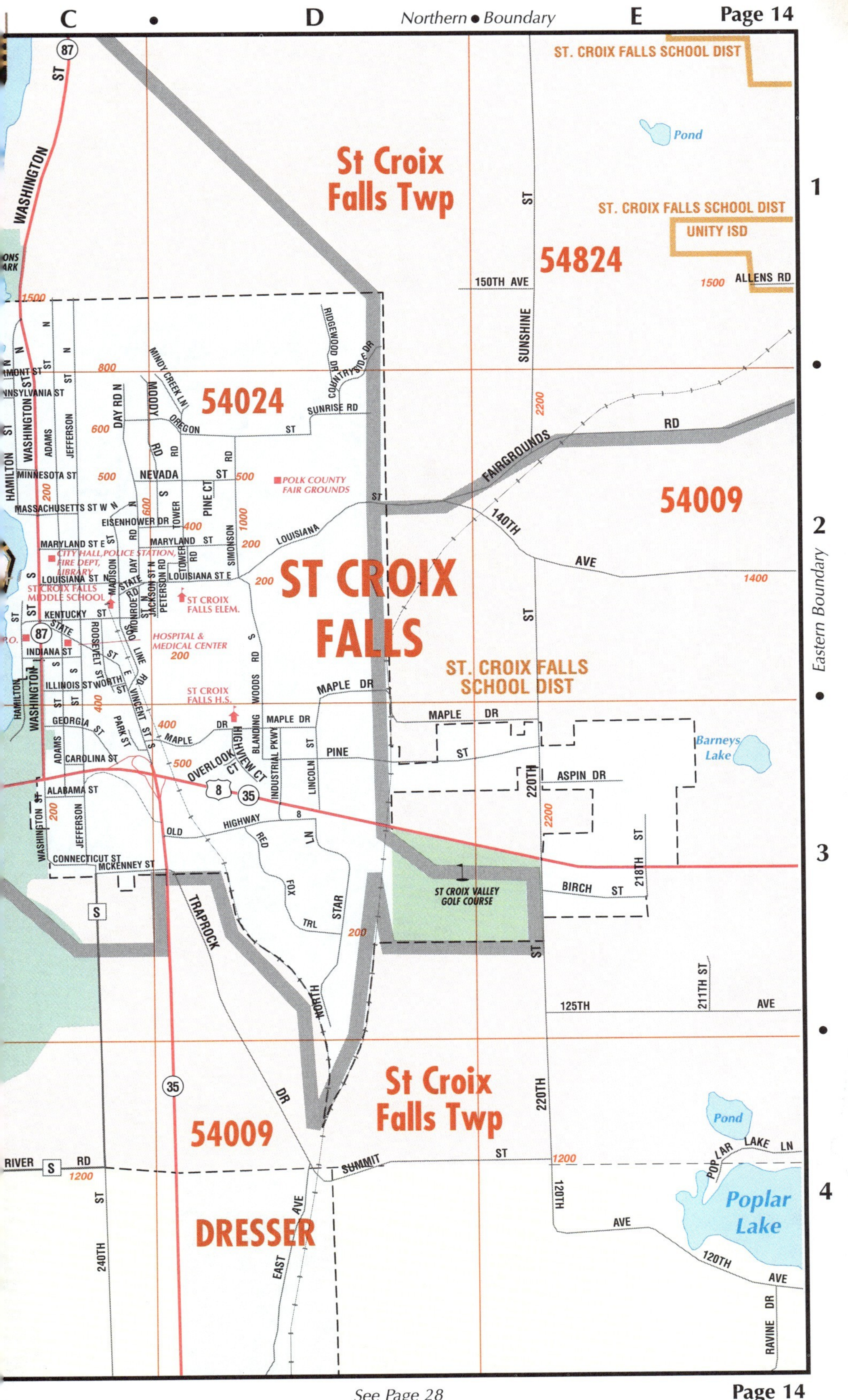

1

2

3

4

St Croix
Falls Twp

ST. CROIX FALLS SCHOOL DIST

Pond

ST. CROIX FALLS SCHOOL DIST

UNITY ISD

54824

1500 ALLENS RD

150TH AVE

Eastern Boundary

54024

SUNRISE RD

NINDY CREEK LN

MOODY RD

OREGON RD

DAY RD N

NEVADA ST

EISENHOWER DR

PINE CT

TOWER

200

500

1000

MADISON ST

LOUISIANA

SIMONSON RD

MARYLAND ST E

LOUISIANA ST E

CITY HALL, POLICE STATION,
FIRE DEPT.
LIBRARY

ST CROIX FALLS
MIDDLE SCHOOL

ST CROIX
FALLS ELEM.

HOSPITAL &
MEDICAL CENTER
200

ST CROIX
FALLS H.S.

MAPLE DR

MAPLE DR

PINE

LINCOLN ST

BLANDING

HIGHVIEW CT

INDUSTRIAL PKWY

OVERLOOK CT

35

8

OLD HIGHWAY

RED

FOX

STAR

TRL

NORTH

TRAPROCK

200

400

500

200

400

MAPLE ST

ASPIN DR

220TH

2200

218TH ST

BIRCH ST

ST CROIX VALLEY
GOLF COURSE

*Barneys
Lake*

ST. CROIX FALLS
SCHOOL DIST

54009

FAIRGROUNDS

140TH

AVE

1400

2200

RD

Polk County
Fair Grounds

RIDGEWOOD DR

COUNTRY RD

SUNSHINE ST

WOODS RD

211TH ST

125TH

AVE

St Croix
Falls Twp

54009

DRESSER

240TH ST

EAST AVE

SUMMIT

220TH

120TH

1200

AVE

Pond

POPLAR LAKE LN

**Poplar
Lake**

120TH AVE

RAVINE DR

RIVER RD

1200

MCKENNEY ST

CONNECTICUT ST

ALABAMA ST

JEFFERSON ST

WASHINGTON ST

200

CAROLINA ST

GEORGIA ST

ADAMS ST

PARK ST

VINCENT ST S

ROOSEVELT ST

MONROE ST

LINE ST

JACKSON ST N

STATE

KENTUCKY ST

INDIANA ST

ILLINOIS ST

WORTH ST

HAMILTON ST

WASHINGTON ST

87

P.O.

MAPLE

OREGON

STATE ST E

PETERSON RD

PINE RD

DAY

**ST CROIX
FALLS**

LOUISIANA ST

KENTUCKY ST

MINNESOTA ST

MASSACHUSETTS ST W

PENNSYLVANIA ST

FREMONT ST

500

600

800

1500

600

400

ADAMS ST

JEFFERSON ST

HAMILTON ST

WASHINGTON ST

87

ST

S

S

35

A ● *See Page 1* B ● C

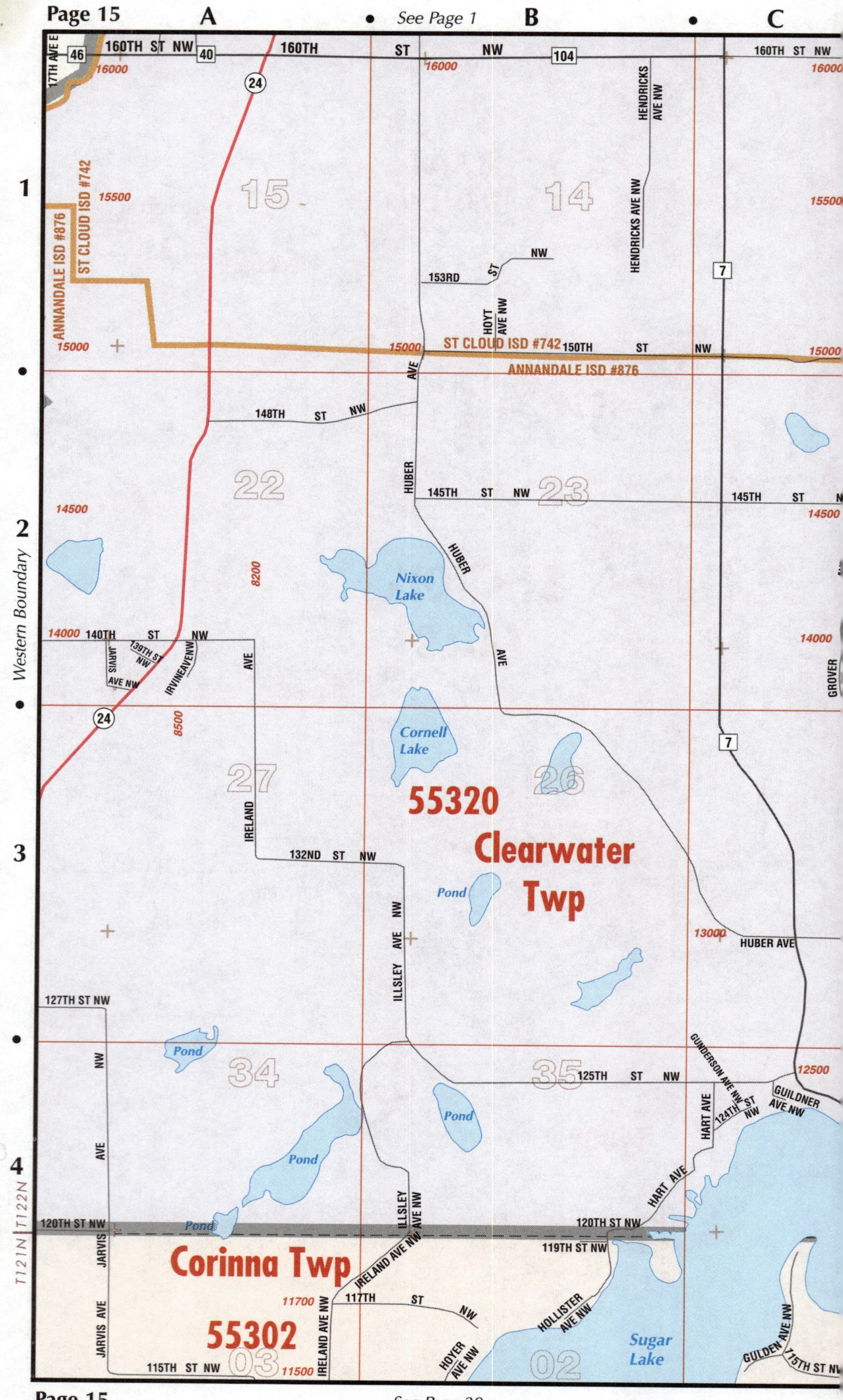

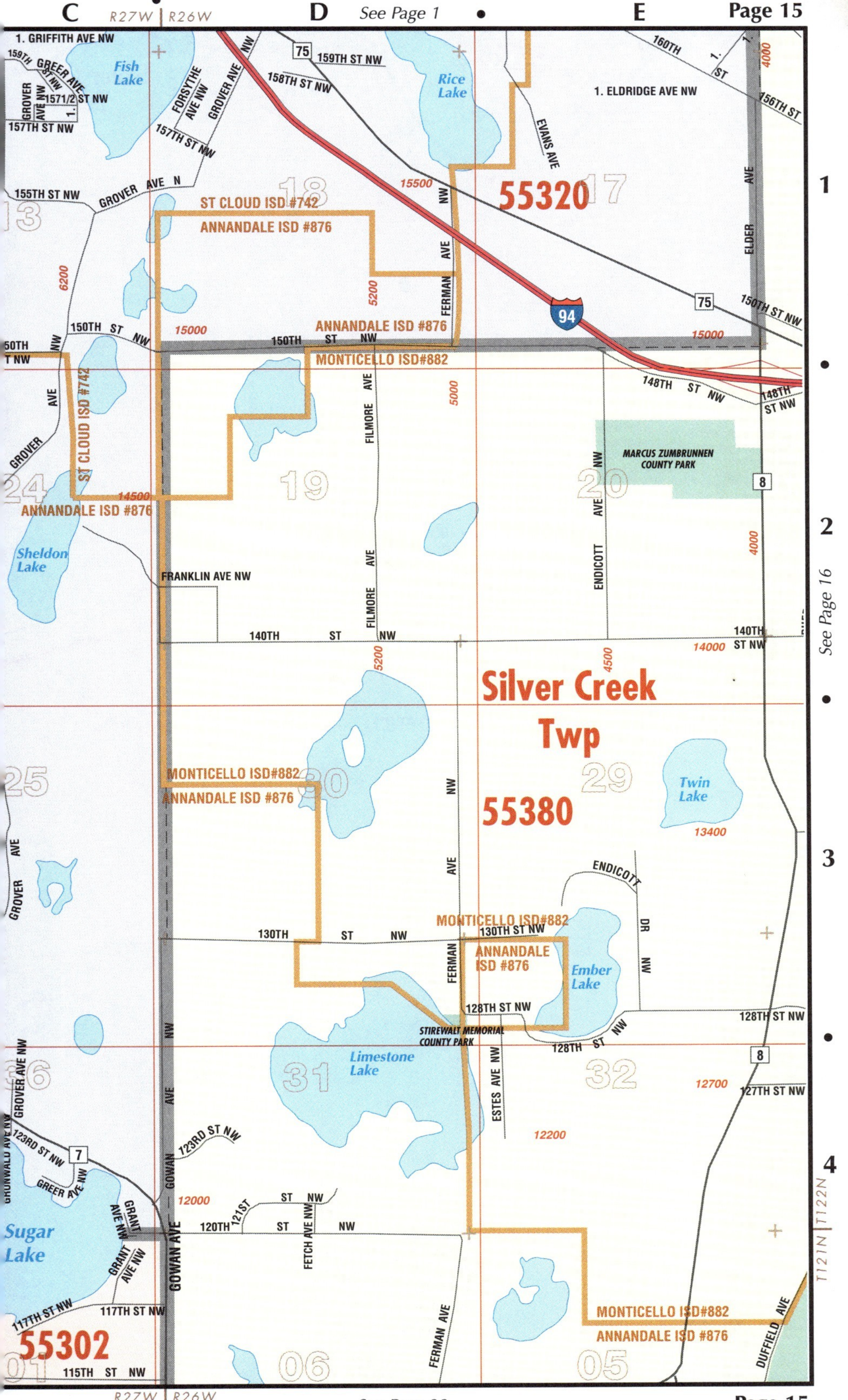
C
D
E
R27W
R26W
See Page 1
1. GRIFFITH AVE NW
Fish Lake
Rice Lake
159TH ST NW
158TH ST NW
157TH ST NW
1571/2 ST NW
GREER AVE
FORSYTHE AVE NW
GROVER AVE NW
160TH
156TH ST
1. ELDRIDGE AVE NW
EVANS AVE
155TH ST NW
GROVER AVE N
15500
55320
ST CLOUD ISD #742
ANNANDALE ISD #876
FERMAN AVE NW
ELDER AVE
6200
5200
150TH ST NW
15000
ANNANDALE ISD #876
MONTICELLO ISD#882
150TH ST NW
148TH ST NW
148TH ST NW
FILMORE AVE
5000
MARCUS ZUMBRUNNEN COUNTY PARK
ENDICOTT AVE NW
GROVER AVE
ST CLOUD ISD #742
14500
ANNANDALE ISD #876
Sheldon Lake
FRANKLIN AVE NW
4000
140TH ST NW
14000
4500
See Page 16
Silver Creek Twp
55380
MONTICELLO ISD#882
ANNANDALE ISD #876
Twin Lake
13400
ENDICOTT DR NW
130TH ST NW
130TH ST NW
MONTICELLO ISD#882
ANNANDALE ISD #876
Ember Lake
128TH ST NW
128TH ST NW
128TH ST NW
STIREWALT MEMORIAL COUNTY PARK
Limestone Lake
ESTES AVE NW
12700
127TH ST NW
12200
GROVER AVE NW
123RD ST NW
123RD ST NW
GREER AVE NW
GRANT AVE NW
GOWAN AVE NW
12000
Sugar Lake
120TH ST NW
121ST ST NW
FETCH AVE NW
117TH ST NW
117TH ST NW
55302
115TH ST NW
FERMAN AVE
MONTICELLO ISD#882
ANNANDALE ISD #876
DUFFIELD AVE
T121N
T122N
1
2
3
4

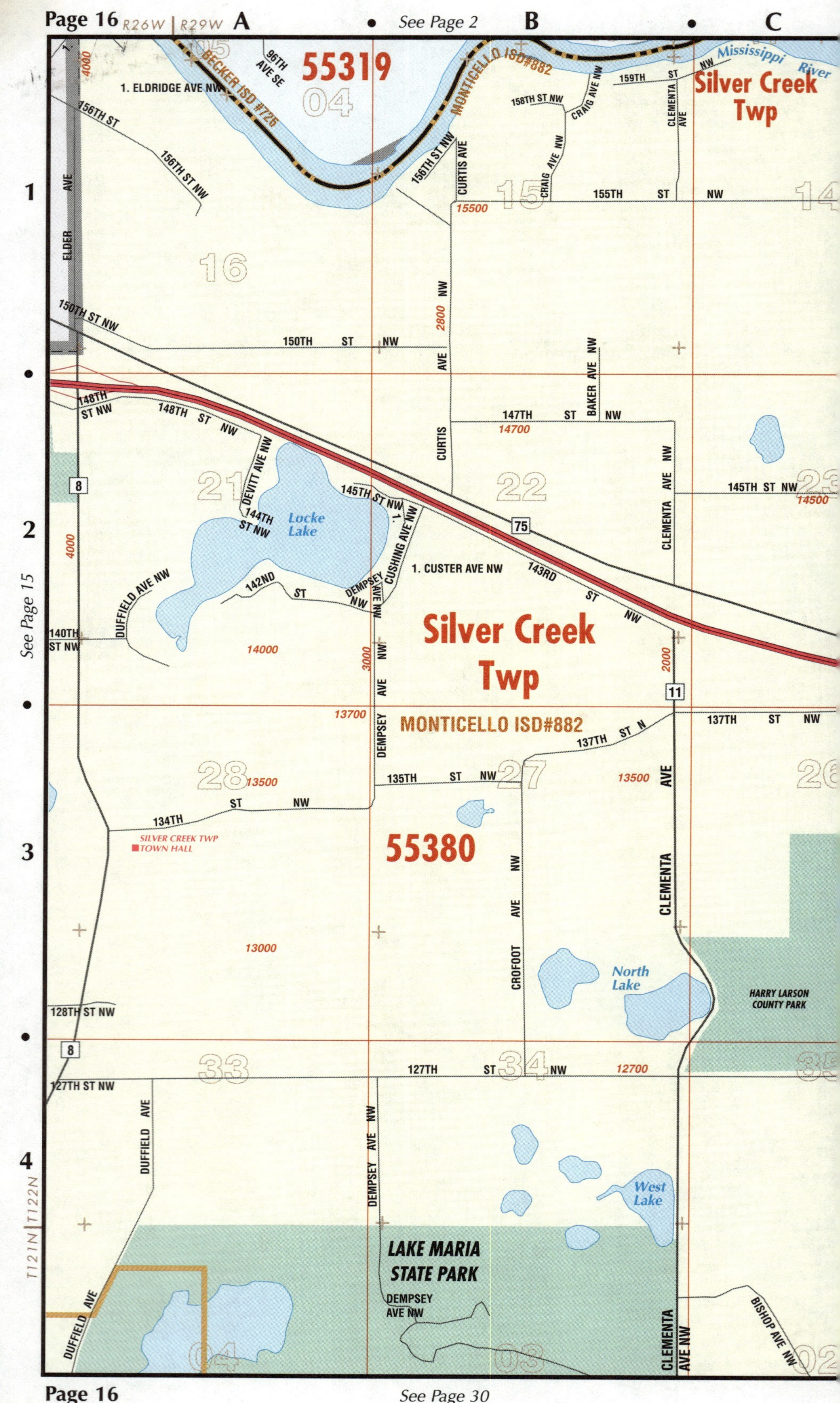

55319

1. ELDRIDGE AVE NW

Silver Creek Twp

Silver Creek Twp

MONTICELLO ISD#882

55380

SILVER CREEK TWP TOWN HALL

Locke Lake

North Lake

HARRY LARSON COUNTY PARK

West Lake

LAKE MARIA STATE PARK

DEMPSEY AVE NW

See Page 15

See Page 30

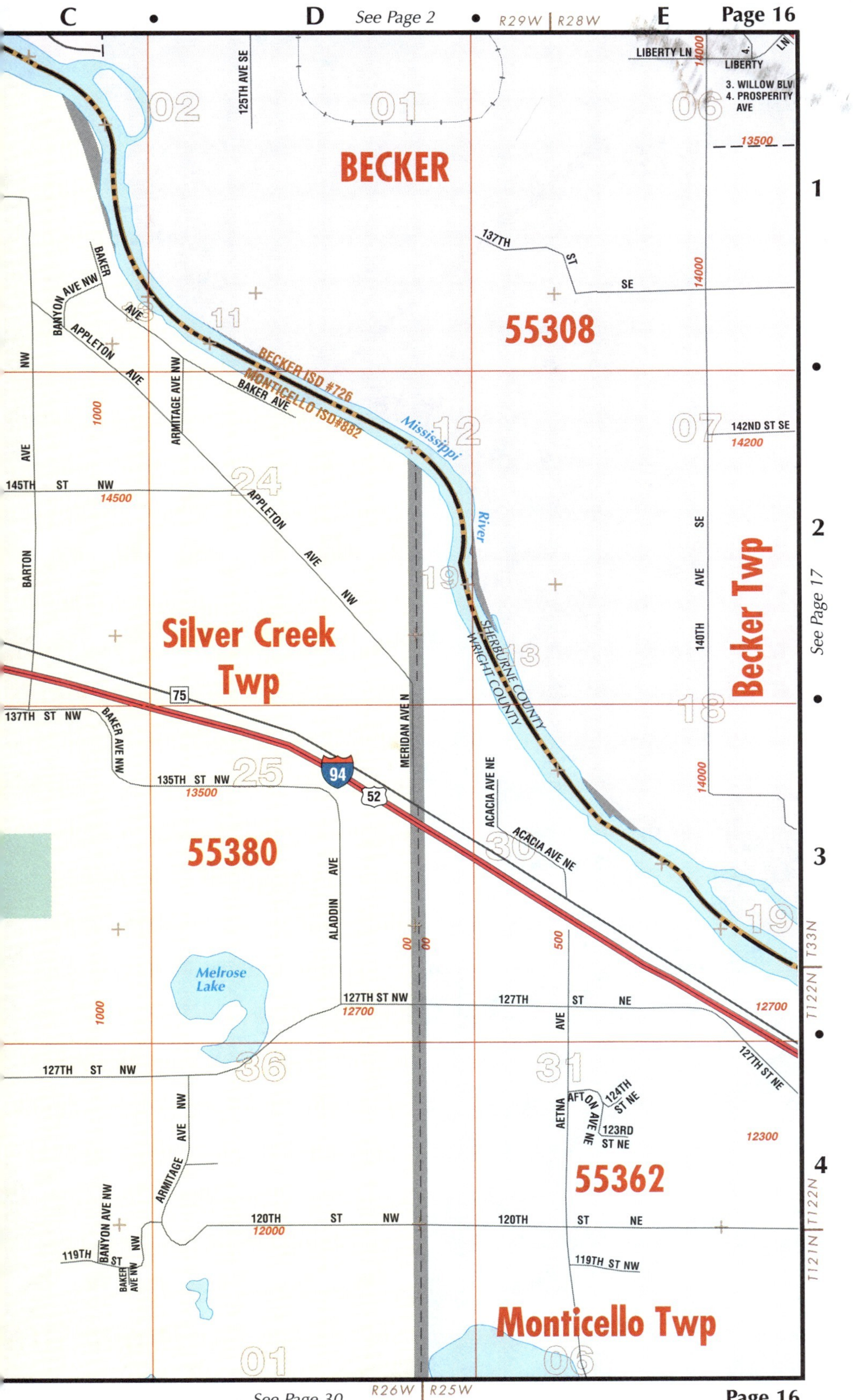

LIBERTY LN
LIBERTY
3. WILLOW BLV
4. PROSPERITY AVE
13500

125TH AVE SE

02

01

BECKER

06

137TH ST SE

14000

55308

BAKER AVE NW

BANYON AVE NW

APPLETON AVE

ARMITAGE AVE NW

11

AVE

NW

BECKER ISD #726
MONTICELLO ISD #882
BAKER AVE

1000

Mississippi

12

07

142ND ST SE
14200

AVE

145TH ST NW
14500

24

APPLETON AVE NW

River

19

13

SHERBURNE COUNTY
WRIGHT COUNTY

SE

140TH AVE SE

Becker Twp

See Page 17

BARTON

2

Silver Creek Twp

75

137TH ST NW

BAKER AVE NW

135TH ST NW
13500

25

94

MERIDAN AVE N

52

ACACIA AVE NE

ACACIA AVE NE

18

14000

19

T33N

3

T122N

55380

ALADDIN AVE

Melrose Lake

00 00

30

500

12700

127TH ST NE

127TH ST NE

4

1000

127TH ST NW
12700

127TH ST NW

127TH ST NE

36

AETNA

AFTON AVE NE

124TH ST NE

123RD ST NE

31

12300

ARMITAGE AVE NW

BANYON AVE NW

119TH ST NW

BAKER AVE NW

120TH ST NW
12000

120TH ST NE

119TH ST NW

55362

01

R26W | R25W

06

Monticello Twp

T121N | T122N

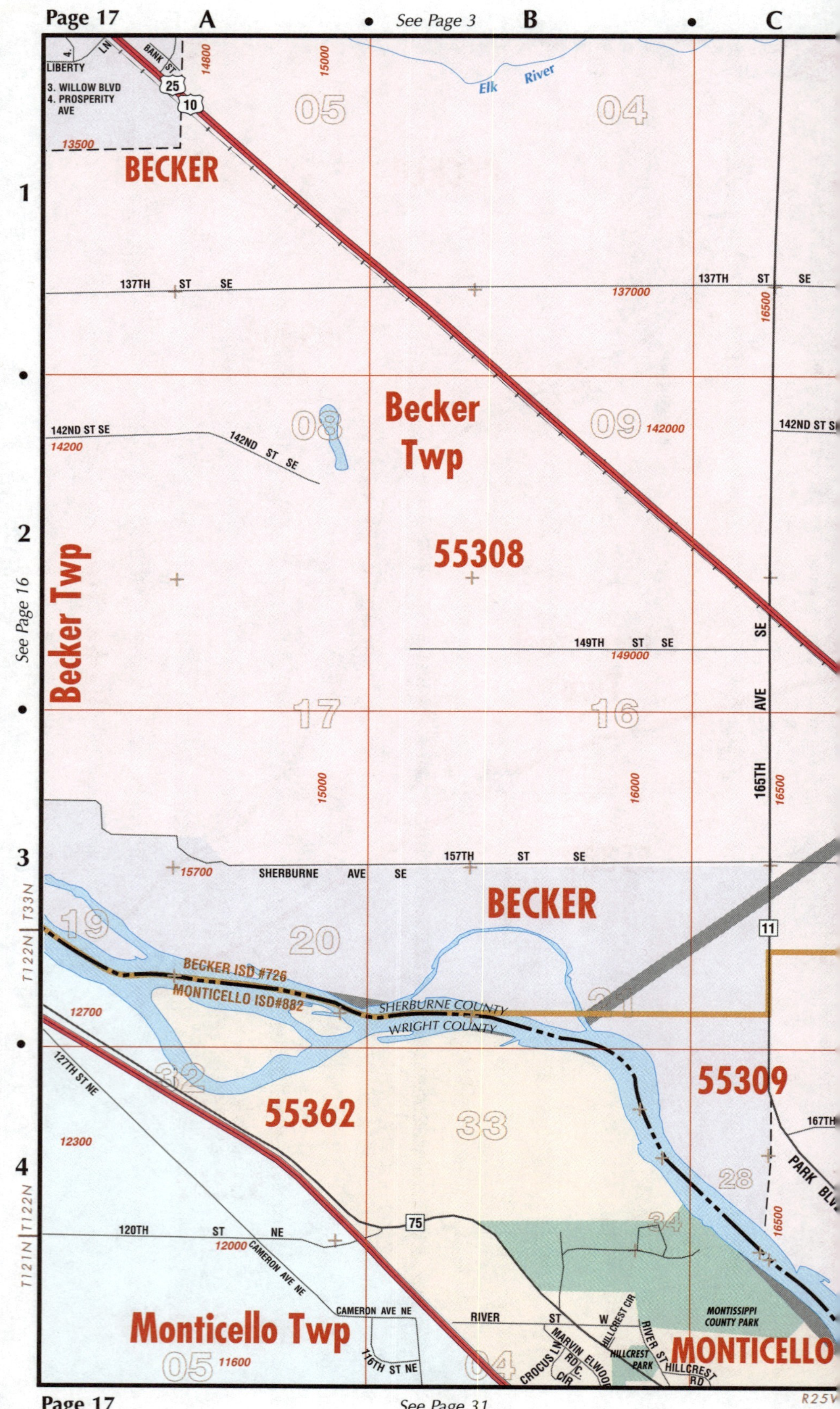

LIBERTY
3. WILLOW BLVD
4. PROSPERITY AVE

14800

15000

Elk River

10 25

13500

BECKER

05

04

1

137TH ST SE

137000

137TH ST SE

16500

142ND ST SE

14200

142ND ST SE

08

Becker Twp

09 142000

142ND ST SE

2

Becker Twp

55308

149TH ST SE

149000

SE

T122N | T33N

17

16

15000

16000

165TH

16500

AVE

3

15700

SHERBURNE AVE SE

157TH ST SE

BECKER

19

20

11

BECKER ISD #726

12700

MONTICELLO ISD#882

SHERBURNE COUNTY

WRIGHT COUNTY

21

55309

127TH ST NE

32

12300

55362

33

167TH

PARK BLV

28

16500

4

T121N | T122N

120TH ST NE

12000

CAMERON AVE NE

75

34

MONTISSIPPI COUNTY PARK

Monticello Twp

05

11600

116TH ST NE

CAMERON AVE NE

RIVER ST W

CROCUS LN

MARVIN ELWOOD RD

HILLCREST CIR

RIVER ST

HILLCREST PARK

HILLCREST RD

MONTICELLO

04

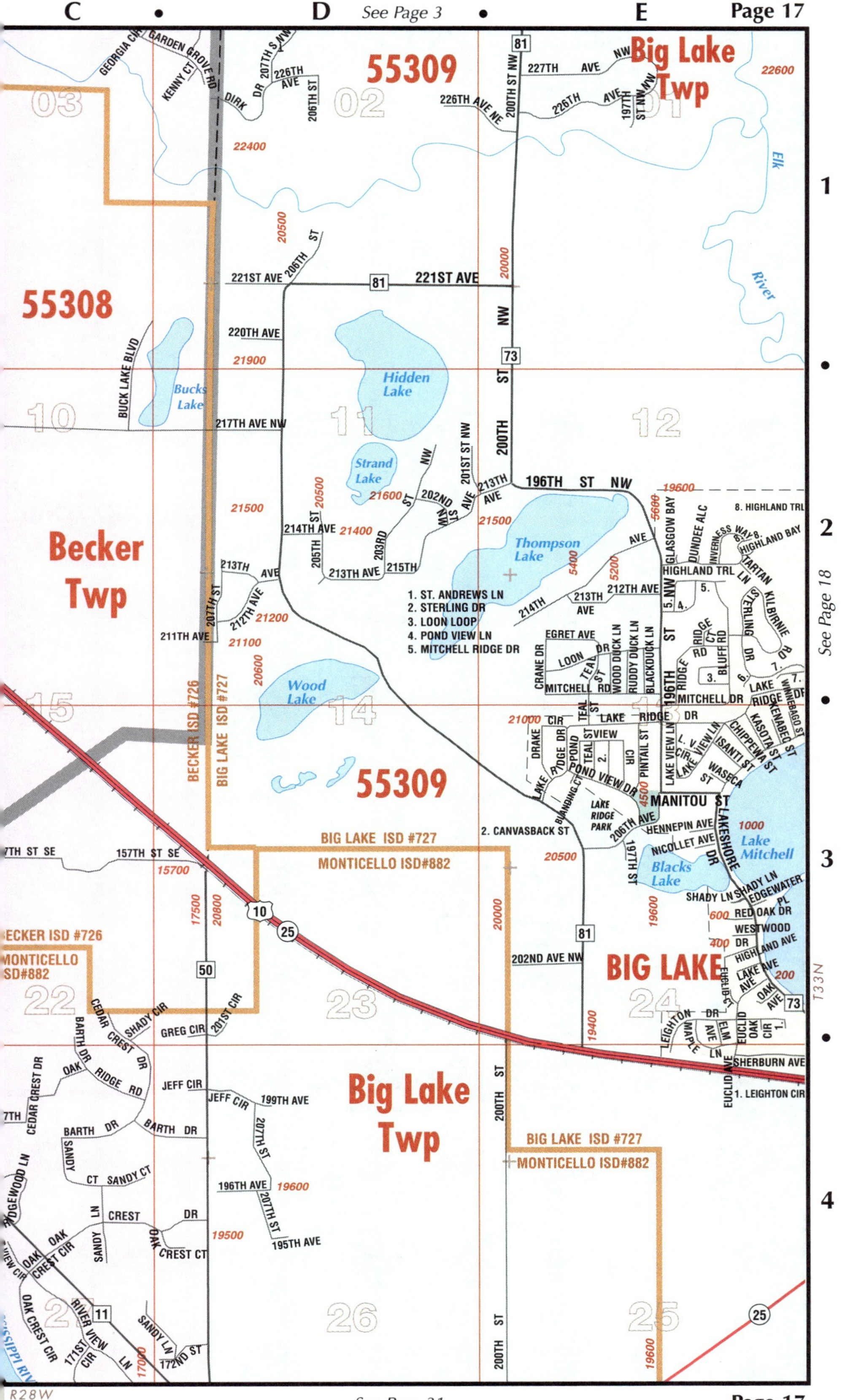
55309
Big Lake Twp
55308
Becker Twp
BIG LAKE
Big Lake Twp
Hidden Lake
Bucks Lake
Strand Lake
Thompson Lake
Wood Lake
Blacks Lake
Lake Mitchell
Elk River
221ST AVE
196TH ST NW
200TH ST NW
217TH AVE NW
220TH AVE
214TH AVE
213TH AVE
211TH AVE
157TH ST SE
202ND AVE NW
MANITOU ST
HENNEPIN AVE
NICOLLET AVE
LAKESHORE DR
SHERBURN AVE
1. ST. ANDREWS LN
2. STERLING DR
3. LOON LOOP
4. POND VIEW LN
5. MITCHELL RIDGE DR
2. CANVASBACK ST
8. HIGHLAND TRL
1. LEIGHTON CIR
BIG LAKE ISD #727
MONTICELLO ISD#882
BECKER ISD #726
1
2
3
4
See Page 18
T33N
R28W

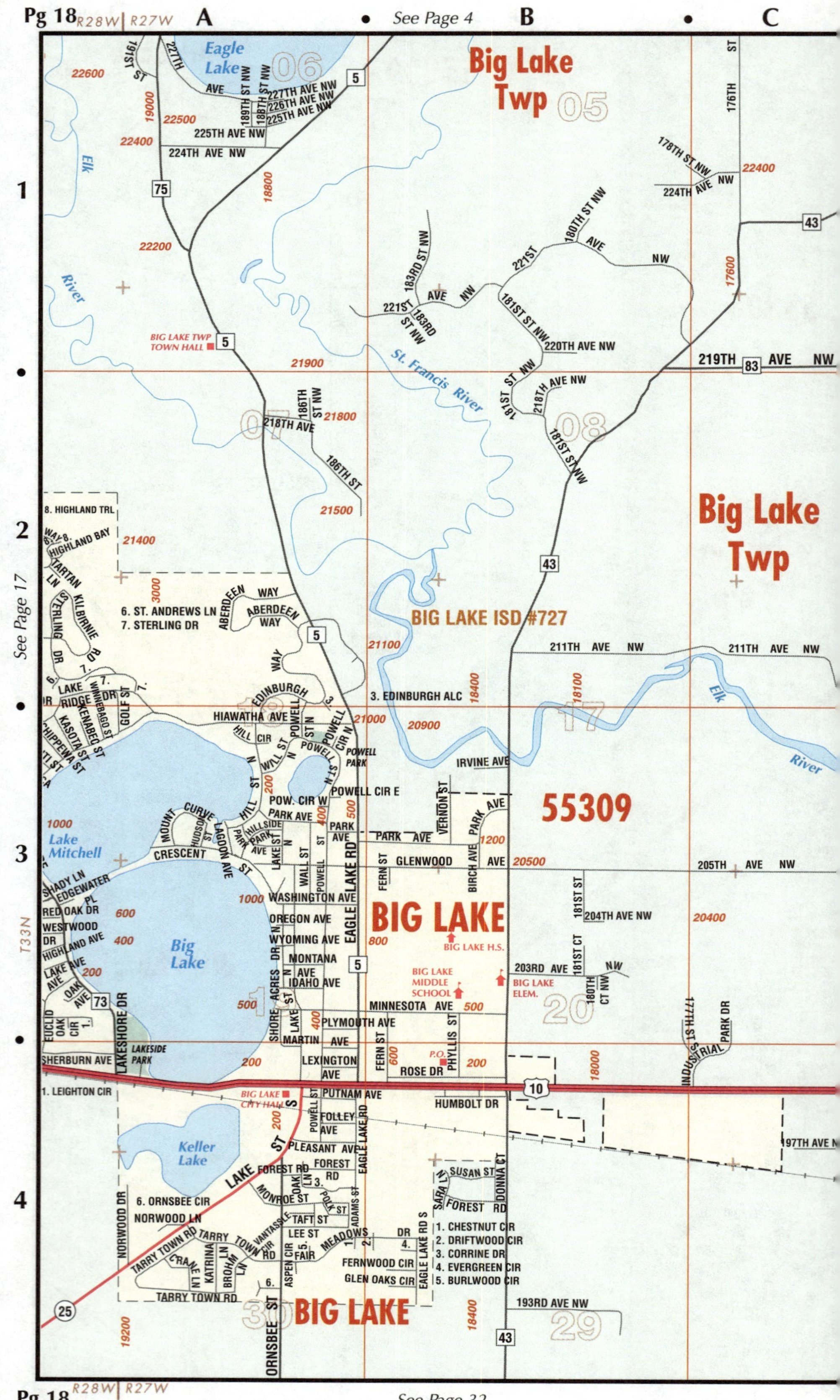

Big Lake Twp
Eagle Lake
Big Lake Twp
BIG LAKE ISD #727
55309
BIG LAKE
Big Lake
Lake Mitchell
Keller Lake
St. Francis River
Elk River
BIG LAKE TWP TOWN HALL
BIG LAKE H.S.
BIG LAKE MIDDLE SCHOOL
BIG LAKE ELEM.
BIG LAKE CITY HALL
P.O.
LAKESIDE PARK
POWELL PARK
3. EDINBURGH ALC
8. HIGHLAND TRL
6. ST. ANDREWS LN
7. STERLING DR
1. LEIGHTON CIR
6. ORNSBEE CIR
1. CHESTNUT CIR
2. DRIFTWOOD CIR
3. CORRINE DR
4. EVERGREEN CIR
5. BURLWOOD CIR
219TH AVE NW
211TH AVE NW
205TH AVE NW
204TH AVE NW
193RD AVE NW
225TH AVE NW
224TH AVE NW
220TH AVE NW
218TH AVE NW
GLENWOOD AVE
WASHINGTON AVE
MINNESOTA AVE
PLYMOUTH AVE
EAGLE LAKE RD
LAKESHORE DR
SHERBURN AVE
ORNSBEE ST
NORWOOD DR
TARRY TOWN RD
HIAWATHA AVE
EDINBURGH
ABERDEEN WAY
IRVINE AVE
PUTNAM AVE
HUMBOLT DR
97TH AVE N
T33N

See Page 17

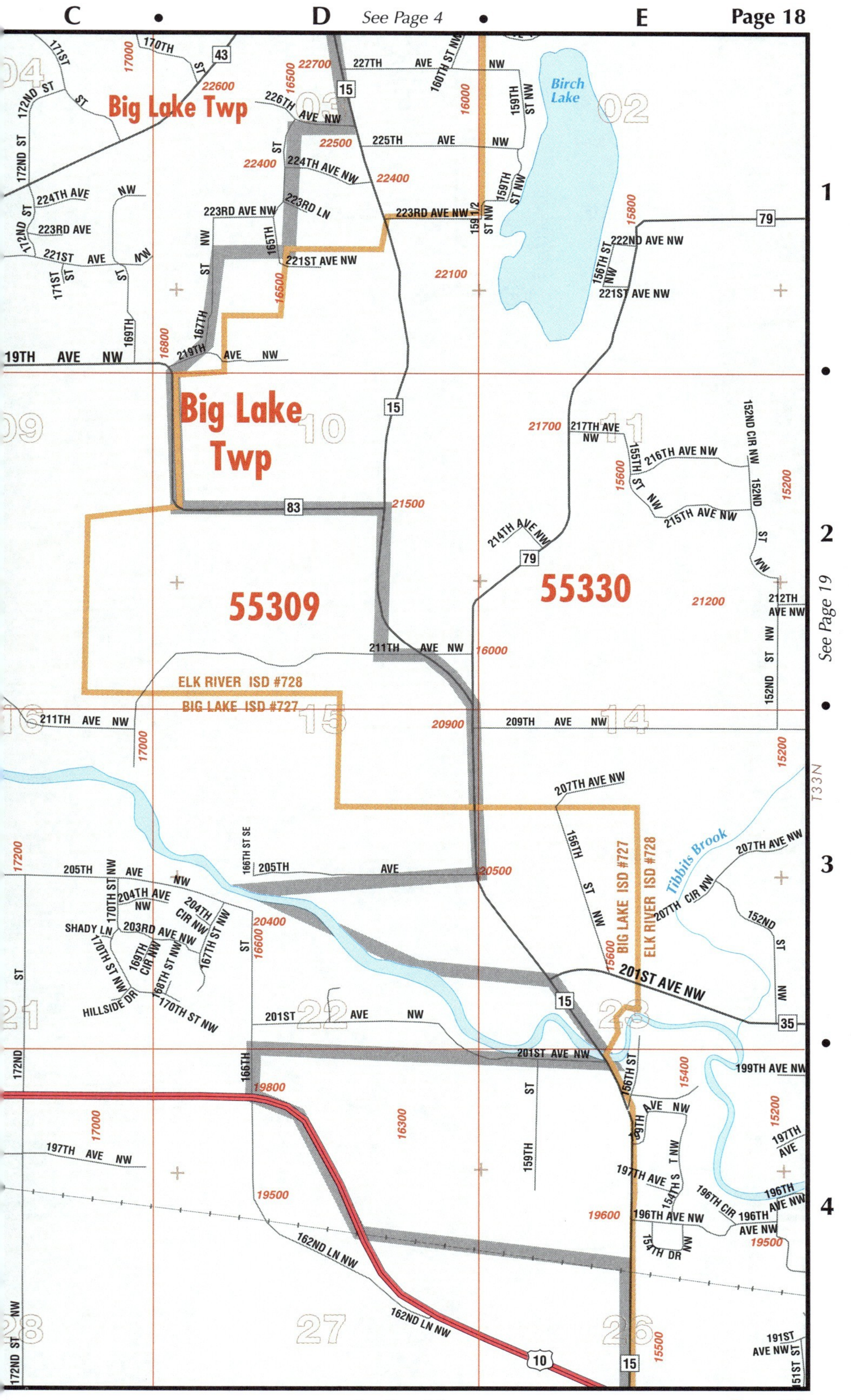

171ST ST
170TH
43
17000
170TH
22600
22700
227TH AVE NW
160TH AVE NW
159TH
Birch Lake
02
172ND ST
ST
172ND ST
22500
226TH AVE NW
15
16500
16000
159TH ST NW
Big Lake Twp
02
22400
225TH AVE
224TH AVE NW
22400
224 ST
22400
223RD LN
225TH AVE
159TH ST NW
1
224TH AVE NW
223RD AVE NW
223RD LN
223RD AVE NW 158 1/2 ST NW
15800
79
223RD AVE
NW
165TH ST NW
222ND AVE NW
172ND
221ST AVE
NW
221ST AVE NW
16500
22100
156TH ST NW
221ST AVE NW
171ST AVE NW
167TH ST NW
16800
169TH
219TH
AVE NW
09
19TH AVE NW
Big Lake Twp
10
21700
217TH AVE NW
11
152ND CIR NW
152ND
15200
15
15600
155TH ST NW
216TH AVE NW
152ND ST NW
15
83
21500
214TH AVE NW
215TH AVE NW
2
79
55309
55330
21200
212TH AVE NW
152ND ST NW
211TH AVE NW
16000
16
211TH AVE NW
17000
ELK RIVER ISD #728
BIG LAKE ISD #727
15
20900
209TH AVE NW
14
15200
207TH AVE NW
207TH AVE NW
166TH ST SE
205TH AVE NW
205TH AVE
156TH ST NW
152ND
207TH CIR NW
3
17200
205TH AVE NW
204TH AVE NW
170TH ST NW
204TH CIR NW
167TH ST NW
20400
20500
156TH ST NW
Tibbits Brook
152ND
SHADY LN
203RD AVE NW
169TH CIR NW
16600
BIG LAKE ISD #727
ELK RIVER ISD #728
HILLSIDE DR
166TH ST NW
170TH ST NW
15600
201ST AVE NW
21
201ST AVE NW
22
AVE NW
15
23
35
166TH ST NW
172ND
201ST AVE NW
199TH AVE NW
19800
159TH ST NW
156TH ST NW
15400
15200
16300
197TH AVE
154TH ST NW
197TH AVE
17000
197TH AVE NW
196TH CIR NW
196TH AVE NW
19500
159TH
196TH AVE NW
154TH DR
19600
28
162ND LN NW
27
162ND LN NW
10
26
15
15500
191ST AVE NW
151ST ST NW

See Page 19

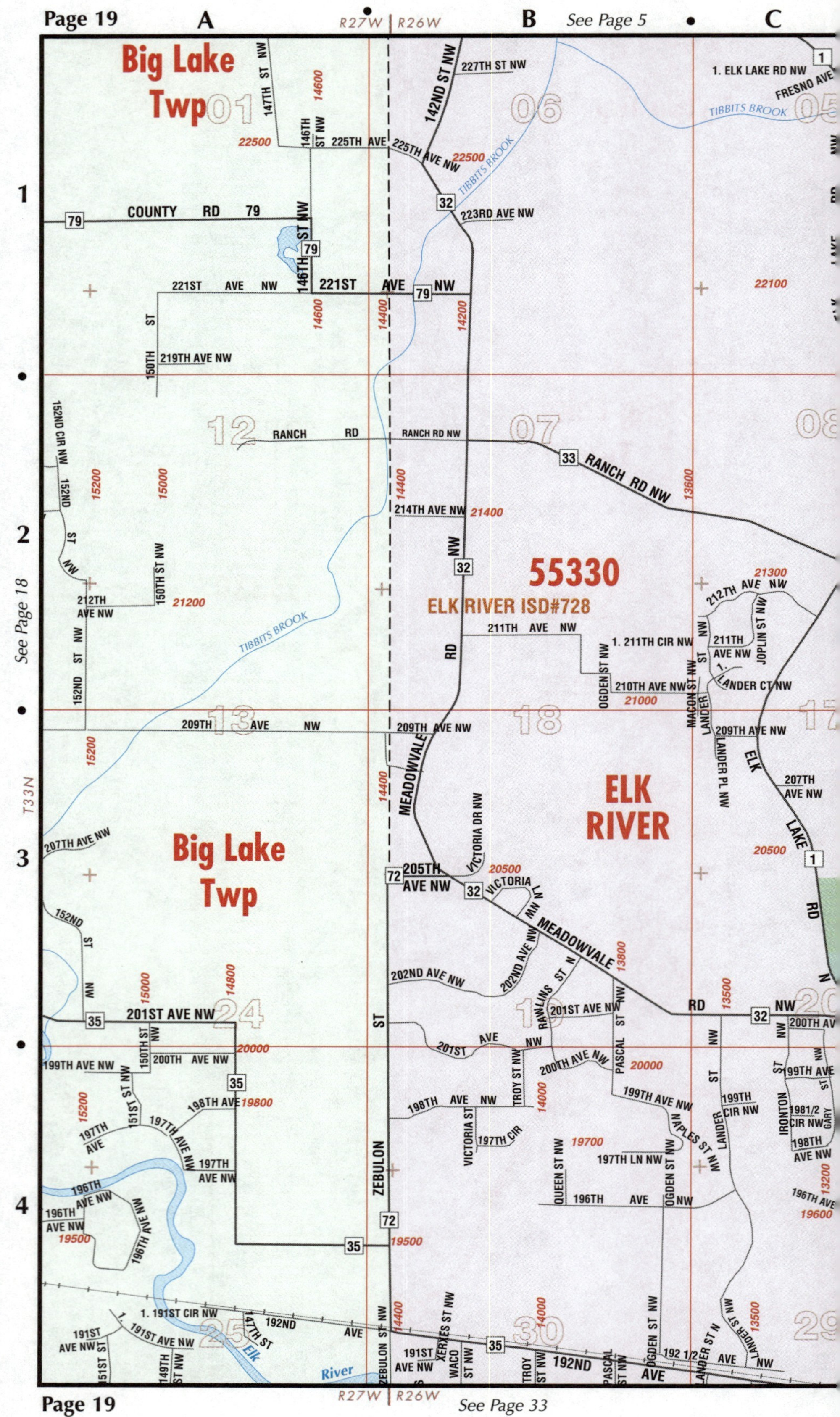

A R27W | R26W B See Page 5 C

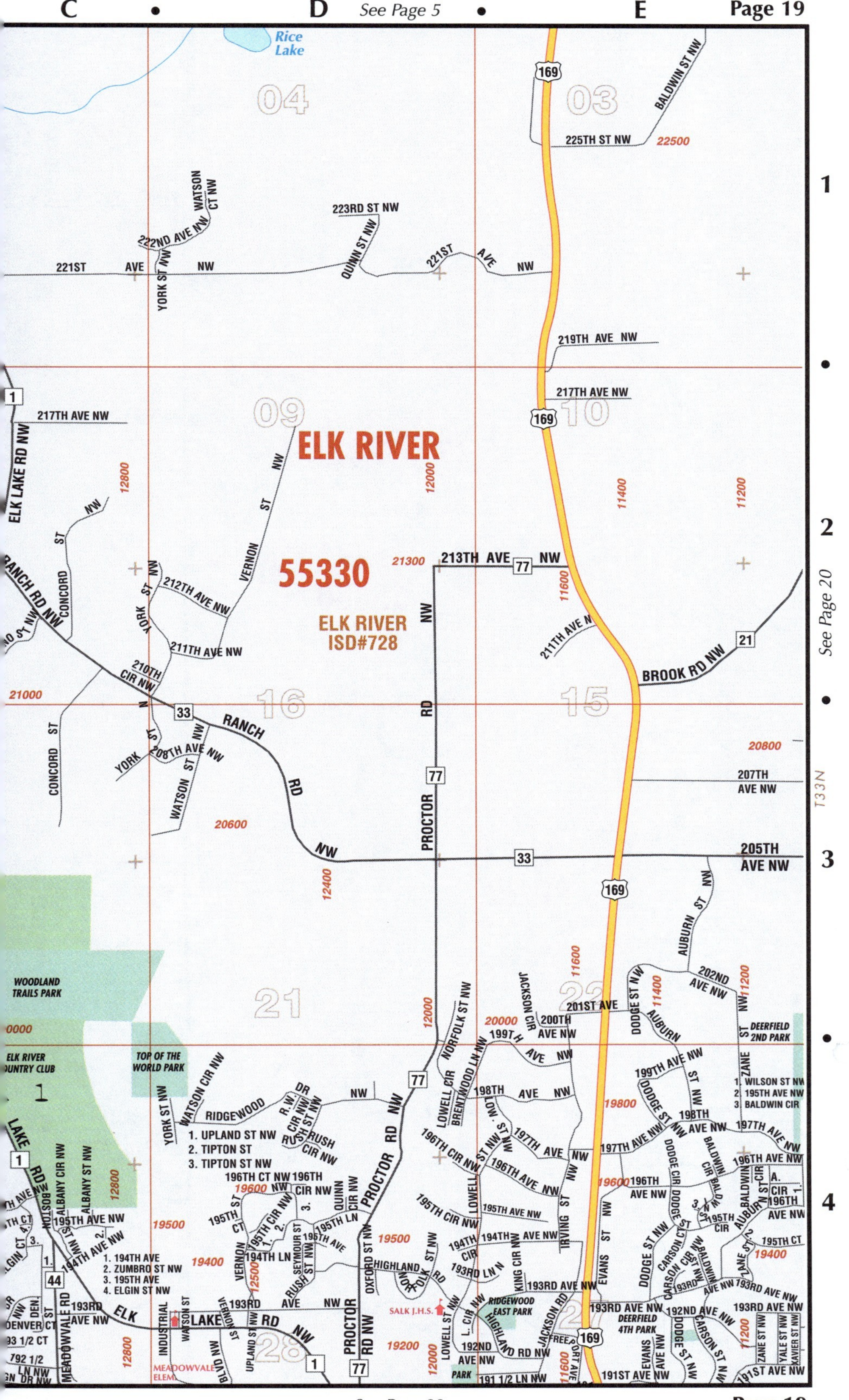

Rice Lake

04

169

03

BALDWIN ST NW

225TH ST NW *22500*

1

222ND AVE NW
WATSON CT NW

223RD ST NW

QUINN ST NW

221ST AVE NW

221ST AVE NW

219TH AVE NW

217TH AVE NW

1

09

217TH AVE NW

ELK RIVER

12800

ELK LAKE RD NW

CONCORD ST NW

VERNON ST NW

YORK ST NW

12000

169

10

11400

11200

2

55330

21300

213TH AVE NW

77

ELK RIVER
ISD#728

11600

211TH AVE N

21

RANCH RD NW

212TH AVE NW

211TH AVE NW

210TH CIR NW

BROOK RD NW

21000

33

16

RANCH RD NW

15

20800

CONCORD ST

YORK ST

208TH AVE NW

WATSON ST

20600

PROCTOR RD NW

77

207TH
AVE NW

12400

NW

33

205TH
AVE NW

3

169

T 33 N

WOODLAND
TRAILS PARK

0000

21

12000

JACKSON CIR

11600

22

201ST AVE

200TH
AVE NW

11400

AUBURN ST NW

202ND
AVE NW

11200

DEERFIELD
2ND PARK

ELK RIVER
COUNTRY CLUB

1

TOP OF THE
WORLD PARK

199TH AVE NW

NORFOLK ST NW

199TH AVE NW

199TH AVE ST NW

DODGE ST NW

198TH

197TH AVE NW

1. WILSON ST NW
2. 195TH AVE NW
3. BALDWIN CIR

YORK ST NW

WATSON CIR NW

RIDGEWOOD DR NW

RUSH CIR NW

198TH AVE NW

LOWELL CIR

BRENTWOOD LN NW

196TH ST NW

197TH AVE NW

DODGE CIR NW

197TH AVE NW

BALDWIN ST NW

197TH AVE NW

LAKE RD NW

1

ALBANY CIR NW

BOSTON

ALBANY ST NW

12800

1. UPLAND ST NW
2. TIPTON ST
3. TIPTON ST NW

196TH CT NW 196TH CIR NW

19600

196TH CIR NW

196TH AVE NW

QUINN ST NW

196TH CIR NW

LOWELL CIR

196TH AVE NW

19600

196TH
AVE NW

ZANE

DODGE CIR NW

CARSON CIR NW

BALDWIN

196TH
AVE NW

A.
CIR

196TH
AVE NW

4

44

195TH CT
3.

195TH AVE NW

19500

195TH
CT NW

1., 2.

195TH AVE

VERNON LN NW

195TH CIR NW

195TH AVE NW

IRVING ST NW

195TH CT NW

DODGE ST NW

195TH CT NW

CARSON ST NW

BALDWIN

195TH CT *19400*

ELGIN
ST NW

1
3.

184TH AVE NW

1. 194TH AVE
2. ZUMBRO ST NW
3. 195TH AVE
4. ELGIN ST NW

19400

VERNON LN NW

194TH LN NW

12500

RUSH SEYMOUR ST NW

OXFORD ST NW

HIGHLAND RD

194TH
AVE NW

194TH LN N

193RD AVE NW

EVANS ST

DODGE ST NW

CARSON ST NW

EVANS ST NW

193RD AVE NW

192ND

CARSON ST NW

193RD AVE NW

MEADOWVALE RD NW

193RD
AVE NW

792 1/2

DEN
ST NW

3 1/2 CT NW

ELK LAKE RD NW

193RD AVE
NW

28

WATSON ST NW

PROCTOR RD NW

SALK J.H.S.

RIDGEWOOD
EAST PARK

LOWELL CIR

HIGHLAND RD NW

JACKSON RD NW

DEERFIELD
4TH PARK

169

FREE

193RD AVE NW

193RD AVE NW

192ND ST NW

ZANE ST NW

YALE ST NW

XAVIER ST NW

191ST AVE NW

MEADOWVALE
ELEM.

12800

UPLAND ST NW

BLVD NW

1

19200

77

191 1/2 LN NW

191ST
AVE NW

12000

191 1/2 LN NW

191ST AVE NW

See Page 20

21

Page 19

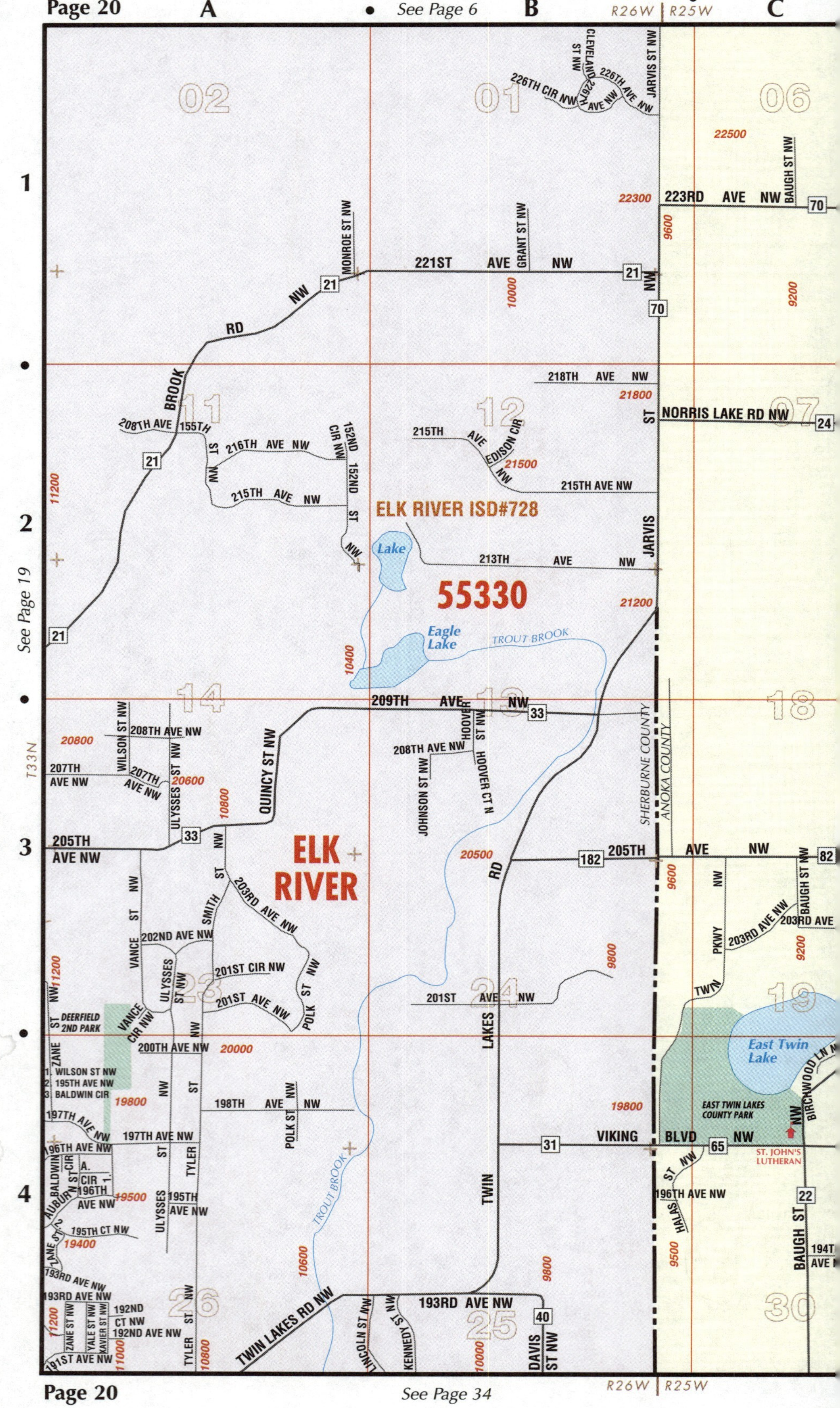

02

01

06

R26W | R25W

22500

223RD   AVE   NW   BAUGH ST NW

70

1

226TH CIR NW
CLEVELAND ST NW
226TH AVE NW
JARVIS ST NW

MONROE ST NW

GRANT ST NW

221ST   AVE   NW

22300

9600

9200

21

70

10000

BROOK   RD   NW

21

See Page 19

218TH   AVE   NW

21800

NORRIS LAKE RD NW   07   24

11   155TH ST NW   12

208TH AVE
216TH AVE NW
152ND CIR NW
152ND ST NW

215TH   AVE   EDISON CIR   NW   21500

215TH   AVE   NW   215TH AVE NW

11200

21

215TH   AVE   NW

ELK RIVER ISD#728

2

Lake

JARVIS

213TH   AVE   NW

55330

21200

21

Eagle
Lake   TROUT BROOK

10400

14   13   18

209TH   AVE   NW   33

208TH AVE NW   WILSON ST NW   207TH AVE NW   QUINCY ST NW

HOOVER ST NW   HOOVER CT N

JOHNSON ST NW

SHERBURNE COUNTY
ANOKA COUNTY

20800

207TH AVE NW   ULYSSES ST NW   20600   10800

205TH   AVE   NW   182   205TH   AVE   NW   82

3

205TH AVE NW   33   SMITH ST NW   203RD AVE NW

20500

9600

203RD AVE NW   BAUGH ST NW   203RD AVE

9200

T33N

ELK RIVER

VANCE ST NW   202ND AVE NW   201ST CIR NW   POLK ST NW

TWIN   PKWY

19

ULYSSES ST NW   201ST AVE NW

0080

9800

11200

23   DEERFIELD 2ND PARK   201ST   AVE   NW   24

East Twin
Lake

20000   VANCE CIR NW   200TH AVE NW   LAKES   RD   NW

ZANE ST NW
1. WILSON ST NW
2. 195TH AVE NW
3. BALDWIN CIR   19800

198TH   AVE   NW   POLK ST NW   19800

EAST TWIN LAKES
COUNTY PARK

BIRCHWOOD LN NW

197TH AVE NW   197TH AVE NW

ST. JOHN'S
LUTHERAN

96TH BALDWIN   ST NW   TYLER ST NW   VIKING   BLVD   NW

65

196TH AVE NW

22

4

96TH ST NW
A. CIR NW
196TH AVE NW   ULYSSES ST NW   195TH AVE NW

9500   HALAS ST NW

9500

BAUGH ST

ZANE ST NW
9500   195TH CT NW   19400

194T AVE NW

TWIN   TROUT BROOK

30

193RD AVE NW   10600   9800

193RD AVE NW   192ND CT NW

11200

26   192ND AVE NW   193RD   AVE   NW   40

191ST AVE NW   ZANE ST NW   YALE ST NW   XAVIER ST NW   TYLER ST NW   TWIN LAKES RD NW   LINCOLN ST NW   KENNEDY ST NW   DAVIS ST NW   25

11000   10800   10000

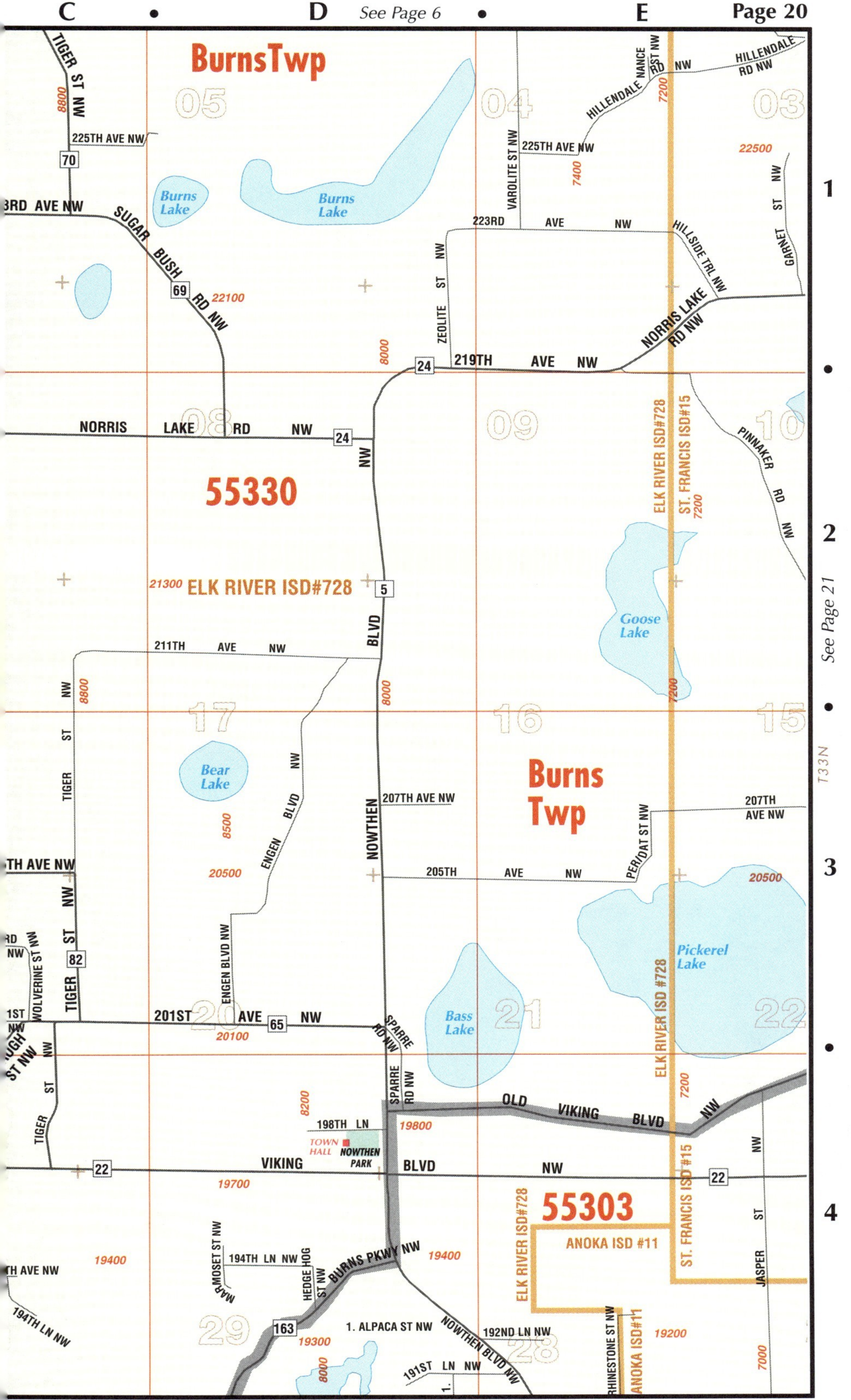
BurnsTwp
Burns Twp
55330
55303
ELK RIVER ISD#728
ST. FRANCIS ISD#15
ANOKA ISD #11
Burns Lake
Burns Lake
Goose Lake
Bear Lake
Bass Lake
Pickerel Lake
TIGER ST NW
225TH AVE NW
SUGAR BUSH RD NW
NORRIS LAKE RD NW
219TH AVE NW
223RD AVE NW
ZEOLITE ST NW
VAROLITE ST NW
225TH AVE NW
HILLENDALE NANCE RD NW
HILLENDALE RD NW
HILLSIDE TRL NW
GARNET ST NW
NORRIS LAKE RD NW
PINNAKER RD NW
NOWTHEN BLVD NW
211TH AVE NW
ENGEN BLVD NW
207TH AVE NW
205TH AVE NW
PERIDAT ST NW
207TH AVE NW
201ST AVE NW
WOLVERINE ST NW
SPARRE RD NW
OLD VIKING BLVD NW
198TH LN
TOWN HALL
NOWTHEN PARK
VIKING BLVD NW
194TH LN NW
MARMOSET ST NW
HEDGEHOG ST NW
BURNS PKWY NW
1. ALPACA ST NW
192ND LN NW
191ST LN NW
RHINESTONE ST NW
JASPER ST NW
194TH LN NW
1
2
3
4
See Page 21
T33N

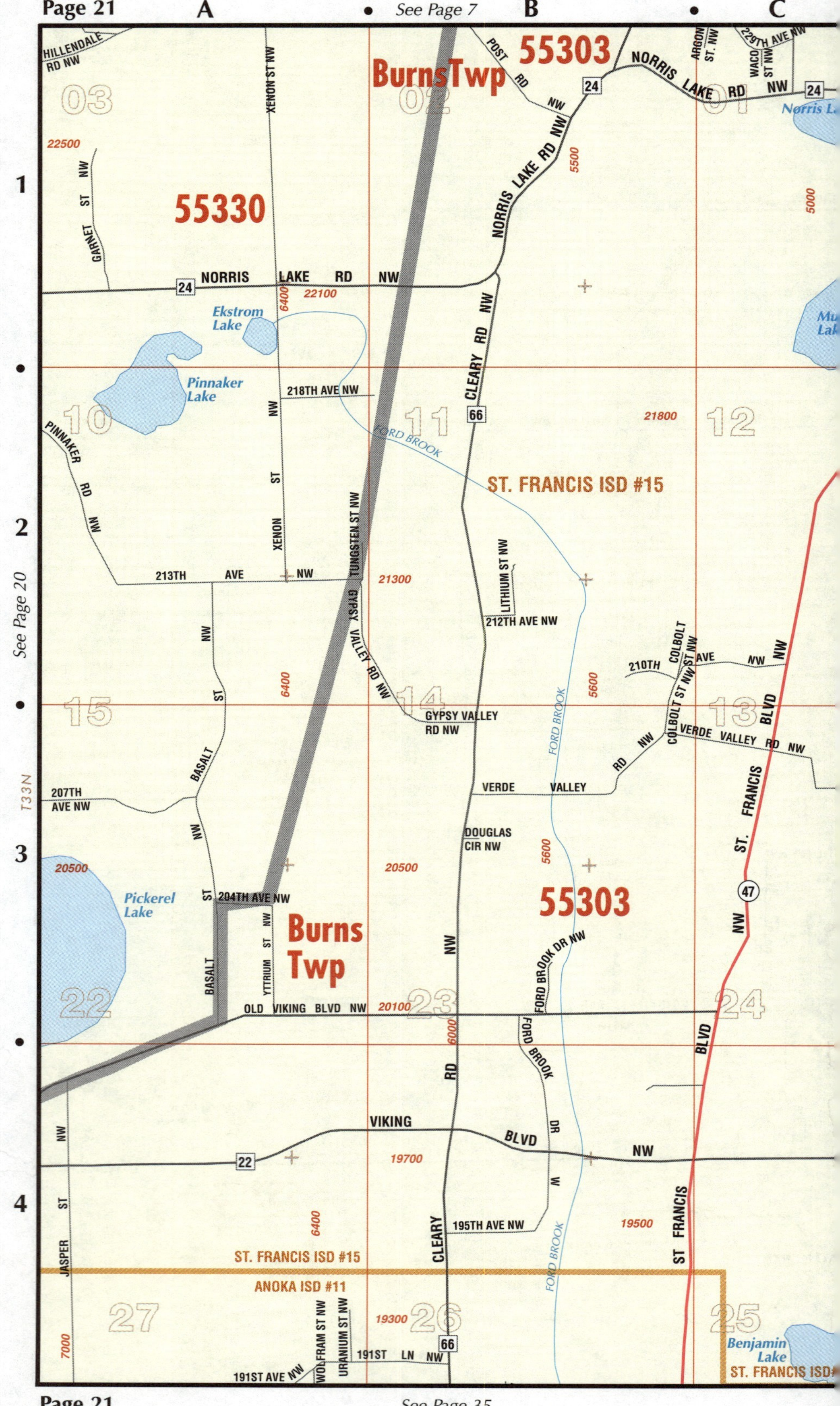

See Page 35

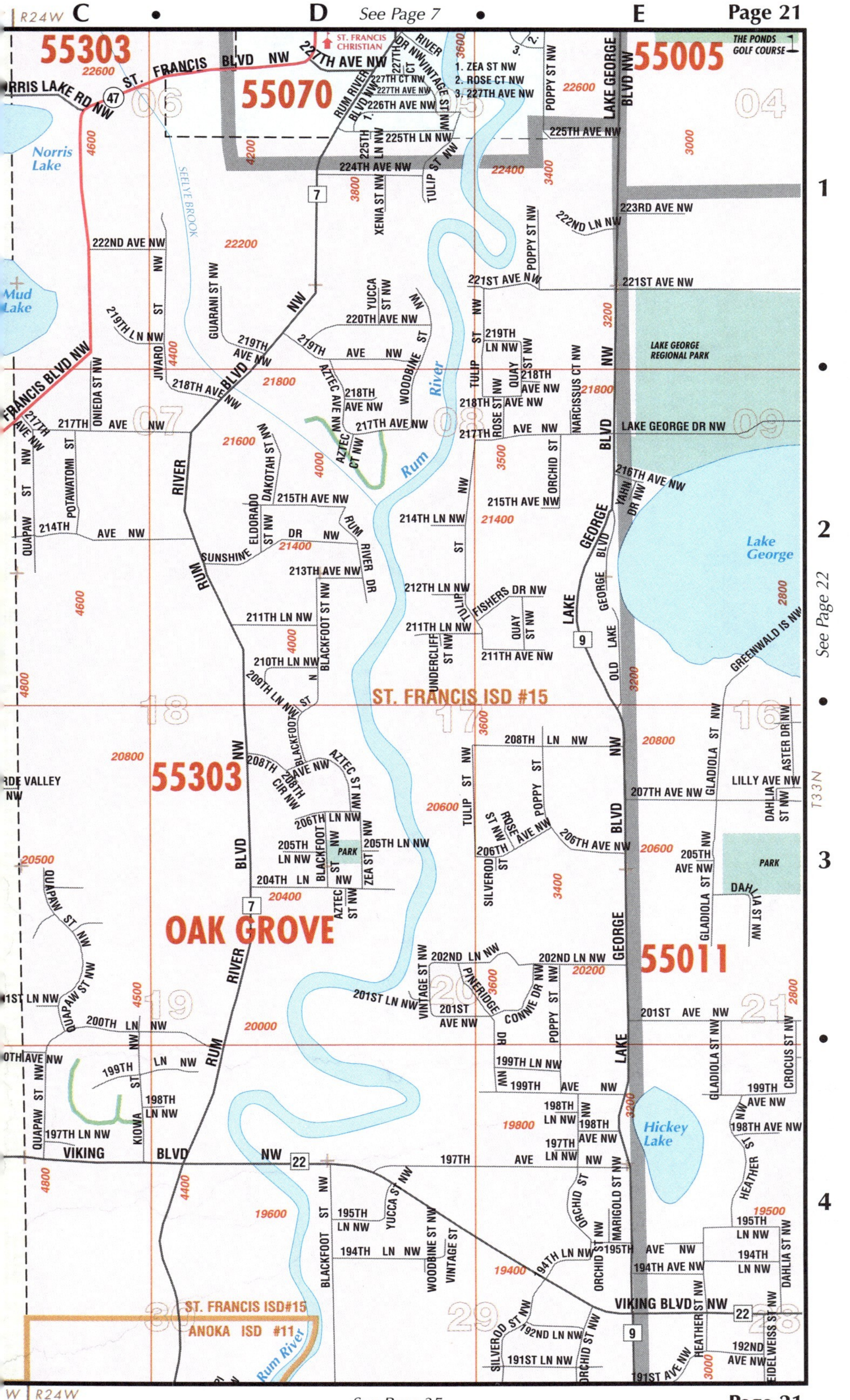

R24W   C   •   D   See Page 7   •   E   Page 21

55303
22600

55070

ST. FRANCIS CHRISTIAN

1. ZEA ST NW
2. ROSE CT NW
3. 227TH AVE NW

THE PONDS
GOLF COURSE

55005

ST. FRANCIS BLVD NW

227TH AVE NW

NORRIS LAKE RD NW

Norris Lake

4600

RUM RIVER BLVD NW

4200

3600

Lake George Blvd NW

22600

04

3000

06

47

3800

225TH AVE NW
224TH AVE NW

7

22400

3400

1

Seelye Brook

222ND AVE NW

NW

22200

GUARANI ST NW

NW

XENIA ST NW

TULIP ST NW

225TH LN NW

226TH AVE NW

223RD AVE NW

222ND LN NW

221ST AVE NW

Mud Lake

219TH LN NW

JIVARO

ST

4400

219TH AVE NW

220TH AVE NW

YUCCA ST NW

WOODBINE ST

River

221ST AVE NW

POPPY ST NW

3200

Lake George Regional Park

•

FRANCIS BLVD NW

218TH BLVD NW

21800

219TH AVE NW

TULIP

219TH AVE NW

218TH AVE NW

Rum

QUAY

218TH AVE NW

NARCISSUS CT NW

21800

217TH AVE NW

ONEIDA ST NW

67

217TH AVE NW

21600

AZTEC AVE NW

AZTEC CT NW

217TH AVE NW

08

ROSE ST

218TH

3500

217TH

AVE NW

ORCHID ST

LAKE GEORGE DR NW

09

POTAWATOMI ST

214TH

RIVER

ELDORADO ST NW

DAKOTAH ST NW

4000

215TH AVE NW

River

215TH AVE NW

216TH AVE NW

YARN

LAKE

GEORGE

BLVD

2

QUAPAW

AVE NW

4600

Sunshine

RUM

RIVER DR

21400

213TH AVE NW

212TH LN NW

214TH LN NW

21400

FISHERS DR NW

Lake George

2800

Greenwald Is NW

See Page 22

211TH LN NW

BLACKFOOT DR NW

4000

210TH LN NW

209TH LN NW

TULIP ST NW

QUAY ST NW

211TH AVE NW

211TH AVE NW

OLD LAKE

3200

9

•

4800

18

20800

55303

208TH BLVD NW

BLACKFOOT CIR NW

AZTEC ST NW

ST. FRANCIS ISD #15

17

3600

208TH LN NW

TULIP ST NW

ROSE AVE NW

POPPY ST

20800

GLADIOLA ST

16

ASTER DR NW

LILLY AVE NW

207TH AVE NW

DAHLIA ST NW

206TH LN NW

BLACKFOOT LN NW

205TH LN NW

204TH LN NW

ZEA ST NW

PARK

20600

SILVEROD NW ST

206TH NW

3400

206TH AVE NW

20600

205TH AVE ST NW

GLADIOLA ST

DAHLIA ST NW

PARK

3

OAK GROVE

7

20400

AZTEC ST NW

55011

QUAPAW ST NW

20500

VERDE VALLEY NW

202ND LN NW

VINTAGE ST NW

PINERIDGE

20

CONNIE DR NW

202ND LN NW

POPPY ST

20200

GEORGE

201ST AVE

21

2800

GLADIOLA ST NW

CROCUS ST NW

•

19

4500

RIVER BLVD NW

RUM

200TH LN NW

20000

201ST LN NW

201ST AVE NW

DR

18600

199TH LN NW

199TH AVE NW

LAKE

199TH AVE NW

1ST LN NW

QUAPAW ST NW

199TH LN NW

KIOWA ST

198TH LN NW

198TH LN NW

198TH AVE NW

197TH AVE NW

ORCHID ST

MARIGOLD ST NW

Hickey Lake

HEATHER

3000

VIKING

BLVD

NW

22

197TH

AVE NW

195TH LN NW

19500

4

4800

4400

19600

BLACKFOOT ST NW

195TH LN NW

YUCCA ST NW

194TH LN NW

WOODBINE ST NW

VINTAGE ST

19400

194TH LN NW

ORCHID ST

195TH AVE NW

194TH AVE NW

194TH LN NW

DAHLIA ST NW

ST. FRANCIS ISD#15
ANOKA ISD #11

30

29

SILVEROD ST NW

ORCHID ST NW

192ND LN NW

191ST LN NW

VIKING BLVD NW

9

22

191ST AVE NW

HEATHER ST NW

EDELWEISS ST

3000

192ND AVE NW

28

Rum River

See Page 35

W   R24W

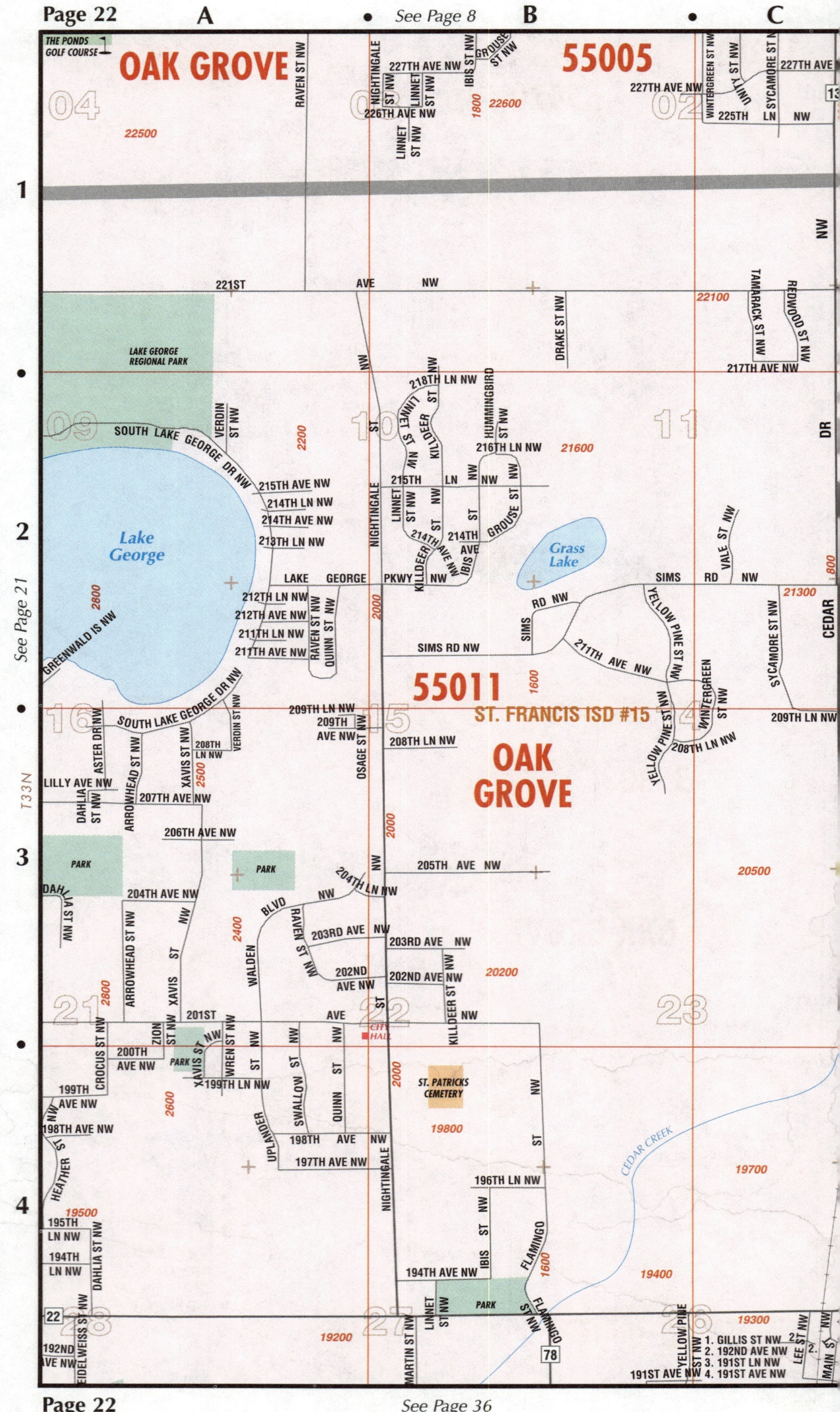

THE PONDS GOLF COURSE

OAK GROVE   **55005**

04

22500

221ST AVE NW

LAKE GEORGE REGIONAL PARK

09   SOUTH LAKE GEORGE DR NW

Lake George

2800

GREENWALD IS NW

10   2200

218TH LN NW
216TH LN NW   21600
215TH AVE NW
214TH LN NW
214TH AVE NW
213TH LN NW
215TH LN
214TH AVE NW

LAKE GEORGE PKWY

212TH LN NW
212TH AVE NW
211TH LN NW
211TH AVE NW

SIMS RD NW

Grass Lake

SIMS   RD   NW

21300

11

16   SOUTH LAKE GEORGE DR NW

209TH LN NW
209TH AVE NW
208TH LN NW

55011
ST. FRANCIS ISD #15

OAK GROVE

15

14   209TH LN NW

LILLY AVE NW
DAHLIA ST NW
207TH AVE NW
206TH AVE NW

2500

208TH LN NW

PARK

PARK   2000

205TH AVE NW

20500

3   PARK   204TH AVE NW   204TH LN NW

203RD AVE NW
203RD AVE NW
202ND AVE NW   202ND AVE NW   20200

2400   WALDEN BLVD   RAVEN ST NW

21   2800   ARROWHEAD ST NW   201ST AVE NW

22   23

ZION
200TH AVE NW   PARK
XAVIS ST NW   199TH LN NW
2600
199TH AVE NW
198TH AVE NW
UPLANDER
SWALLOW ST NW
QUINN ST NW
198TH   AVE   NW
197TH AVE NW

CITY HALL

ST. PATRICKS CEMETERY   19800

2000

19700

HEATHER ST NW
195TH LN NW   19500
194TH LN NW
DAHLIA ST NW

4   196TH LN NW

196TH LN NW

IBIS ST NW   FLAMINGO ST NW   1600

194TH AVE NW   PARK   19400

22   28   19200   27   MARTIN ST NW   LINNET ST NW   FLAMINGO ST NW   78   26   19300

192ND AVE NW
EDELWEISS ST NW

1. GILLIS ST NW
2. 192ND AVE NW
3. 191ST LN NW
4. 191ST AVE NW

191ST AVE NW

See Page 21

T33N

RAVEN ST NW
226TH AVE NW
NIGHTINGALE ST NW
LINNET ST NW
LINNET ST NW
IBIS ST NW
GROUSE ST NW
1800   22600

227TH AVE NW

227TH AVE NW
225TH
WINTERGREEN ST NW
UNITY ST NW
SYCAMORE ST NW
227TH AVE

13

221ST   AVE   NW   22100

DRAKE ST NW
TAMARACK ST NW
REDWOOD ST NW
217TH AVE NW

VERDIN ST NW
NIGHTINGALE ST NW
LINNET ST NW
MN ST NW
KILLDEER ST NW
HUMMINGBIRD ST NW
218TH LN NW

215TH
LINNET ST NW
214TH AVE NW
KILLDEER ST NW
IBIS ST NW
214TH AVE NW
GROUSE ST NW

VALE ST NW
SYCAMORE ST NW
YELLOW PINE ST NW
WINTERGREEN ST NW
211TH AVE NW
208TH LN NW
YELLOW PINE ST NW
CEDAR   DR   1800
1600

RAVEN ST NW
QUINN ST NW
VERDIN ST NW
ASTER DR NW
ARROWHEAD ST NW
XAVIS ST NW
OSAGE ST NW

DAHLIA ST NW
ARROWHEAD ST NW
XAVIS ST
CROCUS ST NW
XAVIS ST NW
WREN ST NW

NIGHTINGALE ST NW
KILLDEER ST NW
QUINN ST NW

CEDAR CREEK

YELLOW PINE
MAIN ST NW
LEE ST NW

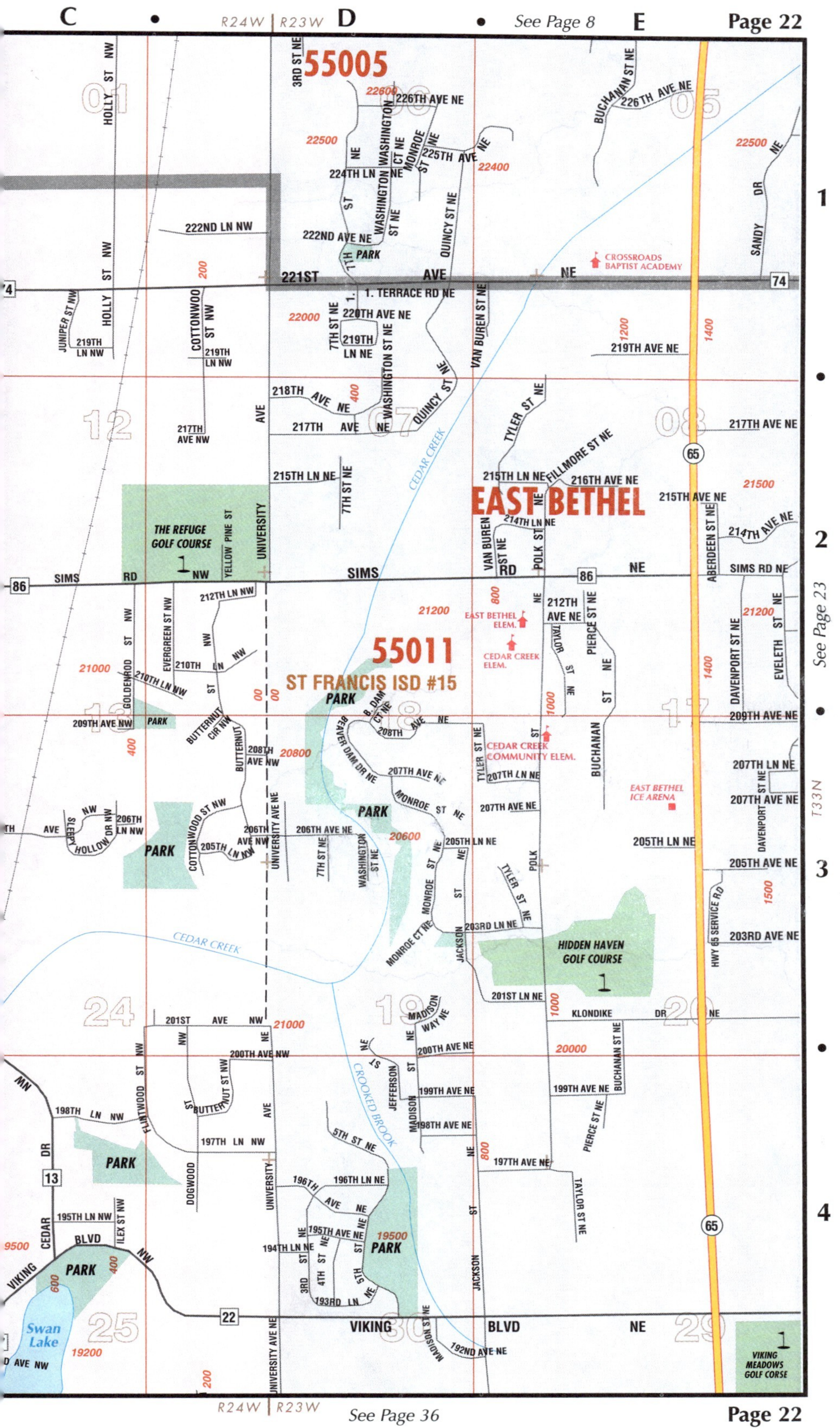

55005

EAST BETHEL

CROSSROADS
BAPTIST ACADEMY

55011
ST FRANCIS ISD #15

EAST BETHEL
ELEM.

CEDAR CREEK
ELEM.

CEDAR CREEK
COMMUNITY ELEM.

EAST BETHEL
ICE ARENA

HIDDEN HAVEN
GOLF COURSE

THE REFUGE
GOLF COURSE

Swan
Lake

VIKING
MEADOWS
GOLF CORSE

See Page 23

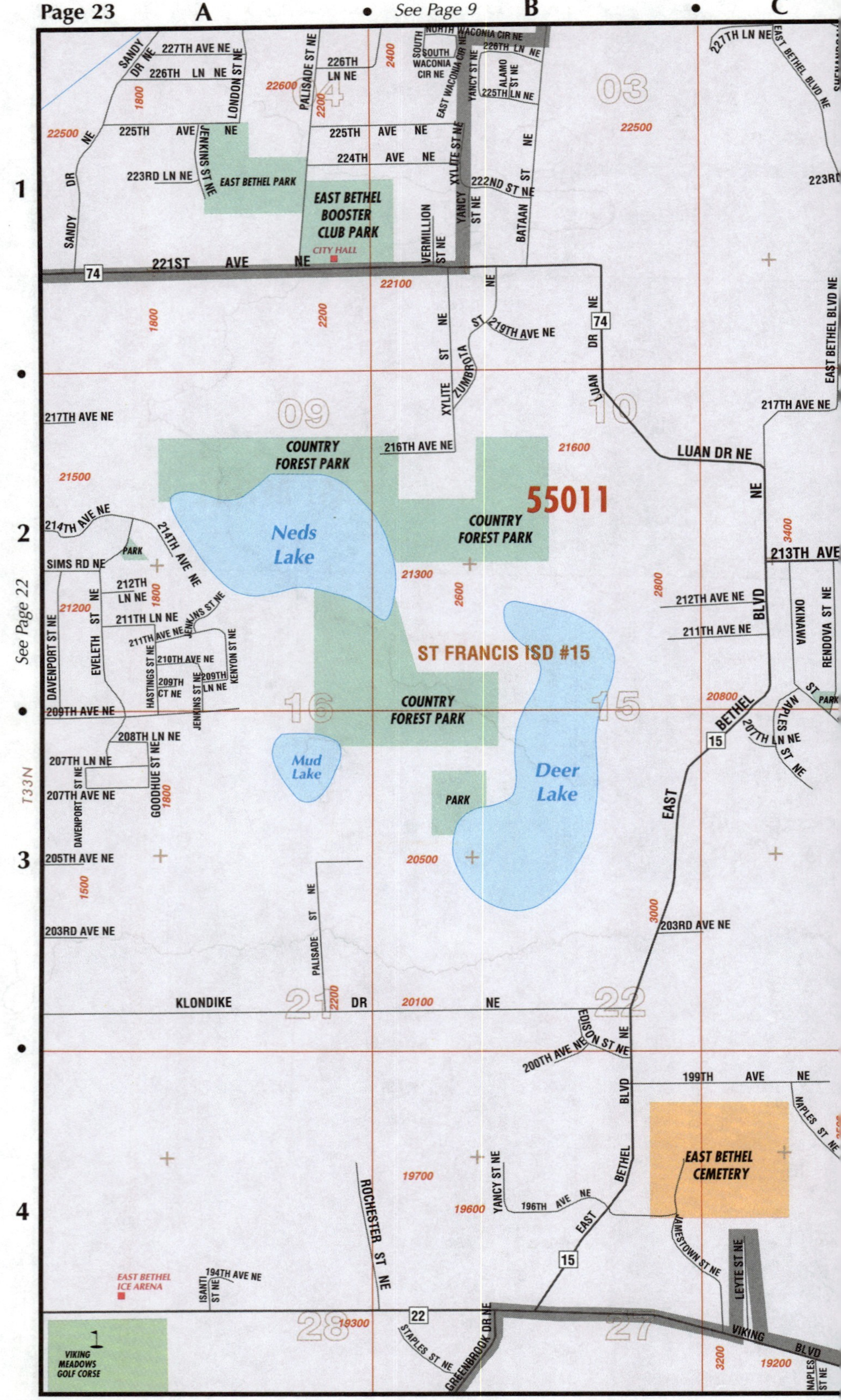

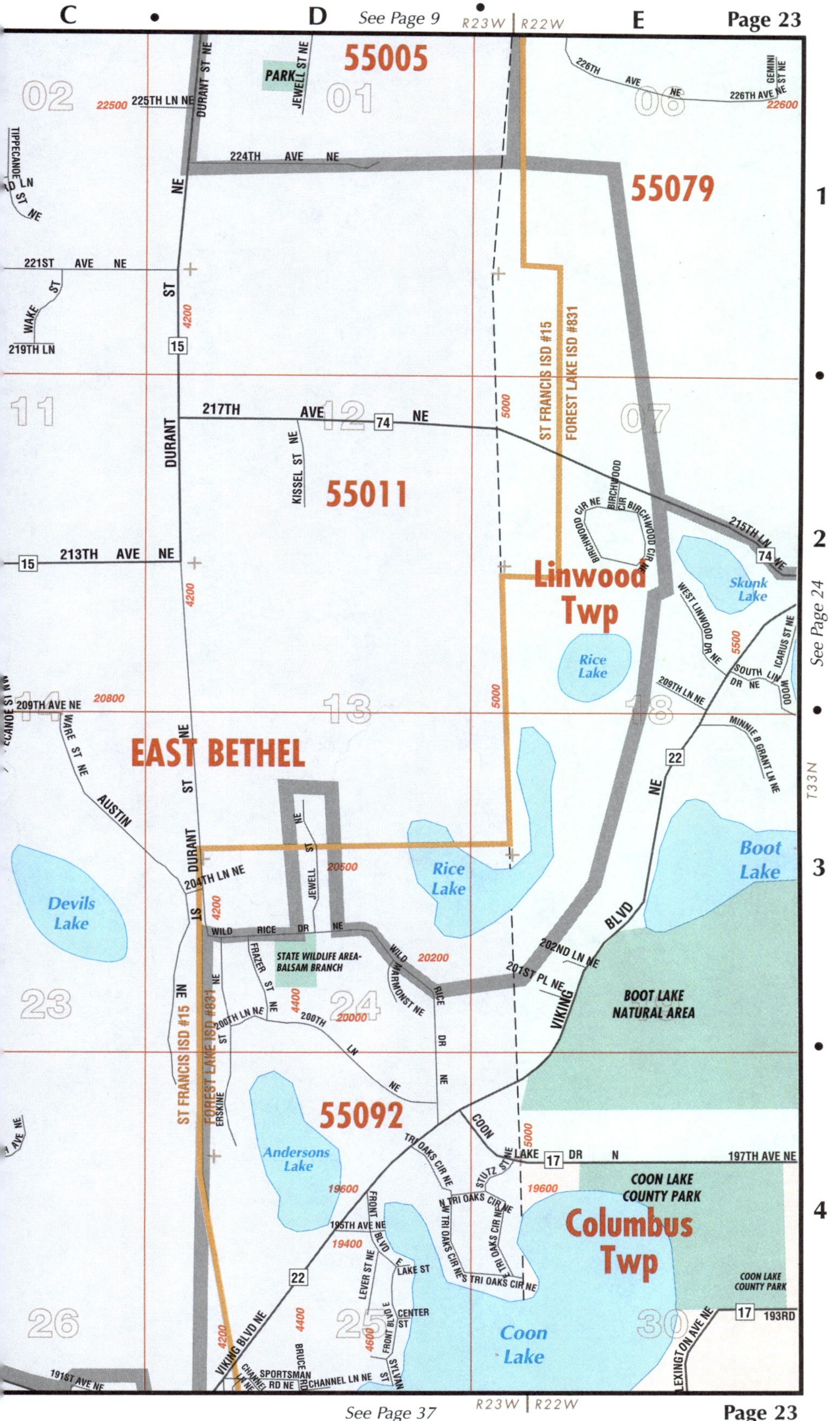

C • D E

See Page 9

R23W | R22W

55005

PARK JEWELL ST NE
01

225TH LN NE
22500
DURANT ST NE

02

TIPPECANOE ST NE

224TH AVE NE

226TH AVE NE

226TH AVE NE
GEMINI ST NE
22600

08

55079

1

221ST AVE NE
ST NE

WAKE ST NE
219TH LN

4200
15

ST FRANCIS ISD #15
FOREST LAKE ISD #831

15 213TH AVE NE

4200

217TH AVE NE 74 NE

DURANT ST NE

KISSEL ST NE

12

55011

5000

BIRCHWOOD CIR NE
BIRCHWOOD CIR NE
BIRCHWOOD CIR NE

07

215TH LN NE
74

2

Linwood
Twp

Skunk
Lake

WEST LINWOOD DR NE

5500

ICARUS ST NE
SOUTH DR NE
ODOM

Rice
Lake

209TH LN NE

209TH AVE NE 20800

ECAPULSOME ST NE

WARE ST NE

AUSTIN

EAST BETHEL

ST NE

13

5000

18

MINNIE B GRANT LN NE

22

NE

T33N

See Page 24

DURANT ST NE
4200
204TH LN NE
JEWELL ST NE
WILD RICE DR NE
FRAZER ST NE

20500

Rice
Lake

VIKING BLVD

Boot
Lake

3

Devils
Lake

State Wildlife Area-
Balsam Branch

WILD
HARMON ST NE
RICE
20200

DR NE

202ND LN NE
201ST PL NE

BOOT LAKE
NATURAL AREA

23

ST FRANCIS ISD #15
FOREST LAKE ISD #831

ERSKINE NE
200TH LN NE
4400
200TH

24

20000

RICE DR NE

LN NE

55092

TRI OAKS CIR NE
STUTZ ST NE

COON LAKE DR N

17

197TH AVE NE

4

Andersons
Lake

19600

FRONT BLVD E
195TH AVE NE
19400

LAKE ST
N TRI OAKS CIR NE
NW TRI OAKS CIR NE
TRI OAKS CIR NE

5000

19600

COON LAKE
COUNTY PARK

Columbus
Twp

COON LAKE
COUNTY PARK

26

191ST AVE NE

4200
VIKING BLVD NE
4400

LEVER ST NE
FRONT BLVD E
22
BRUCE LN NE
CHANNEL RD NE
CHANNEL LN NE

CENTER ST
FRONT BLVD N
SYLVAN
25
4600
SPORTSMAN

Coon
Lake

30

LEXINGTON AVE NE

17 193RD

See Page 37 R23W | R22W Page 23

A • See Page 10 B • C

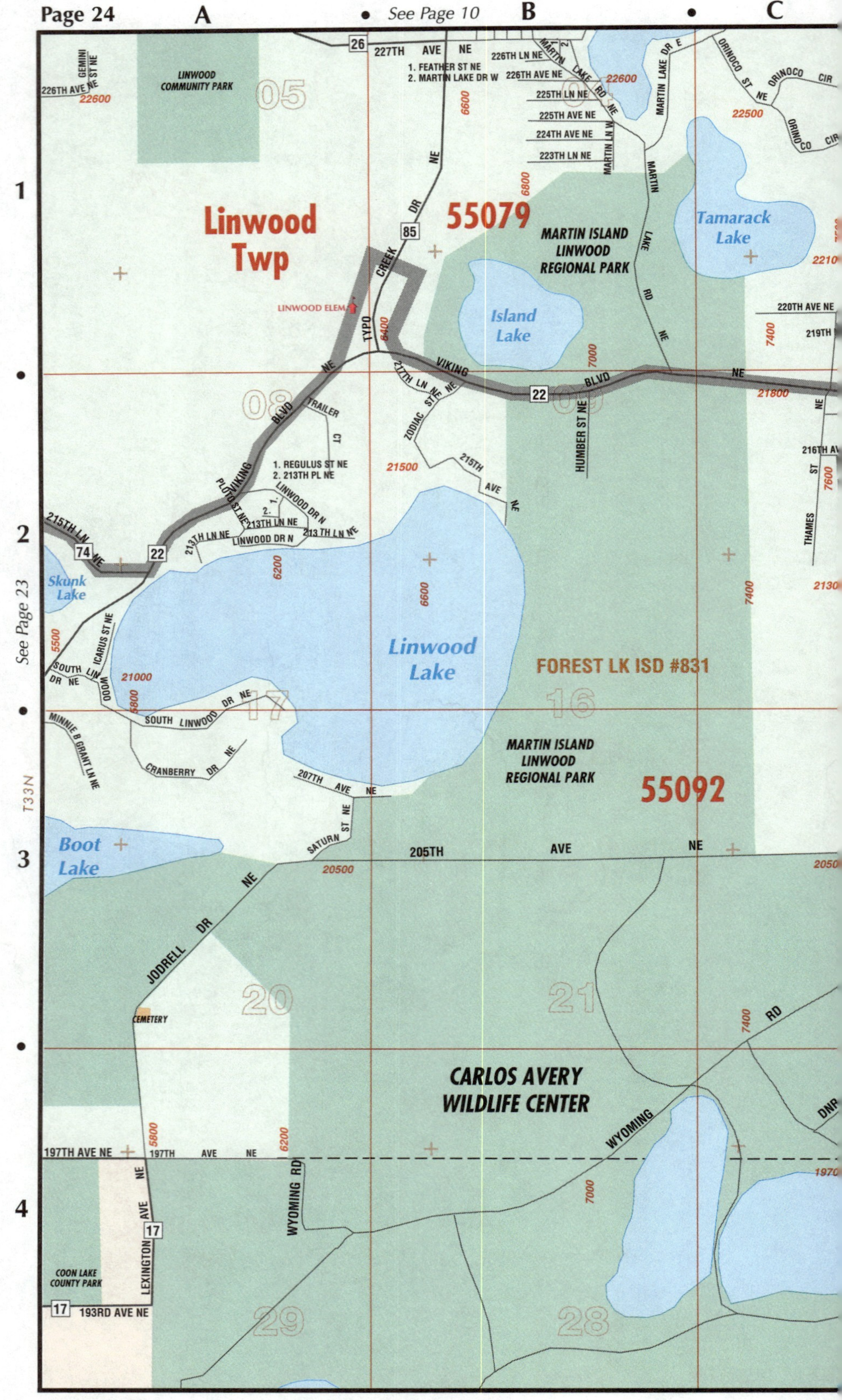

226TH AVE NE 22600
GEMINI ST NE

LINWOOD COMMUNITY PARK

05

26

227TH AVE NE
1. FEATHER ST NE
2. MARTIN LAKE DR W
226TH LN NE
226TH AVE NE
225TH LN NE
225TH AVE NE
224TH AVE NE
223TH LN NE

MARTIN LAKE RD NE
6600
6800

MARTIN LAKE DR E
ORINOCO ST NE
ORINOCO CIR
22500
ORINOCO CIR NE

Linwood Twp

CREEK DR NE

85

55079

MARTIN ISLAND LINWOOD REGIONAL PARK

Tamarack Lake

22100

LINWOOD ELEM

TYPO

6400

Island Lake

MARTIN LAKE RD NE

220TH AVE NE
219TH
7400

7000

1

08

BLVD TRAILER
VIKING

217TH LN NE NE
ZODIAC ST NE NE

VIKING BLVD

22

VIKING

09

HUMBER ST NE
21800
216TH AV
7600

L3
1. REGULUS ST NE
2. 213TH PL NE
LINWOOD DR N
2. 1.
213TH LN NE
LINWOOD DR N
213TH LN NE

215TH AVE NE
21500

215TH LN

74

22

213TH LN NE

2

THAMES ST NE

21300

Skunk Lake

6200

5500

6600

SOUTH DR NE
ICARUS ST NE

21000

5800

WOODMAN

Linwood Lake

FOREST LK ISD #831

7400

MINNIE B GRANT LN NE

SOUTH LINWOOD DR NE

17

16

CRANBERRY DR NE

MARTIN ISLAND LINWOOD REGIONAL PARK

55092

207TH AVE NE

Boot Lake

SATURN ST NE

205TH AVE NE
20500

2050

3

JODRELL DR NE

20

21

7400 RD

CEMETERY

CARLOS AVERY WILDLIFE CENTER

WYOMING

DNR

197TH AVE NE
5800
197TH AVE NE
6200

WYOMING RD

7000

1970

4

LEXINGTON AVE NE

17

COON LAKE COUNTY PARK

17
193RD AVE NE

29

28

See Page 23

T33N

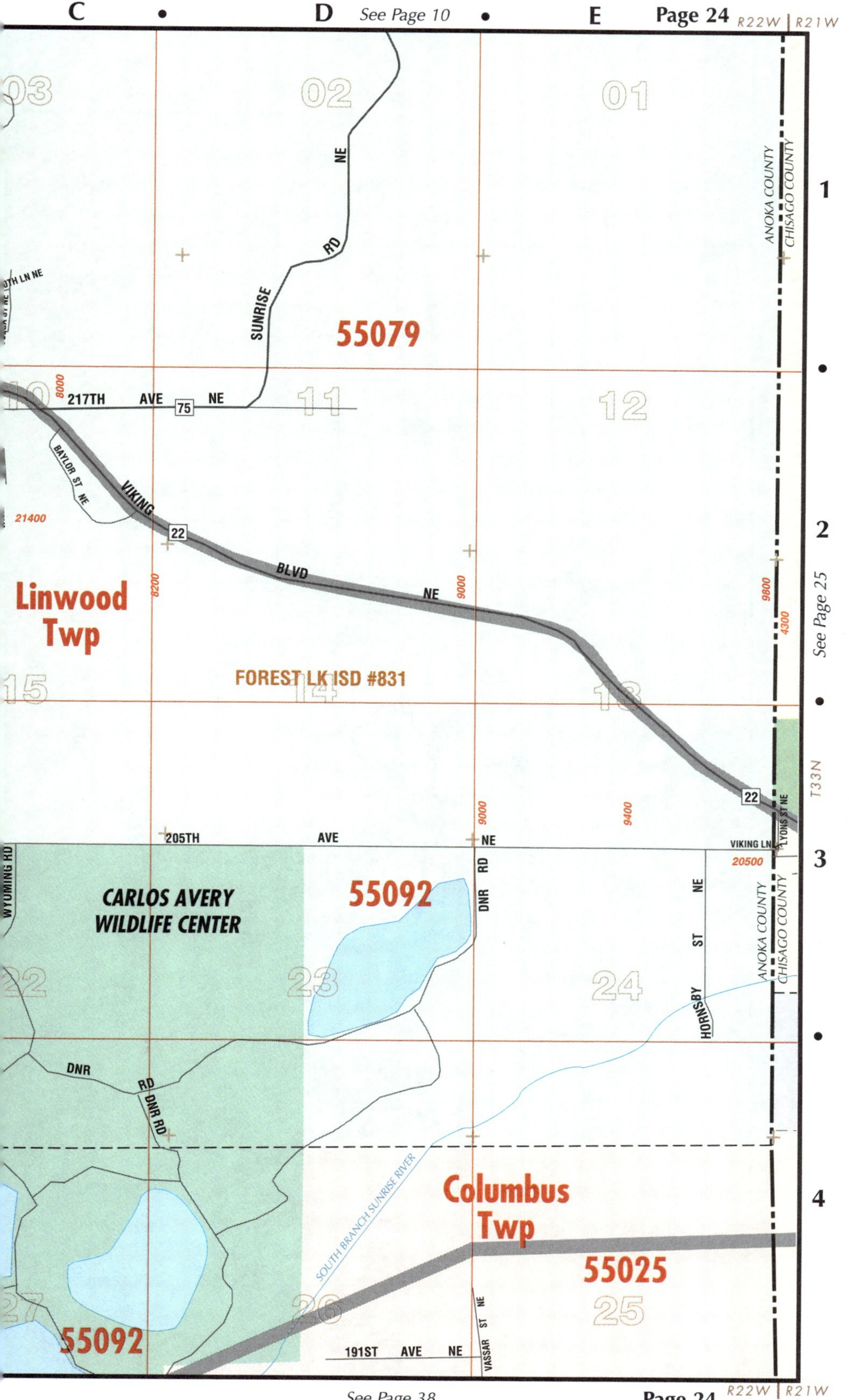

03   02   01

1

SUNRISE RD NE

55079

217TH   AVE   NE   75   11   12

BAYLOR ST NE

VIKING

21400

22

**Linwood
Twp**

8200

BLVD   NE   9000

See Page 25

FOREST LK ISD #831

15   14   13

22   LYONS ST NE

205TH   AVE   NE   9000   9400   VIKING LN   20500

55092

DNR RD

9800

4300

T33N

3

**CARLOS AVERY
WILDLIFE CENTER**

22   23   24

WYOMING RD

HORNSBY ST NE

ANOKA COUNTY   CHISAGO COUNTY

DNR   RD   DNR RD

**Columbus
Twp**

SOUTH BRANCH SUNRISE RIVER

4

27   26   25

55025

55092

191ST   AVE   NE   VASSAR ST NE

R22W | R21W Page 25 A • See Page 11 B • C

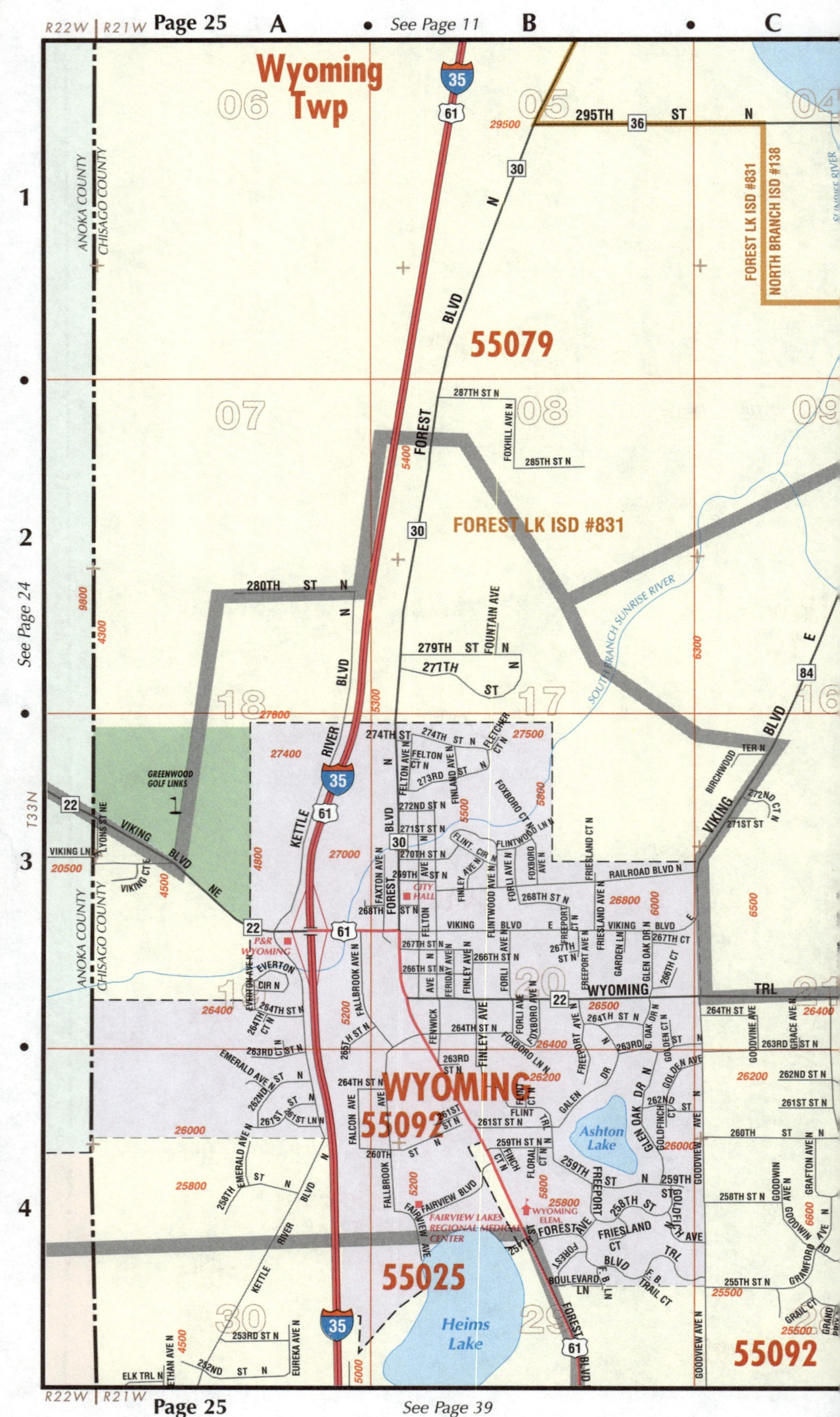

See Page 24

R22W | R21W Page 25 See Page 39

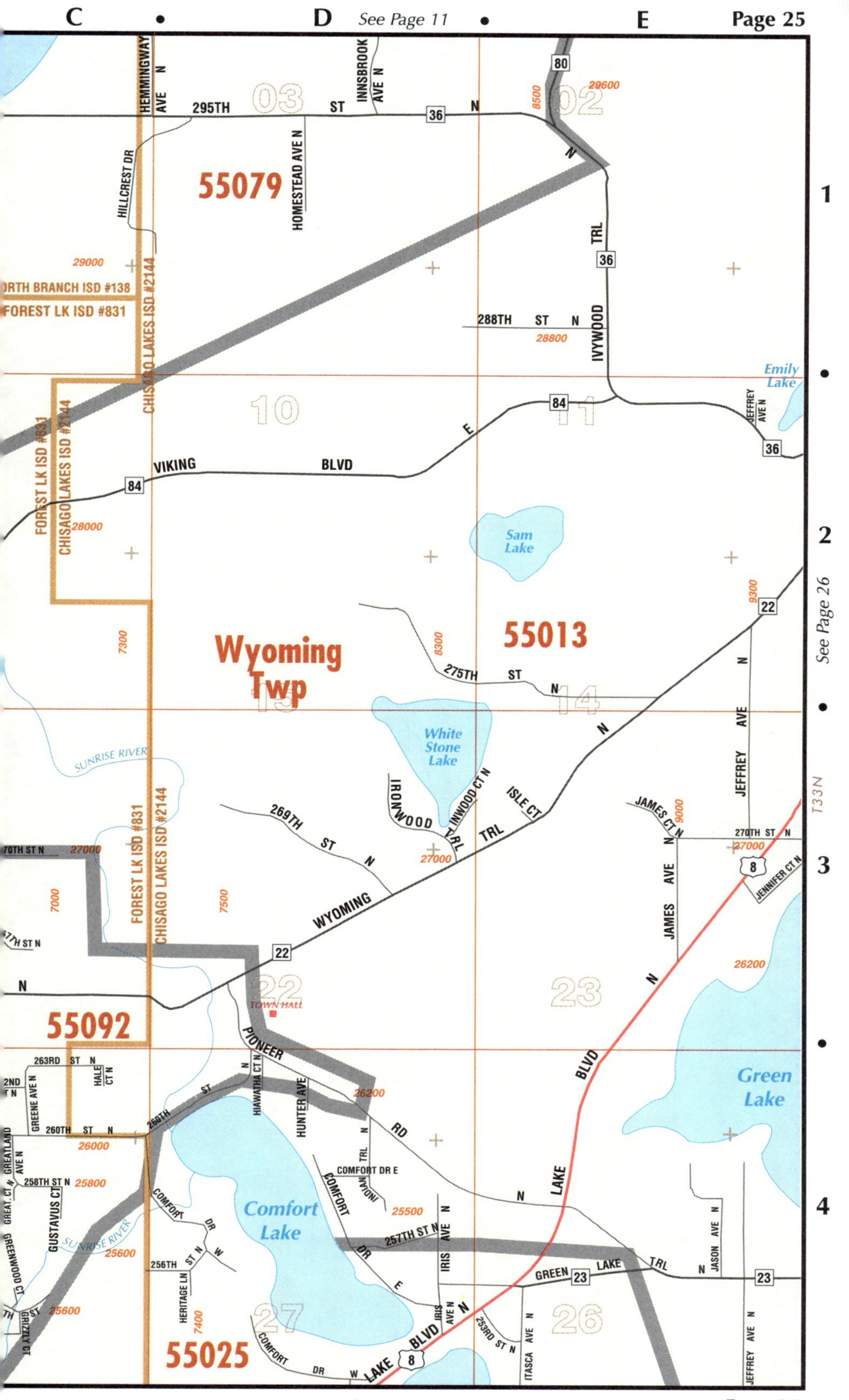

HEMMINGWAY AVE N

295TH ST

03

INNSBROOK AVE N

36 N

8500

80

20600

02

HILLCREST DR

55079

HOMESTEAD AVE N

36

TRL

36

NORTH BRANCH ISD #138

FOREST LK ISD #831

29000

CHISAGO LAKES ISD #2144

288TH ST N

28800

IVYWOOD

Emily Lake

FOREST LK ISD #831

CHISAGO LAKES ISD #2144

10

84

11

Jeffrey AVE N

36

84

VIKING

BLVD

E

Sam Lake

28000

2

7300

Wyoming Twp

19

55013

9300

22

See Page 26

8300

275TH ST

N

14

SUNRISE RIVER

White Stone Lake

JEFFREY AVE

T33N

FOREST LK ISD #831

CHISAGO LAKES ISD #2144

7000

70TH ST N

27000

269TH ST N

IRONWOOD TRL

INWOOD CT N

ISLE CT

N

TRL

JAMES CT N

9000

270TH ST N

27000

7500

27000

WYOMING

N

JAMES AVE N

8

Jennifer CT N

3

67TH ST N

N

22

22

TOWN HALL

23

26200

55092

PIONEER

HIAWATHA CT N

HUNTER AVE N

RD

26200

LAKE BLVD N

Green Lake

263RD ST N

HALE CT N

256TH

GREENE AVE N

2ND

260TH ST N

26000

COMFORT DR E

INDIAN TRL N

25500

IRIS AVE N

N

JASON AVE N

GREAT CT N GREATLAND

258TH ST N 25800

SUNRISE RIVER

COMFORT DR W

Comfort Lake

257TH ST N

N

GREEN 23 LAKE TRL

23

GUSTAVUS CT N

25600

256TH ST N W

HERITAGE LN

7400

COMFORT DR E

GREENWOOD CT N

25600

GRIZZLY LN

27

COMFORT DR W

LAKE BLVD

8

IRIS AVE N

253RD ST N

ITASCA AVE N

26

JEFFREY AVE N

55025

4

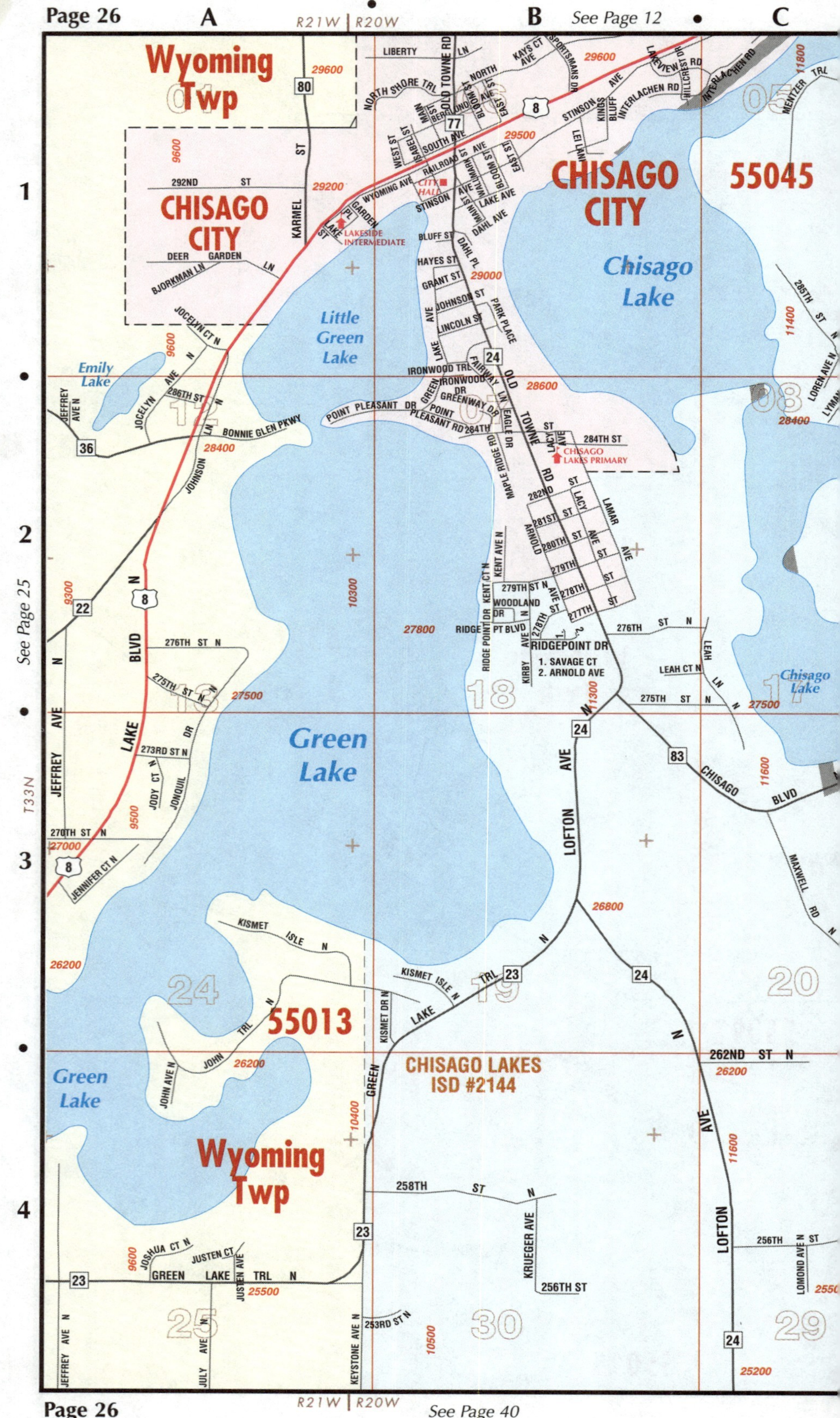
A
B
C
R21W | R20W
See Page 12
Wyoming Twp
CHISAGO CITY
CHISAGO CITY
55045
Chisago Lake
Little Green Lake
Emily Lake
Green Lake
Green Lake
55013
Wyoming Twp
CHISAGO LAKES ISD #2144
LAKESIDE INTERMEDIATE
CHISAGO LAKES PRIMARY
CITY HALL
1. SAVAGE CT
2. ARNOLD AVE
See Page 25
T33N
1
2
3
4
R21W | R20W
See Page 40

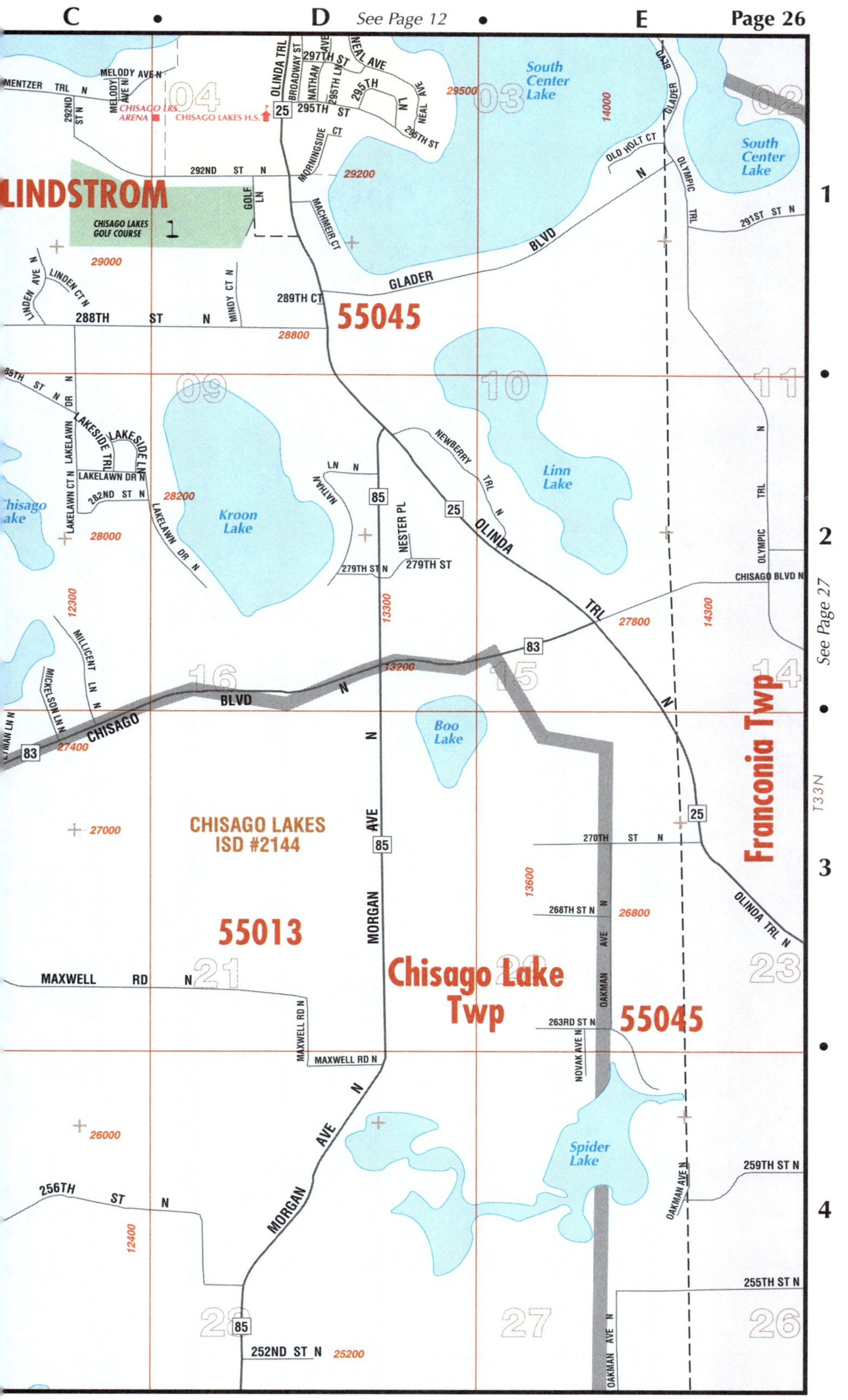

MENTZER TRL

MELODY AVE N

MELODY AVE N

OLINDA TRL
BROADWAY ST
297TH ST
NATHAN AVE
295TH LN
NEAL AVE

04

CHISAGO LKS. ARENA

CHISAGO LAKES H.S.

25

295TH

295TH ST

297TH ST

295TH ST

29500

03

South Center Lake

South Center Lake

OLAR

OLYMPIC TRL

14000

292ND ST N

292ND ST N

MORNINGSIDE CT

29200

OLD HOLT CT

N

291ST ST N

1

LINDSTROM

CHISAGO LAKES GOLF COURSE

1

GOLF LN

MACHMEIR CT

GLADER

BLVD

LINDEN AVE N

LINDEN CT N

29000

288TH ST N

288TH ST N

MINDY CT N

289TH CT N

28800

GLADER

55045

95TH ST N

LAKESIDE TRL

LAKESIDE DR

09

Kroon Lake

NATHAN LN N

85

NESTER PL

NEWBERRY TRL N

10

Linn Lake

25

OLINDA

11

OLYMPIC TRL

2

LAKELAWN CT N

LAKELAWN DR N

282ND ST N

28200

Chisago Lake

28000

LAKELAWN DR N

279TH ST N

279TH ST

13300

TRL

27800

CHISAGO BLVD N

14300

See Page 27

MILLICENT LN N

12300

16

CHISAGO

BLVD

N

13200

83

15

Boo Lake

N

27800

N

14

Franconia Twp

MICKELSON LN N

MAN LN N

83

27400

N

MORGAN

AVE

N

85

27000

CHISAGO LAKES ISD #2144

270TH

25

ST

N

3

13600

268TH ST N

26800

T33N

55013

MAXWELL RD N

MAXWELL RD

N

21

Chisago Lake Twp

OAKMAN AVE N

263RD ST N

NOVAK AVE N

55045

OLINDA TRL N

23

MAXWELL RD N

26000

MORGAN AVE N

Spider Lake

OAKMAN AVE N

259TH ST N

4

256TH ST N

12400

MORGAN AVE N

255TH ST N

28

85

252ND ST N

25200

27

OAKMAN AVE N

26

255TH ST N

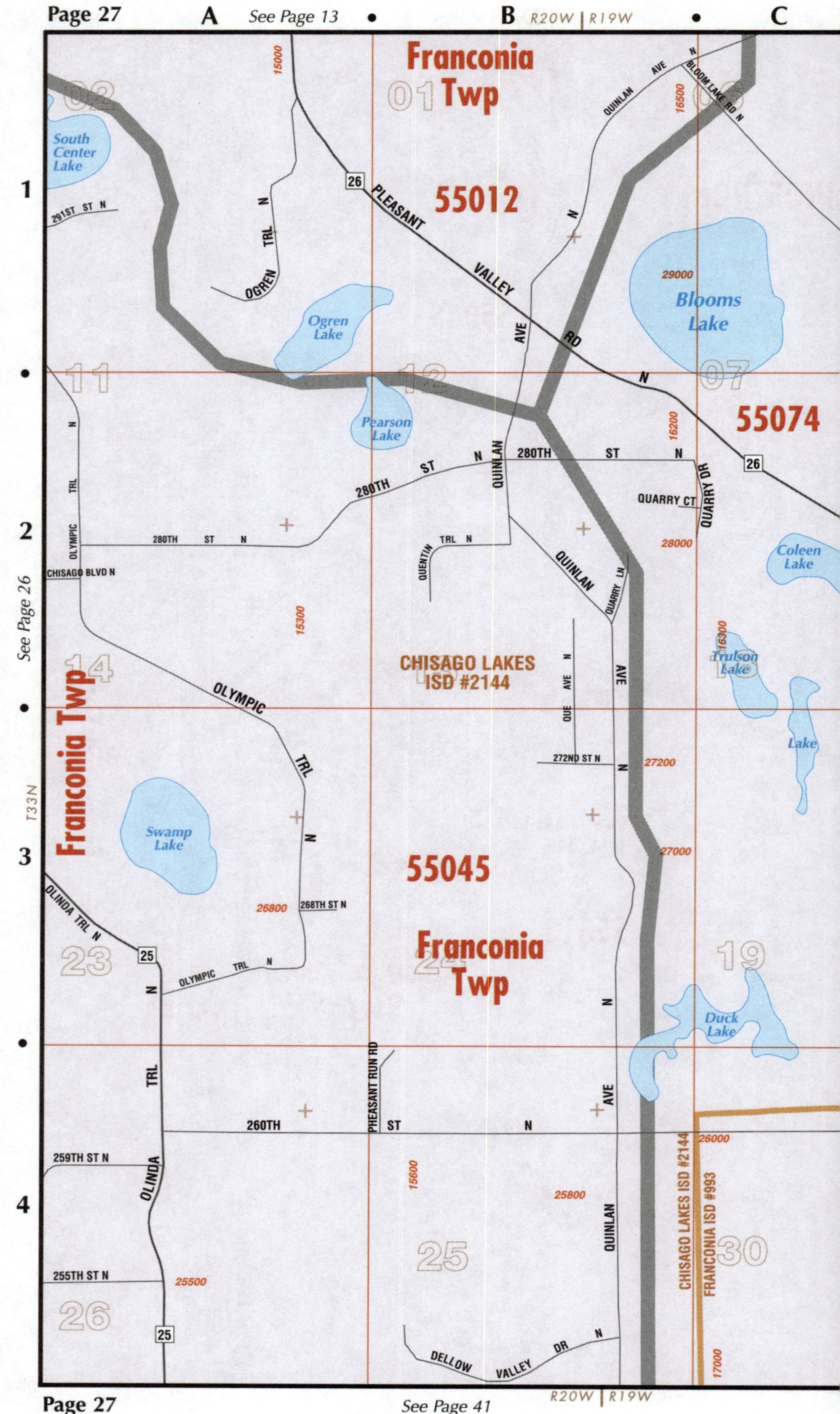

Franconia Twp

01

55012

02

15000

291ST ST N

OGREN TRL N

26 PLEASANT VALLEY AVE RD

QUINLAN AVE N

BLOOM LAKE RD N

16500

03

29000

Blooms Lake

South Center Lake

Ogren Lake

11

12

07

55074

Pearson Lake

N

16200

26

280TH ST N

280TH ST N

QUINLAN AVE N

QUARRY DR

QUARRY CT

280TH ST N

QUENTIN TRL N

QUINLAN AVE N

QUARRY LN

280TH ST N

28000

Coleen Lake

OLYMPIC TRL N

CHISAGO BLVD N

15300

CHISAGO LAKES ISD #2144

QUE AVE N

16300

Trulson Lake

14

Franconia Twp

OLYMPIC TRL N

272ND ST N

27200

Lake

Swamp Lake

26800

268TH ST N

55045

Franconia Twp

27000

19

OLINDA TRL N

23

25

OLYMPIC TRL N

QUINLAN AVE N

Duck Lake

OLINDA TRL N

PHEASANT RUN RD

260TH ST N

QUINLAN AVE N

CHISAGO LAKES ISD #2144

FRANCONIA ISD #993

26000

30

259TH ST N

15600

25800

25

255TH ST N

25500

26

25

DELLOW VALLEY DR N

17000

See Page 26

T33N

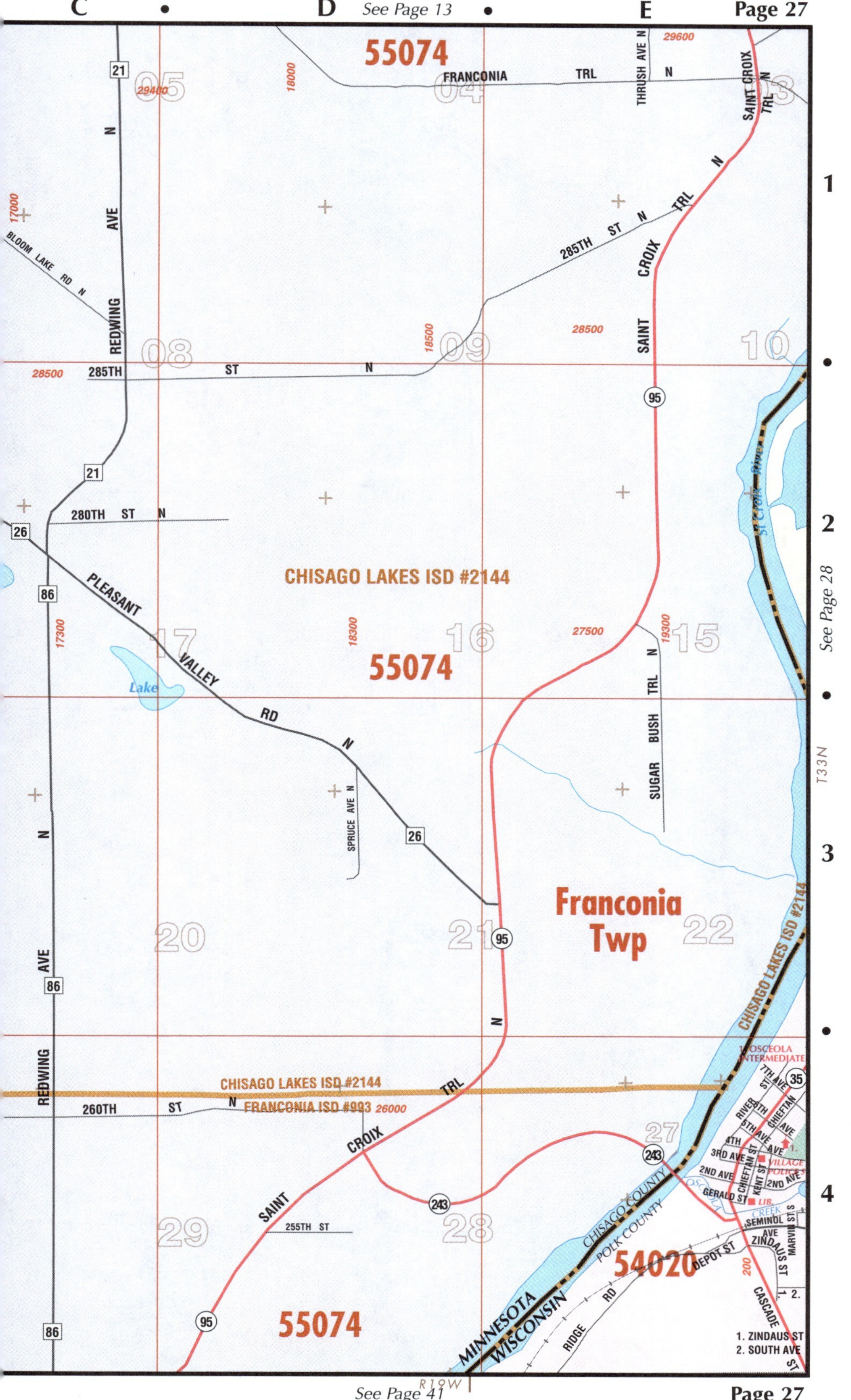
55074
FRANCONIA TRL
THRUSH AVE N
29600
SAINT CROIX TRL N
REDWING AVE N
BLOOM LAKE RD N
285TH ST N
28500
18500
SAINT CROIX
280TH ST N
PLEASANT VALLEY RD N
CHISAGO LAKES ISD #2144
55074
Lake
SPRUCE AVE N
SUGAR BUSH TRL N
27500
19300
St Croix River
Franconia Twp
CHISAGO LAKES ISD #2144
260TH ST N
FRANCONIA ISD #993 26000
SAINT CROIX TRL N
255TH ST
55074
54020
MINNESOTA
WISCONSIN
CHISAGO COUNTY
POLK COUNTY
RIDGE RD
DEPOT ST
OSCEOLA INTERMEDIATE
VILLAGE POLICE
LIB.
CASCADE ST
1. ZINDAUS ST
2. SOUTH AVE
T33N
R19W
1
2
3
4

See Page 28

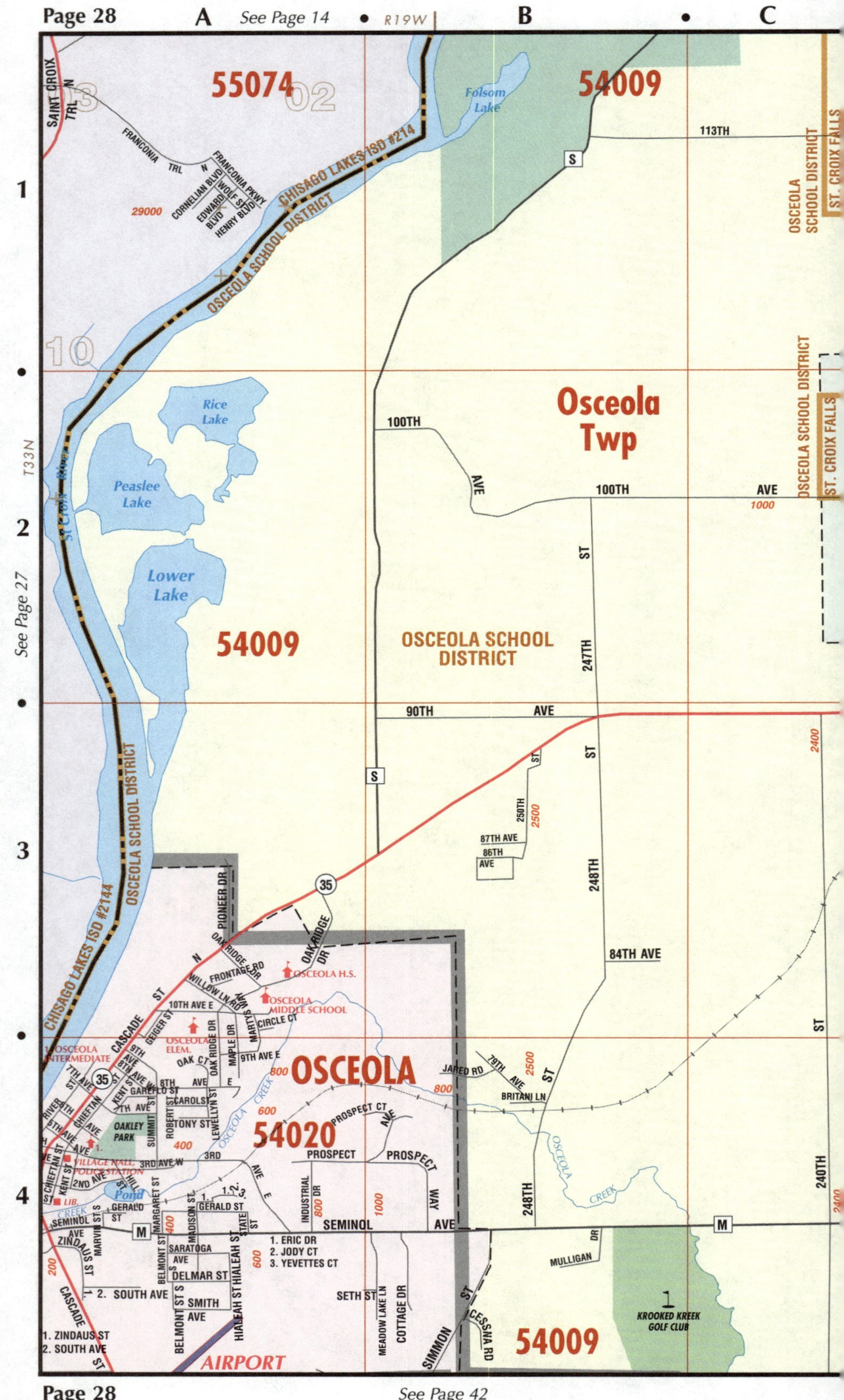

55074 02

54009

Folsom Lake

SAINT CROIX TRL

FRANCONIA TRL

FRANCONIA PKWY N

CORNELIAN BLVD

EDWARD S

WOLF S BLVD

HENRY BLVD

29000

CHISAGO LAKES ISD #214

OSCEOLA SCHOOL DISTRICT

113TH

S

OSCEOLA SCHOOL DISTRICT

ST. CROIX FALLS

1

T33N

St Croix River

Rice Lake

Peaslee Lake

Lower Lake

54009

100TH

AVE

100TH AVE

1000

OSCEOLA SCHOOL DISTRICT

ST. CROIX FALLS

Osceola Twp

2

See Page 27

OSCEOLA SCHOOL DISTRICT

247TH ST

OSCEOLA SCHOOL DISTRICT

OSCEOLA LAKES ISD #2144

90TH   AVE

S

250TH ST

2500

87TH AVE

86TH AVE

248TH ST

84TH AVE

2500

240TH ST

2400

2400

3

CHISAGO LAKES ISD #2144

PIONEER DR

35

OAKRIDGE DR

OAKRIDGE DR

FRONTAGE RD

WILLOW LN RD

Osceola H.S.

Osceola Middle School

CIRCLE CT

MARTY ST

Osceola Elem.

OAK RIDGE DR

MAPLE DR

9TH AVE E

OSCEOLA

800

Osceola Creek

OSCEOLA

JARED RD

79TH AVE

2500

BRITANI LN

OSCEOLA CREEK

248TH ST

240TH ST

2400

4

OSCEOLA INTERMEDIATE

35

CASCADE ST

GREGER S

10TH AVE E

LEWELLYN ST

5TH AVE

7TH AVE

GARFIELD ST

8TH AVE

KENT ST

7TH AVE

ROBERTS ST

SCAROLS ST

6TH AVE

OAK AVE E

TONY AVE

OAKLEY PARK

SUMMIT

5TH AVE

HIAWATHA AVE

CHIETIAN ST

RIVER

4TH AVE

600

800

800

PROSPECT CT

400

PROSPECT AVE

PROSPECT

PROSPECT WAY

SEMINOL AVE

INDUSTRIAL DR

800

1000

54020

VILLAGE HALL

POLICE STATION

3RD AVE W

2ND AVE

CHIETAN ST

KENT ST

Pond

LIB

Osceola Creek

GERALD ST

MADISON ST

GERALD ST

STATE ST

MARGARET ST

400

SEMINOL AVE

ZINDAUS ST

MARVIN ST

200

BELMONT ST S

SARATOGA AVE

DELMAR ST

SMITH AVE

HIALEAH ST

600

1. ERIC DR
2. JODY CT
3. YEVETTES CT

SETH ST

MEADOW LAKE LN

COTTAGE DR

SIMMON ST

CESSNA RD

MULLIGAN DR

M

M

1
KROOKED KREEK GOLF CLUB

54009

1
2. SOUTH AVE

CASCADE ST

1. ZINDAUS ST
2. SOUTH AVE

AIRPORT

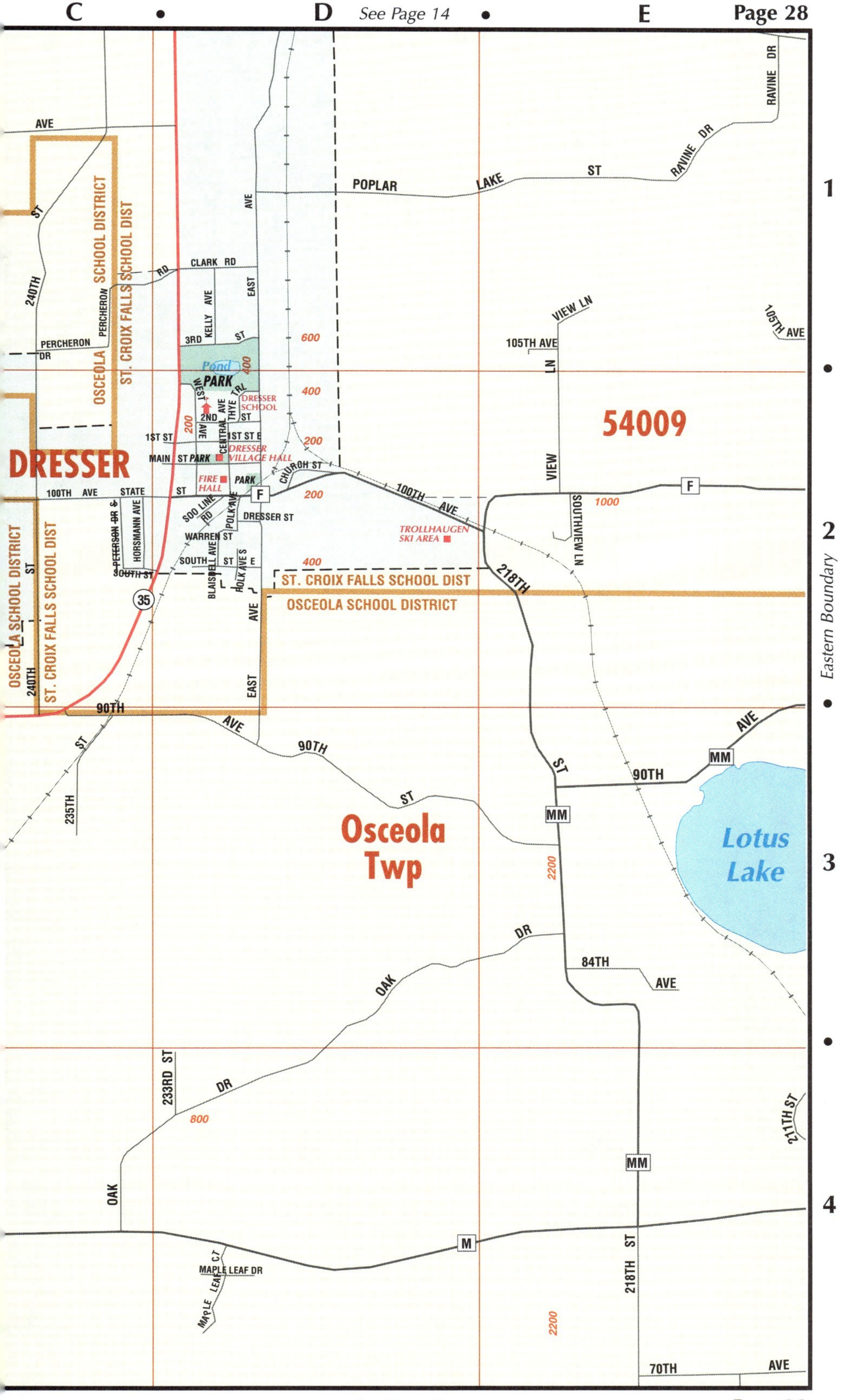

AVE

RAVINE DR

RAVINE DR

POPLAR LAKE ST

RAVINE DR

1

240TH ST

CLARK RD

105TH AVE

OSCEOLA PERCHERON SCHOOL DISTRICT

ST. CROIX FALLS SCHOOL DIST

PERCHERON DR

RD

3RD

KELLY AVE

AVE

ST

EAST AVE

600

VIEW LN

105TH AVE

LN

Pond

400

54009

PARK

DRESSER SCHOOL

400

THYE TRL

1ST ST E

200

VIEW LN

DRESSER

1ST ST

2ND

3RD

CENTRAL AVE

DRESSER VILLAGE HALL

100TH AVE

STATE ST

MAIN ST PARK

CHURCH ST

F

SOUTHVIEW LN

F

PETERSON DR

HORSMANN AVE

FIRE HALL

Park

100TH AVE

1000

100TH AVE

SOO LINE RD

POLK AVE

DRESSER ST

200

TROLLHAUGEN SKI AREA

2

WARREN ST

BLAISDELL AVE

SOUTH

POLK AVE S

400

218TH ST

OSCEOLA SCHOOL DISTRICT

ST. CROIX FALLS SCHOOL DIST

ST. CROIX FALLS SCHOOL DIST

SOUTH ST

35

EAST AVE

OSCEOLA SCHOOL DISTRICT

90TH

90TH AVE

90TH AVE

MM

ST

235TH ST

90TH ST

MM

Osceola Twp

2200

ST

Lotus Lake

3

OAK DR

84TH AVE

233RD ST

DR

800

OAK DR

211TH ST

Eastern Boundary

MM

OAK

MM

4

M

MAPLE LEAF DR

MAPLE LEAF CT

218TH ST

2200

70TH AVE

A • See Page 15 B • C

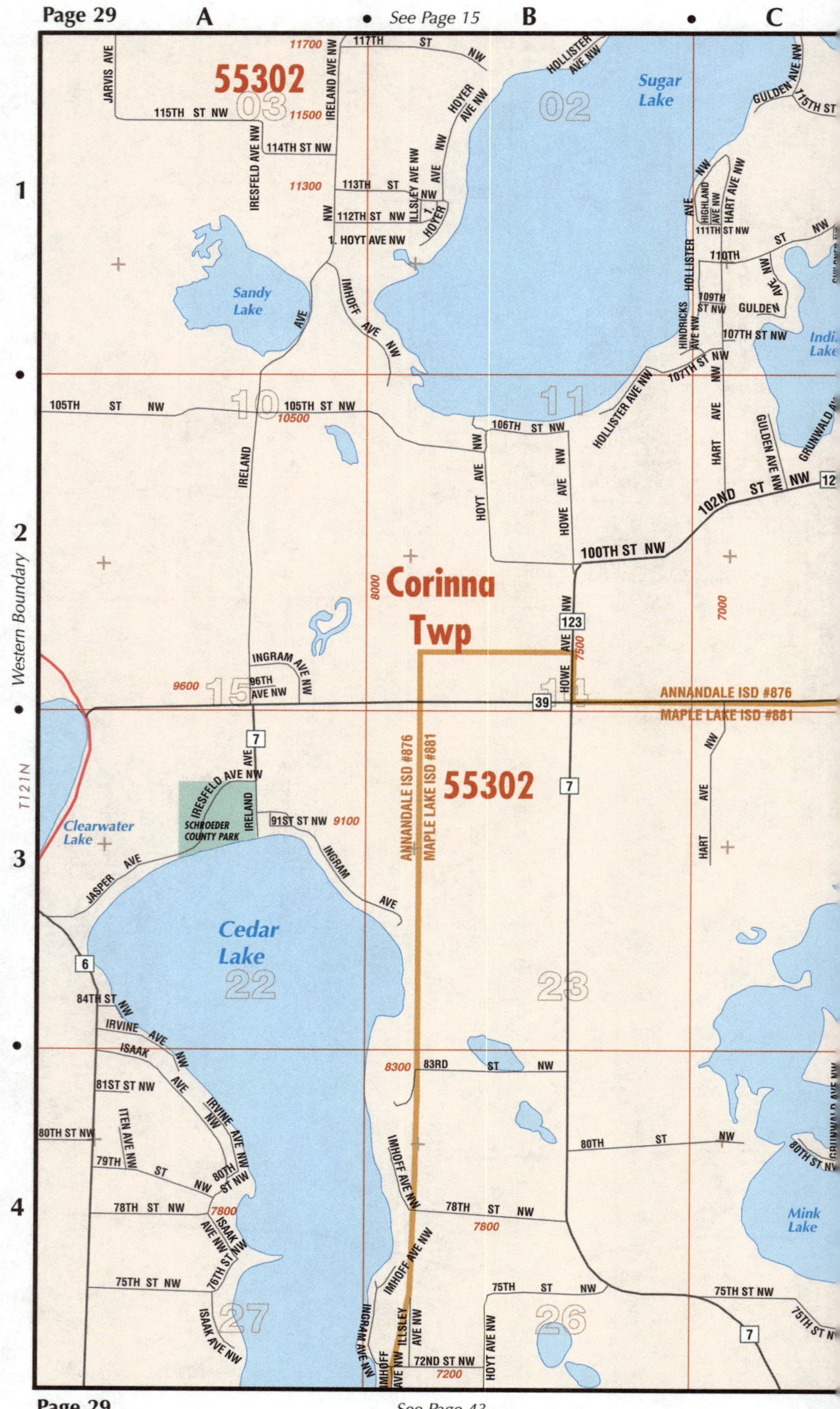

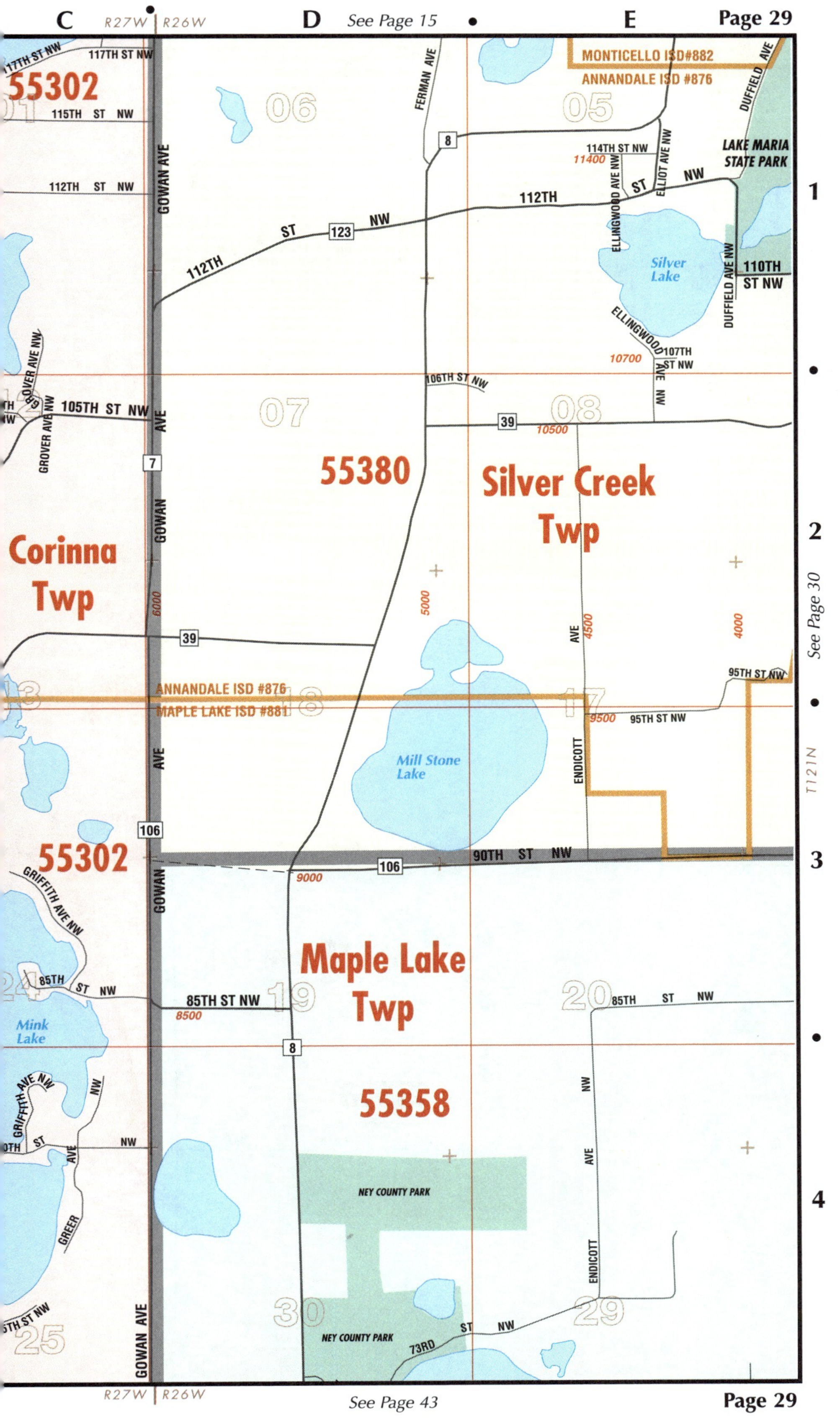

117TH ST NW
117TH ST NW

55302
115TH ST NW

112TH ST NW

GOWAN AVE

06

112TH ST 123 NW

112TH

105TH ST NW

GROVER AVE NW
GROVER AVE NW

7

GOWAN AVE

Corinna Twp

6000

39

39

ANNANDALE ISD #876
MAPLE LAKE ISD #881

AVE

55302

106

GOWAN AVE

GRIFFITH AVE NW

85TH ST NW
8500

Mink Lake

GRIFFITH AVE NW

ST NW

GREER AVE NW

ST NW

25

FERMAN AVE

8

07

55380

5000

39

9000

106

85TH ST NW 19

8

Maple Lake Twp

55358

NEY COUNTY PARK

30

NEY COUNTY PARK

73RD ST NW

See Page 15

MONTICELLO ISD#882
ANNANDALE ISD #876

DUFFIELD AVE

05

LAKE MARIA STATE PARK

114TH ST NW
11400

112TH

ELLINGWOOD AVE NW

ELLIOT AVE NW

ST NW

Silver Lake

110TH ST NW

DUFFIELD AVE NW

ELLINGWOOD AVE NW

107TH ST NW

10700

106TH ST NW

39
10500

08

Silver Creek Twp

AVE

4500

4000

95TH ST NW

17
9500

95TH ST NW

ENDICOTT AVE

90TH ST NW

20
85TH ST NW

NW

AVE

ENDICOTT AVE

29

1

2

See Page 30

T121N

3

4

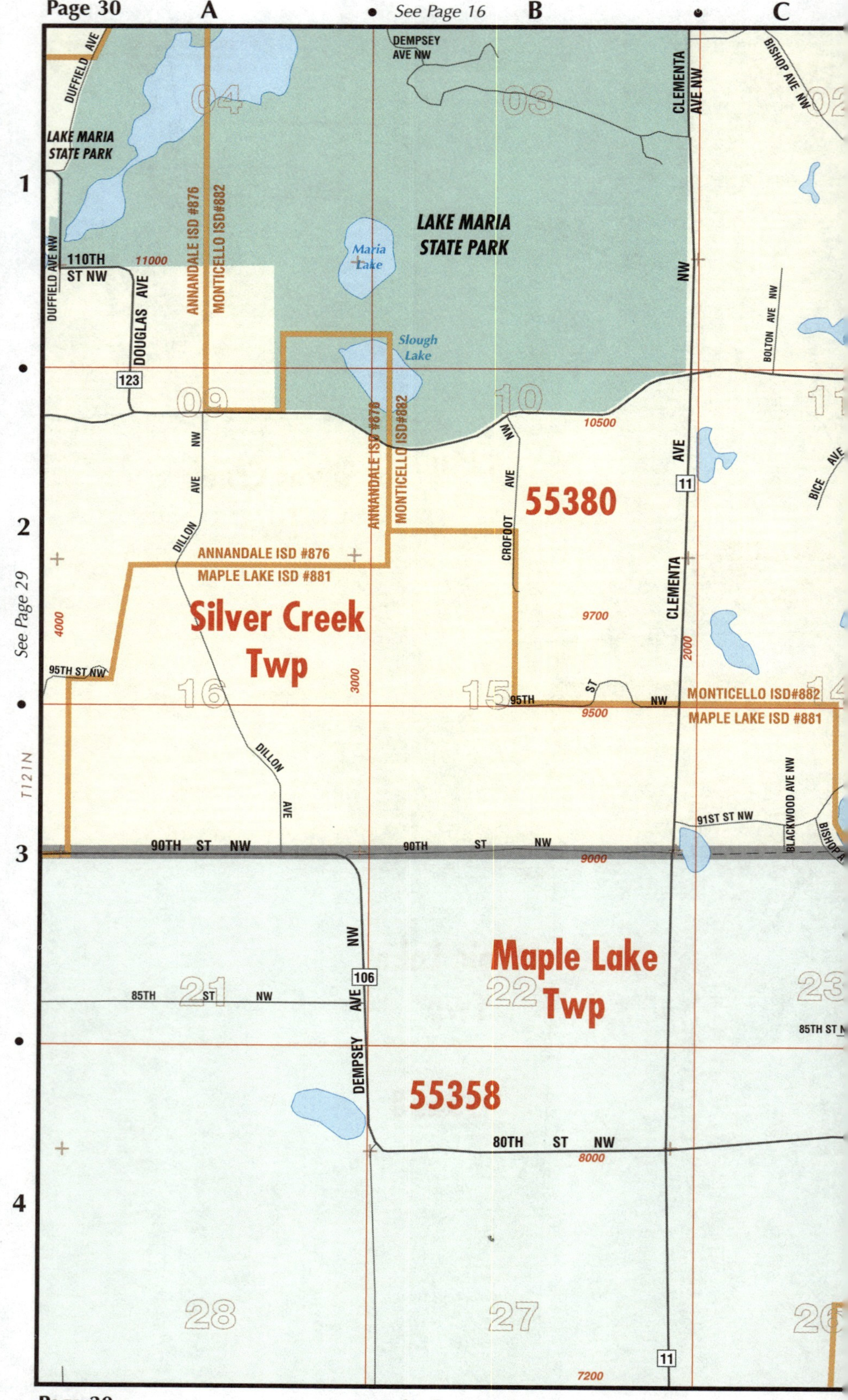

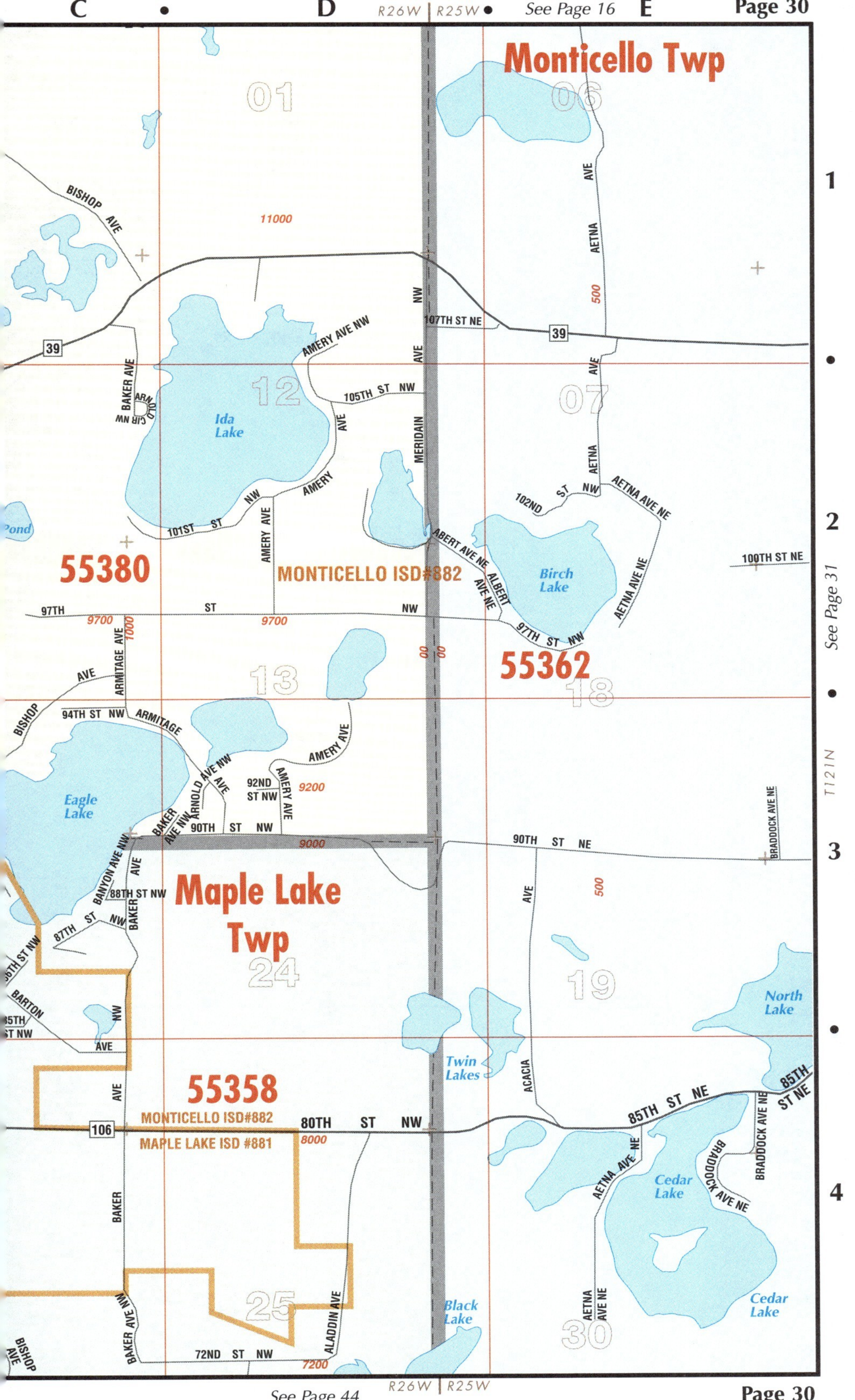

Monticello Twp

01

06

BISHOP AVE

11000

1

AETNA AVE

500

39

BAKER AVE

OLD CIR NW

107TH ST NE

NW

AMERY AVE NW

AVE

39

12

105TH ST NW

MERIDAIN

07

AVE

AETNA AVE

AMERY AVE

Ida Lake

AETNA AVE NE

102ND ST NW

AETNA AVE NE

101ST ST NW

2

100TH ST NE

55380

MONTICELLO ISD#882

ABERT AVE NE

ALBERT AVE NE

Birch Lake

97TH ST NW

Pond

97TH ST

9700

9700

NW

55362

See Page 31

ARMITAGE AVE

1000

13

00 00

18

3

BISHOP AVE

94TH ST NW

ARMITAGE

Eagle Lake

ARNOLD AVE NW

AMERY AVE

92ND ST NW

AMERY AVE

9200

BRADDOCK AVE NE

T121N

BAKER AVE NW

90TH ST NW

9000

90TH ST NE

BANYON AVE NW

AVE

Maple Lake Twp

24

AVE

500

19

88TH ST NW

87TH ST NW

North Lake

86TH ST NW

BARTON

85TH ST NW

AVE

85TH ST NE

85TH ST NE

55358

MONTICELLO ISD#882

MAPLE LAKE ISD#881

BAKER AVE

Twin Lakes

ACACIA

AETNA AVE NE

BRADDOCK AVE NE

BRADDOCK AVE NE

106

80TH ST NW

8000

Cedar Lake

4

BAKER AVE NW

25

ALADDIN AVE

Black Lake

AETNA AVE NE

30

Cedar Lake

BISHOP AVE

72ND ST NW

7200

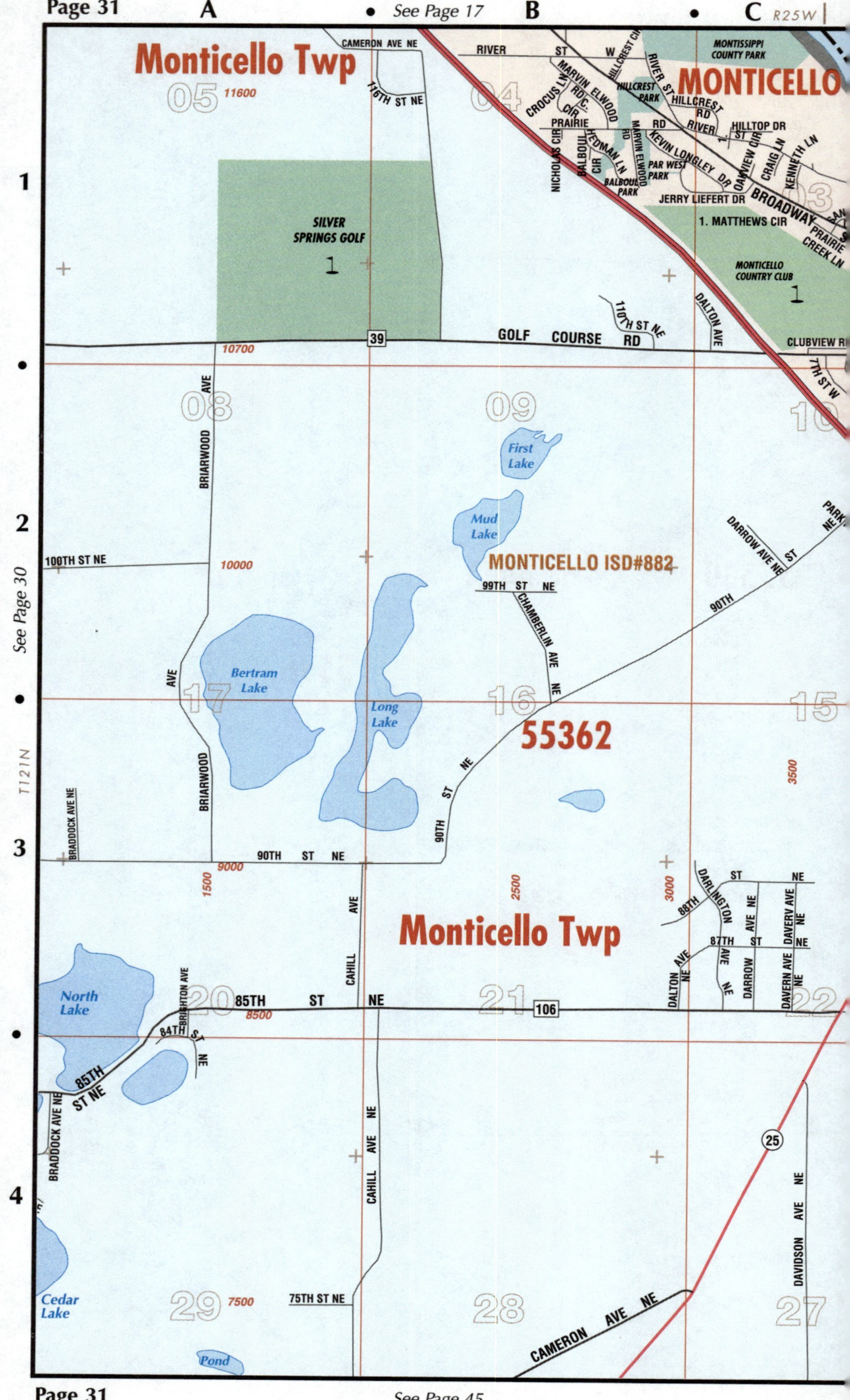

Monticello Twp
05 11600

MONTICELLO

SILVER SPRINGS GOLF

MONTISSIPPI COUNTY PARK

CAMERON AVE NE
RIVER
116TH ST NE

HILLCREST CH
RIVER ST
W
MARVIN ELWOOD RD
CROCUS CIR
NICHOLAS CIR
PRAIRIE
BALBOUL CIR
HEDMAN LN
BALBOUL PARK

HILLCREST PARK
HILLCREST RD
RIVER
RD
MARVIN ELWOOD RD
HILLTOP DR
KEVIN LONGLEY DR
OAKVIEW CIR
CRAIG LN
KENNETH LN
PAR WEST PARK
JERRY LIEFERT DR
BROADWAY
1. MATTHEWS CIR
PRAIRIE CREEK LN

10700
39
GOLF COURSE RD
110TH ST NE
DALTON AVE
7TH ST W
CLUBVIEW R

MONTICELLO COUNTRY CLUB
1

08
BRIARWOOD AVE
100TH ST NE
10000

09
First Lake
Mud Lake
MONTICELLO ISD#882
99TH ST NE
CHAMBERLIN AVE NE
90TH
DARROW AVE NE
ST
PARK NE
10

17
Bertram Lake
AVE
BRIARWOOD AVE
Long Lake
16
55362
15
3500

90TH ST NE
1500 9000
90TH ST NE
2500
3000
88TH
DARLINGTON
ST
NE
87TH
ST
NE
DALTON AVE
DARROW AVE NE
DAVERN AVE
DAVERY AVE NE

Monticello Twp

North Lake
BRADDOCK AVE NE
BRIGHTON AVE
20
85TH ST
8500
84TH ST NE
85TH ST NE
CAHILL AVE
21
106
NE
22

25

Cedar Lake
BRADDOCK AVE NE
29 7500
75TH ST NE
CAHILL AVE NE
28
27
DAVIDSON AVE NE

Pond
CAMERON AVE NE

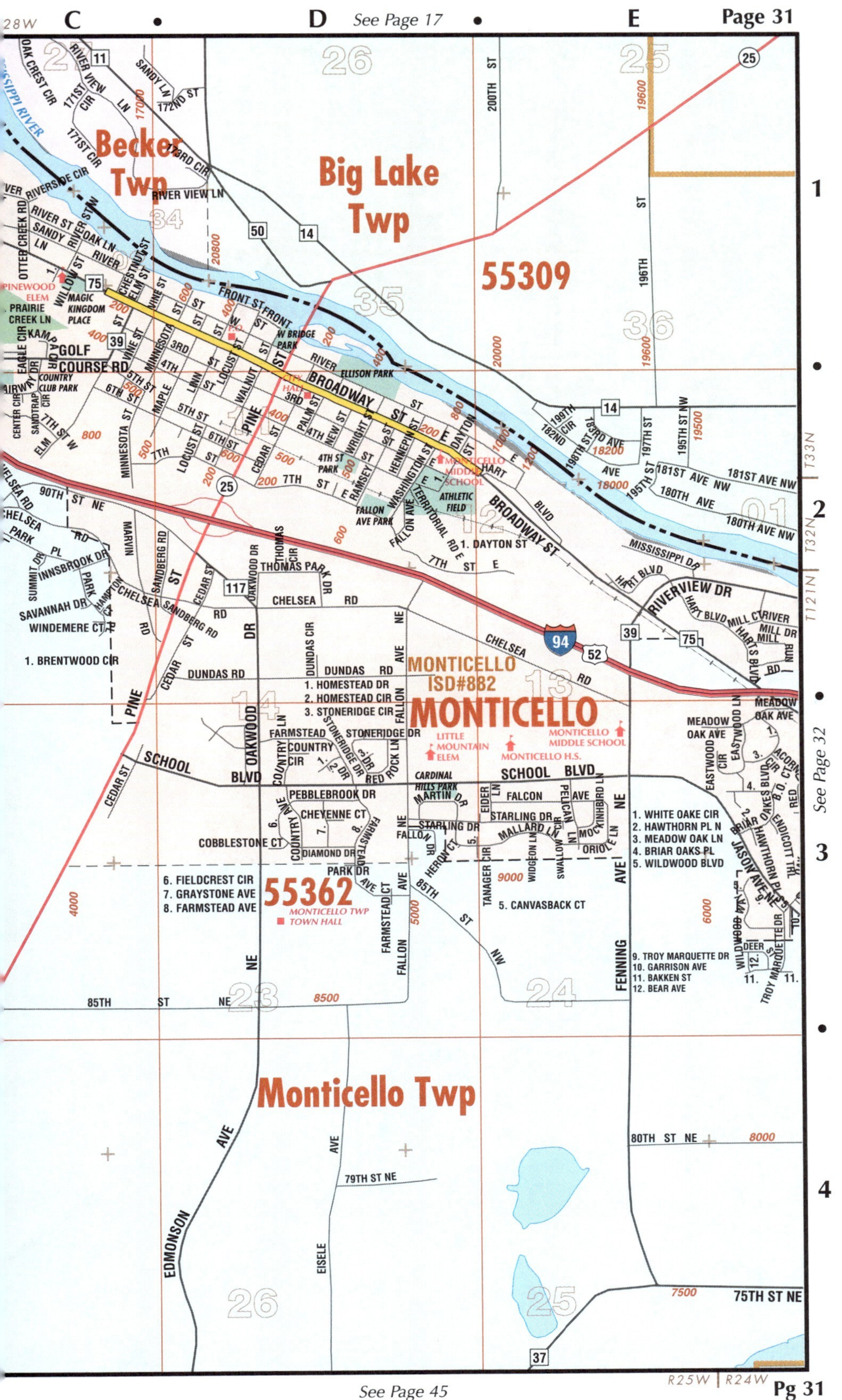

Becker Twp

Big Lake Twp

55309

Monticello ISD#882

MONTICELLO

55362
MONTICELLO TWP
TOWN HALL

Monticello Twp

1. BRENTWOOD CIR

1. HOMESTEAD DR
2. HOMESTEAD CIR
3. STONERIDGE CIR

6. FIELDCREST CIR
7. GRAYSTONE AVE
8. FARMSTEAD AVE

1. WHITE OAKE CIR
2. HAWTHORN PL N
3. MEADOW OAK LN
4. BRIAR OAKS PL
5. WILDWOOD BLVD

5. CANVASBACK CT

9. TROY MARQUETTE DR
10. GARRISON AVE
11. BAKKEN ST
12. BEAR AVE

See Page 32

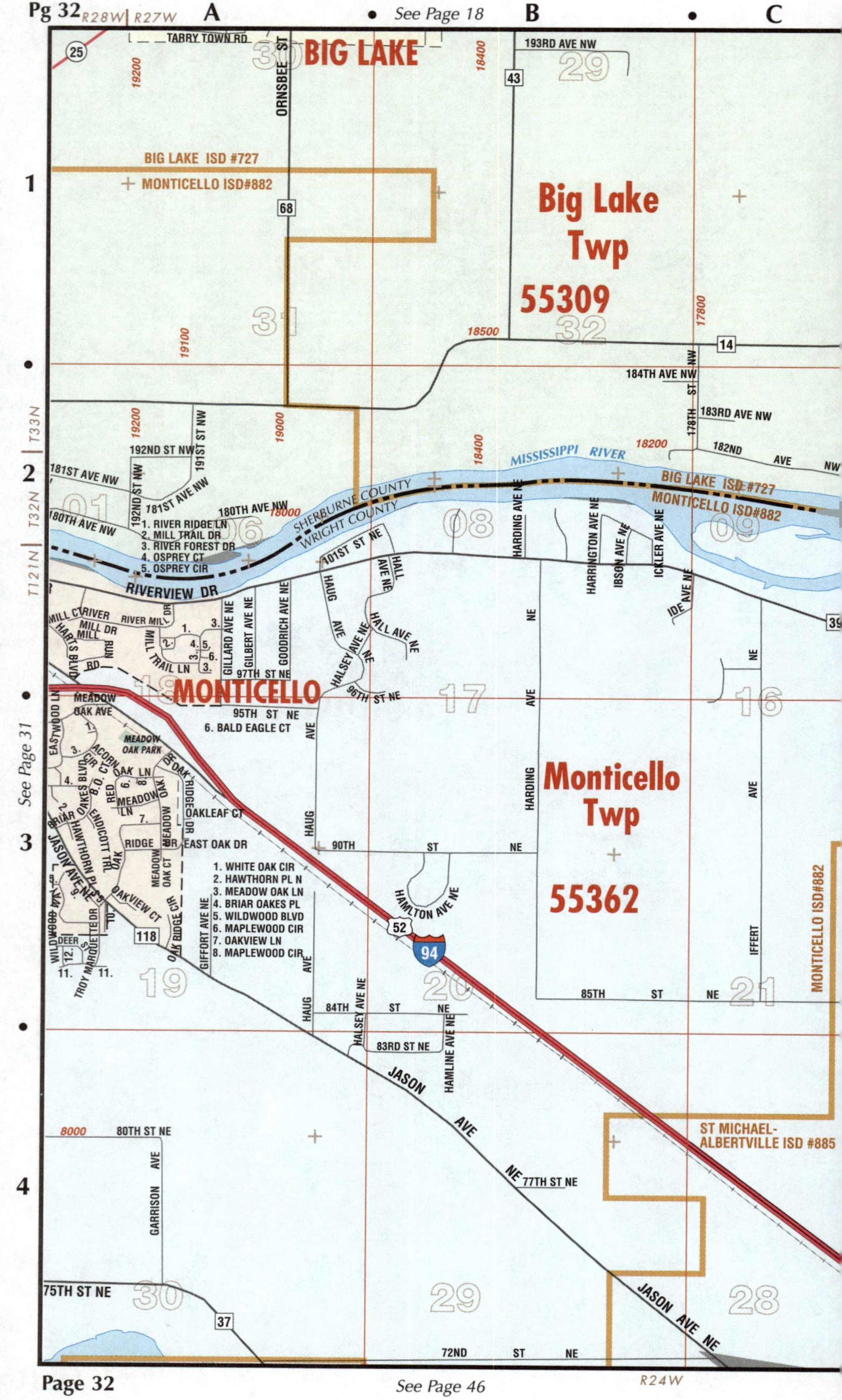

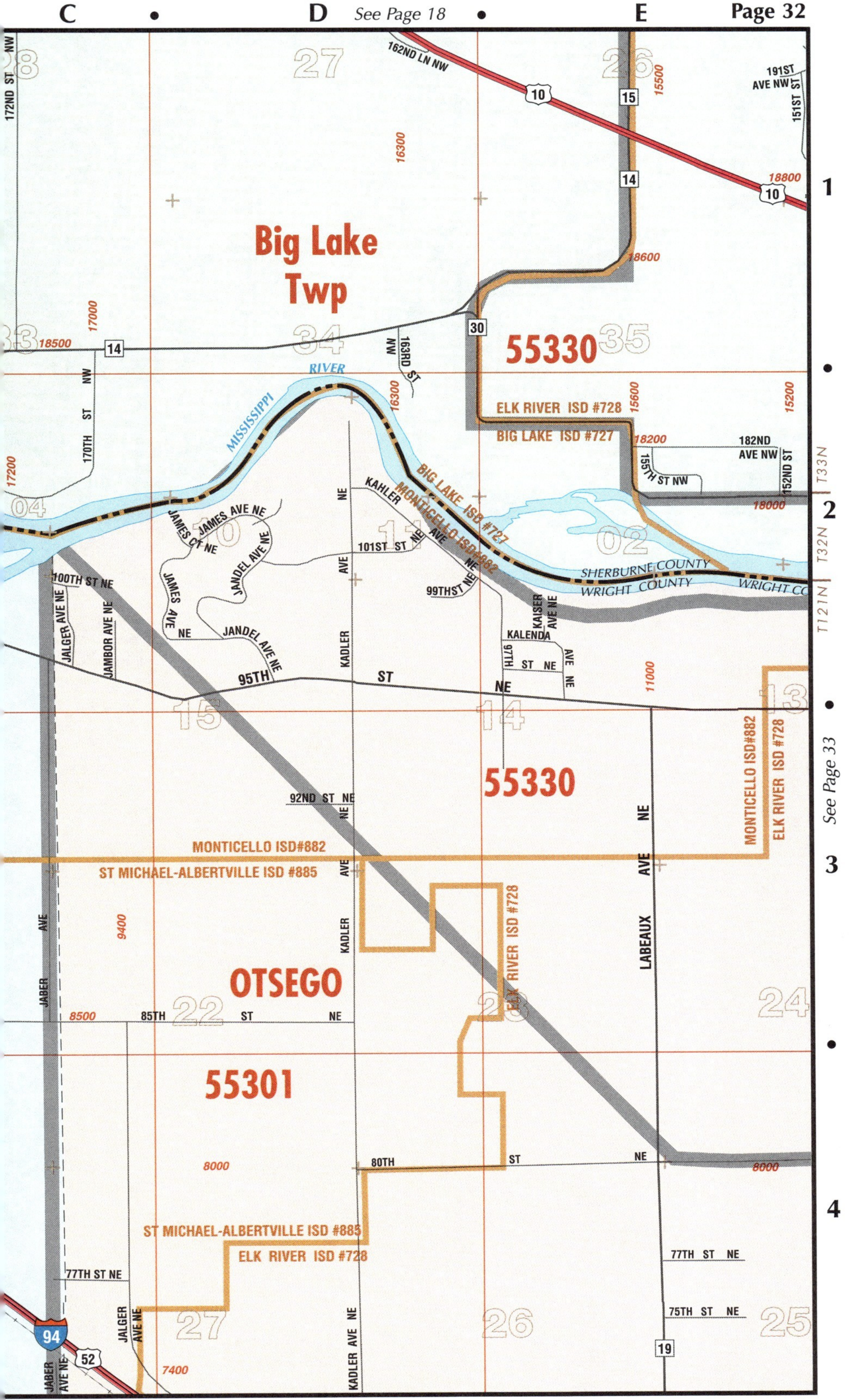

162ND LN NW

10

15 15500

191ST AVE NW

172ND ST NW

151ST ST

27

26

14

16300

10 18800

1

18600

Big Lake Twp

30

55330

35

14 18500

17000

34

163RD ST NW

NW

ELK RIVER ISD #728

15600 15200

33

15500

RIVER

16300

BIG LAKE ISD #727

18200

182ND AVE NW

155TH ST NW

152ND ST NW

T33N

17000

170TH ST NW

MISSISSIPPI

NE

KAHLER AVE NE

MONTICELLO ISD#882

18000

2

17200

04

10

James Ave NE

James Ct NE

Jandel Ave NE

101ST ST NE

11

NE AVE

BIG LAKE ISD #727

18000

02

T32N

T121N

100TH ST NE

James Ave NE

99TH ST NE

KAISER AVE NE

SHERBURNE COUNTY

WRIGHT COUNTY

WRIGHT CO

JALGER AVE NE

JAMBOR AVE NE

Jandel Ave NE

95TH

KADLER

ST

NE

KALENDA AVE NE

6TH ST NE

11000

13

15

14

55330

MONTICELLO ISD#882

ELK RIVER ISD #728

See Page 33

92ND ST NE

NE

LABEAUX AVE NE

3

MONTICELLO ISD#882

ST MICHAEL-ALBERTVILLE ISD #885

KADLER AVE

ELK RIVER ISD #728

9400

OTSEGO

8500

85TH

22

ST

NE

23

24

55301

8000

80TH

ST

NE

8000

JABER AVE NE

4

ST MICHAEL-ALBERTVILLE ISD #885

ELK RIVER ISD #728

77TH ST NE

77TH ST NE

75TH ST NE

94

52

JALGER AVE NE

27

7400

KADLER AVE NE

26

25

19

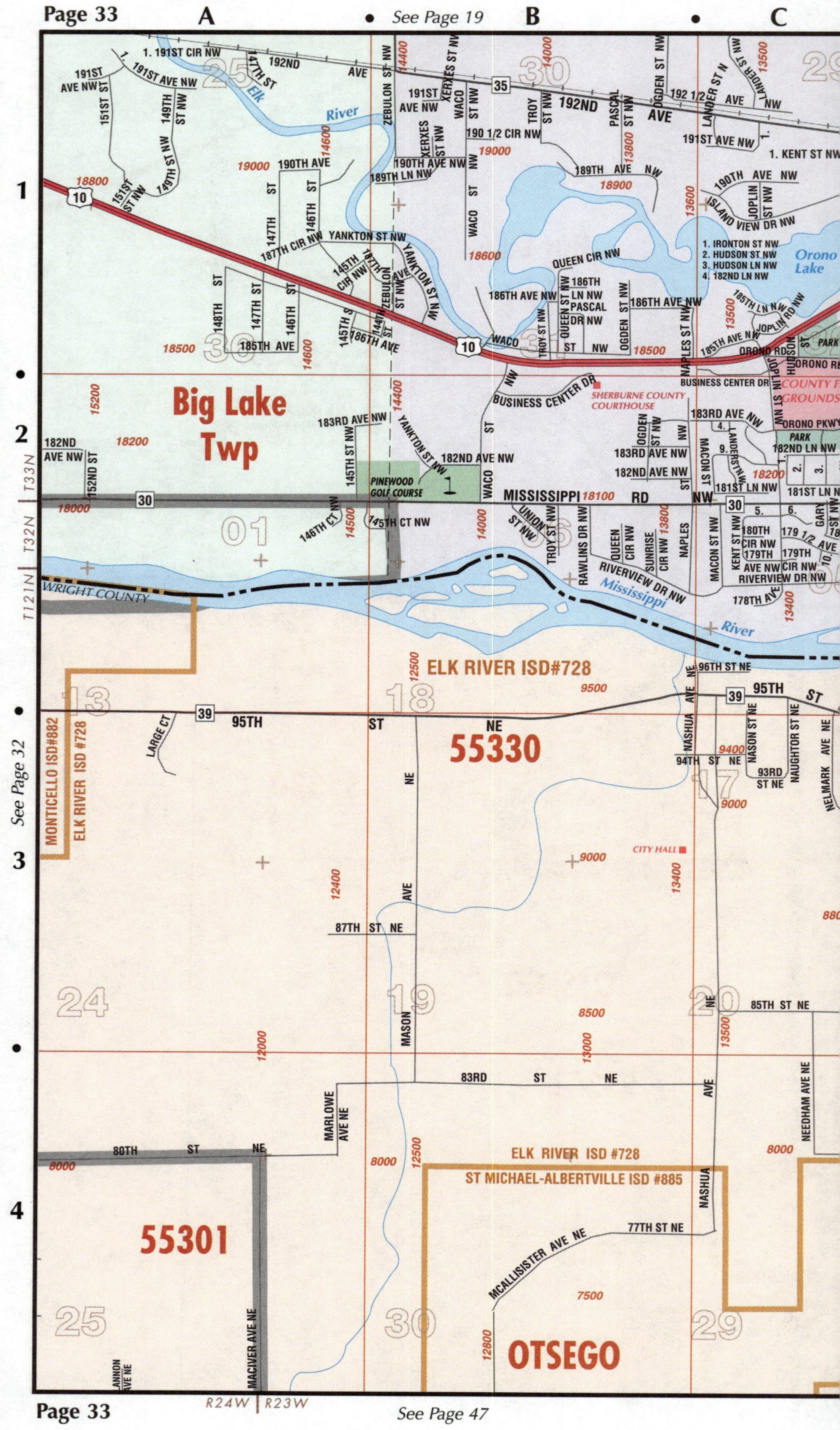

A B C

1

2

3

4

See Page 32

Big Lake Twp

15200

18200

182ND AVE NW

152ND ST

18000

WRIGHT COUNTY

T121N | T32N | T33N

191ST AVE NW
151ST ST

1. 191ST CIR NW
191ST AVE NW
14TH ST
192ND AVE

151ST ST NW
149TH ST NW
149TH ST N

18800
10

19000

190TH AVE

187TH CIR NW
147TH ST
146TH

147TH CIR NW
146TH
145TH
148TH ST
147TH ST
146TH ST
145TH CIR NW
146TH ST
145TH S

18500
185TH AVE

14600

183RD AVE NW

145TH ST NW
182ND AVE NW

PINEWOOD GOLF COURSE

146TH CT NW
145TH CT NW

ZEBULON ST NW
ZEBULON ST NW
YANKTON ST NW
YANKTON ST NW
WACO
WACO ST
YANKTON ST NW
WACO

14400
14600
14500
14000

XERXES ST NW
XERXES ST NW
191ST AVE NW
190TH AVE NW
189TH LN NW

WACO ST NW

QUEEN CIR NW
186TH AVE NW

QUEEN ST NW
QUEEN ST NW

TROY ST NW
OGDEN ST NW

186TH
LN NW
PASCAL
DR NW

TROY ST NW
OGDEN ST NW

35
14000
192ND
190 1/2 CIR NW

19000

18600

18900

18500

BUSINESS CENTER DR

MISSISSIPPI 18100 RD

18200

UNION ST NW
TROY ST NW
QUEEN ST NW

RAWLINS DR NW
RIVERVIEW DR NW

Mississippi

PASCAL AVE
192ND
191ST AVE NW

189TH AVE

ISLAND VIEW DR NW

186TH AVE NW

ORONO RD NW

SHERBURNE COUNTY COURTHOUSE

BUSINESS CENTER DR

183RD AVE NW

183RD AVE NW
OGDEN ST NW
182ND AVE NW

MACON ST NW

SUNRISE CIR NW
QUEEN CIR NW
NAPLES

13800
13600
13500

18500

13800

13400

River

OGDEN ST NW
LANDER ST N
192 1/2 AVE
ANDER ST N

1. KENT ST NW

190TH AVE NW
JOPLIN ST NW

13500

185TH LN N W
185TH LN N W
185TH AVE NW
JOPLIN RD NW

13600

Orono Lake

1. IRONTON ST NW
2. HUDSON ST NW
3. HUDSON LN NW
4. 182ND LN NW

COUNTY
GROUNDS

ORONO RD NW

HUDSON
ORONO PKW
PARK

182ND LN NW

ANDERSTMN

181ST LN NW
181ST LN N

30

KENT ST NW
180TH CIR NW
179TH AVE NW

179 1/2 AVE
179TH CIR NW
RIVERVIEW DR NW

GARY

178TH

13400

96TH ST NE

9500

12500

ELK RIVER ISD#728

95TH ST NE

95TH ST

39

NASHUA AVE NE
MASON ST NE
NAUGHTOR ST NE
NELMARK AVE NE

94TH ST NE
93RD ST NE

9400
9000

12400

9000

55330

CITY HALL

13400

87TH ST NE

MASON AVE NE

24

19

85TH ST NE

20

8500
13500

13000
12500

12000

83RD ST NE

MARLOWE AVE NE

80TH ST NE

8000
8000

NASHUA AVE NE
NEEDHAM AVE NE

8000

ELK RIVER ISD #728
ST MICHAEL-ALBERTVILLE ISD #885

77TH ST NE

55301

MACIVER AVE NE

25

30

12800

MCALLISTER AVE NE

7500

OTSEGO

29

8800

MONTICELLO ISD#882
ELK RIVER ISD #728

13

18

LARGE CT

R24W | R23W

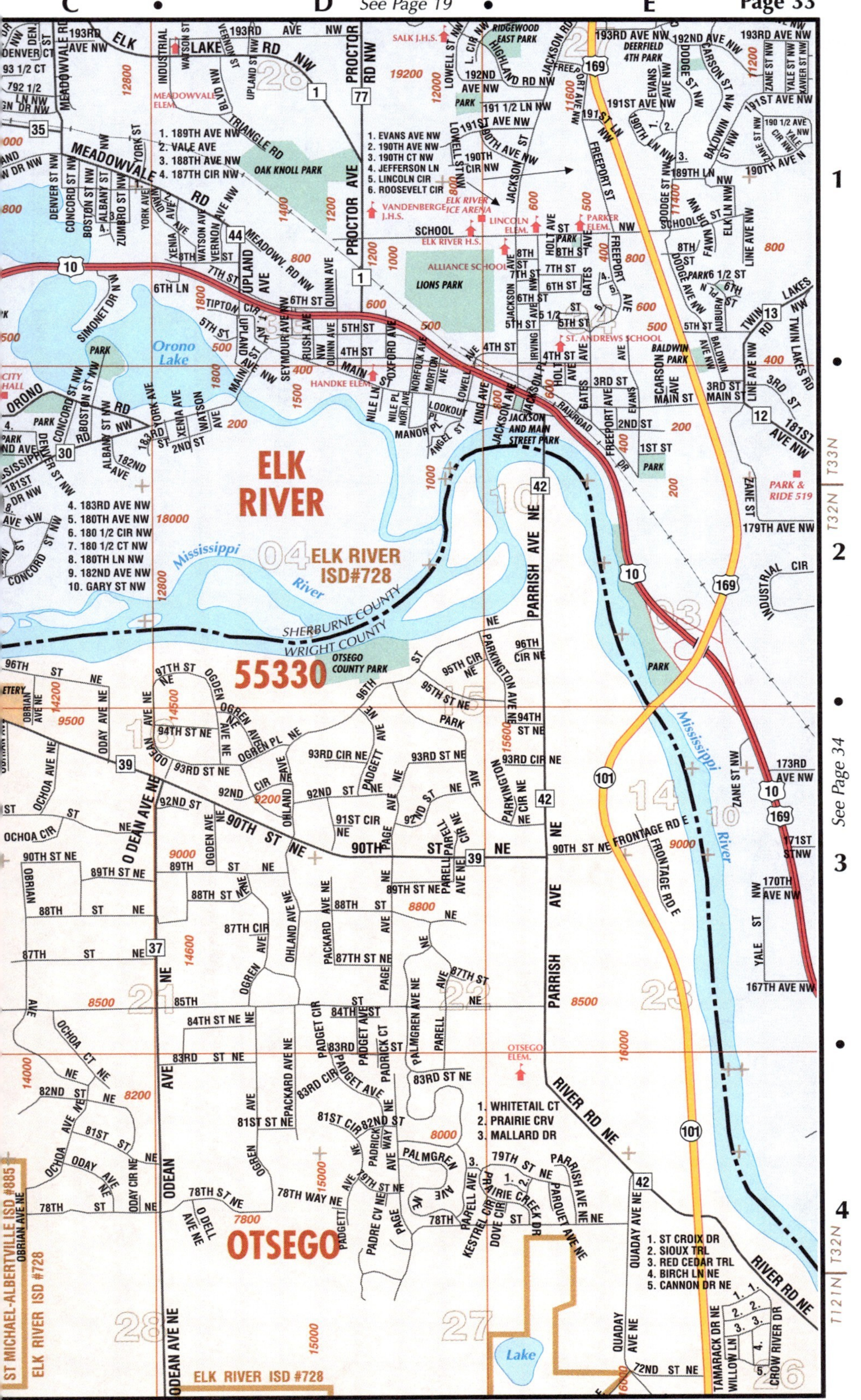
ELK RIVER
OTSEGO
55330
ELK RIVER ISD #728
Mississippi River
Orono Lake
SHERBURNE COUNTY
WRIGHT COUNTY
OAK KNOLL PARK
LIONS PARK
OTSEGO COUNTY PARK
JACKSON AND MAIN STREET PARK
ST MICHAEL-ALBERTVILLE ISD #885
1. 189TH AVE NW
2. VALE AVE
3. 188TH AVE NW
4. 187TH CIR NW
1. EVANS AVE NW
2. 190TH AVE NW
3. 190TH CT NW
4. JEFFERSON LN
5. LINCOLN CIR
6. ROOSEVELT CIR
4. 183RD AVE NW
5. 180TH AVE NW
6. 180 1/2 CIR NW
7. 180 1/2 CT NW
8. 180TH LN NW
9. 182ND AVE NW
10. GARY ST NW
1. WHITETAIL CT
2. PRAIRIE CRV
3. MALLARD DR
1. ST CROIX DR
2. SIOUX TRL
3. RED CEDAR TRL
4. BIRCH LN NE
5. CANNON DR NE

See Page 34

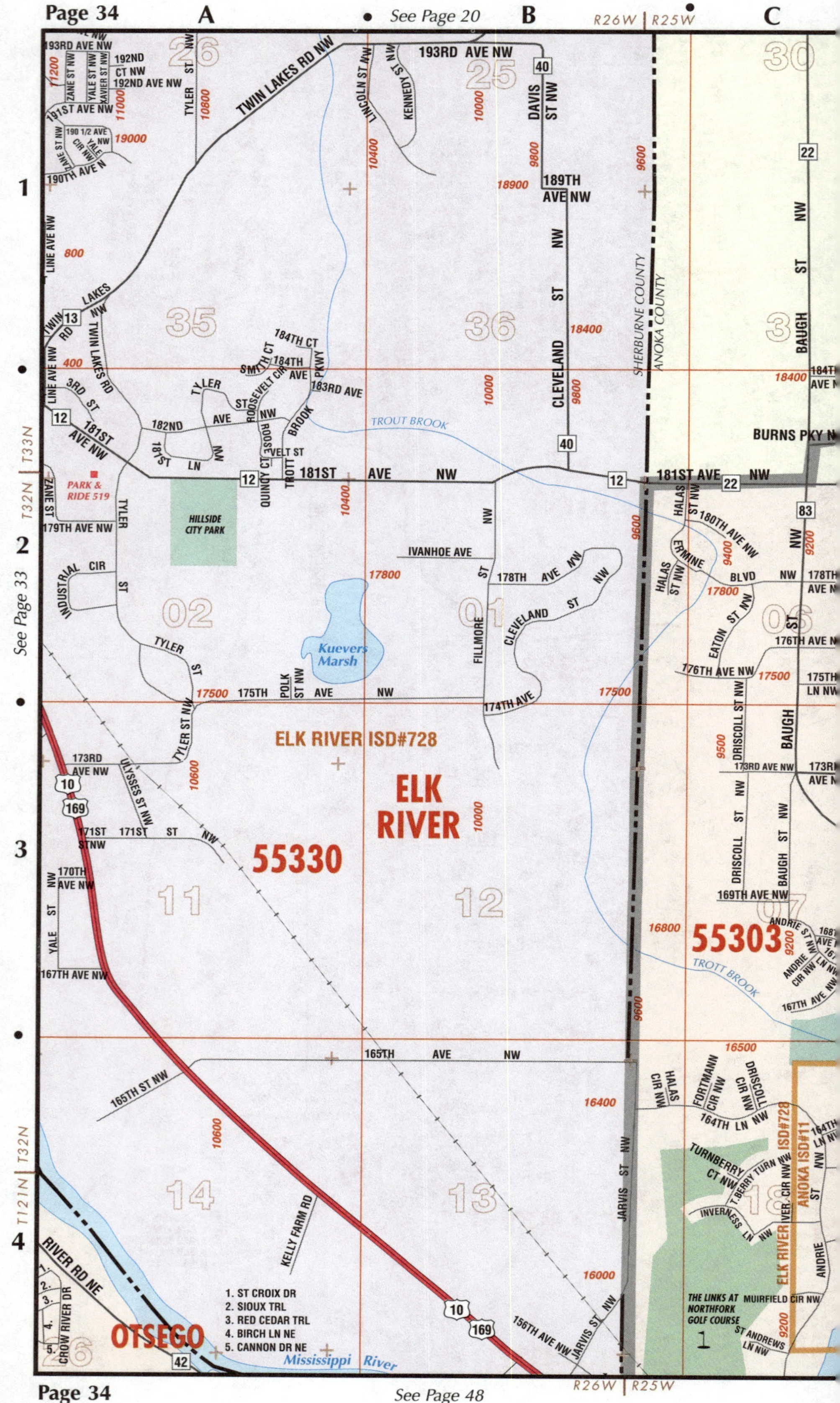

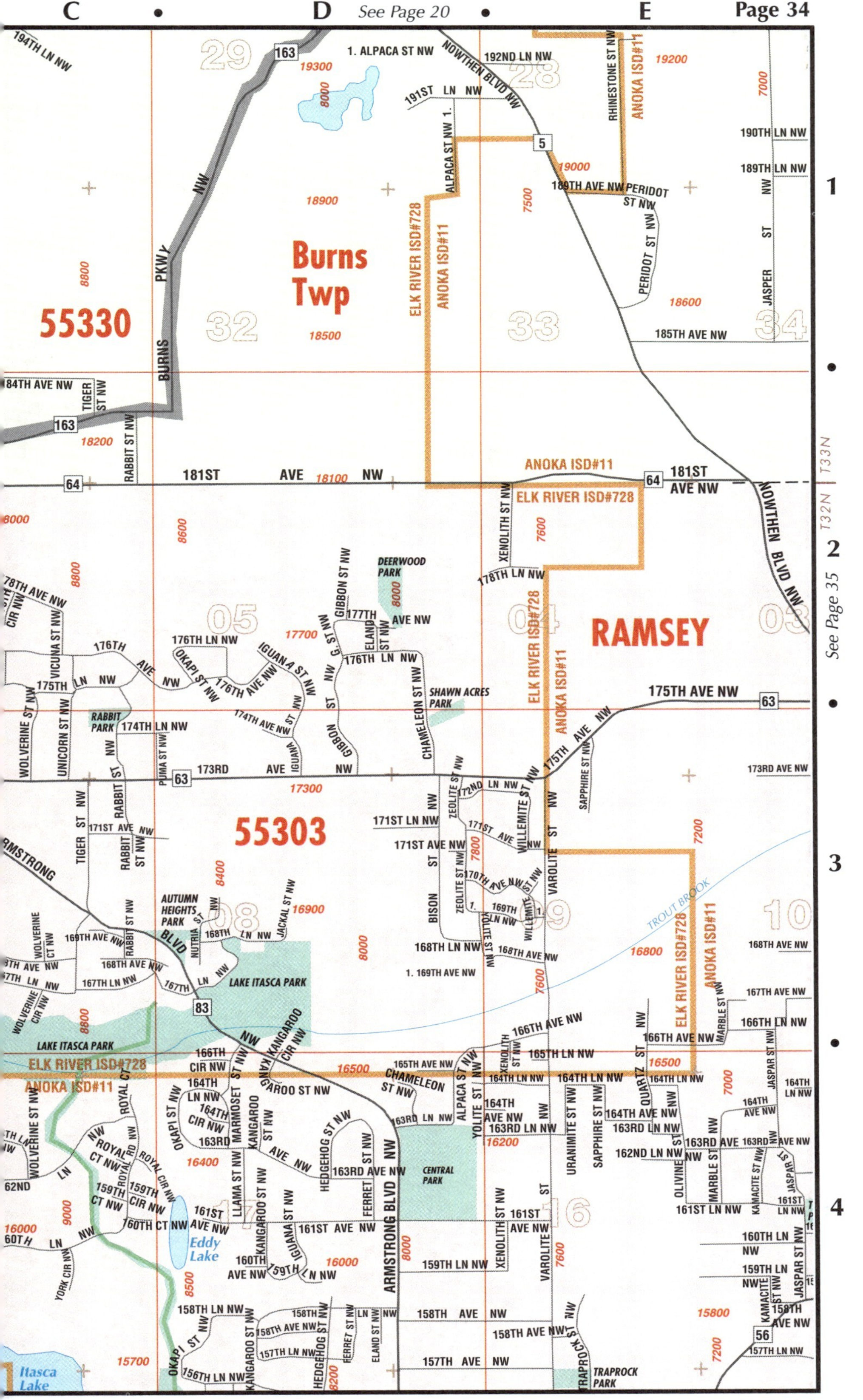

194TH LN NW

29

163
19300

1. ALPACA ST NW
NOWTHEN BLVD NW
192ND LN NW

28

RHINESTONE ST NW
Anoka ISD#11
19200

7000

191ST LN NW

190TH LN NW

ALPACA ST NW

5

189TH LN NW

55330
8800
BURNS PKWY NW

32
18900
18500

Burns Twp

ELK RIVER ISD#728
ANOKA ISD#11

7500

19000
189TH AVE NW PERIDOT ST NW

33

18600

PERIDOT ST NW

185TH AVE NW

34
JASPER ST NW

1

184TH AVE NW
TIGER ST NW

163
18200
RABBIT ST NW

181ST AVE 18100 NW

64

ANOKA ISD#11
ELK RIVER ISD#728

64 181ST AVE NW

NOWTHEN BLVD NW

T32N T33N

8000
8800
78TH AVE NW
VICUNA ST NW CIR NW

8600

DEERWOOD PARK
GIBBON ST NW
8000

XENOLITH ST NW
178TH LN NW

7600

05
17700

04

ELK RIVER ISD#728

RAMSEY

03

See Page 35

2

176TH LN NW
OKAPI ST NW
176TH AVE NW
177TH ELAND ST NW
176TH LN NW

IGUANA ST NW

175TH LN NW
WOLVERINE ST NW
UNICORN ST NW

Rabbit Park
174TH LN NW
174TH AVE NW
IGUANA ST NW
GIBBON ST NW

CHAMELEON ST NW

SHAWN ACRES PARK

ANOKA ISD#11
175TH AVE NW

175TH AVE NW

63

SAPPHIRE ST NW

173RD AVE NW

TIGER ST NW
PIMA ST NW
63 173RD AVE 17300

ZEOLITE ST NW
172ND LN NW
WILLEMITE ST NW
VAROLITE ST NW

173RD AVE NW

3

ARMSTRONG
171ST ST NW
RABBIT ST NW

55303

171ST LN NW
171ST AVE NW
ZEOLITE ST NW
170TH AVE NW
171ST ST NW
WILLEMITE ST NW

7800

7200

10

8400
AUTUMN HEIGHTS PARK
JACKAL ST NW
16900

08
NUTRIA ST NW

8000

BISON ST NW
169TH LN NW
1. 169TH AVE NW

169TH LN NW
168TH AVE NW

09

TROUT BROOK

16800

168TH LN NW

WOLVERINE CT NW
169TH AVE NW
RABBIT ST NW
168TH LN NW
167TH LN NW

ARMSTRONG BLVD
167TH LN NW

Lake Itasca Park

168TH LN NW
1. 169TH AVE NW

7600

167TH AVE NW

WOLVERINE CIR NW
8800

Lake Itasca Park
ELK RIVER ISD#728
ANOKA ISD#11

83
166TH CIR NW
KANGAROO CIR NW

166TH AVE NW
XENOLITH ST NW
165TH LN NW

QUARTZ ST NW

166TH AVE NW
16500

166TH AVE NW

ELK RIVER ISD#728
ANOKA ISD#11

7000
MARBLE ST NW

166TH LN NW

JASPER ST NW

WOLVERINE ST NW
ROYAL RD NW
ROYAL CT NW

OKAPI ST NW
164TH LN NW
MARMOSET CIR NW
KANGAROO ST NW

166TH CIR NW
16500
CHAMELEON ST NW

165TH AVE NW
ALPACA ST NW
YOLITE ST NW

164TH LN NW
164TH LN NW

URANIMITE ST NW
SAPPHIRE ST NW

QUARTZ ST NW
16500
164TH LN NW

7000
164TH AVE NW

164TH LN NW

62ND CT NW
ROYAL CT NW
159TH CT NW
159TH CIR NW

163RD AVE NW

LLAMA ST NW
HEDGEHOG ST NW

163RD LN NW

163RD AVE NW
162ND LN NW

163RD AVE NW
OLIVINE ST NW
MARBLE ST NW
KAMACITE ST NW

163RD AVE NW

16400

161ST AVE NW
IGUANA ST NW

KANGAROO ST NW
FERRET ST NW

CENTRAL PARK

161ST ST NW
XENOLITH ST NW
VAROLITE ST NW

161ST LN NW

KAMACITE ST NW
JASPER ST NW

161ST LN NW

16

4

Eddy Lake
6500
160TH AVE NW
159TH LN NW

16000

ARMSTRONG BLVD NW
8000
159TH LN NW

7600

160TH LN NW
159TH LN NW
KAMACITE ST NW
JASPER ST NW

16000
60TH LN NW
YORK CIR NW
9000

158TH LN NW
158TH AVE NW

158TH AVE NW

158TH AVE NW

15800

56

Itasca Lake
15700
OKAPI ST NW
KANGAROO ST NW
157TH LN NW
HEDGEHOG ST NW
8200
156TH LN NW
FERRET ST NW
ELAND ST NW

157TH AVE NW
158TH AVE NW
157TH AVE NW

TRAPROCK ST NW

TRAPROCK PARK

7200
157TH LN NW

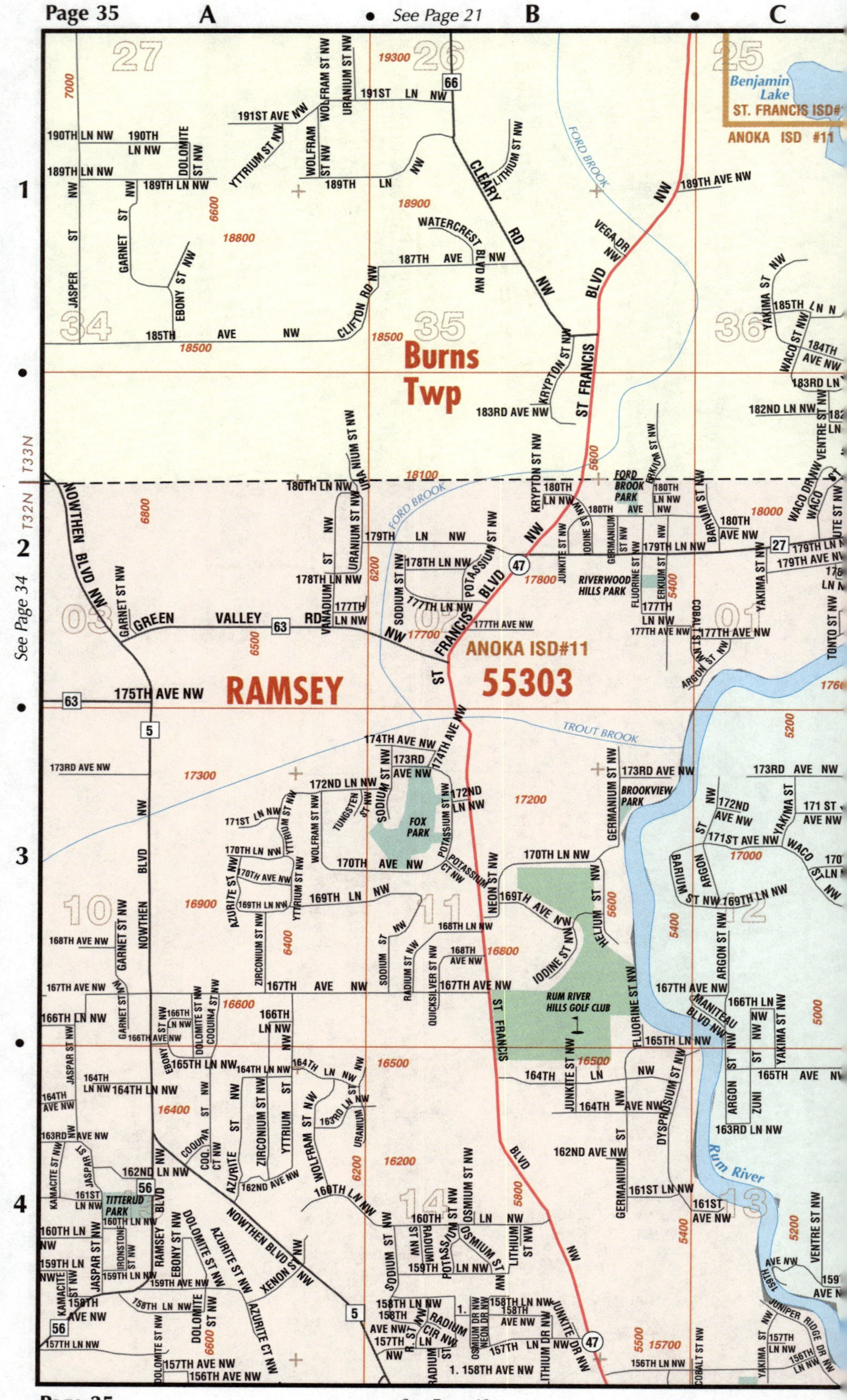

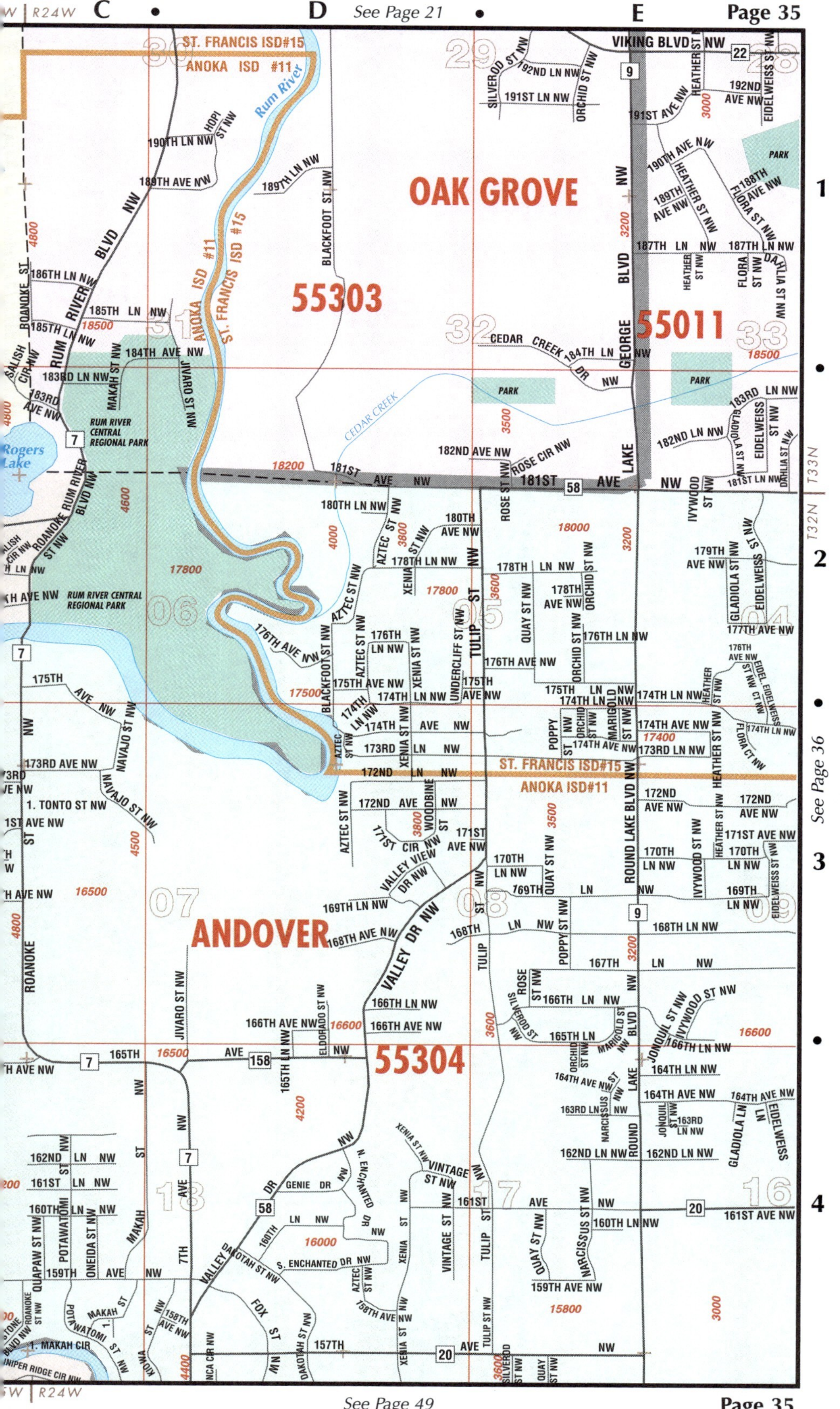

OAK GROVE

55303

55011

ST. FRANCIS ISD#15
ANOKA ISD #11

VIKING BLVD NW

ANDOVER

55304

ST. FRANCIS ISD#15
ANOKA ISD#11

Rogers
Lake

Rum River Central
Regional Park

Rum River Central
Regional Park

PARK

PARK

PARK

CEDAR CREEK

Rum River

1

2

3

4

See Page 36

T32N | T33N

A ● See Page 22 B ● C

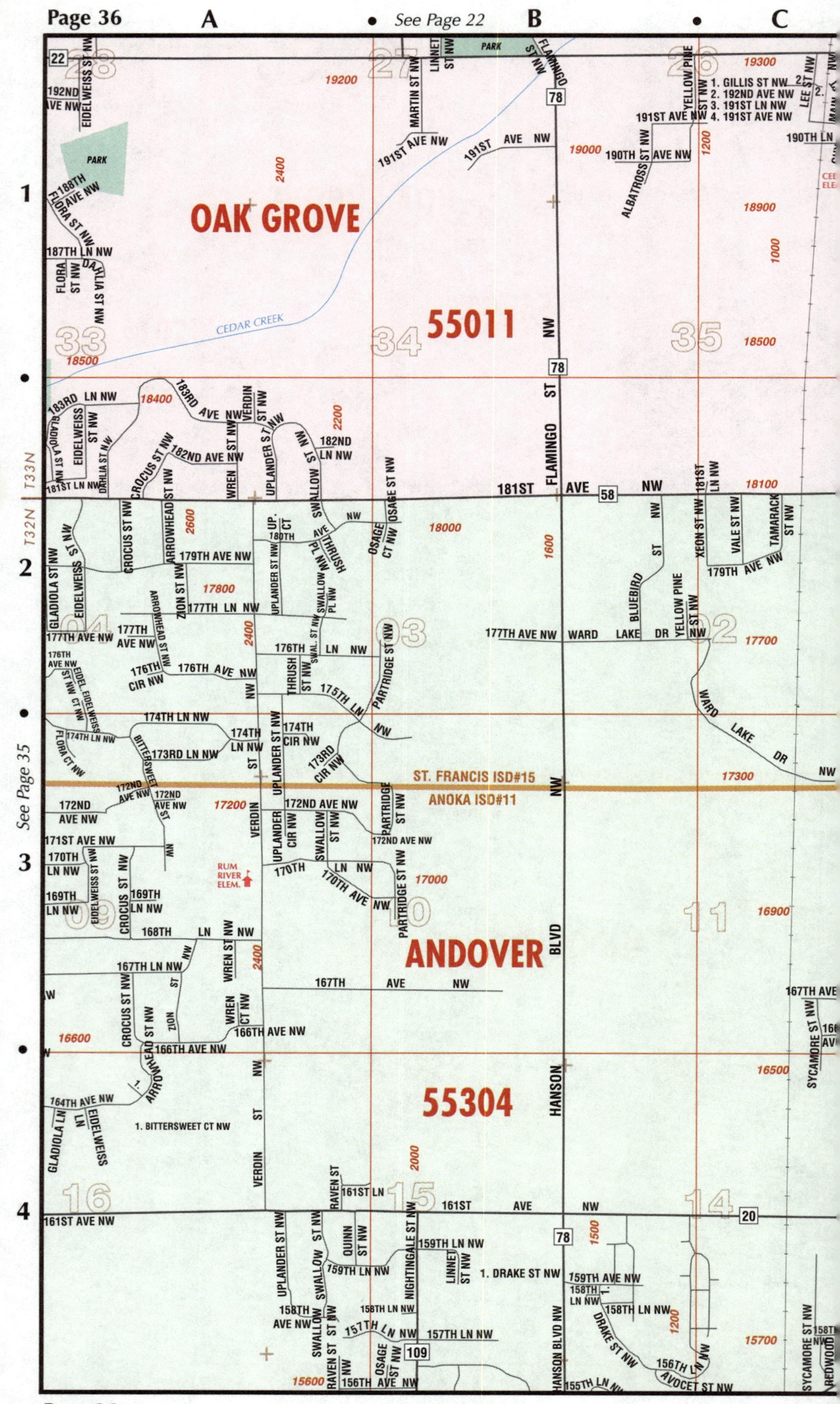

See Page 22
See Page 35

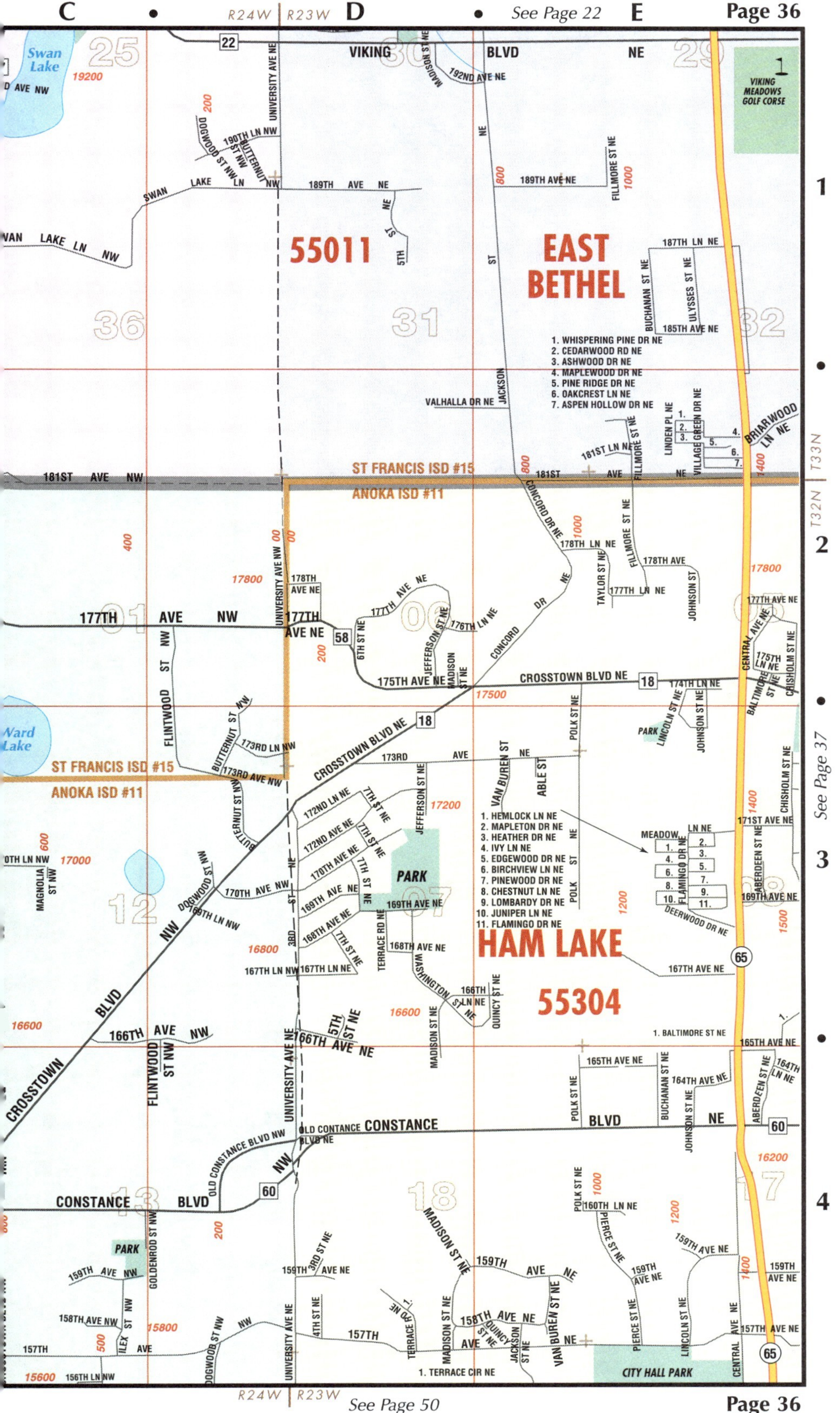

EAST BETHEL

55011

1. WHISPERING PINE DR NE
2. CEDARWOOD RD NE
3. ASHWOOD DR NE
4. MAPLEWOOD DR NE
5. PINE RIDGE DR NE
6. OAKCREST LN NE
7. ASPEN HOLLOW DR NE

HAM LAKE

55304

1. HEMLOCK LN NE
2. MAPLETON DR NE
3. HEATHER DR NE
4. IVY LN NE
5. EDGEWOOD DR NE
6. BIRCHVIEW LN NE
7. PINEWOOD DR NE
8. CHESTNUT LN NE
9. LOMBARDY DR NE
10. JUNIPER LN NE
11. FLAMINGO DR NE

ST FRANCIS ISD #15
ANOKA ISD #11

VIKING MEADOWS GOLF CORSE

1. BALTIMORE ST NE

1. TERRACE CIR NE

CITY HALL PARK

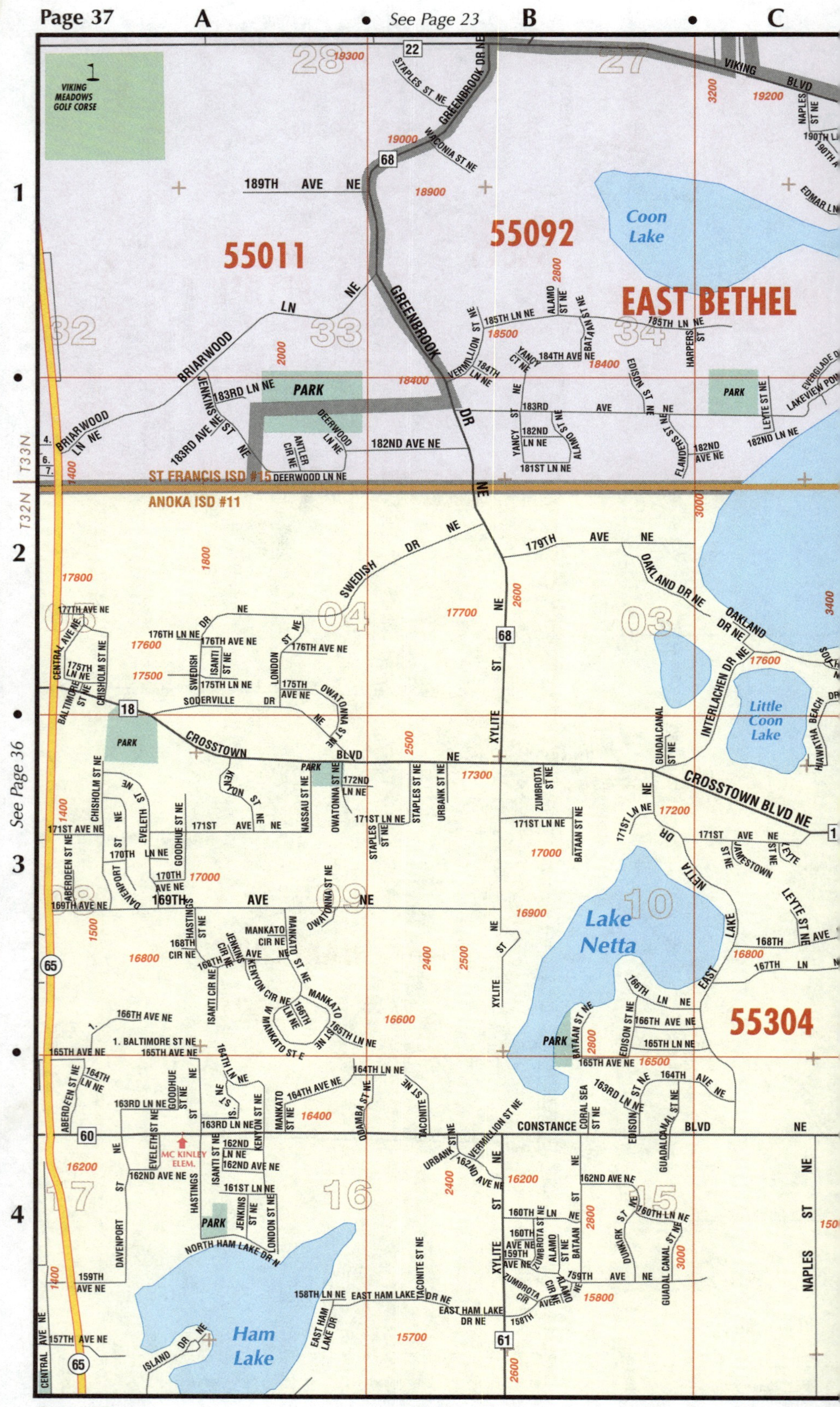

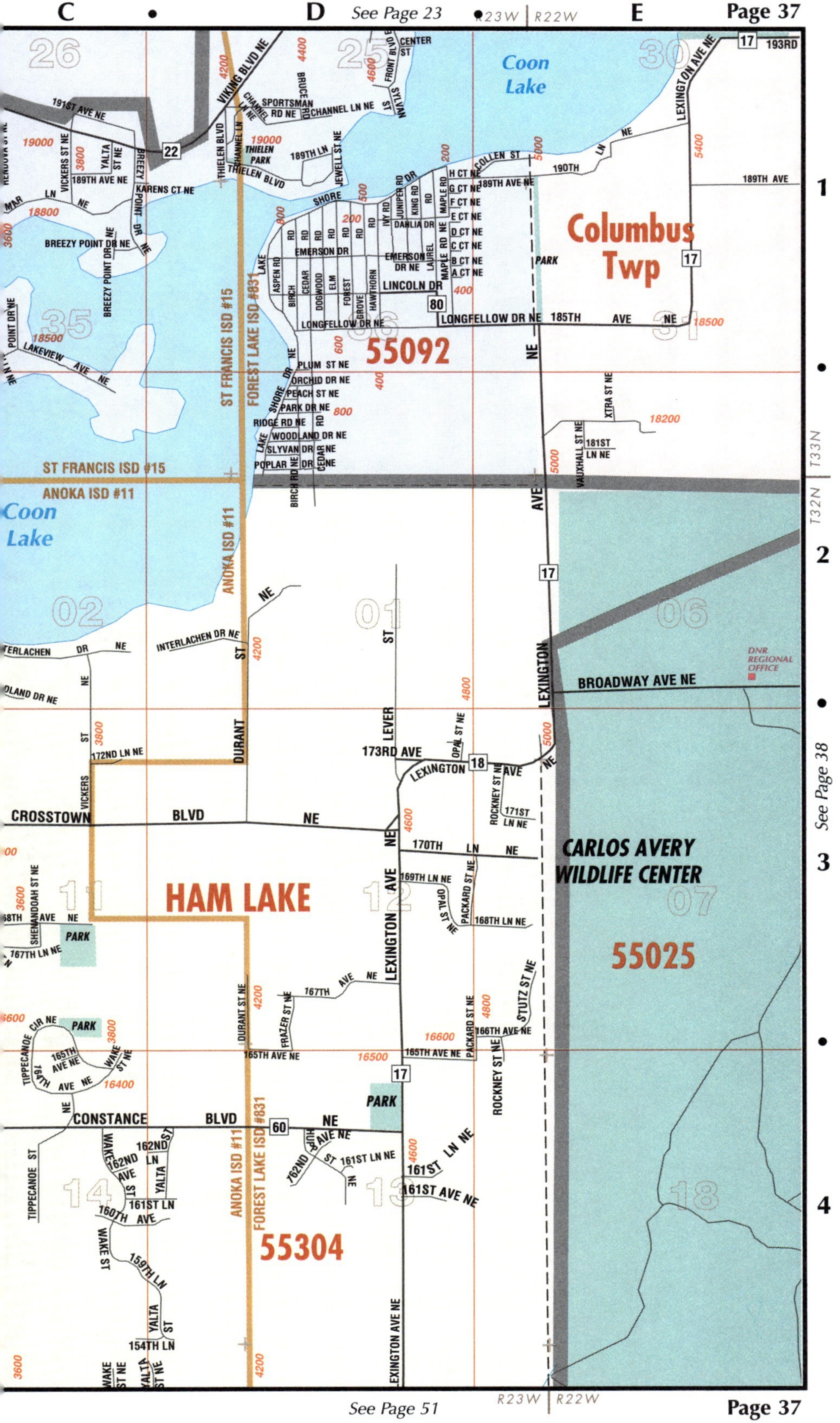

26 25 30 17 193RD

Coon Lake

VIKING BLVD NE
4200 4400 4600 CENTER ST
FRONT BLVD NE
SYLVAN
LEXINGTON AVE NE

191ST AVE NE
19000
VICKERS ST NE
3800
YALTA
189TH AVE NE
19000
SPORTSMAN RD NE
CHANNEL LN NE
189TH LN
JEWELL ST NE
COLLEN NE
190TH
189TH AVE NE
190TH
189TH AVE
5400
5000

18800
BREEZY POINT DR NE
THIELEN PARK
200
H CT NE
G CT NE
F CT NE
17
1

KARENS CT NE
THIELEN BLVD
SHORE
IVY RD NE
JUNIPER RD NE
KING RD NE
MAPLE RD NE
DANLIA DR NE
E CT NE
D CT NE
C CT NE
PARK
5400

3600
BREEZY POINT DR NE
BREEZY POINT DR NE
ASPEN RD
BIRCH
CEDAR
DOGWOOD
ELM
FOREST
HAWTHORN
EMERSON DR NE
LAUREL
DR NE
B CT NE
A CT NE
17

Columbus Twp

35
LAKEVIEW AVE NE
18500
POINT DR NE
LONGFELLOW DR NE
GROVE
80
LINCOLN DR
400
LONGFELLOW DR NE
185TH AVE NE
18500
31

ST FRANCIS ISD #15
FOREST LAKE ISD #831
55092

PLUM ST NE
ORCHID DR NE
PEACH ST NE
PARK DR NE
600
400
800
5000
XTRA ST NE
18200

RIDGE RD NE
WOODLAND DR NE
SLYVAN DR NE
POPLAR DR NE
BIRCH RD NE
ELM NE
181ST LN NE
VAUXHALL ST NE

ST FRANCIS ISD #15

ANOKA ISD #11

Coon Lake

02
NTERLACHEN DR NE
INTERLACHEN ST NE
4200
01
ST NE
NE
5000
06

DURANT
DNR REGIONAL OFFICE
17
2

OLAND DR NE
ST
3800
172ND LN NE
VICKERS
DURANT ST NE
LEVER
173RD AVE
LEXINGTON
18
AVE
OPAL ST NE
ROCKNEY ST NE
171ST LN NE
LEXINGTON
4800
5000
BROADWAY AVE NE

CROSSTOWN BLVD NE
4600
170TH
LN NE
See Page 38

HAM LAKE

11
3800
3600
68TH AVE NE
SHENANDOAH ST NE
167TH LN NE
PARK
12
169TH LN NE
OPAL ST NE
PACKARD ST NE
168TH LN NE

CARLOS AVERY WILDLIFE CENTER

07

55025

3600
600
TIPPECANOE CIR NE
PARK
WAKE ST NE
165TH AVE NE
16400
DURANT ST NE
4200
167TH AVE NE
FRAZIER ST NE
165TH AVE NE
16500
165TH AVE NE
16600
PACKARD ST NE
166TH AVE NE
ROCKNEY ST NE
STUTZ ST NE
4800

CONSTANCE BLVD NE
TIPPECANOE ST
14
162ND LN
162ND AVE
161ST LN
161ST AVE
YALTA ST
160TH AVE
WAKE ST
ANOKA ISD #11
FOREST LAKE ISD #831
60
17
762ND AVE NE
161ST LN NE
PARK
13
161ST AVE NE
4600
161ST LN NE
18
4

55304

159TH LN
YALTA ST
154TH LN
WAKE ST NE
YALTA ST NE
LEXINGTON AVE NE
3600
4200

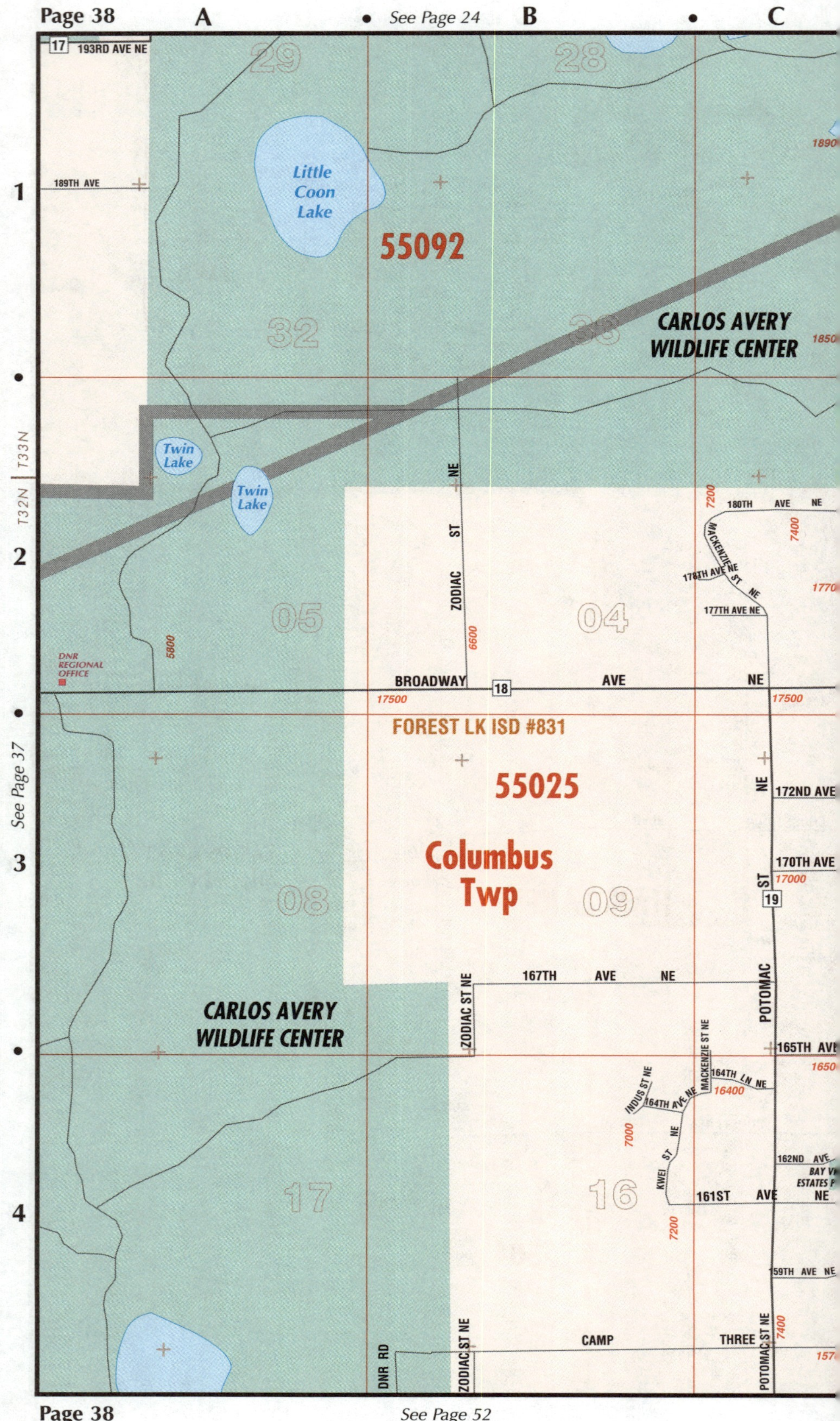

17   193RD AVE NE

189TH AVE

29

28

1890

Little
Coon
Lake

55092

32

30

CARLOS AVERY
WILDLIFE CENTER

1850

1

T33N | T32N

Twin
Lake

Twin
Lake

ZODIAC ST NE

180TH AVE NE

7200

7400

MACKENZIE ST NE

175TH AVE NE

1770

2

DNR
REGIONAL
OFFICE

5800

05

6600

04

177TH AVE NE

BROADWAY   18   AVE   NE

17500

17500

FOREST LK ISD #831

55025

172ND AVE NE

Columbus
Twp

170TH AVE NE

17000

19

3

08

09

POTOMAC ST NE

ZODIAC ST NE

167TH   AVE   NE

CARLOS AVERY
WILDLIFE CENTER

165TH AVE NE

1650

INDUS ST NE

164TH AVE NE

MACKENZIE ST NE

164TH LN NE

16400

KWEI ST NE

7000

162ND AVE
BAY VW
ESTATES P

4

17

16

161ST   AVE   NE

7200

159TH AVE NE

DNR RD

ZODIAC ST NE

CAMP   THREE

POTOMAC ST NE

7400

1570

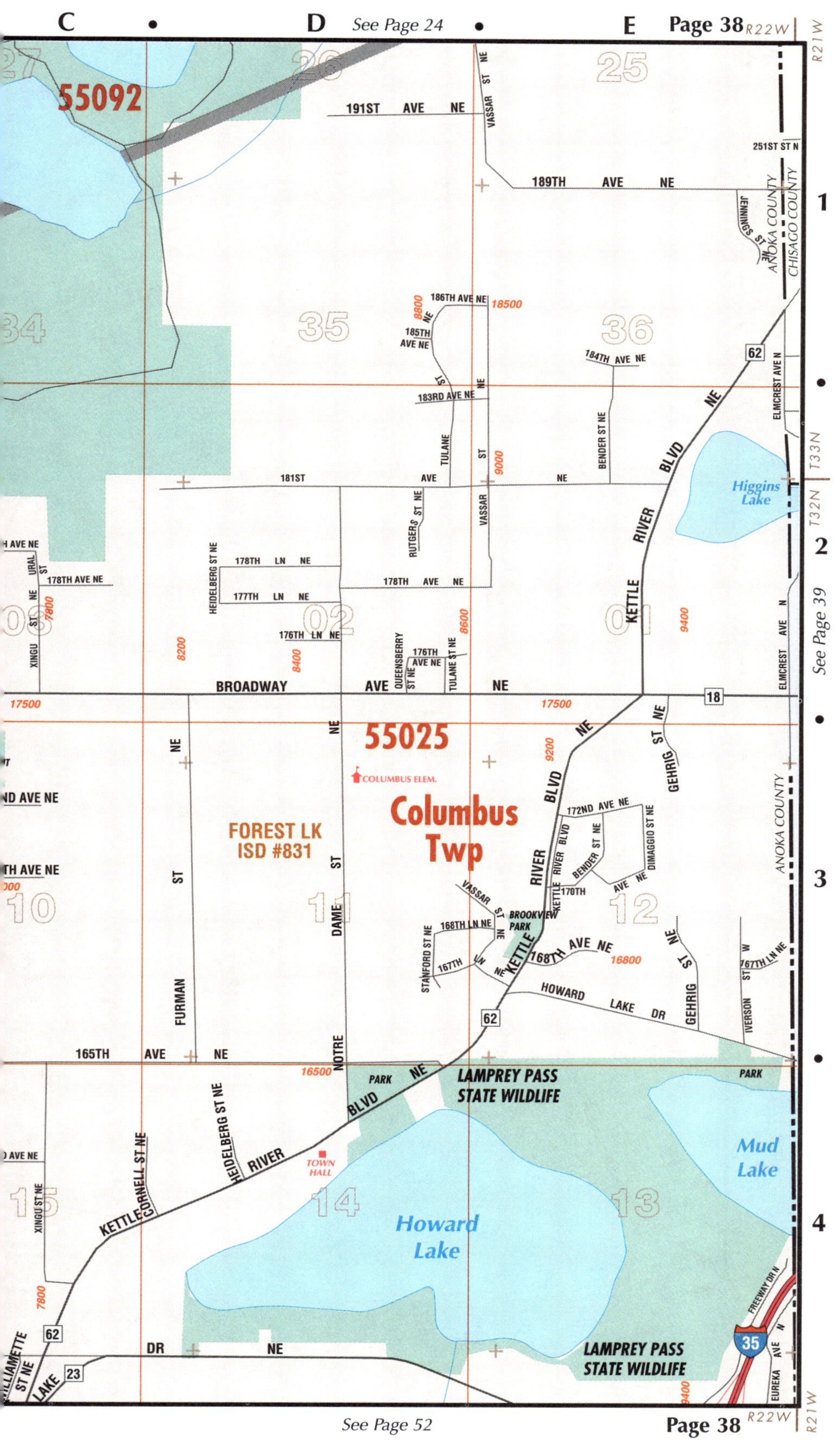

55092

191ST   AVE   NE

VASSAR ST NE

251ST ST N

189TH   AVE   NE

JENNINGS AVE N

ANOKA COUNTY
CHISAGO COUNTY

1

35

186TH AVE NE   8600   18500

185TH AVE NE

184TH AVE NE

62

ELMCREST AVE N

183RD AVE NE

36

BENDER ST NE

RIVER   BLVD   NE

Higgins Lake

T33N

T32N

TULANE ST NE   9000

181ST   AVE   NE

VASSAR ST NE

RUTGERS ST NE

KETTLE

See Page 39

2

URAL ST NE

178TH AVE NE

HEIDELBERG ST NE

178TH LN NE

177TH LN NE

178TH   AVE   NE

9400

ELMCREST AVE N

XINGU ST NE   7800

8200

8400

176TH LN NE   02

QUEENSBERRY ST NE

176TH AVE NE

TULANE ST NE   8600

01

BROADWAY   AVE   NE

17500   17500   18

NE

RIVER   BLVD   NE   9200

GEHRIG ST NE

ANOKA COUNTY

3

NE

↑ COLUMBUS ELEM.

Columbus Twp

772ND AVE NE

DIMAGGIO ST NE

ND AVE NE

FOREST LK ISD #831

DAME   ST   NE

BENDER ST NE

TH AVE NE

VASSAR ST NE

KETTLE RIVER BLVD

170TH AVE NE

12

10

FURMAN   ST   NE

BROOKVIEW PARK

STANFORD ST NE

168TH LN NE

KETTLE

168TH   AVE NE   16800

GEHRIG ST NE

167TH LN NE

IVERSON ST W

177TH LN NE

HOWARD   LAKE   DR

165TH   AVE   NE

62

NOTRE DAME ST NE

16500   PARK   NE

LAMPREY PASS STATE WILDLIFE

PARK

Mud Lake

4

OD AVE NE

KETTLE CORNELL ST NE

HEIDELBERG ST NE

RIVER   BLVD   NE

■ TOWN HALL

14

Howard Lake

13

XINGU ST NE

15

7800

62

WILLIAMETTE ST NE   LAKE   23

DR   NE

LAMPREY PASS STATE WILDLIFE

FREEWAY 195 N

35

EUREKA AVE N

9400

R22W

R21W

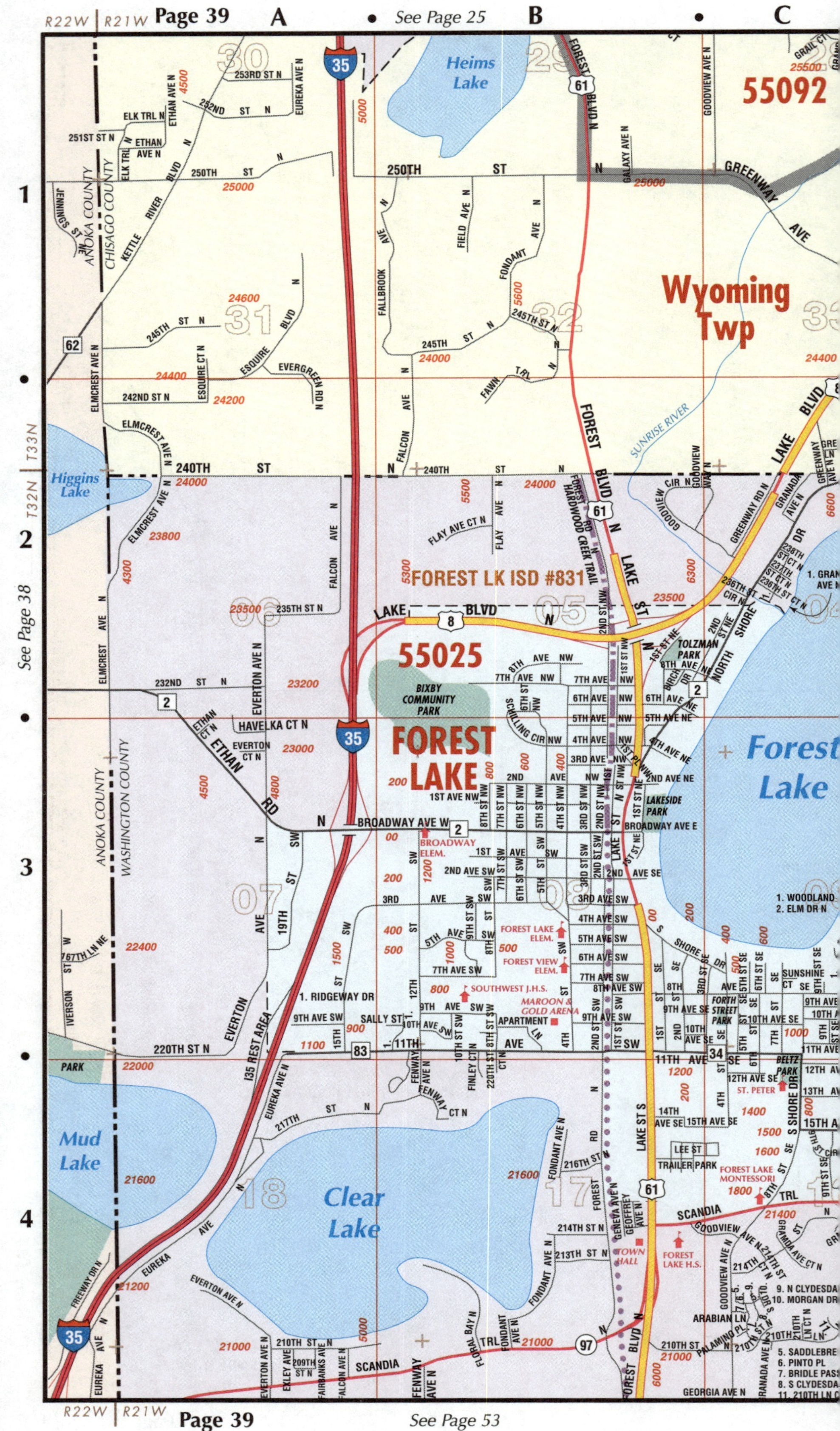

55092

Wyoming Twp

Heims Lake

Higgins Lake

FOREST LK ISD #831

55025

BIXBY COMMUNITY PARK

FOREST LAKE

Forest Lake

Mud Lake

Clear Lake

ANOKA COUNTY / CHISAGO COUNTY

ANOKA COUNTY / WASHINGTON COUNTY

BROADWAY ELEM.

FOREST LAKE ELEM.

FOREST VIEW ELEM.

SOUTHWEST J.H.S.

MAROON & GOLD ARENA

APARTMENT

LAKESIDE PARK

TOLZMAN PARK

1. RIDGEWAY DR

1. GRANDMA AVE N

1. WOODLAND
2. ELM DR N

FORTH STREET PARK

ST. PETER

PELTZ

LEE ST

TRAILER PARK

FOREST LAKE MONTESSORI

TOWN HALL

FOREST LAKE H.S.

SCANDIA

1. N CLYDESDALE
2. MORGAN DR

5. SADDLEBRE
6. PINTO PL
7. BRIDLE PASS
8. S CLYDESDA
11. 210TH

ARABIAN LN

SINGING SUN

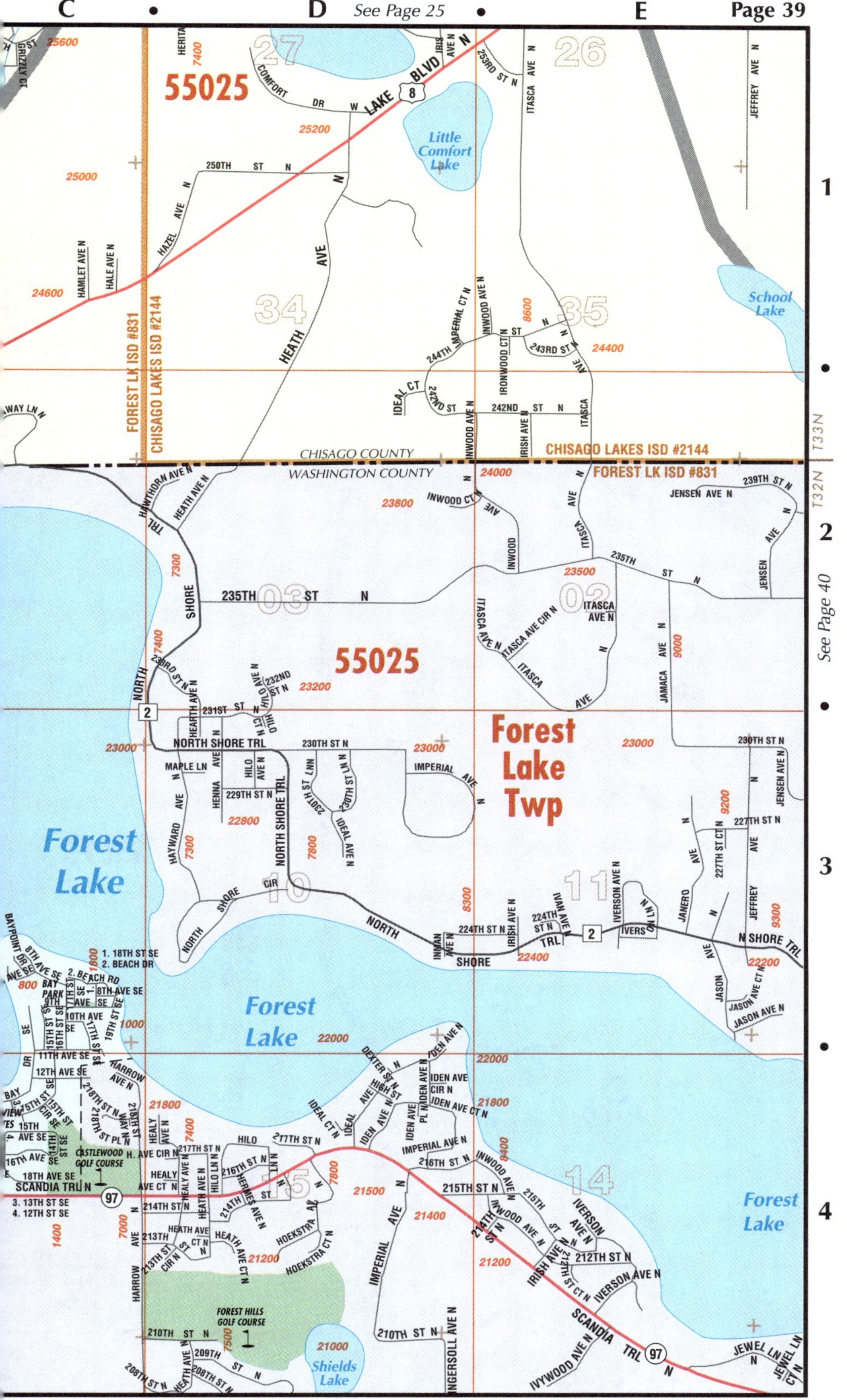

55025

HERITAGE 7400
COMFORT DR W
LAKE BLVD
8
25600
25200
25000
25RD ST N
IRIS AVE N
ITASCA AVE N
27
26
250TH ST N
Little Comfort Lake
JEFFREY AVE N
1
HAZEL AVE N
HAMLET AVE N
HALE AVE N
24600
HEATH AVE
34
244TH ST N
IMPERIAL CT N
INWOOD CTN
8600
243RD ST N
35
24400
School Lake
IDEAL CT N
242ND ST N
IRISH AVE N
ITASCA

FOREST LK ISD #831
CHISAGO LAKES ISD #2144

WAY LN N

CHISAGO COUNTY
WASHINGTON COUNTY
CHISAGO LAKES ISD #2144
FOREST LK ISD #831

T33N
T32N

HAWTHORN AVE N
HEATH AVE N
TRL
24000
23800
INWOOD CT N
INWOOD AVE N
ITASCA AVE
JENSEN AVE N
239TH ST N
2
SHORE
7300
235TH ST N
03
235TH ST N
ITASCA AVE N
235TH ST N
JENSEN AVE N

See Page 40

NORTH
7400
23RD ST N
23200
55025
ITASCA AVE CIR N
02
ITASCA AVE N
JAMACA AVE N
9000
290TH ST N

2
231ST N
232ND ST N
HEARTH AVE N
230TH ST N
23000
Forest Lake Twp
23000
227TH ST CT N
JENSEN AVE N

23000
MAPLE LN
HILO AVE N
230TH ST LN N
IMPERIAL AVE N
9200

HENNA AVE
HILO AVE N
229TH ST N
230TH ST LN N
7800
8300
JANERO AVE N
JEFFREY AVE N
9300

Forest Lake
22800
NORTH SHORE TRL
HAYWARD AVE N
7300
CIR
10
NORTH SHORE
224TH ST N
INMAN AVE N
IRISH AVE N
224TH ST N
11
IVERSON AVE N
2
IVERSON N
N SHORE TRL
22200

BAYPOINT DR SE
1. 18TH ST SE
2. BEACH DR
1600
8TH AVE SE
2. BEACH RD
8TH AVE SE
9TH AVE SE
BAY PARK
10TH AVE SE
800
NORTH SHORE
INMAN AVE N
SHORE
22400
JASON AVE N
JASON AVE CT N
JASON AVE N

15TH ST SE
16TH ST SE
11TH AVE SE
19TH AVE SE
1000
Forest Lake
22000

BAY VIEW ES
11TH AVE SE
12TH AVE SE
22000
21800
DEXTER ST N
HIGH ST N
IDEAL CT N
IDEN AVE N
IDEN AVE N
IDEN AVE CT N
21800
INWOOD AVE N
9400
14

HARROW AVE N
HEALY AVE N
21800
7400
IDEAL CT N
IMPERIAL AVE N
IDEN AVE N
216TH ST N
215TH ST N
215TH N
212TH ST N
IVERSON AVE N
215TH
INWOOD AVE N
Forest Lake

15TH AVE SE
14TH AVE SE
16TH AVE SE
CASTLEWOOD H. GOLF COURSE
SCANDIA TRL N
217TH ST N
HILO
HEALY AVE CIR N
216TH ST N
HILO LN N
HERMES AVE N
7800
21500
21400
4

3. 13TH ST SE
4. 12TH ST SE
97
214TH ST N
213TH AVE N
HEATH AVE N
HOEKSTRA AVE N
HOEKSTRA CT N
HEATH AVE N
21200
IMPERIAL AVE N
INWOOD AVE N
214TH ST N
IRISH AVE N
IRISH AVE CT N
IVERSON AVE N
21200

1400
7000
HARROW AVE N
13TH CIR N
21200
210TH ST N
INGERSOLL AVE N
SCANDIA TRL
97
JEWEL LN N
JEWEL LN N
JEWEL LN CT N

FOREST HILLS GOLF COURSE
7900
210TH ST N
209TH ST N
208TH ST N
21000
Shields Lake
IVYWOOD AVE N

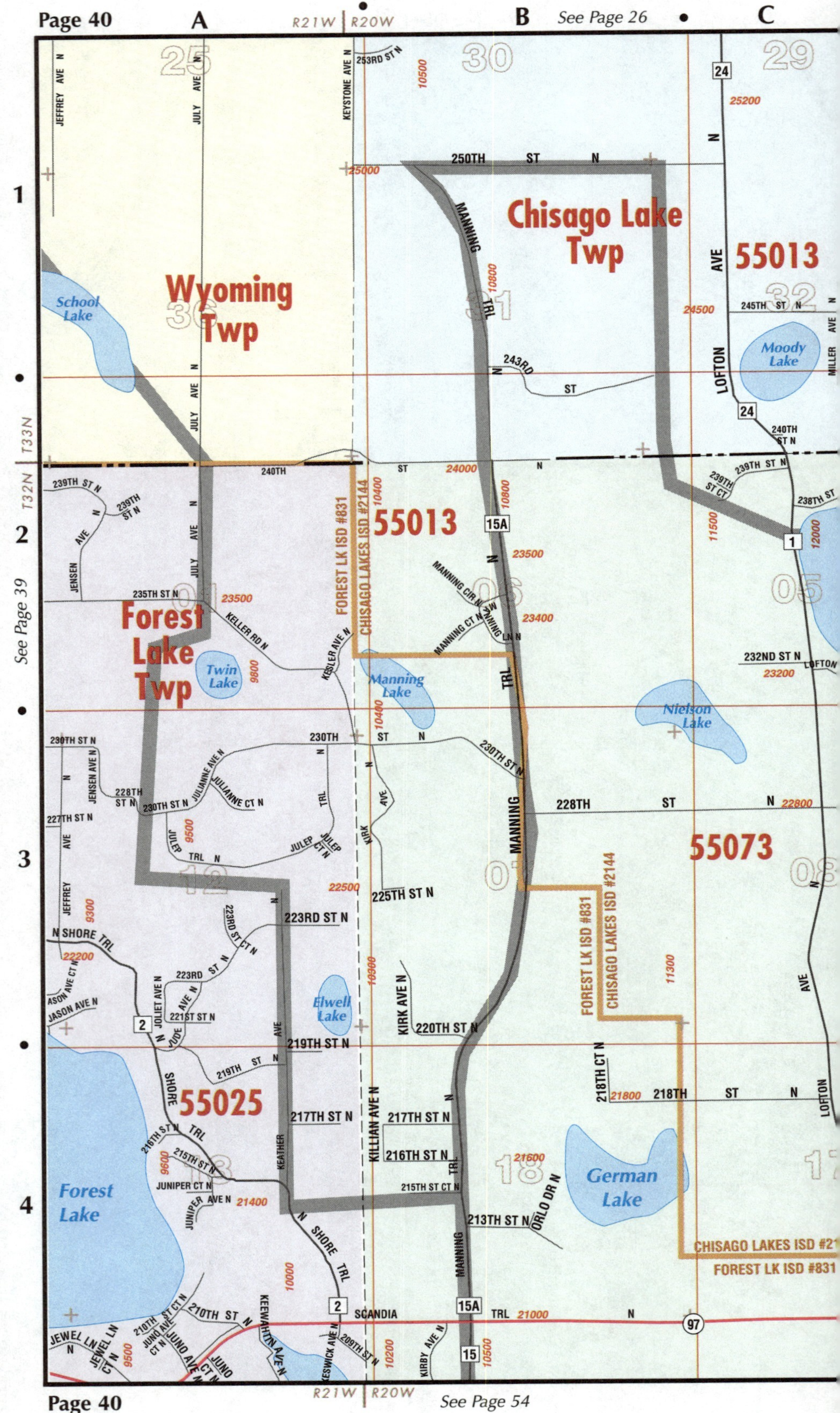

A · R21W | R20W · B *See Page 26* · C

25 · 30 · 29

Wyoming Twp

School Lake

Chisago Lake Twp

55013

Moody Lake

Forest Lake Twp

55013

Twin Lake

Manning Lake

Nielson Lake

Elwell Lake

55073

55025

Forest Lake

German Lake

CHISAGO LAKES ISD #21
FOREST LK ISD #831

SCANDIA

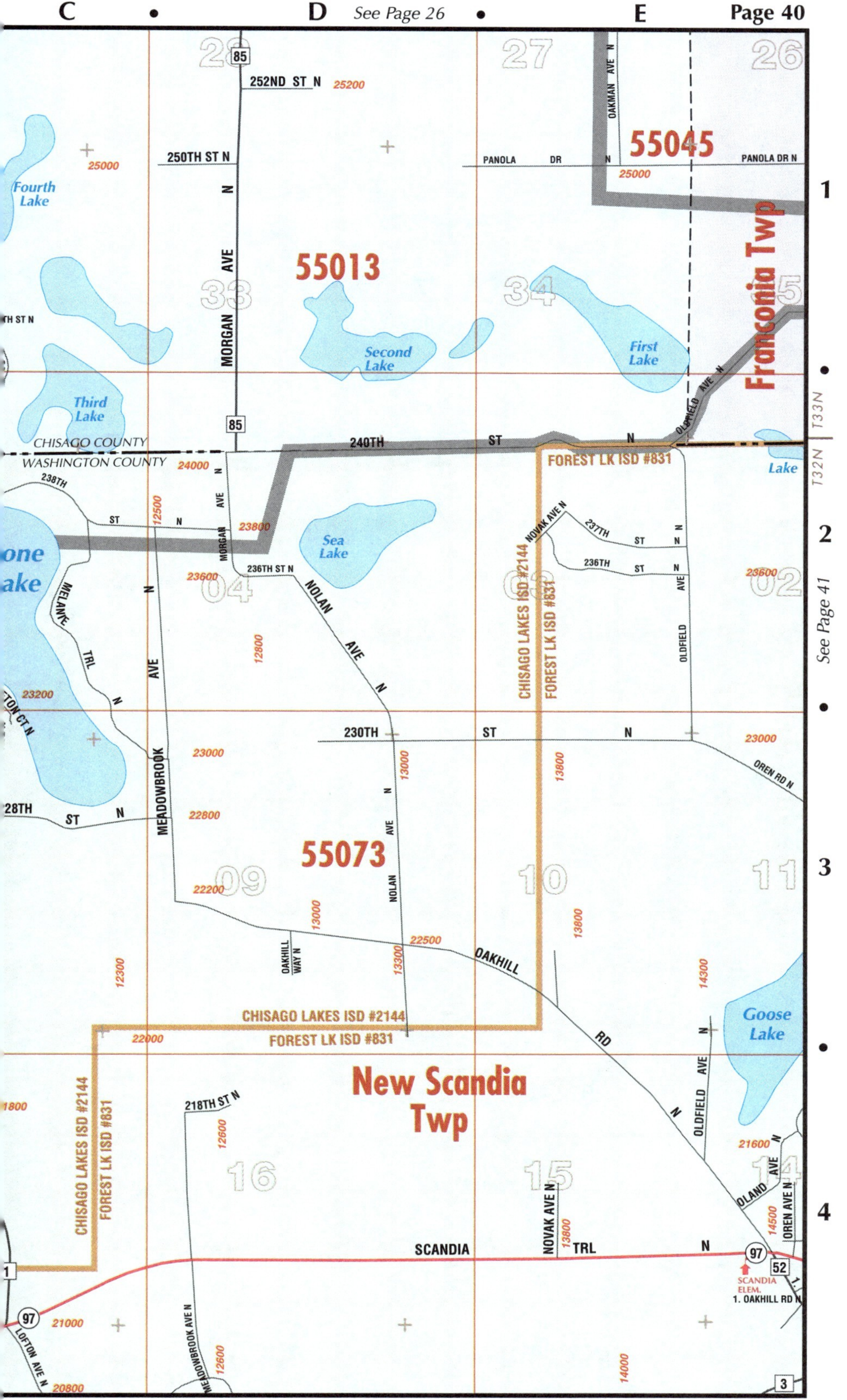

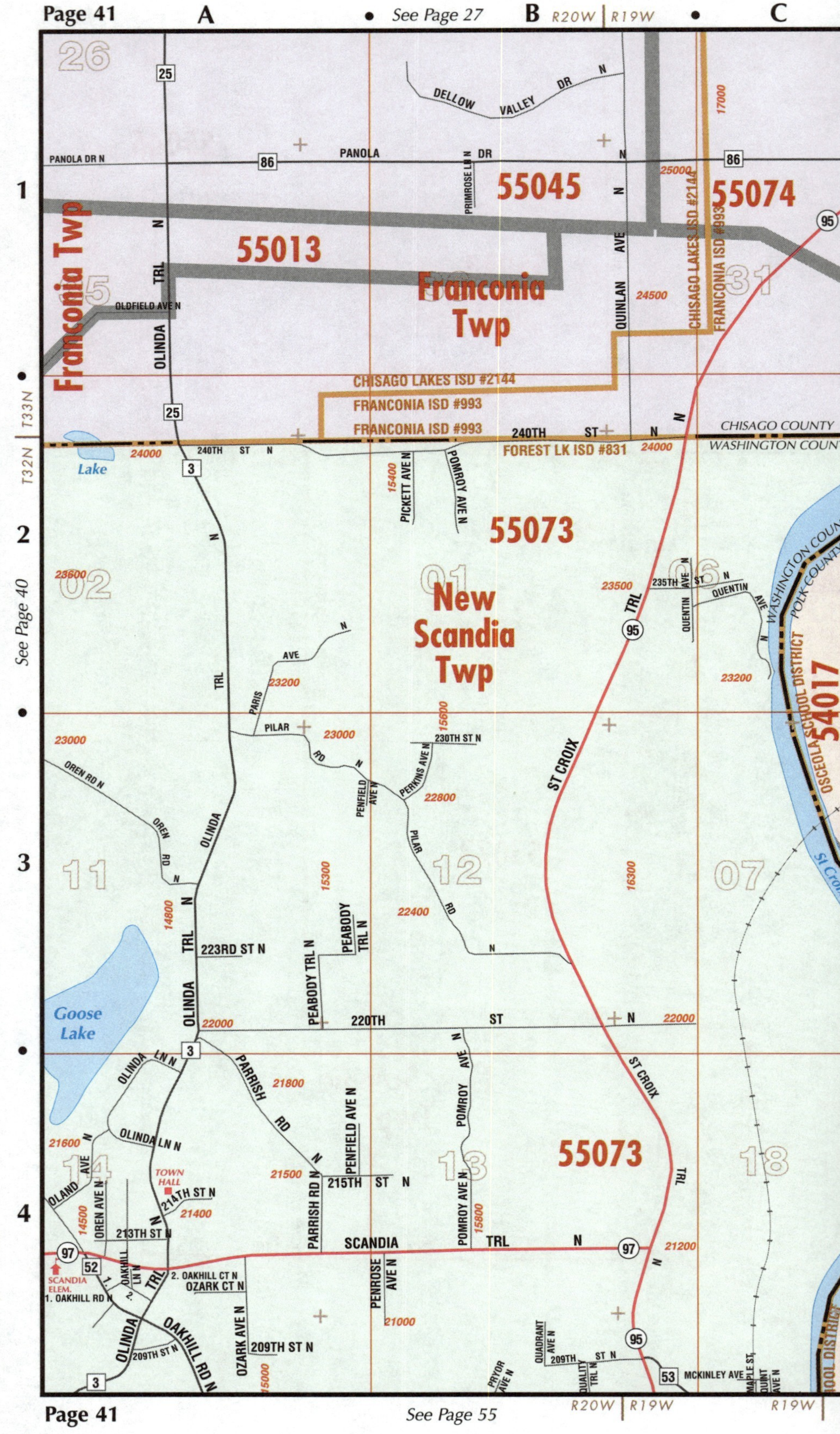
A
See Page 27
B
R20W
R19W
C
1
2
3
4
T33N
T32N
See Page 40
55045
55074
55013
55073
54017
Franconia Twp
New Scandia Twp
PANOLA DR N
PANOLA DR
DELLOW VALLEY DR N
OLINDA TRL N
OLDFIELD AVE N
QUINLAN AVE N
PRIMROSE LN N
CHISAGO LAKES ISD #2144
FRANCONIA ISD #993
FOREST LK ISD #831
240TH ST N
CHISAGO COUNTY
WASHINGTON COUNTY
POLK COUNTY
OSCEOLA SCHOOL DISTRICT
Lake
Goose Lake
PICKETT AVE N
POMROY AVE N
235TH ST N
QUENTIN AVE N
ST CROIX TRL
PARIS AVE N
PILAR RD N
230TH ST N
PERKINS AVE N
PENFIELD AVE N
OREN RD N
223RD ST N
PEABODY TRL N
220TH ST N
PARRISH RD N
OLINDA LN N
215TH ST N
214TH ST N
TOWN HALL
213TH ST N
OLAND AVE N
OREN AVE N
OAKHILL LN N
2. OAKHILL CT N
OZARK CT N
1. OAKHILL RD N
SCANDIA ELEM.
SCANDIA TRL N
PENROSE AVE N
OZARK AVE N
209TH ST N
OAKHILL RD N
PRYOR AVE N
QUADRANT AVE N
QUALITY TRL N
MCKINLEY AVE
MAPLE ST
QUINT AVE N
St Croix

See Page 55

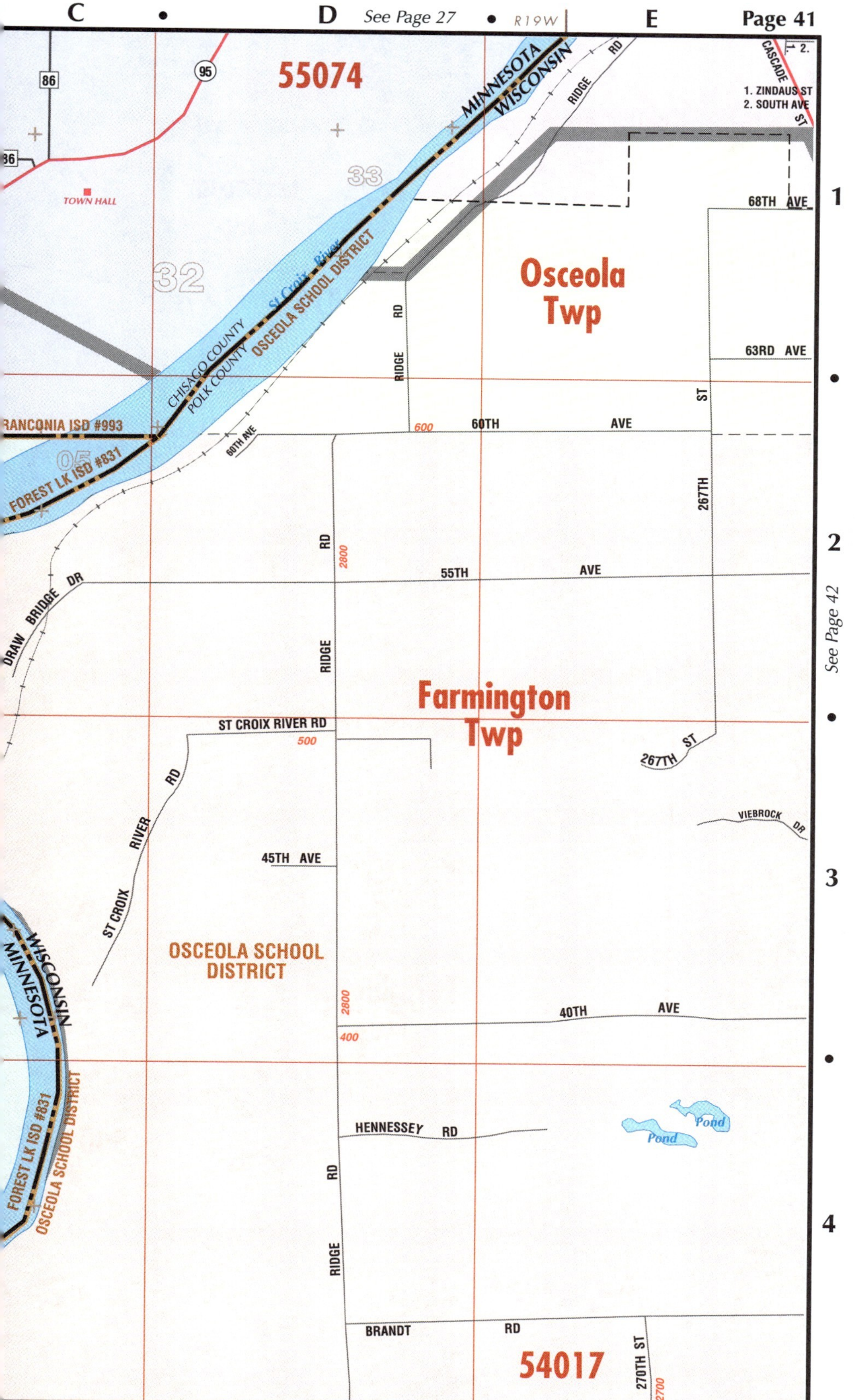

55074

86
95
86

TOWN HALL

MINNESOTA
WISCONSIN

CASCADE ST

1. ZINDAUS ST
2. SOUTH AVE

68TH AVE

1

33

RIDGE RD

32

St Croix River

OSCEOLA SCHOOL DISTRICT

CHISAGO COUNTY
POLK COUNTY

Osceola Twp

63RD AVE

RIDGE RD

267TH ST

FRANCONIA ISD #993

60TH AVE

05

FOREST LK ISD #831

600 60TH AVE

•

55TH AVE

RIDGE RD
2800

DRAW BRIDGE DR

2

Farmington Twp

ST CROIX RIVER RD
500

267TH ST

•

RD

ST CROIX RIVER

VIEBROCK DR

45TH AVE

3

OSCEOLA SCHOOL DISTRICT

2800

40TH AVE

400

•

See Page 42

WISCONSIN
MINNESOTA

FOREST LK ISD #831

OSCEOLA SCHOOL DISTRICT

HENNESSEY RD

Pond
Pond

RIDGE RD

4

BRANDT RD

270TH ST
2700

54017

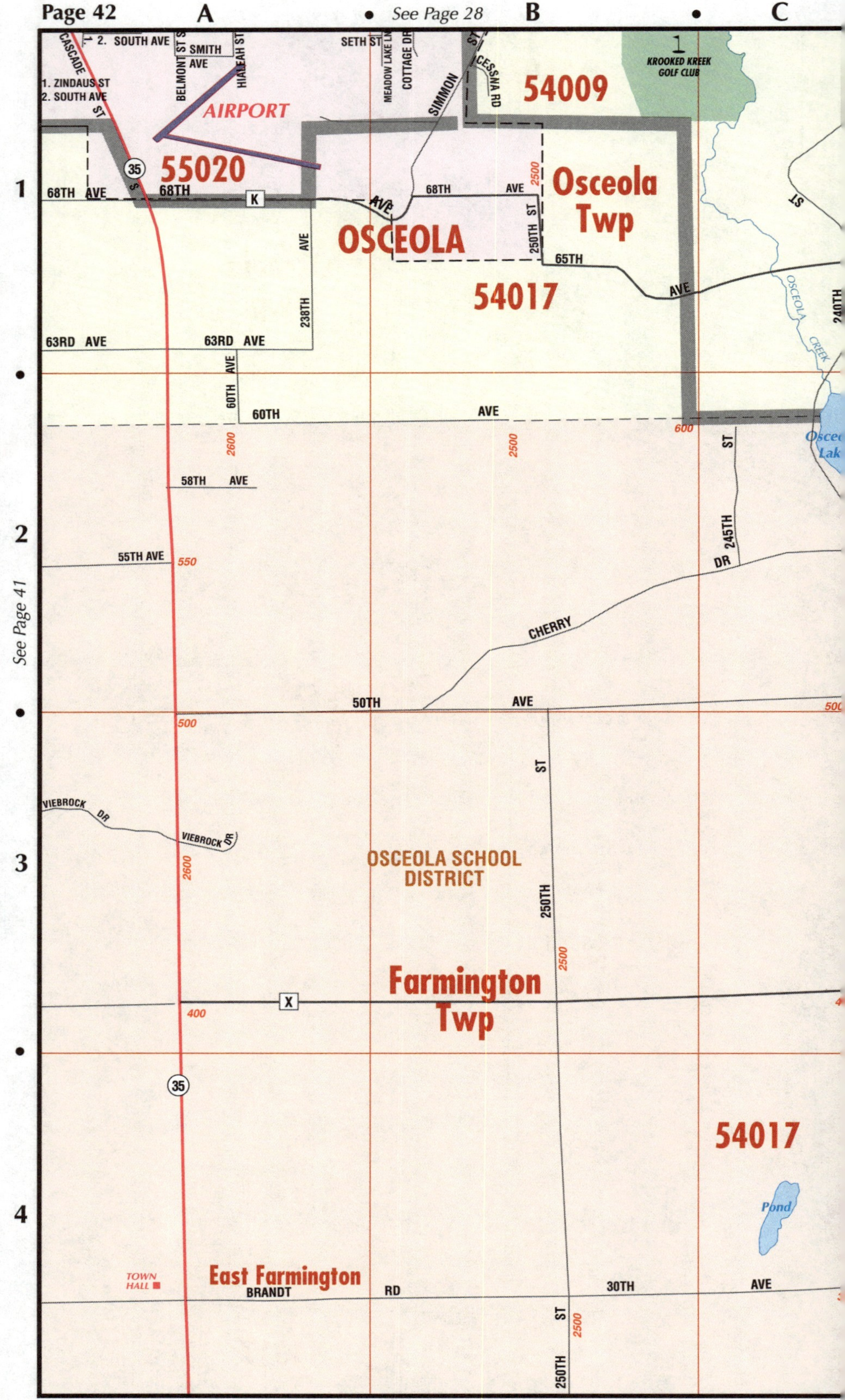

1. ZINDAUS ST
2. SOUTH AVE

1. 2. SOUTH AVE

CASCADE ST

BELMONT ST S

SMITH AVE

HIALEAH ST

SETH ST

MEADOW LAKE LN

COTTAGE DR

SIMMON

CESSNA RD

AIRPORT

KROOKED KREEK GOLF CLUB

54009

55020

68TH

68TH AVE

35

K

AVE

68TH

AVE

2500

250TH ST

65TH

OSCEOLA

Osceola Twp

OSCEOLA CREEK

240TH

ST

238TH

AVE

54017

AVE

63RD AVE

63RD AVE

60TH AVE

60TH

AVE

2600

2500

600

ST

Osceola Lak

58TH AVE

245TH DR

55TH AVE

550

See Page 41

2

CHERRY

50TH

AVE

500

500

VIEBROCK DR

VIEBROCK DR

2600

ST

OSCEOLA SCHOOL DISTRICT

3

250TH

2500

Farmington Twp

400

X

4

54017

Pond

35

TOWN HALL

East Farmington

BRANDT RD

30TH

AVE

250TH ST

2500

250TH ST

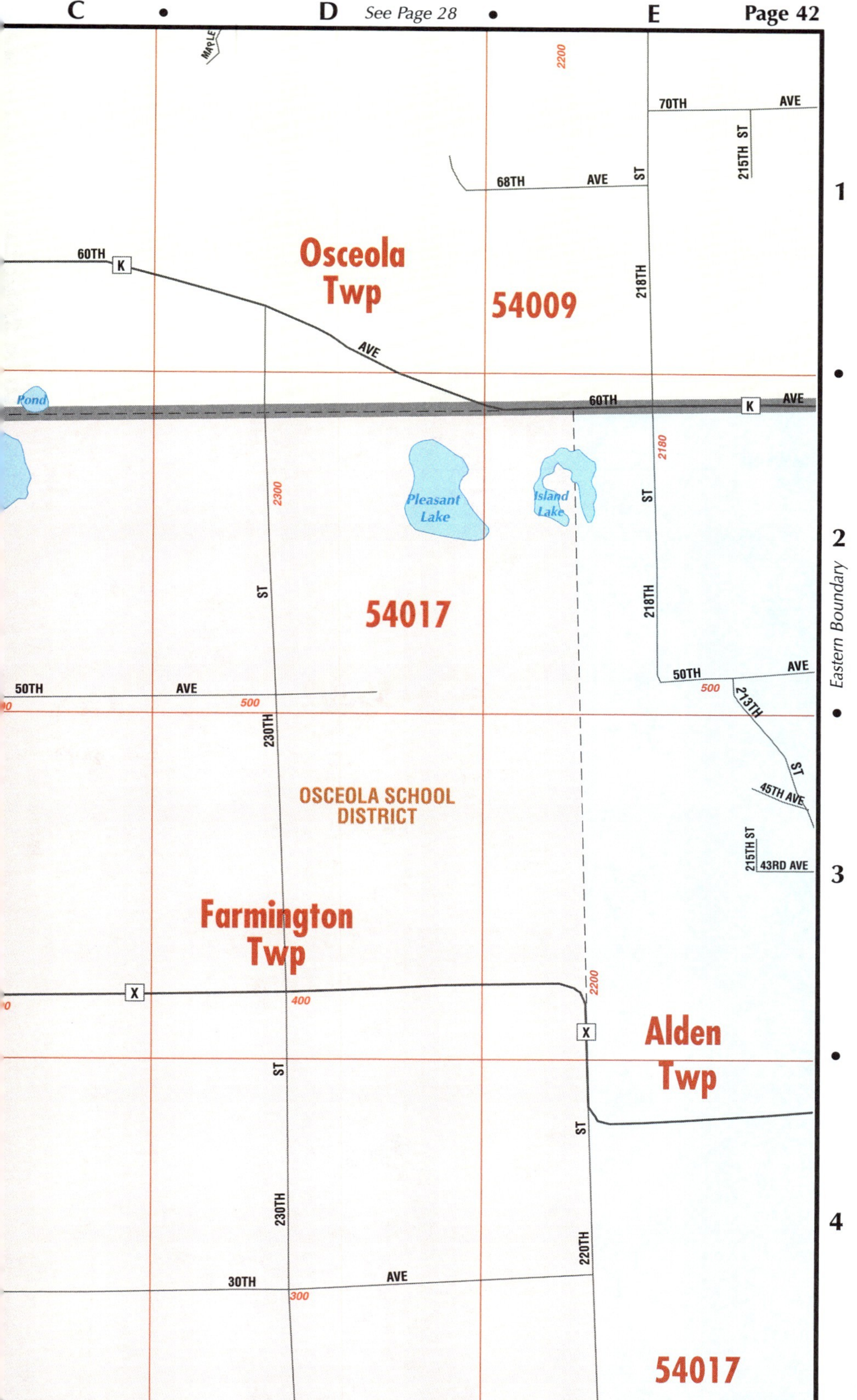

Osceola Twp

54009

70TH   AVE

68TH   AVE

215TH ST

218TH

2200

60TH K

AVE

Pond

60TH K   AVE

2180

ST

Pleasant Lake

Island Lake

218TH

ST

Eastern Boundary

54017

2300

ST

230TH

50TH   AVE

500

50TH   AVE

500

213TH ST

45TH AVE

ST

215TH ST

43RD AVE

OSCEOLA SCHOOL DISTRICT

Farmington Twp

X

400

2200

X

Alden Twp

ST

230TH

ST

220TH

30TH   AVE

300

54017

1

2

3

4

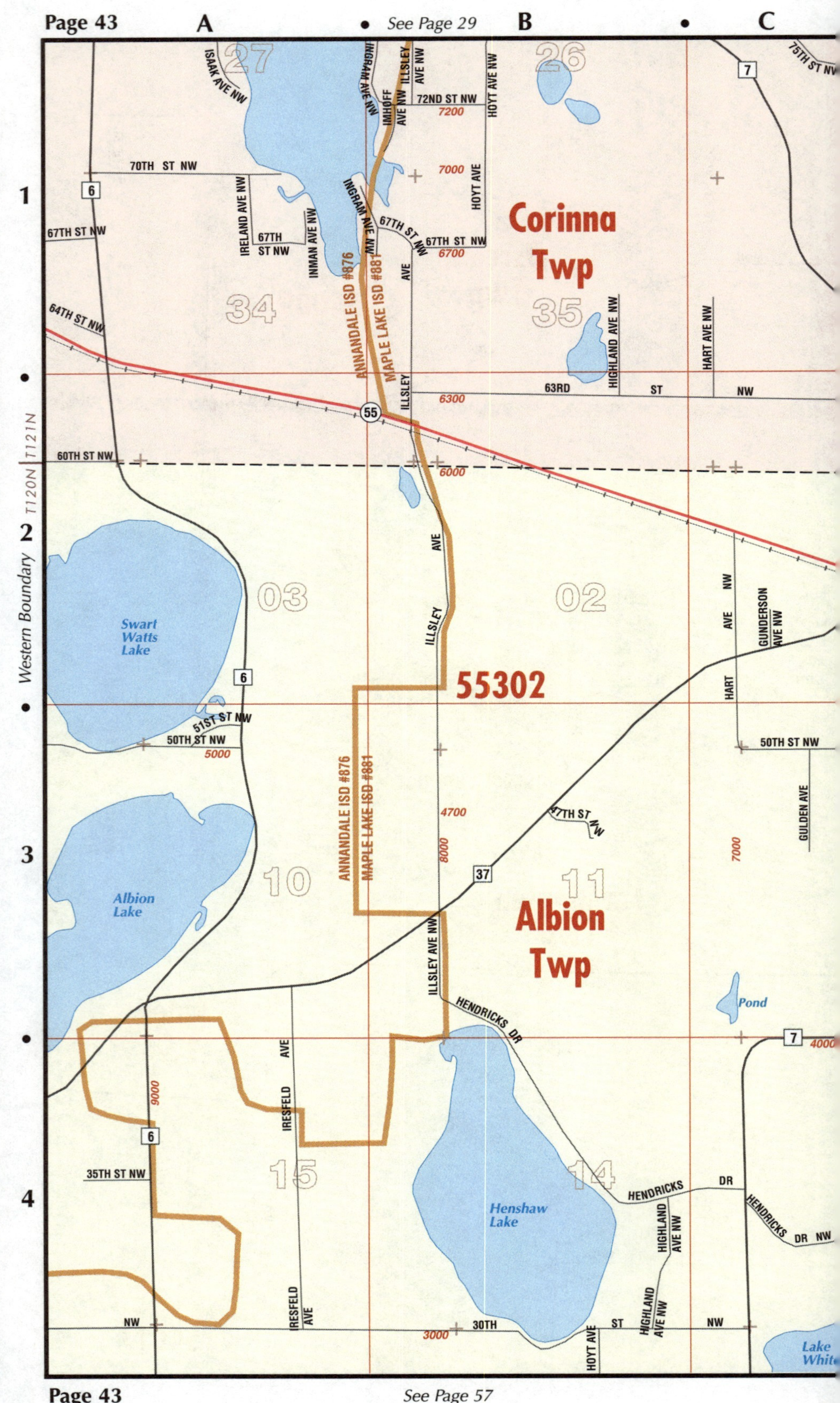

See Page 29

A   B   C

Corinna Twp

27
ISAAK AVE NW
IMHOFF
INGRAM AVE NW
ILLSLEY AVE NW
72ND ST NW
7200
HOYT AVE NW
26

70TH ST NW
7000
HOYT AVE

6
IRELAND AVE NW
67TH ST NW
INMAN AVE NW
67TH ST NW
ANNANDALE ISD #876
MAPLE LAKE ISD #881
67TH ST NW
6700
ILLSLEY AVE

1

67TH ST NW
34
35
HIGHLAND AVE NW
HART AVE NW

64TH ST NW
63RD   ST   NW

55
ILLSLEY
6300

60TH ST NW
6000

T120N | T121N
Western Boundary

2

Swart Watts Lake
03
ILLSLEY AVE
02
AVE NW
GUNDERSON AVE NW

6
55302
HART

51ST ST NW
50TH ST NW
5000
50TH ST NW

ANNANDALE ISD #876
MAPLE LAKE ISD #881
4700
8000
GULDEN AVE

3

Albion Lake
10
37TH ST NW
37
7000
11
Pond

ILLSLEY AVE NW
Albion Twp

HENDRICKS DR
7
4000

9000
IRESFELD AVE

6
HENDRICKS DR

35TH ST NW
15
14
HENDRICKS DR
Henshaw Lake
HIGHLAND AVE NW
HENDRICKS DR NW

4

HIGHLAND AVE NW

NW
IRESFELD AVE
3000
30TH   ST   NW
HOYT AVE
Lake White

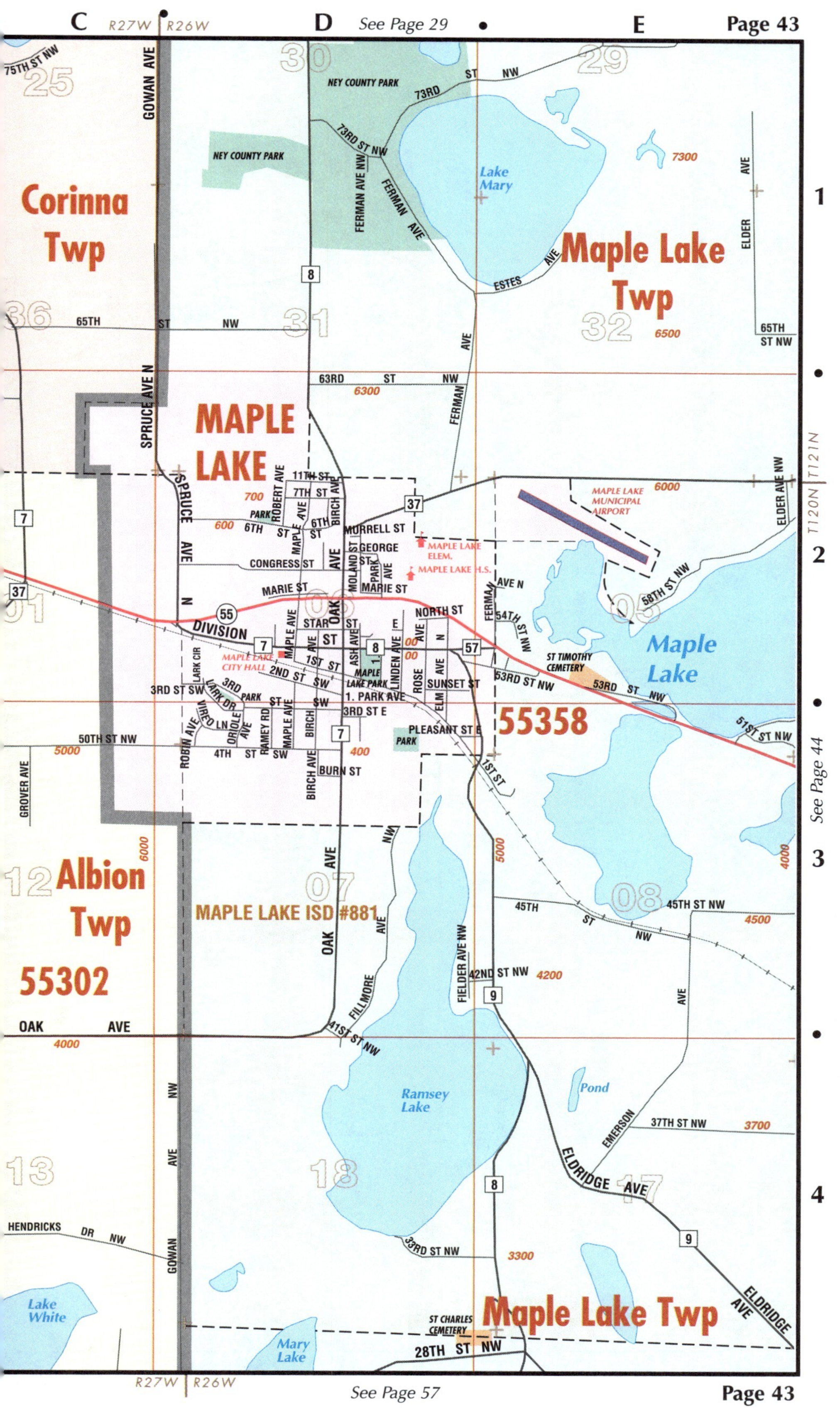

75TH NW
25

Corinna Twp

36   65TH   ST   NW   31

NEY COUNTY PARK

NEY COUNTY PARK

30

73RD   ST   NW

73RD

FERMAN AVE NW

FERMAN   AVE

29

7300

ELDER   AVE

Lake Mary

ESTES   AVE

32

6500

65TH ST NW

1

SPRUCE AVE N

7

MAPLE LAKE

63RD   ST   NW

6300

FERMAN   AVE

T120N | T121N

6000

ELDER AVE NW

•

37

37

91

SPRUCE   AVE   N

11TH   ST

700

ROBERT AVE

7TH   ST

600   6TH   ST

BIRCH AVE

6TH   ST

MAPLE   AVE

PARK AVE

MURRELL ST

MOLAND ST

GEORGE   ST

MAPLE LAKE ELEM.

MAPLE LAKE H.S.

MAPLE LAKE MUNICIPAL AIRPORT

58TH ST NW

2

CONGRESS ST

MARIE ST

MARIE ST

FERMAN   AVE N

DIVISION

55

7

MAPLE AVE

OAK   ST

STAR   ST

1ST ST

ASH AVE

8

MAPLE LAKE CITY HALL

LARK CIR

2ND ST SW

NORTH ST

54TH

ST

57

ST TIMOTHY CEMETERY

Maple Lake

3RD ST SW

3RD ST

PARK

LINDEN ST

ROSE   AVE

SUNSET ST

53RD ST NW

53RD   ST   NW

•

LARK DR

ORIOLE   LN

JIRED RD

ROBIN AVE

RAMEY RD

MAPLE AVE

BIRCH

ELM   ST

MAPLE LAKE PARK

1. PARK AVE

3RD ST E

55358

51ST ST NW

50TH ST NW

5000

4TH   ST SW

BURN ST

400

7

PLEASANT E PARK

1ST ST

5000

4000

See Page 44

3

GROVER AVE

Albion

6000

Twp

55302

OAK   AVE

07

FILLMORE   AVE

45TH   ST   NW

45TH ST NW

4500

MAPLE LAKE ISD #881

FIELDER AVE NW

42ND ST NW   4200

9

OAK   AVE

4000

41ST ST NW

•

12

13

GOWAN   AVE   NW

SPRUCE   AVE   N

8

18

Ramsey Lake

33RD ST NW   3300

Pond

EMERSON

ELDRIDGE   AVE

37TH ST NW   3700

08

AVE

17

9

ELDRIDGE   AVE

4

HENDRICKS   DR   NW

Lake White

Mary Lake

ST CHARLES CEMETERY

28TH   ST   NW

Maple Lake Twp

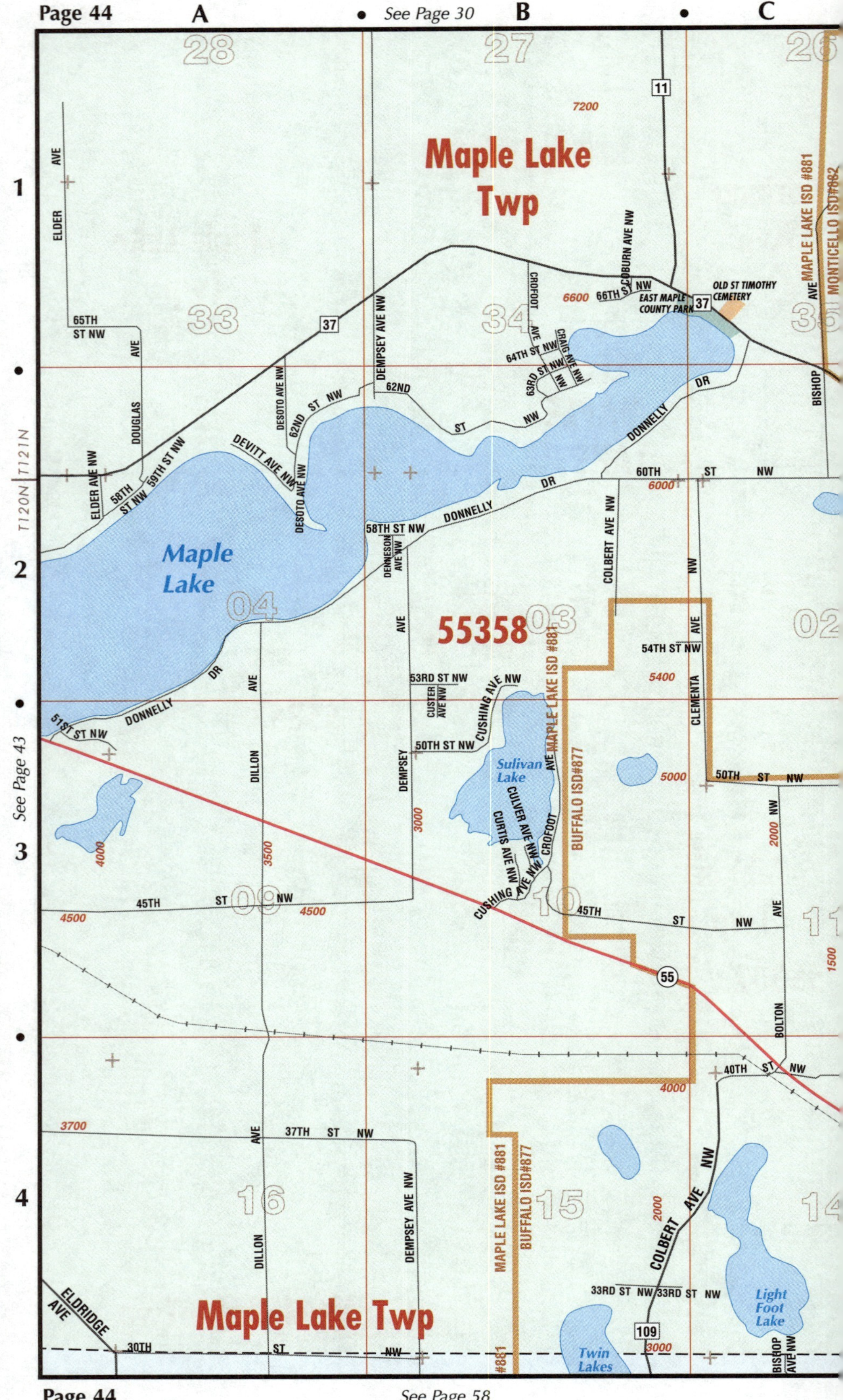

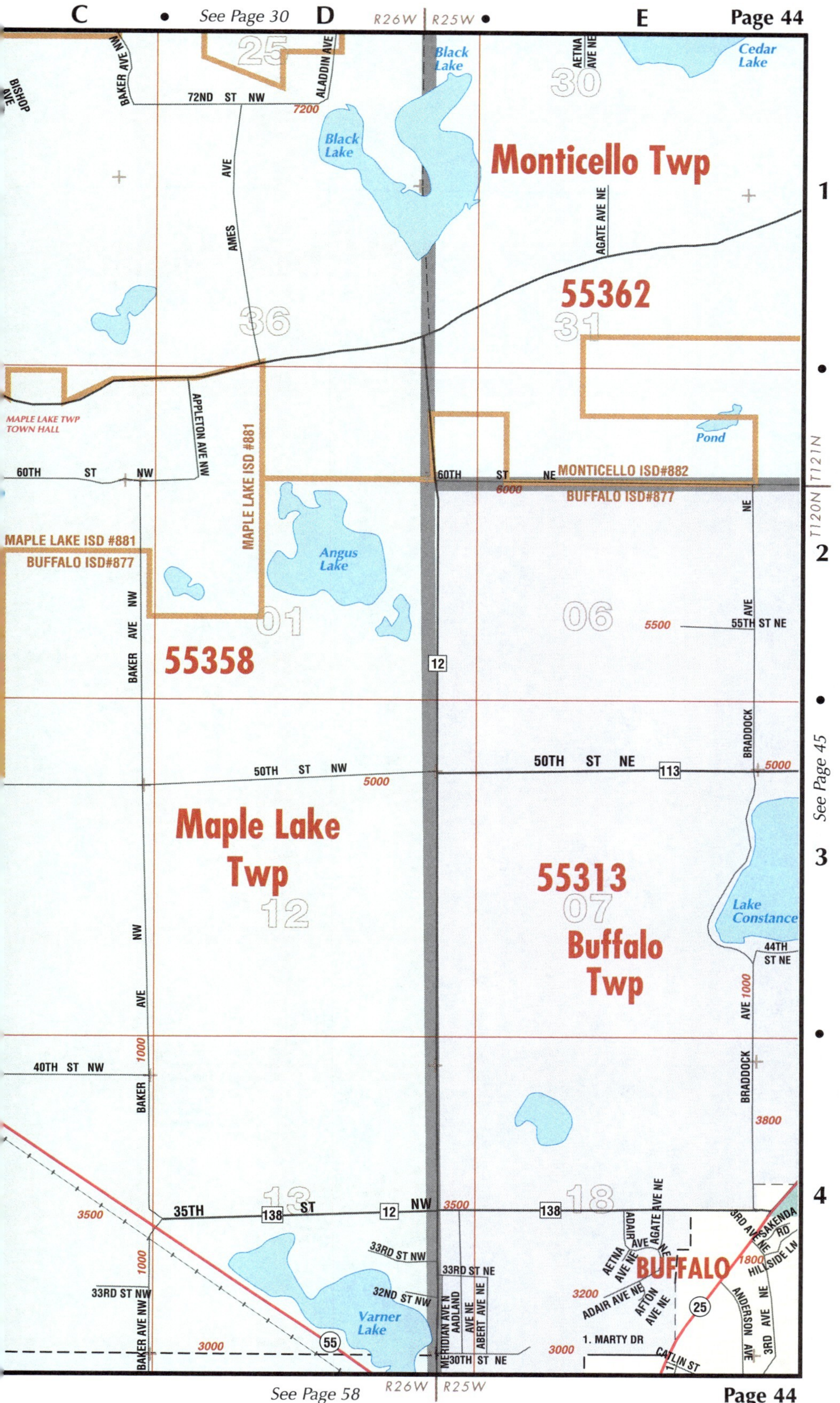

BISHOP AVE

BAKER AVE NW

72ND ST NW
7200

ALADDIN AVE

Black Lake

Cedar Lake

AETNA AVE NE

30

Monticello Twp

AVE

AMES

Black Lake

1

AGATE AVE NE

55362

36

31

T120N | T121N

MAPLE LAKE TWP TOWN HALL

APPLETON AVE NW

MAPLE LAKE ISD #881

Pond

60TH ST NW

60TH ST NE

MONTICELLO ISD#882
6000
BUFFALO ISD#877

NE

2

MAPLE LAKE ISD #881
BUFFALO ISD#877

BAKER AVE NW

Angus Lake

01

06

5500

AVE

55TH ST NE

55358

12

Braddock

See Page 45

50TH ST NW
5000

50TH ST NE
113

5000

Maple Lake Twp

12

NW

AVE

55313

07

Lake Constance

44TH ST NE

Buffalo Twp

AVE 1000

BRADDOCK

3

40TH ST NW
1000

BAKER

3800

35TH ST
138

12 NW
3500

138

18

ADAIR AVE NE

AGATE AVE NE

4

3500

1000

33RD ST NW

32ND ST NW

33RD ST NW

MERIDIAN AVE N
AADLAND AVE NE
ABERT AVE NE

33RD ST NE

AETNA AVE NE
ADAIR AVE NE
AFTON AVE NE

3RD AVE
SAKENDA RD
1800
HILLSIDE LN

BUFFALO

1. MARTY DR

3200

25

Varner Lake

55

3000

3000

CATLIN ST

ANDERSON AVE NE
3RD AVE NE

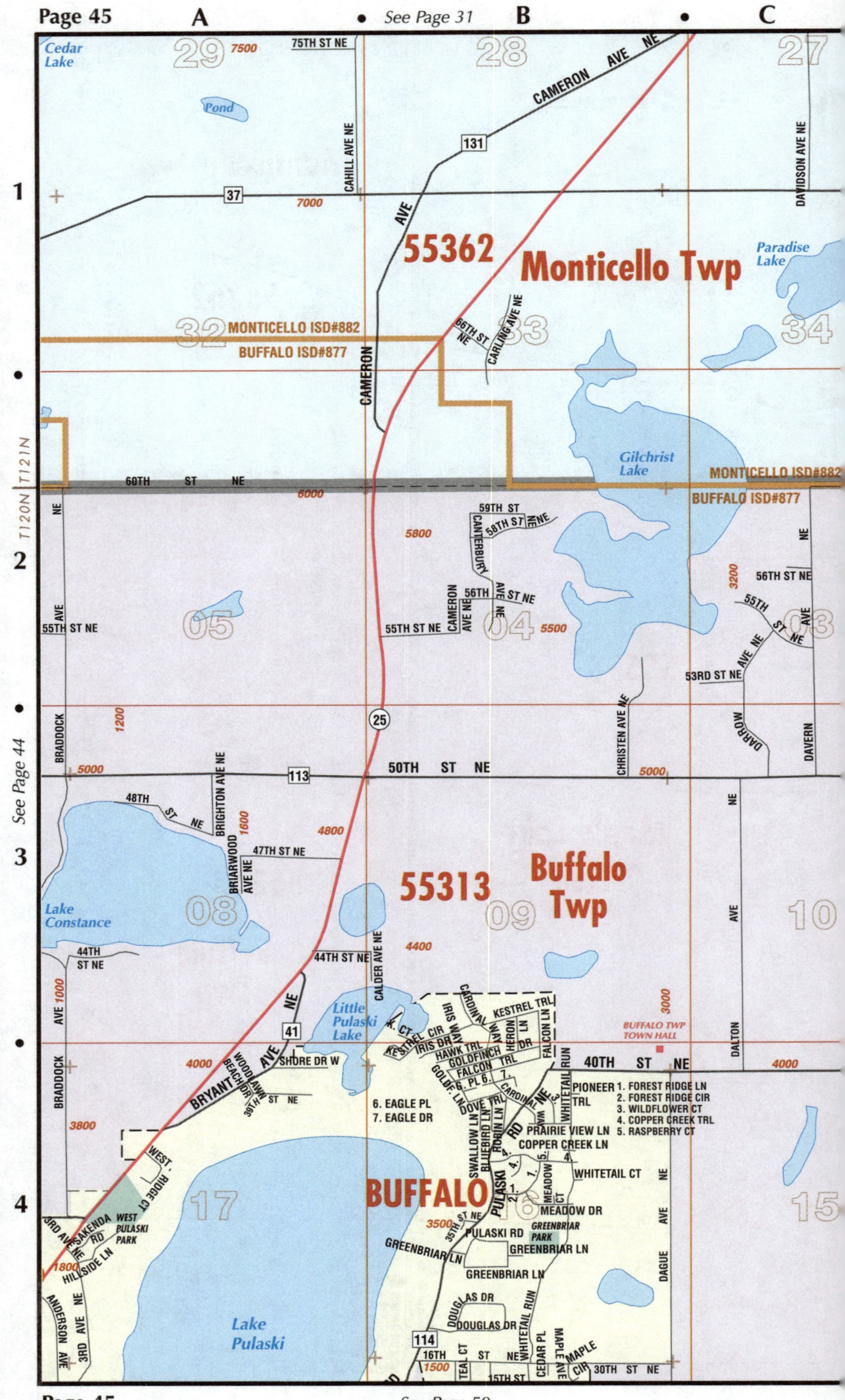

See Page 31

55362

Monticello Twp

MONTICELLO ISD#882

BUFFALO ISD#877

MONTICELLO ISD#882

BUFFALO ISD#877

55313

Buffalo Twp

BUFFALO

BUFFALO TWP TOWN HALL

6. EAGLE PL
7. EAGLE DR

1. FOREST RIDGE LN
2. FOREST RIDGE CIR
3. WILDFLOWER CT
4. COPPER CREEK TRL
5. RASPBERRY CT

PIONEER TRL
PRAIRIE VIEW LN
COPPER CREEK LN

WHITETAIL CT

MEADOW DR

GREENBRIAR LN
GREENBRIAR LN
GREENBRIAR LN

DOUGLAS DR
DOUGLAS DR

West Pulaski Park

Lake Pulaski

Little Pulaski Lake

Lake Constance

Cedar Lake

Paradise Lake

Gilchrist Lake

Pond

See Page 44

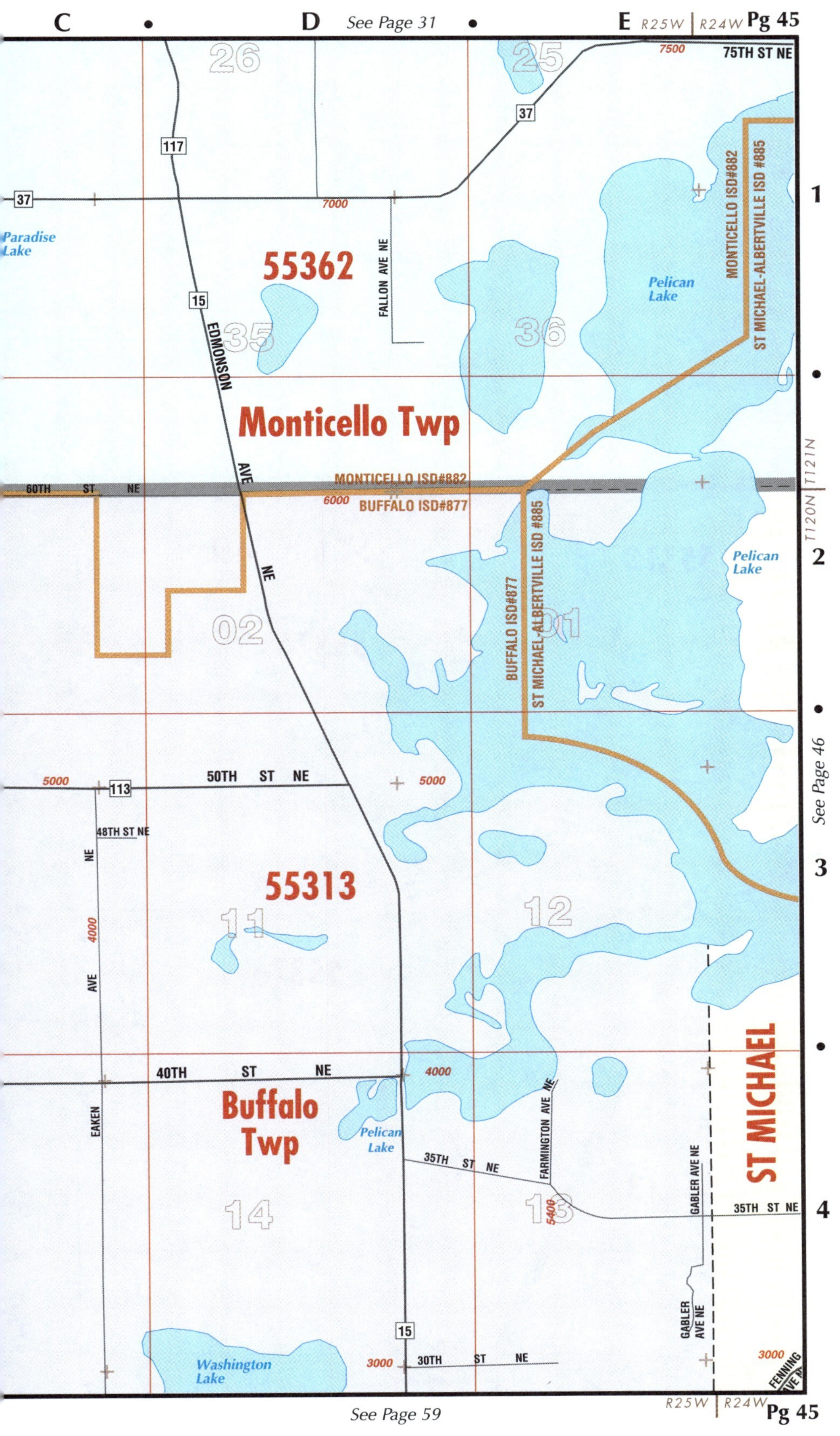

75TH ST NE

7500

37

37

117

37 7000

55362

Paradise
Lake

15

EDMONSON

35

FALLON AVE NE

36

Pelican
Lake

MONTICELLO ISD#882

ST MICHAEL-ALBERTVILLE ISD #885

1

•

Monticello Twp

MONTICELLO ISD#882

60TH ST NE

6000 BUFFALO ISD#877

AVE

NE

02

BUFFALO ISD#877

ST MICHAEL-ALBERTVILLE ISD #885

01

Pelican
Lake

T120N | T121N

2

•

5000

113

50TH ST NE

5000

48TH ST NE

NE

AVE

4000

55313

11

12

3

•

See Page 46

40TH ST NE

4000

EAKEN

**Buffalo
Twp**

Pelican
Lake

14

35TH ST NE

FARMINGTON AVE NE

GABLER AVE NE

13

5400

ST MICHAEL

35TH ST NE

4

15

Washington
Lake

3000 30TH ST NE

GABLER AVE NE

3000

FENNING AVE NE

75TH ST NE 30 37 29 JASON AVE NE 28

72ND ST NE

GIFFORT AVE

55362

7400

Monticello Twp

118

1

31

MONTICELLO ISD#882

ST MICHAEL-ALBERTVILLE ISD #885

Pelican Lake

32 37 65TH ST NE 33

MONTICELLO ISD#882

119 ST MICHAEL-ALBERTVILLE ISD #885

IFFERT AVE

8500

63RD ST NE 6200

6000

60TH ST NE

T120N | T121N

Pelican Lake

55313

06

HALSEY AVE

ST MICHAEL

56TH ST 5500

05

NE

55376

119

2

04

IFFERT AVE

8500

Pelican Lake

8000

07

08

119 119

3

09

IFFERT NE AVE

55376

IBARRA AVE NE

4000

BARBA AVE NE

ST MICHAEL

BUFFALO ISD#877

ST MICHAEL-ALBERTVILLE ISD #885

55313

16

IFFERT 8500

3500 35TH ST NE

4

35TH ST NE

3500

GARRISON AVE NE

GARRISON AVE NE

7500

3000

FENNING AVE NE

30TH ST 35 NE

8500

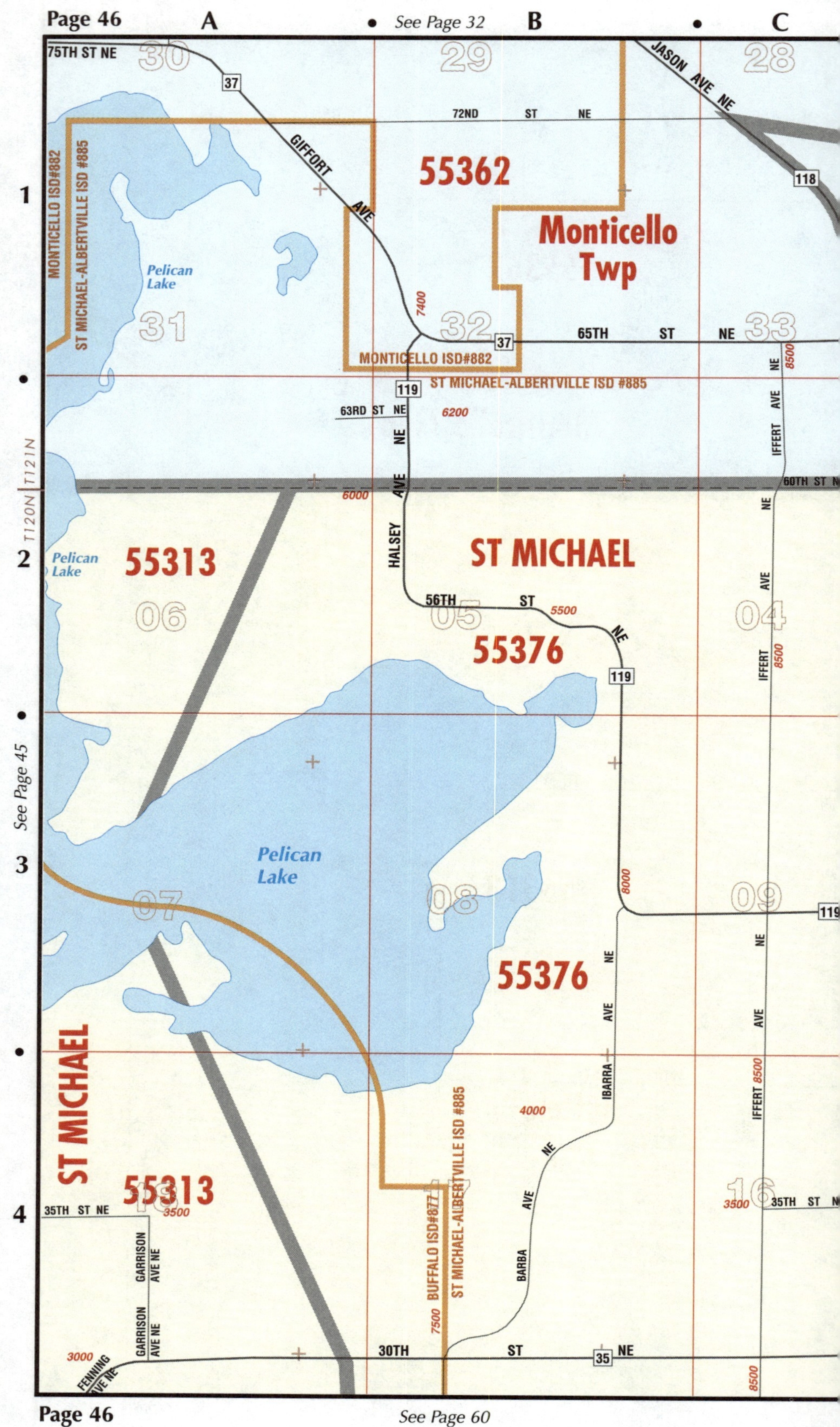

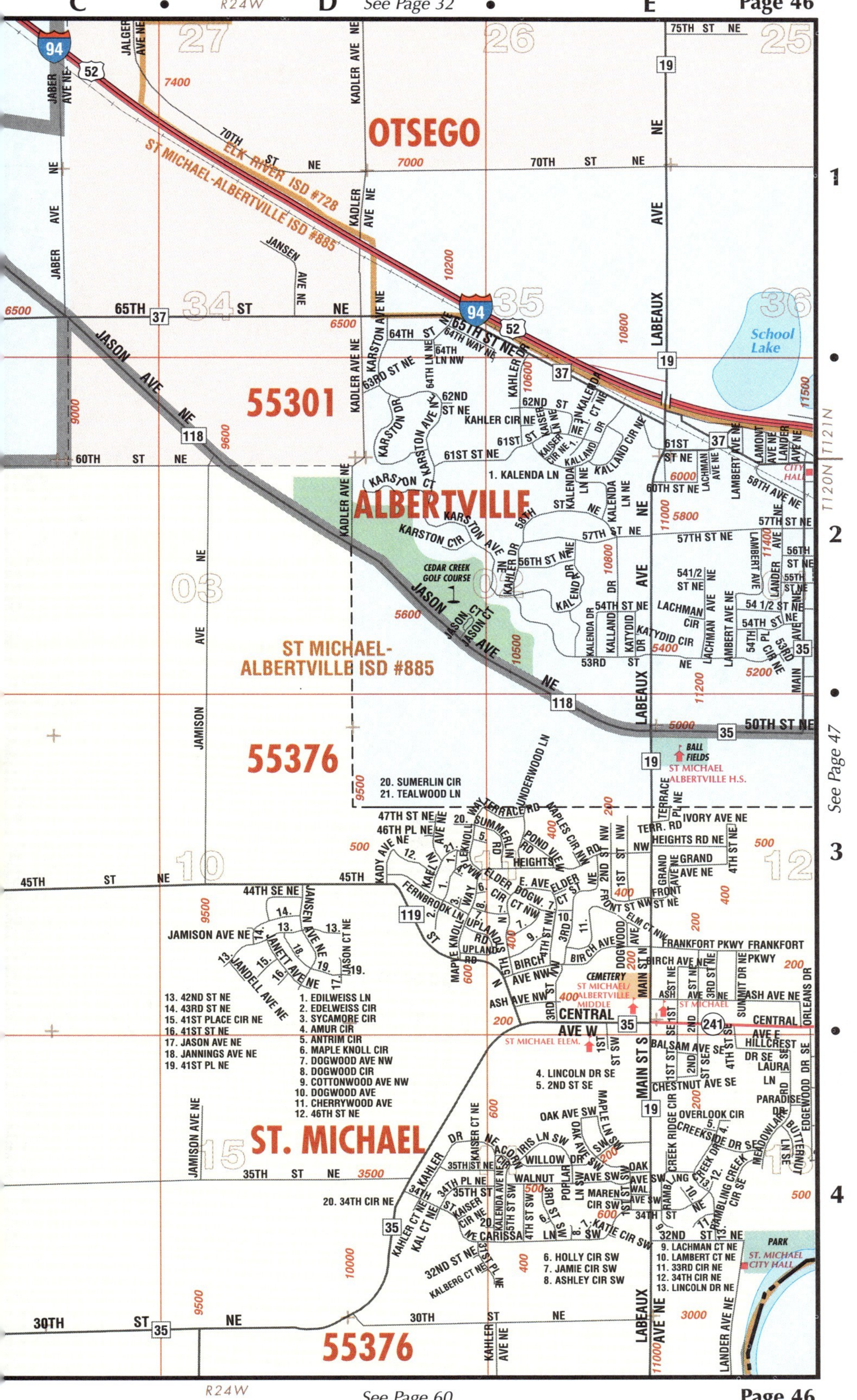
OTSEGO
ALBERTVILLE
ST. MICHAEL
55301
55376
ST MICHAEL-ALBERTVILLE ISD #885
ELK RIVER ISD #728
CEDAR CREEK GOLF COURSE
School Lake
BALL FIELDS
ST MICHAEL ALBERTVILLE H.S.
ST MICHAEL/ALBERTVILLE MIDDLE
ST MICHAEL ELEM.
CEMETERY
CITY HALL
PARK
ST. MICHAEL CITY HALL
JASON AVE NE
LABEAUX AVE NE
KADLER AVE NE
JAMISON AVE NE
70TH ST NE
65TH ST NE
60TH ST NE
50TH ST NE
45TH ST NE
35TH ST NE
30TH ST NE
CENTRAL AVE W
MAIN ST S
13. 42ND ST NE
14. 43RD ST NE
15. 41ST PLACE CIR NE
16. 41ST ST NE
17. JASON AVE NE
18. JANNINGS AVE NE
19. 41ST PL NE
1. EDILWEISS LN
2. EDELWEISS CIR
3. SYCAMORE CIR
4. AMUR CIR
5. ANTRIM CIR
6. MAPLE KNOLL CIR
7. DOGWOOD AVE NW
8. DOGWOOD CIR
9. COTTONWOOD AVE NW
10. DOGWOOD AVE
11. CHERRYWOOD AVE
12. 46TH ST NE
20. SUMERLIN CIR
21. TEALWOOD LN
1. KALENDA LN
4. LINCOLN DR SE
5. 2ND ST SE
6. HOLLY CIR SW
7. JAMIE CIR SW
8. ASHLEY CIR SW
9. LACHMAN CT NE
10. LAMBERT CT NE
11. 33RD CIR NE
12. 34TH CIR NE
13. LINCOLN DR NE
20. 34TH CIR NE
T120N T121N
See Page 47

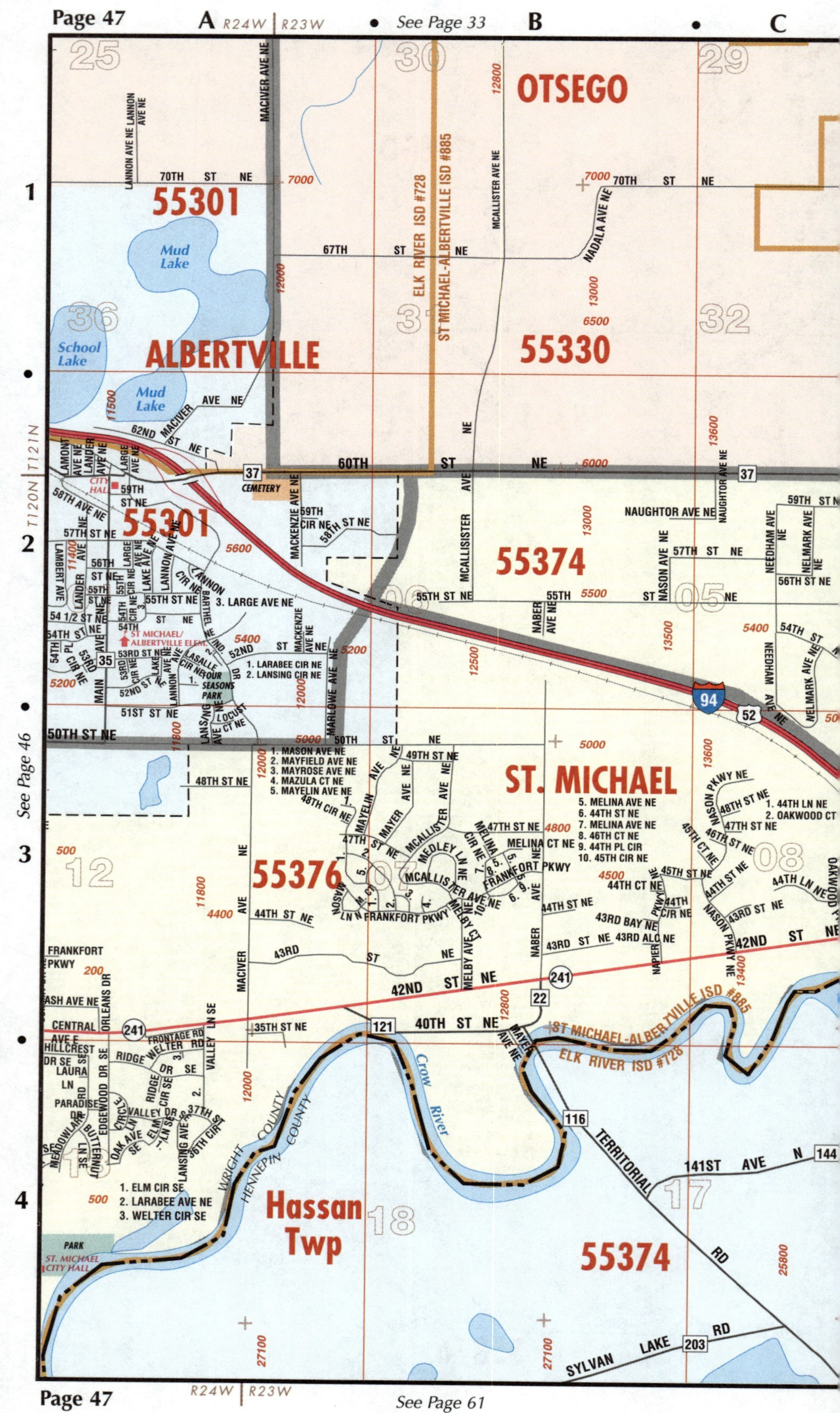

OTSEGO

55301

55330

ALBERTVILLE

ELK RIVER ISD #728

ST MICHAEL-ALBERTVILLE ISD #885

Mud Lake

School Lake

Mud Lake

CITY HALL

CEMETERY

55301

55374

55376

ST. MICHAEL

1. MASON AVE NE
2. MAYFIELD AVE NE
3. MAYROSE AVE NE
4. MAZULA CT NE
5. MAYELIN AVE NE

1. LARABEE CIR NE
2. LANSING CIR NE

5. MELINA AVE NE
6. 44TH ST NE
7. MELINA AVE NE
8. 46TH CT NE
9. 44TH PL CIR NE
10. 45TH CIR NE

1. 44TH LN NE
2. OAKWOOD CT

ST MICHAEL/
ALBERTVILLE ELM.

SEASONS PARK

FRANKFORT PKWY

Hassan Twp

WRIGHT COUNTY

HENNEPIN COUNTY

Crow River

ST MICHAEL-ALBERTVILLE ISD #885

ELK RIVER ISD #728

TERRITORIAL RD

141ST AVE N

55374

PARK

ST. MICHAEL CITY HALL

1. ELM CIR SE
2. LARABEE AVE NE
3. WELTER CIR SE

SYLVAN LAKE RD

See Page 46

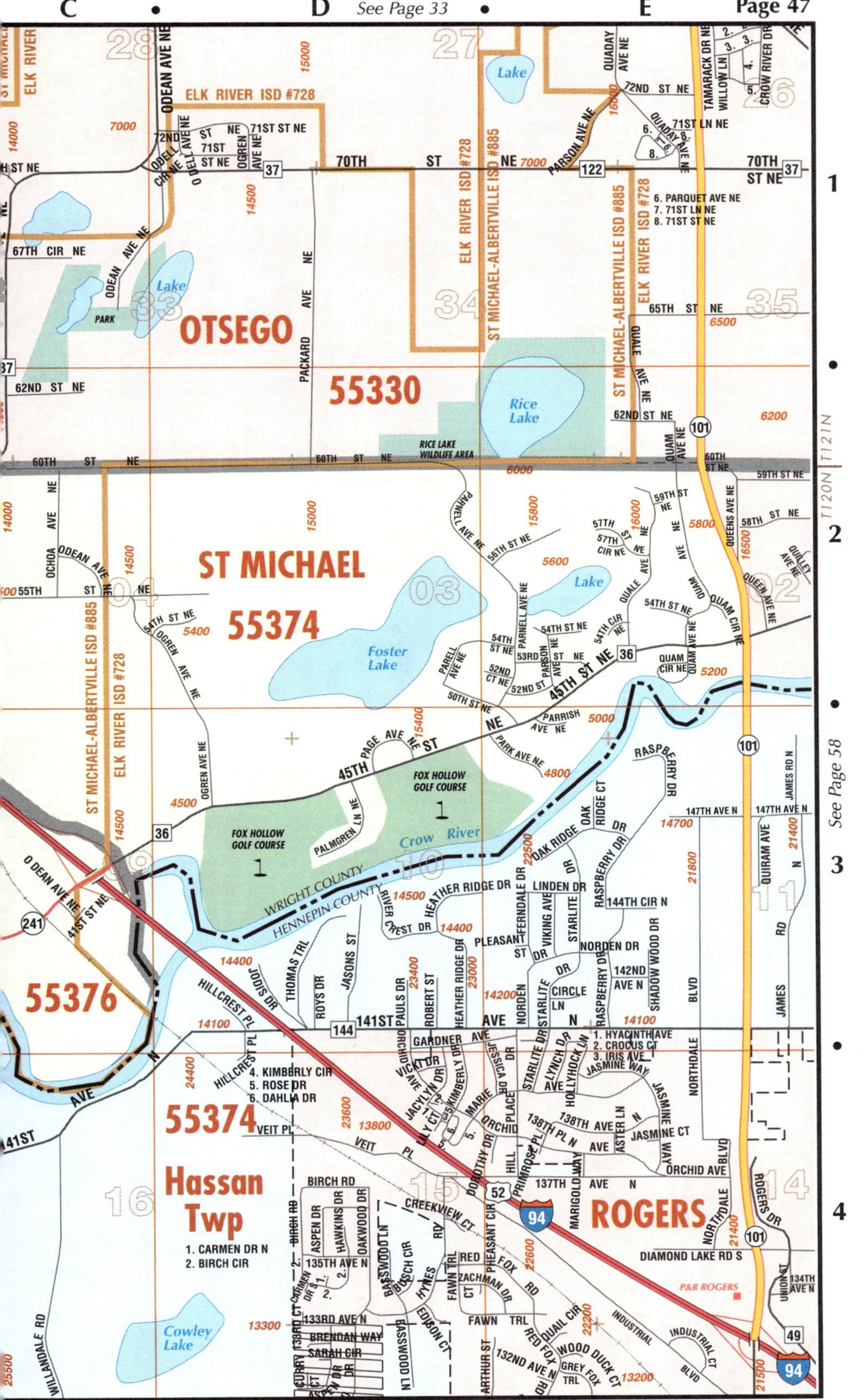

OTSEGO

55330

ELK RIVER ISD #728

ELK RIVER ISD #728

ST MICHAEL-ALBERTVILLE ISD #885

6. PARQUET AVE NE
7. 71ST LN NE
8. 71ST ST NE

Rice Lake

RICE LAKE WILDLIFE AREA

ST MICHAEL

55374

Foster Lake

Fox Hollow Golf Course

Fox Hollow Golf Course

Crow River

WRIGHT COUNTY
HENNEPIN COUNTY

ELK RIVER ISD #728

ST MICHAEL-ALBERTVILLE ISD #885

55376

55374

Hassan Twp

1. CARMEN DR N
2. BIRCH CIR

3. KIMBERLY CIR
4. ROSE DR
6. DAHLIA DR

1. HYACINTH AVE
2. CROCUS CT
3. IRIS AVE

ROGERS

P&R ROGERS

Cowley Lake

See Page 58

See Page 34
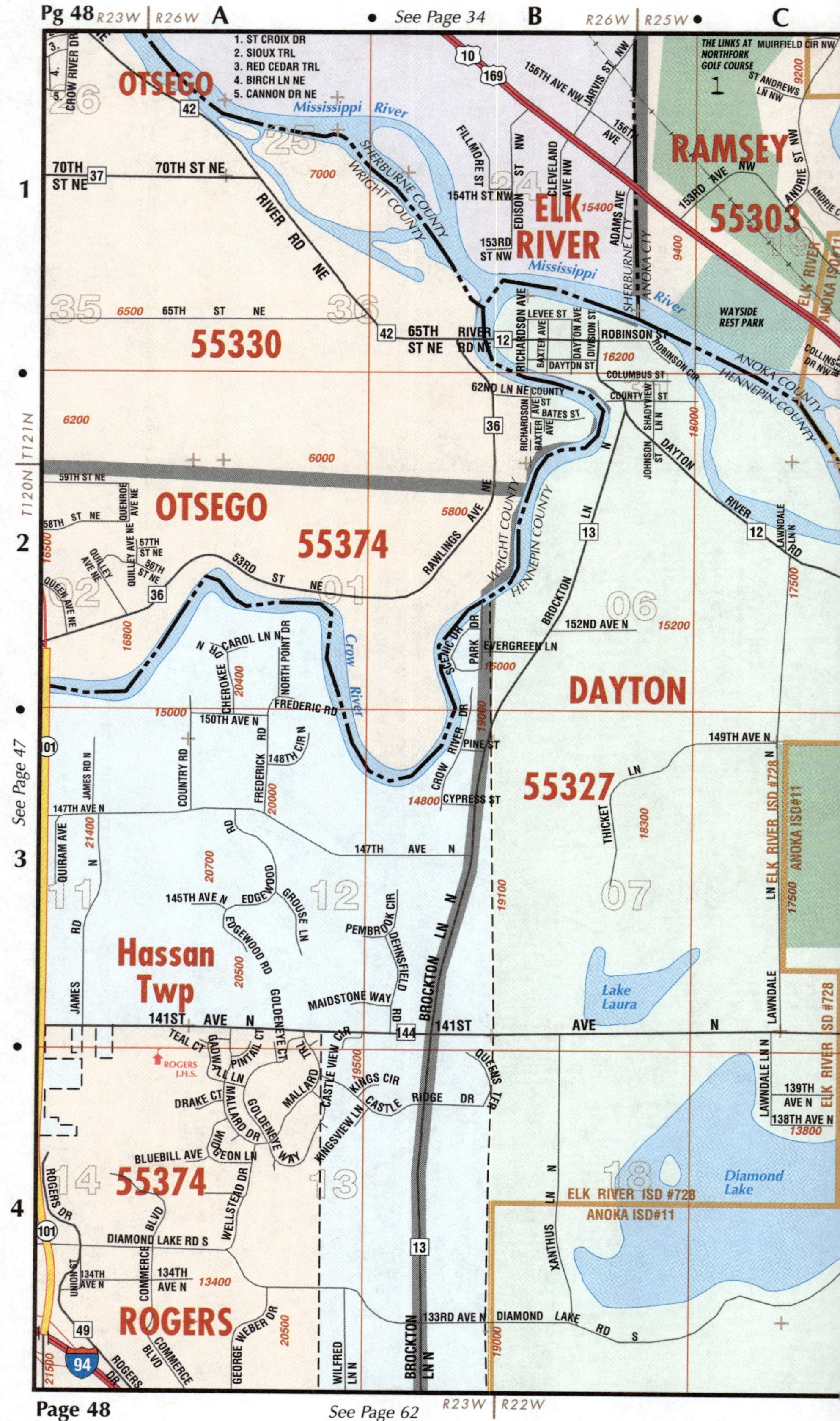

See Page 47

See Page 62
R23W R22W

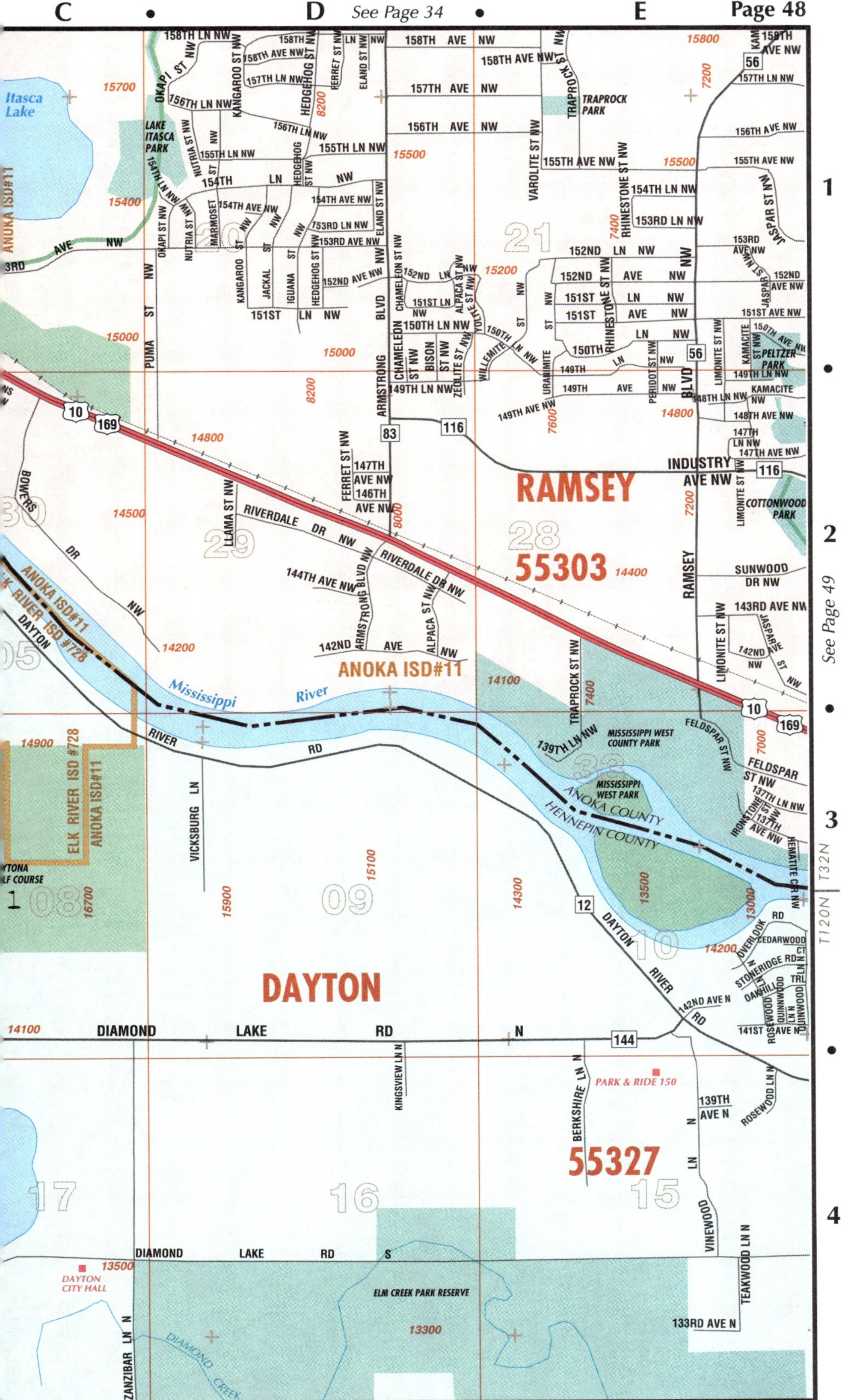

1

2

3

4

See Page 49

T120N T32N

RAMSEY

55303

ANOKA ISD#11

DAYTON

55327

PARK & RIDE 150

Itasca Lake

Lake Itasca Park

Traprock Park

Peltzer Park

Cottonwood Park

Mississippi West County Park

Mississippi West Park

Anoka County

Hennepin County

Dayton River

Elk River ISD #728

Anoka ISD #11

Elm Creek Park Reserve

Daytona Golf Course

DAYTON CITY HALL

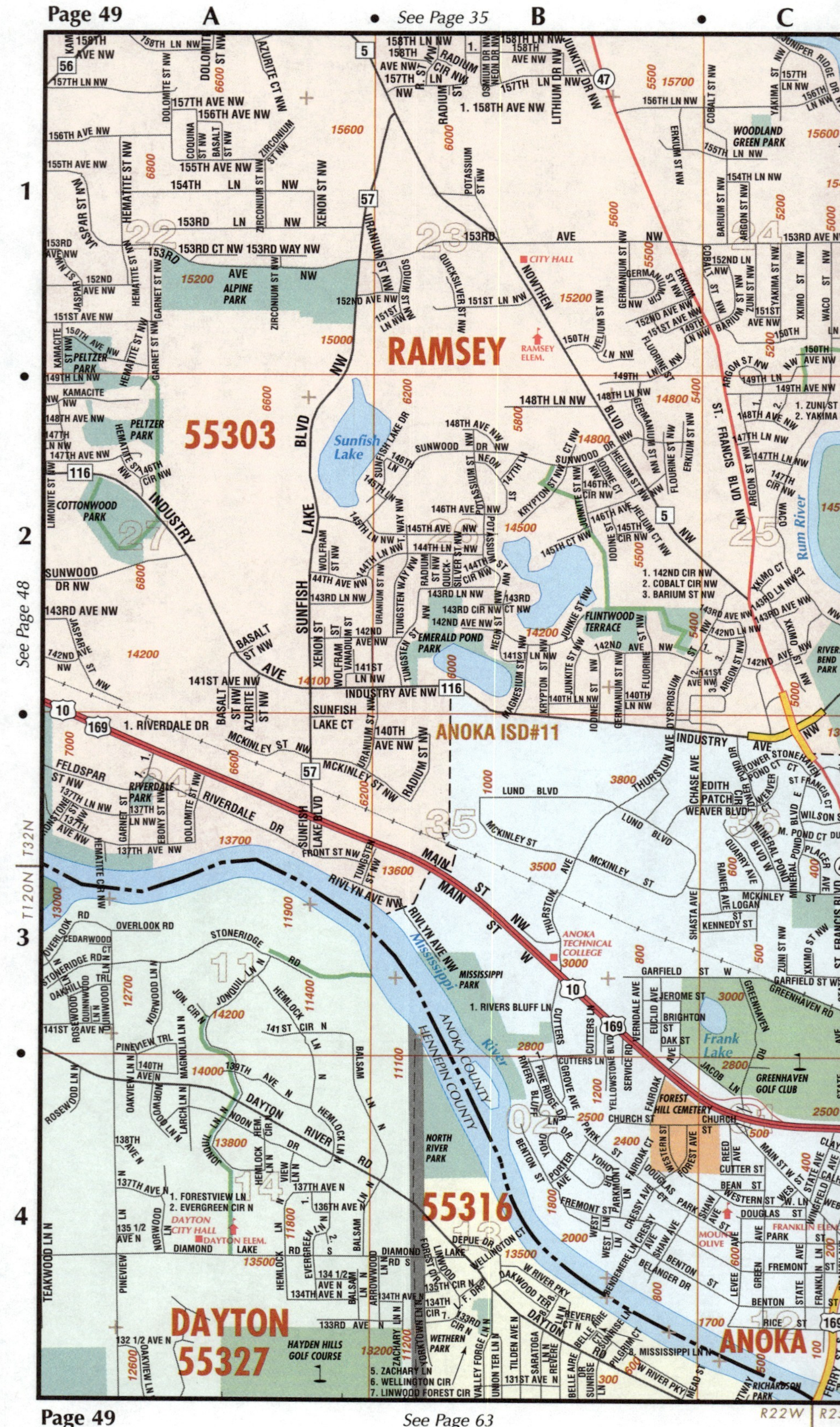

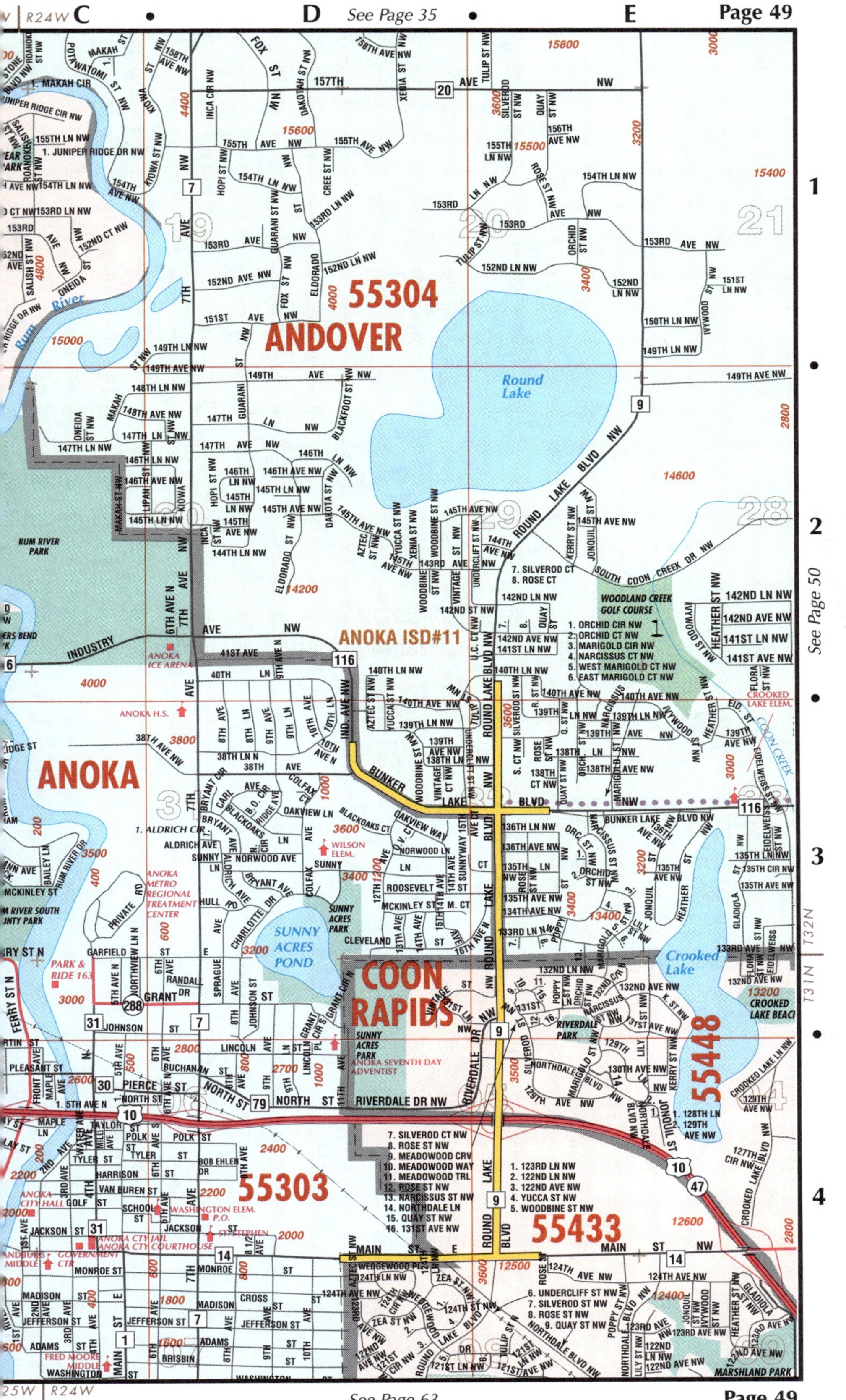
55304
ANDOVER
Round Lake
ANOKA ISD#11
ANOKA
COON RAPIDS
55303
55433
55448
Crooked Lake
SUNNY ACRES POND
SUNNY ACRES PARK
RUM RIVER PARK
Rum River
WOODLAND CREEK GOLF COURSE
ANOKA ICE ARENA
ANOKA H.S.
WILSON ELEM.
ANOKA METRO REGIONAL TREATMENT CENTER
PARK & RIDE 163
RIVERDALE PARK
ANOKA SEVENTH DAY ADVENTIST
CROOKED LAKE ELEM.
CROOKED LAKE BEACH
WASHINGTON ELEM.
P.O.
ST STEPHEN
ANOKA CITY HALL
ANOKA CTY JAIL
ANOKA CTY COURTHOUSE
GOVERNMENT CTR
FRED MOORE MIDDLE
MARSHLAND PARK
COON CREEK
157TH AVE NW
155TH AVE NW
153RD AVE NW
152ND LN NW
151ST AVE NW
149TH AVE NW
147TH AVE NW
146TH AVE NW
145TH AVE NW
144TH LN NW
ROUND LAKE BLVD NW
SOUTH COON CREEK DR NW
INDUSTRY AVE NW
BUNKER LAKE BLVD
140TH LN NW
139TH LN NW
38TH AVE
RIVERDALE DR NW
NORTH ST
MAIN ST NW
124TH AVE NW
123RD AVE NW
122ND AVE NW
NORTHDALE BLVD NW
CROOKED LAKE BLVD
1. MAKAH CIR
1. JUNIPER RIDGE DR NW
1. ORCHID CIR NW
2. ORCHID CT NW
3. MARIGOLD CIR NW
4. NARCISSUS CT NW
5. WEST MARIGOLD CT NW
6. EAST MARIGOLD CT NW
7. SILVEROD CT
8. ROSE CT
1. ALDRICH CIR
7. SILVEROD CT NW
8. ROSE ST NW
9. MEADOWOOD CRV
10. MEADOWOOD WAY
11. MEADOWOOD TRL
12. ROSE ST NW
13. NARCISSUS ST NW
14. NORTHDALE LN
15. QUAY ST NW
16. 131ST AVE NW
1. 123RD LN NW
2. 122ND LN NW
3. 122ND AVE NW
4. YUCCA ST NW
5. WOODBINE ST NW
1. 128TH LN
2. 129TH AVE NW
6. UNDERCLIFF ST NW
7. SILVEROD ST NW
8. ROSE ST NW
9. QUAY ST NW
1. 5TH AVE N
T32N
T31N

See Page 50

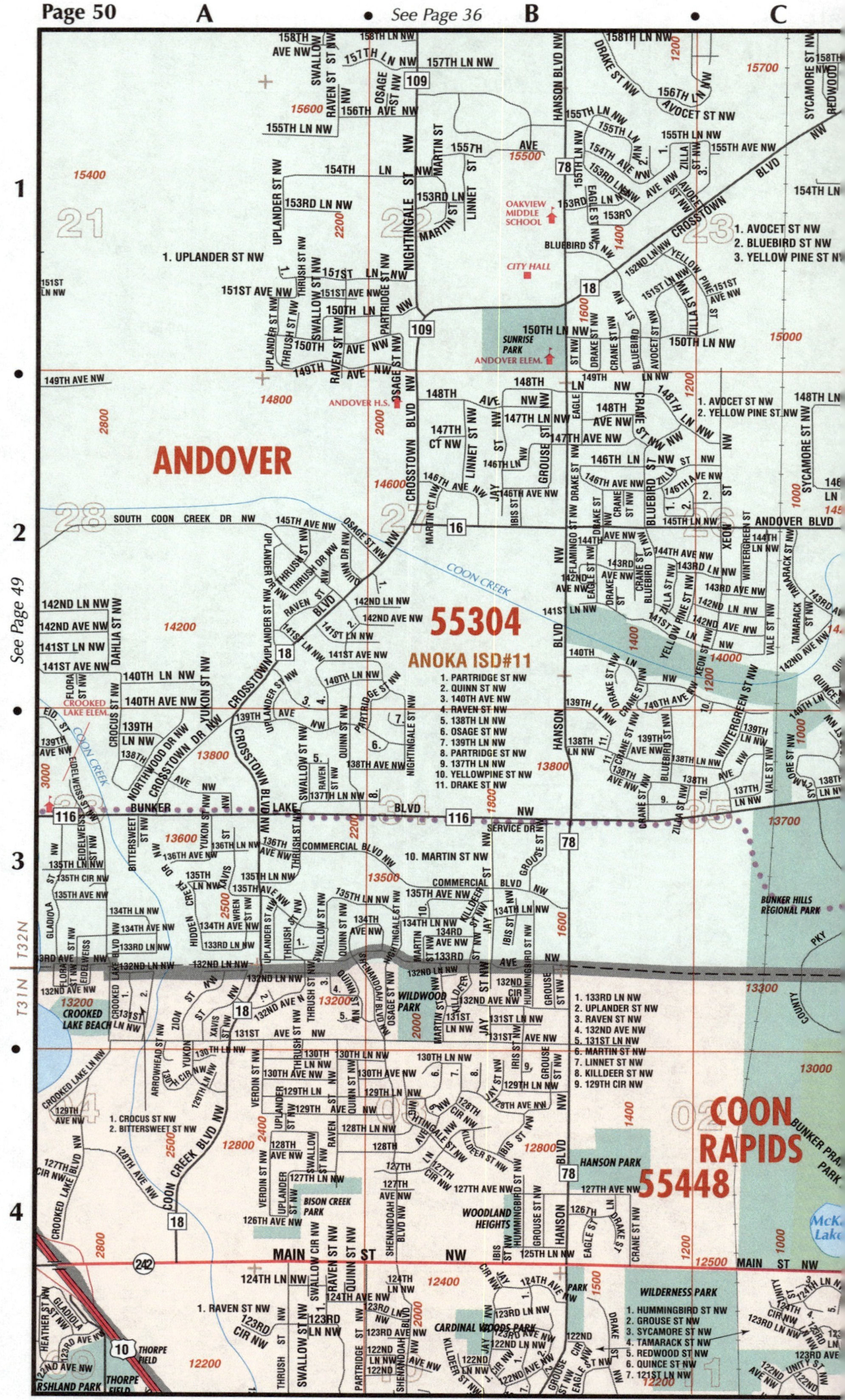

ANDOVER

55304

ANOKA ISD#11

COON RAPIDS

55448

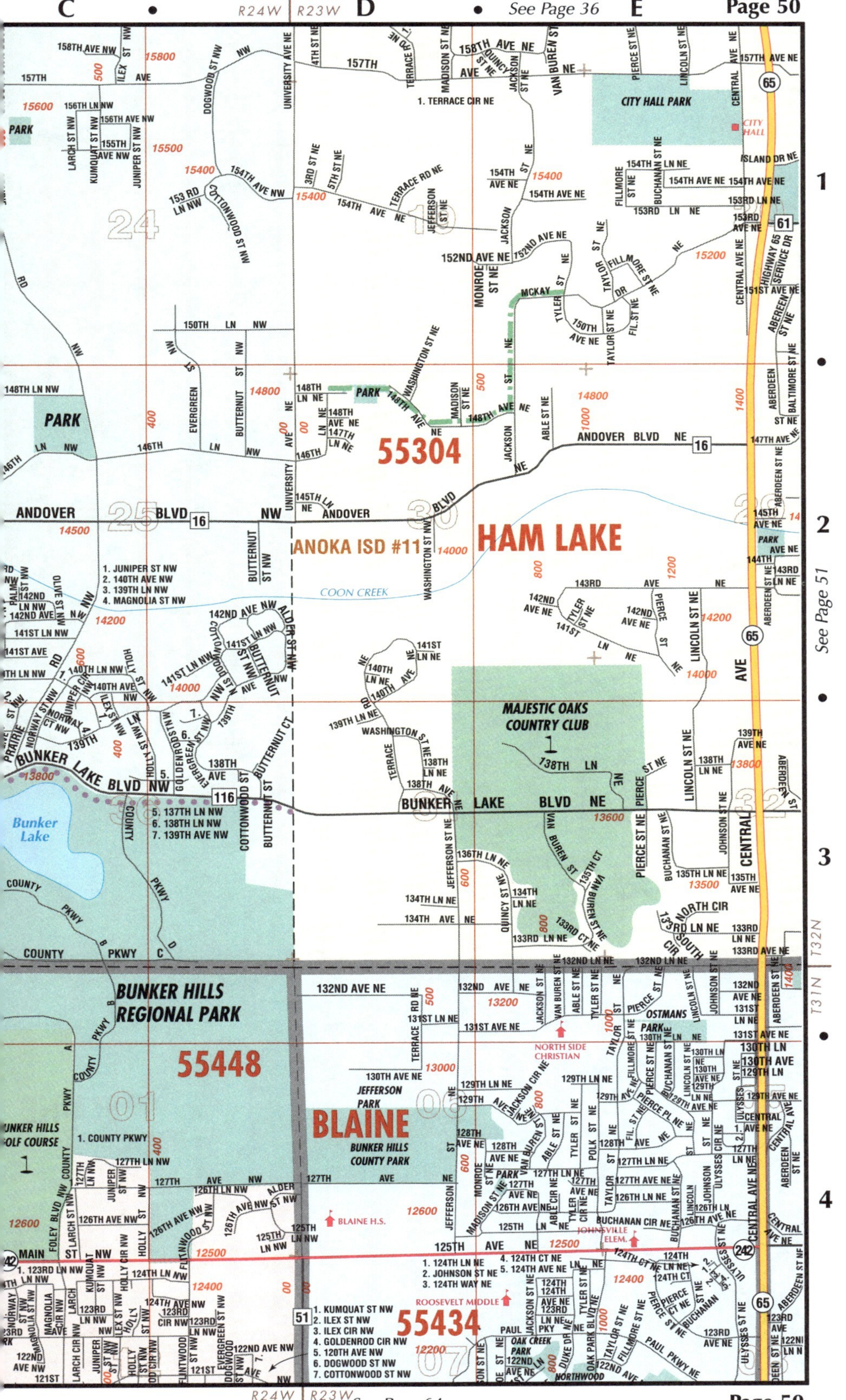
55304
HAM LAKE
ANOKA ISD #11
CITY HALL PARK
CITY HALL
MAJESTIC OAKS COUNTRY CLUB
COON CREEK
Bunker Lake
BUNKER HILLS REGIONAL PARK
55448
BLAINE
JEFFERSON PARK
BUNKER HILLS COUNTY PARK
OSTMANS PARK
NORTH SIDE CHRISTIAN
BLAINE H.S.
JOHNSVILLE ELEM.
ROOSEVELT MIDDLE
55434
BUNKER HILLS GOLF COURSE
OAK CREEK PARK
ANDOVER BLVD NE
ANDOVER BLVD NW
BUNKER LAKE BLVD NE
BUNKER LAKE BLVD NW
UNIVERSITY AVE NE
CENTRAL AVE NE
HIGHWAY 65 SERVICE DR
125TH AVE NE
MAIN ST NW
1. TERRACE CIR NE
1. JUNIPER ST NW
2. 140TH AVE NW
3. 139TH LN NW
4. MAGNOLIA ST NW
5. 137TH LN NW
6. 138TH LN NW
7. 139TH AVE NW
1. COUNTY PKWY
1. 124TH LN NE
2. JOHNSON ST NE
3. 124TH WAY NE
4. 124TH CT NE
5. 124TH AVE NE
1. KUMQUAT ST NW
2. ILEX ST NW
3. ILEX CIR NW
4. GOLDENROD CIR NW
5. 120TH AVE NW
6. DOGWOOD ST NW
7. COTTONWOOD ST NW
1
2
3
4
See Page 51
T32N
T31N

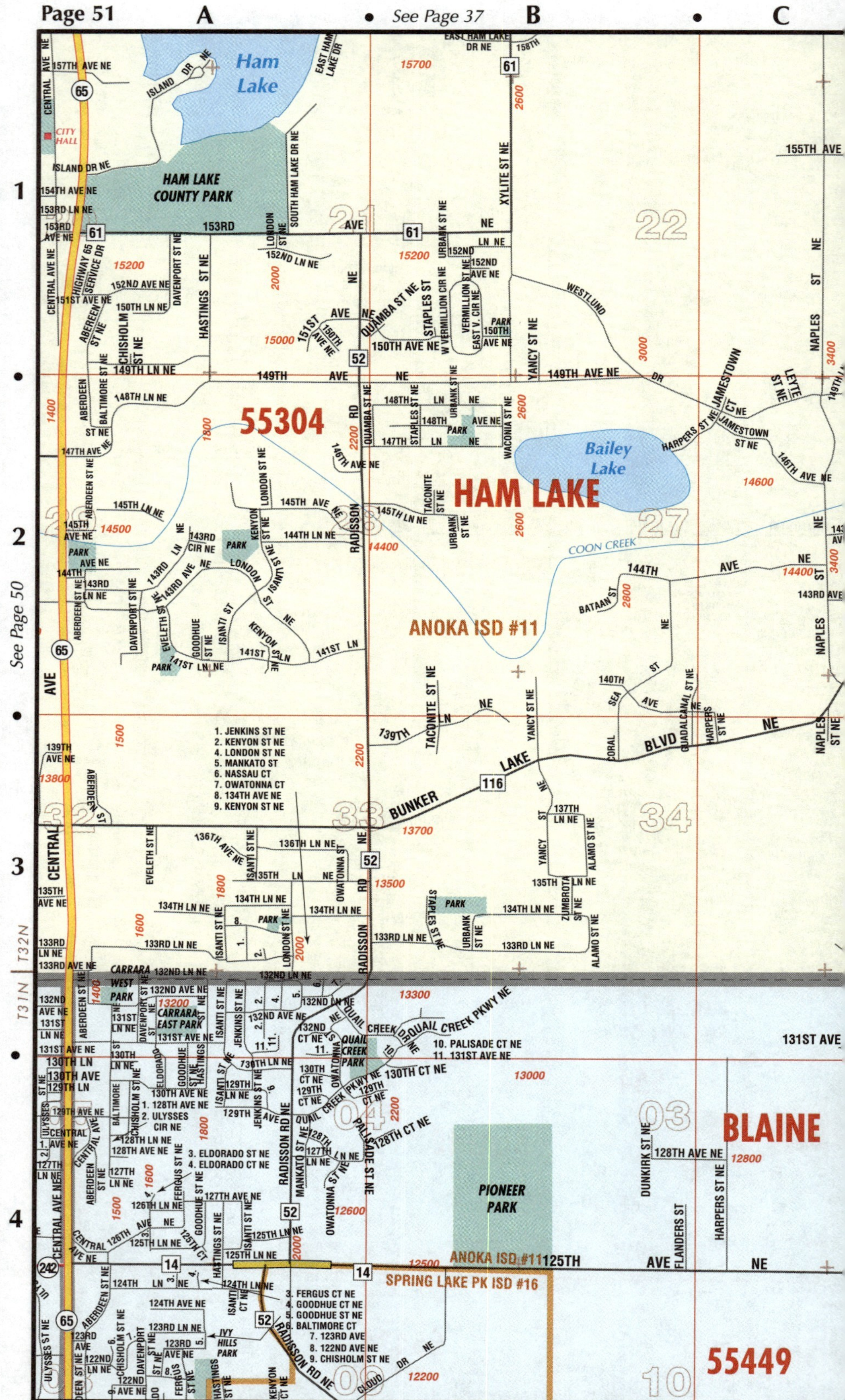

55304

HAM LAKE

Bailey Lake

Ham Lake

HAM LAKE COUNTY PARK

ANOKA ISD #11

1. JENKINS ST NE
2. KENYON ST NE
4. LONDON ST NE
5. MANKATO ST NE
6. NASSAU CT
7. OWATONNA CT
8. 134TH AVE NE
9. KENYON ST NE

BUNKER LAKE BLVD

CARRARA WEST PARK

CARRARA EAST PARK

PIONEER PARK

QUAIL CREEK PARK

BLAINE

ANOKA ISD #11
SPRING LAKE PK ISD #16

1. FERGUS CT NE
2. ULYSSES
CIR NE
3. ELDORADO NE
4. ELDORADO CT NE

3. FERGUS CT NE
4. GOODHUE ST NE
5. GOODHUE ST NE
6. BALTIMORE CT
7. 123RD AVE NE
8. 122ND AVE NE
9. CHISHOLM ST NE

IVY HILLS PARK

55449

1. 132ND AVE NE
5.
11. 131ST AVE NE

10. PALISADE CT NE
11. 131ST AVE NE

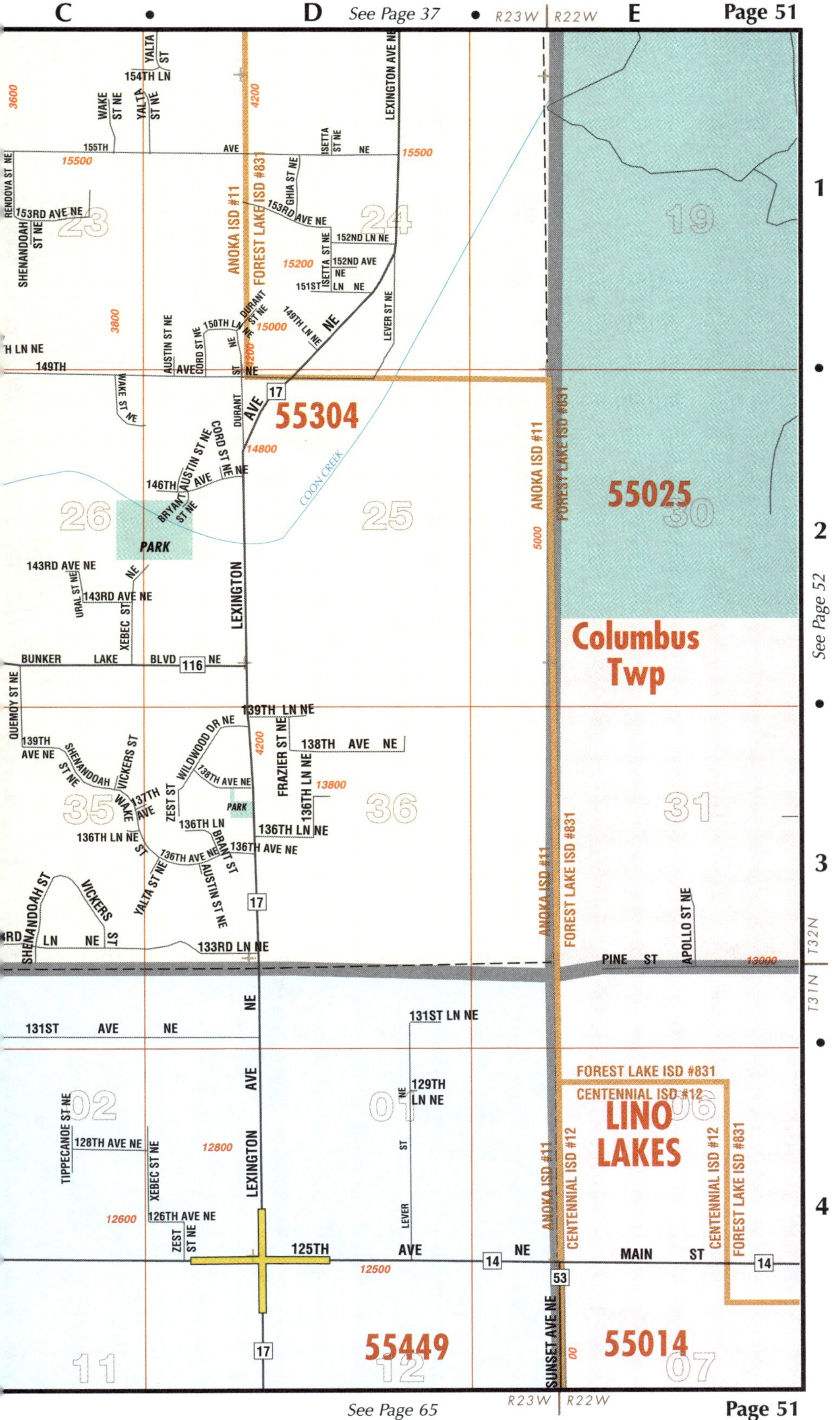

See Page 52

3600
154TH LN
YALTA ST
WAKE ST NE
YALTA ST NE
155TH
AVE
15500
RENDOVA ST NE
153RD AVE NE
SHENANDOAH ST NE
23
ANOKA ISD #11
FOREST LAKE ISD #831
4200
153RD AVE NE
GHIA ST NE
ISETTA ST NE
24
LEXINGTON AVE NE
15500
152ND ST NE
152ND AVE NE
15200
151ST LN NE
3800
150TH LN NE
AUSTIN ST NE
CORD ST NE
DURANT ST NE
149TH AVE NE
LEVER ST NE
NE
15000
H LN NE
149TH
WAKE ST NE
AVE
DURANT AVE
17
55304
14800
146TH AVE
BRYANT ST NE
AUSTIN ST NE
CORD ST NE
26
PARK
COON CREEK
25
ANOKA ISD #11
FOREST LAKE ISD #831
5000
55025
30
143RD AVE NE
NE
URAL ST NE
143RD AVE NE
LEXINGTON
XEBEC ST NE
QUEMOY ST NE
BUNKER LAKE BLVD
116
NE
Columbus Twp
139TH LN NE
139TH AVE NE
SHENANDOAH ST NE
VICKERS ST NE
138TH AVE NE
FRAZIER ST NE
138TH AVE NE
4200
136TH LN NE
13800
35
137TH AVE
WAKE ST NE
ZEST ST
WILDWOOD DR NE
138TH AVE NE
PARK
136TH LN NE
136TH LN NE
36
31
136TH LN NE
BRYANT ST NE
136TH AVE NE
AUSTIN ST NE
YALTA ST NE
136TH AVE NE
VICKERS ST NE
17
SHENANDOAH ST
RD LN NE
133RD LN NE
APOLLO ST NE
ANOKA ISD #11
FOREST LAKE ISD #831
PINE ST
13000
T32N
T31N
NE
131ST AVE NE
131ST LN NE
LEXINGTON
AVE
TIPPECANOE ST NE
02
128TH AVE NE
XEBEC ST NE
12800
129TH LN NE
01
LEVER ST
FOREST LAKE ISD #831
CENTENNIAL ISD #12
LINO LAKES
06
ANOKA ISD #11
CENTENNIAL ISD #12
CENTENNIAL ISD #12
FOREST LAKE ISD #831
12600
126TH AVE NE
ZEST ST NE
125TH AVE
14
12500
MAIN ST
14
17
55
53
00
11
12
55449
SUNSET AVE NE
55014
07

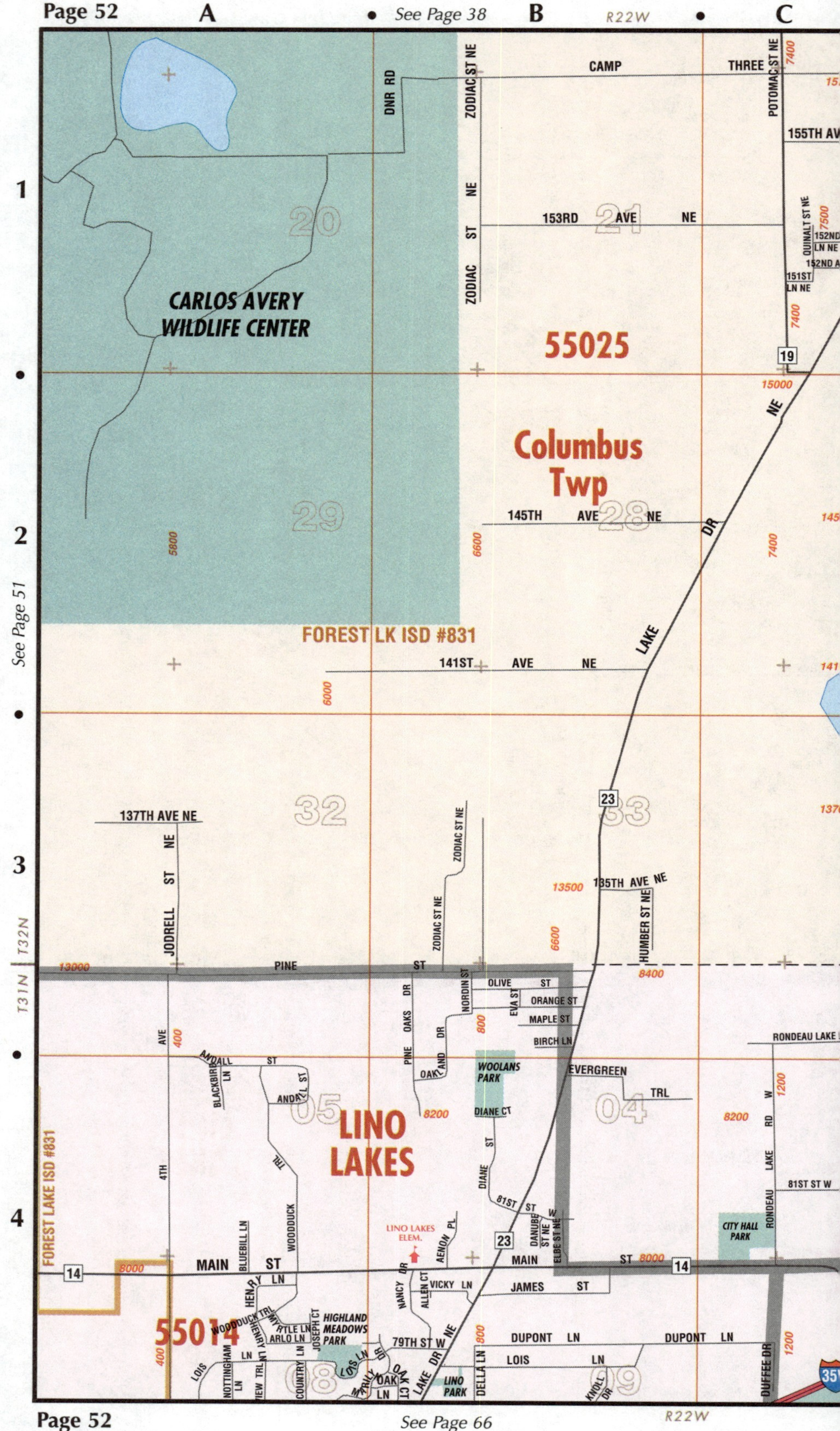

A   See Page 38   B   R22W   C

CAMP   THREE   7400

DNR RD

ZODIAC ST NE

POTOMAC ST NE

155TH AV

15

1

153RD   AVE   NE

21

ZODIAC   ST NE

7500

OUMALT ST NE

152ND
LN NE   152ND A

151ST
LN NE

**CARLOS AVERY
WILDLIFE CENTER**

55025

19

7400

15000

**Columbus
Twp**

NE

2

145TH   AVE   28   NE

5800

6600

DR

7400

145

See Page 51

FOREST LK ISD #831

141ST   AVE   NE

6000

LAKE

141

3

137TH AVE NE

32

ZODIAC ST NE

23

33

137

JODRELL   ST   NE

13500   135TH AVE NE

HUMBER ST NE

6600

RONDEAU LAKE

T31N | T32N

13000   PINE   ST

8400

OLIVE   ST

ORANGE ST

MAPLE ST

NORDIN ST

EVA ST

BIRCH LN

AVE

400

AMDALL
LN

BLACKBIRD LN

ANDAL ST

PINE OAKS DR

OAKLAND DR

800

WOOLANS
PARK

EVERGREEN

TRL

8200

RONDEAU LAKE RD W

1200

05

**LINO
LAKES**

8200

04

81ST ST W

FOREST LAKE ISD #831

4TH

WOODDUCK
TRL

DIANE
ST

DIANE CT

81ST   ST

DIANE
ST

**CITY HALL
PARK**

RONDEAU
LAKE
RD

4

BLUEBILL LN

LINO LAKES
ELEM.

AENIW PL

DANUBE
ST NE

ELBE ST NE

23

14

14

MAIN   ST

8000

HENRY
LN

WOODDUCK TRL

NANCY
DR

ALLEN CT

VICKY   LN

MAIN   ST   8000

JAMES   ST

55014

400

MYRTLE LN

ARLO LN

JOSEPH CT

**HIGHLAND
MEADOWS
PARK**

LAKE DR NE

79TH ST W

DELLA LN

800

DUPONT   LN   DUPONT   LN

DUFFEE DR

1200

LOIS
LN

NOTTINGHAM
LN

NEW TRL

COUNTRY LN

VALLEY LN

OAK
CT

LAKE DR W

LOIS   LN

KNOLL
DR

**LINO
PARK**

08

19

35W

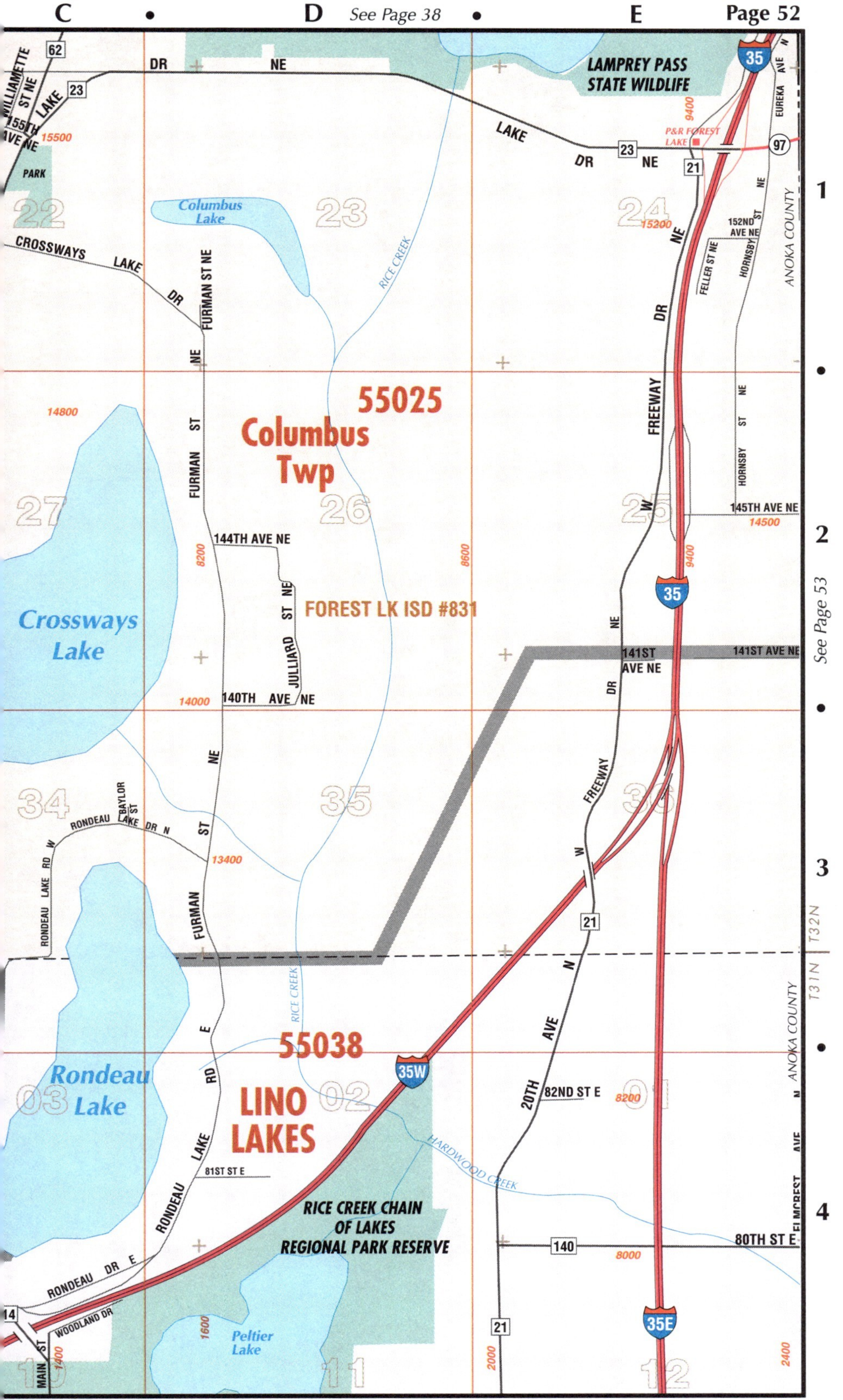

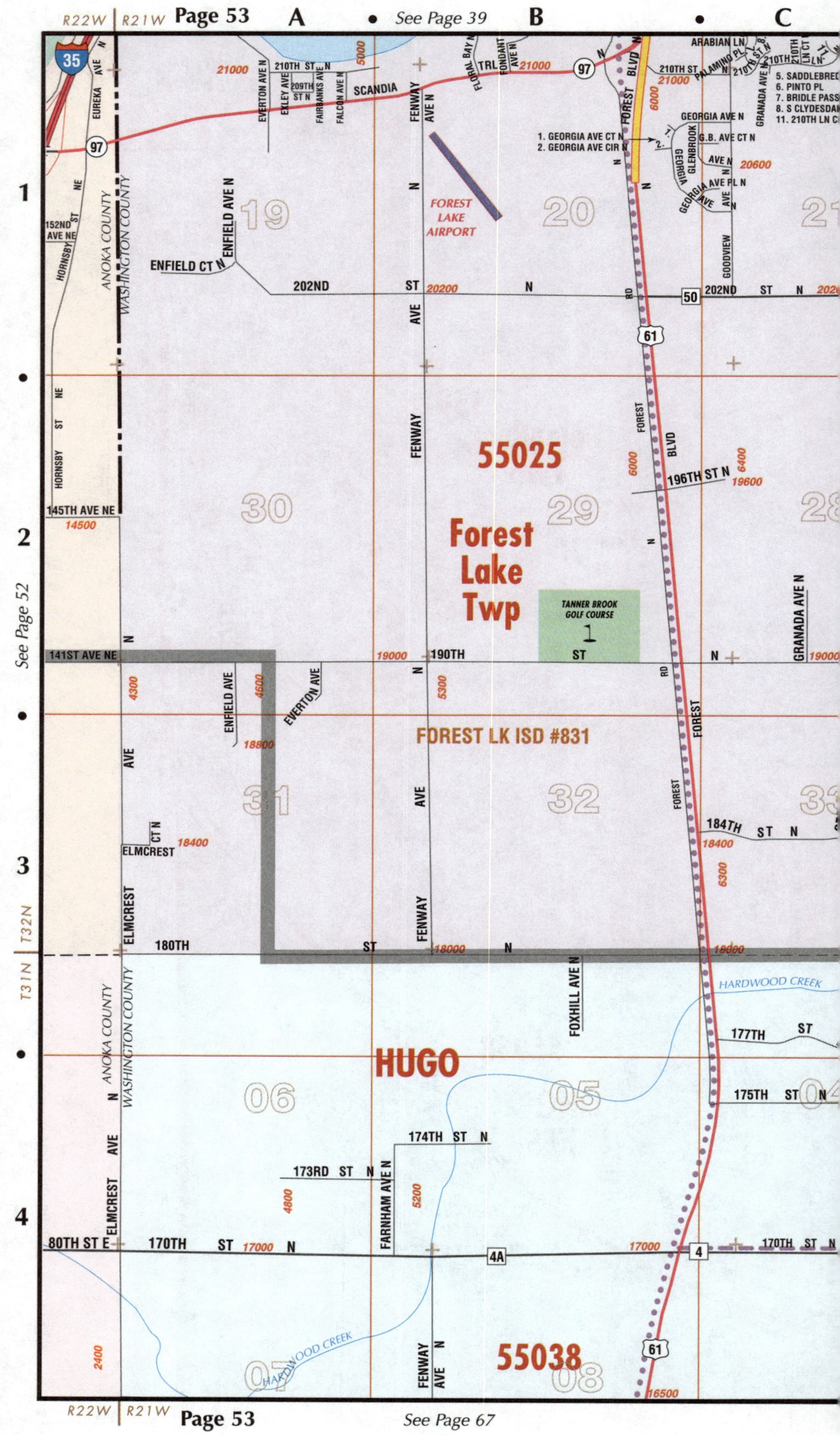
55025
Forest
Lake
Twp
HUGO
55038
FOREST LK ISD #831
FOREST
LAKE
AIRPORT
TANNER BROOK
GOLF COURSE
ANOKA COUNTY
WASHINGTON COUNTY
SCANDIA
210TH ST N
202ND ST N
190TH ST
180TH ST N
170TH ST N
174TH ST N
173RD ST N
177TH ST
175TH ST N
184TH ST N
196TH ST N
FENWAY AVE N
FOREST BLVD N
FOREST RD
ELMCREST AVE N
ENFIELD AVE N
ENFIELD CT N
EVERTON AVE
FARNHAM AVE N
FOXHILL AVE N
GRANADA AVE N
HARDWOOD CREEK
80TH ST E
141ST AVE NE
145TH AVE NE
HORNSBY ST NE
EUREKA AVE N
1. GEORGIA AVE CT N
2. GEORGIA AVE CIR N
5. SADDLEBRED
6. PINTO PL
7. BRIDLE PASS
8. S CLYDESDA
11. 210TH LN C

See Page 52

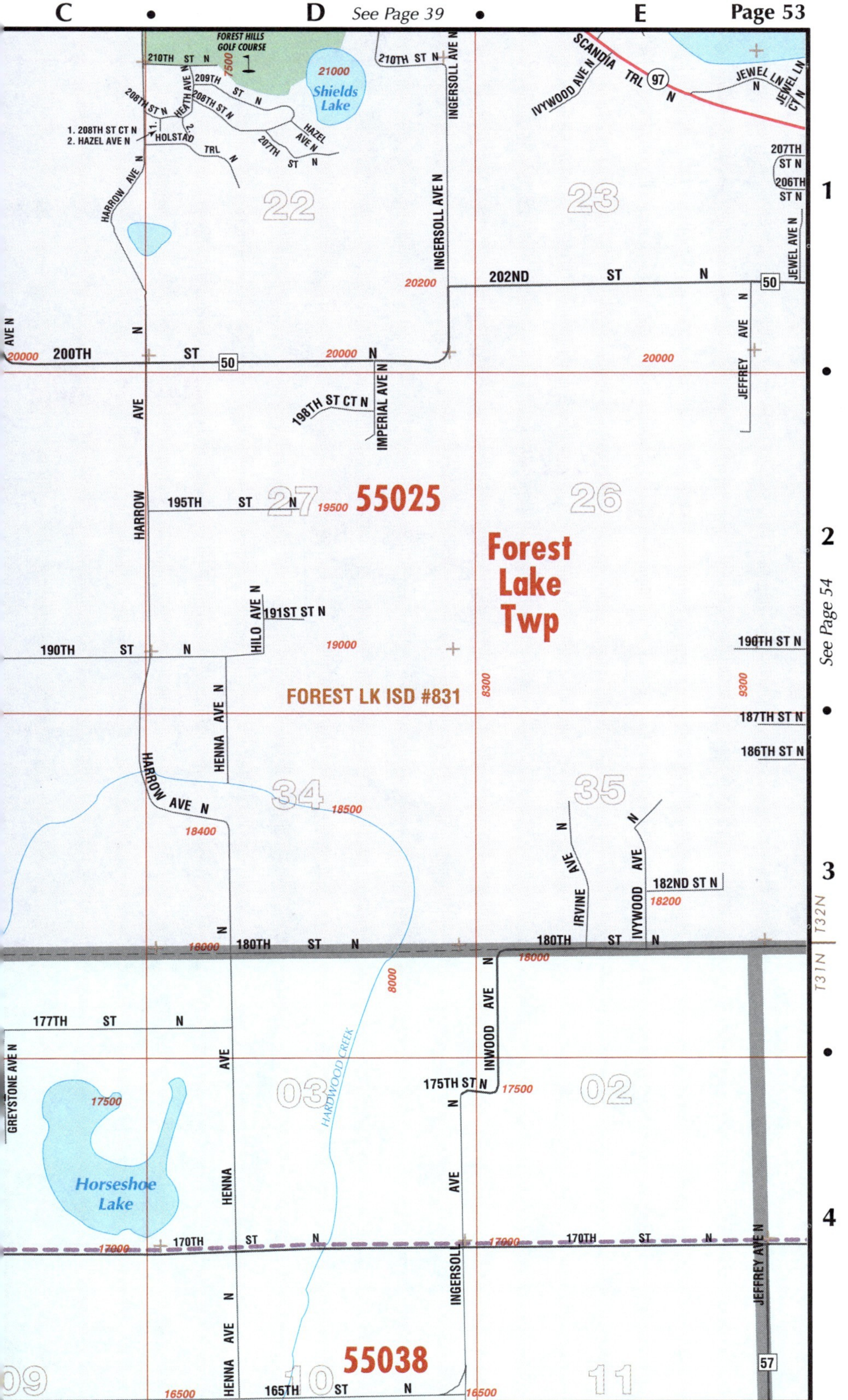

FOREST HILLS
GOLF COURSE

21000

Shields Lake

210TH ST N

210TH ST N

209TH ST N

208TH ST N

207TH ST N

207TH ST N

206TH ST N

1. 208TH ST CT N
2. HAZEL AVE N

HOLSTAD TRL

HAZEL AVE N

HARROW AVE N

HEATH AVE N

INGERSOLL AVE N

IVYWOOD AVE N

SCANDIA TRL 97

JEWEL LN N

JEWEL CT N

JEWEL LN

JEWEL AVE N

22

23

1

202ND ST N 50

20200

JEFFREY AVE N

20000

200TH ST 50

20000

20000 N

HARROW AVE N

198TH ST CT N

IMPERIAL AVE N

27 19500 **55025**

195TH ST

26

**Forest
Lake
Twp**

See Page 54

HILO AVE N

191ST ST N

19000

190TH ST N

190TH ST N

FOREST LK ISD #831

8300

9300

187TH ST N

186TH ST N

HENNA AVE N

HARROW AVE N

34 18500

18400

IRVINE AVE N

IVYWOOD AVE N

35

182ND ST N

18200

2

3

T31N T32N

180TH ST N

18000

8000

180TH ST N

18000

INWOOD AVE N

177TH ST N

GREYSTONE AVE N

HENNA AVE

HARDWOOD CREEK

03

17500

175TH ST N

17500

02

*Horseshoe
Lake*

170TH ST N 17000

17000

170TH ST N

JEFFREY AVE N

4

HENNA AVE N

INGERSOLL AVE N

55038

16500

16500

09

10 165TH ST N

11

57

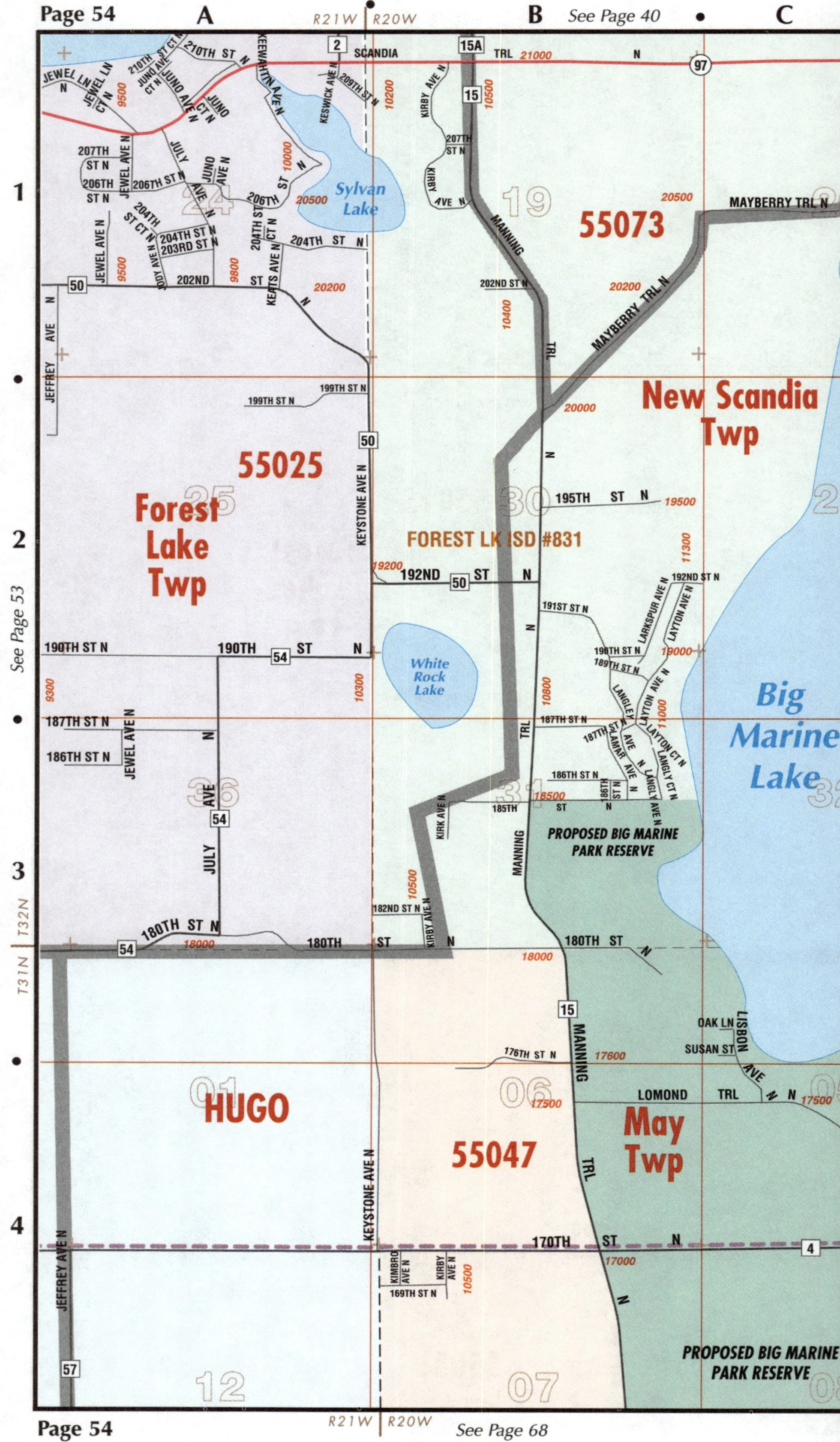

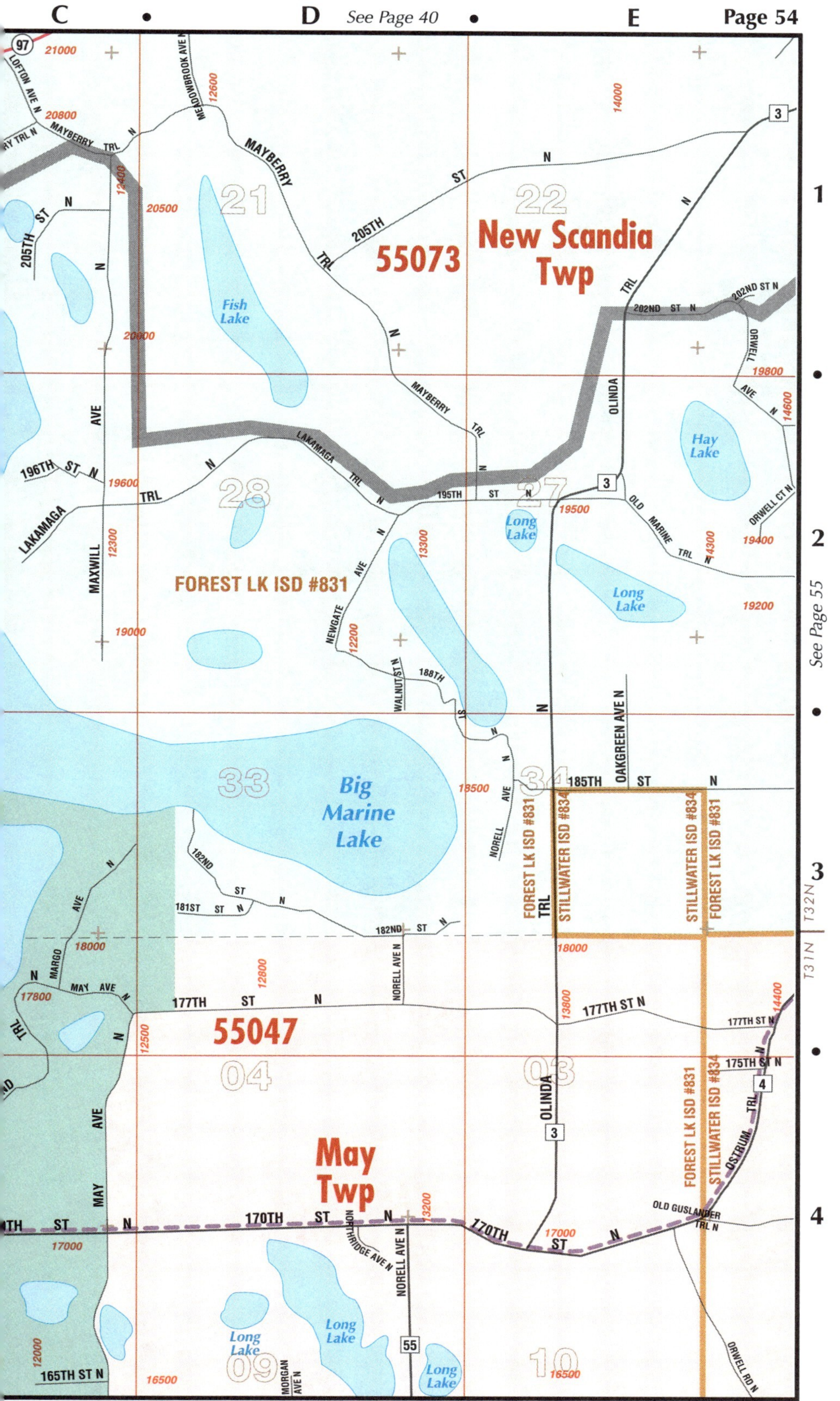
55073
New Scandia Twp
FOREST LK ISD #831
Fish Lake
Hay Lake
Long Lake
Big Marine Lake
55047
May Twp
STILLWATER ISD #834
MAYBERRY TRL N
205TH ST N
202ND ST N
OLINDA TRL
LAKAMAGA TRL N
195TH ST N
OLD MARINE TRL N
MAXWILL AVE N
NEWGATE AVE N
WALNUT ST N
188TH ST N
NORELL AVE N
185TH ST N
OAKGREEN AVE N
182ND ST N
181ST ST N
MARGO AVE N
MAY AVE N
177TH ST N
175TH ST N
170TH ST N
OSTRUM TRL
OLD GUSLANDER TRL N
NORTHRIDGE AVE N
MORGAN AVE N
165TH ST N
ORWELL AVE N
ORWELL CT N
ORWELL RD N
LOFTON AVE N
MEADOWBROOK AVE N
See Page 55
T32N
T31N

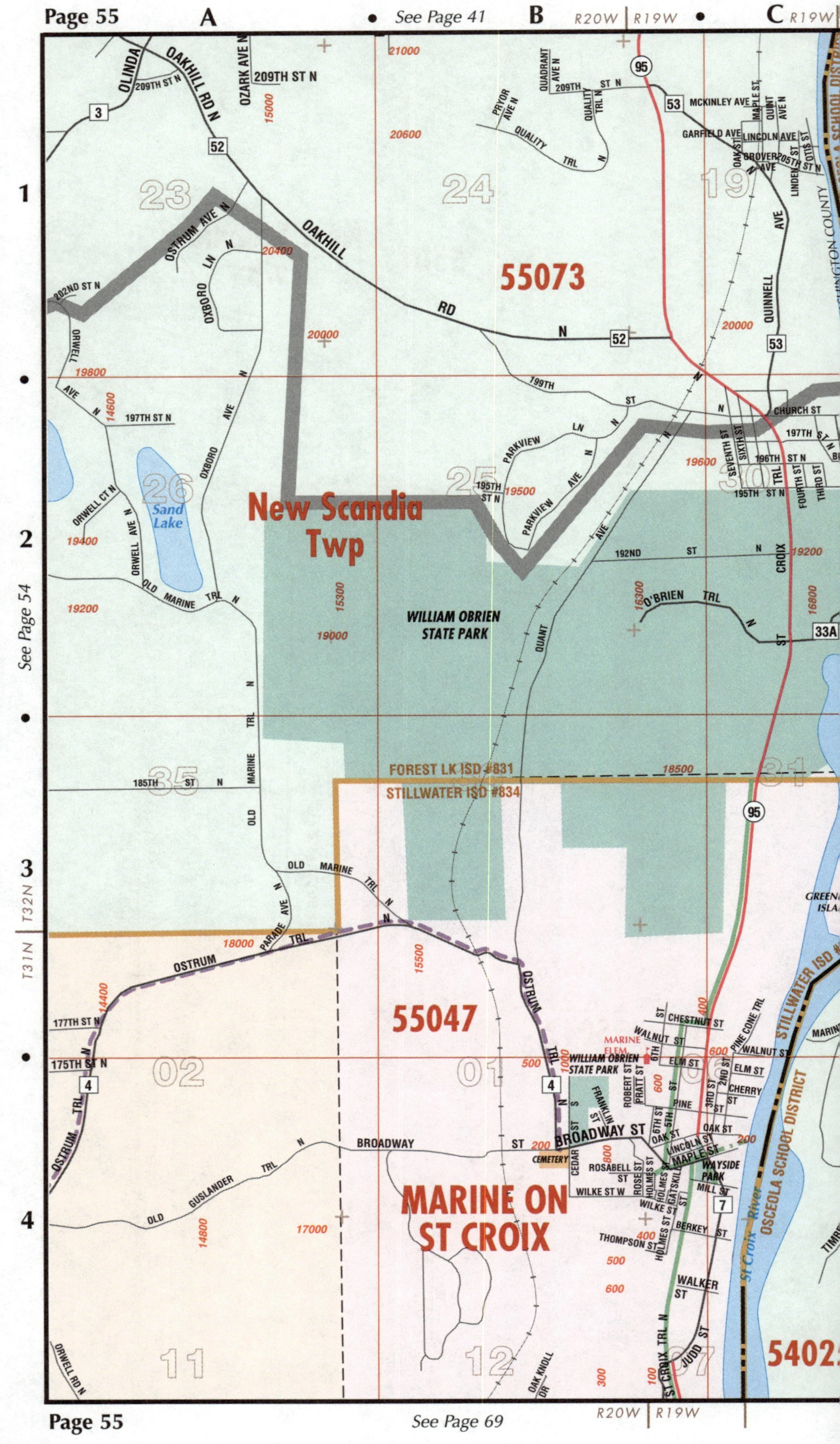

See Page 54

See Page 41

55073

New Scandia Twp

Sand Lake

WILLIAM OBRIEN
STATE PARK

FOREST LK ISD #831

STILLWATER ISD #834

55047

MARINE
ELEM

WILLIAM OBRIEN
STATE PARK

BROADWAY ST

CEMETERY

WAYSIDE PARK

**MARINE ON
ST CROIX**

OSCEOLA SCHOOL DISTRICT

STILLWATER ISD

GREEN ISLA

5402:

T31N | T32N

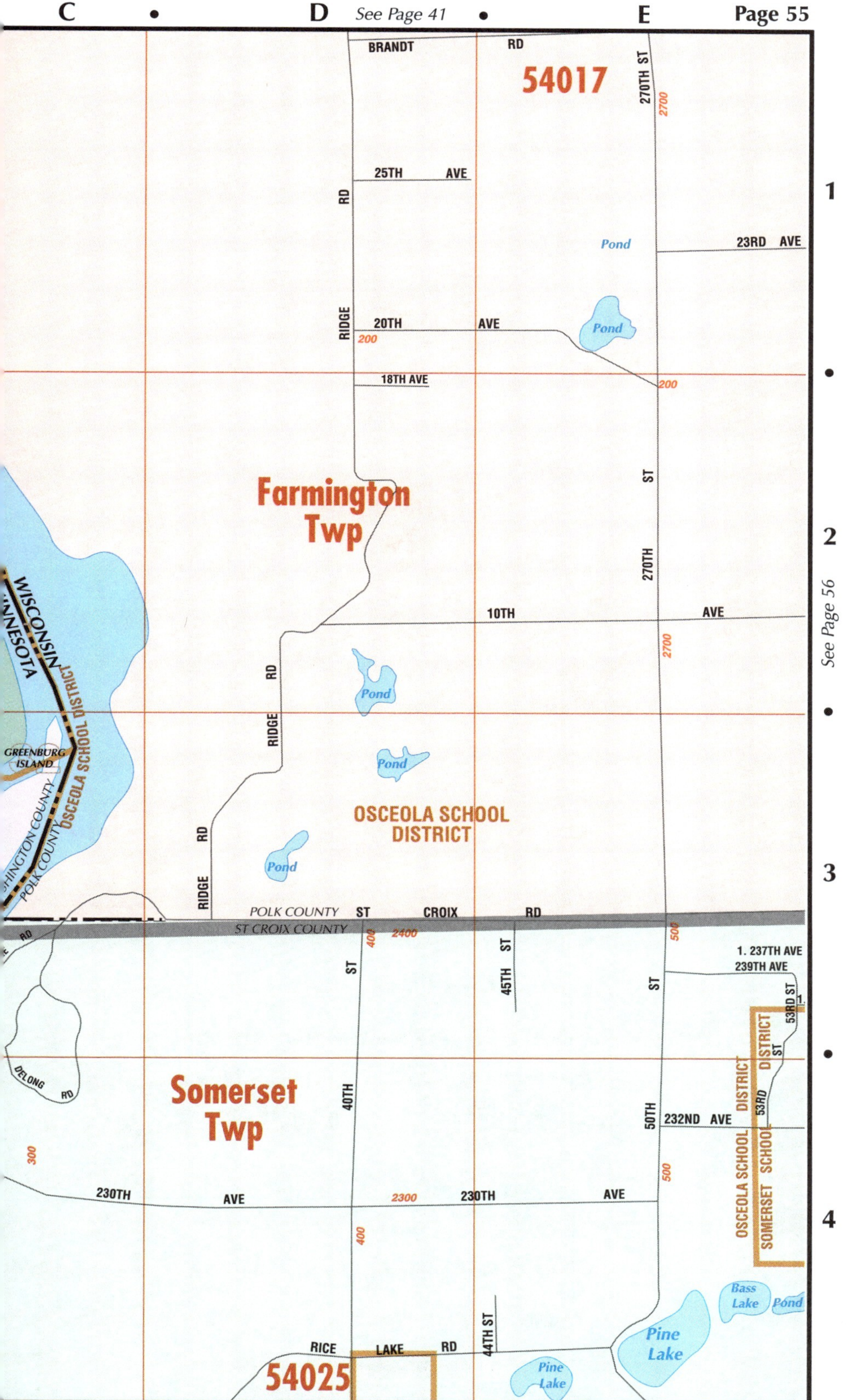

BRANDT   RD

54017

270TH ST

2700

25TH   AVE

RD

1

Pond

23RD   AVE

RIDGE

20TH   AVE

200

Pond

18TH AVE

200

Farmington Twp

ST

See Page 56

2

270TH

10TH   AVE

2700

RD

Pond

RIDGE

Pond

OSCEOLA SCHOOL DISTRICT

RD

RIDGE

Pond

3

POLK COUNTY   ST   CROIX   RD
ST CROIX COUNTY

400 *2400*

500

45TH ST

ST

1. 237TH AVE
239TH AVE

53RD ST

RD

ST

1.

Somerset Twp

40TH

50TH

232ND   AVE

53RD

OSCEOLA SCHOOL   DISTRICT

300

230TH   AVE

2300   230TH   AVE

500

SOMERSET SCHOOL

4

400

44TH ST

Bass Lake *Pond*

RICE   LAKE   RD

Pine Lake

54025

Pine Lake

WISCONSIN
MINNESOTA

GREENBURG ISLAND

OSCEOLA SCHOOL DISTRICT

WASHINGTON COUNTY
POLK COUNTY

DELONG   RD

A • *See Page 42* B • C

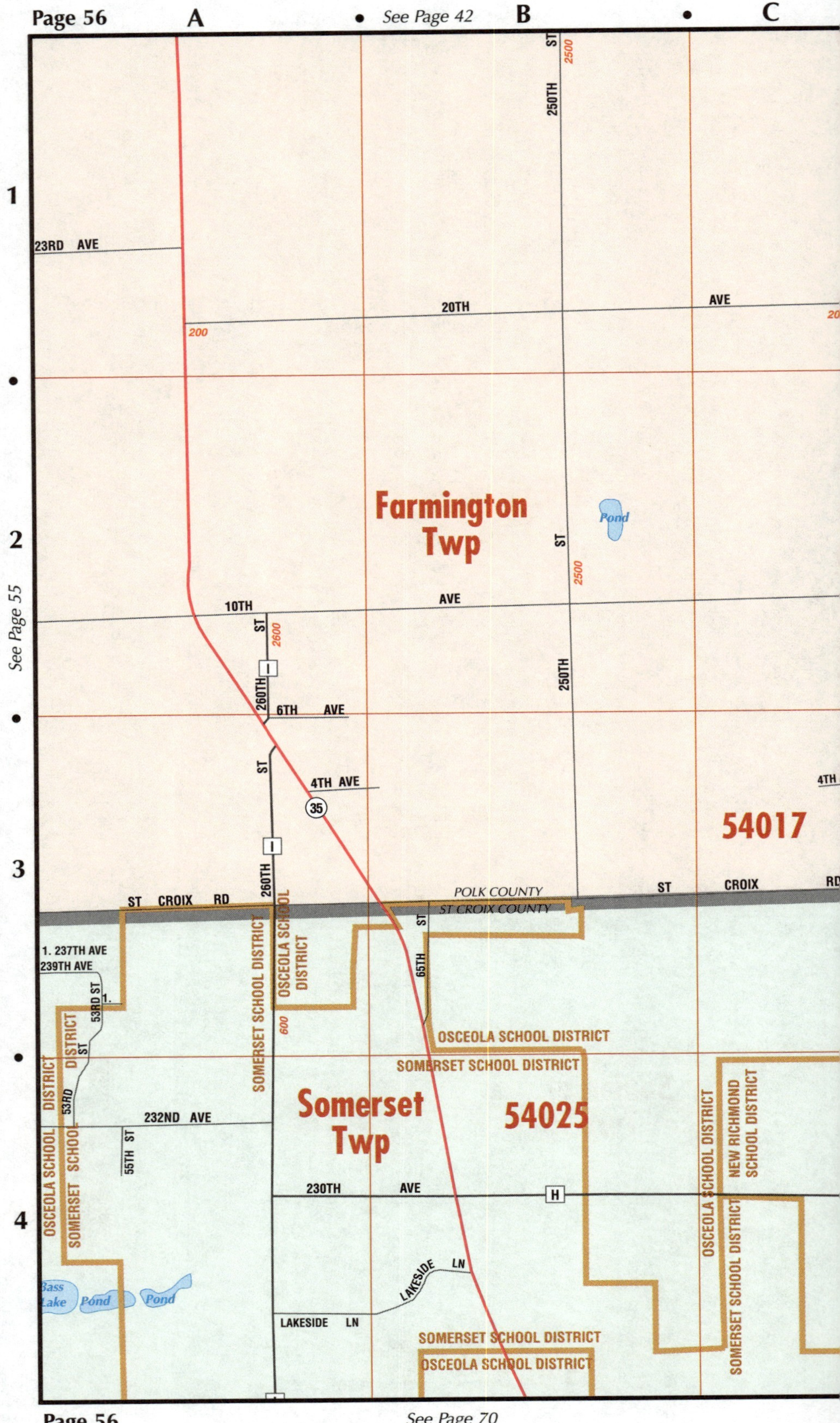

1

23RD   AVE

200

2

Farmington Twp

Pond

10TH

ST

2600

6TH   AVE

260TH

ST

4TH AVE

35

260TH

ST

250TH

ST

20TH   AVE

ST

2500

250TH

AVE

54017

4TH

20

3

ST   CROIX   RD

260TH   ST

ST CROIX COUNTY

POLK COUNTY

ST   CROIX   RD

SOMERSET SCHOOL DISTRICT

OSCEOLA SCHOOL DISTRICT

65TH   ST

600

1. 237TH AVE
239TH AVE

53RD ST

1.

DISTRICT

53RD

ST

OSCEOLA SCHOOL DISTRICT

SOMERSET SCHOOL DISTRICT

OSCEOLA SCHOOL DISTRICT
SOMERSET SCHOOL DISTRICT

Somerset Twp

54025

NEW RICHMOND SCHOOL DISTRICT

4

OSCEOLA SCHOOL DISTRICT   SOMERSET SCHOOL

232ND   AVE

55TH   ST

230TH   AVE

H

OSCEOLA SCHOOL DISTRICT

SOMERSET SCHOOL DISTRICT

Bass Lake   *Pond*   *Pond*

LAKESIDE   LN

LAKESIDE   LN

SOMERSET SCHOOL DISTRICT

OSCEOLA SCHOOL DISTRICT

See Page 55

See Page 70

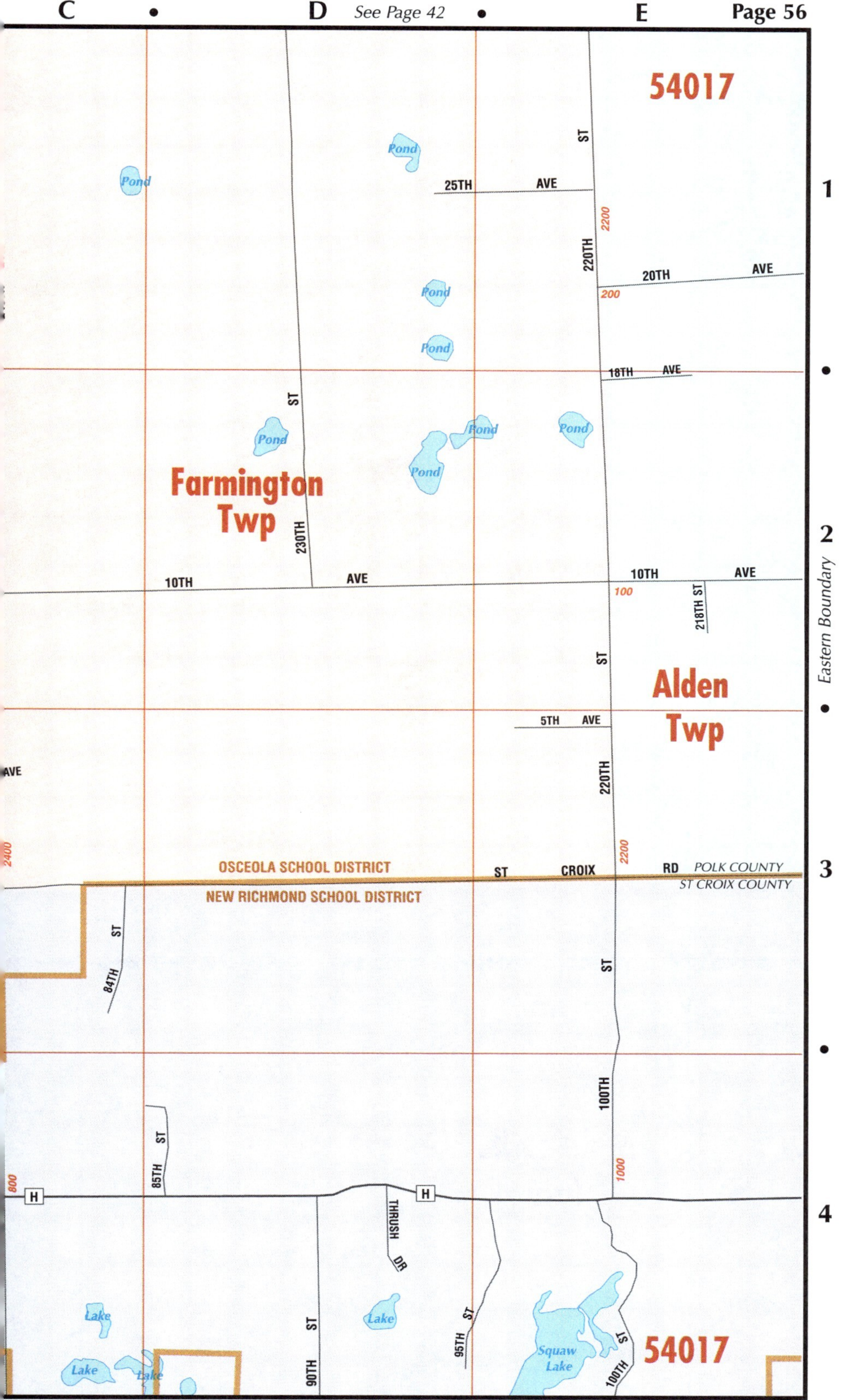

54017

1

25TH AVE

20TH AVE

18TH AVE

Pond

Pond

Pond

Pond

Pond

Pond

Pond

Pond

ST

220TH

2200

200

Farmington Twp

230TH ST

10TH AVE

10TH AVE

218TH ST

100

2

ST

Eastern Boundary

Alden Twp

5TH AVE

220TH

ST

•

2200

2400

AVE

OSCEOLA SCHOOL DISTRICT
NEW RICHMOND SCHOOL DISTRICT

ST CROIX RD POLK COUNTY
ST CROIX COUNTY

3

84TH ST

ST

100TH

ST

•

85TH ST

1000

H

THRUSH DR

H

4

800

Lake

Lake

Lake

Lake

90TH ST

95TH ST

100TH ST

Squaw Lake

54017

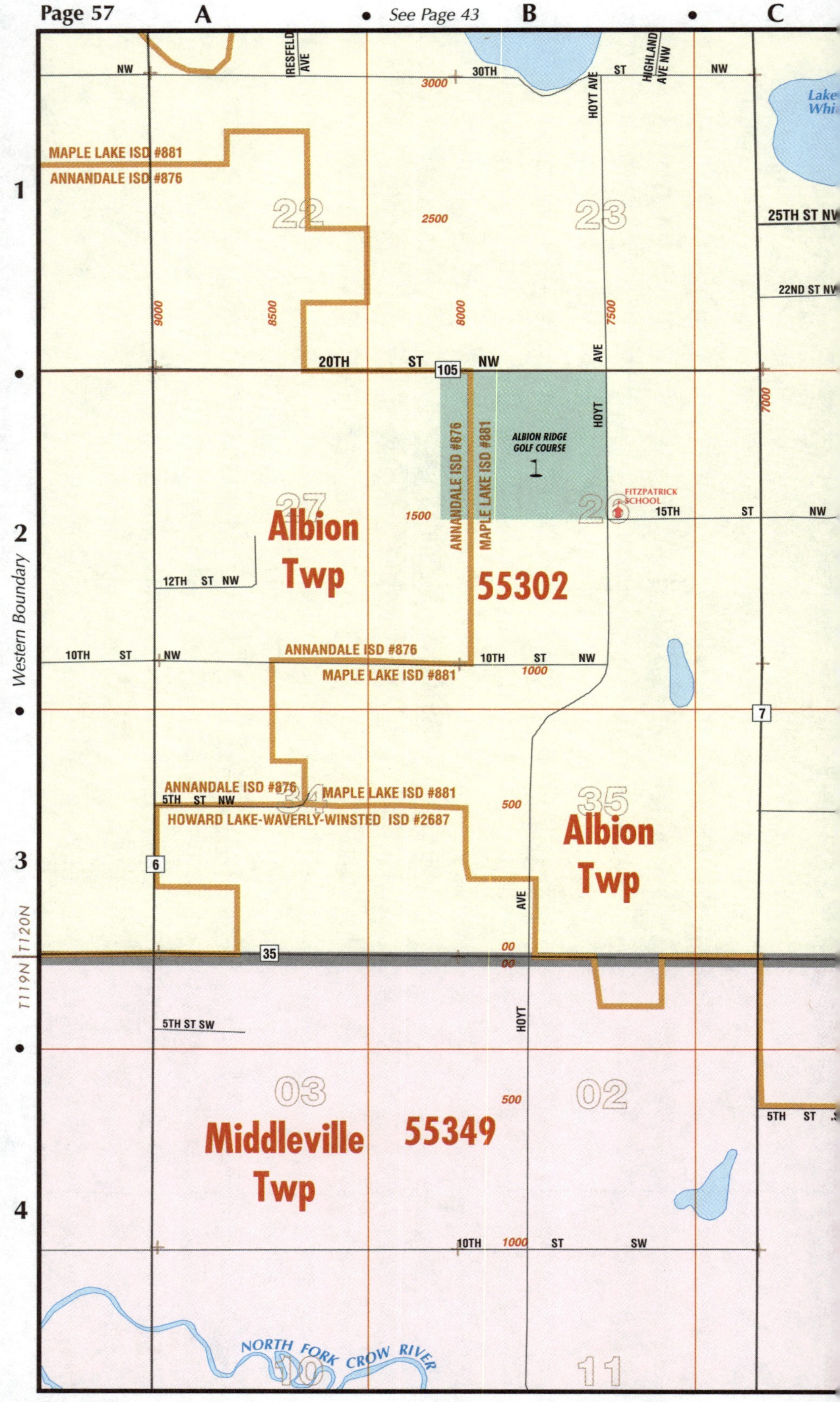

RESFELD AVE

NW

30TH

3000

HOYT AVE

ST

HIGHLAND AVE NW

NW

Lake Whi

MAPLE LAKE ISD #881
ANNANDALE ISD #876

1

22

2500

23

25TH ST NW

22ND ST NW

9000

8500

8000

7500

20TH ST 105 NW

AVE

7000

ANNANDALE ISD #876

MAPLE LAKE ISD #881

ALBION RIDGE GOLF COURSE
1

HOYT

FITZPATRICK SCHOOL

27

Albion Twp

26

15TH ST NW

2

12TH ST NW

1500

55302

Western Boundary

10TH ST NW

ANNANDALE ISD #876

10TH ST NW

1000

MAPLE LAKE ISD #881

7

ANNANDALE ISD #876 **MAPLE LAKE ISD #881**
5TH ST NW

34

HOWARD LAKE-WAVERLY-WINSTED ISD #2687

500

35

Albion Twp

3

6

35

AVE

00
00

T119N | T120N

5TH ST SW

HOYT

03

500

02

5TH ST S

Middleville Twp

55349

4

10TH 1000 ST SW

NORTH FORK CROW RIVER

10

11

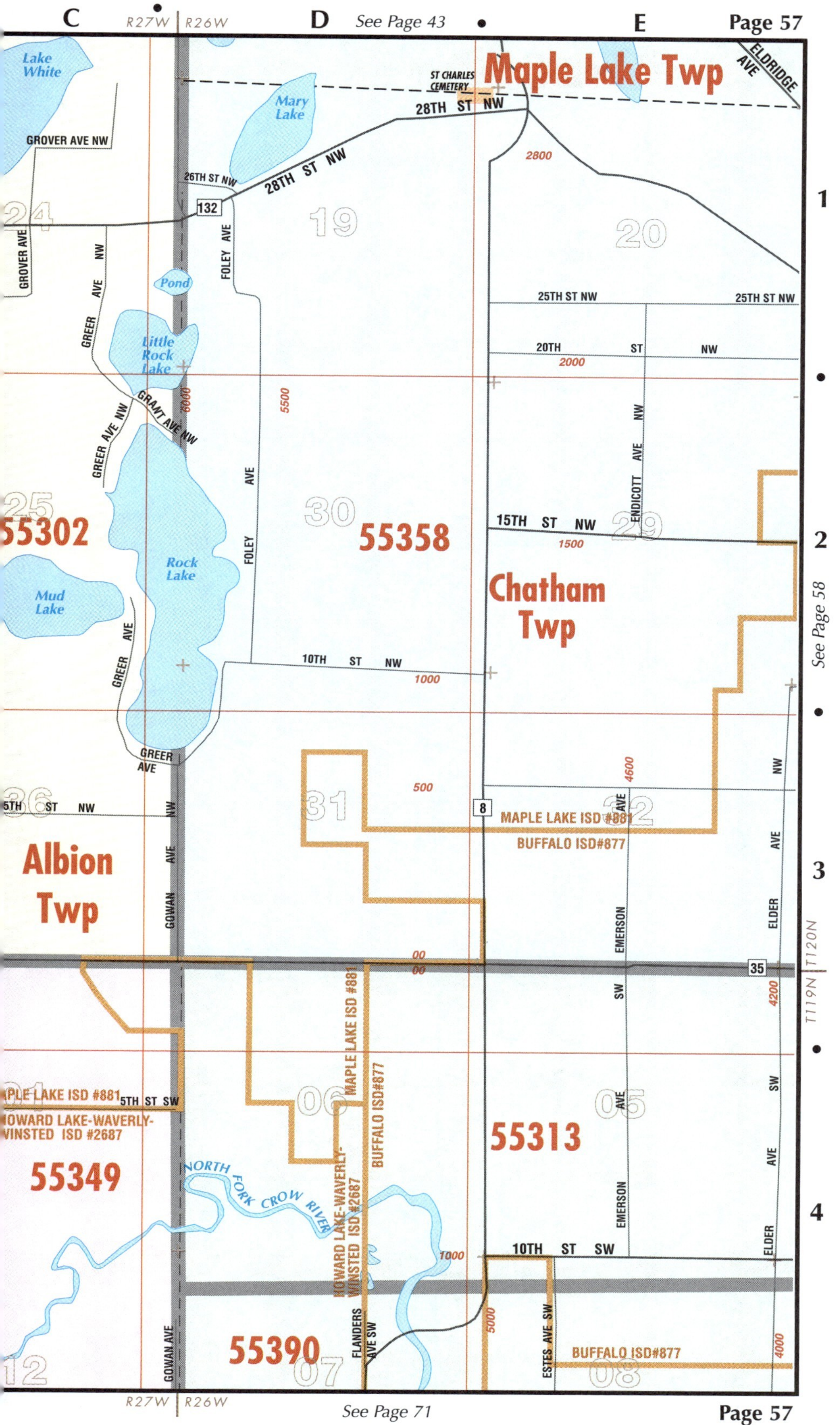

Maple Lake Twp

Lake White

Mary Lake

ST CHARLES CEMETERY

28TH ST NW

GROVER AVE NW

GROVER AVE NW

26TH ST NW

28TH ST NW

2800

132

FOLEY AVE

19

20

1

25TH ST NW

25TH ST NW

Pond

20TH ST NW

2000

ENDICOTT AVE NW

Little Rock Lake

GREER AVE NW

GRANT AVE NW

6000

5500

55302

30

55358

15TH ST NW

1500

29

2

Rock Lake

FOLEY AVE

Chatham Twp

Mud Lake

GREER AVE

10TH ST NW

1000

See Page 58

GREER AVE

500

4600

NW

36

5TH ST NW

NW

31

8

32

AVE

ELDER AVE NW

Albion Twp

GOWAN AVE

MAPLE LAKE ISD #881

BUFFALO ISD#877

EMERSON SW

ELDER AVE SW

3

00
00

35

T119N | T120N

PLE LAKE ISD #881

5TH ST SW

06

MAPLE LAKE ISD#881

BUFFALO ISD#877

AVE SW

05

EMERSON AVE SW

ELDER AVE SW

4200

HOWARD LAKE-WAVERLY-WINSTED ISD #2687

55349

NORTH FORK CROW RIVER

HOWARD LAKE-WAVERLY-WINSTED ISD #2687

55313

4

1000

10TH ST SW

12

55390

FLANDERS AVE SW

07

5000

ESTES AVE SW

BUFFALO ISD#877

08

4000

ELDRIDGE AVE

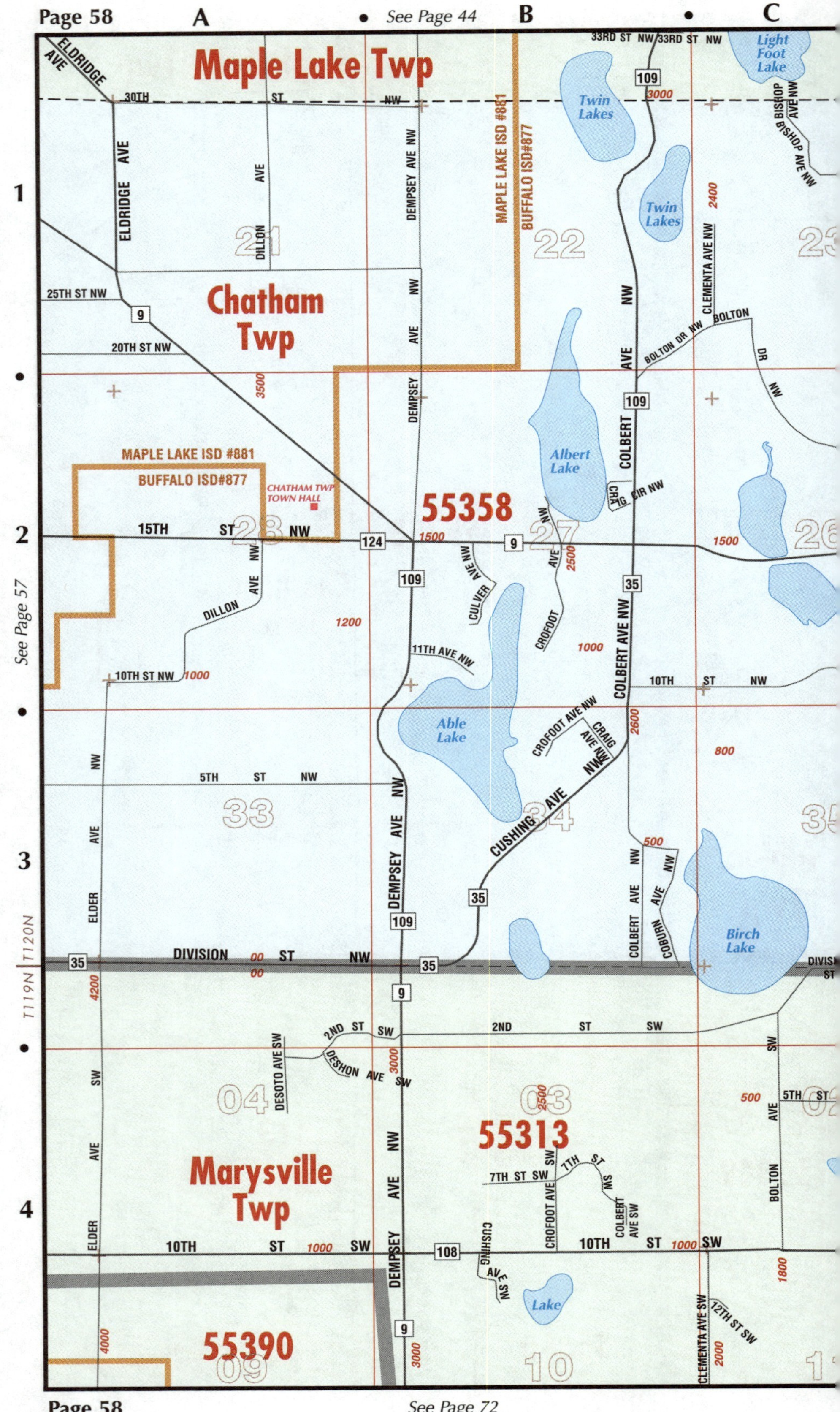

Maple Lake Twp

Chatham Twp

Marysville Twp

55358

55313

55390

MAPLE LAKE ISD #881
BUFFALO ISD #877

MAPLE LAKE ISD #881
BUFFALO ISD#877

CHATHAM TWP
TOWN HALL

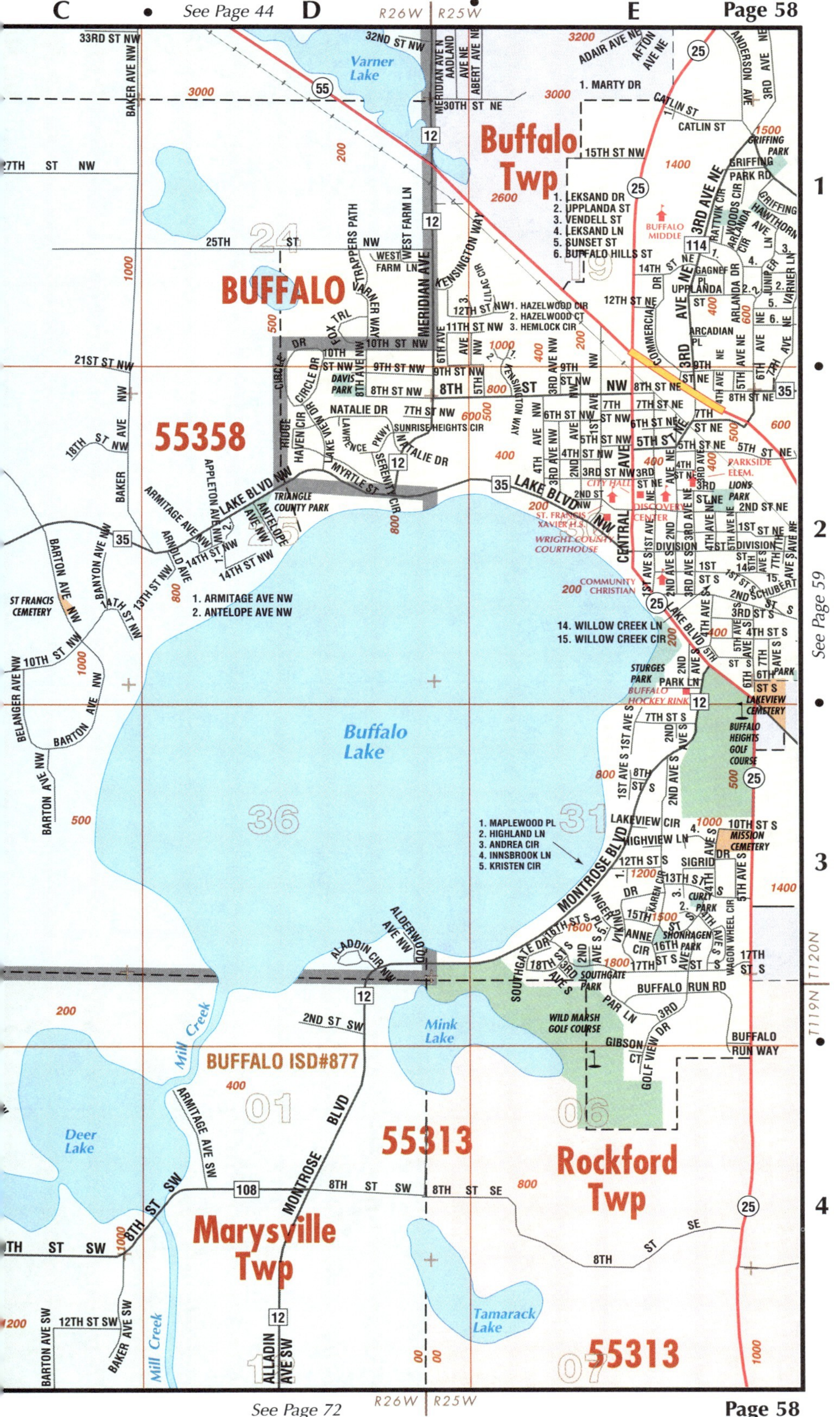

1

33RD ST NW

Baker Ave NW

3000

32ND ST NW

Varner Lake

32ND AVE N

Meridian Ave N

Aadland Ave NE

Abert Ave NE

3200

Adair Ave NE

Afton Ave NE

25

Anderson Ave NE

3RD AVE NE

27TH ST NW

200

55

30TH ST NE

1. Marty Dr

3000

Catlin St

Catlin St

3RD AVE NE

Griffing Park Rd

1500

GRIFFING PARK

Hawthorn Ave NE

12

15TH ST NW

1400

Griffing Ave NE

Aywoods Cir

12

Buffalo Twp

2600

25

Rattvik Cir

Arlanda

Juniper Ln

25TH ST

24

West Farm Ln

West Farm Way

West Farm NW

Kensington Way

Lilac Cir

114

BUFFALO MIDDLE

14TH ST NE

Gagner Ct

Arlanda PL

Varner Ln

1000

Trappers Path

BUFFALO

12TH ST NW

12TH ST NE

Upplanda St

400

600

1. Leksand Dr
2. Upplanda St
3. Vendell St
4. Leksand Ln
5. Sunset St
6. Buffalo Hills St

500

10TH ST NW

10TH ST NW

9TH ST NW

9TH ST NW

5TH ST NW

1. Hazelwood Cir
2. Hazelwood Ct
3. Hemlock Cir

8TH

Commercial Ave NE

Arcadian PL

3RD AVE NE

35

800

Davis Park

8TH ST NW

7TH ST NE

6TH ST NE

600

21ST ST NW

Circle Dr

Circle Dr

Lake View Dr

8TH ST NW

7TH ST NW

Haven Cir

Natalie Dr

Sunrise Heights Cir

6TH AVE NW

6TH ST NW

5TH ST NW

7TH

600

2

55358

Ridge Dr

Lake Blvd NW

Antelope Ave NW

Myrtle St

Serbin Cir

Natalie Dr

800

4TH ST NW

3RD AVE NW

Central Ave

Parkside Elem.

Lions Park

Armitage Ave NW

Arnold Ave

Appleton Ave NW

Triangle County Park

12

800

1. Armitage Ave NW
2. Antelope Ave NW

Lake Blvd NW

35

200

City Hall

St. Francis Xavier H.S.

Discovery Center

1ST ST NE

2ND ST NE

3RD ST NE

1ST ST NE

4TH ST NE

Baker Ave NW

18TH ST NW

Banyon Cir

13TH ST NW

4TH ST NW

14TH ST NW

Wright County Courthouse

Division

Division

35

Barton Ave NW

ST FRANCIS CEMETERY

14TH ST NW

Community Christian

200

14. Willow Creek Ln
15. Willow Creek Cir

3RD ST S

4TH ST S

2ND ST S

Schubert

2ND ST S

See Page 59

10TH ST NW

1000

Belanger Ave NW

Barton Ave NW

Barton

Sturges Park

Park Ln

Buffalo Hockey Rink

7TH ST S

1ST AVE S

2ND AVE S

12

6TH ST S

LAKEVIEW CEMETERY

Buffalo Heights Golf Course

500

500

Buffalo Lake

Barton Ave NW

500

Buffalo Lake

36

7TH ST S

8TH ST S

800

2ND AVE S

25

1. Maplewood PL
2. Highland Ln
3. Andrea Cir
4. Innsbrook Ln
5. Kristen Cir

31

1ST AVE S

Lakeview Cir

Highview Ln

1000

10TH ST S

MISSION CEMETERY

1400

3

Montrose Blvd

12TH ST S

Sigrid Dr

Curly

Shonragen Cir

Wagon Wheel Cir

5TH AVE S

1200

13TH ST S

1500

Aladdin Cir NW

Alderwood Ave NW

15TH ST

Anne Cir

Marsh Park

16TH ST S

17TH ST S

17TH ST S

800

18TH ST S

Southgate Dr

200

2ND AVE S

Southgate Park

Buffalo Run Rd

3RD AVE S

Par Ln

BUFFALO RUN WAY

T119N T120N

12

2ND ST SW

Mink Lake

Wild Marsh Golf Course

Golf View Dr

Gibson

200

Mill Creek

Montrose Blvd

BUFFALO ISD#877

400

01

Deer Lake

Armitage Ave SW

55313

06

55313

Rockford Twp

4

108

8TH ST SW

8TH ST SW

8TH ST SE

800

25

Marysville Twp

SE

8TH

ST SW

Baker Ave SW

1000

Tamarack Lake

00

00

55313

Barton Ave SW

200

12TH ST SW

Mill Creek

Aladdin Ave SW

12

07

1000

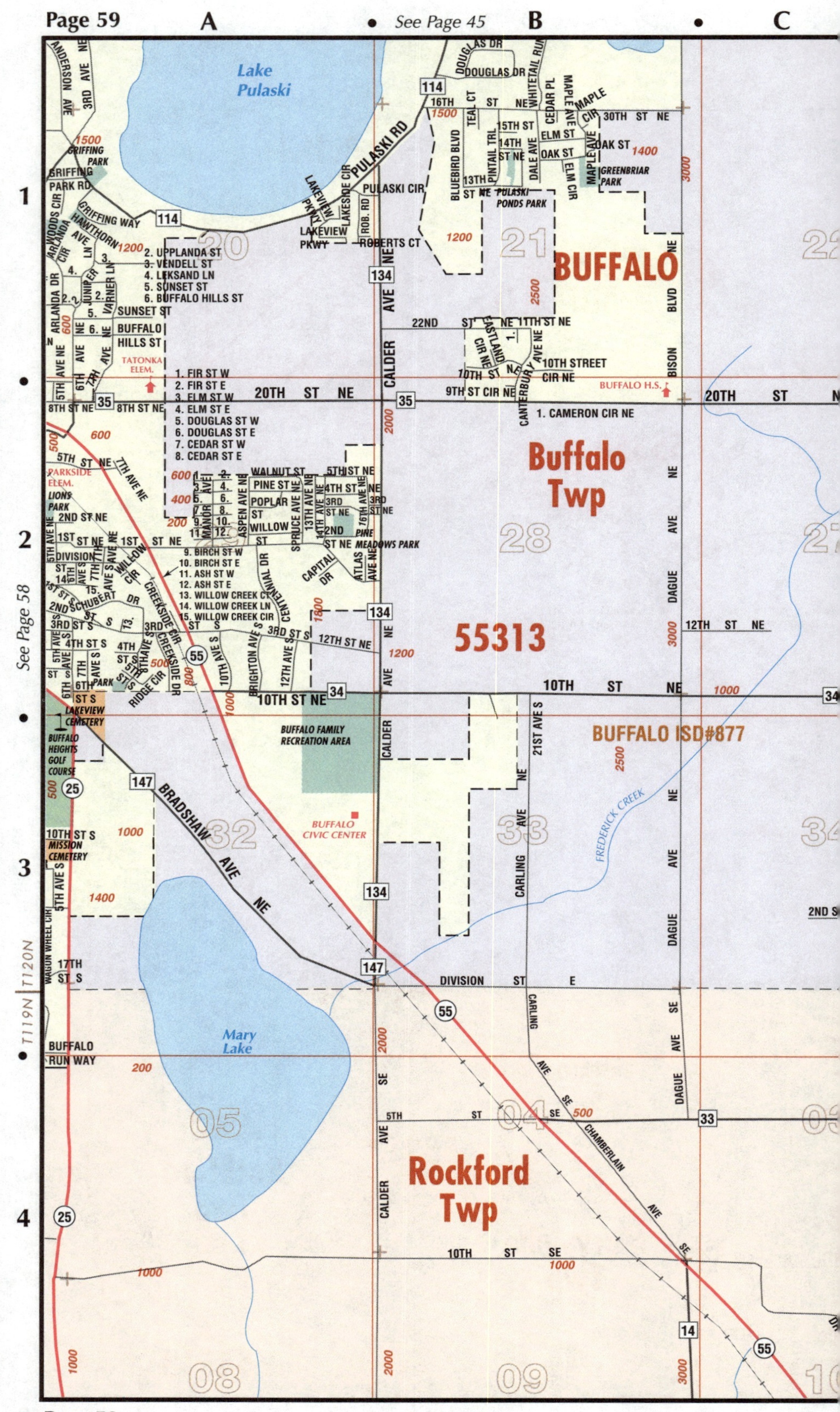

BUFFALO

Buffalo Twp

55313

BUFFALO ISD#877

Rockford Twp

Lake Pulaski

Mary Lake

Frederick Creek

See Page 58

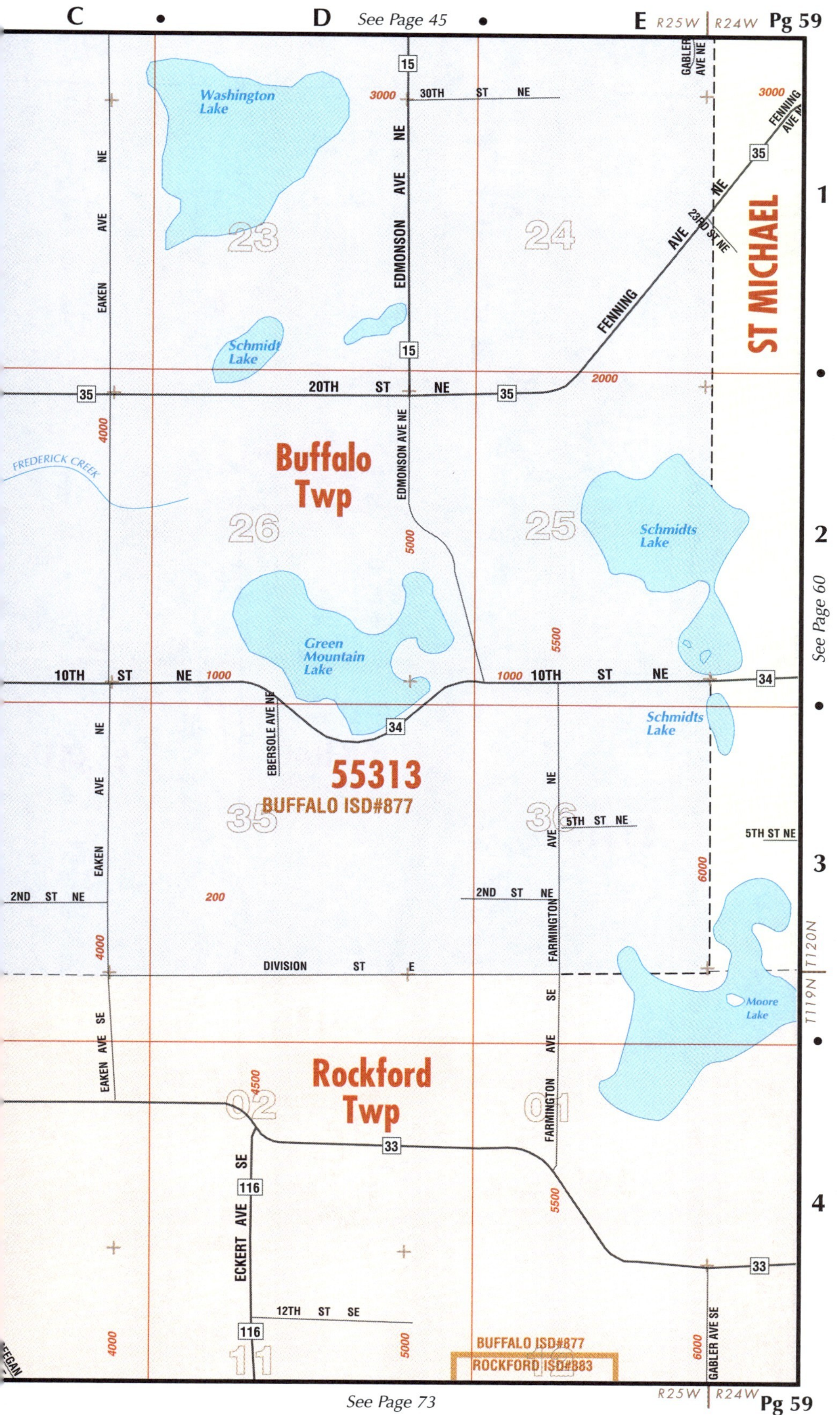

Washington Lake

23

30TH ST NE

3000

15

EDMONSON AVE NE

NE AVE EAKEN

NE AVE

24

GABLER AVE NE

FENNING AVE NE

3000

35

23RD ST NE

ST MICHAEL

1

FENNING AVE NE

Schmidt Lake

15

20TH ST NE

35

35

2000

•

FREDERICK CREEK

Buffalo Twp

26

EDMONSON AVE NE

5000

25

Schmidts Lake

See Page 60

2

Green Mountain Lake

5500

10TH ST NE 1000

1000 10TH ST NE

34

EBERSOLE AVE NE

34

Schmidts Lake

•

55313

BUFFALO ISD#877

NE AVE EAKEN

35

NE AVE

36

5TH ST NE

5TH ST NE

6000

3

2ND ST NE

200

2ND ST NE

FARMINGTON AVE NE

T119N | T120N

DIVISION ST E

•

EAKEN AVE SE

Rockford Twp

02

4500

FARMINGTON AVE SE

01

Moore Lake

ECKERT AVE SE

33

116

5500

4

116

12TH ST SE

4000

5000

11

GABLER AVE SE

6000

33

BUFFALO ISD#877
ROCKFORD ISD#883

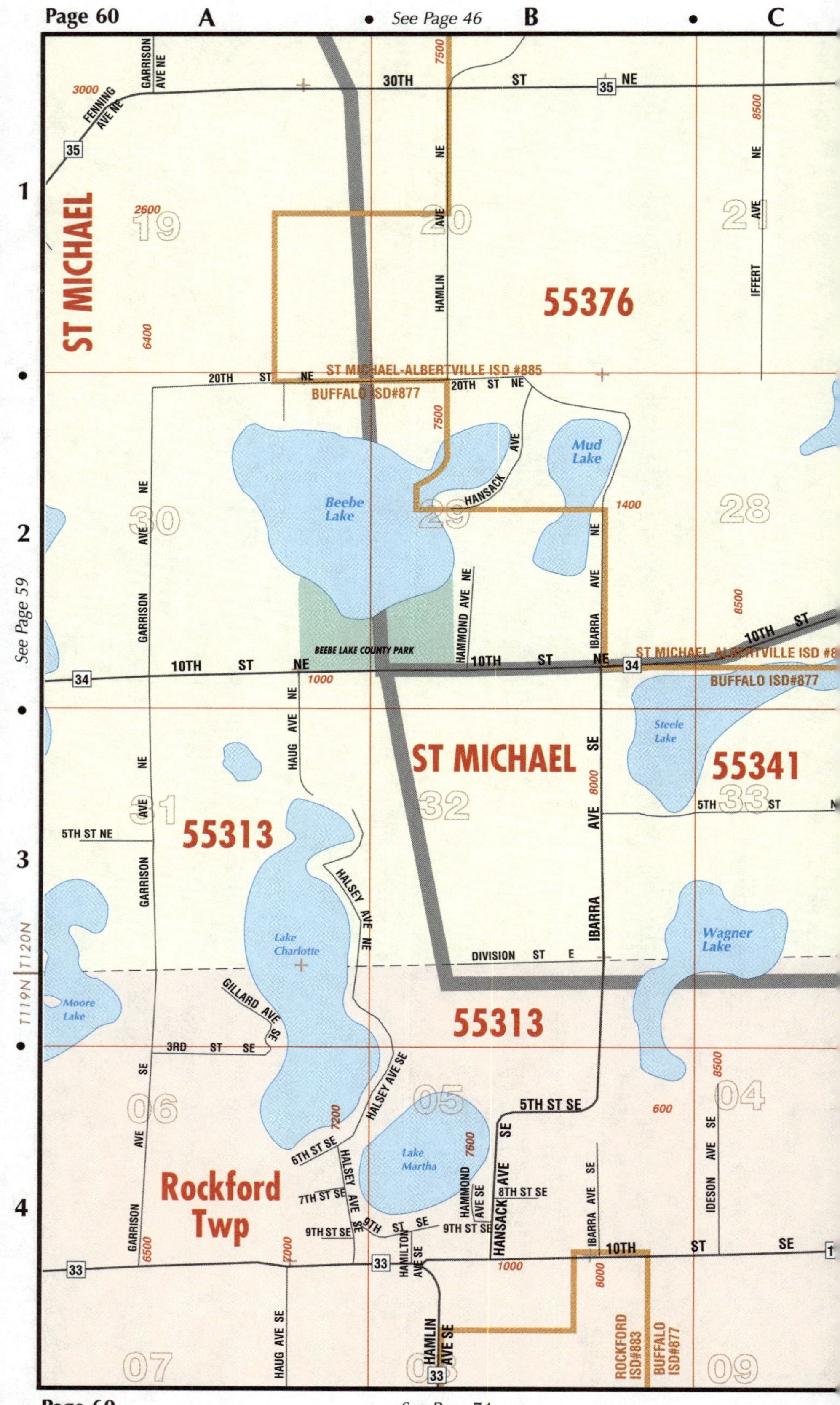

3000

GARRISON AVE NE

FENNING AVE NE

30TH   ST   NE   35

35

7500

1

ST MICHAEL

2600

19

20

HAMLIN   AVE   NE

21

IFFERT   AVE   NE

8500

55376

6400

See Page 59

20TH   ST   NE

ST MICHAEL-ALBERTVILLE ISD #885

BUFFALO ISD#877

20TH ST NE

7500

Mud Lake

30

GARRISON   AVE   NE

Beebe Lake

29

HANSACK   AVE   NE

1400

28

8500

2

HAMMOND AVE NE

IBARRA   AVE   NE

Beebe Lake County Park

10TH   ST   NE   34

34

10TH   ST   NE   34

ST MICHAEL-ALBERTVILLE ISD #8

1000

HAUG   AVE   NE

BUFFALO ISD#877

Steele Lake

10TH   ST

ST MICHAEL

IBARRA   AVE   SE

8000

33   5TH   ST

55341

T119N | T120N

5TH ST NE

31

GARRISON   AVE   NE

55313

HALSEY   AVE   NE

32

3

Lake Charlotte

IBARRA   AVE   SE

Wagner Lake

Moore Lake

GILLARD AVE SE

DIVISION   ST   E

3RD   ST   SE

06

GARRISON   AVE   SE

6500

HALSEY AVE SE

7200

05

55313

5TH ST SE

600

IDESON   AVE   SE

04

8500

4

Rockford Twp

6TH ST SE

7TH ST SE

HALSEY   AVE   SE

9TH ST SE

9TH   ST   SE

HAMMOND   AVE   SE

Lake Martha

7600

9TH ST SE

HANSACK   AVE   SE

8TH ST SE

IBARRA   AVE   SE

10TH   ST   SE

7000

33

HAMILTON AVE SE

33

HAMLIN   AVE   SE

1000

8000

1

07

HAUG   AVE   SE

08   33

HAMLIN AVE SE

ROCKFORD ISD#883

BUFFALO ISD#877

09

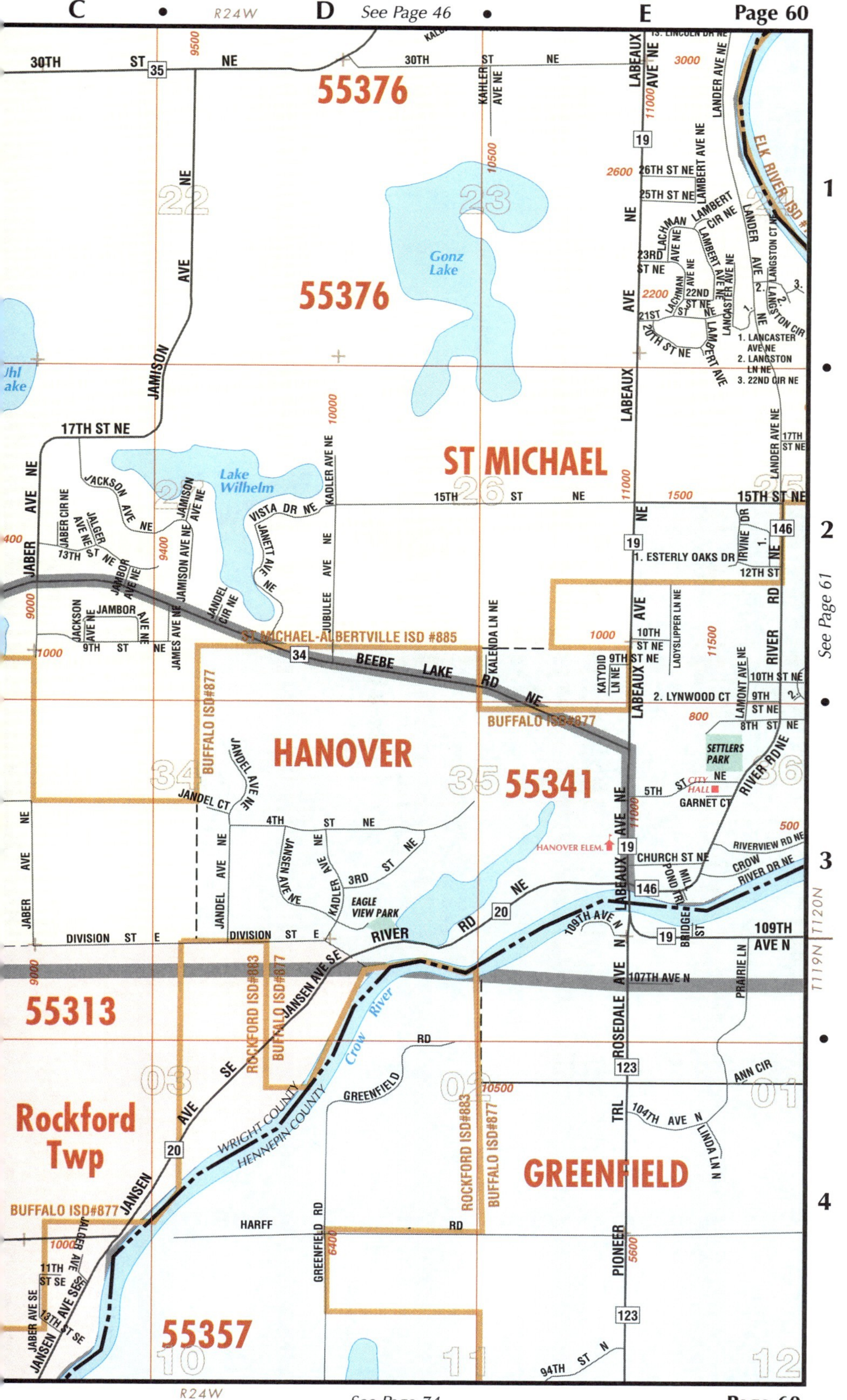

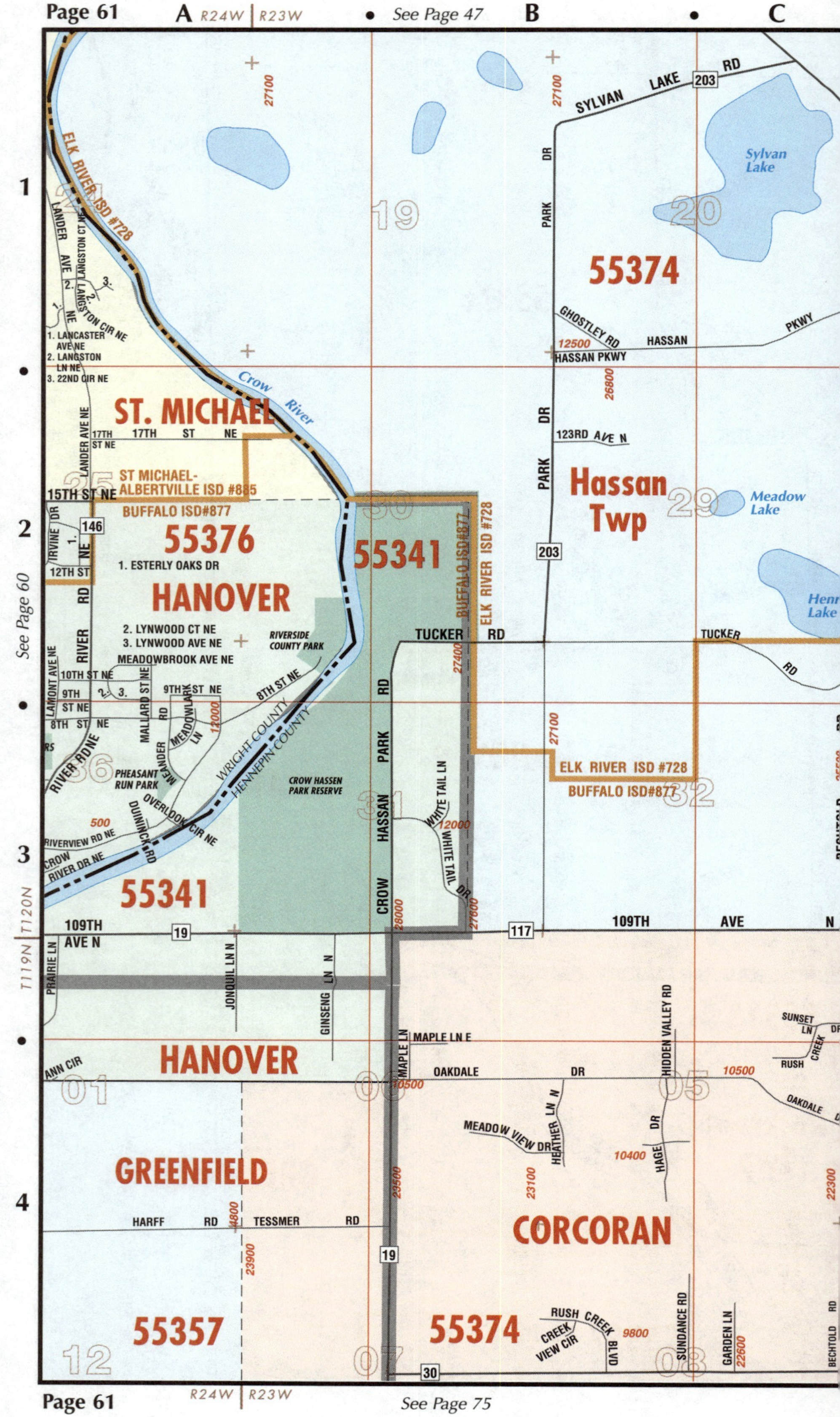

SYLVAN   LAKE   RD   203

27100

Sylvan Lake

19   PARK   DR   20

55374

GHOSTLEY RD   HASSAN   PKWY

12500   *26800*

HASSAN PKWY

123RD   AVE N

ELK RIVER   DR   PARK

Hassan Twp   29   *Meadow Lake*

Crow   River

ST. MICHAEL

LANDER AVE NE   17TH   17TH   ST   NE   ST NE

ST MICHAEL-
ALBERTVILLE ISD #885

15TH ST NE

BUFFALO ISD#877   30   BUFFALO ISD#877

IRVINE DR

146   **55376**   **55341**   ELK RIVER ISD #728   203   *Henr Lake*

12TH ST   NE

HANOVER

1. ESTERLY OAKS DR

1. LANCASTER AVE NE
2. LANGSTON LN NE
3. 22ND CIR NE

1. Langston Ct NE
2. Langston Ln NE
3. 22nd Cir NE

25   **26**   **30**   **29**   **20**

TUCKER   RD   TUCKER   RD

2. LYNWOOD CT NE
3. LYNWOOD AVE NE
MEADOWBROOK AVE NE   *RIVERSIDE COUNTY PARK*   *27000*   *27100*

RIVER   RD   LAMONT AVE NE

10TH ST NE   MALLARD ST NE

9TH   ST NE   MEANDER LN   9TH ST NE   8TH ST NE

8TH   ST NE   MEADOWLARK   *12000*   WRIGHT COUNTY   *CROW HASSEN PARK RESERVE*   PARK   ELK RIVER ISD #728   BUFFALO ISD#877   **32**

RIVER RD NE   **36**   *PHEASANT RUN PARK*   HENNEPIN COUNTY   HASSAN   **31**   WHITE TAIL LN   *12000*   WHITE TAIL DR   **BENTON**

OVERLOOK CIR NE   DUNNICK RD

500   RIVERVIEW RD NE   CROW   RIVER DR NE

55341   *28000*   *27600*   109TH   AVE   N

109TH   19   AVE N   117

PRAIRIE LN   JONQUIL LN N   GINSENG LN N   *22500*

HANOVER

ANN CIR   01   00   *10500*   OAKDALE   DR   HIDDEN VALLEY RD   05   *10500*   SUNSET LN   DR   RUSH   CREEK   DR

MAPLE LN   MAPLE LN E

MEADOW VIEW DR   HEATHER LN N   HAGE   DR   OAKDALE   D

GREENFIELD   *23100*   *10400*   *22300*

HARFF   RD   TESSMER   RD   *4800*   **CORCORAN**

23900   MAPLE LN   *29500*

55357   19   **55374**   RUSH CREEK   BLVD   SUNDANCE RD   GARDEN LN   BECHTOLD   RD

12   **07**   30   CREEK VIEW CIR   *9800*   **08**   *22600*

See Page 60   T119N | T120N

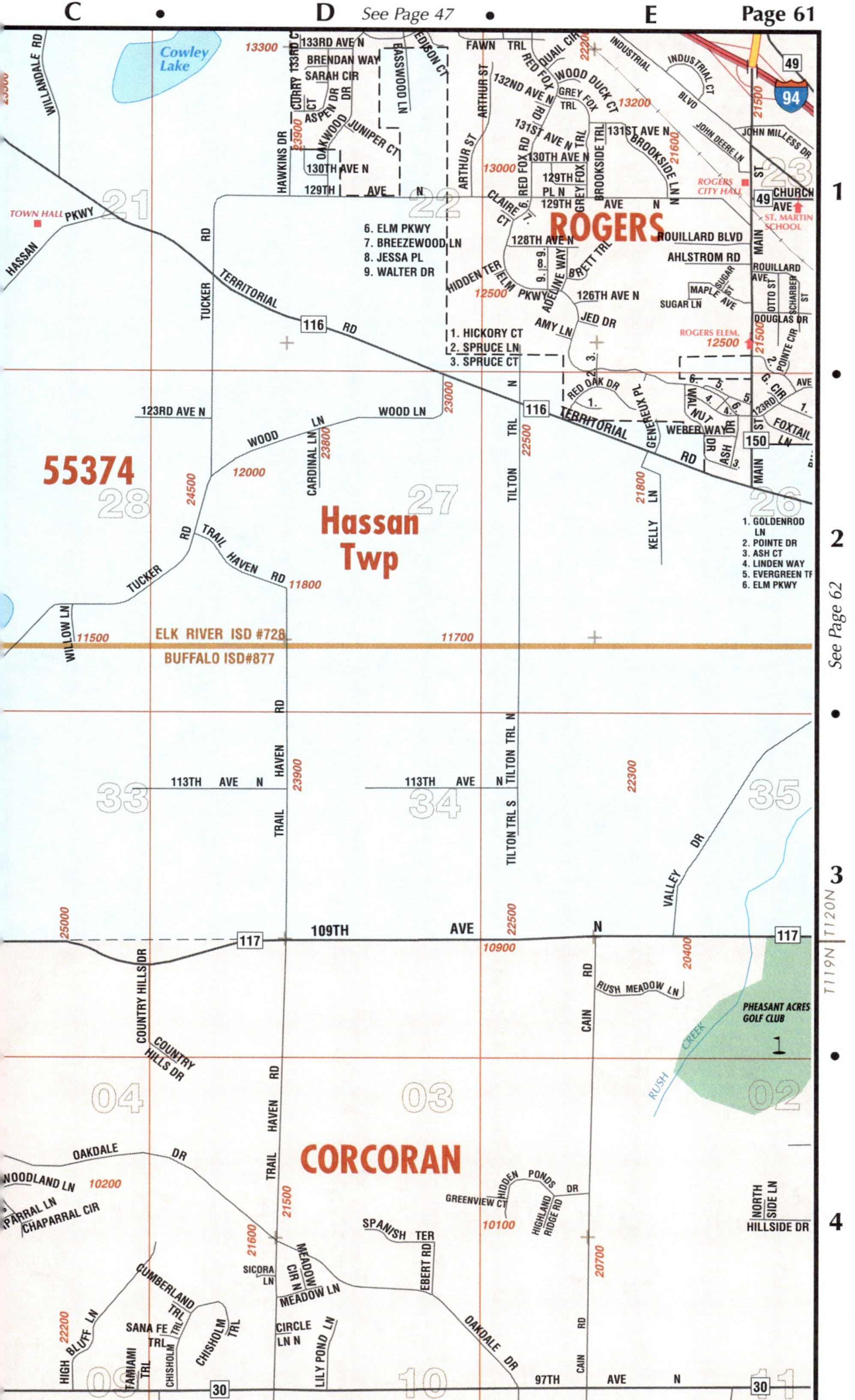

Cowley Lake

13300

133RD AVE N
BRENDAN WAY
SARAH CIR
CURRY 133RD C
EDISON CT
BASSWOOD LN
FAWN TRL
ARTHUR ST
132ND AVE N
RED TO QUAIL CIR
WOOD DUCK CT
GREY FOX TRL
22200
INDUSTRIAL CT
INDUSTRIAL BLVD
21500
94

49

WILLANDALE RD

23900
HAWKINS DR
OAKWOOD DR
ASPEN DR CT
JUNIPER CT
ARTHUR ST
131ST AVE N
130TH AVE N
RED FOX RD
131ST AVE N
BROOKSIDE TRL
21600
JOHN DEERE LN
JOHN MILLESS DR

TOWN HALL PKWY

21

HASSAN

TUCKER RD

TERRITORIAL

116 RD

130TH AVE N
13000
129TH AVE
22
129TH AVE N
GREY FOX
PL N
129TH AVE N
BROOKSIDE TRL
AVE N
ROGERS
ROGERS CITY HALL
23
49 CHURCH AVE N
ST. MARTIN SCHOOL
MAIN ST

6. ELM PKWY
7. BREEZEWOOD LN
8. JESSA PL
9. WALTER DR

CLAIRE S CT
128TH AVE N
ADELINE WAY
BRETT TRL
ROUILLARD BLVD
AHLSTROM RD
ROUILLARD
OTTO ST
SCHARFER ST
DOUGLAS ST

HIDDEN TER ELM PKWY
12500
126TH AVE N
MAPLE AVE
SUGAR LN
SUGAR AVE

1. HICKORY CT
2. SPRUCE LN
3. SPRUCE CT

AMY LN
JED DR
RED OAK DR
ROGERS ELEM. 12500
21500
POINTE CIR

55374

123RD AVE N

WOOD LN
WOOD LN
23000
23800
CARDINAL LN
12000
24500

28

TUCKER RD
TRAIL HAVEN RD
11800

Hassan Twp

27

TILTON TRL
22500
116
TERRITORIAL RD
GENEVIEUX PL
WALNUT
WEBER WAY
ASH LN
21800
KELLY LN

116
RED OAK DR
G CIR
23RD
FOXTAIL
150
MAIN ST

26

1. GOLDENROD LN
2. POINTE DR
3. ASH CT
4. LINDEN WAY
5. EVERGREEN TR
6. ELM PKWY

WILLOW LN
11500

ELK RIVER ISD #728
BUFFALO ISD#877
11700

See Page 62

33

113TH AVE N
23900
HAVEN RD
TRAIL

113TH AVE
34
TILTON TRL S
TILTON TRL N
22500

22300

VALLEY DR

35

T119N T120N

25000

117
109TH AVE N
22500
10900

CAIN RD
RUSH MEADOW LN
20400
117

PHEASANT ACRES GOLF CLUB
1

COUNTRY HILLS DR
COUNTRY HILLS DR

04

TRAIL HAVEN RD

CORCORAN
03

RUSH CREEK

02

OAKDALE DR
WOODLAND LN
10200
CHAPARRAL LN
CHAPARRAL CIR

SICORA LN
21600
MEADOW CIR N
MEADOW LN
21500

SPANISH TER
EBERT RD
GREENVIEW CT
HIDDEN PONDS DR
HIGHLAND RIDGE RD
10100
20700

NORTH SIDE LN
HILLSIDE DR

4

CUMBERLAND TRL
SANA FE TRL
CHISHOLM TRL
CHISHOLM TRL
CIRCLE LN N
LILY POND LN
OAKDALE DR
97TH AVE N

HIGH BLUFF LN
22200
TAMIAMI TRL

09
30
10
11
30

See Page 75

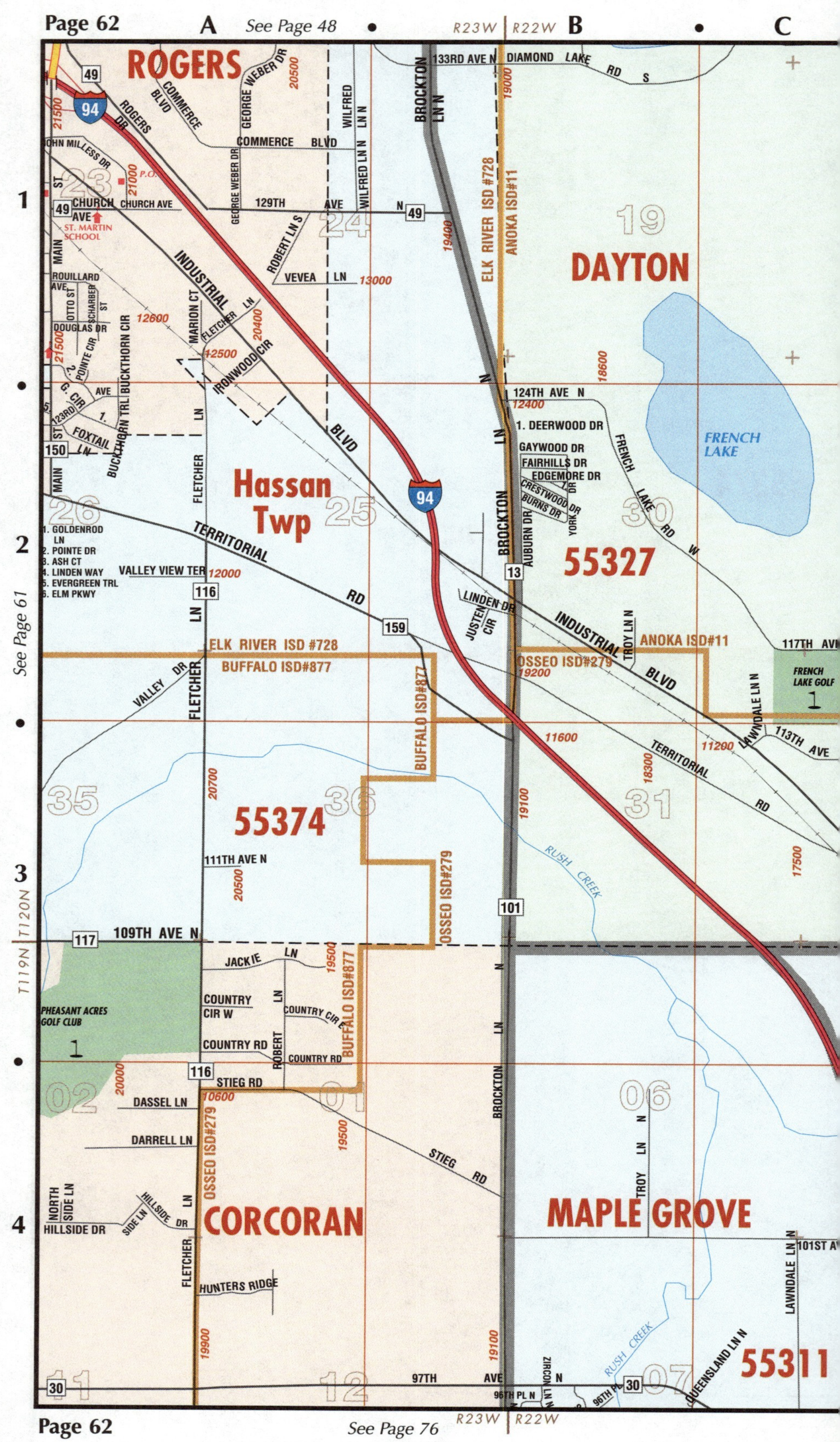

R23W | R22W

ROGERS

49

I-94

21500

COMMERCE BLVD

ROGERS DR

GEORGE WEBER DR   20500

133RD AVE N   DIAMOND LAKE RD S

WILFRED LN N

BROCKTON LN N   19000

ELK RIVER ISD #728

ANOKA ISD #11

DAYTON

19

JOHN MILLESS DR

21000   P.O.

COMMERCE BLVD

1

49   CHURCH AVE   CHURCH AVE

MAIN ST   23

ST. MARTIN SCHOOL

129TH AVE N   49

ROBERT LN S   WILFRED LN N

24

19400

VEVEA LN   13000

ROUILLARD AVE

OTTO ST   SCHAREEF ST

DOUGLAS DR   12600

21500   G. CIR   POINTE CIR   MARION CT

123RD ST   FOXTAIL LN

150   MAIN ST

BUCKHORN TRL   BUCKHORN CIR

FLETCHER LN   20400

IRONWOOD CIR   12500

INDUSTRIAL   FLETCHER LN

BLVD

I-94   25

18600

124TH AVE N   12400

1. DEERWOOD DR

GAYWOOD DR   FRENCH LAKE RD W

FAIRHILLS DR

EDGEMORE DR

FRENCH LAKE

30

Hassan Twp

26

1. GOLDENROD LN
2. POINTE DR
3. ASH CT
4. LINDEN WAY
5. EVERGREEN TRL
6. ELM PKWY

TERRITORIAL   RD

VALLEY VIEW TER   12000

116

FLETCHER LN

2

VALLEY DR

ELK RIVER ISD #728

BUFFALO ISD #877

159

CRESTWOOD DR   BURNS DR

AUBURN DR   YORK LN N

BROCKTON LN N

13

55327

LINDEN DR

JUSTEN CIR   CIR

OSSEO ISD #279   19200

INDUSTRIAL   BLVD

TROY LN N

ANOKA ISD #11

LAWNDALE LN N

117TH AVE

FRENCH LAKE GOLF   1

113TH AVE

11200

35

20700

36

55374

111TH AVE N   20500

BUFFALO ISD #877

OSSEO ISD #279   19100

11600

RUSH CREEK

TERRITORIAL   RD   18300

31

17500

3

117

109TH AVE N

101

JACKIE LN   19504

COUNTRY CIR W

ROBERT LN

COUNTRY CIR E

BUFFALO ISD #877

OSSEO ISD #279

T119N | T120N

PHEASANT ACRES GOLF CLUB   1

20000

116   STIEG RD   10600

DASSEL LN

DARRELL LN

19500

COUNTRY RD

COUNTRY RD

BROCKTON LN N

06

TROY LN N

4

NORTH SIDE LN

HILLSIDE DR   SIDE LN

HILLSIDE DR

FLETCHER LN

HUNTERS RIDGE

CORCORAN

OSSEO ISD #279

STIEG RD

MAPLE GROVE

LAWNDALE LN N

101ST AVE N

101ST A

11   30

20000

12

19900

97TH AVE

19100   ZIRCON LN N

96TH PL N

07   30   96TH LN N

QUEENSLAND LN N

55311

See Page 61

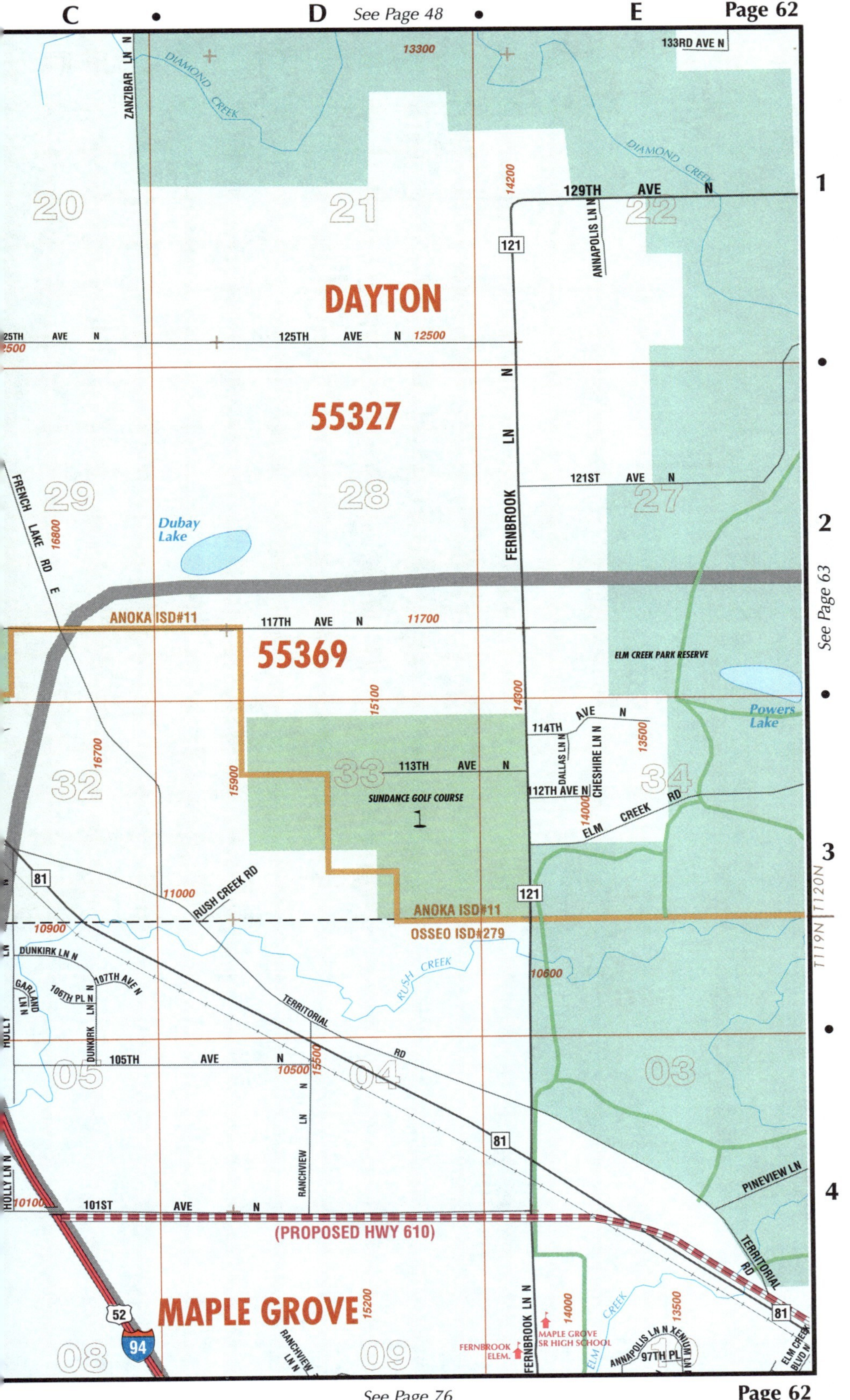

ZANZIBAR LN N

DIAMOND CREEK

13300

133RD AVE N

DIAMOND CREEK

14200

129TH AVE N

121

ANNAPOLIS LN N

20

21

22

1

DAYTON

125TH AVE N

125TH AVE N 12500

12500

55327

N

LN

121ST AVE N

FRENCH LAKE RD E

16900

29

28

FERNBROOK

27

See Page 63

2

Dubay Lake

ANOKA ISD#11

117TH AVE N 11700

ELM CREEK PARK RESERVE

55369

Powers Lake

15100

14900

114TH AVE N

DALLAS LN N

CHESHIRE LN N

13500

16700

32

15900

33

113TH AVE N

112TH AVE N

34

SUNDANCE GOLF COURSE

1

ELM CREEK RD

T119N T120N

3

81

11000

RUSH CREEK RD

121

ANOKA ISD#11

OSSEO ISD#279

10900

DUNKIRK LN N

RUSH CREEK

10600

GARLAND LN N

106TH PL N

107TH AVE N

TERRITORIAL

HOLLY

DUNKIRK

105TH AVE N

10500

15500

05

04

03

LN

81

RANCHVIEW

PINEVIEW LN

4

HOLLY LN

10100

101ST AVE N

(PROPOSED HWY 610)

TERRITORIAL RD

81

52

MAPLE GROVE 15200

94

RANCHVIEW LN N

08

09

FERNBROOK LN N

14000

MAPLE GROVE SR HIGH SCHOOL

CREEK

ELM

13500

ANNAPOLIS LN N

XENIUM LN N

97TH PL N

ELM CREEK BLVD N

FERNBROOK ELEM.

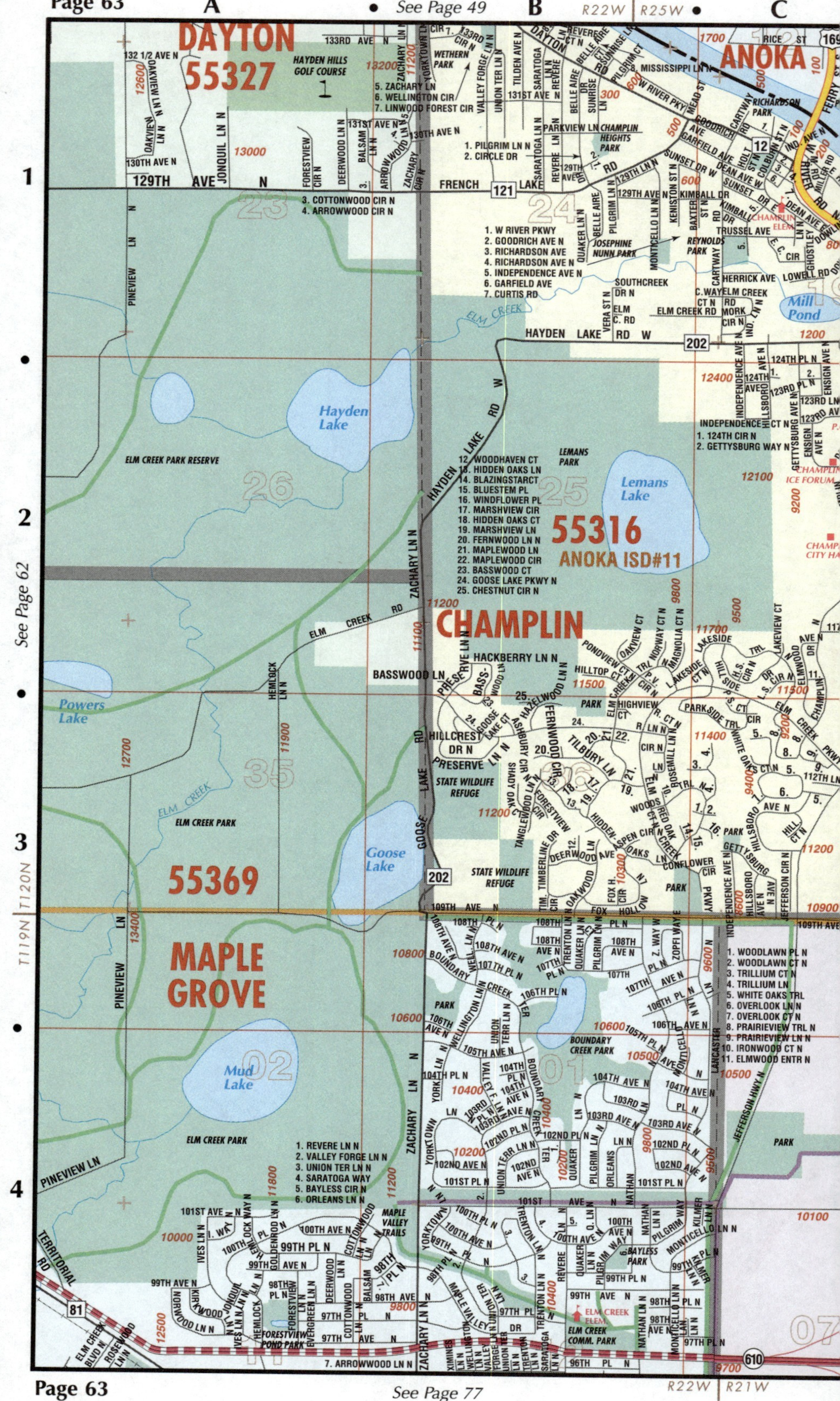

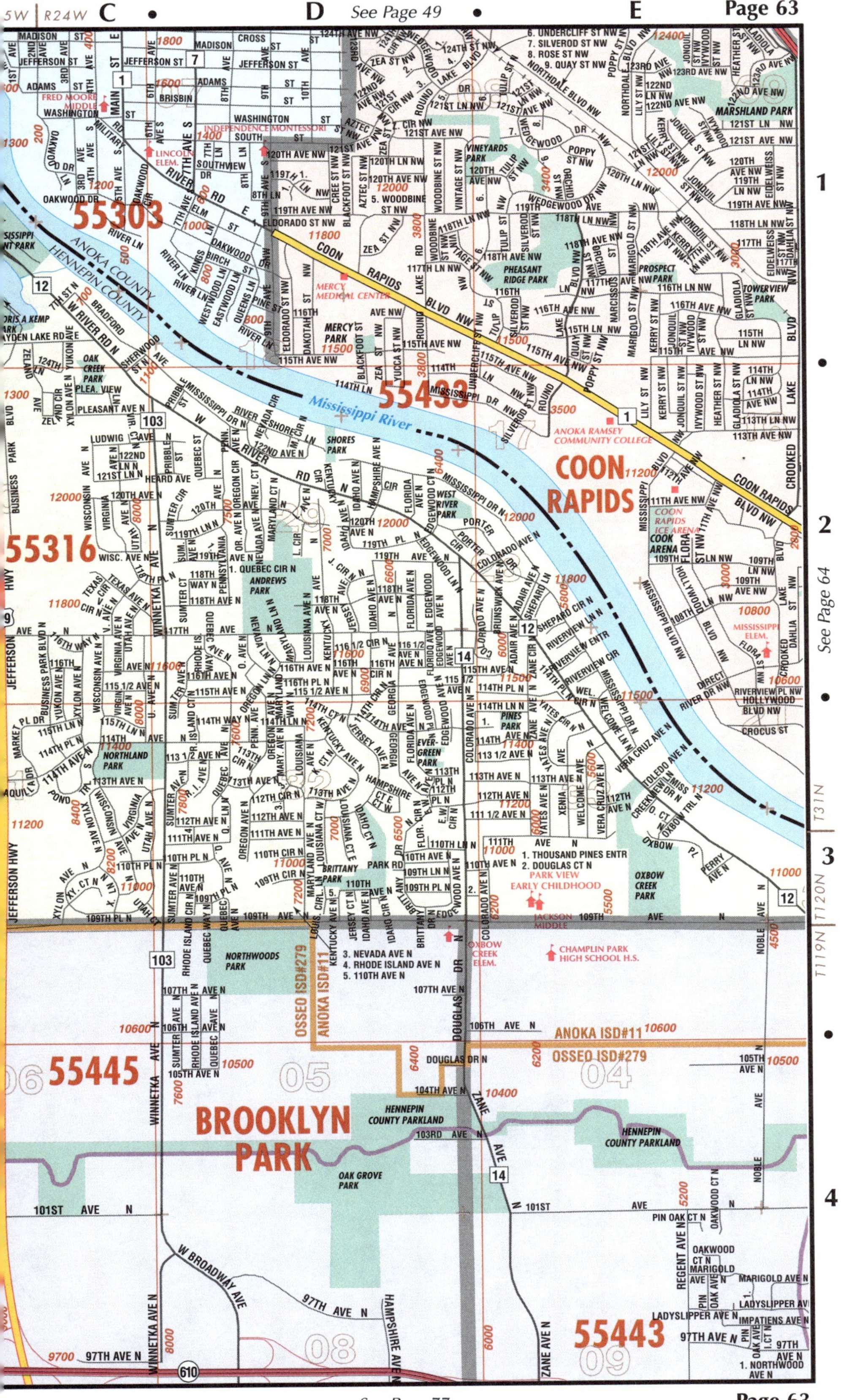
55303
55433
55316
55445
55443
COON RAPIDS
BROOKLYN PARK
Mississippi River
ANOKA COUNTY
HENNEPIN COUNTY
COON RAPIDS BLVD NW
MERCY MEDICAL CENTER
MERCY PARK
ANOKA RAMSEY COMMUNITY COLLEGE
COON RAPIDS ICE ARENA
COOK ARENA
MISSISSIPPI ELEM.
PHEASANT RIDGE PARK
VINEYARDS PARK
MARSHLAND PARK
PROSPECT PARK
TOWERVIEW PARK
SHORES PARK
WEST RIVER PARK
ANDREWS PARK
OAK CREEK PARK
NORTHLAND PARK
PINES PARK
EVER-GREEN PARK
BRITTANY PARK
OXBOW CREEK PARK
PARK VIEW EARLY CHILDHOOD
JACKSON MIDDLE
OXBOW CREEK ELEM.
CHAMPLIN PARK HIGH SCHOOL H.S.
NORTHWOODS PARK
HENNEPIN COUNTY PARKLAND
OAK GROVE PARK
FRED MOORE MIDDLE
LINCOLN ELEM.
INDEPENDENCE MONTESSORI
ANOKA ISD#11
OSSEO ISD#279
WINNETKA AVE
DOUGLAS DR
ZANE AVE
JEFFERSON HWY
W BROADWAY AVE
101ST AVE N
97TH AVE N
109TH AVE
1. THOUSAND PINES ENTR
2. DOUGLAS CT N
3. NEVADA AVE N
4. RHODE ISLAND AVE N
5. 110TH AVE N
6. UNDERCLIFF ST NW
7. SILVEROD ST NW
8. ROSE ST NW
9. QUAY ST NW
1. NORTHWOOD AVE N
See Page 64
T31N
T120N
T119N
1
2
3
4

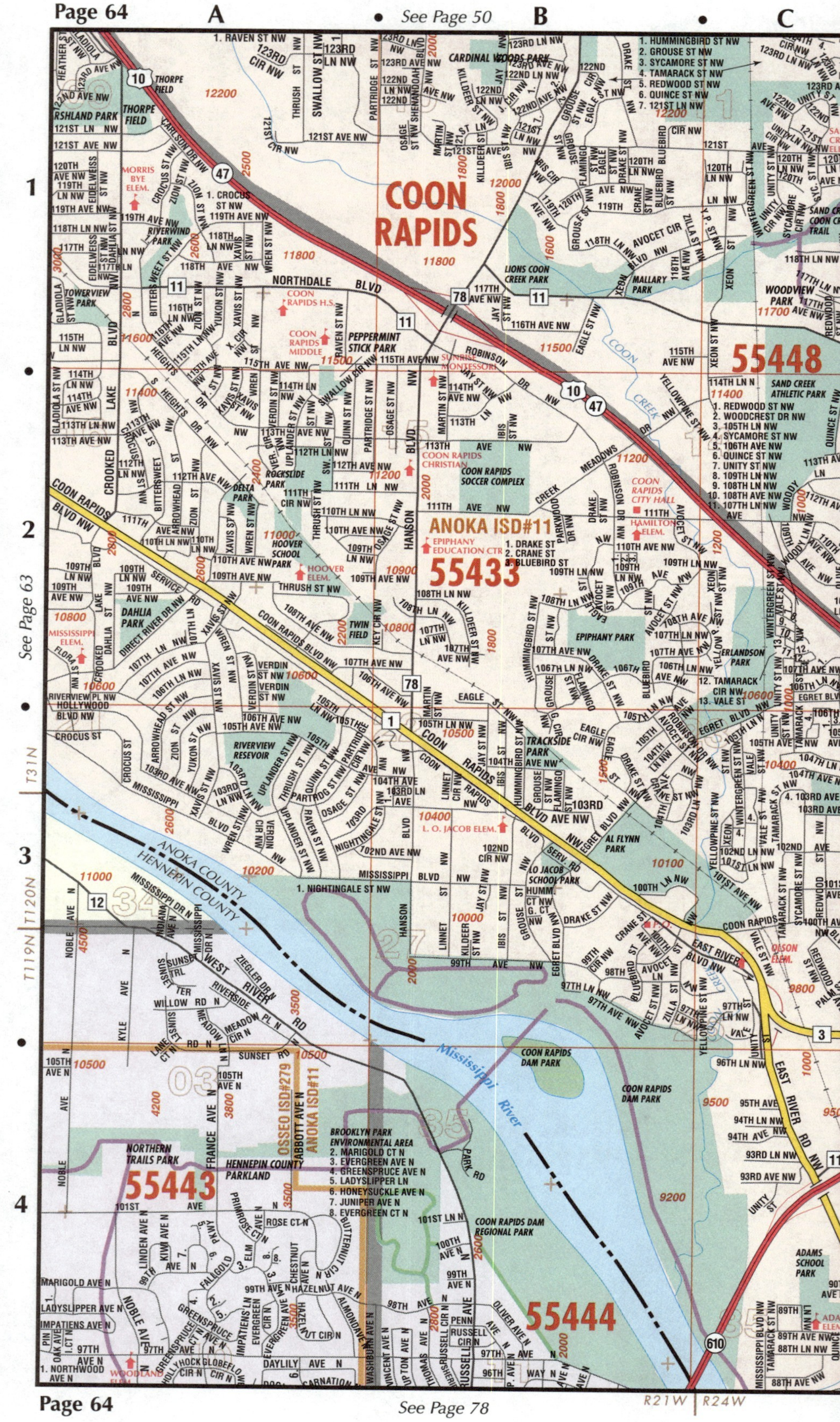

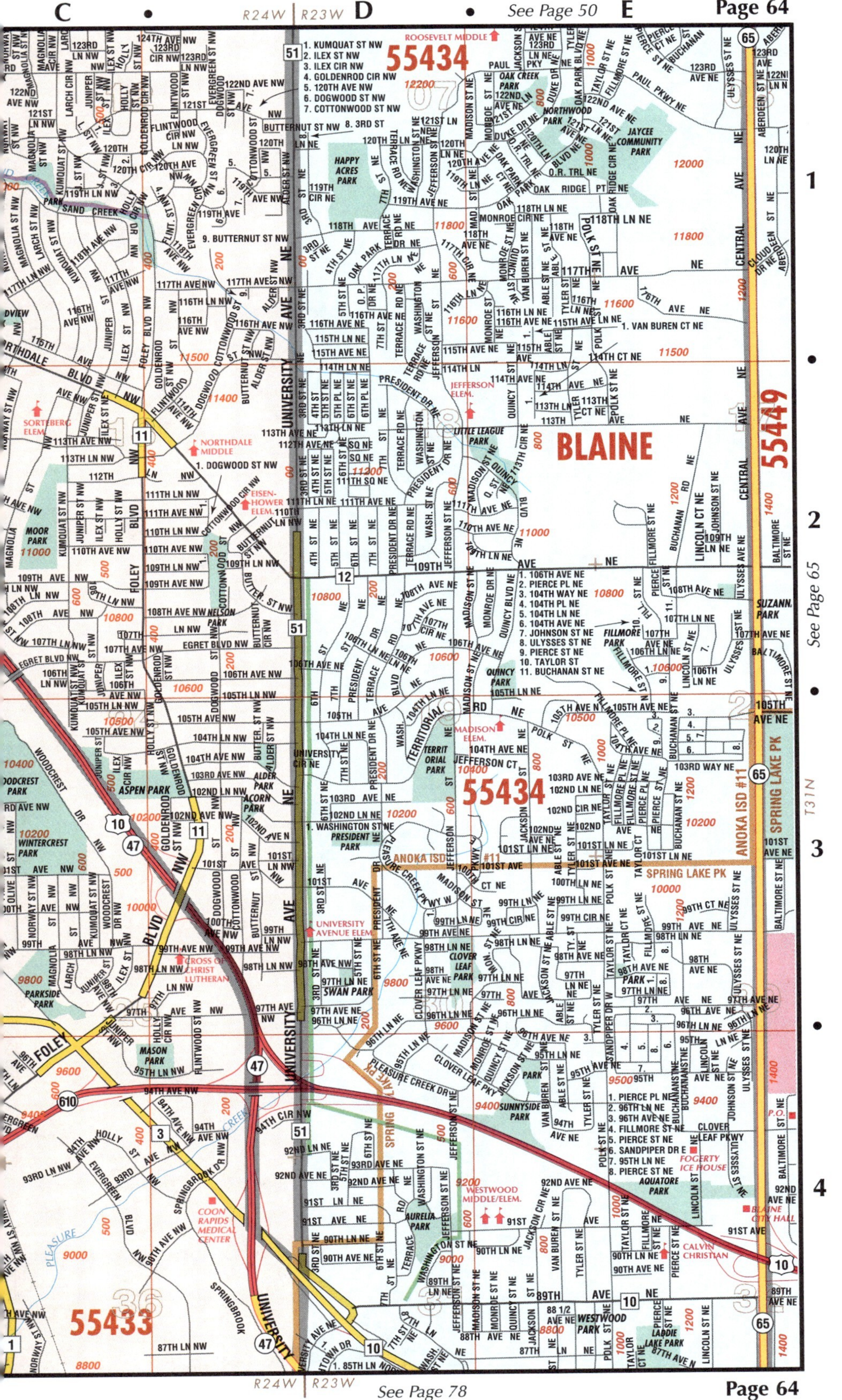
55434
55449
55433
BLAINE
1. KUMQUAT ST NW
2. ILEX ST NW
3. ILEX CIR NW
4. GOLDENROD CIR NW
5. 120TH AVE NW
6. DOGWOOD ST NW
7. COTTONWOOD ST NW
8. 3RD ST
ROOSEVELT MIDDLE
OAK CREEK PARK
NORTHWOOD PARK
JAYCEE COMMUNITY PARK
HAPPY ACRES PARK
JEFFERSON ELEM.
LITTLE LEAGUE PARK
SORTEBERG ELEM.
NORTHDALE MIDDLE
1. DOGWOOD ST NW
EISENHOWER ELEM.
MOOR PARK
1. VAN BUREN CT NE
1. 106TH AVE NE
2. PIERCE PL NE
3. 104TH WAY NE
4. 104TH PL NE
5. 104TH LN NE
6. 104TH AVE NE
7. JOHNSON ST NE
8. ULYSSES ST NE
9. PIERCE ST NE
10. TAYLOR ST
11. BUCHANAN ST NE
SUZANNA PARK
FILLMORE PARK
QUINCY PARK
NELSON PARK
MADISON ELEM.
TERRITORIAL PARK
ASPEN PARK
ALDER PARK
ACORN PARK
WINTERCREST PARK
WOODCREST PARK
1. WASHINGTON ST NE
PRESIDENT PARK
ANOKA ISD #11
SPRING LAKE PK
ANOKA ISD #11
SPRING LAKE PK
UNIVERSITY AVENUE ELEM.
CLOVER LEAF PARK
SWAN PARK
CROSS OF CHRIST LUTHERAN
PARKSIDE PARK
MASON PARK
SUNNYSIDE PARK
1. PIERCE PL NE
2. 96TH LN NE
3. 96TH AVE NE
4. FILLMORE ST NE
5. PIERCE ST NE
6. SANDPIPER DR E
7. 95TH LN NE
8. PIERCE ST NE
FOGERTY ICE HOUSE
AQUATORE PARK
WESTWOOD MIDDLE/ELEM.
AURELIA PARK
COON RAPIDS MEDICAL CENTER
BLAINE CITY HALL
CALVIN CHRISTIAN
WESTWOOD PARK
LADDIE LAKE PARK
P.O.
UNIVERSITY AVE NE
CENTRAL AVE NE
T31N
See Page 65
1. 85TH LN NE

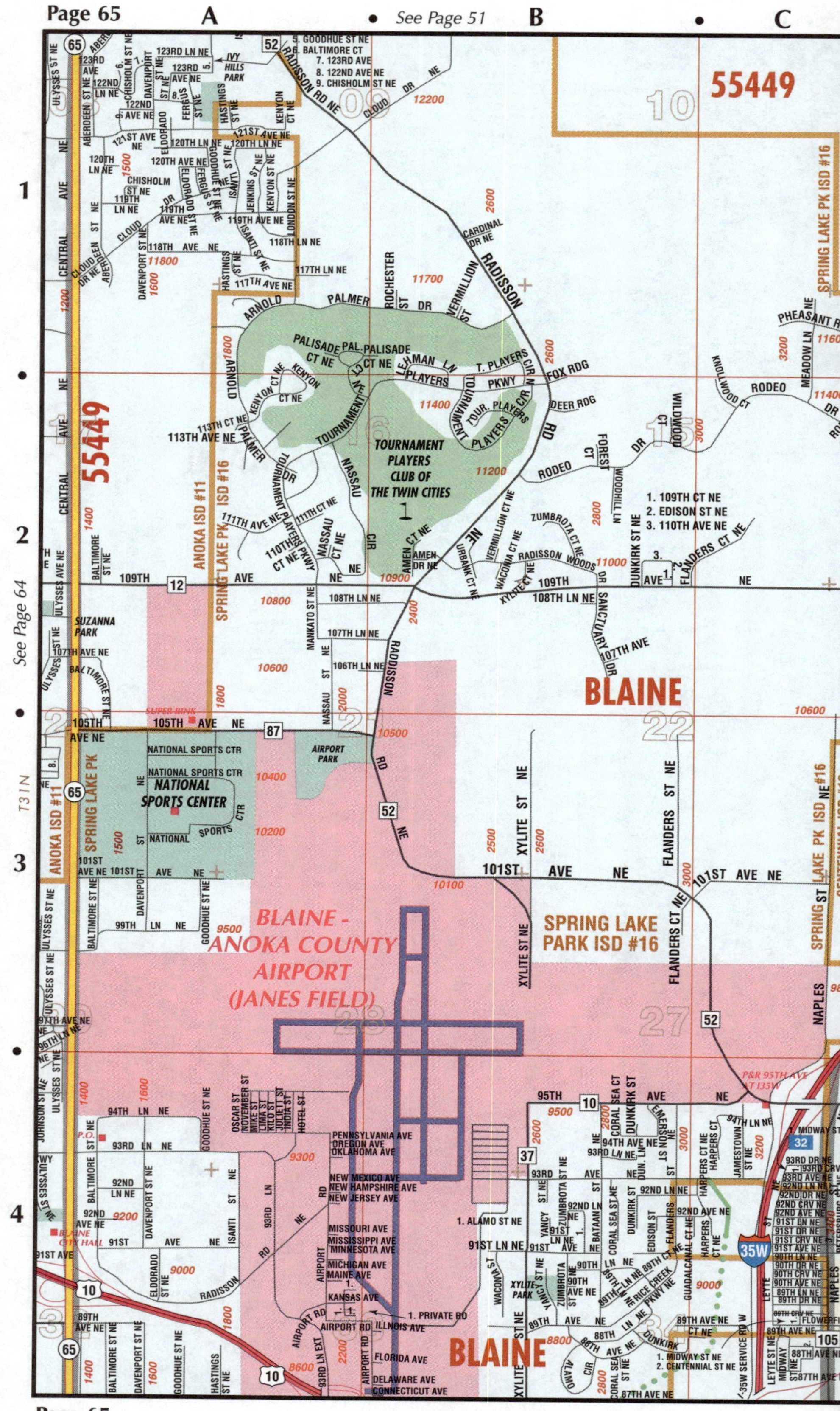

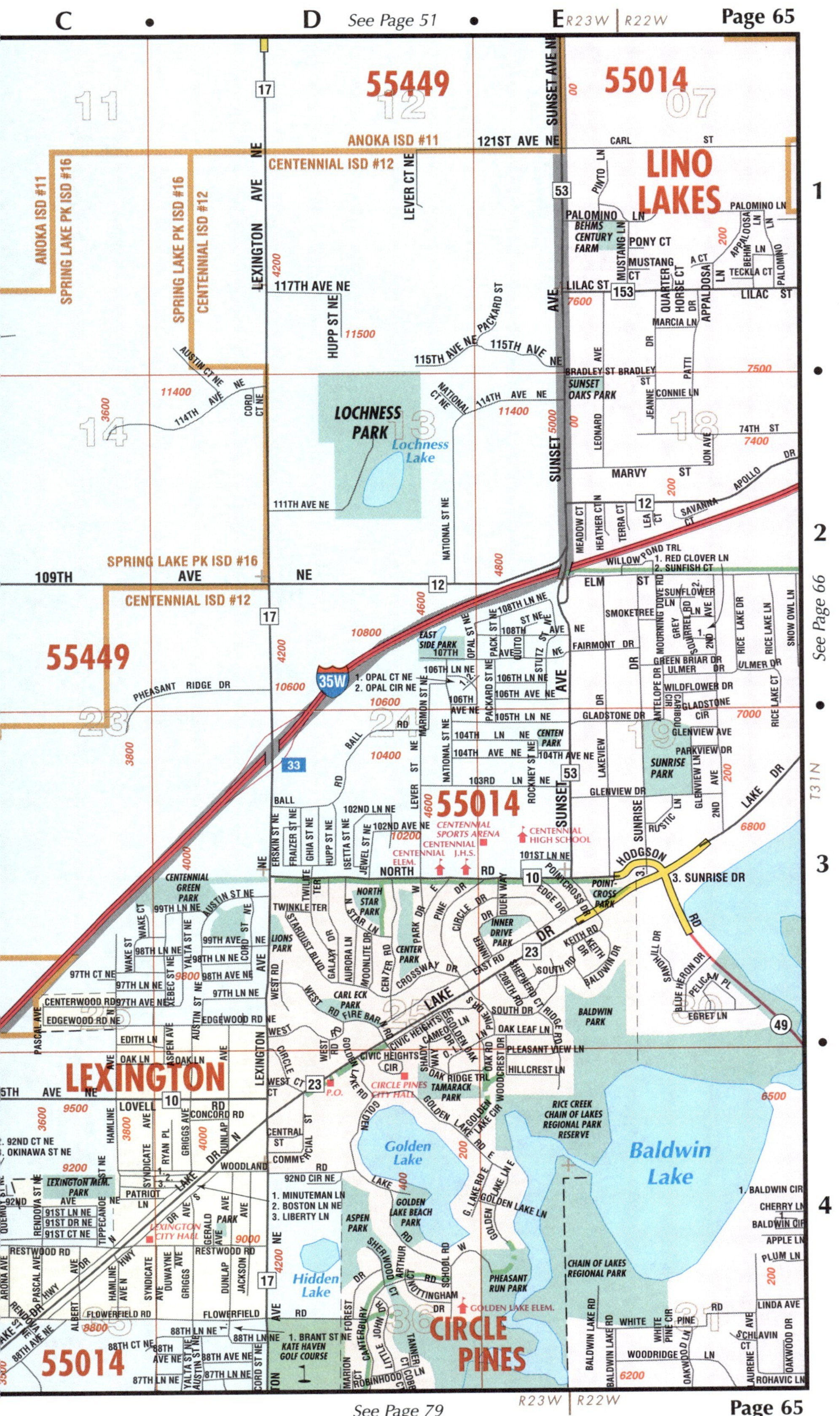

55449
55014
LINO LAKES
ANOKA ISD #11
CENTENNIAL ISD #12
SPRING LAKE PK ISD #16
121ST AVE NE
SUNSET AVE NE
LEXINGTON AVE NE
117TH AVE NE
HUPP ST NE
115TH AVE NE
PACKARD ST
LOCHNESS PARK
Lochness Lake
111TH AVE NE
NATIONAL ST NE
109TH AVE NE
PHEASANT RIDGE DR
BALL RD
NORTH RD
CENTENNIAL SPORTS ARENA
CENTENNIAL HIGH SCHOOL
CENTENNIAL J.H.S.
CENTENNIAL ELEM.
LEXINGTON
CIRCLE PINES
CIRCLE PINES CITY HALL
LEXINGTON CITY HALL
LAKE DR
CENTERWOOD RD
EDGEWOOD RD NE
WOODLAND
RESTWOOD RD
FLOWERFIELD RD
Golden Lake
Hidden Lake
Baldwin Lake
RICE CREEK CHAIN OF LAKES REGIONAL PARK RESERVE
CHAIN OF LAKES REGIONAL PARK
GOLDEN LAKE BEACH PARK
GOLDEN LAKE ELEM.
KATE HAVEN GOLF COURSE
SUNRISE PARK
SUNSET OAKS PARK
BEHMS CENTURY FARM
LIONS PARK
CENTER PARK
CARL ECK PARK
TAMARACK PARK
ASPEN PARK
PHEASANT RUN PARK
BALDWIN PARK
POINT-CROSS PARK
INNER DRIVE PARK
NORTH STAR PARK
LEXINGTON MEM. PARK
CENTENNIAL GREEN PARK
EAST SIDE PARK
HODGSON RD
LILAC ST
APOLLO DR
MARVY ST
CARL ST
PALOMINO LN
1. OPAL CT NE
2. OPAL CIR NE
1. RED CLOVER LN
2. SUNFISH CT
3. SUNRISE DR
1. MINUTEMAN LN
2. BOSTON LN NE
3. LIBERTY LN
1. BRANT ST NE
1. BALDWIN CIR
See Page 66
T31N

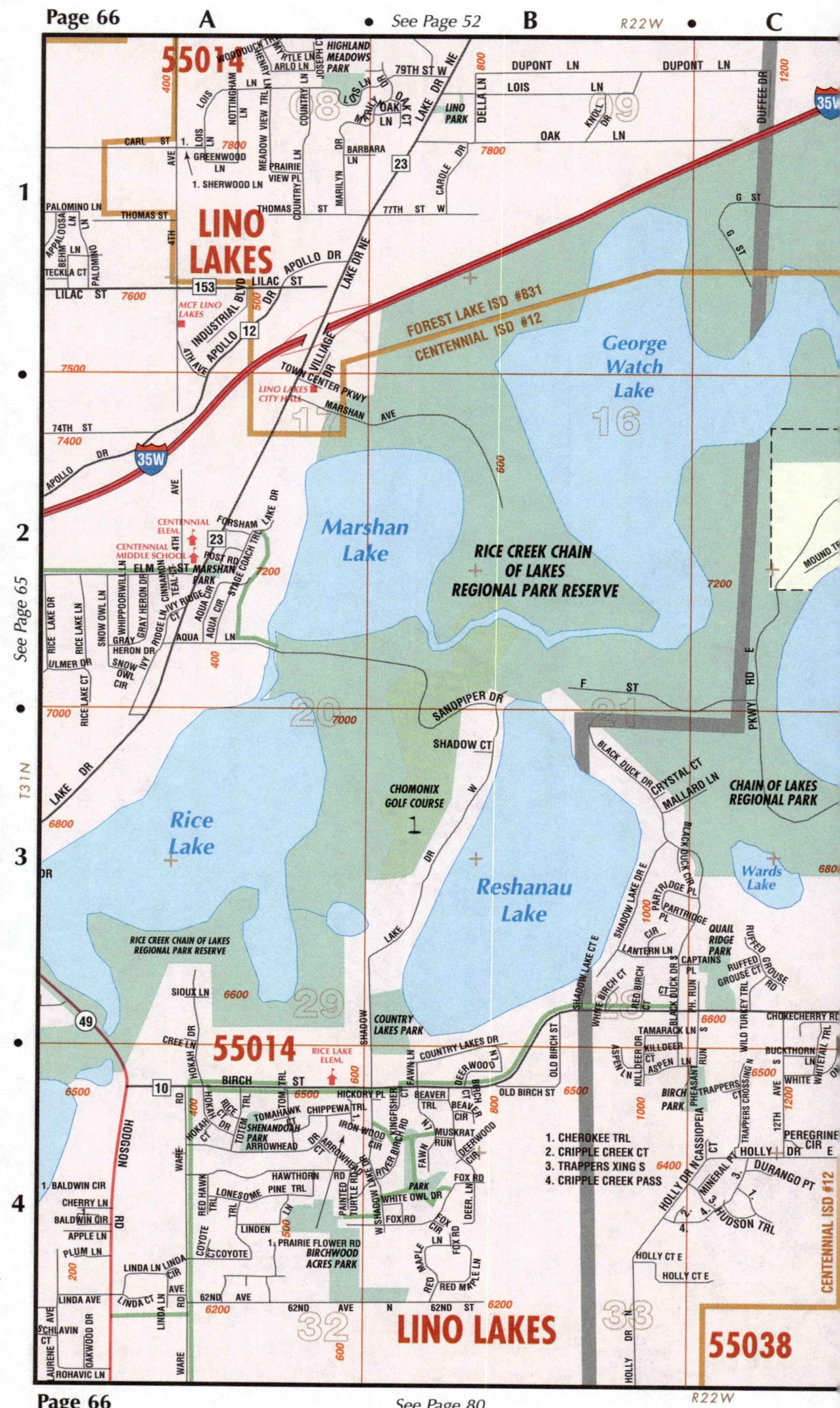

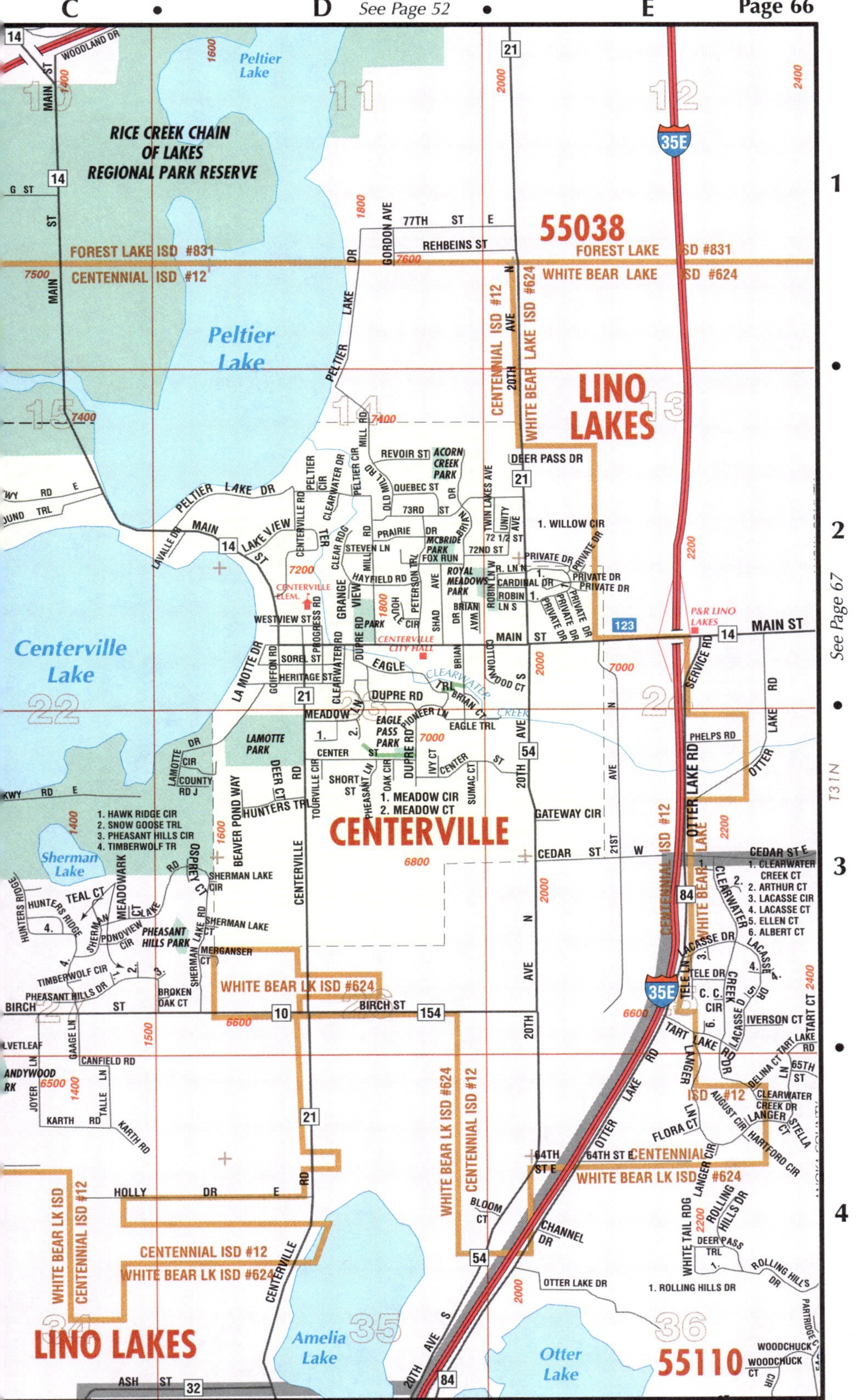

55038

FOREST LAKE ISD #831
CENTENNIAL ISD #12

RICE CREEK CHAIN
OF LAKES
REGIONAL PARK RESERVE

FOREST LAKE ISD #831
WHITE BEAR LAKE ISD #624

Peltier Lake

Peltier Lake

LINO LAKES

Centerville Lake

Sherman Lake

CENTERVILLE

WHITE BEAR LK ISD #624

1. HAWK RIDGE CIR
2. SNOW GOOSE TRL
3. PHEASANT HILLS CIR
4. TIMBERWOLF TR

1. MEADOW CIR
2. MEADOW CT

1. WILLOW CIR

1. CLEARWATER CREEK CT
2. ARTHUR CT
3. LACASSE CIR
4. LACASSE CT
5. ELLEN CT
6. ALBERT CT

WHITE BEAR LK ISD #624
CENTENNIAL ISD #12

WHITE BEAR LK ISD #624

1. ROLLING HILLS DR

LINO LAKES

Amelia Lake

Otter Lake

55110

Page 67 See Page 53

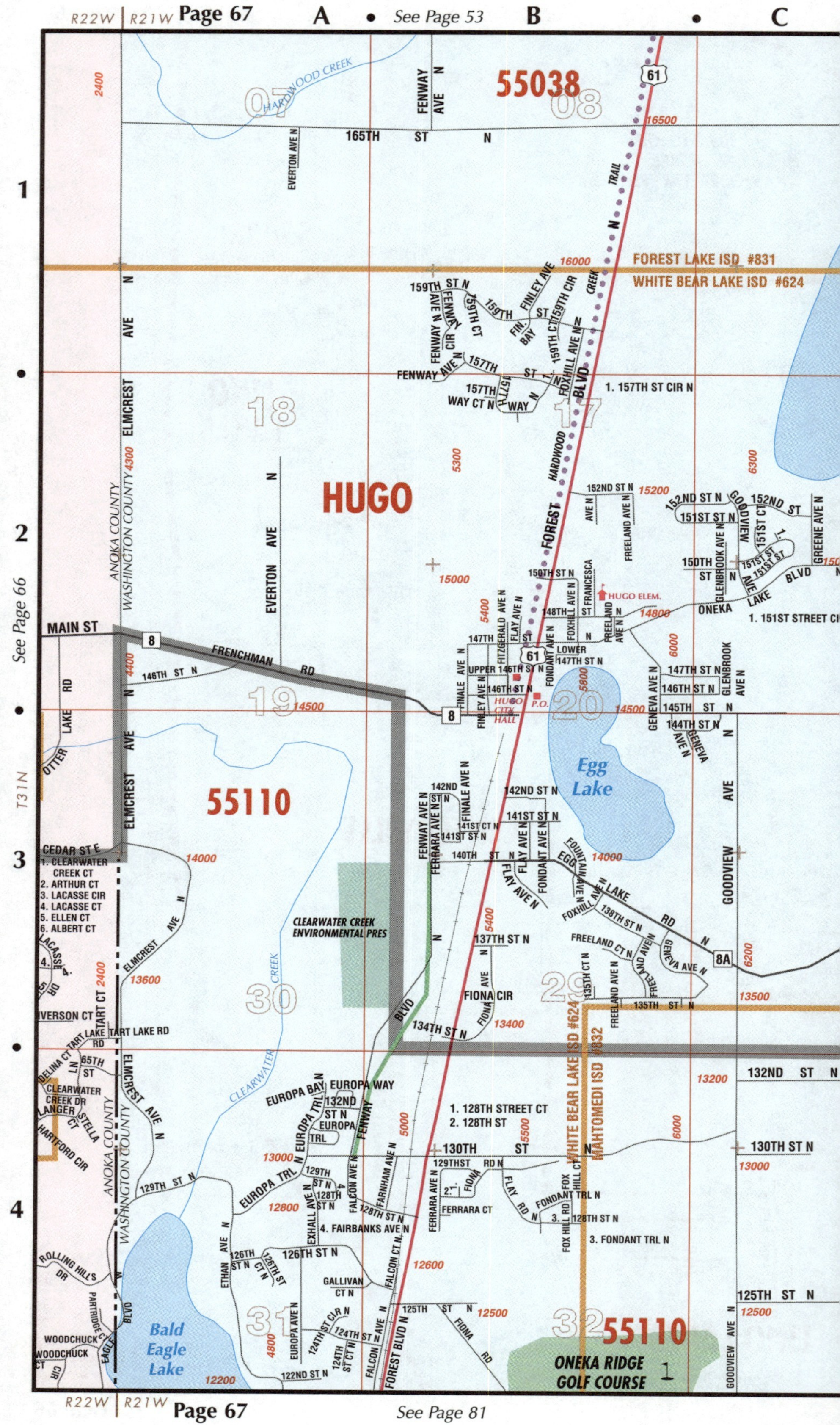

See Page 66

Page 67 See Page 81

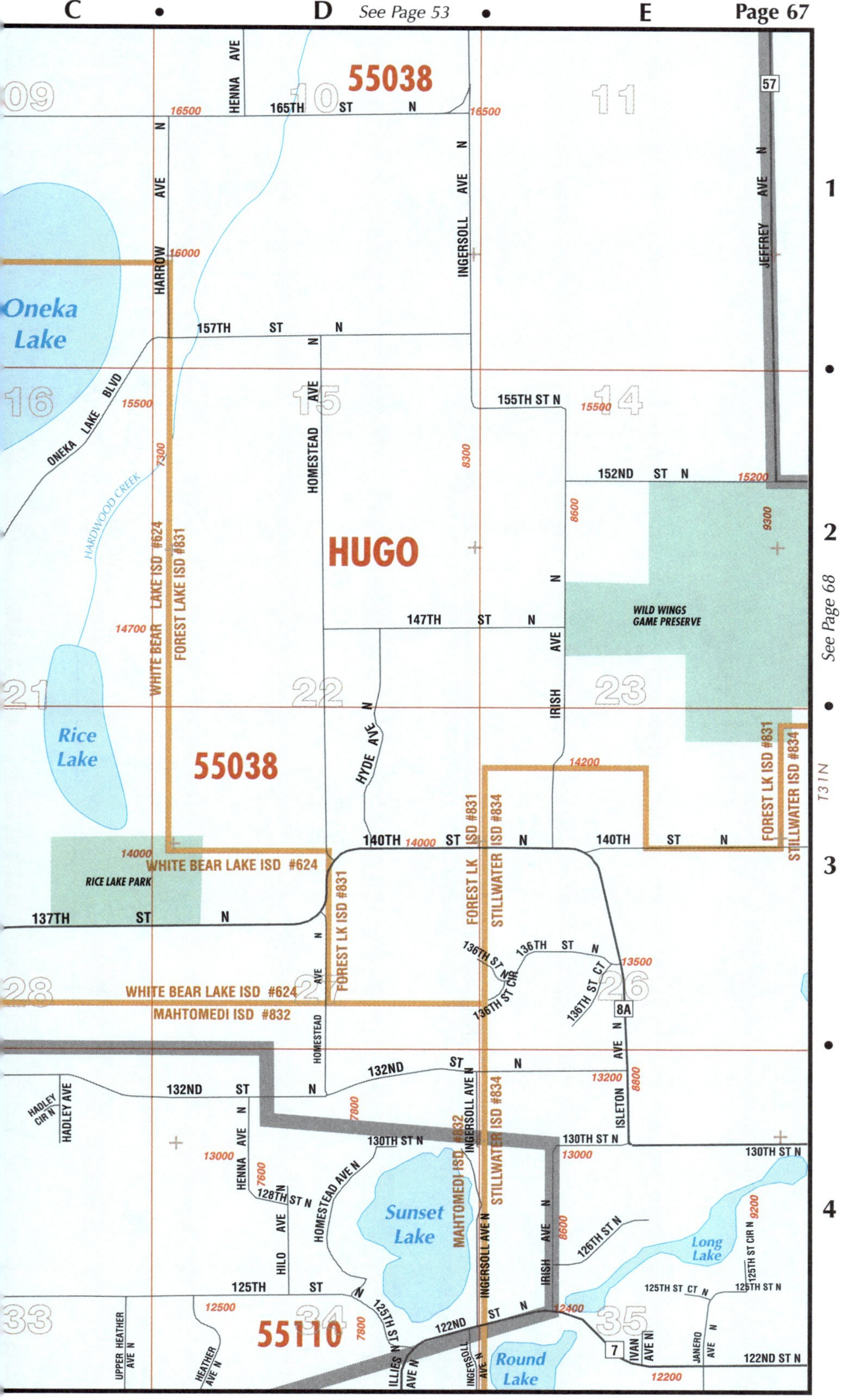

55038

HENNA AVE

165TH ST N

INGERSOLL AVE

11

57

JEFFREY AVE N

16500

16500

1

HARROW AVE

16000

Oneka Lake

157TH ST N

ONEKA LAKE BLVD

15500

HOMESTEAD AVE

15

155TH ST N

14

15500

152ND ST N

15200

9300

7300

HARDWOOD CREEK

HUGO

6300

8600

WILD WINGS GAME PRESERVE

2

WHITE BEAR LAKE ISD #624

FOREST LAKE ISD #831

14700

147TH ST N

IRISH AVE N

21

Rice Lake

22

23

55038

HYDE AVE N

14200

FOREST LK ISD #831

STILLWATER ISD #834

14000

140TH 14000

FOREST LK ISD #831

STILLWATER ISD #834 N

140TH ST N

14000

WHITE BEAR LAKE ISD #624

RICE LAKE PARK

137TH ST N

FOREST LK ISD #831 AVE N

13500

136TH ST N

136TH ST CT N

136TH ST CIR N

136TH ST N

8A

26

3

28

WHITE BEAR LAKE ISD #624

MAHTOMEDI ISD #832

HOMESTEAD AVE N

132ND ST N

INGERSOLL AVE N

ISLETON AVE N

13200

8800

132ND ST N

HADLEY CIR N

HADLEY AVE

7800

130TH ST N

MAHTOMEDI ISD #832

STILLWATER ISD #834

130TH ST N

13000

130TH ST N

13000

HENNA AVE N

7600

13000

128TH ST N

Sunset Lake

126TH ST N

IRISH AVE N

8600

Long Lake

9200

HILO AVE N

125TH ST N

INGERSOLL AVE N

125TH ST CT N

125TH ST N

125TH ST CIR N

12500

7800

55110

33

34

125TH ST N

122ND ST N

Round Lake

IVAN AVE N

7

JANERO AVE N

122ND ST N

35

12400

12200

See Page 81

See Page 68

T31N

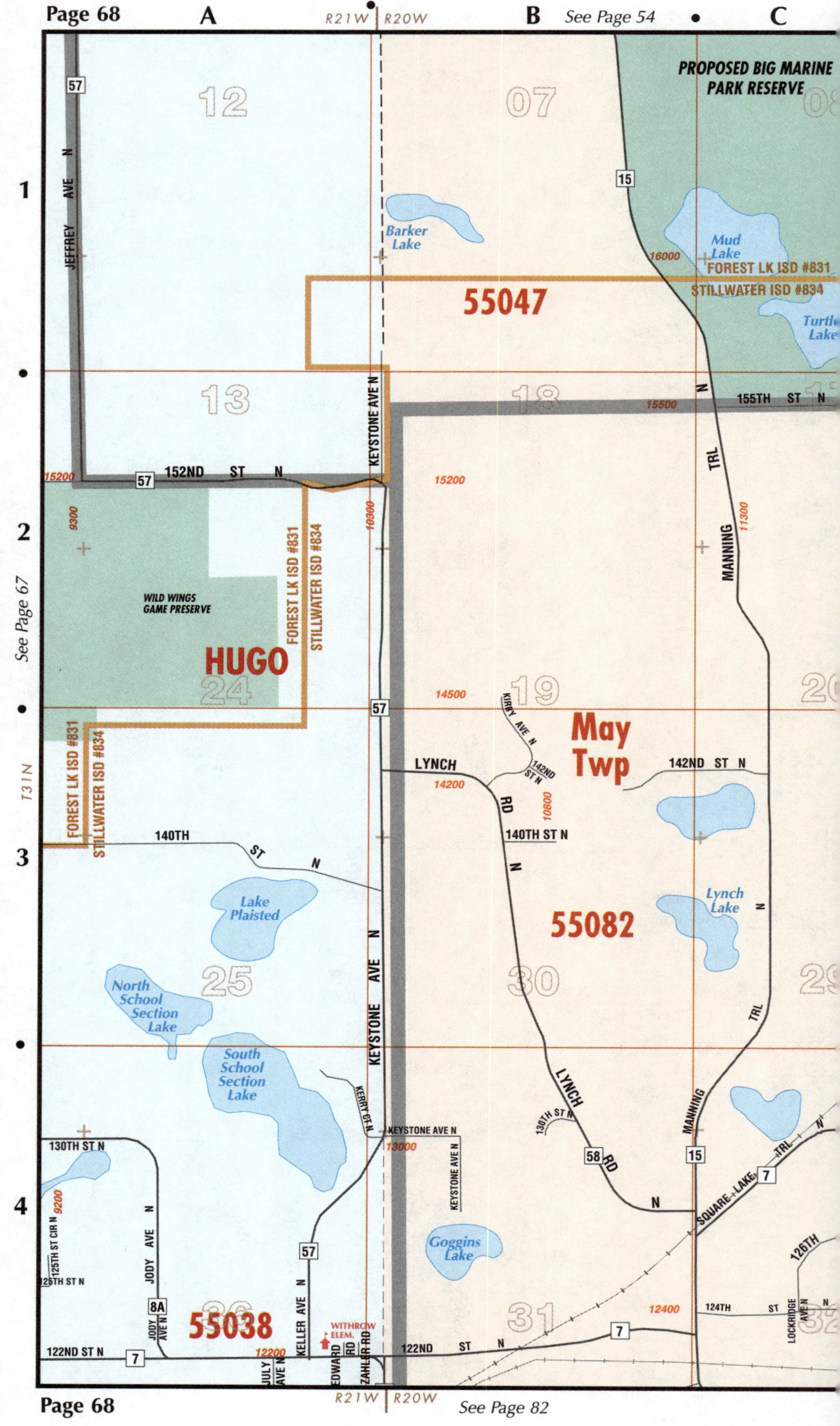

A · R21W | R20W · B *See Page 54* · C

57

JEFFREY AVE N

12

1

Barker Lake

07

PROPOSED BIG MARINE PARK RESERVE

08

15

16000

Mud Lake

FOREST LK ISD #831
STILLWATER ISD #834

Turtle Lake

55047

13

18

15500

155TH ST N

KEYSTONE AVE N

15200

57

152ND ST N

15200

MANNING TRL

11300

See Page 67

9300

2

10300

WILD WINGS GAME PRESERVE

FOREST LK ISD #831
STILLWATER ISD #834

HUGO

24

57

15200

14500

19

KIRBY AVE N

May Twp

20

T31N

FOREST LK ISD #831
STILLWATER ISD #834

LYNCH

14200

142ND ST N

10800

142ND ST N

140TH ST N

140TH

ST

N

RD N

3

Lake Plaisted

55082

Lynch Lake

North School Section Lake

25

LYNCH RD N

30

29

South School Section Lake

KERRY AVE N

139TH ST N

MANNING TRL

130TH ST N

KEYSTONE AVE N

13000

KEYSTONE AVE N

58

15

SQUARE LAKE TRL N

7

126TH AVE N

4

125TH ST CIR N

9200

JODY AVE N

JODY AVE N

Goggins Lake

MANNING

KELLER AVE N

57

8A

55038

26

12200

WITHROW ELEM. RD

EDWARD RD

ZAHLER RD

122ND ST N

7

122ND

ST

N

31

7

12400

124TH

ST

N

LOCKRIDGE AVE N

32

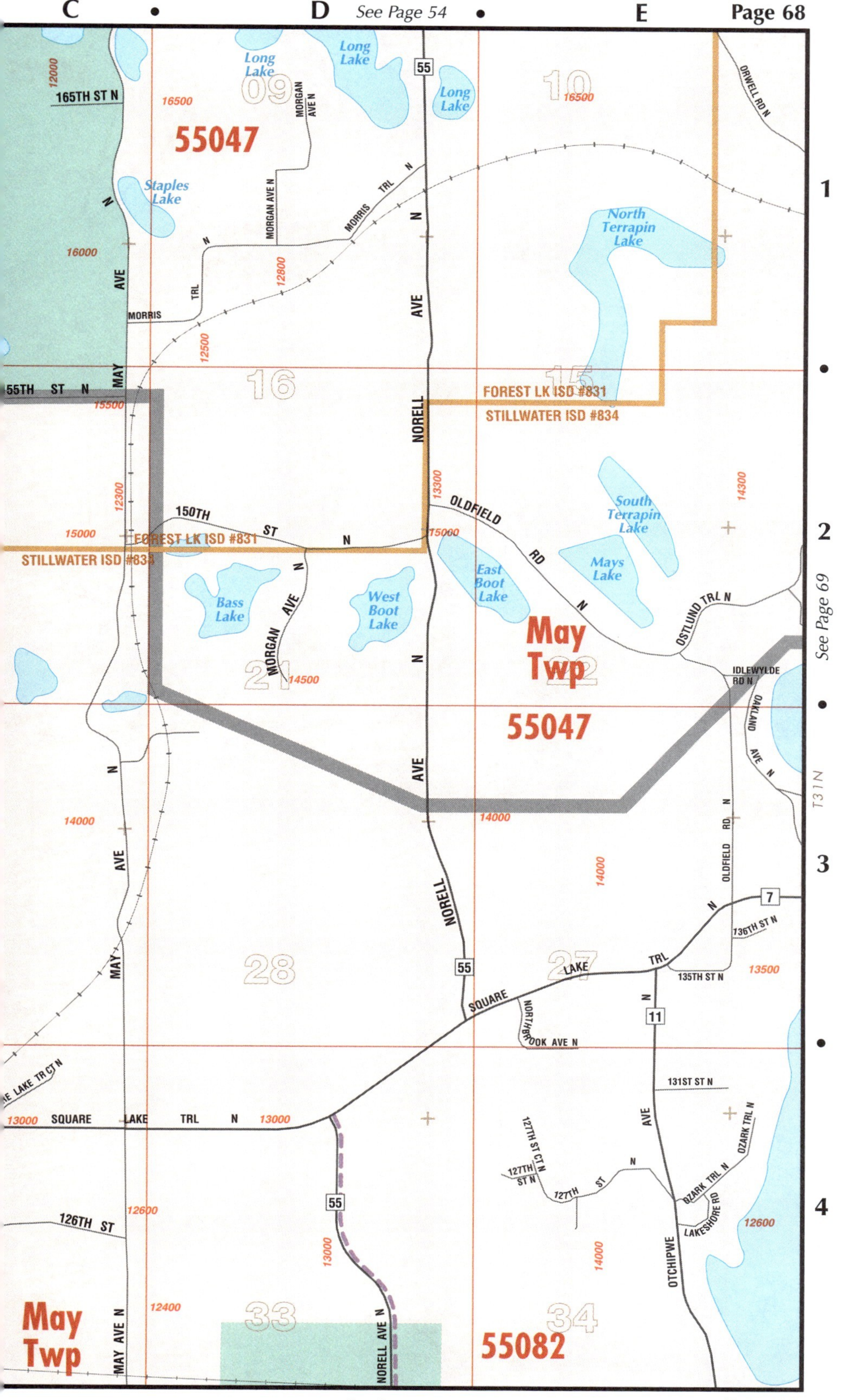

See Page 69

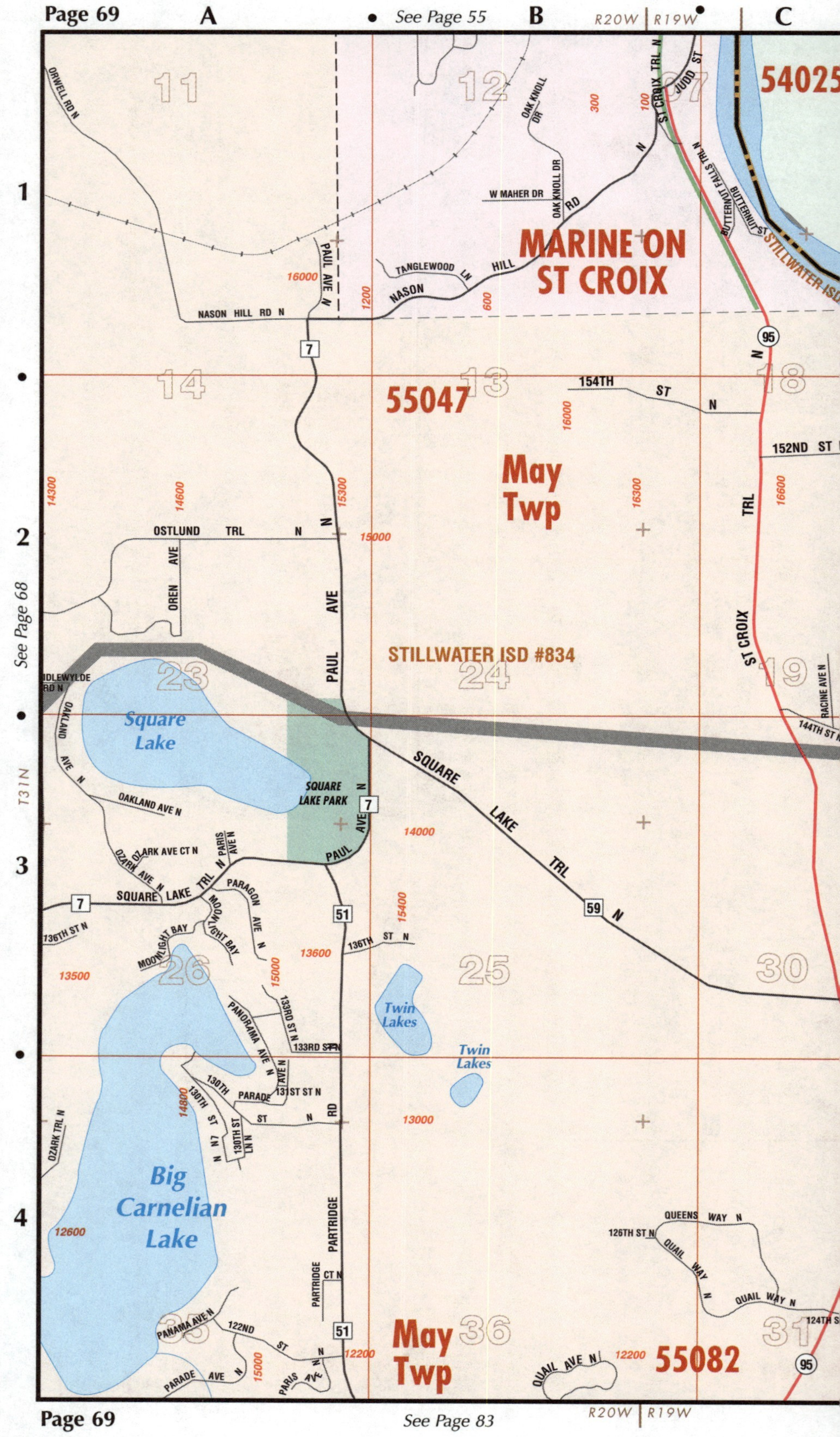

54025

ORWELL RD N

11

12

OAK KNOLL DR

300

100

ST CROIX TRL N

JUDD ST

67

BUTTERNUT FALLS TRL

BUTTERNUT ST

STILLWATER ISL

1

W MAHER DR

OAK KNOLL DR

OAK KNOLL RD

**MARINE ON
ST CROIX**

TANGLEWOOD LN

HILL

PAUL AVE N

1200

NASON

600

95

16000

NASON HILL RD N

7

154TH

ST

N

55047

16000

152ND ST

14

13

18

14300

14600

15300

**May
Twp**

16300

16600

ST CROIX

TRL

2

OREN AVE

PAUL AVE N

OSTLUND TRL N

15000

15000

STILLWATER ISD #834

19

RACINE AVE N

23

24

144TH ST N

DLEWYLDE
RD N

OAKLAND AVE N

*Square
Lake*

SQUARE

LAKE

TRL

ST CROIX

N

OAKLAND AVE N

SQUARE
LAKE PARK

PAUL AVE N

7

14000

59

N

30

3

OZARK AVE CT N

PARIS AVE N

PARAGON AVE N

OZARK AVE N

7

SQUARE LAKE TRL N

51

15400

MOONLIGHT BAY

136TH ST N

136TH ST N

13600

13500

15000

26

25

MOONLIGHT BAY

PANORAMA AVE N

133RD ST N

133RD ST N

*Twin
Lakes*

*Twin
Lakes*

130TH ST N

130TH ST N

131ST ST N

PARADE

130TH ST LN N

ST

PARTRIDGE RD N

13000

14800

**Big
Carnelian
Lake**

QUEENS WAY N

4

12600

OZARK TRL N

126TH ST N

QUAIL WAY N

PARTRIDGE

PARTRIDGE CT N

QUAIL WAY N

QUAIL WAY N

124TH S

PANAMA AVE N

122ND

ST

N

51

36

31

35

PARADE

AVE N

PARIS AVE N

12200

**May
Twp**

QUAIL AVE N

12200

55082

95

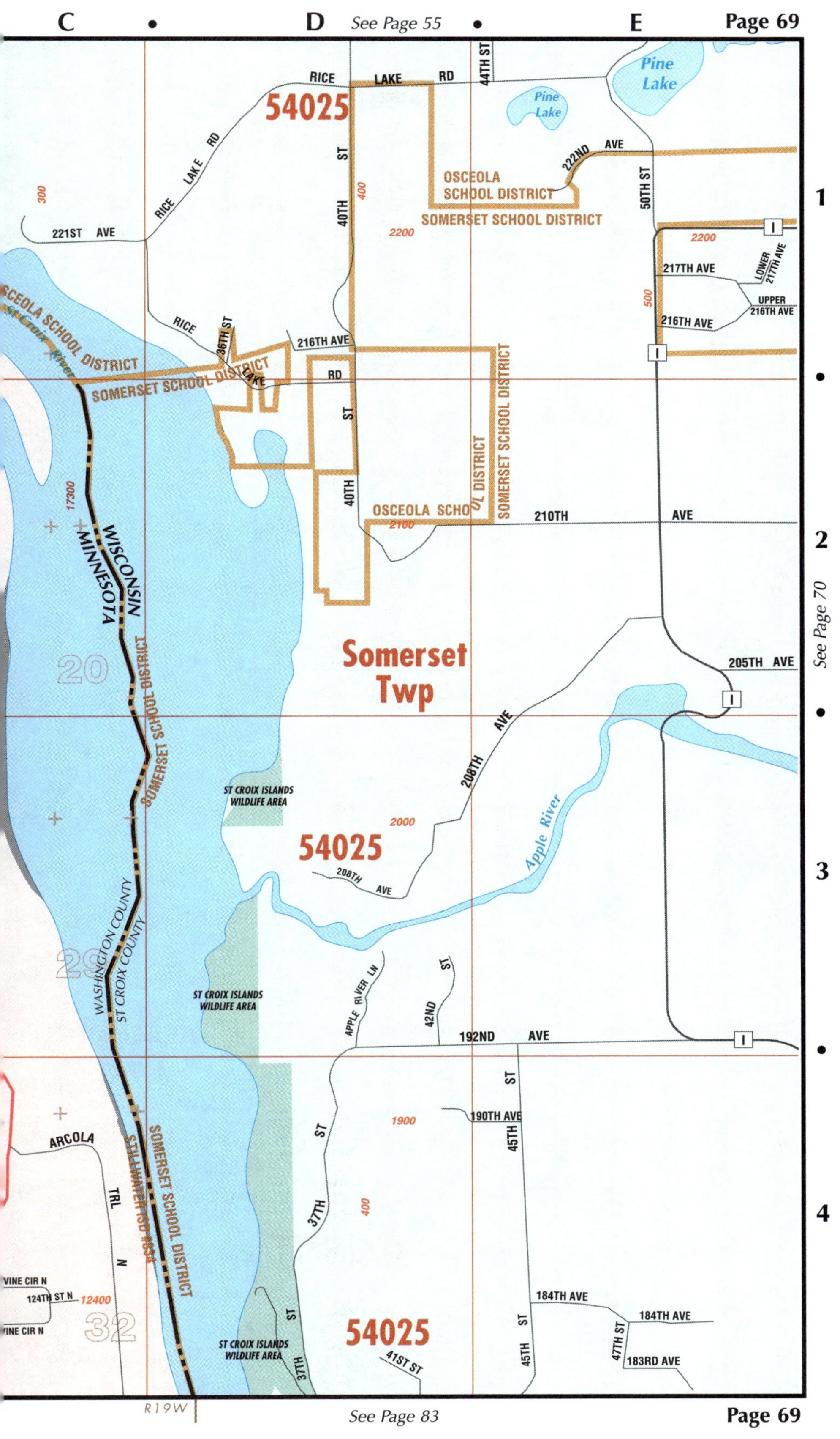

RICE LAKE RD
44TH ST
Pine Lake

54025

Pine Lake

222ND AVE

50TH ST

1

RICE LAKE E RD

300

221ST AVE

40TH ST

400

2200

OSCEOLA
SCHOOL DISTRICT

SOMERSET SCHOOL DISTRICT

2200

217TH AVE

LOWER 217TH AVE

500

216TH AVE

UPPER 216TH AVE

OSCEOLA SCHOOL DISTRICT

St Croix River

RICE 36TH ST

216TH AVE

SOMERSET SCHOOL DISTRICT

LAKE RD

ST

SOMERSET SCHOOL DISTRICT

40TH ST

OSCEOLA SCHOOL DISTRICT

2100

210TH AVE

2

17300

WISCONSIN
MINNESOTA

20

SOMERSET SCHOOL DISTRICT

Somerset Twp

205TH AVE

208TH AVE

ST CROIX ISLANDS
WILDLIFE AREA

2000

54025

Apple River

208TH AVE

See Page 70

3

29

WASHINGTON COUNTY

ST CROIX COUNTY

ST CROIX ISLANDS
WILDLIFE AREA

APPLE RIVER LN

42ND ST

192ND AVE

4

37TH ST

1900

190TH AVE

45TH ST

ARCOLA

STILLWATER RD #64

SOMERSET SCHOOL DISTRICT

400

184TH AVE

VINE CIR N

124TH ST N

12400

VINE CIR N

32

45TH ST

184TH AVE

47TH ST

183RD AVE

ST CROIX ISLANDS
WILDLIFE AREA

37TH ST

54025

41ST ST

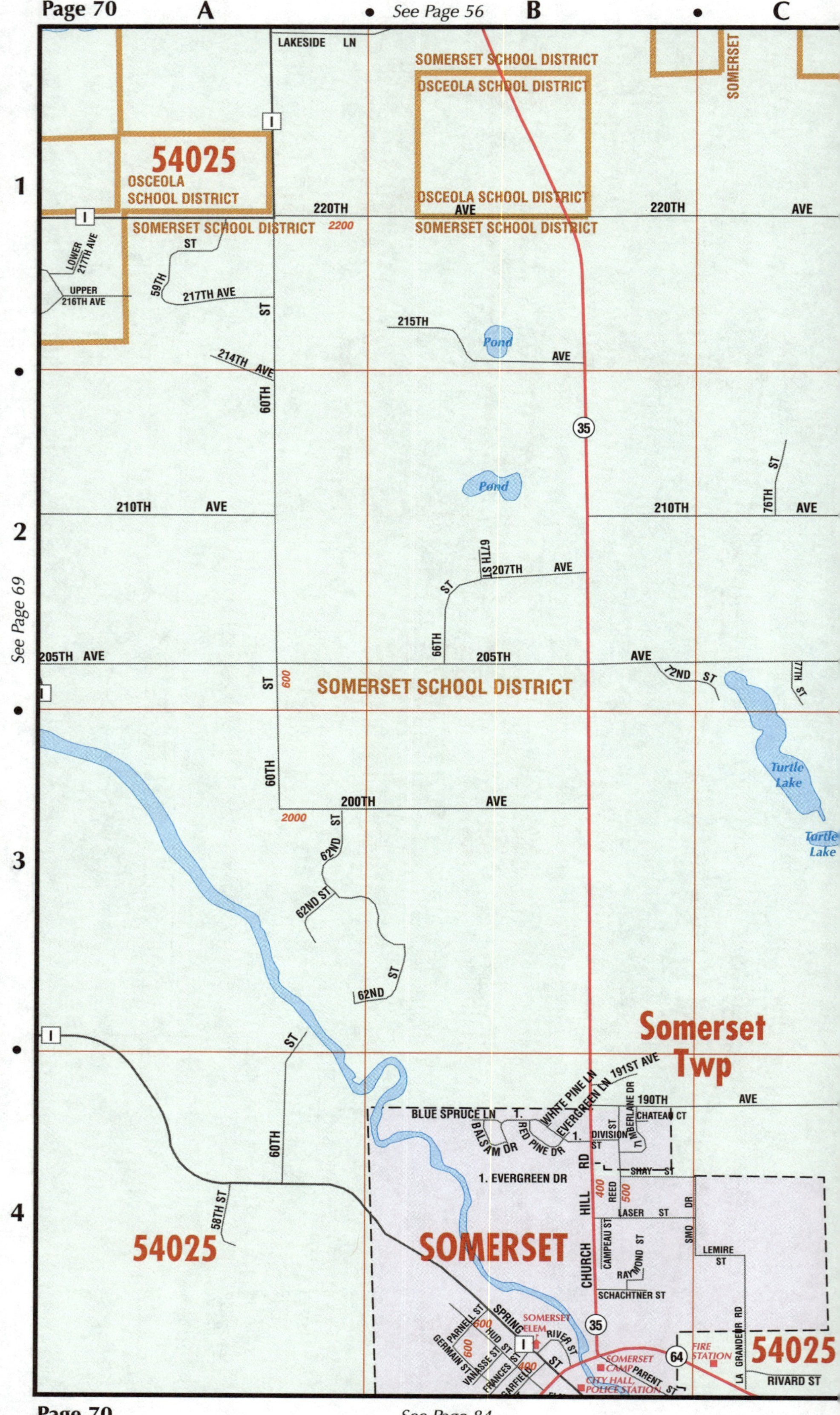

LAKESIDE LN

SOMERSET SCHOOL DISTRICT
OSCEOLA SCHOOL DISTRICT

SOMERSET

54025
OSCEOLA
SCHOOL DISTRICT

OSCEOLA SCHOOL DISTRICT

220TH AVE

220TH AVE

1

LOWER 217TH AVE

SOMERSET SCHOOL DISTRICT *2200*

59TH ST

UPPER 216TH AVE

217TH AVE

SOMERSET SCHOOL DISTRICT

215TH AVE

Pond

214TH AVE

60TH ST

35

210TH AVE

210TH AVE

76TH ST

2

67TH ST

207TH AVE

66TH ST

205TH AVE

205TH AVE

72ND ST

71TH ST

ST *600*

SOMERSET SCHOOL DISTRICT

Turtle Lake

60TH ST

200TH AVE

2000

62ND ST

Turtle Lake

3

62ND ST

62ND ST

ST

Somerset Twp

58TH ST

WHITE PINE LN
191ST AVE

190TH AVE

BLUE SPRUCE LN
EVERGREEN LN
CHATEAU CT

BALSAM DR
RED PINE DR

TIMBERLINE DR

DIVISION ST

60TH ST

1. EVERGREEN DR

SHAY ST

4

54025

SOMERSET

LASER ST

SMO DR

CHURCH HILL RD

REED ST

PARENT ST

CAMPEAU ST

RAY POND ST

LEMIRE ST

SCHACHTNER ST

PARNELL ST *600*

SPRING ST

SOMERSET ELEM *400*

RIVER ST

LA GRANDEUR RD

GERMAIN ST
VANASSE ST
HUD ST

FRANCES ST
GARFIELD ST

35

64

FIRE STATION

54025

SOMERSET CAMP
CITY HALL
POLICE STATION

RIVARD ST

See Page 84
See Page 69

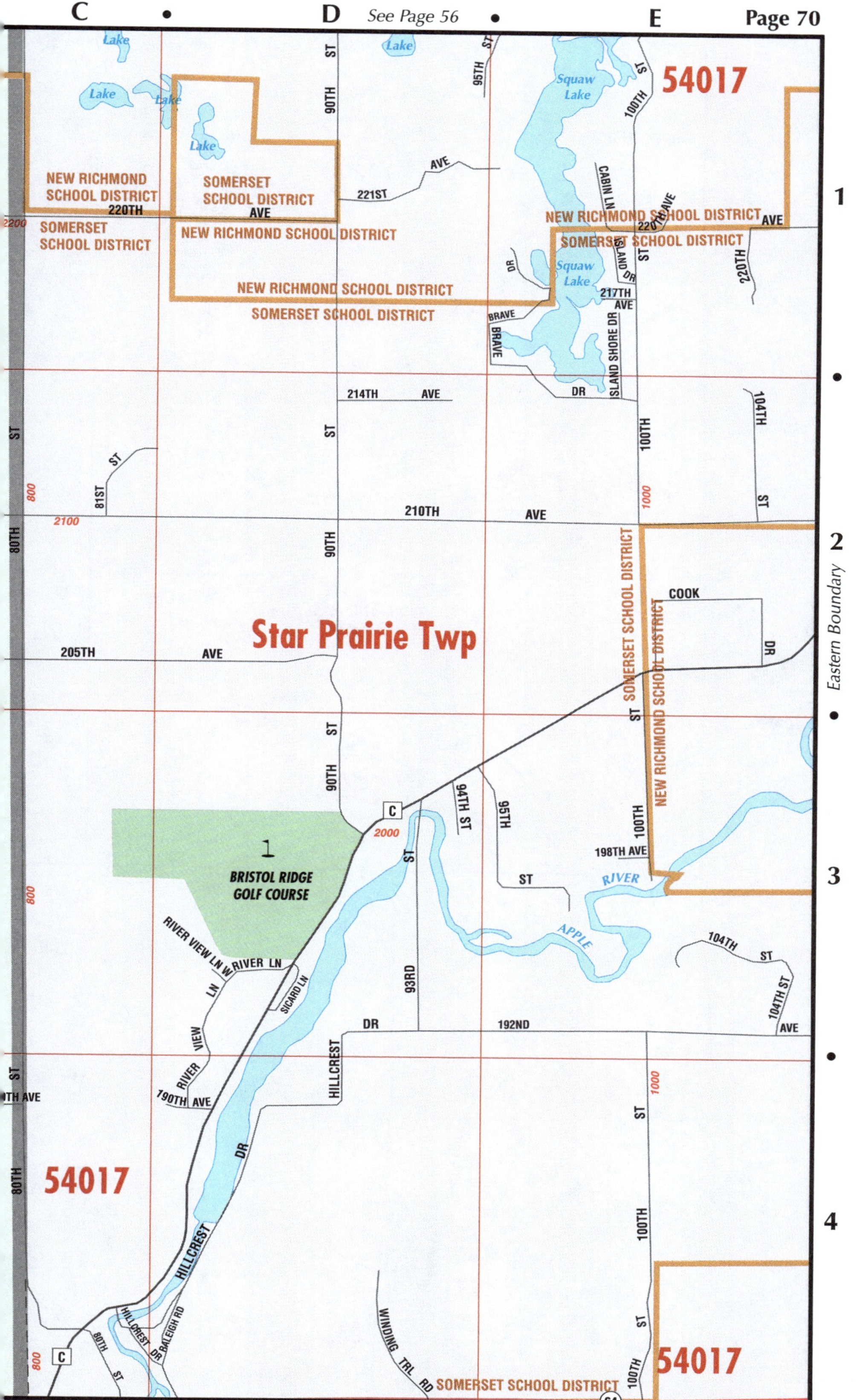

54017

Lake
Lake
Lake
Lake

NEW RICHMOND
SCHOOL DISTRICT

SOMERSET
SCHOOL DISTRICT

90TH ST

95TH ST

100TH ST

Squaw
Lake

221ST AVE

220TH AVE

NEW RICHMOND SCHOOL DISTRICT

SOMERSET SCHOOL DISTRICT

NEW RICHMOND SCHOOL DISTRICT

SOMERSET SCHOOL DISTRICT

CABIN LN

ISLAND DR

NEW RICHMOND SCHOOL DISTRICT
220

SOMERSET SCHOOL DISTRICT

AVE
220TH

Squaw
Lake

217TH AVE

BRAVE

BRAVE

ISLAND SHORE DR

DR

1

214TH AVE

210TH AVE

81ST ST

90TH ST

ST

100TH ST

104TH ST

2100

2

Star Prairie Twp

205TH AVE

COOK DR

SOMERSET SCHOOL DISTRICT

NEW RICHMOND SCHOOL DISTRICT

90TH ST

100TH ST

C
2000

94TH ST

95TH ST

198TH AVE

RIVER

1

**BRISTOL RIDGE
GOLF COURSE**

ST

93RD ST

APPLE

104TH ST

104TH ST AVE

3

RIVER VIEW LN W

RIVER LN

SICARD LN

LN

VIEW

RIVER

790TH AVE

HILLCREST DR

192ND

DR

100TH ST

1000

54017

HILLCREST DR

80TH ST

HILLCREST DR RALEIGH RD

WINDING TRL RD

SOMERSET SCHOOL DISTRICT

100TH ST

4

54017

80TH ST

800

2200

220TH AVE

800

1000

Eastern Boundary

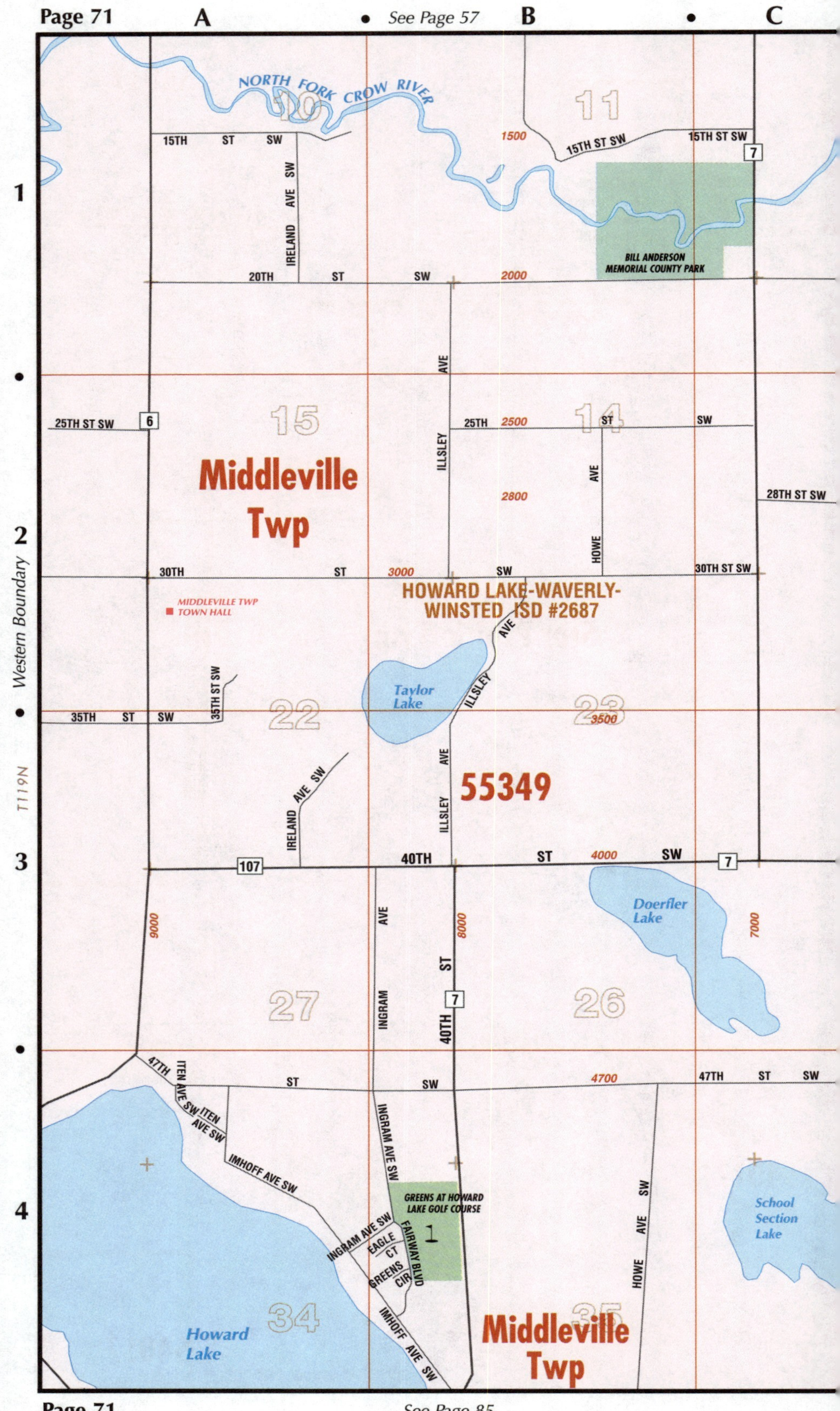

A B C

NORTH FORK CROW RIVER

11

15TH ST SW

15TH ST SW

15TH ST SW

7

1

20TH ST SW

2000

BILL ANDERSON MEMORIAL COUNTY PARK

25TH ST SW 6

15

ILLSLEY AVE

25TH 2500

14

SW

28TH ST SW

Middleville Twp

2800

HOWE AVE

2

30TH ST

3000

SW

30TH ST SW

Western Boundary

HOWARD LAKE-WAVERLY-WINSTED ISD #2687

■ MIDDLEVILLE TWP TOWN HALL

35TH ST SW

ILLSLEY AVE

Taylor Lake

35TH ST SW

22

23

3500

T119N

55349

IRELAND AVE SW

ILLSLEY AVE

3

107

40TH ST

4000

SW

7

9000

8000

INGRAM AVE

40TH ST

7

Doerfler Lake

7000

27

26

4

47TH ST SW

4700

47TH ST SW

ITEN AVE SW ITEN AVE SW

IMHOFF AVE SW

INGRAM AVE SW

HOWE AVE SW

School Section Lake

INGRAM AVE SW

EAGLE CT

GREENS CIR

GREENS AT HOWARD LAKE GOLF COURSE 1

FAIRWAY BLVD

Howard Lake

34

IMHOFF AVE SW

Middleville Twp

35

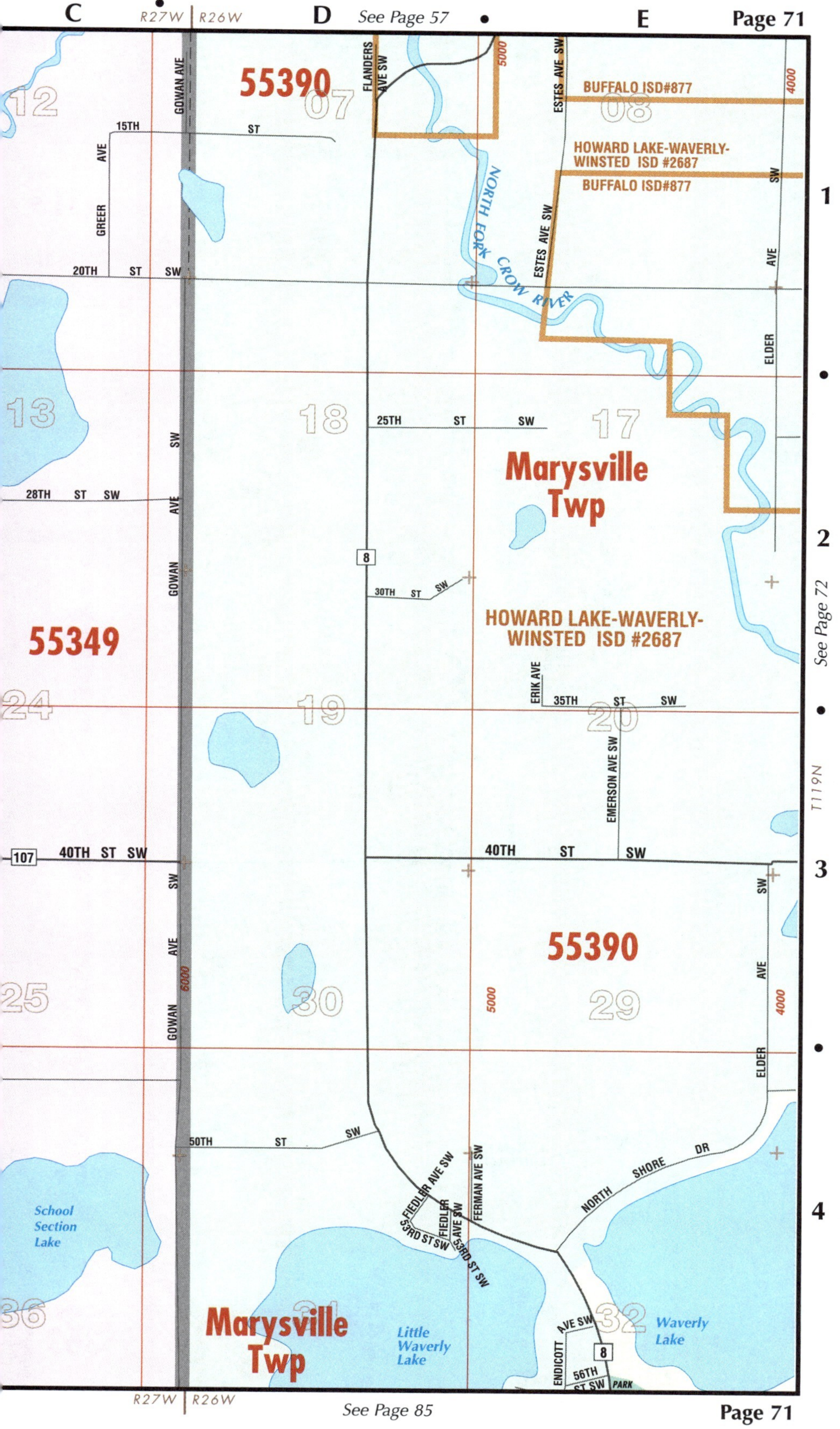

55390
07

08

BUFFALO ISD#877

HOWARD LAKE-WAVERLY-
WINSTED ISD #2687

BUFFALO ISD#877

12

15TH ST
AVE
GREER AVE
GOWAN AVE

20TH ST SW

1

13

18

25TH ST SW

17

**Marysville
Twp**

28TH ST SW
GOWAN AVE SW

8

30TH ST SW

HOWARD LAKE-WAVERLY-
WINSTED ISD #2687

2

55349

24

19

ERIK AVE
35TH ST SW

20

EMERSON AVE SW

107 40TH ST SW

40TH ST SW

3

25

30

55390

29

GOWAN AVE SW
5000

5000
ELDER AVE
4000

50TH ST SW

School
Section
Lake

36

**Marysville
Twp**

31

Little
Waverly
Lake

FIEDLER AVE SW
53RD ST SW
FIEDLER AVE SW
FERMAN AVE SW
53RD ST SW

NORTH SHORE DR

ENDICOTT AVE SW

32

8

56TH ST SW PARK

Waverly
Lake

4

ELDER AVE

North Fork Crow River

ESTES AVE SW
ESTES AVE SW

ELDER AVE SW

See Page 72
T119N

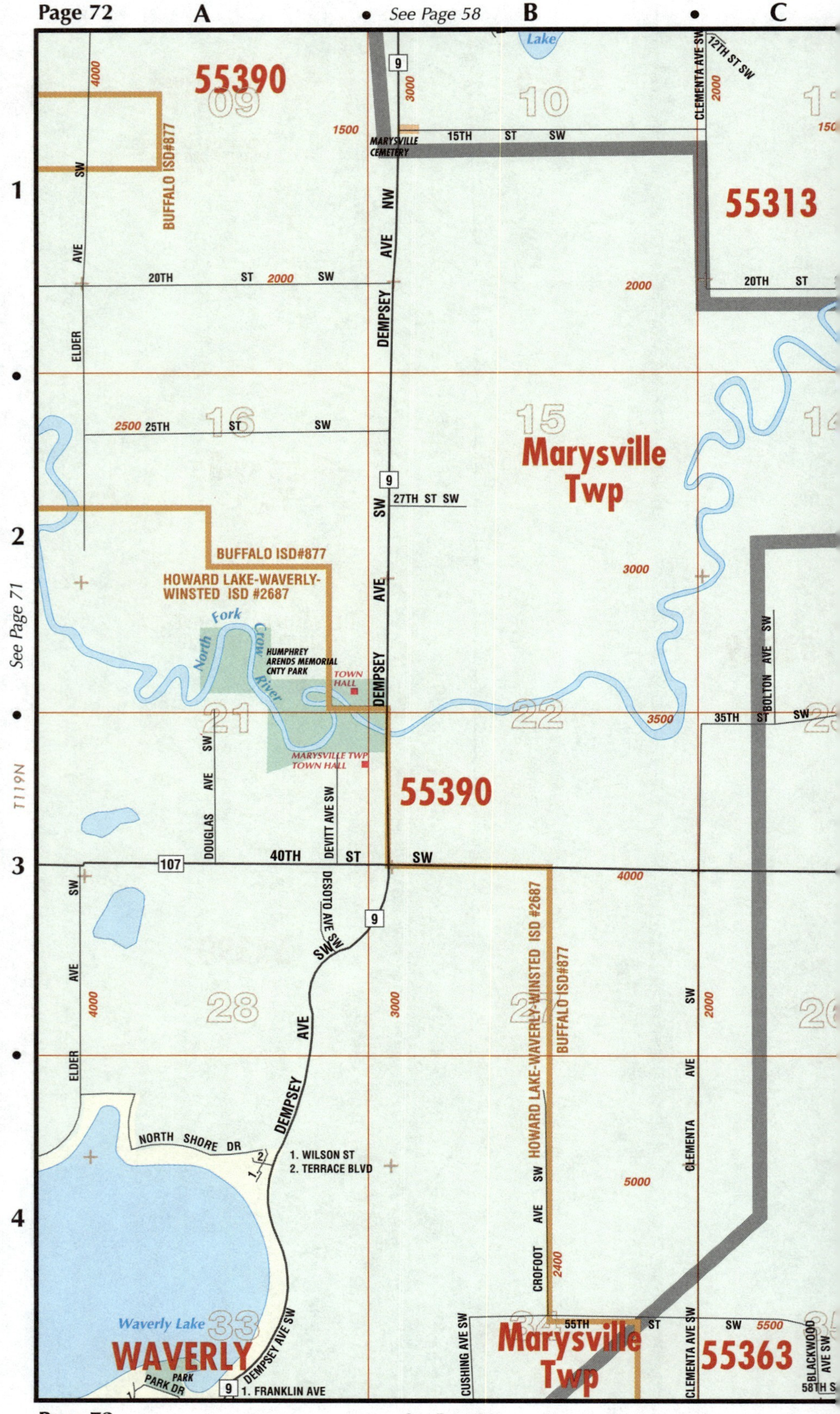

A • *See Page 58* B • C

55390

09

4000

BUFFALO ISD#877

SW

AVE

10

Lake

9

3000

1500

MARYSVILLE
CEMETERY

15TH ST SW

CLEMENTA AVE SW

12TH ST SW

2000

55313

150

1

ELDER

20TH ST 2000 SW

DEMPSEY AVE NW

2000

20TH ST

See Page 71

2500 25TH ST SW

16

9

27TH ST SW

SW

AVE

15

**Marysville
Twp**

14

3000

T119N

2

Buffalo ISD#877

HOWARD LAKE-WAVERLY-
WINSTED ISD #2687

Fork

North

Crow

River

HUMPHREY
ARENDS MEMORIAL
CNTY PARK

TOWN
HALL

SW

AVE

DEMPSEY

21

MARYSVILLE TWP
TOWN HALL

22

3500

BOLTON AVE SW

35TH ST SW

2

DOUGLAS AVE SW

DEVITT AVE SW

55390

DESOTO AVE SW

40TH ST SW

4000

3

107

9

SW

AVE

ELDER

4000

DEMPSEY AVE

28

9

3000

27

HOWARD LAKE-WAVERLY-WINSTED ISD #2687

BUFFALO ISD#877

SW

AVE

SW

CLEMENTA

2000

26

NORTH SHORE DR

2

1. WILSON ST
2. TERRACE BLVD

CROFOOT AVE SW

5000

4

2400

Waverly Lake

33

WAVERLY

DEMPSEY AVE SW

PARK

PARK DR

9

1. FRANKLIN AVE

CUSHING AVE SW

34

55TH ST SW

**Marysville
Twp**

CLEMENTA AVE SW

SW 5500

BLACKWOOD AVE SW

58TH S

55363

3

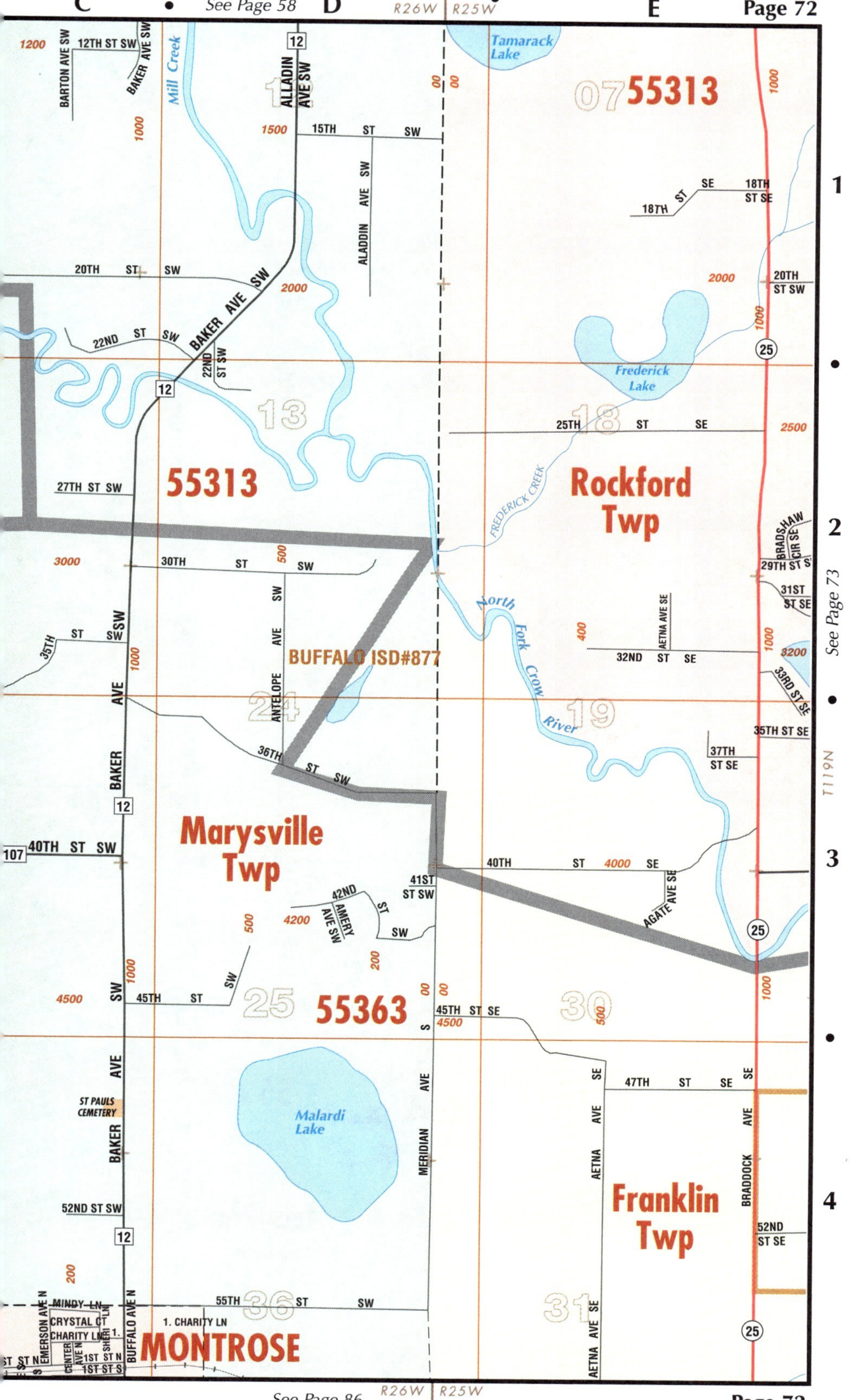

1200 12TH ST SW
BARTON AVE SW
BAKER AVE SW
Mill Creek
ALLADIN AVE SW
12
Tamarack Lake

07 **55313**

1000
1500 15TH ST SW
ALADDIN AVE SW
18TH ST SE 18TH ST SE

1

20TH ST SW
2000
BAKER AVE SW
20TH ST SW
1000
25

22ND ST SW
22ND ST SW
12
Frederick Lake

•

13

Frederick Creek

55313

25TH 18 ST SE 2500

27TH ST SW
Rockford Twp

BRADS-HAW CIR SE

2

3000
30TH ST SW
500
29TH ST SE
31ST ST SE

35TH ST SW
1000
AETNA AVE SE
400
3200
33RD ST SE

BAKER AVE SW
1000
ANTELOPE AVE SW
BUFFALO ISD#877
32ND ST SE

North Fork Crow River

24

35TH ST SE

See Page 73

•

36TH ST SW
19
37TH ST SE

T119N

Marysville Twp

107 40TH ST SW
12
40TH ST 4000 SE

3

42ND ST SW
AMERY AVE SW
41ST ST SW
AGATE AVE SE
25

500
4200
200

4500
1000
45TH ST SW
25
45TH ST SE
4500
30
500
1000

55363

47TH ST SE

•

BAKER AVE N
ST PAULS CEMETERY
Malardi Lake
MERIDIAN AVE
AETNA AVE SE
BRADDOCK AVE SE

52ND ST SW
12
Franklin Twp
52ND ST SE

4

200
MINDY LN
CRYSTAL CT
CHARITY LN
EMERSON AVE N
CENTER AVE N
1ST ST S
55TH ST SW
36
31
AETNA AVE SE
25

MONTROSE
1. CHARITY LN

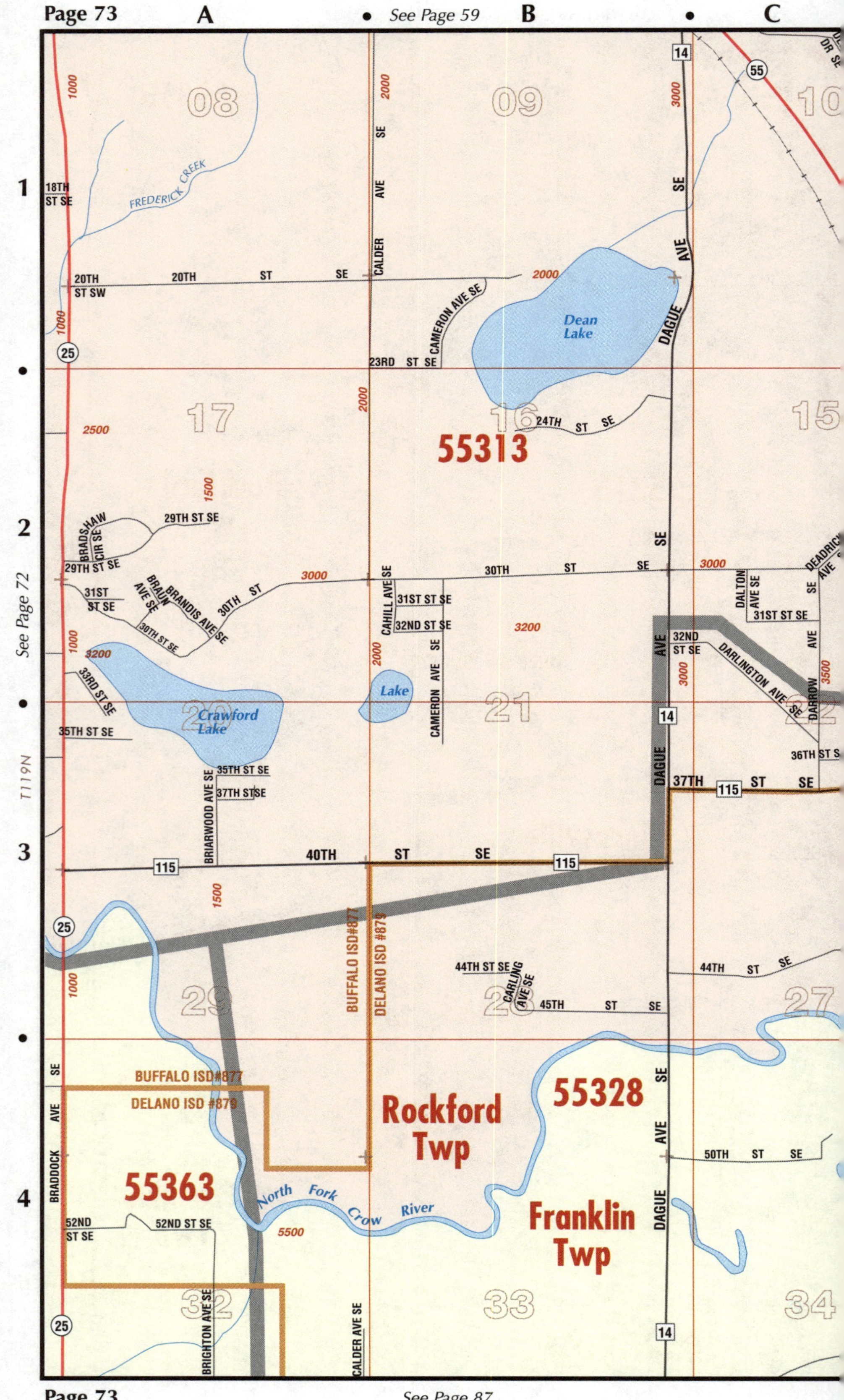

See Page 59

A • B • C

See Page 72

T119N

1000

08

FREDERICK CREEK

18TH ST SE

20TH ST SW
20TH ST SE

25

1000

2500

17

BRADSHAW CIR SE
29TH ST SE

29TH ST SE
31ST ST SE
BRAUN AVE SE
BRANDIS AVE SE
30TH ST
30TH ST SE

1500

3200
33RD ST SE

Crawford Lake
20

35TH ST SE
BRIARWOOD AVE SE
35TH ST SE
37TH ST SE

115

25

1000

1500

115
40TH ST SE

BUFFALO ISD#877
DELANO ISD #879

29

BRADDOCK AVE SE

BUFFALO ISD#877
DELANO ISD #879

55363

52ND ST SE
52ND ST SE

5500

25

BRIGHTON AVE SE

32

2000

CALDER AVE SE

2000

23RD ST SE

CAMERON AVE SE

Dean Lake

2000

24TH ST SE

16

55313

CAHILL AVE SE
30TH ST SE
31ST ST SE
32ND ST SE

2000

Lake

CAMERON AVE SE

3200

21

14

North Fork Crow River

Rockford Twp

44TH ST SE
CARLING AVE SE
45TH ST SE
26

CALDER AVE SE

33

14

14
55

DAGUE AVE SE

3000

SE

SE

DAGUE AVE SE

3000

DALTON AVE SE
31ST ST SE
32ND ST SE
DARLINGTON AVE SE
DARROW

DEADRICK AVE SE

3500

22

36TH ST SE

37TH ST SE
115

115

3000

50TH ST SE

DAGUE AVE SE

55328

Franklin Twp

10

15

27

34

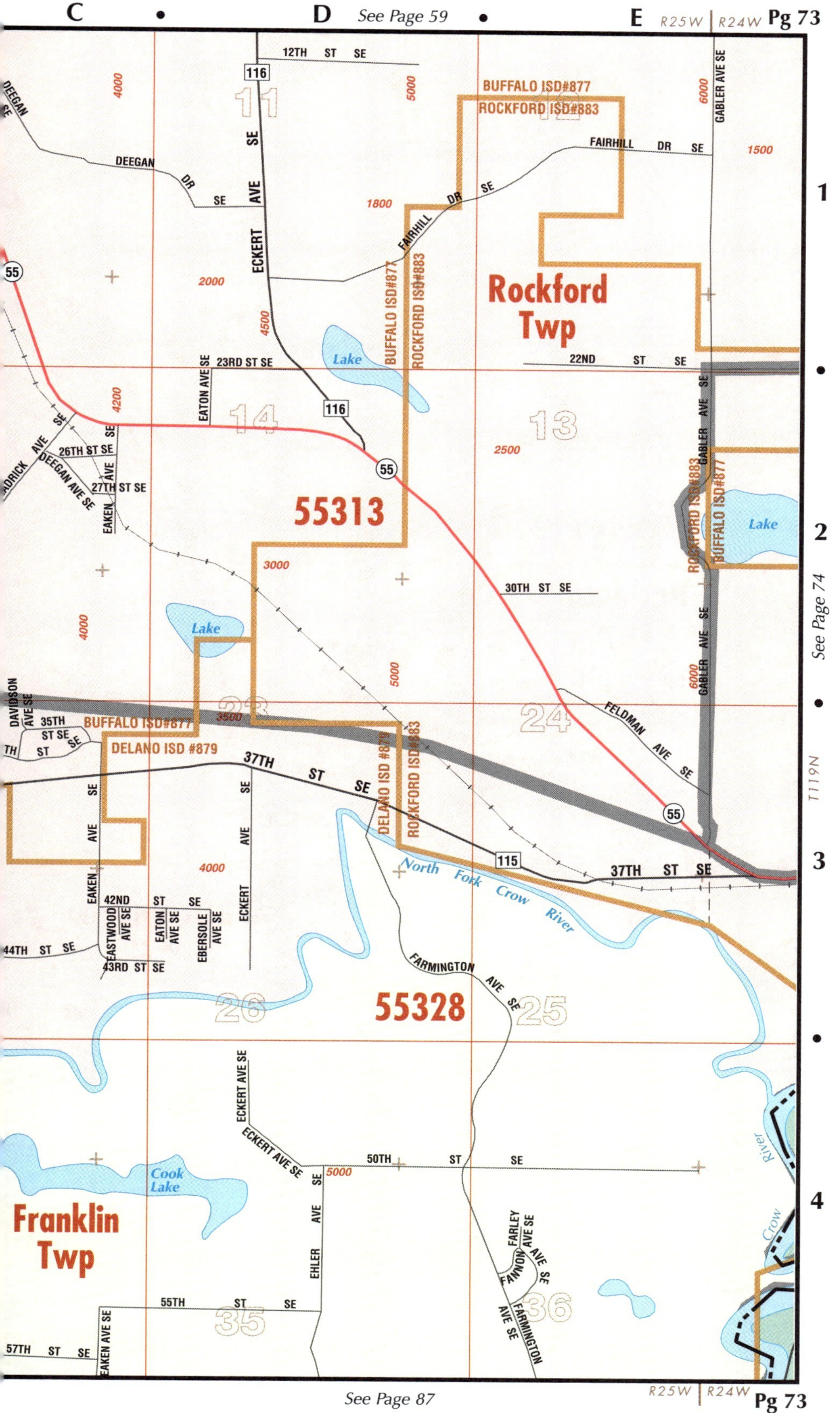

12TH ST SE

116

4000

DEEGAN

5000

6000

GABLER AVE SE

BUFFALO ISD#877
ROCKFORD ISD#883

11

FAIRHILL DR SE

1500

DEEGAN

DR SE

ECKERT AVE SE

1800

FAIRHILL DR SE

1

55

2000

4500

Lake

BUFFALO ISD#877
ROCKFORD ISD#883

Rockford Twp

22ND ST SE

23RD ST SE

4200

EATON AVE SE

14

116

55

13

2500

ROCKFORD ISD#883

GABLER AVE SE

BUFFALO ISD#877

Lake

2

KEDRICK AVE SE

26TH ST SE

DEEGAN AVE SE

EAKEN AVE SE

27TH ST SE

55313

3000

30TH ST SE

4000

Lake

5000

6000

GABLER AVE SE

See Page 74

DAVIDSON AVE SE

35TH ST SE

3500

BUFFALO ISD#877

23

24

FELDMAN AVE SE

•

TH ST SE

DELANO ISD #879

37TH ST SE

EAKEN AVE SE

AVE SE

ECKERT AVE SE

DELANO ISD #879
ROCKFORD ISD#883

115

North Fork Crow River

37TH ST SE

55

3

4000

42ND ST SE

EASTWOOD AVE SE

EATON AVE SE

EBERSOLE AVE SE

ECKERT AVE SE

FARMINGTON AVE SE

55328

25

T119N

44TH ST SE

43RD ST SE

26

ECKERT AVE SE

•

ECKERT AVE SE

50TH ST SE

5000

EHLER AVE SE

Cook Lake

FARLEY AVE SE

FARMON AVE SE

River

Crow

4

Franklin Twp

55TH ST SE

35

FARMINGTON AVE SE

36

EAKEN AVE SE

57TH ST SE

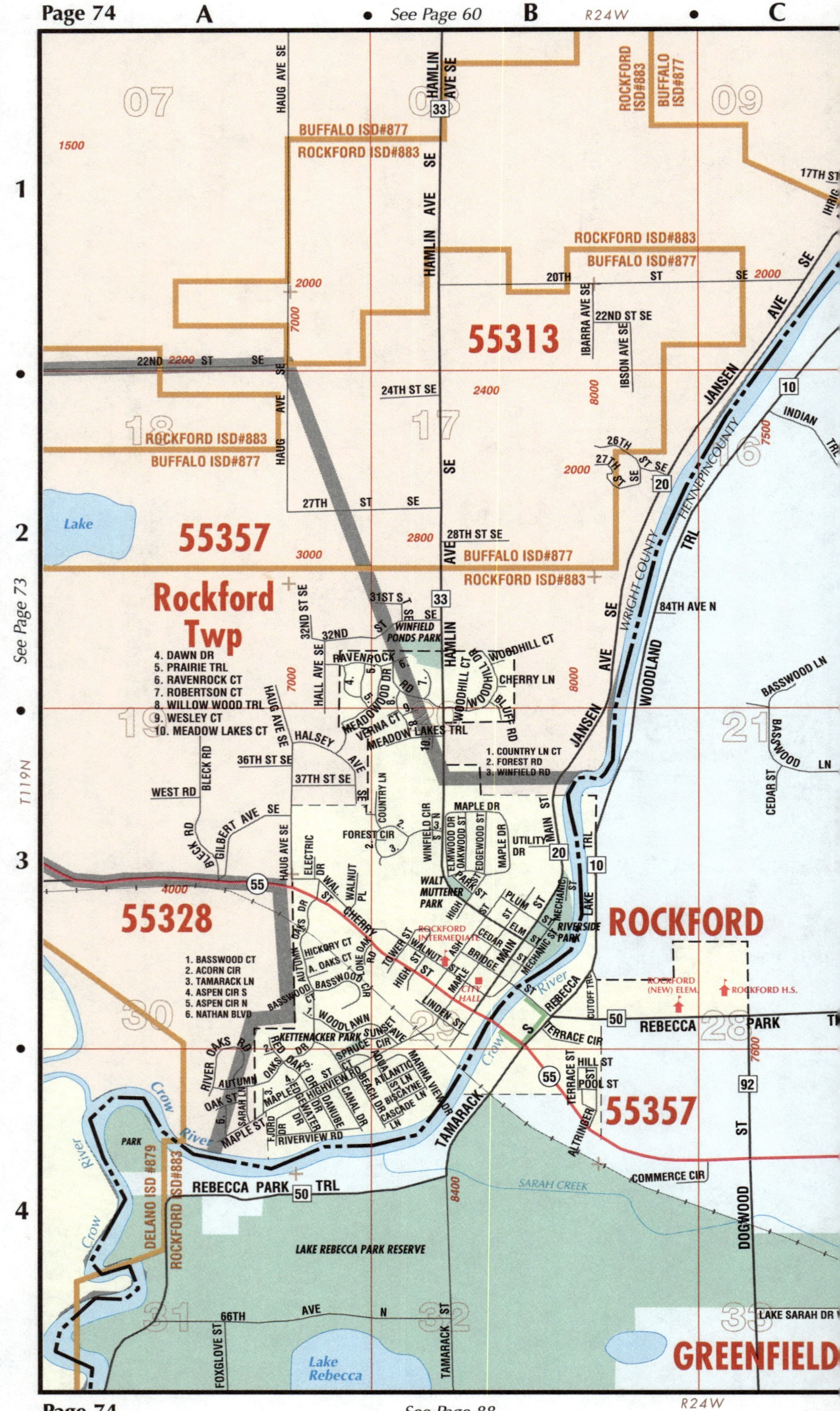

1
2
3
4
07
09
17
18
16
19
21
30
29
28
31
32
33
1500
2000
2200
2400
2800
3000
4000
7000
7500
7600
8000
8400
HAUG AVE SE
HAMLIN AVE SE
BUFFALO ISD#877
ROCKFORD ISD#883
17TH ST
20TH ST SE
22ND ST SE
22ND 2200 ST SE
24TH ST SE
26TH ST SE
27TH ST SE
28TH ST SE
IBARRA AVE SE
IBSON AVE SE
JANSEN AVE SE
INDIAN TRL
55313
55357
55328
Lake
Rockford Twp
4. DAWN DR
5. PRAIRIE TRL
6. RAVENROCK CT
7. ROBERTSON CT
8. WILLOW WOOD TRL
9. WESLEY CT
10. MEADOW LAKES CT
31ST ST SE
32ND ST SE
32ND
WINFIELD PONDS PARK
RAVENROCK
MEADOWOOD DR
VERNA CT
MEADOW LAKES TRL
WOODHILL CT
CHERRY LN
BLUFF RD
HALL AVE SE
HALSEY AVE
36TH ST SE
37TH ST SE
BLECK RD
WEST RD
GILBERT AVE SE
WRIGHT COUNTY
HENNEPIN COUNTY
84TH AVE N
WOODLAND TRL
BASSWOOD LN
CEDAR ST
1. COUNTRY LN CT
2. FOREST RD
3. WINFIELD RD
COUNTRY LN
FOREST CIR
WINFIELD CIR S
MAPLE DR
ELMWOOD DR
OAKWOOD ST
EDGEWOOD ST
UTILITY DR
MAIN ST
WALT MUTTERER PARK
ELECTRIC DR
WALNUT PL
CHERRY ST
PLUM ST
ELM ST
MECHANIC ST
RIVERSIDE PARK
LAKE ST
ROCKFORD
ROCKFORD INTERMEDIATE
CITY HALL
BRIDGE ST
CEDAR ST
ASH ST
1. BASSWOOD CT
2. ACORN CIR
3. TAMARACK LN
4. ASPEN CIR S
5. ASPEN CIR N
6. NATHAN BLVD
AUTUMN OAKS DR
HICKORY CT
A. OAKS CT
LONE OAK CIR
BASSWOOD
TOWER ST
HIGH ST
LINDEN ST
WOODLAWN
SUNSET AVE
KETTENACKER PARK
SPRUCE CIR
RIVER OAKS RD
RED OAK DR
OAK ST
HIGHVIEW RD
EDGEWATER DR
DANUBE
CANAL DR
BEACH DR
ATLANTIC LN
BISCAYNE LN
CASCADE LN
MARINA VIEW DR
SARAH LN
MAPLE ST
FJORD DR
RIVERVIEW RD
TAMARACK
REBECCA PARK TRL
ROCKFORD (NEW) ELEM.
ROCKFORD H.S.
CUTOFF TRL
TERRACE CIR
TERRACE ST
HILL ST
POOL ST
ALTRINGER
COMMERCE CIR
DOGWOOD ST
Crow River
PARK
DELANO ISD #879
ROCKFORD ISD #883
SARAH CREEK
LAKE REBECCA PARK RESERVE
66TH AVE N
FOXGLOVE ST
TAMARACK ST
Lake Rebecca
LAKE SARAH DR
GREENFIELD
T119N

See Page 73

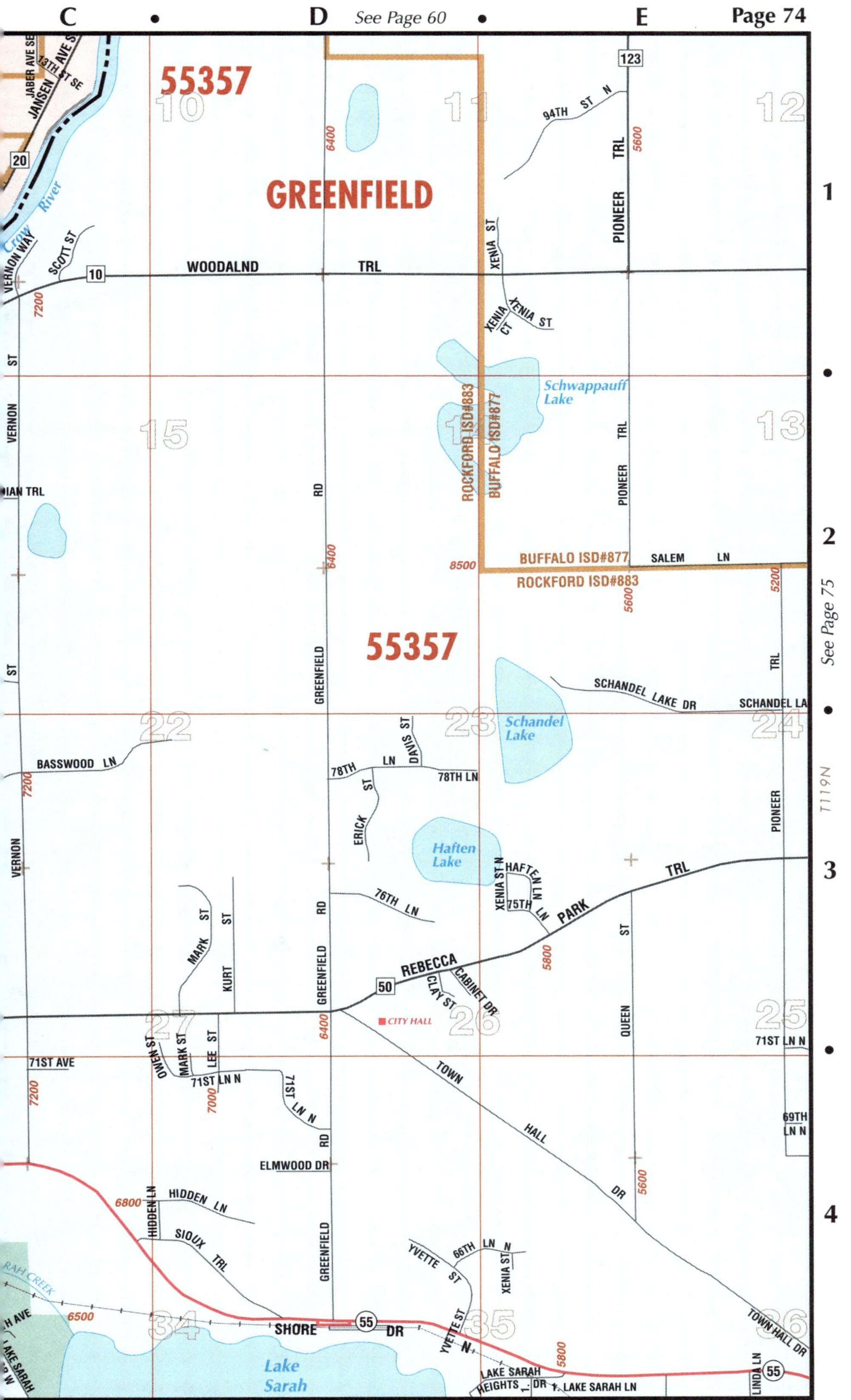

55357

GREENFIELD

55357

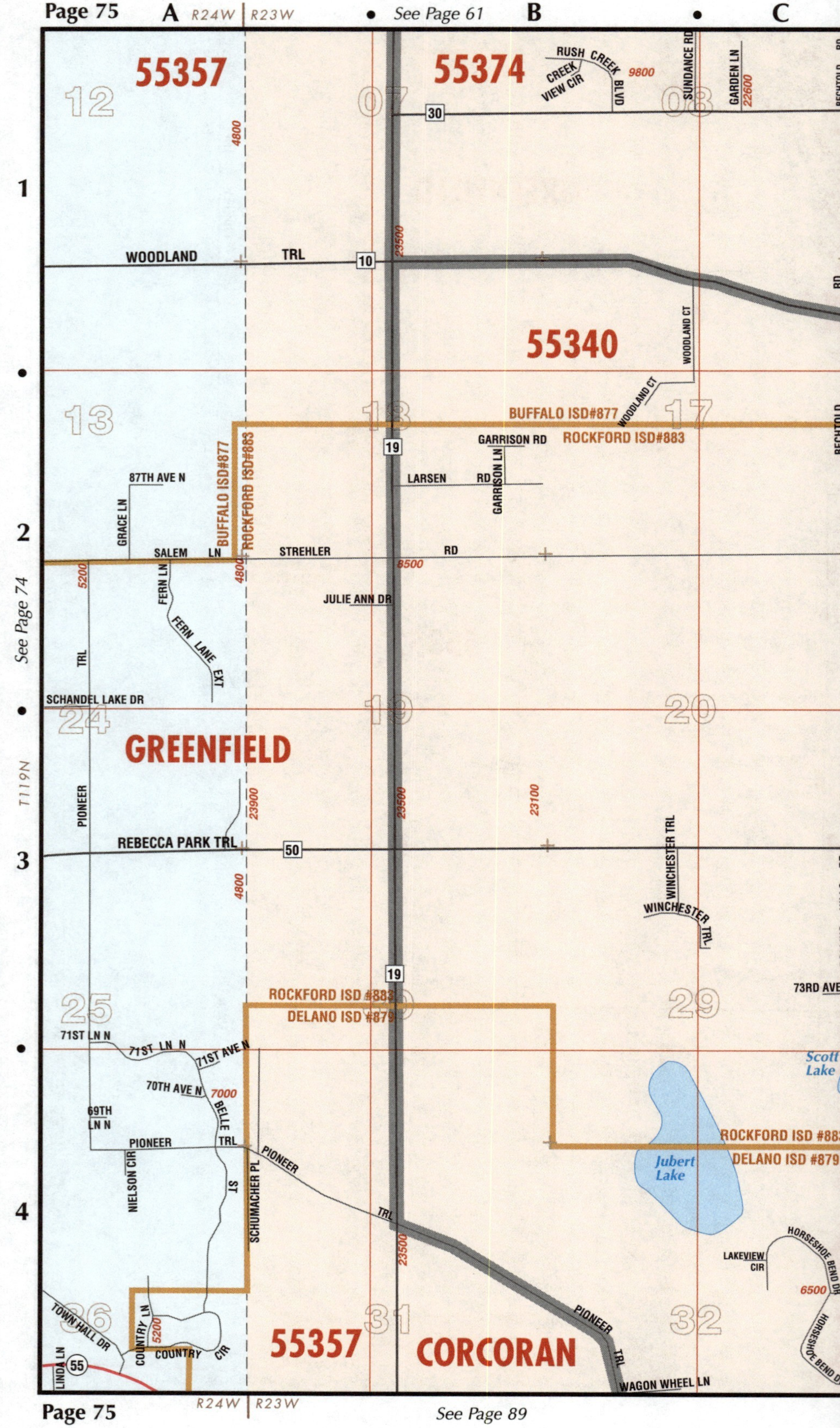

A R24W | R23W • *See Page 61* B • C

55357

12

55374

RUSH CREEK

CREEK VIEW CIR

CREEK BLVD

9800

SUNDANCE RD

GARDEN LN

22600

BECHTOLD RD

30

1

4800

WOODLAND TRL

10

23500

55340

WOODLAND CT

RD

•

13

BUFFALO ISD#877

18

BUFFALO ISD#877

ROCKFORD ISD#883

WOODLAND CT

17

BECHTOLD

87TH AVE N

GRACE LN

SALEM LN

FERN LN

BUFFALO ISD#877

ROCKFORD ISD#883

19

LARSEN RD

GARRISON RD

GARRISON LN

2

5200

4800

STREHLER RD

8500

+

See Page 74

FERN LANE EXT

TRL

JULIE ANN DR

SCHANDEL LAKE DR

•

24

19

20

GREENFIELD

PIONEER

23900

23500

23100

WINCHESTER TRL

WINCHESTER TRL

3

REBECCA PARK TRL

50

+

T119N

4800

19

73RD AVE

RD

25

ROCKFORD ISD #883

DELANO ISD #879

29

•

71ST LN N

71ST LN N

71ST AVE N

70TH AVE N

7000

BELLE TRL

Scott Lake

69TH LN N

PIONEER

NIELSON CIR

TRL

SCHUMACHER PL

SCHUMACHER ST

PIONEER TRL

PIONEER TRL

ROCKFORD ISD #883

DELANO ISD #879

Jubert Lake

4

23500

LAKEVIEW CIR

HORSESHOE BEND DR

6500

HORSESHOE BEND DR

TOWN HALL DR

36

COUNTRY LN

5200

COUNTRY CIR

31

55357

CORCORAN

PIONEER TRL

32

LINDA LN

55

WAGON WHEEL LN

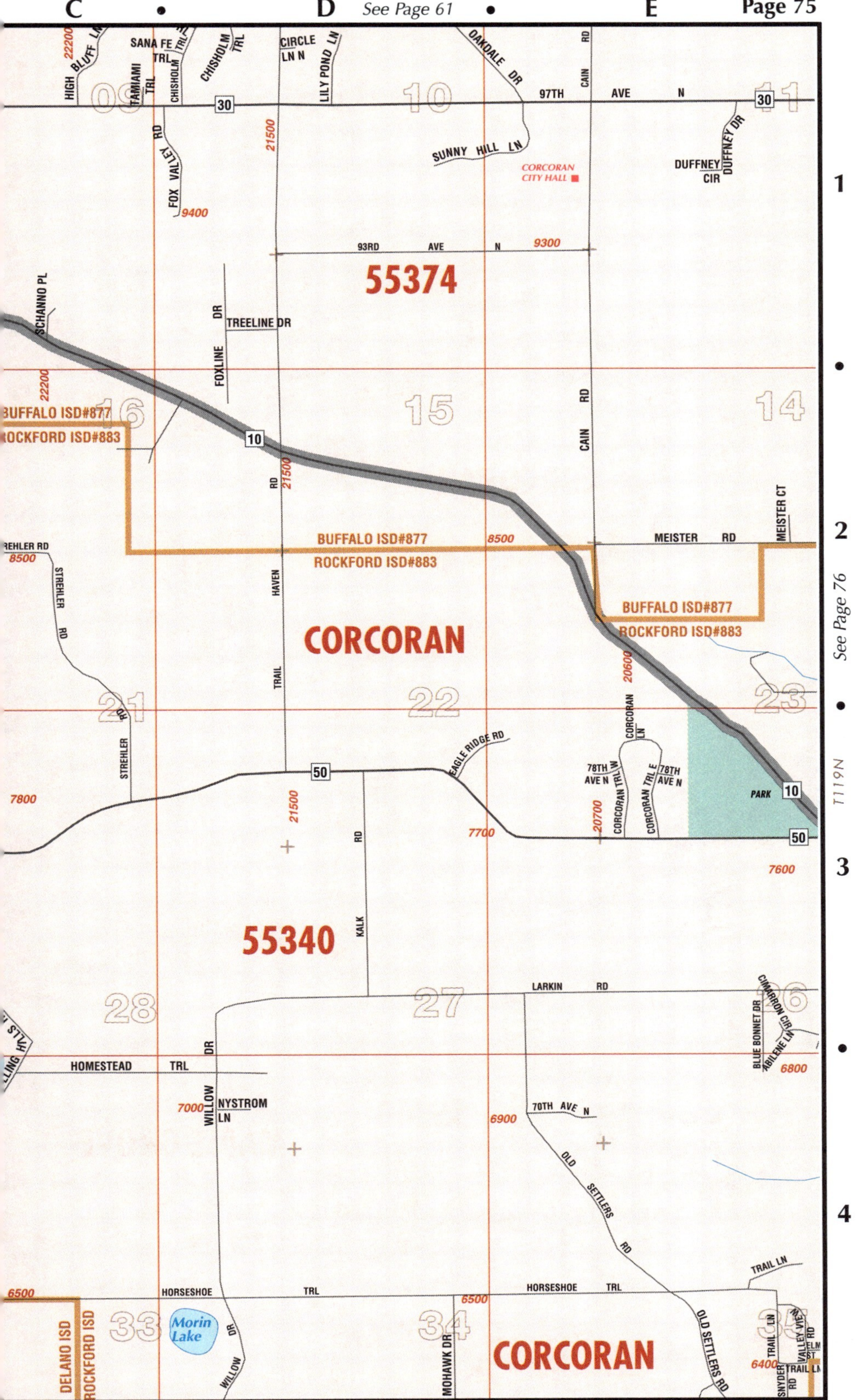
55374
CORCORAN
55340
CORCORAN
BUFFALO ISD#877
ROCKFORD ISD#883
DELANO ISD
ROCKFORD ISD
CORCORAN CITY HALL
97TH AVE N
93RD AVE N
MEISTER RD
LARKIN RD
HOMESTEAD TRL
HORSESHOE TRL
CAIN RD
HAVEN TRAIL RD
KALK RD
WILLOW DR
OLD SETTLERS RD
Morin Lake
PARK
T119N
1
2
3
4

See Page 76

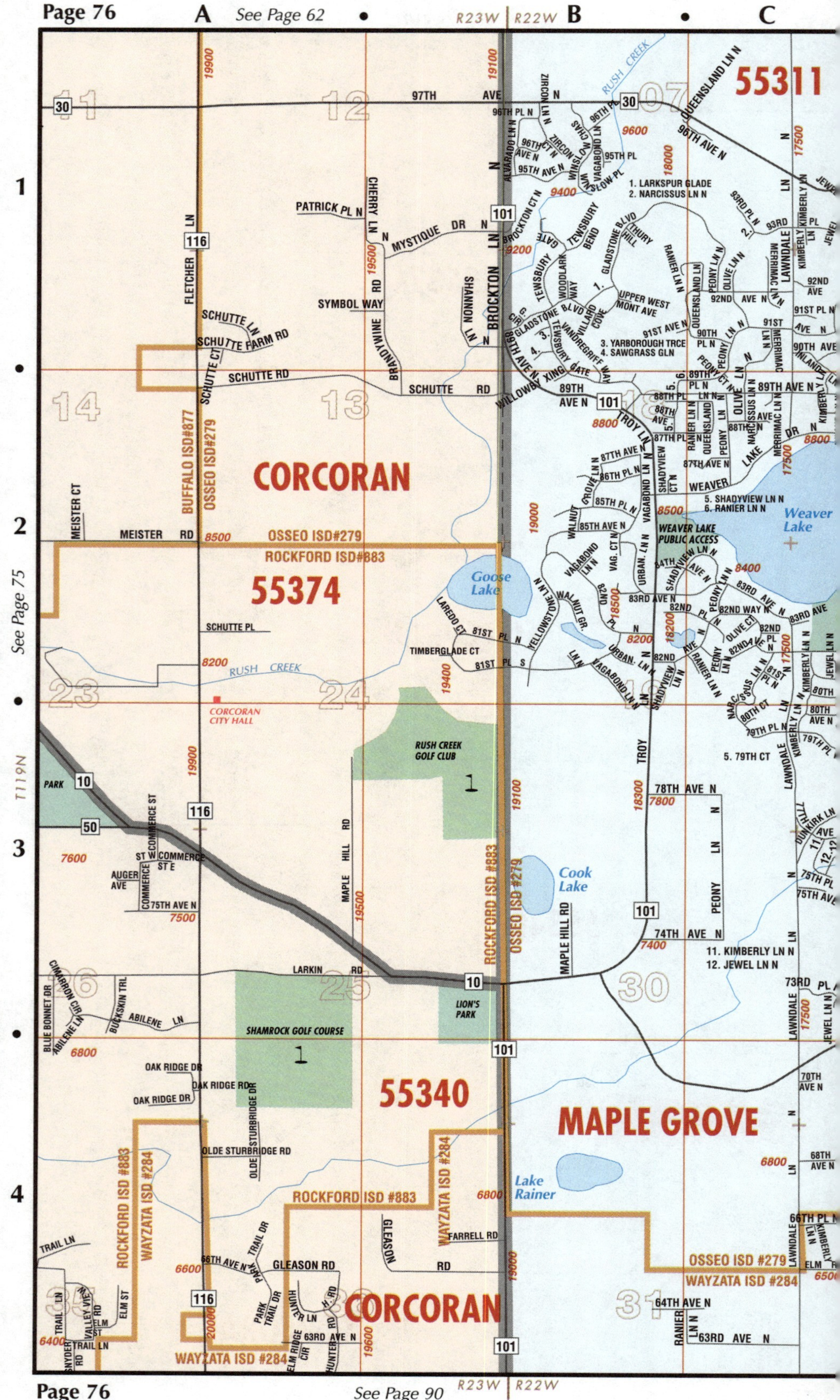

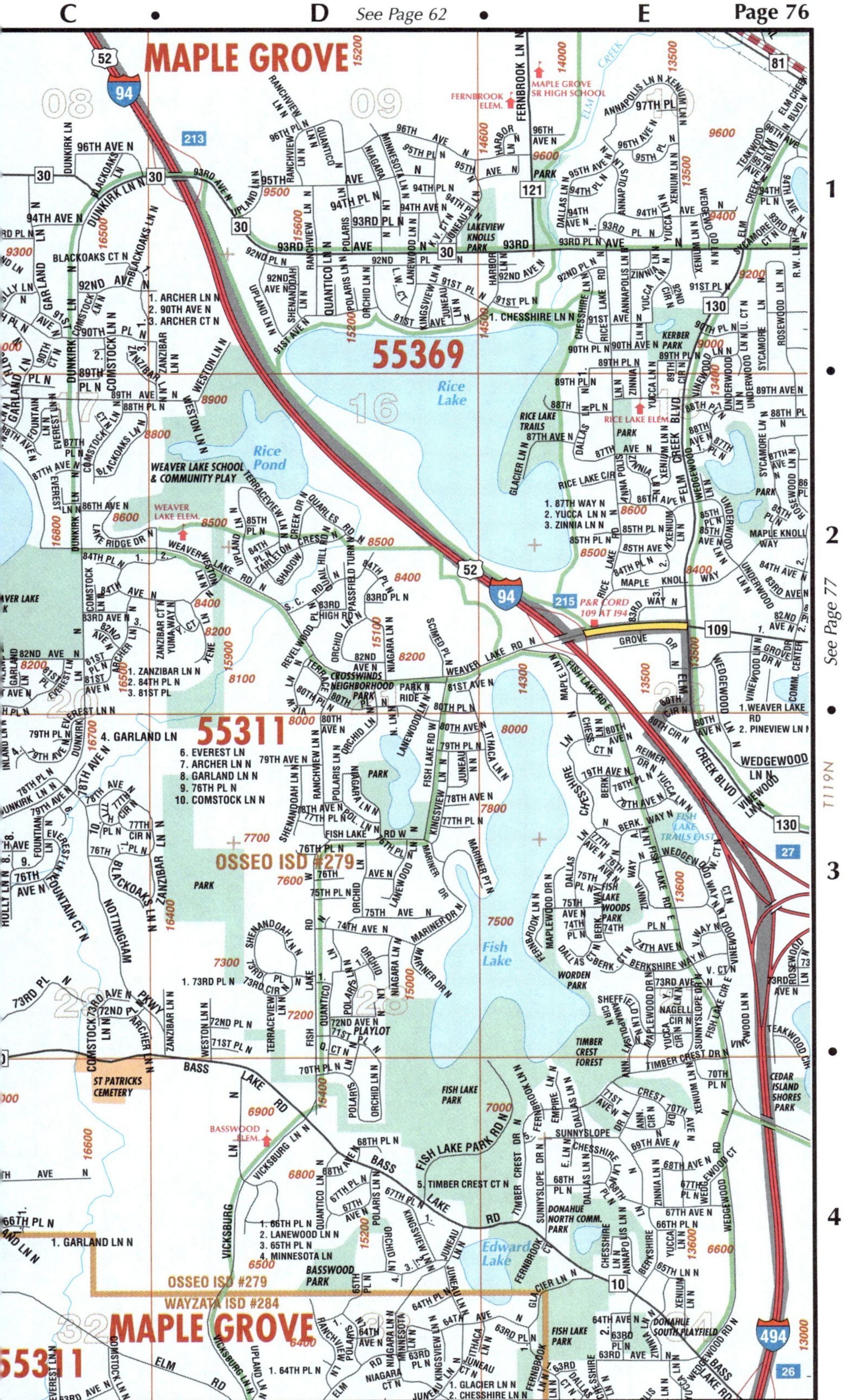

MAPLE GROVE

55369

55311

OSSEO ISD #279

OSSEO ISD #279
WAYZATA ISD #284

MAPLE GROVE

55311

See Page 90

See Page 77

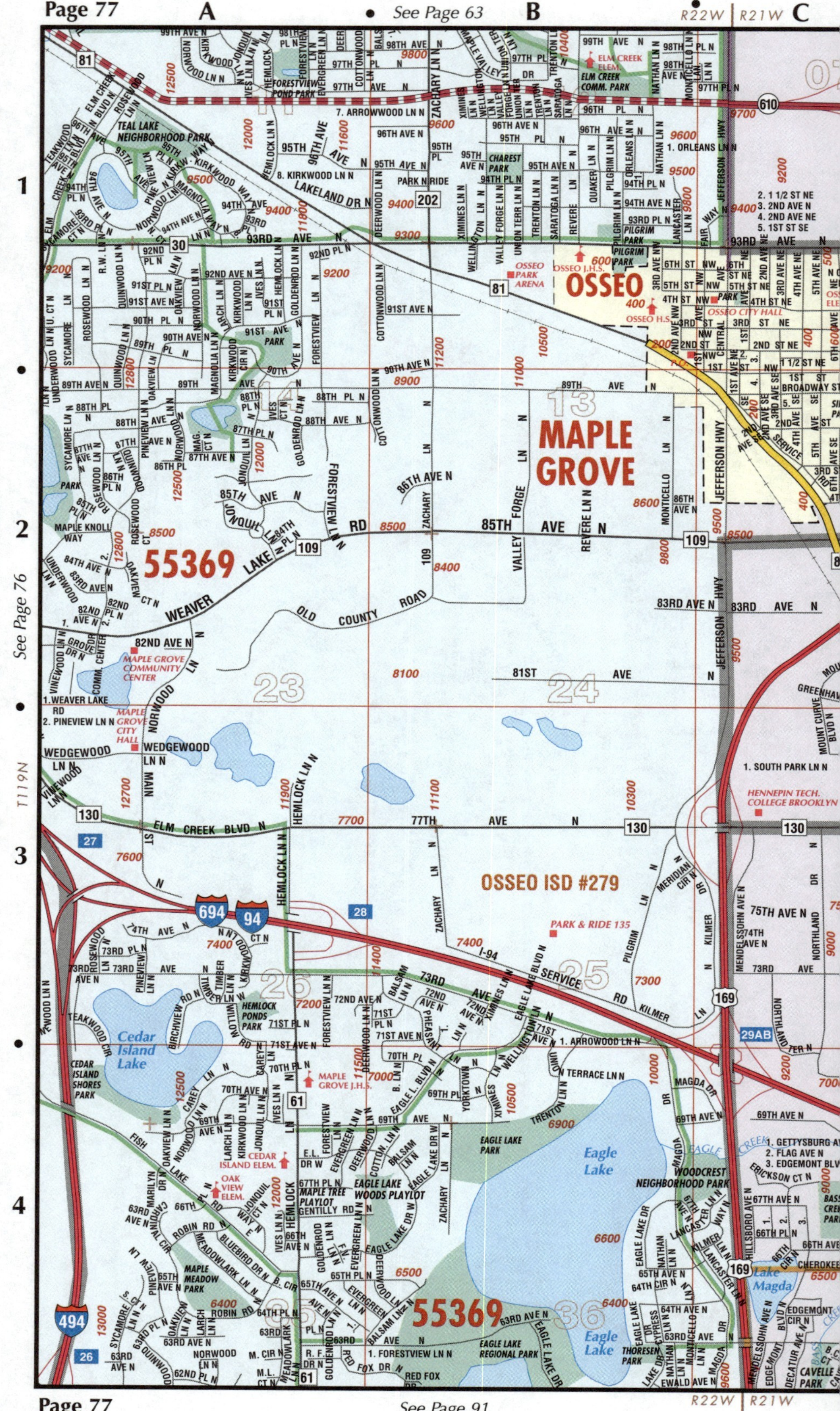
OSSEO
MAPLE GROVE
55369
OSSEO ISD #279
Cedar Island Lake
Eagle Lake
Lake Magda
TEAL LAKE NEIGHBORHOOD PARK
ELM CREEK COMM. PARK
ELM CREEK ELEM.
FORESTVIEW POND PARK
CHAREST PARK
PARK N RIDE
OSSEO PARK ARENA
OSSEO J.H.S.
OSSEO H.S.
OSSEO CITY HALL
PILGRIM PARK
MAPLE GROVE COMMUNITY CENTER
MAPLE GROVE CITY HALL
MAPLE KNOLL WAY
WEAVER LAKE RD
OLD COUNTY ROAD
85TH AVE N
93RD AVE
89TH AVE
81ST AVE N
77TH AVE N
ELM CREEK BLVD N
LAKELAND DR N
JEFFERSON HWY
HENNEPIN TECH. COLLEGE BROOKLYN
PARK & RIDE 135
I-94 SERVICE RD
HEMLOCK PONDS PARK
CEDAR ISLAND SHORES PARK
MAPLE GROVE J.H.S.
CEDAR ISLAND ELEM.
OAK VIEW ELEM.
MAPLE TREE PLAYLOT
EAGLE LAKE WOODS PLAYLOT
EAGLE LAKE PARK
WOODCREST NEIGHBORHOOD PARK
MAPLE MEADOW PARK
EAGLE LAKE REGIONAL PARK
THORESEN PARK
BASS CREEK PARK
CAVELLE PARK
T119N

See Page 76

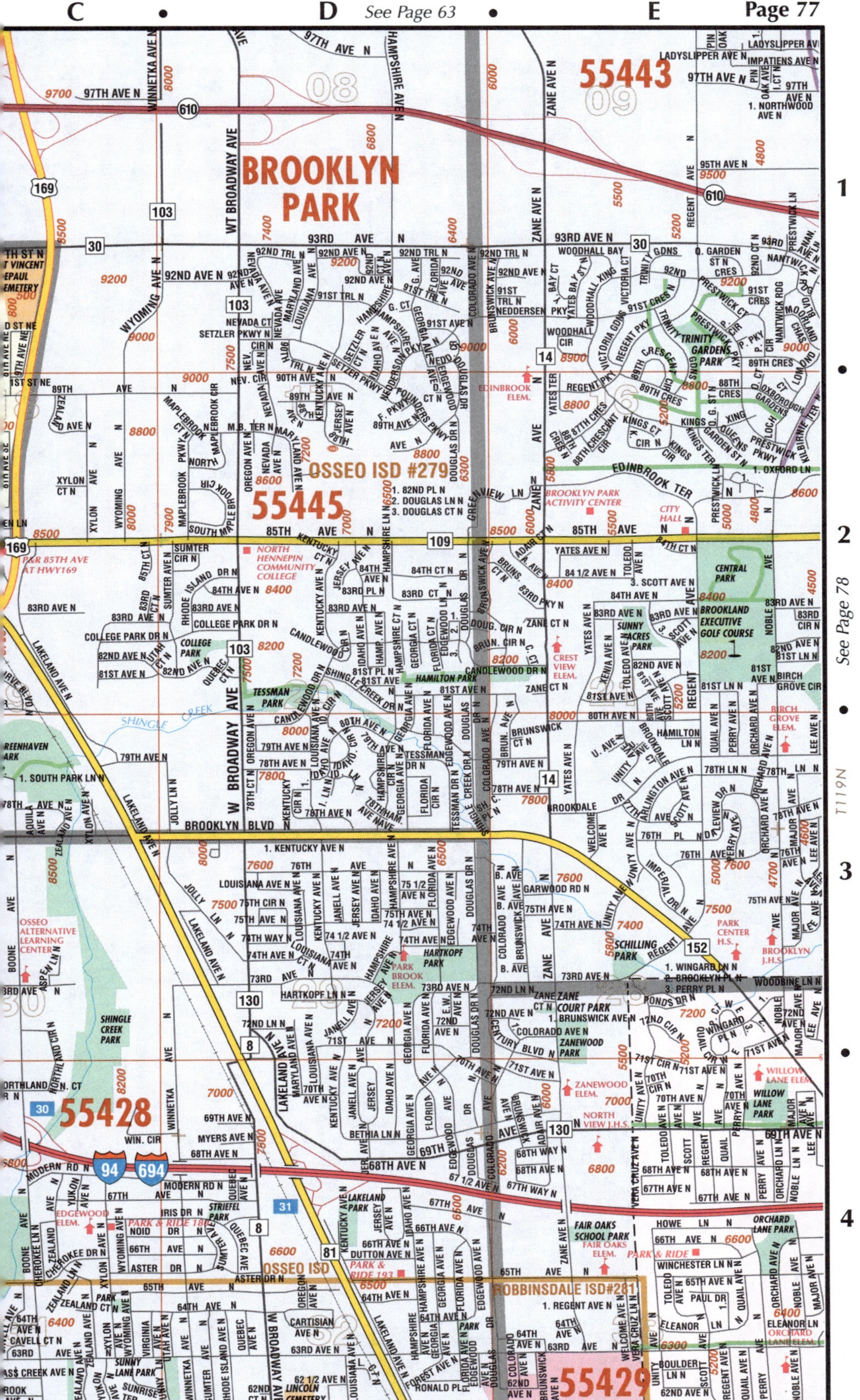
BROOKLYN PARK
55443
55445
55428
55429
OSSEO ISD #279
ROBBINSDALE ISD#281
See Page 78

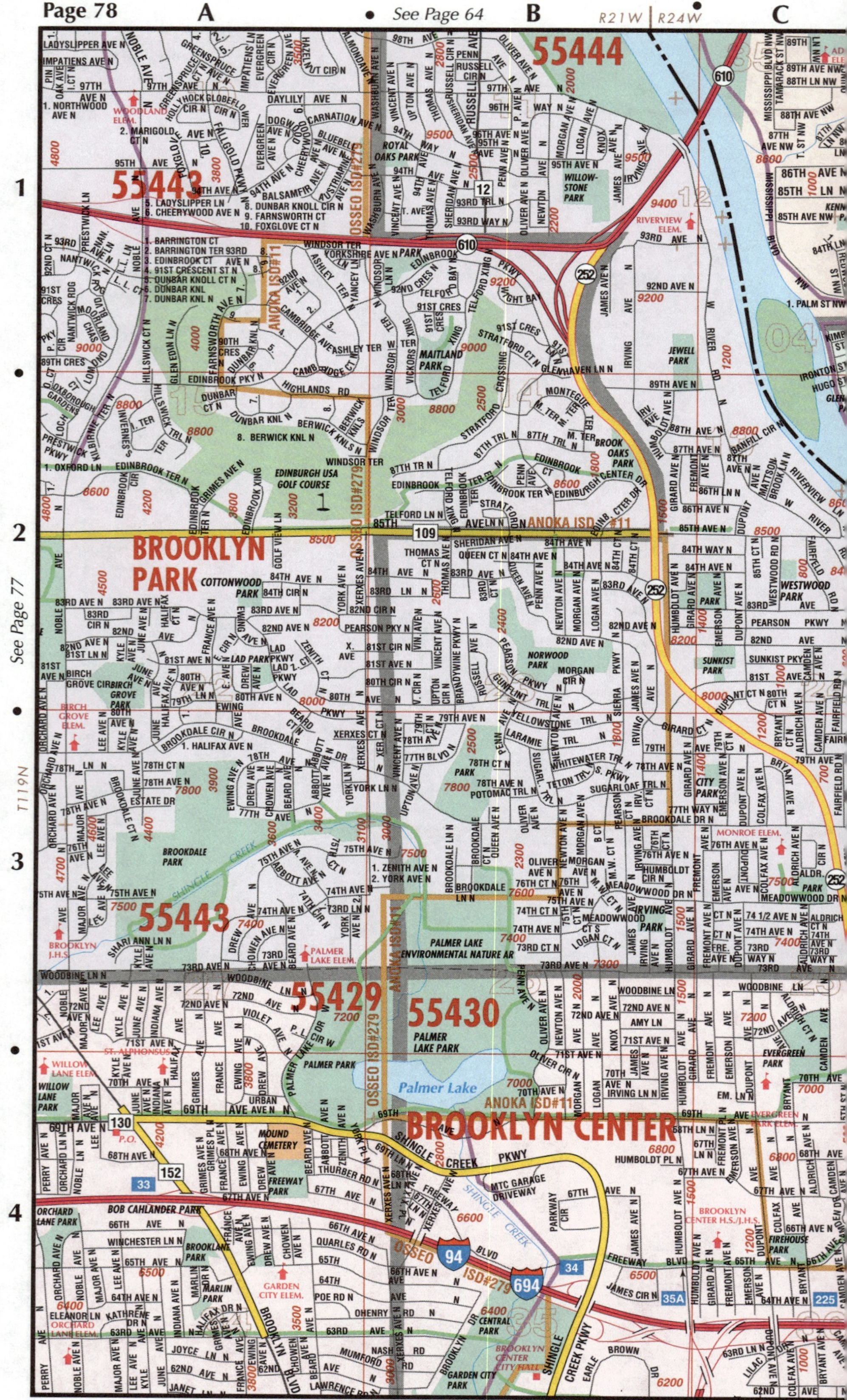

See Page 64

See Page 92

See Page 77

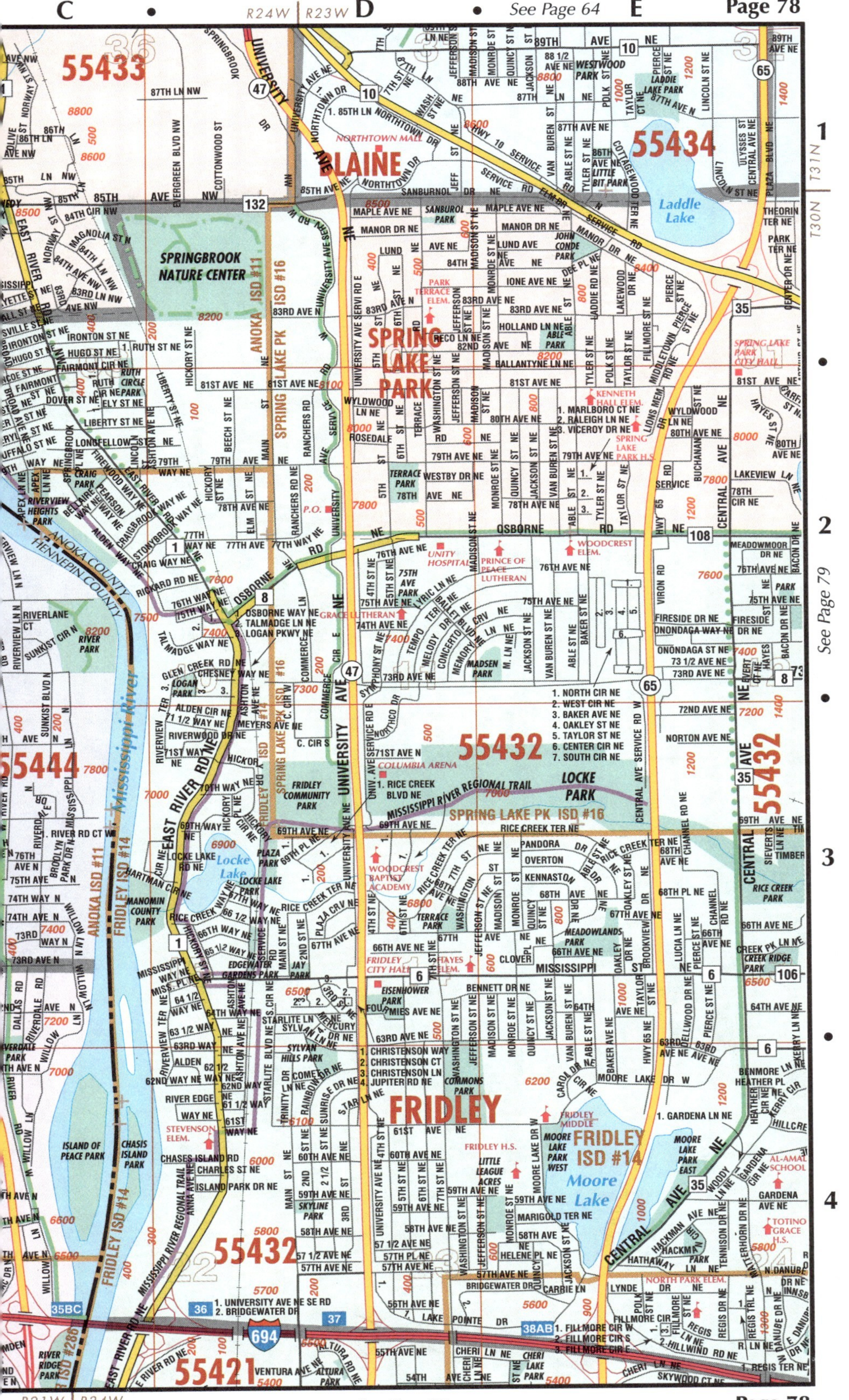

55433

BLAINE

55434

Laddle Lake

SPRINGBROOK NATURE CENTER

ANOKA ISD #11

SPRING LAKE PARK

SPRING LAKE PK

See Page 79

55444

ANOKA COUNTY HENNEPIN COUNTY

Mississippi River

UNITY HOSPITAL

PRINCE OF PEACE LUTHERAN

55432

LOCKE PARK

SPRING LAKE PK ISD #16

ANOKA ISD #11 FRIDLEY ISD #14

55432

FRIDLEY ISD #14

FRIDLEY

Moore Lake

55432

ISLAND OF PEACE PARK

694

55421

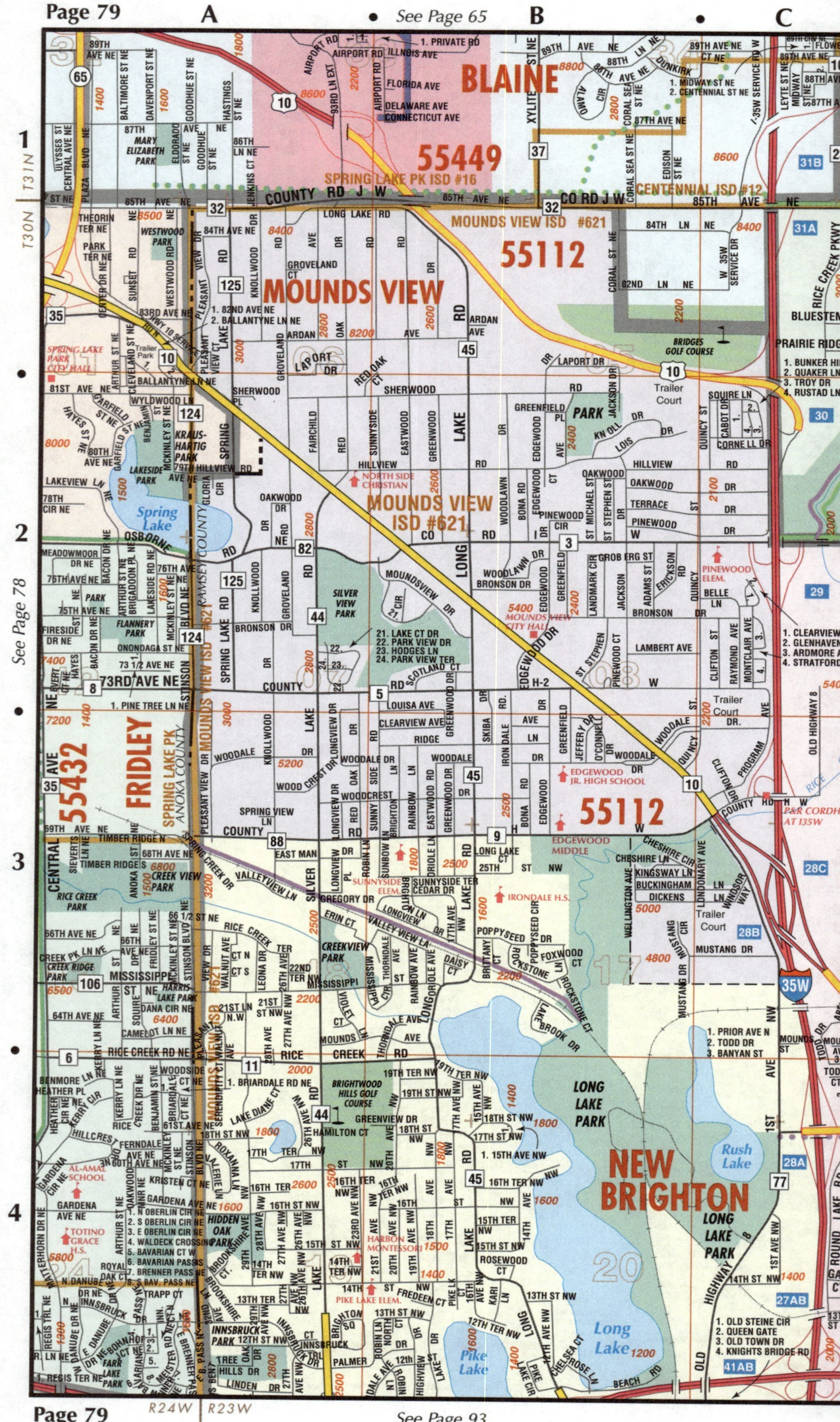

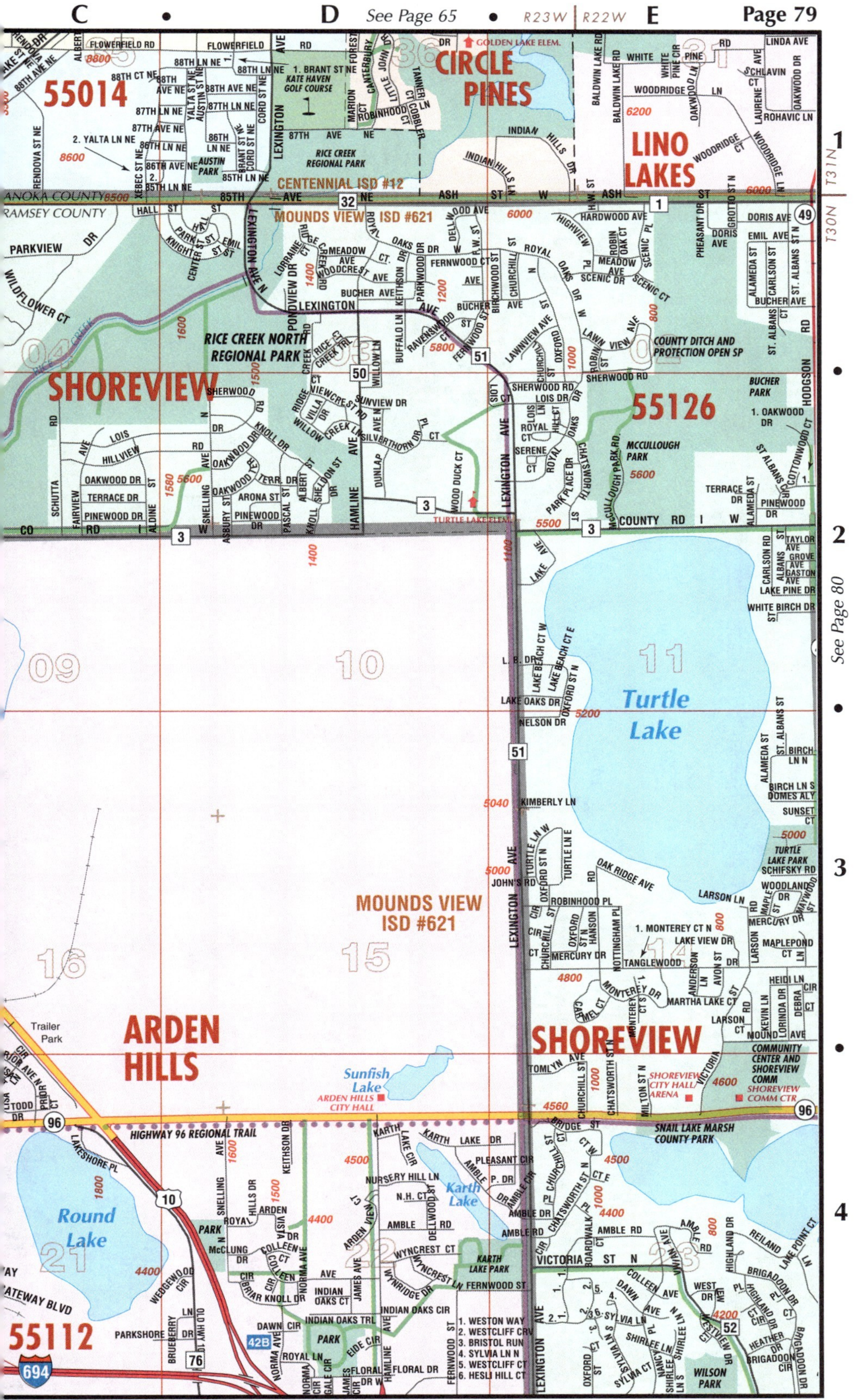

55014
CIRCLE PINES
LINO LAKES
GOLDEN LAKE ELEM.
KATE HAVEN GOLF COURSE
RICE CREEK REGIONAL PARK
CENTENNIAL ISD #12
ANOKA COUNTY
RAMSEY COUNTY
MOUNDS VIEW ISD #621
85TH AVE NE
ASH ST W
PARKVIEW DR
WILDFLOWER CT
RICE CREEK NORTH REGIONAL PARK
SHOREVIEW
55126
COUNTY DITCH AND PROTECTION OPEN SP
BUCHER PARK
McCULLOUGH PARK
SHERWOOD RD
LEXINGTON AVE
HODGSON RD
TURTLE LAKE ELEM.
COUNTY RD I W
CO RD I W
09
10
11
Turtle Lake
See Page 80
T31N
T30N
1
2
3
4
KIMBERLY LN
NELSON DR
LAKE OAKS DR
OAK RIDGE AVE
LARSON LN
MOUNDS VIEW ISD #621
16
15
14
ARDEN HILLS
Trailer Park
Sunfish Lake
ARDEN HILLS CITY HALL
SHOREVIEW
SHOREVIEW CITY HALL ARENA
COMMUNITY CENTER AND SHOREVIEW COMM
SHOREVIEW COMM CTR
SNAIL LAKE MARSH COUNTY PARK
HIGHWAY 96 REGIONAL TRAIL
Round Lake
Karth Lake
KARTH LAKE PARK
VICTORIA ST N
21
22
23
GATEWAY BLVD
55112
PARKSHORE DR
WILSON PARK
1. WESTON WAY
2. WESTCLIFF CRV
3. BRISTOL RUN
4. SYLVIA LN N
5. WESTCLIFF CT
6. HESLI HILL CT

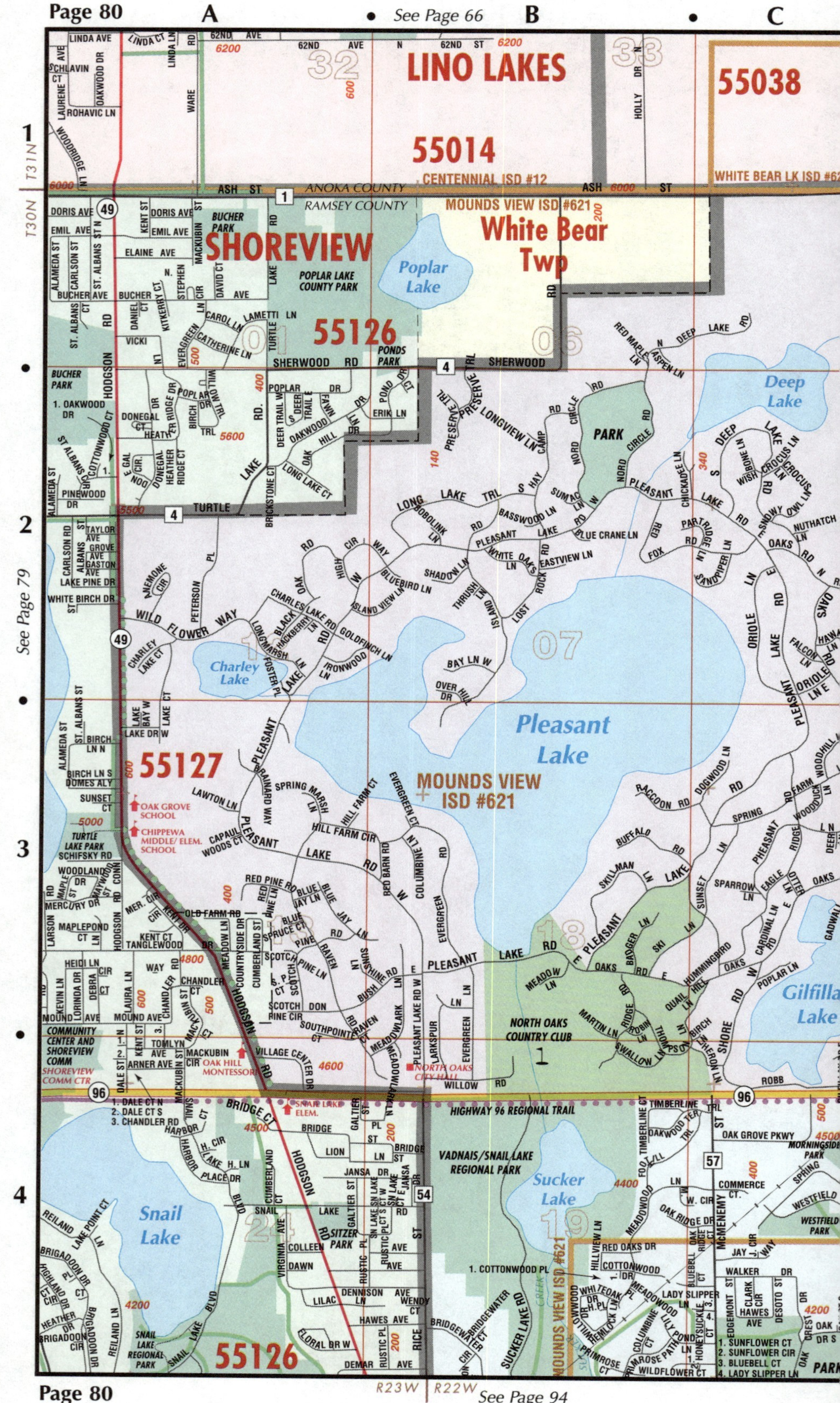

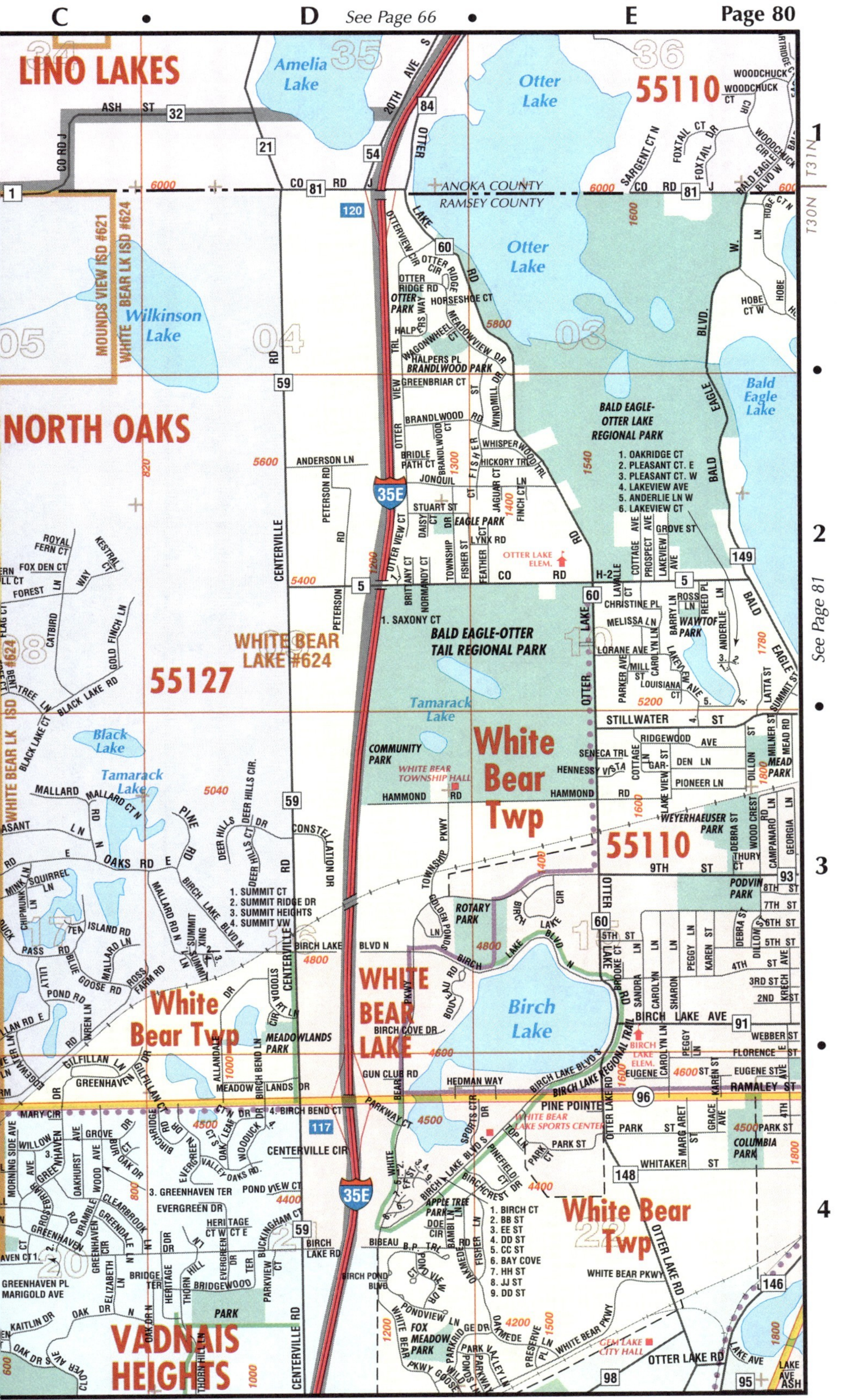

C • D *See Page 66* • E

LINO LAKES

55110

Amelia Lake

Otter Lake

ASH ST 32

CO RD J

21 54

84

CO 81 RD J

ANOKA COUNTY
RAMSEY COUNTY

WOODCHUCK CT
WOODCHUCK CT N

FOXTAIL CT
FOXTAIL DR

BALD EAGLE BLVD W

1

MOUNDS VIEW ISD #621
WHITE BEAR LK ISD #624

Wilkinson Lake

Otter Lake

Bald Eagle Lake

NORTH OAKS

ANDERSON LN

PETERSON RD

CENTERVILLE RD

BALD EAGLE-OTTER LAKE REGIONAL PARK

1. OAKRIDGE CT
2. PLEASANT CT E
3. PLEASANT CT W
4. LAKEVIEW AVE
5. ANDERLIE LN W
6. LAKEVIEW CT

OTTER LAKE ELEM.

149

2

55127

WHITE BEAR LAKE #624

BALD EAGLE-OTTER TAIL REGIONAL PARK

1. SAXONY CT

Tamarack Lake

Black Lake

Tamarack Lake

COMMUNITY PARK

WHITE BEAR TOWNSHIP HALL

STILLWATER ST

RIDGEWOOD AVE

White Bear Twp

MEAD PARK

3

White Bear Twp

1. SUMMIT CT
2. SUMMIT RIDGE DR
3. SUMMIT HEIGHTS
4. SUMMIT VW

CONSTELLATION DR

ROTARY PARK

WEYERHAEUSER PARK

55110

9TH ST

PODVIN PARK

93

60

WHITE BEAR LAKE

Birch Lake

91

MEADOWLANDS PARK

BIRCH LAKE ELEM.

GUN CLUB RD

HEDMAN WAY

96

PINE POINTE

WHITE BEAR LAKE SPORTS CENTER

RAMALEY ST

EUGENE ST E

117

CENTERVILLE CIR

3. GREENHAVEN TER

COLUMBIA PARK

148

35E

1. BIRCH CT
2. BB ST
3. EE ST
4. DD ST
5. CC ST
6. BAY COVE
7. HH ST
8. JJ ST
9. DD ST

White Bear Twp

146

VADNAIS HEIGHTS

GEM LAKE CITY HALL

98

95

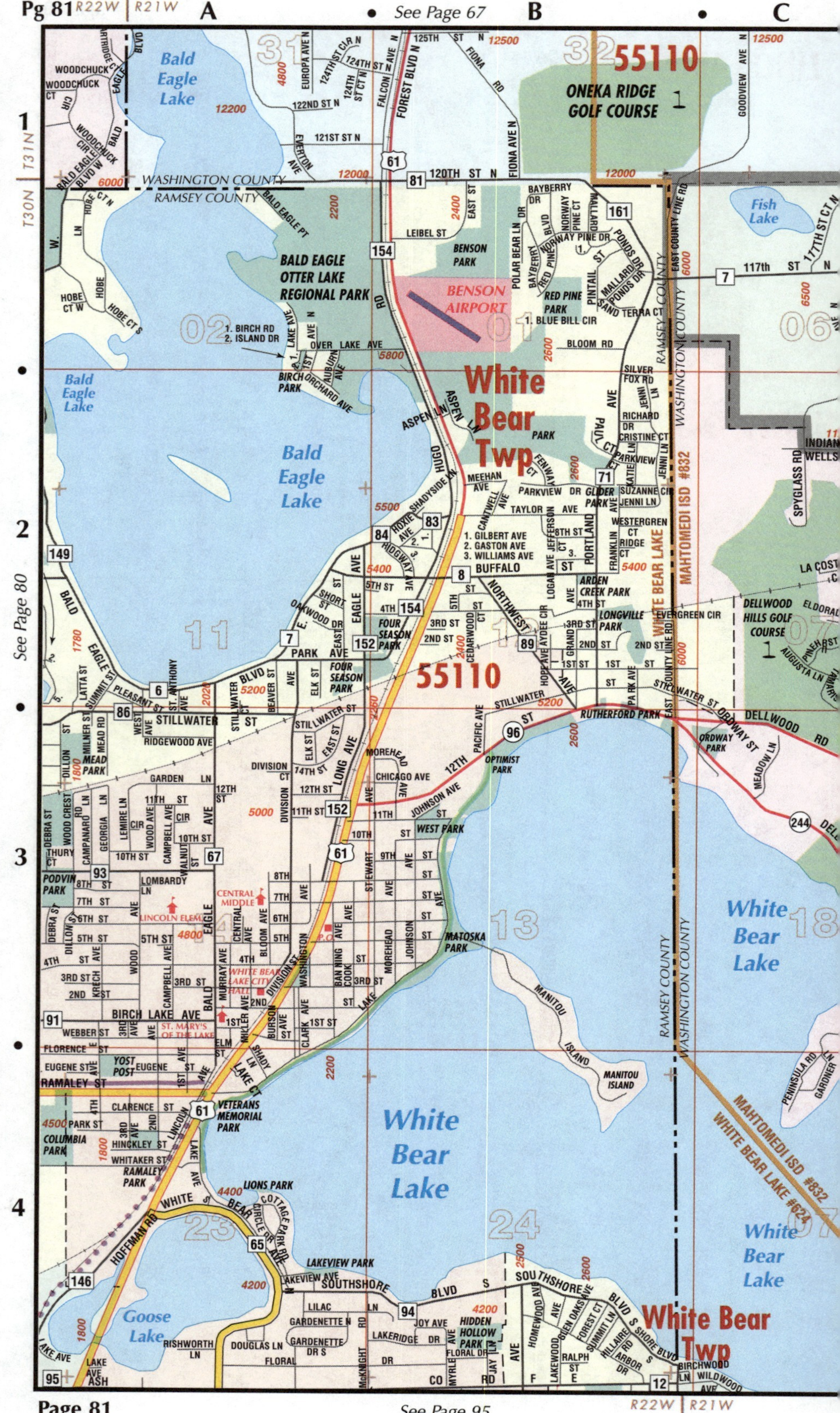
Bald Eagle Lake
55110
ONEKA RIDGE GOLF COURSE
WASHINGTON COUNTY
RAMSEY COUNTY
T31N
T30N
Fish Lake
BALD EAGLE OTTER LAKE REGIONAL PARK
BENSON PARK
BENSON AIRPORT
RED PINE PARK
White Bear Twp
1. BIRCH RD
2. ISLAND DR
BIRCH PARK
ASPEN LN
PARK
1. BLUE BILL CIR
1. GILBERT AVE
2. GASTON AVE
3. WILLIAMS AVE
GLIDER PARK
ARDEN CREEK PARK
LONGVILLE PARK
FOUR SEASON PARK
WHITE BEAR LAKE
MAHTOMEDI ISD #832
DELLWOOD HILLS GOLF COURSE
RUTHERFORD PARK
ORDWAY PARK
OPTIMIST PARK
MEAD PARK
PODVIN PARK
WEST PARK
MATOSKA PARK
CENTRAL MIDDLE
LINCOLN ELEM
WHITE BEAR LAKE CITY HALL
ST. MARY'S OF THE LAKE
YOST POST
VETERANS MEMORIAL PARK
COLUMBIA PARK
RAMALEY PARK
LIONS PARK
White Bear Lake
MANITOU ISLAND
WHITE BEAR LAKE #624
LAKEVIEW PARK
HIDDEN HOLLOW PARK
Goose Lake
INDIAN WELLS
See Page 80

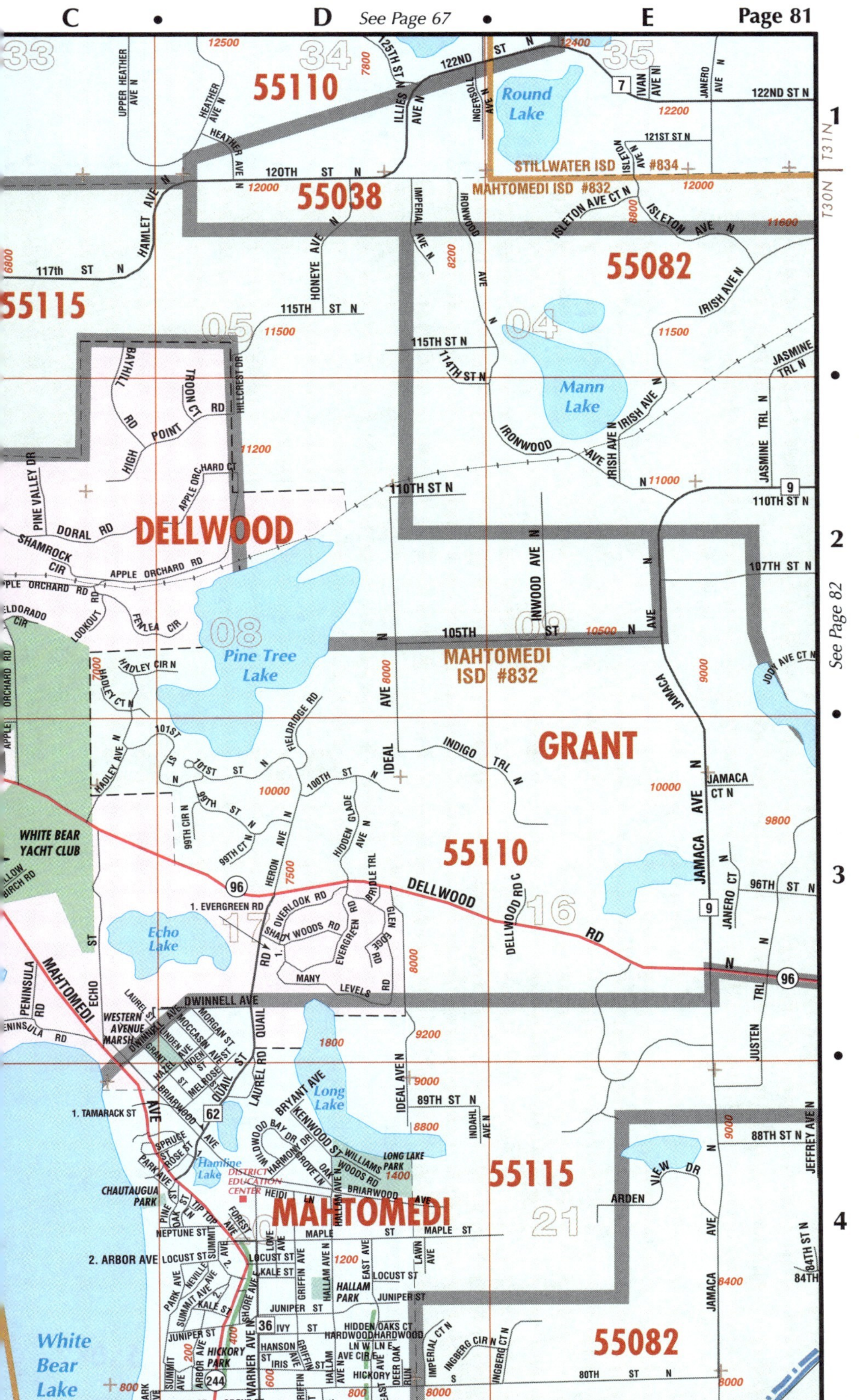

55110
55038
55115
55082
55110
55115
55082

DELLWOOD
GRANT
MAHTOMEDI

STILLWATER ISD #834
MAHTOMEDI ISD #832
MAHTOMEDI ISD #832

Round Lake
Mann Lake
Pine Tree Lake
Echo Lake
Long Lake
Hamline Lake
White Bear Lake

WHITE BEAR YACHT CLUB

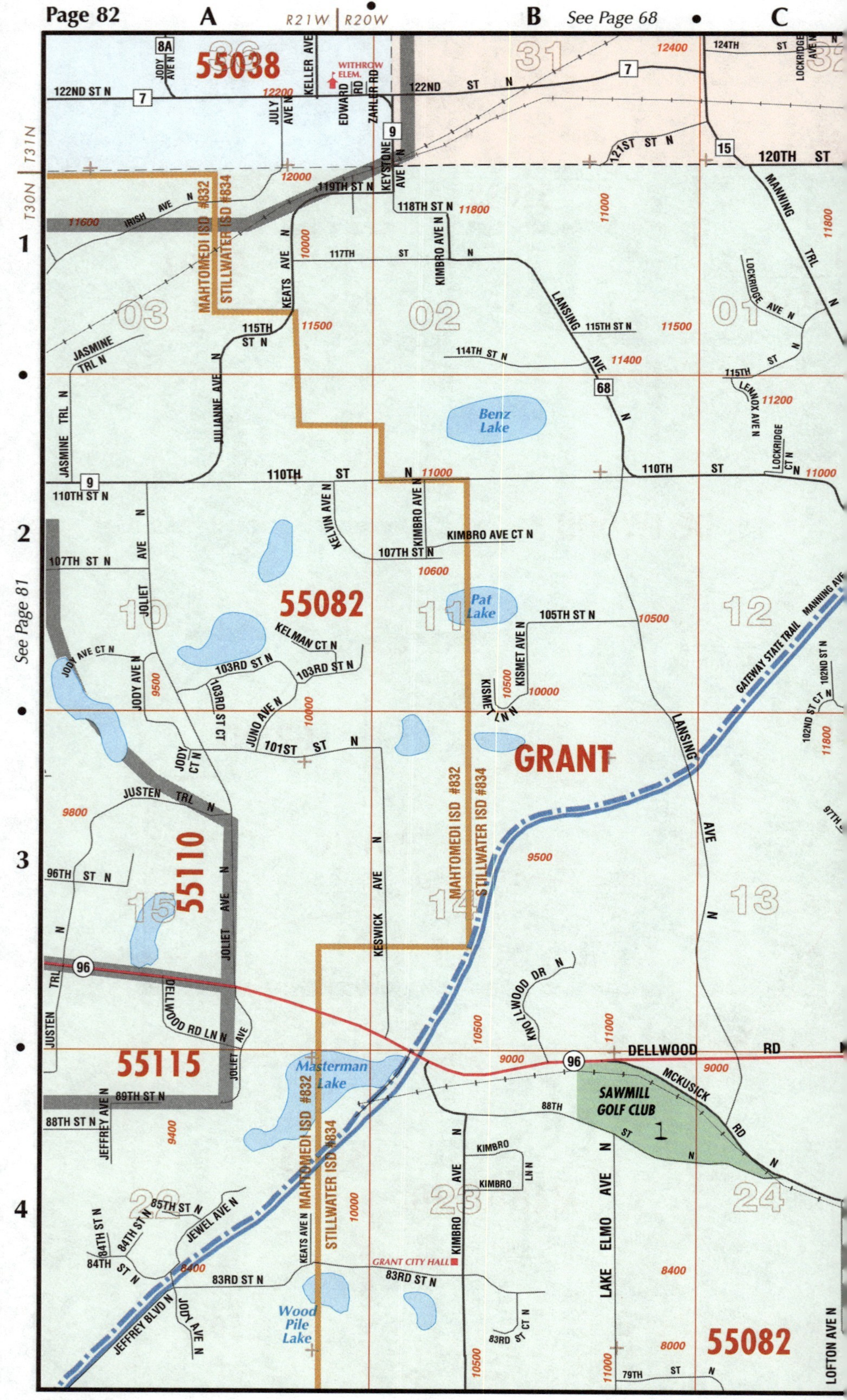

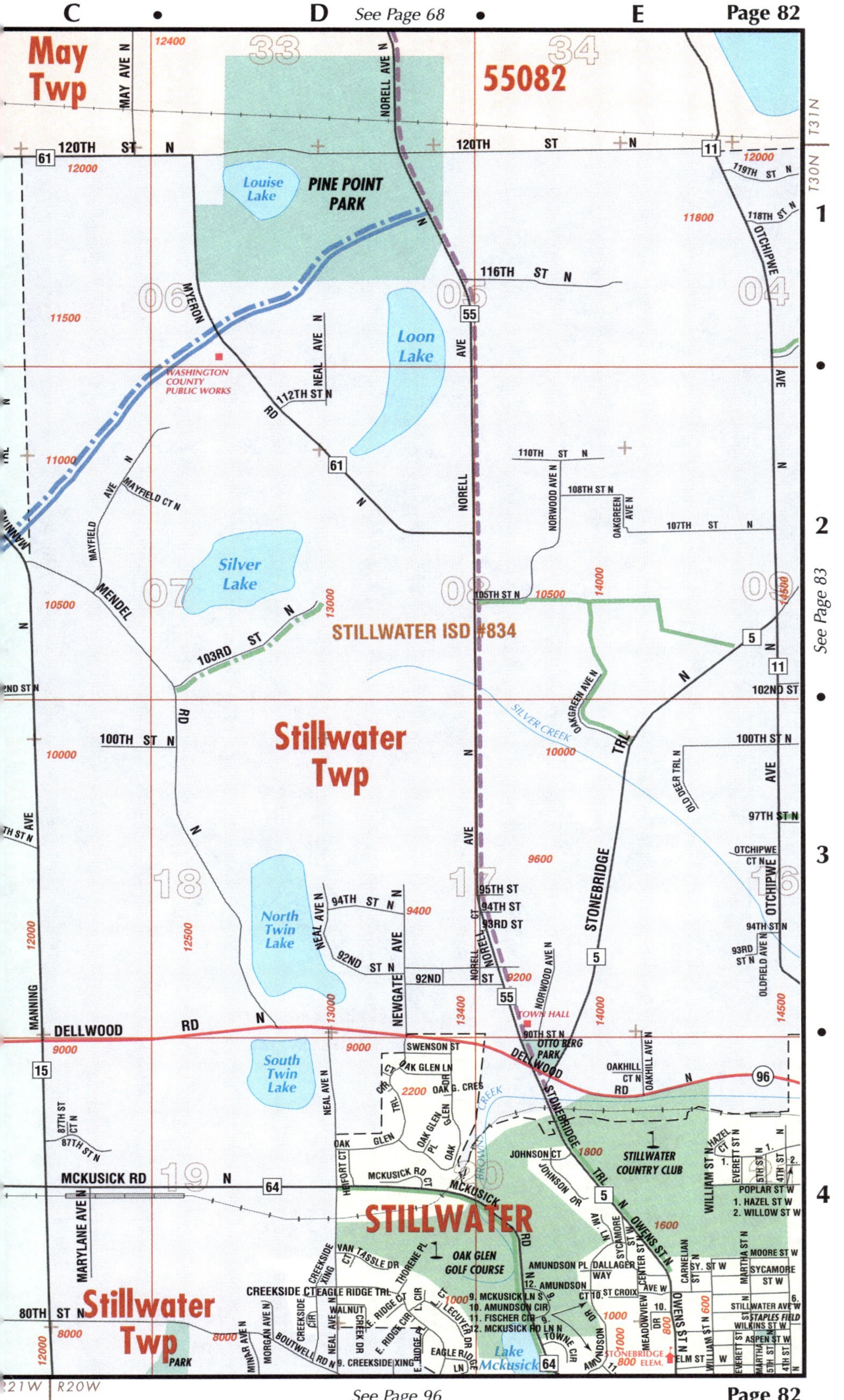
May Twp
55082
120TH ST N
PINE POINT PARK
Louise Lake
Loon Lake
Silver Lake
North Twin Lake
South Twin Lake
WASHINGTON COUNTY PUBLIC WORKS
STILLWATER ISD #834
Stillwater Twp
SILVER CREEK
TOWN HALL
OTTO BERG PARK
STILLWATER COUNTRY CLUB
STILLWATER
OAK GLEN GOLF COURSE
Lake Mckusick
STONEBRIDGE ELEM.
DELLWOOD RD
MCKUSICK RD
STONEBRIDGE TRL
NORELL AVE N
MANNING AVE
OTCHIPWE AVE
1
2
3
4
See Page 83

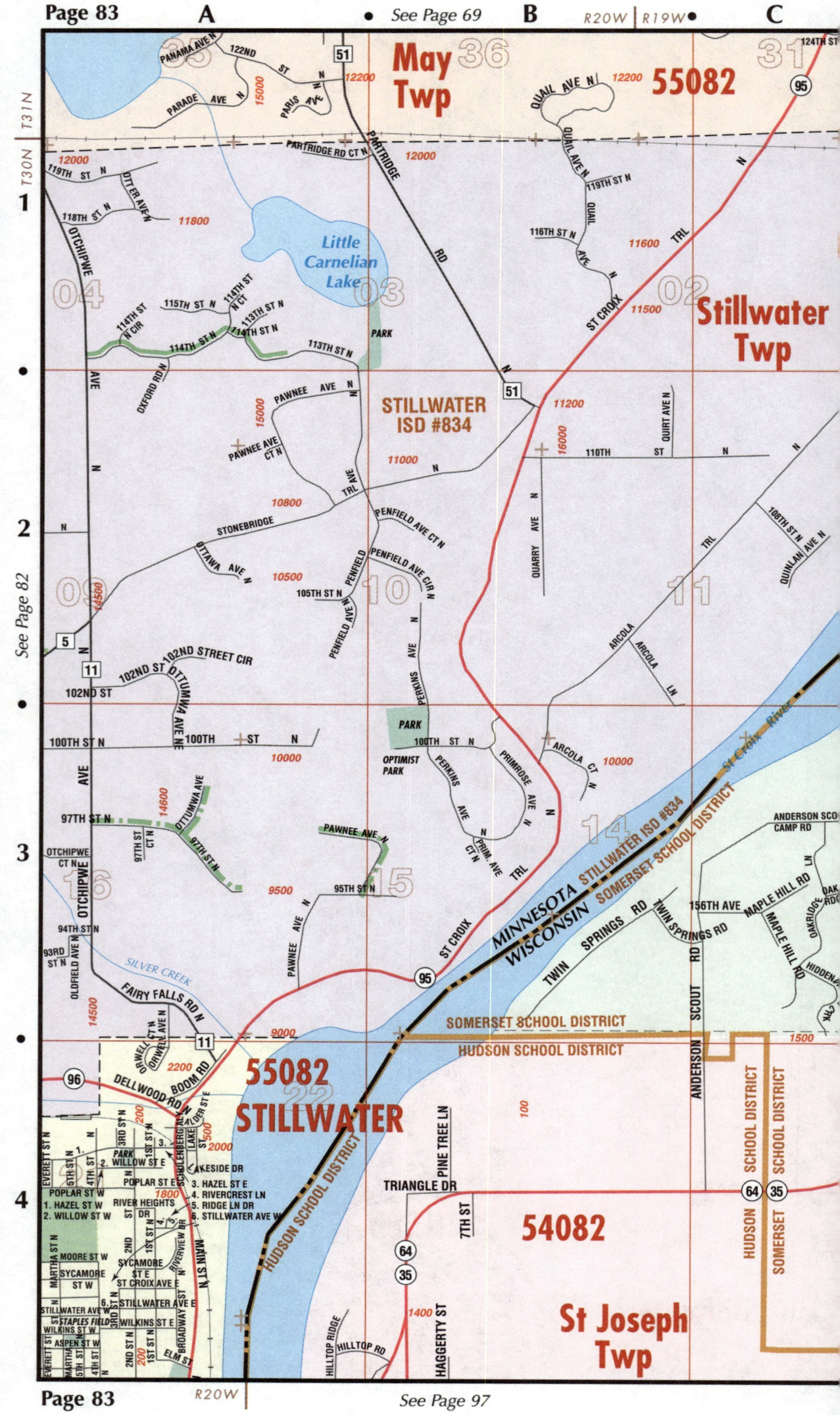

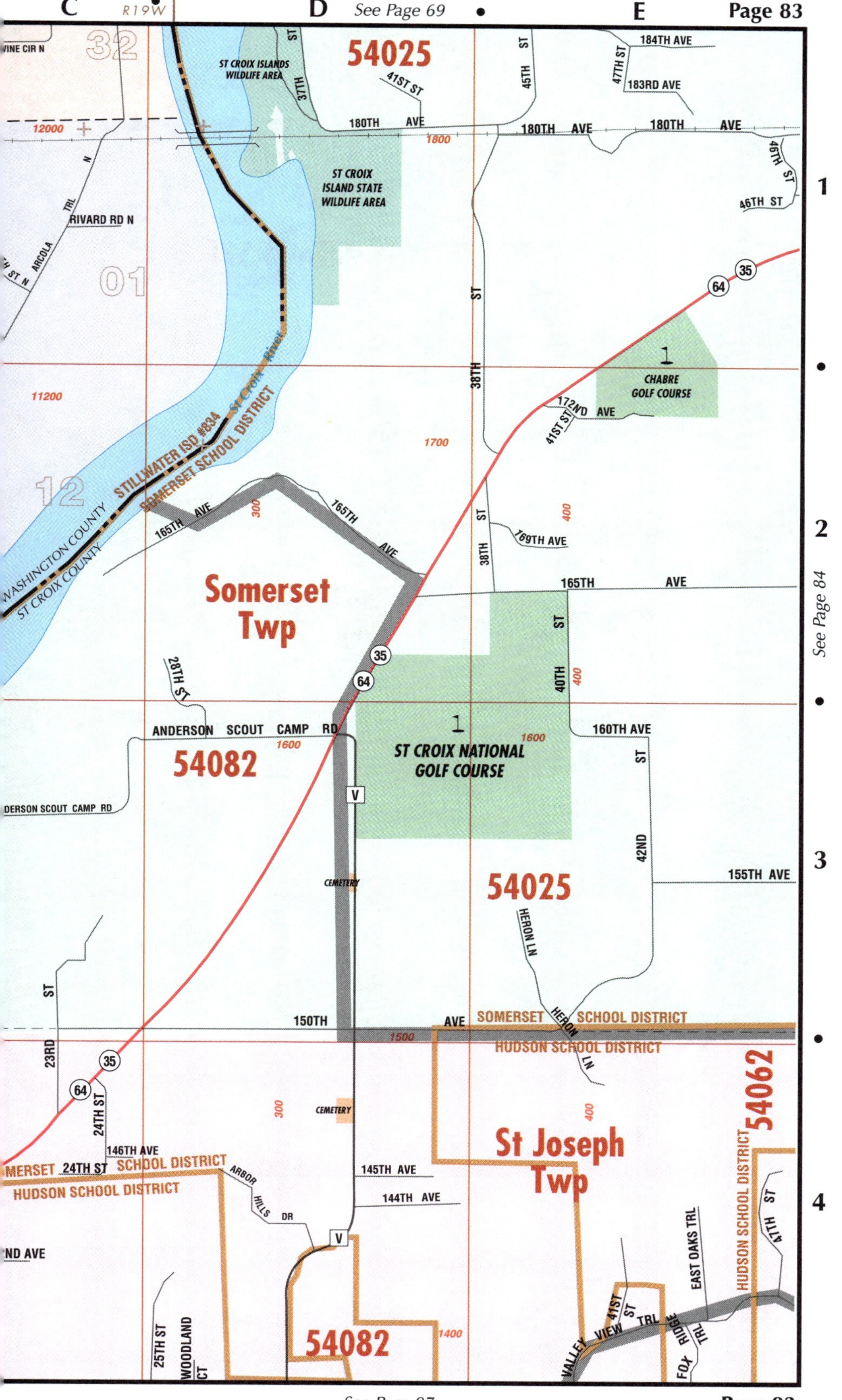

C   R19W

D   *See Page 69*   E

54025

32

WINE CIR N

ST CROIX ISLANDS
WILDLIFE AREA

ST
37TH
ST

41ST ST

180TH   AVE

45TH
ST

47TH
ST

184TH AVE

183RD AVE

12000

180TH   AVE

180TH   AVE

1800

RIVARD RD N

ST CROIX
ISLAND STATE
WILDLIFE AREA

46TH
ST

46TH ST

1

ARGOLA
TRL
N
ST N

01

38TH

64   35

11200

172ND
41ST ST
AVE

CHABRE
GOLF COURSE

1

12

STILLWATER ISD #834

SOMERSET SCHOOL DISTRICT

St Croix River

165TH   AVE

300

165TH   AVE

1700

38TH
ST

769TH AVE

400

**Somerset
Twp**

28TH ST

WASHINGTON COUNTY

ST CROIX COUNTY

165TH   AVE

165TH   AVE

40TH
ST

400

2

See Page 84

35

64

ANDERSON   SCOUT   CAMP   RD

1600

ST CROIX NATIONAL
GOLF COURSE

1

1600

160TH AVE

ST

54082

DERSON SCOUT CAMP RD

V

42ND
ST

155TH   AVE

CEMETERY

ST

150TH

23RD
ST

54025

HERON LN

HERON
LN

3

150TH   AVE

1500

SOMERSET   SCHOOL DISTRICT

HUDSON SCHOOL DISTRICT

35

64

24TH ST

146TH AVE

300

CEMETERY

400

**St Joseph
Twp**

47TH
ST

HUDSON SCHOOL DISTRICT

54062

MERSET

24TH ST

SCHOOL DISTRICT

HUDSON SCHOOL DISTRICT

ARBOR
HILLS
DR

145TH   AVE

144TH   AVE

EAST OAKS TRL

ND AVE

V

41ST
ST

VALLEY VIEW TRL

FOX RIDGE TRL

4

25TH ST
WOODLAND
CT

54082

1400

See Page 97

A • *See Page 70* B • C

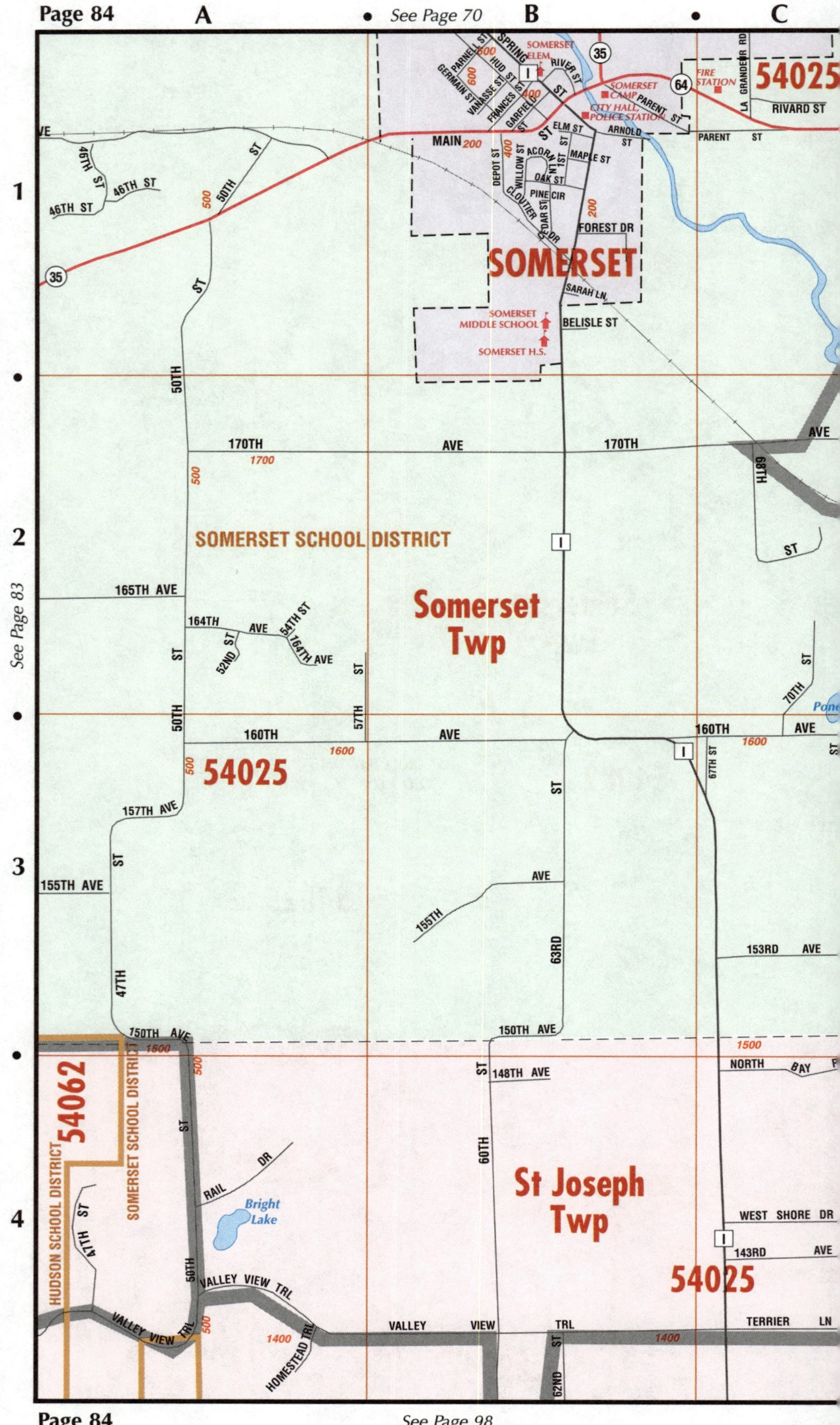

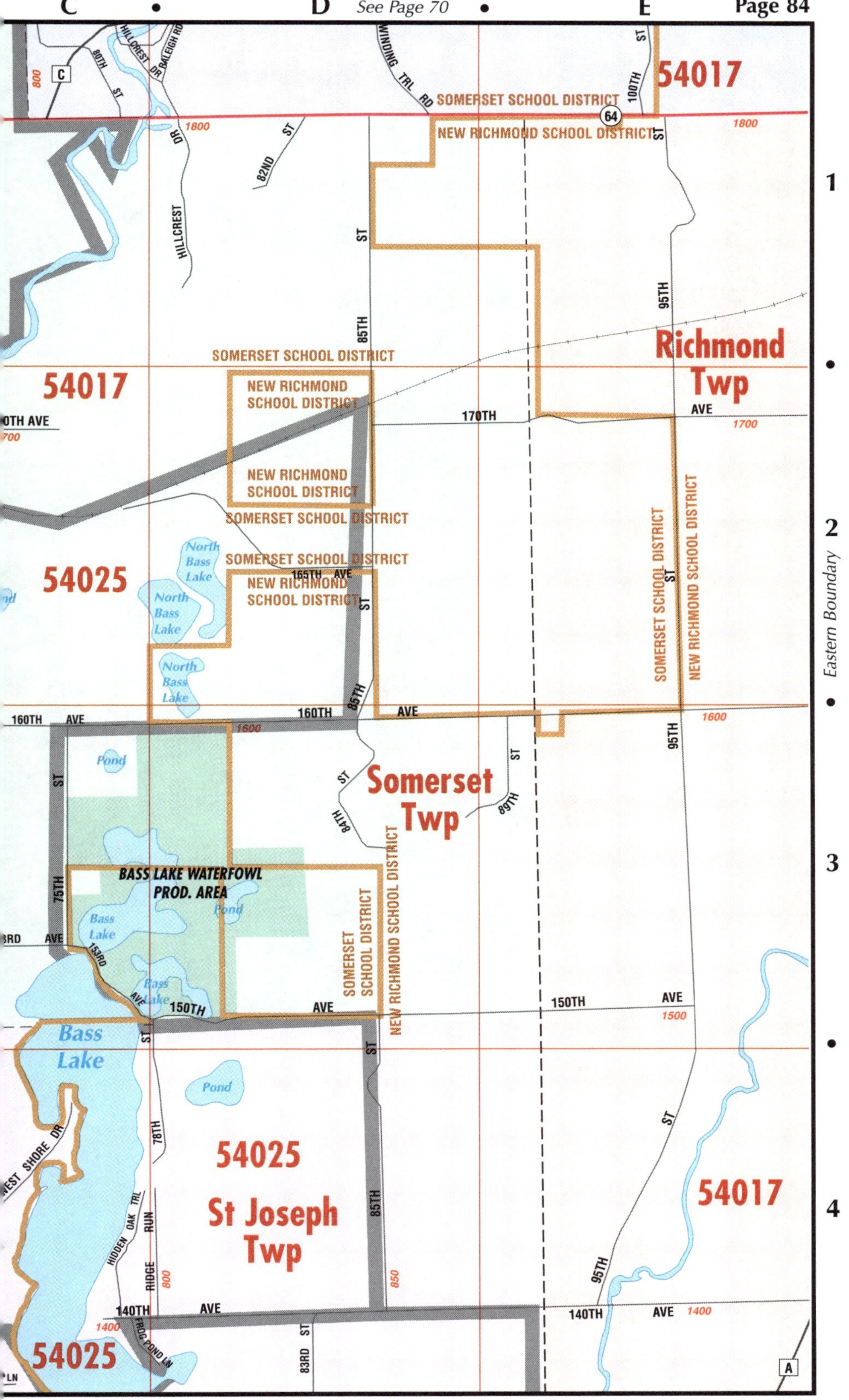

800
C
1800
HILLCREST DR RALEIGH RD
80TH ST
82ND ST
HILLCREST DR
WINDING TRL RD
SOMERSET SCHOOL DISTRICT
64
NEW RICHMOND SCHOOL DISTRICT
1800
100TH ST
95TH ST

54017

1

85TH ST

SOMERSET SCHOOL DISTRICT

54017

0TH AVE
700

NEW RICHMOND
SCHOOL DISTRICT

NEW RICHMOND
SCHOOL DISTRICT

170TH AVE
1700

**Richmond
Twp**

SOMERSET SCHOOL DISTRICT

North
Bass
Lake

54025

North
Bass
Lake

SOMERSET SCHOOL DISTRICT

165TH AVE

NEW RICHMOND
SCHOOL DISTRICT

85TH ST

North
Bass
Lake

2

Eastern Boundary

SOMERSET SCHOOL DISTRICT

NEW RICHMOND SCHOOL DISTRICT

95TH ST

160TH AVE

160TH AVE
1600

85TH AVE

Pond

84TH ST

89TH ST

**Somerset
Twp**

95TH ST

1600

**BASS LAKE WATERFOWL
PROD. AREA**

75TH ST

Pond

Bass
Lake

3

153RD

3RD AVE

Bass
Lake

SOMERSET
SCHOOL DISTRICT

NEW RICHMOND SCHOOL DISTRICT

150TH AVE

150TH AVE
1500

AVE

**Bass
Lake**

78TH ST

Pond

85TH ST

54025

**St Joseph
Twp**

95TH ST

54017

WEST SHORE DR

HIDDEN OAK TRL

RIDGE RUN

800

150TH

850

4

140TH AVE
1400

PROD POND LN

140TH AVE
1400

83RD ST

54025

A

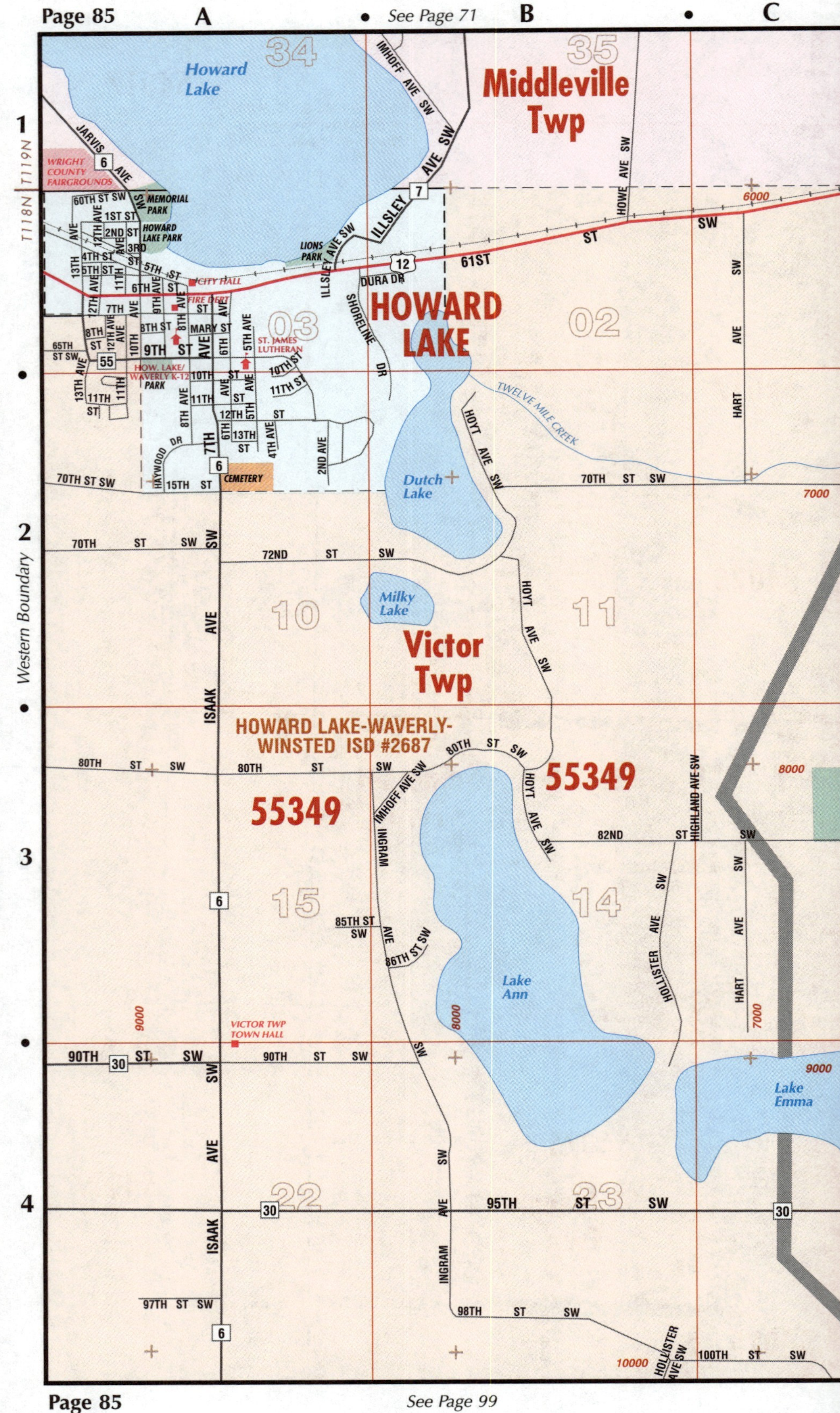

A   B   C

Middleville Twp

Howard Lake

WRIGHT COUNTY FAIRGROUNDS

JARVIS AVE

6

60TH ST SW

MEMORIAL PARK

HOWARD LAKE PARK

LIONS PARK

ILLSLEY

7

HOWE AVE SW

6000

61ST

ST

SW

12

HOWARD LAKE

02

HART AVE

DURA DR

SHORELINE DR

03

ST. JAMES LUTHERAN

TWELVE MILE CREEK

HOYT AVE SW

70TH ST SW

7000

HOW. LAKE/ WAVERLY K-12 PARK

55

CITY HALL

FIRE DEPT

MARY ST

9TH ST

CEMETERY

Dutch Lake

70TH ST SW

70TH ST SW

72ND ST SW

Milky Lake

ISAAK AVE

10

Victor Twp

11

HOYT AVE SW

HOWARD LAKE-WAVERLY-WINSTED ISD #2687

80TH ST SW

80TH ST

80TH ST SW

55349

HOYT AVE SW

55349

HIGHLAND AVE SW

8000

IMHOFF AVE SW

INGRAM

82ND ST SW

6

15

85TH ST SW

86TH ST SW

14

HOLLISTER AVE SW

HART AVE

7000

8000

Lake Ann

9000

VICTOR TWP TOWN HALL

90TH ST SW

30

90TH ST SW

90TH ST SW

9000

Lake Emma

ISAAK AVE

22

30

95TH ST SW

23

SW

30

INGRAM AVE

97TH ST SW

6

98TH ST SW

HOLLISTER AVE SW

10000

100TH ST SW

Western Boundary

65TH ST SW

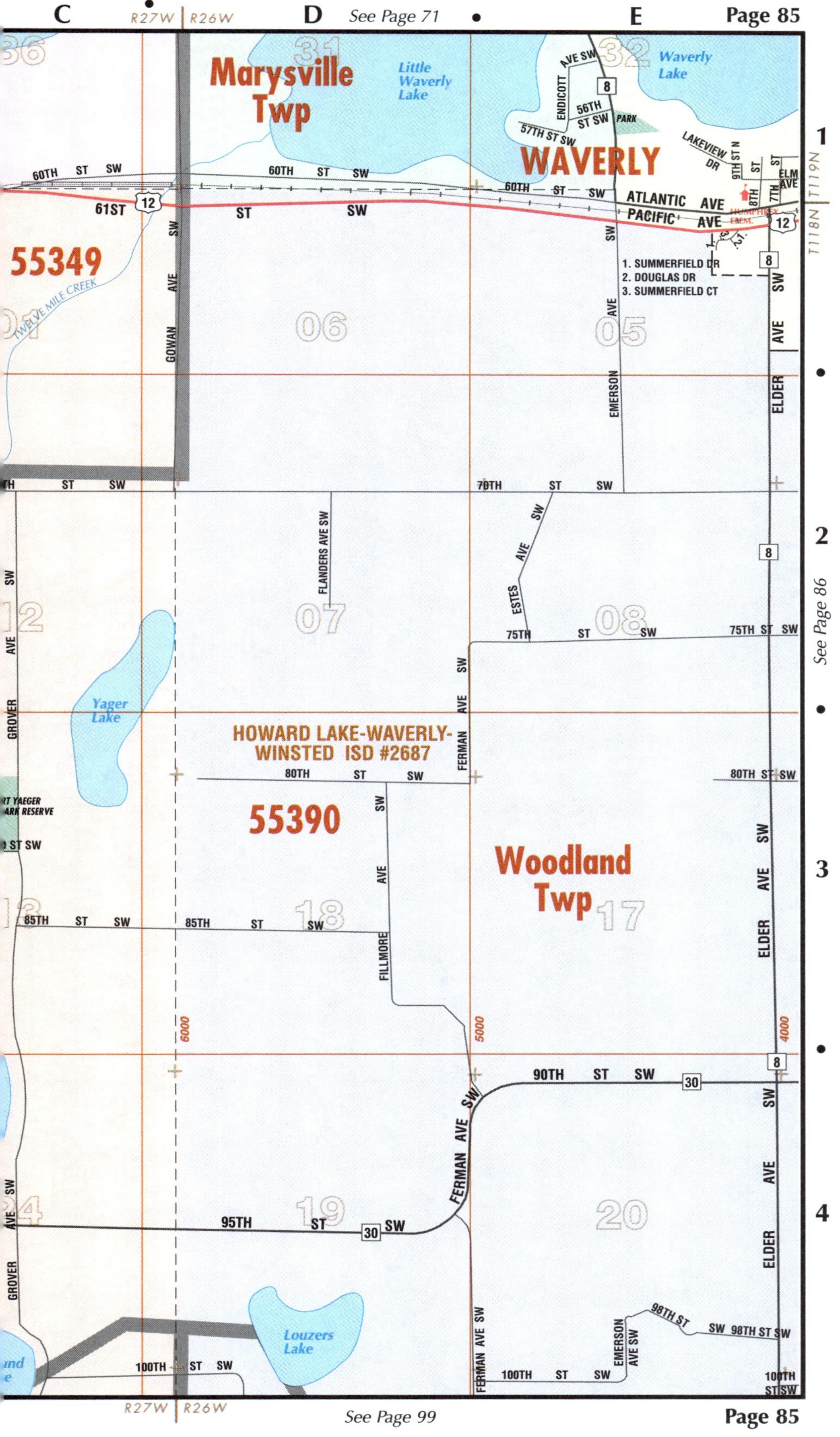

36

31

Marysville Twp

Little Waverly Lake

32

Waverly Lake

ENDICOTT AVE SW

8

56TH ST SW

57TH ST SW

WAVERLY

LAKEVIEW DR

9TH ST N

ELM AVE

8TH

7TH

1

60TH ST SW

60TH ST SW

60TH ST SW

ATLANTIC AVE

T118N | T119N

61ST ST SW

SW

PACIFIC AVE

HUMPHREY MEM.

12

12

55349

TWELVE MILE CREEK

GOWAN AVE SW

06

05

EMERSON AVE SW

1. SUMMERFIELD DR
2. DOUGLAS DR
3. SUMMERFIELD CT

8

ELDER AVE SW

·

ST SW

70TH ST SW

8

2

See Page 86

FLANDERS AVE SW

07

ESTES AVE SW

75TH ST SW

08

75TH ST SW

12

GROVER AVE SW

Yager Lake

FERMAN AVE SW

·

HOWARD LAKE-WAVERLY-WINSTED ISD #2687

80TH ST SW

80TH ST SW

RT YAEGER ARK RESERVE

ST SW

55390

3

Woodland Twp 17

ELDER AVE SW

13

85TH ST SW

85TH ST SW

18

FILLMORE AVE SW

6000

5000

4000

·

8

90TH ST SW

30

ELDER AVE SW

FERMAN AVE SW

4

24

95TH ST SW

30

19

20

GROVER AVE SW

Louzers Lake

FERMAN AVE SW

EMERSON AVE SW

98TH ST SW

98TH ST SW

ELDER AVE SW

und e

100TH ST SW

100TH ST SW

100TH ST SW

A • *See Page 72* B • C

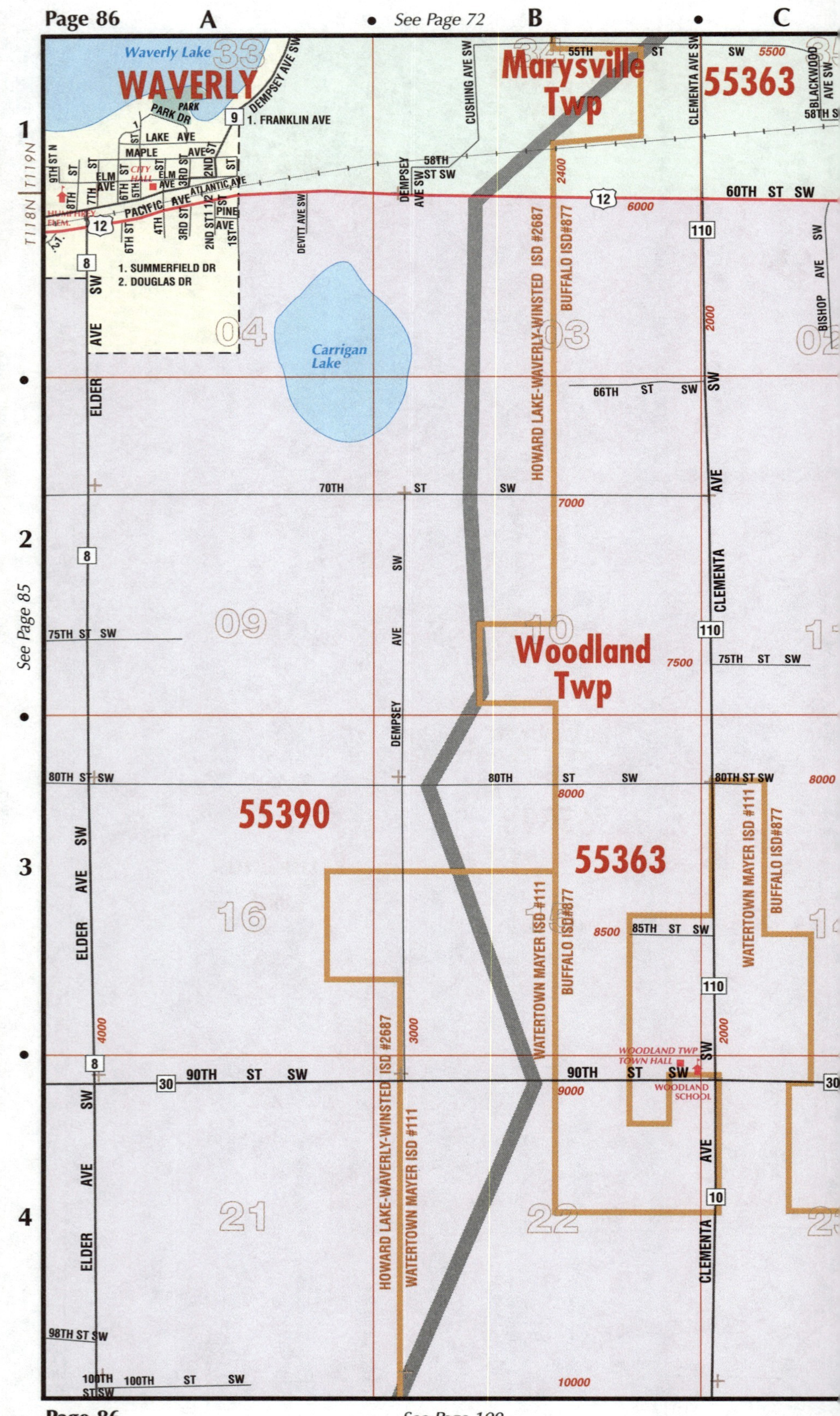

Waverly Lake
WAVERLY 33

Marysville Twp

55363

55TH ST

CUSHING AVE SW

CLEMENTA AVE SW

SW 5500

BLACKWOOD

9TH ST N
DEMPSEY AVE SW
9
1. FRANKLIN AVE
PARK DR
PARK
LAKE AVE
MAPLE AVE
ELM AVE
8TH ST
8TH
ELM AVE
2ND ST
PACIFIC AVE
ATLANTIC AVE
3RD ST
4TH ST
1.12
PINE AVE
1ST ST
6TH ST
5TH
12

1. SUMMERFIELD DR
2. DOUGLAS DR

8

58TH ST

58TH

58TH ST SW

DEMPSEY AVE SW

DEVITT AVE SW

HOWARD LAKE-WAVERLY-WINSTED ISD #2687

BUFFALO ISD #877

2400

12 6000

60TH ST SW

110

BISHOP AVE SW

55363

04

Carrigan Lake

03

2000

02

ELDER AVE

66TH ST SW

SW

70TH ST SW

7000

DEMPSEY AVE SW

CLEMENTA AVE

75TH ST SW

09

Woodland Twp

10

7500

110

75TH ST SW

110

1

80TH ST SW

DEMPSEY AVE

80TH ST SW

8000

80TH ST SW

8000

WATERTOWN MAYER ISD #111

BUFFALO ISD#877

55390

ELDER AVE SW

16

8

4000

3000

WATERTOWN MAYER ISD #2687

55363

WATERTOWN MAYER ISD #111

BUFFALO ISD#877

8500

85TH ST SW

110

WOODLAND TWP TOWN HALL

WATERTOWN MAYER ISD #111

BUFFALO ISD#877

1

90TH ST SW

HOWARD LAKE-WAVERLY-WINSTED ISD #2687

WATERTOWN MAYER ISD #111

9000

90TH ST SW

WOODLAND SCHOOL

2000

CLEMENTA AVE SW

30

21

ELDER AVE SW

22

10

23

98TH ST SW

100TH ST SW

100TH ST SW

10000

See Page 85

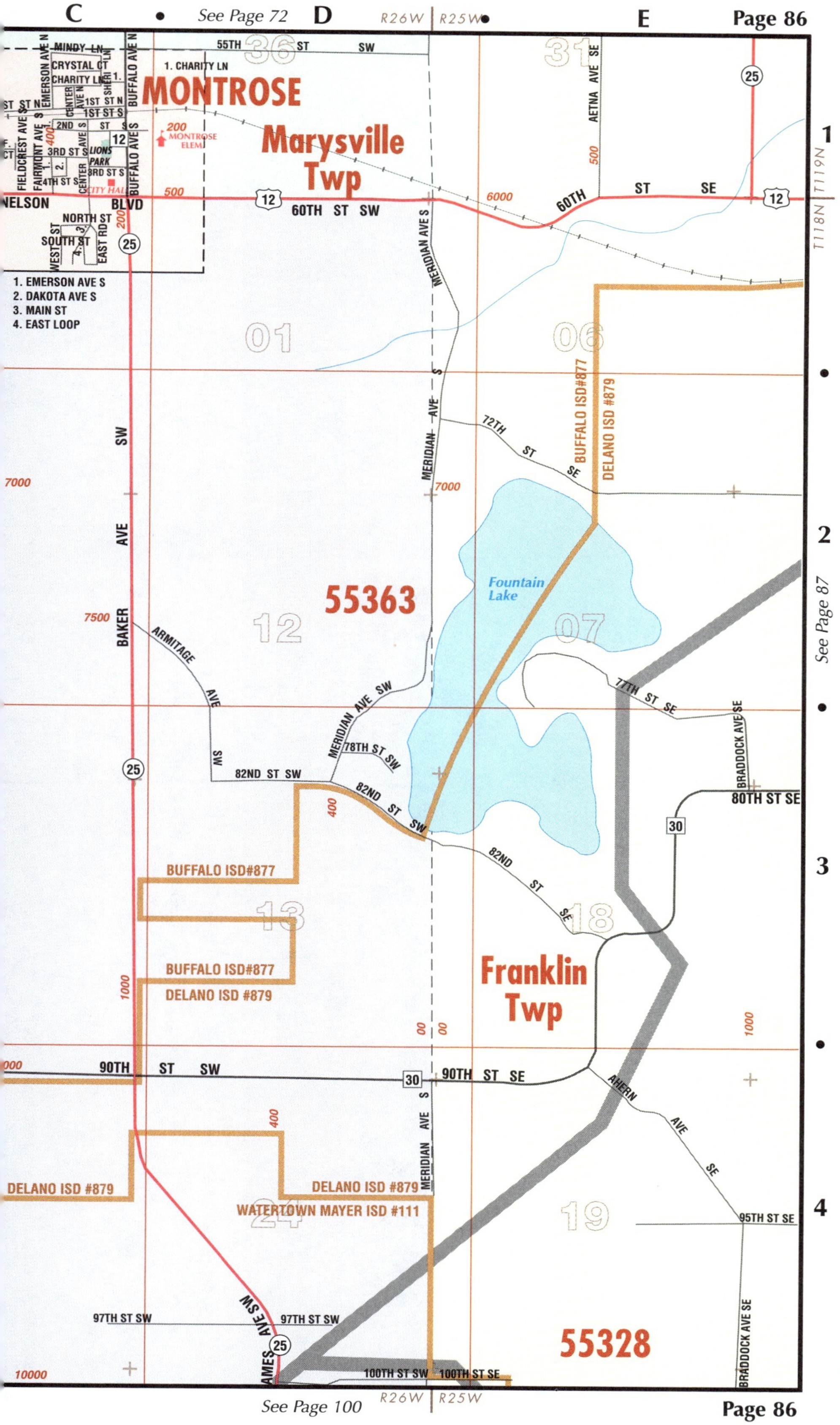

MONTROSE

Marysville Twp

55TH ST SW
1. CHARITY LN
MINDY LN
CRYSTAL CT
CHARITY LN
EMERSON AVE N
CENTER AVE N
1ST ST N
BUFFALO AVE N
2ND ST S
CENTER AVE
1ST ST S
3RD ST S
FAIRMONT AVE S
FIELDCREST AVE S
4TH ST S
400
LIONS PARK
CITY HALL
12
3RD ST S
200 MONTROSE ELEM
NELSON BLVD
NORTH ST
SOUTH ST
WEST ST
EAST RD
25
500
12
60TH ST SW
6000
60TH ST SE
25
AETNA AVE SE
500
T118N T119N
12

1. EMERSON AVE S
2. DAKOTA AVE S
3. MAIN ST
4. EAST LOOP

01

06

7000

MERIDIAN AVE S

72ND ST SE

BUFFALO ISD#877

DELANO ISD #879

7000

55363

Fountain Lake

12

07

7500

BAKER AVE SW

ARMITAGE AVE SW

MERIDIAN AVE SW

77TH ST SE

BRADDOCK AVE SE

78TH ST SW

82ND ST SW

400

82ND ST SW

82ND ST SE

80TH ST SE

30

25

Franklin Twp

18

BUFFALO ISD#877

13

BUFFALO ISD#877
DELANO ISD #879

1000

00 | 00

3

1000

90TH ST SW

30

90TH ST SE

AHERN AVE SE

19

MERIDIAN AVE S

DELANO ISD #879

400

DELANO ISD #879
WATERTOWN MAYER ISD #111

24

95TH ST SE

BRADDOCK AVE SE

4

97TH ST SW

97TH ST SW

JAMES AVE SW

25

10000

100TH ST SW | 100TH ST SE

55328

1

2

3

4

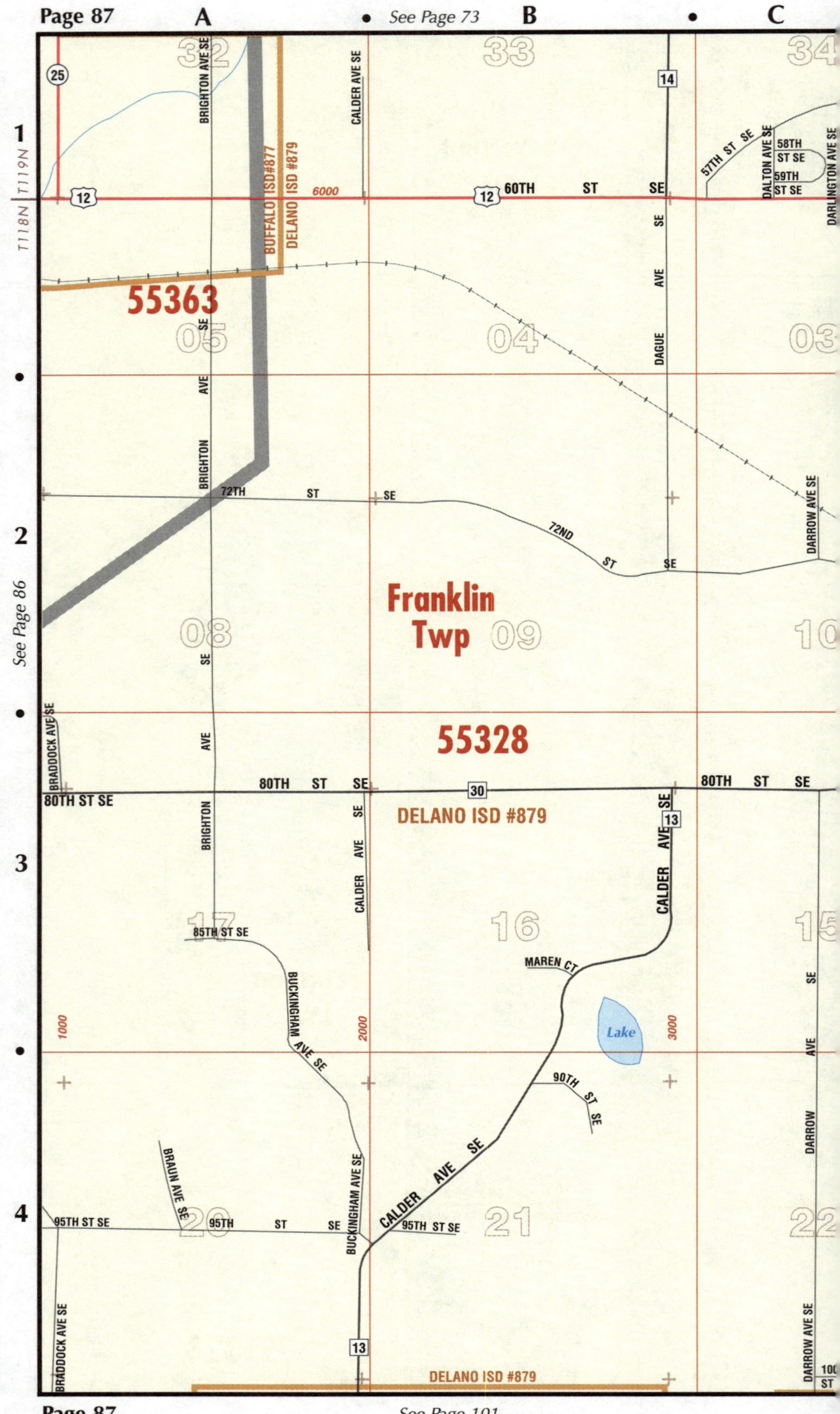

55363

**Franklin
Twp**

55328

DELANO ISD #879

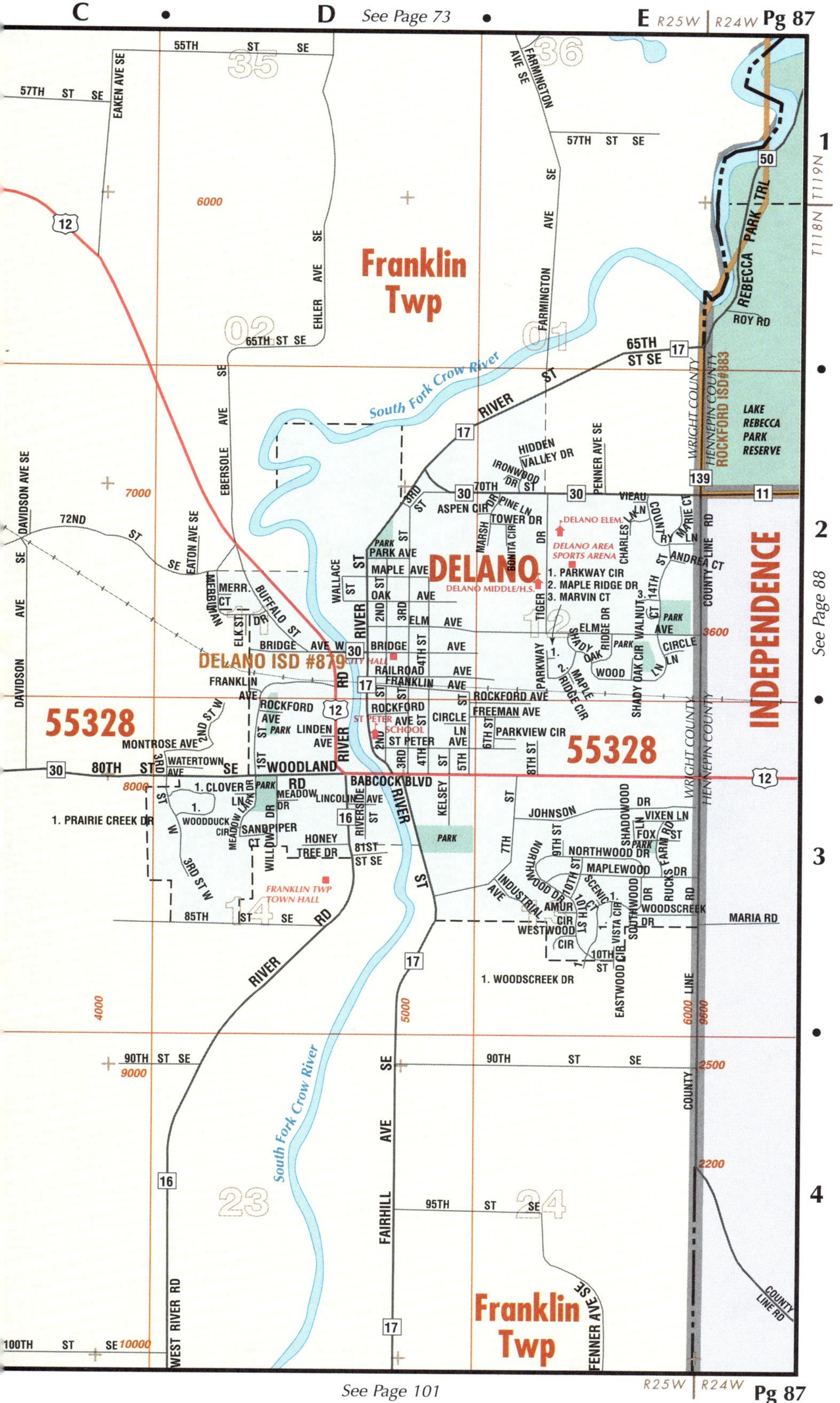
Franklin Twp
DELANO
INDEPENDENCE
55328
55328
DELANO ISD #879
ROCKFORD ISD #883
LAKE REBECCA PARK RESERVE
South Fork Crow River
South Fork Crow River
Franklin Twp
WRIGHT COUNTY
HENNEPIN COUNTY
DELANO ELEM.
DELANO AREA SPORTS ARENA
DELANO MIDDLE/H.S.
CITY HALL
ST PETER SCHOOL
FRANKLIN TWP TOWN HALL
1. PARKWAY CIR
2. MAPLE RIDGE DR
3. MARVIN CT
1. CLOVER LN
1. PRAIRIE CREEK DR
1. WOODSCREEK DR
55TH ST SE
57TH ST SE
65TH ST SE
72ND ST SE
80TH ST SE
85TH ST SE
90TH ST SE
95TH ST SE
100TH ST SE
RIVER ST
RIVER RD
BABCOCK BLVD
WOODLAND RD
FARMINGTON AVE SE
EHLER AVE SE
EBERSOLE AVE SE
EATON AVE SE
DAVIDSON AVE SE
EAKEN AVE SE
FAIRHILL AVE SE
FENNER AVE SE
WEST RIVER RD
COUNTY LINE RD
REBECCA PARK TRL
ROY RD
MARIA RD
See Page 88
1
2
3
4
T119N
T118N

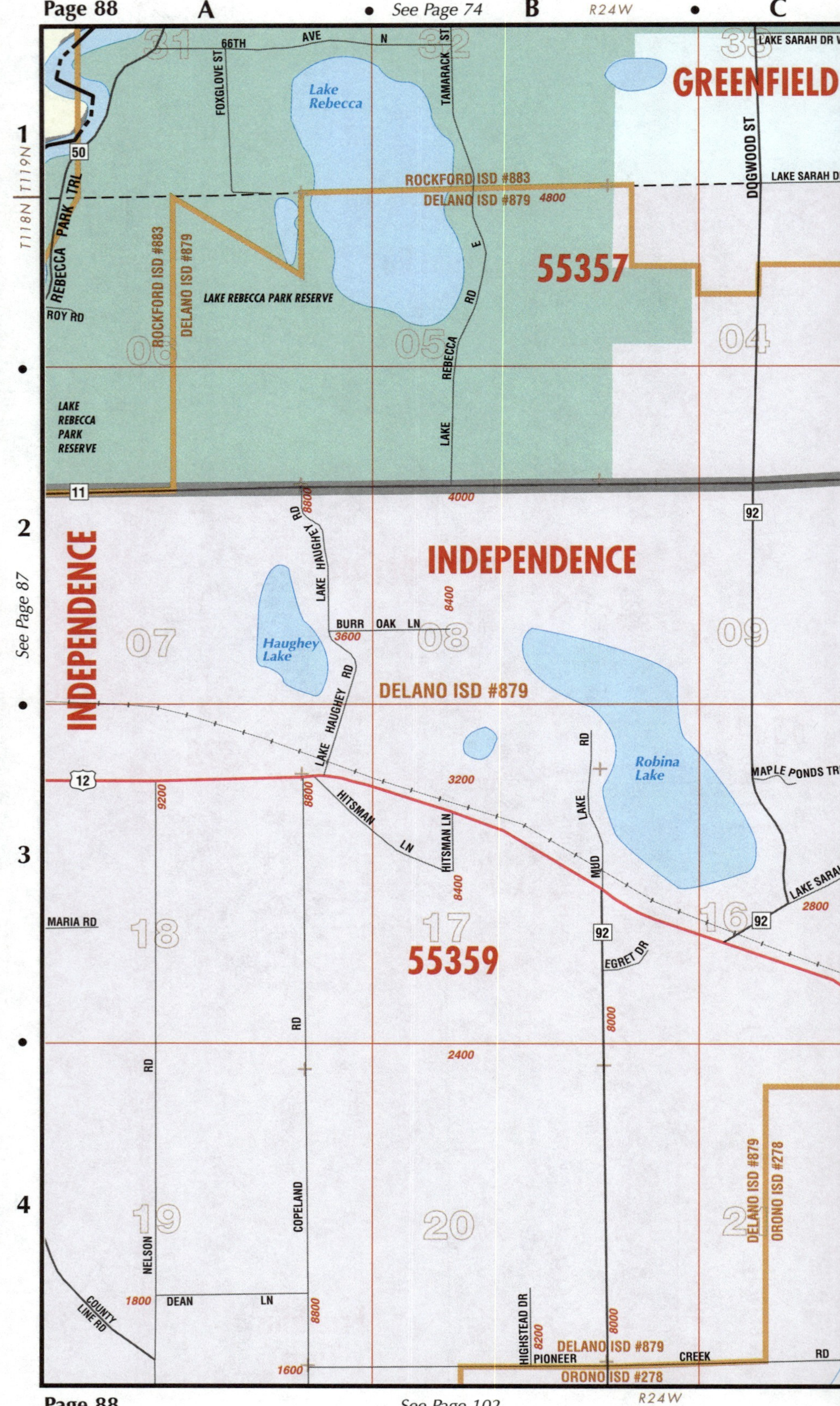

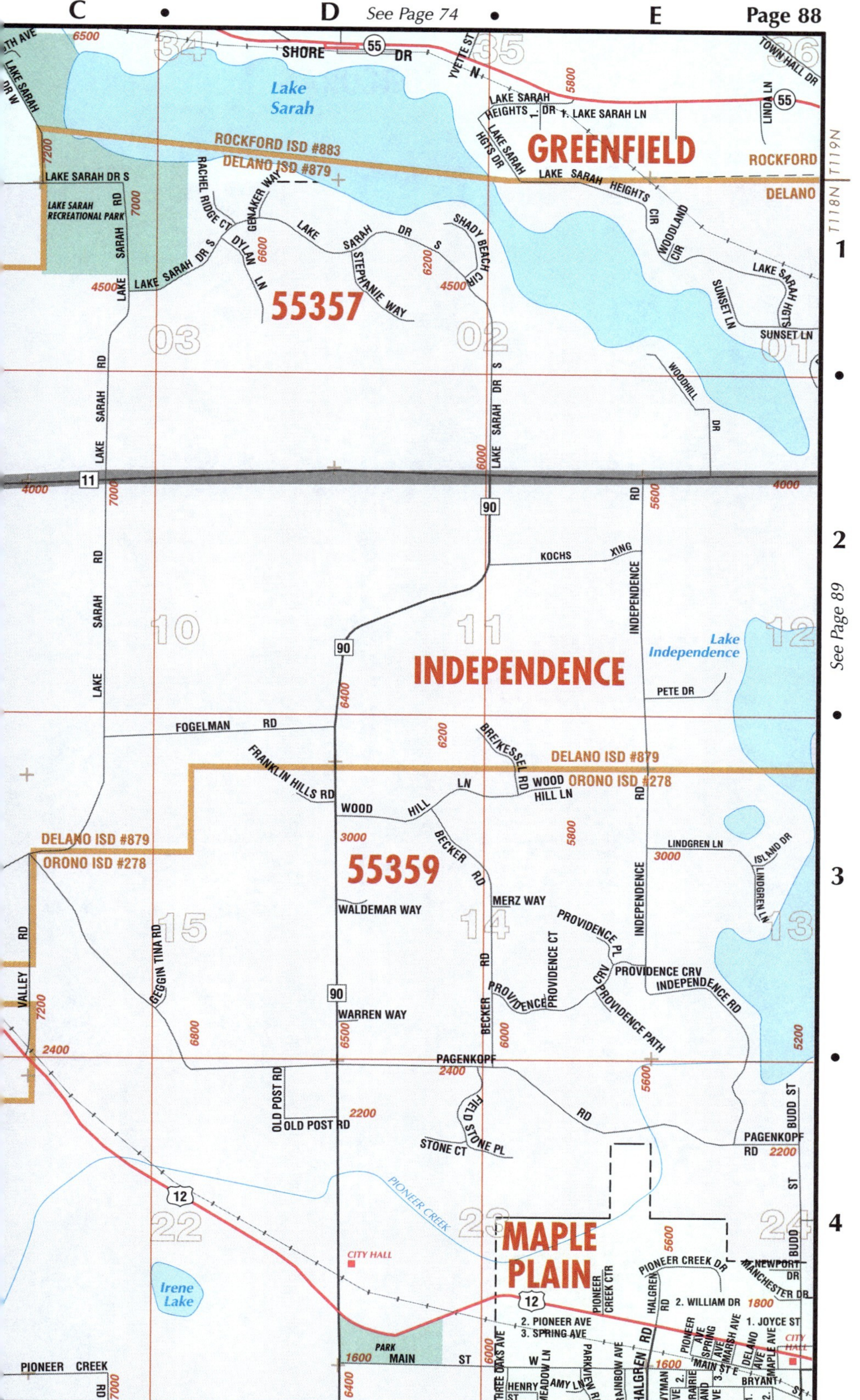

SHORE DR
Lake Sarah
55
34
35
36
YVETTE ST
TOWN HALL DR
LINDA LN
55
LAKE SARAH HEIGHTS DR
1. LAKE SARAH LN
5800
LAKE SARAH HGTS DR
GREENFIELD
ROCKFORD
6500
7200
ROCKFORD ISD #883
DELANO ISD #879
LAKE SARAH HEIGHTS
DELANO
WOODLAND CIR
CIR
Lake Sarah Recreational Park
LAKE SARAH DR S
RACHEL RIDGE CT
GENAKER WAY
7000
LAKE SARAH RD
DYLAN LN
6600
LAKE SARAH DR
SHADY BEACH CIR
6200
LAKE SARAH HGTS LN
SUNSET LN
T118N T119N
4500
LAKE SARAH DR S
STEPHANIE WAY
6200
4500
SUNSET LN
1
55357
03
02
01
WOODHILL DR
LAKE SARAH RD
LAKE SARAH DR S
6000
4000
11
7000
90
5600
RD
4000
2
LAKE SARAH RD
KOCHS XING
See Page 89
10
11
INDEPENDENCE
12
Lake Independence
90
INDEPENDENCE
PETE DR
FOGELMAN RD
6400
6200
BREKKESSEL RD
DELANO ISD #879
WOOD HILL LN
ORONO ISD #278
RD
FRANKLIN HILLS RD
WOOD HILL
LN
LINDGREN LN
3000
ISLAND DR
LINDGREN LN
DELANO ISD #879
3000
BECKER RD
5800
INDEPENDENCE
3
ORONO ISD #278
55359
WALDEMAR WAY
MERZ WAY
PROVIDENCE PL
PROVIDENCE CRV
15
14
13
VALLEY RD
GEGGIN TINA RD
PROVIDENCE CT
PROVIDENCE CRV
INDEPENDENCE RD
7200
6800
90
BECKER RD
PROVIDENCE
PROVIDENCE PATH
5200
2400
WARREN WAY
6500
6000
PAGENKOPF
2400
5600
OLD POST RD
BUDD ST
OLD POST RD
2200
RD
PAGENKOPF
ST
FIELD STONE PL
RD 2200
12
STONE CT
PIONEER CREEK
BUDD ST
22
23
24
4
Irene Lake
CITY HALL
5600
MAPLE PLAIN
PIONEER CREEK CTR
PIONEER CREEK DR
NEWPORT DR
MANCHESTER DR
2. WILLIAM DR
1800
HALGREN RD
1. JOYCE ST
2. PIONEER AVE
12
3. SPRING AVE
1. MAPLE AVE
CITY HALL
PIONEER CREEK RD
7000
PARK
1600
MAIN ST
6400
THREE OAKS AVE
W
HENRY ST
AMY LN
MEADOW LN
PARKVIEW
RAINBOW AVE
HALGREN RD
WYMAN AVE
PIONEER AVE
SPRING AVE
PRAIRIE LN
MAIN ST E
DELANO AVE
MARSH AVE
1600
BRYANT

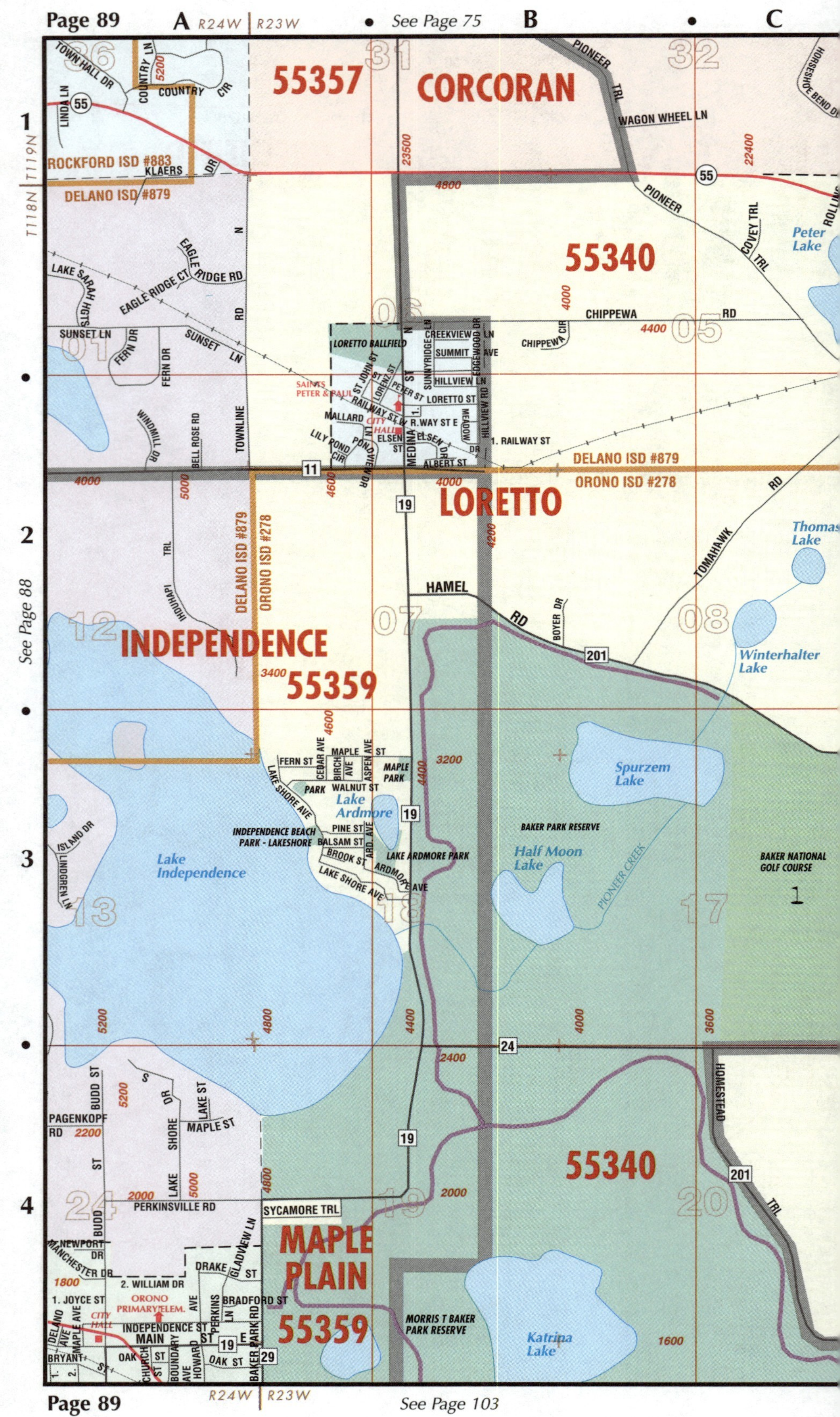

A R24W | R23W • See Page 75 B • C

36 55357 CORCORAN

31 PIONEER TRL 32 HORSESHOE BEND DR

TOWN HALL DR COUNTRY LN 5200 COUNTRY CIR

LINDA LN LINDA LN 55 COUNTRY LN

WAGON WHEEL LN

23500 4800 PIONEER 55

ROCKFORD ISD #883 KLAERS DR

DELANO ISD #879

COVEY TRL ROLLI

Peter Lake

LAKE SARAH HGTS EAGLE RIDGE CT EAGLE RIDGE RD 55340 CHIPPEWA 4400 RD 05

SUNSET LN FERN DR FERN DR WINDHUM DR SUNSET LN TOWNLINE 22400

4000 CHIPPEWA CIR CHIPPEWA

01 FERN DR RD N

CREEKVIEW LN EDGEWOOD LN

Loretto Ballfield SUNNYRIDGE SUMMIT AVE

SAINTS PETER & PAUL RAILWAY ST E HILLVIEW ST HILLVIEW RD

ST JOHN ST ORIEN ST PETER ST LORETTO ST 1. RAILWAY ST

MALLARD CITY HALL R. WAY ST E MEADOW DR DELANO ISD #879

BELL ROSE RD LILY POND CIR PONDVIEW DR ELSEN EL ST ALBERT ST ORONO ISD #278

MEDINA 4000 RD

4000 5000 11 4600 19 LORETTO

INDHIHAPI TRL DELANO ISD #879 ORONO ISD #278 4200 HAMEL RD BOYER DR 201 TOMAHAWK Thomas Lake

12 07 08 Winterhalter Lake

INDEPENDENCE 3400 55359 07 08

4600 FERN ST CEDAR AVE BIRCH AVE MAPLE AVE ASPEN ST ST MAPLE PARK 3200 Spurzem Lake

LAKE SHORE AVE PARK WALNUT ST 4400 19

Lake Ardmore PINE ST BAKER PARK RESERVE

INDEPENDENCE BEACH BALSAM ST ARD AVE Lake Ardmore Park Half Moon Lake BAKER NATIONAL GOLF COURSE

PARK - LAKESHORE BROOK ST ARDMORE AVE PIONEER CREEK

ISLAND DR LINDGREN LN Lake Independence LAKE SHORE AVE 18 17

13

5200 4800 4400 4000 3600

24 2400

BUDD ST 5200 S DR MAPLE ST LAKE ST

PAGENKOPF RD 2200 SHORE DR MAPLE ST 19

SYCAMORE TRL 4800 19 2000 55340 HOMESTEAD

24 LAKE 5000 PERKINSVILLE RD 201 TRL

BUDD ST 2000

NEWPORT DR MANCHESTER DR GLADWIN LN PERKINS AVE DRAKE AVE MAPLE PLAIN 20

1800 2. WILLIAM DR BRADFORD ST 55359

1. JOYCE AVE MAPLE AVE ORONO PRIMARY ELEM. BAKER PARK RD Morris T Baker Park Reserve Katrina Lake 1600

DELANO AVE CITY HALL INDEPENDENCE ST MAIN 19 E

BRYANT CHURCH ST BOUNDARY OAK HOWARD OAK ST 29

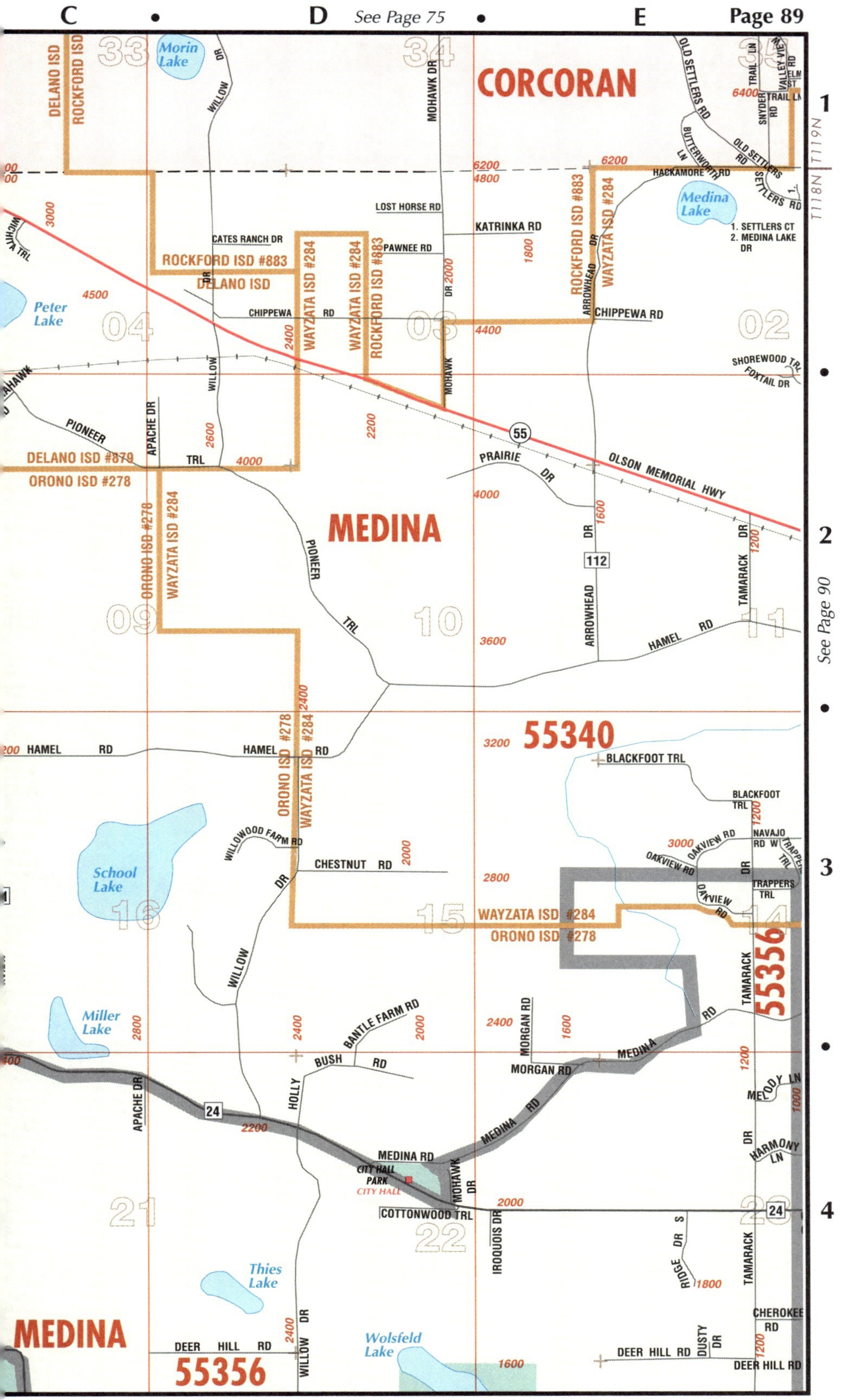

CORCORAN

MEDINA

55340

WAYZATA ISD #284
ORONO ISD #278

55356

MEDINA
55356

1. SETTLERS CT
2. MEDINA LAKE DR

See Page 90
See Page 103

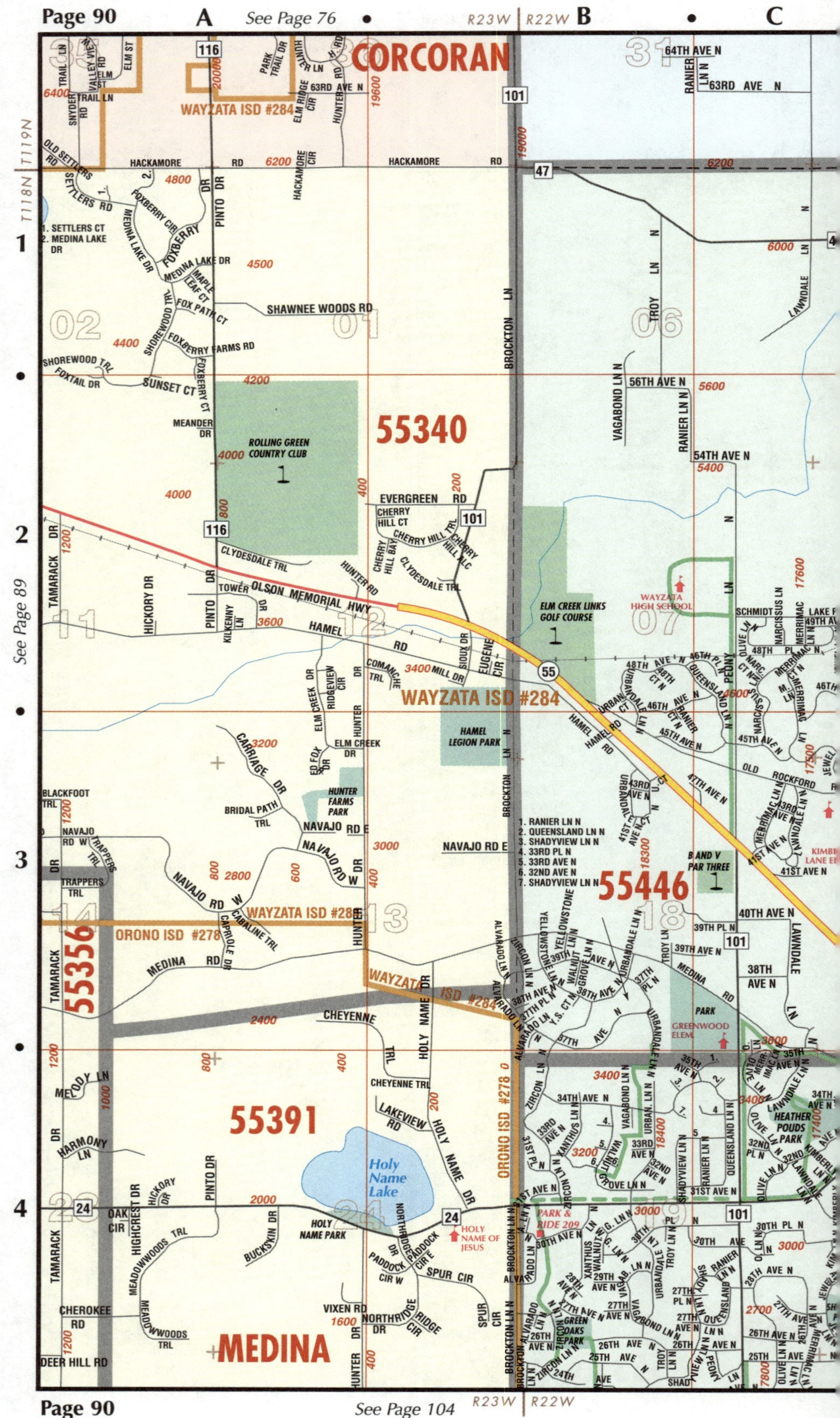
CORCORAN
WAYZATA ISD #284
HACKAMORE RD
6200
6400
4800
4500
4400
4200
4000
3600
3400
3200
3000
2800
2400
2000
1600
1200
1000
800
600
400
200
19600
19000
18300
18400
17600
17500
17400
7800
6000
5600
5400
4600
2700
T118N T119N
1. SETTLERS CT
2. MEDINA LAKE DR
OLD SETTLERS RD
FOXBERRY CIR
MEDINA LAKE DR
PINTO DR
SHAWNEE WOODS RD
FOX PATH CT
FOXBERRY FARMS RD
SHOREWOOD TRL
FOXTAIL DR
SUNSET CT
MEANDER DR
ROLLING GREEN COUNTRY CLUB
55340
EVERGREEN RD
CHERRY HILL CT
CHERRY HILL TRL
CLYDESDALE TRL
OLSON MEMORIAL HWY
HAMEL RD
TAMARACK DR
HICKORY DR
KILKENNY LN
TOWER DR
HUNTER RD
MILL DR
SIOUX DR
EUGENE CIR
BROCKTON LN
WAYZATA ISD #284
HAMEL LEGION PARK
ELM CREEK DR
HUNTER FARMS PARK
CARRIAGE DR
BRIDAL PATH TRL
NAVAJO RD E
NAVAJO RD W
BLACKFOOT TRL
TRAPPERS TRL
ORONO ISD #278
55356
MEDINA RD
CHEYENNE TRL
HOLY NAME DR
55391
LAKEVIEW RD
Holy Name Lake
HOLY NAME PARK
HOLY NAME OF JESUS
MELODY LN
HARMONY LN
HIGHCREST DR
OAK CIR
MEADOWWOODS TRL
CHEROKEE RD
DEER HILL RD
BUCKSKIN DR
NORTHRIDGE DR
PADDOCK CIR E
PADDOCK CIR W
SPUR CIR
VIXEN RD
MEDINA
64TH AVE N
63RD AVE N
RANIER LN N
TROY LN N
VAGABOND LN N
56TH AVE N
54TH AVE N
LAWNDALE LN N
ELM CREEK LINKS GOLF COURSE
WAYZATA HIGH SCHOOL
SCHMIDT LAKE RD
48TH AVE N
46TH AVE N
45TH AVE N
OLD ROCKFORD RD
1. RANIER LN N
2. QUEENSLAND LN N
3. SHADYVIEW LN N
4. 33RD PL N
5. 33RD AVE N
6. 32ND AVE N
7. SHADYVIEW LN N
55446
B AND V PAR THREE
40TH AVE N
39TH PL N
38TH AVE N
37TH AVE
GREENWOOD ELEM.
PARK
35TH AVE N
34TH AVE N
HEATHER POUDS PARK
PARK & RIDE 209
GREEN OAKS PARK
30TH AVE N
28TH AVE N
26TH AVE N
25TH AVE N
24TH AVE N
ORONO ISD #278
KIMBERLY LANE ELEM.
See Page 89

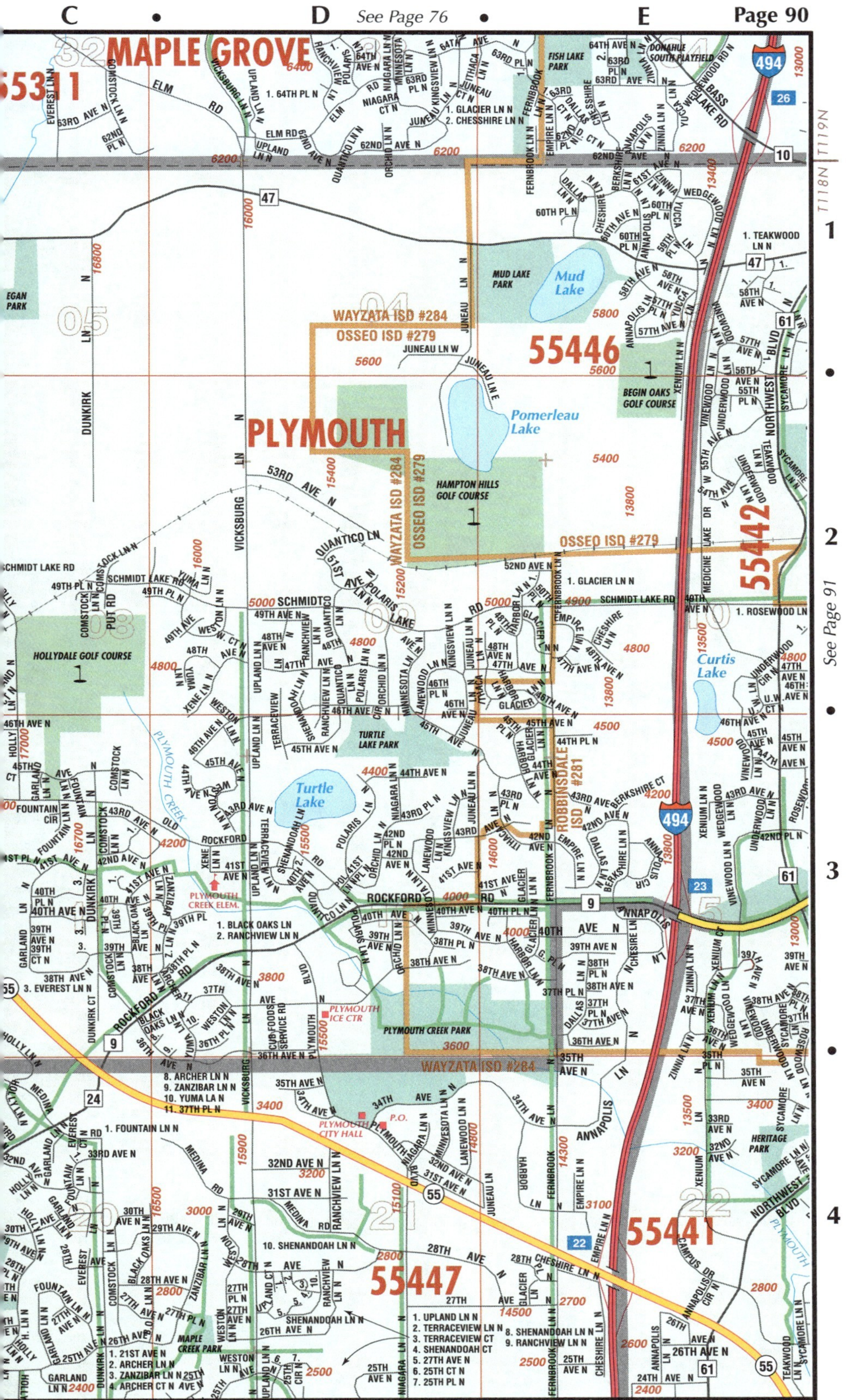

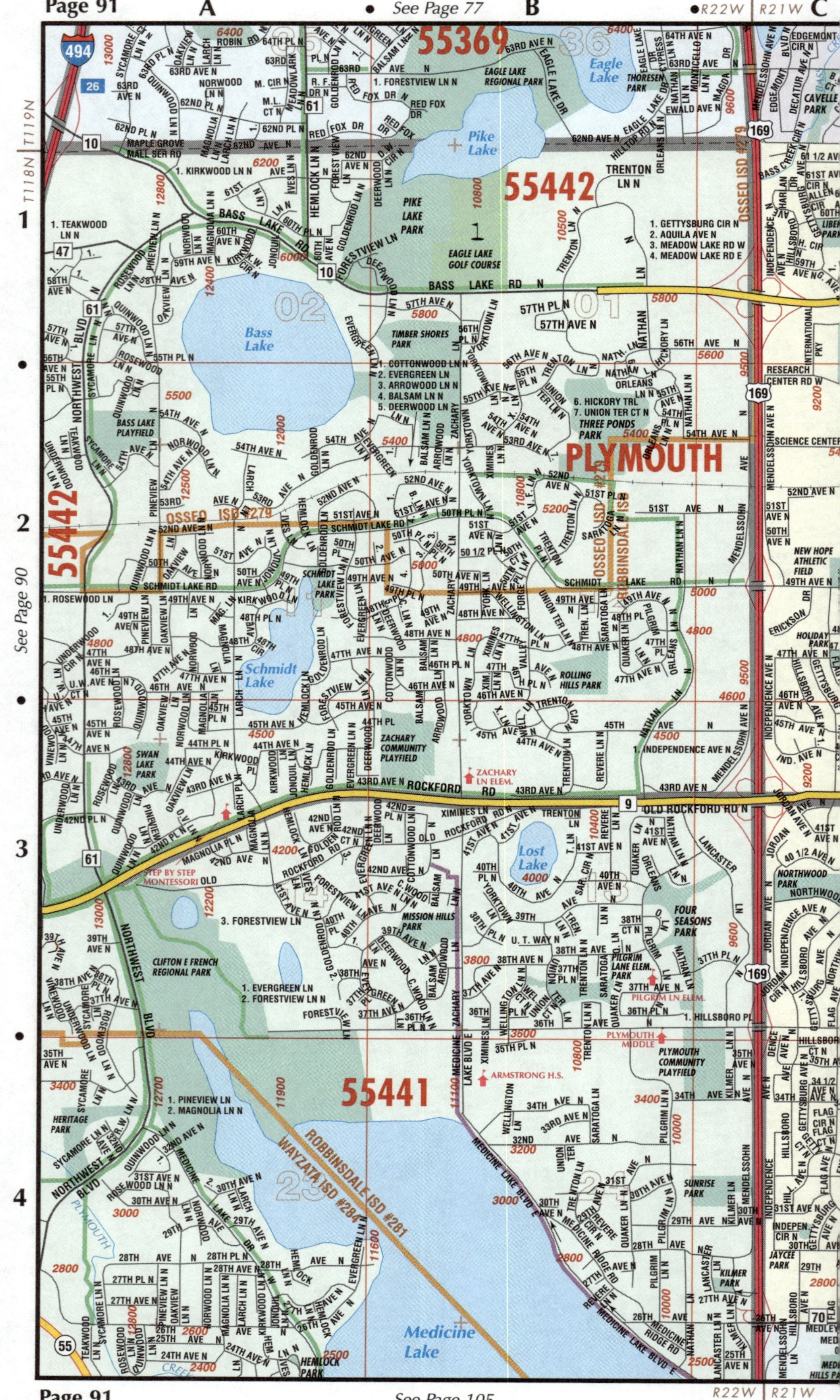

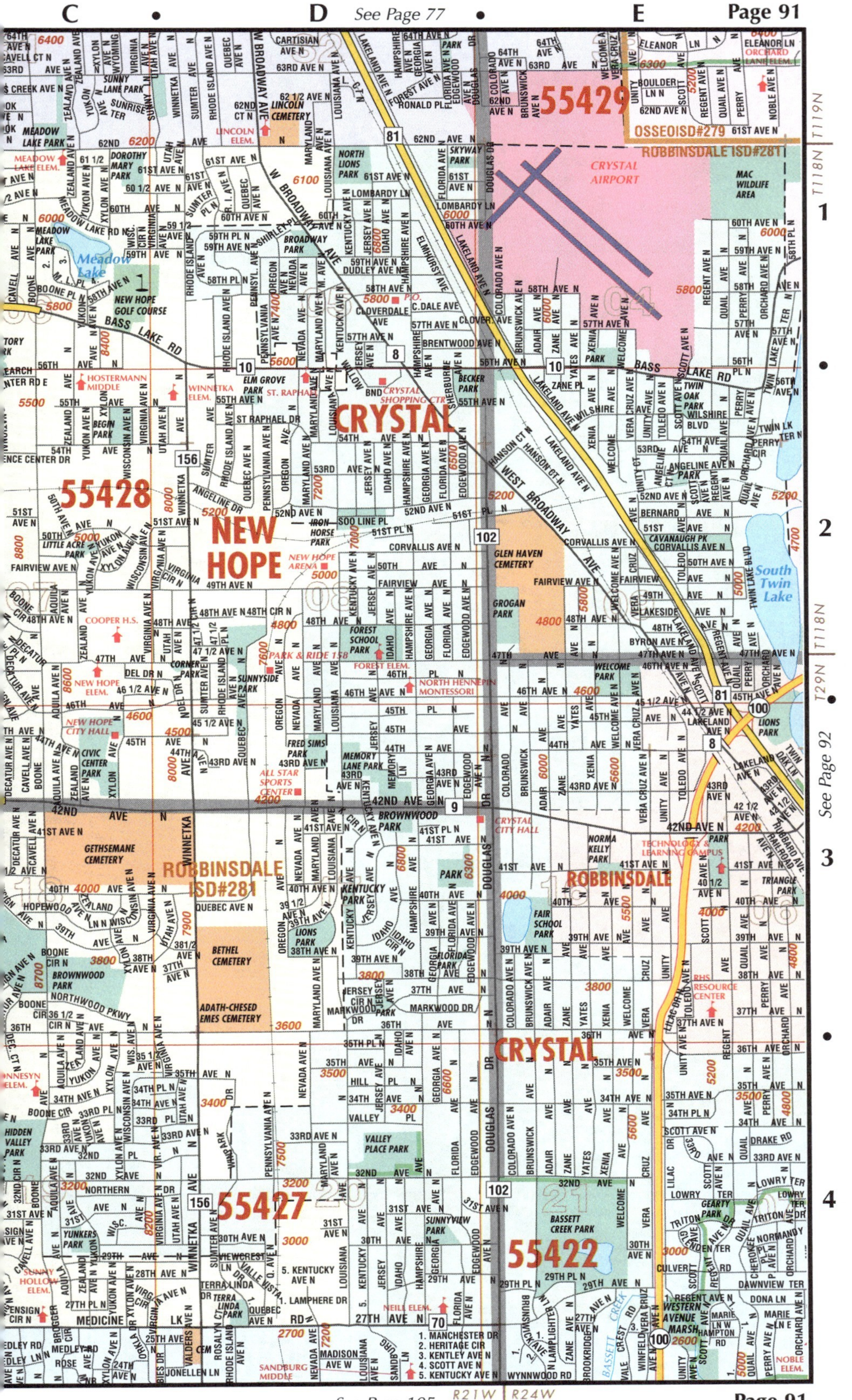

55429
CRYSTAL AIRPORT
ROBBINSDALE ISD#281
OSSEO ISD#279
MAC WILDLIFE AREA
55428
NEW HOPE
CRYSTAL
55427
55422
ROBBINSDALE
ROBBINSDALE ISD#281
Meadow Lake
South Twin Lake
NEW HOPE GOLF COURSE
GLEN HAVEN CEMETERY
GETHSEMANE CEMETERY
BETHEL CEMETERY
ADATH-CHESED EMES CEMETERY
BASSETT CREEK PARK
CRYSTAL SHOPPING CTR
CRYSTAL CITY HALL
NEW HOPE CITY HALL
TECHNOLOGY & LEARNING CAMPUS
BASS LAKE RD
WEST BROADWAY
DOUGLAS DR
WINNETKA
42ND AVE
MEDICINE LK RD
27TH AVE N
T119N
T118N
T29N
R21W
R24W
1
2
3
4

See Page 92

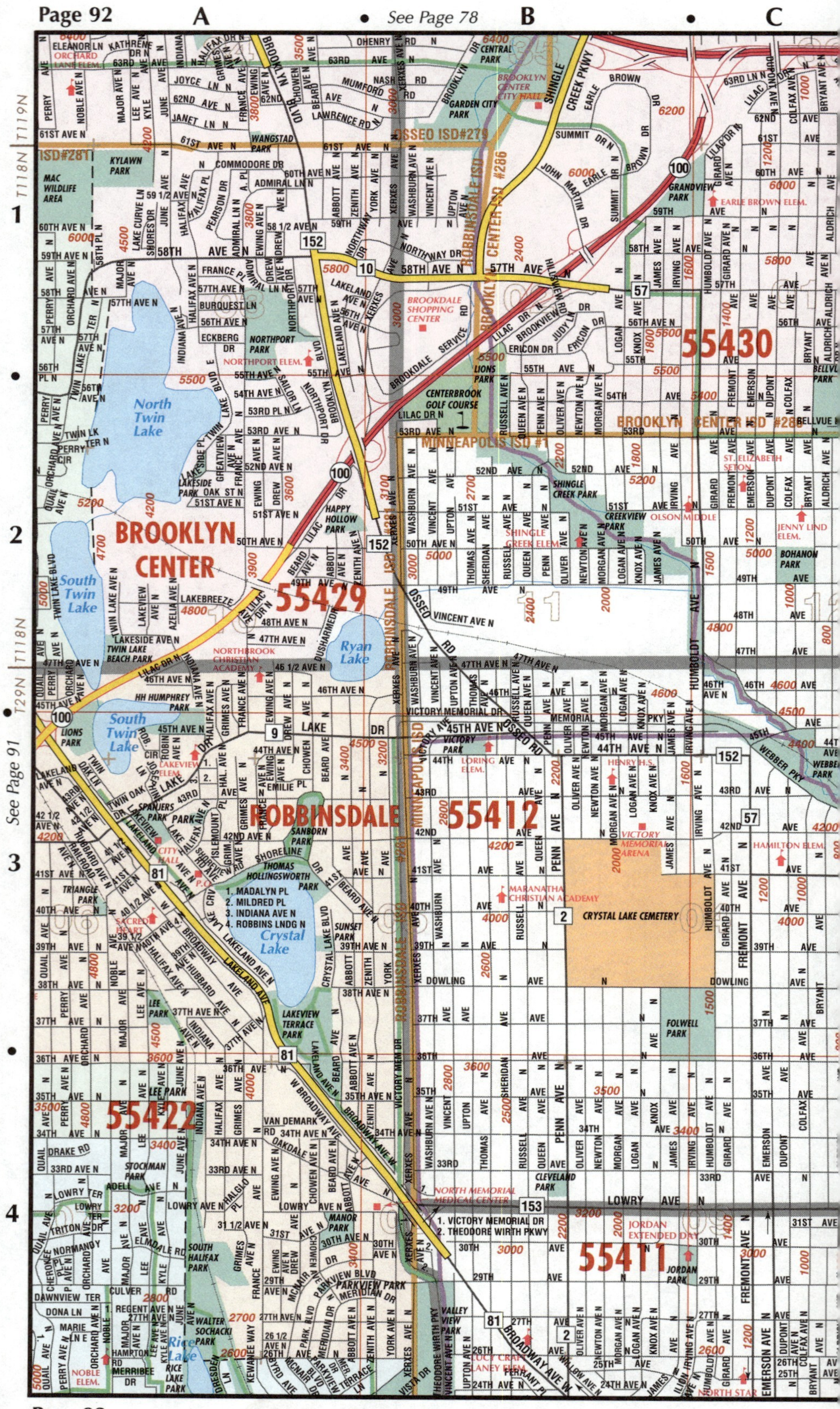

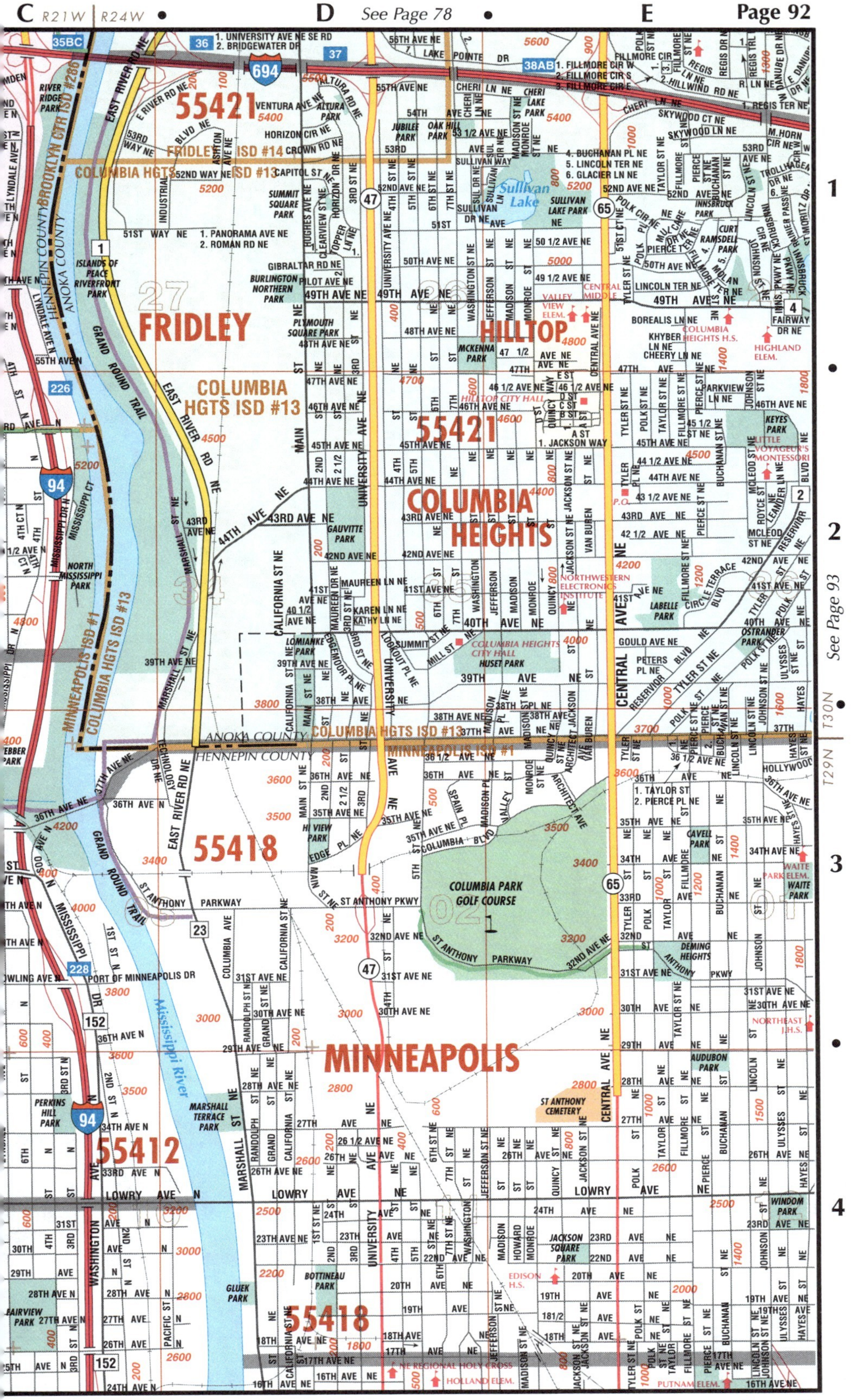
FRIDLEY
COLUMBIA HEIGHTS
HILLTOP
MINNEAPOLIS
55421
55418
55412
Sullivan Lake
Mississippi River
COLUMBIA PARK GOLF COURSE
ANOKA COUNTY
HENNEPIN COUNTY
See Page 93

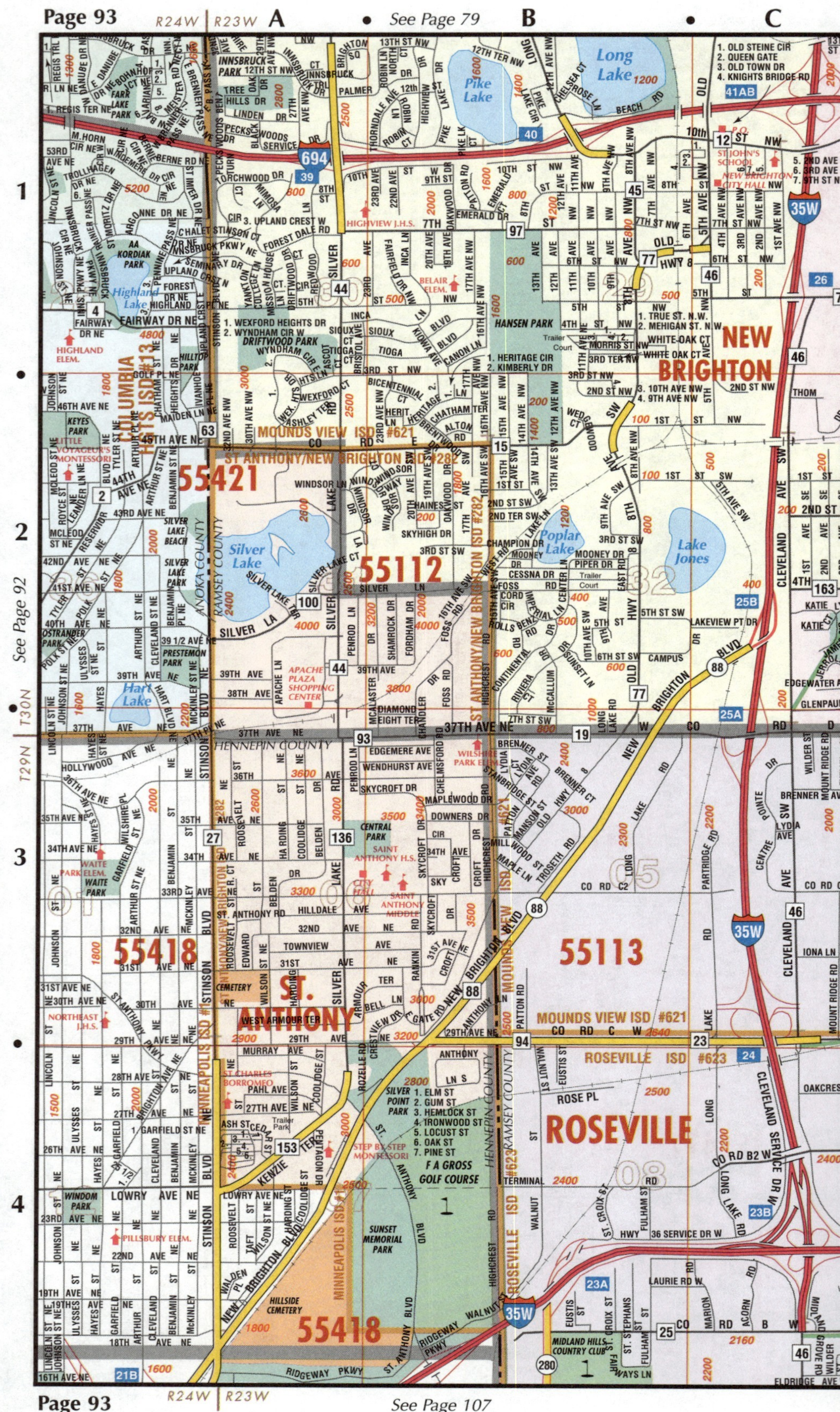
NEW BRIGHTON
ST. ANTHONY
ROSEVILLE
55421
55112
55418
55113
MOUNDS VIEW ISD #621
ST ANTHONY/NEW BRIGHTON ISD #282
COLUMBIA HGTS ISD #13
MINNEAPOLIS ISD #1
ROSEVILLE ISD #623
ANOKA COUNTY
RAMSEY COUNTY
HENNEPIN COUNTY
Silver Lake
Long Lake
Pike Lake
Poplar Lake
Lake Jones
Highland Lake
Hart Lake
HANSEN PARK
F A GROSS GOLF COURSE
SUNSET MEMORIAL PARK
HILLSIDE CEMETERY
MIDLAND HILLS COUNTRY CLUB
APACHE PLAZA SHOPPING CENTER
1. OLD STEINE CIR
2. QUEEN GATE
3. OLD TOWN DR
4. KNIGHTS BRIDGE RD
1. WEXFORD HEIGHTS DR
2. WYNDHAM CIR W
1. HERITAGE CIR
2. KIMBERLY DR
1. TRUE ST. N.W.
2. MEHIGAN ST. N.W.
3. 10TH AVE NW
4. 9TH AVE NW
1. ELM ST
2. GUM ST
3. HEMLOCK ST
4. IRONWOOD ST
5. LOCUST ST
6. OAK ST
7. PINE ST
See Page 92
T30N
T29N
1
2
3
4

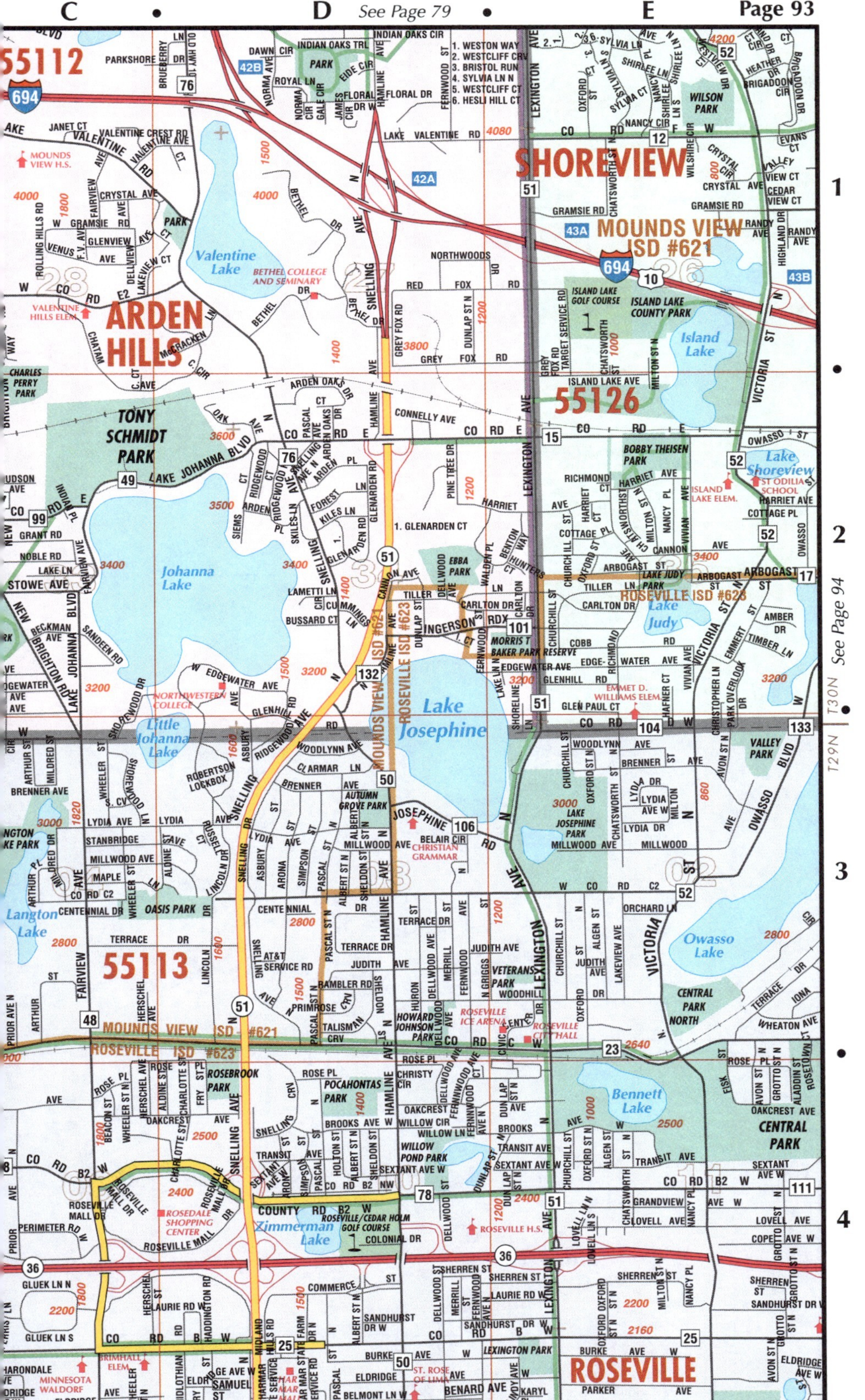

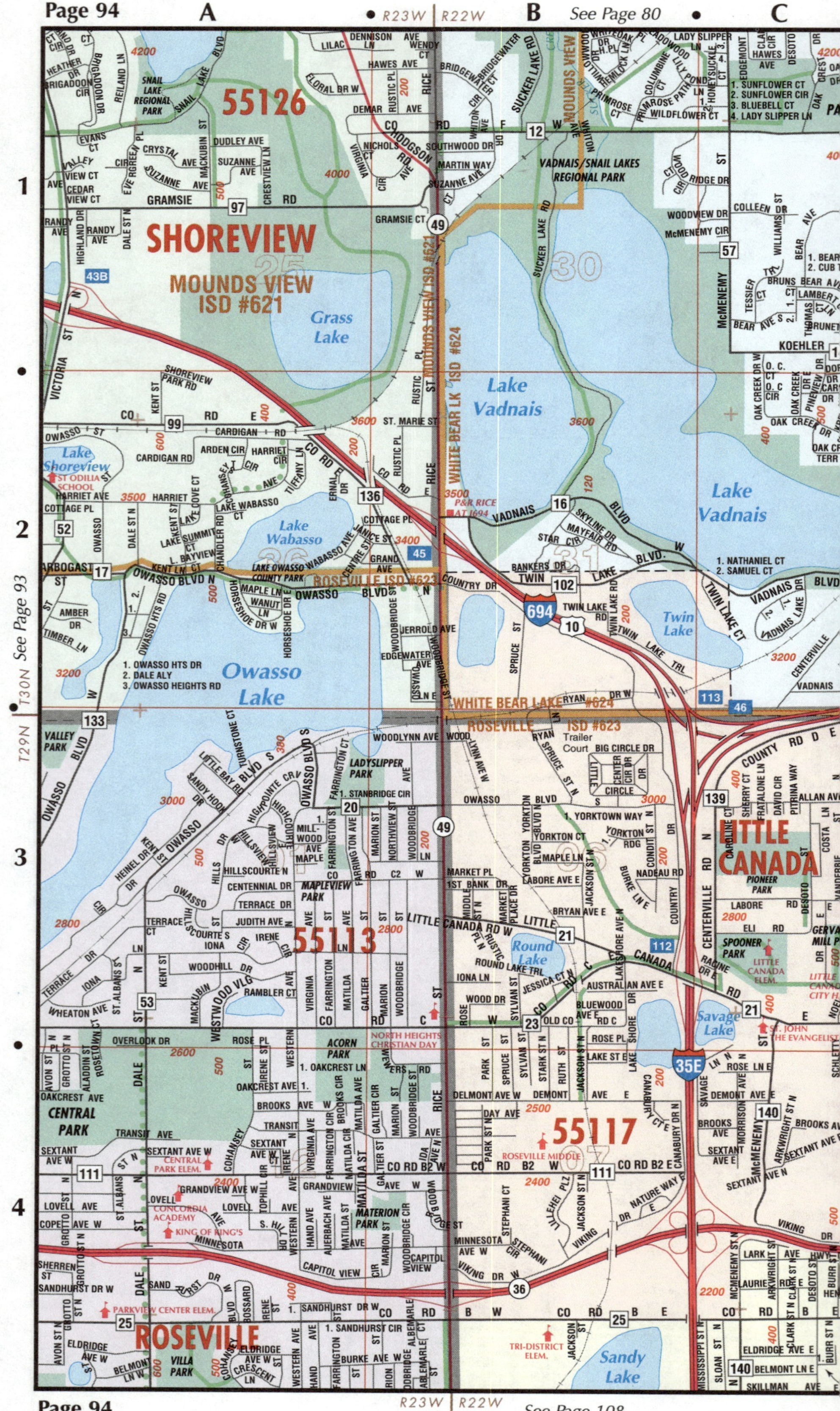

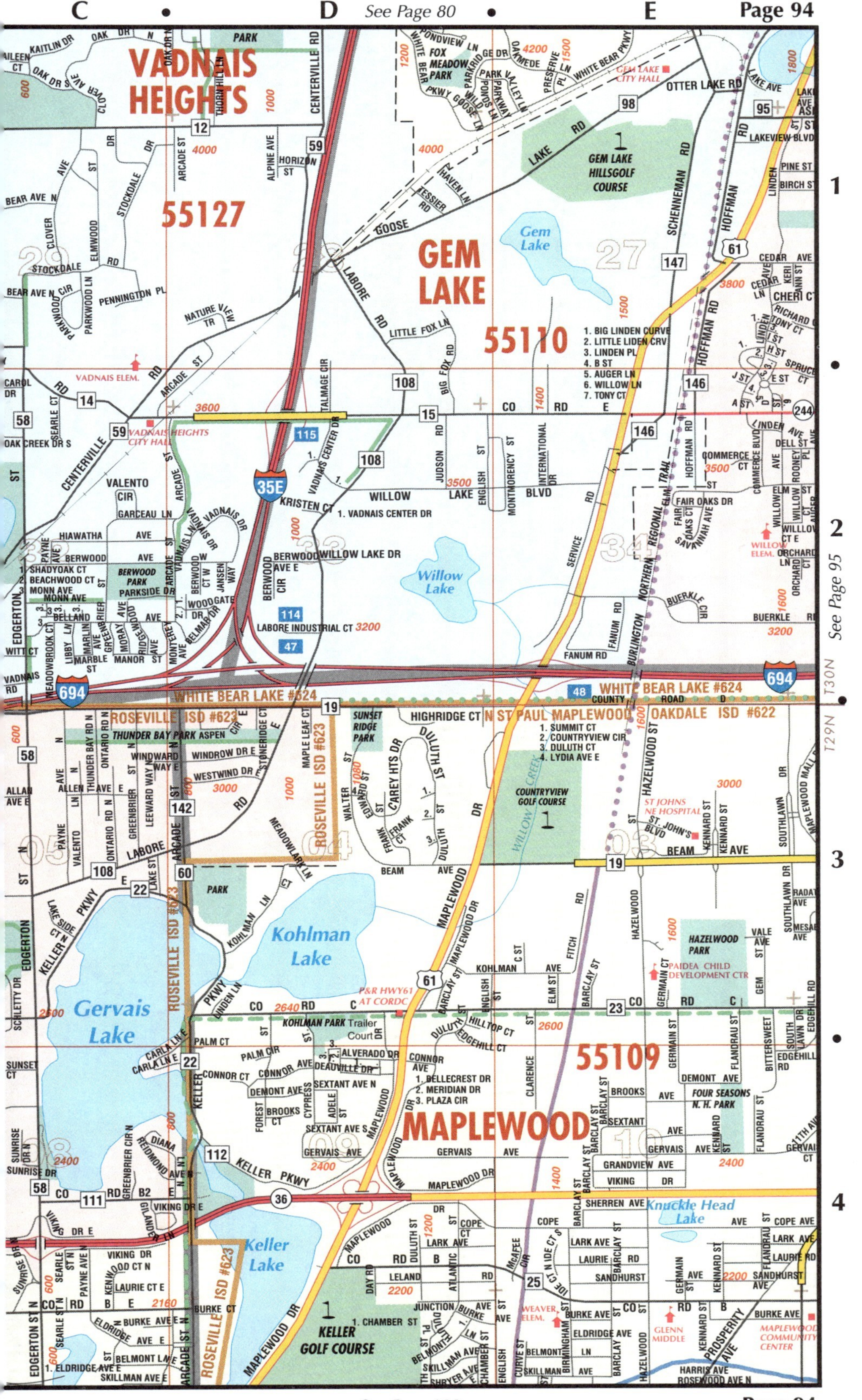

Page 94 is the overall content map. Key labeled features include:

VADNAIS HEIGHTS
55127

GEM LAKE
55110

1. BIG LINDEN CURVE
2. LITTLE LIDEN CRV
3. LINDEN PL
4. B ST
5. AUGER LN
6. WILLOW LN
7. TONY CT E

GEM LAKE HILLS GOLF COURSE

VADNAIS ELEM.

VADNAIS HEIGHTS CITY HALL

GEM LAKE CITY HALL

OTTER LAKE RD

1. VADNAIS CENTER DR

Willow Lake

LABORE INDUSTRIAL CT

WHITE BEAR LAKE #624

ROSEVILLE ISD #623

MAPLE LEAF CT

SUNSET RIDGE PARK

1. SUMMIT CT
2. COUNTRYVIEW CIR
3. DULUTH CT
4. LYDIA AVE E

N ST PAUL MAPLEWOOD OAKDALE ISD #622

COUNTRYVIEW GOLF COURSE

ST JOHNS NE HOSPITAL

HAZELWOOD PARK

Gervais Lake

Kohlman Lake

P&R HWY61 AT CORDC

KOHLMAN PARK Trailer Court

PAIDEA CHILD DEVELOPMENT CTR

55109

1. BELLECREST DR
2. MERIDIAN DR
3. PLAZA CIR

FOUR SEASONS N. H. PARK

MAPLEWOOD

Knuckle Head Lake

Keller Lake

ROSEVILLE ISD #623

1. CHAMBER ST

KELLER GOLF COURSE

WEAVER ELEM.

GLENN MIDDLE

MAPLEWOOD COMMUNITY CENTER

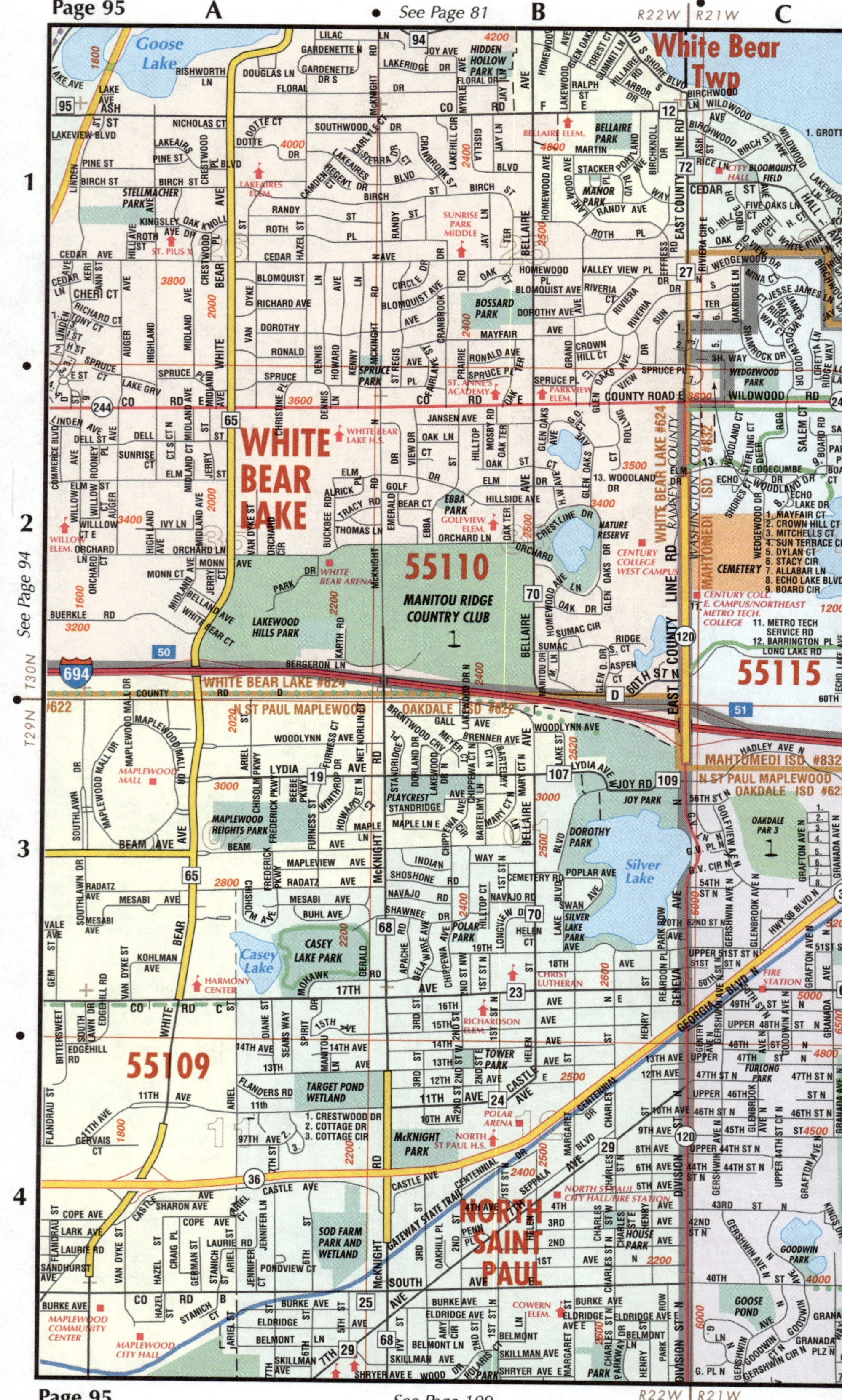

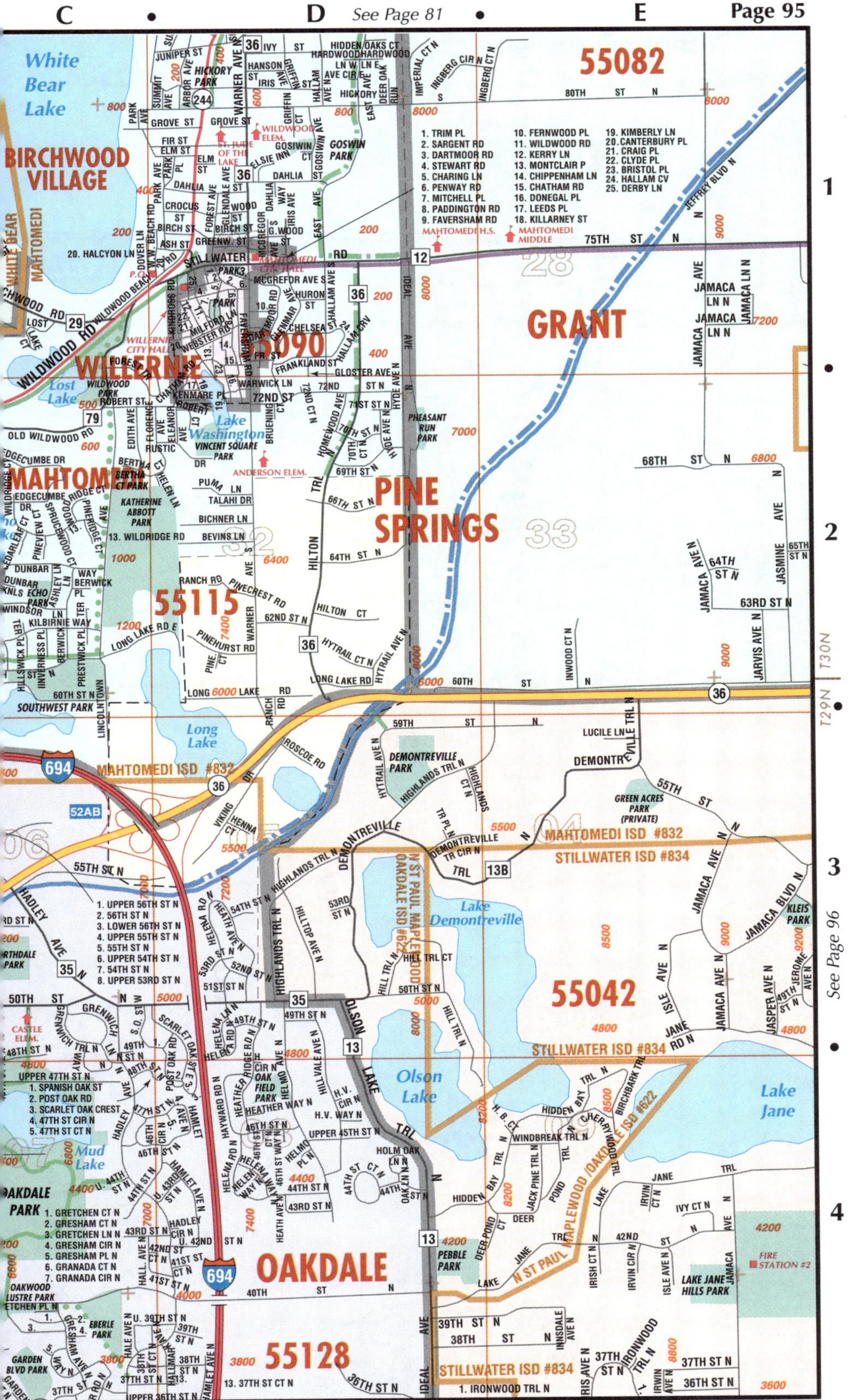
White Bear Lake
BIRCHWOOD VILLAGE
MAHTOMEDI
WILLERNIE
Lost Lake
Lake Washington
Long Lake
GRANT
PINE SPRINGS
OAKDALE
55082
55090
55115
55042
55128
Lake Demontreville
Olson Lake
Lake Jane
Mud Lake
1. TRIM PL
2. SARGENT RD
3. DARTMOOR RD
4. STEWART RD
5. CHARING LN
6. PENWAY RD
7. MITCHELL PL
8. PADDINGTON RD
9. FAVERSHAM RD
10. FERNWOOD PL
11. WILDWOOD RD
12. KERRY LN
13. MONTCLAIR P
14. CHIPPENHAM LN
15. CHATHAM RD
16. DONEGAL PL
17. LEEDS PL
18. KILLARNEY ST
19. KIMBERLY LN
20. CANTERBURY PL
21. CRAIG PL
22. CLYDE PL
23. BRISTOL PL
24. HALLAM CV
25. DERBY LN
MAHTOMEDI H.S.
MAHTOMEDI MIDDLE
GOSWIN PARK
PHEASANT RUN PARK
DEMONTREVILLE PARK
GREEN ACRES PARK (PRIVATE)
KLEIS PARK
KATHERINE ABBOTT PARK
VINCENT SQUARE PARK
ANDERSON ELEM.
SOUTHWEST PARK
MAHTOMEDI ISD #832
STILLWATER ISD #834
N ST PAUL MAPLEWOOD OAKDALE ISD #622
1. UPPER 56TH ST N
2. 56TH ST N
3. LOWER 56TH ST N
4. UPPER 55TH ST N
5. 55TH ST N
6. UPPER 54TH ST N
7. 54TH ST N
8. UPPER 53RD ST N
1. SPANISH OAK ST
2. POST OAK RD
3. SCARLET OAK CREST
4. 47TH ST CIR N
5. 47TH ST CT N
OAK FIELD PARK
CASTLE ELEM.
OAKDALE PARK
1. GRETCHEN CT N
2. GRESHAM CT N
3. GRETCHEN LN N
4. GRESHAM CIR N
5. GRESHAM PL N
6. GRANADA CT N
7. GRANADA CIR N
OAKWOOD LUSTRE PARK
EBERLE PARK
GARDEN BLVD PARK
PEBBLE PARK
LAKE JANE HILLS PARK
FIRE STATION #2
13. 37TH ST CT N
1. IRONWOOD TRL N
80TH ST N
75TH ST N
68TH ST N
60TH ST
59TH ST N
50TH ST
40TH ST N
39TH ST N
38TH ST N
37TH ST N
36TH ST N
IDEAL AVE
HILTON TRL
JAMACA AVE N
HIGHLANDS TRL N
OLSON LAKE TRL N
DEMONTREVILLE TRL N
JANE RD N
694
36
13
35
5
See Page 96

A • See Page 82 B • C

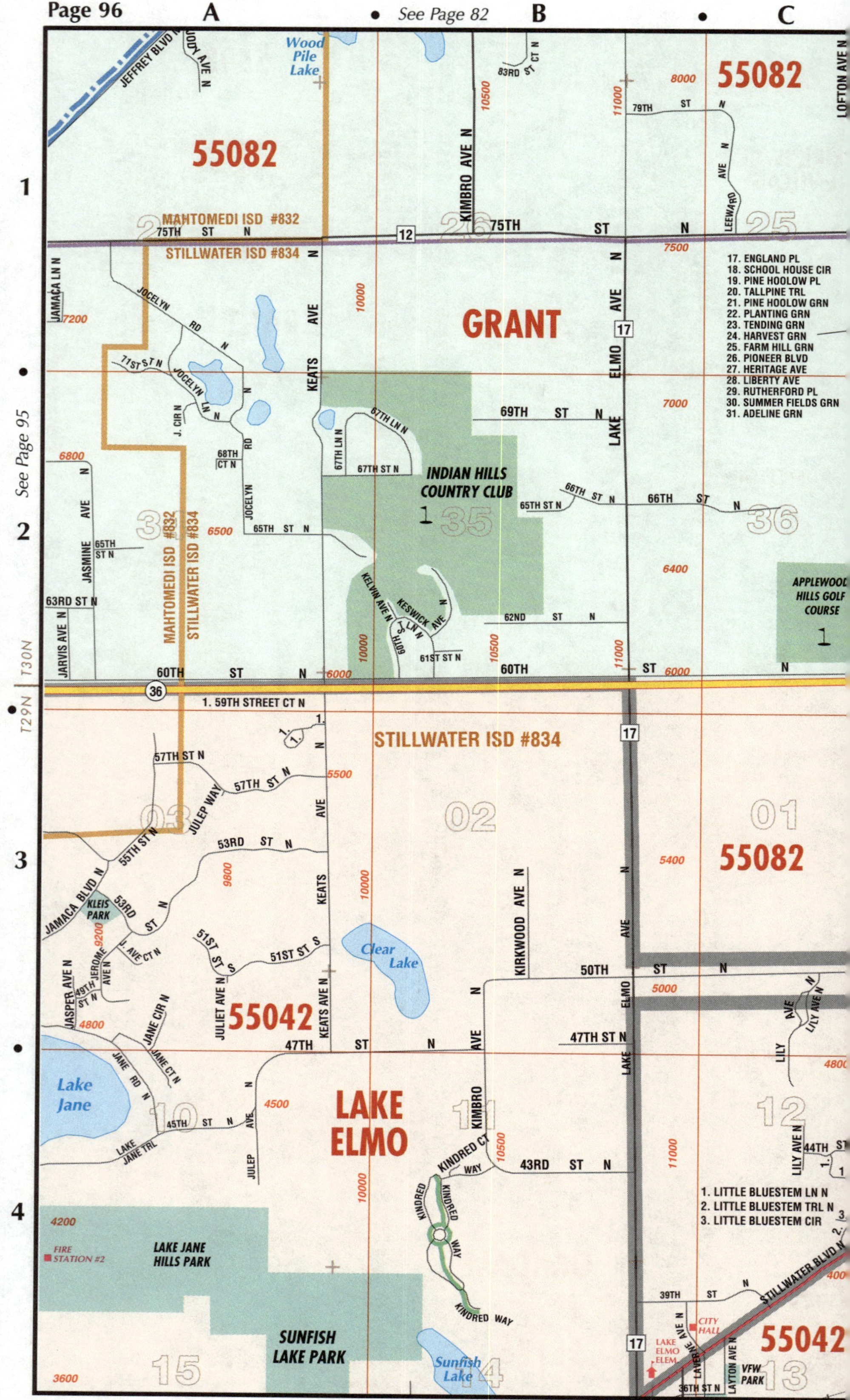

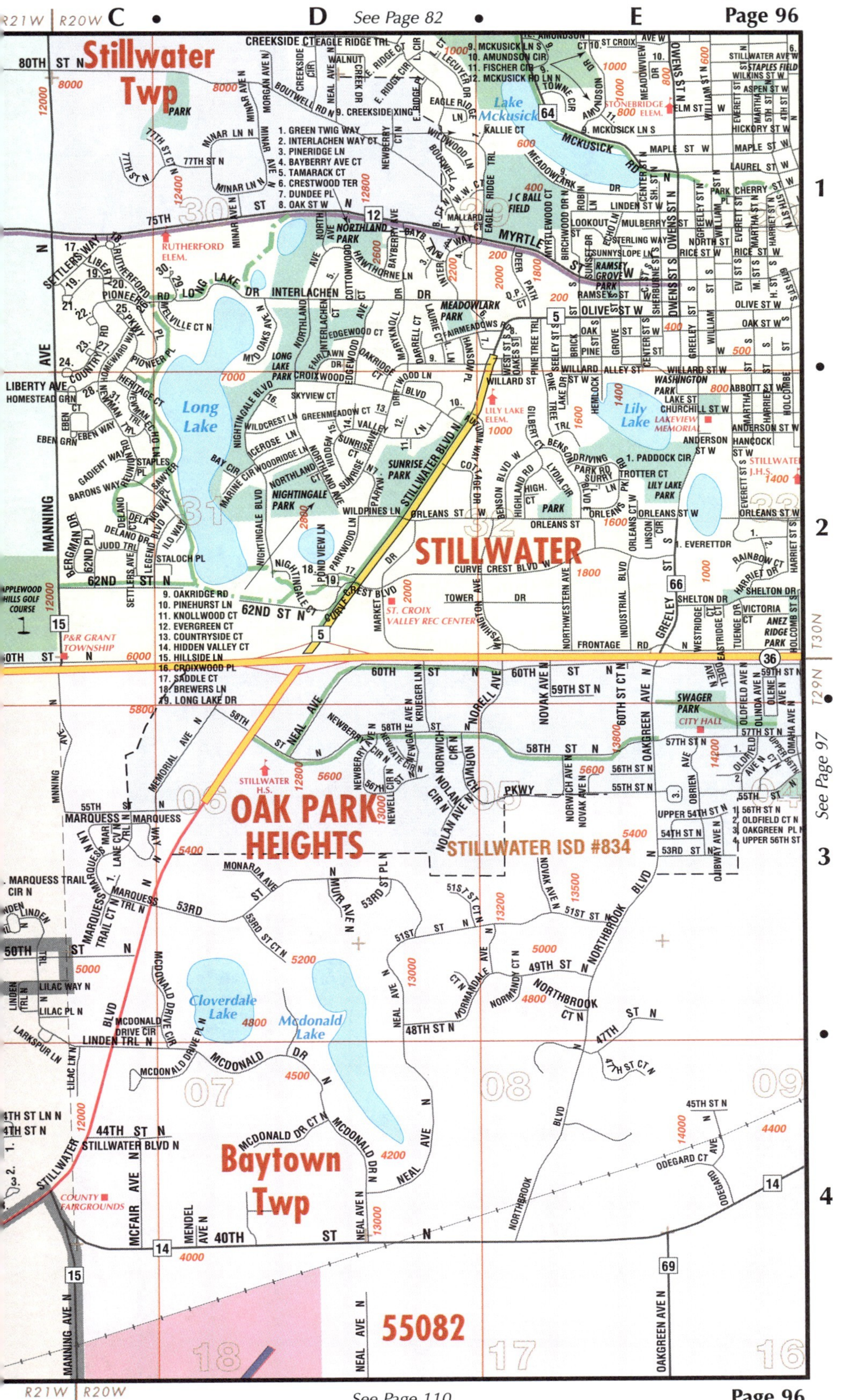
C
D
See Page 82
E
Page 96
R21W
R20W
Stillwater Twp
STILLWATER
OAK PARK HEIGHTS
Baytown Twp
STILLWATER ISD #834
55082
Long Lake
Lily Lake
Lake Mckusick
Cloverdale Lake
Mcdonald Lake
T30N
T29N
See Page 97
See Page 110
1
2
3
4
1. GREEN TWIG WAY
2. INTERLACHEN WAY CT
3. PINERIDGE LN
4. BAYBERRY AVE CT
5. TAMARACK CT
6. CRESTWOOD TER
7. DUNDEE PL
8. OAK ST W
9. OAKRIDGE RD
10. PINEHURST LN
11. KNOLLWOOD CT
12. EVERGREEN CT
13. COUNTRYSIDE CT
14. HIDDEN VALLEY CT
15. HILLSIDE LN
16. CROIXWOOD PL
17. SADDLE CT
18. BREWERS LN
19. LONG LAKE DR
9. MCKUSICK LN S
10. AMUNDSON CIR
11. FISCHER CIR
12. MCKUSICK RD LN N
1. 56TH ST N
2. OLDFIELD CT N
3. OAKGREEN PL N
4. UPPER 56TH ST
RUTHERFORD ELEM.
LILY LAKE ELEM.
STONEBRIDGE ELEM.
STILLWATER H.S.
STILLWATER J.H.S.
ST. CROIX VALLEY REC CENTER
LAKEVIEW MEMORIAL
CITY HALL
COUNTY FAIRGROUNDS
P&R GRANT TOWNSHIP
APPLEWOOD HILLS GOLF COURSE
Page 96

A R20W
See Page 83
B
C

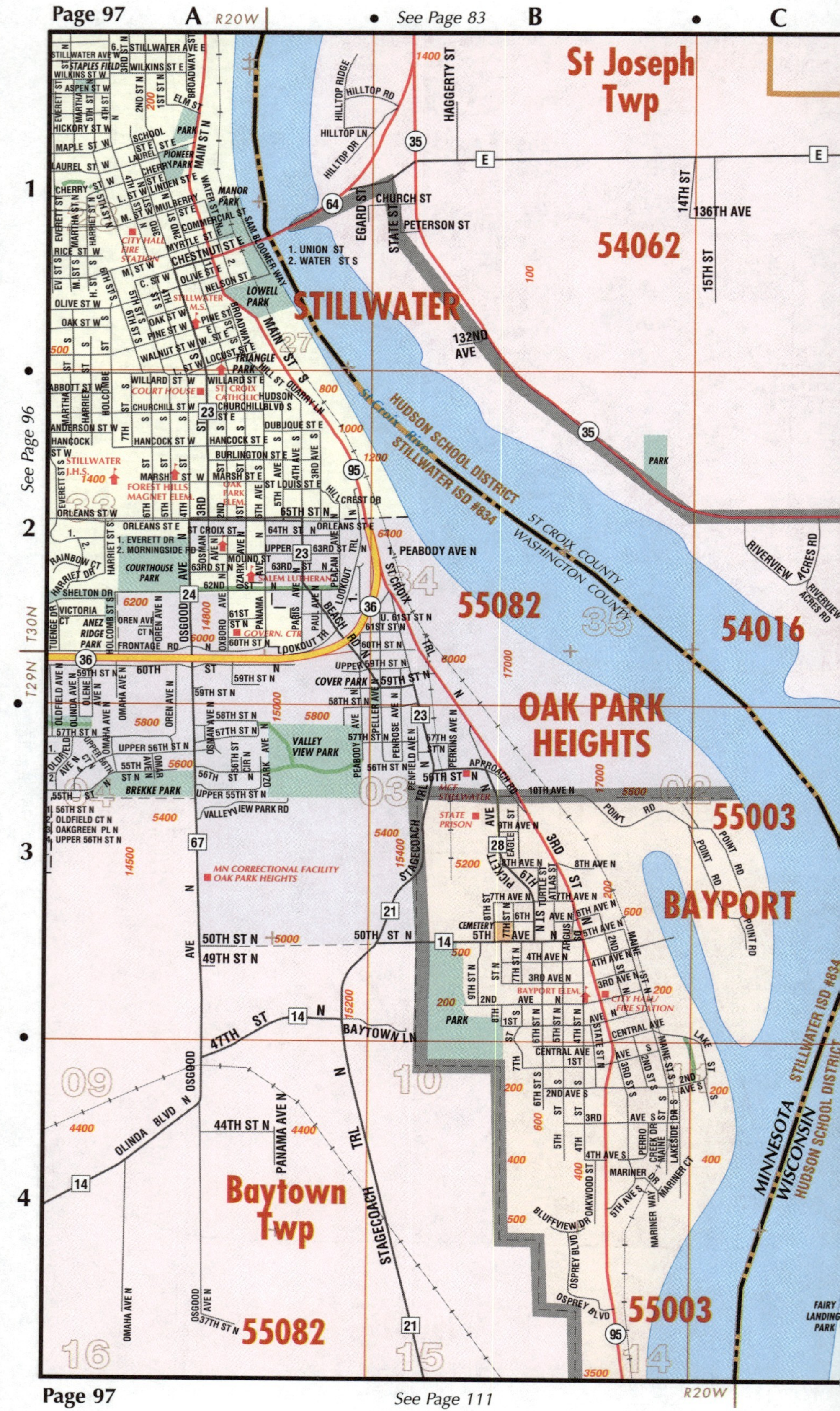

See Page 96
1
2
3
4
T30N
T29N

See Page 111
R20W

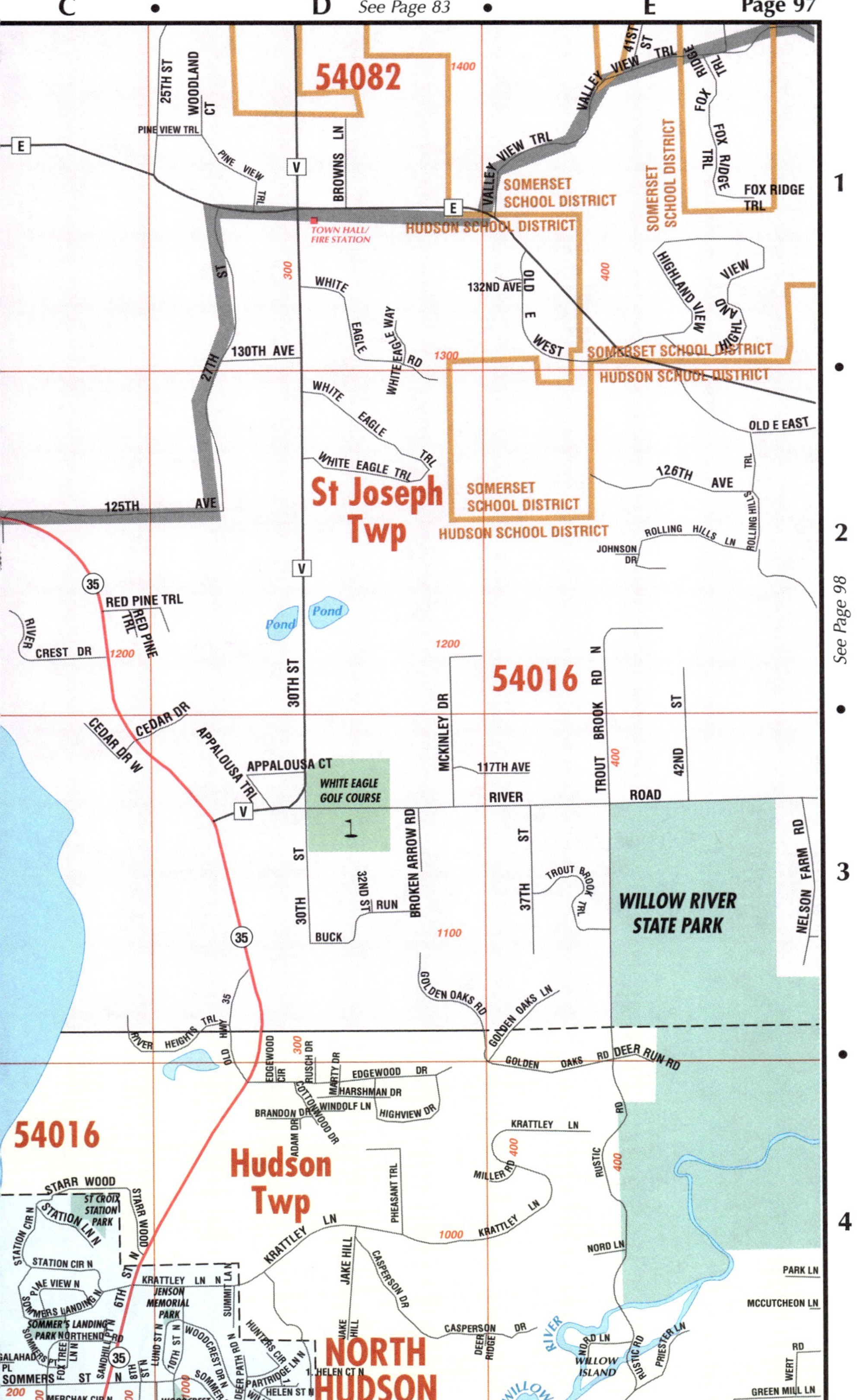

54082

25TH ST

WOODLAND CT

PINE VIEW TRL

PINE VIEW TRL

BROWNS LN

1400

VALLEY VIEW TRL

VALLEY VIEW TRL

VIST ST

FOX RIDGE TRL

FOX RIDGE TRL

FOX RIDGE TRL

SOMERSET SCHOOL DISTRICT

SOMERSET SCHOOL DISTRICT

SOMERSET SCHOOL DISTRICT

HUDSON SCHOOL DISTRICT

TOWN HALL/ FIRE STATION

300

WHITE EAGLE RD

WHITE EAGLE WAY

130TH AVE

132ND AVE

OLD E WEST

1300

400

HIGHLAND VIEW

HIGHLAND VIEW

SOMERSET SCHOOL DISTRICT

HUDSON SCHOOL DISTRICT

OLD E EAST

WHITE EAGLE TRL

WHITE EAGLE TRL

126TH AVE

ROLLING HILLS LN

ROLLING HILLS TRL

St Joseph Twp

SOMERSET SCHOOL DISTRICT

HUDSON SCHOOL DISTRICT

JOHNSON DR

125TH AVE

35

RED PINE TRL

RED PINE TRL

RIVER CREST DR

1200

Pond

Pond

1200

30TH ST

54016

MCKINLEY DR

TROUT BROOK RD N

42ND ST

CEDAR DR W

CEDAR DR

APPALOUSA TRL

APPALOUSA CT

WHITE EAGLE GOLF COURSE

1

117TH AVE

RIVER

400

TROUT BROOK ROAD

NELSON FARM RD

30TH ST

BROKEN ARROW RD

32ND ST RUN

BUCK

1100

37TH ST

TROUT BROOK TRL

WILLOW RIVER STATE PARK

35

RIVER HEIGHTS TRL

OLD HWY 35

GOLDEN OAKS RD

GOLDEN OAKS LN

GOLDEN OAKS RD DEER RUN RD

54016

EDGEWOOD CIR

300

RUSCH DR

MARTY DR

EDGEWOOD DR

HARSHMAN DR

WINDOLF LN

HIGHVIEW DR

BRANDON DR

COTTONWOOD DR

ADAM DR

KRATTLEY LN

MILLER RD

400

KRATTLEY LN

RUSTIC RD

400

Hudson Twp

STARR WOOD

ST CROIX STATION PARK

STATION LN N

STATION CIR N

STATION CIR N

STARR WOOD

PINE VIEW N

6TH ST N

PHEASANT TRL

KRATTLEY LN

1000

KRATTLEY LN

NORD LN

PARK LN

MCCUTCHEON LN

KRATTLEY LN N

JENSON MEMORIAL PARK

SUMMIT LN

SOMMERS LANDING

SOMMER'S LANDING PARK NORTHEND

FOX TREE LN

SANDHILL

32ND ST N

8TH ST

35

KRATTLEY LN

JAKE HILL LN

JAKE HILL

CASPERSON DR

CASPERSON DR

WOODCREST DR N

DEER PATH RD N

HUNTERS CIR N

PARTRIDGE LN

WILLOW CIR N

WOODCREST

DEER RIDGE

WILLOW ISLAND

NORD LN

RUSTIC RD

PRESTER LN

RD

WERT RD

GREEN MILL LN

GALAHAD PL

MERCHAK CIR N

SOMMERS ST

200

800

1000

NORTH HUDSON

HELEN CT N

HELEN ST N

WILLOW RIVER

See Page 111

1

2

3

4

E

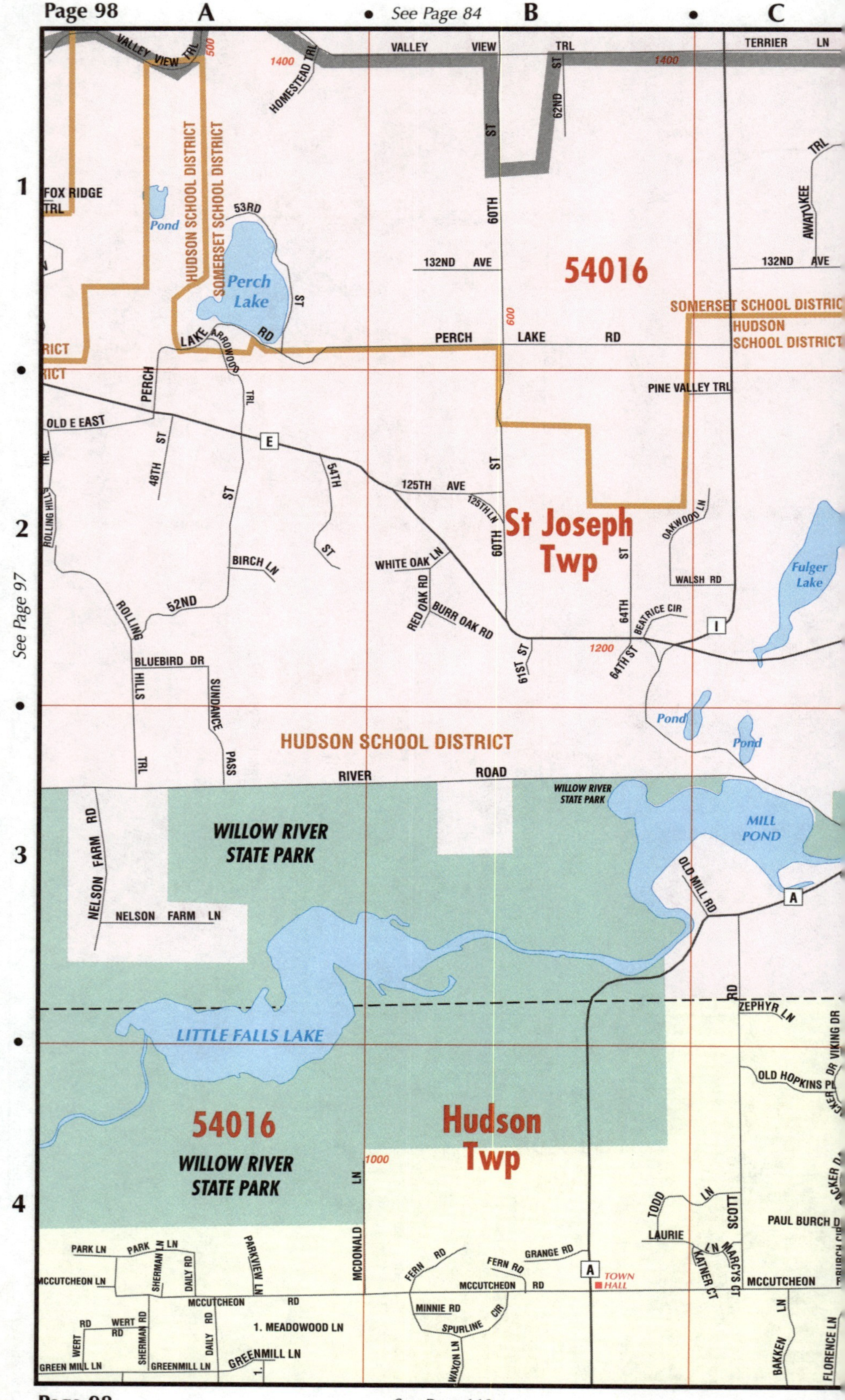

See Page 84

See Page 97

See Page 112

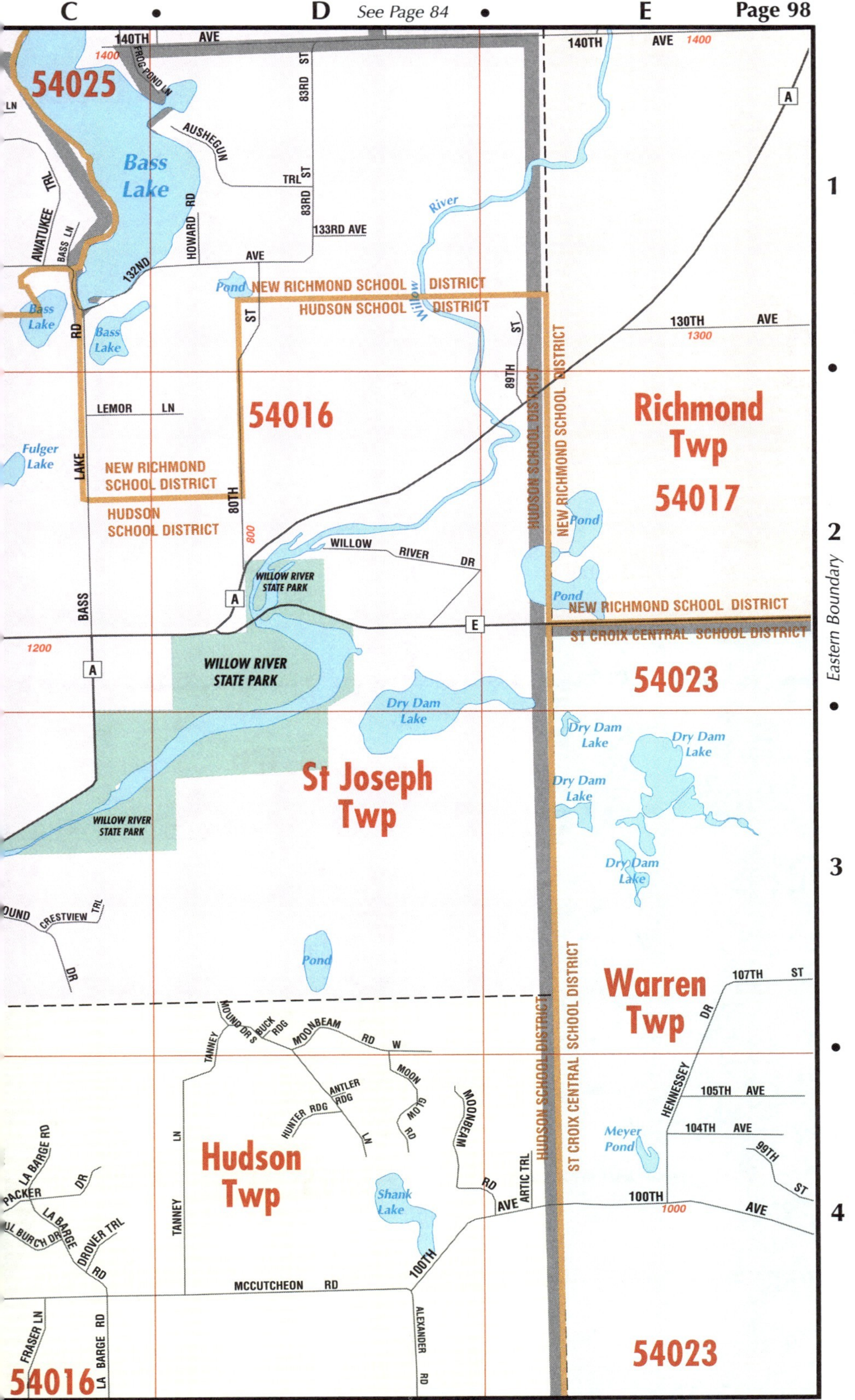

140TH AVE
1400
54025
FROG POND LN
83RD ST
AUSHEGUN
Bass Lake
TRL
133RD AVE
AWATUKEE TRL
BASS LN
HOWARD RD
132ND AVE
Pond
NEW RICHMOND SCHOOL DISTRICT
HUDSON SCHOOL DISTRICT
Willow River
Bass Lake
RD
ST
89TH ST
130TH AVE
1300
A
LEMOR LN
54016
Richmond Twp
54017
Fulger Lake
LAKE
NEW RICHMOND SCHOOL DISTRICT
HUDSON SCHOOL DISTRICT
80TH
800
WILLOW RIVER DR
Pond
HUDSON SCHOOL DISTRICT
NEW RICHMOND SCHOOL DISTRICT
WILLOW RIVER STATE PARK
BASS
A
E
NEW RICHMOND SCHOOL DISTRICT
ST CROIX CENTRAL SCHOOL DISTRICT
1200
WILLOW RIVER STATE PARK
54023
Dry Dam Lake
St Joseph Twp
WILLOW RIVER STATE PARK
CRESTVIEW TRL
DR
Pond
Warren Twp
107TH ST
MOUND DR S
BUCK RDG
MOONBEAM RD W
TANNEY
MOON GLOW RD
ANTLER RDG
HUNTER RDG
LN
MOONBEAM
HENNESSEY DR
105TH AVE
104TH AVE
99TH ST
Meyer Pond
LA BARGE RD
PACKER DR
LA BARGE RD
DROVER TRL
BURCH DR
Hudson Twp
TANNEY
Shank Lake
RD
AVE
ARTIC TRL
HUDSON SCHOOL DISTRICT
ST CROIX CENTRAL SCHOOL DISTRICT
100TH AVE
1000
100TH
MCCUTCHEON RD
ALEXANDER RD
FRASER LN
LA BARGE RD
54016
54023
1
2
3
4
Eastern Boundary

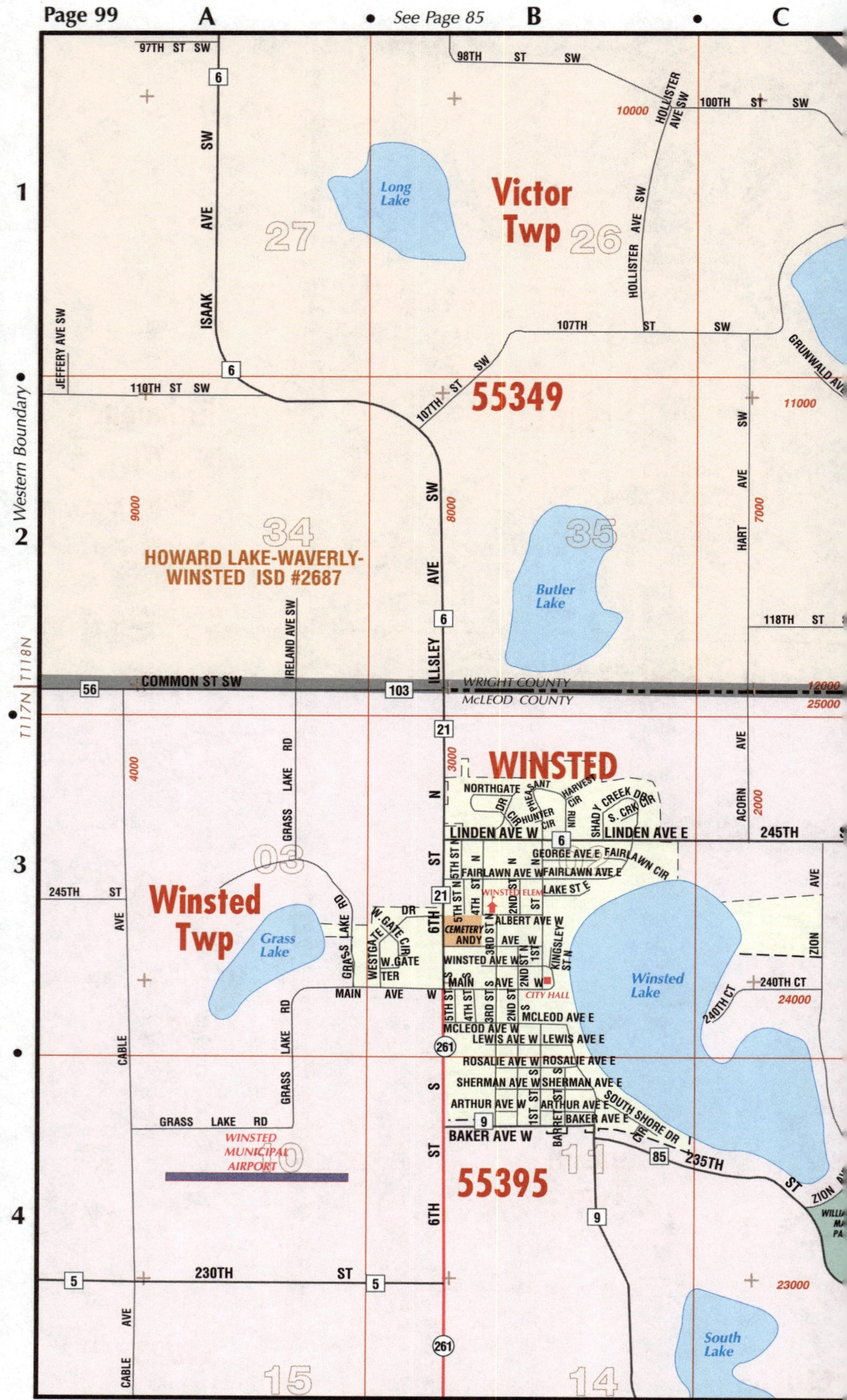

See Page 85

A • B • C

T117N | T118N

97TH ST SW

98TH ST SW

6

HOLLISTER AVE SW

100TH ST SW

10000

Long Lake

Victor Twp

27

26

ISAAK AVE SW

HOLLISTER AVE SW

JEFFERY AVE SW

6

107TH ST SW

107TH ST SW

110TH ST SW

107TH ST SW

55349

HART AVE SW

11000

GRUNWALD AVE

1

9000

34

HOWARD LAKE-WAVERLY-WINSTED ISD #2687

ISAAK AVE SW

ILLSLEY AVE SW

6

35

Butler Lake

7000

118TH ST

IRELAND AVE SW

2

56

COMMON ST SW

103

ILLSLEY

WRIGHT COUNTY
McLEOD COUNTY

12000
25000

4000

03

245TH ST

Winsted Twp

GRASS LAKE RD

GRASS LAKE RD

Grass Lake

GRASS LAKE RD

AVE

21

3000

WINSTED

NORTHGATE DR

PHEASANT CIR

HUNTER CIR

HARVEST CIR

SHADY CREEK DR

S. CRK CIR

ACORN AVE

2000

245TH

LINDEN AVE W

6

LINDEN AVE E

GEORGE AVE E

FAIRLAWN CIR

N 5TH ST

5TH ST N

3RD ST N

FAIRLAWN AVE W

FAIRLAWN AVE E

ZION AVE

21

WINSTED ELEM

LAKE ST E

ALBERT AVE W

WESTGATE DR

W GATE CIR

W. GATE TER

CEMETERY

ANDY AVE

3RD ST

KINGSLEY ST N

240TH CT

24000

240TH CT

Winsted Lake

WINSTED 3RD AVE W

MAIN AVE W

4TH ST S

3RD ST S

2ND ST S

CITY HALL

N 5TH ST S

MCLEOD AVE W

MCLEOD AVE E

261

LEWIS AVE W

LEWIS AVE E

ROSALIE AVE W

ROSALIE AVE E

SHERMAN AVE W

SHERMAN AVE E

ARTHUR AVE W

1ST ST

ARTHUR AVE E

SOUTH SHORE DR

9

BAKER AVE W

BARREL ST

BAKER AVE E

85

235TH ST

ZION AVE

CABLE AVE

GRASS LAKE RD

GRASS LAKE RD

WINSTED MUNICIPAL AIRPORT

10

11

6TH ST S

55395

9

WILLIAM MA PA

5

230TH ST

5

261

CABLE AVE

15

14

South Lake

23000

3

4

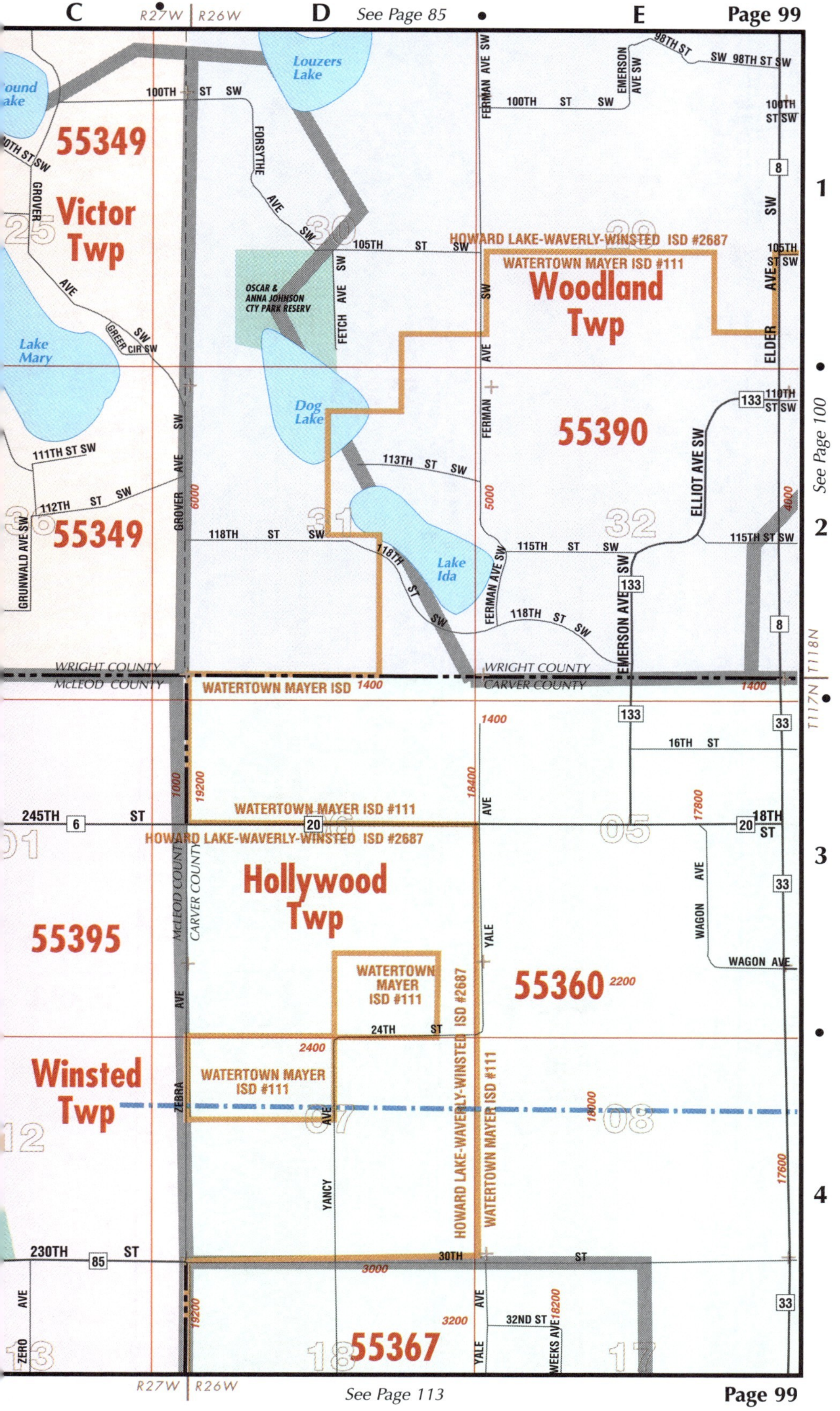

Louzers Lake

Pound Lake

100TH ST SW

55349

Victor Twp

GROVER AVE SW

25

FORSYTHE AVE SW

30

FETCH AVE SW

OSCAR & ANNA JOHNSON CTY PARK RESERV

105TH ST SW

HOWARD LAKE-WAVERLY-WINSTED ISD #2687

WATERTOWN MAYER ISD #111

Woodland Twp

29

FERMAN AVE SW

FERMAN AVE SW

98TH ST

SW 98TH ST SW

EMERSON AVE SW

100TH ST SW

FERMAN AVE SW

100TH ST SW

ELDER AVE SW

105TH ST SW

1

Lake Mary

GREER AVE SW

GREER CIR SW

Dog Lake

113TH ST SW

55390

ELLIOT AVE SW

133

110TH ST SW

See Page 100

111TH ST SW

GROVER AVE SW

6000

31

118TH ST SW

Lake Ida

115TH ST SW

5000

32

115TH ST SW

133

2

GRUNWALD AVE SW

112TH ST SW

55349

118TH ST SW

118TH ST SW

FERMAN AVE SW

118TH ST SW

EMERSON AVE SW

133

8

WRIGHT COUNTY

McLEOD COUNTY

WRIGHT COUNTY

CARVER COUNTY

T117N | T118N

WATERTOWN MAYER ISD 1400

1400

1400

133

33

16TH ST

245TH ST

6

1000

19200

WATERTOWN MAYER ISD #111

20

16

HOWARD LAKE-WAVERLY-WINSTED ISD #2687

18400

AVE

05

17800

18TH ST

20

33

01

McLEOD COUNTY

CARVER COUNTY

Hollywood Twp

55395

WATERTOWN MAYER ISD #111

24TH ST

YALE

WAGON AVE

WAGON AVE

55360 2200

ISD #2687

Winsted Twp

ZEBRA AVE

2400

WATERTOWN MAYER ISD #111

07

YANCY AVE

HOWARD LAKE-WAVERLY-WINSTED ISD #111

WATERTOWN MAYER ISD #111

10000

08

17600

3

12

4

230TH ST

85

3000

30TH ST

ZERO AVE

19200

3200

55367

18

YALE AVE

32ND ST

WEEKS AVE

8200

17

33

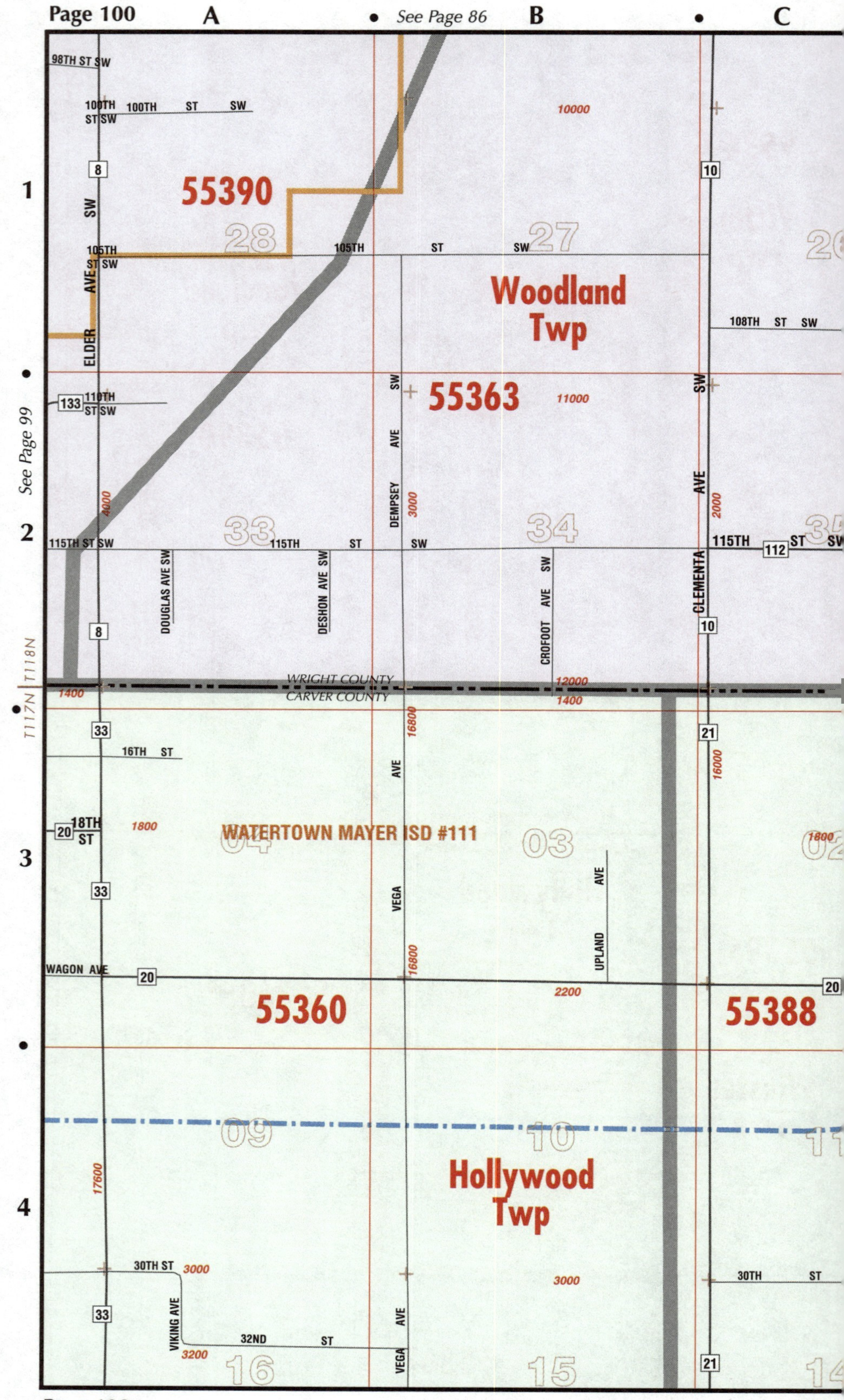

See Page 86

A   B   C

See Page 99

98TH ST SW

100TH ST SW   100TH   ST   SW

8

55390

ELDER   AVE   SW

28

105TH ST SW

105TH   ST   SW   27

10000

10

Woodland
Twp

108TH   ST   SW

133   110TH ST SW

DEMPSEY   AVE   SW

SW   **55363**   11000

SW

CLEMENTA   AVE

4000

3000   2000

33   34

115TH ST SW   115TH   ST   SW   115TH   112   ST   SW

DOUGLAS AVE SW   DESHON AVE SW   CROFOOT   AVE   SW

8   10

T117N | T118N

WRIGHT COUNTY
CARVER COUNTY

1400   12000   1400

33   16800   21

16TH   ST   16000

20   18TH ST   1800   **WATERTOWN MAYER ISD #111**   03   02

04   VEGA   AVE   UPLAND   AVE   1800

33

WAGON AVE   20   16800   2200   20

55360   **55388**

17600   09   10   11

Hollywood
Twp

33   30TH ST   3000   3000   30TH   ST

VIKING AVE

32ND   ST   VEGA   AVE   21

3200   16   15   14

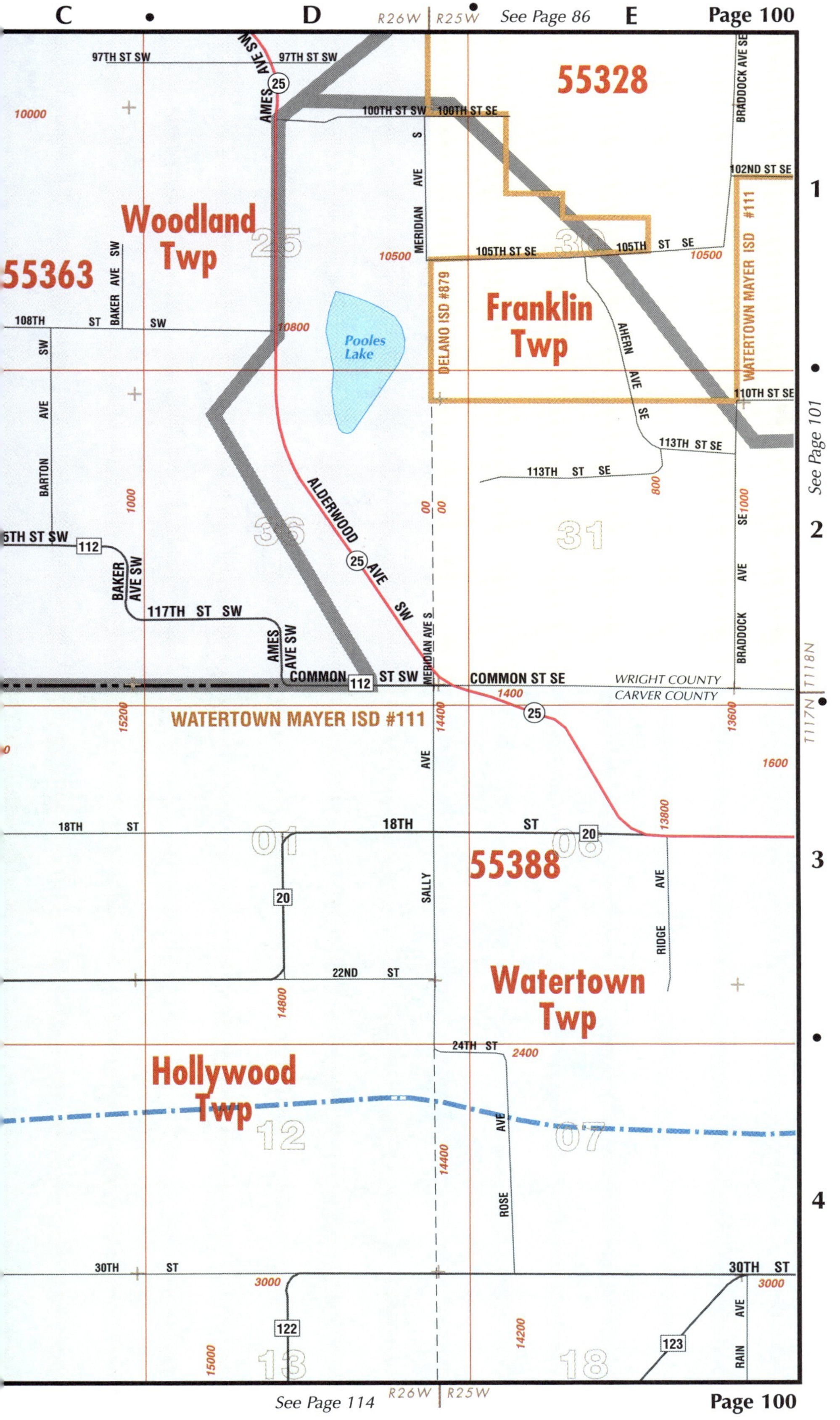

97TH ST SW 97TH ST SW

55328

BRADDOCK AVE SE

10000

100TH ST SW 100TH ST SE

102ND ST SE

Woodland Twp

MERIDIAN AVE S

1

55363

BAKER AVE SW

25

105TH ST SE 105TH ST SE

10500

WATERTOWN MAYER ISD #111

108TH ST SW

10800

Pooles Lake

DELANO ISD #879

Franklin Twp

AHERN AVE SE

•

110TH ST SE

BARTON AVE SW

1000

36

ALDERWOOD AVE SW

113TH ST SE

113TH ST SE

800

SE 1000

BRADDOCK AVE SE

T117N | T118N

5TH ST SW 112

25

00 00

31

2

BAKER AVE SW

117TH ST SW

AMES AVE SW

MERIDIAN AVE S

COMMON ST SW 112

COMMON ST SE

WRIGHT COUNTY
CARVER COUNTY

•

15200

WATERTOWN MAYER ISD #111

14400

1400

25

13600

1600

AVE

18TH ST

18TH ST

20

13800

•

18TH ST

01

SALLY

06

55388

RIDGE AVE

3

20

22ND ST

14800

Watertown Twp

+

AVE

24TH ST

2400

Hollywood Twp

12

07

ROSE AVE

14400

4

30TH ST

30TH ST

15000

3000

122

13

14200

18

123

RAIN AVE

3000

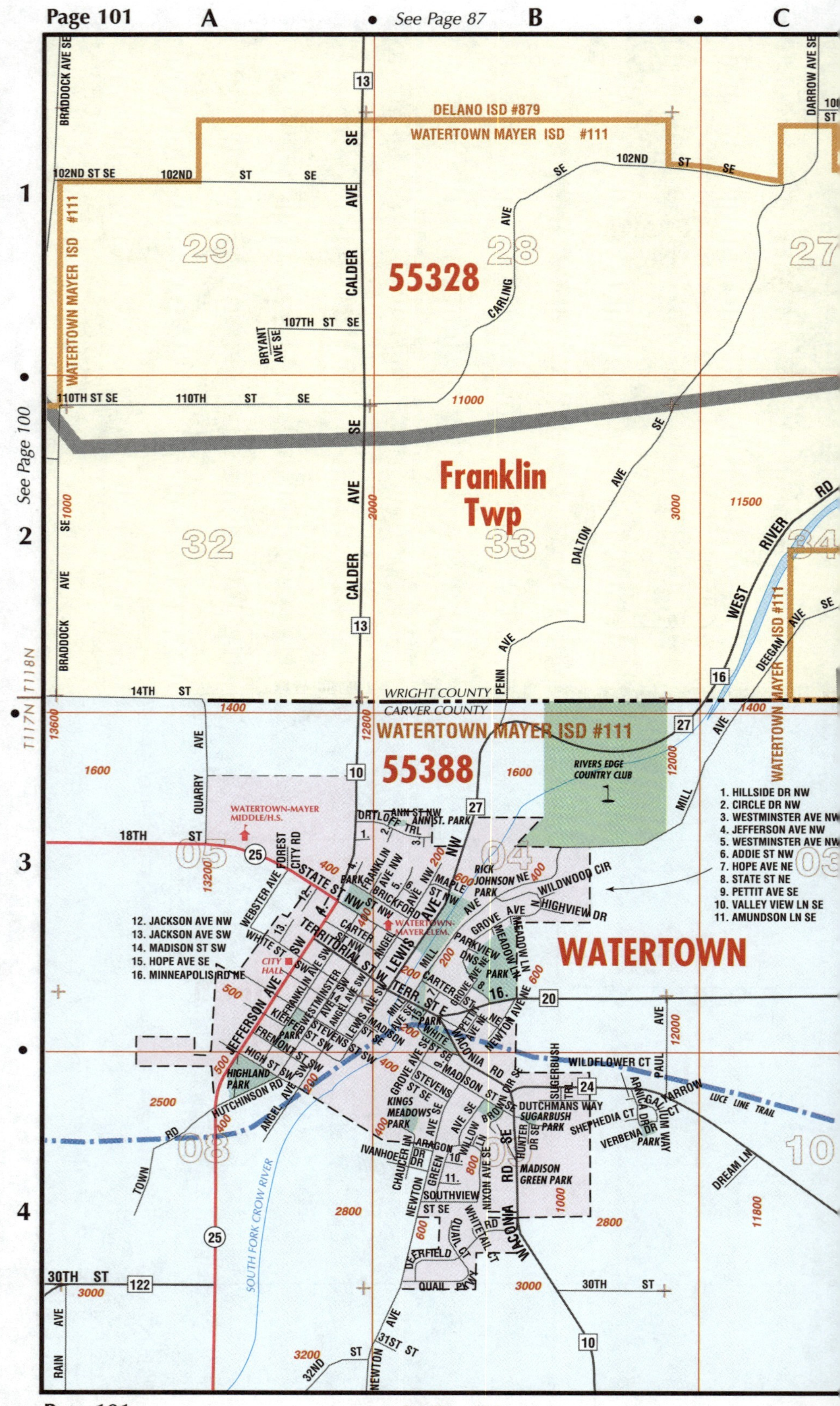

DELANO ISD #879
WATERTOWN MAYER ISD #111

55328

Franklin Twp

WRIGHT COUNTY
CARVER COUNTY

WATERTOWN MAYER ISD #111

55388

RIVERS EDGE
COUNTRY CLUB

1. HILLSIDE DR NW
2. CIRCLE DR NW
3. WESTMINSTER AVE NW
4. JEFFERSON AVE NW
5. WESTMINSTER AVE NW
6. ADDIE ST NW
7. HOPE AVE NE
8. STATE ST NE
9. PETTIT AVE SE
10. VALLEY VIEW LN SE
11. AMUNDSON LN SE

12. JACKSON AVE NW
13. JACKSON AVE SW
14. MADISON ST SW
15. HOPE AVE SE
16. MINNEAPOLIS RD NE

WATERTOWN

WATERTOWN-MAYER MIDDLE/H.S.

WATERTOWN-MAYER ELEM.

CITY HALL

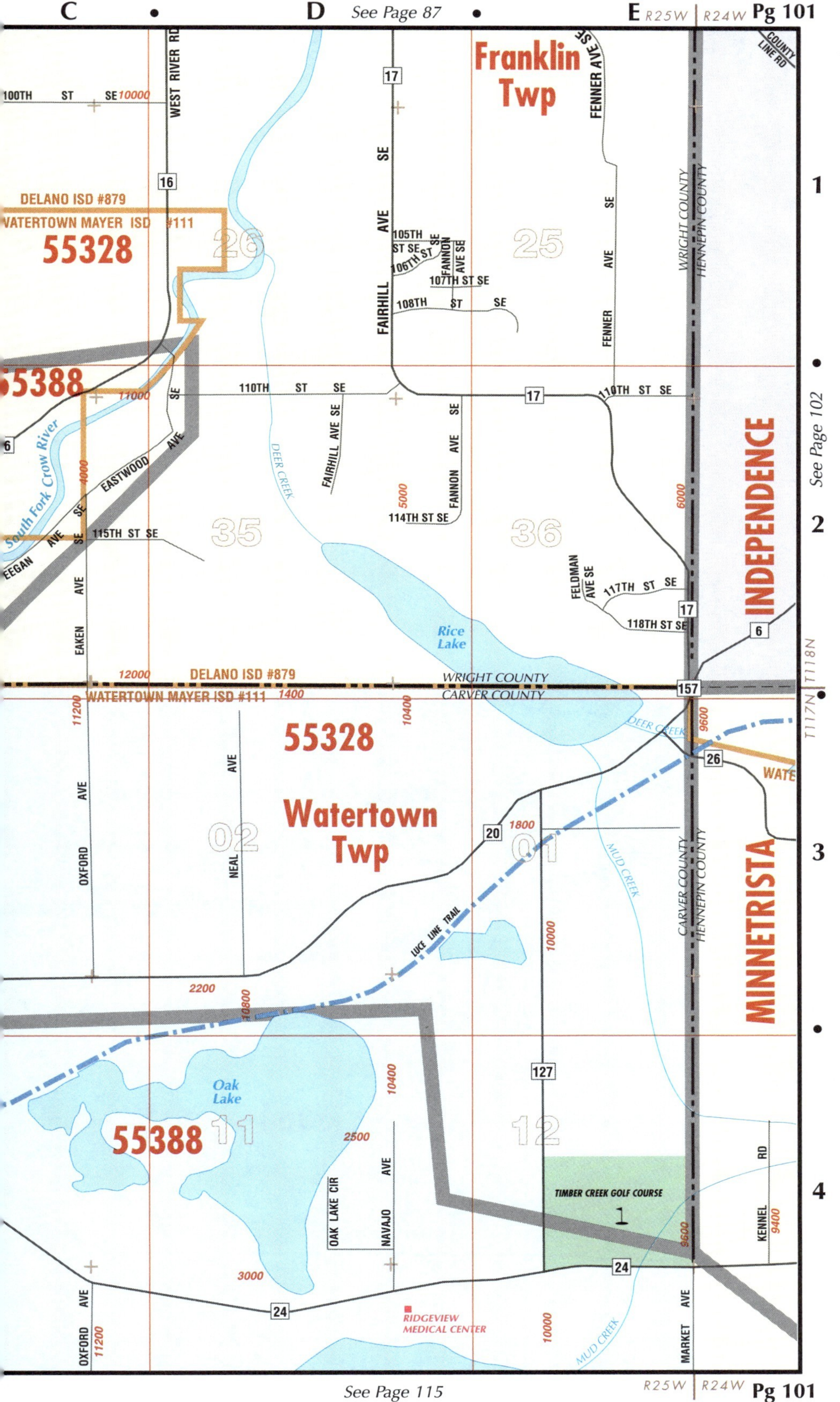
Franklin Twp
Watertown Twp
INDEPENDENCE
MINNETRISTA
55328
55388
DELANO ISD #879
WATERTOWN MAYER ISD #111
WRIGHT COUNTY
HENNEPIN COUNTY
CARVER COUNTY
COUNTY LINE RD
100TH ST SE
WEST RIVER RD
FAIRHILL AVE SE
105TH ST SE
106TH ST
FANNON AVE SE
107TH ST SE
108TH ST SE
FENNER AVE SE
110TH ST SE
114TH ST SE
115TH ST SE
117TH ST SE
118TH ST SE
FELDMAN AVE SE
EASTWOOD AVE
EEGAN AVE SE
EAKEN AVE
OXFORD AVE
NEAL AVE
NAVAJO AVE
OAK LAKE CIR
MARKET AVE
KENNEL RD
LUCE LINE TRAIL
South Fork Crow River
DEER CREEK
MUD CREEK
Rice Lake
Oak Lake
TIMBER CREEK GOLF COURSE
RIDGEVIEW MEDICAL CENTER
T118N
T117N
1
2
3
4

See Page 102

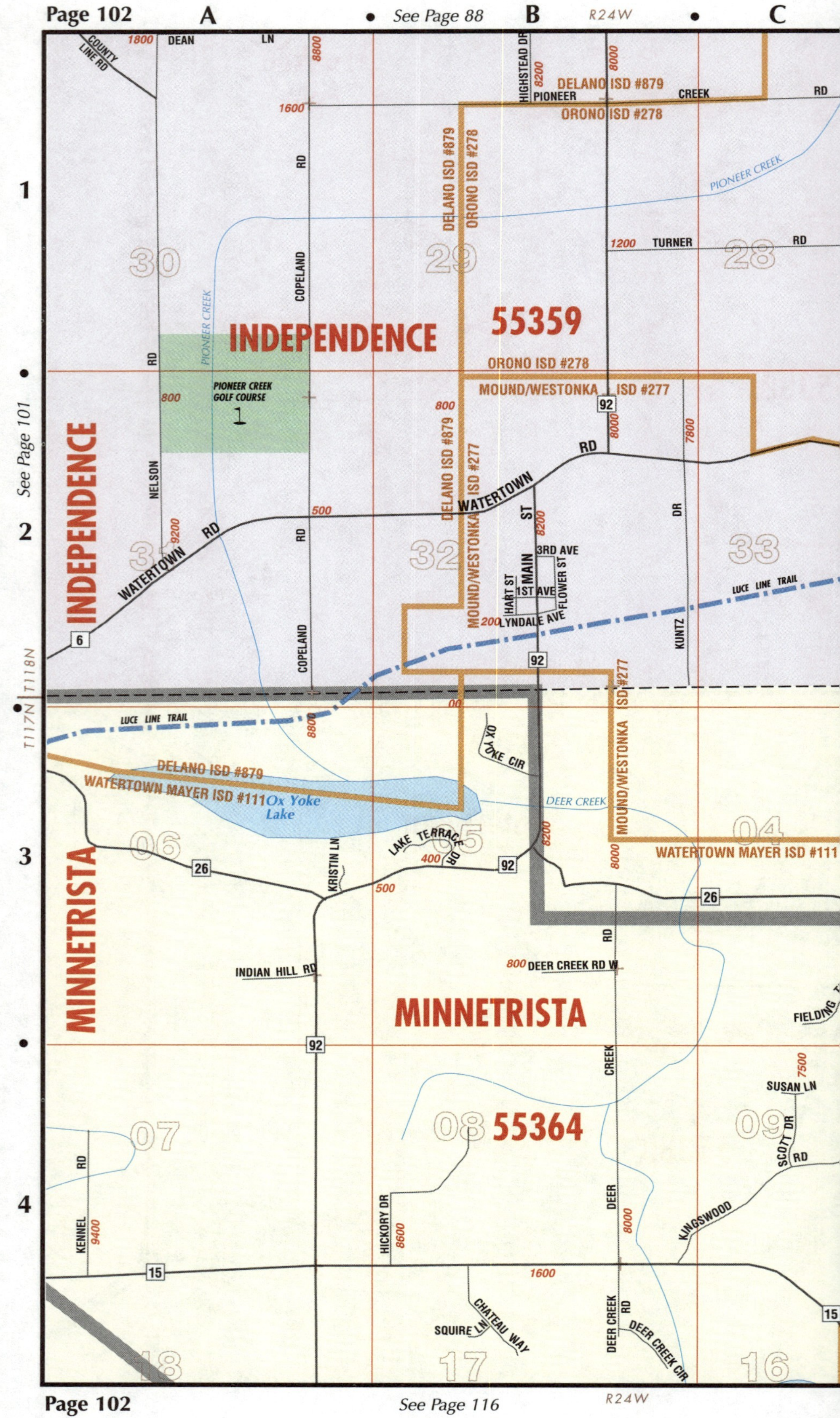

A • See Page 88 • B R24W • C

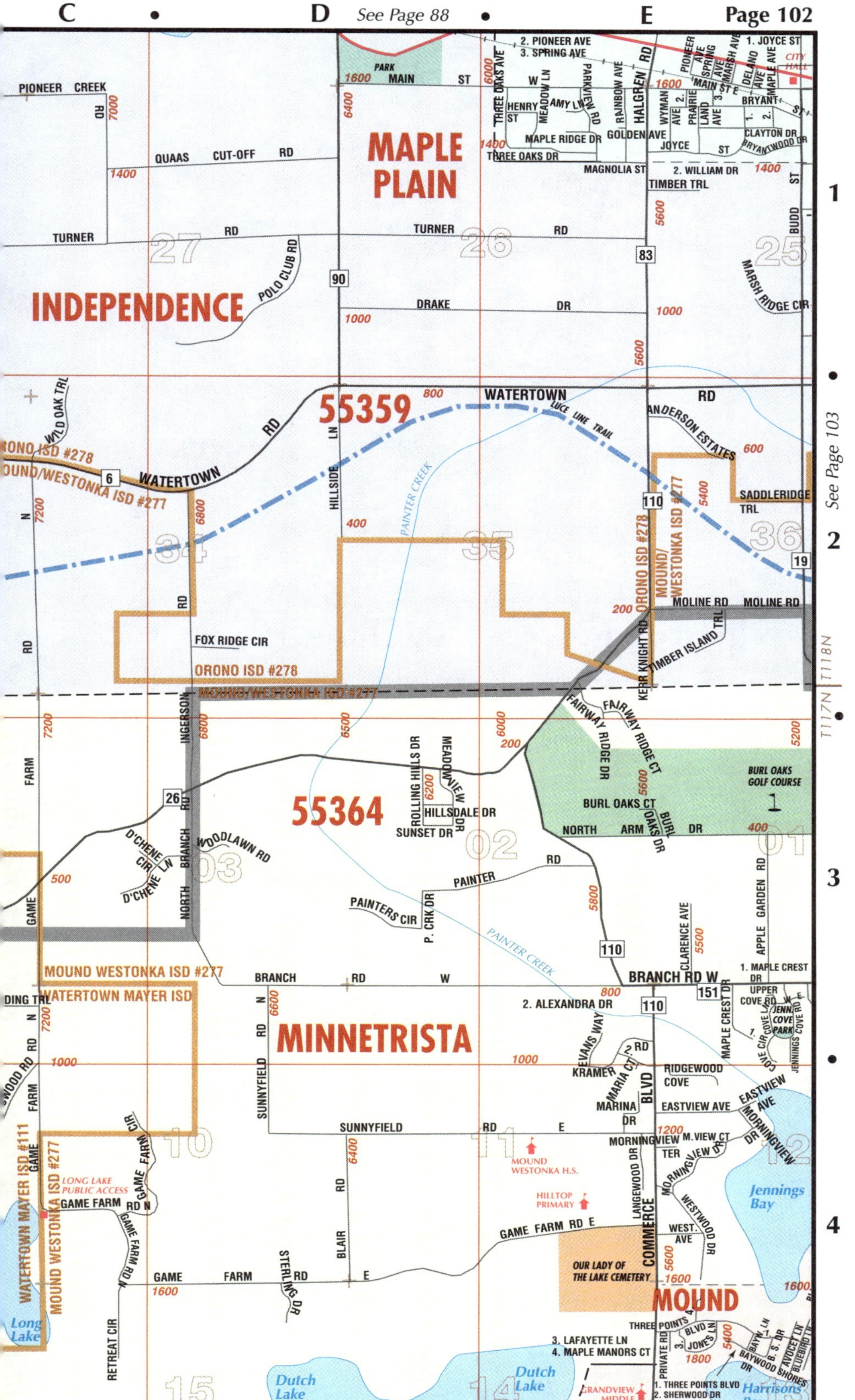

MAPLE PLAIN

INDEPENDENCE

55359

55364

MINNETRISTA

MOUND

BURL OAKS GOLF COURSE

Jennings Bay

Harrison's Bay

Long Lake

Dutch Lake

ORONO ISD #278

MOUND/WESTONKA ISD #277

MOUND WESTONKA ISD #277

WATERTOWN MAYER ISD

WATERTOWN MAYER ISD #111

Mound Westonka H.S.

Hilltop Primary

Our Lady of the Lake Cemetery

Grandview Middle

Long Lake Public Access

See Page 103

T117N | T118N

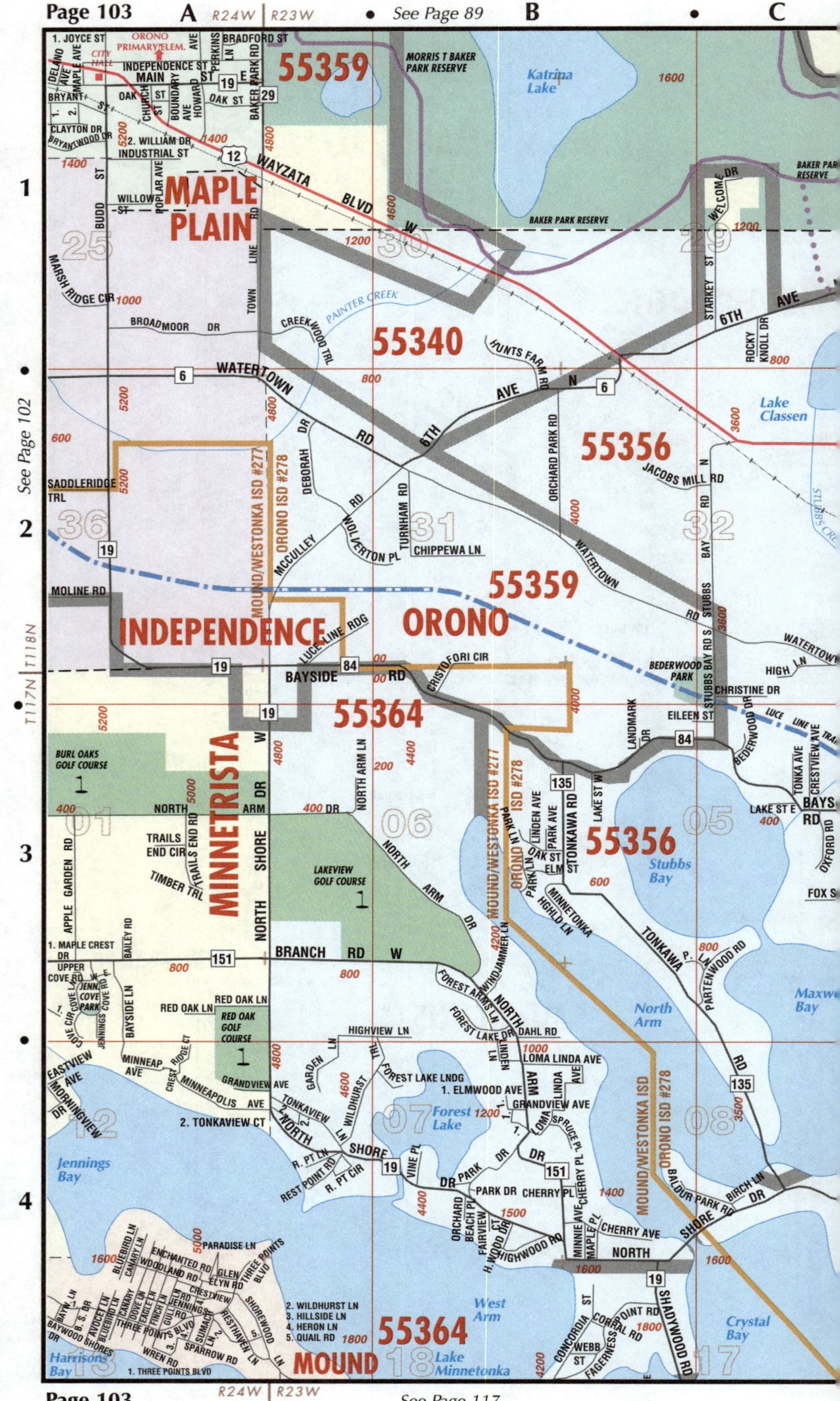

55359

MORRIS T BAKER PARK RESERVE

Katrina Lake

1600

BAKER PARK RESERVE

See Page 102

ORONO PRIMARY/ELEM.

1. JOYCE ST
PERKINS AVE
BRADFORD ST

CITY HALL

IDELAND AVE
MAPLE AVE

INDEPENDENCE ST
MAIN

BAKER PARK RD

OAK ST

BRYANT
1.
2.

OAK ST

CHURCH ST
BOUNDARY AVE
HOWARD

19

29

CLAYTON DR

BRYANTWOOD DR

WILLIAM DR
INDUSTRIAL ST

5200

1400

12

4800

WAYZATA BLVD

4800

MAPLE PLAIN

BUDD ST

POPLAR ST

WILLOW ST

TOWN LINE

30

W

1200

1400

25

MARSH RIDGE CIR 1000

BROADMOOR DR

CREEKWOOD TRL

PAINTER CREEK

HUNTS FARM RD

6TH AVE

STARKEY ST

WELCOME DR

BAKER PARK RESERVE

1200

ROCKY KNOLL DR

800

6

WATERTOWN

800

AVE N

6

5200

4800

55340

5TH AVE N

3600

Lake Classen

600

SADDLERIDGE TRL

5200

ORONO ISD #278

MOUND/WESTONKA ISD #277

DEBORAH RD

WOLVERTON PL

TURNHAM RD

31

CHIPPEWA LN

ORCHARD PARK RD

JACOBS MILL RD

4000

WATERTOWN RD

BAY RD S

32

STILL—R CR

36

19

McCULLEY RD

MOLINE RD

LUCE LINE RDG

55359

ORONO

STUBBS

STUBBS BAY RD S

WATERTOWN

INDEPENDENCE

19

84

BAYSIDE

CRISTO FORI CIR

00

00 RD

BEDERWOOD PARK

HIGH LN

CHRISTINE DR

5200

4800

19

55364

4400

200

4000

LANDMARK DR

EILEEN ST

84

BEDERWOOD DR

LUCE LINE TRL

CRESTVIEW AVE

BURL OAKS GOLF COURSE

5000

400

01

NORTH DR

NORTH ARM LN

TRAILS END RD

TRAILS END CIR

400 DR

06

NORTH ARM DR

135

TONKAWA RD

PARK LN

LINDEN AVE

OAK ST

ELM ST

PARK AVE

LAKE ST W

STONKAWA RD

55356

TONKA AVE

LAKE ST E

400

BAYS RD

OXFORD RD

MINNETRISTA

NORTH SHORE DR W

LAKEVIEW GOLF COURSE

1

NORTH ARM DR

600

Stubbs Bay

05

FOX S

TIMBER TRL

APPLE GARDEN RD

BAILEY RD

151

BRANCH RD

800

W

800

MINNETONKA HIGHLD LN

North Arm

800

Maxwell Bay

1. MAPLE CREST DR

UPPER COVE RD

JENN COVE PK

COVE CIR

COVE PARK DR

BAYSIDE LN

CREST RIDGE CT

RED OAK LN

RED OAK LN

RED OAK GOLF COURSE

1

HIGHVIEW LN

HIGHVIEW LN

FOREST LAKE DR

DAHL RD

FOREST ARMS LN

WINDJAMMER LN

NORTH ARM DR

ORONO ISD #278

MOUND/WESTONKA ISD #277

PARTENWOOD RD

135

3500

EASTVIEW AVE

MORNINGVIEW LN

MINNEAP AVE

MINNEAPOLIS AVE

GRANDVIEW AVE

TONKAVIEW LN

WILDHURST TRL

GARDEN LN

LOMA LINDA AVE

1. ELMWOOD AVE

GRANDVIEW AVE

LOMA LINDA

SPRUCE DR

BALDUR PARK RD

BIRCH LN

DR

12

Jennings Bay

2. TONKAVIEW CT

NORTH SHORE DR

07

Forest Lake

1200

DR

08

Jennings Bay

R. PT LN

REST POINT RD

R. PT CIR

19

VINE PL

PARK DR

151

CHERRY LN

1400

NORTH SHORE DR

4

4400

ORCHARD BEACH PL

FAIRVIEW

H. WOOD RD

1500

HIGHWOOD RD

PARK DR

CHERRY

MINNIE AVE

MAPLE PL

CHERRY PL

CHERRY AVE

1600

1600

19

SHADYWOOD RD

Crystal Bay

BLUEBIRD LN

1600

PARADISE LN

5000

ENCHANTED RD

GLEN ELYN RD

THREE POINTS BLVD

WOODLAND RD

CANARY LN

CRESTVIEW

SHOREWOOD LN

2. WILDHURST LN

3. HILLSIDE LN

4. HERON LN

5. QUAIL RD

1800

55364

West Arm

Lake Minnetonka

CONCORDIA ST

WEBB ST

CORAL RD

COVE POINT RD

1800

PAGENESS RD

SHADYWOOD RD

1600

MOUND

18

4200

17

Harrisons Bay

BAYWOOD SHORES

1. THREE POINTS BLVD

2.
3.

SPARROW LN

WREN RD

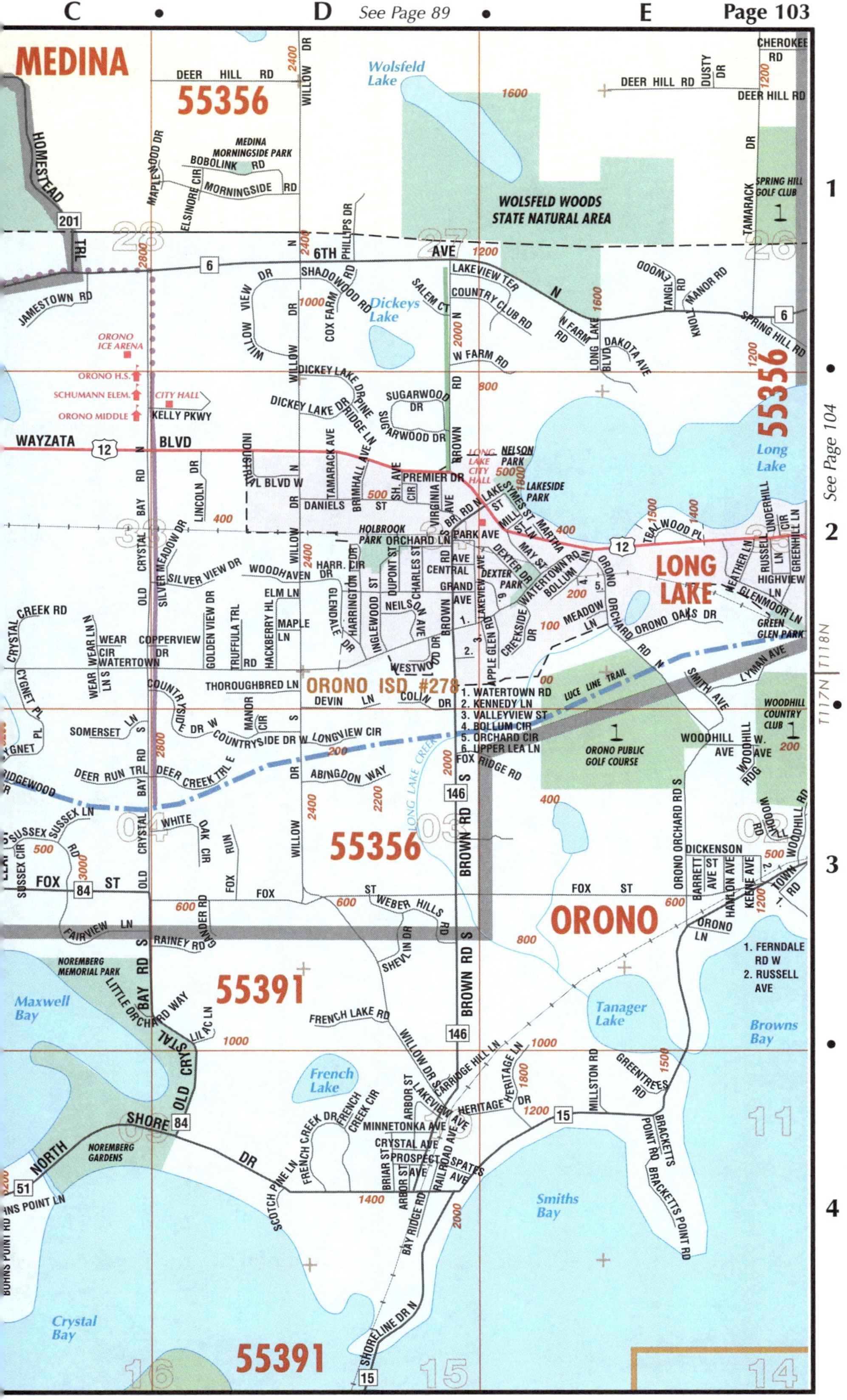
MEDINA
55356
DEER HILL RD
WOLSFELD WOODS STATE NATURAL AREA
Wolsfeld Lake
Dickeys Lake
6TH AVE
WAYZATA BLVD
LONG LAKE
Long Lake
ORONO ISD #278
ORONO
55356
55391
Maxwell Bay
French Lake
Tanager Lake
Browns Bay
Smiths Bay
Crystal Bay
ORONO PUBLIC GOLF COURSE
WOODHILL COUNTRY CLUB
SPRING HILL GOLF CLUB
LUCE LINE TRAIL
NOREMBERG MEMORIAL PARK
NOREMBERG GARDENS
1. WATERTOWN RD
2. KENNEDY LN
3. VALLEYVIEW ST
4. BOLLUM CIR
5. ORCHARD CIR
6. UPPER LEA LN
1. FERNDALE RD W
2. RUSSELL AVE
See Page 104
1
2
3
4

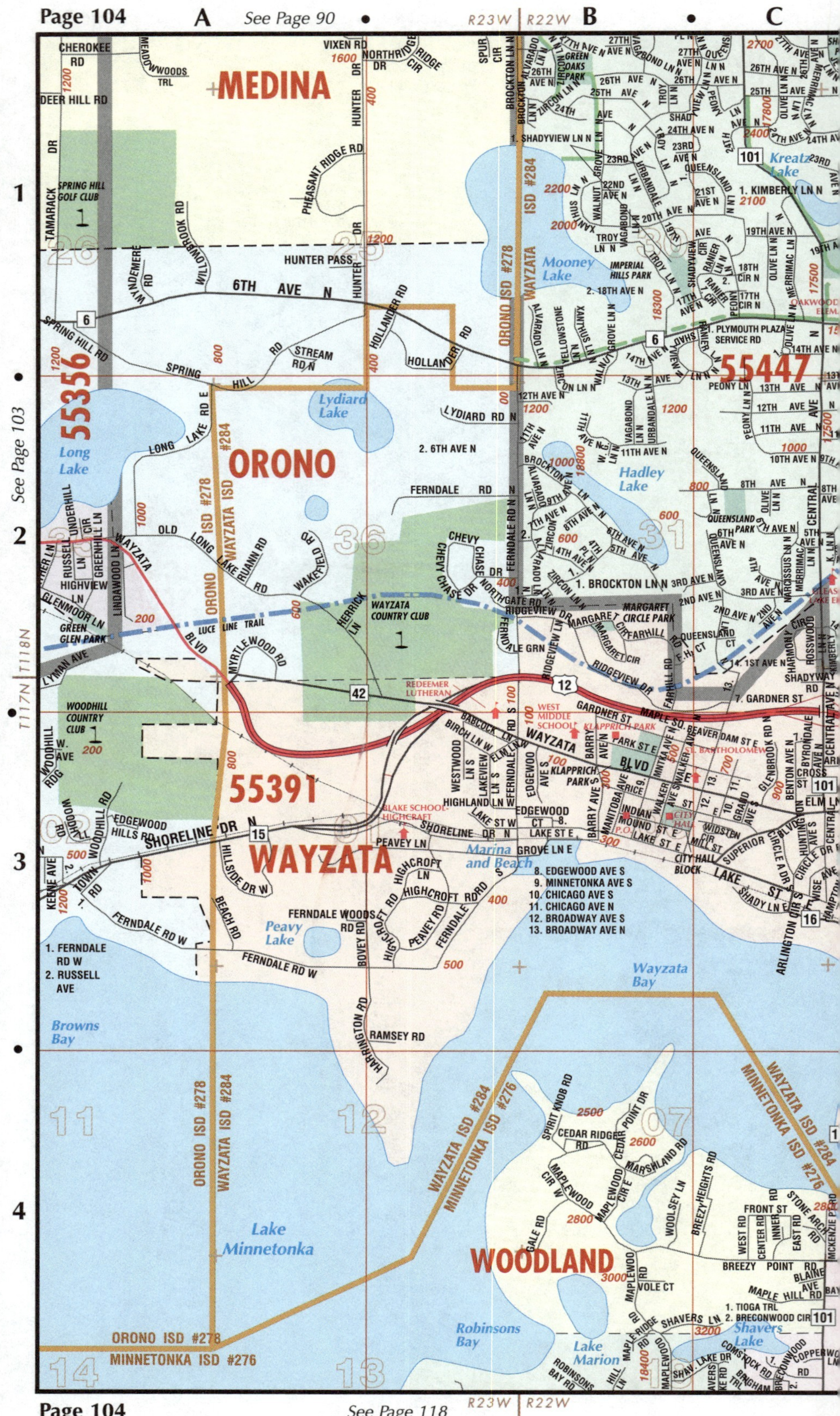
A
See Page 90
R23W R22W
B
C
MEDINA
ORONO
WAYZATA
WOODLAND
55356
55447
55391
Long Lake
Lydiard Lake
Mooney Lake
Hadley Lake
Kreatz Lake
Peavy Lake
Wayzata Bay
Browns Bay
Lake Minnetonka
Robinsons Bay
Lake Marion
Shavers Lake
Marina and Beach
SPRING HILL GOLF CLUB
WAYZATA COUNTRY CLUB
WOODHILL COUNTRY CLUB
6TH AVE N
SHORELINE DR
WAYZATA BLVD
LUCE LINE TRAIL
ORONO ISD #278
WAYZATA ISD #284
MINNETONKA ISD #276
See Page 103
1. FERNDALE RD W
2. RUSSELL AVE
8. EDGEWOOD AVE S
9. MINNETONKA AVE S
10. CHICAGO AVE S
11. CHICAGO AVE N
12. BROADWAY AVE S
13. BROADWAY AVE N
1. TIOGA TRL
2. BRECONWOOD CIR
T117N T118N
1
2
3
4

See Page 118

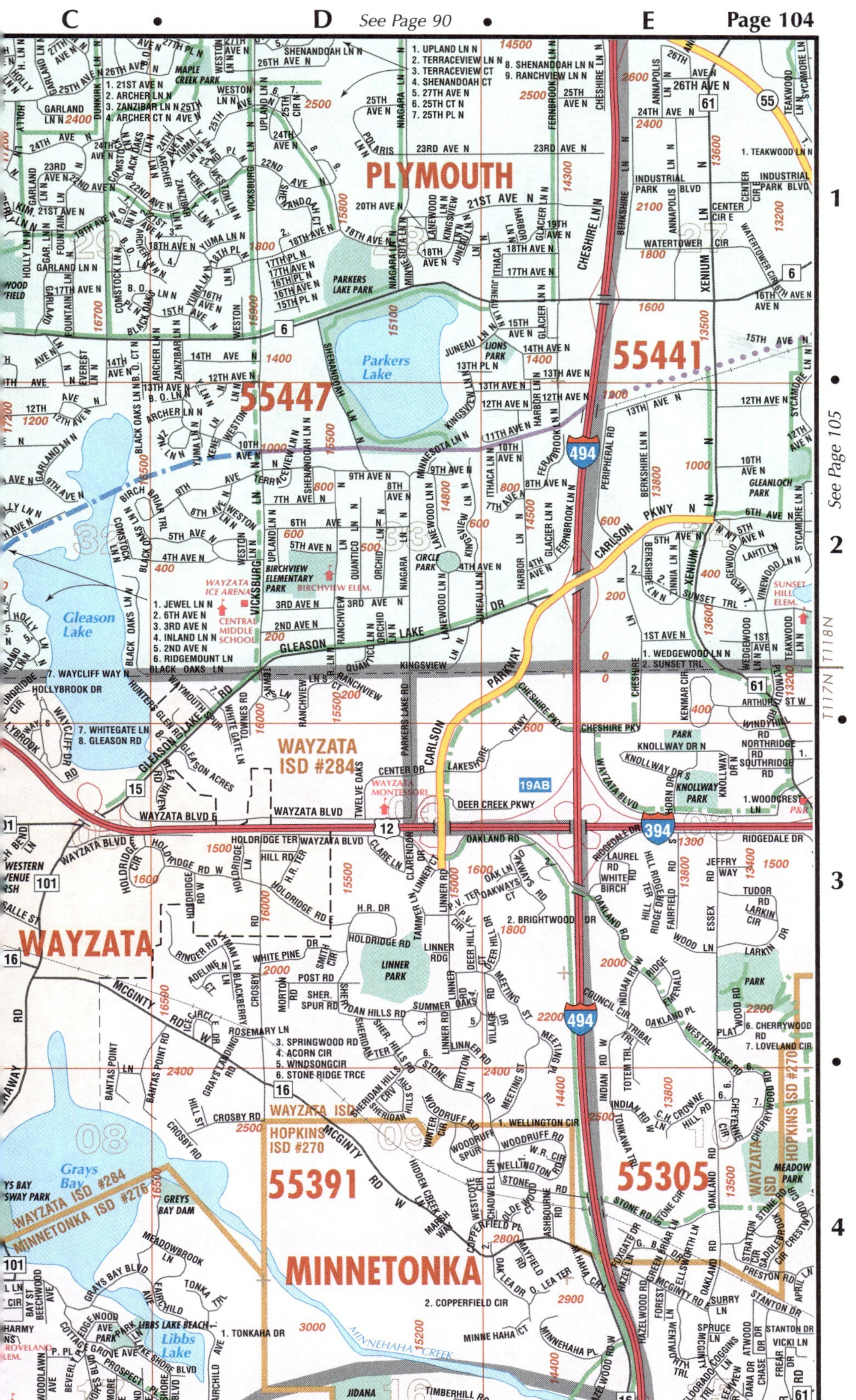
PLYMOUTH
WAYZATA
MINNETONKA
55447
55441
55391
55305
Parkers Lake
PARKERS LAKE PARK
Gleason Lake
Grays Bay
Libbs Lake
WAYZATA ISD #284
HOPKINS ISD #270
MINNETONKA ISD #276
LINNER PARK
LIONS PARK
CIRCLE PARK
KNOLLWAY PARK
MEADOW PARK
JIDANA PARK
BIRCHVIEW ELEMENTARY PARK
WAYZATA ICE ARENA
CENTRAL MIDDLE SCHOOL
WAYZATA MONTESSORI
SUNSET HILL ELEM.
MINNEHAHA CREEK
CARLSON PKWY
WAYZATA BLVD
GLEASON LAKE DR
MCGINTY RD W
1. UPLAND LN N
2. TERRACEVIEW LN N
3. TERRACEVIEW CT
4. SHENANDOAH CT
5. 27TH AVE N
6. 25TH CT N
7. 25TH PL N
8. SHENANDOAH LN N
9. RANCHVIEW LN N
1. 21ST AVE N
2. ARCHER LN N
3. ZANZIBAR LN N
4. ARCHER CT N
1. JEWEL LN N
2. 6TH AVE N
3. 3RD AVE N
4. INLAND LN N
5. 2ND AVE N
6. RIDGEMOUNT LN
7. WAYCLIFF WAY N
7. WHITEGATE LN
8. GLEASON RD
1. WEDGEWOOD LN N
2. SUNSET TRL
1. TEAKWOOD LN N
3. SPRINGWOOD RD
4. ACORN CIR
5. WINDSONGCIR
6. STONE RIDGE TRCE
1. WELLINGTON CIR
2. COPPERFIELD CIR
1. TONKAHA DR
6. CHERRYWOOD RD
7. LOVELAND CIR
T117N
T118N

See Page 105

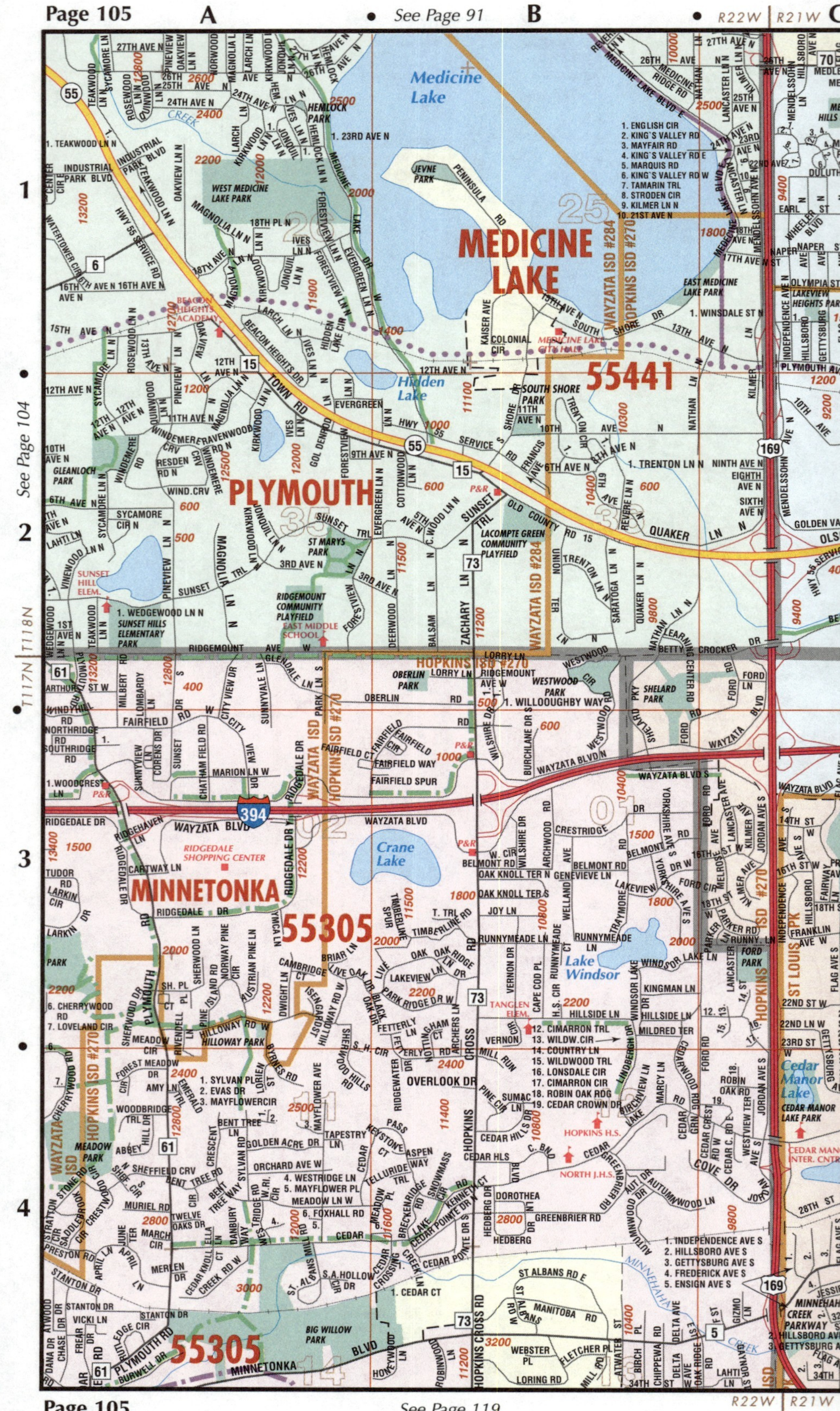

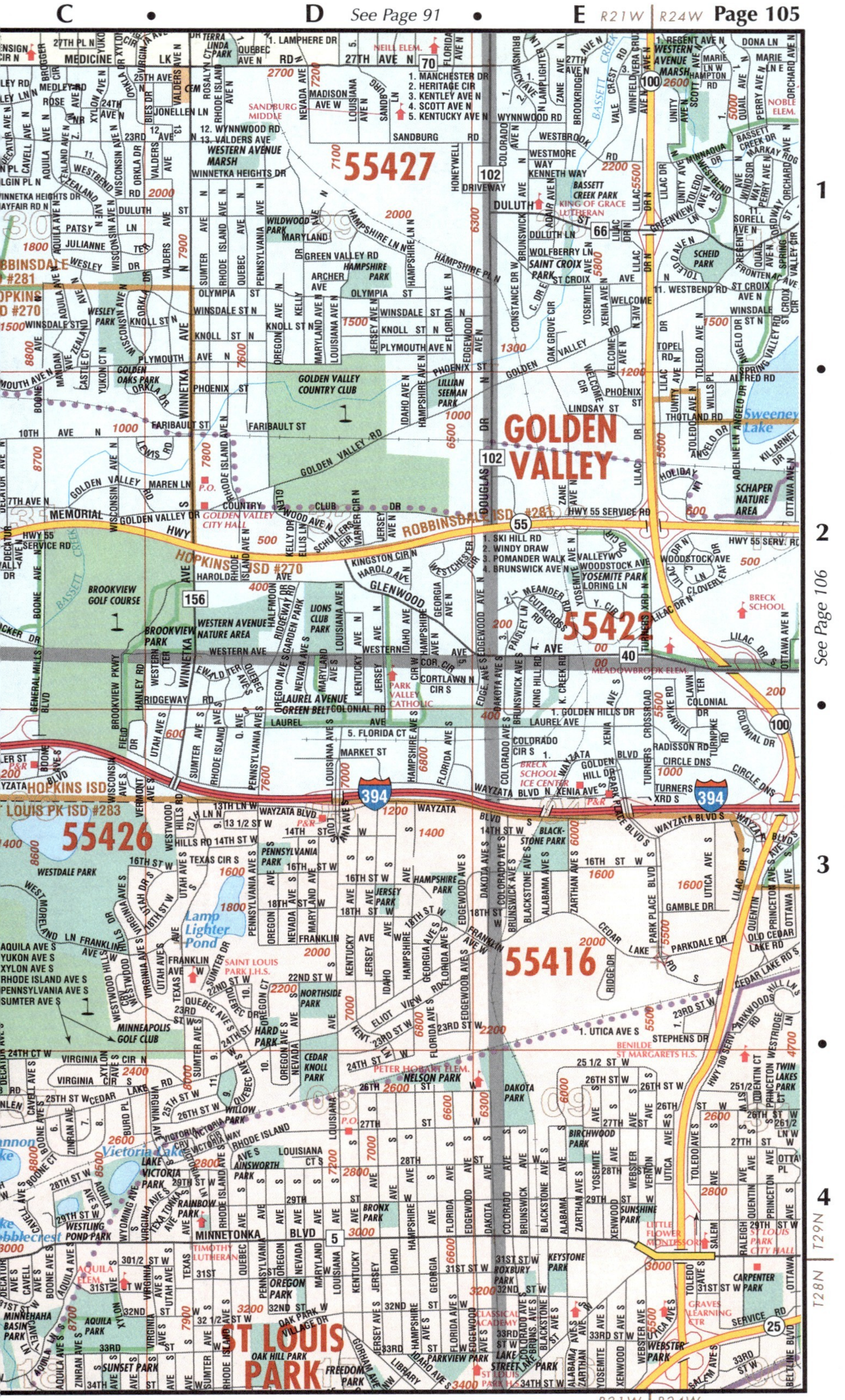
55427
GOLDEN VALLEY
55422
55426
55416
ST LOUIS PARK
GOLDEN VALLEY COUNTRY CLUB
BROOKVIEW GOLF COURSE
MINNEAPOLIS GOLF CLUB
ROBBINSDALE ISD #281
HOPKINS ISD #270
ST LOUIS PK ISD #283
Sweeney Lake
Lamp Lighter Pond
Victoria Lake
GOLDEN VALLEY CITY HALL
SAINT LOUIS PARK J.H.S.
BRECK SCHOOL
MEADOWBROOK ELEM.
BENILDE ST MARGARETS H.S.
SCHAPER NATURE AREA
WESTERN AVENUE NATURE AREA
LAUREL AVENUE GREEN BELT
WESTDALE PARK
NELSON PARK
T29N
T28N
1
2
3
4
See Page 106

A See Page 92 B C

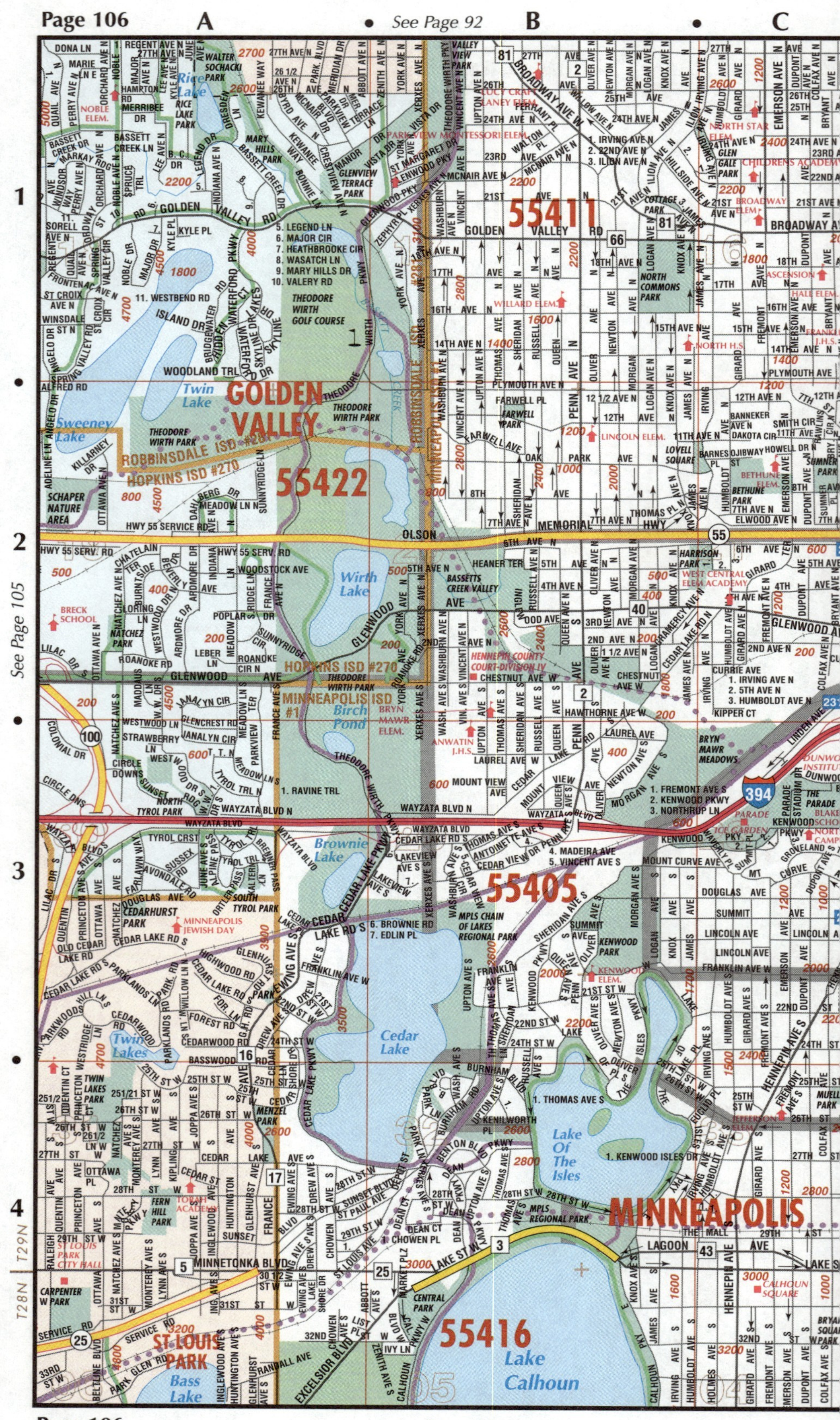

See Page 105

See Page 120

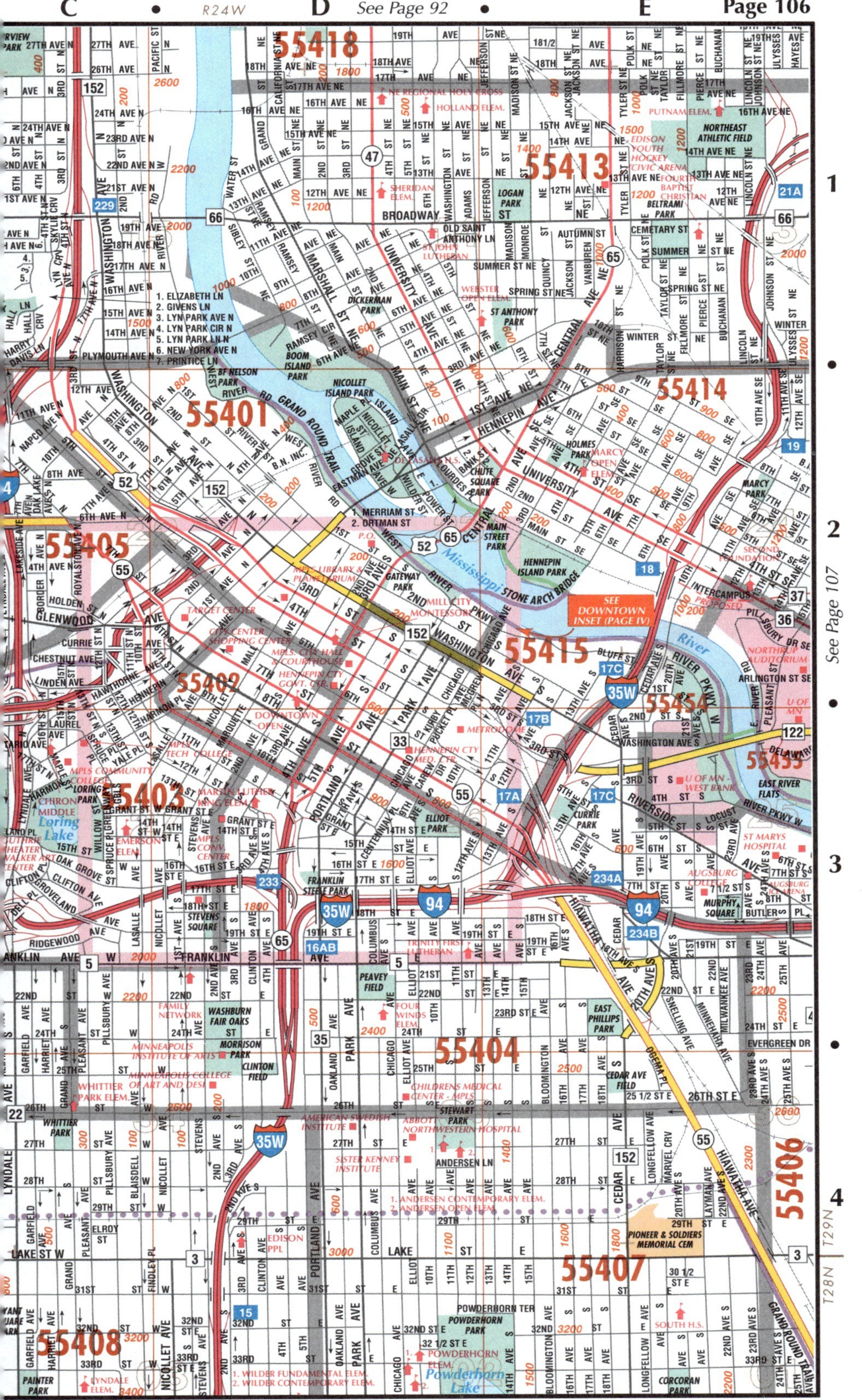

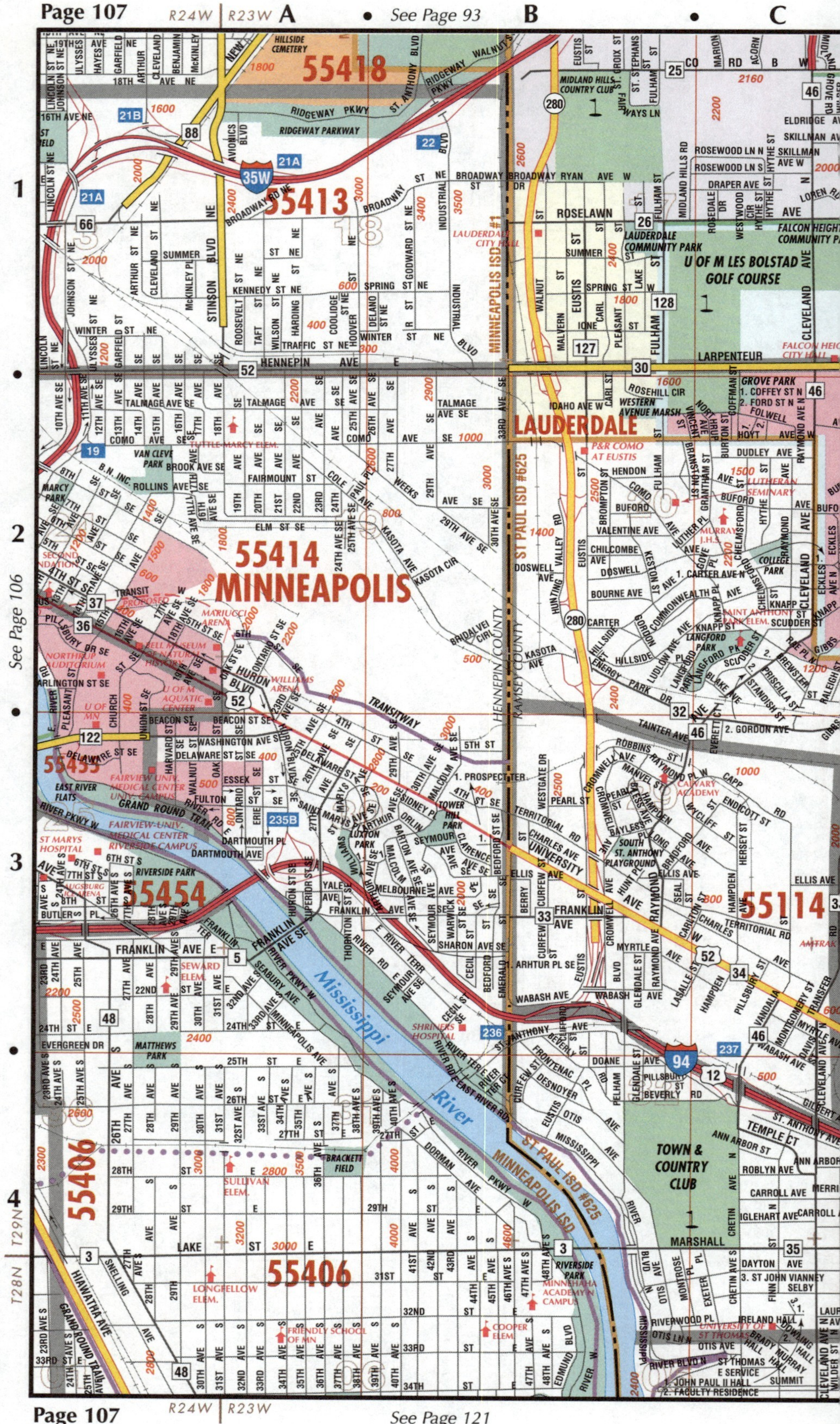
55418
55413
55414
MINNEAPOLIS
55455
55454
55406
55114
LAUDERDALE
HILLSIDE CEMETERY
MIDLAND HILLS COUNTRY CLUB
U OF M LES BOLSTAD GOLF COURSE
LAUDERDALE COMMUNITY PARK
FALCON HEIGHTS COMMUNITY PARK
LAUDERDALE CITY HALL
MINNEAPOLIS ISD #1
ST PAUL ISD #625
HENNEPIN COUNTY
RAMSEY COUNTY
HENNEPIN AVE E
LARPENTEUR
BROADWAY
RIDGEWAY PARKWAY
TRANSITWAY
UNIVERSITY AVE
FRANKLIN AVE
LAKE ST
MARSHALL
Mississippi River
TOWN & COUNTRY CLUB
RIVERSIDE PARK
BRACKETT FIELD
MATTHEWS PARK
SEWARD ELEM.
SULLIVAN ELEM.
LONGFELLOW ELEM.
FRIENDLY SCHOOL OF MN
COOPER ELEM.
MINNEHAHA ACADEMY N CAMPUS
SHRINERS HOSPITAL
ST MARYS HOSPITAL
FAIRVIEW-UNIV. MEDICAL CENTER RIVERSIDE CAMPUS
FAIRVIEW-UNIV. MEDICAL CENTER UNIV. CAMPUS
AUGSBURG ICE ARENA
U OF MN
NORTHROP AUDITORIUM
BELL MUSEUM OF NATURAL HISTORY
U OF M AQUATIC CENTER
MARIUCCI ARENA
WILLIAMS ARENA
TUTTLE MARCY ELEM.
VAN CLEVE PARK
LUTHERAN SEMINARY
MURRAY J.H.S.
COLLEGE PARK
SAINT ANTHONY PARK ELEM.
LANGFORD PARK
CALVARY ACADEMY
SOUTH ST. ANTHONY PLAYGROUND
P&R COMO AT EUSTIS
UNIVERSITY OF ST THOMAS
RIVERSIDE PARK
See Page 106
T29N
T28N

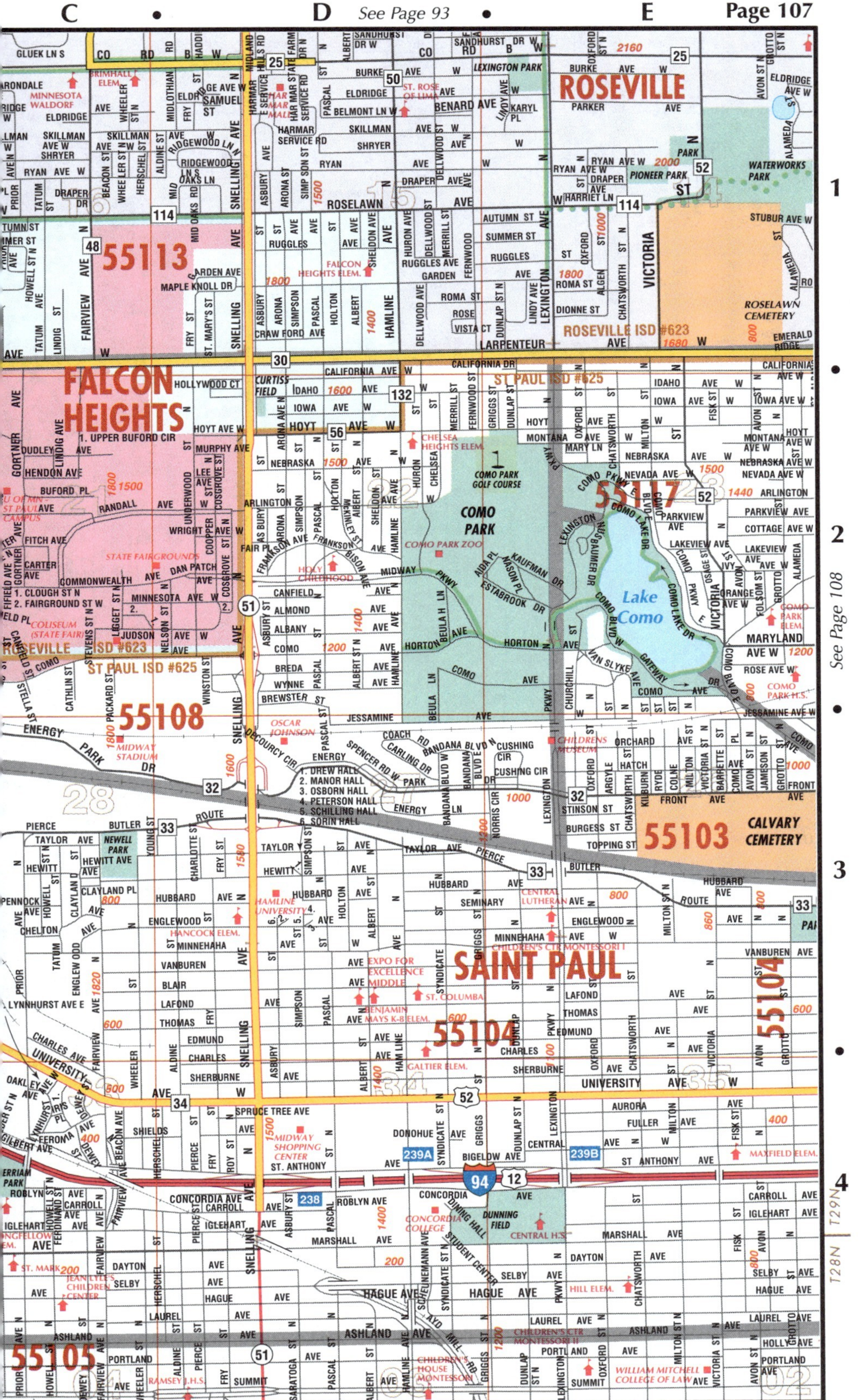
ROSEVILLE
FALCON HEIGHTS
SAINT PAUL
55113
55117
55108
55103
55104
55105
COMO PARK
Lake Como
COMO PARK GOLF COURSE
COMO PARK ZOO
ROSELAWN CEMETERY
CALVARY CEMETERY
STATE FAIRGROUNDS
WATERWORKS PARK
DUNNING FIELD
ROSEVILLE ISD #623
ST PAUL ISD #625
LARPENTEUR
SNELLING
LEXINGTON
VICTORIA
UNIVERSITY
CONCORDIA
MIDWAY SHOPPING CENTER
HAMLINE UNIVERSITY
CONCORDIA COLLEGE
CENTRAL H.S.
WILLIAM MITCHELL COLLEGE OF LAW
MIDWAY STADIUM
1
2
3
4
T29N
T28N
See Page 108

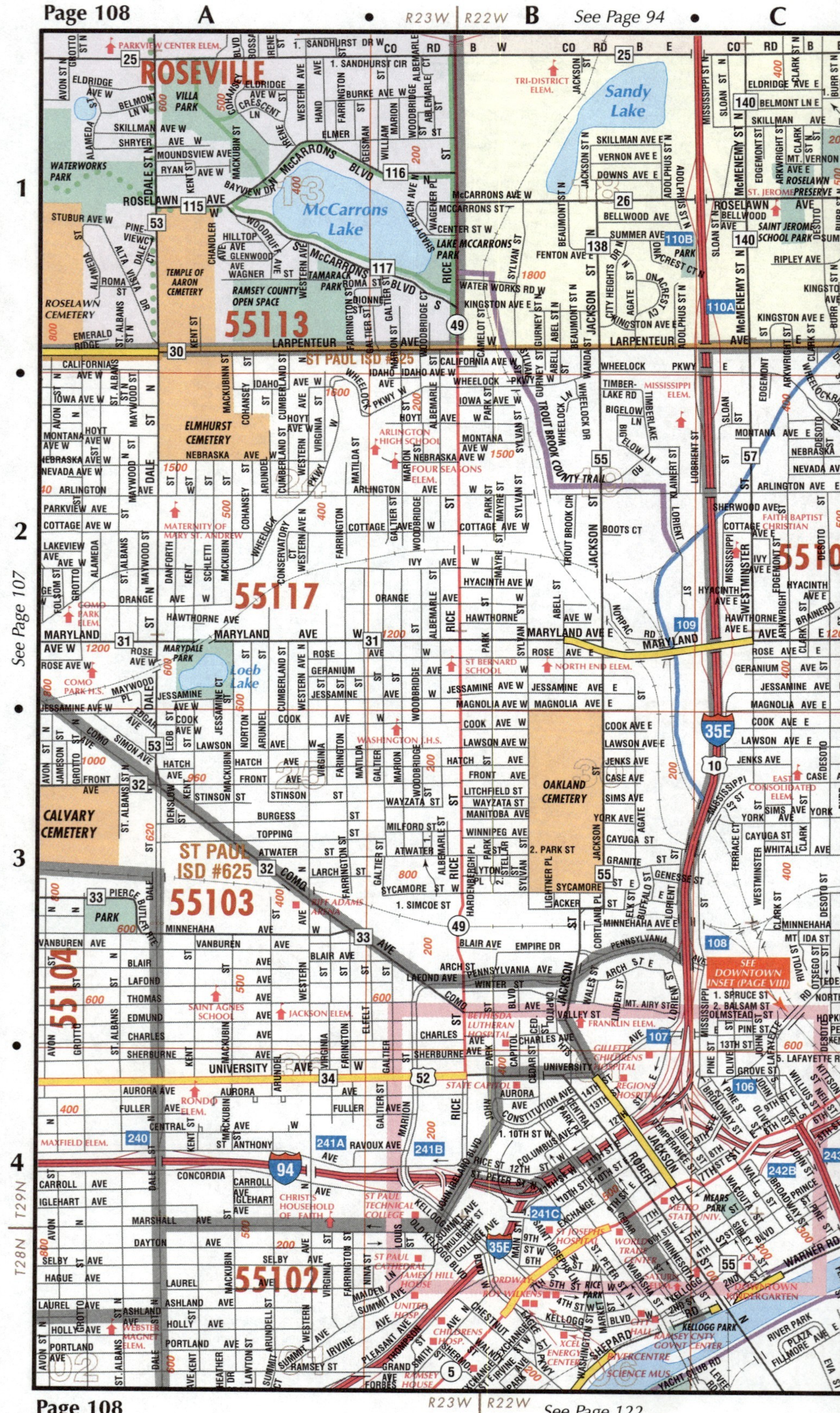
ROSEVILLE
VILLA PARK
WATERWORKS PARK
McCarrons Lake
Sandy Lake
ROSELAWN CEMETERY
TEMPLE OF AARON CEMETERY
RAMSEY COUNTY OPEN SPACE
LAKE McCARRONS PARK
TAMARACK PARK
55113
LARPENTEUR AVE
ST PAUL ISD #625
ELMHURST CEMETERY
ARLINGTON HIGH SCHOOL
FOUR SEASONS ELEM.
MATERNITY OF MARY ST. ANDREW
TROUT BROOK COUNTY TRAIL
MISSISSIPPI ELEM.
FAITH BAPTIST CHRISTIAN
55117
MARYLAND AVE
MARYDALE PARK
Loeb Lake
COMO PARK ELEM.
COMO PARK H.S.
ST BERNARD SCHOOL
NORTH END ELEM.
WASHINGTON J.H.S.
OAKLAND CEMETERY
EAST CONSOLIDATED ELEM.
CALVARY CEMETERY
ST PAUL ISD #625
55103
55104
JIMMY LEE PARK
SAINT AGNES SCHOOL
JACKSON ELEM.
BETHESDA LUTHERAN HOSPITAL
FRANKLIN ELEM.
GILLETTE CHILDRENS HOSPITAL
REGIONS HOSPITAL
STATE CAPITOL
SEE DOWNTOWN INSET (PAGE VIII)
UNIVERSITY AVE
RONDO ELEM.
MAXFIELD ELEM.
CONCORDIA
CHRISTS HOUSEHOLD OF FAITH
ST PAUL TECHNICAL COLLEGE
METRO STATE UNIV.
MEARS PARK
ST JOSEPHS HOSPITAL
WORLD TRADE CENTER
ST PAUL CATHEDRAL
JAMES J HILL HOUSE
UNITED HOSP.
CHILDRENS HOSP.
ORDWAY
ROY WILKINS
XCEL ENERGY CENTER
RIVERCENTRE
SCIENCE MUS.
CITY HALL
RAMSEY CNTY GOVT CENTER
KELLOGG PARK
DOWNTOWN KINDERGARTEN
55102
WEBSTER MAGNET ELEM.
RAMSEY HOUSE
RIVER PARK PLAZA
WARNER RD
SHEPARD RD
See Page 107
T29N
T28N

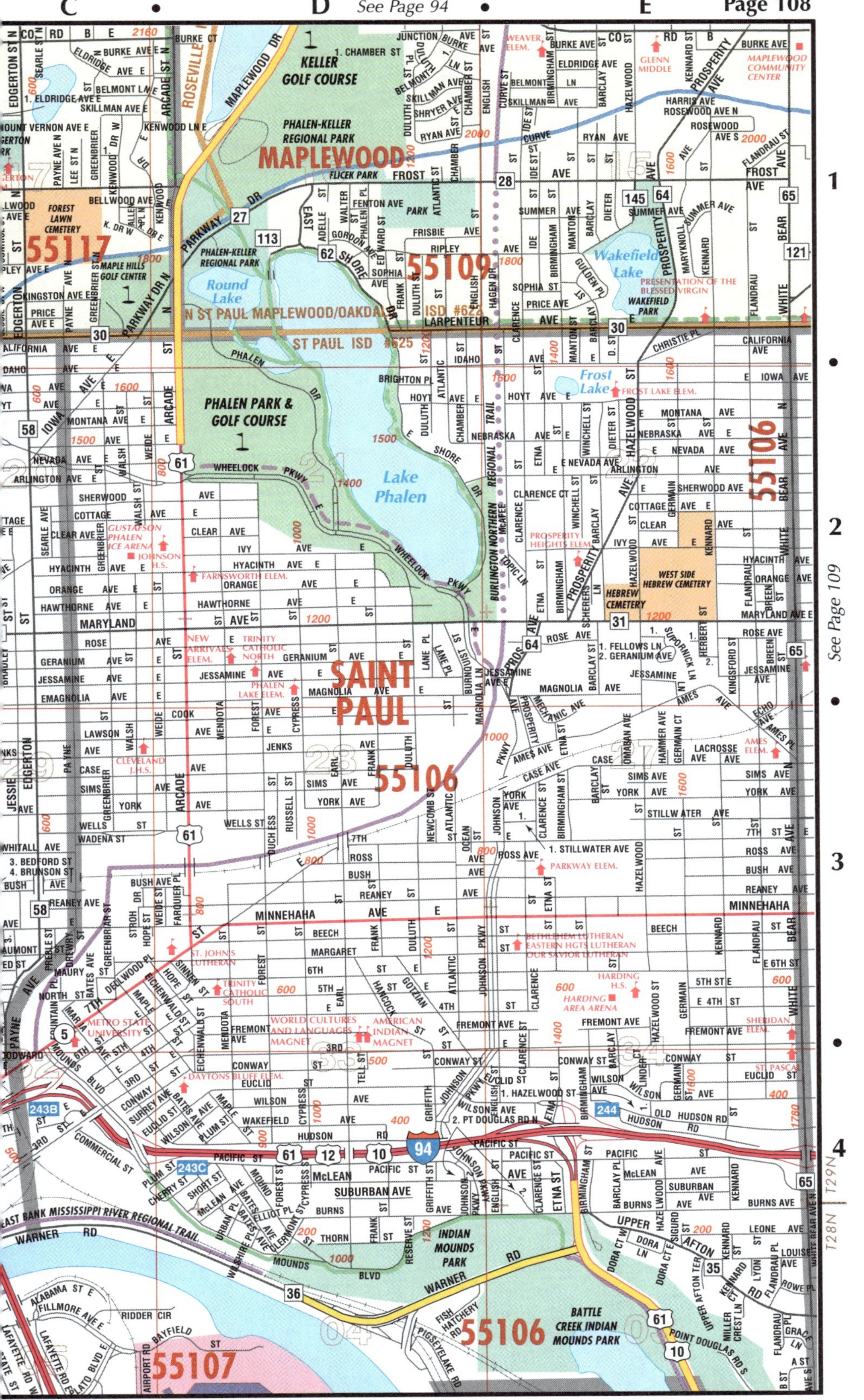

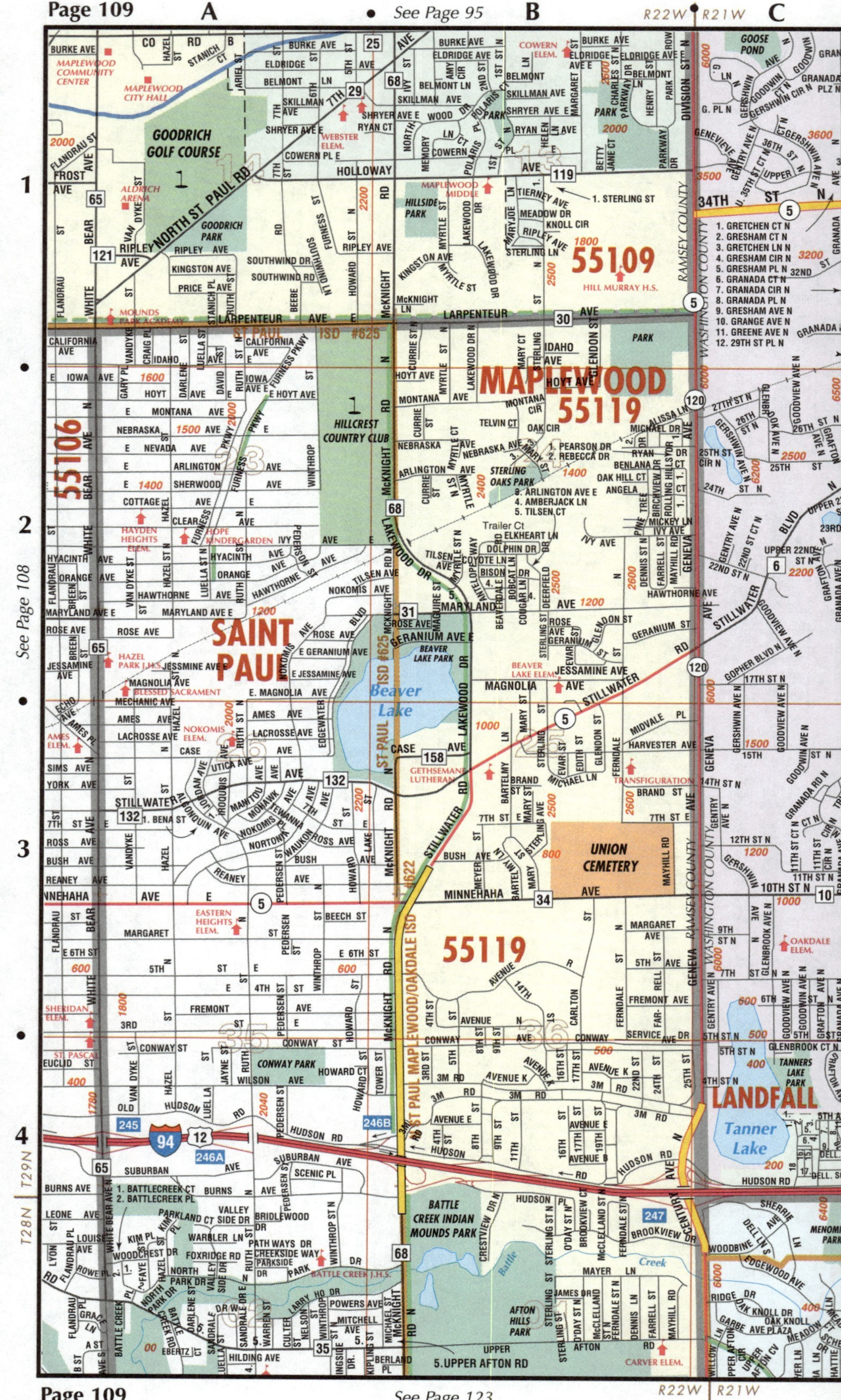

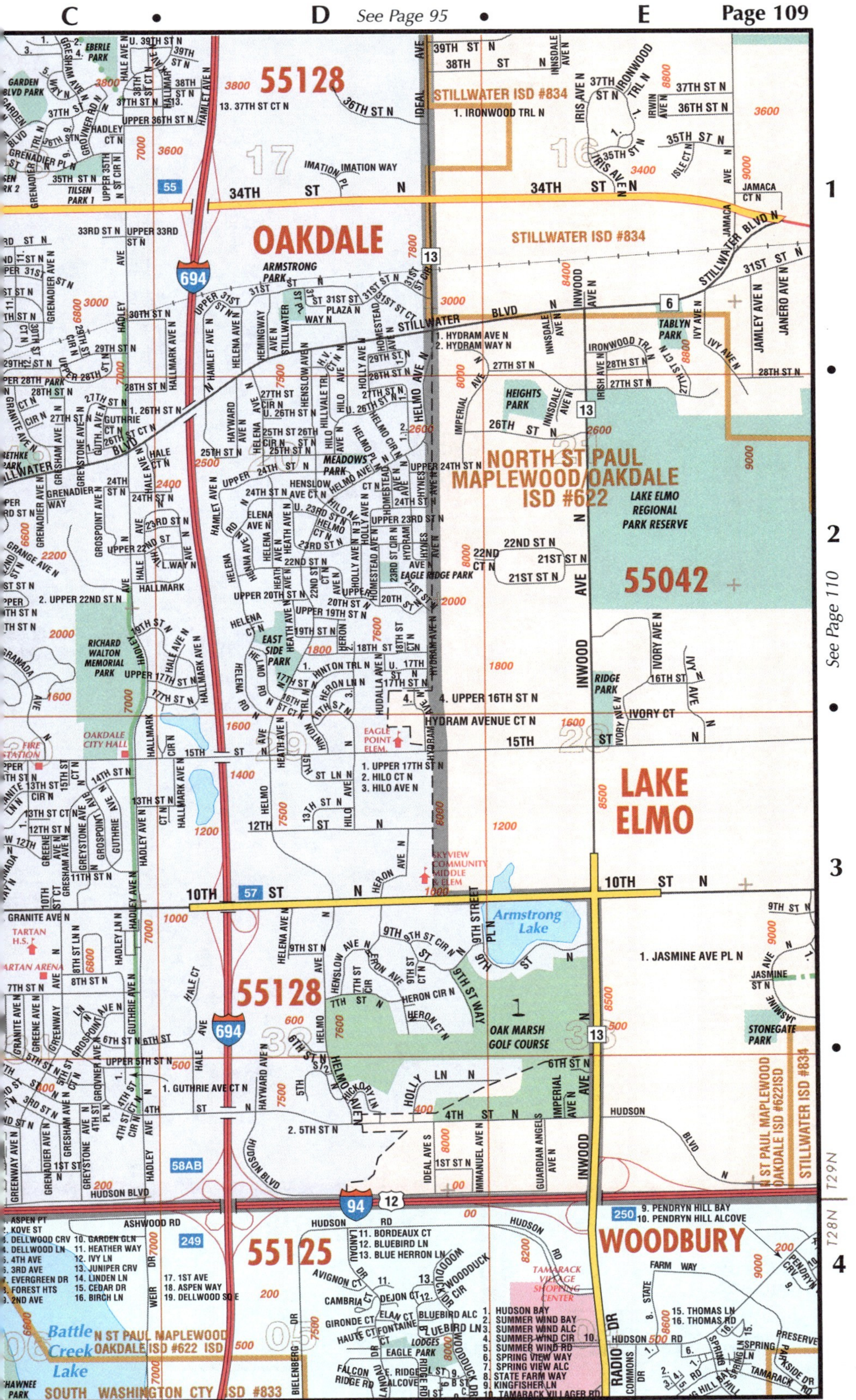

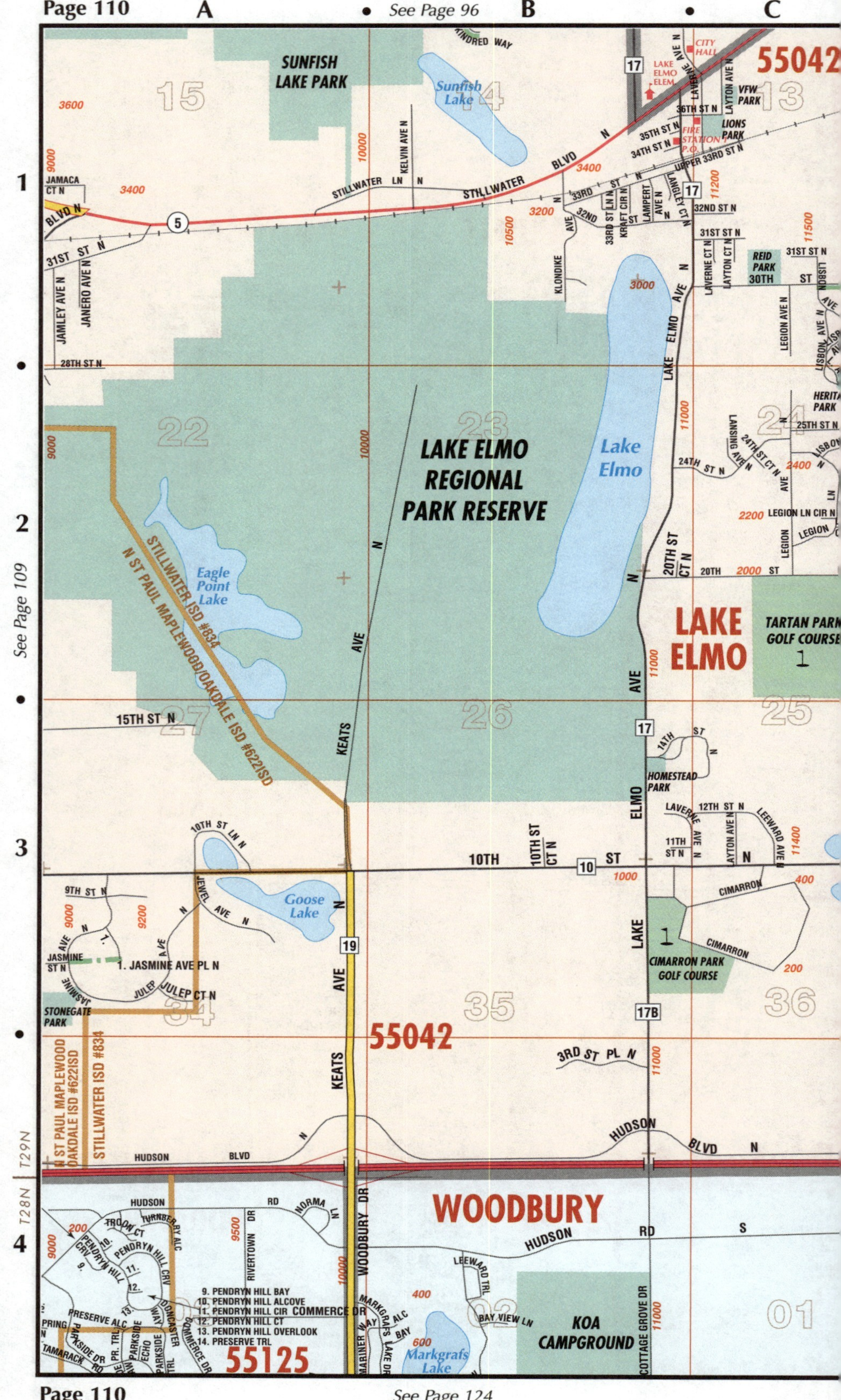
SUNFISH LAKE PARK
Sunfish Lake
55042
CITY HALL
LAKE ELMO ELEM
VFW PARK
LIONS PARK
FIRE STATION P.O.
STILLWATER BLVD N
JAMACA CT N
31ST ST N
JAMLEY AVE N
JANERO AVE N
28TH ST N
KELVIN AVE N
KLONDIKE AVE N
LAVERNE AVE N
LAYTON AVE N
36TH ST N
35TH ST N
34TH ST N
UPPER 33RD ST N
33RD ST N
32ND ST N
31ST ST N
REID PARK
30TH ST
LEGION AVE N
LISBON AVE N
HERITAGE PARK
25TH ST N
24TH ST N
24TH ST CT N
LANSING AVE N
LEGION LN CIR N
20TH ST
20TH ST CT N
LAKE ELMO REGIONAL PARK RESERVE
Lake Elmo
Eagle Point Lake
STILLWATER ISD #834
N ST PAUL MAPLEWOOD/OAKDALE ISD #622ISD
KEATS AVE N
LAKE ELMO AVE N
LAKE ELMO
TARTAN PARK GOLF COURSE
15TH ST N
14TH ST N
HOMESTEAD PARK
12TH ST N
11TH ST N
LEEWARD AVE N
10TH ST N
10TH ST CT N
10TH ST LN N
Goose Lake
9TH ST N
JEWEL AVE N
JASMINE ST N
1. JASMINE AVE PL N
JULEP CT N
STONEGATE PARK
CIMARRON
CIMARRON PARK GOLF COURSE
55042
3RD ST PL N
HUDSON BLVD N
N ST PAUL MAPLEWOOD OAKDALE ISD #622ISD
STILLWATER ISD #834
T29N
T28N
WOODBURY
HUDSON RD
NORMA LN
RIVERTOWN DR
WOODBURY DR
LEEWARD TRL
BAY VIEW LN
KOA CAMPGROUND
COTTAGE GROVE DR
Markgrafs Lake
MARKGRAFS LAKE DR
MARINER WAY
COMMERCE DR
9. PENDRYN HILL BAY
10. PENDRYN HILL ALCOVE
11. PENDRYN HILL CIR
12. PENDRYN HILL CT
13. PENDRYN HILL OVERLOOK
14. PRESERVE TRL
PRESERVE ALC
DONCASTER WAY
TURNBERRY ALC
TROON CT
TAMARACK RD
PARKSIDE DR
55125
01

See Page 109

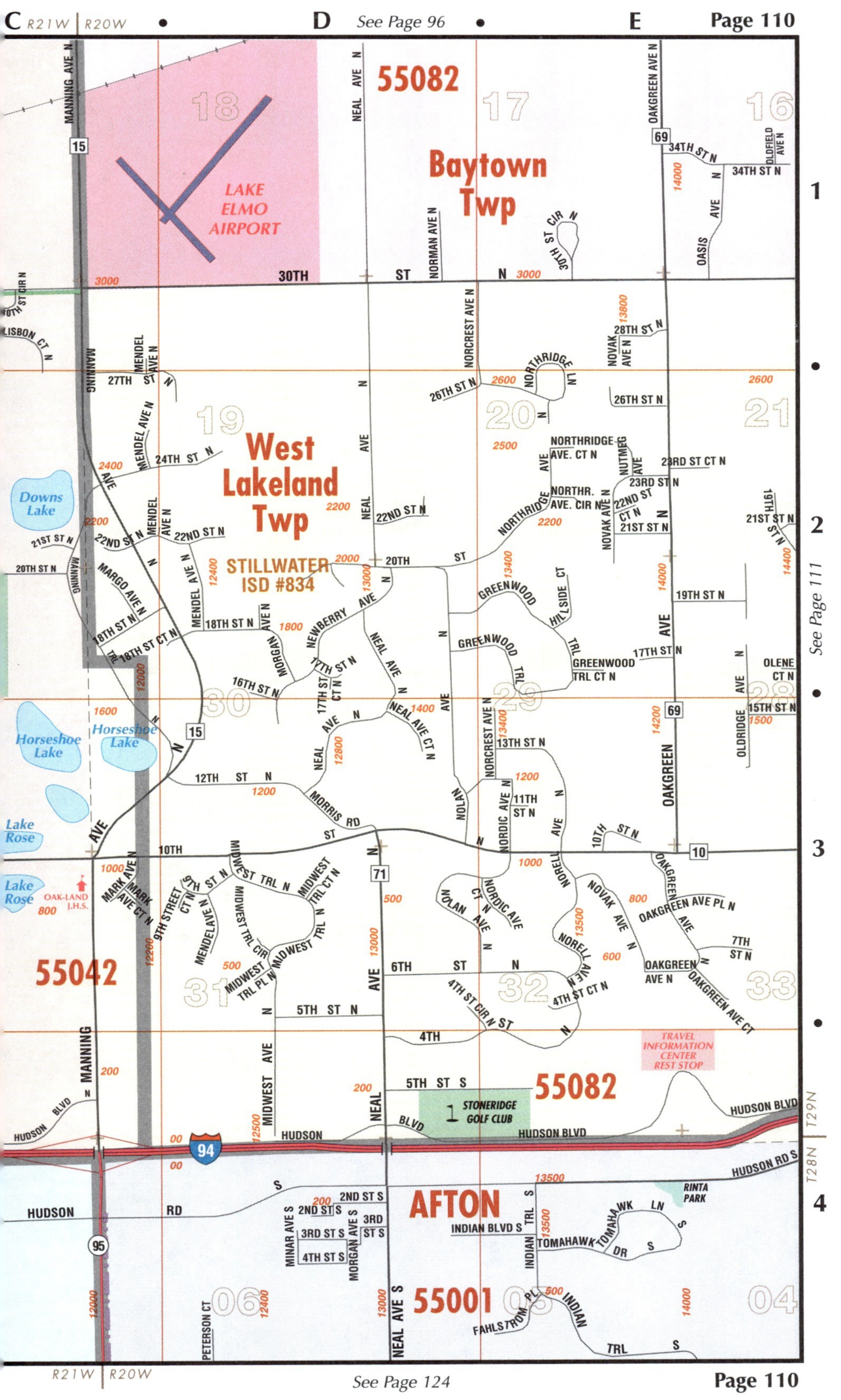
55082
Baytown Twp
LAKE ELMO AIRPORT
West Lakeland Twp
STILLWATER ISD #834
55042
AFTON
55001
STONERIDGE GOLF CLUB
TRAVEL INFORMATION CENTER REST STOP
Downs Lake
Horseshoe Lake
Lake Rose
OAK-LAND J.H.S.
RINTA PARK
30TH ST N
20TH ST
10TH ST
HUDSON BLVD
HUDSON RD
MANNING AVE N
NEAL AVE N
OAKGREEN AVE N
NORCREST AVE N
MIDWEST AVE
INDIAN TRL S
See Page 111

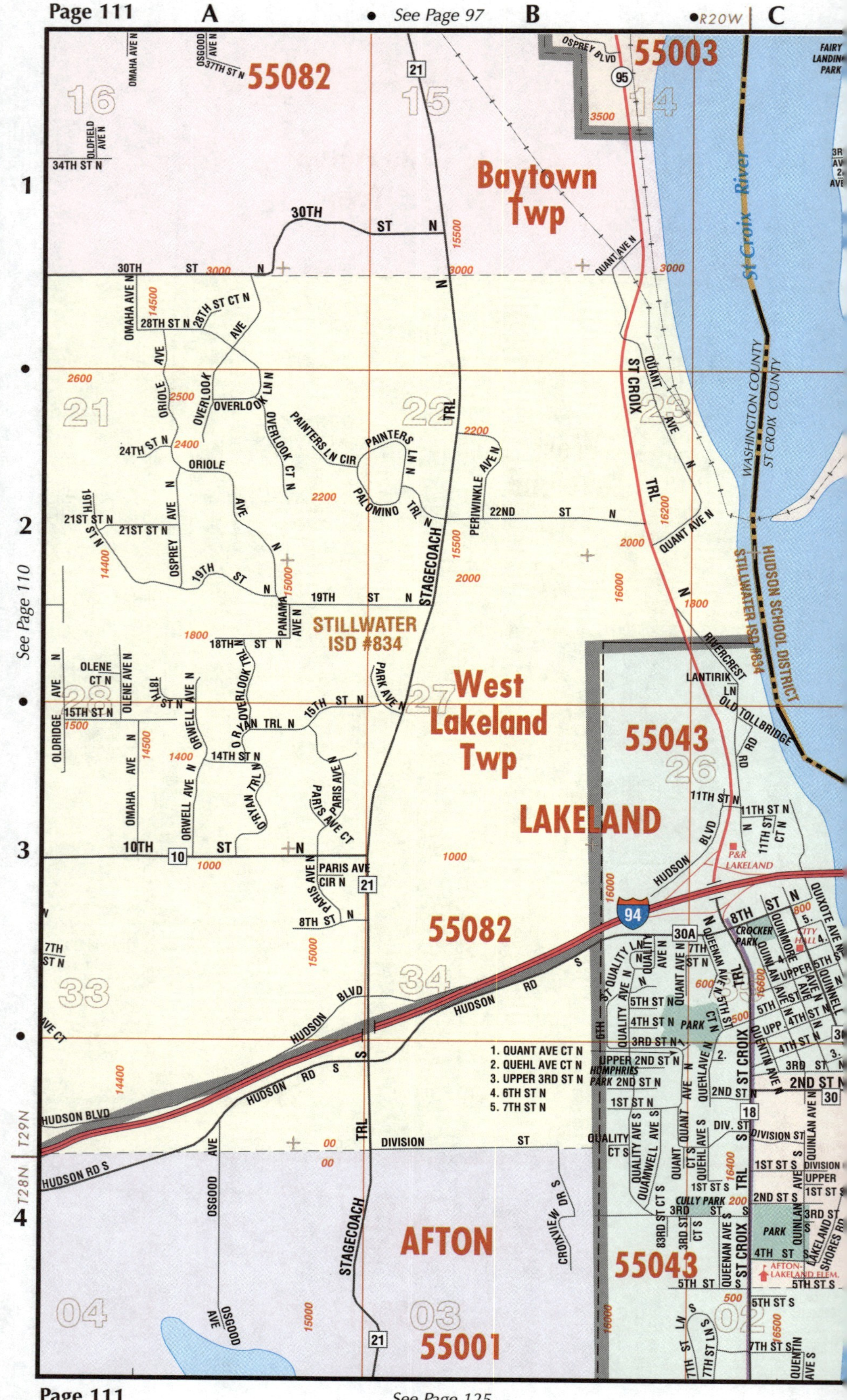

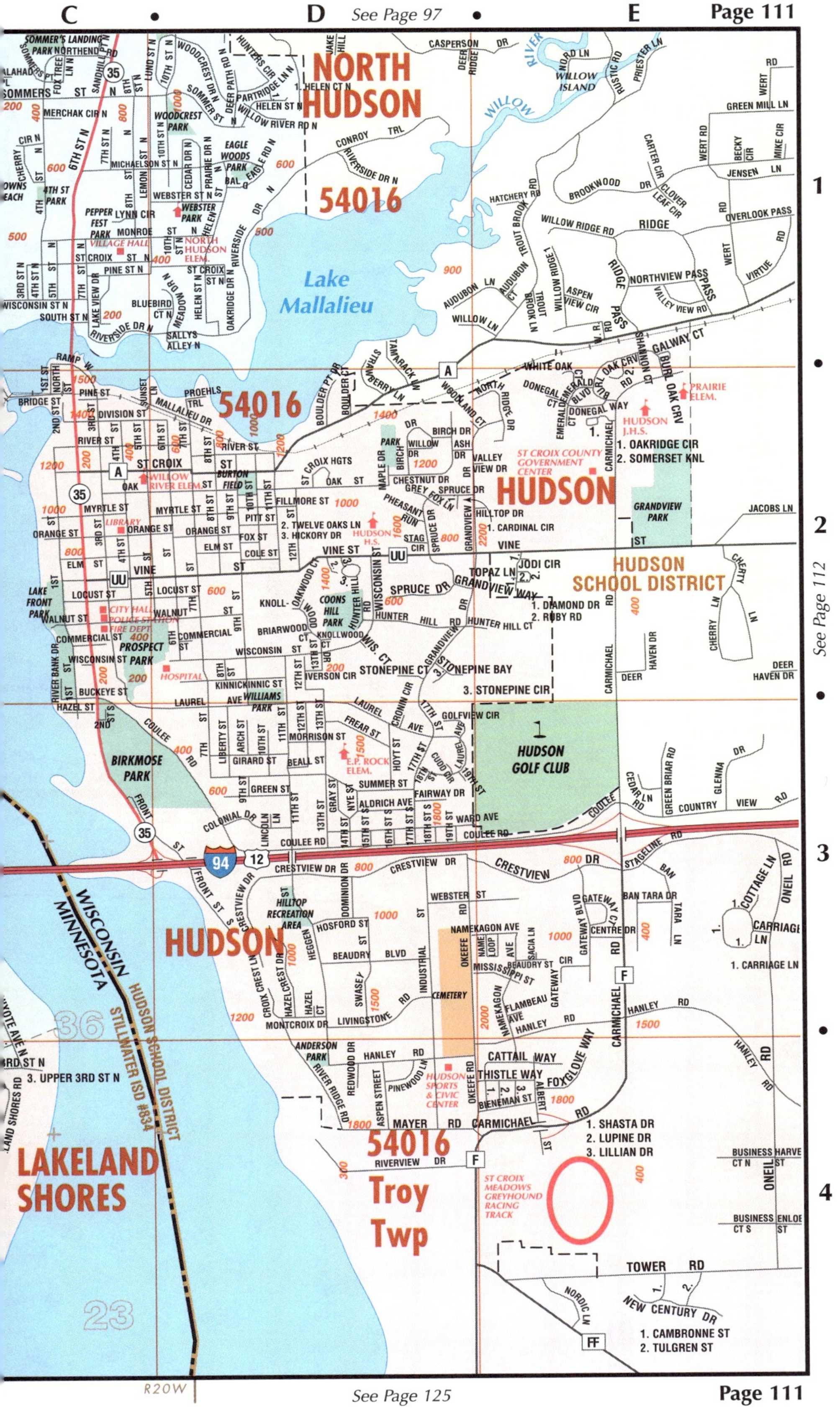
NORTH HUDSON
54016
Lake Mallalieu
HUDSON
HUDSON SCHOOL DISTRICT
HUDSON GOLF CLUB
BIRKMOSE PARK
WISCONSIN
MINNESOTA
HUDSON SCHOOL DISTRICT
STILLWATER ISD #834
LAKELAND SHORES
Troy Twp
ST CROIX MEADOWS GREYHOUND RACING TRACK
1
2
3
4
See Page 112

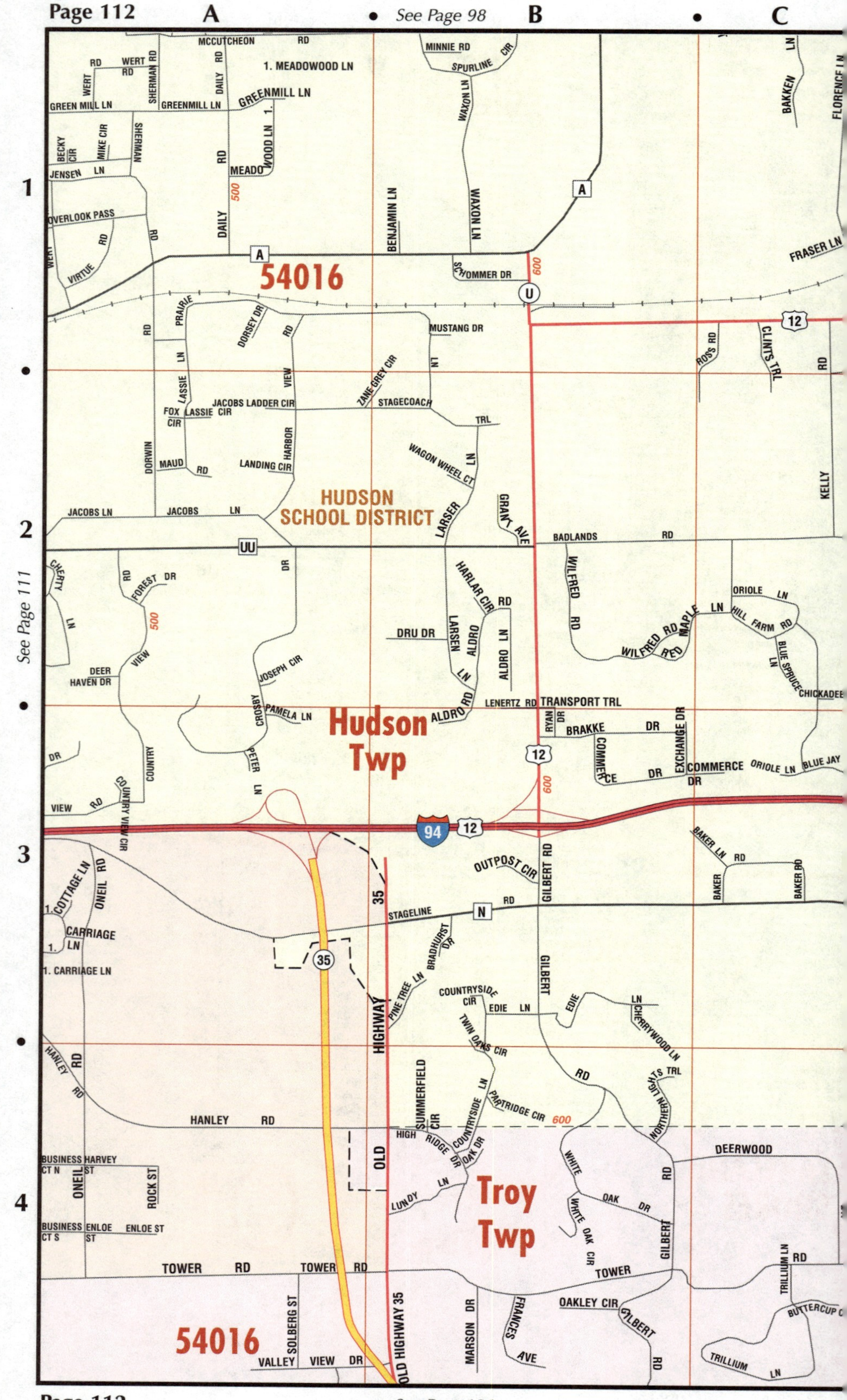

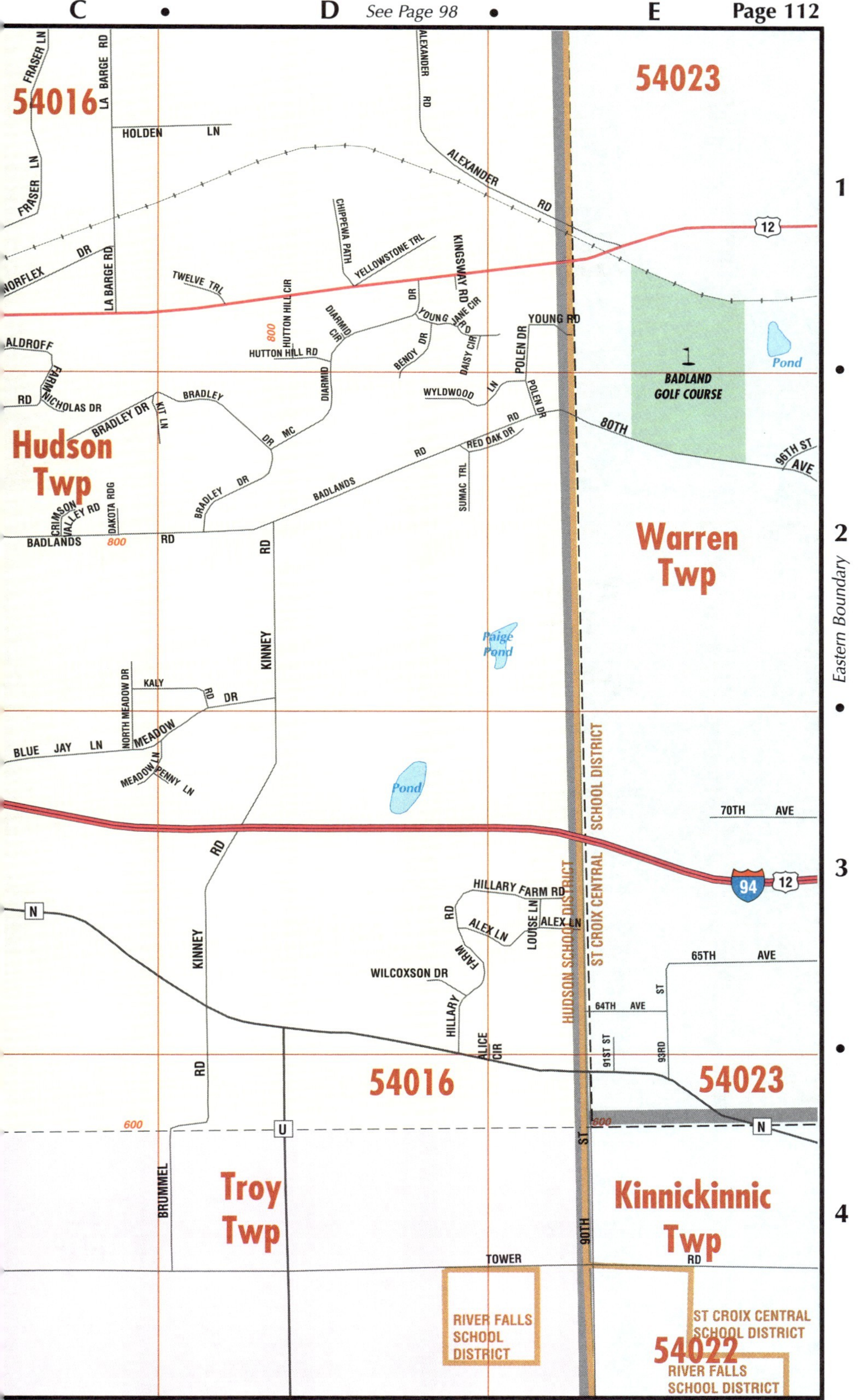

FRASER LN
LA BARGE RD
HOLDEN LN
FRASER LN
NORFLEX DR
LA BARGE RD

54016

ALEXANDER RD

ALEXANDER RD

54023

12

TWELVE TRL
CHIPPEWA PATH
YELLOWSTONE TRL
HUTTON HILL CIR
KINGSWAY RD LN
JANE CIR
YOUNG
DR
DAISY CIR
DIARMID CIR
800
HUTTON HILL RD
YOUNG RD
POLEN DR

Pond

1
BADLAND GOLF COURSE

ALDROFF
NICHOLAS DR
FARM RD
BRADLEY DR
MT LN
BRADLEY
BRADLEY DR MC
DIARMID
BADLANDS RD
WYLDWOOD
LN
POLEN DR
RED OAK DR
SUMAC TRL
80TH
96TH ST AVE

Hudson Twp

CRIMSON VALLEY RD
DAKOTA RDG
BADLANDS 800 RD

KINNEY RD

Warren Twp

2

Paige Pond

NORTH MEADOW DR
KALY
RD
DR
MEADOW
BLUE JAY LN
MEADOW LN
PENNY LN

Pond

KINNEY RD

ST CROIX CENTRAL SCHOOL DISTRICT

70TH AVE

3

94 **12**

N

HILLARY FARM RD
LOUISE LN
ALEX LN
RD
FARM RD
ALEX LN
WILCOXSON DR
HILLARY
ALICE CIR

HUDSON SCHOOL DISTRICT
ST CROIX CENTRAL SCHOOL DISTRICT

65TH AVE

64TH AVE
ST
93RD ST
91ST ST

54016

54023

N

KINNEY RD

600

U

BRUMMEL

Troy Twp

600 ST
90TH ST

Kinnickinnic Twp

4

TOWER
RD

N

RIVER FALLS SCHOOL DISTRICT

ST CROIX CENTRAL SCHOOL DISTRICT

54022
RIVER FALLS SCHOOL DISTRICT

Eastern Boundary

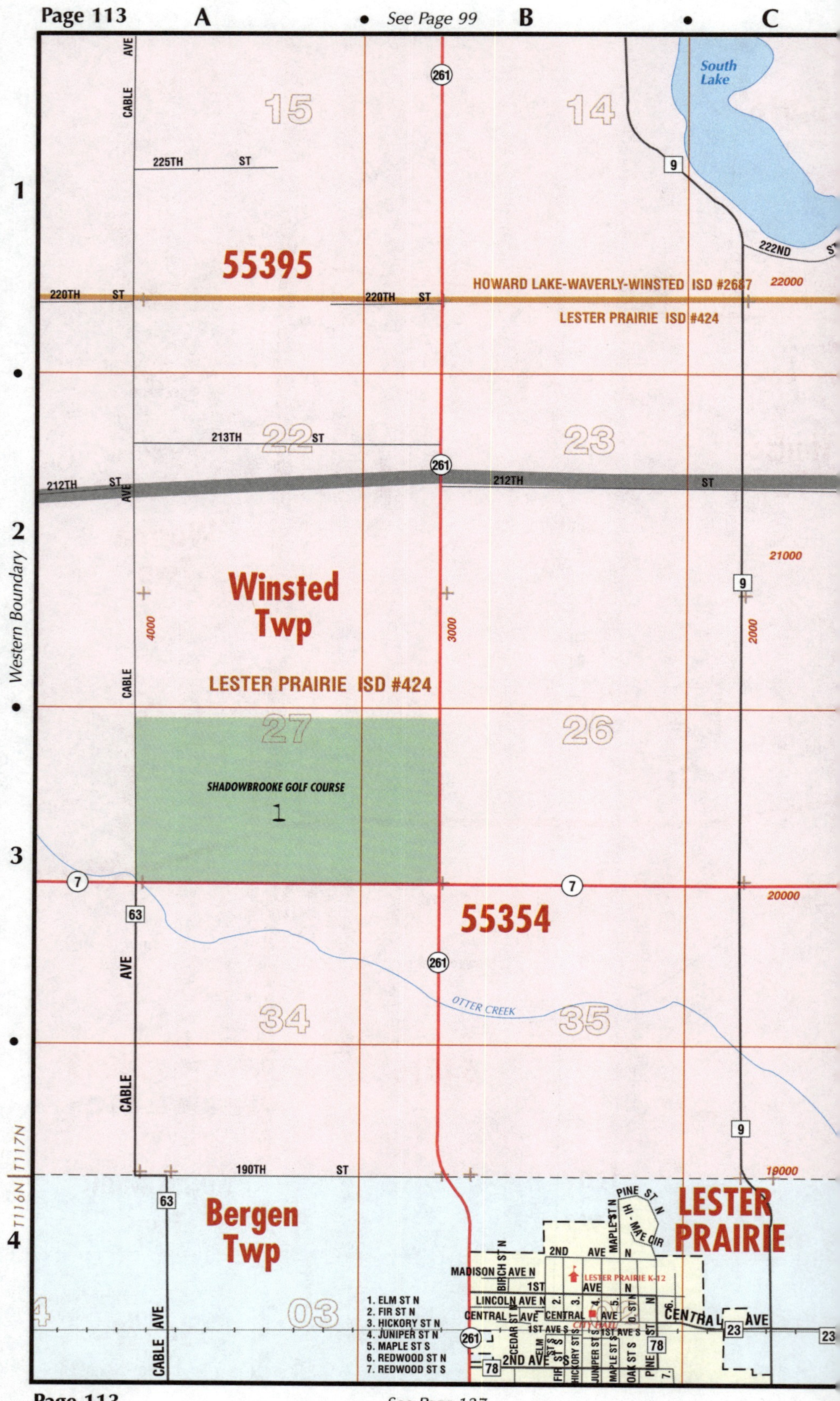

See Page 99

South Lake

15

14

225TH ST

55395

220TH ST

220TH ST

HOWARD LAKE-WAVERLY-WINSTED ISD #2687

LESTER PRAIRIE ISD #424

22000

213TH ST 22

23

212TH ST AVE

261

212TH ST

21000

Winsted Twp

4000

3000

2000

LESTER PRAIRIE ISD #424

CABLE

27

26

SHADOWBROOKE GOLF COURSE

1

7

7

55354

20000

63

261

OTTER CREEK

34

35

CABLE

9

T116N | T117N

190TH ST

19000

Bergen Twp

63

LESTER PRAIRIE

PINE ST N

MAPLE ST N

HI-WAY CIR

2ND AVE

LESTER PRAIRIE K-12

MADISON AVE N

BIRCH ST N

CITY HALL

LINCOLN AVE N

CENTRAL AVE CENTRAL

4

03

CABLE AVE

1. ELM ST N
2. FIR ST N
3. HICKORY ST N
4. JUNIPER ST N
5. MAPLE ST S
6. REDWOOD ST N
7. REDWOOD ST S

1ST AVE S

CENTRAL AVE

23

23

261

2ND AVE

78

78

See Page 127

Western Boundary

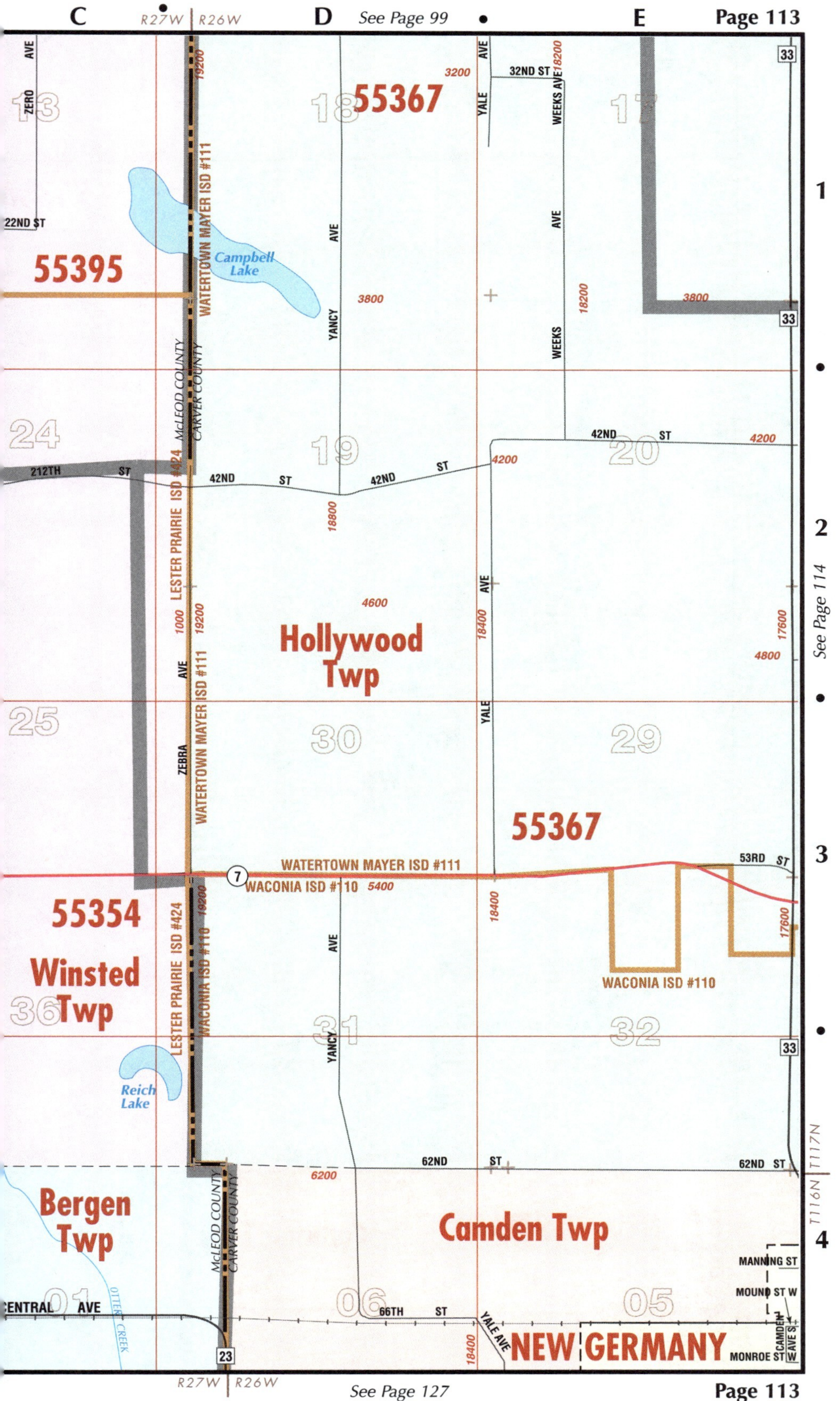

AVE

ZERO

13

22ND ST

55395

24

212TH ST

25

55354

Winsted Twp

36

Reich Lake

Bergen Twp

CENTRAL AVE

OTTER CREEK

See Page 127

WATERTOWN MAYER ISD #111

19200

McLEOD COUNTY
CARVER COUNTY

LESTER PRAIRIE ISD #424

1000

19200

WATERTOWN MAYER ISD #111

ZEBRA

LESTER PRAIRIE ISD #424

WACONIA ISD #110

19200

McLEOD COUNTY
CARVER COUNTY

23

R27W | R26W

18

55367

Campbell Lake

YANCY AVE

3800

19

42ND ST

18800

42ND ST

Hollywood Twp

4600

30

YALE AVE

18400

YALE AVE

WATERTOWN MAYER ISD #111

WACONIA ISD #110   5400

YANCY AVE

31

18400

6200

62ND ST

06

66TH ST

18400

YALE AVE

3200

32ND ST

YALE AVE

WEEKS AVE   18200

3800

18200

WEEKS AVE

4200

42ND ST

20

4200

4800

17600

29

55367

53RD ST

WACONIA ISD #110

17

3800

33

33

1

2

See Page 114

3

18400

32

33

4

62ND ST

Camden Twp

MANNING ST

MOUND ST W

05

MONROE ST

CAMDEN AVE S

T116N | T117N

NEW GERMANY

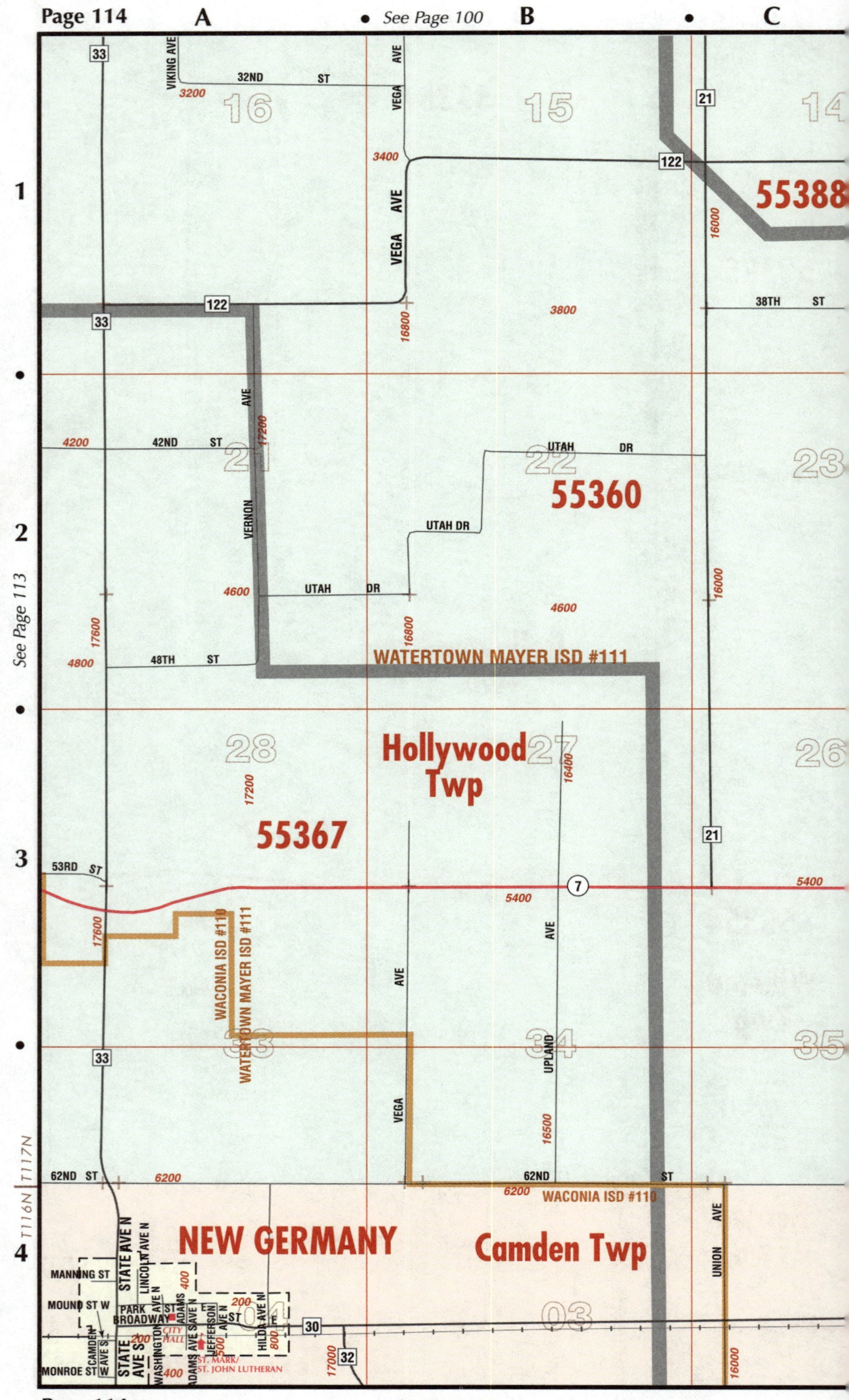

A

33
VIKING AVE
32ND ST
3200
16
15
21
14
3400
122
55388
33
122
16000
38TH ST

1

AVE
4200
42ND ST
17200
21
VERNON
22
UTAH DR
55360
23
UTAH DR
4600
UTAH DR
17600
4600
4800
48TH ST
16800
16000

2

WATERTOWN MAYER ISD #111

28
17200
55367
Hollywood
Twp
27
16400
26
21

3

53RD ST
17600
WACONIA ISD #110
WATERTOWN MAYER ISD #111
AVE
7
5400
5400

33
VEGA
AVE
UPLAND
33
34
16500
35

T116N | T117N

62ND ST
6200
VEGA
62ND ST
6200 WACONIA ISD #110
UNION AVE

4

MANNING ST
STATE AVE N
LINCOLN AVE N
NEW GERMANY
Camden Twp
MOUND ST W
PARK
BROADWAY
ADAMS AVE N
400
200
STATE AVE S
WASHINGTON
CITY HALL
JEFFERSON
ST
HILDA AVE N
800
200
03
16000
30
MONROE ST W
CAMDEN AVE S
200
400
ADAMS AVE S
500
ST. MARK/
ST. JOHN LUTHERAN
17000
32

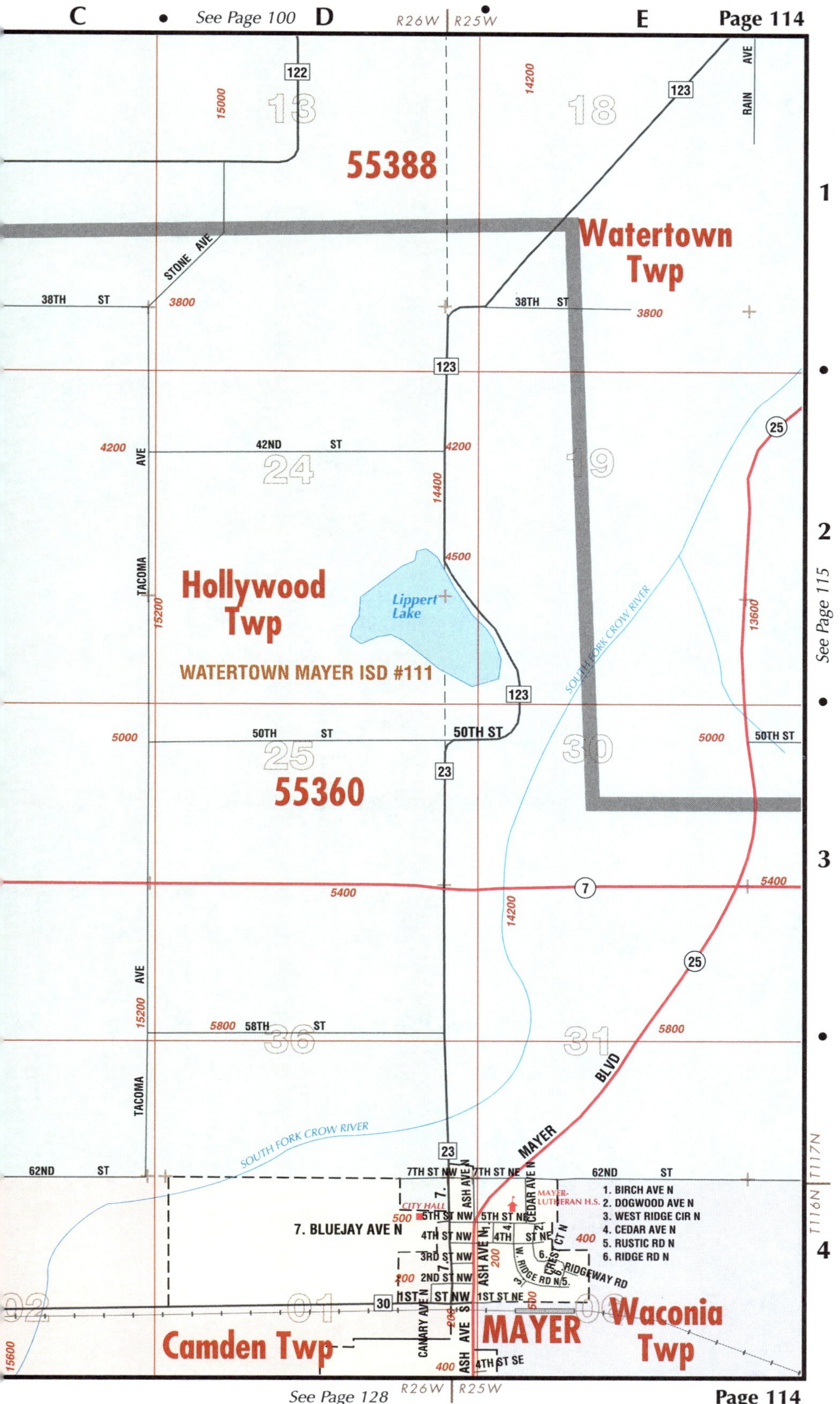

122

15000

13

14200

123

55388

18

RAIN AVE

1

38TH ST 3800

123

38TH ST 3800

Watertown Twp

Watertown Twp

42ND ST 4200

4200

19

AVE

14400

24

•

25

2

TACOMA

15200

4500

Lippert Lake

Hollywood Twp

SOUTH FORK CROW RIVER

13600

WATERTOWN MAYER ISD #111

123

•

5000

50TH ST

50TH ST

30

5000

50TH ST

25

36

55360

23

3

5400

7

5400

TACOMA

15200

AVE

14200

25

•

5800 58TH ST

36

31

5800

BLVD

SOUTH FORK CROW RIVER

MAYER

T116N | T117N

4

62ND ST

23

7TH ST NW | 7TH ST NE

62ND ST

1. BIRCH AVE N
2. DOGWOOD AVE N
3. WEST RIDGE CIR N
4. CEDAR AVE N
5. RUSTIC RD N
6. RIDGE RD N

CITY HALL 500 5TH ST NW | 5TH ST NE

MAYER-LUTHERAN H.S.

CEDAR AVE

7. **BLUEJAY AVE N** 4TH ST NW 4TH ST NE

400

ASH AVE N

3RD ST NW W. RIDGE RD N.5 RIDGEWAY RD

200 2ND ST NW 200

100 1ST ST NW 1ST ST NE

30

02

01

00

CANARY AVE N

ASH AVE S

MAYER

Waconia Twp

Camden Twp

400 4TH ST SE

15600

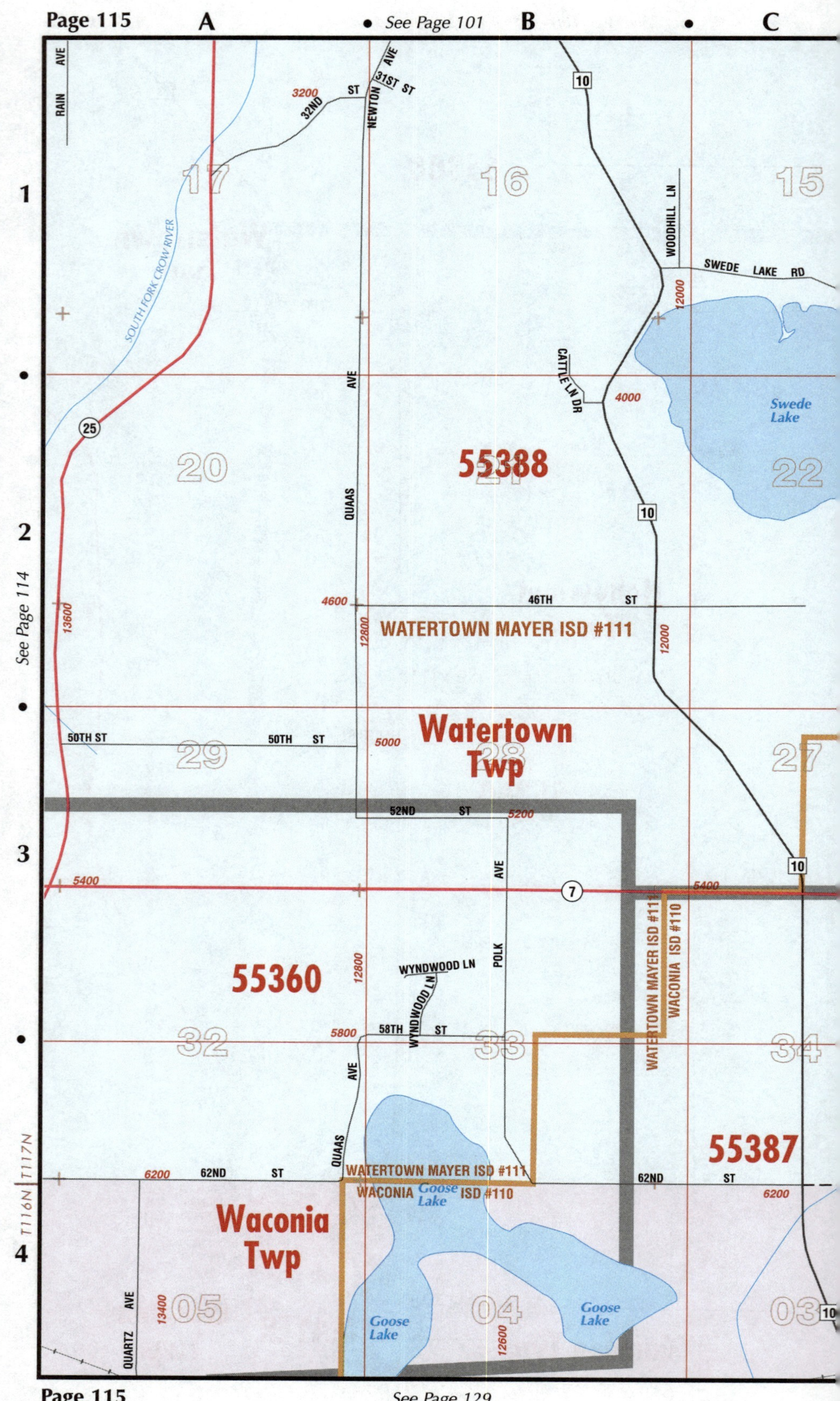

See Page 114

RAIN AVE

NEWTON AVE

31ST ST

32ND ST

3200

10

WOODHILL LN

SWEDE LAKE RD

12000

17

16

15

1

SOUTH FORK CROW RIVER

25

AVE

QUAAS

CATTLE LN DR

4000

Swede Lake

20

55388

22

10

2

13600

4600

46TH ST

4600

12800

WATERTOWN MAYER ISD #111

12000

50TH ST

50TH ST

5000

Watertown Twp

28

27

52ND ST

5200

3

5400

AVE

POLK

7

5400

10

55360

12800

WYNDWOOD LN

WYNDWOOD LN

WATERTOWN MAYER ISD #11

WACONIA ISD #110

32

5800

58TH ST

33

34

AVE

QUAAS

55387

T116N | T117N

6200

62ND ST

6200

62ND ST

WATERTOWN MAYER ISD #111

WACONIA *Goose Lake* ISD #110

Waconia Twp

QUARTZ AVE

13400

05

04

Goose Lake

Goose Lake

12600

03

10

4

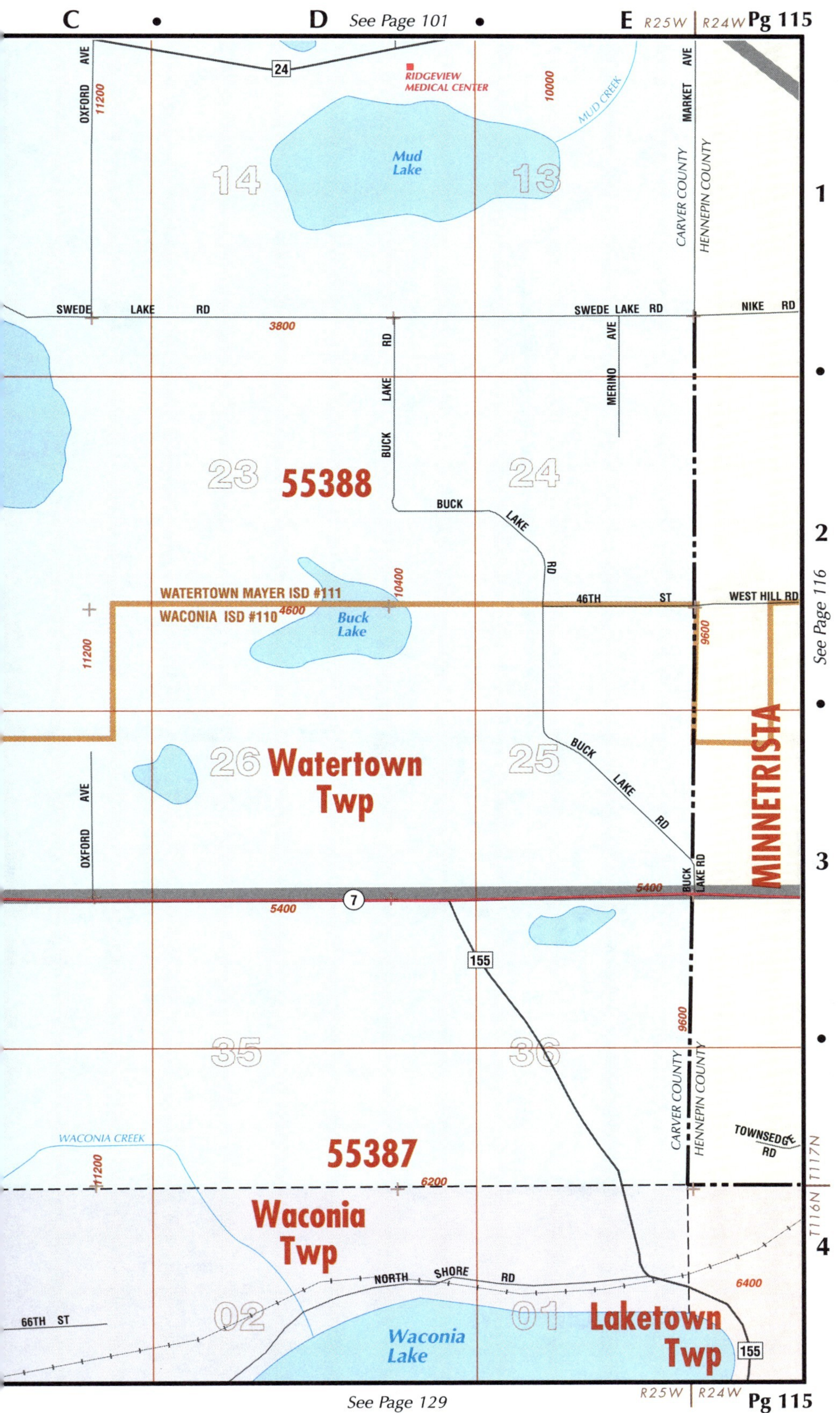

OXFORD AVE
11200

24

■ RIDGEVIEW
MEDICAL CENTER

10000

MUD CREEK

Mud Lake

14

13

MARKET AVE

CARVER COUNTY
HENNEPIN COUNTY

1

SWEDE LAKE RD

3800

SWEDE LAKE RD

NIKE RD

BUCK LAKE RD

MERINO AVE

23 **55388**

24

2

See Page 116

BUCK LAKE RD

46TH ST

WEST HILL RD

WATERTOWN MAYER ISD #111
WACONIA ISD #110

10400

4600

Buck Lake

9600

11200

26 **Watertown Twp**

25

BUCK LAKE RD

OXFORD AVE

MINNETRISTA

BUCK LAKE RD

3

5400

⑦

5400

155

35

36

CARVER COUNTY
HENNEPIN COUNTY

9600

•

WACONIA CREEK

11200

55387

6200

Waconia Twp

TOWNSEDGE RD

T116N | T117N

4

66TH ST

NORTH SHORE RD

6400

02

Waconia Lake

01

Laketown Twp

155

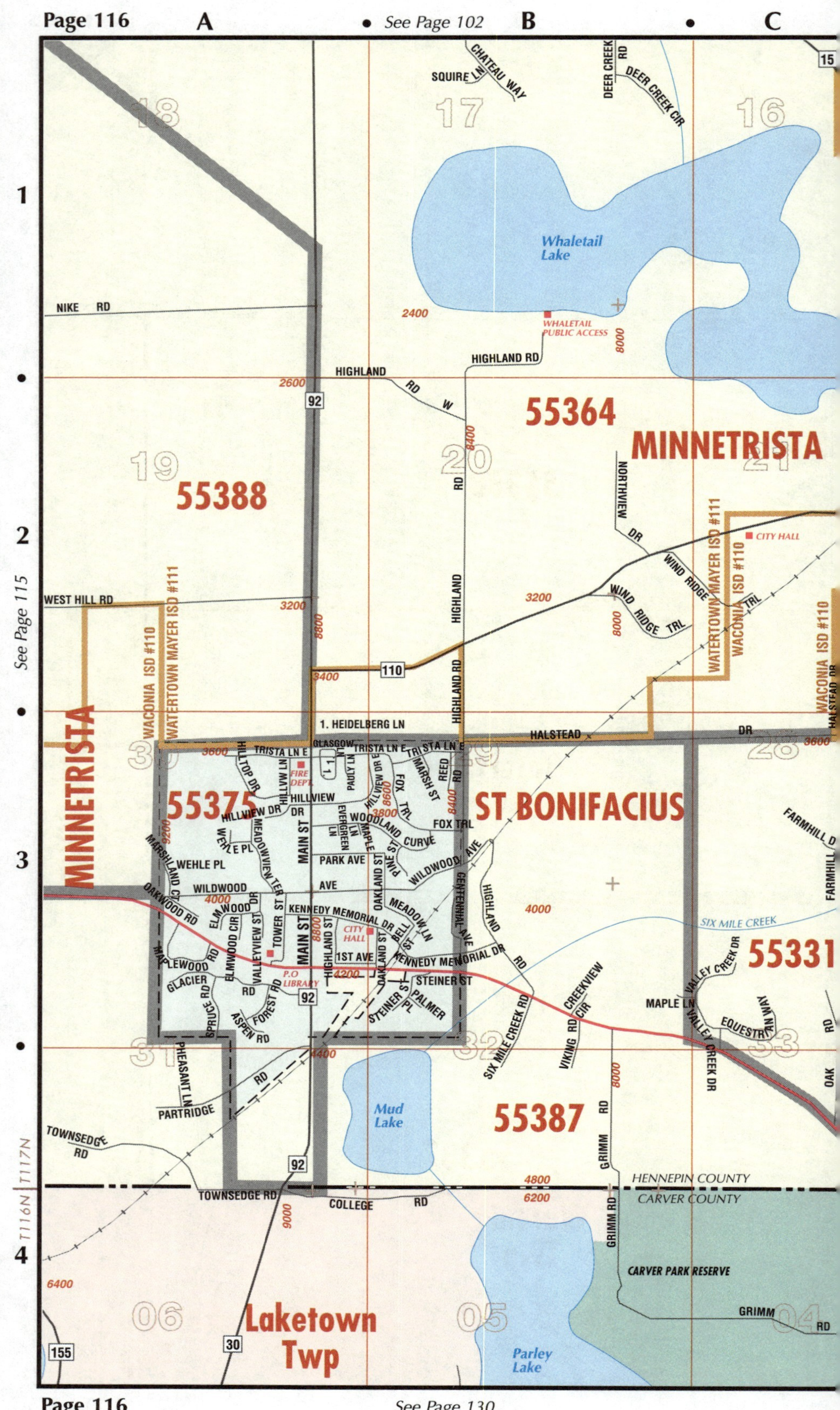

15

CHATEAU WAY

SQUIRE LN

DEER CREEK RD

DEER CREEK CIR

18

17

16

1

Whaletail Lake

NIKE RD

2400

WHALETAIL PUBLIC ACCESS

8000

HIGHLAND RD

HIGHLAND RD W

2600

92

55364

MINNETRISTA

19

20

21

55388

See Page 115

WATERTOWN MAYER ISD #111

WEST HILL RD

3200

NORTHVIEW DR

WIND RIDGE DR

CITY HALL

2

8800

WACONIA ISD #110

3200

WIND RIDGE TRL

WATERTOWN MAYER ISD #111

WACONIA ISD #110

HALSTEAD DR

WACONIA ISD #110

3400

110

HIGHLAND RD

8000

HIGHLAND RD

1. HEIDELBERG LN

GLASGOW

TRISTA LN E

TRISTA LN E

HALSTEAD

DR

3600

30

3600

3600

29

28

3600

MINNETRISTA

55375

HILLTOP DR

HILLVIEW LN

TRISTA LN E

FOX TRL

MARSH ST

REED RD

8400

FARMHILL DR

FARMHILL D

8600

FIRE DEPT.

HILLVIEW DR

PARK AVE

WELLIVIEW ST

EVERGREEN LN

WOODLAND CURVE

3800

FOX TRL

ST BONIFACIUS

9200

MARSHLAND CIR

MEADOWVIEW TER

WEHLE PL

MAIN ST

PARK AVE AVE

OAKLAND ST

PINE ST

WILDWOOD AVE

3

WILDWOOD

4000

ELM WOOD ST

MAPLE ST

MEADOW LN

CENTENNIAL AVE

HIGHLAND RD

4000

SIX MILE CREEK

OAKWOOD RD

ELMWOOD CIR

TOWER ST

KENNEDY MEMORIAL DR

BELL

55331

MAPLEWOOD

VALLEYVIEW ST

MAIN ST

HIGHLAND ST

8800

CITY HALL

1ST AVE

OAKLAND ST

KENNEDY MEMORIAL DR

VALLEY CREEK DR

FARMHILL

VALLEY CREEK DR

GLACIER RD

SPRUCE RD

FOREST RD

P.O LIBRARY

92

4200

STEINER ST

STEINER ST

PALMER

CREEKVIEW CIR

MAPLE LN

EQUESTRIAN WAY

OAK RD

ASPEN RD

4400

SIX MILE CREEK RD

VIKING RD

8000

31

PHEASANT LN

Mud Lake

55387

32

33

PARTRIDGE RD

GRIMM RD

TOWNSEDGE RD

92

4800

HENNEPIN COUNTY

CARVER COUNTY

T116N T117N

6400

TOWNSEDGE RD

COLLEGE RD

9000

6200

GRIMM RD

CARVER PARK RESERVE

4

06

30

05

Laketown Twp

Parley Lake

GRIMM RD

04

155

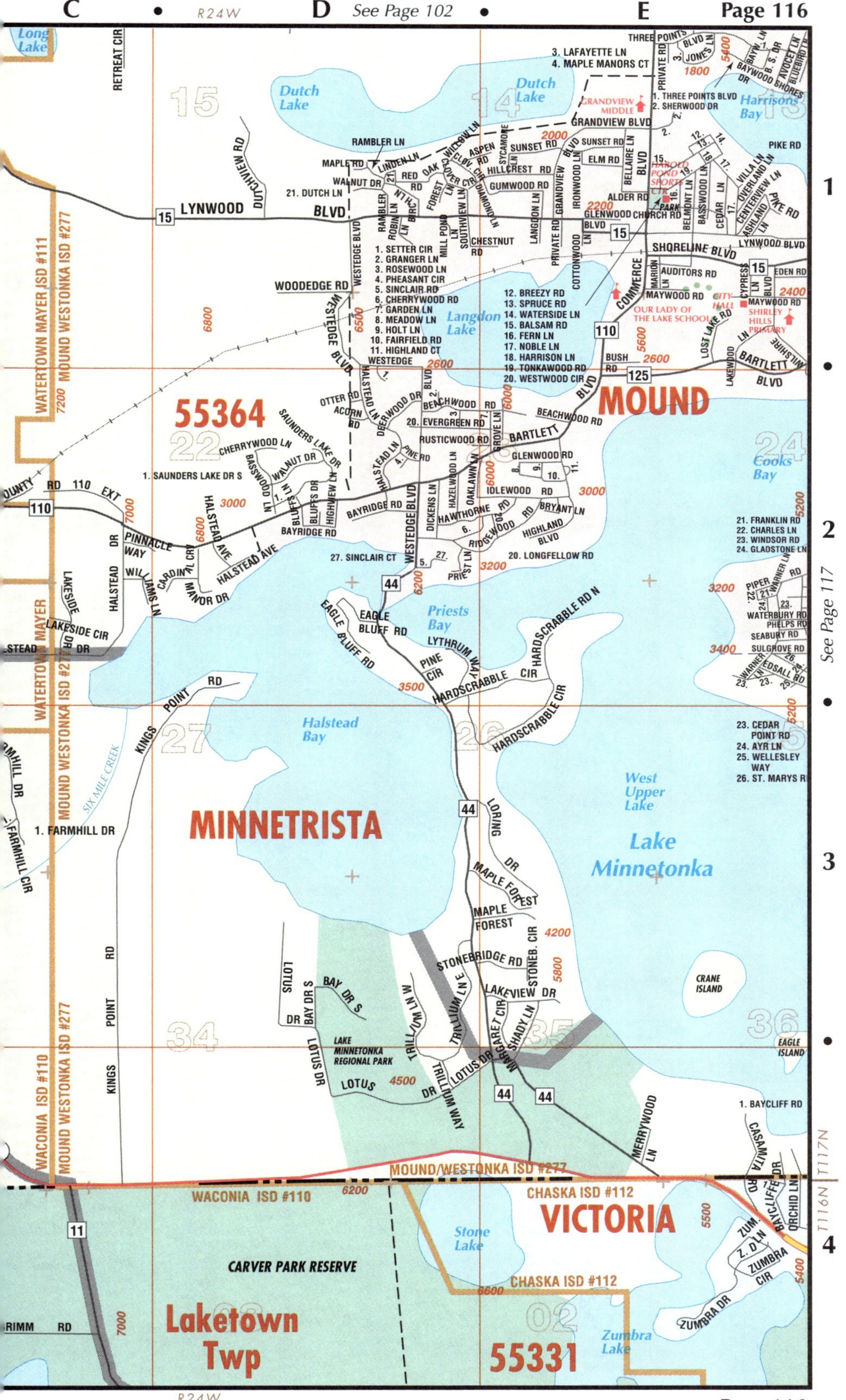

Long Lake

Dutch Lake

Dutch Lake

THREE POINTS

3. LAFAYETTE LN
4. MAPLE MANORS CT

PRIVATE RD

JONE'S

5400

BAYWOOD

BAYWOOD SHORES

1800

GRANDVIEW MIDDLE

1. THREE POINTS BLVD
2. SHERWOOD LN

Harrisons Bay

GRANDVIEW BLVD

15

RETREAT CIR

SOUTHVIEW RD

PIKE RD

RAMBLER LN

WITSON LN

ASPEN

SUNSET RD

SUNSET RD

BLVD

BELLAIRE RD

VILLA LN

OVERLAND RD

CENTERVIEW LN

MAPLE RD

LINDEN LN

SYCAMORE

HILLCREST RD

ELM RD

BASSWOOD LN

ASHLAND RD

PIKE RD

FOREST OAK

RED LN

GRANDVIEW

IRONWOOD RD

CEDAR LN

15 LYNWOOD BLVD

21. DUTCH LN

WALNUT DR

MILL POND LN

GUMWOOD RD

LANGDON LN

ALDER RD

CHURCH RD

BELMONT LN

LYNWOOD BLVD

ROBIN LN

SOUTHVIEW LN

HAMMOND LN

PRIVATE RD

GLENWOOD

15

SHORELINE BLVD

WOODEDGE RD

1. SETTER CIR
2. GRANGER LN
3. ROSEWOOD LN
4. PHEASANT CIR
5. SINCLAIR RD
6. CHERRYWOOD RD
7. GARDEN LN
8. MEADOW LN
9. HOLT LN
10. FAIRFIELD RD
11. HIGHLAND CT
WESTEDGE

CHESTNUT RD

COTTONWOOD

Langdon Lake

12. BREEZY RD
14. WATERSIDE LN
15. BALSAM RD
16. FERN LN
17. NOBLE LN
18. HARRISON LN
19. TONKAWOOD RD
20. WESTWOOD CIR

MAYWOOD RD

COMMERCE

MARION

AUDITORS RD

OUR LADY OF THE LAKE SCHOOL

CITY HALL

CYPRESS

2400

MAYWOOD RD

SHIRLEY HILLS PRIMARY

SUNSHINE

EDEN RD

110

BUSH RD

2600

BARTLETT BLVD

LOST LAKE RD

LAKEWOOD

55364

22 CHERRYWOOD LN

SAUNDERS LAKE DR

6800

6500

WESTEDGE BLVD

HALSTEAD RD

ACORN

DEERWOOD DR

OTTER RD

20. EVERGREEN RD

RUSTICWOOD RD

BEACHWOOD RD

PINE RD

BEACHWOOD RD

GROVE LN

BARTLETT

GLENWOOD RD

MOUND

125

Cooks Bay

24

1. SAUNDERS LAKE DR S

3000

BASSWOOD LN

WALNUT DR

BLUFFS DR

BLUFFS DR

HALSTEAD AVE

DICKENS LN

HAZELWOOD LN

IDLEWOOD

9. 10. 11.

6000

3000

PINNACLE WAY

7000

CARDIN LN

MANOR DR

HALSTEAD AVE

BAYRIDGE RD

HAWTHORNE

RIDGEWOOD

BRYANT LN

HIGHLAND BLVD

21. FRANKLIN RD
22. CHARLES LN
23. WINDSOR RD
24. GLADSTONE LN

COUNTY RD 110 EXT

110

6600

WILSHIRE LN

BAYRIDGE RD

27. SINCLAIR CT

44

6200

5

PRIEST LN

3200

20. LONGFELLOW RD

PIPER RD

GARDNER RD

WATERBURY RD

PHELPS RD

SEABURY RD

SULGROVE RD

3200

LAKESIDE MAYER

WATERTOWN MAYER ISD #111

MOUND WESTONKA ISD #277

HALSTEAD

LAKESIDE CIR

LAKESIDE DR

STEAD

7200

7000

Eagle Bluff

EAGLE BLUFF RD

Priests Bay

LYTHRUM WAY

PINE CIR

3500

HARDSCRABBLE RD N

HARDSCRABBLE CIR

HARDSCRABBLE CIR

MARSH

EDSALL RD

23.

3400

23. CEDAR POINT RD
24. AYR LN
25. WELLESLEY WAY
26. ST. MARYS R

6200

FARMHILL DR

FARMHILL CIR

1. FARMHILL DR

Halstead Bay

27

KINGS POINT RD

SIX MILE CREEK

26

44

HARDSCRABBLE CIR

LORING DR

West Upper Lake

Lake Minnetonka

See Page 117

MINNETRISTA

MAPLE FOREST DR

MAPLE FOREST

STONEBRIDGE RD

STONEB. CIR

4200

5800

CRANE ISLAND

34

KINGS POINT RD

LOTUS DR

BAY DR S

BAY DR S

LAKE MINNETONKA REGIONAL PARK

LOTUS DR

LOTUS

4500

TRILLIUM LN W

TRILLIUM LN E

TRILLIUM WAY

LOTUS DR

LAKEVIEW DR

SHADY LN

MARGARET CIR

35

MERRYWOOD LN

36

EAGLE ISLAND

1. BAYCLIFF RD

CASANITA

BAYCLIFF RD

ORCHID LN

T116N T117N

WACONIA ISD #110

MOUND WESTONKA ISD #277

11

MOUND/WESTONKA ISD #277

WACONIA ISD #110

6200

CHASKA ISD #112

Stone Lake

VICTORIA

5500

ZUM

Z. D LN

ZUMBRA CIR

ZUMBRA DR

CARVER PARK RESERVE

Laketown Twp

7000

RIMM RD

CHASKA ISD #112

6600

55331

Zumbra Lake

ZUMBRIA DR

5400

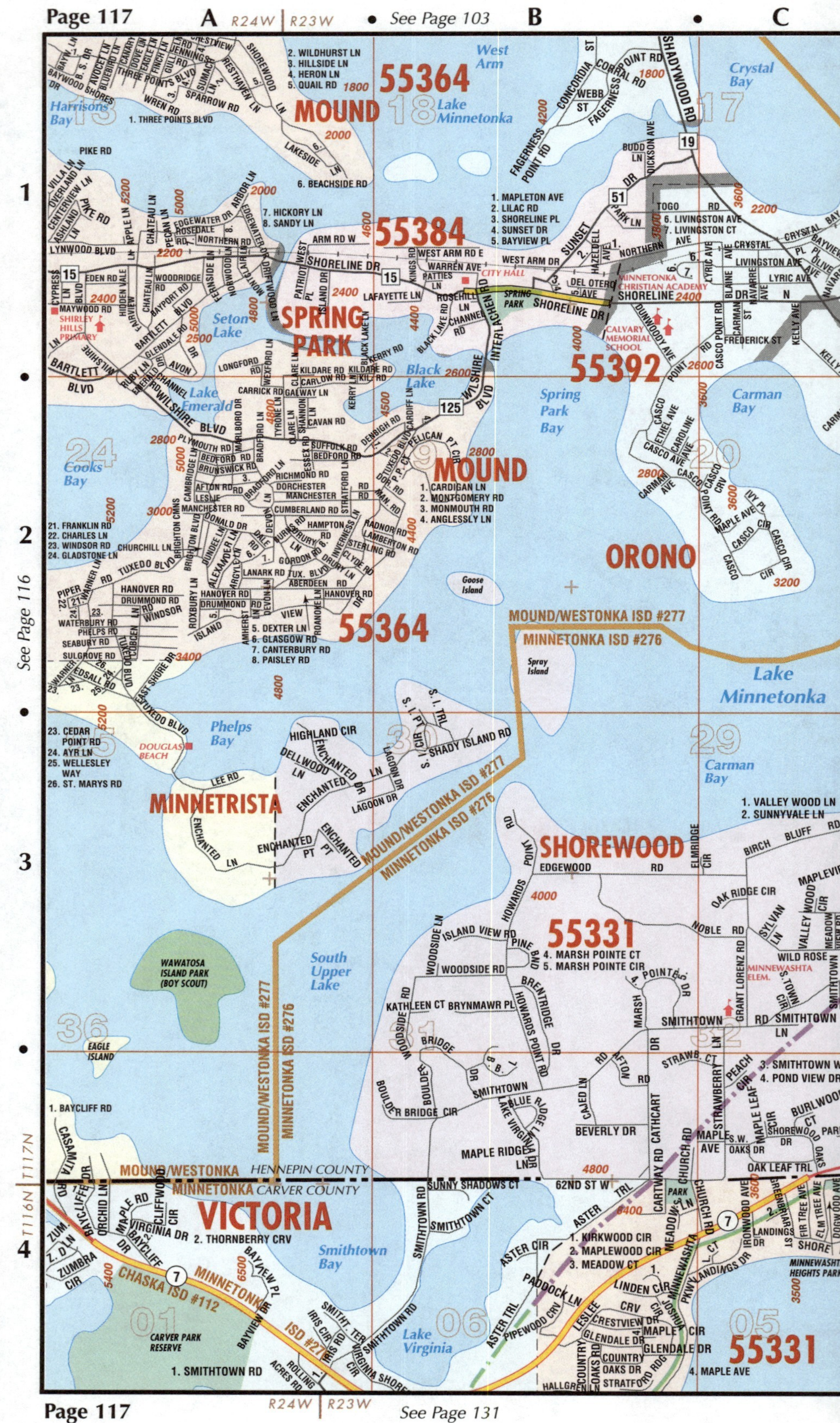

1
2
3
4
See Page 116
55364
MOUND
West Arm
Lake Minnetonka
Crystal Bay
Harrisons Bay
1. THREE POINTS BLVD
2. WILDHURST LN
3. HILLSIDE LN
4. HERON LN
5. QUAIL RD
6. BEACHSIDE RD
7. HICKORY LN
8. SANDY LN
55384
SPRING PARK
CITY HALL
SHORELINE DR
WEST ARM RD E
WARREN AVE
1. MAPLETON AVE
2. LILAC RD
3. SHORELINE PL
4. SUNSET DR
5. BAYVIEW PL
6. LIVINGSTON AVE
7. LIVINGSTON CT
MINNETONKA CHRISTIAN ACADEMY
CALVARY MEMORIAL SCHOOL
SHIRLEY HILLS PRIMARY
Seton Lake
Black Lake
Lake Emerald
Spring Park Bay
Carman Bay
55392
Cooks Bay
MOUND
1. CARDIGAN LN
2. MONTGOMERY RD
3. MONMOUTH RD
4. ANGLESSLY LN
21. FRANKLIN RD
22. CHARLES LN
23. WINDSOR RD
24. GLADSTONE LN
ORONO
Goose Island
5. DEXTER LN
6. GLASGOW RD
7. CANTERBURY RD
8. PAISLEY RD
55364
MOUND/WESTONKA ISD #277
MINNETONKA ISD #276
Spray Island
Lake Minnetonka
Phelps Bay
DOUGLAS BEACH
23. CEDAR POINT RD
24. AYR LN
25. WELLESLEY WAY
26. ST. MARYS RD
MINNETRISTA
Carman Bay
1. VALLEY WOOD LN
2. SUNNYVALE LN
SHOREWOOD
55331
4. MARSH POINTE CT
5. MARSH POINTE CIR
MINNEWASHTA ELEM.
South Upper Lake
WAWATOSA ISLAND PARK (BOY SCOUT)
EAGLE ISLAND
3. SMITHTOWN W
4. POND VIEW DR
1. BAYCLIFF RD
MOUND/WESTONKA
MINNETONKA
HENNEPIN COUNTY
CARVER COUNTY
T117N
T116N
VICTORIA
2. THORNBERRY CRV
Smithtown Bay
CHASKA ISD #112
CARVER PARK RESERVE
1. SMITHTOWN RD
Lake Virginia
1. KIRKWOOD CIR
2. MAPLEWOOD CIR
3. MEADOW CT
MINNEWASHTA HEIGHTS PARK
4. MAPLE AVE
55331

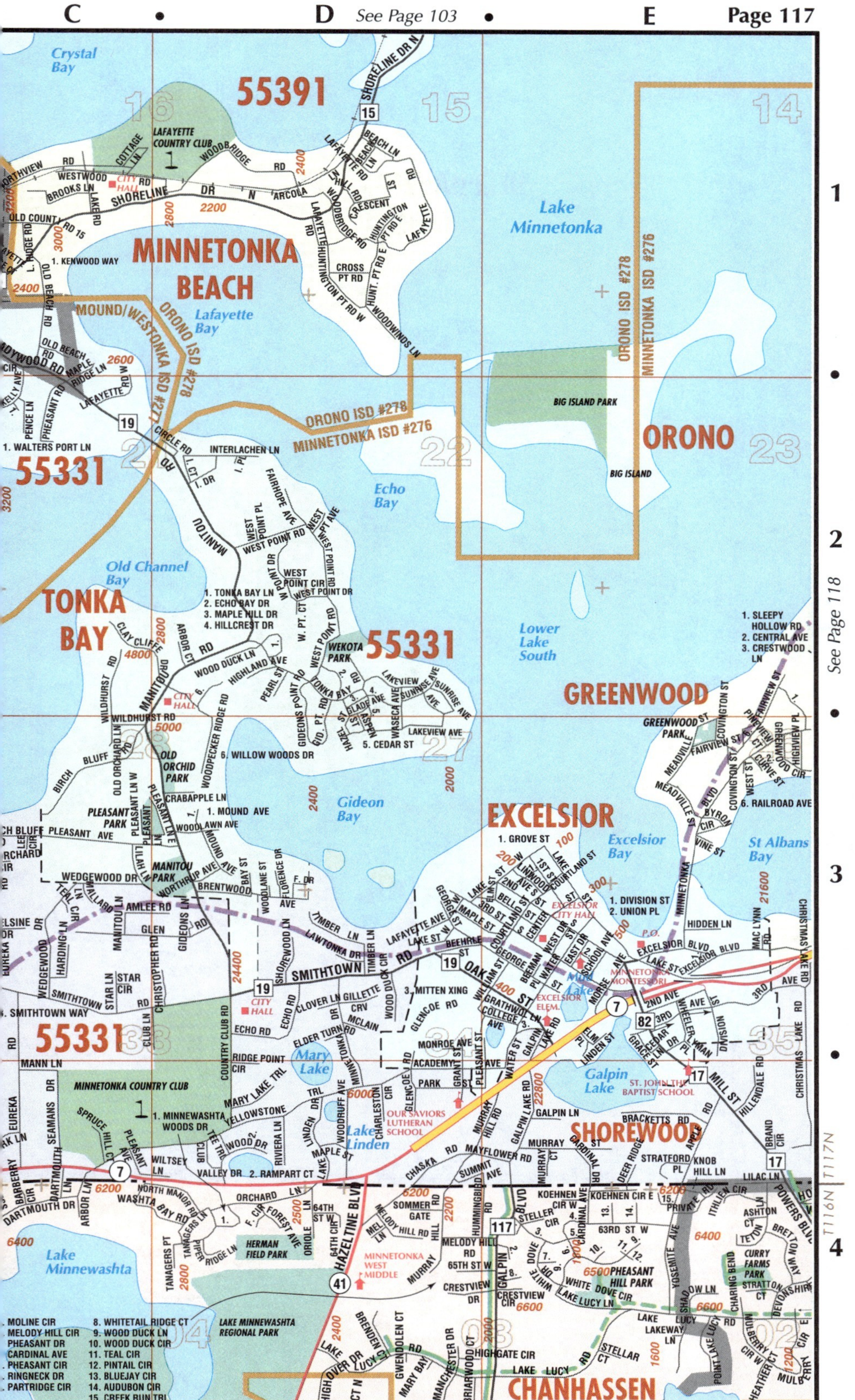
55391
MINNETONKA BEACH
Lafayette Bay
Crystal Bay
Lake Minnetonka
LAFAYETTE COUNTRY CLUB
CITY HALL
MOUND/WESTONKA ISD #277
ORONO ISD #278
MINNETONKA ISD #276
BIG ISLAND PARK
ORONO
BIG ISLAND
Echo Bay
55331
Old Channel Bay
TONKA BAY
WEKOTA PARK
Lower Lake South
GREENWOOD
GREENWOOD PARK
OLD ORCHID PARK
Gideon Bay
EXCELSIOR
Excelsior Bay
St Albans Bay
PLEASANT PARK
MANITOU PARK
EXCELSIOR CITY HALL
P.O.
MINNETONKA MONTESSORI
EXCELSIOR ELEM.
Mud Lake
Mary Lake
MINNETONKA COUNTRY CLUB
Galpin Lake
ST. JOHN THE BAPTIST SCHOOL
OUR SAVIORS LUTHERAN SCHOOL
Lake Linden
SHOREWOOD
HERMAN FIELD PARK
MINNETONKA WEST MIDDLE
Lake Minnewashta
LAKE MINNEWASHTA REGIONAL PARK
CHANHASSEN
See Page 118
1. KENWOOD WAY
1. WALTERS PORT LN
1. TONKA BAY LN
2. ECHO BAY DR
3. MAPLE HILL DR
4. HILLCREST DR
5. CEDAR ST
6. WILLOW WOODS DR
1. MOUND AVE
1. SLEEPY HOLLOW RD
2. CENTRAL AVE
3. CRESTWOOD LN
6. RAILROAD AVE
1. GROVE ST
1. DIVISION ST
2. UNION PL
3. MITTEN XING
1. SMITHTOWN WAY
1. MINNEWASHTA WOODS DR
2. RAMPART CT
MOLINE CIR
MELODY HILL CIR
PHEASANT DR
CARDINAL AVE
PHEASANT CIR
RINGNECK DR
PARTRIDGE CIR
8. WHITETAIL RIDGE CT
9. WOOD DUCK LN
10. WOOD DUCK CIR
11. TEAL CIR
12. PINTAIL CIR
13. BLUEJAY CIR
14. AUDUBON CIR
15. CREEK RUN TRL
T116N T117N

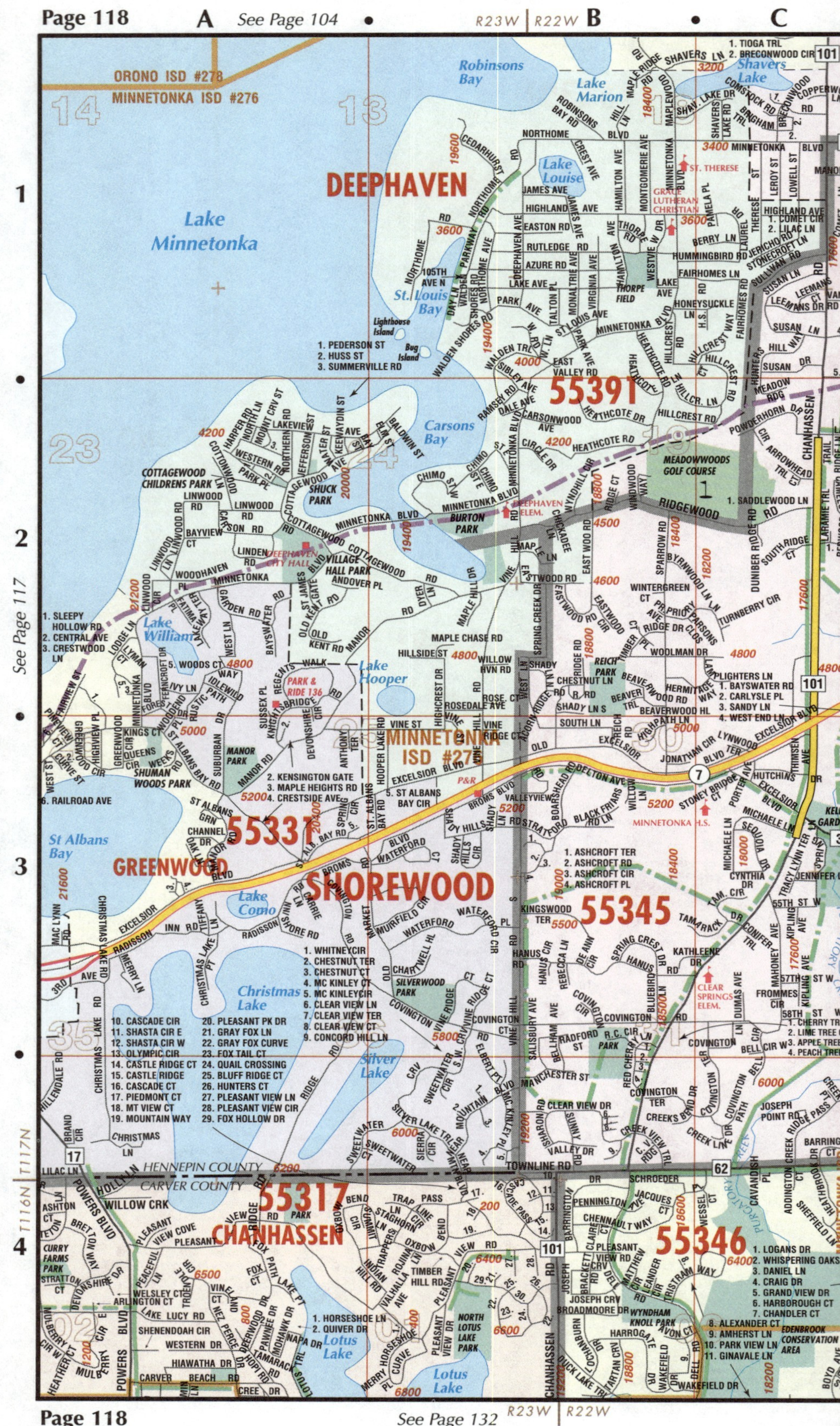

See Page 117
1
2
3
4
ORONO ISD #278
MINNETONKA ISD #276
Lake Minnetonka
Robinsons Bay
Lake Marion
Shavers Lake
Lake Louise
DEEPHAVEN
St. Louis Bay
Lighthouse Island
Bug Island
Carsons Bay
SHUCK PARK
VILLAGE HALL PARK
COTTAGEWOOD CHILDRENS PARK
DEEPHAVEN CITY HALL
DEEPHAVEN ELEM.
BURTON PARK
MEADOWWOODS GOLF COURSE
THORPE FIELD
ST. THERESE
GRACE LUTHERAN CHRISTIAN
Lake William
Lake Hooper
PARK & RIDE 136
MANOR PARK
SHUMAN WOODS PARK
St Albans Bay
GREENWOOD
55391
55331
55345
55317
55346
MINNETONKA ISD #276
SHOREWOOD
MINNETONKA H.S.
CLEAR SPRINGS ELEM.
REICH PARK
SILVERWOOD PARK
R.C. PARK
Lake Como
Christmas Lake
Silver Lake
HENNEPIN COUNTY
CARVER COUNTY
CHANHASSEN
Lotus Lake
NORTH LOTUS LAKE PARK
CURRY FARMS PARK
EDENBROOK CONSERVATION AREA
T117N
T116N
1. TIOGA TRL
2. BRECONWOOD CIR
1. PEDERSON ST
2. HUSS ST
3. SUMMERVILLE RD
1. SLEEPY HOLLOW RD
2. CENTRAL AVE
3. CRESTWOOD LN
1. BAYSWATER RD
2. CARLYSLE PL
3. SANDY LN
4. WEST END LN
1. SADDLEWOOD LN
2. KENSINGTON GATE
3. MAPLE HEIGHTS RD
4. CRESTSIDE AVE
5. ST ALBANS BAY CIR
6. RAILROAD AVE
1. ASHCROFT TER
2. ASHCROFT RD
3. ASHCROFT CIR
4. ASHCROFT PL
1. WHITNEY CIR
2. CHESTNUT TER
3. CHESTNUT CT
4. MC KINLEY CT
5. MC KINLEY CIR
6. CLEAR VIEW LN
7. CLEAR VIEW TER
8. CLEAR VIEW CT
9. CONCORD HILL LN
10. CASCADE CIR
11. SHASTA CIR E
12. SHASTA CIR W
13. OLYMPIC CIR
14. CASTLE RIDGE CT
15. CASTLE RIDGE
16. CASCADE CT
17. PIEDMONT CT
18. MT VIEW CT
19. MOUNTAIN WAY
20. PLEASANT PK DR
21. GRAY FOX LN
22. GRAY FOX CURVE
23. FOX TAIL CT
24. QUAIL CROSSING
25. BLUFF RIDGE CT
26. HUNTERS CT
27. PLEASANT VIEW LN
28. PLEASANT VIEW CIR
29. FOX HOLLOW DR
1. CHERRY TRL
2. LIME TREE CIR
3. APPLE TREE
4. PEACH TREE
1. LOGANS DR
2. WHISPERING OAKS
3. DANIEL LN
4. CRAIG DR
5. GRAND VIEW DR
6. HARBOROUGH CT
7. CHANDLER CT
8. ALEXANDER CT
9. AMHERST LN
10. PARK VIEW LN
11. GINAVALE LN
1. COMET CIR
2. LILAC LN
MINNETONKA BLVD
EXCELSIOR BLVD
HIGHLAND AVE
NORTHOME BLVD
CHANHASSEN RD
TOWNLINE RD
SMITHTOWN RD
POWERS BLVD

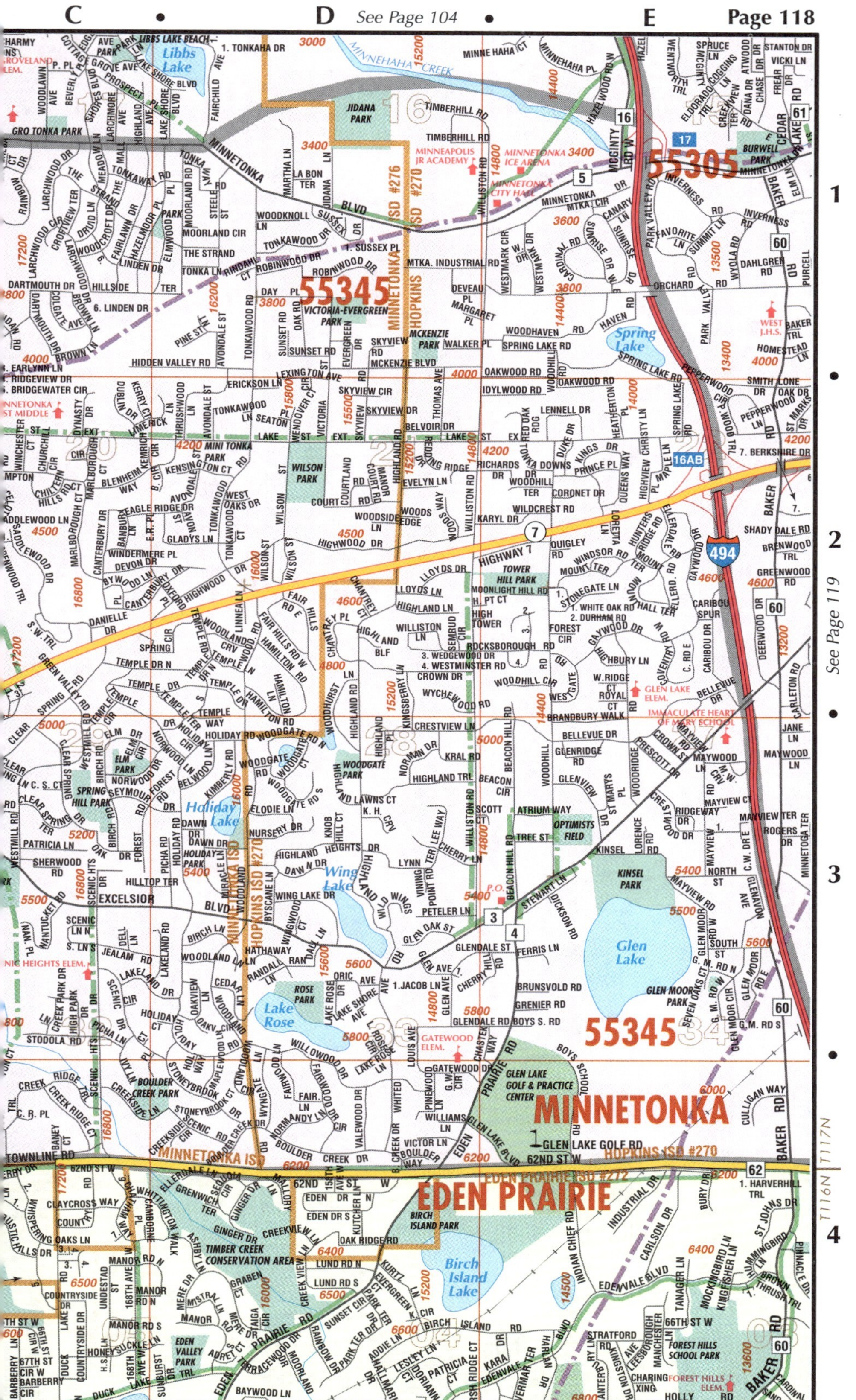

MINNETONKA
EDEN PRAIRIE
55345
55305
Libbs Lake
Spring Lake
Holiday Lake
Wing Lake
Lake Rose
Glen Lake
Birch Island Lake
JIDANA PARK
MINNEAPOLIS JR ACADEMY
MINNETONKA ICE ARENA
MINNETONKA CITY HALL
VICTORIA-EVERGREEN PARK
MCKENZIE PARK
WILSON PARK
MINI TONKA PARK
TOWER HILL PARK
ELM PARK
SPRING HILL PARK
WOODGATE PARK
OPTIMISTS FIELD
KINSEL PARK
GLEN MOOR PARK
ROSE PARK
BOULDER CREEK PARK
GLEN LAKE GOLF & PRACTICE CENTER
GLEN LAKE GOLF RD
BIRCH ISLAND PARK
TIMBER CREEK CONSERVATION AREA
EDEN VALLEY PARK
FOREST HILLS SCHOOL PARK
BURWELL PARK
GRO TONKA PARK
WEST J.H.S.
GLEN LAKE ELEM.
IMMACULATE HEART OF MARY SCHOOL
GATEWOOD ELEM.
FOREST HILLS ELEM.
MINNEHAHA CREEK
MINNETONKA BLVD
EXCELSIOR BLVD
HIGHWAY 7
BAKER RD
MINNETONKA ISD #276
HOPKINS ISD #270
MINNETONKA ISD
EDEN PRAIRIE ISD #272
TOWNLINE RD
62ND ST W
494

See Page 119

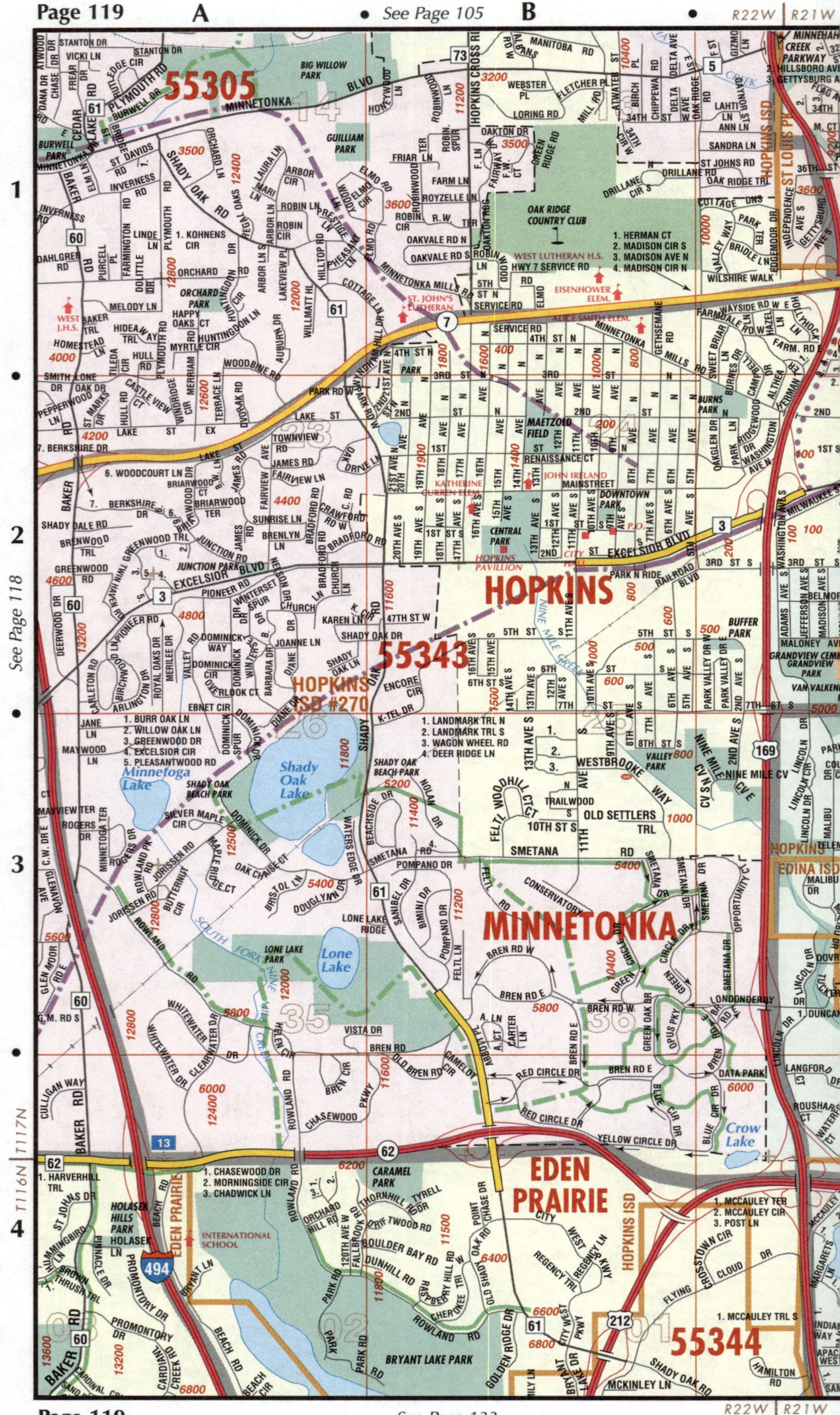
55305
55343
55344
HOPKINS
MINNETONKA
EDEN PRAIRIE
HOPKINS ISD #270
HOPKINS ISD
EDINA ISD
ST LOUIS PK
BIG WILLOW PARK
GUILLIAM PARK
OAK RIDGE COUNTRY CLUB
WEST LUTHERAN H.S.
EISENHOWER ELEM.
ALICE SMITH ELEM.
ST. JOHN'S LUTHERAN
WEST J.H.S.
ORCHARD PARK
MAETZOLD FIELD
JOHN IRELAND
KATHERINE CURREN ELEM.
CENTRAL PARK
HOPKINS PAVILLION
CITY HALL
DOWNTOWN PARK
P.O.
BURNS PARK
BUFFER PARK
VALLEY PARK
GRANDVIEW PARK
Shady Oak Lake
SHADY OAK BEACH PARK
Minnetoga Lake
LONE LAKE PARK
Lone Lake
Crow Lake
CARAMEL PARK
HOLASEK HILLS PARK
INTERNATIONAL SCHOOL
BRYANT LAKE PARK
MINNEHAHA CREEK PARKWAY
NINE MILE CREEK
SOUTH FORK NINE MILE CREEK
MINNETONKA BLVD
EXCELSIOR BLVD
MAINSTREET
SHADY OAK RD
BAKER RD
SMETANA RD
BREN RD E
BREN RD W
RED CIRCLE DR
YELLOW CIRCLE DR
OPUS PKY
WESTBROOKE WAY
OLD SETTLERS TRL
CITY WEST PKWY
FLYING CLOUD DR
CROSSTOWN CIR
ROWLAND RD
1. KOHNENS CIR
1. HERMAN CT
2. MADISON CIR S
3. MADISON AVE N
4. MADISON CIR N
1. BURR OAK LN
2. WILLOW OAK LN
3. GREENWOOD DR
4. EXCELSIOR CIR
5. PLEASANTWOOD RD
1. LANDMARK TRL N
2. LANDMARK TRL S
3. WAGON WHEEL RD
4. DEER RIDGE LN
1. CHASEWOOD DR
2. MORNINGSIDE CIR
3. CHADWICK LN
1. HARVERHILL TRL
1. MCCAULEY TER
2. MCCAULEY CIR
3. POST LN
1. MCCAULEY TRL S
6. WOODCOURT LN
7. BERKSHIRE DR
T116N
T117N
See Page 118
1
2
3
4
7
3
5
61
60
62
13
169
212
494
73

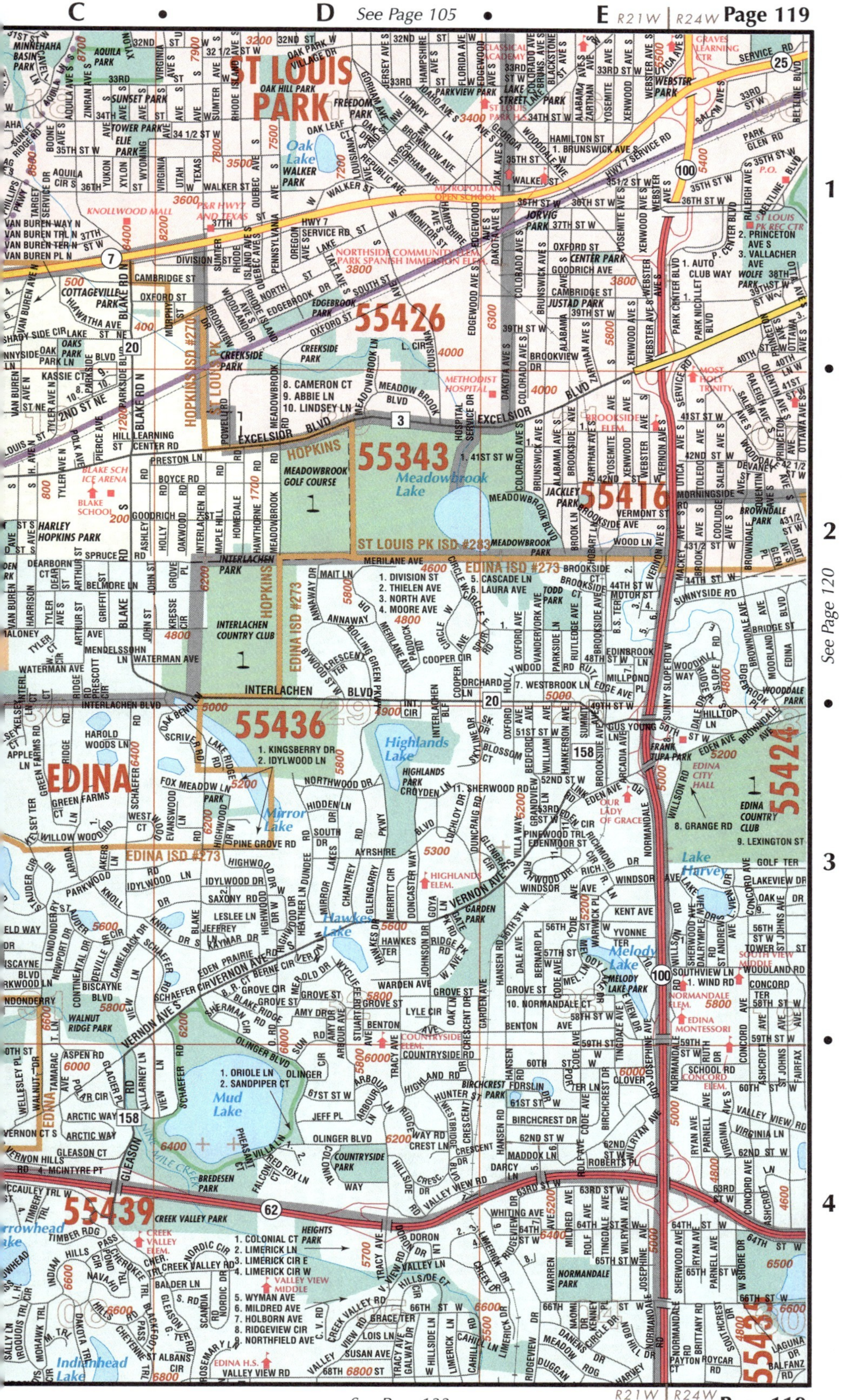

A B C
See Page 106

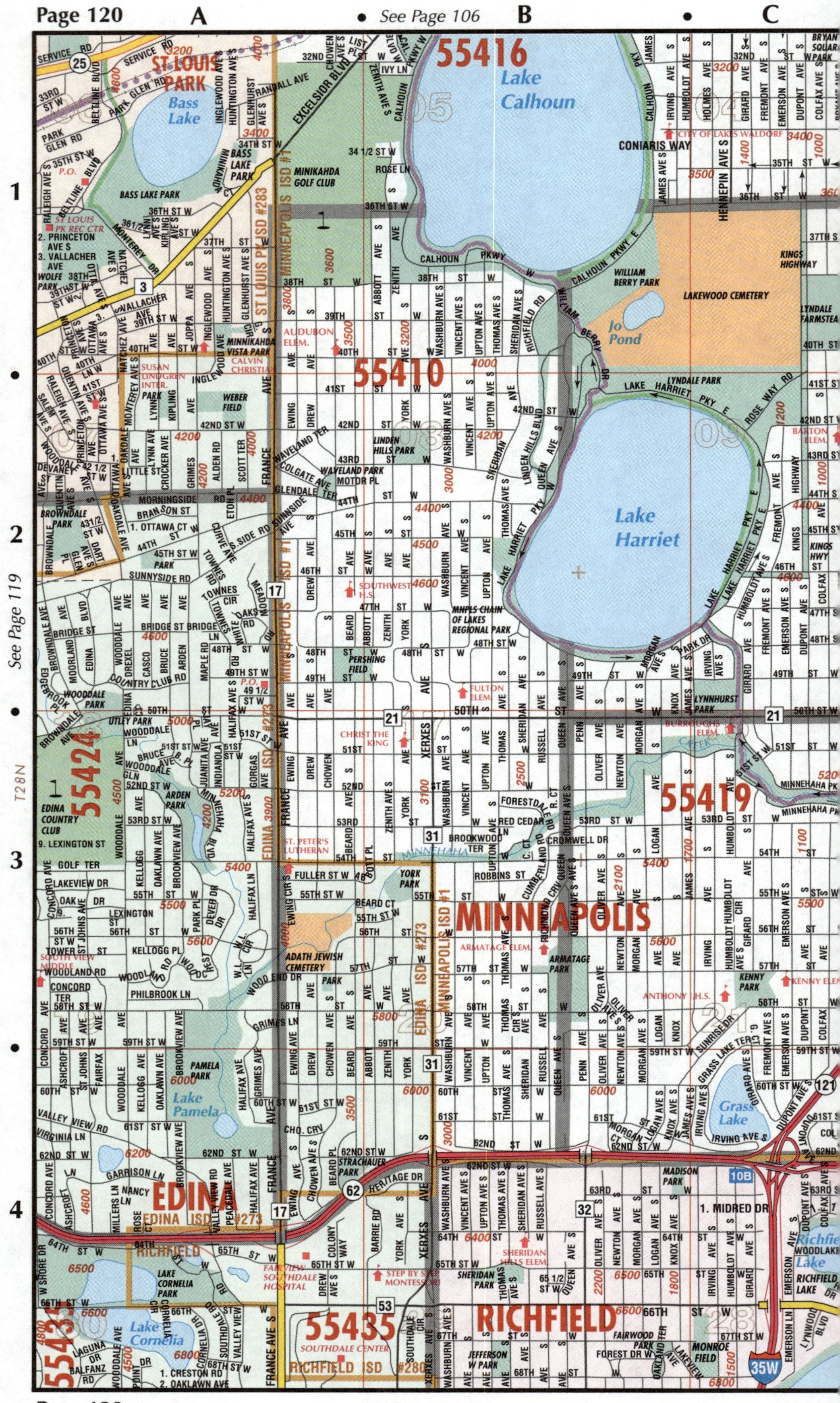

See Page 119

See Page 134

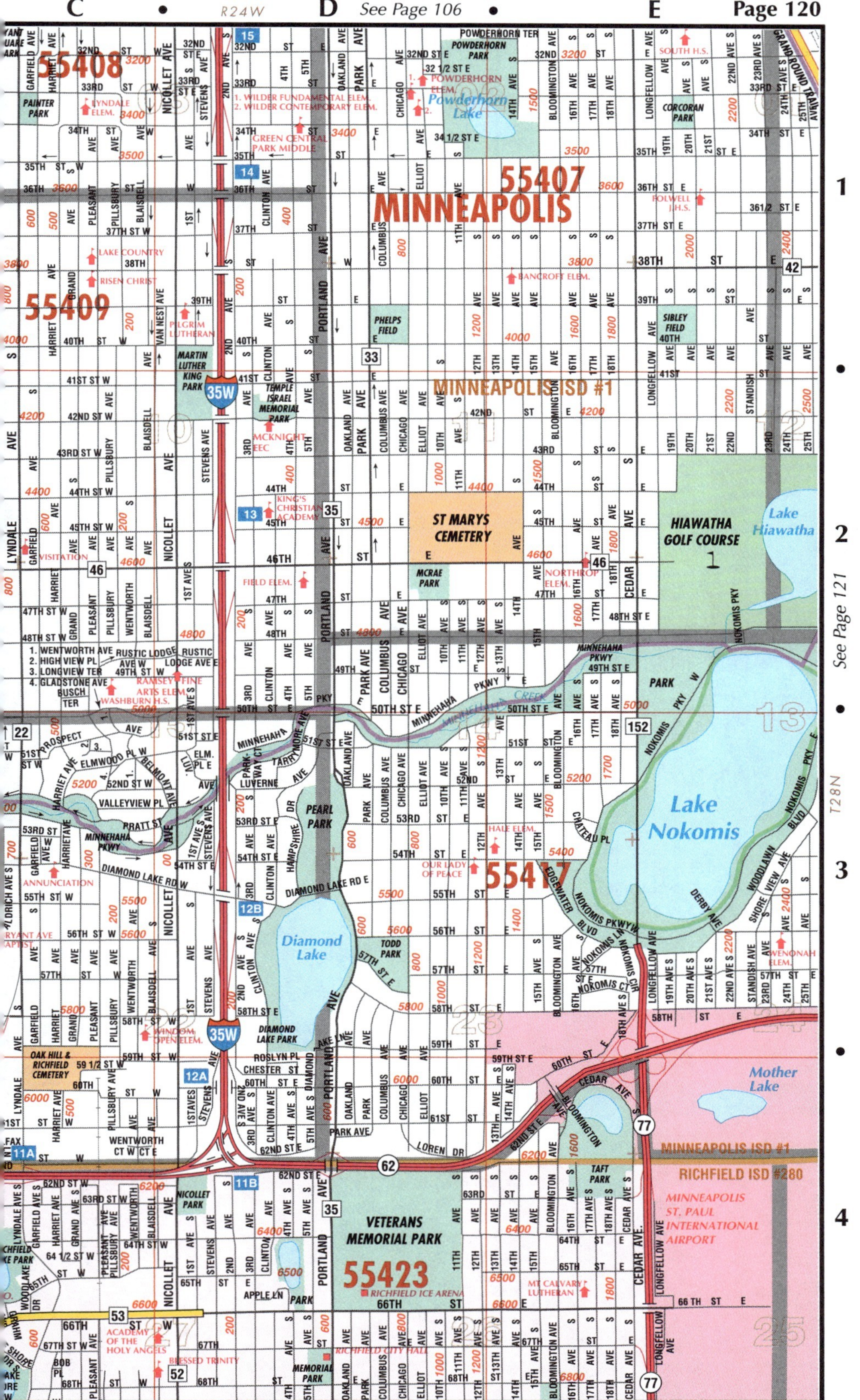

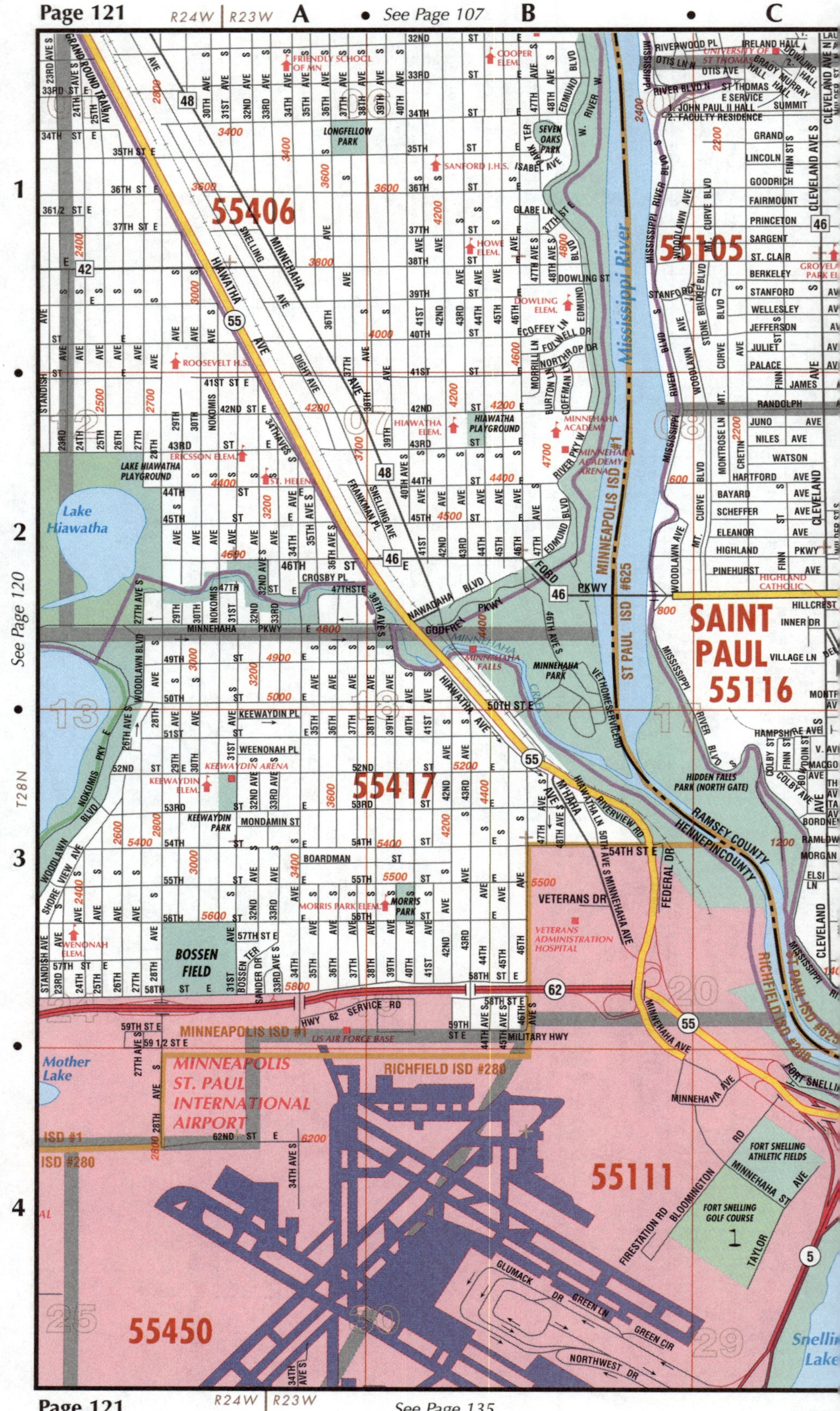

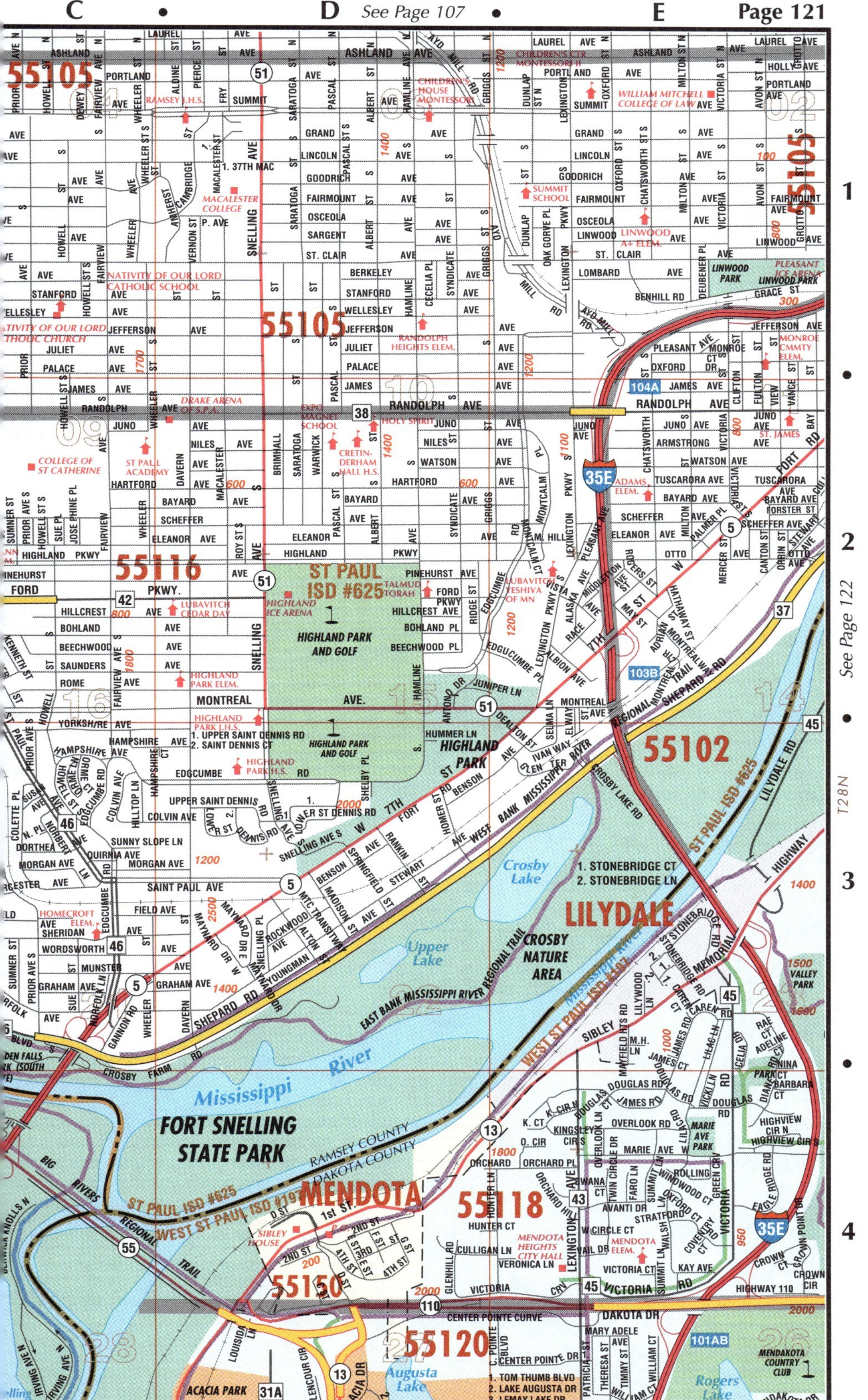

See Page 108

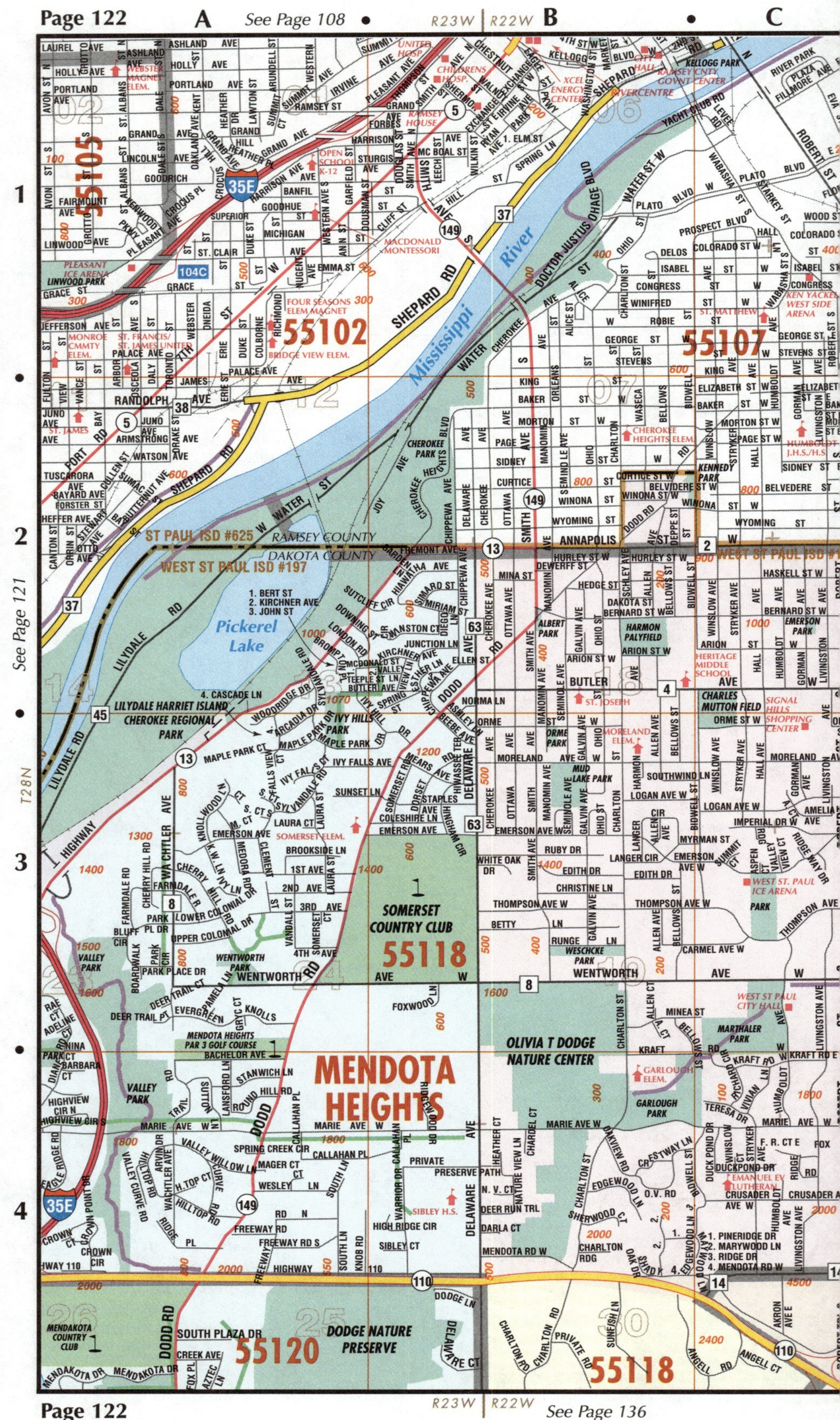

See Page 136
See Page 121

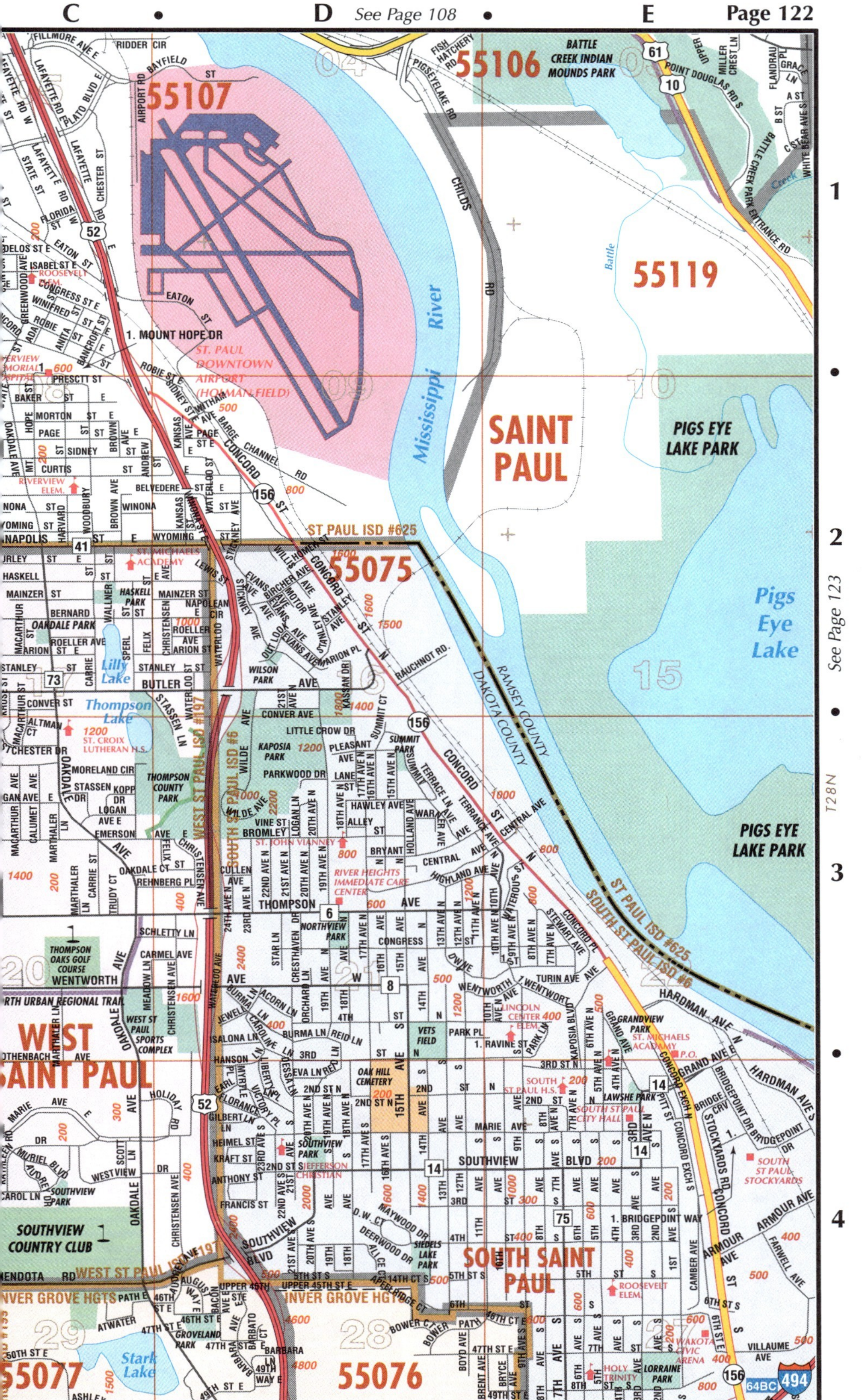

See Page 109

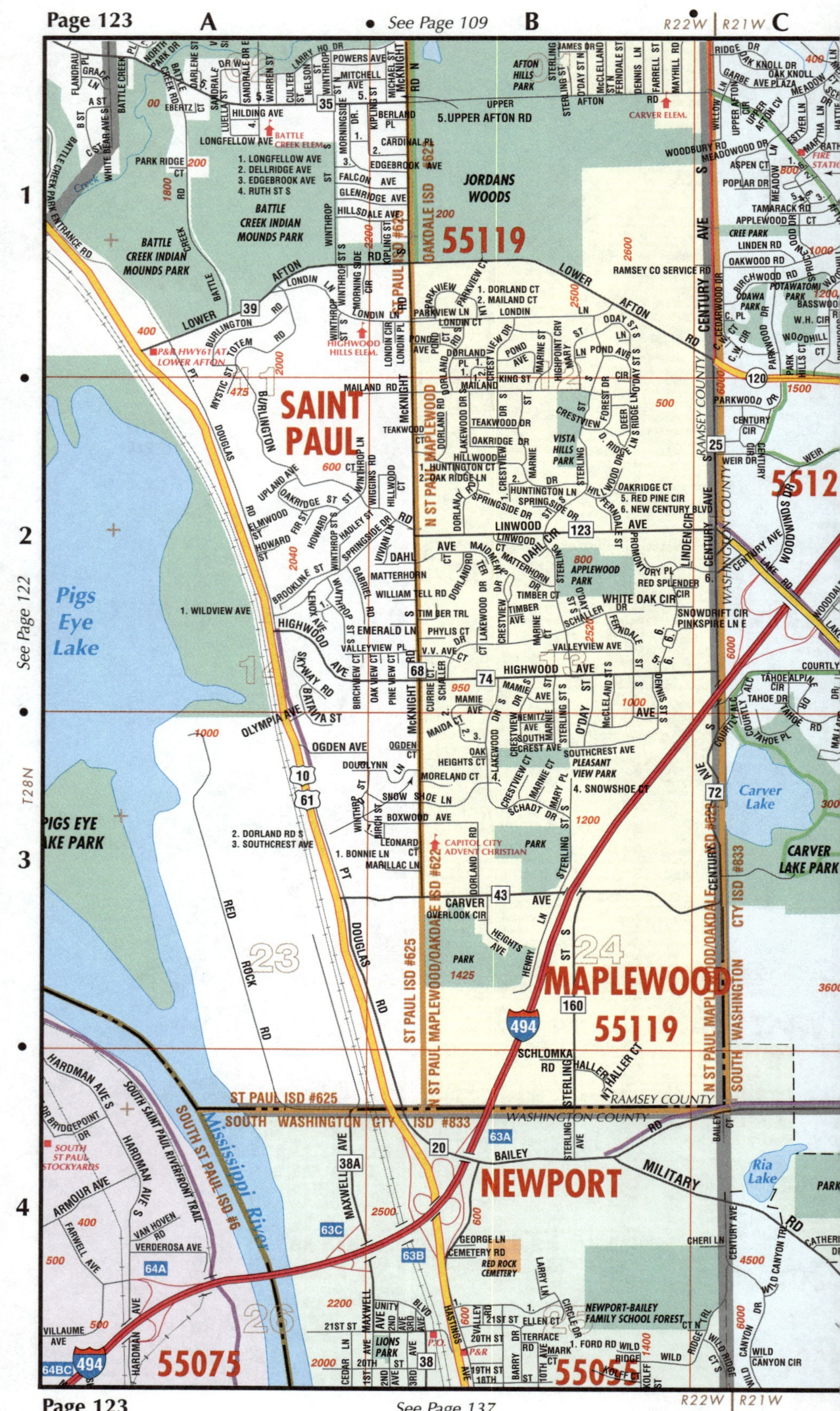

See Page 122

See Page 137

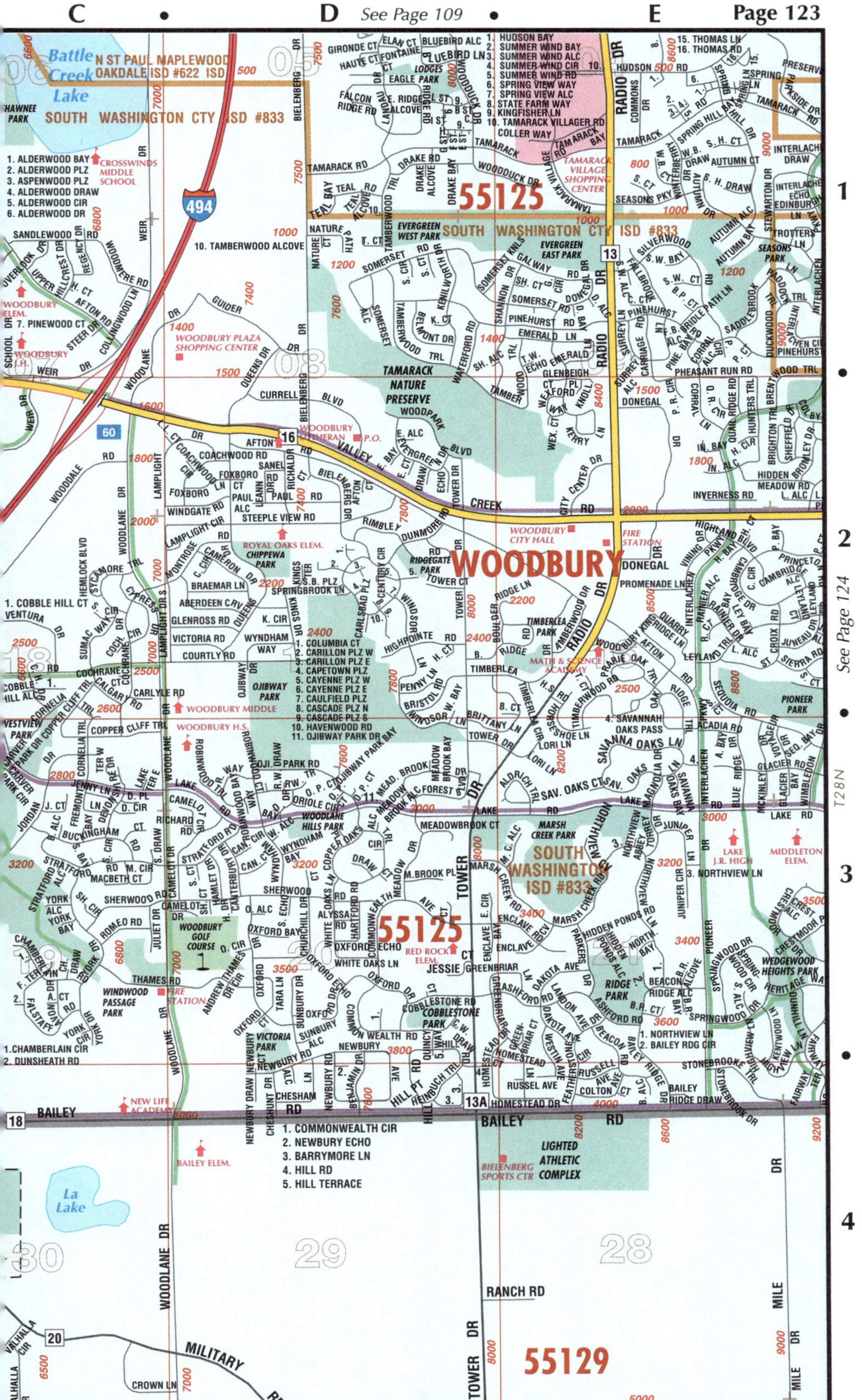
Battle Creek Lake
N ST PAUL MAPLEWOOD OAKDALE ISD #622 ISD
SOUTH WASHINGTON CTY ISD #833
1. ALDERWOOD BAY
2. ALDERWOOD PLZ
3. ASPENWOOD PLZ
4. ALDERWOOD DRAW
5. ALDERWOOD CIR
6. ALDERWOOD DR
CROSSWINDS MIDDLE SCHOOL
494
10. TAMBERWOOD ALCOVE
WOODBURY ELEM.
7. PINEWOOD CT
WOODBURY J.H.
WOODBURY PLAZA SHOPPING CENTER
1. HUDSON BAY
2. SUMMER WIND BAY
3. SUMMER WIND ALC
4. SUMMER WIND CIR
5. SUMMER WIND RD
6. SPRING VIEW WAY
7. SPRING VIEW ALC
8. STATE FARM WAY
9. KINGFISHER LN
10. TAMARACK VILLAGER RD
COLLER WAY
15. THOMAS LN
16. THOMAS RD
TAMARACK VILLAGE SHOPPING CENTER
55125
EVERGREEN WEST PARK
EVERGREEN EAST PARK
SOUTH WASHINGTON CTY ISD #833
RADIO DR
TAMARACK NATURE PRESERVE
VALLEY CREEK RD
WOODBURY LUTHERAN
P.O.
60
16
13
ROYAL OAKS ELEM.
CHIPPEWA PARK
WOODBURY CITY HALL
FIRE STATION
WOODBURY
TIMBERLEA PARK
MATH & SCIENCE ACADEMY
1. COBBLE HILL CT
1. COLUMBIA CT
2. CARILLON PLZ W
3. CARILLON PLZ E
4. CAPETOWN PLZ
5. CAYENNE PLZ W
6. CAYENNE PLZ E
7. CAULFIELD PLZ
8. CASCADE PLZ N
9. CASCADE PLZ S
10. HAVENWOOD RD
11. OJIBWAY PARK DR
OJIBWAY PARK
WOODBURY MIDDLE
WOODBURY H.S.
4. SAVANNAH OAKS PASS
PIONEER PARK
LAKE RD
WOODLANE HILLS PARK
MARSH CREEK PARK
SOUTH WASHINGTON ISD #833
LAKE J.R. HIGH
MIDDLETON ELEM.
3. NORTHVIEW LN
WOODBURY GOLF COURSE
55125
RED ROCK ELEM.
WINDWOOD PASSAGE PARK
FIRE STATION
COBBLESTONE PARK
RIDGE PARK
WEDGEWOOD HEIGHTS PARK
1. NORTHVIEW LN
2. BAILEY RDG CIR
1. CHAMBERLAIN CIR
2. DUNSHEATH RD
NEW LIFE ACADEMY
18
BAILEY RD
13A
1. COMMONWEALTH CIR
2. NEWBURY ECHO
3. BARRYMORE LN
4. HILL RD
5. HILL TERRACE
BAILEY ELEM.
BIELENBERG SPORTS CTR
LIGHTED ATHLETIC COMPLEX
La Lake
30
29
28
T28N
WOODLANE DR
RANCH RD
TOWER DR
MILE DR
20
MILITARY RD
CROWN LN
VALHALLA CIR
55129

See Page 124

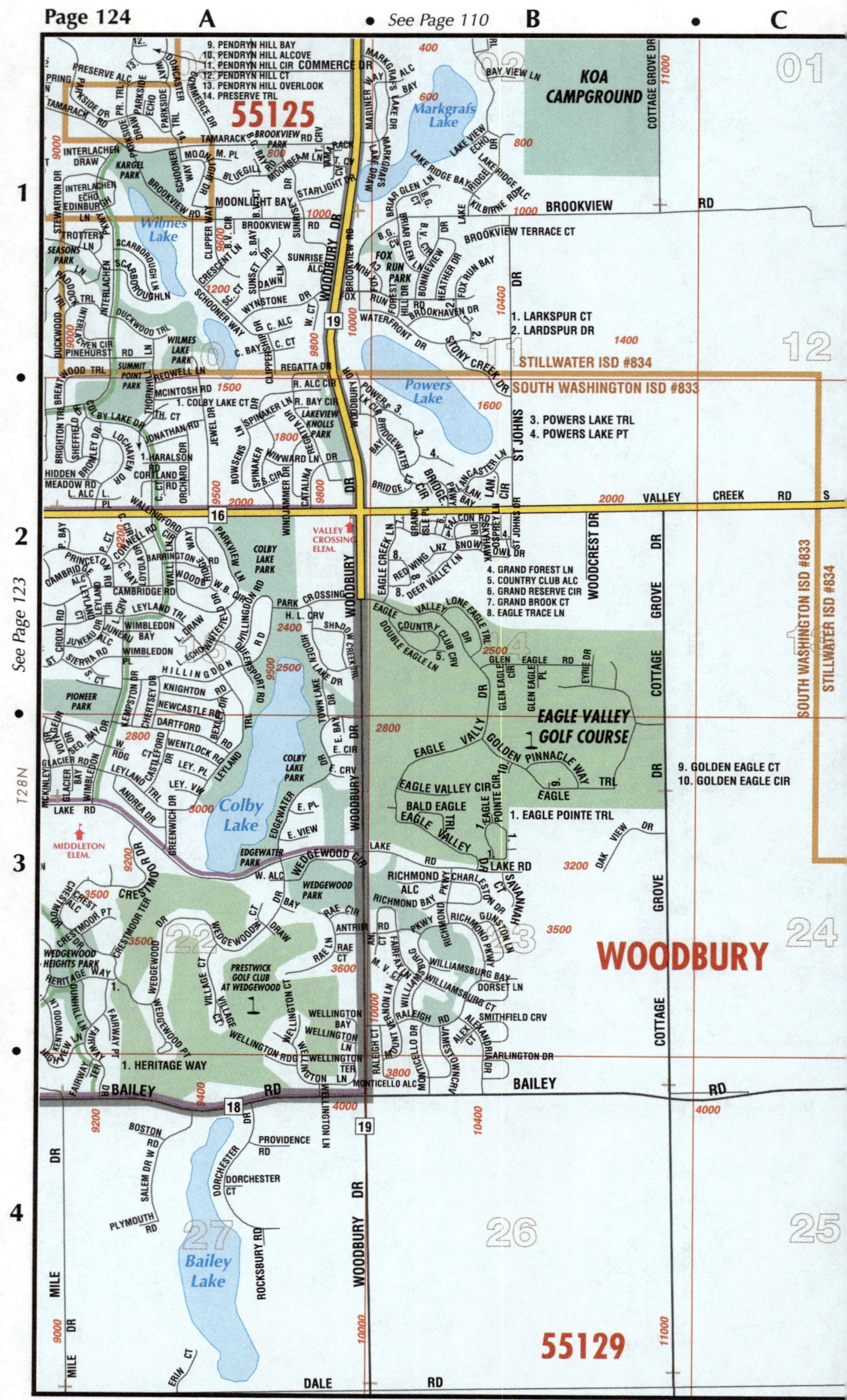

9. PENDRYN HILL BAY
10. PENDRYN HILL ALCOVE
11. PENDRYN HILL CIR **COMMERCE DR**
12. PENDRYN HILL CT
13. PENDRYN HILL OVERLOOK
14. PRESERVE TRL

55125

KOA CAMPGROUND

BROOKVIEW **RD**

1. LARKSPUR CT
2. LARDSPUR DR

STILLWATER ISD #834
SOUTH WASHINGTON ISD #833

3. POWERS LAKE TRL
4. POWERS LAKE PT

Wilmes Lake

Markgrafs Lake

Powers Lake

VALLEY **CREEK** **RD** S

4. GRAND FOREST LN
5. COUNTRY CLUB ALC
6. GRAND RESERVE CIR
7. GRAND BROOK CT
8. EAGLE TRACE LN

EAGLE VALLEY GOLF COURSE

9. GOLDEN EAGLE CT
10. GOLDEN EAGLE CIR

1. EAGLE POINTE TRL

Colby Lake

WOODBURY

1. HERITAGE WAY

BAILEY **RD** **BAILEY** **RD**

Bailey Lake

55129

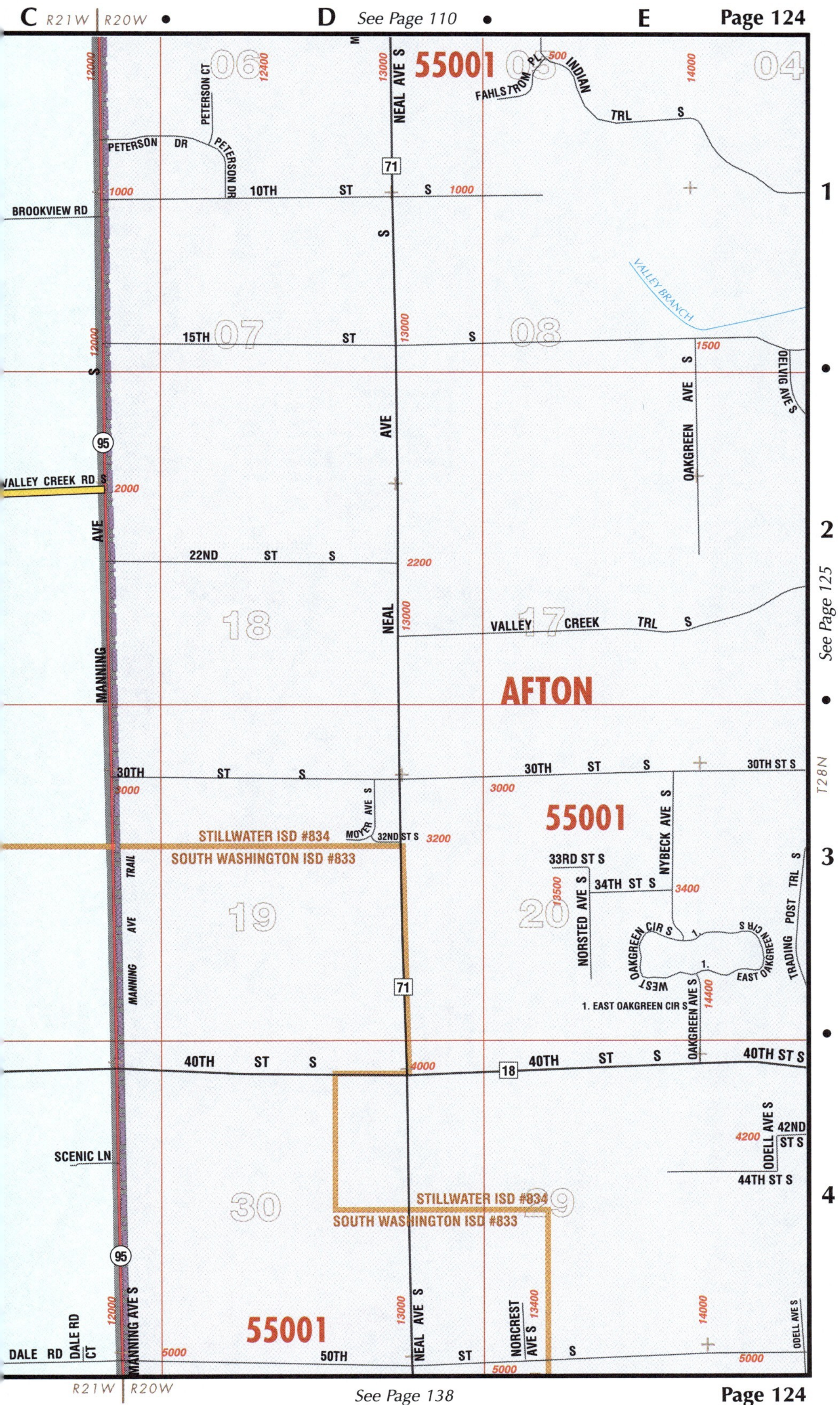
55001
AFTON
NEAL AVE S
MANNING AVE S
PETERSON CT
PETERSON DR
FAHLSTROM PL
INDIAN TRL S
10TH ST S
BROOKVIEW RD
15TH ST S
VALLEY BRANCH
OAKGREEN AVE S
OELVIG AVE S
VALLEY CREEK RD S
22ND ST S
VALLEY CREEK TRL S
30TH ST S
MOYER AVE S
32ND ST S
STILLWATER ISD #834
SOUTH WASHINGTON ISD #833
33RD ST S
34TH ST S
NYBECK AVE S
NORSTED AVE S
WEST OAKGREEN CIR S
EAST OAKGREEN CIR S
1. EAST OAKGREEN CIR S
TRADING POST TRL S
40TH ST S
SCENIC LN
ODELL AVE S
42ND ST S
44TH ST S
NORCREST AVE S
50TH ST S
DALE RD
DALE RD CT
T28N
See Page 125

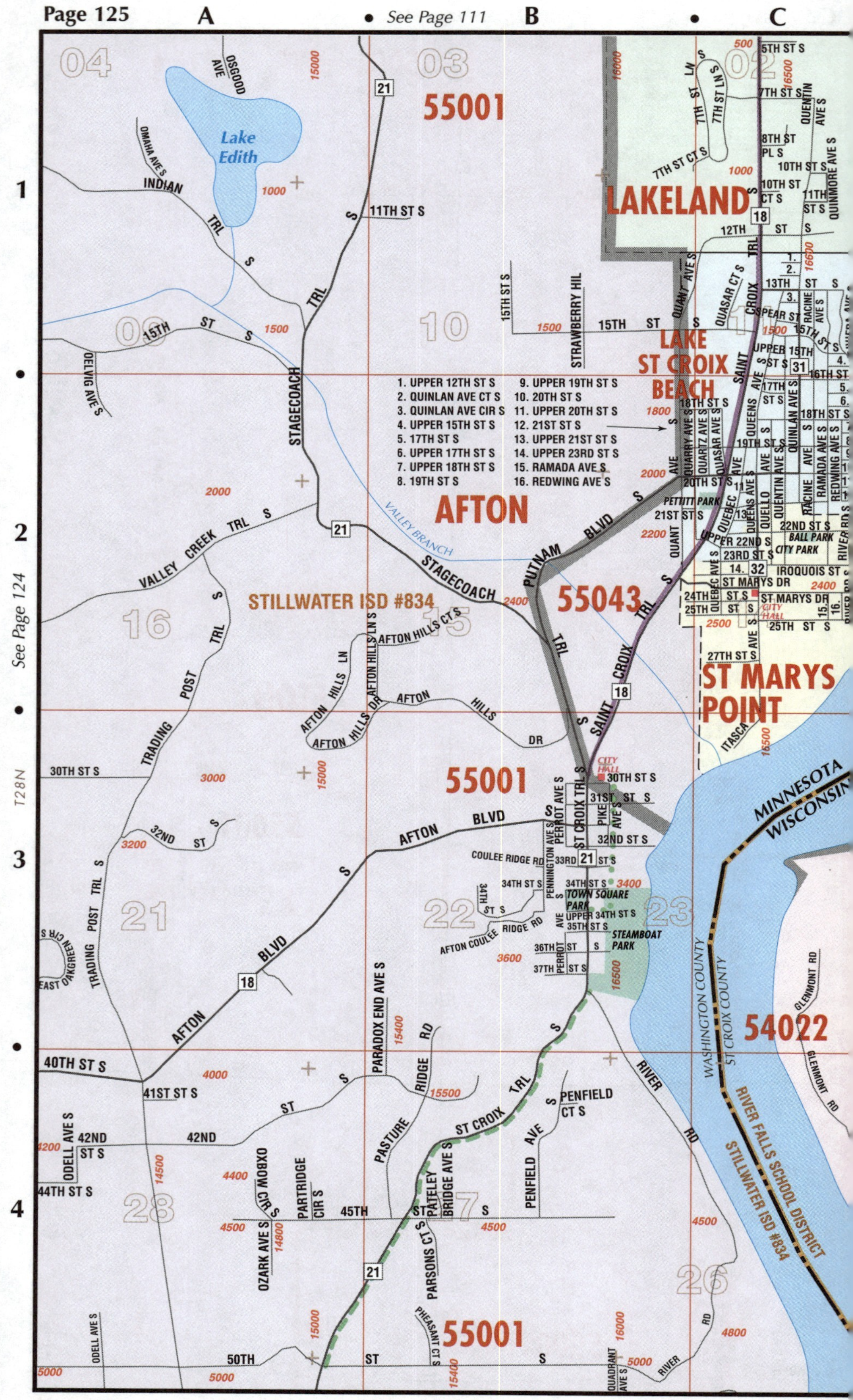

55001

Lake Edith

OSGOOD AVE

21

03

02

5TH ST S
7TH ST LN S
7TH ST LN S
QUENTIN AVE S
QUINMORE AVE S
8TH ST
PL S
10TH ST S
10TH ST S
11TH ST S
500
6500
1000

LAKELAND

OMAH AVE S

INDIAN TRL

1000

12TH
18

1

STAGECOACH TRL

11TH ST S

11TH S

15000

10

STRAWBERRY HIL

15TH ST S

QUANT AVE S

QUASAR CT S
SAINT CROIX TRL
13TH
SPEAR AVE S
RACINE AVE S
16600
1.
2.
QUEENS AVE

1500

OELVIG AVE S

15TH ST S

1500

15TH ST

UPPER 15TH
ST S
31
15TH ST S
QUELLO AVE S
4.
5.
6.

LAKE ST CROIX BEACH

1. UPPER 12TH ST S
2. QUINLAN AVE CT S
3. QUINLAN AVE CIR S
4. UPPER 15TH ST S
5. 17TH ST S
6. UPPER 17TH ST S
7. UPPER 18TH ST S
8. 19TH ST S
9. UPPER 19TH ST S
10. 20TH ST S
11. UPPER 20TH ST S
12. 21ST ST S
13. UPPER 21ST ST S
14. UPPER 23RD ST S
15. RAMADA AVE S
16. REDWING AVE S

16TH ST S
17TH ST S
18TH ST S
QUARTZ AVE S
QUASAR AVE S
QUINLAN AVE S
RAMADA AVE S
REDWING AVE S
RACINE AVE S
1800
19TH ST S

2000

PETTIT PARK

20TH ST S

PUTNAM BLVD

AFTON

2000

VALLEY CREEK TRL S

21

VALLEY BRANCH

STAGECOACH

2400

QUANT

21ST ST S
UPPER 22ND
23RD ST S
ST MARYS DR
QUELLO AVE S
QUEBEC AVE S
QUELL AVE S
QUENTIN AVE S
22ND ST S
BALL PARK
CITY PARK
14. 32
IROQUOIS ST
RIVER RD S
2400

2200

2

STILLWATER ISD #834

AFTON HILLS LN
AFTON HILLS CT S

16

AFTON HILLS LN

15

55043

SAINT CROIX TRL

18

24TH ST S
25TH ST S
ST MARYS DR
QUEBEC AVE S
25TH ST S
15.
16.
2500
CITY HALL

AFTON HILLS DR
AFTON HILLS
AFTON

TRADING POST TRL S

27TH ST

ST MARYS POINT

ITASCA

16500

3

30TH ST S

3000

15000

DR

HILLS

DR

CITY HALL
30TH ST S

PERROT AVE S
ST CROIX TRL

55001

MINNESOTA
WISCONSIN

32ND ST S

3200

AFTON BLVD

31ST ST S
PIKE AVE S
32ND ST S

21

COULEE RIDGE RD

23RD ST S
21 ST S

22

PENNINGTON AVE S
34TH ST S

34TH ST S 3400
TOWN SQUARE PARK
UPPER 34TH ST S
35TH ST S

23

21

EAST OAKGREEN CIR S

TRADING POST TRL S

34TH ST S
AFTON COULEE RIDGE RD

36TH
PERROT ST S
37TH ST S

3600

STEAMBOAT PARK

16500

WASHINGTON COUNTY
ST CROIX COUNTY

GLENMONT RD

BLVD

18

AFTON

PARADOX END AVE S

RIDGE RD

15400

RIVER RD

54022

BLVD

GLENMONT RD

40TH ST S

4000

41ST ST S

15500

ST CROIX TRL

PENFIELD CT S

PENFIELD AVE S

RIVER FALLS SCHOOL DISTRICT

ODELL AVE S

42ND ST S

42ND

4200

4400

PASTURE RIDGE RD

4500

PENFIELD AVE S

4500

STILLWATER ISD #834

4500

44TH ST S

14500

PARTRIDGE CIR S

45TH ST S

PATELEY BRIDGE AVE S

4500

4

OZARK AVE S

28

4500

14800

PARSONS CT S

17

ODELL AVE S

50TH ST S

ST

5000

5000

15000

15400

PHEASANT CT S

55001

QUADRANT AVE S

16000

26

RIVER

RD

4800

5000

5000

See Page 124 T28N

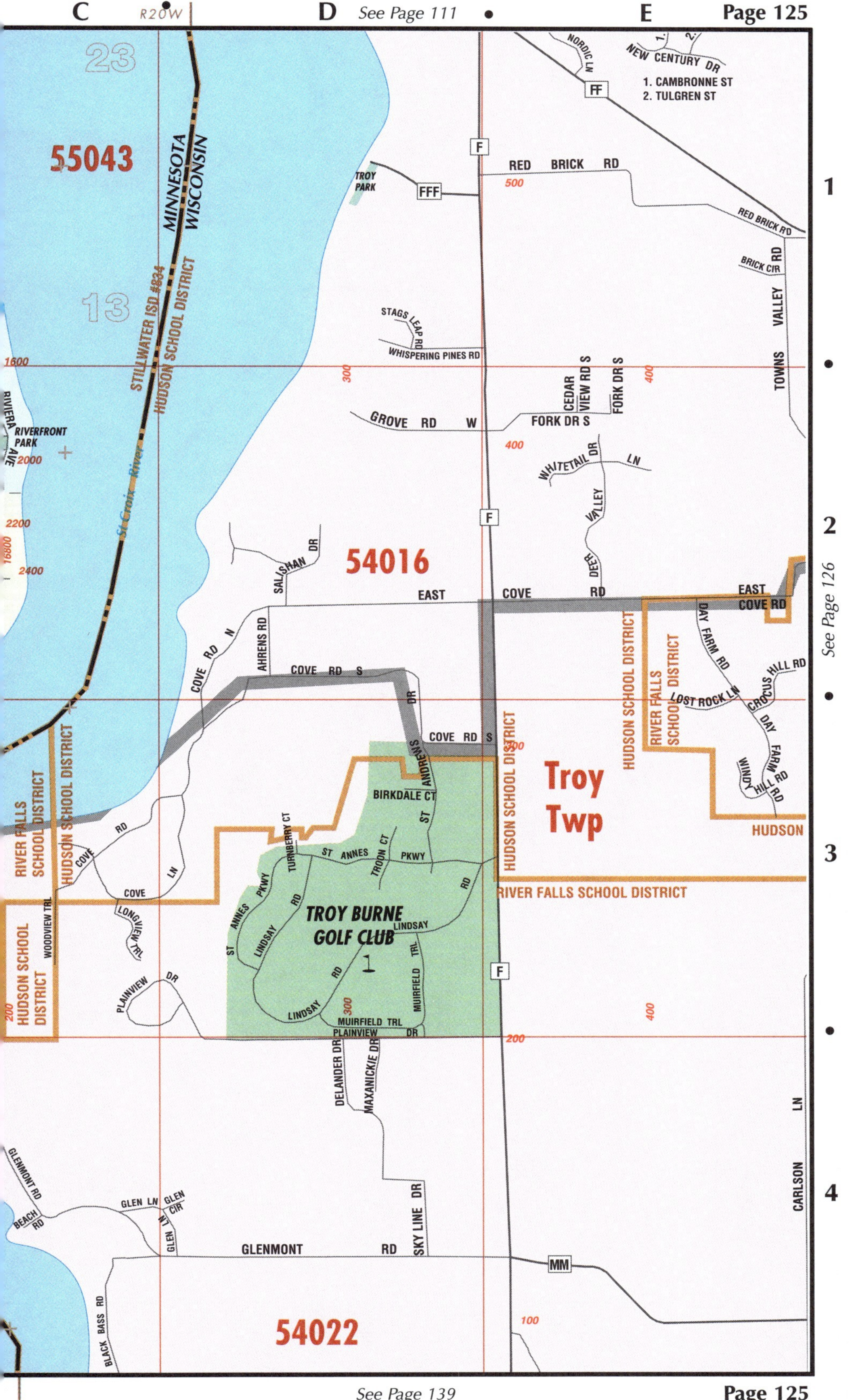

23

55043

13

MINNESOTA
WISCONSIN

STILLWATER ISD 4834

HUDSON SCHOOL DISTRICT

St Croix River

RIVERA AVE

RIVERFRONT PARK

1600
2000
2200
16900
2400
200

NORDIC LN

NEW CENTURY DR
1. CAMBRONNE ST
2. TULGREN ST

FF

F

RED BRICK RD
500

RED BRICK RD

BRICK CIR
BRICK VALLEY RD
TOWNS

TROY PARK

FFF

1

STAGS LEAP RD
WHISPERING PINES RD

300

CEDAR VIEW RD S
FORK DR S
FORK DR S
400

GROVE RD W
FORK DR S
400

WHITETAIL DR
LN
VALLEY
DEER

F

2

SALISHAN DR

54016

EAST COVE RD

EAST COVE RD

COVE RD N

AHRENS RD

COVE RD S

HUDSON SCHOOL DISTRICT

RIVER FALLS SCHOOL DISTRICT

DAY FARM RD

LOST ROCK LN

CROUS HILL RD

DAY FARM RD

WINDY

HILL RD

COVE RD S

ST ANDREWS DR

300

Troy Twp

HUDSON

RIVER FALLS SCHOOL DISTRICT

COVE RD

LN

COVE

LONGVIEW TRL

WOODVIEW TRL

HUDSON SCHOOL DISTRICT

BIRKDALE CT

TURNBERRY CT

ST ANNES PKWY

TRODN CT

PKWY

ST ANNES PKWY

LINDSAY RD

LINDSAY RD

TROY BURNE GOLF CLUB
1

LINDSAY TRL

MUIRFIELD RD

F

400

3

PLAINVIEW DR

LINDSAY RD

MUIRFIELD TRL

300

PLAINVIEW DR

200

HUDSON SCHOOL DISTRICT

200

DELANDER DR

MAXANICKIE DR

GLENMONT RD

BEACH RD

GLEN LN GLEN CIR

GLEN MT

GLENMONT RD

SKY LINE DR

CARLSON LN

4

BLACK BASS RD

54022

MM

100

See Page 126

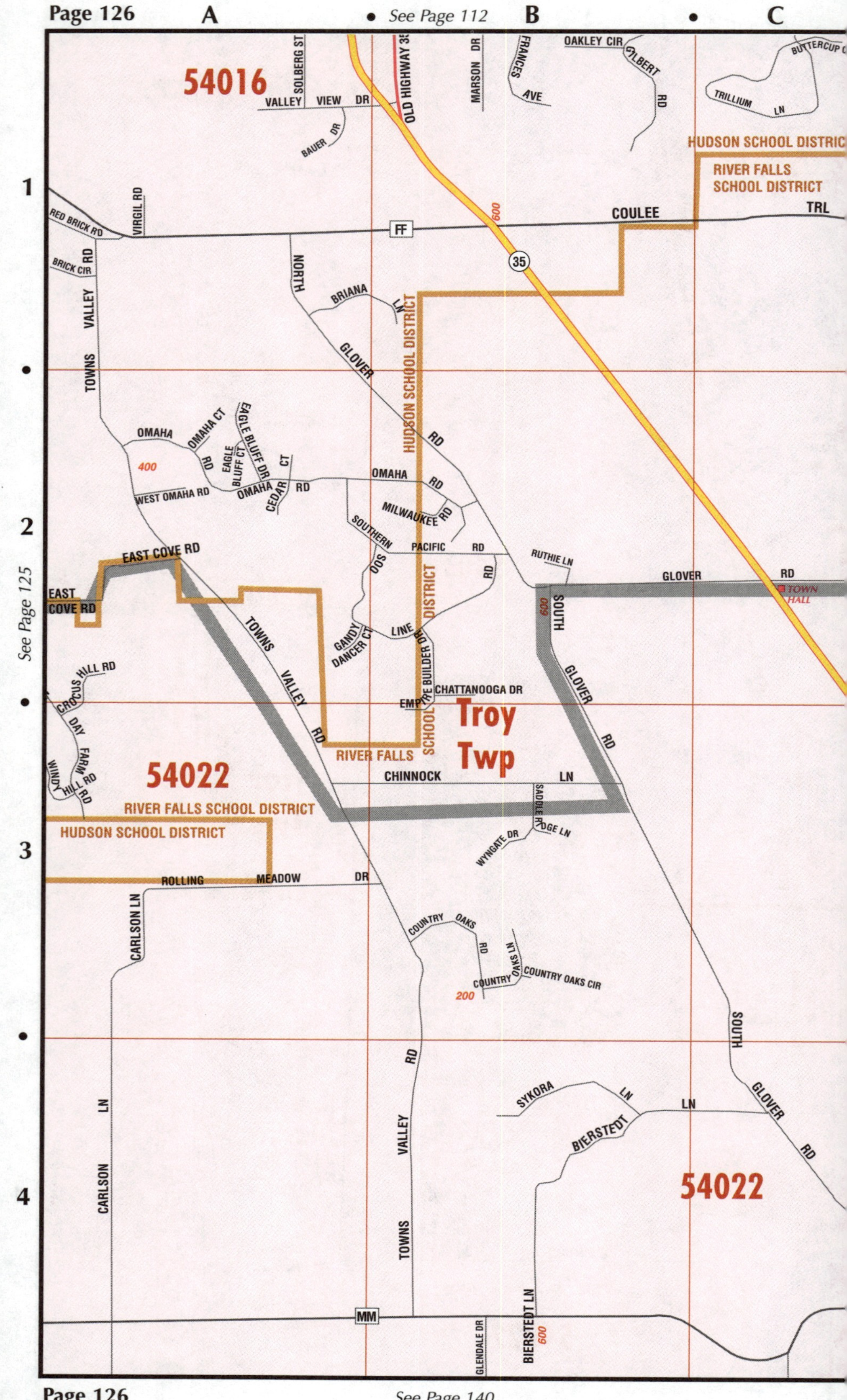
54016
SOLBERG ST
VALLEY VIEW DR
OLD HIGHWAY 35
MARSON DR
FRANCES AVE
OAKLEY CIR
GILBERT RD
BUTTERCUP
TRILLIUM LN
BAUER DR
HUDSON SCHOOL DISTRIC
RIVER FALLS SCHOOL DISTRICT
1
RED BRICK RD
VIRGIL RD
FF
COULEE TRL
600
35
BRICK CIR
TOWNS VALLEY RD
NORTH GLOVER RD
BRIANA LN
HUDSON SCHOOL DISTRICT
OMAHA
OMAHA CT
EAGLE BLUFF DR
EAGLE BLUFF CT
400
OMAHA RD
WEST OMAHA RD
CEDAR CT
MILWAUKEE RD
SOUTHERN
PACIFIC RD
2
EAST COVE RD
EAST COVE RD
RUTHIE LN
GLOVER RD
TOWN HALL
SOO LINE RD
DISTRICT
600
SOUTH GLOVER RD
See Page 125
TOWNS VALLEY RD
GANDY DANCER CT
EMPIRE BUILDER DR
CHATTANOOGA DR
CROCUS HILL RD
DAY FARM RD
WINDY HILL RD
SCHOOL
RIVER FALLS
Troy Twp
54022
CHINNOCK LN
SADDLE RIDGE LN
RIVER FALLS SCHOOL DISTRICT
HUDSON SCHOOL DISTRICT
WYNGATE DR
3
ROLLING MEADOW DR
CARLSON LN
COUNTRY OAKS RD
COUNTRY OAKS LN
COUNTRY OAKS CIR
200
SOUTH GLOVER RD
SYKORA LN
BIERSTEDT LN
TOWNS VALLEY RD
CARLSON LN
4
54022
MM
GLENDALE DR
BIERSTEDT LN
600

See Page 140

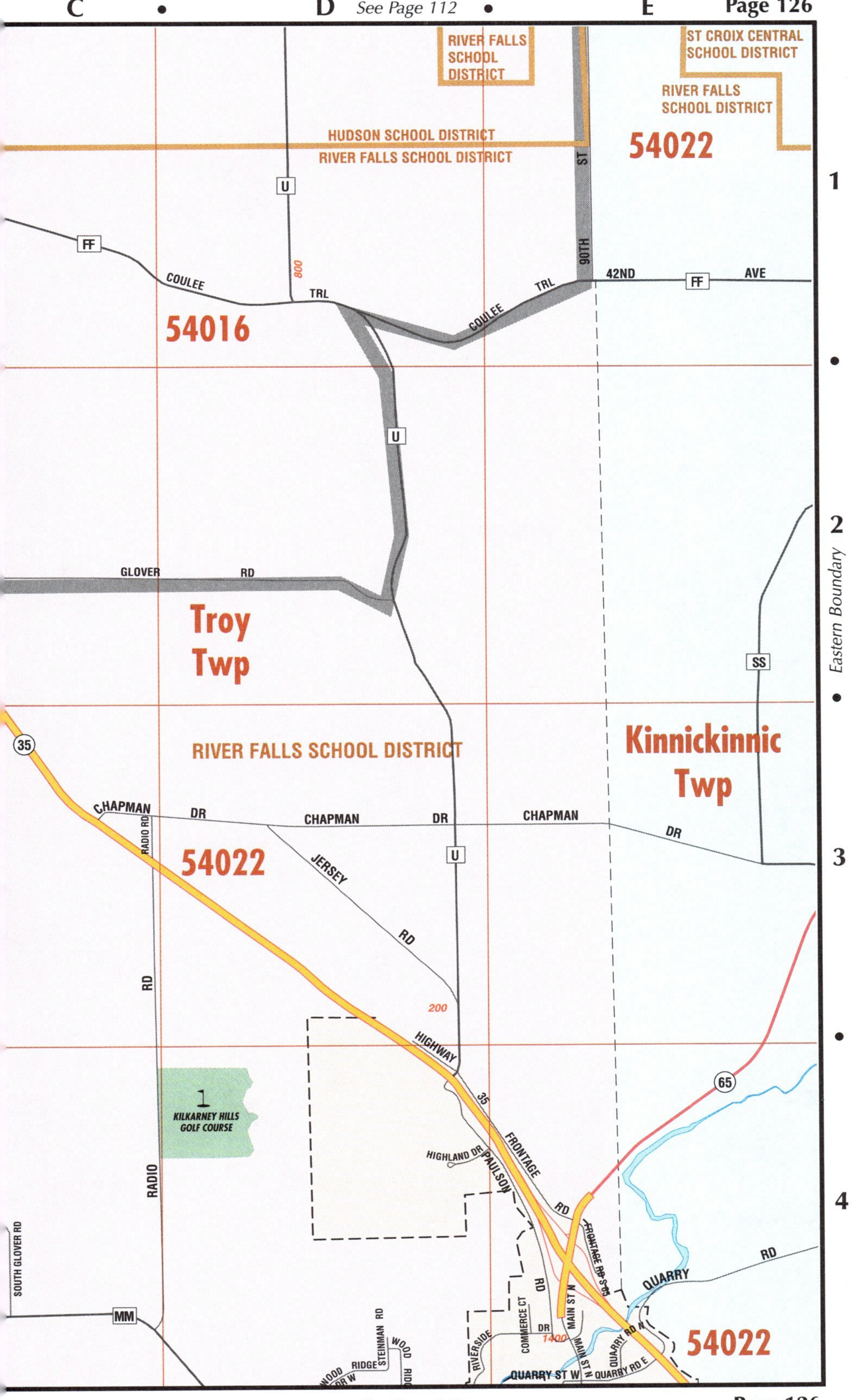
RIVER FALLS SCHOOL DISTRICT
ST CROIX CENTRAL SCHOOL DISTRICT
RIVER FALLS SCHOOL DISTRICT
HUDSON SCHOOL DISTRICT
RIVER FALLS SCHOOL DISTRICT
54022
1
U
FF
COULEE
800
TRL
90TH
ST
42ND
FF
AVE
54016
COULEE
TRL
U
2
Eastern Boundary
GLOVER
RD
Troy Twp
SS
35
RIVER FALLS SCHOOL DISTRICT
Kinnickinnic Twp
CHAPMAN
DR
CHAPMAN
DR
CHAPMAN
DR
RADIO RD
U
54022
JERSEY
RD
3
RD
200
HIGHWAY
35
65
KILKARNEY HILLS GOLF COURSE
FRONTAGE
HIGHLAND DR
PAULSON
RADIO
4
RD
FRONTAGE RD S
SOUTH GLOVER RD
QUARRY
RD
MM
STEINMAN RD
WOOD
RIDGE
WOOD DR W
RIVERSIDE
COMMERCE CT
DR
1400
MAIN ST N
MAIN ST N
QUARRY RD N
QUARRY RD E
QUARRY ST W
54022

See Page 140

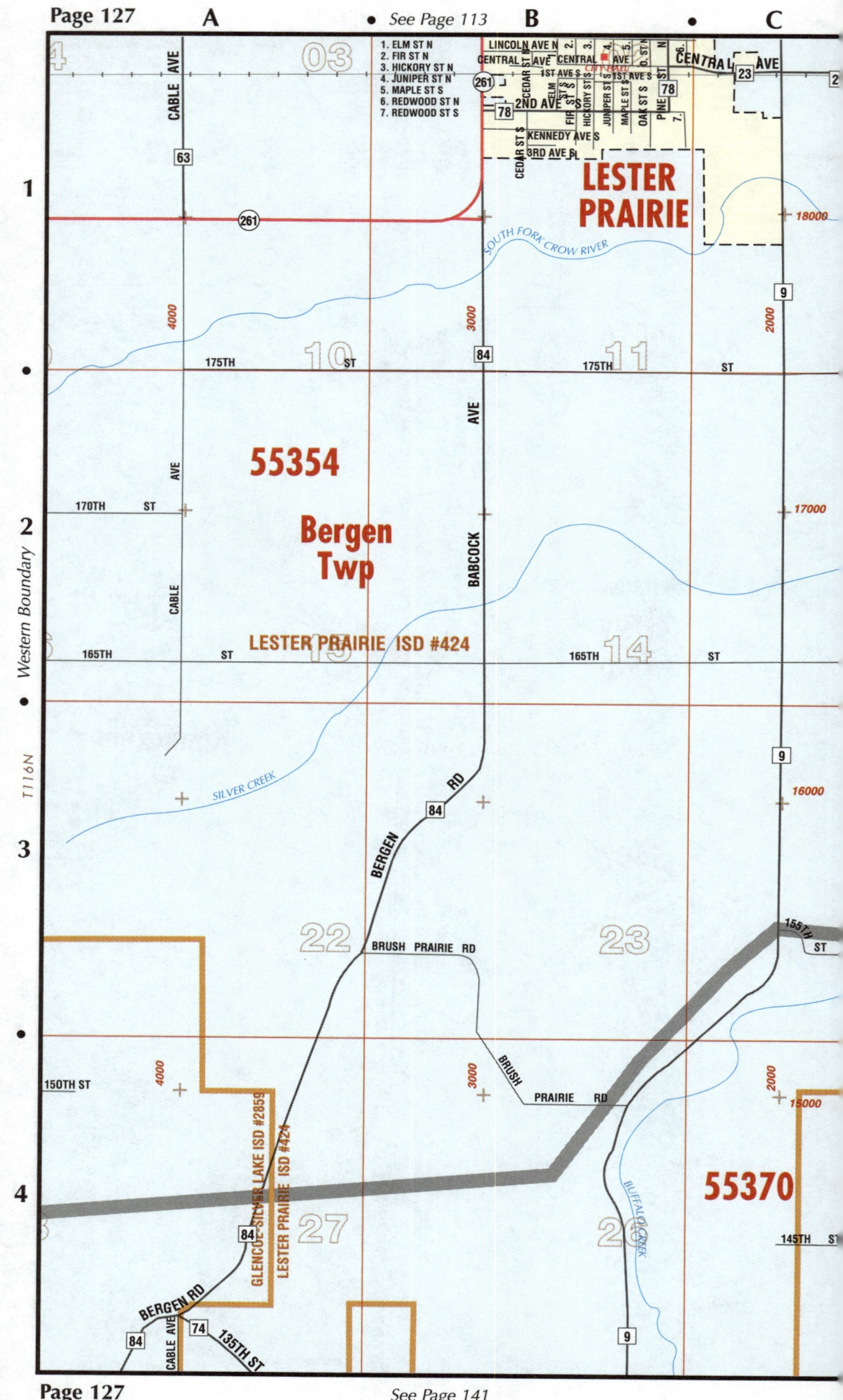

CABLE AVE

1. ELM ST N
2. FIR ST N
3. HICKORY ST N
4. JUNIPER ST N
5. MAPLE ST S
6. REDWOOD ST N
7. REDWOOD ST S

LINCOLN AVE N
CENTRAL ST AVE CENTRAL AVE
CENTRAL AVE

261

78

CEDAR ST S
2ND AVE S
KENNEDY AVE S
3RD AVE S

CEDAR ST S
ELM ST S
FIR ST S
HICKORY ST S
JUNIPER ST S
MAPLE ST S
OAK ST S
PINE ST S

1ST AVE S

78

23

CENTRAL AVE

2

63

**LESTER
PRAIRIE**

1

261

18000

9

175TH   ST

10

84

175TH   ST   ST

11

4000

3000

2000

55354

AVE

BABCOCK

AVE

**Bergen
Twp**

170TH   ST

2

CABLE

17000

LESTER PRAIRIE ISD #424

165TH   ST

13

165TH   ST   ST

14

9

Western Boundary

T116N

SILVER CREEK

BERGEN   RD

84

3

9

16000

155TH
ST

22

BRUSH   PRAIRIE   RD

23

BRUSH

150TH ST

4000

3000

PRAIRIE   RD

2000

15000

BUFFALO CREEK

GLENCOE SILVER LAKE ISD #2859
LESTER PRAIRIE ISD #424

84

27

55370

4

26

145TH   ST

BERGEN RD

84

74

CABLE AVE

135TH ST

9

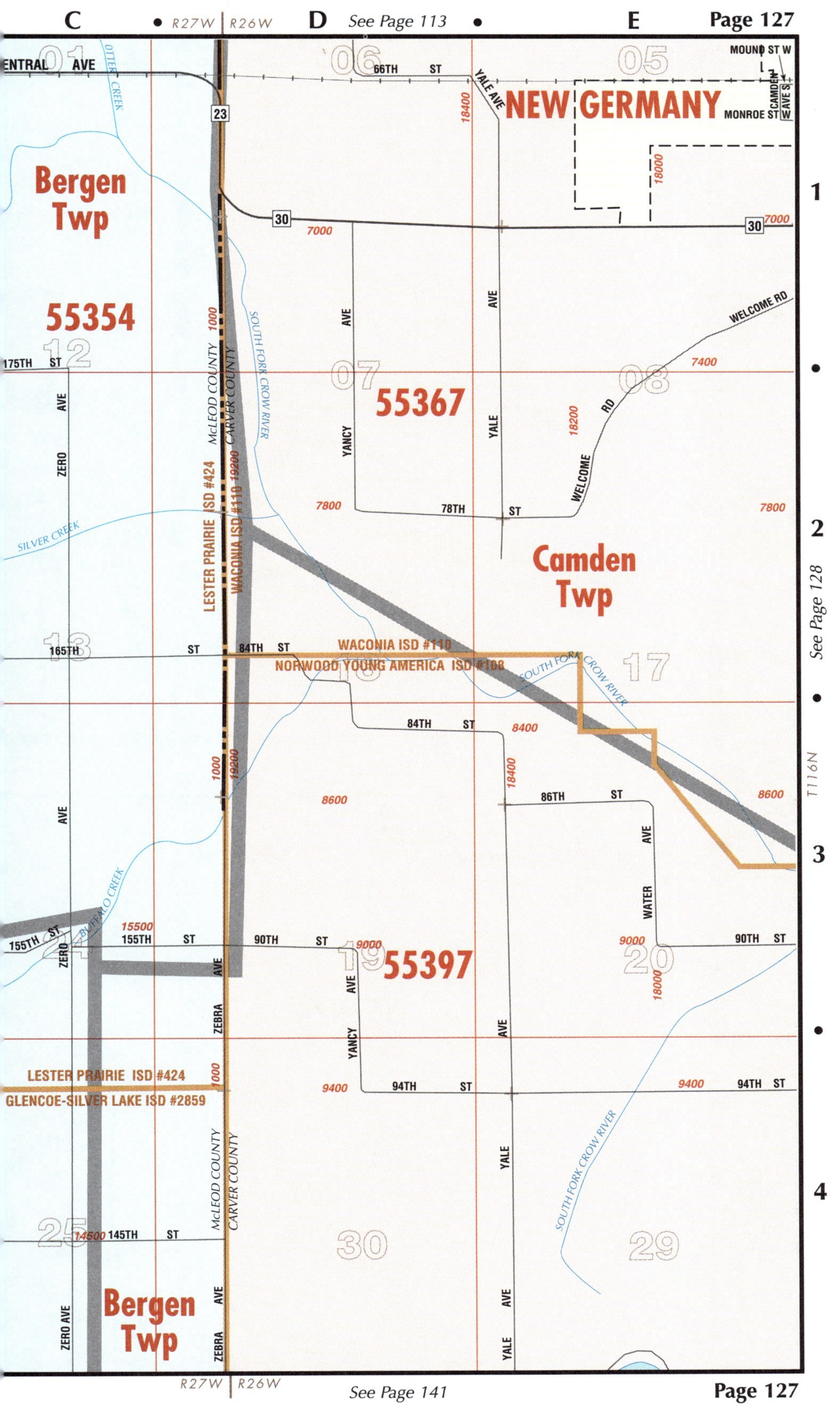

MOUND ST W

CENTRAL AVE

06 66TH ST YALE AVE 05

NEW GERMANY

MONROE ST

CAMDEN AVE S

23

18400

Bergen Twp

30 7000 30 7000

1

55354

WELCOME RD

175TH ST 12

AVE

07 7400 08

55367

YANCY AVE

YALE AVE

18200

WELCOME RD

1000

McLEOD COUNTY

CARVER COUNTY

LESTER PRAIRIE ISD #424

WACONIA ISD #110

SOUTH FORK CROW RIVER

ZERO AVE

SILVER CREEK

7800 78TH ST 7800

2

Camden Twp

165TH ST 84TH ST

WACONIA ISD #110

NORWOOD YOUNG AMERICA ISD #108

13 SOUTH FORK CROW RIVER 17

18

84TH ST 8400

1000

18400

19200

86TH ST

AVE

8600

8600

WATER AVE

3

BUFFALO CREEK

15500

155TH ST 155TH ST 90TH ST 9000 9000 90TH ST

ZERO AVE

ZEBRA AVE

YANCY AVE

19 **55397** 20

AVE

18000

YALE AVE

LESTER PRAIRIE ISD #424

1000

GLENCOE-SILVER LAKE ISD #2859

9400 94TH ST 9400 94TH ST

McLEOD COUNTY

CARVER COUNTY

4

25 14500 145TH ST 30 29

ZERO AVE

ZEBRA AVE

YALE AVE

Bergen Twp

SOUTH FORK CROW RIVER

See Page 128 T116N

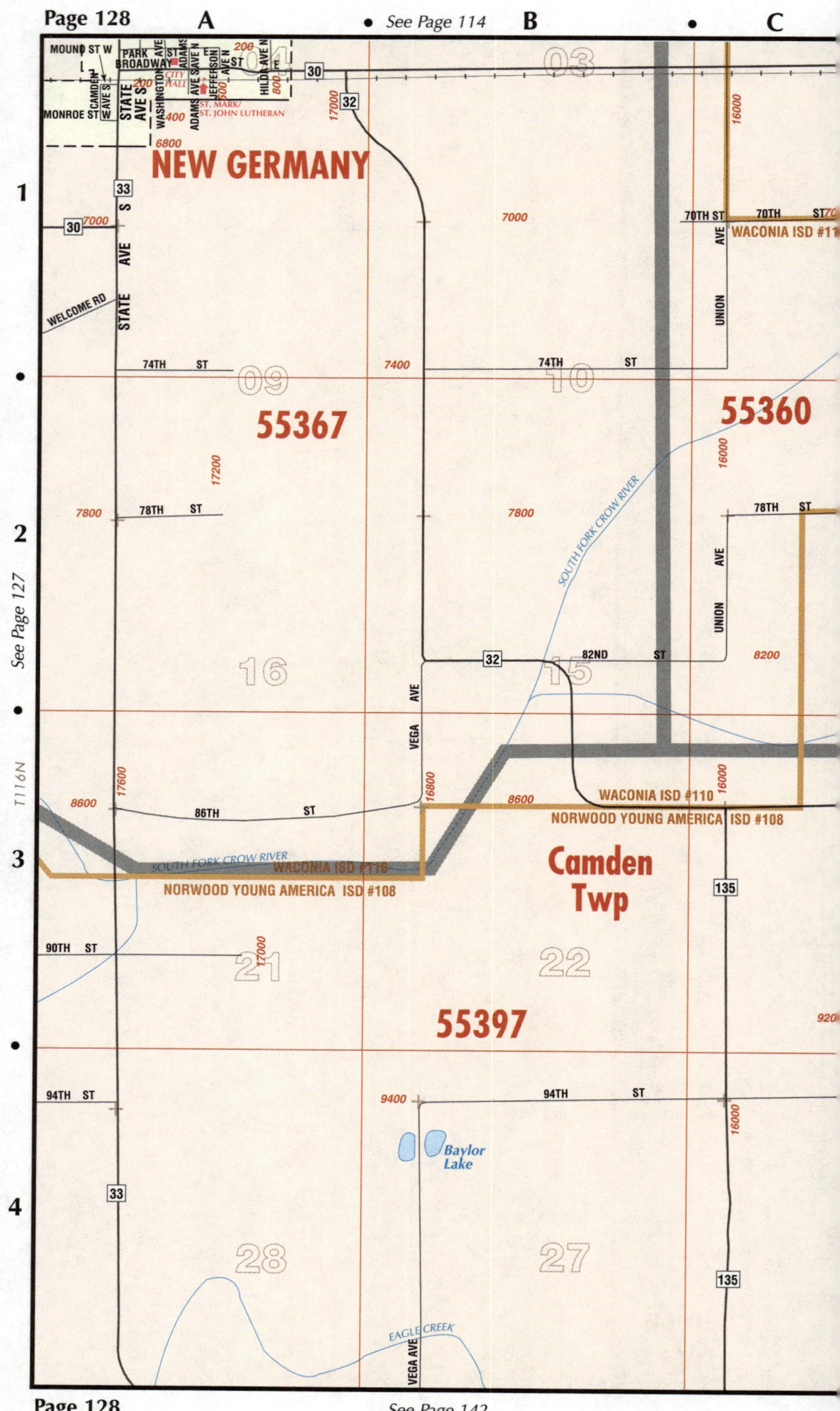

See Page 114

A　　　　B　　　　C

See Page 127

T116N

NEW GERMANY

MOUND ST W

PARK
BROADWAY

STATE AVE S

MONROE ST W

CAMDEN AVE S

WASHINGTON AVE

ADAMS AVE S

ADAMS AVE N

JEFFERSON AVE N

HILDA AVE N

ST. MARK/
ST. JOHN LUTHERAN

CITY HALL

200

200

400

600 AVE E

800

6800

30

17000

32

33

7000

30

WELCOME RD

STATE AVE S

74TH ST

09

55367

17200

7800

78TH ST

16

17600

8600

86TH ST

VEGA AVE

16800

32

15

82ND ST

NORWOOD YOUNG AMERICA ISD #108

WACONIA ISD #110

SOUTH FORK CROW RIVER

NORWOOD YOUNG AMERICA ISD #108

WACONIA ISD #110

**Camden
Twp**

90TH ST

17000

21

55397

22

135

94TH ST

33

94TH ST

9400

Baylor
Lake

28

27

135

EAGLE CREEK

VEGA AVE

7000

7400

7800

8600

55360

70TH ST

70TH ST

WACONIA ISD #11

70

AVE

UNION

16000

74TH ST

16000

78TH ST

AVE

UNION

8200

16000

16000

920

16000

SOUTH FORK CROW RIVER

04

03

30

03

16000

1

2

3

4

See Page 142

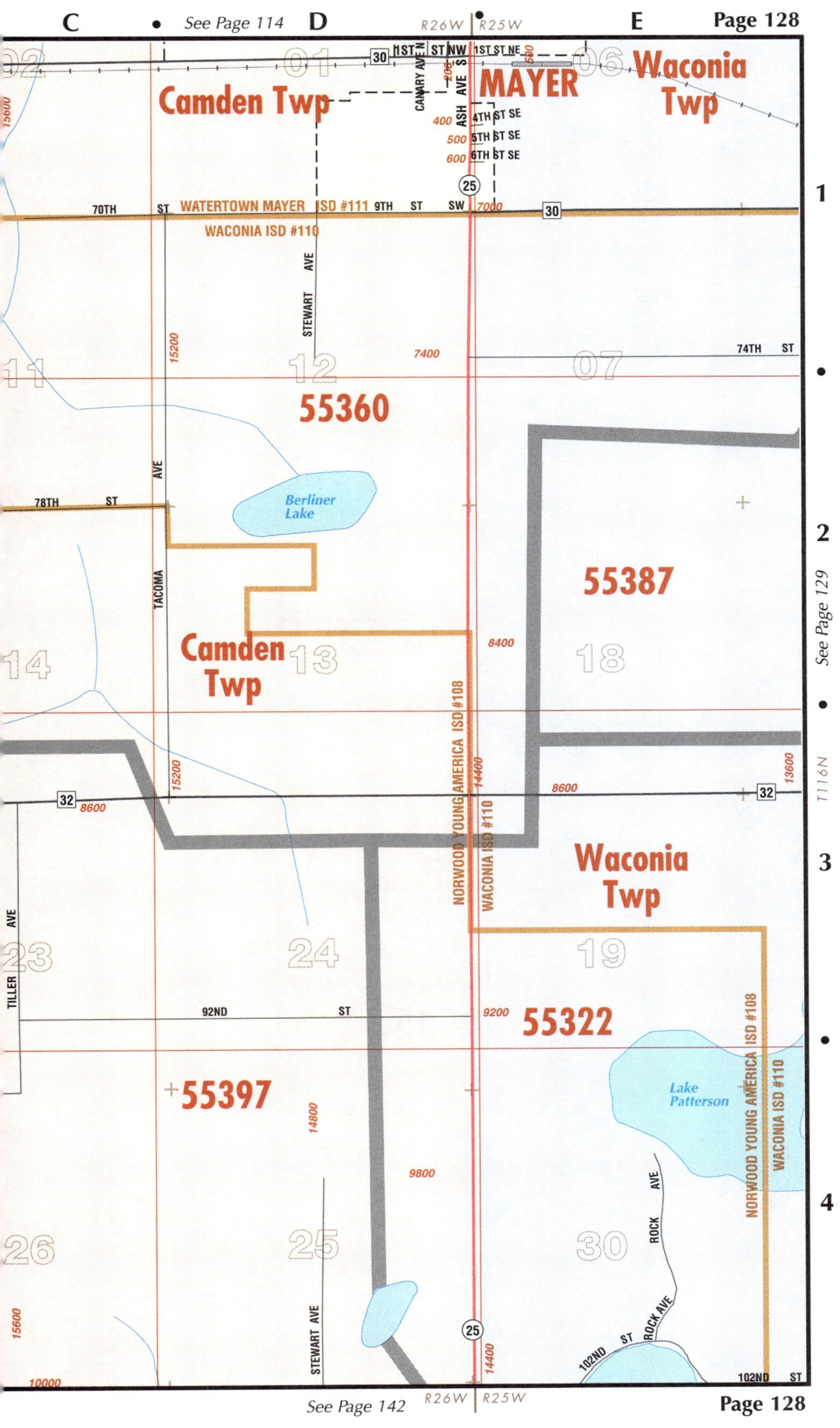

Camden Twp

MAYER

Waconia Twp

92

01

30 1ST N ST NW 1ST ST NE 06

CANARY AVE

ASH AVE S

500

4TH ST SE

5TH ST SE

6TH ST SE

400

500

600

25

70TH ST WATERTOWN MAYER ISD #111 9TH ST SW 7000 30

WACONIA ISD #110

STEWART AVE

15200

11 12 7400 07 74TH ST

55360

AVE

78TH ST

Berliner Lake

TACOMA

Camden Twp 13

NORWOOD YOUNG AMERICA ISD #108

WACONIA ISD #110

8400

55387

18

15200

32 8600

14400

8600 32 13600

Waconia Twp

TILLER AVE

23 24 19

92ND ST 9200 **55322**

+**55397**

14800

Lake Patterson

ROCK AVE

NORWOOD YOUNG AMERICA ISD #108

WACONIA ISD #110

9800

26 25 30 ROCK AVE

STEWART AVE

15600

10000

25

14400

102ND ST 102ND ST

1

2

3

4

See Page 129

T116N

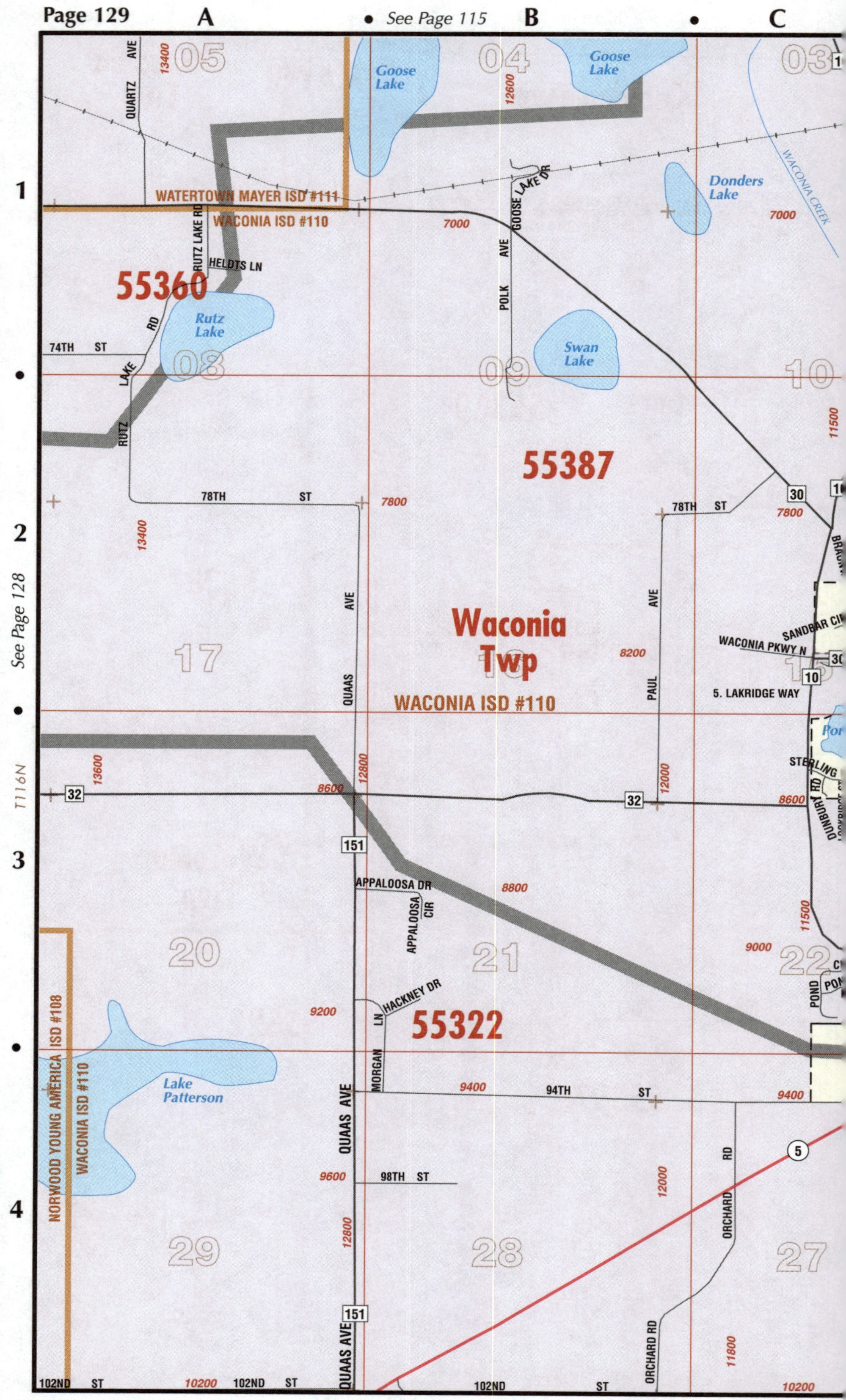

• *See Page 115*

A   B   C

QUARTZ AVE   *13400*   05

Goose Lake

04   *12600*   Goose Lake

03

GOOSE LAKE DR

Donders Lake

WACONIA CREEK

7000

1

See Page 128

WATERTOWN MAYER ISD #111

RUTZ LAKE RD

WACONIA ISD #110

7000

HELDTS LN

POLK   AVE

55360

RUTZ LAKE RD

Rutz Lake

Swan Lake

74TH ST

08

09

10

11500

78TH ST   *7800*

78TH ST   *7800*

30

2

QUAAS AVE

13400

17

55387

Waconia Twp

8200

SANDBAR CIR

WACONIA PKWY N

10

5. LAKRIDGE WAY

PAUL AVE

WACONIA ISD #110

Por

STERLING

DURBIN RD

T116N

13600

32

8600

12800

QUAAS AVE

151

32

8600

12000

3

Appaloosa DR

8800

APPALOOSA CIR

11500

9000

20

21

22

POND

PON

Lake Patterson

9200

HACKNEY DR

MORGAN LN

55322

9400

94TH ST

9400

5

QUAAS AVE

9600

98TH ST

12800

12000

ORCHARD RD

4

29

28

27

151

QUAAS AVE

ORCHARD RD

102ND ST   *10200*   102ND ST

102ND ST

11800

10200

See Page 143

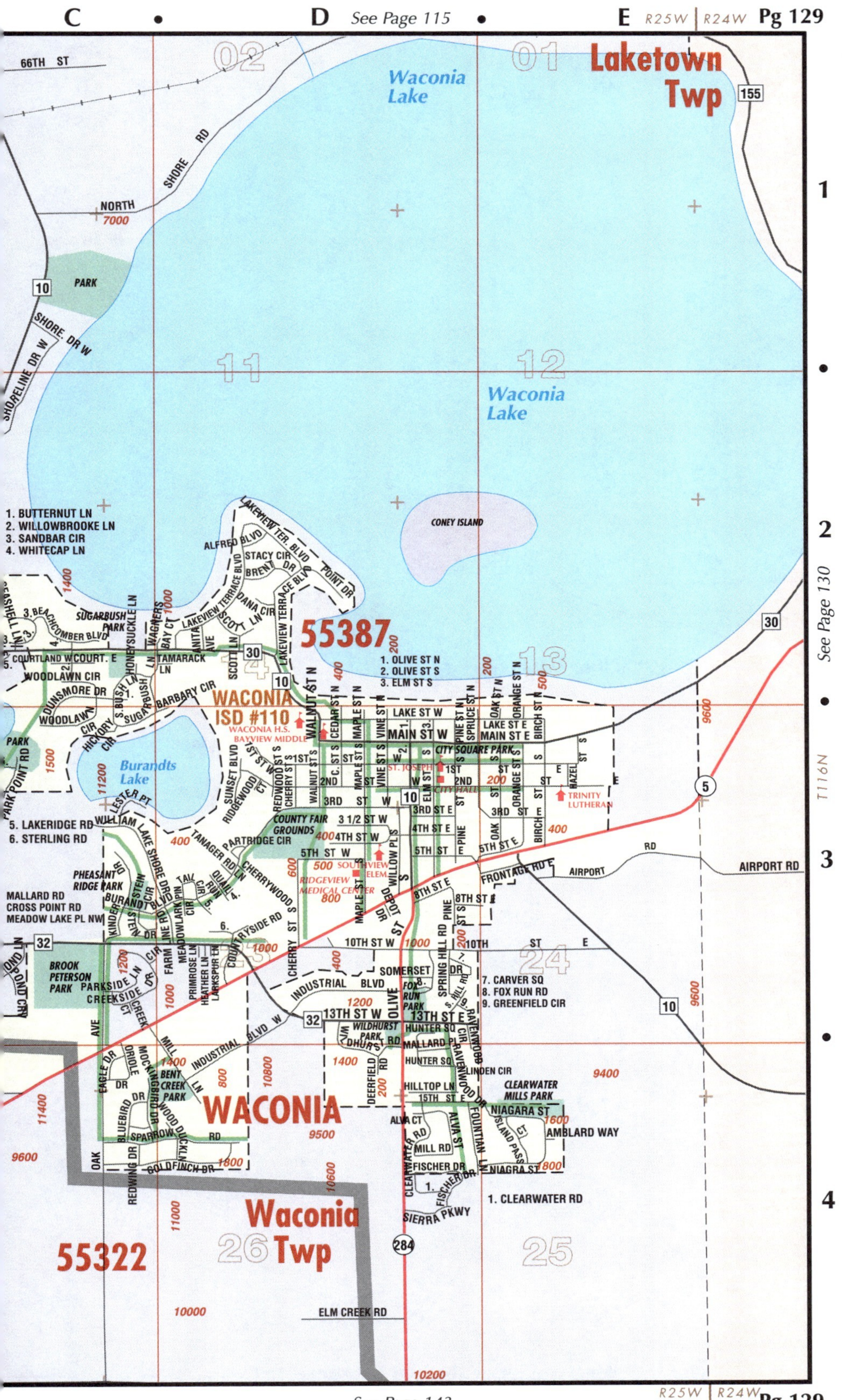

Laketown Twp
155
Waconia Lake
66TH ST
SHORE RD
NORTH
7000
PARK
10
SHORE DR W
SHORELINE DR W
11
12
02
01
1
2
3
4
CONEY ISLAND
1. BUTTERNUT LN
2. WILLOWBROOKE LN
3. SANDBAR CIR
4. WHITECAP LN
LAKEVIEW TER. BLVD
ALFRED BLVD
STACY CIR
BRENT DR
POINT DR
DANA CIR
SCOTT LN
LAKEVIEW TERRACE BLVD
55387
1. OLIVE ST N
2. OLIVE ST S
3. ELM ST S
SUGARBUSH PARK
BEACHCOMBER BLVD
HONEYSUCKLE LN
WAGNERS
BAY CT
TAMARACK LN
COURTLAND W COURT. E
WOODLAWN CIR
DUNSMORE DR
WOODLAWN
BARBARY CIR
WACONIA ISD #110
WACONIA H.S.
BAYVIEW MIDDLE
WALNUT ST N
CEDAR ST N
MAPLE ST N
VINE ST N
LAKE ST W
MAIN ST W
MAIN ST E
LAKE ST E
CITY SQUARE PARK
ST. JOSEPH
CITY HALL
TRINITY LUTHERAN
Burandts Lake
PARK
POINT RD
LESTER PT
HICKORY CIR
SUNSET BLVD
RIDGEWOOD CT
COUNTY FAIR GROUNDS
PARTRIDGE CIR
TANAGER RD
CHERRYWOOD
5. LAKERIDGE RD
6. STERLING RD
WILLIAM LAKE SHORE DR
PHEASANT RIDGE PARK
BURANDT BLVD
MALLARD RD
CROSS POINT RD
MEADOW LAKE PL NW
SOUTHVIEW ELEM.
RIDGEVIEW MEDICAL CENTER
WILLOW PL S
DEPOT DR
8TH ST E
8TH ST E
FRONTAGE RD E
AIRPORT
AIRPORT RD
5
30
10
32
COUNTRYSIDE RD
10TH ST W
10TH ST E
BROOK PETERSON PARK
PARKSIDE DR
CREEKSIDE CT
FARM
MEADOWLARK
PRIMROSE LN
HEATHER LN
LARKSPUR LN
CHERRY ST S
INDUSTRIAL BLVD
SOMERSET DR
FOX RUN PARK
SPRING HILL RD
7. CARVER SQ
8. FOX RUN RD
9. GREENFIELD CIR
13TH ST W
13TH ST E
WILDHURST PARK
HUNTER SQ
MALLARD PL
RAVENWOOD DR
LINDEN CIR
HILLTOP LN
15TH ST E
CLEARWATER MILLS PARK
NIAGARA ST
AMBLARD WAY
ALVA CT
ALVA ST
MILL RD
FISCHER DR
FOUNTAIN LN
ISLAND PASS
1. CLEARWATER RD
SIERRA PKWY
284
EAGLE DR
ORIOLE
MOCKINGBIRD DR
BENT CREEK PARK
BLUEBIRD DR
SPARROW
WOOD DUCK LN
GOLDFINCH DR
REDWING DR
OAK
WACONIA
Waconia Twp
55322
24
25
26
ELM CREEK RD
9400
9500
9600
10000
10200
11000
11400
See Page 130
T116N

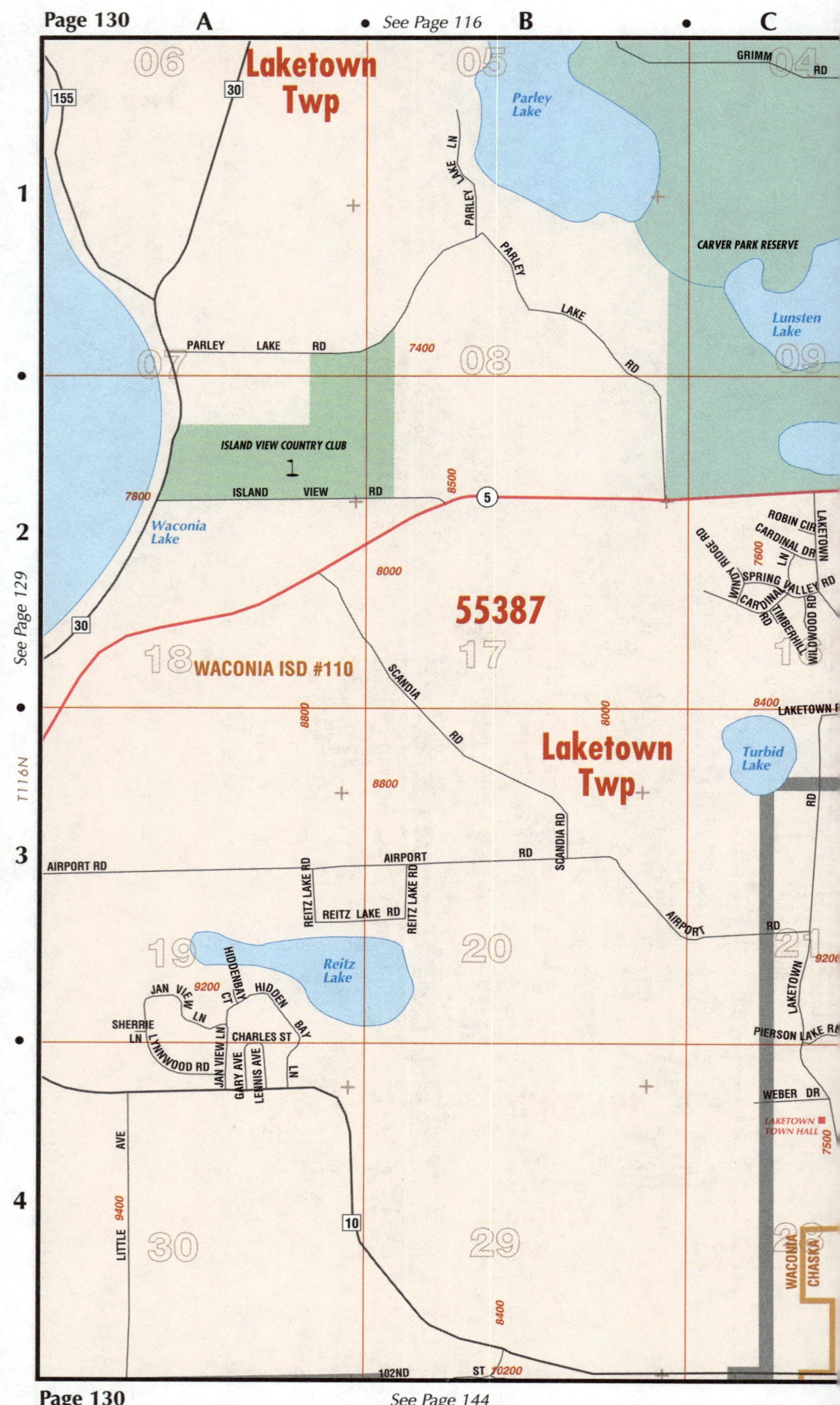

GRIMM RD

06   05   04

Laketown Twp

155

30

Parley Lake

CARVER PARK RESERVE

1

PARLEY LAKE LN

PARLEY LAKE RD

Lunsten Lake

07   7400   08   09

ISLAND VIEW COUNTRY CLUB

1

ISLAND VIEW RD

8500

7800

5

ROBIN CIR
LAKETOWN
CARDINAL DR
LN

7600

WINDY RIDGE RD

SPRING VALLEY RD

TIMBERHILL

WILDWOOD RD

CARDINAL RD

Waconia Lake

2

8000

55387

30

18   **WACONIA ISD #110**   **17**   **1**

8800

SCANDIA RD

8000

8400   LAKETOWN R

Turbid Lake

Laketown Twp

8800

3

AIRPORT RD

REITZ LAKE RD

AIRPORT

REITZ LAKE RD

RD

SCANDIA RD

AIRPORT

RD

RD

9200

21

19   *Reitz Lake*   20

LAKETOWN

JAN VIEW LN

9200

HIDDENBAY CT

HIDDEN BAY

LN

PIERSON LAKE R

SHERRIE LN

LINNWOOD RD

CHARLES ST

GARY AVE

LENNIS AVE

WEBER DR

LAKETOWN TOWN HALL

7500

4

LITTLE AVE

9400

30

10

29

WACONIA

CHASKA

8400

102ND ST 10200

See Page 116

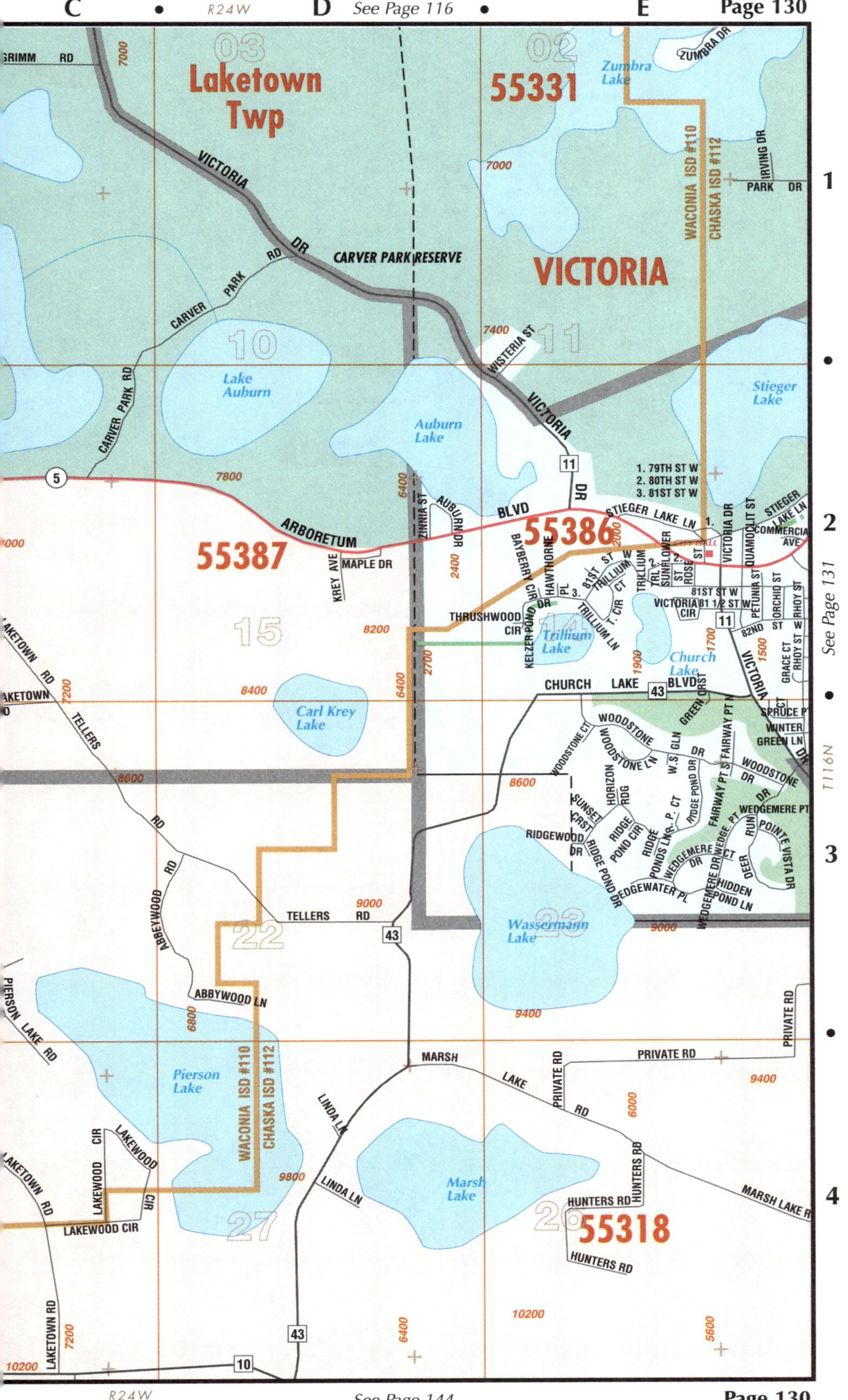

See Page 131
See Page 144

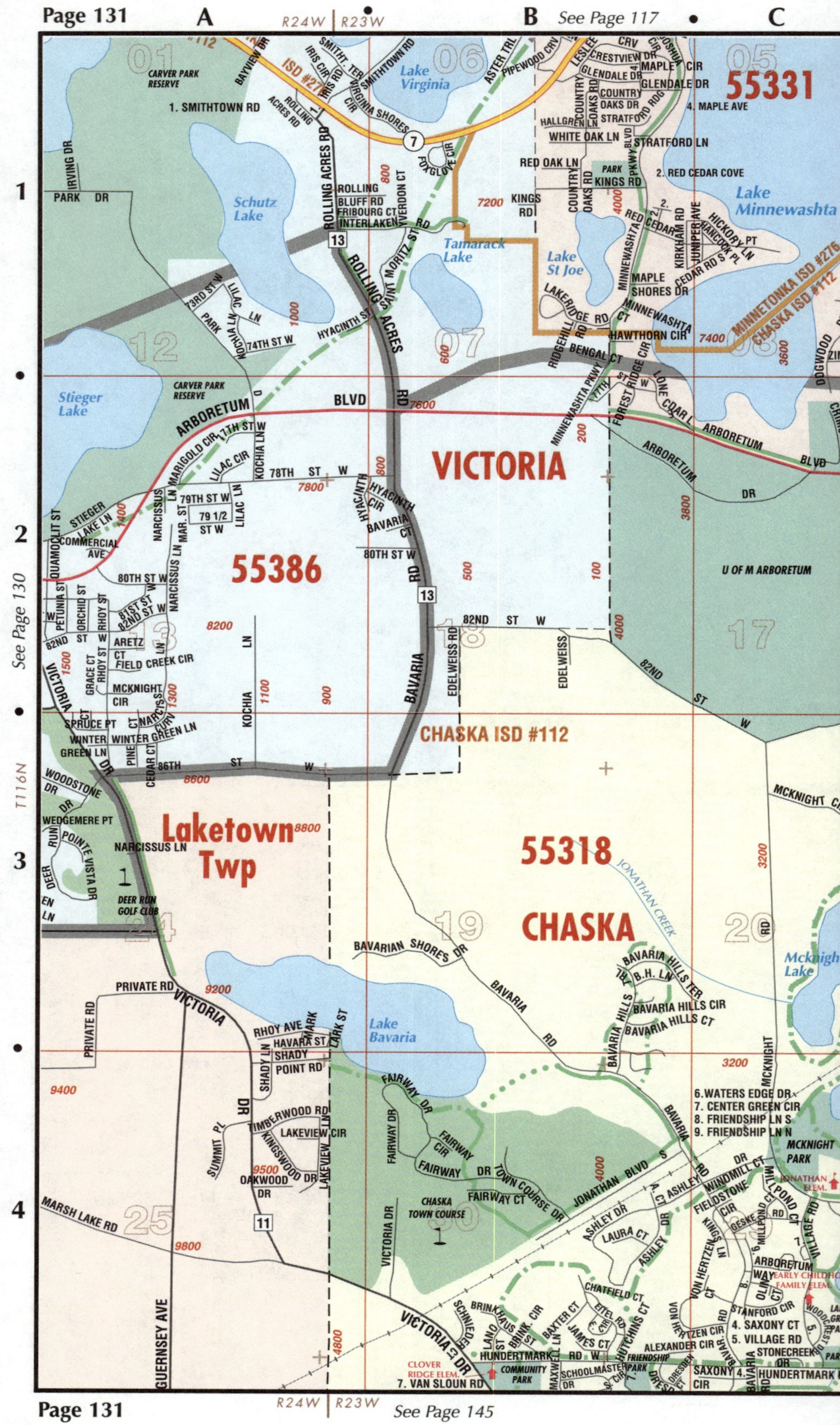

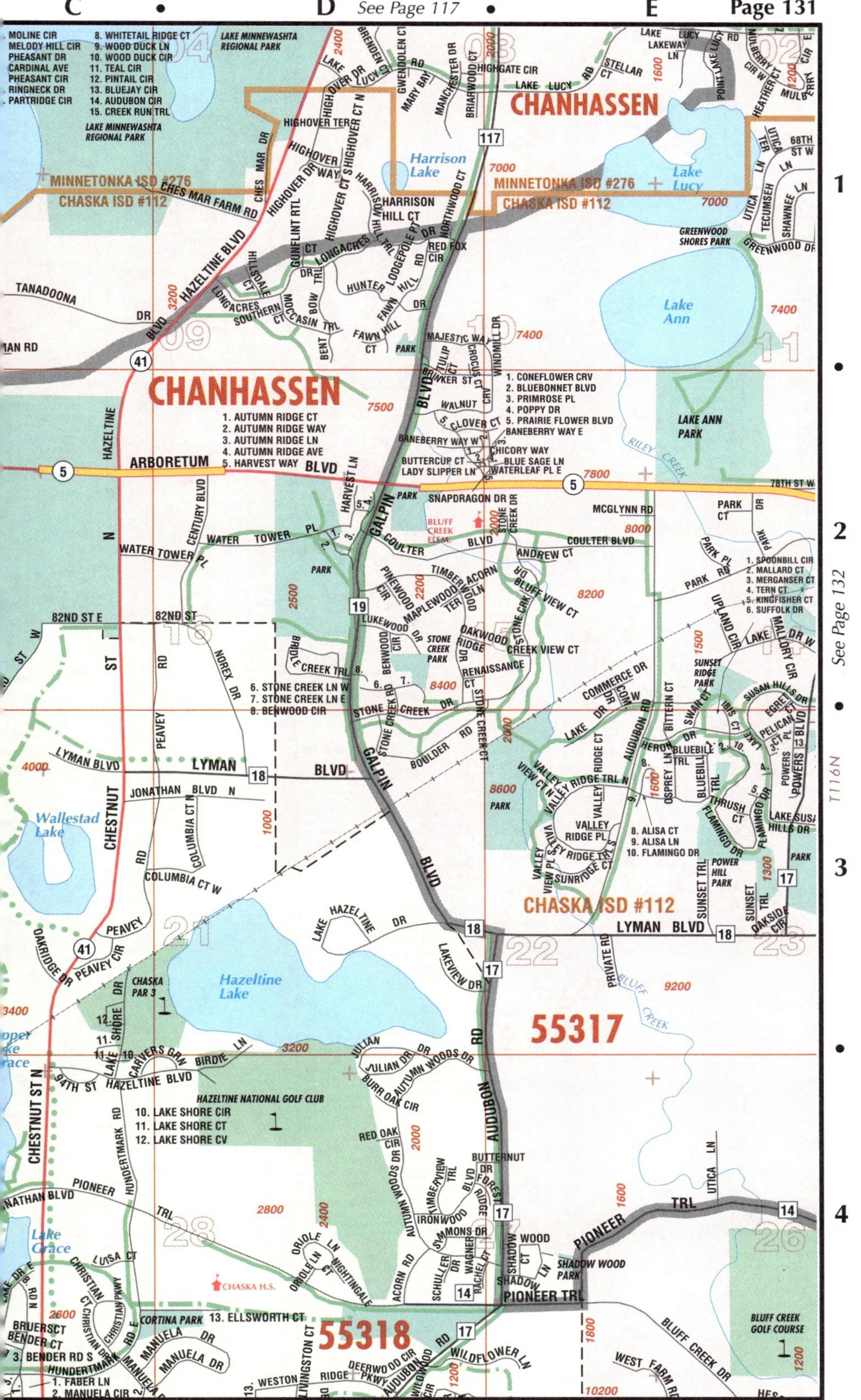

MOLINE CIR
MELODY HILL CIR
PHEASANT DR
CARDINAL AVE
PHEASANT CIR
RINGNECK DR
PARTRIDGE CIR

8. WHITETAIL RIDGE CT
9. WOOD DUCK LN
10. WOOD DUCK CIR
11. TEAL CIR
12. PINTAIL CIR
13. BLUEJAY CIR
14. AUDUBON CIR
15. CREEK RUN TRL

LAKE MINNEWASHTA REGIONAL PARK

CHANHASSEN

MINNETONKA ISD #276
CHASKA ISD #112

LAKE MINNEWASHTA REGIONAL PARK

CHANHASSEN

1. AUTUMN RIDGE CT
2. AUTUMN RIDGE WAY
3. AUTUMN RIDGE LN
4. AUTUMN RIDGE AVE
5. HARVEST WAY

1. CONEFLOWER CRV
2. BLUEBONNET BLVD
3. PRIMROSE PL
4. POPPY DR
5. PRAIRIE FLOWER BLVD
6. BANEBERRY WAY E

MINNETONKA ISD #276
CHASKA ISD #112

LAKE ANN PARK

6. STONE CREEK LN W
7. STONE CREEK LN E
8. BENWOOD CIR

1. SPOONBILL CIR
2. MALLARD CT
3. MERGANSER CT
4. TERN CT
5. KINGFISHER CT
6. SUFFOLK DR

8. ALISA CT
9. ALISA LN
10. FLAMINGO DR

CHASKA ISD #112

55317

CHASKA PAR 3

HAZELTINE NATIONAL GOLF CLUB

10. LAKE SHORE CIR
11. LAKE SHORE CT
12. LAKE SHORE CV

CHASKA H.S.

13. ELLSWORTH CT

55318

BLUFF CREEK GOLF COURSE

1. FABER LN
2. MANUELA CIR

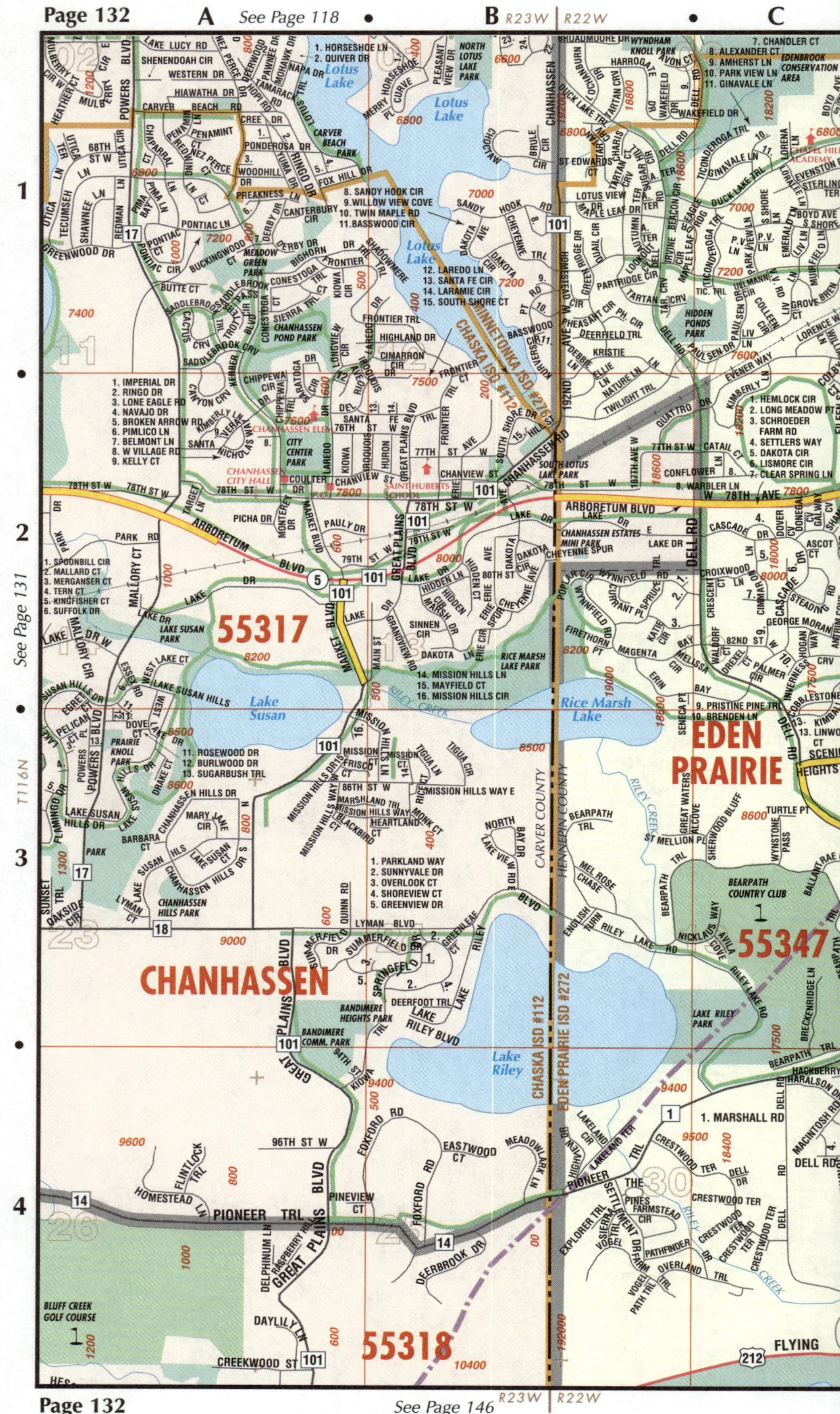

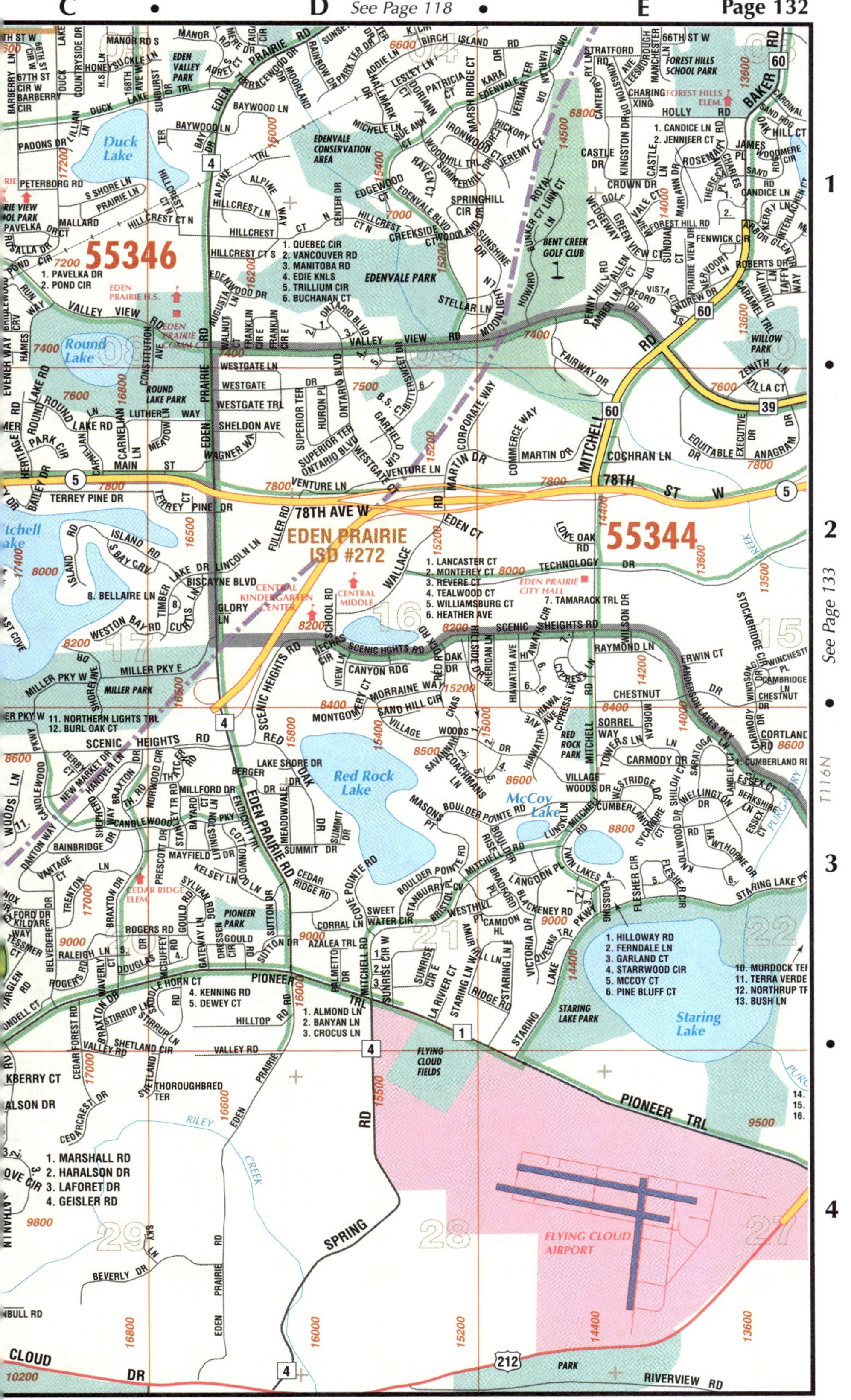

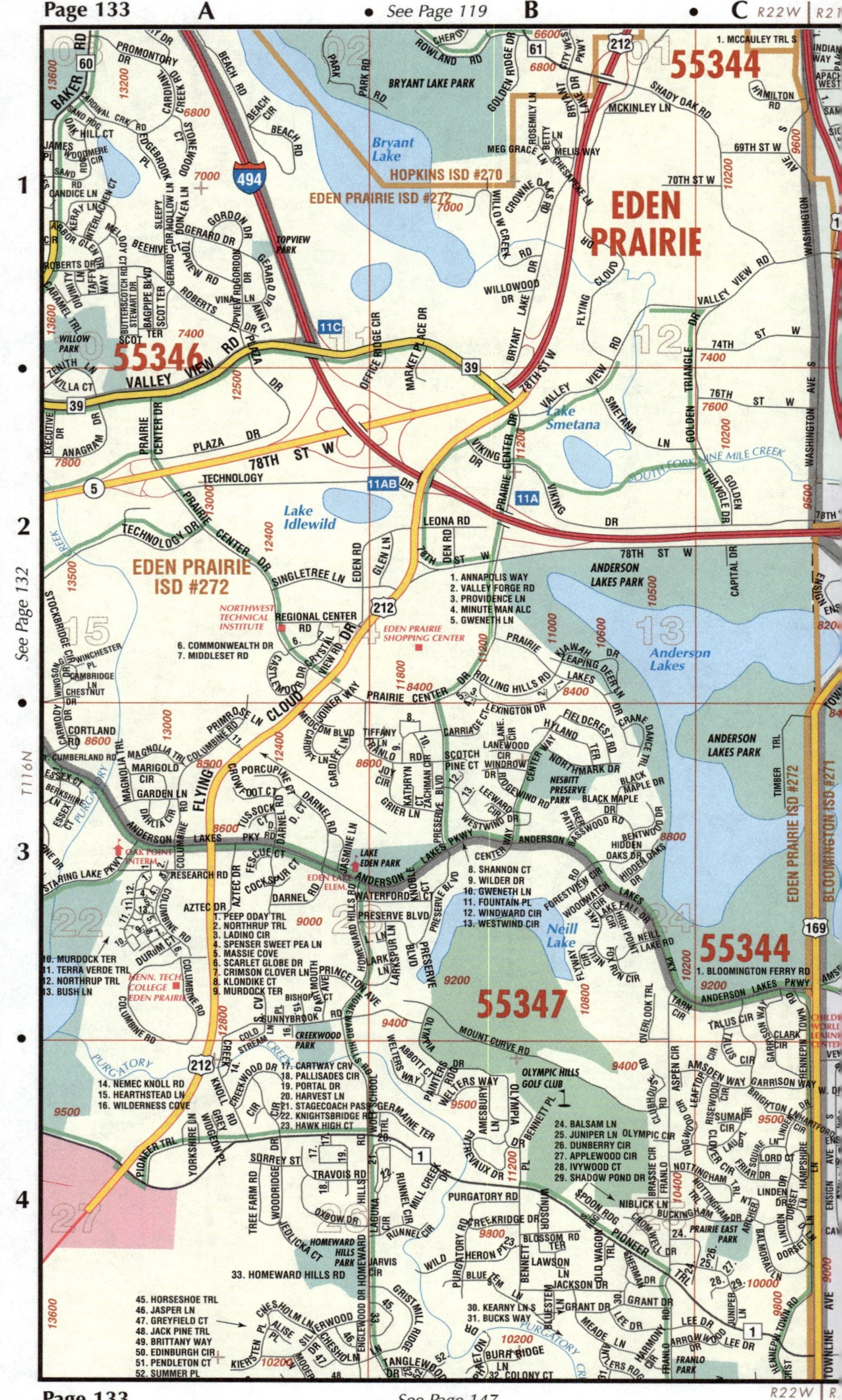

55344
55346
55347
EDEN PRAIRIE
EDEN PRAIRIE ISD #272
HOPKINS ISD #270
EDEN PRAIRIE ISD #272
BLOOMINGTON ISD #271
Bryant Lake
BRYANT LAKE PARK
Lake Idlewild
Lake Smetana
Anderson Lakes
ANDERSON LAKES PARK
Neill Lake
TOPVIEW PARK
WILLOW PARK
NORTHWEST TECHNICAL INSTITUTE
EDEN PRAIRIE SHOPPING CENTER
REGIONAL CENTER RD
NESBITT PRESERVE PARK
LAKE EDEN PARK
EDEN LAKE ELEM.
OAK POINT INTERM.
HENN. TECH. COLLEGE EDEN PRAIRIE
CREEKWOOD PARK
OLYMPIC HILLS GOLF CLUB
HOMEWARD HILLS PARK
PRAIRIE EAST PARK
FRANLO PARK
VALLEY VIEW RD
78TH ST W
PRAIRIE CENTER DR
ANDERSON LAKES PKWY
FLYING CLOUD DR
WASHINGTON AVE S
SHADY OAK RD
PIONEER TRL
MOUNT CURVE RD
PURGATORY CREEK
SOUTH FORK NINE MILE CREEK
1. ANNAPOLIS WAY
2. VALLEY FORGE RD
3. PROVIDENCE LN
4. MINUTE MAN ALC
5. GWENETH LN
6. COMMONWEALTH DR
7. MIDDLESET RD
8. SHANNON CT
9. WILDER DR
10. GWENETH LN
11. FOUNTAIN PL
12. WINDWARD CIR
13. WESTWIND CIR
1. PEEP ODAY TRL
2. NORTHRUP TRL
3. LADINO CIR
4. SPENSER SWEET PEA LN
5. MASSIE COVE
6. SCARLET GLOBE DR
7. CRIMSON CLOVER LN
8. KLONDIKE CT
9. MURDOCK TER
10. MURDOCK TER
11. TERRA VERDE TRL
12. NORTHRUP TRL
13. BUSH LN
14. NEMEC KNOLL RD
15. HEARTHSTEAD LN
16. WILDERNESS COVE
17. CARTWAY CRV
18. PALLISADES CIR
19. PORTAL DR
20. HARVEST LN
21. STAGECOACH PASS
22. KNIGHTSBRIDGE RD
23. HAWK HIGH CT
24. BALSAM LN
25. JUNIPER LN
26. DUNBERRY CIR
27. APPLEWOOD CIR
28. IVYWOOD CT
29. SHADOW POND DR
30. KEARNY LN S
31. BUCKS WAY
32. COLONY CT
33. HOMEWARD HILLS RD
45. HORSESHOE TRL
46. JASPER LN
47. GREYFIELD CT
48. JACK PINE TRL
49. BRITTANY WAY
50. EDINBURGH CIR
51. PENDLETON CT
52. SUMMER PL
1. BLOOMINGTON FERRY RD

See Page 132

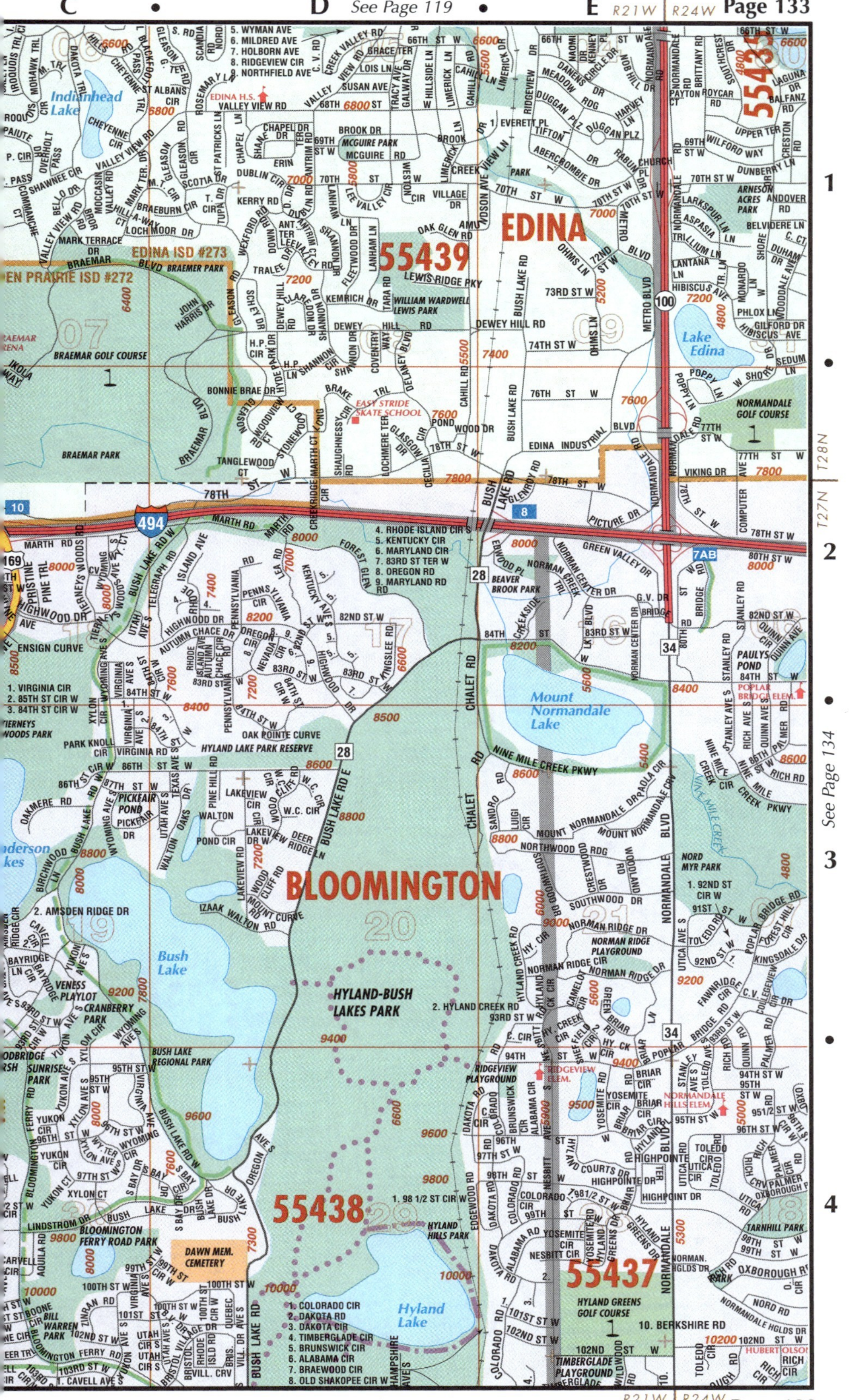

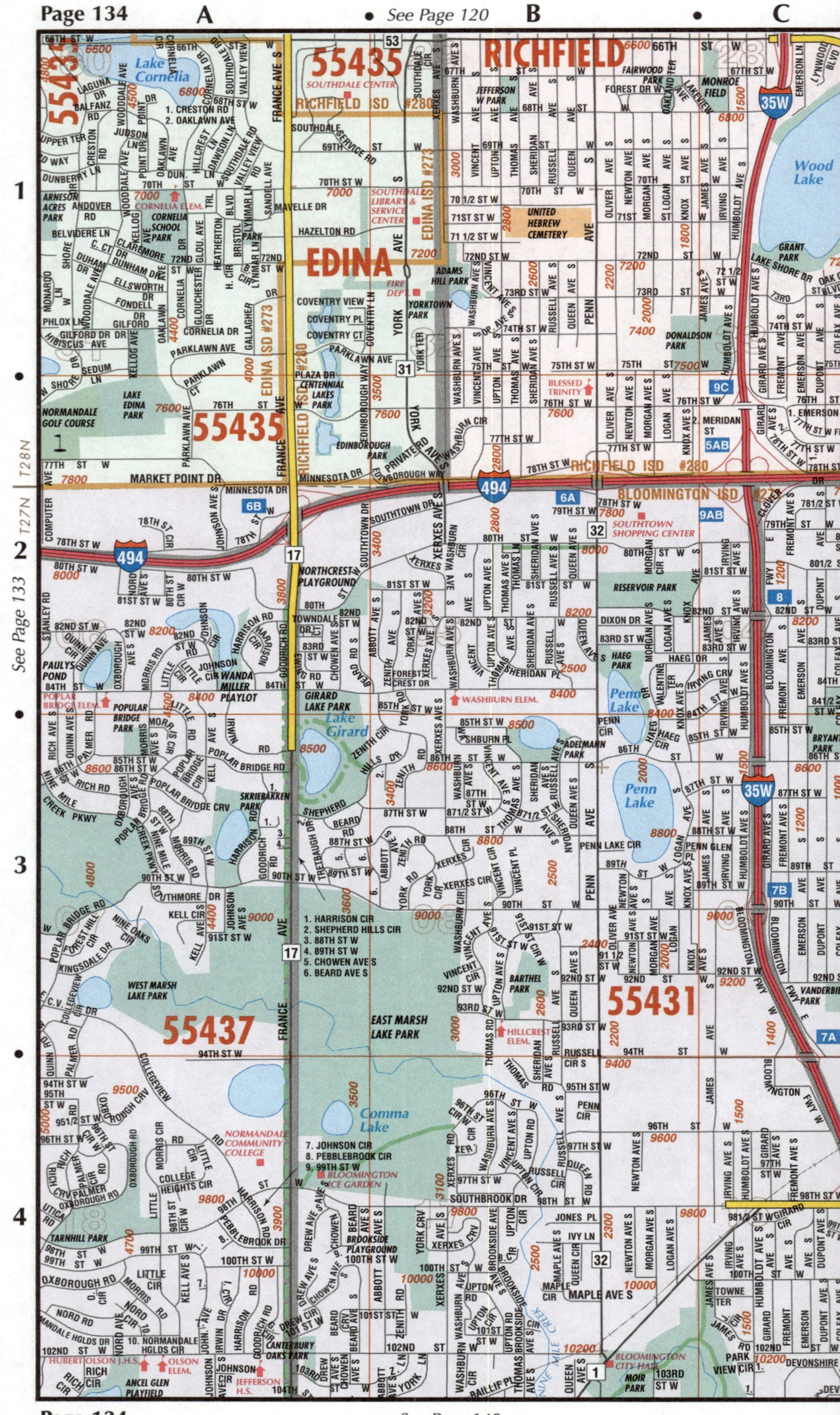

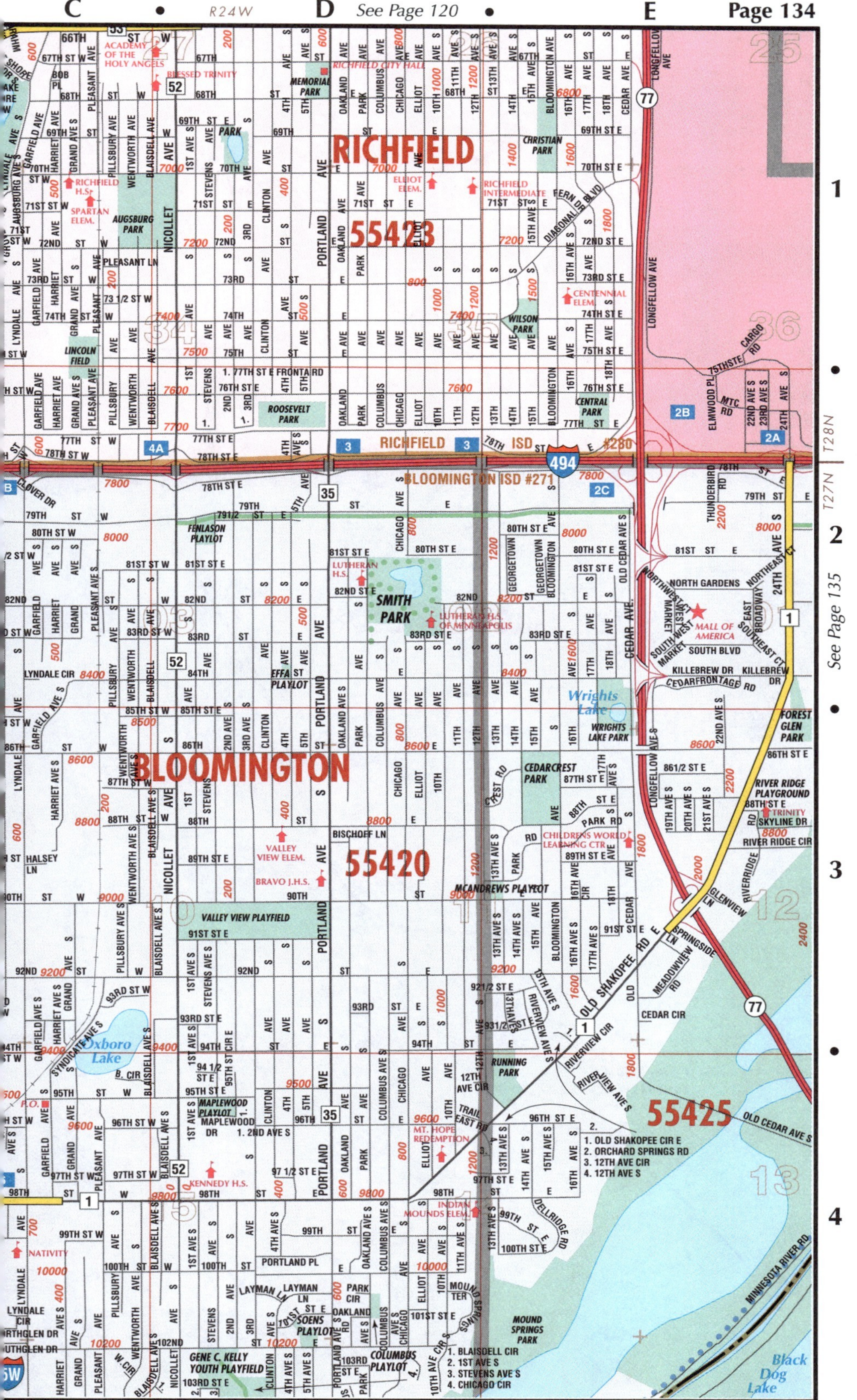
RICHFIELD
55423
BLOOMINGTON
55420
55425
RICHFIELD ISD #280
BLOOMINGTON ISD #271
MALL OF AMERICA
SMITH PARK
AUGSBURG PARK
VALLEY VIEW PLAYFIELD
GENE C. KELLY YOUTH PLAYFIELD
Oxboro Lake
Wrights Lake
Black Dog Lake
MINNESOTA RIVER RD
NICOLLET
PORTLAND
CEDAR AVE.
LONGFELLOW AVE
OLD SHAKOPEE RD E
See Page 135
1. BLAISDELL CIR
2. 1ST AVE S
3. STEVENS AVE S
4. CHICAGO CIR
1. OLD SHAKOPEE CIR E
2. ORCHARD SPRINGS RD
3. 12TH AVE CIR
4. 12TH AVE S
T28N
T27N

A R24W | R23W • *See Page 121* B • C

55450

GREEN LN GREEN CIR

NORTHWEST DR

1

7TH ST E

POST RD

70TH ST E

72ND ST E *7200*

**MINNEAPOLIS
ST PAUL
INTERNATIONAL
AIRPORT**

5

73RD ST E

74TH ST E *7400*

H.H.H.
TERMINAL

AIRLINE DR

7500

**FORT
SNELLING
CEMETERY**

55111

Snelling
Lake

MONTEGUE TER

RICHFIELD ISD #280

WEST ST PAUL ISD #280

HENNEPIN COUNTY

DAKOTA COUNTY

CARGO RD

55423

AIR-

AIRPORT LN AIRLINE LN

2A

22ND AVE S 23RD AVE S

34TH AVE S

494

RICHFIELD ISD #280

BLOOMINGTON ISD #271

MINNESOTA VALLEY STATE TRAIL

1B

1A

T28N T27N

2

78TH ST E METRO PKWY

78TH ST E

ST

79TH ST E

25TH AVE S

2500

INTERNATIONAL DR

3400

80TH

80TH ST E

METRO DR

8000

8000

APPLETREE
SQUARE

**NATIONAL REFUGE
WILDLIFE INTERPRETIVE
CENTER**

BLOOMINGTON

**Gun
Club
Lake**

05

See Page 134

NORTHEAST CT

EAST
SOUTHEAST CT

24TH AVE S

1

26TH AVE S

81ST ST E

8200

82ND ST E

2600

28TH

OLD SHAKOPEE RD E

LONG
MEADOW CIR

KILLEBREW
DR

OAKLAND DR

55425

**FOREST
GLEN
PARK**

86TH ST E

*Long
Meadow
Lake*

Minnesota *River*

3000

MEADOWV
TEX LN

3

RIVERRIDGE

RIVER RIDGE
PLAYGROUND

88TH ST E

TRINITY DR

SKYLINE DR

8800

RIVER RIDGE CIR

12

2400

*Long
Meadow
Lake*

07

River

BLOOMINGTON ISD #271

WEST ST PAUL ISD #197

2000

BURNSVILLE ISD #191

MINNESOTA VALLEY STATE TRAIL

08

3200

SUN DR

TERMINAL DR

1700

LETENG
ST

13

77

YANKEE DOODLE RD

YANKEE DR

3400

**MINNESOTA VALLEY
NATIONAL WILDLIFE REFUGE**

OLD CEDAR AVE S

10000

BLOOMINGTON ISD #271

BURNSVILLE ISD #191

13

MINNESOTA RIVER RD

BLACKDOG RD

18

3600

PLANT RD

COMANCHE RD

BLACKHAWK RD

SIBLEY

WEST ST PAUL ISD #197

KENNEBEC DR

MEMORIAL

BLUE CROSS RD

3500

ASHBURY

DELTA DENTA

**SKY LINE
PARK**

3600

CRESTRIDGE LN

MONTEREY LN

KYLLO LN

BLACKHAWK RD

SHAWNEE RD

RED FOX RD

DEER POND

CAR ROBIN LN

BLUEBILL CIR

BLUEBILL
CIR

4

NICOLS

55122

WUTHERING HEIGHTS RD

WUTHERING
HEIGHTS RD

HAZEL RD

SILVER
BELL

KENNEBEC DR

SENECA RD

VERMILION CT S

VERMILION CURVE

BURGUNDY

MERLOT
CURVE

2000

**5. COUNTRY CREEK WAY
6. RIVERTON CIR**

BROWN CAR ROBIN LN

WILLOW

HEATHER WAY

WOODGREEN

1800

**1. FLAMINGO LN
2. RED ROBIN LN
3. GREY DOVE**

BLUEHILL
CIR

SKATER
CIR SKATER

RIVERTON AVE

**4. SILVER BELL
P. CIR**

13

SILVER
BELL RD

SILVER
BELL

BALLANTRAE RD

LAUREL
CT

DOLOMITE
DR

HEATHER

C. LIR

GOLD PT

PALISADE
LN

LODESTONE LN

55337

TESSERACT
PL

TESSERACT
PL

✚ **TESSERACT**

3800

SILVER
BELL

CEDARVALE BLVD

NEW DR

SERPENTINE

COCHRANE

*Black
Dog
Lake*

3800

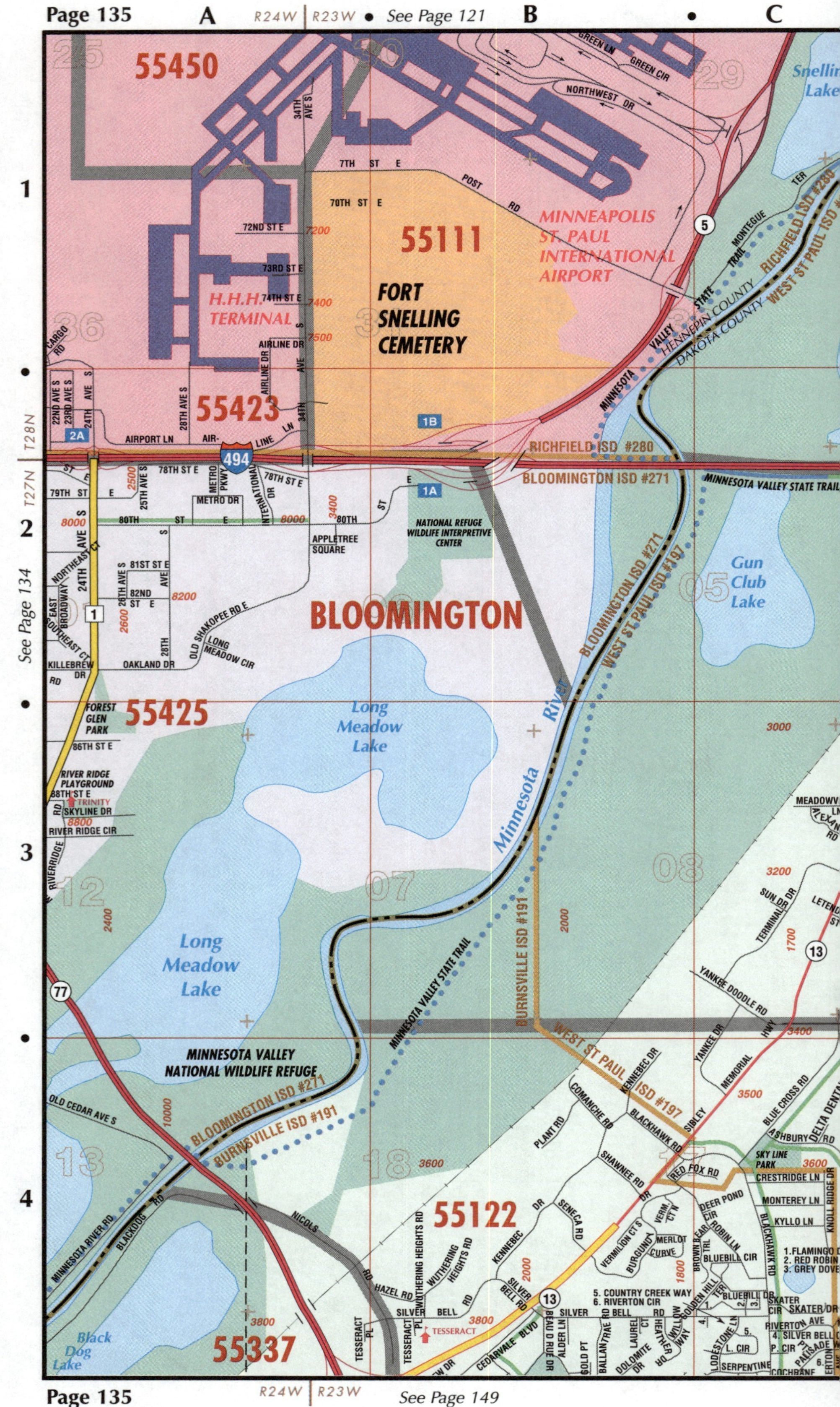

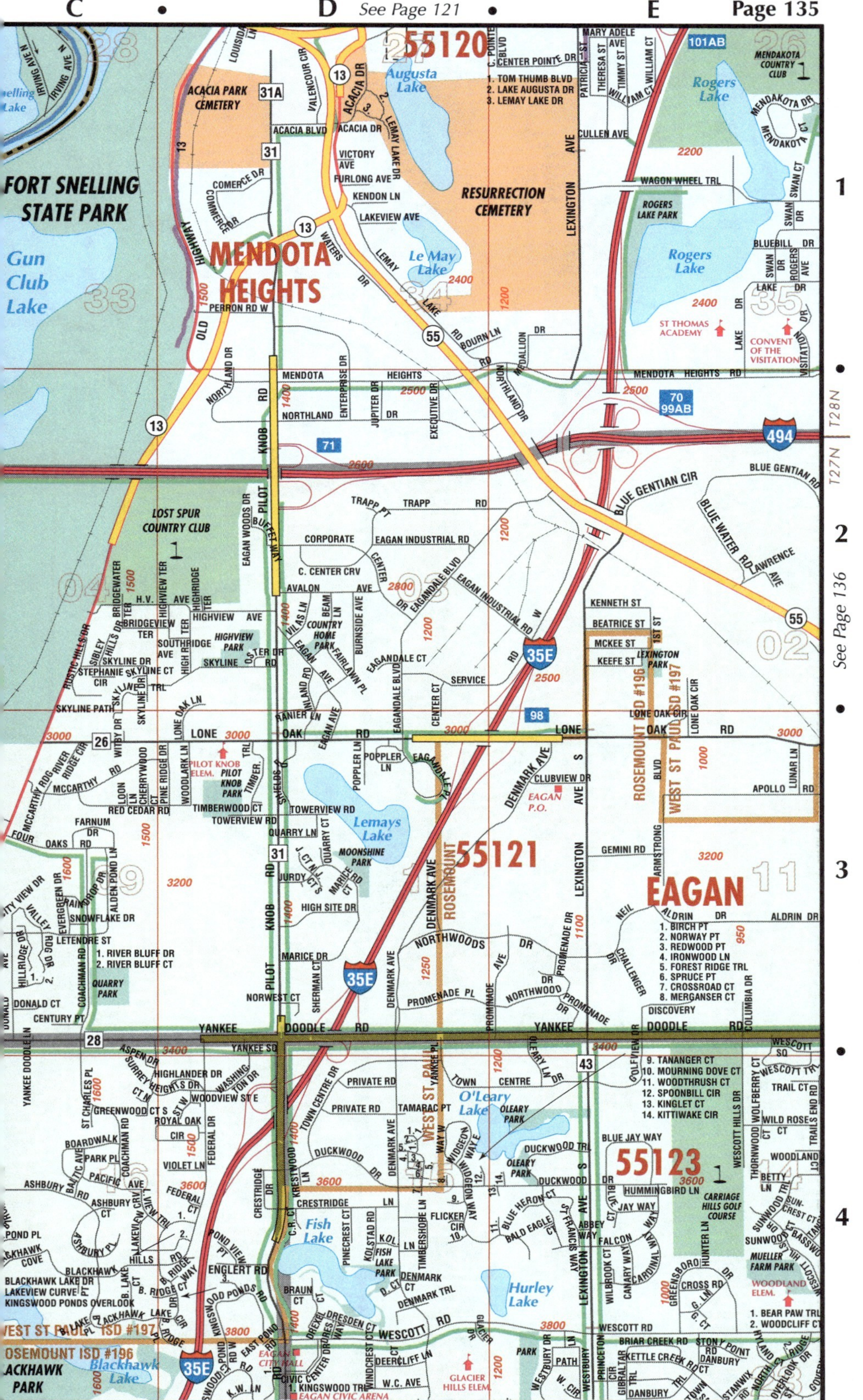
FORT SNELLING STATE PARK
Gun Club Lake
MENDOTA HEIGHTS
55120
Augusta Lake
RESURRECTION CEMETERY
ACACIA PARK CEMETERY
Le May Lake
Rogers Lake
ROGERS LAKE PARK
MENDAKOTA COUNTRY CLUB
ST THOMAS ACADEMY
CONVENT OF THE VISITATION
1. TOM THUMB BLVD
2. LAKE AUGUSTA DR
3. LEMAY LAKE DR
LOST SPUR COUNTRY CLUB
HIGHVIEW PARK
COUNTRY HOME PARK
LEXINGTON PARK
PILOT KNOB ELEM.
PILOT KNOB PARK
EAGAN P.O.
Lemays Lake
MOONSHINE PARK
55121
ROSEMOUNT ISD #196
WEST ST PAUL ISD #197
EAGAN
1. BIRCH PT
2. NORWAY PT
3. REDWOOD PT
4. IRONWOOD LN
5. FOREST RIDGE TRL
6. SPRUCE PT
7. CROSSROAD CT
8. MERGANSER CT
1. RIVER BLUFF DR
2. RIVER BLUFF CT
QUARRY PARK
9. TANANGER CT
10. MOURNING DOVE CT
11. WOODTHRUSH CT
12. SPOONBILL CIR
13. KINGLET CT
14. KITTIWAKE CIR
O'Leary Lake
OLEARY PARK
55123
CARRIAGE HILLS GOLF COURSE
MUELLER FARM PARK
WOODLAND ELEM.
1. BEAR PAW TRL
2. WOODCLIFF CT
Fish Lake
FISH LAKE PARK
Hurley Lake
Blackhawk Lake
BLACKHAWK PARK
EAGAN CITY HALL
EAGAN CIVIC ARENA
GLACIER HILLS ELEM.
YANKEE DOODLE RD
LONE OAK RD
MENDOTA HEIGHTS RD
WESCOTT RD
LEXINGTON AVE
PILOT KNOB RD
T28N
T27N

See Page 136

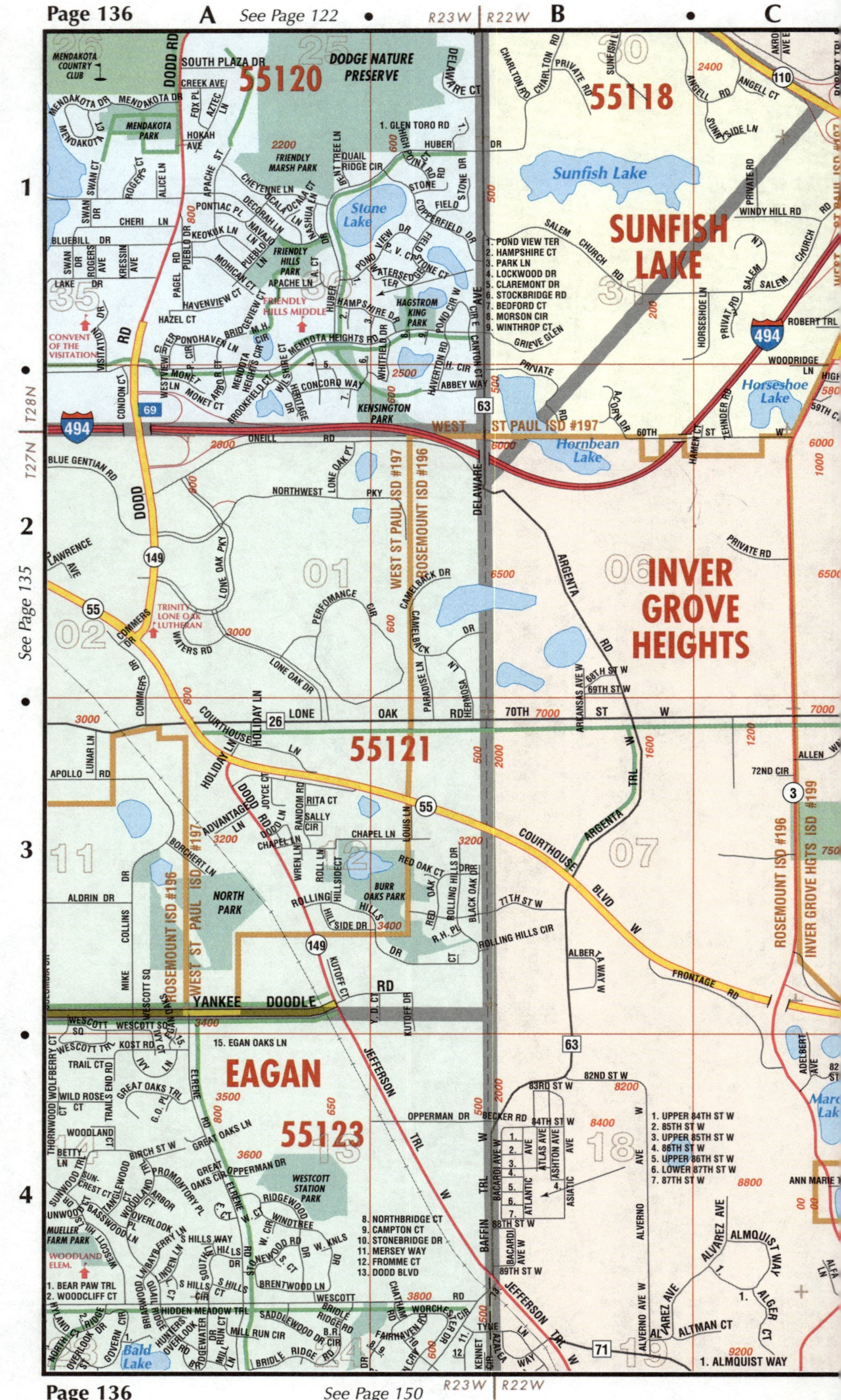

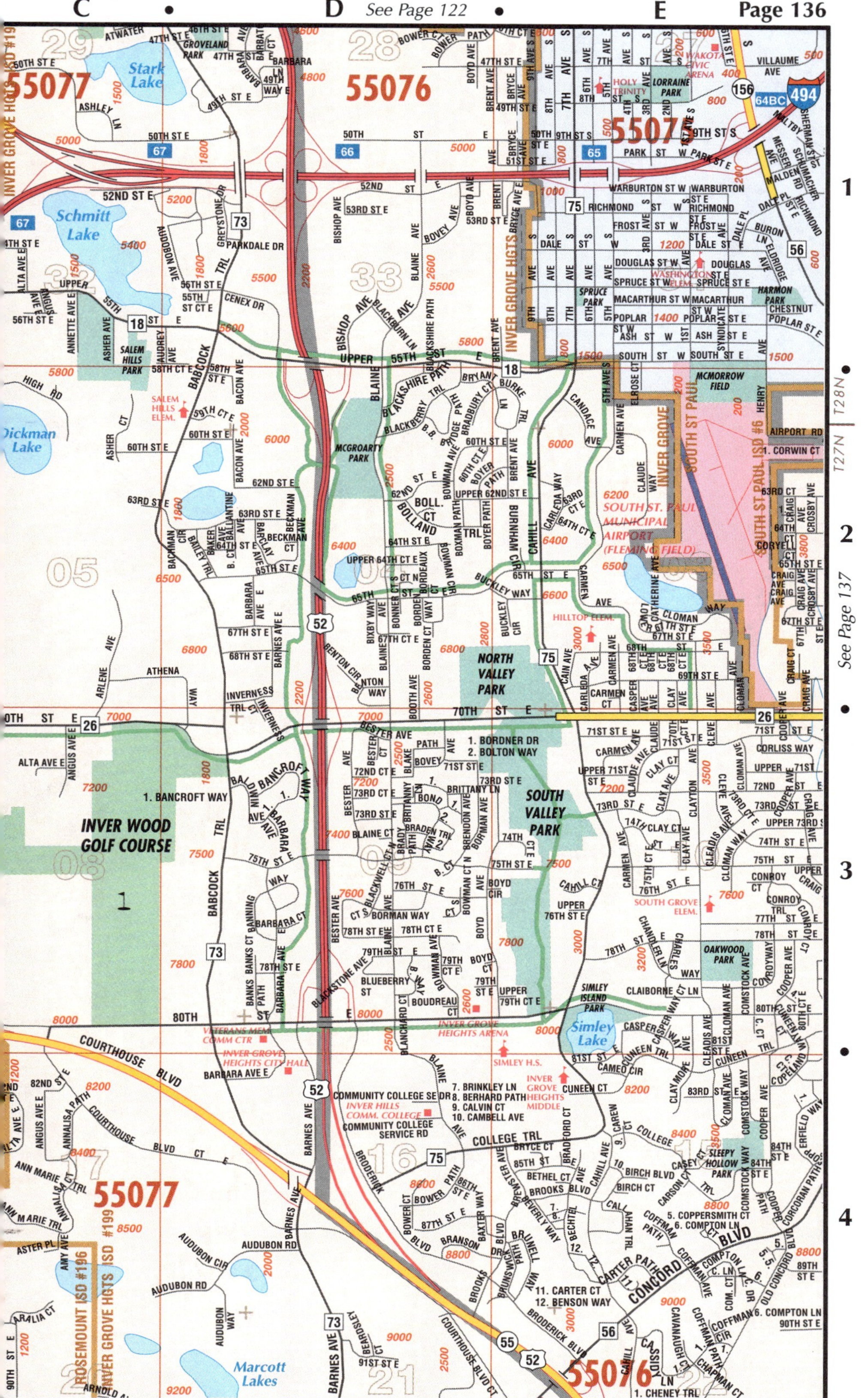

See Page 123

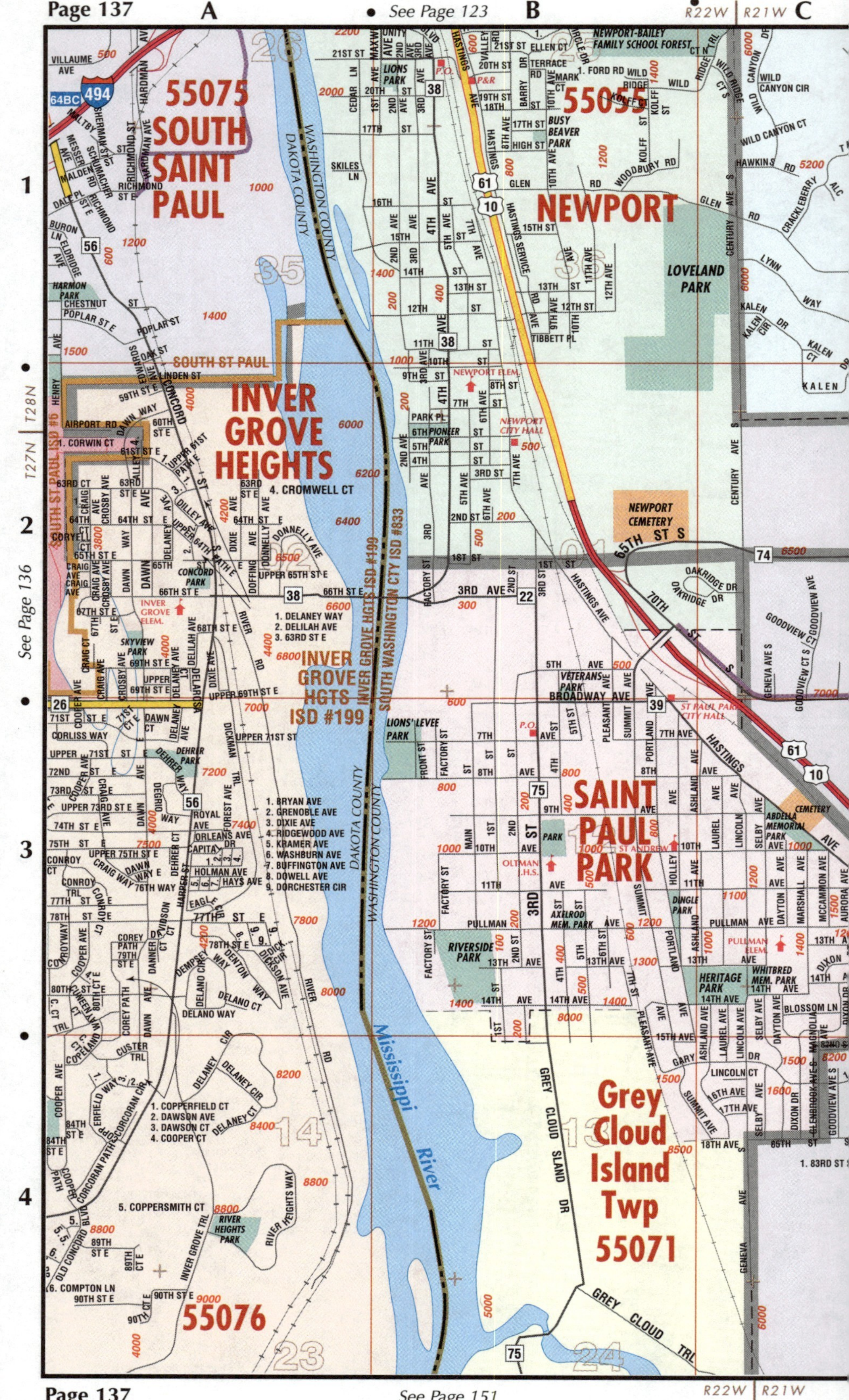

See Page 151
See Page 136
R22W R21W

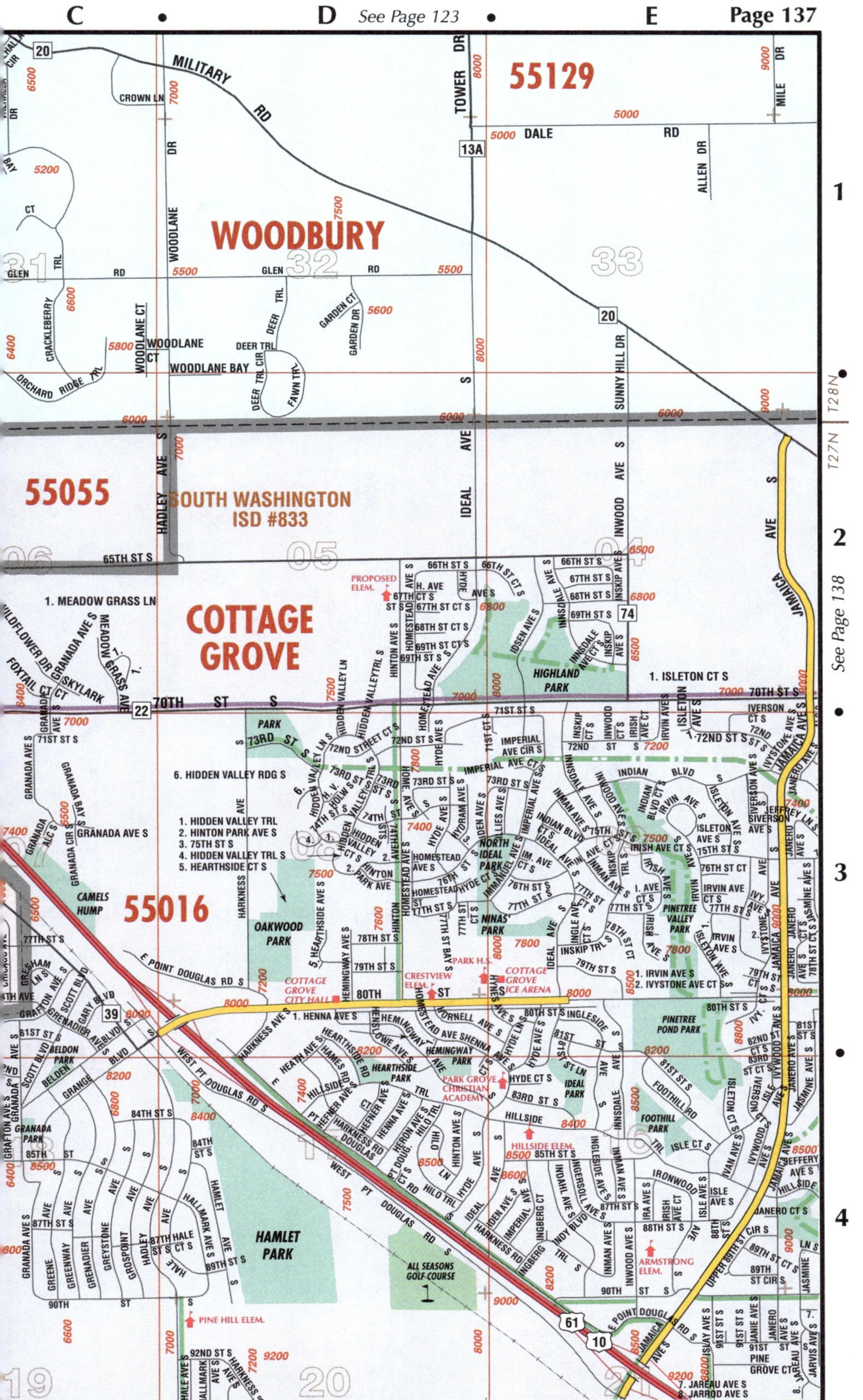

55129

WOODBURY

55055

SOUTH WASHINGTON
ISD #833

COTTAGE
GROVE

55016

See Page 138

HIGHLAND
PARK

CAMELS
HUMP

OAKWOOD
PARK

NINAS
PARK

NORTH
IDEAL
PARK

PINETREE
VALLEY
PARK

COTTAGE
GROVE
ICE ARENA

PINETREE
POND PARK

HEARTHSIDE
PARK

PARK GROVE
CHRISTIAN
ACADEMY

IDEAL
PARK

FOOTHILL
PARK

HAMLET
PARK

ALL SEASONS
GOLF COURSE

ARMSTRONG
ELEM.

PINE
GROVE ELEM

1. MEADOW GRASS LN
6. HIDDEN VALLEY RDG S

1. HIDDEN VALLEY TRL
2. HINTON PARK AVE S
3. 75TH ST S
4. HIDDEN VALLEY TRL S
5. HEARTHSIDE CT S

1. ISLETON CT S

1. IRVIN AVE S
2. IVYSTONE AVE S

1. HENNA AVE S

1. JAREAU AVE S
2. JARROD AVE S

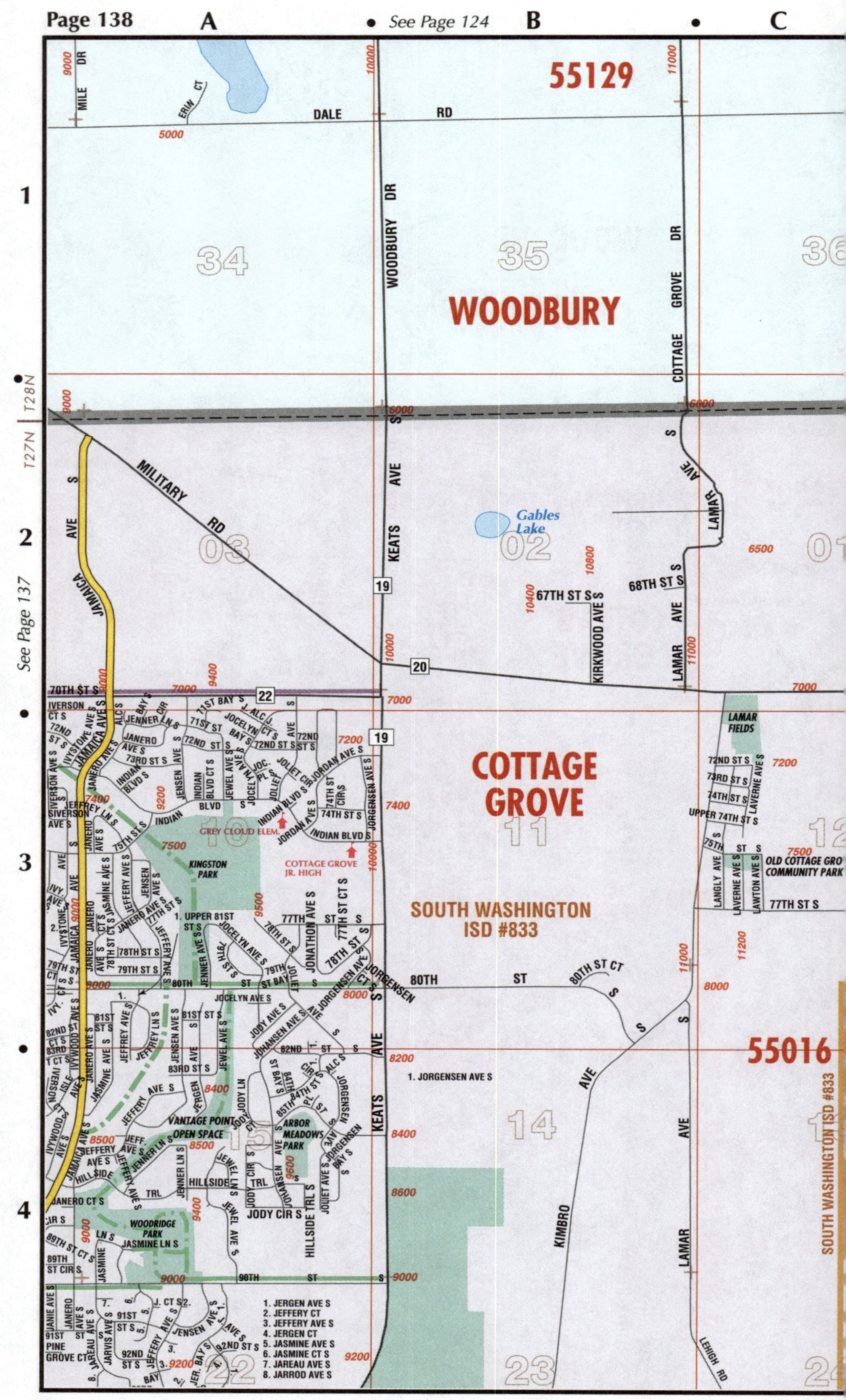

55129

WOODBURY

COTTAGE
GROVE

SOUTH WASHINGTON
ISD #833

55016

LAMAR
FIELDS

OLD COTTAGE GRO
COMMUNITY PARK

Gables
Lake

Kingston
Park

COTTAGE GROVE
JR. HIGH

GREY CLOUD ELEM.

VANTAGE POINT
OPEN SPACE

ARBOR
MEADOWS
PARK

Woodridge
Park

1. JERGEN AVE S
2. JEFFERY CT
3. JEFFERY AVE S
4. JERGEN CT
5. JASMINE AVE S
6. JASMINE CT S
7. JAREAU AVE S
8. JARROD AVE S

1. JORGENSEN AVE S

SOUTH WASHINGTON ISD #833

See Page 137

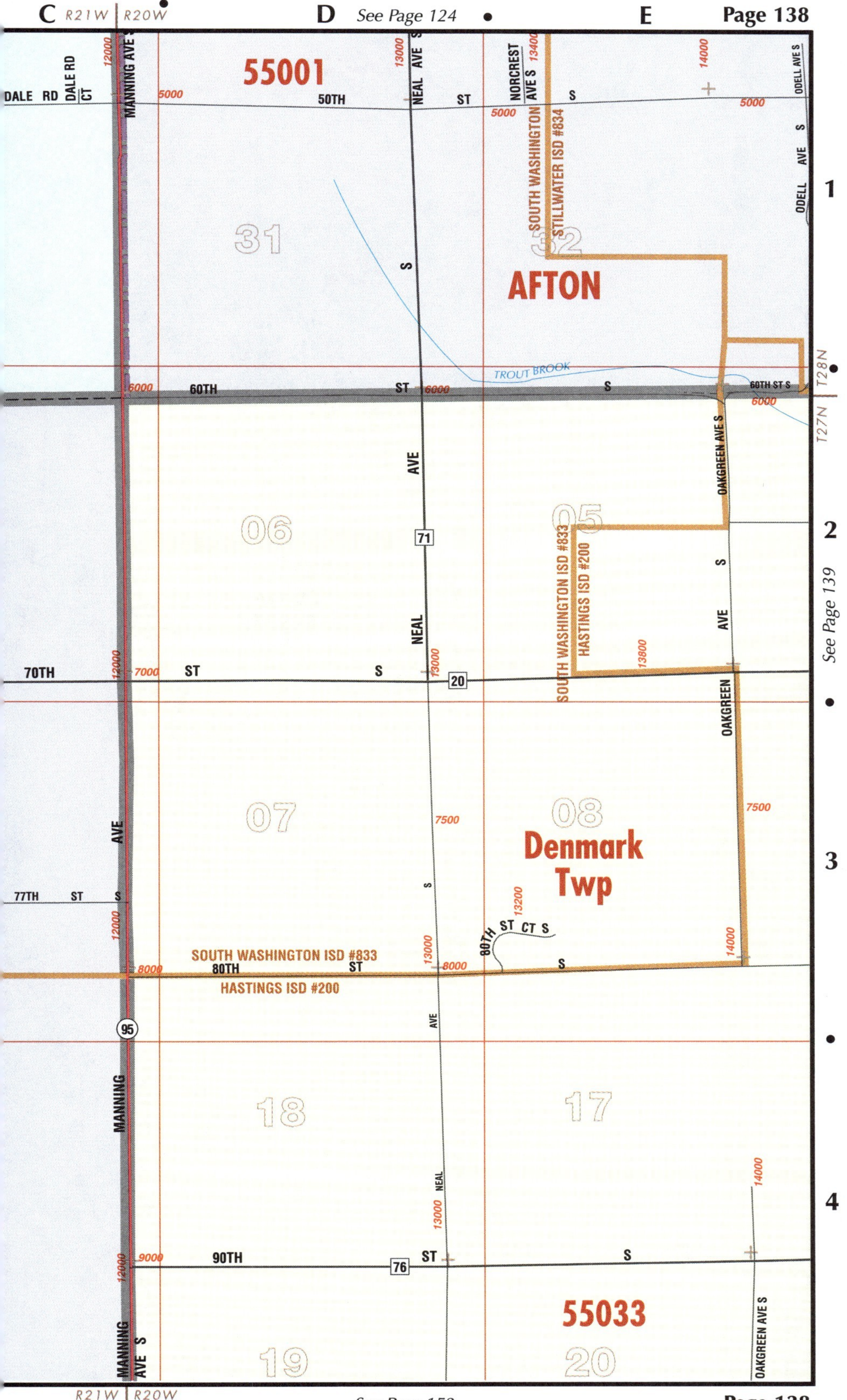

55001

AFTON

DALE RD | DALE RD | CT

MANNING AVE S

50TH ST

NEAL AVE S

NORCREST AVE S

SOUTH WASHINGTON
STILLWATER ISD #834

ODELL AVE S

ODELL AVE S

1

31

32

TROUT BROOK

60TH ST 6000

60TH ST S

T28N | T27N

06

71

NEAL AVE S

05

SOUTH WASHINGTON ISD #833
HASTINGS ISD #200

OAKGREEN AVE S

OAKGREEN AVE S

2

See Page 139

70TH ST S

20

07

08

**Denmark
Twp**

OAKGREEN

MANNING AVE

77TH ST S

7500

7500

3

95

60TH ST CT S

SOUTH WASHINGTON ISD #833
80TH ST S

HASTINGS ISD #200

18

17

NEAL AVE S

MANNING AVE S

NEAL

4

90TH ST S

76

19

20

55033

OAKGREEN AVE S

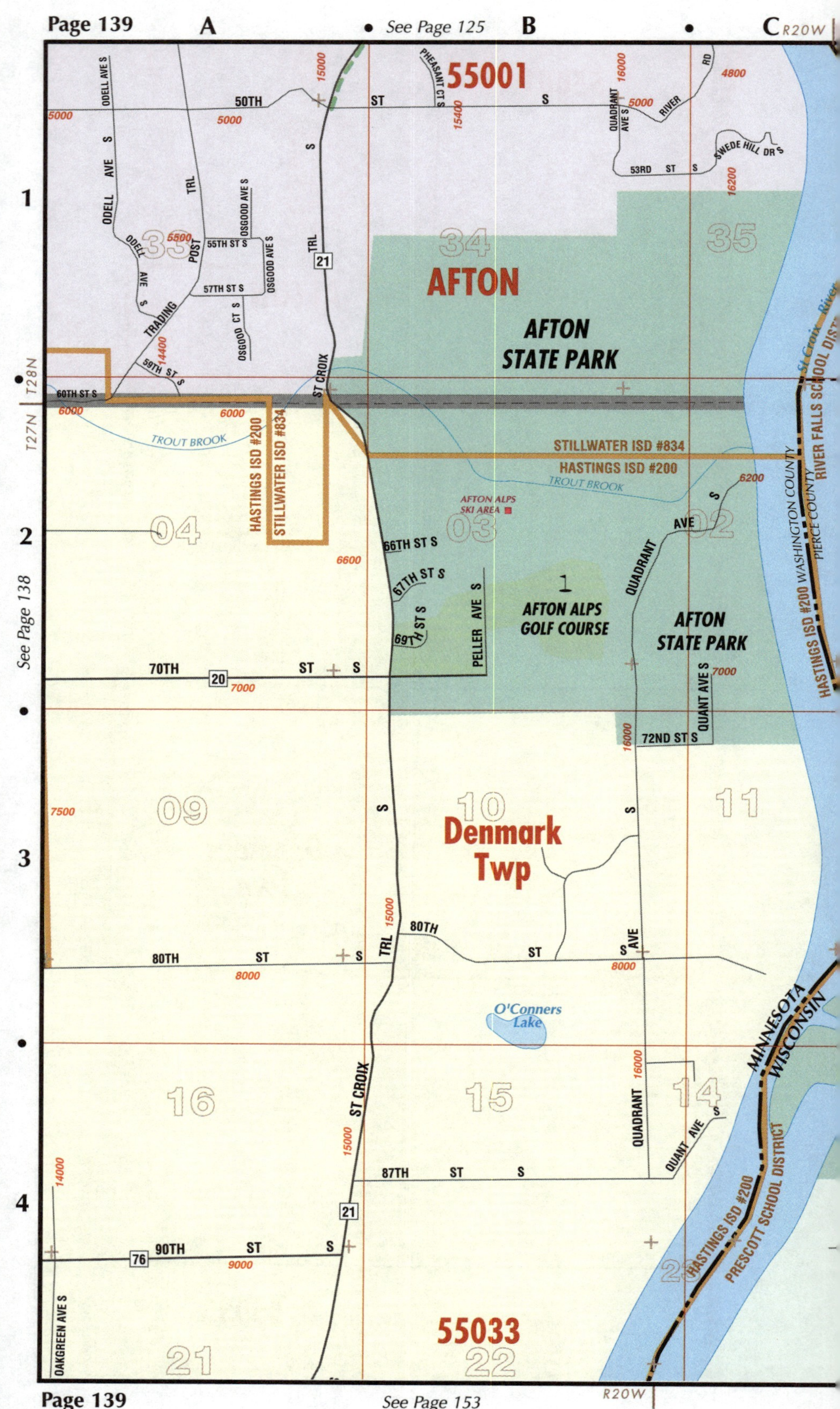

55001

ODELL AVE S

50TH   ST   S

PHEASANT CT S

QUADRANT AVE S

RIVER   RD

4800

5000

53RD   ST

SWEDE HILL DR S

6200

1

ODELL AVE S

TRL

POST

55TH ST S

OSGOOD AVE S

OSGOOD AVE S

5500

33

34

AFTON

35

ODELL AVE S

57TH ST S

OSGOOD CT S

TRADING

21

TRL

AFTON STATE PARK

59TH ST S

14400

60TH ST S

ST CROIX

6000

TROUT BROOK

HASTINGS ISD #200

STILLWATER ISD #834

STILLWATER ISD #834

HASTINGS ISD #200

TROUT BROOK

6200

2

04

6600

66TH ST S

67TH ST S

69TH ST S

PELLER AVE S

AFTON ALPS SKI AREA

03

1

AFTON ALPS GOLF COURSE

QUADRANT AVE

02

AFTON STATE PARK

QUANT AVE S

7000

70TH   ST   S

20   7000

72ND ST S

16000

7500

09

10

Denmark Twp

11

3

ST CROIX

TRL   15000

80TH   ST

80TH   ST   S   AVE

8000

O'Conners Lake

80TH   ST   S

8000

14000

16

ST CROIX

15000

15

O'Conners Lake

QUADRANT

16000

14

QUANT AVE S

4

87TH   ST   S

21

90TH   ST   S

76   9000

OAKGREEN AVE S

21

55033

22

ST CROIX RIVER

RIVER FALLS SCHOOL DISTRICT

HASTINGS ISD #200 WASHINGTON COUNTY

PIERCE COUNTY

MINNESOTA

WISCONSIN

HASTINGS ISD #200

PRESCOTT SCHOOL DISTRICT

See Page 138

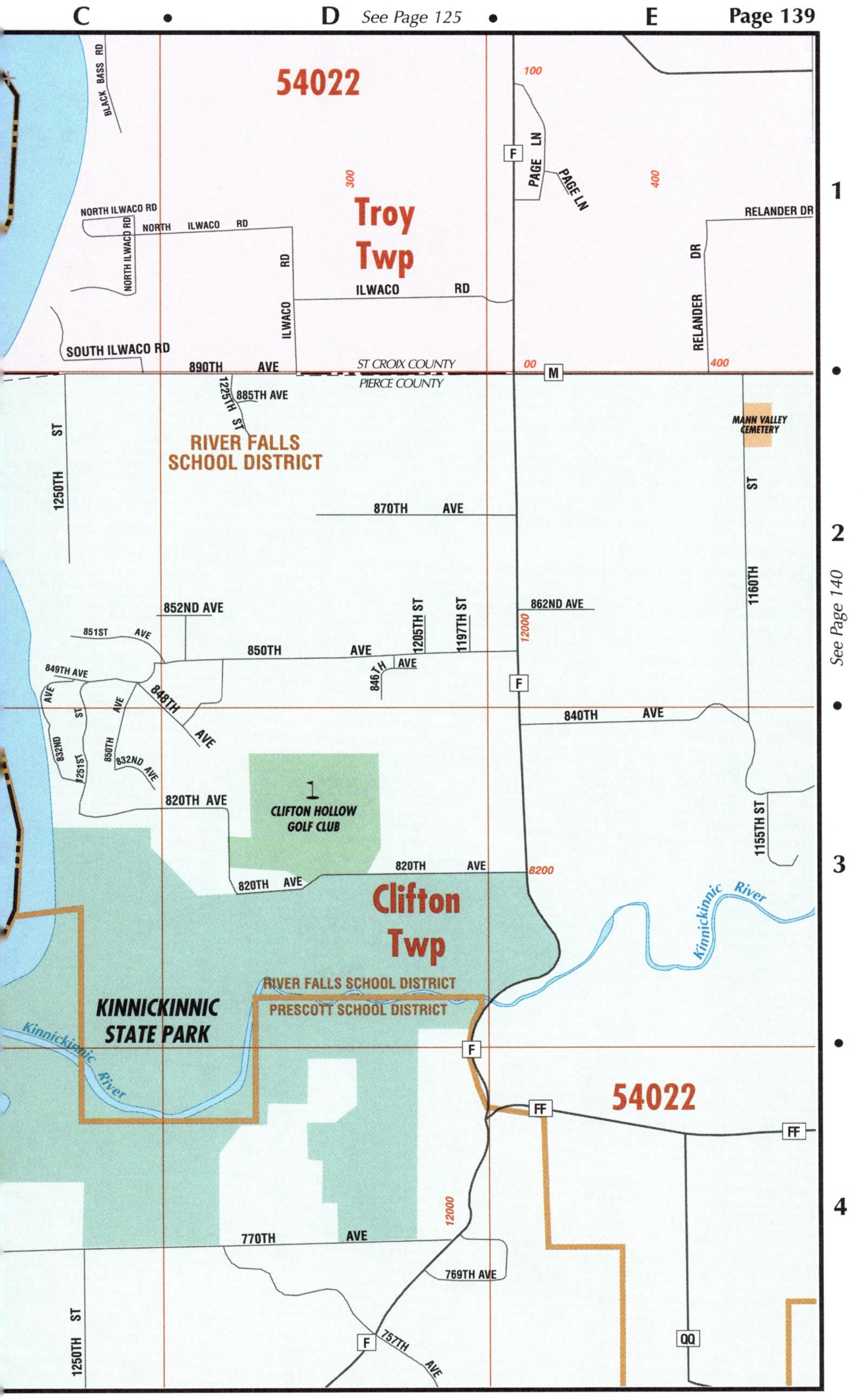

54022

BLACK BASS RD

100

F

PAGE LN

PAGE LN

300

Troy Twp

400

1

NORTH ILWACO RD

NORTH ILWACO RD

NORTH ILWACO RD

RELANDER DR

ILWACO RD

ILWACO RD

RELANDER DR

RELANDER DR

400

SOUTH ILWACO RD

890TH AVE

00 M

ST CROIX COUNTY
PIERCE COUNTY

1250TH ST

1225TH ST

885TH AVE

RIVER FALLS SCHOOL DISTRICT

MANN VALLEY CEMETERY

870TH AVE

1160TH ST

2

See Page 140

852ND AVE

1205TH ST

1197TH ST

862ND AVE

851ST AVE

850TH AVE

12000

849TH AVE

846TH AVE

840TH AVE

832ND AVE

1251ST ST

850TH ST

848TH AVE

832ND AVE

820TH AVE

1155TH ST

1
CLIFTON HOLLOW GOLF CLUB

820TH AVE

820TH AVE

8200

Kinnickinnic River

3

Clifton Twp

KINNICKINNIC STATE PARK

RIVER FALLS SCHOOL DISTRICT
PRESCOTT SCHOOL DISTRICT

Kinnickinnic River

F

54022

FF

FF

770TH AVE

12000

769TH AVE

4

1250TH ST

F

757TH AVE

QQ

See Page 153

• *See Page 126*

A   B   C

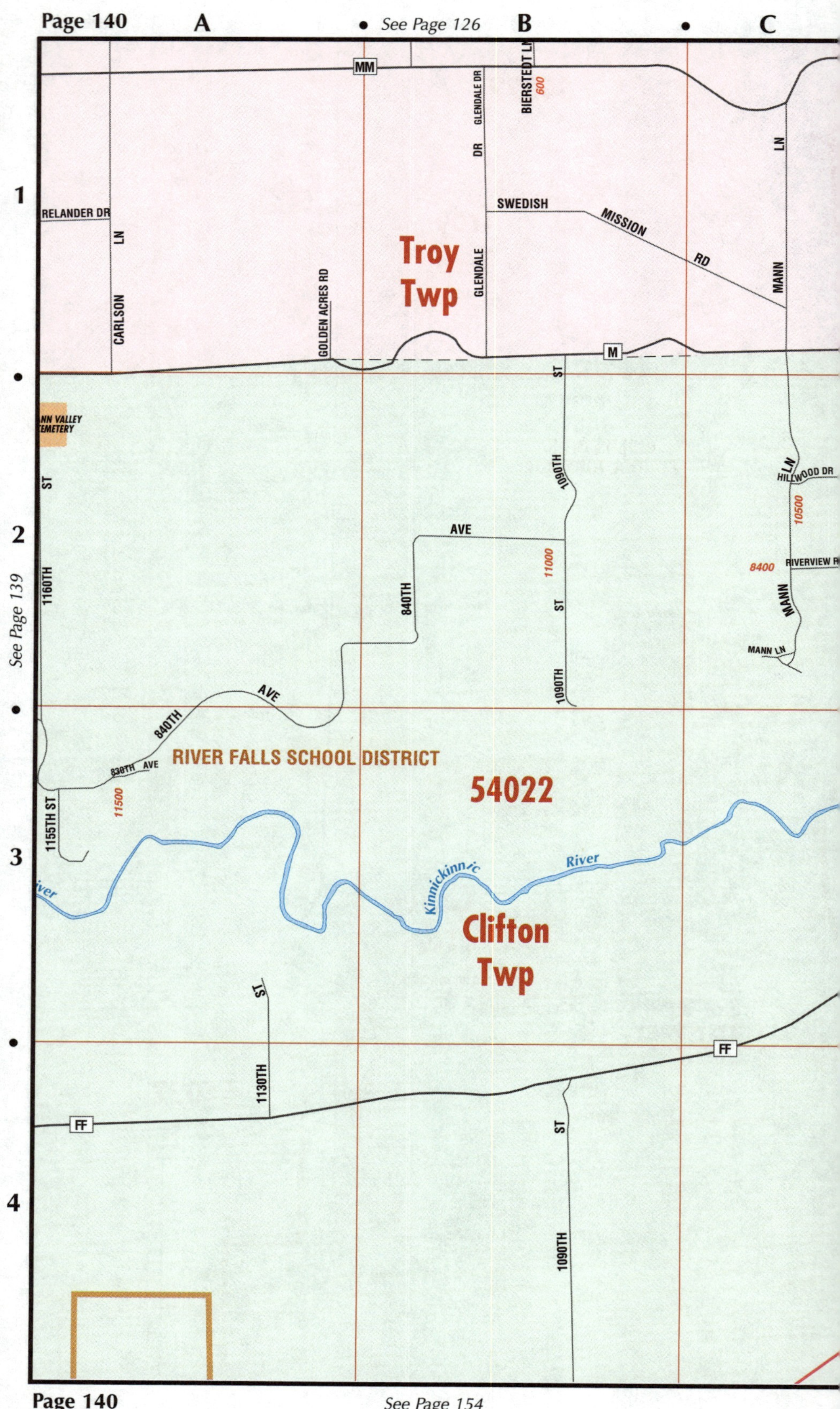

MM

BIERSTEDT LN   *600*

GLENDALE DR

DR

LN

1

RELANDER DR

LN

SWEDISH

MISSION

RD

MANN

See Page 139

CARLSON

GOLDEN ACRES RD

GLENDALE

Troy Twp

ST

M

NN VALLEY EMETERY

ST

1090TH

LN

HILLWOOD DR

10500

2

1160TH

840TH

AVE

ST

11000

8400

RIVERVIEW R

MANN

MANN LN

840TH

AVE

830TH AVE

11500

1090TH

1090TH

RIVER FALLS SCHOOL DISTRICT

54022

1155TH ST

River

Kinnickinnic

River

3

Clifton Twp

ST

FF

1130TH

ST

4

FF

1090TH

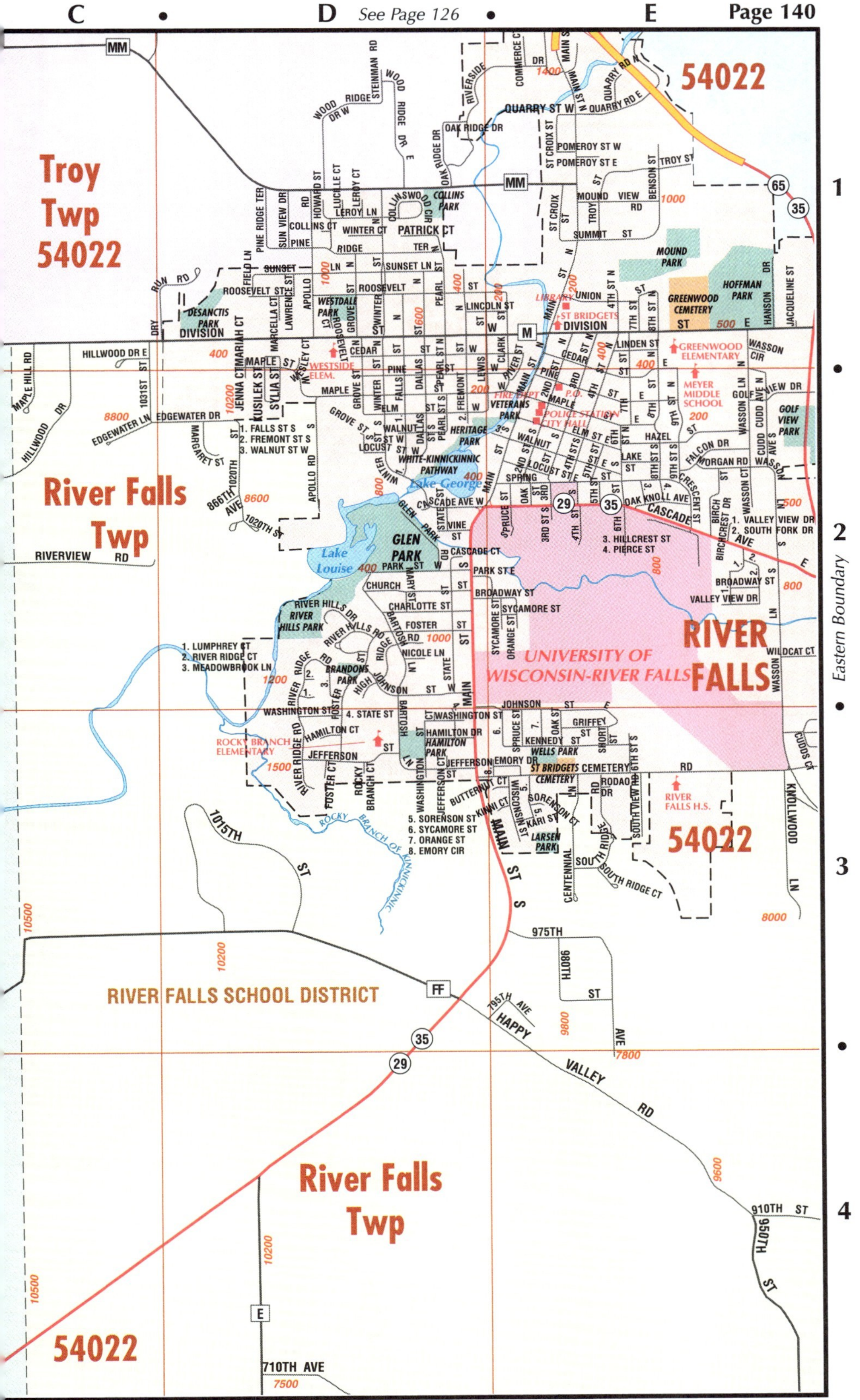

Troy Twp 54022

54022

River Falls Twp

River Falls School District

River Falls Twp

54022

RIVER FALLS

UNIVERSITY OF WISCONSIN-RIVER FALLS

54022

Eastern Boundary

● *See Page 127*

A   B   C

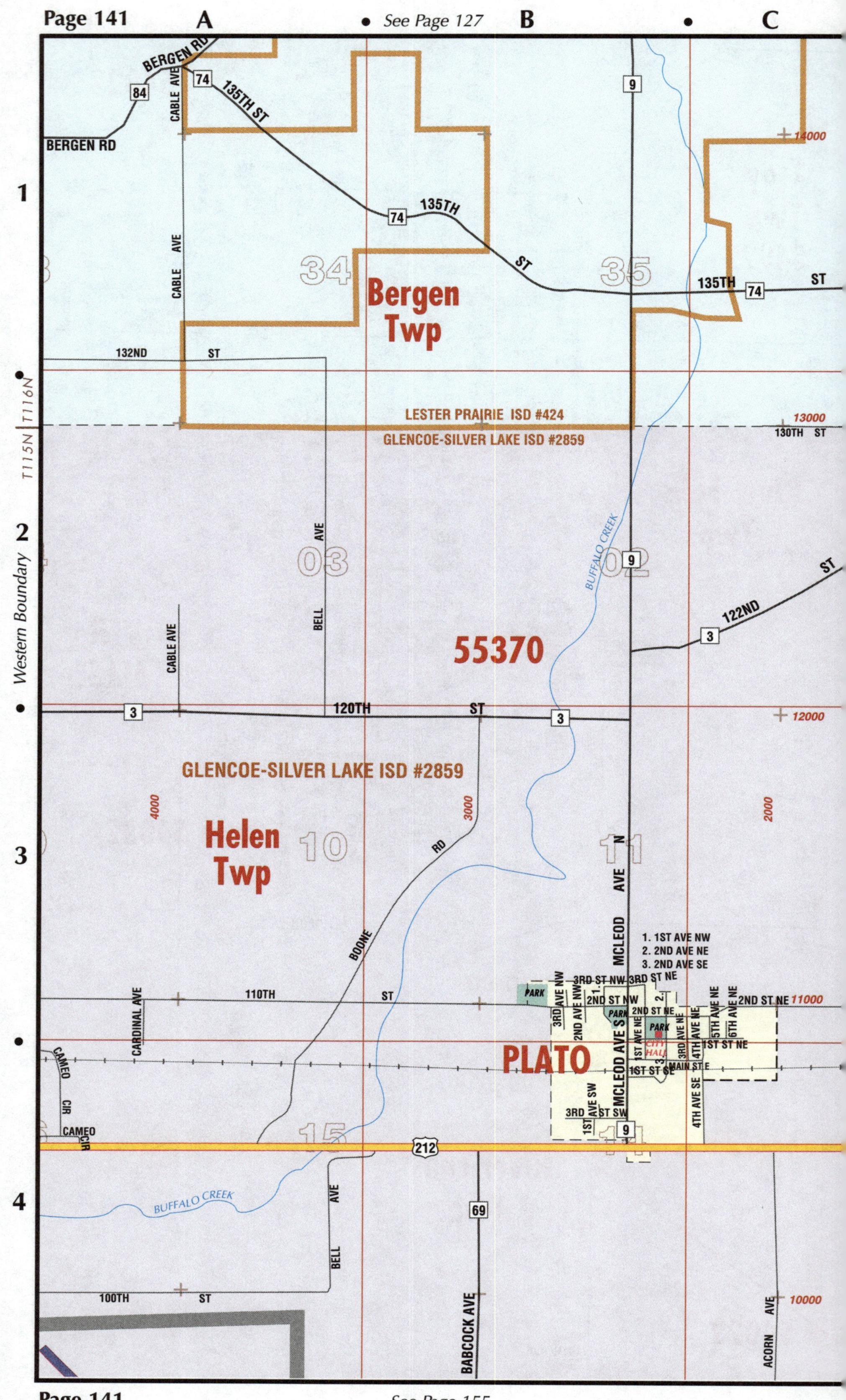

BERGEN RD

84

74

135TH ST

BERGEN RD

74

135TH ST

CABLE AVE

1

34

35

Bergen Twp

135TH 74 ST

9

14000

132ND ST

T115N | T116N

CABLE AVE

LESTER PRAIRIE ISD #424

GLENCOE-SILVER LAKE ISD #2859

13000

130TH ST

Western Boundary

BELL AVE

03

02

BUFFALO CREEK

9

2

CABLE AVE

55370

122ND ST

3

3

120TH ST

3

12000

GLENCOE-SILVER LAKE ISD #2859

4000

3000

2000

Helen Twp

10

BOONE RD

11

MCLEOD AVE N

3

1. 1ST AVE NW
2. 2ND AVE NE
3. 2ND AVE SE

CARDINAL AVE

110TH ST

PARK

3RD AVE NW

2ND AVE NW

3RD ST NE

2ND ST NW

3RD ST NE

11000

2ND ST NE

PARK

CITY HALL

5TH AVE NE

6TH AVE NE

2ND ST NE

MCLEOD AVE S

PLATO

1ST ST E

MAIN ST E

3RD AVE NE

4TH AVE NE

CAMEO CIR

CAMEO CIR

15

3RD AVE SW

1ST AVE SW

4TH AVE SE

212

9

BELL AVE

4

BUFFALO CREEK

69

100TH ST

BABCOCK AVE

ACORN AVE

10000

See Page 155

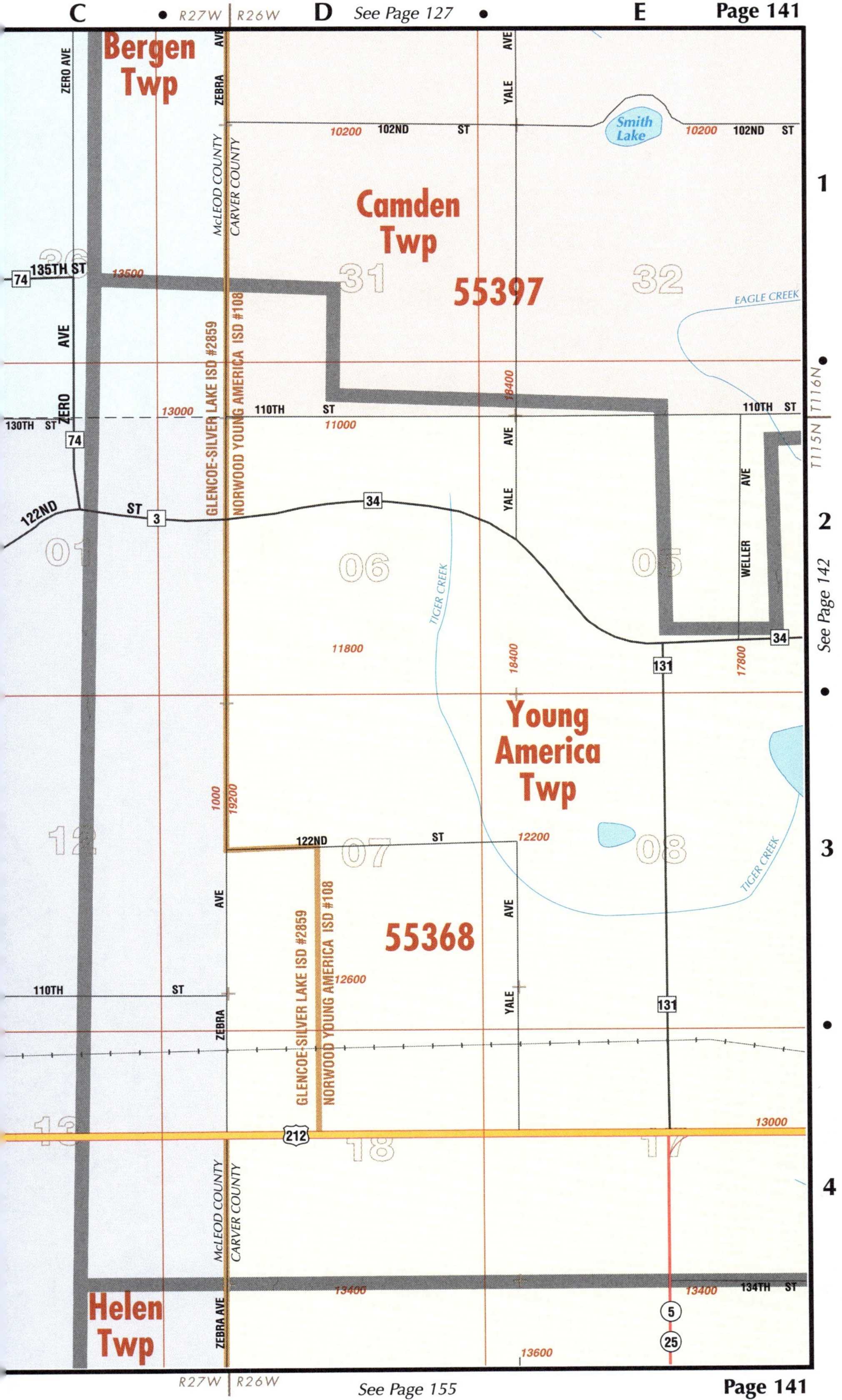

Bergen Twp

ZERO AVE

ZEBRA

McLEOD COUNTY | CARVER COUNTY

10200 102ND ST

Smith Lake

10200 102ND ST

AVE

YALE

Camden Twp

55397

1

26

74 135TH ST 13500

31

32

EAGLE CREEK

AVE

GLENCOE-SILVER LAKE ISD #2859

NORWOOD YOUNG AMERICA ISD #108

ZERO 13000

130TH ST 74

110TH ST 11000

18400

110TH ST

T115N | T116N

AVE

YALE

122ND ST 3

34

01

06

TIGER CREEK

18400

05

WELLER AVE

34

See Page 142

2

11800

131

17800

Young America Twp

1000 19200

12

122ND ST 12200

07

AVE

YALE

08

TIGER CREEK

3

55368

GLENCOE-SILVER LAKE ISD #2859

NORWOOD YOUNG AMERICA ISD #108

12600

AVE

YALE

110TH ST

ZEBRA

131

13

18

212

17

13000

4

McLEOD COUNTY | CARVER COUNTY

Helen Twp

ZEBRA AVE

13400 134TH ST

5

13600

25

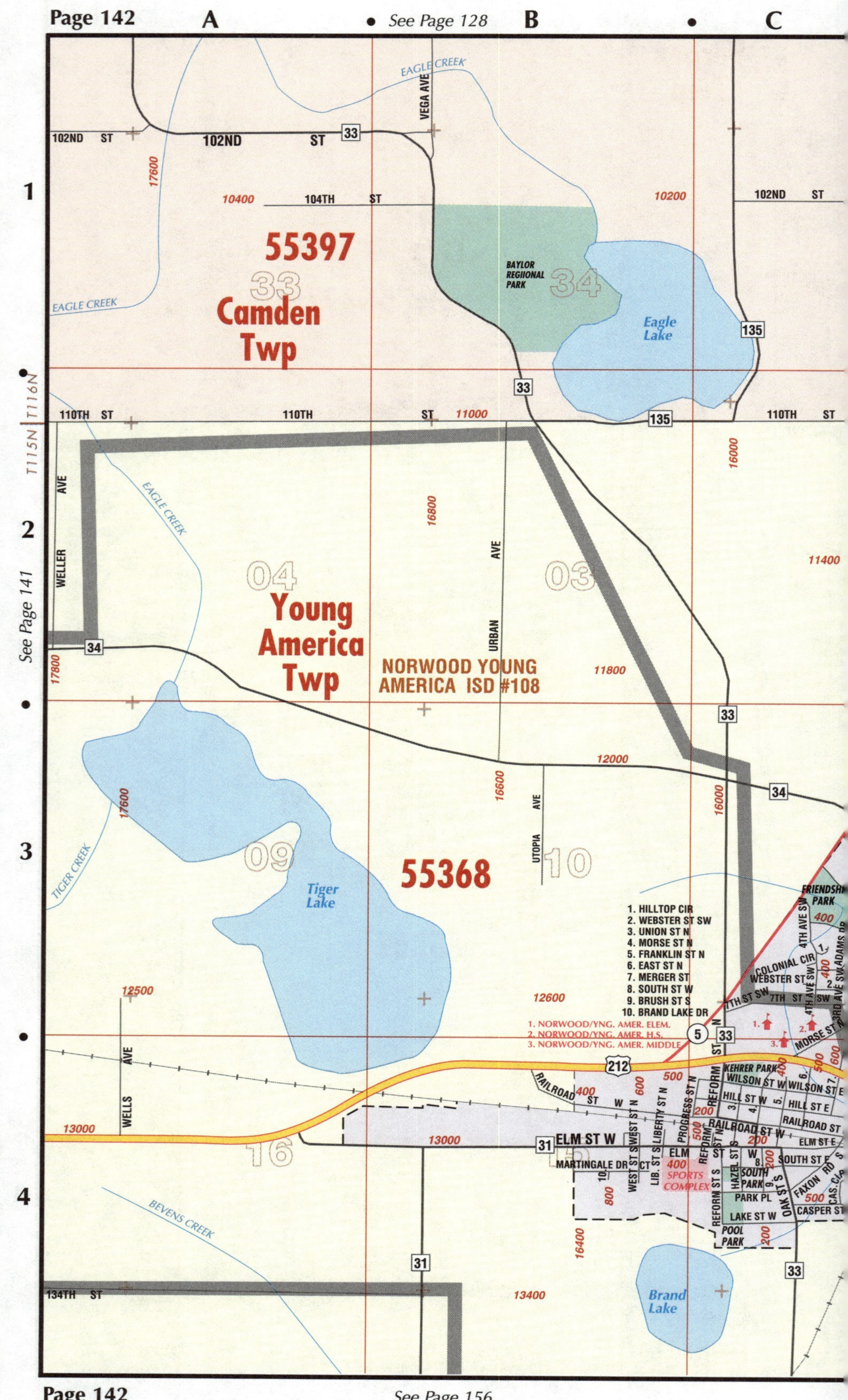

A • See Page 128 B • C

See Page 128

102ND ST
102ND ST 33
VEGA AVE
EAGLE CREEK

1

17600
10400 104TH ST
10200 102ND ST

55397
33
Camden Twp

EAGLE CREEK

BAYLOR REGIONAL PARK
34
Eagle Lake
135

33

110TH ST
110TH ST 11000
135 110TH ST

16000

WELLER AVE
EAGLE CREEK

2

16800

T115N | T116N

See Page 141

04
Young America Twp
34
17800

URBAN AVE
03
11400

NORWOOD YOUNG AMERICA ISD #108
11800

12000
33
34

16600

16000

09
Tiger Lake
TIGER CREEK
17600

3

55368
10
UTOPIA AVE

FRIENDSHIP PARK
400
4TH AVE SW
COLONIAL CIR
WEBSTER ST SW
ADAMS AVE
LAKE SW

1. HILLTOP CIR
2. WEBSTER ST SW
3. UNION ST N
4. MORSE ST N
5. FRANKLIN ST N
6. EAST ST N
7. MERGER ST
8. SOUTH ST W
9. BRUSH ST S
10. BRAND LAKE DR

12500

12600

7TH AVE SW
MORSE ST E

1. NORWOOD/YNG. AMER. ELEM.
2. NORWOOD/YNG. AMER. H.S.
3. NORWOOD/YNG. AMER. MIDDLE

5
33

WELLS AVE

16

13000

212
RAILROAD ST
400 ST
600

KEHRER PARK
WILSON ST W WILSON ST E
HILL ST W HILL ST E
RAILROAD ST W RAILROAD ST
ELM ST W ELM ST E
200

REFORM ST
PROGRESS ST N
LIBERTY ST N

13000
ELM ST W
31
MARTINGALE DR
WEST ST S
WEST ST N
LIB. ST
ELM
400
SPORTS COMPLEX
800

HAZEL ST S
SOUTH ST E
OAK ST S
SOUTH PARK
PARK PL
FAXON RD S
CASPER ST
500
CAS. CAS. CT

4

BEVENS CREEK

16400

LAKE ST W
POOL PARK
200

Brand Lake
33

13400

134TH ST
31

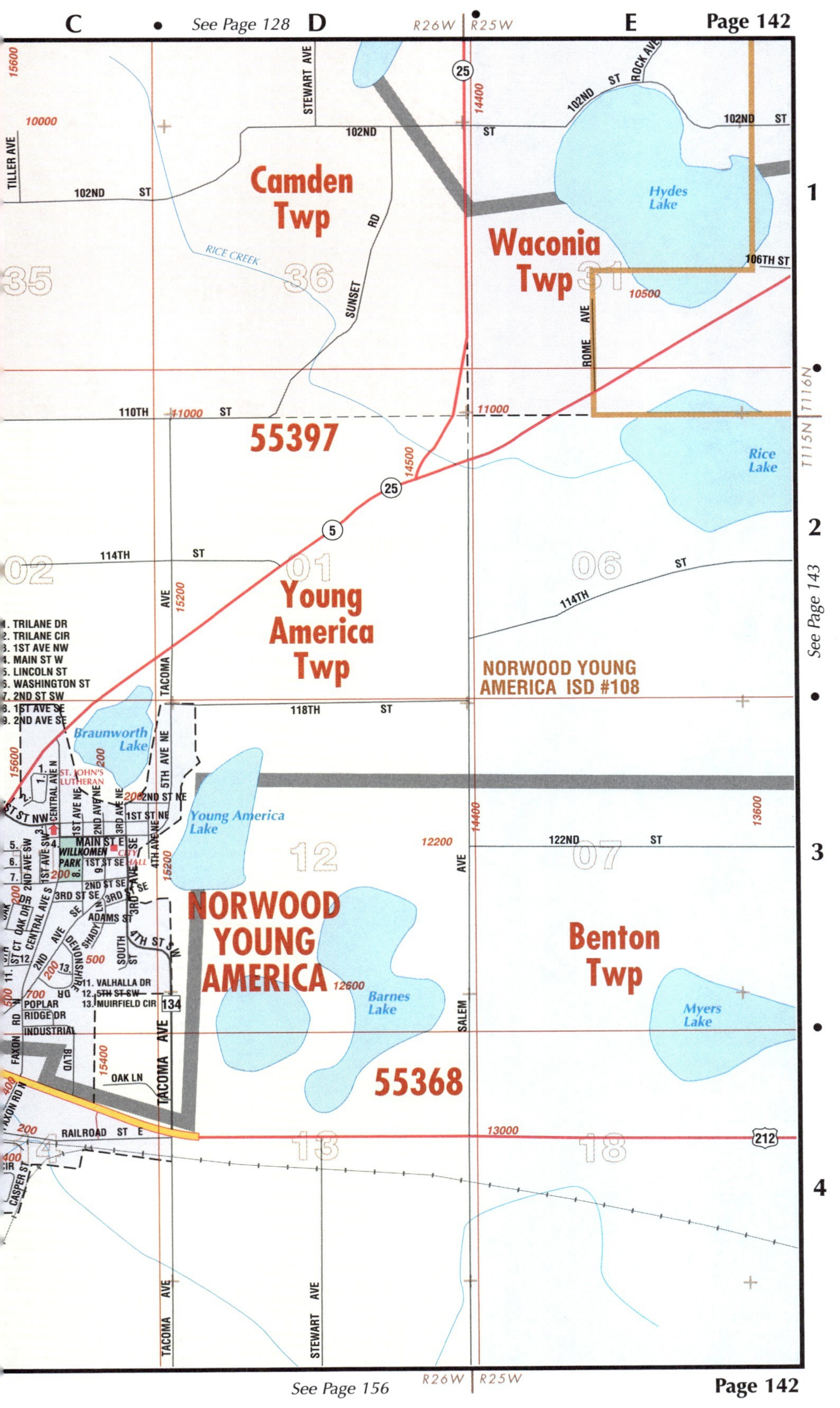

15600
10000
102ND ST
TILLER AVE
STEWART AVE
102ND
102ND ST
ST
ROCK AVE

Camden Twp

14400

25

ST

102ND ST

Hydes Lake

1

Rice Creek

35

36

SUNSET RD

Waconia Twp

31

106TH ST

ROME AVE

10500

110TH 11000 ST

11000

55397

14500

Rice Lake

T115N | T116N

See Page 143

25

5

114TH ST

15200

02

01

06

ST

114TH ST

2

Young America Twp

TACOMA AVE

NORWOOD YOUNG AMERICA ISD #108

118TH ST

Braunworth Lake

5TH AVE NE

118TH ST

15600

ST. JOHN'S LUTHERAN

CENTRAL AVE N

2ND ST NE

1ST ST NE

2ND AVE NE

Young America Lake

14400

13600

NORWOOD YOUNG AMERICA

12

122ND ST

07

12200

AVE

3

MAIN ST E
WILLKOMMEN PARK
CITY HALL
4TH AVE NE

15200

Benton Twp

2ND ST SE

3RD ST

ADAMS ST

SOUTH ST

SHADY LN

12600

Barnes Lake

SALEM AVE

Myers Lake

POPLAR RIDGE DR

VALHALLA DR
5TH ST SW
MUIRFIELD CIR

134

INDUSTRIAL

55368

OAK LN

15400

BLVD

FAXON RD W

RAILROAD ST E

13000

212

400
200

CASPER ST

4

TACOMA AVE

TACOMA AVE

STEWART AVE

13

18

1. TRILANE DR
2. TRILANE CIR
3. 1ST AVE NW
4. MAIN ST W
5. LINCOLN ST
6. WASHINGTON ST
7. 2ND ST SW
8. 1ST AVE SE
9. 2ND AVE SE

A ● *See Page 129* B ● C

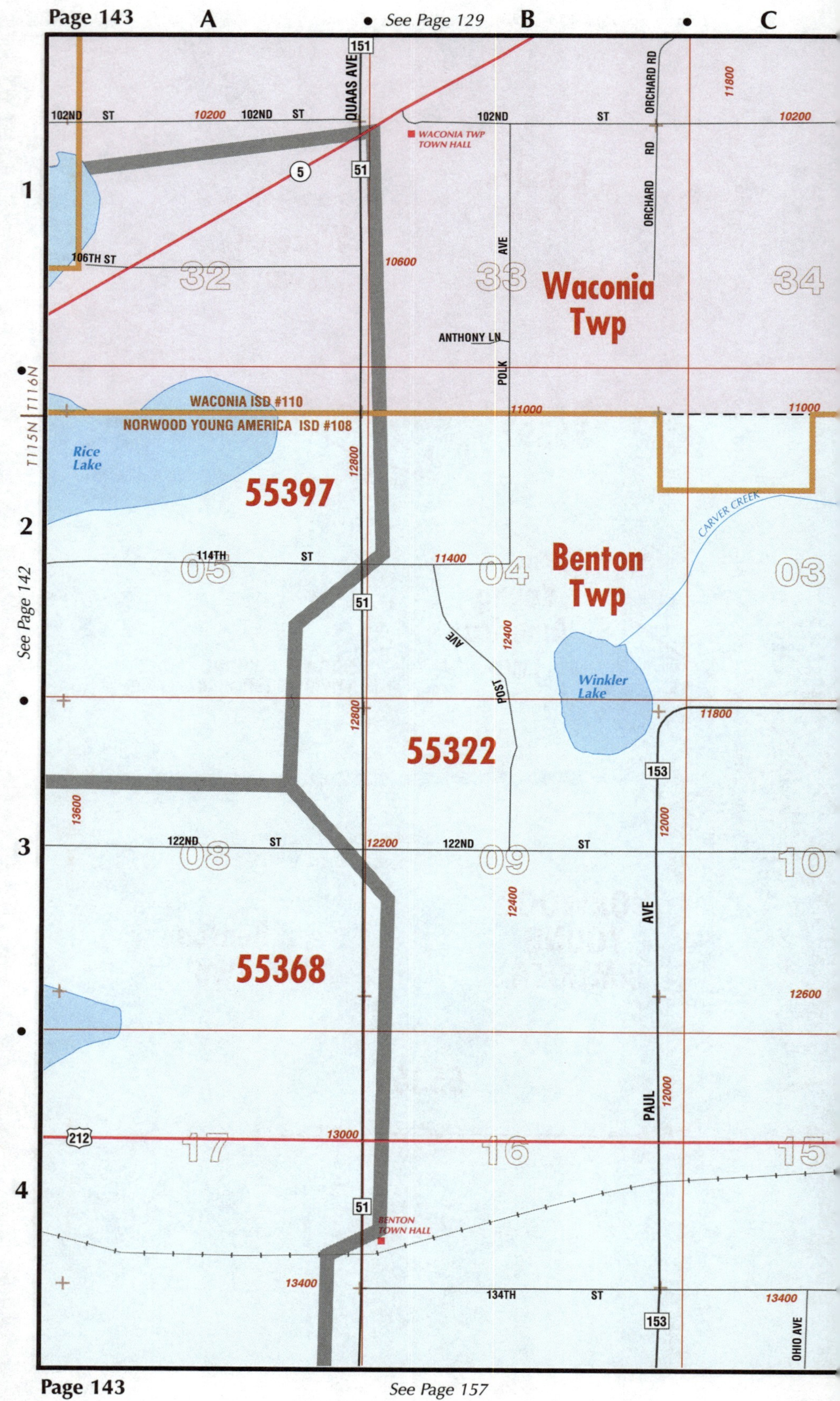

QUAAS AVE

151

102ND ST 10200 102ND ST 102ND ST 10200

⬛ WACONIA TWP TOWN HALL

ORCHARD RD

11800

5

51

1

106TH ST 10600 33 **Waconia Twp** 34

32 ORCHARD RD

ANTHONY LN

POLK AVE

T115N | T116N

WACONIA ISD #110 11000 11000

NORWOOD YOUNG AMERICA ISD #108

Rice Lake

55397

CARVER CREEK

12800

2

114TH ST 05 11400 04 **Benton Twp** 03

51

See Page 142

POST AVE

12400

Winkler Lake

12000

55322

153

11800

13600

12000

3

122ND ST 08 12200 122ND ST 09 ST 10

12400

55368

AVE

12600

PAUL 12000

212 13000 17 16 15

4

51

⬛ *BENTON TOWN HALL*

13400 134TH ST 13400

153

OHIO AVE

10000

ELM CREEK RD

10200

102ND ST

102ND ST

Waconia Twp

35

36

Laketown Twp

1

OAK 11200

AVE

9600

T115N | T116N

110TH ST

ST

11000

110TH ST

ST

110TH ST

140

NORWOOD YOUNG AMERICA ISD #108

WACONIA ISD #110

CARVER CREEK

02

MARKET AVE

11400

AVE

2

See Page 144

Benton Twp

NORWOOD YOUNG AMERICA ISD #108

WACONIA ISD #110

284

9500

153

11800

118TH ST

MARKET

11800

Dahlgren Twp

11200

10400

2000

11

12

55322

9800

NORWOOD YOUNG AMERICA ISD #108

WACONIA ISD #110

9600

36

3

122ND ST

GOLD NUGGET DR

PARKSIDE CREEK ST

PARKSIDE ST

MEADOW ST

MEADOW ST

BENTON ST W

600

BENTON ST E

BENTON ST

BENTON ST 500

Benton Lake

1000

PAUL AVE

ST. BERNARD 400

9600

12800

COLOGNE

Meuwissen Lake

400

CHURCH ST N

PARK ST

VILLA DR

LAKE ST W LAKE ST

EDWARD AVE N

41

Dahlgren Twp

HENRY AVE

PLAYHOUSE ST PLAYHOUSE ST E

PLAYHOUSE ST

MARKET ST W

200

JACOB AVE S

13000

212

14

36

10500

400

LOUIS ST W

CONRAD ST

PAUL AVE S

284

ADAMS RD

SIMON AVE S

EDWARD AVE S

LOUIS ST E 400

2000

200

9600

CITY HALL

PLEASANT CIR

1. VILLA DR
2. JACOB AVE S
3. JACOB AVE N
4. MILL ST E
5. JOHN AVE S
6. JOHN AVE N
7. MARKET LN S

53

4

134TH ST

NAPLES AVE

134TH ST

ST

13400

MARKET AVE

13400

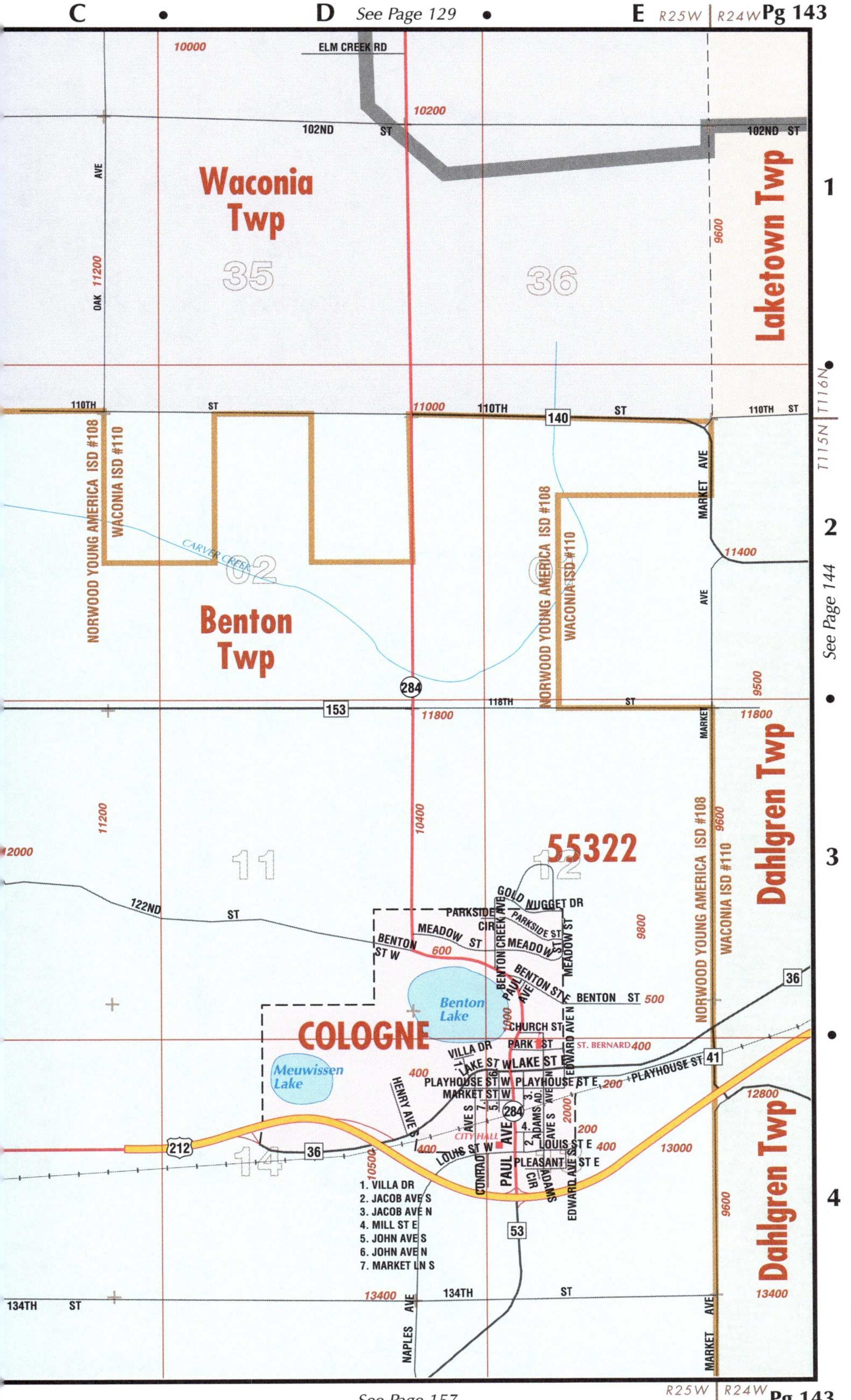

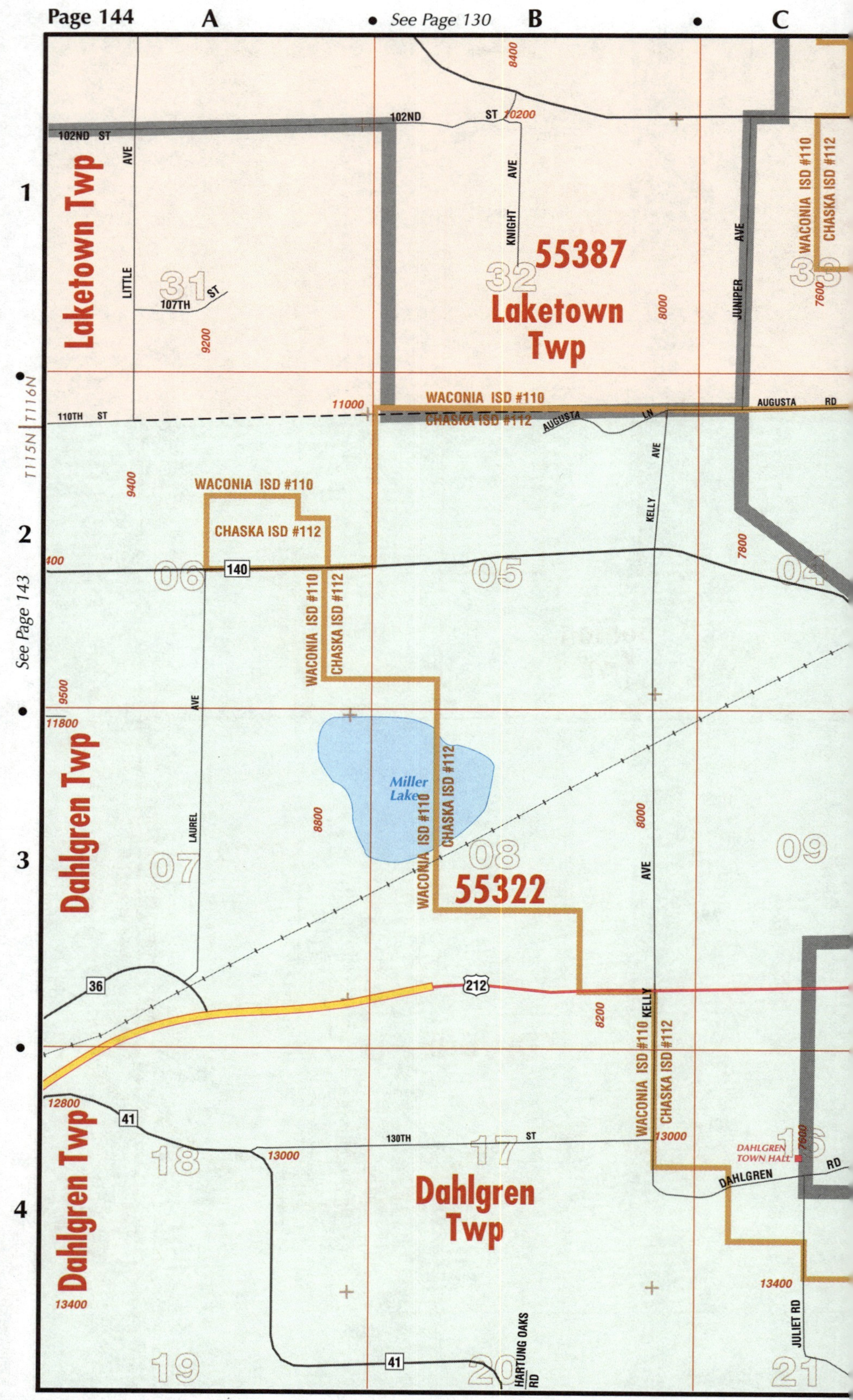

A   B   C

55387
Laketown Twp

Laketown Twp

1

31

102ND ST
102ND ST 10200
107TH ST
9200
8400
KNIGHT AVE
8000
JUNIPER AVE
32
33
7600
WACONIA ISD #110
CHASKA ISD #112

T115N | T116N

WACONIA ISD #110
CHASKA ISD #112
110TH ST
11000
AUGUSTA LN
AUGUSTA RD
KELLY AVE

2

9400
WACONIA ISD #110
CHASKA ISD #112
06
140
05
04
7800
400

See Page 143

9500
11800

3

Dahlgren Twp

07
LAUREL AVE
8800
WACONIA ISD #110
CHASKA ISD #112
Miller Lake
08
09
8000
KELLY AVE

55322

36
212
8200

12800
41
41
13000
130TH ST
17
18
WACONIA ISD #110
CHASKA ISD #112
13000
16
7600
DAHLGREN TOWN HALL
DAHLGREN RD

4

Dahlgren Twp

Dahlgren Twp

13400
13400
JULIET RD

19
41
20
HARTUNG OAKS RD
21

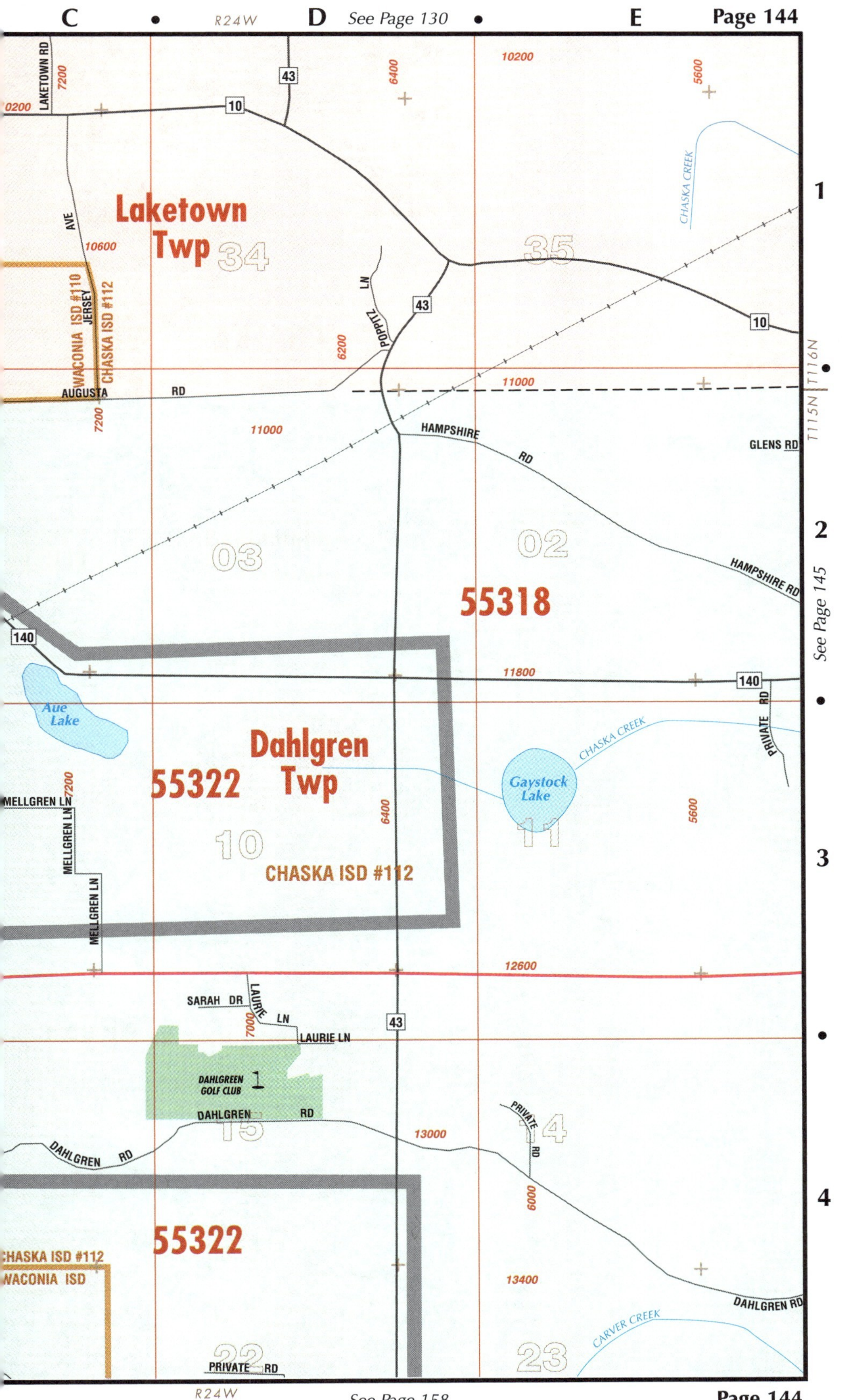

LAKETOWN RD
7200
0200
43
10
6400
10200
5600

Laketown Twp 34
AVE
10600
LN
POPPITZ
43
35
CHASKA CREEK
T115N | T116N
1

WACONIA ISD #110
JERSEY
CHASKA ISD #112
6200
43
10

AUGUSTA RD
7200
11000
11000
HAMPSHIRE RD
GLENS RD

140
03
02
55318
HAMPSHIRE RD
See Page 145
2

Aue Lake
11800
140
PRIVATE RD

Dahlgren Twp
55322
MELLGREN LN
7200
10
6400
CHASKA CREEK
Gaystock Lake
11
5600
3

MELLGREN LN
MELLGREN LN
CHASKA ISD #112

12600

SARAH DR
LAURIE LN
7000
LAURIE LN
43

DAHLGREN GOLF CLUB 1
DAHLGREN RD
15
13000
PRIVATE RD
14
4

DAHLGREN RD

55322
6000

CHASKA ISD #112
WACONIA ISD
13400
DAHLGREN RD

22
PRIVATE RD
23
CARVER CREEK

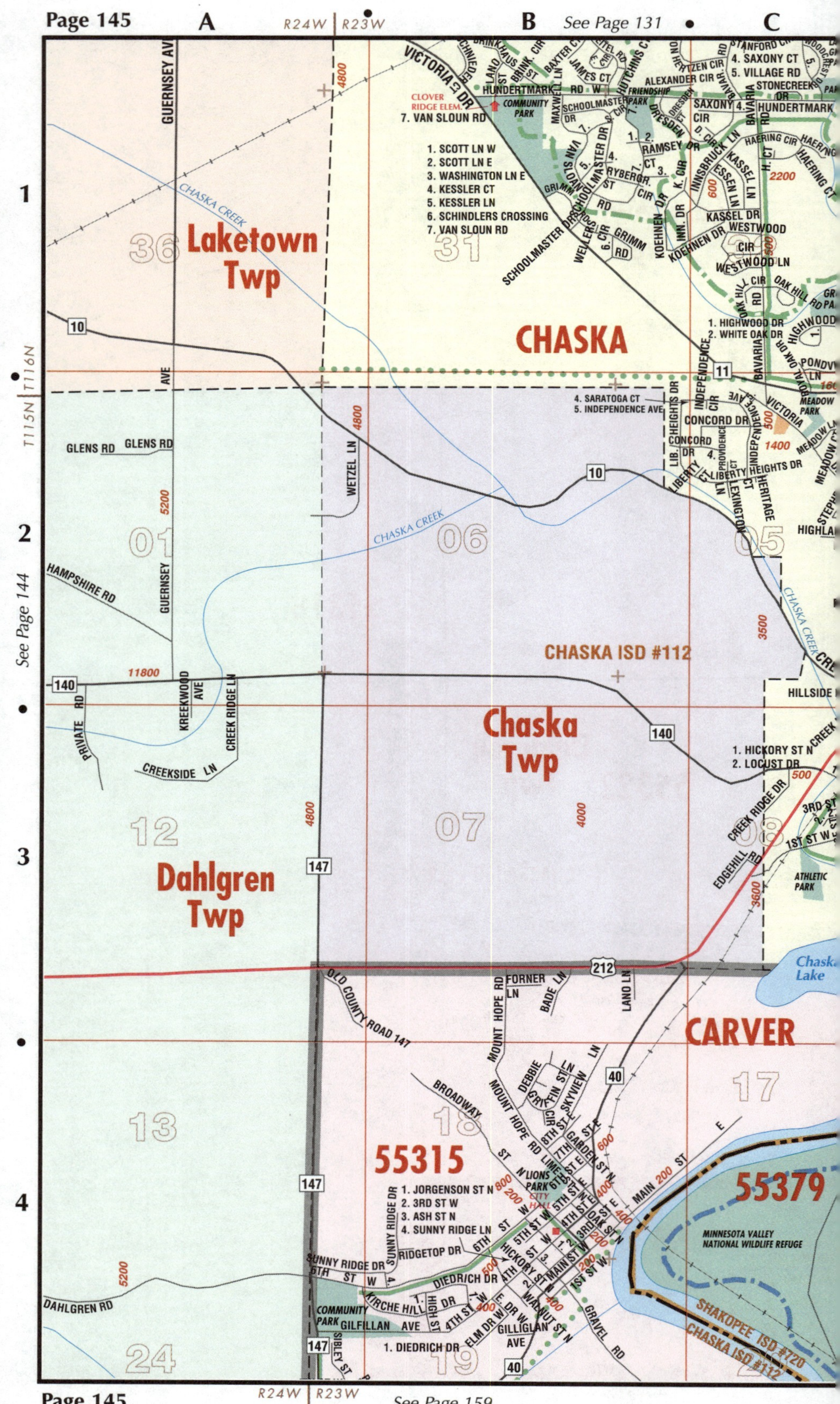

GUERNSEY AVE

VICTORIA ST DR

CHINESE ST

BRINKHAUS ST

BRINK CIR

BAXTER CT

JAMES CT

HUTCHINS CT

STANFORD CT

4. SAXONY CT
5. VILLAGE RD

STONECREEK
DR

CLOVER
RIDGE ELEM.
7. VAN SLOUN RD

COMMUNITY
PARK

MAXWELL

SCHOOLMASTER
DR

ALEXANDER CIR

SAXONY
CIR

BAVARIA
CIR

HAERING CIR

HAERING
CT

HUNDERTMARK

HUNDERTMARK
RD

SCHOOLMASTER DR

DRESDEN

RAMSEY

RYBERG

INNSBRUCK LN

KASSEL LN

HAERING

CHASKA CREEK

**Laketown
Twp**

36

1. SCOTT LN W
2. SCOTT LN E
3. WASHINGTON LN E
4. KESSLER CT
5. KESSLER LN
6. SCHINDLERS CROSSING
7. VAN SLOUN RD

31

GRIMM

WELERS DR

SCHOOLMASTER RD

GRIMM
ST

KOEHNEN DR E

KOEHNEN DR W

600

KASSEL DR

WESTWOOD

WESTWOOD LN

OAK HILL CIR

OAK HILL RD

2200

10

CHASKA

1. HIGHWOOD DR
2. WHITE OAK DR

INDEPENDENCE

INDEPENDENCE

PROVIDENCE DR

HIGHWOOD
DR

HIGHWOOD

11

BAVARIA RD

VICTORIA

PONDVIEW

MEADOW
PARK

MEADOW

T115N | T116N

GLENS RD   GLENS RD

4800

4. SARATOGA CT
5. INDEPENDENCE AVE

LIB. HEIGHTS DR

CONCORD DR

CONCORD
DR

LIBERTY
DR

LIBERTY HEIGHTS DR

4.

1400

500

HERITAGE

HIGHLA

STEPHE

AVE

5200

01

WETZEL LN

CHASKA CREEK

06

10

LEXINGTON

05

See Page 144

HAMPSHIRE RD

GUERNSEY

CHASKA ISD #112

3500

CHASKA CREEK CR

11800

140

KREEKWOOD
AVE

CREEK RIDGE LN

**Chaska
Twp**

HILLSIDE

2

PRIVATE RD

CREEKSIDE LN

140

1. HICKORY ST N
2. LOCUST DR

CREEK

500

3RD ST

12

07

4000

08

1ST ST W

CREEK RIDGE DR

EDGEHILL RD

3600

ATHLETIC
PARK

147

**Dahlgren
Twp**

3

212

FORNER
LN

BADE LN

LANO LN

*Chaska
Lake*

OLD COUNTY ROAD 147

MOUNT HOPE RD

CARVER

DEBBIE LN

GRIFFIN LN

SKYVIEW

GARDEN ST

8TH ST E

40

E

17

13

BROADWAY

MOUNT HOPE RD

18

600

MAIN ST

55379

55315

1. JORGENSON ST N
2. 3RD ST W
3. ASH ST N
4. SUNNY RIDGE LN

N LIONS
PARK
CITY
HALL

800

200

5TH ST N

4TH ST N

6TH ST

5TH ST W

4TH ST W

3RD ST W

2ND ST W

MAIN ST

600

400

**MINNESOTA VALLEY
NATIONAL WILDLIFE REFUGE**

4

SUNNY RIDGE DR

5200

RIDGETOP DR

SUNNY RIDGE DR

6TH

5TH ST W

KIRCHE HILL

HIGH DR

GILFILLAN
AVE

4TH

DIEDRICH DR

HICKORY ST

WALNUT ST

ELM DR E

ELM DR W

WALNUT ST N

1ST ST E

GRAVEL RD

SHAKOPEE ISD #720

CHASKA ISD #112

DAHLGREN RD

24

COMMUNITY
PARK

GILFILLAN
AVE

1. DIEDRICH DR

SIBLEY ST

19

GILLIGAN
AVE

40

147

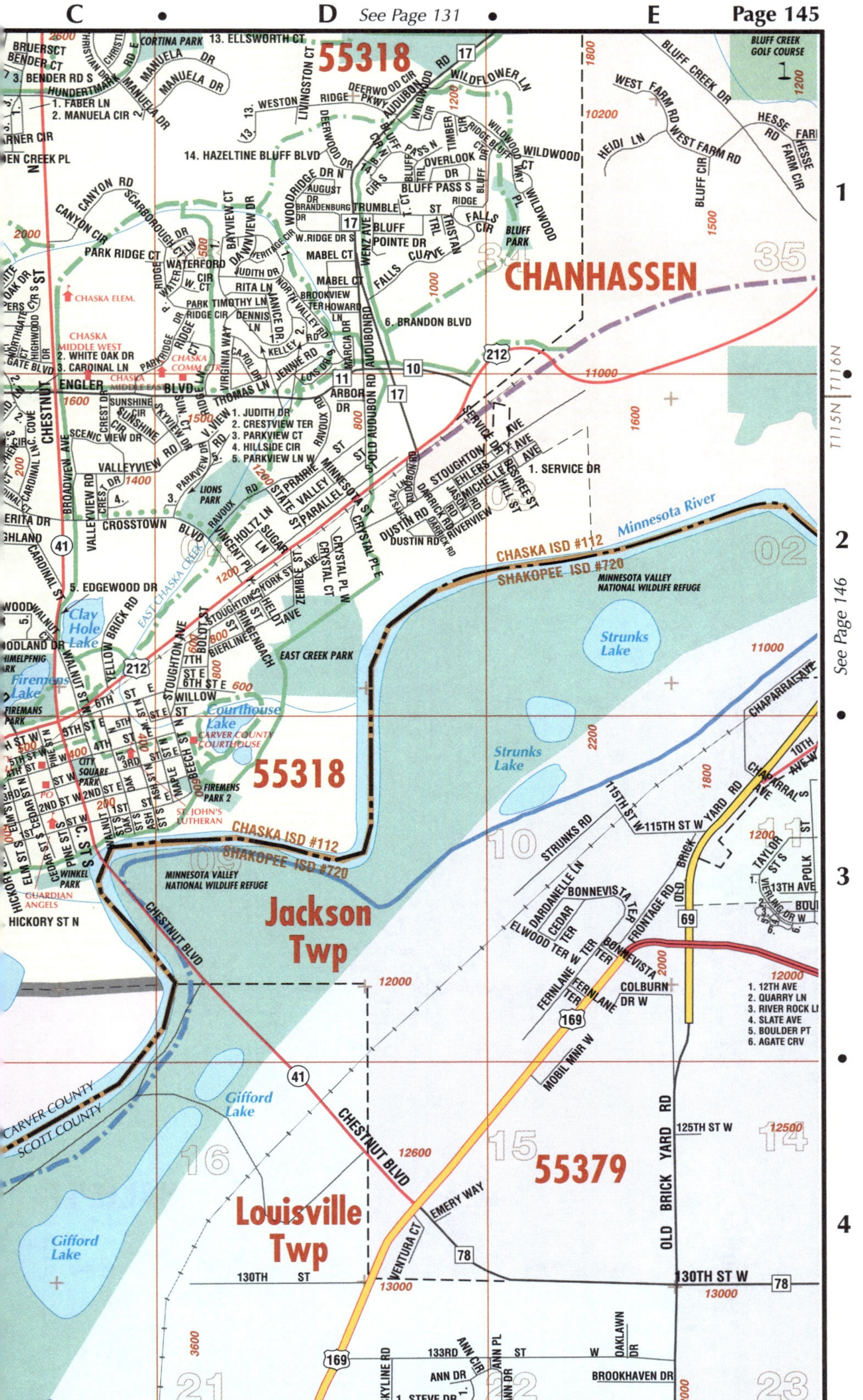

BLUFF CREEK GOLF COURSE

55318

WILDFLOWER LN

CHANHASSEN

35

14. HAZELTINE BLUFF BLVD

6. BRANDON BLVD

CHASKA ELEM.

CHASKA MIDDLE WEST
2. WHITE OAK LN
3. CARDINAL LN

CHASKA COMM

ENGLER BLVD

CHASKA MIDDLE EAST

1. JUDITH DR
2. CRESTVIEW TER
3. PARKVIEW CT
4. HILLSIDE CIR
5. PARKVIEW LN W

1. SERVICE DR

Minnesota River

CHASKA ISD #112

SHAKOPEE ISD #720

MINNESOTA VALLEY NATIONAL WILDLIFE REFUGE

Strunks Lake

5. EDGEWOOD DR

Clay Hole Lake

Firemens Lake

LIONS Park

VALLEYVIEW

CROSSTOWN

East Creek Park

Strunks Lake

Courthouse Lake

Carver County Courthouse

55318

Firemens Park 2

ST JOHN'S LUTHERAN

CHASKA ISD #112

SHAKOPEE ISD #720

MINNESOTA VALLEY NATIONAL WILDLIFE REFUGE

GUARDIAN ANGELS

HICKORY ST N

Winkel Park

Jackson Twp

12000

Gifford Lake

CARVER COUNTY
SCOTT COUNTY

16

Gifford Lake

Louisville Twp

130TH ST

13000

21

55379

125TH ST W

12500

14

130TH ST W

13000

OLD BRICK YARD RD

1. 12TH AVE
2. QUARRY LN
3. RIVER ROCK LI
4. SLATE AVE
5. BOULDER PT
6. AGATE CRV

COLBURN DR W

CHAPARRAL AVE

69

12000

133RD ST

BROOKHAVEN DR

22

23

See Page 159

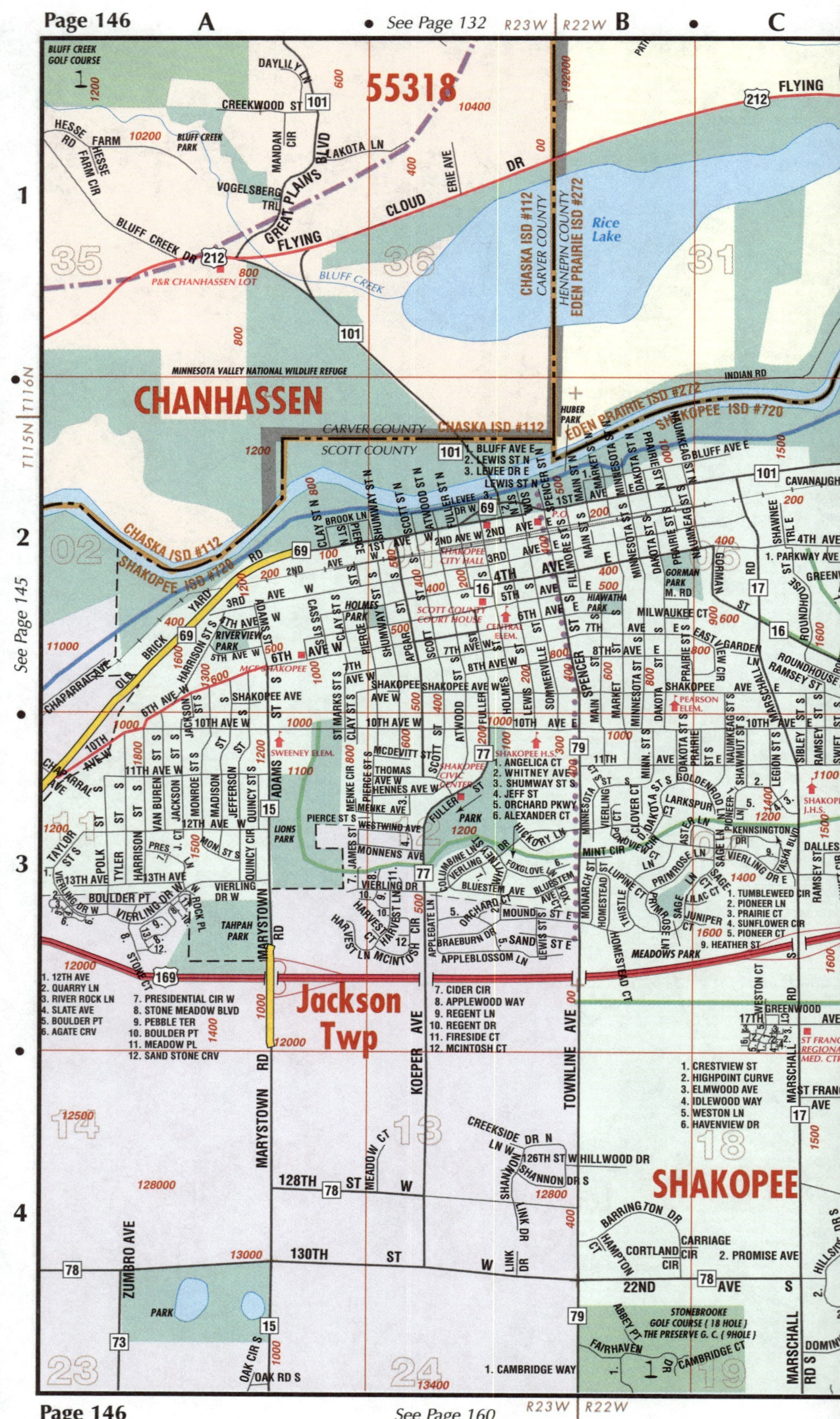

55318
CHANHASSEN
SHAKOPEE
Jackson Twp
BLUFF CREEK GOLF COURSE
BLUFF CREEK PARK
MINNESOTA VALLEY NATIONAL WILDLIFE REFUGE
P&R CHANHASSEN LOT
Rice Lake
CHASKA ISD #112
CARVER COUNTY
HENNEPIN COUNTY
EDEN PRAIRIE ISD #272
SCOTT COUNTY
SHAKOPEE ISD #720
HUBER PARK
FLYING CLOUD DR
GREAT PLAINS BLVD
BLUFF CREEK DR
CREEKWOOD ST
DAYLILY LN
LAKOTA LN
VOGELSBERG TRL
MANDAN CIR
ERIE AVE
HESSE FARM RD
HESSE FARM CIR
BLUFF CREEK
INDIAN RD
CAVANAUGH
1. BLUFF AVE E
2. LEWIS ST N
3. LEVEE DR E
SHAKOPEE CITY HALL
SCOTT COUNTY COURT HOUSE
CENTRAL ELEM.
HOLMES PARK
RIVERVIEW PARK
HIAWATHA PARK
GORMAN PARK
M. RD
PEARSON ELEM.
SWEENEY ELEM.
SHAKOPEE H.S.
SHAKOPEE CIVIC CENTER
SHAKOPEE J.H.S.
LIONS PARK
TAHPAH PARK
FULLER PARK
MEADOWS PARK
1. ANGELICA CT
2. WHITNEY AVE
3. SHUMWAY ST S
4. JEFF ST
5. ORCHARD PKWY
6. ALEXANDER CT
1. 12TH AVE
2. QUARRY LN
3. RIVER ROCK LN
4. SLATE AVE
5. BOULDER PT
6. AGATE CRV
7. PRESIDENTIAL CIR W
8. STONE MEADOW BLVD
9. PEBBLE TER
10. BOULDER PT
11. MEADOW PL
12. SAND STONE CRV
7. CIDER CIR
8. APPLEWOOD WAY
9. REGENT LN
10. REGENT DR
11. FIRESIDE CT
12. MCINTOSH CT
1. TUMBLEWEED CIR
2. PIONEER LN
3. PRAIRIE CT
4. SUNFLOWER CIR
5. PIONEER CT
9. HEATHER ST
1. CRESTVIEW ST
2. HIGHPOINT CURVE
3. ELMWOOD AVE
4. IDLEWOOD WAY
5. WESTON LN
6. HAVENVIEW DR
1. PARKWAY AVE
2. PROMISE AVE
1. CAMBRIDGE WAY
ST FRANCIS REGIONAL MED. CTR
STONEBROOKE GOLF COURSE (18 HOLE)
THE PRESERVE G. C. (9HOLE)
MARYSTOWN RD
KOEPER AVE
TOWNLINE AVE
MARSHALL RD
ZUMBRO AVE
128TH ST W
130TH ST W
22ND AVE S
CREEKSIDE DR N
126TH ST W
HILLWOOD DR
SHANNON DR S
LINK DR
BARRINGTON DR
HAMPTON CT
CORTLAND CIR
CARRIAGE CIR
ABBEY PT
FAIRHAVEN DR
CAMBRIDGE CT
OAK CIR S
OAK RD S
MEADOW CT
10TH AVE W
SHAKOPEE AVE
4TH AVE
VIERLING DR
APPLEBLOSSOM LN
12000
12500
128000
13000
13400
T116N
T115N
35
36
31
02
11
14
13
18
23
24
19

See Page 145

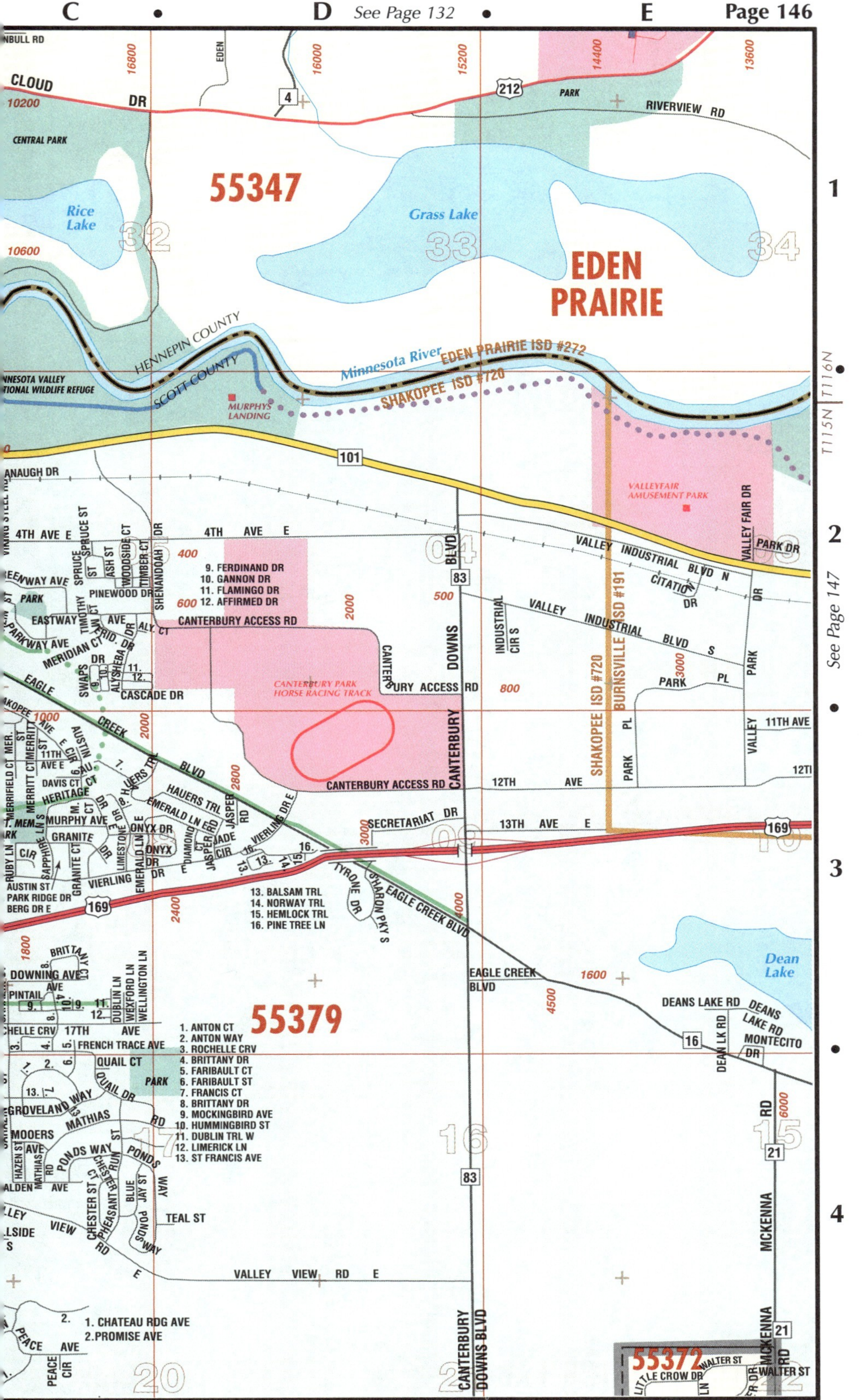
55347
EDEN PRAIRIE
Rice Lake
Grass Lake
Minnesota River
HENNEPIN COUNTY
SCOTT COUNTY
EDEN PRAIRIE ISD #272
SHAKOPEE ISD #720
BURNSVILLE ISD #191
MURPHYS LANDING
VALLEYFAIR AMUSEMENT PARK
CANTERBURY PARK HORSE RACING TRACK
CENTRAL PARK
CLOUD DR
RIVERVIEW RD
4TH AVE E
VALLEY INDUSTRIAL BLVD N
VALLEY INDUSTRIAL BLVD S
CANTERBURY ACCESS RD
CANTERBURY DOWNS BLVD
EAGLE CREEK BLVD
SECRETARIAT DR
12TH AVE
13TH AVE E
9. FERDINAND DR
10. GANNON DR
11. FLAMINGO DR
12. AFFIRMED DR
13. BALSAM TRL
14. NORWAY TRL
15. HEMLOCK TRL
16. PINE TREE LN
55379
1. ANTON CT
2. ANTON WAY
3. ROCHELLE CRV
4. BRITTANY DR
5. FARIBAULT CT
6. FARIBAULT ST
7. FRANCIS CT
8. BRITTANY DR
9. MOCKINGBIRD AVE
10. HUMMINGBIRD ST
11. DUBLIN TRL W
12. LIMERICK LN
13. ST FRANCIS AVE
Dean Lake
DEANS LAKE RD
MCKENNA RD
VALLEY VIEW RD E
TEAL ST
1. CHATEAU RDG AVE
2. PROMISE AVE
PEACE AVE
55372
T116N
T115N

See Page 147

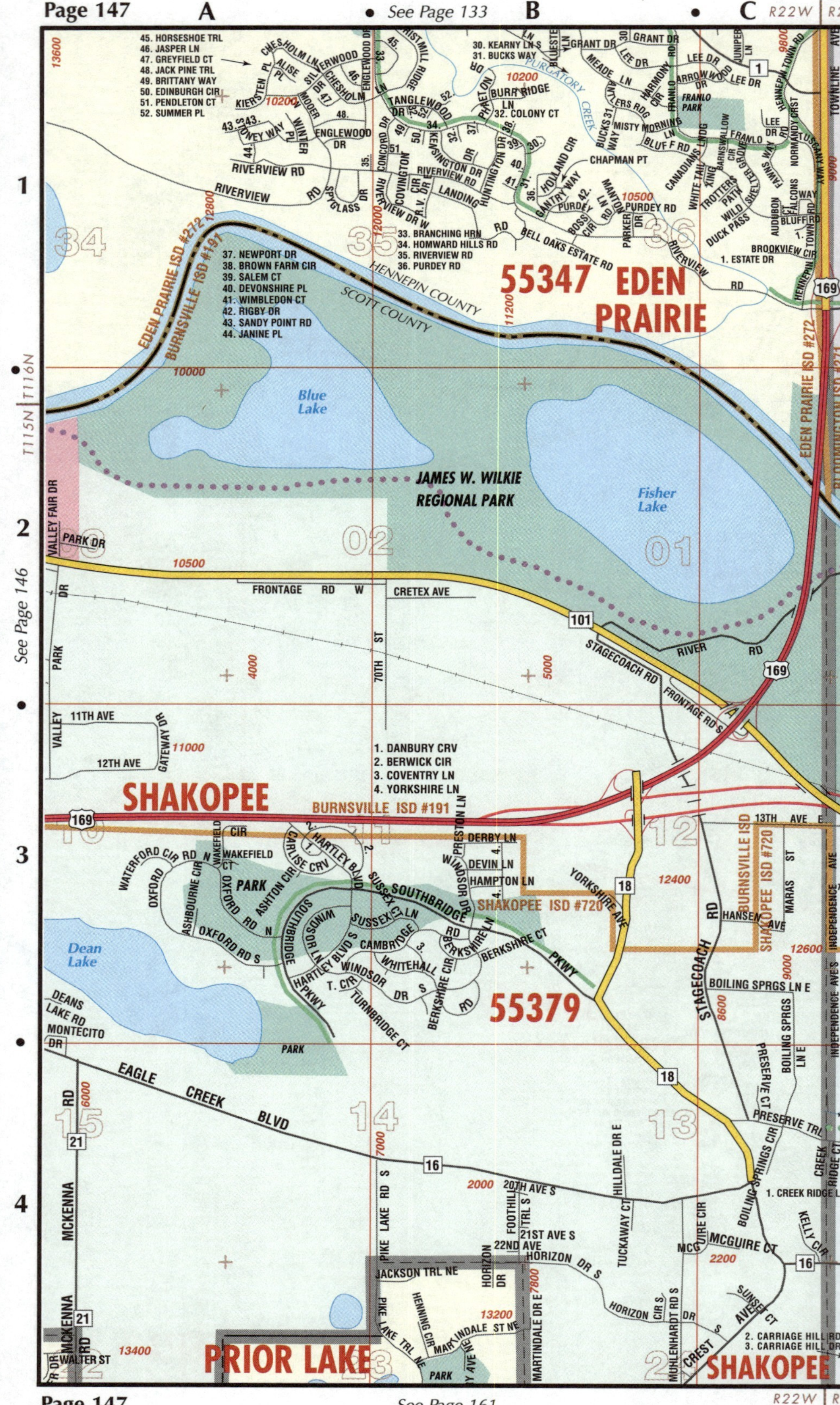

45. HORSESHOE TRL
46. JASPER LN
47. GREYFIELD CT
48. JACK PINE TRL
49. BRITTANY WAY
50. EDINBURGH CIR
51. PENDLETON CT
52. SUMMER PL

30. KEARNY LN S
31. BUCKS WAY
32. COLONY CT

37. NEWPORT DR
38. BROWN FARM CIR
39. SALEM CT
40. DEVONSHIRE PL
41. WIMBLEDON CT
42. RIGBY DR
43. SANDY POINT RD
44. JANINE PL

33. BRANCHING HRM
34. HOMWARD HILLS RD
35. RIVERVIEW RD
36. PURDEY RD

1. ESTATE DR

55347 EDEN PRAIRIE

Blue Lake

Fisher Lake

JAMES W. WILKIE REGIONAL PARK

FRONTAGE RD W   CRETEX AVE

101

STAGECOACH RD

RIVER   RD

169

11TH AVE

12TH AVE

1. DANBURY CRV
2. BERWICK CIR
3. COVENTRY LN
4. YORKSHIRE LN

SHAKOPEE

169

BURNSVILLE ISD #191

DERBY LN

DEVIN LN

HAMPTON LN

SOUTHBRIDGE

SHAKOPEE ISD #720

YORKSHIRE AVE

18

13TH   AVE   E

WATERFORD CIR

PARK

OXFORD

DEAN LAKE

CAMBRIDGE

WHITEHALL

PKWY

55379

BOILING SPRGS LN E

BOILING SPRGS

PRESERVE TRL

PRESERVE CIR

1. CREEK RIDGE L

DEANS LAKE RD

MONTECITO DR

PARK

EAGLE   CREEK   BLVD

16

MCKENNA

15

21

14

16

2000   20TH AVE S

FOOTHILL TRL S

21ST AVE S

22ND AVE

HORIZON DR S

HILLDALE DR E

TUCKAWAY CT

MCGUIRE CIR

13

MCGUIRE CT

2200

16

KELLY CIR

JACKSON TRL NE

HORIZON DR

MARTINDALE ST NE

HORIZON CIR S

HORIZON CIR S

MUHLENHARDT RD S

SUNSET AVE E

CREST

2. CARRIAGE HILL RD
3. CARRIAGE HILL DR

MCKENNA

21

WALTER ST

13400

13200

PRIOR LAKE

SHAKOPEE

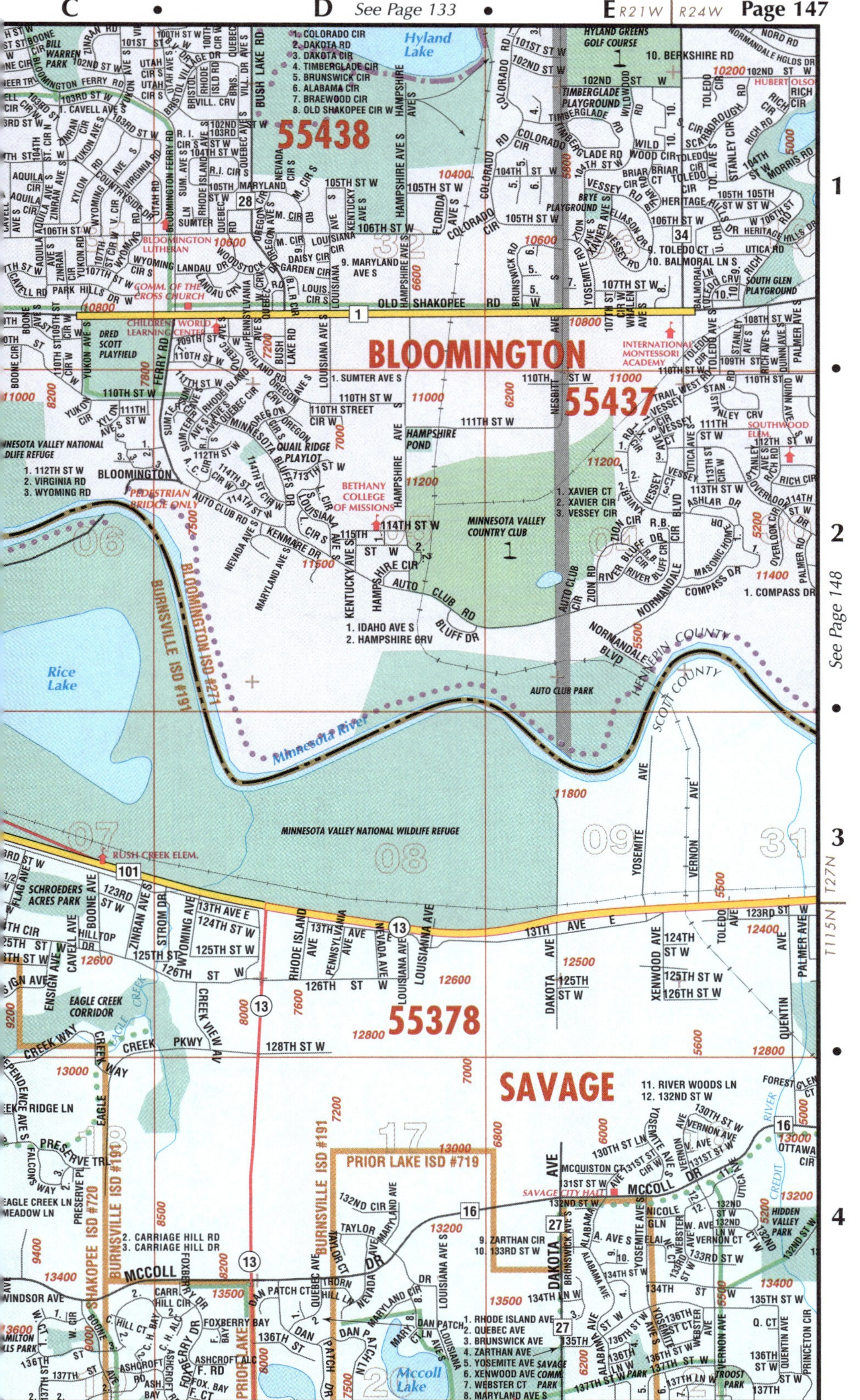
BLOOMINGTON
55438
55437
55378
SAVAGE
Hyland Lake
Rice Lake
Mccoll Lake
Minnesota River
MINNESOTA VALLEY NATIONAL WILDLIFE REFUGE
MINNESOTA VALLEY COUNTRY CLUB
HYLAND GREENS GOLF COURSE
AUTO CLUB PARK
HENNEPIN COUNTY
SCOTT COUNTY
BURNSVILLE ISD #191
BLOOMINGTON ISD #271
PRIOR LAKE ISD #719
SHAKOPEE ISD #720
BETHANY COLLEGE OF MISSIONS
INTERNATIONAL MONTESSORI ACADEMY
RUSH CREEK ELEM.
SAVAGE CITY HALL
EAGLE CREEK CORRIDOR
OLD SHAKOPEE RD
MCCOLL DR
13TH AVE E
1. COLORADO CIR
2. DAKOTA RD
3. DAKOTA CIR
4. TIMBERGLADE CIR
5. BRUNSWICK CIR
6. ALABAMA CIR
7. BRAEWOOD CIR
8. OLD SHAKOPEE CIR W
1. SUMTER AVE S
1. XAVIER CT
2. XAVIER CIR
3. VESSEY CIR
1. IDAHO AVE S
2. HAMPSHIRE CRV
1. COMPASS DR
11. RIVER WOODS LN
12. 132ND ST W
1. RHODE ISLAND AVE
2. QUEBEC AVE
3. BRUNSWICK AVE
4. ZARTHAN AVE
5. YOSEMITE AVE S
6. XENWOOD AVE
7. WEBSTER CT
8. MARYLAND AVE S
2. CARRIAGE HILL RD
3. CARRIAGE HILL DR
9. ZARTHAN CIR
10. 133RD ST W
1. 112TH ST W
2. VIRGINIA RD
3. WYOMING RD
T27N
T115N

See Page 148

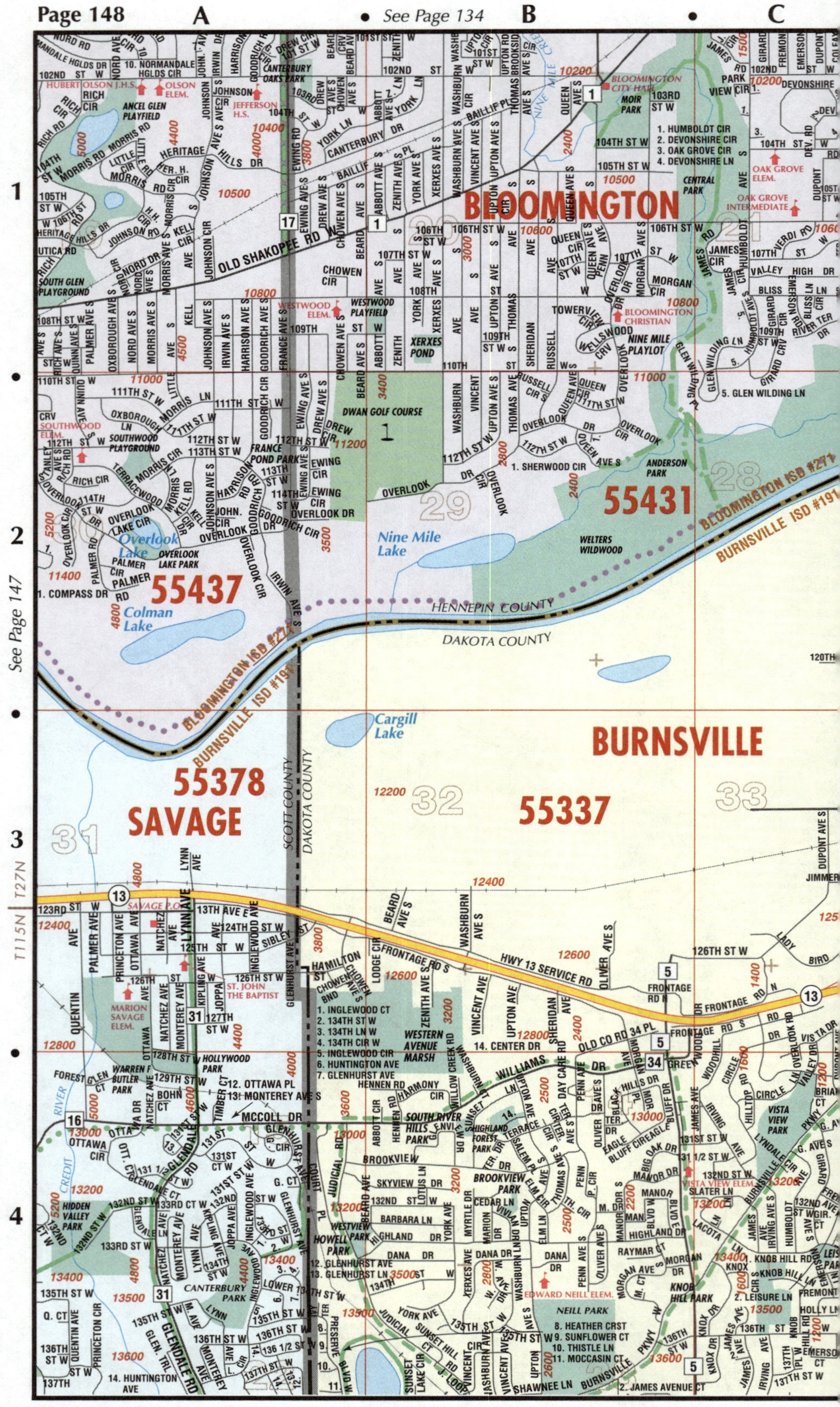
BLOOMINGTON
BURNSVILLE
SAVAGE
55437
55431
55378
55337
HENNEPIN COUNTY
DAKOTA COUNTY
SCOTT COUNTY
BLOOMINGTON ISD #271
BURNSVILLE ISD #191
Nine Mile Lake
Cargill Lake
Colman Lake
Overlook Lake
DWAN GOLF COURSE
ANDERSON PARK
WELTERS WILDWOOD
BLOOMINGTON CITY HALL
MOIR PARK
CENTRAL PARK
OLD SHAKOPEE RD W
HWY 13 SERVICE RD
See Page 147
T27N
T115N

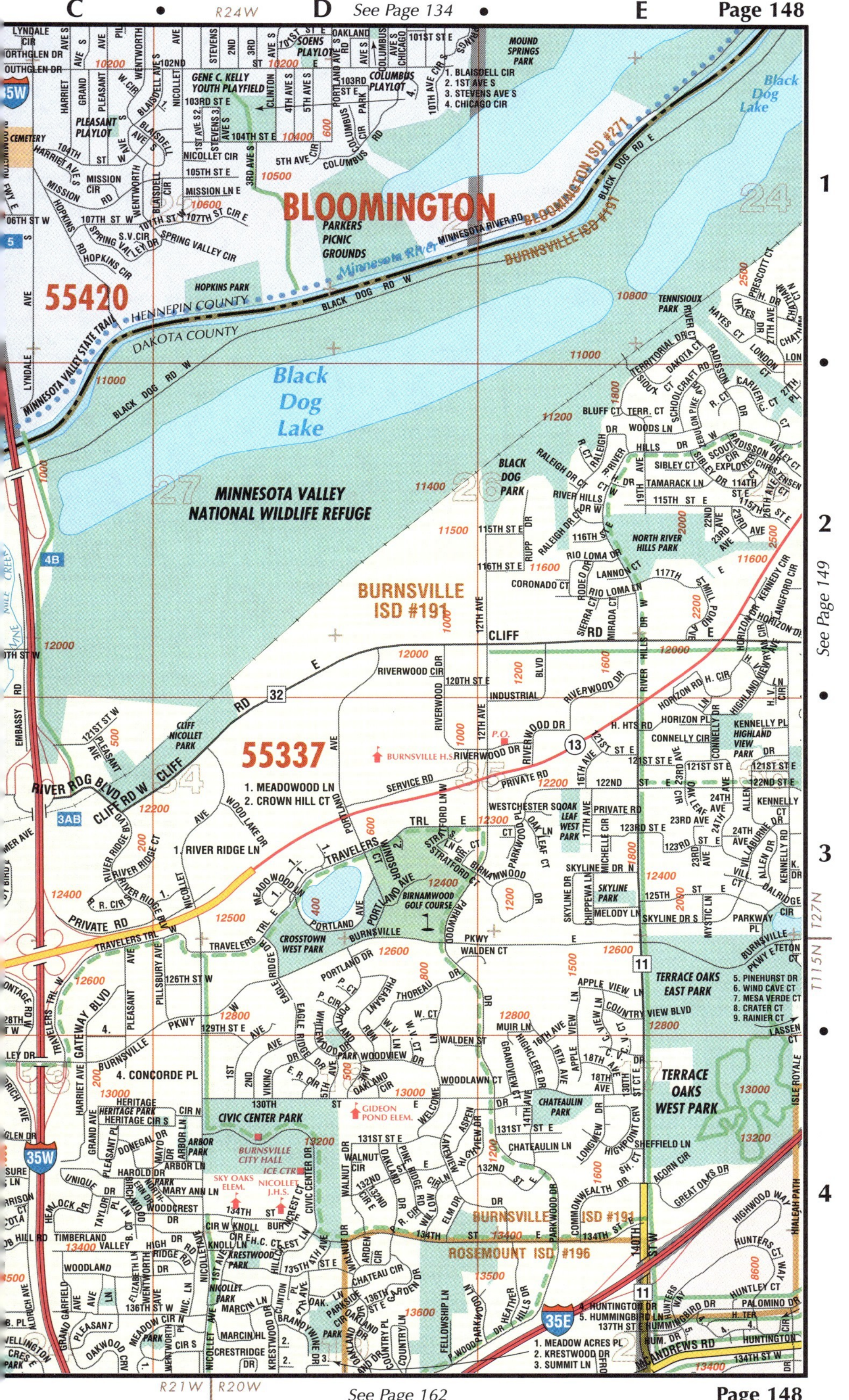
BLOOMINGTON
55420
55337
BLACK DOG LAKE
Black Dog Lake
MINNESOTA VALLEY NATIONAL WILDLIFE REFUGE
BURNSVILLE ISD #191
BLOOMINGTON ISD #271
ROSEMOUNT ISD #196
HENNEPIN COUNTY
DAKOTA COUNTY
Minnesota River
MINNESOTA VALLEY STATE TRAIL
MOUND SPRINGS PARK
GENE C. KELLY YOUTH PLAYFIELD
SOENS PLAYLOT
COLUMBUS PLAYLOT
PLEASANT PLAYLOT
CEMETERY
PARKERS PICNIC GROUNDS
HOPKINS PARK
BLACK DOG PARK
TENNISIOUX PARK
NORTH RIVER HILLS PARK
CLIFF NICOLLET PARK
BURNSVILLE H.S.
P.O.
BIRNAMWOOD GOLF COURSE
CROSSTOWN WEST PARK
SKYLINE PARK
OAK LEAF WEST PARK
HIGHLAND VIEW PARK
TERRACE OAKS EAST PARK
TERRACE OAKS WEST PARK
CHATEAULIN PARK
CIVIC CENTER PARK
BURNSVILLE CITY HALL
ICE CTR
SKY OAKS ELEM.
NICOLLET J.H.S.
GIDEON POND ELEM.
HERITAGE PARK
ARBOR PARK
KRESTWOOD PARK
NICOLLET PARK
MEADOW PARK
1. BLAISDELL CIR
2. 1ST AVE S
3. STEVENS AVE S
4. CHICAGO CIR
1. MEADOWOOD LN
2. CROWN HILL CT
1. RIVER RIDGE LN
4. CONCORDE PL
5. PINEHURST DR
6. WIND CAVE CT
7. MESA VERDE CT
8. CRATER CT
9. RAINIER CT
4. HUNTINGTON DR
5. HUMMINGBIRD LN
1. MEADOW ACRES PL
2. KRESTWOOD DR
3. SUMMIT LN
BLACK DOG RD
MINNESOTA RIVER RD
CLIFF RD
RIVERWOOD DR
TRAVELERS TRL
BURNSVILLE PKWY
NICOLLET AVE
PORTLAND AVE
RIVER HILLS DR
MCANDREWS RD
35W
35E
13
32
11
4B
3AB
5
1
2
3
4
See Page 149
T115N T27N
R24W
R21W R20W

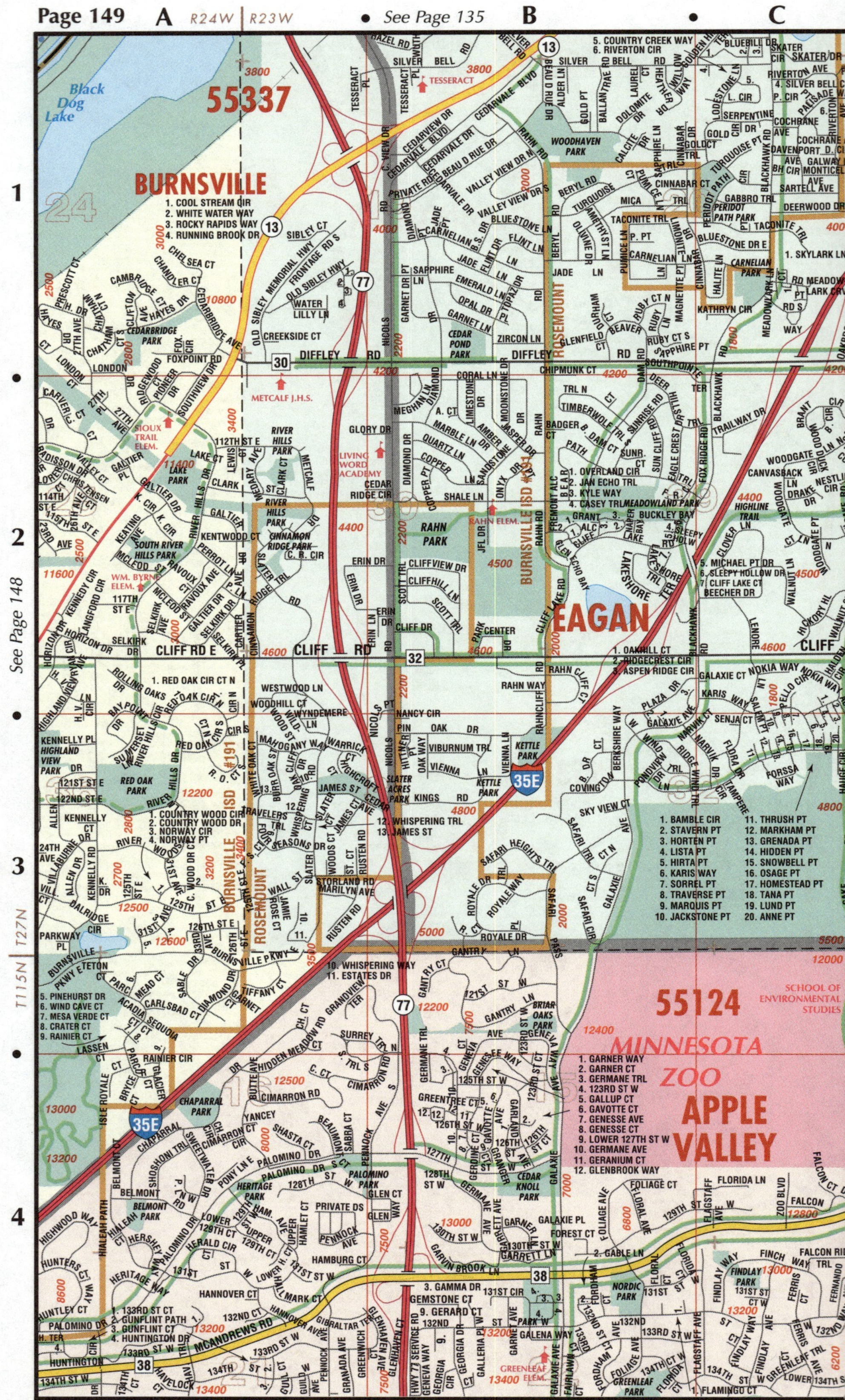

Black Dog Lake
55337
BURNSVILLE
1. COOL STREAM CIR
2. WHITE WATER WAY
3. ROCKY RAPIDS WAY
4. RUNNING BROOK DR
EAGAN
55124
MINNESOTA ZOO
APPLE VALLEY
SCHOOL OF ENVIRONMENTAL STUDIES
5. COUNTRY CREEK WAY
6. RIVERTON CIR
TESSERACT
METCALF J.H.S.
LIVING WORD ACADEMY
SIOUX TRAIL ELEM.
WM. BYRNE ELEM.
RAHN ELEM.
GREENLEAF ELEM.
WOODHAVEN PARK
CEDARBRIDGE PARK
CEDAR POND PARK
RAHN PARK
KETTLE PARK
RED OAK PARK
CHAPARRAL PARK
BELMONT PARK
HERITAGE PARK
PALOMINO PARK
CEDAR KNOLL PARK
NORDIC PARK
FINDLAY PARK
GREENLEAF PARK
BURNSVILLE ISD #191
ROSEMOUNT
DIFFLEY RD
CLIFF RD
MCANDREWS RD
1. OVERLAND CIR
2. JAN ECHO TRL
3. KYLE WAY
4. CASEY TRL
5. MICHAEL PT DR
6. SLEEPY HOLLOW DR
7. CLIFF LAKE CT
1. OAKHILL CT
2. RIDGECREST CIR
3. ASPEN RIDGE CIR
1. RED OAK CIR CT N
1. COUNTRY WOOD CIR
2. COUNTRY WOOD DR
3. NORWAY CIR
4. NORWAY PT
12. WHISPERING TRL
13. JAMES ST
10. WHISPERING WAY
11. ESTATES DR
5. PINEHURST DR
6. WIND CAVE CT
7. MESA VERDE CT
8. CRATER CT
9. RAINIER CT
1. BAMBLE CIR
2. STAVERN PT
3. HORTEN PT
4. LISTA PT
5. HIRTA PT
6. KARIS WAY
7. SORREL PT
8. TRAVERSE PT
9. MARQUIS PT
10. JACKSTONE PT
11. THRUSH PT
12. MARKHAM PT
13. GRENADA PT
14. HIDDEN PT
15. SNOWBELL PT
16. OSAGE PT
17. HOMESTEAD PT
18. TANA PT
19. LUND PT
20. ANNE PT
1. GARNER WAY
2. GARNER CT
3. GERMANE TRL
4. 123RD ST W
5. GALLUP CT
6. GAVOTTE CT
7. GENESSE AVE
8. GENESSE CT
9. LOWER 127TH ST W
10. GERMANE AVE
11. GERANIUM CT
12. GLENBROOK WAY
1. 133RD ST CT
2. GUNFLINT PATH
3. GUNFLINT CT
4. HUNTINGTON DR
3. GAMMA DR
9. GERARD CT
See Page 148
T115N | T27N

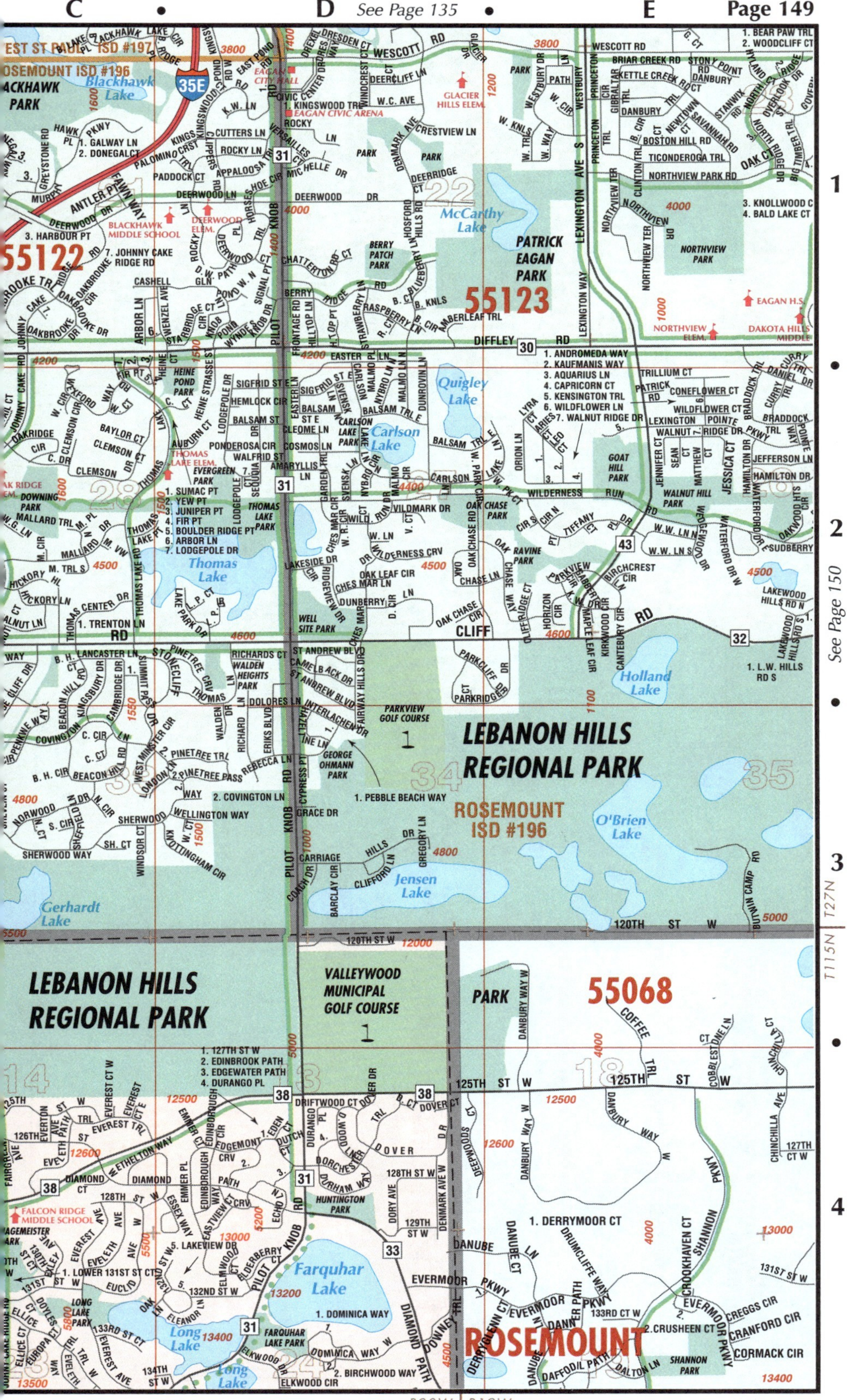

1
2
3
4
See Page 150
T27N
T115N
55122
55123
55068
LEBANON HILLS REGIONAL PARK
LEBANON HILLS REGIONAL PARK
ROSEMOUNT ISD #196
ROSEMOUNT ISD #196
ROSEMOUNT
VALLEYWOOD MUNICIPAL GOLF COURSE
PARKVIEW GOLF COURSE
PATRICK EAGAN PARK
NORTHVIEW PARK
BLACKHAWK PARK
Blackhawk Lake
McCarthy Lake
Quigley Lake
Carlson Lake
Thomas Lake
Holland Lake
O'Brien Lake
Jensen Lake
Gerhardt Lake
Farquhar Lake
Long Lake
EAGAN CITY HALL
EAGAN CIVIC ARENA
GLACIER HILLS ELEM.
BLACKHAWK MIDDLE SCHOOL
DEERWOOD ELEM.
THOMAS LAKE ELEM.
NORTHVIEW ELEM.
EAGAN H.S.
DAKOTA HILLS MIDDLE
FALCON RIDGE MIDDLE SCHOOL
WESCOTT RD
DEERWOOD DR
DIFFLEY RD
CLIFF RD
PILOT KNOB RD
LEXINGTON AVE S
WILDERNESS RUN
120TH ST W
125TH ST W
EVERMOOR PKWY
DIAMOND PATH
35E
31
30
43
32
38
33

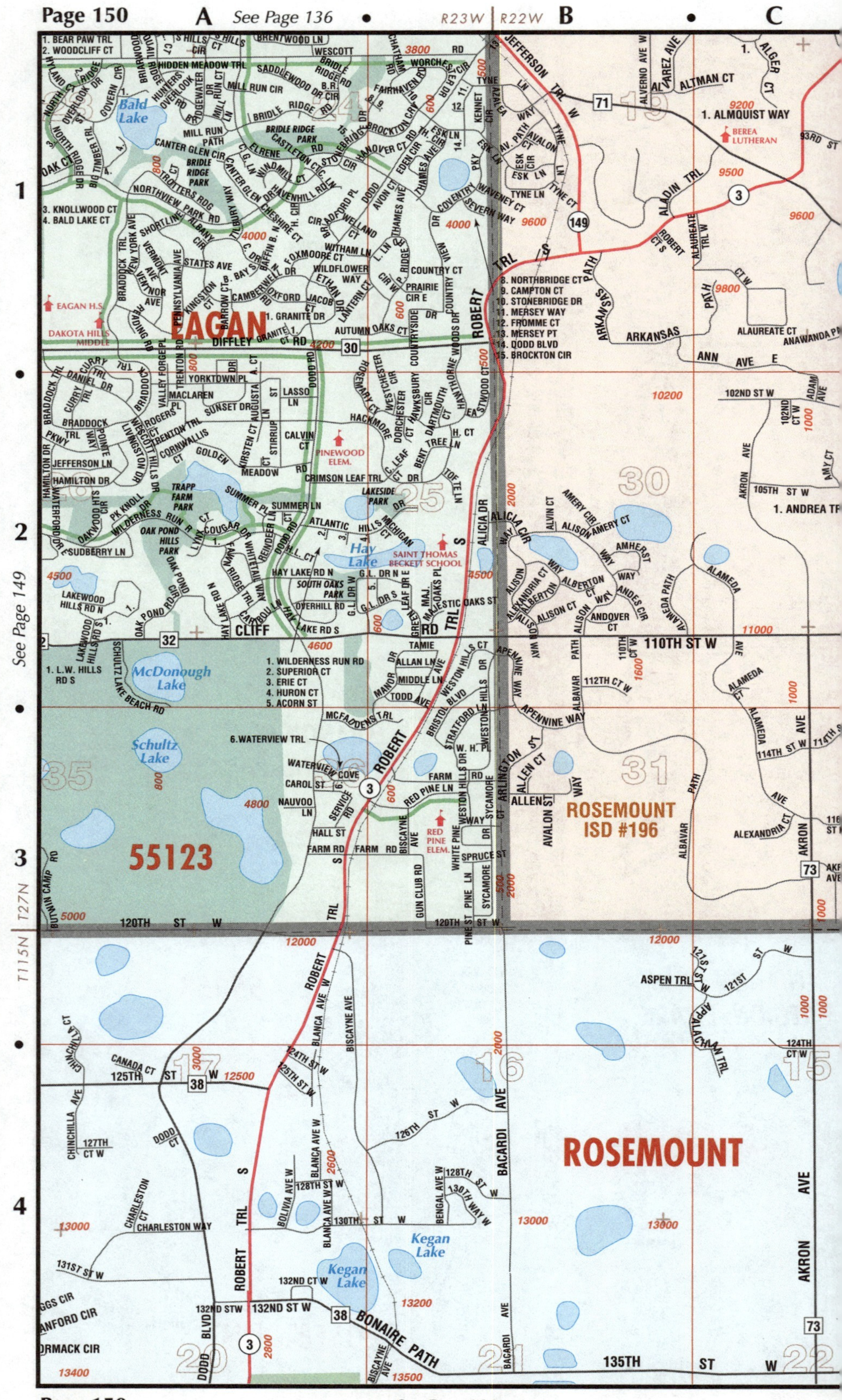

EAGAN

ROSEMOUNT ISD #196

ROSEMOUNT

55123

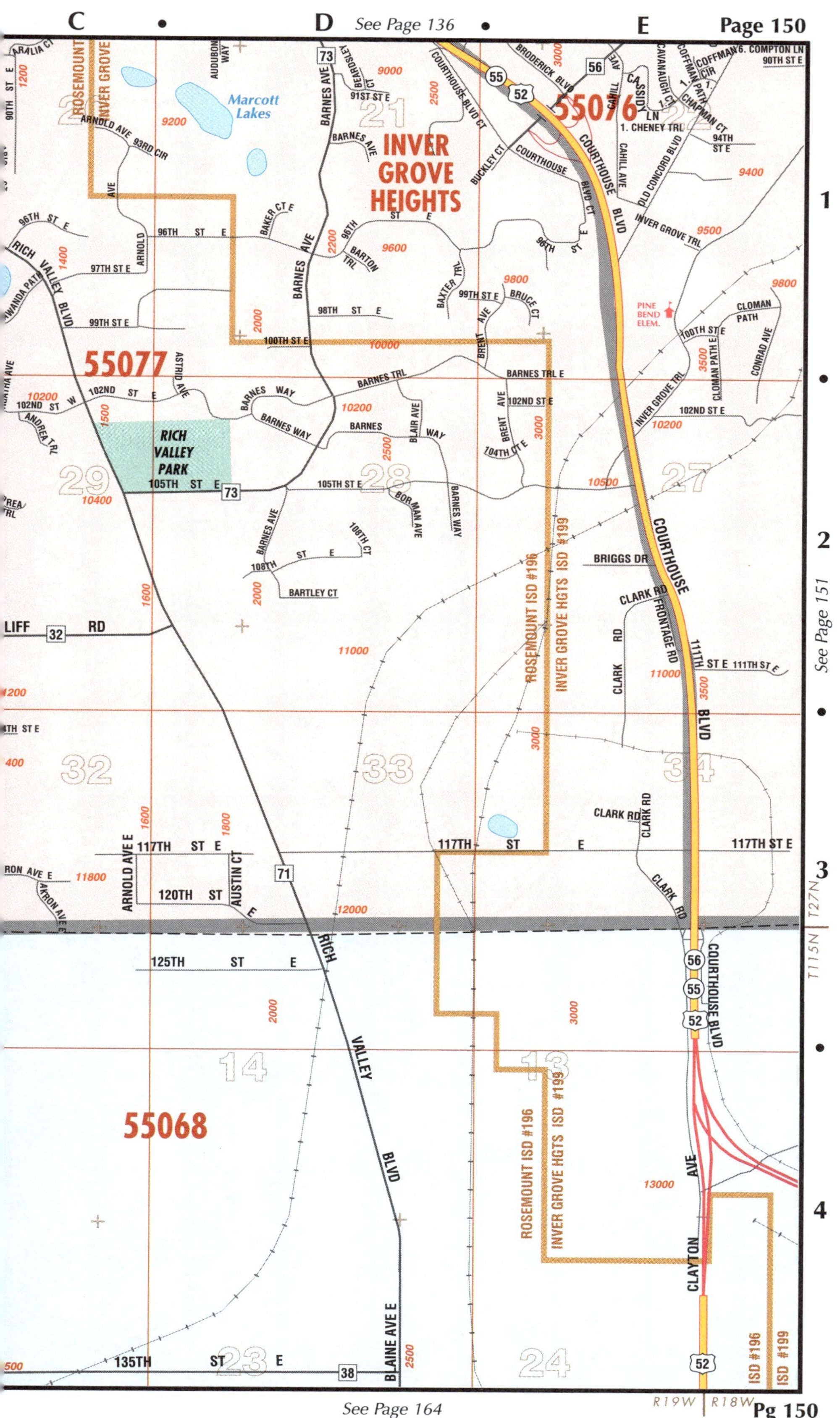

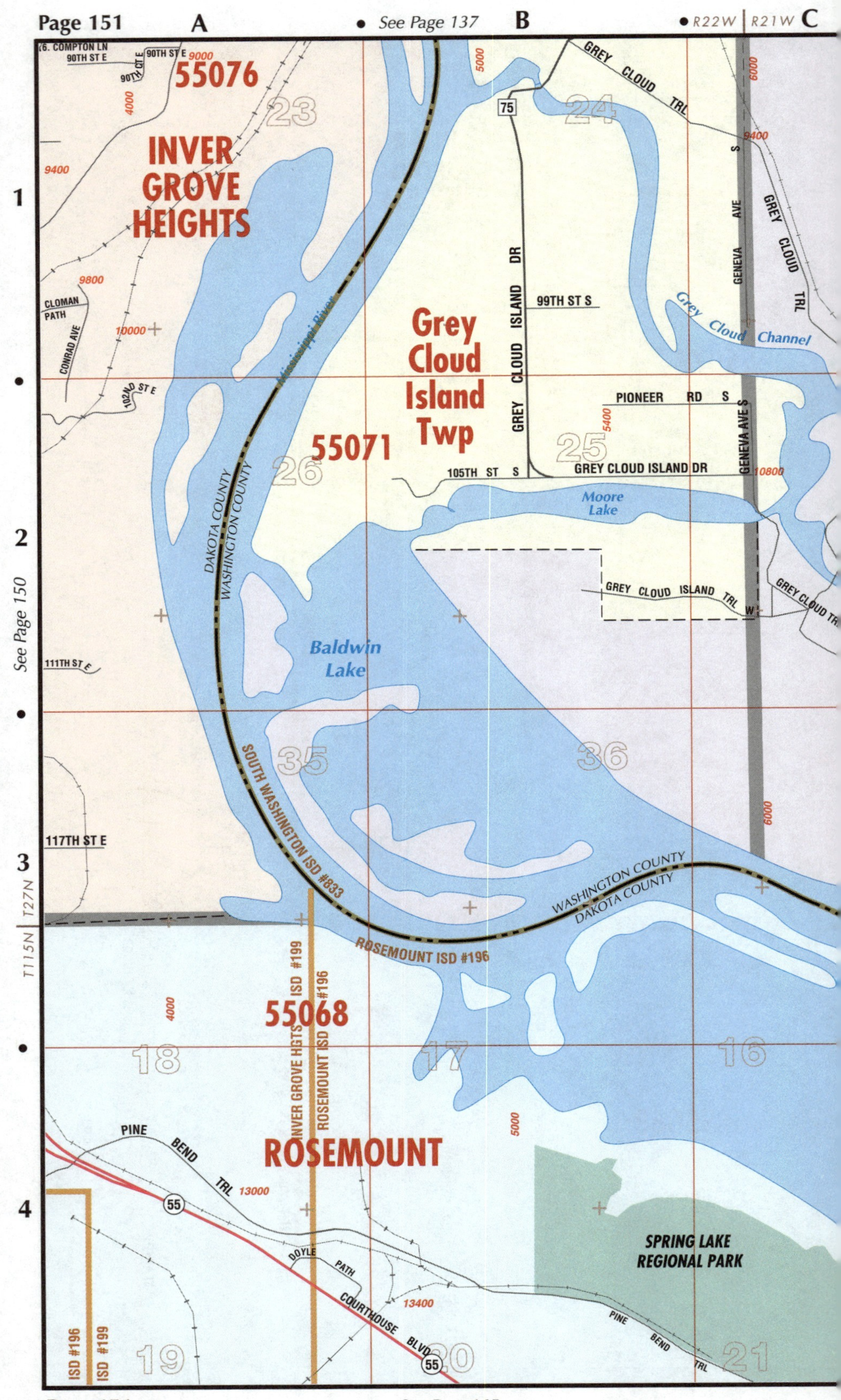

16. COMPTON LN
90TH ST E
90TH ST E   9000
90TH CT E
4000
55076

INVER GROVE HEIGHTS

9400

9800
CLOMAN PATH
CONRAD AVE
10000
192ND ST E

23

GREY CLOUD TRL
5000
75
24
6000
9400
S
GENEVA AVE S
GREY CLOUD TRL

GREY CLOUD ISLAND DR
99TH ST S

Grey Cloud Island Twp

55071

26
DAKOTA COUNTY
WASHINGTON COUNTY

25
PIONEER RD S
5400
GENEVA AVE S
10800
Grey Cloud Channel
105TH ST S   GREY CLOUD ISLAND DR
Moore Lake

GREY CLOUD ISLAND TRL W
GREY CLOUD TRL

111TH ST E

Baldwin Lake

35

36

6000

117TH ST E

SOUTH WASHINGTON ISD #833

T115N | T27N

WASHINGTON COUNTY
DAKOTA COUNTY

ROSEMOUNT ISD #196

4000

INVER GROVE HGTS ISD #199
ROSEMOUNT ISD #196

55068

18

17

16

5000

PINE BEND TRL   13000

ROSEMOUNT

55

DOYLE PATH
COURTHOUSE BLVD
13400

55

SPRING LAKE REGIONAL PARK

PINE BEND TRL

ISD #196
ISD #199

19

20

21

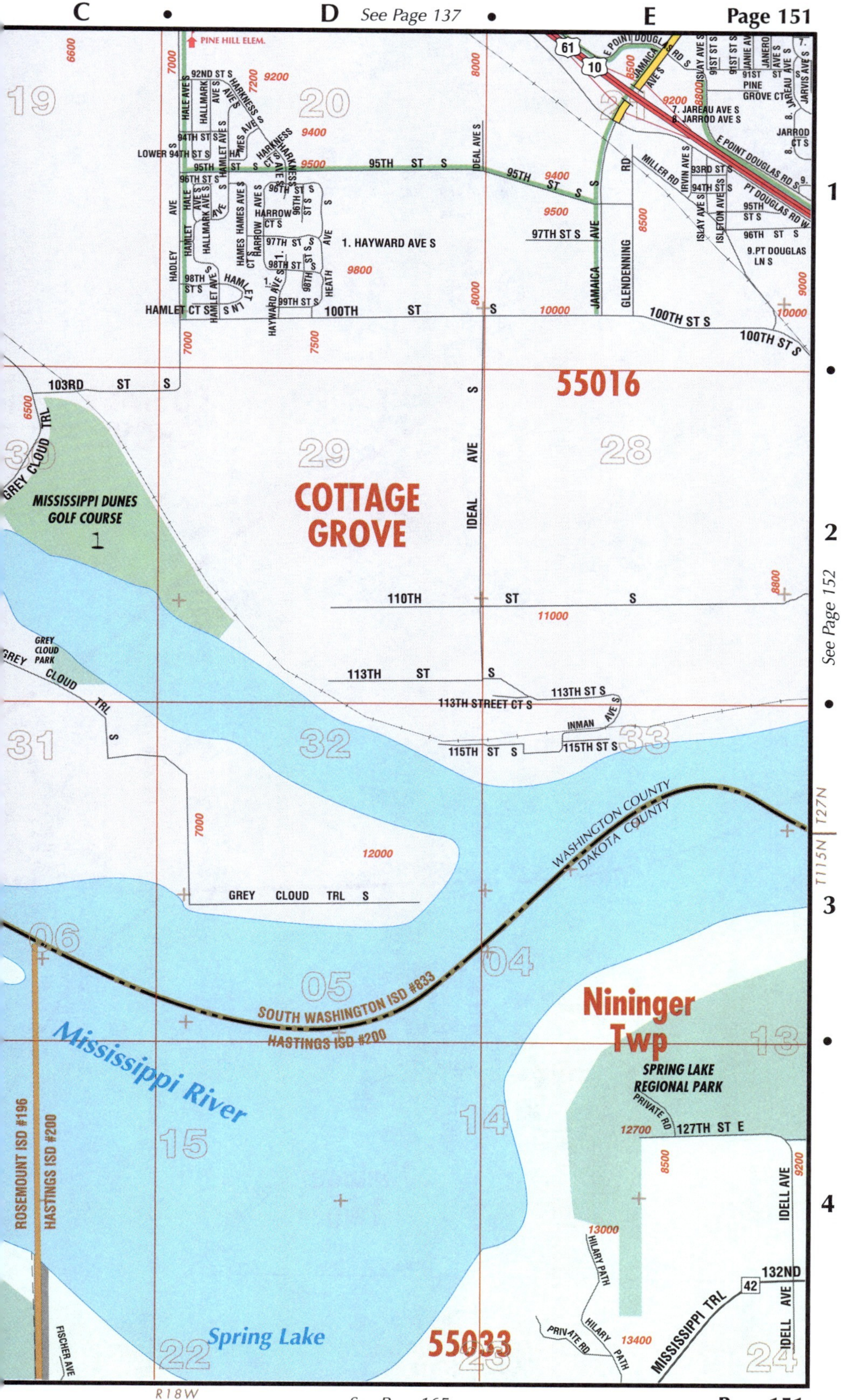

PINE HILL ELEM.
COTTAGE GROVE
55016
MISSISSIPPI DUNES GOLF COURSE
GREY CLOUD PARK
1. HAYWARD AVE S
7. JAREAU AVE S
8. JARROD AVE S
9. PT DOUGLAS LN S
95TH ST S
100TH ST S
103RD ST S
110TH ST S
113TH ST S
113TH STREET CT S
115TH ST S
IDEAL AVE S
JAMAICA AVE S
GLENDENNING RD
GREY CLOUD TRL S
WASHINGTON COUNTY
DAKOTA COUNTY
SOUTH WASHINGTON ISD #833
HASTINGS ISD #200
ROSEMOUNT ISD #196
Mississippi River
Nininger Twp
SPRING LAKE REGIONAL PARK
127TH ST E
IDELL AVE
132ND
MISSISSIPPI TRL
HILARY PATH
PRIVATE RD
FISCHER AVE
Spring Lake
55033
T27N
T115N
R18W

See Page 152

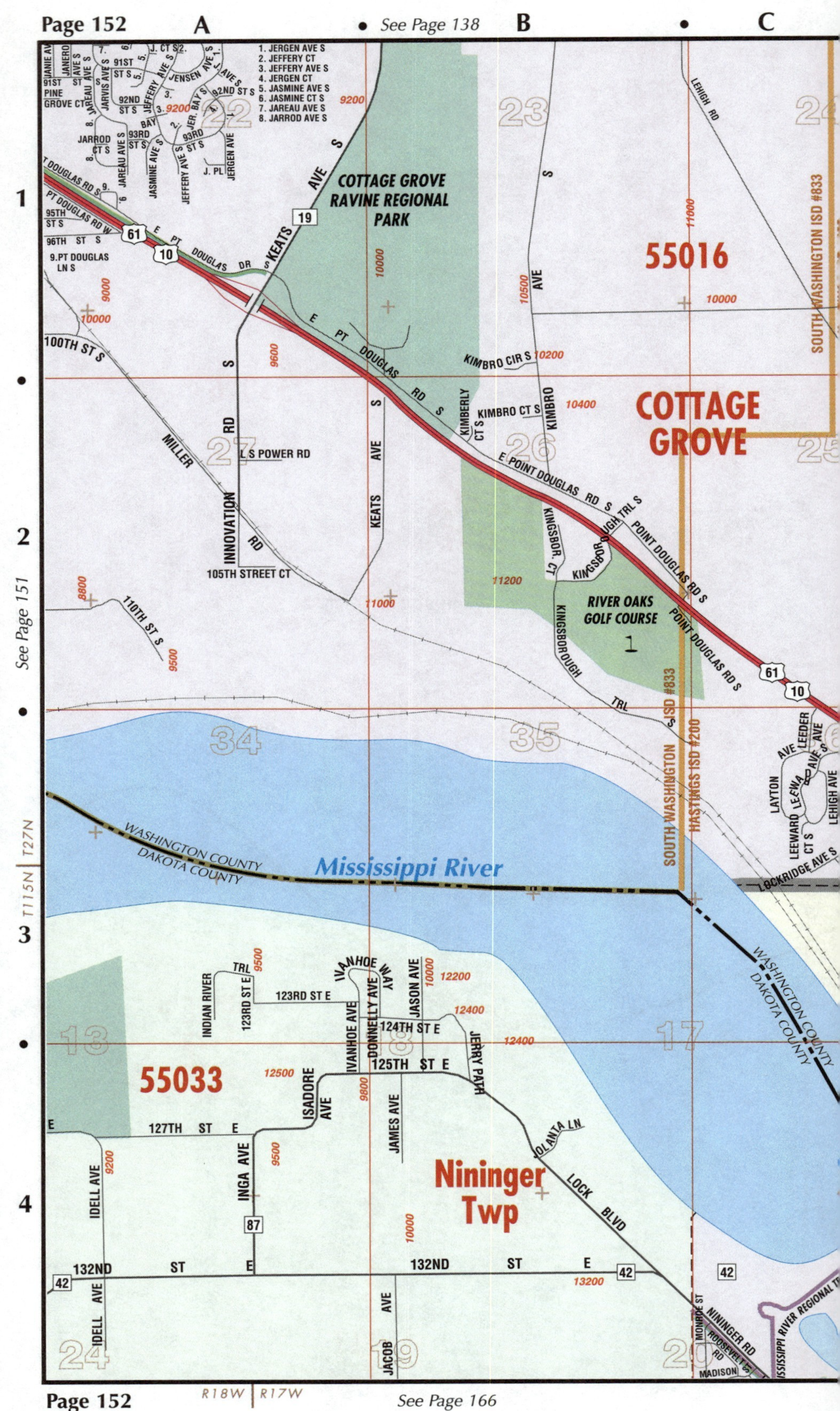

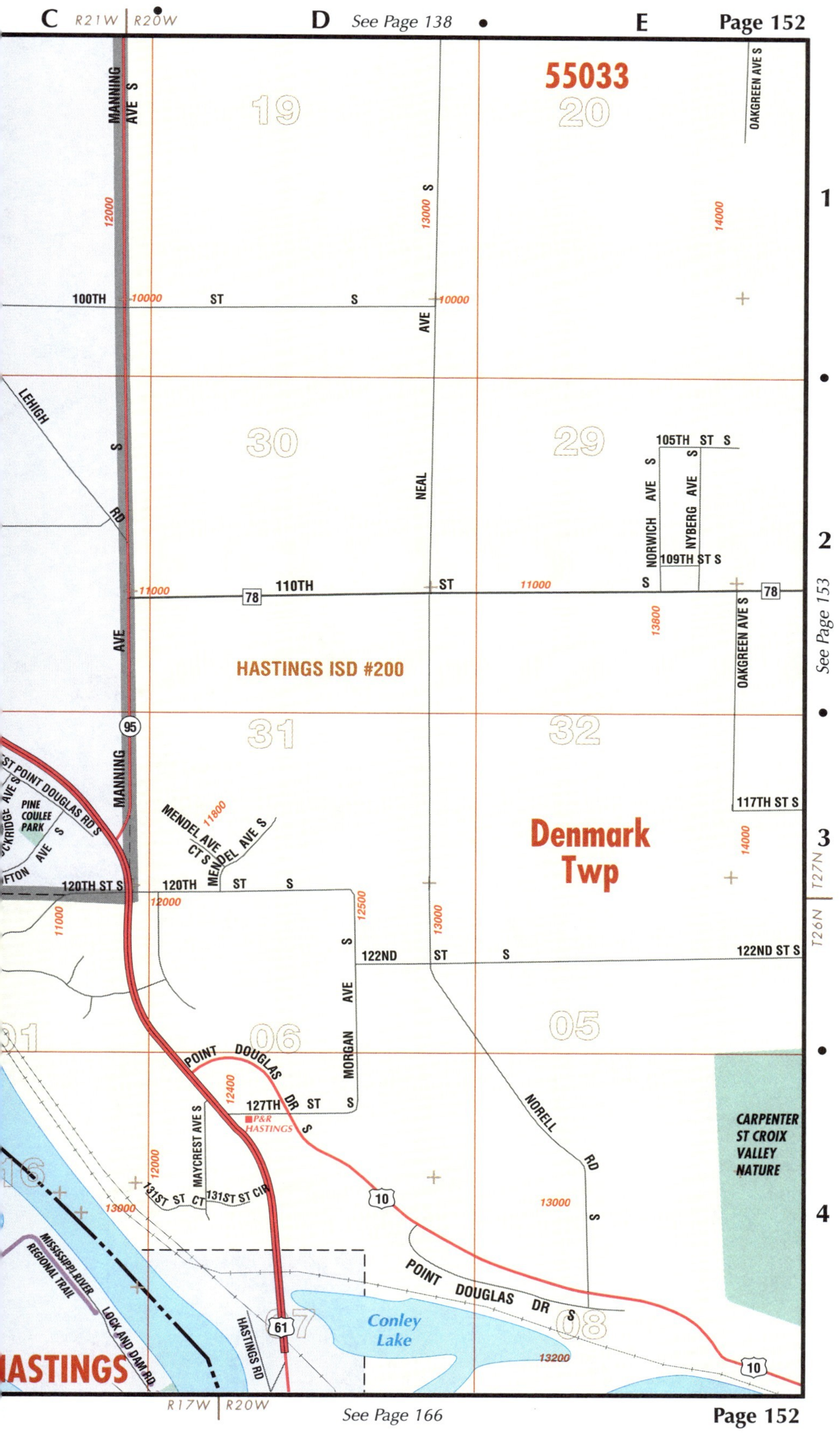

55033

OAKGREEN AVE S

MANNING AVE S

19

20

14000

12000

13000 S

1

LEHIGH

100TH   10000   ST   S   10000

AVE

30

29

105TH ST S

NORWICH AVE S

NYBERG AVE

109TH ST S

NEAL

RD

AVE S

See Page 153

110TH   ST   11000

11000

78

78

13800

OAKGREEN AVE S

HASTINGS ISD #200

95

MANNING

31

32

117TH ST S

14000

Denmark Twp

T26N T27N

ST POINT DOUGLAS RD S

PINE COULEE PARK

CKRIDGE AVE S

FTON AVE S

MENDEL AVE CT S

MENDEL AVE S

11800

3

120TH ST S

120TH   ST   S

12000

12500

13000

122ND   ST   S

122ND ST S

MORGAN AVE S

01

06

05

POINT DOUGLAS DR   ST

12400

127TH   ST   S

P&R HASTINGS

NORELL RD S

CARPENTER ST CROIX VALLEY NATURE

MAYCREST AVE S

12000

131ST ST CT

131ST ST CIR

13000

10

13000

4

MISSISSIPPI RIVER REGIONAL TRAIL

LOCK AND DAM RD

POINT DOUGLAS DR S

16

61

Conley Lake

13200

08

10

HASTINGS

HASTINGS RD

See Page 139

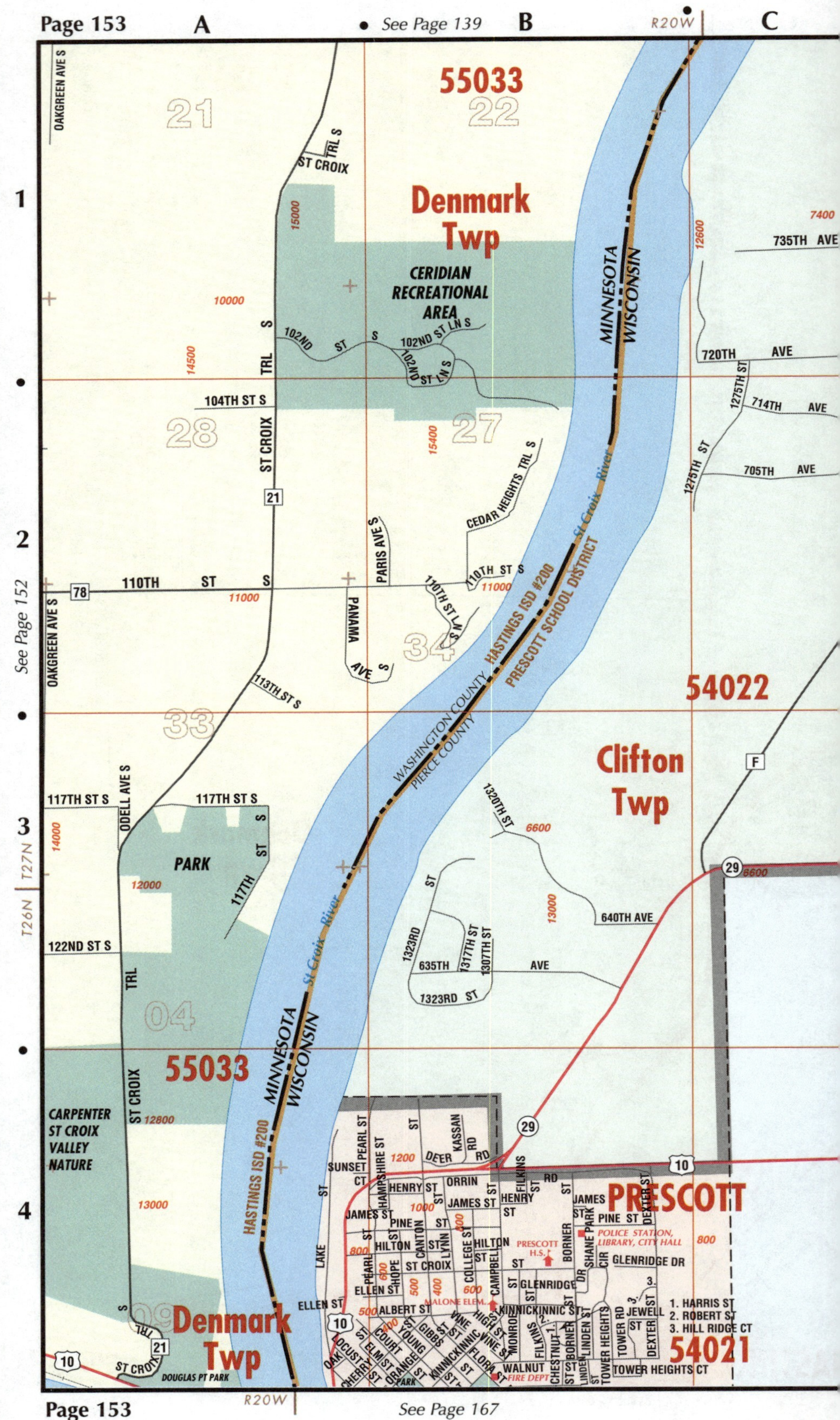

See Page 152

See Page 167

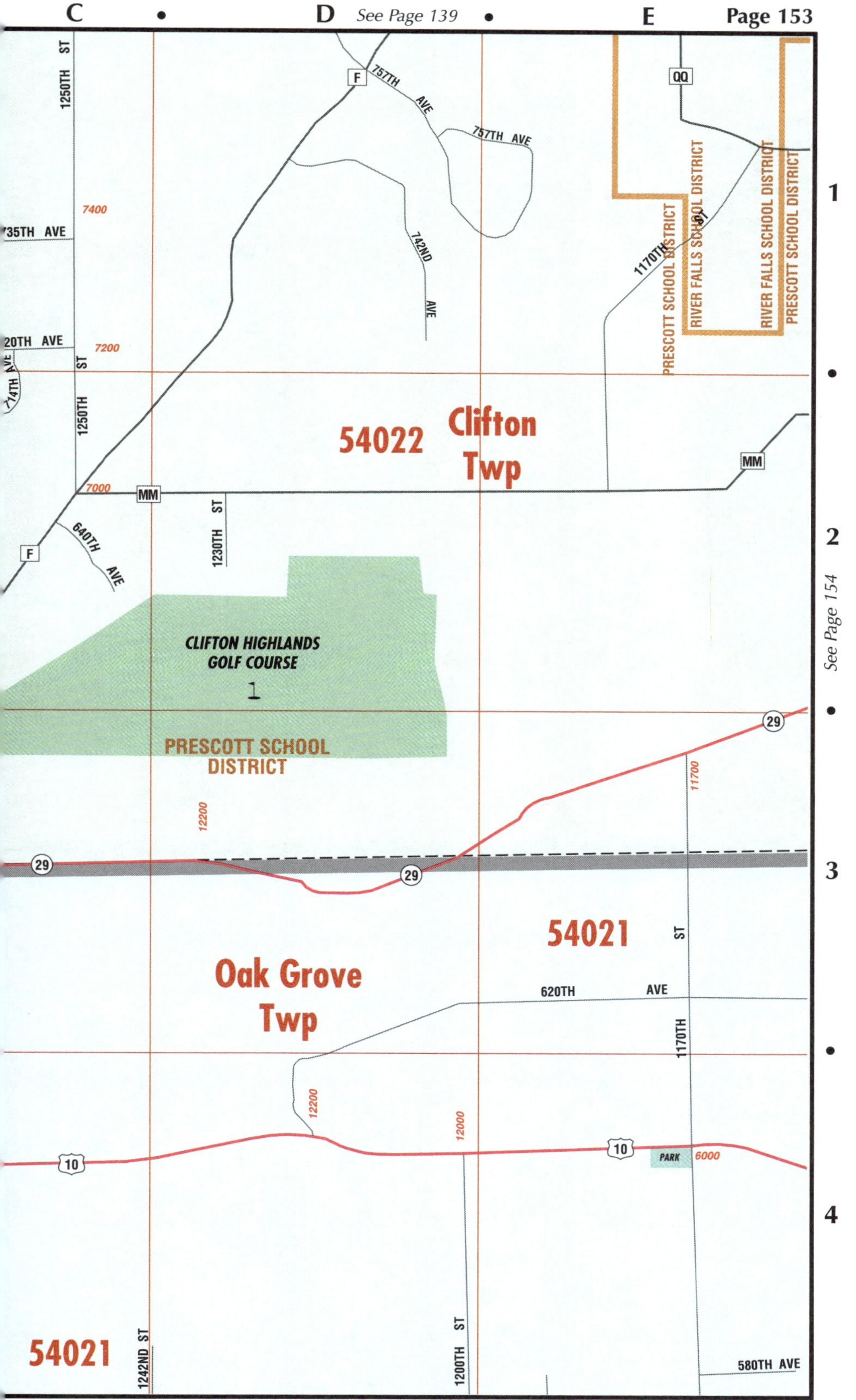

757TH AVE

757TH AVE

1250TH ST

F

QQ

1

PRESCOTT SCHOOL DISTRICT

1170TH

RIVER FALLS SCHOOL DISTRICT

RIVER FALLS SCHOOL DISTRICT

PRESCOTT SCHOOL DISTRICT

742ND AVE

7400

35TH AVE

20TH AVE

7200

74TH AVE

1250TH ST

54022

Clifton Twp

MM

See Page 154

MM

7000

F

640TH AVE

1230TH ST

2

CLIFTON HIGHLANDS GOLF COURSE

1

29

PRESCOTT SCHOOL DISTRICT

12200

11700

29

29

29

3

54021

1170TH ST

Oak Grove Twp

620TH AVE

1170TH

12200

12000

10

10

PARK

6000

4

54021

1242ND ST

1200TH ST

580TH AVE

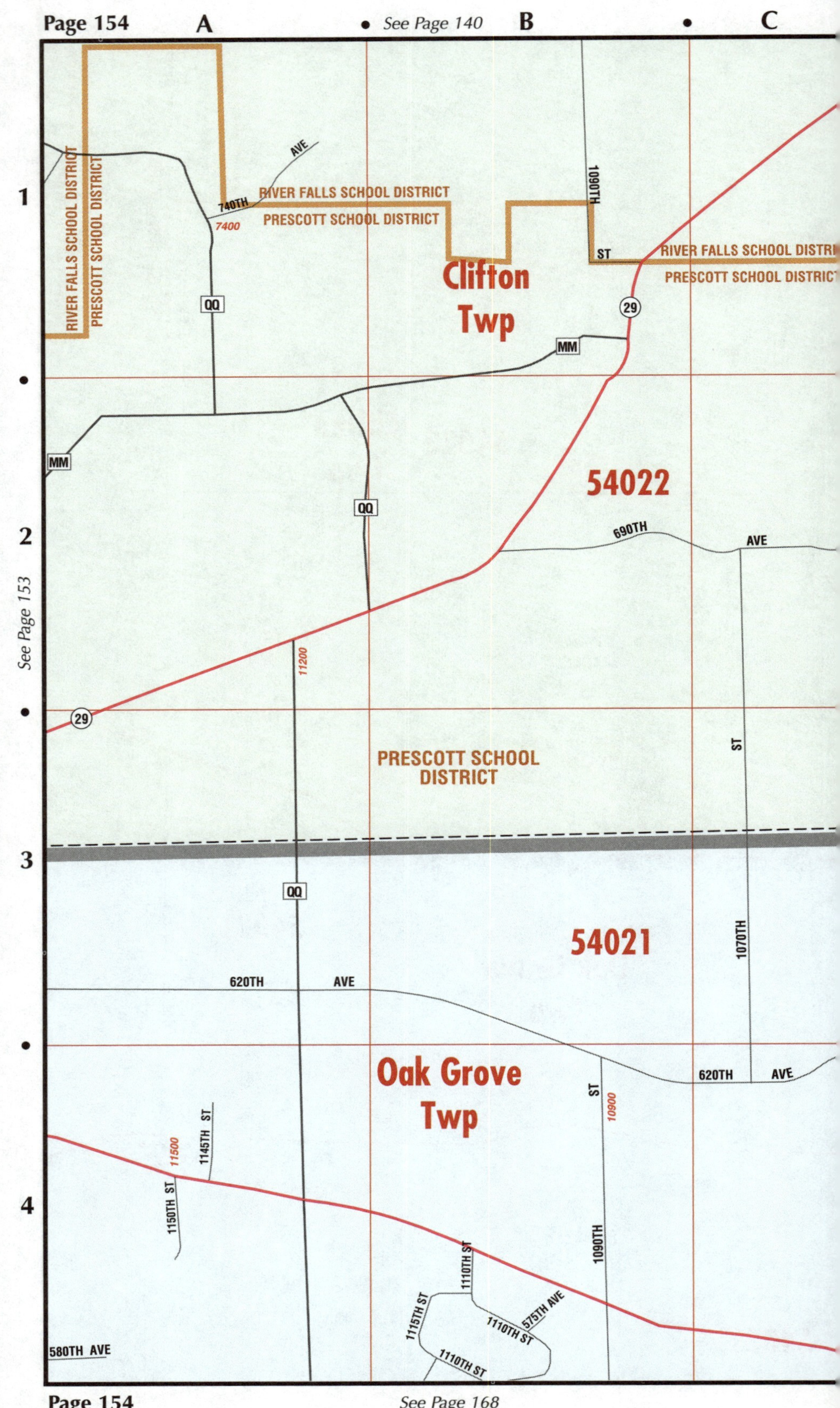

See Page 140

RIVER FALLS SCHOOL DISTRICT

PRESCOTT SCHOOL DISTRICT

AVE

740TH

7400

RIVER FALLS SCHOOL DISTRICT

PRESCOTT SCHOOL DISTRICT

1090TH

ST

RIVER FALLS SCHOOL DISTRI

PRESCOTT SCHOOL DISTRICT

Clifton Twp

QQ

29

MM

MM

54022

QQ

690TH AVE

2

11200

29

See Page 153

ST

PRESCOTT SCHOOL DISTRICT

3

QQ

54021

1070TH

620TH AVE

Oak Grove Twp

ST

10900

620TH AVE

1145TH ST

11500

1150TH ST

4

1090TH ST

1110TH ST

1115TH ST

1110TH ST

575TH AVE

1110TH ST

580TH AVE

54022

710TH AVE
7500

710TH

ST

950TH

AVE

River Falls Twp

1

7000

AVE

690TH

690TH

AVE

9500

2

AVE

Eastern Boundary

PRESCOTT SCHOOL DISTRICT

RIVER FALLS SCHOOL DISTRICT

00

6600

RIVER FALLS SCHOOL DISTRICT

PRESCOTT SCHOOL DISTRICT

ST

6500

3

640TH AVE

9600

AVE

630TH

950TH

ST

10000

620TH AVE
6200

54021

1040TH ST

Oak Grove Twp

1000TH

Trimbelle Twp

4

598TH AVE

1040TH ST

1000TH ST

10

E

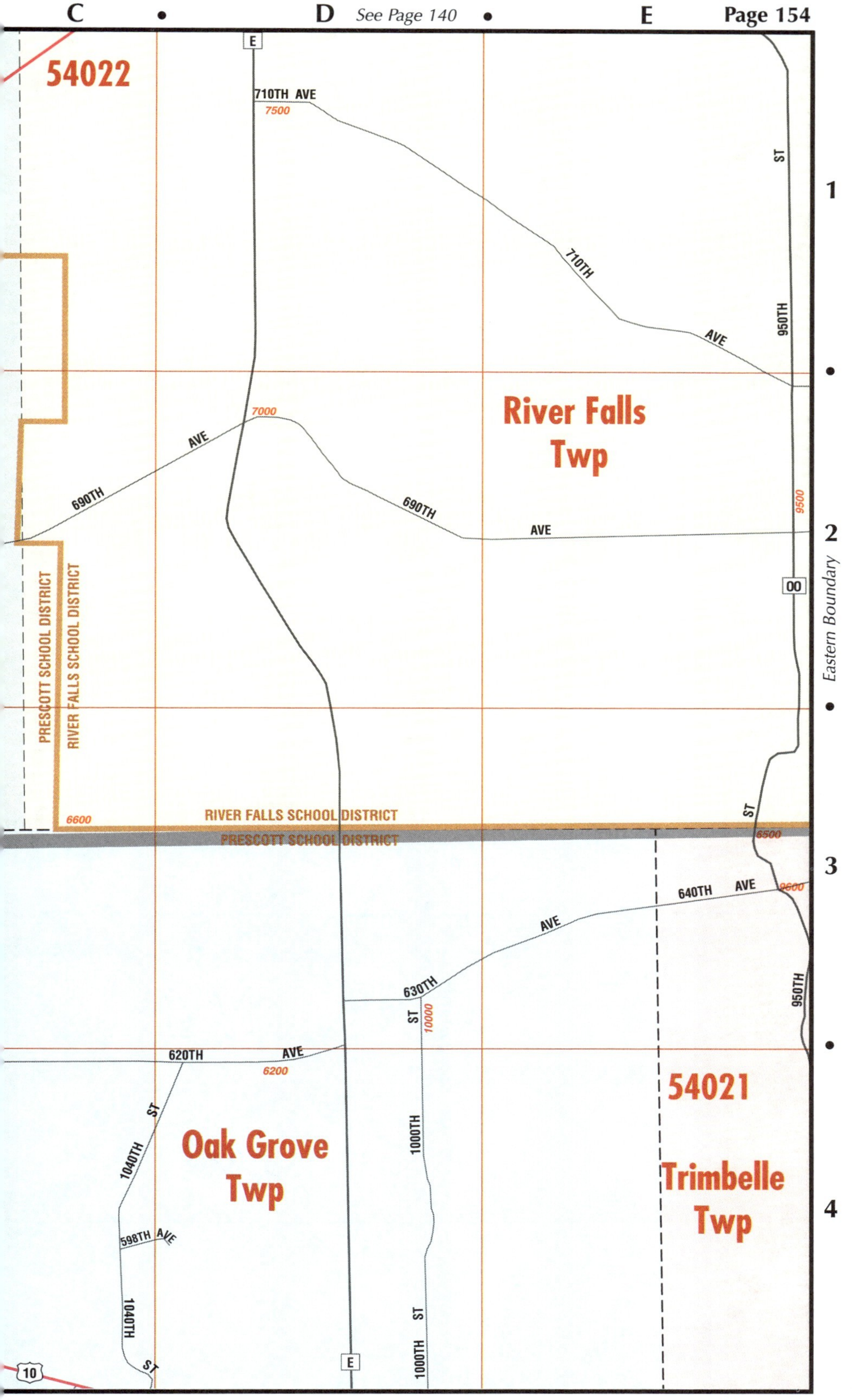

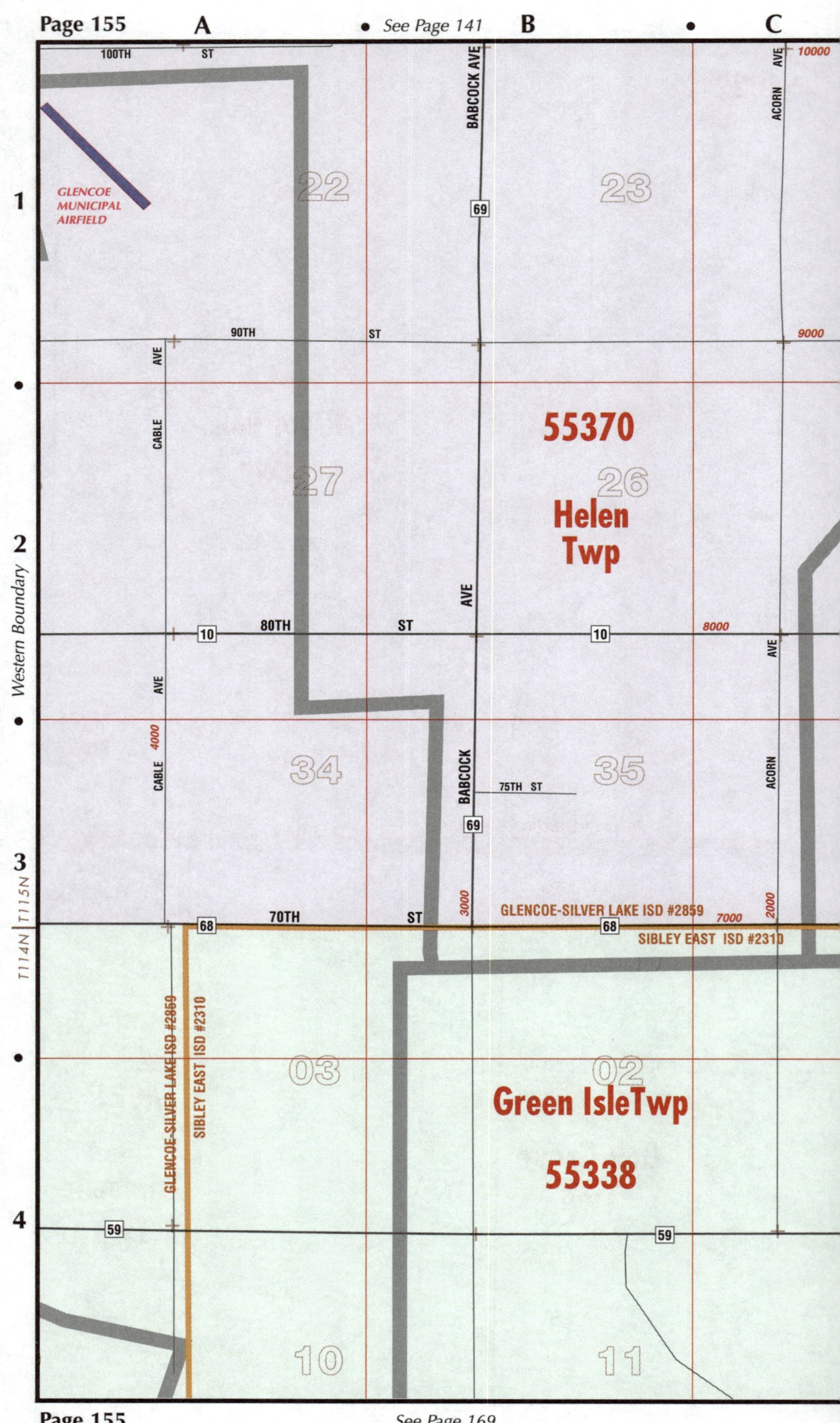

• See Page 141

A   **B**   **C**

100TH   ST

BABCOCK AVE

ACORN   AVE

10000

GLENCOE MUNICIPAL AIRFIELD

1

22

69

23

90TH   ST

9000

AVE

CABLE

55370

27

26

Helen Twp

2

Western Boundary

AVE

80TH   ST

AVE

10

10

8000

AVE

CABLE

4000

34

BABCOCK

75TH ST

ACORN

AVE

35

69

3

T114N | T115N

69

70TH   ST

3000

GLENCOE-SILVER LAKE ISD #2859   7000   2000

68

68

SIBLEY EAST ISD #2310

68

GLENCOE-SILVER LAKE ISD #2859

SIBLEY EAST ISD #2310

03

02

Green Isle Twp

55338

4

59

59

10

11

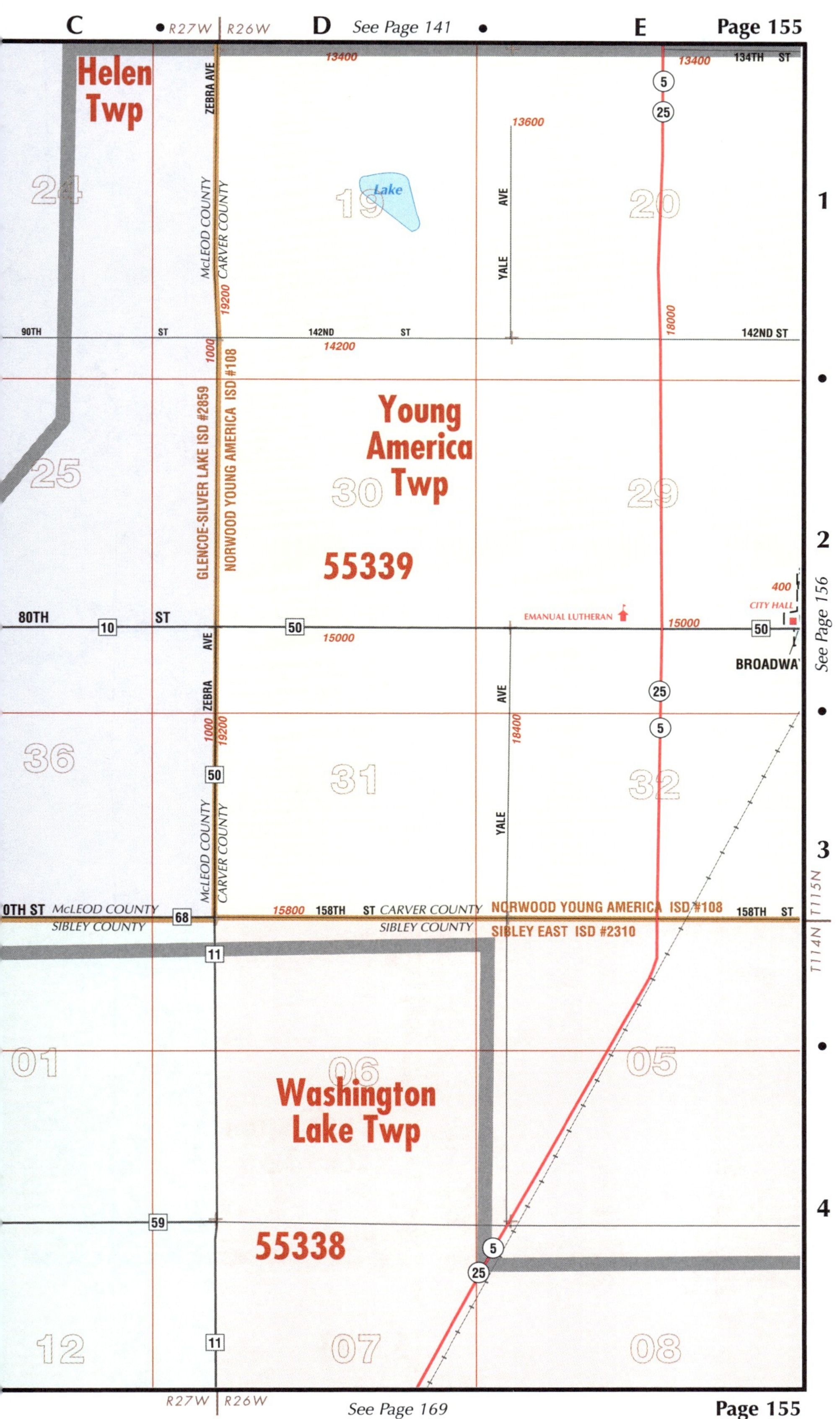

Helen Twp

24

McLEOD COUNTY
CARVER COUNTY

ZEBRA AVE

19200

13400

19 *Lake*

13600

YALE AVE

20

134TH ST
⑤
㉕

18000

1

90TH ST · 142ND ST · 142ND ST

1000

14200

GLENCOE-SILVER LAKE ISD #2859
NORWOOD YOUNG AMERICA ISD #108

25

Young America Twp

30

55339

29

400
CITY HALL
See Page 156

2

80TH ⑩ ST · ㊿ · 15000

EMANUAL LUTHERAN

15000

㊿

BROADWAY

36

1000 ZEBRA AVE 19200

㊿

31

AVE 18400 YALE

㉕
⑤

32

3

T114N T115N

OTH ST *McLEOD COUNTY*
SIBLEY COUNTY

⑥⑧ 15800 158TH ST *CARVER COUNTY*
SIBLEY COUNTY

NORWOOD YOUNG AMERICA ISD #108 158TH ST

SIBLEY EAST ISD #2310

⑪

01

06

Washington Lake Twp

05

4

㊾

55338

⑤
㉕

12

⑪

07

08

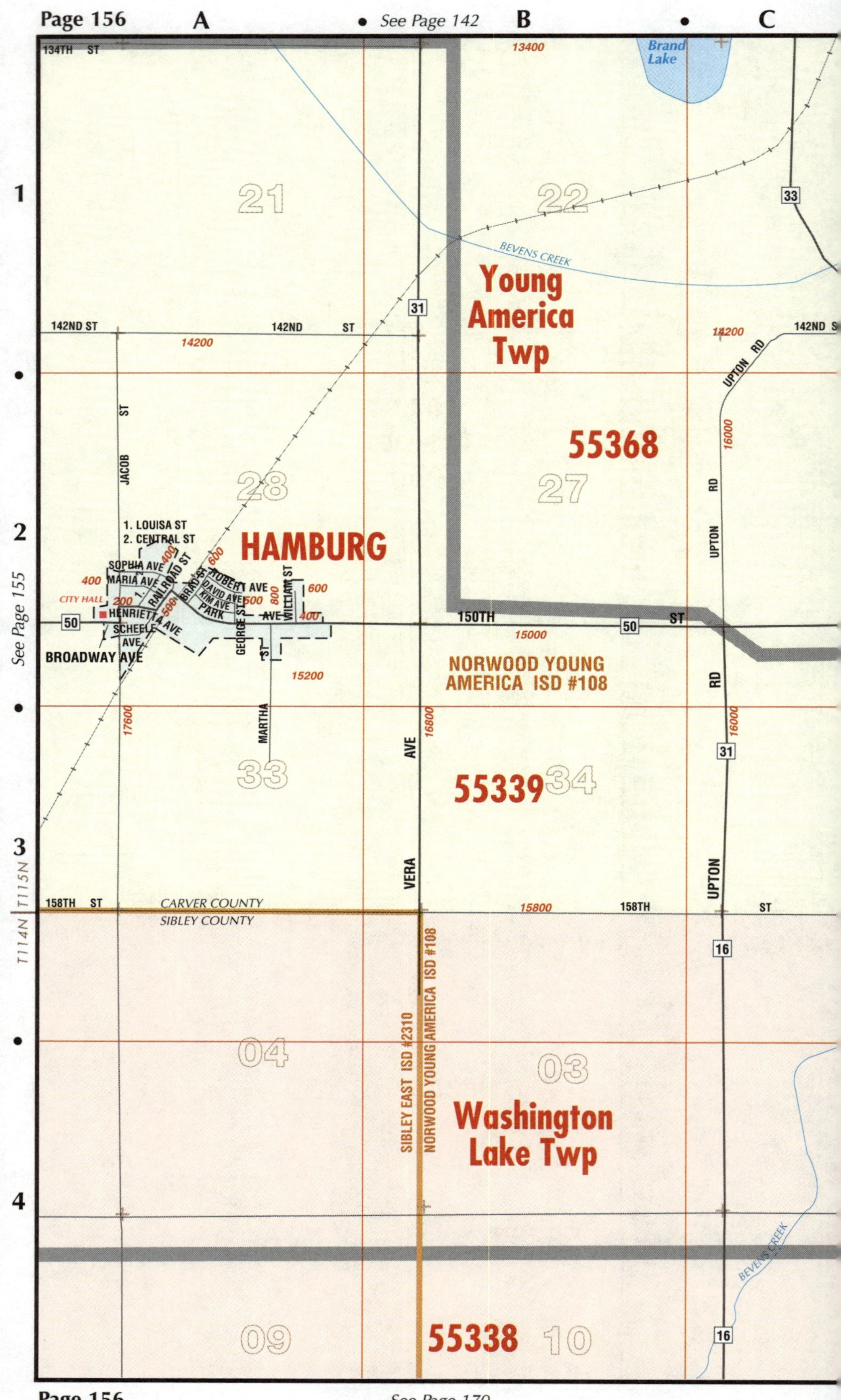

134TH ST

13400

Brand Lake

21

22

33

BEVENS CREEK

31

1

142ND ST   142ND   ST

14200

Young America Twp

142ND S

UPTON RD

14200

See Page 155

JACOB ST

28

55368

27

16000

UPTON RD

UPTON

2

1. LOUISA ST
2. CENTRAL ST

HAMBURG

SOPHIA AVE   400

MARIA AVE

400

RAILROAD ST

BRADLEY ST

600

ROBERT AVE

DAVID AVE   600

KIM AVE

800

WILLIAM ST

600

CITY HALL   200

HENRIETTA AVE

PARK

GEORGE ST

AVE

400

50

SCHEELE AVE

BROADWAY AVE

150TH   ST   50

15000

15200

17600

MARTHA

15200

NORWOOD YOUNG AMERICA ISD #108

RD

3

33

VERA   AVE

16800

55339 34

16000

31

UPTON

T114N | T115N

158TH ST

CARVER COUNTY

SIBLEY COUNTY

VERA

15800

158TH   ST

16

SIBLEY EAST ISD #2310

NORWOOD YOUNG AMERICA ISD #108

04

03

4

Washington Lake Twp

09

55338 10

16

BEVENS CREEK

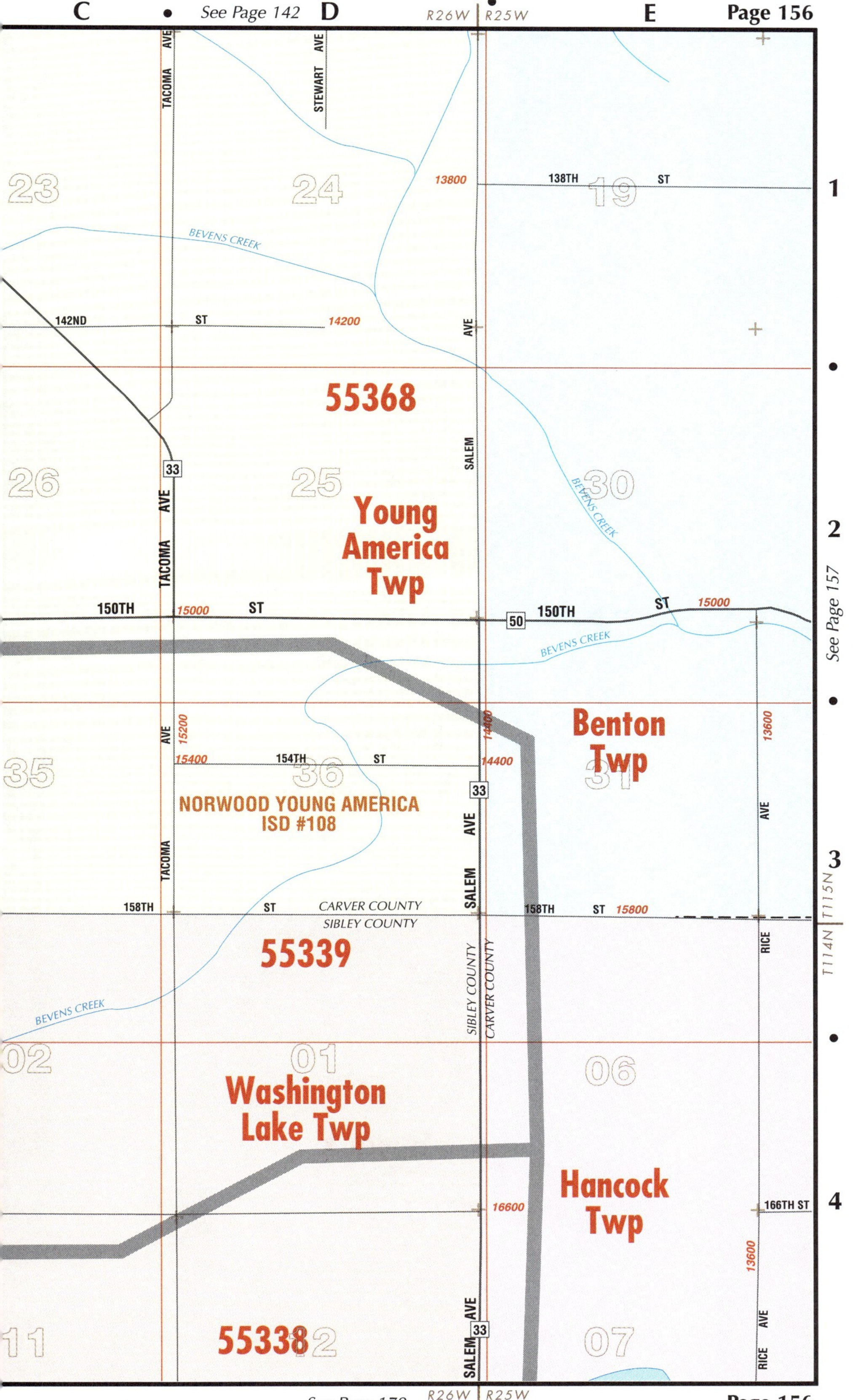

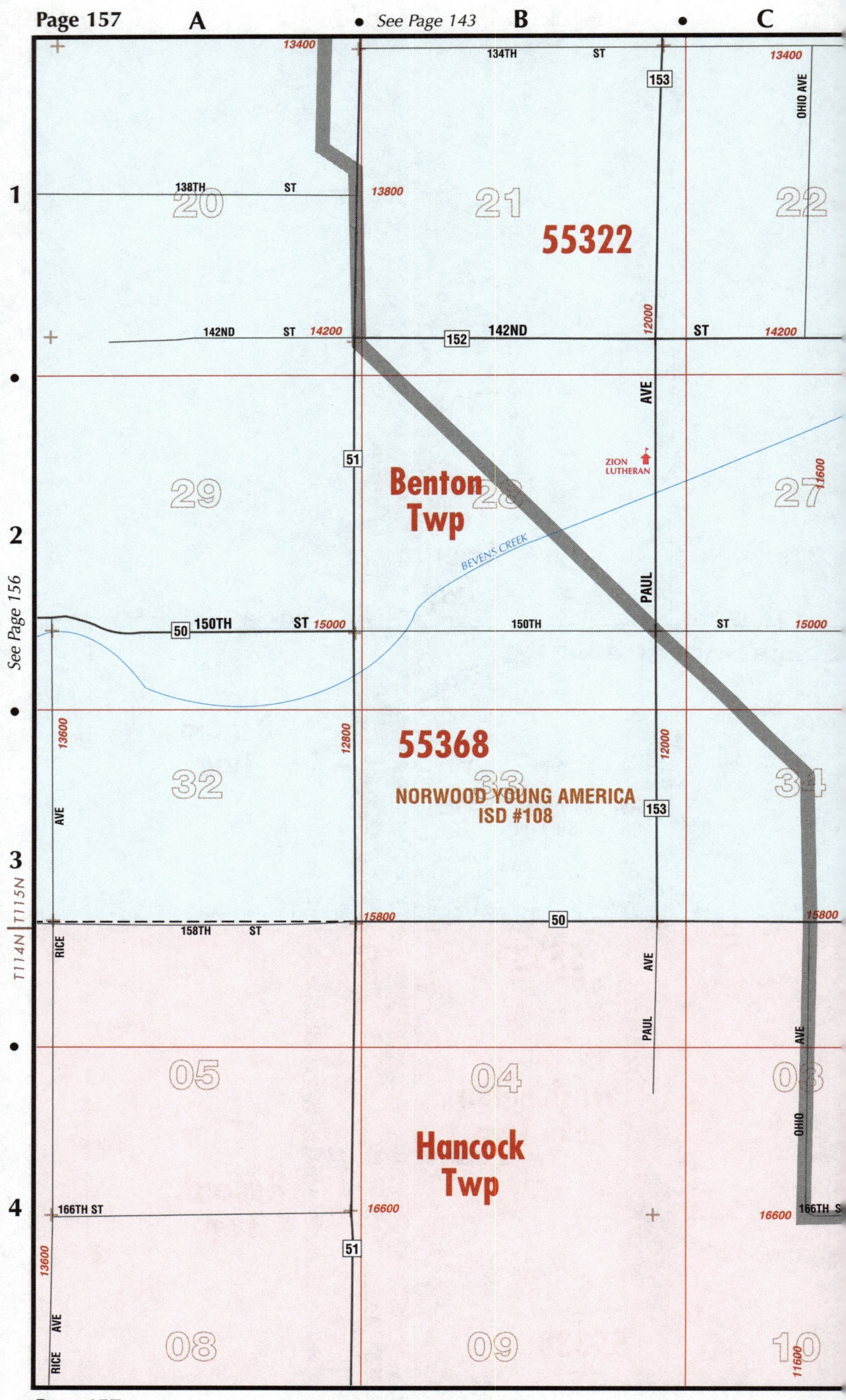

See Page 156

T114N | T115N

13400

134TH ST

153

13400

OHIO AVE

138TH ST

20

13800

21

55322

22

142ND ST 14200

152 142ND ST 14200

12000

AVE

51

Benton Twp

29

28

ZION LUTHERAN

PAUL

27

11600

BEVENS CREEK

50 150TH ST 15000

150TH ST 15000

13600

12800

55368

32

33

NORWOOD YOUNG AMERICA ISD #108

12000

153

34

AVE

158TH ST 15800

50

15800

RICE

PAUL AVE

05

04

AVE

03

OHIO

Hancock Twp

166TH ST

166TH ST 16600

16600

166TH S

51

13600

RICE AVE

08

09

10

11600

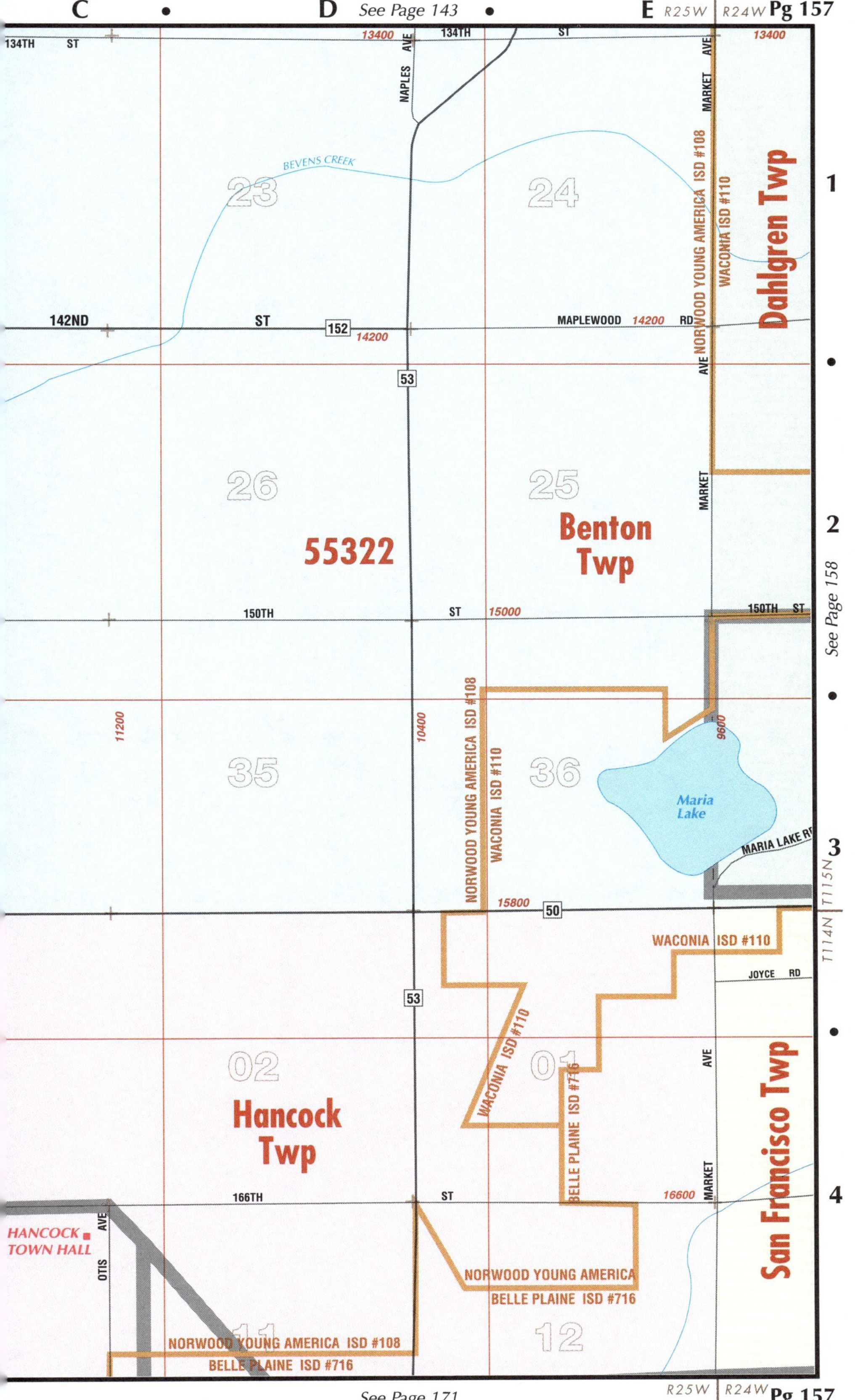

134TH ST   13400 AVE 134TH ST   13400

NAPLES AVE

BEVENS CREEK

23   24

MARKET AVE

NORWOOD YOUNG AMERICA ISD #108

WACONIA ISD #110

Dahlgren Twp

1

142ND ST   152 14200   MAPLEWOOD 14200 RD

53

26   25

MARKET

55322   **Benton Twp**

2

See Page 158

150TH ST 15000   150TH ST

11200   10400

NORWOOD YOUNG AMERICA ISD #108

WACONIA ISD #110

35   36   9600

Maria Lake

MARIA LAKE RD

T114N | T115N

3

15800   50

WACONIA ISD #110

53   JOYCE RD

02   WACONIA ISD #110   01

Hancock Twp   BELLE PLAINE ISD #716

MARKET AVE

San Francisco Twp

166TH ST   16600

HANCOCK ■ TOWN HALL

OTIS AVE

4

NORWOOD YOUNG AMERICA
BELLE PLAINE ISD #716

11

NORWOOD YOUNG AMERICA ISD #108
BELLE PLAINE ISD #716

12

A • *See Page 144* B • C

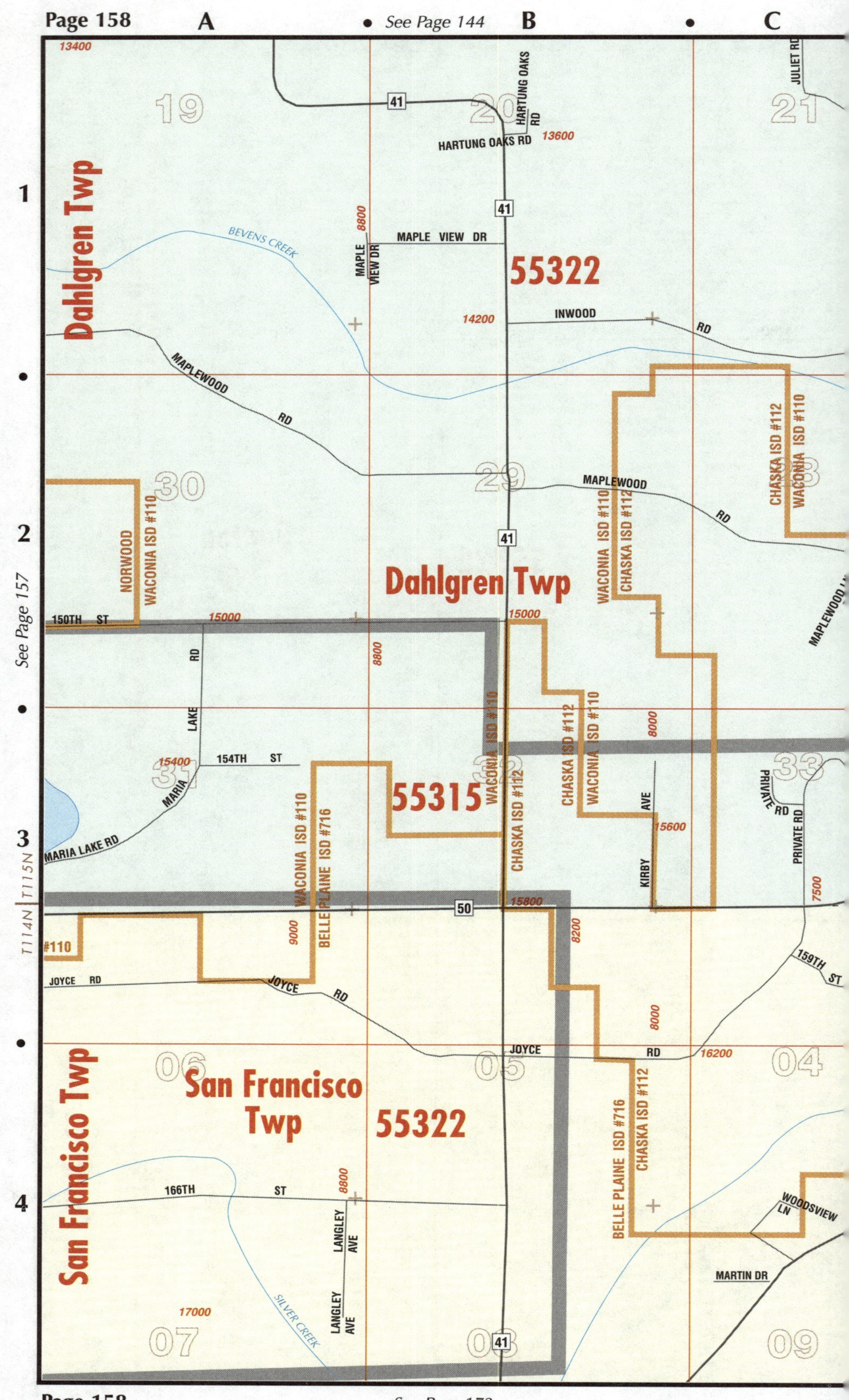

19

Dahlgren Twp

13400

41

HARTUNG OAKS RD

HARTUNG OAKS RD   13600

20

21

JULIET RD

1

BEVENS CREEK

MAPLE VIEW DR

MAPLE VIEW DR

41

55322

14200

INWOOD

RD

See Page 157

MAPLEWOOD

RD

30

NORWOOD

WACONIA ISD #110

29

MAPLEWOOD

RD

WACONIA ISD #110

CHASKA ISD #112

CHASKA ISD #112

WACONIA ISD #110

2

41

Dahlgren Twp

150TH   ST

15000

8800

15000

LAKE   RD

154TH   ST

WACONIA ISD #110

CHASKA ISD #112

CHASKA ISD #112

WACONIA ISD #110

8000

15400

MARIA

MARIA LAKE RD

31

55315

32

WACONIA ISD #110

BELLE PLAINE ISD #716

AVE

15600

KIRBY

PRIVATE RD

33

PRIVATE RD

7500

3

50

15800

9000

8200

8000

159TH   ST

#110

JOYCE   RD

JOYCE   RD

JOYCE

06

05

JOYCE

RD

16200

04

San Francisco Twp

San Francisco Twp

55322

BELLE PLAINE ISD #716

CHASKA ISD #112

WOODSVIEW LN

4

166TH   ST

8800

LANGLEY   AVE

MARTIN DR

17000

LANGLEY AVE

SILVER CREEK

07

03

41

09

T114N | T115N

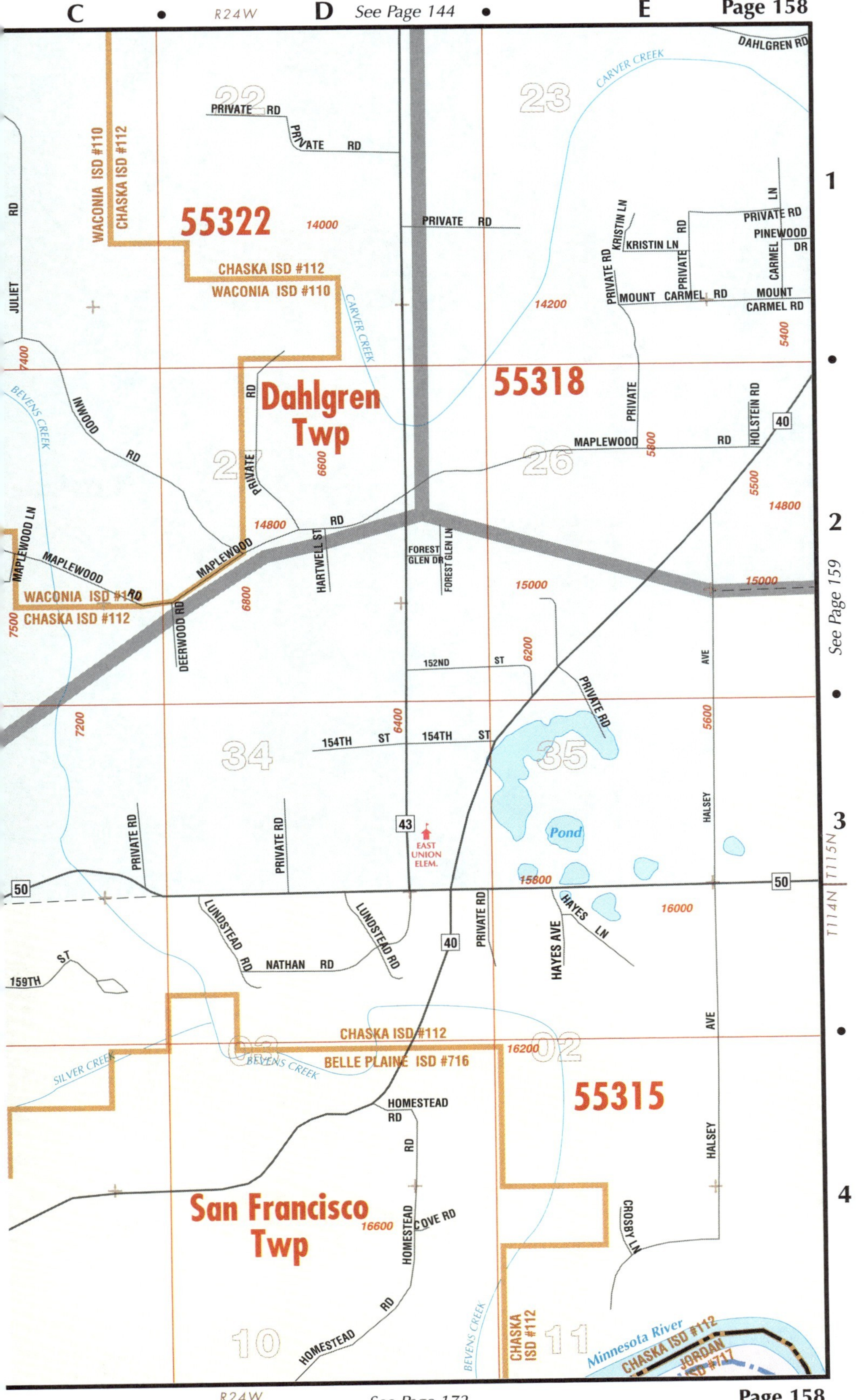

DAHLGREN RD

CARVER CREEK

1

WACONIA ISD #110
CHASKA ISD #112

22 23

PRIVATE RD
PRIVATE RD

55322 *14000*

CHASKA ISD #112
WACONIA ISD #110

JULIET RD

CARVER CREEK

PRIVATE RD

KRISTIN LN
KRISTIN LN
PRIVATE RD
PRIVATE RD
PINEWOOD DR
CARMEL LN

MOUNT CARMEL RD
MOUNT CARMEL RD

14200

5400

7400

Dahlgren Twp

55318 •

BEVENS CREEK

INNWOOD RD

PRIVATE RD

27 *6600*

26

PRIVATE RD

MAPLEWOOD RD
HOLSTEIN RD
5800
40

5500

14800

2

MAPLEWOOD LN

MAPLEWOOD RD

14800

DEERWOOD RD
MAPLEWOOD RD
6800

HARTWELL ST
RD

FOREST GLEN DR
FOREST GLEN LN

15000

See Page 159

WACONIA ISD #110
CHASKA ISD #112
7500

7200

34

PRIVATE RD

PRIVATE RD

152ND ST
6200

154TH ST
6400
154TH ST

AVE

PRIVATE RD

5600

35

Pond

3

50

PRIVATE RD

PRIVATE RD

43
EAST UNION ELEM.

15800

HAYES LN

HALSEY

16000

50

T114N | T115N

159TH ST

LUNDSTEAD RD

NATHAN RD
LUNDSTEAD RD

40

PRIVATE RD

HAYES AVE

HAYES AVE

AVE

•

SILVER CREEK

BEVENS CREEK

03

CHASKA ISD #112
BELLE PLAINE ISD #716

16200

02

55315

HALSEY AVE

4

HOMESTEAD RD

San Francisco Twp

HOMESTEAD COVE RD
16600

HOMESTEAD RD

CROSBY LN

10

HOMESTEAD RD

BEVENS CREEK

CHASKA ISD #112

11

Minnesota River

CHASKA ISD #112
JORDAN ISD #717

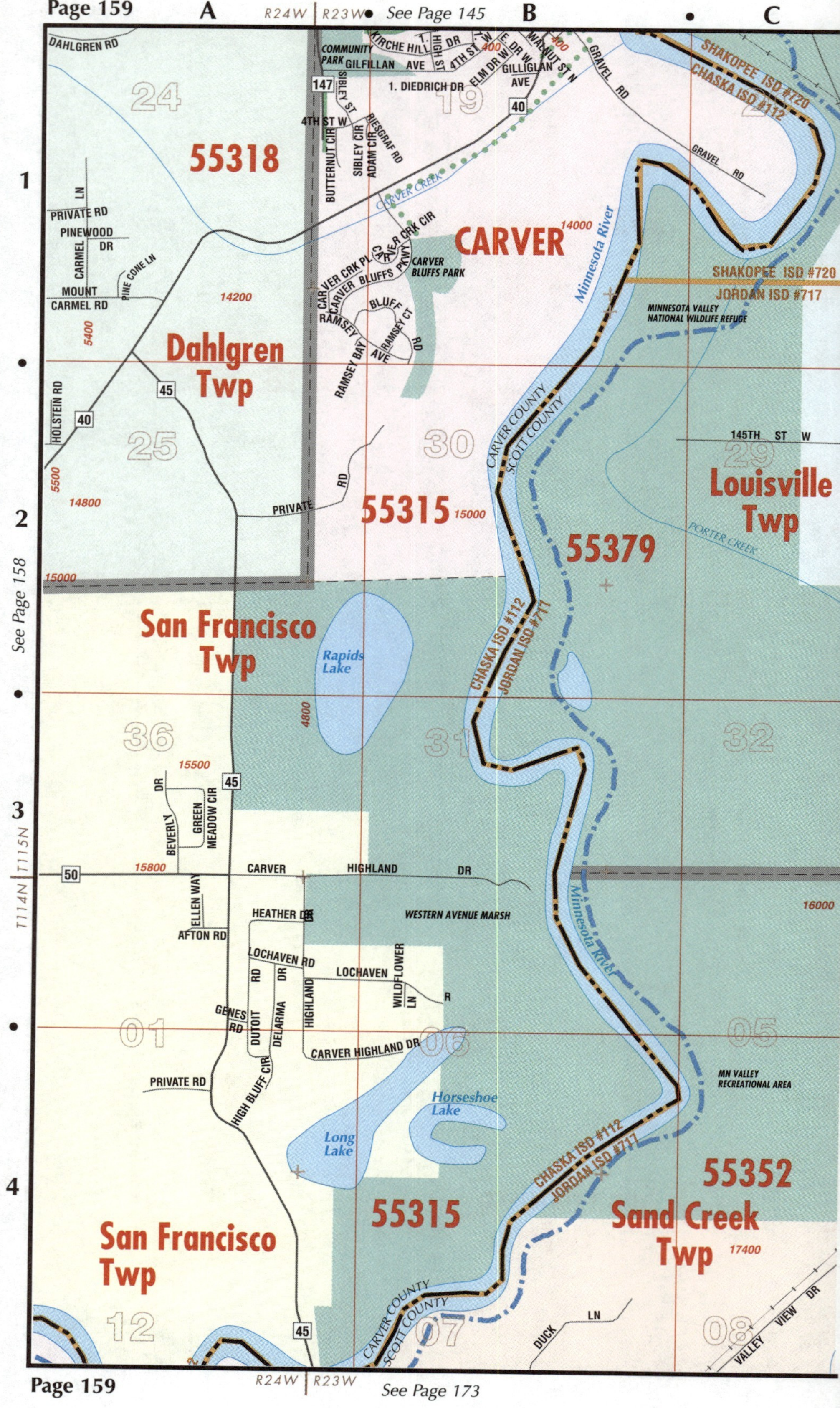

R24W R23W *See Page 145*

A   B   C

DAHLGREN RD

24

55318

COMMUNITY PARK
147
GILFILLAN AVE
SIBLEY ST W
4TH ST W
1. DIEDRICH DR
KIRCHE HILL DR
HIGH DR
4TH ST W
ELM DR W
WALNUT ST N
GILLIGLAN AVE
GRAVEL RD
40
19

SHAKOPEE ISD #720
CHASKA ISD #112
GRAVEL RD

1

PINE LN
PRIVATE RD
PINEWOOD DR
CARMEL RD
MOUNT CARMEL RD
PINE CONE LN
5400
14200

BUTTERNUT CIR
ADAM CIR
RIEGRAF RD
CARVER CRK PL
CARVER BLUFFS
CARVER CRK CIR
RAMSEY
BLUFF
RAMSEY BAY AVE
RAMSEY CT
BLUFF RD
CARVER BLUFFS PARK

CARVER 14000

Minnesota River

SHAKOPEE ISD #720
JORDAN ISD #717
MINNESOTA VALLEY NATIONAL WILDLIFE REFUGE

Dahlgren Twp

45
40
HOLSTEIN RD
5500
14800
25

PRIVATE RD

30

55315 15000

CARVER COUNTY
SCOTT COUNTY

145TH ST W
29

Louisville Twp

2

15000

San Francisco Twp

Rapids Lake
4800

31

55379

CHASKA ISD #112
JORDAN ISD #717

PORTER CREEK

32

16000

36
15500
45
BEVERLY DR
GREEN MEADOW CIR

3

50
15800
CARVER
HIGHLAND DR
ELLEN WAY
AFTON RD
HEATHER DR
LOCHAVEN RD
LOCHAVEN
WILDFLOWER LN
R
WESTERN AVENUE MARSH

Minnesota River

01
GENES RD
DUTOIT RD
DELARMA DR
HIGHLAND DR
HIGH BLUFF CIR
CARVER HIGHLAND DR
06
05

MN VALLEY RECREATIONAL AREA

PRIVATE RD
Horseshoe Lake
Long Lake

4

55315

CHASKA ISD #112
JORDAN ISD #717

55352

Sand Creek Twp 17400

San Francisco Twp

12
45
07
CARVER COUNTY
SCOTT COUNTY
DUCK LN
08
VALLEY VIEW DR

R24W R23W *See Page 173*

See Page 158

T114N | T115N

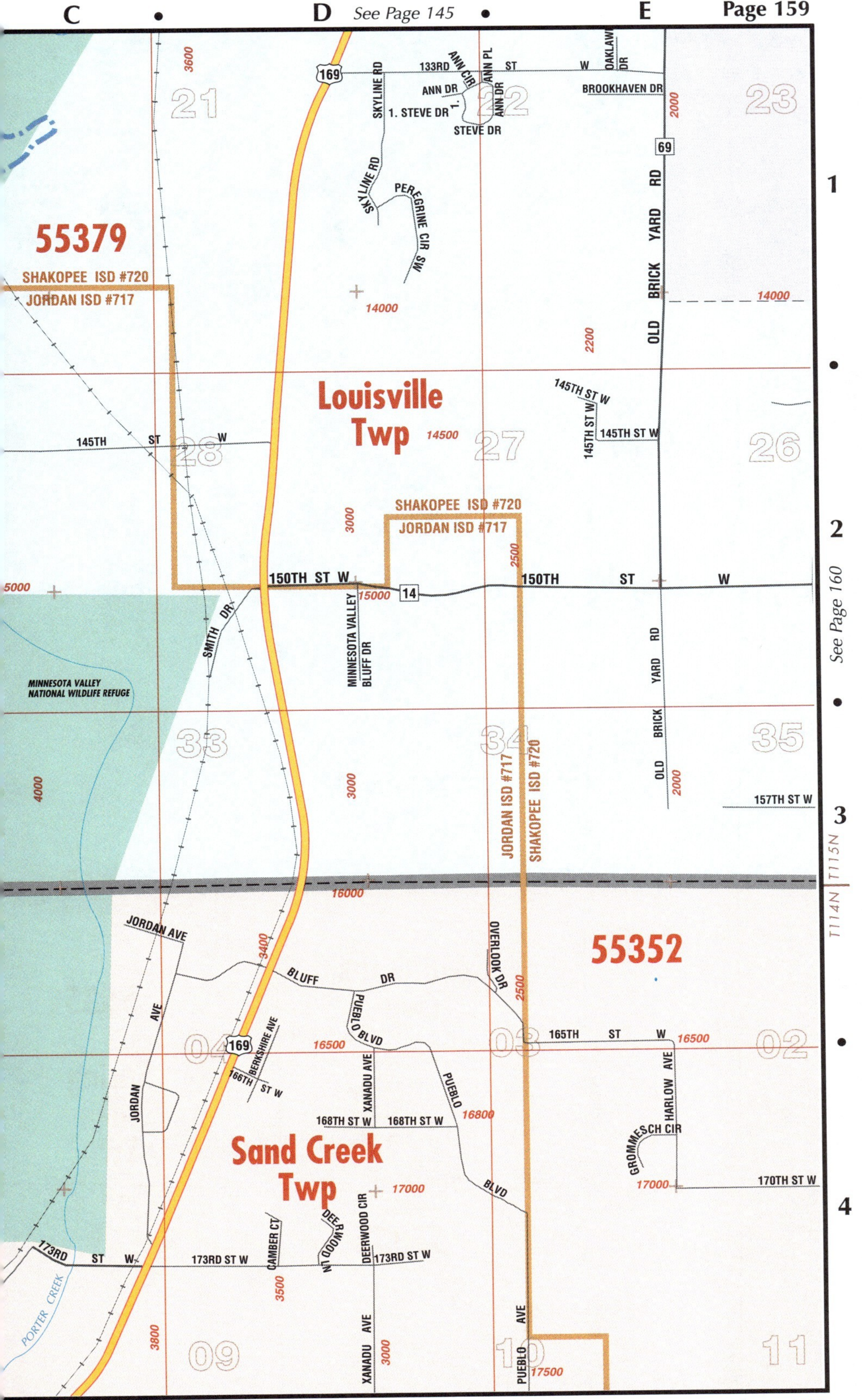

55379

SHAKOPEE ISD #720
JORDAN ISD #717

Louisville Twp

SHAKOPEE ISD #720
JORDAN ISD #717

MINNESOTA VALLEY
NATIONAL WILDLIFE REFUGE

55352

Sand Creek Twp

169

133RD ST W
OAKLAW DR
BROOKHAVEN DR

ANN CIR
ANN PL
ANN DR
ANN ST
ANN DR
1. STEVE DR
STEVE DR

SKYLINE RD
SKYLINE RD
PEREGRINE CIR SW

OLD BRICK YARD RD
69

145TH ST W
145TH ST W
145TH ST W
145TH ST W

145TH ST W

150TH ST W
150TH ST W
14

SMITH DR
MINNESOTA VALLEY BLUFF DR

OLD BRICK YARD RD
157TH ST W

JORDAN ISD #717
SHAKOPEE ISD #720

JORDAN AVE
OVERLOOK DR
BLUFF DR
PUEBLO BLVD
JORDAN AVE
BERKSHIRE AVE
169
166TH ST W
XANADU AVE
168TH ST W
168TH ST W
PUEBLO BLVD
165TH ST W
GROMMESCH CIR
HARLOW AVE
170TH ST W

PUEBLO BLVD
CAMBER CT
DEERWOOD LN
DEERWOOD CIR
173RD ST W
173RD ST W
XANADU AVE
PUEBLO AVE

173RD ST W

PORTER CREEK

T114N | T115N
See Page 160

3600
14000
2000
14000
2200
14500
3000
2500
5000
15000
4000
3000
2000
15000
3400
16500
16800
2500
16500
17000
17000
3500
17000
3000
17500
3800

21
22
23
28
27
26
33
34
35
04
03
02
09
10
11

1
2
3
4

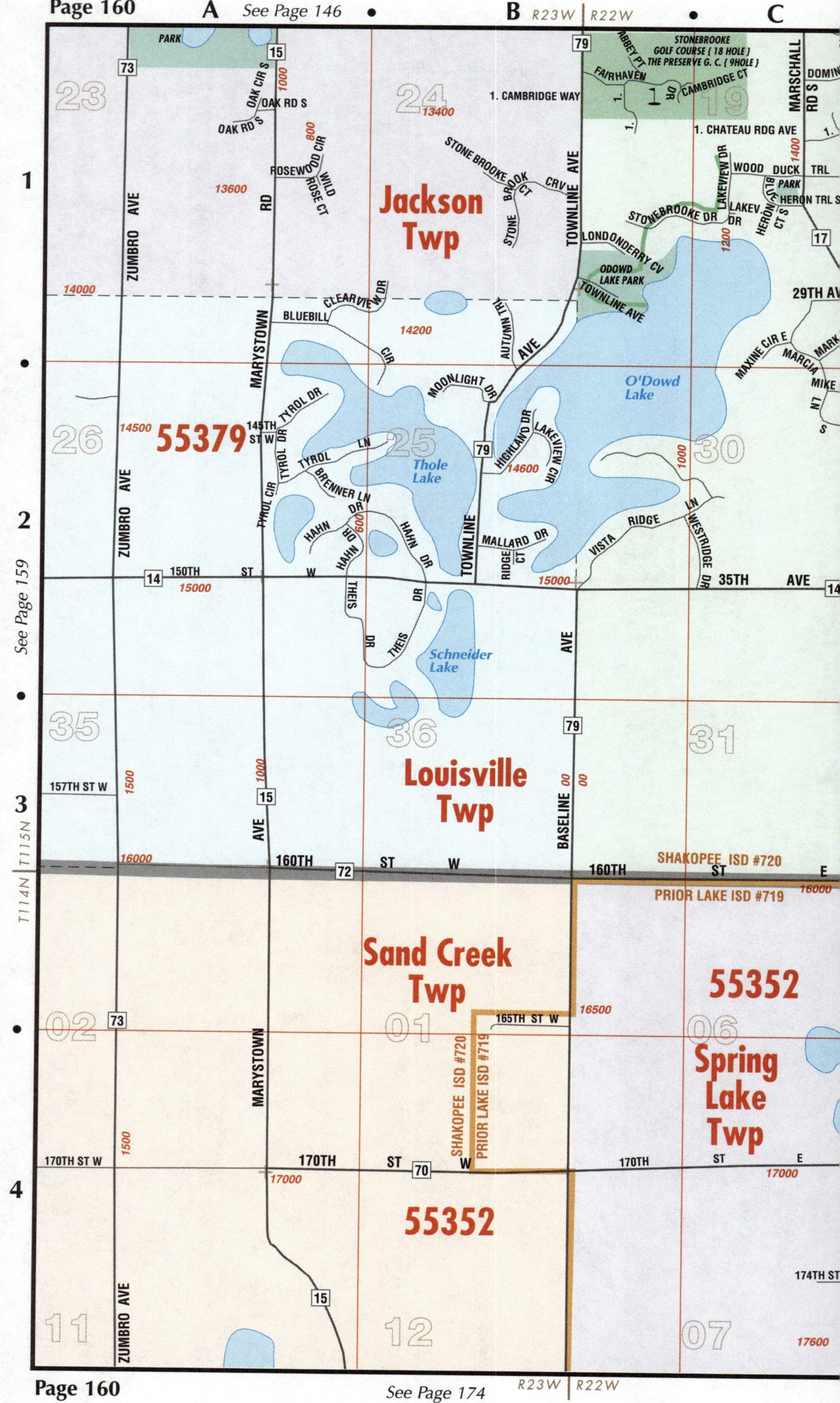

23

73

PARK

15

1000

OAK CIR S
OAK RD S
OAK RD S

ZUMBRO AVE

13600

ROSEWOOD RD

800

WILD ROSE CT

24
13400

Jackson Twp

79

STONEBROOKE GOLF COURSE (18 HOLE)
THE PRESERVE G. C. (9HOLE)

ABBEY PT
FAIRHAVEN

CAMBRIDGE CT
CAMBRIDGE CT

MARSCHALL RD S

19

DOMIN

1. CAMBRIDGE WAY

1. CHATEAU RDG AVE

1400

WOOD DUCK TRL

HERON TRL S

PARK

HERON TRL

17

1

STONE BROOKE CRV

STONE BROOK CT

STONE BROOK

LAKEVIEW DR

STONEBROOKE DR

1200

TOWNLINE AVE

14000

14200

CLEARVIEW DR

BLUEBILL

MARYSTOWN RD

CIR

AUTUMN TRL

LONDONDERRY CV

ODOWD LAKE PARK

TOWNLINE AVE

LAKEV DR

29TH AV

26

14500

55379

145TH ST W

TYROL DR

TYROL CIR

TYROL DR

LN

BRENNER LN

25

MOONLIGHT DR

79

Thole Lake

HIGHLAND DR

LAKEVIEW CIR

14600

O'Dowd Lake

MAXINE CIR E

MARCIA

LN

MARK
MIKE

1000

30

2

ZUMBRO AVE

HAHN DR

HAHN

HAHN DR

600

14

150TH ST W

15000

THEIS DR

THEIS DR

MALLARD DR

RIDGE CT

TOWNLINE

15000

VISTA RIDGE

WESTRIDGE DR

LN

35TH AVE

14

Schneider Lake

AVE

35

1500

1000

36

Louisville Twp

79

BASELINE 00

31

157TH ST W

15

3

16000

160TH

72

ST

W

160TH

ST

E

16000

T114N | T115N

See Page 159

02

73

Sand Creek Twp

MARYSTOWN RD

01

165TH ST W

16500

SHAKOPEE ISD #720

PRIOR LAKE ISD #719

06

55352

Spring Lake Twp

170TH ST W

1500

170TH

ST

70

W

170TH

ST

E

17000

17000

4

17000

55352

ZUMBRO AVE

15

11

12

07

174TH ST

17600

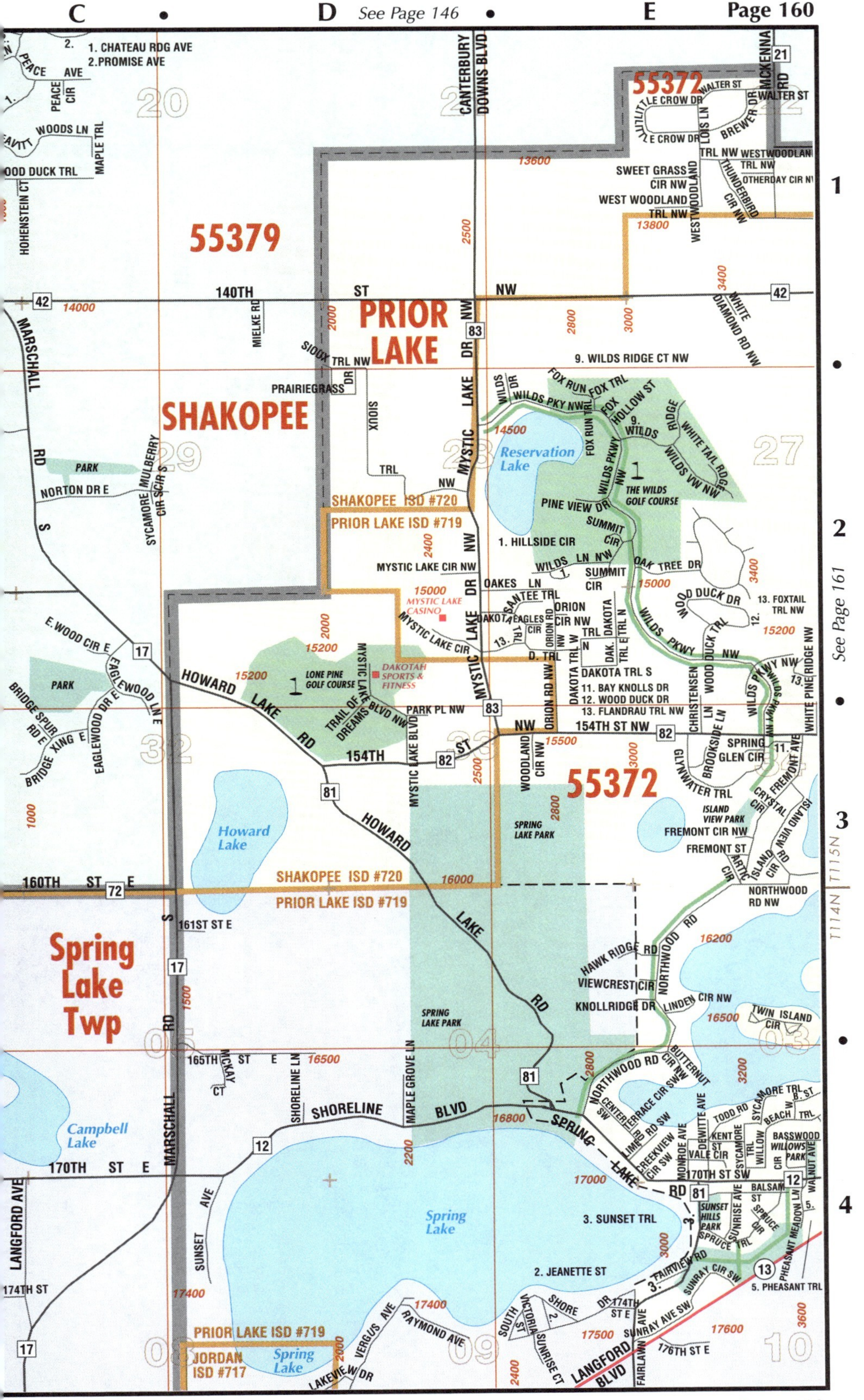

1. CHATEAU RDG AVE
2. PROMISE AVE

55379

PRIOR LAKE

SHAKOPEE

55372

140TH ST NW

PRAIRIEGRASS

9. WILDS RIDGE CT NW

Reservation Lake

THE WILDS GOLF COURSE

SHAKOPEE ISD #720
PRIOR LAKE ISD #719

1. HILLSIDE CIR

MYSTIC LAKE CIR NW

MYSTIC LAKE CASINO

13. FOXTAIL TRL NW

LONE PINE GOLF COURSE

DAKOTAH SPORTS & FITNESS

11. BAY KNOLLS DR
12. WOOD DUCK DR
13. FLANDRAU TRL NW

154TH ST NW

Howard Lake

SPRING GLEN CIR

Spring Lake Park

55372

SHAKOPEE ISD #720
PRIOR LAKE ISD #719

160TH ST E

Spring Lake Twp

161ST ST E

HAWK RIDGE RD

VIEWCREST CIR
KNOLLRIDGE DR

TWIN ISLAND CIR

165TH ST E

Campbell Lake

SHORELINE BLVD

170TH ST E

Spring Lake

3. SUNSET TRL

SUNSET HILLS PARK

BASSWOOD WILLOWS PARK

2. JEANETTE ST

5. PHEASANT TRL

174TH ST

PRIOR LAKE ISD #719
JORDAN ISD #717

176TH ST E

LANGFORD BLVD

See Page 174

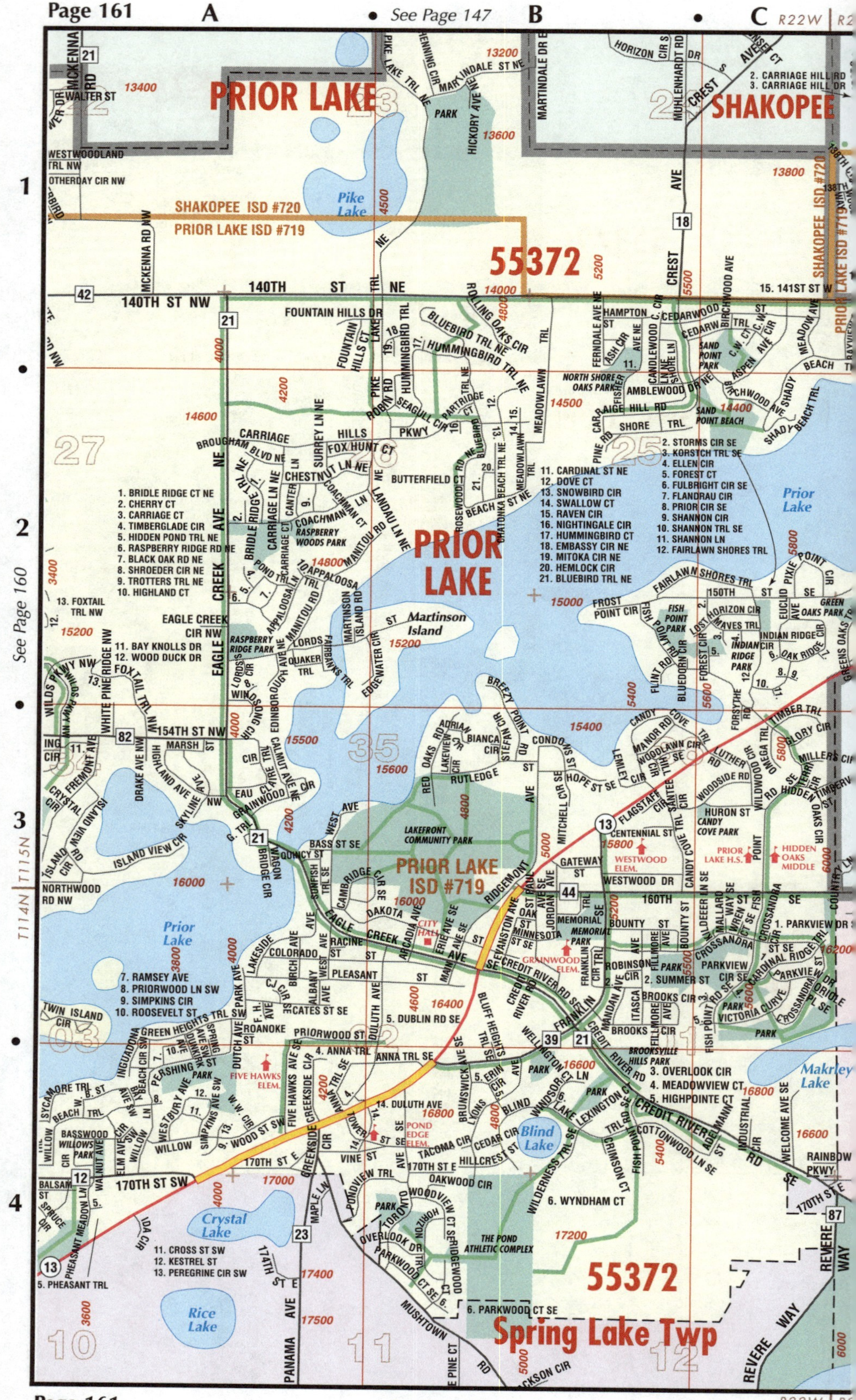

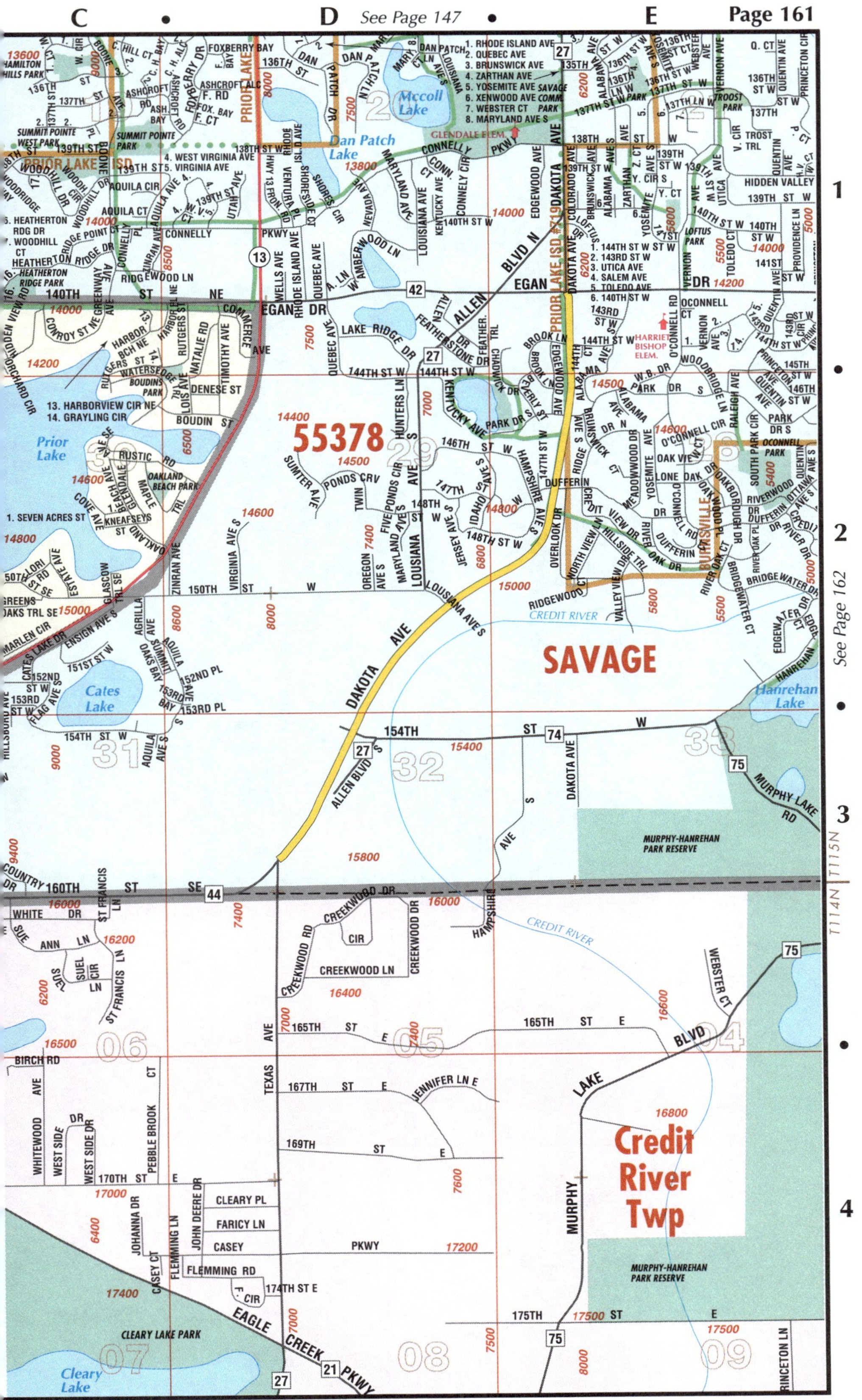

See Page 147

See Page 162

55378

Prior Lake

SAVAGE

Hanrehan Lake

Credit River Twp

MURPHY-HANREHAN PARK RESERVE

MURPHY-HANREHAN PARK RESERVE

Cleary Lake Park

Cleary Lake

See Page 175

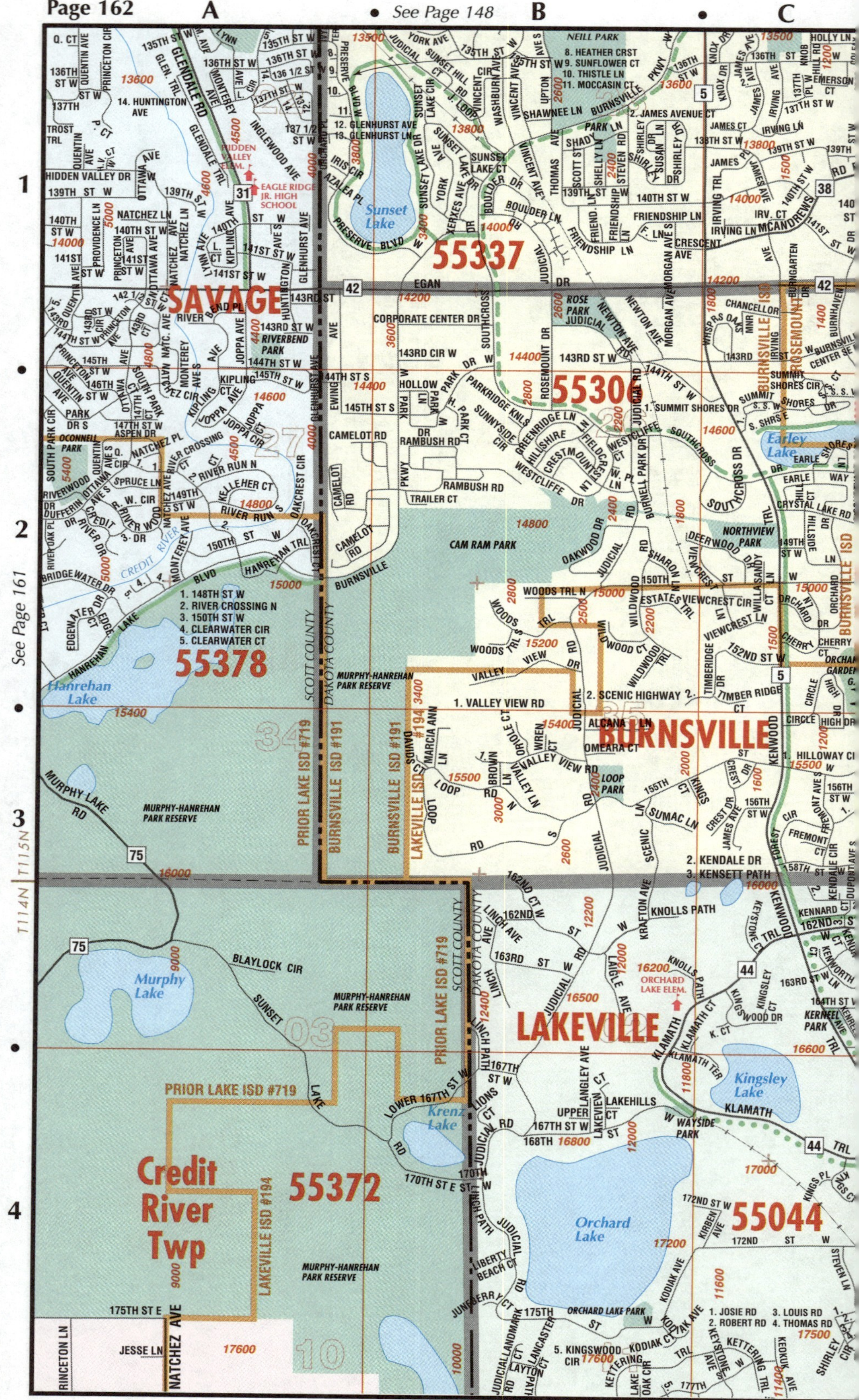

See Page 161

T114N | T115N

SAVAGE

55337

55300

55378

BURNSVILLE

LAKEVILLE

Credit River Twp

55372

55044

Sunset Lake

Hanrehan Lake

Murphy Lake

Krenz Lake

Orchard Lake

Kingsley Lake

Earley Lake

Murphy-Hanrehan Park Reserve

Cam Ram Park

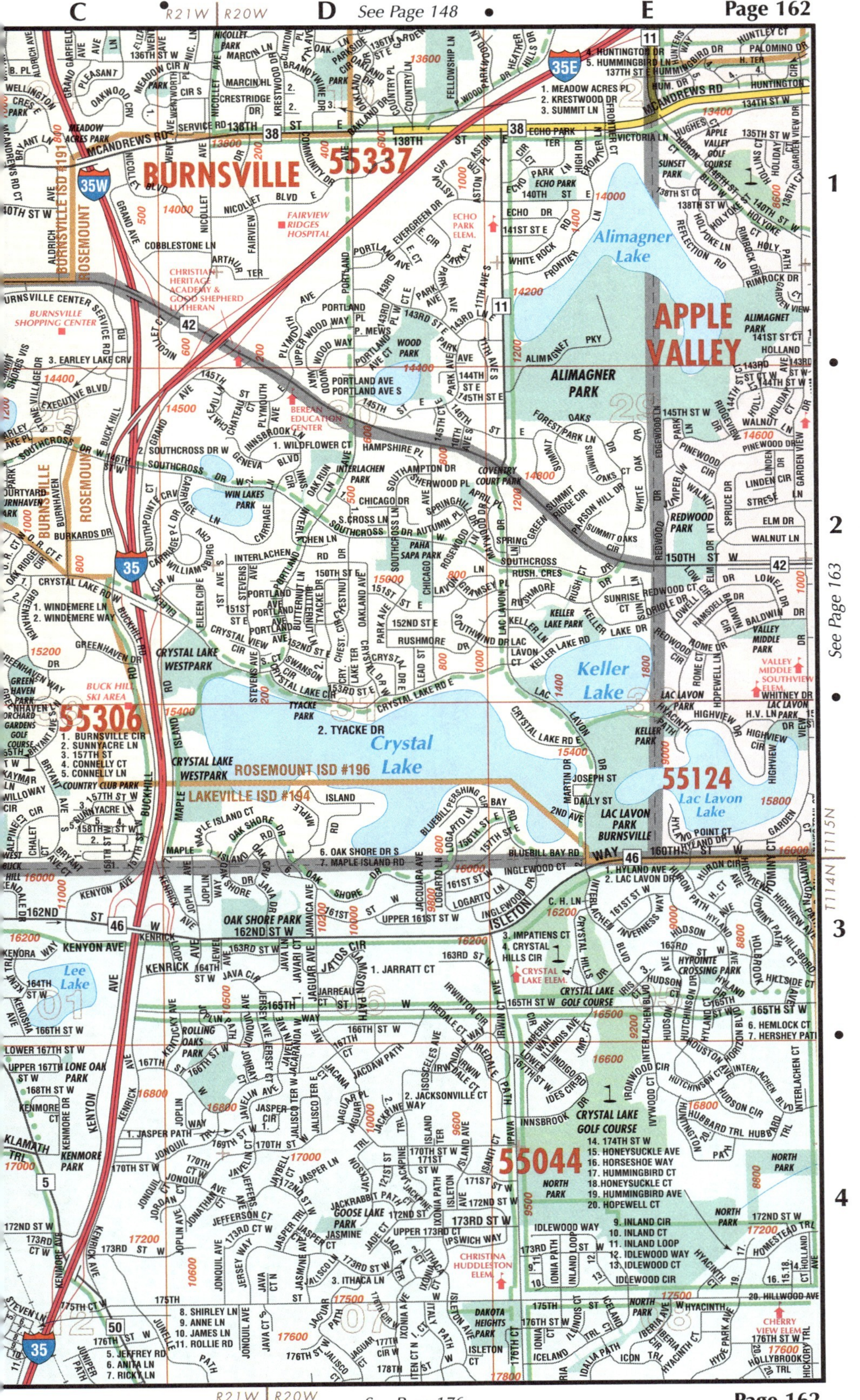

BURNSVILLE
55337
APPLE VALLEY
55306
55124
55044
Alimagner Lake
ALIMAGNER PARK
Keller Lake
Crystal Lake
Lac Lavon Lake
Lee Lake
FAIRVIEW RIDGES HOSPITAL
ECHO PARK ELEM.
CHRISTIAN HERITAGE ACADEMY & GOOD SHEPHERD LUTHERAN
BURNSVILLE SHOPPING CENTER
BEREAN EDUCATION CENTER
BUCK HILL SKI AREA
VALLEY MIDDLE PARK
VALLEY MIDDLE SOUTHVIEW ELEM.
CRYSTAL LAKE ELEM.
CHRISTINA HUDDLESTON ELEM.
CHERRY VIEW ELEM.
CRYSTAL LAKE GOLF COURSE
APPLE VALLEY GOLF COURSE
CRYSTAL LAKE WESTPARK
KELLER LAKE PARK
LAC LAVON PARK BURNSVILLE
WIN LAKES PARK
PAHA SAPA PARK
INTERLACHEN PARK
OAK SHORE PARK
ROLLING OAKS PARK
LONE OAK PARK
KENMORE PARK
GOOSE LAKE PARK
DAKOTA HEIGHTS PARK
NORTH PARK
REDWOOD PARK
ROSEMOUNT ISD #196
LAKEVILLE ISD #194
BURNSVILLE ISD #191
MCANDREWS RD
138TH ST
150TH ST W
160TH ST W
1. MEADOW ACRES PL
2. KRESTWOOD DR
3. SUMMIT LN
1. BURNSVILLE CIR
2. SUNNYACRE LN
3. 157TH ST
4. CONNELLY CT
5. CONNELLY LN
14. 174TH ST W
15. HONEYSUCKLE AVE
16. HORSESHOE WAY
17. HUMMINGBIRD CT
18. HONEYSUCKLE CT
19. HUMMINGBIRD AVE
20. HOPEWELL CT
9. INLAND CIR
10. INLAND CT
11. INLAND LOOP
12. IDLEWOOD WAY
13. IDLEWOOD CT
8. SHIRLEY LN
9. ANNE LN
10. JAMES LN
11. ROLLIE RD
5. JEFFREY RD
6. ANITA LN
7. RICKY LN
T115N
T114N

See Page 163

A • See Page 149 B • C

See Page 162

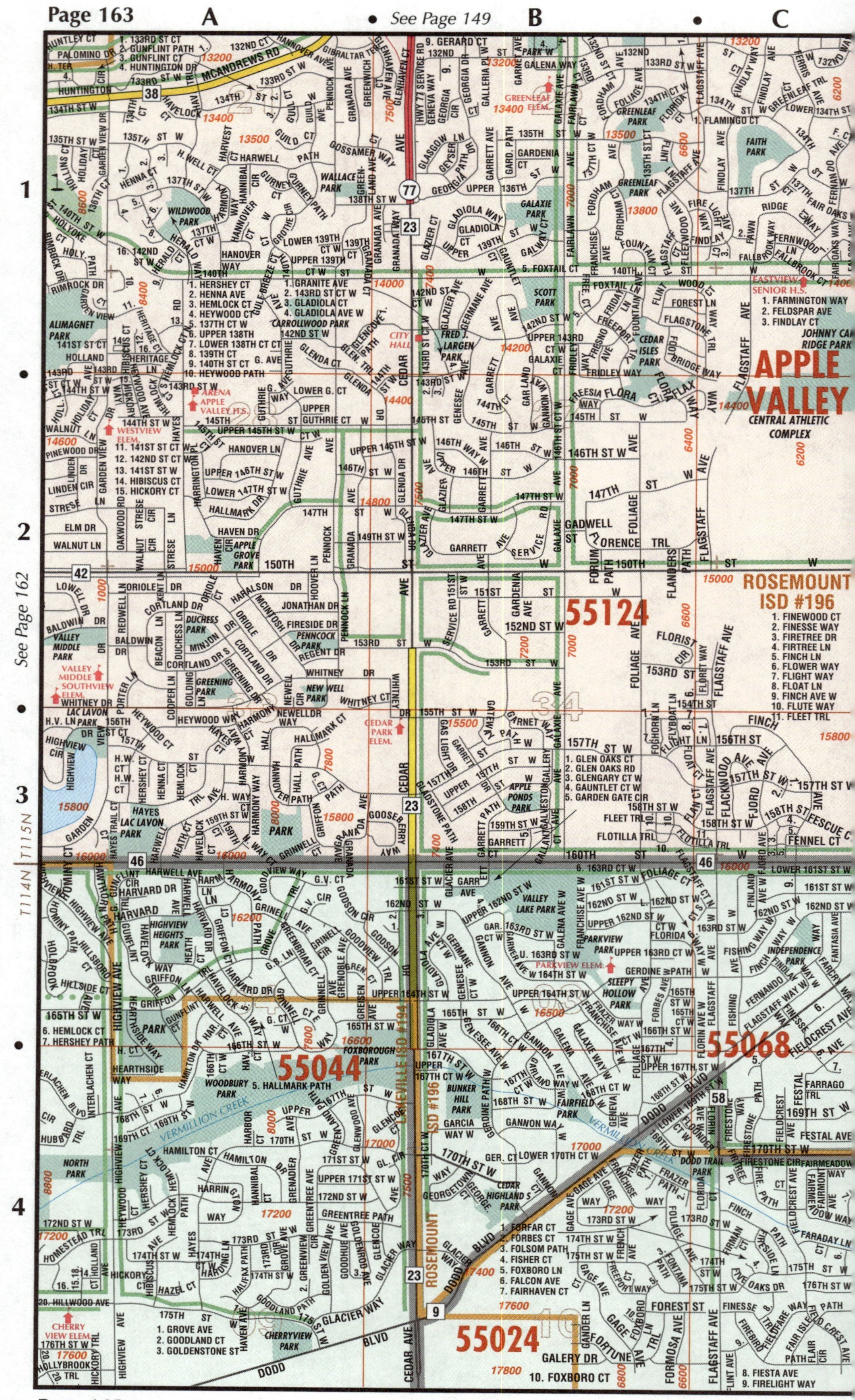

See Page 177

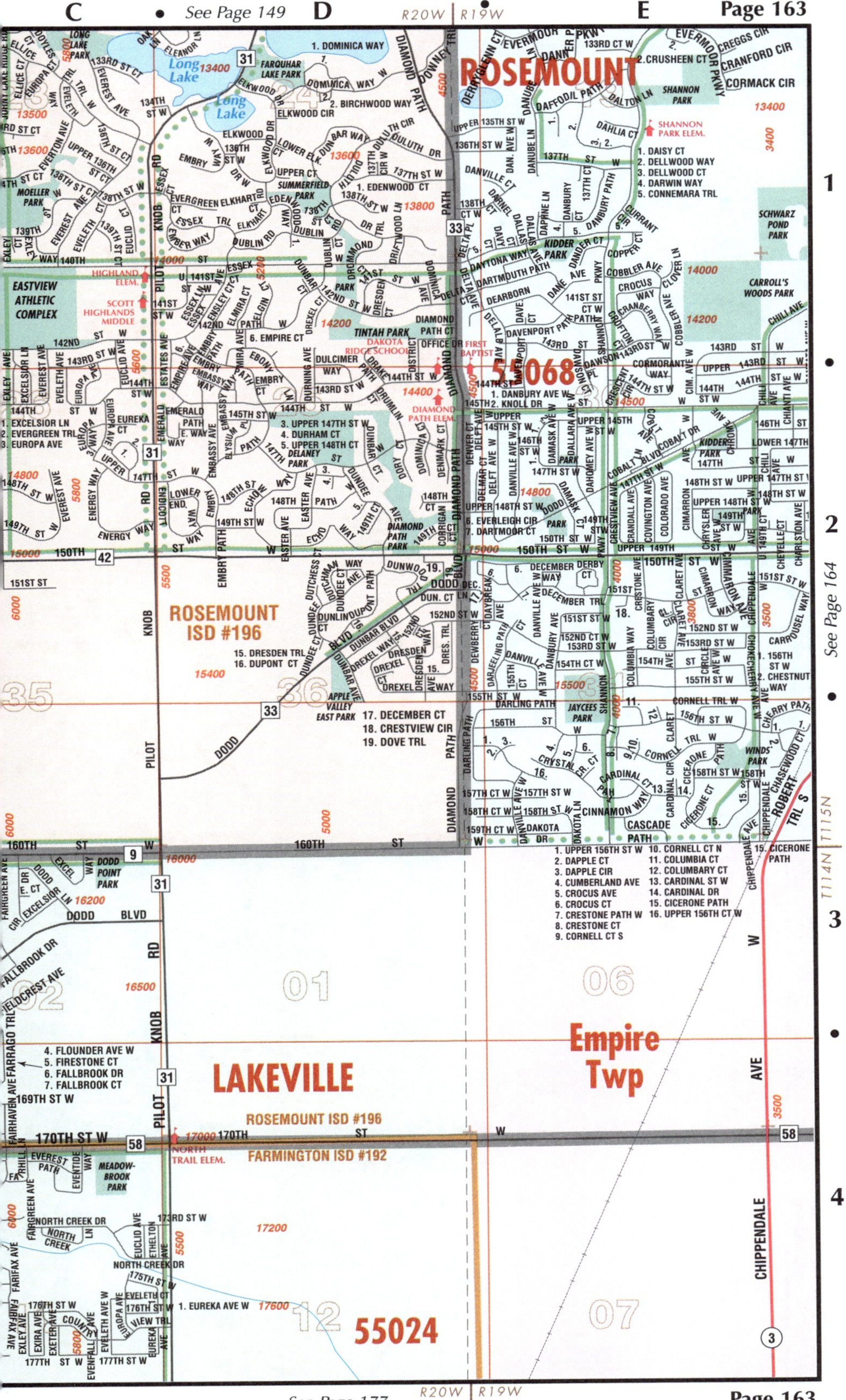
ROSEMOUNT
55068
ROSEMOUNT ISD #196
LAKEVILLE
Empire Twp
ROSEMOUNT ISD #196
FARMINGTON ISD #192
55024
See Page 149
See Page 164
See Page 177

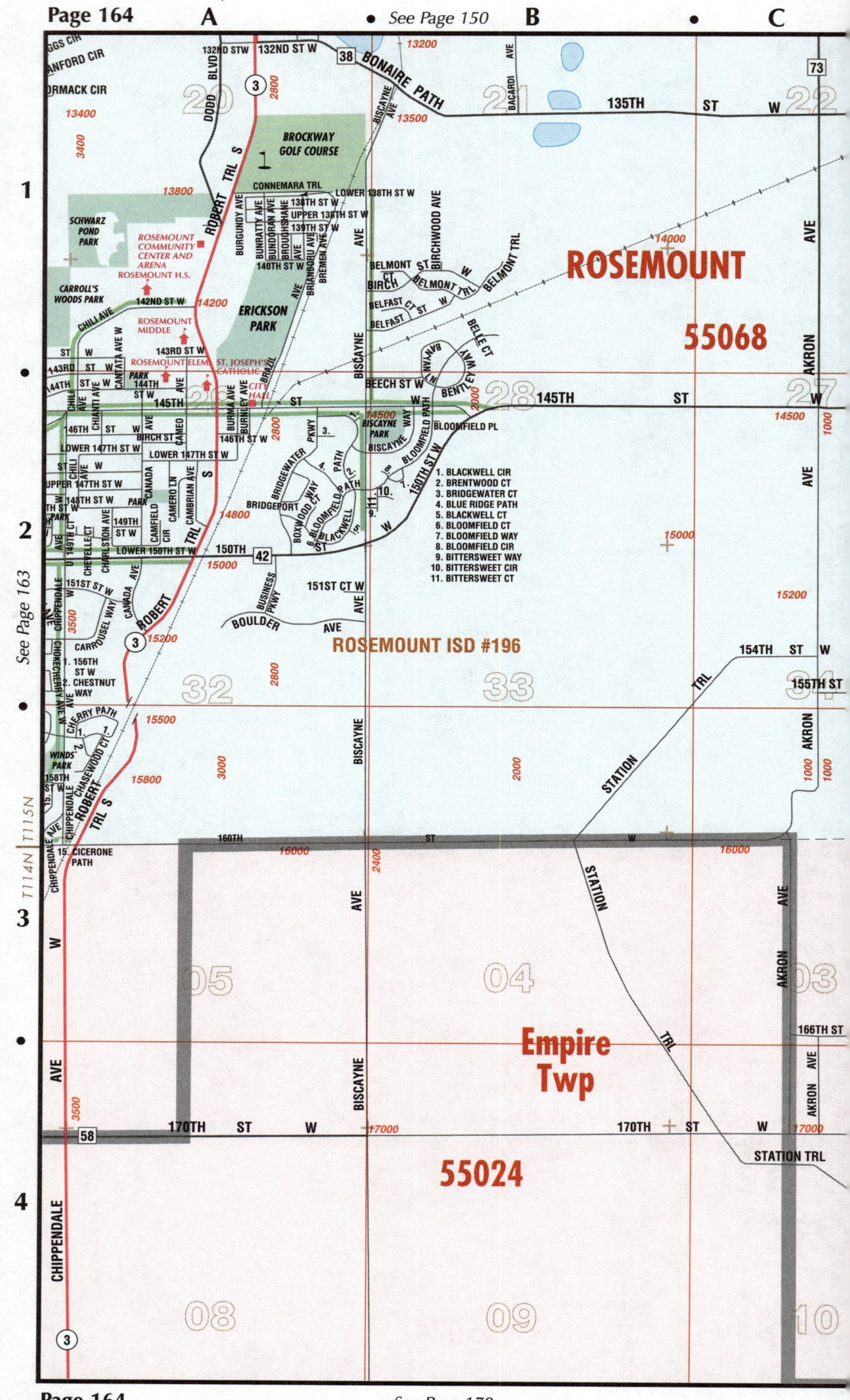

See Page 150

A   B   C

See Page 163

132ND ST W   132ND ST W
DODD BLVD
13200
BONAIRE PATH
BACARDI AVE
BISCAYNE AVE
13500
135TH   ST   W
73
38

20   21   22

13400

3400

1

13800

BROCKWAY GOLF COURSE

SCHWARZ POND PARK

CARROLL'S WOODS PARK

ROSEMOUNT COMMUNITY CENTER AND ARENA
ROSEMOUNT H.S.

CONNEMARA TRL
LOWER 138TH W
UPPER 138TH W
139TH ST W
140TH ST W
BURGUNDY AVE
BUNRATTY AVE
BUNDORAN AVE
BROUGHSHANE
BRIANSBORU AVE
BREMEN AVE

BELMONT ST
BIRCHWOOD AVE
BELMONT CT
BELMONT TRL
BELMONT
BIRCH
BELFAST CT
BELFAST
BELLE CT
BELTRY WAY

14000

ROSEMOUNT

55068

AKRON AVE

142ND ST W

14200

ROSEMOUNT MIDDLE

143RD ST W

ROSEMOUNT ELEM.
PARK

ST. JOSEPH'S CATHOLIC

CITY HALL

ERICKSON PARK

ROBERT TRL S

CHILI AVE
CANATTA AVE W

143RD   ST   W
144TH   ST   W
CHILI AVE
145TH   ST

CHIANTI AVE
144TH AVE
BURMA AVE
BURLEY AVE W

BISCAYNE AVE
BEECH ST W
BENTLEY

145TH   ST   W

2000   28   27

14500   1000

1   •   143RD   ST   •   27

14500

146TH ST W
LOWER 147TH ST W
CHILI AVE
UPPER 147TH ST W
149TH ST W
LOWER 150TH W

BIRCH ST
CAMEO
CAMPFIELD CT
CHETELE CT
CHARLSTON AVE
CANADA AVE
CAMDEN
CAMBRIAN AVE
CAMERON LN
ROBERT TRL S

146TH ST W
BISCAYNE PKWY
BISCAYNE PARK
BISCAYNE
BLOOMFIELD PL

3.
BRIDGEWATER PKWY
BOXWOOD CT
BRIDGEPORT
BLACKWELL CT
BLACKWELL
6.
BLOOMFIELD CT
7.
8.
9.
10.
BLOOMFIELD PATH
150TH AVE W
BLOOMFIELD WAY

1. BLACKWELL CIR
2. BRENTWOOD CT
3. BRIDGEWATER CT
4. BLUE RIDGE PATH
5. BLACKWELL CT
6. BLOOMFIELD CT
7. BLOOMFIELD WAY
8. BLOOMFIELD CIR
9. BITTERSWEET WAY
10. BITTERSWEET CIR
11. BITTERSWEET CT

15000

2800

14800

150TH   ST   42
15000

151ST CT W

BUSINESS PKWY

BOULDER   AVE

ROSEMOUNT ISD #196

15200

15200

3500
CHIPPENDALE CT
151ST ST W
CHESTER
CARROUSEL WAY
1. 156TH ST W
2. CHESTNUT WAY
CHERRY PATH
ROBERT TRL S

ROBERT   3   15200
2800

32   33   34

154TH   ST   W
155TH ST
AKRON AVE

1000   1000

WINDS PARK
158TH
CHIPPENDALE
CHASEWOOD CT
ROBERT TRL S

15500

15800

3000

BISCAYNE AVE

STATION TRL

15. CICERONE PATH

160TH   ST
15000

2400

2000

16000
STATION TRL

AKRON AVE

3

05   04   03

CHIPPENDALE AVE W
3500

Empire Twp

BISCAYNE AVE

STATION TRL

166TH ST

AKRON AVE

170TH   ST   W
17000

170TH   ST   W
17000
STATION TRL

58

55024

4

CHIPPENDALE

08   09   10

3

See Page 178

T114N   T115N

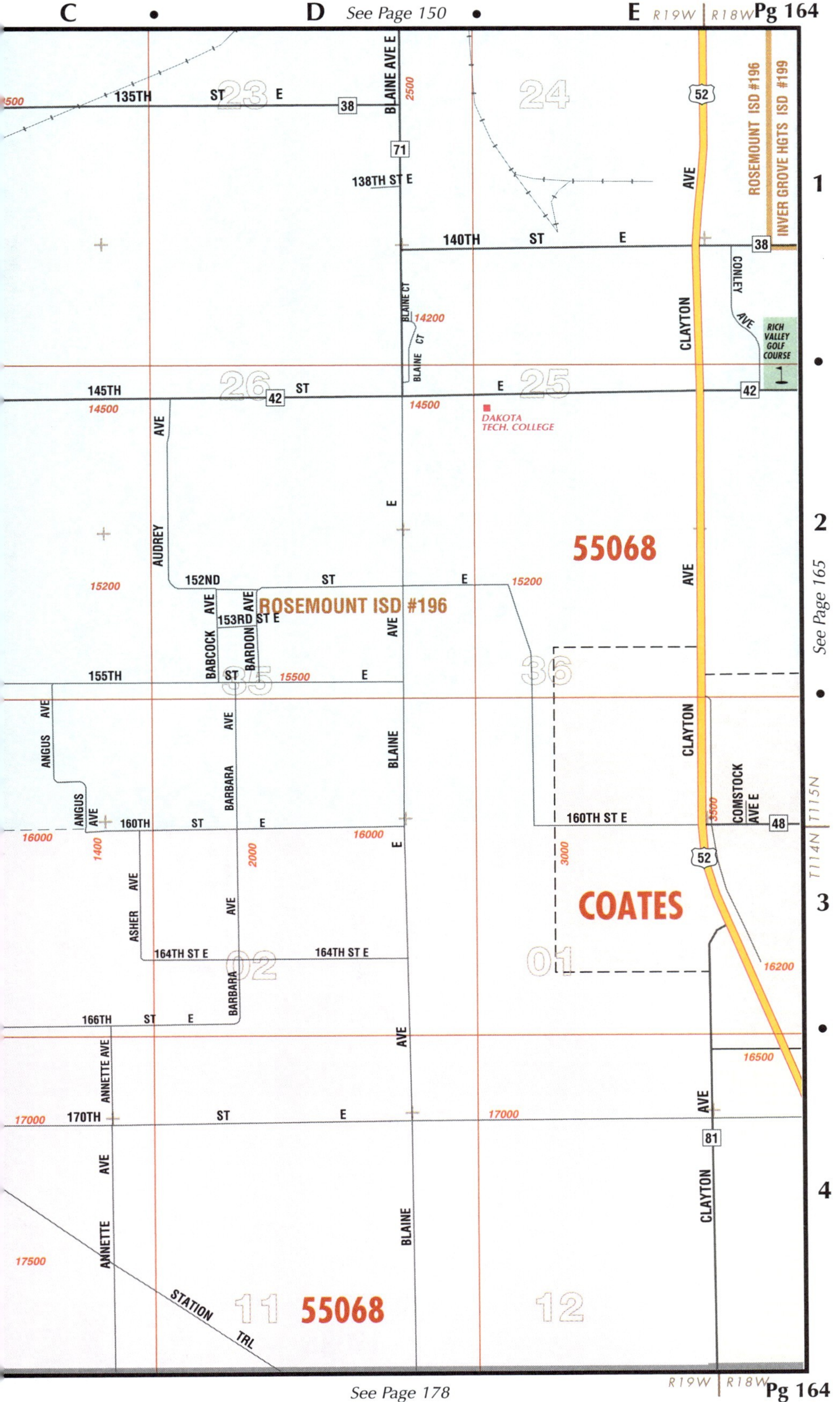

BLAINE AVE E 2500

135TH ST E 23 E [38]

135 00

24

[71]

138TH ST E

140TH ST E [38]

U.S. 52

CLAYTON AVE

CONLEY AVE

ROSEMOUNT ISD #196
INVER GROVE HGTS ISD #199

1

BLAINE CT 14200
BLAINE CT

RICH VALLEY GOLF COURSE

145TH 26 ST E 25 E 42 1 •

14500 [42]

14500

DAKOTA TECH. COLLEGE

55068

See Page 165

AUDREY AVE

2

15200 152ND ST E 15200

ROSEMOUNT ISD #196

BABCOCK AVE
BARDON AVE

153RD ST E

155TH 35 ST E 36 E

15500

ANGUS AVE

BARBARA AVE

BLAINE AVE

CLAYTON AVE

ANGUS AVE

160TH ST E 160TH ST E 48

16000 1400 2000 16000

3000

COMSTOCK AVE E

U.S. 52 3500

COATES

3

ASHER AVE

BARBARA AVE

164TH ST E 02 164TH ST E 01 16200

166TH ST E

ANNETTE AVE

BLAINE AVE

CLAYTON AVE

16500

17000 170TH ST E 17000 [81]

ANNETTE AVE

BLAINE AVE

CLAYTON AVE

4

17500

STATION TRL

11 **55068** 12

R19W | R18W

T114N | T115N

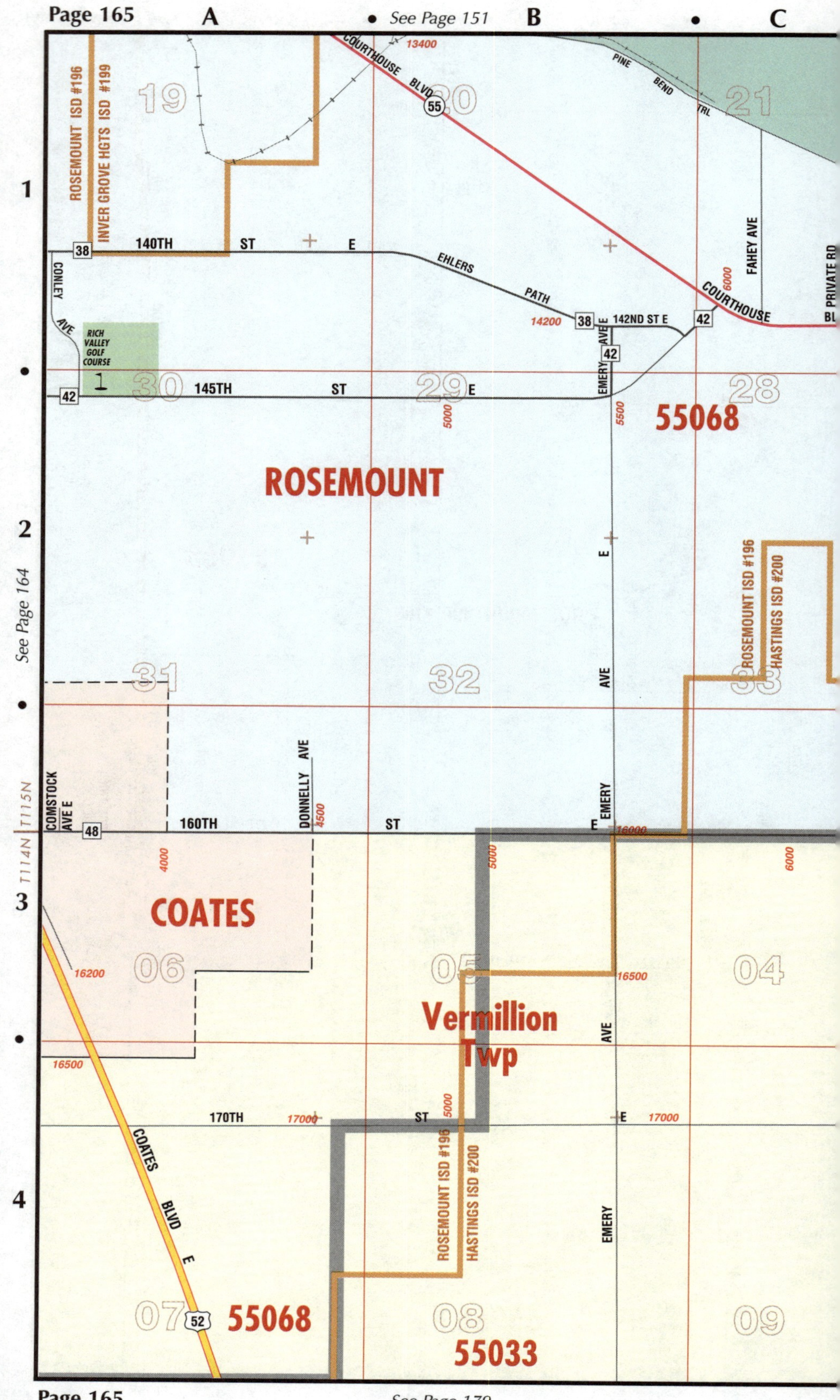

A   B   C

13400

COURTHOUSE BLVD

55

19   20   21

PINE BEND TRL

ROSEMOUNT ISD #196

INVER GROVE HGTS ISD #199

FAHEY AVE

PRIVATE RD

1

38 140TH ST E

CONLEY AVE

EHLERS

PATH

5000

COURTHOUSE

BL

14200 38 142ND ST E 42

EMERY AVE E

RICH VALLEY GOLF COURSE

42

42 1 30 145TH ST 29 E 28

5000 5500

55068

ROSEMOUNT

2

EMERY AVE

ROSEMOUNT ISD #196

HASTINGS ISD #200

31   32   33

See Page 164

DONNELLY AVE

COMSTOCK AVE E

EMERY

48 160TH 4500 ST E 16000

4000 5000 6000

T114N | T115N

3

COATES

16200 06 05 16500 04

Vermillion Twp

AVE

16500 EMERY

170TH 17000 ST 5000 E 17000

ROSEMOUNT ISD #196

HASTINGS ISD #200

EMERY

4

COATES BLVD E

07 52 **55068** 08 09

55033

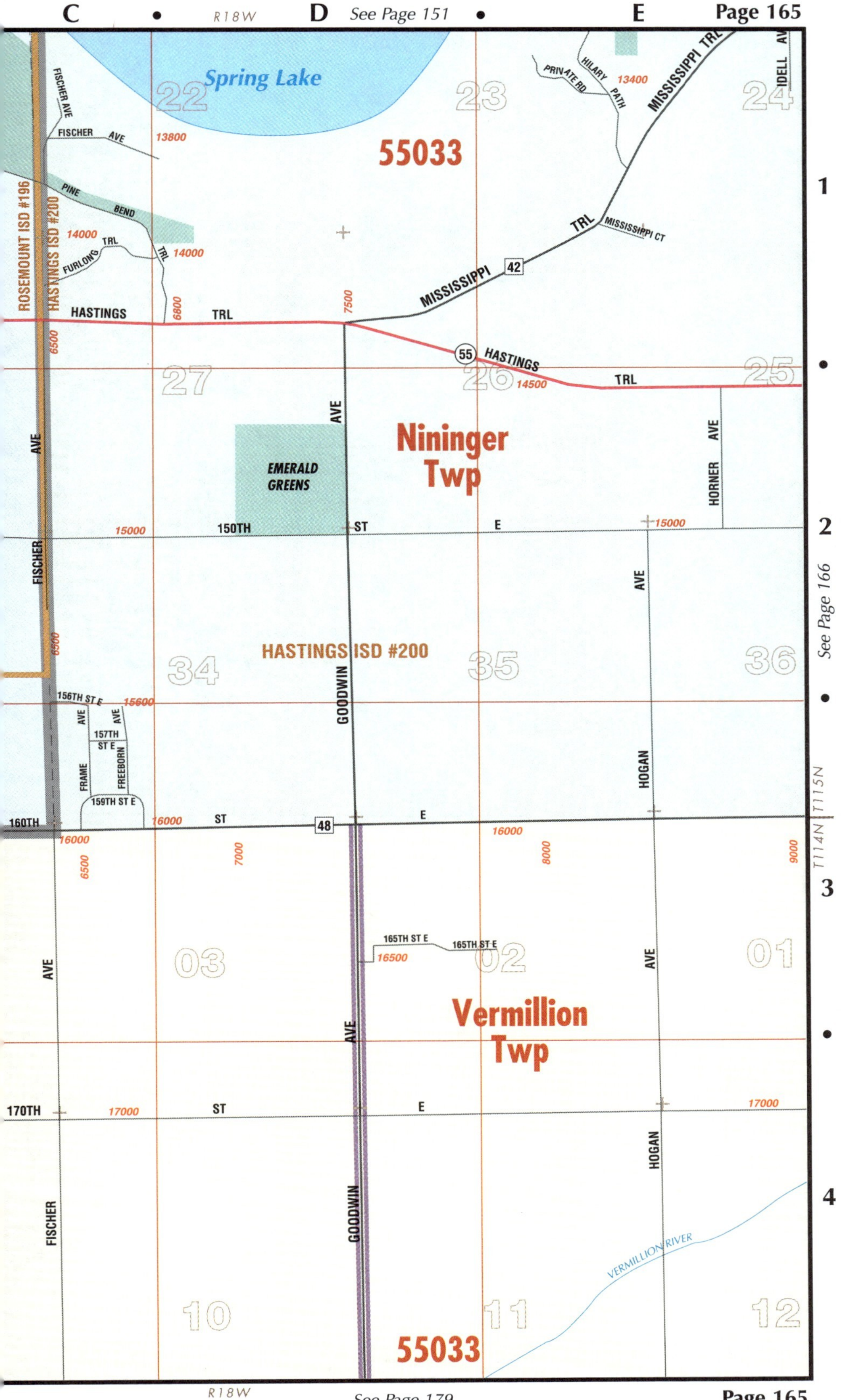

Spring Lake

55033

22   23   24

FISCHER AVE

FISCHER   AVE   *13800*

PINE   BEND

14000

FURLONG   TRL   *14000*

HASTINGS   TRL   *6800*   *7500*

MISSISSIPPI   **42**

TRL   Mississippi CT

PRIVATE RD   HILARY   PATH   *13400*

MISSISSIPPI TRL

IDELL AV

ROSEMOUNT ISD #196

HASTINGS ISD #200

6500

1

55   HASTINGS

27   26   *14500*   25   TRL

AVE

HORNER   AVE

Nininger Twp

EMERALD GREENS

FISCHER   AVE

6900

15000   150TH   ST   E   +   *15000*

2

GOODWIN   AVE

AVE

HASTINGS ISD #200

34   35   36

See Page 166

156TH ST E   *15600*

AVE   AVE

157TH ST E

FRAME   FREEBORN

159TH ST E

HOGAN

T114N | T115N

160TH   *16000*   ST   E   *16000*

48

16000   *7000*   *8000*   *9000*

6500

3

AVE

03   165TH ST E   165TH ST E   *16500*   02   01

GOODWIN   AVE

AVE

Vermillion Twp

HOGAN

170TH   *17000*   ST   E   *17000*

4

FISCHER

GOODWIN

VERMILLION RIVER

10   11   12

55033

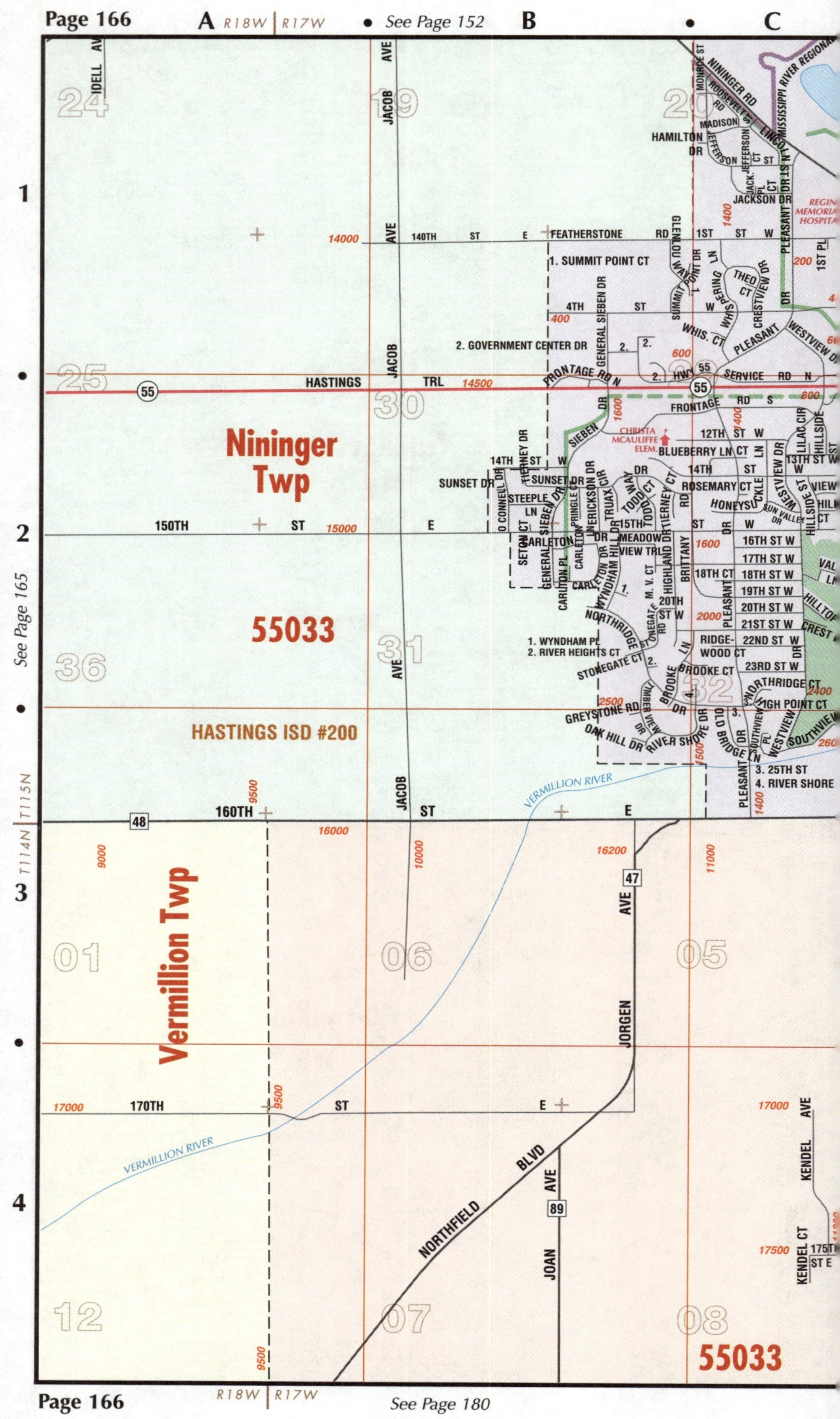

Nininger Twp

55033

HASTINGS ISD #200

Vermillion Twp

55033

See Page 165

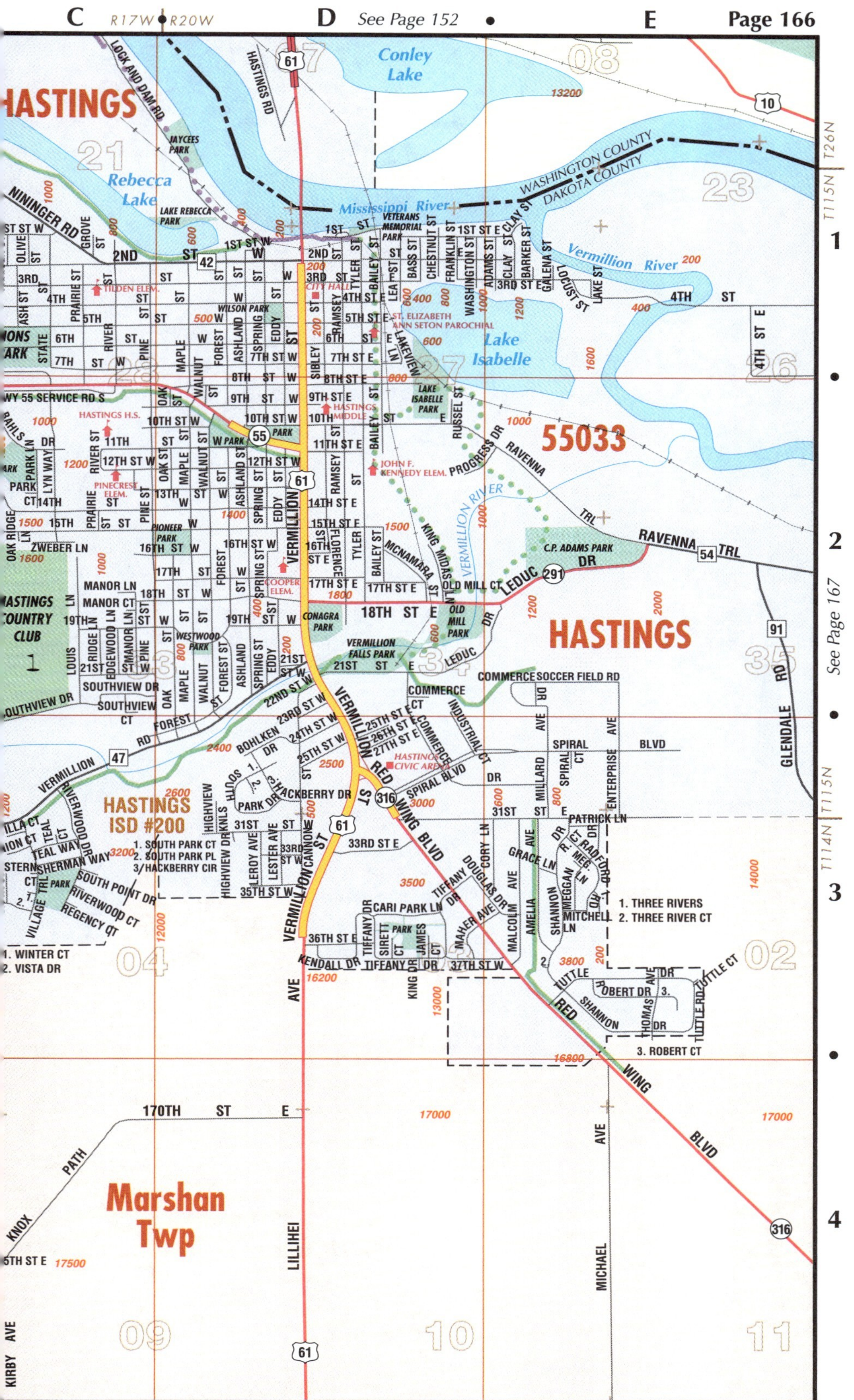

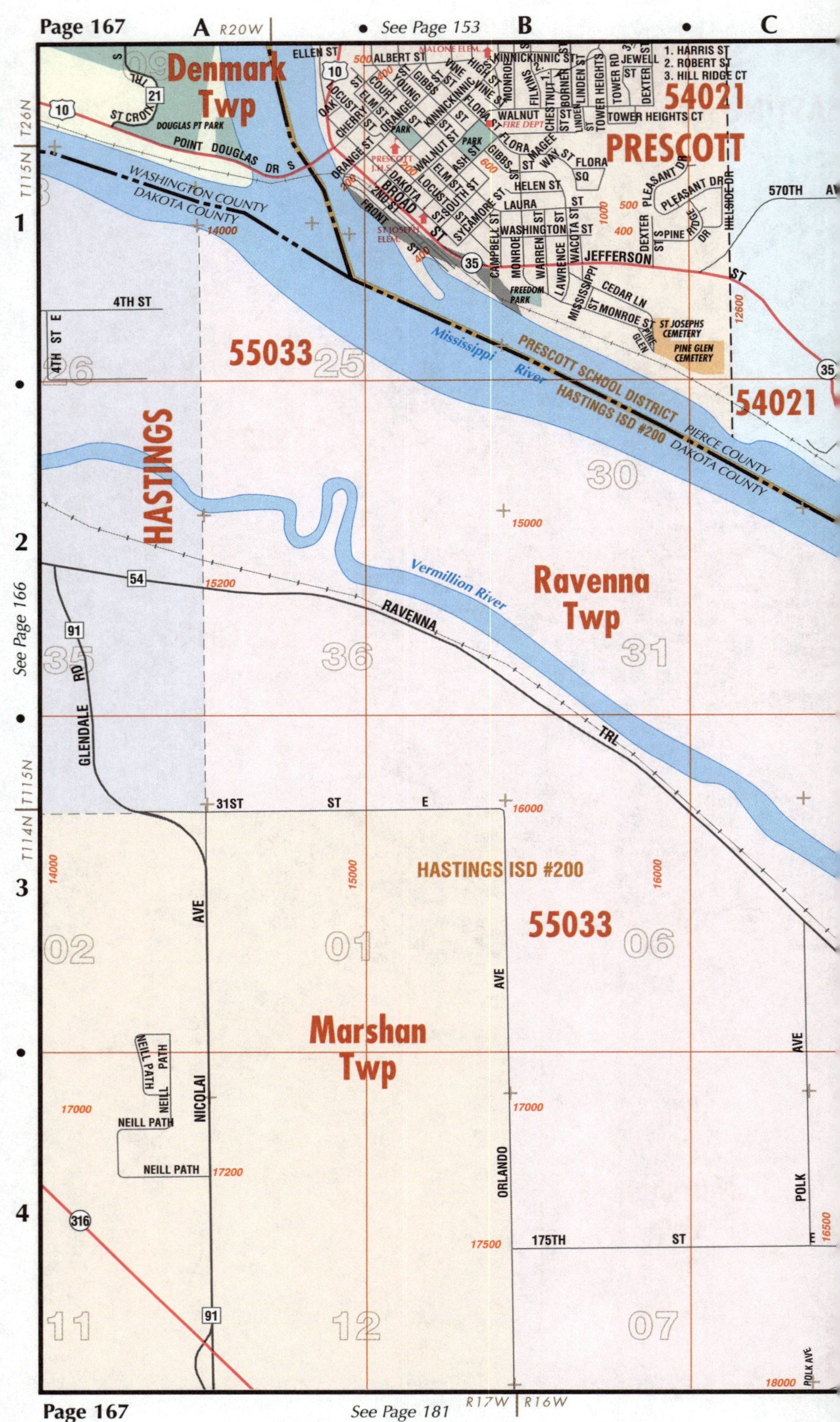

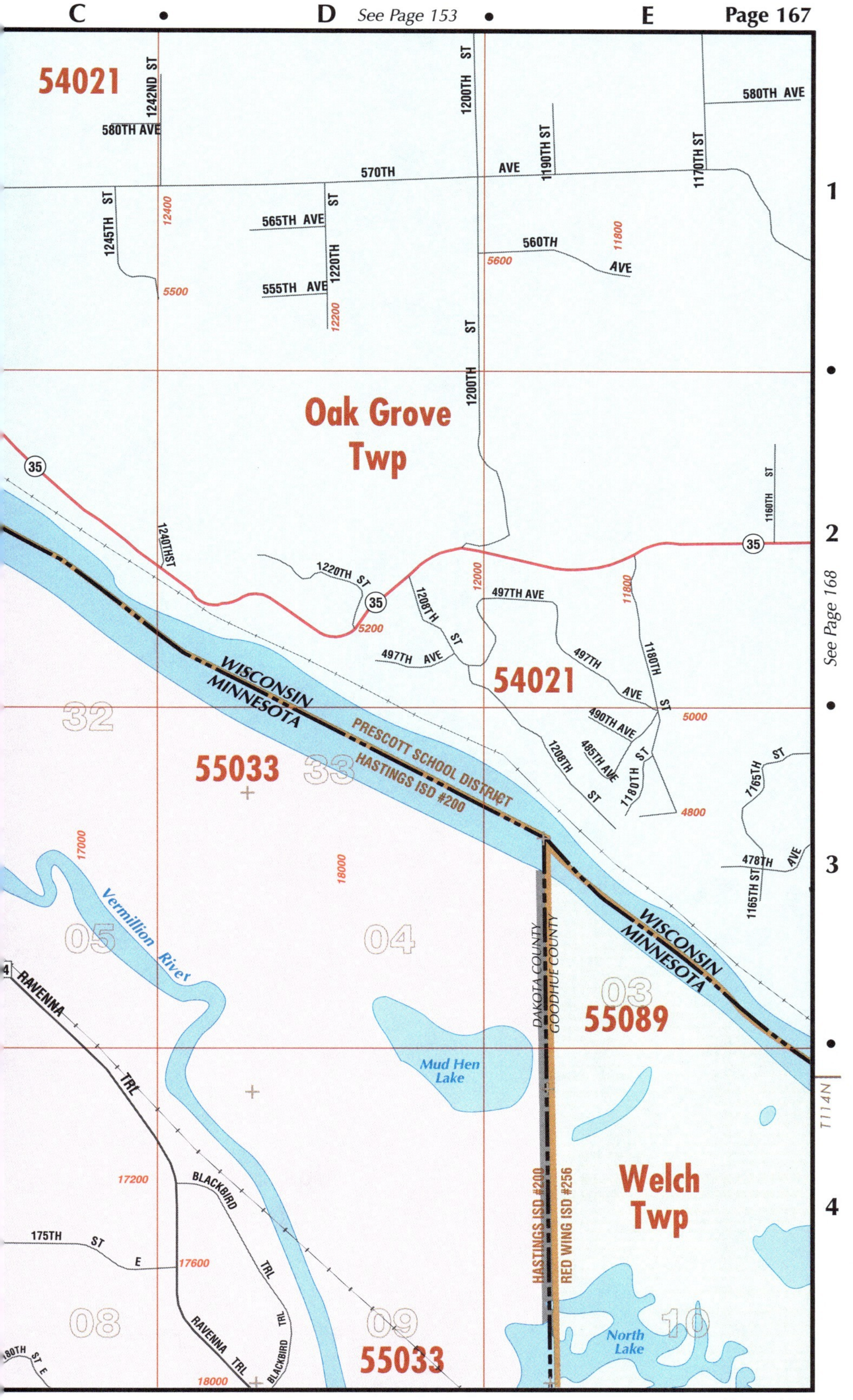

54021

1242ND ST

580TH AVE

580TH AVE

570TH AVE

1200TH ST

1190TH ST

1170TH ST

1

12400

1245TH ST

565TH AVE ST

560TH AVE

5600

11800

1220TH ST

5500

555TH AVE

12200

1200TH ST

Oak Grove Twp

35

1160TH ST

1240TH ST

1220TH ST

35

1200TH ST

12000

497TH AVE

11800

35

2

5200

497TH AVE ST

497TH

54021

1180TH ST

See Page 168

WISCONSIN
MINNESOTA

490TH AVE

AVE

5000

32

PRESCOTT SCHOOL DISTRICT

485TH AVE

775TH ST

55033

33

HASTINGS ISD #200

1208TH ST

1180TH ST

4800

478TH AVE

3

17000

18000

1165TH ST

WISCONSIN
MINNESOTA

05

Vermillion River

04

03

DAKOTA COUNTY
GOODHUE COUNTY

55089

4 RAVENNA

Mud Hen Lake

T114N

TRL

17200

BLACKBIRD

Welch Twp

175TH ST

E

17600

TRL

HASTINGS ISD #200

RED WING ISD #256

4

08

RAVENNA TRL

09

North Lake

10

180TH ST E

BLACKBIRD TRL

55033

18000

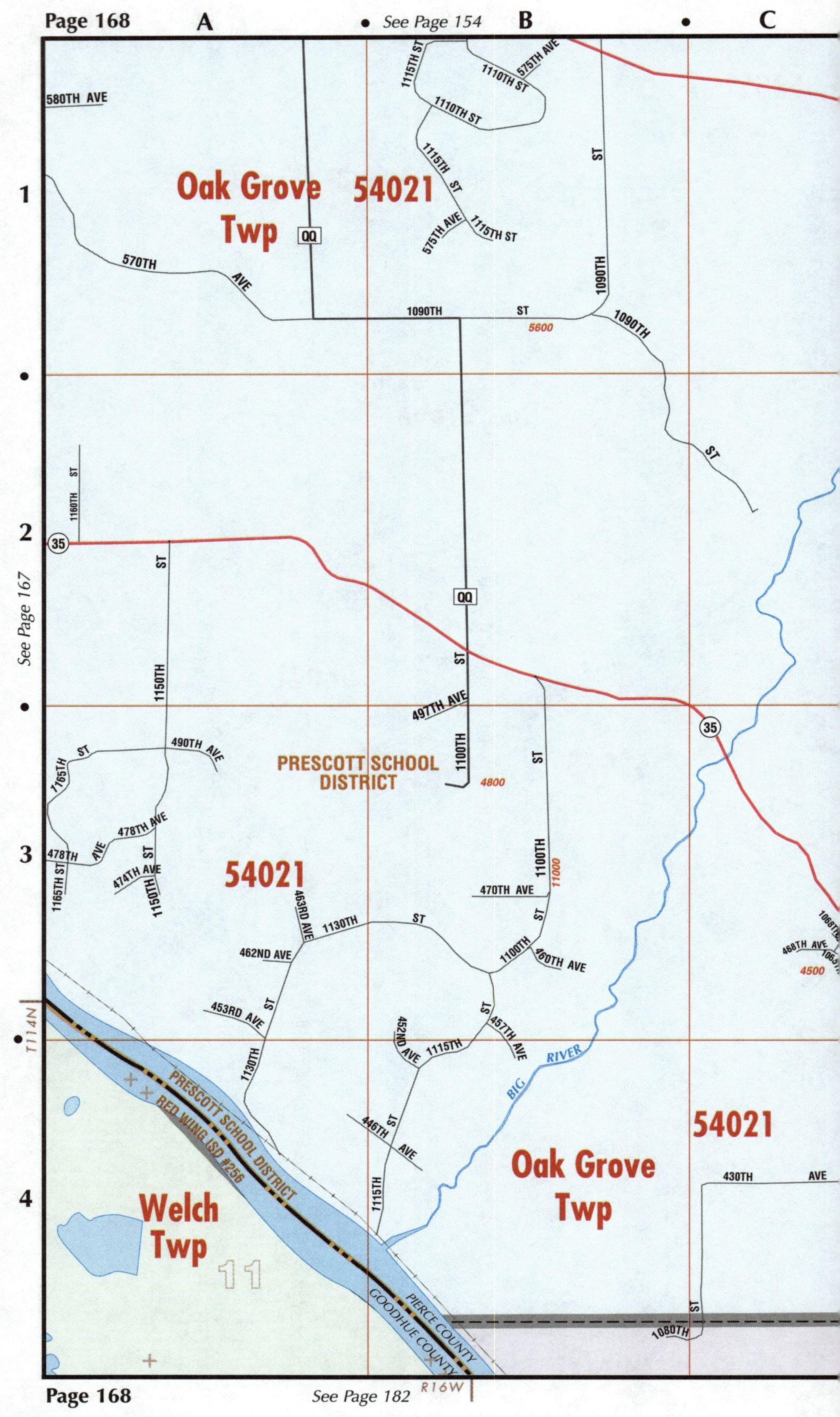

See Page 154

A   B   C

See Page 167

580TH AVE

Oak Grove Twp 54021

570TH AVE

QQ

1115TH ST
1110TH 575TH AVE
1110TH ST
1115TH ST
575TH AVE
1115TH ST

1090TH ST
1090TH
1090TH ST
5600

1160TH ST
35

1150TH ST

35

490TH AVE
1165TH ST
478TH AVE
1150TH ST
478TH ST
474TH AVE
1150TH ST
1165TH ST

PRESCOTT SCHOOL DISTRICT

497TH AVE
1100TH ST
4800

54021

463RD AVE
1130TH ST
462ND AVE
453RD AVE
1130TH ST

470TH AVE
1100TH ST
11000
1100TH ST
460TH AVE

462ND AVE
1115TH ST
457TH AVE
446TH ST
1115TH ST

468TH AVE
4500

BIG RIVER

54021

Oak Grove Twp

430TH AVE

Welch Twp

11

PRESCOTT SCHOOL DISTRICT
RED WING ISD #256

T114N

PIERCE COUNTY
GOODHUE COUNTY

1080TH

See Page 182

R16W

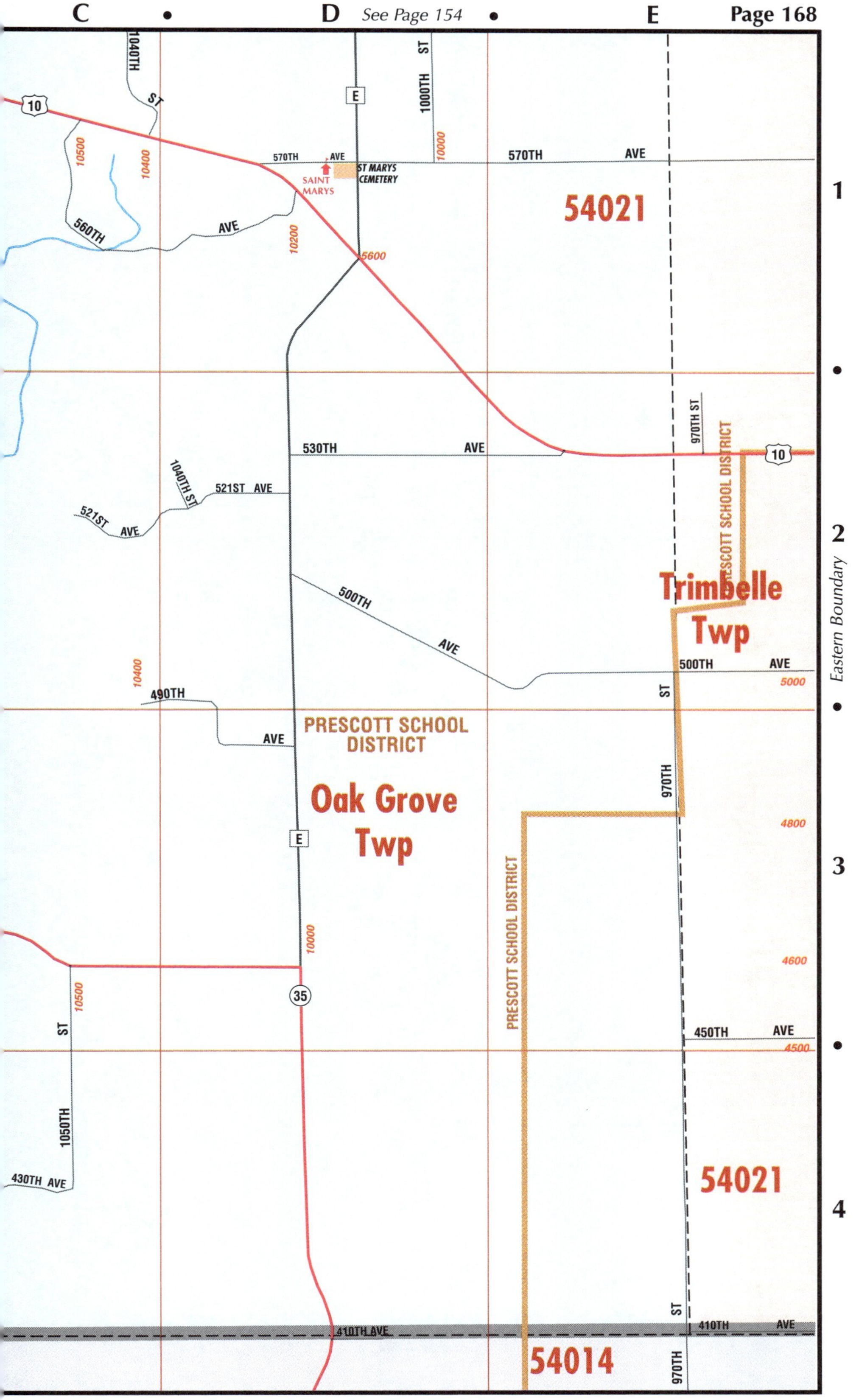

10

1040TH
ST

10500

10400

570TH   AVE
SAINT
MARYS
ST MARYS
CEMETERY

E

ST
1000TH

10000

570TH   AVE

54021

1

560TH   AVE

10200

5600

970TH ST

530TH   AVE

10

1040TH ST

521ST   AVE

521ST   AVE

PRESCOTT SCHOOL DISTRICT

500TH
AVE

**Trimbelle
Twp**

2

10400

490TH

AVE

500TH   AVE

5000

ST

PRESCOTT SCHOOL
DISTRICT

970TH

Eastern Boundary

**Oak Grove
Twp**

E

4800

3

10000

PRESCOTT SCHOOL DISTRICT

4600

10500

35

ST

450TH   AVE

4500

1050TH

430TH   AVE

54021

4

ST

410TH   AVE

410TH   AVE

54014

970TH

Page 169 A See Page 155 B C

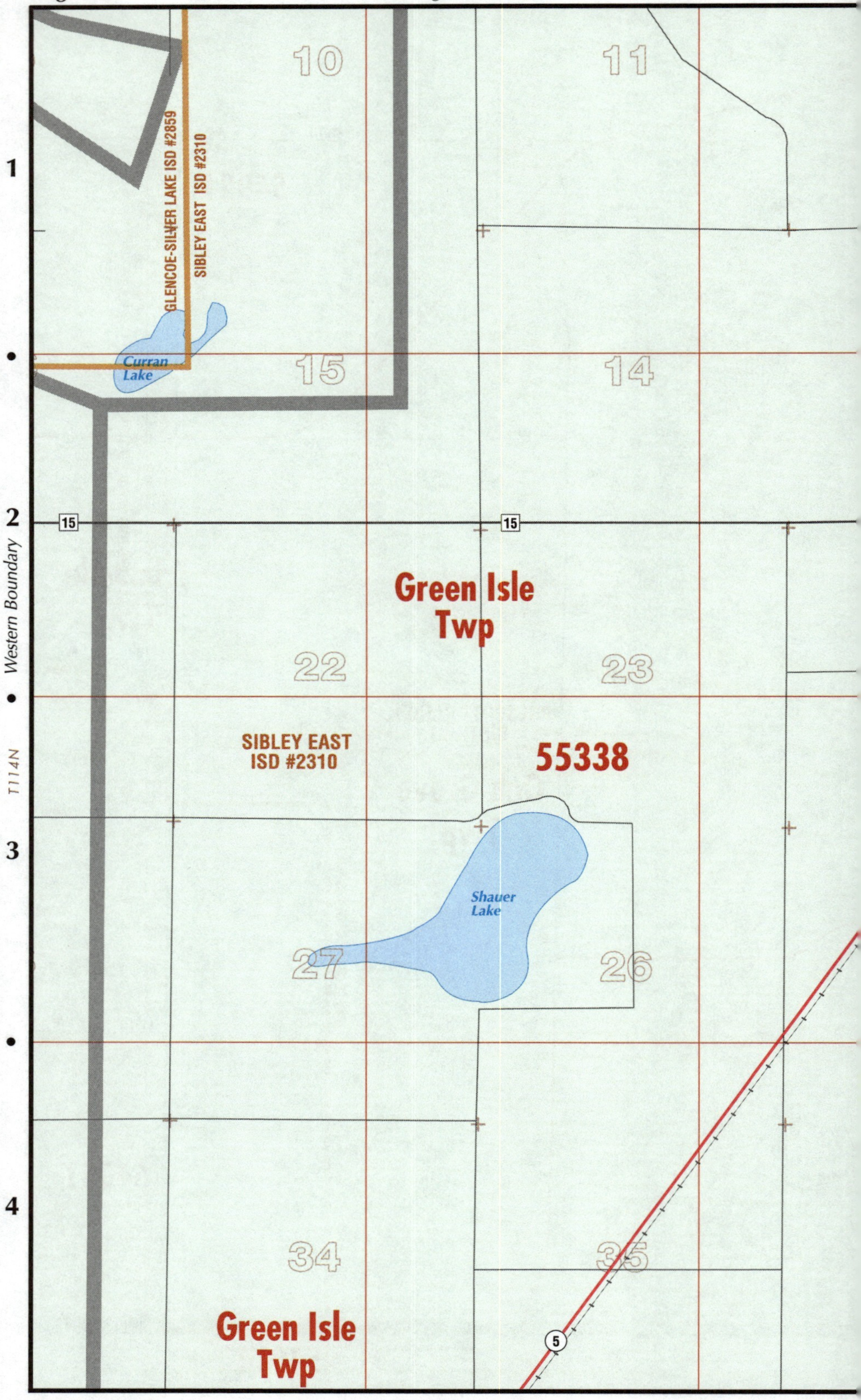
1
2
3
4
Western Boundary
T114N
10
11
GLENCOE-SILVER LAKE ISD #2859
SIBLEY EAST ISD #2310
Curran Lake
15
14
15
15
Green Isle Twp
22
23
SIBLEY EAST ISD #2310
55338
Shauer Lake
27
26
34
35
5
Green Isle Twp

Page 169 See Page 183

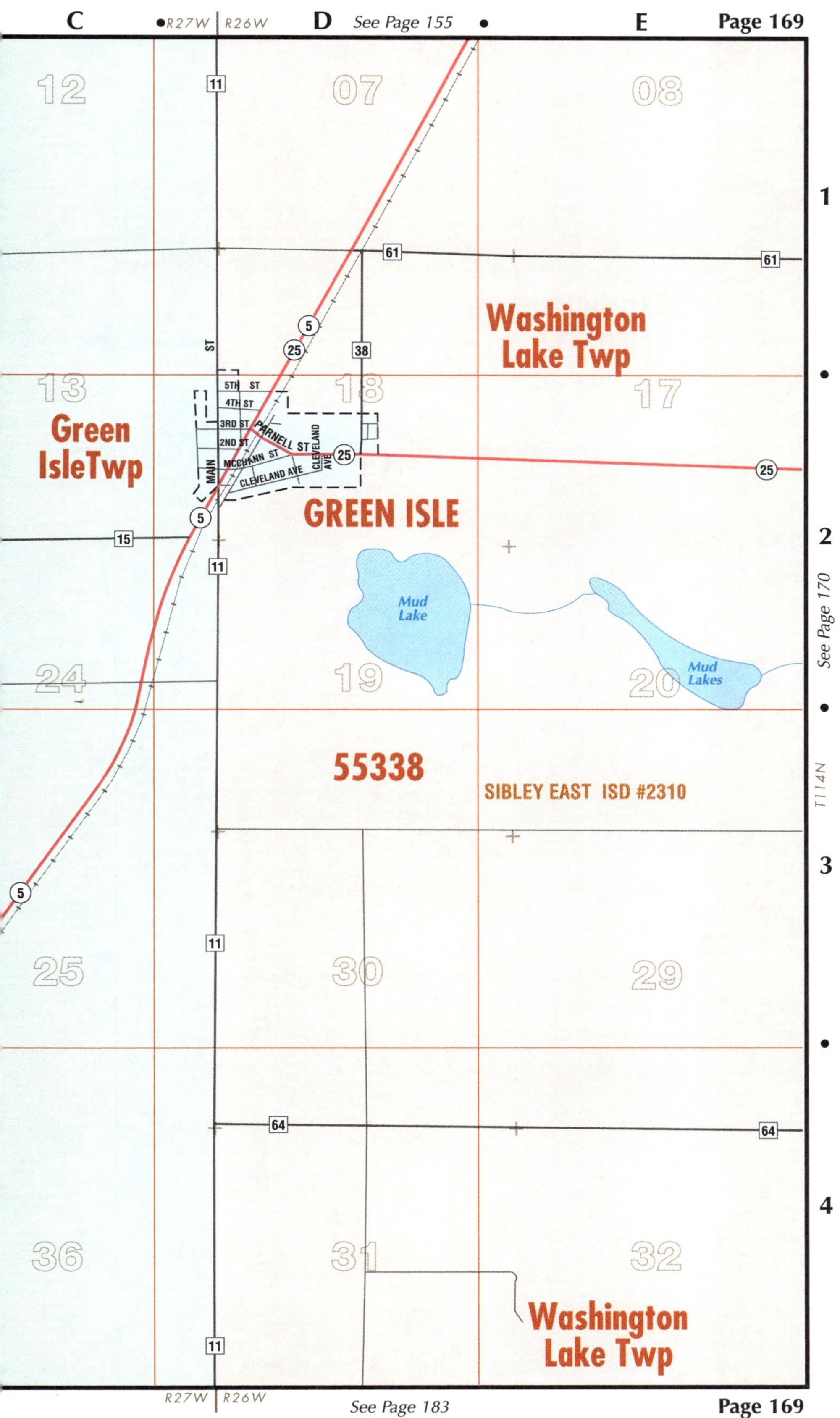

12

11

07

08

1

61

61

Washington Lake Twp

5

25

38

13

18

17

Green Isle Twp

5TH ST
4TH ST
3RD ST
PARNELL ST
2ND ST
CLEVELAND AVE
MCDIANN ST
CLEVELAND AVE

25

MAIN ST

25

5

GREEN ISLE

15

11

2

Mud Lake

24

19

20

Mud Lakes

See Page 170

55338

SIBLEY EAST ISD #2310

T114N

5

3

25

11

30

29

64

64

4

36

31

32

11

Washington Lake Twp

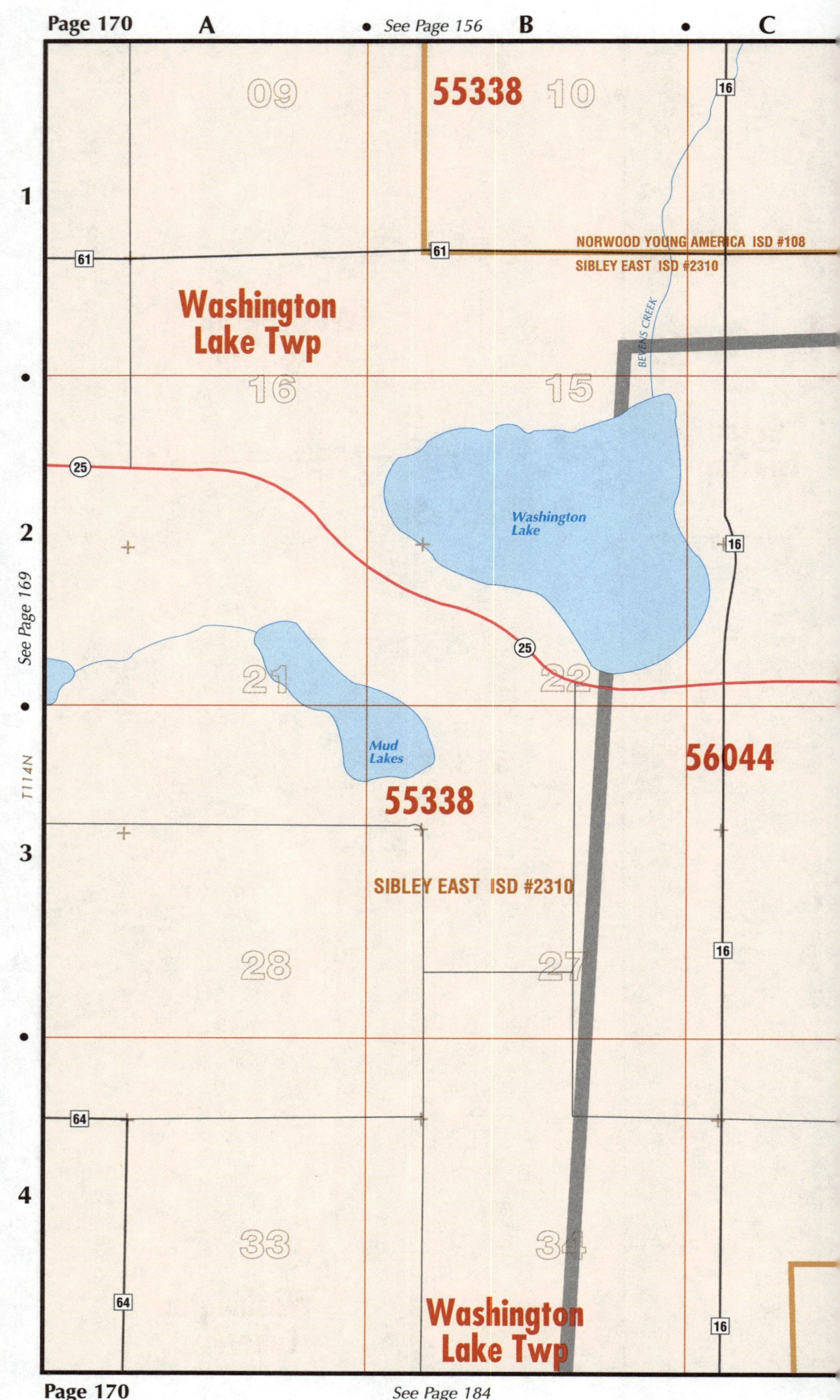

A ● *See Page 156* B ● C

1

55338 10

16

09

NORWOOD YOUNG AMERICA ISD #108

SIBLEY EAST ISD #2310

61 61

**Washington
Lake Twp**

● 16 15

25 *Washington
Lake*

2

25

21 22

Mud
Lakes

● 56044

55338

3

SIBLEY EAST ISD #2310

28 27

●

64

4

33 34

64

**Washington
Lake Twp**

T114N

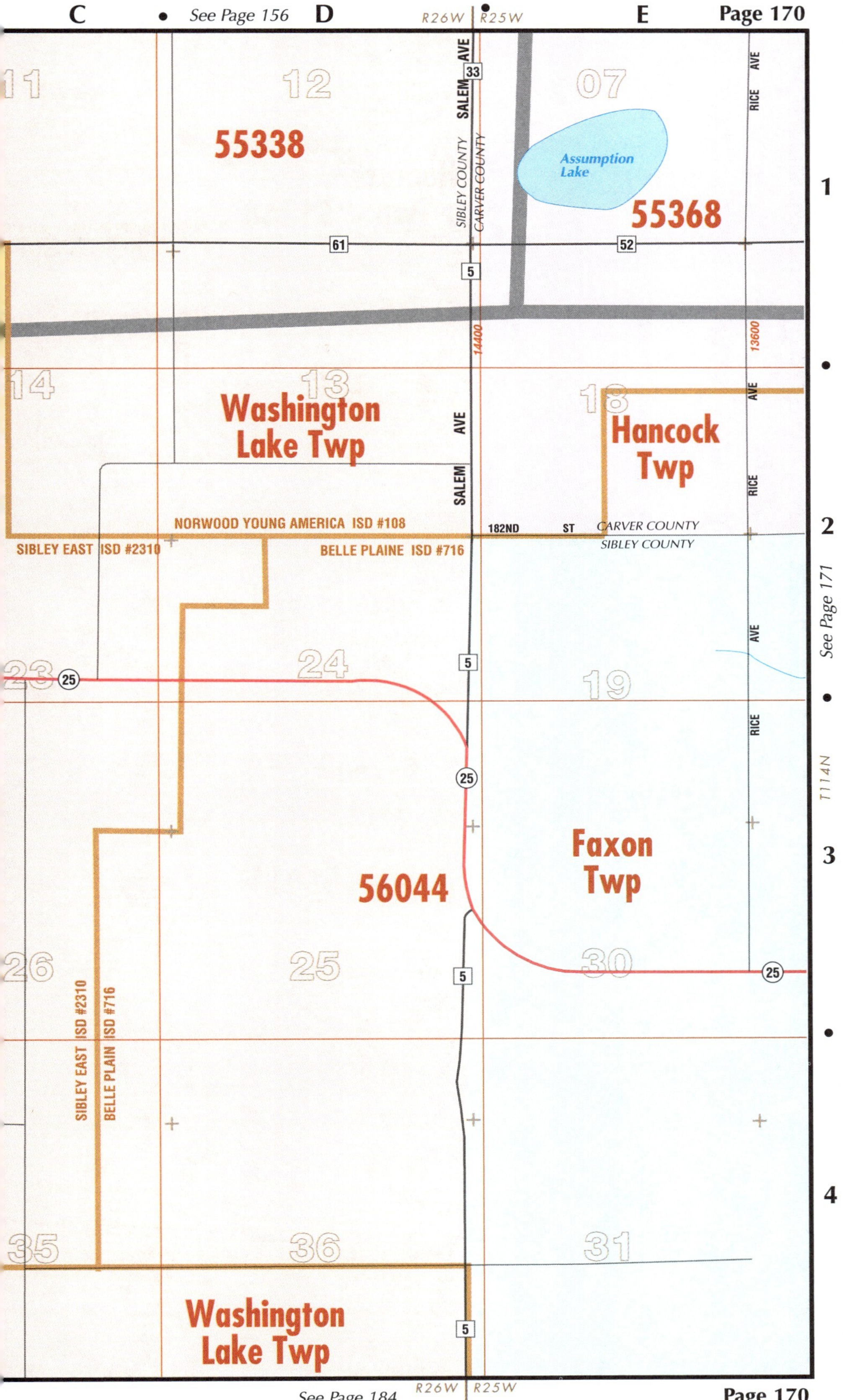

11

12

55338

SALEM AVE

33

R26W | R25W

SIBLEY COUNTY

CARVER COUNTY

07

RICE AVE

Assumption Lake

55368

1

61

52

5

14400

13600

14

13

Washington Lake Twp

SALEM AVE

18

Hancock Twp

AVE

RICE AVE

NORWOOD YOUNG AMERICA ISD #108

SIBLEY EAST ISD #2310

BELLE PLAINE ISD #716

182ND   ST

CARVER COUNTY
SIBLEY COUNTY

2

5

AVE

See Page 171

23

25

24

19

RICE AVE

T114N

25

Faxon Twp

56044

3

26

25

SIBLEY EAST ISD #2310

BELLE PLAIN ISD #716

5

30

25

4

35

36

Washington Lake Twp

5

31

A   B   C

08   09   10

11600

1

51

Hancock
Twp **55368**

17400

NORWOOD YOUNG AMERICA ISD #10

52

BELLE PLAINE ISD #716

151

13600

12800

12000

AVE

RICE AVE

NORWOOD YOUNG AMERICA ISD #108

17   BELLE PLAINE ISD #716   16   15

RICE

OHIO

2   182ND   ST *CARVER COUNTY*   182ND   ST *18200*
SIBLEY COUNTY

See Page 170

60

SILVER CREEK

AVE

20   21   22

RICE

Faxon
Twp

T114N

3   **56044**

56011

60

25   29   28   27

60

25

4

32   33   34   **6**

60

6

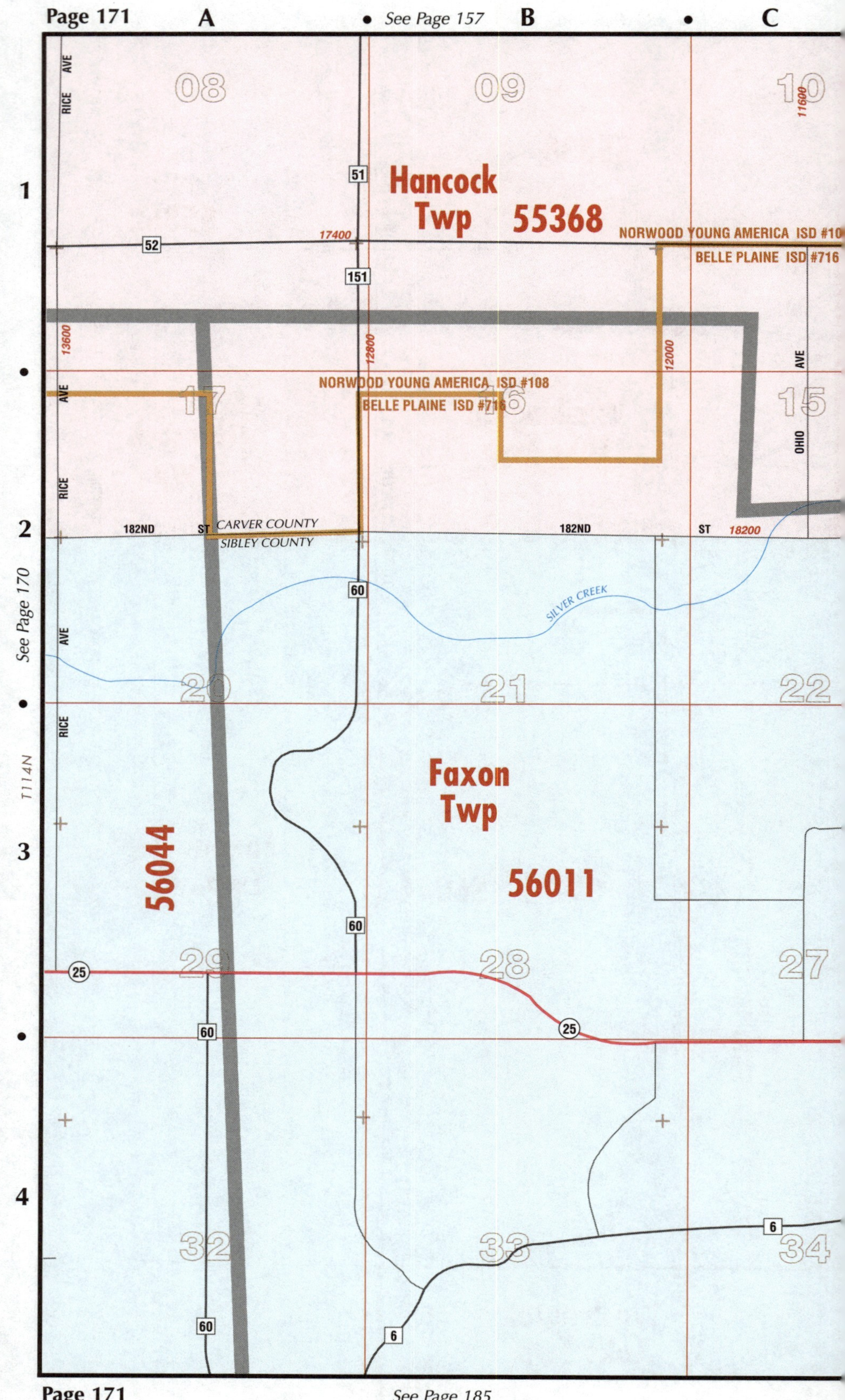

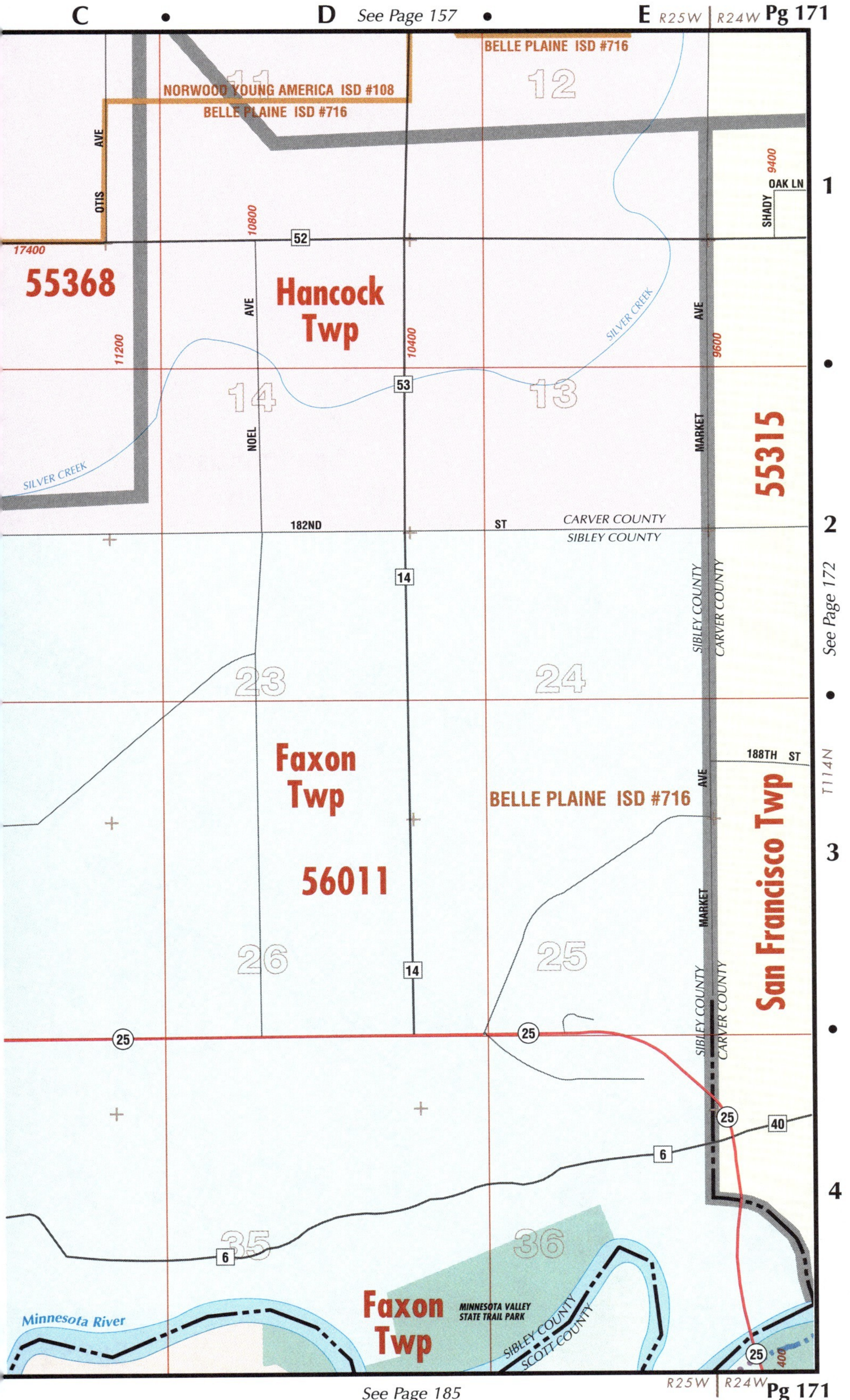

NORWOOD YOUNG AMERICA ISD #108
BELLE PLAINE ISD #716
BELLE PLAINE ISD #716

11

12

OTIS AVE

SHADY OAK LN

9400

1

17400

55368

10800

52

Hancock Twp

AVE

10400

9600

AVE

MARKET

55315

11200

SILVER CREEK

53

14

13

SILVER CREEK

182ND ST

CARVER COUNTY

SIBLEY COUNTY

2

14

23

24

SIBLEY COUNTY

CARVER COUNTY

Faxon Twp

188TH ST

T114N

AVE

BELLE PLAINE ISD #716

San Francisco Twp

3

56011

MARKET

26

25

SIBLEY COUNTY

CARVER COUNTY

25

25

25

40

6

25

4

35

6

36

MINNESOTA VALLEY STATE TRAIL PARK

406

25

Minnesota River

Faxon Twp

SIBLEY COUNTY

SCOTT COUNTY

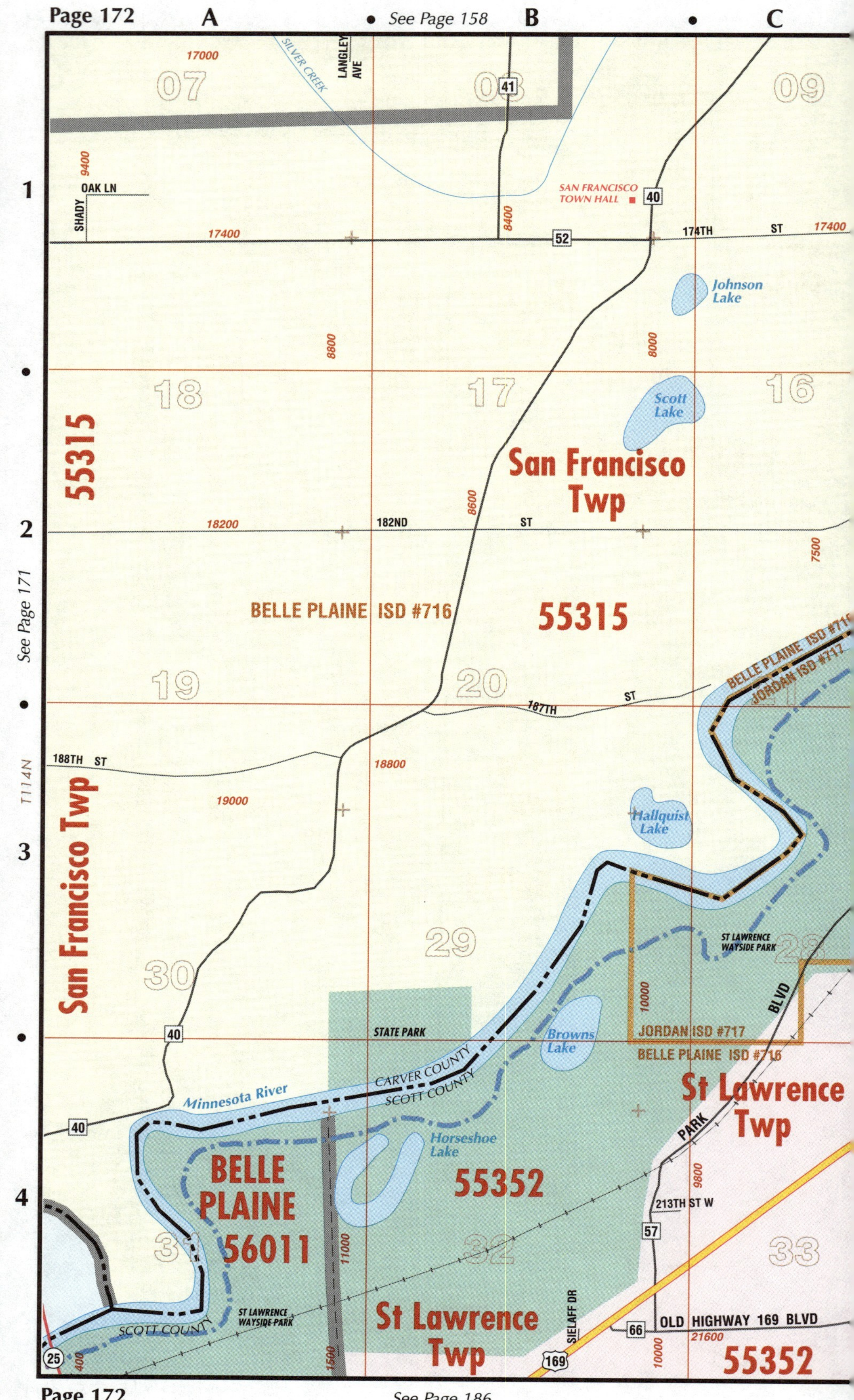

A

B

C

07

08
41

09

17000

SILVER CREEK

LANGLEY AVE

1

OAK LN
9400
SHADY

17400

8400

SAN FRANCISCO
TOWN HALL

40

52

174TH

ST

17400

Johnson
Lake

8800

8000

18

17

16

Scott
Lake

**San Francisco
Twp**

55315

8600

7500

2

18200

182ND

ST

BELLE PLAINE ISD #716

55315

See Page 171

19

20

187TH

ST

188TH ST

18800

BELLE PLAINE ISD #716
JORDAN ISD #717

T114N

19000

Hallquist
Lake

3

San Francisco Twp

30

29

ST LAWRENCE
WAYSIDE PARK

28

10000

BLVD

40

STATE PARK

CARVER COUNTY
SCOTT COUNTY

Browns
Lake

JORDAN ISD #717
BELLE PLAINE ISD #716

**St Lawrence
Twp**

40

Minnesota River

PARK

9800

Horseshoe
Lake

**BELLE
PLAINE**

55352

213TH ST W

4

31

56011

11000

32

57

33

1500

SIELAFF DR

66

OLD HIGHWAY 169 BLVD

ST LAWRENCE
WAYSIDE PARK

**St Lawrence
Twp**

21600

25

400

SCOTT COUNTY

169

10000

55352

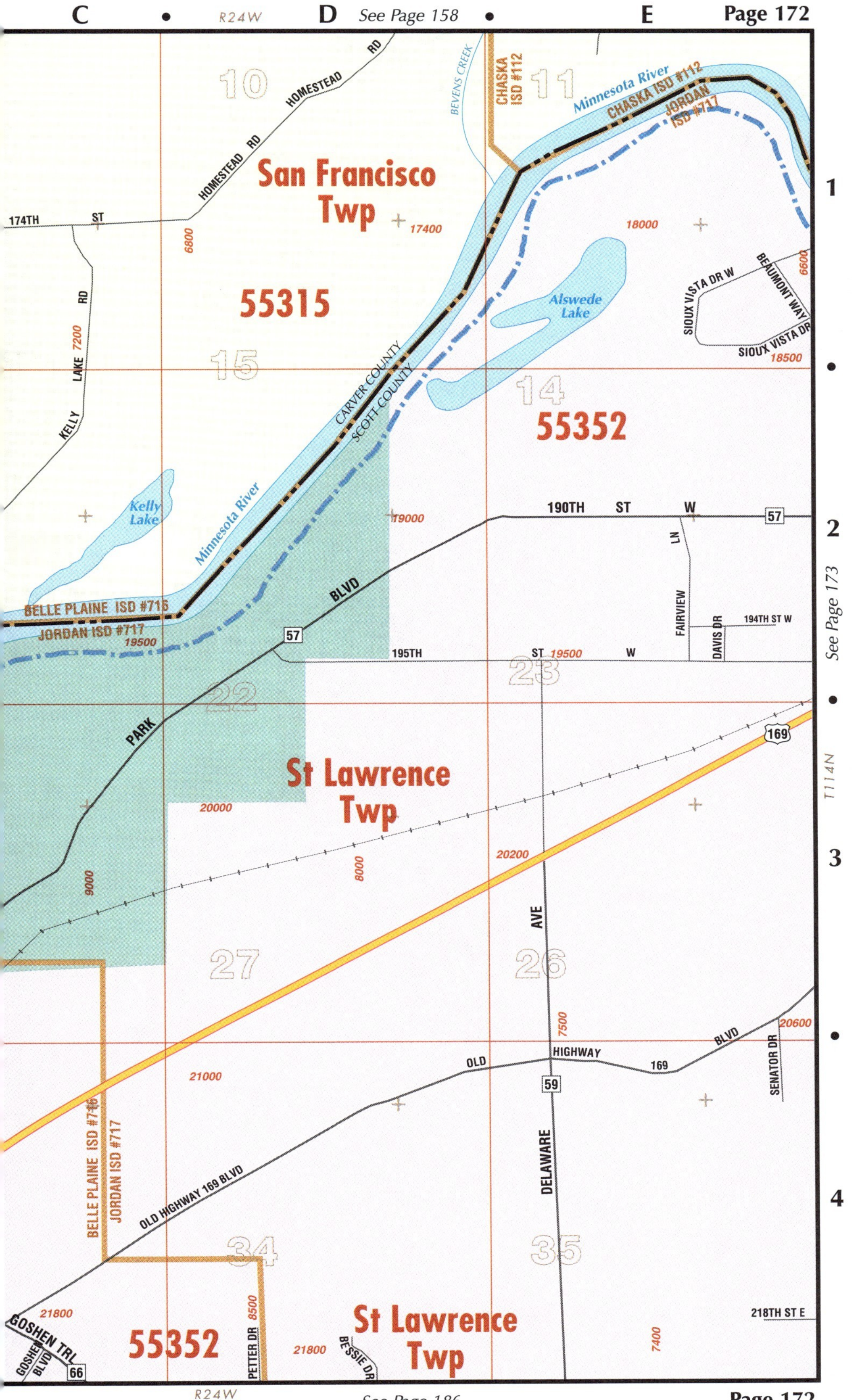

10

HOMESTEAD RD

HOMESTEAD RD

BEVENS CREEK

CHASKA ISD #112

11

Minnesota River

CHASKA ISD #112

JORDAN ISD #717

San Francisco Twp

174TH ST

6800

KELLY LAKE RD 7200

55315

17400

18000

Alswede Lake

SIOUX VISTA DR W

BEAUMONT WAY

6600

SIOUX VISTA DR

18500

CARVER COUNTY

SCOTT COUNTY

15

14

55352

Kelly Lake

Minnesota River

19000

190TH ST W

57 2

FAIRVIEW LN

DAVIS DR

194TH ST W

BELLE PLAINE ISD #716

JORDAN ISD #717

BLVD

57

19500

195TH ST 19500 W

23

22

PARK

St Lawrence Twp

20000

8000

9000

169

T114N

See Page 173

20200

AVE

26

7500

27

21000

OLD

HIGHWAY 169

BLVD

20600

SENATOR DR

59

DELAWARE

BELLE PLAINE ISD #716

JORDAN ISD #717

OLD HIGHWAY 169 BLVD

34

218TH ST E

35

GOSHEN TRL

21800

55352

PETTER DR 8500

BESSIE DR

21800

St Lawrence Twp

7400

GOSHEN BLVD 66

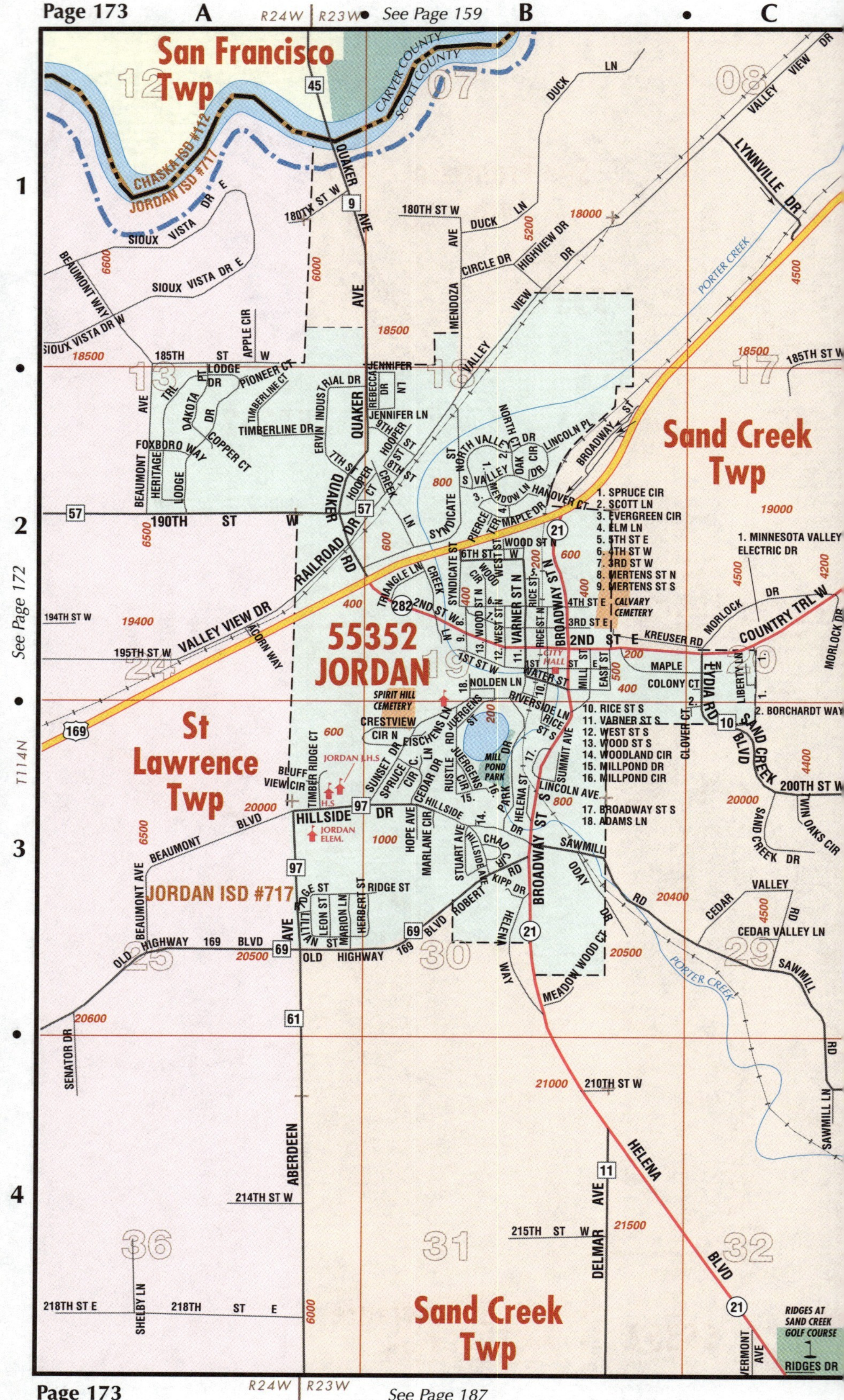

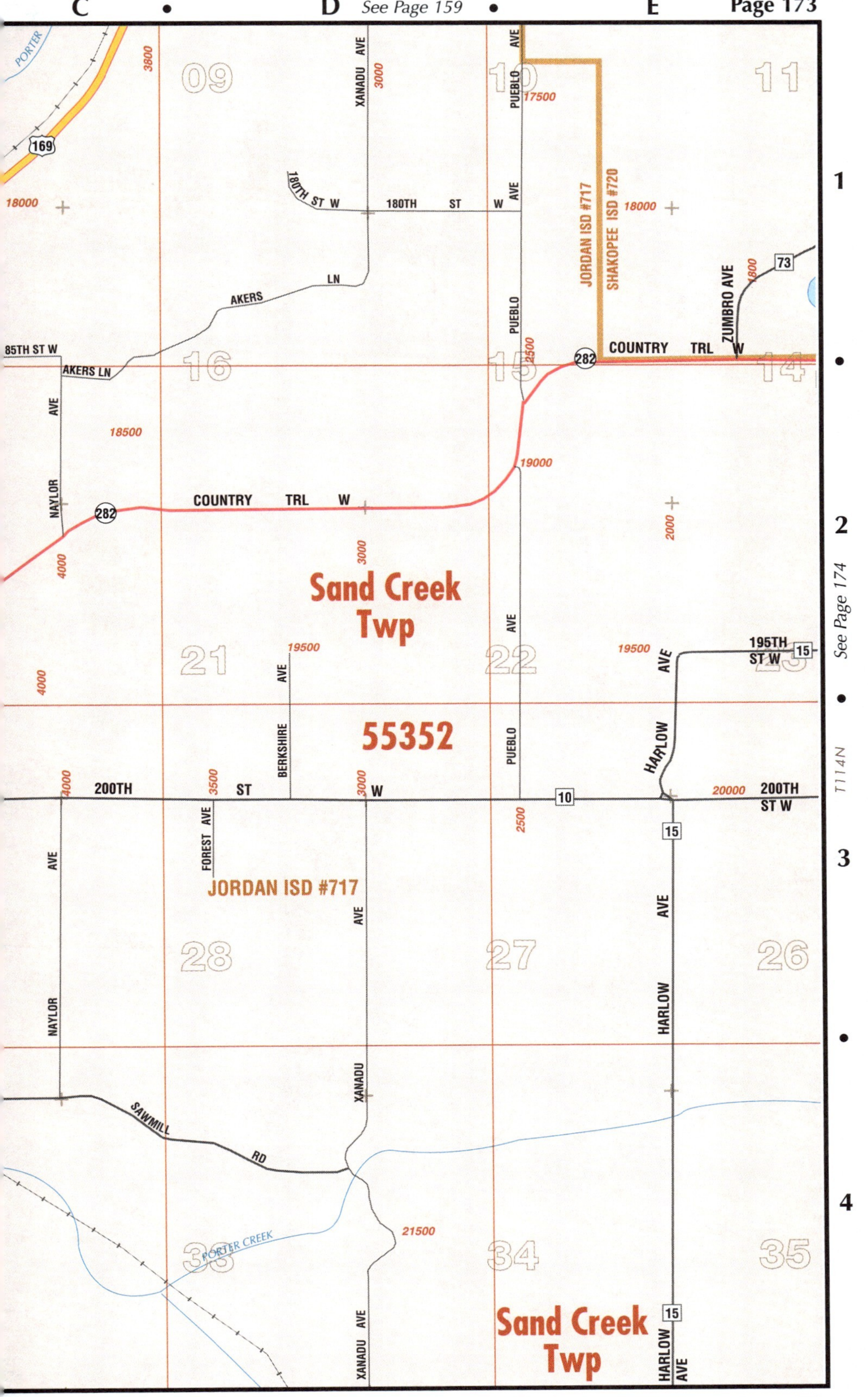

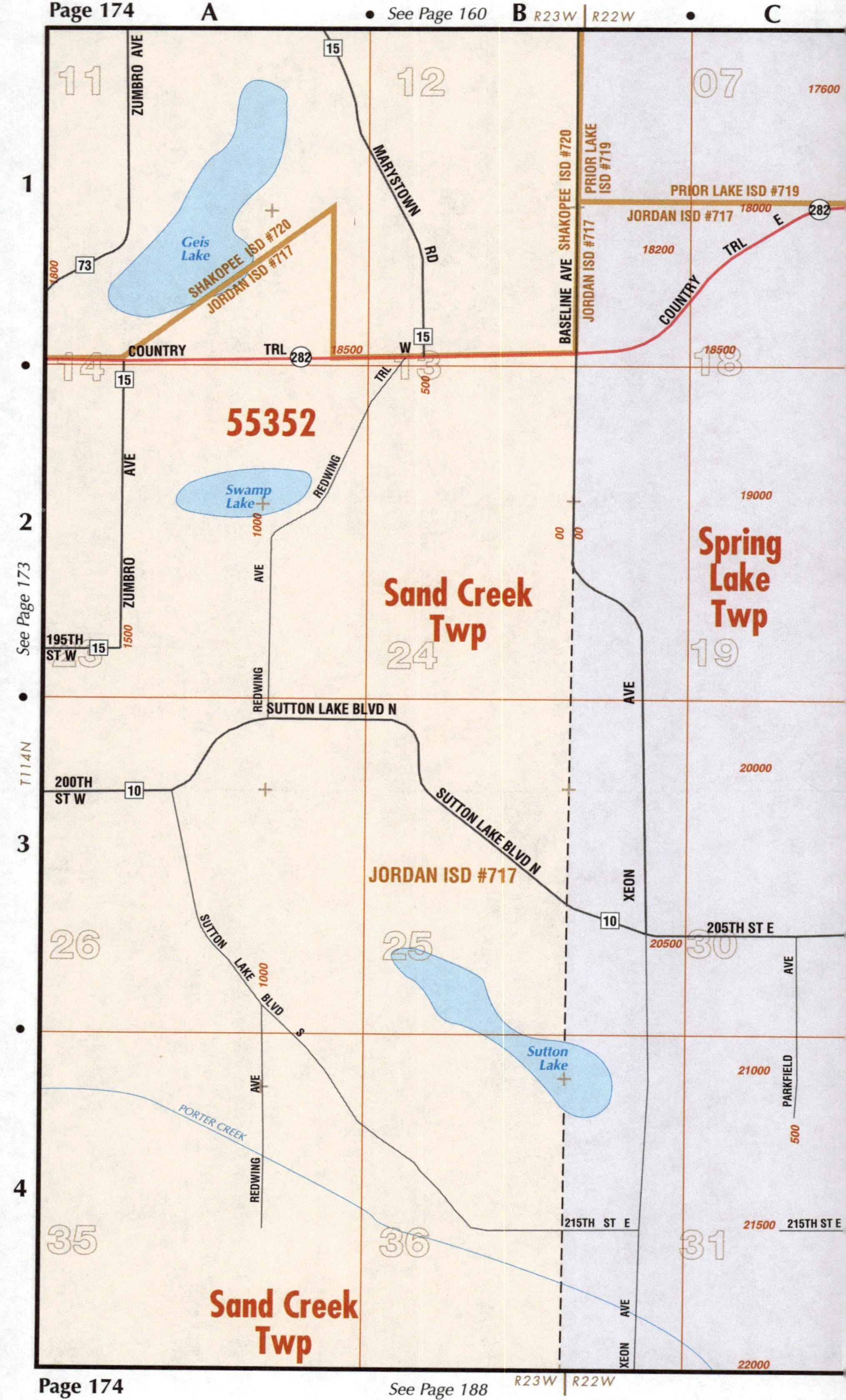

A   B R23W | R22W   C

11   12   07

17600

ZUMBRO AVE

15

MARYSTOWN RD

BASELINE AVE SHAKOPEE ISD #720

PRIOR LAKE ISD #719

PRIOR LAKE ISD #719

JORDAN ISD #717   18000   E 282

1

800   73

Geis Lake

SHAKOPEE ISD #720

JORDAN ISD #717

18200

COUNTRY TRL

COUNTRY   TRL 282   18500   W   15

14   13

18500   18

55352

15

REDWING AVE

ZUMBRO AVE

Swamp Lake   1000

500 TRL

Sand Creek Twp

24

Spring Lake Twp

19000

19

2

1500

See Page 173

195TH ST W   15

REDWING

SUTTON LAKE BLVD N

XEON AVE

20000

200TH ST W   10

T114N

26

SUTTON LAKE BLVD N

JORDAN ISD #717

20500

205TH ST E   30

3

25

1000

SUTTON LAKE BLVD S

10   XEON

Sutton Lake

21000

PARKFIELD AVE

AVE

500

AVE

PORTER CREEK

REDWING AVE

35   36

215TH ST E

215TH ST E   21500   31

4

Sand Creek Twp

XEON AVE

22000

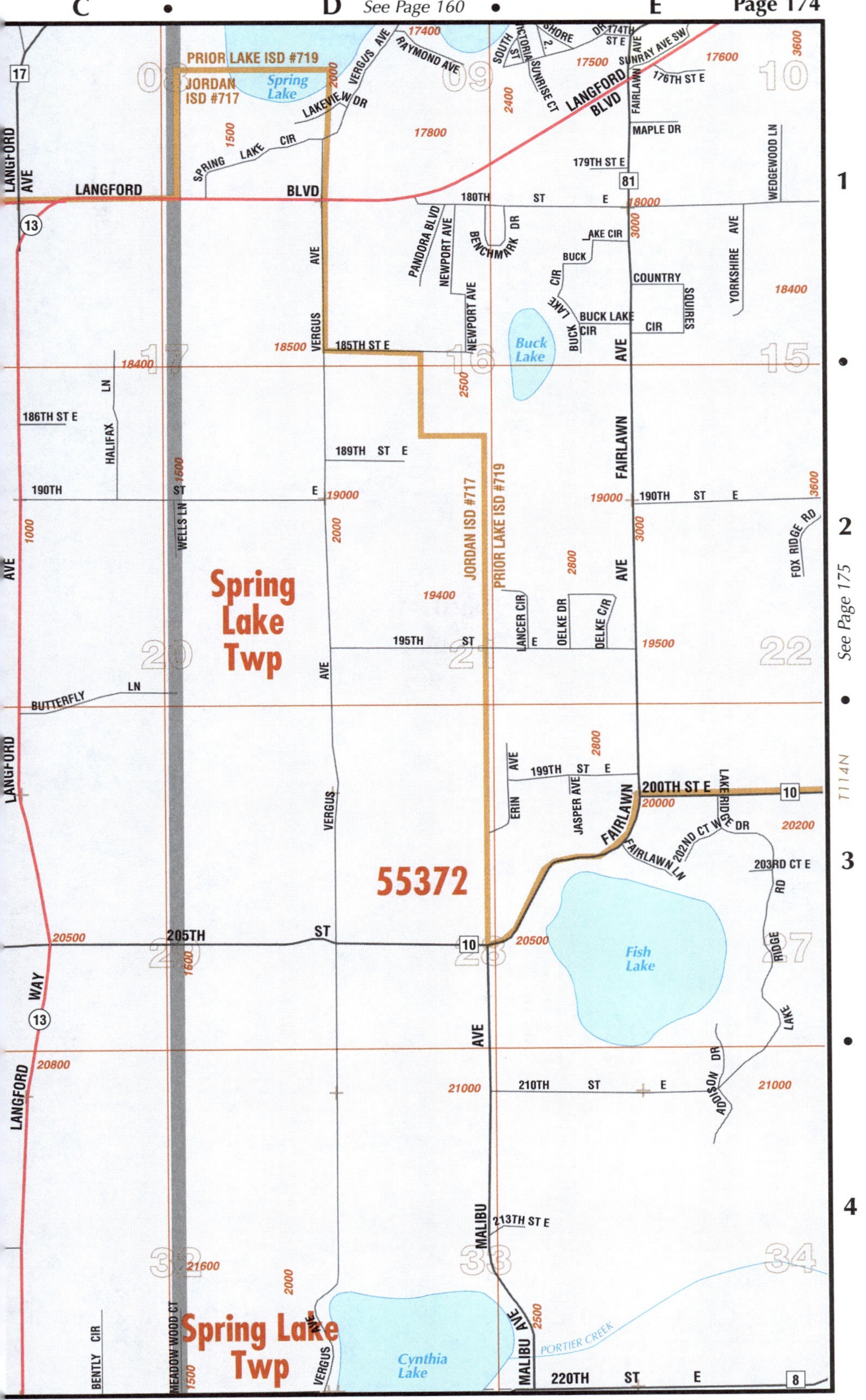

PRIOR LAKE ISD #719

JORDAN ISD #717

Spring Lake

17400

RAYMOND AVE

SOUTH SHORE DR-174TH ST E

174TH ST E

VICTORIA ST S

SUNRISE CT

SUNRAY AVE SW

17500

176TH ST E

17600

3600

LANGFORD BLVD

10

VERGUS AVE

LAKEVIEW DR

2000

2400

MAPLE DR

Spring Lake Cir

1500

17800

179TH ST E

81

LANGFORD

BLVD

LANGFORD AVE

13

PANDORA BLVD

NEWPORT AVE

BENCHMARK DR

180TH ST E

18000

AKE CIR

3000

BUCK

COUNTRY

SQUIRES

WEDGEWOOD LN

YORKSHIRE AVE

18400

VERGUS AVE

BUCK CIR

BUCK LAKE CIR

CIR

Buck Lake

FAIRLAWN AVE

15

18500

185TH ST E

16

NEWPORT AVE

2500

18400

HALIFAX LN

186TH ST E

189TH ST E

19000

190TH ST E

WELLS LN

1500

190TH

ST

E

19000

2000

AVE

1000

Spring Lake Twp

20

17

JORDAN ISD #717

PRIOR LAKE ISD #719

19400

LANCER CIR

OELKE DR

OELKE CIR

2800

19500

FAIRLAWN AVE

3000

FOX RIDGE RD

3600

22

195TH ST

E

21

BUTTERFLY LN

VERGUS AVE

AVE

199TH ST E

2800

ERIN AVE

JASPER AVE

FAIRLAWN AVE

200TH ST E

20000

LAKERIDGE DR

202ND CT W

10

20200

55372

203RD CT E

RIDGE RD

Fish Lake

7

LANGFORD AVE

13

20500

205TH ST

1600

10

28

20500

FAIRLAWN LN

205TH

LAKE

20800

LANGFORD WAY

21000

210TH ST E

ADDISON DR

21000

AVE

4

32

21600

MEADOW WOOD CT

1500

2000

Spring Lake Twp

MALIBU AVE

213TH ST E

33

VERGUS AVE

Cynthia Lake

2500

PORTIER CREEK

34

220TH ST E

8

BENTLY CIR

See Page 175

T114N

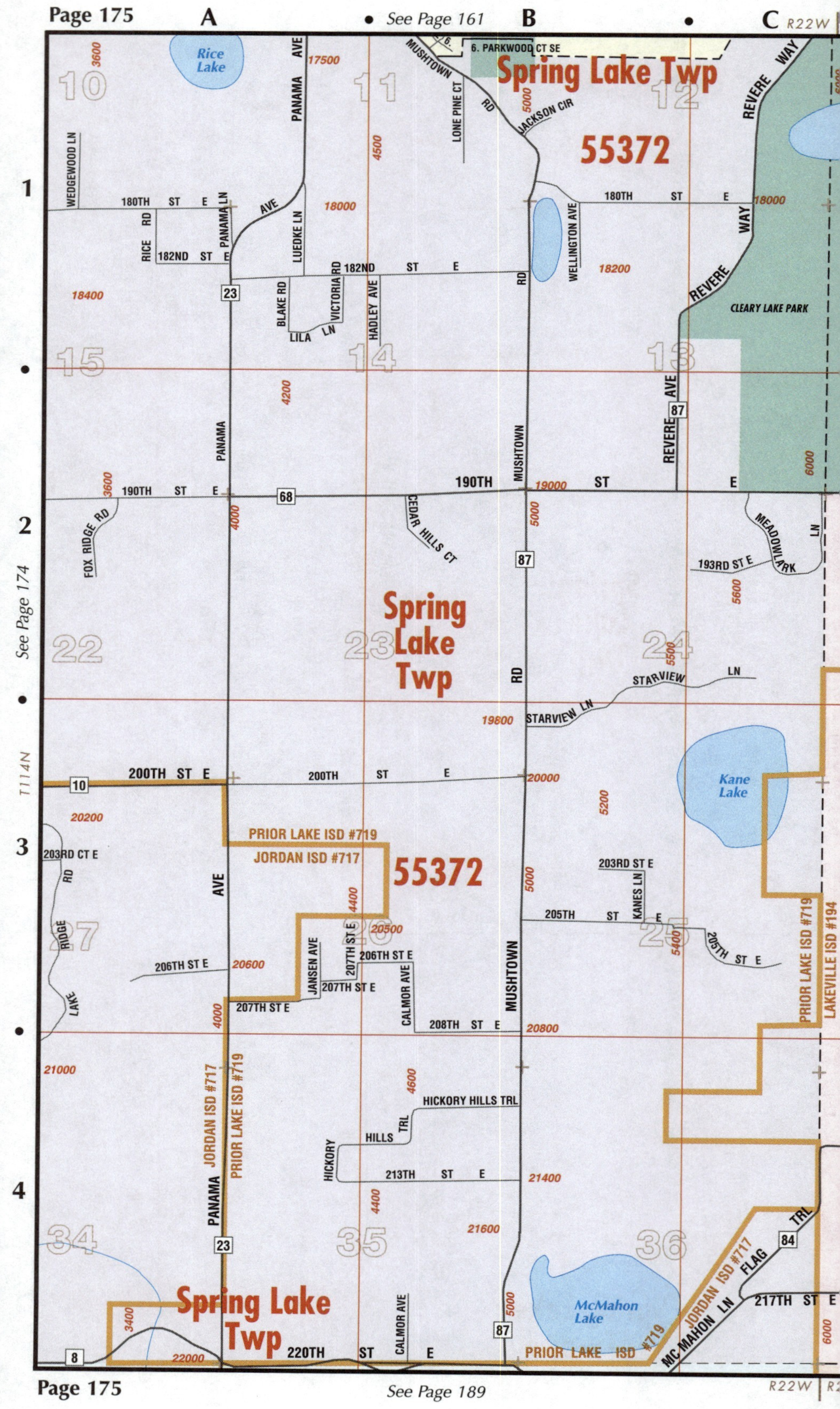

A ● See Page 161 B ● C R22W

Rice Lake

Spring Lake Twp

55372

WEDGEWOOD LN

PANAMA AVE 17500

MUSHTOWN RD

LONE PINE CT

6. PARKWOOD CT SE

JACKSON CIR 5000

REVERE WAY

10

11

12

1

180TH ST E

RICE RD

PANAMA LN

LUEDKE LN

AVE

18000

4500

180TH ST E 18000

WELLINGTON AVE

RD

182ND ST E

BLAKE RD

VICTORIA RD

182ND ST E

HADLEY AVE

18200

WAY

REVERE

18400

LILA LN

23

4200

CLEARY LAKE PARK

15

14

13

● ●

PANAMA

MUSHTOWN

REVERE AVE

87

6000

190TH ST E 3600

FOX RIDGE RD

4000

68

CEDAR HILLS CT

190TH ST 19000

RD

87

5000

MEADOWLARK LN

193RD ST E 5600

See Page 174

T114N

22

Spring Lake Twp

23

RD

STARVIEW LN

24

STARVIEW LN

5500

● 19800 STARVIEW LN ●

Kane Lake

200TH ST E

10

200TH ST E 20000

5200

20200

PRIOR LAKE ISD #719

JORDAN ISD #717

55372

Kane Lake

PRIOR LAKE ISD #719 #194

LAKEVILLE ISD #719

3

203RD CT E

RD

RIDGE

AVE

4400

207TH ST E

20500

5000

203RD ST E

KANES LN

25

205TH ST

205TH ST E

5400

LAKE

206TH ST E 20600

JANSEN AVE

207TH ST E

206TH ST E

CALMOR AVE

MUSHTOWN

4000

207TH ST E

208TH ST E 20800

● 21000 4000 ●

JORDAN ISD #717

PRIOR LAKE ISD #719

4600

HICKORY HILLS TRL

HICKORY HILLS TRL

27

26

JORDAN ISD #717 PRIOR LAKE ISD #719

FLAG LN

TRL

84

4

34

PANAMA

23

213TH ST E 4400

21400

21600

35

5000

36

McMahon Lake

MC MAHON LN

JORDAN ISD #717 PRIOR LAKE ISD #719

6000

Spring Lake Twp

3400

8

22000

CALMOR AVE

220TH ST E

87

PRIOR LAKE ISD

217TH ST E

R2

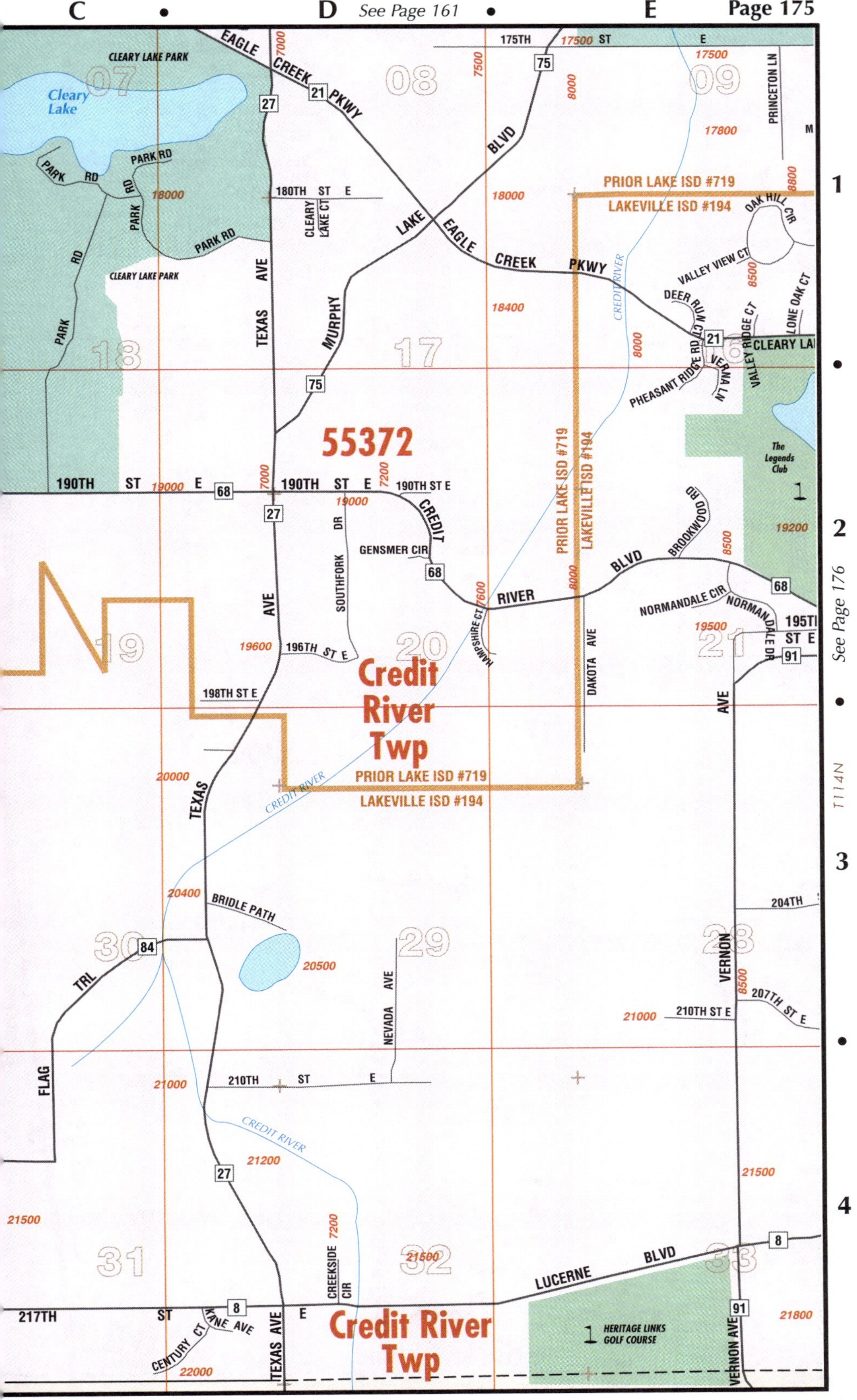

Cleary Lake Park

Cleary Lake

07

Park Rd

Park Rd

18000

Park Rd

Park Rd

Park Rd

Cleary Lake Park

18

EAGLE CREEK PKWY

27

21

08

175TH

17500 ST

17500

7000

7500

75

8000

E

17500

PRINCETON LN

M

09

17800

PRIOR LAKE ISD #719

LAKEVILLE ISD #194

OAK HILL CIR

8800

1

180TH ST E

CLEARY LAKE CT

TEXAS AVE

MURPHY

LAKE

EAGLE CREEK PKWY

18000

18400

Credit River

8000

8500

VALLEY VIEW CT

DEER RUN RD

21

VANLN

PHEASANT RIDGE RD

VALLEY RIDGE CT

LONE OAK CT

CLEARY LA

75

17

•

The Legends Club

1

19200

55372

190TH ST 19000 E

68

7000

190TH ST E

19000

7200

190TH ST E

CREDIT

SOUTHFORK DR

GENSMER CIR

68

RIVER

7600

HAMMSHIRE CT

8000

BLVD

DAKOTA AVE

BROOKWOOD RD

8500

NORMANDALE CIR

19500

NORMANDALE DR

68

91

195TH ST E

2

See Page 176

27

19600

196TH ST E

198TH ST E

19

20

Credit River Twp

PRIOR LAKE ISD #719

LAKEVILLE ISD #194

21

VERNON AVE

T114N

•

20000

Credit River

•

3

20400

BRIDLE PATH

TRL

FLAG

30

84

29

20500

NEVADA AVE

21000

210TH ST E

204TH

28

VERNON

8500

207TH ST E

21500

•

21000

210TH ST

E

CREDIT RIVER

8

4

21500

27

21200

CREEKSIDE CIR

7200

31

21500

32

LUCERNE BLVD

33

91

21800

217TH ST

8

CENTURY CT

KAYNE AVE

TEXAS AVE

E

22000

Credit River Twp

1 HERITAGE LINKS GOLF COURSE

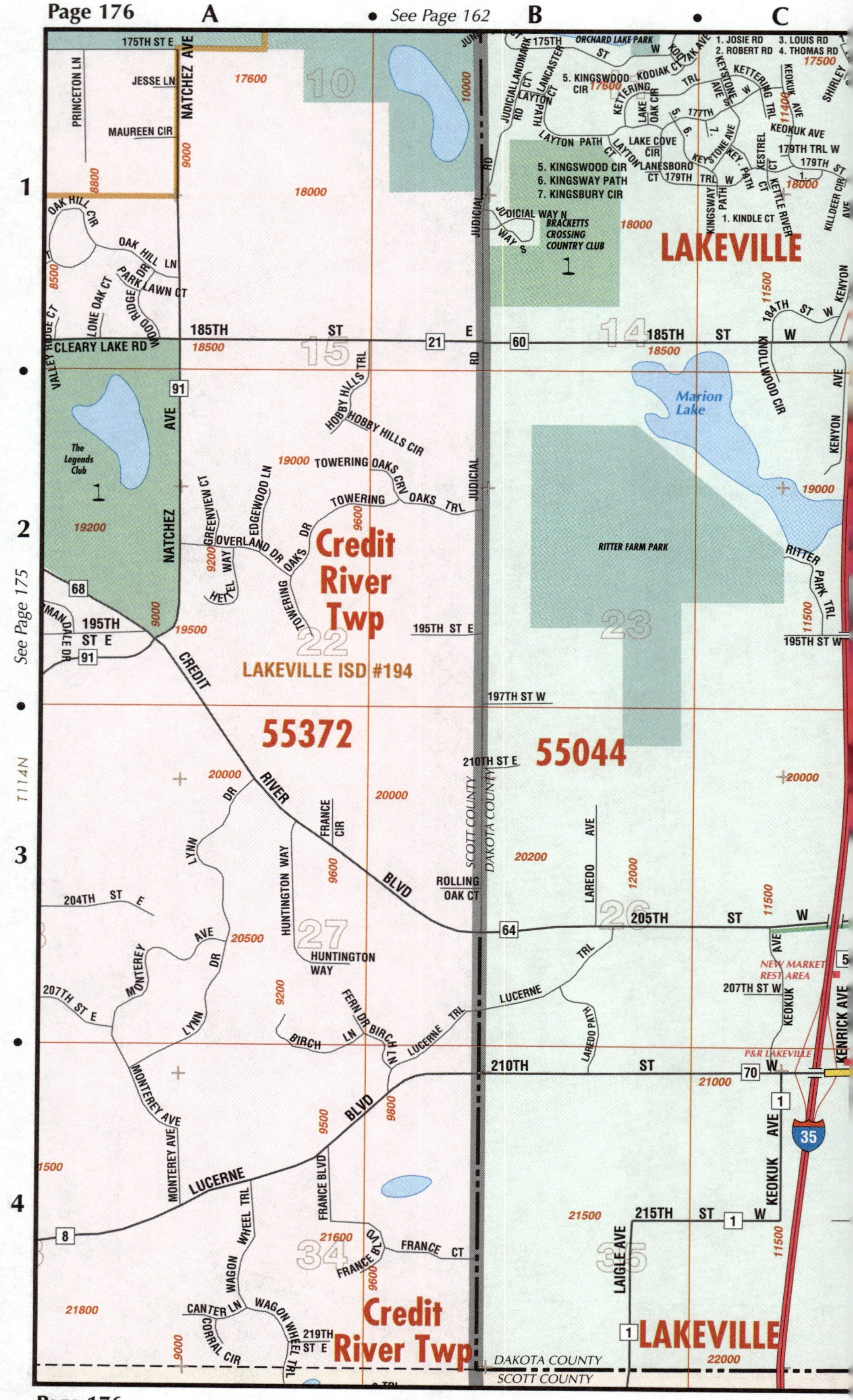

• See Page 162

A   B   C

175TH ST E

PRINCETON LN
JESSE LN
NATCHEZ AVE
17600
10

MAUREEN CIR
9000
8800

18000

1

OAK HILL CIR
OAK HILL LN
OAK HILL DR
PARK LAWN CT
8500
WOOD RIDGE
LONE OAK CT
VALLEY RIDGE CT
CLEARY LAKE RD
185TH   ST   E   21   60   14   185TH   ST   W
18500   15   18500

91
AVE
NATCHEZ
The Legends Club
1
19200

HOBBY HILLS TRL
HOBBY HILLS CIR
19000   TOWERING OAKS CRV
TOWERING   OAKS TRL
9600
GREENVIEW CT
EDGEWOOD LN
OVERLAND DR
HEL WAY
TOWERING OAKS DR

Credit River Twp

Marion Lake
19000

RITTER FARM PARK

RITTER PARK TRL
11500

2

68
91
195TH ST E
9000
19500   22
195TH ST E
LAKEVILLE ISD #194
195TH ST W
23
195TH ST W

197TH ST W

55372

210TH ST E
SCOTT COUNTY
DAKOTA COUNTY

55044

20000
RIVER
20000
FRANCE CIR
20000
20200
LAREDO AVE
12000
11500
20000

3

LYNN DR
HUNTINGTON WAY
9600
BLVD
ROLLING OAK CT
64   26   205TH   ST   W
204TH ST E
AVE
20500
27
HUNTINGTON WAY
9200
NEW MARKET REST AREA
207TH ST W
KEOKUK
207TH ST E
MONTEREY
LYNN DR
FERN DR
BIRCH LN
BIRCH
LUCERNE TRL
LAREDO PATH
KENRICK AVE   5

210TH   ST   W
21000   70

MONTEREY AVE
BLVD
9500
9800
P&R LAKEVILLE
35
1

4

1500
LUCERNE
WAGON WHEEL TRL
FRANCE BLVD
9500
21600
34
FRANCE CT
FRANCE
9600
35
LAIGLE AVE
215TH   ST   W   1
21500
KEOKUK AVE
11500

21800
CANTER LN
CORRAL CIR
WAGON WHEEL TRL
219TH ST E
9000

Credit River Twp

DAKOTA COUNTY
SCOTT COUNTY

LAKEVILLE
1
22000

See Page 190

See Page 175

T114N

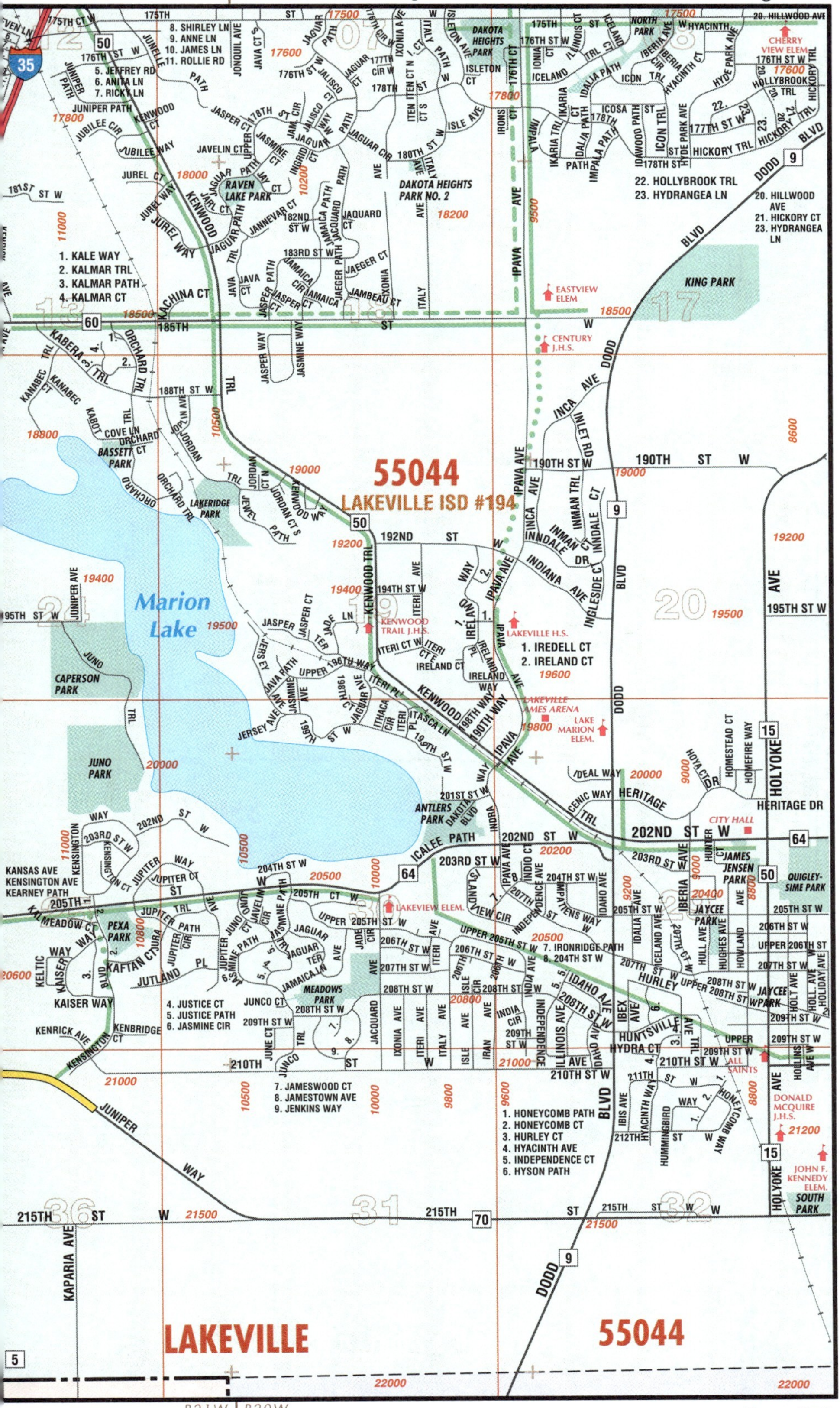
55044
LAKEVILLE ISD #194
LAKEVILLE
55044
Marion Lake
See Page 177
T114N
1
2
3
4
8. SHIRLEY LN
9. ANNE LN
10. JAMES LN
11. ROLLIE RD
5. JEFFREY RD
6. ANITA LN
7. RICKY LN
1. KALE WAY
2. KALMAR TRL
3. KALMAR PATH
4. KALMAR CT
22. HOLLYBROOK TRL
23. HYDRANGEA LN
20. HILLWOOD AVE
21. HICKORY CT
23. HYDRANGEA LN
1. IREDELL CT
2. IRELAND CT
4. JUSTICE CT
5. JUSTICE PATH
6. JASMINE CIR
7. JAMESWOOD CT
8. JAMESTOWN AVE
9. JENKINS WAY
7. IRONRIDGE PATH
8. 204TH ST W
1. HONEYCOMB PATH
2. HONEYCOMB CT
3. HURLEY CT
4. HYACINTH AVE
5. INDEPENDENCE CT
6. HYSON PATH
KANSAS AVE
KENSINGTON AVE
KEARNEY PATH
DAKOTA HEIGHTS PARK
DAKOTA HEIGHTS PARK NO. 2
RAVEN LAKE PARK
NORTH PARK
CHERRY VIEW ELEM.
KING PARK
EASTVIEW ELEM.
CENTURY J.H.S.
LAKERIDGE PARK
BASSETT PARK
CAPERSON PARK
JUNO PARK
KENWOOD TRAIL J.H.S.
LAKEVILLE H.S.
LAKEVILLE AMES ARENA
LAKE MARION ELEM.
ANTLERS PARK
CITY HALL
JAMES JENSEN PARK
QUIGLEY-SIME PARK
JAYCEE PARK
PEXA PARK
LAKEVIEW ELEM.
MEADOWS PARK
ALL SAINTS
DONALD MCQUIRE J.H.S.
JOHN F. KENNEDY ELEM.
SOUTH PARK
175TH ST
185TH ST
190TH ST W
192ND ST
202ND ST W
205TH ST
210TH ST W
215TH ST W
KENWOOD TRL
DODD BLVD
IPAVA AVE
HOLYOKE AVE
JUNIPER WAY
KAPARIA AVE
HERITAGE DR

See Page 163

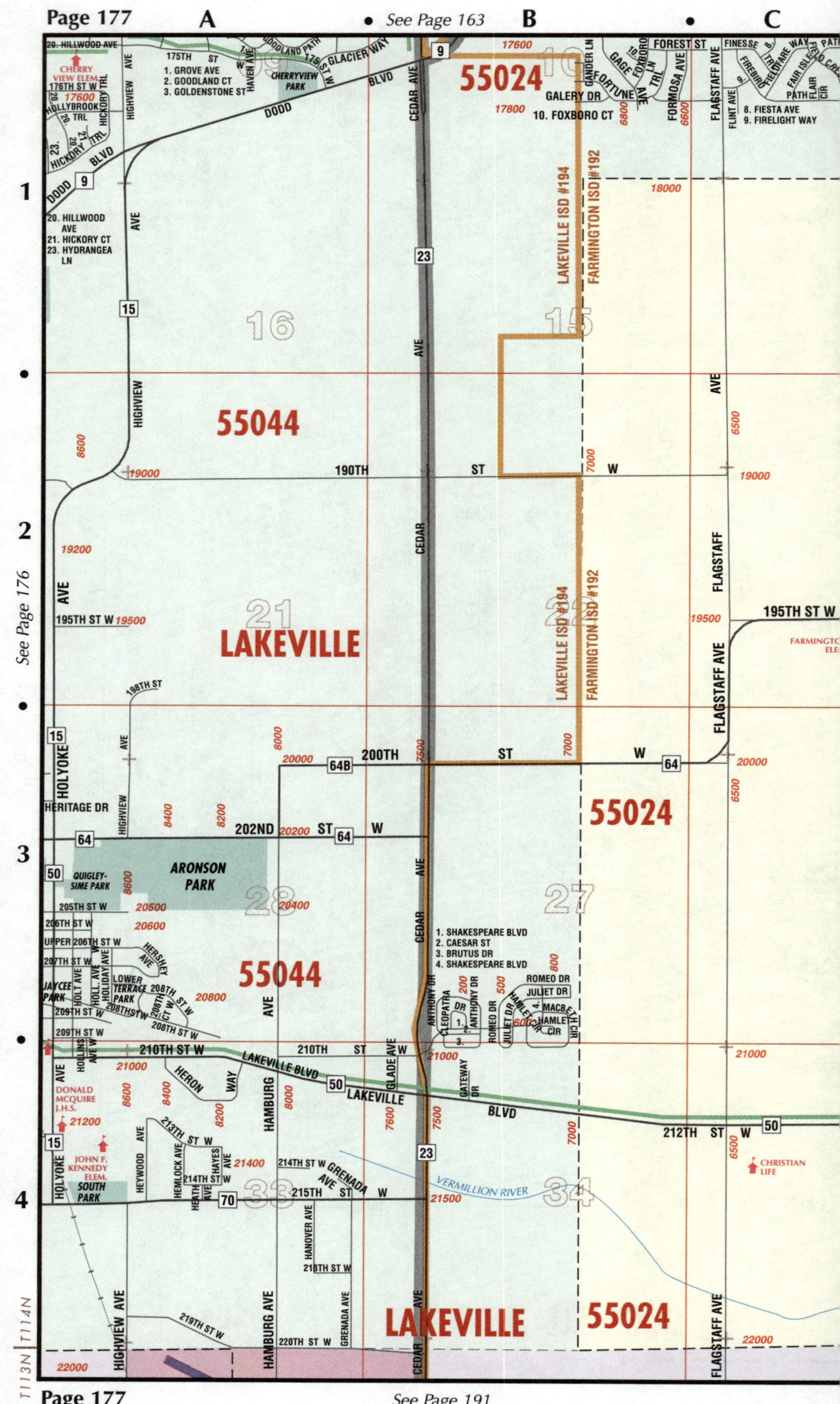

See Page 176
See Page 191

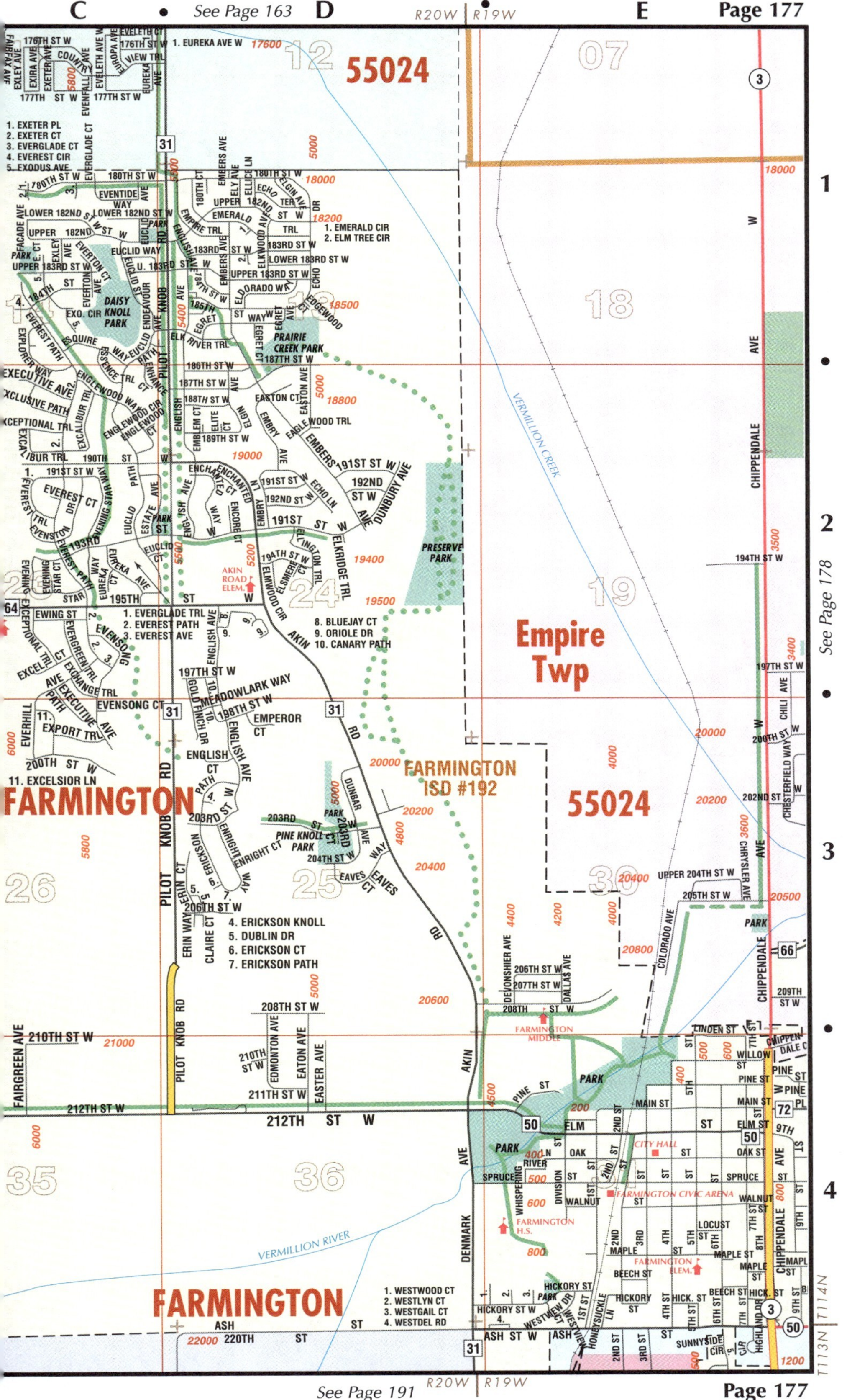

55024

07

3

18000

18

1

55024

Empire
Twp

19

See Page 178

Empire Twp

FARMINGTON

FARMINGTON ISD #192

55024

26

25

2

3

30

66

36

FARMINGTON

35

4

FARMINGTON

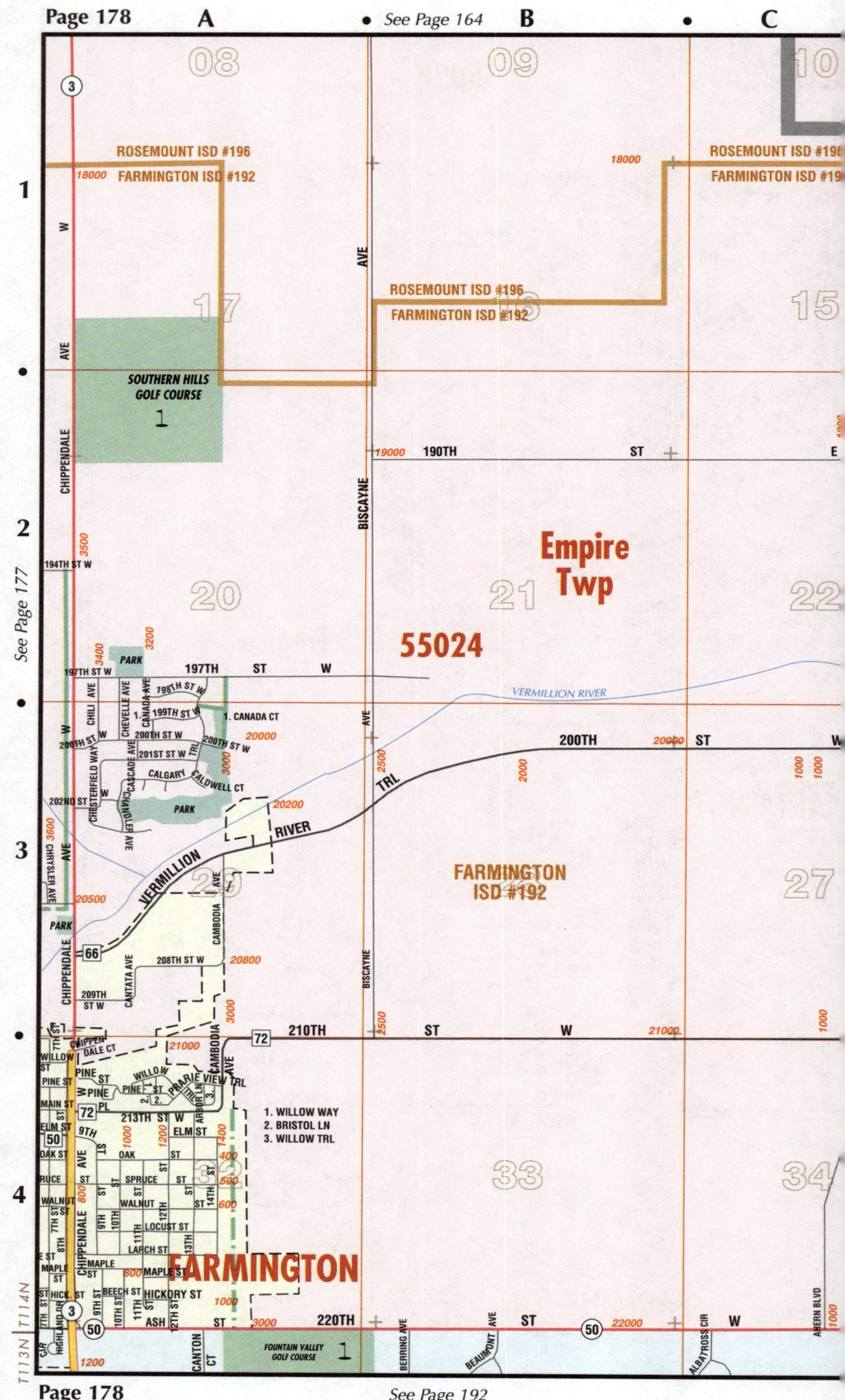

08

09

10

3

ROSEMOUNT ISD #196
FARMINGTON ISD #192
18000

ROSEMOUNT ISD #196
FARMINGTON ISD #1
18000

1

17

ROSEMOUNT ISD #196
FARMINGTON ISD #192

15

W

AVE

AVE

BISCAYNE

SOUTHERN HILLS
GOLF COURSE
1

CHIPPENDALE

19000 190TH ST E

2

3500

194TH ST W

20

21

**Empire
Twp**

22

See Page 177

55024

3200

PARK

197TH ST W

197TH ST W

CHILI AVE

CHEVELLE AVE

CANADA AVE

3400

VERMILLION RIVER

197TH ST W

199TH ST W

1. CANADA CT

CANADA AVE

AVE

200TH ST W

CASCADE AVE

200TH ST W

20000

CHESTERFIELD WAY

201ST ST W

TRL

200TH ST W

2500

200TH ST W

200TH ST 20000 ST W

W

CALGARY

CALDWELL CT

2000

1000
1000

202ND ST W

CALDWELL AVE

PARK

20200

VERMILLION RIVER

3

CHRYSLER AVE

3600

20500

VERMILLION

RIVER

28

AVE

FARMINGTON
ISD #192

27

PARK

CAMBODIA AVE

66

CHIPPENDALE

CANTATA AVE

208TH ST W

20800

209TH
ST W

BISCAYNE

3000

7TH ST

210TH ST W 21000

72

2500

21000

1000

WILLOW
ST

CHIPPEN
DALE CT

21000

CAMBODIA AVE

PINE ST

PINE ST

W PINE ST

WILLOW
ST

PRAIRIE VIEW TRL

1. WILLOW WAY
2. BRISTOL LN
3. WILLOW TRL

MAIN ST

72

213TH ST W

PL

ELM ST

9TH

1000

1200

ELM ST

1400

50

OAK ST W

AVE

OAK ST

400

4

RUCE

ST

SPRUCE ST

500

32

33

34

WALNUT

800

ST

WALNUT ST

14TH

600

7TH ST W

8TH

9TH
10TH

11TH

12TH

LOCUST ST

13TH

LARCH ST

MAPLE ST

CHIPPENDALE

MAPLE

800 MAPLE ST

FARMINGTON

ST HICK ST

BEECH ST

HICKORY ST

1000

3

9TH ST

10TH ST

11TH

12TH

ASH ST

3000

220TH ST

50

22000

W

AHERN BLVD

50

CANTON
CT

FOUNTAIN VALLEY
GOLF COURSE 1

BERRING AVE

BEAUMONT

ALBATROSS CIR

1000

1200

T113N | T114N

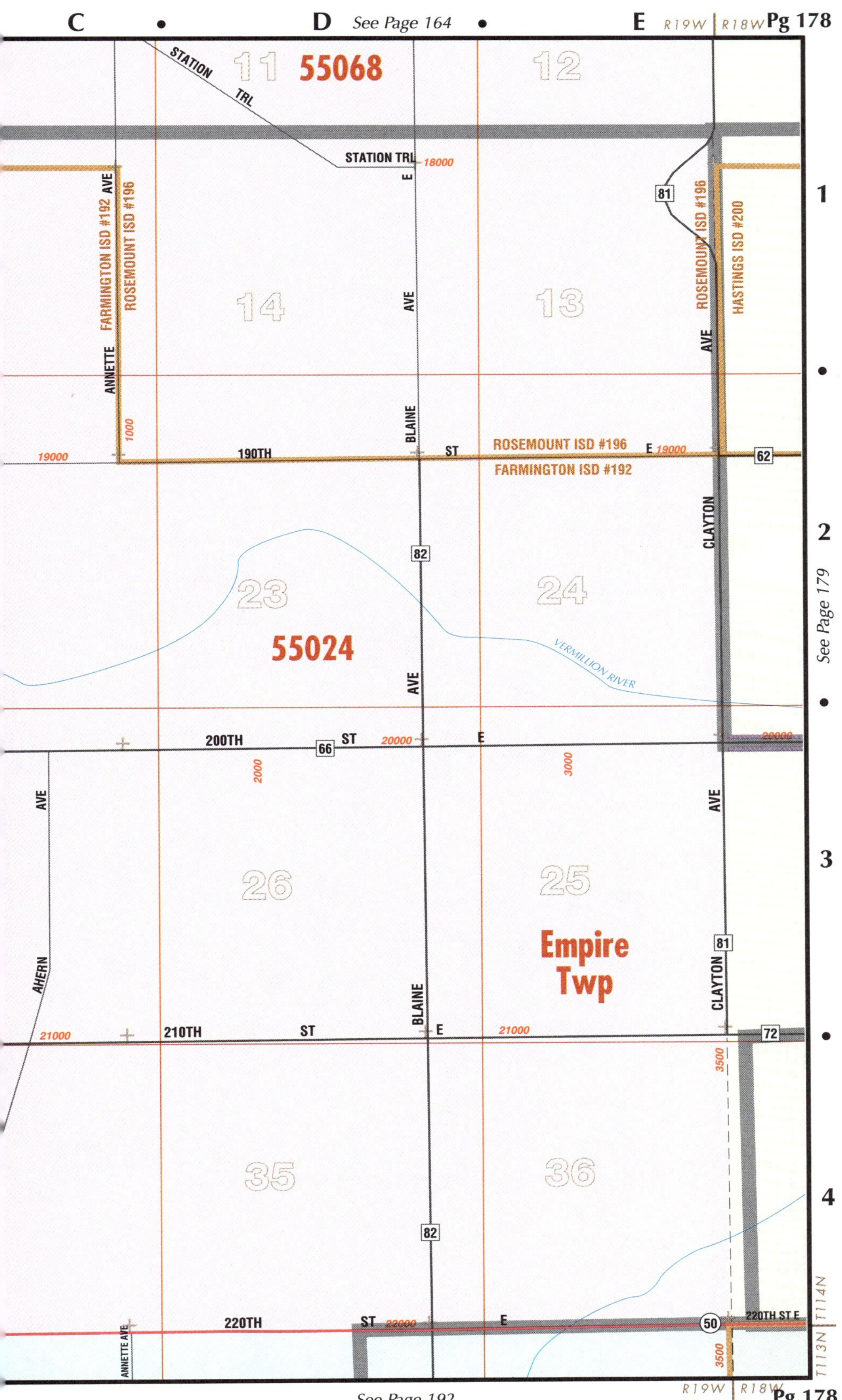

55068

11

12

STATION TRL

STATION TRL — *18000*

E

FARMINGTON ISD #192 AVE

ROSEMOUNT ISD #196

ANNETTE

81

ROSEMOUNT ISD #196

HASTINGS ISD #200

1

14

13

AVE

AVE

1000

BLAINE

19000

190TH

ST

ROSEMOUNT ISD #196

E *19000*

62

FARMINGTON ISD #192

See Page 179

CLAYTON

2

82

23

24

VERMILLION RIVER

55024

AVE

200TH

66

ST

20000

E

20000

AVE

AVE

2000

3000

3

26

25

AHERN

CLAYTON

81

Empire Twp

210TH

ST

BLAINE

E

21000

72

21000

3500

35

36

4

82

T113N | T114N

220TH

ST *22000*

E

50

220TH ST E

ANNETTE AVE

3500

A • B • C

07 55068 08 55033 09

ROSEMOUNT ISD #196
HASTINGS ISD #200

18000 180TH ST E

1

18 17 16

52

AVE

EMERY

AVE

DONNELLY

COATES

52

62 *19000* 190TH ST E
62

2

FARMINGTON ISD #192
HASTINGS ISD #200

19 20 **Vermillion Twp** 21

DONNELLY AVE

BLVD

4600

5600

VERMILLION RIVER

Vermillion River

66 *20000* 200TH ST E *20000* E

4000 *4400* *4500* *5000* *6000*

DOFFING AVE
PRIV
202ND ST E *20200*

3

30 **55024** 29 28

DONNELLY AVE

ELAINE AVE

SOUTH BRANCH VERMILLION RIVER

5400

FARMINGTON ISD #192
HASTINGS ISD #200

20000

DUBARRY TRL

72 DUBARRY TRL *21000* 210TH ST E

81

AVE

FARMINGTON ISD #192
HASTINGS ISD #200

55033

31 *21500* 215TH ST E 32 33

4

DARSOW

COATES BLVD E

81 *4000*

50 220TH ST E

ISD #192 52 *22000* 47

T113N | T114N

See Page 178

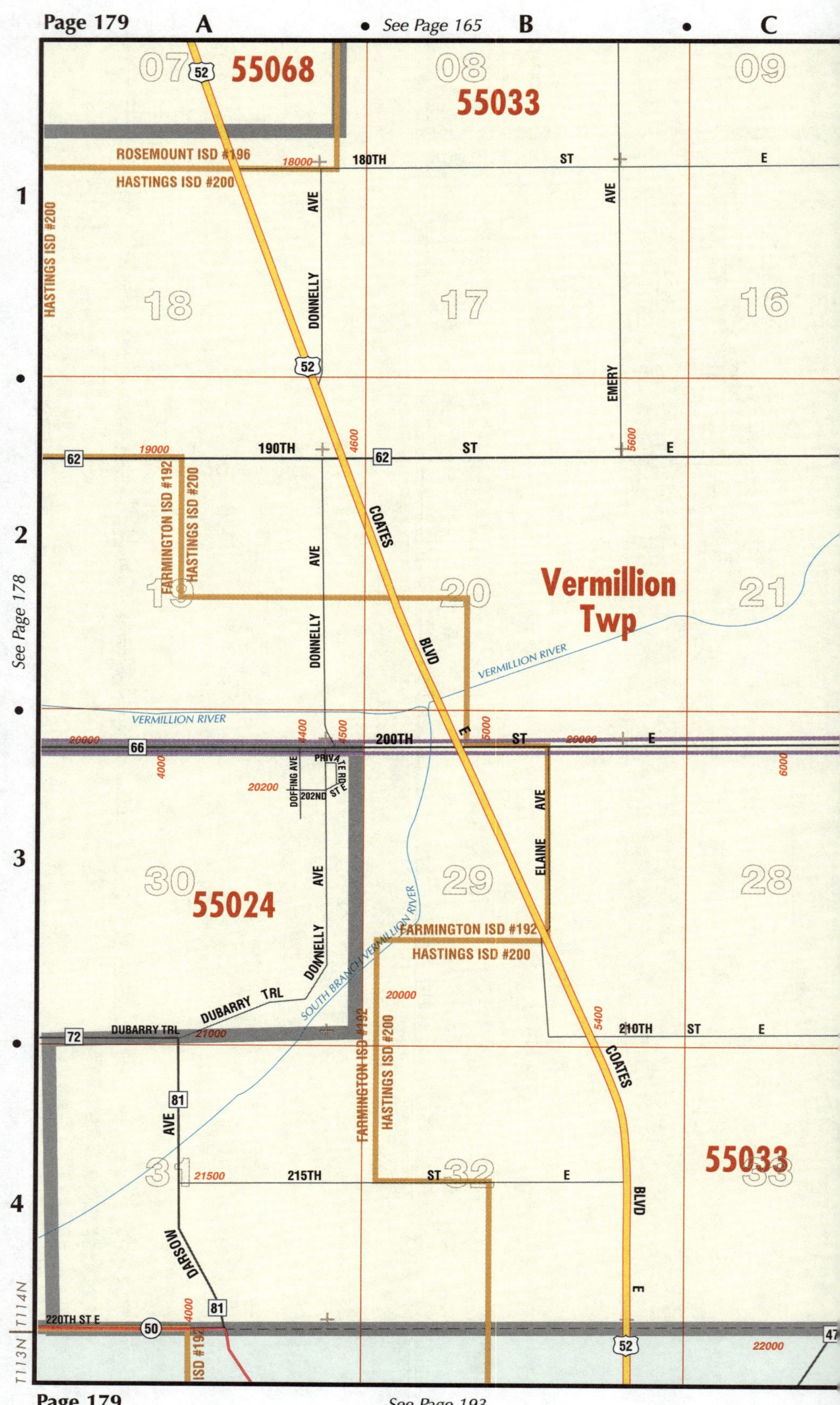

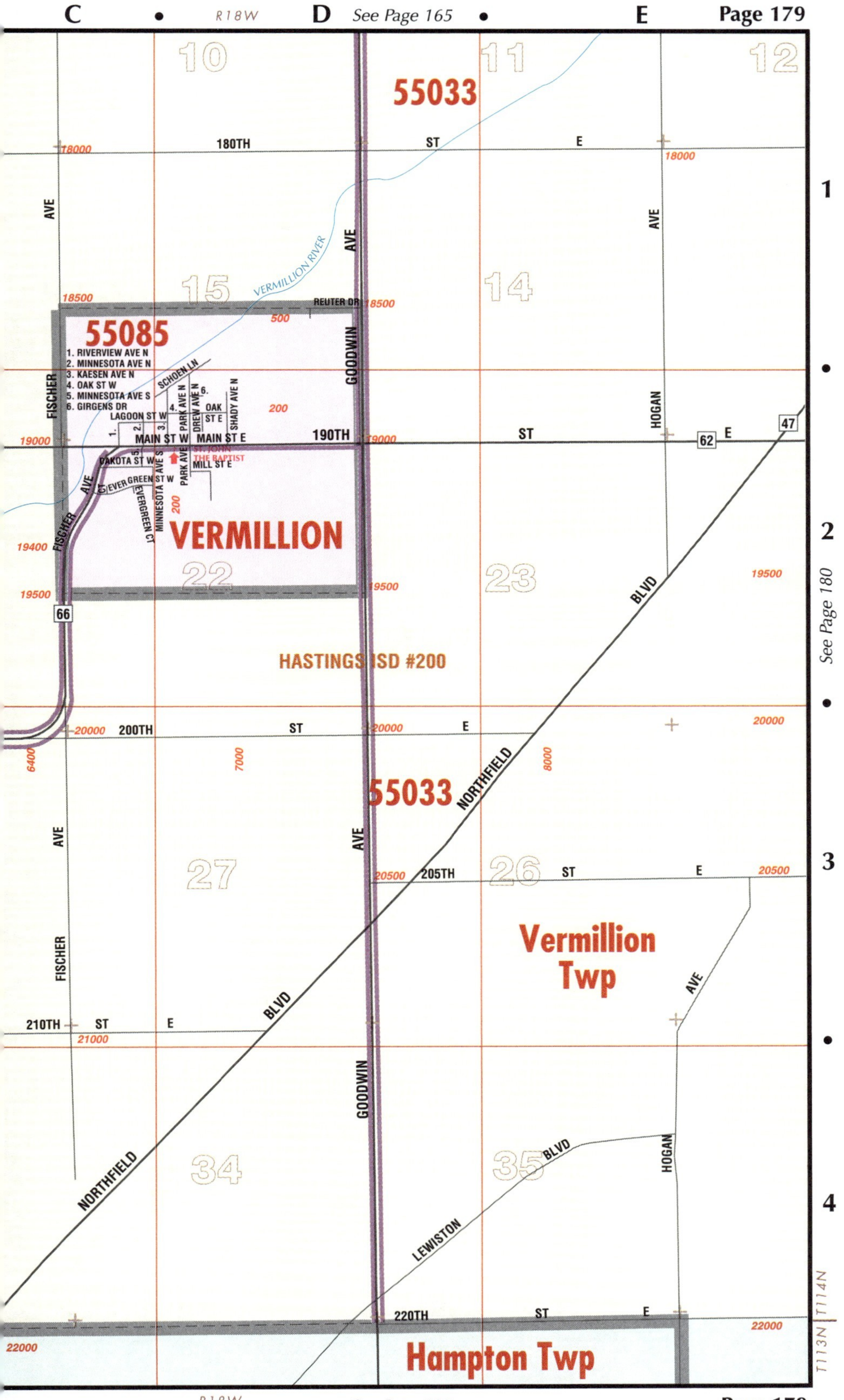

10

55033

11

12

180TH ST E

18000 18000

AVE

AVE

1

AVE

GOODWIN

VERMILLION RIVER

15

14

18500 REUTER DR 18500

500

55085

1. RIVERVIEW AVE N
2. MINNESOTA AVE N
3. KAESEN AVE N
4. OAK ST W
5. MINNESOTA AVE S
6. GIRGENS DR

SCHOEN LN

200

SHADY AVE N

FISCHER

LAGOON ST W

PARK AVE N

DREW AVE N

OAK ST E

MAIN ST W MAIN ST E

190TH ST E 62 E 47

19000 19000

DAKOTA ST W

EVERGREEN AVE

ST JOHN THE BAPTIST

MILL ST E

PARK AVE

MINNESOTA AVE S

HOGAN

FISCHER

EVERGREEN CT

200

VERMILLION

19400

FISCHER

22

23

19500

19500 19500

66

HASTINGS ISD #200

200TH ST E

20000 7000 20000

AVE

8000

55033

NORTHFIELD

BLVD

2

20000

See Page 180

27

205TH ST E

20500 20500 20500

26

3

FISCHER

Vermillion Twp

AVE

210TH ST E

21000

BLVD

GOODWIN

NORTHFIELD

34

35

BLVD

HOGAN

LEWISTON

4

220TH ST E

22000

22000

Hampton Twp

T113N T114N

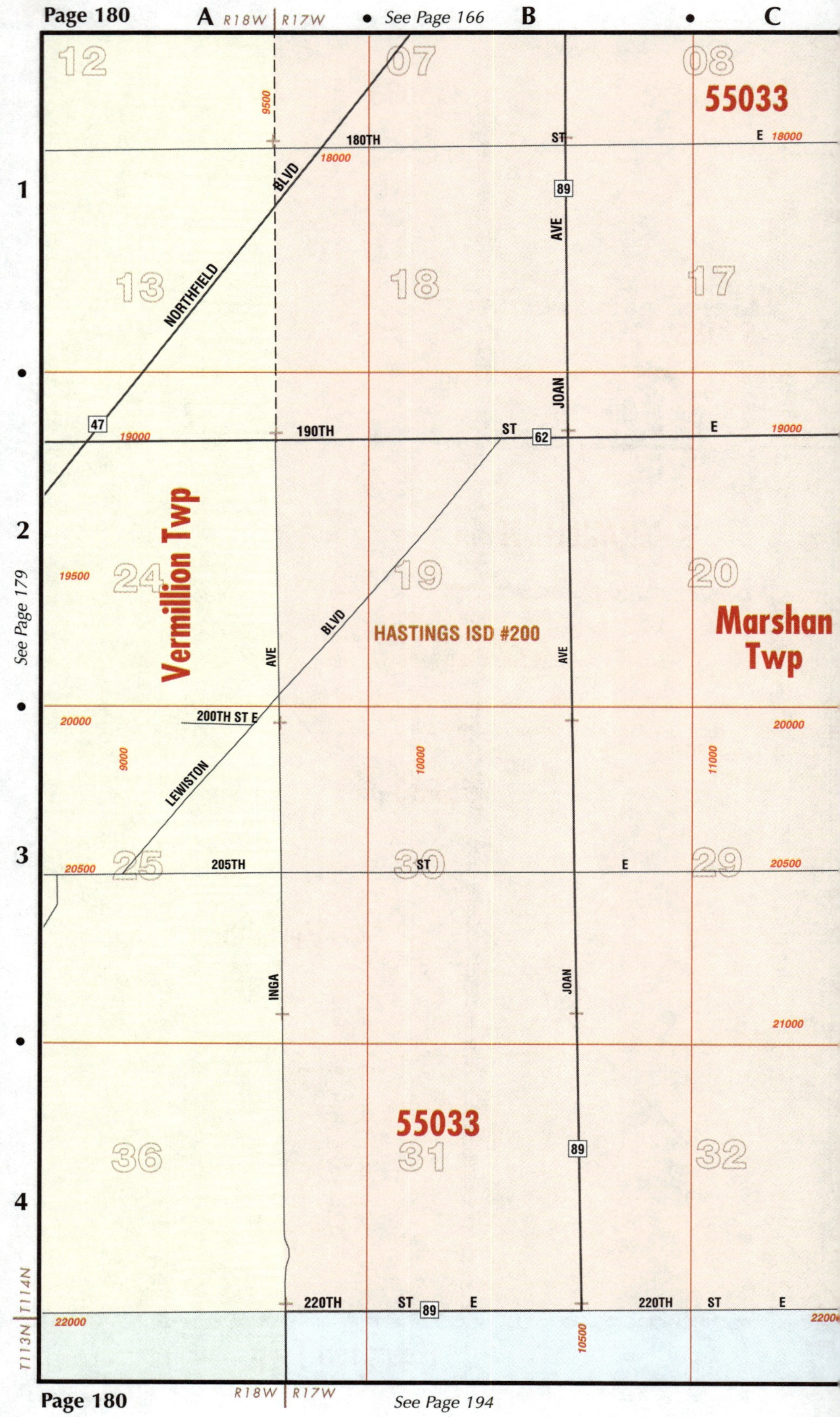

12

07

08

55033

180TH   ST   E *18000*

9500

BLVD

18000

[89]

1

NORTHFIELD

13

18

AVE

17

JOAN

[47] *19000*   190TH   ST [62]   E   *19000*

See Page 179

2

19500   24

BLVD

19

HASTINGS ISD #200

AVE

20

Marshan Twp

Vermillion Twp

AVE

200TH ST E

20000   *9000*   *10000*   *11000*   *20000*

LEWISTON

3

20500   25   205TH   ST   30   E   29   *20500*

INGA

JOAN

21000

•

55033

4

36   31   32

[89]

T113N | *T114N*

220TH   ST [89]   E   220TH   ST   E

22000   *10500*   *2200*

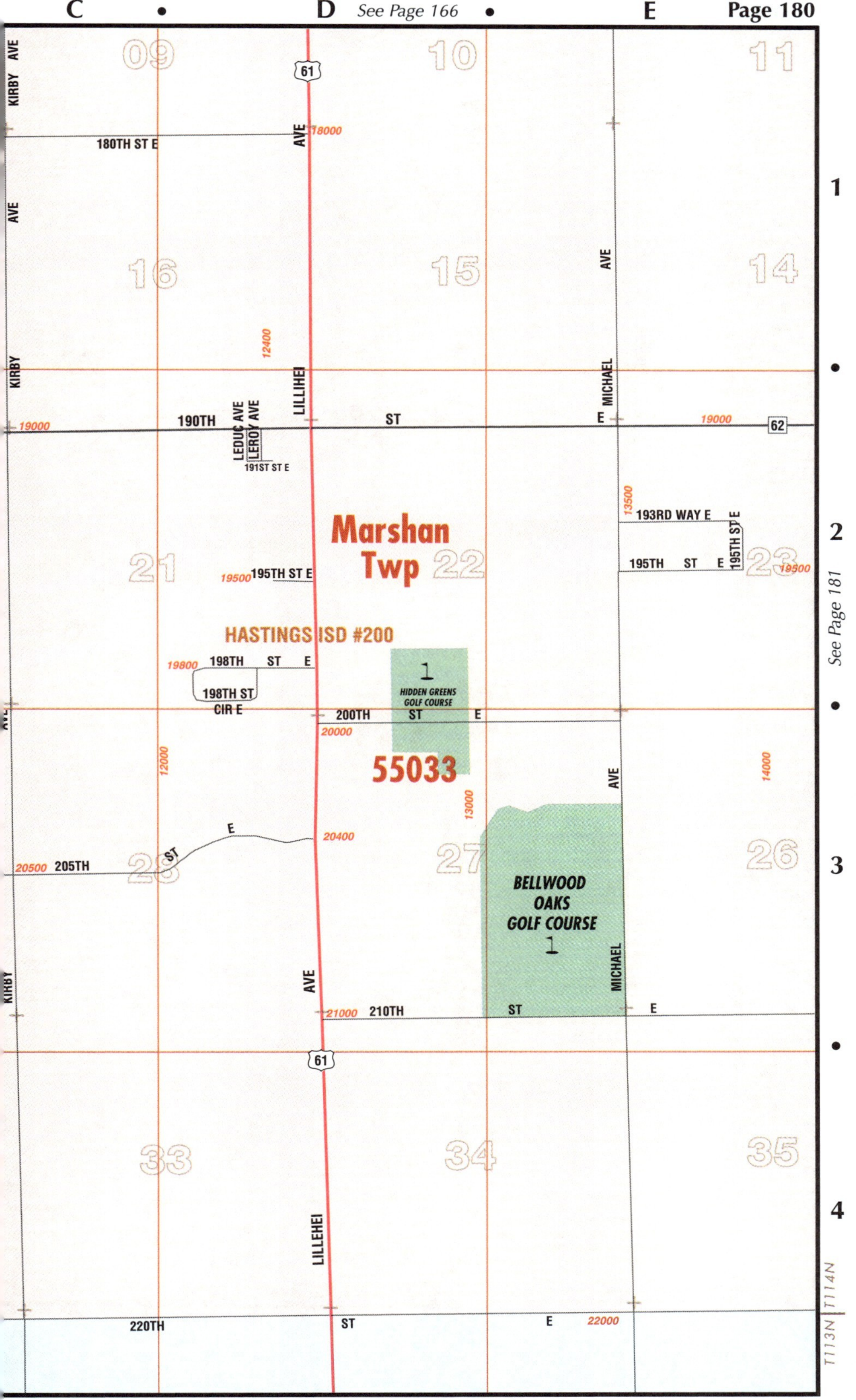

KIRBY AVE

61

180TH ST E

AVE

AVE

1

AVE

16

15

14

KIRBY

12400

MICHAEL

LILLIHEI

LEDUC AVE

LEROY AVE

190TH

ST

E

19000

19000

62

191ST ST E

13500

193RD WAY E

195TH ST E

Marshan Twp

21

22

2

19500

195TH ST E

195TH

ST

E

23

19500

HASTINGS ISD #200

19800

198TH

ST

E

1

HIDDEN GREENS GOLF COURSE

198TH ST

CIR E

200TH

ST

E

20000

55033

12000

13000

14000

AVE

AVE

E

20400

205TH

ST

26

20500

28

27

3

BELLWOOD OAKS GOLF COURSE

1

MICHAEL

KIRBY

AVE

AVE

21000

210TH

ST

E

61

33

34

35

4

LILLEHEI

220TH

ST

E

22000

T113N | T114N

See Page 181

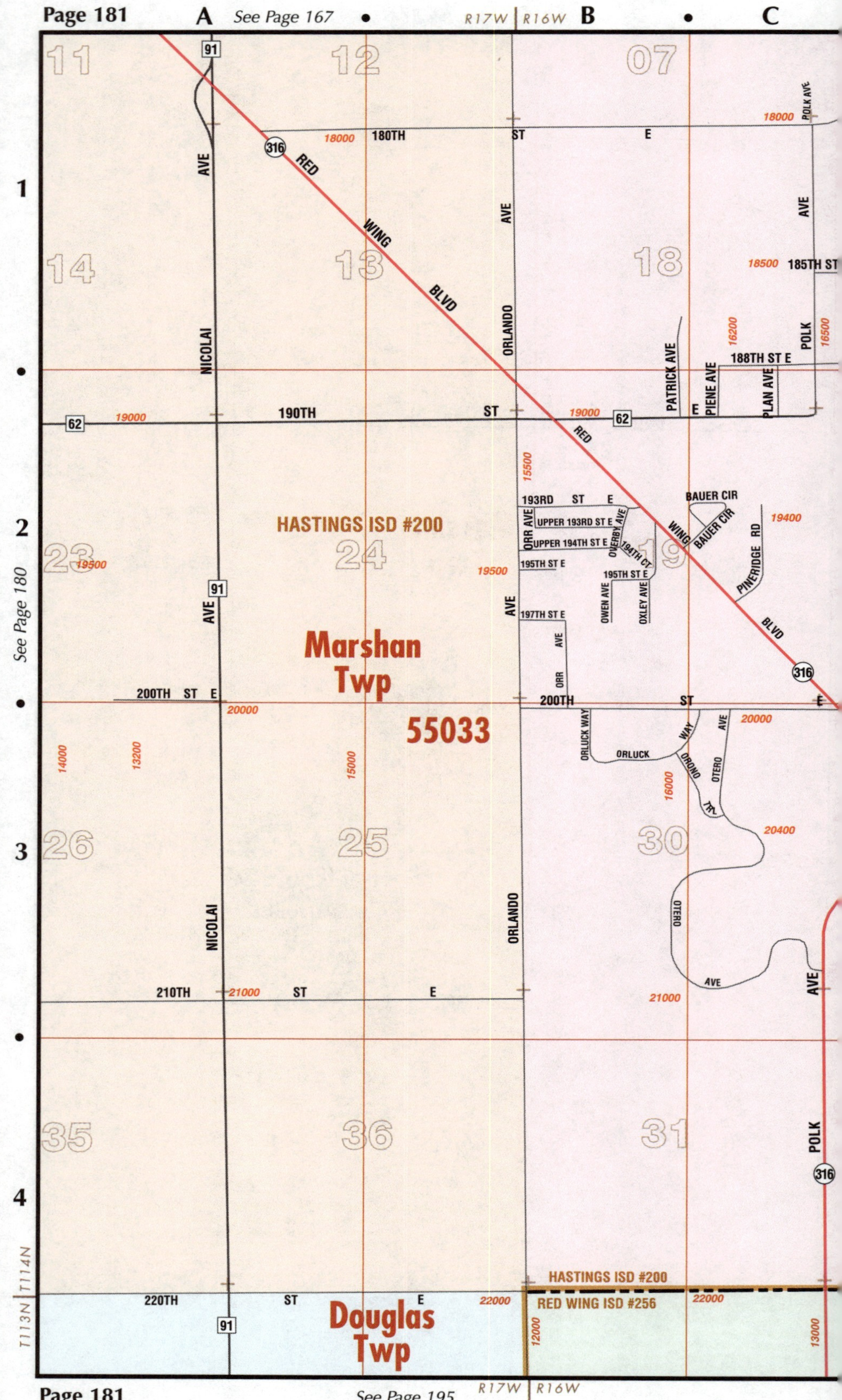

11

91

12

316

AVE

RED

18000   180TH   ST   E

1

14

13

WING

ORLANDO

18000

POLK AVE

07

18

18500   185TH ST

NICOLAI

BLVD

AVE

16200

16500

PATRICK AVE

PIENE AVE

188TH ST E

POLK

PLAN AVE

E

62   19000   190TH   ST +   19000   62

RED

15500

HASTINGS ISD #200

193RD   ST   E

BAUER CIR

19400

2

23

91

AVE

19500

24

**Marshan
Twp**

55033

ORR AVE

UPPER 193RD ST E

OVERBY AVE

194TH CT

UPPER 194TH ST E

BAUER CIR

WING

PINERIDGE RD

19500

195TH ST E

195TH ST E

OWEN AVE

OXLEY AVE

AVE

197TH ST E

AVE

ORR

BLVD

316

200TH ST E   20000   200TH   ST   E

20000

14000

13200

15000

ORLUCK WAY

ORLUCK

WAY

OTERO

AVE

ORONO

TRL

3

26

25

NICOLAI

21000

ORLANDO

30

16000

20400

OTERO

21000

210TH   21000   ST   E

AVE

AVE

4

35

36

31

91

POLK

316

T113N | T114N

220TH   ST   E   22000

HASTINGS ISD #200

**Douglas
Twp**

RED WING ISD #256   22000

12000

13000

See Page 180

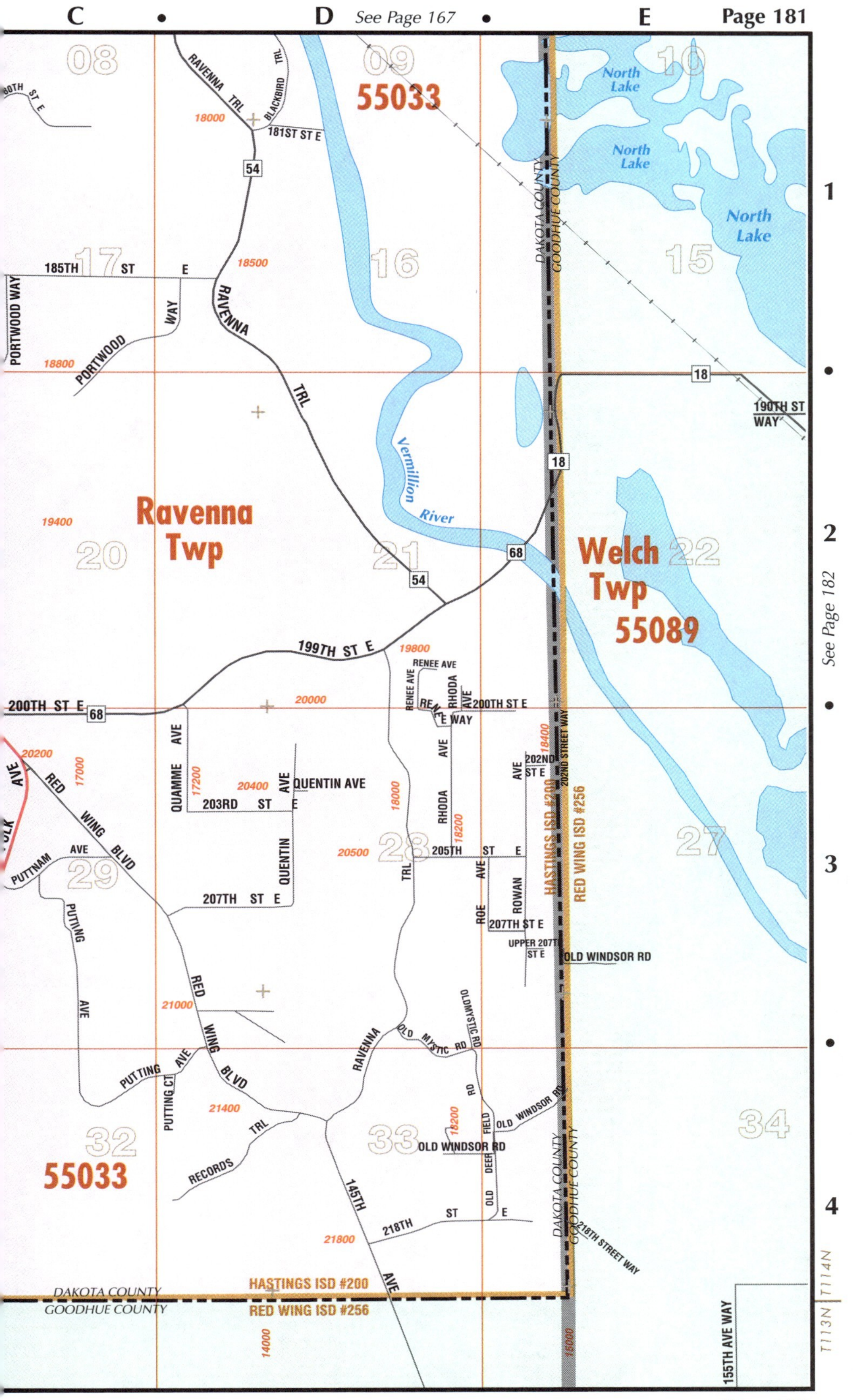

55033

North Lake

North Lake

North Lake

54

181ST ST E

RAVENNA TRL

BLACKBIRD

18000

80TH ST E

08

09

10

15

1

185TH ST E

17

PORTWOOD WAY

PORTWOOD WAY

18500

RAVENNA

16

18

190TH ST WAY

18800

•

Ravenna Twp

20

19400

RAVENNA TRL

Vermillion River

21

54

18

68

2

Welch Twp 55089

22

See Page 182

199TH ST E

19800

RENEE AVE

RENEE AVE

RHODA AVE

200TH ST E

68

200TH ST E

20000

REV E WAY

202ND STREET WAY

18400

•

QUAMME AVE

20200

20400

QUENTIN AVE

RHODA AVE

AVE

202ND ST E

HASTINGS ISD #200

RED WING ISD #256

AVE

17000

17200

203RD ST E

18000

RED WING BLVD

PUTTNAM AVE

29

QUENTIN AVE

20500

28

205TH ST E

18200

ROWAN

207TH ST E

UPPER 207TH ST E

27

3

207TH ST E

ROE AVE

OLD WINDSOR RD

PUTTING AVE

RED WING BLVD

21000

RAVENNA TRL

OLD MYSTIC RD

OLDMYSTIC RD

OLD WINDSOR RD

•

PUTTING CT

PUTTING AVE

21400

RECORDS

32

33

OLD WINDSOR RD

18200

DEER FIELD

OLD WINDSOR RD

34

4

55033

145TH

218TH ST E

21800

218TH STREET WAY

155TH AVE WAY

DAKOTA COUNTY GOODHUE COUNTY

DAKOTA COUNTY GOODHUE COUNTY

HASTINGS ISD #200

RED WING ISD #256

14000

18000

AVE

T113N / T114N

20000

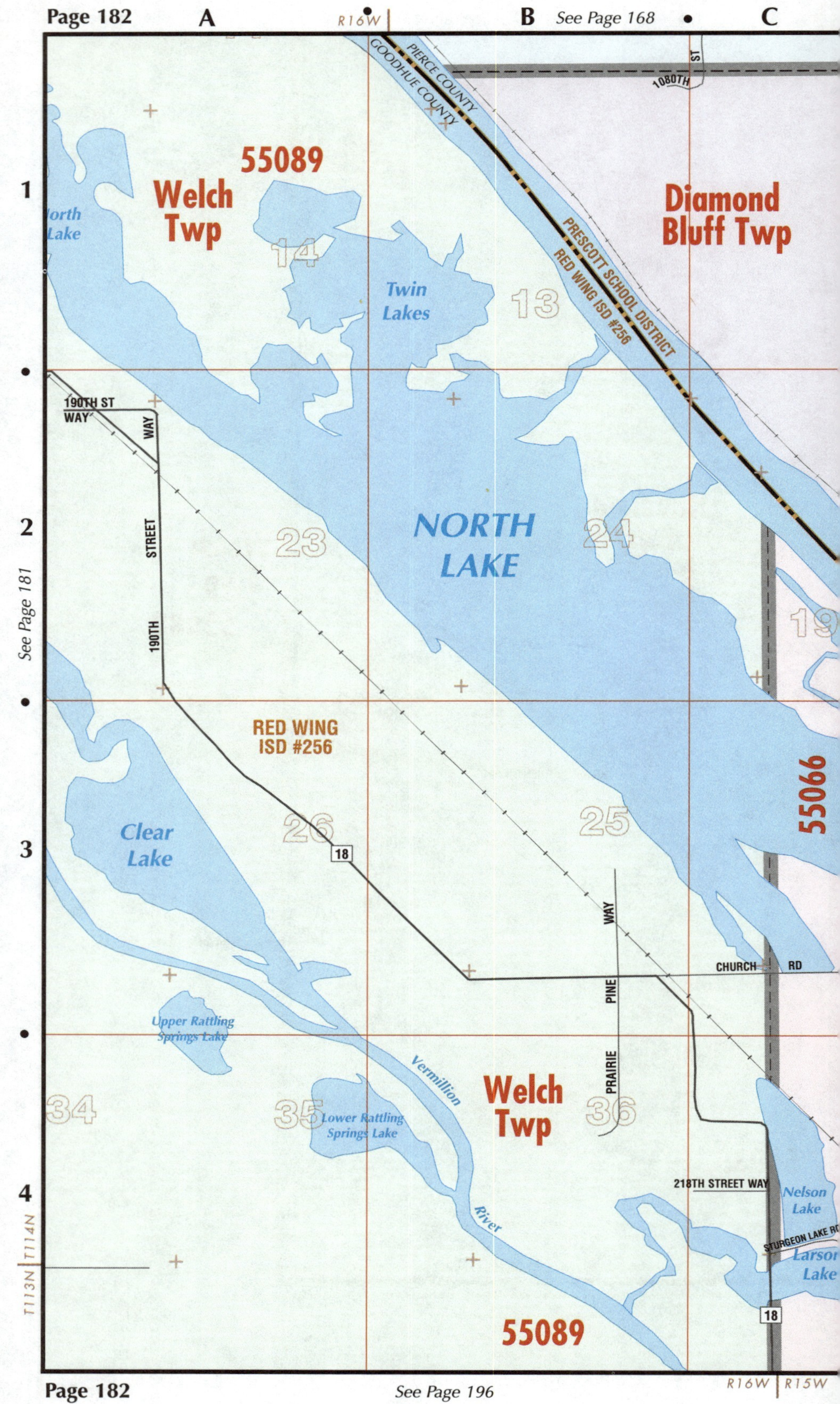

A   B   *See Page 168*   C

R16W

PIERCE COUNTY

GOODHUE COUNTY

1080TH ST

55089

Welch Twp

Diamond Bluff Twp

14

13

Twin Lakes

PRESCOTT SCHOOL DISTRICT

RED WING ISD #256

North Lake

1

190TH ST WAY

WAY

WAY

STREET

190TH

23

NORTH LAKE

24

19

2

See Page 181

RED WING ISD #256

55066

Clear Lake

26

18

25

3

Upper Rattling Springs Lake

CHURCH RD

WAY

PINE

PRAIRIE

34

35

Lower Rattling Springs Lake

Welch Twp

36

218TH STREET WAY

Nelson Lake

Vermillion

River

STURGEON LAKE RD

Larson Lake

4

T113N | T114N

55089

18

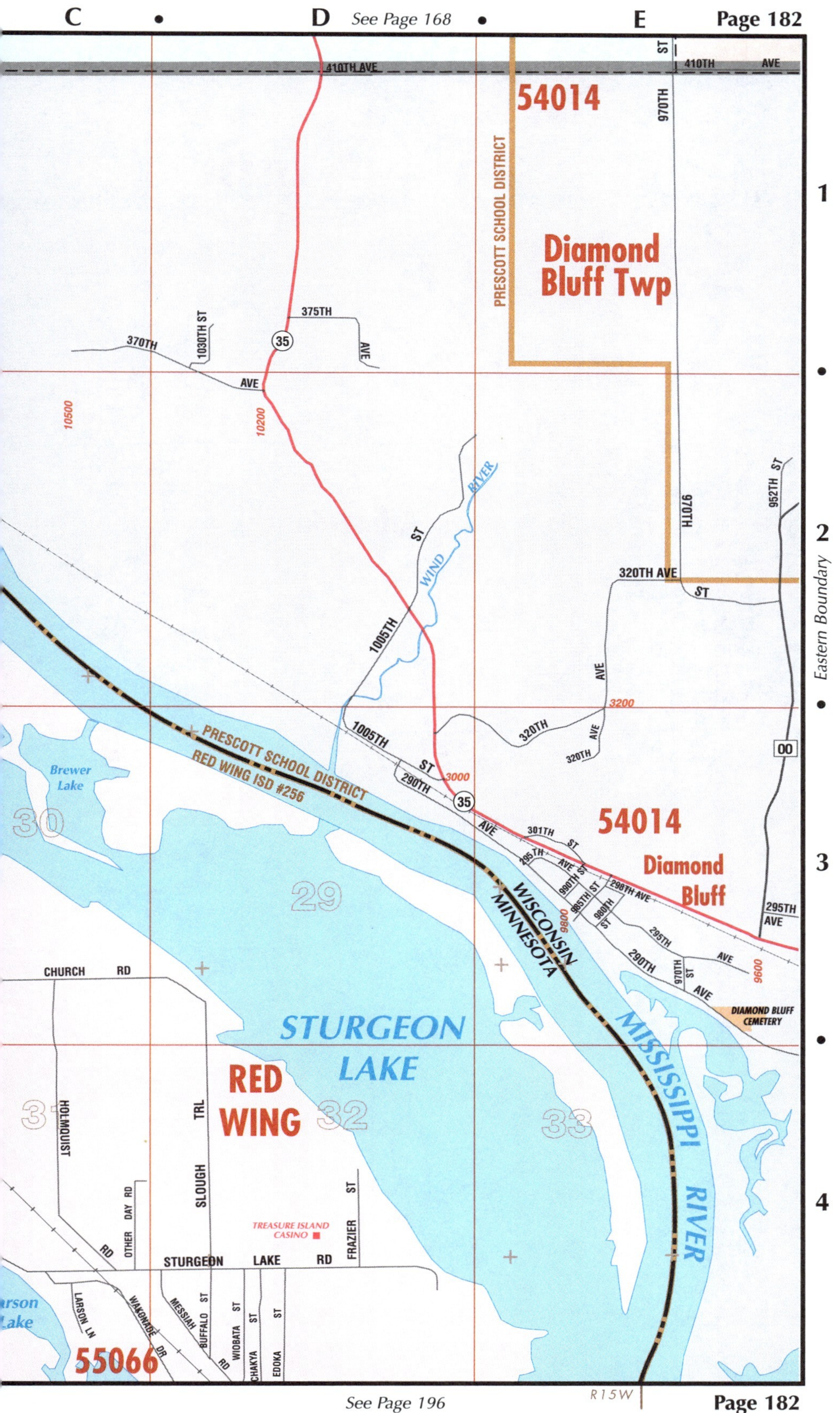

410TH AVE

ST
410TH AVE

54014

970TH

PRESCOTT SCHOOL DISTRICT

1

**Diamond
Bluff Twp**

375TH

1030TH ST

370TH

(35)

AVE

AVE

10500

10200

ST

WIND

RIVER

952TH ST

970TH

2

Eastern Boundary

320TH AVE

ST

1005TH

AVE

320TH

AVE

320TH

3200

1005TH

Brewer
Lake

PRESCOTT SCHOOL DISTRICT
RED WING ISD #256

ST

290TH

3000

(35)

AVE

301TH

ST

54014

00

295TH
AVE

**Diamond
Bluff**

30

295TH ST

AVE ST

290TH ST

298TH AVE

985TH ST

980TH ST

295TH

AVE

29

WISCONSIN

MINNESOTA

9800

290TH

AVE

970TH ST

AVE

9600

CHURCH RD

DIAMOND BLUFF
CEMETERY

**STURGEON
LAKE**

3

HOLMQUIST

**RED
WING**

32

33

MISSISSIPPI

RIVER

4

OTHER DAY RD

SLOUGH TRL

FRAZIER ST

RD

TREASURE ISLAND
CASINO ■

arson
Lake

LARSON LN

WANGMADE DR

STURGEON LAKE RD

MESSIAH ST

BUFFALO ST

WIDBATA ST

CHAKYA ST

EDOKA ST

55066

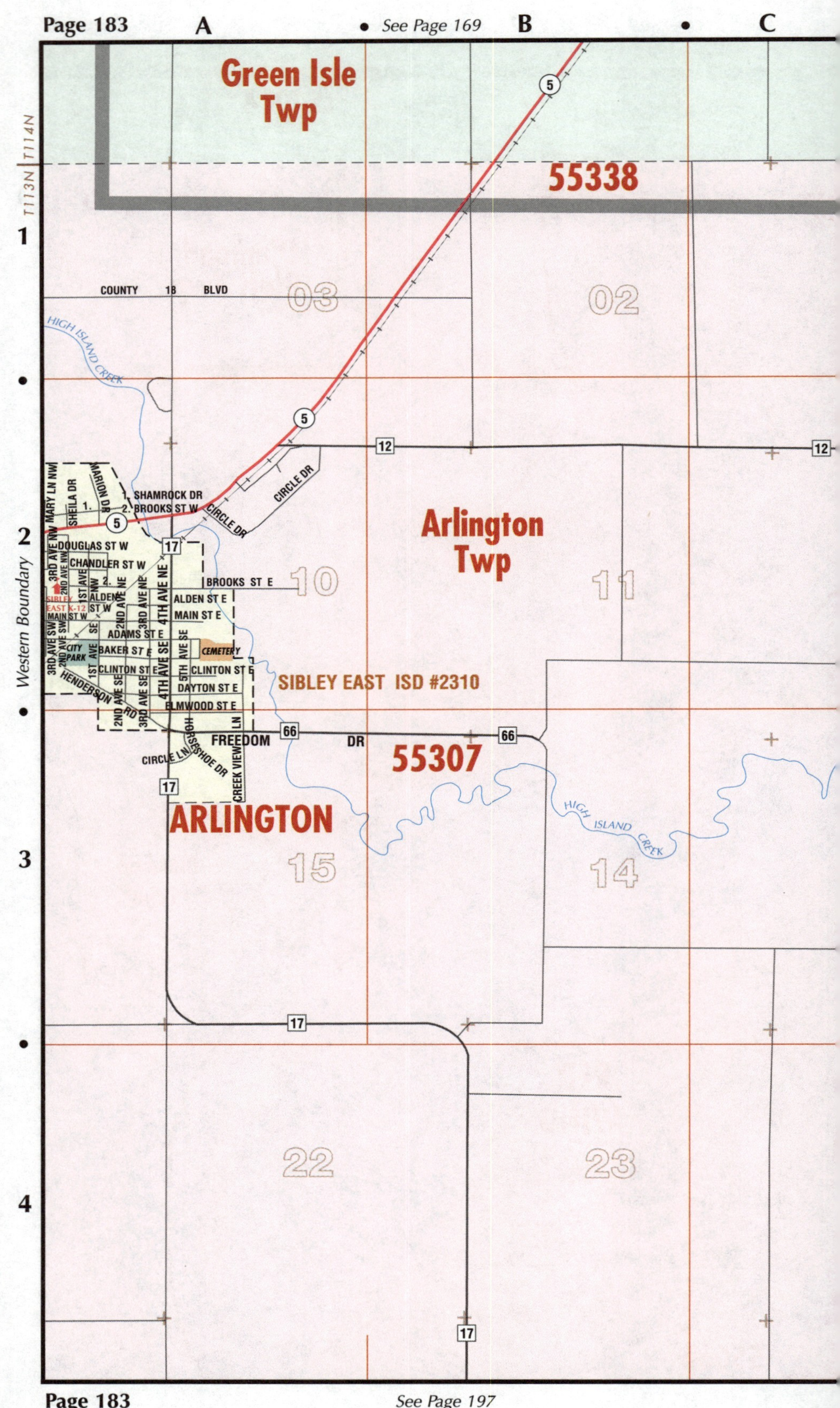

Page 183

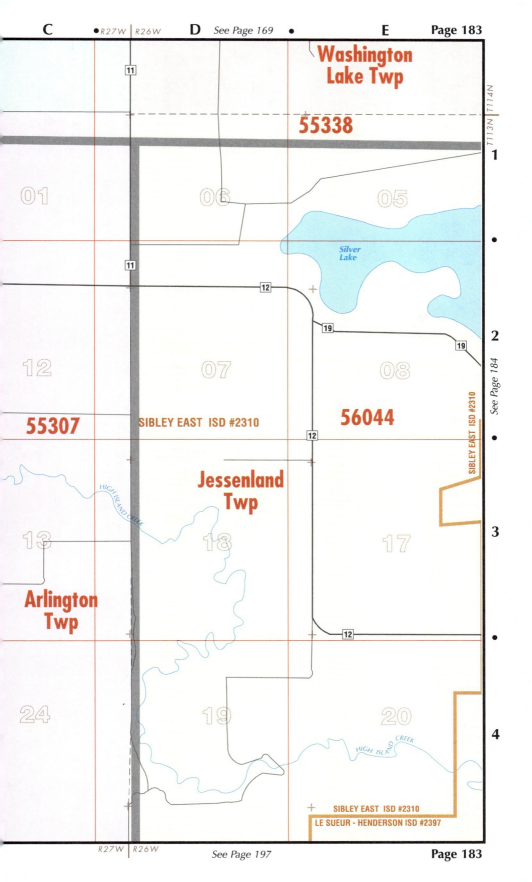
C
R27W
R26W
D
See Page 169
E
Washington Lake Twp
T114N
T113N
55338
1
01
06
05
Silver Lake
11
12
19
2
12
07
08
See Page 184
55307
SIBLEY EAST ISD #2310
56044
SIBLEY EAST ISD #2310
Jessenland Twp
HIGH ISLAND CREEK
3
13
18
17
Arlington Twp
24
19
20
4
HIGH ISLAND CREEK
SIBLEY EAST ISD #2310
LE SUEUR - HENDERSON ISD #2397
R27W
R26W
See Page 197

A • *See Page 170* B • C

64

Washington Lake Twp

16

T113N | T114N

SIBLEY EAST ISD #2310

64

55338

LE SUEUR - HENDERSON ISD #2397

1

04 03

64

Silver Lake

16

27

27

2

19

09

LE SUEUR - HENDERSON ISD #2397

10

19

SIBLEY EAST ISD #2310

See Page 183

SIBLEY EAST ISD #2310

Jessenland Twp

64

19

56044

3

LE SUEUR - HENDERSON ISD #2397

16 15

64

12

64

12

4

21 22

12

HIGH ISLAND CREEK

PARK

6

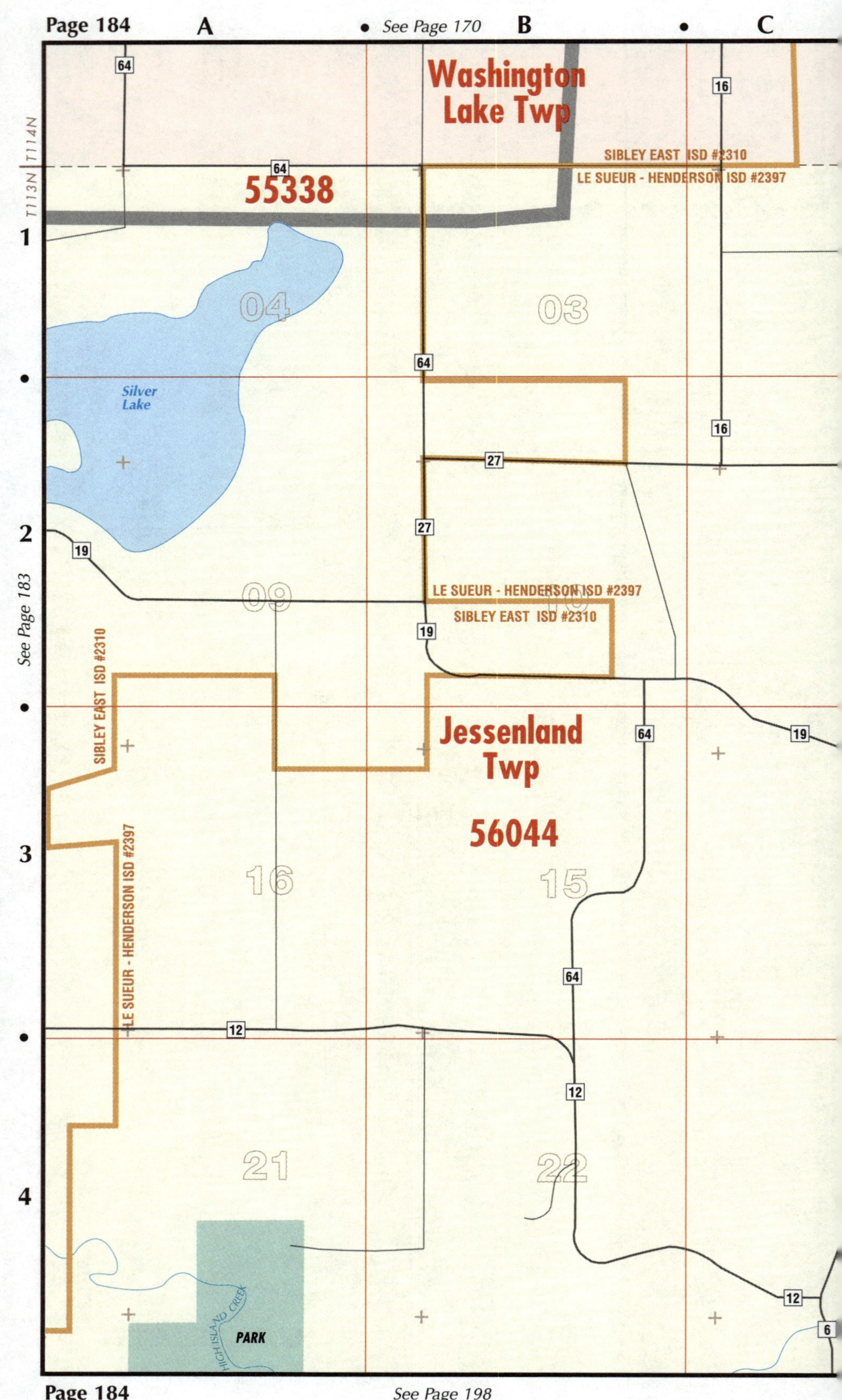

See Page 170

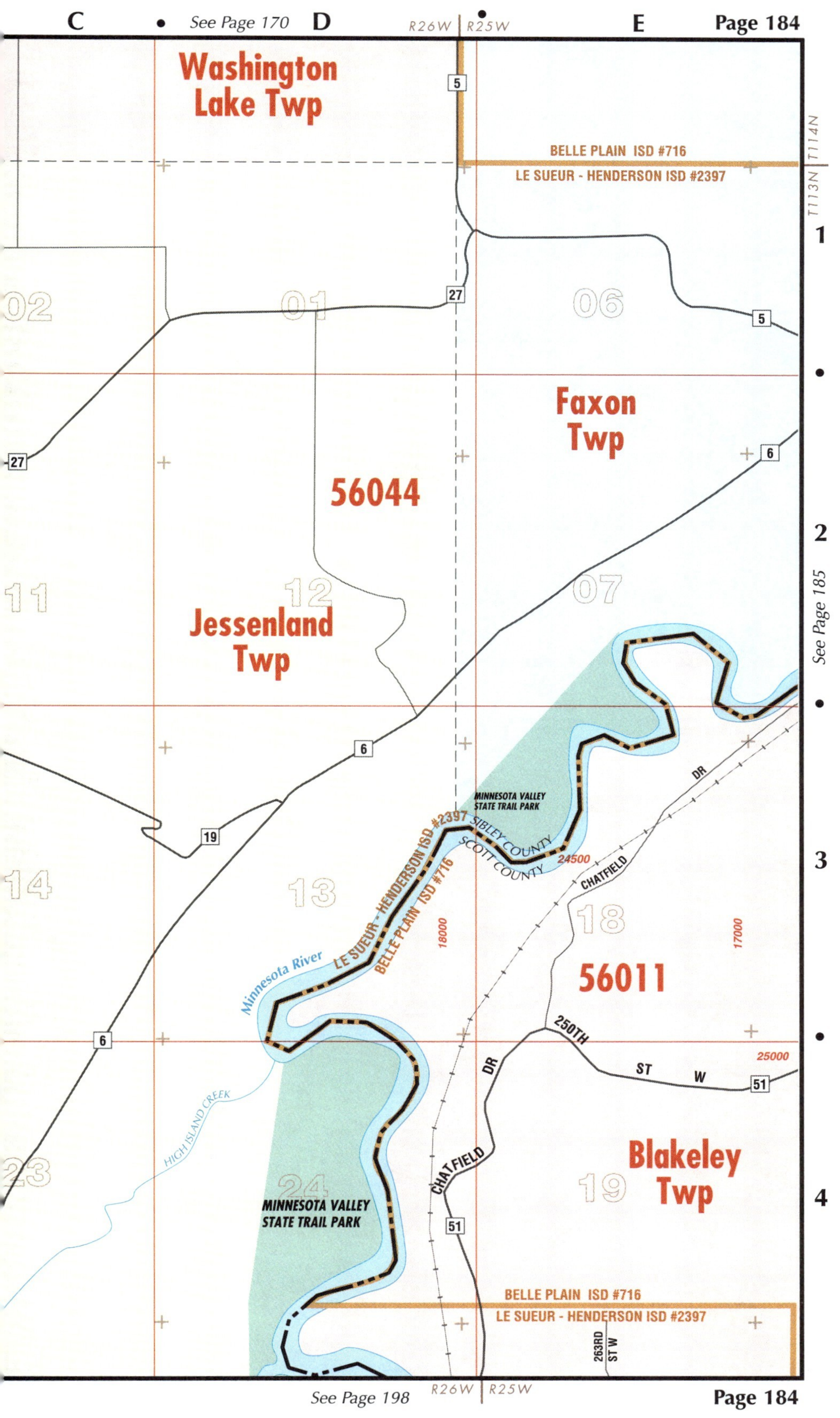

See Page 185

See Page 198

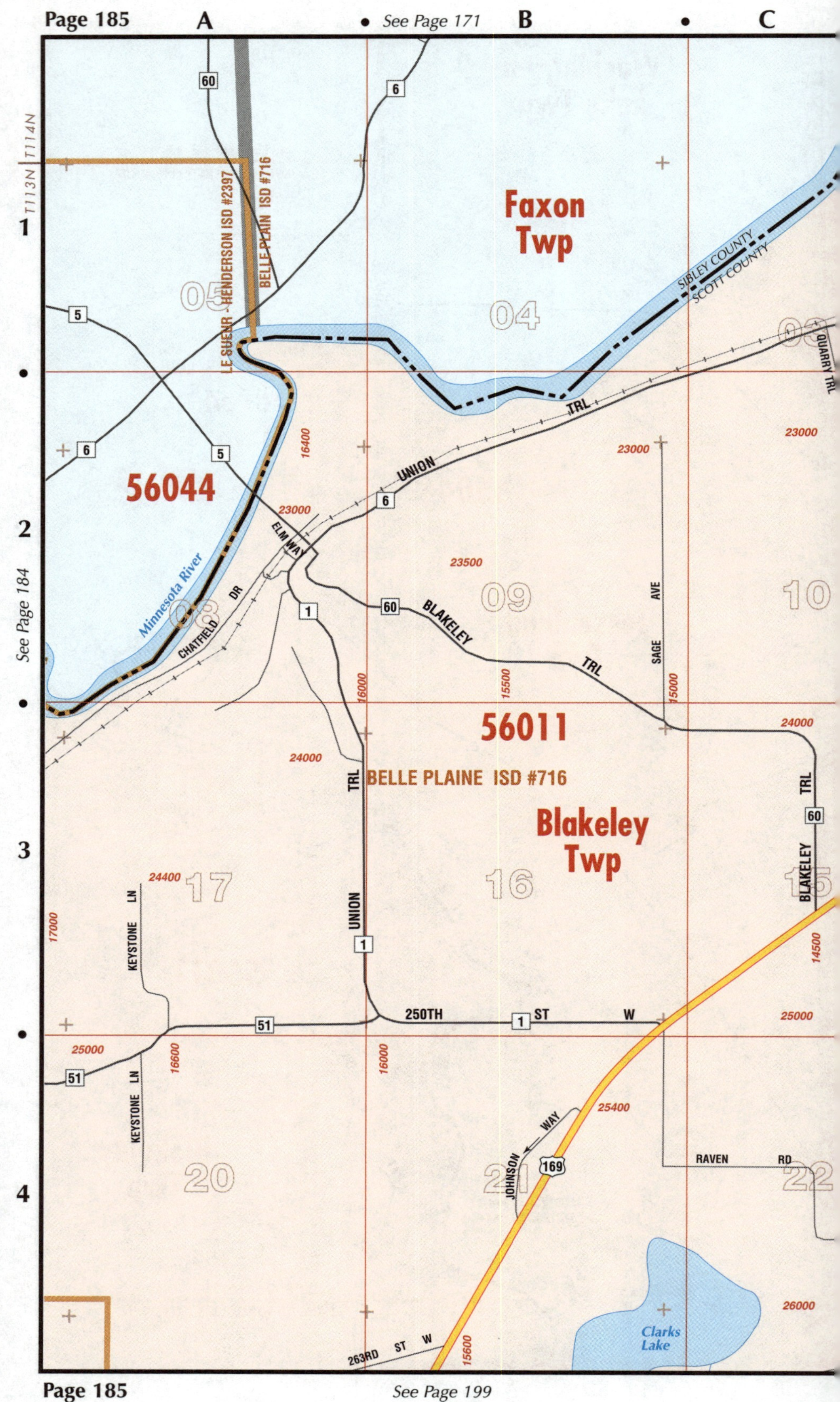

See Page 171

A   B   C

60

6

Faxon Twp

T113N | T114N

05

04

5

SIBLEY COUNTY
SCOTT COUNTY

QUARRY TRL

1

See Page 184

6

5

56044

BELLE PLAIN ISD #716

LE SUEUR-HENDERSON ISD #2397

16400

23000

UNION

TRL

23000

23000

6

Minnesota River

ELM WAY

CHATFIELD DR

08

1

60

BLAKELEY

09

SAGE AVE

10

23500

TRL

15500

15000

2

24000

16000

56011

24000

60

BLAKELEY TRL

BELLE PLAINE ISD #716

Blakeley Twp

24400

17000

KEYSTONE LN

17

UNION

TRL

16

1

15

3

51

250TH

1 ST W

25000

25000

KEYSTONE LN

16600

16000

51

25400

JOHNSON WAY

169

RAVEN RD

20

21

22

14500

26000

263RD ST W

15600

Clarks Lake

4

See Page 199

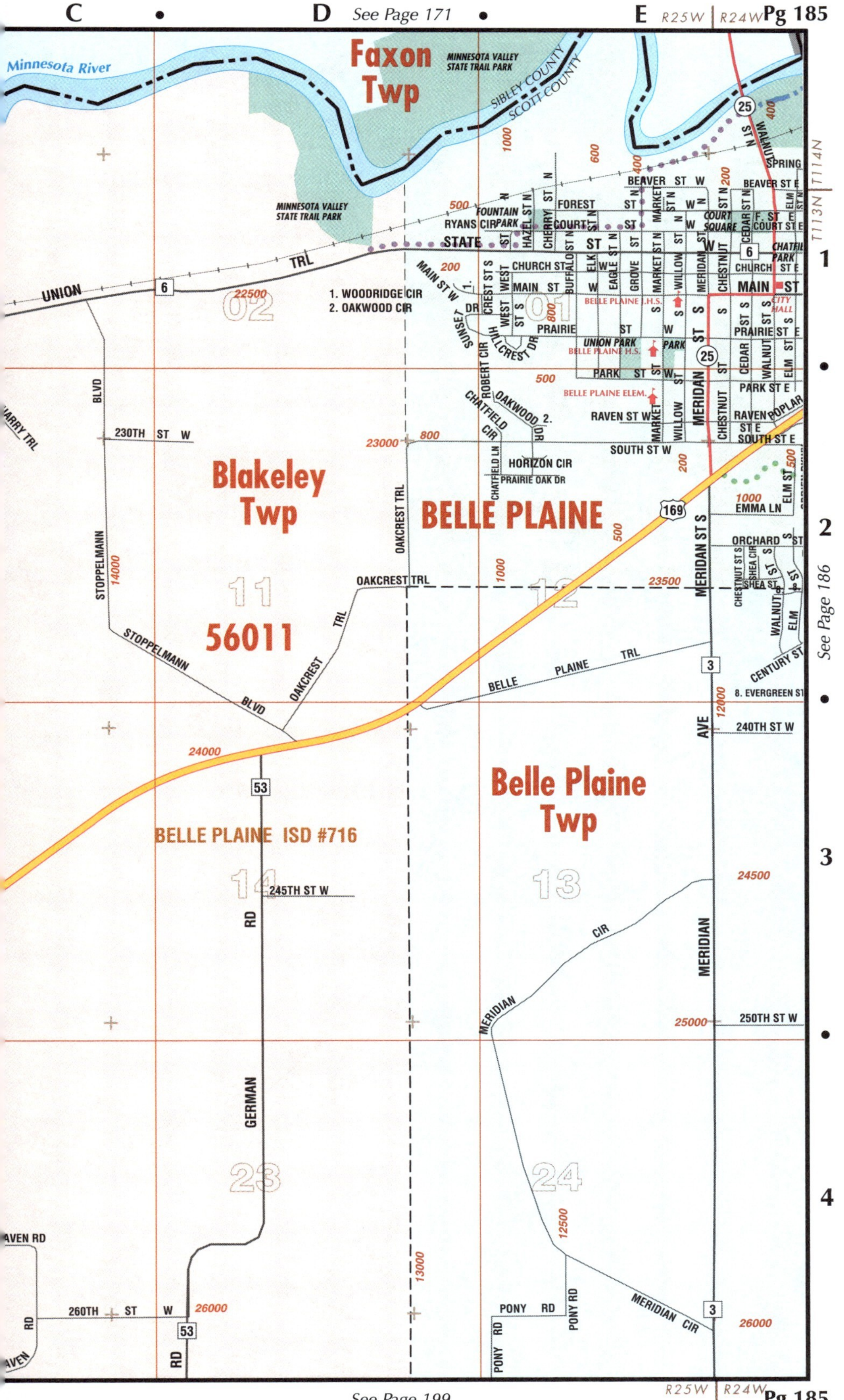

Minnesota River

Faxon Twp

MINNESOTA VALLEY STATE TRAIL PARK

SIBLEY COUNTY
SCOTT COUNTY

1000

600

400

200 N LS

25

400

WALNUT ST

SPRING

BEAVER ST W
BEAVER ST N
BEAVER ST E

500

FOUNTAIN
RYANS CIR PARK
STATE

FOREST

MARKET ST N

COURT SQUARE

CEDAR ST N

F. ST E
COURT ST E

CHATFIELD
PARK

ELM ST N

MINNESOTA VALLEY STATE TRAIL PARK

TRL

UNION

6

22500

02

230TH ST W

HARRY TRL

STOPPELMANN BLVD

14000

STOPPELMANN BLVD

24000

53

BELLE PLAINE ISD #716

14
245TH ST W

RD

GERMAN

23

AVEN RD

AVEN RD

260TH ST W
26000

53

RD

1. WOODRIDGE CIR
2. OAKWOOD CIR

MAIN ST N
200

SUNSET DR

WEST CREST DR

HILLCREST DR

WEST ST S

ROBERT CIR

800

01

CHURCH ST N

MAIN ST

PRAIRIE ST

500

CHATFIELD CIR

OAKWOOD

2.

23000

800

OAKCREST TRL

OAKCREST TRL

OAKCREST TRL

1000

Blakeley Twp

11

56011

HORIZON CIR
PRAIRIE OAK DR

BELLE PLAINE

500

CHERRY ST N
HAZEL ST N
COURT

ELM ST

BUFFALO ST N

EAGLE

GROVE

BELLE PLAINE J.H.S.

UNION PARK
BELLE PLAINE H.S.

PARK ST

BELLE PLAINE ELEM.

RAVEN ST W

SOUTH ST W

WILLOW ST N

MARKET ST S

WILLOW ST S

PARK ST W

MARKET

WILLOW

MERIDIAN ST N

CHESTNUT

MAIN ST

W
6
CHURCH ST E

CITY HALL

PRAIRIE ST E

25

CEDAR

PARK ST E

WALNUT

ELM ST E

CHESTNUT

MERIDIAN ST S

RAVEN ST E
SOUTH ST E

POPLAR

169

200

500

ELM ST

1000
EMMA LN

ORCHARD ST S

CHESTNUT ST S

SHEA ST S

SHEA CIR

WALNUT ST S

ELM ST

CENTURY ST

3

23500

MERIDIAN ST S

8. EVERGREEN ST

BELLE PLAINE TRL

12

500

Belle Plaine Twp

240TH ST W

AVE

12000

24500

CIR

MERIDIAN

13

MERIDIAN

250TH ST W

25000

MERIDIAN

24

12500

PONY RD

PONY RD

PONY RD

MERIDIAN CIR

3

26000

13000

See Page 186

See Page 172

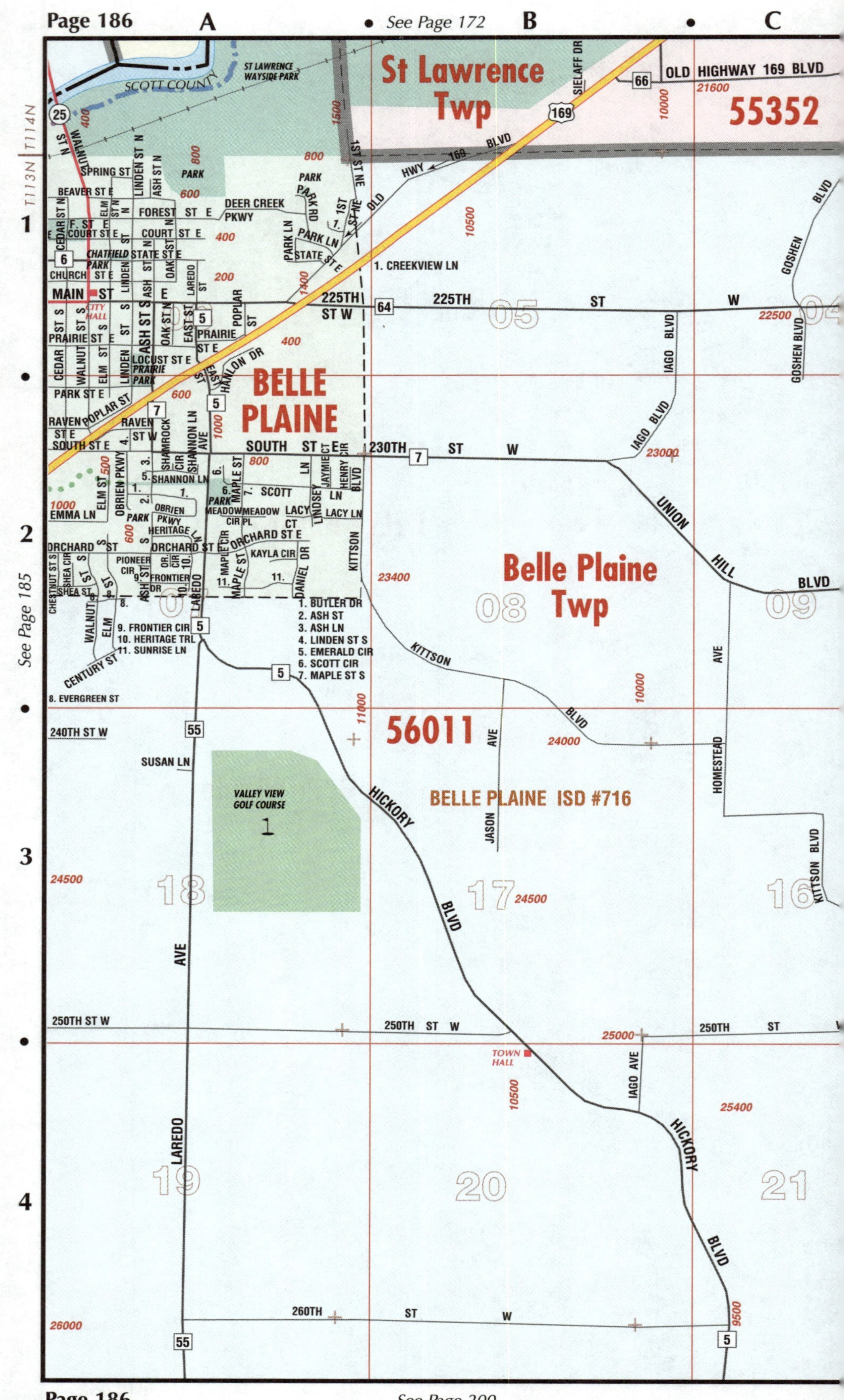

See Page 185

See Page 200

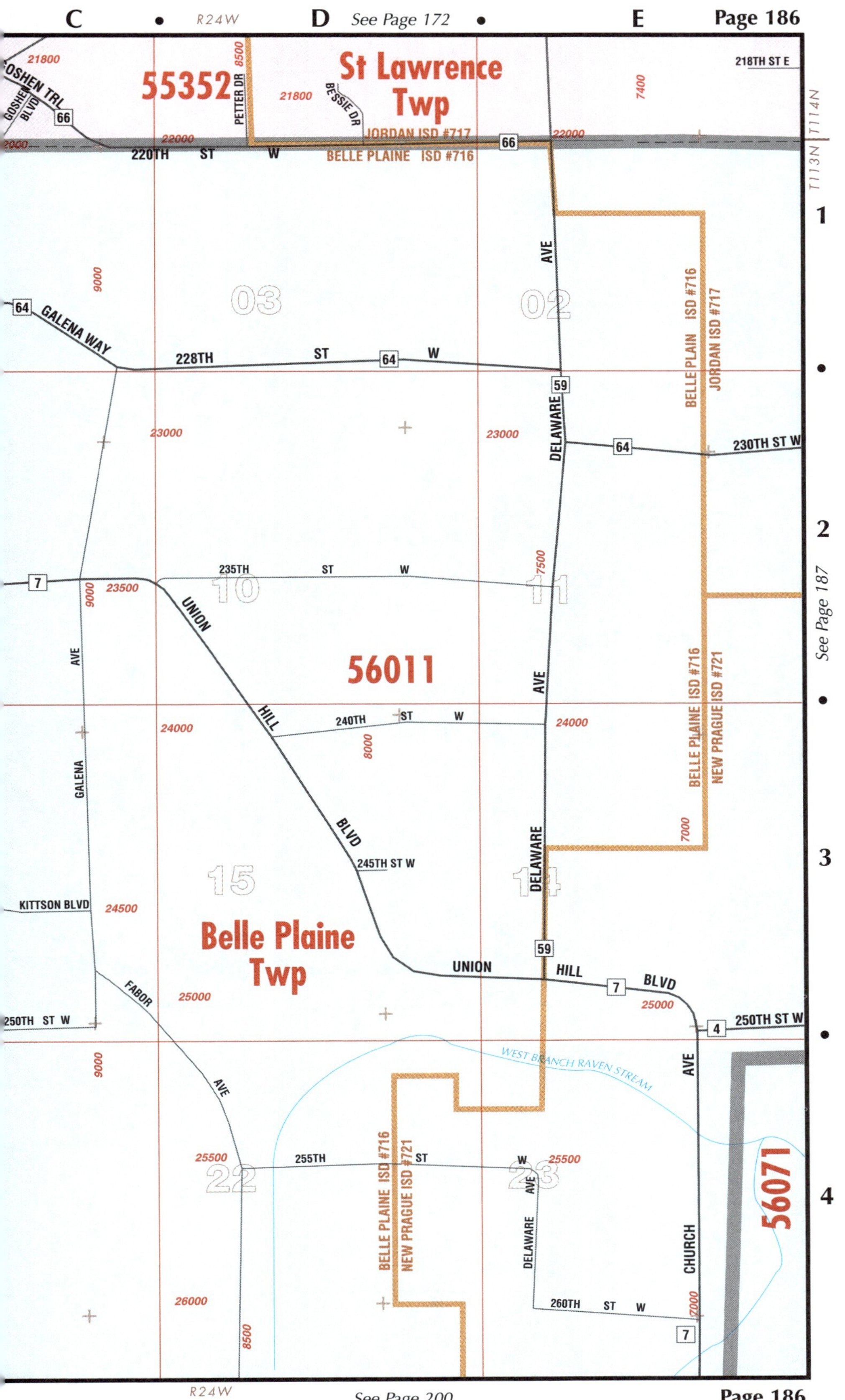

St Lawrence
Twp

55352

21800

GOSHEN TRL
GOSHEN BLVD

66

21800

PETTER DR

BESSIE DR

8500

7400

218TH ST E

JORDAN ISD #717

22000

66

22000

BELLE PLAINE ISD #716

2000

220TH ST W

T113N | T114N

1

9000

64

GALENA WAY

03

02

AVE

BELLE PLAIN ISD #716

JORDAN ISD #717

228TH ST 64 W

59

23000

23000

DELAWARE

64

230TH ST W

2

7

9000

23500

235TH ST W

10

UNION

11

7500

56011

AVE

HILL

GALENA AVE

24000

240TH ST W

8000

24000

BELLE PLAINE ISD #716

NEW PRAGUE ISD #721

7000

See Page 187

BLVD

15

245TH ST W

DELAWARE

14

3

KITTSON BLVD

24500

**Belle Plaine
Twp**

59

250TH ST W

FABOR

25000

UNION HILL BLVD

7

25000

4

250TH ST W

9000

AVE

WEST BRANCH RAVEN STREAM

AVE

4

CHURCH

56071

25500

22

255TH

BELLE PLAINE ISD #716

NEW PRAGUE ISD #721

ST W

25500

23

DELAWARE AVE

26000

8500

260TH ST W

7000

7

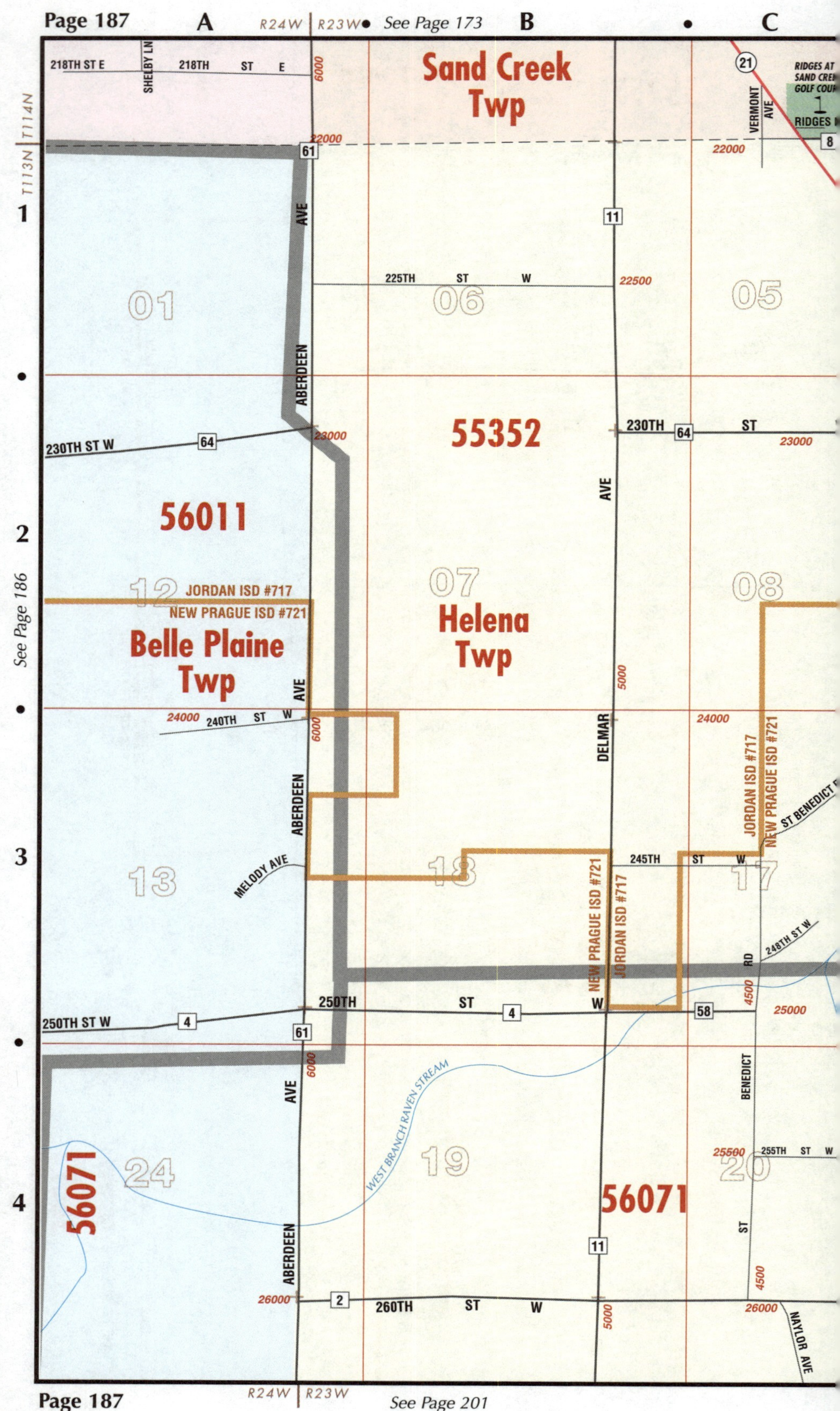

218TH ST E SHELBY LN 218TH ST E

Sand Creek Twp

6000

22000

61

1

T113N | T114N

01

225TH ST W

06

22500

11

21

VERMONT AVE

RIDGES AT SAND CREEK GOLF COURSE

1

RIDGES N

8

05

230TH ST W 64

23000

ABERDEEN AVE

55352

230TH 64 ST

23000

56011

See Page 186

2

12 JORDAN ISD #717

NEW PRAGUE ISD #721

Belle Plaine Twp

07

Helena Twp

AVE

5000

08

24000 240TH ST W

6000

ABERDEEN AVE

DELMAR

24000

JORDAN ISD #717

NEW PRAGUE ISD #721

ST BENEDICT

3

13

MELODY AVE

18

NEW PRAGUE ISD #721

JORDAN ISD #717

245TH ST W

17

250TH ST W 4

61

6000

250TH ST 4 W

RD

58

248TH ST W

4500

25000

4

56071

24

AVE

ABERDEEN

WEST BRANCH RAVEN STREAM

19

11

56071

BENEDICT ST

25500 255TH ST W

20

4500

26000 2

260TH ST W

5000

26000

NAYLOR AVE

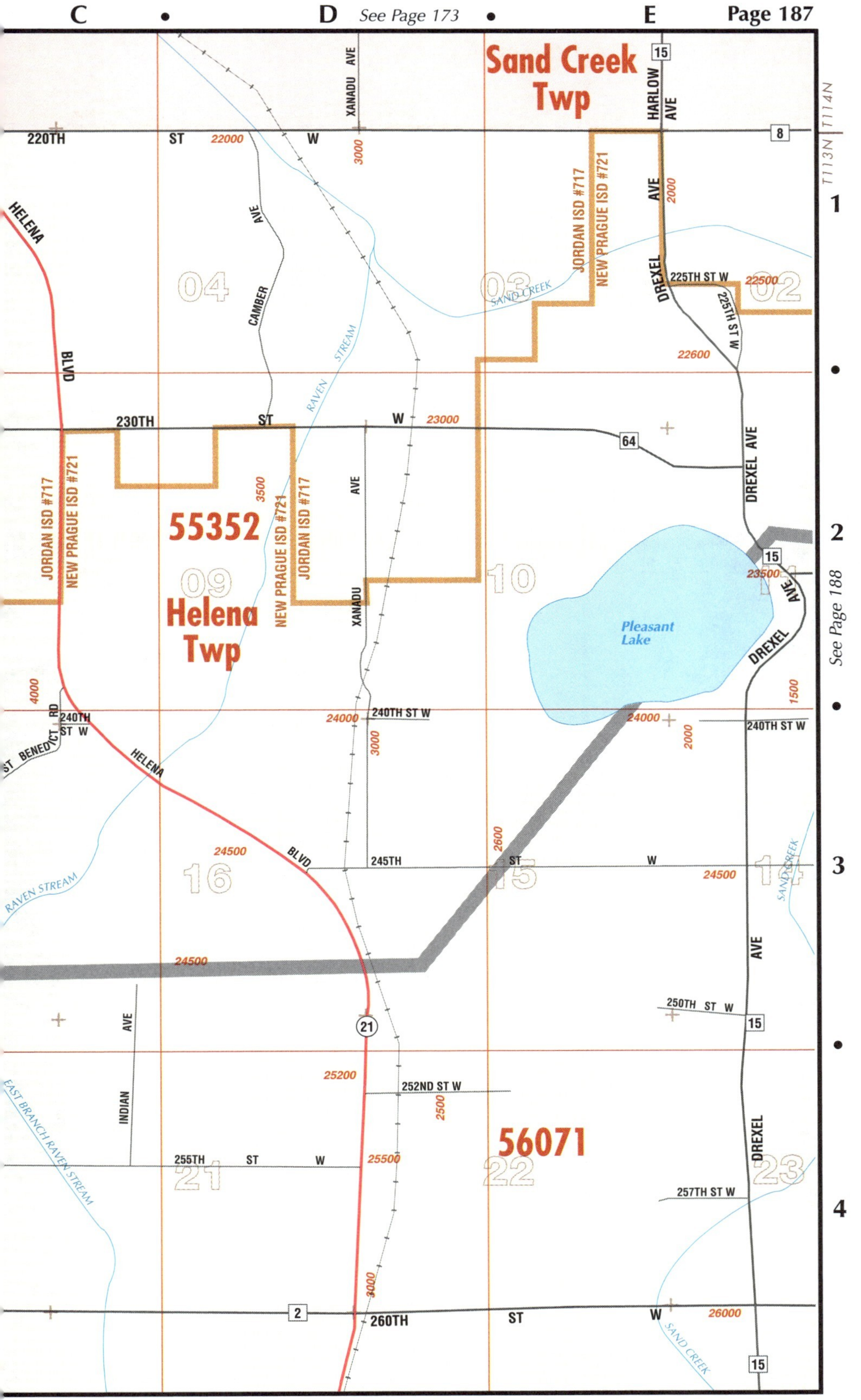

Sand Creek Twp

T113N | T114N

220TH ST 22000 W 3000

HARLOW AVE

15

8

JORDAN ISD #717

NEW PRAGUE ISD #721

DREXEL AVE 2000

1

04

CAMBER AVE

03

SAND CREEK

225TH ST W 22500

225TH ST W

02

22600

55352

230TH ST W 23000

JORDAN ISD #717

NEW PRAGUE ISD #721

RAVEN STREAM

64

DREXEL AVE

2

09

Helena Twp

3500

NEW PRAGUE ISD #721

JORDAN ISD #717

XANADU AVE

10

Pleasant Lake

15

23500

See Page 188

DREXEL AVE

1500

4000

ST BENEDICT RD

240TH ST W

240TH ST W 24000 3000

240TH ST W 24000 2000

240TH ST W

240TH ST W

HELENA

16

24500

BLVD

245TH ST 2600 W

15

14

24500

SAND CREEK

3

RAVEN STREAM

24500

21

INDIAN AVE

250TH ST W

15

DREXEL AVE

25200

252ND ST W 2500

56071

255TH ST W 25500

21

22

257TH ST W

23

4

2

260TH ST W 26000

SAND CREEK

15

See Page 201

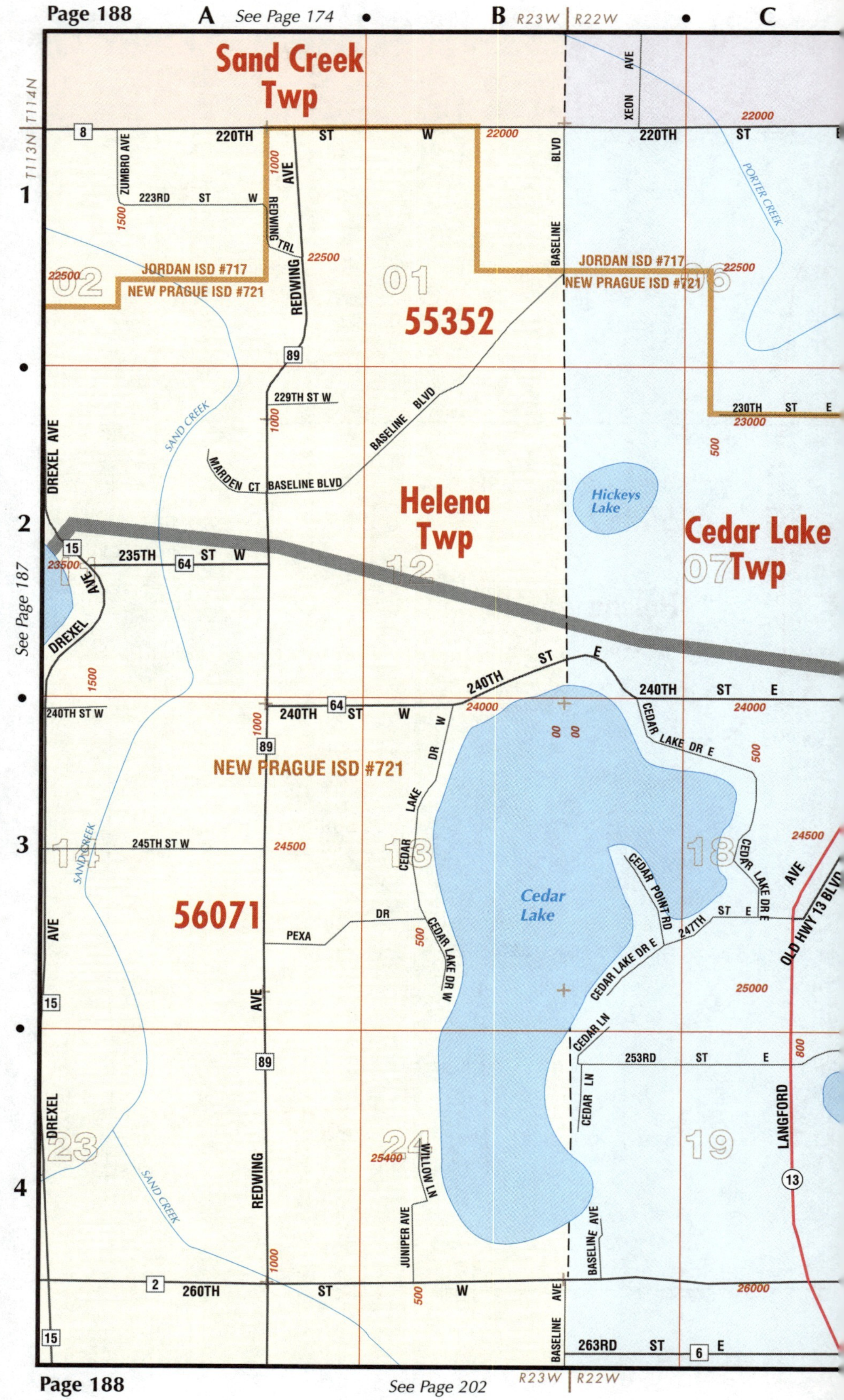

Sand Creek
Twp

8   220TH   ST   W   22000   220TH   ST   E

XEON   AVE

PORTER CREEK

ZUMBRO AVE

REDWING   AVE

1000

223RD   ST   W

1500

REDWING   TRL

22500

BASELINE   BLVD

JORDAN ISD #717
NEW PRAGUE ISD #721

22500

02

01

06

22500

JORDAN ISD #717
NEW PRAGUE ISD #721

55352

89

230TH   ST   E

23000

229TH ST W

1000

BASELINE   BLVD

500

DREXEL AVE

MARDEN CT

BASELINE BLVD

Helena
Twp

Hickeys
Lake

Cedar Lake
Twp

12

07

15   235TH   ST   W   64

23500

DREXEL   AVE

1500

240TH   ST   E

240TH   ST   E

24000

240TH ST W

240TH   ST   W   64

24000

CEDAR LAKE DR E

500

CEDAR LAKE DR E

89

NEW PRAGUE ISD #721

1000

24000

00

00

SAND CREEK

AVE

CEDAR   LAKE   DR   W

245TH ST W

24500

13

Cedar
Lake

18

24500

CEDAR LAKE DR E

CEDAR POINT RD

247TH   ST   E

LANGFORD

OLD HWY 13 BLVD

56071

14

15

PEXA

DR

500

CEDAR LAKE DR W

CEDAR LN

25000

AVE

23

89

DREXEL

253RD   ST   E

800

CEDAR LN

19

24

25400

WILLOW LN

JUNIPER AVE

BASELINE AVE

13

SAND CREEK

REDWING

1000

2   260TH   ST   W

500

BASELINE   AVE

26000

15

263RD   ST   E   6

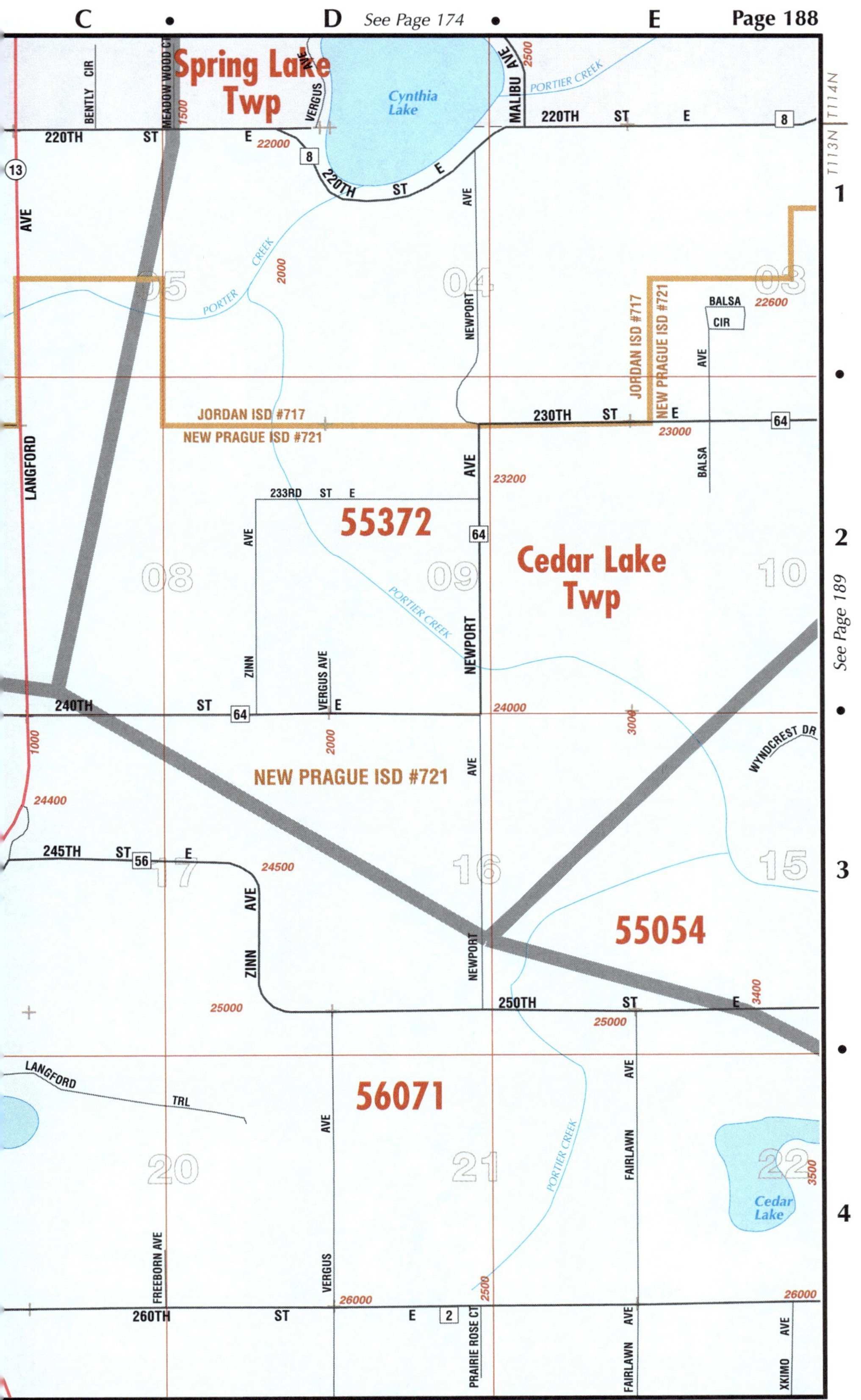

C

• BENTLY CIR

Spring Lake Twp

MEADOW WOOD CT · 1500

Cynthia Lake

MALIBU AVE · 2500

PORTIER CREEK

220TH ST E · 22000

8

220TH ST E · 8

VERGUS AVE

13

AVE

PORTER CREEK · 2000

05

04

NEWPORT AVE

JORDAN ISD #717
NEW PRAGUE ISD #721

03 · 22600

BALSA CIR

AVE

•

JORDAN ISD #717
NEW PRAGUE ISD #721

230TH ST E · 23000

64

BALSA

LANGFORD

233RD ST E

55372

AVE · 23200

64

Cedar Lake Twp

2

08

AVE

ZINN

VERGUS AVE

PORTIER CREEK

09

NEWPORT AVE

10

See Page 189

240TH ST 64 E · 2000

•

24400 · 1000

NEW PRAGUE ISD #721

24000

3004

WYNDCREST DR

245TH ST 56 E · 24500

56

17

ZINN AVE

16

NEWPORT AVE

15

3

55054

3400

25000

250TH ST E · 25000

•

LANGFORD TRL

56071

20

AVE

21

NEWPORT AVE

FAIRLAWN AVE

22

PORTIER CREEK

Cedar Lake

3500

4

FREEBORN AVE

VERGUS AVE

PRAIRIE ROSE CT

2500

260TH ST E 2 · 26000

FAIRLAWN AVE

XKIMO AVE · 26000

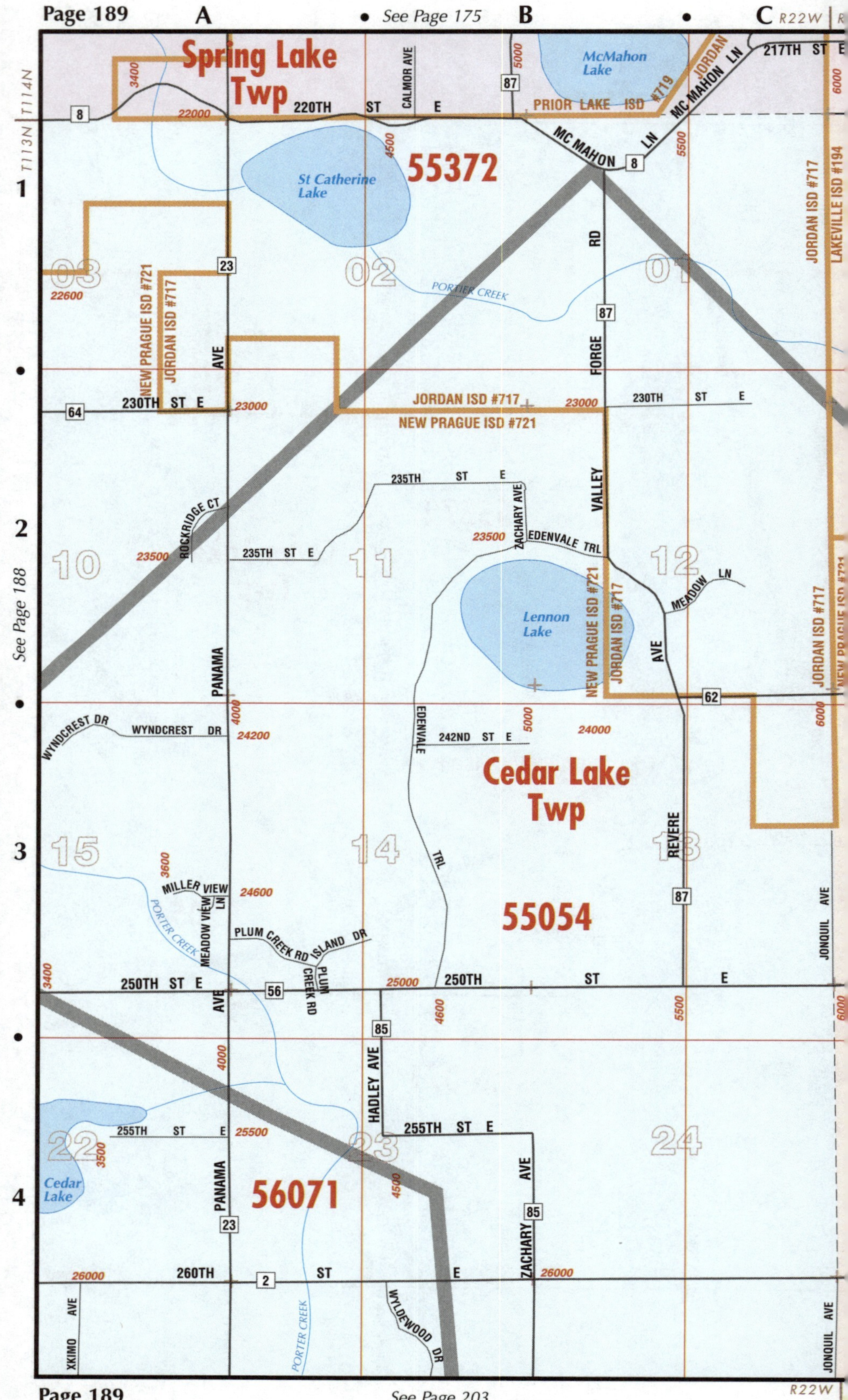

Spring Lake Twp

Spring Lake Twp

220TH ST E

CALMOR AVE

McMahon Lake

PRIOR LAKE ISD

MC MAHON LN

JORDAN MC MAHON LN #719

217TH ST E

JORDAN ISD #717

LAKEVILLE ISD #194

55372

St Catherine Lake

PORTIER CREEK

FORGE RD

1

03

02

01

NEW PRAGUE ISD #721

JORDAN ISD #717

AVE

22600

23

64   230TH ST E   23000   JORDAN ISD #717   23000   230TH ST E
NEW PRAGUE ISD #721

235TH ST E

VALLEY

2

ROCKRIDGE CT

235TH ST E

10   23500   11   23500   ZACHARY AVE   EDENVALE TRL   12   MEADOW LN

Lennon Lake

NEW PRAGUE ISD #721

JORDAN ISD #717

AVE

JORDAN ISD #717   NEW PRAGUE ISD #721

62

PANAMA

4000   24200   5000   24000

WYNDCREST DR   WYNDCREST DR

242ND ST E

Cedar Lake Twp

EDENVALE

3

15   14   13

MILLER VIEW LN   3600   24600   TRL   REVERE

PORTER CREEK

MEADOW VIEW LN   **55054**   87

PLUM CREEK RD ISLAND DR   JONQUIL AVE

PLUM CREEK RD

3400   250TH ST E   56   25000   250TH ST E   5500   6000

4000   85   4600

HADLEY AVE

22   255TH ST E   25500   23   255TH ST E   24

Cedar Lake   3500   PANAMA   4500   ZACHARY AVE   85

4   **56071**   23

26000   260TH ST E   2   26000   JONQUIL AVE

XKIMO AVE   PORTER CREEK   WYLDEWOOD DR

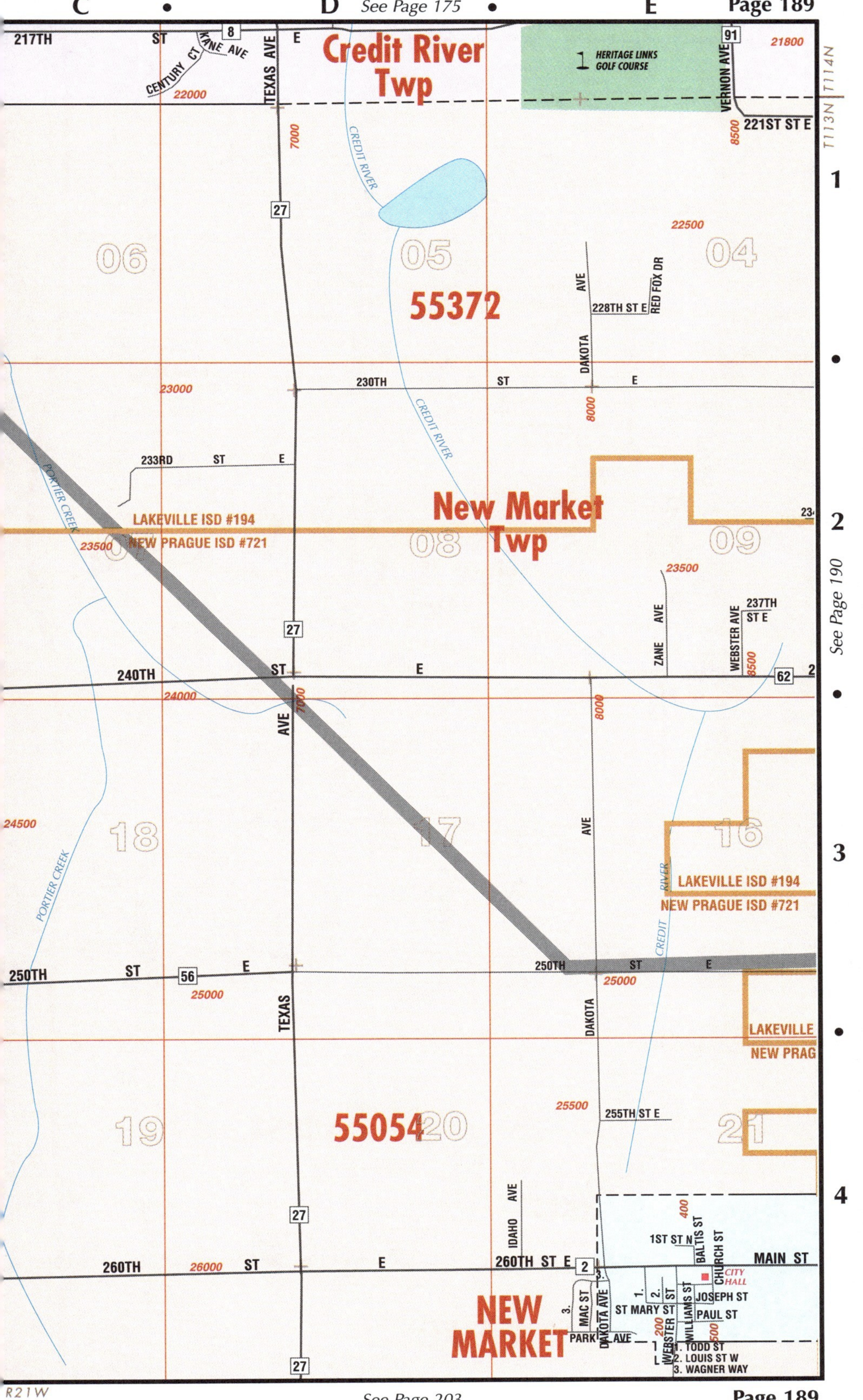

217TH ST

CENTURY CT

KANE AVE

8

TEXAS AVE

E

VERNON AVE

91

21800

Credit River Twp

1 HERITAGE LINKS GOLF COURSE

22000

7000

CREDIT RIVER

8500

221ST ST E

T113N | T114N

T113N | T114N

27

06

05

55372

AVE

DAKOTA

RED FOX DR

22500

04

228TH ST E

1

23000

230TH ST

8000

E

233RD ST E

PORTIER CREEK

New Market Twp

23-

LAKEVILLE ISD #194

23500

NEW PRAGUE ISD #721

08

09

23500

See Page 190

ZANE AVE

WEBSTER AVE

237TH ST E

8500

27

240TH ST

24000

E

7000

AVE

62

2

8000

AVE

CREDIT RIVER

2

24500

18

17

16

3

LAKEVILLE ISD #194

PORTIER CREEK

NEW PRAGUE ISD #721

250TH ST

56

E

250TH ST E

LAKEVILLE

25000

25000

NEW PRAG

TEXAS

DAKOTA

55054

19

20

21

25500

255TH ST E

4

IDAHO AVE

400

BALTIS ST

CHURCH ST

1ST ST N

MAIN ST

27

CITY HALL

260TH ST

26000

E

260TH ST E

2

MAC ST

DAKOTA AVE

ST MARY ST

WEBSTER ST

WILLIAMS ST

JOSEPH ST

PAUL ST

3.

200

PARK AVE

1. 2.

H. TODD ST

500

L

2. LOUIS ST W

3. WAGNER WAY

NEW MARKET

27

See Page 176

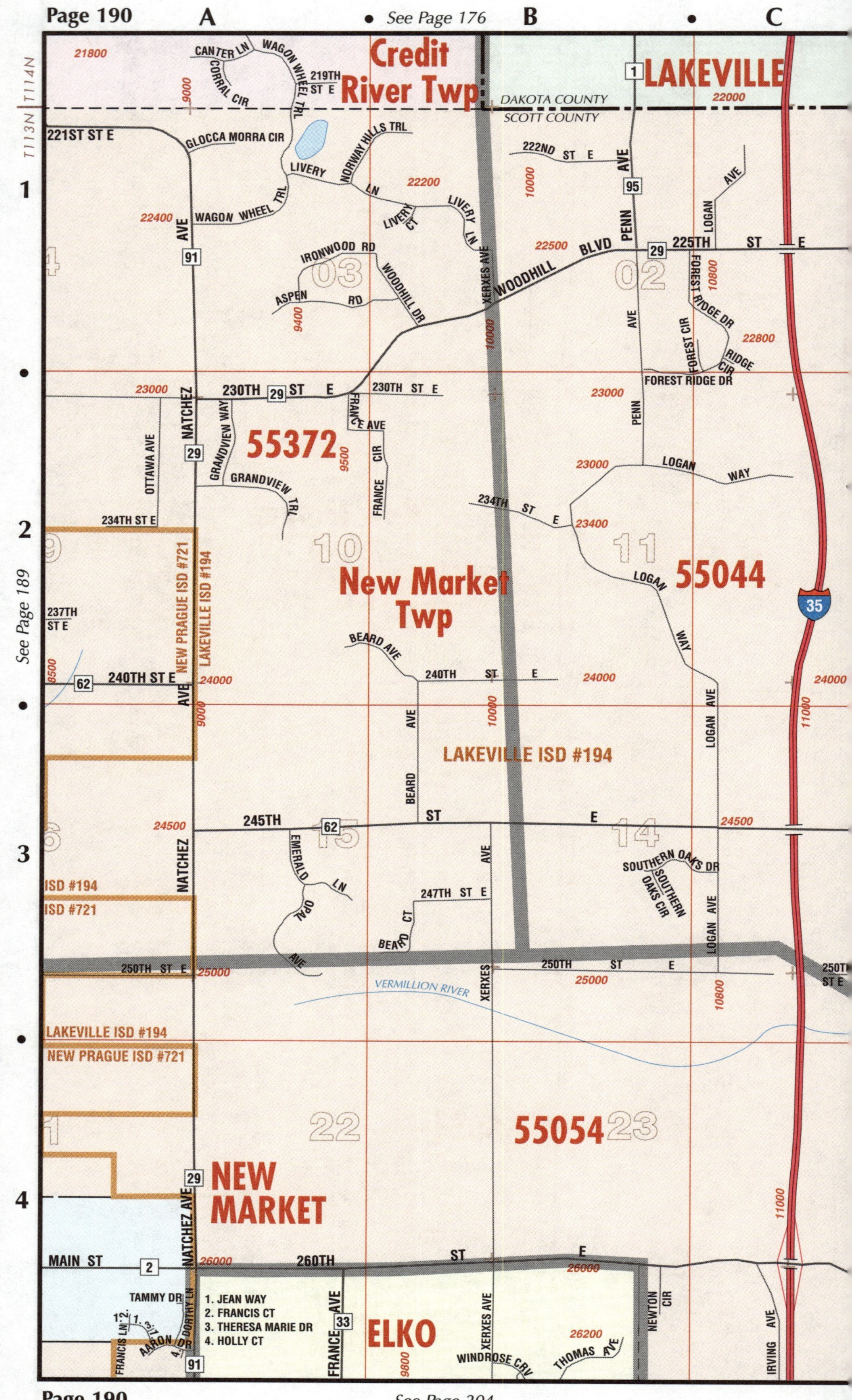

See Page 189

See Page 204

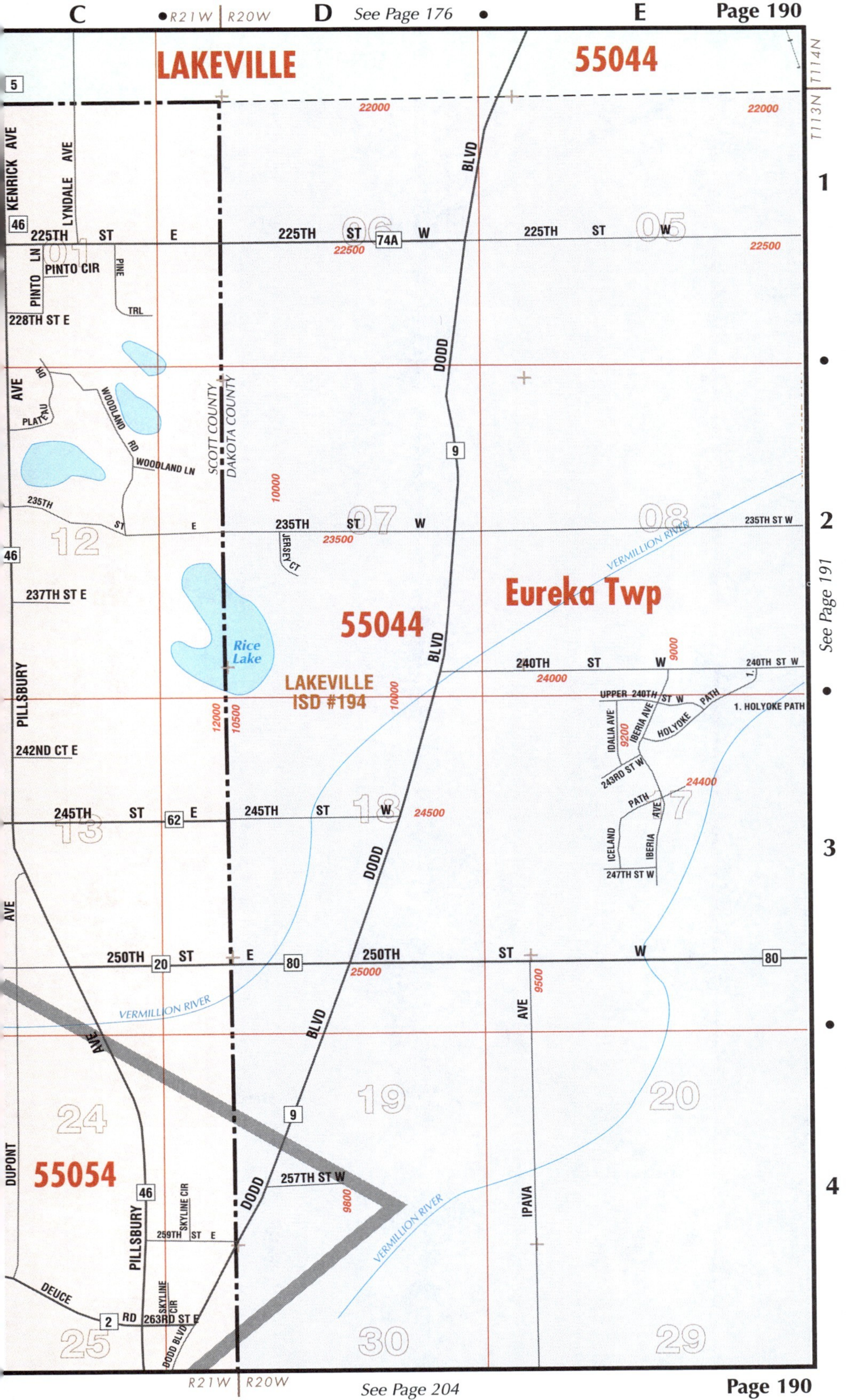

LAKEVILLE

55044

5

22000

22000

KENRICK AVE

LYNDALE AVE

1

46

225TH   ST   E   225TH   ST   06   W   74A   225TH   ST   05   W

22500

22500

01

PINTO LN

PINTO CIR

PINE TRL

228TH ST E

DODD BLVD

•

AVE

DR

PLATEAU

WOODLAND RD

WOODLAND LN

SCOTT COUNTY / DAKOTA COUNTY

9

235TH ST E

12

10000

235TH   ST   07   W   08   235TH ST W

2

46

JERSEY CT

23500

237TH ST E

VERMILLION RIVER

Eureka Twp

PILLSBURY

55044

DODD BLVD

Rice Lake

**LAKEVILLE
ISD #194**

240TH   ST   W   *9000*   240TH ST W

24000

UPPER 240TH ST W

IDALIA AVE

IBERIA AVE

HOLYOKE PATH

1. HOLYOKE PATH

•

242ND CT E

12000

10500

10000

9200

243RD ST W

245TH   ST   62   E   245TH   ST   18   W   *24500*

13

DODD BLVD

PATH

AVE

ICELAND

IBERIA

24400

7

3

247TH ST W

AVE

250TH   20   ST   E   80   250TH   ST   W   80

25000

9500

VERMILLION RIVER

AVE

•

24

DODD BLVD

9

19

20

IPAVA

4

55054

PILLSBURY

46

SKYLINE CIR

259TH ST E

257TH ST W

9600

VERMILLION RIVER

DEUCE

DODD BLVD

SKYLINE CIR

2

RD

263RD ST E

25

30

29

See Page 191

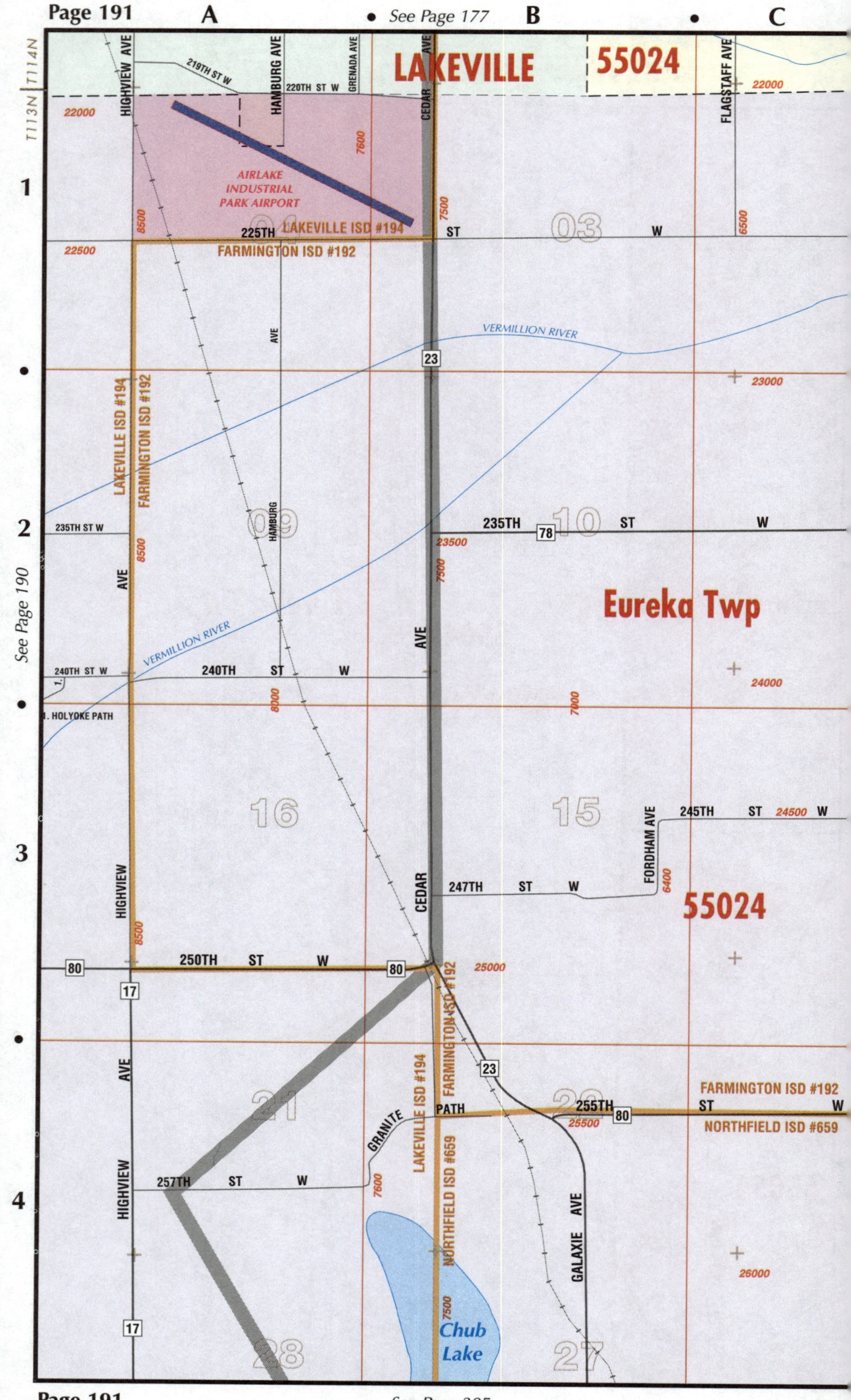

LAKEVILLE 55024

T113N | T114N

HIGHVIEW AVE
219TH ST W
HAMBURG AVE
220TH ST W
GRENADA AVE
CEDAR AVE
FLAGSTAFF AVE

22000

7600

7500

6500

22000

AIRLAKE INDUSTRIAL PARK AIRPORT

8500

225TH ST — LAKEVILLE ISD #194
03 W

22500 **FARMINGTON ISD #192**

AVE

VERMILLION RIVER

23

23000

LAKEVILLE ISD #194
FARMINGTON ISD #192

235TH ST W
8500
HAMBURG
235TH 78 10 ST W

23500
7500

AVE

Eureka Twp

VERMILLION RIVER

240TH ST W
240TH ST W
240TH ST W
8000 7900 24000

1. HOLYOKE PATH

16

245TH ST 24500 W

15

FORDHAM AVE

HIGHVIEW AVE

8500

CEDAR

6400

247TH ST W

55024

80
17

250TH ST W
80
FARMINGTON ISD #192
25000

23

HIGHVIEW AVE

21

LAKEVILLE ISD #194
GRANITE

PATH

20 255TH 80 ST W

FARMINGTON ISD #192

NORTHFIELD ISD #659

257TH ST W
7600
NORTHFIELD ISD #659

GALAXIE AVE

26000

17

7500

28

Chub Lake

27

See Page 190

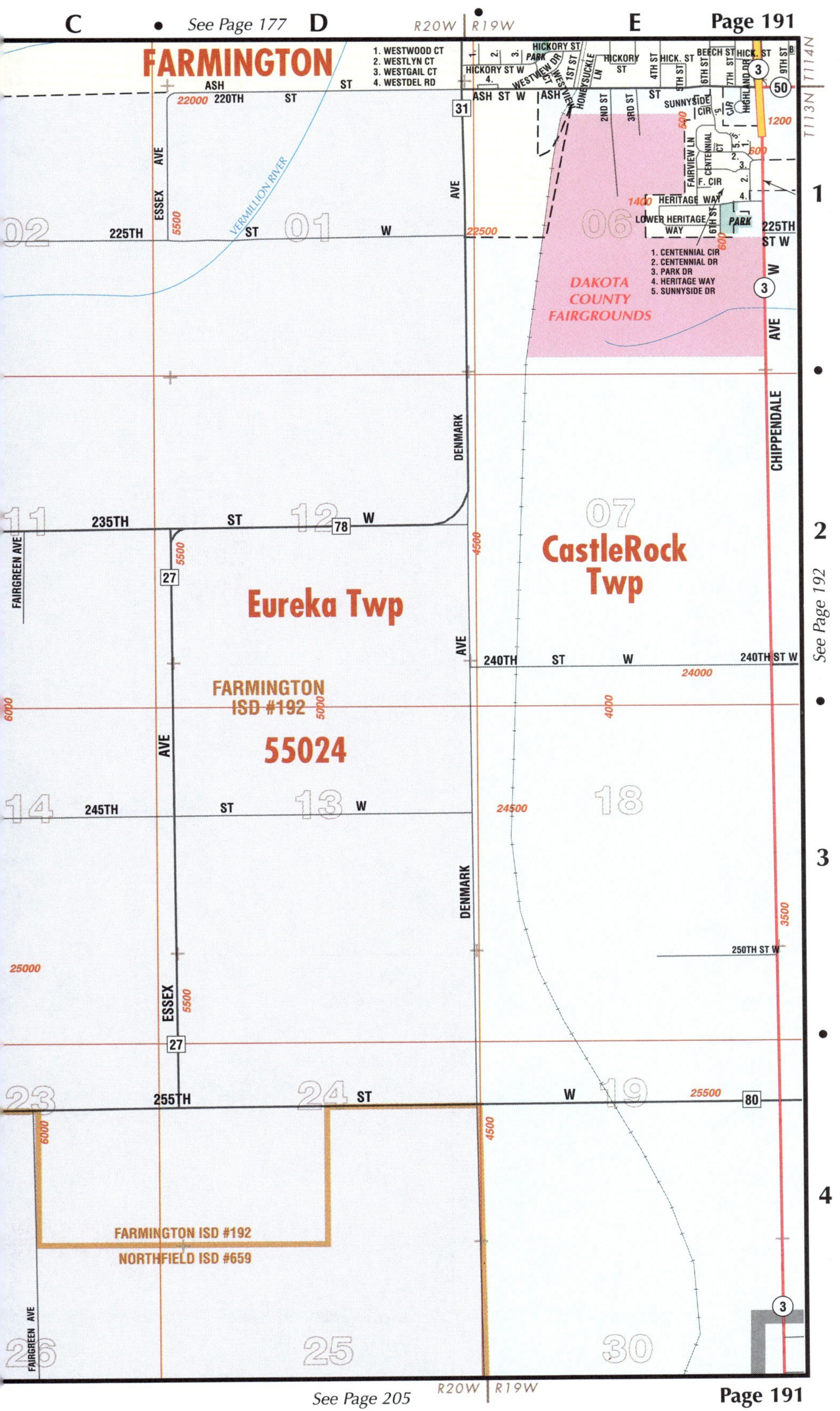

FARMINGTON

1. WESTWOOD CT
2. WESTLYN CT
3. WESTGAIL CT
4. WESTDEL RD

ASH ST
22000 220TH ST ASH ST W ASH

ESSEX AVE
5500
225TH ST W 22500 W

01 06

02

DENMARK

11 235TH ST 12 78 W

FAIRGREEN AVE
5500
27

Eureka Twp

FARMINGTON ISD #192

55024

ESSEX AVE
6000 5500 5000

14 245TH ST 13 W 24500

DENMARK

25000

ESSEX
5500
27

23 255TH 24 ST W 19 25500 80

6000 4500

FARMINGTON ISD #192

NORTHFIELD ISD #659

FAIRGREEN AVE

26 25 30

HICKORY ST
PARK

HICKORY ST W HICKORY

2ND ST
3RD ST

ASH ST W

SUNNYSIDE

FARVIEW LN
CENTENNIAL
F. CIR

1400
HERITAGE WAY
LOWER HERITAGE WAY
PARK
225TH ST W

1. CENTENNIAL CIR
2. CENTENNIAL DR
3. PARK DR
4. HERITAGE WAY
5. SUNNYSIDE DR

DAKOTA COUNTY FAIRGROUNDS

4TH ST 5TH ST 6TH ST
HICK. ST 3
50
1200
800

3

CHIPPENDALE AVE

CastleRock Twp

07

240TH ST W 240TH ST W
24000

4000

3500

18

250TH ST W

3

See Page 192

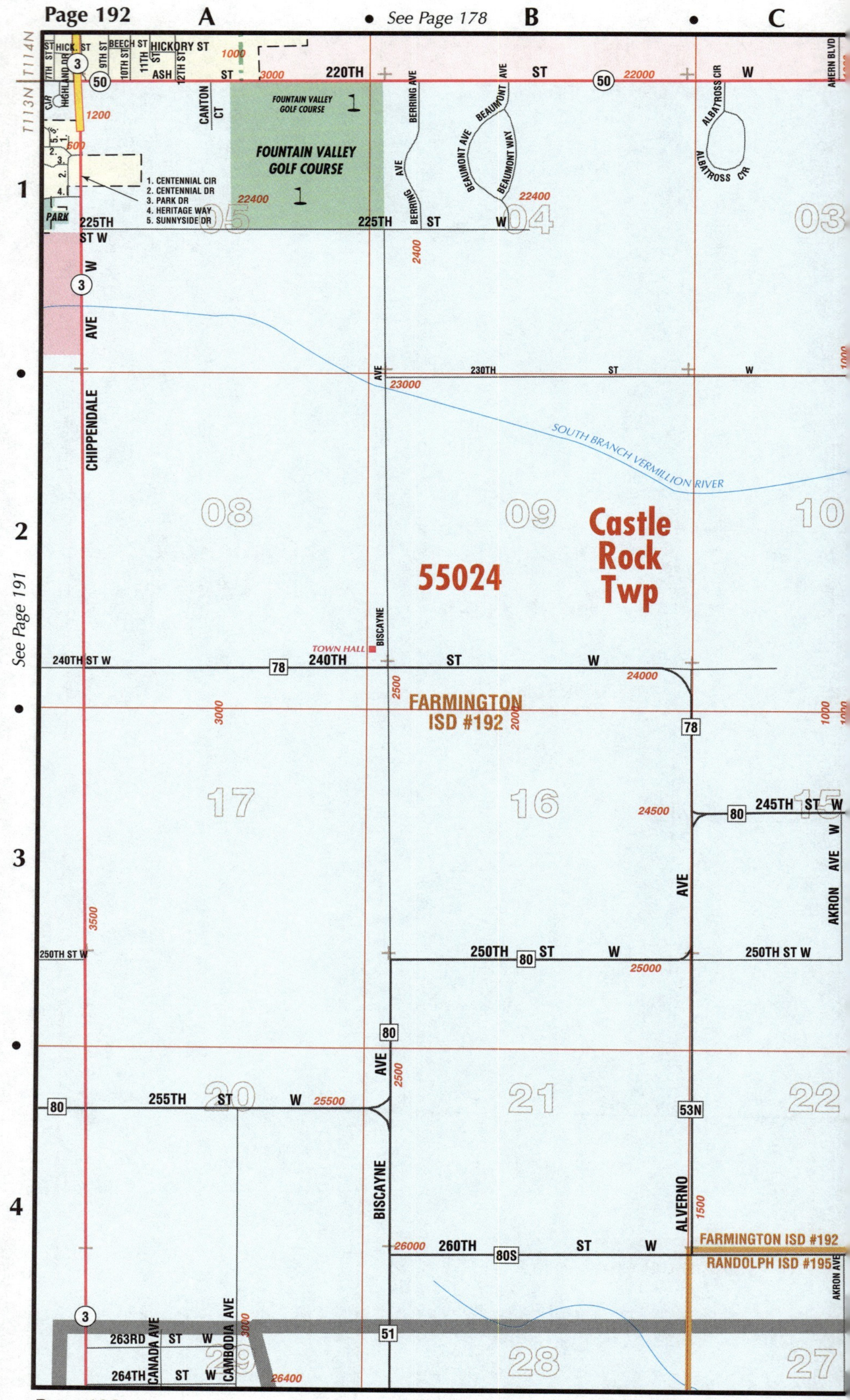

T113N | T114N

ST | HICK ST | 9TH ST
BEECH ST | HICKORY ST
HIGHLAND DR | 10TH ST | 11TH ST | ASH ST
50 | 12TH ST
CANTON CT
1000
220TH
3000
220TH ST | 50 | 22000
AHERN BLVD | W
ALBATROSS CIR
1200
FOUNTAIN VALLEY GOLF COURSE
1
BERRING AVE | BEAUMONT AVE
1 | BEAUMONT AVE
BEAUMONT WAY
600
FOUNTAIN VALLEY GOLF COURSE
1. CENTENNIAL CIR
2. CENTENNIAL DR
3. PARK DR
4. HERITAGE WAY
5. SUNNYSIDE DR
22400
BERRING AVE
22400
ALBATROSS CTR
PARK
225TH ST W
05
1
225TH ST
BERRING ST
04
W
03
1

3
CHIPPENDALE AVE
AVE
2400
W

1000

AVE
230TH ST
W
23000
SOUTH BRANCH VERMILLION RIVER

See Page 191

2
08
09
Castle Rock Twp
10
1000

55024

BISCAYNE
TOWN HALL
240TH ST W
78
240TH ST
W
24000
78

3000
2500
FARMINGTON ISD #192
2000
1000 | 1000

3
17
16
24500
80
245TH ST | W
15
AVE
3500
AKRON AVE | W

250TH ST W
250TH
80
ST
W
25000
250TH ST W

80
255TH
ST
W
25500
BISCAYNE AVE
2500

4
80
20
21
53N
22

BISCAYNE
ALVERNO
1500
260TH
80S
ST
W
26000
FARMINGTON ISD #192
RANDOLPH ISD #195
AKRON AVE

3
263RD ST | W
CANADA AVE
CAMBODIA AVE
3000
51
28
27
264TH ST | W
29
26400

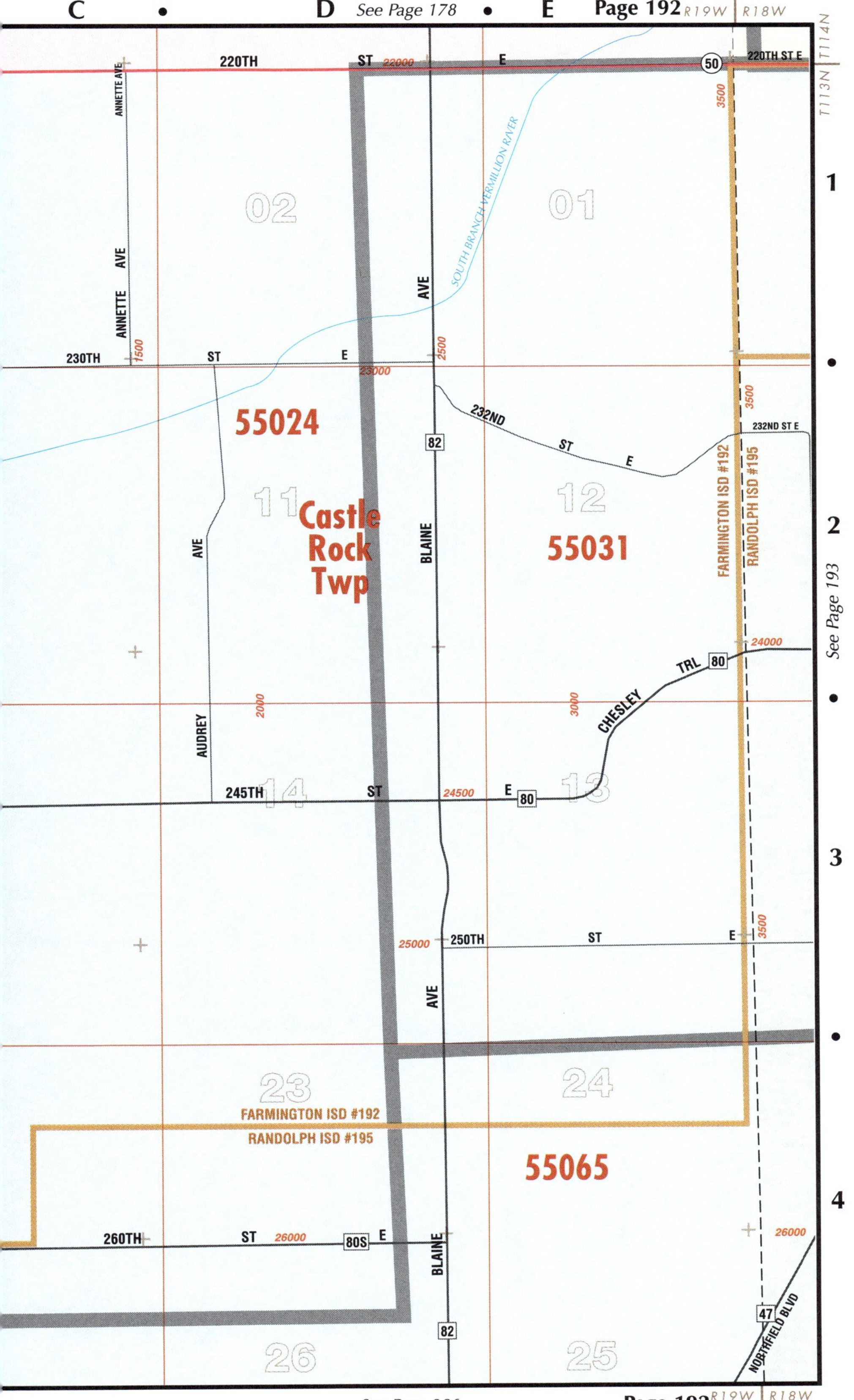

T113N | T114N

ANNETTE AVE

220TH ST 22000 E

50

220TH ST E

3500

02

01

1

ANNETTE AVE

AVE

SOUTH BRANCH VERMILLION RIVER

230TH ST 1500 E 2500 23000 E

3500

55024

232ND ST E

232ND ST E

82

AVE

11 Castle Rock Twp

BLAINE

12

FARMINGTON ISD #192

RANDOLPH ISD #195

See Page 193

55031

2

AUDREY AVE

2000

3000

CHESLEY TRL 80

24000

245TH 14 ST 24500 E 80 13

80

3

25000 250TH ST E

3500

AVE

23

24

FARMINGTON ISD #192

RANDOLPH ISD #195

55065

4

260TH ST 26000 80S E

BLAINE

26000

47

NORTHFIELD BLVD

82

26

25

T113N | T114N

220TH ST E
81
50
4000
22200 222ND ST E
22500 DARK HORSE LAKE LN
22000
52
4
NORTHFIELD BLVD
225TH ST E
22500

HASTINGS ISD #200
FARMINGTON ISD #192

06
05
04

5500
22800

47
23000
23000

1

See Page 192

HASTINGS ISD #200
RANDOLPH ISD #195

3500
232ND ST E

RANDOLPH ISD #195

CONRAD AVE

07

23000

HAMPTON

55031

50
ST. MATHIAS
HAMPTON BLVD
08
WATER ST
SUN VALLEY
MAIN ST
BLVD
5200
GRANT ST
HAMPTON ST
1ST ST
CITY HALL
PARK ST
BELMONT ST
LINCOLN ST
BELMONT ST
BELLE CT
CARDINAL CT
LINCOLN ST
HAMPTON BLVD
23200
23400
23500

RANDOLPH ISD #195
HASTINGS ISD #200

HASTINGS ISD #200
RANDOLPH ISD #195

09

LEWISTON BLVD

4500
24000
240TH ST E
80
24000
NORTHFIELD BLVD
HASTINGS ISD #200
RANDOLPH ISD #195
P&R HAMPTON
MAIN ST
52
50
240TH ST E
5800

2

4000
5000
56
24500
ROCHESTER BLVD
6000

18
17
16

Hampton Twp

47
BLVD
83
250TH ST
25000
LEWISTON
AVE
E
3500

3

19
20
21
NORTHFIELD AVE
DONNELLY AVE
EMERY
55065
55031

26000
260TH ST E
26000

4

47
NORTHFIELD BLVD
83
30
29
56
28

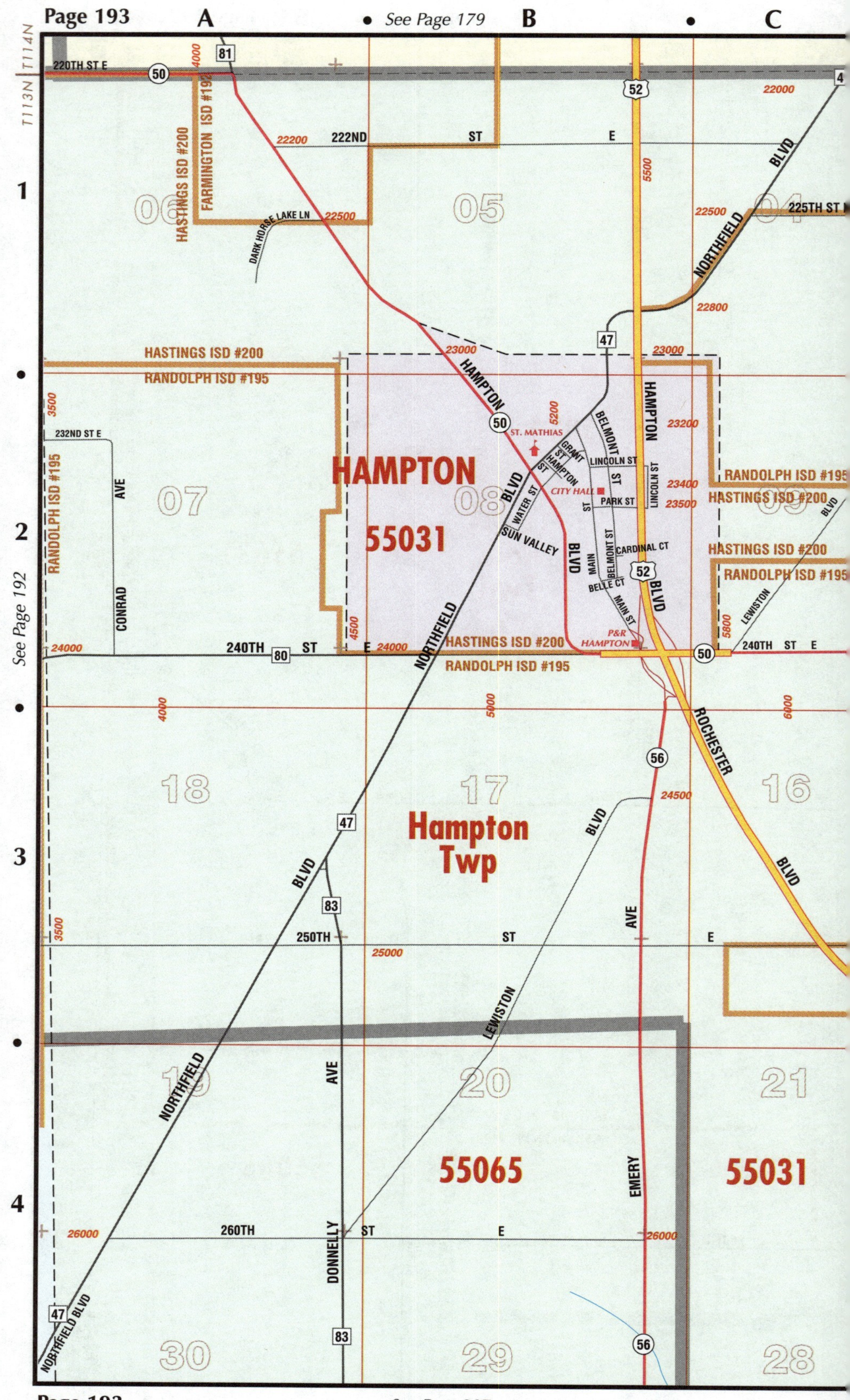

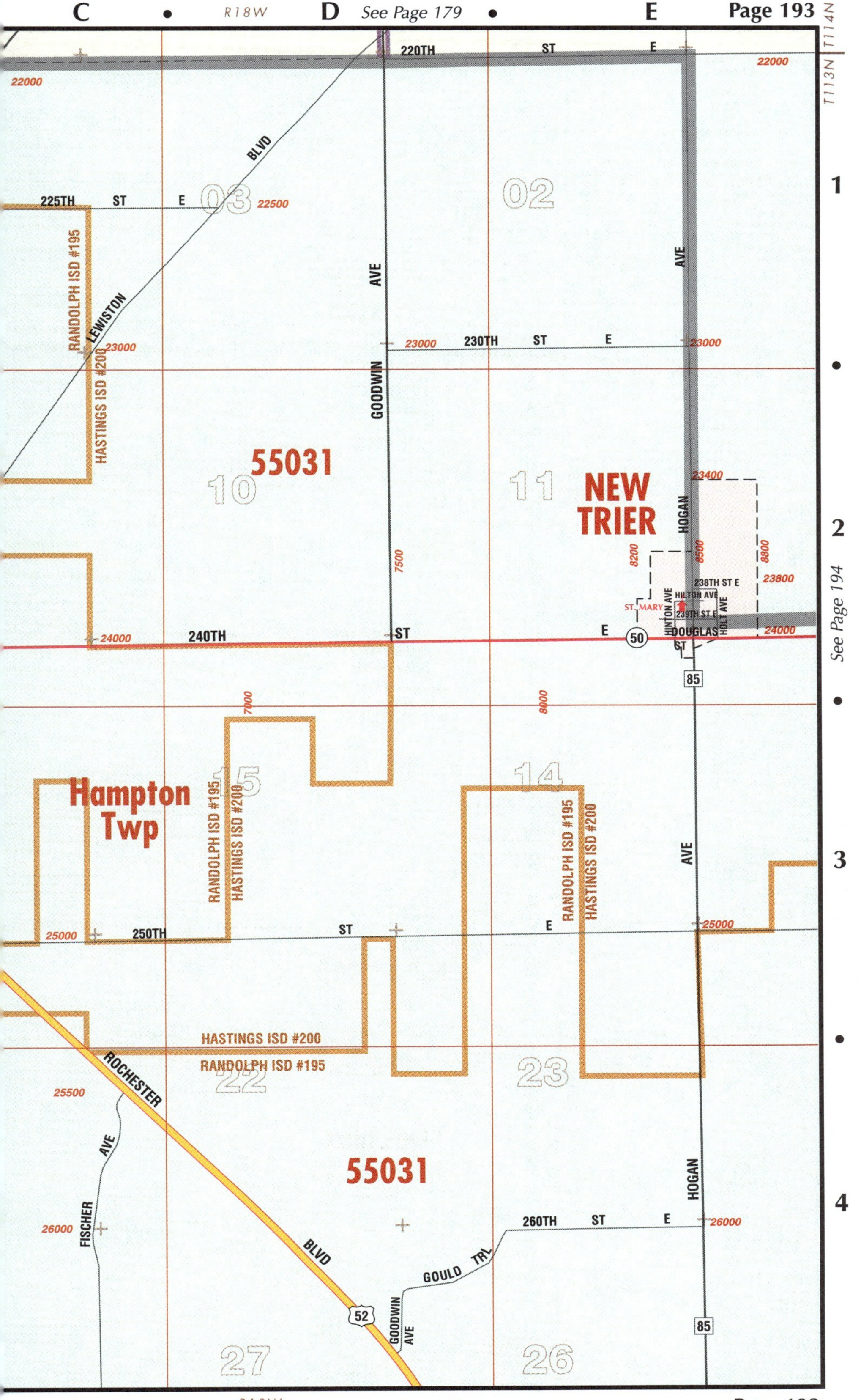

T113N | T114N

220TH ST E

22000

22000

BLVD

225TH ST E 03 22500

02

RANDOLPH ISD #195

LEWISTON

HASTINGS ISD #200

23000

23000 230TH ST E 23000

GOODWIN AVE

55031

10

7500

11

AVE

HOGAN

23400

NEW TRIER

8200

9500

8800

23800

238TH ST E

HILTON AVE

HINTON AVE

ST. MARY

239TH ST E

HILT AVE

24000 240TH ST E 50 DOUGLAS 24000

See Page 194

85

7700

8000

Hampton Twp

15

RANDOLPH ISD #195

HASTINGS ISD #200

14

RANDOLPH ISD #195

HASTINGS ISD #200

AVE

25000 250TH ST E 25000

ROCHESTER AVE

HASTINGS ISD #200

RANDOLPH ISD #195

22

23

25500

FISCHER AVE

55031

HOGAN

26000 GOULD TRL 260TH ST E 26000

BLVD

52

GOODWIN AVE

85

27

26

1

2

3

4

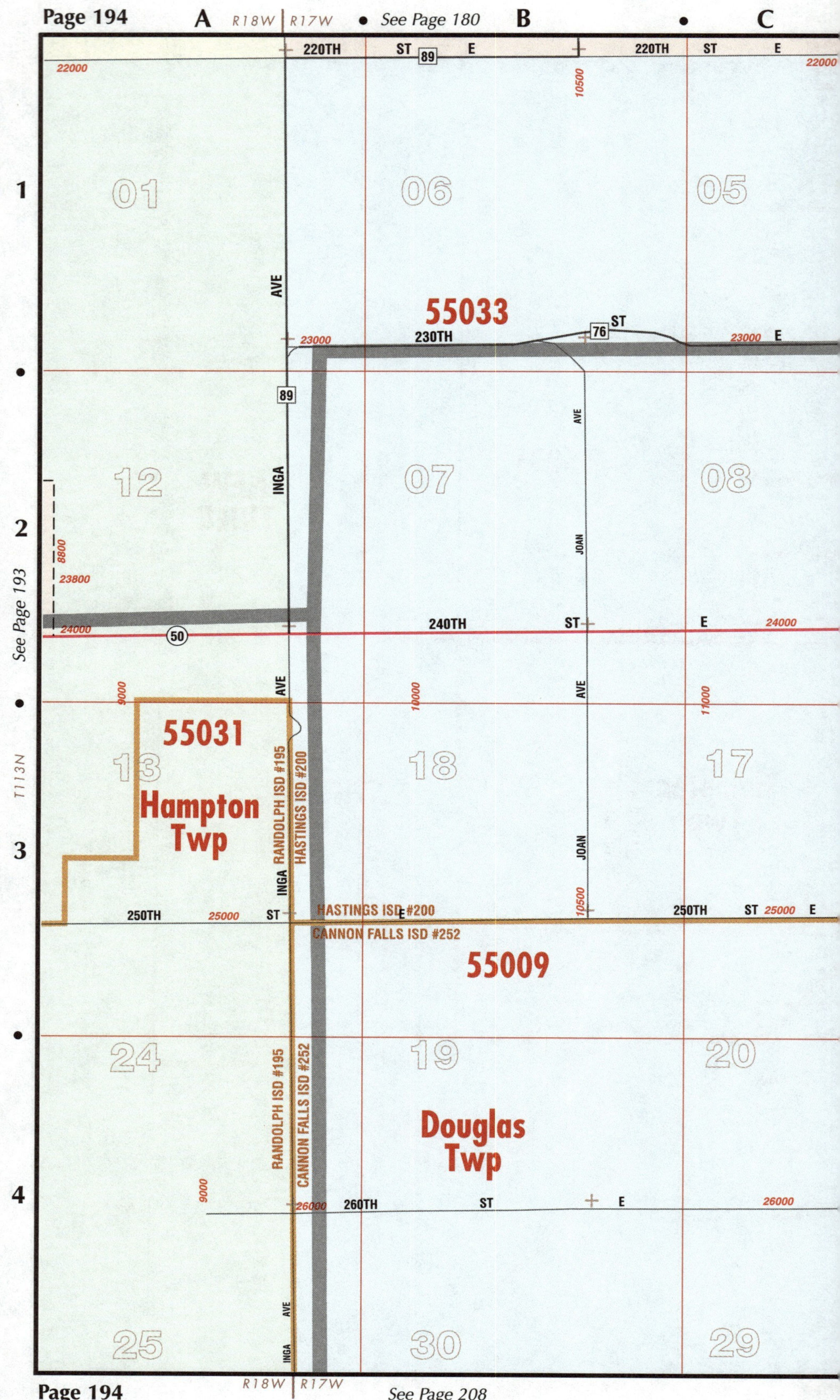

A *R18W* | *R17W* • *See Page 180* B • C

220TH ST **89** E 220TH ST E

22000 *22000*

1

01 06 05

AVE

55033

ST **76** *23000* E
23000 230TH

89

INGA

12 07 08

AVE

23800 *8800* JOAN

2

24000 **50** 240TH ST E *24000*

AVE AVE

9000 *10000* *11000*

55031

3 13 RANDOLPH ISD #195 HASTINGS ISD #200 18 JOAN 17

**Hampton
Twp**

INGA

10500

HASTINGS ISD #200 250TH ST *25000* E
250TH *25000* ST CANNON FALLS ISD #252

55009

24 RANDOLPH ISD #195 CANNON FALLS ISD #252 19 20

**Douglas
Twp**

9000

4 *26000* 260TH ST E *26000*

AVE

25 INGA 30 29

See Page 193 *T113N*

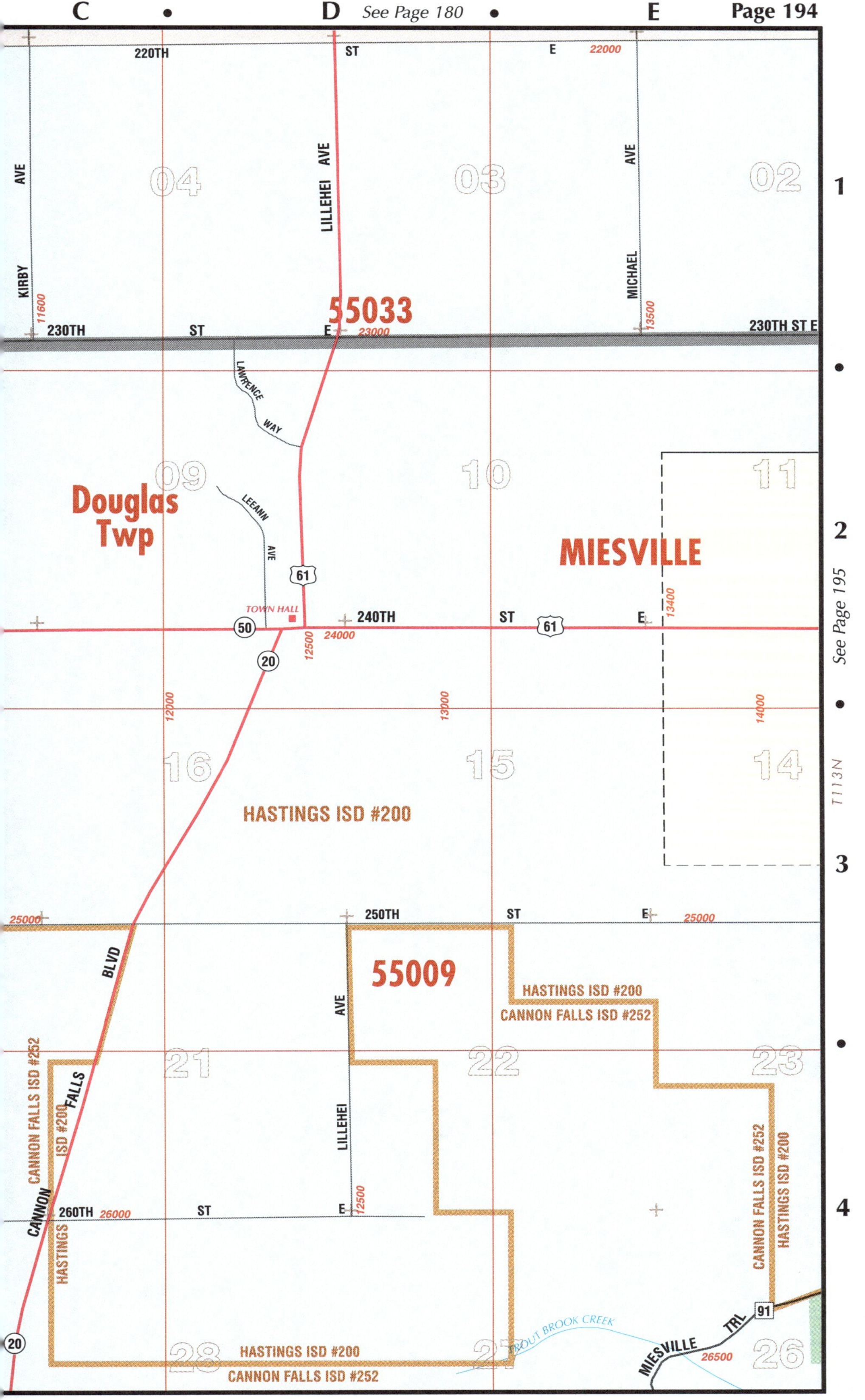

220TH ST E 22000

KIRBY AVE

LILLEHEI AVE

MICHAEL AVE

04 03 02

1

55033

11600

230TH ST E 23000 230TH ST E 13500

LAWRENCE WAY

Douglas Twp

09 10

MIESVILLE

LEEANN AVE

61

11

See Page 195

13400

2

TOWN HALL 50 240TH ST 61 E

20 24000 12500

12000 13900 14000

T113N

16 15 14

HASTINGS ISD #200

3

25000 250TH ST E 25000

BLVD

55009

HASTINGS ISD #200

CANNON FALLS ISD #252

21 22 23

CANNON FALLS ISD #252

CANNON FALLS ISD #200

AVE

LILLEHEI

CANNON FALLS ISD #252

HASTINGS ISD #200

HASTINGS

4

260TH ST E 26000 12500

20 TROUT BROOK CREEK 91

28 25 26

HASTINGS ISD #200

MIESVILLE TRL 26500

CANNON FALLS ISD #252

See Page 181

A • R17W R16W B • C

220TH ST E

91

Douglas Twp

22000 12000 RED WING ISD #256 22000 13000

02 01 06

1

DAKOTA COUNTY GOODHUE COUNTY

230TH ST E 76 230TH 23000 ST E 230TH ST E

55033

NICOLAI AVE 316

23500

11 12 07

MIESVILLE

2

See Page 194

ORLANDO

240TH ST 61 E

24000

Welch Twp

14000 15000 12000 13000

T113N

14 91 13 18

ORLANDO AVE HASTINGS ISD #200 RED WING ISD #256 130TH AVE

3

250TH ST 25000 E

55009

DAKOTA COUNTY GOODHUE COUNTY

NICOLAI

23 24 19

Douglas Twp

CANNON FALLS ISD #252 HASTINGS ISD #200 ORLANDO HASTINGS ISD #200 RED WING ISD #256 AVE

260TH ST E 260TH ST

4

MIESVILLE TRL NICOLAI AVE 26000

1

91 **ELMDALE HILLS GOLF COURSE** 26200

NICOLAI AVE 130TH

55089

26 25 ORLANDO AVE 30

267TH ST

See Page 209

R17W R16W

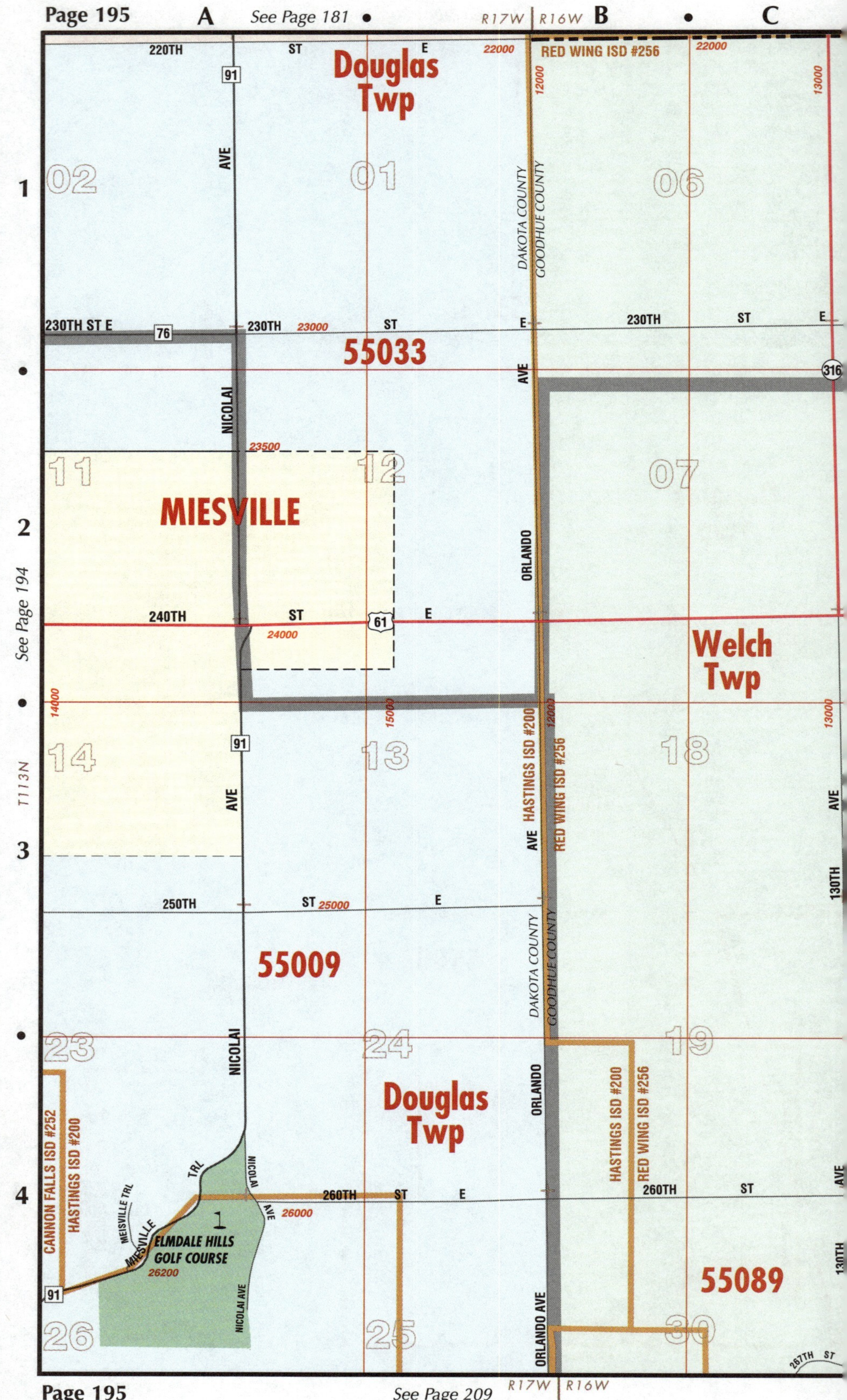

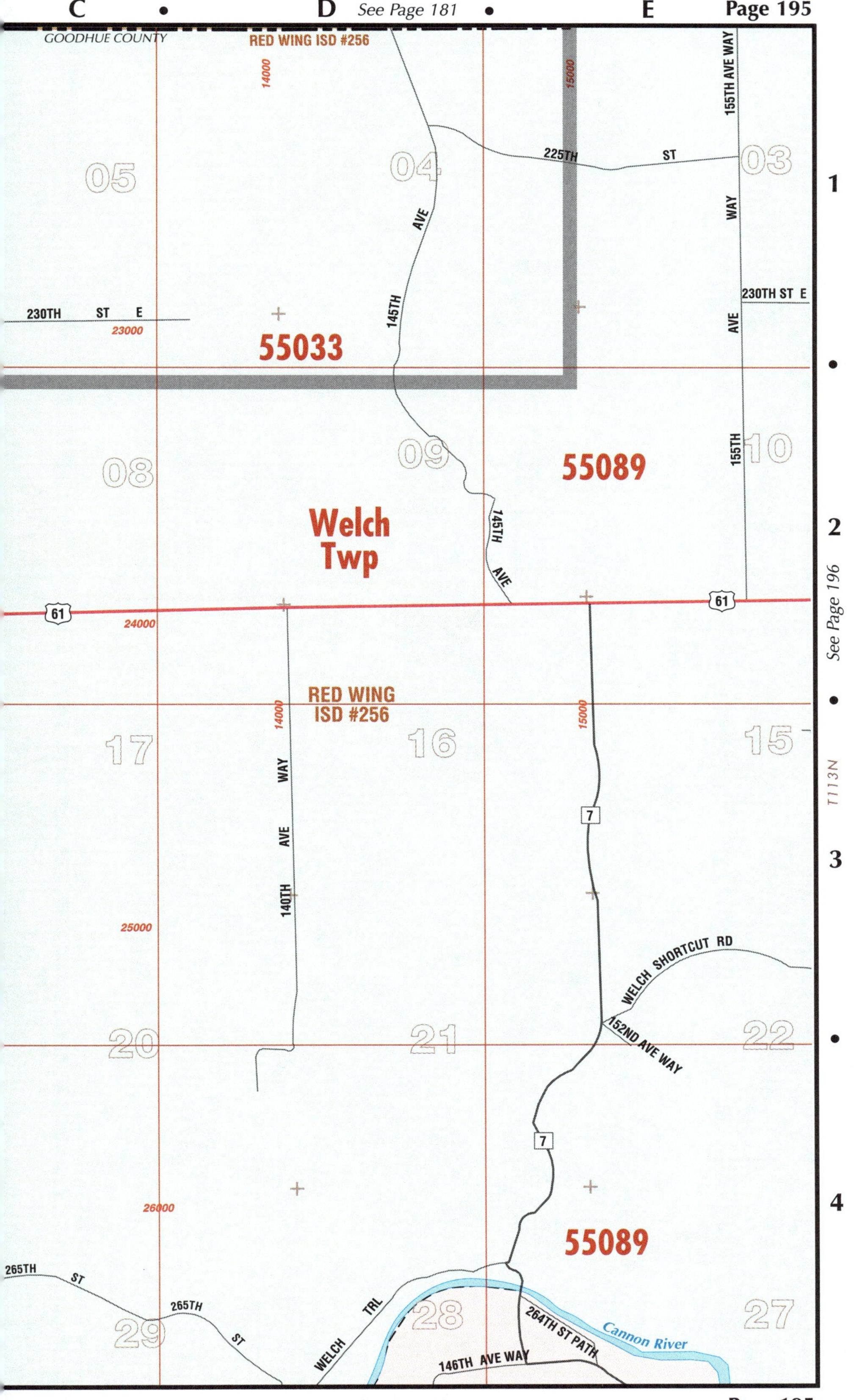

GOODHUE COUNTY

RED WING ISD #256

14000

15000

155TH AVE WAY

05

04

225TH ST

03

1

WAY

145TH AVE

230TH ST E

230TH ST E

23000

55033

AVE

155TH

08

09

55089

10

145TH AVE

Welch Twp

2

See Page 196

61 *24000* 61

RED WING
ISD #256

14000

15000

WAY

17

16

15

7

T113N

140TH AVE

3

25000

WELCH SHORTCUT RD

20

21

152ND AVE WAY

22

7

26000

55089

4

265TH ST

WELCH TRL

265TH ST

29

28

264TH ST PATH

Cannon River

27

146TH AVE WAY

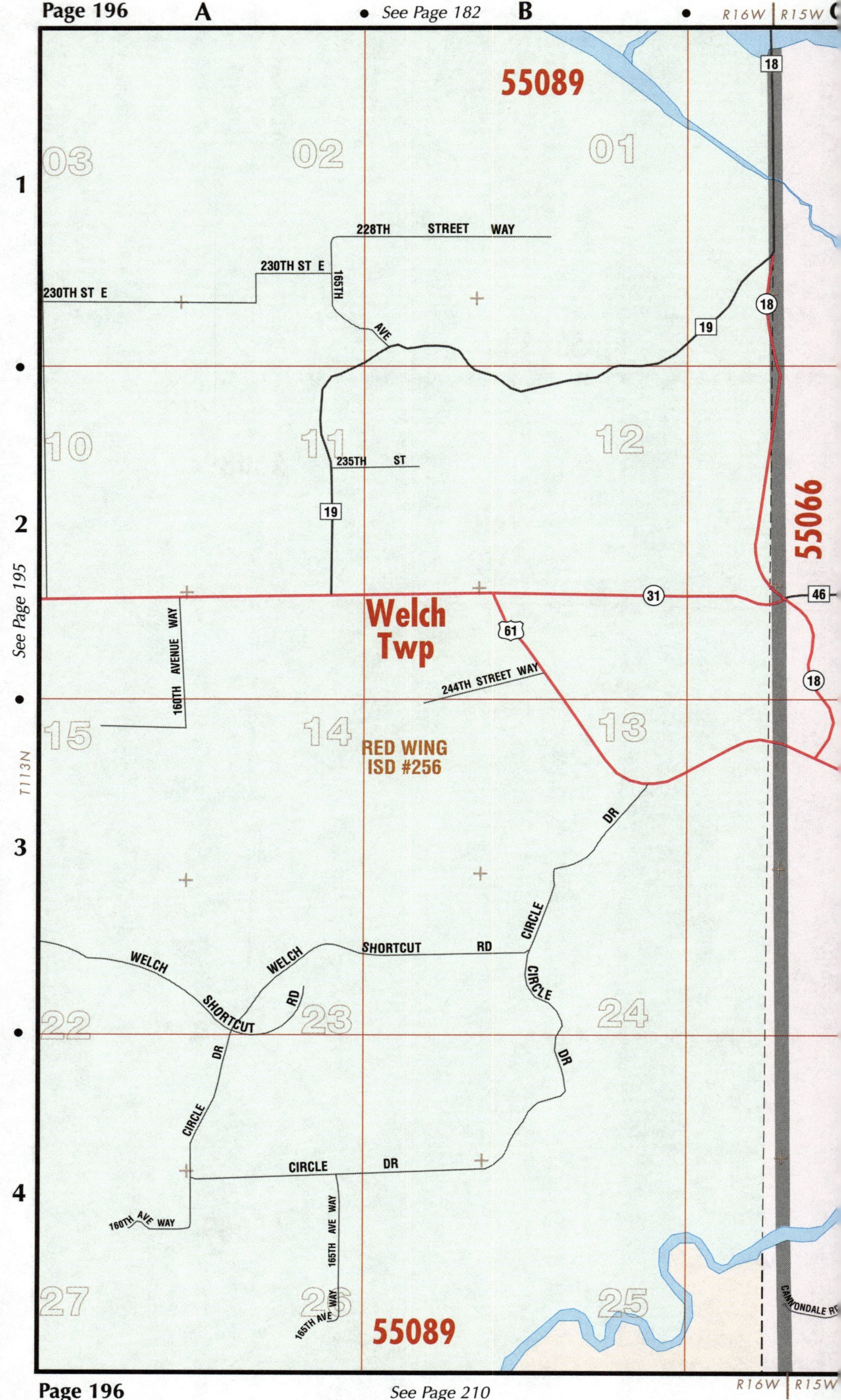

55089

03

02

01

1

228TH STREET WAY

230TH ST E

230TH ST E

165TH

AVE

19

18

19

18

10

11

12

55066

235TH ST

2

19

160TH AVENUE WAY

Welch Twp

31

61

46

18

244TH STREET WAY

15

14

RED WING ISD #256

13

DR

3

CIRCLE

SHORTCUT RD

CIRCLE

WELCH

WELCH

RD

DR

22

SHORTCUT

RD

23

24

CIRCLE

DR

4

CIRCLE

CIRCLE DR

160TH AVE WAY

165TH AVE WAY

27

26

165TH AVE WAY

25

CANNONDALE RD

55089

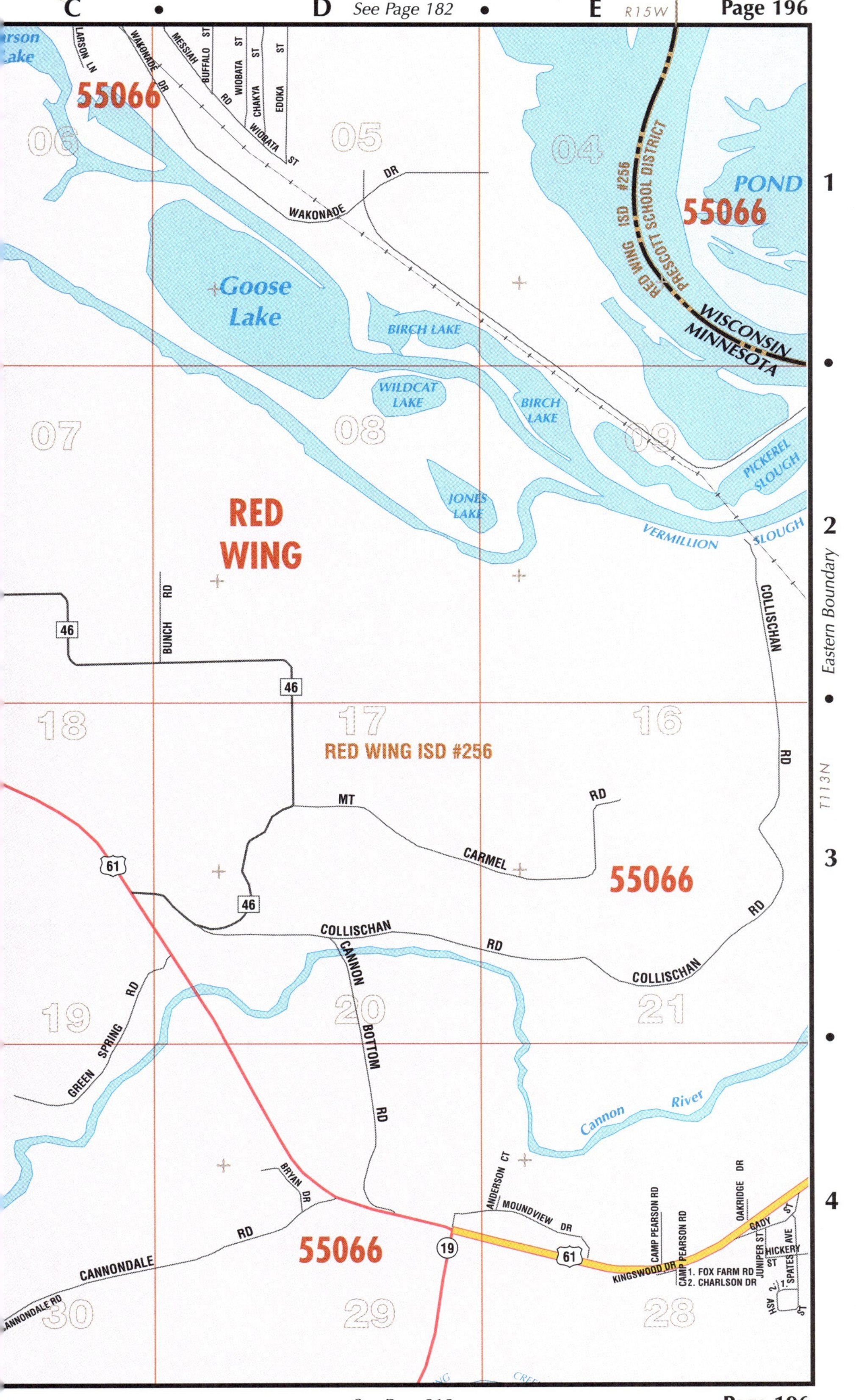
55066
RED WING
Goose Lake
BIRCH LAKE
WILDCAT LAKE
BIRCH LAKE
JONES LAKE
POND
PICKEREL SLOUGH
VERMILLION SLOUGH
WISCONSIN
MINNESOTA
RED WING ISD #256 PRESCOTT SCHOOL DISTRICT
RED WING ISD #256
Eastern Boundary
T113N
LARSON LN
WAKONADE DR
MESSIAH RD
BUFFALO ST
WIOBATA ST
CHAKYA ST
EDOKA ST
WIOBATA ST
WAKONADE DR
BUNCH RD
COLLISCHAN RD
MT CARMEL RD
COLLISCHAN RD
CANNON BOTTOM RD
GREEN SPRING RD
BRYAN DR
CANNONDALE RD
ANDERSON CT
MOUNDVIEW DR
CAMP PEARSON RD
OAKRIDGE DR
KINGSWOOD DR
JUNIPER ST
GADY ST
HICKERY ST
SPATES AVE
HSY
1. FOX FARM RD
2. CHARLSON DR
Cannon River
46
61
19
06
05
04
07
08
09
18
17
16
19
20
21
30
29
28
1
2
3
4

A • *See Page 183* B • C

Western Boundary •

19

1

27 26

19 19

55307 **Arlington Twp**

17

34 35 17

•*T112N* | *T113N*

2

03 02

3

17

SIBLEY EAST ISD #2310

62

62

•

09 62 10 11

56044 **Kelso Twp**

LE SUEUR - HENDERSON ISD #239?

4

RUSH RIVER

56058

6 15 14 17

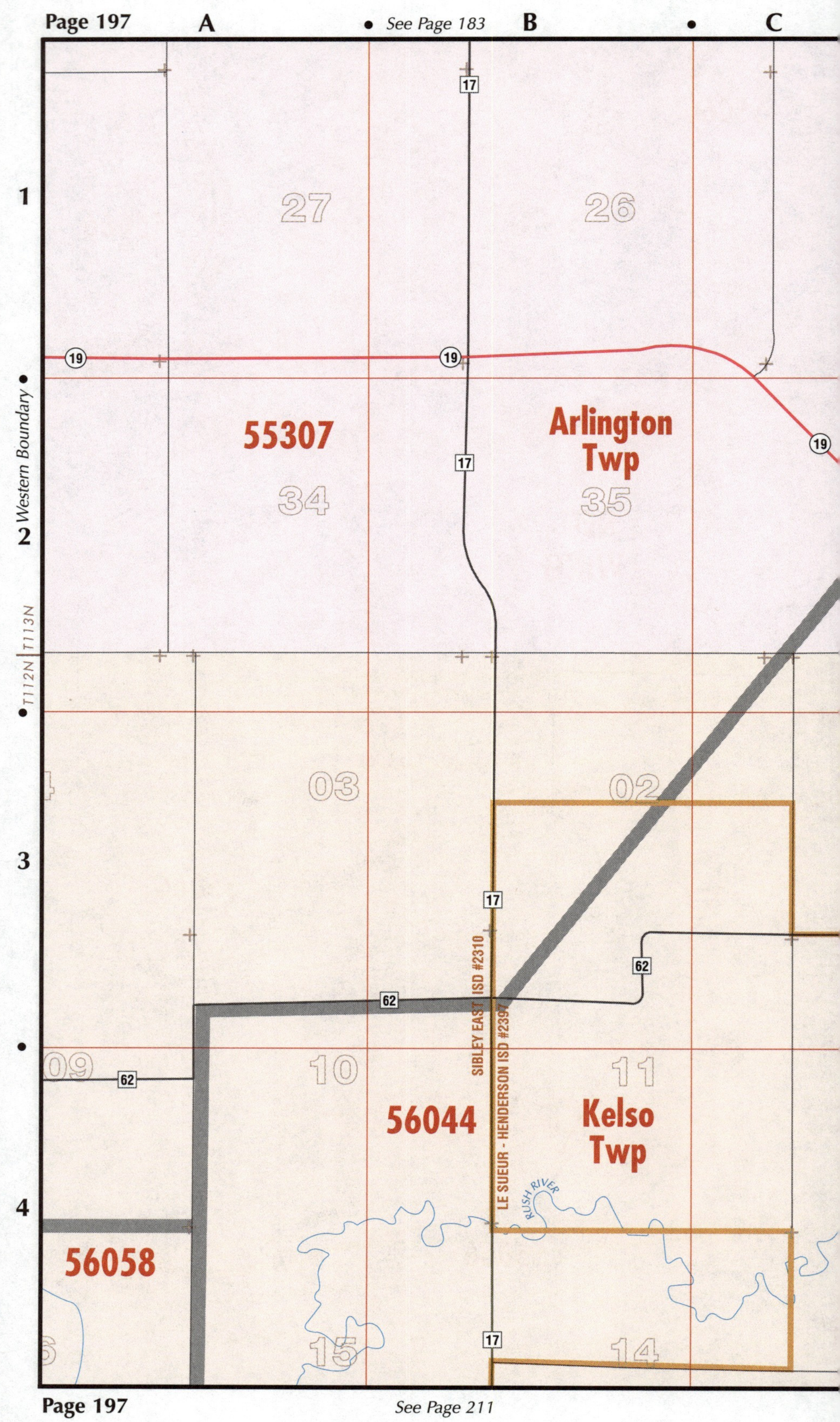

See Page 211

25

Arlington Twp

55307

See Page 198

30

1

Jessenland Twp

SIBLEY EAST ISD #2310

LE SUEUR - HENDERSON ISD #2397

SIBLEY EAST ISD #2310

LE SUEUR - HENDERSON ISD #2397

29

BUFFALO CREEK

36

65

31

32

2

65

T112N | T113N

19

19

56044

01

06

05

3

Kelso Twp

62

62

62

12

Henderson Twp

07

08

4

RUSH RIVER

13

18

RUSH RIVER

17

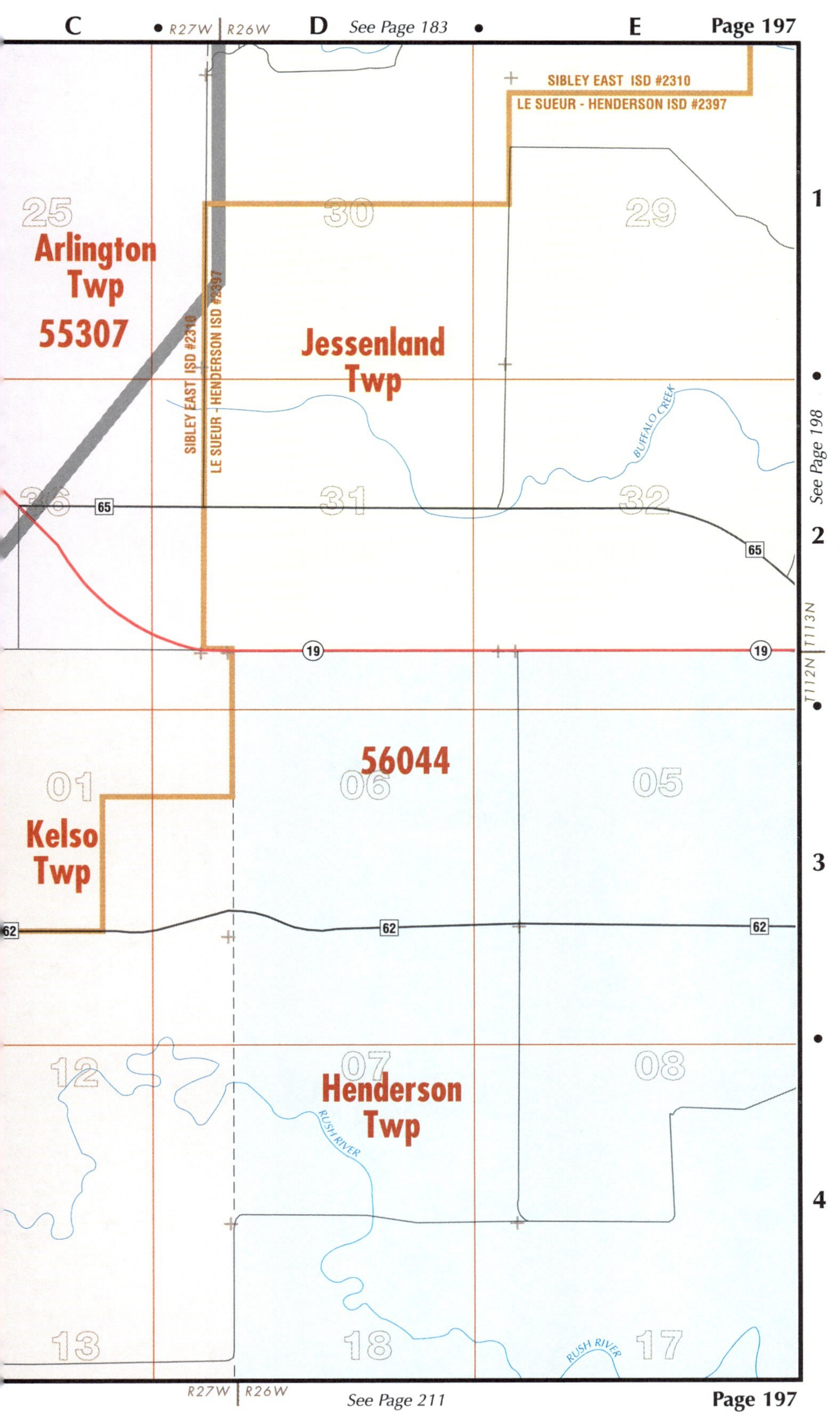

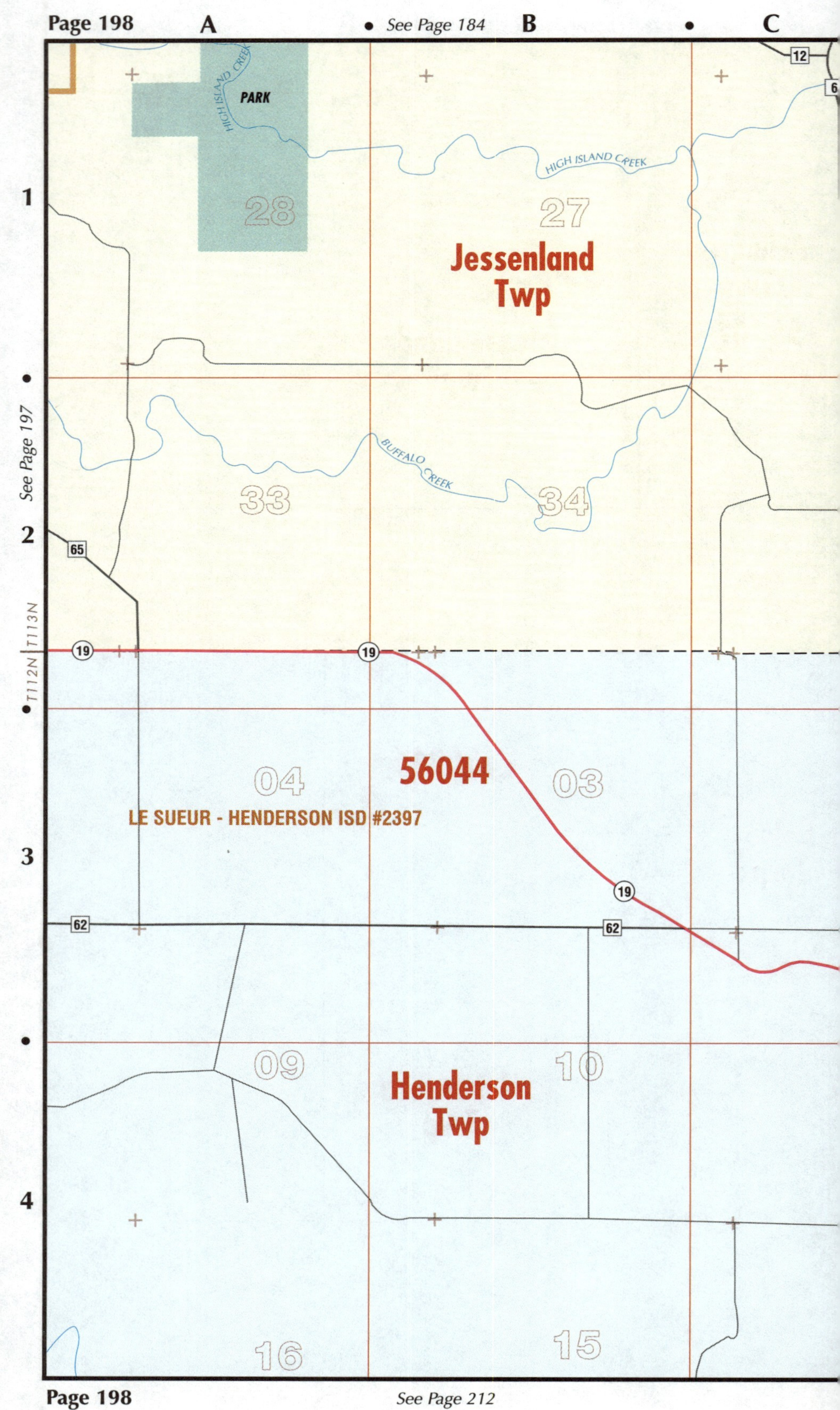

PARK

HIGH ISLAND CREEK

HIGH ISLAND CREEK

12

6

1

28

27

Jessenland Twp

See Page 197

BUFFALO CREEK

33

34

2

65

T112N | T113N

19

19

56044

04

03

LE SUEUR - HENDERSON ISD #2397

3

19

62

62

09

10

Henderson Twp

4

16

15

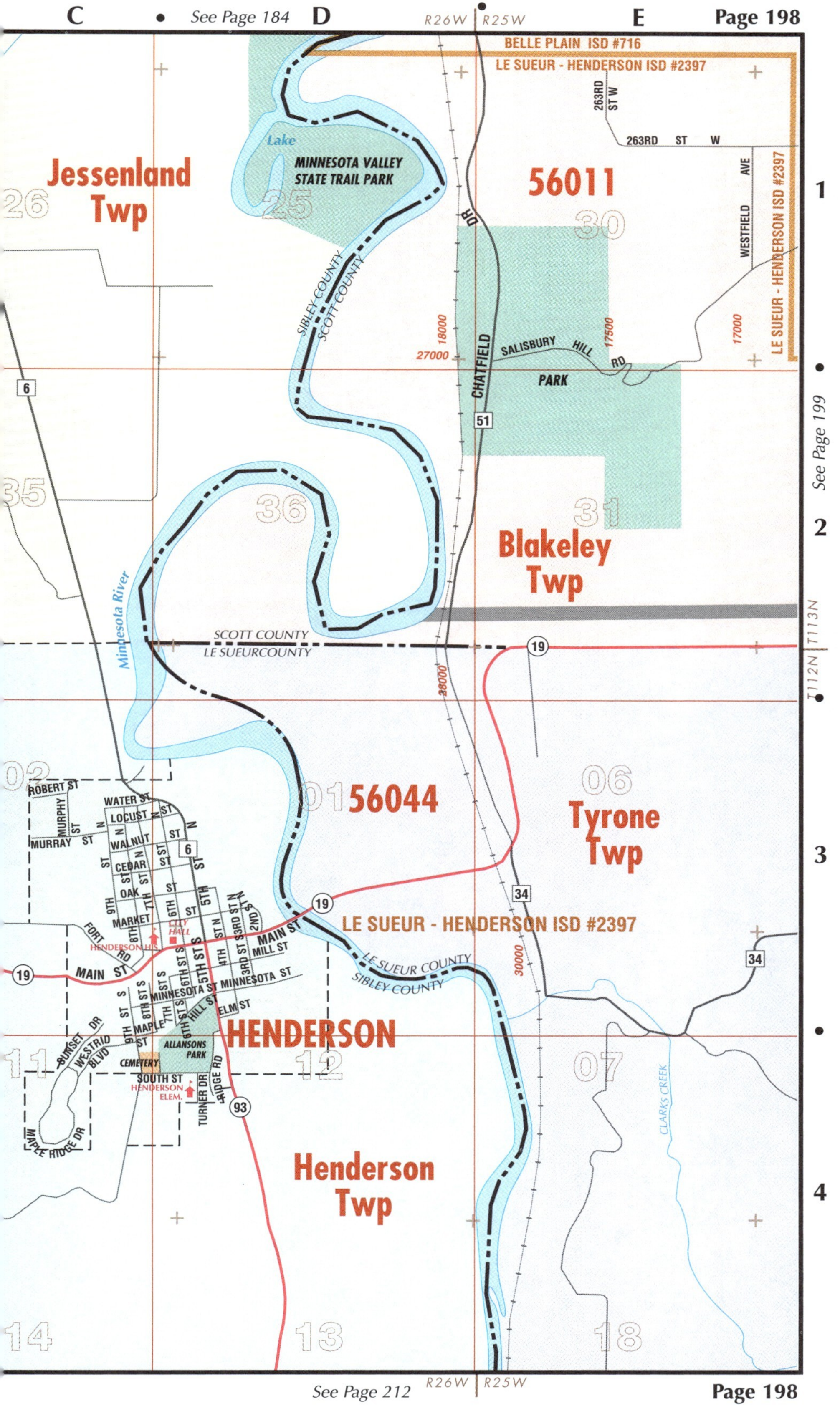

Jessenland Twp

26

35

Lake

MINNESOTA VALLEY STATE TRAIL PARK

25

SIBLEY COUNTY / SCOTT COUNTY

36

Minnesota River

6

BELLE PLAIN ISD #716

LE SUEUR - HENDERSON ISD #2397

56011

263RD ST W

263RD ST W

WESTFIELD AVE

LE SUEUR - HENDERSON ISD #2397

30

18000

27000

17500

17000

CHATFIELD DR

SALISBURY HILL RD

PARK

51

31

Blakeley Twp

1

See Page 199

2

T112N / T113N

SCOTT COUNTY

LE SUEURCOUNTY

19

38000

02

ROBERT ST

WATER ST

MURPHY ST

MURRAY ST

LOCUST ST

WALNUT ST

CEDAR ST

OAK ST

MARKET ST

9TH ST

7TH ST

6TH ST

5TH ST

6

01

56044

06

Tyrone Twp

34

19

FORT RD

HENDERSON H.S.

CITY HALL

MAIN ST

4TH ST N

3RD ST N

2ND S

MILL ST

MAIN ST

19

MAIN ST

MINNESOTA ST

MINNESOTA ST

LE SUEUR COUNTY

SIBLEY COUNTY

30000

34

LE SUEUR - HENDERSON ISD #2397

3

SUNSET DR

WEST RIDGE BLVD

8TH ST S

MAPLE ST

HILL ST

ELM ST

HENDERSON

ALLANSONS PARK

11

CEMETERY

HENDERSON ELEM.

SOUTH ST

RIDGE RD

TURNER DR

93

12

MAPLE RIDGE DR

07

CLARKS CREEK

Henderson Twp

4

14

13

18

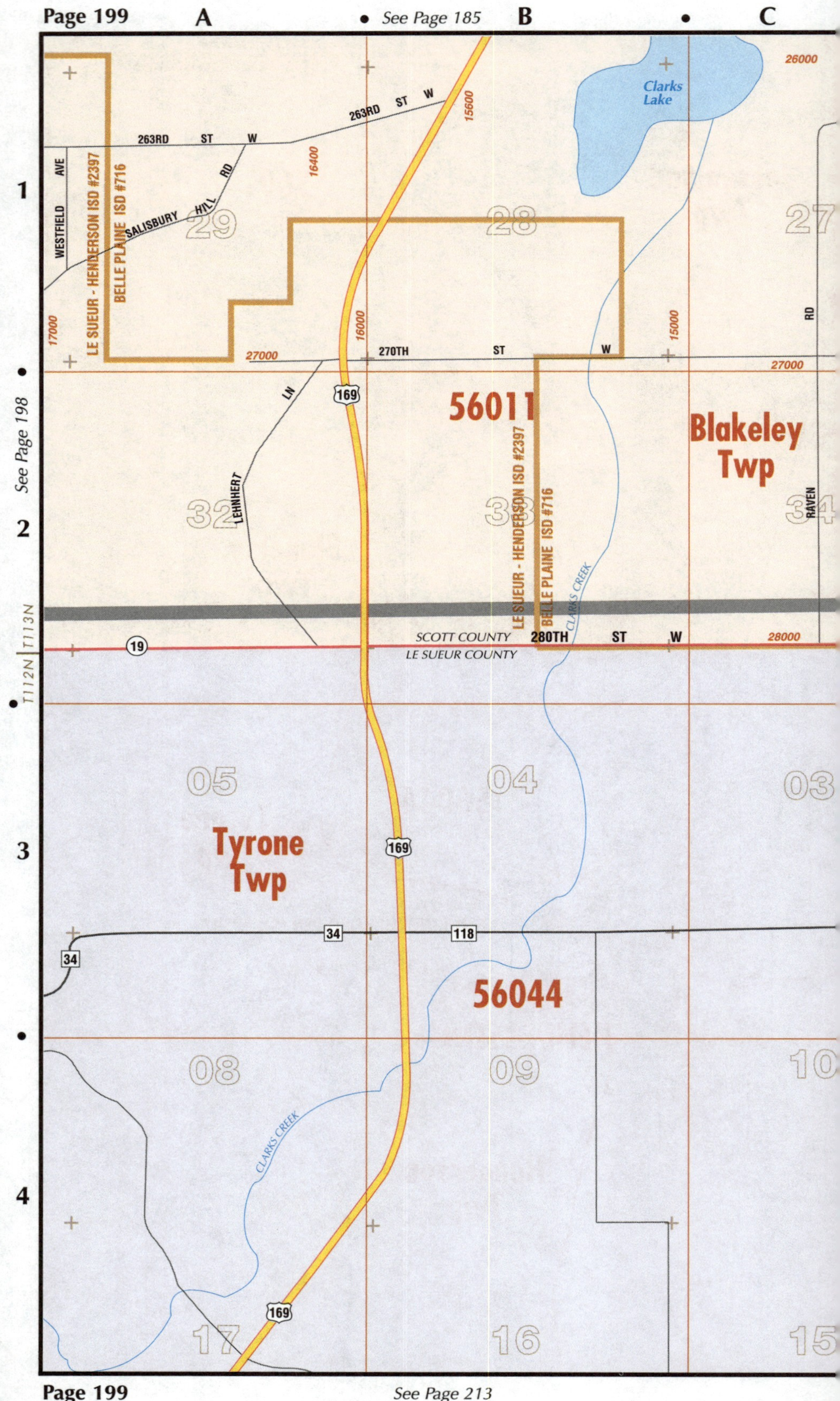

A • See Page 185 B • C

26000

Clarks Lake

263RD ST W

15600

263RD ST W

16400

See Page 198

WESTFIELD AVE

LE SUEUR - HENDERSON ISD #2397

BELLE PLAINE ISD #716

SALISBURY HILL RD

29

28

27

17000

16000

15000

RD

1

27000

270TH ST

W

27000

LN

169

56011

Blakeley Twp

32

LEHNHERT

33

LE SUEUR - HENDERSON ISD #2397

BELLE PLAINE ISD #716

CLARKS CREEK

34

RAVEN

2

T112N | T113N

19

SCOTT COUNTY
LE SUEUR COUNTY

280TH ST W

28000

05

04

03

Tyrone Twp

169

3

34

118

34

56044

08

09

10

CLARKS CREEK

4

169

17

16

15

 See Page 213

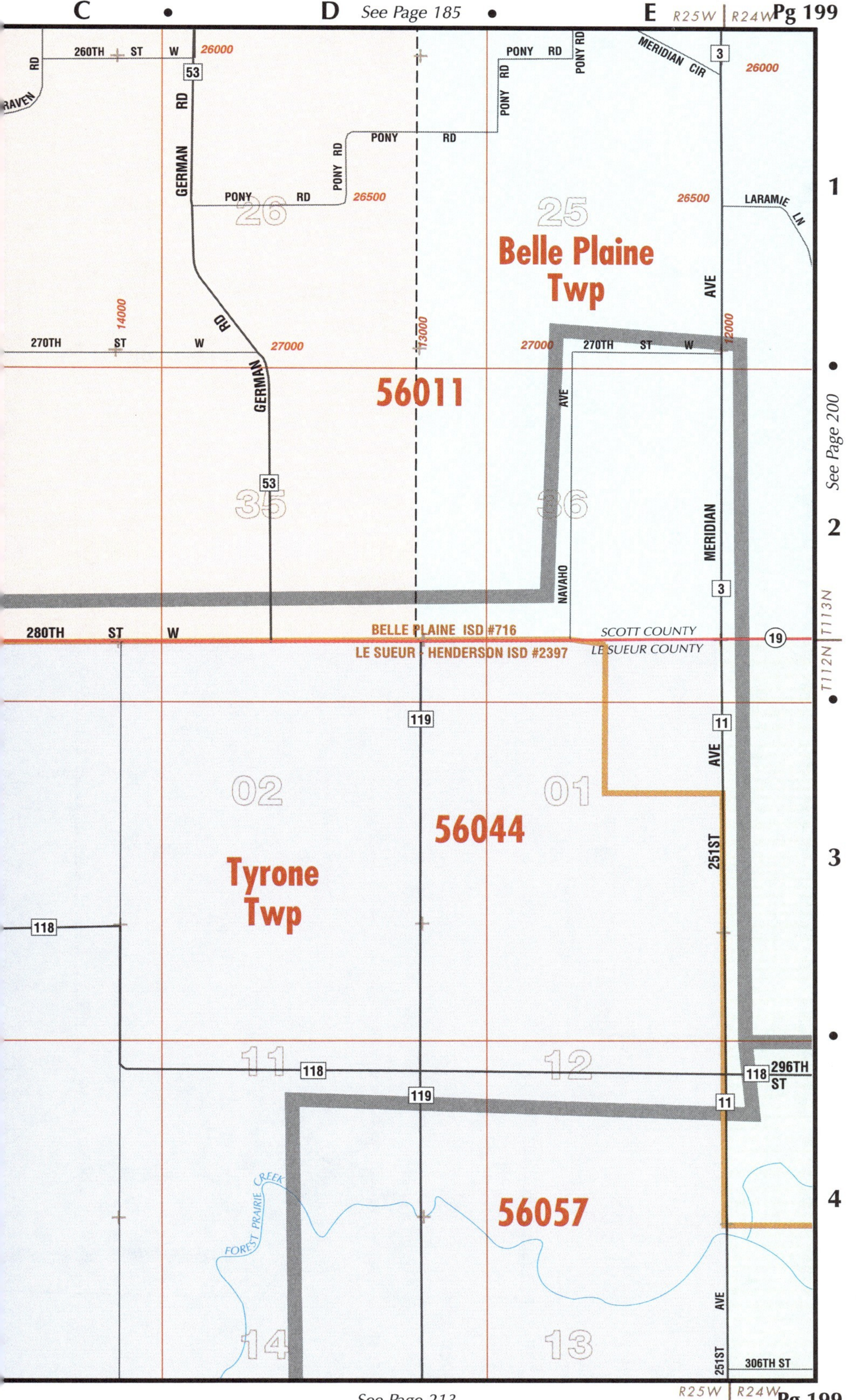

260TH ST W *26000*

RAVEN RD

53

GERMAN RD

PONY RD

PONY RD

PONY RD

PONY RD

MERIDIAN CIR

3

26000

26

PONY RD *26500*

25

1

26500 LARAMIE LN

Belle Plaine Twp

270TH ST W *14000* *27000*

GERMAN RD

27000 AVE *12000*

270TH ST W

See Page 200

56011

53

35

AVE

36

MERIDIAN

3

NAVAHO AVE

2

T112N | T113N

280TH ST W

BELLE PLAINE ISD #716

LE SUEUR - HENDERSON ISD #2397

SCOTT COUNTY
LE SUEUR COUNTY

19

119

11

AVE

02

01

251ST

56044

3

Tyrone Twp

118

118

11

12

118 **296TH ST**

119

11

FOREST PRAIRIE CREEK

56057

4

14

13

AVE

251ST

306TH ST

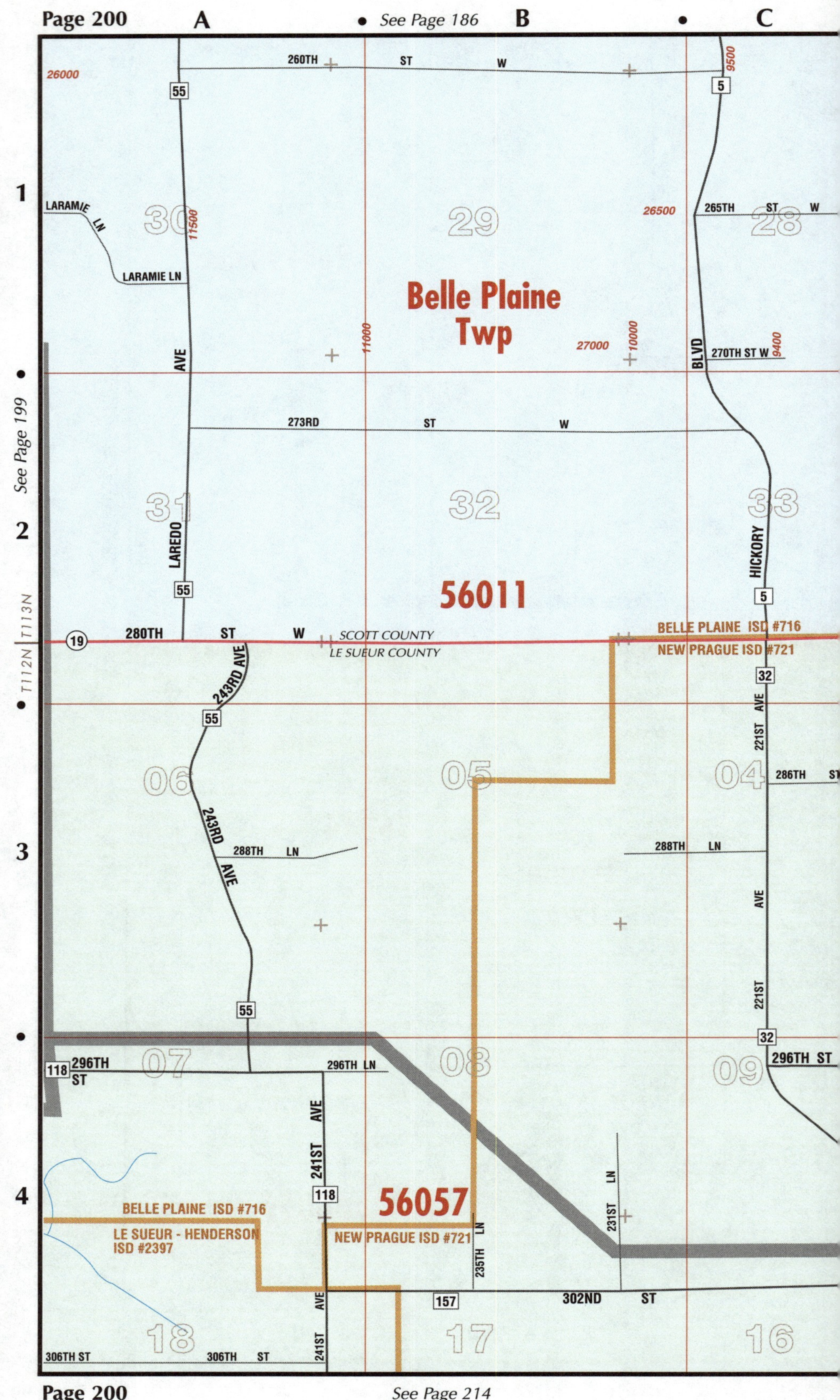

A • *See Page 186* **B** • **C**

260TH ST W

26000

55

9500

5

Laramie Ln

1

30

Laramie Ln

11500

265TH ST W

26500

28

Belle Plaine Twp

AVE

11000

27000

10000

270TH ST W 9400

BLVD

273RD ST W

LAREDO

31

32

33

HICKORY

2

56011

55

5

19 280TH ST W SCOTT COUNTY
LE SUEUR COUNTY

BELLE PLAINE ISD #716
NEW PRAGUE ISD #721

32

T112N | T113N

243RD AVE

55

06

05

04

221ST AVE

286TH ST W

3

243RD AVE

288TH LN

288TH LN

AVE

221ST

32

296TH ST

118 296TH ST

07

296TH LN

08

09

296TH ST

241ST AVE

118

56057

235TH LN

LN

231ST

4

BELLE PLAINE ISD #716

LE SUEUR - HENDERSON
ISD #2397

NEW PRAGUE ISD #721

157

302ND ST

18

241ST AVE

306TH ST 306TH ST

17

16

See Page 199

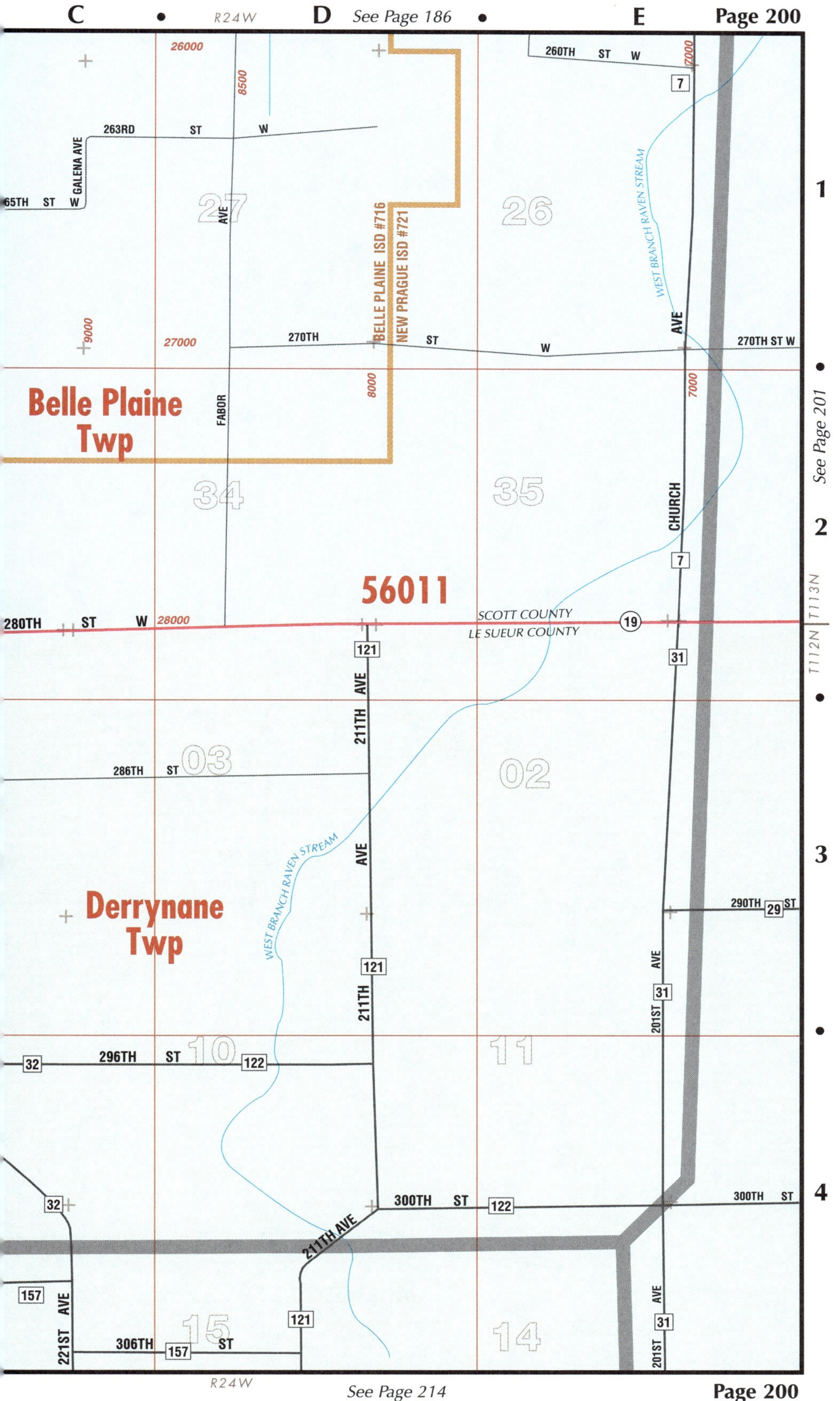

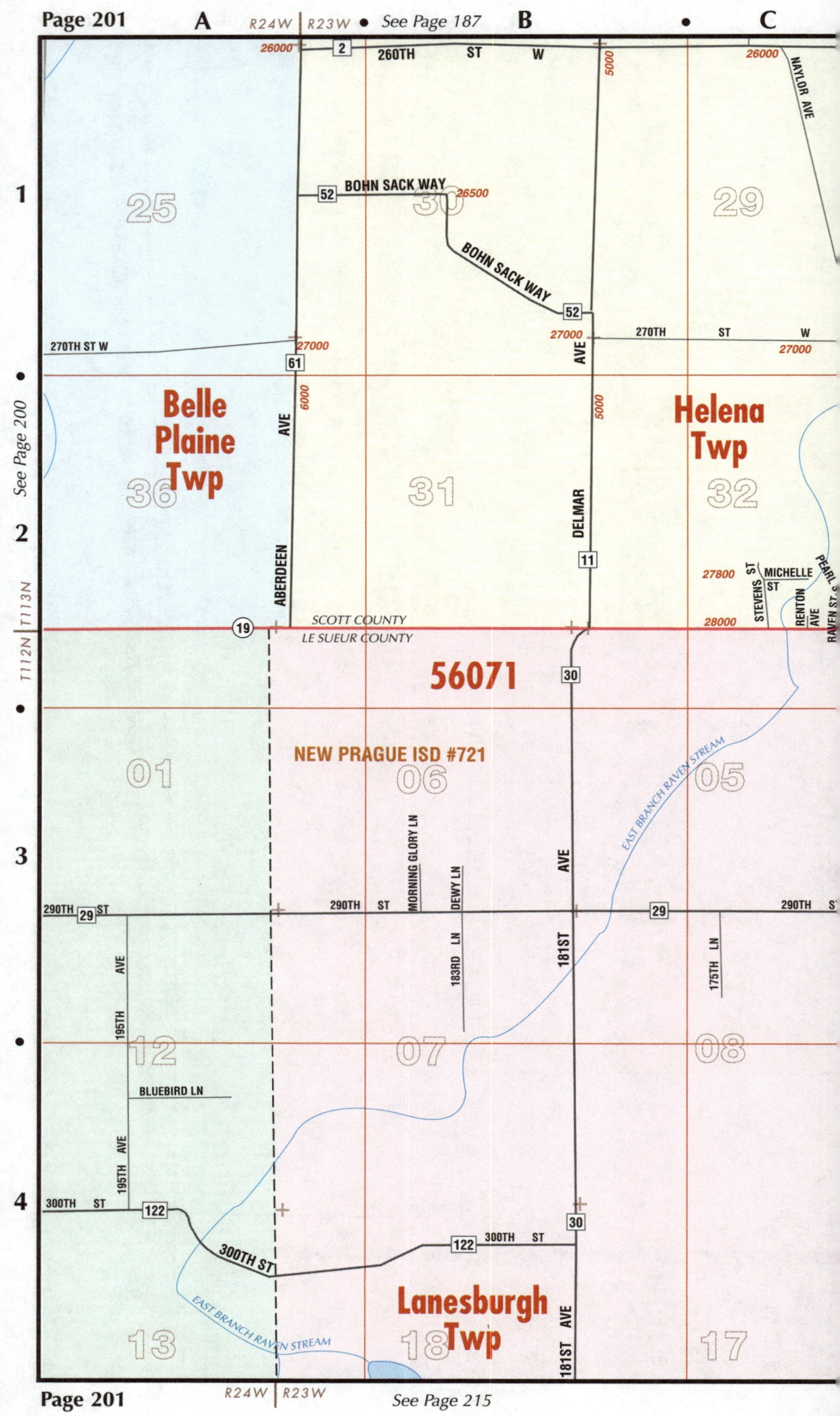

A R24W | R23W • *See Page 187* B • C

26000 [2] 260TH   ST   W   5000 26000 NAYLOR AVE

1

25

[52] **BOHN SACK WAY** 30 26500 29

BOHN SACK WAY

[52]

270TH ST W 27000 [61] 27000 270TH   ST   W   27000

See Page 200

Belle Plaine Twp AVE 6000 **Helena Twp**

36 31 5000 32

2

ABERDEEN DELMAR [11] 27800 STEVENS ST MICHELLE ST RENTON AVE RAVEN ST S TRL S PEARL ST

T112N | T113N [19] *SCOTT COUNTY* 28000
LE SUEUR COUNTY

56071 [30]

NEW PRAGUE ISD #721

01 06 05

3

MORNING GLORY LN DEWY LN AVE EAST BRANCH RAVEN STREAM

290TH [29] ST 290TH   ST [29] 290TH   ST

195TH AVE 183RD LN 181ST 175TH LN

12 07 08

195TH AVE BLUEBIRD LN

4

300TH   ST [122] 300TH ST [122] 300TH   ST [30]

300TH ST

EAST BRANCH RAVEN STREAM **Lanesburgh Twp** 181ST AVE

13 18 17

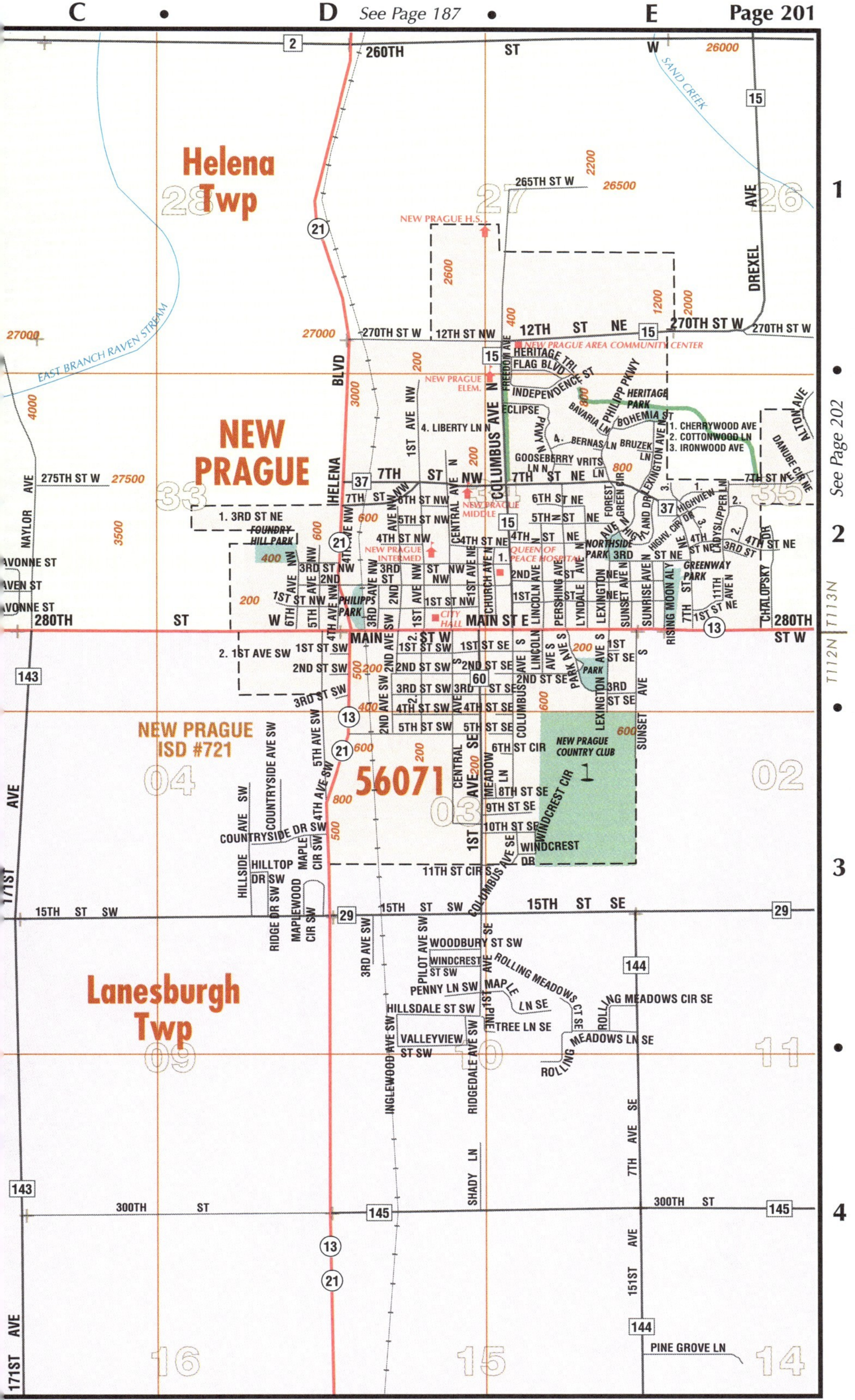

2

260TH ST W 26000

15

Sand Creek

Helena Twp 28

21

265TH ST W 2200 26500

DREXEL AVE 26

1

NEW PRAGUE H.S. 2600

27

27000

EAST BRANCH RAVEN STREAM 4000

27000 270TH ST W 12TH ST NW 400 12TH ST NE 1200 2000 270TH ST W 270TH ST W

15 NEW PRAGUE AREA COMMUNITY CENTER

HERITAGE TRL

FLAG BLVD

NEW PRAGUE ELEM. 200 INDEPENDENCE AVE

ECLIPSE BAVARIA LN PHILIPP PKWY HERITAGE PARK

BOHEMIA LN

4. LIBERTY LN BERNAS LN BRUZEK LN

1. CHERRYWOOD AVE
2. COTTONWOOD LN
3. IRONWOOD AVE

DANUBE CIR NE

ALTON AVE

NEW PRAGUE 3000

HELENA BLVD

GOOSEBERRY VRITS 800

7TH ST NW 200 7TH ST NE

FOREST GREEN LN

32ND DR NE

LEXINGTON CIR NE

HIGHVIEW

LADYSLIPPER LN

7TH ST NE 37

35

See Page 202

33 27500 3500

1. 3RD ST NE 7TH 600 600 6TH ST NE NORTHSIDE PARK 3RD HIGHVIEW 11TH 4TH ST

FOUNDRY HILL PARK 400 6TH ST NW CENTRAL AVE NW NEW PRAGUE MIDDLE 15 4TH ST NE

CHALUPSKY

2

AVONNE ST AVEN ST VONNE ST

200 4TH ST NW 5TH ST NW 3RD AVE NW 2ND 1ST AVE NW

NEW PRAGUE INTERMED. 4. QUEEN OF PEACE MONAS.

GREENWAY PARK

13

280TH ST 27500 3500 200

PHILLIPS PARK

CITY HALL MAIN ST E LINCOLN AVE PERSHING AVE LYNDALE AVE SUNRISE AVE SUNSET AVE RISING MOON ALY

280TH ST W

NEW PRAGUE ISD #721 04

143

171ST AVE

2. 1ST AVE SW MAIN 2ND ST W 1ST ST W 1ST ST SE 60 2ND ST SW 3RD ST SW 500 200 PARK AVE S 200 3RD SUNSET

3RD ST SW 2ND ST SE 4TH ST SW COLUMBUS LINCOLN AVE S PARK AVE S LEXINGTON AVE S 600

13 400 3RD ST SE

21 600 5TH ST SW 4TH ST SE

56071 03 200 800 500 CENTRAL AVE 6TH ST SE 1ST CIR NEW PRAGUE COUNTRY CLUB 1 600

02

MEADOW LN 8TH ST SE 9TH ST SE 10TH ST SE WINDCREST CIR

3

COUNTRYSIDE AVE SW COUNTRYSIDE DR SW MAPLE CIR SW HILLSIDE HILLTOP DR SW MAPLEWOOD CIR SW RIDGE DR SW 5TH AVE SW 4TH AVE SW 21 600 500 800

11TH ST CIR WINDCREST DR

15TH ST SW 29 15TH ST SW 3RD AVE SW 15TH ST SE 29

Lanesburgh Twp 09

PILOT AVE SW WINDCREST ST SW PENNY LN SW HILLSDALE ST SW VALLEYVIEW ST SW INGLEWOOD AVE SW RIDGEDALE AVE SW COLUMBUS AVE SE WOODBURY ST SW MAPLE LN SE PINE TREE LN SE ROLLING MEADOWS CT SE ROLLING MEADOWS LN SE ROLLING MEADOWS CIR SE 144

10 11

143

300TH ST 145 SHADY LN 300TH ST 145 7TH AVE SE

4

13 21 151ST AVE SE 144

16 15 PINE GROVE LN 14

T112N | T113N

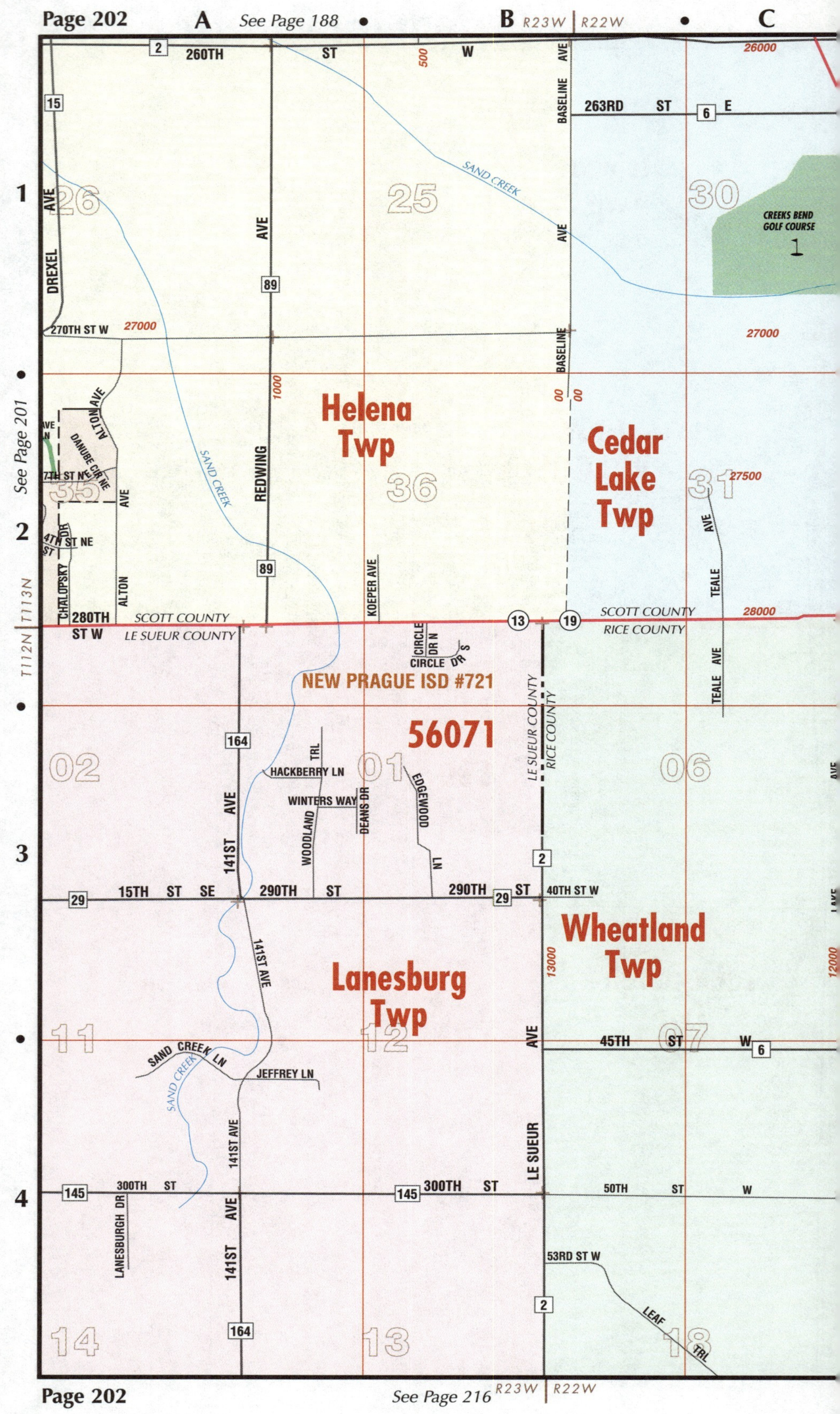

2   260TH   ST   W   500

15

BASELINE   AVE

263RD   ST   6   E

26000

1

DREXEL   AVE

26

AVE

25

89

Sand Creek

AVE

30

CREEKS BEND GOLF COURSE

1

270TH ST W   27000

BASELINE

27000

See Page 201

ALTON AVE

DANUBE CIR NE

7TH ST E

35

AVE

Sand Creek

REDWING

Helena Twp

36

BASELINE

00   00

Cedar Lake Twp

31   27500

TEALE   AVE

2

4TH ST NE

CHALUPSKY

ALTON

89

KOEPER AVE

280TH ST W   SCOTT COUNTY   LE SUEUR COUNTY

13   19   SCOTT COUNTY   RICE COUNTY   28000

TEALE AVE

T112N | T113N

CIRCLE DR N   CIRCLE DR S

NEW PRAGUE ISD #721

56071

164

HACKBERRY LN

WINTERS WAY   DEANS DR

WOODLAND

EDGEWOOD LN

LE SUEUR COUNTY | RICE COUNTY

3

02

141ST   AVE

TRL

01

06

AVE

2

29   15TH   ST   SE   290TH   ST   290TH   29   ST   40TH ST W

141ST   AVE

Wheatland Twp

13000

LAKE   12000

11

SAND CREEK LN

Sand Creek

JEFFREY LN

12

Lanesburg Twp

AVE

45TH   ST   W   6

07

LE SUEUR

4

145   300TH   ST

LANESBURGH DR

141ST   AVE

145   300TH   ST

50TH   ST   W

53RD ST W

2

14

164

13

LEAF TRL

18

260TH ST E 2

PRAIRIE ROSE CT

FAIRLAWN AVE

XKIMO AVE

29

VERGUS AVE

26500 265TH ST E

28

27

267TH ST E XKIMO AVE

270TH ST E

NEWPORT AVE

27000

AVE

3000

1

1000 AVE

13

2000

2500

WEST VIEW DR

EAST VIEW DR

BALSA

See Page 203

LANGFORD

32

SAND CREEK

Cedar Lake Twp

33

COUNTRY HOLLOWS LN

34

T112N | T113N

2

280TH ST E

3000

19

3000

JACKSON AVE

52

56071

05

AVE

NEW PRAGUE ISD #721

04

03

KANABEC AVE

40TH ST W

4000

52

3

11000

10000

Wheatland Twp

KENT AVE

08

09

JACKSON AVE

10

4500

6

48TH CT W

ISLE AVE

CT W

ISLAND AVE

50TH ST W

5000

50TH ST W

6

4

ITASKA CT

ITASKA AVE

49TH

55046

55TH ST W

17

HATCH TRL

Hatch Lake

16

5500

55TH ST W 55TH CT W

52

15

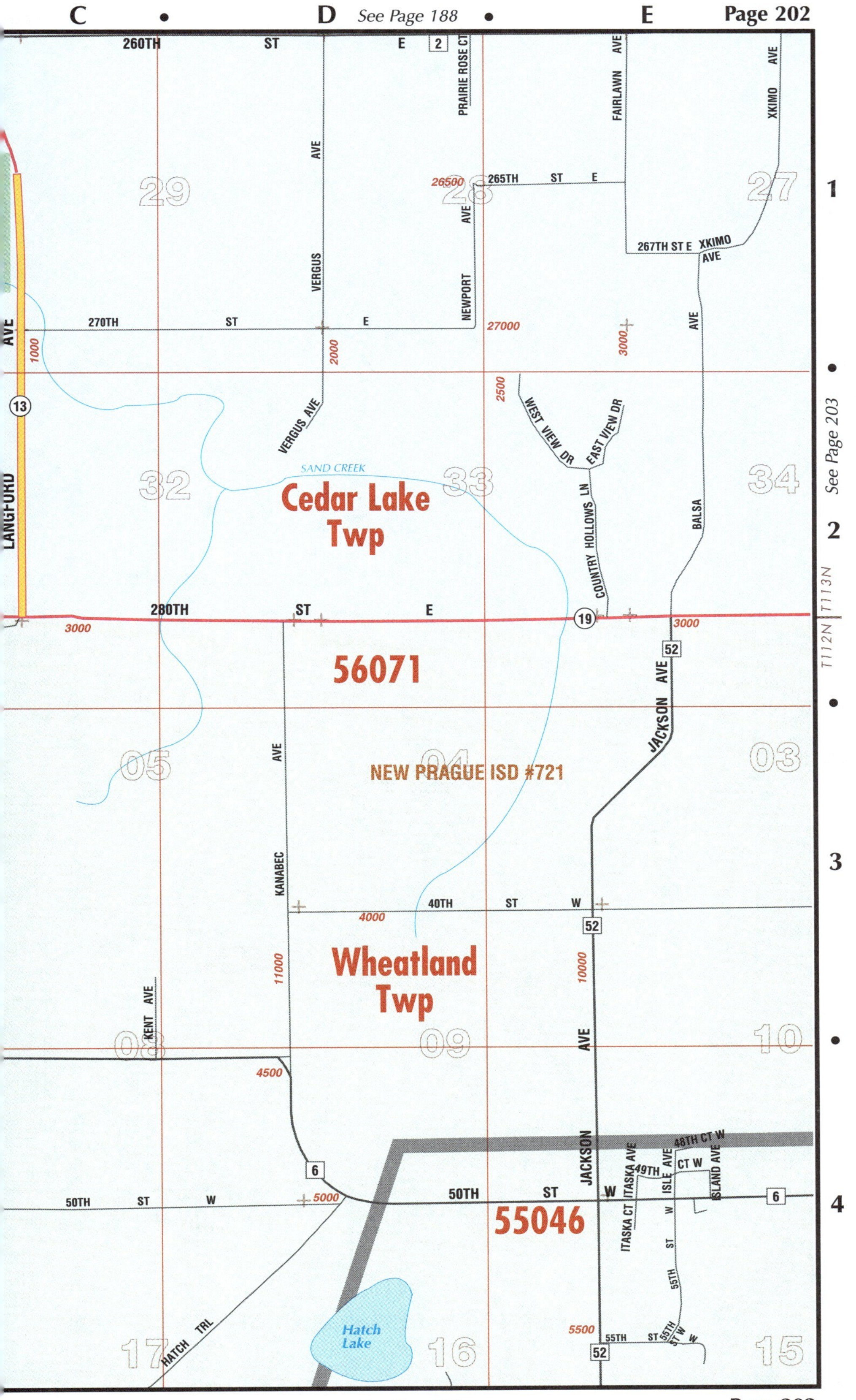

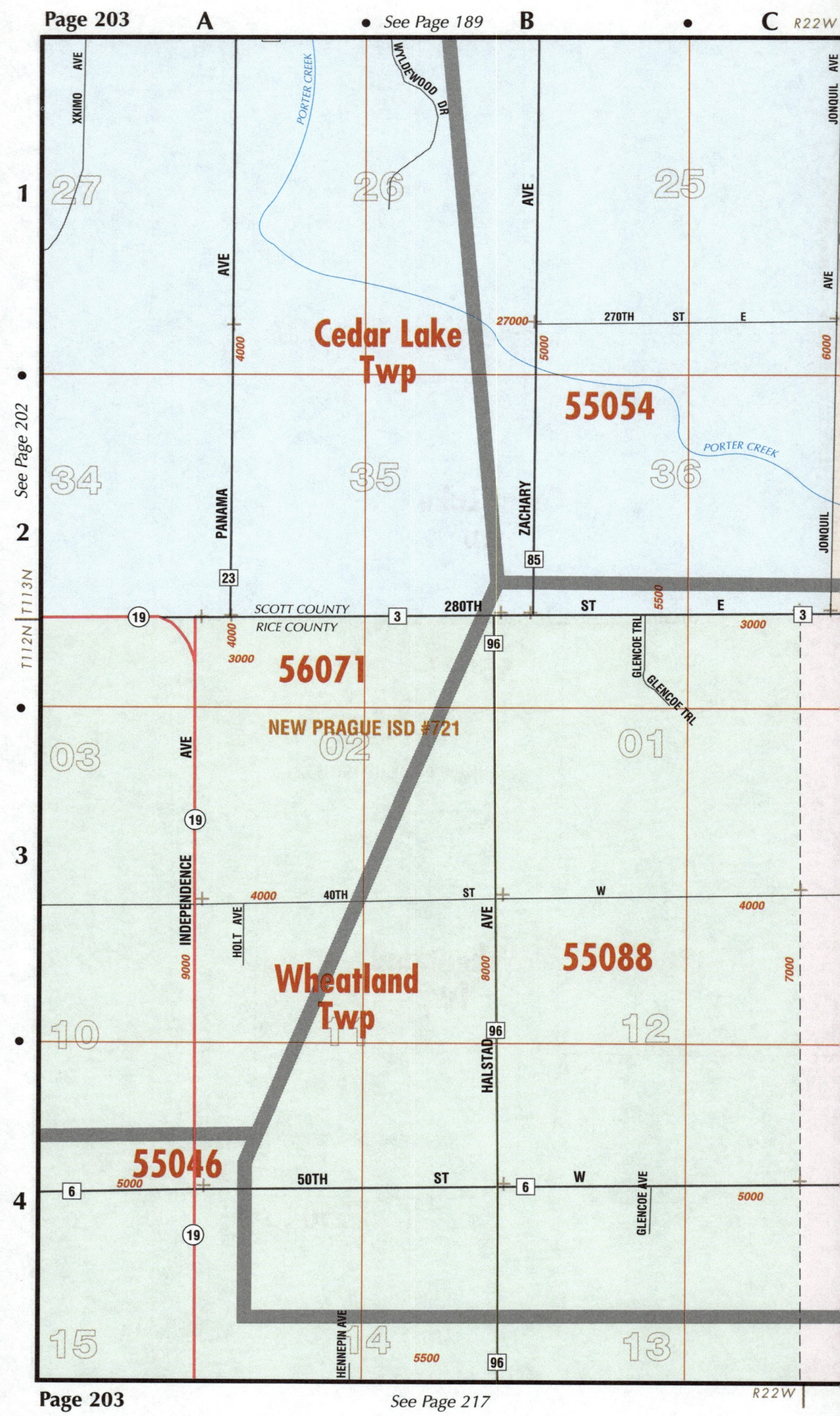

Cedar Lake Twp

55054

56071

NEW PRAGUE ISD #721

Wheatland Twp

55088

55046

XKIMO AVE

PORTER CREEK

WYLDEWOOD DR

JONQUIL AVE

27

26

25

See Page 202

AVE

4000

270TH ST E

27000 5000 6000

AVE

34 35 36

PORTER CREEK

PANAMA AVE

ZACHARY AVE

JONQUIL

23 85

T112N | T113N

19 SCOTT COUNTY / RICE COUNTY 3 280TH ST E 3

4000 3 5500 3000

3000 96 GLENCOE TRL

03 AVE 02 01 GLENCOE TRL

19 INDEPENDENCE AVE

9000

40TH ST W

4000 HOLT AVE AVE 4000

8000 7000

55088

Wheatland Twp

10 HALSTAD 96 12

96

55046

5000 50TH ST W

6 19 6 GLENCOE AVE 5000

15 HENNEPIN AVE 14 5500 96 13

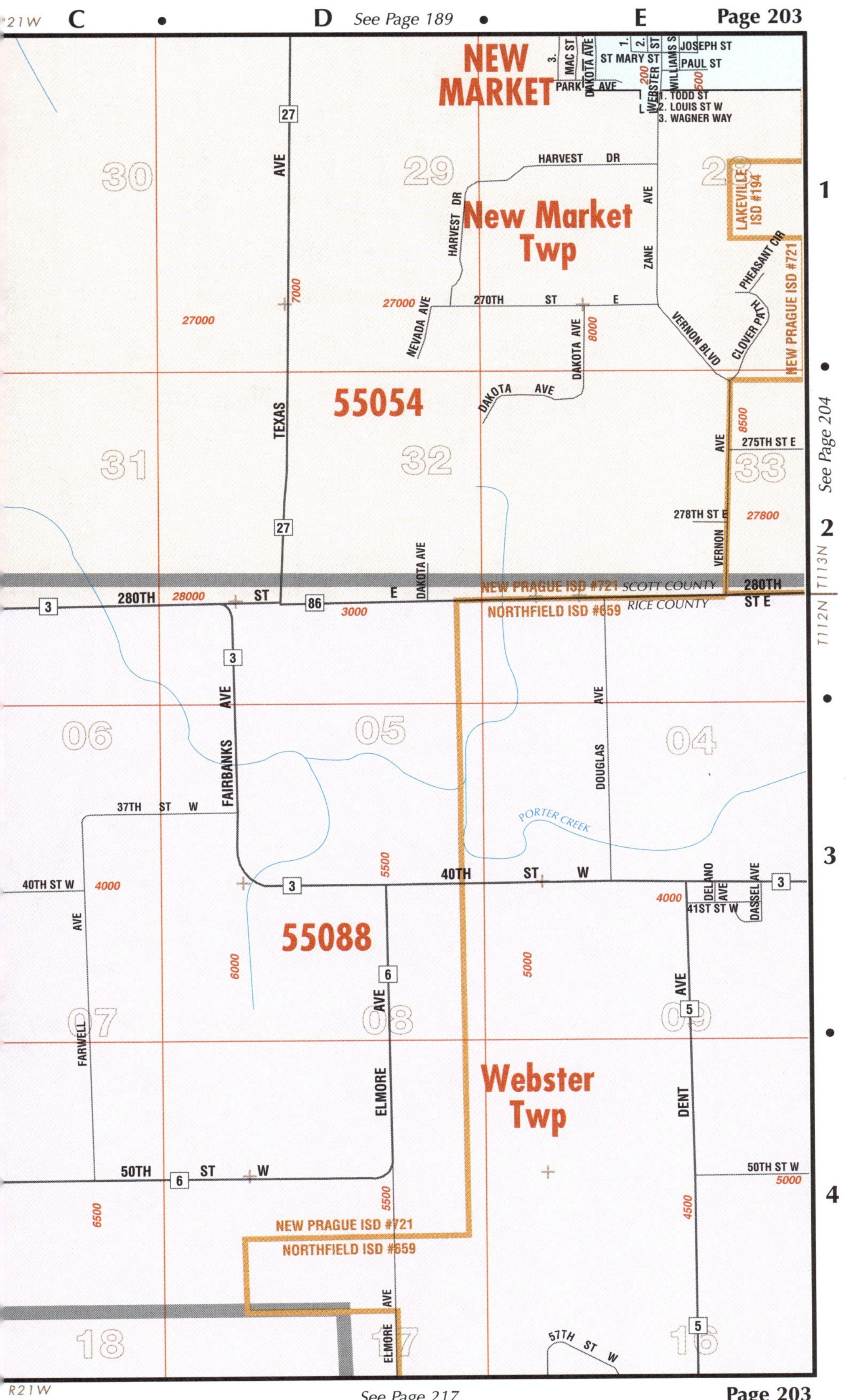
NEW MARKET
New Market Twp
Webster Twp
55054
55088
JOSEPH ST
PAUL ST
ST MARY ST
MAC ST
DAKOTA AVE
WEBSTER ST
WILLIAMS ST
PARK AVE
1. TODD ST
2. LOUIS ST W
3. WAGNER WAY
HARVEST DR
LAKEVILLE ISD #194
NEW PRAGUE ISD #721
PHEASANT CIR
CLOVER PATH
VERNON BLVD
ZANE AVE
NEVADA AVE
270TH ST E
DAKOTA AVE
TEXAS AVE
275TH ST E
278TH ST E
VERNON AVE
280TH ST E
NEW PRAGUE ISD #721 SCOTT COUNTY
NORTHFIELD ISD #659 RICE COUNTY
FAIRBANKS AVE
DOUGLAS AVE
PORTER CREEK
37TH ST W
40TH ST W
DELANO AVE
DASSEL AVE
41ST ST W
FARWELL AVE
ELMORE AVE
DENT AVE
50TH ST W
57TH ST W
See Page 204
T113N
T112N
21W
R21W

A • *See Page 190* B • C

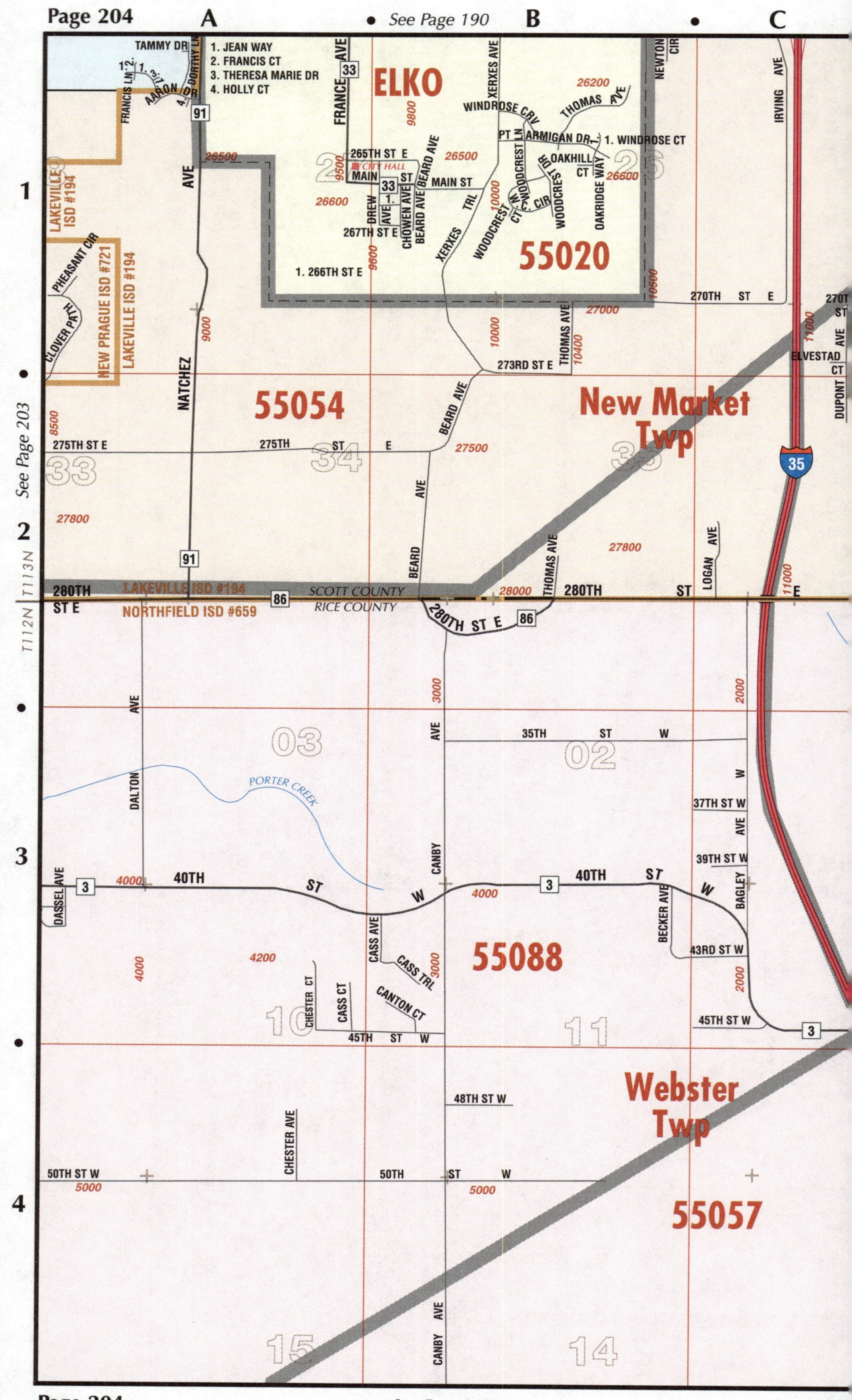

TAMMY DR

1. JEAN WAY
2. FRANCIS CT
3. THERESA MARIE DR
4. HOLLY CT

ELKO

FRANCE AVE

WINDROSE CRV

THOMAS AVE

1. WINDROSE CT

FRANCIS LN

AARON DR

DORTH LN

9800

26200

ARMIGAN DR

26500

26500

265TH ST E

MAIN ST

OAKHILL CT

26600

WOODCREST

267TH ST E

XERXES TRL

WOODCRES CIR

OAKRIDGE WAY

55020

26600

LAKEVILLE ISD #194

PHEASANT CIR

NEW PRAGUE ISD #721

LAKEVILLE ISD #194

CLOVER PATH

NATCHEZ AVE

9000

26500

26600

1. 266TH E

1. 266TH ST E

XERXES AVE

BEARD AVE

10000

270TH ST E

270T

IRVING AVE

10500

11000

I-35

27000

ELVESTAD CT

DUPONT AVE

55054

New Market Twp

8500

275TH ST E

275TH ST E

BEARD AVE

273RD ST E

THOMAS AVE

10400

ELVESTAD CT

33

34

27500

36

27800

BEARD AVE

THOMAS AVE

27800

LOGAN AVE

91

280TH ST E

LAKEVILLE ISD #194

NORTHFIELD ISD #659

86

SCOTT COUNTY

RICE COUNTY

280TH ST E

86

28000

280TH ST

11000

T112N | T113N

3000

2000

03

02

AVE

DALTON AVE

PORTER CREEK

CANBY AVE

35TH ST W

37TH ST W

AVE

39TH ST W

DASSEL AVE

3

4000

40TH ST

4000

3

40TH ST

BAGLEY AVE

BECKER AVE

4000

CASS AVE

4200

CASS TRL

3000

55088

43RD ST W

2000

10

CHESTER CT

CASS CT

CANTON CT

45TH ST W

11

45TH ST W

3

Webster Twp

CHESTER AVE

48TH ST W

50TH ST W

50TH ST W

55057

5000

5000

15

CANBY AVE

14

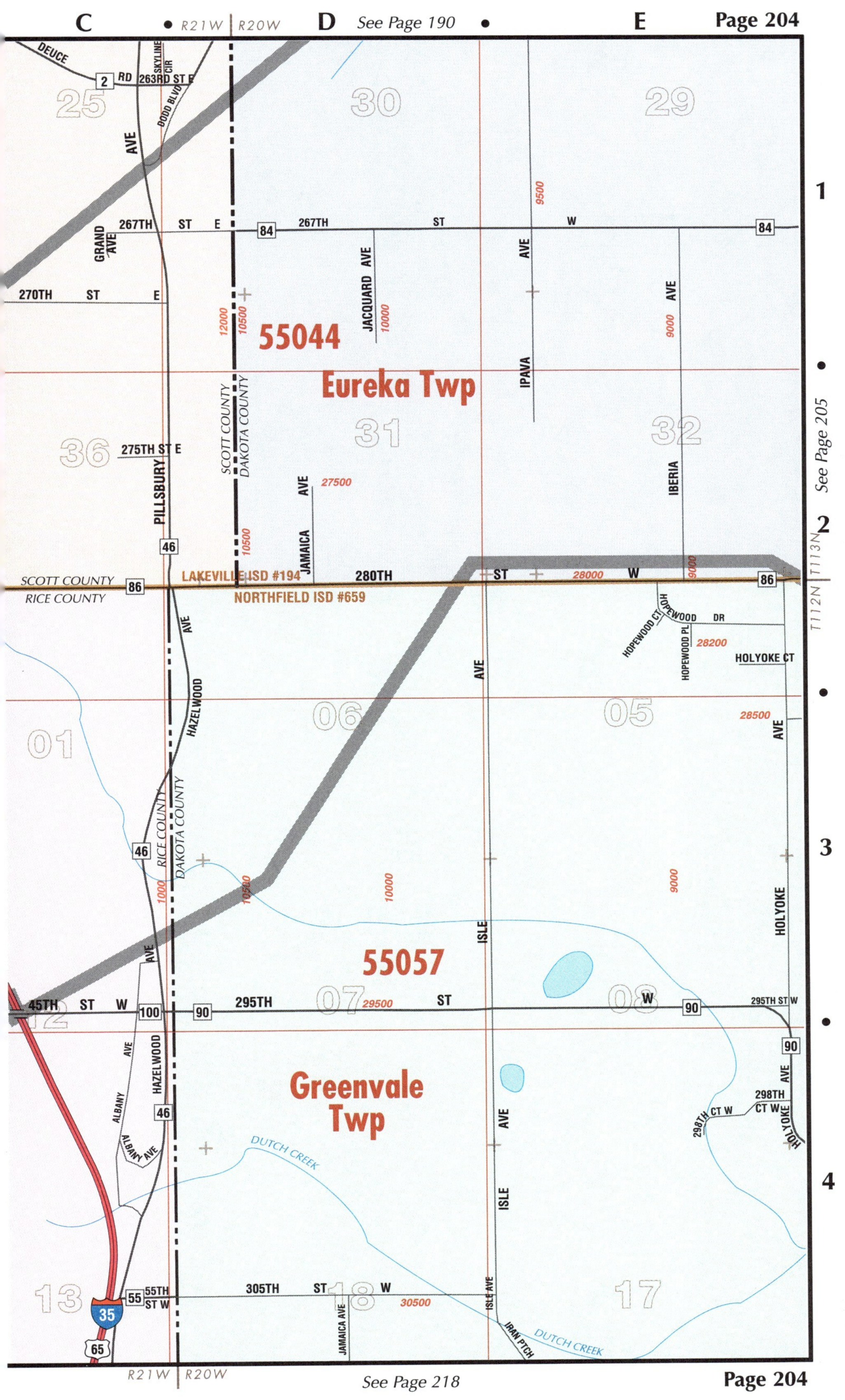

DEUCE

2   RD   263RD ST E

25

SKYLINE CIR

DODD BLVD E

GRAND AVE

267TH   ST   E   84   267TH   ST   W   84

30

29

9500

1

270TH   ST   E

12000

10500

JACQUARD AVE

55044

10000

IPAVA AVE

AVE

9000

9000

Eureka Twp

31

32

See Page 205

36

275TH ST E

PILLSBURY

SCOTT COUNTY | DAKOTA COUNTY

JAMAICA AVE

27500

10500

IBERIA

AVE

9000

2

T112N | T113N

46

SCOTT COUNTY

RICE COUNTY

86   **LAKEVILLE ISD #194**   280TH   ST   28000   W   86

NORTHFIELD ISD #659

HAZELWOOD AVE

AVE

HOPEWOOD CT   HOPEWOOD   DR

HOPEWOOD PL   28200

HOLYOKE CT

01

06

05

28500

AVE

RICE COUNTY | DAKOTA COUNTY

46

1000

10500

10000

ISLE

9000

HOLYOKE

3

55057

AVE

45TH   ST   W   100   90   295TH   07   29500   ST   08   W   90   295TH ST W

12

ALBANY AVE

HAZELWOOD AVE

ALBANY AVE

46

90

HOLYOKE AVE

298TH CT W

Greenvale Twp

DUTCH CREEK

ISLE AVE

299TH CT W

4

ISLE AVE

13

55TH ST W

55   ST W

305TH   ST   18   W

JAMAICA AVE

30500

ISLE AVE

IRAN PTCH

DUTCH CREEK

17

35

65

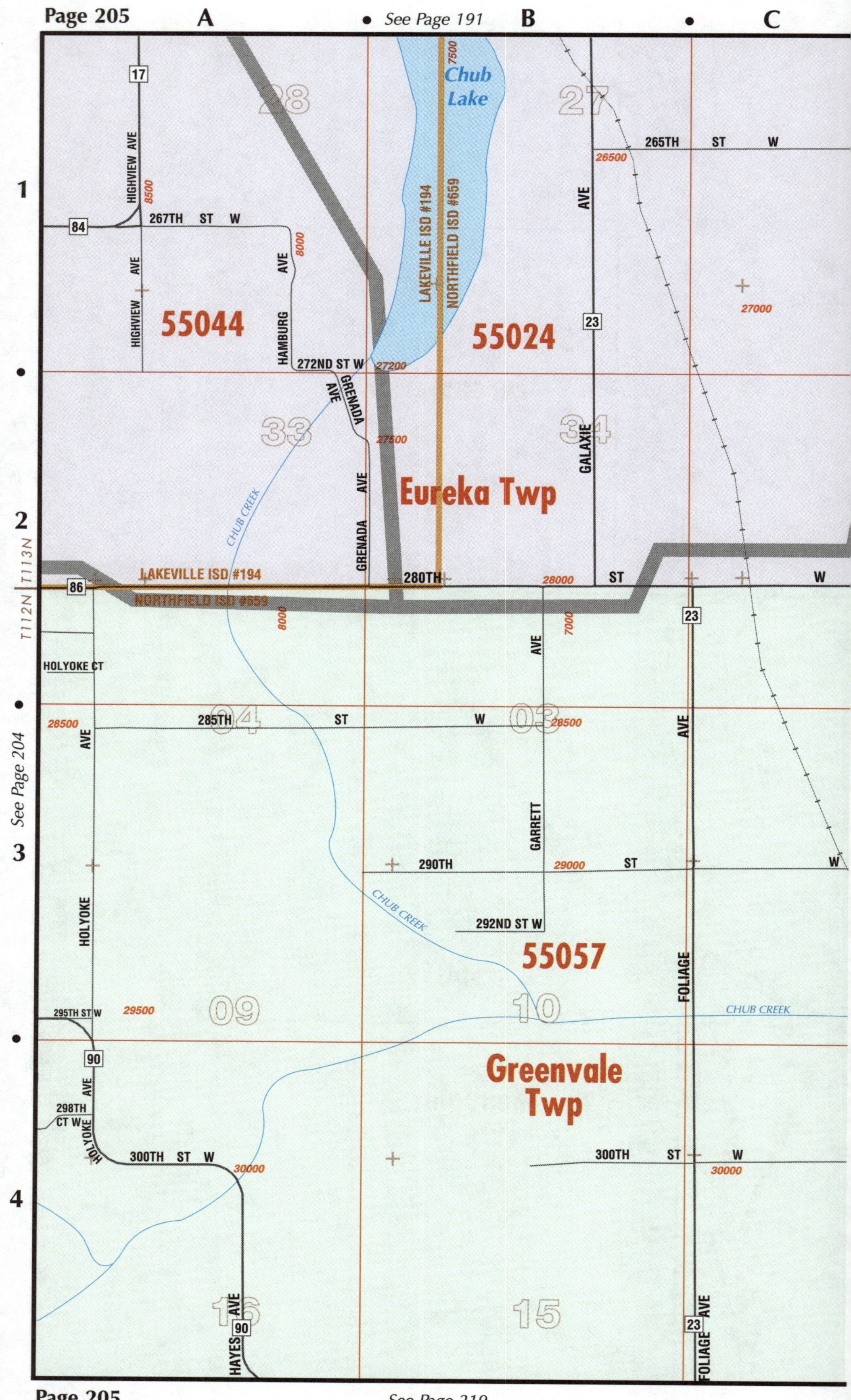

A   B   C

17

Chub
Lake

267TH ST W

84

HIGHVIEW AVE

HIGHVIEW AVE

8500

HAMBURG AVE

8000

28

27

265TH ST W

26500

AVE

23

27000

55044

55024

272ND ST W

27200

GRENADA AVE

33

34

27500

GALAXIE

Eureka Twp

CHUB CREEK

GRENADA AVE

LAKEVILLE ISD #194

NORTHFIELD ISD #659

7500

280TH

ST

W

28000

86

LAKEVILLE ISD #194

NORTHFIELD ISD #659

8000

AVE

7000

23

HOLYOKE CT

285TH

ST

W

04

03

28500

28500

AVE

28500

AVE

290TH

ST

W

29000

GARRETT

HOLYOKE

292ND ST W

55057

FOLIAGE

CHUB CREEK

CHUB CREEK

09

10

295TH ST W

29500

90

298TH
CT W

HOLYOKE AVE

300TH ST W

30000

**Greenvale
Twp**

300TH

ST

W

30000

16

15

90

HAYES AVE

FOLIAGE AVE

23

See Page 204

T112N T113N

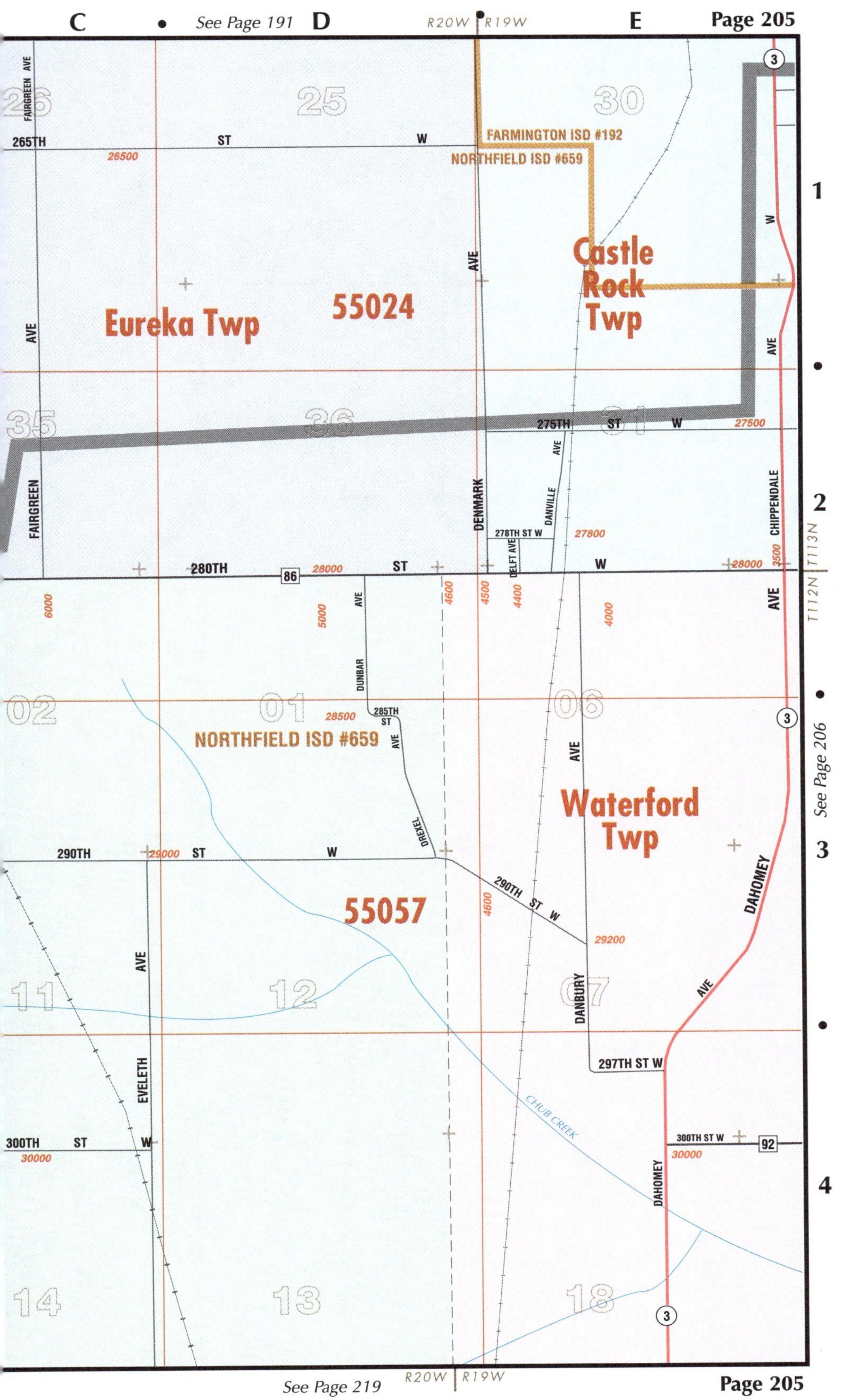

FAIRGREEN AVE

26

25

265TH   ST   W

26500

3

AVE

Eureka Twp   **55024**

FARMINGTON ISD #192

NORTHFIELD ISD #659

Castle Rock Twp

1

W

AVE

35

36

31

FAIRGREEN

275TH   ST   W   27500

DENMARK

AVE

278TH ST W

DANVILLE

DELFT AVE

27800

W

CHIPPENDALE

28000

3500

T112N | T113N

2

AVE

280TH   86   28000   ST   W   28000

6000

5000

AVE

DUNBAR

4600

4500

4400

4000

02

01

28500

NORTHFIELD ISD #659

285TH ST

AVE

06

AVE

3

See Page 206

Waterford Twp

290TH   29000   ST   W

DREXEL

290TH ST W

4600

55057

29200

3

AVE

EVELETH

11

12

DANBURY

AVE

07

DAHOMEY

AVE

297TH ST W

CHUB CREEK

300TH   ST   W

30000

300TH ST W

30000

92

DAHOMEY

4

14

13

18

3

See Page 219   R20W R19W

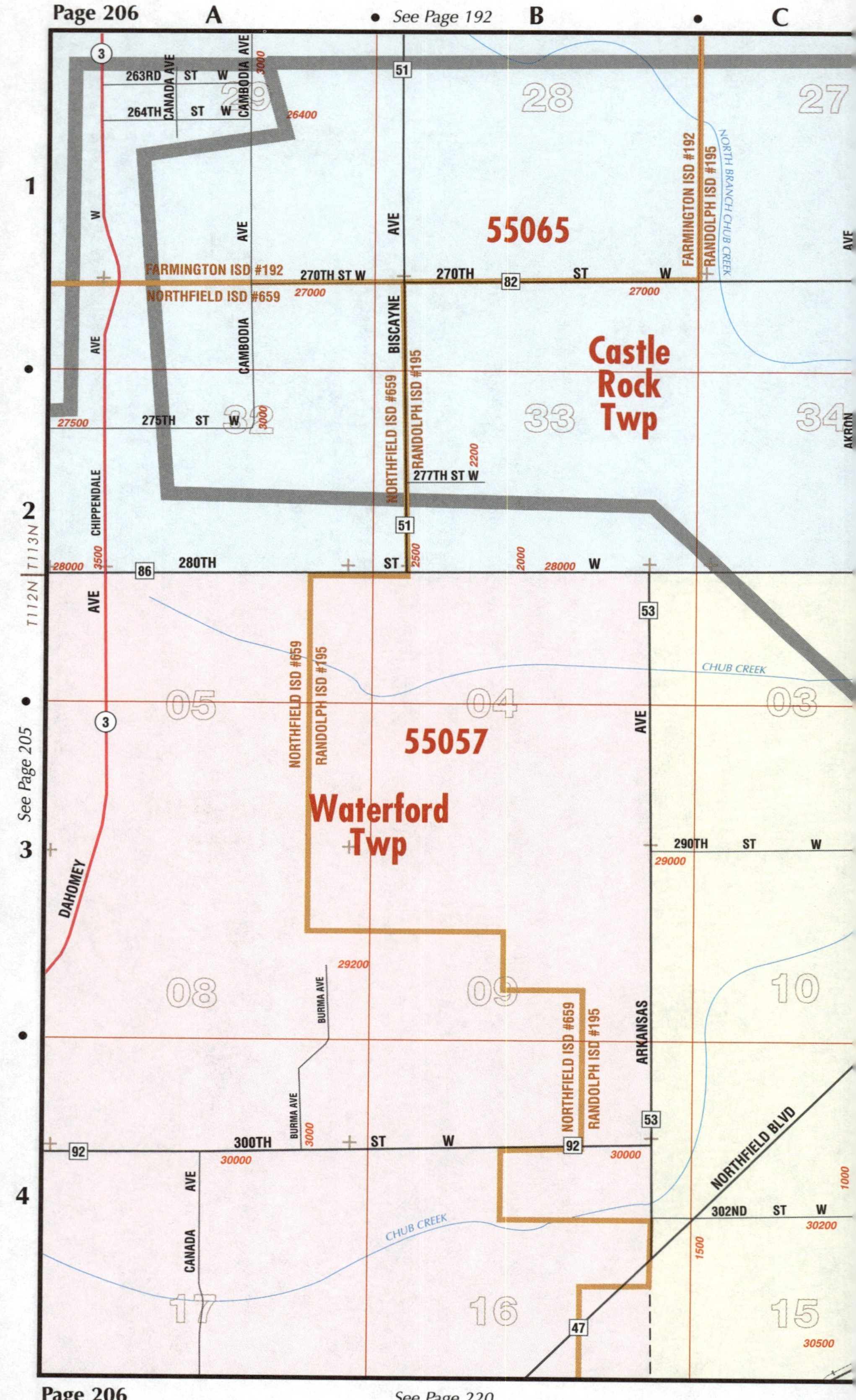

See Page 192

A   B   C

263RD   ST   W
264TH   ST   W
CANADA AVE
CAMBODIA AVE

26400

29

28

27

51

1

55065

FARMINGTON ISD #192
RANDOLPH ISD #195
NORTH BRANCH CHUB CREEK

AVE

AVE

AVE

W

FARMINGTON ISD #192   270TH ST W   270TH   ST   W

NORTHFIELD ISD #659   27000   82   27000

AVE

CAMBODIA

BISCAYNE

NORTHFIELD ISD #659
RANDOLPH ISD #195

Castle Rock Twp

AKRON

27500   275TH   ST   32   3000   33   34

CHIPPENDALE

2200

277TH ST W

2

51

3500   86   280TH   2500   2000   W

28000   ST   28000

See Page 205

T112N | T113N

AVE

53

NORTHFIELD ISD #659
RANDOLPH ISD #195

CHUB CREEK

05   04   03

AVE

3

55057

3   DAHOMEY

Waterford Twp

290TH   ST   W

29000

29200

BURMA AVE

08   09   10

NORTHFIELD ISD #659
RANDOLPH ISD #195

ARKANSAS

53

BURMA AVE   3000

92   300TH   ST   W   92

30000   30000

NORTHFIELD BLVD

4

CANADA AVE

CHUB CREEK

302ND   ST   W   30200

1000

1500

17   16   47   15   30500

See Page 220

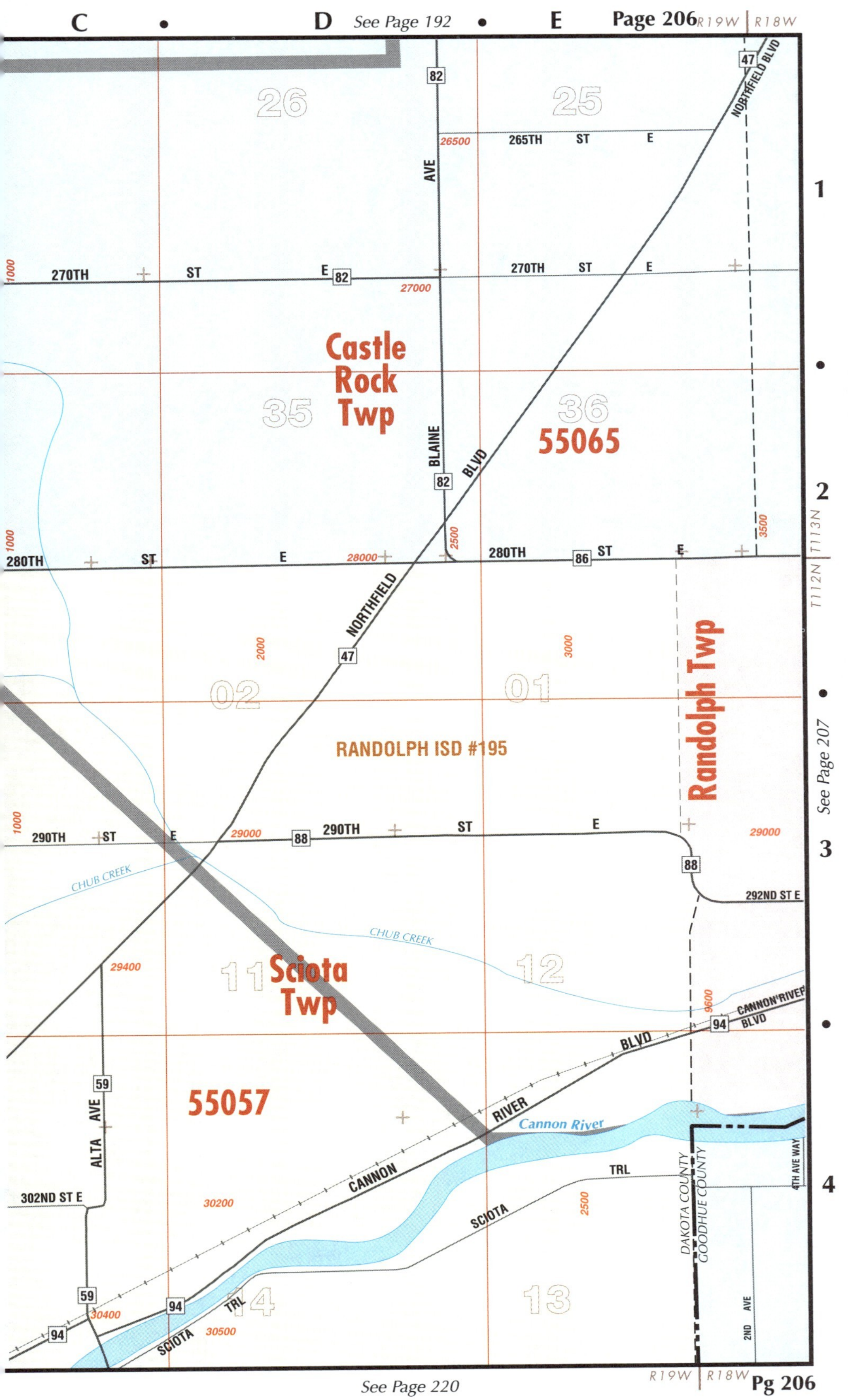

NORTHFIELD BLVD

82

26

25

47

26500   265TH   ST   E

1

AVE

1000   270TH   ST   E 82   270TH   ST   E

27000

Castle Rock Twp

35   36   **55065**

BLAINE   BLVD

82

2500   **2**

1000   280TH   ST   E   28000   280TH   ST 86   E   3500

NORTHFIELD

2000   02   47   01   3000

Randolph Twp

RANDOLPH ISD #195

T112N | T113N

See Page 207

1000   290TH   ST   E   29000 88   290TH   ST   E   29000   **3**

CHUB CREEK   88

292ND ST E

CHUB CREEK

29400   11   **Sciota Twp**   12   9000

CANNON RIVER

94   BLVD   •

55057

ALTA   AVE   59

RIVER   Cannon River   DAKOTA COUNTY | GOODHUE COUNTY   4TH AVE WAY   **4**

302ND ST E   CANNON   TRL

30200   SCIOTA   2500

59   94   TRL   14   13   2ND   AVE

94   30400   SCIOTA   30500

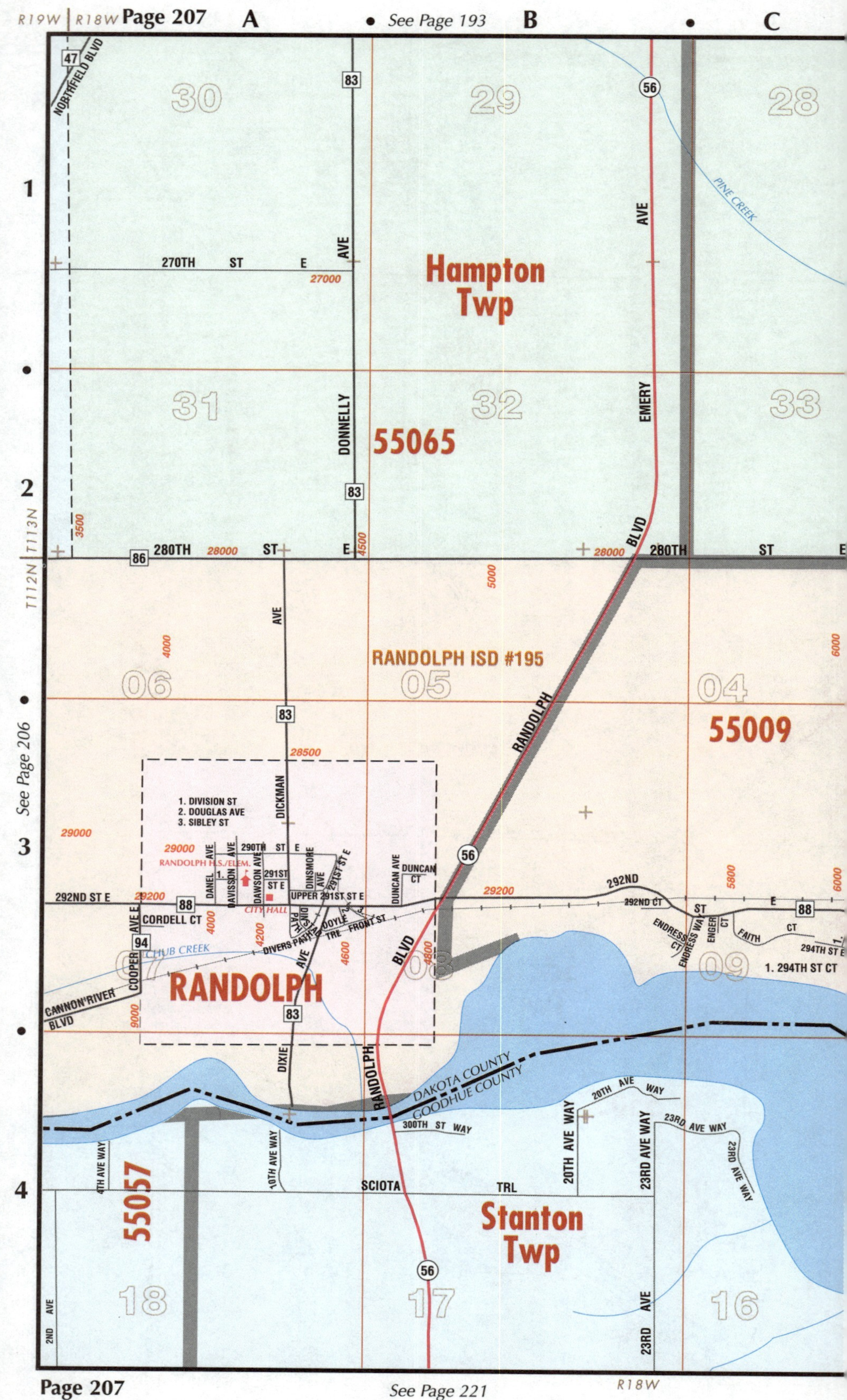

30

83

29

56

28

1

270TH ST E

27000

AVE

Hampton Twp

PINE CREEK

31

DONNELLY

32

EMERY

AVE

33

2

3500

55065

83

T112N T113N

86 280TH 28000 ST E 4500

5000

BLVD

280TH ST E

28000

RANDOLPH ISD #195

AVE

4000

06

05

RANDOLPH

6000

04

See Page 206

29000

83

28500

DICKMAN

1. DIVISION ST
2. DOUGLAS ST
3. SIBLEY ST

55009

3

29000
RANDOLPH H.S./ELEM.

DANEL AVE
DAVISSON AVE

290TH ST E
291ST ST E
UPPER 291ST ST E

DINSMORE AVE
291ST ST E

DUNCAN AVE
DUNCAN CT

56

292ND

5800

6000

ST E

88

292ND ST E

29200

88

DAWSON AVE

CITY HALL

291ST ST E

29200

292ND CT

ENDRESS WAY
ENDRESS CT

ENGER CT
FAITH CT

294TH ST E

94

Cordell Ct

AVE E

4000

DIVERS PATH

AVE

DOYLE PATH

TRL FRONT ST

4600

BLVD

4800

1. 294TH ST CT

09

07

CHUB CREEK

RANDOLPH

COOPER AVE

9000

83

DIXIE

RANDOLPH

DAKOTA COUNTY
GOODHUE COUNTY

CANNON RIVER BLVD

4TH AVE WAY

10TH AVE WAY

300TH ST WAY

20TH AVE WAY

20TH AVE WAY

23RD AVE WAY

23RD AVE WAY

23RD AVE WAY

4

55057

SCIOTA TRL

Stanton Twp

2ND AVE

18

56

17

23RD AVE

16

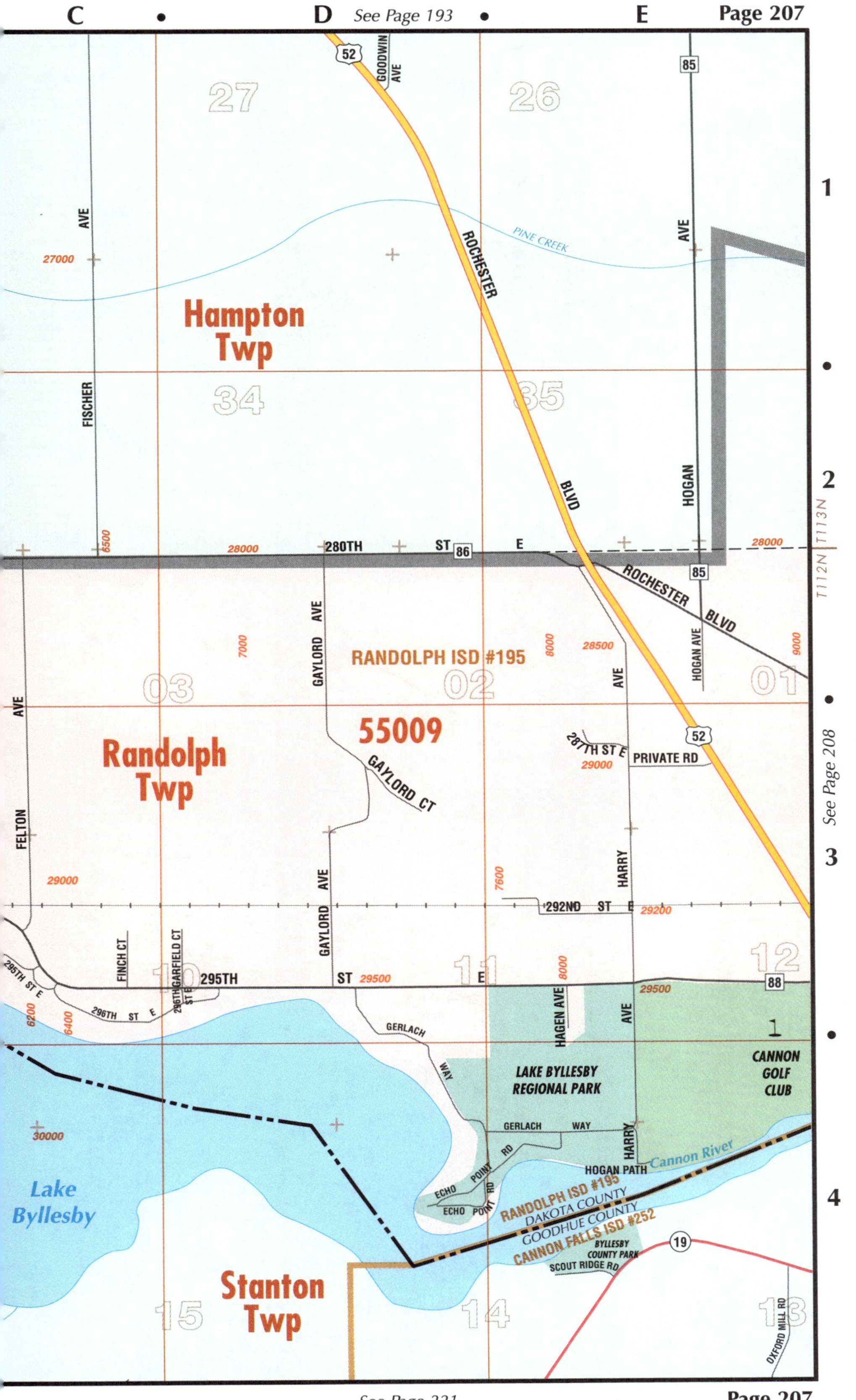

27

26

1

AVE

27000

GOODWIN AVE

ROCHESTER

85

AVE

HOGAN

Hampton Twp

FISCHER

34

35

BLVD

HOGAN

2

6500

28000

280TH **ST** 86 **E**

ROCHESTER BLVD

85

28000

T112N | T113N

7000

GAYLORD AVE

RANDOLPH ISD #195

8000

28500

AVE

9000

HOGAN AVE

03

02

01

AVE

See Page 208

Randolph Twp

55009

GAYLORD CT

287TH ST E

52

29000 **PRIVATE RD**

FELTON

29000

GAYLORD AVE

7600

Harry

3

292ND ST E 29200

295TH ST E

FINCH CT

GARFIELD CT

296TH ST E

10

295TH ST 29500

11

8000 HAGEN AVE

AVE 29500

12

88

296TH ST E

6200

6400

296TH ST E

GERLACH WAY

LAKE BYLLESBY REGIONAL PARK

Harry

1

CANNON GOLF CLUB

30000

GERLACH WAY

HOGAN PATH

Cannon River

ECHO POINT RD

Harry

4

Lake Byllesby

ECHO POINT RD

RANDOLPH ISD #195

DAKOTA COUNTY

GOODHUE COUNTY

CANNON FALLS ISD #252

BYLLESBY COUNTY PARK

SCOUT RIDGE RD.

19

Stanton Twp

15

14

OXFORD MILL RD

13

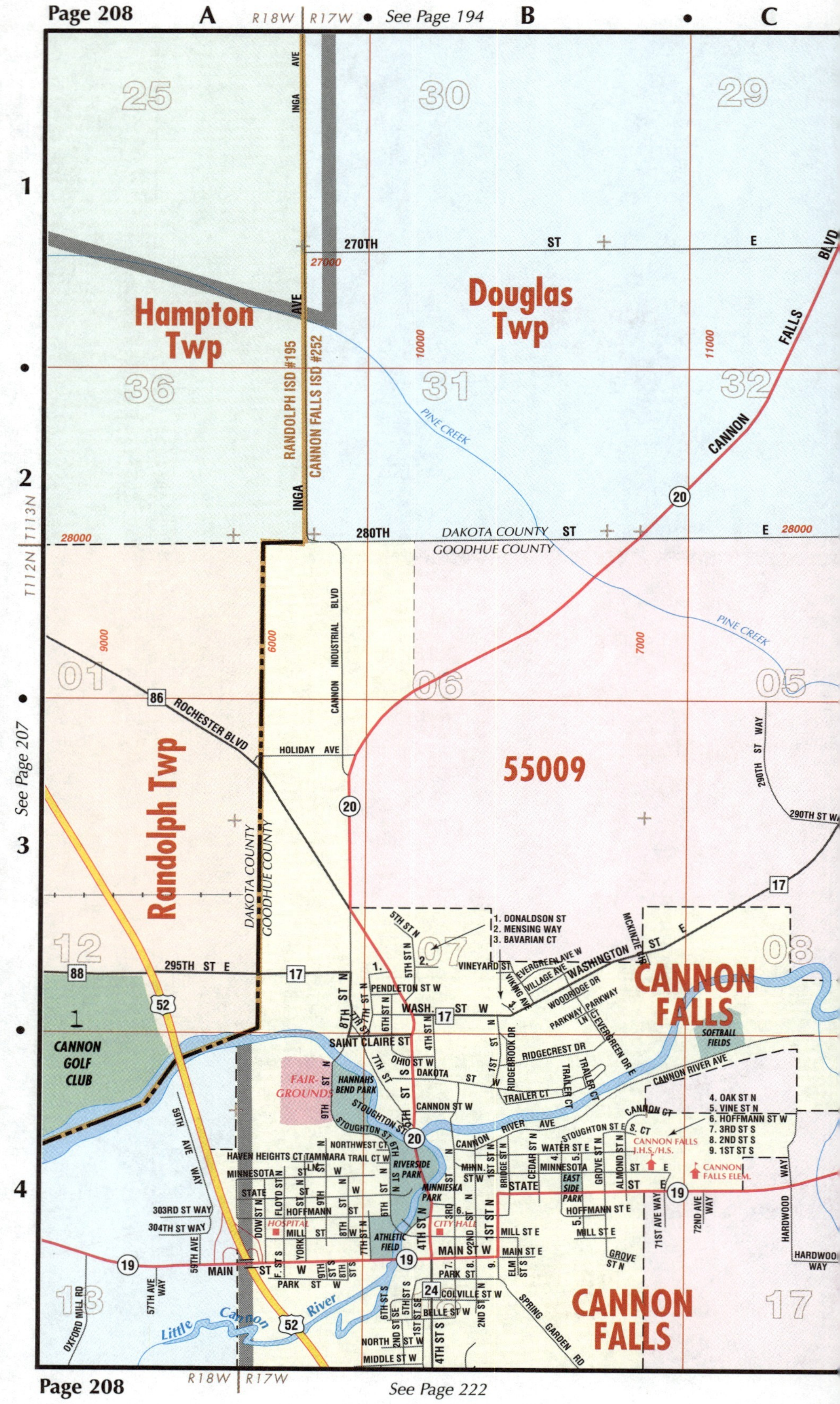

A R18W | R17W • *See Page 194* B • C

25

INGA AVE

30

29

R18W | R17W

1

270TH   ST   E
27000

Hampton Twp

AVE

RANDOLPH ISD #195

CANNON FALLS ISD #252

INGA

10000

Douglas Twp

PINE CREEK

31

11000

FALLS

CANNON

BLVD

36

32

2

280TH   DAKOTA COUNTY   ST   E   28000
28000   GOODHUE COUNTY

20

T112N | T113N

9000

6000

CANNON INDUSTRIAL BLVD

PINE CREEK

7000

01

86 ROCHESTER BLVD

06

05

HOLIDAY   AVE

DAKOTA COUNTY
GOODHUE COUNTY

20

55009

290TH   ST   WAY

290TH ST WAY

3

17

12

5TH ST N

1. Donaldson St
2. Mensing Way
3. Bavarian Ct

MCKINZIE TR

08

88 295TH ST E

VINEYARD ST

EVERGREEN AVE W

VILLAGE AVE

VINING AVE

WASHINGTON

CANNON FALLS

52

17

8TH ST N

7TH ST N

6TH ST N

PENDLETON ST W

WASH.   17   ST   N

WOODBRIDGE DR

PARKWAY

PARKWAY LN

EVERGREEN DR

RIDGEBROOK DR

SOFTBALL FIELDS

1

CANNON GOLF CLUB

SAINT CLAIRE ST

4TH ST N

OHIO ST N

1ST ST N

RIDGECREST DR

TRAILER CT

CANNON RIVER AVE

FAIR-GROUNDS

HANNAHS BEND PARK

9TH ST

DAKOTA

TRAILER CT

4. OAK ST N
5. VINE ST N
6. HOFFMANN ST W
7. 3RD ST S
8. 2ND ST S
9. 1ST ST S

STOUGHTON ST

CANNON ST W

RIVER   AVE

CANNON CT

CANNON FALLS J.H.S./H.S.

4

NORTHWEST CT

TAMNARA TRAIL CT W

20

STOUGHTON ST E

WATER ST E

CANNON FALLS ELEM.

19

95TH AVE WAY

HAVEN HEIGHTS CT

LN

RIVERSIDE PARK

CANNON

BRIDGE ST N

CEDAR ST N

MINNESOTA

GROVE ST N

ALMOND ST N

MINNESOTA

STATE

MINNIESKA PARK

MHN.

STATE

EAST SIDE PARK

71ST AVE WAY

72ND AVE WAY

HARDWOOD WAY

HOFFMANN   ST

8TH ST

7TH ST

303RD ST WAY

DOW ST N

FLOYD ST N

HOFFMANN   ST

HOFFMANN ST E

MILL ST E

304TH ST AVE

HOSPITAL

MILL   ST

3RD

4TH ST N

CITY HALL

1ST ST

MILL ST E

GROVE ST S

HARDWOOD WAY

19

57TH AVE WAY

50TH ST W

MAIN   ST

F. ST S

YORK ST

9TH ST

8TH ST

7TH ST

ATHLETIC FIELD

4TH ST S

3RD

MAIN ST W

MAIN ST E

ELM ST S

SPRING GARDEN RD

CANNON FALLS

13

OXFORD MILL RD

PARK ST

52

Little Cannon River

6TH ST S

3RD ST S

2ND ST S

24 COLVILLE ST

BELLE ST W

NORTH ST W

MIDDLE ST W

1ST ST S

4TH ST S

17

Randolph Twp

See Page 194

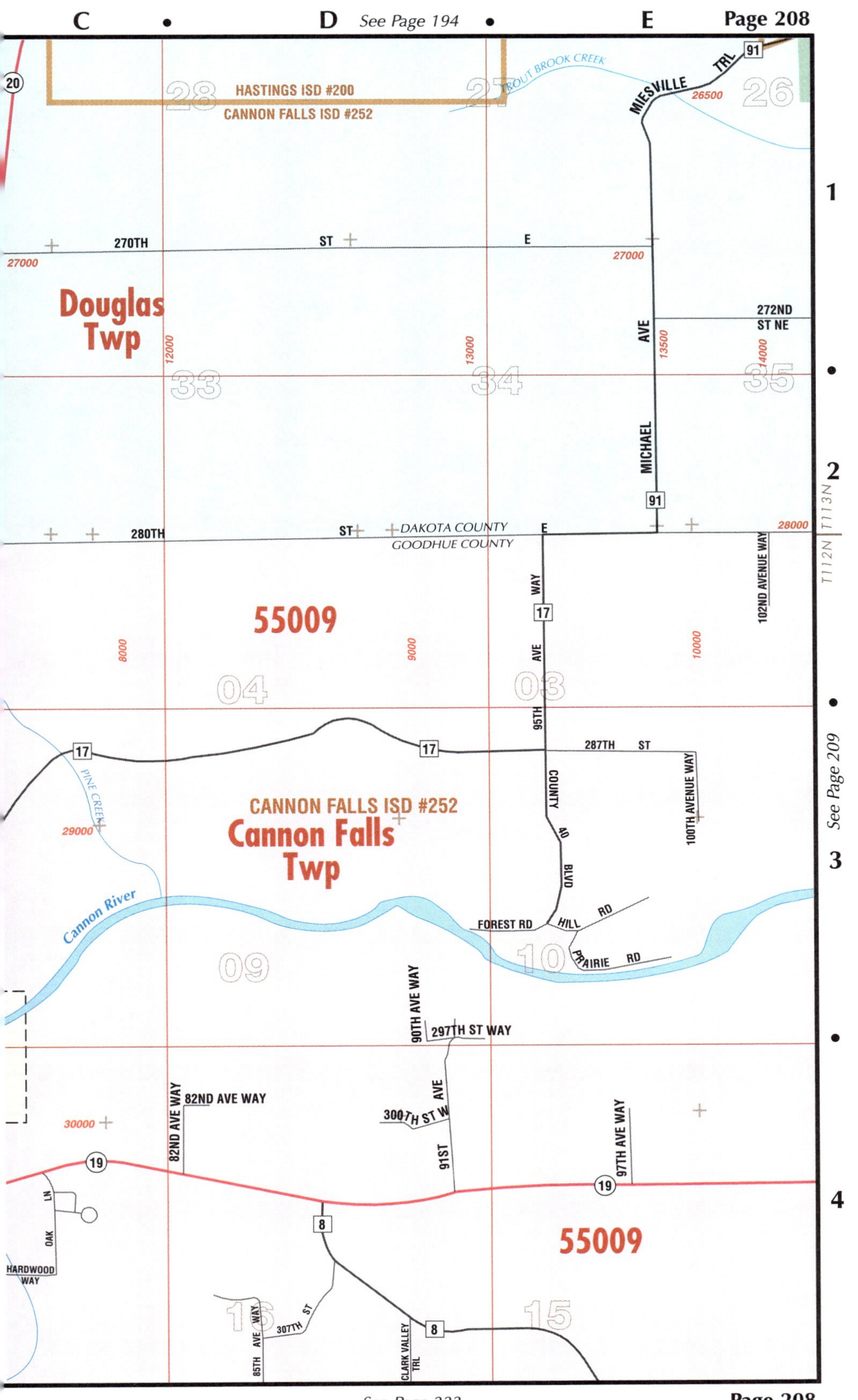

See Page 209
See Page 222

A   See Page 195   •   R17W | R16W   B   •   C

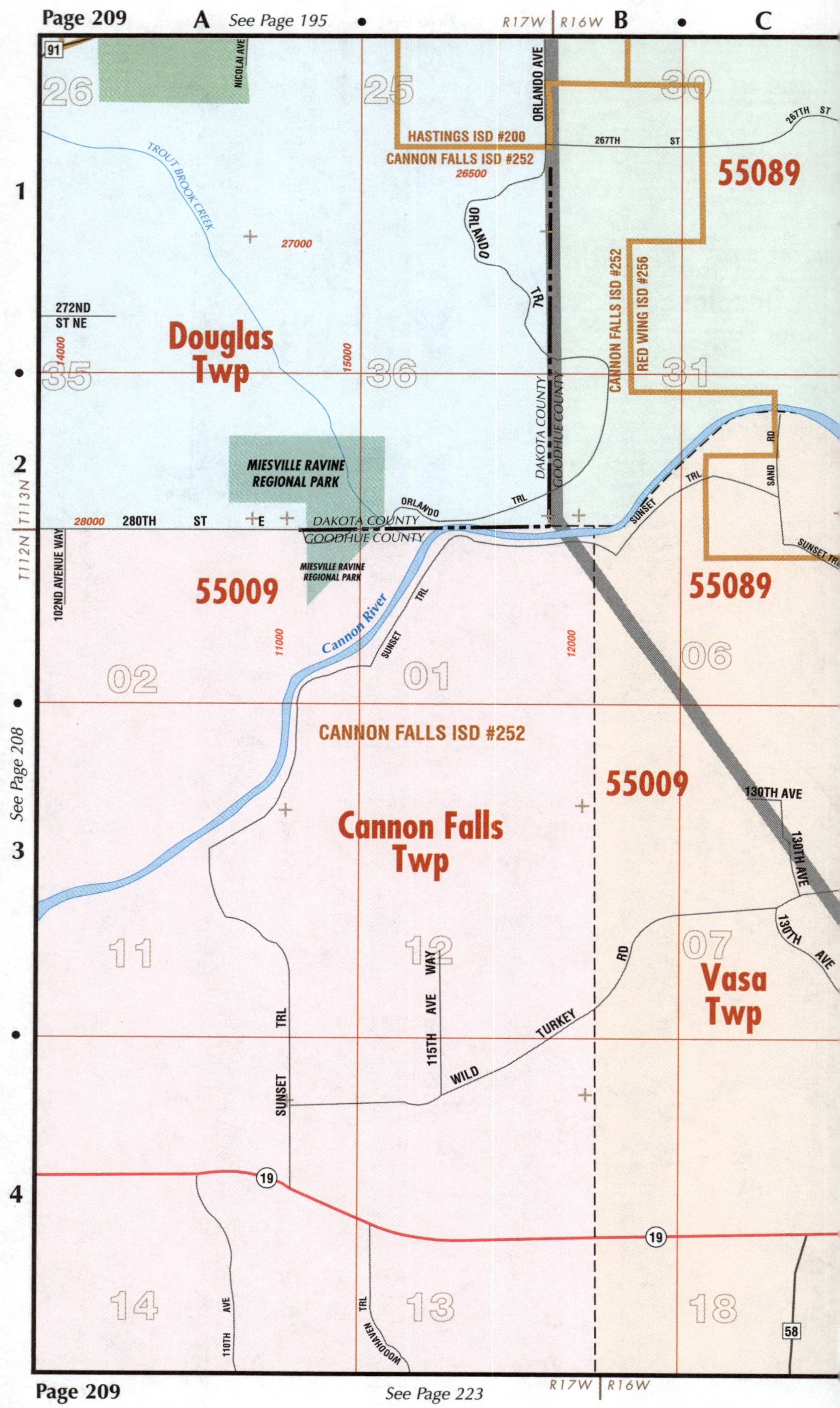

91

26

NICOLAI AVE

25

ORLANDO AVE

30

267TH ST

55089

HASTINGS ISD #200
CANNON FALLS ISD #252
26500

1

27000

ORLANDO

TROUT BROOK CREEK

272ND
ST NE

24000

**Douglas
Twp**

15000

35

36

31

ORLANDO TRL

CANNON FALLS ISD #252

RED WING ISD #256

SAND RD

2

**MIESVILLE RAVINE
REGIONAL PARK**

28000   280TH   ST   E

ORLANDO   TRL

DAKOTA COUNTY

GOODHUE COUNTY

SUNSET TRL

SAND

SUNSET TRL

DAKOTA COUNTY
GOODHUE COUNTY

55009

102ND AVENUE WAY

**MIESVILLE RAVINE
REGIONAL PARK**

Cannon River

SUNSET TRL

11000

12000

55089

02

01

06

CANNON FALLS ISD #252

See Page 208

130TH AVE

55009

3

**Cannon Falls
Twp**

130TH AVE

11

12

07

**Vasa
Twp**

115TH AVE WAY

SUNSET TRL

TURKEY

RD

WILD

130TH AVE

19

4

19

14

110TH AVE

13

WOODHAVEN TRL

18

58

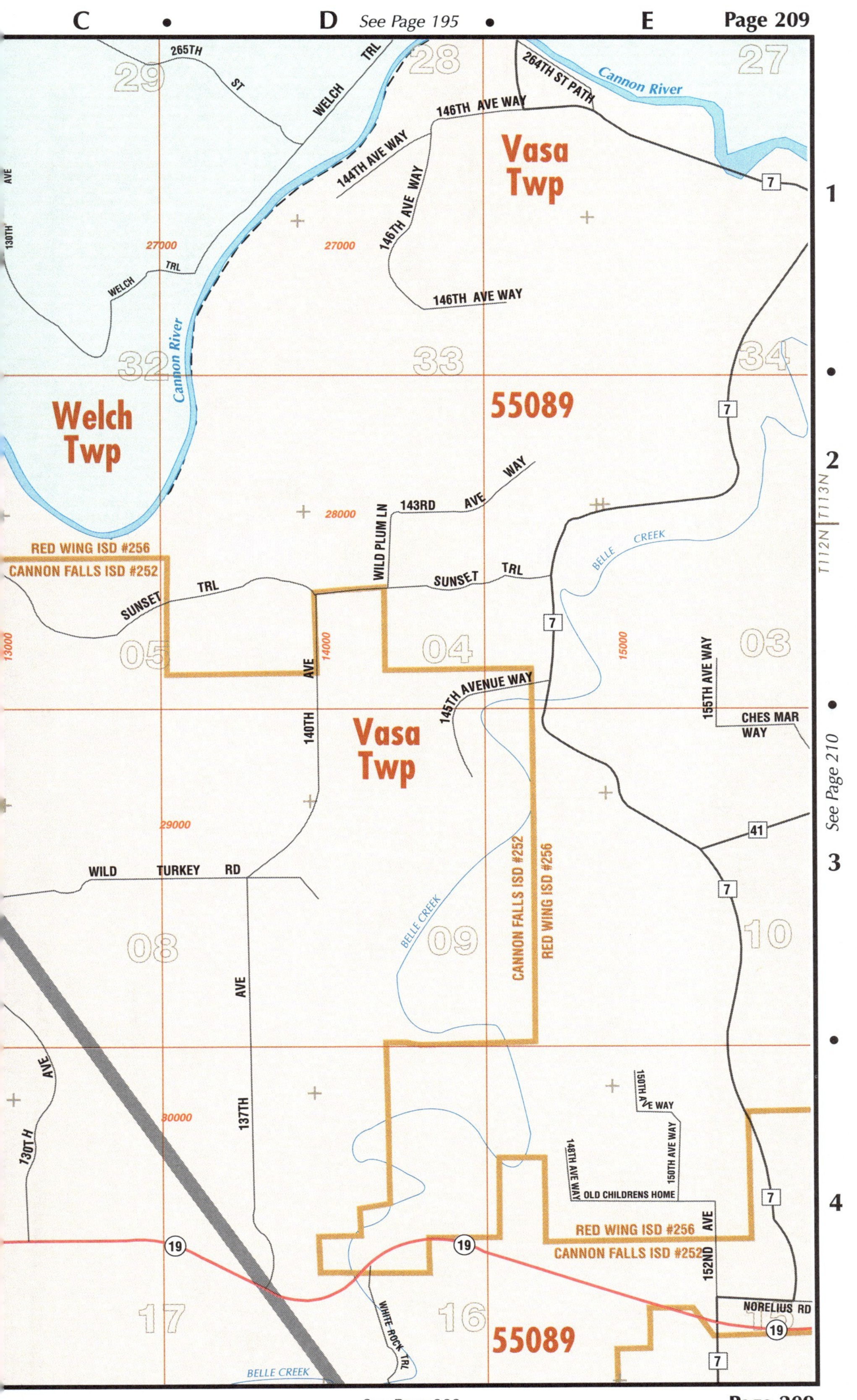

265TH ST

WELCH TRL

28

264TH ST PATH

Cannon River

29

130TH AVE

27

7

1

146TH AVE WAY

144TH AVE WAY

146TH AVE WAY

Vasa Twp

27000

27000

146TH AVE WAY

WELCH TRL

Cannon River

32

33

55089

34

7

2

T112N | T113N

Welch Twp

28000

143RD AVE WAY

WILD PLUM LN

BELLE CREEK

SUNSET TRL

RED WING ISD #256

CANNON FALLS ISD #252

SUNSET TRL

SUNSET TRL

7

13000

05

140TH AVE

14000

04

15000

155TH AVE WAY

03

145TH AVENUE WAY

Vasa Twp

CHES MAR WAY

See Page 210

41

29000

WILD TURKEY RD

BELLE CREEK

CANNON FALLS ISD #252

RED WING ISD #256

7

3

08

AVE

09

10

30000

130TH AVE

13TH AVE

150TH AVE WAY

150TH AVE WAY

148TH AVE WAY

OLD CHILDRENS HOME

7

4

19

19

RED WING ISD #256

152ND AVE

CANNON FALLS ISD #252

7

NORELIUS RD

19

17

WHITE ROCK TRL

16

55089

BELLE CREEK

7

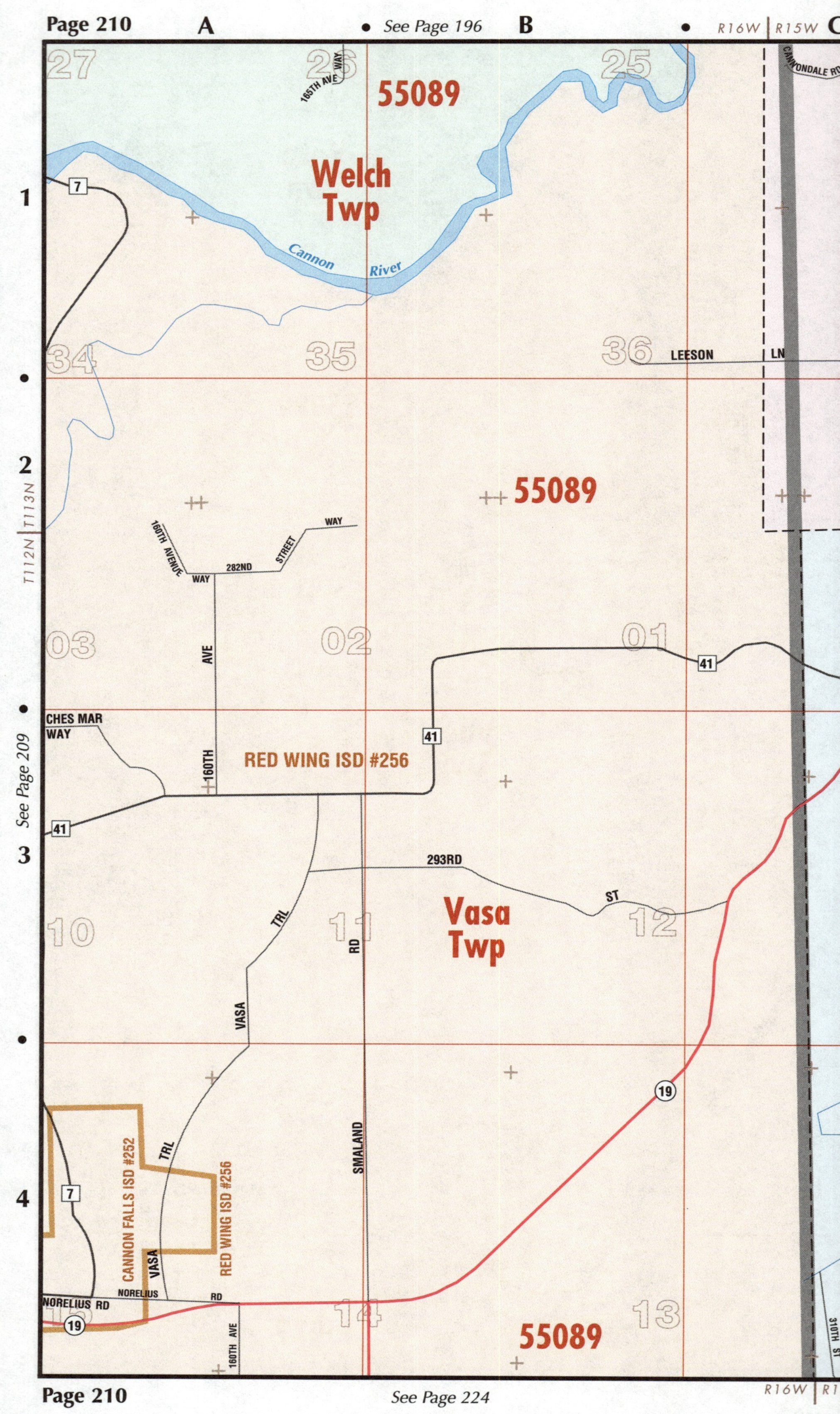

55089

Welch Twp

Cannon River

LEESON LN

55089

RED WING ISD #256

CHES MAR WAY

165TH AVE WAY

160TH AVENUE

282ND STREET WAY

160TH

293RD ST

Vasa Twp

VASA TRL

CANNON FALLS ISD #252

RED WING ISD #256

SMALAND RD

NORELIUS RD

160TH AVE

55089

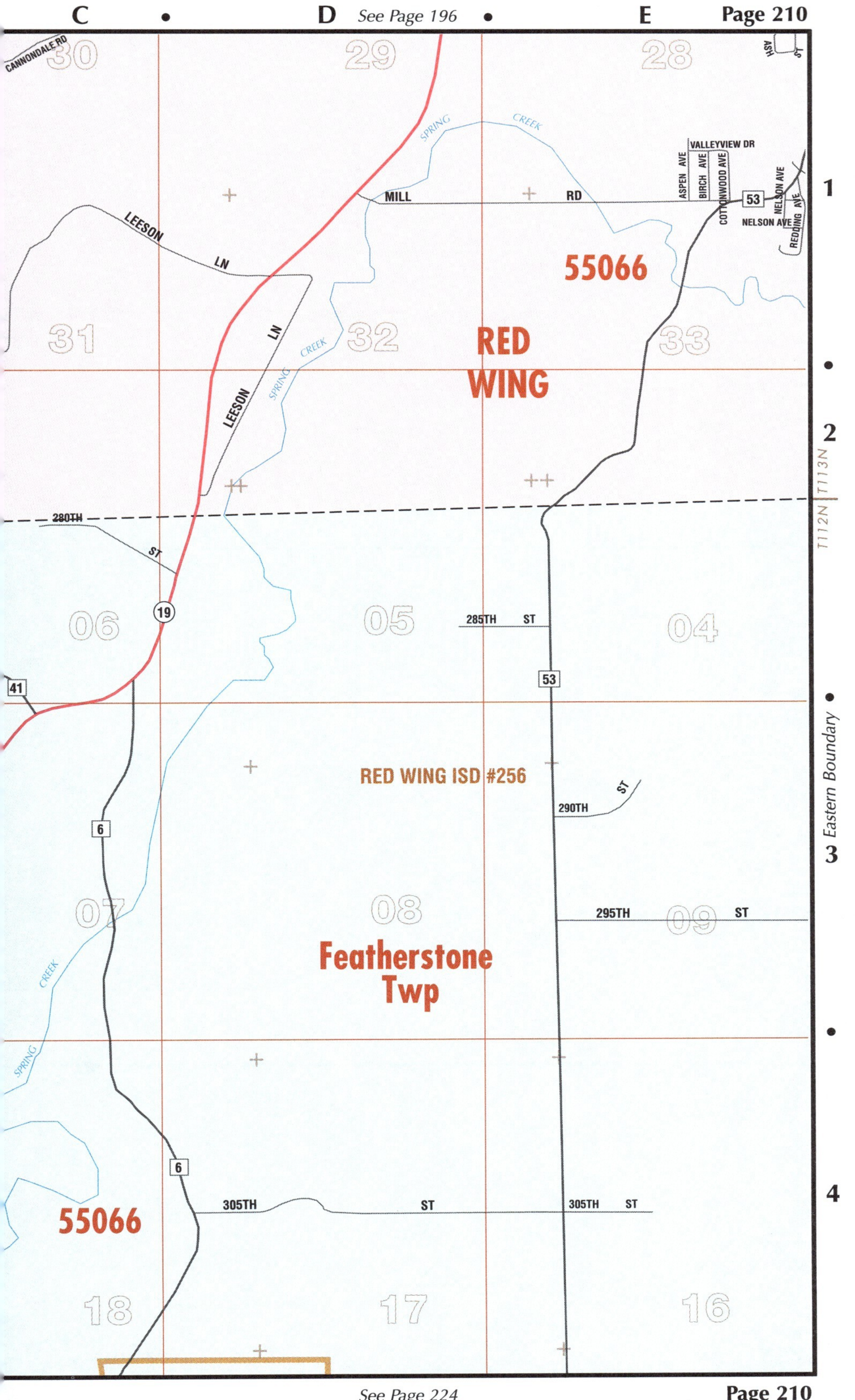

CANNONDALE RD

30

29

28

HSV

LEESON LN

31

SPRING CREEK

LEESON LN

32

SPRING CREEK

33

MILL RD

VALLEYVIEW DR
ASPEN AVE
BIRCH AVE
COTTONWOOD AVE
53
NELSON AVE
NELSON AVE
REDDING AVE

1

55066

RED WING

2

T112N | T113N

280TH ST

06

19

05

285TH ST

04

41

53

3

Eastern Boundary

6

RED WING ISD #256

290TH ST

07

08

Featherstone Twp

295TH 09 ST

SPRING CREEK

6

305TH ST

305TH ST

4

55066

18

17

16

A • *See Page 197* B • C

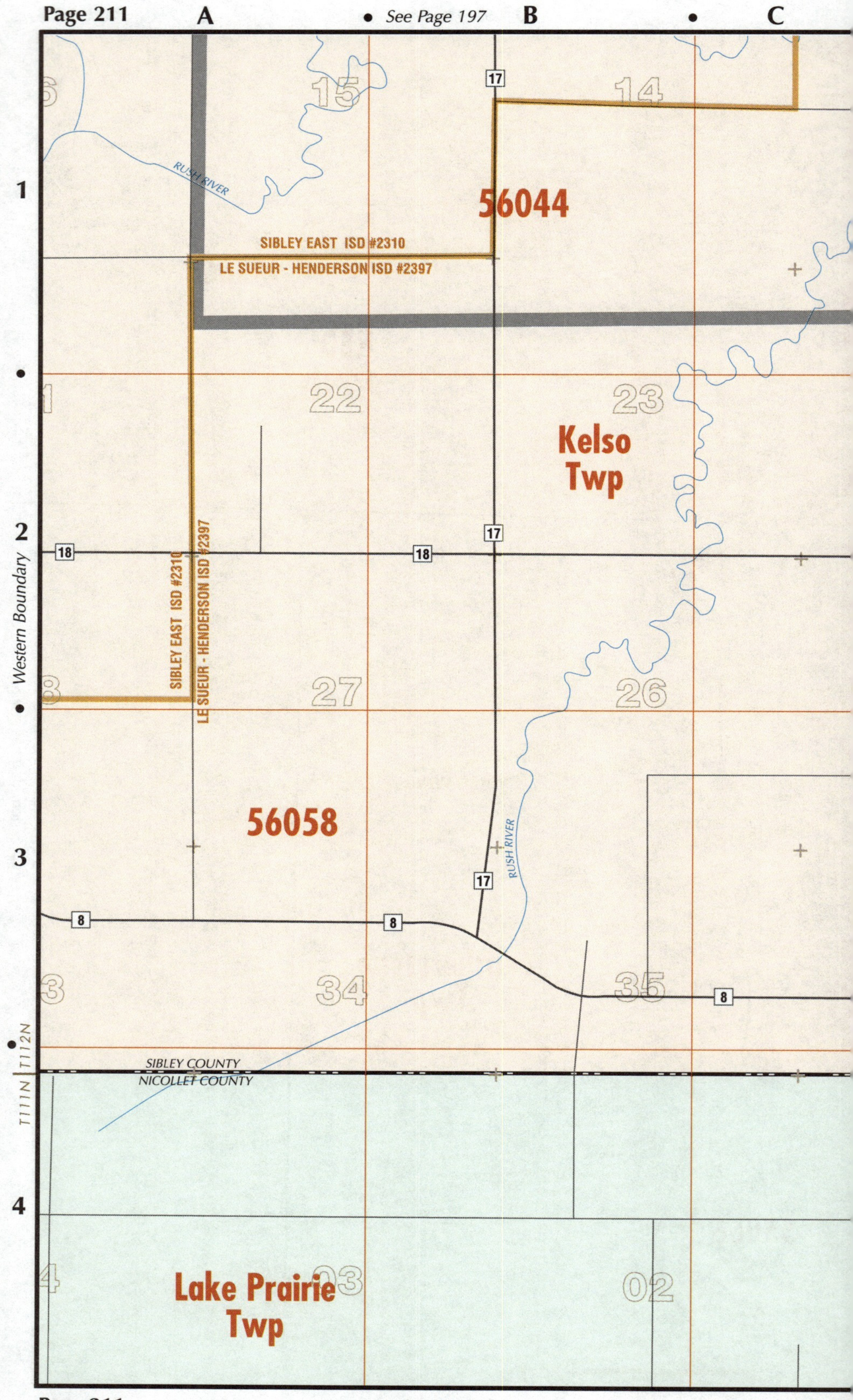

6

15

RUSH RIVER

56044

1

SIBLEY EAST ISD #2310
LE SUEUR - HENDERSON ISD #2397

17

14

21

22

23

**Kelso
Twp**

18

18

17

2

Western Boundary

28

SIBLEY EAST ISD #2310

LE SUEUR - HENDERSON ISD #2397

27

26

56058

RUSH RIVER

3

8

8

17

33

34

35

8

SIBLEY COUNTY
NICOLLET COUNTY

T111N T112N

4

04

03

02

**Lake Prairie
Twp**

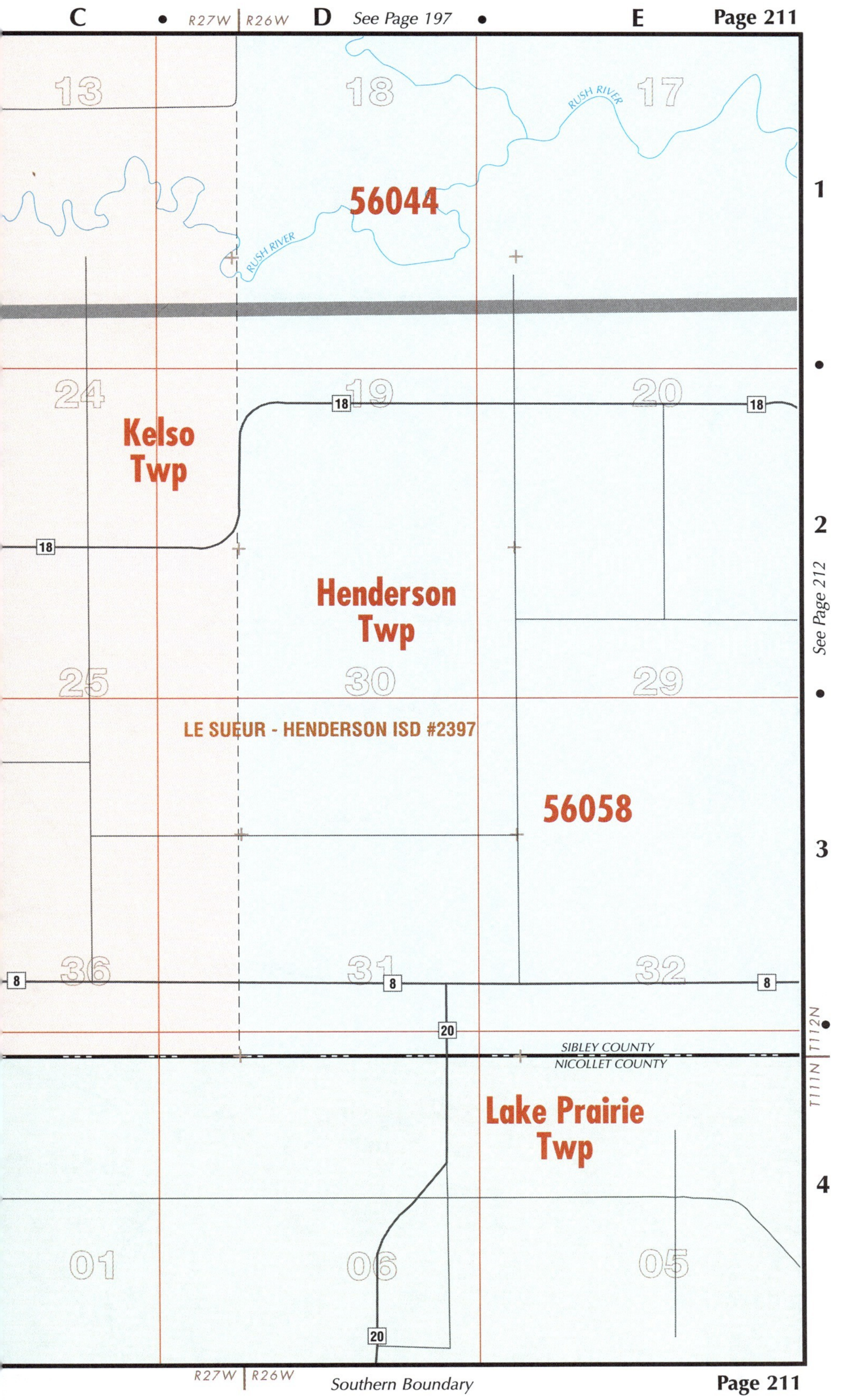

13

18

17

RUSH RIVER

56044

RUSH RIVER

1

24

Kelso Twp

19

18

20

18

2

See Page 212

18

Henderson Twp

25

30

29

LE SUEUR - HENDERSON ISD #2397

56058

3

36

8

31

8

32

8

20

SIBLEY COUNTY
NICOLLET COUNTY

T111N | T112N

Lake Prairie Twp

4

01

06

05

20

A   ● *See Page 198*   B   ●   C

16

15

RUSH RIVER   **56044**

PARK

Henderson Twp

18

21

22

18

2

18

18

28

27

LE SUEUR - HENDERSON ISD #2397

56058

3

18

169

8

33

34   8

93

SIBLEY COUNTY
NICOLLET COUNTY

Minnesota River

Lake Prairie Twp

LE SUEUR

LE SUEUR COUNTY

Ottawa Twp

4

04   169   03

MAIN ST

36

See Page 211

T111N | T112N

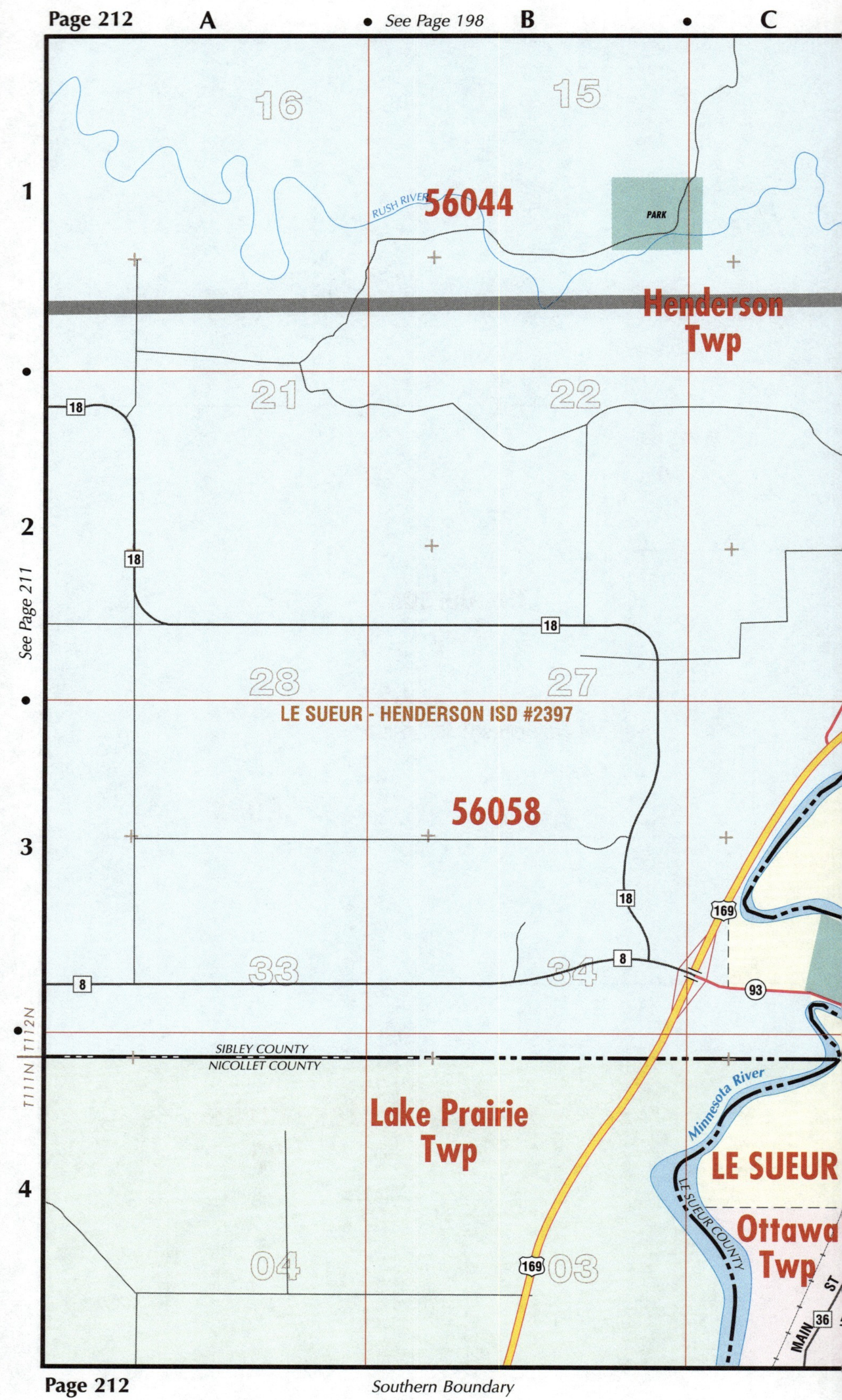

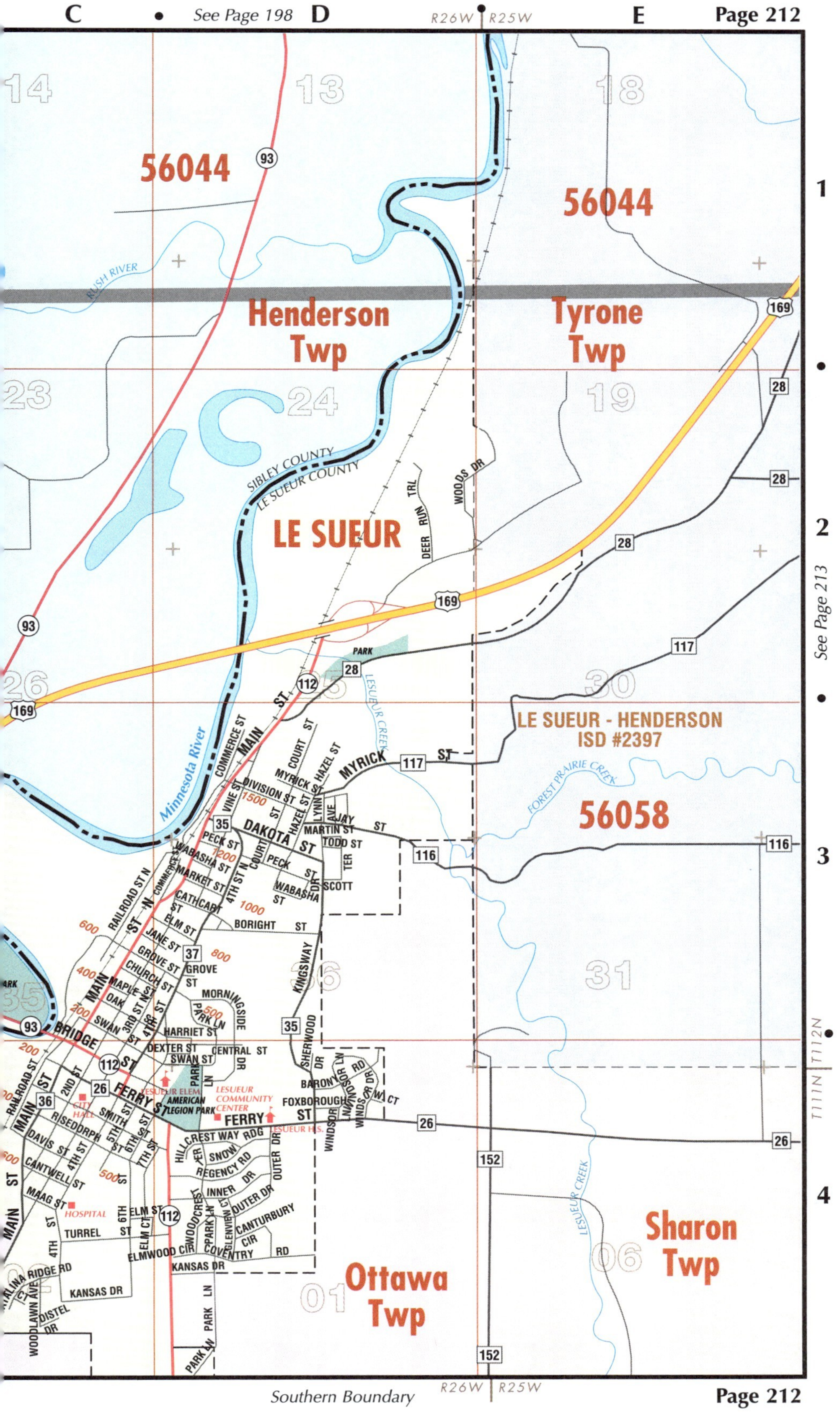
C
See Page 198
D
R26W R25W
E
56044
56044
Henderson Twp
Tyrone Twp
LE SUEUR
SIBLEY COUNTY
LE SUEUR COUNTY
Minnesota River
RUSH RIVER
LE SUEUR - HENDERSON ISD #2397
56058
FOREST PRAIRIE CREEK
LESUEUR CREEK
Ottawa Twp
Sharon Twp
See Page 213
T112N
T111N
Southern Boundary
R26W R25W

• *See Page 199*

A
B
C

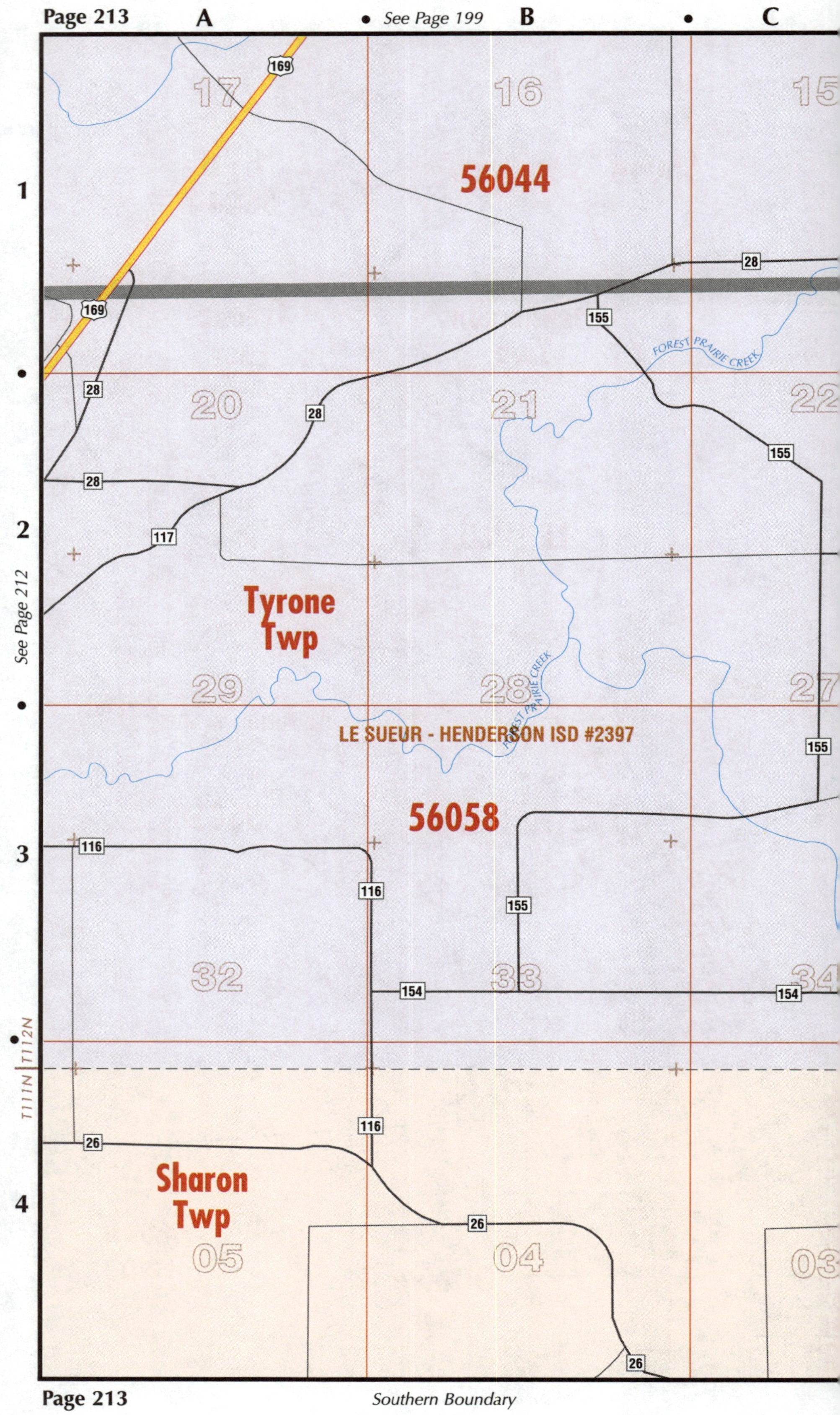

17

169

16

56044

15

28

169

155

FOREST PRAIRIE CREEK

1

28

20

28

21

22

155

28

2

117

155

Tyrone Twp

29

28

FOREST PRAIRIE CREEK

27

LE SUEUR - HENDERSON ISD #2397

155

56058

116

3

116

155

32

33

34

154

154

T111N | T112N

116

26

Sharon Twp

4

26

05

04

03

26

See Page 212

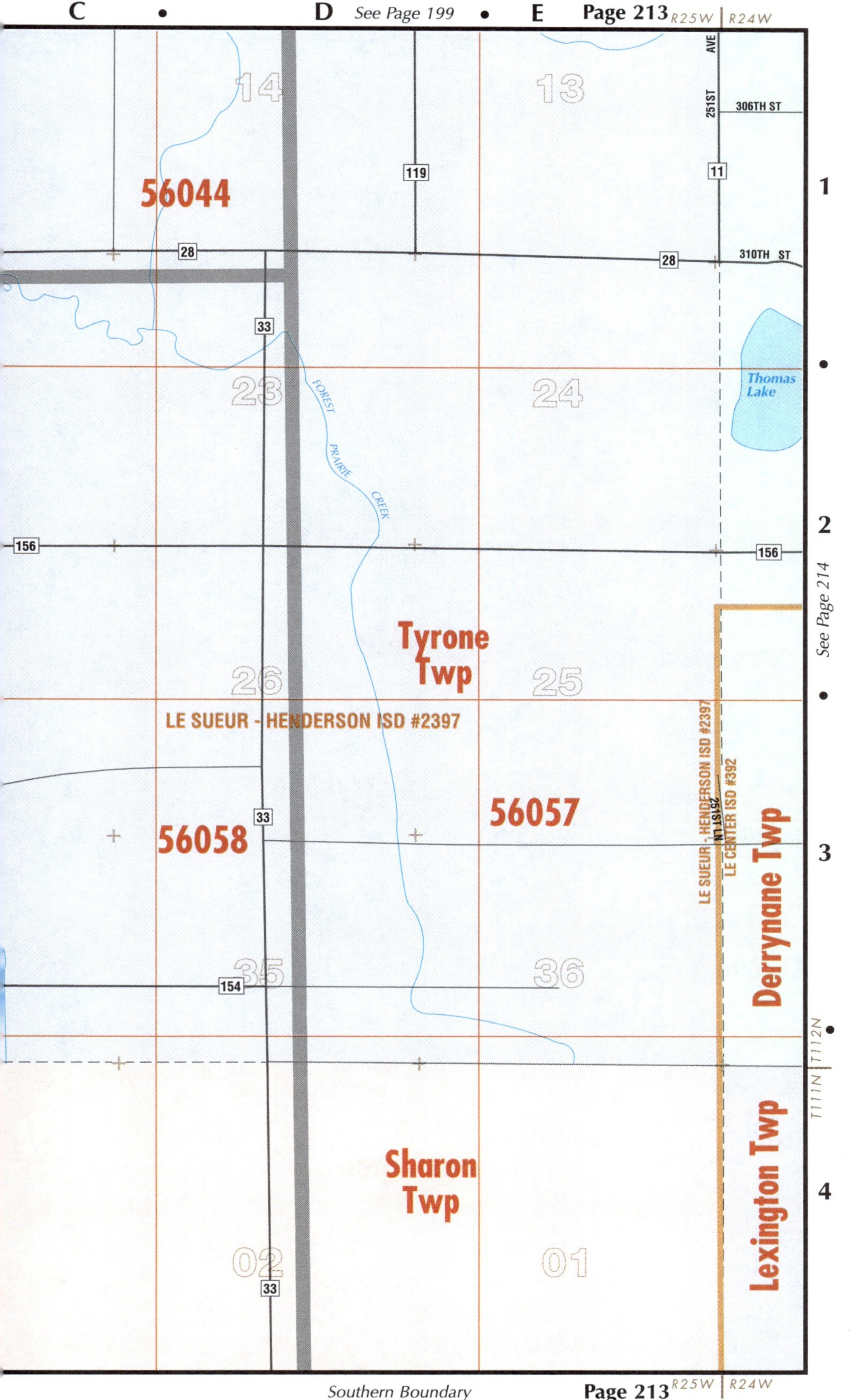

14

56044

13

306TH ST

251ST AVE

119

11

1

28

28

310TH ST

33

Thomas Lake

23

FOREST PRAIRIE CREEK

24

156

156

2

See Page 214

Tyrone Twp

26

25

LE SUEUR - HENDERSON ISD #2397

56058

33

56057

LE SUEUR - HENDERSON ISD #2397

LE CENTER ISD #392

251ST N

Derrynane Twp

3

35

154

36

T111N | T112N

Lexington Twp

Sharon Twp

4

02

33

01

A ● *See Page 200* B ● C

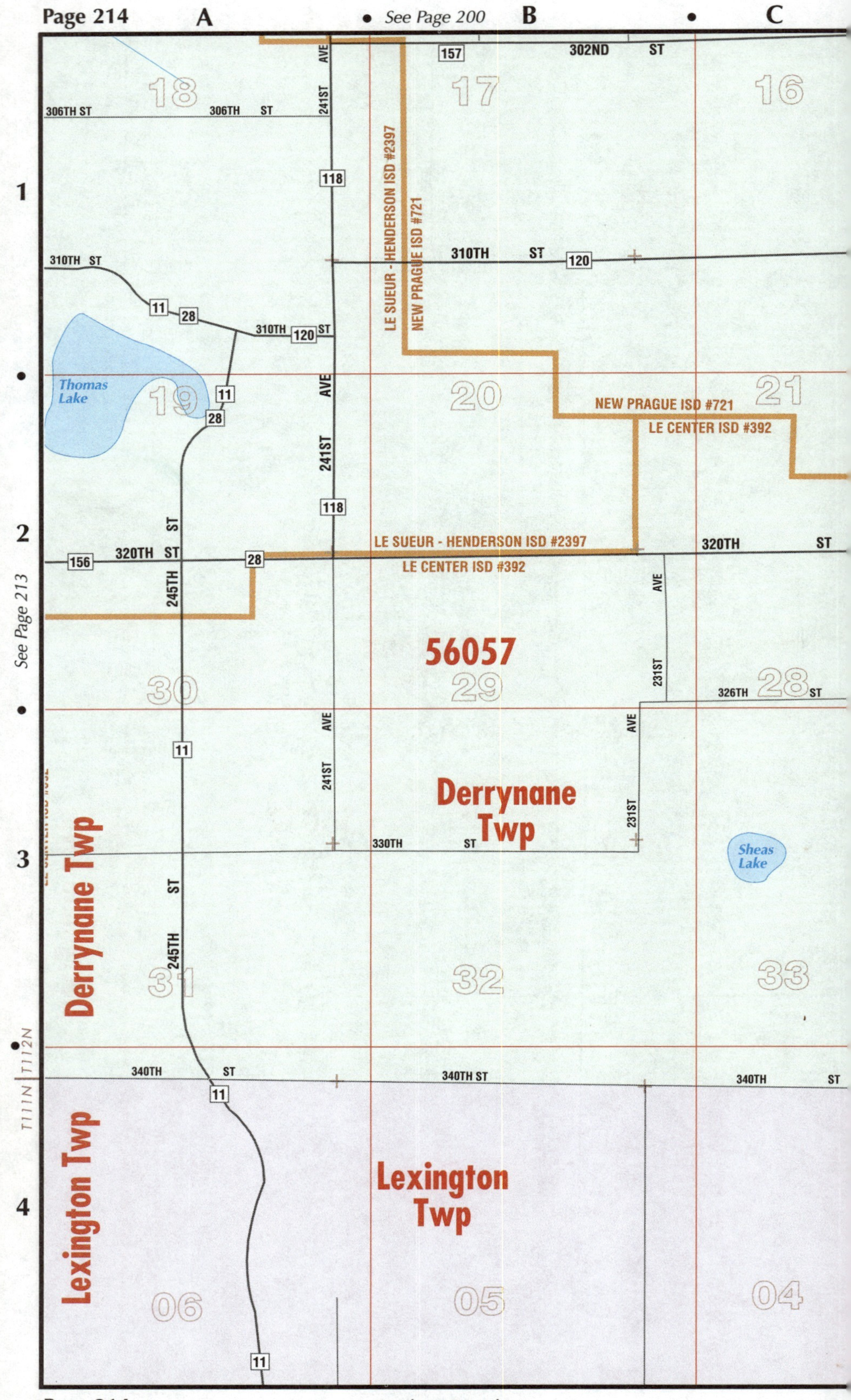

18

306TH ST   306TH   ST

241ST   AVE

157

302ND   ST

17

16

118

1

LE SUEUR - HENDERSON ISD #2397

NEW PRAGUE ISD #721

310TH   ST   120

120

310TH ST

11   28

310TH   120   ST

Thomas Lake

19

11

28

241ST   AVE

20

NEW PRAGUE ISD #721

LE CENTER ISD #392

21

118

2

156   320TH ST   28

245TH   ST

LE SUEUR - HENDERSON ISD #2397

LE CENTER ISD #392

320TH   ST

231ST   AVE

56057

30

11

29

241ST   AVE

231ST   AVE

326TH   ST   28

3

Derrynane Twp

245TH   ST

330TH   ST

231ST

Sheas Lake

See Page 213

Derrynane Twp

31

32

33

T111N | T112N

340TH   ST

11

340TH ST

340TH   ST

Lexington Twp

4

Lexington Twp

06

05

04

11

157

221ST AVE

15

121

306TH 157 ST

157

211TH AVE

14

AVE

201ST

31

310TH ST

1

310TH 120 ST

32

NEW PRAGUE ISD #721
MONTGOMERY-LONSDALE ISD #394

22

23

56071

NEW PRAGUE ISD #721

211TH AVE

211TH AVE

AVE

201ST

31

121

28

320TH ST

AVE

MONTGOMERY-LONSDALE ISD #394

28

320TH ST

2

**Derrynane
Twp**

32

NEW PRAGUE ISD #721

22

MONTGOMERY-LONSDALE ISD #394

56057

26

326TH ST

221ST

LE CENTER ISD #392

MONTGOMERY-LONSDALE ISD #394

•

330TH ST

3

121

211TH AVE

55069

34

MONTGOMERY-LONSDALE ISD #394
LE CENTER ISD #392

35

32

205TH LN

•

221ST AVE

340TH ST

123

340TH ST

123

T111N | T112N

**Lexington
Twp**

4

03

121

02

26

32

26

26

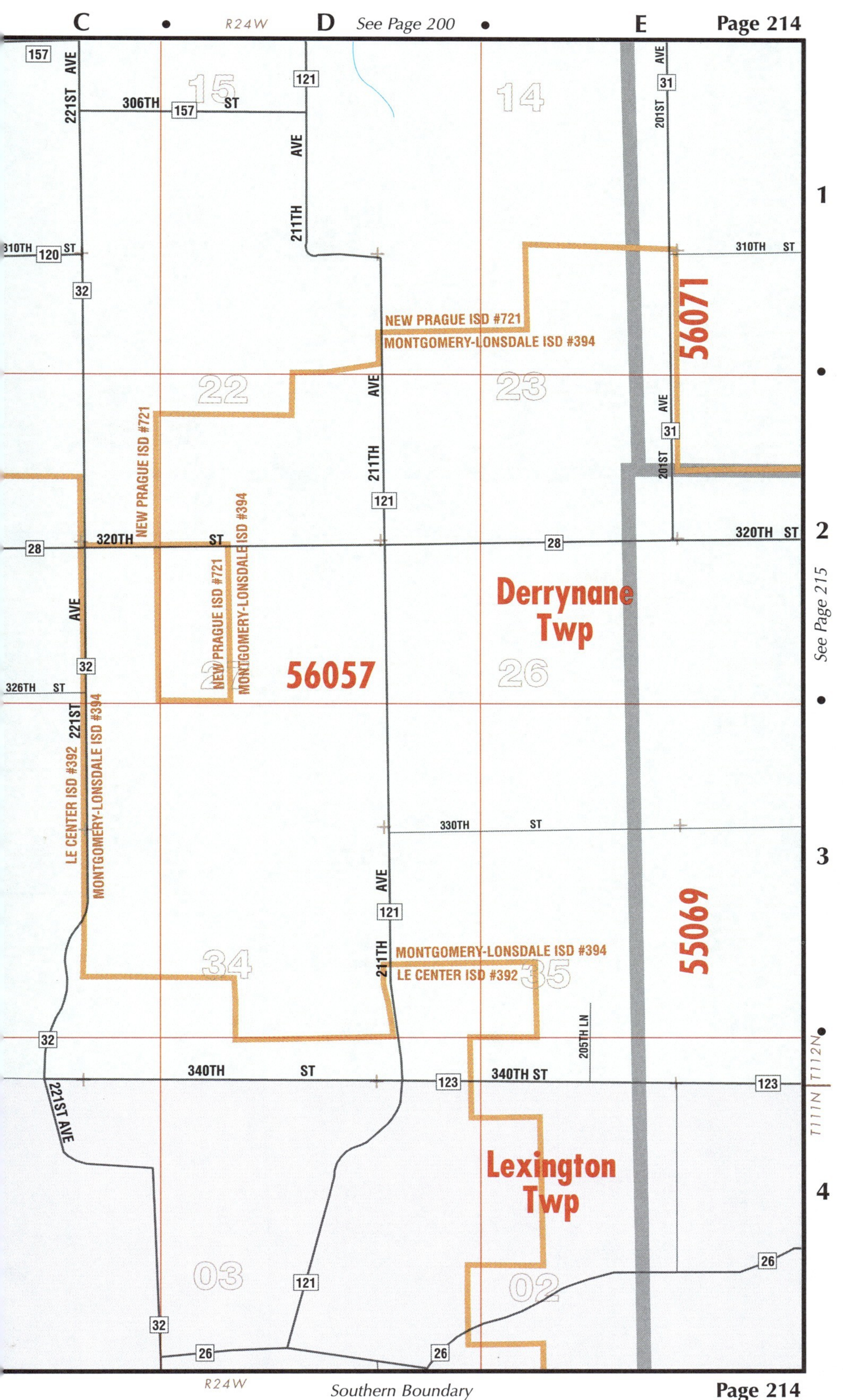

A R24W | R23W ● *See Page 201* B ● C

13

EAST BRANCH RAVEN STREAM

Lanesburgh Twp

181ST AVE

18

17

Mud Lake

1

310TH ST

341ST ST

NEW PRAGUE ISD #721
MONTGOMERY-LONSDALE ISD #394

56071

416TH LOOP

● **24**

NEW PRAGUE ISD #721
MONTGOMERY-LONSDALE ISD #394

19

314TH ST

181ST AVE

20

HEIDELBERG

30

2

320TH ST

28

320TH ST

28

See Page 214

Derrynane Twp

AVE

25

326TH LN

195TH

30

29

●

330TH ST

181ST AVE

Eggert Lake

EGGERT LAKE RD

3

56069

181ST AVE

334TH 142 ST

334TH ST

36

31

336TH ST

30

32

● T111N | T112N

123

340TH ST

4

Lexington Twp

123

Montgomery Twp

AVE

26

01

06

181ST

30

05

26

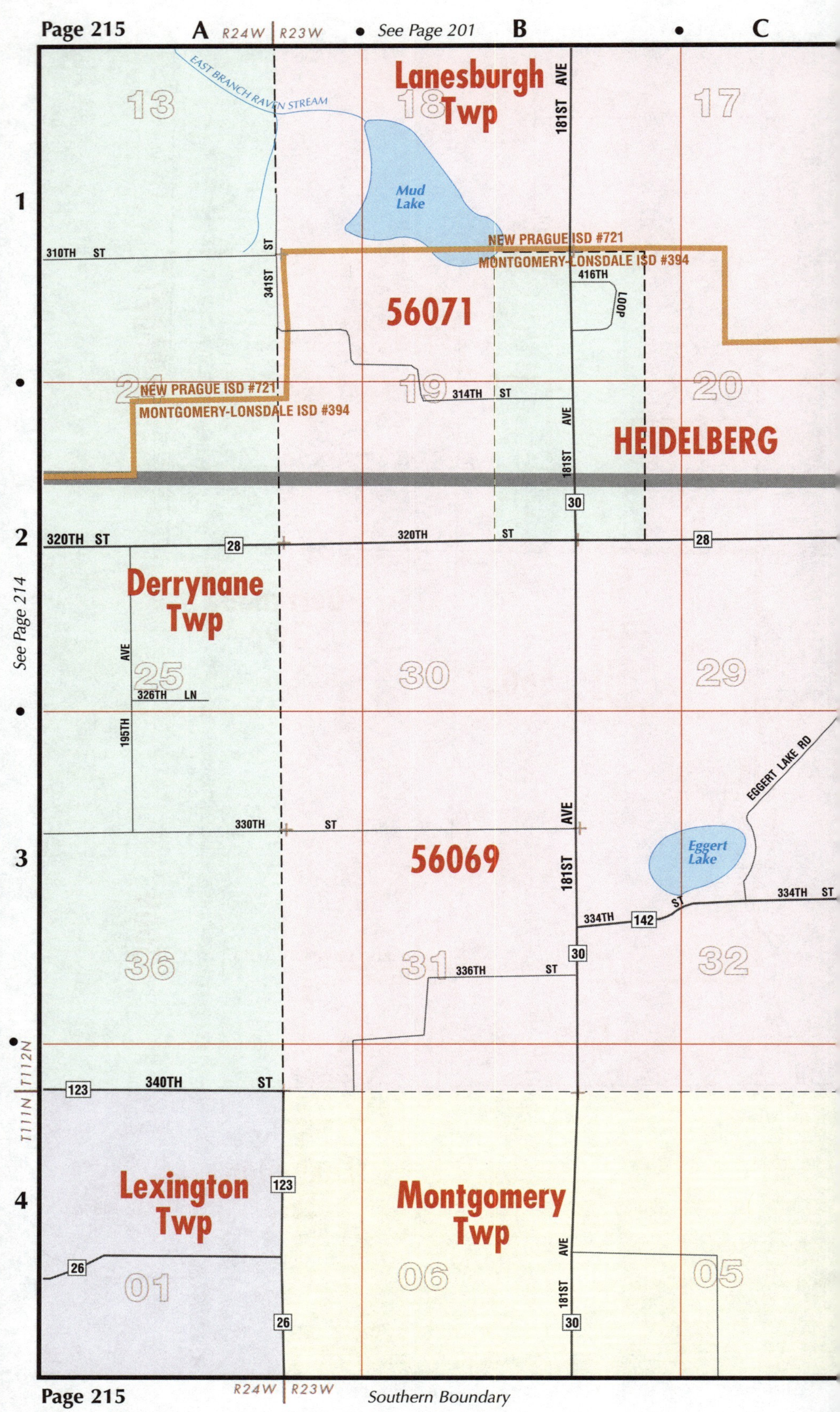

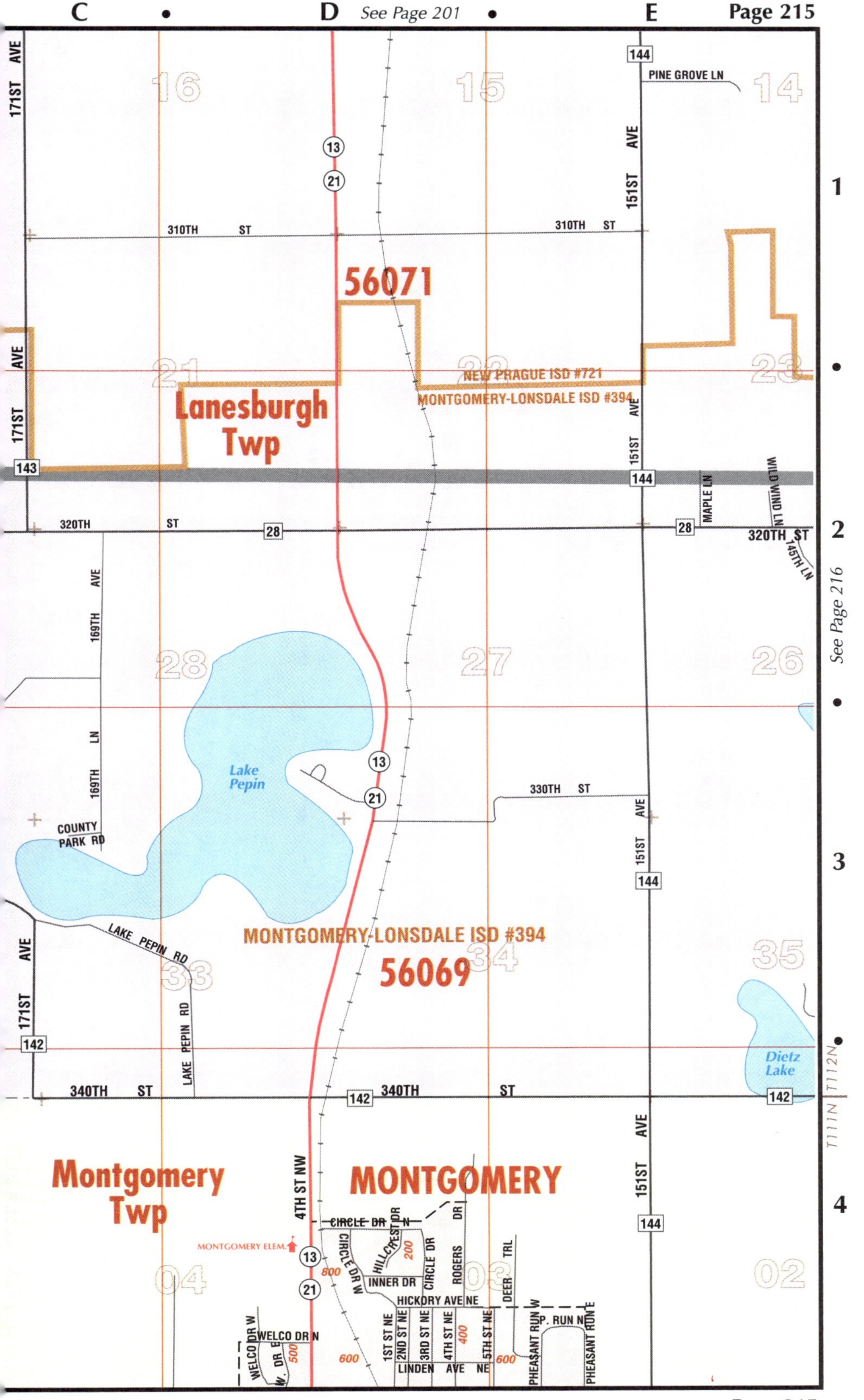

171ST AVE

16

15

14

144

PINE GROVE LN

151ST AVE

1

13
21

310TH ST

310TH ST

56071

171ST AVE

21

22

23

NEW PRAGUE ISD #721

MONTGOMERY-LONSDALE ISD #394

Lanesburgh Twp

151ST AVE

143

144

MAPLE LN

WILD WIND LN

320TH ST

28

28

320TH ST

145TH LN

2

169TH AVE

28

27

26

See Page 216

169TH LN

Lake Pepin

13
21

330TH ST

169TH LN

151ST AVE

3

144

COUNTY PARK RD

171ST AVE

Lake Pepin RD

MONTGOMERY-LONSDALE ISD #394

33

34

35

56069

Lake Pepin RD

Dietz Lake

142

T111N T112N

340TH ST

142

340TH ST

151ST AVE

142

Montgomery Twp

4TH ST NW

MONTGOMERY

151ST AVE

4

144

MONTGOMERY ELEM.

CIRCLE DR N

DR

CIRCLE DR W

HILLCREST DR

200

CIRCLE DR

ROGERS DR

DEER TRL

04

13
21

800

INNER DR

HICKORY AVE NE

03

02

WELCO DR W

WELCO DR N

W. DR E

500

600

1ST ST NE

2ND ST NE

3RD ST NE

4TH ST NE

5TH ST NE

400

600

PHEASANT RUN W

RUN N

PHEASANT RUN E

PHEASANT RUN E

LINDEN AVE NE

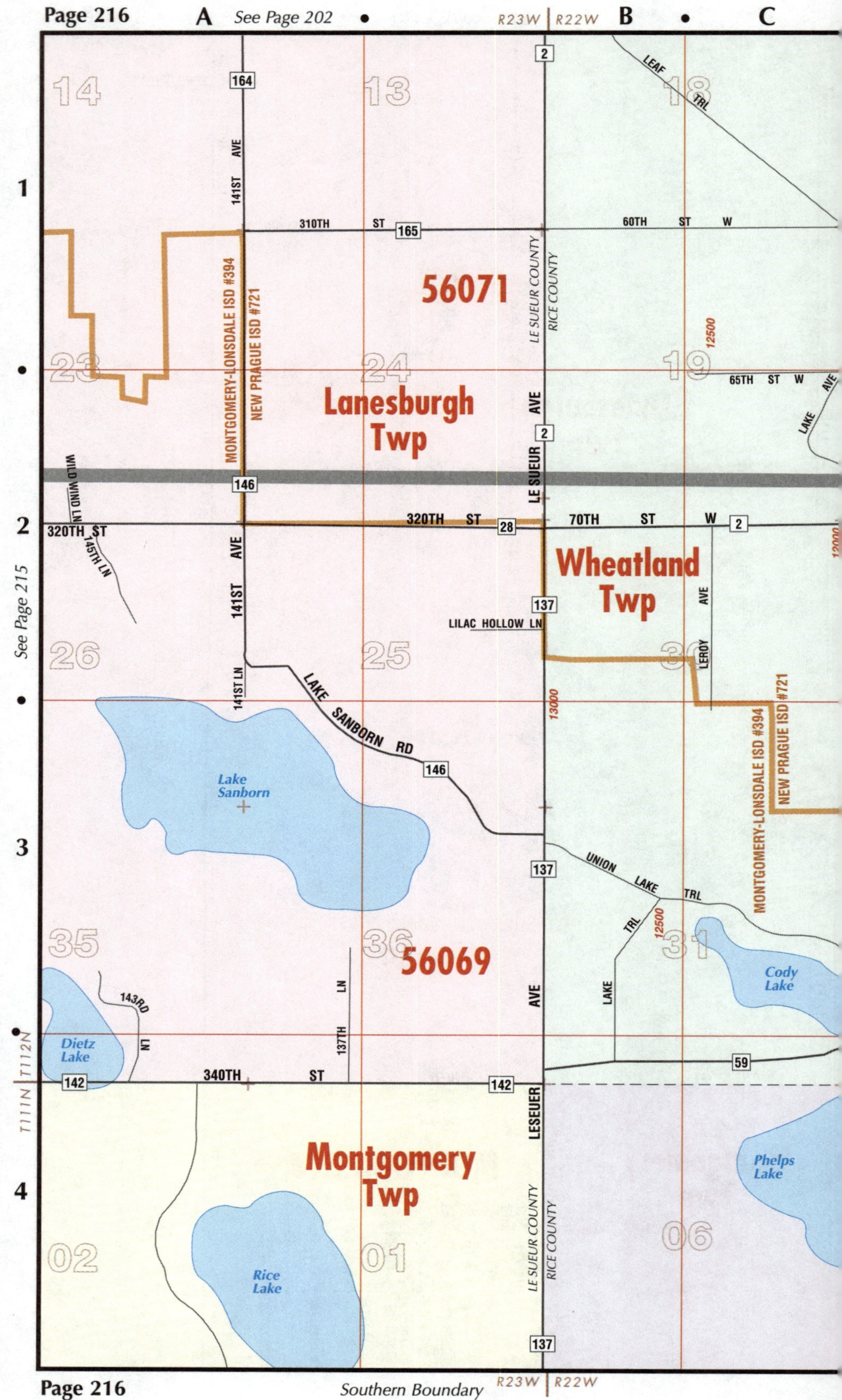

14

164

141ST AVE

13

2

LEAF TRL

18

1

310TH   ST   165

60TH   ST   W

Le Sueur County | Rice County

56071

MONTGOMERY-LONSDALE ISD #394 | NEW PRAGUE ISD #721

23

24

Lanesburgh Twp

LE SUEUR AVE

2

19

12500

65TH   ST   W

LAKE AVE

WILD WIND LN

146

See Page 215

2

320TH ST

141ST AVE

320TH   ST   28

70TH   ST   W   2

Wheatland Twp

145TH LN

26

141ST LN

LILAC HOLLOW LN

137

LEROY AVE

25

LAKE   SANBORN   RD

36

146

Lake Sanborn

13000

MONTGOMERY-LONSDALE ISD #394 | NEW PRAGUE ISD #721

3

137

UNION   LAKE   TRL

35

56069

137TH   LN

36

AVE

LAKE   TRL

12500

31

Cody Lake

143RD

LN

Dietz Lake

T111N | T112N

142

340TH   ST

LESEUER   AVE

142

59

59

Montgomery Twp

LE SUEUR COUNTY | RICE COUNTY

Phelps Lake

4

02

01

Rice Lake

06

137

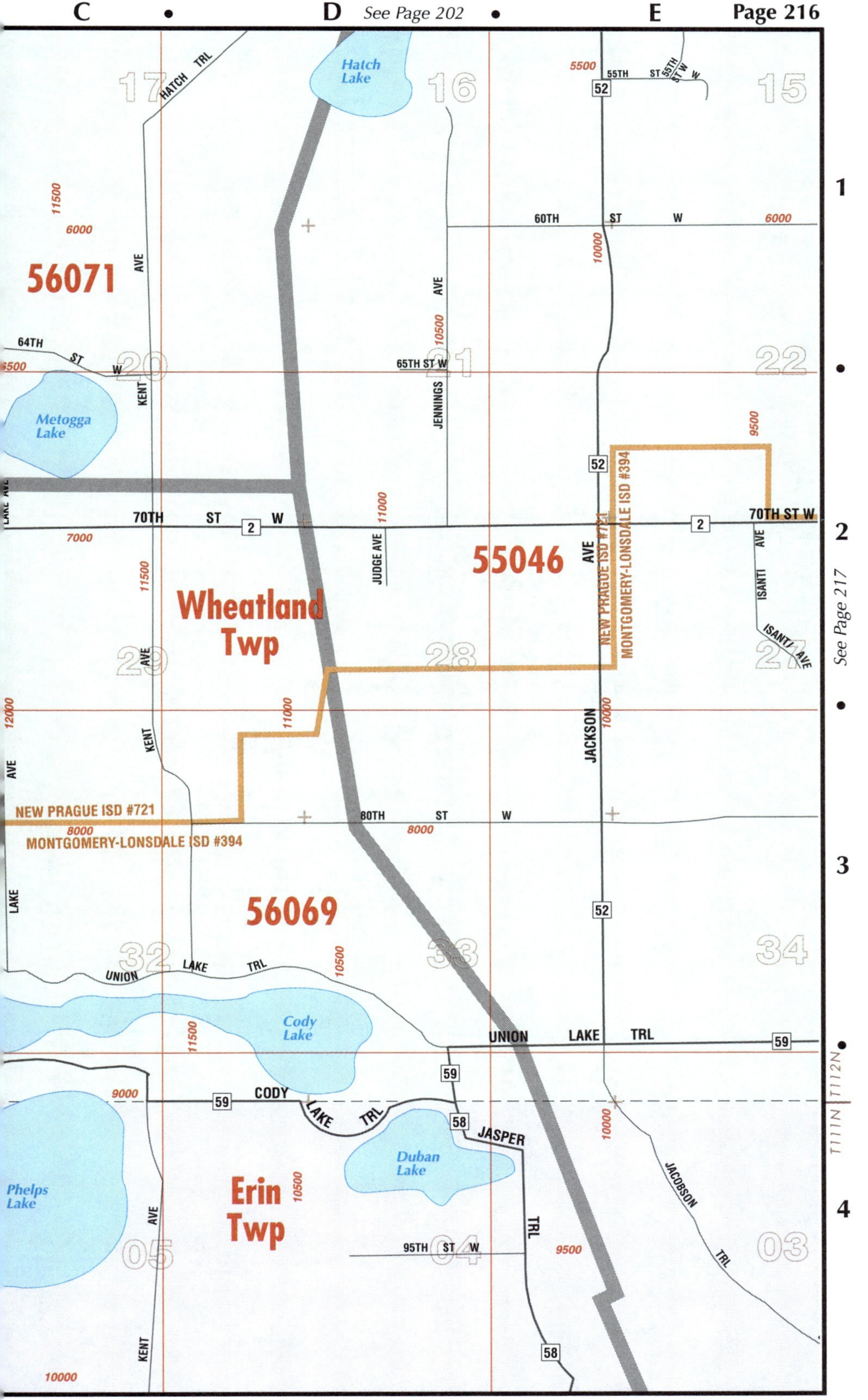

56071

Hatch Lake

HATCH TRL

17

16

15

5500

55TH ST

58TH ST W

52

11500

6000

AVE

60TH ST W

6000

1

10000

AVE

10500

64TH ST W

4500

KENT AVE

20

65TH ST W

JENNINGS AVE

21

22

9500

Metogga Lake

LAKE AVE

7000

70TH ST

2 W

11000

JUDGE AVE

52

MONTGOMERY-LONSDALE ISD #394

NEW PRAGUE ISD #721

AVE

2

70TH ST W

ISANTI AVE

2

Wheatland Twp

11500

KENT AVE

29

11000

28

55046

ISANTI AVE

27

See Page 217

12000

AVE

11000

JACKSON AVE

10000

NEW PRAGUE ISD #721

MONTGOMERY-LONSDALE ISD #394

LAKE AVE

8000

80TH ST W

8000

52

3

56069

32

UNION LAKE TRL

10500

33

34

11500

Cody Lake

UNION LAKE TRL

59

9000

59

CODY LAKE TRL

59

58

Phelps Lake

AVE

10500

58

JASPER

Duban Lake

Erin Twp

JACOBSON TRL

10000

T111N | T112N

05

KENT AVE

95TH ST W

04

TRL

9500

03

10000

58

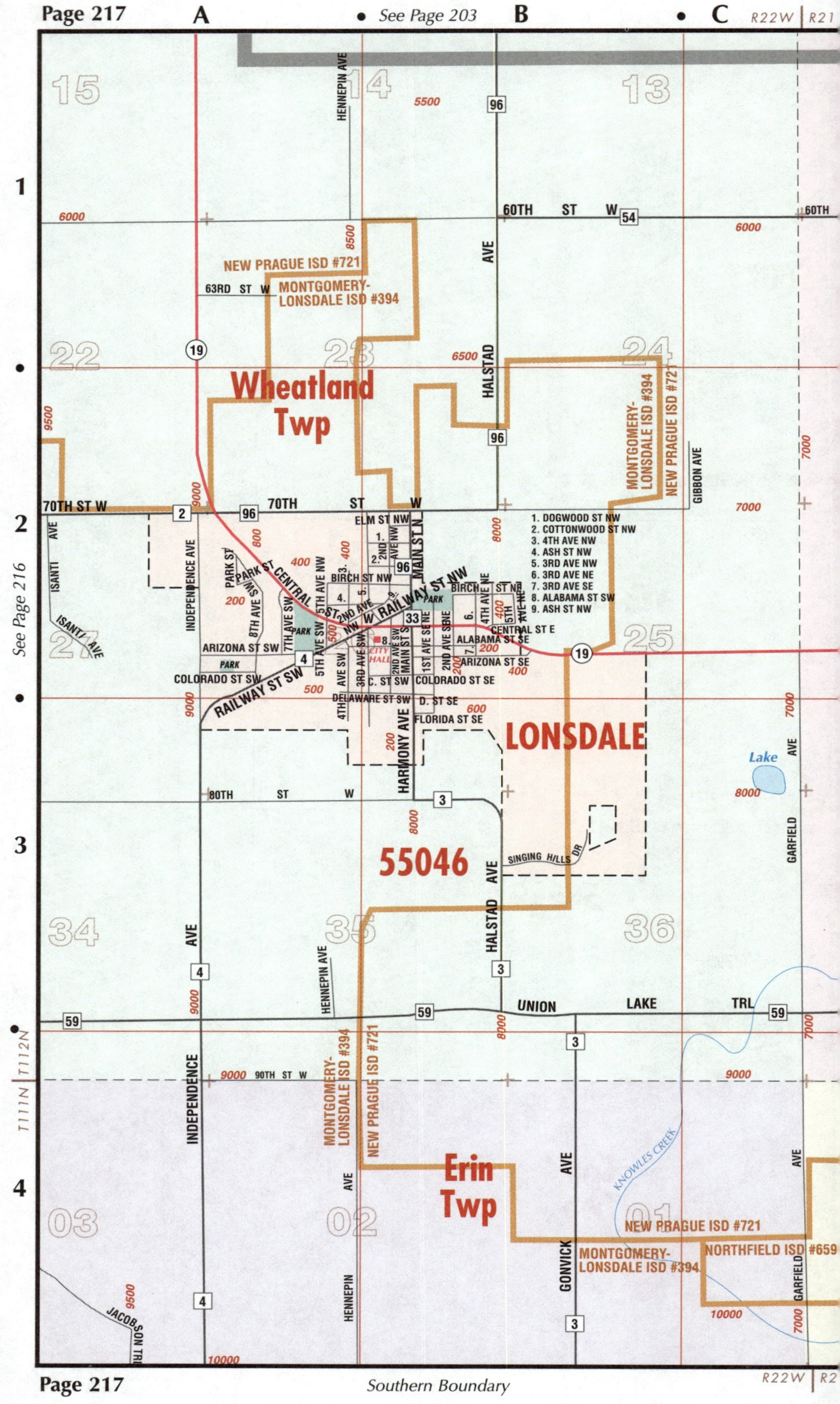

15

14   5500   96

1

6000   60TH   ST   W 54   6000   60TH

8500

NEW PRAGUE ISD #721

63RD   ST   W   MONTGOMERY-
LONSDALE ISD #394

22   23   6500   24

(19)

**Wheatland
Twp**   96

9500

9000

70TH ST W 2   96   70TH   ST   W   8000

See Page 216

2   ELM ST NW   1. DOGWOOD ST NW
2. COTTONWOOD ST NW
3. 4TH AVE NW
4. ASH ST NW
5. 3RD AVE NW
6. 3RD AVE NE
7. 3RD AVE SE
8. ALABAMA ST SW
9. ASH ST NW

400   BIRCH ST NW   96   BIRCH   ST NE

CENTRAL ST E

33   400

CITY HALL 200

4   Arizona st sw   Arizona st se

PARK   400

Colorado st sw   500   Colorado st se

Delaware st sw   D. ST SE

HARMONY AVE   200   Florida st se   600

LONSDALE

Lake
8000

80TH   ST   W   3

3

55046   8000   Singing Hills dr

34   35   36

4   HENNEPIN AVE   3

9000   HALSTAD   AVE   3

59   59   UNION   LAKE   TRL   59

8900   3   7000

T111N | T112N   9000   90TH ST W   9000

INDEPENDENCE   MONTGOMERY-
LONSDALE ISD #394

NEW PRAGUE ISD #721

**Erin
Twp**   KNOWLES CREEK

4   03   02   AVE   01   NEW PRAGUE ISD #721

MONTGOMERY-
LONSDALE ISD #394

NORTHFIELD ISD #659

4   JACOBSON TRL   9500   GONVICK   3   10000   7000

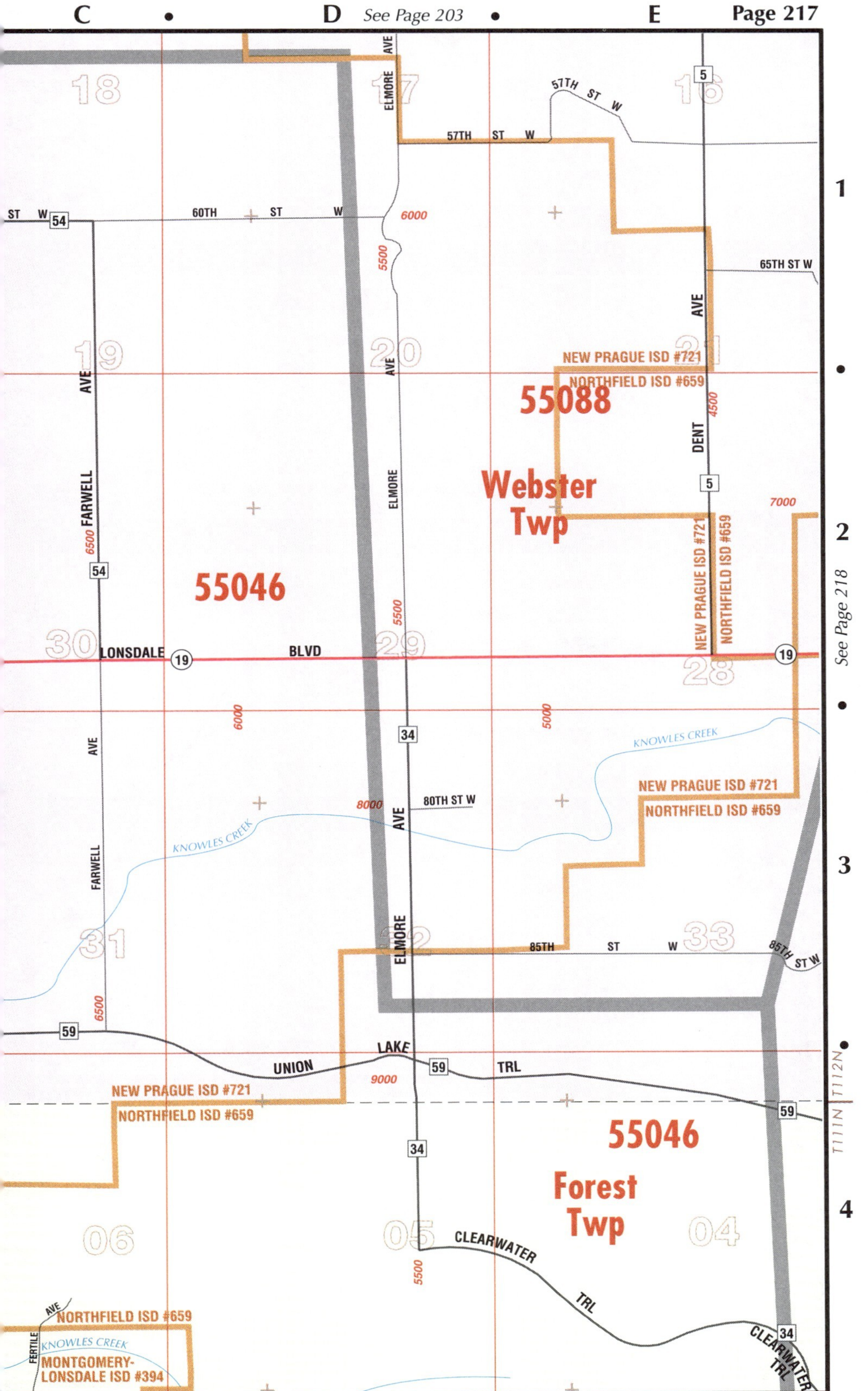

18

17

16

5

57TH ST W

57TH ST W

57TH ST W

1

ST W 54

60TH ST W

6000

5500

65TH ST W

19

20

AVE

AVE

AVE

NEW PRAGUE ISD #721

NORTHFIELD ISD #659

55088

4500

FARWELL

6500

DENT

AVE

Webster Twp

5

7000

54

55046

ELMORE

2

NEW PRAGUE ISD #721

NORTHFIELD ISD #659

See Page 218

30

LONSDALE 19

BLVD

29

5500

28

19

AVE

6000

5000

KNOWLES CREEK

34

NEW PRAGUE ISD #721

NORTHFIELD ISD #659

8000

80TH ST W

AVE

3

FARWELL

KNOWLES CREEK

31

6500

ELMORE

32

85TH ST W

33

85TH ST W

59

LAKE

UNION

9000

59

TRL

NEW PRAGUE ISD #721

NORTHFIELD ISD #659

59

T111N T112N

34

55046

Forest Twp

4

06

05

5500

CLEARWATER

04

TRL

34

AVE

NORTHFIELD ISD #659

FERTILE

KNOWLES CREEK

MONTGOMERY-LONSDALE ISD #394

CLEARWATER TR

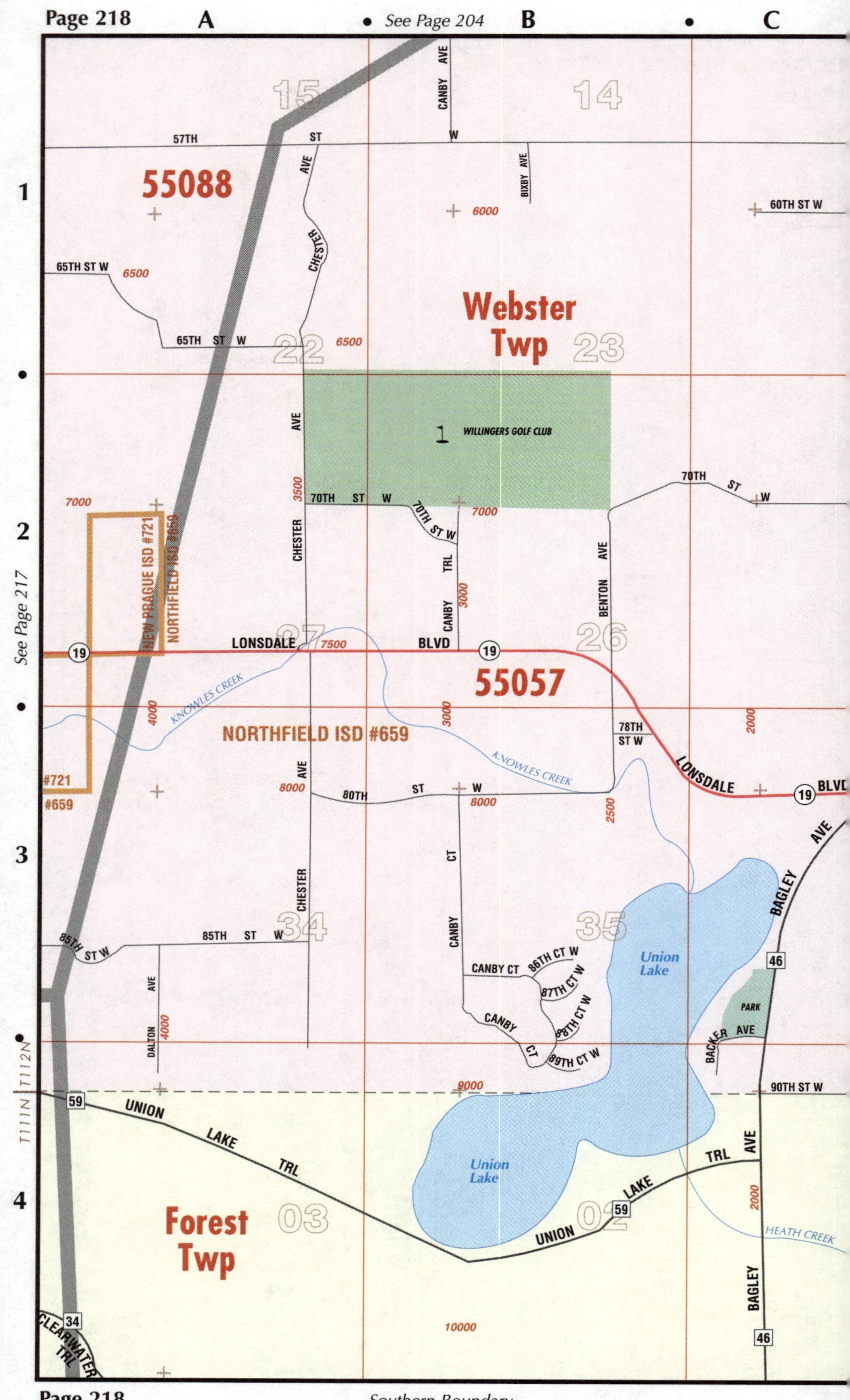

15

CANBY AVE

55088

14

57TH ST W

6000

BIXBY AVE

60TH ST W

1

65TH ST W 6500

CHESTER AVE

65TH ST W 22 6500

Webster Twp

23

See Page 217

7000

NEW PRAGUE ISD #721

NORTHFIELD ISD #659

CHESTER AVE

3500

WILLINGERS GOLF CLUB

70TH ST W

70TH ST W 7000

70TH ST W

BENTON AVE

2

19

LONSDALE 27 7500 BLVD 19

26

CANBY TRL

3000

55057

4000

KNOWLES CREEK

NORTHFIELD ISD #659

3000

KNOWLES CREEK

78TH ST W

2000

#721

#659

AVE

8000

80TH ST W 8000

2500

LONSDALE BLVD 19

3

CHESTER AVE

CANBY CT

CT

35

BAGLEY AVE

85TH ST W

85TH ST W 34

Union Lake

46

DALTON AVE

4000

CANBY CT 86TH CT W

87TH CT W

88TH CT W

CANBY CT

89TH CT W

PARK

BACKER AVE

T111N T112N

9000

90TH ST W

59

UNION LAKE TRL

UNION LAKE TRL

Union Lake

UNION 02 59 LAKE TRL

BAGLEY AVE

2000

HEATH CREEK

Forest Twp

03

4

10000

BAGLEY

34 CLEARWATER TRL

46

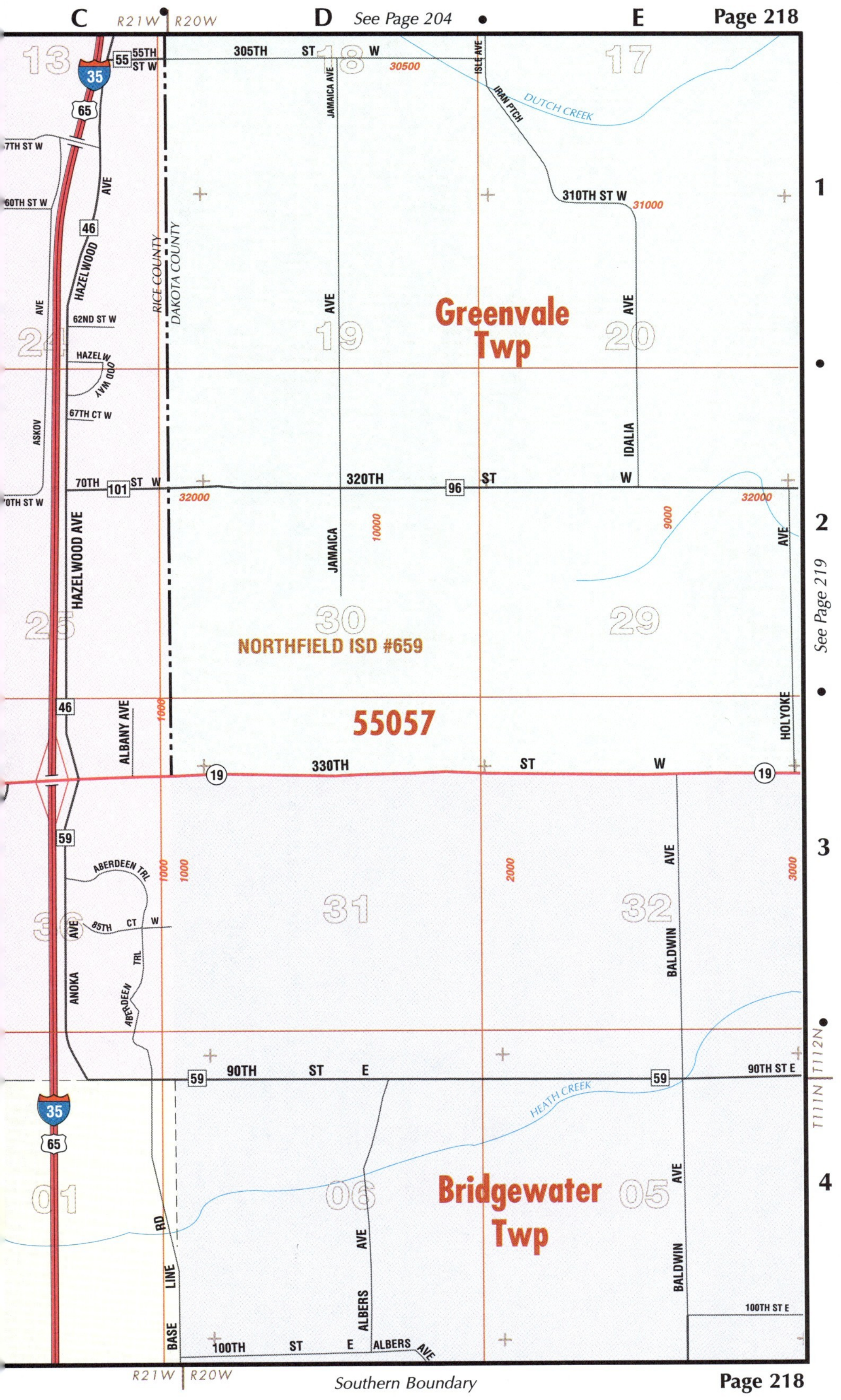

13

I-35
65

55TH ST W
55

305TH ST 18 W
30500
JAMAICA AVE
ISLE AVE
IRAN PTCH
DUTCH CREEK
17

67TH ST W

HAZELWOOD AVE

46

60TH ST W

AVE

62ND ST W

HAZELW OOD WAY

67TH CT W

ASKOV

70TH ST W

RICE COUNTY
DAKOTA COUNTY

310TH ST W
31000

Greenvale Twp

19

AVE

20

IDALIA

AVE

1

24

25

70TH 101 ST W
32000

320TH 96 ST W
32000

JAMAICA
10000

JAMAICA

9000

HOLYOKE

AVE

2

See Page 219

30

29

NORTHFIELD ISD #659

HAZELWOOD AVE

46

ALBANY AVE

1000

1000

55057

19
330TH ST W
19

59

ABERDEEN TRL
1000
1000

85TH CT W

ANOKA AVE

ABERDEEN TRL

36

31

2000

32

BALDWIN AVE

3000

3

59
90TH ST E
59

HEATH CREEK

90TH ST E

T111N | T112N

I-35
65

01

06

Bridgewater Twp

05

BALDWIN AVE

AVE

4

LINE RD

BASE

100TH ST E
ALBERS AVE
ALBERS AVE

100TH ST E

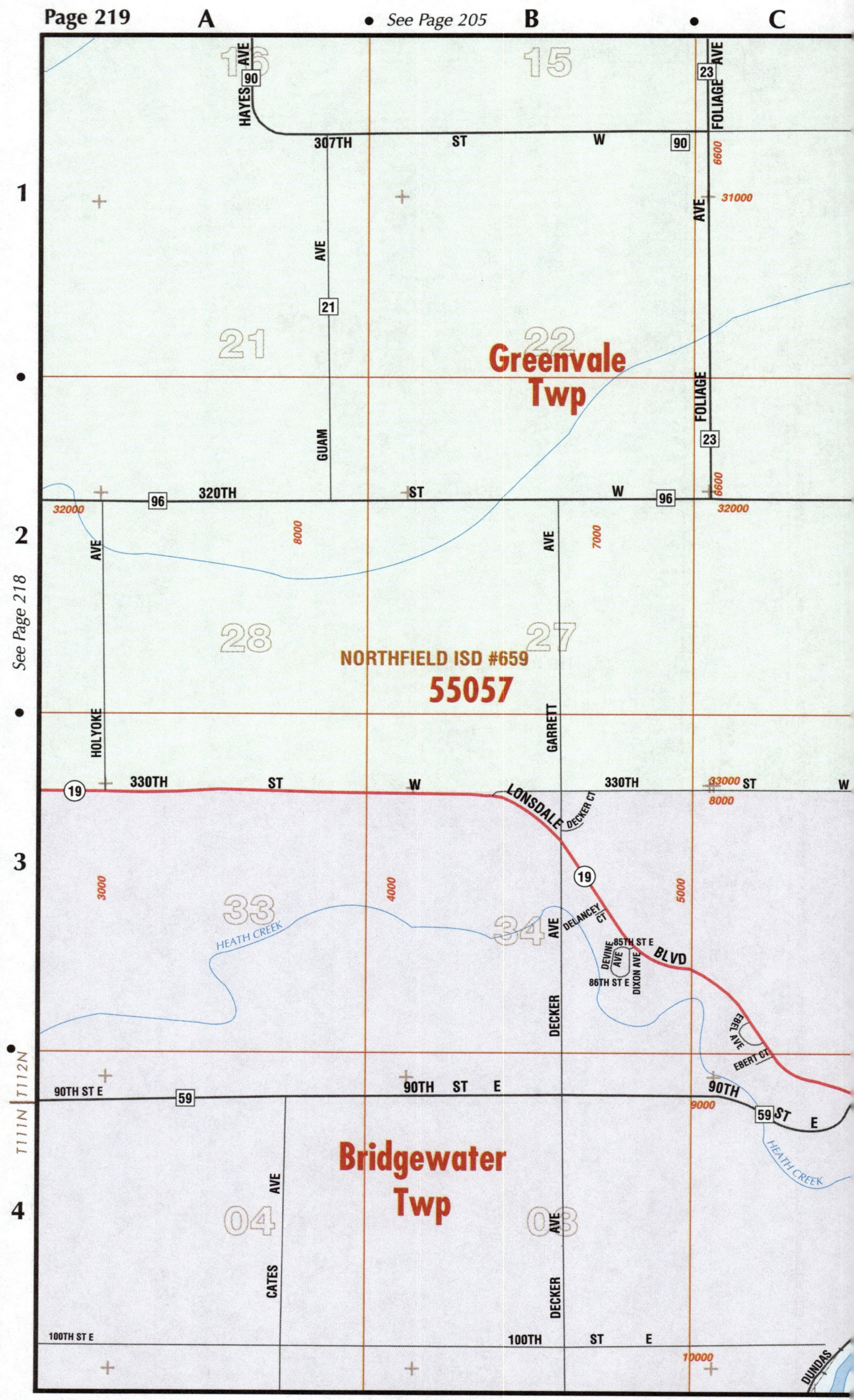

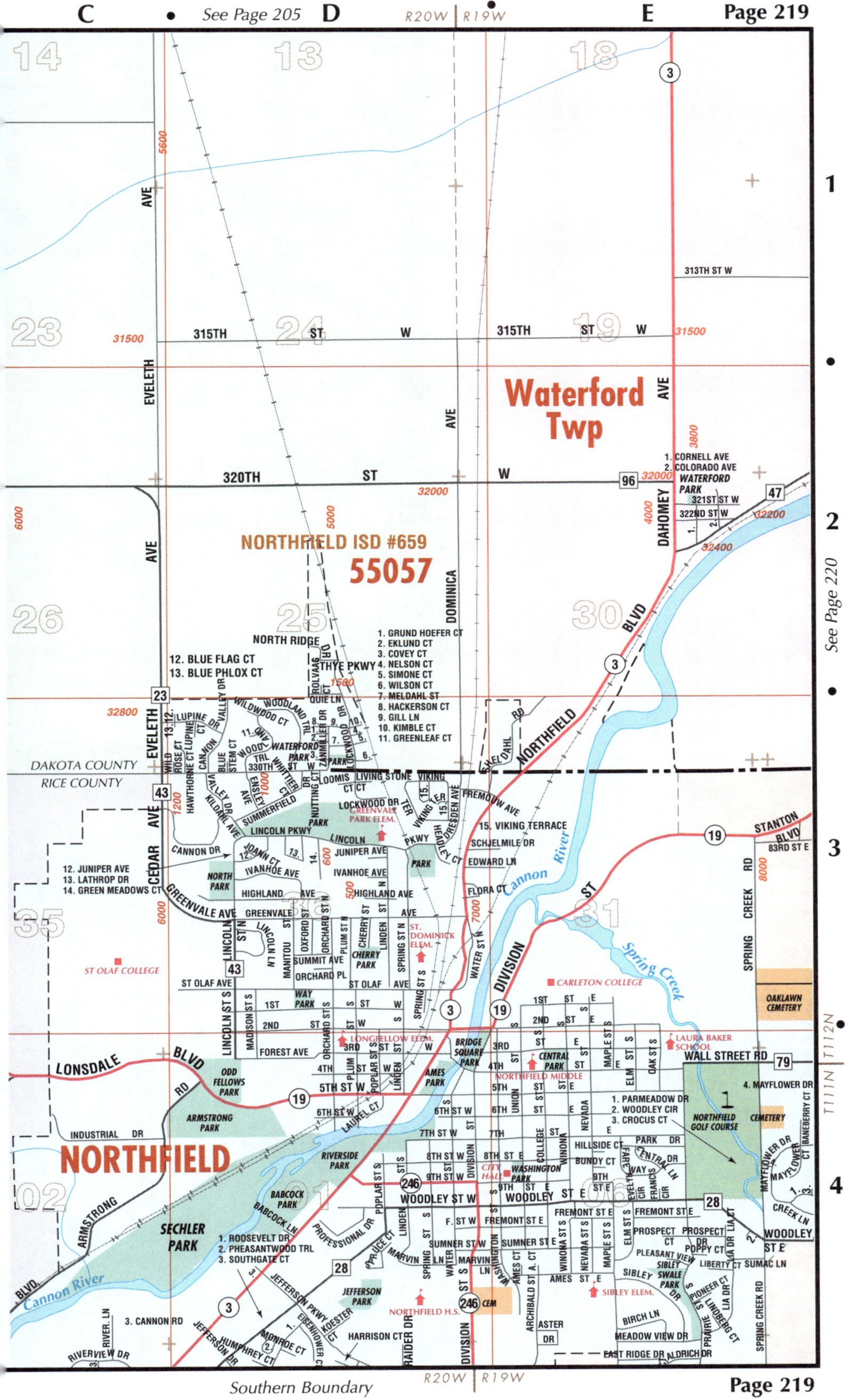

R20W R19W

Waterford Twp

313TH ST W

315TH ST W   315TH ST W

See Page 220

320TH ST W

1. CORNELL AVE
2. COLORADO AVE
WATERFORD PARK

96   32000
321ST ST W
322ND ST W
47

NORTHFIELD ISD #659
55057

NORTH RIDGE

12. BLUE FLAG CT
13. BLUE PHLOX CT

1. GRUND HOEFER CT
2. EKLUND CT
3. COVEY CT
4. NELSON CT
5. SIMONE CT
6. WILSON CT
7. MELDAHL CT
8. HACKERSON CT
9. GILL LN
10. KIMBLE CT
11. GREENLEAF CT

THYE PKWY

DAKOTA COUNTY
RICE COUNTY

15. VIKING TERRACE

LOCKWOOD DR
GREENVALE PARK ELEM.

SCHJELMILE DR
EDWARD LN

STANTON BLVD
83RD ST E

19

12. JUNIPER AVE
13. LATHROP DR
14. GREEN MEADOWS CT

NORTH PARK

IVANHOE AVE

HIGHLAND AVE

Cannon River

FLORA CT

SPRING CREEK RD

OAKLAWN CEMETERY

St OLAF COLLEGE

ST. DOMINICK ELEM.

Spring Creek

CARLETON COLLEGE

WALL STREET RD   79

LONSDALE BLVD

19

ODD FELLOWS PARK

LONGFELLOW ELEM.

BRIDGE SQUARE PARK

NORTHFIELD MIDDLE

CENTRAL PARK

LAURA BAKER SCHOOL

4. MAYFLOWER DR

1. PARMEADOW DR
2. WOODLEY CIR
3. CROCUS CT

NORTHFIELD GOLF COURSE

1

CEMETERY

NORTHFIELD

ARMSTRONG PARK

RIVERSIDE PARK

CITY HALL
WASHINGTON PARK

WOODLEY ST W   WOODLEY ST E

28

WOODLEY ST E

SECHLER PARK

BABCOCK PARK

1. ROOSEVELT DR
2. PHEASANTWOOD TRL
3. SOUTHGATE CT

JEFFERSON PARK

NORTHFIELD H.S.

SIBLEY ELEM.

SIBLEY SWALE PARK

3. CANNON RD

246 CEM

Cannon River

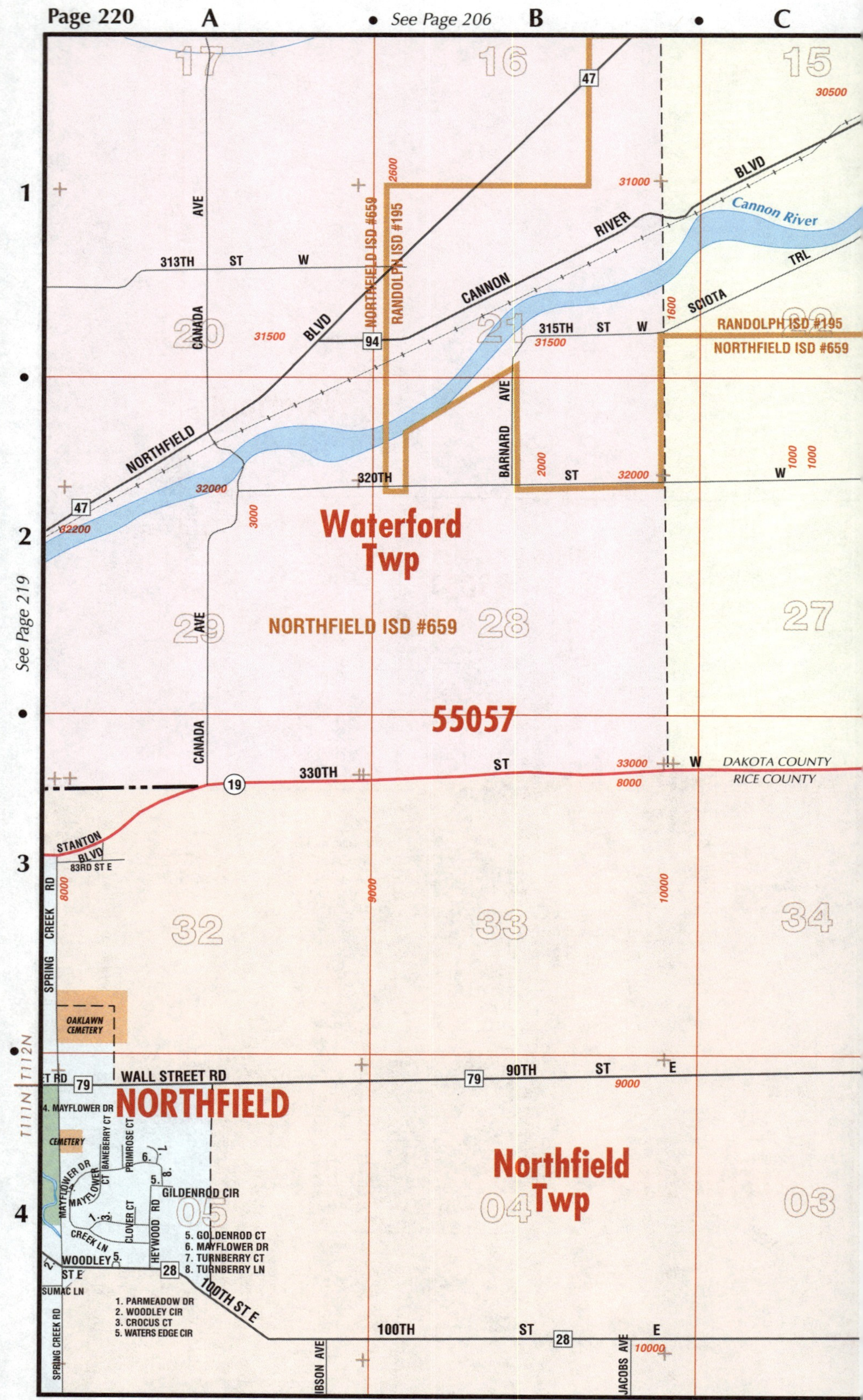

A B C

17 16 15

30500

47

See Page 219

RANDOLPH ISD #195
NORTHFIELD ISD #659

BLVD
Cannon River
TRL

2600

1

313TH ST W

31000

Cannon RIVER

SCIOTA

1600

CANADA AVE

NORTHFIELD BLVD

94

31500

315TH ST W

RANDOLPH ISD #195
NORTHFIELD ISD #659

31500

20 21 22

1000 1000

BARNARD AVE

2000

NORTHFIELD

47
32200 32000 3000

320TH ST 32000 W

Waterford Twp

2

NORTHFIELD ISD #659

CANADA AVE

29 28 27

55057

19 330TH ST 33000 W **DAKOTA COUNTY**
8000 **RICE COUNTY**

STANTON BLVD
83RD ST E

SPRING CREEK RD

8000

9000

10000

3

32 33 34

OAKLAWN CEMETERY

T111N | T112N

ST RD 79 **WALL STREET RD** 79 90TH ST E
9000

4. MAYFLOWER DR **NORTHFIELD**

CEMETERY

MAYFLOWER DR
DANEBERRY CT
PRIMROSE CT

6.
L.
8.
5.
GILDENROD CIR

CLOVER CT
HEYWOOD RD
MAYFLOWER CREEK LN

Northfield Twp

04 03

05

5. GOLDENROD CT
6. MAYFLOWER DR
7. TURNBERRY CT
8. TURNBERRY LN

WOODLEY ST E
28

SUMAC LN

2.

4

1. PARMEADOW DR
2. WOODLEY CIR
3. CROCUS CT
5. WATERS EDGE CIR

SPRING CREEK RD

TOOTH ST E

GIBSON AVE

100TH ST 28 E

JACOBS AVE

10000

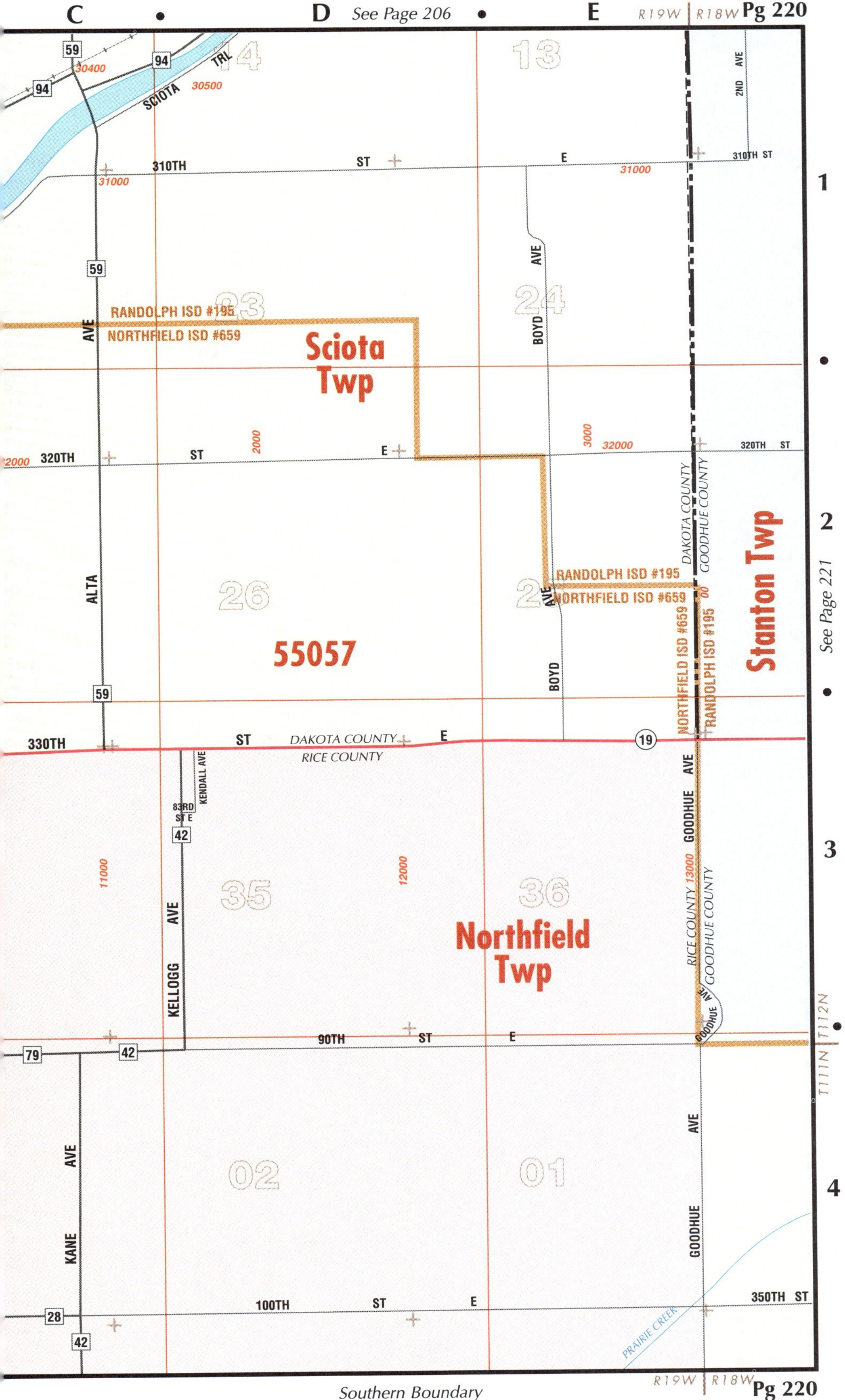

59
94
30400
94
SCIOTA TRL
30500
14
13
2ND AVE

310TH ST
31000
E
31000
310TH ST
1

59
BOYD AVE
24

RANDOLPH ISD #195
NORTHFIELD ISD #659
23
Sciota Twp

AVE
ALTA
2000
320TH ST
2000
E
3000
32000
320TH ST

DAKOTA COUNTY
GOODHUE COUNTY
Stanton Twp
See Page 221
2

26
55057
RANDOLPH ISD #195
NORTHFIELD ISD #659
25
BOYD AVE
NORTHFIELD ISD #659
RANDOLPH ISD #195

59
330TH ST
DAKOTA COUNTY
RICE COUNTY
E
19
GOODHUE AVE

KENDALL AVE
83RD ST E
42
11000
12000
35
36
Northfield Twp
RICE COUNTY
GOODHUE COUNTY
13000
GOODHUE AV
3

KELLOGG AVE
79
42
90TH ST
E
42
GOODHUE AV
T111N | T112N

AVE
KANE
AVE
02
01
GOODHUE AVE
4

28
42
100TH ST
E
350TH ST
PRAIRIE CREEK

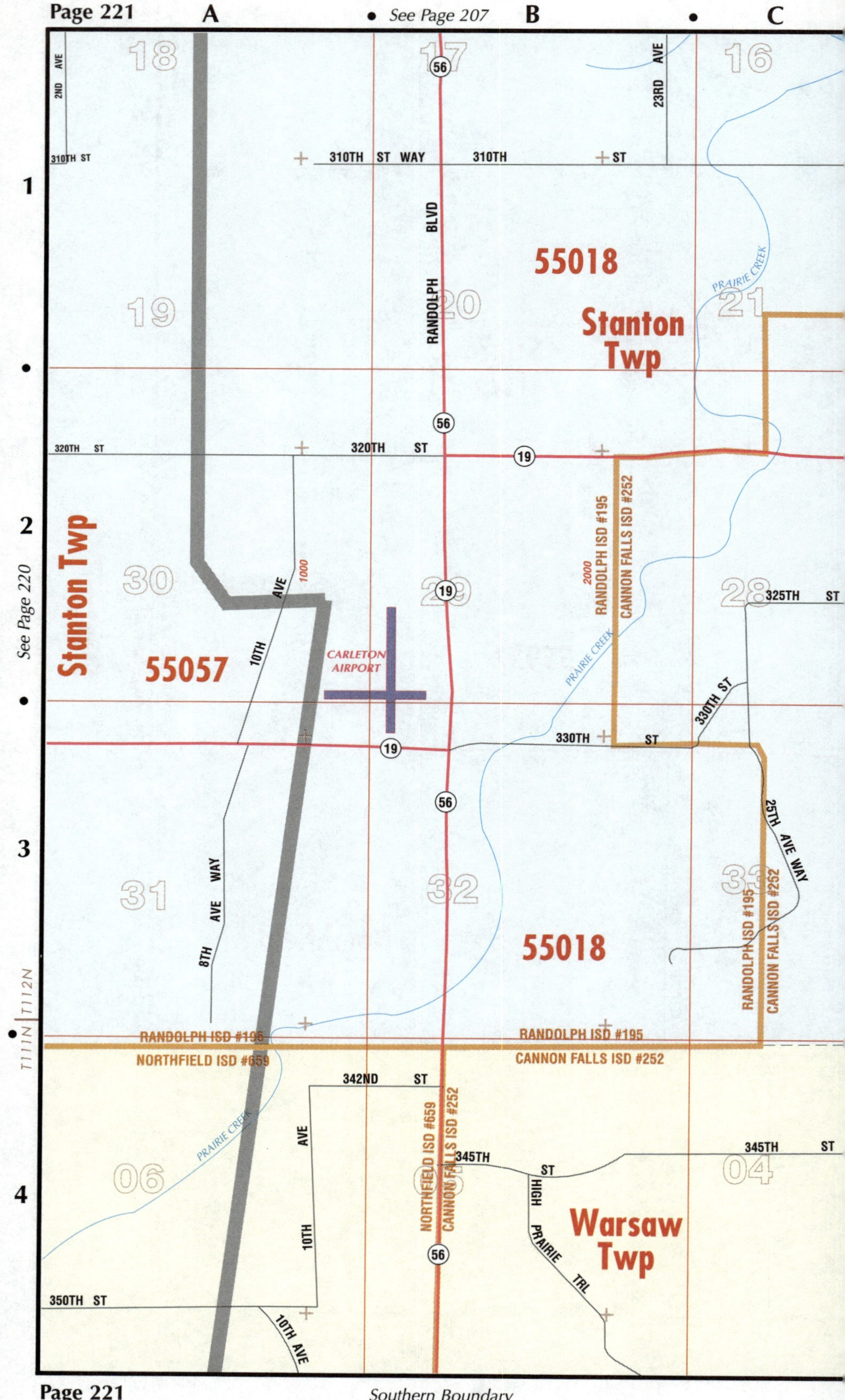

A   • *See Page 207*   B   •   C

18

17
56

310TH ST

2ND AVE

23RD AVE

310TH ST WAY   310TH   ST

16

1

RANDOLPH BLVD

19

20

55018

Stanton Twp

21

PRAIRIE CREEK

320TH ST

320TH   ST

56

19

320TH ST WAY

2

See Page 220

Stanton Twp

30

1000

55057

10TH AVE

29

56

CARLETON AIRPORT

19

28

325TH   ST

2000

PRAIRIE CREEK

RANDOLPH ISD #195

CANNON FALLS ISD #252

330TH ST

19

330TH   ST

3

31

8TH AVE WAY

56

32

55018

33

25TH AVE WAY

RANDOLPH ISD #195

CANNON FALLS ISD #252

T111N | T112N

RANDOLPH ISD #195

NORTHFIELD ISD #659

RANDOLPH ISD #195

CANNON FALLS ISD #252

PRAIRIE CREEK

342ND   ST

10TH AVE

06

NORTHFIELD ISD #659

CANNON FALLS ISD #252

345TH   ST

HIGH PRAIRIE TRL

345TH   ST

4

Warsaw Twp

04

56

350TH ST

10TH AVE

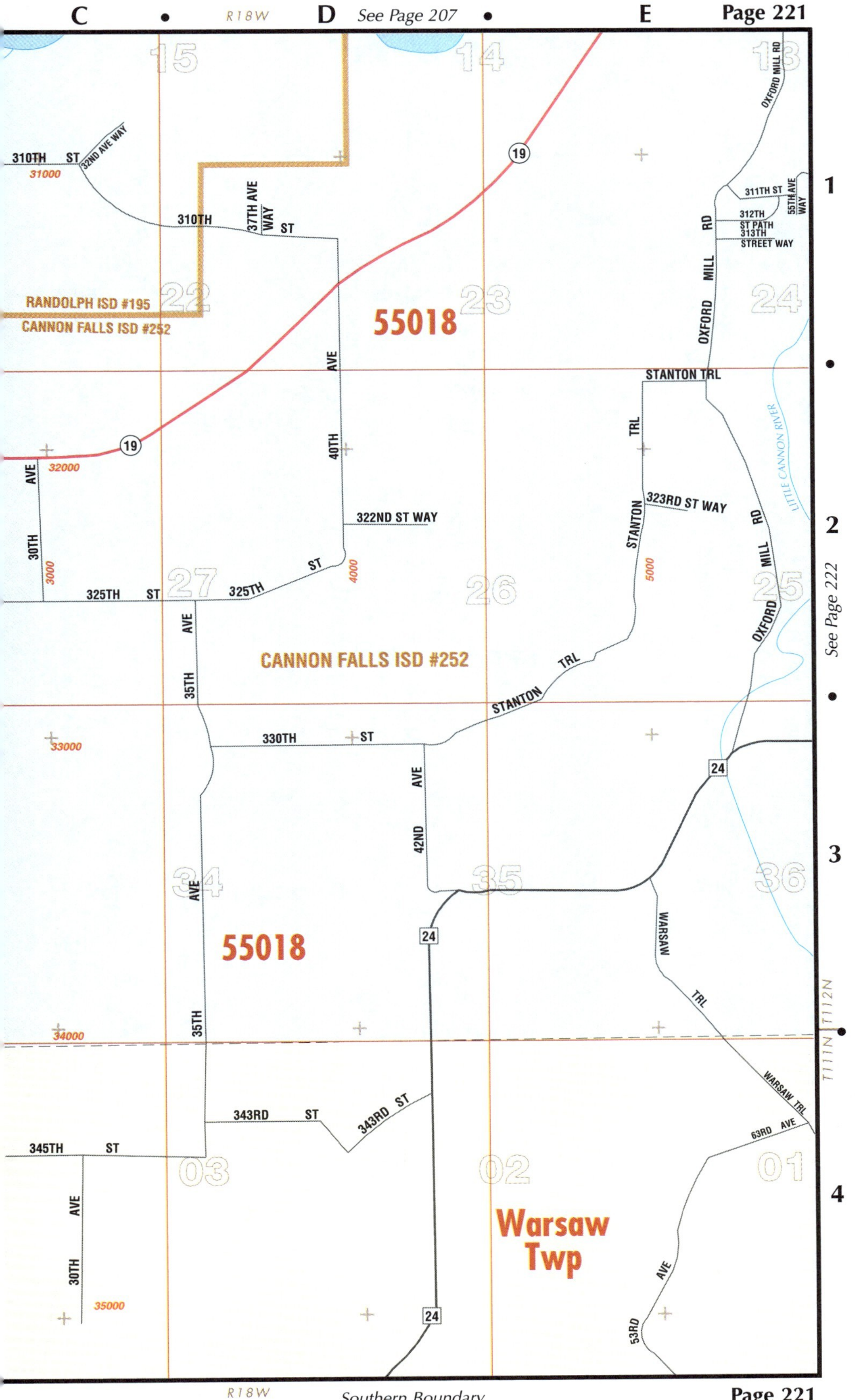

OXFORD MILL RD

310TH ST
31000

32ND AVE WAY

37TH AVE WAY ST

310TH ST

19

311TH ST

55TH AVE WAY

312TH ST PATH
313TH STREET WAY

OXFORD MILL RD

RANDOLPH ISD #195
CANNON FALLS ISD #252

55018

STANTON TRL

19

AVE
32000

40TH AVE

STANTON TRL

323RD ST WAY

30TH AVE
3000

322ND ST WAY

STANTON TRL
5000

OXFORD MILL RD

LITTLE CANNON RIVER

See Page 222

325TH ST

325TH ST
4000

CANNON FALLS ISD #252

35TH AVE

STANTON TRL

STANTON TRL

33000

330TH ST

42ND AVE

24

55018

35TH AVE

34000

24

WARSAW TRL

WARSAW TRL

24

343RD ST

343RD ST

WARSAW TRL AVE

63RD AVE

345TH ST

03

02

01

30TH AVE

Warsaw Twp

35000

24

53RD AVE

T111N | T112N

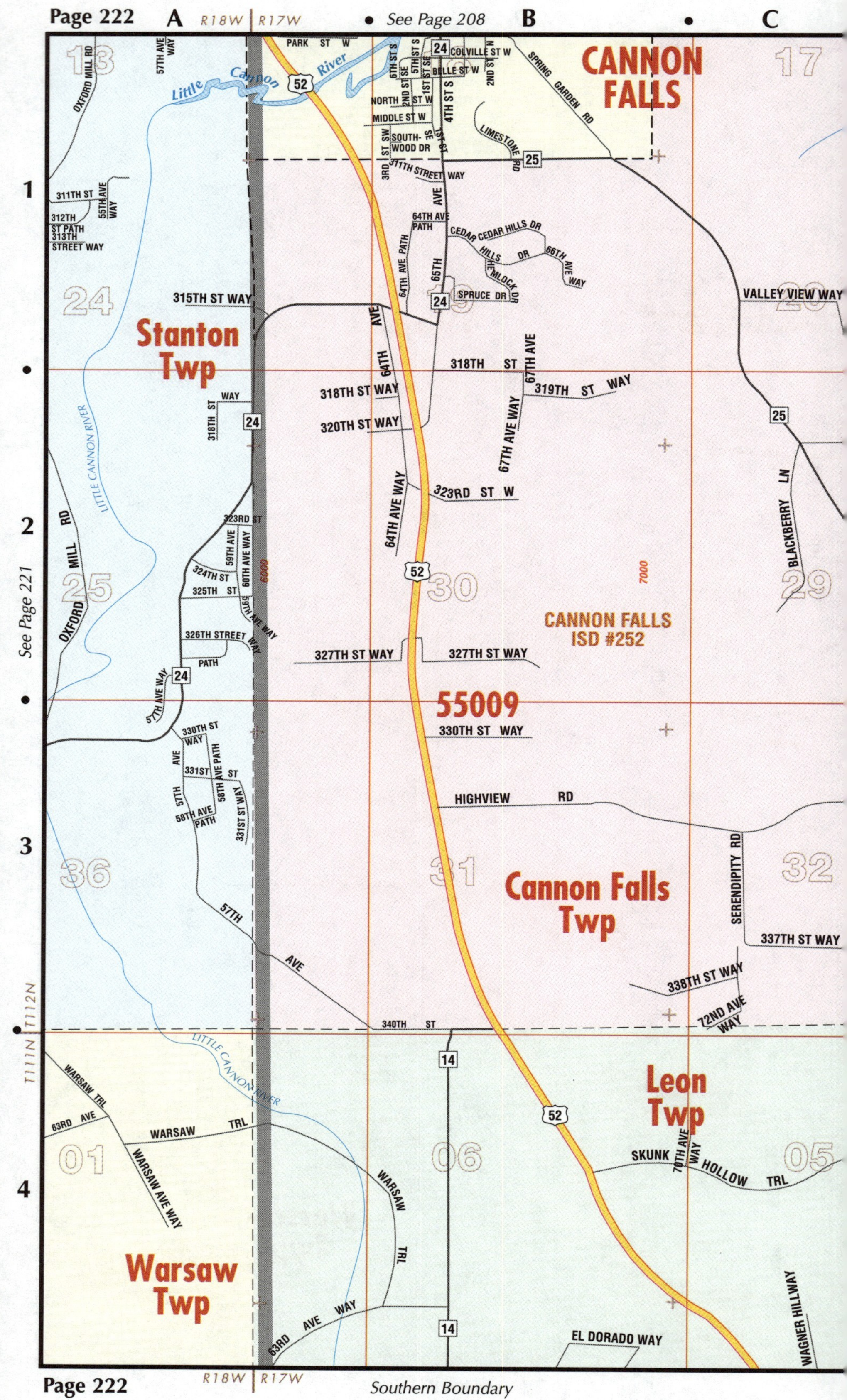

Page 222
A
R18W
R17W
See Page 208
B
C
1
2
3
4
See Page 221
T112N
T111N
Page 222
Southern Boundary
CANNON FALLS
Stanton Twp
Cannon Falls Twp
Leon Twp
Warsaw Twp
CANNON FALLS ISD #252
55009
Little Cannon River
LITTLE CANNON RIVER
PARK ST W
COLVILLE ST W
BELLE ST W
NORTH ST W
MIDDLE ST W
SOUTH-WOOD DR
SPRING GARDEN RD
LIMESTONE RD
311TH STREET WAY
64TH AVE PATH
CEDAR HILLS DR
66TH AVE WAY
HEMLOCK DR
SPRUCE DR
VALLEY VIEW WAY
OXFORD MILL RD
57TH AVE WAY
311TH ST
55TH AVE WAY
312TH ST PATH
313TH STREET WAY
315TH ST WAY
318TH ST
318TH ST WAY
319TH ST WAY
320TH ST WAY
67TH AVE
67TH AVE WAY
64TH AVE
64TH AVE WAY
323RD ST W
323RD ST
324TH ST
325TH ST
326TH STREET PATH
59TH AVE
60TH AVE WAY
327TH ST WAY
330TH ST WAY
331ST ST
58TH AVE PATH
331ST ST WAY
57TH AVE
57TH AVE WAY
BLACKBERRY LN
HIGHVIEW RD
SERENDIPITY RD
337TH ST WAY
338TH ST WAY
72ND AVE WAY
340TH ST
WARSAW TRL
63RD AVE
WARSAW AVE WAY
SKUNK HOLLOW TRL
70TH AVE WAY
63RD AVE WAY
EL DORADO WAY
WAGNER HILLWAY
6000
7000

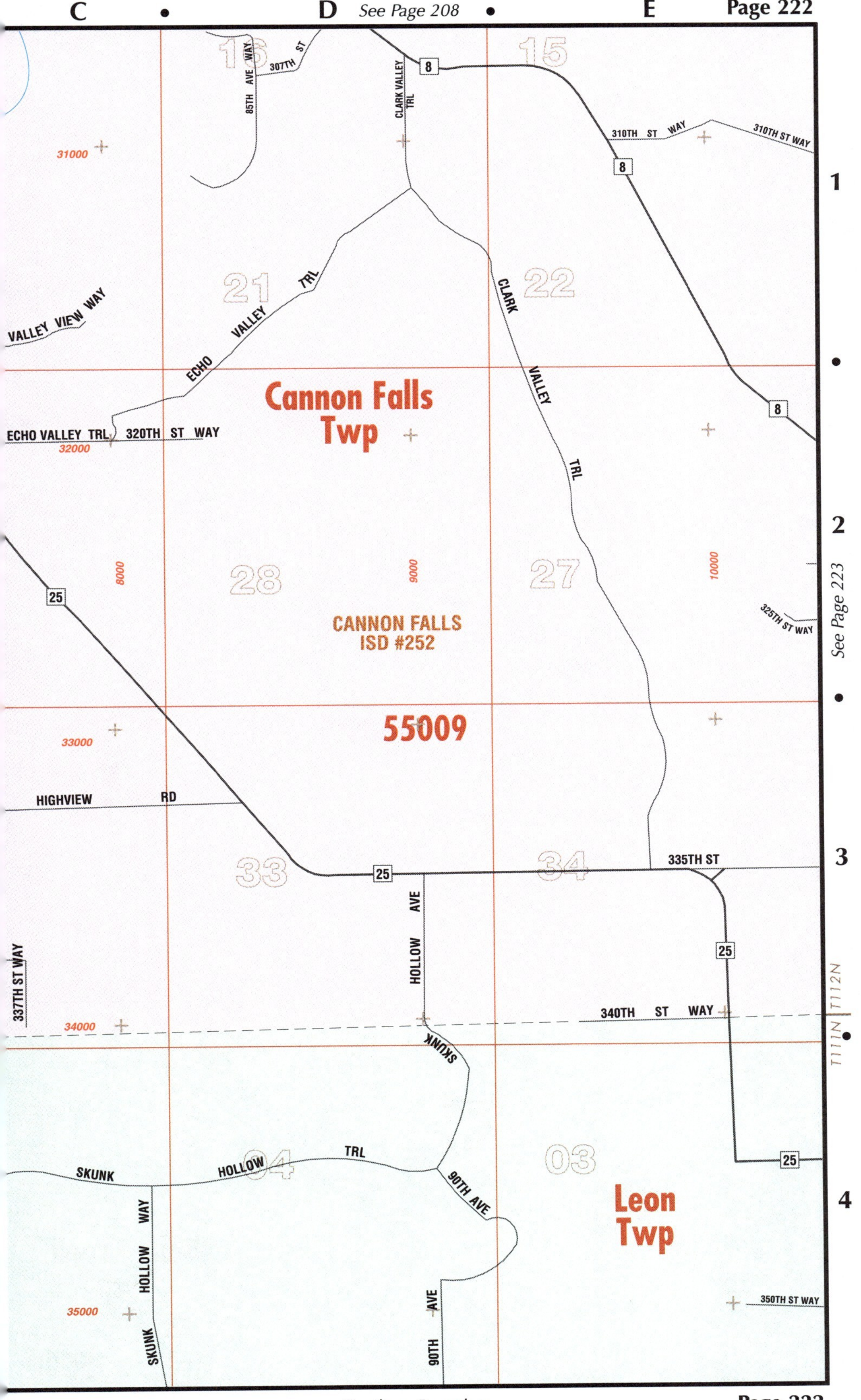

16

85TH AVE WAY
307TH ST
CLARK VALLEY TRL
15

8

31000

310TH ST WAY
310TH ST WAY

8

1

21

ECHO VALLEY TRL

VALLEY VIEW WAY

CLARK VALLEY TRL

22

Cannon Falls Twp

ECHO VALLEY TRL 320TH ST WAY

32000

8

2

See Page 223

25

8000

28

9000

27

10000

325TH ST WAY

CANNON FALLS
ISD #252

55009

33000

HIGHVIEW RD

33

25

34

335TH ST

3

337TH ST WAY

HOLLOW AVE

25

T11N T12N

34000

340TH ST WAY

SKUNK

04

SKUNK HOLLOW TRL

HOLLOW WAY

90TH AVE

03

25

Leon Twp

4

35000

90TH AVE

350TH ST WAY

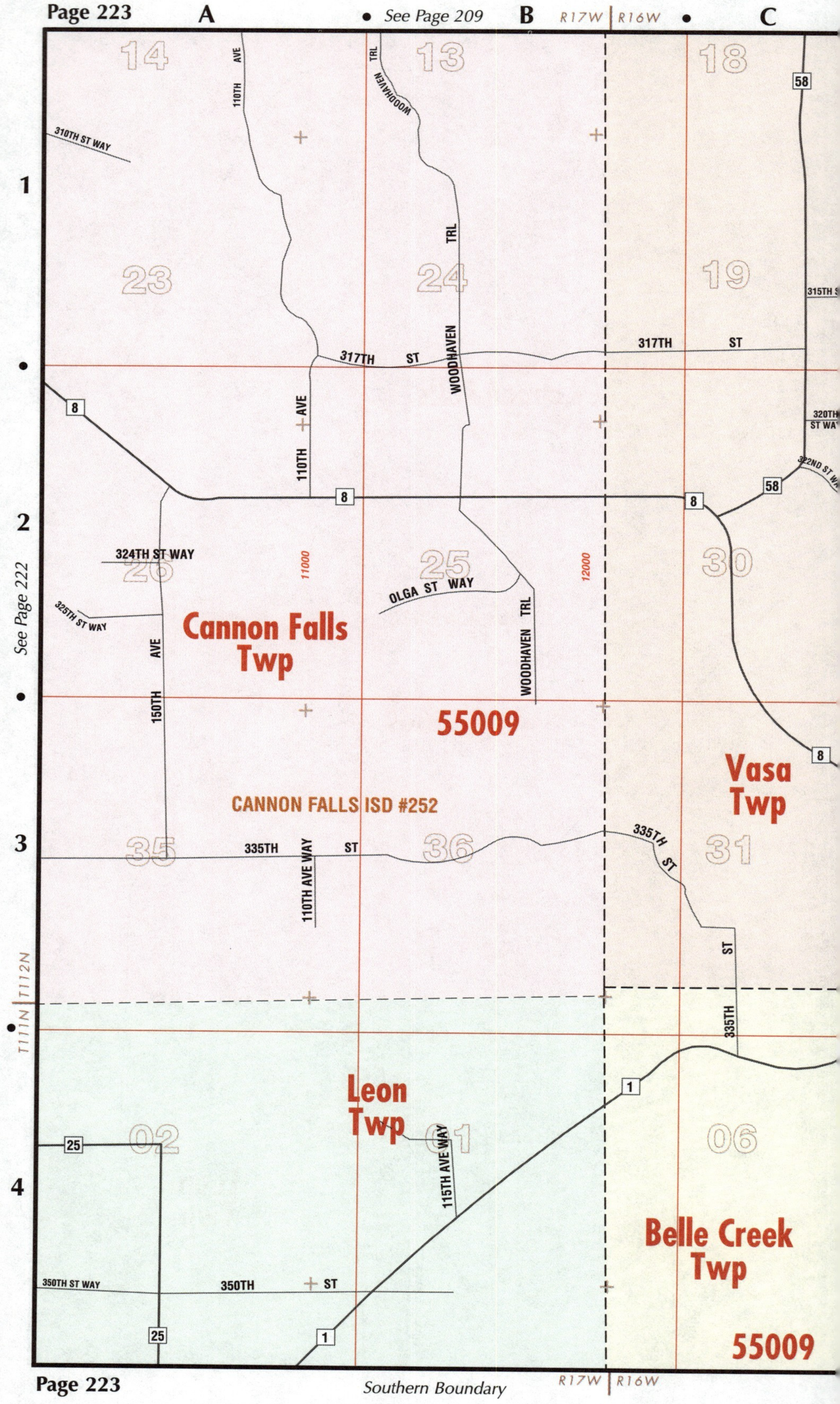

A

See Page 209

B

R17W | R16W

C

14

310TH ST WAY

110TH AVE

WOODHAVEN TRL

13

18

58

1

23

24

19

315TH S

317TH ST

317TH ST

8

110TH AVE

WOODHAVEN ST

320TH ST WA

322ND ST WA

2

8

8

58

324TH ST WAY

26

11000

25

30

325TH ST WAY

150TH AVE

OLGA ST WAY

WOODHAVEN TRL

12000

Cannon Falls Twp

55009

Vasa Twp

CANNON FALLS ISD #252

3

35

335TH AVE WAY

335TH ST

36

335TH ST

31

110TH AVE ST

See Page 222

T111N | T112N

335TH ST

Leon Twp

1

4

25

02

115TH AVE WAY

01

06

Belle Creek Twp

350TH ST WAY

350TH ST

25

1

55009

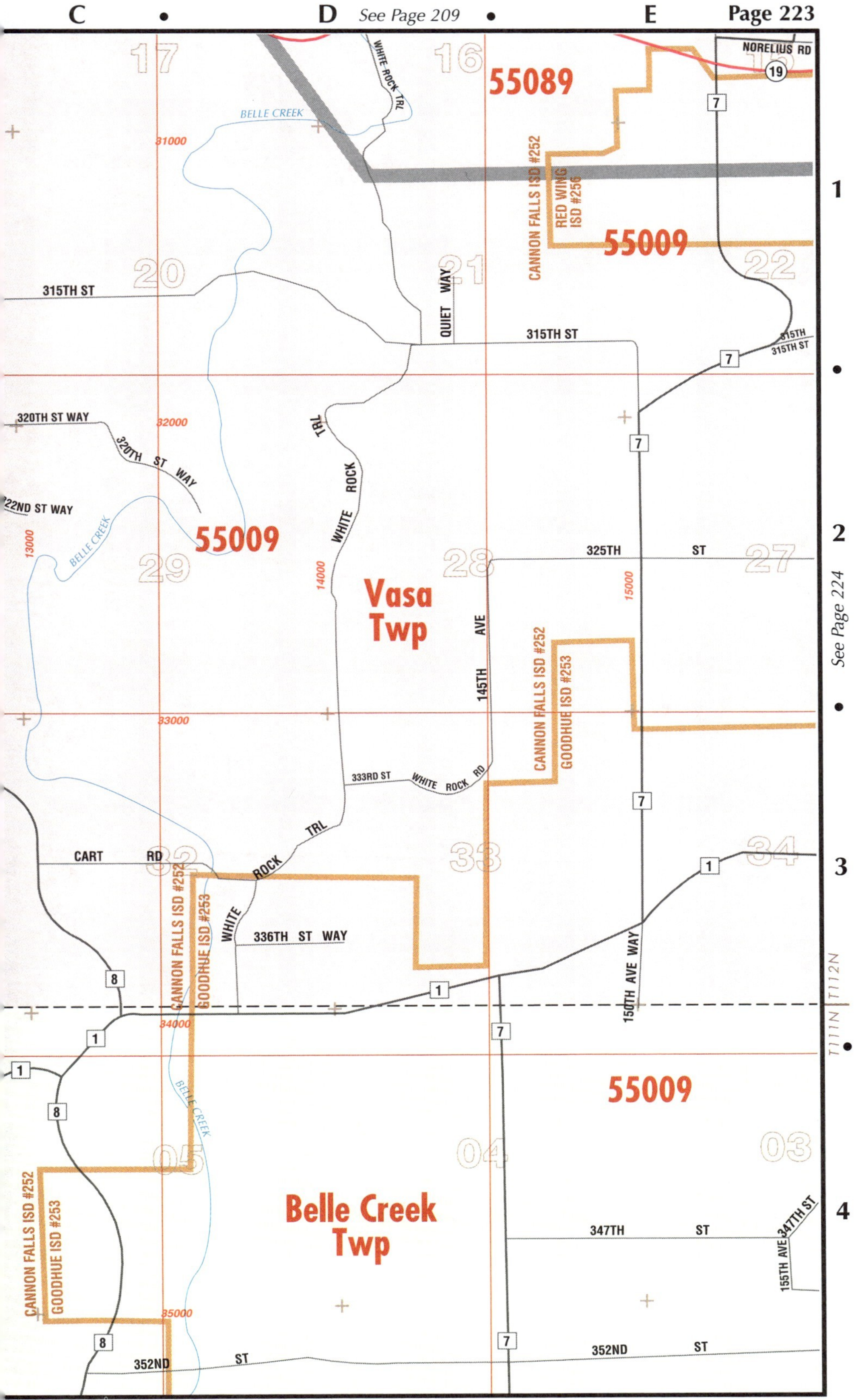

NORELIUS RD

WHITE ROCK TRL

BELLE CREEK

31000

55089

CANNON FALLS ISD #252

RED WING ISD #256

55009

315TH ST

QUIET WAY

315TH ST

315TH
315TH ST

320TH ST WAY

320TH ST WAY

32000

WHITE ROCK TRL

322ND ST WAY

13000

BELLE CREEK

55009

325TH ST

15000

Vasa Twp

14000

145TH AVE

CANNON FALLS ISD #252

GOODHUE ISD #253

33000

333RD ST

WHITE ROCK RD

CART RD

CANNON FALLS ISD #252

GOODHUE ISD #253

WHITE ROCK TRL

336TH ST WAY

150TH AVE WAY

34000

BELLE CREEK

T111N T112N

55009

Belle Creek Twp

CANNON FALLS ISD #252

GOODHUE ISD #253

347TH ST

155TH AVE

347TH ST

35000

352ND ST

352ND ST

A • *See Page 210* B • C R16W R

NORELIUS RD NORELIUS RD
(19)

160TH AVE

AVE

55089

13

51

1

22

315TH ST 23

160TH

315TH ST 315TH ST

160TH ST

315TH ST 24 ST

55009

CANNON FALLS ISD #252

RED WING ISD #256

RED WING ISD #256
GOODHUE ISD #253

RED WING ISD #256
GOODHUE ISD #253

See Page 223

2

27

325TH ST 26

325TH ST 25 ST

**Vasa
Twp**

GOODHUE ISD #253

RED WING ISD #256

GOODHUE ISD #253

GOODHUE ISD #253

51

T111N T112N

3

34

35 RED WING ISD #256 1

GOODHUE ISD #253

36

AVE

180TH

342ND STREET WAY

03

TRL

02

185TH AVENUE WAY

**Belle Creek
Twp**

01

55009

4

155TH AVE 347TH ST

WHEAT

350TH ST

AVE

350TH ST

AVE

165TH

180TH

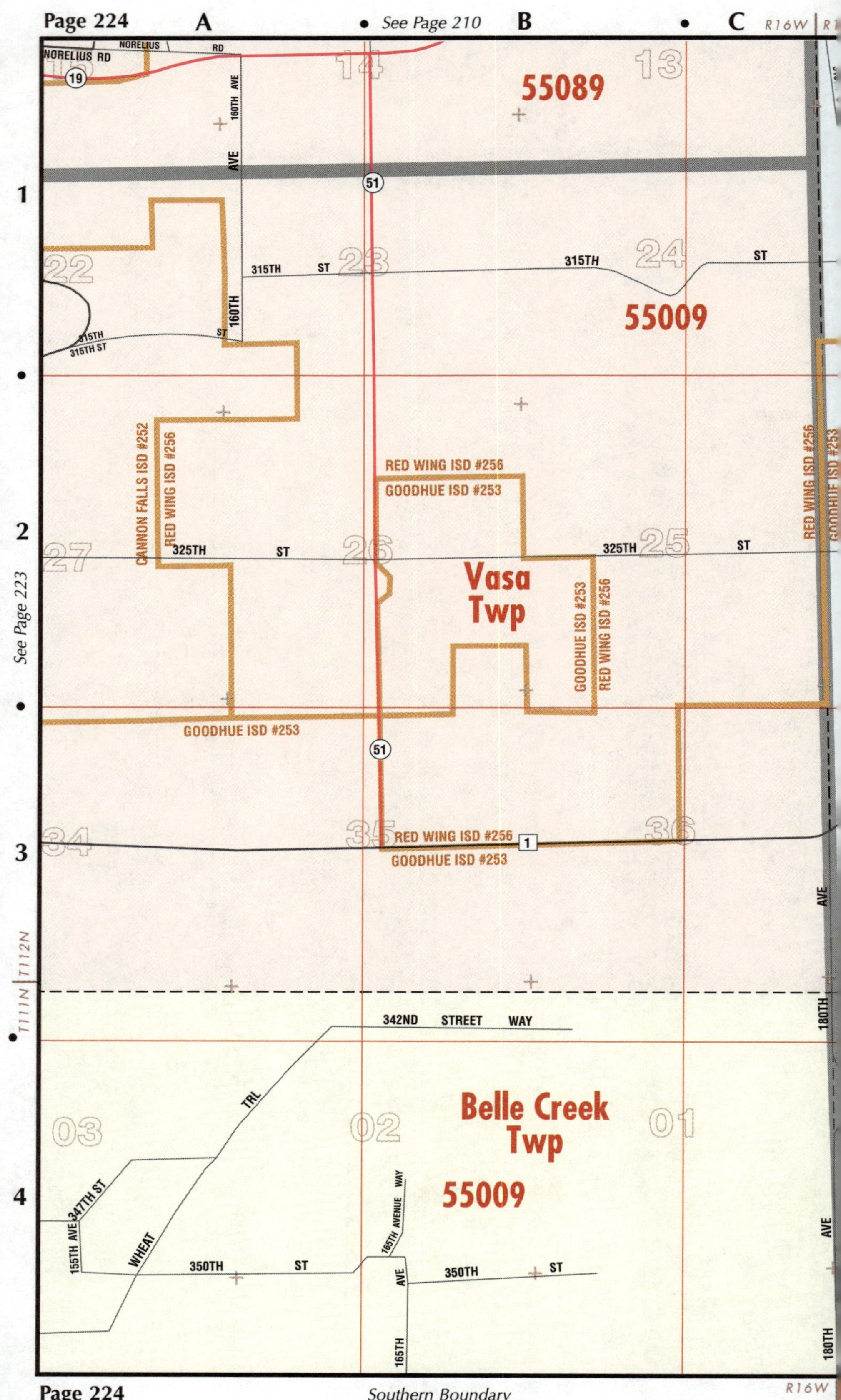

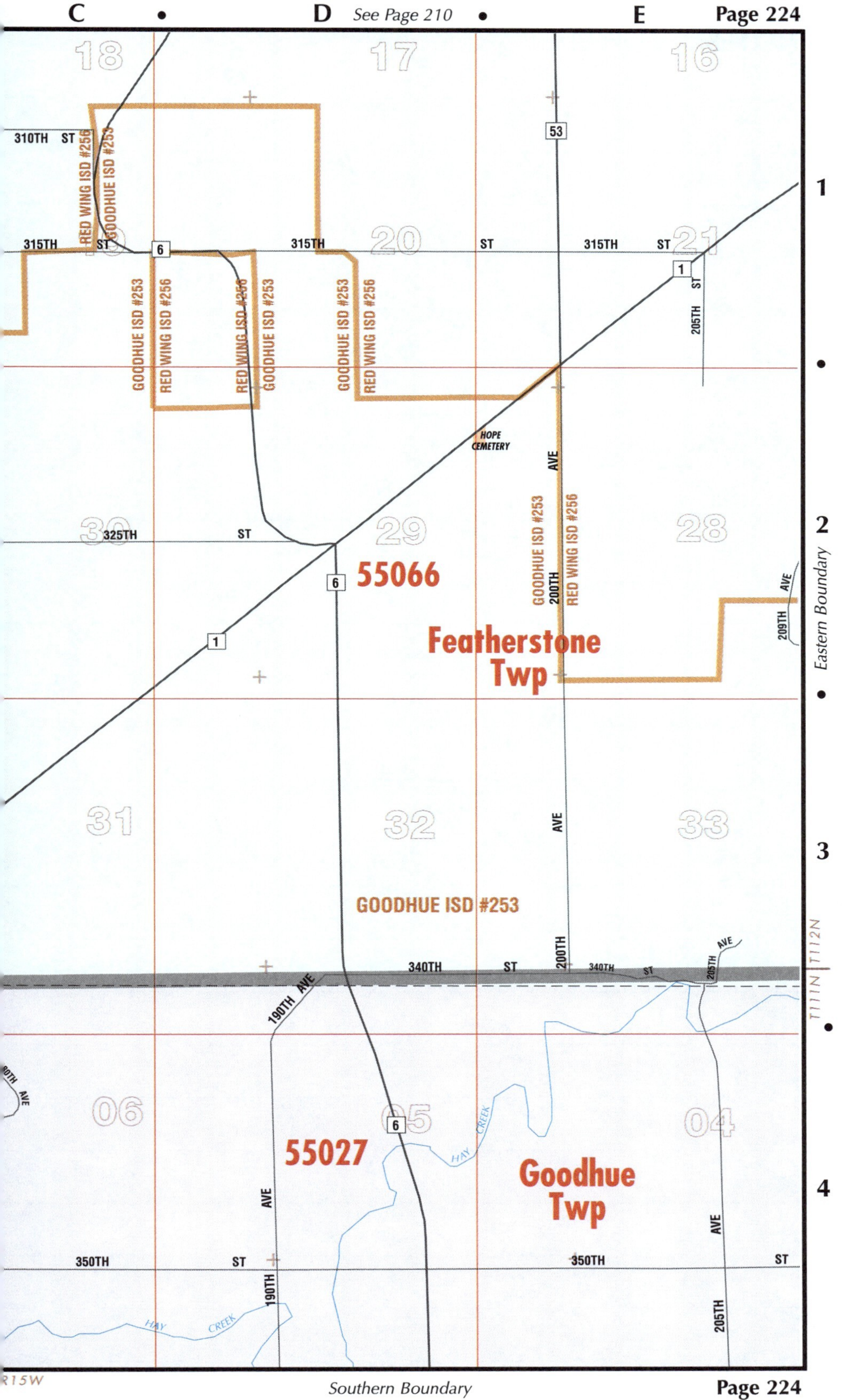

18

17

53

16

310TH ST

RED WING ISD #256
GOODHUE ISD #253

1

315TH ST

6

315TH ST

19

315TH

20

ST

315TH ST

21

1 ST

205TH

GOODHUE ISD #253
RED WING ISD #256
RED WING ISD #256
GOODHUE ISD #253
GOODHUE ISD #253
RED WING ISD #256

HOPE CEMETERY

GOODHUE ISD #253
200TH AVE
RED WING ISD #256

30

325TH ST

29

55066

6

28

AVE

209TH AVE

2

Eastern Boundary

1

Featherstone Twp

31

32

AVE

33

3

GOODHUE ISD #253

200TH

340TH ST

340TH ST

205TH AVE

T111N | T112N

190TH AVE

06

55027

05

6

HAY CREEK

04

Goodhue Twp

AVE

190TH

AVE

205TH

4

350TH ST

350TH ST

ST

HAY CREEK

NOTES:

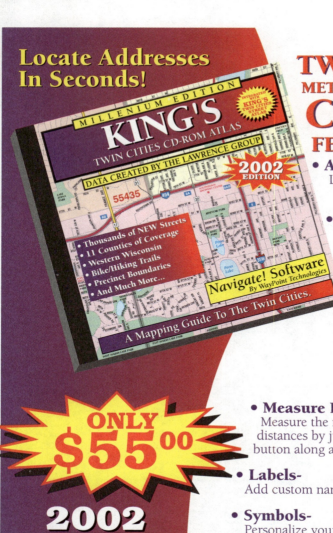

CITY LOCATION GUIDE

CITY (ABRV)	PAGE
AFTON (AFT)	124
ALBERTVILLE (ALB)	46
ALBION TWP (ABT)	43
ALDEN TWP (ADT)	42
ANDOVER (AND)	36
ANOKA (ANO)	49
APPLE VALLEY (APV)	163
ARDEN HILLS (AH)	79
ARLINGTON (ARL)	183
ARLINGTON TWP (ART)	183
ATHENS TWP (ATT)	9
BAYPORT (BAY)	97
BAYTOWN TWP (BYT)	96
BECKER (BEC)	16
BECKER TWP (BKR)	3
BELLE CREEK TWP (BCT)	223
BELLE PLAINE (BEL)	185
BELLE PLAINE TWP (BPT)	186
BENTON TWP (BTT)	143
BERGEN TWP (BNT)	127
BETHEL (BET)	8
BIG LAKE (BL)	18
BIG LAKE TWP (BLT)	18
BIRCHWOOD VILLAGE (BWV)	95
BLAINE (BLA)	65
BLAKELEY TWP (BKT)	185
BLOOMINGTON (BLO)	134
BRIDGEWATER TWP (BWT)	219
BROOKLYN CENTER (BC)	92
BROOKLYN PARK (BP)	78
BUFFALO (BUF)	59
BUFFALO TWP (BUT)	45
BURNS TWP (BT)	20
BURNSVILLE (BUR)	148
CAMDEN TWP (CT)	128
CANNON FALLS (CF)	208
CANNON FALLS TWP (CFT)	208
CARVER (CAR)	159
CASTLE ROCK TWP (CAT)	192
CEDAR LAKE TWP (CLT)	188
CENTER CITY (CNC)	12
CENTERVILLE (CV)	66
CHAMPLIN (CHM)	63
CHANHASSEN (CHN)	131
CHASKA (CHS)	131
CHASKA TWP (CHT)	145
CHATHAM TWP (CMT)	58
CHISAGO CITY (CHC)	26
CHISAGO LAKE TWP (CGT)	12
CIRCLE PINES (CP)	65
CLEAR LAKE (CL)	1
CLEAR LAKE TWP (CLR)	1
CLEARWATER (CW)	1
CLEARWATER TWP (CWT)	15
CLIFTON TWP (CTT)	139
COATES (COA)	164
COLOGNE (COL)	143
COLUMBIA HEIGHTS (CH)	92
COLUMBUS TWP (COT)	38
COON RAPIDS (CR)	64
CORCORAN (COR)	75
CORINNA TWP (CNT)	29
COTTAGE GROVE (CG)	138
CREDIT RIVER TWP (CRT)	175
CRYSTAL (CRY)	91
DAHLGREN TWP (DAT)	144
DAYTON (DAY)	62
DEEPHAVEN (DPH)	118
DELANO (DEL)	87
DELLWOOD (DWD)	81
DENMARK TWP (DET)	152
DERRYNANE TWP (DNT)	214
DIAMOND BLUFF TWP (DBT)	182
DOUGLAS TWP (DT)	194
DRESSER (DRS)	28
EAGAN (EAG)	135
EAST BETHEL (EB)	23
EDEN PRAIRIE (EPR)	132
EDINA (EDI)	119
ELK RIVER (ER)	19
ELKO (EKO)	204
EMPIRE TWP (ET)	178
ERIN TWP (ERT)	216
EUREKA TWP (EUT)	191
EXCELSIOR (EXC)	117
FALCON HEIGHTS (FH)	107
FARMINGTON (FAR)	177
FARMINGTON TWP (FAT)	42
FEATHERSTONE TWP (FET)	210
FOREST LAKE (FL)	39
FOREST LAKE TWP (FLT)	39
FOREST TWP (FOT)	218
FORT SNELLING (FS)	121
FRANCONIA TWP (FRT)	27
FRANKLIN TWP (FKT)	87
FRIDLEY (FRI)	78
GEM LAKE (GL)	94
GOLDEN VALLEY (GV)	105
GOODHUE TWP (GHT)	224
GRANT (GRA)	82
GREEN ISLE (GI)	169
GREEN ISLE TWP (GIT)	169
GREENFIELD (GRF)	74

CITY (ABRV)	PAGE
GREENVALE TWP (GVT)	205
GREENWOOD (GRW)	118
GREY CLOUD ISLAND TWP (GCT)	151
HAM LAKE (HL)	37
HAMBURG (HBG)	156
HAMPTON (HMP)	193
HAMPTON TWP (HMT)	193
HANCOCK TWP (HCT)	157
HANOVER (HAN)	60
HASSAN TWP (HSN)	61
HASTINGS (HAS)	166
HEIDELBERG (HEI)	215
HELEN TWP (HNT)	141
HELENA TWP (HAT)	187
HENDERSON (HEN)	198
HENDERSON TWP (HET)	212
HILLTOP (HIL)	92
HOLLYWOOD TWP (HOT)	114
HOPKINS (HOP)	119
HOWARD LAKE (HWL)	85
HUDSON (HUD)	111
HUDSON TWP (HUT)	112
HUGO (HUG)	67
INDEPENDENCE (IND)	88
INVER GROVE HEIGHTS (IGH)	136
JACKSON TWP (JT)	146
JESSENLAND TWP (JST)	184
JORDAN (JOR)	173
KELSO TWP (KT)	211
KINNICKINNIC TWP (KKT)	126
LAKE ELMO (LE)	110
LAKE PRAIRIE TWP (LPT)	212
LAKE SAINT CROIX BEACH (LSC)	125
LAKELAND (LLD)	111
LAKELAND SHORES (LS)	111
LAKETOWN TWP (LTT)	130
LAKEVILLE (LVL)	176
LANDFALL (LFL)	109
LANESBURGH TWP (LAT)	215
LAUDERDALE (LAU)	107
LE SUEUR (LES)	212
LENT TWP (LET)	11
LEON TWP (LEO)	222
LESTER PRAIRIE (LP)	127
LEXINGTON (LEX)	65
LEXINGTON TWP (LXT)	214
LILYDALE (LIL)	122
LINDSTROM (LND)	12
LINO LAKES (LL)	52
LINWOOD TWP (LWT)	24
LITTLE CANADA (LC)	94
LIVONIA TWP (LIT)	5
LONG LAKE (LOL)	103
LONSDALE (LON)	217
LORETTO (LOR)	89
LOUISVILLE TWP (LVT)	159
LYNDEN TWP (LYT)	1
MAHTOMEDI (MHT)	95
MAPLE GROVE (MG)	76
MAPLE LAKE (ML)	43
MAPLE LAKE TWP (MLT)	44
MAPLE PLAIN (MP)	102
MAPLEWOOD (MPW)	94
MARINE ON SAINT CROIX (MSC)	55
MARSHAN TWP (MT)	180
MARYSVILLE TWP (MVT)	72
MAY TWP (MAY)	68
MAYER (MYR)	114
MEDICINE LAKE (MDL)	105
MEDINA (MED)	89
MENDOTA (MEN)	121
MENDOTA HEIGHTS (MH)	135
MIDDLEVILLE TWP (MIT)	71
MIESVILLE (MIE)	195
MINNEAPOLIS (MPL)	106
MINNETONKA (MTK)	118
MINNETONKA BEACH (MTB)	117
MINNETRISTA (MTA)	116
MONTGOMERY (MGY)	215
MONTGOMERY TWP (MYT)	215
MONTICELLO (MO)	31
MONTICELLO TWP (MOT)	31
MONTROSE (MON)	86
MOUND (MOU)	116
MOUNDS VIEW (MV)	79
NEW BRIGHTON (NB)	79
NEW GERMANY (NG)	128
NEW HOPE (NH)	91
NEW MARKET (NM)	189
NEW MARKET TWP (NMT)	190
NEW PRAGUE (NP)	201
NEW TRIER (NT)	193
NEWPORT (NEW)	137
NININGER TWP (NIT)	165
NORTH HUDSON (NOH)	111
NORTH OAKS (NO)	80
NORTH SAINT PAUL (NSP)	95
NORTHFIELD (NFD)	219
NORTHFIELD TWP (NFT)	220
NORWOOD YOUNG AMERICA (NYA)	142
OAK GROVE (OG)	22
OAK GROVE TWP (OGT)	168
OAK PARK HEIGHTS (OPH)	97

CITY (ABRV)	PAGE
OAKDALE (OKD)	109
ORONO (ORO)	103
ORROCK TWP (ORT)	4
OSCEOLA (OSC)	28
OSCEOLA TWP (OST)	28
OSSEO (OSS)	77
OTSEGO (OTS)	33
OTTAWA TWP (OTT)	212
OXFORD TWP (OXT)	10
PINE SPRINGS (PS)	95
PLATO (PLA)	141
PLYMOUTH (PLY)	90
PRESCOTT (PRE)	167
PRIOR LAKE (PRL)	161
RAMSEY (RAM)	34
RANDOLPH (RAN)	207
RANDOLPH TWP (RAT)	207
RAVENNA TWP (RVT)	167
RED WING (RW)	196
RICHFIELD (RCH)	134
RICHMOND TWP (RDT)	84
RIVER FALLS (RF)	140
RIVER FALLS TWP (RIT)	140
ROBBINSDALE (ROB)	92
ROCKFORD (RFD)	74
ROCKFORD TWP (RFT)	73
ROGERS (ROG)	61
ROSEMOUNT (RMT)	164
ROSEVILLE (RVL)	93
SAINT ANTHONY (SA)	93
SAINT BONIFACIUS (SB)	116
SAINT CROIX FALLS (SCF)	14
SAINT CROIX FALLS TWP (SAT)	14
SAINT FRANCIS (SF)	7
SAINT JOSEPH TWP (SJT)	97
SAINT LAWRENCE TWP (SLW)	172
SAINT LOUIS PARK (SLP)	105
SAINT MARYS POINT (SMP)	125
SAINT MICHAEL (SM)	46
SAINT PAUL (STP)	108
SAINT PAUL PARK (SPP)	137
SAN FRANCISCO TWP (SFT)	172
SAND CREEK TWP (SCT)	173
SAVAGE (SAV)	147
SCIOTA TWP (SIT)	206
SHAFER (SHA)	13
SHAFER TWP (SHT)	13
SHAKOPEE (SHK)	146
SHARON TWP (SNT)	213
SHOREVIEW (SVW)	79
SHOREWOOD (SWD)	117
SILVER CREEK TWP (SVT)	16
SOMERSET (SOM)	70
SOMERSET TWP (SMT)	70
SOUTH SAINT PAUL (SSP)	122
SPRING LAKE PARK (SLK)	78
SPRING LAKE TWP (SLT)	174
SPRING PARK (SPR)	117
STACY (STA)	11
STANFORD TWP (STT)	7
STANTON TWP (STN)	221
STAR PRAIRIE TWP (SPT)	70
STILLWATER (SWR)	96
STILLWATER TWP (SWT)	82
SUNFISH LAKE (SL)	136
TAYLORS FALLS (TF)	14
TONKA BAY (TKB)	117
TRIMBELLE TWP (TLT)	168
TROY TWP (TRT)	126
TYRONE TWP (TYT)	213
VADNAIS HEIGHTS (VH)	94
VASA TWP (VAT)	209
VERMILLION (VER)	179
VERMILLION TWP (VET)	179
VICTOR TWP (VIT)	85
VICTORIA (VIC)	131
WACONIA (WAC)	129
WACONIA TWP (WCT)	129
WARREN TWP (WRT)	112
WARSAW TWP (WST)	221
WASHINGTON LAKE TWP (WLK)	170
WATERFORD TWP (WFT)	206
WATERTOWN (WAT)	101
WATERTOWN TWP (WTT)	101
WAVERLY (WAV)	72
WAYZATA (WAY)	104
WEBSTER TWP (WT)	218
WELCH TWP (WEL)	195
WEST LAKELAND TWP (WLT)	110
WEST SAINT PAUL (WSP)	122
WHEATLAND TWP (WHT)	216
WHITE BEAR LAKE (WBL)	81
WHITE BEAR TWP (WBT)	80
WILLERNIE (WIL)	95
WINSTED (WIN)	99
WINSTED TWP (WIT)	113
WOODBURY (WBY)	123
WOODLAND (WDL)	104
WOODLAND TWP (WDT)	86
WYOMING (WYO)	25
WYOMING TWP (WYT)	25
YOUNG AMERICA TWP (YAT)	156
ZIMMERMAN (ZIM)	5

TWIN CITIES METRO INDEX

CITY ABBREVIATION GUIDE

ABBREVIATION	CITY
ABT	ALBION TWP
ADT	ALDEN TWP
AFT	AFTON
AH	ARDEN HILLS
ALB	ALBERTVILLE
AND	ANDOVER
ANO	ANOKA
APV	APPLE VALLEY
ARL	ARLINGTON
ART	ARLINGTON TWP
ATT	ATHENS TWP
BAY	BAYPORT
BC	BROOKLYN CENTER
BCT	BELLE CREEK TWP
BEC	BECKER
BEL	BELLE PLAINE
BET	BETHEL
BKR	BECKER TWP
BKT	BLAKELEY TWP
BL	BIG LAKE
BLA	BLAINE
BLO	BLOOMINGTON
BLT	BIG LAKE TWP
BNT	BERGEN TWP
BP	BROOKLYN PARK
BPT	BELLE PLAINE TWP
BT	BURNS TWP
BTT	BENTON TWP
BUF	BUFFALO
BUR	BURNSVILLE
BUT	BUFFALO TWP
BWT	BRIDGEWATER TWP
BWV	BIRCHWOOD VILLAGE
BYT	BAYTOWN TWP
CAR	CARVER
CAT	CASTLE ROCK TWP
CF	CANNON FALLS
CFT	CANNON FALLS TWP
CG	COTTAGE GROVE
CGT	CHISAGO LAKE TWP
CH	COLUMBIA HEIGHTS
CHC	CHISAGO CITY
CHM	CHAMPLIN
CHN	CHANHASSEN
CHS	CHASKA
CHT	CHASKA TWP
CL	CLEAR LAKE
CLR	CLEAR LAKE TWP
CLT	CEDAR LAKE TWP
CMT	CHATHAM TWP
CNC	CENTER CITY
CNT	CORINNA TWP
COA	COATES
COL	COLOGNE
COR	CORCORAN
COT	COLUMBUS TWP
CP	CIRCLE PINES
CR	COON RAPIDS
CRT	CREDIT RIVER TWP
CRY	CRYSTAL
CT	CAMDEN TWP
CTT	CLIFTON TWP
CV	CENTERVILLE
CW	CLEARWATER
CWT	CLEARWATER TWP
DAT	DAHLGREN TWP
DAY	DAYTON
DBT	DIAMOND BLUFF TWP
DEL	DELANO
DET	DENMARK TWP
DNT	DERRYNANE TWP
DPH	DEEPHAVEN
DRS	DRESSER
DT	DOUGLAS TWP
DWD	DELLWOOD
EAG	EAGAN
EB	EAST BETHEL
EDI	EDINA
EKO	ELKO
EPR	EDEN PRAIRIE
ER	ELK RIVER
ERT	ERIN TWP
ET	EMPIRE TWP
EUT	EUREKA TWP
EXC	EXCELSIOR
FAR	FARMINGTON
FAT	FARMINGTON TWP
FET	FEATHERSTONE TWP
FH	FALCON HEIGHTS
FKT	FRANKLIN TWP
FL	FOREST LAKE
FLT	FOREST LAKE TWP
FOT	FOREST TWP
FRI	FRIDLEY
FRT	FRANCONIA TWP
FS	FORT SNELLING
GCT	GREY CLOUD ISLAND TWP
GHT	GOODHUE TWP
GI	GREEN ISLE
GIT	GREEN ISLE TWP
GL	GEM LAKE
GRA	GRANT
GRF	GREENFIELD
GRW	GREENWOOD
GV	GOLDEN VALLEY
GVT	GREENVALE TWP
HAN	HANOVER
HAS	HASTINGS
HAT	HELENA TWP
HBG	HAMBURG
HCT	HANCOCK TWP
HEI	HEIDELBERG
HEN	HENDERSON
HET	HENDERSON TWP
HIL	HILLTOP
HL	HAM LAKE
HMP	HAMPTON
HMT	HAMPTON TWP
HNT	HELEN TWP
HOP	HOPKINS
HOT	HOLLYWOOD TWP
HSN	HASSAN TWP
HUD	HUDSON
HUG	HUGO
HUT	HUDSON TWP
HWL	HOWARD LAKE
IGH	INVER GROVE HEIGHTS
IND	INDEPENDENCE
JOR	JORDAN
JST	JESSENLAND TWP
JT	JACKSON TWP
KKT	KINNICKINNIC TWP
KT	KELSO TWP
LAT	LANESBURGH TWP
LAU	LAUDERDALE
LC	LITTLE CANADA
LE	LAKE ELMO
LEO	LEON TWP
LES	LESUEUR
LET	LENT TWP
LEX	LEXINGTON
LFL	LANDFALL
LIL	LILYDALE
LIT	LIVONIA TWP
LL	LINO LAKES
LLD	LAKELAND
LND	LINDSTROM
LOL	LONG LAKE
LON	LONSDALE
LOR	LORETTO
LP	LESTER PRARIE
LPT	LAKE PRARIE TWP
LS	LAKELAND SHORES
LSC	LAKE SAINT CROIX BEACH
LTT	LAKETOWN TWP
LVL	LAKEVILLE
LVT	LOUISVILLE TWP
LWT	LINWOOD TWP
LXT	LEXINGTON TWP
LYT	LYNDEN TWP
MAY	MAY TWP
MDL	MEDICINE LAKE
MED	MEDINA
MEN	MENDOTA
MG	MAPLE GROVE
MGY	MONTGOMERY
MH	MENDOTA HEIGHTS
MHT	MAHTOMEDI
MIE	MIESVILLE
MIT	MIDDLEVILLE TWP
ML	MAPLE LAKE
MLT	MAPLE LAKE TWP
MO	MONTICELLO
MON	MONTROSE
MOT	MONTICELLO TWP
MOU	MOUND
MP	MAPLE PLAIN
MPL	MINNEAPOLIS
MPW	MAPLEWOOD
MSC	MARINE ON SAINT CROIX
MT	MARSHAN TWP
MTA	MINNETRISTA
MTB	MINNETONKA BEACH
MTK	MINNETONKA
MV	MOUNDS VIEW
MVT	MARYSVILLE TWP
MYR	MAYER
MYT	MONTGOMERY TWP
NB	NEW BRIGHTON
NEW	NEWPORT
NFD	NORTHFIELD
NFT	NORTHFIELD TWP
NG	NEW GERMANY
NH	NEW HOPE
NIT	NININGER TWP
NM	NEW MARKET
NMT	NEW MARKET TWP
NO	NORTH OAKS
NOH	NORTH HUDSON
NP	NEW PRAGUE
NSP	NORTH SAINT PAUL
NT	NEW TRIER
NYA	NORWOOD YOUNG AMERICA
OG	OAK GROVE
OGT	OAK GROVE TWP
OKD	OAKDALE
OPH	OAK PARK HEIGHTS
ORO	ORONO
ORT	ORROCK TWP
OSC	OSCEOLA
OSS	OSSEO
OST	OSCEOLA TWP
OTS	OTSEGO
OTT	OTTAWA TWP
OXT	OXFORD TWP
PLA	PLATO
PLY	PLYMOUTH
PRE	PRESCOTT
PRL	PRIOR LAKE
PS	PINE SPRINGS
RAM	RAMSEY
RAN	RANDOLPH
RAT	RANDOLPH TWP
RCH	RICHFIELD
RDT	RICHMOND TWP
RF	RIVER FALLS
RFD	ROCKFORD
RFT	ROCKFORD TWP
RIT	RIVER FALLS TWP
RMT	ROSEMOUNT
ROB	ROBBINSDALE
ROG	ROGERS
RVL	ROSEVILLE
RVT	RAVENNA TWP
RW	RED WING
SA	SAINT ANTHONY
SAT	SAINT CROIX FALLS TWP
SAV	SAVAGE
SB	SAINT BONIFACIUS
SCF	SAINT CROIX FALLS
SCT	SAND CREEK TWP
SF	SAINT FRANCIS
SFT	SAN FRANCISCO TWP
SHA	SHAFER
SHK	SHAKOPEE
SHT	SHAFER TWP
SIT	SCIOTA TWP
SJT	SAINT JOSEPH TWP
SL	SUNFISH LAKE
SLK	SPRING LAKE PARK
SLP	SAINT LOUIS PARK
SLT	SPRING LAKE TWP
SLW	SAINT LAWRENCE TWP
SM	SAINT MICHAEL
SMP	SAINT MARYS POINT
SMT	SOMERSET TWP
SNT	SHARON TWP
SOM	SOMERSET
SPP	SAINT PAUL PARK
SPR	SPRING PARK
SPT	STAR PRAIRIE TWP
SSP	SOUTH SAINT PAUL
STA	STACY
STN	STANTON TWP
STP	SAINT PAUL
STT	STANFORD TWP
SVT	SILVER CREEK TWP
SVW	SHOREVIEW
SWD	SHOREWOOD
SWR	STILLWATER
SWT	STILLWATER TWP
TF	TAYLORS FALLS
TKB	TONKA BAY
TLT	TRIMBELLE TWP
TRT	TROY TWP
TYT	TYRONE TWP
VAT	VASA TWP
VER	VERMILLION
VET	VERMILLION TWP
VH	VADNAIS HEIGHTS
VIC	VICTORIA
VIT	VICTOR TWP
WAC	WACONIA
WAT	WATERTOWN
WAV	WAVERLY
WAY	WAYZATA
WBL	WHITE BEAR LAKE
WBT	WHITE BEAR TWP
WBY	WOODBURY
WCT	WACONIA TWP
WDL	WOODLAND
WDT	WOODLAND TWP
WEL	WELCH TWP
WFT	WATERFORD TWP
WHT	WHEATLAND TWP
WIL	WILLERNIE
WIN	WINSTED
WIT	WINSTED TWP
WLK	WASHINGTON LAKE TWP
WLT	WEST LAKELAND TWP
WRT	WARREN TWP
WSP	WEST SAINT PAUL
WST	WARSAW TWP
WT	WEBSTER TWP
WTT	WATERTOWN TWP
WYO	WYOMING
WYT	WYOMING TWP
YAT	YOUNG AMERICA TWP
ZIM	ZIMMERMAN

ABBEY HILL DR MTK . . . . .81 - A4

Street Name — City/Township Abbreviation — Page Number — Grid Location

A ST - ANN CIR

A

A ST HIL .92-E2
A ST STP 123-A1
A ST WBL .94-E2
AADLAND AVE NE BUT . . .44-D4,58-D1
AARON DR NM 204-A1
ABBEY PT SHK 146-B4,160-B1
ABBEY WAY EAG 135-E4
ABBEY WAY MH 136-B2
ABBEY HILL DR MTK 105-A4
ABBIE LN HOP 119-C2
ABBOTT AVE EDI 120-B3
ABBOTT AVE N BC 78-A4,92-A1
ABBOTT AVE N BP 64-A4,78-A3
ABBOTT AVE N ROB 92-A3,106-A1
ABBOTT AVE S BLO 134-B4,148-B1
ABBOTT AVE S MPL 106-B4,120-B2
ABBOTT CIR BUR 148-B4
ABBOTT CT EPR 133-B4
ABBOTT CT MTK 119-B3
ABBOTT LN MTK 119-B3
ABBOTT PL EDI 120-B3
ABBOTT PL MTK 119-B3
ABBOTT ST W SWR 96-E2,97-A2
ABBY AVE BEC 2-E3
ABBYWOOD LN LTT 130-D3
ABBYWOOD RD LTT 130-D3
ABEL LN MTK 104-C4
ABEL ST N MPW 108-B1
ABELE ST AH 79-C3
ABELL ST STP 108-B2
ABERCROMBIE DR EDI 133-E1
ABERDEEN AVE BPT 187-A3,201-A1
ABERDEEN AVE SLW 173-A4,187-A1
ABERDEEN CRV WBY 123-D2
ABERDEEN RD MOU 117-A2
ABERDEEN ST NE BLA 51-A4,65-A1
ABERDEEN ST NE EB 22-E2
ABERDEEN ST NE HL 37-A4,51-A2
ABERDEEN TRL WT 218-C3
ABERDEEN WAY BL 18-A2
ABERT AVE NE BUT 44-E4,58-E1
ABERT AVE NE MOT 30-D2
ABIGAIL CT IGH 150-C1
ABILENE LN COR 75-E3,76-A3
ABINGDON WAY ORO 103-D3
ABLE CIR NE BLA 50-E4
ABLE ST HL 36-E3
ABLE ST NE BLA 64-E1,78-E1
ABLE ST NE FRI 78-E3
ABLE ST NE HL 50-E2
ABLE ST NE SLK 78-E1
ABLEMARLE ST RVL 108-B1
ABORETUM BLVD LTT . . .129-E3,130-B2
ABORETUM BLVD VIC 130-D2
ACACIA AVE NE MOT 16-E3,30-E3
ACACIA BLVD MH 135-D1
ACACIA DR MH 121-D4,135-D1
ACADEMY AVE EXC 117-D4
ACADEMY AVE SWD 117-D4
ACADIA BAY WBY 123-E3
ACADIA CT BUR 149-A3
ACADIA RD WBY 123-E3
ACKER ST E STP 108-B3
ACKER ST W STP 108-B3
ACORN AVE HNT 141-C4,155-C2
ACORN AVE WIT 99-C3
ACORN CIR BUR 148-E4
ACORN CIR MOT 32-A3
ACORN CIR MTK 104-D3
ACORN CIR RFD 74-A4
ACORN CIR SW SM 46-E4
ACORN DR SL 136-B2
ACORN LN CHN 131-D2
ACORN LN SOM 84-B1
ACORN LN SSP 122-D3
ACORN LN SE BKR 4-A1
ACORN RD CHS 131-D4
ACORN RD MOU 116-D2
ACORN RD RVL 93-C4
ACORN ST EAG 150-B2
ACORN WAY SLW 173-A2
ACORN RIDGE RD MTK 118-B2
ADA ST STP 122-C1
ADAIR AVE N BP 77-E4
ADAIR AVE N CHM 63-E2
ADAIR AVE N CRY 91-E3
ADAIR AVE N GV 105-E1
ADAIR AVE NE BUT 44-E4
ADAIR CT N BP 77-E2
ADAM AVE IGH 150-C2
ADAM CIR CAR 159-A1
ADAM DR HUT 97-D4
ADAMS AVE EDI 119-C2
ADAMS AVE N COL 143-E4
ADAMS AVE N NG 114-A4
ADAMS AVE S COL 143-E4
ADAMS AVE S NG 114-A4,128-A1
ADAMS CIR COL 143-E4
ADAMS DR NYA 142-C3
ADAMS LN JOR 173-B2
ADAMS ST ANO 63-D1
ADAMS ST BL 18-A4
ADAMS ST HAS 166-E1
ADAMS ST MV 79-B2
ADAMS ST NYA 142-C3
ADAMS ST SCF 14-C2
ADAMS ST E ARL 183-A2
ADAMS ST N SCF 14-C2
ADAMS ST NE MPL 92-D4,106-D1
ADAMS ST NW ER 48-B1
ADAMS ST S SCF 14-C2
ADAMS ST S SHK 146-A3
ADAMS ST W ARL 183-A2
ADDIE LN EPR 118-D4,132-D1
ADDIE ST NW WAT 101-B3
ADDINGTON CT EPR 118-C4
ADDISON DR SLT 174-E4
ADELBERT AVE IGH 136-C4
ADELE ST MPW 94-D4,108-D1
ADELINE CT MH 121-E3
ADELINE CT MTK 104-D3
ADELINE GRN SWR 96-C2
ADELINE LN GV 105-E2
ADELINE LN MTK 104-D3
ADELINE WAY ROG 61-E1
ADELL AVE N GV 92-A4
ADELMANN ST PRL 161-C4
ADMIRAL LN N BC 92-A1
ADMIRAL PL BC 92-A1
ADOLPHUS ST N MPW 108-B1
ADRET CT EPR 132-D1
ADRIAN CIR PRL 161-B3
ADRIAN ST STP 121-E2
ADVANTAGE LN EAG 136-A3
AENON PL LL 52-B4
AETNA AVE NE BUT 44-E4
AETNA AVE NE MOT 16-E4,30-E2
AETNA AVE SE FKT 72-E4,86-E1
AETNA AVE SE RFT 72-E2
AFFIRMED DR SHK 146-C2
AFTON AVE NE BUT 44-E4
AFTON AVE NE MOT 16-E4
AFTON BLVD S AFT 125-A3
AFTON COULEE RIDGE RD AFT .125-B3
AFTON CT WBY 123-D2
AFTON RD MOU 117-A2
AFTON RD SFT 159-A3
AFTON RD SWD 117-B4
AFTON RD WBY 123-D2
AFTON HILLS CT S AFT 125-B2
AFTON HILLS DR S AFT 125-B3
AFTON HILLS LN S AFT 125-A2
AGATE AVE NE BUT 44-E4
AGATE AVE NE MOT 44-E1
AGATE AVE SE FKT 72-E3
AGATE AVE SE RFT 72-E3
AGATE CRV SHK 145-E3,146-A3
AGATE ST STP 108-B3
AGATE ST N MPW 108-B1
AGATHA AVE IGH 150-C2
AGLEN ST RVL 93-E3,107-E1
AHERN AVE SE FKT 86-E2
AHERN BLVD ET 178-C4
AHLSTROM RD ROG 61-E1
AHRENS RD TRT 125-D2
AIDA PL STP 107-E2
AILEEN CT VH 80-C4
AIR FORCE BASE FS 121-B3
AIRLINE DR FS 135-A2
AIRLINE LN FS 135-A2
AIRPORT LN FS 135-A2
AIRPORT RD BLA 65-A4,79-B1
AIRPORT RD FS 121-B4,135-B1
AIRPORT RD IGH 136-E2,137-A2
AIRPORT RD LTT 129-E3,130-B3
AIRPORT RD STP 108-C4,122-C1
AIRPORT RD WCT 129-E3
AKERS LN EDI 119-C3
AKERS LN SCT 173-D1
AKERSON CT LND 12-D4
AKERSON ST LND 12-D4
AKIN RD FAR 177-D3
AKRON AVE CAT 192-C3,206-C1
AKRON AVE ET 164-C3
AKRON AVE IGH 122-C4,150-C3
AKRON AVE RMT 150-C4,164-C2
ALABAMA AVE BLA 79-B1
ALABAMA AVE S SAV . . .147-E4,161-E1
ALABAMA AVE S SLP . . .105-E4,119-E1
ALABAMA CIR BLO 133-E4,147-E1
ALABAMA RD BLO 133-E4
ALABAMA ST SCF 14-C3
ALABAMA ST E STP 108-C4
ALABAMA ST SE LON 217-B2
ALABAMA ST SW LON 217-B2
ALADDIN AVE NW MLT 30-D4,44-D1
ALADDIN AVE NW SVT 16-D3
ALADDIN AVE SW MVT 72-D1
ALADDIN CIR NW CMT 58-D3
ALADDIN ST RVL 94-A4
ALADIN TRL IGH 150-B1
ALAMEDA AVE IGH 150-C2
ALAMEDA CT IGH 150-C2
ALAMEDA PATH IGH 150-B2
ALAMEDA ST RVL 94-A4,108-A1
ALAMEDA ST STP 108-A2
ALAMEDA ST SVW 79-E1
ALAMO CIR BLA 65-B4,79-B1
ALAMO CIR NE HL 37-B4
ALAMO ST NE BLA 65-B4
ALAMO ST NE EB 23-B1,37-B2
ALAMO ST NE HL 37-B4,51-B3
ALASKA AVE BLA 79-B1
ALASKA AVE STP 121-E2
ALAUREATE CT IGH 150-C1
ALAUREATE CT W IGH 150-C1
ALAUREATE TRL W IGH 150-C1
ALBANY AVE PRL 161-A3
ALBANY AVE STP 107-D2
ALBANY AVE WT 204-C4,218-C3
ALBANY CIR EAG 150-A1
ALBANY CIR NW ER 19-C4
ALBANY ST ER 33-C2
ALBANY ST NW ER 19-C4,33-C1
ALBATROSS CIR CAT 178-C4,192-C1
ALBATROSS ST NW OG 36-B1
ALBAVAR PATH IGH 150-B3
ALBEMARLE CT RVL 94-B4
ALBEMARLE ST RVL 108-B1
ALBEMARLE ST STP 108-B2
ALBERS AVE BWT 218-D4
ALBERT AVE LEX 65-C4
ALBERT AVE W WIN 99-B3
ALBERT CT LL 66-E3
ALBERT ST HUD 111-E4
ALBERT ST LOR 89-B2
ALBERT ST PRE 153-B4
ALBERT ST SVW 79-D2
ALBERT ST N FH 107-D1
ALBERT ST N RVL 93-D4
ALBERT ST N STP 107-D3,121-D1
ALBERT ST S STP 121-D1
ALBERTA WAY W IGH 136-B3
ALBERTON CT IGH 150-B2
ALBERTON WAY IGH 150-B2
ALBION AVE STP 121-E2
ALCANA LN BUR 162-B3
ALCOVE CIR EPR 132-C4
ALDEN AVE EDI 120-A2
ALDEN AVE SHK 146-C4
ALDEN CIR NE FRI 78-D3
ALDEN ST E ARL 183-A2
ALDEN ST W ARL 183-A2
ALDEN WAY NE FRI 78-C2
ALDEN POND LN EAG 135-C3
ALDER LN EAG 135-B4,149-B1
ALDER RD MOU 116-E1
ALDER ST E SWR 83-A4
ALDER ST NW AND 50-D2
ALDER ST NW BET 8-D3
ALDER ST NW CR 50-D4,64-D1
ALDER WAY NO 80-C2
ALDERWOOD AVE NW CMT 58-D3
ALDERWOOD BAY WBY 123-C1
ALDERWOOD CIR WBY 123-C1
ALDERWOOD DR WBY 123-C1
ALDERWOOD DRAW WBY 123-C1
ALDERWOOD PLZ WBY 123-C1
ALDINE ST RVL 93-D3,107-D1
ALDINE ST STP 107-D4,121-D1
ALDINE ST SVW 79-C2
ALDRICH AVE ANO 49-D3
ALDRICH AVE BUR 148-C4,162-C1
ALDRICH AVE HUD 111-D3
ALDRICH AVE ORT 4-A4
ALDRICH AVE N BC 78-C4,92-C1
ALDRICH AVE N BP 78-C3
ALDRICH AVE N MPL 92-C4,106-C1
ALDRICH AVE S BLO 134-C3
ALDRICH AVE S MPL 106-C4,120-C2
ALDRICH AVE S RCH 120-C4,134-C1
ALDRICH CIR ANO 49-D3
ALDRICH CIR N BP 78-C3
ALDRICH CT N BC 78-C3
ALDRICH CT N BP 78-C3
ALDRICH DR NFD 219-E4
ALDRICH DR N BC 92-C1
ALDRICH TRL WBY 123-E3
ALDRID AVE CHC 12-C4
ALDRIN DR EAG 135-E3,136-A3
ALDRO LN HUT 112-B2
ALDRO RD HUT 112-B2
ALEX LN HUT 112-E3
ALEXANDER CIR CHS . . .131-B4,145-B1
ALEXANDER CT EPR 118-B4
ALEXANDER CT SHK 146-B3
ALEXANDER LN MOU 117-A2
ALEXANDER RD EAG 135-C3
ALEXANDER RD HUT 98-D4,112-E1
ALEXANDRA DR MTA 102-E3
ALEXANDRIA CT IGH 150-C3
ALEXANDRIA CT WBY 124-B3
ALEXANDRIA DR WBY 124-B3
ALFA LN IGH 136-C4
ALFRED BLVD WAC 129-D2
ALFRED RD GV 105-E2
ALGER CT IGH 136-C4,150-C1
ALGONQUIN AVE STP 109-A3
ALICE CIR HUT 112-E3
ALICE CT SSP 122-D4
ALICE LN MH 136-A1
ALICE ST STP 122-B1
ALICIA CIR IGH 150-B2
ALICIA DR EAG 150-B2
ALIMAGNET PKWY BUR 162-E1
ALISA CT CHN 131-E3
ALISA LN CHN 131-E3
ALISE PL EPR 133-A4,147-A1
ALISON CT IGH 150-B2
ALISON WAY IGH 150-B2
ALISSA LN MPW 109-B2
ALLABAR LN WBL 95-B2
ALLAN LN EAG 150-B2
ALLEN AVE WSP 122-B2
ALLEN AVE E LC 94-C3
ALLEN BLVD N SAV 161-D1
ALLEN BLVD S SAV 161-D3
ALLEN CIR NH 91-C1
ALLEN CT EPR 132-E1
ALLEN CT IGH 150-B3
ALLEN CT LL 52-B4
ALLEN CT WSP 122-B3
ALLEN DR BUR 148-E3,149-A3
ALLEN DR SAV 161-D1
ALLEN DR WBY 137-E1
ALLEN DR NE BEB 8-E3
ALLEN PL N MPW 108-C1
ALLEN WAY IGH 136-C3,150-B3
ALLENDALE DR WBT 80-D3
ALLENS RD SAT 14-E1
ALLEY IGH 137-A2
ALLEY SSP 122-D3
ALLEY ST SWR 96-E1
ALMOND AVE STP 107-D2
ALMOND AVE N BP 64-A4,78-A1
ALMOND LN EPR 132-D3
ALMOND ST N CF 208-B4
ALMQUIST WAY IGH 136-C4
ALPACA ST NW BT 34-D1
ALPACA ST NW RAM 34-D4,48-D2
ALPINE AVE VH 94-D1
ALPINE CIR BUR 162-C3
ALPINE DR WBY 123-C2
ALPINE PASS GV 106-A3
ALPINE TRL EPR 132-D1
ALPINE WAY EPR 132-D1
ALPINE CIRCLE CT BUR 162-C3
ALRICK PL WBL 95-A2
ALTA AVE IGH 136-C4
ALTA AVE SIT 206-C4,220-C2
ALTA PT EAG 149-C2
ALTA VISTA DR RVL 108-A1
ALTHEA LN HOP 119-C1
ALTMAN CT IGH 150-C1
ALTMAN CT WSP 122-C3
ALTON AVE HAT 202-A2
ALTON CT IGH 150-B2
ALTON RD NB 93-B2
ALTON ST STP 121-D3
ALTRINGER ST RFD 74-B4
ALTURA RD NE FRI 92-D1
ALVA CT WAC 129-D4
ALVA ST WAC 129-D4
ALVARADO LN PLY 104-B1
ALVARADO LN N NG 76-B1
ALVARADO LN N PLY 90-B3,104-B2
ALVAREZ AVE IGH 136-C4,150-B1
ALVERADO DR MPW 94-D4
ALVERNO AVE CAT 192-C3
ALVERNO AVE W IGH . . .136-B4,150-B1
ALVIN CT IGH 150-B2
ALYSHEBA CT SHK 146-C2
ALYSHEBA DR SHK 146-C2
ALYSHEBA RD SHK 146-C2
ALYSSA RD WBY 123-D3
AMARYLLIS LN EAG 149-D2
AMAZON ST NE LWT 10-B4
AMBASSADOR BLVD NW SF .6-E3,7-B3
AMBER CT EAG 149-B2
AMBER DR EAG 149-B2
AMBER DR SVW 93-E2,94-A2
AMBER LN EPR 132-E1
AMBERJACK LN MPW 109-B2
AMBERLEAF TRL EAG 149-D1
AMBERWOOD DR WBY 123-E2
AMBERWOOD LN SAV 161-D1
AMBERWOOD LN W SAV 161-D1
AMBERWOODS LN SAV 161-D1
AMBLARD WAY WAC 129-E4
AMBLE CIR AH 79-E4
AMBLE CT SVW 79-E4
AMBLE DR AH 79-D4
AMBLE RD AH 79-D4
AMBLE RD SVW 79-E4
AMBLEWOOD DR NE PRL 161-B2
AMELIA AVE HAS 166-E3
AMELIA AVE WSP 122-C3
AMELIA CT WSP 122-C3
AMEN CT NE BLA 65-B2
AMEN DR NE BLA 65-B2
AMERICAN ST RVL 93-D4
AMERY AVE NW SVT 30-D2
AMERY AVE SW MVT 72-D3
AMERY CIR IGH 150-B2
AMERY CT IGH 150-B2
AMES AVE STP 108-E3,109-A3
AMES AVE NW MLT 44-D1
AMES CT NFD 219-E4
AMES PL STP 108-E3,109-A3
AMES ST NFD 219-E4
AMES ST E NFD 219-E4
AMESBURY LN EPR 133-B4
AMETHYST LN EAG 149-B1
AMHERST CT IGH 150-B2
AMHERST LN EPR 118-B4,132-B1
AMHERST LN MOU 117-A2
AMHERST ST STP 121-D1
AMHERST WAY IGH 150-B2
AMLEE RD SWD 117-C3
AMSDEN RD BLO 133-C3
AMSDEN WAY EPR 133-C4
AMSDEN RIDGE CIR BLO 133-C3
AMSDEN RIDGE DR BLO 133-C3
AMUNDSON AVE EDI 133-E1
AMUNDSON CIR SWR 82-E4
AMUNDSON CT SWR 82-E4
AMUNDSON DR SWR 82-E4,96-E1
AMUNDSON LN SWR 82-E4
AMUNDSON LN SE WAT 101-B4
AMUNDSON PL SWR 82-E4
AMUR CIR DEL 87-E3
AMUR CIR NW SM 46-D3
AMUR HILL LN EPR 132-D3
AMY AVE IGH 136-C4
AMY CIR NSP 95-B4,109-B1
AMY CT IGH 150-C2
AMY DR EDI 119-D3
AMY LN BC 78-B3
AMY LN CHC 12-B4
AMY LN MP 102-E1
AMY LN MTK 105-A4
AMY LN ROG 61-E1
ANAGRAM DR EPR 132-E2,133-A2
ANAWANDA PATH IGH 150-C1
ANDALL ST LL 52-A4
ANDERLIE LN WBT 80-E2
ANDERLIE LN W WBT 80-E2
ANDERSEN LN MPL 106-D4
ANDERSON AVE BUF 44-E4,58-E1
ANDERSON CT RW 196-E4
ANDERSON LN SVW 79-E3
ANDERSON LN WBT 80-D2
ANDERSON ST W SWR 96-E2,97-A2
ANDERSON ESTATES RD IND . . .102-E2
ANDERSON LAKES
PKWY EPR 132-E2,133-B3
ANDERSON SCOUT RD SJT 83-C4
ANDERSON SCOUT
CAMP RD SMT 83-C3
ANDES CIR IGH 150-B2
ANDOVER BLVD NE HL 50-E2
ANDOVER BLVD NW AND 50-C2
ANDOVER CT IGH 150-B2
ANDOVER PL DPH 118-A2
ANDOVER RD EDI 134-A1
ANDREA CIR BUF 58-E3
ANDREA CT DEL 87-E2
ANDREA DR WBY 124-A3
ANDREA TRL IGH 150-C2
ANDREW CT CHN 131-E2
ANDREW DR WBY 123-D3
ANDREW ST STP 122-D2
ANDREWS AVE CNC 12-E3
ANDREWS AVE LND 12-D3
ANDRIE CIR NW RAM 34-C3
ANDRIE CT NW RAM 48-C1
ANDRIE ST NW RAM 34-C4,48-C1
ANDROMEDA WAY EAG 149-E2
ANDY AVE W WIN 99-B3
ANEMONE CIR NO 80-A2
ANEMORE CIR NO 80-A2
ANGEL AVE NW WAT 101-B3
ANGEL AVE SW WAT 101-A3
ANGEL AVE SW WTT 101-A4
ANGEL ST NW ER 33-D2
ANGELA CT MPW 109-B2
ANGELICA CT SHK 146-B3
ANGELINE AVE N CRY 91-E2
ANGELINE CT N CRY 91-E2
ANGELINE DR NH 91-D2
ANGELL CT SL 136-C1
ANGELL RD SL 122-B4,136-C1
ANGELO DR GV 105-E2
ANGLESSLY LN MOU 117-B2
ANGUS AVE IGH 136-C3
ANGUS AVE RMT 164-C3
ANITA AVE WAC 129-D2
ANITA LN LVL 162-C4
ANITA ST STP 122-C1
ANN AVE E IGH 150-C1
ANN CIR HAN 60-E4

ANN CIR LVT 159-D1
ANN CT EPR 133-A1
ANN DR LVT 159-E1
ANN LN MTK 119-C1
ANN PL LVT 145-E4,159-E1
ANN ST STP 122-A1
ANN ST NW WAT 101-B3
ANN ARBOR ST STP 107-C4
ANN MARIE TRL IGH 136-C4
ANNA AVE NE FRI 78-D4
ANNA TRL SE PRL 161-A4
ANNALISA CT IGH 136-C4
ANNALISA PATH IGH 136-C4
ANNAPOLIS CIR N MG 76-E3
ANNAPOLIS CIR N PLY 90-E4
ANNAPOLIS LN N DAY 62-E1
ANNAPOLIS LN N MG 76-E1,90-E1
ANNAPOLIS LN N PLY 90-E3,104-E1
ANNAPOLIS ST E SSP 122-D2
ANNAPOLIS ST E STP 122-C2
ANNAPOLIS ST W MH 122-B2
ANNAPOLIS ST W STP 122-B2
ANNAPOLIS ST W WSP 122-B2
ANNAPOLIS WAY EPR 133-B2
ANNAWAY DR EDI 119-D2
ANNE CIR BUF 58-E3
ANNE LN LVL 162-C4,176-C1
ANNE PT EAG 149-C3
ANNETTE AVE CAT 178-C4,192-C1
ANNETTE AVE ET 164-C4,178-C1
ANNETTE AVE IGH 136-C1
ANOKA AVE WT 218-C3
ANOKA ST NE FRI 79-A3
ANTELOPE AVE NW CMT 58-D2
ANTELOPE AVE SW MVT 72-D2
ANTELOPE DR LL 65-E2
ANTELOPE WAY MPW 109-B2
ANTHONY DR LVL 177-B3
ANTHONY LN SA 93-B3
ANTHONY LN WCT 143-B1
ANTHONY LN S SA 93-B4
ANTHONY ST SSP 122-D4
ANTHONY TER SWD 118-A3
ANTLER CIR NE EB 37-A2
ANTLER PT EAG 149-C1
ANTLER RDG HUT 98-D4
ANTLERS RDG EPR 147-B1
ANTOINETTE AVE S MPL 106-B3
ANTON CT SHK 146-C4
ANTON WAY SHK 146-C4
ANTONIO DR STP 121-D2
ANTRIM CIR NW SM 46-D3
ANTRIM CRV EPR 132-C2
ANTRIM CT EDI 133-D1
ANTRIM CT WBY 124-B3
ANTRIM RD EDI 133-D1
ANTRIM RD WBY 124-B3
APACHE CT MH 136-A1
APACHE DR MED 89-D2
APACHE LN MH 136-A1
APACHE LN SA 93-A2
APACHE RD EDI 119-C4
APACHE RD NSP 95-B3
APACHE ST MH 136-A1
APARTMENT LN FL 39-B3
APENNINE WAY EAG 150-B2
APENNINE WAY IGH 150-B3
APEX LN NE FRI 78-C2
APFELRIDGE CT SSP 122-D4
APGAR ST S SHK 146-B2
APOLLO DR LL 65-E2,66-A1
APOLLO RD EAG 135-E3,136-A3
APOLLO RD RF 140-D1
APOLLO RD TRT 140-D1
APOLLO RD S RF 140-D2
APOLLO ST NE COT 51-E3
APOLLO ST NE OXT 9-E1
APPALACHIAN TRL RMT 150-C4
APPALOOSA CIR WCT 129-B3
APPALOOSA CT LL 65-E1
APPALOOSA DR WCT 129-B3
APPALOOSA LN LL 65-E1
APPALOOSA LN PRL 161-A2
APPALOOSA TRL EAG 149-D1
APPALOOSA TRL PRL 161-A2
APPALOUSA CT SJT 97-D3
APPALOUSA TRL SJT 97-D3
APPLE CIR SLW 173-A1
APPLE LN EDI 119-C3
APPLE LN LL 65-E4,66-A4
APPLE LN MOU 117-A1
APPLE LN RCH 120-D4
APPLE RD SWD 117-E4
APPLE GARDEN RD MTA 102-E3
APPLE GLEN RD LOL 103-E2
APPLE ORCHARD CT DWD 81-D2
APPLE ORCHARD RD DWD 81-C2
APPLE ORCHARD RD GRA 81-D2
APPLE RIVER LN SMT 69-D3
APPLE TREE CT MTK 118-B4
APPLE VIEW LN BUR 148-E3
APPLEBLOSSOM LN SHK 146-B3
APPLEGATE LN SHK 146-B3
APPLETON AVE NW CMT 58-D2
APPLETON AVE NW MLT 44-D2
APPLETON AVE NW SVT 16-D2
APPLETREE SQ BLO 135-A2
APPLEWOOD CIR EPR 133-C4
APPLEWOOD CT WBY 123-C1
APPLEWOOD WAY SHK 146-B3
APPROACH RD BAY 97-B3
APPROACH RD OPH 97-B3
APRIL LN MTK 105-A4
APRIL PL BUR 162-D2
AQUA CIR LL 66-A2
AQUA LN LL 66-A2
AQUA ST RFD 74-B4
AQUARIUS LN EAG 149-E2
AQUILA AVE SAV 161-C1
AQUILA AVE N BP 77-C3
AQUILA AVE N CRY 91-C4
AQUILA AVE N GV 91-C4,105-C1
AQUILA AVE N NH 91-C4
AQUILA AVE S BLO 147-C1
AQUILA AVE S SAV 161-D2
AQUILA AVE S SLP 105-C4,119-C1
AQUILA CIR BLO 147-C1
AQUILA CIR SAV 161-C1
AQUILA CIR S SLP 119-C1
AQUILA CT SAV 161-C1
AQUILA LN S SLP 105-C4,119-C1
AQUILA RD BLO 133-C4
AQUILLA DR CHM 63-C3
ARABIAN LN FLT 39-C4
ARAGON DR WAT 101-B4
ARALIA CT IGH 136-C4
ARBOGAST ST SVW 93-E2,94-A2
ARBOR AVE MHT 81-D4,95-D1
ARBOR BLVD BEC 3-A4
ARBOR CIR MTK 119-A1
ARBOR CT EAG 136-A4
ARBOR CT MH 136-A2
ARBOR CT TKB 117-D2
ARBOR DR CHS 145-D2
ARBOR DR WBL 81-B4,95-B1
ARBOR LN BUR 148-D4
ARBOR LN CHN 117-C4
ARBOR LN EAG 149-C1
ARBOR LN ET 178-A4
ARBOR LN MOU 117-A1
ARBOR LN MTK 119-A1
ARBOR LN S MTK 119-A1
ARBOR ST ORO 103-D4
ARBOR ST STP 122-A1
ARBOR GLEN DR EPR 132-E1,133-A1
ARBOR HILLS DR SJT 83-D4
ARBORETUM BLVD CHN 131-C2,132-A2
ARBORETUM BLVD VIC 130-E2,131-A2
ARBORETUM DR CHN 131-B2
ARBORETUM WAY CHS 131-C4
ARBOUR AVE EDI 119-D4
ARBOUR LN EDI 119-D4
ARCADE ST STP 108-D2
ARCADE ST VH 94-D2
ARCADE ST N LC 94-D3
ARCADE ST N MPW 94-D4,108-D1
ARCADIA AVE EDI 119-E3
ARCADIA AVE PRL 161-B3
ARCADIA DR MH 122-A3
ARCADIAN PL BUF 58-E1
ARCH ST HUD 111-D3
ARCH ST STP 108-B3
ARCH ST E STP 108-B3
ARCHER AVE GV 105-D1
ARCHER CT N MG 76-C1
ARCHER CT N PLY 104-D1
ARCHER LN EPR 133-C4
ARCHER LN N MG 76-C2
ARCHER LN N PLY 90-D3,104-D1
ARCHERS LN MTK 105-B3
ARCHIBALD CT NFD 219-E4
ARCHIBALD ST NFD 219-E4
ARCHITECT AVE MPL 92-E3
ARCHWOOD RD MTK 105-B3
ARCOLA CT N SWT 83-B3
ARCOLA LN MTB 117-D1
ARCOLA LN SWT 83-B2
ARCOLA TRL N MAY 69-C4,83-C1
ARCOLA TRL N SWT 83-C1
ARCTIC WAY EDI 119-C4
ARCWOOD RD MHT 95-C2
ARDAN AVE MV 79-B1
ARDEN AVE EDI 120-A2
ARDEN CIR BUR 148-D4
ARDEN CIR SVW 94-A2
ARDEN PL AH 93-D2
ARDEN OAKS CT AH 93-D2
ARDEN OAKS DR AH 93-D2
ARDEN VIEW CT AH 79-D4
ARDEN VIEW DR AH 79-D4
ARDEN VISTA CT AH 79-D4
ARDMORE AVE MED 89-A3
ARDMORE AVE MV 79-C2
ARDMORE DR GV 106-A2
ARETZ CT VIC 131-A2
ARGENTA TRL W IGH 136-B3
ARGON ST NW AND 35-C3
ARGON ST NW BT 7-C4
ARGON ST NW RAM 35-C2,49-C2
ARGONNE DR NE CH 93-A1
ARGUS SQ BAY 97-B3
ARGYLE LN MOU 117-A2
ARGYLE ST STP 107-E3
ARIEL CT MPW 95-A4
ARIEL ST MPW 95-A4
ARIEL ST NSP 95-A4,109-A1
ARIES CT EAG 149-E2
ARION ST E WSP 122-C2
ARION ST W WSP 122-C2
ARIZONA AVE BLA 79-B1
ARIZONA ST SE LON 217-B2
ARIZONA ST SW LON 217-A2
ARKANSAS AVE BLA 79-B1
ARKANSAS AVE SIT 206-B3
ARKANSAS AVE W IGH 136-B2
ARKANSAS PATH IGH 150-B1
ARKWRIGHT ST STP 108-C2
ARKWRIGHT ST N LC 94-C4
ARKWRIGHT ST N MPW 94-C4,108-C1
ARLANDA CIR BUF 58-E1
ARLANDA DR BUF 58-E1
ARLEIGH ST WAY 104-C3
ARLENE AVE IGH 136-C2
ARLINGTON AVE MPW 109-B2
ARLINGTON AVE E MPW 109-B2
ARLINGTON AVE E STP 108-C2,109-A2
ARLINGTON AVE N BP 77-E3
ARLINGTON AVE W STP 107-D2,108-A2
ARLINGTON CIR S WAY 104-C3
ARLINGTON CT CHN 118-A4
ARLINGTON DR MTK 119-A2
ARLINGTON DR WBY 124-B4
ARLINGTON ST IGH 150-B3
ARLINGTON ST SE MPL 106-E2,107-A2
ARLO LN LL 52-A4
ARMITAGE AVE NW CMT 58-D2
ARMITAGE AVE NW SVT 16-D4,30-D3
ARMITAGE AVE SW MVT 58-D4
ARMITAGE AVE SW WDT 86-D2
ARMOUR AVE SSP 122-E4,123-A4
ARMOUR TER SA 93-A3
ARMSTRONG AVE STP 121-E2,122-A2
ARMSTRONG
BLVD NW RAM 34-D4,48-D1
ARMSTRONG RD NFD 219-C4
ARNER AVE SVW 80-A4
ARNICA DR WAT 101-B4
ARNOLD AVE CGT 26-B2
ARNOLD AVE CHC 26-B2
ARNOLD AVE IGH 150-C1
ARNOLD AVE NW CMT 58-D2
ARNOLD AVE NW SVT 30-D3
ARNOLD CIR NW SVT 30-C2
ARNOLD ST SOM 84-B1
ARNOLD PALMER DR BLA 65-A1
ARONA AVE LEX 65-C4
ARONA AVE N FH 107-D2
ARONA ST FH 107-D1
ARONA ST RVL 93-D3,107-D1
ARONA ST STP 107-D2
ARONA ST SVW 79-D2
ARROWHEAD CT LL 66-A4
ARROWHEAD CT MTK 118-C2
ARROWHEAD DR LL 66-A4
ARROWHEAD DR MED 89-E2
ARROWHEAD PASS EDI 119-C4
ARROWHEAD
ST NW AND 36-A2,50-A3
ARROWHEAD ST NW CR 50-A4,64-A2
ARROWHEAD ST NW OG 22-A3
ARROWHEAD ST NW SF 8-A4
ARROWHEAD TRL MTK 118-C2
ARROWOOD TRL SJT 98-A2
ARROWWOOD CIR N DAY 63-B1
ARROWWOOD DR EPR 147-C1
ARROWWOOD LN N DAY 49-B4,63-B1
ARROWWOOD LN N MG 63-B4,77-B3
ARROWWOOD LN N PLY 91-B2
ARTHUR AVE E WIN 99-B4
ARTHUR AVE SE MPL 107-B3
ARTHUR AVE W WIN 99-B4
ARTHUR CT CP 65-D4
ARTHUR CT LL 66-E3
ARTHUR PL RVL 93-C3
ARTHUR PL NE CH 93-A2
ARTHUR PL SE MPL 107-B3
ARTHUR ST EDI 119-C2
ARTHUR ST ROG 47-E4,61-D1
ARTHUR ST RVL 93-C3
ARTHUR ST NE CH 93-A2
ARTHUR ST NE FRI 79-A3
ARTHUR ST NE MPL 93-A4,107-A1
ARTHUR ST NE SLK 93-A3
ARTHUR ST W MTK 104-E2,105-A2
ARTHUR TER BUR 162-D1
ARTIC CIR PRL 160-E3
ARTIC TRL HUT 98-E4
ARUNDEL ST STP 108-A2,122-A1
ARVIN DR MH 122-A4
ASBURY AVE N AH 93-D2
ASBURY AVE N RVL 93-D3
ASBURY ST FH 107-D1
ASBURY ST RVL 93-D3,107-D1
ASBURY ST STP 107-D3
ASBURY ST SVW 79-D2
ASCOT CT EPR 132-C2
ASCOT CT NB 93-A1
ASH AVE N ML 43-D2
ASH AVE N MYR 114-D4
ASH AVE NE SM 46-E3,47-A3
ASH AVE NW SM 46-E3
ASH AVE S ML 43-D2
ASH AVE S MYR 114-D4,128-D1
ASH BLVD BEC 2-E4,3-A4
ASH CIR PRL 161-B1
ASH CT ROG 61-E2
ASH DR HUD 111-D2
ASH DR ROG 61-E2
ASH LN BEL 186-A2
ASH ST BEL 186-A2
ASH ST BWV 95-C1
ASH ST CW 1-B2
ASH ST FAR 191-D1,192-A1
ASH ST HAS 166-C1
ASH ST LL 79-E1,80-B1
ASH ST MHT 95-D1
ASH ST PRE 167-B1
ASH ST RFD 74-B3
ASH ST RW 196-E4
ASH ST SA 93-A4
ASH ST SHK 146-C2
ASH ST WBT 94-E1,95-A1
ASH ST E BUF 59-A2
ASH ST E SSP 136-E1
ASH ST N BEL 186-A1
ASH ST N CAR 145-B4
ASH ST N CHS 145-C3
ASH ST NW LON 217-B2
ASH ST S BEL 186-A2
ASH ST S CHS 145-C3
ASH ST W BUF 59-A2
ASH ST W FAR 191-E1
ASH ST W SSP 136-E1
ASH ST W SVW 79-E1
ASHBOURNE CIR SHK 147-A3
ASHBOURNE RD MTK 104-E4
ASHBURY CIR N CHM 63-B3
ASHBURY CT EAG 135-C4
ASHBURY PL EAG 135-C4
ASHBURY RD EAG 135-C4
ASHBY LN EPR 118-D4
ASHCROFT ALC SAV 147-D4,161-D1
ASHCROFT AVE EDI 119-E3,120-A4
ASHCROFT BAY SAV 161-D1
ASHCROFT CIR MTK 118-B3
ASHCROFT LN EDI 119-E4,120-A4
ASHCROFT PL MTK 118-B3
ASHCROFT RD MTK 118-B3
ASHCROFT RD SAV 161-D1
ASHCROFT TER MTK 118-B3
ASHER AVE ET 164-C3
ASHER AVE IGH 136-C2
ASHER CT IGH 136-C2
ASHFORD RD WBY 123-E3
ASHLAND AVE SPP 137-C3
ASHLAND AVE STP 107-D4,108-A4
ASHLAND LN MOU 116-E1
ASHLAND ST HAS 166-D2
ASHLAR DR BLO 147-E2
ASHLEY CIR SW SM 46-E4
ASHLEY CT CHS 131-B4
ASHLEY DR CHS 131-B4
ASHLEY LN IGH 136-C1
ASHLEY LN MH 122-B3
ASHLEY LN MHT 95-C2
ASHLEY RD HOP 119-C2
ASHLEY TER BP 78-A1
ASHLEY TER NB 93-A2
ASHTON AVE IGH 136-B4
ASHTON AVE NE FRI 78-D3,92-D1
ASHTON CIR SHK 147-A3
ASHTON CT CHN 117-E4
ASHWOOD DR NE EB 36-E2
ASHWOOD RD WBY 109-C4
ASIATIC AVE IGH 136-B4
ASKOV AVE WT 218-C1
ASPASIA LN EDI 133-E1
ASPEN AVE LEX 65-D3
ASPEN AVE MED 89-A3
ASPEN AVE PRL 161-C1
ASPEN AVE RW 196-E4,210-E1
ASPEN AVE NE BUF 59-A2
ASPEN CIR BL 18-A4
ASPEN CIR DEL 87-E2
ASPEN CIR EPR 133-B4
ASPEN CIR E LC 94-D3
ASPEN CIR N CHM 63-B3
ASPEN CIR N RFD 74-A4
ASPEN CIR S RFD 74-A4
ASPEN CT WBL 95-B2
ASPEN CT WBY 123-C1
ASPEN CT WSP 122-C3
ASPEN DR BUR 148-D4
ASPEN DR EAG 135-C4
ASPEN DR ROG 47-D4,61-D1
ASPEN DR SAV 162-A2
ASPEN DR SHA 13-C4
ASPEN LN LL 66-B4
ASPEN LN NO 80-B1
ASPEN LN OSS 77-C2
ASPEN LN WBT 81-B2
ASPEN LN N BP 77-C3
ASPEN PT LFL 109-C4
ASPEN RD EB 37-D1
ASPEN RD EDI 119-C4
ASPEN RD MOU 116-D1
ASPEN RD NMT 190-A1
ASPEN RD SB 116-A3
ASPEN ST HUD 111-D4
ASPEN ST TKB 117-D3
ASPEN ST W SWR 96-E1,97-A1
ASPEN TRL RMT 150-B3
ASPEN WAY LFL 109-C4
ASPEN WAY MTK 105-B4
ASPEN HOLLOW DR NE EB 36-E2
ASPEN RIDGE CIR EAG 149-B2
ASPEN VIEW CIR HUT 111-E1
ASPENWOOD PLZ WBY 123-C1
ASPENWOOD TRL MTK 118-C2
ASPIN DR SCF 14-E3
ASTER CIR VIC 117-B4
ASTER DR BP 77-D4
ASTER DR NFD 219-E4
ASTER DR NW OG 22-A3
ASTER LN ROG 47-E4
ASTER LN SHK 146-C3
ASTER PL IGH 136-C4
ASTER TRL VIC 117-B4
ASTON CIR BUR 162-D1
ASTON PL BUR 162-D1
ASTRID AVE IGH 150-D2
ATHENA WAY IGH 136-D2
ATHERTON WAY EPR 132-C2
ATLANTIC AVE IGH 136-B4
ATLANTIC AVE WAV 85-E1,86-A1
ATLANTIC LN RFD 74-B4
ATLANTIC ST MPW 94-D4,108-D1
ATLANTIC ST STP 108-D3
ATLANTIC HILLS DR EAG 150-A2
ATLAS AVE BUF 59-A2
ATLAS AVE IGH 136-B4
ATLAS ST BAY 97-B3
ATRIUM WAY MTK 118-E3
ATWATER PATH IGH 122-C4
ATWATER ST HOP 105-B4,119-B1
ATWATER ST STP 108-B3
ATWOOD DR MTK 104-E4
ATWOOD ST SHK 146-B3
ATWOOD ST N SHK 146-B2
ATWOOD ST S SHK 146-B2
AUBURN AVE WBT 81-A1
AUBURN CIR ER 20-A4
AUBURN CT EAG 149-D2
AUBURN DR DAY 62-B2
AUBURN DR MTK 119-A1
AUBURN DR VIC 130-D2
AUBURN PL NW ER 33-E1
AUBURN ST ER 19-E4,20-A4
AUBURN ST NW ER 19-E3
AUDITORS RD MOU 116-E1
AUDOBON AVE IGH 136-D1
AUDREY AVE CAT 192-D2
AUDREY AVE IGH 122-D4,136-D1
AUDREY AVE RMT 164-D2
AUDREY DR WSP 122-C4
AUDUBON CIR CHN 117-E4
AUDUBON CIR IGH 136-D4
AUDUBON CT EPR 147-C1
AUDUBON CT HUT 111-E1
AUDUBON LN HUT 111-E1
AUDUBON RD CHN 131-E3
AUDUBON RD CHS 131-E4,145-D1
AUDUBON RD IGH 136-D4
AUDUBON WAY IGH 136-D4
AUERBACH ST RVL 94-A4
AUGER AVE COR 76-A3
AUGER AVE WBL 95-A2
AUGER LN WBL 94-E2
AUGSBURG AVE S RCH 134-C1
AUGUST CIR LL 66-E4
AUGUST DR CHS 145-D1
AUGUST WAY IGH 122-D4
AUGUSTA CT EAG 150-A2
AUGUSTA LN DAT 144-B2
AUGUSTA LN DWD 81-C2
AUGUSTA LN EAG 150-A2
AUGUSTA LN EPR 132-D1
AUGUSTA RD DAT 144-C2
AURORA AVE SPP 137-C3
AURORA AVE STP 107-E4,108-A4
AURORA CIR RW 210-E1
AURORA LN CP 65-D3
AUSHEGUN TRL SJT 98-D1
AUSTIN CIR SHK 146-C3
AUSTIN CT IGH 150-D3
AUSTIN CT SHK 146-C3
AUSTIN CT NE BLA 65-D1
AUSTIN ST SHK 146-C3
AUSTIN ST NE BLA 65-D3,79-D1
AUSTIN ST NE EB 23-D3
AUSTIN ST NE HL 51-D2
AUSTRALIAN AVE E LC 94-B3
AUSTRIAN PINE LN MTK 105-A3
AUSTRIAPINE AVE N BP 78-A1
AUTO CLUB CIR BLO 147-D2
AUTO CLUB RD BLO 147-D2
AUTO CLUB WAY SLP 119-E1
AUTUMN ALC WBY 123-E1
AUTUMN BAY WBY 123-E1
AUTUMN CT WBY 123-E1
AUTUMN DR WBY 123-E1,124-A1
AUTUMN DRAW WBY 123-E1
AUTUMN PL BUR 162-D2
AUTUMN PL RVL 107-C1
AUTUMN RDG BKR 2-E2
AUTUMN ST FH 107-C1
AUTUMN ST MPL 106-E1
AUTUMN ST RVL 107-E1
AUTUMN TER EPR 132-B1
AUTUMN TRL LVT 160-B1
AUTUMN WAY SWR 96-E2
AUTUMN CHACE CIR BLO 133-D2
AUTUMN CHACE DR BLO 133-D2
AUTUMN OAKS CIR RFD 74-A3
AUTUMN OAKS CT EAG 150-B1
AUTUMN OAKS DR RFD 74-A3
AUTUMN RIDGE AVE CHN 131-D2
AUTUMN RIDGE CT CHN 131-D2
AUTUMN RIDGE LN CHN 131-D2
AUTUMN RIDGE WAY CHN 131-D2
AUTUMN WOODS DR CHS 131-D4
AUTUMNWOOD DR MTK 105-B4

AUTUMNWOOD LN MTK 105-B4
AVALON AVE EAG 135-D2
AVALON CT IGH 150-B1
AVALON PATH IGH 150-B1
AVALON ST IGH 136-B1
AVANTI DR MH 121-E4
AVENUE CT E MHT 81-D4
AVENUE E MPW 109-B4
AVENUE E MPW 109-B4
AVENUE K MPW 109-B4
AVENUE M MPW 109-B4
AVENUE M MPW 109-B4
AVENUE R MPW 109-B3
AVIGNON CT WBY 109-B3
AVILA CV EPR 132-C3
AVOCET CIR CR 64-B1
AVOCET LN MOU 103-A4,117-A1
AVOCET ST NW AND 50-B1
AVOCET ST NW CR 64-B3
AVON CT EPR 118-B4
AVON CT WBY 123-C3
AVON DR MOU 117-A1
AVON DR WBY 123-C3
AVON ST ORT 4-A4
AVON ST SW 93-E3,107-E1
AVON ST N RVL 93-E3,107-E1
AVON ST N STP 107-E4,121-E1
AVON ST S STP 121-E1
AVONDALE RD GV 106-A3
AVONDALE ST MTK 118-D2
AWATUKEE TRL SJT 98-C1
AYD MILL RD STP 107-D4,121-E1
AYDEE CIR WBT 81-B2
AYR LN MH 117-A2
AYRSHIRE BLVD EDI 119-D3
AZALEA PL BUR 162-A1
AZALEA TRL EPR 132-D3
AZALEA WAY IGH 150-B1
AZELIA AVE N BC 92-A2
AZTEC CT NW OG 21-D2
AZTEC DR EPR 133-A3
AZTEC LN MH 136-A1
AZTEC ST NW AND 35-D2,49-D2
AZTEC ST NW CR 49-D4,63-D1
AZTEC ST NW OG 21-D3
AZURE RD DPH 118-B1
AZURITE CT NW RAM 35-A4,49-A2
AZURITE ST NW RAM 35-A4,49-A2

B

B CT NE EB 37-D1
B ST HIL 92-E2
B ST WBL 94-E2
B ST STP 123-A1
B ST WBY 123-D1
BABCOCK AVE BNT ....
BABCOCK AVE RMT 141-B4,155-B2
BABCOCK AVE RMT 164-D2
BABCOCK BLVD DEL 87-D3
BABCOCK LN N WAY 104-B3
BABCOCK LN N WAY 219-D4
BACARDI AVE WGH ....
BACHELOR AVE MH 122-A4
BACHMAN CIR IGH 136-D2
BACKER AVE WT 218-C3
BACON AVE IGH 122-D4,136-D2
BACON DR NE FRI 79-C2
BADE LN CAR 145-B3
BADGER CT EAG 149-B2
BADGER LN NO 80-B3
BADLANDS RD HUT 112-D2
BADLANDS RD WRT 112-E2
BAFFIN BAY N EAG 150-A1
BAFFIN BAY S EAG 150-A1
BAFFIN TRL W EAG 136-B4
BAFFIN TRL W IGH 136-B4
BAGLEY AVE FOT 218-C4
BAGLEY AVE W 204-C3,218-C3
BAGPIPE BLVD EPR 133-A1
BAHLS DR HAS ....
BAILEY CT NEW 123-C4
BAILEY DR EPR 132-C2
BAILEY LN ANO 49-C3
BAILEY RD MTA 103-A3
BAILEY RD NEW 123-B4
BAILEY RD WBY 123-D4,124-B4
BAILEY TRL IGH 136-D2
BAILEY RIDGE ALC WBY ..123-E3
BAILEY RIDGE BAY WBY ..123-E3
BAILEY RIDGE CIR WBY ..123-E3
BAILEY RIDGE CT WBY ...123-E3
BAILEY RIDGE DRAW WBY .123-E4
BAILLIF PL BLO 148-B1
BAINBRIDGE DR EPR 132-C3
BAKER AVE IGH 136-D2
BAKER AVE E WT 99-B4
BAKER AVE NE FRI 78-E2
BAKER AVE NW CMT 58-C1
BAKER AVE NW MLT 30-C4,44-C3
BAKER AVE NW SVT 16-C1,30-C2
BAKER AVE SW WDT 58-C4,72-C1
BAKER AVE W WIT 99-B4
BAKER CT IGH 150-D1
BAKER LN HUT 112-C3
BAKER RD EPR 119-A4,132-E1
BAKER RD HUT 112-C3
BAKER RD MTK 118-E3,119-A2
BAKER ST E ARL 183-A2
BAKER ST E STP 122-C2
BAKER ST NE FRI 78-E2
BAKER ST W ARL 183-A2
BAKER ST W STP 122-B2
BAKER TRL MTK 119-A1
BAKER PARK RD IND 89-A4
BAKER PARK RD MP 89-A4,103-A1
BAKKEN LN HUT 98-C4,112-C1
BAKKEN ST MO 31-E3,32-A3
BALBOUL DR MO 31-B1
BALD EAGLE AVE WBL 81-A3
BALD EAGLE BLVD E WBT .81-A2
BALD EAGLE BLVD W HUG .67-A4
BALD EAGLE BLVD W WLL .67-A4,81-A1
BALD EAGLE BLVD W WBT .80-E2,81-A2
BALD EAGLE CT EAG 135-E4
BALD EAGLE CT MO 32-A2
BALD EAGLE IS WBT 80-E2
BALD EAGLE PT WBT 81-A3
BALD EAGLE RD N NOH ...111-E1
BALD EAGLE TRL WBY 124-B3
BALD LAKE CT EAG 150-A1
BALDER LN EDI 119-D4

BALDUR PARK RD ORO 103-C4
BALDWIN AVE BWT 218-E4
BALDWIN AVE IGH 136-D3
BALDWIN AVE NW ER 33-E1
BALDWIN AVE APV 162-E2
BALDWIN CIR ER 19-E4
BALDWIN CIR LL 66-A4
BALDWIN CT BNT 127-B1
BALDWIN CT ER 19-E4
BALDWIN DR APV 162-E2,163-A2
BALDWIN DR CP 65-E3
BALDWIN ST DPH 118-B2
BALDWIN ST ER 19-E4
BALDWIN ST NW ER 5-E4,33-E1
BALDWIN LAKE RD LL 65-E4,79-E1
BALFANZ RD EDI 134-A1
BALL RD BLA 65-D3
BALLANTINE AVE IGH 136-D2
BALLANTINE CT IGH 136-D2
BALLANTRAE RD EAG 135-B4,149-B1
BALLANTYNE LN NE SLK ..78-E2,79-A2
BALLET BLVD NE FRI 78-D2
BALMORAL LN S BLO 147-E1
BALSA AVE CLT 188-E2,202-E2
BALSA CIR CLT 188-E1
BALSA CT MTK 118-C1
BALSAM AVE SE SM 46-E4
BALSAM BLVD BEC 2-E4,3-A4
BALSAM DR SOM 70-B4
BALSAM LN EPR 133-B4
BALSAM LN N DAY 49-A4,63-A1
BALSAM LN N MG 63-B4,77-B4
BALSAM LN N PLY 91-B3,105-B2
BALSAM RD MOU 116-E1
BALSAM ST EAG 149-D2
BALSAM ST MED 89-A3
BALSAM ST PRL 160-E4,161-A4
BALSAM ST STP 149-D2
BALSAM ST E EAG 149-D2
BALSAM TRL SHK 146-D3
BALSAM TRL E EAG 149-D2
BALSAMFIR AVE N BP 78-A1
BALTIC AVE EAG 149-D3
BALTIMORE ST NE BLA ...51-A4,65-A1
BALTIMORE ST NE BLA ...65-A4,79-A1
BALTIMORE ST NE EB 8-E4
BALTIMORE ST NE HL 37-A2,51-A2
BALTIS ST NM 189-E4
BAMBI LN WBT 80-D4
BAMBLE CIR EAG 149-D2
BAN TARA DR HUT 111-E3
BAN TARA LN HUT 111-E3
BANBURY LN HUT 118-C2
BANCROFT AVE STP 122-C1
BANCROFT WAY IGH 136-D3
BANDANA BLVD E STP 107-D3
BANDANA BLVD N STP 107-D3
BANDANA BLVD W STP 107-D3
BANEBERRY CT NFD 220-A4
BANEBERRY WAY CHN 131-D2
BANEBERRY WAY E CHN ...131-E2
BANEY CT MTK 118-C4
BANFIL ST STP 122-A1
BANFILL CIR N BP 78-C2
BANK ST BEC 2-E4,3-A4
BANK ST ORT 3-A4
BANKERS DR VH 94-B2
BANKS CT IGH 136-D3
BANKS PATH IGH 136-D3
BANNEKER AVE N MPL 106-C2
BANNING AVE WBL 81-A3
BANNING WAY IGH 136-D3
BANTAS POINT LN MTK ...104-C4
BANTAS POINT RD MTK ...104-C4
BANTLE FARM RD MED 89-D3
BANYAN LN EPR 132-D3
BANYAN LN RMT 164-B1
BANYON AVE AH 79-C3
BANYON AVE NW CMT 58-C2
BANYON AVE NW MLT 30-C2
BANYON AVE NW SVT 16-C1
BARBARA AVE ET 164-D3
BARBARA AVE IGH 122-D4,136-D3
BARBARA AVE RMT 164-D2
BARBARA CT CHN 132-A3
BARBARA CT IGH 136-D3
BARBARA CT MH 121-E4,122-A4
BARBARA DR MTK 119-A2
BARBARA LN BUR 148-B4
BARBARA LN IGH 122-D4,136-D1
BARBARA LN LL 66-A1
BARBARY CIR WAC 129-D3
BARBATO CT IGH 122-D4
BARBERRY CIR CHN 132-C1
BARBERRY LN EPR 118-C4,132-C1
BARCLAY AVE IGH 136-D2
BARCLAY CIR EAG 149-D3
BARCLAY ST MPW 94-E4,108-E1
BARCLAY ST STP 108-E2
BARDON AVE RMT 164-D2
BARGE CHANNEL RD STP .122-D2
BARIUM ST NW AND 35-C3
BARIUM ST NW RAM 35-C2,49-C1
BARIUM ST NW SF 7-B3
BARKER ST HAS 166-E1
BARNARD AVE WFT 220-B2
BARNES AVE IGH 136-D4,150-D1
BARNES PL MPL 106-C2
BARNES TRL IGH 150-D1
BARNES WAY IGH 150-D2
BARNSWALLOW CIR EPR ...147-C1
BARONS WAY SWR 96-C2
BARONY RD LES 212-D4
BARRET ST S WIN 99-B4
BARRETT AVE STP 121-C2
BARRETT ST STP 107-E3
BARRIE RD EDI 120-B4
BARRINGTON CT BP 78-A1
BARRINGTON CT MTK 118-C4
BARRINGTON DR EPR 118-B4
BARRINGTON DR SHK 146-B4
BARRINGTON PL MHT 95-C2
BARRINGTON RD WBY 124-A2
BARRINGTON TER BP 78-A1
BARROW CT EAG 149-B2
BARRY AVE N WAY 104-B3
BARRY DR NEW 123-B4,137-B1
BARRY LN WBT 80-E2
BARRYMORE LN WBY 123-D2
BARTELMY CT N MPW 95-B3
BARTELMY LN N MPW 95-B3,109-B3
BARTH DR BKR 17-D4
BARTHEL INDUSTRIAL DR ALB ..47-A2

BARTLETT BLVD MOU 116-E2,117-A1
BARTLETT BLVD MTA 116-D2
BARTLEY CT OXT 150-D2
BARTON AVE NW CMT 58-C2
BARTON AVE NW MLT 30-C3
BARTON AVE SE MPL 107-B3
BARTON AVE SW MVT 58-C4,72-C1
BARTON AVE SW WDT C2
BARTON TRL IGH 150-D1
BARTOSH LN RF 140-D2
BASALT ST NW BT 21-A3
BASALT ST NW RAM 49-A2
BASE LINE RD FOT 218-D4
BASELINE AVE CLT 188-B4
BASELINE AVE HAT 188-B4,202-B1
BASELINE AVE LVT 160-B3
BASELINE AVE SCT 160-B4,174-B3
BASELINE BLVD HAT 188-B1
BASIL ST TF 14-C3
BASIL ST SJT 98-C1
BASS ST HAS 166-E1
BASS ST SE PRL 161-A3
BASS CREEK AVE N BP ...91-C1
BASS CREEK CT BP 91-C1
BASS CREEK CIR N NH ...91-C1
BASS LAKE RD CRY 91-E2,92-A2
BASS LAKE RD MG 76-D4,90-E1
BASS LAKE RD NH 91-C1
BASS LAKE RD PLY 91-B1
BASS LAKE RD SJT 98-C2
BASSETT CREEK DR GV ...105-E1,106-A1
BASSETT CREEK LN GV ...106-A1
BASSWOOD CIR CHN 132-B1
BASSWOOD CIR RFD 74-A3
BASSWOOD CIR SW PRL ...160-E4,161-A4
BASSWOOD LN CHM 63-B3
BASSWOOD LN RFD 74-A3
BASSWOOD LN EAG 135-E4,136-A4
BASSWOOD LN GRF 67-C1
BASSWOOD LN HSN 47-D4,61-D1
BASSWOOD LN MOU 116-E1
BASSWOOD LN MTA 116-D2
BASSWOOD LN NO 80-B2
BASSWOOD LN ROG 47-D4
BASSWOOD RD EPR 133-B3
BASSWOOD RD MPL 106-A4
BASSWOOD RD SLP 106-A4
BASSWOOD RD WBY 123-C1
BATAAN ST NE EB 9-B4,23-B1
BATAAN ST NE EB 37-B4,51-B2
BATAVIA ST STP 123-A2
BATES AVE ORT 4-A4
BATES AVE STP 108-D4
BATES ST OTS 48-B2
BATTLE CREEK CT STP ...109-A4
BATTLE CREEK PL STP ...109-A4
BATTLE CREEK RD STP ...109-A4,123-A4
BATTLE CREEK PARK
RD STP 122-E1,123-A1
BAUER CIR RVT 181-C2
BAUGH ST NW BT 20-C4,34-C1
BAUGH ST NW RAM 34-C2
BAUGH ST NW STT 6-C2
BAVARIA CT VIC 131-B2
BAVARIA LN NP 201-E2
BAVARIA RD CHS 131-B3,165-C1
BAVARIA VIC 131-B2
BAVARIA HILLS CIR CHS .131-B3
BAVARIA HILLS CT CHS ..131-B3
BAVARIA HILLS LN CHS ..131-B3
BAVARIA HILLS TRL CHS .131-B3
BAVARIA SHORES DR CHS .131-B3
BAVARIAN CT CF 208-B3
BAVARIAN CT W FRI 93-A1
BAVARIAN PASS S FRI ...93-A1
BAXTER AVE DAY 24-C1
BAXTER CT CHS 131-B4
BAXTER ST N CHM 63-C1
BAXTER TRL IGH 150-D1
BAY AVE SW PRL 161-A4
BAY CIR MTK 104-C4
BAY CIR SWR 96-D2
BAY DR S BLO 133-D4
BAY DR EPR 132-D1
BAY DR S BLO 133-D4
BAY DR S MTA 116-D3
BAY DR SE FL 39-C4
BAY LN MTK 104-C4
BAY LN W NO 80-B2
BAY ST DPH 118-A2
BAY ST MTK 122-A2
BAY ST STP 122-A2
BAY ST TKB 117-D3
BAY KNOLLS DR PRL 160-E3,161-A3
BAY RIDGE RD ORO 103-D4
BAY VIEW LN WBY 110-B4
BAY VIEW PL VIC 117-A4
BAYARD AVE STP 121-C2,122-A2
BAYARD CT EPR 132-D3
BAYBERRY AVE SWR 96-C1
BAYBERRY DR WBT 81-B1
BAYBERRY LN EAG 136-A4
BAYBERRY AVENUE CT SWR .96-D1
BAYBERRY LN MTA 117-A4
BAYCLIFF DR BUR 149-A3
BAYCLIFF RD VIC 116-E4,117-A4
BAYFIELD ST STP 108-D4,122-C1
BAYHILL RD DWD 81-C1
BAYLESS AVE STP 107-B3
BAYLISS PL STP 107-B3
BAYLISS CIR N MG 63-B4
BAYLOR CT EAG 149-C2
BAYLOR CT COT 52-C3
BAYLOR ST NE LWT 10-C3,24-C2
BAYLOR ST NE OXT 10-C2
BAYPOINT DR BUR 149-A3
BAYPOINT RD MOU 117-A1
BAYPORT RD MOU 117-A1
BAYRIDGE LN BLO 150-A1
BAYRIDGE RD MOU 116-D2
BAYSIDE LN MTA 103-A3
BAYSIDE RD ORO 103-B3
BAYSWATER RD MTK 118-C2
BAYSWATER RD SWD 118-A2
BAYTOWN LN BYT 97-B3
BAYVIEW CIR PRL 161-C1
BAYVIEW CT CHS 145-D1
BAYVIEW CT DPH 118-A2

BAYVIEW DR RVL 108-A1
BAYVIEW DR VIC 117-A4
BAYVIEW PL N ORO 117-C1
BAYVIEW PL SPR 117-B1
BAYWOOD LN EPR 132-D1
BAYWOOD LN NE EB 22-D2
BAYWOOD TER EPR 132-D1
BAYWOOD SHORES DR MOU .102-E4
BB ST WBL 80-D4
BEACH CIR EPR 133-A1
BEACH DR FL 39-C3
BEACH RD EPR 119-A4,133-A4
BEACH RD TRT 125-C4
BEACH RD N OPH 37-C1
BEACH RD N WAY 104-A3
BEACH ST NE PRL 161-B2
BEACHCOMBER BLVD WAC .129-C2
BEACHSIDE DR MTK 119-B3
BEACHWOOD RD MOU 116-E2
BEACON ALC WBY 123-A4
BEACON CIR EPR 133-A1
BEACON CT STP 107-C4
BEACON CIR MTK 118-E3
BEACON LN APV 163-A2
BEACON RD WBY 123-E4
BEACON ST MPL 107-A2
BEACON ST N RVL 93-C4,107-C1
BEACON ST SE MPL 107-A2
BEACON HEIGHTS DR PLY .105-A1
BEACON HILL CIR EAG ..149-C3
BEACON HILL CT EAG ...149-C3
BEACON HILL RD EAG ...149-C3
BEACON HILL RD MTK ...118-E3
BEALL ST HUD 111-D3
BEAM AVE MPW 94-E3,95-A3
BEAM LN EAG 135-D2
BEAN ST ANO 49-C4
BEAR AVE MO 31-E3
BEAR AVE N VH 94-C1
BEAR AVE S VH 94-C1
BEAR AVE N ROB 92-A3
BEAR CT WBL 95-B2
BEAR PATH TRL EAG 149-B2
BEAR PAW TRL EAG 150-A1
BEARD AVE BUR 148-B4
BEARD AVE EKO 204-B1
BEARD AVE NMT 190-B3,204-B2
BEARD AVE N BC 78-A4,92-A1
BEARD AVE N BP 78-A3
BEARD AVE N ROB 92-A3
BEARD AVE S BLO 134-A4,148-A1
BEARD AVE S EDI 148-B3
BEARD AVE S EDI 120-A3
BEARD AVE S MPL 120-A2
BEARD CRV BLO 134-A4
BEARD CT EDI 120-A3
BEARD CT NMT 190-B3
BEARD CT N BP 78-A3
BEARD PL EDI 120-A3
BEARD RD BLO 134-A4
BEARDSLEY CT IGH 136-D4,150-D1
BEARPATH TRL EPR 132-C3
BEATRICE CT SJT 98-B2
BEATRICE DR E BKR 2-E1
BEATRICE DR W BKR 2-E1
BEATRICE ST EAG 135-E2
BEATY AVE NW RAM 48-C1
BEAU D RUE DR EAG 135-B4,149-B1
BEAUDRY BLVD HUD 111-D3
BEAUMONT AVE CAT 192-B1
BEAUMONT AVE SLW 173-A2
BEAUMONT BLVD SLW 173-A3
BEAUMONT CT APV 149-A4
BEAUMONT ST STP 108-C3
BEAUMONT ST N MPW 108-B1
BEAUMONT WAY CAT 192-B1
BEAUMONT WAY SLW 172-E1,173-A1
BEAVER CIR LL 66-B4
BEAVER ST E WBT 81-A2
BEAVER ST E BEL 186-A1
BEAVER ST W BEL 185-E1
BEAVER TRL LL 66-B4
BEAVER TRL MTK 118-B2
BEAVER DAM CT EAG 149-B2
BEAVER DAM CT NE EB ..22-D2
BEAVER DAM DR NE EB ..22-D3
BEAVER DAM RD EAG 149-B2
BEAVER DAM RD EAG 104-C3
BEAVER POND WAY CV ...66-D3
BEAVERDALE RD MPW 118-B3
BEAVERWOOD HL MTK 118-B3
BECHTEL AVE EB 136-E4
BECHTOLD RD COR 61-C4,75-C1
BECHTOLD RD HSN 61-C1
BECKER AVE WT 204-B3
BECKER RD IGH 136-B4
BECKER RD IND 88-E3
BECKMAN AVE AH 93-C2
BECKMAN AVE IGH 136-D2
BECKMAN CT IGH 136-D2
BECKY CIR HUT 111-E1
BEDERWOOD DR ORO 103-C3
BEDFORD AVE EDI 119-E3
BEDFORD CT MH 136-A2
BEDFORD DR EPR 132-E1
BEDFORD RD MOU 117-A2
BEDFORD ST STP 108-C3
BEDFORD ST SE MPL 107-B3
BEEBE AVE MH 122-B3
BEEBE PKWY MPW 95-A3
BEEBE LAKE RD NE HAN .60-D2
BEECH ST FAR 177-E4,178-A4
BEECH ST STP 108-D3,109-A3
BEECH ST N CHS 145-D3
BEECH ST NE FRI 78-D2
BEECH ST W RMT 164-B2
BEECHER DR EAG 149-C2
BEECHWOOD AVE MTK 104-C4
BEECHWOOD AVE STP 121-C2
BEECHWOOD PL STP 121-C2
BEEHIVE CT EPR 133-A1
BEEHRLE ST EXC 110-D3
BEEMAN PL EXC 110-D3
BEHM LN LL 65-E1,66-A1
BELAIR CIR RVL 93-D3
BELAIR DR LND 12-D3
BELANGER AVE NW CMT ..58-C3
BELANGER DR ANO 48-B4
BELDEN BLVD S CG 137-C4
BELDEN DR SA 93-A3
BELFAST CT RMT 164-B1

BELFAST CV EPR 132-C2
BELFAST ST RMT 164-B1
BELFAST ST W RMT 164-B1
BELISLE ST SOM 84-B1
BELL AVE BNT 141-A2
BELL AVE HNT 141-A2
BELL CIR MTK 118-C4
BELL CIR W MTK 118-C3
BELL LN SA 93-B3
BELL ST EXC 117-E3
BELL ST SB 116-B3
BELL OAKS ESTATE RD EPR 147-B1
BELL ROSE RD IND 89-A2
BELLAIRE AVE MPW 95-B3
BELLAIRE AVE WBL 81-B4,95-B2
BELLAIRE LN EPR 132-D2
BELLAIRE LN MOU 116-E1
BELLAIRE WAY NE FRI 78-C2
BELLAND AVE VH 94-C2
BELLAND AVE WBL 95-A2
BELLE CT HMP 193-B2
BELLE CT RMT 164-B1
BELLE LN MV 79-C2
BELLE ST GRF 75-A4
BELLE ST W CF 208-B4
BELLE AIRE CT CHM 49-B4
BELLE AIRE DR CHM 49-B4,63-B1
BELLE PLAINE TRL BPT 185-E2
BELLECREST DR MPW 94-D4
BELLEVUE DR MTK 118-E3
BELLHAM AVE MTK 118-B3
BELLO DR EDI 133-C1
BELLOWS ST STP 122-B1
BELLOWS ST WSP 122-B3
BELLVUE LN N BC 92-C2
BELLWOOD AVE E MPW 108-C1
BELMAR DR VH 94-D2
BELMONT AVE S MPL 120-C3
BELMONT CT APV 149-A4
BELMONT CT RMT 164-B1
BELMONT DR WBY 123-D1
BELMONT LN CHN 132-A1
BELMONT LN MOU 116-E1
BELMONT LN MPW 94-D4,108-E1
BELMONT LN NSP 95-B4,109-A1
BELMONT LN E MPW 108-C1
BELMONT LN W RVL 107-D1,108-A1
BELMONT RD APV 149-A4
BELMONT RD MTK 105-B3
BELMONT ST HMP 193-B2
BELMONT ST S OSC 28-A4
BELMONT TRL RMT 164-B1
BELMORE LN EDI 119-C2
BELT LINE BLVD SLP 106-A4,120-A1
BELVEDERE DR EPR 132-C3
BELVIDERE LN EDI 133-E1,134-A1
BELVIDERE ST E STP 122-C2
BELVIDERE ST W STP 122-C2
BELVIDERE ST W WSP 122-B2
BELVOIR DR MTK 118-D2
BELWOOD LN MTK 118-D3
BEN HILL RD STP 121-E1
BENA ST STP 109-A3
BENARD AVE RVL 107-D1
BENCH ST TF 14-C3
BENCHMARK DR SLT 174-E1
BENDEMERE LN ANO 49-B4
BENDER CT CHS 131-C4
BENDER RD N CHS 131-C4,145-C1
BENDER RD S CHS 145-C1
BENDER ST NE COT 38-E2
BENGAL AVE W RMT 150-B4
BENGAL CT VIC 131-B1
BENJAMIN DR WBY 123-D4
BENJAMIN LN HUT 112-B1
BENJAMIN PL NE CH 93-A2
BENJAMIN ST SLK 79-A2
BENJAMIN ST NE CH 93-A2
BENJAMIN ST NE FRI 79-A4
BENJAMIN ST NE MPL 93-A3
BENJAMIN TRL IGH 150-E1
BENLANA CT MPW 109-B2
BENMORE LN NE FRI 79-A4
BENNETT DR NE FRI 78-E3
BENNETT PL EPR 133-B4
BENOY DR HUT 112-D1
BENSON AVE STP 121-D3
BENSON BLVD E SWR 96-E2
BENSON BLVD W SWR 96-E2
BENSON ST RF 140-E1
BENSON WAY IGH 136-E4
BENT BOW TRL CHN 131-D1
BENT TREE CIR MTK 105-A4
BENT TREE CT NO 80-C2
BENT TREE LN EAG 150-B2
BENT TREE LN MH 136-A1
BENT TREE LN MTK 105-A4
BENT TREE LN NO 80-C2
BENT TREE RD MTK 105-A4
BENT TREE WAY MTK 105-A4
BENT TREE HILLS DR NB 93-A1
BENTLEY WAY RMT 164-B2
BENTLY CIR SLT 174-C4,188-C1
BENTON AVE EDI 119-E3
BENTON AVE WT 218-B2
BENTON AVE N WAY 104-C3
BENTON BLVD MPL 106-B4
BENTON CIR IGH 136-D2
BENTON ST ANO 49-B4
BENTON ST BTT 143-E3
BENTON ST E COL 143-E3
BENTON ST W COL 143-D3
BENTON WAY AH 93-E2
BENTON WAY IGH 136-D2
BENTON CREEK AVE COL 143-E3
BENTWOOD DR EPR 133-B3
BENWOOD CIR CHN 131-D2
BENZ RD NB 93-B2
BERG DR E SHK 146-C3
BERGEN RD BNT 127-A4,141-A1
BERGER DR EPR 132-D3
BERGERON LN WBL 95-A2
BERGLUND AVE CHC 26-B1
BERGMAN DR SWR 96-C2
BERKELEY AVE STP 121-C1
BERKELEY PL WIL 95-D1
BERKEY ST MSC 55-B4
BERKSHIRE AVE SCT 159-D4,173-D3
BERKSHIRE CIR SHK 147-B3
BERKSHIRE CT EAG 149-B3
BERKSHIRE CT SHK 147-B3
BERKSHIRE CT N MG 76-E3
BERKSHIRE CT N PLY 90-E3
BERKSHIRE DR EAG 149-B3
BERKSHIRE DR MTK 119-A2
BERKSHIRE LN EPR 132-E3
BERKSHIRE LN SHK 147-B3
BERKSHIRE LN N DAY 48-E4
BERKSHIRE LN N MG 76-E4,90-E1
BERKSHIRE LN N PLY 90-E3,104-E2
BERKSHIRE RD BLO 147-E1
BERKSHIRE WAY EAG 149-B3
BERKSHIRE WAY N MG 76-E3
BERLAND PL STP 123-B1
BERNARD AVE N CRY 91-E2
BERNARD PATH IGH 136-E4
BERNARD PL EDI 119-E3
BERNARD ST E WSP 122-C2
BERNARD ST W WSP 122-B2
BERNAS LN NP 201-E2
BERNE CIR EDI 119-D3
BERNE CIR NE FRI 93-A1
BERNE RD NE FRI 93-A1
BERRING AVE CAT 192-B1
BERRY LN DPH 118-C1
BERRY ST STP 107-B3
BERRY RIDGE RD EAG 149-D1
BERT ST MH 122-A2
BERTHA CT MHT 95-C2
BERWICK CIR SHK 147-A3
BERWICK KNLS BP 78-A2
BERWICK LN MHT 95-C2
BERWICK PL MHT 95-C2
BERWICK PL WIL 95-D1
BERWOOD AVE VH 94-C2
BERWOOD CT W VH 94-D2
BERYL RD EAG 149-B1
BESSIE DR SLW 186-D1
BESTER AVE IGH 136-D3
BESTER CT IGH 136-D3
BETA ST LWT 9-E3
BETA ST NE LWT 9-E3
BETH CT MPW 123-B2
BETHEL CT IGH 136-E4
BETHEL DR AH 93-D1
BETHIA LN BP 77-D4
BETTY LN EAG 135-E4,136-A4
BETTY LN EPR 133-B1
BETTY LN WSP 122-B3
BETTY CROCKER DR GV 105-C2
BETTY CROCKER DR PLY 105-C2
BETTY JANE CT NSP 109-B1
BEULAH LN STP 107-D2
BEVERLY AVE GV 106-A2
BEVERLY DR EPR 132-C4
BEVERLY DR SFT 159-A3
BEVERLY DR SWD 117-B4
BEVERLY PL MTK 104-C4,118-C1
BEVERLY RD STP 107-B4
BEVERLY ST SAV 161-E2
BEVERLY WAY IGH 136-E4
BEVINS LN MHT 95-D2
BEXLEY DR WBY 124-A3
BIANCA CIR PRL 161-B3
BIBEAU RD WBT 80-D4
BICE AVE NW CMT 58-C3
BICE AVE NW SVT 30-C2
BICE AVE SW MVT 58-C4
BICENTENNIAL CT NB 93-B2
BICHNER LN MHT 95-D2
BIDWELL ST STP 122-B1
BIDWELL ST WSP 122-C2
BIELENBERG CT WBY 123-D2
BIELENBERG DR WBY 109-D4,123-D1
BIENEMAN ST HUD 111-E4
BIERLINE AVE CHS 145-D2
BIES DR GV 105-D1
BIG CIRCLE DR LC 94-B3
BIG CIRCLE DR W LC 94-B3
BIG FOX RD GL 94-D1
BIG LINDEN CRV WBL 94-E1
BIG OAK DR BUR 148-B4
BIG OAK RD SVW 79-E3
BIG SKY CT RW 210-E1
BIG TIMBER TRL EAG 150-A1
BIG WOODS LN EPR 132-C3
BIGELOW AVE STP 107-E4
BIGELOW LN STP 108-B2
BIGHORN DR CHN 132-A1
BIMINI DR MTK 119-B3
BIRCH AVE BL 18-B3
BIRCH AVE MED 89-A3
BIRCH AVE PRL 161-A3
BIRCH AVE RW 210-E1
BIRCH AVE N ML 43-D2
BIRCH AVE N MYR 114-E4
BIRCH AVE NE SM 46-E3
BIRCH AVE NW SM 46-E3
BIRCH AVE S ML 43-D3
BIRCH BLVD IGH 136-E4
BIRCH CIR ROG 47-D4
BIRCH CT IGH 136-E4
BIRCH CT LL 66-B4
BIRCH CT WBL 80-D4
BIRCH DR FL 39-B2
BIRCH DR HUD 111-D2
BIRCH LN CRT 176-A3
BIRCH LN LFL 109-C4
BIRCH LN LL 52-B3
BIRCH LN MOU 116-D1
BIRCH LN MTK 118-D3
BIRCH LN NFD 219-E4
BIRCH LN NO 80-C3
BIRCH LN ORO 103-C4
BIRCH LN SJT 98-A2
BIRCH LN N SVW 79-E3,80-A3
BIRCH LN NE OTS 33-E4,47-E1
BIRCH LN S SVW 79-E3,80-A3
BIRCH LN W WAY 104-B3
BIRCH PL MTK 105-B4,119-B1
BIRCH PT EAG 135-D4
BIRCH RD CRT 161-C4
BIRCH RD EB 37-D1
BIRCH RD MTK 118-C3
BIRCH RD ROG 47-D4
BIRCH RD WBT 81-A1
BIRCH RD NE EB 37-D2
BIRCH ST ANO 63-D1
BIRCH ST BWV 95-C1
BIRCH ST LL 66-C3
BIRCH ST MHT 95-D1
BIRCH ST RF 140-E2
BIRCH ST RMT 164-A2
BIRCH ST SCF 14-E3
BIRCH ST STP 123-B3
BIRCH ST WBL 94-E1,95-A1
BIRCH ST E BUF 59-A2
BIRCH ST N LP 113-B4
BIRCH ST N WAC 129-E3
BIRCH ST NE LON 217-B2
BIRCH ST NW LON 217-B2
BIRCH ST S WAC 129-E3
BIRCH ST W BUF 59-A2
BIRCH ST W EAG 136-A4
BIRCH ST W RMT 164-B1
BIRCH TRL SVW 80-A2
BIRCH BEND CT VH 80-D4
BIRCH BEND LN VH 80-D4
BIRCH BEND LN WAY 104-C3
BIRCH BEND LN WBT 80-D4
BIRCH BLUFF RD SWD 117-C3
BIRCH BLUFF RD TKB 117-C3
BIRCH BRIAR TRL PLY 104-C2
BIRCH COVE DR WBL 80-D4
BIRCH GROVE CIR BP 77-E2,78-A2
BIRCH ISLAND RD EPR 118-E4
BIRCH KNOLL DR WBL 95-B1
BIRCH LAKE AVE WBL 80-E3,81-A3
BIRCH LAKE BLVD N NO 80-D3
BIRCH LAKE BLVD N WBL 80-E3
BIRCH LAKE BLVD N WBT 80-D3
BIRCH LAKE BLVD S WBL 80-E4
BIRCH LAKE CIR WBL 80-E3
BIRCH LAKE RD WBL 80-D4
BIRCH POND PL EAG 135-C4
BIRCH POND RD EAG 135-C4
BIRCH POND TRL WBT 80-D4
BIRCH RIDGE RD VH 80-D4
BIRCH VIEW CT STP 123-A2
BIRCHBARK TRL N LE 95-E4
BIRCHCREST CIR EAG 149-E2
BIRCHCREST DR EDI 119-E4
BIRCHCREST DR RF 140-E2
BIRCHCREST DR WBT 80-E4
BIRCHER AVE SSP 122-D2
BIRCHVIEW DR MPW 109-B2
BIRCHVIEW LN MTK 105-B4
BIRCHVIEW LN NE HL 36-E3
BIRCHVIEW RD MG 77-A3
BIRCHWOOD AVE BWV 95-C1
BIRCHWOOD AVE PRL 161-C2
BIRCHWOOD AVE RMT 164-B1
BIRCHWOOD CIR LWT 23-E2
BIRCHWOOD CIR NE LWT 23-E2
BIRCHWOOD CT BUR 148-C4
BIRCHWOOD CT BWV 95-C1
BIRCHWOOD DR N SWR 96-E1
BIRCHWOOD LN BLO 133-C3
BIRCHWOOD LN BUR 148-C4
BIRCHWOOD LN BWV 95-B1
BIRCHWOOD LN MTK 119-A2
BIRCHWOOD LN NW BT 20-C4
BIRCHWOOD RD MHT 95-C1
BIRCHWOOD RD WBY 123-C1
BIRCHWOOD ST SVW 79-E1
BIRCHWOOD TER N WYT 25-C3
BIRCHWOOD WAY APV 163-D1
BIRDIE LN CHS 131-D3
BIRKDALE CT TRT 125-D3
BIRMINGHAM ST MPW 94-E4,108-E1
BIRMINGHAM ST STP 108-E2
BIRNAMWOOD CT BUR 148-D3
BIRNAMWOOD DR BUR 148-E3
BISCAYNE AVE CAT 192-B2,206-B1
BISCAYNE AVE EAG 150-B3
BISCAYNE AVE ET 164-B4,178-B3
BISCAYNE AVE RMT 150-A4,164-A2
BISCAYNE BLVD EDI 119-C3
BISCAYNE BLVD EPR 132-D2
BISCAYNE LN RFD 74-B4
BISCAYNE WAY RMT 164-B2
BISCHOFF LN BLO 134-D3
BISHOP AVE IGH 136-D1
BISHOP AVE NW CMT 58-C1
BISHOP AVE NW MLT 30-C3,44-C1
BISHOP AVE NW SVT 16-C4,30-C1
BISHOP AVE SW WDT 86-C1
BISHOP CT EPR 133-A3
BISON AVE STP 107-D2
BISON DR MPW 109-B2
BISON ST NW RAM 34-D3,48-D1
BITTERN CT CHN 131-E3
BITTERSWEET CIR RMT 164-B2
BITTERSWEET CT EPR 132-D2
BITTERSWEET CT RMT 164-B2
BITTERSWEET CT NW AND 36-A4
BITTERSWEET DR CW 1-B2
BITTERSWEET DR EPR 132-D2
BITTERSWEET DR HUT 111-E3
BITTERSWEET LN MPW 94-E4
BITTERSWEET
ST NW AND 36-A3,50-A3
BITTERSWEET ST NW CR 50-A3,64-A2
BITTERSWEET ST NW SF 8-A4
BITTERSWEET WAY RMT 164-B2
BIXBY AVE WT 218-B1
BIXBY WAY IGH 136-D2
BJERSTEDT LN TRT 126-B4
BLACK BASS RD TRT 125-C4,139-C1
BLACK DOG RD E BUR 135-A4,148-E1
BLACK DOG RD W BUR 148-D1
BLACK DUCK CIR LL 66-B3
BLACK DUCK CT LL 66-B3
BLACK DUCK DR LL 66-B3
BLACK DUCK DR S LL 66-B3
BLACK FRIARS LN MTK 118-B3
BLACK HILLS DR BUR 148-B4
BLACK LAKE CT NO 80-C3
BLACK LAKE LN MOU 117-A1
BLACK LAKE RD NO 80-C2
BLACK LAKE RD SPR 117-B1
BLACK MAPLE DR EPR 133-B3
BLACK OAK DR EAG 136-B3
BLACK OAK DR MTK 105-B3
BLACK OAK DR NB 79-A4,93-A1
BLACK OAK RD NO 80-A2
BLACK OAK RD NE PRL 161-A2
BLACK OAKS CT N PLY 104-C2
BLACK OAKS LN MTK 104-D2
BLACK OAKS LN PLY 90-C3
BLACK OAKS LN N PLY 90-C4,104-C2
BLACK OAKS PL N PLY 104-C1
BLACKBERRY LN CFT 222-C2
BLACKBERRY LN MTK 104-D3
BLACKBERRY TRL IGH 136-D2
BLACKBERRY BRIDGE PATH IGH 136-D2
BLACKBIRD CT CHN 132-A3
BLACKBIRD LN LL 52-A4
BLACKBIRD TRL RVT 167-D4,181-D1
BLACKBURN LN IGH 136-D1
BLACKDUCK LN BLT 17-E2
BLACKENEY RD EPR 132-D3
BLACKFOOT PASS EDI 119-C4,133-C1
BLACKFOOT ST NW AND 35-D2,49-D2
BLACKFOOT ST NW CR 63-D1
BLACKFOOT ST NW OG 21-D4,35-D1
BLACKFOOT TRL MED 89-E3
BLACKHAWK CIR EAG 149-C1
BLACKHAWK CV EAG 135-C4
BLACKHAWK PT EAG 135-C4
BLACKHAWK RD EAG 135-C4,149-C1
BLACKHAWK HILLS RD EAG 135-C4
BLACKHAWK LAKE CT EAG 135-C4
BLACKHAWK LAKE DR EAG 135-D4
BLACKHAWK LAKE PL EAG 135-C4
BLACKHAWK RIDGE CIR EAG 135-D4
BLACKHAWK RIDGE CT EAG 135-D4
BLACKHAWK RIDGE PL EAG 135-D4
BLACKHAWK RIDGE WAY EAG 135-D4
BLACKOAKS CIR ANO 49-D3
BLACKOAKS CT ANO 49-D3
BLACKOAKS CT N MG 76-C1
BLACKOAKS LN ANO 49-D3
BLACKOAKS LN MG 76-C1
BLACKOAKS LN N MG 76-C2
BLACKSHIRE PATH IGH 136-D2
BLACKSTONE AVE IGH 136-D3
BLACKSTONE AVE S SLP 105-E4,119-E1
BLACKWELL CIR RMT 164-A2
BLACKWELL CT N IGH 136-D3
BLACKWELL CT S IGH 136-D3
BLACKWELL PATH RMT 164-A2
BLACKWOOD AVE NW SVT 30-C3
BLACKWOOD
AVE SW MVT 72-C4,86-C1
BLAINE AVE CAT 192-D3,206-D1
BLAINE AVE ET 178-D3
BLAINE AVE IGH 136-D3
BLAINE AVE ORO 117-C1
BLAINE AVE WDL 104-C4
BLAINE AVE E ET 164-D4,178-D1
BLAINE AVE E RMT 150-D4,164-D2
BLAINE CT IGH 136-D3
BLAINE CT RMT 164-D1
BLAIR AVE IGH 150-D2
BLAIR AVE STP 107-D3,108-A3
BLAIR RD MTA 102-D4
BLAISDELL AVE DRS 28-D2
BLAISDELL AVE MPL 106-C4,120-C1
BLAISDELL AVE RCH 120-D4,134-D1
BLAISDELL AVE S BLO 134-D3,148-D1
BLAISDELL CIR BLO 134-C4,148-D1
BLAKE AVE STP 107-C2
BLAKE PATH IGH 136-D3
BLAKE RD SLT 175-A1
BLAKE RD N HOP 119-C1
BLAKE RD N SLP 119-C1
BLAKE RD S EDI 119-D3
BLAKE RD S HOP 119-C2
BLAKE RIDGE CT EDI 119-D3
BLAKE RIDGE RD EDI 119-D3
BLAKELEY TRL BKT 185-C3
BLAKENEY RD EPR 132-E3
BLANCA AVE W RMT 150-A4
BLANCHARD CT IGH 136-D3
BLANCHARD WAY IGH 136-D3
BLANDING CT BL 17-E3
BLANDING WOODS RD N SCF 14-D2
BLANDING WOODS RD S SCF 14-D2
BLAYLOCK CIR CRT 162-A3
BLAZINGSTAR CT CHM 63-B3
BLECK RD RFD 74-A3
BLENHEIM CIR MTK 118-D2
BLENHEIM WAY MTK 118-C2
BLIND LAKE TRL PRL 161-B4
BLISS LN BLO 148-C1
BLISS LANE CIR BLO 148-C1
BLOMQUIST AVE WBL 95-B1
BLOOM AVE WBL 81-A3
BLOOM CT LL 66-D4
BLOOM RD WBT 81-B1
BLOOM ST CHC 26-B1
BLOOM LAKE RD N FRT 13-B4,27-C1
BLOOMFIELD CIR RMT 164-B2
BLOOMFIELD CT RMT 164-A2
BLOOMFIELD PATH RMT 164-B2
BLOOMFIELD PL RMT 164-B2
BLOOMFIELD WAY RMT 164-B2
BLOOMINGTON AVE FS 120-E4
BLOOMINGTON
AVE MPL 106-E4,120-E2
BLOOMINGTON
AVE RCH 120-E4,134-E1
BLOOMINGTON AVE S BLO 134-E3
BLOOMINGTON
FWY E BLO 134-C2,148-C1
BLOOMINGTON
FWY W BLO 134-C4,148-C1
BLOOMINGTON RD FS 121-C4
BLOOMINGTON
FERRY RD BLO 133-C4,147-D1
BLOSSOM CT EDI 119-E3
BLOSSOM LN SPP 137-C3
BLOSSOM RD EPR 133-B4
BLUE BILL CIR WBT 81-B1
BLUE BIRD LN NO 80-B2
BLUE BONNET DR COR 75-E3
BLUE CIRCLE DR EPR 119-B4
BLUE CIRCLE DR MTK 119-C4
BLUE CRANE LN NO 80-B2
BLUE CROSS RD EAG 135-C4
BLUE FLAG CT NFD 219-D3
BLUE FLAG CT NO 80-C2
BLUE GENTIAN CIR EAG 135-E2
BLUE GENTIAN RD EAG 135-E2,136-A2
BLUE GOOSE RD NO 80-C3
BLUE HERON CT EAG 135-E4
BLUE HERON DR LL 65-E3
BLUE HERON TRL S SHK 160-C1
BLUE HERRON LN WBY 109-D4
BLUE JAY CIR CHN 117-E4
BLUE JAY CT EAG 135-E4
BLUE JAY LN HUT 112-C3
BLUE JAY LN NO 80-A3
BLUE JAY ST SHK 146-C4
BLUE JAY WAY EAG 135-E4
BLUE PHLOX CT NFD 219-D3
BLUE RIDGE DR WBY 123-E3
BLUE RIDGE LN SWD 117-B4
BLUE RIDGE PATH RMT 164-A2
BLUE SAGE LN E CHN 131-E2
BLUE SAGE LN W CHN 131-D2
BLUE SPRUCE CT NO 80-A3
BLUE SPRUCE LN HUT 112-C2
BLUE SPRUCE LN SOM 70-B4
BLUE STEM CT NFD 219-D3
BLUE WATER RD EAG 135-E2
BLUEBELL AVE N BP 78-A1
BLUEBELL CT VH 80-C4
BLUEBERRY CIR EAG 149-D1
BLUEBERRY CT EAG 149-D1
BLUEBERRY CT HAS 166-C2
BLUEBERRY KNLS EAG 149-D1
BLUEBERRY LN EAG 149-D1
BLUEBERRY LN HAS 166-C2
BLUEBERRY ST IGH 136-D3
BLUEBILL AVE ROG 48-A4
BLUEBILL BLVD BUF 59-B1
BLUEBILL CIR EAG 135-C4
BLUEBILL CIR LVT 160-A1
BLUEBILL DR EAG 135-C4
BLUEBILL DR MH 135-E1,136-A1

BLUEBILL LN LL 52-A4
BLUEBILL TRL CHN 131-E3
BLUEBILL BAY RD BUR 162-E3
BLUEBILL BAY RD LVL 162-E3
BLUEBIRD ALC WBY 109-D4
BLUEBIRD CIR MG 77-A4
BLUEBIRD CIR NW CR 64-B1
BLUEBIRD CT N NOH 111-D1
BLUEBIRD DR MG 77-A4
BLUEBIRD DR SJT 98-A2
BLUEBIRD DR WAC 129-C4
BLUEBIRD LN BKR 4-A4
BLUEBIRD LN BUF 45-B4
BLUEBIRD LN CW 1-B3
BLUEBIRD LN DNT 201-A4
BLUEBIRD LN MOU 103-A4,117-A1
BLUEBIRD LN MTK 118-B3
BLUEBIRD LN WBY 109-D4
BLUEBIRD ST CR 64-B2
BLUEBIRD ST NW AND 36-B2,50-B2
BLUEBIRD ST NW CR 64-B3
BLUEBIRD ST NW SF 8-B4
BLUEBIRD TRL NE PRL 161-B2
BLUEBONNET BLVD CHN 131-D2
BLUEDORN CIR PRL 161-B2
BLUEGILL BAY WBY 124-A1
BLUEGILL RD WBY 124-A1
BLUEJAY AVE N CT 114-D4
BLUEJAY CT FAR 177-D2
BLUESTEM AVE SHK 146-B3
BLUESTEM LN EPR 133-B4
BLUESTEM LN SVW 79-C1
BLUESTEM PL CHM 63-B3
BLUESTONE DR EAG 149-B1
BLUESTONE DR E EAG 149-C1
BLUESTONE LN EAG 149-B1
BLUFF AVE E SHK 146-B2
BLUFF CIR CHN 145-E1
BLUFF CIR MH 122-A3
BLUFF CIR N CHS 145-D1
BLUFF CIR S CHS 145-D1
BLUFF CT BUR 148-E2
BLUFF DR BLO 147-D2
BLUFF DR SCT 159-D3
BLUFF PASS N CHS 145-D1
BLUFF PASS S CHS 145-D1
BLUFF RD ANN 74-B3
BLUFF RD BLT 17-E2
BLUFF RD CAR 159-B1
BLUFF RD EPR 147-C1
BLUFF ST CHC 26-B1
BLUFF ST CW 1-B2
BLUFF ST MPL 106-E2
BLUFF ST NST 55-C2
BLUFF TRL CHS 145-D1
BLUFF CREEK DR CHN 131-E4,146-A1
BLUFF HEIGHTS TRL SE PRL 161-B4
BLUFF POINTE DR CHS 145-D1
BLUFF RIDGE CT CHN 118-B4
BLUFF VIEW CIR JOR 173-A3
BLUFF VIEW CT CHN 131-E2
BLUFF VIEW DR BAY 97-B4
BLUFFS DR MOU 116-D2
BLUFFS LN MOU 116-D2
BLUFFS LN N MTA 116-D2
BLUWOOD AVE E LC 94-B3
BOARD CIR MHT 95-C2
BOARD CT MHT 95-C2
BOARD RD MHT 95-C2
BOARDMAN ST MPL 121-B3
BOARDWALK EAG 135-C4
BOARDWALK MH 122-A3
BOARDWALK AVE MPL 106-C1
BOARDWALK CT SVW 79-E4
BOARDWALK PL MPL 106-C1
BOARSHEAD RD MTK 118-B3
BOB PL RCH 134-C1
BOB EHLEN DR ANO 49-D4
BOBCAT LN MPW 109-B2
BOBOLINK LN NO 80-B2
BOBOLINK RD MED 103-D1
BOHEMIA ST NP 201-E2
BOHLAND AVE STP 121-C2
BOHLAND PL STP 121-D2
BOHLKEN DR HAS 166-D3
BOHN CT SAV 148-A4
BOHN SACK WAY HAT 201-B1
BOHNHOF JCT NE FRI 79-A4
BOHNS POINT LN ORO 103-C4
BOHNS POINT RD ORO 103-C4
BOILING SPRINGS CIR SHK 147-C4
BOILING SPRINGS LN E SHK 147-C3
BOLDT ST CHS 145-D2
BOLIVIA AVE W RMT 150-A4
BOLLAND CT IGH 136-D2
BOLLAND TRL IGH 136-D2
BOLLUM CIR LOL 103-E2
BOLLUM LN LOL 103-E2
BOLTON AVE NW MLT 44-C3
BOLTON AVE NW SVT 30-C1
BOLTON AVE SW MVT 58-C4,72-C2
BOLTON DR NW CMT 58-C2
BOLTON WAY IGH 136-D3
BONA RD MV 79-B2
BONAIRE PATH RMT 150-A4,164-B1
BOND WAY IGH 136-D3
BONITA CIR DEL 87-E2
BONNER CT N IGH 136-D2
BONNER CT S IGH 136-D2
BONNEVISTA TER JT 145-E3
BONNIE LN GV 106-A1
BONNIE LN STP 123-B3
BONNIE BRAE DR EDI 133-D2
BONNIE GLEN PKWY WYT 26-A2
BONNIEVIEW CIR WBY 124-B1
BONNIEVIEW DR WBY 124-B1
BOOM RD SWR 83-A4
BOONE AVE SAV 147-C3,161-C1
BOONE AVE N BP 77-C4,91-C1
BOONE AVE N GV 105-C2
BOONE AVE N NH 91-C2
BOONE AVE S BLO 147-C1
BOONE AVE S SLP 105-C4,119-C1
BOONE CIR BLO 133-C4,147-C1
BOONE CIR N NH 91-C3
BOONE CT SLP 105-C4
BOONE PL N NH 91-C1
BOONE RD HNT 141-B3
BOOTH AVE IGH 136-D2
BOOTS CT STP 108-B2
BORCHARDT WAY JOR 173-C3
BORCHERT LN EAG 136-A3
BORDEAUX CT IGH 136-D2
BORDEAUX CT WBY 109-D4
BORDEN CT IGH 136-D2
BORDEN WAY IGH 136-D2
BORDER AVE N MPL 106-C2
BORDNER DR IGH 136-D3
BORDNER PL STP 121-C3
BOREALIS LN NE CH 92-E1
BORIGHT ST LES 212-D3
BORMAN AVE IGH 136-D3,150-D2
BORMAN CT IGH 136-D3
BORMAN WAY IGH 136-D3
BORNER ST N PRE 153-B4
BORNER ST S PRE 153-B4,167-B1
BOSS CIR EPR 147-B1
BOSSARD DR RVL 94-A4
BOSSEN TER MPL 121-A3
BOSTON CIR EAG 149-E1
BOSTON CT EAG 149-E1
BOSTON LN NE LEX 65-D4
BOSTON RD WBY 124-A4
BOSTON ST NW ER 19-C4,33-C1
BOSTON HILL RD EAG 149-E1
BOUDIN ST PRL 161-D2
BOUDREAU CT IGH 136-D3
BOULDER AVE RMT 164-A2
BOULDER CT HUD 111-D2
BOULDER DR BUR 162-B1
BOULDER LN BC 91-E1
BOULDER LN BUR 162-B1
BOULDER PT SHK 145-E3,146-A3
BOULDER RD CHN 131-D3
BOULDER RISE EPR 132-E3
BOULDER WAY MTK 118-D4
BOULDER BAY RD EPR 119-B4
BOULDER BRIDGE CIR SWD 117-B4
BOULDER BRIDGE DR SWD 117-B4
BOULDER BRIDGE LN SWD 117-B4
BOULDER CREEK DR MTK 118-D4
BOULDER POINT DR HUD 111-D2
BOULDER POINTE RD EPR 132-D3
BOULDER RIDGE LN WBY 123-E2
BOULDER RIDGE PT EAG 149-C2
BOULDER RIDGE RD WBY 123-E2
BOULEAU RD WBL 80-D3
BOUNDARY AVE MP 103-A1
BOUNDARY CREEK TER MG 63-B4
BOUNTY ST PRL 161-B3
BOURN LN MH 135-D1
BOURNE AVE STP 107-B2
BOUTWELL CT N SWR 96-D1
BOUTWELL PL N SWR 96-D1
BOUTWELL RD N SWR 96-D1
BOUTWELL RD N SWT 96-D1
BOVEY AVE IGH 136-D1
BOVEY RD WAY 104-B3
BOWDOIN ST STP 121-C3
BOWER CT IGH 122-D4,136-D4
BOWER PATH IGH 122-D4,136-D4
BOWERS DR NW RAM 48-C2
BOWMAN AVE IGH 136-D3
BOWMAN CIR IGH 136-D2
BOWMAN CT N IGH 136-D3
BOWMAN CT S IGH 136-D3
BOWSENS LN WBY 124-A2
BOXMAN PATH IGH 136-D2
BOXWOOD AVE MPW 123-B3
BOXWOOD AVE STP 123-B3
BOXWOOD CT RMT 164-A2
BOYCE RD HOP 119-D2
BOYD AVE EPR 118-C4,132-C1
BOYD AVE FH 107-C2
BOYD AVE IGH 122-D4,136-E3
BOYD AVE SIT 220-E2
BOYD CIR IGH 136-E3
BOYD CT IGH 136-D3
BOYER DR MED 89-B2
BOYER DR NW STT 6-C1
BOYER PATH IGH 136-D2
BOYNE ST NE LWT 10-B4
BOYS SCHOOL RD MTK 118-E3
BRACKETT RD EPR 118-B4
BRACKETTS RD SWD 117-E4
BRACKETTS POINT RD ORO 103-E4
BRAD ST HBG 156-A2
BRADBURY CT IGH 136-D2
BRADDOCK AVE NE BUF 58-E3
BRADDOCK AVE NE BUT 44-E3
BRADDOCK AVE NE MOT 30-E4,31-A3
BRADDOCK AVE SE FKT 86-E2
BRADDOCK TRL EAG 149-E2,150-A1
BRADEN TRL IGH 136-D3
BRADFORD AVE CHM 63-C1
BRADFORD CIR EAG 150-A1
BRADFORD CT IGH 136-E4
BRADFORD LN MOU 117-A2
BRADFORD PL EAG 150-A1
BRADFORD PL EPR 132-E3
BRADFORD RD HOP 119-B2
BRADFORD RD MTK 119-A2
BRADFORD ST MP 89-A4
BRADFORD ST STP 107-C3
BRADHURST DR HUT 112-B3
BRADLEY BLVD BEC 2-E3
BRADLEY DR HUT 112-D2
BRADLEY ST LL 65-E2
BRADLEY ST STP 108-C2
BRADLEY ST N MPW 94-C4,108-C1
BRADSHAW AVE NE BUF 58-E3,59-A3
BRADSHAW CIR SE RFT 73-A2
BRADY PATH IGH 136-D3
BRAEBURN CIR EDI 133-D1
BRAEBURN DR SHK 146-B3
BRAEMAR BLVD EDI 133-C1
BRAEMAR LN WBY 123-D2
BRAEWOOD CIR BLO 147-E1
BRAINARD WAY NO 80-A3
BRAINERD AVE STP 108-C2
BRAKKE DR HUT 112-B3
BRAMBLEWOOD AVE VH 80-C4
BRANCH AVE ANO 49-C4
BRANCH RD W MTA 102-E3,103-A3
BRANCH RD W ORO 103-A3
BRANCHING HORN EPR 147-B1
BRAND CIR SWD 117-E4
BRAND ST MPW 109-B3
BRAND LAKE DR NYA 142-B4
BRANDBURY WALK MTK 118-E3
BRANDENBURG DR CHS 145-D1
BRANDIS AVE SE RFT 73-A2
BRANDLWOOD CT WBT 80-D2
BRANDLWOOD RD WBT 80-D2
BRANDON BLVD CHS 145-D1
BRANDON DR HUT 97-D4
BRANDT RD FAT 41-E4,42-A4
BRANDYWINE DR BUR 148-D4,162-D1
BRANDYWINE PKWY N BP 78-B2
BRANDYWINE RD N COR 76-B1
BRANSON DR IGH 136-D4
BRANSON ST EDI 120-A2
BRANSTON ST STP 107-B2
BRANT AVE BEC 2-E3
BRANT CIR EAG 149-C2
BRANT CT BEC 2-E3
BRANT ST HL 51-D3
BRANT ST NE BLA 65-D4,79-D1
BRASSIE CIR EPR 133-B4
BRAUN AVE SE FKT 87-A4
BRAUN AVE SE RFT 73-A2
BRAUN CT EAG 135-D4
BRAUNWARTH CIR WAC 129-C2
BRAVE DR SPT 70-E1
BRAXTON DR EPR 132-C3
BRAZIL AVE RMT 164-A1
BRECKENRIDGE DR RW 210-E1
BRECKENRIDGE LN EPR 132-C3
BRECKENRIDGE RD MTK 105-B4
BRECONWOOD CIR MTK 118-C1
BRECONWOOD RD MTK 118-C1
BREDA AVE STP 107-D2
BREEN ST STP 108-E2,109-A2
BREEZEWOOD LN ROG 61-E1
BREEZY DR MOU 116-E1
BREEZY HEIGHTS RD WDL 104-C4
BREEZY POINT DR NE EB 37-C1
BREEZY POINT RD PRL 161-B3
BREEZY POINT RD WDL 104-C4
BREI KESSEL RD IND 88-E3
BREMEN AVE RMT 164-A1
BREN CIR MTK 119-A4
BREN LN EPR 132-C1
BREN RD MTK 119-B3
BREN RD E MTK 119-B4
BREN RD W MTK 119-B3
BRENDA BLVD BEC 2-E3
BRENDA BLVD BKR 2-E3
BRENDAN WAY ROG 47-D4
BRENDEN CT CHN 117-D4,131-D1
BRENDEN LN EPR 132-C2
BRENDON AVE IGH 136-D3
BRENLYN LN MTK 119-A2
BRENNER AVE MPW 95-B3
BRENNER AVE RVL 93-E3
BRENNER CT RVL 93-B3
BRENNER LN LVT 160-A2
BRENNER PASS GV 106-A3
BRENNER PASS NE FRI 93-A1
BRENNER ST RVL 93-B3
BRENT AVE IGH 136-E1,150-E2
BRENT DR WAC 129-D2
BRENTRIDGE DR SWD 117-B3
BRENTWOOD AVE SWD 117-D3
BRENTWOOD AVE TKB 117-D3
BRENTWOOD AVE N CRY 91-D1
BRENTWOOD CIR MO 31-C2
BRENTWOOD CT RMT 164-A2
BRENTWOOD DR NB 93-B2
BRENTWOOD LN EAG 136-A4
BRENTWOOD LN NW ER 19-E4
BRENTWOOD TRL WBY 123-E2,124-A1
BRENWOOD CRV MPW 95-B3
BRENWOOD TRL MTK 119-A2
BRETT TRL ROG 61-E1
BRETTON WAY CHN 117-E4,118-A4
BREWER DR PRL 160-E1
BREWERS LN SWR 96-D2
BREWSTER AVE IGH 136-E4
BREWSTER ST STP 107-C2
BRIAN CT CV 66-D2
BRIAN DR CV 66-D2
BRIAN WAY CV 66-D2
BRIANA LN TRT 126-A1
BRIANBORU AVE RMT 164-A1
BRIAR CIR BLO 133-E4,147-E1
BRIAR CT BLO 147-E1
BRIAR CT BUR 148-C4
BRIAR CT MO 32-A3
BRIAR LN BLO 133-E3
BRIAR LN MTK 105-A3
BRIAR LN TF 14-C2
BRIAR RD BLO 133-E4,147-E1
BRIAR ST ORO 103-D4
BRIAR CREEK RD EAG 135-E4,149-E1
BRIAR GLEN CT WBY 124-B1
BRIAR GLEN CV WBY 124-B1
BRIAR GLEN LN WBY 124-B1
BRIAR OAKE S PL MO 31-E3,32-A3
BRIAR OAKS BLVD MOT 31-E3,32-A3
BRIAR OAKS PL MO 31-E3
BRIARDALE CT NE FRI 79-A4
BRIARDALE RD NE FRI 79-A4
BRIARGLEN RD EPR 132-C3
BRIARKNOLL CIR AH 79-D4
BRIARKNOLL DR AH 79-D4
BRIARWOOD AVE DWD 81-C3
BRIARWOOD AVE GRA 81-D4
BRIARWOOD AVE MHT 81-D4
BRIARWOOD AVE NE BUT 45-A3
BRIARWOOD AVE NE MOT 31-A2
BRIARWOOD AVE SE RFT 73-A3
BRIARWOOD CT CHN 131-D1
BRIARWOOD CT HUD 111-D2
BRIARWOOD CT MTK 119-A2
BRIARWOOD DR MTK 119-A2
BRIARWOOD LN EAG 136-A4
BRIARWOOD LN MTK 119-A2
BRIARWOOD LN NE EB 36-E2,37-A1
BRIARWOOD TER MTK 119-A2
BRICK CIR TRT 125-E1,126-A1
BRICK ST S SWR 96-E1
BRICKFORD ST NW WAT 101-B3
BRICKSTONE CT SVW 80-A2
BRIDAL CREEK CIR CHN 131-D2
BRIDAL PATH TRL MED 90-A3
BRIDGE AVE DEL 87-D2
BRIDGE AVE W DEL 87-D2
BRIDGE CT SVW 79-E4
BRIDGE CT E SVW 80-A4
BRIDGE XING E SHK 160-C3
BRIDGE LN EDI 120-A2
BRIDGE RD BLO 133-E2
BRIDGE ST EDI 119-E2,120-A2
BRIDGE ST HUD 111-C2
BRIDGE ST LES 212-C4
BRIDGE ST MTK 119-A1
BRIDGE ST RFD 74-B3
BRIDGE ST SVW 79-E4,80-A4
BRIDGE ST N CF 208-B4
BRIDGE ST NW SF 7-E4
BRIDGE SPUR RD E SHK 160-C3
BRIDGE VIEW AVE EAG 135-C2
BRIDGEPOINT CRV SSP 122-E4
BRIDGEPOINT DR SSP 122-E4,123-A4
BRIDGEPOINT WAY SSP 122-E4
BRIDGEPORT AVE RMT 164-A2
BRIDGESTONE RD NW BT 7-B4
BRIDGESTONE RD NW SF 7-B4
BRIDGEVIEW CT MH 136-A1
BRIDGEWATER BAY WBY 124-B2
BRIDGEWATER CIR MTK 118-C1
BRIDGEWATER CIR VH 94-B1
BRIDGEWATER CIR WBY 124-B2
BRIDGEWATER CT RMT 164-A2
BRIDGEWATER CT SAV 161-E2
BRIDGEWATER CT VH 80-B4,94-B1
BRIDGEWATER CT WBY 124-B2
BRIDGEWATER DR EAG 136-A4,150-A1
BRIDGEWATER DR FRI 78-E4
BRIDGEWATER DR SAV 161-E2,162-A2
BRIDGEWATER DR VH 94-B1
BRIDGEWATER PKWY RMT 164-A2
BRIDGEWATER PKWY WBY 124-B2
BRIDGEWATER RD GV 106-A1
BRIDGEWOOD TER VH 80-D4
BRIDLE LN HOP 119-C1
BRIDLE PATH CRT 175-D3
BRIDLE TRL DWD 81-D3
BRIDLE CREEK TRL CHN 131-D2
BRIDLE PASS DR FLT 39-C4
BRIDLE PATH CT WBT 80-D2
BRIDLE PATH CT WBY 123-E1
BRIDLE PATH LN WBY 123-E1
BRIDLE RIDGE CIR EAG 150-A1
BRIDLE RIDGE CT NE PRL 161-A2
BRIDLE RIDGE RD EAG 136-A4,150-A1
BRIDLE RIDGE TRL NE PRL 161-A2
BRIDLEWOOD CRV EPR 132-C1
BRIDLEWOOD DR STP 109-A4
BRIGADOON CIR SVW 93-E1,94-A1
BRIGADOON CT SVW 80-A4
BRIGADOON DR SVW 80-A4,94-A1
BRIGADOON PL SVW 79-E4
BRIGADOON PL NE FRI 79-A2
BRIGGS DR IGH 150-E2
BRIGHAM TRL MTK 118-C1
BRIGHTON AVE NE BUT 45-A3
BRIGHTON AVE NE MOT 31-A3
BRIGHTON AVE NE MPL 93-A4
BRIGHTON AVE S BUF 59-A2
BRIGHTON AVE SE FKT 73-A4,87-A2
BRIGHTON BLVD MOU 117-A2
BRIGHTON CMNS MOU 117-A2
BRIGHTON LN EPR 133-C4
BRIGHTON LN MV 79-B3
BRIGHTON LN NB 79-B3
BRIGHTON PL STP 108-D2
BRIGHTON SQ NB 79-A4
BRIGHTON ST ANO 49-B3
BRIGHTON TRL WBY 123-E2,124-A2
BRIGHTON WAY AH 93-C1
BRIGHTWOOD DR MTK 104-E3
BRIMHALL AVE LOL 103-D2
BRIMHALL ST STP 121-D2
BRINKER ST CHN 131-D2
BRINKHAUS CIR CHS 131-B4
BRINKHAUS ST CHS 131-B4,145-B1
BRINKLEY LN IGH 136-E4
BRISBIN ST ANO 63-D1
BRISTOL AVE NB 93-A1
BRISTOL BLVD EAG 150-B3
BRISTOL BLVD EDI 134-A1
BRISTOL CIR EDI 134-A1
BRISTOL LN ET 178-A4
BRISTOL LN MTK 119-A3
BRISTOL PL EPR 132-D3
BRISTOL PL WIL 95-D1
BRISTOL RD WBY 123-D2
BRISTOL RUN SVW 79-E4
BRISTOL VILLAGE CRV BLO 133-D4,147-D1
BRISTOL VILLAGE DR BLO 133-D4,147-D1
BRITANI LN OST 28-B4
BRITANNY LN IGH 136-D3
BRITTANY CT NB 79-B3
BRITTANY CT SHK 146-C3
BRITTANY CT WBT 80-D2
BRITTANY CT WBY 123-E2
BRITTANY DR SHK 146-C3
BRITTANY DR N CHM 63-D3
BRITTANY LN IGH 136-D3
BRITTANY LN WBY 123-E2
BRITTANY RD EDI 119-E4,133-E1
BRITTANY RD HAS 166-C2
BRITTANY WAY EPR 147-B1
BRITTON LN MTK 104-D4
BROAD AVE NE CR 78-C1
BROAD AVE NE FRI 78-C2
BROAD ST N PRE 167-A1
BROAD ST S PRE 167-B1
BROADBAND BLVD SHK 146-E2
BROADMOOR DR IND 103-A1
BROADMOORE DR EPR 118-B4
BROADVIEW AVE CHS 145-C2
BROADWAY W MO 17-B4
BROADWAY AVE HBG 156-A2
BROADWAY AVE SPP 137-B3
BROADWAY AVE YAT 156-A2
BROADWAY AVE E FL 39-B3
BROADWAY AVE N WAY 104-C3
BROADWAY AVE NE COT 37-E2,38-B2
BROADWAY AVE S WAY 104-B3
BROADWAY AVE W FL 39-B3
BROADWAY DR LAU 107-B1
BROADWAY RD NE MPL 107-A1
BROADWAY ST LND 12-D4,26-D1
BROADWAY ST MO 31-C1
BROADWAY ST MSC 55-B4
BROADWAY ST RF 140-E2
BROADWAY ST SCT 173-B2
BROADWAY ST STP 108-C4
BROADWAY ST E MO 31-D2
BROADWAY ST E NG 114-A4
BROADWAY ST E OSS 77-C2
BROADWAY ST N CAR 145-B4
BROADWAY ST N JOR 173-B2
BROADWAY ST N SWR 83-A4,97-A1
BROADWAY ST NE MPL 106-D1,107-A1
BROADWAY ST NW BET 8-D3
BROADWAY ST S JOR 173-B3
BROADWAY ST S SWR 97-A1
BROADWAY ST W MO 31-D1
BROADWAY ST W OSS 77-B2
BROCKTON CIR EAG 150-A1
BROCKTON CRV EAG 150-B1
BROCKTON CT N MG 76-B1
BROCKTON LN N COR 62-B4,76-B4
BROCKTON LN N DAY 48-B2
BROCKTON LN N HSN 48-B3,62-B2
BROCKTON LN N MED 90-B3,104-B1
BROCKTON LN N PLY 104-B2
BRODERICK BLVD IGH 136-D4,150-E1
BROGGER CIR GV 91-C4,105-C1
BROHM LN BL 18-A4
BROKEN ARROW RD CHN 132-A1
BROKEN ARROW RD SJT 97-D3
BROKEN OAK CT LL 66-D3
BROMLEY DR WBY 124-A2
BROMLEY ST SSP 122-D3
BROMPTON PL MH 122-A2

BROMPTON ST STP 107-B2
BROMS BLVD SWD 118-B3
BRONSON AVE LND 12-C4
BRONSON DR MV 79-B2
BROOK AVE EDI 119-E2
BROOK AVE N BP 91-C1
BROOK AVE S SLP 119-E2
BROOK AVE SE MPL 107-A2
BROOK CIR N BP 91-C1
BROOK DR EDI 133-D1
BROOK LN SAV 161-E1
BROOK LN SHK 146-A2
BROOK LN SLP 119-E2
BROOK RD NW ER 19-E2,20-A2
BROOK ST MED 89-A3
BROOKDALE CIR N BP 78-A3
BROOKDALE CT BP 77-E3
BROOKDALE CT N BP 78-B3
BROOKDALE DR N BP 77-E3,78-B3
BROOKDALE LN N BP 78-B3
BROOKE CT HAS 166-C2
BROOKE CT WBL 80-E3
BROOKE LN HAS 166-B2
BROOKFIELD LN MH 136-A2
BROOKHAVEN DR LVT 159-E1
BROOKHAVEN DR WBY 124-B1
BROOKLINE ST STP 123-A2
BROOKLYN BLVD BC 78-A4,92-A1
BROOKLYN BLVD BP 77-D3
BROOKLYN DR BC 78-B4,92-B1
BROOKLYN PL BC 77-E3
BROOKLYN PARK DR N BP 78-C3
BROOKRIDGE AVE N CRY 91-E4
BROOKRIDGE AVE N GV ...91-E4,105-E1
BROOKS AVE MPW 94-E4
BROOKS AVE E LC 94-C4
BROOKS AVE W RVL 93-E4,94-A4
BROOKS BLVD IGH 136-E4
BROOKS CIR PRL 161-B3
BROOKS CIR RVL 94-A4
BROOKS CT MPW 94-D4
BROOKS LN MTB 117-C1
BROOKS ST ARL 183-A2
BROOKS ST E ARL 183-A2
BROOKS ST E ART 183-A2
BROOKS ST W ARL 183-A2
BROOKSHIRE CT NB 79-A4
BROOKSHIRE LN NB 79-A4
BROOKSIDE AVE EDI 119-E2
BROOKSIDE AVE SLP 119-E2
BROOKSIDE AVE S BLO ..134-B4,148-B1
BROOKSIDE CIR BLO 134-B4
BROOKSIDE CT EDI 119-E2
BROOKSIDE LN MH 122-A3
BROOKSIDE LN PRL 160-E3
BROOKSIDE LN N ROG 61-E1
BROOKSIDE TER EDI 119-E2
BROOKSIDE TRL ROG 61-E1
BROOKVIEW AVE EDI 120-A3
BROOKVIEW CIR EPR 147-C1
BROOKVIEW CIR WBY 124-A1
BROOKVIEW CT MPW 109-B4
BROOKVIEW CT WBY 124-A1
BROOKVIEW DR BC 92-B1
BROOKVIEW DR BUR 148-B4
BROOKVIEW DR MPW 109-B4
BROOKVIEW DR SLP 119-E1
BROOKVIEW DR NE FRI 78-E3
BROOKVIEW PKWY BP 91-C1
BROOKVIEW PKWY GV 105-C2
BROOKVIEW RD WBY 124-B1
BROOKVIEW TER CHS 145-D1
BROOKVIEW TERRACE CT WBY .124-B1
BROOKWOOD DR HUT 111-E1,112-A1
BROOKWOOD RD CRT 175-E2
BROOKWOOD TER MPL 120-B3
BROR RD EDI 133-C1
BROUGHAM BLVD NE PRL 161-A2
BROUGHSHANE AVE RMT 164-A1
BROWN AVE STP 122-C2
BROWN CIR SE WAT 101-B4
BROWN LN BUR 162-B3
BROWN LN MTK 118-C1
BROWN RD N LOL 103-D2
BROWN RD N ORO 103-D2
BROWN RD S ORO 103-D3
BROWN BEAR TRL EAG 135-C4
BROWN FARM CIR EPR 147-B1
BROWN THRUSH TRL EPR 118-E4
BROWNDALE AVE EDI ...119-E2,120-A3
BROWNDALE AVE SLP 119-E2
BROWNIE RD MPL 106-B3
BROWNLOW AVE SLP 119-D1
BROWNS LN SJT 97-D1
BRUCE AVE EDI 120-A2
BRUCE CT IGH 150-E1
BRUCE PL EDI 120-A3
BRUCE RD EB 37-D1
BRUEBERRY LN AH 79-D4
BRUENING CT MHT 95-D2
BRUERS CT CHS 131-C4
BRULE CIR CHN 132-B1
BRUMMEL RD HUT 112-D4
BRUMMEL RD TRT 112-D4
BRUN ST ML 43-D3
BRUNELL WAY IGH 136-E4
BRUNET CT VH 94-C1
BRUNS CT VH 94-C1
BRUNSON ST STP 108-C3
BRUNSVOLD RD MTK 118-E3
BRUNSWICK AVE N BP 77-E3,91-E1
BRUNSWICK AVE N CHM 63-E2
BRUNSWICK AVE N CRY 91-E4
BRUNSWICK AVE N GV ...91-E4,105-E1
BRUNSWICK AVE S GV 105-E2
BRUNSWICK AVE S SAV .147-E4,161-E2
BRUNSWICK AVE S SLP .105-E4,119-E1
BRUNSWICK AVE SE PRL 161-B4
BRUNSWICK CIR BLO ...133-E4,147-E1
BRUNSWICK CIR N BP 77-E2
BRUNSWICK CT N BP 77-E2
BRUNSWICK PATH IGH 136-E4
BRUNSWICK RD BLO 147-E1
BRUNSWICK RD MOU 117-A2
BRUSH ST S NYA 142-C4
BRUSH PRAIRIE RD BNT 127-B3
BRUTUS DR LVL 177-B4
BRUZEK LN NP 201-E2
BRYAN AVE IGH 137-A3
BRYAN AVE E LC 94-B3
BRYAN DR RW 196-D4
BRYANT AVE ANO 49-D3
BRYANT AVE BUR 148-C4
BRYANT AVE MHT 81-D4
BRYANT AVE SSP 122-D3
BRYANT AVE N BC 78-C4,92-C1
BRYANT AVE N BP 78-C3
BRYANT AVE N MPL 92-C3,106-C1
BRYANT AVE NE BUT 45-A3
BRYANT AVE S BLO 134-C3
BRYANT AVE S BUR 162-C3
BRYANT AVE S MPL 106-C4,120-C2
BRYANT AVE S RCH 120-C4,134-C1
BRYANT AVE SE FKT 101-A1
BRYANT CIR ANO 49-D3
BRYANT CT N BP 78-C3
BRYANT LN BUR 162-C1
BRYANT LN EPR 119-A4
BRYANT LN IGH 136-E2
BRYANT LN MOU 116-E2
BRYANT PL BUR 148-C4,162-C1
BRYANT ST MP 102-E1,103-A1
BRYANT ST NE HL 51-D2
BRYANT AVENUE CT BUR 162-C3
BRYANT LAKE DR EPR ...119-B4,133-B1
BRYANTWOOD DR MP 102-E1,103-A1
BRYCE AVE IGH 122-E4,136-E1
BRYCE CT BUR 149-A4
BRYCE CT IGH 136-E4
BRYNMAWR PL SWD 117-B3
BUCHANAN CIR NE BLA 50-E4
BUCHANAN CT EPR 132-D2
BUCHANAN PL NE CH 92-E1
BUCHANAN RD NE BLA 64-E2
BUCHANAN ST ANO 49-D4
BUCHANAN ST NE BLA 50-E4,64-E3
BUCHANAN ST NE CH 92-E2
BUCHANAN ST NE EB 8-E4,22-E3
BUCHANAN ST NE FRI 92-E1
BUCHANAN ST NE HL 36-E4,50-E3
BUCHANAN ST NE MPL ...92-E3,106-E1
BUCHANAN ST NE SLK 78-E2
BUCHER AVE SVW 79-E1,80-A1
BUCK RDG HUT 98-D3
BUCK RUN SJT 97-D3
BUCK HILL RD BUR 162-C2
BUCK HILL RD LVL 162-C3
BUCK LAKE BLVD BKR 17-C2
BUCK LAKE CIR SLT 174-E1
BUCK LAKE RD WTT 115-E3
BUCKBEE RD WBL 95-A2
BUCKEYE ST HUD 111-C2
BUCKHILL RD BUR 162-C2
BUCKINGHAM ALC WBY 123-C3
BUCKINGHAM AVE SE FKT 87-A4
BUCKINGHAM BAY WBY 123-C3
BUCKINGHAM CT VH 80-D4
BUCKINGHAM CT WBY 123-C3
BUCKINGHAM DR EPR 133-C4
BUCKINGHAM LN MV 79-B3
BUCKINGHAM RD WBY 123-C3
BUCKINGWOOD CT CHN 132-A1
BUCKLEY BAY EAG 149-B2
BUCKLEY CIR IGH 136-E2
BUCKLEY CT IGH 150-E1
BUCKLEY WAY IGH 136-E2
BUCKS WAY EPR 147-B1
BUCKSKIN DR MED 90-A4
BUCKSKIN TRL COR 76-A3
BUCKTHORN CIR ROG 62-A2
BUCKTHORN LN LL 66-C4
BUCKTHORN TRL ROG 62-A2
BUDD LN SPR 117-B1
BUDD ST IND 89-A4,103-A1
BUDD ST MP 89-A4,103-A1
BUERKLE CIR WBL 94-E2
BUERKLE RD VH 94-E2
BUERKLE RD WBL 94-E2,95-A2
BUFFALO AVE N MON 72-C4,86-C1
BUFFALO AVE S MON 86-C1
BUFFALO LN SVW 79-D1
BUFFALO RD NO 80-B3
BUFFALO ST DEL 87-D2
BUFFALO ST FKT 87-D2
BUFFALO ST RW 182-D4,196-D1
BUFFALO ST STP 108-B3
BUFFALO ST WBT 81-B2
BUFFALO ST N BEL 185-E1
BUFFALO ST NE FRI 78-C2
BUFFALO ST S BEL 185-E1
BUFFALO HILLS ST BUF ...58-E1,59-A1
BUFFALO RUN RD BUF 58-E3
BUFFALO RUN WAY BUF 58-E3
BUFFET WAY EAG 135-D2
BUFFINGTON AVE IGH 137-A3
BUFORD AVE FH 107-C2
BUFORD AVE STP 107-C2
BUFORD CIR FH 107-C2
BUFORD PL FH 107-C2
BUHL AVE NSP 95-A3
BUNCH RD RW 196-D2
BUNDORAN AVE RMT 164-A1
BUNDY CT NFD 219-E4
BUNKER CIR MO 31-C2
BUNKER CT EPR 132-E1
BUNKER HILL DR MV 79-C2
BUNKER LAKE
BLVD NE HL 50-E3,51-B3
BUNKER LAKE
BLVD NW AND 49-E3,50-C3
BUNKER PRAIRIE PARK DR CR ...50-C4
BUNRATTY AVE RMT 164-A1
BUR OAK CT VH 80-C4
BUR OAK DR VH 80-C4
BUR OAK DR W EAG 136-B3
BUR OAK DR W IGH 136-B3
BURANDT BLVD WAC 129-D3
BURCH CIR HUT 98-C4
BURCHLANE DR S MTK 105-B3
BURD PL SLP 105-C4
BURGESS ST STP 107-E3,108-A3
BURGUNDY AVE RMT 164-A1
BURGUNDY DR EAG 135-B4
BURKARDS DR BUR 162-C2
BURKE AVE MPW 94-E4,95-A4
BURKE AVE NSP 95-B4
BURKE AVE E MPW 94-C4
BURKE AVE W RVL 93-E4,108-B1
BURKE CT MPW 94-D4
BURKE LN E LC 94-B3
BURKE TRL IGH 136-E2
BURL OAK CRV HUD 111-E1
BURL OAK CT EPR 132-C3
BURL OAKS CT MTA 102-E3
BURL OAKS DR MTA 102-E3
BURLINGTON RD STP 123-A2
BURLINGTON ST E SWR 97-A2
BURLWOOD CIR BL 18-A4
BURLWOOD CT SWD 117-C4
BURLWOOD DR CHN 132-A3
BURMA AVE RMT 164-A2
BURMA AVE WFT 206-A4
BURMA LN SSP 122-D3
BURNCREST CT BUR 148-D4
BURNELL PARK DR BUR 162-B2
BURNES AVE CNC 12-E3
BURNES DR HOP 119-C1
BURNGARTEN DR BUR 162-C1
BURNHAM BLVD MPL 106-B4
BURNHAM CIR IGH 136-E2
BURNHAM RD MPL 106-B4
BURNHAVEN DR BUR 162-C2
BURNLEY AVE RMT 164-A2
BURNQUIST ST STP 108-D2
BURNS AVE STP 108-E4,109-A4
BURNS DR DAY 62-B2
BURNS PKWY NW BT 20-D4,34-D1
BURNS RD MOU 117-A2
BURNSIDE AVE EAG 135-D2
BURNSVILLE CIR BUR 162-C3
BURNSVILLE
PKWY E BUR 148-E3,149-A3
BURNSVILLE
PKWY W BUR 148-C4,162-B1
BURNSVILLE
CENTER SE RD BUR 162-C1
BURNTSIDE DR GV 106-A2
BURON LN SSP 136-E1
BURQUEST LN BC 92-A1
BURR ST STP 108-C3
BURR ST N MPW 94-C4,108-C1
BURR OAK CIR CHS 131-D4
BURR OAK LN IND 88-B2
BURR OAK LN MTK 119-A2
BURR OAK RD SJT 98-B2
BURR OAK ST EAG 149-A3
BURR RIDGE LN EPR 147-B1
BURSON AVE WBL 81-A3
BURTON LN MPL 121-B2
BURTON ST FH 107-C2
BURTON HALL NFD 219-E3
BURWELL DR MTK 119-A1
BURY DR EPR 118-E4
BUSCH AVE CNC 12-E3
BUSCH CIR ROG 47-D4
BUSCH TER MPL 120-C2
BUSH AVE MPW 109-B3
BUSH AVE STP 108-D3,109-A3
BUSH LN EPR 133-A3
BUSH RD MOU 116-E1
BUSH LAKE DR BLO 133-D4
BUSH LAKE RD BLO 133-D4,147-D1
BUSH LAKE RD EDI 133-E2
BUSH LAKE RD E BLO 133-D3
BUSH LAKE RD W BLO 133-C3
BUSH LAKE ROAD CIR BLO 147-D1
BUSHAWAY RD WAY 104-C3
BUSINESS PKWY RMT 164-A2
BUSINESS CENTER DR ER 33-C1
BUSINESS PARK BLVD N CHM 63-C2
BUSSARD CT AH 93-D2
BUTLER AVE MH 122-B2
BUTLER AVE SSP 122-D2
BUTLER AVE E WSP 122-C2
BUTLER AVE W WSP 122-B2
BUTLER DR BEL 186-A2
BUTLER PL MPL 106-E3,107-A3
BUTTE AVE APV 149-A4
BUTTE CT CHN 132-A1
BUTTERCUP CT CHN 131-D2
BUTTERCUP CT TRT 112-C4
BUTTERFIELD CT PRL 161-B2
BUTTERFIELD DR NW SF 7-D4
BUTTERFLY LN SLT 174-C2
BUTTERNUT AVE STP 122-A2
BUTTERNUT CIR CAR 159-A1
BUTTERNUT CIR MTK 119-A3
BUTTERNUT CIR N BP 64-A4
BUTTERNUT CIR NW CR 64-D2
BUTTERNUT CIR NW OG 22-D3
BUTTERNUT CIR NW PRL 160-E4
BUTTERNUT CT RF 140-E3
BUTTERNUT CT NW AND 50-D3
BUTTERNUT DR CHS 131-D4
BUTTERNUT LN BUR 162-D2
BUTTERNUT LN WAC 129-C2
BUTTERNUT LN SE SM 47-A4
BUTTERNUT ST MSC 69-C1
BUTTERNUT ST NW AND ..36-D3,50-D2
BUTTERNUT ST NW CR 64-D3
BUTTERNUT ST NW OG ...22-D3,36-D1
BUTTERNUT FALLS TRL N MSC ...69-C1
BUTTERSCOTCH RD EPR 133-A1
BUTTERWORTH LN COR 89-E1
BUTWIN RD EAG 149-E3,150-A3
BUTWIN CAMP RD EAG 149-E3
BWANA CT MH 121-E4
BYRD AVE N GV 106-A1
BYRNES RD MTK 105-A4
BYRNWOOD LN MTK 118-B2
BYRON AVE N CRY 91-E2
BYRON CIR GRW 117-E3
BYRONDALE AVE N WAY 104-C3
BYSCANE LN MTK 118-D3
BYWOOD LN MTK 118-C2
BYWOOD PL MTK 118-C2
BYWOOD ST W EDI 119-D2

C

C CT NE EB 37-D1
C ST HIL 92-E2
C ST MEN 121-D4
C ST STP 123-A1
C ST WBY 123-D1
C J CIR SE PRL 161-A3
CABALINE TRL MED 90-A3
CABIN LN SPT 70-E1
CABINET DR GRF 74-D3
CABLE AVE BNT 127-A2,141-A1
CABLE AVE HNT 141-A2,155-A2
CABLE AVE WIT 99-A3,113-A2
CABOT DR MV 79-C2
CACTUS CRV CHN 132-A1
CADY ST RW 196-E4
CADYS LN TLT 154-E3
CAESAR ST LVL 177-B3
CAHILL AVE IGH 136-E2,150-E1
CAHILL AVE NE MOT 31-B4,45-A1
CAHILL AVE SE RFT 73-B2
CAHILL CT IGH 136-E3
CAHILL LN EDI 119-D4
CAHILL RD EDI 119-E4,133-D1
CAIN AVE IGH 136-E2
CAIN RD COR 61-E4,75-E1
CAJED LN SWD 117-B4
CALCITE DR EAG 149-B1
CALDER AVE NE BUF 59-B3
CALDER AVE NE BUT 59-B2
CALDER AVE SE FKT 87-B4,101-A1
CALDER AVE SE RFT 59-B4,73-B1
CALDWELL CT ET 178-A3
CALGARY RD WBY 123-C2
CALGARY TRL ET 178-A3
CALHOUN BLVD W MPL 106-B4
CALHOUN PKWY E MPL .106-B4,120-B1
CALHOUN PKWY W MPL .106-B4,120-B1
CALHOUN ST ANO 49-C4
CALIFORNIA AVE BLA 79-B1
CALIFORNIA AVE E STP .108-C1,109-A1
CALIFORNIA AVE W FH 107-D2
CALIFORNIA AVE W STP .107-E1,108-A1
CALIFORNIA DR STP 107-E1
CALIFORNIA ST NE CH 92-D2
CALIFORNIA ST NE FRI 92-D2
CALIFORNIA ST NE MPL ..92-D4,106-D1
CALLAHAN PL MH 122-A4
CALLAHAN TRL IGH 136-E4
CALMOR AVE SLT 175-B3,189-B1
CALMUT AVE NE PRL 161-A3
CALUMET AVE WSP 122-C3
CALVIN CT EAG 150-A2
CALVIN CT IGH 136-E4
CAMBER AVE HAT 187-D1
CAMBER AVE SSP 122-E4
CAMBER CT SCT 159-D4
CAMBERWELL DR EAG 150-A1
CAMBERWELL DR N EAG 150-A1
CAMBODIA AVE CAT 192-A4,206-A1
CAMBODIA AVE ET 178-A3
CAMBORNE PL EPR 118-C4
CAMBRIA CT WBY 109-D4
CAMBRIAN AVE RMT 164-A2
CAMBRIDGE ALC WBY ...123-E2,124-A2
CAMBRIDGE AVE BP 78-A1
CAMBRIDGE CIR SE PRL 161-A3
CAMBRIDGE CT BP 78-A2
CAMBRIDGE CT BUR 149-A1
CAMBRIDGE CT MTK 105-A3
CAMBRIDGE CT SHK 160-B1
CAMBRIDGE DR EAG 149-C2
CAMBRIDGE LN EPR 132-E2,133-A2
CAMBRIDGE LN MOU 117-A2
CAMBRIDGE RD SHK 147-B3
CAMBRIDGE RD WBY 123-E2,124-A2
CAMBRIDGE ST HOP 119-C1
CAMBRIDGE ST SLP 119-E1
CAMBRIDGE ST STP 121-D1
CAMBRIDGE WAY SHK 160-B1
CAMBRONNE ST TRT 111-E4
CAMDEN AVE N BC 78-C4,92-C1
CAMDEN AVE N BP 78-C2
CAMDEN AVE N MPL 92-C2
CAMDEN AVE S NG 128-A1
CAMDEN CT BC 92-C1
CAMDEN CT WBL 95-A1
CAMDEN DR BC 78-C4
CAMDON HL EPR 132-E3
CAMELBACK DR EAG 136-B2,149-D2
CAMELBACK DR EDI 119-C3
CAMELOT CIR MTK 119-B4
CAMELOT CIR WBY 123-D3
CAMELOT CIR S BLO 133-E3
CAMELOT DR MTK 118-C2
CAMELOT DR WBY 123-D3
CAMELOT LN NE FRI 79-A3
CAMELOT RD BUR 162-A2
CAMELOT ST STP 108-B1
CAMEO AVE RMT 164-A2
CAMEO CIR HNT 141-A4
CAMEO CIR IGH 136-E4
CAMEO LN CP 65-D3
CAMERO LN RMT 164-A2
CAMERON AVE NE BUT 45-B2
CAMERON AVE NE MOT ...31-B1,45-B1
CAMERON AVE SE RFT 73-B2
CAMERON CIR WBY 123-D2
CAMERON CIR NE BUF 59-B1
CAMERON CT HOP 119-C2
CAMERON DR WBY 123-D2
CAMFIELD CIR RMT 164-A2
CAMP PEARSON RD RW 196-E4
CAMP THREE RD COT 38-C4,52-B1
CAMPANARO LN WBL 81-A3
CAMPBELL AVE IGH 136-E4
CAMPBELL AVE WBL 81-A3
CAMPBELL CIR WBL 81-A3
CAMPBELL DR HOP 119-C1
CAMPBELL ST PRE 153-B4,167-B1
CAMPEAU ST SOM 70-B4
CAMPTON CT EAG 150-B1
CAMPUS DR NB 93-B2
CAMPUS DR PLY 90-E4
CANABURY CT E LC 94-B4
CANABURY DR N LC 94-B4
CANADA AVE CAT 192-A4,206-A1
CANADA AVE ET 178-A3
CANADA AVE RMT 164-A2
CANADA AVE WFT 206-A4,220-A2
CANADA CT ET 178-A3
CANADA CT RMT 150-A4
CANADIANS LNDG EPR 147-C1
CANAL DR RFD 74-A4
CANARY AVE N CT 114-D4
CANARY LN MOU 103-A4,117-A1
CANARY LN MTK 118-E1
CANARY PATH FAR 177-D3
CANARY WAY EAG 135-E4
CANBERRA CT ET 178-A3
CANBY AVE WT 204-B3,218-B1
CANBY CT WT 218-B3
CANBY TRL WT 218-B2
CANDACE AVE IGH 136-E2
CANDICE LN EPR 132-E1
CANDLEWOOD CIR PRL 161-B1
CANDLEWOOD CIR N BP 77-D2
CANDLEWOOD CT N BP 77-E2
CANDLEWOOD DR N BP 77-D2
CANDLEWOOD LN NE PRL 161-B1
CANDLEWOOD PKWY EPR 132-C3
CANDY COVE TRL PRL 161-B3
CANEDAY CT TF 14-B2
CANEDAY ST TF 14-B2
CANFIELD AVE STP 107-D2
CANFIELD RD LL 66-C4
CANFIELD ST STP 107-C2
CANNON AVE AH 93-D2
CANNON AVE SVW 93-E2
CANNON CT CF 208-B4
CANNON DR NFD 219-D3
CANNON DR NE OTS 47-E1
CANNON ST HAS 166-D3
CANNON ST W CF 208-B4
CANNON BOTTOM RD RW 196-D4
CANNON FALLS
BLVD DT 194-C4,208-C1
CANNON INDUSTRIAL
BLVD CF 208-A2
CANNON RIVER AVE CF 208-B4
CANNON RIVER
BLVD RAT 206-E3,207-A3
CANNON RIVER
BLVD SIT 206-D4,220-C1

CANNON RIVER BLVD WFT ...220-B1
CANNON VALLEY DR NFD ...219-D3
CANNONDALE RD RW ...196-C4
CANOPY TRL EPR ...132-C4
CANTATA AVE ET ...178-A3
CANTATA AVE W RMT ...164-A2
CANTER LN CRT ...176-A4
CANTER LN PRL ...161-A2
CANTER GLEN CIR EAG ...150-A1
CANTER GLEN DR EAG ...150-A1
CANTER GLEN LN EAG ...150-A1
CANTERBURY AVE NE BUF ...59-B1
CANTERBURY AVE NE BUT ...45-B2
CANTERBURY CIR CHN ...132-A1
CANTERBURY CIR EAG ...149-E2
CANTERBURY CIR WBY ...123-D3
CANTERBURY CT WBY ...123-D3
CANTERBURY DR BLO ...148-A1
CANTERBURY DR MTK ...118-C2
CANTERBURY DR WBY ...123-D3
CANTERBURY LN EPR ...118-E4,132-E1
CANTERBURY PL WIL ...95-D1
CANTERBURY RD CP ...65-D4,79-D1
CANTERBURY RD MOU ...117-A2
CANTERBURY DOWNS BLVD PRL160-D1
CANTERBURY DOWNS BLVD SHK .146-D3,160-D1
CANTON CT CAT ...192-A1
CANTON CT MH ...136-B1
CANTON CT WT ...204-B3
CANTON ST PRE ...153-B4
CANTON ST STP ...121-E2
CANTURBURY CIR LES ...212-D4
CANTWELL AVE WBT ...81-B2
CANTWELL ST LES ...212-C4
CANVASBACK CT MO ...31-E3
CANVASBACK LN EAG ...149-C2
CANVASBACK ST BL ...17-E3
CANYON CIR CHS ...145-C1
CANYON CRV CHN ...132-A2
CANYON LN NB ...93-B1
CANYON RD CHS ...145-C1
CANYON RDG EPR ...132-D2
CAPAUL WOODS CT NO ...80-A3
CAPE COD PL MTK ...105-B3
CAPELLA ST NE LWT ...9-E3
CAPETOWN PLZ WBY ...123-D2
CAPITAL DR BUF ...59-A2
CAPITAL DR EPR ...133-C2
CAPITAL DR IGH ...137-A3
CAPITAL HTS STP ...108-B3
CAPITOL BLVD STP ...108-B3
CAPITOL ST NE FRI ...92-D1
CAPITOL VW RVL ...94-A4
CAPITOL VIEW CIR RVL ...94-B4
CAPP RD STP ...107-C3
CAPRICORN CT EAG ...149-E2
CAPRIOLE DR MED ...90-A3
CAPTAINS PL LL ...66-B3
CARAMEL TRL EPR ...132-E1,133-A1
CARDIFF LN EPR ...133-A3
CARDIFF LN MOU ...117-B2
CARDIGAN LN MOU ...117-A2
CARDIGAN RD SVW ...94-A2
CARDINAL AVE CHN ...117-E4
CARDINAL AVE HNT ...141-A3
CARDINAL CIR CHS ...145-C2
CARDINAL CIR HUD ...111-D2
CARDINAL CIR MG ...77-A4
CARDINAL CIR RMT ...163-E3
CARDINAL CIR N MG ...77-A4
CARDINAL CT CHS ...145-C2
CARDINAL CT HMP ...193-B2
CARDINAL CT RMT ...163-E3
CARDINAL CV CHS ...145-C2
CARDINAL DR CV ...66-E2
CARDINAL DR LTT ...130-C2
CARDINAL DR SWD ...117-E4
CARDINAL DR NE BLA ...65-B1
CARDINAL LN CHS ...145-C2
CARDINAL LN CW ...1-B3
CARDINAL LN HSN ...61-D2
CARDINAL LN LTT ...130-C2
CARDINAL LN MOU ...116-E1,117-A1
CARDINAL LN NO ...80-C3
CARDINAL PL STP ...123-B1
CARDINAL RD MTK ...118-E1
CARDINAL ST CHS ...145-C2
CARDINAL ST W RMT ...163-E3
CARDINAL WAY BUF ...45-B4
CARDINAL WAY EAG ...135-E4
CARDINAL COVE DR MTA ...116-D2
CARDINAL CREEK
RD EPR ...119-A4,133-A1
CARDINAL RIDGE TRL PRL ...161-C3
CAREN CT MH ...121-E3
CAREN RD MH ...121-E3
CAREW CT IGH ...136-E4
CAREW DR MPL ...106-D3
CAREY LN MG ...77-A4
CAREY LN N MG ...77-A4
CAREY HEIGHTS DR MPW ...94-D3
CARGO RD FS ...134-E1
CARI PARK LN HAS ...166-D3
CARIBOU CIR LL ...65-E2
CARIBOU DR MTK ...118-E2
CARIBOU LN EAG ...150-A2
CARIBOU SPUR MTK ...118-E2
CARILLON PLZ E WBY ...123-D2
CARILLON PLZ W WBY ...123-D2
CARISSA LN SW SM ...46-E4
CARL AVE ANO ...49-D3
CARL ST LAU ...107-B1
CARL ST LL ...65-E1,66-A1
CARLA LN E LC ...94-C4
CARLEDA AVE IGH ...136-E2
CARLEDA WAY IGH ...136-E2
CARLETON DR HAS ...166-B2
CARLETON LN HAS ...166-B2
CARLETON RD MTK ...119-A2
CARLETON ST STP ...107-B3
CARLING AVE NE BUT ...59-B3
CARLING AVE NE MOT ...45-B1
CARLING AVE SE FKT ...101-B1
CARLING AVE SE RFT ...59-B4,73-B3
CARLING DR STP ...107-D3
CARLISE CRV SHK ...147-A3
CARLISLE CRV SHK ...147-A3
CARLISLE CT ET ...178-A3
CARLOW RD MOU ...117-A2
CARLSBAD CT BUR ...149-A3
CARLSBAD PLZ WBY ...123-D2
CARLSON DR EPR ...118-E4
CARLSON DR NW CR ...64-A1
CARLSON LN TRT ...126-A4,140-A1
CARLSON PKWY MTK ...104-D3
CARLSON PKWY PLY ...104-E2
CARLSON RD SVW ...79-E2
CARLSON ST SVW ...79-E1
CARLSON LAKE LN EAG ...149-D2
CARLSON LAKE LN N EAG ...149-D2
CARLTON DR AH ...93-E2
CARLTON DR SVW ...93-E2
CARLTON PL HAS ...166-B2
CARLTON ST MPW ...109-B3
CARLYLE CT WBL ...95-A1
CARLYLE RD WBY ...123-C2
CARLYSLE PL MTK ...118-C2
CARMAN AVE ORO ...117-B2
CARMAN RD ORO ...117-C2
CARMAN ST ORO ...117-C1
CARMEL AVE WSP ...122-D3
CARMEL AVE W WSP ...122-C3
CARMEL CT SVW ...79-E3
CARMEL LN DAT ...159-A1
CARMEN AVE IGH ...136-E2
CARMEN CT IGH ...136-E2
CARMEN DR N ROG ...47-D4
CARMEN DR S ROG ...47-D4
CARMICHAEL RD HUD ...111-E2
CARMICHAEL RD HUT ...111-E3
CARMICHAEL RD S HUT ...111-E3
CARMODY DR EPR ...132-E3
CARNATION AVE N BP ...78-A1
CARNELIAN LN EAG ...149-B1
CARNELIAN LN EPR ...132-C2
CARNELIAN ST N SWR ...82-E4
CAROL CIR NE FRI ...78-E4
CAROL DR CHS ...145-D1
CAROL DR VH ...94-C2
CAROL DR NE FRI ...78-E4
CAROL LN SVW ...80-A1
CAROL LN WSP ...122-C4
CAROL LN N HSN ...48-A2
CAROL ST EAG ...150-A3
CAROL ST OSC ...28-A4
CAROLE CT BEC ...2-E3
CAROLE DR BEC ...2-D3
CAROLE DR LL ...66-B1
CAROLE LN DPH ...118-B1
CAROLINA ST SCF ...14-C3
CAROLINE AVE ORO ...117-B2
CAROLINE CT LC ...94-C3
CAROLINE LN SSP ...122-D3
CAROLYN LN WBL ...80-E3
CAROLYN LN WBT ...80-E2
CARRIAGE CIR SHK ...146-B4
CARRIAGE CT EPR ...133-B3
CARRIAGE CT PRL ...161-A2
CARRIAGE CT WBY ...123-E1
CARRIAGE DR MED ...90-A3
CARRIAGE LN BUR ...162-D2
CARRIAGE LN HUT ...111-E3,112-A3
CARRIAGE LN NE PRL ...161-A2
CARRIAGE RD WBY ...123-E1
CARRIAGE HILL ALC SAV ...147-D4
CARRIAGE HILL BAY SAV ...147-C4
CARRIAGE HILL CIR SAV ...147-C4
CARRIAGE HILL CT SAV ...147-C4
CARRIAGE HILL DR SAV ...147-C4
CARRIAGE HILL PL SAV ...161-C1
CARRIAGE HILL RD SAV .147-C4,161-C1
CARRIAGE HILL RD NE PRL ...161-B2
CARRIAGE HILLS DR EAG ...149-D3
CARRIAGE HILLS LN EAG ...149-D3
CARRIAGE HILLS PKWY PRL ...161-B2
CARRIAGE PLACE DR BUR ...162-D2
CARRICK RD MOU ...117-A2
CARRIDGE HILL LN ORO ...103-D4
CARRIE LN FRI ...78-E4
CARRIE LN SWD ...118-A3
CARRIE ST WSP ...122-C2
CARROLL AVE STP ...107-C4,108-A4
CARROUSEL WAY RMT ..163-E2,164-A2
CARSON CIR NW ER ...19-E4
CARSON CT ER ...19-E4
CARSON CT IGH ...136-E4
CARSON RD DPH ...118-A2
CARSON ST NW ER ...19-E4,33-E1
CARSONWOOD AVE DPH ...118-B2
CART RD VAT ...223-C3
CARTER AVE FH ...107-C2
CARTER AVE STP ...107-B2
CARTER AVE N FH ...107-C2
CARTER CIR HUT ...111-E1
CARTER CT IGH ...136-E4
CARTER LN MTK ...119-B3
CARTER PATH IGH ...136-E4
CARTER ST NE WAT ...101-B3
CARTER ST NW WAT ...101-A3
CARTIER AVE BUR ...149-A2
CARTISIAN AVE BP ...77-D4
CARTWAY CRV EPR ...133-A4
CARTWAY CT N CHM ...63-C1
CARTWAY LN CHN ...117-B4
CARTWAY LN MTK ...105-A3
CARTWAY RD CHM ...63-C1
CARVELL CIR BLO ...133-C4
CARVER AVE MPW ...123-B3
CARVER AVE STP ...123-B3
CARVER CT BUR ...148-E2,149-A2
CARVER SQ WAC ...129-D3
CARVER BEACH RD CHN ...132-A1
CARVER BLUFFS PKWY CAR ...159-B1
CARVER CREEK CIR CAR ...159-B1
CARVER CREEK PL CAR ...159-A1
CARVER HIGHLAND DR SFT ...159-A3
CARVER PARK CIR WBY ...123-C3
CARVER PARK DR WBY ...123-C3
CARVER PARK RD LTT ...130-D1
CARVERS GRN CHS ...131-D3
CASAMITA RD MTA ...116-E4
CASAMITA RD VIC ...116-E4
CASCADE AVE ET ...178-A3
CASCADE AVE E RF ...140-E2
CASCADE AVE W RF ...140-D2
CASCADE CIR CHN ...118-B4
CASCADE CT CHN ...118-B4
CASCADE CT RF ...140-D2
CASCADE DR EPR ...132-C2
CASCADE DR SHK ...146-C2
CASCADE LN EDI ...119-E2
CASCADE LN MH ...122-A3
CASCADE LN RFD ...74-B4
CASCADE PASS CHN ...118-B4
CASCADE PATH RMT ...163-E3
CASCADE PLZ N WBY ...123-D2
CASCADE PLZ S WBY ...123-D2
CASCADE ST N OSC ...27-E4,28-A3
CASCADE ST S OSC ...27-E4,42-A1
CASCO AVE EDI ...120-A2
CASCO AVE ORO ...117-B2
CASCO CIR ORO ...117-C2
CASCO CV ORO ...117-C2
CASCO POINT RD ORO ...117-B2
CASE AVE MPW ...109-B3
CASE AVE STP ...108-E3,109-A3
CASEY CT CRT ...161-C4
CASEY CT IGH ...136-E4
CASEY PKWY CT EPR ...161-D4
CASEY TRL EAG ...149-B2
CASHELL GLN EAG ...149-D1
CASPER AVE IGH ...136-E2
CASPER CIR NYA ...142-C4
CASPER ST NYA ...142-C4
CASPER WAY IGH ...136-E3
CASPER WAY CT IGH ...136-E3
CASPERSON DR HUT ...97-D4
CASS AVE WT ...204-B3
CASS CT WT ...204-A3
CASS ST S SHK ...146-A2
CASS TRL WT ...204-B3
CASSIDY LN IGH ...136-E4,150-E1
CASSIOPEIA CT LL ...66-C4
CASTLE AVE MPW ...95-A4
CASTLE AVE NSP ...95-A4
CASTLE CT GV ...105-C2
CASTLE DR EPR ...132-E1
CASTLE LN EPR ...132-E1
CASTLE RDG CHN ...118-B4
CASTLE RIDGE CT CHN ...118-B4
CASTLE RIDGE DR HSN ...48-B4
CASTLE VIEW CIR HSN ...48-A3
CASTLE VIEW CT MTK ...119-A2
CASTLEFORD CT WBY ...124-A3
CASTLEFORD DR WBY ...124-A3
CASTLEMOOR DR EPR ...133-A2
CASTLETON CT EAG ...150-A1
CASTLETON LN EAG ...150-A1
CATALINA CT LES ...212-C4
CATALINA DR WBY ...124-A2
CATALINA RIDGE RD LES ...212-C4
CATBIRD LN NO ...80-C2
CATES AVE BWT ...219-A4
CATES ST SE PRL ...161-A3
CATES LAKE DR SAV ...161-C2
CATES RANCH DR MED ...89-D1
CATHCART DR SWD ...117-B4
CATHCART ST LES ...212-D3
CATHERINE AVE IGH ...136-E2
CATHERINE DR NEW ...123-C4
CATHERINE LN SVW ...80-A1
CATHLIN ST STP ...107-C2
CATLIN ST BUF ...58-E1
CATTAIL CT EPR ...132-C2
CATTAIL WAY HUD ...111-E4
CATTLE LANE DR WTT ...115-B2
CAULFIELD PLZ WBY ...123-D2
CAVAN RD MOU ...117-A2
CAVANAUGH CT IGH ...136-E4,150-E1
CAVANAUGH DR SHK ...146-C2
CAVANAUGH ST BEC ...2-E4,3-A4
CAVENDISH PL EPR ...118-C4
CAVELL AVE SAV ...147-C3
CAVELL AVE N BP ...77-C4,91-C1
CAVELL AVE N GV ...91-C4,105-C1
CAVELL AVE N NH ...91-C1
CAVELL AVE S BLO ...133-C4,147-C1
CAVELL AVE S SLP ...105-C4
CAVELL CIR BLO ...133-C4,147-C1
CAVELL CT N BP ...77-C4,91-C1
CAVELL LN SLP ...105-C4,119-C1
CAVELL RD BLO ...147-C1
CAYENNE PLZ E WBY ...123-D2
CAYENNE PLZ W WBY ...123-D2
CAYUGA ST STP ...108-B3
CC ST WBL ...80-D4
CECEILA PL STP ...121-D1
CECIL ST SE MPL ...107-B3
CECILIA CIR EDI ...133-D2
CEDAR AVE APV ...149-B4,163-B2
CEDAR AVE EAG ...149-B3
CEDAR AVE EUT ...191-B2
CEDAR AVE LVL ...163-B4,177-B3
CEDAR AVE MED ...89-A3
CEDAR AVE NFD ...219-C3
CEDAR AVE WBL ...94-E1,95-B1
CEDAR AVE N MYR ...114-E4
CEDAR AVE S BLO ...134-E3,135-A4
CEDAR AVE S FS ...120-E4
CEDAR AVE S MPL ...106-E3,120-E3
CEDAR AVE S RCH ...120-E4,134-E1
CEDAR BND MTK ...105-B4
CEDAR CIR BLO ...134-E3
CEDAR CIR PRL ...161-B4
CEDAR CT MTK ...105-B4
CEDAR CT TRT ...126-A2
CEDAR CT VIC ...131-A3
CEDAR CV WBL ...94-E1
CEDAR XING MTK ...105-B4
CEDAR DR JOR ...173-B3
CEDAR DR LFL ...109-C4
CEDAR DR NB ...79-B3
CEDAR DR E SJT ...97-D3
CEDAR DR N NOH ...111-D1
CEDAR DR NW OG ...22-C3,36-C1
CEDAR DR W SJT ...97-C3
CEDAR GRN MTK ...105-B4
CEDAR LN BUR ...148-B4
CEDAR LN CLT ...188-B4
CEDAR LN EXC ...117-E3
CEDAR LN HUT ...111-E3
CEDAR LN JOR ...173-B3
CEDAR LN MOU ...116-E1
CEDAR LN MTK ...118-D3
CEDAR LN NEW ...123-A4,137-A1
CEDAR LN PRE ...167-B1
CEDAR LN SLP ...106-A4
CEDAR LN WBL ...94-E1
CEDAR PASS MTK ...105-B4
CEDAR PL BUF ...59-B1
CEDAR RD EB ...37-D1
CEDAR RD HL ...37-D2
CEDAR RD S CHN ...131-C1
CEDAR ST BWV ...95-C1
CEDAR ST CTT ...153-B4
CEDAR ST GRF ...74-C3
CEDAR ST HEN ...198-C3
CEDAR ST MO ...31-D2
CEDAR ST PRE ...153-B4
CEDAR ST RFD ...74-B3
CEDAR ST SA ...93-A4
CEDAR ST SLP ...106-A4
CEDAR ST SOM ...84-B1
CEDAR ST STP ...108-B4
CEDAR ST TKB ...117-D2
CEDAR ST E BUF ...59-A2
CEDAR ST E LL ...66-E3,67-A3
CEDAR ST E RF ...140-E2
CEDAR ST N BEL ...185-E1
CEDAR ST N CF ...208-B4
CEDAR ST N CHS ...145-C3
CEDAR ST N LP ...113-B4
CEDAR ST N MSC ...55-B4
CEDAR ST N WAC ...129-D3
CEDAR ST S BEL ...185-E2
CEDAR ST S CHS ...145-C3
CEDAR ST S LP ...127-B1
CEDAR ST S MSC ...55-B4
CEDAR ST S WAC ...129-D3
CEDAR ST W BUF ...59-A2
CEDAR ST W CV ...66-E3
CEDAR ST W LL ...66-E3
CEDAR ST W RF ...140-D1
CEDAR TER JT ...145-E3
CEDAR CREEK DR NW OG ...35-E1
CEDAR CREST DR BKR ...17-C4
CEDAR CREST RD E MTK ...105-C4
CEDAR CREST RD W MTK ...105-C4
CEDAR CROWN DR MTK ...105-C4
CEDAR FOREST RD EPR ...132-C4
CEDAR HEIGHTS TRL S DET ...153-B2
CEDAR HILLS BLVD MTK ...105-B4
CEDAR HILLS CT SLT ...175-B2
CEDAR HILLS DR CFT ...222-B1
CEDAR HILLS DR MTK ...105-B4
CEDAR KNOLL CT MTK ...105-A4
CEDAR LAKE AVE MPL ...106-A4
CEDAR LAKE AVE SLP ...106-A4
CEDAR LAKE DR E CLT ...188-C3
CEDAR LAKE DR W HAT ...188-B3
CEDAR LAKE PKWY MPL ...106-A3
CEDAR LAKE PL MPL ...106-A3
CEDAR LAKE RD MTK ...105-B4,119-A1
CEDAR LAKE RD SLP ...105-C4
CEDAR LAKE RD N MPL ...106-B2
CEDAR LAKE RD S MPL ...106-B3
CEDAR LAKE RD S SLP ..105-E3,106-A3
CEDAR POINT DR WDL ...104-B4
CEDAR POINT RD CLT ...188-B3
CEDAR POINT RD MTA ...116-E2
CEDAR POINTE DR N MTK ...105-B4
CEDAR POINTE DR S HOP ...105-B4
CEDAR POINTE DR S MTK ...105-B4
CEDAR RIDGE CIR EAG ...149-B2
CEDAR RIDGE CT LND ...12-D3
CEDAR RIDGE DR LND ...12-D3
CEDAR RIDGE LN LND ...12-D3
CEDAR RIDGE RD EPR ...132-D3
CEDAR RIDGE RD WDL ...104-B4
CEDAR SHORE DR MPL ...106-A4
CEDAR SHORE DR SLP ...106-A4
CEDAR VALLEY LN SCT ...173-C3
CEDAR VALLEY RD SCT ...173-C3
CEDAR VIEW CIR MPL ...106-B3
CEDAR VIEW CT SVW ...93-E1
CEDAR VIEW DR EAG ...149-B1
CEDAR VIEW DR MPL ...106-B3
CEDAR VIEW RD TRT ...125-E1
CEDARBRIDGE AVE BUR ...149-A1
CEDARCREST DR EPR ...132-C4
CEDARHURST DPH ...118-B1
CEDARLEAF CT MHT ...95-C2
CEDARVALE BLVD EAG ..135-B4,149-B1
CEDARVALE DR EAG ...149-B1
CEDARVIEW DR EAG ...149-B1
CEDARWOOD CIR PRL ...161-C1
CEDARWOOD CIR WBY ...123-C1
CEDARWOOD CT DAY ...49-A3
CEDARWOOD CT PRL ...161-C1
CEDARWOOD CT WBT ...81-B2
CEDARWOOD CT WBY ...123-C1
CEDARWOOD DR WBY ...123-C1
CEDARWOOD PL WBY ...123-C1
CEDARWOOD RD SLP ...106-A3
CEDARWOOD RD NE EB ...36-E2
CEDARWOOD RDG MTK ...105-B4
CEDARWOOD ST PRL ...161-C1
CEDARWOOD TRL PRL ...161-C1
CELIA DR MH ...121-E3
CEMETERY RD NEW ...123-B4
CEMETERY RD NSP ...95-B3
CEMETERY RD RF ...140-E3
CEMETERY RD RIT ...140-E3
CEMETERY ST MPL ...106-E1
CENEX DR IGH ...136-D1
CENTENNIAL AVE SB ...116-B3
CENTENNIAL CIR FAR ...191-E1
CENTENNIAL CT FAR ...191-E1
CENTENNIAL DR BUF ...59-A2
CENTENNIAL DR FAR ...191-E1,192-A1
CENTENNIAL DR NSP ...95-B4
CENTENNIAL DR RVL ...93-D3,94-A3
CENTENNIAL LN RIT ...140-E3
CENTENNIAL PL MPL ...106-D3
CENTENNIAL ST PRL ...161-B3
CENTENNIAL ST NE BLA ...65-C4,79-C1
CENTER AVE CNC ...12-E3
CENTER AVE N MON ...86-C1
CENTER AVE S MON ...86-C1
CENTER CIR MO ...31-C2
CENTER CIR E PLY ...104-E1
CENTER CIR NE FRI ...78-E2
CENTER CT EAG ...135-D2
CENTER CT N CGT ...12-D2
CENTER DR BUR ...148-B4
CENTER DR EPR ...132-D1
CENTER DR NE SLK ...79-A1
CENTER LN NB ...93-B2
CENTER LN N CGT ...12-D2
CENTER RD CP ...65-D3
CENTER RD LC ...94-B3
CENTER RD WDL ...104-C4
CENTER RD NW LIT ...6-B1
CENTER RD SW PRL ...160-E4
CENTER ST CLK ...1-D1
CENTER ST CV ...66-D3
CENTER ST EB ...23-D4
CENTER ST EXC ...117-E3
CENTER ST SVW ...79-D1
CENTER ST TF ...14-C3
CENTER ST N SWR ...82-E4,96-E1
CENTER ST S SWR ...96-E1
CENTER ST W RVL ...108-B1
CENTER WAY EPR ...133-B3
CENTER GREEN CIR CHS ...131-C4
CENTERVIEW LN MOU ..116-E1,117-A1
CENTERVILLE CIR VH ...80-D4
CENTERVILLE RD CV ...66-D3
CENTERVILLE RD LL ...66-D4,80-D1
CENTERVILLE RD NO ...80-D2
CENTERVILLE RD VH ...80-D4,94-C2
CENTERVILLE RD WBT ...80-D3
CENTERVILLE RD N LC ...94-C3
CENTERWOOD RD LEX ...65-C3
CENTRAL AVE BAY ...97-B4
CENTRAL AVE BEC ...2-E4,3-A4
CENTRAL AVE BNT ...113-C4
CENTRAL AVE BUF ...58-E2
CENTRAL AVE DRS ...28-D2
CENTRAL AVE EB ...8-E3,22-E3
CENTRAL AVE FRI ...78-E3

CENTRAL AVE GRW 117-E3
CENTRAL AVE HL 36-E3,50-E2
CENTRAL AVE LOL 103-D2
CENTRAL AVE LP 113-B4
CENTRAL AVE OSS 77-C1
CENTRAL AVE SM 47-A3
CENTRAL AVE SSP 122-D3
CENTRAL AVE WBL 81-B3
CENTRAL AVE E SM 46-E3,47-A3
CENTRAL AVE N DRS 28-D2
CENTRAL AVE N NP 201-D2
CENTRAL AVE N NYA 142-C3
CENTRAL AVE N WAY 104-C3
CENTRAL AVE NE BLA 50-E4,64-E1
CENTRAL AVE NE CH 92-E2
CENTRAL AVE NE FRI 78-E4,92-E1
CENTRAL AVE NE HIL 92-E1
CENTRAL AVE NE HL 36-E4,50-E1
CENTRAL AVE NE MPL 92-E3,106-E1
CENTRAL AVE NE SLK 78-E2,79-A1
CENTRAL AVE S DRS 28-D2
CENTRAL AVE S NP 201-D3
CENTRAL AVE S NYA 142-C3
CENTRAL AVE S WAY 104-C3
CENTRAL AVE SE MPL 106-E2
CENTRAL AVE W SM 46-E3
CENTRAL AVE W STP 107-E4,108-A4
CENTRAL LN NFD 219-E4
CENTRAL ST CP 65-D4
CENTRAL ST HBG 156-A2
CENTRAL ST LES 212-D4
CENTRAL ST E LON 217-B2
CENTRAL ST W LON 217-A2
CENTRAL PARK AVE WBL 81-B3
CENTRAL PARK PL STP 108-B4
CENTRE DR HUD 111-E3
CENTRE ST SVW 94-A2
CENTRE POINTE BLVD MH 121-E4
CENTRE POINTE CRV MEN 121-D4
CENTRE POINTE CRV MH 121-D4
CENTRE POINTE DR MH 121-E4
CENTRE POINTE DR RVL 93-C3
CENTURY AVE NEW 123-C4
CENTURY AVE WBY 123-C2
CENTURY AVE N MPW 109-B4
CENTURY AVE N OKD 109-C3
CENTURY AVE N WBL 95-B2
CENTURY AVE S MPW 109-C4,123-C2
CENTURY AVE S NEW 137-C1
CENTURY BLVD BP 77-E3
CENTURY BLVD CHN 131-D2
CENTURY CIR WBY 123-C2
CENTURY CT CRT 175-D4,189-D1
CENTURY PT EAG 135-C3
CENTURY ST BEL 186-A2
CESSNA DR NB 93-B2
CESSNA RD OST 28-B4,42-B1
CHAD CIR JOR 173-B3
CHADWELL CIR MTK 104-E4
CHADWICK CT SAV 161-E1
CHADWICK DR SAV 161-E1
CHADWICK LN EPR 119-A4
CHAKYA ST RW 182-D4,196-D1
CHALET CT BUR 162-C3
CHALET CT RW 210-E1
CHALET DR NE CH 93-A1
CHALET RD BLO 133-E3
CHALLENGER DR EAG 135-E3
CHALUPSKY DR NP 201-E2
CHAMBER ST MPW 94-D4,108-D1
CHAMBER ST STP 108-D2
CHAMBERLAIN AVE NE MOT 31-B2
CHAMBERLAIN AVE SE RFT 59-B4
CHAMBERLAIN CIR WBY 123-C3
CHAMBERLAIN DRAW WBY 123-C3
CHAMBERLAIN RD WBY 123-C3
CHAMELEON ST NW RAM 34-D3,48-D1
CHAMPION DR NB 93-B2
CHAMPLIN DR N CHM 63-C2
CHAN VIEW ST CHN 132-B2
CHANCELLOR MNR BUR 162-C1
CHANDLER AVE ET 178-A3
CHANDLER AVE RVL 108-A1
CHANDLER CT BUR 149-A1
CHANDLER CT EPR 118-C4
CHANDLER CT SVW 80-A3
CHANDLER DR SA 93-B2
CHANDLER LN IGH 136-E3
CHANDLER RD SVW 80-A3,94-A2
CHANDLER ST W ARL 183-A2
CHANHASSEN RD CHN 132-B2
CHANHASSEN RD EPR 118-B4,132-B1
CHANHASSEN HILLS DR N CHN 132-A3
CHANHASSEN HILLS DR S CHN 132-A3
CHANNEL DR GRW 118-A3
CHANNEL DR LL 66-E4
CHANNEL LN EB 37-D1
CHANNEL RD MOU 117-A1
CHANNEL RD SPR 117-B1
CHANNEL RD NE FRI 78-E3
CHANTREY CT MTK 118-D2
CHANTREY PL MTK 118-D2
CHANTREY RD EDI 119-D3
CHAPARRAL AVE JT 145-E3,146-A2
CHAPARRAL CIR APV 149-A4
CHAPARRAL CIR COR 61-C4
CHAPARRAL CT APV 149-A3
CHAPARRAL CT CHN 132-A1
CHAPARRAL DR APV 149-A4
CHAPARRAL LN CHN 132-A1
CHAPARRAL LN COR 61-C4
CHAPEL DR EDI 133-D1
CHAPEL LN EAG 136-A3
CHAPEL LN EDI 133-D1
CHAPMAN CT IGH 150-E1
CHAPMAN DR KKT 126-E3
CHAPMAN DR TRT 126-D3
CHAPMAN PT EPR 147-B1
CHARDEL CT WSP 122-B4
CHARING BND CHN 117-E4
CHARING XING EPR 132-E1
CHARING LN WIL 95-D1
CHARIS CT EPR 132-B1
CHARITY LN MON 86-C1
CHARLES AVE EPR 132-E1
CHARLES AVE STP 107-E3,108-A3
CHARLES LN DEL 87-E2
CHARLES LN MOU 116-E2
CHARLES ST LOL 103-D2
CHARLES ST LTT 130-A4
CHARLES ST N NSP 95-B4,109-B1
CHARLES ST NE FRI 78-D4
CHARLES WAY IGH 136-E3
CHARLES LAKE RD NO 80-A2
CHARLESTON CIR SWD 117-D4
CHARLESTON DR WBY 124-B3
CHARLEY LAKE CT NO 80-A2
CHARLOTTE DR ANO 49-D3
CHARLOTTE ST RVL 93-D4
CHARLOTTE ST STP 107-D3
CHARLOTTE ST E RF 140-E2
CHARLOTTE ST W RF 140-D2
CHARLSON DR RW 196-E4
CHARLSTON AVE RMT 164-A2
CHARLSTON CT RMT 150-A4
CHARLSTON WAY RMT 150-A4
CHARLTON RD SL 122-B4,136-B1
CHARLTON RDG WSP 122-B4
CHARLTON ST STP 122-B2
CHARLTON ST WSP 122-B3
CHARMY DNS MTK 104-C4
CHARTWELL HL SWD 118-B3
CHASE AVE ANO 49-C3
CHASE DR MTK 104-E4,118-E1
CHASES ISLAND RD FRI 78-D4
CHASEWOOD CT RMT 163-E3,164-A3
CHASEWOOD DR EPR 119-A4
CHASEWOOD PKWY MTK 119-A4
CHASKA RD CHN 117-D4
CHASKA RD SWD 117-D4
CHASTEK WAY MTK 118-E3
CHATEAU CIR BUR 148-D4
CHATEAU CT BUR 162-D2
CHATEAU CT SOM 70-B4
CHATEAU LN BUR 162-D2
CHATEAU LN MOU 117-A1
CHATEAU PL MPL 120-E3
CHATEAU WAY MTA 102-B4,116-B1
CHATEAU RIDGE AVE SHK 160-C1
CHATEAULIN LN BUR 148-E4
CHATELAIN TER GV 106-A2
CHATFIELD CIR BEL 185-E2
CHATFIELD CT CHS 131-B4
CHATFIELD DR BKT 184-E3,185-A2
CHATFIELD DR TYT 198-E3
CHATFIELD LN BEL 185-E2
CHATFIELD RD TYT 198-E3
CHATHAM AVE AH 93-C1
CHATHAM CIR AH 93-D1
CHATHAM CT AH 93-C2
CHATHAM CT N BUR 149-A1
CHATHAM CT S BUR 149-A1
CHATHAM RD EAG 136-B4
CHATHAM RD MHT 95-D2
CHATHAM RD WIL 95-D1
CHATHAM ST WIL 95-D1
CHATHAM ST NE CH 93-A2
CHATHAM TER NB 93-B2
CHATHAM WAY EPR 118-C4
CHATHAM FIELD RD MTK 105-A3
CHATHAMFIELD RD MTK 105-A3
CHATONKA BEACH TRL NE PRL 161-B2
CHATSWORTH CIR SVW 79-E4
CHATSWORTH CT E SVW 79-E4
CHATSWORTH CT W SVW 79-E4
CHATSWORTH PL SVW 79-E4
CHATSWORTH ST N RVL 93-E3,107-E1
CHATSWORTH ST N STP 107-E3,121-E1
CHATSWORTH ST N SVW 79-E4,93-E1
CHATSWORTH ST S STP 121-E2
CHATTANOOGA DR TRT 126-B2
CHATTERTON CT EAG 149-D1
CHATTERTON RD EAG 149-D1
CHAUCER LN WAT 101-B4
CHEERY LN NE CH 92-E1
CHEERYWOOD AVE N BP 78-A1
CHELMSFORD RD SA 93-B3
CHELMSFORD ST STP 107-C2
CHELSEA CT BUR 149-A1
CHELSEA CT NB 79-B4,93-B1
CHELSEA RD MO 31-D2
CHELSEA ST MHT 95-D1
CHELSEA ST STP 107-D2
CHELTON AVE STP 107-C3
CHENEY TRL IGH 136-E4,150-E1
CHENNAULT WAY EPR 118-B4
CHERI CT WBL 94-E1,95-A1
CHERI LN MH 135-E1,136-A1
CHERI LN NEW 123-C4
CHERI LN NE FRI 92-E1
CHERITA DR CHS 145-C2
CHEROKEE AVE STP 122-B2
CHEROKEE AVE WSP 122-B2
CHEROKEE DR N BP 77-C4
CHEROKEE DR N HSN 48-A2
CHEROKEE LN N BP 77-C4
CHEROKEE PL GV 91-E4
CHEROKEE RD MED 89-E4,90-A4
CHEROKEE TRL EDI 119-C4
CHEROKEE TRL LL 66-C4
CHEROKEE TRL W EPR 119-B4
CHEROKEE HEIGHTS BLVD STP 122-B2
CHERRY AVE ORO 103-B4
CHERRY CIR N NOH 111-C1
CHERRY CT BUR 162-C2
CHERRY CT PRL 161-A2
CHERRY DR EPR 118-C4
CHERRY DR FAT 42-B2
CHERRY LN ANN 74-B2
CHERRY LN BUR 162-C2
CHERRY LN LL 66-A4
CHERRY LN MTK 118-D3
CHERRY LN N COR 76-B1
CHERRY PATH RMT 163-E3,164-A3
CHERRY PL ORO 103-B4
CHERRY ST MSC 55-C4
CHERRY ST NFD 219-D3
CHERRY ST PRE 153-B4,167-B1
CHERRY ST RFD 74-B3
CHERRY ST STP 108-D4
CHERRY ST E SWR 97-A1
CHERRY ST N BEL 185-E1
CHERRY ST S WAC 129-D3
CHERRY ST W SWR 96-E1,97-A1
CHERRY HILL ALC MED 90-B2
CHERRY HILL BAY MED 90-B2
CHERRY HILL CT MED 90-B2
CHERRY HILL LN HUT 112-B3
CHERRY HILL RD MH 122-A3
CHERRY HILL RD MTK 118-E3
CHERRY HILL TRL MED 90-B2
CHERRY TREE CT MTK 118-B3
CHERRYWOOD AVE NP 201-E2
CHERRYWOOD AVE N BP 78-A1
CHERRYWOOD AVE NW SM 46-E3
CHERRYWOOD CT EAG 135-C3
CHERRYWOOD LN HUT 112-B3
CHERRYWOOD LN MTA 116-D2
CHERRYWOOD LN WAC 129-D3
CHERRYWOOD RD MOU 116-D2
CHERRYWOOD RD MTK 104-E4
CHERRYWOOD TRL N LE 95-E4
CHERTSEY DR WBY 124-A2
CHERYL ST NE FRI 78-C2
CHES MAR CIR EAG 149-D2
CHES MAR DR CHN 131-D1
CHES MAR DR EAG 149-D2
CHES MAR LN EAG 149-D2
CHES MAR WAY VAT 209-E3,210-A3
CHES MAR FARM RD CHN 131-D1
CHESAPEKE LN EPR 133-B1
CHESHAM LN WBY 123-D4
CHESHIRE CIR MV 79-B3
CHESHIRE CT EAG 150-A1
CHESHIRE LN MV 79-B3
CHESHIRE LN N DAY 62-E3
CHESHIRE LN N MTK 104-E2
CHESHIRE LN N PLY 90-E4,104-E2
CHESHIRE PKWY MTK 104-E3
CHESHOLM LN EPR 133-A4,147-A1
CHESHUNT DR WBY 123-D4
CHESIRE LN PLY 90-E3
CHESLEY TRL CAT 192-E2
CHESNEY WAY NE FRI 78-D2
CHESSHIRE CT N MG 76-E3
CHESSHIRE LN N MG 76-E3,90-E1
CHESTER AVE WT 204-A4,218-A2
CHESTER CT SHK 146-C4
CHESTER CT WT 204-A3
CHESTER ST MPL 120-D4
CHESTER ST SHK 146-C4
CHESTER ST STP 122-C1
CHESTERFIELD WAY ET 178-A3
CHESTNUT AVE MPL 106-C2
CHESTNUT AVE N BP 64-A4
CHESTNUT AVE SE SM 46-E4
CHESTNUT AVE W GV 106-B2
CHESTNUT AVE W MPL 106-B2
CHESTNUT BLVD JT 145-D4
CHESTNUT BLVD LVT 145-E4
CHESTNUT CIR BL 18-A4
CHESTNUT CIR BUR 162-D2
CHESTNUT CIR N CHM 63-B3
CHESTNUT CT SWD 118-B4
CHESTNUT DR BUR 162-D2
CHESTNUT DR EPR 132-E2,133-A2
CHESTNUT DR HUD 111-D2
CHESTNUT LN MTK 118-B2
CHESTNUT LN NE HL 36-E3
CHESTNUT LN NE PRL 161-A2
CHESTNUT RD MED 89-D3
CHESTNUT RD MOU 116-E1
CHESTNUT ST HAS 166-D1
CHESTNUT ST MO 31-C1
CHESTNUT ST MSC 55-B3
CHESTNUT ST PRE 167-B1
CHESTNUT ST SSP 136-E1,137-A1
CHESTNUT ST STP 108-B4,122-B1
CHESTNUT ST TF 14-B2
CHESTNUT ST E SWR 97-A1
CHESTNUT ST N BEL 185-E1
CHESTNUT ST N CHS 131-C3,145-C2
CHESTNUT ST S BEL 185-E2
CHESTNUT ST S CHS 145-C3
CHESTNUT ST W SWR 97-A1
CHESTNUT TER SWD 118-B4
CHESTNUT WAY RMT 164-A3
CHEVELLE AVE ET 178-A3
CHEVELLE CT RMT 164-A2
CHEVY CHASE DR ORO 104-B2
CHEYENNE AVE CHN 132-B2
CHEYENNE CIR EDI 133-C1
CHEYENNE CIR MTK 104-E4
CHEYENNE CT MO 31-D3
CHEYENNE LN MH 136-A1
CHEYENNE SPUR CHN 132-B2
CHEYENNE TRL CHN 132-B1
CHEYENNE TRL EDI 119-C4,133-C1
CHEYENNE TRL MED 90-B4
CHIANTI AVE RMT 164-A2
CHICAGO AVE BUR 162-D2
CHICAGO AVE CRY 120-D3
CHICAGO AVE MPL 106-D3,120-D2
CHICAGO AVE RCH 120-D4,134-D1
CHICAGO AVE SPP 137-C3
CHICAGO AVE WBL 81-B3
CHICAGO AVE N WAY 104-C3
CHICAGO AVE S BLO 134-D3
CHICAGO AVE S WAY 104-C3
CHICAGO CIR BLO 134-D4,148-D1
CHICAGO DR BUR 162-D2
CHICKADEE LN DPH 118-B2
CHICKADEE LN HUT 112-C2
CHICKADEE LN NO 80-B2
CHICORY WAY CHN 131-E2
CHIEFTAN ST OSC 27-E4,28-A4
CHILCOMBE AVE STP 107-B2
CHILDS RD STP 122-D1
CHILI AVE ET 178-A3
CHILI AVE RMT 163-E2,164-A1
CHILTERN HILLS RD MTK 118-C2
CHIMO ST E DPH 118-B2
CHIMO ST W DPH 118-B2
CHINCHILLA AVE RMT 149-E4,150-A4
CHINCHILLA CT RMT 149-E4,150-A4
CHINNOCK LN TRT 126-B3
CHIPMUNK CT EAG 149-B2
CHIPMUNK LN NO 80-C3
CHIPPENDALE AVE FAR 177-E4,178-A4
CHIPPENDALE AVE RMT 163-E3
CHIPPENDALE AVE W CAT 192-A2,206-A1
CHIPPENDALE AVE W ET 163-E4,177-E2
CHIPPENDALE AVE W FAR 177-E4,192-A1
CHIPPENDALE AVE W RMT 163-E2
CHIPPENDALE CT FAR 177-E4,178-A4
CHIPPENHAM LN WIL 95-D1
CHIPPEWA AVE MH 122-B2
CHIPPEWA AVE MPW 95-B3
CHIPPEWA AVE NSP 95-B3
CHIPPEWA AVE STP 122-B2
CHIPPEWA CIR CHN 132-A1
CHIPPEWA CIR MED 89-B1
CHIPPEWA CIR MPW 95-B3
CHIPPEWA CT N MPW 95-B3
CHIPPEWA LN BUR 148-E3
CHIPPEWA LN ORO 103-B2
CHIPPEWA PATH HUT 112-D1
CHIPPEWA RD MED 89-B1
CHIPPEWA RD MTK 105-B4,119-B1
CHIPPEWA ST BL 17-E3
CHIPPEWA TRL CHN 132-A2
CHIPPEWA TRL LL 66-A4
CHISAGO BLVD N CGT 26-D2
CHISAGO BLVD N FRT 26-E2
CHISAGO ST N TF 14-C1
CHISHOLM AVE NSP 95-A3
CHISHOLM PKWY MPW 95-A3
CHISHOLM ST NE BLA 51-A4,65-A1
CHISHOLM ST NE HL 37-A3,51-A1
CHISHOLM TRL COR 61-D4,75-D1
CHOCTAW CIR CHN 132-B1
CHOKECHERRY AVE W RMT 163-E2
CHOKECHERRY RD LL 66-C3
CHORLEY AVE W RMT 163-E2
CHOWEN AVE BUR 148-A3
CHOWEN AVE EKO 204-B1
CHOWEN AVE N BC 78-A4,92-A1
CHOWEN AVE N BP 78-A3
CHOWEN AVE N ROB 92-A4
CHOWEN AVE S BLO 134-A4,148-A1
CHOWEN AVE S BUR 148-A3
CHOWEN AVE S EDI 120-A4
CHOWEN AVE S MPL 106-A4,120-A2
CHOWEN BND BUR 148-A3
CHOWEN CIR BLO 148-A1
CHOWEN CRV EDI 120-A4
CHOWEN PL MPL 106-A4
CHRISTEN AVE NE BUT 45-B3
CHRISTENSEN AVE WSP 122-D4
CHRISTENSEN CT BUR 149-A2
CHRISTENSEN LN PRL 160-E3
CHRISTENSON CT FRI 78-D3
CHRISTENSON LN FRI 78-D3
CHRISTENSON WAY FRI 78-D3
CHRISTIAN CT CHS 131-C4
CHRISTIAN DR CHS 131-C4
CHRISTIAN PKWY CHS 131-C4
CHRISTIE PL STP 108-E1
CHRISTINE DR ORO 103-C2
CHRISTINE LN WSP 122-B3
CHRISTINE PL WBL 95-A2
CHRISTMAS LN SWD 118-A4
CHRISTMAS LAKE PT SWD 118-A3
CHRISTMAS LAKE RD SWD 118-A3
CHRISTOPHER LN SVW 93-E2
CHRISTOPHER RD SWD 117-D3
CHRISTY CIR RVL 93-D4
CHRISTY LN MTK 118-E2
CHROME AVE RMT 163-E2
CHRYSLER AVE ET 177-E3
CHRYSLER AVE W RMT 163-E2
CHURCH AVE BPT 186-E1
CHURCH AVE ROG 61-E1,62-A1
CHURCH AVE N NP 201-E2
CHURCH CIR CLK 1-D1
CHURCH LN MTK 119-A2
CHURCH PL EDI 133-E1
CHURCH RD CHN 117-C4
CHURCH RD MOU 116-E1
CHURCH RD RW 182-C3
CHURCH RD SWD 117-B4
CHURCH RD WEL 182-C3
CHURCH ST ANO 49-C4
CHURCH ST CLK 1-D1
CHURCH ST COL 143-E3
CHURCH ST DRS 28-D2
CHURCH ST LES 212-C3
CHURCH ST LND 12-D3
CHURCH ST MP 103-A1
CHURCH ST NM 189-E4
CHURCH ST RF 140-D2
CHURCH ST SJT 97-B1
CHURCH ST E BEL 185-E1,186-A1
CHURCH ST NE HAN 60-E3
CHURCH ST SE MPL 107-A2
CHURCH ST W BEL 185-E1
CHURCH HILL RD SMT 70-B4
CHURCH HILL RD SOM 70-B4,84-B1
CHURCH LAKE BLVD VIC 130-E2
CHURCHILL CIR MTK 118-C2
CHURCHILL CT WBY 123-D3
CHURCHILL DR WBY 123-D3
CHURCHILL LN MOU 117-A2
CHURCHILL PL SVW 79-E4
CHURCHILL ST RVL 93-E3
CHURCHILL ST STP 107-E2
CHURCHILL ST SVW 79-E4,93-E2
CHURCHILL ST E SWR 97-A2
CHURCHILL ST W SWR 96-E2,97-A2
CICERONE CT RMT 163-E3
CICERONE PATH RMT 163-E3
CIDER CIR SHK 146-A3
CIMARRON LE 110-C3
CIMARRON AVE RMT 163-E2
CIMARRON AVE W RMT 163-E2
CIMARRON CIR APV 149-A4
CIMARRON CIR CHN 132-B1
CIMARRON CIR COR 75-E3
CIMARRON CIR MTK 105-C3
CIMARRON CT APV 149-A4
CIMARRON LN EPR 132-C2
CIMARRON RD APV 149-A4
CIMARRON TRL MTK 105-C3
CIMARRON WAY RMT 163-E2
CIMMARON AVE RMT 163-E2
CINNABAR CT EAG 149-B1
CINNABAR DR EAG 149-B1
CINNAMON WAY RMT 163-E3
CINNAMON RIDGE CIR EAG 149-A2
CINNAMON RIDGE TRL EAG 149-A2
CINNAMON RIDGE TRAIL CT EAG 149-A2
CINNAMON TEAL CT LL 66-A2
CIRCLE AVE W RMT 163-E2
CIRCLE CT CP 65-D4
CIRCLE CT OSC 28-A3
CIRCLE DNS GV 105-E3,106-A3
CIRCLE DR ART 183-A2
CIRCLE DR BUF 58-D2
CIRCLE DR BUR 148-C4
CIRCLE DR CHM 63-B1
CIRCLE DR CP 65-E3
CIRCLE DR DPH 118-B2
CIRCLE DR EDI 133-E1
CIRCLE DR NEW 123-B4
CIRCLE DR SCT 173-B1
CIRCLE DR WBL 81-A4,95-B1
CIRCLE DR WEL 196-A4
CIRCLE DR E MGY 215-D4
CIRCLE DR E WAY 104-C3
CIRCLE DR N LAT 202-B2
CIRCLE DR N MGY 215-D4
CIRCLE DR NW WAT 101-B3
CIRCLE DR S LAT 202-B2
CIRCLE DR W MGY 215-D4
CIRCLE LN ARL 183-A3
CIRCLE LN BUR 148-C4
CIRCLE LN DEL 87-D3
CIRCLE LN HSN 47-E3
CIRCLE LN SM 47-A4
CIRCLE LN N COR 61-D4
CIRCLE RD TKB 117-D2
CIRCLE A DR S WAY 104-C3
CIRCLE E EDI 119-D2
CIRCLE HIGH DR BUR 162-C2
CIRCLE TERRACE BLVD CH 92-E2
CIRCLE W EDI 119-D2
CITATION DR SHK 146-E2
CITY CENTRE DR WBY 123-E2

CITY HEIGHTS DR N MPW......108-B1
CITY VIEW DR EAG..........135-C3
CITY VIEW DR MTK..........105-A3
CITY WEST PKWY EPR........119-B4
CIVIC CENTER DR EAG..135-D4,149-D1
CIVIC CENTER DR RVL.........93-E3
CIVIC CENTER PKWY BUR......148-D4
CIVIC HEIGHTS CIR CP.........65-D4
CIVIC HEIGHTS DR CP.........65-D3
CLAIBORNE LN IGH..........136-E3
CLAIRE CT EPR..............118-B4
CLAIRE CT FAR..............177-D3
CLAIRE CT ROG...............61-E1
CLARE LN MOU..............117-A2
CLARE LN MTK..............104-D3
CLAREDON DR EDI...........133-D1
CLAREMONT DR MH..........136-A2
CLAREMORE CT EDI..........134-A1
CLAREMORE DR EDI..........134-A1
CLARENCE AVE MTA..........102-E3
CLARENCE AVE SE MPL.......107-B3
CLARENCE CT STP............108-E2
CLARENCE ST MPW......94-E3,108-E1
CLARENCE ST STP............108-E2
CLARENCE ST WBL.......80-E4,81-A4
CLARENDON DR MTK.........104-D3
CLARET AVE RMT............163-E2
CLARET CIR RMT.............163-E2
CLARK AVE WBL...............81-A3
CLARK CIR EPR..............133-C3
CLARK CIR VH................80-C4
CLARK CT EAG...............149-A2
CLARK RD DRS................28-D1
CLARK RD IGH...............150-E3
CLARK ST BUR...............149-A2
CLARK ST EAG...............149-A2
CLARK ST RF...............140-E1
CLARK ST STP...............108-C2
CLARK ST N MPW.......94-C4,108-C1
CLARK VALLEY TRL CFT.208-D4,222-E2
CLARMAR LN RVL..............93-D3
CLAUDE AVE IGH.............136-E3
CLAUDE WAY IGH............136-E2
CLAY AVE IGH..............136-E3
CLAY CT IGH................136-E3
CLAY ST ANO.................49-C4
CLAY ST GRF.................74-D3
CLAY ST HAS...............166-E1
CLAY ST N SHK.............146-A2
CLAY ST S SHK.............146-A2
CLAY CLIFFE DR TKB........117-C2
CLAYCROSS WAY EPR.........118-C4
CLAYLAND PL STP...........107-C3
CLAYLAND ST STP...........107-C3
CLAYMORE AVE IGH..........136-E4
CLAYTON AVE COA...........164-E2
CLAYTON AVE ET.......164-E4,178-E2
CLAYTON AVE IGH...........136-E3
CLAYTON AVE RMT.....150-E4,164-E1
CLAYTON DR MP.......102-E1,103-A1
CLEADIS AVE IGH............136-E3
CLEAR AVE STP........108-E2,109-A2
CLEAR RDG CV................66-D2
CLEAR SPRING CT MTK.......118-C3
CLEAR SPRING DR MTK.......118-C3
CLEAR SPRING LN EPR.......132-C2
CLEAR SPRING LN MTK.......118-C3
CLEAR SPRING RD MTK.......118-C3
CLEAR SPRING TER MTK......118-C3
CLEAR VIEW CT MTK..........118-B4
CLEAR VIEW DR MTK.........118-B4
CLEAR VIEW LN MTK.........118-B4
CLEAR VIEW TER MTK........118-B4
CLEARBROOK LN VH...........80-C4
CLEARVIEW AVE MV............79-B3
CLEARVIEW DR LVT...........160-A1
CLEARVIEW LN MV.............79-C2
CLEARVIEW ST NE FRI.........92-D1
CLEARWATER CIR SAV........162-A2
CLEARWATER CT SAV.........162-A2
CLEARWATER DR CV............66-D2
CLEARWATER DR MTK.........119-A4
CLEARWATER RD CV............66-D2
CLEARWATER RD WAC.........129-D4
CLEARWATER TRL FOT..217-E4,218-A4
CLEARWATER CREEK CIR LL.....66-E3
CLEARWATER CREEK CT LL.....66-E3
CLEARWATER CREEK DR LL 66-E3,67-A4
CLEARY PL CRT..............161-D4
CLEARY RD NW BT.......21-B2,35-B1
CLEARY LAKE CT CRT........175-D1
CLEARY LAKE RD CRT...175-E1,176-A1
CLEMENT ST MH.............122-A3
CLEMENTA AVE NW CMT.........58-C1
CLEMENTA AVE NW MLT...30-B4,44-C2
CLEMENTA AVE NW SVT...16-B4,30-B2
CLEMENTA AVE SW MVT...72-C3,86-C1
CLEMENTA AVE SW WDT.........86-C2
CLEMSON CIR EAG...........149-C2
CLEMSON CT EAG............149-D2
CLEMSON DR EAG............149-C2
CLEOME LN EAG.............149-D2
CLEOPATRA DR LVL...........177-B3
CLERMONT ST STP...........108-D4
CLEVE AVE IGH..............136-E3
CLEVELAND AVE GI...........169-D2
CLEVELAND AVE N AH..........93-C1
CLEVELAND AVE N FH.........107-C1
CLEVELAND AVE N NB..........93-C2
CLEVELAND AVE N RVL...93-C3,107-C1
CLEVELAND AVE N STP.107-C4,121-C1
CLEVELAND AVE NW ER.........48-B1
CLEVELAND AVE S STP........121-C2
CLEVELAND ST ANO............49-D3
CLEVELAND ST NE CH..........93-A2
CLEVELAND ST NE MPL..93-A4,107-A1
CLEVELAND ST NE SLK.........79-A2
CLEVELAND ST NW ER....20-B1,34-B2
CLIFF DR EAG...............149-B2
CLIFF RD EAG.........149-C2,150-A2
CLIFF RD E BUR.......148-E2,149-A2
CLIFF RD W BUR.............148-C3
CLIFF ST STP...............122-B1
CLIFF LAKE CT EAG.........149-B2
CLIFF LAKE RD EAG.........149-B2
CLIFF RIDGE CT EAG........149-E2
CLIFFHILL LN EAG...........149-B2
CLIFFORD LN EAG...........149-D3
CLIFFORD ST STP...........107-B3
CLIFFVIEW DR EAG...........149-B2
CLIFFWOOD CIR VIC..........117-A4
CLIFTON AVE BUR............149-A1
CLIFTON AVE MPL............106-C3
CLIFTON DR MV...............79-C2
CLIFTON PL MPL.............106-C3
CLIFTON RD BT...............35-A1
CLIFTON RD NW BT............35-A1
CLIFTON ST STP.............121-E1
CLINTON AVE MPL.....106-D4,120-D3
CLINTON AVE RCH.....120-D4,134-D1
CLINTON AVE STP............122-C1
CLINTON AVE S BLO....134-D3,148-D1
CLINTON PL BUR.............148-D4
CLINTON ST E ARL...........183-A2
CLINTON TRL EAG...........149-E1
CLINTS TRL HUT.............112-C1
CLIPPER WAY WBY...........124-A1
CLIPPERS RD EAG...........149-D1
CLIPPERSHIP ALC WBY........124-A1
CLIPPERSHIP BAY WBY........124-A1
CLIPPERSHIP CT WBY.........124-A1
CLIPPERSHIP DR WBY.........124-A1
CLOMAN AVE IGH............136-E3
CLOMAN PATH IGH.....150-E1,151-A1
CLOMAN WAY IGH............136-E2
CLOUD DR NE BLA.......51-B4,65-A1
CLOUGH ST N FH.............107-C2
CLOUTIER CT FAT.............41-D3
CLOUTIER DR SOM.............84-B1
CLOVER AVE VH........80-C4,94-C1
CLOVER CIR EPR............133-C4
CLOVER CIR MOU............116-D1
CLOVER CT CHN.............131-D2
CLOVER CT JOR.............173-C3
CLOVER CT NFD.............220-A4
CLOVER CT SHK.............146-B3
CLOVER DR BLO.............134-C2
CLOVER LN DEL...............87-D3
CLOVER LN EAG.............149-C2
CLOVER LN GV...............105-E2
CLOVER LN RMT.............163-E1
CLOVER LN SWD.............117-D3
CLOVER PATH NMT.....203-E1,204-A1
CLOVER PL NE FRI............78-E3
CLOVER RDG EDI............119-E4
CLOVER LEAF CIR HUT........111-E1
CLOVER LEAF PKWY BLA........64-E4
CLOVERDALE AVE CRY..........91-D1
CLOVERLEAF DR GV...........105-E2
CLUB LN SWD...............117-D3
CLUB RD SLP...............105-C4
CLUB VALLEY DR SWD........117-D4
CLUBHOUSE DR BKR.............3-E4
CLUBHOUSE LN BEC.............2-E3
CLUBHOUSE RD EPR..........133-B4
CLUBVIEW DR EAG...........135-E3
CLUBVIEW DR MO..............31-C1
CLYDE PL WIL................95-D1
CLYDE RD MOU..............117-A2
CLYDESDALE CRV FLT..........39-C4
CLYDESDALE CRV N FLT........39-C4
CLYDESDALE TRL MED..........90-A2
COACH DR EAG..............149-D3
COACH RD STP..............107-D3
COACHMAN CT PRL...........161-A2
COACHMAN LN NE PRL........161-A2
COACHMAN RD EAG...........135-C3
COACHMANS LN EPR..........132-D3
COACHWOOD CIR WBY.........123-D2
COACHWOOD RD WBY.........123-D2
COATES BLVD COA.....164-E3,165-A3
COATES BLVD VET............179-B3
COATES BLVD E COA....164-E3,165-A3
COATES BLVD E VET....165-A4,179-A1
COATS BLVD COA............164-E3
COBALT AVE RMT............163-E2
COBALT CIR NW RAM...........49-B2
COBALT DR RMT.............163-E2
COBALT LN RMT.............163-E2
COBALT ST NW RAM.....35-B2,49-C1
COBALT ST NW STT.............7-B1
COBB RD SVW.................93-E2
COBBLE HILL ALC WBY........123-C2
COBBLE HILL CT WBY.........123-C2
COBBLE HILL DR WBY.........123-C2
COBBLER AVE RMT...........163-E1
COBBLER CT CP...............79-D1
COBBLESTONE CT MO...........31-D3
COBBLESTONE CT RMT........149-E3
COBBLESTONE CT WBY........123-D3
COBBLESTONE LN BUR........162-D1
COBBLESTONE LN RMT........149-E4
COBBLESTONE RD WBY........123-D3
COBBLESTONE WAY EPR.......132-C2
COBCEN LN MOU.............117-A2
COBURN AVE NW CMT...........58-B3
COBURN AVE NW MLT...........44-B1
COBURN CT IGH..............136-E4
COCHRAN LN EPR............132-E2
COCHRANE AVE EAG..........149-C1
COCHRANE CIR WBY..........123-C2
COCHRANE CT WBY...........123-C2
COCHRANE DR WBY...........123-C2
COCHRONE CIR WBY..........123-C2
COCKSPUR CT EPR............133-A3
CODE AVE EDI...............119-E3
CODY LAKE TRL ERT..........216-D4
CODY LAKE TRL WHT..........216-C4
COFFEE TRL RMT.............149-E3
COFFEY LN MPL..............121-B1
COFFEY ST N FH.............107-C2
COFFMAN CIR IGH............136-E4
COFFMAN LN MPL.............121-B2
COFFMAN PATH IGH...........136-E4
COFFMAN ST FH..............107-C2
COGGINS LN MTK......104-E4,118-E1
COHANSEY BLVD RVL....94-A4,108-A1
COHANSEY CIR SVW............94-A4
COHANSEY ST RVL.............94-A4
COHANSEY ST STP............108-A2
COHANSEY ST SVW............94-A2
COLBERT AVE NW CMT..........58-B1
COLBERT AVE NW MLT....44-C4,58-B1
COLBERT AVE SW MVT..........58-B4
COLBOLT ST NW BT............21-B2
COLBORNE ST STP............122-A1
COLBURN DR W JT............145-E3
COLBURN ST N CHM............63-C1
COLBY CT EPR...............132-C2
COLBY ST STP...............121-C3
COLBY ST TF..................14-C3
COLBY LAKE CT WBY..........124-A2
COLBY LAKE DR WBY..........124-A2
COLD STREAM LN EPR.........133-A3
COLE AVE SE MPL............107-A2
COLE ST HUD................111-D2
COLESHIRE LN MH............122-B3
COLETTE PL STP.............121-C3
COLFAX AVE ANO..............49-D3
COLFAX AVE BUR.............148-C4
COLFAX AVE N BC........78-C4,92-C1
COLFAX AVE N BP.............78-C3
COLFAX AVE N MPL.....92-C4,106-C2
COLFAX AVE S BLO.....134-C3,148-C1
COLFAX AVE S MPL.....106-C4,120-C2
COLFAX AVE S RCH.....120-C4,134-C1
COLFAX CT ANO...............49-D3
COLFAX LN S MPL............120-C4
COLGATE AVE MPL............120-A2
COLGATE AVE MTK............118-C1
COLIN DR ORO...............103-D2
COLLEEN AVE AH..............79-D4
COLLEEN AVE SVW.......79-E4,80-B4
COLLEEN CIR AH..............79-D4
COLLEEN CIR EPR............132-C1
COLLEEN CT AH...............79-D4
COLLEEN DR VH...............94-C1
COLLEGE AVE EXC............117-E3
COLLEGE AVE STP............108-B4
COLLEGE RD LTT.............116-A4
COLLEGE ST PRE.............153-B4
COLLEGE ST S NFD...........219-E4
COLLEGE TRL IGH............136-E4
COLLEGE HEIGHTS CIR BLO....134-A4
COLLEGE PARK DR N BP........77-D2
COLLEGEVIEW CIR BLO........133-E3
COLLEGEVIEW RD BLO..133-E3,134-A4
COLLEN ST EB.................37-E1
COLLER WAY WBY............123-E1
COLLINGWOOD LN WBY........123-C1
COLLINS CT RF..............140-D1
COLLINS DR NW RAM...........48-C2
COLLINSWOOD CIR RF.........140-D1
COLLISCHAN RD RW...........196-E3
COLNE ST STP...............107-E3
COLONIAL CIR MDL...........105-B1
COLONIAL CIR NYA...........142-C3
COLONIAL CT EDI............119-D4
COLONIAL DR GV......105-E2,106-A3
COLONIAL DR HUD............111-D3
COLONIAL DR RVL.............93-D4
COLONIAL RD GV.............105-D2
COLONIAL WAY EDI...........119-D4
COLONY CT EPR..............147-B1
COLONY CT JOR..............173-C2
COLONY WAY EDI.............120-A4
COLORADO AVE BLA............79-B1
COLORADO AVE ET............177-E3
COLORADO AVE RMT...........163-E2
COLORADO AVE SAV...........161-E1
COLORADO AVE WFT...........219-E2
COLORADO AVE N BP.....77-E3,91-E1
COLORADO AVE N CHM..........63-E3
COLORADO AVE N CRY..........91-E3
COLORADO AVE N GV..........105-E1
COLORADO AVE S GV..........105-E3
COLORADO AVE S SLP..105-E4,119-E2
COLORADO CIR BLO....133-E4,147-E1
COLORADO CIR S GV...........105-E3
COLORADO RD BLO.....133-E4,147-E1
COLORADO RD S BLO..........133-E4
COLORADO ST LON............217-A2
COLORADO ST PRL............161-A3
COLORADO ST E STP..........122-C1
COLORADO ST SE LON.........217-B2
COLORADO ST SW LON.........217-B2
COLORADO ST W STP..........122-C1
COLTON AVE WBY.............123-E4
COLTON CT WBY..............123-E4
COLUMBARY CIR RMT..........163-E2
COLUMBARY CT RMT...........163-E3
COLUMBIA AVE MPL.............92-D3
COLUMBIA BLVD MPL...........92-E3
COLUMBIA CT RMT............163-E3
COLUMBIA CT WBY............123-D2
COLUMBIA CT N CHS...........131-D3
COLUMBIA CT W CHS...........131-D3
COLUMBIA DR EAG............135-E3
COLUMBIA WAY RMT...........163-E2
COLUMBINE CT VH.......80-B4,94-B1
COLUMBINE LN NO.............80-B3
COLUMBINE LN SHK...........146-B3
COLUMBINE RD EPR...........133-A3
COLUMBUS AVE MPL....106-D4,120-D2
COLUMBUS AVE RCH....120-D4,134-D1
COLUMBUS AVE STP...........108-B4
COLUMBUS AVE N HAT..........201-E1
COLUMBUS AVE N NP...........201-E2
COLUMBUS AVE S BLO..........134-D3
COLUMBUS AVE S NP...........201-E3
COLUMBUS CIR BLO............148-D1
COLUMBUS RD BLO.............148-D1
COLUMBUS ST DAY..............48-B2
COLVILLE ST W CF............208-B4
COLVIN AVE STP..............121-C3
COMANCHE RD EAG............135-B4
COMANCHE TRL MED............90-B2
COMERCE DR MH..............135-D1
COMET CIR MTK...............118-C1
COMET LN MTK................118-C1
COMET LN NE FRI..............78-D4
COMFORT DR E WYT.............25-D4
COMFORT DR W WYT.....25-D4,39-D1
COMMANCHE CT EDI...........133-C1
COMMERCE AVE PRL...........161-D1
COMMERCE BLVD MOU..102-E4,116-E1
COMMERCE BLVD MTA..........102-E4
COMMERCE BLVD ROG....48-A4,62-A1
COMMERCE BLVD WBL...........94-E2
COMMERCE CIR GRF.............74-C4
COMMERCE CIR E FRI...........78-D3
COMMERCE CIR S FRI...........78-D3
COMMERCE CIR W FRI...........78-D3
COMMERCE CT HAS.............166-D2
COMMERCE CT RF..............126-E4
COMMERCE CT VH...............80-C4
COMMERCE CT WBL..............94-E2
COMMERCE DR BEC...............2-E4
COMMERCE DR CHN............131-E2
COMMERCE DR HAS............166-D3
COMMERCE DR HUT............112-B3
COMMERCE DR MH.............135-D1
COMMERCE DR WBY....110-A4,124-A1
COMMERCE LN NE FRI...........78-D2
COMMERCE ST COR..............76-A3
COMMERCE ST LES.............212-D3
COMMERCE ST RVL..............93-D4
COMMERCE ST E COR............76-A3
COMMERCE ST W COR............76-A3
COMMERCE WAY EPR...........132-E2
COMMERCIAL AVE VIC..........131-A2
COMMERCIAL BLVD NW AND......50-B3
COMMERCIAL DR BUF............58-E1
COMMERCIAL ST BUF............58-E1
COMMERCIAL ST CP.............65-D4
COMMERCIAL ST HUD...........111-C2
COMMERCIAL ST STP...........108-C4
COMMERCIAL ST SWR............97-A1
COMMERS DR EAG..............136-A2
COMMODORE DR BC..............92-A1
COMMON ST SE FKT.......-E2,101-A2
COMMON ST SW SKT..............99-A2
COMMONS DR WBY......109-E4,123-E1
COMMONWEALTH AVE FH.........107-C2
COMMONWEALTH AVE STP.......107-B2
COMMONWEALTH AVE WBY.......123-D3
COMMONWEALTH CIR WBY.......123-D3
COMMONWEALTH CT WBY........123-D3
COMMONWEALTH DR BUR........148-E4
COMMONWEALTH DR EPR........133-A2
COMMONWEALTH DRAW WBY.123-D3
COMMONWEALTH RD WBY.......123-D3
COMMUNITY DR BUR...........162-D1
COMMUNITY CENTER DR MG.......77-A2
COMMUNITY CENTER
SERVICE RD RMT..............164-A1
COMMUNITY COLLEGE
SE DR IGH...................136-D4
COMMUNITY COLLEGE
SE RD IGH...................136-D4
COMO AVE STP........107-C2,108-A3
COMO AVE SE MPL............107-A2
COMO BLVD E STP............107-E2
COMO BLVD W STP............107-E2
COMO PL STP................107-E3
COMO LAKE DR E STP.........107-E2
COMPASS DR BLO.............147-E2
COMPTON CT IGH.............136-E4
COMPTON DR IGH.............136-E4
COMPTON LN IGH.............136-E4
COMPUTER AVE BLO...........133-E2
COMPUTER AVE EDI...........133-E2
COMSTOCK AVE IGH...........136-E3
COMSTOCK AVE E COA........164-E3
COMSTOCK CT IGH............136-E3
COMSTOCK CT N MG............76-C2
COMSTOCK LN N MG.....76-C2,90-C1
COMSTOCK LN N PLY.....90-C4,104-C1
COMSTOCK RD MTK............118-C1
COMSTOCK WAY IGH...........136-E4
CONCERTO CRV NE FRI..........78-D2
CONCORD AVE EDI............119-E4
CONCORD BLVD IGH....136-E4,137-A3
CONCORD CT IGH.............136-E4
CONCORD CT NW ER.............33-C2
CONCORD DR CHS.............145-C2
CONCORD DR EPR.............147-B1
CONCORD DR NE HL.............36-E2
CONCORD EXCH N SSP.........122-E4
CONCORD EXCH S SSP.........122-E4
CONCORD PL SSP.............122-E3
CONCORD RD LEX...............65-D4
CONCORD ST STP.............122-D2
CONCORD ST N SSP...........122-E3
CONCORD ST NW ER.......19-C2,33-C2
CONCORD ST S SSP.....122-E4,136-E1
CONCORD TER EDI.......119-E3,120-A3
CONCORD WAY MH.............136-A2
CONCORD HILL LN MTK........118-B4
CONCORDE PL BUR............148-C4
CONCORDIA AVE STP...107-D4,108-A4
CONCORDIA ST ORO....103-B4,117-B1
CONDIT ST N LC...............94-B3
CONDON CT MH...............136-A2
CONDONS ST PRL.............161-B3
CONEFLOWER CIR CHM...........63-C3
CONEFLOWER CRV N CHN.......131-D2
CONEFLOWER CRV S CHN.......131-D2
CONEFLOWER CT EAG..........149-E2
CONEFLOWER LN EPR..........132-C2
CONESTOGA CT CHN...........132-A1
CONESTOGA TRL CHN..........132-A1
CONEY LN WAC...............129-E4
CONGO ST NE LWT..............10-B4
CONGRESS ST SSP.............122-D3
CONGRESS ST E ML.............43-D2
CONGRESS ST E STP...........122-C1
CONGRESS ST W ML.............43-D2
CONGRESS ST W STP...........122-C1
CONIARIS WAY MPL............120-B1
CONIFER TRL MTK.............118-C3
CONLEY AVE RMT..............164-E1
CONNECTICUT AVE BLA...........79-B1
CONNECTICUT ST SCF............14-C3
CONNELLY AVE AH...............93-D2
CONNELLY CIR BUR............148-E3
CONNELLY CT BUR.............162-C3
CONNELLY DR BUR.............148-E3
CONNELLY LN BUR.............162-C3
CONNELLY PKWY SAV...........161-D1
CONNELLY PL SAV.............161-C1
CONNELY CIR SAV.............161-D1
CONNELY CT SAV..............161-D1
CONNEMARA TRL APV...........163-D1
CONNEMARA TRL RMT..163-E1,164-A1
CONNIE DR NW OG...............21-E3
CONNIE LN LL..................65-E2
CONNOR AVE MPW................94-D4
CONNOR CT MPW.................94-D4
CONRAD AVE COL..............143-E4
CONRAD AVE HMT..............193-A2
CONRAD AVE IGH.......150-E1,151-A1
CONROY CT IGH.......136-E3,137-A3
CONROY ST NE PRL............161-C1
CONROY TRL HUT..............111-D1
CONROY TRL IGH.......136-E3,137-A3
CONROY WAY IGH..............136-E3
CONSERVATORY MTK............119-B3
CONSERVATORY CT STP.........108-A2
CONSTANCE BLVD NE HL..36-E4,37-B4
CONSTANCE BLVD NW AND.......36-D4
CONSTANCE DR E GV...........105-E1
CONSTANCE DR W GV...........105-E1
CONSTELLATION DR WBT..........80-D3
CONSTITUTION AVE STP........108-B4
CONTINENTAL DR EDI..........119-C3
CONTINENTAL DR NB.............93-B2
CONTY ROAD 6 FRI...............78-D3
CONVER AVE SSP..............122-D2
CONVER ST WSP...............122-C2
CONWAY AVE MPW..............109-B4
CONWAY ST STP.......108-D4,109-A4
COOK AVE WBL...................81-A3
COOK AVE E STP..............108-D3
COOK AVE W STP..............108-B3
COOK DR SPT....................70-E2
COOL STREAM CIR EAG.........149-A1
COOLIDGE AVE EDI............119-E2
COOLIDGE AVE S SLP..........119-E2
COOLIDGE ST ANO...............49-C3
COOLIDGE ST SA................93-A3
COOLIDGE ST NE MPL...93-A4,107-A1
COON CREEK BLVD NW CR.........50-A4
COON LAKE DR N EB.............23-E4
COON RAPIDS BLVD
NW CR...............63-E2,64-B3
COON RAPIDS BLVD
SER RD CR......................64-B3
COON RAPIDS BOULEVAR
EXT NW CR......................64-C3
COON RAPIDS BOULEVAR
RD CR...........................64-A2

COOPER AVE EDI 119-D2
COOPER AVE IGH 136-E4,137-A3
COOPER AVE RAN 207-A3
COOPER AVE NW BET 8-D3
COOPER CIR EDI 119-D2
COOPER CT IGH 136-E3,137-A3
COOPER LN APV 163-A2
COOPER PATH IGH 136-E4
COOPER ST N FH 107-D2
COPE AVE MPW 94-E4,95-A4
COPE AVE W RVL 93-E4,94-A4
COPE CT MPW 94-D4
COPELAND CT IGH 137-A4
COPELAND RD IND 88-A4,102-A2
COPELAND WAY IGH 136-E4,137-A4
COPPER CT RMT 163-E1
COPPER CT SLW 173-A2
COPPER LN EAG 149-B2
COPPER PT EAG 149-B2
COPPER CLIFF TRL WBY 123-C3
COPPER CREEK LN BUF 45-B4
COPPER CREEK TRL BUF 45-B4
COPPER OAKS ALC WBY 123-D3
COPPER OAKS CIR WBY 123-D3
COPPER OAKS CT WBY 123-D3
COPPER OAKS DRAW WBY 123-D3
COPPER OAKS PL WBY 123-D3
COPPER OAKS TRL WBY 123-D3
COPPER VIEW DR ORO 103-D2
COPPERFIELD CIR MTK 104-E4
COPPERFIELD CT IGH 137-A4
COPPERFIELD DR MH 136-B1
COPPERFIELD PL MTK 104-E4
COPPERFIELD WAY IGH 137-A4
COPPERSMITH CT IGH 136-E4
COPPERWOOD LN MTK 118-C1
COQUINA CT NW RAM 35-A4
COQUINA ST NW RAM 35-A4,49-A1
CORAL LN EAG 149-B2
CORAL SEA CT BLA 65-B4
CORAL SEA ST NE BLA 65-B4,79-B1
CORAL SEA ST NE HL 37-B4,51-B2
CORCORAN CIR IGH 137-A4
CORCORAN LN COR 75-E3
CORCORAN PATH IGH 136-E4,137-A4
CORCORAN TRL E COR 75-E3
CORCORAN TRL W COR 75-E3
CORD CIR NB 93-B2
CORD CT NE BLA 65-D2
CORD ST NE BLA 65-D3,79-D1
CORD ST NE HL 51-D1
CORDELL CT RAN 207-A3
CORENS DR MTK 105-A3
COREY PATH IGH 137-A3
CORLISS WAY IGH 136-E3,137-A3
CORMACK CIR APV 163-E1
CORMORANT WAY RMT 163-E2
CORNELIA CIR EDI 120-A4
CORNELIA DR EDI 120-A4,134-A1
CORNELIA TRL WBY 123-C3
CORNELIAN BLVD FRT 28-A1
CORNELL AVE WFT 219-E2
CORNELL BAY WBY 124-A2
CORNELL CIR WBY 124-A2
CORNELL CT N RMT 163-E3
CORNELL CT S RMT 163-E3
CORNELL DR MV 79-C2
CORNELL RD WBY 124-A2
CORNELL ST NE COT 38-D4
CORNELL TRL W RMT 163-E3
CORNWALLIS CT EAG 150-A2
CORONADO CT BUR 148-E2
CORONET DR MTK 118-E2
CORPORATE WAY EPR 132-D2
CORPORATE CENTER CRV EAG 135-D2
CORPORATE CENTER DR BUR 162-B1
CORPORATE CENTER DR EAG 135-D2
CORRAL ALC WBY 123-E1
CORRAL CIR CRT 176-A4,190-A1
CORRAL LN EPR 132-D3
CORRAL LN WBY 123-E2
CORRAL RD ORO 103-B4
CORRIGAN CT APV 163-D2
CORRINE DR BL 18-A4
CORTLAND CIR SHK 146-B4
CORTLAND CT WBY 124-A2
CORTLAND DR APV 163-A2
CORTLAND DR S APV 163-A2
CORTLAND PL STP 108-B3
CORTLAND RD EPR 132-E3
CORTLAND RD WBY 124-A2
CORTLAWN CIR N GV 105-D2
CORTLAWN CIR S GV 105-D2
CORTLAWN CIR W GV 105-D2
CORVALLIS AVE N CRY 91-E2
CORWIN CT IGH 136-E2,137-A2
CORY LN HAS 166-E3
CORYELL CT IGH 136-E2,137-A2
COSGROVE ST FH 107-D2
COSGROVE ST N FH 107-D2
COSMOS LN EAG 149-D2
COSTA LN LC 94-C3
COTTAGE AVE WBT 80-E2
COTTAGE AVE E STP 108-C2,109-A2
COTTAGE AVE W STP 107-E2,108-A2
COTTAGE CIR NSP 95-A4
COTTAGE CT WBT 80-E2
COTTAGE DNS HOP 119-C1
COTTAGE DR NSP 95-A4
COTTAGE DR OSC 28-B4
COTTAGE DR SWR 96-D2
COTTAGE LN HUT 111-E3
COTTAGE LN MTB 117-C1
COTTAGE LN MTK 119-A1
COTTAGE LN WBT 80-E3
COTTAGE PL SVW 93-E2,94-A2
COTTAGE GROVE AVE MTK 104-C4
COTTAGE GROVE DR WBY 124-B3,138-B1
COTTAGE PARK RD WBL 81-A4
COTTAGEWOOD AVE DPH 118-A2
COTTAGEWOOD RD DPH 118-A2
COTTAGEWOOD TER NE BLA 78-E1
COTTAGEWOOD TER NE SLK 78-E1
COTTONWOOD AVE RW 210-E1
COTTONWOOD AVE NE SM 46-E3
COTTONWOOD AVE NW SM 46-E3
COTTONWOOD BLVD BEC 2-E4,3-A4
COTTONWOOD CIR N DAY 63-A1
COTTONWOOD CIR NW CR 64-D2
COTTONWOOD CT CV 66-D2
COTTONWOOD CT SVW 80-A2
COTTONWOOD CT SWR 96-D1
COTTONWOOD DR HUT 97-D4
COTTONWOOD DR VH 80-B4
COTTONWOOD LN DPH 118-A2
COTTONWOOD LN EPR 132-D3
COTTONWOOD LN MOU 116-E1
COTTONWOOD LN NP 201-E2
COTTONWOOD LN N MG 63-A4,77-B1
COTTONWOOD LN N PLY 91-B3,105-B2
COTTONWOOD LN SE PRL 161-B4
COTTONWOOD PL VH 80-B4
COTTONWOOD ST AND 50-D3
COTTONWOOD ST CR 64-D1,78-D1
COTTONWOOD ST NW AND 50-D2
COTTONWOOD ST NW CR 64-D3
COTTONWOOD ST NW LON 217-B2
COTTONWOOD ST NW OG 22-D3
COTTONWOOD TRL MED 89-D4
COUGAR CT EDI 119-C3
COUGAR DR EAG 150-A2
COUGAR LN MPW 109-B2
COULEE RD HUD 111-D3
COULEE RD HUT 111-E3,112-A3
COULEE TRL TRT 126-D1
COULTER BLVD CHN 131-D2
COULTER DR CHN 132-A2
COUNCIL CIR MTK 104-E3
COUNTRY AVE MO 31-D3
COUNTRY CIR GRF 75-A4,89-A1
COUNTRY CIR MO 31-D3
COUNTRY CIR E COR 62-A3
COUNTRY CIR W COR 62-A3
COUNTRY CT EAG 150-B1
COUNTRY DR LC 94-B2
COUNTRY DR SAV 161-C3
COUNTRY DR W LC 94-B3
COUNTRY LN BUR 148-D4,162-D1
COUNTRY LN DEL 87-E2
COUNTRY LN GRF 75-A4,89-A1
COUNTRY LN LL 66-A1
COUNTRY LN MO 31-D3
COUNTRY LN MTK 105-C3
COUNTRY LN RFD 74-B3
COUNTRY LN SAV 161-C3
COUNTRY PL BUR 148-D4,162-D1
COUNTRY RD COR 62-A3
COUNTRY RD EPR 118-C4
COUNTRY RD HSN 48-A3
COUNTRY RD SWR 96-C1
COUNTRY TRL E SLT 174-C1
COUNTRY TRL W SCT 173-D2,174-A1
COUNTRY CLUB ALC WBY 124-B2
COUNTRY CLUB CIR WBY 124-B2
COUNTRY CLUB CRV WBY 124-B2
COUNTRY CLUB DR GV 105-D2
COUNTRY CLUB RD EDI 120-A2
COUNTRY CLUB RD ORO 103-E1
COUNTRY CLUB RD SWD 117-D4
COUNTRY CREEK WAY EAG 149-C1
COUNTRY HILLS DR COR 61-C3
COUNTRY HOLLOWS LN CLT 202-E2
COUNTRY LAKES DR LL 66-B4
COUNTRY LANE CT RFD 74-B3
COUNTRY OAKS CIR TRT 126-B3
COUNTRY OAKS DR CHN 117-B4,131-B1
COUNTRY OAKS LN TRT 126-B3
COUNTRY OAKS RD CHN 131-B1
COUNTRY OAKS RD TRT 126-B3
COUNTRY SQUIRES CIR SLT 174-E1
COUNTRY VIEW BLVD BUR 148-E3
COUNTRY VIEW CIR HUT 112-A3
COUNTRY VIEW CT BUR 148-E4
COUNTRY VIEW DR BUR 148-E4
COUNTRY VIEW LN BUR 148-E3
COUNTRY VIEW RD HUT 112-A2
COUNTRY VIEW TRL LVL 163-C4,177-C1
COUNTRY WOOD CIR BUR 149-A3
COUNTRY WOOD DR BUR 149-A3
COUNTRY WOOD DRIVE CT BUR 149-A3
COUNTRYSIDE AVE SW LAT 201-D3
COUNTRYSIDE CIR HUT 112-B3
COUNTRYSIDE CT SWR 96-D2
COUNTRYSIDE DR BLO 147-C1
COUNTRYSIDE DR EAG 150-B1
COUNTRYSIDE DR EPR 118-C4,132-C1
COUNTRYSIDE DR SCF 14-D2
COUNTRYSIDE DR SVW 80-A3
COUNTRYSIDE DR SW LAT 201-D3
COUNTRYSIDE DR W ORO 103-D3
COUNTRYSIDE LN HUT 112-B4
COUNTRYSIDE LN TRT 112-B4
COUNTRYSIDE RD EDI 119-D4
COUNTRYSIDE RD WAC 129-D3
COUNTRYVIEW CIR MPW 94-D3
COUNTRYVIEW DR EAG 150-B1
COUNTY PKWY CR 50-C4
COUNTY RD E NB 93-B2
COUNTY RD N HUT 112-C3
COUNTY RD N KKT 112-E4
COUNTY RD N WRT 112-E4
COUNTY RD S OST 14-C4,28-B1
COUNTY RD S SAT 14-C4
COUNTY ST DAY 48-B2
COUNTY ST OTS 48-B2
COUNTY LINE AVE ADT 56-E3
COUNTY LINE AVE FAT 56-C3
COUNTY LINE RD CAR 145-A4
COUNTY LINE RD COT 53-A3
COUNTY LINE RD DEL 87-E4
COUNTY LINE RD IND 87-E3,88-A4
COUNTY PARK RD LAT 215-C3
COUNTY PKWY A AND 50-C3
COUNTY PKWY A CR 50-C3
COUNTY PKWY B AND 50-C3
COUNTY PKWY B CR 50-C3
COUNTY PKWY C AND 50-C3
COUNTY PKWY C CR 50-C3
COUNTY PKWY D AND 50-C3
COUNTY ROAD A RDT 84-E4,98-E1
COUNTY ROAD A SJT 98-D2
COUNTY ROAD B E MPW 94-C4,95-A4
COUNTY ROAD B W MPW 94-B4
COUNTY ROAD B W RVL 93-D4,94-A4
COUNTY ROAD B2 E LC 94-B4
COUNTY ROAD B2 NW RVL 93-D4
COUNTY ROAD B2 W LC 94-B4
COUNTY ROAD B2 W RVL 93-D4,94-A4
COUNTY ROAD C NSP 95-B3
COUNTY ROAD C SPT 70-D3,84-C1
COUNTY ROAD C E LC 94-B3
COUNTY ROAD C E MPW 94-D3,95-A3
COUNTY ROAD C W LC 94-B3
COUNTY ROAD C W RVL 93-C3,94-A3
COUNTY ROAD C2 W RVL 93-D3,94-B3
COUNTY ROAD D E LC 94-C3
COUNTY ROAD D E MPW 94-E2,95-A2
COUNTY ROAD D E VH 94-D2
COUNTY ROAD D E WBL 95-B2
COUNTY ROAD D W AH 93-C3
COUNTY ROAD D W NB 93-B3
COUNTY ROAD D W RVL 93-E3
COUNTY ROAD E AH 93-D2
COUNTY ROAD E GL 94-E2
COUNTY ROAD E NB 93-B2
COUNTY ROAD E OGT 154-D4,168-D2
COUNTY ROAD E RIT 140-D4,154-D2
COUNTY ROAD E SA 93-A2
COUNTY ROAD E SJT 97-D1,98-B2
COUNTY ROAD E SVW 93-E2,94-A2
COUNTY ROAD E VH 94-D2
COUNTY ROAD E WBL 94-E2,95-B2
COUNTY ROAD E WRT 98-E2
COUNTY ROAD E2 W AH 93-C1
COUNTY ROAD F AH 93-C1
COUNTY ROAD F CTT 139-E3,153-C2
COUNTY ROAD F DRS 28-D2
COUNTY ROAD F HUD 111-E4
COUNTY ROAD F HUT 111-E3
COUNTY ROAD F OST 28-E2
COUNTY ROAD F TRT 125-E2,139-E1
COUNTY ROAD F E VH 94-C1
COUNTY ROAD F E WBL 95-B1
COUNTY ROAD F W AH 93-D1
COUNTY ROAD F W SVW 93-E1,94-A1
COUNTY ROAD F W VH 94-B1
COUNTY ROAD FF CTT 139-E4,140-B4
COUNTY ROAD FF RIT 140-D3
COUNTY ROAD FF TRT 125-E1,126-A1
COUNTY ROAD FFF TRT 125-D1
COUNTY ROAD G WBL 81-B3
COUNTY ROAD G WBT 81-B2
COUNTY ROAD G2 W SVW 79-E3,80-A3
COUNTY ROAD H SMT 56-B4
COUNTY ROAD H SPT 56-D4
COUNTY ROAD H W AH 79-C3
COUNTY ROAD H W MV 79-B3
COUNTY ROAD H W NB 79-B3
COUNTY ROAD H2 E WBT 80-E2
COUNTY ROAD H2 W MV 79-B2
COUNTY ROAD I SJT 84-C4,98-C1
COUNTY ROAD I SMT 69-E3,84-B2
COUNTY ROAD I SOM 70-B4,84-B1
COUNTY ROAD I W MV 79-B2
COUNTY ROAD I W SVW 79-D2,80-A2
COUNTY ROAD J HUG 81-B1
COUNTY ROAD J LL 79-E1,80-D1
COUNTY ROAD J E LL 79-E1,80-B1
COUNTY ROAD J W BLA 79-B1
COUNTY ROAD J W LL 79-E1,80-A1
COUNTY ROAD J W SVW 79-D1
COUNTY ROAD K OST 42-E2
COUNTY ROAD M CTT 139-E1,140-C1
COUNTY ROAD M OST 28-D4
COUNTY ROAD M RF 140-E1
COUNTY ROAD M RIT 140-C1
COUNTY ROAD M TRT 139-E1,140-B1
COUNTY ROAD MM CTT 153-D2,154-A2
COUNTY ROAD MM OST 28-E3
COUNTY ROAD MM RF 140-E1
COUNTY ROAD MM TRT 126-B4,140-D1
COUNTY ROAD OO DBT 182-E3
COUNTY ROAD QQ CTT 139-E4,154-A1
COUNTY ROAD QQ OGT 154-A4,168-A1
COUNTY ROAD SS KKT 126-E2
COUNTY ROAD U HUT 112-B1
COUNTY ROAD U RF 126-D4
COUNTY ROAD U TRT 112-D4,126-D1
COUNTY ROAD UU HUD 111-D2
COUNTY ROAD UU HUT 111-E2,112-A2
COUNTY ROAD V SJT 83-D4,97-D2
COUNTY ROAD V SMT 83-D3
COUNTY ROAD X ADT 42-E4
COUNTY ROAD X FAT 42-D3
COUNTY ROAD 1 ANO 49-C4,63-D1
COUNTY ROAD 1 BCT 223-C4
COUNTY ROAD 1 BKT 185-B3
COUNTY ROAD 1 BLO 134-E3,147-D1
COUNTY ROAD 1 CFT 223-D3
COUNTY ROAD 1 CR 63-E2,64-B3
COUNTY ROAD 1 EPR 132-D3,133-B4
COUNTY ROAD 1 ER 19-C2,33-D1
COUNTY ROAD 1 FRI 78-D3,92-D2
COUNTY ROAD 1 LEO 223-B4
COUNTY ROAD 1 LIT 5-B3
COUNTY ROAD 1 NST 40-C3
COUNTY ROAD 1 ORT 5-A1
COUNTY ROAD 1 VAT 223-E3,224-A3
COUNTY ROAD 2 CH 92-E2,93-A2
COUNTY ROAD 2 CLT 188-C4,189-B4
COUNTY ROAD 2 ERT 202-B4
COUNTY ROAD 2 FL 39-B3
COUNTY ROAD 2 FLT 39-D3,40-A4
COUNTY ROAD 2 FRI 92-D2
COUNTY ROAD 2 HAT 187-B4,188-A4
COUNTY ROAD 2 LON 217-A2
COUNTY ROAD 2 MPL 92-B3,106-B2
COUNTY ROAD 2 NM 189-E4,190-A4
COUNTY ROAD 2 NMT 189-D4,190-C4
COUNTY ROAD 2 WHT 202-B4,216-C2
COUNTY ROAD 3 BEL 185-E2
COUNTY ROAD 3 BLA 64-D4,78-D1
COUNTY ROAD 3 BPT 185-E3,199-E1
COUNTY ROAD 3 CKP 1-C2
COUNTY ROAD 3 CR 64-C3
COUNTY ROAD 3 HNT 141-C2
COUNTY ROAD 3 HOP 119-C2
COUNTY ROAD 3 MAY 54-E4
COUNTY ROAD 3 MPL 106-B4,107-A4
COUNTY ROAD 3 MTK 118-D3,119-A2
COUNTY ROAD 3 MV 79-B2
COUNTY ROAD 3 NMT 203-C2
COUNTY ROAD 3 NST 41-A3,54-E2
COUNTY ROAD 3 SLP 119-E1,120-A1
COUNTY ROAD 3 SVW 79-D2,80-A2
COUNTY ROAD 3 WT 203-D3,204-C3
COUNTY ROAD 4 BPT 186-E3,187-A3
COUNTY ROAD 4 CH 92-E1,93-A1
COUNTY ROAD 4 COT 38-C3
COUNTY ROAD 4 EPR 118-D4,132-D4
COUNTY ROAD 4 ERT 217-A4
COUNTY ROAD 4 HAT 187-B3
COUNTY ROAD 4 HIL 92-E1
COUNTY ROAD 4 HL 37-D3
COUNTY ROAD 4 HUG 53-D4,54-A4
COUNTY ROAD 4 LIT 5-E1,6-A1
COUNTY ROAD 4 LON 217-A2
COUNTY ROAD 4 MAY 54-E4,55-A3
COUNTY ROAD 4 MSC 55-B4
COUNTY ROAD 4 MTK 118-E3
COUNTY ROAD 4 ORT 4-E1,5-A1
COUNTY ROAD 4 SSP 122-D2
COUNTY ROAD 4 SVW 80-A2
COUNTY ROAD 4 WBT 80-B1
COUNTY ROAD 4 WHT 217-A3
COUNTY ROAD 4 WSP 122-C2
COUNTY ROAD 4 ZIM 5-C1
COUNTY ROAD 4A HUG 53-B4
COUNTY ROAD 5 ART 170-D4,184-E1
COUNTY ROAD 5 BEL 186-A2
COUNTY ROAD 5 BLT 4-B4,18-A1
COUNTY ROAD 5 BPT 186-B1
COUNTY ROAD 5 BT 20-D3,34-E1
COUNTY ROAD 5 BUR 148-B4,162-C2
COUNTY ROAD 5 HOP 105-B4,119-B1
COUNTY ROAD 5 LVL 162-C4,176-C4
COUNTY ROAD 5 LXT 214-D4
COUNTY ROAD 5 MPL 106-E3,107-A3
COUNTY ROAD 5 MTK 118-D1,119-A1
COUNTY ROAD 5 MV 79-B2
COUNTY ROAD 5 ORT 4-B3
COUNTY ROAD 5 RAM 35-A4,49-B1
COUNTY ROAD 5 SLP 105-E4,106-A4
COUNTY ROAD 5 SWR 82-E4,96-E1
COUNTY ROAD 5 SWT 82-E4
COUNTY ROAD 5 WBT 80-E2
COUNTY ROAD 5 WIT 99-A4
COUNTY ROAD 5 WLK 170-D2,184-D1
COUNTY ROAD 5 WT 203-E4,217-E1
COUNTY ROAD 6 ABT 43-A3,57-A2
COUNTY ROAD 6 ART 171-C4,184-E2
COUNTY ROAD 6 BEL 185-E1,186-A1
COUNTY ROAD 6 BKT 185-B2
COUNTY ROAD 6 CNT 29-A4,43-A1
COUNTY ROAD 6 FRI 78-D3,79-A4
COUNTY ROAD 6 HEN 198-D3
COUNTY ROAD 6 HET 198-C3
COUNTY ROAD 6 HWL 85-A2
COUNTY ROAD 6 IND 102-D2,103-A2
COUNTY ROAD 6 JST 184-D3,198-C1
COUNTY ROAD 6 LE 109-E1,110-A1
COUNTY ROAD 6 MIT 57-A4,71-A3
COUNTY ROAD 6 OKD 109-C2
COUNTY ROAD 6 ORO 103-C1,104-A1
COUNTY ROAD 6 PLY 104-D1,105-A1
COUNTY ROAD 6 SSP 122-D3
COUNTY ROAD 6 VIT 85-A3,99-B2
COUNTY ROAD 6 WBT 80-E2,81-A2
COUNTY ROAD 6 WHT 202-D4,203-B4
COUNTY ROAD 6 WIN 99-B3
COUNTY ROAD 6 WIT 99-C3
COUNTY ROAD 6 WT 203-D4
COUNTY ROAD 7 ABT 43-C4,57-C2
COUNTY ROAD 7 AND 35-C3,49-D1
COUNTY ROAD 7 ANO 49-D2
COUNTY ROAD 7 BCT 223-E4
COUNTY ROAD 7 BEL 186-A2
COUNTY ROAD 7 BPT 186-D1
COUNTY ROAD 7 CNT 29-B3,43-C1
COUNTY ROAD 7 CWT 1-B3,15-C3
COUNTY ROAD 7 GRA 81-C1
COUNTY ROAD 7 HUG 81-E1,82-A1
COUNTY ROAD 7 HWL 85-B1
COUNTY ROAD 7 MAY 68-C4,69-A3
COUNTY ROAD 7 MIT 57-C4,71-B3
COUNTY ROAD 7 MLT 43-D3
COUNTY ROAD 7 MSC 55-C4,69-B1
COUNTY ROAD 7 OG 21-D2,35-C1
COUNTY ROAD 7 RAM 35-C2
COUNTY ROAD 7 SF 7-D4,21-D1
COUNTY ROAD 7 STT 6-E1
COUNTY ROAD 7 SVT 15-D4,29-D1
COUNTY ROAD 7 VAT 209-E2,223-E2
COUNTY ROAD 7 WBT 81-A2
COUNTY ROAD 7 WEL 195-E3
COUNTY ROAD 8 ABT 43-E4,57-E1
COUNTY ROAD 8 BCT 223-C4
COUNTY ROAD 8 BP 77-D4,91-D1
COUNTY ROAD 8 CFT 222-E1,223-A2
COUNTY ROAD 8 CKP 1-B1,2-A3
COUNTY ROAD 8 CLT 188-D1,189-B1
COUNTY ROAD 8 CMT 57-E2
COUNTY ROAD 8 CRT 175-D4,176-A4
COUNTY ROAD 8 CRY 91-E2
COUNTY ROAD 8 FRI 78-D2,79-A2
COUNTY ROAD 8 HET 211-E3,212-A3
COUNTY ROAD 8 HUG 67-A2
COUNTY ROAD 8 KT 211-B3
COUNTY ROAD 8 MH 122-A3
COUNTY ROAD 8 ML 43-D1
COUNTY ROAD 8 MLT 29-D4,43-E4
COUNTY ROAD 8 MVT 57-E4,71-D2
COUNTY ROAD 8 NH 91-D1
COUNTY ROAD 8 ROB 91-E3,92-A3
COUNTY ROAD 8 SCT 187-D1,188-A1
COUNTY ROAD 8 SLK 78-E2
COUNTY ROAD 8 SLT 188-C1,189-A1
COUNTY ROAD 8 SSP 122-D3
COUNTY ROAD 8 STT 6-C1,7-D1
COUNTY ROAD 8 SVT 15-E2,29-D2
COUNTY ROAD 8 VAT 223-C3
COUNTY ROAD 8 WAV 85-E1,86-A1
COUNTY ROAD 8 WBT 81-B2
COUNTY ROAD 8 WDT 86-A2
COUNTY ROAD 8 WSP 122-C3
COUNTY ROAD 8 S ML 43-D2
COUNTY ROAD 8A HUG 67-D3,68-A4
COUNTY ROAD 9 AND 35-E3,49-E2
COUNTY ROAD 9 ANO 49-E3
COUNTY ROAD 9 APV 163-D2
COUNTY ROAD 9 BNT 127-C3,141-B1
COUNTY ROAD 9 CGT 12-E2
COUNTY ROAD 9 CMT 58-A1
COUNTY ROAD 9 CNC 12-E3
COUNTY ROAD 9 CR 49-E4,63-E1
COUNTY ROAD 9 EUT 190-D3
COUNTY ROAD 9 GRA 81-E2,82-A1
COUNTY ROAD 9 HNT 141-B2
COUNTY ROAD 9 HUG 82-B1
COUNTY ROAD 9 IGH 136-B4
COUNTY ROAD 9 JOR 173-A2
COUNTY ROAD 9 LP 127-C1
COUNTY ROAD 9 LVL 163-B4,176-E2
COUNTY ROAD 9 MLT 43-E4,58-A1
COUNTY ROAD 9 MPL 92-B3
COUNTY ROAD 9 MV 79-B3
COUNTY ROAD 9 MVT 58-B4,72-B2
COUNTY ROAD 9 NH 91-C3
COUNTY ROAD 9 OG 21-E2,35-E1
COUNTY ROAD 9 PLA 141-B4
COUNTY ROAD 9 PLY 90-D3,91-B3
COUNTY ROAD 9 RMT 150-A4,164-A1
COUNTY ROAD 9 ROB 92-A3
COUNTY ROAD 9 SCT 173-A1
COUNTY ROAD 9 SF 7-E4
COUNTY ROAD 9 WAV 72-A4,86-A1
COUNTY ROAD 9 WIN 99-B4
COUNTY ROAD 9 WIT 99-B4,113-C3
COUNTY ROAD 10 AH 79-C3
COUNTY ROAD 10 ATT 8-A2
COUNTY ROAD 10 BC 92-B1
COUNTY ROAD 10 BLA 64-E4,78-E1
COUNTY ROAD 10 CHS 145-C2
COUNTY ROAD 10 COR 75-D2,76-A3
COUNTY ROAD 10 CP 65-D3
COUNTY ROAD 10 CR 64-D4
COUNTY ROAD 10 CRY 91-E2,92-A1
COUNTY ROAD 10 GRF 74-D1,75-A1
COUNTY ROAD 10 HNT 155-A2
COUNTY ROAD 10 JOR 173-C2
COUNTY ROAD 10 LE 109-E3,110-B3
COUNTY ROAD 10 LL 66-C3

COUNTY ROAD 10 MG 76-D4,90-E1
COUNTY ROAD 10 MV 79-B2
COUNTY ROAD 10 NH 91-C1
COUNTY ROAD 10 OKD 109-D3
COUNTY ROAD 10 PLY 91-B1
COUNTY ROAD 10 RFD 74-B3
COUNTY ROAD 10 SCT ...173-C3,174-A3
COUNTY ROAD 10 SLK ...78-E1,79-A1
COUNTY ROAD 10 SLT ...174-C3,175-A3
COUNTY ROAD 10 STT 8-A1
COUNTY ROAD 10 WAT 101-B4
COUNTY ROAD 10 WCT ...115-C4,129-C2
COUNTY ROAD 10 WDT 86-C2
COUNTY ROAD 10 WLT ...110-D3,111-A3
COUNTY ROAD 10 WTT ...101-B4,115-C3
COUNTY ROAD 10 E CHT 145-B2
COUNTY ROAD 10 E DAT 145-A2
COUNTY ROAD 10 E LTT .130-A4,144-D1
COUNTY ROAD 10 E WAC 129-E3
COUNTY ROAD 10 E WCT 129-E3
COUNTY ROAD 11 APV ...148-E4,162-E1
COUNTY ROAD 11 ART 148-B3
COUNTY ROAD 11 BUR ...148-E3,162-E1
COUNTY ROAD 11 CHS ..131-B4,145-B1
COUNTY ROAD 11 CKP 17-C4,31-D1
COUNTY ROAD 11 CR 64-B1
COUNTY ROAD 11 DNT ..213-E1,214-A2
COUNTY ROAD 11 GI 169-D2
COUNTY ROAD 11 GIT ...155-D4,169-D3
COUNTY ROAD 11 HAT ..187-B3,201-B1
COUNTY ROAD 11 IND 88-D2,89-A2
COUNTY ROAD 11 LOR 89-B2
COUNTY ROAD 11 LTT ...130-D1,131-A4
COUNTY ROAD 11 LXT 214-A4
COUNTY ROAD 11 MAY ...68-E4,82-E1
COUNTY ROAD 11 MED 89-A2
COUNTY ROAD 11 MLT 30-B3
COUNTY ROAD 11 NB 30-B3
COUNTY ROAD 11 SCT ..173-B4,187-B1
COUNTY ROAD 11 SVT 30-B2
COUNTY ROAD 11 SWR 83-A4
COUNTY ROAD 11 SWT ...82-E1,83-A3
COUNTY ROAD 11 TYT ..199-E3,213-E1
COUNTY ROAD 11 VIC ...130-E2,131-A3
COUNTY ROAD 12 ABT 58-D3
COUNTY ROAD 12 ART 183-B2
COUNTY ROAD 12 ATT 9-C2
COUNTY ROAD 12 BLA ...64-E2,65-B2
COUNTY ROAD 12 BP 64-B4,78-B1
COUNTY ROAD 12 BUF 58-E3
COUNTY ROAD 12 BUT ...64-D4,78-D1
COUNTY ROAD 12 CGT ...12-E3,13-A1
COUNTY ROAD 12 CHM ...49-B4,63-D2
COUNTY ROAD 12 CMT 58-D3
COUNTY ROAD 12 CR 64-C2
COUNTY ROAD 12 DAY ...48-E3,49-A4
COUNTY ROAD 12 ER 33-E2,34-A2
COUNTY ROAD 12 GRA ...95-E1,96-B1
COUNTY ROAD 12 JST ..183-E3,184-B4
COUNTY ROAD 12 LL 65-E2,66-A2
COUNTY ROAD 12 MHT 95-D1
COUNTY ROAD 12 MLT 44-D2
COUNTY ROAD 12 MON ...72-C4,86-C1
COUNTY ROAD 12 MOT 44-D2
COUNTY ROAD 12 MVT ...58-D4,72-C3
COUNTY ROAD 12 NB 93-C1
COUNTY ROAD 12 OXT 9-E1
COUNTY ROAD 12 PRL ..160-E4,161-A4
COUNTY ROAD 12 SLT 160-D4
COUNTY ROAD 12 SVW ...93-E1,94-B1
COUNTY ROAD 12 SWR 96-E1
COUNTY ROAD 12 SWT 96-D1
COUNTY ROAD 12 VH 94-C1
COUNTY ROAD 12 WBL 95-B1
COUNTY ROAD 12 WIL 95-B1
COUNTY ROAD 13 BET 8-D3
COUNTY ROAD 13 DAY 94-E4
COUNTY ROAD 13 ER 20-B4,34-A1
COUNTY ROAD 13 FKT ...87-B3,101-A2
COUNTY ROAD 13 HSN ...48-B3,62-B1
COUNTY ROAD 13 LE 95-D3,109-E2
COUNTY ROAD 13 LVT 159-D2
COUNTY ROAD 13 OG 8-C4,22-C3
COUNTY ROAD 13 OKD ...95-D4,109-E4
COUNTY ROAD 13 SF 8-D4
COUNTY ROAD 13 VIC 131-D2
COUNTY ROAD 13 WBY ..109-E4,123-E1
COUNTY ROAD 13A WBY 123-E2,137-D1
COUNTY ROAD 14 ANO 49-D4
COUNTY ROAD 14 ART 171-D3
COUNTY ROAD 14 BAY 97-B3
COUNTY ROAD 14 BLA ...50-E4,51-B4
COUNTY ROAD 14 BLT ...31-D1,32-D1
COUNTY ROAD 14 BP 63-E4,77-E2
COUNTY ROAD 14 BYT ...90-E3,97-D4
COUNTY ROAD 14 CAT 12-C3
COUNTY ROAD 14 CHM 63-D3
COUNTY ROAD 14 CHN ..131-E4,132-A4
COUNTY ROAD 14 CHS 131-E4
COUNTY ROAD 14 CR 49-E4
COUNTY ROAD 14 CV 66-D2
COUNTY ROAD 14 FKT ...73-B4,87-B1
COUNTY ROAD 14 IGH 122-C4
COUNTY ROAD 14 LE 96-C4
COUNTY ROAD 14 LEO 222-B4
COUNTY ROAD 14 LL 52-B4,66-C1
COUNTY ROAD 14 LND 12-C3
COUNTY ROAD 14 LVT ..159-E2,160-A2
COUNTY ROAD 14 OPH 97-B3
COUNTY ROAD 14 RFT ...59-B4,73-B3
COUNTY ROAD 14 SHK 160-C2
COUNTY ROAD 14 SL 122-C4
COUNTY ROAD 14 SSP 122-E4
COUNTY ROAD 14 VH 94-C1
COUNTY ROAD 14 WSP 122-C4
COUNTY ROAD 15 AH 93-D2
COUNTY ROAD 15 BLT ...4-D4,18-E3
COUNTY ROAD 15 BUT ...45-D3,59-D2
COUNTY ROAD 15 CHS ..131-D4,145-D1
COUNTY ROAD 15 EB 9-D4,23-B3
COUNTY ROAD 15 GIT 169-A2
COUNTY ROAD 15 GL 94-E2
COUNTY ROAD 15 GRA ...82-C2,96-C2
COUNTY ROAD 15 HAT ..187-E3,201-E1
COUNTY ROAD 15 IT ...146-A4,160-A1
COUNTY ROAD 15 LE 64-C4,110-C1
COUNTY ROAD 15 LVL ..176-E2,177-A1
COUNTY ROAD 15 LVT 160-A2
COUNTY ROAD 15 MAY ...54-B4,68-C2
COUNTY ROAD 15 MOT 45-D1
COUNTY ROAD 15 MOU ..116-E1,117-A1
COUNTY ROAD 15 MTA ..102-B4,116-C1
COUNTY ROAD 15 MTB 117-D1
COUNTY ROAD 15 MTK 104-D2
COUNTY ROAD 15 NB 93-B2
COUNTY ROAD 15 NP 22-E2
COUNTY ROAD 15 NST ...40-B4,54-B2
COUNTY ROAD 15 ORO ..103-E4,117-C1

COUNTY ROAD 15 ORT 4-D3
COUNTY ROAD 15 PLY 105-A2
COUNTY ROAD 15 SA 93-A2
COUNTY ROAD 15 SCT ..173-E3,174-A2
COUNTY ROAD 15 SHK 146-A3
COUNTY ROAD 15 SPR 117-B1
COUNTY ROAD 15 SVW 93-E2
COUNTY ROAD 15 VH 94-D2
COUNTY ROAD 15 WAY 104-A3
COUNTY ROAD 15 WLT 110-C2
COUNTY ROAD 15A NST 40-B3
COUNTY ROAD 16 AND ...49-E3,50-C2
COUNTY ROAD 16 DEL 87-D3
COUNTY ROAD 16 FKT ...87-D4,101-C2
COUNTY ROAD 16 HL 50-E2
COUNTY ROAD 16 JST 184-C1
COUNTY ROAD 16 LC 94-B2
COUNTY ROAD 16 MPL 106-A3
COUNTY ROAD 16 MTK ..104-D4,118-E1
COUNTY ROAD 16 SAV ..146-D4,147-A4
COUNTY ROAD 16 SHK ..146-D3,147-B4
COUNTY ROAD 16 SLP 105-E3
COUNTY ROAD 16 TF 14-C1
COUNTY ROAD 16 VH 94-B2
COUNTY ROAD 16 WAY 104-C3
COUNTY ROAD 16 WBY .123-D2,124-A2
COUNTY ROAD 16 WLK ..156-C4,170-C2
COUNTY ROAD 17 ART ..183-A3,197-B1
COUNTY ROAD 17 BLA ...31-D4,65-D2
COUNTY ROAD 17 BLO ..134-A3,148-A1
COUNTY ROAD 17 CF 208-C3
COUNTY ROAD 17 CFT 208-C3
COUNTY ROAD 17 CHN ..118-A4,132-A2
COUNTY ROAD 17 CHS 145-D1
COUNTY ROAD 17 COT ...23-E4,37-E1
COUNTY ROAD 17 DEL 87-D2
COUNTY ROAD 17 EB 23-E4,37-E2
COUNTY ROAD 17 EDI ..120-A4,134-A1
COUNTY ROAD 17 EUT .191-A4,205-A1
COUNTY ROAD 17 FKT ...87-D4,101-E2
COUNTY ROAD 17 GRA 96-B2
COUNTY ROAD 17 HL 37-D3,51-D2
COUNTY ROAD 17 KT ..197-B3,211-B2
COUNTY ROAD 17 LE ...96-B3,110-B1
COUNTY ROAD 17 LEX 65-D4
COUNTY ROAD 17 LVL ..162-E3,163-A3
COUNTY ROAD 17 MPL 120-A2
COUNTY ROAD 17 SHK ..146-C3,160-C1
COUNTY ROAD 17 SLP ..106-A4,120-A1
COUNTY ROAD 17 SLT ..160-C4,174-C1
COUNTY ROAD 17 SVW ...93-E2,94-A2
COUNTY ROAD 17A GRA 96-B2
COUNTY ROAD 17B LE 110-B3
COUNTY ROAD 18 AFT ..124-D4,125-B3
COUNTY ROAD 18 AND ...38-C4,50-B1
COUNTY ROAD 18 BLO ..133-C2,147-C1
COUNTY ROAD 18 CHN ..131-D3,132-A3
COUNTY ROAD 18 CHS 131-D3
COUNTY ROAD 18 COT ...37-E2,38-B2
COUNTY ROAD 18 CR 50-A4,64-A1
COUNTY ROAD 18 EDI 133-C2
COUNTY ROAD 18 ER 133-C4
COUNTY ROAD 18 HET ..211-E2,212-A2
COUNTY ROAD 18 HL 36-E2,37-C3
COUNTY ROAD 18 IGH 136-D1
COUNTY ROAD 18 KT 211-C2
COUNTY ROAD 18 LET 11-D1
COUNTY ROAD 18 LLD ..111-C3,125-C1
COUNTY ROAD 18 LS 111-C4
COUNTY ROAD 18 LSC 125-C2
COUNTY ROAD 18 LTT 131-A3
COUNTY ROAD 18 NEW 123-B4
COUNTY ROAD 18 OXT 10-D1
COUNTY ROAD 18 PRL 161-B1
COUNTY ROAD 18 SHK ..147-B3,161-C1
COUNTY ROAD 18 SMP 125-B2
COUNTY ROAD 18 SVW 94-A2
COUNTY ROAD 18 VIC 131-A3
COUNTY ROAD 18 WBY .123-D4,124-B4
COUNTY ROAD 19 AH 93-C3
COUNTY ROAD 19 ALB 46-E2
COUNTY ROAD 19 CG 138-B2
COUNTY ROAD 19 CGT 12-B3
COUNTY ROAD 19 CHN 131-D2
COUNTY ROAD 19 COR ...61-B4,75-B3
COUNTY ROAD 19 COT ...38-C3,52-C1
COUNTY ROAD 19 EXC 117-E3
COUNTY ROAD 19 HAN ...60-E3,61-A3
COUNTY ROAD 19 IND ...89-A4,103-A2
COUNTY ROAD 19 JST ..183-E2,184-B2
COUNTY ROAD 19 LC 94-D2
COUNTY ROAD 19 LE 110-A3
COUNTY ROAD 19 LET ...11-D3,12-A3
COUNTY ROAD 19 LIT 6-A1
COUNTY ROAD 19 LND 12-C3
COUNTY ROAD 19 LOR 89-B2
COUNTY ROAD 19 MED 89-B3
COUNTY ROAD 19 MP 89-A4,103-A1
COUNTY ROAD 19 MPW ...94-E3,95-A3
COUNTY ROAD 19 MTA 103-A3
COUNTY ROAD 19 NB 93-B3
COUNTY ROAD 19 NSP 95-B3
COUNTY ROAD 19 ORO ..103-B4,117-C1
COUNTY ROAD 19 OTS ...32-E3,46-E1
COUNTY ROAD 19 RFT ...60-C4,74-C1
COUNTY ROAD 19 SA 93-B3
COUNTY ROAD 19 SM 46-E4,60-E1
COUNTY ROAD 19 SPR 117-B1
COUNTY ROAD 19 STA 11-B3
COUNTY ROAD 19 SWD 117-D3
COUNTY ROAD 19 TKB 117-D2
COUNTY ROAD 19 TYT 198-E4
COUNTY ROAD 19 VH 94-D2
COUNTY ROAD 19 WBL 95-B2
COUNTY ROAD 19 WBY .110-A4,124-A2
COUNTY ROAD 19 N IND 103-A2
COUNTY ROAD 19A CG .138-B3,152-A1
COUNTY ROAD 20 AND ...36-E4,49-D1
COUNTY ROAD 20 CG ..137-E2,138-A2
COUNTY ROAD 20 CGT ...12-D2,13-A1
COUNTY ROAD 20 DET ..138-D2,139-A2
COUNTY ROAD 20 EDI 119-D2
COUNTY ROAD 20 HAN 60-E3
COUNTY ROAD 20 HET 211-D3
COUNTY ROAD 20 HOP 19-C2
COUNTY ROAD 20 HOT 99-E3
COUNTY ROAD 20 LND 12-D3
COUNTY ROAD 20 MPL ..106-C3,120-B1
COUNTY ROAD 20 NEW 123-B4
COUNTY ROAD 20 OXT ...9-E2,10-B1
COUNTY ROAD 20 RFD 74-B3
COUNTY ROAD 20 RVL 94-A3
COUNTY ROAD 20 SHT ...13-C1,14-A2
COUNTY ROAD 20 TF 14-B2
COUNTY ROAD 20 WAT 101-B3
COUNTY ROAD 20 WBT 101-A3
COUNTY ROAD 20 WBY .123-C4,137-D1
COUNTY ROAD 20 WTT .....-E3,101-D3

COUNTY ROAD 21 AFT ..125-B4,139-A1
COUNTY ROAD 21 BYT ...97-B4,111-B1
COUNTY ROAD 21 COT 52-E2
COUNTY ROAD 21 CRT ..175-E1,176-A1
COUNTY ROAD 21 CV 66-D3
COUNTY ROAD 21 DET ..139-B3,153-A3
COUNTY ROAD 21 ER ...19-E2,20-A2
COUNTY ROAD 21 ERT ...13-C4,27-C1
COUNTY ROAD 21 HOT ....-C3,114-C2
COUNTY ROAD 21 LC 94-C3
COUNTY ROAD 21 LL 52-E4,66-D4
COUNTY ROAD 21 MPL 120-B3
COUNTY ROAD 21 OPH 97-B3
COUNTY ROAD 21 PRL 161-A2
COUNTY ROAD 21 SHA 13-C4
COUNTY ROAD 21 SHT 13-C2
COUNTY ROAD 21 WIN 99-B3
COUNTY ROAD 21 WLT 111-B3
COUNTY ROAD 22 BT ...20-C4,21-B4
COUNTY ROAD 22 CG ..137-D2,138-A2
COUNTY ROAD 22 CLT 203-B2
COUNTY ROAD 22 EB ...22-E4,23-D4
COUNTY ROAD 22 LC 94-C3
COUNTY ROAD 22 LWT ...23-E3,24-C2
COUNTY ROAD 22 MPL ..106-C4,120-C3
COUNTY ROAD 22 MPW 94-A3
COUNTY ROAD 22 OG ...21-D4,22-C4
COUNTY ROAD 22 SPP 137-B2
COUNTY ROAD 22 WAT 25-A3
COUNTY ROAD 22 WYT 25-A3
COUNTY ROAD 23 APV 163-B2
COUNTY ROAD 23 ATT 8-B2
COUNTY ROAD 23 BEC 2-E3
COUNTY ROAD 23 BKR 2-E2
COUNTY ROAD 23 BLA ...64-C4,79-C1
COUNTY ROAD 23 BNT .113-C4,127-D1
COUNTY ROAD 23 CGT 26-B3
COUNTY ROAD 23 CLT ..189-A3,203-A1
COUNTY ROAD 23 COT ...38-D4,52-C1
COUNTY ROAD 23 CP 64-B4
COUNTY ROAD 23 CT 114-D4
COUNTY ROAD 23 EUT ..191-B2,205-B1
COUNTY ROAD 23 GVT ..205-C3,219-C2
COUNTY ROAD 23 HOT 114-D3
COUNTY ROAD 23 LC 94-B3
COUNTY ROAD 23 LEX 65-C4
COUNTY ROAD 23 LL 52-B4,66-B1
COUNTY ROAD 23 LP 113-B4
COUNTY ROAD 23 LVL ..163-B4,177-B3
COUNTY ROAD 23 MPL ..92-D3,106-D1
COUNTY ROAD 23 MPW ...94-D3,95-A3
COUNTY ROAD 23 OPH 97-A2
COUNTY ROAD 23 PRL 161-A4
COUNTY ROAD 23 RVL ...93-C3,94-A3
COUNTY ROAD 23 SLT ..161-A4,175-A3
COUNTY ROAD 23 SWR 97-A2
COUNTY ROAD 23 WYT ...25-E4,26-A4
COUNTY ROAD 24 BET 8-D3
COUNTY ROAD 24 BT ...20-C4,21-B1
COUNTY ROAD 24 CFT 222-B1
COUNTY ROAD 24 CGT ...26-B3,40-C1
COUNTY ROAD 24 CHC 26-B2
COUNTY ROAD 24 EB 8-E3,9-B3
COUNTY ROAD 24 IGH 37-A3
COUNTY ROAD 24 MGD ..80-D4,90-A4
COUNTY ROAD 24 NMT 204-D2
COUNTY ROAD 24 NSP 95-B4
COUNTY ROAD 24 OG 21-C1
COUNTY ROAD 24 OPH 97-A2
COUNTY ROAD 24 PLY 94-B3
COUNTY ROAD 24 SNT ...7-E4,8-B3
COUNTY ROAD 24 STN ..221-E3,222-A2
COUNTY ROAD 24 SWR 97-A2
COUNTY ROAD 24 WAT 101-B4
COUNTY ROAD 24 WST 221-D4
COUNTY ROAD 25 CFT 222-B1
COUNTY ROAD 25 CGT 26-E2
COUNTY ROAD 25 LEO ..222-E4,223-A4
COUNTY ROAD 25 MPL 106-A4
COUNTY ROAD 25 MPW ...94-C4,123-C2
COUNTY ROAD 25 RVL ...93-D4,94-A4
COUNTY ROAD 25 SLP ..105-E4,106-A4
COUNTY ROAD 26 EAG .135-D3,136-A3
COUNTY ROAD 26 EB 9-B4
COUNTY ROAD 26 FH ...101-C1
COUNTY ROAD 26 FRT ...13-A4,27-C2
COUNTY ROAD 26 IGH ..136-E3,137-A3
COUNTY ROAD 26 LAU 101-B1
COUNTY ROAD 26 LWT ...10-A4,24-B1
COUNTY ROAD 26 LXT ..214-D4,215-A4
COUNTY ROAD 26 MGY 215-A4
COUNTY ROAD 26 MPW 100-C1
COUNTY ROAD 26 MTA .101-E3,102-B3
COUNTY ROAD 26 OTT 212-D4
COUNTY ROAD 26 SNT ..212-E4,213-B4
COUNTY ROAD 26 SPR .136-E3,137-A3
COUNTY ROAD 26 WTT 101-E3
COUNTY ROAD 27 ART 184-D1
COUNTY ROAD 27 CRT ..161-D4,175-D3
COUNTY ROAD 27 EUT 191-D3
COUNTY ROAD 27 JST 184-D2
COUNTY ROAD 27 MPL ...93-A3,107-A1
COUNTY ROAD 27 MPW 108-C1
COUNTY ROAD 27 NMT .189-D2,203-D1
COUNTY ROAD 27 RAM 25-D2
COUNTY ROAD 27 SAV ..147-E4,161-E2
COUNTY ROAD 27 WAT 101-B3
COUNTY ROAD 27 WTT 101-B3
COUNTY ROAD 28 BAY 97-B3
COUNTY ROAD 28 BLO ..133-D3,147-D1
COUNTY ROAD 28 CG ..138-B3,152-A1
COUNTY ROAD 28 EAG .135-D3,136-A3
COUNTY ROAD 28 IGH 136-D3
COUNTY ROAD 28 LAT ..215-C2,216-A2
COUNTY ROAD 28 LES 212-D2
COUNTY ROAD 28 MPW .108-E1,109-A1
COUNTY ROAD 28 NFD ..219-E4,220-A4
COUNTY ROAD 28 NFT 220-B4
COUNTY ROAD 28 OPH 97-A3
COUNTY ROAD 28 SF 6-E3,7-B3
COUNTY ROAD 28 TYT ..212-E2,213-A2
COUNTY ROAD 29 BWV 95-C1
COUNTY ROAD 29 CF 208-A3
COUNTY ROAD 29 DNT ....-E3,201-A3
COUNTY ROAD 29 LAT .201-D3,202-A3
COUNTY ROAD 29 MP 103-A1
COUNTY ROAD 29 NMT 190-B1
COUNTY ROAD 29 NSP ...95-B4,109-A1
COUNTY ROAD 30 ANO 49-C4
COUNTY ROAD 30 BLT ...32-E2,33-A2

COUNTY ROAD 30 BP 77-D1
COUNTY ROAD 30 BUR 149-A1
COUNTY ROAD 30 COR ...75-D1,76-A1
COUNTY ROAD 30 CT ..114-B4,127-D1
COUNTY ROAD 30 DEL 287-C3
COUNTY ROAD 30 EAG .149-D1,150-A1
COUNTY ROAD 30 ER 33-C2
COUNTY ROAD 30 FH 107-C1
COUNTY ROAD 30 FKT ...86-E3,87-B3
COUNTY ROAD 30 HEI 215-B2
COUNTY ROAD 30 LAT .201-B3,215-B3
COUNTY ROAD 30 LAU 107-B1
COUNTY ROAD 30 LET 11-B2
COUNTY ROAD 30 LLD 111-C3
COUNTY ROAD 30 LS 111-C4
COUNTY ROAD 30 LTT ..116-A4,130-A1
COUNTY ROAD 30 MG ...76-D1,77-A1
COUNTY ROAD 30 MGY 215-B4
COUNTY ROAD 30 MPW .108-C1,109-B1
COUNTY ROAD 30 MYR ..114-C4,128-E1
COUNTY ROAD 30 MYT 215-B4
COUNTY ROAD 30 NG ...114-A4,127-E1
COUNTY ROAD 30 OSS 77-C1
COUNTY ROAD 30 RVL ..107-E1,108-A1
COUNTY ROAD 30 STA 11-B3
COUNTY ROAD 30 STP .107-E1,108-A1
COUNTY ROAD 30 VIT 85-C4
COUNTY ROAD 30 WAC 129-C2
COUNTY ROAD 30 WCT ..128-E1,129-B1
COUNTY ROAD 30 WDT ...85-D4,86-C3
COUNTY ROAD 30 WYO 25-B3
COUNTY ROAD 30 WYT ...11-B4,25-B2
COUNTY ROAD 30 N MG 76-D1
COUNTY ROAD 30A LLD 111-B3
COUNTY ROAD 31 ANO 49-C4
COUNTY ROAD 31 APV ..149-D4,163-D2
COUNTY ROAD 31 BLO 134-B2
COUNTY ROAD 31 DNT .....-E3,214-E1
COUNTY ROAD 31 EAG .120-B4,134-B1
COUNTY ROAD 31 EDI ..120-B4,134-B1
COUNTY ROAD 31 ER 20-B4
COUNTY ROAD 31 EUT 191-D1
COUNTY ROAD 31 FAR .177-D3,191-C1
COUNTY ROAD 31 LSC 125-C2
COUNTY ROAD 31 LVL ..163-D4,177-D1
COUNTY ROAD 31 MH 135-D1
COUNTY ROAD 31 MPL 120-B2
COUNTY ROAD 31 MPW 109-B2
COUNTY ROAD 31 NYA 142-B4
COUNTY ROAD 31 SAV ..148-A4,162-A1
COUNTY ROAD 31 STP .107-D2,108-B2
COUNTY ROAD 31 YAT .142-B4,156-B1
COUNTY ROAD 31A MH .121-D4,135-D1
COUNTY ROAD 32 BLA 79-A1
COUNTY ROAD 32 BLO ..134-B3,148-B1
COUNTY ROAD 32 BUR ..148-E2,149-A2
COUNTY ROAD 32 CT ..114-A4,128-B2
COUNTY ROAD 32 DNT ....-C4,214-C3
COUNTY ROAD 32 EAG .149-B2,150-A2
COUNTY ROAD 32 ER 5-B4,19-B3
COUNTY ROAD 32 IGH 150-C2
COUNTY ROAD 32 LIT 5-B4
COUNTY ROAD 32 LL 80-C1
COUNTY ROAD 32 LSC 125-C2
COUNTY ROAD 32 LXT 214-C4
COUNTY ROAD 32 MPL 120-B3
COUNTY ROAD 32 MPW 109-B3
COUNTY ROAD 32 RCH ..120-B4,134-B1
COUNTY ROAD 32 SMP 125-C2
COUNTY ROAD 32 STP .107-D3,108-A3
COUNTY ROAD 32 WAC 129-D3
COUNTY ROAD 32 WCT ..128-E1,129-B3
COUNTY ROAD 33 APV ..149-D4,163-D3
COUNTY ROAD 33 CT ..128-A3,142-B1
COUNTY ROAD 33 EKO .190-A4,204-A1
COUNTY ROAD 33 ER ...19-C2,20-A3
COUNTY ROAD 33 ERT 8-D3
COUNTY ROAD 33 HCT .156-D4,170-D1
COUNTY ROAD 33 HOT ...-A3,114-A3
COUNTY ROAD 33 LON 217-B2
COUNTY ROAD 33 MPL .106-D3,120-D1
COUNTY ROAD 33 NG ..114-A4,128-A1
COUNTY ROAD 33 NYA 142-C4
COUNTY ROAD 33 RFD 74-B3
COUNTY ROAD 33 RFT ...59-E4,74-B2
COUNTY ROAD 33 SNT 213-D4
COUNTY ROAD 33 STP .107-D3,108-B3
COUNTY ROAD 33 TYT 213-D3
COUNTY ROAD 33 WHT 217-B3
COUNTY ROAD 33 YAT .142-C3,156-C1
COUNTY ROAD 34 BET 8-D3
COUNTY ROAD 34 BLO ..133-E3,147-E1
COUNTY ROAD 34 BUF 148-B4
COUNTY ROAD 34 BUT 59-B2
COUNTY ROAD 34 FL 39-C4
COUNTY ROAD 34 FOT .217-E4,218-A4
COUNTY ROAD 34 HAN 60-D2
COUNTY ROAD 34 MPW 109-B3
COUNTY ROAD 34 NYA 142-C3
COUNTY ROAD 34 SM ...59-E2,60-C2
COUNTY ROAD 34 STP .107-D4,108-A4
COUNTY ROAD 34 TYT .198-E3,199-A3
COUNTY ROAD 34 WT 217-D3
COUNTY ROAD 34 YAT .141-E2,142-B3
COUNTY ROAD 34 ABT 58-B3
COUNTY ROAD 35 BLO 134-D3
COUNTY ROAD 35 BLT ...18-E3,19-A4
COUNTY ROAD 35 BUF 59-D2
COUNTY ROAD 35 BUT 59-B2
COUNTY ROAD 35 CMT 68-E2
COUNTY ROAD 35 ER ...19-B4,33-C1
COUNTY ROAD 35 FRI 78-E3
COUNTY ROAD 35 LES 212-D3
COUNTY ROAD 35 MIT 57-A3
COUNTY ROAD 35 MPL .106-D3,120-D3
COUNTY ROAD 35 MVT ..57-E3,58-A3
COUNTY ROAD 35 OKD 95-D3
COUNTY ROAD 35 RCH .120-D4,134-D1
COUNTY ROAD 35 SLK ...78-E2,79-A1
COUNTY ROAD 35 SM ...46-D4,60-B1
COUNTY ROAD 35 STP .107-C4,108-E4
COUNTY ROAD 35 TYT 212-D3
COUNTY ROAD 35 W CMT 58-B3
COUNTY ROAD 36 BTT 143-E4
COUNTY ROAD 36 COL 143-D4
COUNTY ROAD 36 DAT .143-E3,144-A4
COUNTY ROAD 36 EAG 135-D3
COUNTY ROAD 36 LIT 5-E3
COUNTY ROAD 36 LWT ...10-E3,11-A3
COUNTY ROAD 36 MHT ...81-D4,95-D1
COUNTY ROAD 36 MPL .106-E2,107-A4
COUNTY ROAD 36 OTS ...47-E2,48-A2
COUNTY ROAD 36 PS 95-D2
COUNTY ROAD 36 SM 9-E3
COUNTY ROAD 36 STP 108-D4
COUNTY ROAD 36 WIL 95-D1
COUNTY ROAD 36 WYT ...25-D1,26-A2

COUNTY ROAD 37 ABT 43-B3
COUNTY ROAD 37 ALB 46-E2,47-A2
COUNTY ROAD 37 BLA 65-B4,79-B1
COUNTY ROAD 37 CGT 12-E3,13-A3
COUNTY ROAD 37 LES 212-D3
COUNTY ROAD 37 ML 43-E2,44-A2
COUNTY ROAD 37 MLT 43-D2,44-B1
COUNTY ROAD 37 MOT 201-E2
COUNTY ROAD 37 MPL . . .106-E2,107-A2
COUNTY ROAD 37 NP 201-E2
COUNTY ROAD 37 OTS 46-C1,47-D1
COUNTY ROAD 37 SHT 143-A3,157-A2
COUNTY ROAD 37 SM 47-B2
COUNTY ROAD 37 STP 108-C4,122-B1
COUNTY ROAD 37 TF 14-B3
COUNTY ROAD 38 APV . . .149-C4,163-A1
COUNTY ROAD 38 BUR 162-C1
COUNTY ROAD 38 GI 169-D2
COUNTY ROAD 38 MPL . . .120-C1,121-A1
COUNTY ROAD 38 NEW . .123-B4,137-B1
COUNTY ROAD 38 RMT . . .150-A4,164-C1
COUNTY ROAD 38 SPP 137-B2
COUNTY ROAD 38 STP 121-E2,122-A1
COUNTY ROAD 38 WLK 169-C1
COUNTY ROAD 39 CG 137-C3
COUNTY ROAD 39 CNT 29-C2
COUNTY ROAD 39 EPR . . .132-E2,133-A1
COUNTY ROAD 39 LIT 5-E1
COUNTY ROAD 39 MO 31-E2,32-A2
COUNTY ROAD 39 MOT 30-D1,31-B1
COUNTY ROAD 39 MPW 123-B1
COUNTY ROAD 39 OTS 32-D2,33-D3
COUNTY ROAD 39 PRL 161-B3
COUNTY ROAD 39 SPP 137-C3
COUNTY ROAD 39 STP 123-A1
COUNTY ROAD 39 SVT 22-E2,30-E2
COUNTY ROAD 39 NE MOT .30-E1,32-B2
COUNTY ROAD 40 CAR . . .145-B4,159-B1
COUNTY ROAD 40 CHT 145-B3
COUNTY ROAD 40 CWT 1-A4
COUNTY ROAD 40 DAT . . .158-E2,159-A1
COUNTY ROAD 40 ER 20-B4,34-B1
COUNTY ROAD 40 GV 105-E2,106-A2
COUNTY ROAD 40 MPL 106-C2
COUNTY ROAD 40 SFT . . .158-C4,172-A3
COUNTY ROAD 40 STP 122-B1
COUNTY ROAD 41 BTT 143-E4
COUNTY ROAD 41 DAT . . .144-A4,158-B1
COUNTY ROAD 41 SFT 158-B4,172-B1
COUNTY ROAD 41 VAT . . .209-E3,210-B2
COUNTY ROAD 42 APV . . .162-E2,163-C2
COUNTY ROAD 42 HAS . . .152-C4,166-C1
COUNTY ROAD 42 NFT 220-C4
COUNTY ROAD 42 NIT 152-B4,165-E1
COUNTY ROAD 42 OTS 33-E4,48-A1
COUNTY ROAD 42 PRL . . .160-E1,161-C1
COUNTY ROAD 42 RMT . . .163-E2,164-B2
COUNTY ROAD 42 SAV . . .161-E1,162-A1
COUNTY ROAD 42 SHK 160-D1
COUNTY ROAD 42 STP 121-C2
COUNTY ROAD 42 WAY 104-B3
COUNTY ROAD 42 E BUR 162-D2
COUNTY ROAD 42 W BUR 162-C1
COUNTY ROAD 43 BL 18-B3
COUNTY ROAD 43 BLT . . .18-C1,32-B1
COUNTY ROAD 43 DAT . . .144-D2,158-D2
COUNTY ROAD 43 EAG . .135-E3,149-E1
COUNTY ROAD 43 LTT . . .130-D4,144-D1
COUNTY ROAD 43 MH 121-E4,135-E1
COUNTY ROAD 43 MPW 123-B3
COUNTY ROAD 43 NFD 219-D3
COUNTY ROAD 43 ORT 4-D4
COUNTY ROAD 43 STP 123-B3
COUNTY ROAD 43 VIC 130-E2
COUNTY ROAD 44 ER 19-C4,33-D1
COUNTY ROAD 44 LVL 162-C4
COUNTY ROAD 44 MOU 116-D2
COUNTY ROAD 44 MTA 116-E4
COUNTY ROAD 44 MV 79-A2
COUNTY ROAD 44 NB 79-A4,93-A1
COUNTY ROAD 44 PRL 161-E4
COUNTY ROAD 44 SA 93-A2
COUNTY ROAD 44 SAV 161-C3
COUNTY ROAD 45 ATT 9-D1
COUNTY ROAD 45 DAT 159-A2
COUNTY ROAD 45 LIL 121-E3,122-A2
COUNTY ROAD 45 LVL 5-C2
COUNTY ROAD 45 MH 121-E4
COUNTY ROAD 45 NB 79-B4,93-B1
COUNTY ROAD 45 SFT . . .159-A3,173-A1
COUNTY ROAD 46 AH 93-C1
COUNTY ROAD 46 FH 107-C1
COUNTY ROAD 46 FOT 218-C4
COUNTY ROAD 46 LIT 5-B2
COUNTY ROAD 46 LVL . . .162-E3,163-C3
COUNTY ROAD 46 MPL 121-B2
COUNTY ROAD 46 NB 93-C2
COUNTY ROAD 46 NMT . .203-C3,204-D2
COUNTY ROAD 46 RVL . . .93-C3,107-C1
COUNTY ROAD 46 RW 196-D3
COUNTY ROAD 46 STP . . .107-C2,121-C3
COUNTY ROAD 46 WT . . .204-C4,218-C3
COUNTY ROAD 47 AH 93-C2
COUNTY ROAD 47 CAT . . .192-E4,206-E1
COUNTY ROAD 47 HAS 166-C3
COUNTY ROAD 47 HMP 193-B2
COUNTY ROAD 47 MRA . . .192-E4,193-A3
COUNTY ROAD 47 MT . . .166-B4,180-A1
COUNTY ROAD 47 NB 93-C2
COUNTY ROAD 47 NIT 166-C3
COUNTY ROAD 47 PLY 90-C1
COUNTY ROAD 47 SIT 206-C4
COUNTY ROAD 47 VET . . .179-E2,180-A1
COUNTY ROAD 48 COA . . .219-E2,220-B1
COUNTY ROAD 48 N PLY . .90-E1,91-A1
COUNTY ROAD 48 FH 107-C1
COUNTY ROAD 48 MPL . . .107-A4,121-A1
COUNTY ROAD 48 NIT 165-D3,166-B3
COUNTY ROAD 48 RMT 165-B3
COUNTY ROAD 48 RVL . . .93-C4,107-C1
COUNTY ROAD 49 AH 93-C2
COUNTY ROAD 49 HSN 62-B1
COUNTY ROAD 49 LIT 5-C2
COUNTY ROAD 49 ROG . . .48-A4,62-A1
COUNTY ROAD 50 AH 93-D3
COUNTY ROAD 50 BKR . . .17-D4,31-D1
COUNTY ROAD 50 BLT 31-D1
COUNTY ROAD 50 BTT . . .156-E2,157-A2
COUNTY ROAD 50 COR 176-E3,177-A3
COUNTY ROAD 50 DAT 158-C3
COUNTY ROAD 50 FAR 177-D4
COUNTY ROAD 50 FH 107-A1
COUNTY ROAD 50 FLT 53-D1,54-A1
COUNTY ROAD 50 GRF 74-A4,75-A3
COUNTY ROAD 50 HBG 156-A2
COUNTY ROAD 50 HCT 157-D3

COUNTY ROAD 50 IND 87-E1
COUNTY ROAD 50 LVL . . .176-E3,177-A4
COUNTY ROAD 50 NST 54-B2
COUNTY ROAD 50 RFD 74-B3
COUNTY ROAD 50 RVL . . .93-D3,107-D1
COUNTY ROAD 50 SFT . . .158-A3,159-A3
COUNTY ROAD 50 SVW 79-D2
COUNTY ROAD 50 YAT . . .156-E2,156-C2
COUNTY ROAD 51 AH 79-E3,93-E2
COUNTY ROAD 51 BKT . . .184-E4,198-E1
COUNTY ROAD 51 BLA 64-D4
COUNTY ROAD 51 BTT . . .143-A3,157-A2
COUNTY ROAD 51 CAT . . .192-B4,206-B1
COUNTY ROAD 51 CR 50-D4,64-D3
COUNTY ROAD 51 HCT . . .34-A4,171-A1
COUNTY ROAD 51 MAY . . .69-A4,83-A1
COUNTY ROAD 51 ORO 103-C4
COUNTY ROAD 51 RVL . . .93-E3,107-E1
COUNTY ROAD 51 SPR 117-B1
COUNTY ROAD 51 STT 6-D1
COUNTY ROAD 51 SVW 79-D1
COUNTY ROAD 51 SWT 83-B1
COUNTY ROAD 51 WCT 143-A1
COUNTY ROAD 52 BLA . . .51-A4,65-B2
COUNTY ROAD 52 BLO 134-D3
COUNTY ROAD 52 HAT 201-B1
COUNTY ROAD 52 HCT . . .170-E1,171-B1
COUNTY ROAD 52 HL 51-A2
COUNTY ROAD 52 LEX 65-D4
COUNTY ROAD 52 MPL . . .107-A1,120-D3
COUNTY ROAD 52 NST . . .47-A4,59-E1
COUNTY ROAD 52 RCH . . .120-D4,134-D1
COUNTY ROAD 52 SFT . . .133-E3,107-E1
COUNTY ROAD 52 SFT . . .171-E2,172-A1
COUNTY ROAD 52 SVW . . .79-E4,93-E2
COUNTY ROAD 52 WHT . . .202-E3,216-E2
COUNTY ROAD 53 BKT . . .185-D4,199-D1
COUNTY ROAD 53 BLA . . .51-E4,65-E1
COUNTY ROAD 53 BTT . . .143-E4,157-D2
COUNTY ROAD 53 COL 143-E4
COUNTY ROAD 53 EDI 120-B4
COUNTY ROAD 53 FLT . . .210-E2,224-E1
COUNTY ROAD 53 HCT . . .157-D4,171-D1
COUNTY ROAD 53 NST 55-C1
COUNTY ROAD 53 RCH 120-C4
COUNTY ROAD 53 RVL . . .94-A4,108-A1
COUNTY ROAD 53 SIT 206-B3
COUNTY ROAD 53 STT 108-A3
COUNTY ROAD 53N CAT 192-C4
COUNTY ROAD 54 CLT 202-C1
COUNTY ROAD 54 CV 66-E3
COUNTY ROAD 54 FLT 54-A3
COUNTY ROAD 54 FS 121-A3
COUNTY ROAD 54 HAS . . .166-E2,167-A2
COUNTY ROAD 54 LL 66-E4,80-D1
COUNTY ROAD 54 MPL 121-A2
COUNTY ROAD 54 RVT . . .167-C3,181-D3
COUNTY ROAD 54 SVW . . .80-B4,94-B1
COUNTY ROAD 54 WHT 217-B1
COUNTY ROAD 54 WT 217-C1
COUNTY ROAD 55 BPT 186-A1
COUNTY ROAD 55 DNT A3
COUNTY ROAD 55 MAY . . .54-D4,68-D2
COUNTY ROAD 55 STP 108-B3
COUNTY ROAD 55 SWT 82-E3
COUNTY ROAD 55 WT 204-C4
COUNTY ROAD 56 ATT 8-D1,9-B1
COUNTY ROAD 56 CLT . . .188-D3,189-B3
COUNTY ROAD 56 FH 107-D2
COUNTY ROAD 56 IGH 120-B4
COUNTY ROAD 56 NMT 189-C3
COUNTY ROAD 56 RAM . . .35-A4,48-E2
COUNTY ROAD 56 STP . . .136-E1,137-A3
COUNTY ROAD 56 STP 107-D2
COUNTY ROAD 56 WIT 99-A2
COUNTY ROAD 57 BC 92-B1
COUNTY ROAD 57 HUG . . .67-E1,68-A2
COUNTY ROAD 57 JOR 173-A2
COUNTY ROAD 57 MPL . . .92-C3,106-C1
COUNTY ROAD 57 RAM 49-A2
COUNTY ROAD 57 SLW . . .173-C3,173-A2
COUNTY ROAD 57 STP 108-C3
COUNTY ROAD 57 VH 80-C4,94-C1
COUNTY ROAD 57 WAC 129-D3
COUNTY ROAD 58 AND . . .35-E2,36-C2
COUNTY ROAD 58 ERT 216-E4
COUNTY ROAD 58 ET 163-E4,164-A4
COUNTY ROAD 58 HL 36-D2
COUNTY ROAD 58 LVL 163-D4
COUNTY ROAD 58 MAY 68-B3
COUNTY ROAD 58 MPL . . .92-C4,106-C1
COUNTY ROAD 58 MPW . . .94-C4,108-C1
COUNTY ROAD 58 STP 108-C3
COUNTY ROAD 58 VAT . . .209-C4,223-C1
COUNTY ROAD 58 VH 94-C2
COUNTY ROAD 59 BPT 186-E2
COUNTY ROAD 59 BWT . . .218-D4,219-B4
COUNTY ROAD 59 ERT 216-D4
COUNTY ROAD 59 FOT . . .217-E4,218-B4
COUNTY ROAD 59 MAY 69-B3
COUNTY ROAD 59 NO 80-D2
COUNTY ROAD 59 ST 206-C4,220-C1
COUNTY ROAD 59 SLW . . .172-E4,186-E1
COUNTY ROAD 59 VH 80-D4,94-D1
COUNTY ROAD 59 WBT 80-D3
COUNTY ROAD 59 WHT . . .216-C4,217-B3
COUNTY ROAD 60 AND . . .217-D4,218-C3
COUNTY ROAD 60 ART . . .171-A3,185-A1
COUNTY ROAD 60 BKT 185-C3
COUNTY ROAD 60 EPR . . .119-A4,132-E1
COUNTY ROAD 60 HL 36-E4,37-B4
COUNTY ROAD 60 LAT 201-D3
COUNTY ROAD 60 LC 94-D4
COUNTY ROAD 60 LIL 80-D1
COUNTY ROAD 60 MPW . .94-D4,108-D1
COUNTY ROAD 60 MTK . . .118-E3,119-A2
COUNTY ROAD 60 NP 201-D3
COUNTY ROAD 60 WBT 80-E2
COUNTY ROAD 61 BPT . . .187-A3,201-A1
COUNTY ROAD 61 EPR . . .119-B4,133-B1
COUNTY ROAD 61 HL 37-B4,51-B1
COUNTY ROAD 61 HOP 119-B2
COUNTY ROAD 61 JOR 173-B2
COUNTY ROAD 61 MAY 82-C1
COUNTY ROAD 61 MG 77-A4,91-A1
COUNTY ROAD 61 MTK . . .105-A3,119-A1
COUNTY ROAD 61 PLY . . .91-A3,104-E2
COUNTY ROAD 61 SCT 173-B3
COUNTY ROAD 61 SLW . . .173-A4,187-A1
COUNTY ROAD 61 STP 123-A3
COUNTY ROAD 61 SWT 82-D2
COUNTY ROAD 61 WLK . . .169-E1,170-B1

COUNTY ROAD 62 CLT 189-C2
COUNTY ROAD 62 COT . . .38-E2,52-C1
COUNTY ROAD 62 DWD 81-D3
COUNTY ROAD 62 EPR . . .118-D4,119-A4
COUNTY ROAD 62 HET . . .197-E3,198-B3
COUNTY ROAD 62 KT 197-B3
COUNTY ROAD 62 MHT 81-D4
COUNTY ROAD 62 MLK 105-A4
COUNTY ROAD 62 MT 180-C2,181-A2
COUNTY ROAD 62 MTK . . .118-E4,119-A4
COUNTY ROAD 62 NMT . . .189-D2,190-B3
COUNTY ROAD 62 VER 181-B2
COUNTY ROAD 62 VET . . .179-B2,180-A2
COUNTY ROAD 63 BNT . . .113-A4,127-A1
COUNTY ROAD 63 CH 93-A2
COUNTY ROAD 63 EAG 136-B3
COUNTY ROAD 63 GRA . . .82-B4,96-B1
COUNTY ROAD 63 IGH 184-B3
COUNTY ROAD 63 NHR . . .122-B3,136-B1
COUNTY ROAD 63 RAM . . .34-D3,35-A2
COUNTY ROAD 63 SCT 173-C1
COUNTY ROAD 63 WIT 113-A4
COUNTY ROAD 64 BEL 186-A1
COUNTY ROAD 64 BPT . . .186-C1,187-A2
COUNTY ROAD 64 BT 34-C2
COUNTY ROAD 64 CLT . . .188-D2,189-A2
COUNTY ROAD 64 FAR 177-C2
COUNTY ROAD 64 GRA 82-C4
COUNTY ROAD 64 HAT . . .187-D2,188-A2
COUNTY ROAD 64 JST 184-B3
COUNTY ROAD 64 LVL . . .176-D3,177-A3
COUNTY ROAD 64 MPW . . .94-E4,108-E1
COUNTY ROAD 64 RAM 34-E2
COUNTY ROAD 64 STP 108-E2
COUNTY ROAD 64 SWR . . .82-E4,96-E1
COUNTY ROAD 64 SWT 82-D4
COUNTY ROAD 64 WIN 99-B3
COUNTY ROAD 64 WLK . . .169-E4,184-A1
COUNTY ROAD 64B LVL 177-A3
COUNTY ROAD 65 ART 197-C2
COUNTY ROAD 65 BT 20-C4
COUNTY ROAD 65 JST . . .197-E2,198-A2
COUNTY ROAD 65 MPW . .95-A4,109-A1
COUNTY ROAD 65 SCT 159-C4
COUNTY ROAD 65 STP 109-A3
COUNTY ROAD 65 WBL . . .81-A4,95-A2
COUNTY ROAD 66 ART 183-B3
COUNTY ROAD 66 BT 21-B2,35-B1
COUNTY ROAD 66 ET 177-E3,178-B3
COUNTY ROAD 66 GV . . .105-E1,106-A1
COUNTY ROAD 66 MPL 106-D1
COUNTY ROAD 66 SLW . . .172-C4,186-D1
COUNTY ROAD 66 SWR 96-E2
COUNTY ROAD 66 VER 179-C2
COUNTY ROAD 66 VET . . .178-C3,179-B3
COUNTY ROAD 67 BVT 97-A3
COUNTY ROAD 67 OG 22-B3,36-C1
COUNTY ROAD 67 OPH 97-A3
COUNTY ROAD 67 WBL 81-A3
COUNTY ROAD 67 WBT 81-A3
COUNTY ROAD 68 BL 18-A4,32-A1
COUNTY ROAD 68 CRT . . .175-D2,176-A3
COUNTY ROAD 68 GIT 155-B3
COUNTY ROAD 68 HL 37-B2
COUNTY ROAD 68 MPW . . .95-B3,109-B2
COUNTY ROAD 68 NSP . . .95-B4,109-B1
COUNTY ROAD 68 OKD 95-C3
COUNTY ROAD 68 RVT 181-D2
COUNTY ROAD 68 SLT 175-B2
COUNTY ROAD 68 STP . . .109-B4,123-B2
COUNTY ROAD 68 WBL 95-B2
COUNTY ROAD 69 ART 8-A2
COUNTY ROAD 69 BT 20-D1
COUNTY ROAD 69 HNT . . .141-B4,155-B2
COUNTY ROAD 69 JOR 173-B3
COUNTY ROAD 69 JT 145-E3,146-A2
COUNTY ROAD 69 LVT . . .145-E4,159-E1
COUNTY ROAD 69 SCT 173-A3
COUNTY ROAD 69 SHK 146-A2
COUNTY ROAD 69 SLW . . .172-D4,173-A3
COUNTY ROAD 70 BT 6-C4,20-C1
COUNTY ROAD 70 CGT 12-E1
COUNTY ROAD 70 CRY 91-D4
COUNTY ROAD 70 GV 91-C4
COUNTY ROAD 70 LVL . . .176-C4,177-A4
COUNTY ROAD 70 NH 91-C4
COUNTY ROAD 70 NSP 95-B3
COUNTY ROAD 70 PLY 91-C4
COUNTY ROAD 70 SCT 160-B4
COUNTY ROAD 70 SF 6-E3
COUNTY ROAD 70 WBL 95-B2
COUNTY ROAD 71 AFT . . .124-D3,138-D1
COUNTY ROAD 71 DET . . .138-D2,152-D2
COUNTY ROAD 71 IGH 150-C1
COUNTY ROAD 71 RMT . . .150-D4,164-D1
COUNTY ROAD 71 SHT 7-B3
COUNTY ROAD 71 TF 14-B1
COUNTY ROAD 71 WBT 81-B2
COUNTY ROAD 72 BLT 19-B4
COUNTY ROAD 72 ER 177-E4,178-A4
COUNTY ROAD 72 LVT 160-B3
COUNTY ROAD 72 MPW 123-C3
COUNTY ROAD 72 SF 7-E3,8-A3
COUNTY ROAD 72 SLT 160-C3
COUNTY ROAD 72 WBY 123-C2
COUNTY ROAD 73 AH 93-C1
COUNTY ROAD 73 BET 8-D3
COUNTY ROAD 73 BLT . . .3-E4,17-E1
COUNTY ROAD 73 EB 8-D2
COUNTY ROAD 73 HOP . .105-B4,119-B1
COUNTY ROAD 73 IGH . . .136-D4,150-D1
COUNTY ROAD 73 JT 146-A4,160-A1
COUNTY ROAD 73 LVL 163-B4
COUNTY ROAD 73 MTK . .105-B3,119-B1
COUNTY ROAD 73 NB 93-C1
COUNTY ROAD 73 PLY 105-B2
COUNTY ROAD 73 RMT . . .150-C4,164-C1
COUNTY ROAD 73 WSP 122-C3
COUNTY ROAD 74 BNT . . .127-A4,141-B1
COUNTY ROAD 74 CG 137-D2
COUNTY ROAD 74 EB 22-E1,23-D2
COUNTY ROAD 74 FAR 191-E1
COUNTY ROAD 74 HNT 141-C2
COUNTY ROAD 74 LIT 5-E2,6-A2
COUNTY ROAD 74 LWT . . .23-E2,24-A2
COUNTY ROAD 74 MPW 123-B2
COUNTY ROAD 74 NEW 137-B2
COUNTY ROAD 74 OG 22-C1
COUNTY ROAD 74 SAV 161-E3
COUNTY ROAD 74 STP 123-A2
COUNTY ROAD 74A EUT 190-D1
COUNTY ROAD 75 CRT . . .161-E4,175-D1

COUNTY ROAD 75 CW 1-B2
COUNTY ROAD 75 CWT 1-C3,15-E1
COUNTY ROAD 75 GCT . . .137-B4,151-B1
COUNTY ROAD 75 IGH 136-E2
COUNTY ROAD 75 LWT . . .10-D4,24-D1
COUNTY ROAD 75 LYT 1-A2
COUNTY ROAD 75 MO 17-B4,31-B1
COUNTY ROAD 75 MOT . . .16-E3,17-A4
COUNTY ROAD 75 SAV . . .161-E3,162-A3
COUNTY ROAD 75 SSP . . .122-E4,136-E1
COUNTY ROAD 75 STP 107-C2
COUNTY ROAD 75 SVT 15-E1,16-B2
COUNTY ROAD 76 AH 79-D4,93-D1
COUNTY ROAD 76 DET . . .138-D4,139-A4
COUNTY ROAD 76 DT 194-B1,195-A1
COUNTY ROAD 76 EB 9-D3
COUNTY ROAD 76 LWT 9-E3,10-C3
COUNTY ROAD 76 SHT 13-D1
COUNTY ROAD 77 CGT 12-B3
COUNTY ROAD 77 CHC . . .12-B4,26-B1
COUNTY ROAD 77 ER 18-D3,33-D1
COUNTY ROAD 77 JT 146-B4
COUNTY ROAD 77 LWT . . .10-E4,11-A4
COUNTY ROAD 77 MV 79-A2
COUNTY ROAD 77 NB 79-C4,93-B2
COUNTY ROAD 77 SHK 146-B3
COUNTY ROAD 78 AND 36-B3,50-B2
COUNTY ROAD 78 BWT 219-C4
COUNTY ROAD 78 CAT 192-B2
COUNTY ROAD 78 CR 50-B4,64-B2
COUNTY ROAD 78 EUT 192-A2
COUNTY ROAD 78 JT 145-E4,146-A4
COUNTY ROAD 78 LET 11-A1
COUNTY ROAD 78 LP 113-B4,127-B1
COUNTY ROAD 78 LVT 145-E4
COUNTY ROAD 78 NFD 219-C4
COUNTY ROAD 78 OG 22-B4,36-B2
COUNTY ROAD 78 RVL 93-D4
COUNTY ROAD 78 SHK 146-B4
COUNTY ROAD 79 AND 49-D4
COUNTY ROAD 79 BLT . . .18-E2,19-A1
COUNTY ROAD 79 CAT . . .192-D3,206-D1
COUNTY ROAD 79 ER 19-B1
COUNTY ROAD 79 ET 178-D3
COUNTY ROAD 79 JT 146-B4,160-B1
COUNTY ROAD 79 LIT 6-E2
COUNTY ROAD 79 LVT 160-B2
COUNTY ROAD 79 MHT 95-C2
COUNTY ROAD 79 NFD . . .219-E4,220-A4
COUNTY ROAD 79 NFT 220-A4
COUNTY ROAD 79 SCT . . .160-B4,174-B1
COUNTY ROAD 79 SHK 146-B3
COUNTY ROAD 79 SLT 174-B3
COUNTY ROAD 80 CAT . . .191-E4,192-C3
COUNTY ROAD 80 CHC 26-A1
COUNTY ROAD 80 EB 37-D1
COUNTY ROAD 80 EUT . . .190-E3,191-C4
COUNTY ROAD 80 HMP 193-B2
COUNTY ROAD 80 HMT . . .192-E2,193-A2
COUNTY ROAD 80 LET . . .11-E4,12-A4
COUNTY ROAD 80 NMT 190-E2
COUNTY ROAD 80S CAT 192-C4
COUNTY ROAD 81 BLT 17-D2
COUNTY ROAD 81 BP 77-D4,91-D1
COUNTY ROAD 81 COA 164-E3
COUNTY ROAD 81 CRY 91-E2
COUNTY ROAD 81 DAY 62-C3
COUNTY ROAD 81 ET 164-E4,178-E2
COUNTY ROAD 81 HSN 62-B2
COUNTY ROAD 81 HUG 81-B1
COUNTY ROAD 81 LL 80-E1
COUNTY ROAD 81 MG 62-E4,77-B1
COUNTY ROAD 81 MPL . . .92-B4,106-C1
COUNTY ROAD 81 OSS 77-C2
COUNTY ROAD 81 PRL 160-E4
COUNTY ROAD 81 ROB . . .91-E3,92-A3
COUNTY ROAD 81 ROG . . .61-E1,62-A1
COUNTY ROAD 81 SF 7-D4
COUNTY ROAD 81 SLT . . .160-E3,174-E2
COUNTY ROAD 81 VET . . .178-E3,179-A4
COUNTY ROAD 82 BT 206-C3
COUNTY ROAD 82 CAT 206-C1
COUNTY ROAD 82 CGT 13-A4
COUNTY ROAD 82 MV 79-A2
COUNTY ROAD 82 PRL . . .160-E3,161-A3
COUNTY ROAD 82 SWD . . .117-E4,118-A4
COUNTY ROAD 82 SWT . . .82-E3,83-A2
COUNTY ROAD 82 TF 14-B3
COUNTY ROAD 83 BLT 18-D2
COUNTY ROAD 83 CGT 26-D2
COUNTY ROAD 83 FL 39-B3
COUNTY ROAD 83 HMT . . .193-A4,207-A1
COUNTY ROAD 83 IND 102-E1
COUNTY ROAD 83 MP 88-E4,102-E1
COUNTY ROAD 83 PRL 160-E2
COUNTY ROAD 83 RAN . . .34-D4,48-D1
COUNTY ROAD 83 RAT 207-A3
COUNTY ROAD 83 SHK . . .146-D3,160-D1
COUNTY ROAD 83 WBT 81-D2
COUNTY ROAD 84 BNT 127-B2
COUNTY ROAD 84 CRT 175-C4
COUNTY ROAD 84 LL 204-E1,205-A1
COUNTY ROAD 84 LL 66-E3,80-C1
COUNTY ROAD 84 SLT 175-C4
COUNTY ROAD 84 WBT 81-B2
COUNTY ROAD 84 WYT 25-C2
COUNTY ROAD 85 CGT . . .26-D3,40-D1
COUNTY ROAD 85 CLT . . .189-B4,203-B1
COUNTY ROAD 85 LWT . . .10-E4,24-A1
COUNTY ROAD 85 NT 165-D2
COUNTY ROAD 85 RAT 207-E2
COUNTY ROAD 85 VER 179-D2
COUNTY ROAD 85 VET . . .165-D4,179-D3
COUNTY ROAD 85 WBT 81-A2
COUNTY ROAD 85 WIT 99-C4
COUNTY ROAD 86 CAT . . .205-E2,206-D2
COUNTY ROAD 86 DT 208-C2,209-A2
COUNTY ROAD 86 EB 22-E2
COUNTY ROAD 86 EUT . . .204-E2,205-B2
COUNTY ROAD 86 FRT 27-C3,41-B1
COUNTY ROAD 86 HMT . . .206-E2,207-C2
COUNTY ROAD 86 HMT . . .203-E2,204-C2
COUNTY ROAD 86 OG 22-C2
COUNTY ROAD 86 RAT . . .207-E2,208-A3
COUNTY ROAD 86 WBT . . .80-E3,81-A2
COUNTY ROAD 87 BLA . . .64-E3,65-A3
COUNTY ROAD 87 CGT 13-A4
COUNTY ROAD 87 NIT 152-B4
COUNTY ROAD 87 PRL 161-A4
COUNTY ROAD 87 SLT . . .161-C4,175-B2
COUNTY ROAD 88 MPL . . .93-A4,107-A1

COUNTY ROAD 88 MV 79-A3
COUNTY ROAD 88 RAN 207-A3
COUNTY ROAD 88 RAT ..207-C3,208-A3
COUNTY ROAD 88 SA 93-B3
COUNTY ROAD 88 SIT 206-D3
COUNTY ROAD 89 HAT ..188-A2,202-A1
COUNTY ROAD 89 HNT ..180-A4,191-A3
COUNTY ROAD 89 MT 166-B4,180-B4
COUNTY ROAD 89 WBL 81-B2
COUNTY ROAD 89 WBT 81-A2
COUNTY ROAD 90 GVT ..205-A4,219-B1
COUNTY ROAD 90 IND 88-D3,102-D1
COUNTY ROAD 91 CRT ..175-E3,176-A2
COUNTY ROAD 91 DT 195-A4,208-E1
COUNTY ROAD 91 HAS ..166-E2,167-A3
COUNTY ROAD 91 MIE 195-A2
COUNTY ROAD 91 MT 167-A4,181-A3
COUNTY ROAD 91 NM 190-A4,204-A1
COUNTY ROAD 91 NM2 ..190-A4,204-A1
COUNTY ROAD 91 WBL ..80-E3,81-A3
COUNTY ROAD 92 GRF ...74-C4,88-C1
COUNTY ROAD 92 IND 88-C2,102-B2
COUNTY ROAD 92 SB 116-A3
COUNTY ROAD 92 N IND ..88-B4,102-B1
COUNTY ROAD 92 N MTA102-B3,116-A2
COUNTY ROAD 92 S SB 116-A4
COUNTY ROAD 93 DT ...195-B3,209-B1
COUNTY ROAD 93 SB 93-B3
COUNTY ROAD 93 WBL ..80-E3,81-A3
COUNTY ROAD 94 RAN 207-A3
COUNTY ROAD 94 RAT ..206-E3,207-A3
COUNTY ROAD 94 SA 93-B3
COUNTY ROAD 94 WBT ..206-D4,220-C1
COUNTY ROAD 94 WBL ..81-B4,95-B1
COUNTY ROAD 94 WFT 220-B1
COUNTY ROAD 95 NMT 190-B1
COUNTY ROAD 95 WBL 95-A1
COUNTY ROAD 95 WBT ..94-E1,95-A1
COUNTY ROAD 96 GVT ..218-D2,219-C2
COUNTY ROAD 96 LON 217-A2
COUNTY ROAD 96 WFT 219-E2
COUNTY ROAD 96 WHT ..203-B3,217-B1
COUNTY ROAD 96 E NO 80-B4
COUNTY ROAD 96 E WBL ..80-E4,81-A4
COUNTY ROAD 96 E WBT 80-D4
COUNTY ROAD 96 W AH 79-D4
COUNTY ROAD 96 W NB 79-C4
COUNTY ROAD 96 W NO 80-A4
COUNTY ROAD 96 W SVW ..79-E4,80-A4
COUNTY ROAD 97 JOR 173-B3
COUNTY ROAD 97 SLW 173-A3
COUNTY ROAD 97 SVW ..93-E1,94-A1
COUNTY ROAD 98 GL 80-E4,94-E1
COUNTY ROAD 99 AH 93-C2
COUNTY ROAD 99 NB 93-C2
COUNTY ROAD 99 SVW ..93-E2,94-A2
COUNTY ROAD 100 SA 93-D2
COUNTY ROAD 101 AH 93-D2
COUNTY ROAD 101 CHN ..132-A3,146-A1
COUNTY ROAD 101 COR ...62-B4,76-B4
COUNTY ROAD 101 EPR ..118-B4,132-B1
COUNTY ROAD 101 HSN 62-B3
COUNTY ROAD 101 MED 90-B2
COUNTY ROAD 101 MG 76-B2
COUNTY ROAD 101 MTK 118-C2
COUNTY ROAD 101 SAV 104-C3
COUNTY ROAD 101 SHK ..146-D2,147-B2
COUNTY ROAD 101 WAY 104-C3
COUNTY ROAD 101 WT 218-C2
COUNTY ROAD 101 N PLY ..94-C4,104-C1
COUNTY ROAD
   101 S MTK 104-C4,118-C1
COUNTY ROAD 101 W MTK 104-C4
COUNTY ROAD 102 CRY 91-E3
COUNTY ROAD 102 FRI ...78-D4,92-D1
COUNTY ROAD 102 LAU ..91-E4,105-E1
COUNTY ROAD 102 LC 94-B2
COUNTY ROAD 102 VH 94-B2
COUNTY ROAD 103 BP ...63-D4,77-D1
COUNTY ROAD 103 CHM 63-D2
COUNTY ROAD 103 JOR 173-B2
COUNTY ROAD 103 SF 8-B4
COUNTY ROAD 104 CH 92-D1
COUNTY ROAD 104 CWT 1-B4
COUNTY ROAD 104 FRI 92-D1
COUNTY ROAD 104 RVL 93-E3
COUNTY ROAD 105 ABT 57-B1
COUNTY ROAD 105 BLA ...65-C4,79-C1
COUNTY ROAD 106 CNT 29-D3
COUNTY ROAD 106 MLT ..29-D3,30-A3
COUNTY ROAD 106 MOT ...30-E4,31-B3
COUNTY ROAD 106 RVL 93-D3
COUNTY ROAD 106 SAV 104-B3
COUNTY ROAD 107 MIT 71-C3
COUNTY ROAD 107 MPW 95-B3
COUNTY ROAD 107 MVT ...71-E3,72-B3
COUNTY ROAD 107 NSP 95-B3
COUNTY ROAD 107 PLA 141-C4
COUNTY ROAD 108 LC 94-C3
COUNTY ROAD 108 MVT 58-C4
COUNTY ROAD 108 SLK ...78-E2,79-A2
COUNTY ROAD 108 VH 94-D2
COUNTY ROAD 109 AND ...36-B4,50-B1
COUNTY ROAD 109 BP 77-D2,78-B2
COUNTY ROAD 109 CMT 58-B2
COUNTY ROAD 109 LP 113-B4
COUNTY ROAD 109 MG 76-E2,77-B2
COUNTY ROAD 109 MLT ..44-C4,58-B1
COUNTY ROAD 109 MPW 95-B3
COUNTY ROAD 110 CP 65-D4
COUNTY ROAD 110 MOU ..102-E4,116-E1
COUNTY ROAD 110 MTA 102-E3
COUNTY ROAD 110 WDT 86-C2
COUNTY ROAD 110 N IND 102-E2
COUNTY ROAD 110 N MTA 102-E3
COUNTY ROAD 110 W MOU 116-B2
COUNTY ROAD 110 W MTA 116-B2
COUNTY ROAD 110 EXT MTA ..116-C2
COUNTY ROAD 111 LC 94-B4
COUNTY ROAD 111 RVL ..93-E4,94-A4
COUNTY ROAD 111 SVT ...16-C3,30-B1
COUNTY ROAD 112 MPW 94-D4
COUNTY ROAD 112 WDT C2
COUNTY ROAD 113 BUT ..44-E3,45-C3
COUNTY ROAD 113 MPW 108-D1
COUNTY ROAD 114 BUF ..58-E1,59-A1
COUNTY ROAD 114 FH 107-D1
COUNTY ROAD 115 RFT ..72-E3,73-D3
COUNTY ROAD 115 RVL 108-A1
COUNTY ROAD 116 AND ..49-D2,50-C3
COUNTY ROAD 116 ANO 49-D3
COUNTY ROAD 116 COR ..62-A4,76-A2
COUNTY ROAD 116 HL ...50-E3,51-B3
COUNTY ROAD 116 HSN ..61-D1,62-A2
COUNTY ROAD 116 LES 212-D3
COUNTY ROAD 116 MED 90-A1
COUNTY ROAD 116 OTT 212-D3

COUNTY ROAD 116 RAM ...48-E2,49-A2
COUNTY ROAD 116 RFT ...59-D4,73-D1
COUNTY ROAD 116 RVL 108-A1
COUNTY ROAD 116 SNT 213-B4
COUNTY ROAD 116 TYT ..212-E3,213-A3
COUNTY ROAD 116 WIN 99-B3
COUNTY ROAD 117 CHN ..117-E4,131-D1
COUNTY ROAD 117 CHS 131-E4
COUNTY ROAD 117 COR ..61-C3,62-A3
COUNTY ROAD 117 LES 212-D3
COUNTY ROAD 117 MO 31-D2
COUNTY ROAD 117 MOT ...31-D4,45-A1
COUNTY ROAD 117 TYT ..212-E2,213-A2
COUNTY ROAD 118 ALB 46-D2
COUNTY ROAD 118 DNT ...4-A4,214-A2
COUNTY ROAD 118 MO ...31-E3,32-A3
COUNTY ROAD 118 MOT ..32-B4,46-C1
COUNTY ROAD 118 OTS 46-C2
COUNTY ROAD 118 TYT 199-C3
COUNTY ROAD 119 NSP 109-B1
COUNTY ROAD 119 MOT 46-D1
COUNTY ROAD 119 TYT ..199-D3,213-D1
COUNTY ROAD 120 DNT 214-B1
COUNTY ROAD 121 CHM 63-B1
COUNTY ROAD 121 DAY ..62-E1,63-A1
COUNTY ROAD 121 DNT ...D3,214-D1
COUNTY ROAD 121 LXT 214-D4
COUNTY ROAD 121 MG ...62-E4,76-E1
COUNTY ROAD 121 MPW 109-A1
COUNTY ROAD 122 BT 20-E4,21-B3
COUNTY ROAD 122 DNT ...D4,201-A4
COUNTY ROAD 122 HOT ...D4,114-B1
COUNTY ROAD 122 LAT 201-B4
COUNTY ROAD 122 MPL ..106-E3,107-A3
COUNTY ROAD 122 WTT ...E4,101-A4
COUNTY ROAD 123 CNT 29-C2
COUNTY ROAD 123 GRF ...60-E4,74-E1
COUNTY ROAD 123 HAN 60-E3
COUNTY ROAD 123 HOT 114-D2
COUNTY ROAD 123 LXT ..214-E4,215-A4
COUNTY ROAD 123 MGY 215-A4
COUNTY ROAD 123 SVT ...29-E1,30-A1
COUNTY ROAD 123 WTT ...E4,114-E1
COUNTY ROAD 124 FRI 79-A2
COUNTY ROAD 124 SLK 79-A2
COUNTY ROAD 125 MOU ..116-E2,117-A2
COUNTY ROAD 125 MV 79-A2
COUNTY ROAD 125 SLK 79-A2
COUNTY ROAD 125 SPR 117-B1
COUNTY ROAD 127 LAU 107-B1
COUNTY ROAD 127 WTT 101-E3
COUNTY ROAD 128 LAU 107-B1
COUNTY ROAD 130 BC 77-E4,78-A4
COUNTY ROAD 130 BP 77-C3
COUNTY ROAD 130 MG ...76-E2,77-A3
COUNTY ROAD 131 MOT ...31-B4,45-B1
COUNTY ROAD 131 YAT 141-E3
COUNTY ROAD 132 ABT 57-C1
COUNTY ROAD 132 AH 93-D2
COUNTY ROAD 132 BLA 78-D1
COUNTY ROAD 132 CMT 57-C1
COUNTY ROAD 132 CR 78-D1
COUNTY ROAD 132 FH 107-D2
COUNTY ROAD 132 MPW 109-A3
COUNTY ROAD 132 STP 109-A3
COUNTY ROAD 133 HOT 99-E3
COUNTY ROAD 133 RVL ..93-E3,94-A3
COUNTY ROAD 133 SVW 94-A2
COUNTY ROAD 133 WDT 99-E2
COUNTY ROAD 134 BUF 59-B3
COUNTY ROAD 134 BUT 59-B2
COUNTY ROAD 134 NYA 142-C3
COUNTY ROAD 134 YAT 142-D4
COUNTY ROAD 135 CT ..128-C4,142-C1
COUNTY ROAD 135 ORO 103-B3
COUNTY ROAD 136 SA 93-A3
COUNTY ROAD 136 SVW 94-B2
COUNTY ROAD 137 ERT 216-B3
COUNTY ROAD 137 MGY 216-B4
COUNTY ROAD 138 BUF 108-E2
COUNTY ROAD 138 BUT 44-D4
COUNTY ROAD 139 IND 87-E2
COUNTY ROAD 139 LC 94-C3
COUNTY ROAD 140 BTT 143-E2
COUNTY ROAD 140 CHS 145-C3
COUNTY ROAD 140 CNT 145-B2
COUNTY ROAD 140 DAT ..144-C2,145-A2
COUNTY ROAD 140 LC 94-C4
COUNTY ROAD 140 LL ...52-E4,53-A4
COUNTY ROAD 140 MPW ..94-C4,108-C1
COUNTY ROAD 140 WCT 143-E2
COUNTY ROAD 142 LAT 215-C3
COUNTY ROAD 142 LC 54-D3
COUNTY ROAD 142 MGY 215-D4,216-A4
COUNTY ROAD 143 LAT ..201-C3,215-C1
COUNTY ROAD 143 LYT 1-A2
COUNTY ROAD 143 SGV 29-E1
COUNTY ROAD 144 DAY 48-D3
COUNTY ROAD 144 MIE ..47-C4,48-A3
COUNTY ROAD 144 LAT ..201-E4,215-E2
COUNTY ROAD 144 MYT 215-E4
COUNTY ROAD 144 RFT 60-C4
COUNTY ROAD 145 LAT ..201-D4,202-A4
COUNTY ROAD 145 LYT 1-A3
COUNTY ROAD 145 MPW 108-E1
COUNTY ROAD 146 GL ...80-E4,94-E1
COUNTY ROAD 146 LAT ..202-A4,216-A2
COUNTY ROAD 146 LOL 103-D2
COUNTY ROAD 146 ORO 103-D2
COUNTY ROAD 146 SM ...60-E2,61-A2
COUNTY ROAD 146 VH 94-E2
COUNTY ROAD 146 WBL ..81-A4,94-E1
COUNTY ROAD 147 CAR 145-A4
COUNTY ROAD 147 CNT 145-A3
COUNTY ROAD 147 GL 94-E1
COUNTY ROAD 148 GL ...80-E4,94-E1
COUNTY ROAD 148 WBL 80-E4
COUNTY ROAD 148 WBT 80-E4
COUNTY ROAD 149 WBT 80-E2
COUNTY ROAD 150 MPW 109-A1
COUNTY ROAD 150 ROG 61-E1
COUNTY ROAD 151 HCT 171-A2
COUNTY ROAD 151 MTA ..102-E3,103-A3
COUNTY ROAD 151 ORO 103-B4
COUNTY ROAD 151 WBL 81-A3
COUNTY ROAD 151 WBT 81-A3
COUNTY ROAD 151 WCT 129-A4,143-A1
COUNTY ROAD 152 BC ...78-A4,92-A1
COUNTY ROAD 152 BP 77-D3
COUNTY ROAD 152 BTT 157-C1
COUNTY ROAD 152 MPL 92-B3
COUNTY ROAD 152 SNT 212-E4
COUNTY ROAD 152 WBL 81-A3
COUNTY ROAD 152 WBT 81-A2
COUNTY ROAD 153 BTT ..143-B3,157-B2
COUNTY ROAD 153 LL ...65-E1,66-A1
COUNTY ROAD 153 MPL ..92-D4,93-A4

COUNTY ROAD 153 ROB 92-B4
COUNTY ROAD 153 SA 93-A4
COUNTY ROAD 154 LL 66-D3
COUNTY ROAD 154 TYT 213-C3
COUNTY ROAD 154 WBT 81-B2
COUNTY ROAD 155 LTT ..129-E1,130-A1
COUNTY ROAD 155 TYT 213-C2
COUNTY ROAD 155 WCT 115-E4
COUNTY ROAD 156 CRY 91-D3
COUNTY ROAD 156 DNT ..213-D4,214-A2
COUNTY ROAD 156 GV ..91-D4,105-D2
COUNTY ROAD 156 NH 91-D2
COUNTY ROAD 156 TYT 213-B2
COUNTY ROAD 157 DNT ...B4,214-D1
COUNTY ROAD 158 AND 35-D4
COUNTY ROAD 158 EDI 119-D3
COUNTY ROAD 158 MPW 109-B3
COUNTY ROAD 158 STP 109-B3
COUNTY ROAD 159 HSN 62-A2
COUNTY ROAD 160 MPW 123-B3
COUNTY ROAD 160 WBL ..81-B4,95-B1
COUNTY ROAD 161 WBT 81-B1
COUNTY ROAD 163 AN 93-C2
COUNTY ROAD 163 BT ..20-D4,34-D1
COUNTY ROAD 163 NB 93-C2
COUNTY ROAD 164 LAT 202-A3
COUNTY ROAD 165 LAT 216-B1
COUNTY ROAD 182 ER 20-B3
COUNTY ROAD 201 MED ..89-C4,103-C1
COUNTY ROAD 201 ORO 103-C1
COUNTY ROAD 202 DAY 63-B2
COUNTY ROAD 202 DAY 63-B2
COUNTY ROAD 202 MG ..63-B4,77-B1
COUNTY ROAD 203 HAN 61-B3
COUNTY ROAD 203 HSN ..47-C4,61-B1
COUNTY ROAD 204 FS 121-C4
COUNTY ROAD 215 LAT 121-B4
COUNTY ROAD 216 ANO 49-D3
COURT PL BUR 148-A4
COURT RD MTK 118-D2
COURT ST LES 212-D3
COURT ST PRE 153-B4,167-B1
COURT ST E BEL 185-E1,186-A1
COURT ST W BEL 185-E1
COURTHOUSE
   BLVD IGH 136-D4,150-E2
COURTHOUSE
   BLVD RMT 151-A4,165-B1
COURTHOUSE BLVD W IGH ..136-B3
COURTHOUSE LN EAG 136-A3
COURTHOUSE
   BOULEVARD CT IGH ..136-D4,150-E1
COURTLAND E WAC 129-C2
COURTLAND W WAC 129-C2
COURTLAND RD MTK 118-D2
COURTLAND ST EAG 117-E3
COURTLY ALC WBY 123-C3
COURTLY RD WBY 123-C3
COURTYARD PARK BUR 162-C2
COVE AVE PRL 161-C2
COVE CIR MTA 102-E3,103-A3
COVE CT MTK 125-C3
COVE DR MTK 105-C4
COVE LN TRT 125-D3
COVE LN E MTA 103-A3
COVE LN W MTA 102-E3,103-A3
COVE RD SFT 158-D4
COVE RD TRT 125-C3
COVE RD N TRT 125-D2
COVE RD S TRT 125-D2
COVE POINTE RD EPR 132-D3
COVENTRY CT EDI 134-A1
COVENTRY CT NH 121-E4
COVENTRY LN EDI 134-A1
COVENTRY LN SHK 147-B3
COVENTRY PKWY EAG 150-B1
COVENTRY PL EDI 134-A1
COVENTRY RD LES 212-D4
COVENTRY RD E MTK 118-E2
COVENTRY RD W MTK 118-E2
COVENTRY VW EDI 134-A1
COVENTRY WAY EDI 133-D1
COVEY CT NFD 219-D3
COVEY TRL MED 89-C1
COVINGTON AVE RMT 163-E2
COVINGTON CIR EAG 149-C3
COVINGTON CIR EPR 147-B1
COVINGTON CIR MTK 118-B3
COVINGTON CT EAG 149-C3
COVINGTON CT MTK 118-C4
COVINGTON CT SWD 118-B3
COVINGTON LN EAG 149-C3
COVINGTON LN MTK 118-C3
COVINGTON PATH MTK 118-C4
COVINGTON RD MTK 118-B3
COVINGTON RD SWD 118-B3
COVINGTON ST GRW 117-E3
COVINGTON TER MTK 118-C4
COWERN PL E NSP 109-B1
COX FARM RD ORO 103-D1
COYOTE CT LL 66-A4
COYOTE LN MPW 109-B2
COYOTE TRL LL 66-A4
CRABAPPLE LN TKB 117-D1
CRACKLEBERRY ALC WBY ...137-C1
CRACKLEBERRY BAY WBY ...137-C1
CRACKLEBERRY CT WBY 137-C1
CRACKLEBERRY TRL WBY ...137-C1
CRAIG AVE IGH 136-E2,137-A2
CRAIG AVE NW CMT 58-B3
CRAIG AVE NW MLT 44-B1
CRAIG AVE NW WBL ...2-B4,16-B1
CRAIG CIR NW CMT 58-B2
CRAIG CT IGH 137-A2
CRAIG DR EPR 118-C4
CRAIG LN MO 31-C1
CRAIG PL MPW 95-A4
CRAIG PL STP 109-A1
CRAIG PL WIL 95-D1
CRAIG WAY IGH 137-A3
CRAIG WAY NE FRI 78-D2
CRAIGBROOK WAY NE FRI ...78-C2
CRANBERRY DR NE LWT 24-A3
CRANBERRY LN EPR 118-E2
CRANBERRY WAY RMT 163-E1
CRANBROOK DR WBL 95-B1
CRANDALL AVE RMT 163-E2
CRANE DR BLT 17-E2
CRANE LN BL 18-A4
CRANE ST CR 64-B2
CRANE ST NW CR 50-B4,64-B3
CRANE DANCE TRL EPR 133-B3
CRANFORD CIR APV 149-E4
CRATER CT BUR 149-A3
CRAWFORD AVE FH 107-D1
CRAWFORD RD MTK 119-A2

CRAWFORD RD W MTK 119-A2
CREDIT RIVER BLVD CRT .175-E2,176-A3
CREDIT RIVER DR SAV 162-A2
CREDIT RIVER RD PRL 161-B4
CREDIT RIVER RD SE PRL ..161-C4
CREDIT VIEW DR SAV 161-E2
CREE DR CHN 132-A1
CREE LN LL 66-C3
CREE ST NW AND 49-D1
CREE ST NW CR 63-D1
CREE ST NW SF 7-D4
CREEK AVE MH 136-A1
CREEK DR EDI 119-E4
CREEK DR N CHM 63-B1
CREEK LN CHS 145-C3
CREEK LN HOP 105-B4
CREEK LN JOR 173-B2
CREEK LN NFD 220-A4
CREEK LN MTK 118-C3
CREEK LN S JOR 173-B2
CREEK PT MTK 118-C4
CREEK RD CHS 145-C2
CREEK RD CHT 145-C2
CREEK RD W MTK 105-A4
CREEK WAY SAV 147-C3
CREEK KNOLL RD EPR 133-A4
CREEK LINE DR MTK 118-C4
CREEK MEADOWS DR NW CR ..64-B2
CREEK PARK DR MTK 118-C3
CREEK PARK LN MTK 118-C3
CREEK PARK LN NE FRI ..78-E3,79-A3
CREEK RIDGE CIR SM 46-E4
CREEK RIDGE CT SHK 147-C4
CREEK RIDGE LN SAV 147-C4
CREEK RIDGE PASS MTK ..118-C4
CREEK RIDGE PL MTK 118-C4
CREEK RIDGE RL MTK 118-C4
CREEK RUN TRL CHN 117-E4
CREEK VALLEY RD EDI ..119-D4,133-D1
CREEK VIEW AVE SAV 147-B3
CREEK VIEW CIR COR ...61-B4,75-B1
CREEK VIEW CT CHN 131-E2
CREEK VIEW CT NW STT 7-E2
CREEK VIEW LN ARL 183-A3
CREEK VIEW LN CHM 63-E3
CREEK VIEW LN EDI 133-D1
CREEK VIEW LN EPR 118-D4
CREEK VIEW LN WAC 118-B4
CREEK VIEW TRL MTK 118-B4
CREEKRIDGE CIR BLO 133-D2
CREEKRIDGE DR CHS 145-C3
CREEKRIDGE DR EPR 133-B4
CREEKRIDGE LN DAT 145-A3
CREEKS BEND DR MTK 118-B4
CREEKSIDE CIR BLO 133-E2
CREEKSIDE CIR BUF 59-A2
CREEKSIDE CIR CRT 175-D4
CREEKSIDE CIR PRL 161-A4
CREEKSIDE CIR SWT 82-D4
CREEKSIDE CIR WAC 129-D3
CREEKSIDE CT EAG 149-A1
CREEKSIDE CT EPR 132-D1
CREEKSIDE CT SWT 82-D4
CREEKSIDE CT WAC 129-C3
CREEKSIDE XING SWT ..82-D4,96-D1
CREEKSIDE DR BUF 59-A2
CREEKSIDE DR LOL 103-E2
CREEKSIDE DR WAC 129-C3
CREEKSIDE DR SE SM 46-E4
CREEKSIDE LN MTK 118-C4
CREEKSIDE LN MTK 118-C4
CREEKSIDE LN W JT 146-B4
CREEKSIDE WAY STP 109-A4
CREEKSIDE CIRV BLO 133-E2
CREEKVIEW CIR MTA 116-B3
CREEKVIEW CIR SW FRI ..160-E4
CREEKVIEW CT ROG 47-D4
CREEKVIEW LN BEL 186-A1
CREEKVIEW LN BP 77-E2
CREEKVIEW LN EPR 118-D4
CREEKVIEW LN LOR 89-B1
CREEKVIEW TER MTK 118-E1
CREEKWOOD CIR CRT 161-D3
CREEKWOOD DR CRT 161-D3
CREEKWOOD DR EPR 133-A4
CREEKWOOD LN CRT 161-D3
CREEKWOOD RD CRT 161-D3
CREEKWOOD ST CMT 146-A1
CREEKWOOD TRL ORO 103-E3
CREGGS CIR APV 149-E4
CRESCENT AVE BUR 162-B1
CRESCENT CIR RMT 163-E2
CRESCENT CT EPR 132-C2
CRESCENT DR EDI 119-D4
CRESCENT LN RVL 108-A1
CRESCENT LN WBY 124-A1
CRESCENT RD CNC 12-E4
CRESCENT ST BL 18-A3
CRESCENT ST MTB 117-D1
CRESCENT ST RF 140-E2
CRESCENT TER EDI 119-D2
CRESCENT BEACH RD CNC ...12-E4
CRESCENT RIDGE RD MTK ..105-A4
CRESSY AVE ANO 49-B4
CREST AVE DPH 118-B1
CREST AVE PRL 161-B1
CREST AVE SHK 147-C4,161-B1
CREST CT N MYR 114-B3
CREST DR BUR 162-C3
CREST DR CHS 145-C2
CREST DR N MG 76-E4
CREST LN EDI 119-D4
CREST LN HAS 166-C2
CREST RIDGE CT MTA 103-A3
CREST VIEW DR SA 93-B3
CRESTHAVEN DR SSP 122-D3
CRESTLINE DR WBL 95-B2
CRESTMOOR ALC WBY .123-E3,124-A3
CRESTMOOR BAY WBY 124-A3
CRESTMOOR DR WBY ..123-E3,124-A3
CRESTMOOR PT WBY 124-A3
CRESTMOOR TER WBY 124-A3
CRESTMOUNT LN BUR 162-B2
CRESTON RD EDI 134-A1
CRESTONE AVE RMT 163-E2
CRESTONE CIR RMT 163-E2
CRESTONE CT RMT 163-E3
CRESTONE PATH W RMT ..163-E3
CRESTRIDGE CT EAG 135-D4
CRESTRIDGE DR BUR 162-D1
CRESTRIDGE DR EAG 135-D4
CRESTRIDGE DR MTK 105-B3
CRESTRIDGE LN EAG 135-D4

CRESTSIDE AVE GRW 118-A3
CRESTVIEW AVE ORO 103-C3
CRESTVIEW AVE RMT 163-E2
CRESTVIEW AVE N GV 106-A1
CRESTVIEW CIR CHN 117-E4
CRESTVIEW CIR RMT 163-E2
CRESTVIEW CIR N JOR 173-B3
CRESTVIEW CT MPW 123-B3
CRESTVIEW DR CHN 117-D4
CRESTVIEW DR HAS 166-C1
CRESTVIEW DR HUD 111-D3
CRESTVIEW DR N MPW 109-B4
CRESTVIEW DR S MPW 123-B2
CRESTVIEW LN EAG 149-D1
CRESTVIEW LN LOR 89-B1
CRESTVIEW LN MTK 118-D3
CRESTVIEW LN SVW 94-A1
CRESTVIEW RD MOU 103-A4
CRESTVIEW ST SHK 146-C3
CRESTVIEW TER CHS 145-D1
CRESTVIEW TRL SJT 98-C3
CRESTVIEW FOREST DR MPW ..123-B2
CRESTWAY LN WSP 122-B4
CRESTWOOD CIR MTK 105-A4
CRESTWOOD DR BLO 133-E3
CRESTWOOD DR DAY 62-B2
CRESTWOOD DR MTK 118-E3
CRESTWOOD DR NSP 95-A4
CRESTWOOD DR E MTK 118-E3
CRESTWOOD LN GRW 118-A2
CRESTWOOD PL WBL 95-A1
CRESTWOOD TER EPR 132-C4
CRESTWOOD TER SWR 96-E1
CRETEX AVE SHK 147-B2
CRETIN AVE N STP 107-C4,121-C1
CRETIN AVE S STP 121-C1
CRIMSON CT PRL 161-B4
CRIMSON BAY RD CHN 131-C2
CRIMSON CLOVER LN EPR 133-A3
CRIMSON LEAF CT EAG 150-B2
CRIMSON LEAF TRL EAG 150-A2
CRIMSON VALLEY RD HUT 112-C2
CRIPPLE CREEK CT LL 66-B4
CRIPPLE CREEK PASS LL 66-C4
CRISTINE CT WBT 81-B2
CRISTOFORI CIR ORO 103-B2
CROCKER AVE EDI 120-A2
CROCUS AVE RMT 163-E3
CROCUS CIR MO 31-B1
CROCUS CT CHN 131-D1
CROCUS CT NFD 220-A4
CROCUS CT RMT 163-E3
CROCUS CT ROG 47-D4
CROCUS HL STP 122-A1
CROCUS LN EPR 132-D3
CROCUS LN MO 31-B1
CROCUS LN NO 80-C2
CROCUS PL STP 122-A1
CROCUS ST MHT 95-D1
CROCUS ST NW AND 36-A3,50-A3
CROCUS ST NW CR 50-A3,64-A1
CROCUS ST NW OG 22-A4,36-A2
CROCUS WAY RMT 163-E1
CROCUS HILL RD TRT ...125-E3,126-A2
CROFOOT AVE NW CMT 58-B2
CROFOOT AVE NW MLT 44-B3
CROFOOT AVE NW SVT ...16-B3,30-B2
CROFOOT AVE SW MVT ...58-B4,72-B4
CROFOOT AVE SW WDT ....-B2
CROFT DR SA 93-B3
CROFTON CT RMT 163-E1
CROFTVIEW TER MTK 118-C1
CROIX CREST LN HUD 111-D3
CROIXVIEW DR S AFT 111-B4
CROIXWOOD BLVD SWR 96-D2
CROIXWOOD LN EPR 132-C2
CROIXWOOD PL SWR 96-D2
CROMWELL AVE STP 107-B3
CROMWELL CT IGH 137-A2
CROMWELL CT MPL 120-B3
CROMWELL DR EPR 133-B4
CROMWELL DR MPL 120-B3
CRONIN CIR HUD 111-D3
CROOKED LAKE BLVD NW AND ..50-A3
CROOKED LAKE
BLVD NW CR 50-A4,64-A2
CROOKED LAKE
LN NW CR 49-E4,50-A4
CROOKHAVEN CT APV 149-E4
CROSBY AVE IGH 137-A2
CROSBY DR HUT 112-A2
CROSBY LN SFT 158-E4
CROSBY PL MPL 121-A2
CROSBY RD MTK 104-D4
CROSBY RD WAY 104-D3
CROSBY FARM RD STP 121-D3
CROSBY LAKE RD STP 121-E3
CROSS RD EAG 135-E4
CROSS ST ANO 49-D4
CROSS ST LES 212-D4
CROSS ST WAY 104-C3
CROSS ST SW PRL 161-A4
CROSS POINT RD MTB 117-D1
CROSS POINT RD WAC 129-D3
CROSSANDRA CIR PRL 161-C3
CROSSANDRA ST PRL 161-C3
CROSSANDRA ST SE PRL 161-C3
CROSSROAD CT EAG 135-D4
CROSSTOWN BLVD CHS 145-D2
CROSSTOWN BLVD NE HL .36-E2,37-C3
CROSSTOWN
BLVD NW AND 36-C4,50-B1
CROSSTOWN CIR EPR 119-C4
CROSSTOWN DR NW AND 50-A3
CROSSTOWN RD TLT 168-E1
CROSSWAY DR CP 65-D3
CROSSWAYS LAKE DR COT 52-C1
CROW HASSAN PARK RD HAN ...61-B3
CROW RIVER DR HSN 48-B3
CROW RIVER DR NE HAN 60-E3
CROW RIVER DR NE OTS ...33-E4,47-E1
CROWFOOT CT EPR 133-A3
CROWN CIR MH 122-A4
CROWN CIR NW STT 6-E1,7-A1
CROWN CT MH 121-E4
CROWN DR EPR 132-E1
CROWN DR MTK 118-D2
CROWN LN WBY 123-C4,137-C1
CROWN RD NE FRI 92-D1
CROWN ST MTK 118-E3
CROWN HILL CT BUR 148-D3
CROWN HILL CT WBL 95-B1
CROWN POINT DR MH ..121-E4,122-A4
CROWNE HILL LN MTK 104-E4
CROWNE HILL RD MTK 104-E4
CROWNE OAK RD EPR 133-B1
CROYDEN LN EDI 119-D3
CRUSADER AVE E WSP 122-C4
CRUSADER AVE W WSP 122-C4
CRUSHEEN CT APV 149-E4
CRYSTAL AVE AH 93-C1
CRYSTAL AVE ORO 103-D4
CRYSTAL AVE SVW 93-E1,94-A1
CRYSTAL CIR PRL 160-E3
CRYSTAL CIR SVW 93-E1
CRYSTAL CT CHS 145-D2
CRYSTAL CT LL 66-B3
CRYSTAL CT MON 72-C4
CRYSTAL CT RMT 163-E3
CRYSTAL DR E BUR 162-D2
CRYSTAL DR W BUR 162-D2
CRYSTAL LN CHS 145-D2
CRYSTAL PATH RMT 163-E3
CRYSTAL PL ORO 117-C1
CRYSTAL PL E CHS 145-D2
CRYSTAL PL W CHS 145-D2
CRYSTAL BAY RD ORO 117-C1
CRYSTAL CREEK RD ORO 103-C2
CRYSTAL HILLS CIR LVL 162-E3
CRYSTAL HILLS DR LVL 162-E3
CRYSTAL HILLS LN LVL 162-E3
CRYSTAL LAKE BLVD ROB 92-A3
CRYSTAL LAKE CIR BUR 162-D2
CRYSTAL LAKE RD E BUR 162-D2
CRYSTAL LAKE RD W BUR 162-C2
CRYSTAL LAKE TER BUR 162-D2
CRYSTAL VIEW CIR BUR 162-D2
CRYSTAL VIEW RD EPR 133-A2
CUB TRL VH 94-C1
CUDD AVE N RF 140-E2
CUDD AVE S RF 140-E2
CUDD CIR HUD 111-D3
CULLEN AVE MH 135-E1
CULLEN AVE SSP 122-D3
CULLEN ST STP 122-A2
CULLIGAN LN MH 121-D4
CULLIGAN WAY MTK ...118-E4,119-A4
CULVER AVE NW CMT 58-B2
CULVER AVE NW MLT 44-B3
CULVER RD GV 91-E4,92-A4
CUMBERLAND AVE RMT 163-E3
CUMBERLAND CT SVW 80-A4
CUMBERLAND RD EPR 132-E3
CUMBERLAND RD MOU 117-A2
CUMBERLAND RD MPL 120-B3
CUMBERLAND ST STP 108-A2
CUMBERLAND ST SVW 80-A3
CUMBERLAND TRL COR 61-D4
CUMMINGS LN AH 93-D2
CUNEEN CT IGH 136-E4,137-A3
CUNEEN TRL IGH 136-E4,137-A3
CURFEW ST STP 107-B3
CURRANT CIR RMT 163-E1
CURRANT PL EPR 132-B2
CURRELL BLVD WBY 123-D2
CURRIE AVE MPL 106-C2
CURRIE CT MPW 123-B2
CURRIE ST MPW 109-B2
CURRY CT ROG 61-D1
CURRY TRL EAG 149-E2,150-A2
CURTICE ST E STP 122-C2
CURTICE ST W STP 122-B2
CURTICE ST W WSP 122-B2
CURTIS AVE NW MLT 44-B3
CURTIS AVE NW SVT 16-B1
CURTIS LN EPR 132-D2
CURTIS RD CHM 63-C1
CURVE AVE EDI 120-A2
CURVE ST GRW 117-E3
CURVE ST MPW 108-E1
CURVE CREST BLVD SWR 96-D2
CURVE CREST BLVD W SWR 96-E2
CUSHING AVE NW MLT 44-B3
CUSHING AVE NW SVT 16-B2
CUSHING AVE SW MVT ...58-B4,86-B1
CUSHING CIR STP 107-E3
CUSTER AVE NW MLT 44-B3
CUSTER AVE NW SVT 16-B2
CUSTER TRL IGH 137-A4
CUTACROSS RD GV 105-E2
CUTLER ST STP 109-A4,123-A1
CUTOFF TRL RFD 74-B3
CUTTER ST ANO 49-C4
CUTTERS LN ANO 49-B4
CUTTERS LN EAG 149-D1
CUTTERS GROVE AVE ANO 49-B3
CYGNET PL ORO 103-C3
CYNTHIA DR MTK 118-C3
CYPRESS DR CHN 117-C4
CYPRESS DR WBY 123-C2
CYPRESS LN EPR 132-E2
CYPRESS LN MOU 116-E1
CYPRESS LN N MG 77-B4,91-B1
CYPRESS PT EAG 149-D3
CYPRESS ST HSN 48-B3
CYPRESS ST MPW 94-D4
CYPRESS ST STP 108-D3

D

D CT NE EB 37-D1
D ST HIL 92-E2
D ST MEN 121-D4
D ST WBY 123-D1
D N R RD COT 24-C4,52-A1
D N R RD LWT 24-C4
DAFFODIL PATH RMT 149-E4,163-E1
DAGUE AVE NE BUT 45-B4,59-B2
DAGUE AVE SE FKT 73-B4,87-B1
DAGUE AVE SE RFT 59-B4,73-B2
DAHL AVE CHC 26-B1
DAHL AVE MPW 123-B2
DAHL AVE STP 123-B2
DAHL CIR MPW 123-B2
DAHL CT MPW 123-B2
DAHL PL CHC 26-B1
DAHL RD ORO 103-B3
DAHLBERG DR GV 106-A2
DAHLGREN RD DAT 144-D4,145-A4
DAHLGREN RD MTK 118-E1,119-A1
DAHLIA CIR EPR 133-A3
DAHLIA CT RMT 163-E1
DAHLIA DR EB 37-D1
DAHLIA DR ROG 47-D4
DAHLIA ST MHT 95-D1
DAHLIA ST NW AND 50-A2
DAHLIA ST NW CR 64-A2
DAHLIA ST NW OG 22-A4,36-A2
DAHLIA ST NW SF 7-E4
DAHLIA ST NW STT 7-E1
DAHLIA WAY MHT 95-D1
DAHOMEY AVE WFT 205-E4,219-E1
DAHOMEY AVE W RMT 163-E2
DAILY RD HUT 98-A4,112-A1
DAISY CIR BLO 147-D1
DAISY CIR HUT 112-D1
DAISY CIR LYT 1-A4
DAISY CT NB 79-B3
DAISY CT RMT 163-E1
DAISY CT WBT 80-D2
DAKOTA AVE CHN 132-B2
DAKOTA AVE CRT 175-E2
DAKOTA AVE NM 189-E4
DAKOTA AVE NMT 189-E3,203-E2
DAKOTA AVE ORO 103-E1
DAKOTA AVE SAV 147-E4,161-E2
DAKOTA AVE WBY 123-E3
DAKOTA AVE S GV 105-E2
DAKOTA AVE S MON 86-C1
DAKOTA AVE S SLP 105-E4,119-E1
DAKOTA BLVD LVL 176-D3
DAKOTA CIR BLO 133-E4
DAKOTA CIR CHN 132-B1
DAKOTA CIR EPR 132-C2
DAKOTA CIR MPL 106-C2
DAKOTA CIR SHK 146-B3
DAKOTA CT BUR 148-E1
DAKOTA DR MH 121-E4
DAKOTA DR RMT 163-E3
DAKOTA LN CHN 132-B2
DAKOTA LN RMT 163-E3
DAKOTA PT SLW 173-A2
DAKOTA RD BLO 133-E4
DAKOTA RDG HUT 112-C2
DAKOTA ST LES 212-D3
DAKOTA ST PRE 167-B1
DAKOTA ST PRL 161-B3
DAKOTA ST WSP 122-B2
DAKOTA ST N SHK 146-B2
DAKOTA ST NW AND 35-D4,49-D1
DAKOTA ST S SHK 146-B2
DAKOTA ST W CF 208-B4
DAKOTA ST W VER 179-C2
DAKOTA TRL EDI 119-C4,133-C1
DAKOTA TRL PRL 160-E2
DAKOTA TRL E PRL 160-E2
DAKOTA TRL N PRL 160-E2
DAKOTA TRL S PRL 160-E2
DAKOTA TRL W PRL 160-E2
DAKOTAH ST NW AND 49-D2
DAKOTAH ST NW CR 63-D1
DAKOTAH ST NW OG 21-D2
DAKOTAH ST NW SF 7-D3
DALCHOW AVE WTT 101-E4,115-E1
DALE ALY SVW 94-A2
DALE AVE BUF 59-B1
DALE AVE DPH 118-B2
DALE AVE EDI 119-E3
DALE CT RVL 108-A1
DALE CT N SVW 80-A4
DALE CT S SVW 80-A4
DALE DR EDI 119-E3
DALE PL SSP 136-E1,137-A1
DALE RD MOU 117-A2
DALE RD WBY 137-E1,138-B1
DALE ST BEC 2-E4,3-A4
DALE ST SVW 94-A2
DALE ST E SSP 136-E1
DALE ST N RVL 94-A4,108-A1
DALE ST N STP 108-A3,122-A1
DALE ST N SVW 80-A4,94-A2
DALE ST S STP 122-A1
DALE ST W SSP 136-E1
DALE RD CT WBY 138-C1
DALEVIEW DR N BP 77-E3
DALLAGER WAY SWR 82-E4
DALLARA AVE W RMT 163-E2
DALLAS AVE FAR 177-E3
DALLAS AVE RMT 163-E1
DALLAS CT RMT 163-E1
DALLAS CT N MG 76-E3,90-E1
DALLAS LN N DAY 62-E3
DALLAS LN N MG 76-E3
DALLAS LN N PLY 90-E3
DALLAS RD BC 78-C3
DALLAS ST N RF 140-D1
DALLAS ST S RF 140-D2
DALLES DR SHK 146-C3
DALLY ST BUR 162-E3
DALRIDGE CIR BUR 149-A3
DALRYMPLE RD EDI 119-E3
DALTON AVE WT 204-A3,218-A3
DALTON AVE NE BUT 45-C3
DALTON AVE NE MOT 31-C1
DALTON AVE SE FKT 87-C1,101-B2
DALTON AVE SE RFT 73-C2
DALTON LN RMT 163-E1
DALY ST STP 122-A1
DAMASK AVE W RMT 163-E2
DAMASK CT RMT 163-E2
DAMPIER RD CHC 12-B4
DAN PATCH AVE FH 107-D2
DAN PATCH CT SAV 147-D4
DAN PATCH DR SAV 147-D4,161-D1
DAN PATCH LN SAV 147-D4,161-D1
DANA CIR WAC 129-D2
DANA CT NE FRI 79-A3
DANA DR BUR 148-B4
DANA DR MTK 118-E1
DANBURY AVE WFT 205-E3
DANBURY AVE W RMT 163-E2
DANBURY CRV SHK 147-A3
DANBURY CT EAG 149-E1
DANBURY CT RMT 163-E1
DANBURY PATH RMT 163-E1
DANBURY TRL EAG 135-E4,149-E1
DANBURY WAY MTK 105-A4
DANBURY WAY W RMT 149-E4
DANDER CT RMT 163-E1
DANE AVE RMT 163-E1
DANEL AVE RAN 207-A3
DANENS DR EDI 119-E4,133-E1
DANFORTH CIR LYT 1-A4
DANFORTH ST STP 108-A2
DANIEL CT SVW 80-A1
DANIEL DR BEL 186-A2
DANIEL DR EAG 149-E1,150-A2
DANIEL LN EPR 118-C4
DANIELLE DR MTK 118-C2
DANIELS ST LOL 103-D2
DANNER CT IGH 137-A3
DANNER PATH APV 149-E4
DANTON WAY EPR 132-C3
DANUBE CIR NE NP 202-A2
DANUBE CT APV 149-E4
DANUBE DR RFD 74-A4
DANUBE LN APV 149-E4
DANUBE LN RMT 149-E4,163-E1
DANUBE ST LL 52-B4
DANUBE ST NE LWT 10-B4
DANUBE ST NE OXT 10-B1
DANVILLE AVE CAT 205-E2
DANVILLE AVE W RMT 163-E2
DANVILLE CT RMT 163-E1
DAPHNE LN RMT 163-E1
DAPPLE CIR RMT 163-E3
DAPPLE CT RMT 163-E3
DARCY LN EDI 119-E4
DARDANELLE LN JT 145-E3
DARJEELING CT RMT 163-E2
DARJEELING PATH RMT 163-E2
DARK HORSE LAKE LN HMT 193-A1
DARLA CT WSP 122-B4
DARLENE ST STP 109-A1,123-A1
DARLING PATH RMT 163-E3
DARLINGTON AVE NE MOT 31-C3
DARLINGTON AVE SE FKT 87-C1
DARLINGTON AVE SE RFT 73-C2
DARNEL CT RMT 163-E1
DARNEL RD EPR 133-A3
DARRELL CT SWR 96-D1
DARRELL LN COR 62-A4
DARRICK RD CHS 145-D2
DARROW AVE NE BUT 45-C2
DARROW AVE NE MOT 31-C3
DARROW AVE SE FKT 87-C4,101-C1
DARROW AVE SE RFT 73-C2
DARSOW AVE VET 179-A4
DART AVE S SLP 120-A2
DARTFORD RD WBY 124-A3
DARTMOOR CT RMT 163-E2
DARTMOOR RD MHT 95-D1
DARTMOOR RD WIL 95-D1
DARTMOUTH AVE EPR 133-A3
DARTMOUTH AVE MPL 107-A3
DARTMOUTH CT EAG 150-B2
DARTMOUTH DR CHN 117-C4
DARTMOUTH DR MTK 118-C1
DARTMOUTH LN CHN 117-C4
DARTMOUTH PATH RMT 163-E1
DARTMOUTH PL MPL 107-A3
DARWIN WAY RMT 163-E1
DASSEL AVE WT 203-E3
DASSEL LN COR 62-A4
DATA PARK MTK 119-C4
DAVENPORT AVE EAG 149-C1
DAVENPORT AVE RMT 163-E2
DAVENPORT CIR EAG 149-C1
DAVENPORT CT RMT 163-E1
DAVENPORT PATH RMT 163-E1
DAVENPORT RD LYT 1-A3
DAVENPORT ST NE ATT 9-A2
DAVENPORT ST NE BLA ...65-A3,79-A1
DAVENPORT ST NE EB 9-A3,22-E2
DAVENPORT ST NE HL 37-A4,51-A2
DAVERN AVE NE BUT 45-C2
DAVERN AVE NE MOT 31-C3,45-C1
DAVERN ST STP 121-D2
DAVID AVE HBG 156-A2
DAVID CIR LC 94-C3
DAVID CT SVW 80-A1
DAVID ST STP 109-A2
DAVIDS CT BUR 162-B3
DAVIDSON AVE NE MOT ...31-C4,45-C1
DAVIDSON AVE SE FKT 87-C2
DAVIDSON AVE SE RFT 73-C3
DAVIDSON CT IGH 137-A3
DAVIS CT SHK 146-C3
DAVIS DR SLW 172-E2
DAVIS ST GRF 74-D3
DAVIS ST LES 212-C4
DAVIS ST STP 107-C3
DAVIS ST NW ER 20-B4,34-B1
DAVIS HALL NFD 219-E3
DAVISSON AVE RAN 207-A3
DAVY CT RMT 163-E1
DAWN AVE IGH 137-A3
DAWN AVE SVW 79-E4,80-B4
DAWN CIR AH 79-D4
DAWN CT IGH 137-A3
DAWN DR ANN 74-A2
DAWN DR MTK 118-D3
DAWN LN WBY 124-A1
DAWN WAY IGH 137-A2
DAWN WAY SSP 137-A2
DAWNVIEW DR CHS 145-D1
DAWNVIEW TER GV 91-E4,92-A4
DAWSON AVE IGH 137-A4
DAWSON AVE RAN 207-A3
DAWSON CT IGH 137-A4
DAWSON CT RMT 163-E2
DAWSON LN EDI 134-A1
DAWSON PL RMT 163-E2
DAY LN DPH 118-B1
DAY PL MTK 118-D1
DAY RD MPW 94-D4
DAY RD N SCF 14-C2
DAY CARE RD BUR 148-B4
DAY FARM RD TRT 125-E2,126-A3
DAYBREAK AVE RMT 163-E2
DAYLILY AVE N BP 78-A1
DAYLILY LN CHN 132-A4,146-A1
DAYTON AVE DAY 48-B1
DAYTON AVE SPP 137-C3
DAYTON AVE STP 107-C4,108-A4
DAYTON RD CHM 49-B4,63-B1
DAYTON ST DAY 48-B1
DAYTON ST MO 31-D2
DAYTON ST E ARL 183-A2
DAYTON RIVER RD DAY ...48-E3,49-A4
DAYTONA WAY RMT 163-E1
DCHENE CIR MTA 102-D3
DCHENE LN MTA 102-D3
DD ST WBL 80-D4
DE ANN CIR MTK 118-B3
DE LASALLE DR MPL 106-D2
DEADRICK AVE SE RFT 73-C2
DEALTON ST STP 121-E3
DEAN AVE E CHM 63-C1
DEAN AVE W CHM 63-C1
DEAN CT MPL 106-B4
DEAN LN IND 88-A4
DEAN PKWY MPL 106-B4
DEAN LAKE RD SHK 146-E3
DEANS DR LAT 202-A3
DEANS LAKE RD SHK 146-E3
DEARBORN CT EDI 119-C2
DEARBORN PATH RMT 163-E1
DEARBORN ST EDI 119-C2
DEAUVILLE DR MPW 94-D4
DEBBIE LN CAR 145-B4
DEBBIE LN EPR 132-B2
DEBORAH DR ORO 103-A2
DEBRA CIR SVW 80-A3
DEBRA CT SVW 80-A3
DEBRA LN SVW 80-A3
DEBRA ST WBL 80-E3
DECATUR AVE N BP 77-C4,91-C1
DECATUR AVE N GV 91-C4,105-C2
DECATUR AVE N NH 91-C3
DECATUR AVE S BLO 133-C3,147-C1
DECATUR AVE S SLP 105-C4
DECATUR CIR BLO 147-C1

DECATUR CT N NH ... 91-C3
DECATUR LN SLP ... 105-C4,119-C1
DECATUR PL N NH ... 91-C2
DECEMBER CT RMT ... 163-D2
DECEMBER LN RMT ... 163-E2
DECEMBER TRL RMT ... 163-E2
DECEMBER WAY RMT ... 163-E2
DECKER AVE BWT ... 219-B4
DECKER CT BWT ... 219-B3
DECORAH LN MH ... 136-A1
DECOURCY CIR STP ... 107-D3
DEE PL NE SLK ... 78-E1
DEEGAN AVE SE FKT ... 101-C2
DEEGAN AVE SE RFT ... 73-C2
DEEGAN DR SE RFT ... 59-C4,73-C1
DEEP LAKE RD N NO ... 80-C1
DEEP LAKE RD S NO ... 80-C2
DEEPHAVEN AVE DPH ... 118-B1
DEEPWOODS CT RMT ... 149-D4
DEER CT CV ... 66-D3
DEER LN NO ... 80-C3
DEER PATH EPR ... 133-B3
DEER PATH SWR ... 96-E1
DEER RD PRE ... 153-B4
DEER RDG BLA ... 65-B2
DEER RDG CHN ... 117-E4
DEER RDG HUT ... 97-D4
DEER ST MO ... 31-E3,32-A3
DEER TRL MGY ... 215-E4
DEER TRL WBY ... 137-D1
DEER TRL E SVW ... 80-A2
DEER TRL S SVW ... 80-A2
DEER TRL W SVW ... 80-A2
DEER CREEK CIR MTA ... 102-B4,116-B1
DEER CREEK PKWY BEL ... 186-A1
DEER CREEK PKWY MTK ... 104-D3
DEER CREEK RD MTA ... 102-B4
DEER CREEK RD W MTA ... 102-B3
DEER CREEK TRL E ORO ... 103-D3
DEER GARDEN LN CHC ... 26-A1
DEER HAVEN DR HUT ... 111-E2,112-A2
DEER HILL CT MTK ... 104-D3
DEER HILL DR MTK ... 104-E3
DEER HILLS CIR NO ... 80-D3
DEER HILLS CT NO ... 80-D3
DEER HILLS DR NO ... 80-D3
DEER HILLS TRL EAG ... 149-B2
DEER OAK RUN MHT ... 81-D4,95-D1
DEER PASS DR CV ... 66-E2
DEER PASS TRL LL ... 66-E4
DEER PATH CT SWR ... 96-E1
DEER PATH RD N NOH ... 97-D4,111-D1
DEER POND CIR EAG ... 135-C4
DEER POND CT N LE ... 95-E4
DEER POND TRL N LE ... 95-E4
DEER RIDGE LN BLO ... 133-D3
DEER RIDGE LN MPW ... 123-B2
DEER RIDGE LN MTK ... 119-B3
DEER RIDGE LN S MPW ... 123-B2
DEER RUN CT CRT ... 175-E1
DEER RUN DR VIC ... 130-E3,131-A3
DEER RUN RD HUT ... 97-E3
DEER RUN TRL ORO ... 103-C3
DEER RUN TRL WSP ... 122-B4
DEER TRAIL CIR WBY ... 137-D2
DEER TRAIL CT MH ... 122-A3
DEER TRAIL PT MH ... 122-A3
DEER VALLEY DR TRT ... 125-E2
DEER VALLEY LN WBY ... 124-B2
DEERBROOK DR CHN ... 132-B4
DEERCLIFF CT EAG ... 149-D1
DEERCLIFF LN EAG ... 149-D1
DEERFIELD DR MPW ... 109-B2
DEERFIELD RD WAC ... 129-D4
DEERFIELD RD WAT ... 101-B4
DEERFIELD TRL EPR ... 132-B1
DEERFOOT TRL CHN ... 132-B3
DEERHILL RD MED ... 103-E1
DEERRIDGE CT EAG ... 149-D1
DEERWOOD AVE CHM ... 63-B3
DEERWOOD CIR LL ... 66-B4
DEERWOOD CIR SCT ... 159-D4
DEERWOOD CIR N PLY ... 91-B1
DEERWOOD CT EAG ... 149-D1
DEERWOOD CT SSP ... 122-D4
DEERWOOD DR BUR ... 162-C2
DEERWOOD DR CHN ... 118-A4,132-A1
DEERWOOD DR CHS ... 145-D1
DEERWOOD DR DAY ... 62-B2
DEERWOOD DR EAG ... 149-D1
DEERWOOD DR MOU ... 116-D2
DEERWOOD DR MTK ... 118-E2,119-A2
DEERWOOD DR SSP ... 122-D4
DEERWOOD DR TRT ... 112-C4
DEERWOOD DR NE HL ... 36-E3
DEERWOOD LN EAG ... 149-D1
DEERWOOD LN LL ... 66-B4
DEERWOOD LN SCT ... 159-D4
DEERWOOD LN N DAY ... 63-A1
DEERWOOD LN N MG ... 63-A4,77-B4
DEERWOOD LN N PLY ... 91-B1,105-B2
DEERWOOD LN NE EB ... 37-A2
DEERWOOD PATH EAG ... 149-D1
DEERWOOD PL EAG ... 149-D1
DEERWOOD RD DAT ... 158-D2
DEERWOOD TRL EAG ... 149-D1
DEGARDNER CIR NW SF ... 7-D3
DEGRIO WAY IGH ... 137-A3
DEHNSFIELD RD HSN ... 48-B3
DEHRER CT IGH ... 137-A3
DEHRER WAY IGH ... 137-A3
DEJON CT WBY ... 109-D4
DEKALB AVE RMT ... 163-E1
DEL DR N NH ... 91-C2
DEL OTERO AVE SPR ... 117-B1
DEL RIO DR CHN ... 132-A2
DELALB AVE RMT ... 163-E1
DELANCEY CT BWT ... 219-B3
DELANDER DR TRT ... 125-D4
DELANEY AVE IGH ... 137-A2
DELANEY AVE E IGH ... 137-A2
DELANEY BLVD EDI ... 133-D2
DELANEY CIR IGH ... 137-A4
DELANEY CT IGH ... 137-A4
DELANEY WAY IGH ... 137-A2
DELANEY WAY E IGH ... 137-A2
DELANO AVE MP ... 88-E4,102-E1
DELANO AVE WT ... 203-E3
DELANO CIR IGH ... 137-A3
DELANO CT IGH ... 137-A3
DELANO CT SWR ... 96-C2
DELANO DR SWR ... 96-C2
DELANO PL STP ... 121-C2
DELANO ST NE MPL ... 107-B1
DELANO WAY IGH ... 137-A3
DELANO WAY SWR ... 96-C2
DELARMA DR SFT ... 159-A3
DELAROSA CT IGH ... 137-A2
DELAWARE AVE BLA ... 79-B1
DELAWARE AVE BPT ... 186-E2
DELAWARE AVE EAG ... 136-B2
DELAWARE AVE MH ... 122-B3,136-B1
DELAWARE AVE NSP ... 95-B3
DELAWARE AVE SLW ... 172-E3,186-E1
DELAWARE AVE STP ... 122-B2
DELAWARE CT MH ... 136-B1
DELAWARE ST SE LON ... 217-B2
DELAWARE ST SE MPL ... 107-A3
DELAWARE ST SW LON ... 217-B2
DELFT AVE CAT ... 205-E2
DELFT AVE W RMT ... 163-E2
DELILAH AVE IGH ... 137-A2
DELINA CT LL ... 66-E4
DELL CT N WBL ... 95-A2
DELL CT S WBL ... 95-A2
DELL DR EPR ... 132-C4
DELL LN MTK ... 118-C3
DELL LN S WBY ... 109-C4
DELL PL MPL ... 106-C3
DELL RD CHN ... 132-C2
DELL RD EPR ... 118-B4,132-C3
DELL ST WBL ... 94-E2,95-A2
DELLA LN LL ... 52-B4,66-B1
DELLRIDGE AVE STP ... 123-B1
DELLRIDGE RD BLO ... 134-E4
DELLVIEW AVE AH ... 93-C1
DELLWOOD AVE AH ... 93-D2
DELLWOOD AVE DWD ... 81-C3
DELLWOOD AVE RVL ... 93-D3,107-D1
DELLWOOD AVE SVW ... 79-D1
DELLWOOD CRV DWD ... 81-C3
DELLWOOD CRV LFL ... 109-C4
DELLWOOD CT RMT ... 163-E1
DELLWOOD DR NE FRI ... 78-E3
DELLWOOD LN LFL ... 109-C4
DELLWOOD LN SWD ... 117-A3
DELLWOOD PL STP ... 108-C3
DELLWOOD RD N DWD ... 81-C3
DELLWOOD RD N GRA ... 81-D3,82-B4
DELLWOOD RD N SWR ... 83-A4
DELLWOOD RD N SWT ... 82-E4,83-A4
DELLWOOD SQ E LFL ... 109-C4
DELLWOOD SQ N LFL ... 109-C4
DELLWOOD SQ S LFL ... 109-C4
DELLWOOD ST AH ... 79-D4
DELLWOOD ST RVL ... 93-D4
DELLWOOD WAY RMT ... 163-E1
DELLWOOD ROAD CT N GRA ... 81-E3
DELLWOOD ROAD LN N GRA ... 82-A3
DELMAR AVE HAT ... 187-B3,201-B1
DELMAR AVE SCT ... 173-B4,187-B1
DELMAR CT RMT ... 163-D2
DELMAR ST OSC ... 28-A4
DELONG RD SMT ... 55-C3
DELOS ST E STP ... 122-C1
DELOS ST W STP ... 122-C1
DELPHINUM LN CHN ... 132-A4
DELTA AVE MTK ... 105-B4,119-B1
DELTA AVE RMT ... 163-D1
DELTA CT RMT ... 163-D1
DELTA PL RMT ... 163-D1
DELTA DENTAL RD EAG ... 135-C4
DELTON AVE MTK ... 118-B3
DELWOOD RD N DWD ... 81-C3
DEMAR AVE SVW ... 94-B1
DEMONT AVE MPW ... 94-D4
DEMONT AVE E LC ... 94-B4
DEMONT AVE W LC ... 94-B4
DEMONTREVILLE TRL N LE ... 95-D3
DEMONTREVILLE TRAIL CIR N LE 95-D3
DEMONTREVILLE TRAIL PL N LE .95-D3
DEMPSEY AVE WAV ... 72-A4
DEMPSEY AVE NW CMT ... 58-B2
DEMPSEY AVE NW MLT ... 30-B4,44-B1
DEMPSEY AVE NW SVT ... 16-B4
DEMPSEY AVE SW MVT ... 58-B4,72-B2
DEMPSEY AVE SW WAV ... 72-A4,86-A1
DEMPSEY AVE SW WDT ... 86-B2
DEMPSEY WAY IGH ... 137-A3
DEN RD EPR ... 133-B2
DENBIGH RD MOU ... 117-A2
DENESE ST PRL ... 161-D2
DENMARK AVE EAG ... 135-D4,149-D1
DENMARK AVE EUT ... 191-D2,205-E1
DENMARK AVE FAR ... 177-D4,191-D1
DENMARK AVE W APV ... 149-D4
DENMARK CT APV ... 163-D2
DENMARK CT EAG ... 135-D4
DENMARK CT E EAG ... 135-D4
DENMARK TRL EAG ... 135-D4
DENNESON AVE NW MLT ... 44-B2
DENNIS LN CHS ... 145-D1
DENNIS LN MPW ... 109-B4,123-B1
DENNIS LN WBL ... 95-A1
DENNIS ST N MPW ... 109-B2
DENNIS ST S MPW ... 123-B2
DENNISON AVE SVW ... 80-A4
DENSLOW ST STP ... 108-A3
DENT AVE WT ... 203-E4,217-E1
DENTON WAY IGH ... 137-A3
DENVER CT ER ... 19-C4
DENVER CT RMT ... 163-D2
DENVER ST ER ... 19-C4
DENVER ST NW ER ... 19-C4,33-C2
DEPAUL ST NE LWT ... 10-C3
DEPOT DR WAC ... 129-D3
DEPOT ST MPL ... 106-B4
DEPOT ST OSC ... 27-E4
DEPOT ST SOM ... 84-B1
DEPPE ST WSP ... 122-B2
DEPUE DR CHM ... 49-B4
DERBY AVE MPL ... 120-E3
DERBY CIR RMT ... 163-E2
DERBY CT EPR ... 132-C3
DERBY CT RMT ... 163-E2
DERBY DR CHN ... 132-A1
DERBY LN SHK ... 147-B3
DERBY LN WIL ... 95-D1
DERRYGLENN CT APV ... 149-E4
DERRYMOOR CT APV ... 149-D4
DESHON AVE SW MVT ... 58-A4,86-A1
DESHON AVE SW WDT ... -A2
DESIREE ST CHN ... 145-E2
DESNOYER AVE STP ... 107-B4
DESOTO AVE NW MLT ... 44-A2
DESOTO AVE SW MVT ... 58-A4,72-A3
DESOTO ST LC ... 94-C3
DESOTO ST MPW ... 94-C4,108-C1
DESOTO ST STP ... 108-C3
DESOTO ST VH ... 80-C4
DESSA LN SSP ... 122-D4
DEUBENER PL STP ... 121-E1
DEUCE RD NMT ... 190-C4,204-C1
DEVANEY ST SLP ... 119-E2
DEVEAU PL MTK ... 118-D1
DEVER DR EDI ... 120-A3
DEVILLE DR EDI ... 119-C3
DEVIN LN ORO ... 103-D2
DEVIN LN SHK ... 147-B3
DEVINE AVE BWT ... 219-B3
DEVITT AVE NW MLT ... 44-A2
DEVITT AVE NW SVT ... 16-A2
DEVITT AVE SW MVT ... 72-A3,86-A1
DEVON DR MTK ... 118-D2
DEVON LN MOU ... 117-A2
DEVONSHIRE AVE FAR ... 177-E3
DEVONSHIRE CIR BLO ... 148-C1
DEVONSHIRE CIR SWD ... 118-A2
DEVONSHIRE CIR WBY ... 123-C3
DEVONSHIRE CRV BLO ... 148-C1
DEVONSHIRE DR CHN ... 117-E4,118-A4
DEVONSHIRE DR NYA ... 142-C3
DEVONSHIRE DR WBY ... 123-C3
DEVONSHIRE LN BLO ... 148-C1
DEVONSHIRE PL EPR ... 147-B1
DEVONSHIRE PL WBY ... 123-C3
DEVONSHIRE RD BLO ... 148-C1
DEW DROP CT CNC ... 12-D4
DEW DROP LN CNC ... 12-E4
DEWBERRY CT RMT ... 163-D2
DEWERFF ST WSP ... 122-B2
DEWEY CT EPR ... 132-C3
DEWEY LN LAT ... 201-B3
DEWEY ST STP ... 107-C4,121-C1
DEWEY ST NW BET ... 8-D3
DEWEY HILL CIR EDI ... 133-D1
DEWEY HILL RD EDI ... 133-D1
DEWITTE AVE PRL ... 160-E4
DEXTER DR LOL ... 103-E2
DEXTER LN MOU ... 117-A2
DEXTER ST LES ... 212-D4
DEXTER ST PRE ... 153-B4,167-B1
DEXTER ST S PRE ... 167-B1
DIAGONAL BLVD RCH ... 134-E1
DIAMOND CT APV ... 149-C4
DIAMOND CT SHK ... 146-D3
DIAMOND DR BUR ... 149-A3
DIAMOND DR EAG ... 149-B1
DIAMOND DR HUD ... 111-E2
DIAMOND DR MO ... 31-D3
DIAMOND LN MOU ... 116-E1
DIAMOND PATH APV ... 149-D4,163-D1
DIAMOND PATH RMT ... 163-D3
DIAMOND PT EAG ... 149-B1
DIAMOND WAY BKR ... 3-E4
DIAMOND EIGHT TER SA ... 93-B3
DIAMOND LAKE LN MPL ... 120-D4
DIAMOND LAKE RD E MPL ... 120-D3
DIAMOND LAKE RD N DAY ... 48-D3
DIAMOND LAKE RD S CHM ... 49-B4
DIAMOND LAKE RD S DAY .48-C4,49-A4
DIAMOND LAKE RD S ROG .47-E4,48-A4
DIAMOND LAKE RD W MPL ... 120-C3
DIAMOND PATH CT APV ... 163-D1
DIANE AVE BEC ... 2-D3
DIANE CT LL ... 52-B4
DIANE DR MTK ... 119-A2
DIANE RD MH ... 121-E3
DIANE ST LL ... 52-B4
DIANNA LN N LC ... 94-C4
DIANNE ST NSP ... 95-A3
DIARMID CIR HUT ... 112-D1
DICKENS LN MOU ... 116-D2
DICKENS LN MV ... 79-B3
DICKENSON ST ORO ... 103-E3
DICKEY LAKE DR ORO ... 103-D2
DICKMAN AVE RAN ... 207-A3
DICKMAN AVE RAT ... 207-A2
DICKMAN TRL IGH ... 137-A3
DICKSON AVE IGH ... 137-A3
DICKSON AVE SPR ... 117-B1
DICKSON CIR IGH ... 137-A3
DICKSON RD MTK ... 118-E3
DIEDRICH DR CAR ... 145-B4
DIEGO LN MH ... 122-B2
DIETER ST MPW ... 108-E1
DIETER ST STP ... 108-E2
DIFFLEY RD BUR ... 149-A1
DIFFLEY RD EAG ... 149-D1,150-A1
DIGHT AVE MPL ... 121-A1
DILLEY AVE IGH ... 137-A2
DILLON AVE NW CMT ... 58-A2
DILLON AVE NW MLT ... 44-A3,58-A1
DILLON AVE NW SVT ... 30-A2
DILLON ST WBL ... 80-E3
DILLON ST WBT ... 80-E3
DIMAGGIO ST NE COT ... 38-E3
DINSMORE AVE RAN ... 207-A3
DIONNE AVE RVL ... 108-A1
DIONNE ST RVL ... 107-E1
DIRECT RIVER DR NW CR ... 63-E2,64-A2
DIRK DR BKR ... 17-D1
DISCOVERY RD EAG ... 135-E3
DISTAD PATH RAN ... 207-A3
DISTEL DR LES ... 212-C4
DISTRICT OFFICE DR APV ... 163-D1
DIVERS PATH RAN ... 207-A3
DIVINITY LN EPR ... 132-E1,133-A1
DIVISION AVE WBL ... 81-A3
DIVISION AVE WBT ... 81-A2
DIVISION CT LS ... 111-C4
DIVISION CT WBL ... 81-A3
DIVISION ST BUF ... 58-E2,59-A2
DIVISION ST DAY ... 48-B1
DIVISION ST EDI ... 119-E2
DIVISION ST EXC ... 117-E3
DIVISION ST FAR ... 177-E4
DIVISION ST HOP ... 119-D1
DIVISION ST HUD ... 111-C2
DIVISION ST LES ... 212-D3
DIVISION ST LLD ... 111-C4
DIVISION ST LS ... 111-C4
DIVISION ST NFD ... 219-E3
DIVISION ST RAN ... 207-A3
DIVISION ST SLP ... 119-D1
DIVISION ST SOM ... 70-B4
DIVISION ST SWD ... 117-E3
DIVISION ST WBL ... 81-A3
DIVISION ST WLT ... 111-B4
DIVISION ST E ML ... 43-D2
DIVISION ST E RF ... 140-E1
DIVISION ST E RFT ... 59-D3,60-D3
DIVISION ST N MPW ... 95-B3
DIVISION ST N NSP ... 95-B4,109-B1
DIVISION ST S NFD ... 219-D4
DIVISION ST W ML ... 43-D2
DIVISION ST W MVT ... 58-C3
DIVISION ST W RF ... 140-D1
DIXIE AVE IGH ... 137-A2
DIXIE AVE RAN ... 207-A3
DIXIE AVE RAT ... 207-A4
DIXON AVE BWT ... 219-B3
DIXON DR BLO ... 134-B2
DIXON ST SPP ... 137-C3
DNR RD ORT ... 4-E3,5-A3
DO LITTLE DR MTK ... 119-A1
DOANE AVE STP ... 107-B4
DOANE TRL IGH ... 137-A4
DOCTOR JUSTUS
OHAGE BLVD STP ... 122-B1
DODD BLVD APV ... 163-D2
DODD BLVD EUT ... 190-D3
DODD BLVD IGH ... 136-B4
DODD BLVD LVL ... 163-B4,176-E2
DODD BLVD NMT ... 190-D4,204-D1
DODD BLVD RMT ... 150-A4,163-E2
DODD CT RMT ... 150-A4
DODD LN EAG ... 136-A3
DODD LN LVL ... 163-C3
DODD RD EAG ... 136-A2,150-A2
DODD RD MH ... 122-A4,136-A1
DODD RD STP ... 122-C2
DODD RD WSP ... 122-B2
DODGE CIR ER ... 19-E4
DODGE LN MH ... 122-B4
DODGE ST ER ... 19-E4
DODGE ST NW ER ... 19-E4,33-E1
DOE CIR WBT ... 80-D4
DOFFING AVE IGH ... 137-A2
DOFFING AVE VET ... 179-A3
DOGWOOD AVE CHN ... 117-C4
DOGWOOD AVE N BP ... 78-A1
DOGWOOD AVE N MYR ... 114-E4
DOGWOOD AVE NW SM ... 46-E3
DOGWOOD CIR EPR ... 133-B4
DOGWOOD CIR NW SM ... 46-E3
DOGWOOD CT NW SM ... 46-E3
DOGWOOD LN NO ... 80-C3
DOGWOOD RD CHN ... 131-C1
DOGWOOD RD EB ... 37-D1
DOGWOOD ST GRF ... 74-C4,88-C1
DOGWOOD ST NW AND ... 36-D3,50-D1
DOGWOOD ST NW BET ... 8-D3
DOGWOOD ST NW CR ... 64-D2
DOGWOOD ST NW LON ... 217-B2
DOGWOOD ST NW OG ... 22-D4,36-D1
DOGWOOD ST NW SF ... 8-D2
DOLOMITE DR EAG ... 149-B1
DOLOMITE ST NW BT ... 35-A1
DOLOMITE ST NW RAM ... 35-A4,49-A3
DOLORES LN EAG ... 149-D3
DOLPHIN DR MPW ... 109-B2
DOLPHIN ST NW STT ... 6-D1
DOMES ALY SVW ... 79-E3,80-A3
DOMINICA AVE APV ... 163-D1
DOMINICA AVE WFT ... 219-D2
DOMINICA CT APV ... 163-D2
DOMINICA WAY W APV .149-D4,163-D1
DOMINICK CIR MTK ... 119-A2
DOMINICK DR MTK ... 119-A3
DOMINICK SPUR MTK ... 119-A3
DOMINICK WAY MTK ... 119-A2
DOMINION DR HUD ... 111-D3
DOMINION LN SHK ... 146-C4,160-C1
DONA LN GV ... 91-E4,92-A4
DONALD AVE EAG ... 135-C3
DONALD CT EAG ... 135-C3
DONALD DR MOU ... 117-A2
DONALDSON ST CF ... 208-B3
DONBUSH RD NO ... 80-B3
DONCASTER WAY EDI ... 119-D3
DONCASTER WAY WBY ... 110-A4
DONEGAL ALC WBY ... 123-E1
DONEGAL BAY WBY ... 123-E1
DONEGAL CIR SVW ... 80-A2
DONEGAL CRV EPR ... 132-C2
DONEGAL CT EAG ... 149-C1
DONEGAL CT HUD ... 111-E2
DONEGAL CT SVW ... 80-A2
DONEGAL DR BUR ... 148-C4
DONEGAL DR SVW ... 80-A2
DONEGAL DR WBY ... 123-E2
DONEGAL PL WIL ... 95-D2
DONEGAL WAY EAG ... 149-C1
DONEGAL WAY HUD ... 111-E2
DONLEA LN EPR ... 133-A1
DONNA CT BL ... 18-B4
DONNELLY AVE HMT ... 193-A4,207-A1
DONNELLY AVE IGH ... 137-A2
DONNELLY AVE NIT ... 152-B3
DONNELLY AVE RMT ... 165-A3
DONNELLY AVE VET ... 179-A3
DONNELLY DR NW MLT ... 43-E3,44-B2
DONNELLY ST BEC ... 2-E4
DONOHUE AVE STP ... 107-D4
DOOVER LN MHT ... 95-C1
DORA CT E STP ... 108-E4
DORA CT W STP ... 108-E4
DORA LN STP ... 108-E4
DORAL RD DWD ... 81-C2
DORCHESTER CIR IGH ... 137-A3
DORCHESTER CT APV ... 149-D4
DORCHESTER CT EAG ... 150-B2
DORCHESTER CT WBY ... 124-A4
DORCHESTER DR WBY ... 124-A4
DORCHESTER RD MOU ... 117-A2
DORCHESTER TRL APV ... 149-D4
DORIANN CT EPR ... 132-D1
DORIS AVE SVW ... 79-E1,80-A1
DORLAND CT MPW ... 123-B1
DORLAND DR MPW ... 123-B1
DORLAND LN MPW ... 123-B1
DORLAND PL MPW ... 123-B1
DORLAND RD MPW ... 95-B3,123-B2
DORLAND RD S MPW ... 123-B3
DORMAN AVE MPL ... 107-B4
DORON DR EDI ... 119-D4
DORON LN EDI ... 119-D4
DOROTHEA AVE STP ... 121-C3
DOROTHEA LN MTK ... 105-B4
DOROTHY AVE WBL ... 95-B1
DOROTHY DR ROG ... 47-E4
DOROTHY DR VH ... 94-C1
DORSET LN EPR ... 133-C4
DORSET LN WBY ... 124-B3
DORSET RD MH ... 122-B3
DORSEY DR HUT ... 112-A1
DORTHY LN NM ... 190-A4,204-A1
DORWIN RD HUT ... 112-A2
DORY AVE APV ... 149-D4
DORY CT APV ... 163-D2
DOSWELL AVE STP ... 107-B2
DOTTE CT WBL ... 95-A1
DOTTE DR WBL ... 95-A1
DOUBLE EAGLE LN WBY ... 124-B2
DOUGLAS AVE GV ... 105-E3,106-A3
DOUGLAS AVE MPL ... 106-C3
DOUGLAS AVE RAN ... 207-A3
DOUGLAS AVE WT ... 203-E3
DOUGLAS AVE NW MLT ... 44-A2
DOUGLAS AVE NW SVT ... 30-A1
DOUGLAS AVE SW MVT ... 72-A3

DOUGLAS AVE SW WDT .... -A2
DOUGLAS CIR N BP 77-D2
DOUGLAS CIR NW BT 21-B3
DOUGLAS CT ANO 49-B4
DOUGLAS CT MH 121-E4
DOUGLAS CT N BP 77-D2
DOUGLAS CT N CHM 63-D3
DOUGLAS DR BUF 45-B4
DOUGLAS DR EPR 132-C3
DOUGLAS DR HAS 166-E3
DOUGLAS DR ROG 61-E1,62-A1
DOUGLAS DR WAV 85-E1
DOUGLAS DR N BP 63-D3,77-D3
DOUGLAS DR N CHM 63-D3
DOUGLAS DR N CRY 91-E3
DOUGLAS DR N GV 91-E4,105-E1
DOUGLAS LN WBL 81-A4
DOUGLAS LN N BP 77-D2
DOUGLAS RD MH 121-E4,122-A4
DOUGLAS ST ANO 49-C4
DOUGLAS ST HMT 193-E2
DOUGLAS ST NT 193-E2
DOUGLAS ST STP 122-B1
DOUGLAS ST E BUF 59-A2
DOUGLAS ST E SSP 136-E1
DOUGLAS ST W ARL 183-A2
DOUGLAS ST W BUF 59-A2
DOUGLAS ST W SSP 136-E1
DOUGLYNN DR MTK 119-A3
DOUGLYNN LN STP 123-B3
DOUSMAN ST STP 122-B1
DOVE CIR OTS 33-E4
DOVE CT CHN 132-A3
DOVE CT PRL 161-B2
DOVE LN MOU 103-A4,117-A1
DOVE LN NO 80-C4
DOVE TRL APV 163-D2
DOVE TRL BUF 45-B4
DOVER CRV EPR 132-C2
DOVER CT APV 149-D4
DOVER DR APV 149-D4
DOVER ST NE FRI 78-C2
DOVRE DR EDI 119-C3
DOW ST N CF 208-A4
DOWELL AVE IGH 137-A3
DOWLIN ST N CHM 63-C1
DOWLING AVE N MPL 92-B3
DOWLING ST MPL 121-B1
DOWN RD EDI 133-D1
DOWNERS DR SA 93-B3
DOWNEY TRL APV 149-D4
DOWNING AVE SHK 146-C3
DOWNING ST MH 122-A2
DOWNS AVE E MPW 108-B1
DOWNS RD CHM 63-C1
DOYLE PATH RMT 151-A4
DOYLE TRL RAN 207-A3
DOYLES CT APV 149-C4
DOYLES RD RW 196-D3
DRAGONFLY CT SLP 120-A1
DRAKE ALC WBY 123-D1
DRAKE AVE NW PRL 161-A3
DRAKE BAY WBY 123-D1
DRAKE CIR BL 17-E3
DRAKE CT CHN 132-A3
DRAKE CT ROG 48-A4
DRAKE DR EAG 149-C2
DRAKE DR IND 102-E1
DRAKE PATH APV 163-D1
DRAKE RD GV 91-E4,92-A4
DRAKE RD WBY 123-D1
DRAKE ST CR 50-B4,64-B2
DRAKE ST MP 89-A4
DRAKE ST STP 122-A2
DRAKE ST NW AND 36-B4,50-B2
DRAKE ST NW CR 50-B4,64-B3
DRAKE ST NW OG 22-B1
DRAKE ST NW SF 8-B4
DRAPER AVE RVL 107-C1
DRAPER DR RVL 107-C1
DRAW BRIDGE DR FAT 41-C2
DREAM LN WTT 101-C4
DRESDEN AVE APV 163-D2
DRESDEN AVE NFD 219-D3
DRESDEN CIR CHS 145-C1
DRESDEN CT APV 163-D1
DRESDEN CT CHS 145-B1
DRESDEN CT EAG 135-D4
DRESDEN DR CHS 145-C1
DRESDEN LN GV 106-A1
DRESDEN TRL APV 163-D2
DRESDEN WAY APV 163-D2
DRESDEN WAY EAG 135-D4
DRESSEN CIR EPR 132-D3
DRESSER ST DRS 28-D2
DREW AVE EKO 204-B1
DREW AVE N BC 78-A4,92-A2
DREW AVE N BP 78-A3
DREW AVE N ROB 92-A4
DREW AVE N VER 179-D2
DREW AVE S BLO 134-A4,148-A1
DREW AVE S EDI 120-A3
DREW AVE S MPL 106-A3,120-A2
DREW AVE S SLP 106-A3
DREW CIR BLO 134-A4,148-A2
DREWRY ST STP 108-C3
DREXEL AVE EDI 120-A2
DREXEL AVE GVT 205-D3
DREXEL AVE HAT 187-E3,201-E1
DREXEL CT APV 163-D1
DREXEL CT EAG 135-D4
DREXEL CT EPR 132-C2
DREXEL WAY APV 163-D2
DRIFTWOOD CIR BL 18-B4
DRIFTWOOD CIR NB 93-A1
DRIFTWOOD CT APV 149-D4
DRIFTWOOD CT NB 93-A1
DRIFTWOOD LN APV 149-D4,163-D1
DRIFTWOOD LN MOU 117-A1
DRIFTWOOD LN SWR 96-D2
DRIFTWOOD RD EPR 119-B4
DRIFTWOOD RD LYT 1-A4
DRIFTWOOD RD NB 93-A1
DRILLANE CIR HOP 119-B1
DRILLANE RD HOP 119-B1
DRILLANE RD N HOP 119-B1
DRILLANE RD S HOP 119-B1
DRISCOLL CIR NW RAM 34-C4
DRISCOLL ST NW RAM 34-C3
DRIVING PARK RD SWR 96-E2
DROMMOND TRL APV 163-D1
DROVER TRL HUT 98-C4
DRU DR HUT 112-B2
DRUID LN MTK 118-C1
DRUMCLIFFE WAY RMT 149-E4
DRUMLIN CT APV 163-D2
DRUMMOND RD MOU 117-A2
DRURY LN MOU 117-A2
DRY RUN RD TRT 140-D1
DUBARRY TRL VET 179-A3
DUBLIN CIR EDI 133-D1
DUBLIN CT APV 163-D1
DUBLIN DR FAR 177-D3
DUBLIN DR MTK 118-C2
DUBLIN LN SHK 146-C3
DUBLIN RD APV 163-D1
DUBLIN RD EDI 133-D1
DUBLIN RD SE PRL 161-B4
DUBLIN TRL SHK 146-C3
DUBLIN TRL W SHK 146-C3
DUBUQUE ST E SWR 97-A2
DUCHESS LN APV 163-A2
DUCHESS ST STP 108-D3
DUCK LN SCT 159-B4,173-B1
DUCK LAKE RD EPR 118-C4,132-C1
DUCK LAKE TRL EPR 118-B4,132-C1
DUCK PASS RD NO 80-C3
DUCK POND DR WSP 122-C4
DUCKWOOD DR EAG 135-D4
DUCKWOOD TRL EAG 135-E4
DUCKWOOD TRL WBY 123-E1,124-A1
DUDLEY AVE FH 107-C2
DUDLEY AVE STP 107-C2
DUDLEY AVE SVW 94-A1
DUDLEY AVE N CRY 91-D1
DUEN WAY CP 65-E3
DUFFEE DR LL 52-C4,66-C1
DUFFERIN CT SAV 161-E2
DUFFERIN DR SAV 161-E2,162-A2
DUFFIELD AVE NW SVT 16-A4,29-E1
DUFFNEY CIR COR 75-E1
DUFFNEY DR COR 75-E1
DUGGAN PLZ EDI 133-E1
DUININCK RD HAN 61-A3
DUKE DR MTK 118-E2
DUKE DR NE BLA 50-E4,64-E1
DUKE ST STP 122-A1
DULCIMER WAY APV 163-D1
DULUTH AVE PRL 161-B3
DULUTH CIR APV 163-D1
DULUTH CT APV 163-D1
DULUTH CT MPW 94-D3
DULUTH DR APV 163-D1
DULUTH LN GV 105-E1
DULUTH PL MPW 94-D4
DULUTH ST GV 105-E1
DULUTH ST MPW 94-D3,108-D1
DULUTH ST STP 108-D3
DUMAS AVE MTK 118-C3
DUNBAR AVE APV 163-D2
DUNBAR AVE FAR 177-D3
DUNBAR AVE GVT 205-D2
DUNBAR BLVD APV 163-D2
DUNBAR CT APV 163-D2
DUNBAR CT N BP 78-A2
DUNBAR KNL N BP 78-A1
DUNBAR KNLS MHT 95-C2
DUNBAR WAY APV 163-D1
DUNBAR WAY MHT 95-C2
DUNBAR KNOLL CIR N BP 78-A1
DUNBAR KNOLL CT BP 78-A1
DUNBERRY CIR EAG 149-D2
DUNBERRY CIR EPR 133-C4
DUNBERRY LN EAG 149-D2
DUNBERRY LN EDI 133-E1,134-A1
DUNBURY AVE FAR 177-D2
DUNBURY RD WAC 129-C3
DUNCAN AVE RAN 207-B3
DUNCAN CT RAN 207-B3
DUNCAN LN EDI 119-C3
DUNCRAIG RD EDI 119-E3
DUNDAS BLVD BWT 219-C4
DUNDAS BLVD NFD 219-C4
DUNDAS CIR MO 31-D2
DUNDAS RD MO 31-D2
DUNDEE ALC BLT 17-E2
DUNDEE AVE APV 163-D2
DUNDEE CT APV 163-D2
DUNDEE LN MOU 117-A2
DUNDEE PL SWR 96-E1
DUNDEE RD EDI 119-D3
DUNHAM DR ANO 49-C3
DUNHAM DR EDI 133-E1,134-A1
DUNHILL LN WBY 124-A3
DUNHILL RD EPR 119-B4
DUNIBER RIDGE RD MTK 118-C2
DUNKIRK AVE PRL 161-A4
DUNKIRK CT PLY 90-C3
DUNKIRK CT NE BLA 65-B4
DUNKIRK LN BLA 65-B4
DUNKIRK LN MG 76-C1
DUNKIRK LN N MG 62-C3,76-C2
DUNKIRK LN N PLY 90-C3,104-C1
DUNKIRK ST BLA 65-B4
DUNKIRK ST NE BLA 51-B4,65-B2
DUNKIRK ST NE HL 37-B4
DUNLAP AVE LEX 65-D4
DUNLAP AVE N SVW 79-D2
DUNLAP ST N AH 93-D1
DUNLAP ST N RVL 93-E4,107-E1
DUNLAP ST N STP 107-E4,121-E1
DUNLAP ST S STP 121-E1
DUNLIN CT APV 163-D2
DUNMORE RD WBY 123-D2
DUNROVIN LN EAG 149-D2
DUNSHEATH RD WBY 123-C3
DUNSMORE DR WAC 129-C2
DUNWOOD TRL APV 163-D2
DUNWOODY AVE MPL 106-C3
DUNWOODY AVE ORO 117-B1
DUPONT AVE NMT 190-C4,204-C1
DUPONT AVE N BC 78-C4,92-C1
DUPONT AVE N BP 78-C2
DUPONT AVE N MPL 92-C4,106-C1
DUPONT AVE S BLO 134-C3,148-C1
DUPONT AVE S BUR 148-C3,162-C3
DUPONT AVE S MPL 106-C4,120-C2
DUPONT AVE S RCH 120-C4,134-C1
DUPONT CT APV 163-D2
DUPONT CT N BP 78-C2
DUPONT LN LL 52-B4
DUPONT PATH APV 163-D2
DUPONT RD BLO 148-C1
DUPONT ST LOL 103-D2
DUPRE RD CV 66-D2
DURAM CT EPR 133-A3
DURANGO PL APV 149-D4
DURANGO PT LL 66-C4
DURANT DR ATT 9-D1
DURANT DR NE ATT 9-C1
DURANT ST NE ATT 9-D2
DURANT ST NE EB 9-D4,23-D2
DURANT ST NE HL 37-D3,51-D2
DURHAM CT APV 163-D2
DURHAM CT EAG 149-B1
DURHAM RD MTK 118-E2
DURHAM WAY APV 149-D4
DURNING AVE APV 163-D2
DUSHARME DR BC 92-A2
DUSTIN RD CHS 145-D2
DUSTY DR MED 89-E4,103-E1
DUTCH AVE PRL 161-A3
DUTCH CT APV 149-D4
DUTCH LN MOU 116-D1
DUTCH LAKE TRL HWL 85-A2
DUTCHESS CT APV 163-D2
DUTCHMAN WAY APV 163-D2
DUTCHMANS WAY WAT 101-B4
DUTCHVIEW RD MTA 116-D1
DUTOIT RD SFT 159-A3
DUTTON AVE BP 77-D4
DUWAYNE AVE LEX 65-D4
DVORAK RD MTK 119-A2
DWANE ST SSP 122-E3
DWIGHT LN MTK 105-A3
DWINNDELL AVE DWD 81-D3
DWINNELL AVE DWD 81-D3
DWINNELL AVE MHT 81-D3
DYER LN DPH 118-B2
DYLAN CT MHT 95-C1
DYLAN LN IND 88-D1
DYNASTY DR MTK 118-C2
DYSPROSIUM
ST NW RAM 35-B4,49-B2

E

E CT NE EB 37-D1
E ST HIL 92-E2
E ST MEN 121-D4
E ST MTK 105-C4
E ST WBL 94-E2
E ST WBY 123-D1
EAGAN AVE EAG 135-D2
EAGAN INDUSTRIAL RD EAG 135-D2
EAGAN OAKS CT EAG 136-A4
EAGAN OAKS LN EAG 136-A4
EAGAN WOODS DR EAG 135-D2
EAGANDALE BLVD EAG 135-D2
EAGANDALE CT EAG 135-D2
EAGANDALE PL EAG 135-D3
EAGLE CIR BEC 3-A3
EAGLE CIR IGH 137-A3
EAGLE CIR MO 31-C1
EAGLE CIR NW CR 64-B3
EAGLE CT BUF 45-B4
EAGLE CT HWL 71-B4
EAGLE DR BUF 45-B4
EAGLE DR CHC 26-B2
EAGLE DR CW 1-B3
EAGLE DR WAC 129-C4
EAGLE LN MOU 103-A4,117-A1
EAGLE PKWY STP 108-B4,122-B1
EAGLE PL BUF 45-B4
EAGLE RDG BUR 148-D3
EAGLE RDG EPR 132-B1
EAGLE ST BAY 97-B3
EAGLE ST WBT 81-A2
EAGLE ST N BEL 185-E1
EAGLE ST NW AND 50-B2
EAGLE ST NW CR 50-B4,64-B3
EAGLE ST S BEL 185-E1
EAGLE TRL CV 66-D2
EAGLE BLUFF CIR BUR 148-B4
EAGLE BLUFF CT TRT 126-A2
EAGLE BLUFF DR BUR 148-B4
EAGLE BLUFF DR TRT 126-A2
EAGLE BLUFF RD MTA 116-D2
EAGLE CREEK AVE NE PRL 161-A2
EAGLE CREEK AVE SE PRL 161-B3
EAGLE CREEK BLVD SHK 146-D3,147-B4
EAGLE CREEK CIR NW PRL 161-A2
EAGLE CREEK LN SAV 147-C4
EAGLE CREEK LN WBY 124-B2
EAGLE CREEK PKWY CRT 161-C4,175-D1
EAGLE CREEK PKWY PRL 161-C4
EAGLE CREEK PKWY SAV 147-C4
EAGLE CREST DR EAG 149-B2
EAGLE LAKE BLVD N MG 77-B4
EAGLE LAKE DR MG 77-B4,91-B1
EAGLE LAKE DR W MG 77-B4
EAGLE LAKE RD BL 18-A4
EAGLE LAKE RD N BL 18-A3
EAGLE LAKE RD N BLT 18-A3
EAGLE LAKE RD S BL 18-A4
EAGLE POINTE CIR WBY 124-B3
EAGLE POINTE TRL WBY 124-B3
EAGLE RIDGE ALC WBY 123-D1
EAGLE RIDGE CIR BUR 148-D4
EAGLE RIDGE CIR SWR 82-D4
EAGLE RIDGE CRES SWR 82-D4
EAGLE RIDGE CT IND 89-A1
EAGLE RIDGE CT SWR 82-D4
EAGLE RIDGE DR BUR 148-D4
EAGLE RIDGE DR MTK 118-C2
EAGLE RIDGE LN SWR 96-D1
EAGLE RIDGE PL MTK 118-C2
EAGLE RIDGE PL SWR 82-D4,96-D1
EAGLE RIDGE RD COR 75-D3
EAGLE RIDGE RD IND 89-A1
EAGLE RIDGE RD MH 121-E4
EAGLE RIDGE RD NO 80-C3
EAGLE RIDGE RD WBY 123-D1
EAGLE RIDGE TRL SWR 82-D4,96-E1
EAGLE RIDGE TRL SWT 82-D4
EAGLE TRACE LN WBY 124-B2
EAGLE VALLEY CIR WBY 124-B3
EAGLE VALLEY DR WBY 124-B2
EAGLE VALLY DR WBY 124-B3
EAGLES CIR PRL 160-E2
EAGLEWOOD CIR E SHK 160-C2
EAGLEWOOD DR E SHK 160-C3
EAGLEWOOD LN E SHK 160-C2
EAGLEWOOD TRL FAR 177-D2
EAKEN AVE NE BUT 45-C4,59-C2
EAKEN AVE SE FKT 87-C1,101-C2
EAKEN AVE SE RFT 59-C3,73-C3
EARL LN SSP 122-D4
EARL ST GV 105-C1
EARL ST STP 108-D3
EARLE WAY BUR 162-C2
EARLE BROWN DR BC 92-B1
EARLE SHORES LN BUR 162-C2
EARLEY LAKE CRV BUR 162-C2
EARLEY LAKE PL BUR 162-C2
EARLYNN LN MTK 118-C1
EAST AVE DRS 14-D4,28-D1
EAST AVE MHT 81-D4,95-D1
EAST AVE OST 28-D2
EAST AVE N DRS 28-D1
EAST AVE S DRS 28-D2
EAST DR EXC 117-E3
EAST RD CP 65-E3
EAST RD MON 86-C1
EAST RD NB 93-B2
EAST RD WDL 104-C4
EAST ST BEL 186-A1
EAST ST CHC 26-B1
EAST ST JOR 173-B2
EAST ST WBT 81-A2
EAST ST N NYA 142-C4
EAST BANK CT N NOH 111-C1
EAST BAVARIAN
PASS NE FRI 79-A4,93-A1
EAST BETHEL BLVD NE EB 9-C4,23-C2
EAST BRENNER PASS NE FRI 93-A1
EAST COUNTY LINE RD WBL 95-B2
EAST COUNTY LINE RD WBT 81-B1
EAST COVE RD TRT 125-E2,126-A2
EAST DANUBE DR NE FRI 79-A4,93-A1
EAST GATE RD SA 93-B3
EAST HAM LAKE DR NE HL 37-A4
EAST LAKE NETTA DR NE HL 37-C3
EAST MARIGOLD CT NW AND 49-E3
EAST OAK DR MO 32-A3
EAST OAKS RD NO 80-C3
EAST OAKS TRL SJT 83-E4
EAST OBERLIN CIR NE FRI 79-A4,93-A1
EAST ORIOLE LN NO 80-C2
EAST PLEASANT LAKE RD NO 80-B3
EAST POND RD EAG 135-D4
EAST RIDGE CT NFD 219-E4
EAST RIDGE DR NFD 219-E4
EAST RIVER BLVD NW CR 64-C3
EAST RIVER RD MPL 106-E2,107-B4
EAST RIVER RD NE FRI 78-D3,92-C1
EAST RIVER RD NE MPL 92-D3
EAST RIVER RD NW CR 64-C4,78-C1
EAST RIVER RD NW FRI 78-C2
EAST RIVER TER MPL 107-B3
EAST SHORE DR MPW 108-D1
EAST SHORE DR STP 108-D2
EAST VALLEY RD DPH 118-B1
EAST VERMILLION CIR NE HL 51-B1
EAST VIEW DR CLT 202-E2
EAST WACONIA CIR NE EB 9-B4
EASTER AVE APV 163-D2
EASTER AVE FAR 177-D4
EASTER LN EAG 149-D1
EASTLAND CIR NE BUF 59-B1
EASTMAN AVE MPL 106-D2
EASTMAN DR NB 79-A3
EASTON AVE FAR 177-D2
EASTON CT FAR 177-D2
EASTON RD DPH 118-B1
EASTRIDGE CT SWR 96-E2
EASTSHORE DR MTA 117-A2
EASTVIEW AVE MTA 102-E4
EASTVIEW CIR SHK 146-C2
EASTVIEW CRV APV 149-D4
EASTVIEW CT APV 149-D4
EASTVIEW DR EDI 119-E3
EASTVIEW LN NO 80-B2
EASTWAY AVE SHK 146-C2
EASTWOOD AVE SE FKT 101-D2
EASTWOOD AVE SE RFT 73-C3
EASTWOOD CIR DEL 87-E3
EASTWOOD CIR MO 31-E3
EASTWOOD CIR MTK 118-B2
EASTWOOD CT CHN 132-B4
EASTWOOD CT EAG 150-B2
EASTWOOD LN ANO 63-D1
EASTWOOD LN MO 31-E3
EASTWOOD RD DPH 118-B2
EASTWOOD RD MTK 118-B2
EASTWOOD RD MV 79-B2
EATON AVE FAR 177-D4
EATON AVE SE FKT 87-D2
EATON AVE SE RFT 73-D2
EATON ST STP 122-C1
EATON ST NW RAM 34-C2
EAU CLAIRE CIR PRL 161-A3
EAU CLAIRE TRL PRL 161-A3
EAVES CT FAR 177-D3
EAVES WAY FAR 177-D3
EBBA ST WBL 95-B2
EBEL AVE BWT 219-C3
EBEN CT SWR 96-C2
EBEN GRN SWR 96-C2
EBEN WAY SWR 96-C2
EBERSOLE AVE NE BUT 59-D3
EBERSOLE AVE SE FKT 87-D2
EBERSOLE AVE SE RFT 73-D3
EBERT CT BWT 219-C4
EBERT RD COR 61-D4
EBERTZ CT STP 123-A1
EBNET CIR MTK 119-A3
EBONY LN APV 163-D1
EBONY ST NW BT 35-A1
EBONY ST NW RAM 35-A4,49-A3
ECHO AVE STP 108-E3,109-A3
ECHO CT N LET 11-A3
ECHO DR BUR 162-E1
ECHO DR FAR 177-D1
ECHO LN APV 149-D4
ECHO LN FAR 177-D2
ECHO LN SWR 96-E1
ECHO LN N LET 11-A3
ECHO RD SWD 117-D3
ECHO ST DWD 81-C3
ECHO TER FAR 177-D1
ECHO WAY APV 163-D2
ECHO BAY DR TKB 117-D2
ECHO LAKE AVE MHT 95-C2
ECHO LAKE BLVD MHT 95-C2
ECHO LAKE DR MHT 95-C2
ECHO LAKE BLVD DR MHT 95-C2
ECHO PARK CIR BUR 162-E1
ECHO PARK CT BUR 162-E1
ECHO PARK LN BUR 162-E1
ECHO PARK TER BUR 162-E1
ECHO POINT RD RAT 207-E4
ECHO POINT RD7525 RAT 207-D4
ECHO SHORES CT MHT 95-C2
ECHO VALLEY TRL CFT 222-D1
ECKBERG DR BC 92-A1
ECKERT AVE SE FKT 73-D4
ECKERT AVE SE RFT 59-D4,73-D1
ECKLES AVE FH 107-C2
ECKLES AVE N FH 107-C2
ECLIPSE PKWY N NP 201-E2
EDDY ST HAS 166-D2
EDELWEISS CIR NW SM 46-D3
EDELWEISS LN NW SM 46-D3
EDELWEISS RD CHS 131-B2
EDEN AVE EDI 119-E3
EDEN CIR EAG 150-B1
EDEN CIR EDI 119-E3
EDEN CT APV 149-D4
EDEN CT EPR 132-D2
EDEN DR N EPR 118-D4
EDEN DR N MTK 118-D4
EDEN DR S EPR 118-D4

EDEN RD EPR 133-A2
EDEN RD MOU 116-E1,117-A1
EDEN PRAIRIE RD EDI 119-D3
EDEN PRAIRIE RD EPR ..118-D4,132-D3
EDEN PRAIRIE RD MTK 118-E3
EDEN PRARIE CTR EPR 133-A2
EDENMOOR ST EDI 119-E3
EDENVALE BLVD EPR 118-E4,132-D1
EDENVALE TRL CLT 189-B2
EDENWOOD CT APV 163-D1
EDENWOOD DR EPR 132-D1
EDENWOOD WAY APV 163-D1
EDGAR AVE STP 108-A3
EDGCUMBE PL STP 121-E2
EDGCUMBE RD STP 121-C3
EDGE DR CP 65-E3
EDGE PL NE MPL 92-D3
EDGEBROOK AVE STP 123-B1
EDGEBROOK DR SLP 119-D1
EDGEBROOK PL EDI 119-E2
EDGEBROOK PL EPR 133-A1
EDGECUMBE DR MHT 95-C2
EDGEHILL CT MPW 94-D3
EDGEHILL RD CHT 145-C3
EDGEHILL RD MPW 94-E4,95-A4
EDGEMERE AVE SA 93-B3
EDGEMONT BLVD N BP 77-C4,91-C1
EDGEMONT CIR N BP 77-C4
EDGEMONT CRV APV 149-D4
EDGEMONT ST MPW 108-C1
EDGEMONT ST STP 108-C2
EDGEMONT ST VH 80-C4
EDGEMOOR DR HOP 119-C1
EDGEMOOR DR MTK 119-C1
EDGEMOOR PL NE CH 92-D2
EDGEMORE DR DAY 62-B2
EDGERTON ST STP 108-C2
EDGERTON ST VH 94-C2
EDGERTON ST N LC 94-C3
EDGERTON ST N MPW ...94-C4,108-C1
EDGEWATER AVE AH 93-C2
EDGEWATER AVE SVW 93-E2,94-B2
EDGEWATER BAY WBY 124-A3
EDGEWATER BLVD MPL 120-E3
EDGEWATER BLVD STP 109-A2
EDGEWATER CIR PRL 161-B2
EDGEWATER CIR WBY 124-A3
EDGEWATER CRV WBY 124-A3
EDGEWATER CT SAV 162-A2
EDGEWATER DR MOU 117-A1
EDGEWATER DR RFD 74-A4
EDGEWATER DR RIT 140-D2
EDGEWATER DR SAV 161-E2,162-A2
EDGEWATER DR WBY 124-A3
EDGEWATER LN NO 80-C4
EDGEWATER LN RIT 140-C2
EDGEWATER PATH APV 149-D4
EDGEWATER PL BL 17-E3
EDGEWATER PL VIC 130-E3
EDGEWATER PL WBY 124-A3
EDGEWATER VW WBY 124-A3
EDGEWOOD AVE MTK 104-C4
EDGEWOOD AVE SAV 161-E1
EDGEWOOD AVE SWR 96-D1
EDGEWOOD AVE WBY 109-C4
EDGEWOOD AVE N BP 77-D4,91-D1
EDGEWOOD AVE N CHM 63-D3
EDGEWOOD AVE N CRY 91-D2
EDGEWOOD AVE N GV 105-E2
EDGEWOOD AVE S GV 105-E2
EDGEWOOD AVE S SLP ..105-E4,119-D1
EDGEWOOD AVE S WAY 104-B3
EDGEWOOD CIR HUT 97-D4
EDGEWOOD CIR N CHM 63-D3
EDGEWOOD CT EPR 132-D1
EDGEWOOD CT FAR 177-D1
EDGEWOOD CT MV 79-B2
EDGEWOOD CT SWR 96-D1
EDGEWOOD CT WAY 104-B3
EDGEWOOD CT N CHM 63-D2
EDGEWOOD DR CHS 145-C2
EDGEWOOD DR HUT 97-D4
EDGEWOOD DR LOR 89-B1
EDGEWOOD DR MV 79-B2
EDGEWOOD DR NE HL 36-E3
EDGEWOOD DR SE SM 47-A4
EDGEWOOD LN APV 162-E2
EDGEWOOD LN CRT 176-A2
EDGEWOOD LN HAS 166-C2
EDGEWOOD LN LAT 202-B3
EDGEWOOD LN WSP 122-B4
EDGEWOOD LN N CHM 63-D2
EDGEWOOD PL N CHM 63-D3
EDGEWOOD RD BLO 133-D4
EDGEWOOD RD HSN 48-A3
EDGEWOOD RD SWD 117-B3
EDGEWOOD RD NE BLA 65-D3
EDGEWOOD RD NE LEX 65-D3
EDGEWOOD ST BEC 2-D3
EDGEWOOD ST BKR 2-E3
EDGEWOOD ST RFD 74-B3
EDGEWOOD HILLS RD ORO 104-A3
EDIE LN HUT 112-B3
EDINA BLVD EDI 120-A2
EDINA CT EDI 120-A3
EDINA INDUSTRIAL BLVD EDI 133-E2
EDINBOROUGH AVE NE PRL 161-A2
EDINBOROUGH CIR APV 149-D4
EDINBROOK XING BP 78-A2
EDINBOROUGH WAY APV 149-D4
EDINBOROUGH WAY EDI 134-A2
EDINBROOK CIR BP 78-A2
EDINBROOK CT BP 78-B2
EDINBROOK LN EDI 119-E2
EDINBROOK PATH APV 149-D4
EDINBROOK PKWY BP 78-B1
EDINBROOK TER N BP 77-E2,78-A2
EDINBURGH ALC BL 18-A2
EDINBURGH CIR EPR 147-B1
EDINBURGH LN WBY ...123-E1,124-A1
EDINBURGH WAY BL 18-A2
EDINBURGH CENTRE DR BP 78-B2
EDISON CIR ER 20-B2
EDISON CIR LYT 1-A2
EDISON CT ROG 47-D4
EDISON ST BLA 65-B4
EDISON ST NE BLA 65-B2,79-B1
EDISON ST NE EB 23-B3,37-B2
EDISON ST NE HL 37-B3
EDISON ST NW ER 48-B1
EDITH AVE MHT 95-C2
EDITH DR WSP 122-B3
EDITH LN LEX 65-C3
EDITH ST MPW 109-B3
EDITH PATCH CIR ANO 49-C3
EDLIN PL MPL 106-B3
EDMAR LN NE EB 37-C1
EDMONSON AVE NE BUT ..45-D3,59-D2
EDMONSON AVE NE MOT .31-D4,45-D1
EDMONTON AVE FAR 177-D4
EDMUND AVE STP 107-E3,108-A3
EDMUND BLVD MPL 107-B4,121-B1
EDOKA ST RW 182-D4,196-D1
EDSALL RD MTA 116-E2,117-A2
EDWARD AVE N COL 143-E4
EDWARD AVE S COL 143-E4
EDWARD BLVD FRT 28-A1
EDWARD LN NFD 219-D3
EDWARD RD HUG 82-A1
EDWARD ST MPW 94-D3,108-D1
EDWARD ST SA 93-A3
EDWARDS AVE SSP 137-A2
EDWOOD PL BLO 133-E2
EE ST WBL 80-D4
EFFINGHAM AVE MPW 108-C1
EFFRESS RD WBL 95-B1
EGAN DR SAV 161-E1,162-A1
EGARD ST SJT 97-A1
EGG LAKE RD N HUG 67-C3
EGGERT LAKE RD LAT 215-C3
EGRET AVE BLT 17-E2
EGRET BLVD NW CR 64-B3
EGRET CT CHN 131-E2,132-A2
EGRET CT FAR 177-D1
EGRET DR IND 88-B3
EGRET LN LL 65-E3
EGRET WAY FAR 177-D1
EHLER AVE SE FKT 73-D4,87-D1
EHLERS AVE CHN 145-E2
EHLERS AVE CHS 145-D2
EHLERS PATH RMT 165-B1
EICHENWALD ST STP 108-D3
EIDE CIR AH 79-D4,93-D1
EIDE KNLS EPR 132-D1
EIDELWEISS CT NW AND 36-A3
EIDELWEISS LN NW AND 36-A4
EIDELWEISS ST NW AND ..36-A2,50-A3
EIDELWEISS ST NW CR ...50-A3,64-A1
EIDELWEISS ST NW OG ...35-E1,36-A2
EIDELWEISS ST NW SF 7-E4
EIDER LN MO 31-E3
EIFER TRL N LET 11-A3
EIGHTH AVE N GV 106-A2
EIGHTH AVE N HOP 119-B2
EIGHTH AVE N PLY 105-C2
EIGHTH AVE S HOP 119-B2
EIGHTH ST S HOP 119-B3
EILEEN CIR E BUR 162-D2
EILEEN CIR W BUR 162-D2
EILEEN ST EPR 132-C2
EILEEN ST ORO 103-C3
EISCHENS LN JOR 173-B3
EISELE AVE NE MOT 31-D4,45-D1
EISENHOWER CT NFD 219-D4
EISENHOWER DR SCF 14-D2
EITEL CIR CHS 131-B4
EITEL RD CHS 131-B4,145-B1
EKDAHL ST TF 14-B2
EKLUND CT NFD 219-D3
EL DORADO WAY LEO 222-B4
ELAINE AVE SVW 80-A1
ELAINE AVE VET 179-B3
ELAINE CT SAV 147-E4
ELAN CT WBY 109-D4
ELAND ST NW RAM 34-D4,48-D1
ELBE ST NE LL 52-B4
ELBE ST NE LWT 10-B4
ELBERT PT SWD 118-B4
ELDER AVE NW CMT 58-A3
ELDER AVE NW MLT 43-E1,44-A2
ELDER AVE NW SM 46-E3
ELDER AVE NW SVT 15-E1
ELDER AVE SW MVT 58-A4,72-A1
ELDER AVE SW WAV 86-A1
ELDER CIR NW SM 46-E3
ELDER CT NW SM 46-E3
ELDER TURN SWD 117-D3
ELDERBERRY CT APV 149-D4
ELDORADO CIR DWD 81-C2
ELDORADO CT NE BLA 51-A4
ELDORADO DR DWD 81-C2
ELDORADO ST NE BLA 65-A1,79-A1
ELDORADO ST NW AND ...35-D3,49-D1
ELDORADO ST NW CR 63-D1
ELDORADO ST NW OG 21-D2
ELDORADO ST NW SF 7-D3
ELDORADO TRL MTK 118-E1
ELDORADO WAY FAR 177-D1
ELDRIDGE AVE MPW 94-E4,108-E1
ELDRIDGE AVE NSP 95-A4
ELDRIDGE AVE SSP 136-E1
ELDRIDGE AVE E MPW ...94-C4,108-C1
ELDRIDGE AVE E NSP 95-B4
ELDRIDGE AVE NW CMT 58-A1
ELDRIDGE AVE NW CWT 1-E2,2-A4
ELDRIDGE AVE NW MLT ...43-E4,58-A1
ELDRIDGE AVE W RVL ...107-D1,108-A1
ELEANOR AVE STP 121-C2
ELEANOR LN APV 149-D4
ELEANOR LN BC 77-E4,78-A4
ELECTRIC DR RFD 74-A3
ELENA AVE N OKD 109-D2
ELFELT ST STP 108-B3
ELGIN AVE FAR 177-D2
ELGIN CT APV 163-D1
ELGIN CT ER 19-C4
ELGIN DR NW ER 19-C4,33-C1
ELGIN PL N GV 105-C1
ELGIN ST ER 33-C2
ELGIN ST NW ER 19-C4
ELI RD E LC 94-C3
ELIASON DR BLO 147-E1
ELIOT VIEW RD SLP 105-D3
ELITE CT FAR 177-D2
ELIZABETH LN BUR 148-C4
ELIZABETH LN MPL 106-C1
ELIZABETH LN VH 80-C4
ELIZABETH ST E STP 122-C2
ELIZABETH ST W STP 122-C2
ELK CT N LET 11-A2
ELK LN N LET 11-A2
ELK LN NW ER 33-E1
ELK ST DEL 87-D2
ELK ST STP 108-B3
ELK ST WBT 81-A2
ELK ST N BEL 185-E1
ELK ST S BEL 185-E1
ELK TRL N WYT 39-A1
ELK HILLS DR NW ER 33-E1
ELK LAKE RD NW ER 5-C4,19-C2
ELK RIVER TRL FAR 177-D1
ELKHART CT APV 163-D1
ELKHART LN MPW 109-B2
ELKHART RD APV 163-D1
ELKRIDGE TRL FAR 177-D2
ELKWOOD AVE FAR 177-D1
ELKWOOD CIR APV 163-D1
ELKWOOD DR APV 163-D1
ELLA LN MTK 105-A4
ELLEN CIR PRL 161-C2
ELLEN CT LL 66-E3
ELLEN CT NEW 123-B4
ELLEN ST MH 122-B2
ELLEN ST PRE 153-B4
ELLEN WAY SFT 159-A3
ELLERDALE LN EPR 118-D4
ELLERDALE RD MTK 118-E2
ELLICE CT APV 149-C4,163-C1
ELLICE LN FAR 177-D1
ELLICE TRL APV 163-C1
ELLICE TRL W APV 149-C4,163-C1
ELLIE LN EPR 132-B2
ELLINGTON TRL FAR 177-D2
ELLINGWOOD AVE NW SVT 29-E1
ELLIOT AVE MPL 106-D4,120-D3
ELLIOT AVE RCH 120-D4,134-D1
ELLIOT AVE S BLO 134-D3
ELLIOT PL STP 108-D4
ELLIOTT AVE NW SVT 29-E1
ELLIOTT AVE SW WDT 99-E2
ELLIS AVE STP 107-B3
ELLIS LN GV 105-D2
ELLSWORTH CT CHS 145-D1
ELLSWORTH DR EDI 134-A1
ELLSWORTH LN MTK 104-E4
ELM AVE BL 17-E3
ELM AVE DEL 87-E2
ELM AVE PRL 161-A4
ELM AVE WAV 85-E1,86-A1
ELM AVE N BP 64-A4
ELM AVE N ML 43-D2
ELM AVE S ML 43-D2
ELM CIR BUF 59-B1
ELM CIR BUR 148-B4
ELM CIR MTK 118-C3
ELM CIR SE SM 47-A4
ELM CT LES 212-C4
ELM DR APV 162-E2,163-A2
ELM DR BUR 148-D4
ELM DR MTK 118-C3
ELM DR WBL 95-B2
ELM DR N FL 39-C3
ELM DR NE SLK 78-E1
ELM DR W CAR 145-B4,159-B1
ELM LN BUR 148-B4
ELM LN JOR 173-B2
ELM LN MTK 119-A1
ELM LN ORO 103-D2
ELM LN WAY 104-B3
ELM LN SE SM 47-A4
ELM PKWY ROG 61-E1
ELM PL EXC 117-E3
ELM RD EB 37-D1
ELM RD MG 76-C4,90-D1
ELM RD MOU 116-E1
ELM ST ANO 63-D1
ELM ST BEL 186-A2
ELM ST BUF 59-B1
ELM ST COR 76-A4
ELM ST CW 1-B2
ELM ST DPH 118-B2
ELM ST EXC 117-E3
ELM ST FAR 177-E4,178-A4
ELM ST HEN 198-D3
ELM ST HUD 111-C2
ELM ST LES 212-D3
ELM ST LL 65-E2,66-A2
ELM ST LND 12-D4
ELM ST MHT 95-D1
ELM ST MO 31-C2
ELM ST MPW 94-E3
ELM ST MSC 55-B4
ELM ST ORO 103-B3
ELM ST PRE 167-B1
ELM ST RFD 74-B3
ELM ST SA 93-A4
ELM ST SOM 84-B1
ELM ST STP 122-B1
ELM ST SWR 97-A1
ELM ST WBL 94-E2,95-A2
ELM ST E BUF 59-A2
ELM ST E NYA 142-C4
ELM ST E RF 140-E2
ELM ST N BEL 186-A1
ELM ST N CF 208-B4
ELM ST N CHS 145-C3
ELM ST N LP 113-B4
ELM ST N WAC 129-D3
ELM ST NE FRI 78-D2
ELM ST NW LON 217-B2
ELM ST S BEL 186-A2
ELM ST S CF 208-B4
ELM ST S CHS 145-C3
ELM ST S LP 113-B4,127-B1
ELM ST S NFD 219-E4
ELM ST S WAC 129-D3
ELM ST SE MPL 107-A2
ELM ST W BUF 59-A2
ELM ST W NYA 142-B4
ELM ST W RF 140-D2
ELM ST W SWR 96-E1,97-A1
ELM WAY BKT 185-A2
ELM CREEK BLVD N MG 76-E2,77-A3
ELM CREEK CIR CHM 63-C1
ELM CREEK DR MED 90-A2
ELM CREEK PKWY CHM 63-B3
ELM CREEK RD CHM 63-B1
ELM CREEK RD DAY 62-E3,63-A2
ELM CREEK RD WCT 129-D4
ELM CREEK TRL N CHM 63-B2
ELM RIDGE CIR COR 90-A1
ELM RIDGE CIR SWD 117-C3
ELM TREE AVE CHN 117-C4
ELM TREE CIR FAR 177-D1
ELMCREST AVE N COT 39-A2,53-A3
ELMCREST AVE N FL 39-A2
ELMCREST AVE N HUG 67-A3
ELMCREST AVE N LL 53-A4,67-A2
ELMCREST AVE N LWT 11-A3
ELMCREST AVE N WYT 39-A2
ELMCREST CT N FLT 53-A3
ELMDALE RD GV 92-A4
ELMER ST RVL 108-B1
ELMHURST AVE CRY 91-D1
ELMIRA CT APV 163-D1
ELMO AVE N LET 11-A1
ELMO CIR MTK 119-B1
ELMO RD HOP 119-B1
ELMO RD MTK 119-B1
ELMORE AVE WT 203-D4,217-D2
ELMWOOD AVE ORO 103-B4
ELMWOOD AVE SHK 146-C3
ELMWOOD AVE N CHM 63-C2
ELMWOOD CIR FAR 177-D2
ELMWOOD CIR LES 212-D4
ELMWOOD CIR SB 116-A3
ELMWOOD CT APV 149-D4
ELMWOOD DR GRF 74-D4
ELMWOOD DR RFD 74-B3
ELMWOOD DR SB 116-A3
ELMWOOD PL MTK 118-D1
ELMWOOD PL E MPL 120-D3
ELMWOOD PL W MPL 120-C3
ELMWOOD ST STP 123-A2
ELMWOOD ST VH 94-C1
ELMWOOD ST E ARL 183-A3
ELMWOOD TRL LET 11-A3
ELMWOOD ENTR N CHM 63-C2
ELODIE LN MTK 118-D3
ELRENE CT EAG 136-A4
ELRENE RD EAG 136-A4,150-A1
ELROSE CT SSP 136-E2
ELROY ST MPL 106-C4
ELSEN DR LOR 89-B2
ELSEN ST LOR 89-B2
ELSIE LN STP 121-C3
ELSIE INN MHT 95-D1
ELSINORE CIR MED 103-D1
ELSMERE CT FAR 177-D2
ELVESTAD CT NMT 204-C1
ELWAY ST STP 121-E3
ELWOOD AVE N MPL 106-C2
ELWOOD TER W JT 145-E3
ELY AVE FAR 177-D1
ELY ST NE FRI 78-C2
ELYSIUM PL APV 163-D2
EMBASSY AVE APV 163-D2
EMBASSY CIR NE PRL 161-B1
EMBASSY RD BUR 148-C2
EMBASSY WAY APV 163-D2
EMBER CT APV 163-D2
EMBER WAY APV 163-D1
EMBERS AVE FAR 177-D2
EMBLEM CT FAR 177-D2
EMBRY AVE FAR 177-D2
EMBRY CT APV 163-D2
EMBRY LN FAR 177-D2
EMBRY PATH APV 163-D2
EMBRY WAY W APV 163-D1
EMERALD AVE WYO 25-A4
EMERALD AVE N WYT 25-A4
EMERALD BLVD HUD 111-E2
EMERALD CIR BEL 186-A2
EMERALD CIR FAR 177-D1
EMERALD CT HUD 111-E2
EMERALD CT NB 93-B1
EMERALD DR MOU 117-A2
EMERALD DR NB 93-B1
EMERALD DR WBL 95-B2
EMERALD LN EAG 149-B1
EMERALD LN EPR 132-C1
EMERALD LN NMT 190-A3
EMERALD LN STP 123-B2
EMERALD LN WBY 123-E1
EMERALD LN E SHK 146-D3
EMERALD PATH APV 163-D2
EMERALD RDG MTK 104-E3
EMERALD RDG RVL 108-A1
EMERALD ST STP 107-B3
EMERALD ST SE STP 107-B3
EMERALD TRL FAR 177-D1
EMERALD TRL MTK 105-A4
EMERALD WAY APV 163-D2
EMERSON AVE CMT 57-E3
EMERSON AVE MH 122-B3
EMERSON AVE E WSP 122-C3
EMERSON AVE N BC 78-C4,92-C1
EMERSON AVE N BP 78-C3
EMERSON AVE N MON 72-C4,86-C1
EMERSON AVE N MPL ...92-C4,106-C1
EMERSON AVE N WDT 85-E1
EMERSON AVE NW MLT 43-E4
EMERSON AVE S BLO ...134-C3,148-C1
EMERSON AVE S MON 86-C1
EMERSON AVE S MPL ...106-C4,120-C3
EMERSON AVE S RCH ...120-C4,134-C1
EMERSON AVE SW MVT ...57-E4,71-E3
EMERSON AVE SW WAV 85-E1
EMERSON AVE SW WDT ...85-E1,99-E2
EMERSON AVE W WSP 122-B3
EMERSON CT BUR 148-C4,162-C1
EMERSON DR EB 37-D1
EMERSON DR NE EB 37-D1
EMERSON LN BUR 148-C4
EMERSON LN RCH 134-C1
EMERSON LN N BC 78-C4
EMERSON RD BLO 148-C1
EMERSON ST BLA 65-B4
EMERY AVE HMP 193-B2
EMERY AVE HMT 193-B1,207-B1
EMERY AVE VET 165-B4,179-B1
EMERY AVE E RMT 165-B2
EMIL AVE SVW 79-E1,80-A1
EMILIE PL ROB 92-A3
EMILY CIR RF 140-D1
EMILY CT N LET 11-A3
EMILY LN LET 11-B3
EMILY LN N LET 11-A3
EMMA LN BEL 185-E2,186-A2
EMMA ST STP 122-A1
EMMER CT APV 149-D4
EMMER PL APV 149-D4
EMMERT ST SVW 93-E2
EMMITT AVE RW 196-E4
EMORY CIR RF 140-E3
EMORY DR RF 140-E3
EMPEROR CT FAR 177-D3
EMPIRE AVE APV 163-D2
EMPIRE CT APV 163-D1
EMPIRE DR STP 108-B3
EMPIRE LN N MG 76-E4,90-E1
EMPIRE LN N PLY 90-E2
EMPIRE RD LYT 1-A3
EMPIRE TRL FAR 177-D1
EMPIRE BUILDER DR TRT 126-B2
ENCHANTED CT FAR 177-D2
ENCHANTED DR SWD 117-A3
ENCHANTED LN MTA 117-A3
ENCHANTED LN SWD 117-A3
ENCHANTED PT SWD 117-A3
ENCHANTED RD MOU 103-A4
ENCHANTED WAY FAR 177-D2
ENCHANTMENT LN LET 11-A1
ENCLAVE BAY WBY 123-D3
ENCLAVE CIR WBY 123-D3
ENCLAVE CV WBY 123-E3
ENCLAVE RD WBY 123-E3
ENCORE CIR MTK 119-B2
ENCORE CT FAR 177-D2
ENDEAVOUR AVE FAR 177-C1
ENDICOTT AVE NW CMT 57-E2
ENDICOTT AVE NW MLT 29-E4

ENDICOTT AVE NW SVT 15-E2,29-E2
ENDICOTT AVE SW MVT 71-E4,85-E1
ENDICOTT DR NW SVT 15-E3
ENDICOTT ST STP 107-C3
ENDICOTT TRL EPR 132-D3
ENDICOTT TRL MOT 32-A3
ENDICOTT WAY APV 163-D2
ENDRESS CT RAT 207-B3
ENDRESS WAY RAT 207-C3
ENERGY LN STP 107-D3
ENERGY WAY APV 163-C2
ENERGY PARK DR STP 107-D3
ENFIELD AVE FLT 53-A2
ENFIELD AVE N FLT 53-A1
ENFIELD CT N FLT 53-A1
ENGEN BLVD NW BT 20-D3
ENGER CT RAT 207-C3
ENGLAND PL SWR 96-C1
ENGLER BLVD CHS 145-C2
ENGLERT RD EAG 135-D4
ENGLEWOOD AVE STP 107-D3,108-A3
ENGLEWOOD CIR FAR 177-C2
ENGLEWOOD CT FAR 177-C2
ENGLEWOOD DR EPR 133-A4,147-A1
ENGLEWOOD WAY FAR 177-C2
ENGLISH AVE FAR 177-D2
ENGLISH CIR GV 105-C1
ENGLISH CT FAR 177-D3
ENGLISH ST MPW 94-D4,108-E1
ENGLISH ST STP 108-E4
ENGLISH ST VH 94-D2
ENGLISH TURN EPR 132-B3
ENHANCE CT FAR 177-C2
ENLOE ST HUD 111-E4,112-A4
ENRIGHT CT FAR 177-D3
ENRIGHT WAY FAR 177-D3
ENSIGN AVE SAV 147-C3
ENSIGN AVE N CHM 63-C2
ENSIGN AVE N GV 91-C4,105-C1
ENSIGN AVE N NH 91-C4
ENSIGN AVE S BLO 133-C4
ENSIGN AVE S PRL 161-C2
ENSIGN AVE S SAV 161-C2
ENSIGN AVE S SLP 105-C4
ENSIGN CIR BLO 133-C4
ENSIGN CIR N NH 91-C4
ENSIGN CRV BLO 133-C2
ENSIGN CT N NH 91-C4
ENSIGN RD BLO 133-C2
ENSLEY AVE NFD 219-D3
ENSLEY CT APV 163-D1
ENTERPRISE AVE HAS 166-E3
ENTERPRISE DR MH 135-D1
ENTREVAUX DR EPR 133-B4
EQUESTRIAN WAY MTA 116-C3
EQUITABLE DR EPR 132-E2
ERIC DR OSC 28-A4
ERICK ST GRF 74-D3
ERICKSON CT FAR 177-D3
ERICKSON CT N BP 77-C4
ERICKSON DR HAS 166-B2
ERICKSON DR NH 91-C2
ERICKSON KNL FAR 177-D3
ERICKSON LN MTK 118-D2
ERICKSON PATH FAR 177-D3
ERICKSON RD MV 79-B2
ERICON DR BC 92-B1
ERIE AVE CHN 132-B2,146-B1
ERIE AVE SE PRL 161-B3
ERIE CIR CHN 132-B2
ERIE CIR N LET 11-A2
ERIE CT EAG 150-A2
ERIE CT N LET 11-A2
ERIE LN N LET 11-A2
ERIE SPUR CHN 132-B2
ERIE ST STP 122-A1
ERIE ST SE MPL 107-A3
ERIK AVE SW MVT 71-E2
ERIK LN SVW 80-B2
ERIKS BLVD EAG 149-D3
ERIN AVE SLT 174-E3
ERIN BAY EPR 132-B2
ERIN CIR SE PRL 161-B4
ERIN CT FAR 177-D3
ERIN CT NB 79-A3
ERIN CT WBY 138-A1
ERIN DR EAG 149-A2
ERIN LN EAG 149-B2
ERIN TER EDI 133-D1
ERIN WAY FAR 177-D3
ERKIUM ST NW BT 35-B2
ERKIUM ST NW RAM 35-B2,49-B1
ERKIUM ST NW SF 7-B3
ERMINE BLVD NW RAM 34-C2
ERNAL DR SVW 94-A2
ERSKIN ST NE BLA 65-D3
ERSKIN ST NE EB 9-D4,23-D3
ERVIN INDUSTRIAL DR JOR 173-A2
ERWIN CT EPR 132-E2
ESK CIR IGH 150-B1
ESK LN EAG 150-B1
ESK LN IGH 150-B1
ESQUIRE BLVD N WYT 39-A1
ESQUIRE CT N WYT 39-A1
ESQUIRE WAY FAR 177-C1
ESSEN LN CHS 145-C1
ESSENCE TRL FAR 177-C2
ESSEX AVE APV 163-D1
ESSEX AVE EUT 191-D3
ESSEX CT APV 163-D1
ESSEX CT EPR 132-E3,133-A3
ESSEX LN APV 163-D1
ESSEX RD CHN 132-A2
ESSEX RD MOU 117-A2
ESSEX RD MTK 104-E3
ESSEX ST SE MPL 107-A3
ESSEX TRL APV 163-D1
ESSEX WAY APV 149-D4
ESTABROOK DR STP 107-E2
ESTATE AVE FAR 177-C2
ESTATE AVE PRL 161-C2
ESTATE DR BP 78-A3
ESTATE DR EPR 147-C1
ESTATES AVE APV 163-D1
ESTATES DR EAG 149-A3
ESTATES TRL BUR 162-B2
ESTERLY OAKS DR MO 60-E2
ESTES AVE NW MLT 43-E1
ESTES AVE NW SVT 15-E4
ESTES AVE SW MVT 57-E4,71-E1
ESTES AVE SW WDT 85-E2
ESTHER LN MH 122-B2
ESTHER LN WBY 123-C1
ETHAN AVE N HUG 67-A4,81-A1
ETHAN AVE N WYT 39-A1
ETHAN CT N FL 39-A3
ETHAN DR EAG 150-A1
ETHAN RD N FL 39-A3
ETHEL AVE ORO 117-B2
ETHELTON AVE LVL 163-C4
ETHELTON WAY APV 149-C4
ETNA ST STP 108-E4
ETON PL EDI 120-A2
EUCLID AVE ANO 49-B3
EUCLID AVE APV 149-C4,163-C1
EUCLID AVE BL 17-E3
EUCLID AVE FAR 177-C1
EUCLID AVE LVL 163-C4
EUCLID AVE PRL 161-C2
EUCLID CT APV 163-C1
EUCLID CT BL 17-E3
EUCLID CT FAR 177-C2
EUCLID PATH FAR 177-C2
EUCLID PL MPL 106-C4
EUCLID ST FAR 177-C1
EUCLID ST STP 108-D4,109-A4
EUCLID WAY FAR 177-C1
EUGENE CIR MED 90-B2
EUGENE ST WBL 80-E4,81-A4
EUREKA AVE N COT 39-A4,53-A1
EUREKA AVE N FLT 39-A4
EUREKA AVE N WYT 25-A4,39-A1
EUREKA AVE W FAR 177-C2
EUREKA AVE W LVL 163-C4,177-C1
EUREKA CT APV 163-C2
EUREKA CT FAR 177-C2
EUREKA RD SWD 117-C3
EUROPA AVE APV 163-C2
EUROPA AVE LVL 163-C4
EUROPA AVE N HUG 67-A4,81-A1
EUROPA BAY HUG 67-A4
EUROPA CT APV 149-C4
EUROPA TRL HUG 67-A4
EUROPA TRL N HUG 67-A4
EUROPA WAY APV 163-C2
EUROPA WAY HUG 67-A4
EUROPE AVE APV 163-C2
EUSTIS ST LAU 107-B1
EUSTIS ST RVL 93-B4
EUSTIS ST STP 107-B3
EVA LN SSP 122-D4
EVA ST LL 52-B3
EVA ST STP 108-C4,122-C1
EVANS AVE SSP 122-D2
EVANS AVE NW CWT 1-E4,15-E1
EVANS AVE NW ER 19-E4,33-E2
EVANS CT SVW 94-A1
EVANS ST NW ER 19-E4
EVANS WAY MTA 102-E3
EVANS HALL NFD 219-E3
EVANSTON AVE PRL 161-B3
EVANSWOOD LN EDI 119-D3
EVAR ST MPW 109-B2
EVAS DR MTK 105-A4
EVELETH AVE APV 149-C4,163-C2
EVELETH AVE GVT 205-C4,219-C2
EVELETH AVE W LVL 163-C4,177-C1
EVELETH CT APV 163-C1
EVELETH CT LVL 163-C4
EVELETH PATH APV 149-C4
EVELETH ST NE EB 23-A2
EVELETH ST NE HL 37-A3,51-A2
EVELETH WAY APV 163-C1
EVELYN CIR NFD 219-E4
EVELYN LN MTK 118-D2
EVELYN ST RVL 93-C3
EVENER WAY EPR 132-C1
EVENFALL AVE LVL 163-C4,177-C1
EVENING STAR CT FAR 177-C2
EVENING STAR WAY FAR 177-C2
EVENSONG AVE FAR 177-C2
EVENSONG CT FAR 177-C3
EVENSTON DR FAR 177-C2
EVENSTON RD EPR 132-C1
EVENTIDE WAY FAR 177-C1
EVENTIDE WAY LVL 163-C4
EVEREST AVE APV 149-C4,163-C1
EVEREST AVE FAR 177-C2
EVEREST CIR FAR 177-C1
EVEREST CT FAR 177-C2
EVEREST CT E APV 149-C4
EVEREST CT N PLY 90-C4
EVEREST CT W APV 149-C4
EVEREST LN MG 76-C3
EVEREST LN N MG 76-C2,90-C1
EVEREST LN N PLY 90-C4,104-C1
EVEREST PATH FAR 177-C2
EVEREST PATH LVL 163-C4
EVEREST TRL APV 149-C4
EVEREST TRL FAR 177-C2
EVERETT CT STP 107-C3
EVERETT DR SWR 96-E2,97-A2
EVERETT PL EDI 133-E1
EVERETT ST N SWR 82-E4,96-E1
EVERETT ST S SWR 96-E2
EVERGLADE CT FAR 177-C1
EVERGLADE DR NE EB 37-C1
EVERGLADE TRL FAR 177-C2
EVERGREEN ALC WBY 123-D2
EVERGREEN AVE N BP 64-A4,78-A1
EVERGREEN AVE W CF 208-B3
EVERGREEN BAY WBY 123-D2
EVERGREEN BLVD NW CR 64-C4,78-D1
EVERGREEN CIR BL 18-B4
EVERGREEN CIR BUR 162-D1
EVERGREEN CIR JOR 173-B2
EVERGREEN CIR SVW 94-A1
EVERGREEN CIR WBT 81-B2
EVERGREEN CIR N BP 64-A4
EVERGREEN CIR N DAY 49-A4
EVERGREEN CIR NW CR 64-D1
EVERGREEN CT APV 163-D1
EVERGREEN CT BP 64-A4
EVERGREEN CT BUR 162-D1
EVERGREEN CT EPR 118-D4
EVERGREEN CT NO 80-B3
EVERGREEN CT RVL 107-C1
EVERGREEN CT SWR 96-D2
EVERGREEN CT VER 179-C2
EVERGREEN CT WBY 123-D2
EVERGREEN CT N BP 64-A4
EVERGREEN DR BUR 162-D1
EVERGREEN DR EAG 135-C3
EVERGREEN DR LFL 109-C4
EVERGREEN DR MPL 106-E3,107-A3
EVERGREEN DR MTK 118-D1
EVERGREEN DR SOM 70-B4
EVERGREEN DR VH 80-D4
EVERGREEN DR WBY 123-D2
EVERGREEN DR E CF 208-B3
EVERGREEN DRAW WBY 123-D2
EVERGREEN ECHO WBY 123-D2
EVERGREEN KNLS MH 122-A3
EVERGREEN LN NO 80-B3
EVERGREEN LN SB 116-A3
EVERGREEN LN SVW 80-A1
EVERGREEN LN N DAY 48-B2,49-A4
EVERGREEN LN N HSN 48-B2
EVERGREEN LN N MG 63-A4,77-A4
EVERGREEN LN N PLY 91-A3,105-A1
EVERGREEN PL SVW 94-A1
EVERGREEN RD DWD 81-D3
EVERGREEN RD MED 90-B2
EVERGREEN RD MOU 116-D2
EVERGREEN RD NO 80-B3
EVERGREEN RD N WYT 39-A1
EVERGREEN ST BEL 186-A2
EVERGREEN ST NW AND 50-D2
EVERGREEN ST NW CR 50-D4,64-D1
EVERGREEN ST NW OG 22-D2
EVERGREEN ST W VER 179-C2
EVERGREEN TRL APV 163-C2
EVERGREEN TRL FAR 177-C2
EVERGREEN TRL LL 52-B4
EVERGREEN TRL ROG 61-E2
EVERHILL AVE FAR 177-C2
EVERLEIGH CIR RMT 163-E2
EVERMMOR PKWY APV 149-E4
EVERMOOR PKWY APV 149-E4,163-E1
EVERT CT NE FRI 78-E2
EVERTON AVE APV 149-C4,163-C1
EVERTON AVE FAR 177-C1
EVERTON AVE FLT 53-A2
EVERTON AVE HUG 81-A1
EVERTON AVE WYO 25-A3
EVERTON AVE N FL 39-A3
EVERTON AVE N FLT 39-A4,53-A1
EVERTON AVE N HUG 67-A2
EVERTON CIR WYO 25-A3
EVERTON CT FAR 177-C1
EVERTON CT N FL 39-A3
EWALD AVE N MG 91-B1
EWALD TER GV 105-D2
EWING AVE BUR 162-A1
EWING AVE N BC 78-A4,92-A1
EWING AVE N BP 78-A2
EWING AVE N ROB 92-A4
EWING AVE S BLO 148-A2
EWING AVE S EDI 120-A4
EWING AVE S MPL 106-A4,120-A2
EWING CIR BLO 148-A2
EWING CIR N BP 78-A2
EWING CIR S EDI 120-A3
EWING RD BLO 134-A2,148-A1
EWING ST FAR 177-C2
EXCALIBUR TRL FAR 177-C2
EXCEL CT FAR 177-C2
EXCEL WAY LVL 163-C3
EXCELSIOR BLVD DPH 118-B3
EXCELSIOR BLVD EXC 117-E3
EXCELSIOR BLVD GRW 117-E3,118-A3
EXCELSIOR BLVD HOP 119-C2
EXCELSIOR BLVD MPL 106-B4,120-A1
EXCELSIOR BLVD MTK 118-C3,119-A2
EXCELSIOR BLVD SLP 119-E1,120-A1
EXCELSIOR BLVD SWD 118-A3
EXCELSIOR CIR LVL 163-C3
EXCELSIOR CIR MTK 119-A2
EXCELSIOR CT LVL 163-C3
EXCELSIOR DR LVL 163-C3
EXCELSIOR LN APV 163-C2
EXCELSIOR LN FAR 177-C3
EXCELSIRO BLVD MTK 118-B3
EXCEPTIONAL TRL FAR 177-C2
EXCHANGE DR HUT 112-B3
EXCHANGE ST E STP 108-B4
EXCHANGE ST W STP 108-B4,122-B1
EXCHANGE TRL FAR 177-C2
EXCLUSIVE PATH FAR 177-C2
EXECUTIVE AVE FAR 177-C2
EXECUTIVE BLVD BUR 162-C2
EXECUTIVE DR EPR 132-E2
EXECUTIVE DR MH 135-D2
EXECUTIVE PATH FAR 177-C3
EXETER AVE LVL 163-C4,177-C1
EXETER CT FAR 177-C1
EXETER PL FAR 177-C1
EXETER PL STP 107-C4
EXHALL AVE N HUG 67-A4
EXIRA AVE LVL 163-C4,177-C1
EXLEY AVE APV 149-C4,163-C2
EXLEY AVE FAR 177-C1
EXLEY AVE FLT 39-A4,53-A1
EXLEY AVE LVL 163-C4,177-C1
EXLEY CT APV 163-C1
EXLEY WAY APV 163-C1
EXODUS AVE FAR 177-C1
EXODUS CIR FAR 177-C1
EXODUS CT FAR 177-C1
EXPLORER CT BUR 148-E2
EXPLORER WAY FAR 177-C1
EXPORT TRL FAR 177-C3
EYRIE DR WBY 124-B2

F

F CT NE EB 37-D1
F ST LL 66-B2
F ST MEN 121-D4
F ST MTK 105-C4
F ST WBY 123-D1
FABER LN CHS 145-C1
FABOR AVE BPT 186-D1
FACADE AVE FAR 177-C1
FACTORY ST SPP 137-B3
FAGERNESS
POINT RD ORO 103-B4,117-B1
FAHEY AVE RMT 165-C1
FAHLSTROM PL AFT 110-E4,124-E1
FAIR PL STP 107-D2
FAIR WAY N MG 77-C1
FAIR HILLS RD W MTK 118-D2
FAIR ISLE PATH LVL 163-C4,177-C1
FAIR MEADOWS DR BL 18-A4
FAIR OAKS CT APV 163-C1
FAIR OAKS CT WBL 94-E2
FAIR OAKS DR WBL 94-E2
FAIR OAKS LN APV 163-C1
FAIR OAKS WAY APV 163-C1
FAIRBANKS AVE FLT 39-A4,53-A1
FAIRBANKS AVE WT 203-D3
FAIRBANKS AVE N HUG 67-A4
FAIRBANKS TRL PRL 161-A2
FAIRCHILD AVE MTK 104-D4,118-D1
FAIRCHILD AVE MV 79-A1
FAIRFAX AVE EDI 120-A4
FAIRFAX AVE LVL 163-C4
FAIRFAX LN WBY 124-B3
FAIRFIELD CIR MTK 105-B3
FAIRFIELD CIR N BP 78-C3
FAIRFIELD CT MTK 105-A3
FAIRFIELD DR NW NB 93-B1
FAIRFIELD RD MOU 116-E2
FAIRFIELD RD MTK 105-B3
FAIRFIELD RD N BP 78-C3
FAIRFIELD RD S MTK 104-E3
FAIRFIELD RD W MTK 105-A3
FAIRFIELD SPUR MTK 105-B3
FAIRFIELD WAY MTK 105-B3
FAIRGREEN AVE APV 149-C4
FAIRGREEN AVE EUT 191-C4,205-C1
FAIRGREEN AVE FAR 177-C4
FAIRGREEN AVE LVL 163-C3
FAIRGROUND ST W FH 107-D2
FAIRGROUNDS RD SAT 14-E2
FAIRHAVEN AVE LVL 163-C4
FAIRHAVEN CT LVL 163-C4
FAIRHAVEN DR SHK 146-B4,160-B1
FAIRHAVEN RD EAG 136-B4,150-B1
FAIRHILL AVE DEL 87-D3
FAIRHILL AVE FKT 87-D3
FAIRHILL AVE LVL 163-C4
FAIRHILL AVE SE FKT 101-D2
FAIRHILL DR SE RFT 73-E1
FAIRHILL LN LVL 163-C4
FAIRHILLS DR DAY 62-B2
FAIRHILLS RD E MTK 118-D2
FAIRHILLS RD W MTK 118-D2
FAIRHOMES LN DPH 118-C1
FAIRHOMES RD DPH 118-C1
FAIRHOPE AVE TKB 117-D2
FAIRLANE ST WBL 95-B1
FAIRLAWN AVE APV 163-B1
FAIRLAWN AVE CLT 188-E4,202-E1
FAIRLAWN AVE SLT 160-E4,174-E2
FAIRLAWN AVE E WIN 99-B3
FAIRLAWN AVE W WIN 99-B3
FAIRLAWN CIR WIN 99-B3
FAIRLAWN CT APV 163-B1
FAIRLAWN DR MTK 118-C1
FAIRLAWN DR SWR 96-D1
FAIRLAWN LN SLT 174-E3
FAIRLAWN PL EAG 135-D2
FAIRLAWN WAY GV 106-A3
FAIRLAWN SHORES TRL PRL 161-C2
FAIRMEADOW WAY LVL 163-C4
FAIRMEADOWS RD SWR 96-D1
FAIRMONT AVE LVL 163-C4
FAIRMONT AVE MON 86-C1
FAIRMONT CIR NE FRI 78-C2
FAIRMONT DR LL 65-E2
FAIRMONT ST MPL 107-A2
FAIRMONT ST NE FRI 78-C2
FAIRMOUNT AVE STP 121-C1,122-A1
FAIROAK AVE ANO 49-B4
FAIROAK CT ANO 49-B4
FAIRVIEW AVE MTK 119-A2
FAIRVIEW AVE WYO 25-B4
FAIRVIEW AVE WYT 25-B4
FAIRVIEW AVE N AH 93-C1
FAIRVIEW AVE N CRY 91-E2
FAIRVIEW AVE N FH 107-C1
FAIRVIEW AVE N NH 91-C2
FAIRVIEW AVE N RVL 93-C4,107-C1
FAIRVIEW AVE N STP 107-C4,121-C1
FAIRVIEW AVE N SVW 79-C2
FAIRVIEW AVE S STP 121-C2
FAIRVIEW BLVD WYO 25-B4
FAIRVIEW CIR FAR 191-E1
FAIRVIEW CT ORO 103-B4
FAIRVIEW DR BUR 162-D1
FAIRVIEW LN FAR 191-E1
FAIRVIEW LN MOU 117-A1
FAIRVIEW LN MTK 119-A2
FAIRVIEW LN SLW 172-E2
FAIRVIEW RD PRL 160-E4
FAIRVIEW ST GRW 117-E3,118-A2
FAIRWAY BLVD HWL 71-B4
FAIRWAY CIR BEC 2-E3
FAIRWAY CIR CHS 131-B4
FAIRWAY CT CHS 131-B4
FAIRWAY CT MTK 119-B1
FAIRWAY DR CHS 131-B4
FAIRWAY DR EPR 132-E1
FAIRWAY DR HUD 111-D3
FAIRWAY DR MO 31-C2
FAIRWAY DR MTK 119-B1
FAIRWAY DR WBY 124-A3
FAIRWAY DR NE CH 92-E1,93-A1
FAIRWAY LN BEC 2-E3,3-A3
FAIRWAY LN CHC 26-B2
FAIRWAY LN MTK 119-B1
FAIRWAY LN SLP 105-C3
FAIRWAY PT WBY 124-A3
FAIRWAY PT N VIC 130-E3
FAIRWAY PT S VIC 130-E3
FAIRWAY TER WBY 124-A4
FAIRWAY HILLS DR EAG 149-D2
FAIRWAY RIDGE CT MTA 102-E2
FAIRWAY RIDGE DR MTA 102-E2
FAIRWAYS LN RVL 93-B4,107-B1
FAIRWOOD CIR MTK 118-D4
FAIRWOOD DR MTK 118-D4
FAIRWOOD LN MTK 118-D4
FAIRY FALLS RD N SWR 83-A4
FAIRY FALLS RD N SWT 83-A3
FAITH CT RAT 207-C3
FALCON AVE APV 163-C1
FALCON AVE LET 11-A1
FALCON AVE LVL 163-C4
FALCON AVE MO 31-E3
FALCON AVE STP 123-B1
FALCON AVE WYO 25-A4
FALCON AVE N FL 39-A2
FALCON AVE N FLT 39-A4,53-A1
FALCON AVE N HUG 67-B4,81-B1
FALCON AVE N LET 11-B3
FALCON AVE N WYT 39-B2
FALCON CT APV 149-C4
FALCON CT EDI 119-D4
FALCON CT N HUG 67-B4
FALCON DR APV 149-C4
FALCON DR RF 140-E2
FALCON LN BUF 45-B3
FALCON LN NO 80-C2
FALCON RD WBY 124-B2
FALCON TRL BUF 45-B4
FALCON WAY EAG 135-E4
FALCON RIDGE BAY WBY 123-D1
FALCON RIDGE RD WBY 123-D1
FALCON RIDGE TRL APV 149-C4
FALCONS WAY EPR 147-C1
FALCONS WAY SAV 147-C4
FALLBROOK ALC WBY 123-E1
FALLBROOK AVE WYO 25-B4
FALLBROOK AVE N WYT 39-B1
FALLBROOK CT APV 163-C1
FALLBROOK CT LVL 163-C4
FALLBROOK CT WYO 25-A3
FALLBROOK DR LVL 163-C3
FALLBROOK LN WBY 123-E1
FALLBROOK RD EPR 119-A4
FALLBROOK WAY APV 163-C1

FALLGOLD PKWY BP 64-A4
FALLGOLD PKWY N BP 64-A4,78-A1
FALLON AVE MO 31-D2
FALLON AVE NE MO 31-D3
FALLON AVE NE MOT 31-D3,45-D1
FALLON DR MO 31-D3
FALLS CIR CHS 145-E1
FALLS CRV CHS 145-D1
FALLS ST N RF 140-D1
FALLS ST S RF 140-D2
FALLS VIEW CT MH 122-A3
FALSTAFF RD WBY 123-C3
FALSTAFF TER WBY 123-C3
FANNON AVE SE FKT 73-E4,101-D2
FANTASIA AVE LVL 163-C3
FANUM RD VH 94-E2
FAR HILL CT WAY 104-B2
FAR HILL RD WAY 104-B2
FARADAY CT LVL 163-C4
FARADAY LN LVL 163-C4
FARCRY WAY LVL 163-C3
FARCY WAY LVL 163-C3
FAREWAY DR NFD 219-E4
FARIBAULT CT SHK 146-C3
FARIBAULT ST GV 105-D2
FARIBAULT ST SHK 146-C4
FARICY LN CRT 161-D4
FARLEY AVE SE FKT 73-E4
FARM LN MTK 119-B1
FARM RD EAG 150-B3
FARM RD N ORO 103-E1
FARM RD W ORO 103-D1
FARM ST HAS 166-C1
FARM HILL GRN SWR 96-C1
FARM LINE RD WAC 129-D3
FARMDALE RD MH 122-A3
FARMDALE RD E HOP 119-C1
FARMDALE RD W HOP 119-C1
FARMHILL CIR MTA 116-C3
FARMHILL CT MTA 116-C3
FARMHILL DR MTA 116-C3
FARMINGTON AVE NE BUT 45-E4,59-E3
FARMINGTON AVE SE FKT 73-E4,87-E1
FARMINGTON AVE SE RFT 59-E4,73-D3
FARMINGTON RD MTK 119-A1
FARMINGTON WAY APV 163-C1
FARMSTEAD AVE MO 31-D3
FARMSTEAD CIR EPR 132-B4
FARMSTEAD CT MO 31-D3
FARMSTEAD DR MO 31-D3
FARNHAM AVE N HUG 53-B4,67-B4
FARNSWORTH AVE N BP 78-A1
FARNSWORTH CT BP 78-A1
FARNUM DR EAG 135-C3
FARO LN MH 121-E4
FARRAGO TRL LVL 163-C3
FARRELL RD COR 76-B4
FARRELL ST MPW 109-B3,123-B1
FARRINGTON CIR RVL 94-A4
FARRINGTON CT RVL 94-A3
FARRINGTON ST RVL 94-A3,108-A1
FARRINGTON ST STP 108-A3
FARVIEW LN ORO 103-C3
FARWELL AVE MPL 106-B2
FARWELL AVE SSP 122-E4,123-A4
FARWELL AVE WT 203-C3,217-C2
FARWELL PL MPL 106-B2
FATIMA PL SWD 118-A2
FAUQUIER PL STP 108-D3
FAVERSHAM RD WIL 95-D1
FAVORITE LN MTK 118-E1
FAWN CT NE LWT 10-D3
FAWN DR NW ER 33-E1
FAWN LN LL 66-B4
FAWN LN SVW 80-A2
FAWN RD W LWT 10-D3
FAWN TRL ROG 47-D4
FAWN TRL N WYT 39-B2
FAWN WAY EAG 149-C1
FAWN HILL CT CHN 131-D1
FAWN HILL RD CHN 131-D1
FAWN LAKE DR N LET 11-A3
FAWN LAKE DR NE EB 9-B3
FAWN LAKE DR NE LWT 9-E3,10-C3
FAWN LAKE RD BKR 3-E4
FAWN LAKE RD N LWT 10-D2
FAWN LAKE RD NE LWT 10-D2
FAWN RIDGE CT APV 163-C1
FAWN RIDGE TRL EAG 150-A2
FAWN RIDGE WAY APV 163-C1
FAWN TRAIL CIR WBY 137-D2
FAWNRIDGE CIR BLO 133-E3
FAWNS WAY EPR 147-C1
FAXON RD N NYA 142-C4
FAXON RD S NYA 142-C4
FAXTON AVE WYO 25-B3
FAYE ST STP 109-A4
FEATHER CT WBT 80-E2
FEATHER ST NE LWT 10-B4
FEATHER RIDGE DR WBY 123-E3
FEATHERSTONE DR SAV 161-D1
FEATHERSTONE DR WBY 123-E3
FEATHERSTONE RD NIT 166-B1
FEATHERSTONE RD WBY 123-E4
FEATHERSTONE TRL SAV 161-D1
FEDERAL CT EAG 135-D4
FEDERAL DR EAG 135-D4
FEDERAL DR FS 121-B3
FELDMAN AVE SE RFT 73-E3
FELDSPAR AVE RMT 163-C1
FELDSPAR ST NW RAM 48-E3,49-A3
FELDSPAR ST NW STT 7-A2
FELIX ST WSP 122-C2
FELLER ST NE COT 52-E1
FELLOWS LN STP 108-E2
FELLOWSHIP LN BUR 148-D4,162-D1
FELTL CT HOP 119-B3
FELTL LN MTK 119-B3
FELTL RD MTK 119-B3
FELTON AVE RAT 207-C3
FELTON AVE WYO 25-B3
FELTON CT WYO 25-B3
FENLEA CIR DWD 81-C2
FENNEL CT APV 163-C3
FENNER AVE SE FKT 87-E4,101-E1
FENNING AVE NE BUT 59-E1
FENNING AVE NE MO 31-E2
FENNING AVE NE MOT 31-E3
FENNING AVE NE SM 59-E1,60-A1
FENTON AVE MPW 108-D1
FENTON AVE E MPW 108-B1
FENWAY AVE N FLT 39-B4,53-B2
FENWAY AVE N HUG 53-B4,67-B1
FENWAY AVE N STA 11-B3
FENWAY BLVD N HUG 67-B3
FENWAY CIR HUG 67-B1
FENWAY CT WBT 81-B2
FENWAY CT N FLT 39-B4
FENWAY CT N STA 11-B3
FENWICK AVE WYO 25-B3
FENWICK CIR EPR 132-E1
FERDINAND DR SHK 146-C2
FERDINAND ST STP 107-C4
FERG BLVD BC 92-A2
FERGUS CT NE BLA 51-A4
FERGUS ST NE BLA 51-A4,65-A1
FERIDAY AVE WYO 25-B3
FERMAN AVE NW CWT 15-D1
FERMAN AVE NW ML 43-D1
FERMAN AVE NW MLT 43-D1
FERMAN AVE NW SVT 15-D3,29-D1
FERMAN AVE SW MVT 71-E4
FERMAN AVE SW WDT 85-E4,99-E1
FERN DR CRT 176-A3
FERN DR IND 89-A1
FERN DR RCH 134-E1
FERN LN GRF 75-A2
FERN LN MOU 116-E1
FERN RD HUT 98-B4
FERN ST BL 18-B4
FERN ST MED 89-A3
FERN TRL N LET 11-B2
FERN HILL CT NO 80-C2
FERN LANE EXT GRF 75-A2
FERNANDO AVE APV 149-C4,163-C1
FERNANDO CT APV 163-C1
FERNANDO WAY LVL 163-C3
FERNBROOK CT MG 76-E4
FERNBROOK LN SM 46-D3
FERNBROOK LN N DAY 62-E2
FERNBROOK LN N MG 62-E4,76-E1
FERNBROOK LN N PLY 90-E3,104-E1
FERNBROOK LN NW SM 46-D3
FERNCROFT DR SWD 118-A2
FERNDALE AVE NE FRI 79-A4
FERNDALE AVE NE PRL 161-B1
FERNDALE DR HSN 47-E3
FERNDALE DR MTK 119-B3
FERNDALE GRN ORO 104-B2
FERNDALE LN EPR 132-E3
FERNDALE RD N ORO 104-B2
FERNDALE RD N PLY 104-B2
FERNDALE RD N WAY 104-B2
FERNDALE RD S WAY 104-B3
FERNDALE RD W ORO 103-E3,104-A3
FERNDALE RD W WAY 104-A3
FERNDALE ST MPW 123-B2
FERNDALE ST N MPW 109-B3,123-B1
FERNDALE ST S MPW 123-B2
FERNDALE WOODS RD WAY 104-A3
FERNLANE TER JT 145-E3
FERNSIDE LN MOU 117-A1
FERNWOOD AVE RVL 93-D4
FERNWOOD AVE N RVL 93-D4,107-D1
FERNWOOD CIR BL 18-B4
FERNWOOD CIR CHM 63-B3
FERNWOOD CIR N STA 11-B4
FERNWOOD CT RVL 93-D4
FERNWOOD CT SVW 79-D1
FERNWOOD LN APV 163-C1
FERNWOOD LN N CHM 63-B3
FERNWOOD PL MHT 95-D1
FERNWOOD ST AH 79-D4,93-D1
FERNWOOD ST STP 107-D2
FERNWOOD ST SVW 79-D1
FERNWOOD ST N RVL 93-D3
FERONIA AVE STP 107-C4
FERRANT PL MPL 106-B1
FERRARA AVE N HUG 67-B4
FERRARA CT HUG 67-B4
FERRET ST NW RAM 34-D4,48-D2
FERRIS AVE APV 149-C4,163-C1
FERRIS CT APV 149-C4
FERRIS LN MTK 118-E3
FERRIS LN RVL 93-C4
FERRIS TRL N STA 11-B3
FERRY ST LES 212-D4
FERRY ST N ANO 49-C4
FERRY ST S ANO 49-C4,63-C1
FERRY LANDING RD SMT 55-C3
FERTILE AVE FOT 217-C4
FESCUE CT APV 163-C3
FESCUE CT EPR 133-A3
FESTAL AVE LVL 163-C4
FETCH AVE NW SVT 15-D4
FETCH AVE SW WDT 99-D1
FETTERLY LN MTK 105-B3
FETTERLY RD MTK 105-B4
FF ST WBL 80-D4
FIEDLER AVE NW MLT 43-D3
FIEDLER AVE SW MVT 71-D4
FIELD AVE STP 121-C3
FIELD AVE N WYT 39-B1
FIELD DR GV 105-C3
FIELD LN RF 140-D1
FIELD ST BEC 2-E4
FIELD WAY EDI 119-C3
FIELD CREEK CIR VIC 131-A2
FIELD STONE CT MH 136-B1
FIELD STONE DR MH 136-B1
FIELD STONE PL IND 88-D4
FIELDCREST AVE LVL 163-C4,177-C1
FIELDCREST AVE MON 86-C1
FIELDCREST CIR MO 31-D3
FIELDCREST CT LVL 163-C4
FIELDCREST CT MON 86-C1
FIELDCREST LN BUR 162-B2
FIELDCREST RD EPR 133-B3
FIELDFARE WAY LVL 163-C4,177-C1
FIELDING TRL MTA 102-C3
FIELDRIDGE RD GRA 81-D3
FIELDSTONE CIR CHS 131-C4
FIESTA AVE LVL 163-C4
FIFIELD AVE FH 107-C2
FIFIELD PL FH 107-C2
FIFIELD ST FH 107-C2
FIFIELD ST STP 107-C2
FIFTH AVE N GV 106-B2
FIFTH AVE N HOP 119-C2
FIFTH AVE S HOP 119-B2
FIFTH ST N HOP 119-B1
FIFTH ST S HOP 119-B2
FILKINS ST PRE 153-B4,167-B1
FILLMORE AVE PRL 161-B3
FILLMORE AVE E STP 108-C4,122-C1
FILLMORE AVE NW CWT 1-D4,15-D1
FILLMORE AVE NW MLT 43-D3
FILLMORE AVE NW SVT 15-D2
FILLMORE AVE SW WDT 85-D3
FILLMORE CIR FRI 78-E4
FILLMORE CIR E FRI 78-E4
FILLMORE CIR NE EB 8-E3
FILLMORE CIR S FRI 78-E4
FILLMORE CIR W FRI 78-E4
FILLMORE PL NE BLA 64-E3
FILLMORE ST HUD 111-D2
FILLMORE ST NE BLA 50-E4,64-E2
FILLMORE ST NE CH 92-E1
FILLMORE ST NE EB 8-E3,36-E2
FILLMORE ST NE FRI 78-E4,92-E1
FILLMORE ST NE HL 36-E2,50-E1
FILLMORE ST NE MPL 92-E3,106-E1
FILLMORE ST NE SLK 78-E1
FILLMORE ST NW ER 34-B2,48-B1
FILLMORE ST S SHK 146-B2
FILLY TRL SE BKR 2-E1,3-A1
FINALE AVE N HUG 67-B3
FINCH AVE APV 163-C3
FINCH AVE N STA 11-B3
FINCH AVE W LVL 163-C3
FINCH CT RAT 207-C3
FINCH CT WBT 80-E2
FINCH CT WYO 25-B4
FINCH CT N STA 11-B3
FINCH LN APV 163-C3
FINCH LN MOU 103-A4,117-A1
FINCH PATH LVL 163-C4
FINCH WAY APV 149-C4
FINCH WAY W LVL 163-C3
FINDLAY AVE APV 149-C4,163-C1
FINDLAY CT APV 149-C4,163-C1
FINDLAY WAY APV 149-C4,163-C1
FINDLAY WAY W LVL 163-C3
FINDLEY PL MPL 106-C4
FINESSE TRL LVL 163-C4
FINESSE WAY APV 163-C3
FINESSE WAY LVL 163-C3
FINEWOOD CT APV 163-C3
FINLAND AVE WYO 25-B3
FINLAND AVE W LVL 163-C3
FINLEY AVE HUG 67-B1
FINLEY AVE WYO 25-B3
FINLEY AVE N HUG 67-B2
FINLEY BAY HUG 67-B1
FINLEY CT N FLT 39-B4
FINN ST N STP 107-C4
FINN ST S STP 121-C1
FIONA AVE N HUG 67-B3,81-B1
FIONA CIR N HUG 67-B3
FIONA RD HUG 67-B4,81-B1
FIONA RD N HUG 67-B4
FIR PT EAG 149-C2
FIR ST MHT 95-D1
FIR ST STP 123-A2
FIR ST E BUF 59-A2
FIR ST N LP 113-B4
FIR ST S LP 113-B4,127-B1
FIR ST W BUF 59-A2
FIR TRL N LET 11-A4
FIR TREE AVE CHN 117-C4
FIRE BARN RD CP 65-D3
FIREBIRD CT LVL 177-C1
FIREBIRD PATH LVL 163-C4,177-C1
FIRELIGHT CT APV 163-C1
FIRELIGHT WAY APV 163-C1
FIRELIGHT WAY LVL 163-C4,177-C1
FIRESIDE CT SHK 146-B3
FIRESIDE DR APV 163-A2
FIRESIDE DR NE FRI 78-E2,79-A2
FIRESIDE LN LVL 163-C4
FIRESTATION RD FS 121-B4
FIRESTONE CIR LVL 163-C4
FIRESTONE CT LVL 163-C4
FIRESTONE PATH LVL 163-C4
FIRESTONE WAY LVL 163-C4
FIRETHORN PT EPR 132-B2
FIREWOOD WAY NE FRI 78-C2
FIRMAN CT LVL 163-C4
FIRST AVE IND 102-B2
FIRST AVE SB 116-A3
FIRST AVE N MPL 106-D2
FIRST AVE N PLY 104-C2
FIRST AVE NE MPL 106-D2
FIRST AVE NE OSS 77-C1
FIRST AVE NW OSS 77-C1
FIRST AVE S BLO 134-D3,148-D1
FIRST AVE S MPL 106-D4,120-D1
FIRST AVE S RCH 120-D4,134-D1
FIRST ST EXC 117-E3
FIRST ST N HOP 119-B2
FIRST ST N MPL 92-C3,106-D2
FIRST ST N MTK 119-B2
FIRST ST NE HOP 119-C2
FIRST ST NE MPL 92-D4
FIRST ST NE OSS 77-C2
FIRST ST NW OSS 77-C2
FIRST ST NW SLP 119-D1
FIRST ST S HOP 119-B2
FIRST ST S MPL 106-D2
FIRST ST SE OSS 77-C2
FIRTREE DR APV 163-C3
FIRTREE LN APV 163-C3
FIRTREE PL LVL 163-C4
FISCHER AVE HMT 193-C4,207-C1
FISCHER AVE NIT 165-C1
FISCHER AVE RMT 165-C2
FISCHER AVE VER 179-C2
FISCHER AVE VET 165-C4,179-C3
FISCHER CIR SWR 96-E1
FISCHER DR WAC 129-D4
FISH HATCHERY RD STP 108-D4
FISH LAKE CIR E MG 76-E3
FISH LAKE RD E MG 76-E3,77-A4
FISH LAKE RD W MG 76-D3
FISH LAKE PARK RD N MG 76-E4
FISH POINT RD PRL 161-B2
FISH POINT RD SE PRL 161-C3
FISHER AVE NE PRL 161-B1
FISHER CT LVL 163-C4
FISHER CT WBT 80-E2
FISHER LN WBT 80-E4
FISHER ST WBT 80-E2
FISHERS DR NW OG 21-E2
FISHING AVE W LVL 163-C3
FISHING WAY W LVL 163-C3
FISK ST RVL 93-E4
FISK ST STP 107-E4
FITCH AVE FH 107-C2
FITCH RD MPW 94-E3
FITZGERALD AVE N HUG 67-B2
FIVE HAWKS AVE PRL 161-A3
FIVE HAWKS AVE SE PRL 161-A4
FIVE OAKS DR LVL 163-C4
FIVE OAKS LN BWV 95-C1
FIVE PONDS CIR SAV 161-D2
FJORD AVE APV 163-C3
FJORD DR RFD 74-A4
FLACKWOOD AVE APV 163-C3
FLACKWOOD WAY APV 163-C3
FLAG AVE SAV 147-C3
FLAG AVE N BP 77-C4
FLAG AVE N GV 105-C1
FLAG AVE N NH 91-C4
FLAG AVE S GV 105-C3
FLAG AVE S SAV 161-C2
FLAG AVE S SLP 105-C3,119-C1
FLAG BLVD NP 201-E1
FLAG CIR N NH 91-C4
FLAG CT N NH 91-C4
FLAG TRL CRT 175-C4
FLAG TRL SLT 175-C4
FLAGSTAFF AVE APV 149-C4,163-C2
FLAGSTAFF AVE EUT 191-C1
FLAGSTAFF AVE FAR 177-C2,191-C1
FLAGSTAFF AVE LVL 163-C4,177-C1
FLAGSTAFF CIR PRL 161-B3
FLAGSTAFF CT APV 163-B1
FLAGSTAFF CT N LVL 163-C3
FLAGSTAFF CT S LVL 163-C3
FLAGSTAFF WAY W LVL 163-C3
FLAGSTONE TRL APV 163-B1
FLAGTONE TRL APV 163-C1
FLAIR CIR LVL 177-C1
FLAIR CT APV 163-C1
FLAMINGO CT APV 149-B4
FLAMINGO DR CHN 131-E3
FLAMINGO DR EAG 135-C4
FLAMINGO DR SHK 146-C2
FLAMINGO DR NE HL 36-E3
FLAMINGO ST NW AND 50-B2
FLAMINGO ST NW CR 64-B3
FLAMINGO ST NW OG 22-B4,36-B1
FLAMINGO ST NW STT 8-B1
FLAN CT APV 163-C3
FLANDERS AVE SW MVT 57-D4,71-D1
FLANDERS AVE SW WDT 85-D2
FLANDERS CT NE BLA 65-C2
FLANDERS PATH APV 163-B2
FLANDERS RD NSP 95-A4
FLANDERS ST BLA 51-B4
FLANDERS ST NE BLA 65-B3
FLANDERS ST NE EB 37-B2
FLANDRAU CIR PRL 161-C2
FLANDRAU PL STP 108-E4,109-A4
FLANDRAU ST MPW 94-E4,108-E1
FLANDRAU ST STP 108-E3
FLANDRAU TRL NW PRL 160-E2
FLAX WAY APV 163-B2
FLAY AVE N FLT 39-B2
FLAY AVE N HUG 67-B3
FLAY RD N HUG 67-B4
FLAY AVENUE CT N FLT 39-B2
FLEET TRL APV 163-B3
FLEETWOOD AVE APV 163-B1
FLEETWOOD DR EDI 133-D1
FLEMMING CIR CRT 161-D4
FLEMMING LN CRT 161-D4
FLEMMING RD CRT 161-D4
FLESHER CIR EPR 132-E3
FLETCHER CT WYO 25-B3
FLETCHER LN HSN 62-A2
FLETCHER LN ROG 62-A1
FLETCHER PL HOP 119-B1
FLICKER CIR EAG 135-D4
FLIGHT LN APV 163-B3
FLIGHT WAY APV 163-B3
FLINT AVE LVL 177-C1
FLINT CT WYO 25-B4
FLINT DR EAG 149-B1
FLINT LN APV 163-B1
FLINT LN EAG 149-B1
FLINT RD PRL 161-B2
FLINT TRL WYO 25-B4
FLINT TRL N WYO 25-B4
FLINTLOCK TRL CHN 132-A4
FLINTWOOD AVE WYO 25-B3
FLINTWOOD CIR WYO 25-B3
FLINTWOOD CIR NW CR 64-D1
FLINTWOOD CT APV 163-C1
FLINTWOOD LN WYO 25-B3
FLINTWOOD ST NW AND 36-D3
FLINTWOOD ST NW CR 50-D4,64-D1
FLINTWOOD ST NW OG 22-D4
FLINTWOOD ST NW SF 8-D4
FLINTWOOD WAY APV 163-B1
FLOAT CT APV 163-B3
FLOAT LN APV 163-B3
FLORA CT APV 163-B2
FLORA CT LL 66-E4
FLORA CT NFD 219-D3
FLORA CT NW AND 35-E3
FLORA DR EAG 149-C3
FLORA SQ PRE 167-B1
FLORA ST PRE 153-B4,167-B1
FLORA ST NW AND 50-A2
FLORA ST NW CR 49-E3,63-E2
FLORA ST NW OG 35-E1
FLORA ST NW SF 7-E4
FLORA WAY APV 163-B2
FLORAL AVE APV 149-B4
FLORAL AVE N LET 11-B2
FLORAL CT APV 149-B4
FLORAL CT WYO 25-B4
FLORAL DR WBL 95-A1
FLORAL DR W AH 93-D1
FLORAL DR W SVW 80-A4,94-A1
FLORAL BAY DR N FLT 39-B4
FLORENCE AVE MHT 95-D2
FLORENCE DR TKB 117-D3
FLORENCE LN HUT 98-C4,112-C1
FLORENCE LN SSP 122-D4
FLORENCE ST HAS 166-D2
FLORENCE ST WBL 80-E4,81-A4
FLORENCE TRL APV 163-B2
FLORET WAY APV 163-C2
FLORIDA AVE BLA 79-B1
FLORIDA AVE N BP 77-D4,91-D1
FLORIDA AVE N CHM 63-D2
FLORIDA AVE N CRY 91-D4
FLORIDA AVE N GV 91-D4,105-D1
FLORIDA AVE S BLO 147-D1
FLORIDA AVE S GV 105-D3
FLORIDA AVE S SLP 105-D4,119-D1
FLORIDA CIR N BP 77-D3
FLORIDA CIR N CHM 63-D3
FLORIDA CT APV 149-B4,163-B1
FLORIDA CT GV 105-D2
FLORIDA CT LVL 163-C4
FLORIDA CT N BP 77-D2
FLORIDA LN APV 149-C4
FLORIDA ST STP 122-C1
FLORIDA ST SE LON 217-B3
FLORIDA WAY W LVL 163-B3
FLORIN AVE W LVL 163-C3
FLORIST CIR APV 163-B2
FLOTILLA TRL APV 163-B3
FLOUNDER AVE W LVL 163-B3
FLOUNDER CT W LVL 163-B4
FLOWER ST IND 102-B2
FLOWER WAY APV 163-B2
FLOWERFIELD RD BLA 65-C4
FLOWERFIELD RD CP 65-D4

FLOYD ST N CF 208-A4
FLOYD ST S CF 208-A4
FLUORINE ST NW RAM 35-B2,49-B2
FLUTE WAY APV 163-B3
FLYBOAT LN APV 163-B3
FLYING CLOUD DR CHN 146-B1
FLYING CLOUD DR EPR .. 133-A3,146-C1
FLYWAY CIR EPR 133-B3
FOGELMAN RD IND 88-D3
FOGHORN LN APV 163-B3
FOLEY AVE N STA 11-B3
FOLEY AVE NW CMT 57-D2
FOLEY BLVD NW CR 50-C4,64-D3
FOLIAGE AVE APV 149-B4,163-B2
FOLIAGE AVE GVT 205-C3,219-C1
FOLIAGE AVE LVL 163-B3
FOLIAGE CT APV 149-B4
FOLIAGE CT LVL 163-B3
FOLLEY AVE BL 18-A4
FOLSOM AVE CNC 12-E4
FOLSOM PATH LVL 163-B4
FOLSOM ST STP 107-E2
FOLSOM ST TF 14-B3
FOLWELL AVE FH 107-C2
FOLWELL DR MPL 121-B1
FONDANT AVE N FLT 39-B4
FONDANT AVE N HUG 67-B3
FONDANT AVE N WYT 39-B1
FONDANT TRL N HUG 67-B4
FONDELL DR EDI 134-A1
FONTAINE CT WBY 109-D4
FONTANA PATH LVL 163-B4
FONTANA ST NE LWT 9-E4
FONTINA PATH LVL 177-B1
FOOTBRIDGE WAY APV 163-B1
FOOTHILL RD S CG 137-E4
FOOTHILL TRL VH 80-B4
FOOTHILL TRL S SHK 147-B4
FORBES AVE STP 122-B1
FORBES AVE W LVL 163-B3
FORBES CT LVL 163-B4
FORD CIR SLP 105-C3
FORD LN SLP 105-C2
FORD PKWY MPL 121-B2
FORD PKWY STP 121-C2
FORD RD MTK 105-C3
FORD RD NEW 123-B4
FORD RD SLP 105-C2
FORD ST N FH 107-C2
FORD BROOK DR BT 21-B4
FORD BROOK DR NW BT 21-B3
FORDHAM AVE APV 149-B4,163-B1
FORDHAM AVE EUT 191-B3
FORDHAM CT APV 149-B4,163-B1
FORDHAM DR SA 93-B2
FOREST AVE ANO 49-B4
FOREST AVE CHN 117-D4
FOREST AVE IGH 137-A3
FOREST AVE MHT 81-D4,95-D1
FOREST AVE NFD 219-D4
FOREST AVE SCT 173-D3
FOREST AVE N BP 77-D4,91-D1
FOREST BLVD WBY 123-D3
FOREST BLVD WYO 25-B3
FOREST BLVD WYT 25-B2
FOREST BLVD N FLT 39-B4,53-B1
FOREST BLVD N HUG 67-B4,81-B4
FOREST BLVD N LET 11-B2
FOREST BLVD N STA 11-B3
FOREST BLVD N WYO 25-B4
FOREST BLVD N WYT 25-B1,39-B1
FOREST CIR BUR 162-C3
FOREST CIR CHN 117-D4
FOREST CIR MTK 118-E2
FOREST CIR NMT 190-C1
FOREST CIR RFD 74-B3
FOREST CIR SE PRL 161-C2
FOREST CT APV 149-B4
FOREST CT BLA 65-B2
FOREST CT PRL 161-C2
FOREST CT WBL 81-B4
FOREST DR BEC 2-E3
FOREST DR CP 65-D4
FOREST DR HUT 112-A2
FOREST DR SOM 84-B1
FOREST DR SWD 118-A2
FOREST DR NE CH 93-A1
FOREST DR W RCH 134-B1
FOREST HTS LFL 109-C4
FOREST LN AH 93-D2
FOREST LN APV 163-B1
FOREST LN MOU 116-D1
FOREST LN MTK 104-E4
FOREST LN SLP 106-A3
FOREST RD BL 18-A4
FOREST RD CFT 208-E3
FOREST RD EB 37-D1
FOREST RD MTK 118-C3
FOREST RD RFD 74-B3
FOREST RD SB 116-A3
FOREST RD SLP 106-A3
FOREST RD N FLT 39-B4,53-B2
FOREST RD N HUG 53-C3
FOREST RDG CHS 131-D4
FOREST ST HAS 166-D2
FOREST ST LVL 163-B4
FOREST ST MPW 94-D4
FOREST ST STP 108-D3
FOREST ST E BEL 185-E1,186-A1
FOREST ST W BEL 185-E1
FOREST TRL MHT 95-C1
FOREST ARMS LN ORO 103-B3
FOREST BOULEVARD LN WYO 25-B4
FOREST BOULEVARD TRL WYO 25-B4
FOREST BOULEVARD
TRA CT WYO 25-B4
FOREST CITY RD WTT 101-A3
FOREST CREST DR BLO 134-B2
FOREST DALE RD MPL 120-B3
FOREST DALE RD NB 93-A1
FOREST GLEN CT BUR 148-C4
FOREST GLEN CT SAV 148-A4
FOREST GLEN DR BUR 148-C4
FOREST GLEN DR DAT 158-D2
FOREST GLEN LN DAT 158-D2
FOREST GLEN RD BLO 133-D2
FOREST GREEN CIR NP 201-E2
FOREST HILL DR WBY 124-B1
FOREST HILL RD EPR 132-E1
FOREST HILLS CIR BLO .. 133-E3,134-A3
FOREST LAKE DR ORO 103-B3
FOREST LAKE LNDG ORO 103-B4
FOREST MEADOW CIR MTK 105-A4
FOREST MEADOW DR MTK 105-A4
FOREST PARK LN BUR 162-E2
FOREST RIDGE CIR BUF 45-B4
FOREST RIDGE CIR CHN 131-B2
FOREST RIDGE DR NMT 190-C1
FOREST RIDGE LN BUF 45-B4
FOREST RIDGE TRL EAG 135-D4
FORESTVIEW CIR CHM 63-B3
FORESTVIEW CIR EPR 133-B3
FORESTVIEW CIR N DAY 63-A1
FORESTVIEW LN PLY 91-A1
FORESTVIEW LN N DAY 49-A4
FORESTVIEW LN N MG 63-A4,77-A1
FORESTVIEW LN N PLY 91-A2,105-A2
FORFAR CT LVL 163-B4
FORK DR S TRT 125-E1
FORLI AVE WYO 25-B3
FORMOSA AVE LVL 163-B4,177-B1
FORNER LN CAR 145-B3
FORREST DR BEC 2-E3
FORSHAM LAKE DR LL 66-A2
FORSLIN DR EDI 119-E4
FORSSA WAY EAG 149-C3
FORSTER ST STP 121-E2,122-A2
FORSYTHE AVE NW CWT 15-D1
FORSYTHE AVE SW WDT 99-D1
FORSYTHE RD SE PRL 161-C3
FORT RD HEN 198-C3
FORT RD HET 198-C3
FORT SNELLING DR FS 121-C4
FORTMANN CIR NW RAM 34-C4
FORTUNE TRL LVL 163-B4,177-B1
FORUM PATH APV 163-B2
FOSS RD NB 93-B2
FOSS RD SA 93-B2
FOSSIL LN APV 163-B1
FOSTER AVE N STA 11-B3
FOSTER CT RF 140-D3
FOSTER PL NO 80-A2
FOSTER ST RF 140-D2
FOUNDERS PKWY BP 77-D2
FOUNTAIN AVE APV 163-B1
FOUNTAIN AVE WYT 25-B2
FOUNTAIN AVE N HUG 67-B3
FOUNTAIN CIR PLY 90-C3
FOUNTAIN CT APV 163-B1
FOUNTAIN CT N MG 76-C3
FOUNTAIN LN N MG 76-C2
FOUNTAIN LN N PLY 90-C4,104-C1
FOUNTAIN PL EPR 133-A3
FOUNTAIN PL STP 108-C3
FOUNTAIN HILLS CT PRL 161-A1
FOUNTAIN HILLS DR PRL 161-A1
FOUNTIAN LN WAC 129-D4
FOUNTIAN LN N MG 76-C3
FOUR OAKS RD EAG 135-C3
FOUR SEASONS CT EAG 149-A3
FOUR SEASONS DR EAG 149-A3
FOURMIES AVE NE FRI 78-D3
FOURTH AVE NE NYA 142-C3
FOURTH ST N HOP 119-B1
FOURTH ST N LE 109-E4
FOURTH ST N OKD 109-C4
FOX CIR HUT 112-A2
FOX CIR LL 66-B4
FOX CT CHN 118-A4
FOX PATH CHN 118-A4
FOX PL MH 136-A1
FOX RD LL 66-B4
FOX RDG NE BLA 65-B2
FOX RUN CV 66-D2
FOX RUN ORO 103-D3
FOX RUN PRL 160-E2
FOX ST DEL 87-E3
FOX ST HUD 111-D2
FOX ST ORO 103-D3
FOX ST NW AND 35-D4,49-D1
FOX ST NW SF 7-D4
FOX TRL ABT 58-D1
FOX TRL PRL 160-E2
FOX TRL SB 116-B3
FOX DEN CT NO 80-C2
FOX FARM RD RW 196-E4
FOX HILL CT HUG 67-B4
FOX HILL DR CHN 132-A1
FOX HILL RD HUG 67-B4
FOX HOLLOW CIR CHM 63-B3
FOX HOLLOW DR CHN 118-B4
FOX HOLLOW LN CHM 63-B3
FOX HOLLOW ST PRL 160-E2
FOX HUNT CT PRL 161-A2
FOX MEADOW LN EDI 119-D3
FOX PATH CT MED 90-A1
FOX RIDGE CIR IND 102-D2
FOX RIDGE CT EAG 149-B2
FOX RIDGE CT E WSP 122-C4
FOX RIDGE RD EAG 149-C2
FOX RIDGE RD ORO 103-D3
FOX RIDGE RD SLT 175-A2
FOX RIDGE RD WSP 122-C4
FOX RIDGE TRL SJT 83-E4,97-E1
FOX RUN BAY WBY 124-B1
FOX RUN CIR EPR 133-B3
FOX RUN CV WBY 124-B1
FOX RUN RD WAC 129-D3
FOX RUN RD WBY 124-B1
FOX RUN TRL PRL 160-E2
FOX TAIL CT CHN 118-B4
FOX TREE LN N NOH 97-C4
FOX VALLEY RD COR 75-D1
FOXBERRY BAY SAV 147-D4,161-D1
FOXBERRY CIR MED 90-A1
FOXBERRY CT MED 90-A1
FOXBERRY CT SAV 161-D1
FOXBERRY DR MED 90-A1
FOXBERRY DR SAV 161-D1
FOXBERRY RD SAV 147-D4,161-D1
FOXBERRY FARMS RD MED 90-A1
FOXBORO AVE WYO 25-B3
FOXBORO CT LVL 163-B4
FOXBORO CT WBY 123-D2
FOXBORO CT WYO 25-B3
FOXBORO LN LVL 163-B4,177-B1
FOXBORO LN WBY 123-D2
FOXBORO LN WYO 25-B3
FOXBORO WAY SLW 173-A2
FOXBOROUGH LES 212-D4
FOXFORD RD CHN 132-B4
FOXGATE DR MTK 104-E4
FOXGLOVE AVE N BP 78-A1
FOXGLOVE CIR VIC 131-B1
FOXGLOVE CT SHK 146-B3
FOXGLOVE CT N BP 78-A1
FOXGLOVE LN SHK 146-B3
FOXGLOVE ST GRF 74-A4,88-A1
FOXGLOVE WAY HUD 111-E4
FOXHALL RD MTK 105-B4
FOXHILL AVE N HUG 53-B3,67-B2
FOXHILL AVE N LET 11-B3
FOXHILL AVE N STA 11-B3
FOXHILL AVE N WYT 25-B2
FOXLINE DR COR 75-D1
FOXMOORE CT EAG 150-A1
FOXPOINT CIR BUR 149-A1
FOXPOINT RD BUR 149-A1
FOXRIDGE RD STP 109-A4
FOXTAIL CT APV 163-B1
FOXTAIL CT CG 137-C2
FOXTAIL CT LL 80-E1
FOXTAIL CT LYT 1-B2
FOXTAIL DR LL 80-E1
FOXTAIL DR MED 90-A2
FOXTAIL LN APV 163-B1
FOXTAIL LN ROG 61-E2,62-A2
FOXTAIL TRL NW PRL 161-A2
FOXWOOD CT NB 79-B3
FOXWOOD LN MH 122-B3
FRAISER ST HAS 166-C1
FRAIZER ST NE BLA 65-D3
FRAIZER ST NE HL 37-D3,51-D3
FRAME AVE NIT 165-C3
FRANCE AVE EKO 190-A4,204-A1
FRANCE AVE NMT 190-A2
FRANCE AVE N BC 78-A4,92-A2
FRANCE AVE N BP 64-A4,78-A2
FRANCE AVE N GV 106-A2
FRANCE AVE N ROB 92-A4,106-A1
FRANCE AVE S BLO 134-A3,148-A1
FRANCE AVE S EDI 120-A4,134-A1
FRANCE AVE S GV 106-A2
FRANCE AVE S MPL 106-A3,120-A2
FRANCE AVE S SLP 106-A4,120-A1
FRANCE BLVD CRT 176-A4
FRANCE CIR CRT 176-A3
FRANCE CIR NMT 190-B2
FRANCE CT CRT 176-B4
FRANCE PL BC 92-A1
FRANCES AVE TRT 112-B4,126-B1
FRANCES ST SOM 84-B1
FRANCESCA AVE N HUG 67-B2
FRANCHISE AVE APV 163-B1
FRANCHISE AVE W LVL 163-B3
FRANCHISE CT W LVL 163-B3
FRANCHISE WAY LVL 163-B4
FRANCIS AVE PLY 105-B2
FRANCIS CIR NFD 219-E4
FRANCIS CT NM 190-A4
FRANCIS CT SHK 146-C4
FRANCIS LN NM 190-A4
FRANCIS ST SSP 122-D4
FRANCONIA PKWY FRT 28-A1
FRANCONIA TRL N FRT 13-D4,28-A1
FRANK CT MPW 94-D3
FRANK ST MPW 94-D3,108-D1
FRANK ST STP 108-D3
FRANKFORT PKWY SM 46-E3,47-B3
FRANKLAND ST MHT 95-D1
FRANKLIN AVE DEL 87-D2
FRANKLIN AVE STP 107-B3
FRANKLIN AVE WAV 86-A1
FRANKLIN AVE WBT 81-B2
FRANKLIN AVE E MPL 106-E3,107-A3
FRANKLIN AVE N STA 11-B4
FRANKLIN AVE NW CWT 15-D2
FRANKLIN AVE NW WAT 101-A3
FRANKLIN AVE SE MPL 107-A3
FRANKLIN AVE SW WAT 101-A3
FRANKLIN AVE W DEL 87-D2
FRANKLIN AVE W MPL 106-C3
FRANKLIN AVE W SLP 105-D3
FRANKLIN CIR PRL 161-B3
FRANKLIN CIR E EPR 132-D1
FRANKLIN LN ANO 49-C4
FRANKLIN RD LYT 1-A2
FRANKLIN RD MOU 116-E2,117-A2
FRANKLIN ST HAS 166-D1
FRANKLIN ST MSC 55-B4
FRANKLIN ST N NYA 142-C4
FRANKLIN TER MPL 107-A3
FRANKLIN TRL SE PRL 161-B3
FRANKLIN HILLS RD IND 88-D3
FRANKMAN PL MPL 121-A2
FRANKSON AVE STP 107-D2
FRANLO RD EPR 133-B4,147-B1
FRASER LN HUT 98-C4,112-C1
FRATALONE LN LC 94-C3
FRAZER PATH LVL 163-B4
FRAZER ST NE EB 23-D3
FRAZER WAY W LVL 163-B3
FRAZIER ST RW 182-D4
FREAR DR MTK 104-E4,119-A1
FREAR ST HUD 111-D3
FRED ST STP 108-C3
FREDEEN CT NB 79-B4
FREDERIC RD HSN 48-A2
FREDERICK AVE SLP 105-C4
FREDERICK PKWY MPW 95-A3
FREDERICK RD HSN 48-A3
FREDERICK ST MPW 95-A3
FREDERICK ST ORO 117-C1
FREEBORN AVE CLT 188-C4
FREEBORN AVE NIT 165-C3
FREEDOM AVE NP 201-E1
FREEDOM DR ARL 183-A3
FREELAND AVE N HUG 67-B3
FREELAND CT N HUG 67-B3
FREEMAN AVE DEL 87-E3
FREEMOUW AVE NFD 219-D3
FREEPORT AVE WYO 25-B4
FREEPORT AVE NW ER 19-E4,33-E1
FREEPORT CT APV 163-B1
FREEPORT CT LVL 163-B4
FREEPORT CT WYO 25-B3
FREEPORT CT NW ER 19-E4
FREEPORT ST ER 33-E1
FREEPORT TRL APV 163-B1
FREEPORT WAY LVL 163-B4
FREESIA WAY APV 163-B2
FREEWAY BLVD BC 78-B4
FREEWAY DR COT 38-E4,52-E1
FREEWAY DR NE COT 52-E2
FREEWAY RD MH 122-A4
FREEWAY RD N MH 122-A4
FREEWAY RD S MH 122-A4
FREMONT ALC EAG 149-B2
FREMONT AVE MH 122-B2
FREMONT AVE MPW 109-B3
FREMONT AVE PRL 160-E3,161-A3
FREMONT AVE STP 108-E3,109-A3
FREMONT AVE ZIM 5-C1
FREMONT AVE N BC 78-C3,92-C1
FREMONT AVE N BP 78-C3
FREMONT AVE N MPL 92-C3,106-C1
FREMONT AVE S BLO 134-C3,148-C1
FREMONT AVE S BUR 148-C4,162-C3
FREMONT AVE S MPL 106-C4,120-C2
FREMONT AVE S RCH 134-C1
FREMONT CIR NW PRL 160-E3
FREMONT CT BUR 162-C3
FREMONT CT N BP 78-C3
FREMONT LN WBY 123-C3
FREMONT LN ZIM 5-D1
FREMONT PL BUR 148-C4
FREMONT PL N BC 78-C4
FREMONT ST ANO 49-C4
FREMONT ST PRL 160-E3
FREMONT ST E NFD 219-E4
FREMONT ST N RF 140-D1
FREMONT ST S RF 140-D2
FREMONT ST SW WAT 101-A3
FREMONT ST W NFD 219-D4
FRENCH AVE LVL 163-B4
FRENCH CRV EPR 132-C3
FRENCH CREEK CIR ORO 103-D4
FRENCH CREEK DR ORO 103-D4
FRENCH LAKE RD CHM 63-B1
FRENCH LAKE RD ORO 103-D3
FRENCH LAKE RD E DAY 62-C2
FRENCH LAKE RD W DAY 62-B2
FRENCH TRACE AVE SHK 146-C3
FRENCHMAN RD HUG 67-A2
FRESNO AVE APV 163-B1
FRESNO AVE NW ER 5-C4
FRESNO AVE NW LIT 5-C4
FRESNO ST NW ER 19-C2,33-C2
FRIAR DR EPR 133-C4
FRIAR LN MTK 119-B1
FRIBOURG CT VIC 131-A1
FRIDAY LN APV 163-B1
FRIDLEY ST NE FRI 79-A3
FRIDLEY WAY APV 163-B2
FRIENDSHIP LN BUR 162-B1
FRIENDSHIP LN N CHS 131-C4
FRIENDSHIP LN S CHS 131-C4
FRIESLAND AVE WYO 25-B3
FRIESLAND CT WYO 25-B4
FRISBIE AVE MPW 108-D1
FRISCO CT CHN 132-B3
FROG POND LN SJT 84-C4,98-C1
FROMME CT EAG 150-B1
FROMMES CIR MTK 118-C3
FRONDELL CT EPR 132-C3
FRONT AVE ANO 49-C4
FRONT AVE STP 107-E3,108-A3
FRONT BLVD E EB 23-D4,37-D1
FRONT ST HUD 111-C3
FRONT ST MO 31-D1
FRONT ST PRE 167-B1
FRONT ST RAN 207-A3
FRONT ST SPP 137-B3
FRONT ST WDL 104-C4
FRONT ST NE SM 46-E3
FRONT ST NW RAM 49-A3
FRONT ST NW SM 46-E3
FRONT ST S HUD 111-D3
FRONTAGE AVE N STA 11-B3
FRONTAGE RD EAG 149-D1
FRONTAGE RD IGH 136-C3,150-E2
FRONTAGE RD JT 145-E3
FRONTAGE RD OSC 28-A3
FRONTAGE RD RF 126-E4
FRONTAGE RD SLP 105-C3
FRONTAGE RD SM 47-A3
FRONTAGE RD TRT 126-D4
FRONTAGE RD VH 94-E2
FRONTAGE RD E OTS 33-E3
FRONTAGE RD E WAC 129-E3
FRONTAGE RD N BUR 148-B3
FRONTAGE RD N OPH 97-A2
FRONTAGE RD N SWR 96-E2,97-A2
FRONTAGE RD S BUR 148-B3
FRONTAGE RD S EAG 149-A1
FRONTAGE RD S HAS 166-C2
FRONTAGE RD W BUR 148-C3
FRONTAGE RD W SHK 147-A2
FRONTAGE RD W SWR 96-E2
FRONTAGE RD STH 35 RF 126-E4
FRONTENAC AVE N GV 105-E1,106-A1
FRONTENAC PL STP 107-B4
FRONTIER AVE N LET 11-B3
FRONTIER AVE N STA 11-B3
FRONTIER CIR BEC 2-E3
FRONTIER CIR BEL 186-A2
FRONTIER CT BUR 162-E1
FRONTIER CT CHN 132-B2
FRONTIER DR BEL 186-A2
FRONTIER LN BUR 162-E1
FRONTIER TRL CHN 132-A1
FROST AVE MPW 108-E1,109-A1
FROST ST E SSP 136-E1
FROST ST W SSP 136-E1
FROST POINT CIR PRL 161-B2
FRY ST FH 107-D1
FRY ST RVL 93-D4,107-D1
FRY ST STP 107-D4,121-D1
FULBRIGHT CIR SE PRL 161-C2
FULHAM ST LAU 107-B1
FULHAM ST RVL 93-B4,107-B1
FULHAM ST STP 107-B2
FULLER AVE STP 107-E4,108-A4
FULLER RD EPR 132-D2
FULLER ST SHK 146-B3
FULLER ST N SHK 146-B2
FULLER ST S SHK 146-B2
FULLER ST W EDI 120-A3
FULTON CIR LYT 1-B1
FULTON ST STP 121-E1
FULTON ST SE MPL 107-A3
FURLONG AVE MH 135-D1
FURLONG TRL NIT 165-C1
FURMAN ST NE COT 38-D3,52-D2
FURMAN ST NE LWT 10-D3
FURNESS CT MPW 95-A3
FURNESS PKWY STP 109-A2
FURNESS ST MPW 95-A3,109-A1
FURUBY RD CGT 12-E1,13-A1
FURUBY RD SHT 13-C1,14-A2
FURUBY RD TF 14-B2

G

G CT NE EB 37-D1
G ST LL 66-C1
G ST MEN 121-D4
G ST WBY 123-D1
GAAGE LN LL 66-C3
GABBERT CIR EAG 149-E2
GABBRO TRL EAG 149-C1
GABLE AVE N STA 11-B3
GABLE LN APV 149-B4
GABLER AVE NE SM 45-E4
GABLER AVE SE RFT 59-E4,73-E2
GABRIEL RD STP 123-A2
GADIENT WAY SWR 96-C2
GADWALL CT EAG 149-C2
GADWALL LN NO 80-C3
GADWALL LN ROG 48-A4
GADWELL ST APV 163-B2
GAGE AVE LVL 163-B4,177-B1
GAGE CT LVL 163-B4

GAGE WAY LVL 163-B4
GAGNEF PL BUF 58-E1
GALAHAD PL NOH 97-C4
GALAHAD RD N NOH 97-C4,111-C1
GALAXIE AVE APV 149-B4,163-B2
GALAXIE AVE EAG 149-B3
GALAXIE AVE EUT 191-B4,205-B1
GALAXIE CT APV 163-B1
GALAXIE CT EAG 149-C2
GALAXIE PL APV 149-B4
GALAXIE WAY W LVL 163-B3
GALAXY AVE N WYT 39-B1
GALAXY DR CP 65-D3
GALE CIR AH 93-D1
GALE RD WDL 104-B4
GALEN DR WYO 25-B4
GALENA AVE BPT 186-C1
GALENA AVE W LVL 163-B4
GALENA ST HAS 166-E1
GALENA WAY APV 149-B4
GALENA WAY BPT 186-C1
GALERY DR LVL 177-B1
GALIUM WAY WAT 101-B4
GALL AVE MPW 95-B3
GALLAGHER DR EDI 134-A1
GALLANT CT APV 163-B3
GALLERIA PL W APV 149-B4
GALLERY AVE APV 163-B3
GALLIVAN CT N HUG 67-A4
GALLUP CT APV 149-B4
GALPIN BLVD CHN 117-E4,131-D2
GALPIN LN SWD 117-E4
GALPIN LAKE RD SWD 117-E4
GALTIER CIR RVL 94-B4
GALTIER DR BUR 149-A2
GALTIER PL BUR 149-A2
GALTIER PL SVW 80-B4
GALTIER ST RVL 94-B3,108-B1
GALTIER ST STP 108-B3
GALTIER ST SVW 80-A4
GALVESTON AVE APV 163-B3
GALVIN AVE WSP 122-B3
GALWAY CIR WBY 123-E1
GALWAY CRV EPR 132-C2
GALWAY CT APV 163-B1
GALWAY CT HUD 111-E1
GALWAY DR EDI 119-D4,133-D1
GALWAY LN EAG 149-C1
GALWAY LN MOU 117-A2
GALWAY RD WBY 123-E1
GAMBLE DR SLP 105-E3
GAME FARM CIR MTA 102-D4
GAME FARM RD IND 102-C2
GAME FARM RD E MTA 102-D4
GAME FARM RD N MTA 102-C3
GAMMA DR APV 149-B4
GAMMA WAY APV 149-B4
GANDER LN LVL 163-B4
GANDER RD ORO 103-D3
GANDY DANCER CT TRT 126-A2
GANGES ST NW LWT 10-B4
GANNON AVE W LVL 163-B3
GANNON CT LVL 163-B4
GANNON DR SHK 146-C2
GANNON RD STP 121-C3
GANNON WAY APV 163-B2
GANNON WAY W LVL 163-B4
GANTRY CT APV 149-B3
GANTRY LN APV 149-B3
GANTRY WAY EPR 147-B1
GARBE AVE WBY 109-C4,123-C1
GARCEAU LN VH 94-C2
GARCIA WAY W LVL 163-B4
GARDEN AVE EDI 119-D3
GARDEN AVE FH 107-D1
GARDEN AVE RVL 107-D1
GARDEN BLVD OKD 109-C1
GARDEN CIR BLO 147-D1
GARDEN CT WBY 137-D1
GARDEN CT N OKD 109-C1
GARDEN DR BUR 148-D4
GARDEN DR WBY 137-D1
GARDEN GLN LFL 109-C4
GARDEN LN COR 61-C4,75-C1
GARDEN LN EPR 133-A3
GARDEN LN MH 122-B2
GARDEN LN MOU 116-E2
GARDEN LN ORO 103-A4
GARDEN LN SHK 146-C2
GARDEN LN WBL 80-E3,81-A3
GARDEN LN WBT 80-E3
GARDEN LN WYO 25-B3
GARDEN PARK GV 105-D2
GARDEN PL CHC 26-A1
GARDEN RD SWD 118-A2
GARDEN ST N CAR 145-B4
GARDEN TRL EAG 149-D2
GARDEN GATE CIR APV 163-B3
GARDEN GROVE RD BKR 3-C4,17-D1
GARDEN VIEW CT APV 163-A3
GARDEN VIEW DR APV 162-E3,163-A2
GARDENA AVE NE FRI 78-E4,79-A4
GARDENA CIR NE FRI 78-E4
GARDENA LN NE FRI 78-E4
GARDENETTE DR N WBL 81-A4
GARDENETTE DR S WBL 81-A4
GARDENIA AVE APV 163-B2
GARDENIA CT APV 163-B1
GARDENIA PATH APV 163-B1
GARDNER AVE ROG 47-D3
GARDNER LN DWD 81-C4
GARDNER ST BEC 2-E4
GARDNER ST WAY 104-B3
GAREFLO ST OSC 28-A4
GARFIELD AVE BUR 148-C4
GARFIELD AVE CHM 63-C1
GARFIELD AVE FOT 217-C4
GARFIELD AVE MPL 106-C4,120-C2
GARFIELD AVE RCH 120-C4,134-C1
GARFIELD AVE WHT 217-C3
GARFIELD AVE S BLO 134-C2
GARFIELD AVE S MON 86-C1
GARFIELD CIR EPR 132-D2
GARFIELD ST SOM 84-B1
GARFIELD ST STP 122-A1
GARFIELD ST E ANO 49-D3
GARFIELD ST NE MPL 93-A4,107-A1
GARFIELD ST NE SLK 79-A2
GARFIELD ST W ANO 49-C3
GARLAND AVE APV 149-B4,163-B1
GARLAND CT EPR 132-E3
GARLAND LN MG 76-C3
GARLAND LN N MG 62-C3,76-C1
GARLAND LN N PLY 90-C4,104-C1
GARLAND WAY W LVL 163-B4
GARNER AVE W LVL 163-B3
GARNER CT APV 149-B4
GARNER CT W LVL 163-B3
GARNER LN APV 149-B4
GARNER WAY APV 149-B4
GARNET AVE APV 149-B4
GARNET CT BUR 149-A3
GARNET CT HAN 60-E3
GARNET DR EAG 149-B1
GARNET LN EAG 149-B1
GARNET PT EAG 149-B1
GARNET ST NW BT 21-A1,35-A1
GARNET ST NW RAM 35-A3,49-A1
GARNET WAY APV 163-B3
GARRETT AVE APV 149-B4,163-B2
GARRETT AVE GVT 205-B3,219-B2
GARRETT CT APV 163-B3
GARRETT DR APV 163-B3
GARRETT LN APV 149-B4
GARRETT PATH APV 163-B3
GARRISON AVE MO 32-A3
GARRISON AVE NE MOT 32-A4
GARRISON AVE NE SM 46-A4,60-A3
GARRISON AVE SE RFT 60-A4
GARRISON CT BUR 148-C4
GARRISON LN COR 75-B2
GARRISON LN EDI 120-A4
GARRISON RD COR 75-B2
GARRISON WAY EPR 133-C4
GARVIN BROOK LN APV 149-B4
GARWOOD RD BP 77-E3
GARY AVE LTT 130-A4
GARY BLVD S CG 137-C3
GARY DR SPP 137-C4
GARY PL STP 109-A2
GARY ST NW ER 19-C4,33-C2
GAS LIGHT DR APV 163-B3
GASTON AVE SVW 80-A2
GASTON AVE WBT 81-B2
GATE PARK RD EDI 119-D3
GATES AVE NW ER 33-E1
GATEWAY BLVD AH 79-C4
GATEWAY BLVD BUR 148-C3
GATEWAY BLVD HUD 111-E3
GATEWAY CIR CV 66-E3
GATEWAY CIR HUD 111-E3
GATEWAY CT AH 79-C4
GATEWAY CT HUD 111-E3
GATEWAY DR LVL 177-B4
GATEWAY DR SHK 147-A3
GATEWAY DR STP 107-E2
GATEWAY DR ZIM 5-D1
GATEWAY LN EPR 132-D3
GATEWAY PATH APV 163-B3
GATEWAY ST PRL 161-B3
GATEWOOD CIR MTK 118-D4
GATEWOOD DR MTK 118-D4
GATSKILL ST MSC 55-B4
GAUNTLET CT APV 163-B1
GAUNTLET CT W LVL 163-B3
GAVOTTE AVE APV 149-B4
GAVOTTE CT APV 149-B4
GAYLORD AVE RAT 207-D3
GAYLORD CT RAT 207-D3
GAYNOR ST MTK 119-C1
GAYWOOD DR DAY 62-B2
GAYWOOD DR MTK 118-E2
GEGGEN TINA RD IND 88-D3
GEHRIG ST NE COT 38-E3
GEIGER ST OSC 28-A3
GEISLER RD EPR 132-C4
GEM ST MPW 94-E3
GEMINI RD EAG 135-E3
GEMINI ST NE LWT 10-A4,24-A1
GEMSTONE CT APV 149-B4
GENAKER WAY IND 88-D1
GENERAL MILLS BLVD GV 105-C3
GENERAL SIEBEN DR HAS 166-B2
GENEREUX PL HSN 61-E2
GENES RD SFT 159-A3
GENESEE AVE APV 149-B4,163-B2
GENESEE AVE W LVL 163-B3
GENESEE CT APV 149-B4
GENESEE CT W LVL 163-B3
GENESEE WAY APV 149-B4
GENESIS AVE N STA 11-B3
GENESSE ST STP 108-B3
GENEVA AVE APV 149-B3
GENEVA AVE LVL 163-B4
GENEVA AVE N FLT 39-B4
GENEVA AVE N HUG 67-B3
GENEVA AVE N MPW 95-B3,109-C3
GENEVA AVE N NSP 95-B4,109-B1
GENEVA AVE S CG 137-C2,151-C1
GENEVA AVE S GCT 137-C4,151-C2
GENEVA AVE S NEW 137-C2
GENEVA AVE S SPP 137-C2
GENEVA BLVD BUR 162-D2
GENEVA CT APV 149-B3
GENEVA WAY APV 149-B4,163-B1
GENEVIEVE AVE OKD 109-C1
GENEVIEVE LN MTK 105-B3
GENIE DR NW AND 35-D4
GENSMER CIR CRT 175-D2
GENTILLY RD N MG 77-A4
GENTRY AVE N OKD 95-C4,109-C3
GEOFFREY AVE N FLT 39-B4
GEORGE AVE E WIN 99-B3
GEORGE CT APV 149-B4
GEORGE LN NEW 123-B4
GEORGE ST EXC 117-E3
GEORGE ST HBG 156-A2
GEORGE ST ML 43-D2
GEORGE ST E STP 122-C1
GEORGE ST W STP 122-B1
GEORGE MORAN DR EPR 132-C2
GEORGE WEBER DR ROG 48-A4,62-A1
GEORGETOWN BLO 134-E2
GEORGETOWN CT LVL 163-B4
GEORGETOWN WAY LVL 163-B4
GEORGIA AVE BLA 79-B1
GEORGIA AVE N BP 77-D4
GEORGIA AVE N CHM 63-D2
GEORGIA AVE N CRY 91-D3
GEORGIA AVE N FLT 53-B1
GEORGIA AVE N GV 105-D2
GEORGIA AVE S SLP 105-D4,119-E1
GEORGIA BLVD N OKD 95-C3
GEORGIA CIR APV 163-B1
GEORGIA CIR BKR 3-C4
GEORGIA CT APV 163-B1
GEORGIA CT N BP 77-D2
GEORGIA DR APV 149-B4,163-B1
GEORGIA LN WBL 81-A3
GEORGIA ST SCF 14-C3
GEORGIA ST E SCF 14-C3
GEORGIA AVENUE CIR N FLT 53-B1
GEORGIA AVENUE CT N FLT 53-B1
GEORGIA AVENUE PL N FLT 53-C1
GERALD AVE LEX 65-D4
GERALD AVE NSP 95-A3
GERALD ST OSC 27-E4,28-A4
GERANIUM AVE E MPW 109-B2
GERANIUM AVE E STP 108-C2,109-A2
GERANIUM AVE W STP 108-B2
GERANIUM CT APV 149-B4
GERARD CT APV 149-B4,163-B1
GERARD DR EPR 133-A1
GERDINE CT APV 149-B4
GERDINE CT LVL 163-B4
GERDINE PATH W LVL 163-B3
GERLACH WAY RAT 207-E4
GERMAIN CT MPW 94-E3
GERMAIN CT STP 108-E3
GERMAIN ST MPW 94-E4
GERMAIN ST SOM 70-B4,84-B1
GERMAIN ST STP 108-E3
GERMAINE TER EPR 133-B4
GERMAN RD BKT 185-D4,199-D1
GERMAN ST MPW 95-A4
GERMANE AVE APV 149-B4,163-B1
GERMANE CT W LVL 163-B3
GERMANE TRL APV 149-B4
GERMANIUM CIR NW RAM 49-B1
GERMANIUM ST NW RAM 35-B4,49-B2
GERMANIUM ST NW SF 7-B3
GERSHWIN AVE N OKD 95-C4,109-C3
GERSHWIN CIR N OKD 109-C1
GERSHWIN CT N OKD 109-C1
GERSHWIN LN N OKD 95-C4,109-C1
GERSHWIN PL N OKD 109-C1
GERVAIS AVE MPW 94-E4,95-A4
GERVAIS CT MPW 95-A4
GESKE RD CHS 131-C4
GETHSEMANE RD HOP 119-B1
GETTYSBURG AVE N BP 77-C4
GETTYSBURG AVE N CHM 63-C3
GETTYSBURG AVE N GV 105-C1
GETTYSBURG AVE N NH 91-C3
GETTYSBURG AVE S SLP 105-C4,119-C1
GETTYSBURG CIR N NH 91-C1
GETTYSBURG CT N NH 91-C4
GETTYSBURG WAY N CHM 63-C2
GEYSER PATH APV 163-B1
GHERTY LN HUT 111-E2
GHIA ST NE BLA 65-D3
GHIA ST NE HL 51-D1
GHOSTLEY LN N CHM 63-C1
GHOSTLEY RD HSN 61-B1
GIBBON AVE WHT 217-C2
GIBBON ST NW RAM 34-D2
GIBBS AVE FH 107-C2
GIBBS AVE STP 107-C2
GIBBS ST PRE 153-B4,167-B1
GIBRALTAR RD NE FRI 92-D1
GIBRALTAR TER APV 149-A4
GIBRALTAR TRL EAG 135-E4,149-E1
GIBSON CT BUF 58-E4
GIDEONS LN SWD 117-D3
GIDEONS POINT RD TKB 117-D3
GIESMAN ST RVL 108-A1
GIFFORT AVE NE MOT 32-A3
GILANDERI LN LC 94-C4
GILBERT AVE STP 107-C4
GILBERT AVE NE MOT 32-A2
GILBERT AVE SE RFD 74-A3
GILBERT CT SWR 96-E2
GILBERT LN SSP 122-D4
GILBERT RD HUT 112-B3
GILBERT RD TRT 112-B4,126-B1
GILDENROD CIR NFD 220-A4
GILFILLAN AVE CAR 145-B4
GILFILLAN CT WBT 80-C4
GILFILLAN LN WBT 80-C4
GILFILLAN RD E NO 80-C3
GILFORD DR EDI 133-E1,134-A1
GILL LN NFD 219-D3
GILLARD AVE NE MOT 32-A2
GILLARD AVE SE RFT 60-A3
GILLETTE CRV SWD 117-D3
GILLIGAN AVE CAR 145-B4
GILLIS ST NW OG 22-C4,36-C1
GINAVALE LN EPR 132-C1
GINGER DR EPR 118-D4
GINSENG LN N HAN 61-A3
GIRARD AVE N BC 78-C3,92-C1
GIRARD AVE N BP 78-B3
GIRARD AVE N MPL 92-C3,106-C1
GIRARD AVE S BLO 134-C4,148-C1
GIRARD AVE S BUR 148-C4
GIRARD AVE S MPL 106-C4,120-C3
GIRARD AVE S RCH 120-C4,134-C1
GIRARD CIR BLO 134-C4,148-C1
GIRARD CRV BLO 148-C1
GIRARD CT BUR 148-C4
GIRARD CT MPL 120-C3
GIRARD CT N BP 78-B3
GIRARD ST HUD 111-D3
GIRARD TER MPL 106-C2
GIRGEN DR VER 179-D2
GIRONDE CT WBY 109-D4
GISELLA BLVD WBL 95-B1
GIVENS LN MPL 106-C1
GIZMO LN MTK 105-C4
GLABE LN MPL 121-B1
GLACIER AVE APV 163-B3
GLACIER BAY WBY 123-E3
GLACIER CT BUR 149-A4
GLACIER DR EAG 135-D4
GLACIER LN N MG 76-E4,90-E1
GLACIER LN N PLY 90-E3,104-E1
GLACIER LN NE FRI 92-E1,93-A1
GLACIER PL EDI 119-C4
GLACIER PL N PLY 90-E3
GLACIER RD SB 116-A3
GLACIER RD WBY 123-E3,124-A3
GLACIER WAY LVL 163-B4
GLADE AVE LVL 177-B4
GLADE AVE TKB 117-D2
GLADER BLVD CGT 12-E4,26-E1
GLADIOLA AVE W APV 163-B1
GLADIOLA AVE W LVL 163-B3
GLADIOLA CT APV 163-B2
GLADIOLA LN NW AND 35-E4
GLADIOLA ST NW AND 35-E2,49-E3
GLADIOLA ST NW CR 49-E4,63-E1
GLADIOLA ST NW OG 21-E3,35-E2
GLADIOLA ST NW SF 7-E4
GLADIOLA WAY APV 163-B1
GLADSTONE AVE MPL 120-C3
GLADSTONE BLVD MG 76-B1
GLADSTONE CIR LL 65-E3
GLADSTONE CIR MG 76-B1
GLADSTONE DR LL 65-E3
GLADSTONE LN MOU 116-E2
GLADSTONE PATH APV 163-B3
GLADVIEW LN MG 89-A4
GLADYS LN MTK 118-D2
GLASCOW TRL SE PRL 161-C2
GLASGOW BAY BLT 17-E2
GLASGOW DR EDI 133-D2
GLASGOW LN APV 163-B1
GLASGOW LN SB 116-A3
GLASGOW RD MOU 117-A2
GLAZIER AVE APV 163-B2
GLAZIER CT APV 163-B1
GLEAHAVEN RD WAY 104-D3
GLEASON CIR EDI 133-D1
GLEASON CT EDI 119-C4
GLEASON RD COR 76-B4
GLEASON RD EDI 119-C4,133-D1
GLEASON RD MTK 104-D3
GLEASON ACRES DR MTK 104-D3
GLEASON LAKE DR PLY 104-D2
GLEASON LAKE RD MTK 104-D2
GLEASON LAKE RD WAY 104-C3
GLEN AVE MTK 118-D3
GLEN CIR LL 66-A4
GLEN CIR TRT 125-D4
GLEN CT APV 149-B4
GLEN CT TRT 125-C4
GLEN LN EPR 133-B2
GLEN LN TRT 125-D4
GLEN PL SLP 119-E2,120-A2
GLEN RD NEW 137-B1
GLEN RD SWD 117-C3
GLEN RD WBY 137-D1
GLEN TER STP 121-E3
GLEN TRL S LL 66-A4
GLEN WAY APV 149-B4
GLEN CREEK RD NE FRI 78-D2
GLEN EAGLE CIR WBY 124-B2
GLEN EAGLE PL WBY 124-B2
GLEN EAGLE RD WBY 124-B2
GLEN ECHO BAY EAG 149-B2
GLEN EDGE RD DWD 81-D3
GLEN EDIN LN BP 78-A1
GLEN ELYN RD MOU 103-A4
GLEN LAKE BLVD MTK 118-E4
GLEN LAKE GOLF RD MTK 118-E4
GLEN MOOR CIR MTK 118-E3
GLEN MOOR RD E MTK 118-E3
GLEN MOOR RD N MTK 118-E3
GLEN MOOR RD S MTK 118-E3
GLEN MOOR RD W MTK 118-E3
GLEN OAK DR WYO 25-B4
GLEN OAK DR N WYO 25-B3
GLEN OAK ST MTK 118-D3
GLEN OAKS AVE WBL 81-B4,95-B2
GLEN OAKS CIR BL 18-B4
GLEN OAKS CT LVL 163-B3
GLEN OAKS CT WBL 95-B2
GLEN OAKS RD LVL 163-B3
GLEN PARK RD RF 140-D2
GLEN PAUL AVE AH 93-C2
GLEN PAUL CT SVW 93-E2
GLEN TORO RD MH 136-B1
GLEN WILDING LN BLO 148-C1
GLEN WILDING PL BLO 148-C1
GLENARDEN CT AH 93-D2
GLENARDEN RD AH 93-D2
GLENAVON AVE MTK 118-E3
GLENBEIGH CT WBY 123-E2
GLENBEIGH KNLS WBY 123-E2
GLENBEIGH PL WBY 123-E2
GLENBRAE CIR EDI 119-E3
GLENBROOK AVE N FLT 53-B1
GLENBROOK AVE N HUG 67-C2
GLENBROOK AVE N OKD 95-C4,109-C3
GLENBROOK AVE S CG 137-C4
GLENBROOK CT N OKD 109-C4
GLENBROOK RD N WAY 104-C3
GLENBROOK WAY APV 149-B4
GLENBROOK AVENUE CT N FLT 53-C1
GLENCOE AVE LVL 163-B4
GLENCOE AVE WHT 203-B4
GLENCOE CIR LVL 163-B4
GLENCOE CT LVL 163-B4
GLENCOE RD EXC 117-D3
GLENCOE RD SWD 117-D4
GLENCOE ST NE FRI 78-C2
GLENCOE TRL WHT 203-B2
GLENCOVE PATH APV 163-A1
GLENCOVE TRL APV 163-A1
GLENCREST RD GV 106-A3
GLENDA CT APV 163-A1
GLENDA DR APV 163-B2
GLENDALE AVE MHT 95-D1
GLENDALE AVE SE PRL 161-C2
GLENDALE CT SAV 148-A4
GLENDALE DR CHN 117-B4,131-B1
GLENDALE DR LOL 103-D2
GLENDALE DR ORO 103-D2
GLENDALE DR TRT 126-B4,140-B1
GLENDALE LN MTK 105-A2
GLENDALE LN SAV 148-A4
GLENDALE RD HAS 166-E2,167-A3
GLENDALE RD MOU 117-A1
GLENDALE RD MTK 118-D3
GLENDALE RD SAV 148-A4,162-A1
GLENDALE ST MTK 118-D3
GLENDALE ST STP 107-B3
GLENDALE TER MPL 120-A2
GLENDALE TRL SAV 148-A4,162-A1
GLENDEN TER GV 91-E4
GLENDENNING RD S CG 151-E1
GLENDON ST MPW 109-B3
GLENFIELD CT EAG 149-B1
GLENGARRY PKWY EDI 119-D3
GLENGARY CT W LVL 163-B3
GLENHAVEN AVE APV 149-B4
GLENHAVEN CT APV 149-B4,163-B1
GLENHAVEN LN MV 79-C2
GLENHAVEN LN N BP 78-B2
GLENHILL RD AH 93-D3
GLENHILL RD MH 121-D4
GLENHILL RD RVL 93-D3
GLENHILL RD SVW 93-E2
GLENHURST AVE SAV 148-A4,162-A1
GLENHURST AVE S SLP 106-A4,120-A1
GLENHURST CIR SAV 148-A4
GLENHURST CIR SLP 120-A1
GLENHURST CT SAV 148-A4
GLENHURST LN SAV 162-A1
GLENHURST RD SLP 106-A3
GLENLOU WAY HAS 166-B1
GLENMAR AVE MHT 95-D1
GLENMONT RD TRT 125-C4
GLENMOOR LN LOL 103-E2,104-A2
GLENMOUNT RD TRT 125-D4
GLENNA DR HUT 111-E3
GLENRIDGE AVE STP 123-B1
GLENRIDGE DR PRE 153-B4
GLENRIDGE RD MTK 118-E3
GLENROSS RD WBY 123-D2
GLENROY RD BLO 133-E2
GLENS RD DAT 145-A2

GLENVIEW AVE AH 93-C1
GLENVIEW AVE LL 65-E3
GLENVIEW CT AH 93-D1
GLENVIEW CT LES 212-D4
GLENVIEW DR BUR 148-B4
GLENVIEW DR LL 65-E3
GLENVIEW DR MTK 118-E3
GLENVIEW LN BLO 134-E3
GLENVIEW LN LL 65-E3
GLENWOOD AVE BL 18-B3
GLENWOOD AVE BLT 18-C3
GLENWOOD AVE GV 105-E2,106-A2
GLENWOOD AVE LVL 163-A4
GLENWOOD AVE MPL 106-C2
GLENWOOD AVE RVL 108-A1
GLENWOOD AVE NE LWT 10-B4
GLENWOOD BLVD MOU 116-E1
GLENWOOD PKWY GV 106-B1
GLENWOOD RD MOU 116-E2
GLOBEFLOWER CIR N BP 78-A1
GLOCCA MORRA CIR NMT 190-A1
GLORIA CIR MV 79-A2
GLORY CIR PRL 161-C3
GLORY DR EAG 149-B2
GLORY LN EPR 132-D2
GLOSTER AVE MHT 95-D1
GLOUCHESTER AVE EDI 134-A1
GLOUCHESTER DR EDI 134-A1
GLOVER RD TRT 126-C2
GLUEK LN RVL 93-C4
GLUEK LN N RVL 93-C4
GLUEK LN S RVL 93-C4
GLUMACK DR FS 121-B4,135-B1
GLYNWATER TRL PRL 160-E3
GODFREY PKWY MPL 121-B2
GODSON CIR LVL 163-A3
GODSON DR LVL 163-B3
GODWARD ST NE MPL 107-B1
GOIFFON RD CV 66-D2
GOLD CT EAG 149-C1
GOLD PT EAG 149-B1
GOLD TRL EAG 149-B1
GOLD FINCH DR FAR 177-D3
GOLD NUGGET DR COL 143-E3
GOLDEN AVE MP 102-E1
GOLDEN AVE WYO 25-B4
GOLDEN CT WYO 25-B3
GOLDEN ACRE DR MTK 105-A4
GOLDEN ACRES RD TRT 140-A1
GOLDEN EAGLE CIR WBY 124-B3
GOLDEN EAGLE CT WBY 124-B3
GOLDEN EAGLE TRL WBY 124-B3
GOLDEN HILL TER EAG 135-C4
GOLDEN HILLS DR GV 105-E3
GOLDEN LAKE CIR CP 65-D4
GOLDEN LAKE LN CP 65-E4
GOLDEN LAKE LN E CP 65-E4
GOLDEN LAKE RD CP 65-D4
GOLDEN LAKE RD E CP 65-D4
GOLDEN LAKE RD W CP 65-D4
GOLDEN MEADOW CT EAG 150-A2
GOLDEN MEADOW RD EAG 150-A2
GOLDEN OAK DR CP 65-D3
GOLDEN OAKS LN HUT 97-E3
GOLDEN OAKS LN SJT 97-E3
GOLDEN OAKS RD HUT 97-E4
GOLDEN OAKS RD SJT 97-D3
GOLDEN PONDS LN WBL 80-D3
GOLDEN RIDGE DR EPR 119-B4,133-B1
GOLDEN TRIANGLE DR EPR 133-C2
GOLDEN VALLEY DR GV 105-C2
GOLDEN VALLEY RD GV 105-D2,106-A1
GOLDEN VALLEY RD MPL 106-B1
GOLDEN VIEW DR ORO 103-D2
GOLDENEYE CT ROG 48-A4
GOLDENEYE WAY ROG 48-A4
GOLDENROD AVE LVL 163-B4
GOLDENROD CIR ROG 61-E2,62-A2
GOLDENROD CIR NW CR 50-D4,64-D1
GOLDENROD CT NFD 220-A4
GOLDENROD LN ROG 62-A2
GOLDENROD LN SHK 146-C3
GOLDENROD LN N MG 63-A4,77-A1
GOLDENROD LN N PLY 91-A3,105-A2
GOLDENROD ST NW AND 36-C4,50-D3
GOLDENROD ST NW CR 50-D4,64-D1
GOLDENROD ST NW OG 22-C2
GOLDENROD ST NW SF 8-C4
GOLDENSTONE ST LVL 163-A4
GOLDENVIEW AVE LVL 163-A4
GOLDFINCH AVE WYO 25-B4
GOLDFINCH CT WYO 25-B4
GOLDFINCH DR BUF 45-B4
GOLDFINCH DR WAC 129-D4
GOLDFINCH LN BUF 45-B4
GOLDFINCH LN CW 1-B3
GOLDFINCH LN NO 80-A2
GOLDFINCH PL BUF 45-B4
GOLDING LN APV 163-A2
GOLF LN LND 26-D1
GOLF PL NE CH 93-A2
GOLF ST ANO 49-C4
GOLF ST BL 18-A3
GOLF TER BKR 3-E4,4-A4
GOLF TER EDI 119-E3,120-A3
GOLF COURSE RD MO 31-C1
GOLF VIEW DR BUF 58-E3
GOLF VIEW DR EPR 132-E1
GOLF VIEW DR RF 140-E2
GOLF VIEW LN BP 78-A2
GOLFVIEW AVE N OKD 95-C3
GOLFVIEW CIR HUD 111-D3
GOLFVIEW CIR N OKD 95-C3
GOLFVIEW CT WBL 95-B2
GOLFVIEW CT N OKD 95-C3
GOLFVIEW DR EAG 135-E4
GOLFVIEW DR WBL 95-B2
GOLFVIEW LN N OKD 95-C3
GOLFVIEW PL N OKD 95-C3
GONVICK AVE ERT 217-B4
GONVICK AVE WHT 217-B4
GOODHUE AVE LVL 163-A4
GOODHUE AVE NFT 220-E4
GOODHUE AVE STN 220-E3
GOODHUE AVE WST 220-E4
GOODHUE CT NE BLA 51-A4
GOODHUE ST STP 122-A1
GOODHUE ST NE BLA 51-A4,79-A1
GOODHUE ST NE EB 9-A3,23-A3
GOODHUE ST NE HL 37-A3,51-A2
GOODHUE HALL NFD 219-E3
GOODLAND CT LVL 163-A4
GOODLAND PATH LVL 163-A4
GOODRICH AVE SLP 119-E1
GOODRICH AVE STP 121-C1,122-A1
GOODRICH AVE N CHM 63-C1
GOODRICH AVE NE MOT 32-A2
GOODRICH AVE S BLO 148-A1
GOODRICH CIR BLO 134-A4,148-A2
GOODRICH RD BLO 134-A4,148-A2
GOODRICH ST HOP 119-D2
GOODVIEW AVE HUG 67-C2
GOODVIEW AVE N FLT 39-C4,53-C1
GOODVIEW AVE N HUG 67-C3,81-C1
GOODVIEW AVE N OKD 109-C3
GOODVIEW AVE N WYO 25-C4
GOODVIEW AVE N WYT 25-C4,39-C1
GOODVIEW AVE S CG 137-C4
GOODVIEW CIR LVL 163-A3
GOODVIEW CIR N FLT 39-B2
GOODVIEW CT LVL 163-A3
GOODVIEW CT S CG 137-C2
GOODVIEW TRL LVL 163-A3
GOODVIEW WAY LVL 163-A3
GOODVIEW WAY N FLT 39-B2
GOODVINE AVE WYT 25-C3
GOODWIN AVE HMT 193-D1,207-D1
GOODWIN AVE NIT 165-D2
GOODWIN AVE VER 179-D2
GOODWIN AVE VET 165-D4,179-D3
GOODWIN AVE N OKD 95-C4,109-C3
GOODWIN CT N OKD 109-C1
GOODWIN RD N WYT 25-C4
GOOSE LAKE CT CHM 63-B3
GOOSE LAKE DR WCT 129-B1
GOOSE LAKE PKWY N CHM 63-B3
GOOSE LAKE RD DAY 63-B3
GOOSE LAKE RD GL 80-E4,94-E1
GOOSE LAKE RD VH 94-D1
GOOSEBERRY LN N NP 201-E2
GOOSEBERRY WAY APV 163-B3
GOPHER BLVD N OKD 109-C2
GOPHER DR NE EB 9-B4
GOPHER ST BEC 3-A4
GORDON AVE MPW 108-D1
GORDON AVE STP 107-C2
GORDON AVE N LL 66-D1
GORDON DR EPR 133-A1
GORDON PL STP 107-B2
GORDON RD MOU 117-A2
GORGAS AVE EDI 120-A3
GORHAM AVE SLP 105-D4,119-D1
GORMAN AVE STP 122-C2
GORMAN AVE WSP 122-C2
GORMAN ST SHK 146-C2
GORTNER AVE FH 107-C2
GOSHEN BLVD BPT 186-C1
GOSHEN BLVD SLW 186-C1
GOSHEN TRL SLW 172-C4,186-C1
GOSIWIN AVE MHT 95-D1
GOSIWIN CT MHT 95-D1
GOSSAMER CT APV 163-B1
GOSSAMER WAY APV 163-A1
GOTZIAN ST STP 108-D3
GOULD AVE NE CH 92-E2
GOULD RD EPR 132-D3
GOULD TRL HMT 193-D4
GOVE PL STP 107-C2
GOVERN CIR EAG 136-A4,150-A1
GOVERNMENT ST TF 14-C3
GOVERNMENT
CENTER DR HAS 166-B1
GOWAN AVE NW ABT 57-D3
GOWAN AVE NW CMT 57-D2
GOWAN AVE NW CNT 29-D3,43-D1
GOWAN AVE NW CWT 1-D4,15-D1
GOWAN AVE NW MLT 43-D4,57-D1
GOWAN AVE NW SVT 15-D4
GOWAN AVE SW MIT 71-D4,85-D1
GOWAN AVE SW MVT 57-D4,71-D3
GOWAN AVE SW WDT 85-D1
GOYA LN EDI 119-D3
GRABEN CT EPR 118-D4
GRACE AVE N WYT 25-C3
GRACE CT VIC 131-A2
GRACE DR EAG 149-D3
GRACE LN GRF 75-A2
GRACE LN HAS 166-E3
GRACE LN STP 109-A4
GRACE ST EXC 117-E3
GRACE ST STP 121-E1,122-A1
GRACE ST WBT 80-E4
GRACE TER EDI 119-D4
GRAFTON AVE N OKD 95-C3,109-C4
GRAFTON AVE N WYT 25-C4
GRAFTON AVE S CG 137-C3
GRAHAM AVE STP 121-C3
GRAHM AVE RCH 120-C4
GRAIL CT WYT 25-C4
GRAINWOOD CIR PRL 161-A3
GRAINWOOD TRL PRL 161-A3
GRAMERCY AVE N MPL 106-B2
GRAMFORD AVE N WYT 25-C4
GRAMSEY PL BUR 162-D2
GRAMSIE CT SVW 94-B1
GRAMSIE RD AH 93-C1
GRAMSIE RD SVW 93-E1,94-A1
GRANADA ALC S CG 137-C3
GRANADA AVE APV 149-A4,163-A2
GRANADA AVE N FLT 39-C2,53-C2
GRANADA AVE N OKD 95-C3,109-C2
GRANADA AVE N WYT 25-C4
GRANADA AVE S CG 137-C4
GRANADA BAY S CG 137-C3
GRANADA CIR N OKD 109-C3
GRANADA CIR S CG 137-C3
GRANADA CT APV 163-A1
GRANADA CT N OKD 109-C3
GRANADA LN OKD 95-C4
GRANADA LN N OKD 109-C1
GRANADA PL N OKD 109-C1
GRANADA PLZ N OKD 109-C1
GRANADA RD N OKD 109-C3
GRANADA TRL N OKD 109-C3
GRANADA WAY APV 163-B1
GRANADA WAY N OKD 95-C4,109-C3
GRANADA AVENUE CT N FLT 39-C4
GRAND AVE BUR 148-C4,162-C2
GRAND AVE CNC 12-E4
GRAND AVE LOL 103-D2
GRAND AVE NMT 204-C1
GRAND AVE STP 121-D1,122-A1
GRAND AVE SVW 94-A2
GRAND AVE WBL 95-B1
GRAND AVE WBT 81-B2
GRAND AVE E SSP 122-E4
GRAND AVE N LET 11-C1
GRAND AVE N WYT 25-C3
GRAND AVE NE SM 46-E3
GRAND AVE S BLO 134-C4,148-C1
GRAND AVE S MPL 106-C4,120-C2
GRAND AVE S RCH 120-C4,134-C1
GRAND AVE S WAY 104-C3
GRAND AVE W SSP 122-E3
GRAND HL STP 122-A1
GRAND ST NE MPL 92-D4,106-D1
GRAND BROOK CT WBY 124-B2
GRAND ISLE PL WBY 124-B2
GRAND PRIX CT WYT 25-C4
GRAND RESERVE CIR WBY 124-B2
GRAND RESERVE LN WBY 124-B2
GRAND VIEW CT MOU 116-E1
GRAND VIEW DR EPR 118-C4
GRANDVIEW AVE MTA 103-A4
GRANDVIEW AVE ORO 103-B4
GRANDVIEW AVE W MPW 94-E4
GRANDVIEW AVE W RVL 93-E4,94-A4
GRANDVIEW BLVD MOU 116-E1
GRANDVIEW CT BUR 148-E4
GRANDVIEW DR HUD 111-E2
GRANDVIEW LN EDI 119-E3
GRANDVIEW RD CHN 132-B2
GRANDVIEW TER APV 149-B3
GRANDVIEW TRL NMT 190-A2
GRANDVIEW WAY HUD 111-D2
GRANDVIEW WAY NMT 190-A2
GRANGE AVE N OKD 109-C2
GRANGE BLVD S CG 137-C4
GRANGE RD EDI 119-E3
GRANGE RD HUT 98-B4
GRANGE VW CV 66-D2
GRANGER CT APV 149-B4
GRANGER LN MOU 116-D2
GRANITE AVE APV 163-B1
GRANITE AVE N OKD 109-C3
GRANITE CIR N OKD 109-C2
GRANITE CT EAG 150-A1
GRANITE CT SHK 146-C3
GRANITE CT N OKD 109-C2
GRANITE DR EAG 150-A1
GRANITE DR SHK 146-C3
GRANITE LN N OKD 109-C3
GRANITE PATH EUT 191-B4
GRANITE ST STP 108-B3
GRANT ALC EAG 149-B2
GRANT AVE HUT 112-B2
GRANT AVE NW ABT 57-D2
GRANT AVE NW CNT 15-C4
GRANT AVE NW CWT 15-C4
GRANT CIR N ANO 49-D3
GRANT CIR S ANO 49-D3
GRANT DR EPR 133-B4
GRANT RD AH 93-C2
GRANT ST ANO 49-D3
GRANT ST CHC 26-B1
GRANT ST DWD 81-C3
GRANT ST EXC 117-D3
GRANT ST HMP 193-B2
GRANT ST MHT 81-D4
GRANT ST SWD 117-D4
GRANT ST E MPL 106-D3
GRANT ST NW ER 20-B1
GRANT ST W MPL 106-C3
GRANT LORENZ RD SWD 117-C3
GRANTHAM ST STP 107-C2
GRASS LAKE RD WIT 99-A3
GRASS LAKE TER MPL 120-C4
GRATHWOL LN EXC 117-E3
GRAVEL RD CAR 145-B4,159-B1
GRAY ST ANO 49-C4
GRAY ST HUD 111-D3
GRAY CLOUD ISLAND DR GCT 151-B2
GRAY FOX CRV CHN 118-B4
GRAY FOX LN CHN 118-B4
GRAY HERON DR LL 66-A2
GRAYLING CIR PRL 161-C1
GRAYS BAY BLVD MTK 104-C4
GRAYS LANDING RD MTK 104-D3
GRAYSTONE AVE MO 31-D3
GREAT OAKS CIR EAG 136-A4
GREAT OAKS DR BUR 148-E4
GREAT OAKS LN EAG 136-A4
GREAT OAKS PL EAG 136-A4
GREAT OAKS TRL EAG 136-A4
GREAT PLAINS
BLVD CHN 132-A3,146-A1
GREAT WATERS ALC EPR 132-B3
GREATLAND AVE N WYT 25-C4
GREATLAND CT N WYT 25-C4
GREATVIEW AVE BC 92-A2
GREELEY ST N SWR 96-E1
GREELEY ST S SWR 96-E2
GREEN AVE ANO 49-C4
GREEN AVE SE WAT 101-B4
GREEN CIR FS 121-B4,135-B1
GREEN CRST VIC 130-E3
GREEN LN FS 121-B4,135-B1
GREEN ST HUD 111-D3
GREEN BRIAR DR LL 65-E2
GREEN BRIAR DR MTK 104-E4
GREEN BRIAR LN MTK 104-E4
GREEN BRIAR RD BLO 133-E3
GREEN BRIAR RD HUT 111-E3
GREEN CIRCLE DR MTK 119-B3
GREEN FARMS CT EDI 119-C2
GREEN FARMS RD EDI 119-C3
GREEN HAVEN DR BP 77-C2
GREEN HEIGHTS TRL SW PRL 161-A3
GREEN LAKE AVE CHC 26-B1
GREEN LAKE TRL N CGT 26-B3
GREEN LAKE TRL N WYT 25-E4,26-A4
GREEN MEADOW CIR SFT 159-A3
GREEN MEADOWS CT NFD 219-D3
GREEN MILL LN HUT 111-E1,112-A1
GREEN OAK DR MTK 119-B3
GREEN OAKS TRL SE PRL 161-C2
GREEN RIDGE DR EPR 132-B1
GREEN RIDGE RD MTK 119-B1
GREEN SPRING RD RW 196-C4
GREEN TREES RD ORO 103-E4
GREEN TWIG WAY SWR 96-E1
GREEN VALLEY DR BLO 133-E2
GREEN VALLEY RD BLO 133-E2
GREEN VALLEY RD GV 105-D1
GREEN VALLEY RD MTK 118-C2
GREEN VALLEY RD NW RAM 35-A2
GREEN VIEW CT EPR 132-E1
GREENBRIAR CT LVL 163-A3
GREENBRIAR CT WBT 80-D2
GREENBRIAR CT WBY 123-E3
GREENBRIAR LN BUF 45-B4
GREENBRIAR LN LVL 163-A3
GREENBRIAR LN WBY 123-E3
GREENBRIAR ST CHN 117-C4
GREENBRIAR ST STP 108-C2
GREENBRIER CIR N LC 94-C4
GREENBRIER RD MTK 105-B4
GREENBRIER ST STP 108-C3
GREENBRIER ST VH 94-C2
GREENBRIER ST N LC 94-C2
GREENBRIER ST N MPW 94-C4,108-C1
GREENBROOK DR NE EB 23-B4,37-B1
GREENDALE LN VH 80-C4
GREENE AVE N HUG 67-C2
GREENE AVE N OKD 109-C3
GREENE AVE N WYT 25-C4
GREENE AVE S CG 137-C4
GREENFIELD AVE MV 79-B2
GREENFIELD CIR WAC 129-D3
GREENFIELD PL MV 79-B2
GREENFIELD RD GRF 60-D4,74-D3
GREENFIELD ROAD EXT GRF 60-D4
GREENHAVEN CIR VH 80-C4
GREENHAVEN CT VH 80-C4
GREENHAVEN DR BUR 162-C2
GREENHAVEN DR VH 80-C4
GREENHAVEN DR WBT 80-C4
GREENHAVEN LN BUR 162-C2
GREENHAVEN PL VH 80-C4
GREENHAVEN RD ANO 49-C3
GREENHAVEN TER VH 80-C4
GREENHAVEN WAY BUR 162-C2
GREENHILL LN LOL 104-A2
GREENING DR APV 163-A2
GREENLAND AVE APV 163-A1
GREENLAND PATH LVL 163-A4
GREENLEAF CT APV 163-C1
GREENLEAF CT CHN 132-B3
GREENLEAF CT NFD 219-D3
GREENLEAF DR E EAG 150-B2
GREENLEAF DR N EAG 150-B2
GREENLEAF DR S EAG 150-B2
GREENLEAF DR W EAG 150-A2
GREENLEAF TRL APV 163-C1
GREENMEADOW CT SWR 96-D2
GREENMILL LN HUT 112-A1
GREENRIDGE LN BUR 162-B2
GREENS CIR HWL 71-B4
GREENSBORO CT EAG 135-E4
GREENSBORO DR EAG 135-E4
GREENSBORO LN EAG 135-E4
GREENSPRUCE AVE N BP 64-A4
GREENSPRUCE CT N BP 64-A4
GREENTREE AVE LVL 163-A4
GREENTREE CT APV 149-B4
GREENTREE PATH LVL 163-A4
GREENVALE AVE NFD 219-D3
GREENVIEW CIR LVL 163-A4
GREENVIEW CT COR 61-E4
GREENVIEW CT CRT 176-A2
GREENVIEW DR CHN 132-A3
GREENVIEW DR NB 79-B4
GREENVIEW LN GV 105-E1
GREENVIEW RD BKR 2-E2
GREENWALD IS NW OG 21-E2
GREENWAY AVE PRL 161-C1
GREENWAY AVE SHK 146-C2
GREENWAY AVE N FLT 39-C2,53-C3
GREENWAY AVE N OKD 109-C4
GREENWAY AVE N WYT 39-C1
GREENWAY AVE S CG 137-C4
GREENWAY DR CHC 26-B2
GREENWAY LN N WYT 39-C2
GREENWAY RD N FLT 39-C2
GREENWAY GBLS MPL 106-C3
GREENWICH CT APV 149-B4,163-B1
GREENWICH DR WBY 124-A3
GREENWOOD AVE STP 122-C1
GREENWOOD CIR GRW 118-A3
GREENWOOD CT SHK 146-C3
GREENWOOD CT WYT 25-C4
GREENWOOD CT N EAG 135-C4
GREENWOOD CT S EAG 135-C4
GREENWOOD DR BUR 148-B3
GREENWOOD DR CHN 131-E1,132-A1
GREENWOOD DR MTK 119-A2
GREENWOOD DR MV 79-B2
GREENWOOD LN LL 66-A1
GREENWOOD RD MTK 119-A2
GREENWOOD ST MHT 95-D1
GREENWOOD TRL MTK 119-A2
GREENWOOD TRL N WLT 110-E2
GREENWOOD TRAIL CT N WLT 110-E2
GREER AVE NW ABT 57-C2
GREER AVE NW CNT 29-C4
GREER AVE NW CWT 1-C4,15-C4
GREER AVE SW MIT 71-C1
GREER CIR SW VIT 99-C1
GREG CIR BKR 17-D3
GREGORY DR NB 79-A3
GREGORY RD GV 105-D3
GREISEN AVE LVL 163-B3
GRENADA AVE EUT 205-B2
GRENADA AVE LVL 177-A4,191-A1
GRENADA PT EAG 149-C3
GRENADER WAY OKD 109-C2
GRENADIER AVE LVL 163-A4
GRENADIER AVE N OKD 109-C2
GRENADIER AVE S CG 137-C4
GRENADIER PL N OKD 109-C1
GRENADIER TRL N OKD 109-C1
GRENELEFE AVE N DWD 81-C2
GRENELEFE AVE N GRA 81-C1
GRENIER RD MTK 118-E3
GRENOBLE AVE IGH 137-A3
GRENOBLE AVE LVL 163-A3
GRENOBLE CT LVL 163-A3
GRENWICH LN N OKD 95-C3
GRENWICH PL N OKD 95-C3
GRENWICH RD N OKD 95-C3
GRENWICH TER EPR 118-D4
GRENWICH TRL N OKD 95-C3
GRENWICH WAY N OKD 95-C4
GRESHAM AVE N OKD 95-C4,109-C3
GRESHAM CIR N OKD 95-C4
GRESHAM CT N OKD 95-C4
GRESHAM LN S CG 137-C3
GRESHAM PL N OKD 95-C4
GRESHAM WAY N OKD 95-C4,109-C1
GRETCHEN CT N OKD 95-C4
GRETCHEN LN N OKD 95-C4
GRETCHEN PL N OKD 95-C4
GREY CLOUD TRL GCT 137-B4,151-B1
GREY CLOUD TRL S CG 151-C2
GREY CLOUD ISLAND DR CG 151-C2
GREY CLOUD
ISLAND DR GCT 137-B4,151-B1
GREY CLOUD
ISLAND TRL W CG 151-C2
GREY CLOUD
ISLAND TRL W GCT 151-B2
GREY DOVE LN EAG 135-C4
GREY FOX LN HUD 111-D2
GREY FOX RD AH 93-D1
GREY FOX RD SVW 93-E1
GREY FOX TRL ROG 61-E1
GREY SQUIRREL RD LL 65-E2
GREY WIDGEON PL EPR 133-A4
GREYFIELD CT EPR 147-A1
GREYSTONE AVE N FLT 53-C1
GREYSTONE AVE N HUG 53-C4
GREYSTONE AVE N OKD 109-C3

GREYSTONE AVE S CG 137-C4
GREYSTONE DR IGH 136-D1
GREYSTONE RD HAS 166-B3
GREYSTONE RDG EAG 149-C1
GRIER LN EPR 133-B3
GRIEVE GLN SL 136-B1
GRIFFEY ST RF 140-E3
GRIFFIN AVE MHT 81-D4,95-D1
GRIFFIN CIR CAR 145-B4
GRIFFIN CT MHT 95-D1
GRIFFIN ST CAR 145-B4
GRIFFING WAY BUF 58-E1,59-A1
GRIFFING PARK RD BUF ...58-E1,59-A1
GRIFFIT ST EDI 119-C2
GRIFFITH AVE NW CNT 29-C3
GRIFFITH AVE NW CWT 15-C1
GRIFFITH ST STP 108-D4
GRIFFON CT APV 163-A3
GRIFFON CT LVL 163-A3
GRIFFON LN LVL 163-A3
GRIFFON PATH APV 163-A3
GRIFFON TRL LVL 163-A3
GRIGGS AVE BLA 65-D4
GRIGGS AVE LEX 65-D4
GRIGGS ST N RVL 93-E3
GRIGGS ST N STP 107-D3,121-E1
GRIGGS ST S STP 121-E2
GRIMES AVE EDI 120-A2
GRIMES AVE N BC 78-A4
GRIMES AVE N ROB 92-A4
GRIMES LN EDI 120-A3
GRIMES PL N BC 78-A4
GRIMM RD CHS 145-B1
GRIMM RD LTT 116-C4
GRIMM RD MTA 116-B4
GRINELL AVE LVL 163-A3
GRINELL CIR LVL 163-A3
GRINNELL AVE LVL 163-A3
GRINNELL CT APV 163-A3
GRINNELL CT E LVL 163-A3
GRINNELL CT W LVL 163-A3
GRINNELL WAY LVL 163-A3
GRISTMILL RDG EPR 133-B4,147-B1
GRIZZLY CT WYT 25-C4
GROBERG ST MV 79-B2
GROMMESCH CIR SCT 159-E4
GROSPOINT AVE N OKD 109-C3
GROSPOINT AVE S CG 137-C4
GROSPOINT LN N OKD 109-C3
GROTHE CIR APV 163-A1
GROTTO ST BWV 95-C1
GROTTO ST N RVL 93-E4,94-A4
GROTTO ST N STP 108-A2,122-A1
GROTTO ST N SVW 79-E1
GROTTO ST S STP 122-A1
GROUSE CIR NW CR 64-B3
GROUSE CT NW CR 64-B3
GROUSE LN HSN 48-A3
GROUSE ST NW AND 50-B2
GROUSE ST NW CR 50-B4,64-B3
GROUSE ST NW OG 8-B4,22-B2
GROVE AVE LVL 163-A4
GROVE AVE SVW 80-A2
GROVE AVE NE WAT 101-B3
GROVE AVE SE WAT 101-B4
GROVE CIR EDI 119-D3
GROVE CT EPR 132-C1
GROVE DR MG 76-E2,77-A2
GROVE LN MOU 116-E2
GROVE LN E WAY 104-B3
GROVE PL EDI 119-D2
GROVE RD EB 37-D1
GROVE RD W TRT 125-D2
GROVE ST EDI 119-D3
GROVE ST EXC 117-E3
GROVE ST HAS 166-C1
GROVE ST LES 212-C3
GROVE ST MHT 95-D1
GROVE ST MPL 106-D2
GROVE ST STP 108-C4
GROVE ST TF 14-C3
GROVE ST WBT 80-E2
GROVE ST N BEL 185-E1
GROVE ST N CF 208-B4
GROVE ST N RF 140-D1
GROVE ST S BEL 185-E1
GROVE ST S RF 140-D2
GROVE ST S SWR 96-E1
GROVE TRL LVL 163-A3
GROVELAND AVE MPL 106-C3
GROVELAND CT MV 79-A1
GROVELAND RD MV 79-A2
GROVELAND TER MPL 106-C3
GROVELAND WAY SHK 146-C4
GROVELAND SCHOOL RD MTK ...104-C4,118-C1
GROVER AVE NW ABT 43-C3,57-C1
GROVER AVE NW CNT 29-C1
GROVER AVE NW CWT 1-D4,15-C2
GROVER AVE SW VIT 85-C3,99-C1
GROVER AVE SW WDT 99-D2
GROVNER AVE N OKD 109-C4
GROVNER RD N OKD 109-C1
GRUNDHOEFER CT NFD 219-D3
GRUNWALD AVE NW CNT 29-C2
GRUNWALD AVE NW CWT ..1-C4,15-C1
GRUNWALD AVE SW VIT 99-C2
GRYC CT MH 122-A3
GUADALCANAL CT NE BLA 65-C4
GUADALCANAL ST NE HL .37-B4,51-B2
GUAM AVE GVT 219-A1
GUARANI ST SF 7-D4
GUARANI ST NW AND 49-D2
GUARANI ST NW OG 21-D1
GUARANI ST NW SF 7-D4
GUARDIAN ANGELS AVE N OKD 109-E4
GUERNSEY AVE DAT 144-D2,158-D2
GUERNSEY AVE LTT 131-A4,145-A1
GUIDER DR WBY 123-D1
GUILD AVE APV 163-A1
GUILD CT APV 163-A1
GUILDNER AVE NW CNT 29-C1
GUILDNER AVE NW CWT 15-C4
GULDEN AVE NW ABT 43-C3
GULDEN AVE NW CNT 15-C4,29-C1
GULDEN PL MPW 108-E1
GULF BREEZE CT APV 163-A1
GULL CT APV 163-A1
GULL LN MOU 103-A4,117-A1
GUM ST SA 93-A4
GUMWOOD RD MOU 116-E1
GUN CLUB RD EAG 150-B3
GUN CLUB RD WBL 80-D4
GUNDERSON AVE NW ABT 43-C2
GUNDERSON AVE NW CWT 15-C4
GUNFLINT CIR LVL 163-A3
GUNFLINT CT APV 163-A1
GUNFLINT CT CHN 131-D1
GUNFLINT CT LVL 163-A3
GUNFLINT PATH APV 163-A1
GUNFLINT TRL CHN 131-D1
GUNFLINT TRL LVL 163-A3
GUNFLINT TRL N BP 78-B2
GUNFLINT RTL CHN 131-D1
GUNSTON LN WBY 124-B3
GURNEY CT APV 163-A1
GURNEY PATH APV 163-A1
GURNEY ST STP 108-B1
GURNEY ST N MPW 108-B1
GUS YOUNG LN EDI 119-E3
GUSTAVUS CT WYT 25-C4
GUTHRIE AVE APV 163-A2
GUTHRIE AVE N OKD 109-C3
GUTHRIE CT APV 163-A1
GUTHRIE CT N OKD 109-C2
GUTHRIE WAY APV 163-A2
GUTHRIE AVENUE CT N OKD ...109-C4
GUY ST OG 36-C1
GWENDOLEN CT CHN ...117-D4,131-D1
GWENETH LN EPR 133-B3
GYPSY VALLEY RD NW BT 21-B3

H

H CT NE EB 37-D1
H ST WBL 94-E1
H ST WBY 123-D1
H K YLHH NB 79-A4
HABITAT CT EDI 119-C4
HACKAMORE CIR COR 90-A1
HACKAMORE RD MED 89-E1,90-A1
HACKBERRY CIR HAS 166-D3
HACKBERRY CT EPR 132-C4
HACKBERRY DR HAS 166-D3
HACKBERRY HL ORO 103-D2
HACKBERRY LN LAT 202-A3
HACKBERRY LN NO 80-A2
HACKBERRY LN N CHM 63-B2
HACKERSON CT NFD 219-D3
HACKMAN AVE NE FRI 78-E4
HACKMAN CIR NE FRI 78-E4
HACKMORE CT EAG 150-B2
HACKMORE DR EAG 150-A2
HACKNEY DR WCT 129-B3
HADDINGTON RD RVL 93-D4
HADLEY AVE CLT 189-B4
HADLEY AVE SLT 175-B1
HADLEY AVE N DWD 81-C3
HADLEY AVE N GRA 81-C3
HADLEY AVE N OKD 95-C3,109-C2
HADLEY AVE S CG 137-D4,151-D1
HADLEY CIR N GRA 81-C2
HADLEY CIR N HUG 67-C4
HADLEY CIR N OKD 95-D4
HADLEY CT N GRA 81-C2
HADLEY CT N OKD 109-C1
HADLEY DR N OKD 109-C3
HADLEY LN N OKD 109-C3
HADLEY ST STP 123-A2
HAEG CIR BLO 134-B3
HAEG DR BLO 134-B2
HAERING CIR CHS 145-C1
HAERING CT CHS 145-C1
HAERING LN CHS 145-C1
HAFNER CT SVW 93-E2
HAFTEN LN GRF 74-E3
HAGE DR COR 61-B4
HAGEN AVE RAT 207-E3
HAGEN DR MPW 108-E1
HAGGERTY ST SJT 97-B1
HAGUE AVE STP 107-D4,108-A4
HAHN DR LVT 160-A2
HAILEYS CT CGT 12-B4
HAINES ST NB 93-B2
HALAS CIR NW RAM 34-B4
HALAS ST NW BT 20-B4
HALAS ST NW RAM 34-B2
HALCYON LN MHT 95-D1
HALDEN CIR EAG 149-C2
HALE AVE OKD 109-D3
HALE AVE N OKD 95-C4,109-C2
HALE AVE N WYT 39-C1
HALE AVE S CG 137-D4,151-D1
HALE CT OKD 109-D3
HALE CT N OKD 109-D2
HALE CT N WYT 25-C4
HALE CT S CG 137-D4
HALF MOON DR GV 105-D2
HALGLO PL ROB 92-A4
HALGREN RD MP 88-E4,102-E1
HALIFAX AVE N BC 78-A3,92-A1
HALIFAX AVE N BP 78-A2
HALIFAX AVE N ROB 92-A3
HALIFAX AVE S EDI 120-A3
HALIFAX CT N BP 78-A2
HALIFAX DR BC 78-A4
HALIFAX LN EDI 120-A3
HALIFAX LN SLT 174-C2
HALIFAX PATH LVL 163-A4
HALIFAX PL BC 92-A1
HALITE LN EAG 149-C1
HALL AVE BWV 95-C1
HALL AVE STP 122-C2
HALL AVE WSP 122-C2
HALL AVE NE MOT 32-B2
HALL AVE SE RFD 74-A2
HALL AVE SE RFT 74-A3
HALL CRV MPL 106-C1
HALL CT BWV 95-C1
HALL LN MPL 106-C1
HALL LN STP 122-C1
HALL ST CHN 145-E2
HALL ST EAG 150-A3
HALL ST SVW 79-D1
HALLA NURSERY DR W CHN ...132-A4
HALLAM AVE N MHT 81-D4,95-D1
HALLAM AVE S MHT 95-D1
HALLAM CRV MHT 95-D1
HALLER CT MPW 123-B3
HALLER LN MPW 123-B3
HALLGREN LN CHN 131-B1
HALLMARK AVE N OKD ..95-C4,109-D2
HALLMARK AVE S CG ..137-D4,151-D1
HALLMARK CIR N OKD 109-D3
HALLMARK CT APV 149-A4,163-A3
HALLMARK CT N OKD 109-D3
HALLMARK DR APV 163-A2
HALLMARK DR EPR 132-D1
HALLMARK LN N OKD 109-D3
HALLMARK PATH APV 163-A3
HALLMARK PATH LVL 163-A3
HALLMARK WAY APV 163-A3
HALLMARK WAY N OKD 109-D2
HALPERS PL WBT 80-D1
HALPERS WAY WBT 80-D1
HALSEY AVE DAT 158-E2
HALSEY AVE SFT 158-E4
HALSEY AVE NE MOT 32-A2,46-B2
HALSEY AVE NE SM 60-A3
HALSEY AVE SE RFT 60-A4,74-A3
HALSEY LN BLO 134-C3
HALSTAD AVE LON 217-B3
HALSTAD AVE WHT 203-B3,217-B1
HALSTEAD AVE MTA 116-D2
HALSTEAD DR MTA 116-C2
HALSTEAD LN MOU 116-D2
HAM LAKE DR HL 37-B4
HAMBURG AVE EUT 191-A2,205-A1
HAMBURG AVE LVL 177-A4,191-A1
HAMBURG CT APV 149-A4
HAMEL RD MED 89-B2,90-A2
HAMEL RD PLY 90-B3
HAMEN CT SL 136-C2
HAMES AVE S CG 151-D1
HAMES CT S CG 151-D1
HAMES RD S CG 137-D4
HAMES WAY EPR 132-C1
HAMILTON AVE DPH 118-B1
HAMILTON AVE NE MOT 32-B3
HAMILTON AVE SE RFT 60-B4
HAMILTON CT LVL 163-A4
HAMILTON CT NB 79-A4
HAMILTON CT RF 140-D3
HAMILTON DR EAG 149-E2,150-A2
HAMILTON DR HAS 166-C1
HAMILTON DR LVL 163-A4
HAMILTON DR RF 140-D3
HAMILTON LN MTK 118-D2
HAMILTON LN N BP 77-E3
HAMILTON RD EPR 133-C1
HAMILTON RD MTK 118-D2
HAMILTON ST BUR 148-A3
HAMILTON ST SCF 14-C2
HAMILTON ST SLP 119-E1
HAMILTON ST N SCF 14-C2
HAMLET AVE APV 149-A4
HAMLET AVE N GRA 81-C1
HAMLET AVE N OKD 95-D4,109-D2
HAMLET AVE N WYT 39-C1
HAMLET AVE S CG 137-D4,151-D1
HAMLET CIR LVL 177-B3
HAMLET CT S CG 151-D1
HAMLET DR WBY 123-D3
HAMLET LN S CG 151-D1
HAMLIN AVE NE SM 46-B4,60-B1
HAMLIN AVE SE RFD 74-B3
HAMLIN AVE SE RFT 60-B4,74-B2
HAMLINE AVE N AH 79-D4,93-D2
HAMLINE AVE N BLA 65-C4
HAMLINE AVE N FH 107-D1
HAMLINE AVE N LEX 65-C4
HAMLINE AVE N RVL 93-D3,107-D1
HAMLINE AVE N STP ...107-D4,121-D1
HAMLINE AVE N SVW 79-D2
HAMLINE AVE NE MOT 32-B3
HAMLINE AVE S STP 121-D2
HAMMER AVE STP 108-E3
HAMMOND AVE NE SM 60-B2
HAMMOND AVE SE RFT 60-B4
HAMMOND RD WBT 80-E3
HAMPDEN AVE STP 107-C3
HAMPSHIRE AVE BLO 147-D2
HAMPSHIRE AVE CRT 161-D3
HAMPSHIRE AVE STP 121-C3
HAMPSHIRE AVE N BP 63-D4,77-D1
HAMPSHIRE AVE N CHM 63-D2
HAMPSHIRE AVE N CRY 91-D3
HAMPSHIRE AVE N GV 105-D1
HAMPSHIRE AVE S BLO 147-D1
HAMPSHIRE AVE S GV 105-D3
HAMPSHIRE AVE S SAV 161-E3
HAMPSHIRE AVE S SLP .105-D4,119-D1
HAMPSHIRE CIR BLO 147-D2
HAMPSHIRE CIR CHM 63-D2
HAMPSHIRE CIR N BP 77-D3
HAMPSHIRE CRV BLO 147-D2
HAMPSHIRE CT CRT 175-D2
HAMPSHIRE CT MH 136-A1
HAMPSHIRE CT STP 121-D3
HAMPSHIRE CT E CHM 63-D3
HAMPSHIRE CT N BP 77-D2
HAMPSHIRE CT W CHM 63-D3
HAMPSHIRE DR MH 136-A1
HAMPSHIRE DR MPL 120-D3
HAMPSHIRE LN EPR 133-C4
HAMPSHIRE LN N BP 77-D2
HAMPSHIRE LN N GV 105-D1
HAMPSHIRE PL BUR 162-D2
HAMPSHIRE PL N GV 105-D1
HAMPSHIRE RD DAT 144-E2,145-A2
HAMPSHIRE ST PRE 153-B4
HAMPTON AVE HMT 193-A1
HAMPTON BLVD HMP 193-B2
HAMPTON BLVD HMT 193-B1
HAMPTON CIR SHK 146-B4
HAMPTON CT MO 31-C2
HAMPTON CT MTK 118-C2
HAMPTON LN SHK 147-B3
HAMPTON RD GV 105-E1,106-A1
HAMPTON RD MOU 117-A2
HAMPTON ST HMP 193-B2
HAMPTON ST PRL 161-B1
HAMPTON ST WAY 104-C3
HANCOCK ST BEC 2-E4
HANCOCK ST BKR 2-E4
HANCOCK ST STP 108-D3
HANCOCK ST E SWR 97-A2
HANCOCK ST W SWR 96-E2,97-A2
HAND AVE RVL 94-A4,108-A1
HANKERSON AVE EDI 119-E3
HANLEY RD GV 105-C2
HANLEY RD HUD 111-E3
HANLEY RD HUT 111-E3,112-A4
HANLON AVE ORO 103-E3
HANLON DR BEL 186-A1
HANNAH HILL CT HUG 67-C4
HANNIBAL CIR APV 163-A1
HANNIBAL CT LVL 163-A4
HANNOVER AVE APV 149-A4
HANNOVER CT APV 149-A4
HANNOVER PATH APV 163-A3
HANOVER AVE LVL 177-A4
HANOVER CT APV 163-A1
HANOVER CT EAG 150-B1
HANOVER CT JOR 173-B2
HANOVER LN APV 163-A2
HANOVER LN EPR 132-C3
HANOVER RD MOU 117-A2
HANOVER WAY APV 163-A1
HANREHAN TRL SAV 162-A2
HANREHAN LAKE BLVD SAV 161-E2,162-A2
HANSACK AVE NE SM 60-B2
HANSACK AVE SE RFT 60-B4
HANSEN AVE SHK 147-C3
HANSEN RD EDI 119-E3
HANSON BLVD NW AND ...36-B3,50-B2
HANSON BLVD NW CR 50-B4,64-B2
HANSON CT N CRY 91-E2
HANSON DR RF 140-E1
HANSON LN SSP 122-D4
HANSON PL SWR 96-D1
HANSON RD SVW 79-E3
HANSON ST MHT 81-D4
HANUS CIR MTK 118-B3
HANUS RD MTK 118-B3
HAPPY OAKS CT MTK 119-A1
HAPPY VALLEY RD RIT 140-E4
HARALSON DR APV 163-A2
HARALSON DR EPR 132-C4
HARALSON RD WBY 124-A2
HARBOR BCH NE PRL 161-C1
HARBOR CIR SVW 80-A4
HARBOR CT LVL 163-A4
HARBOR CT SVW 80-A4
HARBOR LN SVW 80-A4
HARBOR LN N MG 76-E1
HARBOR LN N PLY 90-E4,104-E2
HARBOR PL NE PRL 161-D1
HARBOR ST STP 122-B1
HARBOR PLACE DR SVW 80-A4
HARBOR VIEW RD HUT 112-A2
HARBOROUGH CT EPR 118-C4
HARBORVIEW CIR NE PRL 161-C1
HARBOUR PT EAG 149-C1
HARDENBERGH PL STP 108-B3
HARDING AVE NE MOT 32-B3
HARDING AVE NE SM 60-B2
HARDING LN LVL 163-A4
HARDING LN SWD 117-C3
HARDING ST SA 93-A3
HARDING ST NE MPL 93-A4,107-A1
HARDMAN AVE N SSP 122-E3
HARDMAN AVE S SSP ...123-A4,137-A1
HARDSCRABBLE CIR MTA 116-E2
HARDSCRABBLE RD N MTA 116-E2
HARDWOOD AVE SVW 79-E1
HARDWOOD LN E MHT 81-D4
HARDWOOD LN W MHT 81-D4
HARDWOOD ST SVW 79-E1
HARDWOOD WAY CF 208-C4
HARDWOOD WAY CFT 208-C4
HARFF RD GRF 60-D4,61-A4
HARKNESS AVE S CG ...137-D3,151-D1
HARKNESS CT S CG 151-D1
HARKNESS RD S CG 137-D4
HARLAN DR EPR 118-E4,132-E1
HARLAN DR NH 91-C1
HARLAR CIR HUT 112-B2
HARLOW AVE SCT 159-E4,173-E3
HARMON AVE WSP 122-B2
HARMON PL MPL 106-C3
HARMONY CIR BUR 148-B4
HARMONY CIR EPR 147-B1
HARMONY CIR WAY 104-C2
HARMONY CT APV 163-A3
HARMONY DR MHT 81-D4
HARMONY LN LVL 163-A3
HARMONY LN MED 89-E4,90-A4
HARMONY PATH LVL 163-A3
HARMONY WAY APV 163-A3
HARMONY WAY CT APV 163-A3
HAROLD AVE GV 105-D2
HAROLD DR BUR 148-C4
HAROLD WOODS LN EDI 119-C3
HARPER RD DPH 118-A2
HARPER ST IGH 137-A3
HARPER ST NE EB 37-B1
HARPERS CT NE BLA 65-C4
HARPERS ST NE BLA 51-C4
HARPERS ST NE HL 51-C2
HARRIET AVE AH 93-E2
HARRIET AVE BUR 148-C4
HARRIET AVE MPL 106-C4,120-C2
HARRIET AVE RCH 120-C4,134-C1
HARRIET AVE SVW 93-E2,94-A2
HARRIET AVE S BLO ...134-C3,148-C1
HARRIET CIR SVW 94-A2
HARRIET CT SVW 93-E2
HARRIET DR S SWR 96-E2,97-A2
HARRIET LN RVL 107-E1
HARRIET ST LES 212-D3
HARRIET ST N SWR 97-A1
HARRIET ST S SWR 97-A2
HARRINGTON AVE NE MOT 32-B2
HARRINGTON CIR LOL 103-D2
HARRINGTON DR LOL 103-D2
HARRINGTON PL APV 163-A2
HARRINGTON RD WAY 104-B3
HARRINGTON WAY LVL 163-A4
HARRIS AVE MPW 108-E1
HARRIS ST PRE 153-B4,167-B1
HARRISON AVE STP 122-A1
HARRISON AVE N HOP 119-C2
HARRISON AVE S BLO 148-A2
HARRISON AVE S EDI 119-C2
HARRISON AVE S HOP 119-C2
HARRISON CIR BLO 134-A3
HARRISON LN MOU 116-E1
HARRISON RD BLO 134-A4,148-A2
HARRISON ST ANO 49-C4
HARRISON ST NE MPL 106-E1
HARRISON ST S SHK 146-A3
HARRISON HILL CT CHN 131-D1
HARRISON HILL TRL CHN 131-D1
HARROGATE DR EPR ...118-B4,132-B1
HARROW AVE N FLT 39-C4,53-D2
HARROW AVE N HUG 67-D1
HARROW AVE S CG 151-D1
HARROW CT S CG 151-D1
HARRY AVE RAT 207-E3
HARRY DAVIS LN MPL 106-C1
HARSHMAN DR HUT 97-D4
HART AVE NW ABT 43-C2
HART AVE NW CNT 29-C1,43-C1
HART AVE NW CWT 15-C4
HART AVE SW VIT 85-C3,99-C2
HART BLVD MO 31-E2
HART BLVD NE CH 93-A3
HART ST IND 102-B2
HARTFORD AVE STP 121-D2
HARTFORD CIR EPR 133-C4
HARTFORD CIR LL 66-E4
HARTFORD RD WBY 123-D3
HARTKOPF LN BP 77-D3
HARTLEY BLVD SHK 147-A3
HARTLEY BLVD N SHK 147-A3
HARTLEY BLVD S SHK 147-A3
HARTMAN CIR NE FRI 78-D3
HARTS BLVD MO 31-E2
HARTUNG OAKS RD DAT 158-B1
HARTWELL ST DAT 158-D2
HARVARD CT LVL 163-A3

HARVARD DR LVL .163-A3
HARVARD LN LVL .163-A3
HARVARD ST STP .122-C2
HARVARD ST SE MPL .107-A3
HARVERHILL TRL EPR .118-E4
HARVEST CIR WIN .99-B3
HARVEST CT APV .163-A1
HARVEST CT SHK .146-B3
HARVEST DR NMT .203-E1
HARVEST GRN SWR .96-C2
HARVEST LN CHN .131-D2
HARVEST LN EPR .133-B4
HARVEST LN SHK .146-B3
HARVEST WAY CHN .131-D2
HARVESTER AVE MPW .109-B3
HARVEY LN EDI .133-E1
HARVEY ST HUD .111-E4,112-A4
HARWELL AVE APV .163-A3
HARWELL AVE LVL .163-A3
HARWELL CT APV .163-A1
HARWELL CT LVL .163-A3
HARWELL PATH APV .163-A1
HASKELL ST E WSP .122-C2
HASKELL ST W WSP .122-C2
HASSAN PKWY HSN .61-C1
HASTINGS AVE NEW .123-B4,137-B1
HASTINGS AVE SPP .137-C3
HASTINGS RD HAS .152-D4,166-D1
HASTINGS ST NE ATT .9-A1
HASTINGS ST NE BLA .51-A4,79-A1
HASTINGS ST NE EB .9-A3,23-A2
HASTINGS ST NE HL .37-A4,51-A1
HASTINGS TRL NIT .165-D1,166-A2
HATCH AVE STP .107-E3,108-A3
HATCH TRL WHT .202-D4,216-C1
HATCHERY RD HUT .111-E1
HATHAWAY LN MTK .118-D3
HATHAWAY LN NE FRI .78-E4
HATHAWAY ST STP .121-E2
HATTIE LN WBY .123-C1
HAUER TRL SHK .146-D3
HAUERS TRL SHK .146-D3
HAUG AVE NE MOT .32-A3
HAUG AVE NE SM .60-A3
HAUG AVE SE RFD .74-A3
HAUG AVE SE RFT .60-A4,74-A1
HAUGE CIR EAG .149-C3
HAUTE CT WBY .109-D4
HAVELKA CT N FL .39-A3
HAVELOCK CT APV .163-A1
HAVELOCK CT LVL .163-A4
HAVELOCK TRL APV .149-A4,163-A1
HAVELOCK WAY LVL .163-A3
HAVEN AVE LVL .163-A4
HAVEN CIR APV .163-A2
HAVEN DR APV .163-A2
HAVEN LN GL .94-D1
HAVEN RD MTK .118-E1
HAVEN HEIGHTS CT CF .208-A4
HAVENHILL CIR EAG .150-A1
HAVENHILL RD EAG .150-A1
HAVENVIEW CT MH .136-A1
HAVENVIEW DR SHK .146-C3
HAVENWOOD RD WBY .123-D2
HAVERTON CIR MH .136-B2
HAVERTON RD MH .136-B1
HAWAII AVE BLA .65-B4
HAWES AVE SVW .80-B4
HAWES AVE VH .80-C4
HAWK LN NO .80-C2
HAWK PL EAG .149-C1
HAWK TRL BUF .45-B4
HAWK HIGH CT EPR .133-B4
HAWK RIDGE CIR LL .66-C3
HAWK RIDGE RD PRL .160-E3
HAWKES DR EDI .119-D3
HAWKES TER EDI .119-D3
HAWKINS DR HSN .61-D1
HAWKINS DR ROG .47-D4
HAWKINS RD WBY .137-C1
HAWKSBURY CIR EAG .150-B2
HAWLEY AVE SSP .122-D3
HAWTHORN AVE BUF .59-A1
HAWTHORN AVE N FLT .39-D2
HAWTHORN PATH LVL .163-A3
HAWTHORN RD EB .37-D1
HAWTHORN RD LL .66-A4
HAWTHORNE AVE MPL .106-C3
HAWTHORNE AVE MPW .109-B2
HAWTHORNE AVE E STP 108-D2,109-A2
HAWTHORNE AVE W MPL .106-B2
HAWTHORNE AVE W STP .108-B2
HAWTHORNE CIR CHN .131-B1
HAWTHORNE CT NFD .219-D3
HAWTHORNE DR EPR .132-E3
HAWTHORNE LN SWR .96-D1
HAWTHORNE PL VIC .130-E2
HAWTHORNE PL N MOT .31-E3
HAWTHORNE PL S MOT .31-E3
HAWTHORNE RD HOP .119-D2
HAWTHORNE RD MOU .116-E2
HAWTHORNE WOODS DR EAG .150-B2
HAY CAMP RD NO .80-B2
HAY LAKE CT EAG .150-A2
HAY LAKE RD N EAG .150-A2
HAY LAKE RD S EAG .150-A2
HAYDEN LAKE RD E CHM .63-C1
HAYDEN LAKE RD W CHM .63-B1
HAYES AVE GVT .205-A4,219-A1
HAYES AVE LVL .163-A4,177-A4
HAYES AVE SFT .158-E3
HAYES CT APV .163-A3
HAYES CT BUR .148-E1
HAYES DR BUR .148-E1,149-A1
HAYES LN SFT .158-E3
HAYES RD APV .163-A2
HAYES ST CHC .26-B1
HAYES ST NE CH .93-A2
HAYES ST NE FRI .79-A2
HAYES ST NE MPL .93-A4
HAYES ST NE SLK .78-E2,79-A2
HAYES TRL APV .163-A3
HAYES TRAIL CT APV .163-A3
HAYFIELD RD CV .66-D2
HAYS AVE IGH .137-A3
HAYWARD AVE N FLT .39-D3
HAYWARD AVE N OKD .109-D2
HAYWARD AVE S CG .151-D1
HAYWARD RD N OKD .95-D4
HAYWOOD DR HWL .85-A2
HAZEL AVE MHT .81-D3
HAZEL AVE N FLT .53-D1
HAZEL AVE N WYT .39-D1
HAZEL CT HUD .111-D3
HAZEL CT LVL .163-A4
HAZEL CT MH .136-A1
HAZEL CT SWR .82-E4
HAZEL LN HOP .119-C1
HAZEL LN MTK .104-E4
HAZEL RD EAG .135-B4
HAZEL ST LES .212-D3
HAZEL ST MPW .95-A4,109-A1
HAZEL ST RF .140-E2
HAZEL ST STP .109-A2
HAZEL ST TKB .117-D3
HAZEL ST WBL .81-A4,95-A1
HAZEL ST E SWR .83-A4
HAZEL ST N BEL .185-E1
HAZEL ST N STP .109-A3
HAZEL ST S NYA .142-C4
HAZEL ST S WAC .129-E3
HAZEL ST W SWR .82-E4,83-A4
HAZEL BUSH TRL NW STT .6-D2
HAZELCREST DR HUD .111-D3
HAZELDELL AVE SPR .117-B1
HAZELMOOR PL MTK .118-C1
HAZELNUT AVE N BP .64-A4
HAZELNUT CIR N BP .64-A4,78-A1
HAZELTINE BLVD CHN .117-D4,131-D1
HAZELTINE BLVD CHS .131-C4
HAZELTINE LN EAG .149-D3
HAZELTINE BLUFF BLVD CHS .145-D1
HAZELTON RD EDI .134-A1
HAZELWOOD AVE WT .204-C4,218-C2
HAZELWOOD CIR BUF .58-E1
HAZELWOOD CT BUF .58-E1
HAZELWOOD LN MOU .116-D2
HAZELWOOD LN N CHM .63-B3
HAZELWOOD RD MTK .104-E4
HAZELWOOD RD W MTK .104-E4,118-E1
HAZELWOOD ST MPW .94-E3,108-E1
HAZELWOOD ST STP .108-E2
HAZELWOOD WAY WT .218-C2
HAZEN ST SHK .146-C4
HEADLEY CT NFD .219-D3
HEALY AVE N FLT .39-D4
HEALY AVENUE CIR N FLT .39-D4
HEALY AVENUE CT N FLT .39-D4
HEANER TER MPL .106-B2
HEARD AVE CHM .63-D2
HEARTH AVE N FLT .39-D3
HEARTHSIDE AVE S CG .137-D3
HEARTHSIDE CT LVL .163-A4
HEARTHSIDE CT S CG .137-D3
HEARTHSIDE RD S CG .137-D3
HEARTHSIDE WAY LVL .163-A4
HEARTHSTEAD LN EPR .133-A3
HEARTLAND CT CHN .132-B3
HEATH AVE LVL .177-A4
HEATH AVE N FLT .39-D4,53-D1
HEATH AVE N OKD .95-D3,109-D2
HEATH AVE N WYT .39-D1
HEATH AVE S CG .137-D3,151-D1
HEATH CT APV .163-A3
HEATH CT LVL .163-A3
HEATH AVENUE CT N FLT .39-D4
HEATHBROOK DR EPR .118-C4
HEATHBROOKE CIR GV .106-A1
HEATHCOTE DR DPH .118-B2
HEATHCOTE LN DPH .118-B2
HEATHCOTE RD DPH .118-B2
HEATHER AVE EPR .132-E2
HEATHER AVE N HUG .67-D4,81-D1
HEATHER CIR N OKD .95-D4
HEATHER CIR NE FRI .78-E4
HEATHER CRST BUR .148-A4
HEATHER CT CHN .131-E1
HEATHER CT WSP .122-B4
HEATHER CT N LL .65-E2
HEATHER DR EAG .135-B4,149-B1
HEATHER DR SFT .159-A3
HEATHER DR STP .122-A1
HEATHER DR SVW .79-E4,93-E1
HEATHER DR WBY .124-B1
HEATHER DR NE HL .36-E3
HEATHER LN COR .61-B4
HEATHER LN EDI .119-D3
HEATHER LN LOL .103-E2
HEATHER LN WAC .129-D3
HEATHER PL STP .122-A1
HEATHER PL NE FRI .78-E4,79-A4
HEATHER ST SHK .146-C3
HEATHER ST NW AND .35-E2,49-E3
HEATHER ST NW CR .49-E4,63-E1
HEATHER ST NW OG .21-E4,35-E1
HEATHER WAY LFL .109-C4
HEATHER WAY N OKD .95-D4
HEATHER HILLS DR BUR .148-E4,162-E1
HEATHER RIDGE CT SVW .80-A2
HEATHER RIDGE DR HSN .47-D3
HEATHER RIDGE DR SVW .80-A2
HEATHER RIDGE RD N OKD .95-D4
HEATHERTON CIR EDI .134-A1
HEATHERTON PL MTK .118-E2
HEATHERTON TRL EDI .134-A1
HEATHERTON RIDGE DR SAV .161-C1
HEATON BLVD CW .1-B3
HEDBERG DR MTK .105-B4
HEDGE ST WSP .122-B2
HEDGEHOG ST NW BT .20-D4
HEDGEHOG ST NW RAM .34-D4,48-D1
HEDMAN LN MO .31-B1
HEDMAN WAY WBL .80-D4
HEFNER AVE S CG .137-D4
HEFNER CT S CG .137-D4
HEGGEN ST HUD .111-D3
HEIDELBERG LN SB .116-A3
HEIDELBERG ST NE COT .38-D4
HEIDI LN CHN .145-E1
HEIDI LN MHT .81-D4
HEIDI LN SVW .79-E3,80-A3
HEIFORT CT SWR .82-D4
HEIGHTS AVE S MPW .123-B3
HEIGHTS DR NE CH .93-A2
HEIGHTS RD NE SM .46-E3
HEIGHTS RD NW SM .46-E3
HEIMEL ST SSP .122-D4
HEINBUCH TRL WBY .123-D4
HEINE CT EAG .149-D1
HEINE STRASSE ST EAG .149-D2
HEINEL CIR RVL .94-A3
HEINEL DR RVL .93-E3,94-A3
HEITEL WAY CRT .176-A2
HELDT LN WCT .129-A1
HELDT ST CHS .145-D2
HELEN CT NSP .95-B3
HELEN CT N NOH .111-D1
HELEN LN MHT .95-D2
HELEN LN NSP .109-B1
HELEN ST MPW .95-B3
HELEN ST NSP .95-B3
HELEN ST PRE .167-B1
HELEN ST N NOH .111-D1
HELEN WAY N OKD .95-D4
HELENA AVE N OKD .109-D2
HELENA BLVD HAT .187-D3,201-D1
HELENA BLVD SCT .173-B4,187-C1
HELENA CT N OKD .109-D2
HELENA LN N OKD .95-D3
HELENA RD N OKD .95-D3,109-D2
HELENA ST JOR .173-B3
HELENA WAY JOR .173-B3
HELENA WAY SCT .173-B3
HELENA WAY N OKD .95-D4
HELENE PL NE FRI .78-E4
HELIUM CT NW RAM .49-B2
HELIUM ST NW RAM .35-B3,49-B2
HELIUM ST NW STT .7-B2
HELMO AVE N OKD .95-D4,109-D2
HELMO CIR N OKD .109-D2
HELMO CT N OKD .109-D2
HELMO PL N OKD .95-D4,109-D2
HELMO RD N OKD .109-D2
HEMATITE CIR NW RAM .49-A3
HEMATITE ST NW RAM .49-A1
HEMINGWAY AVE N LET .11-C1
HEMINGWAY AVE N OKD .109-D1
HEMINGWAY AVE N WYT .11-C4,25-C1
HEMINGWAY AVE S CG .137-D3
HEMLOCK AVE LVL .177-A4
HEMLOCK BLVD WBY .123-C2
HEMLOCK CIR BUF .58-E1
HEMLOCK CIR EAG .149-D2
HEMLOCK CIR EPR .132-B2
HEMLOCK CIR PRL .161-B2
HEMLOCK CIR N DAY .49-A4
HEMLOCK CT APV .163-A1
HEMLOCK CT LVL .163-A4
HEMLOCK CT N APV .163-A2
HEMLOCK CT S APV .163-A2
HEMLOCK DR BUR .148-C4
HEMLOCK DR CFT .222-B1
HEMLOCK LN VH .80-B4
HEMLOCK LN N DAY .49-A4,63-A3
HEMLOCK LN N MG .63-A4,77-A4
HEMLOCK LN N PLY .91-A1,105-A1
HEMLOCK LN NE HL .36-E3
HEMLOCK PATH LVL .163-A4
HEMLOCK PL VH .80-B4
HEMLOCK ST SA .93-A4
HEMLOCK ST S SWR .96-E1
HEMLOCK TRL SHK .146-D3
HEMLOCK WAY N MG .63-A4
HENDERSON RD ARL .183-A2
HENDON AVE FH .107-C2
HENDON AVE STP .107-C2
HENDRICKS AVE NW CNT .29-B1
HENDRICKS AVE NW CWT .1-B4,15-B1
HENDRICKS DR NW ABT .43-C4
HENDRY PL N MPW .94-C4
HENNA AVE APV .163-A1
HENNA AVE N FLT .39-D3,53-D3
HENNA AVE N HUG .53-D4,67-D4
HENNA AVE N OKD .109-D2
HENNA AVE S CG .137-D4
HENNA CT APV .163-A3
HENNA CT PS .95-D3
HENNEN RD BUR .148-B4
HENNEPIN AVE BL .17-E3
HENNEPIN AVE ERT .217-A4
HENNEPIN AVE MPL .106-C3,120-C1
HENNEPIN AVE WHT .217-B2
HENNEPIN AVE E MPL .106-E2,107-A1
HENNEPIN ST MO .31-D2
HENNEPIN TOWN RD EPR133-C4,147-C1
HENNES AVE W SHK .146-B3
HENNESSEY DR WRT .98-E4
HENNESSEY RD FAT .41-D4
HENNESSY VIS WBT .80-E3
HENNING CIR PRL .147-B4,161-B1
HENRIETTA AVE HBG .156-A2
HENRY AVE IGH .136-E2
HENRY AVE SSP .136-E1
HENRY AVE S COL .143-D4
HENRY BLVD FRT .28-A1
HENRY CIR BEL .186-A2
HENRY LN LL .52-A4
HENRY LN MPW .123-B3
HENRY ST CLK .1-D1
HENRY ST MP .102-E1
HENRY ST NSP .95-B4,109-B1
HENRY ST PRE .153-B4
HENSLOW AVE N OKD .109-D2
HENSLOW AVENUE CT N OKD .109-D2
HENSLOWE AVE S CG .137-D3
HERALD CIR APV .149-A4
HERALD CT APV .149-A4,163-A1
HERALD WAY APV .163-A1
HERBERG CT N CGT .12-D2
HERBERG RD SHT .14-A4
HERBERG RD TF .14-B3
HERBERT ST SCT .173-B3
HERBERT ST STP .108-E2
HERITAGE AVE SWR .96-C1
HERITAGE CIR CHS .145-D1
HERITAGE CIR GV .105-E1
HERITAGE CIR NB .93-B2
HERITAGE CIR N BUR .148-D4
HERITAGE CIR S BUR .148-C4
HERITAGE CT APV .163-A1
HERITAGE CT CHS .145-C2
HERITAGE CT SWR .96-C2
HERITAGE CT E VH .80-D4
HERITAGE CT W VH .80-D4
HERITAGE DR EDI .120-B4
HERITAGE DR LVL .176-E3
HERITAGE DR MH .136-A2
HERITAGE DR ORO .103-E4
HERITAGE DR VH .80-D4
HERITAGE DR E SHK .146-C3
HERITAGE LN APV .163-A1
HERITAGE LN BEL .186-A2
HERITAGE LN EAG .135-C3
HERITAGE LN NB .93-B2
HERITAGE LN ORO .103-E4
HERITAGE LN WYT .25-D4
HERITAGE RD EPR .132-C2
HERITAGE ST CV .66-D2
HERITAGE TRL BEL .186-A2
HERITAGE TRL NP .201-E1
HERITAGE TRL SLW .173-A2
HERITAGE WAY APV .149-A4
HERITAGE WAY FAR .191-E1,192-A1
HERITAGE WAY WBY .123-E3,124-A3
HERITAGE HILLS CIR BLO .148-A1
HERITAGE HILLS DR BLO 147-E1,148-A1
HERMAN CT HOP .119-C1
HERMAN TER HOP .119-C2
HERMES AVE N FLT .39-D4
HERMITAGE WAY MTK .118-B2
HERMOSA LN EAG .136-B2
HERON AVE N GRA .81-D3
HERON AVE N OKD .109-D3
HERON AVE S CG .137-D4
HERON CIR N OKD .109-D3
HERON CT MO .31-D3
HERON CT N OKD .109-D3
HERON CT S SHK .160-C1
HERON DR CHN .131-E3
HERON LN BUF .45-B3
HERON LN MOU .103-A4,117-A1
HERON LN NO .80-C4
HERON LN SJT .83-E4
HERON LN SMT .83-E3
HERON LN N OKD .109-D2
HERON WAY LVL .177-A4
HERRICK AVE CHM .63-C1
HERRICK LN ORO .104-A2
HERSCHEL ST RVL .93-C4,107-C1
HERSCHEL ST STP .107-D4
HERSEY ST STP .107-C3
HERSHEY AVE LVL .177-A3
HERSHEY CT APV .163-A1
HERSHEY CT LVL .163-A4
HERSHEY PATH LVL .163-A4
HERSHEY WAY APV .149-A4
HESLI HILL CT SVW .79-E4
HESSE FARM CIR CHN .146-A1
HESSE FARM RD CHN .145-E1,146-A1
HEWITT AVE STP .107-D3
HEYWOOD AVE APV .163-A2
HEYWOOD AVE LVL .177-A4
HEYWOOD CT APV .163-A3
HEYWOOD CT LVL .163-A4
HEYWOOD PATH APV .163-A1
HEYWOOD RD NFD .220-A4
HEYWOOD WAY APV .163-A3
HH ST WBL .80-D4
HI MAE CIR LP .113-B4
HIALEAH CT APV .149-A4
HIALEAH PATH APV .149-A4
HIALEAH ST OSC .28-A4
HIAWATHA AVE BL .17-E3,18-A3
HIAWATHA AVE EPR .132-E3
HIAWATHA AVE FS .121-B3
HIAWATHA AVE HOP .119-C1
HIAWATHA AVE MH .122-B2
HIAWATHA AVE MPL .106-E3,121-A1
HIAWATHA AVE VH .94-C2
HIAWATHA CIR EPR .132-E2
HIAWATHA CT N WYT .25-D4
HIAWATHA DR CHN .132-A1
HIAWATHA LN MPL .121-B3
HIAWATHA BEACH DR NE HL .37-C3
HIBISCUS AVE EDI .133-E1,134-A1
HIBISCUS AVE LVL .163-A4
HIBISCUS CT APV .163-A1
HICKERY ST RW .196-E4
HICKORY AVE NE MGY .215-D4
HICKORY AVE NE PRL .161-B1
HICKORY BLVD BPT .186-B1
HICKORY CIR WAC .129-C3
HICKORY CIR NE FRI .78-D3
HICKORY CT APV .163-A2
HICKORY CT EPR .132-E1
HICKORY CT LVL .163-A4,177-A1
HICKORY CT RFD .74-A3
HICKORY CT ROG .61-E2
HICKORY DR FRI .78-D3
HICKORY DR HUD .111-D2
HICKORY DR MED .90-A4
HICKORY DR MTA .102-B4
HICKORY HL EAG .149-C2
HICKORY LN CHN .131-C1
HICKORY LN EAG .149-C2
HICKORY LN MOU .117-A1
HICKORY LN OKD .109-D4
HICKORY LN PLY .91-B1
HICKORY LN SHK .146-B3
HICKORY PL LL .66-B4
HICKORY PL NE FRI .78-D3
HICKORY ST FAR .177-E4,178-A4
HICKORY ST MHT .95-D1
HICKORY ST N CAR .145-B4
HICKORY ST N CHS .145-C3
HICKORY ST N LP .113-B4
HICKORY ST NE FRI .78-D2
HICKORY ST S CHS .145-C3
HICKORY ST S LP .113-B4,127-B1
HICKORY ST W FAR .177-E4
HICKORY ST W SWR .96-E1,97-A1
HICKORY TRL LVL .176-E1,177-A1
HICKORY TRL PLY .91-B2
HICKORY TRL WBT .80-E2
HICKORY WAY APV .163-A2
HICKORY HILLS TRL SLT .175-B4
HIDDEN CIR CHN .132-B2
HIDDEN CT CHN .132-B2
HIDDEN LN CHN .132-B2
HIDDEN LN EDI .119-D3
HIDDEN LN EXC .117-E3
HIDDEN LN GRF .74-D4
HIDDEN PT EAG .149-C3
HIDDEN TER ROG .61-E1
HIDDEN BAY CT LTT .130-A3
HIDDEN BAY CT N LE .95-E4
HIDDEN BAY LN LTT .130-A3
HIDDEN BAY TRL N LE .95-E4
HIDDEN CREEK DR NW AND .50-A3
HIDDEN CREEK LN MTK .104-D4
HIDDEN CREEK PL CHS .145-C1
HIDDEN GLADE AVE N GRA .81-D3
HIDDEN LAKE CIR PLY .105-A1
HIDDEN LAKE CRV WBY .124-A2
HIDDEN LAKE DR WBY .124-A2
HIDDEN LAKES PKWY GV .106-A1
HIDDEN MEADOW CT APV .149-A3
HIDDEN MEADOW RD APV .149-A4
HIDDEN MEADOW RD WBY123-E2,124-A2
HIDDEN MEADOW TRL EAG .136-A4
HIDDEN OAK TRL SJT .84-C4
HIDDEN OAKS CIR PRL .161-C3
HIDDEN OAKS CT CHM .63-B3
HIDDEN OAKS CT MHT .81-D4
HIDDEN OAKS DR EPR .133-B3
HIDDEN OAKS LN CHM .63-B3
HIDDEN POND LN VIC .130-E3
HIDDEN POND TRL NE PRL .161-A2
HIDDEN PONDS ALC WBY .123-E3
HIDDEN PONDS DR COR .61-E4
HIDDEN PONDS RD WBY .123-E3
HIDDEN VALLEY CRK SMT .83-C3
HIDDEN VALLEY CT SWR .96-D2
HIDDEN VALLEY CT S CG .137-D3
HIDDEN VALLEY CT W SAV .162-A1
HIDDEN VALLEY DR DEL .87-E2
HIDDEN VALLEY DR W SAV161-E1,162-A1
HIDDEN VALLEY HOLW S CG .137-D3
HIDDEN VALLEY LN SWR .96-D2
HIDDEN VALLEY LN S CG .137-D3
HIDDEN VALLEY RD COR .61-B4
HIDDEN VALLEY RD MTK .118-D1

HIDDEN VALLEY RDG S CG 137-D3
HIDDEN VALLEY TRL S CG 137-D3
HIDDEN VIEW RD PRL 161-C1
HIDDENVALE LN MOU 117-A1
HIDEAWAY TRL MTK 119-A1
HIFHWAY 169 ANO 162-E1
HIGH DR BUR 49-B3
HIGH LN ORO 103-C2
HIGH RD IGH 136-C2
HIGH ST CAR 145-B4
HIGH ST FLT 39-D4
HIGH ST NEW 137-B1
HIGH ST PRE 153-B4
HIGH ST RFD 74-B3
HIGH ST SW WAT 101-A4
HIGH ST SW WYT 101-A4
HIGH BLUFF CIR SFT 159-A4
HIGH BLUFF LN COR 61-C4,75-C1
HIGH CIRCLE WAY NO 80-A2
HIGH PARK DR MTK 118-C3
HIGH POINT CIR EPR 133-B3
HIGH POINT CT HAS 166-C2
HIGH POINT CT MH 136-B1
HIGH POINT DR MTK 118-D2
HIGH POINT RD DWD 81-D2
HIGH POINT RD MH 136-B1
HIGH PRAIRIE TRL WST 221-B4
HIGH RIDGE CIR MH 122-B4
HIGH RIDGE DR HUT 112-B4
HIGH RIDGE DR TRT 112-B4
HIGH RIDGE RD RF 140-D2
HIGH SITE DR EAG 135-D3
HIGH TOWER MTK 118-D2
HIGHBURY LN MTK 118-E2
HIGHCLERE DR BUR 148-E4
HIGHCOURTE RVL 94-A3
HIGHCREST DR DPH 118-B2
HIGHCREST DR MED 90-A4
HIGHCREST RD NB 93-B2
HIGHCREST RD RVL 93-B4
HIGHCREST RD SA 93-B3
HIGHCROFT CT EAG 149-A3
HIGHCROFT LN WAY 104-B3
HIGHCROFT RD WAY 104-B3
HIGHGATE CIR CHN 131-D1
HIGHLAND AVE BL 17-E3
HIGHLAND AVE DPH 118-B1
HIGHLAND AVE MTK 118-C1
HIGHLAND AVE NFD 219-D3
HIGHLAND AVE SSP 122-D3
HIGHLAND AVE TKB 117-D2
HIGHLAND AVE WBL 95-A1
HIGHLAND AVE NW ABT 43-B4
HIGHLAND AVE NW CNT ...29-C1,43-B1
HIGHLAND AVE NW PRL 161-A3
HIGHLAND AVE SW VIT 85-C3
HIGHLAND BAY BLT 17-E2
HIGHLAND BAY WBY 123-E2
HIGHLAND BLF MTK 118-D2
HIGHLAND BLVD MOU 116-E2
HIGHLAND BLVD WBY 123-E2
HIGHLAND CIR CAT 191-E1
HIGHLAND CIR SVW 79-E4
HIGHLAND CIR SWD 117-A3
HIGHLAND CIR WBY 123-E2
HIGHLAND CT MOU 116-E2
HIGHLAND CT PRL 161-A2
HIGHLAND CT SVW 79-E4
HIGHLAND CT SWR 96-E2
HIGHLAND CT WBY 123-E2
HIGHLAND DR BUR 148-B4
HIGHLAND DR CAT 191-E1
HIGHLAND DR CHS 132-B1
HIGHLAND DR CHS 145-C2
HIGHLAND DR HAS 166-B2
HIGHLAND DR LVT 160-B2
HIGHLAND DR NP 201-E2
HIGHLAND DR RF 58-E3
HIGHLAND DR SVW 79-E4,94-A1
HIGHLAND LN BUR 148-B3
HIGHLAND LN MTK 118-D2
HIGHLAND LN NW WAY 104-B3
HIGHLAND PKWY STP 121-D2
HIGHLAND PL MTK 118-D3
HIGHLAND PL SVW 79-E4
HIGHLAND PL NE CH 93-A1
HIGHLAND RD BLO 147-D1
HIGHLAND RD EDI 119-D4
HIGHLAND RD MTA 116-B2
HIGHLAND RD MTK 118-D2
HIGHLAND RD SB 116-B3
HIGHLAND RD SWR 96-E2
HIGHLAND RD NW MTA ...19-D4,33-E1
HIGHLAND RD W MTA 116-B2
HIGHLAND ST SB 116-A3
HIGHLAND TRL BLT 17-E2
HIGHLAND TRL MTK 118-D3
HIGHLAND VW SJT 97-E1
HIGHLAND HEIGHTS DR MTK ...118-D3
HIGHLAND LAWNS CT MTK 118-D3
HIGHLAND RIDGE RD COR 61-E4
HIGHLAND VIEW
  AVE BUR 148-E3,149-A2
HIGHLAND VIEW
  CIR BUR 148-E3,149-A2
HIGHLAND VIEW
  LN BUR 148-E3,149-A2
HIGHLANDER DR EAG 135-D4
HIGHLANDS CT N LE 95-D3
HIGHLANDS RD BP 78-A2
HIGHLANDS TRL N LE 95-D3
HIGHOVER CT N CHN 131-D1
HIGHOVER CT S CHN 131-D1
HIGHOVER DR CHN 131-D1
HIGHOVER TER CHN 131-D1
HIGHOVER WAY CHN 131-D1
HIGHPATH LN MTK 118-B3
HIGHPOINT CIR CHS 131-B3
HIGHPOINT CIR BUR 148-E4
HIGHPOINT CRV MPW 123-B1
HIGHPOINT CRV SHK 146-C3
HIGHPOINT DR CHS 131-B4
HIGHPOINTE CRV RVL 94-A3
HIGHPOINTE CT PRL 161-C3
HIGHPOINTE CT WBY 123-D2
HIGHPOINTE RD WBY 123-D2
HIGHPOINTE TER BLO 133-E4
HIGHRIDGE CT MPW 94-D3
HIGHRIDGE TER EAG 135-D2
HIGHSTED DR IND 88-B4,102-B1
HIGHVIEW AVE EAG 135-D4
HIGHVIEW AVE EUT 191-A3,205-A1
HIGHVIEW AVE LVL 163-A4,171-E1
HIGHVIEW CIR APV 162-E3
HIGHVIEW CIR NP 121-E4
HIGHVIEW CIR N MH 121-E4,122-A4
HIGHVIEW CIR S MH 121-E4
HIGHVIEW CT CHM 63-B3

HIGHVIEW CT SCF 14-D3
HIGHVIEW DR APV 162-E3,163-A3
HIGHVIEW DR BUR 148-E4
HIGHVIEW DR EPR 132-B4
HIGHVIEW DR HAS 166-D3
HIGHVIEW DR HUT 97-D4
HIGHVIEW DR NB 79-B4,93-B1
HIGHVIEW DR NP 201-E2
HIGHVIEW DR SCT 173-B1
HIGHVIEW DR WAT 101-B3
HIGHVIEW KNLS HAS 166-D3
HIGHVIEW LN APV 162-E3
HIGHVIEW LN BUF 58-E3
HIGHVIEW LN LOL 104-A2
HIGHVIEW LN MOU 116-D2
HIGHVIEW LN ORO 103-A3
HIGHVIEW LN WBY 123-E3,124-A3
HIGHVIEW PL GRW 120-C3
HIGHVIEW PL MPL 118-E2
HIGHVIEW PL MTK 118-E2
HIGHVIEW PL SVW 79-E1
HIGHVIEW RD RFD 74-A4
HIGHVIEW TER EAG 135-D2
HIGHVIEW DR MPW 94-C4
HIGHVIEW DR N LEX 65-C4
HIGHVIEW DR S LEX 65-C4
HIGHWAY A HUD 111-D2
HIGHWAY A HUT 98-B4,112-B1
HIGHWAY A SJT 98-C3
HIGHWAY 1 FET 224-D2
HIGHWAY 1 VAT 224-B3
HIGHWAY 3 CAT 192-A2,206-A1
HIGHWAY 3 EAG 150-B2
HIGHWAY 3 ET 163-E4,177-E2
HIGHWAY 3 FAR 177-E4,192-A1
HIGHWAY 3 IGH 136-C2,150-B1
HIGHWAY 3 NFD 219-D4
HIGHWAY 3 RMT 150-A4,164-A2
HIGHWAY 3 SL 136-C1
HIGHWAY 3 WFT 205-E4,219-E2
HIGHWAY 5 ARL 183-A2
HIGHWAY 5 ART 183-A2
HIGHWAY 5 BLO 133-E2
HIGHWAY 5 BTT 142-E2
HIGHWAY 5 BYT 96-C3
HIGHWAY 5 CHN 131-C2,132-B2
HIGHWAY 5 EPR 132-D2,133-A2
HIGHWAY 5 FS 121-C4,135-B2
HIGHWAY 5 GI 169-D2
HIGHWAY 5 GIT 169-C3,183-B1
HIGHWAY 5 LE 109-E1,110-B1
HIGHWAY 5 LTT 129-E3,130-B2
HIGHWAY 5 MPW 109-B3
HIGHWAY 5 NYA 142-C3
HIGHWAY 5 OKD 109-C1
HIGHWAY 5 OPH 142-E1
HIGHWAY 5 STP 108-B4,121-D3
HIGHWAY 5 VIC 130-E2,131-A2
HIGHWAY 5 WAC 129-D3
HIGHWAY 5 WCT 129-B4,143-A1
HIGHWAY 5 WLK 155-E4,169-D1
HIGHWAY 5 YAT 141-E4,142-B4
HIGHWAY 5 E WAC 129-E3
HIGHWAY 6 FET 210-C3,224-D2
HIGHWAY 6 GHT 224-D4
HIGHWAY 7 CHN 117-B4,131-B1
HIGHWAY 7 DPH 118-B3
HIGHWAY 7 EXC 113-E3,118-A3
HIGHWAY 7 GRW 118-A3
HIGHWAY 7 HOP 113-E3
HIGHWAY 7 HOT 113-E3,114-B3
HIGHWAY 7 MTA 115-E3,116-C4
HIGHWAY 7 MTK 118-D2,119-A2
HIGHWAY 7 SB 116-A3
HIGHWAY 7 SLP 106-A4,119-D1
HIGHWAY 7 SWD 117-D4,118-A3
HIGHWAY 7 VIC 117-A4,131-B1
HIGHWAY 7 WIT 113-A3
HIGHWAY 7 WTT 114-E3,115-D3
HIGHWAY 8 CGT 12-C4,13-A4
HIGHWAY 8 CNC 12-B4,26-B1
HIGHWAY 8 FLT 12-E4
HIGHWAY 8 FRT 14-A4
HIGHWAY 8 LND 12-D4
HIGHWAY 8 SAT 14-E3
HIGHWAY 8 SCF 13-C4
HIGHWAY 8 SHA 13-C4
HIGHWAY 8 SHT 13-C4,14-B4
HIGHWAY 8 TF 14-B3
HIGHWAY 8 WYT 25-E4,26-A2
HIGHWAY 10 AH 79-C4
HIGHWAY 10 ANO 49-C4
HIGHWAY 10 BL 17-E4,18-A4
HIGHWAY 10 BLA 64-E4,65-A4
HIGHWAY 10 BLT 18-D4,33-A1
HIGHWAY 10 CG 137-C3,152-B2
HIGHWAY 10 CKP 1-E1,2-A1
HIGHWAY 10 CLK 1-D1
HIGHWAY 10 CR 49-E4,64-C2
HIGHWAY 10 CTT 153-B4
HIGHWAY 10 DET 152-D4,167-A1
HIGHWAY 10 ER 33-E2,34-A3
HIGHWAY 10 MV 79-B1
HIGHWAY 10 NEW 123-B4,137-B3
HIGHWAY 10 OGT 154-B4,168-D1
HIGHWAY 10 PRE 153-A4,167-A1
HIGHWAY 10 RAM 48-D2,49-A3
HIGHWAY 10 SPP 108-E4,123-A2
HIGHWAY 10 TLT 168-E2
HIGHWAY 10 NE AH 79-C3,93-D1
HIGHWAY 10 SE AH 79-C3,93-D1
HIGHWAY 10 SE BKR 2-E4,17-A1
HIGHWAY 10 SE BKR 2-C2,17-C2
HIGHWAY 10 SE CKP 2-B1
HIGHWAY 12 DEL 87-E3
HIGHWAY 12 FCT 86-C1
HIGHWAY 12 FKT 86-E1,87-C1
HIGHWAY 12 HUT 112-B2
HIGHWAY 12 HWL 86-B1
HIGHWAY 12 IND 87-E3,88-D4
HIGHWAY 12 LOL 103-E2,104-A2
HIGHWAY 12 MED 103-A1
HIGHWAY 12 MON 86-A1
HIGHWAY 12 MP 88-E4,103-A1
HIGHWAY 12 MVT 86-A1
HIGHWAY 12 ORO 103-C2,104-A2
HIGHWAY 12 VIT 85-B1
HIGHWAY 12 WAY 104-C3
HIGHWAY 12 WDT 85-D1,86-B1
HIGHWAY 12 WRT 112-E1
HIGHWAY 13 CLT 188-C3,202-C2
HIGHWAY 13 EAG 135-C3

HIGHWAY 13 LAT 201-D4,215-D2
HIGHWAY 13 LIL 121-E3,122-A3
HIGHWAY 13 MEN 121-D4
HIGHWAY 13 MH 121-D4,135-D1
HIGHWAY 13 MVT 215-D4
HIGHWAY 13 NP 201-D3
HIGHWAY 13 PRL 160-E4,161-D1
HIGHWAY 13 SAV 147-D4,161-D1
HIGHWAY 13 SLT 161-A4,174-C3
HIGHWAY 13 STP 122-B2
HIGHWAY 13 E BUR 148-D3,149-A2
HIGHWAY 13 E EAG 135-B4,149-A1
HIGHWAY 13 W BUR 148-B3
HIGHWAY 13 W SAV 147-A3,148-B4
HIGHWAY 18 RW 182-C4,196-C2
HIGHWAY 18 WEL 182-B3,196-C1
HIGHWAY 19 ART 197-C2
HIGHWAY 19 BKT 198-E2,199-B2
HIGHWAY 19 BPT 199-E2
HIGHWAY 19 BWT 219-B3
HIGHWAY 19 CF 208-B4
HIGHWAY 19 CFT 208-D4,209-A4
HIGHWAY 19 CLT 202-C2,203-A2
HIGHWAY 19 FET 210-D2
HIGHWAY 19 GVT 218-D3,219-B3
HIGHWAY 19 HAT 201-C2,202-A2
HIGHWAY 19 HEN 198-D3
HIGHWAY 19 HET 197-E2,198-B3
HIGHWAY 19 LON 217-B2
HIGHWAY 19 NFD 219-E3
HIGHWAY 19 NFT 219-E3,220-A3
HIGHWAY 19 NP 201-D2
HIGHWAY 19 RW 196-D4,210-D1
HIGHWAY 19 SIT 220-D3
HIGHWAY 19 STN 207-E4,221-C2
HIGHWAY 19 VAT 209-D4,210-B4
HIGHWAY 19 WEL 196-A2
HIGHWAY 19 WFT 220-B3
HIGHWAY 19 WHT 203-A3,217-A1
HIGHWAY 19 WT 217-D2,218-C3
HIGHWAY 20 CF 208-B4
HIGHWAY 20 CFT 208-B2
HIGHWAY 20 DT 194-C4,208-C1
HIGHWAY 20 LPT 211-D4
HIGHWAY 21 HAT 187-D3,201-D1
HIGHWAY 21 JOR 173-B3
HIGHWAY 21 LAT 201-D4,215-D2
HIGHWAY 21 MGY 215-D4
HIGHWAY 21 MVT 215-D4
HIGHWAY 21 NP 201-D4
HIGHWAY 21 SCT 173-B4,187-C1
HIGHWAY 24 CKP 1-C2
HIGHWAY 24 CLK 1-D1
HIGHWAY 24 CNT 1-B2
HIGHWAY 24 CW 1-B2
HIGHWAY 24 CWT 1-A4,15-A2
HIGHWAY 25 ART 170-E3,171-C4
HIGHWAY 25 BEL 185-E1,186-A1
HIGHWAY 25 BL 18-A4
HIGHWAY 25 BLT 18-A4,31-E1
HIGHWAY 25 BUF 58-E2
HIGHWAY 25 BUF 45-A3,58-E4
HIGHWAY 25 CT 128-D2,142-D1
HIGHWAY 25 FKT 72-E4,86-E1
HIGHWAY 25 GI 169-D2
HIGHWAY 25 MO 31-C3
HIGHWAY 25 MOT 31-C4,45-B1
HIGHWAY 25 MYR 114-D4,128-D1
HIGHWAY 25 NYA 142-C3
HIGHWAY 25 RFT 58-E4,72-E2
HIGHWAY 25 SFT 171-E4
HIGHWAY 25 WAT 101-A3
HIGHWAY 25 WDT 86-C2
HIGHWAY 25 WLK 169-D1,170-B2
HIGHWAY 25 WTT 114-E3,115-A1
HIGHWAY 25 YAT 142-D2,155-E2
HIGHWAY 25 N BUF 58-E1
HIGHWAY 25 NE BUF 44-E4,45-A4
HIGHWAY 25 NE BUT 45-A3
HIGHWAY 29 CTT 153-C3,154-B2
HIGHWAY 29 OGT 153-D3
HIGHWAY 29 PRE 153-B4
HIGHWAY 29 RIT 140-D4
HIGHWAY 31 WEL 196-B2
HIGHWAY 34 STP 108-B4
HIGHWAY 35 CTT 153-C3,154-B2
HIGHWAY 35 DBT 168-D4,182-D2
HIGHWAY 35 DRS 14-D4,28-D2
HIGHWAY 35 FAT 42-A2,56-A2
HIGHWAY 35 HUD 111-C2,112-A4
HIGHWAY 35 HUT 97-D4,112-A3
HIGHWAY 35 KKT 140-E1
HIGHWAY 35 NOH 97-C4,111-C1
HIGHWAY 35 OGT 167-D2,168-C3
HIGHWAY 35 OSC 27-E4,28-A4
HIGHWAY 35 OSC 28-B3
HIGHWAY 35 PRE 153-B4,167-B3
HIGHWAY 35 RF 126-E4,140-E1
HIGHWAY 35 RIT 140-D4
HIGHWAY 35 SAT 14-D3
HIGHWAY 35 SCF 14-D3
HIGHWAY 35 SJT 83-B4,97-C2
HIGHWAY 35 SMT 70-B2,83-D3
HIGHWAY 35 SOM 70-B4,84-B1
HIGHWAY 35 TRT 112-A4,126-B1
HIGHWAY 36 BYT 96-D2
HIGHWAY 36 LE 95-E2,96-B2
HIGHWAY 36 OKD 95-C3
HIGHWAY 36 OPH 96-E2,97-A2
HIGHWAY 36 PS 95-D3
HIGHWAY 36 RVL 93-C4
HIGHWAY 36 SWR 96-D2,97-A2
HIGHWAY 36 E MPW 94-C4
HIGHWAY 36 W LC 94-C4
HIGHWAY 36 W MPW 94-D4,95-A4
HIGHWAY 36 W NSP 95-B4
HIGHWAY 36 W RVL 93-D4,94-A4
HIGHWAY 36 BLVD N OKD 95-C3
HIGHWAY 39 CNT 29-A2
HIGHWAY 39 MOT 32-B2
HIGHWAY 41 CHN 117-D4,131-D1
HIGHWAY 41 CHS 131-C3,145-C2
HIGHWAY 41 JT 145-C4
HIGHWAY 41 LVT 145-D4
HIGHWAY 47 ANO 49-D4
HIGHWAY 47 BLA 78-D1
HIGHWAY 47 BT 21-C3,35-B1
HIGHWAY 47 CR 92-D2
HIGHWAY 47 CR 49-E4,64-C2
HIGHWAY 47 FRI 78-D3,92-D1
HIGHWAY 47 MPL 92-D3,106-D1
HIGHWAY 47 OG 7-D4,21-C1
HIGHWAY 47 RAM 35-B3,49-C2
HIGHWAY 47 SF 7-D4
HIGHWAY 47 SLK 78-D2
HIGHWAY 47 NW BLA 78-D1

HIGHWAY 47 NW CR 64-D4,78-D1
HIGHWAY 47 NW STT 7-D1
HIGHWAY 49 LC 94-B3
HIGHWAY 49 LL 65-E3,66-A2
HIGHWAY 49 MPW 94-B4,108-B1
HIGHWAY 49 NO 80-A3
HIGHWAY 49 STP 108-B3
HIGHWAY 49 SVW 80-A4,94-B1
HIGHWAY 49 VH 94-B2
HIGHWAY 50 DT 178-D4,192-B1
HIGHWAY 50 FAR 191-E1,192-A1
HIGHWAY 50 HMP 193-B2
HIGHWAY 50 HMT 193-A1,194-A2
HIGHWAY 50 NT 193-E2
HIGHWAY 50 VET 178-E4,179-A4
HIGHWAY 51 FH 107-D1
HIGHWAY 51 RVL 93-D3,107-D1
HIGHWAY 51 STP 107-D3,121-D2
HIGHWAY 51 VAT 210-B4,224-B2
HIGHWAY 52 CF 209-A4,222-A1
HIGHWAY 52 CFT 208-A4,222-B3
HIGHWAY 52 COA 164-E3,165-A3
HIGHWAY 52 HMP 193-B2
HIGHWAY 52 HMT 193-C3,207-D1
HIGHWAY 52 IGH 136-D2,150-E2
HIGHWAY 52 LEO 222-B4
HIGHWAY 52 MPL 106-D2
HIGHWAY 52 RAT 207-E2,208-A3
HIGHWAY 52 RMT 150-E4,164-E1
HIGHWAY 52 SSP 122-D2
HIGHWAY 52 STP 108-C4,122-C1
HIGHWAY 52 VET 165-A4,179-B3
HIGHWAY 52 WSP 122-D3
HIGHWAY 53 RW 210-E1
HIGHWAY 55 ABT 43-C2
HIGHWAY 55 BUF 58-E2,59-A2
HIGHWAY 55 BUT 58-E1,59-B3
HIGHWAY 55 CMT 58-D1
HIGHWAY 55 CNT 43-A2
HIGHWAY 55 COR 89-B1
HIGHWAY 55 EAG 135-E2,136-A3
HIGHWAY 55 ES 121-C4
HIGHWAY 55 GRF 74-C4,88-E1
HIGHWAY 55 GV 105-E2,106-A2
HIGHWAY 55 HAS 166-C2
HIGHWAY 55 IGH 136-D4
HIGHWAY 55 MED 89-E2,90-A2
HIGHWAY 55 MH 121-D4,135-D1
HIGHWAY 55 MLT 43-E3,44-B3
HIGHWAY 55 MPL 106-C2,121-A1
HIGHWAY 55 NIT 165-D1,166-A2
HIGHWAY 55 PLY 90-C3,105-B2
HIGHWAY 55 RFD 59-B4,73-D2
HIGHWAY 56 RMT 151-A4,165-B1
HIGHWAY 56 HMT 193-B3,207-B3
HIGHWAY 56 RAN 207-B3
HIGHWAY 56 RAT 207-B3
HIGHWAY 56 STN 207-B4,221-D2
HIGHWAY 56 WST 221-B4
HIGHWAY 61 CG 137-C3,152-B2
HIGHWAY 61 DET 152-D4
HIGHWAY 61 DT 194-D2,195-B2
HIGHWAY 61 FL 39-B3
HIGHWAY 61 FLT 39-B4,53-B1
HIGHWAY 61 GI 94-E1
HIGHWAY 61 HAS 152-D4,166-D2
HIGHWAY 61 HUG 67-B4,81-B1
HIGHWAY 61 MIE 194-E2,195-A2
HIGHWAY 61 MPW 94-D3,108-D1
HIGHWAY 61 MT 166-D4,180-D3
HIGHWAY 61 NEW 123-B4,137-B1
HIGHWAY 61 RW 196-E4
HIGHWAY 61 SPP 137-B2
HIGHWAY 61 SSP 108-E4,123-A2
HIGHWAY 61 VH 94-E2
HIGHWAY 61 WEL 195-C2,196-A2
HIGHWAY 61 N WBL 81-A3,94-E1
HIGHWAY 61 N WBT 81-B2
HIGHWAY 62 EDI 119-D4,120-A4
HIGHWAY 62 EPR 119-B4
HIGHWAY 62 FS 120-E3,121-A3
HIGHWAY 62 MPL 120-B4,121-B3
HIGHWAY 62 MTK 119-B4
HIGHWAY 62 RCH 120-D4
HIGHWAY 64 RDT 84-E1
HIGHWAY 64 SJT 83-B4,97-A1
HIGHWAY 64 SMT 83-D3,84-C1
HIGHWAY 64 SOM 70-B4,84-B1
HIGHWAY 65 ATT 8-E1
HIGHWAY 65 BL 63-E4,64-E1
HIGHWAY 65 BLA 92-E2
HIGHWAY 65 EB 8-E4,22-E3
HIGHWAY 65 FRI 78-E4,92-E1
HIGHWAY 65 HL 50-E3
HIGHWAY 65 KKT 126-E4,140-E1
HIGHWAY 65 MPL 92-E3,106-D3
HIGHWAY 65 RF 126-E4,140-E1
HIGHWAY 65 SLK 78-E2
HIGHWAY 65 TRT 126-E4
HIGHWAY 65 NE BLA 64-E4,65-A4
HIGHWAY 65 NE FRI 78-E3
HIGHWAY 65 NE SLK 78-E2,79-A1
HIGHWAY 75 MO 31-E2
HIGHWAY 75 MOT 31-E2,32-A3
HIGHWAY 77 APV 149-B4,163-B1
HIGHWAY 77 BLO 134-E3,135-A4
HIGHWAY 77 BUR 135-A4
HIGHWAY 77 EAG 135-A4,149-A2
HIGHWAY 77 FS 120-E4,134-E1
HIGHWAY 77 MPL 120-E3
HIGHWAY 77 RCH 120-E4,134-E1
HIGHWAY 87 SAT 14-C1
HIGHWAY 87 SCF 93-C2
HIGHWAY 88 NB 93-B3
HIGHWAY 88 RVL 93-B3
HIGHWAY 93 HEN 198-D3
HIGHWAY 93 HET 198-D4,212-C4
HIGHWAY 95 AFT 124-C4,138-C1
HIGHWAY 95 BAY 97-B4,111-B1
HIGHWAY 95 BYT 111-B1
HIGHWAY 95 CG 152-C3
HIGHWAY 95 DET 138-C3,152-C2
HIGHWAY 95 FRI 27-D4,41-C1
HIGHWAY 95 LLD 111-C3
HIGHWAY 95 MAY 69-C3,83-C1
HIGHWAY 95 MSC 55-B4,69-C1
HIGHWAY 95 NST 41-B5,55-C2
HIGHWAY 95 SHT 13-E1,14-A1
HIGHWAY 95 SWR 83-A4,97-A1
HIGHWAY 95 SWT 83-B3
HIGHWAY 95 TF 14-C2

HIGHWAY 95 WBY 110-C4,124-C2
HIGHWAY 95 WLT 111-B2
HIGHWAY 96 DWD 81-C3
HIGHWAY 96 GRA 81-D3,82-A3
HIGHWAY 96 SWR 83-A4
HIGHWAY 96 SWT 82-E4,83-A4
HIGHWAY 96 WBL 81-A3
HIGHWAY 96 E WBL 81-B3
HIGHWAY 96 E WBT 81-B2
HIGHWAY 97 COT 52-E1,53-A1
HIGHWAY 97 FLT 39-D4,53-A1
HIGHWAY 97 NST 40-C4,41-A4
HIGHWAY 98 WYO 25-B3
HIGHWAY 98 WYT 25-D3,26-A2
HIGHWAY 100 BC 78-C4,92-B1
HIGHWAY 100 BLO 133-E2
HIGHWAY 100 CRY 91-E4
HIGHWAY 100 EDI 119-E3,133-E1
HIGHWAY 100 GV 91-E4,105-E2
HIGHWAY 100 ROB 91-E3,92-A2
HIGHWAY 100 SLP 119-E2
HIGHWAY 100 S GV 105-E3,106-A3
HIGHWAY 100 S SLP 105-E4,119-E1
HIGHWAY 101 HSN 47-E3
HIGHWAY 101 OTS 33-E3,47-E2
HIGHWAY 101 ROG 47-E4,61-E1
HIGHWAY 110 IGH 122-C4,136-C1
HIGHWAY 110 MEN 121-D4
HIGHWAY 110 MH 121-E4,122-A4
HIGHWAY 110 SL 122-C4,136-C1
HIGHWAY 110 WSP 122-B4
HIGHWAY 112 LES 212-D3
HIGHWAY 118 BLA 65-A4,79-A1
HIGHWAY 118 MV 79-B1
HIGHWAY 120 MPW 109-C3,123-C1
HIGHWAY 120 OKD 109-C3
HIGHWAY 120 WBY 123-C2
HIGHWAY 121 MPL 120-C4
HIGHWAY 121 RCH 120-C4
HIGHWAY 122 MPL 106-E3
HIGHWAY 149 EAG 136-A2
HIGHWAY 149 IGH 136-B4,150-B1
HIGHWAY 149 MH 122-A4,136-A1
HIGHWAY 149 STP 122-B1
HIGHWAY 149 WSP 122-B2
HIGHWAY 156 SSP 122-E4,136-E1
HIGHWAY 156 STP 122-D2
HIGHWAY 169 ANO 49-C4,63-C1
HIGHWAY 169 BEL 185-E2,186-A1
HIGHWAY 169 BKT 185-C3,199-A2
HIGHWAY 169 BLO 133-C2,147-C1
HIGHWAY 169 BP 63-C4,77-C2
HIGHWAY 169 BPT 185-E2,186-B1
HIGHWAY 169 CHM 63-C2
HIGHWAY 169 CHN 146-A1
HIGHWAY 169 EDI 119-C4,133-C1
HIGHWAY 169 EPR 133-C3,147-C1
HIGHWAY 169 ER 19-E2,33-E2
HIGHWAY 169 HET 212-C3
HIGHWAY 169 HOP 119-C2
HIGHWAY 169 JOR 173-B2
HIGHWAY 169 JT 145-E3,146-A3
HIGHWAY 169 LES 212-D2
HIGHWAY 169 LIT 5-E3
HIGHWAY 169 LPT 212-B4
HIGHWAY 169 LVT 145-D4,159-D2
HIGHWAY 169 MG 77-C3
HIGHWAY 169 MTK 119-C3
HIGHWAY 169 NH 91-C2
HIGHWAY 169 OSS 77-C2
HIGHWAY 169 RAM 48-D2,49-A3
HIGHWAY 169 SCT 159-D4,173-C1
HIGHWAY 169 SHK 146-C3,147-B3
HIGHWAY 169 SLP 105-C3
HIGHWAY 169 SLW 172-C4,173-A2
HIGHWAY 169 TYT 199-B3,212-E2
HIGHWAY 169 ZIM 5-D1
HIGHWAY 169 N BP 77-C3,91-C1
HIGHWAY 169 N GV 105-C2
HIGHWAY 169 N MG 77-C4,91-C1
HIGHWAY 169 N NH 91-C4
HIGHWAY 169 N PLY 91-C2,105-C1
HIGHWAY 169 S GV 105-C3
HIGHWAY 169 S HOP 119-C1
HIGHWAY 169 S MTK 105-C4
HIGHWAY 169 S SLP 105-C3,119-C1
HIGHWAY 169 BLVD SLW 186-B1
HIGHWAY 201 ER 19-E4,33-E1
HIGHWAY 212 BTT 142-E4,143-E4
HIGHWAY 212 CHN 145-E1,146-A1
HIGHWAY 212 CHS 145-C3
HIGHWAY 212 CHT 145-B3
HIGHWAY 212 COL 143-D4
HIGHWAY 212 DAT 144-A3,145-A3
HIGHWAY 212 EDI 119-C4
HIGHWAY 212 EPR 119-B4,133-A3
HIGHWAY 212 HNT 141-A4
HIGHWAY 212 NYA 142-C4
HIGHWAY 212 PLA 141-B4
HIGHWAY 212 YAT 141-E4,142-B4
HIGHWAY 212 E CHS 145-D2
HIGHWAY 212 W CHS 145-C3
HIGHWAY 212 W CHT 145-C3
HIGHWAY 241 SM 46-E3,47-B3
HIGHWAY 242 BLA 50-E4
HIGHWAY 242 CR 49-E4,50-C4
HIGHWAY 243 FRT 27-E4
HIGHWAY 243 OSC 27-E4
HIGHWAY 244 DWD 81-C3
HIGHWAY 244 GL 94-E2
HIGHWAY 244 MHT 81-D4,95-D1
HIGHWAY 244 WBL 94-E2,95-B2
HIGHWAY 246 NFD 219-D4
HIGHWAY 252 BC 78-C4,92-C1
HIGHWAY 252 BP 78-B2
HIGHWAY 261 BNT 113-B4,127-A1
HIGHWAY 261 WIT 99-B4,113-B2
HIGHWAY 280 LAU 107-B1
HIGHWAY 280 RVL 93-B4,107-B1
HIGHWAY 280 STP 107-B2
HIGHWAY 282 JOR 173-B2
HIGHWAY 282 SCT 173-D2,174-A1
HIGHWAY 282 SLT 174-C1
HIGHWAY 284 BTT 143-D2
HIGHWAY 284 COL 143-E4
HIGHWAY 284 WAC 129-D3
HIGHWAY 284 WCT 129-D4,143-D1
HIGHWAY 288 ANO 49-C3
HIGHWAY 291 HAS 166-E2
HIGHWAY 300 JT 145-E3,146-A3
HIGHWAY 300 SHK 146-A2
HIGHWAY 312 EPR 132-D2
HIGHWAY 316 HAS 166-D3
HIGHWAY 316 MT 166-E4,181-A1
HIGHWAY 316 RVT 181-C3
HIGHWAY 316 BLVD WEL 181-C4,195-C1
HIGHWAY 610 BLA 64-D4
HIGHWAY 610 BP 77-D1,78-B1
HIGHWAY 610 CR 64-C4,78-C1
HIGHWOOD AVE MPW 123-B2
HIGHWOOD AVE STP 123-A2
HIGHWOOD DR BLO 133-D2
HIGHWOOD DR CHS 145-C1
HIGHWOOD DR EDI 119-D3
HIGHWOOD DR MTK 118-D2
HIGHWOOD DR ORO 103-B4
HIGHWOOD DR W EDI 119-D3
HIGHWOOD RD ORO 103-B4
HIGHWOOD RD SLP 106-A3
HIGHWOOD ST BWV 95-C1
HIGHWOOD WAY APV 148-E4,149-A4
HILARY PATH NIT 151-E4,165-E1
HILDA AVE CT 114-A4
HILDA AVE N NG 114-A4
HILDING AVE STP 123-A1
HILL AVE BKR 4-A4
HILL AVE WBL 95-A1
HILL CIR PRL 161-B3
HILL CIR E BL 18-A3
HILL CIR W BL 18-A3
HILL CT SVW 79-E2
HILL LN DPH 118-B1
HILL LN S SLP 106-A3
HILL PL N CRY 91-D4
HILL PT WBY 123-D4
HILL RD CFT 208-E3
HILL RD MTB 117-D1
HILL RD WAY 104-D3
HILL RD WBY 123-D4
HILL ST BKR 4-A4
HILL ST BL 18-A3
HILL ST CHN 132-B2
HILL ST HEN 198-D3
HILL ST HOP 119-C2
HILL ST MTK 104-D4
HILL ST OSC 28-A4
HILL ST RFD 74-B4
HILL ST STP 122-B1
HILL ST SWR 97-A1
HILL ST TF 14-C3
HILL ST E NYA 142-C4
HILL ST N BL 18-A3
HILL ST W NYA 142-C4
HILL TER WBY 123-D3
HILL TRL N LE 95-D3
HILL A WAY CT EDI 133-C1
HILL AND DALE DR NW SF 6-D3
HILL FARM CIR NO 80-A3
HILL FARM CT NO 80-A3
HILL FARM RD HUT 112-C2
HILL PLACE DR ROG 47-E4
HILL RIDGE CT PRE 153-B4
HILL RIDGE DR EAG 135-C3
HILL RIDGE DR MTK 104-E3
HILL RIDGE TER MTK 104-E3
HILL SIDE AVE BL 18-A3
HILL TRAIL CT N LE 95-D3
HILLAIRE RD WBL 81-B4,95-B1
HILLARY FARM RD HUT 112-D3
HILLCREST AVE STP 121-C2
HILLCREST CIR MO 17-B4,31-B1
HILLCREST CT BEC 3-A4
HILLCREST CT BUR 148-D4
HILLCREST CT DPH 118-C1
HILLCREST CT WBY 123-C1
HILLCREST CT N EPR 132-D1
HILLCREST CT S EPR 132-D1
HILLCREST DR BEL 185-E1
HILLCREST DR CHC 12-B4,26-B1
HILLCREST DR DWD 81-D2
HILLCREST DR MGY 215-D4
HILLCREST DR SMT 84-D1
HILLCREST DR TKB 117-D2
HILLCREST DR WBY 123-C1
HILLCREST DR WYT 25-C1
HILLCREST DR N CHM 63-C2
HILLCREST DR NE FRI 78-E4,79-A4
HILLCREST DR S SWR 97-A2
HILLCREST DR SE SM 46-E4,47-A4
HILLCREST LN BUR 148-D4
HILLCREST LN CP 65-E4
HILLCREST LN DPH 118-B2
HILLCREST LN EDI 134-A1
HILLCREST LN EPR 132-D1
HILLCREST PL HSN 47-D3
HILLCREST RD BEC 3-A4
HILLCREST RD DPH 118-B1
HILLCREST RD MO 31-C1
HILLCREST RD MOU 116-E1
HILLCREST ST PRL 161-B4
HILLCREST ST RF 140-E2
HILLCREST WAY DPH 118-C1
HILLCREST WAY LES 212-D4
HILLDALE AVE SA 93-A3
HILLDALE DR E SHK 147-B4
HILLENDALE RD SWD 117-E4
HILLENDALE RD NW BT 6-E4,7-A4
HILLINGDON RD WBY 124-A2
HILLOWAY CIR BUR 162-C3
HILLOWAY RD EPR 132-E3
HILLOWAY RD W MTK 105-A3
HILLRIDGE DR EAG 135-C3
HILLSBORO AVE SAV 147-C4,161-C3
HILLSBORO AVE N BP 77-C4
HILLSBORO AVE N CHM 63-C3
HILLSBORO AVE N GV 91-C4,105-C1
HILLSBORO AVE N NH 91-C4
HILLSBORO AVE S SLP ..105-C3,119-C1
HILLSBORO CIR N NH 91-C1
HILLSBORO CT LVL 163-A3
HILLSBORO CT SAV 161-C1
HILLSBORO CT N CHM 63-C3
HILLSBORO CT N NH 91-C4
HILLSBORO PL NH 91-C3
HILLSCOURTE N RVL 94-A3
HILLSCOURTE S RVL 94-A3
HILLSDALE AVE STP 123-B1
HILLSDALE CT CHN 131-D1
HILLSDALE DR MTA 102-D3
HILLSDALE ST SW LAT 201-D3
HILLSHIRE LN BUR 162-B2
HILLSIDE AVE JOR 173-B3
HILLSIDE AVE SB 116-A3
HILLSIDE AVE STP 107-B2
HILLSIDE AVE N MPL 106-B1
HILLSIDE AVE SW LAT 201-D3
HILLSIDE CIR CHS 145-C2
HILLSIDE CIR EDI 119-D4
HILLSIDE CIR MTK 105-B3
HILLSIDE CIR PRL 160-E2
HILLSIDE CIR N CHM 63-C2
HILLSIDE CT BUR 162-C2
HILLSIDE CT EAG 136-A3
HILLSIDE CT EDI 119-D4
HILLSIDE CT HAS 166-C2
HILLSIDE CT LVL 163-A3
HILLSIDE CT NFD 219-E4
HILLSIDE CT STP 107-B2
HILLSIDE CT WLT 110-E2
HILLSIDE DR BLT 18-C3
HILLSIDE DR CHM 63-C2
HILLSIDE DR COR 61-E4,62-A4
HILLSIDE DR EAG 136-A3
HILLSIDE DR EPR 132-D2
HILLSIDE DR JOR 173-B3
HILLSIDE DR PRE 167-C1
HILLSIDE DR NW WAT 101-A3
HILLSIDE DR S SHK 146-C4
HILLSIDE DR W WAY 104-A3
HILLSIDE LN BUF 45-A4
HILLSIDE LN BUR 162-C2
HILLSIDE LN EDI 119-D4,133-D1
HILLSIDE LN IND 102-D2
HILLSIDE LN MOU 117-A1
HILLSIDE LN MTK 105-B3
HILLSIDE LN ORT 3-A4
HILLSIDE LN SWR 96-D2
HILLSIDE RD EDI 119-D4
HILLSIDE RD WBL 95-B2
HILLSIDE ST DPH 118-B2
HILLSIDE ST HAS 166-C2
HILLSIDE TER MTK 118-C1
HILLSIDE TRL SAV 161-E2
HILLSIDE TRL NW BT 20-E1
HILLSIDE TRL S CG 137-E4,138-A4
HILLSVIEW E RVL 94-A3
HILLSVIEW W RVL 94-A3
HILLSVIEW RD BC 92-B1
HILLSWICK CT N BP 78-A2
HILLSWICK PL MHT 95-C2
HILLSWICK TER MHT 95-C2
HILLSWICK TRL BP 78-A2
HILLTOP AVE RVL 108-A1
HILLTOP AVE N LE 95-D3
HILLTOP CIR NYA 142-C3
HILLTOP CT CHM 63-B2
HILLTOP CT MH 122-A4
HILLTOP CT MPW 94-D3
HILLTOP CT NSP 95-B3
HILLTOP DR HUD 111-E2
HILLTOP DR MO 31-C1
HILLTOP DR SAV 147-C3
HILLTOP DR SB 116-A3
HILLTOP DR SJT 97-A1
HILLTOP DR SW LAT 201-D3
HILLTOP LN EAG 149-D1
HILLTOP LN EDI 119-E3
HILLTOP LN HAS 166-C2
HILLTOP LN SJT 97-A1
HILLTOP LN STP 121-C3
HILLTOP LN WAC 129-D4
HILLTOP PT EAG 149-D1
HILLTOP RD BUR 148-C4
HILLTOP RD EPR 132-D3
HILLTOP RD MH 122-A4
HILLTOP RD MTK 119-A1
HILLTOP RD SJT 97-A1
HILLTOP RD N MG 91-B1
HILLTOP RDG SJT 83-A4,97-A1
HILLTOP ST WBL 95-B2
HILLTOP TER MTK 118-D3
HILLVALE AVE N OKD 95-D4
HILLVALE CIR N OKD 95-D4
HILLVALE CT N OKD 109-D1
HILLVALE TRL OKD 109-D2
HILLVALE WAY N OKD 95-D4
HILLVIEW DR SB 116-A3
HILLVIEW DR E SB 116-A3
HILLVIEW LN LOR 89-B2
HILLVIEW LN SB 116-A3
HILLVIEW LN VH 80-B4
HILLVIEW RD LOR 89-B2
HILLVIEW RD MV 79-B2
HILLVIEW RD SLK 79-A2
HILLVIEW RD SVW 79-C2
HILLWIND RD NE FRI 78-E4,92-E1
HILLWOOD AVE LVL 176-E1
HILLWOOD CT STP 123-B2
HILLWOOD DR CTT 140-C2
HILLWOOD DR MPW 123-B2
HILLWOOD DR RIT 140-C2
HILLWOOD DR SHK 146-B4
HILLWOOD DR STP 123-B2
HILLWOOD DR E RIT 140-C1
HILO AVE N FLT 39-D3,53-D2
HILO AVE N HUG 67-D4
HILO AVE N OKD 109-D2
HILO CT N FLT 39-D3
HILO CT N OKD 109-D2
HILO LN N FLT 39-D4
HILO LN S CG 137-D4
HILO TRL S CG 137-D4
HILTON CT N PS 95-D2
HILTON ST PRE 153-B4
HILTON TRL N MHT 95-D1
HILTON TRL N PS 95-D2
HINCKLEY ST WBL 81-A4
HINGHAM CIR MH 122-B3
HINTON AVE NT 193-E2
HINTON AVE S CG 137-D3
HINTON TRL N OKD 109-D2
HINTON PARK AVE S CG 137-D3
HIRTA PT EAG 149-C3
HITSMAN LN IND 88-B3
HITTNER PT EAG 149-B3
HIWASSEE TER MH 122-B3
HOBART LN SLP 119-E2
HOBBY HILLS CIR CRT 176-A2
HOBBY HILLS TRL CRT 176-A2
HOBE CT N WBT 81-A1
HOBE CT S WBT 81-A1
HOBE CT W WBT 80-E1,81-A1
HOBE LN WBT 80-E1,81-A1
HODGES LN MV 79-A2
HODGSON RD LL 65-E3,66-A4
HODGSON RD NO 80-A3
HODGSON RD SVW 80-A4,94-B1
HODGSON ROAD CONN SVW 80-A3
HOEKSTRA AVE N FLT 39-D4
HOEKSTRA CT N FLT 39-D4
HOFFMAN RD GL 80-E4,94-E1
HOFFMAN RD VH 94-E2
HOFFMAN RD WBL 81-A4,94-E1
HOFFMAN ST CF 208-A4
HOFFMANN ST E CF 208-B4
HOFFMANN ST W CF 208-B4
HOGAN AVE HMT 193-E3,207-E1
HOGAN AVE NIT 165-E2
HOGAN AVE NT 193-E2
HOGAN AVE RAT 207-E2
HOGAN AVE VET 165-E4,179-E1
HOGAN PATH RAT 207-E4
HOGAN WAY EPR 132-C2
HOHENSTEIN CT SHK 160-C1
HOIST RD DBT 182-C1
HOKAH AVE MH 136-A1
HOKAH DR LL 66-A4
HOLASEK AVE BEC 2-E3
HOLASEK LN EPR 119-A4
HOLBORN AVE EDI 119-E4
HOLBROOK AVE LVL 162-E3,163-A3
HOLCOMB ST S OPH 97-A2
HOLCOMBE ST S SWR 97-A2
HOLDEN LN HUT 112-D1
HOLDEN ST N MPL 106-C2
HOLDRIDGE CIR WAY 104-C3
HOLDRIDGE DR MTK 104-D3
HOLDRIDGE LN WAY 104-D3
HOLDRIDGE RD MTK 104-D3
HOLDRIDGE RD E MTK 104-D3
HOLDRIDGE RD E WAY 104-D3
HOLDRIDGE RD W WAY 104-D3
HOLDRIDGE TER WAY 104-D3
HOLIDAY AVE CF 208-A3
HOLIDAY AVE LVL 177-A3
HOLIDAY CIR MTK 118-D3
HOLIDAY CT APV 163-A2
HOLIDAY CT MTK 118-D3
HOLIDAY LN EAG 136-A3
HOLIDAY LN GV 105-E2
HOLIDAY RD MTK 118-D3
HOLIDAY RD WSP 122-D4
HOLIDAY WAY MTK 118-D4
HOLLAND AVE APV 162-E2,163-A2
HOLLAND AVE LVL 163-A4
HOLLAND AVE SSP 122-D3
HOLLAND CIR EPR 147-B1
HOLLAND CT APV 162-E2
HOLLAND CT LVL 163-A4
HOLLAND LN NE SLK 78-E1
HOLLANDER RD ORO 104-B1
HOLLEY AVE SPP 137-B3
HOLLINS AVE W LVL 177-A3
HOLLINS CT APV 162-E1
HOLLISTER AVE NW CNT 15-B4,29-C1
HOLLISTER AVE SW VIT 85-B3,99-B1
HOLLOW LN LL 66-A4
HOLLOW PARK CT BUR 162-B2
HOLLOW PARK LN BUR 162-B2
HOLLOWAY AVE MPW 109-A1
HOLLOWAY AVE NSP 109-B1
HOLLY AVE STP 107-E4,108-A4
HOLLY AVE N OKD 109-D2
HOLLY CIR WAY 104-C2
HOLLY CIR NW CR 50-C4,64-D3
HOLLY CIR SW SM 46-E4
HOLLY CT NM 204-A1
HOLLY CT E LL 66-B4
HOLLY DR E LL 66-C4
HOLLY DR N LL 66-B4,80-B1
HOLLY LN BUR 148-C4
HOLLY LN CHN 118-A4
HOLLY LN N DAY 62-C3
HOLLY LN N MG 62-C3,76-C3
HOLLY LN N OKD 109-D4
HOLLY LN N PLY 90-C4,104-C1
HOLLY RD EPR 132-E1
HOLLY RD HOP 119-D2
HOLLY ST NW AND 50-D3
HOLLY ST NW CR 50-C4,64-C4
HOLLY ST NW OG 8-C4,22-C1
HOLLY BUSH RD MED 89-D4
HOLLYBROOK RD WAY 104-C2
HOLLYBROOK RD WAY 104-C3
HOLLYBROOK TRL LVL 176-E1,177-A1
HOLLYBUSH RD MED 89-D4
HOLLYHOCK CIR N BP 78-A1
HOLLYHOCK LN HOP 119-C1
HOLLYHOCK LN ROG 47-E4
HOLLYWOOD AVE NE MPL ...92-E3,93-A3
HOLLYWOOD BLVD NW CR .63-E2,64-A3
HOLLYWOOD CT FH 107-D2
HOLLYWOOD RD EDI 119-E2
HOLM OAK LN N OKD 95-D4
HOLMAN AVE IGH 137-A3
HOLMES AVE S MPL 106-C4,120-C1
HOLMES ST MSC 55-B4
HOLMES ST N SHK 146-B2
HOLMES ST S SHK 146-B2
HOLMQUIST RD RW 182-C4
HOLSTAD TRL N FLT 53-D1
HOLSTEIN RD DAT 158-E2
HOLT AVE LVL 176-E3
HOLT AVE NT 193-E2
HOLT AVE WHT 203-A3
HOLT AVE NW ER 33-E1
HOLT LN MOU 116-E2
HOLT ST N CHM 63-C1
HOLT ST NW ER 19-E4
HOLTON ST FH 107-D1
HOLTON ST RVL 93-D4
HOLTON ST STP 107-D3
HOLTZ LN CHS 145-D2
HOLY NAME DR MED 90-B4
HOLYOKE AVE GVT 205-A3,219-A2
HOLYOKE AVE LVL 176-E3,177-A2
HOLYOKE CT APV 162-E1
HOLYOKE CT GVT 204-E2,205-A2
HOLYOKE LN APV 162-E1
HOLYOKE PATH APV 162-E1,163-A1
HOLYOKE PATH EUT 190-E3
HOLYOKE ST APV 162-E1,163-A1
HOMEDALE RD HOP 119-D2
HOMEFIRE WAY LVL 176-E3
HOMER ST SSP 122-D2
HOMER ST STP 121-D3
HOMESTEAD AVE BPT 186-C2
HOMESTEAD AVE N HUG 67-D3
HOMESTEAD AVE N OKD 109-D2
HOMESTEAD AVE N WYT 25-D1
HOMESTEAD AVE S CG 137-D3
HOMESTEAD CIR EPR 132-B1
HOMESTEAD CIR MO 31-D3
HOMESTEAD CT LVL 176-E3
HOMESTEAD CT SHK 146-B3
HOMESTEAD CT WBY 123-D3
HOMESTEAD CT N OKD 109-D2
HOMESTEAD CT S CG 137-D4
HOMESTEAD DR MO 31-D3
HOMESTEAD DR WBY 123-E4
HOMESTEAD DR N HUG 67-D4
HOMESTEAD GRN SWR 96-C2
HOMESTEAD LN CHN 132-A4
HOMESTEAD LN MTK 119-A1
HOMESTEAD PT EAG 149-C3
HOMESTEAD RD SFT 158-D4,172-D1
HOMESTEAD ST CG 137-D3
HOMESTEAD ST SHK 146-B3
HOMESTEAD TRL COR 75-C4
HOMESTEAD TRL LVL 162-E4,163-A4
HOMESTEAD TRL MED 89-C4,103-C1
HOMESTEAD TRL ORO 103-C1

HOMESTEAD TRL SJT 84-A4,98-A1
HOMESTEAD AVENUE CT S CG .137-D2
HOMEWARD WAY SWR 96-C1
HOMEWARD HILLS
RD EPR 133-A4,147-B1
HOMEWOOD AVE MHT 95-D2
HOMEWOOD AVE WBL 81-B4,95-B1
HOMEWOOD PL WBL 95-B1
HOMINY CT LVL 162-E3
HOMINY PATH LVL 162-E3
HONEY TREE DR DEL 87-D3
HONEYCOMB CT LVL 176-E4
HONEYCOMB PATH LVL 176-E4
HONEYCOMB WAY LVL 176-E4
HONEYE AVE N GRA 81-D1
HONEYSUCKLE AVE LVL 163-A4
HONEYSUCKLE AVE N BP 64-A4
HONEYSUCKLE CT LVL 163-A4
HONEYSUCKLE CT VH 80-C4,94-C1
HONEYSUCKLE LN DPH 118-B1
HONEYSUCKLE LN EPR . .118-C4,132-C1
HONEYSUCKLE LN FAR . .177-E4,191-E1
HONEYSUCKLE LN HAS 166-C2
HONEYSUCKLE LN WAC 129-C2
HONEYSUCKLE RD DPH 118-C1
HONEYWELL DRIVEWAY GV 105-D1
HONEYWOOD LN MTK 119-B1
HOOPER CT JOR 173-B2
HOOPER ST JOR 173-B2
HOOPER LAKE RD DPH 118-B3
HOOVER CT NW ER 20-B3
HOOVER LN APV 163-A2
HOOVER ST NE MPL 107-A1
HOOVER ST NW ER 20-B3
HOPE AVE JOR 173-B3
HOPE AVE WBT 81-B2
HOPE AVE NE WAT 101-B3
HOPE AVE SE WAT 101-B3
HOPE ST PRE 153-B4
HOPE ST STP 108-D3
HOPE ST WBT 81-B2
HOPE ST SE PRL 161-B3
HOPEWELL CT LVL 162-E4
HOPEWELL LN APV 162-E2
HOPEWOOD CT GVT 204-E2
HOPEWOOD DR GVT 204-E2,205-A2
HOPEWOOD LN N NH 91-C3
HOPEWOOD PL GVT 204-E2
HOPI RD CHN 118-A4,132-A1
HOPI ST NW AND 49-D1
HOPI ST NW OG 35-D1
HOPI ST NW SF 7-D4
HOPKINS CIR BLO 148-C1
HOPKINS RD BLO 148-C1
HOPKINS ST STP 108-C3
HOPKINS XRD HOP 119-B1
HOPKINS XRD MTK 105-B3,119-B1
HOPKINS CROSS
RD HOP 105-B4,119-B1
HOPKINS CROSS
RD MTK 105-B4,119-B1
HORIZON BLVD LVL 162-E3
HORIZON CIR BEL 185-E2
HORIZON CIR BUR 148-E2
HORIZON CIR EAG 149-E2
HORIZON CIR NE FRI 92-D1
HORIZON CIR S SHK 147-B4
HORIZON CT BEL 185-E2
HORIZON DR BUR 148-E2
HORIZON DR PRL 147-B4
HORIZON DR NE FRI 92-D1
HORIZON DR S SHK 147-B4,161-C1
HORIZON HTS BUR 148-E3
HORIZON LN BUR 148-E3
HORIZON PL BUR 148-E3
HORIZON RD BUR 148-E2
HORIZON RDG VIC 130-E3
HORIZON ST VH 94-D1
HORIZON TRL PRL 161-B4
HORN DR MTK 104-E3
HORNELL AVE S CG 137-D3
HORNER AVE NIT 165-E2
HORNSBY ST NE COT 52-E1,53-A1
HORNSBY ST NE LWT 24-E3
HORSESHOE CIR EAG 149-D1
HORSESHOE CRV CHN . .118-B4,132-B1
HORSESHOE CT WBT 80-D1
HORSESHOE DR ARL 183-A3
HORSESHOE DR E SVW 94-A2
HORSESHOE DR W SVW 94-A2
HORSESHOE LN CHN 118-B4
HORSESHOE LN SL 136-C1
HORSESHOE LN WBY 123-E3
HORSESHOE RD WBY 123-E2
HORSESHOE TRL COR 75-D4
HORSESHOE TRL EPR . . .133-B4,147-B1
HORSESHOE WAY LVL . .162-E4,163-A4
HORSESHOE
BEND DR COR 75-C4,89-C1
HORSMANN AVE DRS 28-C2
HORTON AVE STP 107-E2
HORTON PT EAG 149-C3
HOSFORD ST HUD 111-D3
HOSFORD HILLS RD EAG 149-D1
HOTEL ST BLA 65-A4
HOULE CIR CV 66-D2
HOUSTON AVE LVL 162-E4
HOWARD AVE MP 89-A4,103-A1
HOWARD AVE WBL 95-A1
HOWARD CT MPW 95-A3
HOWARD CT STP 109-A4
HOWARD LN CHS 145-D1
HOWARD LN EPR 132-E1
HOWARD RD SJT 98-D1
HOWARD ST RF 140-D1
HOWARD ST N MPW 95-A3,109-A1
HOWARD ST N STP 109-A3,123-A2
HOWARD ST NE MPL 92-E4
HOWARD ST NW SF 8-C4
HOWARD LAKE DR COT . . .38-E3,39-A3
HOWARD LAKE RD PRL 160-E4
HOWARD LAKE RD SLT 160-E3
HOWARD LAKE RD NW PRL 160-D3
HOWARDS POINT RD SWD 117-B3
HOWE AVE NW CNT 29-B2
HOWE AVE SW MIT 71-B4,85-B1
HOWE LN BC 77-E4
HOWELL DR N MPL 106-C2
HOWELL ST N FH 107-C1
HOWELL ST N STP 107-C4,121-C1
HOWELL ST S STP 121-C2
HOWKINS RD WBY 137-C1
HOWLAND AVE LVL 176-E3
HOXIE AVE WBT 81-B2
HOYA CT LVL 176-E3
HOYER AVE NW CNT 29-B1
HOYT AVE MPW 109-B2
HOYT AVE E STP 108-E2,109-A2
HOYT AVE NW ABT 43-B4,57-B2
HOYT AVE NW CNT 29-B2,43-B1
HOYT AVE NW CWT 15-B1
HOYT AVE SW MIT 57-B4,71-B1
HOYT AVE SW VIT 85-B2
HOYT AVE W FH 107-D2
HOYT AVE W STP 107-E2,108-B2
HOYT ST HUD 111-D3
HUBBARD AVE STP 107-D3
HUBBARD AVE N ROB 92-A3
HUBBARD TRL LVL 162-E4
HUBER AVE NW CWT 1-B4,15-B2
HUBER DR MH 136-A1
HUD ST SOM 70-B4,84-B1
HUDALLA AVE N OKD 109-D2
HUDSON AVE LVL 162-E3
HUDSON BAY WBY 109-E4,123-E1
HUDSON BLVD LE 109-E4,110-B4
HUDSON BLVD OKD 109-D4
HUDSON BLVD WLT 110-E4,111-A4
HUDSON BLVD N LLD 111-C3
HUDSON BLVD S SWR 97-A2
HUDSON CIR LVL 162-E4
HUDSON CT LVL 162-E3
HUDSON LN NW ER 33-C2
HUDSON PL MPW 109-B4
HUDSON RD LFL 109-C4
HUDSON RD MPW 109-B4
HUDSON RD OKD 109-C4
HUDSON RD STP 108-D4,109-A4
HUDSON RD WBY 109-E4,110-B4
HUDSON RD S AFT 110-D4,111-A4
HUDSON RD S WLT 111-A4
HUDSON ST BL 18-A3
HUDSON ST NW ER 33-C2
HUDSON TRL LL 66-C4
HUGHES AVE LVL 176-E3
HUGHES AVE NE FRI 92-D1
HUGHES CT APV 162-E1
HUGO RD WBT 81-B2
HUGO ST NE FRI 78-C1
HULL AVE LVL 176-E3
HULL RD ANO 49-D3
HULL RD MTK 119-A2
HUMBER ST NE COT 52-B3
HUMBER ST NE LWT 24-B2
HUMBOLDT AVE BUR 148-C4
HUMBOLDT AVE STP 122-C2
HUMBOLDT AVE WSP 122-C2
HUMBOLDT AVE N BC 78-B4,92-C1
HUMBOLDT AVE N BP 78-B3
HUMBOLDT AVE N MPL . .92-C3,106-C2
HUMBOLDT AVE S BLO . .134-C4,148-C1
HUMBOLDT AVE S MPL .106-C3,120-C3
HUMBOLDT AVE S RCH . .120-C4,134-C1
HUMBOLDT CIR BLO 148-C1
HUMBOLDT CIR MPL 120-C3
HUMBOLDT CIR N BP 78-B3
HUMBOLDT PL N BC 78-B4
HUMBOLT DR BL 18-B4
HUMMER LN STP 121-D3
HUMMINGBIRD AVE LVL 162-E4
HUMMINGBIRD CT CW 1-B3
HUMMINGBIRD CT LVL 162-E4
HUMMINGBIRD CT PRL 161-B1
HUMMINGBIRD CT NW CR 64-B3
HUMMINGBIRD DR APV 162-E1
HUMMINGBIRD HL NO 80-C3
HUMMINGBIRD LN APV . .148-E4,162-E1
HUMMINGBIRD LN CW 1-B3
HUMMINGBIRD LN EAG 135-E4
HUMMINGBIRD LN EPR 118-E4
HUMMINGBIRD LN LVL 176-E4
HUMMINGBIRD RD CHN 117-E4
HUMMINGBIRD RD DPH 118-C1
HUMMINGBIRD RD SWD 117-E4
HUMMINGBIRD ST SHK 146-C3
HUMMINGBIRD ST NW AND 50-B3
HUMMINGBIRD ST NW CR .50-B4,64-B2
HUMMINGBIRD ST NW OG 22-B2
HUMMINGBIRD TRL PRL 161-B2
HUMMINGBIRD TRL NE PRL 161-B1
HUNDERTMARK RD CHS 131-C4
HUNDERTMARK
RD E CHS 131-C4,145-C1
HUNDERTMARK RD W CHS 145-B1
HUNT PL STP 107-B3
HUNTER AVE WYT 25-D4
HUNTER CIR WIN 99-B3
HUNTER CT LVL 176-E3
HUNTER CT MH 121-D4
HUNTER DR CHN 131-D1
HUNTER DR MED 90-A3,104-A1
HUNTER DR ORO 104-A1
HUNTER DR SE WAT 101-B4
HUNTER LN COR 76-A4
HUNTER LN EAG 135-E4
HUNTER LN MH 121-E4
HUNTER PASS ORO 104-A1
HUNTER RD COR 76-A4,90-A1
HUNTER RD MED 90-B2
HUNTER RDG HUT 98-D4
HUNTER SQ WAC 129-D4
HUNTER ST EDI 119-D4
HUNTER HILL CT HUD 111-E2
HUNTER HILL RD HUD 111-D2
HUNTERS CIR NOH 97-D4,111-D1
HUNTERS CIR WBY 123-E2
HUNTERS CT AH 93-E2
HUNTERS CT APV 149-A4
HUNTERS CT CHN 118-B4
HUNTERS LN SAV 161-D2
HUNTERS RD LTT 130-E4
HUNTERS RDG COR 62-A4
HUNTERS RDG LL 66-C3
HUNTERS RUN EPR 132-C1
HUNTERS TRL CV 66-D3
HUNTERS TRL WBY 123-E2
HUNTERS WAY APV 148-E4,149-A4
HUNTERS GLEN RD WAY 104-D3
HUNTERS HILL WAY MTK 118-C1
HUNTERS OVERLOOK EAG 150-A1
HUNTERS RIDGE RD MTK 118-E2
HUNTING VALLEY RD STP 107-B2
HUNTINGDON CIR MTK 119-A1
HUNTINGDON DR MTK 119-A1
HUNTINGDON LN MTK 119-A1
HUNTINGTON AVE SAV .148-A4,162-A1
HUNTINGTON AVE S SAV 162-A1
HUNTINGTON AVE S SLP 106-A4,120-A1
HUNTINGTON AVE S WAY 104-C3
HUNTINGTON CIR APV . .162-E1,163-A1
HUNTINGTON CT MPW 123-B2
HUNTINGTON DR APV . . .148-E4,162-E1
HUNTINGTON DR EPR 147-B1
HUNTINGTON PATH LVL 162-E4
HUNTINGTON TER APV 148-E4
HUNTINGTON WAY CRT 176-A3
HUNTINGTON POINT
RD E MTB 117-D1
HUNTINGTON POINT
RD W MTB 117-D1
HUNTLEY CT APV 148-E4
HUNTS FARM RD ORO 103-B1
HUNTSVILLE TRL LVL 176-E3
HUPP ST NE BLA 65-D1
HUPP ST NE EB 9-D3
HUPP ST NE HL 37-D4
HURLEY AVE LVL 176-E3
HURLEY CT LVL 176-E3
HURLEY ST E WSP 122-C2
HURLEY ST W WSP 122-B2
HURON AVE CHN 132-B2
HURON AVE RVL 107-D1
HURON BLVD SE MPL 107-A3
HURON CIR LVL 162-E3
HURON CT APV 162-E1
HURON CT EAG 150-B2
HURON CT LVL 162-E3
HURON PATH LVL 162-E3
HURON PL EPR 132-D2
HURON ST MHT 95-D1
HURON ST PRL 161-C3
HURON ST RVL 93-D3
HURON ST STP 107-D2
HURON ST SE MPL 107-A3
HUSS ST DPH 118-A2
HUTCHINS CT CHS 131-B4,145-B1
HUTCHINS DR MTK 118-C3
HUTCHINSON CT LVL 162-E4
HUTCHINSON DR LVL 162-E3
HUTCHINSON RD WAT 101-A4
HUTCHINSON RD WTT 101-A4
HUTTON HILL CIR HUT 112-D1
HUTTON HILL RD HUT 112-D1
HYACINTH VIC 131-B2
HYACINTH AVE LVL 176-E4
HYACINTH AVE ROG 47-D4
HYACINTH AVE E STP . . .108-D2,109-A2
HYACINTH AVE W STP 108-B2
HYACINTH CIR VIC 131-B2
HYACINTH CT LVL 162-E4,176-E1
HYACINTH PATH APV 162-E3
HYACINTH ST VIC 131-A1
HYACINTH WAY LVL 162-E4,176-E4
HYDE AVE N HUG 67-D3
HYDE AVE N MHT 95-D2
HYDE AVE S CG 137-D3
HYDE CT S CG 137-E4
HYDE LN S CG 137-E3
HYDE PARK AVE LVL 162-E4,176-E1
HYDE PARK CIR EDI 133-D1
HYDE PARK DR EDI 133-D1
HYDE PARK LN EDI 133-D2
HYDRA CT LVL 176-E4
HYDRAM AVE N OKD 109-D2
HYDRAM AVE S CG 137-D3
HYDRAM WAY N OKD 109-D2
HYDRAM AVENUE CT N OKD . . .109-D3
HYDRANGEA LN LVL 176-E1
HYLAND AVE APV 162-E3
HYLAND AVE LVL 162-E3
HYLAND CIR LVL 162-E3
HYLAND CT EAG 135-E4,149-E1
HYLAND CT LVL 162-E3
HYLAND DR APV 162-E3
HYLAND PL BLO 133-E4
HYLAND TER EPR 133-B3
HYLAND COURTS DR BLO 133-E4
HYLAND CREEK CIR BLO 133-E3
HYLAND CREEK RD BLO 133-E3
HYLAND GREENS DR BLO 133-E4
HYLAND POINT CT APV 162-E3
HYNES AVE N OKD 109-D2
HYNES AVE S CG 137-E3
HYNES RD HSN 47-D4
HYNES RD ROG 47-D4
HYSON PATH LVL 176-E3
HYTHE ST RVL 107-C1
HYTHE ST STP 107-C2
HYTRAIL AVE N LE 95-D3
HYTRAIL AVE N PS 95-D2
HYTRAIL AVENUE CT N PS 95-D2

I

I ST WBL .94-E1
I ST WBY 123-D1
IAGO AVE BPT 186-B4
IAGO BLVD BPT 186-B2
IBARRA AVE NE SM 46-B3,60-B2
IBARRA AVE SE RFT 60-B4,74-B1
IBERIA AVE EUT 190-E3,204-E2
IBERIA AVE LVL 162-E4,176-E3
IBERIA CIR LVL 176-E1
IBEX AVE LVL 176-E3
IBIS AVE LVL 176-E4
IBIS CIR NW CR 64-B1
IBIS CT CHN 131-E3
IBIS DR BUF 45-B3
IBIS ST NW AND 50-B3
IBIS ST NW CR 50-B4,64-B3
IBIS ST NW OG 8-B4,22-B2
IBSON AVE NFT 220-A4
IBSON AVE NE MOT 32-B2
IBSON AVE SE RFT 74-B1
ICALEE PATH LVL 176-D3
ICARUS ST NE LWT 24-A2
ICE CIRCLE DR MTK 104-D3
ICELAND AVE LVL 176-E3
ICELAND CT LVL 162-E4
ICELAND PATH EUT 190-E3
ICELAND TRL LVL 162-E4,176-E1
ICENIC WAY LVL 176-E3
ICEROSE LN SWR 96-D2
ICKLER AVE NE MOT 32-B2
ICON TRL LVL 176-E1
ICOSA ST LVL 176-E1
IDA AVE N RVL 94-B4
IDA CIR SLT 161-A4
IDAHO AVE BL 18-A3
IDAHO AVE BLA 65-B4
IDAHO AVE LVL 176-E3
IDAHO AVE MPW 109-B1
IDAHO AVE NMT 189-E4
IDAHO AVE STP 108-B2
IDAHO AVE E STP 108-E1,109-A1
IDAHO AVE N BP 77-D3
IDAHO AVE N CHM 63-D2
IDAHO AVE N CRY 91-D4
IDAHO AVE N GV 105-D2
IDAHO AVE S BLO 147-D2
IDAHO AVE S SAV 161-E2
IDAHO AVE S SLP 105-D4,119-D1
IDAHO AVE W FH 107-D2
IDAHO AVE W LAU 107-B2
IDAHO AVE W STP 107-E2,108-A2
IDAHO CIR N BP 77-D3
IDAHO CIR N CHM 63-D3
IDAHO CIR N CRY 91-D3
IDAHO CT N CHM 63-D3
IDAHO LN N BP 77-D3
IDALIA AVE EUT 190-E3
IDALIA AVE GVT 218-E1
IDALIA AVE LVL 176-E3
IDALIA PATH LVL 176-E1
IDAWOOD PATH LVL 176-E1
IDE AVE NE MOT 32-B2
IDE CT N MPW 94-E4
IDE CT S MPW 94-E4
IDE ST MPW 108-E1
IDEAL AVE N DWD 81-D3
IDEAL AVE N FLT 39-D4
IDEAL AVE N GRA 81-D2
IDEAL AVE N MHT 81-D4,95-D1
IDEAL AVE N OKD 95-D4,109-D1
IDEAL AVE N PS 95-D2
IDEAL AVE S CG 137-D2,151-D2
IDEAL AVE S OKD 109-D4
IDEAL CT WYT 39-D2
IDEAL CT N FLT 39-D4
IDEAL WAY LVL 176-E3
IDELL AVE NIT 152-A4,166-A1
IDELWYLDE RD N MAY 68-E2
IDEN AVE N FLT 39-D4
IDEN AVE S CG 137-E4
IDEN AVENUE CIR N FLT 39-D4
IDEN AVENUE CT N FLT 39-D4
IDEN AVENUE PL N FLT 39-D4
IDES CIR LVL 162-E4
IDESON AVE SE SM 60-C4
IDLEWILD PATH SWD 118-A2
IDLEWOOD CIR LVL 162-E4
IDLEWOOD CT LVL 162-E4
IDLEWOOD RD MOU 116-E2
IDLEWOOD WAY LVL 162-E4
IDLEWOOD WAY SHK 146-C3
IDSEN AVE S CG 137-E2
IDYLWOOD DR EDI 119-D3
IDYLWOOD LN EDI 119-D3
IDYLWOOD RD MTK 118-E2
IFFERT AVE NE MOT 32-C3,46-C2
IFFERT AVE NE SM 46-C4,60-C1
IGLEHART AVE STP 107-C4,108-A4
IGUANA ST NW RAM 34-D2,48-D1
IHDUHAPI TRL IND 89-A2
IHRIG AVE SE SM 74-C1
IKARIA CT LVL 176-E1
IKARIA TRL LVL 176-E1
IKOLA WAY EDI 133-C2
ILEX CIR NW CR 64-C1
ILEX ST NE CR 64-C2
ILEX ST NW AND 36-C4,50-C2
ILEX ST NW CR 50-C4,64-C1
ILEX ST NW OG 22-C4
ILION AVE N MPL 106-B1
ILLIES AVE N HUG 81-D1
ILLIES AVE S CG 137-E3
ILLINOIS AVE LVL 162-E4,176-E3
ILLINOIS CT LVL 162-E4
ILLINOIS ST SCF 14-C2
ILLION AVE N MPL 106-B1
ILLSLEY AVE NW ABT 43-B3
ILLSLEY AVE NW CNT 29-B4,43-B1
ILLSLEY AVE NW CWT 15-B4
ILLSLEY AVE SW HWL 85-B1
ILLSLEY AVE SW MIT 71-B2
ILO WAY SWR 96-D2
ILWACO RD TRT 139-D1
IMATION PL OKD 109-D1
IMATION WAY OKD 109-D1
IMHOFF AVE NW CNT 29-B4,43-B1
IMHOFF AVE SW HWL 71-B4,85-B1
IMHOFF AVE SW MIT 71-A4
IMHOFF AVE SW VIT 85-B3
IMMANUEL AVE N OKD 109-D4
IMMANUEL AVE S CG 137-E3
IMMANUEL AVENUE CT S CG 137-E3
IMPALA PATH LVL 176-E1
IMPATIENS AVE N BP 63-E4,64-A4
IMPATIENS CT LVL 162-E3
IMPATIENS CT N BP 63-E4,77-E1
IMPATIENS LN BP 64-A4,78-A1
IMPATIENS WAY LVL 176-E3
IMPERIAL AVE N FLT 39-D3,53-D2
IMPERIAL AVE N GRA 81-D1
IMPERIAL AVE N LE 109-D2
IMPERIAL AVE N OKD 109-E4
IMPERIAL AVE S CG 137-E3
IMPERIAL CIR LVL 162-E3
IMPERIAL CT LVL 162-E3
IMPERIAL CT N GRA 81-D4,95-D1
IMPERIAL CT N WYT 39-D1
IMPERIAL DR CHN 132-A1
IMPERIAL DR E WSP 122-C3
IMPERIAL DR N BP 77-E3
IMPERIAL DR W WSP 122-C3
IMPERIAL LN NB 93-B2
IMPERIAL RDG WSP 122-C3
IMPERIAL WAY LVL 162-E3
IMPERIAL AVENUE CIR S CG 137-E3
IMPERIAL AVENUE CT S CG 137-E3
INCA AVE LVL 176-E2
INCA CIR NW AND 49-D1
INCA LN NB 93-B1
INCA ST NW AND 49-D2
INCA ST NW SF 7-D4
INDAHL AVE N GRA 81-D4
INDAHL AVE S CG 137-E4
INDEPENDENCE AVE CHS 145-C2
INDEPENDENCE AVE ERT 217-A4
INDEPENDENCE AVE LON 217-A2
INDEPENDENCE AVE LVL 176-E3
INDEPENDENCE AVE SAV 147-C3
INDEPENDENCE
AVE WHT 203-A3,217-A1
INDEPENDENCE AVE N CHM 63-C1
INDEPENDENCE AVE N GV 105-C1
INDEPENDENCE AVE N NH 91-C3
INDEPENDENCE AVE S SAV 147-C4
INDEPENDENCE
AVE S SLP 105-C3,119-C1
INDEPENDENCE CIR CHS 145-C2
INDEPENDENCE CIR N NH 91-C4
INDEPENDENCE CT LVL 176-E3
INDEPENDENCE CT N CHM 63-C2
INDEPENDENCE LN N CHM 63-C1
INDEPENDENCE RD IND 88-E3
INDEPENDENCE ST MP 89-A4
INDEPENDENCE ST NP 201-E2
INDIA AVE LVL 176-E3
INDIA CIR LVL 176-E3
INDIA ST BLA 65-A4
INDIAN AVE HAT 187-C4
INDIAN BAY S CG 138-A3

INDIAN BLVD S AFT ... 110-E4
INDIAN BLVD S CG ... 137-E3,138-A3
INDIAN PL AH ... 93-C2
INDIAN RD EPR ... 146-C1
INDIAN RD W MTK ... 104-E3
INDIAN TRL GRF ... 74-C2
INDIAN TRL N WYT ... 25-D4
INDIAN TRL S AFT ... 124-E1,125-A1
INDIAN WAY NSP ... 95-B3
INDIAN WAY W EDI ... 119-C4
INDIAN BOULEVARD CT S CG ... 137-E3,138-A3
INDIAN CHIEF RD EPR ... 118-E4
INDIAN HILL RD CHN ... 118-B4
INDIAN HILL RD MTA ... 102-A3
INDIAN HILLS CIR EDI ... 119-C4
INDIAN HILLS DR CP ... 79-E1
INDIAN HILLS LN CP ... 79-E1
INDIAN HILLS PASS EDI ... 119-C4
INDIAN HILLS RD EDI ... 119-C4
INDIAN MOUND ST E WAY ... 104-B3
INDIAN OAKS CIR AH ... 79-D4
INDIAN OAKS CT AH ... 79-D4
INDIAN OAKS TRL AH ... 79-D4
INDIAN POND CIR EDI ... 119-C4
INDIAN RIDGE CIR PRL ... 161-C2
INDIAN RIVER TRL NIT ... 152-A3
INDIAN WELLS TRL DWD ... 81-C2
INDIANA AVE BLA ... 65-A4
INDIANA AVE LVL ... 176-E2
INDIANA AVE N BC ... 78-A4,92-A1
INDIANA AVE N BP ... 64-A3
INDIANA AVE N CHM ... 64-A3
INDIANA AVE N GV ... 106-A1
INDIANA AVE N ROB ... 92-A4
INDIANA ST SCF ... 14-C2
INDIANOLA AVE EDI ... 120-A3
INDIGO RD LVL ... 162-E4
INDIGO TRL N GRA ... 81-E3
INDIO CT LVL ... 176-E3
INDRA WAY LVL ... 176-E3
INDUS ST NE COT ... 38-B4
INDUSTRIAL AVE DEL ... 87-E3
INDUSTRIAL BLVD BEC ... 2-E4
INDUSTRIAL BLVD HSN ... 62-B2
INDUSTRIAL BLVD LL ... 66-A1
INDUSTRIAL BLVD MPL ... 93-B4,107-B1
INDUSTRIAL BLVD NYA ... 142-C4
INDUSTRIAL BLVD ROG ... 47-E4,62-A1
INDUSTRIAL BLVD SWR ... 96-E2
INDUSTRIAL BLVD WAC ... 129-D3
INDUSTRIAL BLVD YAT ... 142-C4
INDUSTRIAL BLVD NE FRI ... 92-D1
INDUSTRIAL BLVD NW ER ... 19-D4,33-D1
INDUSTRIAL BLVD W LOL ... 103-D2
INDUSTRIAL BLVD W WAC ... 129-D3
INDUSTRIAL CIR ER ... 33-E2,34-A2
INDUSTRIAL CIR PRL ... 161-C4
INDUSTRIAL CIR S SHK ... 146-E2
INDUSTRIAL CT HAS ... 166-D3
INDUSTRIAL CT ROG ... 47-E4,61-E1
INDUSTRIAL DR EPR ... 118-E4
INDUSTRIAL DR NFD ... 219-C4
INDUSTRIAL DR OSC ... 28-A4
INDUSTRIAL PKWY SCF ... 14-D3
INDUSTRIAL ST HUD ... 111-D3
INDUSTRIAL ST MP ... 103-A1
INDUSTRIAL PARK BLVD PLY ... 104-E1,105-A1
INDUSTRIAL PARK DR BLT ... 18-C4
INDUSTRY AVE ANO ... 49-B3
INDUSTRY AVE BEC ... 2-E4
INDUSTRY AVE NW AND ... 49-D2
INDUSTRY AVE NW ANO ... 49-C2
INDUSTRY AVE NW RAM ... 48-E2,49-A2
INDY BLVD S CG ... 137-E4
INGA AVE HMT ... 194-A3,208-A1
INGA AVE NIT ... 152-A4
INGA AVE VET ... 180-A3
INGBERG CIR N GRA ... 81-D4
INGBERG CT N GRA ... 81-E4,95-E1
INGBERG CT S CG ... 137-E4
INGBERG TRL S CG ... 137-E4
INGER PL BUF ... 58-E3
INGERSOLL AVE N FLT ... 39-D4,53-D1
INGERSOLL AVE N HUG ... 53-D4,67-D1
INGERSOLL AVE S CG ... 137-E4
INGERSON CT AH ... 93-D2
INGERSON RD AH ... 93-D2
INGERSON RD IND ... 102-D2
INGERSON RD MTA ... 102-D3
INGERSON RD SVW ... 93-E2
INGLE AVENUE CT S CG ... 137-E3
INGLESIDE AVE S CG ... 137-E4
INGLESIDE CT LVL ... 176-E2
INGLEWOOD AVE EDI ... 120-A1
INGLEWOOD AVE MPL ... 106-B2
INGLEWOOD AVE SAV ... 148-A4,162-A1
INGLEWOOD AVE S SLP ... 106-A4,120-A1
INGLEWOOD AVE SW LAT ... 201-D3
INGLEWOOD CIR SAV ... 148-A4
INGLEWOOD CT LVL ... 162-E3
INGLEWOOD CT SAV ... 148-A4
INGLEWOOD DR LVL ... 162-E3
INGLEWOOD ST LOL ... 103-D2
INGRAM AVE NW CNT ... 29-A3,43-B1
INGRAM AVE SW MIT ... 71-B4
INGRAM AVE SW VIT ... 85-B4
INGRID CT LVL ... 176-D1
INGUADONA BEACH CIR PRL ... 161-A4
INGUADONA BEACH CIR SW PRL ... 161-A4
INLAND CIR LVL ... 162-E4
INLAND CT LVL ... 162-E4
INLAND CT N PLY ... 90-C2
INLAND LN MG ... 76-C1
INLAND LN N MG ... 76-C2
INLAND LN N PLY ... 104-C2
INLAND RD EAG ... 135-D2
INLET RD LVL ... 176-E2
INMAN AVE N FLT ... 39-D3
INMAN AVE NW CNT ... 43-A1
INMAN AVE S CG ... 137-E3,151-E3
INMAN CT LVL ... 176-E2
INMAN TRL LVL ... 176-E2
INMAN AVENUE CT S CG ... 137-E3
INMANN AVE N FLT ... 39-D3
INNDALE CT LVL ... 176-E2
INNDALE DR LVL ... 176-E2
INNER DR CP ... 65-E3
INNER DR LES ... 212-D4
INNER DR MGY ... 215-D4
INNER RD WDL ... 104-C4
INNOVATION RD CG ... 152-A2
INNSBROOK AVE N WYT ... 11-D4,25-D1
INNSBROOK CIR BUR ... 162-D2
INNSBROOK DR LVL ... 162-E4
INNSBROOK DR MO ... 31-C2
INNSBROOK LN BUF ... 58-E3
INNSBROOK LN BUR ... 162-D2
INNSBRUCK CIR NE CH ... 92-E1
INNSBRUCK CT NB ... 79-A4
INNSBRUCK CT N FRI ... 79-A4
INNSBRUCK DR CHS ... 145-C1
INNSBRUCK DR NB ... 79-A4,93-A1
INNSBRUCK LN CHS ... 145-C1
INNSBRUCK PKWY NE CH ... 92-E1,93-A1
INNSBRUCK TRL NB ... 79-A4,93-A1
INNSDALE AVE N LE ... 95-E4,109-E2
INNSDALE AVE S CG ... 137-E3
INNSDALE AVENUE CT S CG ... 137-E2
INSKIP AVE S CG ... 137-E2
INSKIP CT S CG ... 137-E3
INSKIP TRL S CG ... 137-E3
INTERLACHEN ALC WBY ... 123-E2
INTERLACHEN BAY WBY ... 123-E2
INTERLACHEN BLF EDI ... 119-D3
INTERLACHEN BLVD EDI ... 119-D2
INTERLACHEN BLVD LVL ... 162-E4,163-A4
INTERLACHEN CIR EDI ... 119-D3
INTERLACHEN CIR WBY ... 124-A1
INTERLACHEN CT EDI ... 119-C2
INTERLACHEN CT EPR ... 133-A1
INTERLACHEN CT LVL ... 163-A4
INTERLACHEN CT SWR ... 96-D1
INTERLACHEN CT TKB ... 117-D2
INTERLACHEN DR EAG ... 149-D3
INTERLACHEN DR SWR ... 96-D1
INTERLACHEN DR TKB ... 117-D2
INTERLACHEN DR NE HL ... 37-C2
INTERLACHEN DRAW WBY ... 123-E1,124-A1
INTERLACHEN ECHO WBY ... 124-A1
INTERLACHEN LN BUR ... 162-D2
INTERLACHEN LN TKB ... 117-D2
INTERLACHEN PKWY WBY ... 123-E2,124-A1
INTERLACHEN PL TKB ... 117-D2
INTERLACHEN RD BUR ... 162-D2
INTERLACHEN RD CHC ... 12-C4,26-B1
INTERLACHEN RD HOP ... 119-D2
INTERLACHEN RD SPR ... 117-B1
INTERLACHEN WAY SWR ... 96-D1
INTERLACHEN WAY CT SWR ... 96-D1
INTERLAKEN VIC ... 131-B1
INTERNATIONAL DR BLO ... 135-A2
INTERNATIONAL DR VH ... 94-E2
INTERNATIONAL PKWY NH ... 91-C2
INTERSTATE 35 BUR ... 162-C2
INTERSTATE 35 COT ... 39-A4,52-E2
INTERSTATE 35 FL ... 39-A3
INTERSTATE 35 FLT ... 39-A4
INTERSTATE 35 FOT ... 218-C4
INTERSTATE 35 LET ... 11-B2
INTERSTATE 35 LVL ... 162-C4,176-C3
INTERSTATE 35 NMT ... 190-C2,204-C1
INTERSTATE 35 STA ... 11-B3
INTERSTATE 35 WT ... 204-C3,218-C2
INTERSTATE 35 WYO ... 25-A3
INTERSTATE 35 WYT ... 25-B2,39-A1
INTERSTATE 35E APV ... 148-E4,149-A4
INTERSTATE 35E BUR ... 148-E4,162-D1
INTERSTATE 35E COT ... 52-E3
INTERSTATE 35E EAG ... 135-D3,149-C1
INTERSTATE 35E LC ... 94-B3
INTERSTATE 35E LIL ... 121-E3
INTERSTATE 35E LL ... 52-E4,66-E3
INTERSTATE 35E MH ... 121-E4,135-E1
INTERSTATE 35E MPW ... 94-C4,108-C1
INTERSTATE 35E STP ... 121-E2,122-A1
INTERSTATE 35E VH ... 80-D4,94-D2
INTERSTATE 35E WBL ... 80-D4
INTERSTATE 35E WBT ... 80-D2
INTERSTATE 35E PKWY STP ... 122-A1
INTERSTATE 35W AH ... 79-C2
INTERSTATE 35W BLA ... 65-C4,79-C1
INTERSTATE 35W BLO ... 134-C3,148-C1
INTERSTATE 35W BUR ... 148-C3,162-C1
INTERSTATE 35W COT ... 52-E3
INTERSTATE 35W LL ... 52-D4,66-B1
INTERSTATE 35W MPL ... 106-E2,120-D3
INTERSTATE 35W MV ... 79-C3
INTERSTATE 35W NB ... 79-C4,93-C2
INTERSTATE 35W RCH ... 120-C4,134-C1
INTERSTATE 35W RVL ... 93-C3
INTERSTATE 35W SVW ... 79-C1
INTERSTATE 35W N RVL ... 93-C4
INTERSTATE 94 AFT ... 110-D4
INTERSTATE 94 ALB ... 46-E2,47-A2
INTERSTATE 94 BC ... 78-B4,92-C1
INTERSTATE 94 BP ... 77-D4
INTERSTATE 94 CW ... 1-B3
INTERSTATE 94 CWT ... 1-B3,15-D1
INTERSTATE 94 DAY ... 62-B3
INTERSTATE 94 HSN ... 47-D3,62-B2
INTERSTATE 94 HUD ... 111-D3
INTERSTATE 94 HUT ... 111-E3,112-B3
INTERSTATE 94 LE ... 110-C4
INTERSTATE 94 LLD ... 111-C3
INTERSTATE 94 LYT ... 1-A2
INTERSTATE 94 MG ... 62-C4,77-B3
INTERSTATE 94 MO ... 17-B4,31-D2
INTERSTATE 94 MOT ... 16-E3,17-A4
INTERSTATE 94 MPL ... 92-C3,106-C2
INTERSTATE 94 MPW ... 109-B4
INTERSTATE 94 OKD ... 109-D4
INTERSTATE 94 OTS ... 32-C4,46-D1
INTERSTATE 94 ROG ... 47-E4,62-A1
INTERSTATE 94 SM ... 47-C3
INTERSTATE 94 STP ... 107-C4,108-C4
INTERSTATE 94 SVT ... 15-E2,16-B2
INTERSTATE 94 WBY ... 109-E4,110-B4
INTERSTATE 94 WLT ... 110-E4,111-A4
INTERSTATE 94 WRT ... 112-E3
INTERSTATE 394 GV ... 105-C3,106-A3
INTERSTATE 394 MPL ... 106-B3
INTERSTATE 394 MTK ... 104-E3,105-A3
INTERSTATE 394 SLP ... 105-E3
INTERSTATE 394 WAY ... 104-C3
INTERSTATE 494 BLO ... 133-D2,134-A2
INTERSTATE 494 EAG ... 135-D2,136-B2
INTERSTATE 494 EPR ... 119-A4,133-B2
INTERSTATE 494 FS ... 134-E2,135-B2
INTERSTATE 494 IGH ... 136-D1
INTERSTATE 494 MG ... 76-E4,90-E1
INTERSTATE 494 MH ... 135-E2,136-A2
INTERSTATE 494 MPW ... 123-B3
INTERSTATE 494 MTK ... 104-E3,118-E2
INTERSTATE 494 NEW ... 123-B4
INTERSTATE 494 PLY ... 90-E3,104-E1
INTERSTATE 494 RCH ... 134-D2
INTERSTATE 494 SL ... 136-C1
INTERSTATE 494 SSP ... 123-A4,136-E1
INTERSTATE 494 WBY ... 109-D4,123-C2
INTERSTATE 694 AH ... 93-D1
INTERSTATE 694 BC ... 78-C4
INTERSTATE 694 FRI ... 78-D4,92-E1
INTERSTATE 694 LC ... 94-B2
INTERSTATE 694 MPW ... 95-B3
INTERSTATE 694 NB ... 93-B1
INTERSTATE 694 OKD ... 95-D4,109-D2
INTERSTATE 694 PS ... 95-D3
INTERSTATE 694 SVW ... 93-E1,94-A1
INTERSTATE 694 VH ... 94-D2
INTERSTATE 694 WBL ... 94-E2,95-A2
INVER GROVE TRL IGH ... 137-A4,150-E1
INVERNESS CIR NW RAM ... 34-C4
INVERNESS CRV EPR ... 132-C2
INVERNESS CT IGH ... 136-D3
INVERNESS LN MOU ... 117-A2
INVERNESS LN N BP ... 78-A2
INVERNESS LN NW RAM ... 34-C4
INVERNESS PL MHT ... 95-C2
INVERNESS RD MTK ... 118-E1,119-A1
INVERNESS RD WBY ... 123-E2
INVERNESS TER BP ... 78-A2
INVERNESS TRL IGH ... 136-D2
INVERNESS WAY BLT ... 18-C4
INVERNESS WAY LVL ... 162-E3
INWOOD AVE N FLT ... 39-E4
INWOOD AVE N GRA ... 81-E2
INWOOD AVE N HUG ... 53-E3
INWOOD AVE N LE ... 109-E2
INWOOD AVE N OKD ... 109-E4
INWOOD AVE N WYT ... 39-D2
INWOOD AVE S CG ... 137-E2
INWOOD CT N FLT ... 39-D2
INWOOD CT N GRA ... 95-E2
INWOOD CT N WYT ... 25-D3
INWOOD CT S CG ... 137-E3
INWOOD RD DAT ... 158-C1
INWOOD RD MTK ... 118-C2
IODINE CT NW RAM ... 49-B2
IODINE ST NW RAM ... 35-B3,49-B2
IONA CIR RVL ... 94-A3
IONA LN LC ... 94-B3
IONA LN RVL ... 94-A3
IONE AVE NE SLK ... 78-E1
IONE ST LAU ... 107-B1
IONIA CT LVL ... 162-E4,176-E1
IONIA PATH LVL ... 162-E4
IOWA AVE BLA ... 65-A4
IOWA AVE E STP ... 108-C2,109-A2
IOWA AVE W FH ... 107-D2
IOWA AVE W STP ... 107-E2,108-A2
IPAVA AVE EUT ... 190-E4,204-E1
IPAVA AVE LVL ... 162-E4,176-E2
IPSWICH WAY LVL ... 162-E4
IRA AVE S CG ... 137-E4
IRAN AVE LVL ... 176-D3
IRAN PTCH GVT ... 218-E1
IREDALE CT LVL ... 162-D3
IREDALE PATH LVL ... 162-D4
IREDELL CT LVL ... 176-D2
IRELAND AVE NW CNT ... 15-A4,29-A2
IRELAND AVE NW CWT ... 15-A3
IRELAND AVE SW MIT ... 71-A1
IRELAND AVE SW VIT ... 99-A2
IRELAND CT LVL ... 176-D2
IRELAND PL LVL ... 176-D2
IRELAND WAY LVL ... 176-D2
IRENE CIR RVL ... 94-A3
IRENE CT LND ... 12-D3
IRENE CT RVL ... 94-A4
IRENE ST LND ... 12-D3
IRENE ST RVL ... 94-A4,108-A1
IRESFELD AVE NW ABT ... 43-A4
IRESFELD AVE NW CNT ... 29-A3
IRESFELD AVE NW CWT ... 1-A4
IRIS AVE MHT ... 95-D1
IRIS AVE ROG ... 47-D4
IRIS AVE N LE ... 109-E1
IRIS AVE N LET ... 11-D1
IRIS AVE N WYT ... 25-D4,39-D1
IRIS CIR BUR ... 162-A1
IRIS CIR VIC ... 117-A4
IRIS CT LVL ... 162-E3
IRIS DR N BP ... 77-D4
IRIS LN SW SM ... 46-E4
IRIS PL STP ... 107-C4
IRIS RD VIC ... 117-A4,131-A1
IRIS ST BWV ... 95-C1
IRIS ST MHT ... 95-D1
IRIS WAY BUF ... 45-B3
IRISH AVE N FLT ... 39-E3
IRISH AVE N GRA ... 81-E1,82-A1
IRISH AVE N HUG ... 67-E2
IRISH AVE N LE ... 109-E1
IRISH AVE N WYT ... 39-E2
IRISH AVE S CG ... 137-E3
IRISH CT N LE ... 95-E4
IRISH AVENUE CT S CG ... 137-E3
IRONDALE RD MV ... 79-B3
IRONRIDGE PATH LVL ... 176-E3
IRONS CT LVL ... 176-E1
IRONSTONE ST NW RAM ... 35-A4,48-E3
IRONTON ST NE FRI ... 78-C1
IRONTON ST NW ER ... 19-C4,33-C2
IRONWOOD AVE CHN ... 117-C4
IRONWOOD AVE NP ... 201-E2
IRONWOOD AVE N GRA ... 81-E2
IRONWOOD AVE S CG ... 137-E4
IRONWOOD BLVD CHS ... 131-D4
IRONWOOD CIR BKR ... 2-E2
IRONWOOD CIR LL ... 66-B4
IRONWOOD CIR LVL ... 162-E4
IRONWOOD CIR ROG ... 62-A1
IRONWOOD CT EPR ... 132-E1
IRONWOOD CT WYT ... 39-E1
IRONWOOD CT N CHM ... 63-B3
IRONWOOD DR CHC ... 26-B2
IRONWOOD DR DEL ... 87-E2
IRONWOOD LN EAG ... 135-D4
IRONWOOD LN MOU ... 116-E1
IRONWOOD LN NO ... 80-A2
IRONWOOD RD NMT ... 190-A1
IRONWOOD ST SA ... 93-A4
IRONWOOD TRL WYT ... 25-D3
IRONWOOD TRL N LE ... 109-E1
IROQUOIS AVE CHN ... 132-B2
IROQUOIS AVE STP ... 109-A3
IROQUOIS CIR EDI ... 133-C1
IROQUOIS DR MED ... 89-E4
IROQUOIS ST SMP ... 125-C2
IROQUOIS TRL EDI ... 119-C4,133-C1
IRVIN AVE S CG ... 137-E3,151-E1
IRVIN CIR N LE ... 95-E4
IRVIN CT N LE ... 95-E4
IRVIN AVENUE CT S CG ... 137-E3
IRVINE AVE BLT ... 18-B3
IRVINE AVE STP ... 108-B4,122-A1
IRVINE AVE N FLT ... 53-E3
IRVINE AVE NW CNT ... 29-A4
IRVINE AVE NW CWT ... 1-A4,15-A2
IRVINE CIR EPR ... 132-B1
IRVINE DR MO ... 60-E2
IRVINE PARK STP ... 122-B1
IRVING AVE BUR ... 148-C4,162-C1
IRVING AVE NMT ... 190-C4,204-C1
IRVING AVE N BC ... 78-B4,92-B1
IRVING AVE N BP ... 78-B2
IRVING AVE N MPL ... 92-C4,106-C1
IRVING AVE NW ER ... 33-E1
IRVING AVE S BLO ... 134-C2
IRVING AVE S BUR ... 148-C4
IRVING AVE S MPL ... 106-B4,120-C3
IRVING AVE S RCH ... 120-C4,134-C1
IRVING CIR NW ER ... 19-E4
IRVING CRV BLO ... 134-C2
IRVING CT BUR ... 162-C1
IRVING CT N BP ... 78-B3
IRVING DR VIC ... 130-E1
IRVING LN BUR ... 162-C1
IRVING LN N BC ... 78-B4
IRVING ST NW ER ... 19-E4
IRVING TRL BUR ... 162-C1
IRWIN AVE N LE ... 109-E1
IRWIN AVE S BLO ... 148-A2
IRWIN CIR BLO ... 134-A4
IRWIN CT LVL ... 162-E3
IRWIN RD BLO ... 134-A3,148-A1
IRWINDALE CT LVL ... 162-D4
IRWINDALE WAY LVL ... 162-D4
IRWINTON CIR LVL ... 162-D3
ISAAK AVE NW CNT ... 29-A4,43-A1
ISAAK AVE NW CWT ... 1-A4
ISABEL AVE MPL ... 121-B1
ISABEL ST CHC ... 26-B1
ISABEL ST E STP ... 122-C1
ISABEL ST W STP ... 122-C1
ISADORE AVE NIT ... 152-A4
ISALONA LN SSP ... 122-D3
ISANTI AVE WHT ... 216-E2,217-A2
ISANTI CIR NE HL ... 37-A3
ISANTI CT LVL ... 162-D4
ISANTI CT NE BLA ... 51-A4
ISANTI ST BL ... 17-E3
ISANTI ST NE BLA ... 51-A4,65-A4
ISANTI ST NE EB ... 23-A4
ISANTI ST NE HL ... 37-A4,51-A2
ISENGAARD ST MTK ... 105-A3
ISETTA ST NE BLA ... 65-D3
ISETTA ST NE EB ... 9-D3
ISETTA ST NE HL ... 51-D1
ISLAND AVE LVL ... 162-D4
ISLAND AVE WHT ... 202-E4
ISLAND AVE E MPL ... 106-D2
ISLAND AVE W MPL ... 106-D2
ISLAND CIR PRL ... 160-E3
ISLAND CT WAC ... 129-E4
ISLAND DR CLT ... 189-A3
ISLAND DR GV ... 106-A1
ISLAND DR IND ... 88-E3
ISLAND DR SPR ... 117-A1
ISLAND DR SPT ... 70-E1
ISLAND DR WBT ... 81-A1
ISLAND DR NE HL ... 37-A4,51-A1
ISLAND PASS WAC ... 129-E4
ISLAND RD EPR ... 132-C2
ISLAND RD NO ... 80-B2
ISLAND TER LVL ... 162-D4
ISLAND LAKE AVE SVW ... 93-E1
ISLAND PARK DR NE FRI ... 78-D4
ISLAND SHORE DR SPT ... 70-E1
ISLAND VIEW CIR PRL ... 161-A3
ISLAND VIEW DR MOU ... 117-A2
ISLAND VIEW DR NW ER ... 33-C1
ISLAND VIEW LN NO ... 80-B2
ISLAND VIEW RD LTT ... 130-A2
ISLAND VIEW RD PRL ... 160-E3,161-A3
ISLAND VIEW RD SWD ... 117-B3
ISLANDVIEW CIR LVL ... 176-D3
ISLAY AVE S CG ... 137-E4,151-E1
ISLE AVE GVT ... 204-E3,218-E1
ISLE AVE LVL ... 176-D3
ISLE AVE WHT ... 202-E4
ISLE AVE N LE ... 95-E3
ISLE AVE S CG ... 137-E4,138-A4
ISLE CIR LVL ... 176-D3
ISLE CT WYT ... 25-E3
ISLE CT N LE ... 109-E1
ISLE CT S CG ... 137-E4
ISLE DR WYT ... 25-E3
ISLE ROYALE CT BUR ... 149-A4
ISLEMOUNT PL ROB ... 92-A3
ISLETON AVE LVL ... 162-D4,176-D1
ISLETON AVE N GRA ... 81-E1
ISLETON AVE N HUG ... 67-E3,81-E1
ISLETON AVE S CG ... 137-E3,151-E1
ISLETON CT LVL ... 176-D1
ISLETON CT S CG ... 137-E4
ISLETON WAY LVL ... 162-E3
ISLETON AVENUE CT N GRA ... 81-E1
ISOSCELES AVE LVL ... 162-D4
ITALY AVE LVL ... 176-D1
ITALY CT LVL ... 162-D4,176-D1
ITALY PATH LVL ... 162-D4,176-D1
ITASCA AVE PRL ... 161-B3
ITASCA AVE STP ... 121-C3
ITASCA AVE N FLT ... 39-E2
ITASCA AVE N WYT ... 25-E4,39-E1
ITASCA AVE S SMP ... 125-C2
ITASCA LN LVL ... 176-D3
ITASCA AVE CIR N FLT ... 39-E2
ITASKA AVE WHT ... 202-E4
ITEN AVE NW CNT ... 29-A4
ITEN AVE SW MIT ... 71-A4
ITEN CIR NW CWT ... 1-A4
ITEN CT N LVL ... 176-D1
ITEN CT S LVL ... 176-D1
ITERI AVE LVL ... 176-D2
ITERI CT E LVL ... 176-D2
ITERI CT W LVL ... 176-D2
ITERI PL LVL ... 176-D3
ITHACA CIR LVL ... 176-D3
ITHACA CT LVL ... 162-D4
ITHACA LN LVL ... 162-D4
ITHACA LN N MG ... 76-E3
ITHACA LN N PLY ... 90-E2,104-E1
ITHILIEN CHN ... 117-E4
IVAN AVE N FLT ... 39-E3
IVAN AVE N HUG ... 67-E4,81-E1
IVAN AVE S CG ... 137-E4
IVAN CT N FLT ... 39-E3
IVAN WAY STP ... 121-E3
IVANHOE AVE ER ... 34-B2
IVANHOE AVE NFD ... 219-D3
IVANHOE AVE NIT ... 152-A3
IVANHOE DR WAT ... 101-B4
IVANHOE PL NE CH ... 93-A2
IVANHOE WAY NIT ... 152-A3
IVERSON AVE N FLT ... 39-E4

IVERSON AVE S CG 137-E3
IVERSON CIR HUD 111-D2
IVERSON CT LL 66-E3,67-A3
IVERSON CT S CG 137-E3
IVERSON LN N FLT 39-E3
IVERSON ST W COT 38-E3
IVES CT N MG 77-A2
IVES LN PLY 91-A3
IVES LN N MG 63-A4,77-A4
IVES LN N PLY 91-A1,105-A1
IVES WAY N MG 63-A4
IVORY AVE N LE 109-E2
IVORY AVE NE SM 46-E3
IVORY CT LE 109-E3
IVY AVE MPW 109-B2
IVY AVE E STP 108-E2,109-A2
IVY AVE N LE 109-E1
IVY AVE W STP 107-E2,108-B2
IVY CT CV 66-D3
IVY CT EAG 136-A4
IVY CT N LE 95-E4
IVY LN BLO 134-B4
IVY LN EAG 136-A4
IVY LN LFL 109-C4
IVY LN MH 122-A3
IVY LN MPL 106-B4
IVY LN MTK 118-C3
IVY LN SWD 118-A2
IVY LN WBL 95-A2
IVY LN NE HL 36-E3
IVY PL ORO 117-C2
IVY RD EB 37-D1
IVY ST MHT 81-D4
IVY ST NSP 95-B4,109-B1
IVY TER BUR 148-A4
IVY FALLS AVE MH 122-A3
IVY FALLS CT MH 122-A3
IVY HILL DR MH 122-B3
IVY RIDGE CT LL 66-A2
IVY RIDGE LN LL 66-A2
IVYSTONE AVE S CG 137-E3,138-A3
IVYSTONE CT S CG 137-E3
IVYSTONE AVENUE CT S CG 137-E3
IVYWOOD AVE N FLT 39-E4,53-E3
IVYWOOD AVE S CG 137-E4,138-A3
IVYWOOD CIR NW SF 7-E4
IVYWOOD CT EPR 133-C4
IVYWOOD CT LVL 162-E4
IVYWOOD ST NW AND 35-E3,49-E1
IVYWOOD ST NW CR 49-E4,63-E1
IVYWOOD ST NW OG 35-E2
IVYWOOD ST NW SF 7-E4
IVYWOOD TRL N CGT 12-B2
IVYWOOD TRL N LET 11-E3,12-A2
IVYWOOD TRL N WYT 11-E4,25-E1
IXONIA AVE LVL 162-D4,176-D1
IXONIA CT LVL 162-D4
IXONIA PATH LVL 162-D4
IZAAK WALTON RD W BLO 133-D3

J

J ST WBL 94-E2
J ST WBY 123-D1
JABER AVE NE MOT 46-C1
JABER AVE NE OTS 32-C3
JABER AVE NE SM 60-C2
JABER AVE SE RFT 60-C4
JACAMAR WAY LVL 162-D3
JACANA CT LVL 162-D4
JACARANDA WAY LVL 162-D4
JACK PINE TRL EPR 147-A1
JACK PINE TRL N LE 95-E4
JACKAL ST NW RAM 34-D3,48-D1
JACKDAW PATH LVL 162-D4
JACKIE LN COR 62-A3
JACKPINE CT LVL 162-D4
JACKPINE TRL LVL 162-D4
JACKPINE WAY LVL 162-D4
JACKRABBIT PATH LVL 162-D4
JACKSON AVE LEX 65-D4
JACKSON AVE WHT 202-E3,216-E2
JACKSON AVE N HOP 119-C2
JACKSON AVE NE SM 60-C2
JACKSON AVE NW ER 33-E1
JACKSON AVE NW WAT 101-A3
JACKSON AVE S EDI 119-C2
JACKSON AVE S HOP 119-C2
JACKSON AVE SW WAT 101-A3
JACKSON CIR ER 19-E3
JACKSON CIR SLT 175-B1
JACKSON CIR NE BLA 50-E4,64-E4
JACKSON CT HAS 166-C1
JACKSON CT SHK 146-A3
JACKSON DR EPR 133-B4
JACKSON DR HAS 166-C1
JACKSON DR MV 79-B2
JACKSON PL HAS 166-C1
JACKSON PL NW ER 33-E2
JACKSON RD ER 19-E4,33-E1
JACKSON ST ANO 49-D4
JACKSON ST STP 108-B3
JACKSON ST N LC 94-B3
JACKSON ST N MPW 108-B1
JACKSON ST N SCF 14-D2
JACKSON ST NE BLA 50-E4,64-E3
JACKSON ST NE CH 92-E2
JACKSON ST NE EB 22-E4,36-E1
JACKSON ST NE FRI 78-E2
JACKSON ST NE HL 36-E4,50-E1
JACKSON ST NE MPL 92-E4,106-E1
JACKSON ST NE SLK 78-E2
JACKSON ST S SHK 146-A3
JACKSON TRL LVL 162-D4
JACKSON TRL NE PRL 147-B4
JACKSON WAY HIL 92-E2
JACKSONVILLE CT LVL 162-D4
JACKSTONE PT EAG 149-C3
JACOB AVE MT 166-B3
JACOB AVE NIT 152-B4,166-B2
JACOB AVE N COL 143-E4
JACOB AVE S COL 143-E4
JACOB CT EAG 150-A1
JACOB LN ANO 49-C4
JACOB LN MTK 118-D3
JACOB ST HBG 156-A2
JACOB ST YAT 156-A2
JACOBS AVE NFT 220-B4
JACOBS LN HUT 111-E2,112-A2
JACOBS LADDER CIR HUT 112-A2
JACOBS MILL RD ORO 103-B2
JACOBSON TRL ERT 216-E4
JACOBSON TRL WHT 216-E4
JACQUARA AVE LVL 162-D3
JACQUARD AVE EUT 204-D1
JACQUARD AVE LVL 176-D3
JACQUARD PATH LVL 176-D1
JACQUELINE ST RF 140-E1
JACQUES CT EPR 118-B4
JACYLYN DR ROG 47-D4
JADE CIR LVL 176-D3
JADE CIR SHK 146-D3
JADE CT LVL 162-D4
JADE LN EAG 149-B1
JADE LN LVL 176-D2
JADE PT EAG 149-B1
JADE TER LVL 162-D4
JAEGER CT LVL 176-D1
JAEGER PATH LVL 176-D1
JAGUAR AVE LVL 162-D3,176-D3
JAGUAR CIR LVL 176-D1
JAGUAR CT LVL 176-D1
JAGUAR CT WBT 80-E2
JAGUAR PATH LVL 162-D4,176-D1
JAGUAR PL LVL 162-D4
JAGUAR TER LVL 176-D3
JAKE HL HUT 97-D4
JALGER AVE NE OTS 32-C4
JALGER AVE NE SM 60-C2
JALGER AVE SE RFT 60-C4
JALISCO CT LVL 176-D1
JALISCO LN LVL 162-D4
JALISCO TER E LVL 162-D4
JALISCO TER W LVL 162-D4
JALISCO WAY LVL 176-D1
JAMACA AVE N FLT 39-E2
JAMACA AVE N GRA 81-E3,95-E1
JAMACA AVE N LE 95-E3,109-E1
JAMACA BLVD N LE 95-E3,96-A3
JAMACA CT N GRA 81-E3
JAMACA CT N LE 109-E1,110-A1
JAMACA LN N GRA 95-E1
JAMAICA AVE EUT 204-D2
JAMAICA AVE GVT 204-D4,218-D1
JAMAICA AVE LVL 162-D3
JAMAICA AVE S CG 137-E4,151-E1
JAMAICA CIR LVL 176-D1
JAMAICA CT LVL 176-D1
JAMAICA LN LVL 176-D3
JAMAICA PATH LVL 176-D1
JAMBEAU CT LVL 176-D1
JAMBOR AVE NE OTS 32-C2
JAMBOR AVE NE SM 60-C2
JAMBOR CIR NE SM 60-C2
JAMES AVE AH 79-D4
JAMES AVE BUR 148-C4,162-C1
JAMES AVE DPH 118-B1
JAMES AVE NIT 152-B4
JAMES AVE STP 121-C2,122-A2
JAMES AVE N BC 78-B4,92-B1
JAMES AVE N BP 78-B1
JAMES AVE N MPL 92-B4,106-B1
JAMES AVE N WYT 25-E3
JAMES AVE NE OTS 32-D2
JAMES AVE NE SM 60-D2
JAMES AVE S BLO 134-C3
JAMES AVE S BUR 148-C4
JAMES AVE S MPL 106-B4,120-C3
JAMES AVE S RCH 120-C4,134-C1
JAMES CIR AH 93-D1
JAMES CIR BLO 134-C4,148-C1
JAMES CIR N BC 78-B4
JAMES CT BUR 162-C1
JAMES CT CHS 131-B4
JAMES CT EAG 149-A3
JAMES CT HAS 166-D3
JAMES CT MH 121-E3
JAMES CT MHT 95-C1
JAMES CT N WYT 25-E3
JAMES CT NE OTS 32-D2
JAMES DR MPW 109-B4
JAMES LN LVL 176-C1
JAMES PL BUR 162-C1
JAMES PL EPR 132-E1
JAMES RD BLO 134-C4,148-C1
JAMES RD MH 121-E4
JAMES RD MTK 119-A2
JAMES RD N HSN 48-A3
JAMES ST EAG 149-A3
JAMES ST LL 52-B4
JAMES ST PRE 153-B4
JAMES ST SHK 146-A3
JAMES WAY MHT 95-C1
JAMES AVENUE CT BUR 162-C1
JAMESON ST STP 107-E3
JAMESTOWN AVE LVL 176-D3
JAMESTOWN CRV WBY 124-B4
JAMESTOWN RD ORO 103-C1
JAMESTOWN ST NE ATT 9-C2
JAMESTOWN ST NE BLA 65-C4
JAMESTOWN ST NE EB 23-B4
JAMESTOWN ST NE HL 37-C3,51-C2
JAMESWOOD CT LVL 176-D3
JAMIE CIR SW SM 46-E4
JAMIE ROSE CT EAG 149-A3
JAMISON AVE NE OTS 46-D2
JAMISON AVE NE SM 46-D4,60-D1
JAMISON PATH LVL 162-D3
JAMLEY AVE N LE 109-E1
JAN ECHO TRL EAG 149-B2
JAN VIEW LN LTT 130-A3
JANALYN CIR GV 106-A3
JANDEL AVE NE HAN 60-D3
JANDEL AVE NE OTS 32-D2
JANDEL CIR NE SM 60-D2
JANDEL CT HAN 60-D3
JANDELL AVE NE SM 46-D3
JANE CIR HUT 112-D1
JANE CIR N LE 96-A3
JANE CT N LE 96-A4
JANE LN MTK 119-A3
JANE RD N LE 95-E3,96-A4
JANE ST LES 212-D3
JANELL AVE N BP 77-D3
JANERO AVE N FLT 39-E3
JANERO AVE N HUG 67-E4,81-E1
JANERO AVE N LE 109-E1
JANERO AVE S CG 137-E4,138-A3
JANERO CT N GRA 81-E3
JANERO CT S CG 137-E4,138-A3
JANESVILLE ST NE FRI 78-C1
JANET CT AH 93-C1
JANET LN BC 92-A1
JANETT AVE NE SM 46-D3,60-D2
JANICE DR CHS 145-D1
JANICE ST SVW 94-A2
JANIE AVE S CG 137-E4
JANINE PL EPR 147-A1
JANNEVAR CT LVL 176-D1
JANNINGS AVE NE SM 46-D3
JANSA DR SVW 80-B4
JANSEN AVE SLT 175-A3
JANSEN AVE WBL 95-B2
JANSEN AVE NE OTS 46-D1
JANSEN AVE NE SM 46-D3
JANSEN AVE SE HAN 60-D3
JANSEN AVE SE RFT 60-C4,74-C1
JANSEN WAY VH 94-D2
JAPURA ST NE LWT 10-B3
JAQUARD CT LVL 176-D1
JAREAU AVE S CG 138-A4,152-A1
JARED RD OST 28-B4
JARL CT LVL 176-D1
JARRATT CT APV 162-D3
JARREAU CT LVL 162-D3
JARROD AVE S CG 152-A1
JARROD CT S CG 152-A1
JARVIS AVE N GRA 95-E2
JARVIS AVE NW CNT 15-A4,29-A1
JARVIS AVE NW CWT 15-A4
JARVIS AVE S CG 138-A4,152-A1
JARVIS AVE SW HWL 85-A1
JARVIS CIR EPR 133-B4
JARVIS ST NW ER 20-B1,34-B4
JARVIS ST NW LIT 6-B3
JASMINE AVE LVL 162-D4,176-D2
JASMINE AVE N GRA 96-A2
JASMINE AVE N LE 109-E3,110-A3
JASMINE AVE S CG 138-A3,152-A1
JASMINE CIR LVL 176-D3
JASMINE CT LVL 162-D4,176-D1
JASMINE CT ROG 47-E4
JASMINE CT S CG 138-A4
JASMINE LN EPR 133-A3
JASMINE LN S CG 138-A4
JASMINE PATH LVL 176-D3
JASMINE ST N LE 109-E3
JASMINE TRL N GRA 81-E2,82-A1
JASMINE WAY LVL 176-D2
JASMINE WAY ROG 47-E4
JASMINE AVENUE PL N LE 110-A3
JASON AVE BPT 186-B3
JASON AVE NIT 152-B3
JASON AVE N FLT 39-E3,40-A3
JASON AVE N WYT 25-E4
JASON AVE NE ALB 46-D2
JASON AVE NE MO 31-E3,32-A3
JASON AVE NE MOT 32-B4,46-C1
JASON AVE NE OTS 46-D2
JASON AVE NE SM 46-D3
JASON CT ALB 46-D2
JASON CT NE SM 46-D3
JASON RD CHS 145-D2
JASON AVENUE CT N FLT 39-E3
JASONS ST HSN 47-D3
JASPAR ST NW BT 20-E4,35-A1
JASPAR ST NW RAM 35-A4,49-A1
JASPER AVE SLT 174-E3
JASPER AVE N LE 95-E3
JASPER AVE NW CNT 29-A3
JASPER CIR LVL 162-D4
JASPER CT LVL 162-D4,176-D1
JASPER DR EAG 149-B2
JASPER LN EPR 133-A4,147-A1
JASPER LN LVL 162-D4
JASPER PATH LVL 162-D4,176-D1
JASPER RD SHK 146-D3
JASPER TER LVL 176-D2
JASPER TRL ERT 216-E4
JASPER TRL LVL 162-D4
JASPER TRL WHT 216-D4
JASPER WAY LVL 176-D1
JASPERS CIR N CHS 145-C1
JASPERS CIR S CHS 145-C1
JATOS CIR LVL 162-D3
JAVA CIR LVL 162-D3
JAVA CT LVL 176-D1
JAVA CT N LVL 162-D4
JAVA CT S LVL 162-D4
JAVA DR LVL 162-D3
JAVA LN LVL 162-D3
JAVA PATH LVL 176-D2
JAVA TRL LVL 176-D1
JAVARI CT LVL 162-D3
JAVELIN AVE LVL 162-D4
JAVELIN CIR LVL 176-D3
JAVELIN CT LVL 162-D4,176-D1
JAY CIR VH 80-C4
JAY CIR NW CR 50-B4,64-B1
JAY CT LVL 176-D1
JAY LN WBL 95-B1
JAY PL EDI 120-A3
JAY ST BWV 95-C1
JAY ST LES 212-D3
JAY ST NW AND 50-B3
JAY ST NW CR 50-B4,64-B3
JAY WAY VH 80-C4
JAYBELL CT LVL 162-D4
JAYMIE CT BEL 186-A2
JAYNE ST STP 109-A4
JEALAM RD MTK 118-C3
JEAN WAY NM 190-A4,204-A1
JEANETTE ST SLT 160-E4
JEANNE DR LL 65-E1
JED DR ROG 61-E1
JEDLICKA CT EPR 133-A4
JEFF CIR BKR 17-D4
JEFF CIR BLT 17-D4
JEFF PL EDI 119-D4
JEFF ST SHK 146-B3
JEFFERSON AVE LVL 162-D4
JEFFERSON AVE STP 121-E1,122-A1
JEFFERSON AVE N NG 114-A4
JEFFERSON AVE NW WAT 101-A3
JEFFERSON AVE S EDI 119-C2
JEFFERSON AVE SW WAT 101-A3
JEFFERSON CIR N CHM 63-C3
JEFFERSON CT BLA 64-D3
JEFFERSON CT HAS 166-C1
JEFFERSON CT LVL 162-D4
JEFFERSON CT RF 140-D3
JEFFERSON CT WBT 81-B2
JEFFERSON DR NFD 219-D4
JEFFERSON HWY BP 63-C4
JEFFERSON HWY CHM 63-C2
JEFFERSON HWY MG 63-C4,77-C2
JEFFERSON HWY OSS 77-C2
JEFFERSON LN EAG 149-E2,150-A2
JEFFERSON LN NW ER 33-E1
JEFFERSON PKWY NFD 219-D4
JEFFERSON RD NFD 219-D4
JEFFERSON ST ANO 49-D4
JEFFERSON ST DPH 118-A2
JEFFERSON ST HAS 166-C1
JEFFERSON ST PRE 167-B1
JEFFERSON ST RF 140-D3
JEFFERSON ST SCF 14-C2
JEFFERSON ST N SCF 14-C2
JEFFERSON ST NE BLA 50-D4,64-D2
JEFFERSON ST NE CH 92-E2
JEFFERSON ST NE EB 22-D4
JEFFERSON ST NE FRI 78-E4
JEFFERSON ST NE HL 36-D2,50-D3
JEFFERSON ST NE MPL 92-E4,106-E1
JEFFERSON ST NE SLK 78-D2
JEFFERSON ST S SCF 14-C3
JEFFERSON ST S SHK 146-A3
JEFFERSON TRL W EAG 136-B4
JEFFERSON TRL W IGH 136-B4,150-B1
JEFFERY AVE S CG 138-A4,152-A1
JEFFERY BAY S CG 152-A1
JEFFERY CT S CG 138-A4,152-A1
JEFFERY DR MV 79-B3
JEFFERY LN S CG 138-A3
JEFFREY AVE N FLT 39-E3,53-E1
JEFFREY AVE N GRA 82-A4
JEFFREY AVE N HUG 67-E1,68-A2
JEFFREY AVE N WYT 25-E3,39-E1
JEFFREY AVE SW VIT 99-A1
JEFFREY BLVD N GRA 82-A4,95-E1
JEFFREY LN COR 61-C4
JEFFREY LN EDI 119-D3
JEFFREY LN LAT 202-A4
JEFFREY RD LVL 162-C4
JEFFRY WAY MTK 104-E3
JENKINS CIR NE HL 37-A3
JENKINS CT BLA 79-A1
JENKINS DR BEC 2-E3
JENKINS ST NE BLA 51-A3,65-A1
JENKINS ST NE EB 23-A2,37-A2
JENKINS ST NE HL 37-A4,51-A3
JENKINS WAY LVL 176-D3
JENKS AVE STP 108-D3
JENNA CT RF 140-D2
JENNER ALC S CG 138-A3
JENNER AVE S CG 138-A3
JENNER BAY S CG 138-A3
JENNER CIR S CG 138-A3
JENNER LN CG 138-A4
JENNER LN S CG 138-A4
JENNI LN WBT 81-B2
JENNIE RD CHS 145-D1
JENNIFER CT EAG 149-E2
JENNIFER CT EPR 132-E1
JENNIFER CT NSP 95-A4
JENNIFER CT N WYT 25-E3,26-A3
JENNIFER LN JOR 173-B2
JENNIFER LN MTK 118-C3
JENNIFER LN NSP 95-A4
JENNIFER RD LN E CRT 161-D4
JENNINGS AVE WHT 216-D1
JENNINGS RD MOU 103-A4
JENNINGS ST NE COT 38-E1
JENNINGS COVE RD MTA 103-A3
JENNY LN WBY 123-C3
JENSEN AVE N FLT 40-A2
JENSEN AVE S CG 138-A3
JENSEN AVE SE HAN 60-D4
JENSEN LN HUT 111-E1,112-A1
JEREMY CT EPR 132-E1
JERGEN AVE S CG 138-A4,152-A1
JERGEN BAY S CG 138-A4,152-A1
JERGEN CT S CG 152-A1
JERGEN PL S CG 152-A1
JERICHO RD DPH 118-C1
JEROME AVE N LE 96-A3
JEROME ST ANO 49-B3
JEROME AVENUE CT N LE 96-A3
JERROLD AVE AH 93-C2
JERROLD AVE SVW 94-B2
JERRY CT WBL 95-A2
JERRY PATH NIT 152-B4
JERRY ST WBL 95-A2
JERRY LIEFERT DR MO 31-C1
JERSEY AVE LTT 144-C1
JERSEY AVE LVL 162-D3,176-D2
JERSEY AVE N BP 77-D4
JERSEY AVE N CHM 63-D3
JERSEY AVE N CRY 91-D3
JERSEY AVE N GV 105-D2
JERSEY AVE S GV 105-D2
JERSEY AVE S SAV 161-D2
JERSEY AVE S SLP 105-D4,119-D1
JERSEY CIR N CHM 63-D2
JERSEY CIR N CRY 91-D3
JERSEY CT EUT 190-D2
JERSEY CT LVL 162-D4
JERSEY CT N CHM 63-D3
JERSEY RD TRT 126-D3
JERSEY WAY LVL 162-D4
JESSA PL ROG 61-E1
JESSAMINE AVE MPW 109-B2
JESSAMINE AVE E STP 108-D2,109-A2
JESSAMINE AVE W STP 107-E3,108-B2
JESSAMINE CT STP 108-A2
JESSAMINE LN STP 108-E2
JESSE LN CRT 176-A1
JESSE ST BKR 2-E3
JESSE ST MPW 108-C1
JESSE JAMES LN MHT 95-C1
JESSICA CT EAG 149-E2
JESSICA CT N LC 94-B3
JESSICA DR ROG 47-E4
JESSIE AVE SLP 105-C4
JESSIE CT WBY 123-D3
JESSIE ST STP 108-C2
JESSIE ST N MPW 108-C1
JEWEL AVE LVL 162-D3
JEWEL AVE N FLT 54-A1
JEWEL AVE N GRA 82-A4
JEWEL AVE N LE 110-A3
JEWEL AVE S CG 138-A4
JEWEL CT LET 11-E1
JEWEL CT MG 76-C1
JEWEL CT PLY 90-C3
JEWEL DR WBY 124-A2
JEWEL LN LET 11-E2,12-A2
JEWEL LN MG 76-C1
JEWEL LN SSP 122-D3
JEWEL LN N FLT 53-E1,54-A1
JEWEL LN N MG 76-C1
JEWEL LN N PLY 90-C4,104-C1
JEWEL LN S CG 138-A4
JEWEL PATH LVL 176-D2
JEWEL LANE CT N FLT 54-A1
JEWELL ST PRE 153-B4
JEWELL ST NE BLA 65-D3
JEWELL ST NE EB 9-D4,23-D3
JFL DR EAG 149-B2
JIDANA LN MTK 118-D1
JIMMER AVE BUR 148-C3
JIVARO ST SF 7-D4
JIVARO ST NW AND 35-D3
JIVARO ST NW OG 21-D1,35-D1
JIVARO ST NW SF 7-D4
JJ ST WBL 80-D4
JOAN AVE DT 194-B2
JOAN AVE MT 166-B4,180-B3
JOANN CT NFD 219-D3
JOANNE LN MTK 119-A2
JOCELYN ALC S CG 138-A3
JOCELYN AVE N WYT 26-A2
JOCELYN AVE S CG 138-A3

JOCELYN BAY S CG .138-A3
JOCELYN CIR N GRA .96-A2
JOCELYN CT N WYT .26-A2
JOCELYN CT S CG .138-A3
JOCELYN LN N GRA .96-A2
JOCELYN PL S CG .138-A3
JOCELYN RD N GRA .96-A1
JODI CIR HUD .111-E2
JODIS DR HSN .47-D3
JODRELL DR NE LWT .24-A3
JODRELL ST NE COT .52-A3
JODY AVE N FLT .54-A1
JODY AVE N GRA .82-A3,96-A1
JODY AVE N HUG .68-A4,82-A1
JODY AVE S CG .138-A3
JODY CIR S CG .138-A4
JODY CT OSC .28-A4
JODY CT N GRA .82-A3
JODY CT N WYT .26-A3
JODY CT S CG .138-A4
JODY LN S CG .138-A4
JODY AVENUE CT N GRA .82-A2
JOHANNA DR CRT .161-C4
JOHANSEN AVE S CG .138-A4
JOHN AVE N COL .143-E4
JOHN AVE N WYT .26-A4
JOHN AVE S COL .143-E4
JOHN ST EDI .119-D2
JOHN ST MH .122-B2
JOHN ST STP .108-C4
JOHN TRL N CGT .26-A3
JOHN TRL N WYT .26-A3
JOHN DEERE DR CRT .161-D4
JOHN DEERE LN ROG .61-E1
JOHN HARRIS DR EDI .133-D1
JOHN IRELAND BLVD STP .108-B4
JOHN MARTIN DR BC .92-B1
JOHN MILLESS DR ROG .61-E1,62-A1
JOHNATHAN LN EPR .132-C4
JOHNNY CAKE RD APV .163-C2
JOHNNY CAKE
RIDGE RD APV .149-C4,163-C1
JOHNNY CAKE
RIDGE RD EAG .149-C2
JOHNNY CAKE
RIDGE WAY EAG .149-C1
JOHNS RD SVW .79-E3
JOHNSON AVE WBL .81-B3
JOHNSON AVE S BLO .134-A2,148-A1
JOHNSON CIR BLO .134-A4,148-A1
JOHNSON CT SWR .82-E4
JOHNSON DR DEL .87-E3
JOHNSON DR EDI .119-D3
JOHNSON DR SJT .97-E2
JOHNSON DR SWR .82-E4
JOHNSON LN N WYT .26-A2
JOHNSON PKWY STP .108-E3
JOHNSON RD BLO .148-A1
JOHNSON RD OGT .167-C1
JOHNSON RD PRE .167-C1
JOHNSON ST ANO .49-D3
JOHNSON ST CHC .26-B1
JOHNSON ST DAY .48-B2
JOHNSON ST E RF .140-E3
JOHNSON ST NE BLA .50-E4,64-E2
JOHNSON ST NE CH .92-E2,93-A2
JOHNSON ST NE EB .8-E3
JOHNSON ST NE HL .36-E4,50-E3
JOHNSON ST NE MPL .92-E3,106-E1
JOHNSON ST NW ER .20-B3
JOHNSON ST W RF .140-D2
JOHNSON WAY BKT .185-B4
JOHNSON
MEMORIAL DR BEL .185-E2,186-A1
JOHNSON
MEMORIAL DR BKT .185-C3,199-A2
JOHNSON
MEMORIAL DR BPT .185-E2,186-B1
JOHNSON MEMORIAL DR JOR .173-B2
JOHNSON MEMORIAL DR JT .145-E3
JOHNSON MEMORIAL DR LVT .145-D4,159-D2
JOHNSON
MEMORIAL DR SCT .159-D4,173-C1
JOHNSON
MEMORIAL DR SLW .172-C4,173-A2
JOINER WAY EPR .133-A2
JOLANTA LN NIT .152-B4
JOLIET AVE GRA .82-A3
JOLIET AVE N FLT .40-A3
JOLIET AVE N GRA .82-A3
JOLIET AVE S CG .138-A3
JOLIET CIR S CG .138-A3
JOLLY LN BP .77-D3
JON AVE LL .65-E2
JONATHAN AVE S CG .138-A3
JONATHAN BLVD N CHS .131-D3
JONATHAN BLVD S CHS .131-B4
JONATHAN CIR MTK .118-B3
JONATHAN CT LVL .162-D4
JONATHAN DR APV .163-A2
JONATHAN LN EPR .132-C4
JONATHAN RD WBY .124-A2
JONATHAN TRL NE EB .8-E3
JONELLEN LN N GV .105-D1
JONES LN MOU .102-E4
JONES PL W BLO .134-B4
JONQUIL AVE CLT .189-C3,203-C1
JONQUIL AVE LVL .162-D4,176-D1
JONQUIL CIR N DAY .49-A3
JONQUIL CT N MG .77-A4
JONQUIL DR N WYT .26-A3
JONQUIL LN WBT .80-E2
JONQUIL LN N DAY .49-A4,63-A1
JONQUIL LN N HAN .61-A3
JONQUIL LN N MG .63-A4,77-A2
JONQUIL LN N PLY .91-A2,105-A1
JONQUIL ST CR .49-E4
JONQUIL ST NW AND .35-E4,49-E3
JONQUIL ST NW CR .49-E4,63-E1
JONQUIL ST NW SF .7-E4
JONQUIL TRL LVL .162-D4
JONQUIL WAY MG .77-A4
JONRAY CT LVL .162-D4
JONSEN AVE NE HAN .60-D3
JOPLIN AVE BUR .162-D3
JOPLIN AVE LVL .162-D3,176-D2
JOPLIN AVE S CG .138-A3
JOPLIN PATH LVL .162-D3
JOPLIN RD NW ER .33-C1
JOPLIN ST NW ER .19-C2,33-C2
JOPLIN WAY LVL .162-D4
JOPPA AVE SAV .148-A3,162-A2
JOPPA AVE S SLP .106-A4,120-A1
JOPPA CIR SAV .162-A2
JOPPA CT SAV .162-A2
JORDAN AVE PRL .161-B3
JORDAN AVE SCT .159-C4
JORDAN AVE STP .109-A3
JORDAN AVE N NH .91-C3
JORDAN AVE S MTK .105-C4
JORDAN AVE S SLP .105-C3
JORDAN CIR N NH .91-C3
JORDAN CT LVL .162-D4
JORDAN CT WBY .123-C3
JORDAN CT N LVL .176-D2
JORDAN CT S LVL .176-D2
JORDAN DR WBY .123-C3
JORDAN TRL LVL .176-D2
JORDON AVE S CG .138-A3
JORGEN AVE MT .166-B3
JORGENSEN ALC S CG .138-A4
JORGENSEN AVE S CG .138-A4
JORGENSEN BAY S CG .138-A4
JORGENSEN CT S CG .138-A3
JORGENSON ST N CAR .145-B4
JORISSEN RD MTK .119-A3
JOSEPH AVE BKR .2-E3
JOSEPH CIR HUT .112-A2
JOSEPH CRV EPR .118-B4
JOSEPH CT LL .52-A4
JOSEPH ST BUR .162-E3
JOSEPH ST NM .189-E4
JOSEPH POINT RD MTK .118-C4
JOSEPHINE AVE EDI .119-E4
JOSEPHINE LN ROB .92-A3
JOSEPHINE PL STP .121-C2
JOSEPHINE RD RVL .93-D3
JOSHUA CIR CHN .117-B4
JOSHUA CT N WYT .26-A4
JOSIE RD LVL .162-C4
JOSTENS RD BLO .133-E2
JOY AVE STP .122-B2
JOY AVE WBL .81-B4
JOY CIR EPR .133-B3
JOY LN MTK .105-B3
JOY RD MPW .95-B3
JOYCE CT EAG .136-A3
JOYCE LN BC .92-A1
JOYCE RD SFT .157-E3,158-A3
JOYCE ST MP .102-E1
JOYER LN LL .66-C4
JUANITA AVE EDI .120-A3
JUBILEE CIR LVL .176-C1
JUBILEE WAY LVL .176-C1
JUDD ST MSC .55-C4,69-B1
JUDD TRL SWR .96-C2
JUDE AVE N FLT .40-A3
JUDGE AVE WHT .216-D2
JUDICIAL RD BUR .148-A4,162-B1
JUDICIAL RD CRT .176-B2
JUDICIAL RD LVL .162-B4,176-B1
JUDICIAL WAY N LVL .176-B1
JUDICIAL WAY S LVL .176-B1
JUDITH AVE RVL .93-D3,94-A3
JUDITH DR CHS .145-D1
JUDSON AVE W FH .107-C2
JUDSON LN EDI .134-A1
JUDSON RD VH .94-D2
JUDY LN BC .92-B1
JUERGENS CIR JOR .173-B3
JUERGENS ST JOR .173-B3
JULEP AVE N LE .96-A4,110-A3
JULEP CT N FLT .40-A3
JULEP CT N LE .110-A3
JULEP TRL N FLT .40-A3
JULEP WAY LE .96-A3
JULIA LN BEC .2-E3
JULIAN DR CHS .131-D4
JULIANNE AVE N FLT .40-A3
JULIANNE AVE N GRA .82-A2
JULIANNE CT N FLT .40-A3
JULIANNE TER GV .105-C1
JULIE ANN DR COR .75-B2
JULIET AVE STP .121-C1
JULIET AVE N LE .96-A3
JULIET DR LVL .177-B3
JULIET DR WBY .123-C3
JULIET RD DAT .144-C4,158-C1
JULIETT ST BLA .65-A4
JULLIARD ST NE COT .52-D2
JULLIARD ST NE LWT .10-D3
JULY AVE N FLT .40-A2,54-A3
JULY AVE N GRA .82-A1
JULY AVE N HUG .82-A1
JULY AVE N WYT .26-A4,40-A1
JUNCO CT LVL .176-D3
JUNCO TRL LVL .176-D3
JUNCTION AVE MPW .94-D4
JUNCTION LN MH .122-B2
JUNCTION RD MTK .119-A2
JUNE AVE N BC .78-A4,92-A1
JUNE AVE N BP .78-A3
JUNE AVE N CRY .92-A4
JUNE AVE N GV .92-A4
JUNE AVE N ROB .92-A4
JUNE AVE S GV .106-A3
JUNE CT LVL .176-D3
JUNE ST LND .12-D3
JUNE TER MTK .105-A4
JUNEAU ALC WBY .124-A2
JUNEAU CT N MG .90-D1
JUNEAU DR WBY .123-E2,124-A2
JUNEAU LN E PLY .90-E2
JUNEAU LN N MG .76-D4,90-D1
JUNEAU LN N PLY .90-D3,104-D1
JUNEAU LN W PLY .90-D1
JUNEBERRY CT LVL .162-B4
JUNELLE PATH LVL .162-C4,176-D1
JUNIPER AVE CHN .131-C1
JUNIPER AVE HAT .188-B4
JUNIPER AVE LTT .144-C1
JUNIPER AVE LVL .176-C2
JUNIPER AVE NFD .219-D3
JUNIPER AVE N BP .64-A4
JUNIPER AVE N FLT .40-A4
JUNIPER CIR WBY .123-E3
JUNIPER CIR NW AND .50-C2
JUNIPER CRV LFL .109-C4
JUNIPER CT ROG .61-D1
JUNIPER CT SHK .146-C3
JUNIPER CT N FLT .40-A4
JUNIPER LN APV .162-E2
JUNIPER LN BUF .59-A1
JUNIPER LN EPR .133-C4
JUNIPER LN STP .121-D2
JUNIPER LN WBY .123-E3
JUNIPER LN NE HL .36-E3
JUNIPER PATH LVL .176-C1
JUNIPER PT EAG .149-C1
JUNIPER RD EB .37-D1
JUNIPER ST MHT .81-D4
JUNIPER ST RW .196-E4
JUNIPER ST N LP .113-B4
JUNIPER ST NW AND .50-C2
JUNIPER ST NW CR .50-C4,64-C1
JUNIPER ST NW OG .22-C1
JUNIPER ST S LP .113-B4,127-B1
JUNIPER WAY LVL .176-C4
JUNIPER RIDGE CIR NW RAM .49-C1
JUNIPER RIDGE
DR NW RAM .35-C4,49-C1
JUNKITE DR NW RAM .35-B4
JUNKITE ST NW RAM .35-B2,49-B2
JUNO AVE STP .121-E2,122-A2
JUNO AVE N FLT .40-A4,54-A1
JUNO AVE N GRA .82-A3
JUNO CT LVL .176-D3
JUNO CT N FLT .54-A1
JUNO TRL LVL .176-C2
JUPITER AVE LVL .176-D3
JUPITER CIR LVL .176-D3
JUPITER CT LVL .176-C3
JUPITER DR MH .135-D2
JUPITER PATH LVL .176-D3
JUPITER RD NE FRI .78-D4
JUPITER WAY LVL .176-D3
JURA TRL LVL .176-D3
JURDY CT N EAG .135-D3
JURDY CT S EAG .135-D3
JURDY RD EAG .135-D3
JUREL CT LVL .176-C1
JUREL WAY LVL .176-D1
JUSTEN AVE WYT .26-A4
JUSTEN CIR HSN .62-B2
JUSTEN CT WYT .26-A4
JUSTEN TRL N GRA .81-E3,82-A3
JUSTICE CT LVL .176-D3
JUSTICE PATH LVL .176-D3
JUTLAND PL LVL .176-D3

K

K ST WBY .123-D1
K TEL DR MTK .119-B2
KABERA TRL LVL .176-C2
KABOT CV LVL .176-C2
KACHINA CT LVL .176-D1
KADLER AVE NE ALB .46-D2
KADLER AVE NE HAN .60-D3
KADLER AVE NE OTS .32-D3,46-D1
KADLER AVE NE SM .60-D2
KADY AVE NE SM .46-D3
KAELIN AVE NE SM .46-D3
KAESEN AVE N VER .179-D2
KAFTAN CT LVL .176-C3
KAHL AVE NE SM .46-D4
KAHLER AVE NE OTS .32-D2
KAHLER AVE NE SM .46-E4,60-E1
KAHLER CIR NE ALB .46-E2
KAHLER CT NE SM .46-D4
KAHLER DR ALB .46-E2
KAHLER DR NE ALB .46-E2
KAHLER DR NE SM .46-D4
KAISER AVE MDL .105-B1
KAISER AVE NE OTS .32-E2
KAISER CIR NE ALB .46-E2
KAISER CIR NE SM .46-D4
KAISER CT NE SM .46-D4
KAISER LN NE ALB .46-E2
KAISER WAY LVL .176-C3
KAITLIN DR VH .80-C4,94-C1
KAL CT NE SM .46-D4
KALBERG CT NE SM .46-D4
KALE AVE LET .12-A1
KALE ST MHT .81-D4
KALE WAY LVL .176-C1
KALEN CIR WBY .137-C1
KALEN CT WBY .137-C1
KALEN DR WBY .137-C1
KALENA LN NE ALB .46-E2
KALENDA AVE NE OTS .32-E2
KALENDA AVE NE SM .46-E4
KALENDA CT NE ALB .46-E2
KALENDA DR ALB .46-E2
KALENDA DR NE ALB .46-E2
KALK RD COR .75-D3
KALLAND AVE NE ALB .46-E2
KALLAND CIR NE ALB .46-E2
KALLAND DR NE ALB .46-E2
KALLIE CT SWR .96-E1
KALMAR CT LVL .176-C1
KALMAR PATH LVL .176-C2
KALMAR TRL LVL .176-C2
KALMEADOW CT LVL .176-C3
KALTERN LN GV .106-A3
KALY RD HUT .112-D2
KAMACITE ST NW RAM .34-E4,48-E2
KAMPA CIR MO .31-C1
KANABEC AVE WHT .202-D3
KANABEC CT LVL .176-C2
KANABEC ST BL .18-A3
KANABEC ST NW SF .7-C3
KANABEC TRL LVL .176-C2
KANE AVE CRT .175-D4
KANE AVE NFT .220-C4
KANES LN SLT .175-B3
KANGAROO CIR NW RAM .34-D4
KANGAROO ST NW RAM .34-D4,48-D1
KANSAS AVE BLA .65-A4
KANSAS AVE LVL .176-C3
KANSAS DR LES .212-C4
KANSAS ST STP .122-D2
KAPARIA AVE LVL .176-C4,190-C1
KAPOSIA BLVD SSP .122-E3
KARA DR EPR .118-E4,132-E1
KAREN CIR BUF .58-E3
KAREN CIR MTK .119-A2
KAREN LN MTK .119-A2
KAREN LN NE CH .92-D2
KAREN PL WBL .80-E3
KARENS CT NE EB .37-C1
KARI LN NB .79-B4
KARI ST RF .140-E3
KARIS WAY EAG .149-C2
KARMEL AVE N CGT .12-B3
KARMEL AVE N LET .12-A4
KARMEL AVE N WYT .12-A4,26-A1
KARMEL ST CHC .26-A1
KARSTON AVE NE ALB .46-D2
KARSTON CIR ALB .46-D2
KARSTON CT ALB .46-D2
KARSTON DR ALB .46-D2
KARSTON ST ALB .46-E2
KARTH RD LL .66-C4
KARTH RD WBL .95-A2
KARTH LAKE CIR AH .79-D4
KARTH LAKE DR AH .79-D4
KARYL DR MTK .118-E2
KARYL PL RVL .107-E1
KASOTA AVE MPL .107-B2
KASOTA AVE STP .107-B2
KASOTA CIR MPL .107-B2
KASOTA ST BL .17-E3
KASSAN CRES SSP .122-D2
KASSAN DR SSP .122-D2
KASSAN RD PRE .153-B4
KASSEL DR CHS .145-C1
KASSEL LN CHS .145-C1
KASSIE CT HOP .119-C2
KATHERINE AVE BKR .2-E3
KATHERINE DR BC .78-A4
KATHLEEN CT SWD .117-B3
KATHLEEN DR WSP .122-C4
KATHLEENE DR MTK .118-B3
KATHRYN CIR EAG .149-C1
KATHRYN CT EPR .133-B3
KATHY LN NE CH .92-D2
KATIE CIR EPR .132-B2
KATIE CIR SW SM .46-E4
KATIE CT AH .93-C2
KATIE LN AH .93-C2
KATIE LN WBT .81-B2
KATNER CT HUT .98-C4
KATRINA LN BL .18-A4
KATRINKA RD MED .89-E1
KATYDID CIR ALB .46-E2
KATYDID DR ALB .46-E2
KATYDID LN NE HAN .60-E2
KAUFMAN DR STP .107-E2
KAUFMANIS WAY EAG .149-E2
KAY AVE MH .121-E4
KAYLA CIR BEL .186-A2
KAYMAR DR EDI .119-D3
KAYMAR LN BUR .162-C3
KAYS CT CHC .12-B4
KEARNEY PATH LVL .176-C3
KEARNY LN S EPR .133-B4
KEATHER AVE N FLT .40-A3
KEATING AVE BUR .149-A2
KEATING CIR BUR .149-A2
KEATING CT BUR .149-A2
KEATS AVE N FLT .54-A1
KEATS AVE N GRA .82-A1,96-A2
KEATS AVE N LE .96-A3,110-A3
KEATS AVE N WBY .110-A4
KEATS AVE S CG .138-B3,152-A1
KEEFE ST EAG .135-E2
KEENE AVE ORO .103-E3
KEEWAHTIN AVE N FLT .40-A4,54-A1
KEEWAYDIN PL MPL .121-A3
KEEWAYDIN ST DPH .118-A2
KEITH DR CP .65-E3
KEITH RD CP .65-E3
KEITHSON DR AH .79-D4
KEITHSON DR SVW .79-D1
KELL AVE S BLO .134-A3,148-A1
KELL CIR BLO .134-A3,148-A2
KELL RD BLO .148-A2
KELLEHER CT SAV .162-A2
KELLER AVE N HUG .68-A4,82-A1
KELLER LN BUR .162-E2
KELLER PKWY MPW .94-D4
KELLER PKWY E LC .94-C3
KELLER RD N FLT .40-A2
KELLER LAKE DR BUR .162-E2
KELLER LAKE RD BUR .162-E2
KELLEY PKWY ORO .103-D2
KELLEY RD CHS .145-D1
KELLOGG AVE EDI .120-A3,134-A1
KELLOGG AVE NFT .220-D3
KELLOGG BLVD E STP .108-C4
KELLOGG BLVD W STP .108-B4
KELLOGG PL EDI .120-A3
KELLY AVE DAT .144-B3
KELLY AVE DRS .28-D1
KELLY AVE ORO .117-C1
KELLY CIR SAV .147-C4
KELLY CT CHN .132-A2
KELLY DR GV .105-D1
KELLY LN HSN .61-E2
KELLY RD HUT .112-C2
KELLY FARM RD ER .34-A4
KELLY LAKE RD SFT .172-C2
KELMAN CT N GRA .82-A2
KELSEY CT EDI .119-C3
KELSEY LN EDI .119-C3
KELSEY LN EPR .132-D3
KELSEY ST DEL .87-D3
KELSEY TER EDI .119-C3
KELTIC WAY LVL .176-C3
KELVIN AVE N GRA .82-A2,96-B2
KELVIN AVE N LE .110-B1
KELZER POND DR VIC .130-E2
KEMPSTON DR WBY .124-A2
KEMRICH CIR MTK .118-C2
KEMRICH DR EDI .133-D1
KENBRIDGE CT LVL .176-C3
KENDALE CIR LVL .162-C3
KENDALE DR LVL .162-C3
KENDALL AVE NFT .220-D3
KENDALL DR HAS .166-D3
KENDEL AVE MT .166-C4
KENDEL CT MT .166-C4
KENDON LN MH .135-D1
KENDRICK AVE LVL .176-C4
KENILWORTH CT WBY .123-D1
KENILWORTH DR WBY .123-D1
KENILWORTH PL MPL .106-B4
KENISTON ST N CHM .63-B1
KENMAR CIR MTK .104-E2
KENMARE DR BLO .147-D2
KENMARE PL WIL .95-D2
KENMORE AVE LVL .162-C4
KENMORE CT LVL .162-C4
KENMORE DR LVL .162-C4
KENNARD CT LVL .162-C3
KENNARD CT STP .108-E4
KENNARD ST MPW .94-E4,108-E1
KENNARD ST STP .108-E2
KENNASTON DR NE FRI .78-E3
KENNEBEC DR EAG .135-B4
KENNEDY AVE S LP .127-B1
KENNEDY CIR BUR .148-E2
KENNEDY LN LOL .103-D2
KENNEDY ST ANO .49-C3
KENNEDY ST RF .140-E3
KENNEDY ST NE MPL .107-A1
KENNEDY ST NW ER .20-B4,34-B1
KENNEDY MEMORIAL DR MTA .116-B3
KENNEDY MEMORIAL DR SB .116-B3
KENNEL RD MTA .102-A4
KENNELLY CT BUR .149-A3
KENNELLY DR BUR .149-A3
KENNELLY PL BUR .148-E3,149-A3
KENNELLY RD BUR .148-E3,149-A3
KENNET CIR EAG .150-B1
KENNETH CT MTK .105-B4
KENNETH LN MO .31-C1
KENNETH ST EAG .135-E2
KENNETH ST STP .121-C2
KENNETH WAY GV .105-E1
KENNEY PL EDI .119-E4

KENNING RD EPR 132-D3
KENNSINGTON DR SHK 146-C3
KENNY CT BKR 3-D4,17-D1
KENNY LN WBL 95-A1
KENNY RD STP 108-C3
KENORA CT LVL 162-C3
KENORA WAY LVL 162-C3
KENOSHA AVE LVL 162-C3
KENREEL AVE LVL 162-C3
KENRICK AVE LVL 162-C4,176-C3
KENSETT PATH LVL 162-C3
KENSINGTON AVE LVL 176-C3
KENSINGTON BLVD LVL 176-C3
KENSINGTON CT LVL 176-C3
KENSINGTON CT MTK 118-D2
KENSINGTON DR EPR 147-B1
KENSINGTON GATE SWD 118-A3
KENSINGTON TRL EAG 149-E2
KENSINGTON WAY BUF 58-E2
KENSINGTON WAY LVL 176-C3
KENT AVE CHC 26-B2
KENT AVE EDI 119-E3
KENT AVE ERT 216-C4
KENT AVE WHT 202-C3,216-C2
KENT CIR SVW 80-A3
KENT CT SVW 80-A3
KENT CT N CHC 26-B2
KENT DR SVW 80-A3
KENT LN APV 163-A2
KENT LN SVW 94-A2
KENT ST OSC 27-E4,28-A4
KENT ST PRL 160-E4
KENT ST RVL 94-A3,108-A1
KENT ST STP 108-A3,122-A1
KENT ST SVW 80-A3,94-A2
KENT ST NW ER 33-C2
KENT TRL LVL 162-C3
KENT WAY SVW 80-A3
KENTLEY AVE N GV 91-E4
KENTUCKY AVE BLA 65-A4
KENTUCKY AVE LVL 162-D3
KENTUCKY AVE SAV 161-D2
KENTUCKY AVE N BP 77-D3
KENTUCKY AVE N CHM 63-D2
KENTUCKY AVE N CRY 91-D3
KENTUCKY AVE N GV 105-D2
KENTUCKY AVE S BLO 133-D2,147-D1
KENTUCKY AVE S GV 105-D2
KENTUCKY AVE S SLP 105-D4
KENTUCKY CIR CHM 63-D2
KENTUCKY CIR N BP 77-D3
KENTUCKY CIR N CRY 91-D3
KENTUCKY CIR S BLO 133-D2
KENTUCKY CT N BP 77-D2
KENTUCKY CT N CHM 63-D3
KENTUCKY LN SLP 105-D3
KENTUCKY ST E SCF 14-C2
KENTWOOD CT BUR 149-A2
KENTWOOD LN WBY 123-E3
KENWOOD CT LVL 176-C1
KENWOOD CT N MPW 94-C4
KENWOOD DR E MPW 94-D4,108-C1
KENWOOD DR W MPW 108-C1
KENWOOD LN E MPW 108-D1
KENWOOD PKWY MPL 106-B3
KENWOOD PKWY STP 122-A1
KENWOOD ST MHT 81-D4
KENWOOD TRL BUR 148-B4,162-C2
KENWOOD TRL LVL 162-C4,176-D2
KENWOOD WAY LVL 176-D2
KENWOOD WAY ORO 117-C1
KENWOOD ISLES DR MPL 106-C4
KENWORTH CT LVL 162-C3
KENWORTH LN LVL 162-C3
KENYON AVE LVL 162-C4,176-C1
KENYON CIR NE HL 37-A3
KENYON CT NE BLA 65-A2
KENYON ST NE BLA 51-A3,65-A1
KENYON ST NE EB 23-A2
KENYON ST NE HL 37-A4,51-A2
KENZIE TER SA 93-A4
KEOKUK AVE LVL 162-C4,176-C4
KEOKUK LN MH 136-A1
KERBER BLVD CHN 132-A1
KERELS ST VH 94-C2
KERI ANN LN WBL 95-A1
KERR KNIGHT RD IND 102-E2
KERRY CIR NE FRI 79-A4
KERRY CT MTK 118-C2
KERRY CT N HUG 68-A4
KERRY LN EPR 132-E1,133-A1
KERRY LN MOU 117-A2
KERRY LN WBY 123-E2
KERRY LN WIL 95-D1
KERRY LN NE FRI 79-A4
KERRY RD EDI 133-D1
KERRY RD MOU 117-A1
KERRY ST CR 49-E4
KERRY ST NW AND 49-E2
KERRY ST NW CR 49-E3,63-E1
KERRY ST NW SF 7-E4
KERRY ST NW STT 7-E1
KESLER AVE N FLT 40-A2
KESSLER CT CHS 145-B1
KESSLER LN CHS 145-B1
KESTON ST STP 107-B2
KESTRAL CT NO 80-C2
KESTREL CIR BUF 45-B4
KESTREL CIR OTS 33-D4
KESTREL CT BUF 45-B3
KESTREL CT LVL 176-C1
KESTREL ST PRL 161-A4
KESTREL TRL BUF 45-B3
KESWICK AVE N FLT 40-A4,54-A1
KESWICK AVE N GRA 82-B3,96-B2
KETTENACKER DR RFD 74-A4
KETTERING TRL LVL 162-C4,176-B1
KETTLE CREEK RD EAG 149-E1
KETTLE RIVER BLVD COT 38-E3,52-C1
KETTLE RIVER BLVD N WYO 25-A3
KETTLE RIVER
BLVD N WYT 25-A4,39-A1
KETTLE RIVER
BLVD NE COT 38-E2,52-C1
KETTLE RIVER CT LVL 176-C1
KEVIN LN SVW 79-E3
KEVIN LONGLEY DR MO 31-B1
KEWANEE WAY GV 106-A1
KEY CIR NW CR 64-B2
KEYSTONE AVE LVL 162-C4,176-C1
KEYSTONE AVE N CGT 26-A4,40-A1
KEYSTONE AVE N FLT 54-A2
KEYSTONE AVE N GRA 82-B1
KEYSTONE AVE N HUG 54-B4,68-B2
KEYSTONE AVE N MAY 68-B4
KEYSTONE CT LVL 162-C3
KEYSTONE CT MTK 105-B4
KEYSTONE LN BKT 185-A3
KEYSTONE PATH LVL 176-C1
KHYBER LN NE CH 92-E1
KIAWAH DR EPR 133-B2
KIEFFER ST SW WAT 101-A3
KIERSTEN PL EPR 133-A4,147-A1
KILBIRNE RD WBY 124-B1
KILBIRNIE RD BL 17-E2,18-A2
KILBIRNIE TER BP 78-A2
KILBIRNIE WAY MHT 95-C2
KILBURN ST STP 107-E3
KILDAHL AVE NFD 219-D3
KILDARE RD MOU 117-A1
KILDARE WAY EPR 132-C3
KILKENNEY LN MED 90-A2
KILLARNEY DR GV 106-A2
KILLARNEY LN EDI 119-C4
KILLARNEY RD WIL 95-D2
KILLDEER CIR LVL 176-C1
KILLDEER CT LL 66-B4
KILLDEER DR LL 66-B4
KILLDEER LN SE PRL 161-C3
KILLDEER ST NW AND 50-B3
KILLDEER ST NW CR 50-B4,64-B1
KILLDEER ST NW OG 22-B2
KILLEBREW DR BLO 134-E2,135-A2
KILLIAN AVE N NST 40-B4
KILMER AVE EPR 132-C2
KILMER AVE SLP 105-C3
KILMER DR N MG 77-C3
KILMER LN PLY 91-C4,105-C1
KILMER LN N MG 63-C4,77-C3
KILMER LN N PLY 91-C4,105-C1
KILMER WAY N MG 77-C4
KILO ST BLA 65-A4
KIM AVE HBG 156-A2
KIM PL STP 109-A4
KIMBALL DR CHM 63-C1
KIMBALL DR EPR 132-C2
KIMBALL ST NE CR 78-C1
KIMBALL ST NE FRI 78-C1
KIMBERLY CIR ROG 47-D4
KIMBERLY CT N PLY 104-C1
KIMBERLY CT S CG 152-B2
KIMBERLY DR NB 93-B2
KIMBERLY LN CHN 132-A2
KIMBERLY LN EPR 132-C2
KIMBERLY LN MG 76-C1
KIMBERLY LN SVW 79-E3
KIMBERLY LN WIL 95-D2
KIMBERLY LN N MG 76-C2
KIMBERLY LN N PLY 90-C4,104-C1
KIMBERLY RD MTK 118-D3
KIMBERLY RD WIL 95-D1
KIMBLE CT NFD 219-D3
KIMBRO AVE N GRA 82-B4,96-B1
KIMBRO AVE N LE 96-B4
KIMBRO AVE N MAY 54-B4
KIMBRO AVE S CG 138-B4,152-B1
KIMBRO CIR S CG 152-B1
KIMBRO CT S CG 152-B2
KIMBRO LN N GRA 82-B4
KIMBRO AVENUE CT N GRA 82-B2
KINDER DR WAC 129-C3
KINDLE CT LVL 176-C1
KINDRED CT LE 96-B4
KINDRED WAY LE 96-B4
KINDROSS RD MHT 95-D1
KINDROSS RD WIL 95-D1
KING AVE MPW 123-B1
KING AVE NW ER 33-E2
KING CIR NW ER 19-E4
KING DR HAS 166-D3
KING RD EB 37-D1
KING ST E STP 122-C1
KING ST W STP 122-B2
KING CREEK RD GV 105-E2
KING HILL RD GV 105-E2
KING MIDAS LN HAS 166-D2
KINGFISHER CT CHN 131-E3
KINGFISHER CT LL 66-B4
KINGFISHER LN BUF 45-B4
KINGFISHER LN EPR 118-E4
KINGFISHER LN WBY 123-D1
KINGLET CT EAG 135-E4
KINGMAN LN MTK 105-B3
KINGS BLF CHC 26-B1
KINGS CIR BP 77-E2
KINGS CIR HSN 48-B4
KINGS CIR WBY 123-D2
KINGS CRST EAG 149-D1
KINGS CT BP 77-E2
KINGS CT BUR 162-B3
KINGS CT GRW 118-A3
KINGS CT LVL 162-C4
KINGS XING BP 77-E2
KINGS DR MTK 118-E2
KINGS DR OKD 95-C4
KINGS DR WBY 123-D2
KINGS HWY NW SF 7-E2
KINGS LN ANO 63-D1
KINGS LN CHS 131-C4
KINGS PL LVL 162-C4
KINGS RD CHN 131-B1
KINGS RD EAG 149-B3
KINGS RD SPR 117-B1
KINGS RD VIC 131-B1
KINGS TER BP 77-E2
KINGS TER WBY 123-D2
KINGS POINT RD MTA 116-C3
KINGS VALLEY RD GV 105-C1
KINGS VALLEY RD E GV 105-C1
KINGS VALLEY RD W GV 105-C1
KINGSBERRY DR EDI 119-C3
KINGSBOROUGH LN MTK 118-D2
KINGSBOROUGH CT S CG 152-B2
KINGSBOROUGH TRL S CG 152-B2
KINGSBURY CIR LVL 176-C1
KINGSBURY DR EAG 149-C2
KINGSDALE DR BLO 133-E3,134-A3
KINGSFORD ST STP 108-E2
KINGSLEE RD BLO 133-D2
KINGSLEY AVE WBL 95-A1
KINGSLEY CIR N MH 121-E4
KINGSLEY CIR S MH 121-E4
KINGSLEY CT LVL 162-C3
KINGSLEY CT MH 121-E4
KINGSLEY ST N WIN 99-B3
KINGSLEY ST S WIN 99-B4
KINGSLEY ST S WIT 99-B4
KINGSTON AVE MPW 108-C1,109-A1
KINGSTON AVE E MPW 108-C1
KINGSTON CIR N GV 105-D2
KINGSTON CT EAG 150-A1
KINGSTON DR EPR 118-E4,132-E1
KINGSVIEW CT MG 76-D1
KINGSVIEW LN HSN 48-A4
KINGSVIEW LN N DAY 48-D4
KINGSVIEW LN N MG 76-D1,90-D1
KINGSVIEW LN N PLY 90-D3,104-D2
KINGSWAY DR LES 212-D3
KINGSWAY DR TYT 212-D3
KINGSWAY LN MV 79-B3
KINGSWAY PATH LVL 176-B1
KINGSWAY RD HUT 112-D1
KINGSWOOD CIR LVL 176-B1
KINGSWOOD CT EAG 149-D1
KINGSWOOD CT LVL 162-C3
KINGSWOOD DR LTT 131-A4
KINGSWOOD DR LVL 162-C3
KINGSWOOD DR RW 196-E4
KINGSWOOD LN EAG 149-D1
KINGSWOOD RD EAG 149-D1
KINGSWOOD RD MTA 102-C4
KINGSWOOD TER MTK 118-B3
KINGSWOOD TRL EAG 135-D4,149-D1
KINGSWOOD PONDS RD EAG 135-D4
KINGSWOOD
PONDS OVER EAG 135-D4
KINNEY RD HUT 112-D3
KINNI CT RF 140-E3
KINNICKINNIC ST HUD 111-D2
KINNICKINNIC ST PRE 153-B4,167-B1
KINSEL RD MTK 118-E3
KINSHIP GRN SWR 96-C2
KIOWA AVE CHN 132-A2
KIOWA AVE NB 93-B1
KIOWA CIR CHN 132-A1
KIOWA ST NW AND 35-D4,49-D1
KIOWA ST NW OG 21-C4
KIOWA ST NW SF 7-D4
KIOWA ST NW STT 7-D1
KIOWA TRL CHN 132-A4
KIPLING AVE EDI 120-A2
KIPLING AVE MTK 118-C3
KIPLING AVE SAV 148-A4,162-A1
KIPLING AVE S SLP 106-A4,120-A1
KIPLING CT SAV 162-A2
KIPLING ST STP 123-A1
KIPP DR JOR 173-B3
KIRBEN AVE LVL 162-C4
KIRBY AVE CGT 26-B2
KIRBY AVE CHC 26-B2
KIRBY AVE DAT 158-B3
KIRBY AVE DT 180-C4,194-C1
KIRBY AVE MT 166-C4,180-C3
KIRBY AVE N MAY 54-B4,68-B3
KIRBY AVE N NST 40-B4,54-B1
KIRBY PUCKETT PL MPL 106-D3
KIRCHE HILL DR CAR 145-B4
KIRCHNER AVE MH 122-B2
KIRK AVE N NST 40-B3,54-B3
KIRKHAM RD CHN 131-B1
KIRKWOOD AVE N LE 96-B3
KIRKWOOD AVE S CG 138-B2
KIRKWOOD CIR CHN 117-B4
KIRKWOOD CIR EAG 149-E2
KIRKWOOD CIR MG 77-A1
KIRKWOOD CIR N PLY 91-A1
KIRKWOOD CT MG 77-A3
KIRKWOOD DR EAG 149-E2
KIRKWOOD LN N MG 63-A4,77-A3
KIRKWOOD LN N PLY 91-A1,105-A1
KIRKWOOD PL PLY 91-A3
KIRKWOOD WAY N MG 77-A1
KIRSTEN CT EAG 150-A2
KISMET AVE N GRA 82-B2
KISMET DR N CGT 26-B3
KISMET ISLE N CGT 26-B3
KISMET ISLE N WYT 26-A3
KISMET LN N GRA 82-B2
KISSEL ST NE EB 9-D4,23-D2
KISSELL ST NE BLA 65-D3
KIT LN HUT 112-C2
KITKERRY CT N SVW 80-A1
KITKERRY CT S SVW 80-A1
KITTIWAKE CIR EAG 135-E4
KITTSON BLVD BEL 186-A2
KITTSON BLVD BPT 186-C3
KITTSON ST STP 108-C4
KITTY DR CW 1-B3
KIWI AVE N BP 64-A4
KLAERS DR GRF 89-A1
KLAINERT ST STP 108-B2
KLAMATH CT LVL 162-B3
KLAMATH TER LVL 162-B3
KLAMATH TRL LVL 162-C4
KLICKITAT AVE BL 18-A3
KLONDIKE AVE N LE 110-B1
KLONDIKE CT EPR 133-A3
KLONDIKE DR NE EB 22-E3,23-A3
KNAPP PL STP 107-C2
KNAPP ST FH 107-C2
KNAPP ST STP 107-C2
KNEAFSEYS ST PRL 161-C2
KNIGHT AVE LTT 144-B1
KNIGHT ST SVW 79-D1
KNIGHTON RD WBY 124-A2
KNIGHTS BRIDGE RD NB 93-B1
KNIGHTSBRIDGE RD EPR 133-B4
KNIGHTSBRIDGE RD NB 93-B1
KNIGHTSBRIDGE RD SWD 118-A2
KNOB CIR EAG 149-D1
KNOB DR EAG 149-D1
KNOB LN EAG 149-D1
KNOB RD MH 122-A4
KNOB HILL CRV MTK 118-D3
KNOB HILL CT MTK 118-D3
KNOB HILL DR BKR 3-E4
KNOB HILL LN BUR 148-C4
KNOB HILL LN CHN 117-E4
KNOB HILL RD BUR 148-C4
KNOBLE CT EPR 133-B3
KNOLL CIR MPW 109-B1
KNOLL CIR E BUR 148-D4
KNOLL CIR W BUR 148-D4
KNOLL DR EDI 119-C3
KNOLL DR LL 66-B1
KNOLL DR MV 79-B2
KNOLL DR RMT 163-E2
KNOLL DR SVW 79-D2
KNOLL DR S EDI 119-D3
KNOLL LN BUR 148-D4
KNOLL ST N GV 105-D1
KNOLL MANOR RD ORO 103-E1
KNOLL RIDGE DR EAG 135-C4
KNOLLRIDGE DR PRL 160-E3
KNOLLS PATH LVL 162-B3
KNOLLWAY DR N MTK 104-E3
KNOLLWAY DR S MTK 104-E3
KNOLLWOOD CIR LVL 176-C1
KNOLLWOOD CT BLA 65-C2
KNOLLWOOD CT EAG 149-E1
KNOLLWOOD CT HUD 111-D2
KNOLLWOOD CT MH 122-A3
KNOLLWOOD CT SWR 96-D2
KNOLLWOOD DR EPR 132-E3
KNOLLWOOD DR HUD 111-D2
KNOLLWOOD DR MV 79-A2
KNOLLWOOD DR NB 79-A3
KNOLLWOOD DR N GRA 82-B3
KNOLLWOOD LN MH 122-A3
KNOLLWOOD LN RIT 140-E3
KNOTTINGHAM CIR EAG 149-D3
KNOX AVE N BC 78-B3,92-B1
KNOX AVE N BP 78-B1
KNOX AVE N MPL 92-B4,106-B2
KNOX AVE S BLO 134-B3
KNOX AVE S MPL 106-B3,120-B3
KNOX AVE S RCH 120-B4,134-B1
KNOX CIR S BUR 148-C4
KNOX DR BUR 148-C4,162-C1
KNOX PATH MT 166-C4
KOCHIA LN VIC 131-A2
KOCHS XING IND 88-E2
KODIAK AVE LVL 162-B4
KODIAK CT LVL 162-B4
KOEHLER ST MTA 116-D2
KOEHNEN CIR CHN 117-E4
KOEHNEN CIR CHS 145-C1
KOEHNEN DR CHS 145-B1
KOEPER AVE HAT 202-B2
KOEPER AVE JT 146-B4
KOEPER AVE SHK 146-B3
KOESTER CT NFD 219-D4
KOHLER RD VH 94-C1
KOHLMAN AVE MPW 94-E3,95-A3
KOHLMAN CT MPW 94-D3
KOHLMAN LN MPW 94-D3
KOHNENS CIR MTK 119-A1
KOLFF CT NEW 137-B1
KOLFF ST NEW 137-B1
KOLSTAD LN EAG 135-D4
KOLSTAD RD EAG 135-D4
KOPP DR WSP 122-C3
KORTSCH TRL SE PRL 161-C2
KOST RD EAG 136-A4
KOTHMANN CIR CW 1-B3
KOVE ST LFL 109-C4
KRAFT CIR N LE 110-B1
KRAFT RD E WSP 122-C4
KRAFT RD W WSP 122-C4
KRAFT ST SSP 122-D4
KRAFTON AVE LVL 162-B3
KRAL RD MTK 118-D3
KRAMER AVE IGH 137-A3
KRAMERS RD MTA 102-E3
KRATTLEY LN HUT 97-E4
KRATTLEY LN N HUT 97-D4
KRATTLEY LN N NOH 97-D4
KRECH AVE WBL 81-A3
KREEKWOOD AVE DAT 145-A2
KRESSE CIR EDI 119-D2
KRESSIN AVE MH 136-A1
KRESTWOOD DR BUR 148-D4,162-D1
KRESTWOOD LN EAG 135-D4
KREUSER RD SCT 173-B2
KREY AVE LTT 130-D2
KREY AVE VH 94-C2
KRISTEN CIR BUF 58-E3
KRISTEN CT VH 94-D2
KRISTEN CT NE FRI 79-A4
KRISTIE LN EPR 132-B1
KRISTIN LN DAT 158-E1
KRISTIN LN MTA 102-A3
KRUEGER AVE CGT 26-B4
KRUEGER LN N OPH 96-D2
KRUSE ST WSP 122-C3
KRYPTON CT NW RAM 49-B2
KRYPTON ST NW BT 35-B2
KRYPTON ST NW RAM 35-B2,49-B2
KUMQUAT ST CR 64-C2
KUMQUAT ST NW AND 50-C1
KUMQUAT ST NW BET 8-C3
KUMQUAT ST NW CR 50-C4,64-C2
KUNTZ DR IND 102-B2
KURT ST GRF 74-D3
KURTZ CIR EPR 118-D4
KURTZ LN EPR 118-D4
KURVERS POINT RD CHN 132-B1
KUSILEK ST RF 140-D2
KUTCHER LN EPR 118-D4
KUTOFF CT EAG 136-A3
KUTOFF DR EAG 136-B3
KUTZ XING IND 101-E2,102-A2
KWEI ST NE COT 38-B4
KYLE AVE N BC 78-A4,92-A1
KYLE AVE N BP 64-A3,78-A3
KYLE AVE N CRY 92-A4
KYLE AVE N GV 92-A4,106-A1
KYLE PL GV 106-A1
KYLE WAY EAG 149-B2
KYLLO LN EAG 135-C4

L

L ST WBY 123-D1
L S POWER RD CG 152-A2
LA BARGE RD HUT 98-C4,112-C1
LA BON TER MTK 118-D1
LA COSTA DR DWD 81-C2
LA GRANDEUR RD SMT 70-C4,84-C1
LA GRANDEUR RD SOM 70-C4
LA RIVER CT EPR 132-D3
LA SALLE ST WAY 104-C3
LABEAUX AVE NE ALB 46-E2
LABEAUX AVE NE HAN 60-E3
LABEAUX AVE NE OTS 32-E3,46-E1
LABEAUX AVE NE SM 46-E4,60-E1
LABORE AVE E LC 94-B3
LABORE RD VH 94-D2
LABORE RD E LC 94-C3
LABORE INDUSTRIAL CT VH 94-D2
LAC LAVON CT BUR 162-E2
LAC LAVON DR BUR 162-E2
LAC LAVON DR LVL 162-E3
LACASSE CIR LL 66-E3
LACASSE CT LL 66-E3
LACASSE DR LL 66-E3
LACHMAN AVE SM 60-E1
LACHMAN AVE NE ALB 46-E2
LACHMAN AVE NE SM 60-E1
LACHMAN CIR ALB 46-E2
LACHMAN CT NE SM 46-E4
LACKAWANNA ST NW SF 7-C4
LACOSTA CIR DWD 81-C2
LACOSTA DR DWD 81-C2
LACOTA CIR BUR 148-C4
LACOTA LN BUR 148-C4
LACROSSE AVE STP 108-E3,109-A3
LACY AVE CHC 26-B2
LACY CT BEL 186-A2
LACY LN BEL 186-A2
LAD PKWY BP 78-A2
LADDIE RD NE SLK 78-E1
LADINO CIR EPR 133-A3

LADY BIRD LN BUR 148-C3
LADY SLIPPER LN CHN 131-D2
LADY SLIPPER LN NP 201-E2
LADY SLIPPER LN VH 80-C4
LADYSLIPPER AVE N BP ...63-E4,64-A4
LADYSLIPPER LN BP 64-A4
LADYSLIPPER LN NE HAN 60-E2
LAFAYETTE AVE EXC 117-D3
LAFAYETTE FWY OKD 95-C3
LAFAYETTE FWY SSP 122-D3
LAFAYETTE FWY STP ...108-C4,122-C1
LAFAYETTE FWY WSP 122-D3
LAFAYETTE LN MOU 102-E4
LAFAYETTE LN SPR 117-B1
LAFAYETTE RD MTB 117-D1
LAFAYETTE RD STP 108-C4
LAFAYETTE RD E STP ...108-C4,122-C1
LAFAYETTE RD S STP 108-C4
LAFAYETTE RD W ORO 117-C2
LAFAYETTE RD W STP ...108-C4,122-C1
LAFAYETTE ST NE CR 78-C1
LAFAYETTE RIDGE CT ORO 117-C1
LAFAYETTE RIDGE RD MTB 117-C1
LAFOND AVE STP 107-D3,108-A3
LAFORET DR EPR 132-C4
LAGOON AVE BL 18-A3
LAGOON AVE MPL 106-C4
LAGOON DR SWD 117-B3
LAGOON ST W VER 179-C2
LAGUNA CIR EPR 133-B4
LAGUNA DR EDI 134-A1
LAHTI LN MTK 119-C1
LAHTI LN PLY 104-E2,105-A2
LAIGLE AVE LVL 162-B3,176-B4
LAKAMAGA TRL N NST 54-D2
LAKE AVE BL 17-E3
LAKE AVE BWV 95-C1
LAKE AVE CHC 26-B1
LAKE AVE DPH 118-B1
LAKE AVE SVW 79-E2
LAKE AVE WAV 86-A1
LAKE AVE WBL 81-B3,95-A1
LAKE AVE WBT 80-E4,81-A1
LAKE AVE WHT 202-C3,216-C2
LAKE AVE NE ALB 47-A2
LAKE AVE S WBL 81-A4
LAKE BAY W NO 80-A2
LAKE BLVD CGT 12-C4,13-A4
LAKE BLVD CHC 12-B4,26-B1
LAKE BLVD CNC 12-E4
LAKE BLVD FRT 14-A4
LAKE BLVD LND 12-D4
LAKE BLVD MPW 95-B3
LAKE BLVD NSP 95-B3
LAKE BLVD SHA 13-C4
LAKE BLVD SHT 13-D4,14-A4
LAKE BLVD WYT 26-A1
LAKE BLVD N CGT 12-C4,13-B4
LAKE BLVD N FL 39-B2
LAKE BLVD N FLT 39-C2
LAKE BLVD N SHT 13-B4
LAKE BLVD N WYT 25-E4,39-D1
LAKE BLVD NW BUF 58-D2
LAKE BLVD S BUF 58-E2
LAKE CRV ROB 92-A3
LAKE CT BUR 149-A2
LAKE CT NO 80-A2
LAKE CT WBL 81-A4
LAKE DR BLA 65-C4,79-C1
LAKE DR CHN 132-A2
LAKE DR CP 65-E3
LAKE DR LEX 65-C4
LAKE DR LL 65-E3,66-A2
LAKE DR MH 135-E1,136-A1
LAKE DR ROB 92-A3
LAKE DR SWR 96-E2
LAKE DR E CHN 132-B2
LAKE DR E CHS 131-C4
LAKE DR NE COT 38-D4,52-C1
LAKE DR NE LL 52-B4,66-B1
LAKE DR W CHN 131-E2,132-A2
LAKE DR W NO 80-A2
LAKE GRV WBL 95-A2
LAKE LN AH 93-C2
LAKE LN CGT 12-C3
LAKE LN LND 12-C3
LAKE LN NB 93-B2
LAKE LN N AH 93-E2
LAKE PL MPL 106-B4
LAKE PT CHN 118-A4
LAKE RD MTB 117-C1
LAKE RD WBY 123-C2,124-A3
LAKE ST CHC 26-A1
LAKE ST CNC 12-E3
LAKE ST EB 23-D4
LAKE ST EXC 117-E3
LAKE ST HAS 166-E1
LAKE ST IND 89-A4
LAKE ST LAU 107-B1
LAKE ST LC 94-C3
LAKE ST LND 12-C4
LAKE ST LOL 103-E2
LAKE ST MPW 95-B3
LAKE ST PRE 153-A4,167-A1
LAKE ST RF 140-E2
LAKE ST RVL 107-B1
LAKE ST STP 109-B3
LAKE ST SWR 83-A4,96-E2
LAKE ST E COL 143-E4
LAKE ST E LC 94-B4
LAKE ST E MPL 106-D4,107-A4
LAKE ST E ORO 103-C3
LAKE ST E WAC 129-E3
LAKE ST E WAY 104-B3
LAKE ST E WIN 99-B3
LAKE ST N BL 18-A3
LAKE ST N FL 39-B2
LAKE ST NE HOP 119-C1
LAKE ST S BAY 97-C4
LAKE ST S BL 18-A4
LAKE ST S FL 39-B3
LAKE ST S FLT 39-B4
LAKE ST W COL 143-D4
LAKE ST W EXC 117-E3
LAKE ST W MPL 106-B4
LAKE ST W NYA 142-C4
LAKE ST W ORO 103-B3
LAKE ST W SLP 105-E4,119-D1
LAKE ST W WAC 129-D3
LAKE ST W WAY 104-B3
LAKE TER E WBY 123-C3
LAKE TER W WBY 123-C3
LAKE TRL WHT 216-B3
LAKE AUGUSTA DR MH 135-D1
LAKE BAYVIEW CT SVW 94-A2
LAKE BEACH CT E SVW 79-E2
LAKE BEACH CT W SVW 79-E2
LAKE BEACH DR SVW 79-E2
LAKE BREEZE AVE BC 92-A2
LAKE COURT CIR MV 79-B2
LAKE COURT DR MV 79-B2
LAKE COVE CIR LVL 176-B1
LAKE COVE CT SVW 94-A2
LAKE CURVE LN BC 92-A1
LAKE DIANE CT NB 79-A4
LAKE ELMO AVE N GRA 82-B4,96-B2
LAKE ELMO AVE N LE 96-B3,110-B2
LAKE FALL DR EPR 133-B3
LAKE GEORGE
BLVD NW OG 21-E2,35-E1
LAKE GEORGE BLVD NW SF 7-E4
LAKE GEORGE DR NW OG 21-E2,22-A2
LAKE GEORGE PKWY NW OG 22-A2
LAKE HARRIET PKWY E MPL 120-C2
LAKE HARRIET PKWY W MPL 120-B2
LAKE HAUGHEY RD IND 88-A2
LAKE HAZELTINE DR CHS 131-D3
LAKE JANE TRL N LE 95-E4,96-A4
LAKE JOHANNA BLVD AH 93-C2
LAKE LAND AVE CRY 91-E1
LAKE LINDEN DR SWD 117-D4
LAKE LUCY LN CHN 117-E4
LAKE LUCY RD CHN 117-E4,131-D1
LAKE OAK CIR LVL 176-B1
LAKE OAKS DR SVW 79-E2
LAKE OF THE ISLES
PKWY E MPL 106-B4
LAKE OF THE ISLES
PKWY W MPL 106-B4
LAKE PARK CIR EAG 149-D2
LAKE PARK CT EAG 149-D2
LAKE PARK DR EAG 149-D2
LAKE PEPIN RD LAT 215-C3
LAKE PINE DR SVW 79-E2,80-A2
LAKE POINT CT SVW 80-A4
LAKE POINTE DR FRI 78-E4
LAKE PULASKI DR BUF 45-A4
LAKE REBECCA RD E IND 88-B1
LAKE RIDGE ALC WBY 124-B1
LAKE RIDGE BAY WBY 124-B1
LAKE RIDGE DR BL 17-E3,18-A2
LAKE RIDGE DR SAV 161-D1
LAKE RIDGE DR SLT 174-E3
LAKE RIDGE DR WBY 124-B1
LAKE RIDGE DR N MG 76-C2
LAKE RIDGE RD EDI 119-D3
LAKE RILEY BLVD CHN 132-B3
LAKE ROAD AVE ROB 92-A3
LAKE ROSE CIR MTK 118-D3
LAKE ROSE DR MTK 118-D3
LAKE ROSE LN MTK 118-D3
LAKE SANDBORN RD LAT 216-B3
LAKE SARAH DR S GRF 88-C1
LAKE SARAH DR S IND 88-D1
LAKE SARAH DR W GRF 74-C4,88-C1
LAKE SARAH LN GRF 88-E1
LAKE SARAH RD IND 88-C2
LAKE SARAH HEIGHTS CIR IND 88-E1
LAKE SARAH HEIGHTS DR GRF 88-E1
LAKE SARAH HEIGHTS
DR IND 88-E1,89-A1
LAKE SHORE AVE MED 89-A3
LAKE SHORE AVE MTK 118-D3
LAKE SHORE BLVD MTK 104-C4,118-D1
LAKE SHORE CIR CHS 131-C3
LAKE SHORE CT CHS 131-C3
LAKE SHORE CV CHS 131-C3
LAKE SHORE DR CHS 131-C3
LAKE SHORE DR EB 37-D1
LAKE SHORE DR MPL 106-A4
LAKE SHORE DR NE EB 37-D2
LAKE SHORE DR S IND 89-A4
LAKE SHORE DR S RCH 120-C4,134-C1
LAKE SHORE DR W RCH 120-C4,134-C1
LAKE STREET EXT MTK 118-D2,119-A2
LAKE SUMMIT CT SVW 94-A2
LAKE SUSAN CT CHN 132-A3
LAKE SUSAN DR CHN 132-A3
LAKE SUSAN
HILLS DR CHN 131-E3,132-A3
LAKE TERRACE DR MTA 102-B3
LAKE VALENTINE RD AH 93-C1
LAKE VIEW CIR BL 17-E3
LAKE VIEW DR BUF 58-D2
LAKE VIEW DR NOH 111-C1
LAKE VIEW DR WBY 110-B4,124-B1
LAKE VIEW ECHO WBY 124-B1
LAKE VIEW LN BL 17-E3
LAKE VIRGINIA DR SWD 117-B4
LAKE WABASSO CT SVW 94-A2
LAKEAIRES BLVD GL 94-E1
LAKEAIRES BLVD WBL 95-A1
LAKEBROOK DR NB 79-B3
LAKEHILL CIR WBL 95-B1
LAKEHILLS CT LVL 162-B4
LAKELAND AVE N BC 92-A1
LAKELAND AVE N BP 77-C2,91-D1
LAKELAND AVE N CRY 91-E2
LAKELAND AVE N ROB 91-E2,92-A3
LAKELAND CIR CV 66-D2
LAKELAND CIR EPR 132-B4
LAKELAND DR MTK 118-C3
LAKELAND DR N MG 77-A1
LAKELAND RD MTK 118-D3
LAKELAND TER EPR 132-B4
LAKELAND SHORES RD LS 111-C4
LAKELAWN CT N CGT 26-C2
LAKELAWN DR N CGT 26-C2
LAKERIDGE DR WBL 81-B4
LAKERIDGE RD CHN 131-B1
LAKERIDGE WAY WAC 129-C2
LAKESHORE AVE N LC 94-B3
LAKESHORE DR BL 17-E3,18-A3
LAKESHORE DR EPR 132-D3
LAKESHORE DR LC 94-B3
LAKESHORE PKWY MTK 104-D3
LAKESHORE PL AH 79-C4
LAKESHORE RD MAY 68-E4
LAKESHORE TER EAG 149-B2
LAKESIDE AVE MPL 106-C2
LAKESIDE AVE PRL 161-A3
LAKESIDE AVE N BC 92-A2
LAKESIDE AVE N CRY 91-E2
LAKESIDE CIR BUF 59-A1
LAKESIDE CIR EAG 149-D2
LAKESIDE CIR MTA 116-C2
LAKESIDE CIR N CHM 63-C2
LAKESIDE CT N CHM 63-C2
LAKESIDE CT N LC 94-C3
LAKESIDE DR EAG 149-D2
LAKESIDE DR MTA 116-C2
LAKESIDE DR SWR 83-A4
LAKESIDE DR N BAY 97-B4
LAKESIDE DR S BAY 97-B4
LAKESIDE LN CGT 26-C2
LAKESIDE LN MOU 117-A1
LAKESIDE LN SMT 56-B4
LAKESIDE PL BC 92-A2
LAKESIDE RD NE FRI 79-A2
LAKESIDE TRL CGT 26-C2
LAKESIDE TRL N CHM 63-C2
LAKETOWN RD LTT 130-C3,144-C1
LAKEVIEW AVE DPH 118-A2
LAKEVIEW AVE LOL 103-D2
LAKEVIEW AVE MH 135-D1
LAKEVIEW AVE ORO 103-D4
LAKEVIEW AVE RCH 120-B4,134-B1
LAKEVIEW AVE RVL 93-E3
LAKEVIEW AVE STP 107-E2,108-A2
LAKEVIEW AVE TKB 117-D2
LAKEVIEW AVE WBL 81-A4
LAKEVIEW AVE WBT 80-E2
LAKEVIEW AVE N BC 92-A2
LAKEVIEW AVE N ROB 92-A3
LAKEVIEW AVE NE EB 37-C1
LAKEVIEW AVE S MPL 106-B3
LAKEVIEW CIR BLO 133-D3
LAKEVIEW CIR BUF 58-E3
LAKEVIEW CIR COR 75-C4
LAKEVIEW CIR LTT 131-A4
LAKEVIEW CIR LVT 160-B2
LAKEVIEW CIR PRL 161-B3
LAKEVIEW CRV EAG 135-C4
LAKEVIEW CT AH 93-C1
LAKEVIEW CT CHM 63-C2
LAKEVIEW CT LVL 162-B4
LAKEVIEW CT WBT 80-E2
LAKEVIEW DR APV 149-D4
LAKEVIEW DR BKR 3-E4
LAKEVIEW DR BUR 148-D4
LAKEVIEW DR CHN 131-D3
LAKEVIEW DR EDI 119-E3,120-A3
LAKEVIEW DR LL 65-E3
LAKEVIEW DR MTA 116-E3
LAKEVIEW DR SHK 160-C1
LAKEVIEW DR SLT 174-D1
LAKEVIEW DR SVW 79-E3
LAKEVIEW DR WAV 85-E1
LAKEVIEW DR S BLO 133-D3
LAKEVIEW DR W MTK 105-B3
LAKEVIEW LN LTT 131-A4
LAKEVIEW LN MTK 105-B3
LAKEVIEW LN NE SLK 78-E2,79-A2
LAKEVIEW LN S WAY 104-B3
LAKEVIEW PKWY BUF 59-A1
LAKEVIEW PL MTK 119-A1
LAKEVIEW RD BLO 133-D3
LAKEVIEW RD CHC 12-B4,26-B1
LAKEVIEW RD MED 90-B4
LAKEVIEW RD E CHN 132-B3
LAKEVIEW TER ORO 103-E1
LAKEVIEW TRL EAG 135-C4
LAKEVIEW TRL HUT 111-D1
LAKEVIEW POINT DR NB 93-C2
LAKEVIEW POINT DR NE EB 37-C2
LAKEVIEW TERRACE BLVD WAC 129-D2
LAKEVILLE BLVD LVL 177-B4
LAKEWAY CT CHN 117-E4
LAKEWAY DR CHN 117-E4,131-E1
LAKEWAY LN CHN 117-E4
LAKEWAY TER SWD 118-A2
LAKEWOOD AVE WBL 81-B4,95-B1
LAKEWOOD CIR LTT 130-C4
LAKEWOOD CT MPW 123-B2
LAKEWOOD DR MPW 109-B2
LAKEWOOD DR N MPW 95-B3,109-B1
LAKEWOOD DR NE SLK 78-E1
LAKEWOOD DR S MPW 123-B2
LAKEWOOD LN BWV 95-C1
LAKEWOOD LN MOU 116-E1
LAKEWOOD HILLS RD N EAG 150-A2
LAKEWOOD HILLS RD S EAG 150-A2
LAKOTA LN CHN 146-A1
LAMAR AVE CHC 26-B2
LAMAR AVE N NST 54-B3
LAMAR AVE S CG 138-B4
LAMBERT AVE ALB 46-E2
LAMBERT AVE MV 79-B2
LAMBERT AVE SM 60-E1
LAMBERT AVE NE ALB 46-E2
LAMBERT AVE NE SM 60-E1
LAMBERT CIR NE SM 60-E1
LAMBERT CT NE SM 46-E4
LAMBERT CREEK LN VH 94-C1
LAMBERTON RD MOU 117-A2
LAMETTI CIR AH 93-D2
LAMETTI LN AH 93-D2
LAMETTI LN SVW 80-A1
LAMONT AVE NE ALB 46-E2
LAMONT AVE NE HAN 60-E2
LAMOTTE CIR LL 66-D3
LAMOTTE DR CV 66-D2
LAMOTTE DR LL 66-D3
LAMPERT AVE N LE 110-B1
LAMPHERE DR NH 91-D4
LAMPLIGHT CIR WBY 123-D2
LAMPLIGHT CT WBY 123-D2
LAMPLIGHT DR WBY 123-D2
LAMPLIGHT DR S WBY 123-D2
LAMPLIGHTER LN CRY 91-E4
LAMPLIGHTER LN GV 91-E4,105-E1
LAMPLIGHTERS LN MTK 118-C2
LANARK RD MOU 117-A2
LANCASTER AVE SLP 105-C3
LANCASTER AVE NE SM 60-E1
LANCASTER BAY WBY 124-B2
LANCASTER CIR WBY 124-B2
LANCASTER CT EPR 132-E3
LANCASTER CT LVL 176-B1
LANCASTER LN EAG 149-C2
LANCASTER LN WBY 124-B2
LANCASTER LN N MG 63-C4,77-C4
LANCASTER LN N PLY 91-C3,105-C1
LANCASTER ST MTK 105-C3
LANCELOT CT MTK 118-C2
LANCELOT DR MTK 118-C2
LANCER CIR SLT 174-E2
LANDAU CRV BLO 147-D1
LANDAU DR BLO 147-D1
LANDAU DR WBY 109-D4,123-D1
LANDAU LN NE PRL 161-A2
LANDER AVE NE ALB 47-A2
LANDER AVE NE SM 60-E1,61-A2
LANDER CT NW ER 19-C2
LANDER PL NW ER 19-C3
LANDER ST NW ER 19-C4,33-C1
LANDING CIR HUT 112-A2
LANDING RD EPR 147-B1
LANDINGS CT CHN 117-C4
LANDINGS DR CHN 117-C4
LANDMARK CIR MV 79-B2
LANDMARK CT LVL 162-B4,176-B1
LANDMARK DR ORO 103-B3
LANDMARK TRL N HOP 119-B3
LANDMARK TRL S HOP 119-B3
LANDON AVE WBY 123-E3
LANE CT N BP 64-A4
LANE PL STP 108-D2
LANE ST SSP 122-D3
LANESBORO CT LVL 176-B1
LANESBURGH DR LAT 202-A4
LANEWOOD CIR EPR 133-B3
LANEWOOD CT MG 76-D1
LANEWOOD LN N MG 76-D1
LANEWOOD LN N PLY 90-D4,104-D2
LANGDON LN MOU 116-E1
LANGDON PL EPR 132-E3
LANGER AVE DBT 182-E2
LANGER CIR LL 66-E4
LANGER CIR WSP 122-B3
LANGER LN LL 66-E4,67-A4
LANGEWOOD DR MTA 102-E4
LANGFORD AVE CLT 188-C3,202-C2
LANGFORD AVE SLT 160-C4,174-C3
LANGFORD BLVD PRL 160-E4
LANGFORD BLVD SLT 174-D1
LANGFORD CIR BUR 148-E2,149-A2
LANGFORD CT EDI 119-C4
LANGFORD DR EDI 119-C4
LANGFORD PARK STP 107-C2
LANGFORD TRL CLT 188-C4
LANGFORD WAY SLT 174-C3
LANGLEY AVE LVL 162-B4
LANGLEY AVE SFT 158-A4
LANGLEY CT EPR 132-E3
LANGLY AVE N NST 54-B2
LANGLY AVE S CG 138-C3
LANGLY CT N LE 110-B1
LANGLY CT N NST 54-B3
LANGSTON CIR NE SM 60-E1
LANGSTON CT NE SM 60-E1
LANGSTON LN NE SM 60-E1,61-A1
LANHAM LN EDI 133-D1
LANNON AVE NE ALB 47-A2
LANNON AVE NE OTS 47-A1
LANNON CIR NE ALB 47-A2
LANNON CT BUR 148-E2
LANO LN CAR 145-B3
LANO ST CHS 131-B4,145-B1
LANSFORD LN MH 122-A4
LANSING AVE SM 47-A4
LANSING AVE N GRA 82-B2
LANSING AVE N LE 110-C2
LANSING AVE NE ALB 47-A3
LANSING CIR NE ALB 47-A2
LANTANA LN EDI 133-E1
LANTERN CIR LL 66-B3
LANTERN CT EAG 150-A1
LANTERN LN EAG 150-B1
LANTERN LN LL 66-B3
LANTIRIK LN LLD 111-C2
LAPORT DR MV 79-B1
LARABEE AVE NE SM 47-A4
LARABEE CIR NE ALB 47-A2
LARADA LN EDI 119-C3
LARAMIE LN BPT 199-E1
LARAMIE TRL MTK 118-C2
LARAMIE TRL N BP 78-B3
LARC INDUSTRIAL BLVD BUR 148-E2
LARCH CIR NW CR 64-C1
LARCH LN N DAY 49-A4
LARCH LN N MG 77-A1,91-A1
LARCH LN N PLY 91-A2,105-A1
LARCH PL N PLY 91-A3
LARCH ST FAR 177-E4,178-A4
LARCH ST STP 108-A3
LARCH ST NW AND 50-C1
LARCH ST NW ATT 8-C2
LARCH ST NW CR 50-C4,64-C1
LARCHMORE AVE MTK 118-C1
LARCHWOOD CIR MTK 118-C1
LARCHWOOD DR MTK 118-C1
LAREDO AVE BEL 186-A2
LAREDO AVE BPT 186-A1
LAREDO AVE LVL 176-B3
LAREDO CT COR 76-B2
LAREDO DR CHN 132-A2
LAREDO LN CHN 132-A2
LAREDO PATH LVL 176-B3
LAREDO ST BEL 186-A2
LARGE AVE NE ALB 47-A2
LARGE CT OTS 33-A3
LARK AVE MPW 94-E4,95-A4
LARK AVE E MPW 94-C4
LARK CIR ML 43-D2
LARK DR ML 43-D3
LARK ST LTT 131-A3
LARKIN CIR MTK 104-E3
LARKIN DR MTK 104-E3,105-A3
LARKIN RD COR 75-E3,76-A3
LARKSPUR AVE N NST 54-B2
LARKSPUR CT SHK 146-B3
LARKSPUR CT WBY 124-B1
LARKSPUR DR WBY 124-B1
LARKSPUR LN EDI 133-E1
LARKSPUR LN EPR 133-B3
LARKSPUR LN NO 80-B3
LARKSPUR LN WAC 129-D3
LARKSPUR LN N LE 96-C3
LARKSPUR GLADE MG 76-B1
LARPENTEUR
AVE E MPW 108-C1,109-B1
LARPENTEUR AVE W FH 107-C1
LARPENTEUR AVE W LAU 107-B1
LARPENTEUR AVE W RVL 107-E1,108-A1
LARPENTEUR AVE W STP 107-E1,108-A1
LARRY LN NEW 123-B4
LARRY HO DR STP 109-A4
LARSEN LN HUT 112-B2
LARSEN RD COR 75-B2
LARSER LN HUT 112-B2
LARSON CT SVW 79-E3
LARSON LN RW 182-C4
LARSON LN SVW 79-E3
LARSON RD SVW 79-E3
LASALLE AVE MPL 106-C3
LASALLE CIR NE ALB 47-A2
LASALLE ST STP 107-C3
LASER ST SOM 70-B4
LASSEN CT BUR 149-A3
LASSIE CIR HUT 112-A2
LASSIE LN HUT 112-A2
LASSO LN EAG 150-A2
LATHROP DR NFD 219-D3
LATTA ST WBT 80-E2
LAURA AVE EDI 119-E2
LAURA CT CHS 131-B4
LAURA CT MH 122-A3
LAURA LN MTK 119-A1
LAURA LN SM 47-A4
LAURA LN SVW 80-A3
LAURA ST MH 122-A3

LAURA ST PRE 167-B1
LAUREL AVE DAT 144-A3
LAUREL AVE GV 105-D3
LAUREL AVE HUD 111-D3
LAUREL AVE MPL 106-B3
LAUREL AVE SPP 137-C3
LAUREL AVE STP 107-D4,108-A4
LAUREL CT EAG 135-B4,149-B1
LAUREL CT NFD 219-D4
LAUREL DR DPH 118-C1
LAUREL DR EPR 133-C4
LAUREL RD EB 37-D1
LAUREL RD MHT 81-D4
LAUREL RD MTK 104-E3
LAUREL ST DWD 81-C3
LAUREL ST E SWR 97-A1
LAUREL ST W SWR 96-E1,97-A1
LAURENE AVE LL 65-E4,79-E1
LAURIE CT SWR 96-D1
LAURIE CT E MPW 94-C4
LAURIE LN DAT 144-D3
LAURIE LN HUT 98-C4
LAURIE LN SWR 96-D1
LAURIE RD MPW 94-E4,95-A4
LAURIE RD NSP 95-A4
LAURIE RD E MPW 94-C4
LAURIE RD W RVL 93-E4
LAVALLE CT WBT 80-E2
LAVALLE DR CV 66-D2
LAVERNE AVE N LE 96-B4,110-C1
LAVERNE AVE S CG 138-C3
LAVERNE CT N LE 110-C1
LAVON LN BUR 162-D2
LAVONNE ST HAT 201-C2
LAWN AVE GRA 81-D4
LAWN TER GV 105-E2
LAWN VIEW DR WBY 110-A4
LAWNDALE LN N DAY 48-C3,62-C3
LAWNDALE LN N MG 62-C4,76-C3
LAWNDALE LN N PLY 90-C3
LAWNVIEW AVE SVW 79-E1
LAWRENCE AVE EAG 135-E2,136-A2
LAWRENCE PKWY BUF 58-D2
LAWRENCE RD BC 92-A1
LAWRENCE ST PRE 167-B1
LAWRENCE ST RF 140-D1
LAWRENCE WAY DT 194-D2
LAWRENCE CREEK RD FRT 13-E4,14-A4
LAWSON AVE E STP 108-C3
LAWSON AVE W STP 108-A3
LAWSON LN EPR 133-B4
LAWTON AVE S CG 138-C3
LAWTON LN NO 80-A3
LAWTON ST STP 122-A1
LAWTONKA DR SWD 117-D3
LAYMAN AVE MPL 106-E4
LAYMAN LN BLO 134-D4
LAYTON AVE N LE 96-C4,110-C3
LAYTON AVE N NST 54-B2
LAYTON AVE S CG 152-C3
LAYTON CT LVL 176-B1
LAYTON CT N LE 110-C1
LAYTON CT N NST 54-B3
LAYTON PATH LVL 176-B1
LE SUEUR AVE ERT 202-B4,216-B3
LE SUEUR AVE WHT 202-B4
LEA CT LL 65-E2
LEA RD BLO 133-D2
LEA ST HAS 166-D1
LEAD ST BUR 162-D2
LEAF ST ORO 103-C3
LEAF TRL WHT 202-B4,216-C1
LEAFTOP CIR EPR 133-C4
LEAH CT N CGT 26-B2
LEAH LN N CGT 26-B2
LEANDER CIR EPR 118-B4
LEANDER LN NE CH 92-E2,93-A2
LEANN DR WBY 123-D2
LEAPING DEER DR EPR 133-B2
LEARNING LN RW 196-E4
LEARNING CENTER RD HOP 119-C2
LEARNING CENTER RD PLY 105-B2
LEAVITT WOODS LN SHK 160-C1
LEBER LN GV 106-A2
LECUYER CIR SWR 82-D4
LECUYER CT SWR 82-D4
LECUYER DR SWR 82-D4,96-D1
LEDUC AVE MT 180-D2
LEDUC DR HAS 166-E2
LEE AVE FH 107-D2
LEE AVE N BC 78-A4,92-A1
LEE AVE N BP 78-A3
LEE AVE N CRY 92-A4
LEE AVE N GV 92-A4,106-A1
LEE AVE N ROB 92-A3
LEE CIR SWD 117-C3
LEE DR EPR 133-B4,147-C1
LEE RD MTA 117-A3
LEE ST BEC 2-E4
LEE ST BL 18-A4
LEE ST FL 39-B4
LEE ST GRF 74-D3
LEE ST N MPW 108-C1
LEE ST NW OG 22-C4,36-C1
LEE WAY MTK 118-D3
LEE VALLEY CIR EDI 133-D1
LEE VALLEY RD EDI 133-D1
LEEANN AVE DT 194-D2
LEECH ST STP 122-B1
LEEDER AVE S CG 152-C3
LEEDS PL WIL 95-D2
LEEMANS CT MTK 118-C1
LEEMANS DR MTK 118-C1
LEESBOROUGH AVE EPR 118-E4,132-E1
LEESON LN RW 210-C1
LEESON LN VAT 210-C1
LEEWARD AVE N GRA 96-C1
LEEWARD AVE N LE 110-C3
LEEWARD AVE S CG 152-C3
LEEWARD CIR EPR 133-B3
LEEWARD CT S CG 152-C3
LEEWARD TRL WBY 110-B4
LEEWARD WAY N LC 94-C3
LEGEND BLVD SWR 96-D2
LEGEND DR GV 106-A1
LEGEND LN GV 106-A1
LEGION AVE N LE 110-C2
LEGION LN N LE 110-C2
LEGION ST S SHK 146-C3
LEGION LN CIR N LE 110-C2
LEGION LN CT N LE 110-C2
LEHIGH AVE CGT 12-C4
LEHIGH AVE S CG 152-C3
LEHIGH CT CGT 12-C4
LEHIGH RD S CG 138-B4,152-C1
LEHMAN LN BLA 65-B1
LEHNHERT LN BKT 199-A2
LEIBEL ST WBT 81-B1
LEIGHTON DR BL 17-E3,18-A3
LEILANI LN CHC 26-B1
LEISURE CT BUR 148-C4
LEISURE LN BUR 148-C4
LEKSAND LN BUF 58-E1
LELAND RD MPW 94-D4
LEMAY LAKE DR MH 135-D1
LEMAY LAKE RD MH 135-D1
LEMCROW DR RFD 74-B3
LEMIRE CIR WBL 81-A3
LEMIRE LN WBL 81-A3
LEMIRE ST SOM 70-C4
LEMLEY CIR PRL 161-B3
LEMON ST N NOH 111-D1
LEMOR LN SJT 98-C2
LENERTZ RD HUT 112-B3
LENNELL DR MTK 118-E2
LENNIS AVE LTT 130-A4
LENNOX AVE N GRA 82-C2
LENORE LN EAG 149-C2
LENOX AVE STP 123-A2
LENOX CIR EPR 132-C3
LENT TRL N LET 11-D1
LEO CT EAG 149-E2
LEON ST SCT 173-A3
LEONA DR NB 79-A3
LEONA RD EPR 133-B2
LEONARD AVE LL 65-E2
LEONARD CT STP 123-B3
LEONE AVE STP 108-E4,109-A4
LEROY AVE HAS 166-D3
LEROY AVE MT 180-D2
LEROY AVE WHT 216-C2
LEROY CT RF 140-D1
LEROY LN RF 140-D1
LEROY ST DPH 118-C1
LEROY ST MTK 118-C1
LESLEE CRV CHN 117-B4,131-B1
LESLEE LN EDI 119-D3
LESLEY LN EPR 132-D1
LESLIE RD MOU 117-A2
LESTER AVE HAS 166-D3
LESTER PT WAC 129-C3
LETENDRE ST EAG 135-C3
LEVEE AVE ANO 49-C4
LEVEE DR E SHK 146-B2
LEVEE DR W SHK 146-B2
LEVEE RD STP 122-C1
LEVEE ST DAY 48-B1
LEVER CT NE BLA 65-D1
LEVER ST HL 37-D2
LEVER ST NE ATT 9-D1
LEVER ST NE BLA 51-D4,65-D3
LEVER ST NE EB 23-D4
LEVER ST NE HL 51-D1
LEWELLYN ST OSC 28-A4
LEWIS AVE E WIN 99-B3
LEWIS AVE NW WAT 101-B3
LEWIS AVE SW WAT 101-A3
LEWIS AVE W WIN 99-B3
LEWIS CT BUR 149-A2
LEWIS RD GV 105-D2
LEWIS ST RF 140-E1
LEWIS ST SSP 122-D2
LEWIS ST N SHK 146-B2
LEWIS ST S SHK 146-B2
LEWIS RIDGE PKWY EDI 133-D1
LEWISTON BLVD HMT 179-D4,193-C2
LEWISTON BLVD MT 180-B2
LEWISTON BLVD VET 179-E4,180-A3
LEXIE CT EAG 150-A1
LEXINGTON AVE AH 79-E3,93-E1
LEXINGTON AVE BL 18-A4
LEXINGTON AVE MH 121-E4,135-E1
LEXINGTON AVE MTK 118-D2
LEXINGTON AVE N AH 93-E2
LEXINGTON AVE N NP 201-E2
LEXINGTON AVE N RVL 93-E3,107-E1
LEXINGTON AVE N SVW 79-D1
LEXINGTON AVE NE BLA 51-D4,65-D2
LEXINGTON AVE NE COT 24-A4,37-E1
LEXINGTON AVE NE EB 37-E2
LEXINGTON AVE NE HL 37-D3,51-D2
LEXINGTON AVE NE LEX 65-D4
LEXINGTON AVE S EAG 135-E3,149-E1
LEXINGTON AVE S NP 201-E2
LEXINGTON CIR MTK 118-D2
LEXINGTON CT PRL 161-B4
LEXINGTON DR EPR 133-B2
LEXINGTON LN CHS 145-C2
LEXINGTON PKWY N STP 107-E3,121-E1
LEXINGTON PKWY S STP 121-E2
LEXINGTON ST EDI 119-E3,120-A3
LEXINGTON WAY EAG 149-E1
LEXINGTON POINTE PKWY EAG 149-E2,150-A2
LEYLAND ALC WBY 123-E2
LEYLAND BAY WBY 123-E2
LEYLAND CIR WBY 124-A2
LEYLAND CT WBY 124-A2
LEYLAND CV WBY 124-A2
LEYLAND DRAW WBY 124-A2
LEYLAND ECHO WBY 124-A2
LEYLAND PL WBY 124-A3
LEYLAND TRL WBY 123-E2,124-A2
LEYLAND VW WBY 124-A3
LEYTE ST NE BLA 65-C4,79-C1
LEYTE ST NE EB 23-C4,37-C2
LEYTE ST NE HL 37-C3,51-C2
LIA CT NFD 219-E4
LIA DR NFD 219-E4
LIBBY LN VH 94-C2
LIBERTY AVE SWR 96-C2
LIBERTY CT CHS 145-C2
LIBERTY CT NFD 219-E4
LIBERTY LN BEC 2-E4,3-A4
LIBERTY LN CHC 12-B4
LIBERTY LN JOR 173-C2
LIBERTY LN LEX 65-C4
LIBERTY LN N NP 201-E2
LIBERTY PKWY SWR 96-C1
LIBERTY PL SSP 122-D4
LIBERTY ST HUD 111-D3
LIBERTY ST N NYA 142-B4
LIBERTY ST NE FRI 78-C2
LIBERTY ST S NYA 142-B4
LIBERTY BEACH CT LVL 162-B4
LIBERTY HEIGHTS DR CHS 145-C2
LIBRARY LN SLP 105-D4,119-D1
LIGGETT ST N FH 107-C2
LIGHTNER PL STP 108-B3
LILA LN SLT 175-A1
LILAC CIR BUF 58-E1
LILAC CIR HAS 166-C2
LILAC CIR VIC 131-A2
LILAC CT SHK 146-C3
LILAC CT WAC 129-D3
LILAC DR N BC 78-C4,92-A2
LILAC DR N CRY 91-E4
LILAC DR N GV 91-E4,105-E2
LILAC DR N ROB 91-E3,92-A2
LILAC DR S SLP 105-E3
LILAC LN MH 121-E3
LILAC LN MTK 118-C1
LILAC LN ORO 103-D3
LILAC LN SVW 80-A4
LILAC LN SWD 117-E4,118-A4
LILAC LN VIC 131-A1
LILAC LN WBL 81-A4
LILAC LN N LE 96-C4
LILAC PL N LE 96-C3
LILAC RD MH 121-E4
LILAC RD SPR 117-B1
LILAC ST LL 65-E1,66-A1
LILAC WAY N LE 96-C3
LILAC HOLLOW LN LAT 216-B2
LILAH LN TKB 117-C3
LILLEHEI AVE DT 180-D4,194-D1
LILLEHEI AVE MT 166-D4,180-D3
LILLEHEI PLZ LC 94-B4
LILLIAN DR HUD 111-E4
LILLIAN LN EPR 132-C1
LILLIAN ST SCT 173-A3
LILLY AVE NW OG 22-A3
LILY AVE N LE 96-C3
LILY CT ROG 47-D4
LILY ST NW AND 49-E3
LILY ST NW CR 49-E4,63-E1
LILY ST NW STT 7-E1
LILY POND CIR LOR 89-A2
LILY POND LN VH 80-B4,94-C1
LILY POND RD NO 80-C3
LILYDALE RD LIL 121-E3,122-A2
LILYPOND LN COR 61-D4,75-D1
LILYWOOD LN LIL 121-E3
LIMA ST BLA 65-A4
LIME RD SW PRL 160-E4
LIME ST CW 1-B2
LIME ST N CAR 145-B4
LIME TREE CT MTK 118-B4
LIMERICK CIR E EDI 119-D4
LIMERICK CIR W EDI 119-D4
LIMERICK DR EDI 119-E4,133-E1
LIMERICK LN EDI 119-D4,133-D1
LIMERICK LN MTK 118-D2
LIMERICK LN SHK 146-C3
LIMESTONE DR EAG 149-B2
LIMESTONE DR SHK 146-C3
LIMESTONE RD CF 222-B1
LIMONITE LN EAG 149-B1
LIMONITE ST NW RAM 48-E2
LINCH AVE LVL 162-B3
LINCH PATH LVL 162-B4
LINCOLN AVE DEL 87-D3
LINCOLN AVE JOR 173-B3
LINCOLN AVE LND 12-C3
LINCOLN AVE MPL 106-C3
LINCOLN AVE SPP 137-C3
LINCOLN AVE STP 121-E1,122-A1
LINCOLN AVE WBL 81-A4
LINCOLN AVE N LP 113-B4
LINCOLN AVE N NG 114-A4
LINCOLN AVE N NP 201-E2
LINCOLN AVE S NP 201-E2
LINCOLN CIR EDI 119-C3
LINCOLN CIR NW ER 33-E1
LINCOLN CT SPP 137-C4
LINCOLN CT NE ATT 8-E2
LINCOLN CT NE BLA 64-E2
LINCOLN CT NE EB 8-E3
LINCOLN DR EB 37-D1
LINCOLN DR EDI 119-C3
LINCOLN DR ORO 103-D2
LINCOLN DR RVL 93-D3
LINCOLN DR SM 46-E4
LINCOLN DR NE SM 46-E4
LINCOLN DR SE SM 46-E4
LINCOLN LN EPR 132-D2
LINCOLN LN HUD 111-D3
LINCOLN LN NFD 219-D3
LINCOLN PKWY NFD 219-D3
LINCOLN PL ANO 49-D4
LINCOLN PL JOR 173-B2
LINCOLN RD LND 12-C3
LINCOLN RD N CGT 12-C3
LINCOLN ST ANO 49-D4
LINCOLN ST BL 18-A4
LINCOLN ST CHC 26-B1
LINCOLN ST HAS 166-C1
LINCOLN ST HMP 193-B2
LINCOLN ST MSC 55-B4
LINCOLN ST NYA 142-C3
LINCOLN ST RF 140-E1
LINCOLN ST SCF 14-D3
LINCOLN ST N NFD 219-D3
LINCOLN ST NE BLA 64-E4,78-E1
LINCOLN ST NE CH 92-E3
LINCOLN ST NE EB 8-E3
LINCOLN ST NE FRI 92-E1
LINCOLN ST NE HL 36-E4,50-E2
LINCOLN ST NE MPL 92-E4,106-E1
LINCOLN ST NW ER 20-A4,34-B1
LINCOLN ST S NFD 219-D4
LINCOLN TER NE CH 92-E1
LINCOLNTOWN AVE MHT 95-C2
LINDA AVE LL 65-E4,66-A4
LINDA CIR LL 66-A4
LINDA CT LL 66-A4
LINDA LN GRF 88-E1
LINDA LN LL 66-A4
LINDA LN LTT 130-D4
LINDA LN N GRF 60-E4
LINDAWOOD LN LOL 104-A2
LINDBERG CT NFD 219-E4
LINDBERGH DR MTK 105-B4
LINDE LN EAG 136-A2
LINDE LN MTK 119-A1
LINDEKE AVE CNC 12-E3
LINDEN AVE DEL 87-D3
LINDEN AVE LND 12-C4
LINDEN AVE MPL 106-C2
LINDEN AVE ORO 103-B3
LINDEN AVE WBL 94-E1
LINDEN AVE E WIN 99-B3
LINDEN AVE N BP 64-A4,78-A1
LINDEN AVE N CGT 26-C1
LINDEN AVE N ML 43-D2
LINDEN AVE NE MGY 215-D4
LINDEN AVE S ML 43-D2
LINDEN AVE W WIN 99-B3
LINDEN CIR APV 162-E2
LINDEN CIR CHN 117-B4
LINDEN CIR MPW 123-B2
LINDEN CIR WAC 129-D4
LINDEN CIR NW PRL 160-E3
LINDEN CT EAG 136-A4
LINDEN CT N CGT 26-C1
LINDEN CV WBL 94-E1
LINDEN DR APV 162-E2
LINDEN DR EPR 133-C4
LINDEN DR HSN 47-E3,62-B2
LINDEN DR MTK 118-C1
LINDEN DR NB 93-A1
LINDEN LN EAG 136-A4
LINDEN LN LFL 109-C4
LINDEN LN LL 66-A4
LINDEN LN MOU 116-D1
LINDEN LN MPW 94-D3
LINDEN LN ORO 103-B4
LINDEN PL WBL 94-E2
LINDEN PL NE EB 36-E2
LINDEN RD DPH 118-A2
LINDEN RD WBY 123-C1
LINDEN ST EXC 117-E3
LINDEN ST FAR 177-E4
LINDEN ST MHT 81-D3
LINDEN ST PRE 153-B4,167-B1
LINDEN ST RF 140-E1
LINDEN ST RFD 74-B3
LINDEN ST SSP 137-A2
LINDEN ST STP 108-B3
LINDEN ST TF 14-C2
LINDEN ST WBL 94-E1,95-A1
LINDEN ST E SWR 97-A1
LINDEN ST N BEL 186-A1
LINDEN ST N NFD 219-D3
LINDEN ST S BEL 186-A1
LINDEN ST S NFD 219-D4
LINDEN ST W SWR 96-E1,97-A1
LINDEN TRL LE 96-C3
LINDEN TRL N LE 96-C3
LINDEN WAY ROG 61-E2
LINDEN HILLS BLVD MPL 120-B2
LINDER CT STP 108-E4
LINDGREN LN IND 88-E3
LINDIG AVE FH 107-C2
LINDIG ST FH 107-C1
LINDO TRL N CGT 12-B1
LINDSAY RD TRT 125-D3
LINDSAY ST GV 105-E2
LINDSEY LN BEL 186-A2
LINDSEY LN HOP 119-C2
LINDSTROM DR BLO 133-C4
LINDY AVE RVL 93-E4,107-E1
LINE AVE NW ER 33-E1
LINK DR JT 146-B4
LINK RD EDI 119-E3
LINN ST CW 1-B2
LINN ST MO 31-D1
LINNEA LN MTK 118-D2
LINNER CT MTK 104-D3
LINNER RD MTK 104-D3
LINNER RDG MTK 104-D3
LINNET CIR NW CR 64-B3
LINNET ST AND 50-B1
LINNET ST NW AND 36-B4,50-B2
LINNET ST NW CR 50-B4,64-B3
LINNET ST NW OG 8-B4,22-B2
LINSON CIR SWR 96-E2
LINWOOD AVE MPW 123-B2
LINWOOD AVE STP 121-E1,122-A1
LINWOOD AVE S EXC 117-E3
LINWOOD CIR DPH 118-A2
LINWOOD CT EPR 132-C3
LINWOOD CT MPW 123-B2
LINWOOD DR N LWT 24-A2
LINWOOD LN DPH 118-A2
LINWOOD RD DPH 118-A2
LINWOOD RD SWD 118-A2
LINWOOD FOREST CIR CHM 49-B4
LINWOOD FOREST DR CHM 49-B4
LIOBRIENT ST STP 108-C2
LION LN SVW 80-A4
LIONS CT LVL 162-B4
LIONS MEMORIAL DR SLK 78-E2
LIPAN ST NW AND 49-D2
LISA CT AH 79-C4
LISA LN AH 79-C4
LISBON AVE N LE 110-C1
LISBON AVE N MAY 54-C4
LISBON CT N LE 110-C1
LISMORE CIR EPR 132-C2
LIST PL MPL 106-A4
LISTA PT EAG 149-C3
LITCHFIELD ST STP 108-B3
LITHIUM DR NW RAM 35-B4
LITHIUM ST NW BT 21-B2,35-B1
LITTLE AVE LTT 130-A4,144-A1
LITTLE AVE S BLO 148-A1
LITTLE CIR BLO 134-A4,148-A1
LITTLE RD BLO 134-A4,148-A1
LITTLE ST EDI 120-A2
LITTLE BAY RD RVL 94-A3
LITTLE BLUESTEM CIR N LE 96-C4
LITTLE BLUESTEM LN N LE 96-C4
LITTLE BLUESTEM TRL N LE 96-C4
LITTLE CANADA RD E LC 94-C3
LITTLE CANADA RD W LC 94-B3
LITTLE CIR DR W LC 94-B3
LITTLE CROW DR PRL 160-E1
LITTLE CROW DR SSP 122-D3
LITTLE FOX LN GL 94-D1
LITTLE JOHN DR CP 65-D4,79-D1
LITTLE LAKE RD N CGT 13-A2
LITTLE LINDEN CRV WBL 94-E1
LITTLE ORCHARD WAY MED 103-C3
LIV LN EPR 132-C1
LIVE OAK DR MTK 105-B3
LIVERY CT NMT 190-B1
LIVERY LN NMT 190-B1
LIVING STONE CT NFD 219-D3
LIVINGSTON AVE ORO 117-C1
LIVINGSTON AVE STP 122-C2
LIVINGSTON AVE WSP 122-C4
LIVINGSTON CT CHS 145-D1
LIVINGSTON CT ORO 117-B1
LIVINGSTON DR EAG 150-A2
LIVINGSTON LN EPR 132-D3
LIVINGSTONE RD HUD 111-D3
LLAMA ST NW RAM 34-D4,48-D2
LLAMA ST NW STT 6-D1
LLOYDS DR MTK 118-D2
LLOYDS LN MTK 118-D2
LOCH LOMOND BLVD BP 77-E2,78-A1
LOCH LOMOND CT BP 77-E2,78-A1
LOCH LOMOND LN BP 78-A1
LOCH MOOR DR EDI 133-D1
LOCHANBURN RD EPR 118-B4,132-B1
LOCHAVEN ALC WBY 123-E2,124-A2
LOCHAVEN PL WBY 124-A2
LOCHAVEN RD SFT 159-A3
LOCHLOY DR EDI 119-D3
LOCHMERE TER EDI 133-D2
LOCK BLVD NIT 152-B4

LOCK AND DAM RD HAS 152-C4,166-D1
LOCKE AVE CNC 12-E3
LOCKE LAKE RD NE FRI 78-D3
LOCKHAVEN DR WBY 124-A2
LOCKRIDGE AVE N GRA 82-C1
LOCKRIDGE AVE N MAY 68-C4
LOCKRIDGE AVE S CG 152-C3
LOCKRIDGE CT N GRA 82-C2
LOCKRIDGE TRL CGT 12-B3
LOCKSLIE TRL SAV 161-D2
LOCKSLIE WAY SAV 161-D2
LOCKWOOD DR MH 136-A2
LOCKWOOD DR NFD 219-D3
LOCUST CT NE ALB 47-A3
LOCUST DR CHS 145-C3
LOCUST LN TF 14-C2
LOCUST ST FAR 177-E4,178-A4
LOCUST ST HAS 166-E1
LOCUST ST HEN 198-C3
LOCUST ST HUD 111-C2
LOCUST ST MHT 81-D4
LOCUST ST MO 31-D1
LOCUST ST MPL 106-E3
LOCUST ST PRE 167-B1
LOCUST ST SA 93-A4
LOCUST ST E BEL 186-A1
LOCUST ST E RF 140-E2
LOCUST ST E SWR 97-A1
LOCUST ST W RF 140-D2
LOCUST ST W SWR 97-A2
LODESTONE CIR EAG 149-C1
LODESTONE LN EAG 135-C4,149-C1
LODGE CIR BUR 148-B3
LODGE DR JOR 173-A2
LODGE DR SLW 173-A2
LODGE LN GRW 118-A2
LODGEPOLE CT EAG 149-D2
LODGEPOLE DR EAG 149-D2
LODGEPOLE PT CHN 131-D1
LOEB ST STP 108-A3
LOFTON AVE CGT 12-B4
LOFTON AVE CHC 12-B4,26-B1
LOFTON AVE N CGT 12-B3,26-B3
LOFTON AVE N GRA 82-C4
LOFTON AVE N NST 40-C3,54-C1
LOFTON AVE S CG 152-C3
LOFTON CT N NST 40-C2
LOFTON LN N CGT 12-B2
LOFTUS DR SAV 161-E1
LOGAN AVE NMT 190-C3,204-C2
LOGAN AVE WBT 81-B2
LOGAN AVE WSP 122-C3
LOGAN AVE E WSP 122-C3
LOGAN AVE N BC 78-B3,92-B1
LOGAN AVE N BP 78-B2
LOGAN AVE N MPL 92-B4,106-B2
LOGAN AVE S BLO 134-B3
LOGAN AVE S MPL 106-B3,120-B3
LOGAN AVE S RCH 120-B4,134-B1
LOGAN AVE W WSP 122-C3
LOGAN CT N BP 78-B3
LOGAN LN SSP 122-D3
LOGAN PKWY NE FRI 78-D2
LOGAN ST ANO 49-C3
LOGAN WAY NMT 190-B2
LOGANS DR EPR 118-C4
LOGARTO LN BUR 162-D3
LOGARTO LN LVL 162-D3
LOIS AVE PRL 161-D2
LOIS CT SVW 79-E2
LOIS DR CHS 145-D2
LOIS DR MV 79-B2
LOIS DR SVW 79-C2
LOIS LN EDI 133-D1
LOIS LN LL 52-B4,66-A1
LOIS LN PRL 160-E1
LOIS LN SVW 79-E2
LOMA LINDA AVE ORO 103-B4
LOMBARD AVE STP 121-E1
LOMBARDY DR NE HL 36-E3
LOMBARDY LN CRY 91-D1
LOMBARDY LN MTK 105-A2
LOMBARDY LN NH 91-D1
LOMBARDY LN WBL 81-A3
LOMOND AVE N CGT 26-C4
LOMOND TRL N MAY 54-C4
LONDIN CIR STP 123-B1
LONDIN CT MPW 123-B1
LONDIN LN MPW 123-B1
LONDIN LN STP 123-A1
LONDIN PL STP 123-B1
LONDON CT BUR 148-E1,149-A2
LONDON DR BUR 149-A2
LONDON LN EAG 149-D3
LONDON RD MH 122-A2
LONDON ST NE BLA 51-A3,65-A1
LONDON ST NE EB 9-A4,23-A1
LONDON ST NE HL 37-A2,51-A2
LONDONARY AVE MV 79-B3
LONDONDERRY CV SHK 160-B1
LONDONDERRY DR EDI 119-C3
LONDONDERRY DR MTK 119-C3
LONDONDERRY RD EDI 119-C3
LONE CEDAR LN CHN 131-B2
LONE EAGLE DR CHN 132-A1
LONE EAGLE TRL WBY 124-B2
LONE LAKE RDG MTK 119-B3
LONE OAK CIR EAG 135-E3
LONE OAK CT CRT 176-A1
LONE OAK DR EAG 136-A2
LONE OAK DR MTK 119-A2
LONE OAK DR RFD 74-A3
LONE OAK DR SAV 161-E2
LONE OAK LN EAG 135-D3
LONE OAK PKWY EAG 136-A2
LONE OAK PT EAG 136-A2
LONE OAK RD EAG 135-D3,136-A3
LONE OAK RD EPR 132-E2
LONE PINE CT SLT 161-B4,175-B1
LONESOME PINE TRL LL 66-A4
LONG AVE STP 107-B3
LONG AVE WBL 81-A3
LONG BRAKE CIR EDI 133-D2
LONG BRAKE TRL EDI 133-D2
LONG LAKE BLVD ORO 103-E1
LONG LAKE CT NB 79-B3
LONG LAKE CT SVW 80-A2
LONG LAKE DR SWR 96-D1
LONG LAKE RD BLA 79-A1
LONG LAKE RD MHT 95-C2
LONG LAKE RD MV 79-B2
LONG LAKE RD NB 79-B4,93-B1
LONG LAKE RD PS 95-D2
LONG LAKE RD RVL 93-C4
LONG LAKE RD E ORO 104-A2
LONG LAKE TRL S NO 80-B2
LONG MARSH LN NO 80-A2
LONG MEADOW CIR BLO 135-A2
LONG MEADOW PT EPR 132-B2
LONGACRES DR CHN 131-D1
LONGFELLOW AVE FS 120-E4,134-E1
LONGFELLOW AVE MPL 106-E4,120-E1
LONGFELLOW AVE RCH 120-E4,134-E1
LONGFELLOW AVE STP 123-A1
LONGFELLOW AVE S BLO 134-E3
LONGFELLOW DR NE EB 37-D1
LONGFELLOW RD MOU 116-E2
LONGFELLOW ST NE FRI 78-C2
LONGFORD RD MOU 117-A1
LONGVIEW CIR CHN 132-A1
LONGVIEW CIR ORO 103-D3
LONGVIEW DR BUR 148-E4
LONGVIEW DR MV 79-A3
LONGVIEW DR NB 79-B3
LONGVIEW DR NSP 95-B3
LONGVIEW LN NO 80-B2
LONGVIEW TER MPL 120-C3
LONGVIEW TRL TRT 125-C3
LONSDALE BLVD BWT 219-B3
LONSDALE BLVD LON 217-B2
LONSDALE BLVD NFD 219-D4
LONSDALE BLVD WHT 217-C2
LONSDALE BLVD WT 217-D2,218-C3
LONSDALE CIR MTK 105-C3
LOOKOUT CT EPR 132-B1
LOOKOUT PL NE CH 92-D2
LOOKOUT PL NW ER 33-D2
LOOKOUT RD DWD 81-C2
LOOKOUT ST SWR 96-E1
LOOKOUT TRL N OPH 97-A2
LOOKRIDGE CT WAC 129-C3
LOOMIS CT NFD 219-D3
LOON DR BLT 17-E2
LOON LN EAG 135-C3
LOOP RD N BUR 162-B3
LOOP RD S BUR 162-B3
LORALEE LN EPR 132-C1
LORANE AVE WBT 80-E2
LORD CT EPR 133-C4
LORDS CIR PRL 161-A2
LORDS ST PRL 161-A2
LOREN AVE N CGT 26-C2
LOREN DR MPL 120-D4
LOREN RD RVL 107-C1
LORENA LN EPR 132-C1
LORENCE RD MTK 118-E3
LORENCE WAY EPR 132-C1
LORENZ CT LON 217-A2
LORENZ ST LOR 89-B2
LORETTA LN MHT 95-C1
LORETTA LN MTK 118-E2
LORETTO ST LOR 89-B2
LORI AVE RW 196-D4
LORI LN WBY 123-E3
LORI RD PRL 161-C2
LORIEN ST MTK 105-A4
LORIENT ST STP 108-B2
LORINDA DR SVW 80-A3
LORING DR MTA 116-E3
LORING LN GV 105-E2,106-A2
LORING RD HOP 105-B4,119-B1
LORRAINE CT SVW 79-D1
LORRY LN MTK 105-B2
LOST HORIZON CIR PRL 161-C2
LOST HORSE RD MED 89-D1
LOST LAKE CT MHT 95-C1
LOST LAKE RD MHT 95-C2
LOST LAKE RD MOU 116-E1
LOST ROCK LN NO 80-B2
LOST ROCK LN TRT 125-E3
LOTHENBACH AVE WSP 122-C4
LOTUS DR MTA 116-D4
LOTUS LN BUR 148-B4
LOTUS TRL CHN 118-A4,132-A1
LOTUS VIEW DR EPR 132-B1
LOUIS AVE MTK 118-D3
LOUIS LN EAG 136-B3
LOUIS LN HAS 166-C2
LOUIS RD LVL 162-C4
LOUIS ST STP 108-B4
LOUIS ST E COL 143-E4
LOUIS ST W COL 143-E4
LOUIS ST W NM 189-E4
LOUISA AVE MV 79-B2
LOUISA ST HBG 156-A2
LOUISE AVE CNC 12-E3
LOUISE AVE STP 108-E4,109-A4
LOUISE LN HUT 112-E3
LOUISIANA AVE BLA 65-A4
LOUISIANA AVE SAV 147-D3,161-D1
LOUISIANA AVE N BP 77-D3,91-D1
LOUISIANA AVE N CHM 63-D2
LOUISIANA AVE N CRY 91-D2
LOUISIANA AVE N GV 105-D1
LOUISIANA AVE N NH 91-D3
LOUISIANA AVE S BLO 147-D1
LOUISIANA AVE S GV 105-D3
LOUISIANA AVE S SAV 147-D4,161-D2
LOUISIANA AVE S SLP 105-D4,119-D1
LOUISIANA CIR CHM 63-D2
LOUISIANA CIR SLP 119-D1
LOUISIANA CIR S BLO 147-D2
LOUISIANA CT WBT 80-E2
LOUISIANA CT E CHM 63-D3
LOUISIANA CT N BP 77-D3,91-D1
LOUISIANA CT S SLP 105-D4
LOUISIANA CT W CHM 63-D3
LOUISIANA LN N CHM 63-D3
LOUISIANA ST SAT 14-D2
LOUISIANA ST SCF 14-D2
LOUISIANA ST E SCF 14-C2
LOUISIANA ST N SCF 14-C2
LOURDES PL MPL 106-D2
LOUSIANA AVE N BP 77-D1
LOVE AVE MHT 81-D4
LOVELAND CIR MTK 104-E4
LOVELL AVE RVL 93-E4,94-A4
LOVELL LN N RVL 93-E4
LOVELL LN S RVL 93-E4
LOVELL RD BLA 65-C4
LOVELL RD LEX 65-D4
LOWELL AVE NW ER 33-D2
LOWELL CIR APV 162-E2
LOWELL CIR NW ER 19-D4
LOWELL DR APV 162-E2,163-A2
LOWELL RD CHM 63-C1
LOWELL ST DPH 118-C1
LOWELL ST MTK 118-C1
LOWELL ST NW ER 19-D4,33-D1
LOWER 12TH ST N OKD 109-C3
LOWER 56TH ST N OKD 95-C3
LOWER 67TH ST E IGH 136-E2
LOWER 87TH ST W IGH 136-B4
LOWER 94TH ST S CG 151-D1
LOWER 127TH ST W APV 149-B4
LOWER 129TH CT APV 149-A4
LOWER 131ST STREET CT APV 149-C4
LOWER 134TH ST W APV 163-C1
LOWER 134TH ST W SAV 148-A4
LOWER 138TH CT APV 163-A1
LOWER 138TH ST W RMT 164-A1
LOWER 139TH CT W APV 163-A1
LOWER 147TH ST N HUG 67-B2
LOWER 147TH ST W APV 163-A2
LOWER 147TH ST W RMT 163-E2,164-A2
LOWER 150TH ST W RMT 164-A2
LOWER 161ST ST W LVL 163-C3
LOWER 162ND ST W LVL 163-B3
LOWER 167TH ST E CRT 162-B4
LOWER 167TH ST W LVL 162-C4
LOWER 169TH ST W LVL 163-B4
LOWER 170TH CT W LVL 163-B4
LOWER 182ND ST W FAR 177-C1
LOWER 183RD ST W FAR 177-D1
LOWER 208TH ST W LVL 177-A3
LOWER 217TH AVE SMT 69-E1,70-A1
LOWER AFTON RD MPW 123-B1
LOWER AFTON RD STP 123-A1
LOWER COLONIAL DR MH 122-A3
LOWER ELKWOOD CT APV 163-D1
LOWER ENDICOTT WAY APV 163-D2
LOWER GUTHRIE CT APV 163-A2
LOWER HAMLET CT APV 149-A4
LOWER HERITAGE WAY FAR 191-E1
LOWER RIVER RD DBT 182-E3
LOWER SAINT DENNIS RD STP 121-D3
LOWRY AVE N MPL 92-C4
LOWRY AVE N ROB 92-A4
LOWRY AVE NE MPL 92-E4,93-A4
LOWRY AVE NE SA 93-A4
LOWRY TER GV 91-E4,92-A4
LOYOLA DR WBY 124-A2
LOYOLA ST NE LWT 10-D3
LUAN DR NE EB 23-B2
LUCE LINE RDG ORO 103-A2
LUCERNE BLVD CRT 175-E4,176-A4
LUCERNE TRL CRT 176-B4
LUCERNE TRL LVL 176-B3
LUCIA LN NE FRI 78-E3
LUCILE LN LE 95-E3
LUCILLE CT RF 140-D1
LUDLOW AVE STP 107-B2
LUDWIG AVE N CHM 63-C2
LUEDKE LN SLT 175-A1
LUEDKELA LN SLT 175-A1
LUELLA ST N STP 109-A2
LUELLA ST S STP 123-A1
LUIGI CIR S BLO 133-E3
LUISA CT CHS 131-C4
LUKEWOOD DR CHN 131-D2
LUMPHREY CT RF 140-D2
LUNAR LN EAG 136-A3
LUND AVE NE SLK 78-E1
LUND BLVD ANO 49-B3
LUND PT EAG 149-C3
LUND RD N EPR 118-D4
LUND RD S EPR 118-D4
LUND ST N NOH 97-D4
LUNDSTEAD RD DAT 158-D3
LUNDY LN TRT 112-B4
LUNSKI CT EPR 132-E3
LUNSKI LN EPR 132-E3
LUPINE CT NFD 219-B3
LUPINE CT SHK 146-B3
LUPINE DR HUD 111-E4
LUPINE DR NFD 219-D3
LUTHER PL STP 107-B2
LUTHER RD PRL 161-C3
LUTHER WAY EPR 132-D2
LUVERNE AVE MPL 120-D3
LYDIA AVE E MPW 94-D3
LYDIA AVE W MPW 95-B3
LYDIA AVE W NSP 95-B3
LYDIA AVE W RVL 93-D3
LYDIA CIR SWR 96-E2
LYDIA CT RVL 93-B3
LYDIA DR RVL 93-E3
LYDIA RD JOR 173-C2
LYDIA RD SCT 173-C2
LYDIARD AVE ORO 117-C2
LYDIARD CIR ORO 117-C1
LYLE CIR EDI 119-D3
LYMAN AVE ORO 103-E2,104-A2
LYMAN AVE N CGT 26-C2
LYMAN BLVD CHN 131-E3,132-A3
LYMAN BLVD CHS 131-C3
LYMAN CT CHN 132-A3
LYMAN CT GRW 118-A2
LYMAN LN MTK 104-D3
LYMAN LN N CGT 26-C3
LYMAN PL EXC 117-E3
LYN WAY HAS 166-C2
LYN CURVE AVE N MPL 106-C1
LYN PARK AVE N MPL 106-C1
LYN PARK CIR N MPL 106-C1
LYN PARK LN N MPL 106-C1
LYNCH DR ROG 47-E4
LYNCH RD N MAY 68-B3
LYNDALE AVE IND 102-B2
LYNDALE AVE NMT 190-C1
LYNDALE AVE N BC 92-C1
LYNDALE AVE N MPL 92-C3,106-C2
LYNDALE AVE N NP 201-E2
LYNDALE AVE S BLO 134-C3,148-C1
LYNDALE AVE S MPL 106-C3,120-C2
LYNDALE AVE S RCH 120-C4,134-C1
LYNDALE CIR BLO 134-C4
LYNDALE CIR BUR 148-C4
LYNDE DR NE FRI 78-E4
LYNMAR LN EDI 134-A1
LYNN AVE EDI 120-A2
LYNN AVE LES 212-D3
LYNN AVE SAV 148-A3,162-A1
LYNN AVE S SLP 106-A4,120-A1
LYNN CIR NOH 111-C1
LYNN CIR SAV 162-A1
LYNN CT SAV 162-A1
LYNN DR CRT 176-A3
LYNN DR NE EB 9-D3
LYNN ST PRE 153-B4
LYNN TER MTK 118-D3
LYNN WAY WBY 137-C1
LYNNHURST AVE E STP 107-C4
LYNNHURST AVE W STP 107-C4
LYNNVILLE DR SCT 173-C1
LYNNWOOD RD LTT 130-A4
LYNWOOD AVE NE OTS 61-A2
LYNWOOD BLVD MOU 116-E1,117-A1
LYNWOOD BLVD RCH 120-C4,134-C1
LYNWOOD CT NE OTS 61-A2
LYNWOOD TER MTK 118-C3
LYNX CT EAG 150-A2
LYNX RD WBT 80-E2
LYON ST STP 108-E4
LYONS AVE PRL 161-B4
LYONS ST NE LWT 11-A3,25-A3
LYONS ST NE OXT 10-E1
LYRA CT EAG 149-E2
LYRIC AVE ORO 117-C1
LYRIC LN NE FRI 78-D2
LYTHRUM WAY MTA 116-D2
LYTON PL STP 108-B3

M

M ST WBY 123-D1
MAAG ST LES 212-C4
MABEL CT CHS 145-D1
MAC ST NM 189-E4
MACALASTER DR SA 93-B2
MACALESTER ST STP 121-D2
MACARTHUR AVE WSP 122-C3
MACARTHUR ST WSP 122-C2
MACARTHUR ST E SSP 136-E1
MACARTHUR ST W SSP 136-E1
MACBETH CIR LVL 177-B3
MACBETH CIR WBY 123-C3
MACBETH CT WBY 123-C3
MACGOFFIN AVE STP 121-C3
MACHMEIR CT LND 26-D1
MACINTOSH RD EPR 132-C4
MACIVER AVE NE ALB 47-A2
MACIVER AVE NE OTS 33-A4,47-A1
MACIVER AVE NE SM 47-A3
MACKENZIE AVE NE ALB 47-A2
MACKENZIE ST NE COT 38-C2
MACKEY AVE EDI 119-E2
MACKEY AVE S SLP 119-E2
MACKUBIN CIR SVW 80-A4
MACKUBIN CT SVW 80-A3
MACKUBIN ST RVL 94-A3,108-A1
MACKUBIN ST STP 108-A3,122-A1
MACKUBIN ST SVW 80-A4,94-A1
MACLAREN PL EAG 150-A2
MACLYNN RD EXC 117-E3
MACON ST ER 33-C2
MACON ST NW ER 19-C2,33-C2
MADALYN PL ROB 92-A3
MADDAUS LN GV 106-A2
MADDOX LN EDI 119-E4
MADEIRA AVE MPL 106-B3
MADISON AVE N HOP 119-C1
MADISON AVE N LP 113-B4
MADISON AVE S EDI 119-C2
MADISON AVE W GV 105-D1
MADISON CIR N HOP 119-C1
MADISON CIR S HOP 119-C2
MADISON PL MPL 92-E3
MADISON PL NE CH 92-E3
MADISON ST ANO 49-D4
MADISON ST HAS 166-C1
MADISON ST OSC 28-A4
MADISON ST STP 121-D3
MADISON ST N NFD 219-D3
MADISON ST N SCF 14-C2
MADISON ST NE BLA 50-E4,64-E1
MADISON ST NE CH 92-E2
MADISON ST NE EB 22-D4
MADISON ST NE FRI 78-E3,92-E1
MADISON ST NE HL 36-D4,50-D2
MADISON ST NE MPL 92-E4,106-E1
MADISON ST NE SLK 78-D2
MADISON ST NW SF 8-C4
MADISON ST S NFD 219-D4
MADISON ST S SCF 14-C2
MADISON ST S SHK 146-A3
MADISON ST SE WAT 101-B4
MADISON ST SW WAT 101-A3
MADISON WAY NE EB 22-D3
MAGDA DR MG 77-B4,91-C1
MAGEE WAY PRE 167-B1
MAGENTA BAY EPR 132-B2
MAGER CT MH 122-A4
MAGNESIUM ST NW RAM 49-B2
MAGNESIUM ST NW SF 7-B3
MAGNETITE PT EAG 149-B1
MAGNOLIA AVE MPW 109-B2
MAGNOLIA AVE SPP 137-C3
MAGNOLIA AVE E STP 108-C2,109-A2
MAGNOLIA AVE W STP 108-B2
MAGNOLIA CIR NW CR 50-C4
MAGNOLIA CT N CHM 63-B2
MAGNOLIA CT N MG 77-A2
MAGNOLIA DR WBY 123-E3
MAGNOLIA LN STP 108-E2
MAGNOLIA LN N DAY 49-A4
MAGNOLIA LN N MG 77-A1,91-A1
MAGNOLIA LN N PLY 91-A4,105-A2
MAGNOLIA PL N PLY 91-A3
MAGNOLIA ST IND 102-E1
MAGNOLIA ST MP 102-E1
MAGNOLIA ST NW AND 36-C3,50-C3
MAGNOLIA ST NW CR 50-C4,64-C1
MAGNOLIA TRL EPR 133-A3
MAGNOLIA WAY N MG 77-A1
MAGOFFIN AVE STP 121-C3
MAGUIRE ST MPW 109-B2
MAHER AVE HAS 166-D3
MAHOGANY WAY EAG 149-A3
MAHONEY AVE MTK 118-C3
MAHTOMEDI AVE MHT 81-D4,95-D1
MAIDA CT MPW 123-B3
MAIDEN LN STP 108-B4
MAIDEN LN NE CH 93-A2
MAIDSTONE WAY HSN 48-B3
MAILAND CT MPW 123-B1
MAILAND RD MPW 123-B2
MAILAND RD STP 123-B2
MAIN AVE NE ALB 47-A2
MAIN AVE SE PRL 161-B3
MAIN AVE W WIN 99-B3
MAIN AVE W WIT 99-B3
MAIN ST CHC 26-B1
MAIN ST CHN 132-B2
MAIN ST CNC 12-E3
MAIN ST CV 66-D2
MAIN ST CW 1-B2
MAIN ST DRS 28-D2
MAIN ST EKO 204-B1
MAIN ST EPR 132-D2
MAIN ST ER 33-D2
MAIN ST FAR 177-E4
MAIN ST GI 169-D2
MAIN ST GIT 169-D2
MAIN ST HEN 198-D3
MAIN ST HMP 193-B2
MAIN ST HOP 119-B2
MAIN ST IND 102-B2
MAIN ST LES 212-C4
MAIN ST LL 52-B4,66-C1
MAIN ST MON 86-C1
MAIN ST NM 189-E4,190-A4

MAIN ST OTT 212-C4
MAIN ST RFD 74-B3
MAIN ST ROG 61-E1
MAIN ST SB 116-A3
MAIN ST SM 46-E4
MAIN ST SOM 84-B1
MAIN ST SPP 137-B3
MAIN ST STP 108-B4
MAIN ST ZIM 5-D1
MAIN ST E ANO 49-D4
MAIN ST E ARL 183-A2
MAIN ST E BEL 185-E1,186-A1
MAIN ST E CAR 145-B4
MAIN ST E CF 208-B4
MAIN ST E CR 49-D4
MAIN ST E DRS 28-D2
MAIN ST E MP 102-E1,103-A1
MAIN ST E NP 201-E2
MAIN ST E NYA 142-C3
MAIN ST E PLA 141-B4
MAIN ST E VER 179-D2
MAIN ST E WAC 129-E3
MAIN ST N LES 212-C3
MAIN ST N LON 217-B2
MAIN ST N MG 77-A3
MAIN ST N RF 126-E4,140-E1
MAIN ST N SHK 146-B2
MAIN ST N SM 46-E3
MAIN ST N SWR 83-A4,97-A1
MAIN ST NE CH 92-D2
MAIN ST NE FRI 78-D4,92-D1
MAIN ST NE MPL 92-D3,106-D1
MAIN ST NW ANO 49-B3
MAIN ST NW BET 8-D3
MAIN ST NW CR 49-E4,50-C4
MAIN ST NW OG 22-C4,36-C1
MAIN ST S LON 217-B3
MAIN ST S RF 140-D2
MAIN ST S SHK 146-B2
MAIN ST S SM 46-E4
MAIN ST S SWR 97-A1
MAIN ST SE MPL 106-E2
MAIN ST W ANO 49-B3
MAIN ST W ARL 183-A2
MAIN ST W BEL 185-E1
MAIN ST W CAR 145-B4
MAIN ST W CF 208-B4
MAIN ST W DRS 28-D2
MAIN ST W IND 102-D1
MAIN ST W MP 102-E1
MAIN ST W NP 201-D2
MAIN ST W NYA 142-C3
MAIN ST W VER 179-C2
MAIN ST W WAC 129-D3
MAINE AVE BLA 65-A4
MAINE ST N BAY 97-B3
MAINE ST S BAY 97-B4
MAINSTREET HOP 119-B2
MAINZER ST WSP 122-C2
MAIT LN EDI 119-D2
MAJESTIC OAKS EAG 150-B2
MAJESTIC WAY CHN 131-D1
MAJESTIC OAKS CT EAG 150-B2
MAJESTIC OAKS PL EAG 150-B2
MAJOR AVE N BC 78-A4,92-A1
MAJOR AVE N BP 78-A3
MAJOR AVE N CRY 92-A4
MAJOR AVE N GV 92-A4,106-A1
MAJOR AVE N ROB 92-A3
MAJOR CIR GV 106-A1
MAJOR DR GV 106-A1
MAKAH ST NW AND 35-D4,49-C2
MAKAH ST NW OG 35-C2
MAKAH ST NW SF 7-C4
MALCOLM AVE HAS 166-E3
MALCOLM AVE SE MPL 107-B3
MALDEN ST SSP 136-E1,137-A1
MALIBU AVE SLT 174-D4,188-E1
MALIBU DR EDI 119-C3
MALLALIEU DR HUD 111-D2
MALLARD AVE N NST 40-C3
MALLARD CIR EAG 149-C2
MALLARD CT CHN 131-E3
MALLARD CT EAG 149-C2
MALLARD CT EPR 132-C1
MALLARD CT SWR 96-E1
MALLARD CT N NO 80-C3
MALLARD DR EAG 149-C2
MALLARD DR LVT 160-B2
MALLARD DR ROG 48-A4
MALLARD DR WBY 123-C3
MALLARD DR SE BKR 2-D3
MALLARD LN LL 66-B3
MALLARD LN LOR 89-A2
MALLARD LN MO 31-E3
MALLARD LN NO 80-C3
MALLARD LN SWD 117-C3
MALLARD PL EAG 149-C2
MALLARD PL WAC 129-D4
MALLARD RD WAC 129-D3
MALLARD RD N NO 80-C3
MALLARD ST NE MO 61-A2
MALLARD ST NE MOT 61-A2
MALLARD TER LIT 5-D1
MALLARD TRL ROG 48-A4
MALLARD TRL N EAG 149-C2
MALLARD TRL S EAG 149-C2
MALLARD VW EAG 149-C2
MALLARD WAY ROG 48-A4
MALLARD WAY SE PRL 161-C3
MALLARD PASS TRL HWL 85-A2
MALLARD PONDS DR WBT 81-B1
MALLORY CIR CHN 131-E2
MALLORY CT CHN 132-A2
MALLORY LN EPR 118-D4
MALMBERG AVE N CGT 12-D1
MALMBERG CT N CGT 12-D1
MALMO CIR EAG 149-D2
MALMO LN N EAG 149-D2
MALMO PL EAG 149-D1
MALONEY AVE EDI 119-C2
MALTBY ST SSP 136-E1,137-A1
MALVERN ST LAU 107-B1
MAMIE AVE MPW 123-B2
MANCHESTER DR CHN 117-D4,131-D1
MANCHESTER DR GV 105-E1
MANCHESTER DR MP 88-E4,89-A4
MANCHESTER LN EPR 118-E4,132-E1
MANCHESTER RD MOU 117-A2
MANCHESTER ST MTK 118-B4
MANDAN AVE GV 105-C1
MANDAN AVE PRL 161-B3
MANDAN CIR CHN 146-A1
MANITEAU BLVD NW AND 35-C3
MANITOBA AVE STP 108-B3
MANITOBA AVE S WAY 104-B3
MANITOBA RD EPR 132-D1
MANITOBA RD HOP 105-B4
MANITOU AVE STP 109-A3
MANITOU DR WBL 95-B2
MANITOU IS WBL 81-B3
MANITOU LN SWD 117-C3
MANITOU LN WBL 95-B2
MANITOU RD PRL 161-A2
MANITOU RD SWD 117-D3
MANITOU RD TKB 117-D2
MANITOU RD NE PRL 161-A2
MANITOU ST BL 17-E3
MANITOU ST NFD 219-D3
MANKATO CIR NE HL 37-A3
MANKATO ST NE BLA 51-A4,65-A2
MANKATO ST NE HL 37-A3
MANKATO ST W HL 37-A3
MANN LN SWD 117-C4
MANN LN TRT 140-C1
MANNING AVE N GRA 82-C3,96-C2
MANNING AVE N LE 96-C4,110-C1
MANNING AVE N WLT 110-C2
MANNING AVE S AFT 124-C4,138-C1
MANNING AVE S CG 152-C3
MANNING AVE S DET 138-C3,152-C2
MANNING AVE S WBY 110-C4,124-C2
MANNING CIR N NST 40-B2
MANNING CT N NST 40-B2
MANNING LN N NST 40-B2
MANNING ST NG 114-A4
MANNING TRL N CGT 40-B1
MANNING TRL N GRA 82-C1
MANNING TRL N LE 110-C2
MANNING TRL N MAY 54-B4,68-C2
MANNING TRL N NST 40-B3,54-B2
MANNING TRL N WLT 110-C2
MANNING AVENUE CT N GRA 82-C2
MANOMIN AVE STP 122-B2
MANOMIN AVE WSP 122-B3
MANOR AVE BUF 59-A2
MANOR BLVD E BUR 148-B4
MANOR BLVD W BUR 148-B4
MANOR CIR ORO 103-D3
MANOR CT HAS 166-C2
MANOR DR BUR 148-B4
MANOR DR CW 1-B3
MANOR DR EAG 150-B2
MANOR DR GV 106-B1
MANOR DR MTA 116-D2
MANOR DR NE SLK 78-E1
MANOR DR S BUR 148-B4
MANOR LN HAS 166-C2
MANOR PL NW ER 33-D2
MANOR RD DPH 118-B2
MANOR RD GRW 118-A3
MANOR RD MTK 118-C1
MANOR RD PRL 161-B3
MANOR RD SWD 118-A3
MANOR RD N CHN 117-D4
MANOR RD N EPR 118-C4
MANOR RD S EPR 118-D4,132-D1
MANOR ST VH 94-C2
MANOR COURT RD MTK 118-D2
MANSON ST RVL 93-B3
MANTON LN EPR 147-B1
MANTON ST MPW 108-E1
MANTON ST STP 108-E1
MANUELA CIR CHS 145-C1
MANUELA DR CHS 131-D4,145-C1
MANVEL ST STP 107-B3
MANY LEVELS RD DWD 81-D3
MAPLE AVE ANO 49-C4
MAPLE AVE BUF 59-B1
MAPLE AVE CHN 117-B4,131-B1
MAPLE AVE DEL 87-D2
MAPLE AVE MP 89-A4,103-A1
MAPLE AVE ORO 117-C2
MAPLE AVE ROG 61-E1
MAPLE AVE SWD 117-C4
MAPLE AVE WAV 86-A1
MAPLE AVE N ML 43-D2
MAPLE AVE NE SLK 78-E1
MAPLE AVE S BLO 134-B4
MAPLE AVE S ML 43-D3
MAPLE CIR BEL 186-A2
MAPLE CIR BLO 134-B4
MAPLE CIR BUF 59-B1
MAPLE CIR CHN 117-B4
MAPLE CIR SW LAT 201-D3
MAPLE CT FH 107-C1
MAPLE DR HUD 111-D2
MAPLE DR JOR 173-B2
MAPLE DR LTT 130-D2
MAPLE DR OSC 28-A4
MAPLE DR RFD 74-B3
MAPLE DR SAT 14-D3
MAPLE DR SCF 14-D3
MAPLE DR SLT 174-E1
MAPLE FRST MTA 116-E3
MAPLE LN ANO 49-C4
MAPLE LN BL 17-E3
MAPLE LN DPH 118-B2
MAPLE LN FLT 39-D3
MAPLE LN JOR 173-B2
MAPLE LN LAT 215-E2
MAPLE LN LC 94-B3
MAPLE LN MPW 95-A3
MAPLE LN MTA 116-B3
MAPLE LN MTK 118-E2
MAPLE LN ORO 103-D2
MAPLE LN RVL 93-C3,94-B3
MAPLE LN SB 116-A3
MAPLE LN SLT 161-A4
MAPLE LN SVW 94-A2
MAPLE LN E COR 61-B4
MAPLE LN E MPW 95-B3
MAPLE LN N MG 76-E2
MAPLE LN SE LAT 201-E3
MAPLE LN SW SM 46-E4
MAPLE PL MPL 106-D2
MAPLE PL ORO 103-B4
MAPLE RD EB 37-D1
MAPLE RD EDI 120-A2
MAPLE RD MOU 116-D1
MAPLE RD NE EB 37-D1
MAPLE RDG VIC 117-A4
MAPLE SQ WAY 104-B3
MAPLE ST BEL 186-A2
MAPLE ST BUF 59-B1
MAPLE ST CW 1-B2
MAPLE ST EXC 117-D3
MAPLE ST FAR 177-E4,178-A4
MAPLE ST GRA 81-D4
MAPLE ST HAS 166-D2
MAPLE ST HEN 198-C3
MAPLE ST IND 89-A4
MAPLE ST LES 212-C3
MAPLE ST LL 52-B3
MAPLE ST LND 12-D4
MAPLE ST MED 89-A3
MAPLE ST MHT 81-D4
MAPLE ST MO 31-D2
MAPLE ST MPL 106-C3
MAPLE ST MSC 55-B4
MAPLE ST RFD 74-B3
MAPLE ST SOM 84-B1
MAPLE ST STP 108-D4
MAPLE ST SVW 79-E3
MAPLE ST SWD 117-D4
MAPLE ST TF 14-C2
MAPLE ST E RF 140-E2
MAPLE ST N BNT 113-B4
MAPLE ST N CHS 145-D3
MAPLE ST N LP 113-B4
MAPLE ST N WAC 129-D3
MAPLE ST NW WAT 101-B3
MAPLE ST S LP 113-B4,127-B1
MAPLE ST S NFD 219-E4
MAPLE ST S WAC 129-D3
MAPLE ST W RF 140-D2
MAPLE ST W SWR 96-E1,97-A1
MAPLE TRL PRL 161-C2
MAPLE TRL SHK 160-C1
MAPLE CHASE RD DPH 118-B2
MAPLE CREST DR MTA 102-E3
MAPLE GROVE LN SLT 160-D4
MAPLE GROVE MALL SER RD MG 91-A1
MAPLE HEIGHTS RD GRW 118-A3
MAPLE HILL DR DPH 118-B2
MAPLE HILL DR TKB 117-D2
MAPLE HILL RD COR 76-A3
MAPLE HILL RD HOP 119-D2
MAPLE HILL RD RIT 140-C2
MAPLE HILL RD SMT 83-C3
MAPLE HILL RD WDL 104-C4
MAPLE ISLAND CT BUR 162-D3
MAPLE ISLAND RD BUR 162-D3
MAPLE ISLAND RD LVL 162-D3
MAPLE KNOLL CIR NW SM 46-D3
MAPLE KNOLL DR FH 107-D1
MAPLE KNOLL WAY MG 76-E2,77-A2
MAPLE KNOLL WAY NW SM 46-D3
MAPLE LANE CT RVL 94-A3
MAPLE LEAF CIR EAG 149-E2
MAPLE LEAF CIR SWD 117-C4
MAPLE LEAF CT MED 90-A1
MAPLE LEAF CT OST 28-D4
MAPLE LEAF DR EPR 132-B1
MAPLE LEAF DR OST 28-D4
MAPLE MANORS CT MOU 102-E4
MAPLE PARK CT MH 122-A3
MAPLE PARK DR MH 122-A3
MAPLE POND CT SVW 79-E3,80-A3
MAPLE PONDS TRL IND 88-C3
MAPLE RIDGE CIR DEL 87-E2
MAPLE RIDGE CT MTK 119-A3
MAPLE RIDGE DR DEL 87-E2
MAPLE RIDGE DR HEN 198-C4
MAPLE RIDGE DR MP 102-E1
MAPLE RIDGE LN ORO 117-C1
MAPLE RIDGE LN SWD 117-B4
MAPLE RIDGE RD CHC 26-B2
MAPLE RIDGE RD DPH 104-B4,118-B1
MAPLE SHORES DR CHN 131-B1
MAPLE VALLEY DR MG 63-B4,77-B1
MAPLE VIEW DR DAT 158-B1
MAPLEBROOK CT N BP 77-D2
MAPLEBROOK PKWY N BP 77-D2
MAPLEBROOK TER N BP 77-D2
MAPLELEAF CT LC 94-D3
MAPLETON AVE SPR 117-B1
MAPLETON DR NE HL 36-E3
MAPLEVIEW AVE MPW 95-A3
MAPLEVIEW CT SWD 117-C3
MAPLEWOOD CIR CHM 63-B3
MAPLEWOOD CIR CHN 117-C4
MAPLEWOOD CIR MOT 32-A3
MAPLEWOOD CIR E WDL 104-B4
MAPLEWOOD CIR SW LAT 201-D3
MAPLEWOOD CIR W WDL 104-B4
MAPLEWOOD DR BLO 134-D4
MAPLEWOOD DR DEL 87-E3
MAPLEWOOD DR MED 103-D1
MAPLEWOOD DR MPW 94-D4,108-D1
MAPLEWOOD DR SA 93-B3
MAPLEWOOD DR VH 94-E2
MAPLEWOOD DR N MG 76-E3
MAPLEWOOD DR NE EB 36-E2
MAPLEWOOD LN CHM 63-B3
MAPLEWOOD LN DAT 158-C2
MAPLEWOOD LN MTK 118-D4
MAPLEWOOD PL BUF 58-E3
MAPLEWOOD RD DAT 157-E1,158-D2
MAPLEWOOD RD DPH 104-B4,118-B1
MAPLEWOOD RD SB 116-A3
MAPLEWOOD RD WDL 104-B4
MAPLEWOOD TER CHN 131-D2
MAPLEWOOD MALL DR MPW 95-A3
MARAS ST SHK 147-C3
MARBLE LN EAG 149-B2
MARBLE ST VH 94-C2
MARBLE ST NW RAM 34-E4
MARCELLA CT RF 140-D1
MARCH CIR MTK 105-A4
MARCIA DR CHS 145-D1
MARCIA LN LL 65-E1
MARCIA LN S SHK 160-C2
MARCIA ANN LN BUR 162-B3
MARCIN HL BUR 148-D4,162-D1
MARCIN LN BUR 148-D4
MARCY LN MTK 105-B4
MARCYS CT HUT 98-C4
MARDEN CT HAT 188-A2
MAREN CIR SW SM 46-E4
MAREN CT FKT 87-B3
MAREN LN GV 105-D2
MARGARET CIR MTA 116-E3
MARGARET CIR WAY 104-B2
MARGARET PL MTK 118-D1
MARGARET ST MPW 109-B3
MARGARET ST NSP 95-B4,109-B1
MARGARET ST OSC 28-A4
MARGARET ST RIT 140-D2
MARGARET ST STP 108-D3,109-A3
MARGARET ST WBT 80-E4
MARGARETS LN EDI 119-C4
MARGO AVE N MAY 54-C3
MARGO AVE N NST 54-C3
MARGO AVE N WLT 110-C2
MARI LN MTK 119-A1
MARIA AVE DAY 48-B2
MARIA AVE HBG 156-A2
MARIA AVE STP 108-D4
MARIA CT MTA 102-E4
MARIA RD IND 87-E3,88-A3
MARIA LAKE RD DAT 157-E3,158-A3
MARIAH CT RF 140-D1
MARIAN CT CP 79-D1
MARIANN DR EPR 132-E1
MARICE CT EAG 135-D3
MARICE DR EAG 135-D3
MARIE AVE ROG 47-E4
MARIE AVE SSP 122-D4
MARIE AVE E WSP 122-C4
MARIE AVE W MH 121-E4,122-A4
MARIE AVE W WSP 122-B4
MARIE CT DEL 87-E2
MARIE LN E GV 92-A4
MARIE LN W GV 91-E4
MARIE ST E ML 43-D2
MARIE ST W ML 43-D2
MARIGOLD AVE VH 80-C4
MARIGOLD AVE N BP 63-E4,64-A4
MARIGOLD CIR CGT 12-C3
MARIGOLD CIR EPR 133-A3
MARIGOLD CIR VIC 131-A2
MARIGOLD CIR NW AND 49-E3
MARIGOLD CT N BP 64-A4
MARIGOLD LN CGT 12-C3
MARIGOLD PL CGT 12-C3
MARIGOLD ST VIC 131-A2
MARIGOLD ST NW AND 35-E3,49-E3
MARIGOLD ST NW CR 49-E3,63-E1
MARIGOLD ST NW OG 21-E4
MARIGOLD TER NE FRI 78-E4
MARIGOLD WAY CGT 12-C3
MARIGOLD WAY ROG 47-E4
MARILLAC LN STP 123-B3
MARILYN AVE EAG 149-A3
MARILYN DR LL 52-B4,66-A1
MARILYN DR N MG 77-A4
MARINA DR MTA 102-E4
MARINA VIEW DR RFD 74-B4
MARINE CIR SWR 96-D2
MARINE CT LND 12-D4
MARINE RD SMT 55-C4
MARINE ST LND 12-D4
MARINER CT BAY 97-B4
MARINER DR BAY 97-B4
MARINER DR N MG 76-D3
MARINER PT N MG 76-D3
MARINER WAY BAY 97-B4
MARINER WAY WBY 110-B4,124-B1
MARION CT ROG 62-A1
MARION DR ARL 183-A2
MARION DR BUR 148-B4
MARION LN MOU 116-E1
MARION LN SCT 173-A3
MARION LN W MTK 105-A3
MARION PL SSP 122-D2
MARION RD RVL 93-C4
MARION ST RVL 94-B3,108-B1
MARION ST STP 108-B2
MARK AVE N WLT 110-C3
MARK CT NEW 137-B1
MARK CT SHK 160-C1
MARK ST GRF 74-D4
MARK ST LTT 131-A3
MARK ST MED 74-D3
MARK AVENUE CT N WLT 110-C3
MARK TERRACE CIR EDI 133-D1
MARK TERRACE DR EDI 133-C1
MARKAY RDG GV 105-E1,106-A1
MARKET AVE BTT 143-E3,157-E1
MARKET AVE DAT 143-E4
MARKET AVE HCT 157-E4,171-E1
MARKET AVE SFT 171-E3
MARKET AVE WTT 101-E4,115-E1
MARKET BLVD CHN 132-A2
MARKET DR RCH 134-C2
MARKET DR SWR 96-D2
MARKET LN S COL 143-E4
MARKET PL LC 94-B3
MARKET PLZ MPL 106-B4
MARKET ST CLK 1-D1
MARKET ST COL 143-E4
MARKET ST GV 105-D3
MARKET ST HEN 198-D3
MARKET ST LES 212-D3
MARKET ST MPL 106-C2
MARKET ST STP 108-B4
MARKET ST N BEL 185-E1
MARKET ST N SHK 146-B2
MARKET ST S BEL 185-E1
MARKET ST S SHK 146-B2
MARKET PLACE DR CHM 63-C3
MARKET PLACE DR EPR 133-B1
MARKET PLACE DR LC 94-B3
MARKET POINT DR BLO 134-A2
MARKGRAFS LAKE ALC WBY 110-B4
MARKGRAFS LAKE BAY WBY 124-B1
MARKGRAFS LAKE DR WBY 110-B4,124-B1
MARKGRAFS LAKE DRAW WBY 124-B1
MARKHAM PT EAG 149-C3
MARKWOOD DR CRY 91-D3
MARLANE CIR JOR 173-B3
MARLBORO CT NE SLK 78-E2
MARLBORO DR MOU 117-A2
MARLBOROUGH CIR MTK 118-C2
MARLBOROUGH CT MTK 118-C2
MARLEN CIR PRL 161-C2
MARLIN AVE VH 94-C2
MARLIN DR BC 78-A4
MARLOWE AVE NE ALB 47-A2
MARLOWE AVE NE OTS 33-A4
MARLYLAND AVE S SAV 147-D4
MARMON ST NE BLA 65-D2
MARMON ST NE BOT 23-D3
MARMOSET ST NW BT 20-D4
MARMOSET ST NW RAM 34-D4,48-D1
MARNIE CIR MPW 123-B2
MARNIE CT MPW 123-B3
MARNIE ST MPW 123-B2
MARNIE ST S MPW 123-B2
MARQUESS LN N LE 96-C3
MARQUESS TRL N LE 96-C3
MARQUESS WAY N LE 96-C3
MARQUESS LANE CV N LE 96-C3
MARQUESS TRAIL CIR N LE 96-C3
MARQUESS TRAIL CT N LE 96-C3
MARQUETTE AVE MPL 106-D2
MARQUIS PT EAG 149-C3
MARQUIS RD GV 105-C1
MARSCHALL RD SLT 160-C4,174-C1
MARSCHALL RD S SHK 146-C3,160-C2
MARSCHALL RD S SLT 160-D3
MARSH AVE MP 88-E4,102-E1
MARSH DR CHN 132-B2
MARSH DR DEL 87-E2
MARSH ST PRL 161-A3
MARSH ST SB 116-B3
MARSH ST E SWR 97-A2
MARSH ST NW PRL 161-A3
MARSH ST W SWR 97-A2
MARSH WAY MTK 118-D4

MARSH CREEK ALC WBY 123-E3
MARSH CREEK RD WBY 123-E3
MARSH LAKE RD LTT . . .130-E4,131-A4
MARSH POINTE CIR SWD 117-B3
MARSH POINTE CT SWD 117-B3
MARSH POINTE DR SWD 117-B3
MARSH RIDGE CIR IND . .102-E1,103-A1
MARSH RIDGE CT EPR 132-E1
MARSHALL AVE SPP 137-C3
MARSHALL AVE STP 107-D4,108-A4
MARSHALL RD EPR 132-C4
MARSHALL ST NE FRI 92-D2
MARSHALL ST NE MPL . . .92-D4,106-D1
MARSHAN LN LL 66-B2
MARSHLAND CT SB 116-A3
MARSHLAND RD WDL 104-B4
MARSHLAND TRL CHN 132-A3
MARSHVIEW CIR CHM 63-B3
MARSHVIEW LN CHM 63-B3
MARSON DR TRT 112-B4,126-B1
MARTH CT EDI 133-D2
MARTH RD BLO 133-D2
MARTHA LN LOL 103-E2
MARTHA LN MTK 118-D1
MARTHA LN WBY 123-C1
MARTHA ST HBG 156-A2
MARTHA ST YAT 156-A3
MARTHA ST N SWR 82-E4,96-E1
MARTHA ST S SWR 96-E2
MARTHA LAKE CT SVW 79-E3
MARTHALER LN WSP 122-C3
MARTIN AVE BL 18-A4
MARTIN CT NW AND 50-B2
MARTIN DR BEC 2-D3
MARTIN DR BUR 162-E3
MARTIN DR EPR 132-E2
MARTIN DR MO 31-D3
MARTIN DR SFT 158-C4
MARTIN LN NO 80-B3
MARTIN LN W LWT 24-B1
MARTIN ST AND 50-B1
MARTIN ST ANO 49-C4
MARTIN ST NW AND 50-B1
MARTIN ST NW CR 50-B3,64-B2
MARTIN ST NW OG 22-B4,36-B1
MARTIN WAY VH 94-B1
MARTIN WAY WBL 95-B1
MARTIN LAKE DR E LWT . . .10-C4,24-B1
MARTIN LAKE DR W LWT . . .10-B4,24-B1
MARTIN LAKE RD NE LWT . .10-B4,24-B1
MARTINDALE DR E SHK 147-B4
MARTINDALE ST NE PRL 147-B4,161-B1
MARTINGALE CT NYA 142-B4
MARTINGALE DR NYA 142-B4
MARTINSON ISLAND RD PRL . . .161-A2
MARTY DR BUF 58-E1
MARTY DR HUT 97-D4
MARTYS WAY OSC 28-A4
MARVEL CRV MPL 106-E4
MARVIN CT DEL 87-E2
MARVIN LN NFD 219-D4
MARVIN RD MO 31-C2
MARVIN ST S OSC 28-A4
MARVIN ELWOOD RD MO . .17-B4,31-B1
MARVY ST LL 65-E2
MARY BAY CHN 131-D1
MARY CIR VH 80-C4
MARY CT MPW 109-B1
MARY CT N MPW 95-B3
MARY LN MPW 95-B3,123-B1
MARY LN STP 107-E2
MARY LN NW ARL 183-A2
MARY PL MPW 123-B3
MARY ST MPW 95-B3,109-B3
MARY ST RF 140-D2
MARY ADELE AVE MH 121-E4
MARY ANN LN BUR 148-D4
MARY HILLS DR GV 106-A1
MARY JANE CIR CHN 132-A3
MARY LAKE TRL SWD 117-D4
MARYJOE LN NSP 109-B1
MARYKNOLL AVE MPW 108-E1
MARYKNOLL DR SWR 96-D1
MARYLAND AVE BLA 65-A4
MARYLAND AVE MPW 109-B2
MARYLAND AVE OKD 109-C2
MARYLAND AVE SAV . . .147-D4,161-D1
MARYLAND AVE E STP . .108-C2,109-A2
MARYLAND AVE N BP 77-D2,91-D1
MARYLAND AVE N CHM 63-D3
MARYLAND AVE N CRY 91-D2
MARYLAND AVE N GV 105-D1
MARYLAND AVE N NH 91-D3
MARYLAND AVE S BLO 147-D1
MARYLAND AVE S GV 105-D2
MARYLAND AVE S SAV . .147-D4,161-D2
MARYLAND AVE S SLP 105-D4
MARYLAND AVE W STP . .107-E2,108-A2
MARYLAND CIR SAV 147-D4
MARYLAND CIR N CHM 63-D2
MARYLAND CIR S BLO . .133-D2,147-D1
MARYLAND CT SAV 147-D4
MARYLAND CT N BP 77-D2
MARYLAND CT N CHM 63-D2
MARYLAND LN N CHM 63-D2
MARYLAND RD BLO 133-D2,147-D1
MARYLAND ST SCF 14-D2
MARYLAND ST E SCF 14-C2
MARYLAND WAY N CHM 63-D3
MARYLANE AVE N SWT 82-C4
MARYSTONE BLVD
NW AND 35-C4,49-C1
MARYSTOWN RD JT . . .146-A4,160-A1
MARYSTOWN RD LVT 160-A2
MARYSTOWN RD SCT . .160-A4,174-B1
MARYSTOWN RD SHK 146-A3
MARYWOOD LN WSP 122-B4
MASON AVE NE OTS 33-B3
MASON AVE NE SM 47-A3
MASON CT SM 47-A3
MASON LN NE SM 47-A3
MASONIC HOME DR BLO 147-E2
MASONS PT EPR 132-D3
MASSACHUSETTS ST SCF 14-C2
MASSACHUSETTS ST W SCF 14-C2
MASSIE CRV EPR 133-A3
MATHIAS RD SHK 146-C4
MATILDA CIR RVL 94-A4
MATILDA ST RVL 94-A3
MATILDA ST STP 108-A2
MATTERHORN CIR NE FRI . .92-E1,93-A1
MATTERHORN DR MPW 123-B2
MATTERHORN DR NE CH 92-E1
MATTERHORN DR NE FRI . .78-E4,92-E1
MATTERHORN LN STP 123-B2
MATTHEW CIR EPR 118-B4
MATTHEW CT EAG 149-E2
MATTHEW DR CGT 12-B4
MATTHEW DR MO 31-C1
MATTHEWS CIR MO 31-C1
MATTSON CT N CGT 12-B3
MATTSON LN N CGT 12-B3
MATTSON BROOK LN N BP 78-C2
MAUD RD HUT 112-A2
MAUREEN CIR CRT 176-A1
MAUREEN DR NE CH 92-D2
MAUREEN LN NE CH 92-D2
MAURY ST STP 108-C3
MAVELLE DR EDI 134-A1
MAVES TRL PRL 161-C2
MAXANICKIE DR TRT 125-D4
MAXINE CIR E SHK 160-C1
MAXWELL AVE NEW 123-A4
MAXWELL LN CHS 145-B1
MAXWELL RD N CGT 26-C3
MAXWILL AVE N NST 54-C2
MAY AVE N MAY 54-C4,68-C3
MAY ST LOL 103-E2
MAY ST STP 121-E2
MAYBERRY TRL N NST 54-D1
MAYCREST AVE S DET 152-D4
MAYCREST AVENUE CT S DET . .152-D4
MAYELIN AVE NE SM 47-B3
MAYER AVE NE SM 47-B3
MAYER BLVD WTT 114-E4
MAYER LN MPW 109-B4
MAYER RD HUD 111-E4
MAYER RD TRT 111-D4
MAYFAIR AVE WBL 95-B1
MAYFAIR CT WBL 95-B1
MAYFAIR RD GV 105-C1
MAYFAIR RD VH 94-B2
MAYFAIR RD N GV 105-C1
MAYFIELD AVE SM 47-A3
MAYFIELD AVE N SWT 82-C2
MAYFIELD AVE NE SM 47-B3
MAYFIELD CT CHN 132-A3
MAYFIELD CT N SWT 82-C2
MAYFIELD DR EPR 132-D3
MAYFIELD RD MTK 104-E4
MAYFIELD HEIGHTS LN MH 121-E3
MAYFIELD HEIGHTS RD LIL 121-E3
MAYFLOWER AVE MTK 105-A4
MAYFLOWER CIR MTK 105-A4
MAYFLOWER CT NFD 220-A4
MAYFLOWER DR NFD . . .219-E4,220-A4
MAYFLOWER PL MTK 105-A4
MAYFLOWER RD SWD 117-E4
MAYHILL RD MPW 109-B3,123-B1
MAYNARD DR STP 121-D3
MAYNARD DR E STP 121-D3
MAYNARD DR W STP 121-D3
MAYO DR BUR 148-D4
MAYRE ST STP 108-B2
MAYROSE AVE NE SM 47-B3
MAYVIEW CT MTK 118-E3
MAYVIEW RD MTK 118-E3
MAYVIEW TER MTK 118-E3
MAYWOOD CRV MTK 118-E3
MAYWOOD DR BUR 162-E2
MAYWOOD DR SSP 122-D4
MAYWOOD LN MTK 118-E3,119-A3
MAYWOOD LN WSP 122-B4
MAYWOOD PL STP 108-A2
MAYWOOD RD MOU 116-E1,117-A1
MAYWOOD ST STP 108-A2
MAYWOOD ST SVW 80-A3
MAZULA CT NE SM 47-B3
MC DIARMID DR HUT 112-D1
MCAFEE CIR MPW 94-E4
MCAFEE ST STP 108-E2
MCALLISTER AVE NE OTS . .33-B4,47-B1
MCALLISTER AVE NE SM 47-B3
MCANDREWS RD APV . . .149-C4,163-A1
MCANDREWS RD BUR 162-C1
MCANDREWS RD E BUR 162-C1
MCANDREWS ROAD CT BUR . . .162-C1
MCBOAL ST STP 122-B1
MCCALLUM DR NB 93-B2
MCCAMMON AVE SPP 137-C3
MCCANN AVE ANO 49-C3
MCCARRONS BLVD N RVL 108-A1
MCCARRONS BLVD S RVL 108-A1
MCCARRONS ST RVL 108-B1
MCCARTHY RD EAG 135-C3
MCCARTHY RDG EAG 135-C3
MCCAULEY CIR EDI 119-C4
MCCAULEY TER EDI 119-C4
MCCAULEY TRL S EDI . . .119-C4,133-C1
MCCAULEY TRL W EDI 119-C4
MCCHANN ST GI 169-D2
MCCLELLAND
ST N MPW 109-B4,123-B1
MCCLELLAND ST S MPW 123-B2
MCCLUNG DR AH 79-D4
MCCOLL DR SAV 147-D4,148-A4
MCCOLL DR SHK 147-C4
MCCOY CT EPR 132-E3
MCCRACKEN LN AH 93-D1
MCCULLEY RD ORO 103-A2
MCCUTCHEON LN HUT 98-A4
MCCUTCHEON RD HUT 98-C4
MCDEVITT ST SHK 146-B3
MCDONALD DR N BYT 96-D4
MCDONALD LN HUT 98-B4
MCDONALD ST MH 122-A2
MCDONALD DR CT N BYT 96-D4
MCDONALD DRIVE CIR BYT 96-D3
MCDONALD DRIVE PL N BYT 96-C4
MCDONALD DRIVE OVERL BYT . .96-D3
MCDONALD OVERLOOK DR BYT .96-D3
MCDOUGAL GRN SWR 96-C2
MCFADDENS TRL EAG 150-A3
MCFAIR AVE N BYT 96-C4
MCGINTY RD WAY 104-C3
MCGINTY RD E MTK 104-E4,118-E1
MCGINTY RD W MTK 104-D4,118-E1
MCGLYNN DR CHN 131-E2
MCGREGOR AVE N MHT 95-D1
MCGREGOR AVE N WIL 95-D1
MCGREGOR AVE S MHT 95-D1
MCGREW PL N MPL 106-D2
MCGUFFEY RD EPR 132-D3
MCGUIRE CIR SHK 147-C4
MCGUIRE CT SHK 147-C4
MCGUIRE RD EDI 133-D1
MCINTOSH CIR SHK 146-B3
MCINTOSH CT SHK 146-B3
MCINTOSH DR APV 163-A2
MCINTOSH RD WBY 124-A2
MCINTYRE PT EDI 119-C4
MCKAY CT SLT 160-D4
MCKAY DR NE HL 50-E1
MCKEE ST EAG 135-E2
MCKENNA RD PRL 160-E1,161-A1
MCKENNA RD SHK 146-E4
MCKENNA RD NW PRL 160-E1
MCKENNEY ST SCF 14-C3
MCKENZIE BLVD MTK 118-D1
MCKENZIE POINT RD WDL 104-C4
MCKINLEY CIR ANO 49-C3
MCKINLEY CIR SWD 118-B4
MCKINLEY CT ANO 49-D3
MCKINLEY CT SWD 118-B4
MCKINLEY DR SJT 97-D3
MCKINLEY DR WBY 123-E3
MCKINLEY PL MPL 107-A1
MCKINLEY PL SWD 118-B4
MCKINLEY ST ANO 49-B3
MCKINLEY ST STP 107-D2
MCKINLEY ST NE CH 93-A2
MCKINLEY ST NE FRI 79-A2
MCKINLEY ST NE MPL 93-A3
MCKINLEY ST NE SLK 79-A2
MCKINLEY ST NW RAM 49-A3
MCKINZIE CIR CF 208-B3
MCKNIGHT CIR CHS 131-C3
MCKNIGHT CIR VIC 131-A2
MCKNIGHT LN MPW 109-B1
MCKNIGHT RD CHS 131-C3
MCKNIGHT RD MPW 95-B3,109-B1
MCKNIGHT RD NSP 95-B4,109-B1
MCKNIGHT RD STP 109-B4
MCKNIGHT RD N STP . . .109-B3,123-B1
MCKNIGHT RD N WBL . . .81-B4,95-B2
MCKNIGHT RD S STP 123-B2
MCKUSICK LN S SWR 96-E1
MCKUSICK RD GRA 82-C4
MCKUSICK RD SWR 82-E4,96-E1
MCKUSICK RD SWT 82-D4
MCKUSICK ROAD CT SWR 82-D4
MCKUSICK ROAD LN N SWR 82-E4
MCLAIN RD SWD 117-D3
MCLEAN AVE STP 108-D4
MCLEOD AVE E WIN 99-B3
MCLEOD AVE N PLA 141-B3
MCLEOD AVE S HNT 141-B4
MCLEOD AVE S PLA 141-B4
MCLEOD AVE W WIN 99-B3
MCLEOD ST BUR 149-A2
MCLEOD ST NE CH 92-E2,93-A2
MCMAHON LN CLT 189-B1
MCMAHON LN SLT 175-C4,189-C1
MCMENEMY CIR VH 94-C1
MCMENEMY RD VH 80-C4,94-C1
MCMENEMY ST N LC 94-C4
MCMENEMY ST N MPW . .94-C4,108-C1
MCNAIR AVE MPL 106-B1
MCNAIR AVE N MPL 106-B1
MCNAIR DR GV 106-A1
MCNAIR DR ROB 92-A4,106-A1
MCNAMARA ST HAS 166-D2
MCQUISTON CT SAV 147-E4
MEAD CT BUR 149-A3
MEAD RD WBT 81-A3
MEAD ST CHM 63-B1
MEADE LN EPR 133-B4,147-B1
MEADOW AVE PRL 161-C1
MEADOW AVE SVW 79-D1
MEADOW CIR BEL 186-A2
MEADOW CIR CV 66-D3
MEADOW CIR MTK 105-A3
MEADOW CIR ORT 3-A4
MEADOW CIR N BP 64-A3
MEADOW CIR N BUR . . .148-D4,162-C1
MEADOW CIR N COR 61-D4
MEADOW CIR S BUR 162-D1
MEADOW CRV N LND 12-C3
MEADOW CT BUF 45-B4
MEADOW CT CHN 117-B4
MEADOW CT CHS 145-C2
MEADOW CT CV 66-D3
MEADOW CT JT 146-B4
MEADOW CT LL 65-E2
MEADOW CT SVW 79-D1
MEADOW CT WBY 109-C4
MEADOW DR BUF 45-B4
MEADOW DR DEL 87-D3
MEADOW DR HUT 112-D2
MEADOW DR LOR 89-B2
MEADOW DR NSP 109-B1
MEADOW DR N NOH 111-D1
MEADOW LN CHN 117-B4
MEADOW LN CLT 189-C2
MEADOW LN COR 61-D4
MEADOW LN CV 66-D3
MEADOW LN DWD 81-C3
MEADOW LN EPR 132-D2
MEADOW LN HUT 112-C3
MEADOW LN JOR 173-B2
MEADOW LN LOL 103-E2
MEADOW LN MOT 32-A3
MEADOW LN MOU 116-E2
MEADOW LN MP 102-E1
MEADOW LN MTK 118-C1
MEADOW LN NO 80-B3
MEADOW LN NP 201-E3
MEADOW LN SAV 147-C4
MEADOW LN SB 116-B3
MEADOW LN SVW 80-A3
MEADOW LN WAT 101-B3
MEADOW LN WBY 109-C4,123-C1
MEADOW LN WSP 122-C3
MEADOW LN N BP 64-A3
MEADOW LN N CHS 145-C2
MEADOW LN N GV 106-A2
MEADOW LN NE BLA 65-C1
MEADOW LN NE HL 36-E3
MEADOW LN S GV 106-A3
MEADOW LN W MTK 105-A4
MEADOW PL BEL 186-A2
MEADOW PL MTK 105-B4
MEADOW PL SHK 146-A3
MEADOW RD EDI 120-A2
MEADOW RDG EDI 133-E1
MEADOW RDG MTK 118-C2
MEADOW ST COL 143-E3
MEADOW ACRES PL BUR 162-C1
MEADOW BROOK ALC WBY 123-D3
MEADOW BROOK BAY WBY 123-D3
MEADOW BROOK CT VH 94-C2
MEADOW BROOK CT WBY 123-D3
MEADOW BROOK DR WBY 123-D3
MEADOW BROOK PL WBY 123-D3
MEADOW GRASS AVE CG 137-C2
MEADOW GRASS LN CG 137-C2
MEADOW LAKE LN OSC 28-B4
MEADOW LAKE PL NH 91-C1
MEADOW LAKE PL NW WAC 129-D3
MEADOW LAKE RD E NH 91-C1
MEADOW LAKE RD N NH 91-C1
MEADOW LAKE RD W NH 91-C1
MEADOW LAKES CT RFD 74-B3
MEADOW LAKES TRL RFD 74-B3
MEADOW LARK DR DEL 87-D3
MEADOW OAK AVE MOT . .31-E3,32-A3
MEADOW OAK CT MO 32-A3
MEADOW OAK DR MOT 32-A3
MEADOW OAK LN MOT 31-E3,32-A3
MEADOW VIEW CT HAS 166-B2
MEADOW VIEW DR COR 61-B4
MEADOW VIEW DR NFD 219-E4
MEADOW VIEW LN CLT 189-A3
MEADOW VIEW TRL HAS 166-B2
MEADOW VIEW TRL LL 66-A1
MEADOW WOOD CT SCT 173-B3
MEADOW WOOD CT SLT 174-D4,188-D1
MEADOWARK CT LL 66-C3
MEADOWBROOK
AVE N NST 40-D4,54-D1
MEADOWBROOK AVE NE MOT . .61-A2
MEADOWBROOK AVE NE OTS . . .61-A2
MEADOWBROOK BLVD SLP 119-E2
MEADOWBROOK LN MTK 104-D4
MEADOWBROOK LN RF 140-D2
MEADOWBROOK LN SLP 119-D2
MEADOWBROOK RD HOP 119-D2
MEADOWBROOK RD SLP 119-D2
MEADOWLANDS DR WBT 80-D4
MEADOWLARK BLVD BEC 3-A4
MEADOWLARK CIR MG 91-A1
MEADOWLARK CIR WAC 129-D3
MEADOWLARK CRV EAG 149-C1
MEADOWLARK CT BEC 3-A4
MEADOWLARK CT EAG 149-C1
MEADOWLARK CT N MG 91-A1
MEADOWLARK DR SWR 96-E1
MEADOWLARK LN CHN 132-B4
MEADOWLARK LN EAG 149-C1
MEADOWLARK LN HAN 61-A3
MEADOWLARK LN MPW 94-D3
MEADOWLARK LN NO 80-B3
MEADOWLARK LN SLT 175-C2
MEADOWLARK LN N MG . .77-A4,91-A1
MEADOWLARK PT EAG 149-C1
MEADOWLARK RD EAG 149-C1
MEADOWLARK RD S EAG 149-C1
MEADOWLARK RD SE SM . .46-E4,47-A4
MEADOWLARK WAY EAG 149-C1
MEADOWLARK WAY FAR 177-D3
MEADOWLAWN TRL PRL 161-B2
MEADOWMOOR
DR NE FRI 78-E2,79-A2
MEADOWOOD CIR VH 80-B4
MEADOWOOD CRV CR 49-E3
MEADOWOOD DR ANN 74-B2
MEADOWOOD DR RFD 74-A3
MEADOWOOD DR WBY 123-C1
MEADOWOOD LN BUR 148-D3
MEADOWOOD LN HUT 112-A1
MEADOWOOD LN VH 80-B4
MEADOWOOD PL VH 80-B4
MEADOWOOD TRL CR 49-E3
MEADOWOOD WAY CR 49-E3
MEADOWOODS TRL MED 90-A4
MEADOWVALE DR EPR 132-D3
MEADOWVALE RD NW ER . .19-B3,33-C1
MEADOWVIEW CT PRL 161-C3
MEADOWVIEW DR MTA 102-D3
MEADOWVIEW DR SWR . . .82-E4,96-E1
MEADOWVIEW DR WBT 80-D1
MEADOWVIEW LN EAG 135-C3
MEADOWVIEW RD BLO 134-E3
MEADOWVIEW RD SWD 117-C3
MEADOWVIEW TER SB 116-A3
MEADOWWOOD CT SAV 161-E2
MEADOWWOOD CT N BP 78-B3
MEADOWWOOD DR SAV 161-E2
MEADOWWOOD DR N BP 78-B3
MEADVILLE ST GRW 117-E3
MEANDER DR MED 90-A2
MEANDER RD GV 105-E2
MEANDER RD HAN 61-A3
MEARS AVE MH 122-B3
MECHANIC AVE STP 108-E3,109-A3
MECHANIC ST RFD 74-B3
MEDALLION DR MH 135-E1
MEDARY AVE EAG 149-A2
MEDCOM BLVD EPR 133-A3
MEDICINE LAKE
BLVD E PLY 91-B4,105-C1
MEDICINE LAKE
DR W PLY 91-A4,105-A1
MEDICINE LAKE RD CRY 91-D4
MEDICINE LAKE RD NH 91-C4
MEDICINE RIDGE RD PLY .91-B4,105-B1
MEDINA RD MED 89-E4,90-A3
MEDINA RD PLY 90-B3
MEDINA ST N LOR 89-B2
MEDINA LAKE DR MED 90-A1
MEDLEY CIR GV 91-C4,105-C1
MEDLEY LN N GV 105-C1
MEDLEY LN NE SM 47-B3
MEDLEY RD GV 91-C4,105-C1
MEDORA CT MH 122-A3
MEDORA RD MH 122-A3
MEEHAN DR WBT 81-B2
MEETING PL MTK 104-E3
MEETING ST MTK 104-E3
MEG GRACE LN EPR 133-B1
MEGGAN CT HAS 166-E3
MEGGAN DR HAS 166-E3
MEGHANS LN EAG 149-B2
MEHIGAN ST NW NB 93-B1
MEISTER CT COR 76-A2
MEISTER RD COR 75-E2,76-A2
MEISTER RD NE FRI 79-A4,93-A1
MEISVILLE TRL DT 195-A4
MELANIE TRL N NST 40-C2
MELBOURNE AVE SE MPL 107-B3
MELBY AVE NE SM 47-B3
MELBY CT NE SM 47-B3
MELDAHL LN NFD 219-D3
MELINA AVE NE SM 47-B3
MELINA CIR NE SM 47-B3
MELINA CT NE SM 47-B3
MELIS WAY EPR 133-B1
MELISSA CIR EPR 132-B2
MELISSA LN WBT 80-E2
MELLGREN LN DAT 144-C3
MELODY AVE N CGT 12-C4,26-C1
MELODY CT EPR 133-A1
MELODY DR NE FRI 78-D2
MELODY LN BPT 187-A3
MELODY LN BUR 148-E3
MELODY LN CHN 117-D4
MELODY LN EDI 119-E3
MELODY LN MED 89-E4,90-A4
MELODY LN MTK 119-A1
MELODY HILL CIR CHN 117-E4
MELODY HILL RD CHN 117-D4
MELODY LAKE DR EDI 119-E3

MELROSE AVE SLP 105-C3
MELROSE ST MHT 81-D4
MELROSE CHAS EPR 132-B3
MELVILLE CT N SWR 96-D1
MEMORIAL AVE N BYT 96-D3
MEMORIAL PKWY MPL 92-B3
MEMORIAL TRL PRL 161-B3
MEMORY CT NSP 109-B1
MEMORY LN CRY 91-D3
MEMORY LN NSP 109-B1
MEMORY LN NE FRI 78-E2
MENDAKOTA CT MH 135-E1,136-A1
MENDAKOTA DR MH 136-A1
MENDEL AVE N BYT 96-D4
MENDEL AVE N WLT 110-D2
MENDEL AVE S DET 152-D3
MENDEL RD N GRA 82-C2
MENDEL RD N SWT 82-D3
MENDEL AVENUE CT S DET 152-D3
MENDELSSOHN AVE N BP .77-C3,91-C1
MENDELSSOHN AVE N GV 105-C2
MENDELSSOHN
AVE N PLY 91-C2,105-C1
MENDELSSOHN LN EDI 119-C2
MENDELSSOHN LN GV 105-C1
MENDOTA BRG FS 121-C4
MENDOTA RD IGH 122-C4
MENDOTA RD SL 122-C4
MENDOTA RD WSP 122-C4
MENDOTA RD W IGH 122-C4
MENDOTA RD W MH 122-A4
MENDOTA RD W WSP 122-B4
MENDOTA ST STP 108-D3
MENDOTA HEIGHTS CIR MH 136-A1
MENDOTA HEIGHTS
RD MH 135-D2,136-A2
MENDOZA AVE JOR 173-B1
MENDOZA AVE SCT 173-B1
MENKE AVE SHK 146-B3
MENKE CIR SHK 146-A3
MENSING WAY CF 208-B3
MENTZER TRL LND 12-D4
MENTZER TRL N CGT 12-C4,26-C1
MERCER ST STP 121-E2
MERCHAK CIR N NOH 111-C1
MERCURY CIR SVW 80-A3
MERCURY DR NE FRI 78-D3
MERCURY DR W SVW 79-E3,80-A3
MERE DR EPR 118-D4
MERGANSER CT CHN 131-E3
MERGANSER CT EAG 135-D4
MERGANSER CT LL 66-D3
MERGER ST NYA 142-C4
MERIDAN ST N BEL 185-E1
MERIDAN ST S BEL 185-E2
MERIDIAN AVE BPT 185-E3,199-E1
MERIDIAN AVE BUF 58-D2
MERIDIAN AVE BUT 44-D4,58-D1
MERIDIAN AVE MLT 44-D2
MERIDIAN AVE MOT 44-D2
MERIDIAN AVE N BUT 44-D4,58-D1
MERIDIAN AVE N MOT 16-D3,30-D2
MERIDIAN AVE S FKT 86-D1
MERIDIAN AVE S MVT 72-D4
MERIDIAN AVE S WDT 86-D1
MERIDIAN CIR BPT 185-E4
MERIDIAN CIR N MG 77-B3
MERIDIAN CT SHK 146-C2
MERIDIAN DR GV 106-A1
MERIDIAN DR MPW 94-D4
MERIDIAN DR ROB 92-A4,106-A1
MERIDIAN DR SHK 146-C2
MERIDIAN ST RCH 134-C2
MERILANE AVE EDI 119-D2
MERILEE DR MTK 119-A2
MERINO AVE WTT 115-E2
MERLEN DR MTK 105-A4
MERLOT CRV EAG 135-B4
MEROLD DR EDI 119-D3
MERRIAM LN STP 107-C4
MERRIAM RD MTK 119-A2
MERRIAM ST MPL 106-D2
MERRIBEE DR GV 106-A1
MERRIFIELD CT SHK 146-C3
MERRIFIELD ST SHK 146-C3
MERRILL ST RVL 93-D3,107-D1
MERRILL ST STP 107-D2
MERRIMAC CT N PLY 90-C2
MERRIMAC LN PLY 90-C2
MERRIMAC LN N MG 76-C1
MERRIMAC LN N PLY 90-C3,104-C1
MERRIMAN CT DEL 87-D2
MERRIMAN DR DEL 87-D2
MERRIMAN DR FKT 87-D2
MERRITT CIR EDI 119-D3
MERRITT CT SHK 146-C3
MERRITT ST SHK 146-C3
MERRY LN SWD 118-A3
MERRYWOOD LN MTA 116-E4
MERSEY PT EAG 150-B1
MERSEY WAY EAG 150-B1
MERTENS ST N JOR 173-B2
MERTENS ST S JOR 173-B2
MERZ WAY IND 88-E3
MESA VERDE CT BUR 149-A3
MESABI AVE MPW 95-A3
MESABI AVE NSP 95-A3
MESABI RD MPW 95-A3
MESSER AVE SSP 136-E1
MESSIAH RD RW 182-D4,196-D1
METCALF DR EAG 149-A2
METRO BLVD EDI 133-E1
METRO DR BLO 135-A2
METRO PKWY BLO 135-A2
MEYER CT N MPW 95-B3
MEYER ST MPW 109-B3
MEYERS AVE NE FRI 78-D3
MICA TRL EAG 149-B1
MICHAEL AVE DT 194-E1,208-E1
MICHAEL AVE MT 166-E4,180-E3
MICHAEL DR MPW 109-B2
MICHAEL LN HAS 166-E3
MICHAEL LN MPW 109-B3
MICHAEL ST STP 109-B4,123-B1
MICHAEL POINT DR EAG 149-B2
MICHAELE LN MTK 118-C3
MICHAELSON ST N NOH 111-D1
MICHELE LN EPR 132-D1
MICHELLE AVE CHN 145-E2
MICHELLE AVE CHS 145-E2
MICHELLE CIR BUR 148-E3
MICHELLE DR EAG 149-D1
MICHELLE ST HAT 201-C2
MICHIGAN AVE BLA 65-A4
MICHIGAN CT EAG 150-B2
MICHIGAN ST STP 122-A1
MICKELSON LN N CGT 26-C3
MICKEY LN MPW 109-B2
MID OAKS AVE N SWR 96-D1
MID OAKS LN RVL 107-D1
MID OAKS RD RVL 107-D1
MIDDLE LN EAG 150-B2
MIDDLE ST N LC 94-B3
MIDDLE ST W CF 222-B1
MIDDLESET RD EPR 133-A2
MIDDLETON AVE STP 121-E2
MIDDLETOWN RD NE SLK 78-E1
MIDLAND AVE WBL 95-A2
MIDLAND CT WBL 95-A2
MIDLAND GROVE RD RVL 93-C4
MIDLAND HILLS RD RVL 107-B1
MIDLOTHIAN RD RVL 93-D4,107-D1
MIDVALE PL MPW 109-B3
MIDWAY PKWY STP 107-D2
MIDWAY ST NE BLA 65-C4,79-C1
MIDWEST AVE N WLT 110-D4
MIDWEST TRL N WLT 110-D3
MIDWEST TRAIL CIR N WLT 110-D3
MIDWEST TRAIL CT N WLT 110-D3
MIDWEST TRAIL PL N WLT 110-D3
MIELKE RD SHK 160-D1
MIESVILLE TRL DT 194-E4,195-A4
MIKE CIR HUT 112-A1
MIKE CT SHK 160-C2
MIKE ST BLA 65-A4
MIKE COLLINS DR EAG 136-A3
MILBERT RD MTK 105-A2
MILDRED AVE EDI 119-E4
MILDRED AVE N CGT 12-C3
MILDRED DR RCH 120-C4
MILDRED DR RVL 93-C3
MILDRED PL ROB 92-A3
MILDRED TER MTK 105-B3
MILE DR WBY 123-E4,137-E1
MILFORD LN WIL 95-D1
MILFORD ST STP 108-B3
MILITARY HWY FS 121-B3
MILITARY RD ANO 63-C1
MILITARY RD CG 137-E2,138-A2
MILITARY RD NEW 123-B4
MILITARY RD TF 14-B3
MILITARY RD WBY 123-C4,137-D1
MILL AVE ANO 49-C4
MILL AVE WTT 101-B3
MILL AVE NE WAT 101-B3
MILL AVE SE WAT 101-B3
MILL CT MO 31-E2,32-A2
MILL DR MED 90-B2
MILL LN WAC 129-D4
MILL RD CV 66-D2
MILL RD HOP 105-B4,119-B1
MILL RD RW 210-E1
MILL RD WAC 129-D4
MILL RUN MTK 105-B4
MILL ST CLK 1-D1
MILL ST COL 143-E4
MILL ST EXC 117-E3
MILL ST HEN 198-D3
MILL ST JOR 173-B2
MILL ST LOL 103-E2
MILL ST MSC 55-C4
MILL ST SWD 117-E4,118-A4
MILL ST TF 14-C3
MILL ST WAY 104-C3
MILL ST WBT 80-E2
MILL ST E CF 208-B4
MILL ST E VER 179-D2
MILL ST NE CH 92-D2
MILL ST W CF 208-B4
MILL CREEK DR EPR 133-B4
MILL POND DR JOR 173-B3
MILL POND LN MOU 116-D1
MILL POND TRL HAN 60-E3
MILL RUN CIR EAG 150-A1
MILL RUN CT EAG 136-A4,150-A1
MILL RUN LN EAG 150-A1
MILL RUN PATH EAG 150-A1
MILL RUN RD MO 31-E2,32-A2
MILL TRAIL DR MO 32-A2
MILL TRAIL LN MO 32-A2
MILLARD AVE HAS 166-E3
MILLER AVE WBL 81-A3
MILLER AVE N CGT 40-C1
MILLER PKWY E EPR 132-D2
MILLER PKWY W EPR 132-C2
MILLER RD CHM 63-C1
MILLER RD HUT 97-E4
MILLER RD S CG 151-E1,152-A2
MILLER ST GV 105-C3
MILLER ST SHK 146-C3
MILLER ST S SHK 146-C3
MILLER CREST LN STP 108-E4
MILLER VIEW RD CLT 189-A3
MILLERS CIR PRL 161-C3
MILLERS LN EDI 120-A4
MILLFORD DR EPR 132-D3
MILLICENT LN N CGT 26-C2
MILLPOND AVE BUR 148-E2
MILLPOND CT CHS 131-C4
MILLPOND PL EDI 119-E2
MILLSTON RD ORO 103-E4
MILLWOOD AVE RVL 93-E3,94-A3
MILLWOOD RD MTK 118-C3
MILNER ST WBT 81-A3
MILTON ST N RVL 93-E4
MILTON ST N STP 107-E4,121-E1
MILTON ST N SVW 79-E4,93-E2
MILTON ST S STP 121-E1
MILWAUKEE AVE MPL 106-E3
MILWAUKEE RD SHK 146-B2
MILWAUKEE RD TRT 126-B2
MILWAUKEE ST HOP 119-C2
MIMOSA LN NB 93-A1
MINA CT MHT 95-C1
MINA ST WSP 122-B2
MINAR AVE N SWT 96-D1
MINAR AVE S AFT 110-D4
MINAR LN N SWT 96-D1
MINDY CT N CGT 26-D1
MINDY LN MON 72-C4
MINDY CREEK LN SCF 14-D2
MINEA ST WSP 122-B3
MINERAL PT LL 66-C4
MINERAL POND BLVD E ANO 49-C3
MINERAL POND BLVD W ANO 49-C3
MINERAL POND CT ANO 49-C3
MINIKAHDA CT SLP 120-A1
MINJON DR APV 163-A2
MINK LN NO 80-C3
MINNAQUA DR GV 105-E1
MINNEAPOLIS AVE MPL 107-A3
MINNEAPOLIS AVE MTA 103-A4
MINNEAPOLIS RD NE WAT 101-B3
MINNEHAHA AVE FS 121-B3
MINNEHAHA AVE MPL ..106-E3,121-A1
MINNEHAHA AVE MPW 109-B3
MINNEHAHA AVE E STP .108-D3,109-A3
MINNEHAHA AVE W STP 107-D3,108-A3
MINNEHAHA BLVD EDI 120-A3
MINNEHAHA CIR N SLP 119-C1
MINNEHAHA CIR S SLP 119-C1
MINNEHAHA CRV MTK 104-E4
MINNEHAHA CT MTK 104-E4
MINNEHAHA CT SLP 119-C1
MINNEHAHA PKWY E MPL120-D3,121-A2
MINNEHAHA PKWY W MPL 120-C3
MINNEHAHA PL MTK 104-E4
MINNEHAHA ST FS 121-C4
MINNEHAHA
ACADEMY DR MPL 121-B2
MINNESOTA AVE BL 18-B3
MINNESOTA AVE BLA 65-A4
MINNESOTA AVE RVL 94-A4
MINNESOTA AVE N CGT 12-C3
MINNESOTA AVE N VER 179-C2
MINNESOTA AVE S VER 179-C2
MINNESOTA AVE W FH 107-D2
MINNESOTA AVE W LC 94-B4
MINNESOTA CT S SHK 146-B3
MINNESOTA DR BLO 134-A2
MINNESOTA LN N MG 76-D1
MINNESOTA LN N PLY ...90-D3,104-D1
MINNESOTA ST CHS 145-D2
MINNESOTA ST HEN 198-D3
MINNESOTA ST MO 31-C2
MINNESOTA ST SCF 14-C2
MINNESOTA ST STP 108-B4
MINNESOTA ST E CF 208-B4
MINNESOTA ST N SHK 146-B2
MINNESOTA ST S BAY 97-B4
MINNESOTA ST S SHK 146-B2
MINNESOTA ST SE PRL 161-B3
MINNESOTA ST W CF 208-A4
MINNESOTA BLUFFS DR BLO ...147-D2
MINNESOTA
RIVER RD BLO 135-A4,148-E1
MINNESOTA VALLEY
BLU DR LVT 159-D2
MINNESOTA VALLEY
ELE DR JOR 173-C2
MINNETOGA TER MTK 119-A3
MINNETONKA AVE ORO 103-D4
MINNETONKA AVE N WAY 104-B3
MINNETONKA AVE S WAY 104-B3
MINNETONKA BLVD DPH 118-B1
MINNETONKA BLVD EXC 117-E3
MINNETONKA BLVD GRW117-E3,118-A2
MINNETONKA BLVD HOP 105-B4,119-B1
MINNETONKA BLVD MTK 118-D1,119-A1
MINNETONKA BLVD SLP .105-E4,106-A4
MINNETONKA BLVD SWD 118-A2
MINNETONKA CIR MTK 118-E1
MINNETONKA DR MTK ...118-E1,119-A1
MINNETONKA DR SWD 117-D3
MINNETONKA
HIGHLANDS LN ORO 103-B3
MINNETONKA INDUSTRIAL
RD MTK 118-D1
MINNETONKA MILLS RD HOP ..119-B1
MINNETONKA MILLS RD MTK ..119-B1
MINNEWASHTA CT CHN 131-B1
MINNEWASHTA
PKWY CHN 117-B4,131-B1
MINNEWASHTA PKWY VIC 131-B2
MINNEWASHTA
WOODS DR CHN 117-D4
MINNIE AVE ORO 103-B4
MINNIE RD HUT 98-B4
MINNIE B GRANT
LN NE LWT 23-E3,24-A3
MINT CIR SHK 146-B3
MINUTE MAN ALC EPR 133-B2
MINUTEMAN LN LEX 65-C4
MIRA AVE APV 163-D1
MIRACLE LN MTK 118-D3
MIRADA CT BUR 148-E2
MIRIAM ST MH 122-B2
MIRROR LAKES DR EDI 119-D3
MISSION CIR BLO 148-C1
MISSION CT CHN 132-B3
MISSION CT NB 93-A1
MISSION LN E BLO 148-D1
MISSION RD BLO 148-C1
MISSION HILLS CIR CHN 132-B3
MISSION HILLS DR CHN 132-A3
MISSION HILLS LN CHN 132-B3
MISSION HILLS WAY E CHN 132-B3
MISSION HILLS WAY W CHN ...132-A3
MISSION HOUSE LN NB 93-A1
MISSISSIPPI AVE BLA 65-A4
MISSISSIPPI BLVD NW CR ..63-E2,64-A3
MISSISSIPPI CIR NB 79-B3
MISSISSIPPI CT MPL 92-C2
MISSISSIPPI CT NIT 165-E1
MISSISSIPPI DR MO 31-E2
MISSISSIPPI DR N BP 64-A3
MISSISSIPPI DR N CHM ...63-E2,64-A3
MISSISSIPPI DR N MPL 92-C2
MISSISSIPPI DR NW CR 63-E2
MISSISSIPPI LN N BP 78-C3
MISSISSIPPI LN N CHM 49-B4
MISSISSIPPI PL NE FRI 78-D3
MISSISSIPPI RD NW ER 33-C2
MISSISSIPPI ST HUD 111-E3
MISSISSIPPI ST NB 79-B3
MISSISSIPPI ST PRE 167-B1
MISSISSIPPI ST STP 108-C3
MISSISSIPPI ST N MPW ..94-C4,108-C1
MISSISSIPPI ST NE FRI 78-D3,79-A3
MISSISSIPPI TRL NIT 151-E4,165-E1
MISSISSIPPI WAY NE FRI 78-D3
MISSISSIPPI RIVER
BLVD N STP 107-B4,121-B1
MISSISSIPPI RIVER BLVD S STP .121-C3
MISSOURI AVE BLA 65-A4
MISTRAL LN EPR 118-D4
MISTY MORNING LN EPR 147-B1
MITCHELL AVE STP 109-A4
MITCHELL CIR SE PRL 161-B3
MITCHELL DR BLT 17-E3
MITCHELL PL WIL 95-D1
MITCHELL RD BLT 17-E2
MITCHELL RD EPR 132-E2
MITCHELL RIDGE DR BLT 17-E2
MITCHELLS CT MHT 95-B1
MITOKA CIR NE PRL 161-B1
MITTEN XING EXC 117-E3
MOBECK AVE CNC 12-E3
MOBIL MNR W JT 145-E4
MOCCASIN AVE MHT 81-D3
MOCCASIN CT BUR 162-A1
MOCCASIN TRL CHN 131-D1
MOCCASIN VALLEY RD EDI 133-C1
MOCKINGBIRD AVE SHK 146-C3
MOCKINGBIRD DR WAC 129-C4
MOCKINGBIRD LN EPR 118-E4
MOCKINGBIRD LN MO 31-E3
MODERN RD BP 77-C4
MOHAWK AVE STP 109-A3
MOHAWK DR CHN 118-A4,132-A1
MOHAWK DR COR 75-D4,89-D1
MOHAWK DR MED 89-D1
MOHAWK RD NSP 95-A3
MOHAWK TRL EDI 119-C4,133-C1
MOHICAN CT MH 136-A1
MOHICAN ST NW SF 7-C3
MOLAN TER NE CH 92-E1
MOLAND AVE ML 43-D2
MOLINE CIR CHN 117-E4
MOLINE RD IND 102-E2,103-A2
MONALTRIE AVE DPH 118-B1
MONARCH ST SHK 146-B3
MONARDA AVE BYT 96-D3
MONARDO LN EDI 133-E1
MONDAMIN ST MPL 121-A3
MONET CT MH 136-A2
MONET LN MH 136-A2
MONITOR ST SLP 119-D1
MONK CT CHN 132-B3
MONMOUTH RD MOU 117-A2
MONN AVE VH 94-C2
MONN AVE WBL 95-A2
MONN CT WBL 95-A2
MONNENS AVE SHK 146-B3
MONROE AVE EXC 117-D3
MONROE AVE PRL 160-E4
MONROE AVE N HOP 119-C2
MONROE AVE S EDI 119-C2
MONROE AVE S HOP 119-C2
MONROE CIR NE BLA 64-E1
MONROE CT BEC 2-E3
MONROE CT NFD 219-D4
MONROE CT STP 121-E1
MONROE CT NE EB 22-D3
MONROE DR BEC 2-E3
MONROE DR NE BLA 64-E2
MONROE PL HOP 119-C1
MONROE ST ANO 49-D4
MONROE ST BL 18-A4
MONROE ST HAS 152-C4,166-C1
MONROE ST PRE 153-B4,167-B1
MONROE ST N NOH 111-C1
MONROE ST N SCF 14-C2
MONROE ST NE ATT 8-D1
MONROE ST NE BLA 50-E4,64-E1
MONROE ST NE CH 92-E2
MONROE ST NE EB 8-D3,22-D3
MONROE ST NE FRI 78-E3,92-E1
MONROE ST NE HL 50-E1
MONROE ST NE MPL 92-E4,106-E1
MONROE ST NE SLK 78-E2
MONROE ST NW ER 20-A1
MONROE ST NW SF 8-C4
MONROE ST S SHK 146-A3
MONROE ST W NG 128-A1
MONTANA AVE BL 18-A3
MONTANA AVE BLA 65-A4
MONTANA AVE MPW 109-B2
MONTANA AVE E STP ...108-C2,109-A2
MONTANA AVE W STP ...107-E2,108-B2
MONTANA CIR MPW 109-B2
MONTCALM CT STP 121-E2
MONTCALM HL STP 121-E2
MONTCALM PL STP 121-E2
MONTCLAIR AVE MV 79-C2
MONTCLAIR DR LND 12-D3
MONTCLAIR LN MOU 117-A1
MONTCLAIR PL WIL 95-D1
MONTCROIX DR HUD 111-D3
MONTECITO DR SHK 146-E3
MONTEGUE TER BP 78-B2
MONTEREY AVE CRT 176-A3
MONTEREY AVE EDI 120-A2
MONTEREY AVE SAV 162-A2
MONTEREY AVE VH 94-C2
MONTEREY AVE S SAV ..148-A4,162-A1
MONTEREY AVE S SLP ..106-A4,120-A1
MONTEREY CT EPR 132-E3
MONTEREY CT N SVW 79-E3
MONTEREY CT S SVW 79-E3
MONTEREY DR CHN 132-A2
MONTEREY DR SLP 120-A1
MONTEREY DR SVW 79-E3
MONTEREY LN EAG 135-C4
MONTEREY PKWY SLP 106-A4
MONTGOMERIE AVE DPH 118-B1
MONTGOMERY CT EPR 132-D3
MONTGOMERY RD MOU 117-B2
MONTGOMERY ST STP 107-C3
MONTGOMERY
ELEMENTAR MGY 215-D4
MONTICELLO ALC WBY 124-B4
MONTICELLO AVE EAG 149-C1
MONTICELLO DR WBY 124-B4
MONTICELLO LN N CHM 63-B1
MONTICELLO LN N MG 63-B4,77-B2
MONTMORENCY ST VH 94-E2
MONTREAL AVE STP 121-D2
MONTREAL CIR STP 121-E2
MONTREAL WAY STP 121-E2
MONTROSE AVE DEL 87-D3
MONTROSE BLVD BUF 58-E3
MONTROSE LN STP 121-C2
MONTROSE PL STP 107-B4
MONTROSE RD WBY 123-D2
MOODY AVE CNC 12-E4
MOODY LN N CGT 40-C1
MOODY RD S SCF 14-D2
MOOER LN EPR 147-A1
MOOERS AVE SHK 146-C4
MOON GLOW RD HUT 98-D4
MOONBEAM DR W HUT 98-D3
MOONBEAM LN WBY 124-A1
MOONBEAM RD HUT 98-D4
MOONBEAM RD W HUT 98-D3
MOONEY DR NB 93-B2
MOONLIGHT BAY MAY 69-A3
MOONLIGHT BAY WBY 124-A1
MOONLIGHT DR LVT 160-B2
MOONLIGHT DR WBY 124-A1
MOONLIGHT LN EPR 132-E1
MOONLIGHT PL WBY 124-A1
MOONLIGHT HILL RD MTK 118-E2
MOONLITE DR CP 65-D3
MOONSTONE DR EAG 149-B2
MOORE AVE EDI 119-E2
MOORE ST FH 107-C1
MOORE ST STP 107-C4,121-C1
MOORE ST W SWR 82-E4,83-A4
MOORE LAKE DR W FRI 78-E4
MOORLAND AVE EDI 119-E2,120-A2
MOORLAND CIR MTK 118-D1

MOORLAND DR EPR 118-D4,132-D1
MOORLAND RD E MTK 118-D1
MOORLAND CHAS BP 77-E1,78-A1
MORAY AVE VH 94-C2
MOREHEAD AVE WBL 81-B3
MORELAND AVE E WSP 122-C3
MORELAND AVE W WSP 122-B3
MORELAND CIR WSP 122-C3
MORELAND CT MPW 123-B3
MORGAN AVE BUR 162-B1
MORGAN AVE STP 121-C3
MORGAN AVE N BC 78-B3,92-B2
MORGAN AVE N BP 78-B2
MORGAN AVE N CGT 26-D3,40-D1
MORGAN AVE N MAY 68-D1
MORGAN AVE N MPL 92-B4,106-B2
MORGAN AVE N NST 40-D2
MORGAN AVE N SWT 82-D4,96-D1
MORGAN AVE N WLT 110-D2
MORGAN AVE S AFT 110-D4
MORGAN AVE S BLO 134-B4,148-B1
MORGAN AVE S BUR 148-B4,162-B1
MORGAN AVE S DET 152-D3
MORGAN AVE S MPL 106-B3,120-B3
MORGAN AVE S RCH 120-B4,134-B1
MORGAN CIR BLO 134-B2,148-B1
MORGAN CIR N BP 78-B2
MORGAN CT BUR 148-B4
MORGAN CT MPL 120-B4
MORGAN DR BUR 148-B4
MORGAN DR N FLT 39-C4
MORGAN DR S FLT 39-C4
MORGAN LN EPR 132-E3
MORGAN LN WCT 129-B3
MORGAN PL BUR 148-B4
MORGAN RD MED 89-E4
MORGAN RD RF 140-E2
MORGAN ST MHT 81-D3
MORK CIR N CHM 63-C1
MORLEY DR LND 12-C3
MORLOCK DR SCT 173-C2
MORNING DOVE DR BEC 3-A3
MORNING GLORY LN LAT 201-B3
MORNINGSIDE AVE VH 80-C4
MORNINGSIDE CIR EPR 119-A4
MORNINGSIDE CIR STP 123-A1
MORNINGSIDE CT LND 26-D1
MORNINGSIDE DR LES 212-D3
MORNINGSIDE DR STP 123-A1
MORNINGSIDE PL VH 80-C4
MORNINGSIDE RD EDI 120-A2
MORNINGSIDE RD MED 103-D1
MORNINGSIDE RD SLP 119-E2,120-A2
MORNINGSIDE RD SWR 96-E2
MORNINGVIEW CT MTA 102-E4
MORNINGVIEW DR MTA 102-E4
MORNINGVIEW TER MTA 102-E4
MORRAINE WAY EPR 132-D2
MORRILL LN MPL 121-B2
MORRIS AVE S BLO 134-A3,148-A1
MORRIS CIR BLO 134-A4,148-A2
MORRIS LN BLO 148-A2
MORRIS RD BLO 134-A3,148-A1
MORRIS RD N WLT 110-D3
MORRIS ST BEC 2-E4
MORRIS ST NW NB 93-B1
MORRIS TRL N MAY 67-D1
MORRISON AVE N LC 94-C4
MORRISON ST HUD 111-D3
MORSE AVE EXC 117-E3
MORSE ST N NYA 142-C4
MORSON CIR MH 136-B1
MORTON AVE NW ER 33-D2
MORTON RD MTK 104-D3
MORTON ST E STP 122-C2
MORTON ST W STP 122-B2
MOSBY RD WBL 95-B2
MOTOR AVE SSP 122-D2
MOTOR PL MPL 120-A2
MOTOR ST EDI 119-E2
MOUND AVE SVW 79-E3,80-A3
MOUND AVE TKB 117-D3
MOUND DR SJT 98-C3
MOUND DR S HUT 98-D3
MOUND ST SHK 146-B3
MOUND ST STP 108-D4
MOUND ST SWR 97-A2
MOUND ST E SHK 146-B3
MOUND ST W NG 128-A1
MOUND TRL CV 66-C2
MOUND SPRINGS TER BLO 134-D4
MOUND VIEW RD RF 140-E1
MOUNDS AVE NB 79-B3
MOUNDS BLVD STP 108-D4
MOUNDS ST NB 79-C3
MOUNDSVIEW AVE RVL 108-A1
MOUNDSVIEW DR MV 79-B2
MOUNDVIEW DR RW 196-E4
MOUNT CRV BL 18-A3
MOUNT TER MTK 118-E2
MOUNT AIRY ST STP 108-B3
MOUNT CARMEL RD DAT 158-E1,159-A1
MOUNT CURVE AVE MPL 106-C3
MOUNT CURVE BLVD STP 121-C2
MOUNT CURVE BLVD N BP 77-C2
MOUNT CURVE RD BLO 133-D3
MOUNT CURVE RD EPR 133-B4
MOUNT CURVE ST DPH 118-A2
MOUNT HOPE DR STP 122-C1
MOUNT HOPE RD CAR 145-B4
MOUNT HOPE ST STP 122-C2
MOUNT IDA ST STP 108-C3
MOUNT NORMANDALE
CRV BLO 133-E3
MOUNT NORMANDALE DR BLO 133-E3
MOUNT RIDGE RD RVL 93-C3
MOUNT VERNON AVE E MPW 108-B1
MOUNT VERNON CT WBY 124-B3
MOUNT VERNON LN WBY 124-B3
MOUNT VIEW AVE MPL 106-B3
MOUNTAIN WAY CHN 118-B4
MOUNTAIN VIEW CT CHN 118-B4
MOUNTHALL TER MTK 118-E2
MOURNING DOVE CT EAG 135-D4
MOURNING DOVE RD LL 65-E2
MOYER AVE S AFT 124-D3
MT CARMEL RD RW 196-E3
MT HOOD LN RW 210-E1
MTC RD FS 134-E2
MUD LAKE RD IND 88-B3
MUHLENHARDT
RD S SHK 147-B4,161-B1
MUIR AVE N BYT 96-D3
MUIR LN BUR 148-E3
MUIRFIELD CIR NYA 142-C3
MUIRFIELD CIR SWD 118-B3
MUIRFIELD CIR NW RAM 34-C4
MUIRFIELD LN EPR 132-C1
MUIRFIELD TRL TRT 125-D3
MULBERRY CIR E CHN 118-A4,132-A1
MULBERRY CIR S SHK 160-C2
MULBERRY CIR W CHN 117-E4,131-E1
MULBERRY ST STP 108-B4
MULBERRY ST TF 14-B2
MULBERRY ST E SWR 97-A1
MULBERRY ST W SWR 96-E1,97-A1
MULCARE DR NE CH 92-E1
MULLIGAN DR OST 28-B4
MUMFORD RD BC 92-B1
MUNSTER AVE STP 121-C3
MURDOCK TER EPR 133-A3
MURIEL BLVD WSP 122-C4
MURIEL RD MTK 105-A4
MURPHY AVE FH 107-D2
MURPHY AVE SHK 146-C3
MURPHY CT SHK 146-C3
MURPHY PKWY EAG 149-C1
MURPHY ST HEN 198-C3
MURPHY ST HOP 119-D1
MURPHY LAKE
BLVD CRT 161-E4,175-D1
MURPHY LAKE RD CRT 162-A3
MURPHY LAKE RD SAV 161-E3,162-A3
MURRAY AVE SA 93-A4
MURRAY AVE WBL 81-A3
MURRAY CT SWD 117-E4
MURRAY ST HEN 198-C3
MURRAY ST STP 121-C3
MURRAY ST SWD 117-E4
MURRAY HILL RD CHN 117-D4
MURRAY HILL RD SWD 117-D4
MURRELL ST ML 43-D2
MUSHTOWN RD PRL 161-A4
MUSHTOWN RD SLT 161-B4,175-B3
MUSKRAT RUN LL 66-B4
MUSSER HALL NFD 219-E3
MUSTANG CT LL 65-E1
MUSTANG CT MV 79-B3
MUSTANG DR HUT 112-B1
MUSTANG DR MV 79-C3
MUSTANG LN LL 65-E1
MYERON RD N SWT 82-D2
MYERS AVE N BP 77-D4
MYERS HALL NFD 219-E3
MYHRE ST BEC 2-E3,3-A3
MYRICK ST LES 212-D3
MYRLE AVE WBL 81-B4,95-B1
MYRMAN ST WSP 122-B3
MYRTLE AVE STP 107-B3
MYRTLE CIR MTK 119-A1
MYRTLE CT MPW 109-B2
MYRTLE DR BUR 148-B4
MYRTLE LN LL 52-A4
MYRTLE PL SSP 122-D4
MYRTLE ST BUF 58-D2
MYRTLE ST HUD 111-D2
MYRTLE ST MPW 109-B1
MYRTLE ST E SWR 97-A1
MYRTLE ST N MPW 109-B2
MYRTLE ST W SWR 96-E1,97-A1
MYRTLEWOOD CT SWR 96-E1
MYRTLEWOOD RD ORO 104-A2
MYSTIC LN BUR 148-E3
MYSTIC ST STP 123-A2
MYSTIC LAKE BLVD NW PRL 160-D3
MYSTIC LAKE CIR PRL 160-D2
MYSTIC LAKE CIR NW PRL 160-D2
MYSTIC LAKE DR NW PRL 160-D2
MYSTIQUE DR N COR 76-B1

N

N ST WBY 123-D1
NAARCISSUS LN N MG 76-C1
NABER AVE NE SM 47-B3
NACRE ST NW SF 6-E3
NACRE ST NW STT 6-E2
NADALA AVE NE OTS 47-B1
NADEAU RD LC 94-B3
NAGELL CIR N MG 76-E3
NAMEKAGON ST HUD 111-E3
NANCE ST NW BT 6-E4,20-E1
NANCY CIR EAG 149-B3
NANCY CIR SVW 93-E1
NANCY DR LL 52-B4
NANCY LN EDI 120-A4
NANCY PL RVL 93-E4
NANCY PL SVW 79-E4,93-E2
NANTUCKET PL MTK 118-C3
NANTUCKET RD MTK 118-C3
NANTWICK LN BP 78-A1
NANTWICK RDG BP 77-E1,78-A1
NAOMI DR EDI 119-E4,133-E1
NAPA DR CHN 118-A4
NAPCO AVE N MPL 106-C2
NAPER BAY EAG 149-B2
NAPER ST GV 105-C1
NAPIER AVE NE OTS 33-C3
NAPIER PKWY NE SM 47-B3
NAPLES AVE BTT 143-D4,157-D1
NAPLES CIR NW SM 46-E3
NAPLES ST NE ATT 9-C2
NAPLES ST NE BLA 65-C3,79-C1
NAPLES ST NE EB 23-C4,37-C1
NAPLES ST NE HL 37-C4,51-C2
NAPLES ST NW ER 19-B4,33-B2
NAPOLEAN CIR SSP 122-D2
NARCISIS ST NW STT 7-E2
NARCISSIUS LN N MG 76-C3
NARCISSUS CRV VIC 131-A3
NARCISSUS CT VIC 131-A2
NARCISSUS CT N PLY 90-C2
NARCISSUS CT NW AND 49-E3
NARCISSUS CT NW OG 21-E2
NARCISSUS LN PLY 90-C2
NARCISSUS LN VIC 131-A2
NARCISSUS LN N MG 76-C2
NARCISSUS LN N PLY 104-C2
NARCISSUS ST VIC 131-A2
NARCISSUS ST NW AND 35-E4,49-E3
NARCISSUS ST NW CR 49-E3,63-E1
NARSISUS ST NW AND 35-E4
NARVIK CT EAG 149-C3
NARVIK DR EAG 149-C3
NASH RD BC 92-B1
NASHUA AVE NE OTS 33-C3
NASHUA LN MH 136-A1
NASON AVE NE SM 47-B2
NASON PKWY NE SM 47-C3
NASON PL STP 107-E2
NASON ST NE OTS 33-C3
NASON HILL RD N MAY 69-A1
NASON HILL RD N MSC 69-B1
NASSAU CIR NE BLA 65-A2
NASSAU CT NE BLA 51-A3,65-A2
NASSAU CT NE EB 9-A4
NASSAU ST NE BLA 65-A2
NASSAU ST NE HL 37-A3
NATALIE DR BUF 58-D2
NATALIE RD PRL 161-D1
NATCHEZ AVE CRT 162-A4,176-A1
NATCHEZ AVE NM 190-A4,204-A1
NATCHEZ AVE NMT 190-A2,204-A1
NATCHEZ AVE SAV 148-A3,162-A1
NATCHEZ AVE N GV 106-A2
NATCHEZ AVE S EDI 120-A2
NATCHEZ AVE S GV 106-A3
NATCHEZ AVE S SLP 106-A4,120-A1
NATCHEZ CIR SAV 162-A2
NATCHEZ CT SAV 162-A1
NATCHEZ LN SAV 162-A1
NATCHEZ PL SAV 162-A2
NATHAN AVE LND 12-D4,26-D1
NATHAN BLVD RFD 74-A4
NATHAN CT LND 12-D4
NATHAN LN PLY 91-B2
NATHAN LN N CGT 26-D2
NATHAN LN N MG 63-B4,77-B1
NATHAN LN N PLY 91-B2,105-B2
NATHAN RD SFT 158-D3
NATHANIEL CT VH 94-C2
NATIONAL CT NE BLA 65-D2
NATIONAL ST NE BLA 65-D2
NATIONAL SPORTS CTR BLA 65-A3
NATURE CT WBY 123-D1
NATURE LN EPR 132-B2
NATURE PATH WBY 123-D1
NATURE VIEW CT WSP 122-B4
NATURE VIEW LN WSP 122-B4
NATURE VIEW TRL VH 94-D1
NATURES WAY E LC 94-B4
NAUGHTOR AVE NE SM 47-C2
NAUGHTOR ST NE OTS 33-C3
NAUMKEAG ST N SHK 146-B2
NAUMKEAG ST S SHK 146-C3
NAUVOO LN EAG 150-A3
NAVAHO BPT 199-E2
NAVAHO TRL EDI 119-C4
NAVAJO AVE WTT 101-D4
NAVAJO DR CHN 132-A1
NAVAJO LN MH 136-A1
NAVAJO RD NSP 95-B3
NAVAJO RD E MED 90-B3
NAVAJO RD W MED 89-E3,90-A3
NAVAJO ST NW AND 35-C3
NAVAJO ST NW SF 7-C4
NAVARRE AVE ORO 117-C1
NAVARRE LN MTB 117-C1
NAVARRE LN ORO 117-C1
NAWADAHA BLVD MPL 121-B2
NAYLOR AVE HAT 187-C4,201-C1
NAYLOR AVE SCT 173-C3
NEAL AVE LND 12-D4,26-D1
NEAL AVE OPH 96-D3
NEAL AVE WTT 101-D3
NEAL AVE N BYT 96-D4,110-D1
NEAL AVE N SWT 82-D4,96-D1
NEAL AVE N WLT 110-D3
NEAL AVE S AFT 124-D3,138-D1
NEAL AVE S DET 138-D3,152-D2
NEAL CT N WLT 110-D3
NEAR MOUNTAIN BLVD CHN 118-B4
NEAR MOUNTAIN BLVD SWD 118-B4
NEBRASKA AVE BLA 65-A4
NEBRASKA AVE MPW 109-B2
NEBRASKA AVE E STP 108-E2,109-A2
NEBRASKA AVE W STP 107-E2,108-A2
NEBULA ST NE OXT 10-A2
NECHAS CIR EPR 132-D2
NEDDERSEN CIR N BP 77-D1
NEDDERSEN PKWY N BP 77-D1
NEEDHAM AVE NE OTS 33-C4
NEEDHAM AVE NE SM 47-C2
NEIL ARMSTRONG BLVD EAG 135-E3
NEILL PATH MT 167-A4
NEILL LAKE RD EPR 133-B3
NEILSON AVE LOL 103-D2
NELMARK AVE NE OTS 33-C3
NELMARK AVE NE SM 47-C2
NELSINE DR SWD 117-C3
NELSON AVE RW 210-E1
NELSON BLVD FCT 86-C1
NELSON BLVD MON 86-C1
NELSON CT CGT 12-E3
NELSON CT CNC 12-E3
NELSON CT NFD 219-D3
NELSON DR CW 1-B3
NELSON DR MTK 119-A2
NELSON DR SVW 79-E3
NELSON LN CNC 12-E3
NELSON RD IND 88-A4,102-A1
NELSON ST STP 109-A4,123-A1
NELSON ST SWR 97-A1
NELSON ST N FH 107-D2
NELSON FARM LN SJT 98-A3
NELSON FARM RD SJT 98-A3
NEMEC KNOLL RD EPR 133-A4
NEMITZ AVE MPW 123-B3
NEON DR NW RAM 35-B4,49-B1
NEON ST NW RAM 35-B3,49-B2
NEON ST NW SF 7-B3
NEPTUNE DR LND 12-D4
NEPTUNE ST MHT 81-D4
NESBITT AVE S BLO 133-E4,147-E1
NESBITT CIR BLO 133-E4
NESBITT RD BLO 133-E3
NESTER PL CGT 26-D2
NESTLING CIR EAG 149-C2
NET NORLIN CT MPW 95-A3
NEUMAN CIR CGT 12-D1
NEVADA AVE BLA 65-A4
NEVADA AVE BP 77-D1
NEVADA AVE CRT 175-D3
NEVADA AVE NMT 203-D1
NEVADA AVE SAV 147-D4,161-D1
NEVADA AVE E STP 108-C2,109-A2
NEVADA AVE N BP 77-D2
NEVADA AVE N CHM 63-D2
NEVADA AVE N CRY 91-D1
NEVADA AVE N GV 91-D4,105-D1
NEVADA AVE N NH 91-D3
NEVADA AVE S BLO 147-D2
NEVADA AVE S GV 105-D2
NEVADA AVE S SLP 105-D4
NEVADA AVE W STP 107-E2,108-A2
NEVADA CIR BP 77-D2
NEVADA CIR CHM 63-D2
NEVADA CIR N BP 77-D1
NEVADA CIR S BLO 133-D2,147-D1
NEVADA CT BP 77-D1
NEVADA CT N CHM 63-D2
NEVADA LN N CHM 63-D2
NEVADA ST SCF 14-D2
NEVADA ST S NFD 219-E4
NEVILLE AVE MHT 81-D4
NEW ST MO 31-D2
NEW BRIGHTON
BLVD MPL 93-A4,107-A1
NEW BRIGHTON BLVD NB 93-C2
NEW BRIGHTON BLVD RVL 93-B3
NEW BRIGHTON BLVD SA 93-B3
NEW BRIGHTON RD AH 93-C2
NEW BRIGHTON RD NB 93-C2
NEW CENTURY BLVD MPW 123-B2
NEW CENTURY DR TRT 111-E4
NEW CENTURY LN E MPW 123-C2
NEW CENTURY TER E MPW 123-B2
NEW JERSEY AVE BLA 65-A4
NEW MARKET DR EPR 132-C3
NEW MEXICO AVE BLA 65-A4
NEW PRAGUE BLVD WHT 203-A2
NEW YORK AVE BLA 65-A4
NEW YORK AVE EAG 150-A1
NEW YORK AVE N MPL 106-C1
NEWBERRY AVE N OPH 96-D3
NEWBERRY AVE N WLT 110-D2
NEWBERRY CIR N OPH 96-D3
NEWBERRY CT N SWT 96-D1
NEWBERRY TRL N CGT 26-D2
NEWBURY ALC WBY 123-D4
NEWBURY CT WBY 123-D4
NEWBURY DRAW WBY 123-D4
NEWBURY ECHO WBY 123-D4
NEWBURY RD WBY 123-D4
NEWCASTLE RD WBY 124-A3
NEWCOMBE ST STP 108-D3
NEWELL AVE LND 12-D4
NEWELL CIR APV 163-A2
NEWELL CIR N OPH 96-D3
NEWELL DR APV 163-A2
NEWGATE AVE N NST 54-D2
NEWGATE AVE N OPH 96-D3
NEWGATE AVE N SWT 82-D3
NEWGATE CIR N OPH 96-D3
NEWLANDER AVE CGT 12-E4
NEWLANDER AVE LND 12-D4
NEWLANDER CT CGT 12-E4
NEWMAN TRL SWR 96-C2
NEWPORT AVE CLT 188-D2,202-D1
NEWPORT AVE SLT 174-D1
NEWPORT DR EDI 119-C3
NEWPORT DR EPR 147-B1
NEWPORT DR MP 88-E4,89-A4
NEWTON AVE BUR 162-B1
NEWTON AVE WTT 101-B4,115-A1
NEWTON AVE N BC 78-B3,92-B2
NEWTON AVE N BP 78-B3
NEWTON AVE N MPL 92-B4,106-B2
NEWTON AVE NE WAT 101-B3
NEWTON AVE S BLO 134-B4
NEWTON AVE S MPL 106-B3,120-B3
NEWTON AVE S RCH 120-B4,134-B1
NEWTON AVE SE WAT 101-B4
NEWTON AVE SE WTT 101-B4
NEWTON CIR EKO 190-B4
NEWTOWN CT EAG 149-E1
NEZ PERCE CT CHN 132-A1
NEZ PERCE DR CHN 118-A4,132-A1
NIAGARA CT N MG 90-D1
NIAGARA LN N MG 76-D3,90-D1
NIAGARA LN N PLY 90-D4,104-D1
NIAGARA ST WAC 129-E4
NIBLICK LN EPR 133-B4
NICHOLAS CIR MO 31-B1
NICHOLAS CT WBL 95-A1
NICHOLAS DR HUT 112-C2
NICHOLAS WAY CHN 132-A2
NICHOLS CT SVW 94-A1
NICKLAUS WAY EPR 132-C3
NICOLAI AVE DT 181-A4,195-A4
NICOLAI AVE MIE 195-A2
NICOLAI AVE MT 167-A3,181-A3
NICOLE GLN SAV 147-E4
NICOLE LN RF 140-D2
NICOLLET AVE BL 17-E3
NICOLLET AVE BUR 148-D3,162-D1
NICOLLET AVE MPL 106-D4,120-D3
NICOLLET AVE RCH 120-D4,134-D1
NICOLLET AVE S BLO 134-D3,148-D1
NICOLLET BLVD E BUR 162-D1
NICOLLET BLVD W BUR 162-C1
NICOLLET CIR BLO 148-D1
NICOLLET CT BUR 162-D1
NICOLLET LN BUR 148-D4
NICOLLET MALL MPL 106-D2
NICOLLET ST MPL 106-D2
NICOLS PT EAG 149-B2
NICOLS RD BUR 135-A4
NICOLS RD EAG 135-A4,149-B2
NIELSON CIR GRF 75-A4
NIGHTHAWK DR SPT 70-E3
NIGHTINGALE BLVD SWR 96-D2
NIGHTINGALE CIR PRL 161-B2
NIGHTINGALE CT CHS 131-D4
NIGHTINGALE CT SWR 96-D2
NIGHTINGALE ST CR 64-B3
NIGHTINGALE ST NW AND 36-B4,50-B1
NIGHTINGALE ST NW CR 50-B4,64-A3
NIGHTINGALE ST NW OG 8-B4,22-B2
NIGHTINGALE ST NW SF 8-B3
NIKE RD MTA 115-E1,116-A1
NILE LN NW ER 33-D2
NILE PL NW ER 33-D2
NILES AVE STP 121-D2
NINA CT MH 121-E3,122-A3
NINA ST STP 108-B4
NINE MILE CV HOP 119-C3
NINE MILE CV E HOP 119-C3
NINE MILE CV N HOP 119-C3
NINE MILE CV S HOP 119-C3
NINE MILE CREEK CIR BLO 133-E3
NINE MILE CREEK
PKWY BLO 133-E3,134-A3
NINE OAKS CIR BLO 134-A3
NININGER RD HAS 152-C4,166-C1
NINTH AVE N HOP 119-B2
NINTH AVE N PLY 105-C2
NINTH AVE S HOP 119-B2
NIXON AVE SE WAT 101-B4
NOB HILL DR EDI 119-E4,133-E1
NOBLE AVE N BC 78-A4,92-A1
NOBLE AVE N BP 63-E4,77-E3
NOBLE AVE N CHM 63-E3
NOBLE AVE N CRY 92-A4
NOBLE AVE N GV 92-A4,106-A1
NOBLE AVE N ROB 92-A3
NOBLE DR GV 106-A1
NOBLE LN MOU 116-E1
NOBLE LN N BC 78-A4
NOBLE PKWY N BP 64-A4,78-A1
NOBLE RD AH 93-C2
NOBLE RD SWD 117-B3
NOEL AVE HCT 171-D2

NOEL DR E LC 94-C3
NOID DR BP 77-D4
NOKIA WAY EAG 149-C2
NOKOMIS AVE STP 109-A3
NOKOMIS AVE S MPL 121-A2
NOKOMIS CIR MPL 120-E3
NOKOMIS CT MPL 120-E3
NOKOMIS LN MPL 120-E3
NOKOMIS PKWY W MPL .120-E3,121-A3
NOLAN AVE N NST 40-D3
NOLAN AVE N OPH 96-D3
NOLAN AVE N WLT 110-D3
NOLAN CIR N OPH 96-D3
NOLAN DR MTK 119-B3
NOLDEN LN JOR 173-B2
NOON DR DAY 49-A4
NORBERT LN STP 121-C3
NORBERT PL STP 121-C3
NORCREST AVE N WLT 110-E1
NORCREST AVE S AFT ...124-E4,138-E1
NORD AVE S BLO 134-A2,148-A1
NORD CIR BLO 134-A4,148-A1
NORD DR BLO 148-A1
NORD LN HUT 97-E4,111-E1
NORD RD BLO 133-E4,134-A4
NORD CIRCLE RD NO 80-B2
NORDEN DR HSN 47-E3
NORDIC AVE N WLT 110-E3
NORDIC CIR EDI 119-D4
NORDIC DR EDI 119-D4
NORDIC DR RW 210-E1
NORDIC LN TRT 111-E4
NORDIC AVENUE CT N WLT 110-E3
NORDIN ST LL 52-B3
NORELIUS DR LND 12-D4
NORELIUS LN LND 12-D4
NORELIUS RD VAT 209-E4,210-A4
NORELL AVE OPH 96-E2
NORELL AVE N MAY 54-D4,68-D2
NORELL AVE N NST 54-E3
NORELL AVE N SWT 82-E3
NORELL AVE N WLT 110-E3
NORELL CT SWT 82-E3
NORELL RD S DET 152-E4
NOREX DR CHS 131-D2
NORFLEX DR HUT 112-C1
NORFOLK AVE STP 121-C3
NORFOLK AVE NW ER 33-D2
NORFOLK LN STP 121-C3
NORFOLK ST NW ER 19-D4
NORMA AVE AH 79-D4,93-D1
NORMA CIR AH 93-D1
NORMA LN MH 122-B2
NORMA LN WBY 110-A4
NORMAN AVE N BYT 110-D1
NORMAN DR MTK 118-D3
NORMAN LN CNC 12-E4
NORMAN CENTER DR BLO 133-E2
NORMAN CREEK TRL BLO 133-E2
NORMAN RIDGE CIR BLO 133-E3
NORMAN RIDGE DR BLO 133-E3
NORMANDALE AVE N BYT 96-E3
NORMANDALE BLVD BLO 133-E3,147-E2
NORMANDALE CIR CRT 175-E2
NORMANDALE CT EDI 119-E3
NORMANDALE CT N BYT 96-D3
NORMANDALE DR CRT 175-E2
NORMANDALE RD BLO 133-E2
NORMANDALE RD EDI ...119-E3,133-E1
NORMANDALE
HIGHLANDS CIR BLO 134-A4
NORMANDALE
HIGHLANDS DR BLO ..133-E4,134-A4
NORMANDY CRST EPR 147-C1
NORMANDY CT WBT 80-D2
NORMANDY CT N BYT 96-E3
NORMANDY LN MTK 118-D4
NORMANDY PL GV 91-E4,92-A4
NORRIS CIR STP 107-E3
NORRIS LAKE RD NW BT ..20-C2,21-B1
NORRIS LAKE RD NW OG 21-C1
NORSTED AVE S AFT 124-E3
NORTH AVE CGT 12-C4
NORTH AVE CHC 12-B4,26-B1
NORTH AVE EDI 119-E2
NORTH CIR HL 50-E3
NORTH CIR NE FRI 78-E2
NORTH CT JOR 173-B2
NORTH CT NB 79-B4
NORTH LN DPH 118-A2
NORTH RD CP 65-D3
NORTH ST ANO 49-D4
NORTH ST HUD 111-C2
NORTH ST ML 43-D2
NORTH ST MON 86-C1
NORTH ST MTK 118-E3
NORTH ST SLP 119-D1
NORTH ST STP 108-C3
NORTH ST SWR 96-E1
NORTH ST W CF 222-B1
NORTH ARM DR MTA ...102-E3,103-A3
NORTH ARM DR ORO 103-B3
NORTH ARM LN ORO 103-A3
NORTH BAY DR CHN 132-B3
NORTH BAY RD SJT 84-C4
NORTH BRANCH RD MTA 102-D3
NORTH CAROLINA AVE BLA 65-A4
NORTH CREEK DR LVL 163-C4
NORTH CREEK LN LVL 163-C4
NORTH DAKOTA AVE BLA 65-A4
NORTH DANUBE DR NE FRI 79-A4
NORTH DEEP LAKE RD NO 80-C1
NORTH ENCHANTED
DR NW AND 35-D4
NORTH GLOVER RD TRT 126-B2
NORTH HEIGHTS DR NW CR 64-A2
NORTH ILWACO RD TRT 139-C1
NORTH INNSBRUCK
DR NE FRI 78-E4,79-A4
NORTH LAKES CT LND 12-D3
NORTH LAKES LN CGT 12-D2
NORTH LAKES TRL CGT 12-D3
NORTH LAKES TRL LND 12-D3
NORTH LAKES TRL N CGT 12-D2
NORTH MALLARD CT NO 80-C3
NORTH MALLARD RD NO 80-C3
NORTH MAPLEBROOK CIR BP 77-D2
NORTH MEADOW DR HUT 112-C2
NORTH NORTH VALLEY DR JOR .173-B2
NORTH OAKS RD NO 80-C2
NORTH OBERLIN CIR NE FRI 79-A4
NORTH PARK DR STP 109-A4
NORTH POINT DR HSN 48-A2
NORTH RIDGE DR EAG ..136-A4,149-E1
NORTH RIDGE DR HUD 111-E2
NORTH RIDGE DR NFD 219-D2
NORTH SAINT PAUL RD MPW ..109-A1
NORTH SHORE CIR FLT 39-D3
NORTH SHORE DR FL 39-C2
NORTH SHORE DR ORO 103-B4
NORTH SHORE DR WAV ...71-E4,72-A4
NORTH SHORE DR W IND 103-A2
NORTH SHORE DR W MTA 103-A3
NORTH SHORE RD WCT .115-D4,129-D1
NORTH SHORE TRL CHC 26-B1
NORTH SHORE TRL FL 39-C2
NORTH SHORE TRL FLT ...39-D3,40-A4
NORTH SIDE LN COR 61-E4
NORTH STAR LN CP 65-D3
NORTH STAR LN SCF 14-D3
NORTH VALLEY RD CHS 145-D1
NORTH VIEW LN SAV 161-E2
NORTH VIEW LN WBY 123-E3
NORTH WACONIA CIR NE EB 9-B4
NORTHBRIDGE CT EAG 150-A1
NORTHBROOK AVE N MAY 68-E4
NORTHBROOK BLVD N BYT 96-E4
NORTHBROOK CT N BYT 96-E3
NORTHCO DR FRI 78-D3
NORTHDALE BLVD HSN 47-E3
NORTHDALE BLVD ROG 47-E4
NORTHDALE BLVD NW CR ..49-E4,63-E1
NORTHDALE LN CR 49-E4
NORTHEND RD NOH 97-C4,111-C1
NORTHERN AVE ORO 117-B1
NORTHERN AVE SPR 117-B1
NORTHERN DR BUR 148-D4
NORTHERN DR CRY 91-C4
NORTHERN RD DPH 118-A2
NORTHERN RD MOU 117-A1
NORTHERN LIGHTS TRL EPR 132-C3
NORTHERN LIGHTS TRL TRT 112-B4
NORTHFIELD AVE EDI 119-E4
NORTHFIELD BLVD CAT ..192-E4,206-E1
NORTHFIELD BLVD HMP 193-B2
NORTHFIELD BLVD HMT .192-E4,193-A3
NORTHFIELD BLVD MT ..166-B4,180-A1
NORTHFIELD BLVD SIT 206-C4
NORTHFIELD BLVD VET ..179-E2,180-A1
NORTHFIELD BLVD WFT .219-E2,220-B1
NORTHGATE BLVD CHS 145-C1
NORTHGATE CIR WIN 99-B3
NORTHGATE CT CHS 145-C1
NORTHGATE DR WIN 99-B3
NORTHGATE RD ORO 104-B2
NORTHGLEN DR BLO 134-C4
NORTHLAND AVE SWR 96-D1
NORTHLAND CIR N BP 77-C3
NORTHLAND CT SWR 96-D2
NORTHLAND CT N BP 77-C4
NORTHLAND CT N CGT 12-D2
NORTHLAND DR MH 135-D2
NORTHLAND DR N BP 77-C3
NORTHLAND TER N BP 77-C3
NORTHLAND TRL N CGT 12-D1
NORTHMARK DR EPR 133-B3
NORTHOME AVE DPH 118-B1
NORTHOME BLVD DPH 118-B1
NORTHOME RD DPH 118-B1
NORTHPORT DR BC 92-A1
NORTHRIDGE AVE N MAY 54-D4
NORTHRIDGE AVE N WLT 110-E2
NORTHRIDGE CT HAS 166-C2
NORTHRIDGE DR HAS 166-B2
NORTHRIDGE DR MED 90-B4
NORTHRIDGE LN N WLT 110-E2
NORTHRIDGE RD MTK ...104-E3,105-A3
NORTHRIDGE AVENUE
CIR N WLT 110-E2
NORTHRIDGE
AVENUE CT N WLT 110-E2
NORTHROP DR MPL 121-B1
NORTHRUP AVE FH 107-C2
NORTHRUP AVE TKB 117-D3
NORTHRUP LN MPL 106-C3
NORTHRUP TER EPR 133-A3
NORTHRUP TRL EPR 133-A3
NORTHSHIRE CT N CGT 12-D2
NORTHTOWN DR BLA 78-D1
NORTHVIEW BAY WBY 123-E3
NORTHVIEW CV WBY 123-E3
NORTHVIEW DR EAG 149-E1
NORTHVIEW DR HUT 111-E2
NORTHVIEW DR MTA 116-B2
NORTHVIEW LN ANO 49-C3
NORTHVIEW LN WBY 123-E3
NORTHVIEW PASS HUT 111-E1
NORTHVIEW RD MTB 117-C1
NORTHVIEW ST RVL 94-B3
NORTHVIEW TER EAG 149-E1
NORTHVIEW ABBEY WBY 123-E3
NORTHVIEW PARK
RD EAG 149-E1,150-A1
NORTHWAY CIR BEC 2-E3
NORTHWAY DR BC 92-B1
NORTHWEST AVE WBL 81-B2
NORTHWEST AVE WBT 81-B2
NORTHWEST BLVD PLY 90-E4,91-A2
NORTHWEST CT CF 208-B4
NORTHWEST CT FS 121-B4,135-B1
NORTHWEST DR FS 121-B4,135-B1
NORTHWEST PKWY EAG 136-A2
NORTHWESTERN AVE SWR 96-E2
NORTHWOOD AVE N BP 63-E4
NORTHWOOD CIR NH 91-C3
NORTHWOOD CT CHN 131-D1
NORTHWOOD DR DEL 87-E3
NORTHWOOD DR EAG 135-E3
NORTHWOOD DR EDI 119-D3
NORTHWOOD DR NSP 109-B1
NORTHWOOD DR NW AND 50-A3
NORTHWOOD PKWY NH 91-C3
NORTHWOOD
RD NW PRL 160-E3,161-A3
NORTHWOOD RDG BLO 133-E3
NORTHWOODS DR AH 93-D1
NORTHWOODS DR EAG 135-D3
NORTON AVE NE FRI 78-E3
NORTON DR E SHK 160-C2
NORTON ST STP 108-A2
NORTONIA AVE STP 109-A3
NORWAY AVE LND 12-D4
NORWAY CIR BUR 149-A3
NORWAY CT N CHM 63-B2
NORWAY CT NW AND 50-C3
NORWAY LN SOM 70-B4
NORWAY PT BUR 149-A3
NORWAY PT EAG 135-D4
NORWAY ST NW AND 50-C3
NORWAY ST NW CR 64-C2,78-C1
NORWAY TRL SHK 146-D3
NORWAY HILLS TRL NMT 190-B1
NORWAY PINE CIR MTK 105-A3
NORWAY PINE CT WBT 81-B1
NORWAY PINE DR WBT 81-B1
NORWEST CT EAG 135-D3
NORWICH AVE N OPH 96-E3
NORWICH AVE S DET 152-E2
NORWICH CIR N OPH 96-D3
NORWICH PKWY OPH 96-E3
NORWOOD AVE ANO 49-D3
NORWOOD AVE N SWT 82-E2
NORWOOD CIR ANO 49-D3
NORWOOD CIR EAG 149-C3
NORWOOD CIR EPR 132-D3
NORWOOD CT EAG 149-C3
NORWOOD CT N MG 77-A1
NORWOOD DR BL 18-A4
NORWOOD DR EAG 149-C3
NORWOOD DR MTK 118-C3
NORWOOD LN ANO 49-D3
NORWOOD LN BL 18-A4
NORWOOD LN MOU 117-A1
NORWOOD LN MTK 118-D3
NORWOOD LN N DAY 49-A4
NORWOOD LN N MG 77-A2,91-A1
NORWOOD LN N PLY 91-A2
NOTRE DAME ST NE COT 38-D3
NOTRE DAME ST NE LWT 10-D3
NOTTINGHAM CT MTK 105-B3
NOTTINGHAM CT N CGT 12-D2
NOTTINGHAM DR CP 65-D4
NOTTINGHAM LN LL 66-A1
NOTTINGHAM PKWY MG 76-C3
NOTTINGHAM PL SVW 79-E3
NOTTINGHAM TRL EPR 133-C4
NOURSE HALL NFD 219-E3
NOVAK AVE N BYT 96-E3
NOVAK AVE N CGT 26-E3
NOVAK AVE N NST 40-E4
NOVAK AVE N OPH 96-E2
NOVAK AVE N WLT 110-E3
NOVEMBER ST BLA 65-A4
NOWTHEN BLVD NW BT ...20-D3,34-E1
NOWTHEN BLVD
NW RAM 35-A4,49-B1
NSP RD BEC 2-E4
NUEMAN CT N CGT 12-D1
NUEMAN TRL N CGT 12-D1
NUGENT AVE STP 122-A1
NURSERY DR MTK 118-D3
NURSERY HILL CT AH 79-D4
NURSERY HILL LN AH 79-D4
NUSBAUMER DR STP 107-E2
NUTHATCH LN NO 80-C2
NUTRIA ST NW RAM 34-D3,48-D1
NUTTING CT NFD 219-D3
NYBECK AVE S AFT 124-E3
NYBERG AVE S DET 152-E2
NYBRO CIR EAG 149-D2
NYBRO LN N EAG 149-D2
NYE ST HUD 111-D3
NYSTROM LN LND 12-D3
NYSTROM RD COR 75-D4

O

O ST WBY 123-D1
O BRIAN AVE NE OTS 33-C2
O BRIEN AVE NE OTS 33-C3
O CONNELL DR HAS 166-B2
O DAY AVE NE OTS 33-C4
O DAY CIR NE OTS 33-C4
O DEAN AVE NE OTS 33-D3,47-D1
O DEAN AVE NE SM 47-C2
O DELL AVE NE OTS 33-D3,47-D1
O DELL CIR NE OTS 47-D1
O RYAN TRL N WLT 111-A3
OAK AVE AH 93-D2
OAK AVE BL 17-E3,18-A3
OAK AVE DEL 87-D2
OAK AVE WAC 129-C3
OAK AVE WCT 129-C4,143-C1
OAK AVE N ML 43-D2
OAK AVE S ML 43-D3
OAK AVE SE SM 47-A4
OAK AVE SW SM 46-E4
OAK CIR BL 17-E3
OAK CIR CV 66-D3
OAK CIR JOR 173-B2
OAK CIR MED 90-A4
OAK CIR MPW 109-B2
OAK CIR NW STT 7-E2
OAK CIR S JT 160-A1
OAK CRV BUR 162-D3
OAK CRV LVL 162-D3
OAK CT EAG 149-E1
OAK CT LL 66-B1
OAK CT OSC 28-A4
OAK CT WBL 95-B2
OAK CT S VH 80-C4
OAK DR EDI 119-E3,120-A3
OAK DR EPR 132-D2
OAK DR MTK 118-C3
OAK DR NYA 142-C3
OAK DR OST 28-D4
OAK DR TF 14-C2
OAK DR TRT 112-B4
OAK DR WBL 95-B2
OAK DR N VH 80-C4
OAK DR S VH 80-C4,94-C1
OAK LN APV 149-D4
OAK LN BKR 2-D1,4-A4
OAK LN BL 18-A4
OAK LN CFT 208-C4
OAK LN EDI 119-D3
OAK LN GRW 118-A3
OAK LN LEX 65-C4
OAK LN LL 66-B1
OAK LN MAY 54-C3
OAK LN MO 31-C1
OAK LN MTK 104-E3
OAK LN WBL 95-B2
OAK LN YAT 142-C4
OAK LN N OKD 95-D4
OAK RD CP 65-E4
OAK RD MTA 116-C4
OAK RD MTK 118-D1
OAK RD S JT 160-A1
OAK ST ANO 49-B3
OAK ST BEC 2-E4
OAK ST BUF 59-B1
OAK ST CGT 12-C4
OAK ST CHC 12-C4
OAK ST CW 1-B2
OAK ST EXC 117-E3
OAK ST FAR 177-E4,178-A4
OAK ST HAS 166-D2
OAK ST HEN 198-D3
OAK ST HUD 111-D2
OAK ST LES 212-C3
OAK ST LND 12-D4
OAK ST MHT 81-D4
OAK ST MP 102-E1,103-A1
OAK ST MSC 55-B4
OAK ST ORO 103-B3
OAK ST PRE 153-B4,167-A1
OAK ST PRL 161-B3
OAK ST RF 140-E3
OAK ST RFD 74-A4
OAK ST SA 93-A4
OAK ST SOM 84-B1
OAK ST SSP 137-A1
OAK ST SWD 117-E3
OAK ST TF 14-C2
OAK ST WBL 95-B2
OAK ST E VER 179-D2
OAK ST N BC 92-A2
OAK ST N BEL 186-A1
OAK ST N CAR 145-B4
OAK ST N CF 208-B4
OAK ST N CHS 145-C3
OAK ST N LP 113-B4
OAK ST N WAC 129-E3
OAK ST S CHS 145-C3
OAK ST S LP 127-B1
OAK ST S NFD 219-E4
OAK ST S NYA 142-C4
OAK ST S WAC 129-E3
OAK ST SE MPL 107-A3
OAK ST W SWR 96-E1,97-A1
OAK ST W VER 179-D2
OAK TER WBL 81-B4,95-B2
OAK WAY BKT 185-A2
OAK WAY EAG 149-B3
OAK BEND LN EDI 119-D3
OAK CHAISE CT MTK 119-A3
OAK CHASE CIR EAG 149-D2
OAK CHASE LN EAG 149-D2
OAK CHASE RD EAG 149-D2
OAK CHASE WAY EAG 149-E2
OAK CLIFF DR EAG 149-A3
OAK CREEK CIR VH 94-C2
OAK CREEK CT VH 94-C1
OAK CREEK DR E VH 94-C2
OAK CREEK DR S VH 94-C2
OAK CREEK DR W VH 94-C2
OAK CREEK TER VH 94-C2
OAK CREST CIR BKR 17-C4
OAK CREST CT BKR 17-D4
OAK CREST DR BKR 17-C4
OAK DRIVE LN MTK 119-A2
OAK GLEN CIR SWR 82-D4
OAK GLEN CRES SWR 82-D4
OAK GLEN CT SWR 82-D4
OAK GLEN DR HOP 119-C2
OAK GLEN DR SWR 82-D4
OAK GLEN LN SWR 82-D4
OAK GLEN PL SWR 82-D4
OAK GLEN RD EDI 133-D1
OAK GLEN TRL SWR 82-D4
OAK GROVE BLVD RCH 134-C1
OAK GROVE CIR BLO 148-C1
OAK GROVE CIR GV 105-E1
OAK GROVE LN MHT 81-D4
OAK GROVE PKWY VH 80-C4
OAK GROVE PL STP 121-E1
OAK GROVE ST MPL 106-C3
OAK HEIGHTS CT MPW 123-B3
OAK HILL CIR CHS 145-C1
OAK HILL CIR CRT 175-E1,176-A1
OAK HILL CT EPR 132-E1,133-A1
OAK HILL CT MPW 109-B2
OAK HILL DR HAS 166-B3
OAK HILL DR SVW 80-A2
OAK HILL LN CRT 176-A1
OAK HILL RD CHS 145-C1
OAK KNOLL AVE RF 140-E2
OAK KNOLL DR MSC 69-B1
OAK KNOLL DR WBL 95-A1
OAK KNOLL DR WBY 109-C4
OAK KNOLL PLZ WBY 109-C4
OAK KNOLL TER N MTK 105-B3
OAK KNOLL TER S MTK 105-B3
OAK LAKE AVE N MPL 106-C2
OAK LAKE CIR WTT 101-D4
OAK LANE DR RW 196-E4
OAK LEA DR MTK 104-E4
OAK LEA TER MTK 104-E4
OAK LEAF CIR BUR 148-E3
OAK LEAF CIR EAG 149-D2
OAK LEAF CT BUR 148-E3
OAK LEAF CT SLP 119-D1
OAK LEAF CT N VH 80-D4
OAK LEAF CT S VH 80-D4
OAK LEAF DR SLP 119-D1
OAK LEAF DR VH 80-D4
OAK LEAF LN BUR 148-E3
OAK LEAF LN CP 65-E3
OAK LEAF TRL SWD 117-C4
OAK PARK AVE N MPL 106-B2
OAK PARK BLVD NE BLA ...50-E4,64-E1
OAK PARK CT NE BLA 64-E1
OAK PARK DR NE BLA 64-D1
OAK PARK LN HOP 119-C1
OAK PARK VILLAGE DR SLP 105-D4
OAK POINTE CRV BLO 133-D3
OAK POND CIR EAG 150-A2
OAK POND RD EAG 150-A2
OAK RIDGE AVE SVW 79-E3
OAK RIDGE CIR BUR 162-C2
OAK RIDGE CIR EAG 149-C2
OAK RIDGE CIR MO 32-A3
OAK RIDGE CIR PRL 161-C2
OAK RIDGE CIR SWD 117-C3
OAK RIDGE CIR NE BLA 64-E1
OAK RIDGE CT HSN 47-E3
OAK RIDGE CT VH 80-C4
OAK RIDGE CT WBT 80-E2
OAK RIDGE CT E BUR 162-C2
OAK RIDGE CT W BUR 162-C2
OAK RIDGE DR COR 76-A4
OAK RIDGE DR DEL 87-E2
OAK RIDGE DR HSN 47-E3
OAK RIDGE DR MO 32-A3
OAK RIDGE DR OSC 28-A3
OAK RIDGE DR TRT 140-D1
OAK RIDGE DR VH 80-C4
OAK RIDGE LN HAS 166-C2
OAK RIDGE LN MTK 105-B3
OAK RIDGE LN SMT 83-C3
OAK RIDGE PT NE BLA 64-E1
OAK RIDGE RD BKR 17-C4
OAK RIDGE RD COR 76-A4
OAK RIDGE RD DBT 168-E4,182-E1
OAK RIDGE RD EPR 118-D4
OAK RIDGE RD HOP 119-C1
OAK RIDGE RD MTK 105-C4,119-C1
OAK RIDGE RD TLT 168-E3
OAK RIDGE TRL CP 65-D4
OAK RIDGE TRL MTK 119-C1
OAK RIDGE TRL WBY 123-E2
OAK RIDGE TRL NE BLA 64-E1

OAK RUN LN BUR 162-D2
OAK SHORE DR BUR 162-D3
OAK SHORE DR LVL 162-D3
OAK SHORE DR S LVL 162-D3
OAK SIDE CIR CHN 131-E3,132-A3
OAK TERRACE CT WBL 95-B1
OAK TREE DR PRL 160-E2
OAK VIEW CT SAV 161-E2
OAK VIEW CT STP 123-B2
OAK VIEW DR WBY 124-B3
OAKBOROUGH DR SAV 161-E2
OAKBROOKE CIR EAG 149-C1
OAKBROOKE DR EAG 149-C1
OAKBROOKE TRL EAG 149-C1
OAKBROOKE WAY EAG 149-C1
OAKCREST AVE RVL 93-C4,94-A4
OAKCREST CIR SAV 162-A2
OAKCREST CT SAV 162-A2
OAKCREST DR VH 80-C4,94-C1
OAKCREST LN RVL 94-A4
OAKCREST LN NE EB 36-E2
OAKCREST TRL BKT 185-D2
OAKDALE AVE EDI 120-A2
OAKDALE AVE STP 122-C2
OAKDALE AVE WSP 122-C3
OAKDALE AVE N ROB 92-A4
OAKDALE CT WSP 122-C3
OAKDALE DR COR 61-D4,75-E1
OAKDALE DR MHT 95-C3
OAKES LN PRL 160-E2
OAKES ST SWR 96-E1
OAKGREEN AVE N BYT 96-E4,110-E1
OAKGREEN AVE N NST 54-E3
OAKGREEN AVE N OPH 96-E2
OAKGREEN AVE N SWR 96-E3
OAKGREEN AVE N SWT 82-E3
OAKGREEN AVE N WLT 110-E3
OAKGREEN AVE S AFT 124-E2
OAKGREEN AVE S DET 138-E2,152-E2
OAKGREEN CIR S AFT 124-E3
OAKGREEN PL N OPH 96-E3
OAKGREEN AVE CT WLT 110-E3
OAKGREEN AVENUE PL N WLT 110-E3
OAKHILL AVE N SWT 82-E4
OAKHILL CT BWV 95-C1
OAKHILL CT EAG 149-B3
OAKHILL CT EKO 204-B1
OAKHILL CT N NST 41-A4
OAKHILL CT N SWT 82-E4
OAKHILL LN N NST 41-A4
OAKHILL PL NSP 95-B4
OAKHILL RD N NST 40-D3,55-B1
OAKHILL TRL DAY 48-E3,49-A3
OAKHILL WAY N NST 40-D3
OAKHURST AVE VH 80-C4
OAKLAND AVE BUR 162-D2
OAKLAND AVE MPL 106-D4,120-D2
OAKLAND AVE RCH 120-D4,134-D1
OAKLAND AVE STP 122-A1
OAKLAND AVE N MAY 68-E3,69-A3
OAKLAND AVE S BLO 134-D3
OAKLAND CIR BUR 148-D4
OAKLAND DR BUR 148-D4,162-D1
OAKLAND DR LL 52-B3
OAKLAND DR NE HL 37-B2
OAKLAND LN BUR 148-D4
OAKLAND PL MTK 104-E3
OAKLAND RD BLO 134-D4
OAKLAND RD MTK 104-E3
OAKLAND ST SB 116-B3
OAKLAND TER RCH 134-B1
OAKLAND BEACH AVE PRL 161-C2
OAKLAWN AVE EDI 120-A3,134-A1
OAKLAWN DR LVT 145-E4
OAKLAWN LN MOU 116-D2
OAKLEAF CT MO 32-A3
OAKLEY AVE STP 107-C4
OAKLEY CIR TRT 112-B4
OAKLEY DR NE FRI 78-E3
OAKLEY ST NE FRI 78-E2
OAKMAN AVE N CGT 26-E3,40-E1
OAKMEDE LN WBT 80-E4,94-E1
OAKMERE RD BLO 133-C3
OAKRIDGE CIR HUD 111-E2
OAKRIDGE CT MPW 123-B2
OAKRIDGE CT SWR 96-D2
OAKRIDGE DR BWV 95-C1
OAKRIDGE DR CHS 131-C3
OAKRIDGE DR MPW 123-B2
OAKRIDGE DR NEW 137-C2
OAKRIDGE DR RW 196-E4
OAKRIDGE DR N NOH 111-D1
OAKRIDGE LN MHT 95-C1
OAKRIDGE LN MPW 123-B2
OAKRIDGE LN WBL 95-C1
OAKRIDGE RD SWR 96-D1
OAKRIDGE ST STP 123-A2
OAKRIDGE WAY EKO 204-B1
OAKS DR N OSS 77-C1
OAKS RD E NO 80-C3
OAKS RD N NO 80-C2
OAKTON DR MTK 119-B1
OAKTON RDG MTK 119-B1
OAKVALE RD N MTK 119-B1
OAKVALE RD S MTK 119-B1
OAKVIEW AVE BEC 2-E4
OAKVIEW CIR MO 31-C1
OAKVIEW CIR MTK 118-D3
OAKVIEW CT ANO 49-D3
OAKVIEW CT BWV 95-C1
OAKVIEW CT CHM 63-B2
OAKVIEW CT CHS 145-C1
OAKVIEW CT MO 32-A3
OAKVIEW CT N MG 77-A2
OAKVIEW LN ANO 49-D3
OAKVIEW LN MOT 32-A3
OAKVIEW LN MTK 118-D3
OAKVIEW LN N DAY 49-A4,63-A1
OAKVIEW LN N MG 77-A1
OAKVIEW LN N PLY 91-A4,105-A1
OAKVIEW RD MED 89-E3
OAKVIEW RD WSP 122-B4
OAKVIEW WAY ANO 49-D3
OAKWAYS CT MTK 104-E3
OAKWAYS RD MTK 104-E3
OAKWOOD AVE NE OTS 33-C4,47-C1
OAKWOOD CIR ANO 63-C1
OAKWOOD CIR BEL 185-E2
OAKWOOD CIR PRL 161-B4
OAKWOOD CRV BUR 162-C1
OAKWOOD CT HUD 111-D2
OAKWOOD CT N BP 63-E4
OAKWOOD CT NE SM 47-C3
OAKWOOD DR ANO 63-C1
OAKWOOD DR BEL 185-E2
OAKWOOD DR BKR 2-D1
OAKWOOD DR BUR 162-B2
OAKWOOD DR CR 63-D1
OAKWOOD DR LL 66-A4,80-A1
OAKWOOD DR LTT 131-A4
OAKWOOD DR MO 31-D2
OAKWOOD DR MOT 31-D3
OAKWOOD DR MV 79-B2
OAKWOOD DR NB 93-B2
OAKWOOD DR ROG 47-D4,61-D1
OAKWOOD DR SA 93-B2
OAKWOOD DR SVW 79-C2,80-A2
OAKWOOD DR WBT 81-A2
OAKWOOD LN ANO 63-C1
OAKWOOD LN CHM 63-B3
OAKWOOD LN LL 65-E4,79-E1
OAKWOOD LN SJT 98-B2
OAKWOOD MNR NE FRI 79-A4
OAKWOOD PKWY SM 47-C3
OAKWOOD PL SAV 161-E2
OAKWOOD RD APV 163-A2
OAKWOOD RD HOP 119-D2
OAKWOOD RD MTK 118-E1
OAKWOOD RD SB 116-A3
OAKWOOD RD WBY 123-C1
OAKWOOD RDG CHN 131-D2
OAKWOOD ST BAY 97-B4
OAKWOOD ST RFD 74-B3
OAKWOOD TER CHM 49-B4
OAKWOOD TER SVW 79-D2
OAKWOOD TER VH 80-B4
OAKWOOD HEIGHTS CIR EAG 150-A2
OASIS AVE N BYT 110-E1
OASIS RD CGT 12-D1
OASIS RD N CGT 12-E2
OBERLIN RD MTK 105-B2
OBERLIN ST LWT 10-D3
OBRIAN AVE OTS 33-C3
OBRIAN AVE NE OTS 33-C3
OBRIEN AVE N NST 55-C2
OBRIEN AVE N OPH 96-E3
OBRIEN PKWY BEL 186-A2
OBRIEN TRL N NST 55-C2
OCALA CT MH 136-A1
OCALA LN MH 136-A1
OCEAN ST STP 108-D3
OCHOA AVE NE OTS 33-C4
OCHOA AVE NE SM 47-C2
OCHOA CIR NE OTS 33-C3
OCHOA CT NE OTS 33-C3
OCONNELL CIR SAV 161-E2
OCONNELL CT SAV 161-E1
OCONNELL DR MV 79-B3
OCONNELL RD SAV 161-E2
ODAY CIR MPW 123-B1
ODAY DR JOR 173-B3
ODAY DR SCT 173-B3
ODAY LN MPW 123-B1
ODAY ST N MPW 109-B4,123-B1
ODAY ST S MPW 123-B1
ODEGARD AVE N BYT 96-E4
ODEGARD CT BYT 96-E4
ODELL AVE N OPH 96-E2
ODELL AVE S AFT 125-A4,139-A1
ODELL AVE S DET 153-A3
OELKE CIR SLT 174-E2
OELKE DR SLT 174-E2
OELVIG AVE AFT 125-A2
OFFICE RIDGE CIR EPR 133-B1
OGDEN AVE STP 123-A3
OGDEN AVE NE OTS 33-D3
OGDEN CT STP 123-B3
OGDEN ST NW ER 19-B4,33-B1
OGEMA PL MPL 106-E4
OGREN AVE NE OTS 33-D3,47-D1
OGREN AVE NE SM 47-D3
OGREN PL NE OTS 33-D3
OGREN TRL N FRT 27-A1
OHENRY RD BC 78-B4
OHENRY RD N BC 78-B4
OHIO AVE BTT 143-C4,157-C1
OHIO AVE HCT 157-C4,171-C2
OHIO ST STP 122-B1
OHIO ST WSP 122-B2
OHIO ST W CF 208-B4
OHLAND AVE NE OTS 33-D3
OHMS LN EDI 133-E1
OJIB WAY N OPH 96-E3
OJIBWAY DR WBY 123-D2
OJIBWAY ST MPL 106-C2
OJIBWAY PARK BAY WBY 123-D3
OJIBWAY PARK CT WBY 123-D3
OJIBWAY PARK DR WBY 123-D3
OJIBWAY PARK DRAW WBY 123-D3
OJIBWAY PARK RD WBY 123-D3
OKAPI ST NW RAM 34-D4,48-D1
OKEEFE RD HUD 111-D3
OKINAWA ST NE BLA 65-C4
OKINAWA ST NE EB 23-C2
OKLAHOMA AVE BLA 65-A4
OLAND AVE N NST 40-E4,41-A4
OLD AUDUBON RD CHS 145-D2
OLD BEACH RD MTB 117-C1
OLD BEACH RD ORO 117-C1
OLD BIRCH ST LL 66-B4
OLD BREN RD MTK 119-B4
OLD BRICK YARD RD JT 145-E3,146-A2
OLD BRICK YARD RD LVT 145-E4,159-E2
OLD BRICK YARD RD SHK 146-A2
OLD BRIDGE LN HAS 166-C3
OLD CEDAR AVE S BLO 134-E3,135-A4
OLD CEDAR LAKE
RD SLP 105-E3,106-A3
OLD CHILDRENS HOME VAT 209-E4
OLD CONCORD
BLVD IGH 136-E4,150-E1
OLD CONSTANCE BLVD NE HL 36-D4
OLD CONSTANCE BLVD NW AND 36-D4
OLD COUNTRY CLUB RD MO 31-C2
OLD COUNTY ROAD 109 MG 77-A2
OLD COUNTY ROAD 147 CAR 145-A3
OLD COUNTY ROAD 15 MTB 117-C1
OLD COUNTY ROAD 15 PLY 105-B2
OLD COUNTY ROAD 18 SHK 147-C3
OLD COUNTY ROAD 34 PL BUR 148-B3
OLD COUNTY ROAD C E LC 94-B3
OLD CRYSTAL BAY RD N ORO 103-C2
OLD CRYSTAL BAY RD S ORO 103-C3
OLD DEER TRL N SWT 82-E3
OLD DEER FIELD RD RVT 181-E4
OLD E E SJT 97-E2,98-A2
OLD E W SJT 97-E1
OLD EXCELSIOR BLVD MTK 118-B3
OLD FARM RD SVW 80-A3
OLD GUSLANDER
TRL N MAY 54-E4,55-A4
OLD HIGHWAY 10 AH 79-D4
OLD HIGHWAY 13 BLVD CLT 188-C3
OLD HIGHWAY 169 BLVD BEL 186-A1
OLD HIGHWAY 169 BLVD BPT 186-B1
OLD HIGHWAY 169
BLVD SLW 173-A3,186-B1
OLD HIGHWAY 35 HUT 97-D3,112-B3
OLD HIGHWAY 35 SJT 97-D3
OLD HIGHWAY 35 TRT 112-B4,126-B1
OLD HIGHWAY 8 AH 79-C3
OLD HIGHWAY 8 MV 79-C3
OLD HIGHWAY 8 NB 79-C4,93-B2
OLD HIGHWAY 8 RVL 93-B3
OLD HIGHWAY 8 SA 93-B3
OLD HIGHWAY 8 SCF 14-D3
OLD HOLT CT CGT 26-E1
OLD HOPKINS PL HUT 98-C4
OLD HUDSON RD STP 108-E4,109-A4
OLD KELLOGG BLVD STP 108-B4
OLD KENT RD DPH 118-A2
OLD LAKE GEORGE
BLVD NW OG 21-E2
OLD LONG LAKE RD LOL 104-A2
OLD LONG LAKE RD ORO 104-A2
OLD LONG LAKE RD WAY 104-B2
OLD MARINE TRL N MSC 55-B3
OLD MARINE TRL N NST 54-E2,55-A2
OLD MARKET RD SWD 118-B3
OLD MILL CT HAS 166-D2
OLD MILL RD CV 66-D2
OLD MILL RD SJT 98-C3
OLD MYSTIC RD RVT 181-D3
OLD ORCHARD LN TKB 117-C3
OLD POST RD IND 88-D4
OLD ROCKFORD RD N PLY 90-C3,91-B3
OLD SAINT ANTHONY LN MPL 106-D1
OLD SETTLERS RD COR 75-E4,89-E1
OLD SETTLERS TRL HOP 119-B3
OLD SHADY OAK RD EPR 119-B4
OLD SHAKOPEE CIR E BLO 134-E3
OLD SHAKOPEE CIR W BLO 147-E1
OLD SHAKOPEE
RD E BLO 134-D4,135-A2
OLD SHAKOPEE
RD W BLO 134-C4,147-D1
OLD SIBLEY HWY EAG 149-A1
OLD SIBLEY MEMORIAL
HWY EAG 149-A1
OLD STEINE CIR NB 93-C1
OLD TOLLBRIDGE RD LLD 111-C3
OLD TOWN DR NB 93-C1
OLD TOWNE RD CHC 26-B1
OLD VIKING BLVD NW BT 20-E4,21-B3
OLD WAGON TRL EPR 133-B4
OLD WHITE BEAR AVE WBL 81-A4
OLD WILDWOOD RD MHT 95-C2
OLD WINDSOR RD RVT 181-E4
OLD WINDSOR RD WEL 181-E4
OLDE STURBRIDGE DR COR 76-A4
OLDE STURBRIDGE RD COR 76-A4
OLDE WOOD CT MTK 104-E4
OLDFIELD AVE N BYT 111-A1
OLDFIELD AVE N CGT 40-E2
OLDFIELD AVE N FRT 40-E1,41-A1
OLDFIELD AVE N NST 40-E2
OLDFIELD AVE N OPH 96-E3
OLDFIELD AVE N SWT 82-E3
OLDFIELD CT N OPH 96-E3
OLDFIELD RD N MAY 68-E2
OLDRIDGE AVE N WLT 110-E3
OLEARY LN EAG 135-E4
OLENE AVE N OPH 97-A2
OLENE AVE N WLT 111-A2
OLENE CT N WLT 111-A2
OLGA STREET WAY CFT 223-B2
OLIN CT CHS 131-C4
OLINDA AVE N OPH 96-E2
OLINDA BLVD N BYT 96-E4,97-A4
OLINDA LN N NST 41-A4
OLINDA TRL N CGT 12-D3,26-E1
OLINDA TRL N FRT 27-A4,41-A1
OLINDA TRL N LND 12-D4,26-D1
OLINDA TRL N MAY 54-E4
OLINDA TRL N NST 41-A3,54-E2
OLINGER BLVD EDI 119-D4
OLINGER CIR EDI 119-D4
OLINGER RD EDI 119-D3
OLIVE AVE ORO 117-C1
OLIVE CT MG 76-C2
OLIVE LN N MG 76-C1
OLIVE LN N PLY 90-C4,104-C1
OLIVE ST CR 78-C1
OLIVE ST HAS 166-C1
OLIVE ST LL 52-B3
OLIVE ST STP 108-C3
OLIVE ST E SWR 97-A1
OLIVE ST N WAC 129-D3
OLIVE ST NW AND 50-C3
OLIVE ST NW CR 50-C4,64-C1
OLIVE ST S WAC 129-D3
OLIVE ST W SWR 96-E1,97-A1
OLIVER AVE N BC 78-B3,92-B2
OLIVER AVE N BP 64-B4,78-B1
OLIVER AVE N MPL 92-B4,106-B1
OLIVER AVE S BLO 134-B3
OLIVER AVE S BUR 148-B4
OLIVER AVE S MPL 106-B3,120-B3
OLIVER AVE S RCH 120-B4,134-B1
OLIVER CIR N BC 78-B4
OLIVER PL S MPL 106-B3
OLIVIA CT BEC 2-E3
OLIVINE DR EAG 149-B1
OLIVINE ST NW RAM 34-E4
OLMSTEAD ST STP 108-C3
OLSON LAKE TRL N OKD 95-D4
OLSON MEMORIAL
HWY GV 105-D2,106-A2
OLSON MEMORIAL
HWY MED 89-E2,90-A2
OLSON MEMORIAL HWY MPL 106-B2
OLSON MEMORIAL
HWY PLY 90-C3,105-B2
OLYMIPIA AVE STP 123-A2
OLYMPIA AVE STP 123-A3
OLYMPIA DR EPR 133-B4
OLYMPIA ST GV 105-D1
OLYMPIC CIR CHN 118-B4
OLYMPIC CIR EPR 133-B4
OLYMPIC TRL CGT 26-E1
OLYMPIC TRL N CGT 26-E1
OLYMPIC TRL N FRT 26-E2,27-A3
OMABAN ST STP 108-E3
OMAHA AVE N BYT 97-A4
OMAHA AVE N OPH 97-A2
OMAHA AVE N SWR 97-A2
OMAHA AVE N WLT 111-A3
OMAHA AVE S AFT 125-A1
OMAHA CT TRT 126-A2
OMAHA RD TRT 126-A2
OMAR AVE N OPH 97-A3
OMEARA CT BUR 162-B3
OMEGA TRL PRL 161-C3
ONACREST CRV MPW 108-B1
ONACREST CT N MPW 108-B1
ONEIDA ST STP 122-A1
ONEIDA ST NW AND 35-C4,49-C2
ONEIDA ST NW OG 21-C2
ONEIDA ST NW RAM 49-C1
ONEIDA ST NW SF 7-C4
ONEIL RD HUD 112-A4
ONEIL RD HUT 112-A3
ONEILL RD EAG 136-B2
ONEILL RD MH 136-A2
ONEKA LAKE BLVD N HUG 67-C2
ONONDAGA ST NE FRI 78-E2,79-A2
ONONDAGA WAY NE FRI 78-E2
ONTARIO AVE MPL 106-C3
ONTARIO BLVD EPR 132-D2
ONTARIO RD N LC 94-C3
ONTARIO ST SE MPL 107-A3
ONYX DR EAG 149-B2
ONYX DR SHK 146-D3
ONYX PT EAG 149-B2
OPAL AVE NMT 190-A3
OPAL CIR NE BLA 65-D2
OPAL CT NE BLA 65-D2
OPAL DR EAG 149-B1
OPAL PL EAG 149-B1
OPAL ST NE BLA 65-D2
OPAL ST NE HL 37-D3
OPPERMAN DR EAG 136-B4
OPPORTUNITY CT MTK 119-C3
OPUS PKWY MTK 119-B3
ORANGE AVE E STP 108-D2,109-A2
ORANGE AVE W STP 107-E2,108-A2
ORANGE ST HUD 111-C2
ORANGE ST LL 52-B3
ORANGE ST PRE 153-B4,167-B1
ORANGE ST RF 140-E3
ORANGE ST N WAC 129-E3
ORANGE ST S WAC 129-E3
ORCHARD AVE STP 107-E3,108-A3
ORCHARD AVE WBT 81-A2
ORCHARD AVE N BC 77-E4,78-A4
ORCHARD AVE N BP 77-E3
ORCHARD AVE N CRY 91-E2,92-A1
ORCHARD AVE N GV 92-A4,106-A1
ORCHARD AVE N ROB 92-A3
ORCHARD AVE W MTK 105-A4
ORCHARD CIR BEL 186-A2
ORCHARD CIR LOL 103-E2
ORCHARD CIR MH 121-E4
ORCHARD CIR PRL 161-C1
ORCHARD CIR SWD 117-C3
ORCHARD CIR WBL 95-A2
ORCHARD CT LVL 176-C2
ORCHARD CT SHK 146-B3
ORCHARD CT WBL 95-A2
ORCHARD DR BUR 162-C2
ORCHARD DR WBY 124-A2
ORCHARD HL EPR 119-A4
ORCHARD HL MH 121-E4
ORCHARD LN CHN 117-D4
ORCHARD LN EDI 119-D2
ORCHARD LN LOL 103-D2
ORCHARD LN MTK 119-A1
ORCHARD LN RVL 93-E3
ORCHARD LN SSP 122-D3
ORCHARD LN WBL 94-E2,95-A2
ORCHARD LN N BC 77-E4
ORCHARD PKWY SHK 146-B3
ORCHARD PL BUR 162-A1
ORCHARD PL MH 121-E4
ORCHARD PL NFD 219-D3
ORCHARD RD MTK 118-E1,119-A1
ORCHARD RD WCT 129-C4,143-B1
ORCHARD ST BEL 185-E2,186-A2
ORCHARD ST E BEL 186-A2
ORCHARD ST N NFD 219-D3
ORCHARD ST S NFD 219-D4
ORCHARD TRL LVL 176-C2
ORCHARD BEACH PL ORO 103-B4
ORCHARD PARK RD ORO 103-B2
ORCHARD RIDGE TRL WBY 137-C2
ORCHARD SPRINGS RD BLO 134-E4
ORCHID AVE ROG 47-E4
ORCHID CIR PLY 90-D2
ORCHID CIR NW AND 49-E3
ORCHID CT NW AND 49-E3
ORCHID DR NE EB 37-D2
ORCHID LN VIC 117-A4
ORCHID LN N MG 76-D3,90-D1
ORCHID LN N PLY 90-D3,104-D2
ORCHID ST VIC 131-A2
ORCHID ST NW AND 35-E2,49-E3
ORCHID ST NW CR 49-E3,63-E1
ORCHID ST NW OG 21-E4,35-E1
ORCHID ST NW STT 7-E2
ORDWAY ST DWD 81-C3
ORDWAY ST GV 106-A1
OREGON AVE BL 18-A3
OREGON AVE BLA 65-A4
OREGON AVE N BP 77-D2
OREGON AVE N CHM 63-D3
OREGON AVE N CRY 91-D1
OREGON AVE N GV 105-D1
OREGON AVE N NH 91-D3
OREGON AVE S BLO 133-D4,147-D2
OREGON AVE S GV 105-D2
OREGON AVE S SAV 161-D2
OREGON AVE S SLP 105-D4,119-D1
OREGON CIR CHM 63-D2
OREGON CIR S BLO 133-D2,147-D2
OREGON CRV BLO 147-D2
OREGON CT SLP 105-D3
OREGON LN N CHM 63-D2
OREGON RD BLO 133-D2
OREGON ST SCF 14-D2
OREN AVE MAY 69-A2
OREN AVE N NST 41-A4
OREN AVE N OPH 97-A2
OREN RD N NST 40-E3,41-A3
OREN AVENUE CT N OPH 97-A2
ORIC AVE MTK 118-D3
ORINCO ST NE OXT 10-B2
ORINOCO CIR N LWT 24-C1
ORINOCO CIR S LWT 24-C1
ORINOCO ST NE LWT 10-C4,24-C1
ORIOLE AVE NB 79-B3
ORIOLE AVE N CGT 12-E1
ORIOLE AVE N WLT 111-A2
ORIOLE AVE S ML 43-D3
ORIOLE BAY WBY 123-D3
ORIOLE CIR WBY 123-D3
ORIOLE CT APV 163-A2
ORIOLE CT BUR 162-B3
ORIOLE DR APV 162-E2,163-A2
ORIOLE DR BUR 162-E2
ORIOLE DR FAR 177-D2
ORIOLE DR WAC 129-C4
ORIOLE DR WBY 123-D3

ORIOLE LN CHN 117-D4
ORIOLE LN CHS 131-D4
ORIOLE LN EDI 119-D4
ORIOLE LN HUT 112-C2
ORIOLE LN MO 31-E3
ORIOLE LN NB 79-B3
ORIOLE LN NO 80-C2
ORIOLE LN E NO 80-C2
ORIOLE PL SE PRL 161-C3
ORION CIR NW PRL 160-E2
ORION LN EAG 149-E2
ORION RD NW PRL 160-E2
ORION ST NE LWT 10-A3
ORKLA DR GV 91-C4,105-C1
ORLANDO AVE DT 195-B2,209-B1
ORLANDO AVE MT 167-B4,181-B2
ORLANDO TRL DT 209-B1
ORLEANS AVE IGH 137-A3
ORLEANS CT W SWR 96-E2
ORLEANS DR NE SM 47-A3
ORLEANS LN N MG 63-B4,77-B1
ORLEANS LN N PLY 91-B2
ORLEANS ST STP 122-B1
ORLEANS ST SWR 96-E2
ORLEANS ST E OPH 97-A2
ORLEANS ST E SWR 97-A2
ORLEANS ST W OPH 97-A2
ORLEANS ST W SWR 96-E2,97-A2
ORLIN AVE SE MPL 107-B3
ORLO DR N NST 40-B4
ORLUCK WAY RVT 181-B3
ORME CT STP 121-C3
ORME LN STP 121-C3
ORME ST E WSP 122-C3
ORME ST W WSP 122-B3
ORNSBEE CIR BL 18-A4
ORNSBEE ST BL 18-A4,32-A1
ORONO LN ORO 103-E3
ORONO PKWY NW ER 33-C2
ORONO RD NW ER 33-C2
ORONO TRL RVT 181-C3
ORONO OAKS DR ORO 103-E2
ORONO ORCHARD RD N LOL 103-E2
ORONO ORCHARD RD N ORO 103-E2
ORONO ORCHARD RD S ORO 103-E3
ORR AVE RVT 181-B2
ORRIN RD PRE 153-B4
ORRIN ST STP 121-E2,122-A2
ORTLER PASS GV 106-A3
ORTLOFF TRL NW WAT 101-B3
ORTMAN ST MPL 106-D2
ORWELL AVE N NST 54-E1,55-A2
ORWELL AVE N SWR 83-A4
ORWELL AVE N SWT 83-A3
ORWELL AVE N WLT 111-A3
ORWELL CT N NST 55-A2
ORWELL CT N SWR 83-A4
ORWELL RD N MAY 54-E4,69-A1
OSAGE CT NW AND 36-B2
OSAGE PT EAG 149-C3
OSAGE ST STP 107-E2
OSAGE ST NW AND 36-B2,50-B1
OSAGE ST NW CR 50-B3,64-B2
OSAGE ST NW OG 22-A3
OSBORNE RD NE FRI 78-D2
OSBORNE RD NE SLK 78-E2,79-A2
OSBORNE WAY NE FRI 78-D2
OSCAR ST BLA 65-A4
OSCEOLA AVE STP 121-E1,122-A1
OSCEOLA AVE S STP 122-A2
OSCEOLA RD FRT 27-E4
OSGOOD AVE AFT 111-A4
OSGOOD AVE WLT 111-A4
OSGOOD AVE N BYT 97-A4
OSGOOD AVE N OPH 97-A2
OSGOOD AVE N SWR 97-A2
OSGOOD AVE S AFT 139-A1
OSGOOD CT S AFT 139-A1
OSMAN AVE N OPH 97-A2
OSMAN AVE N SWR 97-A2
OSMIUM DR NW RAM 35-B4,49-B1
OSMIUM ST NW RAM 35-B4
OSMIUM ST NW SF 7-B3
OSPREY AVE N WLT 111-A2
OSPREY CIR MO 32-A2
OSPREY CT LL 66-D3
OSPREY CT MO 32-A2
OSPREY DR BAY 97-B4
OSPREY LN CHN 131-E3
OSPREY LN WBY 124-B2
OSSEO RD MPL 92-B2
OSTER DR EAG 135-D2
OSTLUND TRL N MAY 68-E2,69-A2
OSTRUM AVE N NST 55-A1
OSTRUM TRL N MAY 54-E4,55-A3
OSTRUM TRL N MSC 55-B3
OTCHIPWE AVE N MAY 68-E4,82-E1
OTCHIPWE AVE N SWT 82-E1,83-A2
OTCHIPWE CT N SWT 82-E3,83-A3
OTERO AVE RVT 181-C3
OTHER DAY RD RW 182-C4
OTHERDAY CIR NW PRL 160-E1
OTIS AVE HCT 157-C4,171-C1
OTIS AVE STP 107-B4
OTIS LN STP 107-B4
OTSEGO ST STP 108-C3
OTTAWA AVE NMT 190-A2
OTTAWA AVE SAV 148-A3,162-A1
OTTAWA AVE STP 122-B2
OTTAWA AVE WSP 122-B2
OTTAWA AVE N GV 106-A2
OTTAWA AVE N SWT 83-A2
OTTAWA AVE S GV 106-A3
OTTAWA AVE S SAV 162-A2
OTTAWA AVE S SLP 106-A4,120-A2
OTTAWA CIR SAV 148-A4
OTTAWA CT SAV 148-A4
OTTAWA CT SLP 120-A2
OTTAWA DR SAV 148-A4
OTTAWA PL SAV 148-A4
OTTAWA PL SLP 106-A4
OTTER AVE N SWT 83-A1
OTTER LN NO 80-C3
OTTER RD MOU 116-D2
OTTER CREEK RD MO 31-C1
OTTER LAKE DR LL 66-E4
OTTER LAKE RD GL 80-E4,94-E1
OTTER LAKE RD LL 66-E3,80-D1
OTTER LAKE RD WBL 80-E3
OTTER LAKE RD WBT 80-E2
OTTER RIDGE CIR WBT 80-D1
OTTER RIDGE RD WBT 80-D1
OTTER VIEW CIR WBT 80-D1
OTTER VIEW CT WBT 80-D2
OTTER VIEW TRL WBT 80-D1
OTTO AVE STP 121-E2,122-A2
OTTO ST ROG 61-E1,62-A1
OTTUMWA AVE N SWT 83-A3
OTTUMWA AVE NE SWT 83-A3
OUTER DR LES 212-D4
OUTLOOK AVE SSP 122-D2
OUTPOST CIR HUT 112-B3
OVERBY AVE RVT 181-B2
OVERHILL DR NO 80-B2
OVERHILL RD EAG 150-A2
OVERHOLT PASS EDI 133-C1
OVERLAKE RD WBT 81-A1
OVERLAND CIR EAG 149-B2
OVERLAND DR CRT 176-A2
OVERLAND LN MOU 116-E1
OVERLAND TRL EPR 132-C4
OVERLOOK AVE N WLT 111-A1
OVERLOOK CIR BLO 147-E2,148-A2
OVERLOOK CIR MPW 123-B3
OVERLOOK CIR PRL 161-C3
OVERLOOK CIR SM 46-E4
OVERLOOK CIR NE HAN 61-A3
OVERLOOK CT CHN 132-B3
OVERLOOK CT MTK 119-A2
OVERLOOK CT SCF 14-D3
OVERLOOK CT N CHM 63-C3
OVERLOOK CT N WLT 111-A2
OVERLOOK DR BLO 147-E2,148-B2
OVERLOOK DR CHS 145-D1
OVERLOOK DR MTK 105-B4
OVERLOOK DR PRL 161-B4
OVERLOOK DR RVL 94-A3
OVERLOOK DR SAV 161-E2
OVERLOOK DR SCT 159-D3
OVERLOOK DR WBY 123-C1
OVERLOOK LN MH 121-E4
OVERLOOK LN N CHM 63-C3
OVERLOOK LN N WLT 111-A2
OVERLOOK PASS HUT 111-E1,112-A1
OVERLOOK PL EAG 136-A4
OVERLOOK RD BUR 148-C4
OVERLOOK RD DAY 48-E3,49-A3
OVERLOOK RD DWD 81-D3
OVERLOOK RD MH 121-E4
OVERLOOK ST EAG 149-E1,150-A1
OVERLOOK TRL EPR 133-B3
OVERLOOK TRL N WLT 111-A2
OVERLOOK LAKE CIR BLO 148-A2
OVERTON DR NE FRI 78-E3
OWASSO BLVD N SVW 94-A2
OWASSO BLVD S LC 94-B3
OWASSO BLVD S RVL 94-A3
OWASSO BLVD W RVL 93-E3,94-A3
OWASSO BLVD W SVW 94-A2
OWASSO LN E SVW 94-B2
OWASSO ST SVW 93-E2,94-A2
OWASSO HEIGHTS DR SVW 94-A2
OWASSO HEIGHTS RD SVW 94-A2
OWASSO HILLS DR RVL 94-A3
OWATONNA CT NE BLA 51-A3
OWATONNA ST NE BLA 51-A4
OWATONNA ST NE HL 37-A3,51-A3
OWEN AVE RVT 181-B2
OWEN ST GRF 74-D4
OWENS ST N SWR 82-E4,96-E1
OWENS ST S SWR 96-E1
OX YOKE CIR MTA 102-B3
OXBORO AVE N NST 55-A2
OXBORO AVE N OPH 97-A2
OXBORO AVE N SWR 97-A2
OXBORO LN N NST 55-A1
OXBOROUGH AVE S BLO 134-A2,148-A1
OXBOROUGH CIR BLO 134-A4
OXBOROUGH CRV BLO 134-A4
OXBOROUGH CT BP 77-E2
OXBOROUGH GDNS BP 77-E2,78-A2
OXBOROUGH LN BLO 148-A2
OXBOROUGH RD BLO 133-E4,134-A4
OXBOW BND CHN 118-A4
OXBOW CIR S AFT 125-A4
OXBOW CT N CHM 63-E3
OXBOW DR EPR 133-A4
OXBOW PL CHM 63-E3
OXBOW TRL N CHM 63-E3
OXFORD ALC WBY 123-D3
OXFORD AVE EDI 119-E2
OXFORD AVE WTT 101-C3,115-C1
OXFORD AVE NW ER 33-D1
OXFORD BAY WBY 123-D3
OXFORD CIR WBY 123-D3
OXFORD CT MH 121-E4
OXFORD CT WBY 123-D3
OXFORD CT N SVW 79-E4,93-E1
OXFORD DR WBY 123-D3
OXFORD ECHO WBY 123-D3
OXFORD LN BP 77-E2
OXFORD PL MTK 118-D2
OXFORD PL SHK 147-A3
OXFORD RD EAG 150-A1
OXFORD RD ORO 103-C3
OXFORD RD N SHK 147-A3
OXFORD RD N SWT 83-A2
OXFORD RD S SHK 147-A3
OXFORD ST HOP 119-D1
OXFORD ST NFD 219-D3
OXFORD ST SLP 119-D1
OXFORD ST SVW 93-E2
OXFORD ST N RVL 93-E3,107-E1
OXFORD ST N STP 107-E3,121-E1
OXFORD ST N SVW 79-E1,93-E1
OXFORD ST NW ER 19-D4
OXFORD ST S STP 121-E1
OXFORD MILL RD STN 208-A4,221-E2
OXLEY AVE RVT 181-B2
OZARK AVE N MAY 69-A3
OZARK AVE N NST 41-A4,55-A1
OZARK AVE N OPH 97-A3
OZARK AVE N SWR 97-A2
OZARK AVE S AFT 125-A4
OZARK CT N NST 41-A4
OZARK TRL N MAY 68-E4
OZARK AVENUE CT N MAY 69-A3

P

PACIFIC AVE EAG 135-C4
PACIFIC AVE WAV 85-E1,86-A1
PACIFIC AVE WBL 81-B3
PACIFIC ST MPL 92-D4,106-D1
PACIFIC ST STP 108-D4,109-A4
PACKARD AVE NE OTS 33-D3,47-D1
PACKARD ST BLA 65-E1
PACKARD ST STP 107-C2
PACKARD ST NE BLA 65-E2
PACKARD ST NE EB 9-D4
PACKARD ST NE HL 37-E3
PACKER DR HUT 98-C4
PADDINGTON RD WIL 95-D1
PADDOCK CIR 96-E2
PADDOCK CIR E MED 90-B4
PADDOCK CIR W MED 90-B4
PADDOCK CT EAG 149-D1
PADDOCK LN CHN 117-B4
PADDOCK RD EDI 119-D2
PADDOCK TRL WBY 123-E1
PADGET AVE OTS 33-D4
PADGET CIR OTS 33-D3
PADGETT AVE NE OTS 33-D3
PADON DR EPR 132-C1
PADONS DR EPR 132-C1
PADRE CV NE OTS 33-D4
PADRICK CIR OTS 33-D3
PADRICK CT OTS 33-D4
PADRICK WAY OTS 33-D4
PAGE AVE NE OTS 33-D3
PAGE AVE NE SM 47-D3
PAGE LN TRT 139-E1
PAGE ST E STP 122-C2
PAGE ST W STP 122-B2
PAGEL RD MH 136-A1
PAGENKOPF RD IND 88-E4,89-A4
PAHL AVE SA 93-A4
PAINTED TURTLE RD LL 66-A4
PAINTER CIR MTA 102-D3
PAINTER RD MTA 102-E3
PAINTERS LN N WLT 111-B2
PAINTERS RDG EPR 133-B4
PAINTERS CREEK DR MTA 102-D3
PAINTERS LANE CIR N WLT 111-A2
PAISLEY LN GV 105-E2
PAISLEY RD MOU 117-A2
PAIUTE CIR EDI 133-C1
PAIUTE DR EDI 133-C1
PAIUTE PASS EDI 133-C1
PALACE AVE STP 121-D1,122-A1
PALAMINO PL FLT 39-C4
PALISADE CIR EAG 149-C1
PALISADE CT NE BLA 51-B3,65-A1
PALISADE PT EAG 149-C1
PALISADE ST NE BLA 51-A4
PALISADE ST NE EB 9-A4,23-A1
PALISADE WAY EAG 149-C1
PALLISADES CIR EPR 133-A4
PALM CIR MPW 94-D4
PALM CT MPW 94-D4
PALM ST MO 31-D2
PALM ST NW AND 36-C2,50-C2
PALM ST NW ATT 8-C1
PALM ST NW CR 64-C3,78-C1
PALMER AVE SAV 148-A3
PALMER AVE S BLO 148-A1
PALMER CIR BLO 134-A4,148-A2
PALMER CT LND 12-D3
PALMER DR NB 79-B4,93-A1
PALMER PL SB 116-B3
PALMER PL STP 121-E2
PALMER RD BLO 134-A3,148-A2
PALMER LAKE CIR BC 78-A3
PALMER LAKE DR W BC 78-A3
PALMER LAKE DR W BP 78-A3
PALMETTO DR EPR 132-D3
PALMGREN AVE NE OTS 33-D4
PALMGREN LN NE SM 47-D3
PALOMINO DR APV 148-E4,149-A4
PALOMINO DR S APV 149-A4
PALOMINO LN LL 65-E1,66-A1
PALOMINO TRL EAG 149-D1
PALOMINO TRL N WLT 111-B2
PAMELA LN HUT 112-A3
PAMELA LN MH 122-A3
PAMELA PL DPH 118-C1
PANAMA AVE CLT 189-A3,203-A1
PANAMA AVE SLT 161-A4,175-A3
PANAMA AVE N BYT 97-A4
PANAMA AVE N MAY 69-A4
PANAMA AVE N OPH 97-A2
PANAMA AVE N SWR 97-A2
PANAMA AVE N WLT 111-A2
PANAMA AVE S DET 153-A2
PANAMA LN SLT 175-A1
PANDORA BLVD SLT 174-D1
PANDORA DR NE FRI 78-E3
PANOLA DR CGT 40-E1
PANOLA DR N CGT 40-E1
PANOLA DR N FRT 40-E1,41-B1
PANORAMA AVE N MAY 69-A3
PANORAMA AVE NE FRI 92-D1
PAOLA CIR S BLO 133-E3
PAR LN BUF 58-E3
PARADE AVE N MAY 69-A4,83-A1
PARADE AVE N NST 55-A3
PARADE STADIUM DR MPL 106-C3
PARADISE DR SM 47-A4
PARADISE LN EAG 136-B2
PARADISE LN MOU 103-A4
PARADOX END AVE S AFT 125-B3
PARAGON AVE N MAY 69-A3
PARALLEL ST CHS 145-D2
PARC DR BUR 149-A3
PARELL AVE NE OTS 33-D3
PARELL AVE NE SM 47-D2
PARENT ST SOM 84-B1
PARIS AVE N MAY 69-A3,83-A1
PARIS AVE N NST 41-A2
PARIS AVE N OPH 97-A2
PARIS AVE N SWR 97-A2
PARIS AVE N WLT 111-A3
PARIS AVE S DET 153-B2
PARIS AVENUE CIR N WLT 111-A3
PARIS AVENUE CT N WLT 111-A3
PARK AVE BL 18-B3
PARK AVE BUR 162-D1
PARK AVE DEL 87-D2
PARK AVE DPH 118-B1
PARK AVE HBG 156-A2
PARK AVE LOL 103-D2
PARK AVE MHT 81-D4,95-D1
PARK AVE MPL 106-D3,120-D2
PARK AVE NM 189-E4,203-E1
PARK AVE ORO 103-B3
PARK AVE PRL 161-A3
PARK AVE RCH 120-D4,134-D1
PARK AVE SB 116-A3
PARK AVE VER 179-D2
PARK AVE WBL 80-E4
PARK AVE WBT 81-A2
PARK AVE N ML 43-D2
PARK AVE N NOH 111-C1
PARK AVE N VER 179-D2
PARK AVE N WLT 111-B2
PARK AVE NE OTS 33-D3
PARK AVE NE SM 47-E3
PARK AVE S BLO 134-D3,148-D1
PARK AVE S ML 43-D2
PARK AVE S NP 201-E2
PARK BLVD SLW 172-C3
PARK CIR BLO 134-D4
PARK CIR EPR 132-C2
PARK CIR MH 122-A3
PARK CT CF 208-A4
PARK CT CHN 131-E2
PARK CT HAS 166-C2
PARK CT WBL 80-E4
PARK XING WBY 124-A2
PARK DR CHN 131-E2
PARK DR CP 65-D3
PARK DR FAR 191-E1
PARK DR HSN 48-B2,61-B2
PARK DR JOR 173-B3
PARK DR MO 31-D3
PARK DR MPL 120-C2
PARK DR NFD 219-E4
PARK DR ORO 103-B4
PARK DR SHK 146-E2,147-A2
PARK DR VIC 130-E1,131-A1
PARK DR WAV 86-A1
PARK DR E CP 65-D3
PARK DR NE EB 37-D2
PARK DR S SAV 161-E2,162-A2
PARK DR W BUR 162-B2
PARK DR W CP 65-D3
PARK LN APV 162-E2
PARK LN BEL 186-A1
PARK LN HAS 166-C2
PARK LN HOP 119-C2
PARK LN HUT 98-A4
PARK LN LES 212-D4
PARK LN MH 136-B1
PARK LN MPL 106-B4
PARK LN MTK 104-C4
PARK LN ORO 103-B3
PARK LN OTT 212-D4
PARK LN SPR 117-B1
PARK LN SSP 122-E3
PARK LN SWD 117-C4
PARK LN S MTK 105-A2
PARK PL BKR 3-E4
PARK PL BUR 162-D1
PARK PL CHC 26-B1
PARK PL CHN 131-E2
PARK PL DPH 118-A2
PARK PL EAG 135-C4
PARK PL EDI 120-A3
PARK PL MHT 95-D1
PARK PL MO 31-C2
PARK PL NEW 137-B2
PARK PL NYA 142-C4
PARK PL SHK 146-E2
PARK PL SSP 122-D3
PARK PL SWR 96-E1
PARK PL NW PRL 160-D3
PARK RD BEL 186-A1
PARK RD BLO 134-E3
PARK RD CHM 63-D3
PARK RD CHN 131-E2,132-A2
PARK RD CRT 175-C1
PARK RD EPR 119-A4,133-A1
PARK RD W HOP 119-B2
PARK RD W MTK 119-A2
PARK ROW NSP 95-B4,109-B1
PARK ST ANO 49-B4
PARK ST COL 143-E4
PARK ST EXC 117-D4
PARK ST HMP 193-B2
PARK ST LC 94-B4
PARK ST LND 12-D4
PARK ST LON 217-A2
PARK ST RFD 74-B3
PARK ST SCF 14-C3
PARK ST STP 108-B3
PARK ST SVW 79-D1
PARK ST SWD 117-D4
PARK ST WBL 81-A4
PARK ST WBT 80-E4
PARK ST E BEL 185-E2,186-A2
PARK ST E NG 114-A4
PARK ST E RF 140-D2
PARK ST E SSP 136-E1
PARK ST E WAY 104-B3
PARK ST N LC 94-B4
PARK ST W BEL 185-E2
PARK ST W CF 208-B4
PARK ST W RF 140-D2
PARK ST W SSP 136-E1
PARK TER EDI 119-C3
PARK TER HOP 119-C1
PARK TER MPL 121-B1
PARK TER NE SLK 79-A1
PARK TRL N CGT 12-E3,13-A1
PARK CENTER BLVD SLP 119-E1
PARK CENTER DR EAG 149-B2
PARK GLEN RD SLP 119-E1,120-A1
PARK HILLS CT WBY 123-C1
PARK HILLS DR W BLO 147-C1
PARK ISLAND RD CNC 12-E4
PARK KNOLL CIR BLO 133-C3
PARK KNOLL DR EAG 150-A2
PARK LAWN CT CRT 176-A1
PARK MANOR CIR BEC 2-E3
PARK N RIDE HOP 119-B2
PARK N RIDE MG 76-D2,77-B1
PARK NICOLLET BLVD SLP 119-E1
PARK OVERLOOK DR SVW 93-E2
PARK PLACE BLVD S GV 105-E3
PARK PLACE BLVD S SLP 105-E3
PARK PLACE DR MH 122-A3
PARK PLACE DR SVW 79-E2
PARK POINT RD WAC 129-C3
PARK RIDGE CIR CHS 145-D1
PARK RIDGE CT CHS 145-D1
PARK RIDGE CT STP 123-A1
PARK RIDGE DR CHS 145-D1
PARK RIDGE DR SHK 146-C3
PARK RIDGE DR W MTK 105-B3
PARK TERRACE DR EPR 118-D4,132-D1
PARK VALLEY DR E HOP 119-C2
PARK VALLEY DR W HOP 119-C2
PARK VALLEY LN WBT 80-D4,94-E1
PARK VALLEY RD MTK 118-E1
PARK VIEW CIR BLO 148-C1
PARK VIEW DR MV 79-A2
PARK VIEW LN EPR 132-C1
PARK VIEW TER MV 79-A2
PARKCLIFF DR EAG 149-D2
PARKDALE DR IGH 136-D1
PARKDALE DR SLP 105-E3
PARKER AVE RVL 107-E1
PARKER AVE WBT 80-E2
PARKER DR EPR 147-B1
PARKER LN SLP 105-C3
PARKER PL MHT 95-C2
PARKER RD SLP 105-C3
PARKERS DR WBY 123-E3
PARKERS LAKE RD MTK 104-D3
PARKFIELD AVE SLT 174-C3
PARKINGTON AVE NE OTS 33-E2
PARKINGTON CIR NE OTS 33-E3

PARKLAND CT STP .109-A4
PARKLAND WAY CHN .132-B3
PARKLANDS LN SLP .106-A3
PARKLANDS RD SLP .106-A3
PARKLAWN AVE EDI .134-A1
PARKLAWN CT EDI .134-A2
PARKMONT LN ANO .49-B4
PARKRIDGE CT EAG .149-D2
PARKRIDGE DR EAG .149-E2
PARKRIDGE DR WBT .80-D4,94-D1
PARKRIDGE KNLS BUR .162-B2
PARKSHORE DR AH .79-D4
PARKSIDE BLVD HOP .119-C2
PARKSIDE CIR BUR .148-D4
PARKSIDE CIR CHM .63-C3
PARKSIDE CIR COL .143-E3
PARKSIDE CT CHM .63-C3
PARKSIDE DR STP .109-A4
PARKSIDE DR VH .94-C2
PARKSIDE DR WBY .109-E4,124-A1
PARKSIDE DRAW WBY .124-A1
PARKSIDE ECHO WBY .124-A1
PARKSIDE LN EDI .119-E2
PARKSIDE LN WAC .129-C3
PARKSIDE ST COL .143-E3
PARKSIDE TRL CHM .63-C3
PARKVIEW AVE STP .107-E2,108-A2
PARKVIEW AVE N NST .55-B2
PARKVIEW BLVD GV .106-A1
PARKVIEW BLVD ROB .92-A4,106-A1
PARKVIEW CIR DEL .87-E3
PARKVIEW CIR SE PRL .161-C3
PARKVIEW CT CHS .145-D2
PARKVIEW CT MPW .123-B1
PARKVIEW CT VH .80-D4
PARKVIEW DNS WAT .101-B3
PARKVIEW DR BEC .2-E3
PARKVIEW DR CHS .145-D2
PARKVIEW DR LL .65-E3
PARKVIEW DR MED .89-C3
PARKVIEW DR PRL .161-C3
PARKVIEW DR SVW .79-C1
PARKVIEW DR WBT .81-B2
PARKVIEW DR SE PRL .161-C3
PARKVIEW LN CHM .63-B1
PARKVIEW LN EAG .149-E2
PARKVIEW LN MPW .123-B1
PARKVIEW LN NOH .98-A4
PARKVIEW LN WBY .124-A2
PARKVIEW LN N NST .55-B2
PARKVIEW LN NE CH .92-E2
PARKVIEW LN W CHS .145-D2
PARKVIEW RD MP .102-E1
PARKVIEW TER GV .106-A3
PARKWAY DEL .87-E2
PARKWAY AVE SHK .146-C2
PARKWAY CIR BC .78-B4
PARKWAY CIR DEL .87-E2
PARKWAY CT CF .208-B3
PARKWAY CT MPL .120-D3
PARKWAY CT WBL .80-D4
PARKWAY DR MPW .108-D1
PARKWAY DR NSP .109-B1
PARKWAY DR STP .108-C2
PARKWAY LN CF .208-B3
PARKWAY PL BUR .148-E3
PARKWAY RD DPH .118-B1
PARKWAY RD E CV .66-C2
PARKWAY RD E LL .66-C3
PARKWAY ST DEL .87-E2
PARKWAY PONDS LN WBT .80-D4,94-E1
PARKWOOD CIR VH .94-C1
PARKWOOD CT BUR .148-E3
PARKWOOD DR BUR .148-E4,162-D1
PARKWOOD DR SSP .122-D3
PARKWOOD DR SVW .79-D1
PARKWOOD DR WBY .123-C1
PARKWOOD DR NW CR .64-B2
PARKWOOD DR SE PRL .161-B4
PARKWOOD LN BUR .148-E4,162-E1
PARKWOOD LN EDI .119-C3
PARKWOOD LN SWR .96-D2
PARKWOOD LN VH .94-C1
PARKWOOD PL BUR .148-E3
PARKWOOD RD EDI .119-C3
PARKWOODS RD SLP .105-E3,106-A3
PARLEY LAKE LN LTT .130-B1
PARLEY LAKE RD LTT .130-B1
PARMEADOW DR NFD .219-E4,220-A4
PARNELL AVE EDI .119-E4
PARNELL AVE NE SM .47-E2
PARNELL ST GI .169-D2
PARNELL ST SOM .70-B4
PARQUET AVE NE OTS .33-E4,47-E1
PARRISH AVE NE ER .33-E2
PARRISH AVE NE OTS .33-E3
PARRISH AVE NE SM .47-E3
PARRISH RD N NST .41-A4
PARRISH AVAE NE OTS .33-E4
PARSON AVE NE OTS .47-E1
PARSON AVE NE SM .47-E2
PARSON HILL DR BUR .162-E2
PARSONS AVE NE OTS .47-E1
PARSONS CLOS MTK .118-B2
PARSONS CT S AFT .125-B4
PARTENWOOD LN ORO .103-C3
PARTENWOOD RD ORO .103-C3
PARTRIDGE CIR CHN .117-E4
PARTRIDGE CIR EPR .132-B1
PARTRIDGE CIR HUT .112-B4
PARTRIDGE CIR WAC .129-D3
PARTRIDGE CIR NW CR .64-A3
PARTRIDGE CIR S AFT .125-A4
PARTRIDGE CT LL .67-A4
PARTRIDGE CT PRL .161-B2
PARTRIDGE CT N MAY .69-A4
PARTRIDGE LN NO .80-C2
PARTRIDGE LN N NOH .97-D4,111-D1
PARTRIDGE PL LL .66-B3
PARTRIDGE RD RVL .93-C3
PARTRIDGE RD SB .116-A4
PARTRIDGE RD N MAY .69-A4,83-A1
PARTRIDGE RD N SWT .83-B1
PARTRIDGE ST NW AND .36-B3,50-B3
PARTRIDGE ST NW CR .50-B4,64-A2
PARTRIDGE ST NW SF .8-A3
PARTRIDGE ST NW STT .8-A1
PARTRIDGE RD CT N SWT .83-A1
PASCAL AVE LEX .65-C4
PASCAL AVE N AH .93-D2
PASCAL DR NW ER .33-B1
PASCAL ST STP .107-D2
PASCAL ST SVW .79-D2
PASCAL ST N FH .107-D1
PASCAL ST N RVL .93-D3,107-D1
PASCAL ST N STP .107-D4,121-D1
PASCAL ST NW ER .19-B3,33-B1
PASCAL ST S STP .121-D1
PASSFIELD TURN N MG .76-D2
PASTURE RIDGE RD AFT .125-B4
PATELEY BRIDGE AVE S AFT .125-B4
PATHFINDER DR EPR .132-B4
PATHWAYS DR STP .109-A4
PATRICIA CT EPR .132-D1
PATRICIA LN MTK .118-C3
PATRICIA ST MH .121-E4,135-E1
PATRICK AVE RVT .181-B1
PATRICK CT RF .140-D1
PATRICK LN HAS .166-E3
PATRICK PL N COR .76-A1
PATRICK RD EAG .149-E2
PATRIOT LN LEX .65-C4
PATRIOT PL SPR .117-A1
PATSY LN GV .105-C1
PATTI DR LL .65-E1
PATTIES LN SPR .117-B1
PATTON RD NB .93-B1
PATTON RD RVL .93-B3
PAUL ALC WBY .123-D2
PAUL AVE BTT .143-B3,157-B2
PAUL AVE COL .143-E3
PAUL AVE HCT .157-B3
PAUL AVE WCT .129-B2
PAUL AVE WTT .101-B3
PAUL AVE N COL .143-E4
PAUL AVE N MAY .69-A2
PAUL AVE N OPH .97-A2
PAUL AVE S COL .143-E4
PAUL CT WBT .81-B2
PAUL DR BC .77-E4
PAUL PKWY NE BLA .50-E4,64-E1
PAUL PL WBT .81-B2
PAUL RD WBY .123-D2
PAUL BURCH DR HUT .98-C4
PAULS DR HSN .47-D3
PAULSEN DR EPR .132-C1
PAULSON RD RF .126-E4
PAULY DR CHN .132-A2
PAULY LN SB .116-A3
PAVELKA DR EPR .132-C1
PAWNEE AVE N SWT .83-A2
PAWNEE DR CHN .118-A4
PAWNEE RD EDI .119-C4
PAWNEE RD MED .89-D1
PAWNEE AVENUE CT N SWT .83-A2
PAYNE AVE STP .108-C3
PAYNE AVE VH .94-C2
PAYNE AVE N LC .94-C3
PAYNE AVE N MPW .94-C4,108-C1
PAYTON CT EDI .133-E1
PEABODY AVE N OPH .97-A2
PEABODY TRL N NST .41-A3
PEACAN AVE N OPH .97-A2
PEACE AVE SHK .146-C4,160-C1
PEACE CIR SHK .160-C1
PEACEDALE AVE EDI .120-A4
PEACEFUL LN CHN .118-A4
PEACEFUL RIDGE RD RW .210-E1
PEACH CIR SWD .117-C4
PEACH ST NE EB .37-D2
PEACH TREE CT MTK .118-B4
PEARL ST HAT .201-C2
PEARL ST PRE .153-B4
PEARL ST STP .107-B3
PEARL ST TKB .117-D2
PEARL ST N RF .140-D1
PEARL ST S RF .140-D2
PEARSON CT N BP .78-B3
PEARSON DR BC .92-A1
PEARSON DR MPW .109-B2
PEARSON PKWY BP .78-A2
PEARSON PKWY N BP .78-B2
PEARSON WAY NE FRI .78-C2
PEAVEY CIR CHS .131-C3
PEAVEY LN WAY .104-B3
PEAVEY RD CHS .131-C3
PEAVEY RD WAY .104-B3
PEBBLE TER SHK .146-A3
PEBBLE BEACH WAY EAG .149-D3
PEBBLE BROOK CT CRT .161-C4
PEBBLEBROOK CIR BLO .134-A4
PEBBLEBROOK DR BLO .134-A4
PEBBLEBROOK DR MO .31-D3
PECAN LN MOU .117-A1
PECK ST LES .212-D3
PECKS WOODS TURN NB .93-A1
PEDERSEN ST STP .109-A3
PEDERSON DR NW SF .7-D4
PEDERSON ST DPH .118-A2
PEEP O DAY TRL EPR .133-A3
PEGGY LN WBL .80-E3
PELHAM BLVD STP .107-B3
PELICAN CT CHN .131-E3
PELICAN LN MO .31-E3
PELICAN PL LL .65-E3
PELICAN POINT CIR MOU .117-B2
PELICAN POINT CT MOU .117-B2
PELLER AVE N OPH .97-B2
PELLER AVE S DET .139-B2
PELLO CIR EAG .149-C2
PELTIER CIR CV .66-D2
PELTIER LAKE DR CV .66-D2
PELTIER LAKE DR LL .66-D1
PEMBROOK CIR HSN .48-B3
PENAMINT CT CHN .132-A1
PENAMINT LN CHN .132-A1
PENCE LN ORO .117-C2
PENDLETON CT EPR .147-B1
PENDLETON ST W CF .208-B3
PENDRYN HILL ALC WBY .110-A4
PENDRYN HILL BAY WBY .110-A4
PENDRYN HILL CIR WBY .110-A4
PENDRYN HILL CRV WBY .110-A4
PENDRYN HILL CT WBY .110-A4
PENDRYN HILL OVERLOO WBY .110-A4
PENFIELD AVE N NST .41-A4
PENFIELD AVE N OPH .97-B3
PENFIELD AVE N SWT .83-A2
PENFIELD AVE S AFT .125-B4
PENFIELD CT S AFT .125-B4
PENFIELD AVENUE CIR N SWT .83-B2
PENFIELD AVENUE CT N SWT .83-B2
PENINSULA AVE LND .12-D3
PENINSULA RD DWD .81-C3
PENINSULA RD MDL .105-B1
PENINSULA POINT DR SAV .161-D1
PENKWE CIR EAG .149-C3
PENKWE WAY EAG .149-C2
PENN AVE NMT .190-B1
PENN AVE WTT .101-B2
PENN AVE N BC .78-B3,92-B2
PENN AVE N BP .64-B4,78-B3
PENN AVE N MPL .92-B3,106-B2
PENN AVE S BLO .134-B3,148-B1
PENN AVE S BUR .148-B4
PENN AVE S MPL .106-B3,120-B3
PENN AVE S RCH .120-B4,134-B1
PENN CIR BLO .134-B4
PENN CIR BUR .148-B4
PENN PL NSP .95-B4
PENN GLEN PL BLO .134-B3
PENN LAKE CIR BLO .134-B3
PENNINE PASS NE CH .93-A1
PENNINGTON AVE EPR .118-B4
PENNINGTON AVE S AFT .125-B3
PENNINGTON PL VH .94-C1
PENNOCK AVE APV .149-B4,163-A1
PENNOCK AVE STP .107-C3
PENNOCK CT APV .163-A1
PENNOCK LN APV .163-A2
PENNSYLVANIA AVE BLA .65-A4
PENNSYLVANIA AVE CHM .63-D2
PENNSYLVANIA AVE EAG .150-A1
PENNSYLVANIA AVE SAV .147-D3
PENNSYLVANIA AVE STP .108-B3
PENNSYLVANIA AVE N CHM .63-D2
PENNSYLVANIA AVE N CRY .91-D1
PENNSYLVANIA AVE N GV .105-D1
PENNSYLVANIA AVE N NH .91-D2
PENNSYLVANIA AVE S BLO .147-D1
PENNSYLVANIA AVE S GV .105-D3
PENNSYLVANIA AVE S SLP .105-D3,119-D1
PENNSYLVANIA CIR BLO .133-D2
PENNSYLVANIA PL NSP .95-B4
PENNSYLVANIA RD BLO .133-D2
PENNSYLVANIA ST SCF .14-C2
PENNY LN HUT .112-D3
PENNY LN WBY .123-D2
PENNY LN SW LAT .201-D3
PENNY HILL RD EPR .132-E1
PENROD LN SA .93-A2
PENROSE AVE N NST .41-B4
PENROSE AVE N OPH .97-B3
PENTAGON DR SA .93-A4
PENWAY RD WIL .95-D1
PEONY CT N MG .76-C2
PEONY LN PLY .104-C2
PEONY LN N MG .76-C3
PEONY LN N PLY .90-C2,104-C1
PEPPERWOOD CIR MTK .118-E2
PEPPERWOOD LN MTK .118-E2
PEPPERWOOD TRL MTK .118-E2
PERCH LAKE RD SJT .98-B1
PERCHERON DR OST .28-C1
PERCHERON RD DRS .28-C1
PEREGRINE CIR LL .66-C4
PEREGRINE CIR SW LVT .159-D1
PEREGRINE CIR SW PRL .161-A4
PERFORMANCE CIR EAG .136-A2
PERIDOT PATH EAG .149-C1
PERIDOT ST NW BT .20-E3,34-E1
PERIDOT ST NW RAM .48-E1
PERIMETER RD W RVL .93-C4
PERIPHERAL RD PLY .104-E2
PERIWINKLE AVE N WLT .111-B2
PERKINS AVE N NST .41-B3
PERKINS AVE N OPH .97-B3
PERKINS AVE N SWT .83-B3
PERKINS LN MP .89-A4
PERKINSVILLE RD IND .89-A4
PERRO CREEK DR BAY .97-B4
PERRON RD MH .135-D1
PERRON RD W MH .135-D1
PERROT AVE S AFT .125-B3
PERROT LN BUR .149-A2
PERRY AVE N BC .77-E4,91-E1
PERRY AVE N BP .77-E3
PERRY AVE N CHM .63-E3
PERRY AVE N CRY .91-E1,92-A4
PERRY AVE N GV .92-A4,106-A1
PERRY AVE N ROB .91-E3,92-A3
PERRY CIR CRY .91-E2
PERRY CT E BC .77-E3
PERRY CT W BC .77-E3
PERRY PL N BC .77-E3
PERSHING AVE N NP .201-E2
PERSHING CIR BUR .162-D3
PERSHING ST PRL .161-A4
PETE DR IND .88-E2
PETELER LN MTK .118-D3
PETER LN HUT .112-A3
PETERBORG RD EPR .132-C1
PETERS PL NE CH .92-E2
PETERSBURG ST NE ATT .9-C2
PETERSBURG ST NE BLA .65-C4
PETERSBURG ST NE HL .37-C4
PETERSON CT AFT .124-D1
PETERSON DR AFT .124-D1
PETERSON DR S DRS .28-C2
PETERSON PL NO .80-A2
PETERSON RD SCF .14-D2
PETERSON RD WBT .80-D2
PETERSON ST SJT .97-B1
PETERSON TRL CV .66-D2
PETIT ST STP .108-C3
PETTER DR SLW .172-D4,186-D1
PETTIT AVE NE WAT .101-B3
PETTIT AVE SE WAT .101-B4
PETUNIA ST VIC .130-E2
PEXA DR HAT .188-A3
PHAETON DR EPR .133-B4,147-B1
PHALEN DR STP .108-D2
PHALEN PL MPW .108-D1
PHEASANT CIR CHN .117-E4
PHEASANT CIR EPR .132-B1
PHEASANT CIR MOU .116-D2
PHEASANT CIR NMT .203-E1
PHEASANT CIR ROG .47-D4
PHEASANT CT EDI .119-D4
PHEASANT CT S AFT .125-B4,139-B1
PHEASANT DR CHN .117-E4
PHEASANT DR SVW .79-E1
PHEASANT LN CV .66-D3
PHEASANT LN MTK .119-A1
PHEASANT LN NO .80-C3
PHEASANT LN SB .116-A4
PHEASANT LN N MG .77-B3
PHEASANT RD ORO .117-C2
PHEASANT RUN BUR .148-D3
PHEASANT RUN HUD .111-D2
PHEASANT RUN WIN .99-B3
PHEASANT RUN E MGY .215-E4
PHEASANT RUN N MGY .215-E4
PHEASANT RUN NE BLA .65-C1
PHEASANT RUN S LL .66-C3
PHEASANT RUN W MGY .215-E4
PHEASANT TRL HUT .97-D4
PHEASANT TRL PRL .161-A4
PHEASANT HILLS CIR LL .66-D3
PHEASANT HILLS DR LL .66-C3
PHEASANT MEADOW LN PRL .161-A4
PHEASANT RIDGE DR BLA .65-D2
PHEASANT RIDGE RD CRT .175-E2
PHEASANT RIDGE RD MED .104-A1
PHEASANT RUN CIR WBY .123-E2
PHEASANT RUN RD FRT .27-B4
PHEASANT RUN RD WBY .123-E2
PHEASANT RUN ST SHK .146-C4
PHEASANTWOOD TRL NFD .219-D4
PHELPS RD LL .66-E3
PHELPS RD MOU .117-A2
PHILBROOK LN EDI .120-A3
PHILIPP PKWY NP .201-E2
PHILLIPS DR MED .103-D1
PHILLIPS DR ORO .103-D1
PHILLIPS PKWY SLP .119-C1
PHLOX LN EDI .133-E1
PHOENIX ST GV .105-D2
PHYLIS CT MPW .123-B2
PHYLLIS ST BL .18-B4
PICHA DR CHN .132-A2
PICHA LN MTK .118-C3
PICHA RD MTK .118-D3
PICKETT AVE N BAY .97-B3
PICKETT AVE N NST .41-B2
PICKETT AVE N OPH .97-B3
PICKFAIR DR BLO .133-C3
PICTURE DR BLO .133-E2
PIEDMONT CT CHN .118-B4
PIENE AVE RVT .181-C2
PIERCE AVE HOP .119-C2
PIERCE CT NE BLA .50-E4
PIERCE PATH NE EB .8-E3
PIERCE PL NE BLA .50-E4,64-E3
PIERCE PL NE MPL .92-E3
PIERCE ST ANO .49-C4
PIERCE ST RF .140-E2
PIERCE ST SHK .146-B3
PIERCE ST STP .107-D4,121-D1
PIERCE ST N SHK .146-A2
PIERCE ST NE BLA .50-E4,64-E3
PIERCE ST NE CH .92-E2
PIERCE ST NE EB .8-E3,22-E4
PIERCE ST NE FRI .78-E3,92-E1
PIERCE ST NE HL .36-E4,50-E2
PIERCE ST NE MPL .92-E3,106-E1
PIERCE ST NE SLK .78-E1
PIERCE ST NW HL .50-E3
PIERCE ST S SHK .146-B3
PIERCE TER JOR .173-B2
PIERCE TER NE CH .92-E1
PIERCE BUTLER RTE STP .107-D3,108-A3
PIERCE PATH CIR EB .8-E3
PIERSON LAKE DR LTT .130-C3
PIERSON LAKE RD LTT .130-C3
PIGEON LOFT RD NE OXT .10-C1
PIGSEYE LAKE RD STP .108-D4,122-D1
PIKE AVE S AFT .125-B3
PIKE RD MOU .116-E1,117-A1
PIKE LAKE CIR NB .93-B1
PIKE LAKE CT NB .79-B4,93-B1
PIKE LAKE DR NB .79-B4,93-B1
PIKE LAKE RD S SHK .147-B4
PIKE LAKE TRL NE PRL .147-B4,161-B1
PILAR RD N NST .41-B3
PILGRIM CT CHM .49-B4,63-B1
PILGRIM LN N CHM .63-B1
PILGRIM LN N MG .63-B4,77-B3
PILGRIM LN N PLY .91-B4
PILGRIM WAY MG .63-B4
PILLSBURY AVE BUR .148-D3
PILLSBURY AVE MPL .106-C4,120-C1
PILLSBURY AVE NMT .190-C3,204-D2
PILLSBURY AVE RCH .120-C4,134-C1
PILLSBURY AVE S BLO .134-C2
PILLSBURY DR SE MPL .106-E2,107-A2
PILLSBURY ST STP .107-B4
PILOT AVE NE FRI .92-D1
PILOT AVE SW LAT .201-D3
PILOT KNOB RD APV .149-D4,163-C2
PILOT KNOB RD EAG .135-D4,149-D2
PILOT KNOB RD FAR .177-D3
PILOT KNOB RD LVL .163-D4,177-D1
PILOT KNOB RD MH .121-D4,135-D1
PIMA BAY CHN .132-A1
PIMA LN CHN .132-A1
PIMLICO LN CHN .132-A1
PIN OAK AVE BP .63-E4,77-E1
PIN OAK CT N BP .63-E4
PIN OAK DR EAG .149-B3
PINE AVE WAV .86-A1
PINE BND SWD .117-B3
PINE CIR MTA .116-D2
PINE CIR MTK .105-B4
PINE CIR SOM .84-B1
PINE CT SCF .14-D2
PINE CT VIC .131-A3
PINE DR CP .65-D3
PINE DR S CP .65-E3
PINE GLN PRE .167-B1
PINE LN DEL .87-E2
PINE LN EAG .150-B3
PINE LN MTK .118-D1
PINE PL ET .178-A4
PINE PT WBL .80-E4
PINE RD MOU .116-D2
PINE RD NO .80-D3
PINE RD PRL .161-B2
PINE ST ANO .63-D1
PINE ST BEC .2-E4
PINE ST BUF .59-A2
PINE ST COT .51-E3,52-A3
PINE ST CW .1-B2
PINE ST EAG .150-B3
PINE ST ET .178-A4
PINE ST FAR .177-E4
PINE ST HAS .166-C2
PINE ST HSN .48-B3
PINE ST HUD .111-C2
PINE ST MED .89-A3
PINE ST MHT .81-D4
PINE ST MO .31-D2
PINE ST MSC .55-B4
PINE ST MTK .118-D1
PINE ST PRE .153-B4
PINE ST SA .93-A4
PINE ST SB .116-B3
PINE ST SCF .14-D3
PINE ST STP .108-C4
PINE ST TF .14-B2
PINE ST WBL .95-A1
PINE ST E RF .140-E2
PINE ST E SWR .97-A1
PINE ST N CHS .145-C3
PINE ST N LP .113-B4
PINE ST N NOH .111-C1
PINE ST N WAC .129-D3
PINE ST S CHS .145-C3
PINE ST S LP .113-B4,127-B1
PINE ST S WAC .129-D3

PINE ST W RF 140-D2
PINE ST W SWR 96-E1,97-A1
PINE TRL NMT 190-C1
PINE VW N NOH 97-C4
PINE BEND TRL NIT 165-C1
PINE BEND TRL RMT 151-A4,165-C1
PINE BLUFF CT EPR 132-E3
PINE CONE LN DAT 159-A1
PINE CONE TRL N MSC 55-C3
PINE COULEE DR S CG 152-C3
PINE GROVE CT CG 151-E1
PINE GROVE LN LAT 215-E1
PINE GROVE RD EDI 119-D3
PINE HILL RD BLO 133-D3
PINE HOLLOW GRN SWR 96-C1
PINE HOLLOW PL SWR 96-C1
PINE ISLAND RD MTK 105-A3
PINE OAKS DR LL 52-B3
PINE RIDGE CIR BUR 148-D4
PINE RIDGE DR ANO 49-B4
PINE RIDGE DR EAG 135-D3
PINE RIDGE DR PRE 167-C1
PINE RIDGE DR NE EB 36-E2
PINE RIDGE LN ORO 103-D2
PINE RIDGE RD BUR 148-D4
PINE RIDGE RD RVT 181-C2
PINE RIDGE TER RF 140-D1
PINE RIDGE TER TRT 140-D1
PINE TREE DR AH 93-D2
PINE TREE DR MPW 109-B2
PINE TREE LN HUT 112-B3
PINE TREE LN SHK 146-D3
PINE TREE LN SJT 83-B4
PINE TREE LN NE FRI 79-A2
PINE TREE LN SE LAT 201-D3
PINE TREE TRL SWR 96-E2
PINE VALLEY DR DWD 81-C2
PINE VALLEY TRL SJT 98-C2
PINE VIEW CT CHN 132-A4
PINE VIEW CT STP 123-B2
PINE VIEW DR PRL 160-E2
PINE VIEW TRL SJT 97-D1
PINECREST CT EAG 135-D4
PINECREST RD PS 95-D2
PINEFIELD CT WBT 80-E4
PINEHURST AVE STP 121-C2
PINEHURST BAY WBY 123-E1
PINEHURST CIR WBY 123-E1
PINEHURST CT PS 95-D2
PINEHURST CT WBY 123-E1
PINEHURST DR BUR 149-A3
PINEHURST DR DWD 81-C2
PINEHURST LN SWR 96-D2
PINEHURST RD PS 95-D2
PINEHURST RD WBY 123-E1,124-A1
PINERIDGE CT MHT 95-C2
PINERIDGE DR WSP 122-B4
PINERIDGE DR NW OG 21-D3
PINERIDGE LN SWR 96-D1
PINETREE CRV EAG 149-D2
PINETREE PASS EAG 149-D3
PINETREE TRL EAG 149-D3
PINEVIEW CT GRW 117-E3
PINEVIEW CT MHT 95-C2
PINEVIEW CT RVL 108-A1
PINEVIEW DR BEC 2-E4,3-A4
PINEVIEW DR VH 94-C1
PINEVIEW LN DAY 63-A3
PINEVIEW LN LND 12-D4
PINEVIEW LN N DAY 49-A4,63-A1
PINEVIEW LN N MG 63-A4,77-A2
PINEVIEW LN N PLY 91-A2,105-A2
PINEVIEW PL LND 12-D4
PINEVIEW RD BEC 3-A4
PINEVIEW TRL DAY 49-A3
PINEWOOD CIR APV 162-E2
PINEWOOD CIR CHN 131-D2
PINEWOOD CIR MV 79-B2
PINEWOOD CT MV 79-B2
PINEWOOD CT WBY 123-C1
PINEWOOD DR APV 162-E2,163-A2
PINEWOOD DR DAT 159-A1
PINEWOOD DR MV 79-B2
PINEWOOD DR SHK 146-C2
PINEWOOD DR SVW 79-C2,80-A2
PINEWOOD DR WBY 123-C1
PINEWOOD DR NE HL 36-E3
PINEWOOD LN HUD 111-D4
PINEWOOD LN MTK 118-D4
PINEWOOD TRL EDI 119-E3
PINKSPIRE LN E MPW 123-B2
PINNACLE DR EPR 119-A4
PINNACLE WAY MTA 116-C2
PINNACLE WAY WBY 124-B3
PINNAKER RD NW BT 20-E2,21-A2
PINR RIDGE DR PRE 167-B1
PINTAIL AVE SHK 146-C3
PINTAIL CIR CHN 117-E4
PINTAIL CIR WAC 129-D3
PINTAIL CT EAG 149-C2
PINTAIL CT ROG 48-A4
PINTAIL ST BL 17-E3
PINTAIL ST WBT 81-B1
PINTAIL TRL BUF 59-B1
PINTO CIR NMT 190-C1
PINTO CIR NW ATT 8-B2
PINTO DR MED 90-A2
PINTO DR NW ATT 8-B2
PINTO LN LL 65-E1
PINTO LN NMT 190-C1
PINTO PL FLT 39-C4
PIONEER AVE MP 88-E4,102-E1
PIONEER AVE N CGT 13-B1
PIONEER BLVD SWR 96-C1
PIONEER CIR BEL 186-A2
PIONEER CIR CHN 132-B4
PIONEER CT JOR 173-A2
PIONEER CT NFD 219-E4
PIONEER CT SHK 146-C3
PIONEER DR BUR 149-A2
PIONEER DR OSC 28-A3
PIONEER DR WBY 123-E3
PIONEER LN CV 66-D2
PIONEER LN SHK 146-C3
PIONEER LN WBT 80-E3,81-A3
PIONEER PL SWR 96-C1
PIONEER RD MTK 119-A2
PIONEER RD WYT 25-D4
PIONEER RD N WYT 25-D4
PIONEER RD S GCT 151-B2
PIONEER TRL BLO 147-C1
PIONEER TRL BUF 45-B4
PIONEER TRL CHN 131-E4,132-A4
PIONEER TRL CHS 131-D4
PIONEER TRL COR 75-B4,89-B1
PIONEER TRL EPR 132-D3,133-B4
PIONEER TRL GRF 74-E1,75-A3
PIONEER TRL MED 89-D2
PIONEER CREEK CTR MP 88-E4
PIONEER CREEK DR MP 88-E4
PIONEER CREEK RD IND 102-C1
PIPER DR NB 93-B2
PIPER RD MOU 116-E2,117-A2
PIPER RIDGE LN CHN 117-D4
PIPEWOOD CRV CHN 117-B4
PITRINA WAY LC 94-C3
PITT ST HUD 111-D2
PITT ST SSP 122-E4
PIXIE POINT CIR PRL 161-C2
PLACER AVE ANO 49-C3
PLAINVIEW DR TRT 125-D4
PLAN AVE RVT 181-C2
PLANT RD EAG 135-B4
PLANTING GRN SWR 96-C1
PLATEAU DR NMT 190-C2
PLATEAU ST TF 14-C3
PLATO BLVD E STP 108-C4,122-C1
PLATO BLVD W STP 122-B1
PLATWOOD RD MTK 104-E3
PLAYHOUSE ST BTT 143-E4
PLAYHOUSE ST E COL 143-E4
PLAYHOUSE ST W COL 143-D4
PLAZA BLVD NE SLK 79-A1
PLAZA CIR MPW 94-D4
PLAZA CRV NE FRI 78-D3
PLAZA DR EAG 149-B2
PLAZA DR EDI 134-A2
PLAZA DR EPR 133-A2
PLAZA DR S MH 122-A4
PLEASANT AVE BEC 2-E4
PLEASANT AVE BKR 3-E4,4-A4
PLEASANT AVE BL 18-A4
PLEASANT AVE BLO 134-C4,148-C1
PLEASANT AVE BUR 148-C3
PLEASANT AVE LND 12-D4
PLEASANT AVE MPL 106-C4,120-C2
PLEASANT AVE RCH 120-C4,134-C1
PLEASANT AVE SPP 137-B3
PLEASANT AVE SSP 122-D3
PLEASANT AVE STP 121-E2,122-A1
PLEASANT AVE SWD 117-C4
PLEASANT AVE TKB 117-C3
PLEASANT AVE WBT 81-A2
PLEASANT AVE N CHM 63-C2
PLEASANT CIR AH 79-E4
PLEASANT CT E WBT 80-E2
PLEASANT CT W WBT 80-E2
PLEASANT DR AH 79-E4
PLEASANT DR HAS 166-C2
PLEASANT DR PRE 167-B1
PLEASANT KNLS CNC 12-E4
PLEASANT LN BUR 148-C4,162-C1
PLEASANT LN RCH 134-C1
PLEASANT LN E TKB 117-D3
PLEASANT LN W TKB 117-C3
PLEASANT PL BUR 148-C4
PLEASANT ST ANO 49-C4
PLEASANT ST EXC 117-E3
PLEASANT ST HSN 47-E3
PLEASANT ST LAU 107-B1
PLEASANT ST PRL 161-A3
PLEASANT ST E COL 143-E4
PLEASANT ST E ML 43-D3
PLEASANT ST SE MPL 106-E3,107-A2
PLEASANT VW NFD 219-E4
PLEASANT KNOLL DR CNC 12-E4
PLEASANT LAKE RD E NO 80-B3
PLEASANT LAKE RD W NO 80-B2
PLEASANT PARK DR CHN 118-B4
PLEASANT VALLEY RD N CGT 13-A4
PLEASANT VALLEY
RD N FRT 13-A4,27-C2
PLEASANT VIEW CIR CHN 118-B4
PLEASANT VIEW CT MV 79-A1
PLEASANT VIEW CV CHN 118-A4
PLEASANT VIEW DR CHN 118-B4,132-B1
PLEASANT VIEW DR MV 79-A1
PLEASANT VIEW DR NB 79-A3
PLEASANT VIEW DR NE SLK 79-A2
PLEASANT VIEW LN CHM 63-C2
PLEASANT VIEW LN CHN 118-B4
PLEASANT VIEW LN CP 65-E4
PLEASANT VIEW RD CHN 118-A4
PLEASANT VIEW RD EPR 118-B4
PLEASANTWOOD RD MTK 119-A2
PLEASURE CREEK DR BLA 64-D4
PLEASURE CREEK PKWY BLA 64-D3
PLEASURE CREEK PKWY E BLA 64-E3
PLEASURE CREEK PKWY W BLA 64-D3
PLUM LN LL 66-A4
PLUM ST RFD 74-B3
PLUM ST STP 108-D4
PLUM ST N NFD 219-D3
PLUM ST NE EB 37-D2
PLUM ST S NFD 219-D4
PLUM CREEK RD CLT 189-A3
PLUTO ST NE LWT 24-A2
PLYMOUTH AVE BL 18-A3
PLYMOUTH AVE BUR 162-D1
PLYMOUTH AVE N GV 105-D1,106-B2
PLYMOUTH AVE N MPL 106-C1
PLYMOUTH AVE N PLY 105-C1
PLYMOUTH BLVD PLY 90-D4
PLYMOUTH RD MOU 117-A2
PLYMOUTH RD MTK 105-A3,119-A1
PLYMOUTH RD WBY 124-A4
POE RD BC 78-A4
POINT DR EDI 134-A1
POINT DR WAC 129-D2
POINT DR NE EB 37-C1
POINT RD BAY 97-C3
POINT CHAS EPR 119-B4
POINT DOUGLAS CT S CG 137-D4
POINT DOUGLAS DR S CG 152-B2
POINT DOUGLAS
DR S DET 152-D4,167-A1
POINT DOUGLAS LN S CG 152-A1
POINT DOUGLAS RD N STP 108-E4
POINT DOUGLAS RD S CG137-D4,152-A1
POINT DOUGLAS RD S SPP 137-C2
POINT DOUGLAS
RD S STP 122-E1,123-A2
POINT PLEASANT DR CHC 26-A2
POINT PLEASANT RD CHC 26-B2
POINTCROSS DR CP 65-E3
POINTE CIR ROG 62-A1
POINTE DR ROG 61-E1,62-A2
POINTE WAY EAG 150-A2
POINTE LAKE LUCY CHN 117-E4,131-E1
POINTE VISTA DR VIC 130-E3,131-A3
POLAR CIR EDI 119-C4
POLAR BEAR LN WBT 81-B1
POLARIS CT NSP 109-B1
POLARIS LN N MG 76-D4,90-D1
POLARIS LN N PLY 90-D3,104-D1
POLARIS PL NSP 109-B1
POLEN DR HUT 112-E1
POLK AVE BTT 143-B2
POLK AVE DRS 28-D2
POLK AVE HOP 119-C2
POLK AVE RVT 167-C4,181-C3
POLK AVE WCT 129-B1,143-B1
POLK AVE WTT 115-B3
POLK AVE S DRS 28-D2
POLK CIR NE CH 92-E1
POLK PL NE CH 92-E1
POLK RD FAT 55-D3,56-C3
POLK ST ANO 49-D4
POLK ST BL 18-A4
POLK ST NE ATT 8-E1
POLK ST NE BLA 50-E4,64-E3
POLK ST NE CH 92-E2,93-A2
POLK ST NE EB 8-E3,22-E3
POLK ST NE FRI 78-E4
POLK ST NE HL 36-E3
POLK ST NE MPL 92-E3,106-E1
POLK ST NE SLK 78-E1
POLK ST NW ER 20-A3,34-A2
POLK ST S SHK 146-A3
POLO CLUB RD IND 102-D1
POMANDER WALK GV 105-E2
POMEROY ST E RF 140-E1
POMEROY ST W RF 140-E1
POMPANO DR MTK 119-B3
POMROY AVE N NST 41-B4
POND AVE MPW 123-B1
POND CIR EPR 132-C1
POND CIR E MH 136-B1
POND CIR W MH 136-B1
POND CRV WCT 129-C3
POND CT MPW 123-B1
POND CT SVW 80-B2
POND DR SVW 80-B2
POND LN WCT 129-C3
POND RD W EAG 135-D4,149-D1
POND TRL PRL 161-A2
POND TRL S CHM 63-C3
POND VIEW CIR BL 17-E3
POND VIEW CT MH 136-B1
POND VIEW CT VH 80-D4
POND VIEW CT WBT 80-D4
POND VIEW DR BL 17-E3
POND VIEW DR MH 136-B1
POND VIEW DR SWD 117-C4
POND VIEW DR WBT 80-D4
POND VIEW LN BLT 17-E2
POND VIEW LN SWR 96-D2
POND VIEW LN WBT 80-D4
POND VIEW PT EAG 135-D4
POND VIEW RD NW SM 46-E3
POND VIEW TER MH 136-A1
POND WYNDE N EAG 149-D1
POND WYNDE S EAG 149-D1
PONDEROSA CIR EAG 149-D2
PONDEROSA DR CHN 132-A1
PONDHAVEN CIR MH 136-A1
PONDHAVEN LN MH 136-A1
PONDRIDGE CIR WAY 104-C2
PONDS DR N BC 77-E3
PONDS WAY SHK 146-C4
PONDVIEW CIR LL 66-C3
PONDVIEW CIR MTK 104-D3
PONDVIEW CIR N CHM 63-B2
PONDVIEW CT NSP 95-A4
PONDVIEW CT SHK 146-B3
PONDVIEW CT N CHM 63-B2
PONDVIEW DR EAG 149-B3
PONDVIEW DR LOR 89-B2
PONDVIEW DR SVW 79-D1
PONDVIEW LN CHS 145-C1
PONDVIEW TER MTK 104-D3
PONDVIEW TRL PRL 161-B4
PONDVIEW TRL SLT 161-A4
PONDWOOD DR EDI 133-D2
PONTIAC CIR CHN 132-A1
PONTIAC CT CHN 132-A1
PONTIAC LN CHN 132-A1
PONTIAC PL MH 136-A1
PONY CT LL 65-E1
PONY LN E APV 149-A4
PONY LN W APV 149-A4
PONY RD BKT 199-D1
PONY RD BPT 185-E4,199-D1
POOL ST RFD 74-B4
POPLAR AVE MP 103-A1
POPLAR AVE NSP 95-B3
POPLAR CIR EPR 132-B2
POPLAR DR GV 106-A2
POPLAR DR SVW 80-A2
POPLAR DR WBY 123-C1
POPLAR DR NE EB 37-D2
POPLAR LN NO 80-C3
POPLAR LN SW SM 46-E4
POPLAR ST BEL 186-A2
POPLAR ST BUF 59-A2
POPLAR ST SSP 137-A1
POPLAR ST E SSP 136-E1,137-A1
POPLAR ST E SWR 83-A4
POPLAR ST S NFD 219-D4
POPLAR ST W SSP 136-E1
POPLAR ST W SWR 82-E4,83-A4
POPLAR BRIDGE CIR BLO 134-A3
POPLAR BRIDGE CRV BLO 134-A3
POPLAR BRIDGE RD BLO .133-E3,134-A3
POPLAR LAKE LN OST 14-E4
POPLAR RIDGE DR NYA 142-C3
POPPITZ LN LTT 144-D1
POPPLER LN EAG 135-D3
POPPY CT NFD 219-E4
POPPY DR CHN 131-E2
POPPY LN EDI 133-E2
POPPY ST NW AND 35-E3,49-E3
POPPY ST NW CR 49-E4,63-E1
POPPY ST NW OG 21-E3
POPPY ST NW SF 7-E4,21-E1
POPPYSEED CT NB 79-B3
POPPYSEED DR NB 79-B3
PORCUPINE CT EPR 133-A3
PORT OF MINNEAPOLIS DR MPL 92-C3
PORTAL DR EPR 133-A4
PORTER AVE ANO 49-B4
PORTER AVE MTK 118-C3
PORTER CIR CHM 63-D2
PORTER CIR CW 1-B3
PORTER DR CHM 63-E2
PORTER LN APV 163-A2
PORTER LN EDI 119-E4
PORTER ST CW 1-B3
PORTLAND AVE BUR 148-D3,162-D2
PORTLAND AVE MPL 106-D3,120-D3
PORTLAND AVE RCH 120-D4,134-D1
PORTLAND AVE SPP 137-B3
PORTLAND AVE STP 121-D1,122-A1
PORTLAND AVE WBL 95-B1
PORTLAND AVE WBT 81-B2
PORTLAND AVE S BLO 134-D3,148-D1
PORTLAND AVE S BUR 162-D2
PORTLAND AVE S MPL 120-D3
PORTLAND CIR BUR 148-D3
PORTLAND CT BUR 148-D3
PORTLAND DR E BUR 148-D3
PORTLAND MEWS BUR 162-D1
PORTLAND PL BLO 134-D4
PORTLAND PL BUR 162-D1
PORTLAND AVENUE CT BUR 162-D1
PORTWOOD WAY RVT 181-C2
POST AVE BTT 143-B2
POST LN EDI 119-C4
POST RD FS 135-B1
POST RD LL 66-A2
POST RD MTK 104-D3
POST RD NW BT 7-B4,21-B1
POST OAK RD OKD 95-D4
POTASSIUM CT NW RAM 35-B3
POTASSIUM ST NW RAM 35-B3,49-B2
POTAWATOMI
ST NW AND 35-C4,49-C1
POTAWATOMI ST NW OG 21-C2
POTOMAC ST NE COT 38-C3,52-C1
POTOMAC ST NE LWT 10-C3
POTOMAC ST NE OXT 10-B1
POTOMAC TRL N BP 78-B3
POWDER RIDGE CT RW 210-E1
POWDERHORN CIR MTK 118-C2
POWDERHORN DR MTK 118-C2
POWDERHORN TER MPL 106-E4
POWELL CIR E BL 18-A3
POWELL CIR N BL 18-A3
POWELL CIR W BL 18-A3
POWELL RD HOP 119-D2
POWELL RD SLP 119-D2
POWELL ST N BL 18-A3
POWELL ST S BL 18-A4
POWER ST MPL 106-D2
POWERS AVE STP 109-A4
POWERS BLVD CHN 118-A4,132-A2
POWERS PL CHN 132-A3
POWERS LAKE CIR WBY 124-B2
POWERS LAKE PT WBY 124-B2
POWERS LAKE TRL WBY 124-B2
PRAIRIE CIR NFD 219-E4
PRAIRIE CIR E EAG 150-B1
PRAIRIE CIR W EAG 150-B1
PRAIRIE CRV OTS 33-E4
PRAIRIE CT BEC 2-E3
PRAIRIE CT SHK 146-C3
PRAIRIE DR CV 66-D2
PRAIRIE DR MED 89-E2
PRAIRIE DR N NOH 111-D1
PRAIRIE LN EPR 132-C1
PRAIRIE LN HAN 60-E3
PRAIRIE LN HUT 112-A1
PRAIRIE LN SHK 146-C3
PRAIRIE RD BEC 2-E3
PRAIRIE RD CFT 208-E3
PRAIRIE RD MO 31-B1
PRAIRIE RD WBL 95-B1
PRAIRIE RD NW AND 50-C2
PRAIRIE ST CHS 145-D2
PRAIRIE ST CW 1-B2
PRAIRIE ST HAS 166-C1
PRAIRIE ST NFD 219-E4
PRAIRIE ST E BEL 185-E1,186-A1
PRAIRIE ST N SHK 146-B2
PRAIRIE ST S NFD 219-E4
PRAIRIE ST S SHK 146-B2
PRAIRIE ST W BEL 185-E1
PRAIRIE TRL ANN 74-A2
PRAIRIE TRL RFD 74-A2
PRAIRIE CENTER DR EPR 133-A2
PRAIRIE CREEK DR DEL 87-D3
PRAIRIE CREEK DR OTS 33-E4
PRAIRIE CREEK LN MO 31-C1
PRAIRIE FLOWER BLVD CHN 131-D2
PRAIRIE FLOWER RD LL 66-A4
PRAIRIE LAKES DR EPR 133-B2
PRAIRIE LAND AVE MP 102-E1
PRAIRIE OAK DR BEL 185-E2
PRAIRIE OAK TRL WBY 123-E2
PRAIRIE PINE WAY WEL 182-B3
PRAIRIE RIDGE DR SVW 79-C1
PRAIRIE RIDGE RD EAG 150-B1
PRAIRIE ROSE CT CLT 188-D4,202-D1
PRAIRIE VIEW DR EPR 132-E1
PRAIRIE VIEW LN BUF 45-B4
PRAIRIE VIEW PL LL 66-A1
PRAIRIE VIEW TRL ET 178-A4
PRAIRIEGRASS DR PRL 160-D2
PRAIRIEVIEW LN N CHM 63-C3
PRAIRIEVIEW TRL N CHM 63-C3
PRARIE RIDGE DR SVW 79-C1
PRARIE VIEW TRL ET 178-A4
PRATT ST MPL 120-C3
PRATT ST MSC 55-B4
PREAKNESS LN CHN 132-A1
PREBLE ST STP 108-C3
PREMIER DR LOL 103-D2
PRESCOTT CIR EDI 119-C2
PRESCOTT CT BUR 148-E1
PRESCOTT DR EPR 132-D3
PRESCOTT DR MTK 118-E3
PRESCOTT ST STP 122-C2
PRESERVE ALC SAV 147-C4
PRESERVE ALC WBY 110-A4,124-A1
PRESERVE BLVD EPR 133-B3
PRESERVE BLVD W BUR .148-A4,162-A1
PRESERVE CIR SAV 147-C4
PRESERVE CT SHK 147-C4
PRESERVE LN N CHM 63-B3
PRESERVE PATH WSP 122-B4
PRESERVE PL SAV 147-C4
PRESERVE PL WBT 94-E1
PRESERVE TRL NO 80-B2
PRESERVE TRL SAV 147-C4
PRESERVE TRL SHK 147-C4
PRESERVE TRL WBY 110-A4,124-A1
PRESIDENT DR NE BLA 64-D2
PRESIDENTIAL CIR W SHK 146-A3
PRESIDENTIAL LN SHK 146-A3
PRESIDENTIAL LN W SHK 146-A3
PRESTIGE LN MTK 119-A1
PRESTON LN HOP 119-D2
PRESTON LN SHK 147-B3
PRESTON RD MTK 104-E4,105-A4
PRESTWICK CIR BP 77-E1
PRESTWICK CT BP 77-E1
PRESTWICK LN BP 77-E2,78-A1
PRESTWICK PKWY BP 77-E2,78-A2
PRESTWICK PL MHT 95-C2
PRESTWICK TER BP 77-E1,78-A1
PRESTWICK TER MHT 95-C2
PRIBBLE ST N CHM 63-D2

PRICE AVE MPW 108-E1,109-A1
PRIEST LN MOU 116-D2
PRIESTER LN HUT 97-E4,111-E1
PRIMROSE AVE N SWT 83-B3
PRIMROSE CRV RVL 93-D3
PRIMROSE CT NFD 220-A4
PRIMROSE CT VH 94-B1
PRIMROSE CT N BP 64-A4
PRIMROSE LN EPR 133-A3
PRIMROSE LN SHK 146-B3
PRIMROSE LN WAC 129-D3
PRIMROSE LN N FRT 41-B1
PRIMROSE PATH VH 94-B1
PRIMROSE PL CHN 131-E2
PRIMROSE PL ROG 47-E4
PRIMROSE AVENUE CT N SWT 83-B3
PRINCE PL MTK 118-E2
PRINCE ST STP 108-C4
PRINCETON AVE EPR 133-A3
PRINCETON AVE SAV 148-A3,162-A1
PRINCETON AVE STP 121-C1
PRINCETON AVE S GV 106-A3
PRINCETON AVE S SLP 106-A4,120-A1
PRINCETON BAY WBY 123-E2
PRINCETON CIR EAG 149-E1
PRINCETON CIR SAV 148-A4,162-A1
PRINCETON CT SAV 162-A1
PRINCETON CT SLP 106-A4
PRINCETON CT WBY 124-A2
PRINCETON LN CRT 162-A4,176-A1
PRINCETON RD WBY 123-E2,124-A2
PRINCETON TRL EAG 149-E1
PRINGLE CT HAS 166-B2
PRINTICE LN MPL 106-C1
PRIOR AVE AH 79-C3
PRIOR AVE N AH 79-C4,93-C2
PRIOR AVE N FH 107-C1
PRIOR AVE N RVL 93-C4,107-C1
PRIOR AVE N STP 107-C4,121-C1
PRIOR AVE S STP 121-C1
PRIOR CIR RVL 93-C3
PRIOR CIR SE PRL 161-C2
PRIOR CT AH 79-C4
PRIORWOOD LN SW PRL 161-A4
PRIORWOOD ST PRL 161-A3
PRIORY AVE MTK 118-B2
PRIORY LN MTK 118-C2
PRISCILLA ST STP 107-C2
PRISTINE PINE TRL BLO 133-C2
PRISTINE PINE TRL EPR 132-C2
PROCTOR AVE NW ER 19-D4,33-D1
PROCTOR RD NW ER 19-D3,33-D1
PROEHLS TRL HUD 111-D2
PROFESSIONAL DR NFD 219-D4
PROGRAM AVE MV 79-C3
PROGRESS DR HAS 166-D2
PROGRESS RD CV 66-D2
PROGRESS ST N NYA 142-C4
PROMENADE AVE EAG 135-E3
PROMENADE DR EAG 135-E3
PROMENADE LN WBY 123-E2
PROMENADE PL EAG 135-D3
PROMISE AVE SHK 146-C4
PROMONTORY DR EPR 119-A4
PROMONTORY PL EAG 136-A4
PROMONTORY PL MPW 123-B2
PROSPECT AVE MPL 120-C3
PROSPECT AVE ORO 103-D4
PROSPECT AVE OSC 28-B4
PROSPECT AVE WBT 80-E2
PROSPECT BLVD STP 122-C1
PROSPECT CT NFD 219-E4
PROSPECT CT OSC 28-B4
PROSPECT DR NFD 219-E4
PROSPECT PL MTK 104-C4,118-C1
PROSPECT TER MPL 107-B3
PROSPECT WAY OSC 28-B4
PROSPERITY AVE BEC 2-E4
PROSPERITY AVE MPW 94-E4,108-E1
PROSPERITY AVE STP 108-E2
PROVIDENCE CRV IND 88-E3
PROVIDENCE CT CHS 145-C2
PROVIDENCE CT IND 88-E3
PROVIDENCE LN EPR 133-B2
PROVIDENCE LN SAV 162-A1
PROVIDENCE PATH IND 88-E3
PROVIDENCE PL IND 88-E3
PROVIDENCE RD WBY 124-A4
PRYOR AVE N NST 55-B1
PTARMIGAN DR EKO 204-B1
PUEBLO AVE SCT 159-E4,173-E1
PUEBLO BLVD SCT 159-D4
PUEBLO DR MH 136-A1
PUEBLO LN MH 136-A1
PULASKI CIR BUF 59-A1
PULASKI RD BUF 45-B4,59-A1
PULASKI RD NE BUF 45-B4
PULLMAN AVE SPP 137-B3
PUMA LN MHT 95-D2
PUMA ST NW RAM 34-D3,48-D1
PUMICE CT EAG 149-B1
PUMICE LN EAG 149-B1
PUMICE PT EAG 149-B1
PURCELL PL MTK 119-A1
PURDEY RD EPR 147-B1
PURDUE ST NE LWT 10-D3
PURGATORY RD EPR 133-B4
PUT RD PLY 90-C2
PUTNAM AVE BL 18-A4
PUTNAM BLVD S AFT 125-B2
PUTNAM PATH RVT 181-C3
PUTTING AVE RVT 181-C3
PUTTING CT RVT 181-D4
PUTTNAM AVE RVT 181-C3

Q

QUAAS AVE WCT 129-A3,143-A1
QUAAS AVE WTT 115-A2
QUAAS CUTOFF RD IND 102-D1
QUADAY AVE NE OTS 33-E4,47-E1
QUADRANT AVE N NST 41-B4,55-B1
QUADRANT AVE S AFT 139-B1
QUADRANT AVE S DET 139-B3
QUAGGA ST NW STT 6-C1
QUAIL AVE N BC 77-E4,91-E1
QUAIL AVE N BP 77-E3
QUAIL AVE N CRY 91-E2
QUAIL AVE N GV 91-E4,105-E1
QUAIL AVE N ROB 91-E3
QUAIL AVE N SWT 83-B1
QUAIL CIR EPR 132-B1
QUAIL CIR ROG 47-E4
QUAIL CIR E BC 77-E3
QUAIL CIR W BC 77-E3
QUAIL CT SHK 146-C4
QUAIL CT WAT 101-B4
QUAIL XING CHN 118-B4
QUAIL DR SHK 146-C4
QUAIL LN NO 80-B3
QUAIL PKWY WAT 101-B4
QUAIL RD DWD 81-D3
QUAIL RD MHT 81-D3
QUAIL RD MOU 117-A1
QUAIL RUN WAC 129-D3
QUAIL ST MHT 81-D4
QUAIL WAY N MAY 69-C4
QUAIL CREEK DR NE BLA 51-A3
QUAIL CREEK PKWY NE BLA 51-A4
QUAIL HILL RD N MG 76-D2
QUAIL RIDGE CIR MH 136-A1
QUAIL RIDGE CIR WBY 123-E2
QUAIL RIDGE RD EAG 136-A4,150-A1
QUAIL RIDGE RD WBY 123-E2
QUAKER AVE JOR 173-B2
QUAKER AVE SCT 173-A1
QUAKER CT MG 63-B3
QUAKER LN MV 79-C2
QUAKER LN N CHM 63-B3
QUAKER LN N MG 63-B4,77-B1
QUAKER LN N PLY 91-B3,105-B2
QUAKER RD JOR 173-A2
QUAKER TRL PRL 161-A2
QUALE AVE NE OTS 47-E2
QUALE AVE NE SM 47-E2
QUALITY AVE N LLD 111-B3
QUALITY AVE S LLD 111-B4
QUALITY CT S LLD 111-B4
QUALITY LN N LLD 111-B3
QUALITY TRL N NST 55-B1
QUAM AVE NE OTS 47-E2
QUAM AVE NE SM 47-E2
QUAM CIR NE SM 47-E2
QUAMBA ST NE HL 37-B4,51-B2
QUAMME AVE RVT 181-D3
QUAMOCLIT ST VIC 130-E2
QUAMWELL AVE N LLD 111-B4
QUAMWELL AVE S LLD 111-B4
QUANDAM LN N SHT 13-B4
QUANT AVE N BYT 111-B1
QUANT AVE N LLD 111-B4
QUANT AVE N MSC 55-B3
QUANT AVE N NST 55-B2
QUANT AVE N WLT 111-B2
QUANT AVE S AFT 125-B2
QUANT AVE S DET 139-C4
QUANT AVE S LLD 125-C1
QUANT AVE S LSC 125-B1
QUANT CT S LLD 111-B4
QUANT AVENUE CT N LLD 111-B4
QUANTICO CT N MG 76-D3
QUANTICO LN N MG 76-D3,90-D1
QUANTICO LN N PLY 90-D2,104-D2
QUAPAW ST NW AND 35-C4
QUAPAW ST NW OG 21-C3
QUARLES RD BC 78-A4
QUARLES RD N MG 76-D2
QUARRY AVE ANO 49-C3
QUARRY AVE WTT 101-A3
QUARRY AVE N SWT 83-B2
QUARRY AVE S LSC 125-B2
QUARRY CT EAG 135-D3
QUARRY CT FRT 27-B2
QUARRY DR FRT 27-B2
QUARRY LN EAG 135-D3
QUARRY LN FRT 27-B2
QUARRY LN SHK 145-E3,146-A3
QUARRY LN SWR 97-A2
QUARRY RD KKT 126-E4,140-E1
QUARRY RD RF 140-E1
QUARRY RD E RF 140-E1
QUARRY RD N RF 140-E1
QUARRY ST W RF 140-E1
QUARRY TRL BLO 185-C2
QUARRY RIDGE LN WBY 123-E2
QUARTER HORSE CT LL 65-E1
QUARTZ AVE WCT 115-A4,129-A1
QUARTZ AVE S LSC 125-C2
QUARTZ LN EAG 149-B2
QUARTZ ST NW RAM 34-E4
QUASAR AVE S LSC 125-C2
QUASAR CT S LSC 125-C1
QUATTRO DR CHN 132-B2
QUAY ST NW AND 35-E2,49-E3
QUAY ST NW CR 49-E3,63-E1
QUAY ST NW OG 21-E2
QUAY ST NW SF 7-E4
QUE AVE N FRT 27-B3
QUEBEC AVE SAV 147-D4,161-D1
QUEBEC AVE N BP 63-D3,77-D4
QUEBEC AVE N CHM 63-D3
QUEBEC AVE N CRY 91-D1
QUEBEC AVE N GV 105-D1
QUEBEC AVE N NH 91-D3
QUEBEC AVE S BLO 133-D4,147-D1
QUEBEC AVE S GV 105-D3
QUEBEC AVE S LSC 125-C2
QUEBEC AVE S SLP 105-D4,119-D1
QUEBEC AVE S SMP 125-C2
QUEBEC CIR BLO 147-D2
QUEBEC CIR EPR 132-D1
QUEBEC CIR N CHM 63-D2
QUEBEC CT N BP 77-D2
QUEBEC DR SLP 105-D3
QUEBEC LN N CHM 63-D3
QUEBEC RD BLO 147-D1
QUEBEC ST CV 66-D2
QUEBEC WAY N CHM 63-D3
QUEEN AVE N BC 92-B2
QUEEN AVE N BP 78-B2
QUEEN AVE N MPL 92-B3,106-B2
QUEEN AVE NE OTS 47-E2
QUEEN AVE S BLO 134-B3,148-B1
QUEEN AVE S MPL 106-B3,120-B2
QUEEN AVE S RCH 120-B4,134-B1
QUEEN CIR BLO 134-B4,148-B2
QUEEN CIR NW ER 33-B1
QUEEN CT N BP 78-B2
QUEEN RD BLO 134-B4
QUEEN ST GRF 74-E4
QUEEN ST NW ER 19-B4,33-B1
QUEENAN AVE N LLD 111-C3
QUEENAN AVE S LLD 111-C4
QUEENS AVE NE OTS 47-E2
QUEENS AVE S LSC 125-C2
QUEENS CIR GRW 118-A3
QUEENS DR WBY 123-D2
QUEENS GATE NB 93-C1
QUEENS GDN N BP 77-E1
QUEENS GDNS N BP 77-E2
QUEENS LN ANO 63-D1
QUEENS TER HSN 48-B4
QUEENS TRL EPR 132-E3
QUEENS WAY MTK 118-E2
QUEENS WAY N MAY 69-C4
QUEENSBERRY ST NE COT 38-D2
QUEENSLAND CT PLY 104-C2
QUEENSLAND LN MG 76-C1
QUEENSLAND LN N MG 76-C2
QUEENSLAND LN N PLY 90-C4,104-C2
QUEENSPORT RD WBY 124-A2
QUEHL AVE N LLD 111-C4
QUEHL AVE S LLD 111-C4
QUEHL AVENUE CT N LLD 111-C4
QUELLO AVE S LSC 125-C2
QUELLO AVE S SMP 125-C2
QUEMAY CT NE ATT 9-C2
QUEMOY CT NE BLA 65-C4
QUEMOY ST NE BLA 65-C4
QUEMOY ST NE HL 51-C2
QUENROE AVE NE OTS 48-A2
QUENTIN AVE RVT 181-D3
QUENTIN AVE SAV 148-A3,162-A1
QUENTIN AVE N LLD 111-C4
QUENTIN AVE N NST 41-C2
QUENTIN AVE S GV 105-E3,106-A3
QUENTIN AVE S LLD 125-C1
QUENTIN AVE S LSC 125-C2
QUENTIN AVE S SAV 162-A2
QUENTIN AVE S SLP 105-E4,119-E1
QUENTIN AVE S SMP 125-C2
QUENTIN CIR SAV 162-A2
QUENTIN CT SAV 147-E4
QUENTIN CT SLP 105-E4
QUENTIN TRL N FRT 27-B2
QUICKSILVER ST NW RAM 35-B3,49-B2
QUIE LN NFD 219-D2
QUIET WAY VAT 223-D1
QUIET VALLEY RD FRT 27-B4,41-B1
QUIGLEY RD MTK 118-E2
QUILLEY AVE NE OTS 48-A2
QUINALT ST NE COT 52-C1
QUINCE ST NW AND 50-C2
QUINCE ST NW CR 50-C4,64-C3
QUINCY BLVD NE BLA 64-E2
QUINCY CIR SHK 146-A3
QUINCY CIR NW ER 20-A3
QUINCY CT ER 34-A2
QUINCY ST MV 79-B2
QUINCY ST PRL 161-A3
QUINCY ST NE BLA 50-E3,64-E2
QUINCY ST NE CH 92-E2
QUINCY ST NE EB 22-D1
QUINCY ST NE FRI 78-E3
QUINCY ST NE HL 36-E3,50-E3
QUINCY ST NE MPL 92-E4,106-E1
QUINCY ST NE SLK 78-E2
QUINCY ST NW ER 20-A3
QUINCY ST S SHK 146-A3
QUINCY WAY HIL 92-E2
QUINCY WAY WBY 123-D3
QUINLAN AVE N CGT 13-B2
QUINLAN AVE N FRT 27-B2,41-B1
QUINLAN AVE N LLD 111-C3
QUINLAN AVE N LS 111-C4
QUINLAN AVE N SWT 83-C2
QUINLAN AVE S LLD 111-C4,125-C1
QUINLAN AVE S LS 111-C4
QUINLAN AVE S LSC 125-C2
QUINLAN LN N FRT 13-C4
QUINLAN AVENUE CIR S LSC 125-C1
QUINLAN AVENUE CT S LSC 125-C1
QUINMORE AVE N LLD 111-C3
QUINMORE AVE S LLD 125-C1
QUINN AVE BLO 133-E2,134-A2
QUINN AVE NW ER 33-D1
QUINN AVE S BLO 133-E3,148-A2
QUINN CIR BLO 133-E2,134-A2
QUINN CIR ER 19-D4
QUINN DR NW AND 50-A2
QUINN RD BLO 133-E3
QUINN RD CHN 132-A3
QUINN ST NW AND 36-A4,50-A3
QUINN ST NW CR 50-A4,64-A3
QUINN ST NW ER 19-D1
QUINN ST NW OG 22-A2
QUINNELL AVE N LLD 111-C3
QUINNELL AVE N LS 111-C4
QUINNELL AVE N NST 55-C1
QUINNWOOD LN N DAY 49-A3
QUINT AVE N NST 55-C2
QUINTON AVE N SHT 13-B1
QUINWOOD LN N DAY 49-A3
QUINWOOD LN N MG 77-A1,91-A1
QUINWOOD LN N PLY 91-A1,105-A1
QUIRAM AVE HSN 47-E3
QUIRNIA AVE STP 121-C3
QUIRT AVE N SWT 83-B2
QUITO ST NE BLA 65-E2
QUIVER DR CHN 118-A4
QUIXOTE AVE N LLD 111-C3
QUIXOTE AVE N LS 111-C4

R

RABBIT ST NW BT 34-C2
RABBIT ST NW RAM 34-C3
RABUN DR EDI 133-E1
RACCOON RD NO 80-B3
RACE ST STP 121-E2
RACHEL CT CHS 131-D4
RACHEL RIDGE CT IND 88-D1
RACINE AVE N MAY 69-C2
RACINE AVE S LSC 125-C2
RACINE DR E LC 94-C3
RACINE ST PRL 161-A3
RADATZ AVE MPW 95-A3
RADFORD CT HAS 166-E3
RADFORD RD HAS 166-E3
RADFORD ST MTK 118-B3
RADIO DR WBY 109-E4,123-E2
RADIO RD TRT 126-C4
RADISSON CT BUR 148-E2
RADISSON DR BUR 148-E2,149-A2
RADISSON RD GV 105-E3
RADISSON RD NE BLA 51-A4,65-B2
RADISSON RD NE HL 51-A2
RADISSON ENTRANCE SWD 118-A3
RADISSON INN RD SWD 118-A3
RADISSON WOODS DR BLA 65-B2
RADIUM CIR NW RAM 35-B4
RADIUM ST NW RAM 35-B4,49-B3
RADNOR RD MOU 117-B2
RAE CIR WBY 124-A3
RAE CT MH 121-E3
RAE CT WBY 124-A3
RAE DR RCH 120-C4
RAE LN WBY 124-A3
RAE PL N STP 107-C2
RAHN RD EAG 149-B1
RAHN WAY EAG 149-B2
RAHNCLIFF CT EAG 149-B2
RAHNCLIFF RD EAG 149-B2
RAIDER DR NFD 219-D4
RAIL DR SJT 84-A4
RAILROAD AVE CHC 26-B1
RAILROAD AVE DEL 87-D2
RAILROAD AVE GRW 117-E3
RAILROAD AVE HWL 85-A1
RAILROAD AVE ORO 103-D4
RAILROAD AVE N ROB 91-E3,92-A3
RAILROAD BLVD HOP 119-B2
RAILROAD BLVD WYO 25-B3
RAILROAD DR JOR 173-A2
RAILROAD DR NW ER 33-E2
RAILROAD ST HBG 156-A2
RAILROAD ST LES 212-C4
RAILROAD ST E NYA 142-C4
RAILROAD ST N LES 212-C3
RAILROAD ST W NYA 142-B4
RAILROAD ST W YAT 142-B4
RAILWAY ST LOR 89-B2
RAILWAY ST E LOR 89-B2
RAILWAY ST NW LON 217-B2
RAILWAY ST SW LON 217-A2
RAILWAY ST W LOR 89-B2
RAIN AVE WTT .... -E4,114-E1
RAINBOW AVE CGT 13-C3
RAINBOW AVE MP 102-E1
RAINBOW AVE NB 79-B3
RAINBOW CT SWR 96-E2
RAINBOW DR EPR 118-D4,132-D1
RAINBOW DR MTK 118-C1
RAINBOW DR NE FRI 78-D4
RAINBOW LN MV 79-B3
RAINBOW LN NB 79-B3
RAINBOW PKWY PRL 161-C4
RAINDROP DR EAG 135-C3
RAINER AVE ANO 49-C3
RAINEY RD ORO 103-D3
RAINIER ALC WBY 123-E2
RAINIER BAY WBY 123-E2
RAINIER CIR BUR 149-A4
RAINIER CT BUR 149-A4
RAINIER CT WBY 123-E2
RAINIER DR WBY 123-E2
RAINIER LN N MG 76-C2
RAINIER PASS NE CH 93-A1
RAINIER PASS NE FRI 93-A1
RALEIGH AVE SAV 161-E2
RALEIGH AVE S SLP 105-E4,119-E2
RALEIGH CT BUR 148-E2
RALEIGH CT WBY 124-B4
RALEIGH DR BUR 148-E2
RALEIGH LN EPR 132-C3
RALEIGH LN NE SLK 78-E2
RALEIGH RD SPT 70-D4,84-D1
RALEIGH RD WBY 104-B3
RALEIGH ST STP 107-C2
RALEIGH DRIVE CT BUR 148-E2
RALPH ST WBL 95-B1
RAMADA AVE S LSC 125-C2
RAMADA AVE S SMP 125-C2
RAMBLER CT RVL 94-A3
RAMBLER LN MOU 116-D1
RAMBLER RD RVL 93-D3
RAMBLING CREEK CIR SE SM 46-E4
RAMBLING CREEK DR SE SM 46-E4
RAMBUSH RD BUR 162-B2
RAMEY RD ML 43-D3
RAMLOW PL STP 121-C3
RAMP EAG 136-A2
RAMP E HUT 111-C1
RAMP W HUD 111-C1
RAMPART CT SWD 117-D4
RAMSDELL DR APV 162-E2
RAMSEY AVE CAR 159-A1
RAMSEY AVE PRL 161-A4
RAMSEY BAY CAR 159-A1
RAMSEY BLVD NW RAM 35-A4,48-E2
RAMSEY CIR MPL 106-D1
RAMSEY CT CAR 159-B1
RAMSEY CT CHS 145-B1
RAMSEY RD DPH 118-B2
RAMSEY RD WAY 104-B3
RAMSEY ST BEC 2-E4
RAMSEY ST HAS 166-D2
RAMSEY ST MO 31-D2
RAMSEY ST SHK 146-C2
RAMSEY ST STP 122-A1
RAMSEY ST NE MPL 106-D1
RAMSEY ST S SHK 146-C3
RAMSEY ST W SWR 96-E1,97-A1
RANCH RD PS 95-D2
RANCH RD WBY 123-E4
RANCH RD NW BLT 19-A2
RANCH RD NW ER 19-C2
RANCH TRL N SHT 13-C2
RANCHERS RD FRI 78-D2
RANCHERS RD NE FRI 78-D2
RANCHVIEW CT MTK 104-D2
RANCHVIEW LN N MG 62-D4,76-D1
RANCHVIEW LN N PLY 90-D4,104-D2
RANCHVIEW LN S MTK 104-D2
RANDALL AVE SLP 120-A1
RANDALL AVE W FH 107-C2
RANDALL DR ANO 49-D3
RANDALL LN MTK 118-D3
RANDOLPH AVE STP 121-E2,122-A2
RANDOLPH BLVD RAN 207-B3
RANDOLPH BLVD RAT 207-B3
RANDOLPH ST NE MPL 92-D4
RANDOM RD EAG 136-A3
RANDY AVE SVW 93-E1,94-A1
RANDY AVE WBL 95-B1
RANIER CIR PLY 104-C1
RANIER CT N PLY 90-C3
RANIER LN EAG 135-D3
RANIER LN N MG 76-C1,90-C1
RANIER LN N PLY 90-C4,104-C1
RANKIN RD SA 93-B3
RANKIN ST STP 121-D3
RASPBERRY CT BUF 45-B4
RASPBERRY CT EAG 149-D1
RASPBERRY DR HSN 47-E3
RASPBERRY HL CHN 132-A4
RASPBERRY LN EAG 149-D1
RASPBERRY HILL RD EPR 119-B4
RASPBERRY RIDGE RD NE PRL 161-A2
RATH DR WBY 123-C1
RATTVIK CIR BUF 58-E1
RAVEN CIR PRL 161-B2
RAVEN CT EPR 132-D1
RAVEN RD BKT 185-C4,199-C1
RAVEN RD NO 80-A3
RAVEN ST HAT 201-C2
RAVEN ST E BEL 185-E2,186-A2
RAVEN ST NW AND 36-A4,50-A2
RAVEN ST NW CR 50-A4,64-A3
RAVEN ST NW OG 8-A4,22-A1
RAVEN ST NW SF 8-A3
RAVEN ST W BEL 185-E2
RAVENNA TRL HAS 166-E2,167-A2
RAVENNA TRL RVT 167-C3,181-D3

RAVENROCK CT RFD .74-B2
RAVENROCK RD RFD .74-B2
RAVENSWOOD CT SVW .79-D1
RAVENSWOOD ST SVW .79-D1
RAVENWOOD CIR WAC .129-D3
RAVENWOOD DR WAC .129-D4
RAVENWOOD RD N PLY .105-A2
RAVINE CIR N MAY .69-C4
RAVINE DR DRS .28-D1
RAVINE DR OST .14-E4,28-E1
RAVINE ST SSP .122-E3
RAVINE ST TF .14-C3
RAVINE TRL GV .106-A3
RAVOUX AVE BUR .149-A2
RAVOUX AVE STP .108-B4
RAVOUX CT BUR .149-A2
RAVOUX RD CHS .145-D2
RAWLIINGS AVE NE OTS .48-B2
RAWLINGS AVE NE OTS .48-B2
RAWLINS CIR N MPL .106-C2
RAWLINS DR NW ER .33-B2
RAWLINS ST NW ER .19-B3
RAYMAR CT BUR .148-B4
RAYMOND AVE MV .79-C2
RAYMOND AVE SLT .160-D4
RAYMOND AVE STP .107-C2
RAYMOND AVE N FH .107-C2
RAYMOND LN EPR .132-E2
RAYMOND PL W STP .107-B3
RAYMOND ST SOM .70-B4
READING RD EAG .150-A1
REANEY AVE STP .108-D3,109-A3
REARDON PL NSP .95-B3
REBECCA DR JOR .173-B2
REBECCA DR MPW .109-B2
REBECCA LN EAG .149-D3
REBECCA LN MTK .118-B3
REBECCA LAKE TRL RFD .74-B3
REBECCA PARK TRL GRF .74-A4,75-A3
REBECCA PARK TRL RFD .74-B3
RECO LN NE SLK .78-D1
RECORDS TRL RVT .181-D4
RED BARN RD NO .80-B3
RED BIRCH CT LL .66-B3
RED BRICK RD TRT .125-E1,126-A1
RED CEDAR CV CHN .131-B1
RED CEDAR LN MPL .120-B3
RED CEDAR PT CHN .131-C1
RED CEDAR RD EAG .135-C3
RED CEDAR TRL NE OTS .33-E4
RED CHERRY CIR MTK .118-B3
RED CHERRY LN MTK .118-B4
RED CIRCLE DR MTK .119-B4
RED CLOVER LN LL .65-E2
RED FOREST WAY NO .80-C2
RED FOX CIR CHN .131-D1
RED FOX CT EDI .119-D4
RED FOX DR MED .90-A3
RED FOX DR MG .91-A1
RED FOX DR NMT .189-E1
RED FOX LN EDI .119-D4
RED FOX RD AH .93-D1
RED FOX RD EAG .135-C4
RED FOX RD NO .80-B2
RED FOX RD ROG .47-E4,61-E1
RED FOX RD SVW .93-E1
RED FOX TRL SCF .14-D3
RED HAWK TRL LL .66-A4
RED MAPLE LN HUT .112-B2
RED MAPLE LN LL .66-B4
RED MAPLE LN NO .80-B1
RED OAK CIR CHS .131-D4
RED OAK CIR MOT .32-A3
RED OAK CIR N BUR .149-A2
RED OAK CIR S BUR .149-A3
RED OAK CT EAG .136-B3
RED OAK CT MV .79-A2
RED OAK CT N BUR .149-A3
RED OAK CT N CHM .63-B3
RED OAK CT S BUR .149-A3
RED OAK DR BL .17-E3
RED OAK DR EAG .136-B3
RED OAK DR EPR .132-D3
RED OAK DR HUT .112-E2
RED OAK DR MV .79-A1
RED OAK DR RFD .74-A4
RED OAK DR ROG .61-E2
RED OAK LN CHN .131-B1
RED OAK LN MOT .32-A3
RED OAK LN MTA .103-A3
RED OAK RD MOU .116-D1
RED OAK RD SJT .98-B2
RED OAK RDG MTK .118-E2
RED OAK CIRCLE CT N BUR .149-A2
RED OAKS DR VH .80-B4
RED OAKS RD PRL .161-B3
RED PINE BLVD WBT .81-B1
RED PINE CIR MPW .123-B2
RED PINE DR SOM .70-B4
RED PINE LN EAG .150-B3
RED PINE LN NO .80-A3
RED PINE RD NO .80-A3
RED PINE TRL SJT .97-C2
RED ROBIN LN EAG .135-C4
RED ROCK LN MO .31-D3
RED ROCK RD EPR .132-D2
RED ROCK RD STP .123-A3
RED SPLENDER CIR MPW .123-B2
RED WING BLVD HAS .166-D3
RED WING BLVD MT .166-E4,181-A1
RED WING BLVD RVT .181-C3
RED WING LN WBY .124-B2
REDDING AVE RW .210-E1
REDDING RIDGE DR MTK .118-D2
REDFIELD AVE N SHA .13-C4
REDFIELD CIR SHA .13-C4
REDMAN LN CHN .132-A1
REDWELL LN APV .163-A2
REDWELL LN WBY .124-A1
REDWING AVE HAT .188-A2,202-A1
REDWING AVE SCT .174-A4
REDWING AVE N FRT .13-C4,27-C3
REDWING AVE N SHA .13-C4
REDWING AVE N SHT .13-C2
REDWING AVE S LSC .125-C2
REDWING AVE S SMP .125-C2
REDWING CT CHN .132-A1
REDWING DR WAC .129-C4
REDWING LN CHN .132-A1
REDWING TRL HAT .188-A1
REDWING TRL SCT .174-A2
REDWOOD CIR APV .162-E2
REDWOOD CIR MTK .118-C2
REDWOOD CT APV .162-E2
REDWOOD CT NW SF .8-C4
REDWOOD DR APV .162-E2
REDWOOD DR HUD .111-D4
REDWOOD LN NB .93-A1
REDWOOD PT EAG .135-D4
REDWOOD ST CR .64-C2
REDWOOD ST N LP .113-B4
REDWOOD ST NW AND .36-C4,50-C3
REDWOOD ST NW CR .64-C3,78-C1
REDWOOD ST NW OG .22-C1
REDWOOD ST S LP .127-B1
REDWOOD ST S WAC .129-D3
REED AVE ANO .49-C4
REED PL WBT .80-E2
REED RD SB .116-B3
REED ST SOM .70-B4
REFLECTION RD APV .162-E1
REFORM ST N NYA .142-C4
REFORM ST N YAT .142-C3
REFORM ST S NYA .142-C4
REGAL AVE N SHA .13-C4
REGAL OAKS MTK .119-A1
REGATTA DR WBY .124-A2
REGATTA ALC CIR WBY .124-A2
REGATTA BAY CIR WBY .124-A2
REGENCY CT HAS .166-C3
REGENCY DR WBY .123-C1
REGENCY LN EPR .119-B4
REGENCY RD LES .212-D4
REGENCY TRL EPR .119-B4
REGENT AVE N BC .77-E4,91-E1
REGENT AVE N BP .63-E4,77-E3
REGENT AVE N CRY .91-E1
REGENT AVE N GV .91-E4,105-E1
REGENT AVE N ROB .91-E3
REGENT DR APV .163-A2
REGENT DR SHK .146-B3
REGENT DR WBL .95-A1
REGENT LN SHK .146-B3
REGENT PKWY BP .77-E1
REGENTS WALK SWD .118-A2
REGIONAL CENTER RD EPR .133-A2
REGIS DR NE FRI .78-E4,92-E1
REGIS LN NE FRI .78-E4,92-E1
REGIS TER NE FRI .78-E4
REGIS TRL NE FRI .78-E4,92-E1
REGULUS ST NE LWT .24-A2
REHBEINS ST LL .66-D1
REHNBERG PL WSP .122-D3
REICH RD MTK .118-B3
REID LN SSP .122-D4
REIDMOND AVE N LC .94-C4
REILAND LN SVW .79-E4,80-A4
REILING RD LL .66-E4
REIMER DR N MG .76-E3
REINDEER LN EAG .150-A2
REISLING BLVD NW CR .49-E4,63-D1
REITZ LAKE RD LTT .130-A3
RELANDER DR TRT .139-E1,140-A1
RENAISSANCE CT CHN .131-D2
RENAISSANCE CT HOP .119-B2
RENDOVA CT NE ATT .63-E1
RENDOVA ST NE BLA .65-C4,79-C1
RENDOVA ST NE EB .23-C2,37-C1
RENDOVA ST NE HL .51-C1
RENEE AVE RVT .181-D2
RENEE WAY RVT .181-D3
RENO ST WAY .104-C3
RENTON AVE HAT .201-C2
REPUBLIC AVE SLP .119-D1
RESDEN RD N PLY .105-A2
RESEARCH CENTER RD E NH .91-C2
RESEARCH CENTER RD W NH .91-C2
RESERVE ST STP .108-D4
RESERVOIR BLVD NE CH .92-E2,93-A2
REST POINT CIR ORO .103-A4
REST POINT LN ORO .103-A4
REST POINT RD ORO .103-A4
RESTHAVEN LN MOU .103-A4,117-A1
RESTWOOD RD BLA .65-C4
RESTWOOD RD LEX .65-D4
RETREAT CIR MTA .102-C4
RETURN CT STP .121-C3
REUNION RD SWR .96-C2
REUTER DR VET .179-D1
REVELWOOD PL N MG .76-D2
REVERE AVE CLT .189-B3
REVERE AVE SLT .175-B2
REVERE CIR N PLY .91-B4
REVERE CT EPR .132-D3
REVERE CT N CHM .49-B4
REVERE LN PLY .105-B2
REVERE LN N CHM .49-B4,63-B1
REVERE LN N MG .63-B4,77-B1
REVERE LN N PLY .91-B3,105-B2
REVERE WAY SLT .161-C4,175-C1
REVOIR ST CV .66-D2
RHINESTONE ST NW BT .20-E4,34-E1
RHINESTONE ST NW RAM .48-E1
RHODA AVE RVT .181-D3
RHODE ISLAND AVE SAV 147-D3,161-D1
RHODE ISLAND AVE N BP .63-D3,91-D1
RHODE ISLAND AVE N CHM .63-D3
RHODE ISLAND AVE N CRY .91-D1
RHODE ISLAND AVE N GV .91-D4,105-D1
RHODE ISLAND AVE N NH .91-D2
RHODE ISLAND AVE S BLO133-D2,147-D1
RHODE ISLAND AVE S GV .105-D3
RHODE ISLAND AVE S SLP .105-D4,119-D1
RHODE ISLAND CIR N CHM .63-D3
RHODE ISLAND CIR S BLO .133-D2,147-D1
RHODE ISLAND CT N CHM .63-D3
RHODE ISLAND DR N BP .77-D2
RHODE ISLAND RD BLO .133-D4,147-D1
RHODE ISLAND WAY CHM .63-D2
RHOY AVE LTT .131-A3
RHOY ST VIC .131-A2
RICE AVE ART .170-E3
RICE AVE BTT .156-E3
RICE AVE HCT .156-E4,170-E1
RICE CT CHN .132-B3
RICE CT LL .66-A4
RICE LN BWV .95-C1
RICE RD SLT .175-A1
RICE ST ANO .49-C4
RICE ST JOR .173-B2
RICE ST LC .94-B3
RICE ST MPW .94-B4,108-B1
RICE ST STP .108-B3
RICE ST SVW .80-B4,94-B1
RICE ST VH .94-B2
RICE ST E WAY .104-B3
RICE ST N JOR .173-B2
RICE ST S JOR .173-B2
RICE ST W SWR .96-E1,97-A1
RICE CREEK BLVD NE FRI .78-D3
RICE CREEK DR NE FRI .79-A4
RICE CREEK PKWY SVW .79-C1
RICE CREEK PKWY NE BLA .65-B4
RICE CREEK RD NB .79-A4
RICE CREEK RD NE FRI .78-E4,79-A4
RICE CREEK TER NB .79-A3
RICE CREEK TER NE FRI .78-D3
RICE CREEK TRL SVW .79-D1
RICE CREEK WAY NE FRI .78-D3
RICE CREEK TRAIL CT SVW .79-D1
RICE LAKE CIR MG .76-E2
RICE LAKE CT LL .66-A2
RICE LAKE DR LL .65-E2
RICE LAKE LN LL .66-A2
RICE LAKE RD MG .76-E2
RICE LAKE RD SMT .55-E4,69-D1
RICE LAKE RD N MG .76-E2
RICH AVE S BLO .133-E3,147-E1
RICH CIR BLO .147-E2,148-A1
RICH CRV BLO .133-E4
RICH RD BLO .133-E4,147-E1
RICH VALLEY BLVD IGH .150-C1
RICH VALLEY BLVD RMT .150-D4
RICHAL DR WBY .123-D2
RICHARD AVE WBL .95-A1
RICHARD CIR WSP .122-C4
RICHARD CT WBL .95-A1
RICHARD DR WBT .81-B2
RICHARD LN EAG .149-D3
RICHARD RD WBY .123-D3
RICHARDS CT EAG .149-D2
RICHARDS DR MTK .118-D2
RICHARDSON AVE DAY .48-B1
RICHARDSON AVE OTS .48-B2
RICHARDSON AVE N CHM .63-C1
RICHFIELD RD MPL .120-B1
RICHMOND ALC WBY .124-B3
RICHMOND AVE SVW .93-E2
RICHMOND BAY WBY .124-B3
RICHMOND CIR EDI .119-E3
RICHMOND CRV MPL .120-B3
RICHMOND CT SVW .93-E2
RICHMOND DR EDI .119-E3
RICHMOND LN EDI .119-E3
RICHMOND PKWY WBY .124-B3
RICHMOND RD MOU .117-A2
RICHMOND ST SSP .137-A1
RICHMOND ST STP .122-A1
RICHMOND ST E SSP .136-E1,137-A1
RICHMOND ST W SSP .136-E1
RICHWOOD DR EDI .119-E3
RICKARD RD NE FRI .78-D2
RICKY LN LVL .162-C4
RIDDER CIR STP .108-C4
RIDGE AVE ANO .49-D3
RIDGE AVE WTT .-E3
RIDGE CIR MED .90-B4
RIDGE CIR NMT .190-C1
RIDGE CIR SE SM .47-A4
RIDGE CT BLT .17-E2
RIDGE CT CHS .145-D1
RIDGE CT LVT .160-B2
RIDGE CT MTK .118-B2
RIDGE CT WBT .81-B2
RIDGE DR MED .89-E4
RIDGE DR ORT .4-A3
RIDGE DR SLP .105-E3
RIDGE DR WBY .109-C4
RIDGE DR WSP .122-C4
RIDGE DR N SAV .161-E2
RIDGE DR SE SM .47-A4
RIDGE DR SW LAT .201-D3
RIDGE LN CHS .145-D1
RIDGE LN HAS .166-C2
RIDGE LN MV .79-B3
RIDGE PASS HUT .111-E1
RIDGE PL EDI .119-E2
RIDGE PL MH .122-A4
RIDGE RD BLT .17-E2
RIDGE RD BUR .148-D4
RIDGE RD CHN .118-A4
RIDGE RD CP .65-E4
RIDGE RD EDI .119-C3
RIDGE RD EPR .132-E3
RIDGE RD FAT .41-D3,55-D2
RIDGE RD HEN .198-D4
RIDGE RD MTK .118-B2
RIDGE RD NO .80-B3
RIDGE RD OSC .27-E4,41-E1
RIDGE RD SWD .118-A4
RIDGE RD N MYR .114-E4
RIDGE RD NE EB .37-D2
RIDGE RUN SJT .84-D4
RIDGE ST SCT .173-A3
RIDGE ST STP .121-D2
RIDGE WAY MHT .95-C1
RIDGE BLUFF CT CHS .145-E1
RIDGE BLUFF DR CHS .145-E1
RIDGE CLIFF DR EAG .149-C2
RIDGE CREEK RD SVW .79-D1
RIDGE CREEK ROAD CT SVW .79-D1
RIDGE HAVEN CIR BUF .58-D2
RIDGE LANE DR SWR .83-A4
RIDGE PARK RD EDI .119-D3
RIDGE POINT BLVD CGT .26-B2
RIDGE POINT CIR SWD .117-D4
RIDGE POINT CT SAV .161-C1
RIDGE POINT DR CGT .26-B2
RIDGE POND CIR VIC .130-E3
RIDGE POND CT VIC .130-E3
RIDGE POND DR VIC .130-E3
RIDGE PONDS LN VIC .130-E3
RIDGE WAY DR WSP .122-C3
RIDGE WIND TRL EAG .149-B3
RIDGEBROOK DR CF .208-B4
RIDGECREST CIR EAG .149-B3
RIDGECREST DR CF .208-B4
RIDGEDALE AVE SW LAT .201-D3
RIDGEDALE DR MTK .104-E3,105-A3
RIDGEHAVEN LN MTK .105-A3
RIDGEHILL RD CHN .131-B1
RIDGEMONT AVE PRL .161-B3
RIDGEMOUNT AVE W PLY .104-E2,105-A2
RIDGEMOUNT LN PLY .104-C2
RIDGEPOINT DR CHC .26-B2
RIDGETOP DR CAR .145-B4
RIDGEVIEW CIR EDI .119-E4
RIDGEVIEW CIR MED .90-A2
RIDGEVIEW DR APV .162-E2
RIDGEVIEW DR EAG .149-D2
RIDGEVIEW DR EDI .119-E4,133-E1
RIDGEVIEW DR MTK .118-C1
RIDGEVIEW DR WAY .104-B2
RIDGEVIEW LN WAY .104-B2
RIDGEWATER DR MTK .105-B4
RIDGEWAY AVE WBT .81-B2
RIDGEWAY CT MHT .95-C1
RIDGEWAY DR FL .39-B3
RIDGEWAY DR MTK .118-E3
RIDGEWAY PKWY MPL .93-B4,107-A1
RIDGEWAY RD EDI .119-D4
RIDGEWAY RD GV .105-D2
RIDGEWAY RD MYR .114-E4
RIDGEWIND RD EPR .133-B3
RIDGEWOOD AVE IGH .137-A3
RIDGEWOOD AVE MPL .106-C3
RIDGEWOOD AVE VH .94-C2
RIDGEWOOD AVE WBT .80-E3,81-A3
RIDGEWOOD AVE N SHA .13-C4
RIDGEWOOD CIR ORO .103-C3
RIDGEWOOD CIR NW ER .19-D4
RIDGEWOOD CT AH .93-D2
RIDGEWOOD CT BUR .149-A2
RIDGEWOOD CT HAS .166-C2
RIDGEWOOD CT PRL .161-B4
RIDGEWOOD CT SAV .161-E2
RIDGEWOOD CT WAC .129-D3
RIDGEWOOD CV MTA .102-E4
RIDGEWOOD DR CHS .145-C2
RIDGEWOOD DR EAG .136-A4
RIDGEWOOD DR HOP .119-C2
RIDGEWOOD DR MH .122-B4
RIDGEWOOD DR SCF .14-D1
RIDGEWOOD DR VIC .130-E3
RIDGEWOOD DR NW ER .19-D4
RIDGEWOOD LN BEC .17-C4
RIDGEWOOD LN SAV .161-C1
RIDGEWOOD LN N RVL .107-D1
RIDGEWOOD LN S RVL .107-D1
RIDGEWOOD RD AH .93-D2
RIDGEWOOD RD DPH .118-B2
RIDGEWOOD RD MOU .116-E2
RIDGEWOOD RD MTK .118-C2
RIDGEWOOD RD RVL .93-D3
RIESGRAF RD CAR .159-A1
RIGBY DR EPR .147-B1
RILEY AVE BEC .3-A4
RILEY AVE ORT .3-A4
RILEY LAKE RD EPR .132-C3
RIMBLEY RD WBY .123-D2
RIMROCK DR APV .162-E1,163-A1
RINDAHL CT MTK .118-D1
RINGENBACH ST CHS .145-D2
RINGER RD MTK .104-D3
RINGNECK DR CHN .117-E4
RINGO DR CHN .132-A1
RIO LOMA DR BUR .148-E2
RIO LOMA LN BUR .148-E2
RIPLEY AVE MPW .108-E1,109-A1
RIPLEY AVE NSP .109-B1
RIPLEY AVE E MPW .108-C1
RISEDORPH ST LES .212-C4
RISEWOOD CIR EPR .133-C4
RISHWORTH LN WBL .95-A1
RISING MOON ALY NP .201-E2
RITA CT EAG .136-A3
RITA LN CHS .145-D1
RITTER PARK TRL LVL .176-C2
RIVARD RD N SWT .83-C1
RIVARD ST SOM .84-C1
RIVENDELL LN MTK .105-A3
RIVER AVE ANO .49-C4
RIVER CIR BEC .3-A3
RIVER CIR NW STT .7-E2
RIVER CT BUR .148-E1
RIVER XING N SAV .162-A2
RIVER DR NW SF .7-D4
RIVER LN ANO .63-D1
RIVER LN SPT .70-D3
RIVER PKWY E CHM .63-C1
RIVER PKWY W CHM .49-B4,63-C1
RIVER PKWY W MPL .107-A3,121-B1
RIVER RD AFT .125-C4,139-B1
RIVER RD IGH .137-A3
RIVER RD OST .14-C4,28-B1
RIVER RD SAT .14-C4
RIVER RD SAV .147-C2
RIVER RD SHK .147-C2
RIVER RD SJT .97-E3,98-B3
RIVER RD E ANO .63-D1
RIVER RD E MPL .106-E3,107-A3
RIVER RD N DEL .87-D2
RIVER RD NE HAN .60-E3,61-A2
RIVER RD NE OTS .33-E4,48-A1
RIVER RD S DEL .87-D3
RIVER RD S SMP .125-C2
RIVER RD W BC .78-C4
RIVER RD W CHM .63-E3,64-A3
RIVER RD W MPL .106-D1
RIVER RUN N SAV .162-A2
RIVER RUN S SAV .162-A2
RIVER ST BEC .3-A4
RIVER ST DEL .87-D2
RIVER ST FKT .87-D3
RIVER ST HAS .166-C1
RIVER ST HUD .111-D2
RIVER ST MO .17-B4,31-C1
RIVER ST MPL .106-D2
RIVER ST OSC .27-E4,28-A4
RIVER ST RF .140-E2
RIVER ST SOM .70-B4,84-B1
RIVER ST TF .14-C2
RIVER ST E MO .31-D2
RIVER ST N DEL .87-D2
RIVER ST S DEL .87-D3
RIVER ST W MO .17-B4,31-C1
RIVER TER BLO .148-C1
RIVER TER E MPL .107-B4
RIVER BEND PL SAV .162-A1
RIVER BIRCH PL LL .66-B4
RIVER BLUFF CIR BLO .147-E2
RIVER BLUFF CRV BLO .147-E2
RIVER BLUFF CT EAG .135-C3
RIVER BLUFF DR BLO .147-E2
RIVER BLUFF DR EAG .135-C3
RIVER CREST CIR SJT .97-C2
RIVER CREST DR HSN .47-D3
RIVER CREST DR SJT .97-C2
RIVER CROSSING CT SAV .162-A2
RIVER EDGE WAY NE FRI .78-D4
RIVER FOREST DR MO .32-A2
RIVER HEIGHTS CT HAS .166-B2
RIVER HEIGHTS DR SWR .83-A4
RIVER HEIGHTS TRL HUT .97-D3
RIVER HEIGHTS TRL SJT .97-D3
RIVER HEIGHTS WAY IGH .137-A4
RIVER HILLS CIR BUR .149-A2
RIVER HILLS DR BUR .149-A2
RIVER HILLS DR RF .140-D2
RIVER HILLS DR NW STT .7-E2,8-A2
RIVER HILLS DR W BUR .148-E2,149-A2
RIVER HILLS RD RF .140-D2
RIVER HILLS DRIVE CT W BUR .148-E2
RIVER MILL DR MO .31-E2,32-A2
RIVER OAK CT SAV .161-E2
RIVER OAK DR SAV .161-E2
RIVER OAK PL SAV .161-E2
RIVER OAKS RD RFD .74-A4

RIVER PARK PLZ STP 108-C4,122-C1
RIVER RIDGE BLVD BUR 148-C3
RIVER RIDGE CIR BLO . .134-E3,135-A3
RIVER RIDGE CIR EAG 135-C3
RIVER RIDGE CT BLO 148-C3
RIVER RIDGE CT BUR 148-C3
RIVER RIDGE CT RF 140-D2
RIVER RIDGE LN BUR 148-D3
RIVER RIDGE LN MO 32-A2
RIVER RIDGE RD BLO 134-E3
RIVER RIDGE RD HUD 111-D4
RIVER RIDGE RD RF 140-D2
RIVER ROAD CT W BP 78-C3
RIVER ROCK LN SHK 145-E3
RIVER RUN CT SAV 162-A2
RIVER SHORE CT HAS 166-C2
RIVER SHORE DR HAS 166-B3
RIVER SHORE LN CHM 63-D2
RIVER TERRACE CT MPL 107-B4
RIVER TERRACE DR BLO 148-C1
RIVER VIEW CIR BKR 17-C4
RIVER VIEW LN BKR 17-C4,31-C1
RIVER VIEW LN SPT 70-D3
RIVER VIEW LN W SPT 70-D3
RIVER WOOD DR SAV 162-A2
RIVER WOOD DR SAV . .161-E2,162-A2
RIVER WOODS LN BUR 149-A3
RIVERBANK LN NW SF 7-E3
RIVERBANK LN NW STT 7-E2
RIVERCREST LN SWR 83-A4
RIVERCREST RD N LLD 111-C3
RIVERDALE DR N BP 78-C3
RIVERDALE DR NW CR 49-D4
RIVERDALE DR NW RAM . .48-D2,49-A3
RIVERDALE BC 78-C3
RIVERLANE CT BP 78-C3
RIVERS BLUFF LN ANO 49-B4
RIVERSIDE AVE MPL . .106-E3,107-A3
RIVERSIDE AVE N MAY 69-C2
RIVERSIDE CIR MO 31-C1
RIVERSIDE DR BKR 2-D1
RIVERSIDE DR RF 126-E4,140-D1
RIVERSIDE DR TRT 140-D1
RIVERSIDE DR N NOH 111-D1
RIVERSIDE LN JOR 173-B2
RIVERSIDE PL N BP 64-A3
RIVERSIDE RD BC 87-D3
RIVERTON AVE EAG . . .135-C4,149-C1
RIVERTON CIR EAG 149-C1
RIVERTON PT EAG 135-C4
RIVERTOWN DR WBY 110-A4
RIVERVIEW AVE STP 122-C2
RIVERVIEW AVE N VER 179-C2
RIVERVIEW AVE S BLO 134-E4
RIVERVIEW CIR BLO 134-E4
RIVERVIEW CIR CHM 63-E2
RIVERVIEW DR MO . . .31-E2,32-A2
RIVERVIEW DR MOT 32-A2
RIVERVIEW DR SWR 83-A4
RIVERVIEW DR TRT 111-D4
RIVERVIEW DR E EPR 147-B1
RIVERVIEW DR W EPR 147-B1
RIVERVIEW DR RF 33-B2
RIVERVIEW LN NFD 219-C4
RIVERVIEW LN N BP 78-C2
RIVERVIEW LN N CHM 63-E2
RIVERVIEW PL NW CR 64-A2
RIVERVIEW RD CHS 145-D2
RIVERVIEW RD CTT 145-D2
RIVERVIEW RD EPR . . .146-E1,147-B1
RIVERVIEW RD MPL 121-B3
RIVERVIEW RD RFD 74-A4
RIVERVIEW RD RIT 140-C2
RIVERVIEW RD NE HAN . .60-E3,61-A3
RIVERVIEW TER NE FRI 78-D3
RIVERVIEW ACRES RD SJT 97-C2
RIVERVIEW ENTR N CHM 63-E2
RIVERWOOD CIR BUR 148-D2
RIVERWOOD DR HAS 166-C3
RIVERWOOD DR BUR 148-E3
RIVERWOOD DR HAS 166-C3
RIVERWOOD DR NE FRI 78-D3
RIVERWOOD LN SAV 162-A4
RIVERWOOD PL STP 107-C4
RIVIERA AVE S LSC 125-C2
RIVIERA CIR E WBL 95-C1
RIVIERA CT NB 93-B2
RIVIERA CT WBL 95-B1
RIVIERA DR N WBL 93-B2
RIVIERA DR N WBL 95-B1
RIVIERA DR S WBL 95-B1
RIVIERA LN SWD 117-D4
RIVIERIA DR N WBL 95-C1
RIVLYN AVE NW RAM 49-B3
RIVOLI ST STP 108-C3
ROANOKE CIR N GV 106-A2
ROANOKE LN MOU 117-A2
ROANOKE RD GV 106-A2
ROANOKE ST SL 136-C1
ROANOKE ST PRL 161-A3
ROANOKE ST NW AND 35-C3
ROANOKE ST NW BT 35-C1
ROANOKE ST NW RAM . .35-C2,49-C1
ROANOKE ST NW SF 7-C3
ROANOKE ST NW STT 7-C1
ROBB FARM RD NO 80-C4
ROBB FARM RD WBT 80-C3
ROBBINS LNDG N ROB 92-A3
ROBBINS ST MPL 120-B3
ROBBINS ST STP 107-B3
ROBERT AVE HBG 156-A2
ROBERT AVE N ML 43-D2
ROBERT CIR BEL 185-E2
ROBERT CT HAS 166-E3
ROBERT CT MHT 95-D2
ROBERT CT S IGH 150-B1
ROBERT DR HAS 166-E3
ROBERT LN COR 62-A3
ROBERT LN S ROG 62-A1
ROBERT LN S JOR 173-B3
ROBERT RD LVL 162-C4
ROBERT ST HEN 166-E3
ROBERT ST HSN 47-D3
ROBERT ST MHT 95-C2
ROBERT ST MSC 55-B4
ROBERT ST OSC 28-A4
ROBERT ST PRE 153-B4
ROBERT ST WSP 122-C3
ROBERT ST N S STP . . .108-B4,122-C1
ROBERT ST S STP 122-C1
ROBERT TRL S EAG 150-B2
ROBERT TRL S RMT . . .150-A4,164-A2
ROBERT TRL S SL 136-D1
ROBERTS CT BUF 59-A1
ROBERTS DR EPR 132-E1,133-A1
ROBERTS PL EDI 119-E4
ROBERTS RD BUF 59-A1

ROBERTSON CT RFD 74-B2
ROBIE ST E STP 122-C1
ROBIE ST W STP 122-B1
ROBIN AVE N ROB 92-A3
ROBIN AVE S ML 43-D3
ROBIN CIR LTT 130-C2
ROBIN CIR MTK 119-A1
ROBIN CT NB 93-B1
ROBIN LN BUF 45-B4
ROBIN LN EAG 135-C4
ROBIN LN MOU 116-D1
ROBIN LN MTK 119-A1
ROBIN LN NB 79-B4,93-B1
ROBIN LN NO 80-B3
ROBIN LN SWR 96-E1
ROBIN LN N CV 66-E2
ROBIN LN S CV 66-E2
ROBIN LN W CV 66-E2
ROBIN RD MG 77-A4
ROBIN RD PRL 161-B2
ROBIN ST SVW 79-E1
ROBIN OAK CT SVW 79-E1
ROBIN OAK RD MTK 105-C4
ROBIN OAK RDG MTK 105-C4
ROBINHOOD LN CP 79-D1
ROBINHOOD CT SVW 79-E3
ROBINHOOD PL SVW 79-E3
ROBINSON CIR DAY 48-B1
ROBINSON CIR PRL 161-B3
ROBINSON DR NW CR 64-B2
ROBINSON DR S DAY 48-B1
ROBINSONS BAY RD DPH 118-B1
ROBINWOOD BAY WBY 123-D3
ROBINWOOD CIR MTK 119-B1
ROBINWOOD CT WBY 123-D3
ROBINWOOD DR MTK 118-D1
ROBINWOOD DRAW WBY 123-D3
ROBINWOOD LN HOP 119-B1
ROBINWOOD LN MTK . .105-B4,119-B1
ROBINWOOD SPUR MTK 119-B1
ROBINWOOD TER MTK 119-B1
ROBINWOOD TRL WBY 123-D3
ROBINWOOD WAY WBY 123-D3
ROBLYN AVE STP 107-C4
ROCHELLE CRV SHK 146-C3
ROCHESTER BLVD HMT .193-C3,207-D1
ROCHESTER BLVD RAT .207-E2,208-A3
ROCHESTER ST BLA 65-B1
ROCHESTER ST NE EB 23-A4
ROCKFORD RD PLY . . .90-D3,91-B3
ROCKFORD RD ROB . .91-E3,92-A3
ROCKFORD RD NH 91-C3
ROCKNEY ST NE BLA 65-E3
ROCKNEY ST NE HIL 37-E3
ROCKRIDGE CT CLT 189-A2
ROCKSBOROUGH RD MTK 118-E2
ROCKSBURY RD WBY 124-A4
ROCKSTONE CT NB 79-B3
ROCKSTONE LN NB 79-B3
ROCKWOOD AVE STP 108-C1
ROCKY LN EAG 149-D1
ROCKY KNOLL DR ORO 103-C1
ROCKY BRANCH CT RF 140-D3
ROCKY RAPIDS WAY EAG 149-A1
ROD GUN CLUB RD HUT .97-D4,111-D1
RODAO DR RF 140-E3
RODEO CT NE BLA 65-C2
RODEO DR BLA 65-C2
RODEO DR BUR 148-E2
ROE AVE RVT 181-E3
ROELLER AVE WSP 122-C2
ROGERS AVE MH 136-A1
ROGERS CT EAG 150-A2
ROGERS CT MH 136-A1
ROGERS DR MGY 215-D4
ROGERS DR MTK 119-A3
ROGERS RD ROG 47-E4,62-A1
ROGERS RD EPR 132-C3
ROGERS ST STP 121-E2
ROHAVIC LN LL 79-E1,80-A1
ROJINA LN CHN 118-B4
ROLF AVE EDI 119-E4
ROLL LN EAG 136-A3
ROLLIE RD LVL 162-C4,176-C1
ROLLING BLF VIC 131-A1
ROLLING GREEN CRV MH 121-E4
ROLLING HILLS CIR EAG 136-B3
ROLLING HILLS CT EAG 136-B3
ROLLING HILLS DR EAG 136-B3
ROLLING HILLS DR LL . .66-E4,67-A4
ROLLING HILLS DR MPW 109-B2
ROLLING HILLS DR MTA 102-D3
ROLLING HILLS LN SJT 97-E2
ROLLING HILLS PL EAG 136-B3
ROLLING HILLS RD AH 93-C1
ROLLING HILLS RD COR . .75-C4,89-C1
ROLLING HILLS RD MED 89-C1
ROLLING HILLS TRL SJT . .97-E2,98-A2
ROLLING MEADOWS CIR SE LAT .201-E3
ROLLING MEADOWS DR SE LAT .201-E3
ROLLING MEADOWS LN SE LAT .201-E3
ROLLING OAK CT CRT 176-B3
ROLLING OAKS CIR PRL 161-B1
ROLLING OAKS RD BUR 149-A2
ROLLING RIDGE RD BEC 3-A4
ROLLING RIDGE RD ORT 3-A4
ROLLING VIEW CT WBL 95-B2
ROLLINS AVE SE MPL 107-A2
ROLLS RD NB 93-B2
ROLVAAG CT NFD 219-D2
ROMA ST RVL 107-E1,108-A1
ROMAN RD NE FRI 92-D1
ROME AVE STP 121-C2
ROME CT APV 162-E2
ROME DR APV 162-E2
ROMEO DR LVL 177-B3
ROMEO RD WBY 123-C3
RONALD AVE WBL 95-A1
RONALD ST STP 91-D1
RONDEAU LAKE DR N COT 52-C3
RONDEAU LAKE RD E COT 52-C2
RONDEAU LAKE RD E LL 52-D4
RONDEAU LAKE RD W COT 52-C3
RONDEAU LAKE RD W LL 52-C3
ROONEY PL WBL 95-A2
ROOSEVELT CIR ER 34-A2

ROOSEVELT CIR NW ER 33-E1
ROOSEVELT CT RF 140-D1
ROOSEVELT CT SA 93-A3
ROOSEVELT DR NFD 219-D4
ROOSEVELT RD HAS 166-C1
ROOSEVELT ST ANO 49-D3
ROOSEVELT ST ER 34-A2
ROOSEVELT ST PRL 161-A4
ROOSEVELT ST RF 140-D1
ROOSEVELT ST SA 93-A3
ROOSEVELT ST NE MPL .93-A4,107-A1
ROOSEVELT ST S SCF 14-C2
ROS EMILY LN EPR 133-B1
ROSABELL ST MSC 55-B4
ROSALE AVE E WIN 99-B4
ROSALE AVE W WIN 99-B4
ROSALLA DR EPR 132-C1
ROSALYN CT NH 91-D4
ROSCOE RD PS 95-D3
ROSE AVE MPW 109-B2
ROSE AVE WTT E4
ROSE AVE E STP 108-C2,109-B3
ROSE AVE W WIN 99-B4
ROSE AVE S ML 43-D2
ROSE AVE W STP 107-E2,108-B2
ROSE AVE NW OG 35-E2
ROSE CT EDI 120-A4
ROSE CT N BP 64-A4
ROSE CT NW SF 7-E4
ROSE DR BL 10-B4
ROSE DR ROG 47-D4
ROSE LN MPL 120-B1
ROSE LN NB 93-B1
ROSE LN E LC 94-C4
ROSE MNR GV 105-C1
ROSE PL RVL 93-E4,94-A3
ROSE PL E LC 94-B3
ROSE ST MHT 81-D4
ROSE ST MSC 55-B4
ROSE ST VIC 118-B3
ROSE ST NW AND 35-E3,49-E3
ROSE ST NW CR 49-E4,63-E1
ROSE ST NW RAM 21-E2,35-E2
ROSE HILL CIR LAU 107-B2
ROSE VISTA CT RVL 107-D1
ROSE WAY RD MPL 120-D2
ROSEBERRY PL ANO 49-C3
ROSEBRIAR AVE VH 80-C4
ROSEDALE AVE DPH 118-B2
ROSEDALE AVE N HAN 60-E3
ROSEDALE CT DPH 118-B2
ROSEDALE DR RVL 107-C1
ROSEDALE RD NE RVL 78-D2
ROSEDALE MALL DR RVL 93-D4
ROSEGATE RVL 93-C4
ROSEHILL LN SPR 117-B1
ROSELAWN AVE E MPW 108-C1
ROSELAWN AVE W FH 107-C1
ROSELAWN AVE W LAU 107-B1
ROSELAWN AVE W RVL . .107-E1,108-A1
ROSELAWN AVE W RVL .107-E1,108-A1
ROSEMARY CT EAG 150-A2
ROSEMARY CT HAS 166-C2
ROSEMARY LN EDI 133-D1
ROSEMARY LN MTK 104-D3
ROSEMARY RD EPR 132-E1
ROSEMILL CIR N CHM 63-B3
ROSEMILL CT N CHM 63-B3
ROSEMILL LN N CHM 63-B3
ROSEMOUNT DR BUR 162-B1
ROSETOWN CT RVL 94-A3
ROSEVILLE MALL DR RVL 93-D4
ROSEWOOD AVE N MPW 108-E1
ROSEWOOD AVE S MPW 108-E1
ROSEWOOD CIR JT 160-A1
ROSEWOOD CT MG 77-A4
ROSEWOOD CT NB 79-B4
ROSEWOOD DR CHM 132-A3
ROSEWOOD DR LC 94-B3
ROSEWOOD LN BUR 162-D2
ROSEWOOD LN MOU 116-D2
ROSEWOOD LN N PLY 91-A4
ROSEWOOD LN N DAY . .48-E3,49-A4
ROSEWOOD LN N MG 77-A1
ROSEWOOD LN N PLY . .91-A3,95-A1
ROSEWOOD LN S RVL 107-C1
ROSEWOOD LN S RVL 107-C1
ROSEWOOD RD NE PRL 161-B2
ROSLYN PL MPL 120-D4
ROSS AVE STP 108-D3,109-A3
ROSS LN WBT 80-E2
ROSS RD HUT 112-C1
ROSSWOOD LN N WAY 104-C2
ROTH PL WBL 95-B1
ROTH ST WBL 95-A1
ROUILLARD AVE ROG 61-E1
ROUILLARD BLVD ROG 61-E1
ROUND HILL RD MH 122-A4
ROUND LAKE
BLVD NW AND 35-E3,49-E3
ROUND LAKE BLVD NW ANO 49-E3
ROUND LAKE
BLVD NW CR 49-E4,63-E1
ROUND LAKE RD AH 132-C2
ROUND LAKE RD W AH 79-C4
ROUND LAKE TRL LC 94-B3
ROUNDHOUSE CIR SHK 146-C2
ROUNDHOUSE CT SHK 146-C2
ROUNDHOUSE ST SHK 146-C2
ROWAN AVE RVT 181-E3
ROWE PL STP 109-A4
ROWLAND RD EPR 119-B4
ROWLAND RD MTK 119-A3
ROWLAND PARK RD MTK 119-A3
ROXANNA LN NB 79-A4
ROXBURY LN MOU 117-A2
ROY AVE CNC 12-E4
ROY ST N STP 107-D4
ROY ST S STP 121-D2
ROYAL AVE IGH 137-A3
ROYAL CIR NW RAM 34-C4
ROYAL CT MTK 118-E2
ROYAL CT SVW 79-E2
ROYAL LN NW RAM 34-C4
ROYAL LN AH 93-D1
ROYAL RD NW RAM 34-C4
ROYAL FERN CT NO 80-C2
ROYAL HILLS DR AH 79-D4
ROYAL LINK CT EPR 132-E1
ROYAL OAK CIR EAG 135-D4
ROYAL OAK CT FRI 79-A4
ROYAL OAK DR CHS 145-C1
ROYAL OAKS DR MTK 119-A2
ROYAL OAKS DR SVW 79-E2
ROYAL OAKS DR W SVW 79-D1
ROYALE CT EAG 149-B3

ROYALE DR EAG 149-B3
ROYALE PL EAG 149-B3
ROYALE TRL EAG 149-B3
ROYALE WAY EAG 149-B3
ROYALSTON AVE N MPL 106-C2
ROYCAR RD EDI 133-E1
ROYCE ST NE CH 92-E2
ROYS DR HSN 47-D3
ROYZELLE LN MTK 119-B1
ROZELLE RD SA 93-A4
RUANN RD ORO 104-A2
RUBY CIR SHK 146-C3
RUBY CT N EAG 149-B1
RUBY CT S EAG 149-B1
RUBY DR WSP 122-B3
RUBY LN EAG 149-B1
RUBY LN MOU 117-A4
RUBY LN SHK 146-C3
RUBY RD HUD 111-E2
RUCKS FARM RD DEL 87-E3
RUDDY DUCK LN BLT 17-E2
RUFFED GROUSE CT EPR 66-C3
RUFFED GROUSE RD LL 66-C3
RUGGLE AVE FH 107-D1
RUGGLES AVE RVL 107-E1
RUGGLES ST FH 107-D1
RUGGLES ST RVL 107-E1
RUM RIVER BLVD NW OG .21-D2,35-C1
RUM RIVER BLVD NW RAM 35-C2
RUM RIVER BLVD NW SF .7-E3,21-D1
RUM RIVER DR ANO 49-C3
RUM RIVER DR NW ATT 8-B1
RUM RIVER DR NW OG 21-D2
RUNGE LN WSP 122-B3
RUNNEL CIR EPR 133-B4
RUNNING BROOK DR EAG 149-A1
RUNNYMEADE CT MTK 105-B3
RUNNYMEADE LN MTK 105-B3
RUPP DR BUR 148-E2
RUSCH DR HUT 97-D4
RUSH AVE NW ER 33-D1
RUSH CIR NW ER 19-D4
RUSH ST NW ER 19-D4
RUSH CREEK BLVD COR .61-B4,75-B1
RUSH CREEK DR COR 61-C4
RUSH CREEK LN COR 61-B4
RUSH CREEK RD DAY 62-D3
RUSH MEADOW LN COR 61-C3
RUSHMORE CRES BUR 162-E2
RUSHMORE DR BUR 162-E2
RUSSEL ST HAS 166-D2
RUSSELL AVE ORO 103-E3
RUSSELL AVE WBY 123-E4
RUSSELL AVE N BC 92-B2
RUSSELL AVE N BP 64-B4,78-B1
RUSSELL AVE S BLO . . .106-B3,120-B1
RUSSELL AVE S BLO . .134-B3,148-B1
RUSSELL AVE S MPL . .106-B3,120-B3
RUSSELL AVE S RCH . .120-B4,134-B1
RUSSELL CIR N BC 64-B4,78-B1
RUSSELL CIR S BLO . .134-B4,148-B2
RUSSELL CT MPL 120-B3
RUSSELL LN LOL 103-E2,104-A2
RUSSELL ST PRL 161-D1
RUSSELL ST STP 108-D3
RUSTAD LN MV E2
RUSTEN RD EAG 149-A3
RUSTIC DR MHT 95-D2
RUSTIC LDG E MPL 120-D2
RUSTIC LDG W MPL 120-C2
RUSTIC LN LL 65-E3
RUSTIC PL SVW 80-B4,94-B1
RUSTIC PL N LC 94-B3
RUSTIC RD PRL 161-D2
RUSTIC RD N MYR 114-E4
RUSTIC WAY SWD 118-A2
RUSTIC HILLS DR EAG 135-C2
RUSTIC HILLS DR EPR 118-C4
RUSTICWOOD RD MOU 116-E2
RUSTLE RD JOR 173-B3
RUTGERS ST LWT 10-D3
RUTGERS ST PRL 161-D1
RUTGERS ST NE COT 38-D2
RUTGERS ST NE OXT 10-D2
RUTH CIR NE FRI 78-C2
RUTH DR EDI 119-E4
RUTH ST MPW 109-A1
RUTH ST N STP 109-A3,123-A1
RUTH ST NE FRI 78-C2
RUTH ST S STP 123-A1
RUTHERFORD PL SWR 96-D1
RUTHERFORD RD SWR 96-C1
RUTHIE LN TRT 126-B2
RUTLEDGE AVE EDI 119-E2
RUTLEDGE CIR MTK . .105-A4,119-A1
RUTLEDGE RD DPH 118-B1
RUTLEDGE ST PRL 161-B3
RUTZ LAKE RD WCT 129-A1
RYAN AVE EDI 119-E4
RYAN AVE MPW 108-D1
RYAN AVE NSP 109-B1
RYAN AVE STP 122-B1
RYAN AVE W LAU 107-B1
RYAN AVE W RVL 107-D1,108-A1
RYAN CIR BUR 148-E2,149-A2
RYAN CT NSP 109-B1
RYAN DR HUT 112-B3
RYAN DR MPW 109-B2
RYAN DR W LC 94-B2
RYAN LN LC 94-B3
RYAN PL LEX 93-E2
RYAN LAKE DR NE LWT . .10-D4,11-A4
RYANS CIR BEL 185-E1
RYBERG CIR CHS 145-B1
RYBERG ST CHS 145-B1
RYDE ST STP 107-E3
RYDEEN AVE N FRT 13-D4
RYDEEN AVE N SHT 13-D4
RYE ST BEC 2-E4

S
SABLE DR BUR 149-A3
SABRA CT APV 149-A4
SACIA LN HUD 111-E3
SADDLE CT SWR 96-D2
SADDLE HORN CT EPR 132-D3
SADDLE RIDGE LN TRT 126-B3
SADDLEBRED WAY FLT 39-C4
SADDLEBROOK CIR MTK .104-E2,105-A4
SADDLEBROOK CRV CHN 132-A1
SADDLEBROOK LN WBY .123-E1,124-A1
SADDLEBROOK PASS CHN 132-A1
SADDLEBROOK TRL CHN 132-A1
SADDLERIDGE TRL IND .102-E2,103-A2
SADDLEWOOD DR EAG .136-A4,150-A1

SADDLEWOOD DR MTK 118-C2
SADDLEWOOD LN MTK 118-C2
SADDLEWOOD TRL MTK 118-C2
SAFARI CIR EAG 149-B3
SAFARI CT N EAG 149-B3
SAFARI CT S EAG 149-B3
SAFARI PASS APV 149-B3
SAFARI PASS EAG 149-B3
SAFARI TRL EAG 149-B3
SAFARI HEIGHTS TRL EAG 149-B3
SAGE AVE BKT 185-B2
SAGE CT SHK 146-C3
SAGE LN SHK 146-C3
SAILOR LN BC 92-A2
SAINT ALBANS CIR EDI 133-D1
SAINT ALBANS CIR SVW 79-E2,80-A2
SAINT ALBANS CT SVW 79-E1
SAINT ALBANS GRN GRW 118-A3
SAINT ALBANS RD E HOP 105-B4
SAINT ALBANS RD W HOP 105-B4
SAINT ALBANS ST N RVL 94-A4,108-A1
SAINT ALBANS ST N STP 108-A4,122-A1
SAINT ALBANS ST N SVW 80-A1
SAINT ALBANS ST S STP 122-A1
SAINT ALBANS BAY CIR SWD 118-A3
SAINT ALBANS BAY RD GRW 118-A3
SAINT ALBANS BAY RD SWD 118-A3
SAINT ALBANS HOLLOW CIR MTK 105-A4
SAINT ALBANS HOLLOW DR MTK 105-A4
SAINT ALBANS MILL RD MTK 105-A4
SAINT ANDREW BLVD EAG 149-D2
SAINT ANDREW DR EPR 132-E1
SAINT ANDREWS AVE EDI 119-E3
SAINT ANDREWS DR TRT 125-D3
SAINT ANDREWS LN BL 17-E2
SAINT ANDREWS LN RAM 48-C1
SAINT ANDREWS LN NW RAM 48-C1
SAINT ANNES PKWY TRT 125-D3
SAINT ANTHONY AVE MPL 107-B4
SAINT ANTHONY AVE STP 107-D4,108-A4
SAINT ANTHONY AVE WBT 81-A3
SAINT ANTHONY BLVD SA 93-B4
SAINT ANTHONY PKWY MPL 92-D3,93-A3
SAINT ANTHONY RD SA 93-A3
SAINT BENEDICT RD HAT 187-C3
SAINT CHARLES PL EAG 135-C4
SAINT CLAIR AVE STP 121-C1,122-A1
SAINT CLAIR ST CF 208-B4
SAINT CROIX AVE LND 12-D4
SAINT CROIX AVE E SWR 83-A4
SAINT CROIX AVE N GV 105-E1,106-A1
SAINT CROIX AVE W SWR 82-E4,83-A4
SAINT CROIX CIR GV 106-A1
SAINT CROIX DR OTS 33-E4
SAINT CROIX HTS HUD 111-D2
SAINT CROIX RD FAT 55-D3,56-A3
SAINT CROIX RD WBY 123-E2
SAINT CROIX ST HUD 111-D2
SAINT CROIX ST OPH 97-A2
SAINT CROIX ST PRE 153-B4
SAINT CROIX ST RF 140-E1
SAINT CROIX ST RVL 93-B4
SAINT CROIX ST N NOH 111-C1
SAINT CROIX TRL N BAY 97-B4,111-B1
SAINT CROIX TRL N BYT 111-B1
SAINT CROIX TRL N FRT 27-D4,41-C1
SAINT CROIX TRL N LLD 111-C3
SAINT CROIX TRL N LS 111-C4
SAINT CROIX TRL N MAY 69-C3,83-C1
SAINT CROIX TRL N MSC 55-B4,69-C1
SAINT CROIX TRL N NST 41-B3,55-C2
SAINT CROIX TRL N OPH 97-B2
SAINT CROIX TRL N SHT 13-E1,14-A1
SAINT CROIX TRL N SWR 83-A4
SAINT CROIX TRL N SWT 83-B3
SAINT CROIX TRL N WLT 111-B2
SAINT CROIX TRL S AFT 125-B3,139-A1
SAINT CROIX TRL S DET 139-B3,153-A3
SAINT CROIX TRL S LLD 111-C4,125-C1
SAINT CROIX TRL S LS 111-C4
SAINT CROIX TRL S LSC 125-C2
SAINT CROIX TRL S SMP 125-B2
SAINT CROIX RIVER RD FAT 41-D3
SAINT DAVIDS RD MTK 119-A1
SAINT DENNIS CT STP 121-D3
SAINT EDWARDS CT EPR 132-B1
SAINT FRANCIS AVE SHK 146-C4
SAINT FRANCIS AVE NW BET 8-D3
SAINT FRANCIS BLVD ANO 49-C3
SAINT FRANCIS BLVD RAM 49-C3
SAINT FRANCIS BLVD NW BT 21-C3,35-B1
SAINT FRANCIS BLVD NW OG 7-D4,21-C1
SAINT FRANCIS BLVD NW RAM 35-B3,49-C2
SAINT FRANCIS BLVD NW SF 7-D4
SAINT FRANCIS CT ANO 49-C3
SAINT FRANCIS LN CRT 161-C3
SAINT FRANCIS WAY EAG 135-E4
SAINT IMIER DR NE FRI 93-A1
SAINT JAMES GATE DPH 118-A2
SAINT JOHN ST LOR 89-A2
SAINT JOHNS AVE EDI 120-A4
SAINT JOHNS BLVD MPW 94-E3
SAINT JOHNS DR EPR 118-E4,119-A4
SAINT JOHNS DR WBY 124-B2
SAINT JOHNS RD MTK 119-C1
SAINT JOSEPHS LN STP 108-B4
SAINT LOUIS AVE DPH 118-B1
SAINT LOUIS AVE MPL 106-B4
SAINT LOUIS ST HOP 119-C2
SAINT LOUIS ST E SWR 97-A2
SAINT MARGARET DR GV 106-B1
SAINT MARIE ST SVW 94-B2
SAINT MARKS DR MTK 119-A2
SAINT MARKS RD S SHK 146-A2
SAINT MARKS ST S SHK 146-A2
SAINT MARY ST NM 189-E4
SAINT MARYS AVE MPL 107-A3
SAINT MARYS DR SMP 125-C2
SAINT MARYS PL MPL 107-A3
SAINT MARYS PL MTK 118-E3
SAINT MARYS RD MTA 116-E2,117-A2
SAINT MARYS ST FH 107-D1
SAINT MELLION PL EPR 132-B3
SAINT MICHAEL ST MV 79-B2
SAINT MORITZ VIC 131-A1
SAINT MORITZ DR NE CH 93-A1
SAINT MORITZ DR NE FRI 93-A1
SAINT OLAF AVE NFD 219-D3
SAINT PATRICKS LN EDI 133-D1
SAINT PAUL AVE MPL 106-A4
SAINT PAUL AVE STP 121-C3
SAINT PAUL AVE SE PRL 161-B3
SAINT PAUL ST NM 189-E4
SAINT PETER AVE DEL 87-D3
SAINT PETER ST LOR 89-B2
SAINT PETER ST STP 108-B4
SAINT RAPHAEL DR NH 91-D2
SAINT REGIS DR WBL 95-B1
SAINT STEPHEN ST RVL 93-B4
SAINT STEPHENS ST MV 79-B2
SAINTS ST CRT 161-E4
SAKENDA RD BUF 44-E4,45-A4
SALEM AVE HCT 156-D4,170-D1
SALEM AVE SAV 161-E1
SALEM AVE YAT 142-D3,156-D2
SALEM AVE S SLP 105-E4,119-E2
SALEM CT EPR 147-B1
SALEM CT MHT 95-C2
SALEM CT ORO 103-D1
SALEM DR W WBY 124-A4
SALEM LN GRF 74-E2,75-A2
SALEM LN SL 136-C1
SALEM PL BUR 148-B4
SALEM PL MHT 95-C2
SALEM PT EAG 149-C3
SALEM CHURCH RD IGH 136-C1
SALEM CHURCH RD SL 136-B1
SALISBURY AVE MTK 118-B3
SALISBURY HILL RD BKT 198-E1,199-A1
SALISH CIR NW BT 35-C2
SALISH CIR NW RAM 35-C2
SALISH ST NW RAM 49-C1
SALISH ST NW SF 7-C4
SALISHAN DR TRT 125-D2
SALLY AVE WTT -D3
SALLY CIR EAG 136-A3
SALLY LN EDI 119-C4,133-C1
SALLY ST FL 39-B3
SALLYS ALY N NOH 111-D1
SAMUEL CT VH 94-C2
SAMUEL RD EDI 133-C1
SAMUEL ST RVL 107-D1
SANA FE TRL COR 61-D4
SANBURNOL DR NE BLA 78-D1
SANCTUARY DR BLA 65-B2
SAND RD VAT 209-C2
SAND ST E SHK 146-B3
SAND CREEK BLVD SCT 173-C3
SAND CREEK DR NW CR 64-C1
SAND CREEK LN LAT 202-A4
SAND CREEK RD SCT 173-C3
SAND HILL CIR EPR 132-D3
SAND RIDGE RD EPR 132-E1,133-A1
SAND STONE CRV SHK 146-A3
SAND TERRA CT WBT 81-B1
SANDBAR CIR WAC 129-C2
SANDBERG RD MO 31-C2
SANDBURG LN GV 91-D4,105-D1
SANDBURG RD GV 105-D1
SANDEEN RD AH 93-C2
SANDELL AVE EDI 134-A1
SANDER DR MPL 121-A3
SANDHILL DR LL 65-E3
SANDHILL PT N NOH 97-C4
SANDHILL RD NO 80-C2
SANDHURST AVE MPW 94-E4
SANDHURST CIR RVL 94-A4
SANDHURST DR W RVL 93-E4,94-A4
SANDLEWOOD RD WBY 123-C1
SANDPIPER CT DEL 87-D3
SANDPIPER CT EDI 119-D4
SANDPIPER DR LL 66-B2
SANDPIPER DR E BLA 64-E4
SANDPIPER DR W BLA 64-E4
SANDPIPER LN NO 80-C2
SANDPIPER TRL CHN 117-D4
SANDRA LN MTK 119-C1
SANDRA LN WBL 80-E3
SANDRALEE DR E STP 109-A4,123-A1
SANDRALEE DR W STP 109-A4,123-A1
SANDRO RD BLO 133-E3
SANDSTONE DR EAG 149-B2
SANDTRAP CIR MO 31-C2
SANDY CT BKR 17-C4
SANDY DR ORT 3-A4
SANDY DR NE EB 9-A4,23-A1
SANDY LN BKR 17-C4,31-D1
SANDY LN BUR 162-C2
SANDY LN MO 31-C1
SANDY LN MOU 117-A1
SANDY LN MTK 118-C2
SANDY BEACH AVE N RVL 108-B1
SANDY HOOK CIR CHN 132-B1
SANDY HOOK DR RVL 94-A3
SANDY HOOK RD CHN 132-B1
SANDY POINT RD EPR 147-A1
SANEL RD WBY 123-D2
SANIBEL DR MTK 119-B3
SANTA FE CIR CHN 132-B2
SANTA FE TRL CHN 132-B2
SANTA VERA DR CHN 132-A2
SANTEE CIR PRL 161-B3
SANTEE TRL PRL 160-E2
SAPPHIRE LN EAG 149-B1
SAPPHIRE LN S SHK 146-C3
SAPPHIRE PT EAG 149-B1
SAPPHIRE ST NW RAM 34-E3
SARA LN BL 18-B4
SARAH CIR ROG 61-D1
SARAH DR DAT 144-C3
SARAH LN RFD 74-A4
SARAH LN SOM 84-B1
SARAH L RFD 74-A4
SARATOGA AVE OSC 28-A4
SARATOGA CIR CHN 132-A2
SARATOGA CIR N PLY 91-B3
SARATOGA CT CHS 145-C2
SARATOGA DR CHN 132-A1
SARATOGA LN EPR 132-E3
SARATOGA LN N CHM 49-B4,63-B1
SARATOGA LN N MG 77-B1
SARATOGA LN N PLY 91-B3,105-B2
SARATOGA ST N STP 107-D4,121-D1
SARATOGA ST S STP 121-D1
SARATOGA WAY MG 63-B4
SARAZIN ST SHK 146-C4
SARGENT AVE STP 121-C1
SARGENT CT N LL 80-E1
SARGENT RD WIL 95-D1
SARTELL AVE EAG 149-C1
SATELLITE LN NE FRI 78-D3
SATURN ST NE LWT 24-A3
SAUNDERS AVE STP 121-C2
SAUNDERS LAKE DR S MTA 116-D2
SAVAGE CT CHC 26-B2
SAVAGE LN N LC 94-C4
SAVANAH AVE WBL 94-E2
SAVANNA CT LL 65-E2
SAVANNA OAKS BAY WBY 123-E3
SAVANNA OAKS CT WBY 123-E3
SAVANNA OAKS LN WBY 123-E3
SAVANNA OAKS PASS WBY 123-E3
SAVANNAH AVE WBL 94-E2
SAVANNAH CT WBY 124-B3
SAVANNAH DR MO 31-C2
SAVANNAH RD EAG 149-E1
SAVANNAH CHAS EPR 132-D3
SAWGRASS GLN MG 76-B1
SAWMILL LN SCT 173-C4
SAWMILL RD JOR 173-B3
SAWMILL RD SCT 173-C4
SAWYER PL SWR 96-D2
SAXONY CIR CHS 145-C1
SAXONY CT CHS 145-C1
SAXONY CT WBT 80-D2
SAXONY RD EDI 119-D3
SCANDIA RD EDI 119-D4
SCANDIA RD LTT 130-B3
SCANDIA TRL N FLT 39-D4,53-A1
SCANDIA TRL N NST 40-C4,41-A4
SCARBOROUGH CIR BLO 147-E1
SCARBOROUGH CT CHS 145-D1
SCARBOROUGH LN WBY 124-A1
SCARBOROUGH RD BLO 147-E1
SCARLET GLOBE DR EPR 133-A3
SCARLET OAK CRES OKD 95-D4
SCARLET OAK ST E OKD 95-D3
SCARLET OAK ST W OKD 95-C3
SCENIC CIR MTK 118-C3
SCENIC CT DEL 87-E3
SCENIC CT MTK 118-C3
SCENIC CT SVW 79-E1
SCENIC DR HSN 48-B2
SCENIC DR MTK 118-C3
SCENIC DR SVW 79-E1
SCENIC HWY BUR 162-B2
SCENIC LN BUR 162-B3
SCENIC LN WBY 124-C4
SCENIC LN N MTK 118-C3
SCENIC LN S MTK 118-C3
SCENIC PL MTK 118-C4
SCENIC PL STP 109-A4
SCENIC PL SVW 79-E1
SCENIC RD MTK 118-D4
SCENIC HEIGHTS DR MTK 118-C3
SCENIC HEIGHTS RD EPR 132-C3
SCENIC VIEW DR CHS 145-C2
SCHACHTNER ST SOM 70-B4
SCHADT DR MPW 123-B3
SCHAEFER CIR EDI 119-D3
SCHAEFER RD EDI 119-C3
SCHALLER DR MPW 123-B2
SCHANDEL LAKE DR GRF 74-E2,75-A2
SCHANNO PL COR 75-C1
SCHAPER RD GV 105-E2,106-A2
SCHARBER ST ROG 61-E1,62-A1
SCHEEL DR WBY 109-C4,123-C1
SCHEELE AVE HBG 156-A2
SCHEFFER AVE STP 121-D2,122-A2
SCHERERS LN STP 108-E2
SCHEUNEMAN RD GL 94-E1
SCHEUNEMANN AVE STP 107-D4
SCHEY DR EDI 133-D1
SCHIFSKY RD SVW 79-E3,80-A3
SCHILLING CIR NW FL 39-B3
SCHINDLERS XING CHS 145-B1
SCHJELMILE DR NFD 219-D3
SCHLAVIN CT LL 65-E4,79-E1
SCHLETTI ST STP 108-A2
SCHLETTY DR LC 94-C3
SCHLETTY LN WSP 122-D3
SCHLEY AVE WSP 122-B2
SCHLOMKA RD MPW 123-B3
SCHMAHL AVE CNC 12-E3
SCHMIDT RD FAT 42-B2
SCHMIDT LAKE RD PLY 90-D2,91-B2
SCHNEIDER CT CHS 131-B4
SCHOEN LN VER 179-D2
SCHOMMER DR HUT 112-B1
SCHOOL AVE EXC 117-E3
SCHOOL BLVD MO 31-D3
SCHOOL DR WBY 123-C1
SCHOOL RD CP 65-D4
SCHOOL RD EDI 119-E4
SCHOOL RD EPR 132-D2
SCHOOL RD LND 12-D4
SCHOOL ST ANO 49-D4
SCHOOL ST E SWR 97-A1
SCHOOL ST NW ER 33-E1
SCHOOL ST W SWR 97-A1
SCHOOL HOUSE CIR SWR 96-C1
SCHOOLCRAFT RD BUR 148-E2
SCHOOLMASTER CIR CHS 145-B1
SCHOOLMASTER DR CHS 145-B1
SCHOOLMASTER RD CHS 145-B1
SCHOONER CT WBY 124-A1
SCHOONER WAY WBY 124-A1
SCHROEDER CIR NE PRL 161-A2
SCHROEDER PL EPR 118-B4
SCHROEDER FARM RD EPR 132-B2
SCHUBERT DR BUF 59-A2
SCHULENBERG ALY SWR 83-A4
SCHULLER CT CHS 131-D4
SCHULLERS CIR GV 105-D2
SCHULTZ AVE CNC 12-E3
SCHULTZ LAKE BEACH RD EAG 150-A2
SCHUMACHER PL COR 75-A4
SCHUMACHER RD SSP 137-A1
SCHUTTA RD SVW 79-C2
SCHUTTE CT COR 76-A1
SCHUTTE LN COR 76-A1
SCHUTTE PL COR 76-A2
SCHUTTE RD COR 76-A2
SCHUTTE FARM RD COR 76-A1
SCIENCE CENTER DR NH 91-C2
SCIMED PL N MG 76-D2
SCIOTA TRL SIT 206-D4,220-C1
SCIOTA TRL STN 206-E4,207-B4
SCOT TER EPR 133-A1
SCOTCH PINE CT EPR 133-B3
SCOTCH PINE CT NO 80-A3
SCOTCH PINE LN NO 80-A3
SCOTCH PINE LN ORO 103-D4
SCOTCH PINE RD NO 80-A3
SCOTIA DR EDI 133-D1
SCOTLAND CT MV 79-B2
SCOTT AVE N BC 77-E4,91-E1
SCOTT AVE N BP 77-E3
SCOTT AVE N CRY 91-E2
SCOTT AVE N GV 91-E4,105-E1
SCOTT AVE N ROB 91-E3
SCOTT BLVD S CG 137-C3
SCOTT CIR BEL 186-A2
SCOTT CT MTK 118-E3
SCOTT DR MTA 102-C4
SCOTT LN BEL 186-A2
SCOTT LN JOR 173-B2
SCOTT LN WAC 129-D2
SCOTT LN WSP 122-C4
SCOTT LN E CHS 145-B1
SCOTT LN W CHS 145-B1
SCOTT RD HUT 98-C4
SCOTT RD SJT 98-C3
SCOTT ST BUR 162-B1
SCOTT ST GRF 74-C1
SCOTT ST SHK 146-B3
SCOTT ST N SHK 146-B2
SCOTT ST S SHK 146-B2
SCOTT TER EDI 120-A2
SCOTT TER LES 212-D3
SCOTT TRL EAG 149-B2
SCOUT CIR BUR 148-E2
SCOUT RIDGE RD STN 207-E4
SCRIVER RD EDI 119-D3
SCUDDER ST STP 107-C2
SEA ST NE MV 79-B1
SEABURY AVE MPL 107-A3
SEABURY RD MOU 117-A2
SEAGULL CIR PRL 161-B2
SEAL ST STP 107-B3
SEAMANS DR SWD 117-C4
SEAN CT EAG 149-E2
SEANS WAY NSP 95-A3
SEARLE AVE STP 108-C2
SEARLE CT VH 94-C2
SEARLE ST N MPW 94-C4
SEASHELL LN WAC 129-C2
SEASONS CT WBY 123-E1
SEASONS PKWY WBY 123-E1
SEATON PL MTK 118-D2
SECOND AVE S HOP 119-C2
SECOND ST N HOP 119-B2
SECOND ST NE HOP 119-C2
SECOND ST S EDI 119-C2
SECOND ST S HOP 119-B2
SECRETARIAT DR SHK 146-D3
SEDUM LN EDI 134-A1
SEELEY ST S SWR 96-E1
SEELYE BROOK DR NW SF 7-B3
SELBY AVE SPP 137-C3
SELBY AVE STP 107-D4,108-A4
SELKIRK AVE BUR 149-A2
SELKIRK DR BUR 149-A2
SELKIRK PL BUR 149-A2
SELMA LN STP 121-E3
SEMINARY AVE STP 107-E3
SEMINARY DR NB 93-A1
SEMINOL AVE OSC 27-E4,28-A4
SEMINOL AVE OST 28-B4
SEMINOLE AVE STP 122-B2
SEMINOLE AVE WSP 122-B2
SEMRUD CIR MTK 118-D2
SENATOR DR SLW 172-E3,173-A4
SENECA PT EPR 132-B2
SENECA RD EAG 135-B4
SENECA TRL WBT 80-E3
SENJA CT EAG 149-C3
SEPPALA BLVD NSP 95-B4
SEQUOIA BAY WBY 124-A3
SEQUOIA CIR EPR 118-D4
SEQUOIA CT BUR 149-A3
SEQUOIA CT WBY 123-E2
SEQUOIA DR EAG 149-D2
SEQUOIA DR MTK 118-C3
SEQUOIA RD WBY 123-E2,124-A3
SERENDIPITY CT NB 79-A4
SERENDIPITY RD CFT 222-C3
SERENE CT SVW 79-E2
SERENITY CIR BUF 58-D2
SERPENTINE CIR EAG 149-C1
SERPENTINE DR EAG 149-C1
SERVICE DR AND 50-B3
SERVICE DR CHN 145-E2
SERVICE DR EAG 150-A3
SERVICE RD AH 79-C4
SERVICE RD ANO 49-B3
SERVICE RD APV 163-B2
SERVICE RD BUR 148-C3,162-D1
SERVICE RD EPR 132-D2
SERVICE RD FRI 78-D3
SERVICE RD LL 66-E3
SERVICE RD MPW 94-B4
SERVICE RD SLP 119-E2
SERVICE RD WSP 122-C4
SERVICE RD W EAG 135-E2
SETH ST OSC 28-B4
SETON CT HAS 166-B2
SETTER CIR MOU 116-D2
SETTLEMENT DR EPR 132-B4
SETTLERS AVE SWR 96-C2
SETTLERS CT MED 90-A1
SETTLERS RD MED 90-A1
SETTLERS WAY EPR 132-C2
SETTLERS WAY SWR 96-C1
SETZLER CT N BP 77-D1
SETZLER PKWY N BP 77-D1
SEVEN ACRES ST PRL 161-C2
SEVEN OAKS CT MTK 118-E3
SEVENTH AVE N GV 105-C2
SEVENTH AVE N HOP 119-B2
SEVENTH AVE S HOP 119-B2
SEVENTH ST S EDI 119-C2
SEVENTH ST S HOP 119-B2
SEVERANCE HALL NFD 219-E3
SEVERN WAY EAG 150-B1
SEXTANT AVE MPW 94-E4
SEXTANT AVE E LC 94-C4
SEXTANT AVE N LC 94-C4
SEXTANT AVE S MPW 94-D4
SEXTANT AVE W RVL 93-E4,94-A4
SEYMOUR AVE NW ER 33-D1
SEYMOUR AVE SE MPL 107-B3
SEYMOUR DR MTK 118-C3
SEYMOUR ST NW ER 19-D4
SHAD AVE CV 66-D2
SHADOW CT LL 66-B3
SHADOW LN CHN 117-E4
SHADOW LN CHS 131-E4
SHADOW LN NO 80-B2
SHADOW CREEK DR N MG 76-D2
SHADOW CREEK RD N MG 76-D2
SHADOW CREEK TRL WBY 124-A2
SHADOW LAKE CT E LL 66-B3
SHADOW LAKE DR E LL 66-B3
SHADOW LAKE DR W LL 66-B3
SHADOW POND CIR EPR 133-C4
SHADOW WOOD CT CHS 131-E4
SHADOW WOOD DR HSN 47-E3
SHADOWMERE TER CHN 132-A1
SHADOWOOD LN DEL 87-E3
SHADOWOOD RD ORO 103-D1
SHADY AVE N SHT 13-D3
SHADY AVE N VER 179-D2

SHADY CIR BKR 17-C3
SHADY LN BL 17-E3
SHADY LN BLT 18-C3
SHADY LN BUR 162-B1
SHADY LN LAT 201-D4
SHADY LN LTT 131-A4
SHADY LN MTA 116-E3
SHADY LN NYA 142-C3
SHADY LN SWD 118-B3
SHADY LN WBL 81-A4
SHADY LN E WAY 104-C3
SHADY LN N MTK 118-B2
SHADY LN S MTK 118-B2
SHADY WAY CP 65-D3
SHADY BEACH CIR IND 88-D1
SHADY BEACH TRL PRL 161-C1
SHADY CREEK CIR WIN 99-B3
SHADY CREEK DR WIN 99-B3
SHADY DALE RD MTK 119-A2
SHADY HILLS CIR SWD 118-B3
SHADY HILLS RD SWD 118-B3
SHADY ISLAND CIR SWD 117-B3
SHADY ISLAND PT SWD 117-B3
SHADY ISLAND RD SWD 117-B3
SHADY ISLAND TRL SWD 117-B3
SHADY OAK CIR DEL 87-E2
SHADY OAK CIR MO 31-E3
SHADY OAK CT CHM 63-B3
SHADY OAK CT VH 94-D2
SHADY OAK DR MTK 119-A2
SHADY OAK DR WSP 122-B4
SHADY OAK LN MTK 119-A2
SHADY OAK LN SFT 171-E1,172-A1
SHADY OAK RD EPR 119-B4,133-C1
SHADY OAK RD HOP 119-B2
SHADY OAK RD MTK 119-A1
SHADY OAK TRL N SHT 13-D1
SHADY POINT RD LTT 131-A4
SHADY SIDE CIR HOP 119-C1
SHADY WOOD LN DEL 87-E2
SHADY WOODS RD DWD 81-D3
SHADYSIDE LN WBT 81-B2
SHADYVIEW CIR PLY 104-C1
SHADYVIEW CT N MG 76-B2
SHADYVIEW LN N DAY 48-B2
SHADYVIEW LN N MG 76-B2
SHADYVIEW LN N PLY 90-B4,104-B1
SHADYWAY RD WAY 104-C2
SHADYWOOD RD ORO 103-B4,117-C1
SHADYWOOD RD SPR 117-B1
SHAKESPEARE BLVD LVL 177-B3
SHAKOPEE AVE SHK 146-A2
SHAKOPEE AVE E SHK 146-C2
SHAKOPEE AVE W SHK 146-B2
SHALE LN EAG 149-B2
SHAMROCK CIR BEL 186-A2
SHAMROCK CIR DWD 81-C2
SHAMROCK DR ARL 183-A2
SHAMROCK DR MHT 95-C1
SHAMROCK DR SA 93-B2
SHAMROCK TRL EPR 132-C2
SHAMROCK WAY MHT 95-C1
SHANE DR EDI 133-D1
SHANE PARK CIR PRE 153-B4
SHANNON ALC WBY 123-E1
SHANNON CIR EDI 133-D1
SHANNON CIR PRL 161-C2
SHANNON CT EPR 133-B3
SHANNON CT HUD 111-E1
SHANNON CT WBY 123-E1
SHANNON DR EDI 133-D1
SHANNON DR HAS 166-E3
SHANNON DR WBY 123-E1
SHANNON DR N JT 146-B4
SHANNON DR S JT 146-B4
SHANNON LN BEL 186-A2
SHANNON LN COR 76-B1
SHANNON LN MOU 117-A2
SHANNON LN PRL 161-C2
SHANNON PKWY RMT 149-E4,163-E2
SHANNON TRL SE PRL 161-C2
SHARI ANN LN BP 78-A3
SHARON AVE SE MPL 107-B3
SHARON LN BUR 162-B2
SHARON LN WBL 80-E3
SHARON PKWY S SHK 146-D3
SHARON RD MTK 118-B4
SHARONDALE AVE RVL 107-C1
SHARONS WAY CGT 12-B4
SHASTA AVE ANO 49-B3
SHASTA CIR E CHN 118-B4
SHASTA CIR W CHN 118-B4
SHASTA CT APV 149-A4
SHASTA DR HUD 111-E4
SHAUGHNESSY AVE LOL 103-D2
SHAUGHNESSY RD EDI 133-D2
SHAVERS LN DPH 104-B4
SHAVERS LN WDL 104-C4
SHAVERS LAKE DR DPH 118-C1
SHAVERS LAKE RD DPH 118-C1
SHAW AVE ANO 49-B4
SHAWMUT ST S SHK 146-C3
SHAWNEE CIR EDI 133-C1
SHAWNEE DR NSP 95-B3
SHAWNEE LN BUR 162-B1
SHAWNEE LN CHN 132-A1
SHAWNEE RD EAG 135-B4
SHAWNEE TRL E SHK 146-C2
SHAWNEE WOODS RD MED 90-A1
SHAY ST SOM 70-B4
SHEA CIR BEL 185-E2
SHEA ST BEL 185-E2,186-A2
SHEFFIELD CIR BLO 133-E3
SHEFFIELD CIR EAG 149-C3
SHEFFIELD CIR N MTK 105-A4
SHEFFIELD CIR S MTK 105-A4
SHEFFIELD CRV MTK 105-A4
SHEFFIELD CT BUR 148-E4
SHEFFIELD DR WBY 124-A2
SHEFFIELD LN BUR 148-E4
SHEFFIELD LN EAG 149-C3
SHEFFIELD LN EPR 118-C4
SHEFFIELD LN MAY 69-C2
SHEFFIELD LN N MG 76-E3
SHEILA DR ARL 183-A2
SHELARD PKWY SLP 105-B3
SHELBY LN SLW 173-A4
SHELBY PL STP 121-D3
SHELDAHL RD NFD 219-E3
SHELDON AVE EPR 132-D2
SHELDON ST FH 107-D1
SHELDON ST RVL 93-D3
SHELDON ST STP 107-D2
SHELDON ST SVW 79-D2
SHELLY LN BUR 162-B1
SHELTER GRV EPR 147-C1
SHELTON DR SWR 96-E2,97-A2
SHENANDOAH BLVD NW CR 50-B4,64-B1
SHENANDOAH CT PLY 90-D4,104-D1
SHENANDOAH DR SHK 146-C2
SHENANDOAH LN N MG 76-D3
SHENANDOAH LN N PLY 90-D4,104-D1
SHENANDOAH RD NE EB 9-C4
SHENANDOAH ST HL 51-C3
SHENANDOAH ST NE ATT 9-C2
SHENANDOAH ST NE HL 37-C3,51-C3
SHENENDOAH CIR CHN 132-A1
SHEPARD CIR N CHM 63-E2
SHEPARD LN CHM 63-E2
SHEPARD RD STP 121-D3,122-B1
SHEPHEDIA CT WAT 101-B4
SHEPHERD CT CP 65-E3
SHEPHERD WAY EPR 132-C3
SHEPHERD HILLS CIR BLO 134-B3
SHEPHERD HILLS DR BLO 134-A3
SHERBURN AVE BL 17-E4,18-A4
SHERBURNE AVE BEC 2-E4,16-E1
SHERBURNE AVE STP 107-D4,108-A4
SHERBURNE AVE N CRY 91-D2
SHERBURNE CIR BEC 2-E3
SHERBURNE ST N SWR 96-E1
SHERBURNE ST S SWR 96-E1
SHERI LN MON 72-C4,86-C1
SHERIDAN AVE BUR 148-B3
SHERIDAN AVE STP 121-C3
SHERIDAN AVE N BP 78-B2
SHERIDAN AVE N MPL 92-B3,106-B1
SHERIDAN AVE S BLO 134-B2,148-B1
SHERIDAN AVE S MPL 106-B3,120-B3
SHERIDAN AVE S RCH 120-B4,134-B1
SHERIDAN LN EPR 132-E2
SHERIDAN PL BLO 134-B2
SHERIDAN TER MTK 104-D3
SHERIDAN HILLS CRV MTK 104-D4
SHERIDAN HILLS RD MTK 104-D3
SHERIDAN SPUR RD MTK 104-D3
SHERMAN AVE E WIN 99-B4
SHERMAN AVE W WIN 99-B4
SHERMAN CIR EDI 119-D3
SHERMAN CT EAG 135-D3
SHERMAN DR EPR 133-B4
SHERMAN LN HUT 98-A4
SHERMAN RD HUT 98-A4,112-A1
SHERMAN ST STP 122-B1
SHERMAN WAY HAS 166-C3
SHERMAN LAKE CIR LL 66-D3
SHERMAN LAKE CT LL 66-D3
SHERMAN LAKE RD LL 66-D3
SHERMAN OAKS RD N STA 11-B3
SHERREN AVE MPW 94-E4
SHERREN AVE RVL 93-E4
SHERREN ST RVL 93-E4
SHERRIE LN LTT 130-A3
SHERRIE LN WBY 109-C4
SHERRY CT LC 94-C3
SHERWOOD AVE EDI 119-E4
SHERWOOD AVE STP 108-C2,109-A2
SHERWOOD BLF EPR 132-C3
SHERWOOD CIR BLO 148-B2
SHERWOOD CIR WBY 123-C3
SHERWOOD CT CP 65-D4
SHERWOOD CT EAG 149-C3
SHERWOOD CT MTK 105-A3
SHERWOOD CT WBY 123-D3
SHERWOOD CT WSP 122-B4
SHERWOOD DR LES 212-D4
SHERWOOD DR MOU 116-E1
SHERWOOD DR MTK 105-A3
SHERWOOD DR SAV 161-D1
SHERWOOD ECHO WBY 123-D3
SHERWOOD LN LL 66-A1
SHERWOOD LN MTK 105-A3
SHERWOOD PL BUR 162-D2
SHERWOOD PL MTK 105-A3
SHERWOOD PL MV 79-A2
SHERWOOD RD EDI 119-E3
SHERWOOD RD MTK 118-C3
SHERWOOD RD MV 79-B2
SHERWOOD RD SVW 79-E1,80-A1
SHERWOOD RD WBT 80-B1
SHERWOOD RD WBY 123-D3
SHERWOOD ST N CHM 63-C1
SHERWOOD WAY EAG 149-C3
SHERWOOD HILLS CIR MTK 105-A4
SHERWOOD HILLS RD MTK 105-A4
SHETLAND CIR EPR 132-D4
SHETLAND RD EPR 132-D3
SHEVLIN CT EAG 149-C3
SHEVLIN DR ORO 103-D3
SHIELDS AVE STP 107-D4
SHIELDS DR EAG 135-D3
SHILOH CT EPR 132-E3
SHINGLE CREEK DR BP 77-D3
SHINGLE CREEK DR MPL 92-C2
SHINGLE CREEK DR N BP 77-D2
SHINGLE CREEK PKWY BC 78-B4,92-B1
SHINGLE CREEK PL BP 77-D3
SHIRLEE LN SVW 79-E4,93-E1
SHIRLEE LN N SVW 79-E4,93-E1
SHIRLEE LN S SVW 93-E1
SHIRLEY CIR LVL 162-C4,176-C1
SHIRLEY DR BUR 162-B1
SHIRLEY LN LVL 162-C4,176-C1
SHIRLEY PL CRY 91-D1
SHORE AVE E MHT 81-D4
SHORE BLVD S WBL 81-B4,95-B1
SHORE DR CHN 117-C4
SHORE DR N GRF 74-D4
SHORE DR N ORO 103-C4
SHORE DR W NO 80-C3
SHORE LN PRL 161-B2
SHORE RD SWD 118-A3
SHORE TRL PRL 161-B2
SHORE ACRES DR BL 18-A3
SHORE ACRES DR N BL 18-A3
SHORELINE BLVD MOU 116-E1,117-A1
SHORELINE BLVD PRL 160-E4
SHORELINE BLVD SLT 160-D4
SHORELINE DR EPR 132-C2
SHORELINE DR HWL 85-A1
SHORELINE DR ORO 117-C1
SHORELINE DR ROB 92-A3
SHORELINE DR SPR 117-B1
SHORELINE DR N MTB 117-D1
SHORELINE DR N ORO 103-E4,104-A3
SHORELINE DR N WAY 104-A3
SHORELINE DR W WCT 129-C1
SHORELINE LN AH 93-E2
SHORELINE LN SLT 160-D4
SHORELINE PL SPR 117-B1
SHORES BLVD MTK 104-C4,118-C1
SHORES DR BC 92-A1
SHORESIDE CIR SAV 161-D1
SHORESIDE CT SAV 161-D1
SHOREVIEW AVE MPL 120-E3,121-A3
SHOREVIEW CT CHN 132-B3
SHOREVIEW RD ROB 92-A3
SHOREVIEW PARK RD SVW 94-A2
SHOREWOOD CRV RVL 93-C3
SHOREWOOD DR AH 93-C2
SHOREWOOD LN MOU 103-A4,117-A1
SHOREWOOD LN RVL 93-C3
SHOREWOOD LN SWD 117-D3
SHOREWOOD TRL MED 90-A1
SHOREWOOD OAKS DR SWD 117-C4
SHORT ST BKR 4-A4
SHORT ST CV 66-D3
SHORT ST RF 140-E3
SHORT ST STP 108-D4
SHORT ST WBT 81-A2
SHORTLINE EAG 150-A1
SHORTY ST CW 1-B3
SHOSHONE RD NSP 95-B3
SHOSHONI TRL APV 149-A4
SHRYER AVE E MPW 108-D1
SHRYER AVE E NSP 109-B1
SHRYER AVE W RVL 107-E1,108-A1
SHUMWAY ST N SHK 146-B2
SHUMWAY ST S SHK 146-B2
SIBLEY AVE DPH 118-B2
SIBLEY CIR CAR 159-A1
SIBLEY CT BUR 148-E2
SIBLEY CT EAG 149-A1
SIBLEY CT MH 122-B4
SIBLEY DR BUR 148-E2
SIBLEY DR NFD 219-E4
SIBLEY ST BUR 148-A3
SIBLEY ST CAR 159-A1
SIBLEY ST HAS 166-D1
SIBLEY ST RAN 207-A3
SIBLEY ST STP 108-C4
SIBLEY ST NE MPL 106-D1
SIBLEY ST S SHK 146-C3
SIBLEY HILLS DR EAG 135-C2
SIBLEY MEMORIAL HWY EAG 135-B4,149-B1
SIBLEY MEMORIAL HWY LIL 121-E3,122-A3
SIBLEY MEMORIAL HWY MEN 121-D4
SIBLEY MEMORIAL HWY MH 121-D4,135-D1
SICARD LN SPT 70-D3
SICORA LN COR 61-D4
SIDE LN COR 62-A4
SIDNEY PL MPL 107-B3
SIDNEY ST E STP 122-C2
SIDNEY ST W STP 122-B2
SIEBEN DR HAS 166-C3
SIELAFF DR SLW 172-B4,186-B1
SIEMS CT AH 93-D2
SIERRA CIR SWD 118-B4
SIERRA CT BUR 148-E2
SIERRA CT CHN 132-A1
SIERRA CT WBL 95-B1
SIERRA CT WBY 124-A2
SIERRA DR WBL 95-A1
SIERRA PKWY BP 78-B3
SIERRA PKWY WAC 129-D4
SIERRA PKWY N BP 78-B2
SIERRA RD WBY 123-E2,124-A2
SIERRA TRL CHN 132-A1
SIERRA TRL EPR 132-B4
SIEVERTS LN NE FRI 79-A3
SIGFRID ST E EAG 149-D2
SIGNAL PT EAG 149-D1
SIGNE ST LND 12-D3
SIGRID DR BUF 58-E3
SIGURD ST STP 108-E4
SILVER LN NB 93-B2
SILVER LN SA 93-A2
SILVER BELL CIR EAG 135-C4
SILVER BELL RD EAG 135-B4
SILVER FOX RD WBT 81-B1
SILVER LAKE CT SA 93-A2
SILVER LAKE RD NB 93-A1
SILVER LAKE RD SA 93-A3
SILVER LAKE RD NW MV 79-A2
SILVER LAKE RD NW NB 79-A4,93-A1
SILVER LAKE TER SA 93-A2
SILVER LAKE TRL SWD 118-B4
SILVER MAPLE CIR MTK 119-A3
SILVER MEADOW DR ORO 103-D2
SILVER VIEW DR ORO 103-D2
SILVEROD CT NW AND 49-E3
SILVEROD ST NW AND 35-E3,49-E1
SILVEROD ST NW CR 49-E4,63-E1
SILVEROD ST NW OG 21-E4,35-E1
SILVEROD ST NW SF 7-E4
SILVERTHORN CT SVW 79-D2
SILVERTHORN DR SVW 79-D2
SILVERTHORN PL SVW 79-D2
SILVERWOOD ALC WBY 123-E1
SILVERWOOD BAY WBY 123-E1
SILVERWOOD CT WBY 123-E1
SILVERWOOD DR EPR 133-A4,147-A1
SILVERWOOD RD WBY 123-E1
SIMARD ST MH 122-B2
SIMCOE ST STP 108-B3
SIMMON ST FAT 42-B1
SIMMON ST OST 28-B4,42-B1
SIMON AVE STP 108-A3
SIMONE CT NFD 219-D3
SIMONET DR NW ER 33-C1
SIMONS DR CHS 131-D4
SIMONSON RD SCF 14-D2
SIMPKINS AVE SW PRL 161-A4
SIMPKINS CIR PRL 161-A4
SIMPKINS DR SW PRL 161-A4
SIMPSON ST FH 107-D1
SIMPSON ST RVL 93-D3,107-D1
SIMPSON ST STP 107-D3
SIMS AVE STP 108-D3,109-A3
SIMS RD NE EB 22-E2,23-A2
SIMS RD NW OG 22-B2
SINCLAIR CT MOU 116-D2
SINCLAIR RD MOU 116-D2
SINGING HILLS DR LON 217-B3
SINGLETREE LN EPR 133-A2
SINNEN CIR CHN 132-B2
SINNEN ST STP 108-D3
SIOUX AVE RW 196-D4
SIOUX BLVD NB 93-B1
SIOUX CT BUR 148-E2
SIOUX CT NB 93-A1
SIOUX DR MED 90-B2
SIOUX LN LL 66-A3
SIOUX TRL EDI 133-C1
SIOUX TRL GRF 74-D4
SIOUX TRL OTS 33-E4
SIOUX TRL NW PRL 160-D2
SIOUX VISTA DR E SLW 172-E1,173-A1
SIOUX VISTA DR W SLW 172-E1,173-A1
SIRETT CT HAS 166-D3
SIX MILE CREEK RD MTA 116-B3
SIXTH AVE N HOP 119-B2
SIXTH AVE N PLY 105-B2
SIXTH AVE S HOP 119-B2
SIXTH ST S HOP 119-B2
SKATER CIR EAG 135-C4
SKATER DR EAG 135-C4
SKI LN NO 80-B3
SKI HILL RD GV 105-E2
SKIBA DR MV 79-B2
SKILES LN AH 93-D2
SKILES LN NEW 137-A1
SKILLMAN AVE NSP 109-B1
SKILLMAN AVE E MPW 108-C1
SKILLMAN AVE W RVL 107-D1,108-A1
SKILLMAN LN NO 80-B3
SKUNK HOLLOW AVE CFT 222-D3
SKUNK HOLLOW AVE LEO 222-D4
SKUNK HOLLOW TRL LEO 222-C4
SKUNK HOLLOW WAY LEO 222-C4
SKY LN EPR 132-C4
SKY HIGH DR NB 93-B2
SKY LINE DR TRT 125-D4
SKY VIEW CT EAG 149-B3
SKYCROFT CIR SA 93-B3
SKYCROFT DR SA 93-B3
SKYHAWK DR WBY 124-B2
SKYLARK CT CG 137-C2
SKYLARK DR NE EB 8-E3
SKYLARK LN EAG 149-C1
SKYLINE AVE PRL 161-A3
SKYLINE CIR LVT 145-D4,159-D1
SKYLINE CIR NMT 190-D4,204-D1
SKYLINE CRV MPL 106-C1
SKYLINE CT EAG 135-C2
SKYLINE DR BLO 134-E3,135-A3
SKYLINE DR BUR 148-E3
SKYLINE DR EAG 135-C2
SKYLINE DR EDI 119-D3
SKYLINE DR GV 106-A1
SKYLINE DR VH 94-B2
SKYLINE DR N BUR 148-E3
SKYLINE DR S BUR 148-E3
SKYLINE PATH EAG 135-C3
SKYLINE RD EAG 135-D2
SKYLINE TRL EAG 135-C2
SKYVIEW CIR MTK 118-D2
SKYVIEW CT SWR 96-D2
SKYVIEW DR BUR 148-B4
SKYVIEW DR CHS 145-C2
SKYVIEW DR MTK 118-D2
SKYVIEW LN CAR 145-B4
SKYVIEW RD MTK 118-D2
SKYWAY RD STP 123-A2
SKYWOOD CT NE FRI 92-E1
SKYWOOD LN NE FRI 92-E1
SLATE AVE SHK 145-E3
SLATER CT EAG 149-A3
SLATER LN BUR 148-C4
SLATER RD EAG 149-A2
SLEEPY HOLW EAG 149-B2
SLEEPY HOLLOW DR NW OG 22-C3
SLEEPY HOLLOW LN EPR 133-A1
SLEEPYHOLLOW RD GRW 118-A2
SLOAN PL MPW 108-C1
SLOAN ST STP 108-C2
SLOAN ST N MPW 94-C4,108-C1
SLOTH ST NW STT 6-C1
SLOUGH TRL RW 182-D4
SLYVAN DR NE EB 37-D2
SMALAND RD VAT 210-A3
SMETANA DR MTK 119-C3
SMETANA LN EPR 133-B2
SMETANA RD MTK 119-B3
SMITH AVE ORO 103-E2
SMITH AVE OSC 28-A4
SMITH AVE WSP 122-B3
SMITH AVE N STP 108-B4,122-B1
SMITH AVE S STP 122-B2
SMITH CIR MPL 106-C2
SMITH CIR MTK 104-D3
SMITH CT ER 34-A2
SMITH DR LVT 159-D2
SMITH DR MTK 118-E2,119-A2
SMITH ST LES 212-C4
SMITH ST NW ER 20-A3
SMITHFIELD CRV WBY 124-B3
SMITHTOWN CIR SWD 117-C3
SMITHTOWN CT VIC 117-B4
SMITHTOWN LN SWD 117-C3
SMITHTOWN RD SWD 117-C3
SMITHTOWN RD TKB 117-D3
SMITHTOWN RD VIC 117-B4,131-A1
SMITHTOWN TER VIC 117-A4
SMITHTOWN WAY SWD 117-C3
SMO DR SOM 70-C4
SMOKETREE LN LL 65-E2
SNAIL LAKE BLVD SVW 80-A4,94-A1
SNAIL LAKE CT E SVW 80-B4
SNAIL LAKE CT S SVW 80-B4
SNAIL LAKE CT W SVW 80-B4
SNAIL LAKE RD SVW 80-A4
SNAPDRAGON DR CHN 131-D2
SNELLING AVE MPL 107-A4,121-A1
SNELLING AVE N AH 79-D4,93-D2
SNELLING AVE N FH 107-D1
SNELLING AVE N RVL 93-D3,107-D1
SNELLING AVE N STP 107-D3,121-D1
SNELLING AVE N SVW 79-D2
SNELLING AVE S STP 121-D2
SNELLING CRV RVL 93-D4
SNELLING DR RVL 93-D3
SNELLING PL STP 121-D3
SNOW RDG LES 212-D4
SNOW GOOSE TRL LL 66-C3
SNOW OWL CIR LL 66-A2
SNOW OWL DR WBY 124-B2
SNOW OWL LN LL 66-A2
SNOWBELL PT EAG 149-C3
SNOWBIRD CIR PRL 161-B2
SNOWBIRD DR RW 210-E1
SNOWDRIFT CIR MPW 123-B2
SNOWFLAKE DR EAG 135-C3
SNOWMASS CIR MTK 105-B4
SNOWSHOE CT MPW 123-B3
SNOWSHOE LN MPW 123-B3
SNOWSHOE LN STP 123-B3
SNOWY OWL LN NO 80-C2
SNYDER RD COR 90-A1
SOCCER FIELD RD HAS 166-E2
SODERVILLE DR NE HL 37-A2
SODIUM ST NW RAM 35-B3,49-B1
SOLBERG ST TRT 112-A4,126-A1
SOMERSET ALC WBY 123-D1
SOMERSET CIR EPR 132-C2
SOMERSET CIR WBY 123-D1
SOMERSET CT MH 122-A3
SOMERSET CT WBY 123-D1

SOMERSET DR WAC 129-D3
SOMERSET KNL HUD 111-E2
SOMERSET KNLS WBY 123-D1
SOMERSET LN ORO 103-C3
SOMERSET RD MH 122-B3
SOMERSET RD WBY 123-D1
SOMMERGATE CHN 117-D4
SOMMERS LNDG N NOH 97-C4
SOMMERS PT N NOH 97-C4
SOMMERS ST N NOH 111-C1
SOMMERVILLE ST S SHK 146-B2
SOO AVE N MPL 92-C3
SOO LN BUF 58-E2
SOO ST SVW 94-B2
SOO LINE PL CRY 91-D2
SOO LINE RD DRS 28-D2
SOO LINE RD TRT 126-B2
SOPHIA AVE HBG 156-A2
SOPHIA AVE MPW 108-D1
SOREL ST CV 66-D2
SORELL AVE N GV 105-E1,106-A1
SORENSON CT RF 140-E3
SORENSON ST RF 140-E3
SORREL PT EAG 149-C3
SORREL WAY EPR 132-E3
SOUTH AVE CHC 26-B1
SOUTH AVE OSC 28-A4
SOUTH AVE E NSP 95-B4
SOUTH CIR HL 50-E3
SOUTH CIR NE FRI 78-E2
SOUTH DR CP 65-E3
SOUTH DR EDI 119-D3
SOUTH DR NE HL 37-C2
SOUTH LN MH 122-A4
SOUTH LN MTK 118-B3
SOUTH RD CP 65-E3
SOUTH ST ANO 63-D1
SOUTH ST CR 63-D1
SOUTH ST HEN 198-D4
SOUTH ST MON 86-C1
SOUTH ST MTK 118-E3
SOUTH ST NYA 142-C3
SOUTH ST PRE 167-B1
SOUTH ST SLP 119-D1
SOUTH ST E BEL 185-E2,186-A2
SOUTH ST E DRS 28-D2
SOUTH ST E NYA 142-C4
SOUTH ST E SSP 136-E1
SOUTH ST N NOH 111-C1
SOUTH ST W BEL 185-E2
SOUTH ST W DRS 28-D2
SOUTH ST W NYA 142-C4
SOUTH ST W SSP 136-E1
SOUTH BAVARIAN PASS NE FRI 93-A1
SOUTH BAY CRV EPR 132-C2
SOUTH COON CREEK
DR NW AND 49-E2,50-A2
SOUTH DEEP LAKE RD NO 80-C2
SOUTH ENCHANTED
DR NW AND 35-D4
SOUTH FORK DR RF 140-E2
SOUTH GLEN TRL LL 66-A4
SOUTH GLOVER RD TRT 126-C4
SOUTH HAM LAKE DR NE HL 51-A1
SOUTH HEIGHTS DR NW CR 64-A2
SOUTH HILL DR N RVL 94-A4
SOUTH HILLS CIR EAG 136-A4
SOUTH HILLS CT EAG 136-A4
SOUTH HILLS DR EAG 136-A4
SOUTH HILLS LN EAG 136-A4
SOUTH HILLS WAY EAG 136-A4
SOUTH ILWACO RD TRT 139-C1
SOUTH LAKE
GEORGE DR NW OG 22-A3
SOUTH LINWOOD
DR NE LWT 23-E2,24-A3
SOUTH LONG LAKE TRL NO 80-B2
SOUTH MAPLEBROOK CIR BP 77-D2
SOUTH OBERLIN CIR NE FRI 93-A1
SOUTH PARK CIR SAV 161-E2
SOUTH PARK CT HAS 166-D3
SOUTH PARK CT SAV 162-A2
SOUTH PARK DR HAS 166-D3
SOUTH PARK LN N BP 77-C3
SOUTH PARK PL HAS 166-D3
SOUTH PLAZA DR MH 122-A4
SOUTH POINTE DR HAS 166-C3
SOUTH RIDGE CT RIT 140-E3
SOUTH RIDGE RD RIT 140-E3
SOUTH SHORE CIR WIN 99-B4
SOUTH SHORE CT CHN 132-B2
SOUTH SHORE DR CHN 132-B2
SOUTH SHORE DR EPR 132-C1
SOUTH SHORE DR FL 39-C3
SOUTH SHORE DR MDL 105-B1
SOUTH SHORE DR PLY 105-B1
SOUTH SHORE DR SLT 160-E4
SOUTH SHORE DR WIN 99-B4
SOUTH SHORE LN EPR 132-C1
SOUTH VALLEY DR JOR 173-B2
SOUTH VIEW RD RIT 140-E3
SOUTH WACONIA CIR NE EB 9-B4
SOUTHAMPTON DR BUR 162-D2
SOUTHBRIDGE PKWY SHK 147-B3
SOUTHBROOK DR BLO 134-B4
SOUTHCREST AVE MPW 123-B3
SOUTHCREST DR EDI 119-E4,133-E1
SOUTHCROSS DR W BUR 162-D2
SOUTHCROSS LN BUR 162-D2
SOUTHDALE CIR EDI 120-B4
SOUTHDALE RD EDI 120-A4,134-A1
SOUTHERN CT CHN 131-D1
SOUTHERN OAKS CIR NMT 190-B3
SOUTHERN OAKS DR NMT 190-B3
SOUTHERN PACIFIC RD TRT 126-B2
SOUTHFORK DR CRT 175-D2
SOUTHGATE CT NFD 219-D4
SOUTHGATE DR BUF 58-E3
SOUTHGLEN DR BLO 134-C4
SOUTHLAWN DR MPW 94-E3,95-A3
SOUTHMORE DR BLO 134-A3
SOUTHPOINTE CRV BUR 162-C2
SOUTHPOINTE CT BUR 162-C2
SOUTHPOINTE CT NO 80-A3
SOUTHPOINTE TER EAG 149-B1
SOUTHRIDGE AVE EAG 135-D2
SOUTHRIDGE CT MTK 118-C2
SOUTHRIDGE RD MTK 104-E3,105-A3
SOUTHRIDGE RD RF 140-E3
SOUTHTOWN DR BLO 134-B2
SOUTHVIEW BLVD SSP 122-D4
SOUTHVIEW CT HAS 166-C2
SOUTHVIEW DR ANO 63-D1
SOUTHVIEW DR BUR 149-A2
SOUTHVIEW DR HAS 166-C3
SOUTHVIEW LN EDI 119-E3
SOUTHVIEW LN MOU 116-D1
SOUTHVIEW LN OST 28-E2
SOUTHVIEW PL HAS 166-C3
SOUTHVIEW ST SE WAT 101-B4
SOUTHWIND DR BUR 162-D2
SOUTHWIND DR MPW 109-A1
SOUTHWIND LN MPW 109-A1
SOUTHWIND LN WSP 122-B3
SOUTHWIND RD MPW 109-A1
SOUTHWOOD DR BLO 133-E3
SOUTHWOOD DR CF 222-B1
SOUTHWOOD DR DEL 87-E3
SOUTHWOOD DR VH 94-B1
SOUTHWOOD DR WBL 95-A1
SPAIN PL MPL 92-D3
SPANISH OAK OKD 95-D4
SPANISH TER COR 61-D4
SPANISH OAK ST OKD 95-D3
SPARRE RD NW BT 20-D4
SPARROW LN NO 80-C3
SPARROW RD MOU 117-A1
SPARROW RD MTK 118-B2
SPARROW RD WAC 129-D4
SPATES AVE ORO 103-D4
SPATES AVE RW 196-E4
SPEAR ST LSC 125-C1
SPENCER RD W STP 107-D3
SPENCER ST N SHK 146-B2
SPENCER ST S SHK 146-B2
SPENSER SWEET PEA LN EPR 133-A3
SPERL ST WSP 122-C2
SPINAKER CIR WBY 124-A2
SPINAKER DR WBY 124-A2
SPINAKER LN WBY 124-A2
SPIRAL BLVD HAS 166-E3
SPIRAL CT HAS 166-E3
SPIRIT DR NSP 95-A3
SPIRIT HILLS LN NSP 95-A4
SPIRIT KNOB RD WDL 104-B4
SPOON RDG EPR 133-B4
SPOONBILL CIR CHN 131-E3
SPOONBILL CIR EAG 135-D4
SPORTS CENTER DR WBL 80-E4
SPORTSMAN RD NE EB 37-D1
SPORTSMANS DR CHC 12-B4,26-B1
SPRAGUE AVE ANO 49-D3
SPRING AVE MP 88-E4,102-E1
SPRING AVE N SHT 13-E1
SPRING AVE SW PRL 161-A4
SPRING CIR MTK 118-D2
SPRING CIR SWD 118-A3
SPRING LN MTK 118-C3
SPRING LN STP 122-B1
SPRING LN WBY 109-E4,123-E1
SPRING RD EPR 132-D4,146-D1
SPRING ST BEL 186-A1
SPRING ST CW 1-B2
SPRING ST HAS 166-D2
SPRING ST MH 122-B2
SPRING ST RF 140-E2
SPRING ST SOM 70-B4,84-B1
SPRING ST SPR 117-B1
SPRING ST N NFD 219-D3
SPRING ST NE MPL 106-E1,107-B1
SPRING ST S NFD 219-D4
SPRING ST W LAU 107-B1
SPRING CREEK CIR MH 122-A4
SPRING CREEK DR DPH 118-B2
SPRING CREEK DR FRI 79-A3
SPRING CREEK DR NB 79-A3
SPRING CREEK RD NFD 219-E4
SPRING CREEK RD NFT 219-E3
SPRING CREST DR MTK 118-B3
SPRING FARM LN NO 80-C3
SPRING GLEN CIR PRL 160-E3
SPRING GREEN LN BUR 162-E2
SPRING HILL BAY WBY 123-E1
SPRING HILL CIR WAC 129-D3
SPRING HILL CT WBY 123-E1
SPRING HILL DR WBY 109-E4,123-E1
SPRING HILL DRAW WBY 123-E1
SPRING HILL RD ORO 103-E1,104-A1
SPRING HILL RD VH 80-C4
SPRING HILL RD WAC 129-D3
SPRING LAKE CIR SLT 174-D1
SPRING LAKE RD MTK 118-E1
SPRING LAKE RD MV 79-A2
SPRING LAKE RD SLK 79-A2
SPRING LAKE RD SW PRL 160-E4
SPRING MARSH LN NO 80-A3
SPRING VALLEY CIR BLO 148-C1
SPRING VALLEY CIR GV 106-A1
SPRING VALLEY DR BLO 148-C1
SPRING VALLEY RD GV 105-E1,106-A1
SPRING VALLEY RD LTT 130-C2
SPRING VIEW ALC WBY 123-E1
SPRING VIEW LN MV 79-A3
SPRING VIEW WAY WBY 109-E4,123-E1
SPRINGBROOK DR NW CR 64-D4,78-D1
SPRINGBROOK LN WBY 123-D2
SPRINGBROOK PL NE FRI 78-C2
SPRINGBROOK PLZ WBY 123-D2
SPRINGFIELD DR CHN 132-B3
SPRINGFIELD ST STP 121-D3
SPRINGHILL CIR EPR 132-D1
SPRINGHILL DR BUR 162-D2
SPRINGHILL RD NW BT 6-E4,7-A4
SPRINGHILL RD NW SF 6-E4
SPRINGS RD SMT 83-B3
SPRINGSIDE DR MPW 123-B2
SPRINGSIDE DR STP 123-A2
SPRINGSIDE LN BLO 134-E3
SPRINGWOOD ALC WBY 123-E3
SPRINGWOOD CIR WBY 123-E3
SPRINGWOOD DR WBY 123-E3
SPRINGWOOD RD MTK 104-D3
SPRUCE AVE N FRT 27-D3
SPRUCE AVE N ML 43-D2
SPRUCE AVE NE BUF 59-A2
SPRUCE CIR JOR 173-B3
SPRUCE CIR PRL 160-E4
SPRUCE CT NFD 219-D4
SPRUCE CT RFD 74-A4
SPRUCE CT ROG 61-E1
SPRUCE CT VIC 131-A3
SPRUCE CT WBL 95-A2
SPRUCE DR APV 162-E2
SPRUCE DR CFT 222-B1
SPRUCE DR HUD 111-D2
SPRUCE LN MTK 104-E4
SPRUCE LN ROG 61-E2
SPRUCE LN SAV 162-A2
SPRUCE PL MPL 106-C3
SPRUCE PL ORO 103-B4
SPRUCE PL WBL 95-A2
SPRUCE PT EAG 135-D4
SPRUCE PT VIC 131-A3
SPRUCE RD EDI 119-C2
SPRUCE RD MOU 116-E1
SPRUCE RD SB 116-A3
SPRUCE ST CHS 145-C3
SPRUCE ST EAG 150-B3
SPRUCE ST FAR 177-E4,178-A4
SPRUCE ST MHT 81-C4
SPRUCE ST RF 140-E3
SPRUCE ST SHK 146-C2
SPRUCE ST STP 108-C4
SPRUCE ST E SSP 136-E1
SPRUCE ST N LC 94-B3
SPRUCE ST N WAC 129-D3
SPRUCE ST S RF 140-E2
SPRUCE ST S WAC 129-D3
SPRUCE ST W SSP 136-E1
SPRUCE TRL EPR 132-B2
SPRUCE TRL GV 106-A1
SPRUCE TRL PRL 160-E4
SPRUCE HILL CT SWD 117-C4
SPRUCE TREE AVE STP 107-D4
SPRUCEWOOD CT MHT 95-C2
SPRUCEWOOD DR WBY 123-C1
SPUR CIR MED 90-B4
SPUR RD EDI 119-E2
SPURLINE CIR HUT 98-B4
SPYGLASS DR EPR 147-A1
SPYGLASS RD DWD 81-C2
SQUARE LAKE TRL N MAY 68-C4,69-B3
SQUARE LAKE TRAIL CT N MAY 68-C4
SQUIRE DR NE FRI 79-A3
SQUIRE LN EPR 133-C4
SQUIRE LN MTA 102-B4
SQUIRE LN MV 79-C2
SQUIRREL LN NO 80-C3
STACKER BLVD WBL 95-B1
STACKER PL WBL 95-B1
STACY CIR WAC 129-D2
STACY CIR WBL 95-C1
STACY LN N LET 11-D3
STACY TRL N CGT 12-B3
STACY TRL N LET 11-D3,12-A3
STACY TRL N LND 12-C3
STACY TRL N STA 11-B3
STAG CIR HUD 111-D2
STAGECOACH PASS EPR 133-B4
STAGECOACH RD SHK 147-C3
STAGECOACH TRL HUT 112-B2
STAGECOACH TRL LL 66-A2
STAGECOACH TRL N BYT 97-B4,111-B1
STAGECOACH TRL N OPH 97-B3
STAGECOACH TRL N WLT 111-B3
STAGECOACH TRL S AFT 111-A4,125-B2
STAGELINE RD HUT 111-E3,112-A3
STAGHORN LN CHN 118-B4
STAGS LEAP RD TRT 125-D1
STALOCH PL SWR 96-D2
STANBRIDGE AVE RVL 93-C3
STANBRIDGE CIR RVL 94-A3
STANBRIDGE ST RVL 93-B3
STANBURRY CRV EPR 132-D3
STANDISH AVE MPL 120-E1
STANDISH ST STP 107-C2
STANDRIDGE AVE MPW 95-B3
STANDRIDGE PL MPW 95-B3
STANFORD AVE STP 121-D1
STANFORD CIR CHS 131-C4
STANFORD CT STP 121-B1
STANFORD ST NE COT 38-D3
STANICH CT MPW 95-A4
STANICH PL MPW 109-A1
STANICH ST MPW 95-A4
STANLEN RD SLP 105-C4
STANLEY AVE SSP 122-D4
STANLEY AVE S BLO 133-E4,147-E2
STANLEY CIR BLO 147-E1
STANLEY CRV BLO 147-E2
STANLEY RD BLO 133-E2,147-E2
STANLEY ST WSP 122-C2
STANLEY TRL EPR 132-D3
STANTON BLVD NFT 219-E3,220-A3
STANTON DR MTK 104-E4,105-A4
STANTON TRL STN 221-E2
STANWICH LN MH 122-A4
STANWIX RD EAG 149-E1
STAPLES AVE MH 122-B3
STAPLES PL SWR 96-C2
STAPLES ST HL 51-B1
STAPLES ST NE EB 9-B4,37-B1
STAPLES ST NE HL 37-B3,51-B3
STAR CIR SWD 117-C3
STAR CIR VH 94-B2
STAR LN SSP 122-D3
STAR LN SWD 117-C3
STAR LN NE FRI 78-D4
STAR ST E ML 43-D2
STAR ST W ML 43-D2
STARBRIDGE CT EAG 149-D1
STARDUST BLVD CP 65-D3
STARING LN E EPR 132-E3
STARING LN W EPR 132-E3
STARING LAKE
PKWY EPR 132-E3,133-A3
STARK DR NW SF 7-D3
STARK ST N LC 94-B4
STARKEY ST ORO 103-C1
STARKEY ST STP 122-C1
STARLIGHT DR WBY 124-A1
STARLING DR MO 31-E3
STARLITE BLVD NE FRI 78-D4
STARLITE CIR NE FRI 78-D3
STARLITE DR HSN 47-E3
STARLITE DR ROG 47-E4
STARLITE SHOPPING CE RD BP 77-D3
STARR WOOD HUT 97-C4
STARRWOOD CIR EPR 132-E3
STARVIEW LN SLT 175-B3
STASSEN DR WSP 122-C3
STASSEN LN WSP 122-D2
STATE AVE ANO 49-C4
STATE AVE N NG 114-A4
STATE AVE S CT 114-A4
STATE AVE S NG 114-A4,128-A1
STATE RD SCF 14-C2
STATE ST BEL 186-A1
STATE ST CHS 145-D2
STATE ST CKP 1-E1,2-A1
STATE ST CLK 1-D1
STATE ST DRS 28-D2
STATE ST HAS 166-C1
STATE ST OSC 28-A4
STATE ST RF 140-D2
STATE ST SJT 97-B1
STATE ST STP 108-C4,122-C1
STATE ST E BEL 185-E1,186-A1
STATE ST E CF 208-B4
STATE ST E SCF 14-C2
STATE ST N BAY 97-B3
STATE ST NE WAT 101-B3
STATE ST NW WAT 101-A3
STATE ST NW WTT 101-A3
STATE ST S BAY 97-B4
STATE ST W BEL 185-E1
STATE ST W CF 208-A4
STATE FARM DR N RVL 93-D4
STATE FARM WAY WBY 109-E4
STATELINE RD TLT 154-E3
STATES AVE EAG 150-A1
STATION CIR N NOH 97-C4
STATION LN N NOH 97-C4
STATION TRL ET 164-C4,178-D1
STATION TRL RMT 164-B3
STAUDER CIR EDI 119-C3
STAVERN PT EAG 149-C2
STEADING RD EPR 132-C2
STEAMBOAT DR RW 210-E1
STEELE ST MTK 118-D1
STEEPLE LN HAS 166-B2
STEEPLEVIEW RD WBY 123-D2
STEER DR WBY 123-C1
STEFAN CIR PRL 161-B3
STEIGER LAKE LN VIC 130-E2,131-A2
STEIN CIR WAC 129-C3
STEIN DR WAC 129-C3
STEINER ST SB 116-B3
STEINMAN RD TRT 126-D4,140-D1
STELLA CT LL 67-A4
STELLA ST STP 107-C2
STELLAR LN EPR 132-D1
STELLAR ST STP 108-B3
STELLER CIR CHN 117-E4
STELLER CT CHN 131-E1
STEPHANI CIR LC 94-B4
STEPHANI CT LC 94-B4
STEPHANIE CIR EAG 135-C2
STEPHANIE WAY IND 88-D1
STEPHEN CIR SVW 80-A1
STEPHEN CT CHS 145-C2
STEPHEN LN CHS 145-C2
STEPHENS DR SLP 105-E3
STERLING AVE NEW 123-B4
STERLING CT MHT 95-C2
STERLING DR BL 17-E2,18-A2
STERLING DR MTA 102-D4
STERLING LN NSP 109-B1
STERLING RD MOU 117-A2
STERLING RD WAC 129-C3
STERLING ST N MPW 109-B2,123-B1
STERLING ST N NSP 109-B1
STERLING ST S MPW 123-B2
STERLING TER EPR 132-C1
STERLING WAY SWR 96-E1
STEVE DR LVT 159-D1
STEVEN LN CV 66-D2
STEVEN LN LVL 162-C4,176-C1
STEVEN RD BUR 162-B1
STEVENS AVE BEC 2-E3
STEVENS AVE BUR 162-D2
STEVENS AVE MPL 106-D4,120-D2
STEVENS AVE RCH 120-D4,134-D1
STEVENS AVE S BLO 134-D3,148-D1
STEVENS CT BUR 162-D2
STEVENS ST HAT 201-C2
STEVENS ST E STP 122-C1
STEVENS ST N FH 107-C2
STEVENS ST SE WAT 101-B4
STEVENS ST SW WAT 101-A3
STEVENS ST W STP 122-B1
STEWART AVE CT 128-D4,142-D1
STEWART AVE SSP 122-E3
STEWART AVE STP 121-D3,122-A2
STEWART AVE WBL 81-B3
STEWART AVE YAT 142-D4,156-D1
STEWART DR EPR 133-A1
STEWART LN MTK 118-E3
STEWART LN SSP 122-E3
STEWART RD WIL 95-D1
STEWARTON DR WBY 123-E1,124-A1
STICKNEY AVE SSP 122-D2
STICKNEY ST STP 122-D2
STIEG RD COR 62-A4
STIEGER LAKE LN VIC 130-E2
STILLWATER AVE MPW 109-B3
STILLWATER AVE STP 108-E3,109-A3
STILLWATER AVE E SWR 83-A4
STILLWATER AVE W SWR 82-E4,83-A4
STILLWATER BLVD N BYT 96-C3
STILLWATER BLVD N LE 109-E1,110-B1
STILLWATER BLVD N OKD 109-C2
STILLWATER BLVD N OPH 96-D3
STILLWATER BLVD N SWR 96-D2
STILLWATER CT WBT 81-A2
STILLWATER LN N LE 110-B1
STILLWATER RD DWD 81-B2
STILLWATER RD MHT 95-D1
STILLWATER RD MPW 109-B3
STILLWATER RD WIL 95-D1
STILLWATER ST WBL 81-B2
STILLWATER ST WBT 80-E3,81-A2
STILLWATER WAY N OKD 109-D1
STINSON AVE CHC 12-B4,26-B1
STINSON BLVD CH 93-A1
STINSON BLVD FRI 79-A3
STINSON BLVD MPL 93-A3
STINSON BLVD NE CH 93-A2
STINSON BLVD NE FRI 79-A4
STINSON BLVD NE MPL 93-A4,107-A1
STINSON CT NB 93-A1
STINSON ST STP 107-E3,108-A3
STIRRUP LN EPR 132-C3
STIRRUP ST EAG 150-A2
STOCKBRIDGE CIR EPR 132-E2
STOCKBRIDGE RD MH 136-A2
STOCKDALE DR VH 94-C1
STOCKDALE RD VH 94-C1
STOCKYARDS RD SSP 122-E4
STODDART CIR WBT 80-D3
STODDART LN WBT 80-D3
STODOLA RD MTK 118-C3
STONE AVE HOT 114-D1
STONE CIR MTK 104-E4
STONE CT IND 88-D4
STONE CT SHK 146-A3
STONE RD MH 136-B1
STONE RD MTK 104-E4,105-A4
STONE ARCH RD WDL 104-C4
STONE BRIDGE BLVD STP 121-C1
STONE BROOK CRV JT 160-B1
STONE BROOKE CRV JT 160-B1
STONE BROOKE CT JT 160-B1
STONE CREEK CT CHN 131-D2
STONE CREEK DR CHN 131-E2
STONE CREEK DR CHS 145-C1
STONE CREEK LN E CHN 131-D2
STONE CREEK LN W CHN 131-D2
STONE CREEK RD CHN 131-D3
STONE MEADOW BLVD SHK 146-A3
STONE MEADOWN BLVD SHK 146-A3
STONE RIDGE TRCE MTK 104-D3

STONE VILLAGE DR BUR 162-C2
STONEBRIDGE CIR EAG 150-A1
STONEBRIDGE CIR MTA 116-E3
STONEBRIDGE CT LIL 121-E3
STONEBRIDGE DR EAG 150-A1
STONEBRIDGE LN LIL 121-E3
STONEBRIDGE RD LIL 121-E3
STONEBRIDGE RD MTA 116-E3
STONEBRIDGE TRL N SWR 82-E4
STONEBRIDGE TRL N SWT .82-E3,83-A2
STONEBROOKE CT WBY 123-E4
STONEBROOKE DR SHK 160-B1
STONEBROOKE TRL WBY 123-E4
STONECLIFF DR EAG 149-D2
STONECROFT LN DPH 118-C1
STONEGATE CT HAS 166-B2
STONEGATE LN MTK 118-E2
STONEGATE RD HAS 166-B2
STONEHAVEN CT ANO 49-C3
STONEPINE AVE HUD 111-E2
STONEPINE BAY HUD 111-D2
STONEPINE CIR HUD 111-D2
STONEPINE CT HUD 111-D2
STONERIDGE CIR MO 31-D3
STONERIDGE CT LC 94-D3
STONERIDGE DR MO 31-D3
STONERIDGE LN MO 31-D3
STONERIDGE RD DAY 48-E3,49-A3
STONEWOOD CT EAG 136-A4
STONEWOOD CT EDI 133-D2
STONEWOOD CT EPR 133-A1
STONEWOOD RD EAG 136-A4
STONEY WAY EPR 147-A1
STONEY BRIDGE CT MTK 118-C3
STONEYBROOK CT MTK 118-D4
STONEYBROOK DR MTK 118-D4
STONY CREEK DR WBY 124-B1
STONY POINT RD EAG ..135-E4,149-E1
STONYBROOK WAY NE FRI 78-D2
STOPPELMANN BLVD BKT 185-C2
STORLAND CT EAG 149-A3
STORLAND RD EAG 149-A3
STORMS CIR SE PRL 161-C2
STOUGHTON AVE CHN 145-E2
STOUGHTON AVE CHS 145-D2
STOUGHTON CT CF 208-B4
STOUGHTON ST CF 208-B4
STOUGHTON ST E CF 208-B4
STOWE AVE AH 93-C2
STOWE AVE NB 93-C2
STRATFORD ALC WBY 123-C3
STRATFORD AVE MV 79-C2
STRATFORD BAY WBY 123-C3
STRATFORD BLVD CHN 131-B1
STRATFORD CT BUR 148-D3
STRATFORD CT WBY 123-C3
STRATFORD CT N BP 78-B1
STRATFORD XING BP 78-B2
STRATFORD DRAW WBY 123-C3
STRATFORD ECHO WBY 123-D3
STRATFORD LN CHN 131-B1
STRATFORD LN EAG 150-B3
STRATFORD LN IGH 150-B2
STRATFORD LN MOU 117-A2
STRATFORD LN E BUR 148-D3
STRATFORD LN N BP 78-B2
STRATFORD LN W BUR 148-D3
STRATFORD PL SWD 117-E4
STRATFORD RD EPR 118-E4
STRATFORD RD MH 121-E4
STRATFORD RD MTK 118-B3
STRATFORD RD WBY 123-C3
STRATFORD RDG CHN 131-B1
STRATTON CIR MTK 104-E4
STRATTON CT CHN 117-E4,118-A4
STRAWBERRY CT SWD 117-C4
STRAWBERRY LN EAG 149-D1
STRAWBERRY LN GV 106-A3
STRAWBERRY LN HUT 111-D2
STRAWBERRY LN SWD 117-C4
STRAWBERRY HILL RD AFT 125-B1
STREAM RD N ORO 104-A1
STREHLER RD COR 75-C2
STRESE CIR APV 163-A2
STRESE LN APV 162-E2,163-A2
STRODEN CIR GV 105-C1
STROH DR STP 108-C3
STROM DR SAV 147-D3
STRONG DR WAC 129-D3
STRUNKS RD JT 145-E3
STRYKER AVE STP 122-C2
STRYKER AVE WSP 122-C2
STUART AVE EDI 119-D3
STUART AVE JOR 173-B3
STUART ST WBT 80-D2
STUBBS BAY RD N ORO 103-C2
STUBBS BAY RD S ORO 103-C2
STUBUR AVE W RVL 108-A1
STUNKS RD LVT 145-C4,159-C1
STURGEON LAKE RD RW 182-D4
STURGIS AVE STP 122-A1
STUTZ ST NE BLA 65-E2
STUTZ ST NE EB 23-E4
STUTZ ST NE HL 37-E3
SUBURBAN AVE STP ...108-D4,109-A4
SUBURBAN DR SWD 118-A3
SUCKER LAKE RD VH 80-B4,94-B1
SUDBERRY LN EAG 150-A2
SUE PL STP 121-C2
SUE ST STP 121-C3
SUE ANN CT EPR 132-D1
SUE ANN LN CRT 161-C3
SUEL CIR CRT 161-C3
SUEL LN CRT 161-C3
SUFFOLK DR CHN 132-A2
SUFFOLK RD MOU 117-A2
SUGAR LN CHS 145-D2
SUGAR LN ROG 61-E1
SUGAR ST ROG 61-E1
SUGAR BUSH RD NW BT 20-D1
SUGAR BUSH TRL N FRT 27-E2
SUGAR HILL CIR EPR 132-B1
SUGARBUSH LN WAC 129-C2
SUGARBUSH RD NW BT 6-C4,20-C1
SUGARBUSH RD NW SF 6-C4
SUGARBUSH TRL WAT 101-B4
SUGARLOAF TRL N BP 78-B3
SUGARWOOD DR ORO 103-D2
SUGERBUSH TRL CHN 132-A3
SUGERBUSH TRL WAT 101-B4
SULGROVE RD MOU 116-E2,117-A2
SULLIVAN DR NE CH 92-D1
SULLIVAN LN CH 92-E1
SULLIVAN RD DPH 118-C1
SULLIVAN WAY CH 92-E1
SUMAC CIR EPR 133-C4
SUMAC CIR WBL 95-B2
SUMAC CIR WBY 123-C2
SUMAC CT CV 66-D3
SUMAC CT WBL 95-B2
SUMAC LN BUR 162-B3
SUMAC LN MTK 105-B4
SUMAC LN NFD 219-E4
SUMAC LN NO 80-B2
SUMAC PT EAG 149-C1
SUMAC RDG WBL 95-B2
SUMAC ST STP 122-A2
SUMAC TRL HUT 112-D2
SUMAC WAY WBY 123-C2
SUMACH LN MOU 103-A4,117-A1
SUMERLIN CIR NW SM 46-D3
SUMERLIN RD NW SM 46-E3
SUMMER AVE FH 107-C1
SUMMER AVE LAU 107-B1
SUMMER AVE MPW 108-E1
SUMMER AVE RVL 107-E1
SUMMER CT EAG 150-A2
SUMMER CT MPW 108-C1
SUMMER LN EAG 150-A2
SUMMER PL EAG 150-A2
SUMMER PL EPR 147-B1
SUMMER ST FH 107-C1
SUMMER ST HUD 111-D3
SUMMER ST LAU 107-B1
SUMMER ST PRL 161-B3
SUMMER ST RVL 107-E1
SUMMER ST NE MPL 106-E1,107-A1
SUMMER FIELDS GRN SWR 96-D1
SUMMER OAKS DR MTK 104-D3
SUMMER WIND ALC WBY 123-E1
SUMMER WIND BAY WBY 123-E1
SUMMER WIND CIR WBY 123-E1
SUMMER WIND RD WBY 123-E1
SUMMERFIELD CIR HUT 112-B4
SUMMERFIELD CT WAV 85-E1
SUMMERFIELD DR CHN 132-A3
SUMMERFIELD DR NFD 219-D3
SUMMERFIELD DR WAV 85-E1
SUMMERHILL DR EPR 132-D1
SUMMERSET LN BUR 149-A3
SUMMERVILLE RD DPH 118-A2
SUMMIT AVE CNC 12-E3
SUMMIT AVE EDI 119-E3
SUMMIT AVE JOR 173-B3
SUMMIT AVE LND 12-D4
SUMMIT AVE LOR 89-B1
SUMMIT AVE MHT 81-D4,95-D1
SUMMIT AVE MPL 106-C3
SUMMIT AVE NFD 219-D3
SUMMIT AVE SPP 137-B3
SUMMIT AVE SSP 122-D3
SUMMIT AVE STP 121-D1,122-A1
SUMMIT AVE SWD 117-D4
SUMMIT CIR CHN 118-A4
SUMMIT CIR PRL 160-E2
SUMMIT CT MPW 94-D3
SUMMIT CT NO 80-D3
SUMMIT CT SSP 122-D3
SUMMIT CT STP 122-A1
SUMMIT CT WSP 122-C3
SUMMIT XING NO 80-D3
SUMMIT DR EPR 132-D3
SUMMIT DR MO 31-C2
SUMMIT DR N BC 92-B1
SUMMIT DR NE SM 46-E3
SUMMIT HTS NO 80-D3
SUMMIT LN BUR 162-D1
SUMMIT LN MH 121-E4
SUMMIT LN MTK 118-E1
SUMMIT LN NO 80-D3
SUMMIT LN WBL 81-B4,95-B1
SUMMIT LN N NOH 97-D4
SUMMIT PASS EAG 149-C2
SUMMIT PL LTT 131-A4
SUMMIT PL MPL 106-C3
SUMMIT SHRS E BUR 162-C2
SUMMIT SHRS W BUR 162-C2
SUMMIT ST OSC 28-A4
SUMMIT ST OST 14-D4
SUMMIT ST RF 140-E1
SUMMIT ST WBT 81-A2
SUMMIT ST NE CH 92-D2
SUMMIT VW NO 80-D3
SUMMIT OAKS BAY SAV 161-C2
SUMMIT OAKS CIR BUR 162-E2
SUMMIT OAKS CT BUR 162-E2
SUMMIT OAKS DR BUR 162-E2
SUMMIT POINT CT HAS 166-B1
SUMMIT POINT DR HAS 166-B1
SUMMIT RIDGE CIR BUR 162-E2
SUMMIT RIDGE DR NO 80-D3
SUMMIT SHORES CIR BUR 162-C2
SUMMIT SHORES CT BUR 162-C2
SUMMIT SHORES DR BUR 162-C2
SUMMIT SHORES VIS BUR 162-C2
SUMNER PL MPL 106-C2
SUMNER ST HAS 166-D2
SUMNER ST STP 121-C3
SUMNER ST E NFD 219-E4
SUMNER ST W NFD 219-D4
SUMTER AVE SAV 161-D2
SUMTER AVE N BP 77-D2,91-D1
SUMTER AVE N CHM 63-D3
SUMTER AVE N CRY 91-D4
SUMTER AVE N GV 105-D1
SUMTER AVE N NH 91-D2
SUMTER AVE S BLO 147-D2
SUMTER AVE S GV 105-D3
SUMTER AVE S SLP 105-D4,119-D1
SUMTER CIR BLO 147-D2
SUMTER CIR CHM 63-D2
SUMTER CIR N BP 77-D2
SUMTER CT CHM 63-D2
SUMTER DR SLP 105-D3
SUMTER LN BLO 147-D1
SUMTER PL N NH 91-D1
SUN DR EAG 135-C3
SUN RD EDI 119-D3
SUN TER WBL 95-B1
SUN CLIFF RD EAG 149-B2
SUN RISE DR SOM 84-B1
SUN TERRACE CIR WBL 95-C1
SUN VALLEY DR HAS 166-C2
SUN VALLEY LN HMP 193-B2
SUN VIEW DR TRT 140-D1
SUNBOW LN NB 79-B3
SUNBURST DR EPR 132-D1
SUNBURY ALC WBY 123-D3
SUNBURY DR WBY 123-D3
SUNCREST CT EAG 135-E4,136-A4
SUNDANCE PASS SJT 98-A3
SUNDANCE RD COR 61-B4,75-B1
SUNDIAL CT EPR 132-E1
SUNFISH CT LL 65-E2
SUNFISH LN SL 122-B4,136-B1
SUNFISH TRL SE PRL 161-A3
SUNFISH LAKE BLVD NW RAM 49-A2
SUNFISH LAKE CT RAM 49-A3
SUNFISH LAKE DR NW RAM 49-B2
SUNFLOWER CIR SHK 146-C3
SUNFLOWER CIR VH 94-C1
SUNFLOWER CT BUR 162-A1
SUNFLOWER CT VH 94-C1
SUNFLOWER LN LL 65-E2
SUNFLOWER ST VIC 130-E2
SUNKIST BLVD N BP 78-C2
SUNKIST CIR N BP 78-C2
SUNKIST PKWY BP 78-C2
SUNNE PT EAG 149-C3
SUNNY LN ANO 49-D3
SUNNY LN BP 77-D4,91-D1
SUNNY RD MTK 118-B4
SUNNY HILL DR WBY 137-E2
SUNNY HILL LN COR 75-E1
SUNNY RIDGE DR CAR 145-B4
SUNNY RIDGE LN CAR 145-B4
SUNNY SHADOWS CT VIC 117-B4
SUNNY SLOPE LN STP 121-C3
SUNNY WAY CT ANO 49-E3
SUNNYACRE LN BUR 162-C3
SUNNYBROOK CV EPR 133-A3
SUNNYBROOK PL EPR 133-A3
SUNNYBROOK RD EPR 133-A3
SUNNYFIELD RD E MTA 102-D4
SUNNYFIELD RD N MTA 102-D3
SUNNYRIDGE CIR GV 106-A2
SUNNYRIDGE LN GV 106-A2
SUNNYRIDGE LN LOR 89-B1
SUNNYSIDE AVE MPL 120-A2
SUNNYSIDE CIR BUR 162-B2
SUNNYSIDE CIR FAR 191-E1
SUNNYSIDE DR FAR 191-E1
SUNNYSIDE LN HOP 119-C1
SUNNYSIDE LN SL 136-C1
SUNNYSIDE RD EDI 119-E2,120-A2
SUNNYSIDE RD MV 79-B2
SUNNYSIDE RD SLP 120-A2
SUNNYSIDE TER NB 79-B3
SUNNYSLOPE DR N MG 76-E4
SUNNYSLOPE LN SWR 96-E1
SUNNYSLOPE RD E EDI 119-E2
SUNNYSLOPE RD W EDI 119-E2
SUNNYVALE DR CHN 132-B3
SUNNYVALE LN MTK 105-A2
SUNNYVALE LN SWD 117-C3
SUNNYVIEW LN MTK 105-A3
SUNRAY AVE SW PRL ...160-E4,174-E1
SUNRAY CIR SW PRL 160-E4
SUNRIDGE CT CHN 131-E3
SUNRISE ALC WBY 124-A1
SUNRISE AVE PRL 160-E4
SUNRISE AVE SWR 96-D2
SUNRISE AVE TKB 117-D2
SUNRISE AVE N NP 201-E2
SUNRISE CIR E EPR 132-D3
SUNRISE CIR NW ER 33-B2
SUNRISE CIR W EPR 132-D3
SUNRISE CT BUR 162-E2
SUNRISE CT EAG 149-B2
SUNRISE CT MPW 108-C1
SUNRISE CT SLT 160-E4,174-E1
SUNRISE CT SWR 96-D2
SUNRISE CT WBL 95-A2
SUNRISE DR LC 94-C4
SUNRISE DR LL 65-E3
SUNRISE DR MPL 120-C3
SUNRISE DR WBY 124-A1
SUNRISE DR E MTK 118-E1
SUNRISE DR N LC 94-C4
SUNRISE DR N MPW 94-C4
SUNRISE DR NE FRI 78-D4
SUNRISE DR W MTK 118-E1
SUNRISE LN BEL 186-A2
SUNRISE LN BUR 162-E2
SUNRISE LN CHM 49-B4,63-B1
SUNRISE LN MTK 119-A2
SUNRISE RD EAG 149-B2
SUNRISE RD SCF 14-D2
SUNRISE RD NE LWT 10-D4,24-D1
SUNRISE TER BP 77-C4,91-C1
SUNRISE HEIGHTS CIR BUF 58-D2
SUNSET AVE BLA 51-E4,65-E2
SUNSET AVE SLT 160-D4
SUNSET AVE N NP 201-E2
SUNSET AVE S LAT 201-E2
SUNSET BAY WBY 124-A1
SUNSET BLVD MPL 106-A4
SUNSET BLVD SLP 106-A4
SUNSET BLVD WAC 129-D3
SUNSET CIR EPR 118-D4
SUNSET CIR LES 212-D4
SUNSET CIR RFD 74-B3
SUNSET CRST VIC 130-E3
SUNSET CT CW 1-B2
SUNSET CT LC 94-C4
SUNSET CT MED 90-A2
SUNSET CT PRE 153-A4
SUNSET CT SHK 147-C4
SUNSET CT SVW 80-A3
SUNSET DR BEC 2-E3
SUNSET DR BEL 185-E1
SUNSET DR EAG 150-A2
SUNSET DR HAS 166-B2
SUNSET DR HEN 198-C4
SUNSET DR JOR 173-B3
SUNSET DR MTA 102-D3
SUNSET DR SPR 117-B1
SUNSET DR SWR 96-E1
SUNSET DR WBY 124-A1
SUNSET DR E CHM 63-C1
SUNSET DR S MTK 105-A3
SUNSET DR W CHM 63-C1
SUNSET LN BUR 148-B4
SUNSET LN COR 61-C3
SUNSET LN HUD 111-D2
SUNSET LN IND 88-E1,89-A1
SUNSET LN MH 122-A3
SUNSET LN NB 93-B2
SUNSET LN NO 80-C3
SUNSET LN RF 140-D1
SUNSET RD CT 142-D1
SUNSET RD MOU 116-E1
SUNSET RD MTK 118-D1
SUNSET RD N BP 64-A4
SUNSET RD NE EB 9-E3
SUNSET RD NE SLK 79-A1
SUNSET RDG GV 106-A3
SUNSET ST BUF 58-E1,59-A1
SUNSET ST ML 43-D2
SUNSET TER BP 64-A3
SUNSET TRL BP 64-A3
SUNSET TRL CFT 209-A3
SUNSET TRL CHN 131-E3
SUNSET TRL PLY 104-E2,105-A2
SUNSET TRL PRL 160-E4
SUNSET TRL VAT 209-C2
SUNSET HILL CT BUR 162-B1
SUNSET LAKE CIR BUR 162-B1
SUNSET LAKE CT BUR 162-B1
SUNSET LAKE DR BUR 162-B1
SUNSET LAKE RD CRT 162-A3
SUNSET RIDGE RD SLP 119-C1
SUNSHINE CIR CHS 145-C2
SUNSHINE CT CHS 145-D2
SUNSHINE CT FL 39-C3
SUNSHINE DR EPR 132-E1
SUNSHINE DR NW OG 21-D2
SUNSHINE LN NO 80-B3
SUNSHINE ST SAT 14-E1
SUNVIEW CT SVW 79-D2
SUNVIEW DR SVW 79-D2
SUNWOOD CT EAG 135-E4,136-A4
SUNWOOD DR NW RAM 48-E2,49-B2
SUNWOOD TRL EAG 135-E4,136-A4
SUPERIOR BLVD WAY 104-C3
SUPERIOR CT EAG 150-A2
SUPERIOR ST STP 122-A1
SUPERIOR ST SE MPL 107-A3
SUPERIOR TER EPR 132-D2
SUPORNICK LN STP 108-E2
SURREY ALC WBY 123-E1
SURREY AVE STP 108-C4
SURREY LN WBY 123-E1
SURREY LN NE PRL 161-A2
SURREY ST EPR 133-A4
SURREY TRL N APV 149-A3
SURREY TRL S APV 149-A4
SURREY HEIGHTS DR EAG 135-D4
SURRY LN MTK 104-E4
SURRY LN SWR 96-E2
SUSAN AVE EDI 133-D1
SUSAN AVE STP 121-C3
SUSAN DR MTK 118-C1
SUSAN LN BPT 186-A3
SUSAN LN BUR 162-B1
SUSAN LN MTA 102-C4
SUSAN LN MTK 118-C1
SUSAN ST BL 18-B4
SUSAN ST MAY 54-C3
SUSSEX CIR ORO 103-C3
SUSSEX CT SHK 147-B3
SUSSEX DR MTK 118-D1
SUSSEX LN ORO 103-C3
SUSSEX LN SHK 147-B3
SUSSEX PL MTK 118-D1
SUSSEX PL SWD 118-A3
SUSSEX RD GV 106-A3
SUSSEX RD ORO 103-C3
SUTCLIFF CIR MH 122-B2
SUTTON DR EPR 132-D3
SUTTON LN MH 122-A4
SUTTON LAKE BLVD N SCT 174-B3
SUTTON LAKE BLVD S SCT 174-A3
SUZANNE AVE SVW 94-A1
SUZANNE AVE VH 94-B1
SUZANNE CIR WBT 81-B2
SUZANNE CT VH 94-B1
SVENSK LN EAG 149-D2
SWALLOW CIR MO 31-E3
SWALLOW CIR NW CR 50-A4,64-A2
SWALLOW CT PRL 161-B2
SWALLOW LN BUF 45-B4
SWALLOW LN NO 80-B4
SWALLOW PL NW AND 36-A2
SWALLOW ST NW AND ...36-A4,50-A3
SWALLOW ST NW CR 50-A4,64-A2
SWALLOW ST NW OG 22-A4,36-A2
SWAN AVE NSP 95-B3
SWAN CT CHN 131-E3
SWAN CT MH 135-E1,136-A1
SWAN DR MH 135-E1,136-A1
SWAN ST LES 212-D4
SWAN LAKE LN NW OG 36-C1
SWANSON CIR BUR 162-D2
SWAPS DR SHK 146-C2
SWASEY ST HUD 111-D3
SWEDE HILL DR S AFT 139-C1
SWEDE LAKE RD WTT 115-C1
SWEDISH DR NE HL 37-A2
SWEDISH MISSION RD TRT 140-B1
SWEET BRIAR LN HOP 119-C1
SWEETGRASS CIR PRL 160-E1
SWEETWATER CIR EPR 132-D3
SWEETWATER CIR SWD 118-B4
SWEETWATER CRV SWD 118-B4
SWEETWATER CT SWD 118-B4
SWEETWATER DR APV 149-A4
SWENSON ST SWR 82-D4
SWIFT CIR SHK 146-C3
SWIFT ST S SHK 146-C3
SYCAMORE CIR N PLY 105-A2
SYCAMORE CIR NW CR 64-C1
SYCAMORE CIR NW SM 46-D3
SYCAMORE CIR S SHK 160-C2
SYCAMORE CT EAG 150-B3
SYCAMORE CT EPR 132-E3
SYCAMORE CT N MG 76-E1,77-A4
SYCAMORE DR EAG 150-B3
SYCAMORE LN MOU 116-E1
SYCAMORE LN N MG 76-E1,91-A1
SYCAMORE LN N PLY 91-A4,105-A2
SYCAMORE ST CR 64-C2
SYCAMORE ST PRE 167-B1
SYCAMORE ST RF 140-E2
SYCAMORE ST E STP 108-B3
SYCAMORE ST E SWR 83-A4
SYCAMORE ST NW AND ...36-C4,50-C2
SYCAMORE ST NW CR 50-C4,64-C3
SYCAMORE ST NW OG 8-C4,22-C2
SYCAMORE ST W STP 108-B3
SYCAMORE ST W SWR 82-E4,83-A4
SYCAMORE TRL MED 89-A4
SYCAMORE TRL PRL 160-E4
SYCAMORE TRL WBY 123-C2
SYKORA LN TRT 126-B4
SYLIA ST RF 140-D2
SYLVAN AVE LND 12-D4
SYLVAN LN SWD 117-C3
SYLVAN LN NE FRI 78-D3
SYLVAN PL MTK 105-A4
SYLVAN RD MTK 105-A4
SYLVAN RDG EPR 132-D3
SYLVAN ST EB 37-D1
SYLVAN ST LC 94-B3
SYLVAN ST MPW 108-B1
SYLVAN ST STP 108-B2
SYLVAN LAKE RD HSN ...47-C4,61-B1
SYLVANDALE CT MH 122-A3
SYLVANDALE CT S MH 122-A3
SYLVANDALE RD MH 122-A3
SYLVIA CT SVW 93-E1
SYLVIA LN SVW 79-E4

SYLVIA LN N SVW 79-E4
SYLVIA LN S SVW 79-E4,93-E1
SYMBOL WAY COR 76-B1
SYMES ST LOL 103-E2
SYMPHONY ST NE FRI 78-D2
SYNDICATE AVE LEX 65-C4
SYNDICATE AVE SSP 136-E1
SYNDICATE AVE S BLO 134-C3
SYNDICATE ST JOR 173-B2
SYNDICATE ST N STP 107-D4,121-D1
SYNDICATE ST S STP 121-D2

T

TACOMA AVE CT 128-D2
TACOMA AVE HOT 114-C2
TACOMA AVE NYA 142-D3
TACOMA AVE YAT 142-D4,156-D2
TACOMA CIR PRL 161-B4
TACONITE PT EAG 149-C1
TACONITE ST NE HL 37-B4,51-B2
TACONITE TRL EAG 149-C1
TAFFY WAY EPR 133-A1
TAFT AVE S SLP 119-D1
TAFT ST BL 18-A4
TAFT ST NE MPL 93-A4,107-A1
TAHOE CIR WBY 123-C2
TAHOE DR WBY 123-C2
TAHOE PL WBY 123-C3
TAHOE RD WBY 123-C3
TAIGA CIR EPR 118-D4
TAILDRAGGER LN BUF 59-B2
TAINTER AVE STP 107-B3
TALAHI DR MHT 95-D2
TALISMAN CRV RVL 93-D3
TALLE LN LL 66-C4
TALLPINE TRL SWR 96-C1
TALMADGE LN NE FRI 78-D2
TALMADGE WAY NE FRI 78-D2
TALMAGE AVE SE MPL 107-A2
TALMAGE CIR VH 94-D2
TALTON PL DPH 118-B1
TALUS CIR EPR 133-C4
TAMARAC AVE EDI 119-C4
TAMARAC LN EDI 119-C3
TAMARAC PT EAG 135-D4
TAMARACK AVE LOL 103-D2
TAMARACK BAY WBY 123-E1
TAMARACK CIR MTK 118-C3
TAMARACK CIR NW CR 64-C2
TAMARACK CRV WBY 124-A1
TAMARACK CT SWR 96-D1
TAMARACK CV WBY 124-A1
TAMARACK DR MED 89-E4,103-E1
TAMARACK DR MTK 118-C3
TAMARACK DR ORO 103-E1
TAMARACK DR NE OTS 33-E4,47-E1
TAMARACK LN BUR 148-E2
TAMARACK LN HUT 111-D1
TAMARACK LN LL 66-B3
TAMARACK LN RFD 74-A4
TAMARACK LN WAC 129-D2
TAMARACK RD CHN 118-A4,132-A1
TAMARACK RD WBY 123-E1,124-A1
TAMARACK ST GRF 74-B4,88-B1
TAMARACK ST MHT 81-D4
TAMARACK ST NW AND 36-C2,50-C2
TAMARACK ST NW CR 50-C4,64-C3
TAMARACK ST NW OG 22-C1
TAMARACK ST NW SF 8-C4
TAMARACK TRL EPR 132-E2
TAMARACK VLG WBY 123-E1
TAMARACK VILLAGE
RD WBY 109-E4,123-E1
TAMARIN TRL GV 105-C1
TAMARISK RD DWD 81-C2
TAMBERWOOD ALC WBY 123-D1
TAMBERWOOD CT WBY 123-D1
TAMBERWOOD ECHO WBY 123-E1
TAMBERWOOD TRL WBY 123-D1
TAMIAMI TRL COR 75-C1
TAMIE AVE EAG 150-B2
TAMMARA LN CF 208-A4
TAMMER LN MTK 104-D3
TAMMY DR NM 190-A4
TAMPERE CIR EAG 149-C3
TANA PT EAG 149-C3
TANADOONA DR CHN 131-C1
TANAGER CIR MO 31-E3
TANAGER LN EPR 118-E4
TANAGER RD WAC 129-D3
TANAGERS LN CHN 117-D4
TANAGERS PT CHN 117-D4
TANANGER CT EAG 135-D4
TANGLEWOOD CT EAG 136-A4
TANGLEWOOD CT EDI 133-D2
TANGLEWOOD DR EPR 147-B1
TANGLEWOOD DR SVW 79-E3,80-A3
TANGLEWOOD LN CHM 63-B3
TANGLEWOOD LN MSC 69-B1
TANGLEWOOD LN N CHM 63-B3
TANGLEWOOD RD ORO 103-E1
TANNER CT CP 79-D1
TANNEY LN HUT 98-D4
TAPESTRY LN MTK 105-A4
TARA LN WBY 123-D3
TARA RD EDI 133-D1
TARLETON CRES N MG 76-D2
TARN CIR EPR 133-B3
TARRY TOWN RD BL 18-A4
TARRYMORE AVE MPL 120-D3
TARRYTOWN RD BL 18-A4
TART CT LL 67-A3
TART LAKE RD LL 66-E3,67-A3
TARTAN CRV EPR 118-B4,132-B1
TARTAN LN BLT 17-E2
TASHA BLVD SHK 146-C3
TATUM ST FH 107-C1
TATUM ST RVL 107-C1
TATUM ST STP 107-C3
TAYLOR AVE FS 121-C4
TAYLOR AVE STP 107-D3
TAYLOR AVE SVW 80-A2
TAYLOR AVE WBT 81-B2
TAYLOR CT BLA 64-E3
TAYLOR CT SAV 147-D4
TAYLOR CT NE BLA 64-E3,78-E1
TAYLOR DR SAV 147-D4
TAYLOR PL BUR 148-C4
TAYLOR ST ANO 49-C4
TAYLOR ST NE BLA 50-E4,64-E3
TAYLOR ST NE CH 92-E2
TAYLOR ST NE EB 8-E4,22-E2
TAYLOR ST NE FRI 78-E2,92-E1
TAYLOR ST NE HL 36-E2,50-E1
TAYLOR ST NE MPL 92-E4,106-E1
TAYLOR ST NE SLK 78-E2
TAYLOR ST S SHK 145-E3,146-A3
TEA ISLAND RD NO 80-C3
TEAKWOOD CIR MG 76-E3,77-A3
TEAKWOOD CT MPW 123-B2
TEAKWOOD DR MPW 123-B2
TEAKWOOD LN N DAY 48-E4
TEAKWOOD LN N MG 76-E1,77-A3
TEAKWOOD LN N PLY 90-E1,105-A1
TEAL ALC WBY 123-D1
TEAL AVE N SHT 13-E3
TEAL BAY WBY 123-D1
TEAL CIR CHN 117-E4
TEAL CIR SWD 117-C3
TEAL CT BUF 59-B1
TEAL CT HAS 166-C3
TEAL CT LL 66-C3
TEAL CT ROG 48-A3
TEAL CV EAG 149-C2
TEAL RD WBY 123-D1
TEAL ST BL 17-E3
TEAL ST BLT 17-E2
TEAL ST SHK 146-D4
TEAL WAY HAS 166-C3
TEALE AVE CLT 202-C2
TEALE AVE WHT 202-C2
TEALWOOD CT EPR 132-E3
TEALWOOD LN NW SM 46-D3
TEALWOOD PL ORO 103-E2
TECHNOLOGY DR EPR 132-E2,133-A2
TECHNOLOGY DR MPL 92-D3
TECHNOLOGY DR NE MPL 92-D3
TECKLA CT LL 65-E1
TECUMSEH LN CHN 131-E1,132-A1
TEDESCO ST STP 108-C3
TEE TRL SWD 117-D4
TEEPLE ST MH 122-A2
TELE DR LL 66-E3
TELE LN LL 66-E3
TELEGRAPH RD BLO 133-D2
TELEMARK TRL EDI 119-C3
TELFORD BAY N BP 78-B1
TELFORD XING BP 78-B1
TELFORD LN N BP 78-B2
TELL ST STP 108-D4
TELLERS RD LTT 130-D3
TELLURIDE TRL MTK 105-B4
TELVIN CT MPW 109-B2
TEMPERANCE ST STP 108-B4
TEMPLE CIR MTK 118-C2
TEMPLE CT STP 107-C4
TEMPLE DR MTK 118-D2
TEMPLE DR N MTK 118-D2
TEMPLE DR S MTK 118-C2
TEMPLE LN MTK 118-D2
TEMPLE RD MTK 118-D2
TEMPLE TER MTK 118-D2
TEMPLE WAY MTK 118-D3
TEMPO TER NE FRI 78-D2
TENDING GRN SWR 96-C1
TENNISON DR NE FRI 78-E4
TERESA DR WSP 122-C4
TERMINAL DR EAG 135-C3
TERMINAL LN FS 121-B4,135-B1
TERMINAL RD RVL 93-B4
TERN AVE N SHT 13-E3
TERN CT CHN 131-E3
TERRA CT LL 65-E2
TERRA LINDA DR NH 91-D4
TERRA VERDE TRL EPR 133-A3
TERRACE BLVD WAV 72-A4
TERRACE CIR BUR 148-B4
TERRACE CIR RFD 74-B3
TERRACE CIR NE HL 36-D4
TERRACE CIR SW PRL 160-E4
TERRACE CT STP 108-C3
TERRACE DR BUR 148-B4
TERRACE DR MV 79-B2
TERRACE DR RVL 93-D3,94-A3
TERRACE DR SVW 79-C2
TERRACE LN GV 106-A1
TERRACE LN MTK 119-A2
TERRACE LN SSP 122-D3
TERRACE PL NE SM 46-E3
TERRACE RD NEW 123-B4
TERRACE RD SM 46-E3
TERRACE RD NE BLA 50-D3,64-D2
TERRACE RD NE EB 22-D1
TERRACE RD NE HL 36-D4,50-D3
TERRACE RD NE SLK 78-D2
TERRACE RD NW SM 46-E3
TERRACE ST RFD 74-B4
TERRACE COURTE RVL 94-A3
TERRACE VIEW LN N MG 76-D2
TERRACEVIEW CT N PLY 90-D4
TERRACEVIEW LN N MG 76-D2
TERRACEVIEW LN N PLY 90-D3,104-D1
TERRACEWOOD DR BLO 147-E2,148-A2
TERRACEWOOD DR EPR 132-D1
TERRANCE AVE SSP 122-D3
TERRE VERDE TRL EPR 133-A3
TERREY PINE CT EPR 132-D2
TERREY PINE DR EPR 132-C2
TERRI CIR PRL 161-C3
TERRIER LN SJT 84-C4,98-C1
TERRITORIAL CT BUR 148-E2
TERRITORIAL DR BUR 148-E2
TERRITORIAL RD DAY 62-C3
TERRITORIAL RD HSN 61-D1,62-A2
TERRITORIAL RD MG 62-E4
TERRITORIAL RD STP 107-B3
TERRITORIAL RD E MO 31-D2
TERRITORIAL RD NE BLA 64-D3
TERRITORIAL ST E WAT 101-B3
TERRITORIAL ST W WAT 101-A3
TERRYLL ST LND 12-D4
TESSERACT PL EAG 135-B4,149-A1
TESSIER CIR VH 94-C1
TESSIER RD GL 94-D1
TESSIER TRL VH 94-C1
TESSMAN DR N BP 77-D3
TESSMER CT EPR 132-C3
TESSMER RD COR 61-A4
TETON CT BUR 149-A3
TETON LN CHN 117-E4
TETON TRL N BP 78-B3
TEWANNA PL STP 109-A3
TEWSBURY BND MG 76-B1
TEWSBURY GATE MG 76-B1
TEXA TONKA AVE SLP 105-D4
TEXAS AVE CRT 161-D4,175-D3
TEXAS AVE NMT 189-D2,203-D1
TEXAS AVE SAV 161-D3
TEXAS AVE N CHM 63-C2
TEXAS AVE S BLO 133-D3
TEXAS AVE S HOP 119-D1
TEXAS AVE S SLP 105-D3,119-D1
TEXAS CIR CHM 63-C2
TEXAS CIR S SLP 105-D3
THAMES AVE EAG 150-B1
THAMES CIR EAG 150-B1
THAMES CIR WBY 123-D3
THAMES RD WBY 123-D3
THAMES ST NE LWT 10-C3,24-C2
THATCHER RD EPR 132-D3
THE MALL MPL 106-B4
THE MALL MTK 118-C1
THE PNES EPR 132-B4
THE PINES EPR 132-B4
THE STRAND MTK 118-C1
THEIS DR LVT 160-B2
THEO CT HAS 166-C1
THEODORE WIRTH PKWY GV 106-A2
THEODORE WIRTH
PKWY MPL 92-B4,106-A3
THEODORE WIRTH PKWY ROB 92-B4
THEORIN TER NE SLK 79-A1
THERESA PL EPR 132-E1
THERESA ST MH 121-E4,135-E1
THERESA MARIE DR NM 190-A4
THERESE ST DPH 118-C1
THERESE ST MTK 118-C1
THICKET LN DAY 48-B3
THIELEN AVE EDI 119-E2
THIELEN BLVD EB 37-D1
THIMSEN AVE MTK 118-C3
THIRD ST N HOP 119-B2
THIRD ST S EDI 119-C2
THIRD ST S HOP 119-C2
THIRTEENTH ST HUD 111-D2
THISTLE LN BUR 162-A1
THISTLE LN SHK 146-B3
THISTLE WAY HUD 111-E4
THOM CT AH 93-C2
THOM DR AH 93-C2
THOMAS AVE BUR 162-B1
THOMAS AVE EKO 204-B1
THOMAS AVE HAS 166-E3
THOMAS AVE MTK 118-D2
THOMAS AVE NMT 204-B1
THOMAS AVE STP 107-D3,108-A3
THOMAS AVE N BP 64-B4,78-B1
THOMAS AVE N MPL 92-B3,106-B1
THOMAS AVE S BLO 134-B2,148-B1
THOMAS AVE S BUR 148-B4
THOMAS AVE S MPL 106-B3,120-B3
THOMAS AVE S RCH 120-B4,134-B1
THOMAS AVE W SHK 146-B3
THOMAS CIR BUR 148-B4
THOMAS CIR MO 31-D2
THOMAS CIR S MPL 120-B3
THOMAS CT VH 94-C1
THOMAS CT N BP 78-B2
THOMAS DR WBY 109-E4
THOMAS LN BLO 134-B2
THOMAS LN CHS 145-D2
THOMAS LN EAG 149-D2
THOMAS LN MPL 106-B3
THOMAS LN WBL 95-A2
THOMAS LN WBY 109-E4
THOMAS PL N MPL 106-B2
THOMAS RD BLO 134-B3
THOMAS RD LVL 162-C4
THOMAS RD S BLO 134-B4
THOMAS ST LL 66-A1
THOMAS TRL HSN 47-D3
THOMAS CENTER DR EAG 149-C2
THOMAS LAKE RD EAG 149-C2
THOMAS LAKE POINTE RD EAG 149-C2
THOMAS PARK DR MO 31-D2
THOMPSON AVE SSP 122-D3
THOMPSON AVE E WSP 122-C3
THOMPSON AVE W WSP 122-B3
THOMPSON LN NO 80-B3
THOMPSON ST STP 108-B4,122-B1
THOREAU DR BUR 148-D3
THORENE PL SWR 82-D4
THORN ST STP 108-D4
THORN HILL LN SAV 147-D4
THORNBERRY CRV VIC 117-A4
THORNDALE AVE NB 79-B3,93-B1
THORNHILL CT WBY 124-A2
THORNHILL LN VH 80-D4,94-D1
THORNHILL LN WBY 124-A2
THORNHILL RD EPR 119-B4
THORNTON ST SE MPL 107-A3
THORNWOOD CT EAG 135-E4
THOROUGHBRED LN ORO 103-D2
THOROUGHBRED TER EPR 132-D4
THORPE RD DPH 118-B1
THOTLAND RD GV 105-E2
THOUSAND PINES ENTR CHM 63-E3
THREE OAKS AVE MP 102-E1
THREE OAKS DR MP 102-E1
THREE POINTS BLVD MOU 102-E4,103-A4
THREE RIVER CT HAS 166-E3
THREE RIVERS HAS 166-E3
THRUSH AVE N FRT 13-E4
THRUSH CT CHN 131-E3
THRUSH DR SPT 56-D4
THRUSH LN NO 80-B2
THRUSH PL NW AND 36-A2
THRUSH PT EAG 149-C3
THRUSH ST NW AND 36-A2,50-A3
THRUSH ST NW CR 50-A4,64-A2
THRUSHWOOD CIR VIC 130-E2
THRUSHWOOD LN MTK 118-D2
THUNDER BAY RD N LC 94-C3
THUNDERBIRD CIR NW PRL 160-E1
THUNDERBIRD RD BLO 134-E2
THURBER RD BC 78-A4
THURE AVE STP 121-C3
THURSTON AVE ANO 49-B3
THURY CT WBL 80-E3
THURY HL MG 76-B1
THYE PKWY NFD 219-D2
THYE TRL DRS 28-D2
TIBBETT PL NEW 137-B1
TICONDEROGA TRL EAG 149-E1
TICONDEROGA TRL EPR 132-C1
TIERNEY AVE NSP 109-B1
TIERNEY CT HAS 166-B2
TIERNEY DR HAS 166-B2
TIERNEYS WOODS CRV BLO 133-C2
TIERNEYS WOODS RD BLO 133-C2
TIFFANY CIR N EAG 149-E2
TIFFANY CIR S EAG 149-E2
TIFFANY CT BUR 149-A3
TIFFANY CT EAG 149-E2
TIFFANY DR EAG 149-E2
TIFFANY DR HAS 166-D3
TIFFANY LN EPR 133-B3
TIFFANY LN SVW 94-A2
TIFFANY LN SWD 118-A3
TIFFANY PL EAG 149-E2
TIFFANY PT EAG 149-E2
TIFTON DR EDI 133-E1
TIGER DR DEL 87-E2
TIGER ST NW BT 20-C3,34-C2
TIGER ST NW RAM 34-C3
TIGER ST NW STT 6-C2
TIGUA CIR CHN 132-B3
TILBURY LN CHM 63-B3
TILBURY WAY EAG 150-A1
TILDEN AVE N CHM 49-B4,63-B1
TILEDA CIR MTK 119-A1
TILLER AVE CT 128-C3,142-C1
TILLER LN AH 93-D2
TILLER LN SVW 93-E2
TILSEN AVE MPW 109-B2
TILSEN AVE STP 109-B2
TILSEN CT MPW 109-B2
TILTON TRL N HSN 61-E2
TILTON TRL S HSN 61-E3
TIMBER AVE MPW 123-B2
TIMBER CIR CHS 145-D1
TIMBER CT MPW 123-B2
TIMBER CT SAV 148-A4
TIMBER CT SHK 146-C2
TIMBER LN SVW 93-E2
TIMBER LN SWD 117-D3
TIMBER LN N MG 77-A3
TIMBER LN W MG 77-A3
TIMBER RD SMT 55-C4
TIMBER RDG EDI 119-C4
TIMBER RDG N FRI 79-A3
TIMBER RDG S FRI 79-A3
TIMBER TRL EDI 119-C4
TIMBER TRL EPR 133-C3
TIMBER TRL IND 102-E1
TIMBER TRL MPW 123-B2
TIMBER TRL MTA 103-A3
TIMBER TRL PRL 161-C3
TIMBER CREST CT N MG 76-E4
TIMBER CREST DR N MG 76-E4
TIMBER HILL RD CHN 118-B4
TIMBER ISLAND TRL IND 102-E2
TIMBER LAKE DR EPR 132-D2
TIMBER RIDGE CT BUR 162-C2
TIMBER RIDGE CT MTK 118-B2
TIMBER RIDGE DR MTK 118-B2
TIMBER RIDGE PL MTK 118-B2
TIMBER VIEW DR HAS 166-B2
TIMBER WOLF CT EAG 149-B2
TIMBERGLADE CIR BLO 147-E1
TIMBERGLADE CIR PRL 161-A2
TIMBERGLADE CT COR 76-B2
TIMBERGLADE DR BLO 147-E1
TIMBERGLADE RD BLO 147-E1
TIMBERHILL RD LTT 130-C2
TIMBERHILL RD MTK 118-D1
TIMBERIDGE CT JOR 173-A3
TIMBERIDGE DR BUR 162-C2
TIMBERLAKE RD STP 108-B2
TIMBERLAND DR BUR 148-C4
TIMBERLANE DR SOM 70-B4
TIMBERLEA CIR WBY 123-E2
TIMBERLEA DR WBY 123-E2
TIMBERLINE CIR CHM 63-B3
TIMBERLINE CT JOR 173-A2
TIMBERLINE CT VH 80-B4
TIMBERLINE DR CHM 63-B3
TIMBERLINE DR JOR 173-A2
TIMBERLINE RD MTK 105-B3
TIMBERLINE SPUR MTK 105-B3
TIMBERLINE TRL MTK 105-B3
TIMBERLINE TRL VH 80-B4
TIMBERSHORE LN EAG 135-D4
TIMBERVIEW ST PRL 161-C3
TIMBERVIEW TRL CHS 131-D4
TIMBERWOLF CIR LL 66-C3
TIMBERWOLF TRL LL 66-C3
TIMBERWOLF TRL N EAG 149-B2
TIMBERWOLF TRL S EAG 149-B2
TIMBERWOOD CT EAG 135-D3
TIMBERWOOD CT WBY 123-E2
TIMBERWOOD DR CHN 131-D2
TIMBERWOOD RD LTT 131-A4
TIMBERWOOD RD WBY 123-E2
TIMBERWOOD TRL EAG 135-D3
TIMMY ST MH 121-E4,135-E1
TIMOTHY AVE PRL 161-D1
TIMOTHY CT SHK 146-C2
TIMOTHY LN CHS 145-D1
TINGDALE AVE EDI 119-E4
TIOGA BLVD NB 93-B1
TIOGA CT NB 93-A1
TIOGA TRL MTK 118-C1
TIP TOP LN MHT 81-D4
TIPPECANOE ST NE BLA 51-C4,65-C4
TIPPECANOE ST NE EB 9-C4,23-C1
TIPPECANOE ST NE HL 37-C4
TIPPECANOE ST NW EB 23-C3
TIPTON CIR NW ER 33-D1
TIPTON ST NW ER 19-D4,33-D1
TODD AVE EAG 150-B2
TODD CT AH 79-C4
TODD CT HAS 166-B2
TODD DR AH 79-C4
TODD LN HUT 98-B4
TODD RD PRL 160-E4
TODD ST LES 212-D3
TODD ST NM 189-E4
TODD WAY HAS 166-B2
TOFT CV EPR 132-C2
TOFTE LN EAG 150-B2
TOGO RD ORO 117-B1
TOGO RD SPR 117-B1
TOLEDO AVE SAV 147-E3,161-E1
TOLEDO AVE N BC 77-E4
TOLEDO AVE N BP 77-E2
TOLEDO AVE N CHM 63-E3
TOLEDO AVE N CRY 91-E2
TOLEDO AVE N GV 105-E1
TOLEDO AVE N ROB 91-E3
TOLEDO AVE S BLO 133-E4,147-E1
TOLEDO AVE S SLP 105-E4,119-E2
TOLEDO CIR BLO 133-E4,147-E1
TOLEDO CRV BLO 147-E1
TOLEDO CT BLO 147-E1
TOLEDO CT SAV 161-E1
TOLEDO RD BLO 133-E3
TOM THUMB BLVD MH 121-E4
TOMAH CT LON 217-A2
TOMAHAWK CT LL 66-A4
TOMAHAWK DR S AFT 110-E4
TOMAHAWK LN S AFT 110-E4
TOMAHAWK RD MED 89-C2
TOMAHAWK TRL LL 66-A4
TOMLYN AVE SVW 79-E4,80-A4
TONKA AVE ORO 103-C3
TONKA LN MTK 118-D1
TONKA TRL MTK 104-D4
TONKA BAY LN TKB 117-D2
TONKA BAY RD TKB 117-D2
TONKA DOWNS DR MTK 118-E2
TONKAHA DR MTK 104-D4

TONKAVIEW CT ORO 103-A4
TONKAVIEW LN ORO 103-A4
TONKAWA RD ORO 103-B3
TONKAWA TRL MTK 104-E4
TONKAWAY RD MTK 118-D1
TONKAWOOD CT MTK 118-D2
TONKAWOOD DR MTK 118-D1
TONKAWOOD LN MTK 118-D2
TONKAWOOD RD MOU 116-E1
TONKAWOOD RD MTK 118-D2
TONTO ST NW AND 35-C3
TONTO ST NW RAM 35-C2,49-C1
TONY CT WBL 94-E1
TONY ST OSC 28-A4
TOP LN WBT 80-E4
TOPAZ DR EAG 149-B1
TOPAZ LN HUD 111-E2
TOPEL RD GV 105-E1
TOPHILL CIR RVL 94-A4
TOPIC LN STP 108-E2
TOPPER LN NE FRI 92-D1
TOPPING ST STP 107-E3,108-A3
TOPVIEW RD EPR 133-A1
TORCHWOOD CIR NB 93-A1
TORCHWOOD CT NB 93-A1
TORCHWOOD DR NB 93-A1
TORONTO AVE SE PRL 161-B4
TORONTO ST STP 122-A1
TORREY DR WBY 123-E3
TOTEM RD STP 123-A1
TOTEM TRL LL 66-A4
TOTEM TRL MTK 104-E3
TOURNAMENT
PLAYERS CIR BLA 65-B2
TOURNAMENT
PLAYERS CIR N BLA 65-B1
TOURNAMENT
PLAYERS CT BLA 65-B2
TOURNAMENT
PLAYERS PKWY BLA 65-A2
TOURVILLE CIR CV 66-D3
TOWER AVE HOT -C3
TOWER CT WBY 123-D2
TOWER DR DEL 87-E2
TOWER DR MED 90-A2
TOWER DR SWR 96-E2
TOWER DR WBY 123-D3,137-D1
TOWER HTS PRE 153-B4,167-B1
TOWER PL NW CR 64-C2
TOWER RD KKT 112-E4
TOWER RD PRE 153-B4,167-B1
TOWER RD SCF 14-D2
TOWER RD TRT 111-E4,112-B4
TOWER ST ANN 74-B3
TOWER ST EDI 119-E3,120-A3
TOWER ST RFD 74-B3
TOWER ST SB 116-A3
TOWER ST STP 109-B4
TOWER ST SE PRL 161-B4
TOWER HEIGHTS CT PRE 167-B1
TOWER POND BLVD ANO 49-C3
TOWER POND CT ANO 49-C3
TOWER POND DR ANO 49-C3
TOWERING OAKS CRV CRT 176-B2
TOWERING OAKS DR CRT 176-A2
TOWERING OAKS TRL CRT 176-B2
TOWERS LN EPR 132-E3
TOWERVIEW CIR BLO 148-B1
TOWERVIEW RD EAG 135-D3
TOWN RD COT 24-A4,38-A1
TOWN RD ORO 104-A3
TOWN RD WTT 101-A4
TOWN CENTER PKWY LL 66-A2
TOWN CENTRE DR EAG 135-D4
TOWN COURSE DR CHS 131-B4
TOWN HALL DR GRF 74-E4,75-A4
TOWN LAKE DR WBY 124-A2
TOWN LINE RD IND 103-A1
TOWNDALE CT BLO 134-A2
TOWNDALE DR BLO 134-A2
TOWNE CIR SWR 96-E1
TOWNE TER BLO 134-C4
TOWNES CIR EDI 120-A2
TOWNES LN MTK 104-D2
TOWNES RD EDI 120-A2
TOWNES RD MTK 104-D2
TOWNLINE AVE BLO 133-C3
TOWNLINE AVE EPR 133-C3
TOWNLINE AVE JT 146-B4,160-B1
TOWNLINE AVE LVT 160-B2
TOWNLINE AVE SHK 146-B3
TOWNLINE RD BLO 133-C4,147-C1
TOWNLINE RD EPR 118-E4,147-C1
TOWNLINE RD MTK 118-B4
TOWNLINE RD N IND 89-A1
TOWNS VALLEY RD TRT 126-A2
TOWNSEDGE RD LTT 116-A4
TOWNSEDGE RD MTA 115-E4,116-A4
TOWNSHIP DR WBT 80-D2
TOWNSHIP PKWY WBT 80-D2
TOWNSHIP ROAD 120 SM 46-D4,60-D1
TOWNSHIP ROAD 16 SHK 146-B2
TOWNVIEW AVE SA 93-A3
TOWNVIEW RD MTK 119-A2
TR NST 40-C2
TRACY AVE EDI 119-D4,133-D1
TRACY RD WBL 95-A2
TRACY LYNN TER MTK 118-C3
TRADING POST
TRL S AFT 125-A3,139-A1
TRAFFIC ST NE MPL 107-A1
TRAIL CT EAG 136-A4
TRAIL CT W CF 208-B4
TRAIL LN COR 75-E4,76-A4
TRAIL RD MH 122-A4
TRAIL EAST RD BLO 134-D4
TRAIL HAVEN RD COR 61-D4,75-D2
TRAIL HAVEN RD HSN 61-D2
TRAIL OF DREAMS PRL 160-D3
TRAIL RIDGE LN MTK 118-C2
TRAIL WEST RD BLO 147-E2
TRAILER CT LWT 24-A2
TRAILER CT NFD 219-D3
TRAILER PARK RD NE EB 8-E3
TRAILS END CIR MTA 103-A3
TRAILS END RD EAG 136-A4
TRAILS END RD MTA 103-A3
TRAILWAY DR EAG 149-C2
TRAILWOOD N HOP 119-B3
TRAILWOOD S HOP 119-B3
TRALEE DR EDI 133-D1
TRAMMEL LN LWT 10-B3
TRANSFER RD STP 107-C3
TRANSIT AVE RVL 93-E4,94-A4
TRANSPORT TRL HUT 112-B3
TRAP LINE CIR CHN 118-B4
TRAP LINE LN CHN 118-B4
TRAPP CT FRI 79-A4
TRAPP PT EAG 135-D2
TRAPP RD EAG 135-D2
TRAPPERS CT LL 66-C4
TRAPPERS XING N LL 66-C4
TRAPPERS XING S LL 66-C4
TRAPPERS PASS CHN 118-B4
TRAPPERS PATH ABT 58-D1
TRAPPERS TRL MED 89-E3,90-A3
TRAPROCK DR SAT 14-D3
TRAPROCK ST NW RAM 34-E4,48-E1
TRAVELERS TRL EAG 149-A3
TRAVELERS TRL E BUR 148-D3
TRAVELERS TRL W BUR 148-C3
TRAVERSE PT EAG 149-C3
TRAVOIS RD EPR 133-A4
TRAYMORE RD MTK 105-B3
TREE ST MTK 118-E3
TREE FARM RD EPR 133-A4
TREELINE DR COR 75-D1
TRENTON CIR N PLY 91-B3,105-B2
TRENTON LN EAG 149-C2
TRENTON LN EPR 132-C3
TRENTON LN N MG 63-B4,77-B1
TRENTON LN N PLY 91-B1,105-B2
TRENTON PL N PLY 91-B2
TRENTON RD EAG 150-A1
TRENTON TRL EAG 150-A2
TRETBAUGH DR BLO 134-A3
TRI OAKS CIR NE EB 23-D4
TRIANGLE DR SJT 83-B4
TRIANGLE LN JOR 173-B2
TRIANGLE RD NW ER 33-D1
TRIBAL TRL MTK 104-E3
TRILANE CIR NYA 142-C3
TRILANE DR NYA 142-C3
TRILLIUM CIR EPR 132-D1
TRILLIUM CIR VIC 130-E2
TRILLIUM CT EAG 149-E2
TRILLIUM CT VIC 130-E2
TRILLIUM CT N CHM 63-C3
TRILLIUM LN EDI 133-E1
TRILLIUM LN TRT 112-C4,126-C1
TRILLIUM LN VIC 130-E2
TRILLIUM LN E MTA 116-D3
TRILLIUM LN N CHM 63-C3
TRILLIUM LN W MTA 116-D3
TRILLIUM TRL VIC 130-E2
TRILLIUM WAY MTA 116-D4
TRIM PL WIL 95-D1
TRINITY DR NE FRI 78-D4
TRINITY GDNS BP 77-E1
TRISTA CT SB 116-A3
TRISTA LN SB 116-A3
TRISTA LN E SB 116-B3
TRISTAN TRL CHS 145-D1
TRISTRAM WAY EPR 118-C4
TRITON DR GV 91-E4,92-A4
TROENDLE CIR CHN 118-A4
TROLLHAGEN DR NE FRI 92-E1,93-A1
TROON CT DWD 81-D2
TROON CT TRT 125-D3
TROON CT WBY 110-A4
TROSETH RD RVL 93-B3
TROST TRL SAV 161-E1
TROTT BROOK PKWY ER 34-A2
TROTTER CT SWR 96-E2
TROTTERS CIR CHN 132-A1
TROTTERS CT EAG 150-A1
TROTTERS LN WBY 123-E1,124-A1
TROTTERS PATH EPR 147-C1
TROTTERS RDG EAG 150-A1
TROTTERS TRL NE PRL 161-A2
TROUT BROOK CIR STP 108-B2
TROUT BROOK RD HUT 97-E4,111-E1
TROUT BROOK RD SJT 97-E3
TROUT BROOK RD N SJT 97-E2
TROUT BROOK TRL SJT 97-E3
TROY DR MV 79-C2
TROY LN N DAY 62-B2
TROY LN N MG 62-B4,76-B2
TROY LN N PLY 90-B1,104-B1
TROY ST RF 140-E1
TROY ST NW ER 19-B4,33-B1
TROY MARQUETTE
DR MO 31-E3,32-A3
TRUAX CIR HAS 166-B3
TRUDY CT WSP 122-C3
TRUE ST NW NB 93-B1
TRUFFULA TRL ORO 103-D2
TRUMBLE CT CHS 145-D1
TRUMBLE ST CHS 145-D1
TRUSSEL AVE CHM 63-C1
TUCKAWAY CT SHK 147-B4
TUCKER LN EDI 119-C3
TUCKER RD HAN 61-B2
TUCKER RD HSN 61-C2
TUDOR RD MTK 104-E3
TUENGE DR SWR 96-E2
TULANE ST NE COT 38-D2
TULGREN ST TRT 111-E4
TULIP CT CHN 131-D1
TULIP ST NW AND 35-E3,49-E1
TULIP ST NW CR 63-E1
TULIP ST NW OG 21-D2
TULIP ST NW SF 7-D2,21-D1
TUMBLEWEED CIR SHK 146-C3
TUNGSTEN ST NW BT 21-A2
TUNGSTEN ST NW RAM 35-A3,49-B2
TUNGSTEN WAY NW RAM 49-B2
TUPA CIR EDI 133-D1
TUPA DR EDI 133-D1
TURIN AVE SSP 122-E3
TURNBERRY ALC WBY 110-A4
TURNBERRY CIR MTK 118-C2
TURNBERRY CT NFD 220-A4
TURNBERRY CT TRT 125-D3
TURNBERRY CT NW RAM 34-C4
TURNBERRY LN NFD 220-A4
TURNBERRY TURN NW RAM 34-C4
TURNBRIDGE CIR SHK 147-A3
TURNBRIDGE CT SHK 147-A3
TURNER DR HEN 198-D4
TURNER RD IND 102-D1
TURNERS XRD N GV 105-E2
TURNERS XRD S GV 105-E3
TURNHAM RD ORO 103-B2
TURNPIKE RD GV 105-E3
TURNSTONE CT RVL 94-A3
TURQUOISE CIR EAG 149-C1
TURQUOISE PT EAG 149-C1
TURQUOISE TRL EAG 149-B1
TURREL ST LES 212-C4
TURTLE LN E SVW 79-E3
TURTLE LN W SVW 79-E3
TURTLE PT EPR 132-C3
TURTLE ST BAY 97-B3
TURTLE LAKE RD SVW 80-A2
TUSCANY WAY EPR 147-C1
TUSCARORA AVE STP 121-E2,122-A2
TUSSOCK CT EPR 133-A3
TUTTLE CT HAS 166-E3
TUTTLE DR HAS 166-E3
TUTTLE RD HAS 166-E3
TUXEDO BLVD MOU 117-A2
TUXEDO RD MTA 117-A3
TWELVE TRL HUT 112-D1
TWELVE OAKS DR MTK 105-A4
TWELVE OAKS LN HUD 111-D2
TWELVE OAKS CENTER DR MTK 104-D3
TWILIGHT TRL EPR 132-B2
TWILITE TER BLA 65-D3
TWILITE TER CP 65-D3
TWILLA AVE BEC 2-D3
TWIN PKWY NW BT 20-C3
TWIN CIRCLE DR MH 121-E4
TWIN HAVEN RD MTK 119-A2
TWIN ISLAND CIR PRL 160-E3,161-A3
TWIN LAKE AVE BC 92-A2
TWIN LAKE BLVD CRY 91-E2
TWIN LAKE BLVD LC 94-B2
TWIN LAKE BLVD VH 94-B2
TWIN LAKE BLVD E BC 92-A2
TWIN LAKE CT LC 94-C2
TWIN LAKE RD LC 94-B2
TWIN LAKE TER N CRY 91-E2,92-A1
TWIN LAKE TRL LC 94-B2
TWIN LAKES AVE CV 66-E2
TWIN LAKES XING EPR 132-E3
TWIN LAKES RD ER 34-A2
TWIN LAKES RD NW ER 20-B4,34-A1
TWIN MAPLE LN CHN 132-B1
TWIN OAK DR ROB 92-A3
TWIN OAK LN ROB 92-A3
TWIN OAKS CIR HUT 112-B4
TWIN OAKS CIR SCT 173-C3
TWIN PONDS CRV SAV 161-D2
TWIN SPRINGS RD SMT 83-B3
TWINKLE TER CP 65-D3
TYACKE DR BUR 162-D2
TYLER AVE BEC 3-A4
TYLER AVE N HOP 119-C2
TYLER AVE S EDI 119-C2
TYLER CIR NE BLA 50-E4
TYLER CT EDI 119-C2
TYLER PL NE CH 92-E2
TYLER ST ANO 49-C4
TYLER ST ER 34-A2
TYLER ST HAS 166-D2
TYLER ST NE BLA 50-E4,64-E4
TYLER ST NE CH 92-E2,93-A2
TYLER ST NE EB 22-E2
TYLER ST NE HL 50-E1
TYLER ST NE MPL 92-E3,106-E1
TYLER ST NE SLK 78-E2
TYLER ST NW ER 20-A4,34-A1
TYLER ST S SHK 146-A3
TYNE CT IGH 150-B1
TYNE LN EAG 150-B1
TYNE LN IGH 150-B1
TYPO DR E LWT 10-B3
TYPO DR W LWT 10-B3
TYPO CREEK DR NE LWT 10-B3,24-B1
TYPO CREEK DR NE OXT 10-B2
TYRELL DR EPR 119-B4
TYROL CIR LVT 160-A2
TYROL CRST GV 106-A3
TYROL DR LVT 160-A2
TYROL LN LVT 160-A2
TYROL TRL N GV 106-A3
TYROL TRL S GV 106-A3
TYRONE DR SHK 146-D3
TYRONE LN MOU 117-A2

U

ULLMANN CIR EPR 132-C1
ULMER DR LL 65-E2,66-A2
ULSSES CIR NE BLA 50-E4
ULYSSES CIR NE BLA 50-E4
ULYSSES CT NE ATT 8-E2
ULYSSES PATH NE EB 8-E3
ULYSSES ST ER 20-A4
ULYSSES ST NE ATT 8-E2
ULYSSES ST NE BLA 50-E4,64-E3
ULYSSES ST NE CH 93-A2
ULYSSES ST NE EB 8-E3,36-E1
ULYSSES ST NE MPL 93-A4,107-A1
ULYSSES ST NW ER 20-A3,34-A3
UMBRIA LN MG 76-B2
UNDERCLIFF ST NW CR 63-E1
UNDERCLIFF ST NW AND 49-E2
UNDERCLIFF ST NW AND 35-D2,49-D3
UNDERCLIFF ST NW OG 21-D2
UNDERHILL CIR LOL 104-A2
UNDERWOOD CIR N PLY 90-E2
UNDERWOOD CT N MG 76-E1
UNDERWOOD CT N PLY 90-E2
UNDERWOOD LN N MG 76-E2
UNDERWOOD LN N PLY 90-E2
UNDERWOOD LN NW SM 46-E3
UNDERWOOD ST N FH 107-D2
UNDESTAD ST EPR 118-C4
UNICORN PL SAV 161-E2
UNICORN ST NW RAM 34-C3
UNION AVE CT 114-C4,128-C1
UNION CT HAS 166-C3
UNION PL EXC 117-E3
UNION ST RF 140-E1
UNION ST SWR 97-A1
UNION ST N NYA 142-C4
UNION ST NW ER 33-B2
UNION ST S NFD 219-E4
UNION ST SE MPL 107-A2
UNION TRL BKT 185-B2
UNION HILL BLVD BPT 186-D3
UNION LAKE BLVD WHT 216-D3,217-B3
UNION LAKE TRL FOT 217-E4,218-B4
UNION LAKE TRL WT 217-D4
UNION TERRACE CT N PLY 91-B2
UNION TERRACE
LN N CHM 49-B4,63-B1
UNION TERRACE LN N MG 63-B4,77-B1
UNION TERRACE
LN N PLY 91-B2,105-B2
UNION TERRACE WAY N PLY 91-B3
UNIQUE DR BUR 148-C4
UNITY AVE CV 66-E2
UNITY AVE FRT 14-A4
UNITY AVE SHT 14-A1
UNITY AVE N BC 77-E4,91-E1
UNITY AVE N BP 77-E3
UNITY AVE N CRY 91-E2
UNITY AVE N GV 105-E1
UNITY AVE N ROB 91-E3
UNITY BLVD NEW 123-B4
UNITY CIR NW CR 64-C1
UNITY CT CRY 91-E2
UNITY ST NW CR 50-C4,64-C1
UNITY ST NW OG 8-C4,22-C1
UNITY ST NW SF 8-C3
UNIVERSITY AVE BEC 2-E4
UNIVERSITY AVE E STP 108-B4
UNIVERSITY AVE NE AND 36-D4,50-D1
UNIVERSITY AVE NE BLA 64-D4,78-D1
UNIVERSITY AVE NE CH 92-D2
UNIVERSITY AVE NE CR 50-D4,64-D3
UNIVERSITY AVE NE EB 22-D3
UNIVERSITY AVE NE FRI 78-D3,92-D1
UNIVERSITY AVE NE MPL 92-D3,106-D1
UNIVERSITY AVE NE OG 22-D4,36-D1
UNIVERSITY AVE NE SLK 78-D2
UNIVERSITY AVE NW AND 36-D2
UNIVERSITY
AVE SE MPL 106-E2,107-A2
UNIVERSITY AVE W STP 107-D4,108-A4
UNIVERSITY CIR NE BLA 64-D3
UNIVERSITY AVE EXT BET 8-D3
UNIVERSITY AVE EXT EB 8-D2
UNIVERSITY AVE EXT OG 8-D4,22-D1
UNIVERSITY AVE EXT SF 8-D4
UNIVERSITY AVE NE DR FRI 78-D3
UNIVERSITY AVE NE SE RD FRI 78-D4
UNIVERSITY AVENUE EXT ATT 8-D1
UNSER ST NE LWT 9-E4
UPLAND AVE HOT -B3,114-B3
UPLAND AVE STP 123-A2
UPLAND AVE NW ER 33-D1
UPLAND CIR CHN 131-E2
UPLAND CRST E CH 93-A1
UPLAND CRST N CH 93-A1
UPLAND CRST W CH 93-A1
UPLAND CT N PLY 90-D4
UPLAND LN N MG 76-D1,90-D1
UPLAND LN N PLY 90-D3,104-D2
UPLAND RD SHT 14-A2
UPLAND RD NW SM 46-D3
UPLAND ST NW ER 19-D4
UPLANDER CIR NW AND 36-A3
UPLANDER DR NW AND 50-A2
UPLANDER ST NW AND 36-A2,50-A1
UPLANDER ST NW CR 50-A4,64-A3
UPLANDER ST NW OG 22-A4,36-A2
UPPER 1ST ST S LS 111-C4
UPPER 2ND ST N LLD 111-B4
UPPER 3RD ST N LLD 111-C4
UPPER 4TH ST N LLD 111-C3
UPPER 5TH ST N LLD 111-C3
UPPER 5TH ST N OKD 109-C4
UPPER 12TH ST S LSC 125-C1
UPPER 14TH ST N OKD 109-C3
UPPER 15TH ST S LSC 125-C1
UPPER 16TH ST N OKD 109-D2
UPPER 17TH ST N OKD 109-D2
UPPER 17TH ST S LSC 125-C2
UPPER 18TH ST S LSC 125-C2
UPPER 19TH ST N OKD 109-D2
UPPER 19TH ST S LSC 125-C2
UPPER 20TH ST N OKD 109-D2
UPPER 20TH ST S LSC 125-C2
UPPER 21ST ST S LSC 125-C2
UPPER 22ND ST N OKD 109-C2
UPPER 22ND ST S LSC 125-C2
UPPER 23RD ST N OKD 109-D2
UPPER 23RD ST S SMP 125-C2
UPPER 24TH ST N OKD 109-D2
UPPER 26TH ST N OKD 109-D1
UPPER 28TH ST N OKD 109-C2
UPPER 33RD ST N LE 110-B1
UPPER 33RD ST N OKD 109-C1
UPPER 34TH ST S AFT 125-B3
UPPER 35TH ST N OKD 109-C1
UPPER 35TH STREET
CIR N OKD 109-C1
UPPER 35TH STREET
CT N OKD 109-C1
UPPER 36TH ST N OKD 109-D1
UPPER 39TH ST N OKD 95-C4
UPPER 42ND ST N OKD 95-D4
UPPER 43RD ST N OKD 95-D4
UPPER 44TH ST N OKD 95-C4
UPPER 44TH STREET CT N OKD 95-C4
UPPER 45TH ST E IGH 122-D4
UPPER 45TH ST N OKD 95-D4
UPPER 46TH ST N OKD 95-C4
UPPER 47TH ST N OKD 95-C4
UPPER 48TH ST N OKD 95-C3
UPPER 51ST ST N OKD 95-C3
UPPER 53RD ST N OKD 95-C3
UPPER 54TH ST N OKD 95-C3
UPPER 54TH ST N OPH 96-E3
UPPER 55TH ST E IGH 136-D1
UPPER 55TH ST N OKD 95-C3
UPPER 55TH ST N OPH 97-A3
UPPER 56TH CT N OPH 97-A3
UPPER 56TH ST N OKD 95-C3
UPPER 56TH ST N OPH 96-E3,97-A3
UPPER 59TH ST N OPH 97-B2
UPPER 61ST PATH E IGH 137-A2
UPPER 61ST ST N OPH 97-A2
UPPER 62ND ST E IGH 136-E2
UPPER 63RD ST N OPH 97-A2
UPPER 64TH CT E IGH 136-D2
UPPER 64TH PATH E IGH 137-A2
UPPER 65TH ST E IGH 137-A2
UPPER 69TH ST E IGH 137-A2
UPPER 71ST ST IGH 137-A3
UPPER 71ST ST E IGH 136-E3,137-A3
UPPER 73RD ST E IGH 136-E3,137-A3
UPPER 74TH ST S CG 138-C3
UPPER 75TH ST E IGH 137-A3
UPPER 76TH ST E IGH 136-E3
UPPER 79TH CT E IGH 136-E3
UPPER 81ST ST S CG 138-A3
UPPER 84TH ST W IGH 136-B4
UPPER 85TH ST W IGH 136-B4
UPPER 86TH ST W IGH 136-B4
UPPER 89TH STREET CIR S CG 137-E4
UPPER 91ST ST SWT 82-D3
UPPER 129TH CT APV 149-A4
UPPER 135TH ST W APV 163-D1
UPPER 135TH ST W RMT 163-E1
UPPER 136TH ST W APV 163-B1
UPPER 136TH STREET CT APV 163-C1
UPPER 138TH CT APV 163-A1
UPPER 138TH ST W RMT 164-A1
UPPER 139TH CT W APV 163-A1
UPPER 139TH ST W APV 163-B1
UPPER 141ST ST W APV 163-D1
UPPER 143RD CT W APV 163-B1
UPPER 143RD ST W RMT 163-E2,164-A2
UPPER 145TH CT W APV 163-A2
UPPER 145TH ST W APV 163-A2
UPPER 145TH ST W RMT 163-E2
UPPER 146TH ST N HUG 67-B2
UPPER 146TH ST W APV 163-B2

UPPER 147TH ST W APV 163-C2
UPPER 147TH ST W RMT 163-E2,164-A2
UPPER 148TH CT APV 163-D2
UPPER 148TH ST W RMT 163-E2
UPPER 149TH CT RMT 163-E2
UPPER 149TH ST W RMT 163-E2,164-A2
UPPER 156TH CT W RMT 163-E3
UPPER 156TH ST W RMT 163-E3
UPPER 157TH ST W APV 163-B3
UPPER 161ST ST W LVL 162-D3
UPPER 162ND ST W LVL 163-B3
UPPER 163RD CT W LVL 163-B3
UPPER 163RD ST W LVL 163-B3
UPPER 164TH ST W LVL 163-B3
UPPER 167TH CT W LVL 163-B4
UPPER 167TH ST W LVL .162-C4,163-B4
UPPER 171ST ST W LVL 163-A4
UPPER 173RD CT LVL 162-D4
UPPER 178TH ST W LVL 176-D1
UPPER 182ND ST FAR 177-C1
UPPER 182ND ST W FAR 177-D1
UPPER 183RD ST W FAR 177-D1
UPPER 193RD ST E RVT 181-B2
UPPER 194TH ST E RVT 181-B2
UPPER 196TH WAY W LVL 176-D2
UPPER 204TH ST W ET 177-E3
UPPER 205TH ST W LVL 176-D3
UPPER 206TH ST W LVL .176-E3,177-A3
UPPER 207TH ST E RVT 181-E3
UPPER 208TH ST W LVL 176-E3
UPPER 209TH ST W LVL .176-E3,177-A3
UPPER 216TH AVE SMT ...69-E1,70-A1
UPPER 240TH ST W EUT 190-E3
UPPER 291ST ST E RAN 207-A3
UPPER TER EDI 133-E1,134-A1
UPPER AFTON CIR WBY 123-C1
UPPER AFTON CV WBY 123-C1
UPPER AFTON RD MPW 123-B1
UPPER AFTON RD STP ..108-E4,123-A1
UPPER AFTON RD WBY 123-C1
UPPER AFTON TER STP 108-E4
UPPER BUFORD CIR FH 107-C2
UPPER COLONIAL DR MH 122-A3
UPPER COVE RD MTA ...102-E3,103-A3
UPPER ELKWOOD CT APV 163-D1
UPPER GUTHRIE CT APV 163-A2
UPPER HAMLET CT APV 149-A4
UPPER HEATHER
AVE N HUG 67-C4,81-C1
UPPER LEA LN LOL 103-E2
UPPER SAINT DENNIS RD STP ..121-D3
UPPER VALLEY CREEK RD WBY .123-D2
UPPER WESTMONT AVE MG 76-B1
UPPER WOOD WAY BUR 162-D1
UPPLANDA ST BUF 58-E1,59-A1
UPTON AVE BUR 148-B4,162-B1
UPTON AVE N BC 92-B1
UPTON AVE N BP 64-B4,78-B1
UPTON AVE N MPL 92-B3,106-B1
UPTON AVE S BLO 134-B2,148-B1
UPTON AVE S BUR 148-B4
UPTON AVE S MPL 106-B3,120-B2
UPTON AVE S RCH 120-B4,134-B1
UPTON CIR BLO 134-B4,148-B1
UPTON CIR N BP 78-B2
UPTON PL BLO 148-B1
UPTON RD BLO 134-B4,148-B1
UPTON RD YAT 156-C2
URAL ST NE COT 38-C2
URAL ST NE HL 51-C2
URANIMITE ST NW RAM ..34-E4,48-E1
URANIUM ST NW BT 21-A4,35-A2
URANIUM ST NW RAM 35-A2,49-A2
URBAN AVE YAT 142-B2
URBAN AVE N BC 78-A4
URBAN PL STP 108-D4
URBANDALE CT PLY 90-B3
URBANDALE CT N PLY 90-B3
URBANDALE LN N MG 76-B2
URBANDALE LN N PLY ...90-B4,104-B1
URBANK CT NE BLA 65-B2
URBANK ST NE HL 37-B3,51-B2
US HIGHWAY 61 WYO 25-B4
US HIGHWAY 61 WYT 25-B4,39-B1
US HIGHWAY 8 WYT 39-D1
UTAH AVE SAV 161-D1
UTAH AVE N BP 77-D4
UTAH AVE N CHM 63-C2
UTAH AVE N CRY 91-D4
UTAH AVE N NH 91-D2
UTAH AVE S BLO 133-D4,147-D1
UTAH AVE S GV 105-D3
UTAH AVE S SLP 105-D3,119-D1
UTAH CIR S BLO 133-D4,147-D1
UTAH CT N BP 77-C2
UTAH DR HOT 114-B2
UTAH DR S SLP 105-D3
UTAH RD BLO 147-D1
UTE ST NW RAM 35-C2,49-C1
UTE ST NW SF 7-C3
UTICA AVE SAV 147-E4,161-E1
UTICA AVE STP 109-A3
UTICA AVE S BLO 133-E3,147-E2
UTICA AVE S SLP 105-E4,119-E2
UTICA CIR BLO 133-E4,147-E1
UTICA CIR CHN 132-A1
UTICA LN CHN 131-E1
UTICA RD BLO 133-E4,147-E1
UTICA TER CHN 131-E1
UTILITY DR RFD 74-B3
UTOPIA AVE YAT 142-B3

V

VADNAIS BLVD LC 94-C2
VADNAIS BLVD VH 94-B2
VADNAIS BLVD W VH 94-B2
VADNAIS DR VH 94-D2
VADNAIS LN VH 94-D2
VADNAIS RD VH 94-C2
VADNAIS CENTER DR VH 94-D2
VADNAIS LAKE DR VH 94-C2
VAGABOND CT MG 76-B2
VAGABOND LN MG 76-B1
VAGABOND LN N MG 76-B2
VAGABOND LN N PLY ...90-B2,104-B2
VAIL DR MH 121-E4
VALDERS AVE GV 105-D1
VALE AVE MPW 94-E3
VALE AVE NW ER 33-D1
VALE CIR PRL 160-E4
VALE CT EPR 132-E1
VALE ST CR 64-C2
VALE ST NW AND 36-C2,50-C2
VALE ST NW CR 64-C3
VALE ST NW OG 22-C2
VALE CREST RD CRY 91-E4
VALE CREST RD GV 91-E4,105-E1
VALENCOUR CIR MH 135-D1
VALENTINE AVE AH 93-D1
VALENTINE AVE STP 107-B2
VALENTINE CT AH 93-D1
VALENTINE TER BLO 134-B2
VALENTINE CREST RD AH 93-C1
VALENTO CIR VH 94-C2
VALENTO LN N LC 94-C3
VALERIE LN NB 79-A4
VALERY RD GV 106-A1
VALEWOOD DR MTK 118-D4
VALHALLA CIR WBY 123-C4
VALHALLA DR NYA 142-C3
VALHALLA DR WBY 123-C4,137-C1
VALHALLA DR NE EB 36-E2
VALLACHER AVE SLP 119-E1,120-A1
VALLE VISTA ST NH 91-D4
VALLEY CT BUR 149-A2
VALLEY DR BUR 148-C4
VALLEY DR HSN 61-E3,62-A2
VALLEY DR MTK 118-B4
VALLEY DR NFD 219-D3
VALLEY DR NW AND 35-D4
VALLEY DR SE SM 47-A4
VALLEY LN BUR 162-B3
VALLEY LN EDI 119-D4
VALLEY LN HAS 166-C2
VALLEY LN MH 122-B2
VALLEY LN SE SM 47-A4
VALLEY PL CRY 91-D4
VALLEY RD EPR 132-D4
VALLEY RD IND 88-C3
VALLEY RD MTK 119-A2
VALLEY RD NEW 123-B4
VALLEY ST CHS 145-D2
VALLEY ST MPL 92-E3
VALLEY ST STP 108-B3
VALLEY WAY HOP 119-C1
VALLEY CREEK DR MTA 116-C3
VALLEY CREEK PLZ WBY 123-D1
VALLEY CREEK RD WBY .123-D2,124-B2
VALLEY CREEK
TRL S AFT 124-E2,125-A2
VALLEY CURVE RD MH 122-A4
VALLEY FAIR DR SHK 146-E2
VALLEY FORGE LN N CHM .49-B4,63-B1
VALLEY FORGE LN N MG ..63-B4,77-B2
VALLEY FORGE LN N PLY 91-B2
VALLEY FORGE PL EAG 150-A2
VALLEY FORGE RD CLT 189-B1
VALLEY FORGE RD EPR 133-B2
VALLEY HIGH DR BLO 148-C1
VALLEY HIGH RD BUR 148-C4
VALLEY INDUSTRIAL
BLVD N SHK 146-E2
VALLEY INDUSTRIAL
BLVD S SHK 146-E2
VALLEY OAKS RD VH 80-D4
VALLEY PARK DR SHK 146-E2
VALLEY RIDGE CT CHN 131-E3
VALLEY RIDGE CT CRT 175-E1
VALLEY RIDGE DR EAG 135-C3
VALLEY RIDGE PL CHN 131-E3
VALLEY RIDGE TRL N CHN 131-E3
VALLEY RIDGE TRL S CHN 131-E3
VALLEY SIDE DR STP 109-A4
VALLEY VIEW CT CHN 131-E3
VALLEY VIEW CT CRT 175-E1
VALLEY VIEW CT SVW 93-E1,94-A1
VALLEY VIEW CT WSP 122-C3
VALLEY VIEW DR BUR 162-B2
VALLEY VIEW DR HUD 111-E2
VALLEY VIEW DR JOR 173-B2
VALLEY VIEW DR RF 140-E2
VALLEY VIEW DR SAV 161-E2
VALLEY VIEW DR SCT ...159-C4,173-B1
VALLEY VIEW DR SLW 173-A2
VALLEY VIEW DR TRT 126-A1
VALLEY VIEW DR N EAG 149-B1
VALLEY VIEW DR NW AND 35-D3
VALLEY VIEW DR S EAG 149-B1
VALLEY VIEW LN FRT 14-B4
VALLEY VIEW LN NB 79-A3
VALLEY VIEW LN SE WAT 101-B4
VALLEY VIEW PL S CHN 131-E3
VALLEY VIEW RD BUR 162-B3
VALLEY VIEW RD COR 76-A4,90-A1
VALLEY VIEW RD EDI ..120-A4,133-C1
VALLEY VIEW RD EPR ..132-C1,133-B1
VALLEY VIEW RD HUT 111-E1
VALLEY VIEW RD MTK 118-B3
VALLEY VIEW RD E SHK 146-D4
VALLEY VIEW TER HSN 62-A2
VALLEY VIEW TRL SJT 84-A4,97-E1
VALLEY VIEW WAY CFT 222-C1
VALLEY VIEW PARK RD OPH 97-A3
VALLEYVIEW AVE MPW 123-B2
VALLEYVIEW DR RW 210-E1
VALLEYVIEW PL MPL 120-C3
VALLEYVIEW PL STP 123-B2
VALLEYVIEW PL WBL 95-B1
VALLEYVIEW RD CHS 145-C2
VALLEYVIEW ST LOL 103-E2
VALLEYVIEW ST SB 116-A3
VALLEYVIEW ST SW LAT 201-D3
VALLEYWOOD CIR GV 105-E2
VALLEYWOOD CIR SWD 117-C3
VALLEYWOOD LN SWD 117-C3
VAN BUREN AVE STP ...107-D3,108-A3
VAN BUREN AVE N HOP 119-C1
VAN BUREN AVE S EDI 119-C2
VAN BUREN AVE S HOP 119-C2
VAN BUREN CT NE BLA 64-E1
VAN BUREN PL N HOP 119-C1
VAN BUREN ST ANO 49-C4
VAN BUREN ST HL 36-E3
VAN BUREN ST NE BLA 64-E4,78-E1
VAN BUREN ST NE CH 92-E2
VAN BUREN ST NE EB 22-E1
VAN BUREN ST NE FRI 78-E2
VAN BUREN ST NE HL 36-E4,50-E3
VAN BUREN ST NE MPL ..92-E3,106-E1
VAN BUREN ST NE SLK 78-E2
VAN BUREN ST S SHK 146-A3
VAN BUREN TER N HOP 119-C1
VAN BUREN TRL N HOP 119-C1
VAN BUREN WAY N HOP 119-C1
VAN DEMARK RD ROB 92-A4
VAN DYKE ST MPW 95-A4,109-A1
VAN DYKE ST STP 109-A3
VAN DYKE ST WBL 95-A1
VAN HOVEN RD SSP 123-A4
VAN NEST AVE MPL 120-D1
VAN SLOAN RD CHS 145-B1
VAN SLYKE AVE STP 107-E2
VAN TASSEL CT SWR 82-D4
VAN TASSEL DR SWR 82-D4
VAN TASSLE CIR BL 18-A4
VANADIUM ST NW RAM ...35-A2,49-A2
VANASSE ST SOM 84-B1
VANCE CIR NW ER 20-A3
VANCE ST STP 122-A1
VANCE ST NW ER 20-A3
VANCOUVER RD EPR 132-D1
VANDALIA ST STP 107-C3
VANDALL ST MH 122-A3
VANDAN RD MTK 118-C1
VANDERBIE ST N LC 94-C3
VANDERVORK AVE EDI 119-E2
VANDREGRIFF WAY MG 76-B2
VANTAGE CT EPR 132-C3
VARIOLITE ST NW BT 6-E4,20-E1
VARIOLITE ST NW RAM 34-E4,48-E1
VARIOLITE ST NW SF 6-E4
VARIOLITE ST NW STT 6-E1
VARNER CIR N GV 105-D2
VARNER LN BUF 59-A1
VARNER ST N JOR 173-B2
VARNER ST S JOR 173-B2
VARNER WAY ABT 58-D1
VASA TRL VAT 210-A4
VASSAR ST NE COT 24-E4,38-E2
VASSAR ST NE OXT 10-D1
VAUXHALL ST NE COT 37-E2
VEGA AVE CT 128-B2,142-B1
VEGA AVE HOT ....-B3,114-B3
VEGA DR NW BT 35-B1
VEIT PL ROG 47-D4
VELMA ST LND 12-D4
VELVETLEAF LN LL 66-C3
VENDELL ST BUF 58-E1,59-A1
VENESS RD BLO 133-C3
VENTNOR AVE EAG 150-A1
VENTRE ST NW AND 35-C4
VENTRE ST NW BT 35-C2
VENTURA AVE NE FRI 92-D1
VENTURA CT JT 145-D4
VENTURA DR WBY 123-C2
VENTURA PL SAV 161-D1
VENTURE LN EPR 132-D2
VENUS AVE AH 93-C1
VERA AVE YAT 156-B3
VERA ST N CHM 63-B1
VERA CRUZ AVE N BC 77-E4
VERA CRUZ AVE N CHM 63-E3
VERA CRUZ AVE N CRY 91-E4
VERA CRUZ AVE N GV 91-E4
VERA CRUZ AVE N ROB 91-E3
VERA CRUZ LN N BC 77-E4
VERBENA DR WAT 101-B4
VERDE VALLEY RD NW BT 21-B3
VERDEROSA AVE SSP 123-A4
VERDI RD BLO 148-C1
VERDIN CIR NW CR 64-A3
VERDIN ST NW AND 36-A3
VERDIN ST NW ATT 8-A2
VERDIN ST NW CR 50-A4,64-A2
VERDIN ST NW OG 22-A2,36-A2
VERDIN ST NW SF 8-A3
VERDIN ST NW STT 8-A1
VERGUS AVE CLT 188-D4,202-D1
VERGUS AVE SLT 160-D4,174-D3
VERMAR TER EPR 132-E1
VERMILLION CT N EAG 135-B4
VERMILLION CT NE BLA 65-B2
VERMILLION CT S EAG 135-B4
VERMILLION ST BLA 65-B1
VERMILLION ST HAS 166-D2
VERMILLION ST NE EB 23-B1,37-B1
VERMILLION ST NE HL 37-B4,51-B1
VERMILLION
RIVER TRL ET 177-E3,178-A3
VERMONT AVE EAG 150-A1
VERMONT AVE HAT 187-C1
VERMONT AVE SCT 173-C4,187-C1
VERMONT AVE S GV 105-C3
VERMONT ST SCF 14-C2
VERMONT ST SLP 119-E2
VERNA CT RFD 74-B3
VERNA LN CRT 175-E2
VERNDALE AVE ANO 49-B3
VERNON AVE CRT 175-E3,189-E1
VERNON AVE HOT 114-A2
VERNON AVE NMT 189-E1,203-E2
VERNON AVE SAV 147-E4,161-E1
VERNON AVE NW ER 33-D1
VERNON AVE S EDI 119-D3
VERNON AVE S SLP 105-E4,119-E2
VERNON BLVD NMT 203-E1
VERNON CIR MTK 105-B3
VERNON CIR SAV 161-E1
VERNON CT SAV 147-E4
VERNON CT S EDI 119-C4
VERNON DR MTK 105-B3
VERNON LN EDI 119-D3
VERNON ST BLT 18-B3
VERNON ST GRF 74-C3
VERNON ST STP 121-D1
VERNON ST NW ER 19-D2
VERNON WAY GRF 74-C1
VERNON HILLS RD EDI 119-C4
VERONICA LN MH 121-E4
VERSAILLES CT EAG 149-D1
VERVOORT LN EPR 132-E1
VESSEY AVE S BLO 147-E2
VESSEY CIR BLO 147-E2
VESSEY CT BLO 147-E2
VESSEY RD BLO 147-E1
VETERANS DR MPL 121-B3
VEVEA LN ROG 62-A1
VIBURNUM TRL EAG 149-B3
VICEROY DR NE SLK 78-E2
VICKERS ST HL 51-C3
VICKERS ST NE ATT 9-C1
VICKERS ST NE EB 37-C1
VICKERS ST NE HL 37-C3
VICKI CIR ROG 47-D4
VICKI DR ROG 47-D4
VICKI LN MH 121-E4
VICKI LN MTK 105-A4
VICKI LN SVW 80-A1
VICKORS XING BP 78-B1
VICKSBURG LN N DAY 48-D3
VICKSBURG LN N MG 76-D4,90-D1
VICKSBURG LN N PLY ...90-D2,104-D1
VICKY LN LL 52-B4
VICTOR LN MTK 118-D4
VICTORIA CIR SLP 105-D4
VICTORIA CIR VIC 130-E2
VICTORIA CRV MEN 121-D4
VICTORIA CRV MH 121-E4
VICTORIA CRV PRL 161-C3
VICTORIA CRV SLP 105-D4
VICTORIA CT BP 77-E1
VICTORIA CT MH 121-E4
VICTORIA CT SWR 96-E2,97-A2
VICTORIA DR CHS 131-B4,145-B1
VICTORIA DR EPR 132-E3
VICTORIA DR LTT 131-A4
VICTORIA DR VIC 130-E2,131-A3
VICTORIA DR NW ER 19-B3
VICTORIA GDNS BP 77-E1
VICTORIA LN BUR 162-E1
VICTORIA LN SLP 105-D4
VICTORIA LN NW ER 19-B3
VICTORIA RD LIL 121-E3
VICTORIA RD MH 121-E4
VICTORIA RD SLT 175-A1
VICTORIA RD WBY 123-D2
VICTORIA ST ER 19-B4
VICTORIA ST MTK 118-D2
VICTORIA ST SLT 160-E4
VICTORIA ST N RVL 93-E3,107-E1
VICTORIA ST N STP 107-E4,121-E1
VICTORIA ST N SVW 79-E4,93-E2
VICTORIA ST S STP 121-E1
VICTORIA WAY SLP 105-D4
VICTORY AVE MH 135-D1
VICTORY AVE MPL 92-B3
VICTORY LN SHT 14-B2
VICTORY PL SSP 122-D4
VICTORY MEMORIAL DR MPL 92-B3
VICTORY MEMORIAL DR ROB 92-B3
VICUNA ST NW RAM 34-C2
VIEAU LN DEL 87-E2
VIEBROCK DR FAT 41-E3,42-A3
VIENNA LN EAG 149-B3
VIERLING CT SHK 146-B3
VIERLING DR SHK 146-B3
VIERLING DR E SHK 146-C3
VIERLING DR W SHK 145-E3,146-A3
VIEW CT HAS 166-C2
VIEW LN EDI 119-C3
VIEW LN EPR 132-D2
VIEW LN MH 122-B2
VIEW LN OST 28-E2
VIEW LN N DAY 49-A4
VIEW RD MHT 95-C1
VIEW ST STP 121-E2
VIEWCREST CIR BUR 162-C2
VIEWCREST CIR PRL 160-E3
VIEWCREST LN BUR 162-C2
VIEWCREST LN NH 91-D4
VIEWCREST RD SVW 79-D2
VIKING AVE CF 208-B3
VIKING AVE HOT ....-A4,114-A1
VIKING AVE HSN 47-E3
VIKING BLVD E WYO 25-B3
VIKING BLVD E WYT 25-C2
VIKING BLVD N WYT 25-D2,26-A2
VIKING BLVD NE EB 22-E4,23-D4
VIKING BLVD NE LWT 23-E3,24-C2
VIKING BLVD NE WYT 25-A3
VIKING BLVD NW BT 20-D4,21-B4
VIKING BLVD NW ER 20-B4
VIKING BLVD NW OG 21-D4,22-C4
VIKING CT E WYT 25-A3
VIKING DR BLO 133-E2
VIKING DR BUF 58-E3
VIKING DR BUR 148-D4
VIKING DR EDI 133-E2
VIKING DR EPR 133-B2
VIKING DR HUT 98-C4
VIKING DR MPW 94-C4
VIKING DR PS 95-D3
VIKING DR E LC 94-C4
VIKING DR W LC 94-B4
VIKING LN E WYT 25-A3
VIKING RD MTA 116-B3
VIKING TER NFD 219-D3
VIKING STEEL RD SHK 146-C2
VILAS LN EAG 135-D2
VILDMARK CT EAG 149-D2
VILDMARK DR EAG 149-D2
VILLA CT EDI 119-D4
VILLA CT EPR 132-E2
VILLA CT HAS 166-C3
VILLA DR COL 143-D4
VILLA DR SVW 79-D2
VILLA LN EDI 119-D4
VILLA LN MOU 116-E1
VILLA WAY EDI 119-E3
VILLABURNE CT BUR 148-E3
VILLABURNE DR BUR 148-E3,149-A3
VILLAGE AVE CF 208-B3
VILLAGE CT WBY 124-A3
VILLAGE DR EDI 133-D1
VILLAGE LN STP 121-C2
VILLAGE RD CHS 131-C4,145-C1
VILLAGE TRL HAS 166-C3
VILLAGE CENTER DR NO 80-A4
VILLAGE GREEN DR NE EB 36-E2
VILLAGE WOODS DR EPR 132-E3
VILLARD AVE STP 121-C3
VILLARD CV MG 76-B1
VILLARD PL STP 121-C3
VILLAUME AVE SSP 122-E4,123-A4
VILLIAGE DR LL 66-A1
VINA LN EPR 133-A1
VINCENT AVE BUR 148-B3,162-B1
VINCENT AVE N BC 92-B1
VINCENT AVE N BP 64-B4,78-B1
VINCENT AVE N MPL 92-B3,106-B1
VINCENT AVE S BLO 134-B3,148-B1
VINCENT AVE S MPL 106-B3,120-B3
VINCENT AVE S RCH 120-B4,134-B1
VINCENT CIR BLO 134-B3
VINCENT CIR BUR 162-B1
VINCENT CIR N BP 78-B2
VINCENT CIR S BLO 134-B3
VINCENT PL BLO 134-B3
VINCENT PL CHS 145-D2
VINCENT ST FH 107-B2
VINCENT ST SCF 14-C3
VINCENT ST S SCF 14-C3
VINE PL ORO 103-B4
VINE ST DPH 118-B3
VINE ST GRW 117-E3
VINE ST HUD 111-D2
VINE ST HUT 111-E2
VINE ST LES 212-D3
VINE ST LND 12-C4
VINE ST MO 31-C1
VINE ST PRE 153-B4,167-B1
VINE ST PRL 161-A4
VINE ST RF 140-D2
VINE ST SSP 122-D3
VINE ST SWD 118-A3
VINE ST N CF 208-B4
VINE ST N WAC 129-D3
VINE ST S WAC 129-D3
VINE HILL RD DPH 118-B2
VINE HILL RD S MTK 118-B3
VINE RIDGE CT DPH 118-B3
VINE RIDGE CT SWD 118-B3

VINELAND CT CHN 118-A4
VINELAND PL MPL 106-C3
VINEWOOD CT N MG 76-E3
VINEWOOD LN N DAY 48-E4
VINEWOOD LN N MG 76-E3
VINEWOOD LN N PLY 90-E3,104-E2
VINEWOOD WAY N MG 76-E3
VINEYARD ST CF 208-B3
VINING DR WBY 123-E2
VINING POINT RD MTK 118-D3
VINTAGE CT NW AND 49-D3
VINTAGE ST NW AND 35-D4,49-D2
VINTAGE ST NW CR 49-D3,63-D1
VINTAGE ST NW OG 21-D3
VINTAGE ST NW SF 7-D4,21-D1
VINTAGE ST NW STT 7-D1
VIOLET AVE N BC 78-A3
VIOLET CT NB 79-A3
VIOLET LN EAG 135-D4
VIOLET LN NB 79-A3
VIREO LN ML 43-D3
VIRGIL RD TRT 126-A1
VIRGINIA AVE DPH 118-B1
VIRGINIA AVE LOL 103-D2
VIRGINIA AVE RVL 94-A3
VIRGINIA AVE SAV 161-D1
VIRGINIA AVE SVW 80-A4,94-B1
VIRGINIA AVE N BP 77-C4
VIRGINIA AVE N CHM 63-C2
VIRGINIA AVE N CRY 91-D4
VIRGINIA AVE N NH 91-D2
VIRGINIA AVE S BLO 133-C4
VIRGINIA AVE S EDI 119-E4
VIRGINIA AVE S SAV 161-D2
VIRGINIA AVE S SLP 105-D4,119-D1
VIRGINIA CIR BLO 133-C3,147-C1
VIRGINIA CIR RVL 94-A4
VIRGINIA CIR SVW 94-B1
VIRGINIA CIR N CHM 63-C2
VIRGINIA CIR N NH 91-D2
VIRGINIA CIR N SLP 105-C4
VIRGINIA CIR S SLP 105-C4
VIRGINIA CT N CHM 63-C2
VIRGINIA DR VIC 117-A4
VIRGINIA LN EDI 119-E4,120-A4
VIRGINIA RD BLO 133-C3,147-C1
VIRGINIA ST STP 108-A2
VIRGINIA WAY CHS 145-D1
VIRGINIA SHORES CIR VIC 131-B1
VIRON RD NE FRI 78-E2
VIRTUE RD HUT 111-E1,112-A1
VISITATION DR MH 136-A1
VISTA AVE STP 121-E2
VISTA CIR DEL 87-E3
VISTA CT EPR 132-E1
VISTA CT HAS 166-C3
VISTA DR BUR 148-C3
VISTA DR GV 106-B1
VISTA DR HAS 166-C3
VISTA DR MTK 119-A3
VISTA DR NE SM 60-D2
VISTA RD SHT 14-B1
VISTA RD TF 14-B1
VISTA RIDGE LN SHK 160-B2
VIVIAN AVE SVW 79-E4,93-E2
VIVIAN DR BUR 148-B4
VIVIAN LN STP 123-B2
VIVIAN LN WSP 122-C4
VIXEN LN DEL 87-E3
VIXEN RD MED 90-A4
VOGEL FARM TRL EPR 132-B4
VOGELSBERG TRL CHN 146-A1
VOLE CT WDL 104-B4
VOLGA ST NE COT 38-C2
VOLGA ST NE LWT 24-C2
VON HERTZEN CIR CHS 131-C4
VON HERTZEN CT CHS 131-C4
VOYAGEUR DR WBY 123-E3
VRITS LN NP 201-E2

W

WABASH AVE STP 107-B3
WABASHA ST LES 212-D3
WABASHA ST N STP 108-B4
WABASHA ST S STP 108-B4,122-C1
WABASSO AVE SVW 94-A2
WACHTLER AVE MH 122-A3
WACO DR NW BT 35-C2
WACO DR NW RAM 35-C2
WACO ST NW AND 35-C3
WACO ST NW BT 7-C4,35-C2
WACO ST NW ER 33-B1
WACO ST NW RAM 35-C2,49-C2
WACONIA CIR NE EB 9-B4
WACONIA CT NE BLA 65-B2
WACONIA PKWY N WAC 129-C2
WACONIA PKWY N WCT 129-C3
WACONIA PKWY S WAC 129-C3
WACONIA PKWY S WCT 129-C3
WACONIA RD WAT 101-B3
WACONIA RD SE WAT 101-B4
WACONIA ST BLA 65-B4
WACONIA ST NE EB 37-B1
WACONIA ST NE HL 51-B2
WACOTA ST PRE 167-B1
WACOUTA ST STP 108-C4
WADENA ST STP 108-C3
WAGENER PL RVL 108-B1
WAGNER DR CHS 131-D4
WAGNER ST RVL 108-A1
WAGNER WAY EPR 132-D2
WAGNER WAY NM 189-E4
WAGNER HILLWAY LEO 222-C4
WAGNERS BAY CT WAC 129-D2
WAGON AVE HOT 99-E3
WAGON BRIDGE CIR PRL 161-A3
WAGON WHEEL CIR BUF 58-E3
WAGON WHEEL CT HUT 112-B2
WAGON WHEEL LN COR 89-B1
WAGON WHEEL RD HOP 119-B3
WAGON WHEEL TRL CRT 176-A4,190-A1
WAGON WHEEL TRL MH 135-E1,136-A1
WAGON WHEEL TRL NMT 190-A1
WAGONWHEEL CT WBT 80-D1
WAKE CT BLA 65-C3
WAKE ST BLA 65-C3
WAKE ST EB 23-C1
WAKE ST HL 37-C4,51-C3
WAKE ST NE HL 51-C2
WAKEFIELD AVE STP 108-D4
WAKEFIELD CIR SHK 147-A3
WAKEFIELD CT SHK 147-A3
WAKEFIELD DR EPR 132-B1
WAKEFIELD RD ORO 104-A2
WAKONADE DR RW 182-C4,196-D1
WALDECK XING FRI 79-A4
WALDEMAR WAY IND 88-D3
WALDEN BLVD NW OG 22-A3
WALDEN CT BUR 148-D3
WALDEN DR EAG 149-D3
WALDEN LN DPH 118-B1
WALDEN PL AH 93-E2
WALDEN PL MPL 93-A4
WALDEN RD DPH 118-B1
WALDEN ST BUR 148-D4
WALDEN TRL DPH 118-B1
WALDEN SHORES RD DPH 118-B1
WALDORF CT EPR 132-C2
WALDROFF FARM RD HUT 112-C1
WALES ST STP 108-B3
WALFRID ST EAG 149-D2
WALKER AVE N WAY 104-B3
WALKER AVE S WAY 104-B3
WALKER DR VH 80-C4
WALKER PL MTK 118-D1
WALKER ST MSC 55-B4
WALKER ST SLP 119-D1
WALL RD NFD 219-E4,220-A4
WALL ST BL 18-A3
WALL ST EAG 149-A3
WALL ST STP 108-C4
WALL STREET RD NFD 219-E4
WALL STREET RD NFT 220-A4
WALLACE RD EPR 132-D2
WALLACE ST DEL 87-D2
WALLINGFORD CIR WBY 124-A2
WALLINGFORD LN WBY 124-A2
WALLMARK ST CHC 26-B1
WALLMARK LAKE DR CGT 12-B4
WALLNER ST WSP 122-C2
WALLY DR GV 105-C2
WALNUT CHN 131-D2
WALNUT AVE NB 79-A3
WALNUT AVE PRL 161-A4
WALNUT AVE SW SM 46-E4
WALNUT CIR APV 163-A2
WALNUT CIR BUR 148-D4
WALNUT CIR EAG 149-C2
WALNUT CT CHS 145-C2
WALNUT CT DEL 87-E2
WALNUT CT EAG 149-C2
WALNUT CT EPR 132-D1
WALNUT CT N NB 79-A3
WALNUT CT S NB 79-A3
WALNUT DR BUR 148-D4
WALNUT DR EDI 119-C4
WALNUT DR MOU 116-D1
WALNUT DR MTA 116-D2
WALNUT DR ROG 61-E2
WALNUT LN APV 162-E2,163-A2
WALNUT LN EAG 149-C2
WALNUT LN SVW 94-A2
WALNUT PL RFD 74-A3
WALNUT RD SB 116-A3
WALNUT ST BUF 59-A2
WALNUT ST CAR 145-B4
WALNUT ST FAR 177-E4,178-A4
WALNUT ST HAS 166-D2
WALNUT ST HEN 198-C3
WALNUT ST HUD 111-C2
WALNUT ST LAU 107-B1
WALNUT ST MED 89-A3
WALNUT ST MO 31-D2
WALNUT ST MSC 55-B3
WALNUT ST PRE 167-B1
WALNUT ST RFD 74-B3
WALNUT ST RVL 93-B4
WALNUT ST STP 108-B4,122-B1
WALNUT ST TF 14-C3
WALNUT ST WBL 81-A3
WALNUT ST E RF 140-E2
WALNUT ST E SWR 97-A1
WALNUT ST N BEL 185-E1,186-A1
WALNUT ST N CAR 145-B4
WALNUT ST N CHS 145-C3
WALNUT ST N NST 54-D2
WALNUT ST N WAC 129-D3
WALNUT ST S BEL 186-A2
WALNUT ST S CHS 145-C3
WALNUT ST S CW 1-B2
WALNUT ST S WAC 129-D3
WALNUT ST SE MPL 107-A3
WALNUT ST W RF 140-D2
WALNUT ST W SWR 97-A1
WALNUT STA FAR 178-A4
WALNUT CREEK DR SWR 82-D4,96-D1
WALNUT GROVE LN N MG 76-B2
WALNUT GROVE
LN N PLY 90-B4,104-B1
WALNUT RIDGE DR EAG 149-E2
WALSH LN MH 121-E4
WALSH RD SJT 98-C2
WALSH ST STP 108-C2
WALTER DR ROG 61-E1
WALTER ST MPW 94-D3,108-D1
WALTER ST PRL 160-E1
WALTERS PORT LN ORO 117-C2
WALTON PL MPL 106-B1
WALTON OAKS DR BLO 133-D3
WALTON POND CIR BLO 133-D3
WAND AVE NW ER 33-D1
WANDA ST STP 108-B1
WARBLER LN EPR 132-C2
WARBLER LN STP 109-A4
WARBURTON ST E SSP 136-E1
WARBURTON ST W SSP 136-E1
WARD AVE HUD 111-D3
WARD LAKE DR NW AND 36-C3
WARDEN AVE EDI 119-D3
WARE RD LL 66-A4,80-A1
WARNER AVE SSP 122-D3
WARNER AVE N MHT 81-D4,95-D1
WARNER AVE N WIL 95-D1
WARNER AVE S MHT 95-D2
WARNER AVE S PS 95-D2
WARNER AVE S WIL 95-D1
WARNER CIR CHS 145-C1
WARNER LN MOU 116-E2,117-A2
WARNER LN MTA 116-E2
WARNER RD STP 108-D4
WARREN AVE BEC 2-E3
WARREN AVE EDI 119-E4
WARREN AVE SPR 117-B1
WARREN ST DRS 28-D2
WARREN ST PRE 167-B1
WARREN ST STP 109-A4,123-A1
WARREN WAY IND 88-D3
WARRICK CT EAG 149-A3
WARRIOR DR MH 122-B4
WARSAW TRL LEO 222-B4
WARSAW TRL STN 221-E3
WARSAW TRL WST 221-E4,222-A4
WARSAW AVENUE WAY WST 222-A4
WARWICK LN WIL 95-D2
WARWICK PL EDI 119-E3
WARWICK ST STP 121-D2
WARWICK ST SE MPL 107-B3
WASATCH LN GV 106-A1
WASECA AVE TKB 117-D2
WASECA ST BL 17-E3
WASECA ST STP 122-B2
WASECA ST WSP 122-B2
WASHBURN AVE BUR 148-B4,162-B1
WASHBURN AVE IGH 137-A3
WASHBURN AVE N BC 92-B1
WASHBURN AVE N BP 64-B4,78-B1
WASHBURN AVE N MPL 92-B3,106-B2
WASHBURN AVE S BLO 134-B4,148-B1
WASHBURN AVE S BUR 148-B3
WASHBURN AVE S MPL 106-B4,120-B3
WASHBURN AVE S RCH 120-B4,134-B1
WASHBURN CIR BLO 134-B3,148-B1
WASHBURN CIR S RCH 134-B2
WASHBURN CT BUR 148-B4
WASHBURN DR BUR 148-B4
WASHBURN LN BUR 148-B4
WASHBURN PL BLO 134-B3
WASHINGTON AVE BL 18-A3
WASHINGTON AVE OPH 96-E2
WASHINGTON AVE SWR 96-E2
WASHINGTON AVE WBL 81-A3
WASHINGTON AVE N HOP 119-C2
WASHINGTON
AVE N MPL 92-C4,106-C1
WASHINGTON AVE N NG 114-A4
WASHINGTON AVE S EDI 119-C4,133-C1
WASHINGTON AVE S EPR 133-C1
WASHINGTON AVE S HOP 119-C2
WASHINGTON AVE S MPL 106-D2
WASHINGTON
AVE SE MPL 106-E3,107-A3
WASHINGTON BLVD NE BLA 64-D2
WASHINGTON CT ER 33-E1
WASHINGTON CT RF 140-D3
WASHINGTON CT NE EB 8-D4,22-D1
WASHINGTON DR EAG 135-D4
WASHINGTON LN E CHS 145-B1
WASHINGTON ST ANO 63-D1
WASHINGTON ST HAS 166-D1
WASHINGTON ST MO 31-D2
WASHINGTON ST NYA 142-C3
WASHINGTON ST PRE 167-B1
WASHINGTON ST RF 140-D3
WASHINGTON ST SCF 14-C1
WASHINGTON ST STP 108-B4
WASHINGTON ST E CF 208-B3
WASHINGTON ST E CFT 208-B3
WASHINGTON ST N SCF 14-C2
WASHINGTON ST NE BLA 64-D2,78-D1
WASHINGTON ST NE CH 92-D2
WASHINGTON ST NE EB 8-D3,22-D1
WASHINGTON ST NE FRI 78-D3
WASHINGTON ST NE HL 36-D3,50-D3
WASHINGTON
ST NE MPL 92-D4,106-D1
WASHINGTON ST NE SLK 78-D2
WASHINGTON ST S NFD 219-E4
WASHINGTON ST S SCF 14-C3
WASHINGTON ST W CF 208-B3
WASHTA BAY RD CHN 117-C4
WASSON CIR RF 140-E1
WASSON CT RF 140-E2
WASSON LN N RF 140-E2
WASSON LN S RF 140-E2
WASSON LN S RIT 140-E3
WATER AVE ANO 49-C4
WATER AVE CT 127-E3
WATER ST DPH 118-A2
WATER ST EXC 117-E3
WATER ST HEN 198-C3
WATER ST HMP 193-B2
WATER ST JOR 173-B2
WATER ST MPL 106-D1
WATER ST E CF 208-B4
WATER ST E STP 122-C1
WATER ST N NFD 219-D3
WATER ST N SWR 97-A1
WATER ST S NFD 219-D4
WATER ST S SWR 97-A1
WATER ST W STP 122-B1
WATER LILLY LN EAG 149-A1
WATER TOWER PL CHN 131-D2
WATER WORKS RD W MPW 108-B1
WATERBURY RD MOU 116-E2,117-A2
WATERCREST BLVD NW BT 35-B1
WATERFORD CIR CHS 145-D1
WATERFORD CIR SHK 147-A3
WATERFORD CIR SWD 118-B3
WATERFORD CT CHS 145-D1
WATERFORD CT EDI 119-C4
WATERFORD CT EPR 133-B3
WATERFORD CT GV 106-A1
WATERFORD CT SWD 118-B3
WATERFORD DR GV 106-A1
WATERFORD DR E EAG 149-E2
WATERFORD DR W EAG 149-E2
WATERFORD LN CHS 145-D1
WATERFORD PL SWD 118-B3
WATERFORD RD WBY 123-D1
WATERFRONT DR WBY 124-B1
WATERLEAF PL E CHN 131-E2
WATERLEAF PL W CHN 131-D2
WATERLOO AVE SSP 122-D3
WATERLOO AVE WSP 122-D3
WATERLOO ST STP 122-D2
WATERLOO ST WSP 122-D2
WATERMAN AVE EDI 119-C2
WATERMAN CIR EDI 119-C2
WATEROUS ST SSP 122-E3
WATERS DR MH 135-D1
WATERS RD EAG 136-A2
WATERS EDGE CIR NFD 220-A4
WATERS EDGE DR CHS 131-C4
WATERS EDGE DR MTK 119-A3
WATERSEDGE TER MH 136-B1
WATERSEDGE TRL PRL 161-C2
WATERSIDE LN MOU 116-E1
WATERTOWER CIR PLY 104-E1
WATERTOWN AVE DEL 87-D3
WATERTOWN RD IND 102-D2,103-A2
WATERTOWN RD LOL 103-D2
WATERTOWN RD ORO 103-B2
WATERVIEW CV EAG 150-A3
WATERVIEW TRL EAG 150-A3
WATSON AVE STP 121-E2,122-A2
WATSON AVE NW ER 33-D2
WATSON CIR NW ER 19-D4
WATSON CT NW ER 19-D1
WATSON ST NW ER 19-D3
WATSON HALL NFD 219-E3
WAUKON AVE STP 109-A3
WAVELAND TER MPL 120-A2
WAVENEY CT EAG 150-B1
WAVERLY CT EPR 132-C3
WAVERLY PL MPL 106-C3
WAXON LN HUT 98-B4,112-B1
WAYCLIFFE DR WAY 104-C3
WAYCLIFFE DR N WAY 104-C3
WAYCLIFFE DR S WAY 104-C3
WAYMOUTH SPUR WAY 104-D2
WAYSIDE RD E HOP 119-C1
WAYSIDE RD W HOP 119-C1
WAYZATA BLVD GV 105-D3,106-A3
WAYZATA BLVD MPL 106-B3
WAYZATA BLVD MTK 104-E3,105-A3
WAYZATA BLVD SLP 105-D3
WAYZATA BLVD WAY 104-D3
WAYZATA BLVD E MTK 104-D3
WAYZATA BLVD E WAY 104-C3
WAYZATA BLVD W LOL 103-E2,104-A2
WAYZATA BLVD W MED 103-A1
WAYZATA BLVD W ORO 103-C2,104-A2
WAYZATA BLVD W WAY 104-A2
WAYZATA ST STP 108-B3
WEAR CIR ORO 103-C2
WEAR LN N ORO 103-C2
WEAR LN S ORO 103-C2
WEAVER BLVD ANO 49-C3
WEAVER CT ANO 49-C3
WEAVER LAKE DR N MG 76-C2
WEAVER LAKE RD MG 76-E2,77-A2
WEAVER LAKE RD N MG 76-D2,77-A2
WEBB ST ORO 117-B1
WEBBER PKWY MPL 92-C3
WEBBER ST WBL 80-E3,81-A3
WEBBER HILLS RD ORO 103-D3
WEBER DR LTT 130-C4
WEBER WAY ROG 61-E2
WEBSTER AVE NMT 189-E2
WEBSTER AVE SAV 147-E4
WEBSTER AVE WTT 101-A3
WEBSTER AVE S SLP 105-E4,119-E2
WEBSTER CT CRT 161-E3
WEBSTER CT SAV 161-E1
WEBSTER PL HOP 119-B1
WEBSTER RD WIL 95-D1
WEBSTER ST ANO 49-C4
WEBSTER ST HUD 111-D3
WEBSTER ST NM 189-E4,203-E1
WEBSTER ST NYA 142-C3
WEBSTER ST SHK 146-A2
WEBSTER ST STP 122-A1
WEBSTER ST N NOH 111-D1
WEBSTER ST SW NYA 142-C3
WEDGEMERE DR VIC 130-E3
WEDGEMERE PT VIC 130-E3
WEDGEWAY CT EPR 132-E1
WEDGEWOOD ALC WBY 124-A3
WEDGEWOOD BAY WBY 124-A3
WEDGEWOOD CIR AH 79-D4
WEDGEWOOD CIR WBY 124-A3
WEDGEWOOD CT MG 76-E4
WEDGEWOOD CT NB 93-B2
WEDGEWOOD CT WBY 124-A3
WEDGEWOOD DR EAG 149-E2
WEDGEWOOD DR MHT 95-C2
WEDGEWOOD DR MTK 118-E2
WEDGEWOOD DR SWD 117-C3
WEDGEWOOD DR TKB 117-C3
WEDGEWOOD DR WBY 124-A3
WEDGEWOOD DR NW CR 49-D4,63-E1
WEDGEWOOD DRAW WBY 124-A3
WEDGEWOOD LN SLT 174-E1
WEDGEWOOD LN N EAG 149-E2
WEDGEWOOD LN N MG 76-E3,77-A3
WEDGEWOOD LN N PLY 90-E1,104-E2
WEDGEWOOD LN S EAG 149-E2
WEDGEWOOD PL CR 49-D4
WEDGEWOOD PT WBY 124-A3
WEDGEWOOD RD N MG 76-E4,90-E1
WEDGEWOOD WAY MG 76-E3
WEEKS AVE HOT 113-E1
WEEKS AVE SE MPL 107-B2
WEEKS RD GRW 118-A3
WEENONAH PL MPL 121-A3
WEHLE PL SB 116-A3
WEIDE ST STP 108-D2
WEIR DR OKD 109-C4
WEIR DR WBY 109-C4,123-C1
WELCH TRL WEL 195-D4,209-D1
WELCH SHORTCUT
RD WEL 195-E3,196-A3
WELCO DR E MGY 215-D4
WELCO DR N MGY 215-D4
WELCO DR W MGY 215-D4
WELCOME AVE BKR 3-E4,4-A4
WELCOME AVE N BP 77-E4
WELCOME AVE N CHM 63-E3
WELCOME AVE N CRY 91-E2
WELCOME AVE N GV 105-E1
WELCOME AVE N ROB 91-E3
WELCOME AVE SE PRL 161-C4
WELCOME CIR GV 105-E2
WELCOME CIR N CHM 63-E2
WELCOME CT BUR 148-D3
WELCOME DR MED 103-C1
WELCOME LN BUR 148-D4
WELCOME LN N CHM 63-E3
WELCOME RD CT 127-E2,128-A1
WELLAND AVE MTK 105-B3
WELLAND CT EAG 150-A1
WELLER AVE YAT 141-E2
WELLERS CIR CHS 145-B1
WELLESLEY AVE STP 121-C1
WELLESLEY PL EDI 119-C4
WELLESLEY WAY MTA 117-A2
WELLINGTON AVE MV 79-B3
WELLINGTON AVE SLT 175-B1
WELLINGTON BAY WBY 124-A3
WELLINGTON CIR CHM 49-B4
WELLINGTON CIR MTK 104-E4
WELLINGTON CRES BUR 148-C4,162-C1
WELLINGTON CRES E BUR 162-C1
WELLINGTON CT CHM 49-B4
WELLINGTON CT EAG 149-D3
WELLINGTON CT PRL 161-B4
WELLINGTON CT WBY 124-A3
WELLINGTON CT N PLY 91-B3
WELLINGTON DR EPR 132-E3
WELLINGTON LN SHK 146-C3
WELLINGTON LN WBY 124-A4
WELLINGTON LN N MG 63-B3,77-B1
WELLINGTON LN N PLY 91-B3
WELLINGTON RD MTK 104-E4
WELLINGTON RDG WBY 124-A4
WELLINGTON TER WBY 124-A4
WELLINGTON WAY EAG 149-D3
WELLS AVE YAT 142-A4
WELLS LN SLT 174-D2
WELLS ST STP 108-C3
WELLS WOOD CRV BLO 148-B1
WELLSTEAD DR ROG 48-A4

WELSLEY CT CHN 118-A4
WELTER CIR SE SM 47-A4
WELTER RD SE SM 47-A4
WELTERS WAY EPR 133-B4
WENDHURST AVE SA 93-B3
WENDOVER CT MTK 118-D2
WENDY CT SVW 80-B4
WENTLOCK RD WBY 124-A3
WENTWORTH AVE BUR .148-D4,162-D1
WENTWORTH AVE MPL 120-C2
WENTWORTH AVE RCH ..120-C4,134-C1
WENTWORTH AVE SSP 122-D3
WENTWORTH AVE E WSP 122-C3
WENTWORTH
AVE S BLO 134-C3,148-C1
WENTWORTH AVE W MH 122-A3
WENTWORTH AVE W WSP 122-B3
WENTWORTH CIR BLO 148-C1
WENTWORTH CT E MPL 120-C4
WENTWORTH CT W MPL 120-C4
WENTWORTH PL BUR ..148-D4,162-D1
WENTWORTH TRL MTK 104-E4
WENZ AVE CHS 145-D1
WENZEL AVE EAG 149-D1
WERT RD HUT 98-A4,111-E1
WESCOTT RD EAG 135-E4,136-A4
WESCOTT SQ EAG 135-E3,136-A3
WESCOTT TRL EAG 135-E4,136-A4
WESCOTT HILLS
DR EAG 135-E4,136-A4
WESLEY CT MH 122-A4
WESLEY CT RF 140-D1
WESLEY CT RFD 74-B3
WESLEY DR GV 105-C1
WESLEY LN MH 122-A4
WESSEL CT EPR 118-C4
WEST AVE PRL 161-A3
WEST AVE WBT 81-A3
WEST AVE N DRS 28-D2
WEST AVE S DRS 28-D2
WEST CIR NE FRI 78-E2
WEST CT CP 65-D4
WEST DR EXC 117-E3
WEST LN ANO 49-B4
WEST LN MTK 118-B2
WEST LN SWD 118-A2
WEST RD CP 65-D3
WEST RD NB 93-B2
WEST RD RFD 74-A3
WEST RD WDL 104-C4
WEST ST CHC 26-B1
WEST ST GRW 117-E3
WEST ST JOR 173-B2
WEST ST MON 86-C1
WEST ST TF 14-C3
WEST ST N BEL 185-E1
WEST ST N JOR 173-B2
WEST ST N NYA 142-B4
WEST ST S BEL 185-E1
WEST ST S JOR 173-B2
WEST ST S NYA 142-B4
WEST ST S SWR 96-E1
WEST TRL EDI 133-C1
WEST ARM DR SPR 117-B1
WEST ARM RD SPR 117-B1
WEST ARMOUR TER SA 93-A3
WEST BAVARIAN
PASS NE FRI 79-A4,93-A1
WEST BAY LN NO 80-B2
WEST BRENNER PASS NE FRI 93-A1
WEST BROADWAY BP 63-D4,77-D2
WEST BROADWAY AVE CRY 91-E2
WEST BROADWAY AVE MPL92-B4,106-C1
WEST BROADWAY AVE NH 91-D1
WEST BROADWAY AVE ROB91-E3,92-A3
WEST CIRCLE CT MH 121-E4
WEST DANUBE DR NE FRI .79-A4,93-A1
WEST END LN MTK 118-C2
WEST FARM LN ABT 58-D1
WEST FARM RD CHN 145-E1
WEST HILL RD MTA 115-E2,116-A2
WEST LAKE CT CHN 132-A2
WEST LAKE DR CHN 132-A3
WEST LINWOOD DR NE LWT 23-E2
WEST MAHER DR MSC 69-B1
WEST MARIGOLD CT NW AND ...49-E3
WEST OAKS DR MTK 118-D2
WEST OMAHA RD TRT 126-A2
WEST PLEASANT LAKE RD NO ..80-B2
WEST POINT AVE TKB 117-D2
WEST POINT CIR TKB 117-D2
WEST POINT CT TKB 117-D2
WEST POINT DR TKB 117-D2
WEST POINT PL TKB 117-D2
WEST POINT RD TKB 117-D2
WEST RIDGE CIR N MYR 114-E4
WEST RIDGE RD N MYR 114-E4
WEST RIVER RD BP 64-A3,78-C2
WEST RIVER RD MPL 106-D2
WEST RIVER RD N CHM 63-C1
WEST SHADOW LAKE DR LL 66-B4
WEST SHORE DR BUF 45-A4
WEST SHORE DR EDI ..119-E4,134-A1
WEST SHORE DR SJT 84-C4
WEST SHORE RD NO 80-C3
WEST SIDE DR CRT 161-C4
WEST SKYLARK DR NE EB 8-D3
WEST VERMILLION CIR NE HL ..51-B1
WEST VIEW DR CLT 202-E2
WEST VILLAGE RD CHN 132-A2
WEST VIRGINIA AVE SAV 161-D1
WEST VIRGINIA CT SAV 161-D1
WEST WIND TRL EAG 149-B3
WESTBEND RD GV 105-C1,106-A1
WESTBROOK LN EDI 119-E2
WESTBROOK RD GV 105-E1
WESTBROOKE WAY HOP 119-B3
WESTBURY AVE PRL 161-A4
WESTBURY CIR EAG 149-E1
WESTBURY DR EAG 135-E4,149-E1
WESTBURY KNLS EAG 149-E1
WESTBURY LN EAG 135-E4,149-E1
WESTBURY PATH EAG 149-E1
WESTBURY TRL EAG 149-E1
WESTBURY WAY EAG 149-E1
WESTBY DR NE SLK 78-D2
WESTCHESTER CIR EAG 150-B2
WESTCHESTER CIR GV 105-D2
WESTCHESTER DR WSP 122-C3
WESTCHESTER PL WSP 122-C2
WESTCHESTER SQ BUR 148-E3
WESTCLIFF CRV SVW 79-E4
WESTCLIFF CT SVW 79-E4
WESTCLIFFE CT BUR 162-B2
WESTCLIFFE DR BUR 162-B2
WESTCLIFFE PL BUR 162-B2
WESTCOTE CIR MTK 104-D4
WESTDEL RD FAR 177-E4,191-E1
WESTEDGE BLVD MOU 116-D2
WESTEDGE BLVD MTA 116-D1
WESTERGREN CT WBT 81-B2
WESTERN AVE GV 105-D2
WESTERN AVE N RVL 94-A4,108-A1
WESTERN AVE N STP ...108-A3,122-A1
WESTERN AVE S STP 122-A1
WESTERN CT HAS 166-C3
WESTERN DR CHN 132-A1
WESTERN LN ANO 49-C4
WESTERN RD DPH 118-A2
WESTERN ST ANO 49-C4
WESTERN TER GV 105-D2
WESTERNESSE RD MTK 104-E3
WESTFIELD AVE BKT 198-E1
WESTFIELD LN VH 80-C4
WESTGAIL CT FAR 177-E4
WESTGATE CIR WIN 99-B3
WESTGATE CT EPR 132-D2
WESTGATE DR EPR 132-D2
WESTGATE DR STP 107-B3
WESTGATE DR WIN 99-B3
WESTGATE LN EPR 132-D2
WESTGATE RD MTK 118-E2
WESTGATE TER WIN 99-B3
WESTGATE TRL EPR 132-D2
WESTHILL PT EPR 132-E3
WESTIN AVE WBY 123-E3
WESTLUND DR NE HL 51-B1
WESTLYN CT FAR 177-E4
WESTMARK CIR MTK 118-E1
WESTMARK DR MTK 118-E1
WESTMILL RD MTK 118-C3
WESTMINSTER AVE NW WAT 101-B3
WESTMINSTER AVE SW WAT ...101-A3
WESTMINSTER CIR EAG 149-C3
WESTMINSTER RD MTK 118-E2
WESTMINSTER ST STP 108-C2
WESTMORE WAY GV 105-E1
WESTMORELAND LN SLP 105-C3
WESTON CIR EDI 133-D1
WESTON CT SHK 146-C3
WESTON CT N PLY 90-D2
WESTON LN SHK 146-C3
WESTON LN N MG 76-D3
WESTON LN N PLY 90-D4,104-D1
WESTON WAY SVW 79-E4
WESTON BAY RD EPR 132-C2
WESTON HILLS CT EAG 150-B2
WESTON HILLS DR EAG 150-B3
WESTON HILLS PL EAG 150-B3
WESTON RIDGE PKWY CHS 145-D1
WESTRIDGE BLVD EDI 119-D4
WESTRIDGE BLVD HEN 198-C4
WESTRIDGE CIR MTK 105-A4
WESTRIDGE CT BUF 45-A4
WESTRIDGE CT SWR 96-E2
WESTRIDGE DR EPR 132-E3
WESTRIDGE DR SHK 160-C2
WESTRIDGE LN MTK 105-A4
WESTRIDGE LN SLP 106-A3
WESTRIDGE RD MTK 105-A4
WESTVIEW CIR MH 136-A1
WESTVIEW CT FAR 177-E4
WESTVIEW CT SVW 79-E4
WESTVIEW DR DPH 118-B1
WESTVIEW DR FAR 177-E4
WESTVIEW DR HAS 166-C2
WESTVIEW DR SVW 79-E4
WESTVIEW DR WSP 122-C4
WESTVIEW ST CV 66-D2
WESTVIEW TER MH 136-A1
WESTVIEW TER MTK 105-C4
WESTWIND AVE SHK 146-B3
WESTWIND CIR EPR 133-B3
WESTWIND DR EPR 133-B3
WESTWIND DR E LC 94-D3
WESTWOOD AVE MTA 102-E4
WESTWOOD CIR DEL 87-E3
WESTWOOD CIR MOU 116-D2
WESTWOOD CIR MTK 105-B2
WESTWOOD CIR PLY 105-B2
WESTWOOD CIR RVL 107-C1
WESTWOOD CT EDI 119-C3
WESTWOOD CT FAR 177-E4
WESTWOOD DR BL 17-E3
WESTWOOD DR LOL 103-D2
WESTWOOD DR MTA 102-E4
WESTWOOD DR PRL 161-B3
WESTWOOD DR N GV 106-A2
WESTWOOD DR S GV 106-A3
WESTWOOD LN ANO 63-D1
WESTWOOD LN CHS 145-C1
WESTWOOD LN EAG 149-A2
WESTWOOD LN GV 106-A3
WESTWOOD LN S WAY 104-B3
WESTWOOD RD MTB 117-C1
WESTWOOD RD MTK 105-B2
WESTWOOD RD N BP 78-C2
WESTWOOD RD NE SLK 79-A1
WESTWOOD VLG RVL 94-A3
WESTWOOD HILLS CRV SLP 105-C3
WESTWOOD HILLS DR SLP 105-C3
WESTWOOD HILLS RD SLP 105-D3
WESTWOODLAND TRL NW PRL .160-E1
WETZEL LN CHT 145-B2
WEWERS RD RVL 94-B4
WEXFORD CIR EAG 149-C2
WEXFORD CT EAG 149-C2
WEXFORD CT NB 93-A2
WEXFORD CT WBY 123-E2
WEXFORD DR EPR 132-C3
WEXFORD LN MOU 117-A1
WEXFORD LN SHK 146-C3
WEXFORD RD EDI 133-D1
WEXFORD WAY EAG 149-C2
WEXFORD WAY WBY 123-E2
WEXFORD HEIGHTS DR NB 93-A2
WEXFORD HEIGHTS LN NB 93-A2
WHALEN AVE S BLO 147-E1
WHEAT TRL BCT 224-A4
WHEATON AVE RVL 93-E3,94-A3
WHEELER BLVD GV 105-C1
WHEELER DR EXC 117-E3
WHEELER ST N RVL 93-C3,107-C1
WHEELER ST N STP 107-C4,121-C1
WHEELER ST S STP 121-C1
WHEELOCK DR STP 108-B2
WHEELOCK LN STP 108-B2
WHEELOCK PKWY E STP 108-D2
WHEELOCK PKWY W STP 107-E2,108-A2
WHEELOCK RIDGE RD STP 108-C2
WHIPPOORWILL LN LL 66-A2
WHISPERING CT EAG 149-A3
WHISPERING CT HAS 166-C1
WHISPERING LN HAS 166-C1
WHISPERING OAKS BUR 162-C1
WHISPERING TRL EAG 149-A3
WHISPERING WAY EAG 149-A3
WHISPERING OAKS LN EPR 118-C4
WHISPERING PINE DR NE EB 36-E2
WHISPERING PINES RD TRT 125-D1
WHISPERING RIVER LN FAR 177-E4
WHISPERWOOD TRL WBT 80-E2
WHITAKER ST WBL 80-E4,81-A4
WHITAKER ST WBT 80-E4
WHITALL ST STP 108-C3
WHITE DR CRT 161-C3
WHITE ST SE WAT 101-B3
WHITE ST SW WAT 101-A3
WHITE ST SW WTT 101-A3
WHITE BEAR AVE MPW ..95-A4,109-A1
WHITE BEAR AVE WBL 95-A2
WHITE BEAR AVE N STP .109-A3,123-A1
WHITE BEAR AVE N WBL ..81-A4,95-A2
WHITE BEAR AVE S STP 123-A1
WHITE BEAR CT WBL 95-A2
WHITE BEAR PKWY VH 80-D4
WHITE BEAR PKWY WBL 80-D4
WHITE BEAR PKWY WBT 80-E4,94-E1
WHITE BIRCH CT LL 66-B3
WHITE BIRCH DR SVW 79-E2,80-A2
WHITE BIRCH RD MTK 104-E3
WHITE DIAMOND RD NW PRL ..160-E1
WHITE DOVE CIR CHN 117-E4
WHITE DOVE DR CHN 117-E4
WHITE EAGLE RD SJT 97-D1
WHITE EAGLE TRL SJT 97-D2
WHITE EAGLE WAY SJT 97-D1
WHITE GATE LN MTK 104-D3
WHITE OAK CIR MOT 32-A3
WHITE OAK CIR MPW 123-B2
WHITE OAK CIR ORO 103-D3
WHITE OAK CIR TRT 112-B4
WHITE OAK CT EAG 149-A3
WHITE OAK CT HUD 111-E2
WHITE OAK CT NB 93-B1
WHITE OAK DR BUR 162-E2
WHITE OAK DR CHS 145-C1
WHITE OAK DR HUT 112-B4
WHITE OAK DR TRT 112-B4
WHITE OAK DR VH 80-B4
WHITE OAK DR WSP 122-B3
WHITE OAK LN CHN 131-B1
WHITE OAK LN SJT 98-B2
WHITE OAK RD LL 66-C4
WHITE OAK RD MTK 118-E2
WHITE OAKS CT N CHM 63-C3
WHITE OAKS LN NO 80-B2
WHITE OAKS LN WBY 123-D3
WHITE OAKS RD EDI 120-A2
WHITE OAKS TRL CHM 63-C3
WHITE OWL DR LL 66-B4
WHITE PINE CIR HUD 111-E2
WHITE PINE CIR LL 65-E4,79-E1
WHITE PINE CT HUD 111-E2
WHITE PINE DR HUD 111-E2
WHITE PINE DR MTK 104-D3
WHITE PINE LN BWV 95-C1
WHITE PINE LN SOM 70-B4
WHITE PINE RD HUD 111-E2
WHITE PINE RD LL 65-E4
WHITE PINE RDG NW PRL 161-A3
WHITE PINE WAY EAG 150-B3
WHITE ROCK RD BUR 162-E1
WHITE ROCK TRL VAT ..209-D4,223-D2
WHITE TAIL XING EPR 147-C1
WHITE TAIL DR HAN 61-B3
WHITE TAIL LN HAN 61-B3
WHITE TAIL RDG PRL 160-E2
WHITE WATER WAY EAG 149-A1
WHITECAP LN WAC 129-C2
WHITED AVE MTK 118-D3
WHITEFIELD DR WBY 124-A2
WHITEGATE LN WAY 104-D2
WHITEHALL RD SHK 147-B3
WHITETAIL CT BUF 45-B4
WHITETAIL CT OTS 33-E4
WHITETAIL CT WAT 101-B4
WHITETAIL LN TRT 125-E2
WHITETAIL RDG LL 66-E4
WHITETAIL RUN BUF 45-B4,59-B1
WHITETAIL TRL LL 66-C4
WHITETAIL WAY EAG 150-A2
WHITETAIL RIDGE CT CHN 117-E4
WHITEWATER DR MTK 119-A3
WHITEWATER TRL N BP 78-B3
WHITEWOOD AVE CRT 161-C4
WHITEWOOD DR BUR 148-D4
WHITFIELD DR MH 136-B2
WHITING AVE EDI 119-E4
WHITNEY AVE SHK 146-B3
WHITNEY CIR SWD 118-B4
WHITNEY CT APV 163-A2
WHITNEY DR APV 162-E3,163-A2
WHITNEY ST SHK 146-B3
WHITON AVE VH 94-B1
WHITTIER CT NFD 219-D3
WHITTINGTON WALK EPR 118-D4
WICHITA TRL MED 89-C1
WIDGEON LN MO 31-E3
WIDGEON LN ROG 48-A4
WIDGEON WAY BUF 59-B1
WIDGEON WAY EAG 135-D4
WIDGEON WAY E EAG 135-D4
WIDGEON WAY W EAG 135-D4
WIDSTEN CIR WAY 104-C3
WIGGINS RD STP 123-B2
WIGHT BAY BP 78-B1
WILBROOK CT EAG 135-E4
WILCOXSON DR HUT 112-D3
WILD CANYON CIR WBY 137-C1
WILD CANYON CT WBY 137-C1
WILD CANYON DR WBY .123-C4,137-C1
WILD CANYON TRL WBY 123-C4
WILD DUCK PASS EPR 147-C1
WILD GOOSE LN WBT 94-D1
WILD HERON PT EPR 133-B4
WILD OAK TRL IND 102-C2
WILD PLUM LN VAT 209-D2
WILD RICE DR NE EB 23-D3
WILD RIDGE CT N NEW 123-C4
WILD RIDGE CT S NEW ..123-C4,137-C1
WILD RIDGE TRL NEW ...123-C4,137-B1
WILD ROSE CT EAG 135-E4,136-A4
WILD ROSE CT JT 160-A1
WILD ROSE CT NFD 219-D3
WILD TURKEY RD CFT 209-B4
WILD TURKEY RD VAT 209-C3
WILD TURKEY TRL LL 66-C3
WILD WIND LN LAT 215-E2
WILD WINGS MTK 118-D3
WILDCAT CT RF 140-E2
WILDCREST LN SWR 96-D2
WILDCREST RD MTK 118-E2
WILDE AVE SSP 122-D3
WILDER DR EPR 133-B3
WILDER ST MPL 106-D2
WILDER ST N RVL 93-C3,107-C1
WILDER ST N STP 107-C4,121-C1
WILDER ST S STP 121-C2
WILDERNESS CRV EAG 149-D2
WILDERNESS CV EPR 133-A3
WILDERNESS LN EAG 149-D2
WILDERNESS TRL SE PRL 161-B4
WILDERNESS PARK CIR EAG ...149-D2
WILDERNESS PK CT EAG 149-E2
WILDERNESS RUN CIR EAG 149-D2
WILDERNESS RUN CT EAG 149-D2
WILDERNESS RUN DR EAG 149-D2
WILDERNESS
RUN RD EAG 149-E2,150-A2
WILDFLOWER CT BUF 45-B4
WILDFLOWER CT BUR 162-D2
WILDFLOWER CT EAG 149-E2
WILDFLOWER CT SVW 79-C1
WILDFLOWER CT VH 94-B1
WILDFLOWER CT WAT 101-B4
WILDFLOWER DR CG 137-C2
WILDFLOWER DR LL 65-E2
WILDFLOWER LN CHS 145-E1
WILDFLOWER LN EAG 149-E2
WILDFLOWER LN SFT 159-B3
WILDFLOWER TRL SFT 159-B3
WILDFLOWER WAY EAG 150-A1
WILDFLOWER WAY NO 80-A2
WILDHURST LN MOU ..103-A4,117-A1
WILDHURST RD TKB 117-C2
WILDHURST RD WAC 129-D4
WILDHURST TRL ORO 103-A4
WILDPINES LN SWR 96-D2
WILDRIDGE CT MHT 95-C2
WILDRIDGE RD MHT 95-C2
WILDROSE LN SWD 117-C3
WILDS DR PRL 160-E2
WILDS LN NW PRL 160-E2
WILDS PKWY NW PRL 160-E2
WILDS RDG PRL 160-E2
WILDS VW PRL 160-E2
WILDS VW NW PRL 160-E2
WILDS RIDGE CT NW PRL 160-E2
WILDVIEW AVE STP 123-A2
WILDWOOD AVE BWV 95-C1
WILDWOOD AVE MTA 116-A3
WILDWOOD AVE SB 116-A3
WILDWOOD BLVD MO 31-E3,32-A3
WILDWOOD CIR BLO 147-E1
WILDWOOD CIR CHS 145-D1
WILDWOOD CIR MTK 105-C3
WILDWOOD CIR PRL 161-C3
WILDWOOD CIR WAT 101-B3
WILDWOOD CT BLA 65-B2
WILDWOOD CT BUR 162-B2
WILDWOOD CT CHS 145-E1
WILDWOOD CT NFD 219-D3
WILDWOOD CT SWR 96-D1
WILDWOOD DR NE HL 51-D3
WILDWOOD LN SWR 96-D1
WILDWOOD PL CHS 145-E1
WILDWOOD RD BLO 147-E1
WILDWOOD RD BUR 162-B2
WILDWOOD RD LTT 130-C2
WILDWOOD RD MHT 95-C2
WILDWOOD RD WIL 95-D1
WILDWOOD ST EAG 149-A3
WILDWOOD TRL BUR 162-B2
WILDWOOD TRL MTK 105-C3
WILDWOOD WAY CHS 145-E1
WILDWOOD WAY MO 31-E3,32-A3
WILDWOOD BAY DR MHT 81-D4
WILDWOOD BEACH RD MHT 95-D1
WILFORD WAY EDI 133-E1,134-A1
WILFRED LN N ROG 48-A4,62-A1
WILFRED RD HUT 112-B2
WILKE ST MSC 55-B4
WILKE ST W MSC 55-B4
WILKIN ST STP 122-B1
WILKINS ST E SWR 83-A4
WILKINS ST W SWR 83-A4,96-E1
WILL ST N BL 18-A3
WILLA CT BUR 162-C2
WILLANDALE RD HSN 47-C4,61-C1
WILLARD ST SWR 96-E2
WILLARD ST E SWR 97-A2
WILLARD ST W SWR 96-E2,97-A2
WILLEMITE ST NW RAM ...34-E3,48-E1
WILLIAM AVE EDI 119-E3
WILLIAM CT MH 121-E4,135-E1
WILLIAM DR MP 102-E1
WILLIAM ST EXC 117-E3
WILLIAM ST HBG 156-A2
WILLIAM ST RVL 94-B4,108-B1
WILLIAM ST N SWR 82-E4,96-E1
WILLIAM ST S SWR 96-E1
WILLIAM BERRY DR MPL 120-B1
WILLIAM LAKE SHORE DR WAC .129-C3
WILLIAM TELL RD STP 123-B2
WILLIAMETTE ST NE COT ..38-C4,52-C1
WILLIAMETTE ST NE LWT ..10-C2,24-C2
WILLIAMS AVE WBT 81-B2
WILLIAMS AVE SE MPL 107-A3
WILLIAMS DR BUR 148-B4
WILLIAMS LN EPR 132-C1
WILLIAMS LN MTA 116-C2
WILLIAMS LN MTK 118-D4
WILLIAMS ST NM 189-E4
WILLIAMS ST VH 94-C1
WILLIAMS WOODS RD MHT 81-D4
WILLIAMSBURG BAY WBY 124-B3
WILLIAMSBURG CRV BUR 162-D2
WILLIAMSBURG CT EPR 132-E3
WILLIAMSBURG CT WBY 124-B3
WILLIAMSBURG PKWY WBY 124-B3
WILLIS AVE SSP 122-D2
WILLISTON LN MTK 118-D2
WILLISTON RD MTK 118-D2
WILLIUS ST STP 108-C4
WILLMATT HL MTK 119-A1
WILLOOUGHBY WAY E MTK 105-B2
WILLOUGHBY WAY E PLY 105-B2
WILLOW AVE WBL 94-E2
WILLOW AVE N MPL 106-B1
WILLOW BLVD BEC 2-E4
WILLOW BND CRY 91-D2
WILLOW CIR BUF 59-A2
WILLOW CIR CV 66-E2
WILLOW CIR RVL 93-D4
WILLOW CRK CHN 118-A4
WILLOW CT WBL 95-A2
WILLOW CT E WBL 94-E2,95-A2
WILLOW DR COR 75-D4,89-D1
WILLOW DR DEL 87-D3
WILLOW DR HUD 111-D2
WILLOW DR MED 89-D3,103-D1

WILLOW DR N LOL .103-D2
WILLOW DR N ORO .103-D2
WILLOW DR S ORO .103-D3
WILLOW DR SW SM .46-E4
WILLOW INLT HUT .111-E1
WILLOW LN BC .78-C4
WILLOW LN BUR .148-D4
WILLOW LN HAT .188-B4
WILLOW LN HSN .61-C2
WILLOW LN HUT .111-E1
WILLOW LN MH .122-A4
WILLOW LN MOU .116-D1
WILLOW LN MTK .118-B3
WILLOW LN OTS .33-E4,47-E1
WILLOW LN PRL .161-A4
WILLOW LN RVL .93-D4
WILLOW LN WAT .101-B4
WILLOW LN WBL .94-E2
WILLOW LN WBY .109-C4,123-C1
WILLOW LN N BP .78-C3
WILLOW LN N SLP .106-A3
WILLOW LN N SVW .79-D1
WILLOW LN S SLP .106-A3
WILLOW PL S WAC .129-D3
WILLOW RD MG .77-A3
WILLOW RD NO .80-B4
WILLOW RD N BP .64-A3
WILLOW ST BEC .2-E4
WILLOW ST BUF .59-A2
WILLOW ST CHS .145-D2
WILLOW ST FAR .177-E4
WILLOW ST MO .31-C1
WILLOW ST MP .103-A1
WILLOW ST MPL .106-C3
WILLOW ST SOM .84-B1
WILLOW ST E SWR .83-A4
WILLOW ST N BEL .185-E1
WILLOW ST S BEL .185-E1
WILLOW ST W SWR .83-A4
WILLOW TRL ET .178-A4
WILLOW TRL SVW .80-A2
WILLOW WAY EAG .135-B4,149-B1
WILLOW WAY ET .178-A4
WILLOW BEACH ST PRL .161-A4
WILLOW BEACH TRL PRL 160-E4,161-A4
WILLOW CREEK CT BUF .59-A2
WILLOW CREEK LN BUF .58-E2,59-A2
WILLOW CREEK LN SVW .79-D2
WILLOW CREEK RD BUR .148-B4
WILLOW CREEK RD EPR .133-B1
WILLOW GROVE LN VH .80-C4
WILLOW HAVEN RD DPH .118-B2
WILLOW LAKE BLVD VH .94-D2
WILLOW LAKE DR VH .94-D2
WILLOW LANE CIR BUR .148-D4
WILLOW LN RD OSC .28-A3
WILLOW OAK LN MTK .119-A2
WILLOW POND TRL LL .65-E2
WILLOW RIDGE 1 HUT .111-E1
WILLOW RIDGE INLT HUT .111-E1
WILLOW RIDGE RD HUT .111-E1
WILLOW RIVER DR SJT .98-D2
WILLOW RIVER RD N NOH .111-D1
WILLOW VIEW CV CHN .132-B1
WILLOW VIEW DR ORO .103-D1
WILLOW WOOD CIR PRL .161-A4
WILLOW WOOD DR VH .80-B4
WILLOW WOOD RD EDI .119-C3
WILLOW WOOD ST SW PRL .161-A4
WILLOW WOOD TRL RFD .74-B3
WILLOW WOODS DR TKB .117-D2
WILLOWAY CIR BUR .162-C3
WILLOWBROOK DR MED .104-A1
WILLOWBROOK RD ORO .104-A1
WILLOWBROOKE LN WAC .129-C2
WILLOWBY XING MG .76-B2
WILLOWOOD DR EPR .133-B1
WILLOWOOD DR MTK .118-D4
WILLOWOOD FARM RD MED .89-D3
WILLS PL GV .105-E2
WILLSON RD EDI .119-E3
WILRYAN AVE EDI .119-E4
WILSHIRE BLVD CRY .91-E2
WILSHIRE BLVD MOU .116-E1,117-A2
WILSHIRE CIR MTK .105-B3
WILSHIRE CIR SVW .93-E1
WILSHIRE CT MH .136-A2
WILSHIRE DR MTK .105-B3
WILSHIRE PL MPL .93-A3
WILSHIRE PL STP .108-D4
WILSHIRE WALK HOP .119-C1
WILSON AVE STP .108-D4,109-A4
WILSON CIR MTK .118-D2
WILSON CT NFD .219-D3
WILSON DR EPR .132-E2
WILSON ST ANO .49-C3
WILSON ST MTK .118-D2
WILSON ST SA .93-A3
WILSON ST WAV .72-A4
WILSON ST E NYA .142-C4
WILSON ST NE MPL .93-A4,107-A1
WILSON ST NW ER .20-A3
WILSON ST W NYA .142-C4
WILTSEY LN SWD .117-D4
WIMBLEDON BAY WBY .124-A2
WIMBLEDON CT EPR .147-B1
WIMBLEDON DR WBY .124-A2
WIMBLEDON PL WBY .124-A2
WIMBLEDON RDG WBY .124-A3
WINCHELL ST STP .108-E2
WINCHESTER CT MTK .118-C2
WINCHESTER LN BC .77-E4,78-A4
WINCHESTER PL EPR .132-E2,133-A2
WINCHESTER TRL COR .75-B3
WIND RD EDI .119-E3
WIND CAVE CT BUR .149-A3
WIND RIDGE TRL MTA .116-B2
WIND RIVER RD DBT .182-D2
WINDBREAK TRL N LE .95-E4
WINDCREST AVE EAG .149-D1
WINDCREST CIR NP .201-E3
WINDCREST CT EAG .149-D1
WINDCREST DR NP .201-E3
WINDCREST ST SW LAT .201-D3
WINDEMERE CIR NE FRI .93-A1
WINDEMERE CIR W FRI .93-A1
WINDEMERE CRV PLY .105-A2
WINDEMERE CT MO .31-C2
WINDEMERE DR PLY .105-A2
WINDEMERE DR NE FRI .93-A1
WINDEMERE LN BUR .162-C2
WINDEMERE WAY BUR .162-C2
WINDERMERE PL MTK .118-C2
WINDFLOWER PL CHM .63-C3
WINDGATE RD WBY .123-D2
WINDING TRAIL RD SPT .70-D4,84-D1
WINDJAMMER DR WBY .124-A2
WINDJAMMER LN ORO .103-B3
WINDMILL CT CHS .131-C4
WINDMILL CT EAG .150-A1
WINDMILL DR CHN .131-E1
WINDMILL DR IND .89-A2
WINDMILL DR WBT .80-E2
WINDOLF LN HUT .97-D4
WINDRIDGE CIR MTK .119-A2
WINDROSE CRV EKO .204-B1
WINDROSE CT EKO .204-B1
WINDROW DR EPR .133-B3
WINDROW DR E LC .94-D3
WINDSONG CIR MTK .104-D3
WINDSONG CIR PRL .161-A2
WINDSONG DR EPR .132-E2
WINDSOR AVE EDI .119-E3
WINDSOR AVE SAV .147-C4
WINDSOR BAY WBY .123-D2
WINDSOR CIR SAV .147-C4
WINDSOR CT BUR .148-D3
WINDSOR CT EAG .149-C3
WINDSOR CT LES .212-D4
WINDSOR CT NB .93-B2
WINDSOR CT SAV .147-C4
WINDSOR DR LES .212-D4
WINDSOR DR NB .93-A2
WINDSOR DR SHK .147-B3
WINDSOR DR S SHK .147-A3
WINDSOR LN LES .212-D4
WINDSOR LN MHT .95-C2
WINDSOR LN NB .93-A2
WINDSOR LN PRL .161-B4
WINDSOR LN SA .93-A2
WINDSOR LN SHK .147-A3
WINDSOR LN WBY .123-D2
WINDSOR LN N BP .78-B1
WINDSOR RD MOU .117-A2
WINDSOR RD MTK .118-E2
WINDSOR TER BP .78-B1
WINDSOR TER EPR .133-B4
WINDSOR TER N BP .78-B1
WINDSOR WAY GV .105-E1
WINDSOR WAY MV .79-C3
WINDSOR WAY NB .93-B2
WINDSOR LAKE DR MTK .105-B3
WINDSOR LAKE LN MTK .105-B3
WINDTREE CIR EAG .136-A4
WINDTREE CT EAG .136-A4
WINDTREE DR EAG .136-A4
WINDTREE KNLS EAG .136-A4
WINDWARD CIR EPR .133-B3
WINDWARD LN WBY .124-A2
WINDWARD WAY E LC .94-D3
WINDWOOD CT MH .121-E4
WINDWOOD WAY MTK .118-B2
WINDY DRAW GV .105-E2
WINDY HILL RD SL .136-C1
WINDY HILL RD TRT .125-E3
WINDY RIDGE RD LTT .130-C2
WINDYHILL RD MTK .104-E3,105-A3
WINFIELD AVE N GV .91-E4,105-E1
WINFIELD CIR N RFD .74-B3
WINFIELD CIR S RFD .74-B3
WINFIELD RD RFD .74-B3
WING LAKE DR MTK .118-D3
WINGARD LN BC .77-E3
WINGARD PL BC .77-E3
WINGDING TRAIL RD SPT .70-D4,84-D1
WINGFIELD AVE ANO .49-C4
WINGWOOD CT MTK .118-D3
WINHROP ST S STP .123-A3
WINIFRED ST E STP .122-C1
WINIFRED ST W STP .122-B1
WINNEBAGO ST BL .18-A3
WINNETKA AVE N BP .63-D4,77-D4
WINNETKA AVE N CHM .63-D2
WINNETKA AVE N CRY .91-D3
WINNETKA AVE N GV .91-D4,105-D1
WINNETKA AVE N NH .91-D2
WINNETKA AVE S GV .105-D3
WINNETKA CIR BP .77-C4
WINNETKA HEIGHTS DR GV .105-D1
WINNIPEG AVE STP .108-B3
WINONA ST E STP .122-C2
WINONA ST S NFD .219-E4
WINONA ST W STP .122-B2
WINONA ST W WSP .122-B2
WINPARK DR NH .91-D4
WINSDALE ST N GV .105-D1,106-A1
WINSLOW AVE STP .122-C2
WINSLOW AVE WSP .122-C2
WINSLOW CT WSP .122-C4
WINSLOW PL MG .76-B1
WINSLOW CHAS MG .76-B1
WINSTED AVE E WIN .99-B3
WINSTED AVE W WIN .99-B3
WINSTON CIR MH .122-B2
WINSTON CT MH .122-B2
WINSTON ST STP .107-D2
WINTER CIR MTK .104-D4
WINTER CT HAS .166-C3
WINTER CT RF .140-D1
WINTER PL EPR .147-A1
WINTER ST STP .108-B3
WINTER ST N RF .140-D1
WINTER ST NE MPL .106-E1,107-A1
WINTER ST S RF .140-D2
WINTERBERRY CT WBY .123-E1
WINTERBERRY DR WBY .123-E1
WINTERBERRY DRAW WBY .123-E1
WINTERGREEN CT MTK .118-B2
WINTERGREEN CT VIC .131-A3
WINTERGREEN LN VIC .131-A3
WINTERGREEN ST NW AND .50-C3
WINTERGREEN ST NW CR .64-C3
WINTERGREEN ST NW OG .8-C4,22-C1
WINTERS WAY LAT .202-A3
WINTERSET DR MTK .119-A2
WINTERSET SPUR MTK .119-A2
WINTHROP CT MH .136-B1
WINTHROP CT STP .123-A2
WINTHROP DR MPW .95-A3
WINTHROP LN STP .123-A2
WINTHROP ST N STP .109-A4,123-A1
WINTHROP ST S STP .123-A1
WIOBATA ST RW .182-D4,196-D1
WISCONSIN AVE N CHM .63-C3
WISCONSIN AVE N CRY .91-C4
WISCONSIN AVE N GV .105-C1
WISCONSIN AVE N NH .91-C2
WISCONSIN AVE S GV .105-C3
WISCONSIN CIR N NH .91-C1
WISCONSIN CT HUD .111-D2
WISCONSIN ST HUD .111-D2
WISCONSIN ST RF .140-E3
WISCONSIN ST N NOH .111-C1
WISE AVE S WAY .104-C3
WISHBONE LN NO .80-C2
WISTERIA ST VIC .130-E1
WITBY DR EAG .135-C3
WITHAM AVE STP .122-D2
WITHAM LN EAG .150-A1
WITT CT VH .94-C2
WOLF CIR LL .66-C3
WOLF ST FRT .28-A1
WOLF SCHOOL TRL EPR .133-B4
WOLFARM ST NW RAM .49-A2
WOLFBERRY CT EAG .135-E4
WOLFBERRY LN GV .105-E1
WOLFRAM ST NW BT .35-A1
WOLFRAM ST NW RAM .35-A4,49-A2
WOLVERINE CIR NW RAM .34-C3
WOLVERINE CT NW RAM .34-C3
WOLVERINE ST NW BT .20-C3
WOLVERINE ST NW RAM .34-C3
WOLVERTON PL ORO .103-A2
WOOD AVE WBL .81-A3
WOOD CIR JOR .173-B2
WOOD DR SWD .117-D4
WOOD LN HSN .61-D2
WOOD LN MTK .104-E3
WOOD LN SLP .119-E2
WOOD ST MHT .95-D1
WOOD ST STP .122-C1
WOOD ST N JOR .173-B2
WOOD ST S JOR .173-B2
WOOD WAY BUR .162-D1
WOOD CLIFF CIR S BLO .133-D3
WOOD CLIFF RD BLO .133-D3
WOOD DUCK CIR CHN .117-E4
WOOD DUCK CIR EAG .149-C2
WOOD DUCK CIR SWD .117-D3
WOOD DUCK CT ROG .61-E1
WOOD DUCK CT SVW .79-D2
WOOD DUCK DR PRL .160-E2
WOOD DUCK DR VH .80-D4
WOOD DUCK LN BLT .17-E2
WOOD DUCK LN CHN .117-E4
WOOD DUCK LN NO .80-C3
WOOD DUCK LN TKB .117-D2
WOOD DUCK LN WAC .129-D4
WOOD DUCK TRL LL .52-A4
WOOD DUCK TRL PRL .160-E2
WOOD DUCK TRL SHK .160-C1
WOOD DUCK TRL E SHK .160-C1
WOOD END DR EDI .120-A3
WOOD HAVEN TRL CFT .209-B4,223-B2
WOOD HIL LN IND .88-E3
WOOD HILL LN IND .88-D3
WOOD LAKE DR BUR .148-D3
WOOD LAKE DR RCH .120-C4
WOOD RIDGE DR CRT .176-A1
WOOD RIDGE DR E TRT .140-D1
WOOD RIDGE DR W TRT .140-D1
WOODALE DR MV .79-B3
WOODBINE AVE WBY .109-C4
WOODBINE LN BC .78-C3
WOODBINE LN N BC .77-E3,78-A3
WOODBINE RD MTK .119-A1
WOODBINE ST NW AND .35-D3,49-D2
WOODBINE ST NW CR .63-D1
WOODBINE ST NW OG .21-D1
WOODBINE ST NW SF .7-D4
WOODBRIDGE CIR RVL .94-B4
WOODBRIDGE CIR WBY .124-A2
WOODBRIDGE CT RVL .108-B1
WOODBRIDGE DR BLO .133-C4
WOODBRIDGE DR SAV .161-E2
WOODBRIDGE LN SAV .161-E1
WOODBRIDGE RD BLO .133-C4
WOODBRIDGE RD MTB .117-D1
WOODBRIDGE ST RVL .94-B3,108-B1
WOODBRIDGE ST STP .108-B2
WOODBRIDGE ST SVW .94-B2
WOODBRIDGE TRL MTK .105-A4
WOODBRIDGE WAY WBY .124-A2
WOODBURY XING WBY .123-E2
WOODBURY DR WBY .110-A4,124-A2
WOODBURY RD NEW .137-B1
WOODBURY RD WBY .123-C1
WOODBURY ST STP .122-C2
WOODBURY ST SW LAT .201-D3
WOODCHUCK CIR LL .80-E1,81-A1
WOODCHUCK CT LL .80-E1
WOODCLIF CT EAG .135-E4,150-A1
WOODCOURT LN MTK .119-A2
WOODCREST AVE SVW .79-D1
WOODCREST CIR EKO .204-B1
WOODCREST CT EKO .204-B1
WOODCREST DR BUR .148-D4
WOODCREST DR CHS .131-C4
WOODCREST DR CP .65-E4
WOODCREST DR EDI .120-A3
WOODCREST DR EKO .204-B1
WOODCREST DR MV .79-B3
WOODCREST DR STP .109-A4
WOODCREST DR WBY .124-B2
WOODCREST DR N NOH .97-D4,111-D1
WOODCREST DR NW CR .64-C3
WOODCREST LN BKR .2-D1
WOODCREST LN EKO .204-B1
WOODCREST LN MTK .105-A3
WOODCREST RD WBL .80-E3
WOODCREST TER LES .212-D4
WOODCROFT DR MTK .118-C1
WOODDALE AVE EDI .120-A3,134-A1
WOODDALE AVE SLP .119-E1,120-A2
WOODDALE AVE S SLP .119-E1,120-A2
WOODDALE DR WBY .123-C2
WOODDALE GLN EDI .120-A3
WOODDALE LN EDI .120-A3
WOODDUCK CIR DEL .87-D3
WOODDUCK CIR WBY .109-D4
WOODDUCK DR WBY .109-D4,123-D1
WOODDUCK TRL LL .52-A4
WOODEDGE RD MTA .116-D1
WOODEND PL SWD .118-A3
WOODGATE CT EAG .149-C2
WOODGATE CT MTK .118-D3
WOODGATE DR VH .94-D2
WOODGATE LN EAG .149-C2
WOODGATE LN N EAG .149-C2
WOODGATE PT EAG .149-C2
WOODGATE RD MTK .118-D3
WOODGATE RD N MTK .118-D3
WOODGATE RD S MTK .118-D3
WOODHALL BAY BP .77-E1
WOODHALL CIR BP .77-E1
WOODHALL XING BP .77-E1
WOODHAVEN CT CHM .63-B3
WOODHAVEN DR ORO .103-D2
WOODHAVEN PL DPH .118-A2
WOODHAVEN RD MTK .118-E1
WOODHILL AVE ORO .103-E3
WOODHILL BLVD NMT .190-B1
WOODHILL CIR MTK .118-E2
WOODHILL CIR SAV .161-C1
WOODHILL CIR WBY .123-C1
WOODHILL CT ANN .74-B2
WOODHILL CT EAG .149-A2
WOODHILL CT HOP .119-B3
WOODHILL CT SAV .161-C1
WOODHILL CT WBY .123-C1
WOODHILL DR ANN .74-B2
WOODHILL DR CHN .132-A1
WOODHILL DR IND .88-E2
WOODHILL DR NMT .190-B1
WOODHILL DR RVL .93-E3,94-A3
WOODHILL DR SAV .161-C1
WOODHILL DR WBY .123-C1
WOODHILL LN BLA .65-B2
WOODHILL LN NO .80-C3
WOODHILL LN WTT .115-B1
WOODHILL RD BUR .148-C3
WOODHILL RD MTK .118-E2
WOODHILL RD ORO .103-E3,104-A3
WOODHILL RDG ORO .103-E3
WOODHILL TER MTK .118-E2
WOODHILL TRL EPR .132-D1
WOODHILL WAY EDI .119-E2
WOODHURST LN MTK .118-D2
WOODKNOLL LN MTK .118-D1
WOODLAKE LN RCH .120-C4
WOODLAND CIR EDI .120-A3
WOODLAND CIR IND .88-E1
WOODLAND CIR JOR .173-B3
WOODLAND CIR MTK .118-D4
WOODLAND CIR NW PRL .160-E3
WOODLAND CRV MTK .118-D2
WOODLAND CRV SB .116-B3
WOODLAND CT COR .75-B1
WOODLAND CT EAG .135-E4,136-A4
WOODLAND CT HUD .111-E2
WOODLAND CT MHT .95-C2
WOODLAND CT SJT .97-D1
WOODLAND DR BUR .148-C4
WOODLAND DR CGT .26-B2
WOODLAND DR CHS .145-C2
WOODLAND DR EPR .132-E1
WOODLAND DR FL .39-C3
WOODLAND DR LL .52-C4
WOODLAND DR MHT .95-C2
WOODLAND DR SLP .119-D1
WOODLAND DR SVW .79-E3,80-A3
WOODLAND DR NE EB .37-D2
WOODLAND DR NE HL .37-C2
WOODLAND LN BEC .2-E3
WOODLAND LN BKR .2-E1
WOODLAND LN COR .61-C4
WOODLAND LN EDI .120-A3
WOODLAND LN MTK .118-D3
WOODLAND LN NMT .190-C2
WOODLAND RD BLO .133-E3
WOODLAND RD CP .65-D4
WOODLAND RD DEL .87-D3
WOODLAND RD EDI .119-E3,120-A3
WOODLAND RD GRF .74-E1
WOODLAND RD LEX .65-D4
WOODLAND RD MOU .103-A4
WOODLAND RD MTK .118-D3
WOODLAND RD NMT .190-C2
WOODLAND TRL EAG .136-A4
WOODLAND TRL GRF .74-D1,75-A1
WOODLAND TRL GV .106-A1
WOODLAND TRL LAT .202-A3
WOODLAND TRL NFD .219-D3
WOODLANDS PKWY LIT .5-B1
WOODLANE BAY WBY .137-D2
WOODLANE CT WBY .137-C1
WOODLANE DR WBY .123-C2,137-D1
WOODLANE ST TKB .117-D3
WOODLARK LN EAG .135-D3
WOODLARK WAY MG .76-B1
WOODLAWN AVE LES .212-C4
WOODLAWN AVE MTK .104-C4,118-C1
WOODLAWN AVE STP .121-B1
WOODLAWN AVE TKB .117-D3
WOODLAWN BCH BUF .45-A4
WOODLAWN BLVD MPL .120-E3,121-A3
WOODLAWN CIR WAC .129-C3
WOODLAWN CIR SE PRL .161-B3
WOODLAWN CT BUR .148-D4
WOODLAWN CT RFD .74-A3
WOODLAWN CT N CHM .63-C3
WOODLAWN DR MV .79-B2
WOODLAWN DR RFD .74-A3
WOODLAWN PL N CHM .63-C3
WOODLAWN RD MTA .102-D3
WOODLEY CIR NFD .219-E4
WOODLEY ST E NFD .219-E4,220-A4
WOODLEY ST W NFD .219-D4
WOODLYNN AVE MPW .95-A3
WOODLYNN AVE RVL .93-E3,94-B3
WOODLYNN AVE W LC .94-B3
WOODMERE CIR EPR .132-E1,133-A1
WOODMERE RD WBY .123-C1
WOODPARK BLVD WBY .123-D2
WOODPECKER RIDGE RD TKB .117-D3
WOODRIDGE CIR BEL .185-D1
WOODRIDGE CIR EPR .133-A4
WOODRIDGE CIR VH .94-B1
WOODRIDGE CT LL .79-E1
WOODRIDGE CT MHT .95-C2
WOODRIDGE CT MTK .118-E2
WOODRIDGE CT VH .94-B1
WOODRIDGE DR CF .208-B3
WOODRIDGE DR CHS .145-D1
WOODRIDGE DR EPR .133-A4
WOODRIDGE DR MH .122-A2
WOODRIDGE DR VH .94-B1
WOODRIDGE DR N CHS .145-D1
WOODRIDGE DR S CHS .145-D1
WOODRIDGE LN LL .79-E1
WOODRIDGE LN SL .136-C2
WOODRIDGE LN SWR .96-D2
WOODRIDGE RD MOU .117-A1
WOODRIDGE RD MTK .118-E2
WOODRIDGE WAY SAV .161-C1
WOODRUFF AVE RVL .108-A1
WOODRUFF AVE SWD .117-D4
WOODRUFF CIR MTK .104-E4
WOODRUFF RD MTK .104-E4
WOODRUFF SPUR MTK .104-D4
WOODS CIR BUF .58-E1
WOODS CT EAG .149-A3
WOODS CT GRW .118-A2
WOODS DR LES .212-D2
WOODS LN BUR .148-E2
WOODS TRL BUR .162-B2
WOODS TRL CHM .63-B3
WOODS TRL N BUR .162-B2
WOODS TRL N CHM .63-C3
WOODS TRL S BUR .162-B2
WOODS WAY MTK .118-D2
WOODS CREEK DR DEL .87-E3

WOODS EDGE MTK ... 118-D2
WOODSCREEK DR DEL ... 87-E3
WOODSIDE CT SHK ... 146-C2
WOODSIDE CT NE FRI ... 79-A4
WOODSIDE LN MTK ... 118-D2
WOODSIDE LN SWD ... 117-B3
WOODSIDE RD PRL ... 161-C3
WOODSIDE RD SWD ... 117-B3
WOODSTOCK AVE GV ... 105-E2,106-A2
WOODSTOCK CRV BLO ... 147-D1
WOODSTOCK DR BLO ... 147-D1
WOODSTONE CT VIC ... 130-E3
WOODSTONE DR VIC ... 130-E3,131-A3
WOODSTONE GLN VIC ... 130-E3
WOODSTONE LN VIC ... 130-E3
WOODSVIEW LN SFT ... 158-C4
WOODTHRUSH CT EAG ... 135-E4
WOODVIEW CT BUR ... 148-D4
WOODVIEW CT EDI ... 133-D2
WOODVIEW CT VH ... 94-B1
WOODVIEW CT SE PRL ... 161-B4
WOODVIEW DR BUR ... 148-D4
WOODVIEW DR VH ... 94-C1
WOODVIEW LN BUR ... 148-D4
WOODVIEW LN ZIM ... 5-C1
WOODVIEW ST E EAG ... 135-D4
WOODVIEW ST W EAG ... 135-D4
WOODVIEW TRL TRT ... 125-C3
WOODWARD AVE STP ... 108-C4
WOODWATCH CIR EPR ... 133-B3
WOODWINDS DR WBY ... 123-C2
WOODWINDS LN MTB ... 117-D1
WOODY LN MTK ... 119-A1
WOODY LN NE FRI ... 78-E4
WOODY LN NW CR ... 64-C2
WOOLMAN DR MTK ... 118-B2
WOOLSEY LN WDL ... 104-B4
WORCESTER AVE STP ... 121-C3
WORCHESTER CIR EAG ... 136-B4
WORCHESTER DR EAG ... 136-B4,150-B1
WORDSWORTH AVE STP ... 121-C3
WORTH ST E SCF ... 14-C2
WREN CT BUR ... 162-B3
WREN CT NW AND ... 36-A3
WREN CT SE PRL ... 161-C3
WREN LN BUF ... 45-B4
WREN LN EAG ... 136-A3
WREN LN NO ... 80-C3
WREN RD MOU ... 117-A1
WREN ST NW AND ... 36-A3,50-A3
WREN ST NW CR ... 64-A2
WREN ST NW OG ... 22-A4,36-A2
WRIGHT AVE W FH ... 107-D2
WRIGHT ST MO ... 31-D2
WUTHERING HEIGHTS RD EAG ... 135-B4
WYATT ST NW BET ... 8-D3
WYCHEWOOD RD MTK ... 118-D2
WYCLIFF ST STP ... 107-C3
WYCLIFFE RD EDI ... 119-D3
WYLDEWOOD DR CLT ... 189-B4,203-B1
WYLDWOOD LN HUT ... 112-D2
WYLDWOOD LN SLK ... 79-A2
WYLDWOOD LN NE SLK ... 78-D2
WYMAN AVE EDI ... 119-E4
WYMAN AVE MP ... 102-E1
WYNCREST CT AH ... 79-D4
WYNCREST LN AH ... 79-D4
WYNDCREST DR CLT ... 188-E3,189-A3
WYNDEMERE LN EAG ... 149-A3
WYNDHAM ALC WBY ... 123-D3
WYNDHAM BAY WBY ... 123-D3
WYNDHAM CIR E NB ... 93-A1
WYNDHAM CIR W NB ... 93-A2
WYNDHAM CT PRL ... 161-B4
WYNDHAM PL HAS ... 166-B2
WYNDHAM WAY WBY ... 123-D3
WYNDHAM HILL DR HAS ... 166-B2
WYNDHAM HILL DR MTK ... 119-B1
WYNDHILL CIR DPH ... 118-B2
WYNDMERE RD ORO ... 104-A1
WYNDWOOD LN WTT ... 115-B3
WYNGATE DR TRT ... 126-B3
WYNGATE LN MTK ... 118-D4
WYNNE AVE STP ... 107-D2
WYNNFIELD RD EPR ... 132-B2
WYNNWOOD RD GV ... 105-E1
WYNRIDGE DR AH ... 79-D4
WYNSTONE CT WBY ... 124-A1
WYNSTONE DR WBY ... 124-A1
WYNSTONE PASS EPR ... 132-C3
WYOLA RD MTK ... 118-E1
WYOMING AVE BL ... 18-A3
WYOMING AVE CHC ... 26-A1
WYOMING AVE SAV ... 147-D3
WYOMING AVE N BP ... 77-C2
WYOMING AVE S BLO ... 133-C2,147-C1
WYOMING AVE S SLP ... 105-C4,119-C1
WYOMING CIR S BLO ... 133-C4,147-C1
WYOMING CT BLO ... 133-C2
WYOMING RD BLO ... 147-C2
WYOMING RD COT ... 24-B4
WYOMING RD LWT ... 24-C3
WYOMING ST E STP ... 122-C2
WYOMING ST W STP ... 122-B2
WYOMING TER BLO ... 133-C4
WYOMING TRL WYO ... 25-B3
WYOMING TRL N WYT ... 25-D3,26-A2

X

XANADU AVE HAT ... 187-D2
XANADU AVE SCT ... 159-D4,173-D4
XANTHUS LN N DAY ... 48-B4
XANTHUS LN N PLY ... 90-B4,104-B1
XAVIER AVE S BLO ... 147-E1
XAVIER CIR BLO ... 147-E2
XAVIER CT BLO ... 147-E2
XAVIER RD BLO ... 147-E2
XAVIER ST NW ER ... 20-A4,34-A1
XAVIS CIR NW CR ... 64-A1
XAVIS ST NW AND ... 50-A3
XAVIS ST NW CR ... 50-A3,64-A2
XAVIS ST NW OG ... 22-A3
XEBEC ST NE ATT ... 9-C1
XEBEC ST NE BLA ... 51-D4,79-C1
XEBEC ST NE HL ... 51-C2
XENE LN N MG ... 76-D2
XENE LN N PLY ... 90-D2,104-D2
XENIA AVE N BP ... 77-E2
XENIA AVE N CHM ... 63-E3
XENIA AVE N CRY ... 91-E2
XENIA AVE N GV ... 105-E1
XENIA AVE N ROB ... 91-E3
XENIA AVE NW ER ... 33-D1
XENIA AVE S GV ... 105-E3
XENIA CT GRF ... 74-E1
XENIA ST GRF ... 74-E1
XENIA ST NW AND ... 35-D4,49-D1
XENIA ST NW OG ... 21-D1
XENIUM CT PLY ... 90-E3
XENIUM LN N MG ... 76-E1
XENIUM LN N PLY ... 90-E4,104-E2
XENOLITH ST NW RAM ... 34-E2
XENON ST NW BT ... 7-A4,21-A1
XENON ST NW RAM ... 35-A4,49-A2
XENON ST NW STT ... 7-A1
XENWOOD AVE SAV ... 147-E3,161-E1
XENWOOD AVE S SLP ... 105-E4,119-E1
XEON AVE SCT ... 174-B2
XEON AVE SLT ... 174-B3,188-B1
XEON BLVD NW CR ... 64-B1
XEON ST NW AND ... 36-C2,50-C2
XEON ST NW ATT ... 8-B2
XEON ST NW CR ... 64-C1
XERUS ST NW RAM ... 34-C2
XERXES AVE BUR ... 148-B4,162-B1
XERXES AVE EKO ... 190-B4,204-B1
XERXES AVE NMT ... 190-B3
XERXES AVE N BC ... 78-B4,92-B1
XERXES AVE N BP ... 78-A2
XERXES AVE N GV ... 106-B1
XERXES AVE N MPL ... 106-B1
XERXES AVE N ROB ... 92-B3,106-B1
XERXES AVE S BLO ... 134-B2,148-B1
XERXES AVE S BUR ... 148-B4
XERXES AVE S EDI ... 120-B4,134-B1
XERXES AVE S GV ... 106-B2
XERXES AVE S MPL ... 106-B3,120-B2
XERXES CIR BLO ... 134-B3
XERXES CRV BLO ... 134-B4
XERXES CT N BP ... 78-B3
XERXES PL N BC ... 78-B4
XERXES RD BLO ... 134-B4
XERXES ST NW ER ... 19-B4,33-B1
XERXES TRL EKO ... 204-B1
XERXES TRL NMT ... 204-B1
XIMINES LN N MG ... 77-B4
XIMINES LN N PLY ... 91-B2
XINGU ST NE COT ... 38-C4
XKIMO AVE CLT ... 202-E1,203-A1
XKIMO CT NW RAM ... 49-C2
XKIMO ST NW ANO ... 49-C3
XKIMO ST NW RAM ... 49-C2
XKIMO ST NW SF ... 7-C3
XTRA ST NE COT ... 37-E2
XYLITE CT NE BLA ... 65-B2
XYLITE ST NE ATT ... 9-B1
XYLITE ST NE BLA ... 65-B4,79-B1
XYLITE ST NE EB ... 23-B1
XYLITE ST NE HL ... 37-B3,51-B1
XYLON AVE N BP ... 77-C4
XYLON AVE N CHM ... 63-C3
XYLON AVE N CRY ... 91-C4
XYLON AVE N GV ... 91-C4,105-C1
XYLON AVE N NH ... 91-C3
XYLON AVE S BLO ... 133-C4,147-C2
XYLON AVE S SLP ... 105-C4,119-C1
XYLON CIR S BLO ... 133-C3
XYLON CT BLO ... 133-C4
XYLON CT N BP ... 77-C2
XYLON CT N CHM ... 63-C3
XYLON LN N CHM ... 63-C3
XYLON RD BLO ... 147-C1

Y

YACHT CLUB RD STP ... 122-B1
YAHN DR NW OG ... 21-E2
YAKIMA ST NW AND ... 35-C3
YAKIMA ST NW BT ... 35-C1
YAKIMA ST NW RAM ... 35-C2,49-C1
YAKIMA ST NW SF ... 7-C3
YALE AVE CT ... 127-E3,141-E1
YALE AVE HOT ... 99-E3,113-E2
YALE AVE MPL ... 107-A3
YALE AVE YAT ... 141-E3,155-E1
YALE CIR NW ER ... 34-A1
YALE PL MPL ... 106-C3
YALE ST NW ER ... 20-A4,33-E3
YALTA LN NE BLA ... 79-D1
YALTA ST HL ... 37-D4
YALTA ST NE BLA ... 65-D3,79-D1
YALTA ST NE EB ... 37-C1
YALTA ST NE HL ... 51-D1
YANCEY CT APV ... 149-A4
YANCEY LN BP ... 78-A1
YANCY AVE CT ... 113-D4,127-D1
YANCY AVE HOT ... 99-D4,113-D1
YANCY ST NE EB ... 37-B1
YANCY ST NE BLA ... 65-B4
YANCY ST NE EB ... 23-B4,37-B2
YANCY ST NE HL ... 51-B3
YANKEE DR EAG ... 135-C4
YANKEE PL EAG ... 135-D3
YANKEE SQ EAG ... 135-D3
YANKEE DOODLE CT EAG ... 136-B3
YANKEE DOODLE LN EAG ... 135-C3
YANKEE DOODLE RD EAG ... 135-D3,136-A3
YANKTON ST NW BLT ... 33-A1
YANKTON ST NW ER ... 33-B1
YANKTON COLLEGE LN NB ... 93-A1
YARBOROUGH TRCE MG ... 76-B1
YARROW CT WAT ... 101-B4
YATES AVE N BP ... 77-E2
YATES AVE N CHM ... 63-E3
YATES AVE N CRY ... 91-E2
YATES AVE N ROB ... 91-E3
YATES CIR N CHM ... 63-E3
YATES TER BP ... 77-E2
YATES BAY CT BP ... 77-E1
YATES BAY ST N BP ... 77-E1
YELLOW BIRCH RD DWD ... 81-C3
YELLOW BRICK RD CHS ... 145-C2
YELLOW CIRCLE DR MTK ... 119-B4
YELLOW PINE ST NW AND ... 36-B2,50-C1
YELLOW PINE ST NW CR ... 64-C3
YELLOW PINE ST NW OG ... 22-B2,36-B1
YELLOWSTONE BLVD ANO ... 49-B4
YELLOWSTONE CT N PLY ... 90-B3
YELLOWSTONE LN N MG ... 76-B2
YELLOWSTONE LN N PLY ... 90-B3,104-B1
YELLOWSTONE TRL HUT ... 112-D1
YELLOWSTONE TRL SWD ... 117-D4
YELLOWSTONE TRL N BP ... 78-B3
YERKS ST LWT ... 10-B2
YEVETTES CT OSC ... 28-A4
YEW PT EAG ... 149-C1
YMCA LN MTK ... 105-A3
YOHO DR ANO ... 49-B4
YOLITE ST NW RAM ... 34-D4,48-E1
YORK ALC WBY ... 123-C3
YORK AVE BUR ... 148-B4,162-B1
YORK AVE EDI ... 120-B3
YORK AVE GV ... 106-B2
YORK AVE STP ... 108-C3,109-A3
YORK AVE N BC ... 92-B1
YORK AVE N BP ... 78-A3
YORK AVE N GV ... 106-B1
YORK AVE N ROB ... 92-B3,106-B1
YORK AVE NW ER ... 33-D2
YORK AVE S BLO ... 134-B2,148-B1
YORK AVE S BUR ... 148-B4
YORK AVE S EDI ... 120-B4,134-B1
YORK AVE S MPL ... 120-B2
YORK BAY WBY ... 123-C3
YORK CIR BLO ... 134-B3
YORK CIR WBY ... 123-C3
YORK CIR NW RAM ... 34-C4
YORK CRV BLO ... 134-B4
YORK DR DAY ... 62-B2
YORK DR WBY ... 123-C3
YORK LN BLO ... 148-B1
YORK LN N BP ... 78-A3
YORK PL N BC ... 78-B4
YORK RD BLO ... 134-B3
YORK ST CHS ... 145-D2
YORK ST N CF ... 208-A4
YORK ST NW ER ... 19-D2,33-D1
YORK TER EDI ... 134-B1
YORKSHIRE AVE SLT ... 174-E1
YORKSHIRE AVE STP ... 121-C3
YORKSHIRE AVE N BP ... 78-A1
YORKSHIRE AVE S MTK ... 105-B3
YORKSHIRE LN BP ... 78-A1
YORKSHIRE LN EPR ... 133-A4
YORKSHIRE LN SHK ... 147-B3
YORKTON RDG E LC ... 94-B3
YORKTOWN BLVD LC ... 94-B3
YORKTOWN CT LC ... 94-B3
YORKTOWN DR EAG ... 150-A1
YORKTOWN LN PLY ... 91-B1
YORKTOWN LN N CHM ... 49-B4,63-B1
YORKTOWN LN N MG ... 63-B4,77-B4
YORKTOWN LN N PLY ... 91-B2
YORKTOWN PL EAG ... 150-A2
YORKTOWN WAY LC ... 94-B3
YOSEMITE AVE CHN ... 117-E4
YOSEMITE AVE N GV ... 105-E2
YOSEMITE AVE S SAV ... 147-E4,161-E1
YOSEMITE AVE S SLP ... 105-E4,119-E1
YOSEMITE CIR BLO ... 133-E4
YOSEMITE CIR N GV ... 105-E2
YOSEMITE CIR S SAV ... 161-E1
YOSEMITE CT SAV ... 161-E1
YOSEMITE RD BLO ... 133-E4,147-E1
YOUNG RD HUT ... 112-E1
YOUNG ST PRE ... 153-B4,167-B1
YOUNG ST STP ... 107-D3
YOUNGMAN AVE STP ... 121-D3
YTTRIUM ST NW BT ... 21-A3,35-A1
YTTRIUM ST NW RAM ... 35-A3
YUCCA CIR N MG ... 76-E3
YUCCA LN N MG ... 76-E1,90-E1
YUCCA LN N PLY ... 90-E1
YUCCA ST NW AND ... 49-D3
YUCCA ST NW CR ... 49-D4,63-D1
YUCCA ST NW OG ... 21-D1
YUCCA ST NW SF ... 7-D4
YUKON AVE CHM ... 63-C1
YUKON AVE N BP ... 77-C4,91-C1
YUKON AVE N CHM ... 63-C2
YUKON AVE N CRY ... 91-C4
YUKON AVE N NH ... 91-C4
YUKON AVE S BLO ... 133-C4,147-C1
YUKON AVE S SLP ... 105-C4,119-C1
YUKON CIR S BLO ... 133-C4,147-C2
YUKON CT BLO ... 133-C4
YUKON CT N GV ... 105-C2
YUKON RD BLO ... 147-C1
YUKON ST NW AND ... 50-A3
YUKON ST NW CR ... 50-A3,64-A2
YUMA CT MG ... 76-D2
YUMA DR CHN ... 132-A1
YUMA LN N PLY ... 90-D2,104-D1
YUMA WAY N MG ... 76-D2
YVERDON CT VIC ... 131-B1
YVETTE ST GRF ... 74-D4
YVONNE TER EDI ... 119-E3

Z

ZACHARY AVE CLT ... 189-B4,203-B1
ZACHARY CIR N DAY ... 63-B1
ZACHARY LN N DAY ... 49-B4,63-B3
ZACHARY LN N MG ... 63-B4,77-B1
ZACHARY LN N PLY ... 91-B2,105-B2
ZACHMAN CIR EPR ... 133-B3
ZACHMAN CT ROG ... 47-D4
ZACHMAN DR ROG ... 47-E4
ZAHLER RD HUG ... 82-A1
ZANE AVE NMT ... 189-E2,203-E1
ZANE AVE N BP ... 63-E4,77-E3
ZANE AVE N CHM ... 63-E3
ZANE AVE N CRY ... 91-E3
ZANE AVE N GV ... 91-E4,105-E2
ZANE AVE N ROB ... 91-E3
ZANE CIR N CHM ... 63-E2
ZANE CT N BP ... 77-E2
ZANE PL CRY ... 91-E2
ZANE ST ER ... 19-E4,33-E2
ZANE ST NW ER ... 19-E4,33-E1
ZANE GREY CIR HUT ... 112-B2
ZANMILLER DR NFD ... 219-D3
ZANZIBAR CT N MG ... 76-D2
ZANZIBAR LN N DAY ... 48-C4,62-C1
ZANZIBAR LN N MG ... 76-D3
ZANZIBAR LN N PLY ... 90-D4,104-D1
ZARTHAN AVE SAV ... 147-E4,161-E1
ZARTHAN AVE S SLP ... 105-E4,119-E1
ZARTHAN CIR SAV ... 147-E4
ZARTHAN CT SAV ... 161-E1
ZEA CIR NW CR ... 63-D1
ZEA ST NW CR ... 49-D4,63-D1
ZEA ST NW OG ... 21-D3
ZEA ST NW SF ... 7-D3,21-D1
ZEALAND AVE CHM ... 63-C2
ZEALAND AVE N BP ... 77-C4,91-C1
ZEALAND AVE N GV ... 105-C1
ZEALAND AVE N NH ... 91-C2
ZEALAND CT N BP ... 77-C4
ZEALAND LN N BP ... 77-C4
ZEBRA AVE CT ... 127-D4,141-D1
ZEBRA AVE HOT ... 99-D4,113-D2
ZEBRA AVE YAT ... 141-D3,155-D1
ZEBULON ST NW BLT ... 19-B4,33-B1
ZEBULON PIKE AVE BUR ... 148-E2
ZEHNDER RD SL ... 136-C2
ZELAND CIR CHM ... 63-C2
ZEMBLE ST CHS ... 145-D2
ZENITH AVE EDI ... 120-B3
ZENITH AVE N BC ... 78-A4,92-A1
ZENITH AVE N BP ... 78-A3
ZENITH AVE N GV ... 106-B1
ZENITH AVE N ROB ... 92-B3,106-B1
ZENITH AVE S BLO ... 134-B2,148-B1
ZENITH AVE S BUR ... 148-B3
ZENITH AVE S EDI ... 120-B3
ZENITH AVE S MPL ... 106-B4,120-B2
ZENITH CIR BLO ... 134-B3
ZENITH CT N BP ... 78-A2
ZENITH LN BLO ... 148-B1
ZENITH LN EPR ... 132-E2,133-A2
ZENITH RD BLO ... 134-B3
ZEOLITE ST NW BT ... 20-D1
ZEOLITE ST NW RAM ... 34-D3,48-D1
ZEPHYR LN HUT ... 98-C3
ZEPHYR PL GV ... 106-B1
ZERO AVE BNT ... 127-C3,141-C1
ZERO AVE HNT ... 141-C2
ZERO AVE WIT ... 99-C4,113-C1
ZEST ST NE BLA ... 51-D4
ZEST ST NE HL ... 51-D3
ZIEGLERS DR N BP ... 64-A3
ZILLA ST NW AND ... 50-B2
ZILLA ST NW CR ... 64-B3
ZIMMERMAN RD CHN ... 131-C1
ZINDAUS ST OSC ... 27-E4,28-A4
ZINN AVE CLT ... 188-D2
ZINNIA LN N MG ... 76-E4,90-E1
ZINNIA LN N PLY ... 90-E3,104-E2
ZINNIA ST VIC ... 130-D2
ZINNIA WAY N MG ... 76-E3
ZINRAN AVE SAV ... 147-C3,161-D2
ZINRAN AVE S BLO ... 147-C1
ZINRAN AVE S SAV ... 147-C3
ZINRAN AVE S SLP ... 105-C4,119-C1
ZINRAN CIR S BLO ... 147-C1
ZINRAN RD BLO ... 133-C4,147-C1
ZION AVE WIT ... 99-C3
ZION AVE S BLO ... 147-E1
ZION CIR BLO ... 147-E2
ZION RD BLO ... 147-E2
ZION ST NW AND ... 36-A3
ZION ST NW CR ... 50-A3,64-A1
ZION ST NW OG ... 22-A3
ZION ST NW STT ... 8-A2
ZIRCON CT N MG ... 76-B1
ZIRCON LN EAG ... 149-B1
ZIRCON LN N MG ... 76-B1
ZIRCON LN N PLY ... 90-B4,104-B2
ZIRCONIUM ST NW RAM ... 35-A4,49-A1
ZODIAC ST NE COT ... 38-B2,52-B1
ZODIAC ST NE LWT ... 24-B2
ZOO BLVD APV ... 149-C4
ZOPFI WAY E MG ... 63-B3
ZOPFI WAY W MG ... 63-B3
ZUMBRA CIR VIC ... 116-E4
ZUMBRA DR VIC ... 116-E4,117-A4
ZUMBRA LN VIC ... 116-E4
ZUMBRO AVE HAT ... 188-A1
ZUMBRO AVE JT ... 146-A4,160-A1
ZUMBRO AVE LVT ... 160-A2
ZUMBRO AVE SCT ... 160-A4,174-A2
ZUMBRO ST NE LWT ... 10-C3
ZUMBRO ST NW ER ... 19-C4,33-C1
ZUMBROTA CT NE BLA ... 65-B2
ZUMBROTA ST NE BLA ... 65-B4
ZUMBROTA ST NE EB ... 23-B1
ZUMBROTA ST NE HL ... 37-B4,51-B3
ZUNI ST NW AND ... 35-C4
ZUNI ST NW ANO ... 49-C3
ZUNI ST NW RAM ... 49-C1
ZUNI ST NW STT ... 7-C1
ZWEBER LN HAS ... 166-C2

NUMBERED STREETS

1ST AVE ANO ... 49-C4,63-C1
1ST AVE BUR ... 148-D4
1ST AVE IND ... 102-B2
1ST AVE LFL ... 109-C4
1ST AVE MH ... 122-A3
1ST AVE NEW ... 123-B4,137-B1
1ST AVE SB ... 116-A3
1ST AVE WBL ... 81-A4
1ST AVE E SHK ... 146-B2
1ST AVE N BAY ... 97-B3
1ST AVE N LND ... 12-D4
1ST AVE N LP ... 113-B4
1ST AVE N MPL ... 106-D2
1ST AVE N NSP ... 95-B4
1ST AVE N PLY ... 104-C2
1ST AVE N WBT ... 81-A1
1ST AVE NE BUF ... 58-E2
1ST AVE NE LON ... 217-B2
1ST AVE NE MPL ... 106-D2
1ST AVE NE NP ... 201-D2
1ST AVE NE NYA ... 142-C3
1ST AVE NE OSS ... 77-C1
1ST AVE NE PLA ... 141-B3
1ST AVE NW ARL ... 183-A2
1ST AVE NW BUF ... 58-E2
1ST AVE NW FL ... 39-B3
1ST AVE NW NB ... 79-C4,93-C1
1ST AVE NW NP ... 201-D2
1ST AVE NW NYA ... 142-C3
1ST AVE NW PLA ... 141-B3
1ST AVE S BAY ... 97-B4
1ST AVE S BLO ... 134-D3,148-D1
1ST AVE S BUF ... 58-E3
1ST AVE S BUR ... 162-D2
1ST AVE S LP ... 113-B4
1ST AVE S MPL ... 106-D4,120-D1
1ST AVE S OSS ... 77-C2
1ST AVE S RCH ... 120-D4,134-D1
1ST AVE S SSP ... 122-E4,136-E1
1ST AVE S ZIM ... 5-C1
1ST AVE SE ARL ... 183-A2
1ST AVE SE LAT ... 201-D3
1ST AVE SE LON ... 217-B2
1ST AVE SE NB ... 93-C2
1ST AVE SE NP ... 201-D3
1ST AVE SE NYA ... 142-C3
1ST AVE SW FL ... 39-B3
1ST AVE SW NP ... 201-D2
1ST AVE SW NYA ... 142-C3
1ST AVE SW PLA ... 141-B4
1ST AVE W OSS ... 77-C1
1ST AVE W SHK ... 146-B2
1ST PL HAS ... 166-C1
1ST PL NW FL ... 39-B3
1ST ST BEC ... 2-E4
1ST ST CNC ... 12-E3
1ST ST DEL ... 87-D3
1ST ST EAG ... 135-E2
1ST ST ER ... 33-E2
1ST ST EXC ... 117-E3
1ST ST FAR ... 177-E4,191-E1
1ST ST HUD ... 111-C2
1ST ST HWL ... 85-A1
1ST ST LND ... 12-D4
1ST ST ML ... 43-D2

1ST ST NEW .137-B2
1ST ST SOM .84-B1
1ST ST SPP .137-B3
1ST ST WBL .81-A3
1ST ST WBT .81-B2
1ST ST E CHS .145-C3
1ST ST E DRS .28-D2
1ST ST E HAS .166-D1
1ST ST E JOR .173-B2
1ST ST E ML .43-D2
1ST ST E MLT .43-E3
1ST ST E NFD .219-E3
1ST ST E WAC .129-E3
1ST ST N CF .208-B4
1ST ST N HOP .119-D2
1ST ST N LLD .111-B4
1ST ST N MON .86-C1
1ST ST N MPL .92-C3,106-D2
1ST ST N MTK .119-B2
1ST ST N NM .189-E4
1ST ST N NSP .95-B4,109-B1
1ST ST N OKD .109-C4
1ST ST N OSS .77-C2
1ST ST N SWR .83-A4,97-A1
1ST ST N WAV .86-A1
1ST ST N WIN .99-B3
1ST ST NE BEL .186-A1
1ST ST NE BUF .58-E2,59-A2
1ST ST NE FL .39-B2
1ST ST NE HOP .119-C2
1ST ST NE MGY .215-D4
1ST ST NE MPL .92-D4
1ST ST NE MYR .114-E4
1ST ST NE NP .201-E2
1ST ST NE NYA .142-C3
1ST ST NE OSS .77-C2
1ST ST NE PLA .141-B3
1ST ST NE SM .46-E3
1ST ST NW FL .39-B3
1ST ST NW MYR .114-D4
1ST ST NW NB .93-B2
1ST ST NW NP .201-D2
1ST ST NW NYA .142-C3
1ST ST NW SLP .119-D1
1ST ST NW SM .46-E3
1ST ST S BUF .58-E2,59-A2
1ST ST S CF .208-B4
1ST ST S HOP .119-B2
1ST ST S LLD .111-C4
1ST ST S LS .111-C4
1ST ST S MON .86-C1
1ST ST S MPL .106-D2
1ST ST S OPH .97-A2
1ST ST S SWR .97-A2
1ST ST S TF .14-C3
1ST ST S WAV .86-A1
1ST ST S WIN .99-B4
1ST ST SE CF .208-B4,222-B1
1ST ST SE FL .39-B3
1ST ST SE NB .93-C2
1ST ST SE NP .201-E2
1ST ST SE NYA .142-C3
1ST ST SE OSS .77-C2
1ST ST SE PLA .141-B4
1ST ST SE SM .46-E4
1ST ST SW FL .39-B3
1ST ST SW NB .93-B2
1ST ST SW NP .201-D2
1ST ST SW SM .46-E4
1ST ST W CAR .145-B4
1ST ST W CHS .145-C3
1ST ST W CHT .145-C3
1ST ST W DRS .28-D2
1ST ST W HAS .166-C1
1ST ST W JOR .173-B2
1ST ST W ML .43-D2
1ST ST W NFD .219-D3
1ST ST W SHK .146-B2
1ST ST W WAC .129-D3
1ST BANK DR E LC .94-B3
1 1/2 AVE N MPL .106-B2
1 1/2 ST WAV .86-A1
1 1/2 ST NE OSS .77-C1
2ND AVE ANO .49-C4,63-C1
2ND AVE BUR .148-D4,162-E3
2ND AVE EXC .117-E3
2ND AVE HWL .85-A2
2ND AVE LFL .109-C4
2ND AVE LL .65-E2
2ND AVE MH .122-A3
2ND AVE NEW .123-B4,137-B1
2ND AVE NSP .95-B4
2ND AVE OSC .27-E4,28-A4
2ND AVE STN .206-E4,220-E1
2ND AVE WBL .81-A4
2ND AVE E SHK .146-B2
2ND AVE N BAY .97-B3
2ND AVE N LND .12-D3
2ND AVE N LP .113-B4
2ND AVE N MPL .106-B2
2ND AVE N NOH .111-C1
2ND AVE N OSS .77-C1
2ND AVE N PLY .104-C2
2ND AVE N SWR .97-A2
2ND AVE N ZIM .5-C1
2ND AVE NE ARL .183-A2
2ND AVE NE BUF .58-E2
2ND AVE NE FL .39-B3
2ND AVE NE LON .217-B2
2ND AVE NE NYA .142-C3
2ND AVE NE OSS .77-C1
2ND AVE NE PLA .141-B3
2ND AVE NW ARL .183-A2
2ND AVE NW BUF .58-E2
2ND AVE NW FL .39-B3
2ND AVE NW LON .217-B2
2ND AVE NW NB .93-C1
2ND AVE NW NP .201-D2
2ND AVE NW OSS .77-B1
2ND AVE NW PLA .141-B3
2ND AVE NW SM .46-E3
2ND AVE S BAY .97-B4
2ND AVE S BLO .134-D3
2ND AVE S BUF .58-E3
2ND AVE S HOP .119-C2
2ND AVE S LP .127-B1
2ND AVE S MPL .106-D4,120-D2
2ND AVE S OSS .77-C2
2ND AVE S RCH .120-D4,134-D1
2ND AVE S SSP .122-E4,136-E1
2ND AVE S ZIM .5-C1
2ND AVE SE ARL .183-A2
2ND AVE SE FL .39-B3
2ND AVE SE LON .217-B2
2ND AVE SE MPL .106-E2
2ND AVE SE NB .93-C2
2ND AVE SE NYA .142-C3

2ND AVE SE OSS .77-C2
2ND AVE SE PLA .141-B4
2ND AVE SW ARL .183-A2
2ND AVE SW BUF .58-E3
2ND AVE SW FL .39-B3
2ND AVE SW LON .217-B2
2ND AVE SW NYA .142-C3
2ND AVE W SHK .146-B2
2ND ST BEC .2-E4
2ND ST CAT .191-E1
2ND ST CNC .12-E3
2ND ST DRS .28-D2
2ND ST ER .28-E2
2ND ST FAR .177-E4,191-E1
2ND ST GI .169-D2
2ND ST HUD .111-C2
2ND ST HWL .85-A1
2ND ST JOR .173-B2
2ND ST LES .212-C4
2ND ST LND .12-D4
2ND ST MEN .121-D4
2ND ST MSC .55-C4
2ND ST NEW .137-B2
2ND ST NSP .95-B4,109-B1
2ND ST PRE .167-B1
2ND ST SPP .137-B3
2ND ST STP .137-B4
2ND ST WBL .80-E3,81-A3
2ND ST WBT .81-B2
2ND ST ZIM .5-D1
2ND ST E CHS .145-C3
2ND ST E HAS .166-D1
2ND ST E JOR .173-B2
2ND ST E NFD .219-E3
2ND ST E NSP .95-B4
2ND ST E WAC .129-E3
2ND ST E ZIM .5-D1
2ND ST N BAY .97-B3
2ND ST N CF .208-B4
2ND ST N DEL .87-D2
2ND ST N HEN .198-D3
2ND ST N HOP .119-B2
2ND ST N LES .212-C3
2ND ST N LLD .111-B4
2ND ST N LS .111-C4
2ND ST N MON .86-C1
2ND ST N MPL .92-C4,106-C1
2ND ST N OKD .109-C4
2ND ST N RF .140-E2
2ND ST N SSP .122-D4
2ND ST N SWR .83-A4,97-A1
2ND ST N WAV .86-A1
2ND ST N WIN .99-B3
2ND ST NE BUT .59-C3
2ND ST NE CH .92-D2
2ND ST NE FL .39-C2
2ND ST NE FRI .78-D4,92-D2
2ND ST NE HOP .119-C2
2ND ST NE MGY .215-D4
2ND ST NE MPL .92-D4,106-D1
2ND ST NE NP .201-E2
2ND ST NE NYA .142-C3
2ND ST NE OSS .77-C1
2ND ST NE PLA .141-C3
2ND ST NE SM .46-E3
2ND ST NW BUF .58-E2
2ND ST NW FL .39-B2
2ND ST NW HNT .141-B3
2ND ST NW MYR .114-D4
2ND ST NW NB .93-B2
2ND ST NW NP .201-D2
2ND ST NW NSP .95-B3
2ND ST NW OSS .77-C1
2ND ST NW PLA .141-B3
2ND ST NW SLP .119-D1
2ND ST NW SM .46-E3
2ND ST S AFT .110-D4
2ND ST S BAY .97-B4
2ND ST S BUF .58-E2,59-A2
2ND ST S CF .208-B4
2ND ST S DEL .87-D3
2ND ST S EXC .119-C2
2ND ST S HOP .119-B2
2ND ST S HUD .111-C3
2ND ST S LS .111-C4
2ND ST S MON .86-C1
2ND ST S MPL .106-D2
2ND ST S RF .140-E2
2ND ST S SSP .122-D4
2ND ST S SWR .97-A2
2ND ST S WAV .86-A1
2ND ST S WIN .99-B4
2ND ST SE CF .208-B4,222-B1
2ND ST SE FL .39-B3
2ND ST SE MPL .106-E2
2ND ST SE NB .93-C2
2ND ST SE NP .201-E2
2ND ST SE NYA .142-C3
2ND ST SE OSS .77-C2
2ND ST SE SM .46-E4
2ND ST SW FL .39-B3
2ND ST SW MVT .59-B3
2ND ST SW NB .93-B2
2ND ST SW NP .201-D2
2ND ST SW NYA .142-C3
2ND ST W CHS .145-C3
2ND ST W DEL .87-D3
2ND ST W HAS .166-C1
2ND ST W JOR .173-B2
2ND ST W ML .43-D2
2ND ST W NFD .219-D3
2ND ST W WAC .129-D3
2ND TER SW NB .93-B2
2 1/2 ST NE CH .92-D2
2 1/2 ST NE FRI .78-D4,92-D2
2 1/2 ST NE MPL .92-D3
3M RD MPW .109-B4
3RD AVE ANO .49-C4,63-C1
3RD AVE EXC .117-E3,118-A3
3RD AVE IND .117-B2
3RD AVE LFL .109-C4
3RD AVE MH .122-A3
3RD AVE NEW .123-B4,137-B1
3RD AVE NSP .95-B4
3RD AVE OSC .27-E4,28-A4
3RD AVE SPP .137-B2
3RD AVE SWD .107-B4
3RD AVE WBL .81-A4
3RD AVE ZIM .5-C1
3RD AVE E OSC .28-A4
3RD AVE E SHK .146-B2
3RD AVE N BAY .97-B3
3RD AVE N LND .12-D3
3RD AVE N MPL .106-D2

3RD AVE N NOH .111-C1
3RD AVE N PLY .104-D2,105-A2
3RD AVE N SSP .122-E4
3RD AVE NE ARL .183-A2
3RD AVE NE BUF .45-A4,58-E1
3RD AVE NE LON .217-B2
3RD AVE NE MPL .106-C1
3RD AVE NE NYA .142-C3
3RD AVE NE OSS .77-C1
3RD AVE NE PLA .141-B4
3RD AVE NW ARL .183-A2
3RD AVE NW BUF .58-E2
3RD AVE NW FL .39-B3
3RD AVE NW LON .217-B2
3RD AVE NW NB .93-C1
3RD AVE NW NP .201-D2
3RD AVE NW OSS .77-B1
3RD AVE NW PLA .141-B3
3RD AVE S BLO .134-D3,148-D1
3RD AVE S BUF .58-E3
3RD AVE S LP .127-B1
3RD AVE S MPL .106-D3,120-D2
3RD AVE S OPH .97-A2
3RD AVE S RCH .120-D4,134-D1
3RD AVE S SSP .122-E4,136-E1
3RD AVE S SWR .97-A2
3RD AVE S ZIM .5-C1
3RD AVE SE ARL .183-A2
3RD AVE SE LON .217-B2
3RD AVE SE MPL .106-E2
3RD AVE SE NB .93-C2
3RD AVE SE NYA .142-C3
3RD AVE SE OSS .77-C2
3RD AVE SW ARL .183-A2
3RD AVE SW LAT .201-D3
3RD AVE SW LON .217-B2
3RD AVE SW NYA .142-C3
3RD AVE W OSC .28-A4
3RD AVE W SHK .146-B2
3RD ST BEC .2-E3
3RD ST BLA .64-D1
3RD ST CAT .191-E1
3RD ST CLK .1-D1
3RD ST DEL .87-D2
3RD ST DRS .28-D2
3RD ST ER .33-E2,34-A2
3RD ST FAR .177-E4,191-E1
3RD ST GI .169-D2
3RD ST HUD .111-C2
3RD ST HWL .85-A1
3RD ST LES .212-C4
3RD ST LND .12-D4
3RD ST MEN .121-D4
3RD ST MPW .109-B4
3RD ST MSC .55-C4
3RD ST NEW .137-B2
3RD ST NSP .95-B4,109-B1
3RD ST SPP .137-B3
3RD ST WBL .80-E3,81-A3
3RD ST WBT .81-B2
3RD ST ZIM .5-C1
3RD ST E CAR .145-B4
3RD ST E CHS .145-C3
3RD ST E HAS .166-D1
3RD ST E JOR .173-B2
3RD ST E ML .43-D2
3RD ST E MO .31-D2
3RD ST E NFD .219-E4
3RD ST E WAC .129-E3
3RD ST E ZIM .5-D1
3RD ST N BAY .97-B3
3RD ST N CF .208-B4
3RD ST N DEL .87-D2
3RD ST N HEN .198-D3
3RD ST N HOP .119-B2
3RD ST N LES .212-C3
3RD ST N LLD .111-B4
3RD ST N LS .111-C4
3RD ST N MPL .92-C4,106-C1
3RD ST N NOH .111-C1
3RD ST N OKD .109-C4
3RD ST N OPH .97-B3
3RD ST N RF .140-E2
3RD ST N SSP .122-D4
3RD ST N SWR .83-A4,97-A1
3RD ST N WIN .99-B3
3RD ST NE AND .36-D3
3RD ST NE BLA .64-D1
3RD ST NE BUF .58-E2,59-A2
3RD ST NE CH .92-D2
3RD ST NE EB .8-D4,22-D4
3RD ST NE FRI .78-D4,92-D1
3RD ST NE HAN .36-D3,50-D1
3RD ST NE HL .36-D3,50-D1
3RD ST NE MGY .215-D4
3RD ST NE MPL .92-D4,106-D1
3RD ST NE NP .201-E2
3RD ST NE OSS .77-C1
3RD ST NE PLA .141-B3
3RD ST NE SM .46-E3
3RD ST NW BUF .58-E2
3RD ST NW FL .39-B3
3RD ST NW MYR .114-D4
3RD ST NW NB .93-B1
3RD ST NW NP .201-D2
3RD ST NW OSS .77-C1
3RD ST NW PLA .141-B3
3RD ST NW SM .46-E3
3RD ST S AFT .110-D4
3RD ST S BAY .97-B4
3RD ST S BUF .58-E2,59-A2
3RD ST S CF .208-B4
3RD ST S DEL .87-D3
3RD ST S EDI .119-C2
3RD ST S EXC .117-E3
3RD ST S HEN .198-D3
3RD ST S HOP .119-C2
3RD ST S LLD .111-B4
3RD ST S LS .111-C4
3RD ST S MON .86-C1
3RD ST S MPL .106-D2
3RD ST S RF .140-E2
3RD ST S SSP .122-E4
3RD ST S SWR .97-A2
3RD ST S WAV .86-A1
3RD ST S WIN .99-B4
3RD ST SE CH .39-C3
3RD ST SE NP .201-E2
3RD ST SE NYA .142-C3
3RD ST SE OSS .77-C2
3RD ST SE RFT .60-A4
3RD ST SW CF .222-B1
3RD ST SW DEL .87-D3
3RD ST SW FL .39-B3

3RD ST SW NB .93-B2
3RD ST SW PLA .141-B4
3RD ST SW WAC .129-D3
3RD ST W CAR .145-B4
3RD ST W CHS .145-C3
3RD ST W DEL .87-D3
3RD ST W HAS .166-C1
3RD ST W JOR .173-B2
3RD ST W ML .43-D3
3RD ST W MO .31-D1
3RD ST W NFD .219-D3
3RD ST W WAC .129-D3
3RD TER NW NB .93-B1
3RD STREET CT N OKD .109-C4
3RD STREET PL N LE .110-B4
3 1/2 ST W WAC .129-D3
4TH AVE ANO .49-C4,63-C1
4TH AVE BUR .148-D4,162-D1
4TH AVE FAT .56-C3
4TH AVE HWL .85-A2
4TH AVE LFL .109-C4
4TH AVE LL .52-A4,66-A1
4TH AVE MH .122-A3
4TH AVE NEW .123-B4,137-B1
4TH AVE NSP .95-B4
4TH AVE OSC .27-E4,28-A4
4TH AVE SPP .137-B2
4TH AVE WBL .81-A4
4TH AVE E SHK .146-C2
4TH AVE N ANO .49-C4
4TH AVE N BAY .97-B3
4TH AVE N LND .12-D3
4TH AVE N MPL .106-B2
4TH AVE N PLY .104-D2
4TH AVE N SSP .122-E4
4TH AVE NE ARL .183-A2
4TH AVE NE ART .183-A2
4TH AVE NE BUF .58-E2
4TH AVE NE FL .39-B3
4TH AVE NE LON .217-B2
4TH AVE NE MPL .106-D1
4TH AVE NE OSS .77-C1
4TH AVE NE PLA .141-C4
4TH AVE NW BUF .58-E2
4TH AVE NW FL .39-B3
4TH AVE NW LON .217-B2
4TH AVE NW NP .201-D2
4TH AVE S ANO .63-C1
4TH AVE S BAY .97-B4
4TH AVE S BLO .134-D3,148-D1
4TH AVE S BUF .58-E3
4TH AVE S MPL .106-D3,120-D2
4TH AVE S RCH .120-D4,134-D1
4TH AVE S SSP .122-E4,136-E1
4TH AVE S SWR .97-A2
4TH AVE S ZIM .5-C1
4TH AVE SE ARL .183-A2
4TH AVE SE ART .183-A3
4TH AVE SE MPL .106-E2
4TH AVE SE OSS .77-C2
4TH AVE SE PLA .141-C4
4TH AVE SW FL .39-B3
4TH AVE SW LON .217-A2
4TH AVE SW NP .201-D3
4TH AVE SW NYA .142-C3
4TH AVE W SHK .146-B2
4TH CT N MPL .92-C2
4TH PL N PLY .104-B2
4TH ST BAY .97-B3
4TH ST CLK .1-D1
4TH ST FAR .177-E4,191-E1
4TH ST GCT .137-B3
4TH ST GI .169-D2
4TH ST HWL .85-A1
4TH ST LES .212-C4
4TH ST MEN .121-D4
4TH ST MPW .109-B4
4TH ST NEW .137-B2
4TH ST SPP .137-B3
4TH ST WBL .80-E3,81-A3
4TH ST WBT .81-B2
4TH ST ZIM .5-C1
4TH ST E CHS .145-B4
4TH ST E HAS .166-E1,167-A1
4TH ST E JOR .173-B2
4TH ST E MO .31-D2
4TH ST E STP .108-C4,109-A3
4TH ST E WAC .129-D3
4TH ST N BAY .97-B3
4TH ST N BC .92-C2
4TH ST N CF .208-B4
4TH ST N DEL .87-D2
4TH ST N HEN .198-D3
4TH ST N HOP .119-B1
4TH ST N HUD .111-C2
4TH ST N LES .212-D3
4TH ST N LLD .111-C4
4TH ST N MPL .92-C4,106-C1
4TH ST N NOH .111-C1
4TH ST N OKD .109-C4
4TH ST N RF .140-E1
4TH ST N SSP .122-D3
4TH ST N SWR .83-A4,97-A1
4TH ST N WAV .86-A1
4TH ST N WIN .99-B3
4TH ST N WLT .110-D4
4TH ST NE BLA .64-D2
4TH ST NE BUF .58-E2,59-A2
4TH ST NE CH .92-D2
4TH ST NE EB .22-D4
4TH ST NE HAN .78-D4,92-D1
4TH ST NE HL .36-D4,50-D2
4TH ST NE MGY .215-D4
4TH ST NE MPL .92-D4,106-D1
4TH ST NE MYR .114-E4
4TH ST NE NP .201-E2,202-A2
4TH ST NE OSS .77-C1
4TH ST NE SM .46-E3
4TH ST NW BUF .58-E2
4TH ST NW FL .39-B3
4TH ST NW MGY .215-D4
4TH ST NW MYR .114-D4
4TH ST NW NB .93-B1
4TH ST NW NP .201-D2
4TH ST NW SM .46-E3
4TH ST S AFT .110-D4
4TH ST S BAY .97-B4
4TH ST S BUF .58-E2,59-A2
4TH ST S CF .208-B4,222-B1

20TH ST SE RFT 73-A1,74-B1
20TH ST SW MIT 71-B1
20TH ST SW MVT 71-E1,72-C1
20TH ST W HAS 166-C2
20TH AVENUE WAY STN 207-B4
20TH STREET CT N LE 110-B2
21ST AVE N CV 66-E2
21ST AVE N HOP 119-B2
21ST AVE N LL 66-E3
21ST AVE N MPL 106-C1
21ST AVE N MTK 119-B2
21ST AVE N PLY 104-E1,105-C1
21ST AVE N SSP 122-D3
21ST AVE NW NB 79-B4
21ST AVE S BLO 134-E3
21ST AVE S BUT 59-B3
21ST AVE S MPL 106-E3,120-E1
21ST AVE S SHK 147-B4
21ST AVE S SSP 122-D4
21ST AVE SE MPL 107-A2
21ST LN NW NB 79-A3
21ST ST NEW 123-B4,137-B1
21ST ST E HAS 166-D2
21ST ST E MPL 106-D3
21ST ST N LE 109-E2,110-C2
21ST ST N OKD 109-D2
21ST ST N WLT 110-E2,111-A2
21ST ST NE SM 60-E1
21ST ST NW CMT 58-C1
21ST ST NW NB 79-A3
21ST ST S LSC 125-C2
21ST ST W HAS 166-C2
21ST ST W MPL 106-B3
22ND AVE BUR 148-E2
22ND AVE N MPL 106-C1
22ND AVE N PLY 104-D1
22ND AVE N SSP 122-D3
22ND AVE NE MPL 92-E4,93-A4
22ND AVE NW NB 93-B1
22ND AVE S BLO 134-E3
22ND AVE S FS 134-E2
22ND AVE S MPL 106-E3,120-E1
22ND AVE S SHK 146-C4,147-B4
22ND AVE S SSP 122-D4
22ND AVE SE MPL 107-A2
22ND CIR NE SM 61-A1
22ND CT N LE 109-D2
22ND LN W SLP 105-C3
22ND PL N PLY 104-D1
22ND ST HOT . . . .-D3
22ND ST MPW 109-B4
22ND ST E MPL 106-D3,107-A3
22ND ST N LE 109-E2
22ND ST N OKD 109-C2
22ND ST N WLT 110-D2,111-B2
22ND ST NE BUT 59-B1
22ND ST NE SM 60-E1
22ND ST NW ABT 57-C1
22ND ST S AFT 124-D2
22ND ST S LSC 125-C2
22ND ST S SMP 125-C2
22ND ST SE RFT 73-E1,74-A1
22ND ST SW MVT 72-C1
22ND ST W HAS 166-C2
22ND ST W MPL 106-C3
22ND ST W SLP 105-D3
22ND TER NW NB 79-A3
22ND STREET CT N OKD 109-D2
22ND STREET CT N WLT 110-E2
23RD AVE BUR 148-E3
23RD AVE FAT 55-E1,56-A1
23RD AVE STN 207-B4,221-B1
23RD AVE N GV 105-C1
23RD AVE N MPL 106-C1
23RD AVE N PLY 104-E1,105-A1
23RD AVE N SSP 122-D3
23RD AVE NE MPL 92-E4,93-A4
23RD AVE NW NB 79-A4,93-B1
23RD AVE S FS 134-E2
23RD AVE S MPL 106-E3,120-E1
23RD AVE S SSP 122-D4
23RD AVE SE MPL 107-A2
23RD ST SJT 83-C4
23RD ST SMT 83-C3
23RD ST E MPL 106-E3
23RD ST N OKD 109-D2
23RD ST N WLT 110-E2
23RD ST NE BUT 59-E1
23RD ST NE SM 60-E1
23RD ST S LSC 125-C2
23RD ST SE RFT 73-D2
23RD ST W HAS 166-C2
23RD ST W SLP 105-D3
23RD AVENUE WAY STN 207-C4
23RD STREET CIR N OKD 109-D2
23RD STREET CT N WLT 110-E2
24TH AVE BUR 148-E3
24TH AVE N GV 105-C1
24TH AVE N LL 53-A4,67-A1
24TH AVE N MPL 106-C1
24TH AVE N PLY 104-C1,105-A1
24TH AVE N SSP 122-D3
24TH AVE NE MPL 92-E4
24TH AVE S BLO 135-A2
24TH AVE S FS 135-A2
24TH AVE S LL 67-A3
24TH AVE S MPL 106-E3,121-A1
24TH AVE SE MPL 107-A2
24TH CT W SLP 105-C4
24TH PL W SLP 105-C4
24TH ST HOT 99-D3
24TH ST MPW 109-B4
24TH ST SJT 83-C4
24TH ST WTT . . . .-D4
24TH ST E MPL 106-D3,107-A3
24TH ST N LE 110-C2
24TH ST N OKD 109-C2
24TH ST N WLT 110-D2,111-A2
24TH ST S SMP 125-C2
24TH ST SE RFT 73-B2,74-B2
24TH ST W HAS 166-D3
24TH ST W MPL 106-C3
24TH ST W SLP 105-D4,106-A3
24TH STREET CT N LE 110-C2
25TH AVE FAT 55-D1,56-E1
25TH AVE N GV 105-D1
25TH AVE N MPL 106-C1
25TH AVE N PLY 104-C1,105-A1
25TH AVE NW LIT 5-D1
25TH AVE S BLO 135-A2
25TH AVE S MPL 107-A3,121-A1
25TH AVE SE MPL 107-A2
25TH CIR N PLY 104-D1
25TH CT N PLY 104-D1
25TH PL N PLY 104-D1
25TH ST HAS 166-C2
25TH ST MPW 109-C4
25TH ST SJT 83-D4,97-D1
25TH ST E HAS 166-D3
25TH ST E MPL 106-D4,107-A4
25TH ST N LE 110-C2
25TH ST N OKD 109-C2
25TH ST NE SM 60-C1
25TH ST NW ABT 57-C1,58-D1
25TH ST NW CMT 57-E1,58-C1
25TH ST NW HAS 166-C2
25TH ST NW NB 79-B3
25TH ST S SMP 125-C2
25TH ST SE RFT 72-E2
25TH ST SW MIT 71-B2
25TH ST SW MVT 71-D2,72-A2
25TH ST W HAS 166-D3
25TH ST W MPL 106-C4
25TH ST W SLP 105-D4,106-A4
25TH AVENUE WAY STN 221-C3
25TH STREET CIR N OKD 109-C2
25 1/2 AVE NE MPL 93-A4
25 1/2 ST E MPL 106-E4
25 1/2 ST W MPL 106-C4
25 1/2 ST W SLP 105-E4,106-A4
26TH AVE BUR 149-A2
26TH AVE N GV 91-C4,106-A1
26TH AVE N MPL 106-C1
26TH AVE N PLY 90-D4,91-A4
26TH AVE NE MPL 92-E4,93-A4
26TH AVE NW NB 79-A4
26TH AVE S BLO 135-A2
26TH AVE S FS 121-A3,135-A2
26TH AVE S MPL 107-A4,121-A1
26TH AVE SE MPL 107-B2
26TH ST E HAS 166-D3
26TH ST E MPL 106-D4,107-A4
26TH ST N LE 109-E2
26TH ST N OKD 109-C2
26TH ST N WLT 110-E2
26TH ST NE SM 60-E1
26TH ST NW CMT 57-D1
26TH ST SE RFT 73-C2,74-B2
26TH ST W MPL 106-C4
26TH ST W SLP 105-D4,106-A4
26TH STREET CT N OKD 109-C2
26 1/2 AVE N ROB 92-A4
26 1/2 AVE NE MPL 92-D4
26 1/2 LN W SLP 106-A4
27TH AVE BUR 149-A1
27TH AVE E LYT 1-A2
27TH AVE N CRY 91-E4
27TH AVE N GV 92-A4
27TH AVE N MPL 92-B4
27TH AVE N PLY 90-D4,91-A4
27TH AVE N ROB 92-A4
27TH AVE NE MPL 92-E4,93-A4
27TH AVE NE SA 93-A4
27TH AVE NW NB 79-A4,93-A1
27TH AVE S FS 121-A3
27TH AVE S MPL 107-A4,121-A3
27TH AVE SE MPL 107-A3
27TH PL BUR 149-A2
27TH PL N NH 91-C4
27TH PL N PLY 90-D4,91-A4
27TH ST SJT 97-D1
27TH ST E HAS 166-D3
27TH ST E MPL 106-D4,107-A4
27TH ST N LE 109-E2
27TH ST N OKD 109-C2
27TH ST N WLT 110-C2
27TH ST NW CMT 58-C1
27TH ST S SMP 125-C2
27TH ST SE RFT 73-C2,74-B2
27TH ST SW MVT 72-C2
27TH ST W MPL 106-C4
27TH ST W SLP 105-E4,106-A4
27TH STREET CIR N OKD 109-D2
27TH STREET CT N LE 109-E2
28TH AVE N MPL 92-C4
28TH AVE N NH 91-C4
28TH AVE N PLY 90-D4,91-A4
28TH AVE NE MPL 92-E4,93-A4
28TH AVE NW NB 79-A4
28TH AVE S BLO 135-A2
28TH AVE S FS 121-A4
28TH AVE S MPL 107-A4,121-A2
28TH PL N PLY 90-E4,91-A4
28TH ST SMT 83-D3
28TH ST E MPL 106-D4,107-A4
28TH ST N LE 109-E1,110-A2
28TH ST N OKD 109-D1
28TH ST N WLT 110-E1,111-A1
28TH ST NW CMT 57-D1
28TH ST SE RFT 74-B2
28TH ST SW MVT 71-C2
28TH ST W MPL 106-C4
28TH ST W SLP 105-D4,106-A4
28TH STREET CT N WLT 111-A1
29TH AVE SHK 160-C1
29TH AVE N CRY 91-E4
29TH AVE N MPL 92-C4
29TH AVE N NH 91-C4
29TH AVE N PLY 90-C4,91-A4
29TH AVE N ROB 92-A4
29TH AVE NE MPL 92-E4,93-A3
29TH AVE NE SA 93-B3
29TH AVE NW NB 79-A4
29TH AVE S MPL 107-A4,121-A2
29TH AVE SE MPL 107-B2
29TH PL N CRY 91-E4
29TH ST E MPL 106-E4,107-A4
29TH ST N OKD 109-C1
29TH ST SE RFT 72-E2,73-A2
29TH ST W MPL 106-C4
29TH ST W SLP 105-D4,106-A4
29TH STREET CIR N OKD 109-C1
29TH STREET PL N OKD 109-C1
30TH AVE FAT 42-D4
30TH AVE STN 221-C2
30TH AVE WST 221-C4
30TH AVE N CRY 91-D4
30TH AVE N MPL 92-C4
30TH AVE N NH 91-C4
30TH AVE N PLY 90-C4,91-A4
30TH AVE N ROB 92-A4
30TH AVE NE MPL 92-E3,93-A3
30TH AVE NE SA 93-A3
30TH AVE NW NB 93-A2
30TH AVE S MPL 107-A4,121-A2
30TH AVE SE MPL 107-B2
30TH PL N PLY 90-B4
30TH ST HOT 99-E4
30TH ST SJT 97-D3
30TH ST WTT . . . .-E4,101-A4
30TH ST N BYT 110-D1,111-A1
30TH ST N LE 110-C1
30TH ST N OKD 109-C1
30TH ST NE BUT 58-E1,59-B1
30TH ST NE SM 46-D4,60-B1
30TH ST NW ABT 43-A4,58-A1
30TH ST NW MLT 58-B1
30TH ST S AFT 124-D3,125-A3
30TH ST SE RFT 72-E2,73-A2
30TH ST SW MIT 71-B2
30TH ST SW MVT 71-D2,72-D2
30TH STREET CIR N BYT 110-E1
30TH STREET CIR N LE 110-C1
30TH STREET CT N OKD 109-C1
30 1/2 ST E MPL 106-E4
30 1/2 ST W MPL 106-A4
30 1/2 ST W SLP 105-C4
31ST AVE BUR 149-A3
31ST AVE N CRY 91-D4
31ST AVE N MPL 92-C4
31ST AVE N NH 91-C4
31ST AVE N PLY 90-D4,91-B4
31ST AVE N ROB 92-A4
31ST AVE NE MPL 92-E3,93-A3
31ST AVE NE SA 93-A3
31ST AVE S MPL 107-A4,121-A2
31ST PL N PLY 90-B4
31ST PL NE SM 46-D4
31ST ST WTT 101-B4
31ST ST E HAS 166-E3,167-A3
31ST ST E MPL 106-D4,107-A4
31ST ST E RVT 167-A3
31ST ST N LE 109-E1,110-A1
31ST ST N OKD 109-D1
31ST ST S AFT 125-B3
31ST ST SE RFT 73-C2,74-B2
31ST ST W HAS 166-D3
31ST ST W MPL 106-C4
31ST ST W SLP 105-D4,106-A4
31ST STREET CIR OKD 109-D1
31ST STREET CT N OKD 109-D1
31ST STREET PL N OKD 109-D1
31ST STREET PLZ N OKD 109-D1
31 1/2 AVE N ROB 92-A4
32ND AVE N CRY 91-D4
32ND AVE N NH 91-C4
32ND AVE N PLY 90-C4,91-B4
32ND AVE NE MPL 92-E3,93-A3
32ND AVE NE SA 93-A3
32ND AVE NW NB 79-A4,93-A2
32ND AVE S MPL 107-A4,121-A2
32ND CIR N NH 91-C4
32ND CT N NH 91-C4
32ND PL N CRY 91-C4
32ND PL N NH 91-C4
32ND PL N PLY 90-C4
32ND ST HOT 99-E4,114-A1
32ND ST SJT 97-D3
32ND ST WTT 115-A1
32ND ST E MPL 106-E4,107-A4
32ND ST N LE 110-B1
32ND ST N OKD 109-C1
32ND ST NE SM 46-E4
32ND ST NW MLT 44-D4
32ND ST S AFT 124-D3,125-A3
32ND ST SE RFT 72-E2,74-A2
32ND ST W MPL 106-C4
32ND ST W SLP 105-D4
32ND AVENUE WAY STN 221-C1
32 1/2 ST E MPL 106-D4
32 1/2 ST W SLP 105-D4
33RD AVE BUR 149-A3
33RD AVE N CRY 91-C4
33RD AVE N GV 91-E4,92-A4
33RD AVE N MPL 92-C4
33RD AVE N NH 91-C4
33RD AVE N PLY 90-C4,91-B4
33RD AVE N ROB 92-A4
33RD AVE NE MPL 92-E3,93-A3
33RD AVE NE SA 93-A3
33RD AVE S MPL 107-A4,121-A2
33RD AVE SE MPL 107-B2
33RD CIR NE SM 46-E4
33RD PL N CRY 91-D4
33RD PL N NH 91-C4
33RD PL N PLY 90-C4
33RD ST E HAS 166-D3
33RD ST E MPL 120-E1,121-A1
33RD ST N LE 110-B1
33RD ST N OKD 109-C1
33RD ST NE BUT 44-D4
33RD ST NW BUT 44-D4
33RD ST NW MLT 43-D4,44-B4
33RD ST S AFT 124-E3,125-B3
33RD ST SE RFT 72-E2,73-A2
33RD ST W HAS 166-D3
33RD ST W MPL 120-C1
33RD ST W SLP 105-E4,119-D1
33RD STREET LN N LE 110-B1
34TH AVE N CRY 91-E4
34TH AVE N GV 91-E4,92-A4
34TH AVE N MPL 92-B4
34TH AVE N NH 91-C4
34TH AVE N PLY 90-D4,91-B4
34TH AVE N ROB 92-A4
34TH AVE NE MPL 92-E3,93-A3
34TH AVE NE SA 93-A3
34TH AVE S BLO 135-A2
34TH AVE S FS 121-A4,135-A1
34TH AVE S MPL 107-A4,121-A2
34TH CIR NE SM 46-E4
34TH CIR W MTK 119-B1
34TH PL N CRY 91-E4
34TH PL NE SM 46-D4
34TH ST E MPL 120-D1,121-A1
34TH ST N BYT 110-E1,111-A1
34TH ST N LE 109-E1,110-B1
34TH ST N OKD 109-C1
34TH ST NE SM 46-D4
34TH ST S AFT 124-E3,125-B3
34TH ST W MPL 120-C1
34TH ST W MTK 119-B1
34TH ST W SLP 119-C1,120-A1
34 1/2 AVE N NH 91-C4
34 1/2 ST E MPL 120-D1
34 1/2 ST W MPL 120-B1
34 1/2 ST W SLP 119-D1
35TH AVE ADT 42-E4
35TH AVE SHK 160-C2
35TH AVE STN 221-D3
35TH AVE WST 221-D4
35TH AVE N CRY 91-D4,92-A4
35TH AVE N MPL 92-B4
35TH AVE N NH 91-C4
35TH AVE N PLY 90-E4,91-C4
35TH AVE N ROB 92-A4
35TH AVE NE MPL 92-E3,93-A3
35TH AVE NE SA 93-A3
35TH AVE S MPL 107-A4,121-A3
35TH PL N CRY 91-D4
35TH PL N PLY 90-E4,91-B4
35TH ST E MPL 120-D1,121-A1
35TH ST N LE 109-E1,110-B1
35TH ST N OKD 109-C1
35TH ST NE BUF 44-E4,45-B4
35TH ST NE BUT 44-E4,45-E4
35TH ST NE SM 45-E4,46-D4
35TH ST NW ABT 43-A4
35TH ST NW BUT 44-D4
35TH ST S AFT 125-B3
35TH ST SE RFT 72-E3,73-C3
35TH ST SW MIT 71-A3
35TH ST SW MVT 71-E2,72-C2
35TH ST W HAS 166-D3
35TH ST W MPL 120-C1
35TH ST W SLP 119-E1,120-A1
35TH ST W WT 204-B3
35 1/2 AVE N NH 91-C4
35 1/2 ST W SLP 119-E1
36TH AVE N CRY 91-E3,92-A4
36TH AVE N MPL 92-B4
36TH AVE N NH 91-C3
36TH AVE N PLY 90-D3,91-B3
36TH AVE N ROB 91-E4,92-A4
36TH AVE NE MPL 92-E3,93-A3
36TH AVE NE SA 93-A3
36TH AVE S MPL 107-A4,121-A1
36TH CIR SM 47-A4
36TH PL N PLY 90-D3,91-B3
36TH ST SMT 69-D1
36TH ST E HAS 166-D3
36TH ST E MPL 120-D1,121-A1
36TH ST N LE 109-E1,110-C1
36TH ST N OKD 109-D1
36TH ST S AFT 125-B3
36TH ST SE RFT 73-C3,74-A3
36TH ST SW MVT 72-D3
36TH ST W MPL 120-C1
36TH ST W SLP 119-E1,120-A1
36 1/2 AVE NE MPL 92-E3
36 1/2 CIR N NH 91-C3
36 1/2 ST E MPL 120-E1,121-A1
36 1/2 ST W SLP 120-A1
37TH AVE N CRY 91-D3
37TH AVE N MPL 92-B3
37TH AVE N NH 91-D3
37TH AVE N PLY 90-D3,91-B3
37TH AVE N ROB 91-E3,92-A3
37TH AVE NE CH 92-E3,93-A3
37TH AVE NE FRI 92-D3
37TH AVE NE MPL 92-C3
37TH AVE NE SA 93-A3
37TH AVE S MPL 107-A4,121-A1
37TH PL N PLY 90-E3,91-C3
37TH PL NE CH 93-A3
37TH ST SJT 97-E3
37TH ST SM 47-A4
37TH ST SMT 69-D4,83-D1
37TH ST E MPL 120-E1,121-A1
37TH ST N BYT 97-A4
37TH ST N LE 109-E1
37TH ST N OKD 109-C1
37TH ST NW MLT 43-E4,44-A4
37TH ST S AFT 125-B3
37TH ST SE RFT 72-E3,73-D3
37TH ST W HAS 166-D3
37TH ST W MPL 120-C1
37TH ST W SLP 119-D1,120-A1
37TH ST W WT 203-C3,204-C3
37TH AVENUE WAY STN 221-D1
37TH STREET CT N OKD 109-D1
38TH AVE ANO 49-D3
38TH AVE SA 93-A2
38TH AVE N ANO 49-D3
38TH AVE N CRY 91-E3
38TH AVE N NH 91-D3
38TH AVE N PLY 90-D3,91-B3
38TH AVE N ROB 91-E3,92-A3
38TH AVE NE CH 92-D2
38TH AVE NW ANO 49-C3
38TH AVE S MPL 107-A4,121-B3
38TH CT N PLY 91-B3
38TH LN ANO 49-D3
38TH PL N PLY 90-D3,91-B3
38TH PL NE CH 92-E3
38TH ST HOT 114-C1
38TH ST SMT 83-E1
38TH ST WTT 114-E1
38TH ST E MPL 120-D1,121-A1
38TH ST N LE 95-E4
38TH ST N OKD 109-D1
38TH ST W MPL 120-C1
38TH ST W SLP 120-A1
38TH STREET CT N OKD 109-C1
38 1/2 AVE N NH 91-D3
39TH AVE N CRY 91-D3
39TH AVE N MPL 92-C3
39TH AVE N NH 91-C3
39TH AVE N PLY 90-B3,91-B3
39TH AVE N ROB 91-E3,92-A3
39TH AVE NE CH 92-E2,93-A2
39TH AVE NE FRI 92-D2
39TH AVE NE SA 93-A2
39TH AVE NW SF 8-C4
39TH AVE S MPL 107-B4,121-B1
39TH CT N PLY 90-C3
39TH PL N PLY 90-C3
39TH ST E MPL 120-E1,121-A1
39TH ST N LE 95-E4,96-C4
39TH ST N OKD 95-D4
39TH ST NE SM 47-A3
39TH ST W MPL 120-C1
39TH ST W SLP 119-E1,120-A1
39TH ST W WT 204-C3
39 1/2 AVE N NH 91-D3
39 1/2 AVE N ROB 92-A3
39 1/2 AVE NE CH 93-A2
40TH AVE FAT 41-E3,42-D3
40TH AVE STN 221-D2
40TH AVE N CRY 91-D3
40TH AVE N MPL 92-C3
40TH AVE N NH 91-C3
40TH AVE N PLY 90-C3,91-B3
40TH AVE N ROB 91-E3,92-A3
40TH AVE NE CH 92-E2,93-A2
40TH AVE S MPL 107-B4,121-B1
40TH LN ANO 49-D2
40TH LN W SLP 119-E2,120-A1
40TH PL N PLY 90-E3,91-B3
40TH ST SMT 55-D4,69-D1
40TH ST E MPL 120-E1,121-A1
40TH ST N BYT 96-D4
40TH ST N LE 96-C4
40TH ST N OKD 95-C4
40TH ST NE BUF 45-B4
40TH ST NE BUT 45-C4
40TH ST NE SM 47-B3
40TH ST NW MLT 44-C4

40TH ST S AFT 124-D4,125-A4
40TH ST SE MVT 72-E3
40TH ST SE RFT 72-E3,73-B3
40TH ST SW MIT 71-B3
40TH ST SW MVT 71-E3,72-B3
40TH ST W MPL 120-C1
40TH ST W SLP 119-E1,120-A1
40TH ST W WHT 202-E3,203-B3
40TH ST W WT 203-D3,204-B3
40 1/2 AVE N NH 91-C3
40 1/2 AVE N ROB 91-E3,92-A3
40 1/2 AVE NE FRI 92-D2
41ST AVE AND 49-D2
41ST AVE N AND 49-D2
41ST AVE N CRY 91-D3
41ST AVE N MPL 92-C3
41ST AVE N NH 91-C3
41ST AVE N PLY 90-D3,91-A3
41ST AVE N ROB 91-E3,92-A3
41ST AVE NE CH 92-E2,93-A2
41ST AVE S MPL 107-B4,121-B1
41ST PL N CRY 91-D3
41ST PL N PLY 90-C3
41ST PL NE SM 46-D3
41ST ST E MPL 120-E2,121-A2
41ST ST N OKD 95-D4
41ST ST NE SM 46-D3,47-C3
41ST ST NW MLT 43-D3
41ST ST S AFT 125-A4
41ST ST SW MVT 72-D3
41ST ST W MPL 120-C2
41ST ST W SLP 119-E3,120-A2
41ST ST W WT 203-E3
41ST PLACE CIR NE SM 46-D3
41ST STREET CT N OKD 95-C4
41 1/2 AVE N ROB 92-A3
42ND AVE KKT 126-E1
42ND AVE STN 221-D3
42ND AVE N CRY 91-D3
42ND AVE N MPL 92-B3
42ND AVE N NH 91-C3
42ND AVE N PLY 90-E3,91-A3
42ND AVE N ROB 91-E3,92-A3
42ND AVE NE CH 92-E2,93-A2
42ND AVE NW AND 50-D2
42ND AVE S FS 121-B3
42ND AVE S MPL 107-B4,121-B1
42ND CT N PLY 91-A3
42ND PL N PLY 90-E3,91-A3
42ND ST HOT 113-E2,114-D2
42ND ST SJT 97-C3
42ND ST SMT 69-D3,83-E3
42ND ST E MPL 120-E2,121-A2
42ND ST N LE 95-E4
42ND ST N OKD 95-C4
42ND ST NE SM 46-D3,47-B3
42ND ST S AFT 125-A4
42ND ST SE RFT 73-D3
42ND ST SW MVT 72-D3
42ND ST W MPL 120-C2
42ND ST W SLP 119-E2,120-A2
42ND STREET CT N OKD 95-C4
42 1/2 AVE N ROB 91-E3,92-A3
42 1/2 AVE NE CH 92-E2
42 1/2 ST W SLP 120-A2
43RD ALC NE SM 47-B3
43RD AVE ADT 42-E2
43RD AVE N CRY 91-E3
43RD AVE N MPL 92-B3
43RD AVE N NH 91-D3
43RD AVE N PLY 90-E3,91-B3
43RD AVE N ROB 91-E3,92-A3
43RD AVE NE CH 92-E2,93-A2
43RD AVE S MPL 107-B4,121-B1
43RD BAY NE SM 47-B3
43RD PL N PLY 90-D3
43RD ST E MPL 120-E2,121-A2
43RD ST N LE 96-B4
43RD ST N OKD 95-C4
43RD ST NE SM 46-D3,47-B3
43RD ST SE RFT 73-C3
43RD ST W MPL 120-C2
43RD ST W WT 204-C3
43 1/2 AVE NE CH 92-E2
43 1/2 ST W SLP 119-E2,120-A2
44TH AVE N MPL 92-B3
44TH AVE N NH 91-D3
44TH AVE N PLY 90-D3,91-A3
44TH AVE N ROB 91-E3,92-A3
44TH AVE NE CH 92-E2,93-A2
44TH AVE NE FRI 92-D2
44TH AVE S MPL 107-B4,121-B3
44TH CIR N NH 91-C3
44TH CIR NE SM 47-B3
44TH CT NE SM 47-B3
44TH LN N PLY 90-E3,91-A3
44TH PL NE SM 47-B3
44TH ST SMT 55-E4
44TH ST E MPL 120-D2,121-A2
44TH ST N BYT 96-C4,97-A4
44TH ST N LE 96-B4
44TH ST N OKD 95-D4
44TH ST NE BUT 44-E3,45-A3
44TH ST S AFT 124-E4,125-A4
44TH ST SE RFT 73-C3
44TH ST W EDI 119-E2,120-A2
44TH ST W MPL 120-C2
44TH ST W SLP 120-A2
44TH PL CIR SM 47-B3
44TH SE NE SM 46-D3
44TH ST LN N LE 96-C4
44TH STREET CT N OKD 95-D4
44 1/2 AVE N ROB 91-E3
44 1/2 AVE NE CH 92-E2
44TH AVE FAT 41-D3
45TH AVE ADT 42-E3
45TH AVE N CRY 91-D3
45TH AVE N MPL 92-B3
45TH AVE N NH 91-C3
45TH AVE N PLY 90-C3,91-A3
45TH AVE N ROB 91-E3,92-A3
45TH AVE NE CH 92-E2,93-A3
45TH AVE NE FRI 92-D2
45TH AVE NE HIL 92-E2
45TH AVE S MPL 107-B4,121-B1
45TH CIR NE SM 47-B3
45TH CT NE SM 47-C3

45TH PL N CRY 91-D3
45TH PL N PLY 90-E3,91-A3
45TH ST SMT 55-E3,69-E4
45TH ST E MPL 120-D2,121-A2
45TH ST N BYT 96-E4
45TH ST N LE 96-A4
45TH ST N OKD 95-C4
45TH ST NE OTS 47-E2
45TH ST NW MLT 43-E3,44-A3
45TH ST S AFT 125-B4
45TH ST SE MVT 72-E4
45TH ST SE RFT 73-B3
45TH ST SW MVT 72-D3
45TH ST W EDI 120-A2
45TH ST W WHT 202-C3
45TH ST W WT 204-C3
45 1/2 AVE N NH 91-D3
45 1/2 AVE N ROB 91-E3
45 1/2 AVE NE CH 92-E2
46TH AVE N CRY 91-D2
46TH AVE N NH 91-C2
46TH AVE N MPL 92-B3
46TH AVE N PLY 90-D2,91-A2
46TH AVE N ROB 91-E2,92-A2
46TH AVE NE CH 92-E2
46TH AVE NE FRI 92-D2
46TH AVE NE HIL 92-E2
46TH AVE S MPL 107-B4,121-B1
46TH CIR N OKD 95-D4
46TH CT CIR E IGH 122-E4
46TH CT NE SM 47-B3
46TH PL N CRY 91-D2
46TH PL N PLY 90-C2,91-A2
46TH PL NE SM 46-D3
46TH ST SMT 83-E1,84-A1
46TH ST WTT 115-B2
46TH ST E IGH 122-D4
46TH ST E MPL 120-D2,121-A2
46TH ST N OKD 95-C4
46TH ST NE SM 46-D3,47-C3
46TH ST W MPL 120-C2
46TH STREET CT N OKD 95-C4
46TH STREET WAY N OKD 95-D4
46 1/2 AVE N NH 91-C2
46 1/2 AVE N ROB 92-A2
46 1/2 AVE NE CH 92-E2
46 1/2 AVE NE HIL 92-E2
47TH AVE N BC 92-A2
47TH AVE N CRY 91-D2
47TH AVE N MPL 92-C2
47TH AVE N NH 91-C2
47TH AVE N PLY 90-D2,91-B2
47TH AVE NE CH 92-E2
47TH AVE NE HIL 92-E2
47TH AVE S MPL 107-B4,121-B1
47TH PL N PLY 91-A2
47TH ST SJT 83-E4,84-A4
47TH ST SMT 69-E4,84-A3
47TH ST E IGH 122-D4
47TH ST E MPL 120-D2,121-A2
47TH ST E SSP 122-E4
47TH ST N BYT 96-E3,97-A3
47TH ST N LE 96-B3
47TH ST N OKD 95-C4
47TH ST NE BUT 45-A3
47TH ST NE SM 46-D3,47-B3
47TH ST NW ABT 46-B3
47TH ST SE FKT 72-E4
47TH ST SW MIT 71-B4
47TH ST W EDI 120-A2
47TH ST W MTK 119-B2
47TH STREET CIR N OKD 95-D4
47TH STREET CT N BYT 96-E4
47TH STREET CT N OKD 95-D4
47 1/2 AVE N NH 91-C2
47 1/2 AVE NE CH 92-E1
47 1/2 AVE NE HIL 92-E1
47 1/2 CIR N NH 91-D2
47 1/2 PL N NH 91-D2
48TH AVE MPL 121-B3
48TH AVE N BC 92-A2
48TH AVE N CRY 91-D2
48TH AVE N MPL 92-C2
48TH AVE N PLY 91-D2
48TH AVE NE CH 92-D1
48TH AVE NE FRI 92-D1
48TH AVE S MPL 107-B4,121-B1
48TH CIR N NH 91-D2
48TH CIR NE SM 47-A3
48TH CT N PLY 90-B2
48TH CT N PLY 90-C2,91-A2
48TH ST HOT 114-A2
48TH ST SJT 98-A1
48TH ST E MPL 120-D2
48TH ST N BYT 96-D3
48TH ST N OKD 95-C4
48TH ST NE SM 47-A3
48TH ST W EDI 119-E2,120-A2
48TH ST W MPL 120-C2
48TH ST W WT 204-B3
48TH STREET PL N OKD 95-C3
49TH AVE N BC 92-A2
49TH AVE N CRY 91-D2
49TH AVE N MPL 92-B2
49TH AVE N NH 91-C2
49TH AVE N PLY 90-E2,91-B2
49TH AVE NE CH 92-E1,93-A1
49TH AVE NE FRI 92-D1
49TH AVE NE HIL 92-E1
49TH AVE NW WHT 202-E4
49TH CT N PLY 90-C2,91-A2
49TH PL N PLY 83-E1
49TH ST E IGH 136-D1
49TH ST E MPL 120-D2,121-A2
49TH ST E SSP 136-E1
49TH ST N BYT 96-E3,97-A3
49TH ST N LE 95-E3,96-A3
49TH ST N OKD 95-C3
49TH ST NE SM 47-B3
49TH ST W EDI 119-E2,120-A2
49TH ST W MPL 120-C2
49TH WAY N EDI 120-D1
49TH STREET CT N OKD 95-C3
49 1/2 AVE N MPL 92-C2
49 1/2 AVE NE CH 92-E1
49 1/2 ST W EDI 120-A2
50TH AVE ADT 42-E2
50TH AVE FAT 41-D3,42-A2

50TH AVE N BC 92-A2
50TH AVE N CRY 91-D2
50TH AVE N MPL 92-B2
50TH AVE N NH 91-C2
50TH AVE N PLY 91-C2
50TH AVE NE CH 92-E1
50TH AVE S MPL 121-B3
50TH CT N PLY 91-B2
50TH PL N PLY 90-E2,91-B2
50TH ST FAT 42-C2
50TH ST HOT 114-D3
50TH ST SJT 84-A4
50TH ST SMT 55-E4,84-A2
50TH ST E IGH 122-C4,136-D1
50TH ST E MPL 120-D3,121-A2
50TH ST E SSP 136-E1
50TH ST N LE 95-D3,96-C3
50TH ST N OKD 95-C3
50TH ST N OPH 97-B3
50TH ST NE ALB 46-E3,47-A3
50TH ST NE BUT 44-E3,45-A3
50TH ST NE SM 47-B3
50TH ST NW ABT 43-C3
50TH ST NW BUT 44-D3
50TH ST NW MLT 44-C3
50TH ST S AFT 138-D1,139-A1
50TH ST SE FKT 73-E4
50TH ST SW MVT 71-D4
50TH ST W EDI 119-E3,120-A3
50TH ST W MPL 120-A3
50TH ST W WHT 202-C4,203-B4
50TH ST W WT 203-D4,204-A4
50 1/2 AVE NE CH 92-E1
50 1/2 PL N PLY 91-B2
51ST AVE N BC 92-A2
51ST AVE N CRY 91-E2
51ST AVE N MPL 92-B2
51ST AVE N NH 91-C2
51ST AVE N PLY 90-D2,91-B2
51ST AVE NE CH 92-E1
51ST CT NE CH 92-E1
51ST PL N CRY 91-D2
51ST PL N PLY 91-B2
51ST ST SSP 136-E1
51ST ST E IGH 136-E1
51ST ST E MPL 120-D3,121-A3
51ST ST N BYT 96-E3
51ST ST N OKD 95-C3
51ST ST NE ALB 47-A3
51ST ST NW ABT 43-A3
51ST ST NW MLT 43-E3,44-A3
51ST ST W EDI 119-E3,120-A3
51ST ST W MPL 120-B3
51ST WAY NE FRI 92-D1
51ST STREET CT N BYT 96-D3
52ND AVE N BC 92-A2
52ND AVE N CRY 91-D2
52ND AVE N MPL 92-B2
52ND AVE N NH 91-C2
52ND AVE N PLY 90-E2,91-B2
52ND AVE NE FRI 92-D1
52ND AVE NE SM 47-E2
52ND CT NE SM 47-E2
52ND ST SJT 98-A2
52ND ST SMT 84-A2
52ND ST WTT 115-B3
52ND ST E IGH 136-D1
52ND ST E MPL 120-D3,121-A3
52ND ST E SSP 136-E1
52ND ST N OKD 95-C3
52ND ST NE SM 47-A2
52ND ST SE FKT 72-E4,73-A4
52ND ST SW MVT 72-C4
52ND ST W EDI 119-E3,120-A3
52ND ST W MPL 120-B3
52ND WAY NE FRI 92-D1
53RD AVE N BC 92-B2
53RD AVE N CRY 91-D2
53RD AVE N NH 91-D2
53RD AVE N PLY 91-A2
53RD CIR NE ALB 47-A2
53RD PL N BC 92-A2
53RD ST HOT 113-E3,114-A3
53RD ST SJT 98-A1
53RD ST SMT 55-E4,56-A3
53RD ST E IGH 136-D1
53RD ST E MPL 120-D3,121-A3
53RD ST N BYT 96-D3
53RD ST N LE 95-D3,96-A3
53RD ST N OKD 95-C3
53RD ST NE ALB 46-E2,47-A2
53RD ST NE BUT 45-C2
53RD ST NE OTS 47-E2,48-A2
53RD ST NE SM 47-E2
53RD ST NW ML 43-E2
53RD ST NW MLT 43-E2,44-B2
53RD ST W EDI 119-E3,120-A3
53RD ST W MPL 120-B3
53RD ST W WHT 202-B4
53RD WAY NE FRI 92-C1
53RD STREET CT N BYT 96-D3
53RD STREET PL N BYT 96-D3
53 1/2 AVE NE FRI 92-C1
54TH AVE N BC 92-B2
54TH AVE N CRY 91-D2
54TH AVE N NH 91-C2
54TH AVE N PLY 90-E2,91-A2
54TH AVE NE FRI 92-D1
54TH CIR NE ALB 47-A2
54TH PL N ALB 46-E2
54TH PL N PLY 91-B2
54TH ST SJT 98-A2
54TH ST SMT 84-A2
54TH ST E IGH 136-C1
54TH ST E MPL 120-D3,121-B3
54TH ST E SSP 136-E1
54TH ST N OKD 95-C3
54TH ST N OPH 96-E3
54TH ST NE ALB 46-E2,47-A2
54TH ST NE SM 47-E2
54TH ST NW MLT 43-E2,44-C2
54TH ST W EDI 120-A3
54TH ST W MPL 120-B3
54 1/2 ST NE ALB 46-E2,47-A2
54 1/2 ST NE FAT 41-D2,42-A2
55TH AVE N BC 92-B1
55TH AVE N CRY 91-D2
55TH AVE N NH 91-C2

55TH AVE N PLY 90-E2,91-B2
55TH AVE NE FRI 92-D1
55TH CIR NE ALB 47-A2
55TH PL N PLY 90-E2,91-A1
55TH ST SMT 56-A4
55TH ST E IGH 136-D1
55TH ST E MPL 120-D3,121-A3
55TH ST N LE 95-E3,96-A3
55TH ST N OPH 95-C3
55TH ST N PS 95-C3
55TH ST NE BUT 46-E2,47-A2
55TH ST NE OTS 44-E2,45-A2
55TH ST S AFT 139-A1
55TH ST SE FKT 73-D4
55TH ST SW MVT 72-D4
55TH ST W EDI 120-A3
55TH ST W MPL 120-C3
55TH ST W MTK 202-E4,216-E1
55TH ST W WT 204-C4
55TH AVENUE WAY STN 222-A1
55TH STREET CT E IGH 136-D1
56TH AVE N BC 92-C1
56TH AVE N CRY 91-D1,92-A2
56TH AVE N NH 91-C1
56TH AVE N PLY 90-B2,91-A1
56TH AVE NE FRI 78-D4
56TH AVE NE SM 47-E2
56TH PL N CRY 91-E1
56TH ST E IGH 136-C1
56TH ST E MPL 120-E3,121-A3
56TH ST N OKD 95-C3
56TH ST N OPH 96-E3,97-B3
56TH ST NE ALB 46-E2,47-A2
56TH ST NE BUT 45-B2
56TH ST NE MOT 46-B2
56TH ST NE OTS 48-A2
56TH ST NE SM 47-E2
56TH ST SW WAV 85-E1
56TH ST W EDI 119-E3,120-A3
56TH ST W MPL 120-C3
56TH STREET CIR N OPH 97-A3
57TH AVE CFT 222-A3
57TH AVE STN 222-A3
57TH AVE N BC 92-B1
57TH AVE N CRY 91-E1,92-A1
57TH AVE NE FRI 78-D4
57TH PL N PLY 90-E1,91-B1
57TH PL NE FRI 78-D4
57TH ST SMT 84-A2
57TH ST E MPL 120-E3,121-A3
57TH ST N LE 96-A3
57TH ST N OPH 96-E3,97-A3
57TH ST NE ALB 46-E2,47-A2
57TH ST NE OTS 48-A2
57TH ST NE SM 47-D2
57TH ST S AFT 139-A1
57TH ST SE FKT 87-C1
57TH ST SW MVT 85-E1
57TH ST W EDI 119-E3,120-A3
57TH ST W MPL 120-C3
57TH ST W MTK 118-C3
57TH AVENUE WAY STN 217-E1,218-B1
57TH AVENUE WAY STN 208-A4,222-A2
57 1/2 AVE NE FRI 78-D4
58TH AVE CKP 1-B1
58TH AVE FAT 42-A2
58TH AVE N BC 92-A1
58TH AVE N CRY 91-D1,92-A1
58TH AVE N NH 91-C1
58TH AVE N OPH 118-C3
58TH AVE N PLY 90-E1,91-A1
58TH AVE NE ALB 46-E2,47-A2
58TH AVE NE FRI 78-E4
58TH CT E IGH 136-D1
58TH PL N CRY 91-D1,92-A1
58TH ST HOT 114-A2
58TH ST SMT 70-A4
58TH ST WTT 115-B3
58TH ST E FS 120-E3,121-A3
58TH ST E MPL 120-D3,121-B3
58TH ST N BYT 96-D3
58TH ST N OPH 96-E3,97-A3
58TH ST NE ALB 46-E2
58TH ST NE BUT 45-B2
58TH ST NE OTS 47-E2,48-A2
58TH ST NE SM 47-E2
58TH ST NW MLT 43-E2,44-A2
58TH ST SE FKT 87-C1
58TH ST W EDI 119-E3,120-A3
58TH ST W MPL 120-C3
58TH ST W MTK 118-C3
58TH AVENUE PATH STN 222-A3
58 1/2 AVE N BC 92-A1
59TH AVE STN 208-A4,222-A2
59TH AVE N BC 92-C1
59TH AVE N CRY 91-D1,92-A1
59TH AVE N NH 91-C1
59TH AVE N PLY 91-A1
59TH AVE NE FRI 78-D4
59TH CIR NE ALB 47-A2
59TH CT E IGH 136-C2
59TH PL N CRY 91-D1
59TH PL N PLY 90-E1
59TH ST SMT 70-A4
59TH ST E FS 120-E3,121-A3
59TH ST E IGH 137-A2
59TH ST E MPL 120-D3,121-B3
59TH ST N LE 95-D3
59TH ST N OPH 96-E2,97-A2
59TH ST NE ALB 47-A2
59TH ST NE BUT 45-B2
59TH ST NE OTS 47-E2,48-A2
59TH ST NW MLT 44-A2
59TH ST S AFT 139-A1
59TH ST SE FKT 87-C1
59TH ST W EDI 119-E3,120-A3
59TH ST W MPL 120-B3
59TH AVENUE WAY STN 208-A4,222-A2
59TH STREET CT N LE 96-A3
59 1/2 AVE N BC 92-A1
59 1/2 AVE N NH 91-D1
59 1/2 ST E FS 121-A4
59 1/2 ST W MPL 120-C4
60TH AVE FAT 41-D2,42-A2
60TH AVE OST 42-E2
60TH AVE N BC 92-C1
60TH AVE N CRY 91-D1
60TH AVE N NH 91-C1

60TH AVE N PLY 90-E1,91-A1
60TH AVE N FRI 78-D4,79-A4
60TH CT E IGH 136-D2
60TH PL N PLY 90-E1,91-A1
60TH ST SJT 84-B4,98-B1
60TH ST SMT 70-A2
60TH ST E FS 120-E4
60TH ST E IGH 136-D2,137-A2
60TH ST E MPL 120-D4
60TH ST N BYT 96-D2
60TH ST N GRA 95-E2,96-B2
60TH ST N LE 95-E2,96-B2
60TH ST N MHT 95-C2
60TH ST N OPH 96-E2,97-A2
60TH ST N PS 95-D2
60TH ST N SWR 96-E2,97-A2
60TH ST NE ALB 46-E2,47-A2
60TH ST NE BUT 44-E2,45-A2
60TH ST NE MLT 44-E2
60TH ST NE MOT 46-C2
60TH ST NE OTS 46-C2,47-C2
60TH ST NE SM 47-B2
60TH ST NW ABT 43-A2
60TH ST NW MLT 44-C2
60TH ST S AFT 138-E2,139-A2
60TH ST SW HWL 85-A1
60TH ST SW MIT 85-C1
60TH ST SW VIT 85-B1
60TH ST SW WDT 85-E1,86-C1
60TH ST W EDI 119-E4,120-A4
60TH ST W MPL 120-B4
60TH ST W SL 136-C2
60TH ST W WHT 216-E1,217-B1
60TH ST W WT 217-D1,218-C1
60TH AVENUE WAY STN 222-A2
60TH STREET CT N OPH 96-E2
60TH STREET LN N GRA 96-B2
60 1/2 AVE N NH 91-C1
61ST AVE N BC 91-E1,92-A1
61ST AVE N CRY 91-D1
61ST AVE N NH 91-D1
61ST AVE N PLY 90-E1,91-A1
61ST AVE NE FRI 78-D4,79-A4
61ST ST ALB 46-D2
61ST ST SJT 98-B2
61ST ST E FS 120-E4
61ST ST E IGH 137-A2
61ST ST E MPL 120-D4
61ST ST N GRA 96-B2
61ST ST N OPH 97-B2
61ST ST N SWR 97-A2
61ST ST NE ALB 46-E2
61ST ST SW HWL 85-A1
61ST ST W EDI 119-E4,120-A4
61ST ST W MPL 120-C4
61ST WAY NE FRI 78-D4
61ST AVENUE CIR N NH 91-C1
61 1/2 AVE N NH 91-C1
61 1/2 WAY NE FRI 78-D4
62ND AVE LL 66-A4
62ND AVE N BC 91-E1,92-A1
62ND AVE N BP 91-D1
62ND AVE N LL 66-A4
62ND AVE N MG 90-D1,91-B1
62ND AVE N PLY 91-A1
62ND CT N BP 91-D1
62ND LN NE OTS 48-B2
62ND PL SWR 96-C2
62ND PL N MG 90-E1,91-A1
62ND ST CT 113-E4,114-B4
62ND ST LL 66-B4
62ND ST SJT 84-B4,98-B1
62ND ST SMT 70-A3
62ND ST WCT 114-E4,115-A4
62ND ST E FS 120-E4,121-A4
62ND ST E IGH 136-D2
62ND ST E MPL 120-D4
62ND ST E RCH 120-D4
62ND ST N GRA 96-B2
62ND ST N OPH 97-A2
62ND ST N PS 95-D2
62ND ST N SWR 96-D2,97-A2
62ND ST NE ALB 46-E2,47-A2
62ND ST NE OTS 47-C2
62ND ST NW MLT 44-B2
62ND ST SW HWL 86-A1
62ND ST SW CHN 117-B4
62ND ST W EDI 119-E4,120-A4
62ND ST W EPR 118-D4
62ND ST W MPL 120-B4
62ND ST W MTK 118-D4
62ND ST W VIC 120-B4
62ND ST W WHT 117-B4
62ND ST W WT 218-C1
62ND WAY NE FRI 78-D4
62 1/2 AVE N BP 91-D1
62 1/2 WAY NE FRI 78-D4
63RD AVE FAT 41-E1,42-A1
63RD AVE N BC 77-E4,78-A4
63RD AVE N BP 77-D4,91-C1
63RD AVE N COR 90-A1
63RD AVE N MG 90-C1,91-B1
63RD AVE NE FRI 78-D3
63RD AVE SE CKP 1-C2
63RD CT E IGH 136-E2,137-A2
63RD CT E RCH 138-E2
63RD LN N BC 78-C4,92-C1
63RD PL N MG 76-E4,77-A4
63RD ST SMT 84-B3
63RD ST E IGH 136-D2,137-A3
63RD ST E RCH 120-E4
63RD ST N GRA 95-E2,96-A2
63RD ST N OPH 97-A2
63RD ST N SWR 97-A2
63RD ST NE ALB 46-D2
63RD ST NE MOT 46-A2
63RD ST NW CNT 43-B2
63RD ST NW MLT 43-D2,44-B2
63RD ST W CHN 117-E4
63RD ST W EDI 119-E4
63RD ST W RCH 120-C4
63RD ST W WHT 217-A1
63RD WAY NE FRI 78-D4
63RD AVENUE WAY LEO 222-A4
63 1/2 WAY NE FRI 78-D3
64TH AVE CFT 222-B2
64TH AVE FAT 41-E2
64TH AVE WRT 112-E3
64TH AVE N BC 77-E4,78-A4
64TH AVE N BP 77-D4
64TH AVE N MG 76-D4,77-B4
64TH AVE NE FRI 78-E3,79-A3
64TH AVE SE CKP 1-C2
64TH CIR N CHN 117-D4
64TH CT CKP 1-C3

64TH CT IGH 136-E2,137-A2
64TH CT E IGH 136-E2
64TH LN NE ALB 46-D1
64TH LN NW ALB 46-D1
64TH PL N MG 76-E4
64TH ST LL 66-E4
64TH ST SJT 98-B2
64TH ST E IGH 136-E2,137-A2
64TH ST E LL 66-E4
64TH ST E RCH 120-D4
64TH ST N GRA 95-E2
64TH ST N OPH 97-A2
64TH ST N PS 95-D2
64TH ST NE ALB 46-D1
64TH ST NW CNT 43-A1
64TH ST NW MLT 44-B1
64TH ST W CHN 117-D4
64TH ST W EDI 119-E4,120-A4
64TH ST W WHT 216-C2
64TH WAY NE ALB 46-D1
64TH WAY NE FRI 78-D3
64TH AVENUE PATH CFT 222-B1
64TH AVENUE WAY CFT 222-B2
64 1/2 ST W RCH 120-C4
64 1/2 WAY NE FRI 78-D3
65TH AVE CFT 222-B1
65TH AVE FAT 42-B1
65TH AVE GRF 74-C4
65TH AVE WRT 112-E3
65TH AVE N BC 77-E4,78-A4
65TH AVE N BP 77-D4
65TH AVE N MG 77-A4
65TH PL N MG 76-D4,77-B4
65TH ST LL 67-A4
65TH ST SMT 56-B3
65TH ST E IGH 136-D2,137-A2
65TH ST E RCH 120-E4
65TH ST N GRA 96-A2
65TH ST N SWR 96-E2,97-A2
65TH ST NE ALB 46-D1,48-A1
65TH ST NE OTS 46-D1,48-A1
65TH ST NW CNT 43-C1
65TH ST NW ML 43-E1,44-A1
65TH ST S CG 137-D2
65TH ST S NEW 137-B2
65TH ST SE FKT 87-E1
65TH ST SW HWL 85-A1
65TH ST W CHN 117-D4
65TH ST W EDI 119-E4,120-A4
65TH ST W RCH 120-B4
65TH ST W WHT 216-D1
65TH ST W WT 217-D1,218-A1
65 1/2 ST W RCH 120-B4
65 1/2 WAY NE FRI 78-D3
66TH AVE N BC 77-E4,78-A4
66TH AVE N BP 77-D4
66TH AVE N MG 77-A4
66TH AVE NE FRI 78-E3,79-A3
66TH CIR N BP 77-C4
66TH LN NE GRF 74-E4
66TH PL N BP 77-C4
66TH PL N MG 76-C4,77-A4
66TH ST CT 113-D4
66TH ST SMT 70-B2
66TH ST WCT 115-C4,129-C1
66TH ST E IGH 137-A2
66TH ST E RCH 120-D4
66TH ST N GRA 96-B2
66TH ST N PS 95-D2
66TH ST NE MOT 45-B1
66TH ST NW MLT 44-B1
66TH ST S CG 137-E2
66TH ST S DET 139-B2
66TH ST SW WDT 86-B2
66TH ST W EDI 119-E4,120-A4
66TH ST W EPR 118-E4
66TH ST W RCH 120-C4
66TH WAY NE FRI 78-D3
66TH AVENUE WAY CFT 222-B1
66TH STREET CIR W EPR 118-C4
66TH STREET CT S CG 137-E2
66 1/2 AVE NE FRI 79-A3
66 1/2 WAY NE FRI 78-D3
67TH AVE CFT 222-B2
67TH AVE N BC 77-E4,78-C4
67TH AVE N BP 77-D4
67TH AVE N MG 76-E4,77-B4
67TH AVE NE OTS 47-C1
67TH CT E IGH 136-D2
67TH CT W WHT 218-C2
67TH LN N BC 78-B4
67TH LN N GRA 96-A2
67TH PL N MG 76-D4,77-A4
67TH ST SMT 70-B2,84-C3
67TH ST E IGH 136-E2,137-A2
67TH ST E RCH 120-D4
67TH ST N GRA 96-A2
67TH ST NE OTS 47-B1
67TH ST NW CNT 43-B1
67TH ST S CG 137-E2,138-B2
67TH ST S DET 139-B2
67TH ST W EPR 132-C1
67TH ST W RCH 120-B4
67TH WAY NE FRI 78-D3
67TH AVENUE WAY CFT 222-B2
67TH STREET CIR W EPR 132-C1
67TH STREET CT S CG 137-D2
67 1/2 AVE N BP 77-C4
68TH AVE FAT 41-E1,42-A1
68TH AVE OST 42-E1
68TH AVE N BC 77-E4,78-A4
68TH AVE N BP 77-D4
68TH AVE N MG 76-C4
68TH AVE NE FRI 78-E3,79-A3
68TH CT E IGH 136-E2
68TH CT N GRA 96-A2
68TH LN N BC 78-B4
68TH PL N MG 76-E4
68TH PL NE FRI 78-E3
68TH ST CT 84-C2
68TH ST E IGH 136-E2,137-A2
68TH ST N GRA 95-E2,96-A2
68TH ST S CG 137-E2,138-B2
68TH ST W CHN 131-E1,132-A1
68TH ST W EDI 133-D1,134-A1
68TH ST W IGH 136-B2
68TH ST W RCH 134-B1
68TH WAY BP 77-E4
68TH STREET CT S CG 137-D2
69TH AVE N BC 77-E4,78-B4

69TH AVE N BP 77-E4
69TH AVE N MG 76-E4,77-A4
69TH AVE NE FRI 78-D3,79-A3
69TH DR NE FRI 78-D3
69TH LN N BC 78-B4
69TH LN N GRF 75-A4
69TH PL N MG 77-B4
69TH PL NE FRI 78-D3
69TH ST E IGH 136-E2,137-A2
69TH ST E RCH 134-D1
69TH ST N GRA 96-B2
69TH ST N MHT 95-D2
69TH ST S CG 137-E2
69TH ST S DET 139-B2
69TH ST W EDI 133-E1,134-A1
69TH ST W EPR 133-C1
69TH ST W IGH 136-B2
69TH ST W RCH 134-B1
69TH WAY NE FRI 78-D3
69TH STREET CT S CG 137-D2
70TH AVE CKP 1-C1
70TH AVE OST 42-E1
70TH AVE WRT 112-E3
70TH AVE N BC 77-E4,78-C4
70TH AVE N BP 77-D4
70TH AVE N COR 75-E4
70TH AVE N GRF 75-A4
70TH AVE N MG 76-E4,77-A4
70TH AVE SE CKP 1-C2
70TH CIR N BC 77-E4
70TH CT E IGH 136-E3
70TH CT N MHT 95-D2
70TH PL N MG 76-D4,77-B4
70TH ST CT 128-C1
70TH ST DEL 87-D2
70TH ST FKT 87-E2
70TH ST GIT 155-B3
70TH ST SHK 147-B2
70TH ST SMT 84-C2
70TH ST E FS 135-A1
70TH ST E IGH 136-E3,137-A3
70TH ST E RCH 134-D1
70TH ST E SSP 136-E3,137-A3
70TH ST N MHT 95-D2
70TH ST NE ALB 46-E1,47-A1
70TH ST NE OTS 46-D1,47-C1
70TH ST NW CNT 43-A1
70TH ST S CG 137-D2,138-B2
70TH ST S DET 138-D2,139-A2
70TH ST S SPP 137-C2
70TH ST SW VIT 85-B2
70TH ST SW WDT 86-B2
70TH ST W EDI 133-E1,134-A1
70TH ST W EPR 133-B1
70TH ST W IGH 136-B3
70TH ST W LON 217-A2
70TH ST W RCH 134-B1
70TH ST W WHT 216-C2,217-B2
70TH ST W WT 218-C2
70TH WAY NE FRI 78-D3
70TH AVENUE WAY LEO 222-C4
70 1/2 ST W RCH 134-B1
71ST AVE GRF 74-C4
71ST AVE N BC 77-E3,78-A3
71ST AVE N BP 77-D3
71ST AVE N GRF 74-D4,75-A4
71ST AVE NE FRI 78-D3
71ST BAY S CG 138-A3
71ST CIR N BC 77-E4
71ST CT E IGH 137-A3
71ST CT S CG 137-E3
71ST LN N GRF 74-D4,75-A4
71ST PL N MG 76-D3,77-B3
71ST ST E IGH 136-E3,137-A3
71ST ST E RCH 134-D1
71ST ST N GRA 96-A1
71ST ST N MHT 95-D2
71ST ST NE OTS 47-D1
71ST ST S CG 137-E3,138-A3
71ST ST SE FKT 86-E2
71ST ST SW VIT 85-A2
71ST ST W EDI 133-E1,134-A1
71ST ST W RCH 134-B1
71ST WAY NE FRI 78-D3
71ST AVENUE WAY CFT 208-B4
71 1/2 ST W RCH 134-B1
72ND AVE N BC 77-E3,78-C3
72ND AVE N BP 77-D3
72ND AVE N MG 76-D3,77-B3
72ND AVE NE FRI 78-D3
72ND CIR IGH 136-C3
72ND CIR N BC 77-E3
72ND CT E IGH 136-D3
72ND CT N MHT 95-D2
72ND LN N BP 77-D3
72ND PL N MG 76-C3
72ND ST CV 66-E2
72ND ST MHT 95-D2
72ND ST SMT 70-B2,84-C3
72ND ST E FS 135-A1
72ND ST E IGH 136-E3,137-A3
72ND ST E RCH 134-D1
72ND ST NE MOT 46-B1
72ND ST NE OTS 47-D1
72ND ST NW MLT 44-D1
72ND ST S CG 137-E3,138-A3
72ND ST S DET 139-B3
72ND ST SE FKT 86-E2,87-B2
72ND ST SW VIT 85-A2
72ND ST W EDI 133-E1,134-A1
72ND AVENUE WAY CFT 208-C4,222-C3
72 1/2 ST W RCH 134-B1
72 1/2 ST CV 66-E2
73RD AVE N BC 78-C3
73RD AVE N COR 75-C3
73RD AVE N MG 76-E3,77-B3
73RD AVE NE FRI 78-E2,79-A2
73RD CIR N MG 76-D3
73RD CT E IGH 136-D3
73RD CT N BP 78-B3
73RD LN N BP 78-C3
73RD PL N MG 76-C3,77-A3
73RD ST CV 66-D2
73RD ST E FS 135-A1
73RD ST E IGH 136-E3,137-A3
73RD ST E RCH 134-C1
73RD ST NW MLT 29-E4,43-D1
73RD ST S CG 137-D3,138-A3
73RD ST W EDI 133-E1
73RD ST W VIC 131-A1
73RD WAY N BP 78-C3

73 1/2 AVE NE FRI 78-E2,79-A2
73 1/2 ST W RCH 134-C1
74TH AVE N BP 77-D3,78-A3
74TH AVE N MG 76-D3,77-A3
74TH AVE NE FRI 78-D2
74TH CIR N BP 78-A3
74TH CT E IGH 136-E3
74TH CT N BP 78-B3
74TH PL N MG 76-E3
74TH ST CT 128-B1
74TH ST LL 65-E2,66-A2
74TH ST N LL 128-E1,129-A1
74TH ST WCT 135-A1
74TH ST E RCH 134-D1
74TH ST S CG 137-D3,138-A3
74TH ST W EDI 133-E1,134-B1
74TH ST W EPR 133-C1
74TH ST W RCH 134-C1
74TH ST W VIC 131-A1
74TH WAY N BP 77-D3,78-C3
74TH STREET CIR S CG 138-A3
74 1/2 AVE N BP 77-D3,78-A3
75TH AVE N COR 76-A3
75TH AVE N MG 76-D3
75TH AVE NE FRI 78-E2,79-A2
75TH CIR N BP 77-D3
75TH CIR N IGH 136-E3
75TH CT N BP 78-A3
75TH LN GRF 74-E3
75TH LN N MG 76-D3
75TH ST HNT 155-B3
75TH ST SMT 84-C3
75TH ST WDT 86-C2
75TH ST E FS 134-E1,135-A1
75TH ST E IGH 136-D3,137-A3
75TH ST E RCH 134-D1
75TH ST N GRA 95-E1,96-B1
75TH ST N SWT 96-D1
75TH ST NE MOT 31-A4
75TH ST NE OTS 32-E4, 29-C4
75TH ST S CG 137-E3,138-A3
75TH ST SW WDT 85-E2,86-A2
75TH ST W EDI 134-B1
75TH ST W RCH 134-B1
75TH WAY NE FRI 78-D2
75 1/2 AVE N BP 77-D3
76TH AVE N BP 77-D3,78-C3
76TH AVE N MG 76-D3
76TH AVE NE FRI 78-E2,79-A2
76TH CT N BP 78-A3
76TH LN MED 77-E3
76TH PL N MG 76-C3
76TH ST SMT 70-C2
76TH ST E IGH 136-D3
76TH ST E RCH 134-D2
76TH ST NE OTS 33-E4, 29-A4
76TH ST NW CNT 29-A4
76TH ST S CG 137-D3
76TH ST W CHN 132-B2
76TH ST W EDI 133-E2,134-A2
76TH ST W EPR 133-C2
76TH ST W RCH 134-C2
76TH WAY NE FRI 137-A3
76TH STREET CT S CG 137-E3
77TH AVE N BP 77-E3,78-A3
77TH AVE N MG 76-C3,77-B3
77TH BLVD N BP 78-C3
77TH CIR N MG 76-D3
77TH PL N MG 76-D3
77TH ST SMT 70-C2
77TH ST E IGH 136-E3,137-A3
77TH ST E LL 66-D1
77TH ST E RCH 134-D2
77TH ST N SWT 96-D1
77TH ST NE MOT 32-E4
77TH ST NE ALB 32-E4,33-B4
77TH ST S CG 137-E3,138-C3
77TH ST SE FKT 86-E2
77TH ST W CHN 131-B1,132-B2
77TH ST W EAG 136-B3
77TH ST W EDI 133-E2,134-A2
77TH ST W IGH 136-B3
77TH ST W LL 66-B1
77TH ST W RCH 134-C2
77TH ST W VIC 131-A2
77TH WAY NE FRI 78-D2
77TH ST CT S CG 137-D3
77TH STREET BAY S CG 137-D3
77TH STREET CT N SWT 96-D1
77TH STREET CT S CG 137-D3
78TH AVE N BP 77-D3,78-A3
78TH AVE N COR 75-E3
78TH AVE N MG 76-C3
78TH AVE NE FRI 78-D2
78TH AVE NE SLK 78-E2,79-A2
78TH CIR NE SLK 78-E2,79-A2
78TH CT E IGH 136-D3
78TH CT N BP 77-D3,78-A3
78TH LN GRF 74-D3
78TH LN N BP 77-E3,78-A3
78TH ST CT 127-D2,128-C2
78TH ST SJT 84-D4
78TH ST WCT 129-A2
78TH ST E BLO 134-D2,135-A2
78TH ST E IGH 136-E3,137-A3
78TH ST E RCH 134-D2
78TH ST NE OTS 33-D4
78TH ST NW CNT 29-B4
78TH ST S CG 137-D3,138-A3
78TH ST SW WDT 86-D3
78TH ST W BLO 133-E2,134-A2
78TH ST W CHN 132-B2
78TH ST W EDI 132-D2,133-A2
78TH ST W RCH 134-B2
78TH ST W VIC 131-A2
78TH WAY NE OTS 33-D4
78TH STREET CIR W BLO 134-A2
78TH STREET CIR S CG 137-E3,138-A3
78 1/2 ST W BLO 134-C2
79TH AVE OST 28-B4
79TH AVE N BP 77-D3,78-D3
79TH AVE N MG 76-C3
79TH AVE NE SLK 78-E2,79-A2
79TH CT MG 76-C3

79TH CT E IGH ...136-D3
79TH CT N BP ...78-C3
79TH LN N BP ...78-A2
79TH PL MG ...76-C3
79TH PL N MG ...76-C3
79TH ST E BLO ...134-D2,135-A2
79TH ST E IGH ...136-D3,137-A3
79TH ST N GRA ...96-B1
79TH ST NE MOT ...31-D4
79TH ST NE OTS ...33-E4
79TH ST NW CNT ...29-A4
79TH ST S CG ...137-E3,138-A3
79TH ST W BLO ...134-C2
79TH ST W CHN ...132-B2
79TH ST W LL ...52-B4
79TH ST W VIC ...130-E2,131-A2
79TH WAY NE FRI ...78-C2
79TH STREET BAY S CG ...138-A3
79TH TH NE OTS ...33-D4
79 1/2 ST VIC ...131-A2
79 1/2 ST E BLO ...134-D2
80TH AVE HUT ...112-E2
80TH AVE WRT ...112-E2
80TH AVE N BP ...77-E3,78-B2
80TH AVE N MG ...76-E3
80TH AVE NE SLK ...78-E2,79-A2
80TH AVE SE CKP ...1-D2
80TH AVE SE CLK ...1-D1
80TH CIR N BP ...78-B2
80TH CIR N MG ...76-C3
80TH CT MG ...76-C3
80TH CT E IGH ...137-A3
80TH CT N BP ...78-C2
80TH PL N MG ...76-D2
80TH PL N MHT ...155-A2
80TH ST SJT ...98-D2
80TH ST SMT ...56-C4,70-C3
80TH ST SPT ...56-C4
80TH ST E BLO ...134-E2,135-A2
80TH ST E IGH ...136-D3,137-A3
80TH ST E LL ...52-E4,53-A4
80TH ST N GRA ...82-C4,95-E1
80TH ST N MHT ...95-C2
80TH ST N SWT ...82-C4,96-D1
80TH ST NE MOT ...30-E4,31-E4
80TH ST NE OTS ...32-E4,33-A4
80TH ST NW CNT ...29-C4
80TH ST NW MLT ...30-C4
80TH ST S CG ...137-D3,138-B3
80TH ST S DET ...138-D3,139-B3
80TH ST SW VIT ...85-A3
80TH ST SW WHT ...85-D3,86-B3
80TH ST W VIC ...130-E2,131-A2
80TH ST W WHT ...217-D3,218-B3
80TH STREET CIR W BLO ...134-A2
80TH STREET CT S DET ...138-B3
80 1/2 ST W BLO ...134-C2
81ST AVE N BP ...77-E2,78-C2
81ST AVE N FRI ...78-D2
81ST AVE N MG ...76-C2,77-B2
81ST AVE NE FRI ...78-D2
81ST AVE NE SLK ...78-E2,79-A2
81ST CIR N BP ...78-B2
81ST CIR N BP ...77-E2,78-A2
81ST PL N BP ...77-D2
81ST PL N COR ...76-B2
81ST PL S COR ...76-B2
81ST PL S MG ...76-B2
81ST SPT ...70-C2
81ST ST E BLO ...134-D2,135-A2
81ST ST E IGH ...136-E4
81ST ST E LL ...52-D4
81ST ST NE OTS ...33-C4
81ST ST S CG ...137-D3,138-A3
81ST ST SE FKT ...87-D3
81ST ST W BLO ...134-B2
81ST ST W LL ...52-C4
81ST ST W VIC ...130-E2,131-A2
81ST STREET IN S CG ...137-E4
81 1/2 ST W VIC ...130-E2
82ND AVE N BP ...77-D2,78-C2
82ND AVE N MG ...76-C2,77-A2
82ND AVE NE SLK ...78-E1,79-A1
82ND LN NE BLA ...79-B1
82ND PL MG ...76-C3
82ND PL N BP ...77-D2
82ND PL N MG ...76-B2,77-A2
82ND ST CHS ...131-C2
82ND ST CT ...128-B2
82ND ST OTS ...33-D4
82ND ST SMT ...84-D1
82ND ST E BLO ...134-D2,135-A2
82ND ST E CHN ...131-C2
82ND ST E IGH ...136-C4
82ND ST E LL ...52-E4
82ND ST NE OTS ...33-C4
82ND ST S CG ...137-C4,138-A4
82ND ST SE FKT ...86-E3
82ND ST SW WDT ...85-C3
82ND ST SW WDT ...86-D3
82ND ST W BLO ...133-E2,134-C2
82ND ST W CHN ...131-B2
82ND ST W EPR ...132-C2
82ND ST W IGH ...136-B4
82ND ST W VIC ...130-E2,131-A2
82ND WAY N MG ...76-C2
82ND AVENUE WAY CFT ...208-D4
82ND STREET CT S CG ...137-E3

83RD AVE N BP ...77-C2,78-A2
83RD AVE N MG ...76-C2,77-B2
83RD AVE NE FRI ...78-D1
83RD AVE NE SLK ...78-E1,79-A1
83RD AVE NW CR ...78-D1
83RD CIR OTS ...33-D4
83RD CT N BP ...77-D2,78-B2
83RD LN N BP ...78-B2
83RD PL N BP ...77-E2
83RD PL N MG ...76-D2
83RD PKWY N BP ...77-E2
83RD ST OTS ...33-D4
83RD ST SJT ...84-D4,98-D1
83RD ST E BLO ...134-D2
83RD ST E IGH ...136-E4
83RD ST E NFT ...219-E3,220-A3
83RD ST N GRA ...82-A4
83RD ST NE MOT ...32-B4
83RD ST NE OTS ...33-B4
83RD ST NW CNT ...29-B4
83RD ST S CG ...137-E4,138-A4
83RD ST W BLO ...133-D2,134-C2
83RD ST W IGH ...136-B4
83RD HIGH RD MG ...76-D2
83RD STREET CT N GRA ...82-B4
83RD STREET CT S CG ...137-E4
83RD STREET CT S LLD ...111-B4
83RD STREET TER W BLO ...133-D2
84TH AVE OST ...28-E3
84TH AVE N BP ...77-E2,78-B2
84TH AVE N GRF ...75-B4
84TH AVE N MG ...76-C2,77-A2
84TH AVE NE MV ...79-A1
84TH AVE NE SLK ...78-E1
84TH AVE NW CR ...78-C1
84TH AVE SE CKP ...1-E3
84TH CIR N BP ...78-A2
84TH CT N BP ...77-D2,78-B2
84TH LN NE BLA ...79-B1
84TH LN NW CR ...78-C1
84TH PL N MG ...76-D2,77-A2
84TH ST CT ...127-D2
84TH ST OTS ...33-D3
84TH ST SMT ...84-D3
84TH ST SPT ...56-C3
84TH ST E BLO ...134-E4
84TH ST E IGH ...136-E4,137-A4
84TH ST N GRA ...82-A4
84TH ST NE MOT ...31-A4,32-B3
84TH ST NE OTS ...33-D3
84TH ST NW CNT ...29-C4
84TH ST S CG ...137-C4,138-A4
84TH ST W BLO ...133-E2,134-A2
84TH ST W IGH ...136-B4
84TH WAY N BP ...78-C2
84TH STREET BAY S CG ...138-A4
84TH STREET CIR W BLO ...133-D2
84 1/2 AVE N BP ...77-E2
84 1/2 ST W BLO ...134-C2
85TH AVE CKP ...1-E1
85TH AVE N BP ...77-D2,78-B2
85TH AVE N MG ...76-C2,77-B2
85TH AVE NE BLA ...78-D1,79-B1
85TH AVE NE CR ...78-D1
85TH AVE NE SVW ...79-D1
85TH AVE NW CR ...78-C1
85TH AVE SE CKP ...1-E3
85TH CT N BP ...77-C2,78-C2
85TH CT W WT ...218-C3
85TH LN BLA ...78-D1
85TH LN CT ...78-C1
85TH LN NE BLA ...79-D1
85TH LN NW CR ...78-C1
85TH PL MG ...77-B1
85TH PL N MG ...76-B2
85TH ST SJT ...98-A4
85TH ST SMT ...84-D4
85TH ST SPT ...56-D4
85TH ST E BLO ...134-D3
85TH ST E BWT ...219-B3
85TH ST E IGH ...136-E4
85TH ST NE MOT ...31-D3,32-C4
85TH ST NE OTS ...32-D3,33-D3
85TH ST NW MLT ...29-C3,30-A3
85TH ST S CG ...137-C4,138-A4
85TH ST SE FKT ...87-D3
85TH ST SW VIT ...85-D3
85TH ST SW WDT ...
85TH ST W BLO ...133-D3,134-C3
85TH ST W IGH ...136-B4
85TH ST W WT ...217-E3,218-A3
85TH AVENUE
WAY CFT ...208-D4,222-D1
85TH STREET CIR W BLO ...133-D3
86TH AVE OST ...28-B3
86TH AVE N BP ...78-C2
86TH AVE N MG ...76-C2,77-B2
86TH AVE NE BLA ...78-E1,79-C1
86TH AVE NW CR ...78-C1
86TH CT W WT ...218-B3
86TH LN CR ...78-C1
86TH LN N BP ...78-C2
86TH LN NE BLA ...79-D1
86TH LN NW CR ...78-C1
86TH PL MG ...77-A2
86TH PL N MG ...76-B2,77-A2
86TH ST CT ...127-E3,128-A3
86TH ST VIC ...131-A3
86TH ST E BLO ...134-D3,135-A3
86TH ST E IGH ...136-D4
86TH ST NW MLT ...30-C3
86TH ST SW VIT ...85-D3
86TH ST W BLO ...133-D3,134-C3
86TH ST W CHN ...132-A3
86TH ST W IGH ...136-B4
86TH ST W LTT ...131-A3
86TH STREET CIR W BLO ...133-C3
86 1/2 ST E BLO ...134-E3
87TH AVE BLA ...79-B1
87TH AVE OST ...28-B3
87TH AVE N BP ...77-D2
87TH AVE N GRF ...75-A2
87TH AVE N MG ...76-C2,77-A2
87TH AVE NE BLA ...78-E1,79-A1
87TH AVE NW CR ...78-C1
87TH CT W WT ...218-C3
87TH LN NE BLA ...78-E1,79-D1
87TH LN NW CR ...78-C1
87TH PL N MG ...76-B2,77-A2
87TH ST CKP ...2-B1
87TH ST OTS ...33-D3
87TH ST E BLO ...134-E3
87TH ST E IGH ...136-D4
87TH ST N SWT ...82-C4
87TH ST NE MOT ...31-D3
87TH ST NE OTS ...33-C3
87TH ST NW MLT ...30-C3
87TH ST S CG ...137-C4,138-A4
87TH ST SE BKR ...2-C1,3-D1
87TH ST W BLO ...133-C3,134-C3
87TH ST W IGH ...136-B4
87TH TRL N BP ...78-B2
87TH WAY N MG ...76-E2
87TH STREET CT N SWT ...82-C4
87 1/2 ST W BLO ...134-B3

88TH AVE N BP ...77-D2,78-B2
88TH AVE N MG ...76-C2,77-A2
88TH AVE NE BLA ...65-C4,79-D1
88TH AVE NW CR ...78-C1
88TH CRES BP ...77-E2
88TH CT NE BLA ...79-C1
88TH CT W WT ...218-B3
88TH LN NE BLA ...65-D4
88TH LN NW CR ...78-C1
88TH PL N MG ...76-E2,77-A2
88TH ST E BLO ...134-D3
88TH ST N GRA ...81-E4,82-B4
88TH ST NE MOT ...31-C3
88TH ST NE OTS ...33-D3
88TH ST NW MLT ...30-C3
88TH ST S CG ...137-E4
88TH ST W IGH ...134-B3
88TH CRESCENT CIR BP ...77-E2
88 1/2 AVE NE BLA ...64-E4
89TH AVE N BP ...77-D2,78-B2
89TH AVE N MG ...76-C2,77-A2
89TH AVE N OSS ...77-B2
89TH AVE NE BLA ...64-E4,65-C4
89TH AVE NW CR ...64-C4
89TH CIR N MG ...76-C2
89TH CRES BP ...77-E2,78-A1
89TH CRV NE BLA ...65-C4
89TH CT E IGH ...137-A4
89TH CT NE BLA ...65-B4
89TH CT W WT ...218-B4
89TH DR NE BLA ...65-C4
89TH LN NE BLA ...64-D4,65-B4
89TH LN NW CR ...64-C4
89TH PL N MG ...76-C2,77-A1
89TH ST SJT ...98-E1
89TH ST SMT ...84-E3
89TH ST E BLO ...134-D3
89TH ST E IGH ...136-E4,137-A4
89TH ST N GRA ...81-D4,82-A4
89TH ST NE OTS ...33-D3
89TH ST S CG ...137-D4
89TH ST W BLO ...134-C3
89TH ST W IGH ...136-B4
89TH CRESCENT CIR BP ...77-E1
89TH STREET CIR S CG ...137-E4
89TH STREET CIR S CG ...137-E4
90TH AVE LEO ...222-D4
90TH AVE OST ...28-E3
90TH AVE N BP ...77-D2
90TH AVE N MG ...76-C1,77-A1
90TH AVE NE BLA ...64-D4,65-C4
90TH AVE NW CR ...64-C4
90TH AVE SE CKP ...1-E2
90TH CRES N BP ...78-A1
90TH CRV NE BLA ...65-C4
90TH CT E IGH ...137-A4
90TH CT N MG ...76-C2
90TH DR NE BLA ...65-C4
90TH LN NE BLA ...64-D4,65-B4
90TH PL N MG ...76-C1,77-A1
90TH ST CKP ...1-C1
90TH ST CT ...127-D3,128-A3
90TH ST HNT ...155-A1
90TH ST OST ...28-D3
90TH ST SPT ...56-D4,70-D2
90TH ST TRT ...112-E4,126-E1
90TH ST WRT ...112-E4
90TH ST E BLO ...134-D3
90TH ST E BWT ...218-D4,219-B4
90TH ST E IGH ...137-A4,150-C1
90TH ST E NFT ...220-C4
90TH ST N SWT ...82-E4
90TH ST NE MO ...31-C2
90TH ST NE OTS ...30-E3,31-A3
90TH ST NW MLT ...29-E3,30-A3
90TH ST NW MOT ...30-D3
90TH ST NW SVT ...30-D3
90TH ST S CG ...137-E4,138-A4
90TH ST S DET ...138-D4,139-A4
90TH ST SE CKP ...2-C1
90TH ST SE FKT ...87-E4
90TH ST SW VIT ...85-A4
90TH ST W ERT ...217-A4
90TH ST W WHT ...217-C4
90TH ST W WT ...218-C4
90TH TRL N BP ...78-B2
90TH AVENUE WAY CFT ...208-D3
91ST AVE CFT ...208-D4
91ST AVE N BP ...77-D1
91ST AVE NE BLA ...64-D1,77-A1
91ST AVE NE BLA ...64-D4,65-C4
91ST CRES BP ...77-E1,78-B1
91ST CRV NE BLA ...65-C4
91ST CT NE BLA ...65-C4
91ST DR NE BLA ...65-C4
91ST LN N BP ...78-B1
91ST LN NE BLA ...64-D4,65-C4
91ST PL N MG ...76-C1,77-A1
91ST ST WRT ...112-E4
91ST ST E BLO ...134-D3
91ST ST E IGH ...136-D4,150-D1
91ST ST NE OTS ...33-C3
91ST ST NW SVT ...29-A3
91ST ST NW SVT ...30-C3
91ST ST S CG ...137-E4,138-A4
91ST ST SE CKP ...2-C1
91ST ST W BLO ...133-E3,134-B3
91ST TRL N BP ...77-D1
91ST STREET CIR W BLO ...134-B3
91 1/2 ST W BLO ...134-B3
92ND AVE CKP ...A2
92ND AVE MG ...77-A1
92ND AVE N BP ...77-D1,78-B1
92ND AVE N MG ...76-C1,77-A1
92ND AVE NE BLA ...64-D4,65-C4
92ND AVE NE LEX ...65-C4
92ND CIR N MG ...76-E1
92ND CIR NE BLA ...65-D4
92ND CIR NE OTS ...33-D3
92ND CRES BP ...77-E1
92ND CRES N BP ...78-B1
92ND CRV NE BLA ...65-C4
92ND CT N BP ...77-D1
92ND CT NE BLA ...65-C4
92ND DR NE BLA ...65-C4
92ND LN NE BLA ...64-D4,65-B4
92ND PL N MG ...76-D1,77-A1
92ND ST CKP ...1-B1
92ND ST CT ...128-D3
92ND ST OTS ...33-D3
92ND ST SWT ...82-D3

92ND ST E BLO ...134-D3
92ND ST NE OTS ...32-D3,33-D3
92ND ST S CG ...151-D1,152-A1
92ND ST SE BKR ...2-E1,3-B1
92ND ST W BLO ...133-E3,134-C3
92ND TRL N BP ...77-D1
92ND STREET CIR W BLO ...133-E3
92 1/2 ST E BLO ...134-D3
93RD AVE N BP ...77-D1,78-A1
93RD AVE N COR ...75-D1
93RD AVE N MG ...76-D1,77-A1
93RD AVE N OSS ...77-C1
93RD AVE NE BLA ...64-D4,65-B4
93RD AVE NW CR ...64-C4
93RD CIR NE OTS ...33-D3
93RD CRV NE BLA ...65-C4
93RD DR NE BLA ...65-C4
93RD LN NE BLA ...64-E4,65-A4
93RD LN NW CR ...64-C4
93RD PL N MG ...76-C1,77-B1
93RD ST BKR ...2-E1,3-E1
93RD ST SPT ...70-D3
93RD ST SWT ...82-E3
93RD ST WRT ...112-E3
93RD ST E BLO ...134-D3
93RD ST E IGH ...150-C1
93RD ST N SWT ...82-E3
93RD ST N NE OTS ...33-D3
93RD ST S CG ...151-E1,152-A1
93RD ST W BLO ...133-E3,134-B3
93RD TRL BP ...78-B1
93RD WAY BP ...78-B1
93RD LN EXT BLA ...65-A4,79-A1
93RD STREET CIR W BLO ...133-E3
93 1/2 ST E BLO ...134-E3
94TH AVE N BP ...78-A1
94TH AVE N MG ...76-E1,77-B1
94TH AVE NE BLA ...64-E4,65-B4
94TH AVE NW CR ...64-D4
94TH CIR NW CR ...64-D4
94TH LN NE BLA ...65-A4
94TH LN NW CR ...64-C4
94TH ST CHS ...131-C4
94TH ST CT ...127-E4,128-B4
94TH ST SPT ...70-D3
94TH ST SWT ...82-E3
94TH ST WAC ...129-C4
94TH ST WCT ...129-B4
94TH ST E BLO ...150-E1
94TH ST N GRF ...74-E1
94TH ST N SWT ...82-D3,83-A3
94TH ST NE OTS ...33-D3
94TH ST NW SVT ...30-C3
94TH ST S CG ...151-D1
94TH ST SE BKR ...2-E1
94TH ST W BLO ...133-E4,134-C4
94TH ST W CHN ...132-A4
94TH WAY N BP ...78-B1
94 1/2 ST E BLO ...134-D4
95TH AVE N BP ...77-E1,78-B1
95TH AVE N MG ...76-D1,77-B1
95TH AVE NE BLA ...64-E4,65-B4
95TH AVE NW CR ...64-C4
95TH AVE SE CKP ...2-A4
95TH CIR NE OTS ...33-D2
95TH LN CR ...64-C4
95TH LN NE BLA ...64-E4
95TH LN NW CR ...64-D4
95TH PL MG ...76-B1
95TH PL N MG ...76-E1,77-B1
95TH RDT ...84-E3
95TH ST SPT ...56-E4,70-D3
95TH ST SWT ...82-E3
95TH ST E BLO ...134-D4
95TH ST N SWT ...83-A3
95TH ST NE MOT ...32-A3
95TH ST NE OTS ...32-D2,33-B3
95TH ST NW SVT ...29-E3,30-B2
95TH ST SE BKR ...2-E1
95TH ST SE FKT ...86-E4,87-A4
95TH ST W BLO ...133-E4,134-C4
95TH ST W ERT ...216-D4
95TH STREET CIR E BLO ...134-D4
95 1/2 ST W BLO ...134-A4
96TH AVE CR ...64-C4
96TH AVE MG ...77-A1
96TH AVE N BP ...78-B1
96TH AVE N MG ...76-D1,77-B1
96TH AVE SE CKP ...2-A4
96TH CIR NE OTS ...33-E2
96TH LN NE BLA ...64-E4
96TH LN NW CR ...64-C4
96TH PL N MG ...76-B1,77-B1
96TH ST BKR ...3-C1
96TH ST LIT ...6-B4
96TH ST WRT ...112-E2
96TH ST E BLO ...134-D4
96TH ST E IGH ...150-D1
96TH ST N GRA ...81-E3,82-A3
96TH ST NE MOT ...32-B2
96TH ST NE OTS ...33-C2
96TH ST NW CNT ...29-A2
96TH ST NW ER ...6-B4
96TH ST NW LIT ...6-B1
96TH ST S CG ...151-D1,152-A1
96TH ST SE BKR ...3-D1
96TH ST W BLO ...133-E4,134-B4
96TH ST W CHN ...132-A4
96TH WAY BP ...78-B1
96TH STREET CIR W BLO ...134-B4
97TH AVE NSP ...95-A4
97TH AVE N BP ...63-D4,78-A1
97TH AVE N MG ...76-E1,77-A1
97TH AVE NE BLA ...64-E3,65-C3
97TH AVE NW CR ...64-B3
97TH CT NE BLA ...65-C3
97TH LN NE BLA ...64-E3,65-D3
97TH LN NW CR ...64-D3
97TH PL MG ...76-E1
97TH PL N MG ...63-D4,77-B1
97TH ST CKP ...1-E2,2-A2
97TH ST E BLO ...134-E4
97TH ST E IGH ...150-C1
97TH ST N GRA ...82-C3
97TH ST N SWT ...83-A3
97TH ST NE MOT ...30-E2,32-A2
97TH ST NE OTS ...32-E2,33-D2
97TH ST NW LIT ...6-B1
97TH ST NW SVT ...30-D2

97TH ST S CG 151-E1
97TH ST SE BKR 2-D2,3-D2
97TH ST SE CKP 2-C2
97TH ST SE SOT 2-B2
97TH ST SW VIT 85-A4
97TH ST SW WDT 86-D4
97TH ST W BLO 133-C4,134-C4
97TH AVENUE WAY CFT 208-E4
97TH STREET CIR W BLO 133-C4
97TH STREET CT N SWT 83-A3
97 1/2 ST E BLO 134-D4
97 1/2 ST NW LIT 6-B1
97 1/2 ST W BLO 133-C4
98TH AVE N BP 64-B4
98TH AVE N MG 63-B4
98TH AVE NE BLA 64-E3,65-D3
98TH AVE NW CR 64-C3
98TH LN NE BLA 64-E3,65-D3
98TH LN NW CR 64-B3
98TH PL N MG 63-B4
98TH ST LIT 6-B3
98TH ST WCT 129-B4
98TH ST E BLO 134-D4
98TH ST NW LIT 6-B1
98TH ST S CG 151-D1
98TH ST SW VIT 85-B4,99-B1
98TH ST SW WDT 85-E4,86-A4
98TH ST W BLO 133-E4,134-C4
98TH STREET CIR W BLO 134-A4
98 1/2 ST NW LIT 6-B1
98 1/2 ST W BLO 133-E4,134-C4
98 1/2 STREET CIR W BLO 133-E4
99TH AVE N BP 64-A4
99TH AVE N MG 63-A4
99TH AVE NE BLA 64-E3,65-D3
99TH AVE NW CR 64-B3
99TH CIR N GRA 81-D3
99TH CIR NE BLA 64-E3
99TH CIR NW CR 64-B3
99TH CT N GRA 81-D3
99TH CT NE BLA 64-E3
99TH LN NE BLA 64-E3,65-A3
99TH LN NW CR 64-D3
99TH PL N MG 63-B4
99TH ST CKP 1-B2
99TH ST LIT 6-B3
99TH ST WRT 98-E4
99TH ST E BLO 134-D4
99TH ST E IGH 150-D1
99TH ST N GRA 81-D3
99TH ST NE MOT 31-B2
99TH ST NE OTS 32-D2
99TH ST S CG 151-D1
99TH ST S GCT 151-B1
99TH ST W BLO 133-E4,134-A4
99TH STREET CIR W BLO 133-D4
100TH AVE CKP 2-A2
100TH AVE HUT 98-D4
100TH AVE OST 28-B2
100TH AVE WRT 98-E4
100TH AVE N BP 64-B4
100TH AVE N MG 63-B4
100TH AVE NW CR 64-C3
100TH AVE SE CKP 2-A3
100TH CT NE BLA 64-E3
100TH LN NE BLA 64-E3
100TH LN NW CR 64-B3
100TH PL N MG 63-A4
100TH ST HNT 141-A4
100TH ST LIT 6-B2
100TH ST SPT 56-E4,70-E1
100TH ST E BLO 134-D4
100TH ST E BWT 218-D4,219-B4
100TH ST E IGH 150-D1
100TH ST E NFD 220-A4
100TH ST E NFT 220-B4
100TH ST N GRA 81-D3
100TH ST N SWT 82-E3,83-A3
100TH ST NE MOT 30-E2,31-A2
100TH ST NE OTS 32-C2
100TH ST NW CNT 29-B2
100TH ST NW LIT 6-B1
100TH ST S CG 151-D1,152-C1
100TH ST S DET 152-D1
100TH ST SE FKT ....-E1,101-C1
100TH ST SW FKT ....-D1
100TH ST SW VIT 99-C1
100TH ST SW WDT 99-E1
100TH ST W BLO 133-D4,134-C4
100TH AVENUE WAY CFT 208-E3
100TH STREET CIR W BLO 133-D4
100 1/2 ST NW LIT 6-B1
101ST AVE BLA 64-E3
101ST AVE N BP 63-C4,64-A4
101ST AVE N MG 62-C4,63-B4
101ST AVE NE BLA 64-D3,65-B3
101ST AVE NW CR 64-C3
101ST LN N BP 64-B4
101ST LN NE BLA 64-E3,65-E3
101ST LN NW CR 64-D3
101ST PL N MG 63-B4
101ST ST E BLO 134-D4
101ST ST N GRA 81-D3,82-A3
101ST ST NE MOT 32-A2
101ST ST NE OTS 32-D2
101ST ST NW LIT 6-B1
101ST ST NW SVT 30-D2
101ST ST W BLO 133-D4,134-B4
101ST STREET CIR W BLO 133-C4
101 1/2 ST W BLO 134-A4
102ND AVE N MG 63-B4
102ND AVE NE BLA 64-E3,65-D3
102ND AVE NW CR 64-D3
102ND CIR NE BLA 64-E3
102ND CIR NW CR 64-B3
102ND CT W IGH 150-C2
102ND LN NE BLA 64-D3,65-D3
102ND LN NW CR 64-D3
102ND PL N MG 63-B4
102ND ST BKR 3-C2
102ND ST CT 141-E1,142-D1
102ND ST LTT 143-E1,144-A1
102ND ST SWT 83-A2
102ND ST WCT 142-E1,143-D1
102ND ST E BLO 134-D4
102ND ST E IGH 150-C2,151-A2
102ND ST N GRA 82-C2
102ND ST NE MOT 30-E2,32-B2
102ND ST NW CNT 29-C2
102ND ST NW LIT 6-B1
102ND ST S DET 153-A1
102ND ST SE FKT ....-E1,101-A1
102ND ST W BLO 147-E1,148-A1
102ND ST W IGH 150-C2
102ND AVENUE WAY CFT 208-E2
102ND ST LN S DET 153-B1
102ND STREET CIR SWT 83-A2
102ND STREET CT N GRA 82-C2
103RD AVE N BP 63-D4
103RD AVE N MG 63-B4
103RD AVE NE BLA 64-D3
103RD AVE NW CR 64-B3
103RD AVE SE CKP 2-B4
103RD LN CR 64-B3
103RD LN NE BLA 65-E3
103RD LN NW CR 64-A3
103RD PL N MG 63-B4
103RD ST E BLO 148-D1
103RD ST N GRA 82-A2
103RD ST N SWT 82-D2
103RD ST S CG 151-C2
103RD ST SE BKR 2-E2
103RD ST W BLO 147-C1,148-A1
103RD WAY NE BLA 64-E3
103RD STREET CIR W BLO 147-C1
103RD STREET CT N GRA 82-A2
104TH AVE CR 64-B3
104TH AVE WRT 98-E4
104TH AVE N BP 63-D4
104TH AVE N GRF 60-E4
104TH AVE N MG 63-B4
104TH AVE NE BLA 64-E3,65-E3
104TH AVE NW CR 64-B3
104TH CT E IGH 150-E2
104TH LN NE BLA 64-D3,65-E3
104TH LN NW CR 64-D3
104TH PL N MG 63-B4
104TH PL NE BLA 64-E3
104TH ST CT 142-A1
104TH ST LIT 6-A1
104TH ST SPT 70-E3
104TH ST E BLO 148-D1
104TH ST NW LIT 6-A2
104TH ST S DET 153-A2
104TH ST W BLO 147-E1,148-C1
104TH WAY NE BLA 64-E3,65-A3
104TH STREET CIR W BLO 147-C1
105TH AVE OST 28-E1
105TH AVE WRT 98-E4
105TH AVE N BP 63-E4,64-A4
105TH AVE N DPH 118-B1
105TH AVE N MG 62-D4,63-B4
105TH AVE NE BLA 64-E3,65-A3
105TH AVE NW CR 64-A3
105TH AVE SE CKP 2-B3
105TH LN NE BLA 64-E3,65-E3
105TH LN NW CR 64-B3
105TH PL N MG 63-B4
105TH ST E BLO 148-D1
105TH ST E IGH 150-D2
105TH ST N GRA 81-E2,82-B2
105TH ST N SWT 82-E2,83-A2
105TH ST NW CNT 29-A2
105TH ST NW MOT 30-D2
105TH ST S DET 152-E2
105TH ST S GCT 151-B2
105TH ST SE CKP 1-C2
105TH ST SE FKT ....-E1,101-D1
105TH ST SW WDT 99-D1
105TH ST W BLO 147-E1,148-B1
105TH ST W IGH 150-C2
106TH AVE N BP 63-D3
106TH AVE N MG 63-B3
106TH AVE NE BLA 64-D2,65-E2
106TH AVE NW CR 64-B2
106TH LN NE BLA 64-E2,65-E2
106TH LN NW CR 64-C2
106TH PL N MG 62-C3,63-B3
106TH ST WCT 142-E1,143-A1
106TH ST NW CNT 29-B2
106TH ST NW LIT 6-A1
106TH ST NW SVT 29-D2
106TH ST SE CKP 1-C2
106TH ST SE FKT 101-D1
106TH ST W BLO 147-D1,148-B1
107TH AVE BLA 65-B2
107TH AVE N BP 63-D3
107TH AVE N HAN 60-E3
107TH AVE N MG 62-C3,63-B3
107TH AVE NE BLA 64-D2,65-E2
107TH AVE NW CR 64-B2
107TH CIR NE BLA 64-D2
107TH LN NE BLA 64-E2,65-A2
107TH LN NW CR 64-A2
107TH PL N MG 63-B3
107TH ST BKR 2-C2
107TH ST CKP 2-B2
107TH ST LTT 144-A1
107TH ST WRT 98-E3
107TH ST N GRA 81-E2,82-A2
107TH ST N SWT 82-E2,83-A2
107TH ST NE MOT 30-D1
107TH ST NW CNT 29-C1
107TH ST NW SVT 29-E1
107TH ST SE BEC 2-E2,3-A2
107TH ST SE BKR 3-B2
107TH ST SE FKT 101-A1
107TH ST SW VIT 99-B1
107TH ST W BLO 147-C1,148-C1
107TH STREET CIR E BLO 148-D1
107TH STREET CIR W BLO 147-C1
108TH AVE CR 64-C2
108TH AVE N MG 63-B3
108TH AVE NE BLA 64-E2,65-E2
108TH AVE NW CR 64-C2
108TH AVE SE CKP 2-B4
108TH LN NE BLA 65-E2
108TH LN NW CR 63-E2,64-C2
108TH PL N MG 63-B3
108TH ST E IGH 150-D2
108TH ST N SWT 82-E2,83-C2
108TH ST NW CNT 29-C1
108TH ST NW LIT 6-A3
108TH ST SE FKT 101-D1
108TH ST SW WDT ....-C1
108TH ST W BLO 147-E1,148-B1
109TH AVE N BP 63-D3
109TH AVE N COR 61-C3,62-A3
109TH AVE N DAY 62-B3
109TH AVE N HAN 60-E3,61-A3
109TH AVE N MG 63-B3
109TH AVE NE BLA 64-E2,65-B2
109TH AVE NW CR 63-E2,64-C2
109TH CIR N CHM 63-D3
109TH CT NE BLA 65-B2
109TH LN N CHM 63-D3
109TH LN NE BLA 64-E2
109TH LN NW CR 63-E2,64-D2
109TH PL N CHM 63-C3
109TH ST NW CNT 29-C1
109TH ST NW LIT 6-A1
109TH ST S DET 152-E2
109TH ST SE BKR 3-E3,4-A3
109TH ST W BLO 147-D1,148-A1
109TH STREET CIR W BLO 147-C1
110TH AVE CFT 209-A4,223-A1
110TH AVE CR 64-B2
110TH AVE N CHM 63-D3
110TH AVE NE BLA 64-E2,65-B2
110TH AVE NW CR 64-C2
110TH CIR N CHM 63-D3
110TH CT NE BLA 65-A2
110TH CT W IGH 150-B2
110TH LN N CHM 63-D3
110TH LN NW CR 64-A2
110TH PL N CHM 63-D3
110TH ST CKP 2-C3
110TH ST CT 141-E2,142-B2
110TH ST HNT 141-A3
110TH ST LTT 143-E2,144-A2
110TH ST WCT 143-D2
110TH ST E IGH 150-C2
110TH ST N GRA 81-E2,82-B2
110TH ST N SWT 82-E2,83-B2
110TH ST NE MOT 31-B1
110TH ST NW CNT 29-C1
110TH ST NW LIT 6-A1
110TH ST NW SVT 29-E1,30-A1
110TH ST S CG 151-E2,152-A2
110TH ST S DET 152-D2,153-A2
110TH ST SE FKT ....-E2,101-A2
110TH ST SW VIT 99-A2
110TH ST SW WDT 99-E2
110TH ST W BLO 147-D2,148-A2
110TH ST W EAG 150-B2
110TH ST W IGH 150-B2
110TH AVENUE WAY CFT 223-A3
110TH STREET CIR W BLO 147-D2
110TH STREET LN S DET 153-B2
111TH AVE N CHM 63-E3
111TH AVE N HSN 62-A3
111TH AVE NE BLA 64-D2,65-D2
111TH AVE NW CR 63-E2,64-B2
111TH CIR NW CR 64-A2
111TH CT NE BLA 65-A2
111TH LN NE BLA 64-D2
111TH LN NW CR 64-C2
111TH SQ NE BLA 64-D2
111TH ST E IGH 150-E2,151-A2
111TH ST NW CNT 29-C1
111TH ST NW LIT 5-E1
111TH ST SW VIT 99-C2
111TH ST W BLO 147-D2,148-A2
111 1/2 AVE N CHM 63-E3
112TH AVE N CHM 63-D3
112TH AVE N DAY 62-E3
112TH AVE NE BLA 64-D2
112TH AVE NW CR 63-E2,64-A2
112TH CIR N CHM 63-D3
112TH CT W IGH 150-B2
112TH LN N CHM 63-C3
112TH LN NW CR 64-A2
112TH PL N CHM 63-D3
112TH SQ NE BLA 64-D2
112TH ST CKP 2-B3
112TH ST E BUR 149-A2
112TH ST N SWT 82-D2
112TH ST NW CNT 29-C1
112TH ST NW LIT 5-E2
112TH ST NW SVT 29-D1
112TH ST SE BKR 3-D3
112TH ST SE CKP 1-E3
112TH ST SW WDT 99-C2
112TH ST W BLO 147-D2,148-A2
113TH AVE OST 28-C1
113TH AVE N CHM 63-D3
113TH AVE N DAY 62-C3
113TH AVE N HSN 61-D3
113TH AVE NE BLA 64-E2,65-A2
113TH AVE NW CR 63-E2,64-B2
113TH CIR N CHM 63-D3
113TH CIR NE BLA 64-E2
113TH CT NE BLA 64-E2,65-A2
113TH LN BLA 64-E2
113TH LN NE BLA 64-D2
113TH LN NW CR 63-E2,64-B2
113TH PL N CHM 63-D3
113TH SQ NE BLA 64-D2
113TH ST BKR 3-E3
113TH ST N SWT 83-A1
113TH ST NW CNT 29-B1
113TH ST NW LIT 5-E2
113TH ST S CG 151-D2
113TH ST S DET 153-A2
113TH ST SE FKT ....-E2
113TH ST SW WDT 99-D2
113TH ST W BLO 147-D2,148-A2
113TH STREET CIR W BLO 147-E2
113TH STREET CT S CG 151-E2
113 1/2 AVE N CHM 63-E3
114TH AVE BLA 64-E2
114TH AVE N CHM 63-D3
114TH AVE N DAY 62-E3
114TH AVE NE BLA 64-E2,65-D2
114TH AVE NW CR 63-E2,64-C2
114TH CIR N CHM 63-D3
114TH CT N CHM 63-D3
114TH CT NE BLA 64-E2
114TH LN N CHM 63-E3
114TH LN NE BLA 64-D2
114TH LN NW CR 63-E2,64-C2
114TH PL N CHM 63-D2
114TH ST BKR 3-E3,4-A3
114TH ST BTT 142-E2,143-B2
114TH ST YAT 142-C2
114TH ST E BUR 148-E2,149-A2
114TH ST E IGH 150-C3
114TH ST N GRA 81-D2,82-B1
114TH ST N SWT 83-A1
114TH ST NW CNT 29-A1
114TH ST NW LIT 5-E2
114TH ST NW SVT 29-E1
114TH ST SE FKT 101-D2
114TH ST W BLO 147-D2,148-A2
114TH ST W IGH 150-C3
114TH WAY N CHM 63-D3
114TH STREET CIR N SWT 83-A1
114TH STREET CIR W BLO 147-D2
114TH STREET CT N SWT 83-A1
115TH AVE N CHM 63-D2
115TH AVE NE BLA 64-E1,65-E1
115TH AVE NW CR 63-D1,64-A1
115TH AVE SE CKP 2-C1
115TH LN N CHM 63-C3
115TH LN NE BLA 64-D1
115TH LN NW CR 63-E1,64-A1
115TH ST E BUR 148-E2,149-A2
115TH ST N GRA 81-D1,82-C1
115TH ST N SWT 83-A1
115TH ST NW CNT 29-C1
115TH ST NW LIT 5-E2
115TH ST S CG 151-E3
115TH ST SE FKT 101-C2
115TH ST SW WDT 99-E2
115TH ST W BLO 147-D2
115TH ST W JT 145-E3
115TH AVENUE LN NE BLA 64-E1
115TH AVENUE WAY CFT 209-B3
115TH AVENUE WAY LEO 223-B4
115 1/2 AVE N CHM 63-D2
116TH AVE N CHM 63-D2
116TH AVE NE BLA 64-E1
116TH AVE NW CR 63-E1,64-B1
116TH CIR N CHM 63-D2
116TH LN NE BLA 64-E1
116TH LN NW CR 63-E1,64-A1
116TH PL N CHM 63-D2
116TH ST E BUR 148-E2
116TH ST E IGH 150-C3
116TH ST N SWT 82-E1,83-C1
116TH ST NE MOT 17-B4,31-B1
116TH ST NW LIT 5-E2
116TH ST SE CKP 1-E3
116TH WAY N CHM 63-C2
116 1/2 AVE N CHM 63-D2
116 1/2 CIR N CHM 63-D2
117TH AVE SJT 97-E3
117TH AVE N CHM 63-D2
117TH AVE N DAY 62-D2
117TH AVE NE BLA 64-E1,65-D1
117TH AVE NW CR 63-E1,64-D1
117TH AVE SE BEC 2-D3
117TH AVE SE BKR 2-C3
117TH AVE SE CKP 2-C3
117TH CIR NE BLA 64-D1
117TH LN NE BLA 64-D1,65-A1
117TH LN NW CR 63-E1,64-C1
117TH ST E BUR 148-E2,149-A2
117TH ST E IGH 150-D3,151-A3
117TH ST N GRA 81-C1,82-B1
117TH ST NW CNT 15-C4
117TH ST NW LIT 5-E2
117TH ST S DET 152-E3,153-A3
117TH ST SE BKR 3-B3
117TH ST SE CKP 2-B3
117TH ST SE FKT 101-E2
117TH STREET CT N GRA 81-C1
118TH AVE N CHM 63-D2
118TH AVE NE BLA 64-D1,65-A1
118TH AVE NW CR 63-E1,64-A1
118TH LN NE BLA 64-E1,65-A1
118TH LN NW CR 63-E1,64-B1
118TH PL N CHM 63-D2
118TH ST BTT 143-E3
118TH ST DAT 143-E3
118TH ST YAT 142-D3
118TH ST N GRA 82-B1
118TH ST N SWT 82-E1,83-A1
118TH ST SE FKT 101-E2
118TH ST SW VIT 99-C2
118TH ST SW WDT 99-D2
118TH WAY N CHM 63-D2
119TH AVE N CHM 63-D2
119TH AVE NE BLA 64-D1,65-A1
119TH AVE NW CR 63-E1,64-A1
119TH CIR NE BLA 64-D1
119TH LN N CHM 63-D2
119TH LN NE BLA 64-E1,65-A1
119TH LN NW CR 63-D1,64-B1
119TH PL N CHM 63-D2
119TH ST N GRA 82-A1
119TH ST N SWT 82-E1,83-A1
119TH ST NE MOT 16-E4
119TH ST NW CWT 15-B4
119TH ST NW SVT 16-C4
120TH AVE OST 14-E4
120TH AVE N CHM 63-D2
120TH AVE NE BLA 64-E1,65-A1
120TH AVE NW CR 63-E1,64-B1
120TH AVE W EPR 119-A4
120TH CIR NW CR 64-D1
120TH LN NE BLA 64-D1,65-A1
120TH LN NW CR 63-D1,64-C1
120TH ST HNT 141-A3
120TH ST E BUR 148-D2
120TH ST E IGH 150-D3
120TH ST N GRA 81-D1
120TH ST N HUG 81-B1
120TH ST N MAY 82-D1
120TH ST NE MO 17-A4
120TH ST NE MOT 16-E4,17-A4
120TH ST NW CNT 15-A4
120TH ST NW CWT 15-B4
120TH ST NW MOT 16-D4
120TH ST NW SVT 15-D4
120TH ST NW ZIM 5-D1
120TH ST S CG 152-C3
120TH ST S DET 152-D3
120TH ST SE BEC 2-D4
120TH ST SE BKR 3-A4
120TH ST SW WIT 99-A2
120TH ST W APV 149-D3
120TH ST W BUR 148-C2
120TH ST W EAG 149-E3,150-A3
121ST AVE N DAY 62-E2
121ST AVE NE BLA 64-E1,65-A1
121ST AVE NW CR 63-E1,64-C1
121ST CIR NW CR 63-D1,64-A1
121ST LN N CHM 63-C2
121ST LN NE BLA 64-E1
121ST LN NW CR 63-E1,64-B1
121ST ST LVL 162-D4
121ST ST E BUR 148-E3,149-A3
121ST ST N HUG 81-A1
121ST ST N MAY 82-B1
121ST ST NW SVT 15-D4
121ST ST W APV 149-B3
121ST ST W BUR 148-C3
121ST ST W RMT 150-C3
122ND AVE N CHM 63-D2
122ND AVE NE BLA 64-E1,65-A1
122ND AVE NW CR 63-E1,64-B1
122ND CIR NW CR 50-B4,64-B1
122ND LN N CHM 63-C2
122ND LN NE BLA 65-A1
122ND LN NW CR 63-E1,64-B1
122ND ST BTT 142-E3,143-C3
122ND ST HNT 141-C2
122ND ST YAT 141-D3
122ND ST E BUR 148-E3,149-A3
122ND ST N HUG 81-E1,82-A1
122ND ST N MAY 68-B4,82-B1
122ND ST S DET 152-E3,153-A3
122ND ST SE BEC 3-A4

122ND ST SE BKR ...3-B4
123RD AVE BKR ...2-C1
123RD AVE ROG ...61-E2
123RD AVE N CHM ...63-C2
123RD AVE N HSN ...61-B2
123RD AVE N ROG ...61-E2,62-A2
123RD AVE NE BLA ...51-A4,64-E1
123RD AVE NW CR ...50-B4,64-C1
123RD CIR NW CR ...50-A4
123RD LN NE BLA ...50-E4,51-A4
123RD LN NW CR ...49-D4,50-C4
123RD PL N CHM ...63-C2
123RD ST E BUR ...148-E3
123RD ST NE NIT ...152-A3
123RD ST NE MOT ...16-E4
123RD ST NW SVT ...15-D4
123RD ST W SAV ...149-B4
123RD STREET CT SAV ...147-E3,148-A3
123 1/2 ST W SAV ...147-C3
124TH AVE CHM ...63-C2
124TH AVE N CHM ...62-B2
124TH AVE N HSN ...62-B2
124TH AVE NE BLA ...50-E4,51-A4
124TH AVE NW CR ...49-E4,50-B4
124TH CIR CR ...49-D4
124TH CIR SAV ...147-C3
124TH CIR N CHM ...63-C2
124TH CIR N CR ...49-D4,50-C4
124TH CT NE BLA ...50-E4
124TH CT W RMT ...150-C4
124TH LN CHM ...63-C1
124TH LN NE BLA ...50-E4,51-A4
124TH LN NW CR ...49-D4,50-C4
124TH PL N CHM ...63-C1
124TH ST E NIT ...152-B3
124TH ST N HUG ...68-C4,69-C4
124TH ST NE MOT ...16-E4
124TH ST NW CWT ...15-C4
124TH ST W SAV ...150-A4
124TH WAY NE BLA ...50-E4
124TH STREET CIR N HUG ...67-A4
124TH STREET CT N HUG ...67-A4,81-A1
125TH AVE SAT ...14-E3
125TH AVE SJT ...97-C2,98-B2
125TH AVE N DAY ...62-D1
125TH AVE NE BLA ...50-E4,51-B4
125TH AVE SE BKR ...2-D1,16-D1
125TH CT NE BLA ...51-A4
125TH LN SJT ...98-B2
125TH LN NE BLA ...50-E4,51-A4
125TH LN NW CR ...50-B4
125TH ST SAV ...147-D3
125TH ST E BUR ...148-E3,149-A3
125TH ST E NIT ...152-B4
125TH ST E RMT ...150-D3
125TH ST N HUG ...67-C4,81-D1
125TH ST NW CWT ...15-B4
125TH ST NW APV ...149-D4
125TH ST W JT ...146-B4
125TH ST W RMT ...149-E4,150-A4
125TH ST W SAV ...147-C3,148-A3
125TH STREET CIR N HUG ...67-E4
125TH STREET CT N HUG ...67-E4
126TH AVE SJT ...97-E2
126TH AVE N ROG ...61-E1
126TH AVE NE BLA ...50-E4,51-A4
126TH AVE NW CR ...50-D4
126TH LN NE BLA ...50-E4,51-A4
126TH LN NW CR ...50-D4
126TH ST MAY ...68-C4
126TH ST E BUR ...149-A3
126TH ST N HUG ...67-B4
126TH ST N MAY ...69-B4
126TH ST NW APV ...149-C4
126TH ST W BUR ...148-C3
126TH ST W JT ...146-B4
126TH ST W RMT ...150-B4
126TH ST W SAV ...147-D3,148-A3
126TH STREET CT E BUR ...149-A3
126TH STREET CT N HUG ...67-A4
127TH AVE NE BLA ...50-D4,51-A4
127TH AVE NW CR ...50-D4
127TH CIR NW CR ...49-E4,50-B4
127TH CT W RMT ...150-A4
127TH LN NE BLA ...50-E4,51-A4
127TH LN NW CR ...50-D4
127TH ST E NIT ...151-E4,152-A4
127TH ST N MAY ...68-E4
127TH ST NE MOT ...16-E3,17-A4
127TH ST NW CWT ...15-A3
127TH ST NW MOT ...16-D3
127TH ST NW SVT ...15-E4,16-C4
127TH ST S DET ...152-D4
127TH ST SE BKR ...3-C4
127TH ST SE BLT ...3-D4
127TH ST SE CKP ...2-E1
127TH ST W APV ...149-B4
127TH ST W SAV ...148-A3
127TH STREET CT N MAY ...68-E4
128TH AVE N ROG ...61-E1
128TH AVE NE BLA ...50-E4,51-C4
128TH AVE NW CR ...50-B4
128TH CIR NW CR ...50-B4
128TH CT NE BLA ...51-B4
128TH LN CR ...49-E4
128TH LN NE BLA ...51-A4
128TH LN NW CR ...50-A4
128TH ST HUG ...67-B4
128TH ST N HUG ...67-B4
128TH ST NW SVT ...15-E3,16-A3
128TH ST W APV ...149-A4
128TH ST W BUR ...148-C3
128TH ST W JT ...146-B4
128TH ST W RMT ...150-B4
128TH ST W SAV ...147-D3,148-A3
128TH STREET CT HUG ...67-B4
129TH AVE CR ...49-E4
129TH AVE N CHM ...63-B1
129TH AVE N DAY ...62-E1,63-A1
129TH AVE N HSN ...61-D1,62-B1
129TH AVE N ROG ...61-E1,62-A1
129TH AVE NE BLA ...50-E4,51-A4
129TH AVE NW CR ...49-E4,50-B4
129TH CIR NW CR ...51-A4
129TH CT NE BLA ...50-E4
129TH LN N CHM ...63-B1
129TH LN NE BLA ...50-E4,51-A4
129TH LN NW CR ...49-E4,50-B4

129TH PL N ROG ...61-E1
129TH ST HUG ...67-B4
129TH ST E BUR ...148-D3
129TH ST N HUG ...67-A4
129TH ST W APV ...149-B4
129TH ST W SAV ...148-A4
130TH AVE BLA ...50-E4
130TH AVE RDT ...98-E1
130TH AVE VAT ...97-D1
130TH AVE VAT ...209-C3
130TH AVE WEL ...195-C3,209-C1
130TH AVE N DAY ...63-A1
130TH AVE N ROG ...61-E1
130TH AVE NE BLA ...50-D4,51-A4
130TH AVE NW CR ...49-E4,50-A4
130TH CIR NW CR ...50-A4
130TH CT NE BLA ...51-A4
130TH LN BLA ...50-E4
130TH LN NE BLA ...50-E4,51-A4
130TH LN NW CR ...50-A4
130TH ST DAT ...144-B4
130TH ST HNT ...141-C2
130TH ST JT ...145-D4
130TH ST LVT ...145-D4
130TH ST E BUR ...148-D3
130TH ST N HUG ...67-B4,68-A4
130TH ST N MAY ...68-B4,69-A4
130TH ST NW SVT ...15-D3
130TH ST NW APV ...149-B4
130TH ST W JT ...145-E4,146-A4
130TH ST W RMT ...150-A4
130TH ST W SAV ...147-E4
130TH WAY N RMT ...150-A4
130TH STREET CT APV ...149-C4
130TH STREET CT E BUR ...148-E4
130TH STREET CT N SAV ...147-E4
130TH STREET LN N MAY ...69-A4
131ST AVE N CHM ...63-B1
131ST AVE N DAY ...63-B1
131ST AVE NE BLA ...50-E3,51-C3
131ST AVE NW CR ...49-E3,50-B3
131ST CIR APV ...149-B4
131ST CT W SAV ...148-A4
131ST LN NE BLA ...50-E3,51-A3
131ST LN NW CR ...49-E3,50-B3
131ST ST E BUR ...148-D3
131ST ST N MAY ...68-E4,69-A4
131ST ST W APV ...149-A4
131ST ST W BUR ...148-C4
131ST ST W RMT ...149-E4,150-A4
131ST ST W SAV ...147-E4,148-A4
131ST STREET CIR S DET ...152-E4
131ST STREET CIR W SAV ...147-E4
131ST STREET CT S DET ...152-E4
131ST STREET CT W APV ...149-C4
131 1/2 ST W BUR ...148-C4
131 1/2 ST W SAV ...148-A4
132ND AVE SJT ...97-B1,98-C1
132ND AVE N ROG ...61-E1
132ND AVE NE BLA ...50-D3,51-A3
132ND AVE NW CR ...49-E3,50-A3
132ND CIR SAV ...147-D4
132ND CIR NW CR ...49-E3
132ND CT APV ...149-A4
132ND CT NE BLA ...51-A3
132ND CT W RMT ...150-A4
132ND CT W SAV ...147-E4
132ND LN NE BLA ...51-A3
132ND LN NW CR ...49-E3,50-A3
132ND LN W SAV ...147-E4
132ND PL W BUR ...148-C4
132ND ST BNT ...141-A1
132ND ST E BUR ...148-D4
132ND ST E NIT ...151-E4,152-B4
132ND ST NW CWT ...15-A3
132ND ST NW LIT ...5-C3
132ND ST W APV ...149-B4
132ND ST W BUR ...148-B4
132ND ST W RMT ...150-A4
132ND ST W SAV ...147-E4,148-A4
132ND WAY APV ...149-A4
132 1/2 AVE N DAY ...49-A4,63-A1
133RD AVE SJT ...98-D1
133RD AVE N DAY ...48-E4,49-A4
133RD AVE N HSN ...47-D4,48-B4
133RD AVE N ROG ...62-A2
133RD AVE N HL ...51-A3
133RD AVE NW AND ...49-E3,50-B3
133RD CIR N CHM ...49-B4
133RD CT APV ...149-B4,163-B1
133RD CT ROG ...62-163-D3
133RD CT NE HL ...50-E3
133RD CT W RMT ...149-E4
133RD LN NE HL ...50-E3,51-B3
133RD LN NW AND ...49-E3,50-A3
133RD ST N MAY ...69-A3
133RD ST W APV ...149-A4,163-A1
133RD ST W LVT ...145-E4
133RD ST W SAV ...147-E4,148-A4
133RD STREET CT APV ...149-C4,163-C1
134TH AVE BKR ...2-D1
134TH AVE N DAY ...49-A4
134TH AVE N ROG ...47-E4,48-A4
134TH AVE NE HL ...50-D3,51-A3
134TH AVE NW AND ...49-E3,50-A3
134TH CIR N CHM ...49-B4
134TH CIR W SAV ...148-A4
134TH CT APV ...163-A1
134TH CT W APV ...163-B1
134TH LN NE HL ...50-D3,51-A4
134TH LN NW AND ...50-B3
134TH LN W SAV ...147-E4,148-A4
134TH ST BTT ...143-D4
134TH ST YAT ...141-E4,142-A4
134TH ST E BUR ...148-D4
134TH ST N HUG ...67-B3
134TH ST NW SVT ...16-A3
134TH ST NW ZIM ...5-C2
134TH ST W APV ...162-E1,163-C1
134TH ST W BUR ...148-B4
134TH ST W SAV ...147-E4,148-A4
134TH STREET CT APV ...163-C1
134 1/2 CIR BKR ...2-E1
135TH AVE N ROG ...47-D4
135TH AVE NE COT ...52-B3
135TH AVE NE HL ...50-E3
135TH AVE NW AND ...49-E3,50-A3
135TH CIR N CHM ...49-B4
135TH CIR NW AND ...50-A3
135TH CT N HUG ...67-B3

135TH CT NE HL ...50-E3
135TH LN NE HL ...50-E3,51-A3
135TH LN NW AND ...49-E3,50-A3
135TH ST BNT ...127-A4,141-B1
135TH ST E BUR ...148-D4
135TH ST N HUG ...67-B3
135TH ST N MAY ...68-E3
135TH ST NW SVT ...16-A3
135TH ST W APV ...162-E1,163-B1
135TH ST W BUR ...148-B4
135TH ST W RMT ...164-B1
135TH ST W SAV ...147-E4,148-A4
135TH STREET CT APV ...163-B1
135 1/2 AVE N DAY ...49-A4
136TH AVE BKR ...2-E1
136TH AVE SJT ...97-C1
136TH AVE N DAY ...49-A4
136TH AVE NE HL ...51-D3
136TH AVE NW AND ...49-E3,50-A3
136TH CT APV ...163-A1
136TH LN HL ...51-D3
136TH LN NE HL ...50-E3,51-D3
136TH LN NW AND ...49-E3,50-A3
136TH LN W SAV ...147-C4,161-C1
136TH ST E BUR ...148-D4
136TH ST N HUG ...67-B3
136TH ST N MAY ...68-E3,69-B3
136TH ST NW LIT ...5-B1
136TH ST W APV ...163-D1
136TH ST W BUR ...148-C4
136TH ST W RMT ...163-E1
136TH STREET CIR N HUG ...67-E3
136TH STREET CT APV ...163-C1
136TH STREET CT N HUG ...67-E3
136 1/2 ST W SAV ...162-A1
137TH AVE HL ...51-C3
137TH AVE VAT ...209-C3
137TH AVE N DAY ...49-A4
137TH AVE N ROG ...47-E4
137TH AVE NW RAM ...48-E3,49-A3
137TH AVE SE BKR ...2-E1
137TH CT APV ...163-A1
137TH CT RMT ...163-E1
137TH CT W APV ...163-A1
137TH LN LAT ...216-A3
137TH LN NE HL ...51-B3
137TH LN NW AND ...50-A3
137TH PL W BUR ...148-C4,162-C1
137TH ST SAV ...161-C1
137TH ST E APV ...161-C1
137TH ST E BUR ...162-E1
137TH ST N HUG ...67-D3
137TH ST NW SVT ...16-A3
137TH ST SE BKR ...16-E1,17-B1
137TH ST W APV ...163-A1
137TH ST W BUR ...162-C1
137TH ST W RMT ...163-E1
137TH ST W SAV ...161-E1,162-A1
137 1/2 ST W BUR ...162-A1
137 1/2 ST W SAV ...162-A1
138TH AVE N DAY ...48-C4,49-A4
138TH AVE N ROG ...47-E4
138TH AVE NE HL ...50-D3,51-D3
138TH AVE NW AND ...49-E3,50-A3
138TH CT NW AND ...49-E3
138TH CT W RMT ...163-E1
138TH LN NE HL ...50-E3
138TH LN NW AND ...49-E3,50-B3
138TH PL N ROG ...47-E4
138TH ST BTT ...156-E1,157-A1
138TH ST SAV ...161-C1
138TH ST E APV ...162-E1
138TH ST E BUR ...162-D1
138TH ST E RMT ...162-D1
138TH ST N HUG ...67-B3
138TH ST NW LIT ...5-B2
138TH STREET CT APV ...162-E1,163-C1
138TH ST W APV ...162-E1,163-C1
138TH ST W BUR ...162-C1
138TH ST W SAV ...164-A1
138TH ST W SAV ...161-E1
139TH AVE N DAY ...48-E4,49-A4
139TH AVE NE HL ...50-E3,51-C3
139TH AVE NW AND ...49-E3,50-C3
139TH LN NW RAM ...48-E3
139TH CT APV ...163-A1
139TH LN NE HL ...50-D3,51-B3
139TH LN NW AND ...49-E3,50-C3
139TH LN NW RAM ...48-E3
139TH LIT ...5-B1
139TH SAV ...161-C1
139TH ST NW CWT ...15-A3
139TH ST NW LIT ...5-B1
139TH ST W APV ...163-A1
139TH ST W BUR ...162-C1
139TH ST W RMT ...164-A1
139TH ST W SAV ...161-E1,162-A1
139TH STREET CT APV ...163-C1
140TH AVE RDT ...84-E4
140TH AVE SAT ...14-E2
140TH AVE SJT ...84-D4
140TH AVE VAT ...209-D3
140TH AVE N DAY ...49-A4
140TH AVE NE COT ...52-D2
140TH AVE NE HL ...50-D2,51-B2
140TH AVE NW AND ...49-D3,50-A2
140TH AVE NW RAM ...49-B3
140TH AVE SE BKR ...16-E2
140TH CT W APV ...163-A1
140TH LN NE HL ...50-D2
140TH LN NW AND ...49-E2,50-C2
140TH LN NW RAM ...49-B2
140TH ST E BUR ...162-E1
140TH ST E NIT ...166-B1
140TH ST E RMT ...164-E1,165-A1
140TH ST N HUG ...67-E3,68-A3
140TH ST N MAY ...68-B3
140TH ST NE PRL ...161-C1
140TH ST NW CWT ...15-A2
140TH ST NW LIT ...5-B2
140TH ST NW PRL ...160-E1,161-A1
140TH ST W APV ...162-E1,163-B1
140TH ST W BUR ...162-C1
140TH ST W RMT ...164-A1
140TH ST W SAV ...161-E1,162-A1
140TH AVENUE WAY WEL ...195-D3
140TH STREET BLVD W APV ...162-E1

140TH STREET CT APV ...163-A1
141ST AVE LAT ...202-A3,216-A2
141ST AVE N DAY ...48-B3,49-A3
141ST AVE N HSN ...47-C4,48-A3
141ST AVE NE COT ...52-B2,53-A2
141ST AVE NW AND ...49-E2,50-A2
141ST AVE NW RAM ...49-B3
141ST CIR N DAY ...49-A3
141ST CT N HUG ...67-B3
141ST CT W APV ...163-A1
141ST CT W RMT ...163-E1
141ST LN LAT ...216-A2
141ST LN NE HL ...50-E2,51-A2
141ST LN NW AND ...49-E2,50-C2
141ST LN NW RAM ...49-B2
141ST ST LIT ...5-B2
141ST ST E BUR ...162-E1
141ST ST N HUG ...67-B3
141ST ST NW LIT ...5-B1
141ST ST W APV ...163-A1
141ST ST W SAV ...161-E1,162-A1
141ST STREET CT APV ...163-A1
142ND AVE SJT ...83-C4
142ND AVE N DAY ...48-E3
142ND AVE N HSN ...47-E3
142ND AVE NE HL ...50-E2
142ND AVE NW AND ...49-E2,50-C2
142ND AVE NW RAM ...48-D2,49-B3
142ND CIR NW RAM ...49-C2
142ND LN NW AND ...49-E2,50-C2
142ND PATH W APV ...163-D1
142ND ST BTT ...157-D1
142ND ST YAT ...155-E1,156-A1
142ND ST N HUG ...67-B3
142ND ST N MAY ...68-B3
142ND ST NW AND ...49-E2
142ND ST NW ER ...5-B4,19-B1
142ND ST NW LIT ...5-B1
142ND ST NW SVT ...16-A2
142ND ST SE BKR ...16-E2,17-A2
142ND ST W APV ...163-B1
142ND ST W RMT ...164-A1
142ND STREET CT W SAV ...163-A1
142 1/2 ST W SAV ...162-A1
143RD AVE SJT ...84-C4
143RD AVE NE HL ...50-E2,51-A2
143RD AVE NW AND ...49-D2,50-C2
143RD AVE NW RAM ...48-E2,49-C2
143RD CIR SAV ...162-A1
143RD CIR NE HL ...51-A2
143RD CIR NW BUR ...162-B1
143RD CT SAV ...162-A1
143RD CT E BUR ...162-D1
143RD CT NW RAM ...49-B2
143RD LN LAT ...216-A3
143RD LN E BUR ...162-D1
143RD LN NE HL ...51-A2
143RD LN NW AND ...50-C2
143RD LN NW RAM ...49-B2
143RD PL W BUR ...162-D1
143RD ST RMT ...163-E1
143RD ST SAV ...162-A1
143RD ST E BUR ...162-D1
143RD ST NW SVT ...5-B2
143RD ST W APV ...163-A1
143RD ST W BUR ...162-C1
143RD ST W RMT ...163-E1,164-A1
143RD ST W SAV ...161-E1,162-A1
143RD STREET
     CT W APV ...162-E2,163-B1
144TH AVE SJT ...83-D4
144TH AVE NE COT ...52-D2
144TH AVE NE HL ...50-E1,51-C2
144TH AVE NW AND ...49-E2,50-B2
144TH AVE NW RAM ...48-D2,49-A2
144TH CIR N HSN ...47-E3
144TH CIR NW RAM ...49-B2
144TH CT APV ...163-B2
144TH CT SAV ...161-E1
144TH LN NE HL ...51-A2
144TH LN NW AND ...49-D2,50-C2
144TH LN NW RAM ...49-B2
144TH ST RMT ...163-E2
144TH ST SAV ...161-D2
144TH ST E BUR ...162-D2
144TH ST N HUG ...67-B3
144TH ST N MAY ...69-C3
144TH ST NW BLT ...33-B1
144TH ST NW SVT ...16-A2
144TH ST S BUR ...162-A2
144TH ST W APV ...162-E2,163-B2
144TH ST W BUR ...162-B2
144TH ST W RMT ...163-E2,164-A2
144TH ST W SAV ...161-E1,162-A1
144TH AVENUE WAY VAT ...209-D1
144TH STREET CT APV ...162-E2
145TH AVE SJT ...83-D4
145TH AVE VAT ...223-E2
145TH AVE WEL ...181-D4,195-D1
145TH AVE N HSN ...48-A3
145TH AVE NE COT ...52-B2,53-A2
145TH AVE NE HL ...50-E2,51-A2
145TH AVE NW AND ...49-D2,50-B2
145TH AVE SE BKR ...3-A2
145TH CIR NW BLT ...33-A1
145TH CT E BUR ...162-D2
145TH CT NW BLT ...33-B2
145TH LN LAT ...216-A2
145TH LN NE HL ...50-D2,51-B2
145TH LN NW AND ...49-D2,50-B2
145TH ST APV ...163-B2
145TH ST BNT ...127-C4
145TH ST E BUR ...162-D2
145TH ST E RMT ...164-D2,165-A2
145TH ST N HUG ...67-B3
145TH ST NW BLT ...33-A2
145TH ST NW SVT ...15-B2
145TH ST S BUR ...162-B2
145TH ST W APV ...162-E2,163-B2
145TH ST W BUR ...162-B2
145TH ST W LVT ...159-C2,160-A2
145TH ST W RMT ...163-E1,164-A1
145TH ST W SAV ...161-E1,162-A1
145TH AVENUE WAY VAT ...209-D3
145TH STREET CT APV ...163-A2
146TH AVE NE HL ...51-D2
146TH AVE NW AND ...49-D2,50-B2

146TH AVE NW RAM ... 48-D2,49-B2
146TH CIR NW RAM ... 49-C2
146TH CT NW BLT ... 33-A2
146TH LN RAM ... 49-B2
146TH LN NE HL ... 50-D2
146TH LN NW AND ... 49-D2,50-C2
146TH ST BLT ... 33-A1
146TH ST ORT ... 5-A1
146TH ST E BUR ... 162-D2
146TH ST N HUG ... 67-A2
146TH ST NW BLT ... 19-A1,33-A1
146TH ST W APV ... 163-B2
146TH ST W BUR ... 162-C2
146TH ST W RMT ... 163-E2,164-A2
146TH ST W SAV ... 161-D2,162-A2
146TH WAY W APV ... 163-B2
146TH AVENUE WAY VAT ... 209-D1
146TH STREET CT W APV ... 163-B2
147TH AVE N HSN ... 47-E3,48-A3
147TH AVE NE HL ... 50-E2,51-A2
147TH AVE NW AND ... 49-D2,50-B2
147TH AVE NW RAM ... 48-D2,49-A2
147TH AVE SE BKR ... 3-A2
147TH CIR NW RAM ... 49-C2
147TH CT SAV ... 162-A2
147TH CT NW AND ... 50-B2
147TH LN NE HL ... 50-D2,51-B2
147TH LN NW AND ... 49-D2,50-B2
147TH LN NW RAM ... 48-E2,49-C2
147TH ST N HUG ... 67-B2
147TH ST NW BLT ... 5-A4,33-A1
147TH ST NW ORT ... 5-A4
147TH ST NW SVT ... 16-B2
147TH ST W APV ... 163-B2
147TH ST W RMT ... 163-E2,164-A2
147TH ST W SAV ... 161-E2,162-A2
148TH AVE SJT ... 84-B4
148TH AVE NE HL ... 50-D2,51-B2
148TH AVE NW AND ... 49-C2,50-B2
148TH AVE NW RAM ... 48-E2,49-C2
148TH CIR N HSN ... 48-A3
148TH CT APV ... 163-D2
148TH LN NE HL ... 50-D2,51-B2
148TH LN NW AND ... 49-D2,50-B2
148TH LN NW RAM ... 48-E2,49-B2
148TH PATH W APV ... 163-D2
148TH ST N HUG ... 67-B2
148TH ST NW BLT ... 33-A1
148TH ST NW CWT ... 15-A2
148TH ST NW SVT ... 15-E2,16-A2
148TH ST W APV ... 163-C2
148TH ST W RMT ... 163-E2,164-A2
148TH ST W SAV ... 161-D2,162-A2
149TH AVE N DAY ... 48-C3
149TH AVE NE HL ... 51-B2
149TH AVE NW AND ... 49-D2,50-A1
149TH AVE NW RAM ... 48-E2,49-C2
149TH CT APV ... 163-D2
149TH LN NE HL ... 51-A1
149TH LN NW AND ... 49-E1,50-B1
149TH LN NW RAM ... 48-E2,49-B1
149TH ST NW BLT ... 33-A1
149TH ST SE BKR ... 17-B2
149TH ST W APV ... 163-C2
149TH ST W BUR ... 162-C2
149TH ST W RMT ... 163-E2,164-A2
149TH ST W SAV ... 162-A2
150TH AVE CFT ... 223-A2
150TH AVE RDT ... 84-E3
150TH AVE SAT ... 14-E1
150TH AVE SJT ... 84-D3
150TH AVE SMT ... 83-D3
150TH AVE N HSN ... 48-A3
150TH AVE NE HL ... 50-E1,51-B1
150TH AVE NW AND ... 50-A1
150TH AVE NW RAM ... 48-E1,49-A1
150TH AVE SE BKR ... 3-A3
150TH LN NE HL ... 51-A1
150TH LN NW AND ... 49-E1,50-B1
150TH LN NW RAM ... 48-E1,49-C1
150TH ST BNT ... 127-A4
150TH ST BTT ... 156-E2,157-D2
150TH ST DAT ... 157-E2,158-A2
150TH ST YAT ... 156-C2
150TH ST E BUR ... 162-D2
150TH ST E HAS ... 166-B2
150TH ST E NIT ... 165-D2,166-A2
150TH ST E RMT ... 165-C2
150TH ST N HUG ... 67-B2
150TH ST N MAY ... 68-D2
150TH ST NW BLT ... 19-A2
150TH ST NW CWT ... 15-C1
150TH ST NW ORT ... 5-A1
150TH ST NW SVT ... 15-D1,16-A1
150TH ST SE PRL ... 161-C2
150TH ST W APV ... 162-E2,163-A2
150TH ST W BUR ... 162-C2
150TH ST W LVT ... 159-E2,160-A2
150TH ST W PRL ... 161-C2
150TH ST W RMT ... 163-E2,164-A2
150TH ST W SAV ... 161-D2,162-A2
150TH AVENUE WAY VAT 209-E4,223-E3
151ST AVE LAT ... 201-E4,215-E2
151ST AVE NE HL ... 51-A1
151ST AVE NW AND ... 49-D1,50-A1
151ST AVE NW RAM ... 48-E1,49-A1
151ST CT HUG ... 67-C2
151ST CT W RMT ... 164-A2
151ST LN NE COT ... 52-C1
151ST LN NE HL ... 51-D1
151ST LN NW AND ... 49-E1,50-B1
151ST LN NW RAM ... 48-D1,49-B1
151ST ST APV ... 163-C2
151ST ST HUG ... 67-C2
151ST ST RMT ... 163-E2
151ST ST E BUR ... 162-D2
151ST ST N HUG ... 67-C2
151ST ST NW BLT ... 19-A4,33-A1
151ST ST W APV ... 163-B2
151ST ST W RMT ... 163-E2,164-A2
151ST ST W SAV ... 161-C2
151ST STREET CIR HUG ... 67-C2
152ND AVE VAT ... 209-E4
152ND AVE N DAY ... 48-B2
152ND AVE NE COT ... 52-C1
152ND AVE NE HL ... 50-E1,51-A1
152ND AVE NW AND ... 49-D1
152ND AVE NW RAM ... 48-E1,49-B1
152ND CIR NW BLT ... 18-E2
152ND CIR NW ER ... 20-A2
152ND CT APV ... 163-D2
152ND CT NW RAM ... 49-C1
152ND LN NE COT ... 52-C1
152ND LN NE HL ... 51-A1
152ND LN NW AND ... 49-E1,50-B1
152ND LN NW RAM ... 48-E1,49-C1
152ND PL SAV ... 161-D2
152ND ST DAT ... 158-D2
152ND ST HUG ... 67-C2
152ND ST E BUR ... 162-D2
152ND ST E RMT ... 164-D2
152ND ST N HUG ... 67-E2,68-A2
152ND ST N MAY ... 69-C2
152ND ST NW BLT ... 18-E2,19-A2
152ND ST NW HOP ... 20-A2
152ND ST W APV ... 163-D2
152ND ST W BUR ... 162-C2
152ND ST W RMT ... 163-E2
152ND ST W SAV ... 161-C2
152ND AVENUE WAY WEL ... 195-E3
152ND STREET CT W RMT ... 163-E2
153RD AVE SMT ... 84-C3
153RD AVE NE COT ... 52-B1
153RD AVE NE HL ... 50-E1,51-A1
153RD AVE NW AND ... 49-E1,50-B1
153RD AVE NW RAM ... 48-C1,49-B1
153RD AVE SE BKR ... 3-B4
153RD BAY SAV ... 161-D2
153RD CT NW RAM ... 49-A1
153RD LN AND ... 50-B1
153RD LN NE HL ... 50-E1
153RD LN NW AND ... 49-D1,50-B1
153RD LN NW RAM ... 48-D1,49-A1
153RD PL SAV ... 161-D3
153RD ST APV ... 163-B2
153RD ST E BUR ... 162-D2
153RD ST E RMT ... 164-D2
153RD ST NW CWT ... 15-B1
153RD ST NW ER ... 48-B1
153RD ST W APV ... 163-B2
153RD ST W RMT ... 163-E2
153RD ST W SAV ... 161-C2
153RD WAY N RAM ... 49-A1
153RD WAY NW RAM ... 49-A1
154TH AVE ER ... 48-B1
154TH AVE NE HL ... 50-E1
154TH AVE NW AND ... 49-C1,50-D1
154TH AVE NW RAM ... 48-D1,49-C1
154TH CT W RMT ... 163-E2
154TH DR NW BLT ... 18-E4
154TH LN AND ... 50-B1
154TH LN HL ... 37-D4
154TH LN NE HL ... 50-E1
154TH LN NW AND ... 49-E1,50-A1
154TH LN NW RAM ... 48-D1,49-A1
154TH ST APV ... 163-C2
154TH ST DAT ... 158-D3
154TH ST YAT ... 156-D3
154TH ST N MAY ... 69-B2
154TH ST NW BLT ... 18-E4
154TH ST NW ER ... 48-B1
154TH ST NW PRL ... 160-E3,161-A3
154TH ST W RMT ... 163-E2,164-C2
154TH ST W SAV ... 161-E3
155TH AVE AND ... 50-B1
155TH AVE BCT ... 224-A4
155TH AVE SMT ... 83-E3,84-B3
155TH AVE WEL ... 195-E2
155TH AVE NE COT ... 52-C1
155TH AVE NE HL ... 51-D1
155TH AVE NW AND ... 49-D1,50-C1
155TH AVE NW RAM ... 48-E1,49-A1
155TH AVE SE BKR ... 3-B2
155TH CT RMT ... 163-E2
155TH LN NW AND ... 49-E1,50-B1
155TH LN NW RAM ... 48-D1,49-C1
155TH ST BNT ... 127-C3
155TH ST E RMT ... 164-D2
155TH ST N HUG ... 67-E2
155TH ST N MAY ... 68-C2
155TH ST NW BLT ... 18-E2,32-E2
155TH ST NW CWT ... 15-C1
155TH ST NW HOP ... 20-A2
155TH ST NW SVT ... 16-B1
155TH ST W APV ... 163-B3
155TH ST W BUR ... 162-C3
155TH ST W RMT ... 163-E2
155TH AVENUE WAY VAT ... 209-E2
155TH AVENUE WAY WEL 181-E4,195-E1
156TH AVE SMT ... 83-C3
156TH AVE NW AND ... 49-E1,50-B1
156TH AVE NW ER ... 48-B1
156TH AVE NW RAM ... 48-E1,49-A1
156TH LN NW AND ... 50-C1
156TH LN NW RAM ... 48-D1,49-C1
156TH ST APV ... 163-C3
156TH ST BLT ... 18-E4,32-E1
156TH ST E BUR ... 162-D3
156TH ST E NIT ... 165-C2
156TH ST NW BLT ... 18-E1,32-E1
156TH ST NW SVT ... 15-E1,16-A1
156TH ST W BUR ... 162-C3
156TH ST W RMT ... 163-E3,164-A3
156TH STREET CT APV ... 163-A3
157TH AVE SMT ... 84-A3
157TH AVE NE HL ... 36-D4,50-E1
157TH AVE NW AND ... 49-D1,50-C1
157TH AVE NW RAM ... 48-D1,49-A1
157TH AVE SE BKR ... 3-B1
157TH CT W RMT ... 163-E3
157TH LN NW AND ... 36-B4
157TH LN NW RAM ... 48-D1,49-B1
157TH ST APV ... 163-C3
157TH ST BUR ... 162-C3
157TH ST ORT ... 4-E1
157TH ST E BUR ... 162-E3
157TH ST E NIT ... 165-C3
157TH ST N HUG ... 67-D1
157TH ST NW CWT ... 15-C1
157TH ST SE BKR ... 16-E3,17-C3
157TH ST W APV ... 163-B3
157TH ST W BUR ... 162-C3
157TH ST W LVL ... 162-D3
157TH ST W LVT ... 159-E3,160-A3
157TH ST W RMT ... 163-E3
157TH WAY N HUG ... 67-B2
157TH ST CIR N HUG ... 67-B2
157TH WAY CT N HUG ... 67-B2
157 1/2 ST NW CWT ... 15-C1
158TH AVE NE HL ... 36-E4,37-B4
158TH AVE NW AND ... 35-D4,36-C4
158TH AVE NW RAM ... 34-D4,35-B4
158TH AVE W EPR ... 118-D4
158TH CT W RMT ... 163-E3
158TH LN NE HL ... 37-A4
158TH LN NW AND ... 36-B4
158TH LN NW RAM ... 34-D4,35-A4
158TH ST APV ... 163-C3
158TH ST HCT ... 156-E3,157-A3
158TH ST ORT ... 4-E1
158TH ST YAT ... 155-E3,156-B3
158TH ST NW CWT ... 1-D4,15-D1
158TH ST NW SVT ... 16-B1
158TH ST W APV ... 163-B3
158TH ST W BUR ... 162-C3
158TH ST W RMT ... 163-E3
159TH AVE NE COT ... 38-C4
159TH AVE NE HL ... 36-E4,37-B4
159TH AVE NW AND ... 35-C4,36-B4
159TH AVE NW RAM ... 35-A4
159TH CIR HUG ... 67-B1
159TH CT APV ... 163-A3
159TH CT HUG ... 67-B1
159TH CT W RMT ... 163-E3
159TH LN HL ... 37-C4
159TH LN NW AND ... 36-B4
159TH LN NW RAM ... 34-D4,35-B4
159TH ST BLT ... 18-E4
159TH ST ORT ... 4-E1
159TH ST SFT ... 158-C3
159TH ST E NIT ... 165-C3
159TH ST N HUG ... 67-B1
159TH ST NW BLT ... 4-E4,18-E1
159TH ST NW CWT ... 1-D4,15-C1
159TH ST NW SVT ... 2-B4
159TH ST W APV ... 163-A3
159 1/2 ST NW BLT ... 18-E1
160TH AVE HL ... 37-C4
160TH AVE RDT ... 84-E3
160TH AVE SMT ... 83-E3,84-C3
160TH AVE VAT ... 210-A2,224-A1
160TH AVE NE HL ... 37-B4
160TH AVE NW RAM ... 34-D4
160TH CT NW RAM ... 34-C4
160TH LN NE HL ... 36-E4,37-B4
160TH LN NW AND ... 35-D4
160TH LN NW RAM ... 34-C4,35-B4
160TH ST LYT ... 1-A4
160TH ST ORT ... 4-E1
160TH ST E COA ... 164-E3,165-A3
160TH ST E HAS ... 166-C3,167-A3
160TH ST E NIT ... 165-D3,166-B3
160TH ST E RMT ... 164-D3,165-B3
160TH ST E RVT ... 167-A3
160TH ST E SLT ... 160-C3
160TH ST NW BLT ... 4-D4
160TH ST NW CWT ... 1-B4,15-E1
160TH ST SE PRL ... 161-B3
160TH ST SE SAV ... 161-C3
160TH ST W ET ... 163-E3,164-B3
160TH ST W LVL ... 162-E3,163-C3
160TH ST W LVT ... 160-A3
160TH AVENUE WAY VAT ... 210-A2
160TH AVENUE WAY WEL ... 196-A4
161ST AVE NE COT ... 38-C4
161ST AVE NE HL ... 37-D4
161ST AVE NW AND ... 35-E4,36-B4
161ST AVE NW RAM ... 34-D4,35-C4
161ST LN HL ... 37-D4
161ST LN NE HL ... 37-D4
161ST LN NW AND ... 35-C4,36-A4
161ST LN NW RAM ... 34-E4,35-B4
161ST ST E SLT ... 160-D3
161ST ST W LVL ... 162-D3,163-B3
162ND AVE HL ... 37-C4
162ND AVE NE COT ... 38-C4
162ND AVE NE HL ... 37-B4
162ND AVE NW RAM ... 35-A4
162ND CT W LVL ... 162-B3,163-B3
162ND LN HL ... 37-D4
162ND LN NE HL ... 37-A4
162ND LN NW AND ... 35-E4
162ND LN NW BLT ... 18-D4
162ND LN NW RAM ... 34-C4,35-A4
162ND ST ORT ... 4-D3
162ND ST NW ORT ... 4-E3,5-A3
162ND ST NW SVT ... 2-A4
162ND ST W LVL ... 162-D3,163-B3
162NS ST NW CWT ... 1-E4,2-A4
163RD AVE NW AND ... 35-C4
163RD AVE NW RAM ... 34-D4,35-A4
163RD AVE SE BKR ... 3-C3
163RD CT W LVL ... 163-B3
163RD LN NE HL ... 37-A4
163RD LN NW AND ... 35-E4
163RD LN NW RAM ... 34-E4,35-A4
163RD ST NW BLT ... 32-D1
163RD ST NW CWT ... 1-A4
163RD ST W LVL ... 162-E3,163-B3
164TH AVE SMT ... 84-A2
164TH AVE N HL ... 36-E4
164TH AVE NE COT ... 38-B4
164TH AVE NE HL ... 37-C4
164TH AVE NW AND ... 35-E4,36-A4
164TH AVE NW RAM ... 34-E4,35-B4
164TH CIR NW RAM ... 34-D4
164TH LN NE COT ... 38-C4
164TH LN NE HL ... 37-A4
164TH LN NW AND ... 35-E4
164TH LN NW RAM ... 34-C4,35-B4
164TH ST E ET ... 164-D3
164TH ST W LVL ... 162-C3,163-B3
164 1/2 ST NW ORT ... 4-D1
164 3/4 ST NW ORT ... 4-D1
165TH AVE BCT ... 224-B4
165TH AVE SMT ... 83-D2,84-D2
165TH AVE WEL ... 196-A1
165TH AVE NE COT ... 38-D3
165TH AVE NE HL ... 36-E4,37-D4
165TH AVE NW AND ... 35-C4
165TH AVE NW ER ... 34-A4
165TH AVE NW RAM ... 34-D4
165TH AVE SE BKR ... 3-C1,17-C2
165TH CT W LVL ... 163-B3
165TH LN NE HL ... 37-B3
165TH LN NW AND ... 35-E3
165TH LN NW RAM ... 34-E4,35-A4
165TH ST BLT ... 18-D1
165TH ST BNT ... 127-C2
165TH ST ORT ... 4-D2
165TH ST E CRT ... 161-D3
165TH ST E SLT ... 160-D4
165TH ST E VET ... 165-D3
165TH ST N HUG ... 67-D1
165TH ST N MAY ... 68-C1
165TH ST SE ORT ... 4-D3
165TH ST W LVL ... 162-D3,163-B3
165TH ST W SCT ... 159-E3,160-B3
165TH AVENUE WAY BCT ... 224-B4
165TH AVENUE WAY WEL ... 196-A4
165 1/2 ST ORT ... 4-D1
166TH AVE NE HL ... 36-D3,37-B3
166TH AVE NW AND ... 35-D3,36-A3
166TH AVE NW RAM ... 34-E3,35-A3
166TH CIR NW RAM ... 34-D4
166TH CT W LVL ... 163-B3
166TH LN NE HL ... 36-D3,37-B3
166TH LN NW AND ... 35-E3
166TH LN NW RAM ... 34-E3,35-A3
166TH ST BLT ... 18-D4
166TH ST HCT ... 156-E4,157-D4
166TH ST ORT ... 4-D4
166TH ST SFT ... 157-E4,158-A4
166TH ST E ET ... 164-C3
166TH ST SE BLT ... 18-D3
166TH ST W LVL ... 162-D3,163-A4
166TH ST W SCT ... 159-D4
166TH ST CT BKR ... 3-C2
166 1/2 ST ORT ... 4-D1
167TH AVE NE COT ... 38-B3
167TH AVE NE HL ... 36-E3,37-D3
167TH AVE NW AND ... 35-C3,36-B3
167TH AVE NW ER ... 33-E3,34-A3
167TH AVE NW RAM ... 34-C3,35-A3
167TH CT W LVL ... 162-D4,163-B4
167TH LN NE COT ... 38-E3,39-A3
167TH LN NE HL ... 36-D3,37-C3
167TH LN NW AND ... 35-E3,36-A3
167TH LN NW RAM ... 34-C3
167TH ST BKR ... 17-C4
167TH ST BLT ... 18-D1
167TH ST ORT ... 4-D3
167TH ST E CRT ... 161-D4
167TH ST NW ORT ... 4-D1
167TH ST W LVL ... 162-D4,163-B4
167 1/2 ST NW ORT ... 4-D1
168TH AVE NE BKR ... 3-C1
168TH AVE NE COT ... 38-E3
168TH AVE NE HL ... 36-D3,37-C3
168TH AVE NW AND ... 35-D3
168TH AVE NW RAM ... 34-C3,35-B3
168TH AVE W EPR ... 118-C4,132-C1
168TH CIR NE HL ... 37-A3
168TH CT W LVL ... 163-B4
168TH LN NE COT ... 38-D3
168TH LN NE HL ... 37-E3
168TH LN NW AND ... 35-E3,36-A3
168TH LN NW RAM ... 34-D3,35-B3
168TH ST ORT ... 4-D1
168TH ST NW BLT ... 18-D3
168TH ST W LVL ... 162-B4,163-B4
168TH ST W SCT ... 159-D4
169TH AVE LAT ... 215-C2
169TH AVE SMT ... 83-E2
169TH AVE NE HL ... 36-D3,37-A3
169TH AVE NW RAM ... 34-C3,35-B3
169TH CIR NW BLT ... 18-C3
169TH CT LVL ... 163-A4
169TH LN LAT ... 215-C3
169TH LN NE HL ... 37-D3
169TH LN NW AND ... 35-E3,36-A3
169TH LN NW RAM ... 34-E3,35-A3
169TH ST LVL ... 163-C4
169TH ST ORT ... 4-C4
169TH ST E CRT ... 161-D4
169TH ST N MAY ... 54-B4
169TH ST NW BLT ... 18-C1
169TH ST W LVL ... 162-D4,163-C4
170TH AVE RDT ... 84-E2
170TH AVE SMT ... 84-B2
170TH AVE NE AND ... 36-D3
170TH AVE NE COT ... 38-C3
170TH AVE NE HL ... 36-D3,37-A3
170TH AVE NW AND ... 35-C3,36-D3
170TH AVE NW ER ... 33-E3,34-A3
170TH AVE NW RAM ... 34-E3,35-A3
170TH AVE SE BKR ... 17-C1
170TH CT W LVL ... 162-D4,163-B4
170TH LN NE HL ... 36-E3,37-D3
170TH LN NW AND ... 35-E3,36-A3
170TH LN NW RAM ... 35-B3
170TH ST BLT ... 4-D4,18-D1
170TH ST BNT ... 127-A2
170TH ST ORT ... 4-C3
170TH ST E CRT ... 161-C4,162-B4
170TH ST E ET ... 164-D4
170TH ST E MT ... 166-B4
170TH ST E PRL ... 161-A4
170TH ST E SLT ... 160-C4,161-C4
170TH ST E VET ... 165-B4,166-A4
170TH ST N HUG ... 53-D4,54-A4
170TH ST N MAY ... 54-D4
170TH ST NW BLT ... 18-C3,32-C2
170TH ST SW PRL ... 160-E4,161-A4
170TH ST W ET ... 163-E4,164-B4
170TH ST W LVL ... 162-D4,163-D4
170TH ST W SCT ... 159-E4,160-A4
171ST AVE LAT ... 201-C3,215-C1
171ST AVE NE HL ... 36-E3,37-A3
171ST AVE NW AND ... 35-C3,36-A3
171ST AVE NW RAM ... 34-C3
171ST CIR BKR ... 31-C1
171ST CIR NW AND ... 35-D3
171ST LN NE HL ... 37-B3
171ST LN NW RAM ... 34-D3,35-A3
171ST ST BLT ... 4-C4,18-C1
171ST ST NW ER ... 34-A3
171ST ST W LVL ... 162-D4,163-A4
172ND AVE SMT ... 83-E2
172ND AVE NE BKR ... 3-C1
172ND AVE NE COT ... 38-C3
172ND AVE NE HL ... 36-D3
172ND AVE NW AND ... 35-E3,36-A3
172ND LN NE HL ... 36-D3,37-C3
172ND LN NW AND ... 35-D3
172ND LN NW RAM ... 34-E3,35-A3
172ND ST BKR ... 31-D1
172ND ST BLT ... 18-C1
172ND ST LVL ... 162-D4
172ND ST ORT ... 4-C1
172ND ST NW BLT ... 18-C4,32-C1
172ND ST W LVL ... 162-C4,163-A4
173RD AVE HL ... 37-D3
173RD AVE NE HL ... 36-D3
173RD AVE NW AND ... 35-C3,36-D3
173RD AVE NW ER ... 33-E3,34-A3
173RD AVE NW RAM ... 34-D3,35-B3
173RD AVE SE BKR ... 3-C2
173RD CIR BKR ... 31-D1
173RD CIR LVL ... 163-A4
173RD CIR NW AND ... 36-A3
173RD CT W LVL ... 162-D4
173RD LN NW AND ... 35-E3,36-A3
173RD ST N HUG ... 53-A4
173RD ST W LVL ... 162-D4,163-A4
173RD ST W SCT ... 159-D4
174TH AVE NW AND ... 35-E3
174TH AVE NW ER ... 34-B3
174TH AVE NW RAM ... 34-D3,35-B3
174TH CIR NW AND ... 36-A3
174TH CT W LVL ... 163-A4
174TH LN NE HL ... 36-E2
174TH LN NW AND ... 35-E3,36-A3
174TH LN NW RAM ... 34-C3

174TH ST SFT 172-C1
174TH ST E CRT 161-D4
174TH ST E SLT 160-C4,161-A4
174TH ST N HUG 53-B4
174TH ST W LVL 163-A4
175TH AVE NE HL 36-D2,37-A2
175TH AVE NW AND 35-C2
175TH AVE NW ER 34-A2
175TH AVE NW RAM 34-E2,35-A2
175TH AVE SE BKR 3-D1
175TH AVE W EPR 118-C4,132-C1
175TH CT W LVL 162-C4
175TH LN LAT 201-C3
175TH LN NE HL 36-E2,37-A2
175TH LN NW AND 35-E2,36-A2
175TH LN NW RAM 34-C2
175TH ST BNT 127-B1
175TH ST CWT 1-B3
175TH ST E CRT 161-E4,162-A4
175TH ST E MT 166-C4
175TH ST E RVT 167-C4
175TH ST N HUG 53-C4
175TH ST N MAY 54-E4,55-A4
175TH ST W LVL 162-D4,163-A4
175TH AVE WAY WEL 182-B3
176TH AVE NE COT 38-D2
176TH AVE NE HL 37-A2
176TH AVE NW AND 35-D2,36-A2
176TH AVE NW RAM 34-C2
176TH CIR NW AND 36-A2
176TH CIR W LVL 162-D4
176TH CT LVL 162-E4,176-E1
176TH LN NE COT 38-D2
176TH LN NE HL 36-D2,37-A2
176TH LN NW AND 35-E2,36-A2
176TH LN NW RAM 34-D2
176TH ST BLT 4-C4,18-C1
176TH ST ORT 4-C2
176TH ST E SLT 160-E4,174-E1
176TH ST N MAY 54-B3
176TH ST W LVL 163-C4,176-C1
177TH AVE NE COT 38-C2
177TH AVE NE HL 36-D2,37-A2
177TH AVE NW AND 35-E2,36-C2
177TH AVE NW RAM 34-D2,35-C2
177TH AVE SE BKR 3-D2
177TH CIR W LVL 176-D1
177TH LN NE COT 38-D2
177TH LN NE HL 36-E2
177TH LN NW AND 36-A2
177TH LN NW RAM 35-B2
177TH ST LVL 176-E1
177TH ST N HUG 53-C3
177TH ST N MAY 54-D3,55-A3
177TH ST S BLT 18-B3
177TH ST W LVL 176-C1,177-C1
178TH AVE NE COT 38-D2
178TH AVE NE HL 36-E2
178TH AVE NW AND 35-E2
178TH AVE NW ER 33-C2,34-B2
178TH AVE NW RAM 34-C2
178TH CIR NW RAM 34-C2
178TH LN NE COT 38-D2
178TH LN NE HL 36-E2
178TH LN NW AND 35-E2
178TH LN NW RAM 34-E2,35-C2
178TH ST LVL 176-E1
178TH ST NW BLT 18-C1,32-C2
178TH ST W LVL 176-D1
179TH AVE NE COT 38-C2
179TH AVE NE HL 37-B2
179TH AVE NW AND 35-E2,36-A2
179TH AVE NW ER 33-C2,34-A2
179TH AVE NW RAM 35-C2
179TH CIR NW ER 33-C2
179TH CT NW ER 33-C2
179TH LN NW RAM 35-B2
179TH ST E SLT 174-E1
179TH ST NW CWT 1-A3
179TH ST NW ER 33-C2
179TH ST W LVL 176-C1
179TH TRL W LVL 176-C1
179 1/2 AVE NW ER 33-C2
180TH AVE FET 224-C4
180TH AVE GHT 224-C4
180TH AVE SMT 83-E1,84-A1
180TH AVE NE COT 38-C2
180TH AVE NW AND 35-D2,36-A2
180TH AVE NW BLT 31-E2,32-A2
180TH AVE NW ER 33-C2
180TH AVE NW RAM 34-C2,35-B2
180TH AVE SE BKR 3-D1
180TH CIR NW ER 33-C2
180TH CT FAR 177-D1
180TH CT NW BLT 18-B3
180TH LN NW AND 35-D2
180TH LN NW ER 33-C2
180TH LN NW RAM 35-B2
180TH ST FAR 177-C1
180TH ST ORT 4-B2
180TH ST E CRT 175-D1
180TH ST E MT 180-C1,181-B1
180TH ST E RVT 181-C1
180TH ST E SLT 174-E1,175-B1
180TH ST E VET 179-C1,180-A1
180TH ST N FLT 53-B3,54-A3
180TH ST N MAY 54-B3
180TH ST N NST 54-B3
180TH ST NW BLT 18-B1
180TH ST W FAR 177-D1
180TH ST W LVL 176-D1
180TH ST W SCT 173-D1
180TH ST W SLW 173-A1
180 1/2 CIR NW ER 33-C2
180 1/2 CT NW ER 33-C2
181ST AVE HEI 215-B2
181ST AVE LAT 201-B3,215-B3
181ST AVE NE COT 38-D2
181ST AVE NE HL 36-E2
181ST AVE NW AND 35-E2,36-C2
181ST AVE NW BLT 31-E2,32-A2
181ST AVE NW BT 34-C2
181ST AVE NW ER 33-E2,34-A2
181ST AVE NW RAM 34-E2
181ST CT BLT 18-B3
181ST DR NW ER 33-C2
181ST LN NE COT 37-E2
181ST LN NE EB 36-E2,37-B2
181ST LN NW ER 33-C2,34-A2
181ST LN NW OG 35-E2,36-C2
181ST ST BLT 18-B3
181ST ST ORT 4-B3
181ST ST E RVT 181-D1
181ST ST N NST 54-D3
181ST ST NW BLT 18-B2
181ST ST W LVL 176-C1
182ND AVE BLT 31-E2
182ND AVE ER 33-C2,34-A2
182ND AVE SPT 70-C4
182ND AVE NE EB 37-B2
182ND AVE NW BLT 32-C2,33-A2
182ND AVE NW ER 33-B2,34-A2
182ND AVE NW OG 35-E2,36-A2
182ND AVE SE BKR 3-D1
182ND LN NE COT 37-E2
182ND LN NE EB 37-B2
182ND LN NW BT 35-C2
182ND LN NW ER 33-C2
182ND LN NW OG 35-E2
182ND ST HCT 170-E2,171-B2
182ND ST ORT 4-B4
182ND ST SFT 171-E2,172-A2
182ND ST E SLT 175-A1
182ND ST N FLT 53-E3
182ND ST N MAY 54-D3
182ND ST N NST 54-D3
182ND ST NW ORT 4-B4
182ND ST W LVL 176-D1
182NE LN NW OG 36-A2
183RD AVE BLT 31-E2
183RD AVE ER 34-A2
183RD AVE SMT 83-E1
183RD AVE NE COT 38-D2
183RD AVE NE EB 37-B2
183RD AVE NW BLT 32-C2,33-B2
183RD AVE NW BT 35-B2
183RD AVE NW ER 33-C2
183RD AVE NW OG 35-C2,36-A2
183RD AVE SE BKR 3-D1
183RD LN LAT 201-B3
183RD LN NE EB 37-A2
183RD LN NW BT 35-C2
183RD LN NW OG 35-C2,36-A2
183RD ST ER 33-D2
183RD ST ORT 4-B3
183RD ST NW BLT 18-B1
183RD ST W FAR 177-D1
183RD ST W LVL 176-D1
184TH AVE ER 34-A1
184TH AVE SMT 69-E4
184TH AVE NE COT 38-E1
184TH AVE NE EB 37-B1
184TH AVE NW BLT 32-B2
184TH AVE NW BT 34-C2,35-C1
184TH AVE NW OG 35-D1
184TH AVE SE BKR 3-E1
184TH AVE W CHN 132-C2
184TH AVE W EPR 132-C2
184TH CT ER 34-A1
184TH LN NE EB 37-C1
184TH LN NW OG 35-E1
184TH ST FAR 177-C1
184TH ST ORT 4-B1
184TH ST N FLT 53-C3
184TH ST W FAR 177-D1
184TH ST W LVL 176-C1
185TH AVE NE COT 37-E1,38-D1
185TH AVE NE EB 36-E1
185TH AVE NW BLT 33-A1
185TH AVE NW BT 34-E1,35-A1
185TH AVE NW ER 33-C1
185TH AVE SE BKR 3-E3
185TH LN NE EB 37-B1
185TH LN NW BT 35-C1
185TH LN NW ER 33-C1
185TH LN NW OG 35-C1
185TH ST BNT 113-C4,127-D1
185TH ST E CRT 176-A1
185TH ST E RVT 181-C1
185TH ST E SLT 174-D1
185TH ST N NST 54-E3,55-A3
185TH ST NW ORT 4-B4
185TH ST W FAR 177-D1
185TH ST W LVL 176-C1
185TH ST W SCT 173-C1
185TH ST W SLW 173-A1
186TH AVE BLT 33-B1
186TH AVE NE COT 38-D1
186TH AVE NW BLT 33-A1
186TH AVE NW ER 33-B1
186TH LN NW ER 33-B1
186TH LN NW OG 35-C1
186TH ST BLT 18-A2
186TH ST E SLT 174-C2
186TH ST N FLT 53-E3,54-A3
186TH ST N NST 54-B3
186TH ST NW BLT 18-A2
186TH ST W FAR 177-D2
187TH AVE NW BLT 33-B1
187TH AVE NW BT 35-B1
187TH AVE NW ER 33-B1
187TH AVE W CHN 132-B2
187TH CIR NW BLT 33-A1
187TH CIR NW ER 33-C1
187TH LN NE EB 36-E1
187TH LN NW OG 35-E1
187TH ST ORT 4-A1
187TH ST SFT 172-B3
187TH ST N FLT 53-E3,54-A3
187TH ST N NST 54-B3
187TH ST W FAR 177-D2
188TH AVE NW ER 33-C1
188TH AVE NW OG 35-E1
188TH ST BLT 18-A1
188TH ST ORT 4-A2
188TH ST SFT 171-E3,172-A3
188TH ST E LYT 1-A4
188TH ST E RVT 181-C1
188TH ST N NST 54-D2
188TH ST NW BLT 18-A1
188TH ST NW ORT 4-A4
188TH ST W FAR 177-D2
188TH ST W LVL 176-D2
189TH AVE BKR 3-E1
189TH AVE COT 37-E1,38-A1
189TH AVE NE COT 37-E1,38-E1
189TH AVE NE EB 36-D1,37-A1
189TH AVE NW BT 34-E1,35-C1
189TH AVE NW ER 33-B1,34-B1
189TH AVE NW OG 35-D1
189TH LN EB 37-D1
189TH LN NW BLT 33-B1
189TH LN NW BT 35-A1
189TH LN NW ER 33-B1
189TH LN NW OG 35-D1
189TH ST BLT 18-A1
189TH ST ORT 4-A1
189TH ST E LYT 1-A4
189TH ST E SLT 174-D2
189TH ST N NST 54-B2
189TH ST NW BLT 18-A1
189TH ST W FAR 177-D2
190TH AVE BLT 33-A1
190TH AVE GHT 224-D4
190TH AVE SMT 69-E4,70-C4
190TH AVE SPT 70-D4
190TH AVE NE EB 37-C1
190TH AVE NW BLT 33-A1
190TH AVE NW ER 33-E1,34-A1
190TH AVE NW OG 35-E1,36-B1
190TH AVE SE BKR 3-E1
190TH CIR NW ER 33-D1
190TH CT NW ER 33-E1
190TH LN NE COT 37-E1
190TH LN NE EB 37-C1
190TH LN NW BT 34-E1,35-A1
190TH LN NW ER 33-E1
190TH LN NW OG 35-D1,36-D1
190TH ST BLT 4-A4,18-A1
190TH ST BNT 113-A4
190TH ST ORT 4-A4
190TH ST WIT 113-A4
190TH ST E CRT 175-D2
190TH ST E ET 178-D2
190TH ST E MT 180-C2,181-A2
190TH ST E RVT 181-B2
190TH ST E SLT 174-D2,175-B2
190TH ST E VET 179-B2,180-A2
190TH ST N FLT 53-C2,54-A2
190TH ST N NST 54-B2
190TH ST W ET 178-B2
190TH ST W FAR 177-D2
190TH ST W LVL 176-E2,177-A2
190TH ST W SLW 172-E2,173-A2
190TH WAY LVL 176-D3
190TH STREET WAY WEL 181-E2,182-A2
190 1/2 AVE NW ER 33-E1,34-A1
190 1/2 CIR NW ER 33-B1
191ST AVE BKR 3-E1
191ST AVE ER 33-D1
191ST AVE SMT 70-B4
191ST AVE NE COT 38-D1
191ST AVE NE EB 37-C1
191ST AVE NW BLT 19-A4,33-A1
191ST AVE NW BT 35-A1
191ST AVE NW ER 33-E1,34-A1
191ST AVE NW OG 35-E1,36-B1
191ST CIR NW BLT 19-A4
191ST LN NW BT 34-D1,35-B1
191ST LN NW ER 33-E1
191ST LN NW OG 35-E1,36-C1
191ST ST BLT 4-A4
191ST ST E MT 180-D2
191ST ST N FLT 53-D2
191ST ST N NST 54-B2
191ST ST NW BLT 32-A2
191ST ST W FAR 177-D2
191 1/2 LN NW ER 33-E1
192ND AVE SMT 69-E3
192ND AVE SPT 70-E3
192ND AVE NE EB 22-D4,36-D1
192ND AVE NW BLT 19-A4
192ND AVE NW ER 19-B4,33-C1
192ND AVE NW OG 35-E1,36-C1
192ND AVE W EPR 132-B1
192ND CT BKR 3-E1
192ND CT NW ER 20-A4
192ND LN NW BT 20-E4
192ND LN NW OG 21-E4
192ND ST N NST 54-B2,55-B2
192ND ST NW BLT 32-A2
192ND ST W FAR 177-D2
192ND ST W LVL 176-D2
192 1/2 AVE NW ER 33-C1
192 1/2 LN NW ER 33-C1
193RD AVE BKR 3-E1
193RD AVE NE COT 23-E4,24-A4
193RD AVE NW BLT 18-B4,32-B1
193RD AVE NW ER 19-E4,20-B4
193RD LN NE EB 22-D4
193RD LN NW ER 19-D4
193RD ST FAR 177-D2
193RD ST E LYT 1-A3
193RD ST E RVT 181-B2
193RD ST E SLT 175-C2
193RD ST W FAR 177-D2
193RD WAY E MT 180-E2
193 1/2 CT ER 33-C1
194TH AVE NE EB 23-A4
194TH AVE NW BT 20-C4
194TH AVE NW ER 19-E4
194TH AVE NW OG 21-E4,22-B4
194TH CIR NW ER 19-D4
194TH CT RVT 181-B2
194TH LN NE EB 22-D4
194TH LN NW BT 20-D4
194TH LN NW ER 19-D4
194TH LN NW OG 21-E4,22-A4
194TH ST W ET 177-E2
194TH ST W FAR 177-D2
194TH ST W LVL 176-D2
194TH ST W SLW 172-E2
195TH AVE BLT 17-D4
195TH AVE DNT 201-A4,215-A2
195TH AVE ER 19-C4
195TH AVE NE EB 22-D4,23-D4
195TH AVE NW BT 21-B4
195TH AVE NW ER 19-E4,20-A4
195TH AVE NW OG 21-E4
195TH AVE SE BKR 4-A1
195TH CIR ER 19-E4
195TH CIR NW ER 19-D4
195TH CT BKR 4-A1
195TH CT ER 19-C4
195TH CT NW ER 19-E4,20-A4
195TH LN ER 19-D4
195TH LN NW OG 21-E4,22-C4
195TH ST E CRT 175-E2,176-B2
195TH ST E LYT 1-A3
195TH ST E MT 180-E2
195TH ST E RVT 181-B2
195TH ST E SLT 174-D2
195TH ST N FLT 53-D2
195TH ST N NST 54-E2,55-B2
195TH ST NW BLT 31-E2
195TH ST NW ER 19-E4
195TH ST W FAR 177-C2
195TH ST W LVL 176-C2,177-A2
195TH ST W SCT 173-E2,174-A2
195TH ST W SLW 172-E2,173-A2
196TH AVE BLT 17-D4
196TH AVE NE EB 22-D4,23-B4
196TH AVE NW BLT 18-E4,19-A4
196TH AVE NW ER 19-B4,20-A4
196TH CIR BLT 18-E4
196TH CIR NW ER 19-D4
196TH CT NW ER 19-D4
196TH DR BLT 19-A4
196TH LN ER 19-E4
196TH LN NE EB 22-D4
196TH LN NW OG 22-B4
196TH ST BLT 31-E1
196TH ST E CRT 175-D2
196TH ST N FLT 53-B2
196TH ST N NST 54-C2
196TH ST NW BL 17-E3
196TH ST NW BLT 17-E2
196TH ST NW BT 20-B4
196TH ST NW ER 19-E4,20-A4
197TH AVE NE COT 23-E4,24-A4
197TH AVE NE EB 22-E4,23-C4
197TH AVE NW BLT 18-C4,19-A4
197TH AVE NW ER 19-E4,20-A4
197TH AVE NW OG 21-E4,22-A4
197TH CIR ER 19-B4
197TH LN NW ER 19-B4
197TH LN NW OG 21-C4,22-D4
197TH ST BL 17-E3
197TH ST BLT 31-E2
197TH ST E RVT 181-B2
197TH ST N NST 55-A2
197TH ST NW BLT 17-E1
197TH ST W ET 177-E2,178-A2
197TH ST W FAR 177-D2
197TH ST W LVL 176-B2
198TH AVE SPT 70-E3
198TH AVE NE EB 22-D4
198TH AVE NW BLT 19-A4
198TH AVE NW ER 19-E4,20-A4
198TH AVE NW OG 21-E4,22-A4
198TH CT W LVL 176-D3
198TH LN BT 20-D4
198TH LN NW OG 21-E4,22-C4
198TH ST BLT 31-E2
198TH ST LVL 177-A2
198TH ST E CRT 175-D3
198TH ST E MT 180-D2
198TH ST W ET 178-A2
198TH ST W FAR 177-D3
198TH WAY LVL 176-D3
198TH STREET CIR E MT 180-D2
198TH STREET CT N FLT 53-D2
198 1/2 CIR NW ER 19-C4
199TH AVE BLT 17-D4
199TH AVE NE EB 22-E4,23-C4
199TH AVE NW BLT 18-E4,19-A4
199TH AVE NW BT 21-B4
199TH AVE NW ER 19-E4
199TH AVE NW OG 21-E4,22-A4
199TH CIR BLT 31-E2
199TH CIR NW ER 19-C4
199TH LN NW OG 21-E4,22-A4
199TH ST E RVT 181-D2
199TH ST E SLT 174-E3
199TH ST N FLT 54-A2
199TH ST N NST 55-B2
199TH ST W ET 178-A3
199TH ST W LVL 176-D3
200TH AVE FET 224-E2
200TH AVE SMT 70-B3
200TH AVE NE EB 22-D3,23-B4
200TH AVE NW BLT 19-A4
200TH AVE NW ER 19-B4,20-A4
200TH AVE NW OG 21-C4,22-A4
200TH LN NE EB 23-D3
200TH LN NW OG 21-C3
200TH ST BLT 17-E4,31-E1
200TH ST E CRT 175-C3
200TH ST E ET 178-D3
200TH ST E LYT 1-A3
200TH ST E MT 180-D3,181-A2
200TH ST E RVT 181-C3
200TH ST E SLT 174-E3,175-A3
200TH ST E VET 179-D3,180-A3
200TH ST N FLT 53-D1
200TH ST NW BLT 3-E4,17-E1
200TH ST W ET 177-E3,178-A3
200TH ST W FAR 177-C3
200TH ST W LVL 177-B3
200TH ST W SCT 173-D3,174-A3
201ST AVE BLT 18-D3,19-A3
201ST AVE DNT -E3,214-E1
201ST AVE NW BT 20-D3
201ST AVE NW ER 19-B4,20-B3
201ST AVE NW OG 21-E3,22-A3
201ST CIR BLT 17-D3
201ST CIR NW ER 20-A3
201ST LN NE EB 22-E3
201ST LN NW OG 21-D3
201ST PL LWT 23-E3
201ST ST DNT 214-E2
201ST ST NW BLT 17-D2
201ST ST W ET 178-A3
201ST ST W LVL 176-D3
202ND AVE NW BLT 17-E3
202ND AVE NW ER 19-B3,20-A3
202ND AVE NW OG 22-B3
202ND CT W SLT 174-E3
202ND LN NE LWT 23-E3
202ND LN NW OG 21-E3
202ND ST E RVT 181-E3
202ND ST E VET 179-A3
202ND ST N FLT 53-B1,54-A1
202ND ST N NST 54-E1
202ND ST NW BLT 17-D2
202ND ST W ET 177-E3,178-A3
202ND ST W LVL 176-E3,177-A3
202ND STREET WAY WEL 181-E3
203RD AVE NE EB 22-E3,23-B3
203RD AVE NW BLT 18-B3
203RD AVE NW BT 20-C3
203RD AVE NW ER 20-A3
203RD AVE NW OG 22-B3
203RD CT FAR 177-D3
203RD CT E SLT 174-E3
203RD LN NE EB 22-E3
203RD ST E RVT 181-D3
203RD ST E SLT 175-B3
203RD ST N FLT 54-A1
203RD ST NW BLT 17-D2
203RD ST W ET 178-A3
203RD ST W FAR 177-D3
203RD ST W LVL 176-C3
204TH AVE BLT 18-C3
204TH AVE NW BT 21-A3
204TH AVE NW OG 22-A3
204TH CIR BLT 18-D3
204TH LN NE EB 23-D3
204TH LN NW OG 21-D3,22-A3
204TH ST E CRT 175-E3,176-A3
204TH ST N FLT 54-A1
204TH ST W FAR 177-D3
204TH ST W LVL 176-E3
204TH STREET CT N FLT 54-A1

205TH AVE BLT 18-D3
205TH AVE FET 224-E3
205TH AVE GHT 224-E4
205TH AVE SMT 69-E2,70-B2
205TH AVE SPT 70-D2
205TH AVE NE EB 22-E3,23-A3
205TH AVE NE LWT 24-C3,25-A3
205TH AVE NW BT 20-C3
205TH AVE NW ER 19-E3,20-A3
205TH AVE NW OG 21-E3,22-B3
205TH CT W LVL 176-D3
205TH LN DNT 214-E4
205TH LN NE EB 22-E3
205TH LN NW OG 21-D3,22-D3
205TH ST BLT 17-D2
205TH ST FET 224-E1
205TH ST E MT 180-C3
205TH ST E RVT 181-D3
205TH ST E SLT 174-C3,175-B3
205TH ST E VET 179-E3,180-A3
205TH ST N NST 54-E1,55-C1
205TH ST W ET 177-E3
205TH ST W LVL 176-C3,177-A3
206TH AVE BL 17-E3
206TH AVE NE EB 22-D3
206TH AVE NW BLT 17-E3
206TH AVE NW OG 21-E3,22-C3
206TH LN NW OG 21-D3,22-C3
206TH ST BKR 3-D4,17-D1
206TH ST E SLT 175-A3
206TH ST N FLT 54-A1
206TH ST W FAR 177-E3
206TH ST W LVL 176-D3,177-A3
207TH AVE BLT 18-E3
207TH AVE SMT 70-B2
207TH AVE NE EB 22-D3,23-A3
207TH AVE NE LWT 24-A3
207TH AVE NW BLT 18-E3,19-A3
207TH AVE NW BT 20-E3,21-A3
207TH AVE NW ER 19-E3,20-A3
207TH AVE NW OG 21-E3,22-A3
207TH CIR NW BLT 18-E3
207TH CT W LVL 176-E3
207TH LN NE EB 22-E3,23-A3
207TH ST BLT 17-D4
207TH ST E CRT 175-E3,176-A3
207TH ST E RVT 181-D3
207TH ST E SLT 175-A3
207TH ST N FLT 53-D1,54-A1
207TH ST N NST 54-B1
207TH ST NW BLT 3-D4,17-D1
207TH ST W FAR 177-E3
207TH ST W LVL 176-E3,177-A3
208TH AVE ER 20-A2
208TH AVE SMT 69-D3
208TH AVE NE EB 22-D3
208TH AVE NW ER 19-D3,20-A3
208TH AVE NW OG 21-D3,22-D3
208TH CIR NW OG 21-D3
208TH CT W LVL 177-A3
208TH LN NE EB 23-A3
208TH LN NW OG 21-E3,22-B3
208TH RD CP 65-E3
208TH ST E SLT 175-B3
208TH ST N FLT 53-D1
208TH ST NW BLT 3-D4
208TH ST W ET 178-A3
208TH ST W FAR 177-E3
208TH ST W LVL 176-D3,177-A3
208TH STREET CT N FLT 53-D1
209TH AVE FET 224-E2
209TH AVE NE EB 22-E3,23-A3
209TH AVE NW BLT 18-E3,19-A3
209TH AVE NW ER 19-B3,20-B3
209TH AVE NW OG 22-A3
209TH CT NE EB 23-A2
209TH LN NE EB 23-A2
209TH LN NE LWT 23-E2
209TH LN NW OG 21-D3,22-C3
209TH ST N FLT 53-D1,54-A1
209TH ST N NST 41-A4,55-B1
209TH ST W ET 177-E3,178-A3
209TH ST W LVL 176-E3,177-A3
210TH AVE SMT 69-E2,70-A2
210TH AVE SPT 70-E2
210TH AVE NE EB 23-A2
210TH AVE NW BT 21-C2
210TH AVE NW ER 19-B2
210TH CIR NW ER 19-C2
210TH LN N FLT 39-C4
210TH LN NW OG 21-D2,22-D2
210TH ST E CRT 175-D4,176-B4
210TH ST E ET 178-D3
210TH ST E MT 180-E3,181-A3
210TH ST E SLT 174-E4
210TH ST E VET 178-E3,179-C3
210TH ST N FLT 39-D4,40-A4
210TH ST W ET 178-B4
210TH ST W FAR 177-C4
210TH ST W LVL 176-C4,177-A4
210TH ST W SCT 173-B4
210TH LN CIR N FLT 39-C4
210TH LN CT N FLT 39-C4
210TH STREET CT N FLT 40-A4
211TH AVE BLT 17-D2
211TH AVE DNT ....-D3,214-D1
211TH AVE NE EB 23-A2
211TH AVE NW BLT 18-D2
211TH AVE NW BT 20-D2
211TH AVE NW ER 19-B2
211TH AVE NW OG 21-E2,22-B2
211TH CIR NW ER 19-C2
211TH LN NE EB 23-A2
211TH LN NW OG 21-D2,22-A2
211TH ST OST 28-E4
211TH ST SAT 14-E3
211TH ST W FAR 177-D4
211TH ST W LVL 176-E4
212TH AVE BLT 17-E2
212TH AVE NE EB 22-E2,23-C2
212TH AVE NW BLT 19-A2
212TH AVE NW BT 21-B2
212TH AVE NW ER 19-C2
212TH AVE NW OG 22-A2
212TH LN NE EB 23-A2
212TH LN NW OG 21-D2,22-D2
212TH ST WIT 113-C2
212TH ST N FLT 39-E4
212TH ST W FAR 177-C4
212TH ST W LVL 176-E4
212TH STREET CT N FLT 39-E4
213TH AVE BLT 17-D2
213TH AVE NE EB 23-C2
213TH AVE NW BT 21-A2
213TH AVE NW ER 19-E2,20-B2
213TH AVE NW OG 21-D2
213TH LN NE LWT 24-A2
213TH LN NW OG 22-A2
213TH PL NE LWT 24-A2
213TH ST ADT 42-E3
213TH ST E SLT 174-E4,175-B4
213TH ST N FLT 39-D4
213TH ST N NST 40-B4,41-A4
213TH ST W ET 177-E4,178-A4
213TH ST W FAR 177-E4
213TH ST W LVL 177-A4
213TH ST W SLW 172-B4
213TH STREET CIR N FLT 39-D4
214TH AVE BLT 17-E2
214TH AVE SMT 70-A2
214TH AVE SPT 70-D2
214TH AVE NE EB 22-E2,23-A2
214TH AVE NW BLT 18-E2
214TH AVE NW ER 19-B2
214TH AVE NW OG 21-C2,22-B2
214TH LN NE EB 22-E2
214TH LN NW OG 21-D2,22-A2
214TH ST N FLT 39-D4
214TH ST N NST 41-A4
214TH ST W LVL 177-A4
214TH ST W SLW 173-A4
214TH STREET CT N FLT 39-C4
215TH AVE BLT 17-D2
215TH AVE SMT 70-B1
215TH AVE NE EB 22-E2
215TH AVE NE LWT 24-B2
215TH AVE NW BLT 18-E2
215TH AVE NW ER 20-B2
215TH AVE NW HOP 20-A2
215TH AVE NW OG 21-D2,22-A2
215TH LN NE EB 22-D2,23-E2
215TH LN NE LWT 23-E2,24-A2
215TH LN NW OG 22-B2
215TH ST ADT 42-E3
215TH ST OST 42-E1
215TH ST WIT 113-A2
215TH ST E SLT 174-C4
215TH ST E VET 179-B4
215TH ST N FLT 39-E4,40-A4
215TH ST N NST 41-A4
215TH ST W LVL 176-D4,177-A4
215TH ST W SCT 173-B4
215TH STREET CT N NST 40-B4
216TH AVE SMT 69-E1
216TH AVE NE EB 22-E2,23-B2
216TH AVE NE LWT 24-C2
216TH AVE NW BLT 18-E2
216TH AVE NW ER 20-A2
216TH AVE NW OG 21-E2
216TH LN NW OG 22-B2
216TH ST E LYT 1-A1
216TH ST N FLT 39-D4,40-A4
216TH ST N NST 40-B4
217TH AVE SMT 69-E1,70-A1
217TH AVE SPT 70-E1
217TH AVE NE EB 22-D2,23-D2
217TH AVE NE LWT 24-D2
217TH AVE NW BLT 17-D2,18-E2
217TH AVE NW ER 19-C2
217TH AVE NW OG 21-E2,22-D2
217TH LN NE LWT 24-B2
217TH ST ADT 56-E2
217TH ST E CRT 175-D4
217TH ST E SLT 175-C4
217TH ST N FLT 39-A4,40-A4
217TH ST N NST 40-B4
218TH AVE BLT 18-A2
218TH AVE NE EB 22-D2
218TH AVE NW BLT 18-B2
218TH AVE NW BT 21-A2
218TH AVE NW ER 20-B2
218TH AVE NW OG 21-D2
218TH CT N NST 40-B4
218TH LN NW OG 22-B2
218TH ST ADT 42-E2
218TH ST OST 28-E2,42-E1
218TH ST SCF 14-E3
218TH ST E RVT 181-D4
218TH ST E SLW 172-E4,173-A4
218TH ST N FLT 39-C4
218TH ST N NST 40-C4
218TH ST W LVL 177-A4
218TH STREET PL N FLT 39-C4
218TH STREET WAY WEL 181-E4,182-C4
218TH STREET WAY N FLT 39-C4
219TH AVE BLT 18-C1
219TH AVE NE EB 22-E1,23-B1
219TH AVE NW BLT 18-D1,19-A1
219TH AVE NW ER 19-E1
219TH AVE NW OG 21-D1,22-C1
219TH LN EB 23-C1
219TH LN NE EB 22-D1
219TH LN NE LWT 24-C1
219TH LN NW OG 21-C1,22-C1
219TH ST E CRT 190-A1
219TH ST N FLT 40-A4
219TH ST W LVL 177-A4,191-A1
220TH AVE BLT 17-D1
220TH AVE SMT 70-B1
220TH AVE SPT 70-E1
220TH AVE NE EB 22-D1
220TH AVE NE LWT 24-C1
220TH AVE NW BLT 18-B1
220TH AVE NW OG 21-D1
220TH LN NE LWT 24-C1
220TH ST ADT 56-E3
220TH ST FAT 42-E4,56-E1
220TH ST OST 14-E4
220TH ST SAT 14-E3
220TH ST SCF 14-E3
220TH ST WIT 113-A1
220TH ST E CLT 188-D1,189-B1
220TH ST E ET 178-D4
220TH ST E MT 180-D4,181-A4
220TH ST E SLT 188-C1,189-A1
220TH ST E VET 179-E4,180-A4
220TH ST N FL 39-A3
220TH ST N NST 40-B3,41-B3
220TH ST W BPT 186-E1
220TH ST W ET 178-C4,192-B1
220TH ST W LVL 191-A1
220TH ST W SCT 187-D1,188-A1
220TH ST W SLW 186-D1
220TH STREET CT N FLT 39-B4
221ST AVE BLT 17-D1,18-C1
221ST AVE DNT ....-C4,214-C3
221ST AVE SMT 69-C1
221ST AVE SPT 70-D1
221ST AVE NE EB 22-E1,23-A1
221ST AVE NW BLT 18-B1,19-A1
221ST AVE NW ER 19-D1,20-B1
221ST AVE NW OG 21-E1,22-C1
221ST ST E NMT 189-E1,190-A1
221ST ST N FLT 40-A3
222ND AVE SMT 69-E1
222ND AVE NW BLT 18-E1
222ND AVE NW ER 19-D1
222ND AVE NW OG 21-C1
222ND LN NW OG 21-E1,22-D1
222ND ST WIT 113-C1
222ND ST E HMT 193-B1
222ND ST E NMT 190-B1
222ND ST NE EB 23-B1
223RD AVE BLT 18-C1
223RD AVE NE EB 22-D1
223RD AVE NW BLT 18-D1
223RD AVE NW BT 20-C1
223RD AVE NW ER 19-D1
223RD AVE NW OG 21-E1
223RD LN BLT 18-D1
223RD LN EB 23-C1
223RD LN NE EB 23-A1
223RD LN NE LWT 24-B1
223RD ST N FLT 40-A3
223RD ST N NST 41-A3
223RD ST NW ER 19-D1
223RD ST W HAT 188-A1
223RD STREET CT N FLT 40-A3
224TH AVE BLT 18-A1
224TH AVE NE EB 23-D1
224TH AVE NE LWT 24-C1
224TH AVE NW BLT 18-C1
224TH AVE NW OG 21-D1
224TH LN NE EB 22-D1
224TH ST N FLT 39-E3
225TH AVE BLT 18-A1
225TH AVE NE EB 22-E1,23-A1
225TH AVE NE LWT 24-B1
225TH AVE NW BLT 18-D1,19-A1
225TH AVE NW BT 20-C1
225TH AVE NW ER 19-D1
225TH AVE NW OG 21-E1
225TH LN NE EB 23-B1
225TH LN NE LWT 24-C1
225TH LN NW OG 21-D1,22-C1
225TH ST WEL 195-E1
225TH ST WIT 113-A1
225TH ST E HMT 193-C1
225TH ST E NMT 190-C1
225TH ST N NST 40-B3
225TH ST NW ER 19-E1
225TH ST W BEL 186-A1
225TH ST W BPT 186-B1
225TH ST W CAT 192-A1
225TH ST W EUT 190-E1,191-B1
225TH ST W HAT 187-B1
226TH AVE BKR 3-D4,17-D1
226TH AVE BLT 18-D1
226TH AVE NE BLT 17-E1
226TH AVE NE EB 22-E1
226TH AVE NE LWT 23-E1,24-B1
226TH AVE NW BLT 17-E1,18-A1
226TH AVE NW ER 20-B1
226TH AVE NW OG 22-B1
226TH AVE NW SF 21-D1
226TH CIR NW ER 20-B1
226TH LN NE EB 9-B4,23-A1
226TH LN NE LWT 10-B4
227TH AVE BLT 4-A4,18-A1
227TH AVE SF 7-E4
227TH AVE NE EB 9-A4
227TH AVE NE LWT 10-B4
227TH AVE NW BLT 3-E4,4-D4
227TH AVE NW OG 8-B4,22-C1
227TH AVE NW SF 7-D4,21-D1
227TH CT SF 7-D4
227TH CT NW SF 7-D4
227TH LN NE EB 8-D4
227TH LN NE LWT 10-A4
227TH PL NE LWT 10-B4
227TH ST N FLT 39-E3
227TH ST NW ER 5-B4
227TH STREET CT N FLT 39-E3
228TH AVE BLT 4-D4
228TH AVE NE EB 9-C4
228TH AVE NE LWT 10-B4
228TH AVE NW BLT 4-E4
228TH AVE NW SF 7-E4
228TH LN NE LWT 10-B4
228TH LN NW OG 8-C4
228TH PL NE LWT 10-B4
228TH ST E NMT 189-E1,190-C1
228TH ST N FLT 40-A3
228TH ST N NST 40-C3
228TH ST W BPT 186-D1
228TH STREET WAY WEL 196-B1
229TH AVE BLT 4-C4
229TH AVE ORT 4-D4
229TH AVE NE EB 8-E4,9-B4
229TH AVE NE LWT 9-E4,10-B4
229TH AVE NW BLT 3-D4
229TH AVE NW BT 7-C4
229TH AVE NW SF 7-A4,8-C4
229TH LN NE EB 8-E4,9-A4
229TH LN NW SF 7-E4
229TH ST N FLT 39-D3
229TH ST NE EB 8-D4
229TH ST W HAT 188-A2
230TH AVE ORT 4-D4
230TH AVE SMT 55-D4,56-A4
230TH AVE NE LWT 10-B4
230TH AVE NW LIT 6-B4
230TH AVE NW SF 7-D4,8-C4
230TH CT NW SF 7-C4,8-A4
230TH LN NW SF 7-C4,8-A4
230TH ST FAT 42-D3,56-D1
230TH ST OST 42-D1
230TH ST WIT 99-A4
230TH ST E CAT 192-D1
230TH ST E CLT 188-E2,189-A2
230TH ST E DT 194-B1,195-A1
230TH ST E HMT 193-E1
230TH ST E NMT 189-E2,190-A2
230TH ST E WEL 195-B1,196-A1
230TH ST N FLT 39-D3,40-A3
230TH ST N NST 40-E3,41-B3
230TH ST W BKT 185-C2
230TH ST W BPT 186-B2,187-A2
230TH ST W CAT 192-B2
230TH ST W HAT 187-D2
230TH STREET LN N FLT 39-D3
230TH STREET WAY WEL 195-C1
231ST AVE DNT 214-B2
231ST AVE ORT 4-D4
231ST AVE NE LWT 10-B4
231ST AVE NW LIT 5-B4
231ST AVE NW SF 7-C4,8-C4
231ST LN DNT ....-B4
231ST LN NE EB 8-E4,9-D4
231ST LN NE LWT 10-B4
231ST LN NW SF 7-E4,8-B4
231ST ST N FLT 39-D3
231ST ST NW SF 7-E4
232ND AVE ORT 4-C4
232ND AVE SMT 55-E4,56-A4
232ND AVE NE LWT 10-B4
232ND AVE NW ORT 4-A4
232ND AVE NW SF 7-C4
232ND LN NW SF 7-E4,8-A4
232ND ST ORT 4-D4
232ND ST E CAT 192-E2
232ND ST E HMT 192-E2,193-A2
232ND ST N FL 39-A2
232ND ST N FLT 39-D2
232ND ST N NST 40-C2
232 1/2 AVE ORT 4-B4
233RD AVE ORT 4-E4,5-A4
233RD AVE NE EB 8-E4,9-A4
233RD AVE NE LWT 9-E4,10-A4
233RD AVE NW LIT 5-B4
233RD AVE NW ORT 5-A4
233RD AVE NW SF 6-E4,7-D4
233RD CT NW SF 7-C4
233RD LN NW SF 7-E4,8-A4
233RD ST OST 28-D4
233RD ST E CLT 188-D2
233RD ST E NMT 189-D2
233RD ST N FLT 39-D2
233 1/4 AVE NW ORT 4-B4
233 1/2 AVE ORT 4-B4
233 1/2 AVE NW ORT 4-B4
233 3/4 AVE ORT 4-B4
234TH AVE ORT 4-A4
234TH AVE NE EB 8-E4,9-A4
234TH AVE NE LWT 10-B4
234TH AVE NW ORT 4-B4
234TH AVE NW SF 7-D4
234TH CT NW SF 7-C4,8-A4
234TH LN NE EB 8-E3,9-D3
234TH LN NW SF 7-C4
234TH ST E NMT 190-B2
234 1/2 AVE ORT 4-B4
234 1/2 AVE NW ORT 4-B4
235TH AVE ORT 4-B4
235TH AVE NE EB 8-E4
235TH AVE NW SF 7-E3,8-C4
235TH LN DNT ....-B4
235TH LN NE LWT 10-A3
235TH LN NW SF 7-C3
235TH ST OST 28-C3
235TH ST SAT 14-C3
235TH ST WEL 196-B2
235TH ST WIT 99-C4
235TH ST E CLT 189-B2
235TH ST E NMT 190-C2
235TH ST N FL 39-A2
235TH ST N FLT 39-E2,40-A2
235TH ST N NST 41-B2
235TH ST W BPT 186-D2
235TH ST W EUT 190-E2,191-C2
235TH ST W HAT 188-A2
236TH AVE NW SF 7-B3,8-C3
236TH LN NE BET 8-D3
236TH LN NW SF 7-C3
236TH ST N NST 40-E2
236TH ST NW SF 7-D3
236TH STREET CIR N FLT 39-C2
236TH STREET CT N FLT 39-C2
237TH AVE ORT 4-C3
237TH AVE SMT 56-A3
237TH AVE NE BET 8-D3
237TH AVE NE EB 8-E3,9-A3
237TH AVE NE LWT 9-E3,10-B3
237TH AVE NW BET 8-D3
237TH AVE NW LIT 5-E3,6-A3
237TH AVE NW SF 8-B3
237TH ST E NMT 189-E2,190-C2
237TH ST N NST 40-E2
237TH STREET CT N FLT 39-C2
238TH AVE FAT 42-A1
238TH AVE ORT 4-D3
238TH AVE NE BET 8-D3
238TH AVE NE LWT 10-D3,11-A3
238TH AVE NW ORT 4-D3
238TH AVE NW SF 7-B3
238TH LN EB 8-D3
238TH LN NE EB 8-D3
238TH ST E NT 193-E2
238TH ST N NST 40-C2
238TH STREET CT N FLT 39-C2
239TH AVE ORT 4-A3
239TH AVE SMT 55-E3,56-A3
239TH AVE NE EB 9-D3
239TH AVE NE LWT 9-E3,10-B3
239TH AVE NW LIT 5-D3
239TH AVE NW SF 7-E3,8-A3
239TH LN NE LWT 10-D3
239TH ST E NT 193-E2
239TH ST N FLT 39-E2,40-A2
239TH ST N NST 40-C2
239TH STREET CT NST 40-C2
240TH AVE LIT 6-B3
240TH AVE ORT 4-D3
240TH AVE NE LWT 10-D3
240TH AVE NW LIT 5-E3
240TH AVE NW SF 7-B3
240TH CT WIT 99-C3
240TH LN NW SF 7-B3
240TH ST CGT 40-B2
240TH ST FAT 42-C3,56-C2
240TH ST OST 28-C2,42-C1
240TH ST E CLT 188-C2,189-C2
240TH ST E DT 194-D2,195-B2
240TH ST E HMP 193-B2
240TH ST E HMT 193-D2,194-A2
240TH ST E MIE 194-E2,195-A2
240TH ST E NMT 189-D2,190-B2
240TH ST N FLT 39-B2,40-A2
240TH ST N FRT 41-B2
240TH ST N NST 40-D2
240TH ST N WYO 39-A2
240TH ST W BPT 186-D3,187-A3
240TH ST W CAT 191-E2,192-B2
240TH ST W EUT 190-E2,191-A2
240TH ST W HAT 187-E3,188-A3
241ST AVE DNT ....-A4,214-A2
241ST AVE EB 8-E3
241ST AVE ORT 4-B3
241ST AVE NE EB 8-E3,9-A3
241ST AVE NE LWT 10-D3
241ST AVE NW LIT 6-B3
241ST AVE NW SF 7-C3
241ST LN NE BET 8-D3
241ST LN NE EB 8-E3

241ST LN NE LWT .10-C3
241ST WAY NE EB .8-E3
241 1/2 AVE ORT .4-B3
242ND AVE ORT .4-B3
242ND AVE NE EB .8-E3
242ND AVE NE LWT .10-C3
242ND AVE NW SF .8-A3
242ND CT E NMT .190-C3
242ND LN NE EB .8-E3
242ND LN NE LWT .10-D3
242ND ST WYT .39-D2
242ND ST E CLT .189-B3
242ND ST N WYT .39-E2
242ND WAY NE EB .8-E3
243RD AVE DNT .-A3
243RD AVE LIT .5-E3
243RD AVE ORT .4-A3
243RD AVE NE EB .8-D3
243RD AVE NE LWT .10-D3
243RD AVE NW LIT .5-D3
243RD AVE NW SF .8-A3
243RD CIR NE EB .8-E3
243RD CIR NE LWT .10-C3
243RD LN NE EB .8-E3
243RD LN NE LWT .10-C2
243RD ST CGT .40-B2
243RD ST N WYT .39-E2
243RD ST W EUT .190-E3
244TH AVE NE EB .8-E2
244TH AVE NE LWT .10-D2
244TH CIR NE LWT .10-C2
244TH LN NE LWT .10-C2
244TH ST N CGT .40-C1
244TH ST N WYT .39-E1
244TH STREET WAY WEL .196-B2
245TH AVE DNT .214-A2
245TH AVE ORT .4-D2
245TH AVE NE EB .8-E2,9-A2
245TH AVE NE LWT .10-C2
245TH AVE NE OXT .10-E2
245TH AVE NW LIT .5-E2,6-B2
245TH AVE NW SF .6-E3,8-C2
245TH ST FAT .42-C2
245TH ST WIT .99-C3
245TH ST E CAT .192-D3
245TH ST E CLT .188-C3
245TH ST E NMT .190-B3
245TH ST N CGT .40-C1
245TH ST N WYT .39-B1
245TH ST W BKT .185-D3
245TH ST W BPT .186-D3
245TH ST W CAT .192-C3
245TH ST W EUT .190-D3,191-C3
245TH ST W HAT .187-E3,188-A3
246TH AVE NW LIT .5-E2
246TH AVE NW ORT .4-B2
246TH CIR LIT .5-E2
246TH CIR NW ORT .4-B2
247TH AVE LIT .5-E2
247TH AVE NW LIT .5-B2
247TH ST OST .28-B2
247TH ST E CLT .188-C3
247TH ST E NMT .190-B3
247TH ST W EUT .190-E3,191-B3
248TH AVE NW LIT .5-E2,6-B2
248TH ST OST .28-B3
248TH ST W HAT .187-C3
249TH AVE NE ATT .8-E2,9-C2
249TH AVE NE OXT .10-D2
249TH AVE NW ATT .8-B2
249TH AVE NW LIT .5-D2
249TH AVE NW STT .6-D2
250TH AVE NW LIT .5-B2
250TH LN NW STT .7-E2
250TH ST FAT .42-B3,56-B2
250TH ST OST .28-B3
250TH ST E CAT .192-E3
250TH ST E CLT .188-E3,189-B3
250TH ST E DT .194-B3,195-A3
250TH ST E HMT .193-D3,194-A3
250TH ST E NMT .189-D3,190-C3
250TH ST N CGT .40-B1
250TH ST N WYT .39-A1
250TH ST W BKT .184-E4,185-B3
250TH ST W BPT .186-A3,187-A3
250TH ST W CAT .191-E3,192-B3
250TH ST W EUT .190-E3,191-A3
250TH ST W HAT .187-B3
251ST AVE LIT .6-A2
251ST AVE TYT .199-E3,213-E1
251ST AVE NW LIT .5-E2
251ST LN TYT .213-E3
251ST LN NW STT .7-E2
251ST ST N WYT .39-A1
252ND AVE LIT .6-B2
252ND AVE NW LIT .5-E2
252ND ST N CGT .40-D1
252ND ST N WYT .39-A1
252ND ST W HAT .187-D4
252RD AVE NW LIT .5-B2
253RD AVE ORT .4-B2
253RD AVE NE ATT .8-E1,9-D1
253RD AVE NE OXT .9-E1,10-B1
253RD AVE NW LIT .5-C2,6-B2
253RD AVE NW ORT .4-D1
253RD AVE NW STT .6-C2,7-B2
253RD ST CGT .26-B4,40-B1
253RD ST E CLT .188-C4
253RD ST N CGT .26-B4
253RD ST N WYT .25-A4,39-E1
253 1/2 AVE ORT .4-D1
254TH AVE LIT .5-B1
254TH AVE NW LIT .6-B1
254TH AVE NW ORT .4-D1
255TH AVE ORT .4-E1,5-A1
255TH AVE NW LIT .5-B1,6-B1
255TH AVE NW STT .6-C1
255TH ST FRT .27-D4
255TH ST E CLT .189-B4
255TH ST E NMT .189-E4
255TH ST N CGT .26-E4
255TH ST N FRT .26-E4,27-A4
255TH ST N WYT .25-C4,26-A4
255TH ST W BPT .186-D4
255TH ST W CAT .191-E4,192-A4
255TH ST W EUT .191-C4
255TH ST W HAT .187-C4
256TH AVE NW LIT .5-B1,6-A1
256TH AVE NW ORT .4-D1
256TH AVE NW STT .7-E1,8-A1
256TH ST CGT .26-B4
256TH ST WYT .25-C4
256TH ST N CGT .26-C4
256TH ST N WYT .25-D4
257TH AVE ORT .4-D1
257TH AVE NE ATT .9-B1
257TH AVE NW ATT .8-B1
257TH AVE NW LIT .5-B1,6-B1
257TH AVE NW STT .6-C1
257TH ST WYO .25-B4
257TH ST N WYT .25-D4
257TH ST W EUT .190-D4,191-A4
257TH ST W HAT .187-E4
258TH AVE NW LIT .6-A1
258TH LN NW STT .6-C1
258TH ST WYO .25-B4
258TH ST N CGT .26-B4
258TH ST N WYT .25-C4
259TH AVE NE ATT .9-C1
259TH AVE NE OXT .9-E1,10-A1
259TH AVE NW LIT .6-B1
259TH ST WYO .25-B4
259TH ST E NMT .190-D4
259TH ST N CGT .26-E4
259TH ST N FRT .26-E4,27-A4
260TH AVE ORT .4-E1
260TH ST FAT .56-A3
260TH ST WEL .195-C4
260TH ST WYO .25-B4
260TH ST E CAT .192-D4
260TH ST E CLT .188-C4,189-B4
260TH ST E DT .194-B4,195-B4
260TH ST E HMT .193-B4,194-A4
260TH ST E NMT .189-D4,190-B4
260TH ST N FRT .27-B4
260TH ST N WYT .25-C4
260TH ST W BKT .185-C4
260TH ST W BPT .186-B4
260TH ST W CAT .192-B4
260TH ST W HAT .187-B4,188-A4
261ST AVE LIT .5-B1
261ST AVE ORT .4-D1,5-A1
261ST AVE NE ATT .8-E1,9-A1
261ST AVE NE ORT .4-B1
261ST AVE NE OXT .10-B1
261ST AVE NW ATT .8-C1
261ST AVE NW LIT .5-E1,6-A1
261ST AVE NW STT .6-C1,7-D1
261ST LN WYO .25-A4
261ST ST WYO .25-B4
261ST ST N WYT .25-C4
262ND AVE NW LIT .5-E1,6-A1
262ND AVE NW ORT .5-A1
262ND CT LIT .5-E1
262ND ST WYO .25-A4
262ND ST N CGT .26-C4
262ND ST N WYT .25-C4
263RD AVE ORT .4-C1
263RD CT WYO .25-A4
263RD ST WYO .25-B4
263RD ST E CLT .202-C1
263RD ST E NMT .204-D1
263RD ST N CGT .26-E3
263RD ST N WYT .25-C4
263RD ST W BKT .198-E1,199-A1
263RD ST W BPT .-D1
263RD ST W CAT .206-A1
264TH CT WYO .25-A3
264TH ST WYO .25-B3
264TH ST WYT .25-C3
264TH ST W CAT .206-A1
264TH STREET PATH VAT .195-E4,209-E1
265TH ST WEL .195-C4,209-D1
265TH ST E CAT .206-E1
265TH ST E CLT .202-E1
265TH ST E EKO .204-B1
265TH ST W BPT .-C1
265TH ST W EUT .205-D1
265TH ST W HAT .201-E1
266TH CT WYO .25-B3
266TH ST WYO .25-B3
266TH ST E EKO .204-B1
267TH CT WYO .25-B3
267TH ST FAT .41-E2
267TH ST WEL .209-C1
267TH ST WYO .25-B3
267TH ST E CLT .202-E1
267TH ST E EKO .204-B1
267TH ST E NMT .204-D1
267TH ST N WYT .25-C3
267TH ST W EUT .204-E1,205-A1
268TH ST WYO .25-B3
268TH ST N CGT .26-E3
268TH ST N FRT .27-A3
269TH ST WYO .25-B3
269TH ST N WYT .25-D3
270TH ST FAT .41-E4,55-E2
270TH ST WYO .25-B3
270TH ST E CAT .206-D1
270TH ST E CLT .202-D1,203-B1
270TH ST E DT .208-C1
270TH ST E EKO .204-B1
270TH ST E HMT .206-E1,207-A1
270TH ST E NMT .203-E1,204-C1
270TH ST N CGT .26-E3
270TH ST N WYT .25-E3,26-A3
270TH ST W BKT .199-B1
270TH ST W BPT .-E1,201-A1
270TH ST W CAT .206-B1
270TH ST W HAT .201-C1,202-A1
271ST ST WYO .25-B3
271ST ST WYT .25-C3
272ND CT N WYT .25-C3
272ND ST WYO .25-B3
272ND ST N FRT .27-B3
272ND ST NE DT .208-E1,209-A1
272ND ST W EUT .205-A1
273RD ST WYO .25-B3
273RD ST E NMT .204-B1
273RD ST N WYT .26-A3
273RD ST W BPT .-B2
274TH ST WYO .25-B3
275TH ST E NMT .203-E2,204-A2
275TH ST N CGT .26-B2
275TH ST N WYT .25-E2,26-A2
275TH ST W CAT .205-E2,206-A2
275TH ST W HAT .201-C2
276TH ST N CGT .26-B2
276TH ST N WYT .26-A2
277TH ST CHC .26-B2
277TH ST N WYT .25-B2
277TH ST W CAT .206-B2
278TH ST CHC .26-B2
278TH ST E NMT .203-E2
278TH ST W CAT .205-E2
279TH ST CGT .26-D2
279TH ST CHC .26-B2
279TH ST N CGT .26-D2
279TH ST N CHC .26-B2
279TH ST N WYT .25-B2
280TH ST CHC .26-B2
280TH ST FAT .41-D3,55-D2
280TH ST FET .210-C2
280TH ST E CAT .206-D2
280TH ST E CLT .202-C2,203-B2
280TH ST E DT .208-C2,209-A2
280TH ST E HMT .206-E2,207-C2
280TH ST E NMT .203-D2,204-C2
280TH ST N FRT .26-E2,27-A2
280TH ST N WYT .25-A2
280TH ST W BKT .198-E2,199-B2
280TH ST W BPT .199-E2
280TH ST W CAT .205-E2,206-B2
280TH ST W CLT .202-C2
280TH ST W EUT .204-E2,205-B2
280TH ST W HAT .201-C2,202-A2
280TH ST W NMT .204-A2
280TH ST W WT .204-B2
281ST ST CHC .26-B2
282ND ST CHC .26-B2
282ND ST N CGT .26-C2
282ND STREET WAY VAT .210-A2
284TH ST CHC .26-B2
285TH ST FET .210-E2
285TH ST N CGT .26-C1
285TH ST N FRT .27-D1
285TH ST N WYT .25-B2
285TH ST W GVT .205-A3
286TH ST DNT .-C3
286TH ST WYT .26-A2
287TH ST CFT .208-E3
287TH ST E RAT .207-E3
287TH ST N WYT .25-B2
288TH LN DNT .-A3
288TH ST N CGT .26-D1
288TH ST N WYT .25-E1
289TH CT CGT .26-D1
290TH AVE DBT .182-E3
290TH ST DNT .-E3,201-A3
290TH ST FET .210-E3
290TH ST LAT .201-B3,202-B3
290TH ST E RAN .207-A3
290TH ST E SIT .206-D3
290TH ST W GVT .205-D3
290TH ST W SIT .206-C3
290TH ST W WFT .205-E3
290TH STREET WAY CFT .208-C3
291ST ST E RAN .207-A3
291ST ST N FRT .26-E1,27-A1
292ND CT RAT .207-B3
292ND ST CHC .26-A1
292ND ST E RAN .207-A3
292ND ST E RAT .206-E3,207-C3
292ND ST N CGT .26-C1
292ND ST N LND .26-D1
292ND ST W GVT .205-B3
293RD ST VAT .210-B3
294TH ST E RAT .207-C3
294TH ST CT RAT .207-C3
295TH AVE DBT .182-E3
295TH LN LND .26-D1
295TH ST FET .210-E3
295TH ST LND .26-D1
295TH ST E RAT .207-D3,208-A3
295TH ST N WYT .25-D1
295TH ST W GVT .204-D3,205-A3
296TH LN DNT .199-A4
296TH ST DNT .199-E4
296TH ST E RAT .207-C3
297TH ST LND .12-D4
297TH ST N FRT .14-A4
297TH ST W WFT .205-E4
297TH STREET WAY CFT .208-D3
298TH AVE DBT .182-E3
298TH CT W GVT .204-E4,205-A4
299TH ST LND .12-D4
300TH ST DNT .-E4,201-A4
300TH ST LAT .201-D4,202-A4
300TH ST LND .12-D4
300TH ST W GVT .205-C4
300TH ST W WFT .205-E4,206-A4
300TH STREET WAY CFT .208-D4
300TH STREET WAY STN .207-B4
300TH STREET WAY VAT .209-D3
301ST ST DBT .182-E3
302ND ST DNT .-B4
302ND ST E SIT .206-C4
302ND ST N CGT .12-C4
302ND ST N LET .11-E4,12-A4
302ND ST N SHA .13-C4
302ND ST W SIT .206-C4
303RD ST N SHA .13-C4
303RD STREET WAY STN .208-A4
304TH ST N SHA .13-C4
304TH STREET WAY STN .208-A4
305TH ST FET .210-D4
305TH ST LET .11-B4
305TH ST N SHA .13-D4
305TH ST N SHT .13-D3
305TH ST W GVT .204-D4
306TH ST CGT .12-C4
306TH ST DNT .213-E1,214-A1
307TH ST CFT .208-D4,222-D1
307TH ST N STA .11-B3
307TH ST W GVT .219-B1
308TH ST CGT .13-B3
309TH AVE CGT .12-C3
309TH ST N CGT .12-C3
310TH ST DNT .214-B1,215-A1
310TH ST FET .210-C4,224-C1
310TH ST LAT .215-D1,216-B1
310TH ST SHT .13-E3,14-A3
310TH ST STN .220-E1,221-C1
310TH ST TF .14-A3
310TH ST E SIT .206-D4,220-D1
310TH ST N CGT .12-E3,13-A3
310TH ST N SHT .13-C3
310TH ST W GVT .218-E1
310TH STREET WAY CFT .222-E1,223-A1
310TH STREET WAY STN .221-B1
311TH ST STN .221-E1,222-A1
311TH ST N LET .11-A3
311TH ST N STA .11-B3
311TH STREET WAY CFT .222-B1
312TH ST N STA .11-B3
312TH STREET PATH STN .221-E1,222-A1
313TH ST N STA .11-B3
313TH ST W WFT .219-E1,220-A1
313TH STREET WAY STN .221-E1,222-A1
314TH ST HEI .215-B2
314TH ST LAT .215-A1
314TH ST N STA .11-B3
315TH ST FET .224-D1
315TH ST VAT .223-D1,224-B1
315TH ST N CGT .12-E3,13-A3
315TH ST N LET .11-B3
315TH ST N STA .11-B3
315TH ST W GVT .219-D1
315TH ST W WFT .219-E1,220-B1
315TH STREET WAY CFT .222-A1
315TH STREET WAY STN .222-A1
316TH LN LET .11-A3
316TH ST N CGT .12-C3
316TH ST N LET .11-B3
317TH ST CFT .223-B1
317TH ST VAT .223-C1
317TH ST N LET .11-B3
318TH ST CFT .222-B2
318TH ST N CGT .12-D3,13-A2
318TH ST N LET .11-A3
318TH STREET WAY CFT .222-B2
319TH STREET WAY CFT .222-B2
320TH AVE DBT .182-E3
320TH ST CGT .13-C2
320TH ST DNT .214-D2,215-A2
320TH ST LAT .215-C2,216-A2
320TH ST STN .220-E2,221-A2
320TH ST E SIT .220-D2
320TH ST N CGT .12-B2
320TH ST N LET .11-A2
320TH ST W GVT .218-D2,219-C2
320TH ST W SIT .220-C2
320TH ST W WFT .219-E2,220-B2
320TH STREET WAY CFT .222-C2
320TH STREET WAY VAT .223-C2
321ST ST N LET .11-A2
321ST ST W WFT .219-E2
322ND ST N CGT .12-D2,13-A2
322ND ST W WFT .219-E2
322ND STREET WAY STN .221-D2
322ND STREET WAY VAT .223-C2
323RD ST STN .222-A2
323RD STREET WAY CFT .222-B2
323RD STREET WAY STN .221-E2
324TH ST STN .222-A2
324TH ST N LET .11-B2
324TH STREET WAY CFT .223-A2
325TH ST FET .224-C2
325TH ST STN .221-C2,222-A2
325TH ST VAT .223-E2,224-B2
325TH ST N CGT .12-E2
325TH ST N SHT .13-E2
325TH STREET WAY CFT .223-A2
326TH LN DNT .215-A2
326TH ST DNT .214-C2
326TH STREET WAY STN .222-A2
327TH STREET PATH STN .222-A2
327TH STREET WAY CFT .222-B2
330TH ST DNT .214-A3,215-A3
330TH ST LAT .215-B3
330TH ST STN .221-B3
330TH ST E SIT .220-D3
330TH ST N CGT .12-B2
330TH ST W GVT .218-D3,219-B3
330TH ST W NFD .219-D3
330TH ST W SIT .220-C3
330TH ST W WFT .220-B3
330TH STREET WAY CFT .222-B3
330TH STREET WAY STN .222-A3
331ST ST STN .222-A3
331ST STREET WAY STN .222-A3
333RD ST VAT .223-D3
334TH ST LAT .215-C3
335TH ST BCT .223-C3
335TH ST CFT .222-E3,223-A3
335TH ST VAT .223-C3
335TH ST N CGT .12-B1
335TH ST N LET .11-A1
336TH ST LAT .215-B3
336TH ST SHT .14-A1
336TH STREET WAY VAT .223-D3
337TH ST N LET .11-B1
337TH STREET WAY CFT .222-C3
338TH ST N CGT .12-B1
338TH STREET WAY CFT .222-B3
339TH ST LET .11-D1
340TH ST DNT .213-E4,214-A4
340TH ST FET .224-E3
340TH ST LEO .222-B3
340TH ST LXT .214-B4,215-A4
340TH ST MGY .215-D4,216-A4
340TH ST N CGT .12-D1
340TH ST N LET .10-E1,11-B1
340TH ST N SHT .13-C1
340TH STREET WAY LEO .222-E3
341ST ST LET .11-D1
342ND ST WST .221-B4
342ND STREET WAY BCT .224-B3
343RD ST WST .221-D4
345TH ST WST .221-C4
347TH ST BCT .223-E4,224-A4
350TH ST BCT .224-A4
350TH ST GHT .224-E4
350TH ST LEO .223-A4
350TH ST WST .220-E4,221-A4
350TH STREET WAY LEO .222-E4,223-A4
352ND ST BCT .223-D4,224-A4
370TH AVE DBT .182-C1
375TH AVE DBT .182-D1
410TH AVE OGT .168-D4
410TH AVE TLT .168-E4
430TH AVE OGT .168-C4
446TH AVE OGT .168-B4
450TH AVE TLT .168-E3
452ND AVE OGT .168-B4
453RD AVE OGT .168-A3
457TH AVE OGT .168-B3
460TH AVE OGT .168-B3
462ND AVE OGT .168-A3
463RD AVE OGT .168-A3
468TH AVE OGT .168-C3
470TH AVE OGT .168-B3
474TH AVE OGT .168-A3
478TH AVE OGT .167-E3,168-A3
485TH AVE OGT .167-E3
490TH AVE OGT .167-E3,168-D3
497TH AVE OGT .167-E2,168-B3
500TH AVE OGT .168-D2
500TH AVE TLT .168-E2
521ST AVE OGT .168-D2
530TH AVE OGT .168-D2
555TH AVE OGT .167-D1
560TH AVE OGT .167-E1,168-C1
565TH AVE OGT .167-D1
570TH AVE OGT .167-E1,168-A1
570TH AVE TLT .168-E1
575TH AVE OGT .154-B4,168-B1
580TH AVE OGT .167-E1,168-A1
598TH AVE OGT .154-C4
620TH AVE OGT .153-E3,154-C4
630TH AVE OGT .154-E3

635TH AVE CTT 153-B3	850TH AVE CTT 139-D2	990TH ST DBT 182-E3	1160TH ST OGT 167-E2
640TH AVE CTT 153-B3	851ST AVE CTT 139-C2	1000TH ST OGT 154-D4,168-D1	1165TH ST OGT 167-E3,168-A3
640TH AVE TLT 154-E2	852ND AVE CTT 139-C2	1005TH ST DBT 182-D2	1170TH ST CTT 153-E1
690TH AVE CTT 154-D2	860TH AVE CTT 140-C2	1015TH ST RIT 140-D3	1170TH ST OGT 153-E4,167-E1
690TH AVE RIT 154-D2	860TH AVE RIT 140-C2	1020TH ST RIT 140-D2	1180TH ST OGT 167-E2
695TH AVE CTT 153-C2	862ND AVE CTT 139-E2	1025TH ST RIT 140-D2	1190TH ST OGT 167-E1
705TH AVE CTT 153-C2	866TH AVE RIT 139-E2	1030TH ST DBT 182-D1	1197TH ST CTT 139-D2
710TH AVE RIT 154-E1	870TH AVE CTT 139-D2	1031ST ST RIT 140-C2	1200TH ST OGT 153-D4,167-D1
714TH AVE CTT 153-C1	879TH AVE RIT 140-C2	1040TH ST OGT 154-C4,168-C1	1205TH ST CTT 139-D2
720TH AVE CTT 153-C1	880TH AVE CTT 140-C2	1047TH ST RIT 140-C2	1208TH ST OGT 167-E3
735TH AVE CTT 153-C1	880TH AVE RIT 140-C2	1050TH ST OGT 168-C4	1220TH ST OGT 167-D2
740TH AVE CTT 154-A1	885TH AVE CTT 139-D2	1060TH ST CTT 140-C2	1225TH ST CTT 139-D2
742ND AVE CTT 153-C1	887TH AVE RIT 140-C1	1065TH ST OGT 168-C3	1230TH ST CTT 153-B3
757TH AVE CTT 139-D4,153-D1	890TH AVE CTT 139-C2	1068TH ST OGT 168-C3	1242ND ST OGT 153-D4,167-D1
769TH AVE CTT 139-D4	910TH ST RIT 182-E2	1070TH ST CTT 154-C2	1245TH ST OGT 167-C1
770TH AVE CTT 139-D4	948TH ST DBT 182-E2	1070TH ST OGT 168-C3	1250TH ST CTT 139-C2,153-C1
770TH AVE RIT 140-E4	950TH ST RIT 140-E3,154-E2	1080TH ST OGT 168-C4,182-B1	1275TH ST CTT 153-C2
795TH AVE RIT 140-E3	950TH ST TLT 154-E3	1090TH ST CTT 140-B2,154-B1	1307TH ST CTT 153-B3
805TH AVE RIT 140-E3	952TH ST DBT 182-E2	1090TH ST OGT 154-B4,168-B1	1317TH ST CTT 153-B3
818TH AVE RIT 140-E3	965TH ST RIT 182-E2	1100TH ST OGT 168-B3	1320TH ST CTT 153-B3
818TH ST RIT 140-E3	970TH ST DBT 168-E4,182-E2	1110TH ST OGT 154-B4,168-B1	1322ND ST CTT 153-B3
820TH AVE CTT 139-D3	970TH ST RIT 182-E2	1115TH ST OGT 154-B4,168-B4	1323RD ST CTT 153-B3
830TH AVE CTT 139-C3	970TH ST TLT 168-E3	1130TH ST CTT 140-A4	
832TH AVE RIT 139-C3	975TH AVE RIT 140-E3	1130TH ST OGT 168-A3	
840TH AVE CTT 139-E3,140-B2	975TH ST RIT 140-E3	1145TH ST OGT 154-A4	
846TH AVE CTT 139-D2	980TH ST DBT 182-E3	1150TH ST OGT 154-A4,168-A3	
848TH AVE CTT 139-D2	980TH ST RIT 140-E3	1155TH ST CTT 139-E3,140-A3	
849TH AVE CTT 139-C2	985TH ST DBT 182-E3	1160TH ST CTT 139-E2	

SPORT CENTERS & ICE ARENAS

ALDRICH ARENA 109-A1	EAGAN CIVIC ARENA 149-D1	CENTER 212-D4	POLAR ICE ARENA 95-B4
ANOKA ICE ARENA 49-D2	EAST BETHEL ICE ARENA 23-A4	LILY LAKE ARENA 96-E2	RICHFIELD ICE ARENA 120-D4
APPLE VALLEY SPORTS ARENA .163-A2	EASY STRIDE SKATE SCHOOL ..133-D2	MAPLE GROVE COMMUNITY	RIVERCENTRE 108-B4
AUGSBURG ICE ARENA 106-E3	EDEN PRAIRIE COMM CTR 132-D1	CENTER 77-A2	ROSEMOUNT COMM CTR 164-A1
BIELENBERG SPORTS CTR ...123-D4	EDISON YOUTH HOCKEY	MAPLEWOOD COMMUNITY	ROSEVILLE ICE ARENA 93-E3
BIFF ADAMS ARENA 108-A3	CIVIC ARENA 106-E1	CENTER 95-A4	SAINT CROIX VALLEY
BLAKE SCH ICE ARENA 119-C2	ELK RIVER ICE ARENA 33-D1	MARIUCCI ARENA 107-A2	REC CENTER 96-D2
BLOOMINGTON ICE GARDEN ..134-A4	FARMINGTON CIVIC ARENA ...177-E4	MAROON AND GOLD ARENA 39-B3	SAINT LOUIS PK REC CTR 119-E1
BRAEMAR ARENA 133-C2	FOGERTY ICE HOUSE 64-E4	METRODOME 106-D3	SHAKOPEE CIVIC CENTER 148-B3
BRECK SCHOOL ICE CENTER ..105-E3	GUSTAFSON PHALEN	MINNEHAHA ACADEMY ARENA .121-B2	SHOREVIEW ARENA 79-E4
BROOKLYN PARK ACTIVITY	ICE ARENA 108-C2	MINNETONKA ICE ARENA 118-E1	SUPER RINK 106-D2
CENTER 77-E2	HARDING AREA ARENA 108-E3	MUNICIPAL STADIUM 107-C3	TARGET CENTER 106-D2
BUFFALO CIVIC CENTER 59-A3	HAROLD POND SPORTS CTR ...116-E1	NATIONAL SPORTS CENTER 65-A3	TARTAN ARENA 109-C3
BUFFALO HOCKEY RINK 58-E2	HASTINGS CIVIC ARENA 166-D3	NEW HOPE ARENA 91-D2	U OF M AQUATIC CENTER 107-A2
BURNSVILLE ICE CENTER 148-D4	HIGHLAND ICE ARENA 121-D2	NEW PRAGUE AREA	VETERANS MEM COMM CTR ...136-D3
CENTENNIAL SPORTS ARENA ..65-E3	HOPKINS PAVILLION 119-B2	COMMUNITY CENTER 201-E1	VICTORY MEMORIAL ARENA ..92-B3
CHAMPLIN ICE FORUM 63-C2	HUDSON SPORTS &	NORWOOD YNG. AMERICA	WAKOTA CIVIC ARENA 122-E4
CHASKA COMM CTR 145-D2	CIVIC CENTER 111-D4	SPORTS COMPLEX 142-C4	WAYZATA ICE ARENA 104-D2
CHISAGO LKS ARENA 26-C1	HUNT ARENA 140-E2	ORONO ICE ARENA 103-C1	WEST SAINT PAUL ICE ARENA .122-C3
COLUMBIA ARENA 78-D3	INVER GROVE HEIGHTS	OSCAR JOHNSON ARENA 107-D3	WHITE BEAR ARENA 95-A2
COON RAPIDS ICE ARENA 63-E2	ARENA 136-D3	OSSEO PARK ARENA 77-B1	WHITE BEAR LAKE
COTTAGE GROVE ICE ARENA .137-D3	KEN YACKEL WEST	PARADE ICE GARDEN 106-C3	SPORTS CENTER 80-E4
DAKOTAH SPORTS & FITNESS .160-D2	SIDE ARENA 122-C1	PLEASANT ICE ARENA 122-A1	WILLIAMS ARENA 107-A2
DELANO AREA SPORTS ARENA .87-E2	LAKEVILLE AMES ARENA 176-E3	PLYMOUTH ICE CENTER 90-D3	XCEL ENERGY CENTER 108-B4
DRAKE ARENA OF S.P.A 121-D2	LESUEUR COMMUNITY	POLAR ARENA 95-B4	

GOLF COURSES

GOLF COURSES	GRID	CITY	PHONE #	ADDRESS
AFTON ALPS GOLF COURSE 139-B2		DENMARK TWP	(651)436-1320	6600 Peller Ave S
ALBION RIDGES GOLF COURSE ...57-B2		ALBION TWP	(800)430-7888	7771 20th St NW
ALL SEASONS GOLF COURSE 137-D4		COTTAGE GROVE	(651)459-2135	7552 S West Point Douglas R
APPLE VALLEY GOLF COURSE 162-E1		APPLE VALLEY	(952)432-4647	8661 140th St W
APPLEWOOD HILLS GOLF COURSE ..96-C2		GRANT	(651)439-7276	11840 60th St N
ARBOR POINTE GOLF CLUB 136-E4		INVER GROVE HEIGHTS	(651)451-9678	8919 Cahill Ave E
BADLAND GOLF COURSE 112-E1		WARREN TWP	(800)749-4150	1018 80th Ave
BAKER NATIONAL GOLF COURSE ..89-C3		MEDINA	(763)473-0800	2935 Parkview Dr
BEARPATH GOLF AND COUNTRY CLUB .132-C3		EDEN PRAIRIE	(952)975-0123	18100 Pioneer Trl
BEGIN OAKS GOLF COURSE 90-E2		PLYMOUTH	(763)559-7574	5635 Yucca Ln N
BELLWOOD OAKS GOLF COURSE ..180-E3		MARSHAN TWP	(651)437-4141	13239 210 St E
BENT CREEK GOLF CLUB 132-E1		EDEN PRAIRIE	(952)937-9347	14490 Valley View Rd
BIRNAMWOOD GOLF COURSE 148-D3		BURNSVILLE	(952)707-6393	12424 Parkwood Dr
BLUFF CREEK GOLF COURSE 132-A4		CHANHASSEN	(952)445-5685	1025 Creekwood St
BRACKETTS CROSSING COUNTRY CLUB .176-B1		LAKEVILLE	(952)435-7700	17976 Judicial Rd
BRAEMAR GOLF COURSE 133-C1		EDINA	(952)826-6799	6364 John Harris Dr
BRIDGES GOLF COURSE 79-B1		BLAINE	(763)785-9063	2850 82nd Ln NE
BRIGHTWOOD HILLS GOLF COURSE ..79-A4		NEW BRIGHTON	(651)633-7776	1975 Silver Lake Rd
BRISTOL RIDGE GOLF COURSE ...70-D3		STAR PRAIRIE TWP	(715)247-3673	1978 Cty Rd C
BROCKWAY GOLF COURSE 164-A1		ROSEMOUNT	(651)423-5222	13500 South Robert Trl
BROOKLAND EXECUTIVE GOLF COURSE .77-E2		BROOKLYN PARK	(763)561-3800	8232 Regent Ave N
BROOKVIEW GOLF COURSE 105-C2		GOLDEN VALLEY	(763)512-2300	200 Brookview Pkwy
BUFFALO HEIGHTS GOLF COURSE ..58-E3		BUFFALO	(763)682-2854	905 S Hwy 25
BUNKER HILLS GOLF COURSE ...50-C4		COON RAPIDS	(763)755-4141	12800 Bunker Prairie Rd NW
BURL OAKS GOLF COURSE 102-E3		MINNETRISTA	(952)472-7017	5400 North Arm Dr
CANNON GOLF CLUB 207-E4		RANDOLPH TWP	(507)263-3126	8606 295th St E
CAREFREE COUNTRY CLUB 3-E3		BECKER TWP	(763)263-6050	10255 185th Ave SE
CARRIAGE HILLS GOLF COURSE ..135-E4		EAGAN	(651)452-7211	3535 Wescott Woodlands Dr
CASTLEWOOD GOLF COURSE 39-C4		FOREST LAKE TWP	(651)464-6233	7050 N Scandia Trl
CEDAR CREEK GOLF COURSE 46-D2		ALBERTVILLE	(763)497-8245	5700 Jason Dr NE
CENTERBROOK GOLF COURSE 92-B2		BROOKLYN CENTER	(763)561-3239	5500 N Lilac Dr
CHABRE GOLF COURSE 83-E2		SOMERSET TWP	(715)247-5506	407 Hwy 35
CHASKA PAR 3 GOLF COURSE ...131-D3		CHASKA	(952)448-7454	1207 Hazeltine Blvd
CHASKA TOWN COURSE 131-B4		CHASKA	(952)443-3748	3000 Town Course Dr
CHISAGO LAKES GOLF COURSE ..26-B3		CHISAGO LAKE TWP	(651)257-1484	12957 292nd St N
CHOMONIX GOLF COURSE 110-C3		LINO LAKES	(651)482-8484	646 Sandpiper Dr
CIMARRON PARK GOLF COURSE ..136-E4		LAKE ELMO	(651)436-6188	901 Lake Elmo Ave N
CLEARY LAKE GOLF COURSE 175-D1		CREDIT RIVER TWP	(952)447-2171	18106 Texas Ave
CLIFTON HIGHLANDS GOLF COURSE .153-D2		CLIFTON TWP	(800)657-6845	N 6890 1230th St
CLIFTON HOLLOW GOLF CLUB ...139-D3		CLIFTON TWP	(800)487-8879	W 12166 820th Ave
COLUMBIA GOLF COURSE 92-E3		MINNEAPOLIS	(612)789-2627	3300 Central Ave NE
COMO GOLF COURSE 107-E2		SAINT PAUL	(651)488-9673	1432 N Lexington Pkwy
COUNTRY VIEW GOLF COURSE ...94-E3		MAPLEWOOD	(651)484-9809	2926 N Hwy 61
CREEKS BEND GOLF COURSE 202-C1		CEDAR LAKE TWP	(952)758-7200	26826 Langford Ave
CRYSTAL LAKE GOLF COURSE ...162-E4		LAKEVILLE	(952)432-6566	16725 Innsbrook Dr
DAHLGREEN GOLF CLUB 144-D4		DAHLGREN TWP	(952)448-7463	6940 Dahlgren Rd
DAYTONA GOLF COURSE 48-C3		DAYTON	(763)427-6110	14730 Lawndale Ln
DEER RUN GOLF CLUB 130-E3		VICTORIA	(952)443-2351	8661 Deer Run Dr
DELLWOOD HILLS GOLF COURSE ..81-C2		DELLWOOD	(651)426-3218	29 Hwy 96 E
DWAN GOLF COURSE 148-B2		BLOOMINGTON	(952)948-8702	3301 W 110 St
EAGLE LAKE GOLF COURSE 91-B1		PLYMOUTH	(763)268-3181	11000 Cty Rd 10
EAGLE TRACE GOLFERS CLUB ...1-C3		CLEARWATER	(800)842-4386	1100 Main St
EAGLE VALLEY GOLF COURSE ...138-A2		WOODBURY	(651)714-3750	2600 Double Eagle Ln
EDINA COUNTRY CLUB 119-E3		EDINA	(952)927-7151	5100 Wooddale Dr
EDINBURGH USA GOLF COURSE ..78-A2		BROOKLYN PARK	(763)424-0600	8700 Edinbrook Crossing
ELK RIVER COUNTRY CLUB 19-C4		ELK RIVER	(763)441-4111	20015 Elk Lake Rd
ELM CREEK LINKS GOLF COURSE ..90-B2		PLYMOUTH	(763)478-6716	18940 Hwy 55
ELMDALE HILLS GOLF COURSE ..195-A4		DOUGLAS TWP	(888)487-6634	26161 Nicolai Ave
EMERALD GREENS 165-D2		HASTINGS	(651)480-8558	14425 Goodwin Ave

GOLF COURSES

GOLF COURSES	GRID	CITY	PHONE #	ADDRESS
FALCON RIDGE GOLF COURSE	11-A1	LENT TWP	(651)462-5797	33942 Falcon Ave
FOREST HILLS GOLF CLUB	39-D4	FOREST LAKE TWP	(651)464-3097	7530 210th St N
FORT SNELLING GOLF COURSE	121-C4	FORT SNELLING	(612)726-6222	6399 Fort Snelling Ave
FOUNTAIN VALLEY GOLF COURSE	192-A1	CASTLE ROCK TWP	(651)463-2121	2830 W 220th St
FOX HOLLOW GOLF COURSE	47-D3	SAINT MICHAEL	(763)428-4468	4780 Palmgren Ave
FRANCIS A. GROSS GOLF COURSE	93-B4	SAINT ANTHONY	(612)789-2542	2201 St Anthony Blvd
FRED RICHARDS GOLF COURSE	133-E2	EDINA	(952)915-6606	7640 Parklawn Ave
FRENCH LAKE GOLF COURSE	62-C2	DAYTON	(763)428-4544	17500 Cty Rd 81
GEM LAKE GOLF COURSE	94-E1	GEM LAKE	(651)429-8715	4039 Scheuneman Rd
GLEN LAKE GOLF & PRACTICE CENTER	118-E4	MINNETONKA	(952)934-8644	14350 Cty Rd 61
GOLDEN VALLEY COUNTRY CLUB	105-D2	GOLDEN VALLEY	(763)545-2511	7001 Golden Valley Rd
GOODRICH GOLF COURSE	109-A1	MAPLEWOOD	(651)748-2525	1820 N Van Dyke St
GREENHAVEN GOLF CLUB	49-C3	ANOKA	(763)427-3180	2800 Greenhaven Rd
GREENS AT HOWARD LAKE GOLF COURSE	71-B4	HOWARD LAKE	(320)543-3330	5055 Cty Rd 7 SW
GREENWOOD GOLF LINKS	25-A3	WYOMING TWP	(651)462-4653	4520 E Viking Blvd
HAMPTON HILLS GOLF COURSE	90-D2	PLYMOUTH	(763)559-9800	5313 Juneau Ln N
HASTINGS COUNTRY CLUB	166-C2	HASTINGS	(651)437-4612	2015 Westview Dr
HAYDEN HILLS GOLF COURSE	63-A1	DAYTON	(763)421-0060	13150 N Deerwood Ln
HAZELTINE NATIONAL GOLF CLUB	131-D4	CHASKA	(952)448-4929	1900 Hazeltine Blvd
HERITAGE LINKS GOLF COURSE	175-E4	CREDIT RIVER TWP	(952)440-4653	8075 Lucerne Blvd
HIAWATHA GOLF COURSE	120-E2	MINNEAPOLIS	(612)724-7715	4553 Longfellow Ave
HIDDEN GREENS GOLF COURSE	180-D2	MARSHAN TWP	(651)437-3085	12977 E 200th St
HIDDEN HAVEN GOLF COURSE	22-E3	EAST BETHEL	(763)434-6867	20520 NE Polk St
HIGHLAND GOLF COURSE	121-D2	SAINT PAUL	(651)695-3774	1403 Montreal Ave
HILLCREST COUNTRY CLUB	109-A2	SAINT PAUL	(651)774-6088	7200 Larpenteur Ave E
HOLLYDALE GOLF COURSE	90-C2	PLYMOUTH	(763)559-9847	4710 Holly Ln N
HUDSON GOLF CLUB	111-E3	HUDSON TWP	(715)386-3390	378 Frontage Rd
HYLAND GREENS GOLF COURSE	133-E4	BLOOMINGTON	(952)948-8868	10100 Normandale Blvd
INDIAN HILLS GOLF CLUB	96-B2	GRANT	(651)770-2301	6667 Keats Ave N
INTERLACHEN COUNTRY CLUB	119-D2	EDINA	(952)929-1661	6200 Interlachen Blvd
INVER WOOD GOLF COURSE	136-C3	INVER GROVE HEIGHTS	(651)457-3667	1850 70th St E
ISLAND LAKE GOLF COURSE	93-E1	SHOREVIEW	(651)787-0383	1000 Red Fox Rd
ISLAND VIEW COUNTRY CLUB	130-A2	LAKETOWN TWP	(952)442-6116	9150 Island View Rd
KATE HAVEN GOLF COURSE	79-D1	BLAINE	(763)786-2945	8791 Lexington Ave NE
KELLER GOLF COURSE	94-D4	MAPLEWOOD	(651)766-4170	2166 Maplewood Dr
KILKARNEY HILLS GOLF COURSE	126-D4	TROY TWP	(800)466-7999	163 Radio Rd
KROOKED KREEK GOLF CLUB	28-B4	OSCEOLA TWP	(715)294-3673	2448 75th Ave
LAFAYETTE COUNTRY CLUB	117-D1	MINNETONKA BEACH	(952)471-8493	2800 Northview Rd
LAKEVIEW GOLF COURSE	103-A3	ORONO	(952)472-3459	409 North Arm Dr
LONE PINE GOLF COURSE	160-D2	PRIOR LAKE	(952)445-3575	15451 NW Howard Lake Rd
LOST SPUR COUNTRY CLUB	135-D2	EAGAN	(651)454-5681	2750 Hwy 13
MAJESTIC OAKS COUNTRY CLUB	50-E3	HAM LAKE	(763)755-2142	701 NE Bunker Lake Blvd
MANITOU RIDGE GOLF COURSE	95-B2	WHITE BEAR LAKE	(651)777-2987	3200 N McKnight Rd
MAPLE HILLS GOLF CENTER	108-C1	MAPLEWOOD	(651)776-2226	905 Parkway Dr
MEADOWBROOK GOLF COURSE	119-D2	SAINT LOUIS PARK	(952)929-2077	201 Meadowbrook Rd
MEADOWWOODS GOLF COURSE	118-C2	MINNETONKA	(952)470-4000	18300 Ridgewood Rd
MENDAKOTA COUNTRY CLUB	122-A4	MENDOTA HEIGHTS	(651)454-2822	2075 Mendakota Dr
MENDOTA HEIGHTS GOLF COURSE	122-A3	MENDOTA HEIGHTS	(651)454-9822	1695 Dodd Rd
MIDLAND HILLS COUNTRY CLUB	107-B1	ROSEVILLE	(651)631-0440	2001 Fulham St
MINIKAHDA GOLF CLUB	120-A1	MINNEAPOLIS	(612)926-1601	3205 Excelsior Blvd
MINNEAPOLIS GOLF CLUB	105-C3	SAINT LOUIS PARK	(952)544-4471	2001 Flag Ave S
MINNESOTA VALLEY COUNTRY CLUB	147-E2	BLOOMINGTON	(952)884-2400	6300 Auto Club Rd
MINNETONKA COUNTRY CLUB	117-C4	SHOREWOOD	(952)474-5222	24575 Smithtown Rd
MISSISSIPPI DUNES GOLF COURSE	151-C2	COTTAGE GROVE	(651)768-7611	10351 Grey Cloud Trl
MONTICELLO COUNTRY CLUB	1-C1	MONTICELLO	(763)295-4653	1209 Golf Course Rd
NEW HOPE GOLF COURSE	91-C1	NEW HOPE	(763)531-5178	8130 Bass Lake Rd
NEW PRAGUE COUNTRY CLUB	201-A3	NEW PRAGUE	(952)758-3126	400 Lexington Ave S
NORTH OAKS COUNTRY CLUB	80-B3	NORTH OAKS	(651)484-6311	54 East Oaks Rd
NORTHFIELD GOLF CLUB	219-E4	NORTHFIELD	(507)645-4026	707 Prairie St
OAK GLEN GOLF COURSE	82-E4	STILLWATER	(651)439-6963	1599 McKusick Rd
OAK MARSH GOLF COURSE	109-E3	OAKDALE	(651)730-8886	526 Inwood Ave N
OAK RIDGE COUNTRY CLUB	119-B1	HOPKINS	(952)935-7721	700 Oak Ridge Rd
OAKDALE PAR 3	95-C3	OAKDALE	(651)773-3494	5585 Golfview Ave N
OLYMPIC HILLS GOLF CLUB	133-B4	EDEN PRAIRIE	(952)941-6265	10625 Mount Curve Rd
ONEKA RIDGE GOLF COURSE	81-B1	HUGO	(651)429-2390	5610 N 120th St
ORCHARD GARDENS GOLF COURSE	162-C3	BURNSVILLE	(952)435-5771	1020 W 155th St
ORONO PUBLIC GOLF COURSE	103-E3	ORONO	(952)473-9904	265 S Orono Orchard Rd
PARKVIEW GOLF COURSE	149-D2	EAGAN	(651)454-9884	1310 Cliff Rd
PEBBLE CREEK COUNTRY CLUB	3-A3	BECKER	(763)263-4563	14000 Club House Ln
PHALEN GOLF COURSE	108-D2	SAINT PAUL	(651)778-0413	1615 Phalen Park Dr
PHEASANT ACRES GOLF CLUB	62-A3	CORCORAN	(763)428-8244	10705 Cty Rd 116
PINEWOOD GOLF COURSE	33-B2	ELK RIVER	(763)441-3451	14000 182 Ave NW
PIONEER CREEK GOLF COURSE	102-A2	MAPLE PLAIN	(763)955-3982	705 Copeland Rd
PRESTWICK GOLF CLUB AT WEDGEWOOD	124-A3	WOODBURY	(651)731-4779	9555 Wedgewood Dr
RED OAK GOLF COURSE	103-A3	MINNETRISTA	(952)472-3999	855 Red Oak Ln
RICH VALLEY GOLF CLUB	165-A1	ROSEMOUNT	(651)437-4653	3855 145th St E
RIDGES AT SAND CREEK	187-C1	JORDAN	(952)492-2644	21775 Ridges Dr
RIVER OAKS GOLF COURSE	152-B2	COTTAGE GROVE	(651)438-2121	11099 S Hwy 61
RIVERS EDGE COUNTRY CLUB	101-B3	WATERTOWN TWP	(952)955-2223	1455 Cty Rd 27
ROLLING GREEN COUNTRY CLUB	90-A2	MEDINA	(763)478-6021	400 Evergreen Rd
ROSEVILLE CEDARHOLM GOLF COURSE	93-D4	ROSEVILLE	(651)415-2166	2323 N Hamline Ave
RUM RIVER GOLF CLUB	35-B3	RAMSEY	(763)753-3339	16659 NW St Francis Blvd
RUSH CREEK GOLF CLUB	76-B3	MAPLE GROVE	(763)494-8844	7801 Cty Rd 101
SAWMILL GOLF CLUB	82-B4	GRANT	(651)439-7862	11177 N McKusick Rd
SHADOWBROOKE GOLF COURSE	113-A3	WINSTED TWP	(800)450-4250	3192 State Hwy 7
SHAMROCK GOLF COURSE	76-A3	CORCORAN	(763)478-9977	19625 Larkin Rd
SILVER SPRINGS GOLF COURSE	31-A1	MONTICELLO TWP	(763)295-2951	Cty Rd 39 W
SOMERSET COUNTRY CLUB	122-B3	MENDOTA HEIGHTS	(651)457-1416	1416 Dodd Rd
SOUTHERN HILLS GOLF COURSE	178-A2	EMPIRE TWP	(651)463-4653	18950 Chippendale Ave
SOUTHVIEW COUNTRY CLUB	122-C4	WEST SAINT PAUL	(651)451-6856	239 Mendota Rd E
SPRING HILL GOLF CLUB	104-A1	MEDINA	(763)473-2815	725 Cty Rd 6
ST CROIX NATIONAL GOLF COURSE	83-D3	SOMERSET TWP	(715)247-4200	1603 & Cty Rd V
ST CROIX VALLEY GOLF COURSE	14-D3	SAINT CROIX FALLS	(715)483-3377	2200 US Hwy 8
STILLWATER COUNTRY CLUB	82-E4	STILLWATER	(651)439-7979	1421 4th St N
STONEBROOKE GOLF CLUB	146-B4	SHAKOPEE	(952)496-3171	2693 Cty Rd 79
STONERIDGE GOLF CLUB	110-D4	WEST LAKELAND TWP	(651)436-4653	13600 Hudson Blvd N
SUNDANCE GOLF COURSE	62-D3	DAYTON	(763)420-4700	15240 113rd Ave N
TANNER BROOK GOLF COURSE	40-A1	FOREST LAKE	(651)982-6840	5810 190th St
TARTAN PARK GOLF CLUB	110-C2	LAKE ELMO	(651)733-3475	11455 20th Ave N
THE LEGENDS CLUB	176-A2	PRIOR LAKE	(952)226-4777	8670 Credit River Blvd
THE LINKS AT NORTHFORK GOLF COURSE	48-C1	RAMSEY	(763)241-0506	9333 153rd Ave NW
THE PONDS GOLF COURSE	7-E4	ST FRANCIS	(763)753-1100	2881 229th Ave
THE REFUGE GOLF COURSE	22-D2	OAK GROVE	(763)753-8383	2150 Yellow Pine St
THE WILDS GOLF COURSE	160-E2	PRIOR LAKE	(952)445-4455	3151 Wilds Ridge
THEODORE WIRTH GOLF COURSE	106-A1	GOLDEN VALLEY	(763)522-4584	1325 Wirth Pkwy N
THOMPSON OAKS GOLF COURSE	122-C3	WEST SAINT PAUL	(651)457-6064	1555 Oakdale Ave
TIMBER CREEK GOLF COURSE	101-E4	WATERTOWN TWP	(952)955-3600	9750 Cty Rd 24
TOWN & COUNTRY CLUB	107-B4	SAINT PAUL	(651)646-7121	300 Mississippi River Blvd
TPC OF THE TWIN CITIES		BLAINE	(763)795-8508	8990 Springbrook Dr
TROY BURNE GOLF CLUB	125-D3	TROY TWP	(877)888-8633	295 Lindsay Rd
U OF M LES BOLSTAD GOLF COURSE	107-C1	FALCON HEIGHTS	(612)627-4000	Larpenteur Ave W & Fulham
VALLEY VIEW GOLF COURSE	186-A3	BELLE PLAINE TWP	(952)873-4653	23795 Laredo Ave
VALLEYWOOD MUNICIPAL GOLF COURSE	149-D3	APPLE VALLEY	(952)953-2323	4851 125th St W
VIKING MEADOWS GOLF COURSE	37-A1	EAST BETHEL	(763)434-4205	1788 Viking Blvd
WAYZATA COUNTRY CLUB	104-A2	ORONO	(952)473-8846	200 W Wayzata Blvd
WHISPERING PINES GOLF COURSE	43-A1	CORINNA TWP	(320)274-8721	Cty Rd 6 & 70th St NW
WHITE BEAR YACHT CLUB	81-C3	DELLWOOD	(651)429-5002	56 Dellwood Ave
WILD MARSH GOLF COURSE	58-E3	ROCKFORD TWP	(763)682-4476	1710 Montrose Blvd
WHITE EAGLE GOLF COURSE	97-D3	HUDSON	(715)549-4653	1297 Cty Rd V
WILLINGERS GOLF CLUB	218-B2	WEBSTER TWP	(952)440-7000	6900 Canby Trl
WOODBURY GOLF COURSE	123-D3	WOODBURY	(651)735-4401	3351 Woodlane Dr
WOODHILL COUNTRY CLUB	104-A3	ORONO	(952)473-7333	200 Woodhill Rd
WOODLAND CREEK GOLF COURSE	49-E2	ANDOVER	(763)323-0517	3200 Coon Creek Dr S

TOWNSHIP/RANGE NUMBERS

T26N R18W 152-C4
T26N R20W 152-E4
T26N R21W 151-D3
T27N R20W 139-A4
T27N R21W 152-A1
T27N R22W 150-D1
T27N R23W 149-D1
T27N R24W 148-C1
T28N R20W 125-A2
T28N R21W 124-A3
T28N R22W 122-D3
T28N R23W 121-D3
T28N R24W 120-C3
T29N R20W 111-A2
T29N R21W 110-A2
T29N R22W 108-E2
T29N R23W 107-D2
T29N R24W 106-C1
T30N R20W 83-A3
T30N R21W 82-A4
T30N R22W 80-E4
T30N R23W 79-D4
T30N R24W 78-D3
T31N R19W 69-C2
T31N R20W 68-D2
T31N R21W 67-C2
T31N R22W 66-C2
T31N R23W 65-B3
T31N R24W 64-B2
T31N R25W 49-C4
T32N R19W 55-C1
T32N R20W 54-D1
T32N R21W 53-C1
T32N R22W 52-B1
T32N R23W 51-A1
T32N R24W 50-A1
T32N R25W 35-A4
T32N R26W 33-C2
T32N R27W 32-A2
T32N R28W 31-E2
T33N R19W 27-D2
T33N R20W 26-E3
T33N R21W 25-C3
T33N R22W 24-C3
T33N R23W 23-B3
T33N R24W 22-A3
T33N R25W 21-A3
T33N R26W 19-D3
T33N R27W 18-C3
T33N R28W 17-C2
T33N R29W 16-A1
T34N R18W 14-C1
T34N R19W 13-D2
T34N R20W 12-E2
T34N R21W 11-C2
T34N R22W 10-C2
T34N R23W 9-B2
T34N R24W 7-E2
T34N R25W 7-A2
T34N R26W 5-E2
T34N R27W 4-C2
T34N R28W 3-B2
T34N R29W 2-B1
T111N R15W 224-D4
T111N R16W 224-A4
T111N R17W 222-D4
T111N R18W 221-C4
T111N R19W 220-B4
T111N R20W 219-B4
T111N R21W 218-A4
T111N R22W 216-D4
T111N R23W 215-E4
T111N R24W 214-D4
T111N R25W 213-C4
T111N R26W 212-B4
T111N R27W 211-A4
T112N R15W 224-D1
T112N R16W 223-E1
T112N R17W 222-D1
T112N R18W 221-D1
T112N R19W 220-C1
T112N R20W 219-B1
T112N R21W 218-A1
T112N R22W 216-D1
T112N R23W 215-D1
T112N R24W 214-C2
T112N R25W 213-C2
T112N R26W 212-B2
T112N R27W 211-B2
T113N R15W 196-D3
T113N R16W 195-D3
T113N R17W 194-D4
T113N R18W 193-D4
T113N R19W 192-B4
T113N R20W 191-B4
T113N R21W 189-E4
T113N R22W 188-D3
T113N R23W 187-D3
T113N R24W 186-C3
T113N R25W 185-C4
T113N R26W 184-A4
T113N R27W 183-A4
T114N R15W 182-D3
T114N R16W 181-D2
T114N R17W 180-D2
T114N R18W 179-D2
T114N R19W 178-C2
T114N R20W 177-A2
T114N R21W 176-A2
T114N R22W 174-D2
T114N R23W 173-D1
T114N R24W 172-C2
T114N R25W 171-C2
T114N R26W 170-B2
T114N R27W 169-A2
T115N R16W 167-B2
T115N R17W 166-C1
T115N R18W 165-C2
T115N R19W 164-C2
T115N R20W 163-B2
T115N R21W 161-E1
T115N R22W 160-E1
T115N R23W 145-D4
T115N R24W 158-C1
T115N R25W 143-C4
T115N R26W 142-B4
T115N R27W 155-A1
T116N R21W 133-D2
T116N R22W 132-E2
T116N R23W 131-E3
T116N R24W 130-C3
T116N R25W 129-C3
T116N R26W 128-B2
T116N R27W 127-A3
T117N R21W 119-D2
T117N R22W 118-D1
T117N R23W 117-D1
T117N R24W 116-C2
T117N R25W 115-B1
T117N R26W 114-A2
T117N R27W 113-A2
T118N R21W 91-E3
T118N R22W 90-E3
T118N R23W 89-C4
T118N R24W 88-D4
T118N R25W 87-B4
T118N R26W 86-A4
T118N R27W 85-A4
T119N R21W 77-E2
T119N R22W 76-D2
T119N R23W 75-D2
T119N R24W 74-D3
T119N R25W 73-B2
T119N R26W 72-B2
T119N R27W 71-A2
T120N R21W 63-D2
T120N R22W 62-D1
T120N R23W 61-D1
T120N R24W 60-D1
T120N R25W 59-B1
T120N R26W 58-A1
T121N R22W 48-B2
T121N R23W 33-D4
T121N R24W 32-D3
T121N R25W 31-B3
T121N R26W 30-B3
T121N R27W 29-A3
T122N R25W 17-A4
T122N R26W 16-A2
T122N R27W 15-A2
T123N R27W 1-A2

PARKS

4TH ST PARK(MO) 31-D2
4TH ST PARK(NOH) 111-C1
ABDELLA MEMORIAL PARK 137-C3
ABLE PARK 78-E1
ACORN CREEK PARK 66-D2
ACORN PARK(BUR) 162-B1
ACORN PARK(CR) 64-D3
ACORN PARK(RVL) 94-B4
ADAMS HILL PARK 134-B1
ADAMS SCHOOL PARK 64-C4
ADELMANN PARK 134-B3
AFTON HILLS PARK 109-B4
AFTON STATE PARK 139-B2
AINSWORTH PARK 105-D4
AIRPORT PARK 65-A3
AL FLYNN PARK 64-B3
ALBERT PARK 122-B2
ALBERT YAEGER CO PARK RESERVE 85-C3
ALDEN PARK 119-C2
ALDER PARK 64-D3
ALIMAGNET PARK(APV) 162-E1
ALIMAGNET PARK(BUR) 162-E1
ALLANSONS PARK 198-D4
ALPINE PARK 49-A1
ALTURA PARK 92-D1
AMERICAN LEGION PARK 212-D4
AMES PARK 219-D4
ANCEL GLEN PLAYFIELD 147-E1
ANDERSON PARK(BLO) 148-B2
ANDERSON PARK(HUD) 111-D4
ANDREWS PARK 63-D2
ANEZ RIDGE PARK 96-E2
ANN ST. PARK 101-B3
ANOKA - ISANTI COUNTY GAME REFUGE 9-B2
ANOKA COUNTY PARK 49-C2
ANTLERS PARK 176-D3
APPLE GROVE PARK 163-A2
APPLE PONDS PARK 163-B3
APPLE TREE PARK 80-D4
APPLE VALLEY EAST PARK 163-D2
APPLEWOOD PARK 123-B2
AQUATORE PARK 64-E4
AQUILA PARK 105-C4
ARBOR MEADOWS PARK 138-A4
ARBOR PARK 148-D4
ARDEN CREEK PARK 81-B2
ARDEN PARK 120-A3
ARMATAGE PARK 120-B3
ARMSTRONG PARK(NFD) 219-D4
ARMSTRONG PARK(OKD) 109-D1
ARNESON ACRES PARK 133-E1
ARONSON PARK 177-A3
ASPEN PARK(CP) 65-D4
ASPEN PARK(CR) 64-C3
ATHLETIC FIELD(CF) 208-B4
ATHLETIC FIELD(MO) 31-D2
ATHLETIC PARK 145-C3
AUDUBON PARK 92-E4
AUGSBURG PARK 134-C1
AURELIA PARK 64-D4
AUSTIN PARK 79-D1
AUTO CLUB PARK 147-E2
AUTUMN GROVE PARK 93-D3
AUTUMN HEIGHTS PARK 34-D3
AXELROD MEMORIAL PARK 137-B3
BABCOCK PARK 219-D4
BAKER PARK RESERVE 103-B1
BALBOUL PARK 31-B1
BALD EAGLE-OTTER LAKE REGIONAL PARK 81-A1
BALD EAGLE-OTTER TAIL REGIONAL PARK 80-E1
BALDWIN PARK(CP) 65-E3
BALDWIN PARK(ER) 33-E1
BALL FIELDS 46-E3
BALL PARK 125-C2
BANDIMERE COMMUNITY PARK 132-A3
BANDIMERE HEIGHTS PARK 132-A3
BARRINGTON PARK 33-E1
BARTHEL PARK 134-B3
BASS CREEK PARK 77-C4
BASS LAKE PARK 120-A1
BASS LAKE PLAYFIELD 91-A2
BASS LAKE PRESERVE 120-A1
BASS LAKE WATERFOWL PROD. AREA 84-D3
BASSETT CREEK PARK(CRY) 91-E4
BASSETT CREEK PARK(GV) 105-E1
BASSETT PARK 176-C2
BASSETTS CREEK VALLEY 106-B2
BASSWOOD PARK 76-D4
BATTLE CREEK - INDIAN MOUNDS PARK 123-A1
BATTLE CREEK - INDIAN MOUNDS PARK 108-D4,109-A4,123-A1
BATTLE CREEK -INDIAN MOUNDS PARK(MPW) 109-B4
BATTLE CREEK -INDIAN MOUNDS PARK(STP) 109-A4
BAY PARK 39-C3
BAY VIEW ESTATES PARK 39-C4
BAYLESS PLAYLOT 63-B4
BAYLOR REGIIONAL PARK 142-B1
BEAR PARK 49-C1
BEAVER BROOK PARK 133-E2
BEAVER LAKE PARK 109-B2
BECKER PARK 91-E2
BEDERWOOD PARK 103-C2
BEEBE LAKE COUNTY PARK 60-B2
BEGIN PARK 91-C2
BEHMS CENTURY FARM 65-E1
BELDON PARK 137-C4
BELLAIRE PARK 95-B1
BELLVUE PARK 92-C2
BELMONT PARK 149-A4
BELTRAMI PARK 106-E1
BELTZ PARK 39-C4
BENSON PARK(SWR) 96-E2
BENSON PARK(WBT) 81-B1
BENT CREEK PARK 129-D4
BERRY PATCH PARK 149-D1
BERTHA COURT PARK 95-C2
BETHKE PARK 109-C2
BETHUNE PARK 106-C2
BF NELSON PARK 106-D2
BIELENBERG SPORTS CENTER 123-E4
BIG ISLAND PARK 117-E2
BIG WILLOW PARK 105-A4
BILL ANDERSON MEMORIAL COUNTY PARK 71-B1
BILL WARREN PARK 133-C4
BIRCH GROVE PARK 78-A2
BIRCH ISLAND PARK 118-D4
BIRCH PARK(LL) 66-C4
BIRCH PARK(WBT) 81-A1
BIRCHCREST PARK 119-E4
BIRCHVIEW ELEMENTARY PARK 104-D2
BIRCHWOOD ACRES PARK 66-A4
BIRCHWOOD PARK 105-E4
BIRKMOSE PARK 111-C3
BISCAYNE PARK 164-B2
BISON CREEK PARK 50-A4
BIXBY COMMUNITY PARK 39-B2
BLACK DOG PARK 148-E2
BLACKHAWK PARK 149-C1
BLACKSTONE PARK 105-E3
BLOOMINGTON FERRY ROAD PARK 133-C4
BLOOMQUIST FIELD 95-C1
BLUFF CREEK PARK 146-A1
BLUFF PARK 145-E1
BOB CAHLANDER PARK 78-A4
BOBBY THEISEN PARK 93-E2
BOERBOOM PARK 77-C1
BOHANON PARK 92-C2
BOOM ISLAND PARK 106-D2
BOOT LAKE NATURAL AREA(ANO) 49-B4
BOOT LAKE NATURAL AREA(LWT) 23-E3
BOSSARD PARK 95-B1
BOSSEN FIELD 121-A3
BOTTINEAU PARK 92-D4
BOUDINS PARK 161-D1
BOULDER CREEK PARK 118-D4
BOUNDARY CREEK PARK 63-B3
BRACKETT FIELD 107-A4
BRACKETT'S PARK 176-B1
BRAEMER PARK 133-D1
BRANDLWOOD PARK 80-D1
BRANDONS PARK 140-D2
BRANDYWOOD PARK 66-C4
BREDESEN PARK 119-D3
BREKKE PARK 97-A3
BRIAR OAKS PARK 149-B3
BRIDLE RIDGE PARK 136-A4,150-A1
BRITTANY PARK 63-D3
BROADWAY PARK 91-D1
BRONX PARK 105-D4
BROOK OAKS PARK 78-B2
BROOK PETERSON PARK 129-C3
BROOKDALE PARK 78-A3
BROOKLANE PARK 78-A4
BROOKLYN PARK ENVIRONMENTAL AREA 64-B4
BROOKSIDE PLAYGROUND 134-B4
BROOKSVILLE HILLS PARK 161-B4
BROOKVIEW PARK 124-A1
BROOKVIEW PARK(BUR) 148-B4
BROOKVIEW PARK(GV) 105-D2
BROOKVIEW PARK(RAM) 35-B3
BROWNDALE PARK 119-E2
BROWNS BEACH 111-C1
BROWNWOOD PARK 91-D3
BRYANT LAKE PARK 119-A4
BRYANT PARK 134-C3
BRYANT SQUARE PARK 106-C4
BRYE PLAYGROUND 147-E1
BRYN MAWR MEADOWS 106-B3
BUCHER PARK 80-A1
BUFFALO FAMILY RECREATION AREA 59-A3
BUFFER PARK 119-C2
BUNKER HILL PARK 163-B4
BUNKER HILLS COUNTY PARK 50-D4
BUNKER HILLS REGIONAL PARK(AND) 50-C3
BUNKER HILLS REGIONAL PARK(CR) 50-C4
BURNHAVEN PARK 162-C2
BURNS PARK 119-C2
BURNSVILLE HEIGHTS PARK 162-B1
BURR OAKS PARK 136-B3
BURTON FIELD 111-D2
BURTON PARK 118-B2
BURWELL PARK 118-E1
BUSY BEAVER PARK 137-B1
BYLLESBY COUNTY PARK 207-E4
C. P. ADAMS PARK 166-E2
CAM RAM PARK 162-B2
CAMELS HUMP 137-C3
CAMFIELD PARK 164-A2
CANDY COVE PARK 161-B3
CANTERBURY OAKS PARK 148-A1
CANTERBURY PARK(SAV) 148-A4
CANTERBURY PARK(SHK) 146-D2
CAPERSON PARK 176-C2
CAPITAN DODD PARK 150-B1
CARAMEL PARK 119-B4
CARDINAL HILLS PARK 31-D3
CARDINAL WOODS PARK 50-B4
CARL ECK PARK 65-D3
CARLISE PARK 9-D4
CARLOS AVERY WILDLIFE AREA 24-C3
CARLSON LAKE PARK 149-D2
CARNELIAN PARK 149-C1
CARPENTER PARK 105-E4
CARPENTER SAINT CROIX VALLEY NATURE 153-A4
CARRARA EAST PARK 51-A3
CARRARA WEST PARK 51-A3
CARROLL'S WOODS PARK 163-E1
CARROLWOOD PARK 163-A1
CARVER BEACH PARK 132-A1
CARVER BEACH PLAYGROUND 132-A1
CARVER BLUFFS PARK 159-B1
CARVER LAKE PARK 123-C3
CARVER PARK RESERVE(LTT) 130-C1
CARVER PARK RESERVE(VIC) 130-E1
CASEY LAKE PARK 95-A3
CATHCART PARK 117-B4
CAVANAUGH SCHOOL PARK 91-E2
CAVELL PARK 92-E3
CAVELLE PARK 91-C1
CEDAR AVE FIELD 106-E4
CEDAR HIGHLANDS PARK 163-B4
CEDAR ISLAND SHORES PARK 77-A4
CEDAR ISLES PARK 163-B1
CEDAR KNOLL PARK(APV) 149-B4
CEDAR KNOLL PARK(SLP) 105-D4
CEDAR POND PARK 149-B1
CEDARBRIDGE PARK 149-A1
CEDARCREST PARK 134-E3
CEDARHURST PARK 106-A3
CEDARMANOR LAKE PARK 105-C4
CENTENNIAL GREEN PARK 65-D3
CENTENNIAL LAKES PARK 134-A1
CENTENNIAL PARK 65-E3
CENTER PARK(CP) 65-D3
CENTER PARK(SLP) 119-E1
CENTRAL PARK(BC) 92-B1
CENTRAL PARK(BLO) 148-C1
CENTRAL PARK(BP) 77-E2
CENTRAL PARK(EDI) 133-C1
CENTRAL PARK(HOP) 119-B2
CENTRAL PARK(NFD) 219-E4
CENTRAL PARK(RAM) 34-D4

PARKS

CENTRAL PARK(RCH) 134-E2
CENTRAL PARK(RVL) 93-E4,94-A4
CENTRAL PARK(SA) 93-B3
CENTRAL PARK NORTH 93-E3
CHADWICK PARK 161-E2
CHAIN OF LAKES
REGIONAL PARK 65-E4,66-A3,
CHAMPLIN HEIGHTS PARK 63-B1
CHANHASSEN ESTATES
MINI PARK 132-B2
CHANHASSEN HILLS PARK 132-A3
CHANHASSEN POND PARK 132-A1
CHAPARRAL PARK 149-A4
CHAREST PARK 77-B1
CHARLES MUTTON FIELD 122-C2
CHARLIE'S PARK 164-A2
CHASIS ISLAND PARK 78-C4
CHATEAULIN PARK 148-E4
CHATFIELD PARK 186-A1
CHAUTAUGUA PARK 81-C4
CHERRY PARK 219-D3
CHERRYVIEW PARK 163-A4
CHERRYVIEW POND 163-A4
CHIPPENDALE PARK 163-E2
CHIPPEWA PARK 123-D2
CHRISTIAN PARK 134-E1
CHUTE SQUARE PARK 106-E2
CINNAMON RIDGE PARK 149-A2
CIRCLE PARK 104-D2
CITY CENTER PARK 132-A2
CITY HALL BLOCK 104-B3
CITY HALL PARK(ER) 33-C2
CITY HALL PARK(LL) 52-C4
CITY HALL PARK(MED) 89-D4
CITY SQUARE PARK(CHS) 145-C3
CITY SQUARE PARK(WAC) 129-D3
CIVIC CENTER PARK(BUR) 148-D4
CIVIC CENTER PARK(NH) 91-C3
CIVIC PARK 5-D1
CLEARWATER COUNTY PARK 1-B2
CLEARWATER CREEK
ENVIRONMENTAL 67-B3
CLEARWATER MILLS PARK 129-E4
CLEARY LAKE PARK(CRT) 175-C1
CLEARY LAKE PARK(SLT) 175-C1
CLEVELAND PARK 92-B4
CLIFF NICOLLET PARK 148-D3
CLIFTON E FRENCH
REGIONAL PARK 91-A3
CLINTON FIELD 106-D4
CLOVER LEAF PARK 64-D3
COBBLESTONE PARK 123-D3
COLBY LAKE PARK 124-A2
COLLEGE PARK(BP) 77-D2
COLLEGE PARK(STP) 107-C2
COLLINS PARK 140-D1
COLONIAL PARK 162-C1
COLUMBIA PARK 80-E4
COLUMBUS PLAYLOT 134-D4
COMMONS PARK 78-D4
COMMUNITY CENTER
AND SHOREVIEW COMM 79-E4
COMMUNITY PARK(CAR) 145-A4
COMMUNITY PARK(CHS) 145-B1
COMMUNITY PARK(WBT) 80-D3
COMO PARK 107-E2
CON AGRA PARK 166-D2
CONCORD PARK 137-A2
CONWAY PARK 109-A4
CONZEMIUS PARK 166-C2
COOK ARENA 63-E2
COON LAKE COUNTY PARK 23-E4
COON RAPIDS DAM
PARK 64-B3,64-B4
COON RAPIDS DAM
REGIONAL PARK 64-B4
COONS HILL PARK 111-D2
CORCORAN PARK 120-E1
CORNELIA SCHOOL PARK 134-A1
CORNER PARK 91-D2
CORTINA PARK 131-C4
COTTAGE GROVE RAVINE
REGIONAL PARK 152-B1
COTTAGE PARK 106-B1
COTTAGEVILLE PARK 119-C1
COTTAGEWOOD CHILDRENS
PARK 118-A2
COTTONWOOD PARK(BP) 78-A2
COTTONWOOD PARK(RAM) 49-A2
COUNTRY CLUB PARK(BUR) 162-C3
COUNTRY CLUB PARK(MO) 31-C2
COUNTRY CROSSING PARK 33-C2
COUNTRY HOME PARK 135-D2
COUNTRY LAKES PARK 66-B3
COUNTRYSIDE PARK 119-D4
COUNTY DITCH AND
PROTECTION OPEN SP 79-E1
COUNTY FAIR GROUNDS 129-D3
COUNTY FOREST PARK 23-B2
COURT SQUARE 185-E1
COVENTRY COURT PARK 162-D2
COVER PARK 97-B2
COVINGTON PARK 118-B3
CRAIG PARK 78-C2
CRANBERRY PARK 133-C3
CREE PARK 123-C1
CREEK RIDGE PARK 79-A3
CREEK VALLEY PARK 119-D4
CREEK VIEW PARK 79-A3
CREEKSIDE PARK 119-D1
CREEKVIEW PARK(MPL) 92-B2
CREEKVIEW PARK(NB) 79-A3
CREEKWOOD PARK 133-A4
CROCKER PARK 111-C3
CROOKED LAKE BEACH 50-A3
CROSBY NATURE AREA 121-E3
CROSSTOWN WEST PARK 148-D3
CROSSWINDS
NEIGHBORHOOD PARK 76-D2
CROW HASSAN PARK
RESERVE(HAN) 61-A3
CROW HASSAN PARK
RESERVE(HSN) 61-B1
CROW SPRINGS COUNTY PARK .. 72-E3
CRYSTAL HIGHLANDS PARK 91-D3
CRYSTAL LAKE WEST PARK 162-D3
CRYSTAL LAKES WEST PARK .. 162-D2
CULLY PARK 111-C4
CURLY PARK 58-E3
CURRIE PARK 106-E3
CURRY FARMS PARK 117-E4
CURT RAMSDELL PARK 92-E1
CURTISS FIELD 107-D2
DAHLIA PARK 64-A2
DAISY KNOLL PARK 177-C1
DAKOTA HEIGHTS PARK 162-D4
DAKOTA HEIGHTS PARK NO. 2 .. 176-D1
DAKOTA PARK 105-E4
DAVIS PARK 58-D2
DEERFIELD 2ND PARK 20-A4
DEERFIELD 4TH PARK 19-E4
DEERWOOD PARK 34-D2
DEHRER PARK 137-A3
DELANEY PARK 163-D2
DELTA PARK 64-A2
DEMING HEIGHTS 92-E3
DEMONTREVILLE PARK 95-D3
DESANCTIS PARK 140-D1
DEXTER PARK 103-E2
DIAMOND LAKE PARK 120-D3
DIAMOND PATH PARK 163-D2
DICKERMAN PARK 106-D1
DINGLE PARK 137-B3
DODD PARK 122-B2
DODD POINT PARK 163-C3
DODD TRAIL PARK 163-B4
DODGE NATURE PRESERVE 136-A1
DONAHUE NORTH
COMMUNITY PLAYFIELD 76-E4
DONAHUE SOUTH PLAYFIELD .. 76-E4
DONALDSON PARK 134-C1
DORIS A KEMP PARK 63-C1
DOROTHY MARY PARK 91-C1
DOROTHY PARK 95-B3
DOWNING PARK 149-C2
DOWNTOWN PARK(CAR) 145-B4
DOWNTOWN PARK(HOP) 119-B2
DRED SCOTT PLAYFIELD 147-C1
DRIFTWOOD PARK 93-A1
DUCHESS PARK 163-A2
DULLARA PARK 163-E2
DUNNING FIELD 107-E4
EAGLE CREEK CORRIDOR 147-C3
EAGLE LAKE PARK 77-B4,91-B1
EAGLE LAKE WOODS PLAYLOT .. 77-B4
EAGLE PARK 80-D2
EAGLE PASS PARK 66-D3
EAGLE RIDGE PARK 109-D2
EAGLE VIEW PARK 60-D3
EAGLE WOODS PARK 111-D1
EARLY LAKE PARK 162-C2
EAST BETHEL BOOSTER
CLUB PARK 23-A1
EAST BETHEL PARK 23-A1
EAST CREEK PARK 145-D2
EAST MAPLE COUNTY PARK 44-C1
EAST MARSH LAKE PARK 134-A3
EAST MEDICINE LAKE PARK 105-B1
EAST PALMER LAKE PARK 78-B3
EAST PHILLIPS PARK 106-E3
EAST RIVER FLATS 107-A3
EAST SIDE PARK(BLA) 65-D2
EAST SIDE PARK(CF) 208-B4
EAST SIDE PARK(OKD) 109-D2
EBBA PARK 95-B2
EBERLE PARK 95-C4
ECHO PARK(BUR) 162-E1
ECHO PARK(MHT) 95-C2
EDEN VALLEY PARK 118-D4
EDENBROOK CONSERVATION
AREA 118-C4
EDENVALE CONSERVATION
AREA 132-D1
EDENVALE PARK 132-D1
EDGEBROOK PARK 119-D1
EDGEMOOR PARK 92-D2
EDGERTON PARK 108-C1
EDGEWATER GARDENS PARK 78-D3
EDGEWATER PARK 124-A3
EDGEWOOD PARK 77-D4
EDINBOROUGH PARK 134-B2
EDINBROOK PARK 78-B1
EFFA PLAYLOT 134-D2
EGAN PARK 90-C1
ELIE PARK 119-C1
ELLIOT PARK 106-D3
ELLISON PARK 31-D2
ELM CREEK PARK(DAY) ... 62-D1,63-A2
ELM CREEK PARK(MG) 63-A4
ELM CREEK SCHOOL &
COMMUNITY PARK 77-B1
ELM CREEK SPECIAL USE
PARK/ARBORETU 76-E1
ELM GROVE PARK 91-D2
ELMWOOD-STRAND PARK 118-D1
EMERALD POND PARK 49-B2
EMERSON PARK 122-C2
EMERSON WOOD PARK 78-C2
EPIPHANY PARK 64-B2
ERICKSON PARK 164-A1
ERLANDSON PARK 64-C2
EVERGREEN EAST PARK 123-E1
EVERGREEN PARK(BC) 78-C3
EVERGREEN PARK(CHM) 63-D3
EVERGREEN PARK(EAG) 149-D2
EVERGREEN PARK(SAV) 101-B3
EVERGREEN TOT PARK 2-E3
EVERGREEN WEST PARK 123-D1
FAIR OAKS SCHOOL PARK 77-E4
FAIR SCHOOL PARK 91-E3
FAIRFIELD PARK 163-B4
FAIRVIEW PARK 92-C4
FAIRWOOD PARK 134-B1
FAIRY LANDING PARK 97-C4
FAITH PARK 163-C1
FALCON HEIGHTS
COMMUNITY PARK 107-C1
FALLON AVE PARK 31-D2
FARQUHAR LAKE PARK 149-D4
FARR LAKE PARK 93-A1
FARWELL PARK 106-B2
FENLASON PLAYLOT 134-D2
FERN HILL PARK 106-A4
FILLMORE PARK 64-E2
FINDLAY PARK 149-C4
FIREHOUSE PARK 78-C4
FIREMANS PARK 145-C2
FIREMENS PARK 2 .... 145-D3
FISH LAKE PARK(EAG) 135-D4
FISH LAKE PARK(MG) 76-D4,76-E4
FISH LAKE TRAILS EAST 76-E3
FISH LAKE WOODS PARK 76-E3
FISH POINT PARK 161-B2
FLANNERY PARK 79-A2
FLICEK PARK 108-D1
FLINTWOOD TERRACE 49-B2
FLORIDA PARK 91-D3
FLYING CLOUD FIELDS 132-D4
FOLWELL PARK 92-B3
FOOTHILL PARK 137-E4
FORD BROOK PARK 35-B2
FORD PARK 105-C3
FOREST GLEN PARK 135-A3
FOREST HEIGHTS PARK 162-D1
FOREST HILLS SCHOOL PARK ... 118-E4
FOREST SCHOOL PARK 91-D2
FOREST VIEW POND PARK 63-A4
FORT SNELLING ATHLETIC
FIELDS 121-C4
FORT SNELLING STATE
PARK(FS) 121-C4
FORT SNELLING STATE
PARK(MH) 135-C2
FORT SNELLING STATE
PARK(STP) 121-D4
FORTH STREET PARK 39-C3
FOUNDRY HILL PARK 201-D2
FOUNTAIN PARK 185-E1
FOUR SEASON PARK 81-A2,81-B2
FOUR SEASONS N. H. PARK 94-E4
FOUR SEASONS PARK(ALB) 47-A2
FOUR SEASONS PARK(PLY) 91-B3
FOX MEADOW PARK 80-D4
FOX PARK 35-B3
FOX RUN PARK(WAC) 129-D3
FOX RUN PARK(WBY) 124-B1
FOXBOROUGH PARK 163-A4
FRANCE POND PARK 148-A2
FRANK KOLBINGER
MEMORIAL PARK 2-E3
FRANK TUPA PARK 119-E3
FRANKLIN STEELE PARK 106-D3
FRANLO PARK 147-C1
FRED SIMS 91-D3
FREEDOM PARK(PRE) 167-B1
FREEDOM PARK(SLP) 119-D1
FREEWAY PARK 78-A4
FRIDLEY COMMUNITY PARK 78-D3
FRIENDLY HILLS PARK 136-A1
FRIENDLY MARSH PARK 136-A1
FRIENDSHIP PARK(CHS) 145-B1
FRIENDSHIP PARK(NYA) 142-C3
FURLONG PARK 95-C4
GALAXIE PARK 163-B1
GALPIN BLVD PARK 131-D1
GARDEN BLVD PARK 109-C1
GARDEN PARK 119-D3
GARLOUGH PARK 122-B4
GATEWAY PARK 106-D2
GAUVITTE PARK 92-D2
GEARTY PARK 91-E4
GENE C. KELLY
YOUTH PLAYFIELD 148-D1
GEORGE OHMANN PARK 149-D3
GERVAIS MILL PARK 94-C3
GIRARD LAKE PARK 134-A2
GLEANLOCH PARK 105-A2
GLEN GALE PARK 106-C1
GLEN MOOR PARK 118-E3
GLEN PARK 140-D2
GLENCOE PARK 78-C2
GLENDALE PARK 161-E1
GLENVIEW TERRACE PARK 106-B1
GLIDER PARK 81-B2
GLUEK PARK 92-D4
GOAT HILL PARK 149-E2
GOLDEN LAKE BEACH PARK 65-D4
GOLDEN OAKS PARK 105-C2
GOLDEN VALLEY CEMETERY ... 105-D1
GOLDENROD MARSH PARK 76-D3
GOODRICH PARK 109-A1
GOODWIN PARK 95-C4
GOOSE LAKE PARK 162-D4
GOOSE POND 95-C4
GOSWIN PARK 95-D1
GRANADA PARK 137-C4
GRANDVIEW PARK(BC) 92-B1
GRANDVIEW PARK(EDI) 119-C2
GRANDVIEW PARK(HUD) 111-E2
GRANDVIEW PARK(SSP) 122-E3
GRANT PARK 134-C1
GREEN GLEN PARK 104-A2
GREEN OAKS PARK(PLY) 90-B4
GREEN OAKS PARK(PRL) 161-C2
GREENBRIAR PARK(BUF) 59-B1
GREENBRIAR PARK(BUT) 45-B4
GREENHAVEN PARK(BP) 77-C3
GREENHAVEN PARK(BUR) 162-C2
GREENING PARK 163-A2
GREENLEAF PARK 163-B1
GREENWAY PARK 201-E2
GREENWOOD PARK 117-E3
GREENWOOD SHORES PARK ... 131-E1
GREY CLOUD PARK 151-C2
GREYS BAY CAUSWAY PARK ... 104-C4
GREYS BAY DAM 104-D4
GRIEP PARK 145-C1
GRIFFING MEADOWS PARK 58-E1
GRIFFING PARK 59-A1
GRO TONKA PARK 118-C1
GROGAN PARK 91-E2
GROVE PARK 107-C2
GROVELAND PARK(IGH) 122-D4
GROVELAND PARK(MTK) 104-C4
GUILLIAM PARK 119-A1
HACKMANN CIRCLE PARK 78-E4
HAEG PARK 134-B2
HAGEMEISTER PARK 149-C4
HAGSTROM KING PARK 136-B1
HALL PARK 106-C1
HALLAM PARK 81-D4
HAM LAKE COUNTY PARK 51-A1
HAMEL LEGION PARK 90-B3
HAMILTON HILLS PARK 147-C4
HAMILTON PARK(BP) 77-D2
HAMILTON PARK(RF) 140-D3
HAMLET PARK 137-D4
HAMPSHIRE PARK(GV) 105-D1
HAMPSHIRE PARK(SLP) 105-D3
HAMPSHIRE POND 147-D2
HANNAHS BEND PARK 208-A4
HANSEN PARK 93-B1
HANSON PARK 50-B4
HAPPY ACRES PARK 64-D1
HAPPY HOLLOW PARK 92-A2
HARD PARK 105-D3
HARLEY HOPKINS PARK 119-C2
HARMON PALYFIELD 122-B2
HARMON PARK 136-E1
HARRIS LAKE PARK 79-A3
HARRISON PARK 106-B2
HARRY LARSON COUNTY PARK ... 16-C3
HARTKOPF PARK 77-D3
HASKELL PARK 122-C2
HAZELWOOD PARK 94-E3
HEARTHSIDE PARK 137-D4
HEATHER POUDS PARK 90-C4
HEATHERTON RIDGE PARK 161-C1
HEIGHTS PARK(EDI) 119-D4
HEIGHTS PARK(LE) 109-E2
HEINE POND PARK 149-D2
HEMINGWAY PARK 137-D4
HEMLOCK PARK 105-A1
HEMLOCK PONDS PARK 77-A3
HENNEPIN COUNTY
PARKLAND 63-E4,64-A4
HENNEPIN ISLAND PARK 106-E2
HERITAGE PARK(APV) 149-A4
HERITAGE PARK(BUR) 148-D4
HERITAGE PARK(LE) 110-C2
HERITAGE PARK(NP) 201-E2
HERITAGE PARK(PLY) 91-A4
HERITAGE PARK(RF) 140-D2
HERITAGE PARK(SPP) 137-C3
HERMAN FIELD PARK 117-D4
HI VIEW PARK 92-D3
HIAWATHA PARK 146-B2
HIAWATHA PLAYGROUND 121-B2
HICKORY PARK 95-D1
HIDDEN FALLS PARK
(NORTH GATE) 121-C3
HIDDEN FALLS PARK
(SOUTH GATE) 121-C3
HIDDEN HOLLOW PARK 81-B4
HIDDEN OAK PARK 79-A4
HIDDEN PONDS PARK 132-C1
HIDDEN VALLEY PARK(NH) 91-C4
HIDDEN VALLEY PARK(SAV) 148-A4
HIGHLAND FOREST PARK 148-B4
HIGHLAND MEADOWS PARK 66-A1
HIGHLAND PARK(CG) 137-E2
HIGHLAND PARK(SAV) 101-A4
HIGHLAND PARK(STP) 121-D3
HIGHLAND VIEW PARK 148-E3
HIGHLANDS PARK 119-D3
HIGHLINE TRAIL 149-C2
HIGHVIEW HEIGHTS PARK 163-A3
HIGHVIEW PARK 135-D2
HILLCREST PARK 31-B1
HILLOWAY PARK 105-A3
HILLSIDE CITY PARK 34-A2
HILLSIDE PARK 109-B1
HILLTOP PARK(CH) 93-A1
HILLTOP PARK(HOP) 119-B1
HILLTOP RECREATION AREA ... 111-D3
HOFFMAN PARK 140-E1
HOLASEK HILLS PARK 119-A4
HOLBROOK PARK 103-D2
HOLIDAY PARK(MTK) 118-D3
HOLIDAY PARK(NH) 91-C2
HOLLOWS PARK 162-B2
HOLLYWOOD PARK 148-A4
HOLMES PARK 146-B2
HOLMES PARK(MPL) 106-E2
HOLY NAME PARK 90-A4
HOLZ FARM PARK 150-A2
HOMESTEAD PARK 110-B3
HOMEWARD HILLS PARK 133-A4
HOOVER SCHOOL PARK 64-A2
HOPKINS PARK 148-D1
HOUSE PARK 95-B4
HOWARD JOHNSON PARK 93-D3
HOWELL PARK 148-A4
HUBER PARK 146-B2
HUBERT H. HUMPHREY PARK ... 92-A3
HUMPHREY ARENDS
MEMORIAL CNTY PARK 72-A2
HUMPHRIES PARK 111-B4
HUNTER LIONS PARK 90-A3
HUNTINGTON PARK 149-D4
HUSET PARK 92-E2
HYLAND HILLS PARK 133-E4
HYLAND LAKE PARK RESERVE ... 133-D3
HYPOINTE CROSSING PARK 162-E3
I-35 FISHING DOCK 176-C2
IDEAL PARK 137-E4
IMPERIAL HILLS PARK 104-B1
INDEPENDENCE BEACH
PARK - LAKESHORE 89-A3
INDEPENDENCE BEACH
PARK - WALNUT 89-A3
INDEPENDENCE PARK 163-C3
INDIAN RIDGE PARK 161-C2
INNER DRIVE PARK 65-E3
INNSBRUK PARK 93-A1
INTERLACHEN PARK(BUR) 162-D2
INTERLACHEN PARK(HOP) 119-D2
INTERSTATE STATE PARK(SAT) .. 14-B4
INTERSTATE STATE PARK(TF) 14-B3
IRON HORSE PARK 91-D2
IRVING PARK 78-B3
ISLAND LAKE COUNTY PARK 93-E1
ISLAND OF PEACE PARK 78-C4
ISLAND VIEW PARK 160-E3
ISLANDS OF PEACE
RIVERFRONT PARK 92-C2
IVY HILLS PARK(BLA) 65-A1
IVY HILLS PARK(MH) 122-A3
J C BALL FIELD 96-E1
JACKLEY PARK 119-E2
JACKSON AND MAIN
STREET PARK 33-E2
JACKSON SQUARE PARK 92-E4
JAMES JENSEN PARK 176-E3
JAY PARK 78-D3
JAYCEE COMMUNITY PARK 64-E1
JAYCEE PARK(LVL) 176-E3
JAYCEE PARK(NH) 91-C4
JAYCEES PARK(HAS) 166-D1
JAYCEES PARK(RMT) 163-E3
JEFFERSON PARK(BLA) 50-E4
JEFFERSON PARK(NFD) 219-D4
JEFFERSON W PARK 134-B1
JENSON MEMORIAL PARK 97-D4
JERSEY PARK 105-D3
JEVNE PARK 105-B1
JEWELL PARK 78-B1
JIDANA PARK 118-D1
JOHANNA LAKE PARK 93-C2
JOHN ANDERSON
MEMORIAL PARK 8-E4
JOHN CONDE PARK 78-E1
JOHNNY CAKE RIDGE PARK 163-C1
JONQUIL MEADOW
NEIGHBORHOOD PARK 77-A2
JORDAN PARK 92-C4
JORDANS WOODS 123-B1
JORVIG PARK 119-E1
JOSEPHINE NUNN PARK 63-B1
JOY PARK 95-B3
JUBILEE PARK 92-D1
JUDICIAL PARK 162-B2
JUNCTION PARK 119-A2
JUNO PARK 176-C3
JUSTAD PARK 119-E1
KAPOSIA PARK 122-D3
KARGEL PARK 124-A1
KARTH LAKE PARK 79-E4
KATHERINE ABBOTT PARK 95-C2
KEEWAYDIN PARK 121-A3
KEHRER PARK 142-C4
KELLER LAKE PARK 162-E2
KELLER PARK 162-E3
KELLOGG PARK 108-B4
KELLY GARDENS 118-C3
KENMORE PARK 162-C4

KENNEDY PARK(CR) .78-C1
KENNEDY PARK(WSP) .122-B2
KENNY PARK .120-C3
KENSINGTON PARK .136-B2
KENTUCKY PARK .91-D3
KENWOOD PARK .106-B3
KERBER COMMUNITY PARK .76-E1
KERNEEL PARK .162-C3
KETTENACKER PARK .74-A3
KETTLE PARK .149-B3
KEYES PARK .92-E2
KEYSTONE PARK .105-E4
KIDDER PARK .163-E1,163-E2
KILMER PARK .91-C4
KING PARK .176-E1
KINGS HIGHWAY .120-C2
KINGS MEADOWS PARK .101-B4
KINGSTON PARK .138-A3
KINNICKINNIC STATE PARK .139-D3
KINSEL PARK .118-E3
KLAPPRICH PARK .104-B3
KLEIS PARK .96-A3
KNOB HILL PARK .148-C4
KNOLLWAY PARK .104-E3
KNOLLWOOD GREEN PARK .119-C1
KOA CAMPGROUND .124-B1
KOHLMAN PARK .94-D3
KOJETIN PARK .120-A2
KORDIAK PARK .93-A1
KRAUS-HARTIG PARK .79-A2
KRESTWOOD PARK .148-D4
KYLAWN PARK .92-A1
LABELLE PARK .92-E2
LAC LAVON PARK(APV) .163-A3
LAC LAVON PARK(BUR) .162-E3
LAC LAVON/FISHING DOCK SITE PARK .163-A3
LACOMPTE GREEN COMMUNITY PALYFIELD .105-B2
LAD PARK .78-A2
LADDIE LAKE PARK .78-E1
LADYSLIPPER PARK .94-A3
LAKE ANN PARK .131-E2
LAKE ARDMORE PARK .89-B3
LAKE BYLLESBY REGIONAL PARK .207-E4
LAKE CHARLOTTE PARK .118-C3
LAKE CORNELIA PARK .120-A4
LAKE EDEN PARK .133-B3
LAKE EDINA PARK .134-A2
LAKE ELMO REGIONAL PARK RESERVE .110-A2
LAKE GEORGE REGIONAL PARK .21-E2
LAKE GRACE PARK .131-C4
LAKE HIAWATHA PLAYGROUND .121-A2
LAKE ISABELLE PARK .166-D2
LAKE ITASCA PARK .34-C4,34-D3,48-D1
LAKE JANE HILLS PARK .96-A4
LAKE JOSEPHINE PARK .93-E3
LAKE JUDY PARK .93-E2
LAKE MARIA STATE PARK .30-B1
LAKE MCCARRONS PARK .108-B1
LAKE MINNEWASHTA REGIONAL PARK .131-C1
LAKE OWASSO COUNTY PARK .94-A2
LAKE PARK .149-A2
LAKE REBECCA PARK .166-D1
LAKE REBECCA PARK RESERVE(GRF) .74-B4
LAKE REBECCA PARK RESERVE(IND) .88-A1
LAKE RIDGE PARK .17-E3
LAKE ROSE PARK .118-D3
LAKE SARAH RECREATIONAL PARK(GRF) .88-C1
LAKE SARAH RECREATIONAL PARK(IND) .88-C1
LAKE STREET PARK .119-E1
LAKE SUSAN PARK .132-A2
LAKE VICTORIA PARK .105-C4
LAKE VIEW TERRACE PARK .92-A3
LAKEFRONT COMMUNITY PARK .161-B3
LAKEFRONT PARK .111-C2
LAKELAND PARK .77-D4
LAKERIDGE PARK .176-D2
LAKESIDE PARK(BC) .92-A2
LAKESIDE PARK(BL) .18-A4
LAKESIDE PARK(EAG) .150-B2
LAKESIDE PARK(FLT) .39-B3
LAKESIDE PARK(LOL) .103-E2
LAKESIDE PARK(SLK) .79-A2
LAKEVIEW KNOLLS PARK(MG) .76-E1
LAKEVIEW KNOLLS PARK(WBY) .124-A2
LAKEVIEW PARK(GV) .105-C1
LAKEVIEW PARK(WBL) .81-A4
LAKEWOOD HILLS PARK .95-A2
LAMAR FIELDS .138-C3
LAMOTTE PARK .66-D3
LANGFORD PARK .107-C2
LANGTON LAKE PARK .93-C3
LARGEN PARK .163-B1
LARSEN PARK .140-E3
LAUDERDALE COMMUNITY PARK .107-B1
LAUREL AVENUE GREEN BELT .105-D2
LAWSHE PARK .122-E4
LEBANON HILLS REGIONAL PARK(APV) .149-C3
LEBANON HILLS REGIONAL PARK(EAG) .149-D3
LEE PARK(CRY) .92-A4
LEE PARK(ROB) .92-A3
LEISURE PARK .148-C4
LEMANS PARK .63-B2
LEXINGTON DUWAYNE PARK .65-D4
LEXINGTON MEMORIAL PARK .65-C4
LEXINGTON PARK(EAG) .135-E2
LEXINGTON PARK(RVL) .93-E4
LEXINGTON TOT PARK .65-D4
LIBBS LAKE BEACH .104-C4
LIBERTY PARK .91-C1
LILLIAN SEEMAN PARK .105-D2
LILY LAKE PARK .96-E2
LILYDALE-HARRIET IS-CHEROKEE PARK .122-A2
LILYDALE-HARRIET IS-CHEROKEE PARK .122-B2
LINCOLN FIELD .134-C1
LINDEN HILLS PARK .120-B2
LINNER PARK .104-D3
LINO PARK .66-B1
LINWOOD COMMUNITY PARK .24-A1
LINWOOD PARK .121-E1
LIONS CLUB PARK .105-D2
LIONS COON CREEK PARK .64-B1
LIONS PARK(BC) .92-B2
LIONS PARK(BUF) .58-E2
LIONS PARK(CAR) .145-B4
LIONS PARK(CHS) .145-D2
LIONS PARK(CP) .65-D3
LIONS PARK(ER) .33-D1
LIONS PARK(HAS) .166-C1
LIONS PARK(HWL) .85-A1
LIONS PARK(LE) .110-C1
LIONS PARK(MON) .86-C1
LIONS PARK(NEW) .137-B1
LIONS PARK(NH) .91-D3
LIONS PARK(PLY) .104-E1
LIONS PARK(ROB) .92-A3
LIONS PARK(SAT) .14-C1
LIONS PARK(SHK) .146-A3
LIONS PARK(WBL) .81-A4
LIONS SOO LINE PARK .91-E2
LIONS' LEVEE PARK .137-B3
LITTLE ACRE PARK .91-C2
LITTLE BIT PARK .78-E1
LITTLE LEAGUE ACRES .78-E4
LITTLE LEAGUE PARK .64-E2
LO JACOB SCHOOL PARK .64-B3
LOCHNESS PARK .65-D2
LOCKE LAKE PARK .78-D3
LOCKE PARK .78-E3
LODGES PARK .123-D1
LOFTUS PARK .161-E1
LOGAN PARK(FRI) .78-D2
LOGAN PARK(MPL) .106-E1
LOMIANKI PARK .92-D2
LONE LAKE PARK .119-B3
LONE OAK PARK .162-C4
LONG LAKE PARK(APV) .149-C4
LONG LAKE PARK(MHT) .81-D4
LONG LAKE PARK(NB) .79-B3
LONG LAKE PARK(SWR) .96-D1
LONGFELLOW PARK .121-A1
LONGVILLE PARK .81-B2
LOOP PARK .162-B3
LORETTO BALLFIELD .89-A1
LORING PARK .106-C3
LORRAINE PARK .136-E1
LOVELAND PARK .137-B1
LOVELL SQUARE .106-B2
LOWELL PARK .97-A1
LUXTON PARK .107-A3
LYNDALE FARMSTEAD .120-C1
LYNDALE PARK .120-C2
LYNNHURST PARK .120-C2
MAC WILDLIFE AREA .91-E1
MADISON GREEN PARK .101-B4
MADISON PARK .120-B4
MADSEN PARK .78-E2
MAETZOLD FIELD .119-B2
MAGIC KINGDOM PLACE .31-C1
MAIN STREET PARK .106-E2
MAITLAND PARK .78-B1
MALLARY PARK .64-B1
MANITOU PARK .117-D3
MANOMIN COUNTY PARK .78-C3
MANOR PARK(ROB) .92-A4
MANOR PARK(SWD) .118-A3
MANOR PARK(WBL) .95-B1
MAPLE LAKE PARK .43-D2
MAPLE MEADOW PARK .77-A4
MAPLE PARK .89-B3
MAPLE TREE PLAYLOT .77-A4
MAPLE VALLEY TRAILS .63-B4
MAPLECREEK PARK .90-D4
MAPLEVIEW PARK .94-A3
MAPLEWOOD HEIGHTS PARK .95-A3
MAPLEWOOD PLAYLOT .134-D4
MARCUS ZUMBRUNNEN COUNTY PARK .15-E2
MARCY PARK .106-E2
MARGARET CIRCLE PARK .104-B2
MARIE AVE PARK .121-E4
MARLIN PARK .78-A4
MARSH CREEK PARK .123-E3
MARSHALL TERRACE PARK .92-D4
MARSHAN PARK .66-A2
MARSHLAND PARK .63-E1
MARTHALER PARK .122-C3
MARTIN ISLAND LINWOOD REGIONAL PARK .24-B2
MARTIN LUTHER KING PARK .120-D2
MARY ELIZABETH PARK .79-A1
MARY HILLS PARK .106-A1
MARYDALE PARK .108-A2
MASON PARK .64-D4
MATERION PARK .94-B4
MATOSKA PARK .81-B3
MATTHEWS PARK .107-A3
MCANDREWS PLAYLOT .134-E3
MCBRIDE PARK .66-D2
MCCULLOUGH PARK .79-E2
MCGROARTY PARK .136-D2
MCGUIRE PARK .133-D1
MCKENNA PARK .92-D1
MCKENZIE PARK .118-D1
MCKNIGHT PARK(CHS) .131-C4
MCKNIGHT PARK(NSP) .95-B4
MCMORROW FIELD .136-E2
MCRAE PARK .120-D2
MEAD PARK .80-E3
MEADOW GREEN PARK .132-A1
MEADOW LAKE PARK(BP) .91-C1
MEADOW LAKE PARK(NH) .91-C1
MEADOW OAK PARK .32-A3
MEADOW PARK(CHS) .145-C2
MEADOW PARK(MTK) .104-E4
MEADOWBROOK PARK(BLA) .50-E4
MEADOWBROOK PARK(LVL) .163-C4
MEADOWBROOK PARK(SLP) .119-E2
MEADOWLAND PARK .149-B2
MEADOWLANDS PARK(FRI) .78-E3
MEADOWLANDS PARK(WBT) .80-D3
MEADOWLARK PARK .96-D1
MEADOWS PARK .146-B3
MEADOWS PARK(LVL) .176-D3
MEADOWS PARK(OKD) .109-D2
MEARS PARK .108-C4
MEDINA MORNINGSIDE PARK .103-D1
MEDLEY HILLS PARK .105-C1
MEDORA WOODS PARK .106-A3
MELODY LAKE PARK .119-E3
MELROSE LAKE .16-D3
MEMORIAL PARK(HWL) .85-A1
MEMORIAL PARK(PRL) .161-B3
MEMORIAL PARK(RCH) .134-D1
MEMORY LANE PARK .91-D3
MENDAKOTA PARK .136-A1
MENOMINI PARK .109-C4
MENZEL PARK .106-A4
MERCY PARK .63-D1
MERRIAM PARK .107-C4
MIELKE PARK .92-A3
MIESVILLE RAVINE REGIONAL PARK(CFT) .209-A2
MIESVILLE RAVINE REGIONAL PARK(DT) .209-A2
MILL POND PARK .173-B3
MILLER PARK .132-C2
MILLNER PARK .95-D1
MINI TONKA PARK .118-D2
MINNEHAHA BASIN PARK .105-C4
MINNEHAHA CREEK PARKWAY .105-C4
MINNEHAHA PARK .121-B2
MINNEHAHA PKWY .120-D3,121-A2,121-B2
MINNESOTA VALLEY STATE TRAIL PARK .171-D4,184-D4,198-D1
MINNESOTA VALLEY STATE TRAIL PARK(BKT) .185-D1
MINNEWASHTA HEIGHTS PARK .117-C4
MINNIESKA PARK .208-B4
MINNIHAHA PKWY .120-C3
MINNIKAHDA VISTA PARK .120-A1
MISSION HILLS PARK .91-B3
MISSISSIPPI POINT PARK .63-C1
MISSISSIPPI RIVER PARK .49-B3
MISSISSIPPI WEST PARK .48-E3
MN VALLEY RECREATIONAL AREA .159-C4
MOELLER PARK .163-C1
MOIR PARK .148-B1
MOLDENHAUER PARK .33-C2
MONROE FIELD .134-C1
MONTISSIPPI COUNTY PARK .17-B4
MOONSHINE PARK .135-D3
MOOR PARK .64-C2
MOORE LAKE PARK EAST .78-E4
MOORE LAKE PARK WEST .78-E4
MORRIS PARK .121-B3
MORRIS T BAKER PARK RESERVE .89-B4
MORRISON PARK .106-D3
MOUND PARK .140-E1
MOUND SPRINGS PARK .134-E4
MPLS CHAIN OF LAKES REGIONAL PARK .106-B3,120-B2
MUD LAKE PARK(PLY) .90-E1
MUD LAKE PARK(WSP) .122-B3
MUELLER FARM PARK .135-E4
MUELLER PARK .106-C4
MURPHY SQUARE .106-E3
MURPHY-HANREHAN PARK RESERVE(BUR) .162-A3
MURPHY-HANREHAN PARK RESERVE(CRT) .162-A4
MURPHY-HANREHAN PARK RESERVE(SAV) .162-A3
NATCHEZ PARK .106-A2
NATIONAL SPORTS CENTER .65-A3
NATURE RESERVE .95-B2
NEILL PARK .148-B4
NELSON PARK(CR) .64-D2
NELSON PARK(LOL) .103-E2
NELSON PARK(SLP) .105-D4
NESBITT PRESERVE PARK .133-B3
NEW HOPE ATHLETIC FIELD .91-C2
NEWELL PARK .107-C3
NEWPORT-BAILEY FAMILY SCHOOL FOREST .123-B4
NEWWELL PARK .163-A2
NEY COUNTY PARK .29-D4
NICOLLET ISLAND PARK .106-D2
NICOLLET PARK(BUR) .148-D4
NICOLLET PARK(RCH) .120-D4
NIGHTINGALE PARK .96-D2
NINA'S PARK .137-E3
NINE MILE PLAYLOT .148-B1
NORD MYR PARK .133-E3
NORDIC PARK(APV) .149-B4
NORDIC PARK(BUR) .148-D4
NOREMBERG MEMORIAL PARK .103-C4
NORMA KELLY PARK .91-E3
NORMAN RIDGE PLAYGROUND .133-E3
NORMANDALE PARK .119-E4
NORTH BASS LAKE .91-E1
NORTH COMMONS .106-B1
NORTH IDEAL PARK .137-E3
NORTH LIONS PARK .91-D1
NORTH LOTUS LAKE PARK .118-B4
NORTH MISSISSIPPI PARK .92-C2
NORTH PARK(EAG) .136-A3
NORTH PARK(LVL) .162-E4
NORTH PARK(NFD) .219-D3
NORTH RIVER HILLS PARK .148-E2
NORTH RIVER PARK .49-B4
NORTH SHORE OAKS PARK .161-B1
NORTH STAR PARK .65-D3
NORTH TERRACE TOT LOT .33-E1
NORTH TYROL PARK .106-A3
NORTH VALLEY PARK .136-E2
NORTHCREST PLAYGROUND .134-A2
NORTHDALE PARK .95-C3
NORTHEAST ATHLETIC FIELD .106-E1
NORTHERN TRAILS PARK .64-A4
NORTHLAND PARK(CHM) .63-C3
NORTHLAND PARK(SWR) .96-D1
NORTHPORT PARK .92-A1
NORTHSIDE PARK(NP) .201-E2
NORTHSIDE PARK(SLP) .105-D3
NORTHVIEW PARK(BUR) .162-C2
NORTHVIEW PARK(EAG) .149-E1
NORTHVIEW PARK(SSP) .122-D3
NORTHWOOD PARK(BLA) .64-E1
NORTHWOOD PARK(NH) .91-C3
NORTHWOOD PARK(NSP) .109-B1
NORTHWOODS PARK .63-D3
NORWOOD PARK .78-B2
NOWTHEN PARK .20-D4
OAK CHASE PARK .149-D2
OAK CREEK PARK(BLA) .64-E1
OAK CREEK PARK(CHM) .63-C2
OAK FIELD PARK .95-D4
OAK GROVE PARK .63-D4
OAK HILL PARK(FRI) .92-D1
OAK HILL PARK(SLP) .119-D1
OAK KNOLL PARK .33-D1
OAK LEAF WEST PARK .148-E3
OAK POND HILLS PARK .150-A2
OAK SHORES PARK .162-D3
OAKDALE PARK(OKD) .95-C4
OAKDALE PARK(WSP) .122-C2
OAKES PARK .119-C1
OAKLAND BEACH PARK .161-D2
OAKLEY PARK .28-A4
OAKWOOD COMM PLAYFIELD .104-C1
OAKWOOD LUSTRE PARK .95-C4
OAKWOOD PARK(CG) .137-D3
OAKWOOD PARK(IGH) .136-E3
OASIS PARK .93-D3
OBERLIN PARK .105-B2
OCONNELL PARK .161-E2
ODAWA PARK .123-C1
ODD FELLOWS PARK .219-D4
ODOWD LAKE PARK .160-B1
OJIBWAY PARK .123-D2
OLD COTTAGE GROVE COMMUNITY PARK .138-C3
OLD MILL PARK(HAS) .166-D2
OLD MILL PARK(SAV) .101-B3
OLD ORCHID PARK .117-D3
OLEARY PARK .135-E4
OLIVIA T DODGE NATURE CENTER .122-B4
OLYMPIA PARK .64-E3
OPTIMIST PARK .81-B3
OPTIMISTS FIELD .118-E3
ORCHARD GARDENS PARK .162-C3
ORCHARD LAKE PARK .162-B4
ORCHARD LANE PARK .77-E4
ORCHARD PARK .119-A1
OREGON PARK .105-D4
ORME PARK .122-B3
OSCAR & ANNA JOHNSON CO PARK RESERV .99-D1
OSTMANS PARK .50-E3
OSTRANDER PARK .92-E2
OTSEGO COUNTY PARK .33-D2
OTTER PARK .80-D1
OTTO BERG PARK .82-E4
OVERLOOK LAKE PARK .148-A2
OXBOW CREEK PARK .63-E3
PAHA SAPA PARK .162-D2
PAINTER PARK .120-C1
PALMER LAKE ENVIRONMENTAL NATURE AREA .78-B3
PALMER LAKE PARK .78-B4
PALMER PARK .78-B3
PALOMINO PARK .149-A4
PAMELA PARK .120-A4
PAR WEST PARK .31-B1
PARKERS LAKE PARK .104-D1
PARKERS PICNIC GROUNDS .148-D1
PARKSIDE PARK .64-C3
PARKVIEW PARK(LVL) .163-B3
PARKVIEW PARK(ROB) .92-A4
PARKVIEW PARK(SLP) .119-D1
PARKWOOD PARK .148-D4
PATRICK EAGAN PARK .149-E1
PAULYS POND .134-A2
PEARL PARK .120-D3
PEAVEY FIELD .106-D3
PEBBLE PARK .95-D4
PELTZER PARK .49-A1,49-A2
PENNOCK PARK .163-A2
PENNSYLVANIA PARK .105-D3
PEPPER FEST PARK .111-C1
PEPPERMINT STICK PARK .64-A2
PERIDOT PATH PARK .149-C1
PERKINS HILL PARK .92-C4
PERSHING FIELD .120-A2
PETTITT PARK .125-C2
PEXA PARK .176-C3
PHALEN - KELLER REGIONAL PARK .108-D1
PHEASANT HILL PARK .117-E4
PHEASANT HILLS PARK .66-D3
PHEASANT RIDGE PARK(CR) .63-E1
PHEASANT RIDGE PARK(WAC) .129-C3
PHEASANT RUN PARK(CP) .79-D1
PHEASANT RUN PARK(GRA) .95-D2
PHEASANT RUN PARK(HAN) .61-A3
PHELPS FIELD .120-D1
PHILIPPS PARK .201-D2
PICKFAIR POND .133-C3
PIKE LAKE PARK .91-B1
PILGRIM LAKE ELEMENTARY PARK .91-B3
PILGRIM PARK .77-B1
PILOT KNOB PARK .135-D3
PINE COULEE PARK .152-C3
PINE GLEN PARK .151-D1
PINE KNOLL PARK .177-D3
PINE MEADOWS PARK .59-A2
PINE POINT PARK .82-D1
PINES PARK .63-E3
PINETREE POND PARK .137-E3
PINETREE VALLEY PARK .137-E3
PIONEER PARK(BLA) .51-B4
PIONEER PARK(CHS) .131-D4
PIONEER PARK(EPR) .132-D3
PIONEER PARK(HAS) .166-D2
PIONEER PARK(LC) .94-C3
PIONEER PARK(NEW) .137-B2
PIONEER PARK(RVL) .107-E1
PIONEER PARK(SWR) .97-A1
PIONEER PARK(WBY) .124-A2
PLAYCREST PARK .95-B3
PLAZA PARK .78-D3
PLEASANT PARK .117-C3
PLEASANT PLAYLOT .148-C1
PLEASANT VIEW PARK .123-B3
PLYMOUTH COMMUNITY PLAYFIELD .91-C4
PLYMOUTH CREEK PARK .90-D3
PLYMOUTH SQUARE PARK .92-D1
POCAHONTAS PARK .93-D4
PODVIN PARK .80-E3
POINTCROSS PARK .65-E3
POLAR PARK .95-B3
POLARIS PLAYLOT .76-D3
PONDS PARK .80-B2
POOL PARK .142-C4
POPLAR LAKE COUNTY PARK .80-A1
POPULAR BRIDGE PLAYGROUND .134-A3
POTAWATOMI PARK .123-C1
POWDERHORN PARK .120-D1
POWELL PARK .18-A3
POWER HILL PARK .131-E3
PRAIRIE CREEK PARK .177-D1
PRAIRIE EAST PARK .133-C4
PRAIRIE KNOLL PARK .132-A3
PRAIRIE PARK .186-A1
PRAIRIE VIEW SCHOOL PARK .132-C1
PRESERVE PARK .177-D2
PRESIDENT PARK .64-D3
PRESTEMON PARK .93-A2
PROSPECT PARK(CR) .63-E1
PROSPECT PARK(HUD) .111-C2
PUBLIC OPEN SPACE .163-A3
PUDDLES PARK .163-E2
PULASKI PONDS PARK .59-B1
PURGATORY PARK .118-C3
QUAIL CREEK PARK .51-A3
QUAIL RIDGE PARK .66-C3
QUAIL RIDGE PLAYLOT .147-D2
QUARRY PARK .135-C3
QUEENSLAND PARK .104-C2
QUIGLEY-SIME PARK .177-A3
QUINCY PARK .64-E2
RABBIT PARK .34-C3
RAHN PARK .149-B2

PARKS

RAILROAD PARK 81-A3
RAINBOW PARK 105-D4
RAMALEY PARK 81-A4
RAMSEY COUNTY OPEN SPACE 108-A1
RAMSEY GROVE PARK 96-E1
RASPBERRY RIDGE PARK 161-A2
RASPBERRY WOODS PARK 161-A2
RAVEN LAKE PARK 176-D1
RAVINE PARK 149-E2
RED OAK PARK 149-A3
RED PINE PARK 81-B1
RED ROCK PARK 132-E3
REDWOOD PARK 162-E2
REICH PARK 118-B2
REID PARK 110-C1
RESEVOIR PARK 134-B2
REYNOLDS PARK 63-C1
RICE CREEK CHAIN OF
LAKES COUNTY PARK 79-D1
RICE CREEK NORTH
REGIONAL TRAIL COR 79-C2
RICE CREEK PARK 79-A3
RICE LAKE PARK(GV) 106-A1
RICE LAKE PARK(HUG) 67-C3
RICE LAKE SCHOOL &
COMMUNITY PLAYFIELD 76-E2
RICE LAKE TRAILS 76-E2
RICE LAKE WILDLIFE AREA ...47-D2
RICE MARSH LAKE PARK 132-B2
RICE PARK 108-B4
RICH VALLEY PARK 150-D2
RICHARD WALTON
MEMORIAL PARK 109-C2
RICHARDSON PARK 63-C1
RICHFIELD LAKE 120-C4
RICK JOHNSON PARK 101-B3
RIDGE PARK(LE) 109-E2
RIDGE PARK(WBY) 123-E3
RIDGECLIFFE PARK 149-C3
RIDGEGATE PARK 123-D2
RIDGEMOUNT COMMUNITY
PLAYFIELD 105-A2
RIDGEVIEW PLAYGROUND 133-E4
RIDGEWAY PARKWAY 107-A1
RIDGEWOOD EAST PARK 19-E4
RILEY LAKE PARK 132-C3
RINTA PARK 110-E4
RITTER FARM PARK 176-B2
RIVER HEIGHTS PARK 137-A4
RIVER HILLS PARK(EAG) 149-A2
RIVER HILLS PARK(RF) 140-D2
RIVER PARK 78-C2
RIVER RIDGE PARK 92-C1
RIVER RIDGE PLAYGROUND ...135-A3
RIVER'S BEND PARK 49-C2
RIVERBEND PARK 162-A1
RIVERDALE PARK(BC) 78-C3
RIVERDALE PARK(CR) 49-E3
RIVERDALE PARK(RAM) 49-A3
RIVERFRONT PARK 125-C2
RIVERS EDGE PARK 3-A4
RIVERSIDE COUNTY PARK 61-A2
RIVERSIDE PARK(CF) 208-B4
RIVERSIDE PARK(MPL) ..107-A3,121-B1
RIVERSIDE PARK(NFD) 219-D4
RIVERSIDE PARK(RFD) 74-B3
RIVERSIDE PARK(SPP) 137-B3
RIVERVIEW HEIGHTS PARK ...78-C2
RIVERVIEW PARK 146-A2
RIVERVIEW RESERVOIR 64-A3
RIVERWIND PARK 64-A1
RIVERWOOD HILLS PARK 35-B2
ROADSIDE PARK 166-D2
ROCKSLIDE PARK 64-A2
ROGERS LAKE PARK 135-E1
ROLLING HILLS PARK 91-B2
ROLLING MEADOW
ACRES PARK 162-D1
ROLLING OAKS PARK 162-D4
ROOSEVELT PARK 134-D2
ROSE PARK 162-B1
ROSEBROOK PARK 93-D4
ROSELAWN PRESERVE 108-C1
ROTARY PARK 80-E3
ROUND LAKE PARK 132-D2
ROXBURY PARK 105-E4
ROYAL MEADOWS PARK 66-D2
ROYAL OAKS PARK 78-B1
RUM RIVER CENTRAL PARK(OG) .35-C2
RUM RIVER CENTRAL
PARK(RAM) 35-D2
RUM RIVER PRESERVE 21-D2
RUNNING PARK 134-E4
RUTH CIRCLE PARK 78-C2
RUTHERFORD PARK 81-B2,81-B3
SAINT CROIX PARK 105-E1
SAINT JEROME SCHOOL PARK .108-C1
SALEM HILLS PARK 136-C1
SANBORN PARK 92-A3
SANBURNOL PARK 78-D1
SAND CREEK ATHLETIC PARK ..64-C2
SAND CREEK COON
CREEK TRAIL 64-C1
SAND POINT BEACH 161-C2
SAND POINT PARK 161-C1
SAVAGE COMMUNITY PARK 161-E1
SCHEID PARK 105-E1
SCHILLING PARK 77-E3
SCHIMELPFNIG PARK 145-C2
SCHMIDT LAKE PARK 91-A2
SCHROEDER COUNTY PARK 29-A3
SCHROEDERS ACRES PARK 147-C3
SCHULENBURG PARK 83-A4
SCHWARZ POND PARK 164-A1
SCOTT PARK 163-B1
SEASONS PARK 123-E1
SECHLER PARK 219-D4
SETTLERS PARK 60-E3
SEVEN OAKS PARK 121-B1
SHADOW WOOD PARK 131-E4
SHADY ELM PARK 5-C1
SHADY OAK BEACH PARK 119-A3
SHANNON PARK 163-E1
SHAWN ACRES PARK 34-D3
SHAWNEE PARK 123-C1
SHELARD PARK 105-B2
SHENANDOAH PARK 66-A4
SHERIDAN PARK 120-B4
SHILOH PARK 90-C4
SHINGLE CREEK PARK(BP) ...77-C3
SHINGLE CREEK PARK(MPL) ..92-B2
SHONHAGEN PARK 58-E3
SHORES PARK 63-D2
SHUCK PARK 118-A2
SHUMAN WOODS PARK 118-A3
SIBLEY FIELD 120-E1
SIBLEY SWALE PARK 219-E4
SIEDELS LAKE PARK 122-D4
SILVER LAKE BEACH 93-A2
SILVER LAKE PARK(CH) 93-A2
SILVER LAKE PARK(NSP) 95-B3
SILVER POINT PARK 93-B4
SILVERWOOD PARK 118-B3
SIMLEY ISLAND PARK 136-E3
SIPES PARK 77-C2
SITZER PARK 80-A4
SKRIEBAKKEN PARK 134-A3
SKY LINE PARK 135-C4
SKYLINE PARK(BUR) 148-E3
SKYLINE PARK(FRI) 78-D4
SKYVIEW PARK 137-A2
SKYWAY PARK 91-D1
SLATER ACRES PARK 149-A3
SLEEPY HOLLOW PARK(IGH) ..136-E4
SLEEPY HOLLOW PARK(LVL) ..163-B3
SLOUGH LAKE 30-B2
SMITH PARK 134-D2
SNAIL LAKE MARSH
COUNTY PARK 79-E4
SOD FARM PARK AND WETLAND 95-A4
SOENS PLAYLOT 134-D4
SOFTBALL FIELDS 208-C3
SOLBAKKEN PARK 58-E1
SOMMER'S LANDING PARK 97-C4
SOUTH GLEN PLAYGROUND 148-A1
SOUTH HALIFAX PARK 92-A4
SOUTH LOTUS LAKE PARK 132-B2
SOUTH OAKS PARK 150-A2
SOUTH PARK(LVL) 177-A4
SOUTH PARK(NYA) 142-C4
SOUTH RIVER HILLS
PARK 148-B4,149-A2
SOUTH SHORE PARK 105-B2
SOUTH TYROL PARK 106-A3
SOUTH VALLEY PARK 136-E3
SOUTHGATE PARK 58-E3
SOUTHVIEW PARK(SSP) 122-D4
SOUTHVIEW PARK(WSP) 122-C4
SOUTHWEST PARK 95-C2
SOUTHWOOD PARK 109-B1
SOUTHWOOD PLAYGROUND 148-A2
SPANJERS PARK 92-A3
SPOONER PARK 94-C3
SPRING HILL PARK 118-C3
SPRING LAKE PARK(PRL) 160-E3
SPRING LAKE PARK(SLT) 160-E3
SPRING LAKE REGIONAL
PARK(NIT) 151-E4
SPRING LAKE REGIONAL
PARK(RMT) 151-C4
SPRING PARK 117-B1
SPRINGBROOK NATURE CENTER 78-D1
SPRUCE PARK(SSP) 136-E1
SPRUCE PARK(WBL) 95-A2
SQUARE LAKE PARK 69-A3
ST ANTHONY PARK 106-E1
ST CROIX ISLANDS
WILDLIFE AREA 69-D3
ST CROIX STATION PARK 97-C4
ST LAWRENCE WAYSIDE
PARK(BEL) 172-A4
ST LAWRENCE WAYSIDE
PARK(SLW) 172-C3
ST MARYS PARK 105-A2
ST.CROIX BLUFFS
REGIONAL PARK 153-B1
STAPLES FIELD 96-E1
STARING LAKE PARK 132-A2
STATE PARK 172-B3
STATE WILDLIFE REFUGE 63-B3
STEAMBOAT PARK 125-B3
STELLMACHER PARK 95-A1
STERLING OAKS PARK 109-B2
STEVENS SQUARE 106-D3
STEWART PARK 106-D4
STIREWALT MEMORIAL
COUNTY PARK 15-D3
STOCKMAN PARK 92-A4
STONECREEK PARK 131-D2
STONEGATE PARK 109-E3
STRACHAUER PARK 120-A4
STRIEFEL PARK 77-D4
STURGES PARK 58-E2
SUGARBUSH PARK(SAV) 101-B4
SUGARBUSH PARK(WAC) 129-C2
SULLIVAN LAKE PARK 92-E1
SUMMERFIELD PARK 163-D1
SUMMIT PARK 122-D3
SUMMIT POINT PARK 124-A2
SUMMIT POINTE PARK 161-C1
SUMMIT POINTE WEST PARK ..161-C1
SUMMIT SQUARE PARK 92-D1
SUMNER PARK 106-C2
SUNFISH LAKE PARK 96-A4
SUNKIST PARK 78-C2
SUNNY ACRES PARK(ANO) 49-D3
SUNNY ACRES PARK(BP) 77-E2
SUNNY HOLLOW PARK 91-C4
SUNNY LANE PARK 91-D1
SUNNYSIDE PARK(BLA) 64-E4
SUNNYSIDE PARK(NH) 91-D2
SUNNYVIEW PARK 91-D4
SUNRISE PARK(BLO) 133-C4
SUNRISE PARK(LL) 65-E3
SUNRISE PARK(PLY) 91-C4
SUNRISE PARK(SWR) 96-D2
SUNSET HILLS
ELEMENTARY PARK 105-A2
SUNSET HILLS PARK 160-E4
SUNSET MEMORIAL PARK 93-B4
SUNSET OAKS PARK 65-E2
SUNSET PARK(APV) 162-E1
SUNSET PARK(ROB) 92-A3
SUNSET PARK(SLP) 119-C1
SUNSET POND PARK 148-A4
SUNSET RIDGE PARK(CHN) ...131-E2
SUNSET RIDGE PARK(MPW) ...94-D3
SUNSHINE PARK 105-E4
SUZANNA PARK 64-E2
SWAGER PARK 96-E3
SWAN LAKE PARK 91-A3
SWAN PARK 64-D3
SYLVAN HILLS PARK 78-D4
TABLYN PARK 109-E1
TAFT PARK 120-E4
TAHPAH PARK 146-A3
TAMARACK NATURE PRESERVE 123-D2
TAMARACK PARK(CP) 65-D4
TAMARACK PARK(RVL) 108-A1
TANNERS LAKE PARK 109-C4
TARGET POND WETLAND 95-A4
TARNHILL PARK 134-A4
TEAL LAKE NEIGHBORHOOD
PARK 77-A1
TEMPLE ISRAEL MEMORIAL
PARK 120-D2
TENNISIOUX PARK 148-E2
TERRA LINDA PARK 91-D4
TERRACE OAKS EAST PARK ...148-E3
TERRACE OAKS WEST PARK ...148-E4
TERRACE PARK(FRI) 78-D3
TERRACE PARK(LVL) 177-A3
TERRACE PARK(SLK) 78-D2
TERRITORIAL PARK 64-D3
TESSMAN PARK 77-D2
TEXA-TONKA PARK 105-D4
THE PARADE 106-C3
THE PARK 118-A4
THE POND ATHLETIC COMPLEX .161-B4
THEODORE WIRTH PARK(GV) ..106-A2
THEODORE WIRTH PARK(MPL) .106-A3
THOMAS HOLLINGSWORTH
PARK 92-A3
THOMAS LAKE PARK 149-D2
THOMPSON COUNTY PARK 122-D3
THOMPSON HILL 122-C3
THORESEN PARK 91-B1
THORPE FIELD(CR) 64-A1
THORPE FIELD(DPH) 118-B1
THREE PONDS PARK 91-B2
THUNDER BAY PARK 94-D3
TIGHE SCHMITZ PARK 95-C1
TILSEN PARK 1 ....109-C1
TILSEN PARK 2 ....109-C1
TIMBER CREST FOREST 76-E4
TIMBER SHORES PARK 91-B2
TIMBERGLADE PLAYGROUND ...147-E1
TIMBERLAND KNOLLS PARK ...148-C4
TIMBERLEA PARK 123-E2
TINTAH PARK 163-D1
TITTERUD PARK 35-A4
TODD FIELD PARK 166-D2
TODD PARK(EDI) 119-E2
TODD PARK(MPL) 120-D3
TOLZMAN PARK 39-B2
TOP OF THE WORLD PARK 19-D4
TOPVIEW PARK 133-A1
TOWER HILL PARK(MPL) 107-B3
TOWER HILL PARK(MTK) 118-E2
TOWER PARK(NSP) 95-B4
TOWER PARK(SLP) 119-C1
TOWERVIEW PARK 64-A1
TOWN SQUARE PARK 125-B3
TRACKSIDE PARK 64-B3
TRAPP FARM PARK 150-A2
TRAPROCK PARK 48-E1
TRIANGLE COUNTY PARK 58-D2
TRIANGLE PARK(MHT) 95-D1
TRIANGLE PARK(ROB) 92-A3
TRIANGLE PARK(SWR) 97-A1
TRINITY GARDENS PARK 77-E1
TROOST PARK 161-E1
TROY PARK 125-D1
TURTLE LAKE PARK(PLY) 90-D3
TURTLE LAKE PARK(SVW) 80-A3
TWIN FIELD PARK 64-B2
TWIN LAKE BEACH PARK 92-A2
TWIN LAKES 30-D3
TWIN LAKES COUNTY PARK ...20-C4
TWIN LAKES PARK(BUR) 162-D2
TWIN LAKES PARK(SLP) 106-A4
TWIN OAK PARK 91-E2
TYACKE PARK 162-D2
U OF M ARBORETUM 131-C2
UNION PARK 185-E1
UTLEY PARK 120-A3
VADNAIS-SNAIL LAKES
REGIONAL PARK 94-B1
VALLEY HIGHLANDS PARK 148-C4
VALLEY LAKE PARK 163-B3
VALLEY MIDDLE PARK 162-E2
VALLEY PARK(HOP) 119-C3
VALLEY PARK(MH) 122-A4
VALLEY PARK(RVL) 93-E3
VALLEY PLACE PARK 91-D4
VALLEY VIEW PARK(MPL) 106-B1
VALLEY VIEW PARK(OPH) 97-A3
VALLEY VIEW PLAYFIELD 134-D3
VALLEYFAIR AMUSEMENT
PARK 146-E2
VAN BUREN PARK 64-E4
VAN CLEVE PARK 107-A2
VAN VALKENBERG PARK 119-C2
VANDERBIE PARK 134-C3
VANTAGE POINT OPEN SPACE .138-A4
VENESS PLAYLOT 133-C3
VERMILLIAN FALLS PARK 166-D2
VETERANS MEMORIAL
PARK(HAS) 166-D1
VETERANS MEMORIAL
PARK(RCH) 120-D4
VETERANS MEMORIAL
PARK(SHK) 146-C3
VETERANS MEMORIAL
PARK(WBL) 81-A4
VETERANS PARK(RF) 140-E2
VETERANS PARK(RVL) 93-E3
VETERANS PARK(SPP) 137-B2
VETS FIELD 122-D3
VFW PARK 110-C1
VICTORIA HIGHLAND PARK ...121-E4
VICTORIA PARK 123-D3
VICTORIA-EVERGREEN PARK ..118-D1
VICTORY PARK(MPL) 92-B3
VICTORY PARK(NH) 91-C1
VILLA PARK 108-A1
VILLAGE HALL PARK 118-A2
VINCENT SQUARE PARK 95-D2
VINEYARDS PARK 63-E1
VISTA HILLS PARK 123-B2
VISTA VIEW PARK 148-C4
WAITE PARK 93-A3
WALDEN HEIGHTS PARK 149-D2
WALKER PARK 119-D1
WALLACE PARK 163-A1
WALNUT HILL PARK 149-E2
WALNUT RIDGE PARK 119-C3
WALT MUTTERER PARK 74-B3
WALTER SOCHACKI PARK 92-A4
WANDA MILLER PLAYLOT 134-A2
WANGSTAD PARK 92-A1
WARNER PARK 95-D1
WARREN F BUTLER PARK 148-A3
WASHBURN FAIR OAKS 106-D3
WASHINGTON PARK(NFD) 219-E4
WASHINGTON PARK(SWR) 96-E2
WATERFORD PARK 219-E2
WATERWORKS PARK 107-E1
WAVELAND PARK 120-A2
WAWATOSA ISLAND PARK 117-A3
WAWTOF PARK 80-E2
WAY PARK 219-D3
WAYSIDE PARK(LVL) 162-B4
WAYSIDE PARK(MSC) 55-B4
WAYSIDE REST PARK 48-C1
WEAVER LAKE PARK 76-C2
WEAVER LAKE PUBLIC ACCESS ..76-B2
WEAVER LAKE SCHOOL &
COMMUNITY PLAY 76-D2
WEBBER PARK 92-C3
WEBER FIELD 120-A2
WEBSTER PARK(NOH) 111-D1
WEBSTER PARK(SLP) 119-E1
WEDGEWOOD HEIGHTS PARK ...123-E3
WEDGEWOOD PARK 124-B3
WEDGEWOOD PARK(MHT) 95-C2
WEKOTA PARK 117-D2
WELCOME PARK 91-E2
WELL SITE PARK 149-D2
WELLINGTON CRESCENT PARK .162-C1
WELLS PARK 140-E3
WELTERS WILDWOOD 148-B2
WENTWORTH PARK 122-A3
WESCHCKE PARK 122-B3
WESLEY PARK 105-C1
WEST BRIDGE PARK 31-D1
WEST BUCK HILL 162-C3
WEST MARSH LAKE PARK 134-A3
WEST MEDICINE LAKE PARK ..105-A1
WEST PALMER LAKE PARK 78-A3
WEST PARK 81-B3
WEST PULASKI PARK 45-A4
WEST RIVER PARK 63-D2
WEST ST PAUL SPORTS
COMPLEX 122-D3
WESTCOTT STATION PARK 136-A4
WESTDALE PARK(RF) 140-D1
WESTDALE PARK(SLP) 105-C3
WESTERN AVENUE
MARSH(BUR) 148-B3
WESTERN AVENUE
MARSH(GV) 91-E4,105-D1
WESTERN AVENUE
MARSH(LAU) 107-B2
WESTERN AVENUE
MARSH(MHT) 81-D3
WESTERN AVENUE
MARSH(SFT) 159-B3
WESTERN AVENUE
MARSH(WAY) 104-C3
WESTERN HILLS PARK 108-B1
WESTLING POND PARK 105-C4
WESTVIEW PARK 123-C3
WESTVIEW PARK(BUR) 148-A4
WESTWOOD PARK(BLA) 64-E4
WESTWOOD PARK(BP) 78-C2
WESTWOOD PARK(HAS) 166-D2
WESTWOOD PARK(MTK) 105-B2
WESTWOOD PARK(SLK) 79-A1
WESTWOOD PLAYFIELD 148-B1
WETHERN PARK 49-B4
WEYERHAEUSER PARK 80-E3
WHITBRED MEMORIAL PARK ...137-C3
WHITE-KINNICKINNIC
PATHWAY 140-D2
WHITTIER PARK 106-C4
WILD WINGS GAME PRESERVE ..68-A2
WILDERNESS PARK 50-C4
WILDHURST PARK 129-D3
WILDWOOD PARK(APV) 163-A1
WILDWOOD PARK(CR) 50-B3
WILDWOOD PARK(GV) 105-D1
WILDWOOD PARK(MHT) 95-C1
WILLERNIE PARK 95-D1
WILLIAM BERRY PARK 120-B1
WILLIAM MAY PARK 99-C4
WILLIAM OBRIEN
STATE PARK(MSC) 55-B4
WILLIAM OBRIEN
STATE PARK(NST) 55-B2
WILLIAM WARDWELL
LEWIS PARK 133-D1
WILLIAMS PARK 111-D2
WILLKOMEN PARK 142-C3
WILLOW LANE PARK 77-E4
WILLOW PARK(EPR) 133-A1
WILLOW PARK(SLP) 105-D4
WILLOW POND PARK 93-D4
WILLOW RIDGE PARK 59-A2
WILLOW RIVER
STATE PARK(HUT) 98-A4
WILLOW RIVER
STATE PARK(SJT) 98-A3
WILLOWS PARK 161-A4
WILLOWSTONE PARK 78-B1
WILMES LAKE PARK 124-A1
WILSON PARK(HAS) 166-D1
WILSON PARK(MTK) 118-D2
WILSON PARK(RCH) 134-E1
WILSON PARK(SSP) 122-D2
WILSON PARK(SVW) 93-E1
WINDOM PARK 93-A4
WINDS PARK 163-E3
WINDWOOD PASSAGE PARK 123-C3
WINFIELD PONDS PARK 74-B2
WINKEL PARK 145-C3
WINTERCREST PARK 64-C3
WOLFE PARK 120-A1
WOLK PARK 148-D4
WOOD PARK 162-D1,162-D2
WOODBRIDGE MARSH 133-C4
WOODBURY PARK 163-A4
WOODCREST
NEIGHBORHOOD PARK 77-C4
WOODCREST PARK(CR) 64-C3
WOODCREST PARK(NOH) 111-D1
WOODDALE PARK 120-A2
WOODGATE PARK 118-D3
WOODHAVEN PARK 149-B1
WOODLAND GREEN PARK 49-C1
WOODLAND HEIGHTS 50-B4
WOODLAND OAKS PARK 50-B4
WOODLAND TRAILS PARK 19-C3
WOODLANE HILLS PARK 123-D3
WOODLAWN PARK 63-C3
WOODRIDGE PARK 138-A4
WOODVIEW PARK 64-C1
WOOLANS PARK 52-B4
WORDEN SPECIAL USE PARK ..76-E3
WRIGHTS LAKE PARK 134-E2
WYNDHAM KNOLL PARK 118-B4
XERXES POND 148-B1
XYLITE PARK 65-B4
YORK PARK 120-B3
YORKTOWN PARK 134-A1
YOSEMITE PARK 105-E2
YOST POST 81-A4
YUNKERS PARK 91-C4
ZACHARY COMMUNITY
PLAYFIELD 91-B3
ZANE COURT PARK 77-E3
ZANEWOOD PARK 77-E3

POINTS OF INTEREST

ABBOTT NORTHWESTERN HOSPITAL 106-D4
AFTON ALPS SKI AREA 139-B2
AMERICAN SWEDISH INSTITUTE 106-D4
AMTRAK 107-C3
APACHE PLAZA SHOPPING CENTER 93-A2
BECKER COMMUNITY CENTER 2-E3
BELL MUSEUM OF NATURAL HISTORY 107-A2
BETHESDA LUTHERAN HOSPITAL 108-B3
BROOKDALE SHOPPING CENTER 92-B1
BUCK HILL SKI AREA 162-C3
BURNSVILLE SHOPPING CENTER 162-C1
CALHOUN SQUARE 106-C4
CANNON FALLS HOSPITAL 208-A4
CHILDRENS HOSPITAL - SAINT PAUL 108-B4
CHILDRENS MEDICAL CENTER - MPLS . 106-D4
CHILDRENS MUSEUM 107-E3
CITY CENTER SHOPPING CENTER 106-D2
COMO PARK ZOO 107-D2
COON RAPIDS MEDICAL CENTER 64-D4
EDEN PRAIRIE SHOPPING CENTER 133-B2
FAIRVIEW LAKES REGIONAL MEDICAL CENTER 25-B4
FAIRVIEW RIDGES HOSPITAL 162-D1
FAIRVIEW SOUTHDALE HOSPITAL 120-A4
FAIRVIEW-UNIVERSITY MEDICAL CENTER 107-A3
FAIRVIEW-UNIVERSITY-RIVERSIDE CAMPU 107-A3
GILLETTE CHILDRENS HOSPITAL 108-B4
GUTHRIE THEATER 106-C3
HAR MAR MALL 107-D1
HENNEPIN COUNTY MED. CTR ..106-D3
HOSPITAL 111-D2
HOSPITAL & MEDICAL CENTER ..14-C2
JAMES J HILL HOUSE 108-B4
KNOLLWOOD MALL 119-C1
LAKEVIEW MEMORIAL 96-E2
MALL OF AMERICA 134-E2
MAPLEWOOD MALL 95-A3
MCF LINO LAKES 66-A1
MCF OAK PARK HEIGHTS 97-A3
MCF SHAKOPEE 146-A2
MCF STILLWATER 97-B3
MERCY MEDICAL CENTER 63-D1
METHODIST HOSPITAL 119-E2
MIDWAY SHOPPING CENTER 107-D4
MINNEAPOLIS CONVENTION CENTER 106-D3
MINNEAPOLIS INSTITUTE OF ARTS 106-D3
MINNEAPOLIS LIBRARY & PLANETARIUM 106-D2
MINNESOTA ZOO 149-C3
MURPHYS LANDING 146-D2
MYSTIC LAKE CASINO 160-D2
NATIVITY OF OUR LORD CATHOLIC CHURC 121-C1
NORTH MEMORIAL MEDICAL CENTER 92-B4
NORTHRUP AUDITORIUM 107-A2
NORTHTOWN MALL 78-D1
QUEEN OF PEACE HOSPITAL 201-E2
RAMSEY HOUSE 122-B1
REGINA MEMORIAL HOSPITAL ..166-C1
REGIONS HOSPITAL 108-B4
RIDGEDALE SHOPPING CENTER .105-A3
RIDGEVIEW MEDICAL CENTER ..129-D3
RIVER HEIGHTS IMMEDIATE CARE CENTER 122-D3
ROSEDALE SHOPPING CENTER ..93-D4
SAINT FRANCIS REGIONAL MED. CTR 146-C3
SAINT JOHNS NORTHEAST HOSPITAL 94-E3
SAINT JOSEPHS HOSPITAL 108-B4
SAINT MARYS HOSPITAL 107-A3
SAINT PAUL CATHEDRAL 108-B4
SHRINERS HOSPITAL 107-B3
SIBLEY HOUSE 121-D4
SIGNAL HILLS SHOPPING CENTER 122-C3
SISTER KENNEY INSTITUTE 106-D4
SOMERSET CAMP 84-B1
SOUTHDALE SHOPPING CENTER 134-A1
SOUTHTOWN SHOPPING CENTER 134-B2
STATE FAIR COLISEUM 107-C2
TREASURE ISLAND CASINO 182-D4
TROLLHAUGEN SKI AREA 28-D2
UNITED HOSPITAL 108-B4
UNITY HOSPITAL 78-D2
VETERANS ADMINISTRATION HOSPITAL 121-B3
WALKER ART CENTER 106-C3
WELCH VILLAGE SKI AREA 195-E4
WORLD TRADE CENTER 108-B4

PUBLIC & PRIVATE SCHOOLS

ACADEMY OF THE HOLY ANGELS120-C4
ADAMS ELEM.(CR) 64-C4
ADAMS ELEM.(STP) 121-E2
AFTON-LAKELAND ELEM 111-C4
AKIN ROAD ELEM 177-D2
ALICE SMITH ELEM 119-B1
ALLIANCE SCHOOL 33-E1
AMERICAN INDIAN MAGNET ..108-D3
AMES ELEM 109-A3
ANDERSEN CONTEMPORARY ELEM 106-D4
ANDERSEN OPEN ELEM 106-D4
ANDERSON ELEM 95-D2
ANDOVER ELEM 50-B1
ANDOVER H.S 50-B2
ANOKA H.S 49-D3
ANOKA RAMSEY COMMUNITY COLLEGE 63-E2
ANOKA TECHNICAL COLLEGE ..49-C4
ANTHONY J.H.S 120-C3
ANWATIN J.H.S 106-B3
APPLE VALLEY H.S 163-A2
AQUILA ELEM 105-C4
ARLINGTON H.S 108-B2
ARMATAGE ELEM 120-B3
ARMSTRONG ELEM 137-E4
ARMSTRONG H.S 91-B3
AUDUBON ELEM 120-A1
AUGSBURG COLLEGE 106-E3
BAILY ELEM 123-D4
BANCROFT ELEM 120-E1
BARTON ELEM 120-C2
BASSWOOD ELEM 76-D4
BATTLE CREEK ELEM 123-A1
BATTLE CREEK J.H.S 109-A4
BAYPORT ELEM 97-B3
BAYVIEW MIDDLE 129-D3
BEAVER LAKE ELEM 109-B2
BECKER ELEM 2-E4
BECKER H.S 2-E3
BECKER MIDDLE 2-E3
BELAIR ELEM 93-B1
BELLAIRE ELEM 95-B1
BELLE PLAINE ELEM 185-E2
BELLE PLAINE H.S 185-E1
BELLE PLAINE J.H.S 185-E1
BENILDE SAINT MARGARETS H.S 105-E4
BENJAMIN BANNEKER ELEM ..120-D1
BENJAMIN MAYS K-8 ELEM 107-D3
BETHANY ACADEMY 148-B1
BETHANY COLLEGE OF MISSIONS 147-D2
BETHEL COLLEGE AND SEMINARY 93-D1
BETHUNE ELEM 106-C2
BIG LAKE ELEM 18-B3
BIG LAKE H.S 18-B3
BIG LAKE MIDDLE 18-B3
BIRCH GROVE ELEM 77-E3
BIRCH LAKE ELEM 80-E3
BIRCHVIEW ELEM 104-D2
BLACKHAWK MIDDLE 149-D1
BLAINE H.S 50-D4
BLAKE SCHOOL 119-C2
BLAKE SCHOOL - NORTHROP CAMPUS 106-C3
BLUFF CREEK ELEM 131-D2
BRAVO J.H.S 134-D3
BRECK SCHOOL 105-E2
BRIDGE VIEW ELEM 122-A1
BRIMHALL ELEM 93-C4
BROADWAY ELEM 39-B3
BROOKLYN CENTER J.H.S./H.S ..78-C4
BROOKLYN J.H.S 77-E3
BROOKSIDE ELEM 119-E2
BROWN INSTITUTE 106-E4
BRYN MAWR ELEM 106-B2
BUFFALO H.S 59-B2
BUFFALO MIDDLE 58-E1
BURNSVILLE H.S 148-D3
BURROUGHS ELEM 120-C3
CALVARY MEMORIAL SCHOOL ..117-B1
CANNON FALLS ELEM 208-C4
CANNON FALLS J.H.S./H.S 208-B4
CARVER ELEM 123-B1
CASTLE ELEM 95-C3
CAVANAGH EARLY CHILDHOOD ..91-E2
CEDAR CREEK COMMUNITY ELEM 22-E3
CEDAR ELEM 36-C1
CEDAR ISLAND ELEM 77-A4
CEDAR MANOR INTERMEDIATE CNTR 105-C4
CEDAR PARK ELEM 163-B3
CEDAR RIDGE ELEM 132-C3
CENTENNIAL ELEM.(BLA) 65-D3
CENTENNIAL ELEM.(RCH) 134-E1
CENTENNIAL H.S 65-E3
CENTENNIAL J.H.S 65-E3
CENTENNIAL MIDDLE 66-A2
CENTENNIAL NEW ELEM 66-A2
CENTERVILLE ELEM 66-D2
CENTRAL ELEM 146-B2
CENTRAL H.S 107-E4
CENTRAL J.H.S 39-B3
CENTRAL KINDERGARTEN CENTER 132-D2
CENTRAL MIDDLE(CH) 92-E1
CENTRAL MIDDLE(EPR) 132-D2
CENTRAL MIDDLE(WBL) 81-A3
CENTRAL PARK ELEM 94-A4
CENTURY COLLEGE 95-B2
CENTURY J.H.S 176-E1
CHAMPLIN ELEM 63-C1
CHAMPLIN PARK H.S 63-E3
CHANHASSEN ELEM 132-A2
CHAPEL HILL ACADEMY 132-C1
CHASKA ELEM 145-C1
CHASKA H.S 131-D4
CHASKA MIDDLE EAST 145-D2
CHASKA MIDDLE WEST 145-C2
CHELSEA HEIGHTS ELEM 107-D2
CHEROKEE HEIGHTS ELEM 122-B2
CHERRY VIEW ELEM 162-E4
CHILDRENS ACADEMY NORTH ..106-C1
CHIPPEWA MIDDLE 80-A3
CHIRON MIDDLE 106-C3
CHISAGO LAKES H.S 26-D1
CHISAGO LAKES J.H.S 12-E4
CHISAGO LAKES PRIMARY 26-B2
CHRISTA MCAULIFFE ELEM 166-B2
CHRISTINA HUDDLESTON ELEM .162-E4
CLEAR SPRINGS ELEM 118-C3
CLEVELAND J.H.S 108-C3
CLOVER RIDGE ELEM 145-B1
COLLEGE OF SAINT CATHERINE .121-C2
COLUMBIA HTS H.S 92-E1
COLUMBUS ELEM 38-D3
COMO PARK ELEM 107-E2
COMO PARK H.S 107-E2
CONCORD ELEM 119-E4
CONCORDIA ACADEMY 94-A4
CONCORDIA COLLEGE 107-D4
COON RAPIDS H.S 64-A1
COON RAPIDS MIDDLE 64-A1
COOPER ELEM.(HAS) 166-D2
COOPER ELEM.(MPL) 107-B4
COOPER H.S 91-C2
CORNELIA ELEM 134-A1
COTTAGE GROVE J.H.S 138-A3
COUNTRYSIDE ELEM 119-D3
COWERN ELEM 95-B4
CREEK VALLEY ELEM 119-C4
CREST VIEW ELEM 77-E2
CRESTVIEW ELEM 137-D3
CRETIN-DERHAM HALL H.S 121-D2
CROOKED LAKE ELEM 49-E3
CROSSWINDS MIDDLE SCHOOL 123-C1
CRYSTAL LAKE ELEM 162-E3
DAKOTA HILLS MIDDLE 149-E1
DAKOTA TECH. COLLEGE ROSEMOUNT 164-E2
DAYTON ELEM 49-A4
DAYTONS BLUFF ELEM 108-D4
DE LASALLE H.S 106-D2
DEEPHAVEN ELEM 118-B2
DEERWOOD ELEM 149-D1
DELANO ELEM 87-E2
DELANO MIDDLE/H.S 87-E2
DIAMOND PATH ELEM 163-D2
DISCOVERY CENTER 58-E2
DONALD MCQUIRE J.H.S 176-E4
DOWLING ELEM 121-B1
DOWNTOWN KINDERGARTEN ..108-B4
DOWNTOWN OPEN 106-D2
DRESSER SCHOOL 28-D2
DUNWOODY INSTITUTE 106-C3
E.P. ROCK ELEM 111-D3
EAGAN H.S 150-A1
EAGLE POINT ELEM 109-D3
EAGLE RIDGE J.H.S 162-A1
EARLE BROWN ELEM 92-C1
EARLY CHILDHOOD FAMILY ELEM 131-C4
EAST BETHEL CMMTY ELEM 22-E2
EAST CONSOLIDATED ELEM 108-C3
EAST MIDDLE 105-A2
EAST UNION ELEM 158-D3
EASTERN HEIGHTS ELEM 109-A3
EASTSIDE WORKPLACE KDGN ..108-E4
EASTVIEW H.S 163-C1
EASTVIEW ELEM 176-E1
ECHO PARK ELEM 162-E1
EDEN LAKE ELEM 133-A3
EDEN PRAIRIE H.S 132-C1
EDGERTON ELEM 108-C1
EDGEWOOD ELEM 77-C4
EDGEWOOD MIDDLE 79-B3
EDINA H.S 133-D1
EDINBROOK ELEM 77-E2
EDISON H.S 92-E4
EDISON PPL 106-D4
EDWARD NEILL ELEM 148-B4
EISENHOWER ELEM.(CR) 64-D2
EISENHOWER ELEM.(HOP) 119-B1
ELK RIVER H.S 33-E1
ELLIOT ELEM 134-D1
ELM CREEK ELEM 63-B4
EMERSON ELEM 106-C3
EMMET WILLIAMS ELEM 93-E3
ERICSSON ELEM 121-A2
EVERGREEN PARK ELEM 78-C4
EXCELSIOR ELEM 117-E3
EXPO MAGNET SCHOOL 121-D2
FAIR OAKS ELEM 77-E4
FALCON HEIGHTS ELEM 107-D1
FALCON RIDGE MIDDLE 149-C4
FARMINGTON ELEM 177-E4
FARMINGTON H.S 177-E4
FARMINGTON MIDDLE 177-E3
FARMINGTON NEW ELEM 177-C2
FARNSWORTH ELEM 108-D2
FERNBROOK ELEM 76-E1
FIELD ELEM 120-D2
FITZPATRICK SCHOOL 57-B2
FIVE HAWKS ELEM 161-A4
FOLWELL J.H.S 120-E1
FOREST ELEM 91-D2
FOREST HILLS ELEM 132-E1
FOREST HILLS MAGNET ELEM ..97-A2
FOREST LAKE ELEM 39-B3
FOREST LAKE H.S 39-B4
FOREST VIEW ELEM 39-B3
FOUR SEASONS ELEM 108-B2
FOUR WINDS ELEM 106-D3
FRANKLIN ELEM.(ANO) 49-C4
FRANKLIN ELEM.(STP) 108-B3
FRANKLIN J.H.S 106-C1
FRED MOORE MIDDLE 63-C1
FRENCH IMMERSION/ HIGHLAND 121-D2
FRIDLEY H.S 78-E4
FRIDLEY MIDDLE 78-E4
FRIENDLY HILLS MIDDLE 136-A1
FROST LAKE ELEM 108-E2
FULTON ELEM 120-B2
GALTIER ELEM 107-D3
GARDEN CITY ELEM 78-A4
GARLOUGH ELEM 122-B4
GATEWOOD ELEM 118-D4
GIDEON POND ELEM 148-D4
GLACIER HILLS ELEM 149-D1
GLEASON LAKE ELEM 104-C2
GLEN LAKE ELEM 118-E2
GLENDALE ELEM 161-E1
GLENN MIDDLE 94-E4
GOLDEN LAKE ELEM 65-D4
GOLFVIEW ELEM 95-B2
GRAINWOOD ELEM 161-B3
GRANDVIEW MIDDLE 116-E1
GREEN CENTRAL PARK MIDDLE .120-D1
GREENLEAF ELEM 163-B1
GREENWOOD ELEM.(PLY) 90-C3
GREENWOOD ELEM.(RF) 140-E1
GREY CLOUD ELEM 138-A3
GROVELAND ELEM 118-C1
GROVELAND PARK ELEM 121-C1
GUARDIAN ANGELS 145-C3
HALE ELEM 120-E3
HALL ELEM 106-C1
HAMILTON ELEM.(CR) 64-B2
HAMILTON ELEM.(MPL) 92-C3
HAMLINE UNIVERSITY 107-D3
HANCOCK ELEM 107-D3
HANDKE ELEM 33-D2
HANOVER ELEM 60-E3
HARDING H.S 108-E3
HARRIET BISHOP ELEM 161-E1
HASTINGS H.S 166-C2
HASTINGS MIDDLE 166-D2
HAYDEN HEIGHTS ELEM 109-A2
HAYES ELEM 78-E3
HAZEL PARK J.H.S 109-A2
HENDERSON ELEM 198-D4
HENDERSON H.S 198-D3
HENNEPIN TECH. COLLEGE BROOKLYN PK 77-C3
HENNEPIN TECH. COLLEGE EDEN PRAIRIE 133-A3
HENRY H.S 92-B3
HENRY SIBLEY H.S 122-B4
HERITAGE MIDDLE 122-B2
HIAWATHA ELEM 121-B2
HIDDEN OAKS MIDDLE 161-C3
HIDDEN VALLEY ELEM 162-A1
HIGHLAND ELEM.(APV) 163-C1
HIGHLAND ELEM.(CH) 92-E1
HIGHLAND PARK ELEM 121-D2
HIGHLAND PARK H.S 121-D3
HIGHLAND PARK J.H.S 121-D2
HIGHLANDS ELEM 119-D3
HIGHVIEW J.H.S 93-B1
HIGHWOOD HILLS ELEM 123-A1
HILL ELEM 107-E4
HILL MURRAY H.S 109-B1
HILLCREST ELEM 134-B3
HILLSIDE ELEM 137-E4
HILLTOP ELEM 136-E2
HILLTOP PRIMARY 102-E4
HOLLAND ELEM 106-D1
HOMECROFT ELEM 121-C3
HOOVER ELEM 64-A2
HOPKINS H.S 105-B4
HOSTERMANN MIDDLE 91-C2
HOW. LAKE/WAVERLY K-12 ....85-A1
HOWE ELEM 121-B1
HUBERT OLSON J.H.S 148-A1
HUDSON H.S 111-D2
HUDSON J.H.S 111-E2
HUGO ELEM 67-B2
HUMBOLDT J.H.S./H.S 122-C2
HUMPHREY ELEM 85-E1
IMMACULATE HEART OF MARY SCHOOL 118-E3
INDIAN MOUNDS ELEM 134-D4
INTERNATIONAL MONTESSORI ACADEMY 147-E1
INTERNATIONAL SCHOOL 119-A4
INVER GROVE ELEM 137-A2
INVER GROVE HEIGHTS MIDDLE 136-E4
INVER HILLS COMMUNITY COLLEGE 136-D4
IRONDALE H.S 79-B3
ISLAND LAKE ELEM 93-E2
JACKSON ELEM 108-A3
JACKSON MIDDLE 63-E3
JEFFERSON ALTERNATIVE H.S ..122-A1
JEFFERSON ELEM.(BLA) 64-D2
JEFFERSON ELEM.(MPL) 106-C4
JEFFERSON H.S 148-A1
JENNY LIND ELEM 92-C2
JOHN F. KENNEDY ELEM.(HAS) .166-D2
JOHN F. KENNEDY ELEM.(LVL) ..177-A4
JOHN F. KENNEDY H.S 134-D4
JOHNSON H.S 108-D2
JOHNSVILLE ELEM 50-E4
JONATHAN ELEM 131-C4
JORDAN ELEM 173-A3
JORDAN H.S 173-A3
JORDAN J.H.S 173-A3
JORDAN PARK EXTENTED DAY ..92-C4
KAPOSIA EDUCATION CENTER ..136-E1
KATHERINE CURREN ELEM 119-B2
KEEWAYDIN ELEM 121-A3
KENNETH HALL ELEM 78-E2
KENNY ELEM 120-C3
KENWOOD ELEM 106-B3
KENWOOD TRAIL J.H.S 176-D2
KIMBERLY LANE ELEM 90-C3
L. O. JACOB ELEM 64-B3
LAKE ELMO ELEM 110-B1
LAKE J.H.S 123-E3
LAKE MARION ELEM 176-E3
LAKEAIRES ELEM 95-A1
LAKESIDE INTERMEDIATE 26-A1
LAKEVIEW ELEM.(LVL) 176-D3
LAKEVIEW ELEM.(ROB) 92-A3
LAKEVILLE H.S 176-E2
LILY LAKE ELEM 96-E2
LINCOLN CENTER ELEM 122-E3
LINCOLN ELEM.(ANO) 63-C1
LINCOLN ELEM.(BP) 91-D1
LINCOLN ELEM.(ER) 33-E1
LINCOLN ELEM.(MPL) 106-B2
LINCOLN ELEM.(WBL) 81-A3
LINO LAKES ELEM 52-B4
LINWOOD A+ ELEM 121-E1
LINWOOD ELEM 24-A1
LITTLE CANADA ELEM 94-C3

PUBLIC & PRIVATE SCHOOLS

LITTLE MOUNTAIN ELEM 31-D3
LONGFELLOW ELEM.(MPL) 107-A4
LONGFELLOW ELEM.(STP) 107-C4
LORING ELEM 92-B3
LUCY CRAFT LANEY ELEM 92-B4
LUTHERAN H.S. OF
  MINNEAPOLIS 134-D2
LYNDALE ELEM 120-C1
MACALESTER COLLEGE 121-D1
MADISON ELEM 64-E3
MAHTOMEDI H.S 95-D1
MAHTOMEDI MIDDLE 95-D1
MALONE ELEM 153-B4
MANN ELEM 121-C2
MAPLE GROVE H.S 62-E4
MAPLE GROVE J.H.S 77-A4
MAPLE LAKE ELEM 43-D2
MAPLE LAKE H.S 43-D2
MAPLEWOOD MIDDLE 109-B1
MARCY OPEN ELEM 106-E2
MARINE ELEM 55-B4
MARION SAVAGE ELEM 148-A3
MARTIN LUTHER KING ELEM 106-D3
MATH AND SCIENCE ACADEMY .123-E2
MAXFIELD ELEM 107-E4
MAYER-LUTHERAN H.S 114-E4
MC KINLEY ELEM 37-A4
MCKNIGHT EEC 120-D2
MEADOW LAKE ELEM 91-C1
MEADOWBROOK ELEM 105-E2
MEADOWVALE ELEM 19-D4
MENDOTA ELEM 121-E4
METCALF J.H.S 149-A1
METRO STATE UNIVERSITY 108-C3
MEYER MIDDLE 140-E2
MIDELTON ELEM 124-A3
MILL CITY MONTESSORI 106-D2
MINNEAPOLIS COLLEGE
  OF ART AND DESI 106-D4
MINNEAPOLIS
  COMMUNITY COLLEGE 106-C3
MINNEAPOLIS TECHNICAL
  COLLEGE 106-C3
MINNEHAHA ACADEMY
  MIDDLE/LOWER 121-B2
MINNEHAHA ACADEMY
  NO. CAMPUS 107-B4
MINNETONKA EAST MIDDLE 118-C2
MINNETONKA H.S 118-B3
MINNETONKA WEST MIDDLE . . .117-D4
MINNEWASHTA ELEM 117-C3
MISSISSIPPI ELEM.(CR) 63-E2
MISSISSIPPI ELEM.(STP) 108-B2
MONROE CMMTY ELEM 121-E1
MONROE ELEM 78-C3
MONTICELLO H.S 31-D2
MONTICELLO MIDDLE 31-E3
MONTROSE ELEM 86-D1
MORELAND ELEM 122-B3
MORRIS BYE ELEM 64-A1
MORRIS PARK ELEM 121-B3
MOUND WESTONKA H.S 102-E4
MOUNDS PARK ACADEMY 109-A1
MOUNDS VIEW H.S 93-C1
MURRAY J.H.S 107-C2
NATIVITY OF OUR LORD
  CATHOLIC SCHOOL 121-C1
NEILL ELEM 91-D4
NEW ARRIVALS ELEM 108-D2
NEW HOPE ELEM 91-C2
NEW LIFE ACADEMY 123-C4
NEW PRAGUE ELEM 201-E1
NEW PRAGUE H.S 201-D1
NEW PRAGUE INTERMEDIATE . .201-D2
NEW PRAGUE MIDDLE 201-D2
NEWPORT ELEM 137-B2
NICOLLET J.H.S 148-D4
NOBLE ELEM 106-A1
NOKOMIS ELEM 109-A3
NORMANDALE COMMUNITY
  COLLEGE 134-A4
NORMANDALE ELEM 119-E3
NORMANDALE HILLS ELEM 133-E4
NORTH END ELEM 108-B2
NORTH H.S.(MPL) 106-B1
NORTH H.S.(NSP) 95-B4
NORTH HENNEPIN
  COMMUNITY COLLEGE 77-D2
NORTH HUDSON ELEM 111-D1
NORTH J.H.S 105-B4
NORTH PARK ELEM 78-E4
NORTH STAR ELEM 106-C1
NORTH TRAIL ELEM 163-D4
NORTH VIEW J.H.S 77-E4
NORTHDALE MIDDLE 64-D2
NORTHEAST J.H.S 93-A3
NORTHEAST METRO
  TECHNICAL COLLEGE 95-B2
NORTHPORT ELEM 92-A1
NORTHROP ELEM 120-E2
NORTHSIDE COMMUNITY
  ELEM .119-E1
NORTHVIEW ELEM 149-E1
NORTHWEST TECHNICAL
  INSTITUTE 133-A2
NORTHWESTERN COLLEGE 93-D2
NORTHWESTERN
  ELECTRONICS INSTITUTE 92-E2
NORWOOD/YNG. AMER. ELEM . .142-C3

NORWOOD/YNG. AMER. H.S 142-C3
NORWOOD/YNG.
  AMER. MIDDLE 142-C4
OAK GROVE ELEM 148-C1
OAK GROVE INTERMEDIATE 148-C1
OAK GROVE SCHOOL 80-A3
OAK PARK ELEM 97-A2
OAK POINT INTERMEDIATE 133-A3
OAK RIDGE ELEM 149-C2
OAK VIEW ELEM 77-A4
OAK VIEW MIDDLE 50-B1
OAK-LAND J.H.S 110-C3
OAKDALE ELEM 109-C3
OAKLAND ELEM 104-C1
OLSON ELEM 148-A1
OLSON MIDDLE 92-B2
OLTMAN J.H.S 137-B3
ORCHARD LAKE ELEM 162-B3
ORCHARD LANE ELEM 92-A1
ORONO H.S 103-C2
ORONO MIDDLE 103-C2
ORONO PRIMARY ELEM 89-A4
OSCEOLA ELEM 28-A3
OSCEOLA H.S 28-A4
OSCEOLA INTERMEDIATE 28-A4
OSCEOLA MIDDLE 28-A3
OSSEO ELEM 77-C1
OSSEO H.S 77-B1
OSSEO J.H.S 77-B1
OTSEGO ELEM 33-E4
OTTER LAKE ELEM 80-E2
OUR LADY OF THE LAKE
  SCHOOL 116-E1
OUR SAVIORS LUTHERAN
  SCHOOL 117-D4
OXBOW CREEK ELEM 63-D3
PALMER LAKE ELEM 78-A3
PARK BROOK ELEM 77-D3
PARK CENTER H.S 77-E3
PARK H.S 137-E3
PARK SPANISH
  IMMERSION ELEM 119-E1
PARK TERRACE ELEM 78-D1
PARK VIEW EARLY CHILDHOOD .63-E3
PARK VIEW
  MONTESSORI ELEM 106-B1
PARKER ELEM 33-E1
PARKSIDE ELEM 58-E2
PARKVIEW CENTER ELEM 94-A4
PARKVIEW ELEM.(LVL) 163-B3
PARKVIEW ELEM.(WBL) 95-B2
PARKWAY ELEM 109-A3
PEARSON ELEM 148-B2
PETER ENICH KNDG CENTER . . .49-C4
PETER HOBART ELEM 105-D4
PHALEN LAKE ELEM 108-D2
PIKE LAKE ELEM 110-C3
PILGRIM LN ELEM 91-B3
PILLSBURY ELEM 93-A4
PILOT KNOB ELEM 135-D3
PINE BEND ELEM 150-E1
PINE HILL ELEM 137-D4
PINECREST ELEM 162-C2
PINEWOOD ELEM.(EAG) 150-A2
PINEWOOD ELEM.(MO) 31-C1
PINEWOOD ELEM.(MV) 79-C2
PLYMOUTH CREEK ELEM 90-D3
PLYMOUTH MIDDLE 91-B3
POND EDGE ELEM 161-B4
POPLAR BRIDGE ELEM 134-A2
POWDERHORN ELEM 120-D1
PRAIRIE ELEM 111-E2
PRAIRIE VIEW ELEM 132-C1
PRESCOTT H.S 153-B4
PRESCOTT MIDDLE 161-B1
PRIOR LAKE H.S 161-C3
PROSPERITY HEIGHTS ELEM . . .108-E2
PULLMAN ELEM 108-E3
PUTNAM ELEM 106-E1
RAHN ELEM 149-B2
RAMSEY ELEM 49-B1
RAMSEY FINE ARTS ELEM 120-D2
RAMSEY J.H.S 121-D1
RANDOLPH ELEM 207-A3
RANDOLPH H.S 207-A3
RANDOLPH HEIGHTS ELEM 121-D1
RED PINE ELEM 150-B3
RED ROCK ELEM 123-D3
RHS RESOURCE CENTER 91-E3
RICE LAKE ELEM.(LL) 66-A4
RICE LAKE ELEM.(MG) 76-E2
RICHARDSON ELEM 95-B3
RICHFIELD H.S 134-C1
RICHFIELD INTERMEDIATE 134-D1
RIDGEVIEW ELEM 133-E4
RIVER FALLS H.S 140-E3
RIVERVIEW ELEM.(BP) 78-C1
RIVERVIEW ELEM.(STP) 122-C2
ROCKFORD ELEM 74-B3
ROCKFORD H.S 74-C3
ROCKFORD INTERMEDIATE 74-B3
ROCKFORD NEW ELEM 74-B3
ROCKY BRANCH ELEM 140-D3
ROGERS ELEM 61-E1
ROGERS J.H.S 48-A4
RONDO ELEM 108-A4
ROOSEVELT ELEM.(SSP) 122-E4
ROOSEVELT ELEM.(STP) 122-C1

ROOSEVELT H.S 121-A1
ROOSEVELT MIDDLE 50-E4
ROSEMOUNT ELEM 164-A2
ROSEMOUNT H.S 164-A1
ROSEMOUNT MIDDLE 164-A1
ROSEVILLE H.S 93-D4
ROSEVILLE MIDDLE 94-B4
ROYAL OAKS ELEM 123-D2
RUM RIVER ELEM 36-A3
RUSH CREEK ELEM 147-C3
RUTHERFORD ELEM 96-D1
SAINT AGNES SCHOOL 108-A3
SAINT ANDREWS SCHOOL 33-E1
SAINT ANTHONY MIDDLE 93-B3
SAINT ANTHONY PARK ELEM . . .107-C2
SAINT ANTHONY/NEW
  BRIGHTON H.S 93-B3
SAINT BERNARD 143-E4
SAINT BERNARD SCHOOL 108-B2
SAINT CROIX FALLS ELEM 14-D2
SAINT CROIX FALLS H.S 14-D2
SAINT CROIX FALLS MIDDLE 14-D2
SAINT CROIX LUTHERAN H.S . . .122-E4
SAINT ELIZABETH ANN
  SETON PAROCHIAL 166-D1
SAINT FRANCIS ELEM 7-D4
SAINT FRANCIS H.S 7-E4
SAINT FRANCIS J.H.S 7-D4
SAINT FRANCIS SCHOOL 58-E2
SAINT HUBERTS SCHOOL 132-B2
SAINT JOHN THE BAPTIST
  SCHOOL 117-E4
SAINT JOHNS LUTHERAN(CHS) .145-C3
SAINT JOHNS LUTHERAN(NYA) .142-C3
SAINT JOHNS SCHOOL 93-C1
SAINT JOSEPHS 129-D3
SAINT LOUIS PARK H.S 119-D1
SAINT LOUIS PARK J.H.S 105-D3
SAINT MARK/SAINT
  JOHN LUTHERAN 128-A1
SAINT MARTIN SCHOOL 62-A1
SAINT MARYS 168-D1
SAINT MICHAEL
  ALBERTVILLE H.S 46-E3
SAINT MICHAEL SCHOOL 46-A2
SAINT MICHAEL/ALBERTVILLE
  ELEM 47-A2
SAINT MICHAEL/ALBERTVILLE
  MIDDLE 46-E3
SAINT MICHAELS ACADEMY . . .122-C2
SAINT ODELIA SCHOOL 93-E2
SAINT PAUL ACADEMY 121-C2
SAINT PAUL OPEN SCHOOL 122-A1
SAINT PAUL SEMINARY 121-C1
SAINT PAUL TECHNICAL
  COLLEGE 108-B4
SAINT PETER SCHOOL 87-D3
SAINT THOMAS ACADEMY 135-E1
SAINT THOMAS BECKETT 150-B2
SALEM HILLS ELEM 136-D2
SALK J.H.S 19-D4
SAND CREEK ELEM 64-C1
SANDBURG MIDDLE(ANO) 49-C4
SANDBURG MIDDLE(GV) 105-D1
SANFORD J.H.S 121-B1
SATURN ELEM 108-B4
SATURN/RIVER FRONT
  ACADEMY 108-B4
SCANDIA ELEM 40-E4
SCENIC HEIGHTS ELEM 118-C3
SCHOOL OF ENVIRONMENTAL
  STUDIES 149-C3
SCHOOL OF EXTENDED
  LEARNING 105-D1
SCHUMANN ELEM 103-C2
SCOTT HIGHLANDS MIDDLE . . .163-C1
SEWARD ELEM 107-A3
SHAKOPEE H.S 146-B3
SHAKOPEE J.H.S 146-C3
SHANNON PARK ELEM 163-E1
SHERIDAN ELEM.(MPL) 106-D1
SHERIDAN ELEM.(STP) 109-A3
SHERIDAN HILLS ELEM 120-B4
SHINGLE CREEK ELEM 92-B2
SHIRLEY HILLS PRIMARY 117-A1
SIBLEY EAST K-12 . . . . .183-A2
SIMLEY H.S 136-E3
SIOUX TRAIL ELEM 149-A2
SKY OAKS ELEM 148-D4
SKYVIEW COMMUNITY ELEM . . .109-D3
SKYVIEW COMMUNITY
  MIDDLE 109-D3
SNAIL LAKE ELEM 80-A4
SOMERSET H.S 84-B1
SOMERSET ELEM.(MH) 122-A3
SOMERSET ELEM.(SOM) 70-B4
SOMERSET MIDDLE 84-B1
SONNESYN ELEM 91-C4
SORTEBERG ELEM 64-A2
SOUTH GROVE ELEM 136-E3
SOUTH H.S 106-E4
SOUTH SAINT PAUL H.S 122-E4
SOUTH VIEW MIDDLE 119-E3
SOUTHVIEW ELEM.(APV) 162-E2
SOUTHVIEW ELEM.(WAC) 129-D3
SOUTHWEST H.S 120-A2
SOUTHWEST J.H.S 39-B3
SOUTHWOOD ELEM 148-A2
SPARTAN ELEM 134-C1

SPRING LAKE PARK H.S 78-E2
STEVENSON ELEM 78-D4
STILLWATER H.S 96-D3
STILLWATER J.H.S 97-A2
STONEBRIDGE ELEM 96-E1
SULLIVAN ELEM 107-A4
SUMMIT SCHOOL 121-E1
SUN PATH ELEM 146-C3
SUNNY HOLLOW ELEM 91-C4
SUNNYSIDE ELEM 79-B3
SUNRISE PARK MIDDLE 95-B1
SUNSET HILL ELEM 105-A2
SUSAN LINDGREN
  INTERMEDIATE 120-A2
SWEENEY ELEM 146-A3
TALMUD TORAH 121-D2
TANGLEN ELEM 105-B3
TARTAN H.S 109-C3
TATONKA ELEM 59-A2
TAYLORS FALLS ELEM 14-C3
TECHNOLOGY LEARNING
  CAMPUS 91-E3
THOMAS LAKE ELEM 149-D2
TILDEN ELEM 166-C1
TOTINO GRACE H.S 79-A4
TRINITY LUTHERAN 129-E3
TURTLE LAKE ELEM 79-D2
TUTTLE-MARCY ELEM 107-A2
U OF MN - EAST BANK 107-A2
U OF MN - SAINT PAUL
  CAMPUS 107-C2
U OF MN - WEST BANK 106-E3
UNIVERSITY AVENUE ELEM 64-D3
UNIVERSITY OF SAINT
  THOMAS 107-C4
VADNAIS ELEM 94-C2
VALENTINE HILLS ELEM 93-C1
VALLEY MIDDLE 163-A2
VALLEY VIEW ELEM.(BLO) 134-D3
VALLEY VIEW ELEM.(HIL) 92-E1
VALLEY VIEW MIDDLE 133-D1
VANDENBERGE J.H.S 33-D1
VISITATION ACADEMY 136-A1
VISTA VIEW ELEM 148-B4
WACONIA H.S 129-D3
WACONIA J.H.S 129-D3
WAITE PARK ELEM 93-A3
WASHBURN ELEM 134-B2
WASHBURN H.S 120-C2
WASHINGTON ELEM.(ANO) 49-D4
WASHINGTON ELEM.(SSP) 136-E1
WASHINGTON J.H.S 108-B3
WATERTOWN-MAYER ELEM 101-B3
WATERTOWN-MAYER
  MIDDLE/H.S 101-A3
WAYZATA CENTRAL MIDDLE . . .104-D2
WAYZATA H.S 90-B2
WAYZATA WEST MIDDLE 104-B3
WEAVER ELEM 94-E4
WEAVER LAKE ELEM 76-D2
WEBSTER ELEM 109-A1
WEBSTER MAGNET ELEM 108-A4
WEBSTER OPEN ELEM 106-D1
WENONAH ELEM 120-E3
WEST CENTRAL ELEM.
  ACADEMY 106-C2
WEST J.H.S 118-E1
WESTSIDE ELEM 140-D1
WESTVIEW ELEM 163-A2
WESTWOOD ELEM.(BLA) 64-E4
WESTWOOD ELEM.(BLO) 148-A1
WESTWOOD ELEM.(PRL) 161-B3
WESTWOOD MIDDLE 64-E4
WHITE BEAR H.S 95-A2
WHITTIER PARK ELEM 106-C4
WILDER CONTEMPORARY
  ELEM .120-D1
WILDER FUNDAMENTAL ELEM .120-D1
WILDWOOD ELEM 95-D1
WILLARD ELEM 106-B1
WILLOW ELEM 94-E2
WILLOW LANE ELEM 77-E4
WILLOW RIVER ELEM 111-C2
WILSHIRE PARK ELEM 93-B3
WILSON ELEM 49-D3
WILSON EXPO MIDDLE 107-D3
WINDOM OPEN ELEM 120-C3
WINNETKA ELEM 91-D2
WITHROW ELEM 82-A1
WM. BYRNE ELEM 149-A2
WM. MITCHELL COLLEGE
  OF LAW 121-E1
WOODBURY ELEM 123-C1
WOODBURY H.S 123-D3
WOODBURY MIDDLE 123-C2
WOODCREST ELEM 78-E2
WOODLAND ELEM.(BP) 78-A1
WOODLAND ELEM.(EAG) 135-E4
WOODLAND SCHOOL 86-C4
WORLD CULTURES AND
  LANGUAGES MAGNET 108-D3
WYOMING ELEM 25-B4
ZACHARY LN ELEM 91-B3
ZANEWOOD ELEM 77-E4
ZIMMERMAN ELEM 5-C1
ZION LUTHERAN 157-B2

GOVERNMENT OFFICES

AFTON CITY HALL 125-B3
ALBERTVILLE CITY HALL 47-A2
ANDOVER CITY HALL 50-B1
ANOKA CITY HALL 49-C4
ANOKA COUNTY COURTHOUSE .49-C4
ANOKA POST OFFICE 49-D4
APPLE VALLEY CITY HALL 163-B1
ARDEN HILLS CITY HALL 79-D4
BAYPORT CITY HALL 97-B3
BAYPORT FIRE STATION 97-B3
BECKER CITY HALL 2-E4
BECKER TWP HALL 2-E4
BELLE PLAINE CITY HALL 186-A1
BENTON TOWN HALL 143-B4
BETHEL CITY HALL 8-D3
BIG LAKE CITY HALL 18-A4
BIG LAKE POST OFFICE 18-B4
BIG LAKE TWP TOWN HALL 18-A1
BLAINE CITY HALL 65-A4
BLAINE POST OFFICE 65-A4
BLOOMINGTON CITY HALL 148-B1
BLOOMINGTON POST OFFICE . .134-C4

BROOKLYN CENTER CITY HALL . .92-B1
BROOKLYN CENTER
  POST OFFICE 78-A4
BROOKLYN PARK CITY HALL 77-E2
BUFFALO CITY HALL 58-E2
BUFFALO TWP TOWN HALL 45-B4
BURNS TWP TOWN HALL 20-D4
BURNSVILLE CITY HALL 148-D4
BURNSVILLE POST OFFICE 148-E3
CANNON FALLS CITY HALL 208-B4
CARVER CITY HALL 145-B4
CARVER COUNTY
  COURTHOUSE 145-C3
CASTLE ROCK TWP
  TOWN HALL 192-B2
CENTERVILLE CITY HALL 66-D2
CHAMPLIN CITY HALL 63-C2
CHAMPLIN POST OFFICE 63-C2
CHANHASSEN CITY HALL 132-A2
CHANHASSEN POST OFFICE . . .132-A2
CHASKA CITY HALL 145-C3
CHASKA POST OFFICE 145-C3

CHATHAM TWP TOWN HALL 58-A2
CHISAGO CITY HALL 26-B1
CHISAGO COUNTY
  GOVERNMENT CENTER 12-E3
CIRCLE PINES CITY HALL 65-C4
CIRCLE PINES POST OFFICE 65-C4
COLOGNE CITY HALL 143-E4
COLUMBIA HEIGHTS CITY HALL .92-D2
COLUMBIA HEIGHTS
  POST OFFICE 92-E2
COLUMBUS TWP TOWN HALL . . .38-D4
COON RAPIDS CITY HALL 64-B2
COON RAPIDS POST OFFICE 64-B3
CORCORAN CITY HALL 75-E1
COTTAGE GROVE CITY HALL . . .137-D3
CRYSTAL CITY HALL 91-E3
CRYSTAL POST OFFICE 91-D1
DAHLGREN TOWN HALL 144-C4
DAKOTA COUNTY
  GOVERNMENT CENTER 166-B2
DAYTON CITY HALL 49-A4
DEEPHVN/GRNWOOD/WDLAND

CITY HALLS 118-A2
DELANO CITY HALL 87-D2
DOUGLAS TWP TOWN HALL 194-D2
DRESSER VILLAGE HALL 28-D2
EAGAN CITY HALL 135-D4
EAGAN POST OFFICE 135-E3
EAST BETHEL CITY HALL 23-A1
EDEN PRAIRIE CITY HALL 132-E2
EDINA CITY HALL 119-E3
EDINA POST OFFICE 120-A2
ELK RIVER CITY HALL 33-C2
ELKO CITY HALL 204-A1
EXCELSIOR CITY HALL 117-E3
EXCELSIOR POST OFFICE 117-E3
FALCON HEIGHTS CITY HALL . . .107-C1
FARMINGTON CITY HALL 177-E4
FARMINGTON TWP TOWN HALL .42-A4
FOREST LAKE TWP HALL 39-B4
FRANCONIA TWP TOWN HALL . . .41-C1
FRANKLIN TWP TOWN HALL 87-D3
FRIDLEY CITY HALL 78-D3
FRIDLEY POST OFFICE 78-D2

GOVERNMENT OFFICES

GEM LAKE CITY HALL .94-E1
GOLDEN VALLEY CITY HALL .105-D2
GOLDEN VALLEY POST OFFICE .105-D2
GRANT CITY HALL .82-B4
GREENFIELD CITY HALL .74-D3
HAM LAKE CITY HALL .50-E1
HAMBURG CITY HALL .156-A2
HAMPTON CITY HALL .193-B2
HANCOCK TOWN HALL .157-C4
HANOVER CITY HALL .60-E3
HASSAN TOWNSHIP
TOWN HALL .61-C1
HASTINGS CITY HALL .166-D1
HENDERSON CITY HALL .198-D3
HENNEPIN COUNTY
GOVERNMENT CENTER .106-D2
HILLTOP CITY HALL .92-E2
HOPKINS CITY HALL .119-B2
HOPKINS POST OFFICE .119-B2
HOWARD LAKE CITY HALL .85-A1
HOWARD LAKE FIRE DEPT .85-A1
HUDSON CITY HALL .111-C2
HUDSON TWP TOWN HALL .98-B4
HUGO CITY HALL .67-B2
HUGO POST OFFICE .67-B2
INDEPENDENCE CITY HALL .88-C3
INVER GROVE HEIGHTS
CITY HALL .136-D4
JORDAN CITY HALL .173-B2
LAKE ELMO CITY HALL .96-B4
LAKE ELMO FIRE
STATION NO. 1 .110-C1
LAKE ELMO FIRE
STATION NO. 2 .95-E4
LAKE ELMO POST OFFICE .110-B1
LAKELAND CITY HALL .111-C3
LAKETOWN TOWN HALL .130-C4
LAKEVILLE CITY HALL .176-E3
LAUDERDALE CITY HALL .107-B1
LEXINGTON CITY HALL .65-C4
LINDSTROM CITY HALL .12-D4
LINO LAKES CITY HALL .66-A2
LINWOOD TWP TOWN HALL .10-B4
LITTLE CANADA CITY HALL .94-C3
LONG LAKE CITY HALL .103-E2
LONG LAKE POST OFFICE .103-D2
LORETTO CITY HALL .89-B2
MAHTOMEDI CITY HALL .95-D1
MAHTOMEDI POST OFFICE .95-C1
MAIN POST OFFICE .108-C4
MAPLE GROVE CITY HALL .77-A3
MAPLE LAKE CITY HALL .43-D2
MAPLE LAKE TWP TOWN HALL .44-C2
MAPLE PLAIN CITY HALL .89-A4
MAPLEWOOD CITY HALL .109-A1
MARYSVILLE TWP TOWN HALL .72-A3
MAYER CITY HALL .114-D4
MEDICINE LAKE CITY HALL .105-B1
MEDINA CITY HALL .89-D4
MENDOTA HEIGHTS CITY HALL .121-E4
MENDOTA POST OFFICE .121-D4
MIDDLEVILLE TWP TOWN HALL .71-A2
MINNEAPOLIS CITY HALL
& COURTHOUSE .106-D2
MINNEAPOLIS POST OFFICE .106-D2
MINNETONKA BEACH
CITY HALL .117-C1
MINNETONKA CITY HALL .118-E1
MINNETONKA POST OFFICE .118-E3
MINNETRISTA CITY HALL .116-C2
MONTICELLO CITY HALL .31-D2
MONTICELLO POST OFFICE .31-D1
MONTICELLO TWP TOWN HALL .31-D3
MONTROSE CITY HALL .86-C1
MOUND CITY HALL .116-E1
MOUNDS VIEW CITY HALL .79-B2
NEW BRIGHTON CITY HALL .93-C1
NEW BRIGHTON POST OFFICE .93-C1
NEW GERMANY CITY HALL .114-A4
NEW HOPE CITY HALL .91-C3
NEW MARKET CITY HALL .189-E4
NEW PRAGUE CITY HALL .201-D2
NEW SCANDIA TWP HALL .41-A4
NEWPORT CITY HALL .137-B2
NEWPORT POST OFFICE .123-B4
NORTH HUDSON VILLAGE HALL 111-C1
NORTH OAKS CITY HALL .80-B4
NORTH SAINT PAUL CITY HALL .95-B4
NORTH SAINT PAUL
FIRE STATION .95-B4
NORTH ST PAUL POST OFFICE .95-B4
NORWOOD CITY HALL .142-C4
OAK GROVE CITY HALL .22-B3
OAK PARK HTS CITY HALL .96-E3
OAKDALE CITY HALL .109-C3
OAKDALE FIRE STATION .95-C3,109-C3
ORONO CITY HALL .103-D2
OSCEOLA VILLAGE HALL .27-E4
OSSEO CITY HALL .77-C1
OSSEO POST OFFICE .77-B1
OTSEGO CITY HALL .33-B3
PLYMOUTH CITY HALL .90-D4
PLYMOUTH POST OFFICE .90-D4
PRESCOTT CITY HALL .153-B4
PRIOR LAKE CITY HALL .161-B3
RAMSEY CITY HALL .49-B1
RAMSEY COUNTY
GOVERNMENT CENTER .108-B4
RANDOLPH CITY HALL .207-A3
RICHFIELD CITY HALL .120-D4
RICHFIELD POST OFFICE .120-C4
RIVER FALLS CITY HALL .140-E2
RIVER FALLS POST OFFICE .140-E2
ROBBINSDALE CITY HALL .92-A3
ROBBINSDALE POST OFFICE .92-A3
ROCKFORD CITY HALL .74-B3
ROGERS CITY HALL .61-E1
ROGERS POST OFFICE .62-A1
ROSEMOUNT CITY HALL .164-A2
ROSEVILLE CITY HALL .93-E3
SAINT ANTHONY CITY HALL .93-A3
SAINT BONIFACIUS CITY HALL .116-A3
SAINT CROIX COUNTY GOVT
CENTER .111-E2
SAINT CROIX FALLS CITY HALL .14-C2
SAINT CROIX FALLS FIRE DEPT .14-C2
SAINT CROIX FALLS POST OFFICE 14-C2
SAINT FRANCIS CITY HALL .7-D4
SAINT JOESPH TWP FIRE STATION97-D1
SAINT JOSEPH TOWN HALL .97-D1
SAINT LOUIS PARK CITY HALL .105-E4
SAINT LOUIS PARK POST
OFFICE .105-D4,120-A1
SAINT MICHAEL CITY HALL .46-E4
SAINT PAUL CITY HALL .108-B4
SAINT PAUL PARK CITY HALL .137-B3
SAINT PAUL PARK POST OFFICE 137-B3
SAN FRANCISCO TOWN HALL .172-B1
SAVAGE CITY HALL .147-E4
SAVAGE POST OFFICE .148-A3
SCOTT COUNTY COURTHOUSE .146-B2
SHAFER CITY HALL .13-C4
SHAFER TWP TOWN HALL .13-C1
SHAKOPEE CITY HALL .146-B2
SHAKOPEE POST OFFICE .146-B2
SHERBURNE COUNTY
COURTHOUSE .33-B2
SHOREVIEW CITY HALL .79-E4
SHOREWOOD CITY HALL .117-D3
SILVER CREEK TWP TOWN HALL .16-A3
SOMERSET CITY HALL .84-B1
SOMERSET TWP FIRE STATION .84-C1
SOUTH ST PAUL CITY HALL .122-E4
SOUTH ST PAUL POST OFFICE .122-E3
SPRING LAKE PARK CITY HALL .78-E2
SPRING PARK CITY HALL .117-B1
STACY CITY HALL .11-B3
STATE CAPITOL BUILDING .108-B4
STILLWATER CITY HALL .97-A1
STILLWATER FIRE STATION .97-A1
TONKA BAY CITY HALL .117-D2
TROY TWP TOWN HALL .126-C2
VADNAIS HEIGHTS CITY HALL .94-C2
VICTOR TWP TOWN HALL .85-A3
VICTORIA CITY HALL .130-E2
WACONIA CITY HALL .129-D3
WACONIA TWP TOWN HALL .143-B1
WASHINGTON COUNTY
GOVERNMENT CENTER .97-A2
WATERTOWN CITY HALL .101-A3
WAVERLY CITY HALL .86-A1
WAYZATA CITY HALL .104-B3
WAYZATA POST OFFICE .104-B3
WEST ST PAUL CITY HALL .122-C3
WHITE BEAR LAKE CITY HALL .81-A3
WHITE BEAR LAKE POST OFFICE .81-A3
WHITE BEAR TOWNSHIP HALL .80-D3
WILLERNIE CITY HALL .95-D1
WOODBURY CITY HALL .123-E2
WOODBURY FIRE
STATION .123-C1,123-C3,123-E2
WOODBURY POST OFFICE .123-D2
WOODLAND TWP TOWN HALL .86-B4
WRIGHT COUNTY COURTHOUSE .58-E2
WYOMING CITY HALL .25-B3
WYOMING TWP TOWN HALL .25-D3
YOUNG AMERICA CITY HALL .142-C3

LAKES

ABBIE LAKE .58-B3
ALBERT LAKE .58-B2
ALBION LAKE .43-A3
ALIMAGNET LAKE(APV) .162-E1
ALIMAGNET LAKE(BUR) .162-E1
ALSWEDE LAKE .172-E1
AMELIA LAKE .66-D4
ANDERSON LAKES(BLO) .133-C3
ANDERSON LAKES(EPR) .133-C2
ANDERSONS LAKE .23-D4
ANGUS LAKE .44-D2
ARMSTRONG LAKE(LE) .109-E3
ARMSTRONG LAKE(OKD) .109-E3
ARROWHEAD LAKE .119-C4
ASHTON LAKE .25-B4
ASSUMPTION LAKE .170-E1
AUBURN LAKE .130-D2
AUE LAKE .144-C3
AUGUSTA LAKE .135-D1
BAILEY LAKE .124-A4
BALD EAGLE LAKE .81-A2
BALD LAKE .150-A1
BALDWIN LAKE(CG) .151-B3
BALDWIN LAKE(LL) .65-E4
BARKER LAKE .68-B1
BARNES LAKE .142-D3
BARNEYS LAKE .14-E3
BASS LAKE(BT) .20-D3
BASS LAKE(MAY) .68-D2
BASS LAKE(PLY) .91-A1
BASS LAKE(SJT) .84-C4,98-C1
BASS LAKE(SLP) .120-A1
BASS LAKE(SMT) .55-E4,84-C3
BATTLE CREEK LAKE .109-C4
BATTLE CREEK POND .122-E1
BAYLOR LAKE .128-B4
BEAR LAKE .20-D3
BEAVER LAKE .109-B3
BEEBE LAKE .60-A2
BENJAMIN LAKE .35-C1
BENNETT LAKE .93-E4
BENTON LAKE .143-D3
BENZ LAKE .82-B2
BERLINER LAKE .128-D2
BERTRAM LAKE .31-A2
BIG CARNELIAN LAKE .69-A4
BIG LAKE .18-A3
BIG MARINE LAKE .54-C3
BIRCH ISLAND LAKE .118-D4
BIRCH LAKE(BLT) .18-E1
BIRCH LAKE(CMT) .58-C3
BIRCH LAKE(MOT) .30-E2
BIRCH LAKE(RW) .196-D1
BIRCH LAKE(WBL) .80-D4
BIRCH POND .106-A3
BLACK DOG LAKE .148-D2,149-A1
BLACK LAKE(MOT) .44-D1
BLACK LAKE(MOU) .117-B1
BLACK LAKE(NO) .80-C3
BLACKHAWK LAKE .149-C1
BLACKS LAKE .17-E3
BLIND LAKE .161-B4
BLOOMS LAKE .27-C1
BLUE LAKE .147-A2
BONE LAKE .40-C2
BOO LAKE .26-D3
BOOT LAKE .23-E3
BRAND LAKE .142-B4
BRAUNWORTH LAKE .142-C3
BREWER LAKE .182-C3
BRIGHT LAKE .84-A4
BROWNIE LAKE .106-A3
BROWNS LAKE .172-B3
BRYANT LAKE .133-A1
BUCK LAKE(SLT) .174-E1
BUCK LAKE(WTT) .115-D2
BUCKS LAKE .17-D2
BUFFALO LAKE .58-D3
BUNKER LAKE .50-C3
BURANDTS LAKE .129-C3
BURNS LAKE .20-D1
BUSH LAKE .133-D3
BUTLER LAKE .99-B2
CAMP LAKE .2-A1
CAMPBELL LAKE(HOT) .113-D1
CAMPBELL LAKE(SLT) .160-C4
CARGILL LAKE .148-A3
CARL KREY LAKE .130-D3
CARLSON LAKE .149-D2
CARMAN BAY .117-A2
CARRIGAN LAKE .86-A1
CARVER LAKE .123-C3
CASEY LAKE .95-A3
CATES LAKE .161-C2
CEDAR ISLAND LAKE .77-A4
CEDAR LAKE(CLT) .188-E4
CEDAR LAKE(CNT) .29-A4
CEDAR LAKE(HAT) .188-B3
CEDAR LAKE(MOT) .30-E4
CEDAR LAKE(MPL) .106-B3
CEDAR MANOR LAKE .105-C4
CENTENNIAL LAKE .134-A1
CENTERVILLE LAKE .66-C2
CHARLEY LAKE .80-A2
CHASKA LAKE .145-C3
CHISAGO LAKE .26-B2
CHRISTMAS LAKE .118-A4
CHUB LAKE .205-B1
CHURCH LAKE .130-E2
CLARKS LAKE .199-B1
CLAY HOLE LAKE .145-C2
CLEAR LAKE(CLR) .1-B1
CLEAR LAKE(FLT) .39-B4
CLEAR LAKE(LE) .96-B3
CLEAR LAKE(WEL) .182-A3
CLEARY LAKE .175-C1
CLITTY LAKE .2-E2
CLOVERDALE LAKE .96-D3
CODY LAKE .216-C3
COLBY LAKE(SHT) .14-B2
COLBY LAKE(WBY) .124-A3
COLEEN LAKE .27-C2
COLMAN LAKE .148-A2
COLUMBUS LAKE .52-D1
COMFORT LAKE .25-D4
COMMA LAKE .134-A4
CONLEY LAKE .152-D4
CONSTANCE LAKE .45-A3
COOK LAKE(FKT) .73-C4
COOK LAKE(MG) .76-B3
COON LAKE .37-D1
COOPERS LAKE .8-E3
CORNELL LAKE .15-B3
COURTHOUSE LAKE .145-D3
COWLEY LAKE .47-D4
CRAWFORD LAKE .73-A3
CRESCENT LAKE .2-A2
CROOKED LAKE(AND) .49-E3
CROOKED LAKE(CR) .49-E4
CROSBY LAKE .121-E3
CROSSWAYS LAKE .52-C2
CROW LAKE .119-C4
CRYSTAL BAY .103-C4
CRYSTAL LAKE(BUR) .162-D3
CRYSTAL LAKE(ROB) .92-A3
CRYSTAL LAKE(SLT) .161-A4
CURRAN LAKE .169-A1
CURTIS LAKE .90-E2
CYNTHIA LAKE .188-D1
DAN PATCH LAKE .161-D1
DEAN LAKE(HUG) .147-A3
DEAN LAKE(RFT) .73-B1
DEEP LAKE .80-C2
DEER LAKE(EB) .23-B3
DEER LAKE(MVT) .58-C4
DEVILS LAKE .23-C3
DIAMOND LAKE(DAY) .48-C4
DIAMOND LAKE(MPL) .120-D3
DICKEYS LAKE .103-D1
DICKMAN LAKE .136-C2
DIETZ LAKE .215-E3
DOERFLER LAKE .71-B3
DOG LAKE .99-D2
DONDERS LAKE .129-B1
DOWNS LAKE .110-C2
DRY DAM LAKE(SJT) .98-D2
DRY DAM LAKE(WRT) .98-E3
DUBAN LAKE .216-D4
DUBAY LAKE .62-D2
DUCK LAKE(EPR) .132-C1
DUCK LAKE(FRT) .27-C3
DUTCH LAKE(MTA) .116-D1
DUTCH LAKE(VIT) .85-B2
EAGLE LAKE(CT) .142-B1
EAGLE LAKE(ER) .20-B2
EAGLE LAKE(MG) .77-B4
EAGLE LAKE(ORT) .4-B4
EAGLE LAKE(SVT) .30-C3
EAGLE POINT LAKE .110-A2
EARLEY LAKE .162-C2
EAST BOOT LAKE .68-E2
EAST HUNTER LAKE .6-B1
EAST TWIN LAKE .20-C4
ECHO LAKE(DWD) .81-D3
ECHO LAKE(MHT) .95-C2
EDDY LAKE .34-D4
EDS POND .109-C2
EDWARD LAKE .76-E4
EGG LAKE .67-B3
EGGERT LAKE .215-C3
EKSTROM LAKE .21-A1
ELK RIVER .2-C1
ELWELL LAKE .40-A3
EMBER LAKE .15-E3
EMILY LAKE .26-A2
FARQUHAR LAKE .149-D4
FAWN LAKE .10-D3
FIREMENS LAKE .145-C2
FIRST LAKE(CGT) .40-E1
FIRST LAKE(MOT) .31-B2
FISH LAKE(CWT) .1-C4
FISH LAKE(EAG) .135-D4
FISH LAKE(EB) .9-D3
FISH LAKE(GRA) .81-C1
FISH LAKE(MG) .76-E3
FISH LAKE(NST) .54-D1
FISH LAKE(SLT) .174-E3
FISHER LAKE .147-B2
FOLSOM LAKE .28-B1
FOREST LAKE(FLT) .39-D3
FOREST LAKE(ORO) .103-B4
FOSTER LAKE .47-D2
FOUNTAIN LAKE .86-E2
FOURTH LAKE .40-C1
FRANK LAKE .49-C3
FREDERICK LAKE .72-E2
FREDERICKSON SLOUGH .3-E4
FRENCH LAKE(DAY) .62-C2
FRENCH LAKE(ORO) .103-D4
FROST LAKE .108-E2
FULGER LAKE .98-C2
GABLES LAKE .138-B2
GALPIN LAKE .117-E4
GAYSTOCK LAKE .144-E3
GEIS LAKE .174-A1
GEM LAKE .94-E1
GEORGE WATCH LAKE .66-B2
GERHARDT LAKE .149-C3
GERMAN LAKE .40-B4
GERVAIS LAKE .94-C3
GIFFORD LAKE .145-C4,145-D4
GILCHRIST LAKE .45-B2
GILFILLAN LAKE .80-C3
GLEASON LAKE .104-C2
GLEN LAKE .118-E3
GOGGINS LAKE .68-B4
GOLDEN LAKE .65-D4
GOOSE LAKE(BT) .20-E2
GOOSE LAKE(COR) .76-B2
GOOSE LAKE(DAY) .63-B3
GOOSE LAKE(LE) .110-A3
GOOSE LAKE(LVL) .162-D4
GOOSE LAKE(NST) .41-A3
GOOSE LAKE(RW) .196-D1
GOOSE LAKE(WBL) .81-A4
GOOSE LAKE(WBT) .81-A4
GOOSE LAKE(WCT) .115-B4
GRASS LAKE(WIT) .99-A3
GRASS LAKE(EPR) .146-E1
GRASS LAKE(MPL) .120-C4
GRASS LAKE(OG) .22-B2
GRASS LAKE(SVW) .94-A1
GRAYS BAY .104-C4
GREEN LAKE .26-A3
GREEN MOUNTAIN LAKE .59-D2
GUN CLUB LAKE(EAG) .135-C2
GUN CLUB LAKE(MH) .135-C1
HADLEY LAKE .104-B2
HAFFTEN LAKE .74-D3
HALF MOON LAKE .89-B3
HALLQUIST LAKE .172-B3
HALSTEAD BAY .116-D3
HAM LAKE .37-A4
HANNON LAKE .105-C4
HANREHAN LAKE .162-A2
HARRISON LAKE .131-D1
HARRISONS BAY .117-A1
HART LAKE .93-A3
HATCH LAKE .202-D4
HAUGHEY LAKE .88-A2
HAWKES LAKE .119-D3
HAY LAKE(EAG) .150-B2
HAY LAKE(NST) .54-E2
HAYDEN LAKE .63-A2
HAZELTINE LAKE .131-D3
HEIMS LAKE .25-B4
HENRY LAKE .61-C2
HENSHAW LAKE .43-B4
HICKEY LAKE .21-E4
HICKEYS LAKE .188-B2
HIDDEN LAKE(BLA) .65-D4
HIDDEN LAKE(BLT) .17-D2
HIGGINS LAKE(COT) .38-E2
HIGGINS LAKE(FL) .39-A2
HIGHLAND LAKE .93-A1
HIGHLANDS LAKE .119-D3
HOFFMAN LAKE .10-D1
HOLIDAY LAKE .118-D3
HOLLAND LAKE .149-E2
HOLY NAME LAKE .90-B4
HORNBEAN LAKE .136-B2
HORSESHOE LAKE(HUG) .53-C4
HORSESHOE LAKE(LE) .110-C3
HORSESHOE LAKE(SFT) .159-B4
HORSESHOE LAKE(SL) .136-C2
HORSESHOE LAKE(SLW) .172-B4
HORSESHOE LAKE(WLT) .110-C3
HOWARD LAKE(COT) .38-D4
HOWARD LAKE(MIT) .71-A4
HOWARD LAKE(PRL) .160-D3
HURLEY LAKE .135-E4
HYDES LAKE .142-E1
HYLAND LAKE .133-D4
IDA LAKE .30-D2
INDIAN LAKE .29-C1
IRENE LAKE .88-D4
ISLAND LAKE(ADT) .42-E2
ISLAND LAKE(LWT) .24-B1
ISLAND LAKE(SVW) .93-E1
ITASCA LAKE .48-C1
JENNINGS BAY .103-A4
JENSEN LAKE .149-D3
JO POND .120-B1
JOHNSON LAKE .172-B1
JONES LAKE(CLR) .1-E2
JONES LAKE(RW) .196-D2
JUBERT LAKE .75-B4
KANE LAKE .175-C3
KARTH LAKE .79-D4
KATRINA LAKE .103-B1
KEGAN LAKE .150-A4
KELLER LAKE(BL) .18-A4
KELLER LAKE(BUR) .162-E2
KELLER LAKE(MPW) .94-D4
KELLY LAKE .172-C2
KINGSLEY LAKE .162-C4
KNUCKLE HEAD LAKE .94-E4
KOHLMAN LAKE .94-D3
KRAFTZ LAKE .104-C1
KRENZ LAKE .162-B4
KROON LAKE .26-D2
KUEVERS MARSH .34-A2
LA LAKE .123-C4
LABELLE POND .92-E2
LAC LAVON LAKE .162-E3
LADDIE LAKE .78-E1

LAKES

LAKE ALICE 55-C2
LAKE ANN(CHN) ...131-E1
LAKE ANN(ORT) ...4-D2
LAKE ANN(VIT) ...85-B3
LAKE ARDMORE ...89-B3
LAKE AUBURN ...130-D2
LAKE BAVARIA ...131-A3
LAKE BYLLESBY ...207-C4
LAKE CALHOUN ...120-B1
LAKE CHARLOTTE(MTK) ...118-C3
LAKE CHARLOTTE(RFT) ...60-A3
LAKE CLASSEN ...103-C2
LAKE COBBLECREST ...105-C4
LAKE COMO(STP) ...107-E2
LAKE COMO(SWD) ...118-A3
LAKE CORNELIA ...120-A4
LAKE DEMONTREVILLE ...95-D3
LAKE EDINA ...133-E1
LAKE EDITH ...125-A1
LAKE ELMO ...110-B2
LAKE EMERALD ...117-A2
LAKE EMMA ...148-A3
LAKE GEORGE(OG) ...22-A2
LAKE GEORGE(RF) ...140-D2
LAKE GIRARD ...134-A3
LAKE GRACE ...131-C4
LAKE HARRIET ...120-B3
LAKE HARVEY ...119-E3
LAKE HIAWATHA ...121-A2
LAKE HOOPER ...118-B2
LAKE IDA ...99-D2
LAKE IDLEWILD ...133-A2
LAKE INDEPENDENCE ...89-A3
LAKE ISABELLE ...166-D1
LAKE JANE ...95-E4
LAKE JOHANNA ...93-D2
LAKE JONES ...93-C2
LAKE JOSEPHINE(AH) ...93-D3
LAKE JOSEPHINE(RVL) ...93-E3
LAKE LAURA ...48-B3
LAKE LINDEN ...117-D4
LAKE LOUISE(DPH) ...118-B1
LAKE LOUISE(RF) ...140-D2
LAKE LUCY ...131-E1
LAKE MAGDA ...77-C4
LAKE MALLALIEU ...111-D1
LAKE MARION ...104-B4
LAKE MARTHA ...60-B4
LAKE MARY(MLT) ...43-E1
LAKE MARY(VIT) ...99-C1
LAKE MCKUSICK ...96-E1
LAKE MENDAKOTA ...135-E1
LAKE MINNETONKA ...118-A1
LAKE MINNEWASHTA ...131-C1
LAKE MITCHELL ...18-A3
LAKE NETTA ...37-B3
LAKE NOKOMIS ...120-C3
LAKE OF THE DALLES ...14-C3
LAKE OF THE ISLES ...106-B4
LAKE OWASSO ...94-A3
LAKE PAMELA ...120-A4
LAKE PATTERSON ...128-E4
LAKE PEPIN ...215-D3
LAKE PHALEN ...108-D2
LAKE PLAISTED ...68-A3
LAKE PULASKI ...45-A4
LAKE RAINER ...76-E4
LAKE REBECCA(GRF) ...88-A1
LAKE REBECCA(IND) ...88-B1
LAKE RILEY ...132-B3
LAKE ROSE(ILE) ...110-C3
LAKE ROSE(MTK) ...118-D3
LAKE SANBORN ...216-A3
LAKE SARAH ...88-D1
LAKE SMETANA ...133-B2
LAKE ST JOE ...131-B1
LAKE SUSAN ...132-A3
LAKE VADNAIS ...94-B2
LAKE VIRGINIA ...117-B4
LAKE WABASSO ...94-A2
LAKE WASHINGTON ...95-D2
LAKE WHITE ...57-C1
LAKE WILHELM ...60-D2
LAKE WILLIAM ...118-A2
LAKE WINDSOR ...105-B3
LAMP LIGHTER POND ...105-D3
LANGDON LAKE ...116-E1
LARSON LAKE ...182-C4
LEE LAKE ...162-C3
LEMANS LAKE ...63-B2
LEMAY LAKE ...135-D1
LEMAYS LAKE ...135-D3
LENNON LAKE ...189-B2
LIBBS LAKE ...104-D4
LIGHT FOOT LAKE ...78-D3
LILLY LAKE ...122-C2
LILY LAKE ...96-E2
LIMESTONE LAKE ...15-D4
LINN LAKE ...26-E2
LINWOOD LAKE ...24-A2
LIPPERT LAKE ...114-D2
LITTLE CARNELIAN LAKE ...83-A1
LITTLE COMFORT LAKE ...39-D1
LITTLE COON LAKE(COT) ...38-A1
LITTLE COON LAKE(HL) ...37-C3
LITTLE FALLS LAKE ...98-A3
LITTLE GREEN LAKE ...26-A1
LITTLE JOHANNA LAKE ...93-D3
LITTLE LAKE ...13-A2
LITTLE ROCK LAKE ...57-D1
LITTLE WAVERLY LAKE ...71-D4
LOCHNESS LAKE ...65-D2
LOCKE LAKE(FRI) ...78-D3
LOCKE LAKE(SVT) ...16-E4
LOEB LAKE ...108-A2
LONE LAKE ...119-A4
LONG LAKE(APV) ...149-D4,163-D1
LONG LAKE(HUG) ...67-E4
LONG LAKE(MAY) ...54-D4,68-D1
LONG LAKE(MHT) ...81-D4
LONG LAKE(MNT) ...31-B3
LONG LAKE(MTA) ...102-C4
LONG LAKE(NB) ...79-B4
LONG LAKE(NST) ...54-E2
LONG LAKE(ORO) ...103-E2
LONG LAKE(OXT) ...10-E2
LONG LAKE(PS) ...95-D3
LONG LAKE(SFT) ...159-B4
LONG LAKE(SWR) ...96-D2
LONG LAKE(VIT) ...99-B1
LONG MEADOW LAKE ...135-A3
LOON LAKE ...82-D2
LORING LAKE ...106-C3
LOST LAKE(MHT) ...95-C1
LOST LAKE(PLY) ...91-B3
LOTUS LAKE(CHN) ...132-B1
LOTUS LAKE(OST) ...28-E3
LOUISE LAKE ...82-D1

LOUZERS LAKE ...85-D4
LOWER BIRCH LAKE ...10-D1
LOWER LAKE ...28-A2
LOWER RATTLING
  SPRINGS LAKE ...182-A4
LUNSTEN LAKE ...130-C1
LYDIARD LAKE ...104-A2
LYNCH LAKE ...68-C3
MAKRLEY LAKE ...161-C4
MALARDI LAKE ...172-D4
MANN LAKE ...81-E1
MANNING LAKE ...40-B2
MAPLE LAKE ...44-A2
MARCOTT LAKES ...136-C4,150-D1
MARIA LAKE(BTT) ...157-E3
MARIA LAKE(SVT) ...30-A1
MARION LAKE ...176-D2
MARKGRAFS LAKE ...124-B1
MARKLEY LAKE ...161-C3
MARSH LAKE ...130-D4
MARSHAN LAKE ...66-A2
MARTIN LAKE ...55-A4
MARY LAKE(CMT) ...57-D1
MARY LAKE(RFT) ...59-A3
MARY LAKE(SWD) ...117-D4
MASTERMAN LAKE ...82-A4
MATTSON LAKE ...22-E3
MAXWELL BAY ...103-C4
MAYS LAKE ...68-E2
MCCARRONS LAKE ...108-A1
MCCARTHY LAKE ...149-E1
MCCOLL LAKE ...161-D1
MCCOY LAKE ...132-E3
MCDONALD LAKE ...96-D3
MCDONOUGH LAKE ...150-A2
MCKAY LAKE ...50-C4
MCKNIGHT LAKE ...131-C3
MCMAHON LAKE ...175-B4
MEADOW LAKE(HSN) ...61-C2
MEADOW LAKE(NH) ...91-C1
MEADOWBROOK LAKE ...119-D2
MEDICINE LAKE ...105-B1
MEDINA LAKE ...89-E1
MELODY LAKE ...119-E3
METOGGA LAKE ...216-C2
MEUWISSEN LAKE ...143-D4
MEYER POND ...98-E4
MILKY LAKE ...85-B2
MILL POND(CHM) ...63-C1
MILL POND(JOR) ...173-B3
MILL POND(SJT) ...95-C3
MILLER LAKE ...144-B3
MILLSTONE LAKE ...29-D3
MINARD LAKE ...8-E3
MINK LAKE(CNT) ...29-C4
MINK LAKE(RFT) ...58-D3
MINNEHAHA CREEK ...104-D4
MINNETOGA LAKE ...119-A3
MIRROR LAKE ...119-D3
MISSISSIPPI RIVER ...16-E3
MITCHELL LAKE ...132-C2
MOODY LAKE ...40-C1
MOONEY LAKE(EAG) ...149-D1
MOONEY LAKE(PLY) ...104-B1
MOORE LAKE(FRI) ...78-E4
MOORE LAKE(GCT) ...151-B2
MOORE LAKE(RFT) ...59-E3
MORIN LAKE ...75-D4
MOSFORD LAKE ...2-A1
MOTHER LAKE ...120-E4
MOUNT NORMANDALE LAKE ...133-E3
MUD HEN LAKE ...167-D4
MUD LAKE(ABT) ...57-C2
MUD LAKE(ALB) ...47-A1
MUD LAKE(BT) ...21-C1
MUD LAKE(COT) ...39-A4
MUD LAKE(EB) ...23-A3
MUD LAKE(EDI) ...119-D4
MUD LAKE(EXC) ...117-E3
MUD LAKE(LAT) ...215-B1
MUD LAKE(LET) ...11-C3
MUD LAKE(LWT) ...10-C3
MUD LAKE(MAY) ...68-C1
MUD LAKE(MG) ...63-A4
MUD LAKE(MOT) ...31-B2
MUD LAKE(MTA) ...116-B4
MUD LAKE(OKD) ...95-C4
MUD LAKE(PLY) ...90-E1
MUD LAKE(SM) ...60-B2
MUD LAKE(WLK) ...169-D2
MUD LAKE(WTT) ...115-D1
MUD LAKES ...169-A2,170-A3
MURPHY LAKE ...162-A3
MYERS LAKE ...142-E3
NEDS LAKE ...23-A2
NEILL LAKE ...133-B3
NELSON LAKE ...182-C4
NIELSON LAKE ...40-B3
NINE MILE LAKE ...148-B2
NIXON LAKE ...15-B2
NORRIS LAKE ...21-C1
NORTH ARM ...103-A3
NORTH BASS LAKE ...84-D2
NORTH CENTER LAKE ...12-D3
NORTH LAKE(MOT) ...31-A3
NORTH LAKE(RVT) ...167-D4
NORTH LAKE(SVT) ...16-B3
NORTH LAKE(WEL) ...182-B2
NORTH LINDSTROM LAKE ...12-C3
NORTH SCHOOL
  SECTION LAKE ...68-A3
NORTH TERRAPIN LAKE ...68-E1
NORTH TWIN LAKE(BC) ...92-A2
NORTH TWIN LAKE(SWT) ...82-D4
OAK LAKE(SLP) ...119-D1
OAK LAKE(WTT) ...101-D4
OBRIEN LAKE ...149-E3
OCONNERS LAKE ...139-B3
ODOWD LAKE ...160-B2
OGREN LAKE ...27-A1
OLEARY LAKE ...135-E4
OLSON LAKE ...95-D4
ONEKA LAKE ...67-C1
ORCHARD LAKE ...162-B4
ORONO LAKE ...33-C1
OSCEOLA LAKE ...42-C2
OTTER LAKE ...80-E1
OVERLOOK LAKE ...148-A2
OX YOKE LAKE ...102-A3
OXBORO LAKE ...134-C3
PAIGE POND ...112-E2
PALMER LAKE ...78-B4
PARADISE LAKE ...45-C1
PARKERS LAKE ...104-D1
PARLEY LAKE ...130-B1
PAT LAKE ...82-B2
PEARSON LAKE ...27-B2
PEASLEE LAKE ...28-A2

PEAVY LAKE ...104-A3
PELICAN LAKE(BUT) ...45-D4
PELICAN LAKE(SM) ...60-D4
PELTIER LAKE ...66-D1
PENN LAKE ...134-B2
PERCH LAKE ...98-A1
PET LAKE ...10-D3
PETER LAKE ...89-C1
PHELPS LAKE ...216-C4
PICKEREL LAKE(BT) ...20-E3
PICKEREL LAKE(LIL) ...122-A2
PIERSON LAKE ...130-D4
PIGS EYE LAKE ...122-E2
PIKE LAKE(MG) ...91-B1
PIKE LAKE(NB) ...93-B1
PIKE LAKE(PLY) ...91-B1
PIKE LAKE(PRL) ...161-A1
PINE LAKE ...55-E4,69-E1
PINE TREE LAKE ...81-D2
PINNAKER LAKE ...21-A2
PIONEER LAKE ...12-E3
PLEASANT LAKE(FAT) ...42-D2
PLEASANT LAKE(HAT) ...187-E2
PLEASANT LAKE(NO) ...80-B3
POMERLEAU LAKE ...90-D2
POOLES LAKE ...100-D1
POPLAR LAKE(NB) ...93-B2
POPLAR LAKE(OST) ...14-E4
POPLAR LAKE(SVW) ...80-B1
POPLAR LAKE(WBT) ...80-B1
POWDERHORN LAKE ...120-E1
POWERS LAKE(DAY) ...63-A2
POWERS LAKE(WBY) ...124-B2
PRAIRIE LAKE ...2-C1
PRIOR LAKE ...161-B2
QUIGLEY LAKE ...149-D2
RAMSEY LAKE ...43-D4
RAPIDS LAKE ...159-A2
RAVEN LAKE ...176-D1
REBECCA LAKE ...166-C1
RED ROCK LAKE ...132-D3
REICH LAKE ...113-C4
REITZ LAKE ...130-A3
RESERVATION LAKE ...160-E2
RESHANAU LAKE ...66-B3
RIA LAKE ...123-C4
RICE LAKE(BTT) ...143-A2
RICE LAKE(CWT) ...15-D1
RICE LAKE(EB) ...23-D3
RICE LAKE(EPR) ...146-B1
RICE LAKE(ER) ...5-D4
RICE LAKE(FKT) ...101-D2
RICE LAKE(GV) ...106-A1
RICE LAKE(HUG) ...67-C2
RICE LAKE(LLL) ...66-A3
RICE LAKE(MG) ...76-D2
RICE LAKE(MYT) ...216-A4
RICE LAKE(NMT) ...190-D2
RICE LAKE(OST) ...28-A2
RICE LAKE(OTS) ...47-E2
RICE LAKE(SAV) ...147-C2
RICE LAKE(SLT) ...161-A4
RICE LAKE(WTT) ...101-E3
RICE MARSH LAKE ...132-B3
RICE POND ...76-D2
RICHFIELD LAKE ...120-C4
ROBINA LAKE ...88-B3
ROCK LAKE ...57-D2
ROGERS LAKE(BT) ...35-C2
ROGERS LAKE(MH) ...135-E1
RONDEAU LAKE ...52-C4
ROUND LAKE(AN) ...79-C4
ROUND LAKE(AND) ...49-E2
ROUND LAKE(EPR) ...132-C1
ROUND LAKE(HUG) ...81-E1
ROUND LAKE(LC) ...94-B3
ROUND LAKE(MPW) ...100-B1
ROUND LAKE(VIT) ...99-C1
RUSH LAKE ...79-C4
RUTZ LAKE ...129-A1
RYAN LAKE(LWT) ...10-C3
RYAN LAKE(ROB) ...92-A2
SAINT FRANCIS RIVER(BLT) ...11-B1
SAINT FRANCIS RIVER(ORT) ...5-A2
SAM LAKE ...25-E2
SAND LAKE ...55-A2
SANDSHORE LAKE ...8-C3
SANDY LAKE(CNT) ...29-A1
SANDY LAKE(MPW) ...100-B1
SAVAGE LAKE ...94-B3
SCHANDEL LAKE ...74-E3
SCHMIDT LAKE(BUT) ...59-D1
SCHMIDT LAKE(PLY) ...91-A2
SCHMIDTS LAKE(BUT) ...59-E2
SCHMIDTS LAKE(SM) ...59-E3
SCHMITT LAKE ...59-E2
SCHNEIDER LAKE ...160-B2
SCHOOL LAKE(ALB) ...46-E1
SCHOOL LAKE(CGT) ...12-A4
SCHOOL LAKE(MED) ...89-C3
SCHOOL LAKE(NYT) ...40-A1
SCHOOL SECTION LAKE ...71-C4
SCHULTZ LAKE ...150-A3
SCHUTZ LAKE ...131-A1
SCHWAPPAUFF LAKE ...74-E2
SCHWARZ POND ...164-A1
SCOTT LAKE(COR) ...75-C4
SCOTT LAKE(SFT) ...172-B2
SEA LAKE ...40-D2
SECOND LAKE ...40-D1
SETON LAKE ...117-A1
SHADY OAK LAKE ...119-A3
SHANK LAKE ...98-D4
SHARP MUSKRAT
  LAKE(RVT) ...167-E4,181-E1
SHARP MUSKRAT LAKE(WEL) ...181-E1
SHAUER LAKE ...169-B3
SHAVERS LAKE ...104-C4
SHEAS LAKE ...214-C3
SHELDEN LAKE ...15-C2
SHERMAN LAKE ...66-C3
SHIELDS LAKE ...53-D1
SILVER LAKE(JST) ...184-A2
SILVER LAKE(NSP) ...95-B3
SILVER LAKE(SA) ...29-E1
SILVER LAKE(SVT) ...29-E1
SILVER LAKE(SWD) ...118-A4
SILVER LAKE(SWT) ...82-D2
SIMLEY LAKE ...136-E3
SKUNK LAKE ...23-E2
SMITH LAKE ...141-E1
SNAIL LAKE ...94-A3
SNELLING LAKE ...135-C1
SOUTH CENTER LAKE ...12-E4
SOUTH LAKE ...113-C1
SOUTH LINDSTROM LAKE ...12-C4
SOUTH SCHOOL SECTION LAKE ...68-A4

SOUTH TERRAPIN LAKE ...68-E2
SOUTH TWIN LAKE(CRY) ...92-A2
SOUTH TWIN LAKE(ROB) ...92-A3
SOUTH TWIN LAKE(SWT) ...82-D4
SPIDER LAKE ...26-E4
SPRING LAKE(NIT) ...151-D4
SPRING LAKE(SLK) ...79-A2
SPRING LAKE(SLT) ...160-D4
SPURZEM LAKE ...89-B3
SQUARE LAKE ...69-A3
SQUAW LAKE ...70-E1
ST ALBANS BAY ...118-A3
ST CATHERINE LAKE ...189-A1
STAPLES LAKE ...68-C1
STARING LAKE ...132-E3
STARK LAKE ...122-C4
STEELE LAKE ...60-C3
STIEGER LAKE ...130-E2
STONE LAKE(LIT) ...6-B3
STONE LAKE(MH) ...136-A1
STONE LAKE(VIC) ...116-D4
STRAND LAKE ...117-D2
STRATTON LAKE ...8-E1
STRUNKS LAKE ...145-E2
STUBBS BAY ...103-C3
STURGEON LAKE ...182-D4
SUCKER LAKE ...80-B4
SUGAR LAKE ...29-B1
SULLIVAN LAKE(CH) ...92-E1
SULLIVAN LAKE(MLT) ...44-B3
SUNFISH LAKE(AH) ...79-D4
SUNFISH LAKE(LE) ...110-B1
SUNFISH LAKE(RAM) ...49-A2
SUNFISH LAKE(SL) ...136-B1
SUNNY ACRES POND ...49-D3
SUNRISE LAKE ...12-C1
SUNRISE POOL NO 1 ...11-C4
SUNRISE POOL NO 3 ...11-C4
SUNSET LAKE ...87-D4
SUNSET POND ...162-B1
SUTTON LAKE ...174-B4
SWAMP LAKE(FRT) ...27-A3
SWAMP LAKE(SCT) ...174-A2
SWAN LAKE(OG) ...36-C1
SWAN LAKE(WCT) ...15-E3
SWARTOUT LAKE ...43-A2
SWEDE LAKE ...115-C2
SWEENEY LAKE ...106-A1
SYLVAN LAKE(FLT) ...54-A1
SYLVAN LAKE(HSN) ...61-C1
TAMARACK LAKE(LWT) ...24-C1
TAMARACK LAKE(NO) ...80-C3
TAMARACK LAKE(OXT) ...10-E1
TAMARACK LAKE(RFT) ...58-D4
TAMARACK LAKE(VIC) ...131-B1
TAMARACK LAKE(WBT) ...80-B1
TANAGER LAKE ...103-E3
TANNERS LAKE ...109-C4
TAYLOR LAKE ...71-B2
THIES LAKE ...89-D4
THIRD LAKE ...40-C2
THOLE LAKE ...160-B2
THOMAS LAKE(DNT) ...214-A2
THOMAS LAKE(EAG) ...149-D2
THOMAS LAKE(MED) ...89-C2
THOMPSON LAKE(BLT) ...17-E2
THOMPSON LAKE(WSP) ...122-C3
TIGER LAKE ...142-A3
TRILLIUM LAKE ...130-E2
TRULSON LAKE ...27-C2
TURBID LAKE ...130-C3
TURNER POND ...162-B2
TURTLE LAKE(MAY) ...68-C1
TURTLE LAKE(PLY) ...90-D3
TURTLE LAKE(SMT) ...70-C3
TURTLE LAKE(SVW) ...79-E2
TWIN LAKE(COT) ...38-A2
TWIN LAKE(FLT) ...40-A2
TWIN LAKE(GV) ...106-A1
TWIN LAKE(LC) ...94-D1
TWIN LAKE(SVT) ...15-E3
TWIN LAKES(CMT) ...130-E3
TWIN LAKES(MAY) ...69-B3,69-B4
TWIN LAKES(MOT) ...30-E3
TWIN LAKES(SLP) ...106-A3
TWIN LAKES(WEL) ...182-B1
TYPO LAKE ...10-B2
UHL LAKE ...60-C2
UNION LAKE ...218-B4
UPPER LAKE ...121-D3
UPPER LAKE GRACE ...131-C4
UPPER RATTLING
  SPRINGS LAKE ...182-A3
VALENTINE LAKE ...93-D1
VALLEY LAKE ...163-B3
VARNER LAKE ...44-D4
VICTORIA LAKE ...105-C4
WACONIA LAKE ...129-D1
WAKELEY LAKE ...60-C3
WALLESTAD LAKE ...131-C3
WALLMARK LAKE ...12-B4
WARD LAKE ...36-C3
WARDS LAKE ...66-C3
WASHINGTON LAKE(WLK) ...170-B2
WASHINGTON LAKE(BUT) ...59-D1
WASSERMANN LAKE ...130-E3
WAVERLY LAKE ...72-A4
WEAVER LAKE ...76-C2
WEST ARM BAY ...117-B1
WEST BOOT LAKE ...68-D2
WEST HUNTER LAKE ...6-B1
WEST LAKE ...16-B4
WHALETAIL LAKE ...116-B1
WHITE BEAR LAKE ...81-B4
WHITE ROCK LAKE ...54-B2
WHITE STONE LAKE ...25-D3
WILDCAT LAKE ...196-D2
WILKINSON LAKE ...80-D1
WILLOW LAKE ...94-D2
WILMES LAKE ...124-A1
WING LAKE ...118-D3
WINKLER LAKE ...143-B2
WINSTED LAKE ...99-B3
WINTERHALTER LAKE ...89-C2
WIRTH LAKE ...106-A2
WOLSFELD LAKE ...103-D1
WOOD LAKE(BLT) ...17-D2
WOOD LAKE(RCH) ...134-C1
WOOD PILE LAKE ...82-A4
WOODGATE POND ...118-D3
WRIGHTS LAKE ...134-E3
WYCKSTROM LAKE ...14-B2
YAGER LAKE ...10-C4
YOUNG AMERICA LAKE ...142-D3
ZUMBRA LAKE ...130-E1

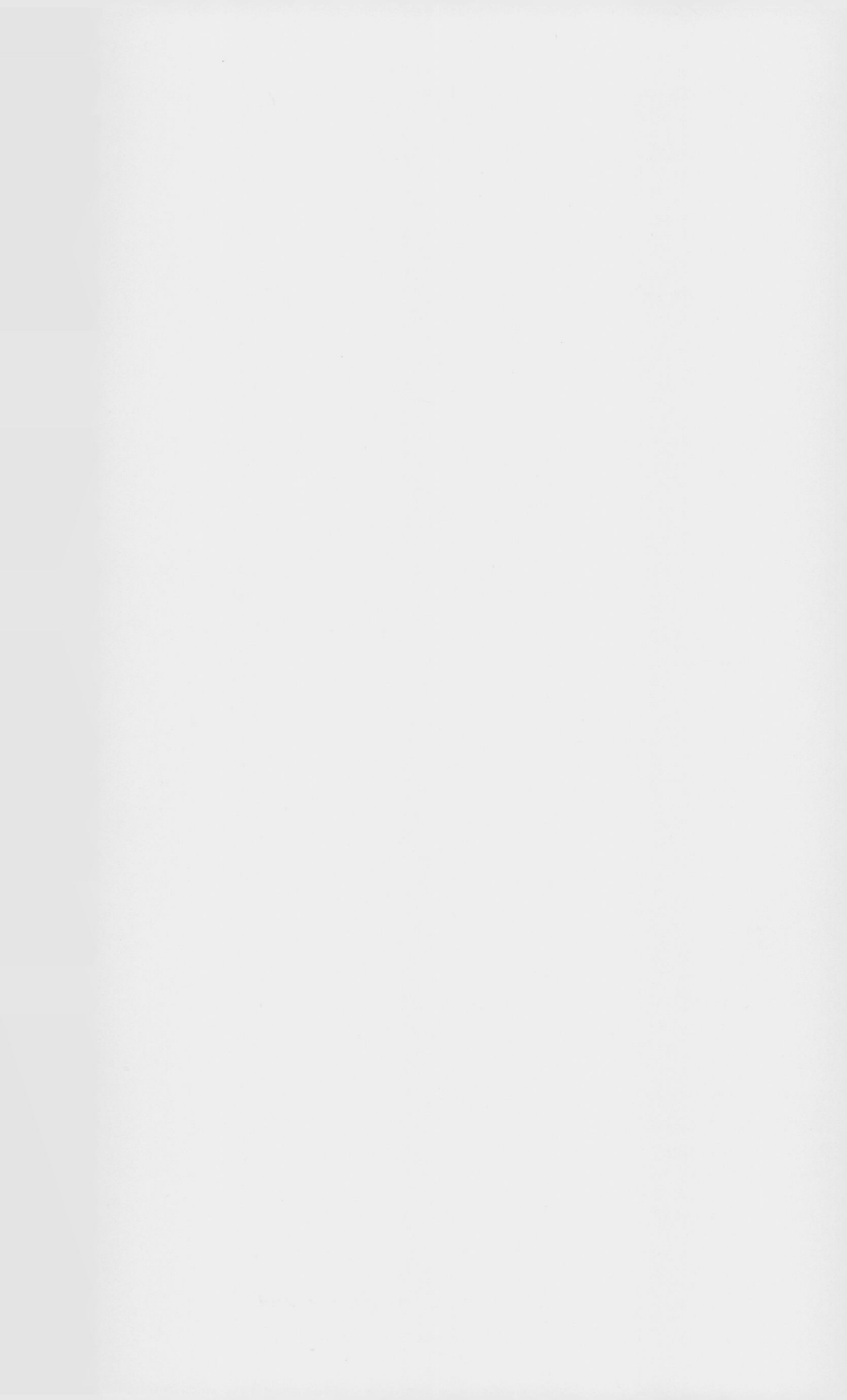

ST. CLOUD PAGE LOCATION GUIDE

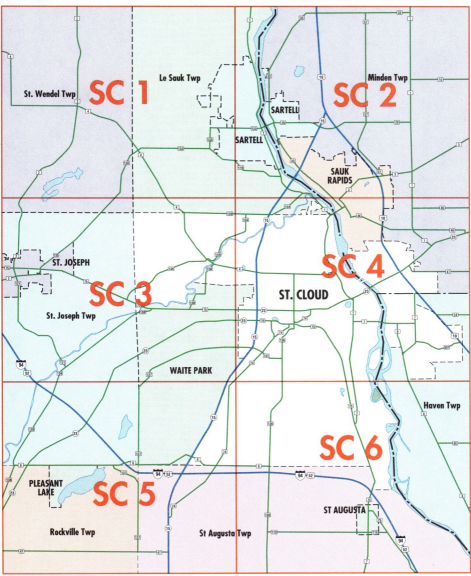

SC 1

St. Wendel Twp
Le Sauk Twp

SC 2

Minden Twp

SARTELL

SARTELL

SAUK RAPIDS

SC 4

SC 3

ST. JOSEPH

St. Joseph Twp

ST. CLOUD

WAITE PARK

SC 6

Haven Twp

SC 5

PLEASANT LAKE

Rockville Twp

St Augusta Twp

ST AUGUSTA

ST. CLOUD LEGEND

Road Classification

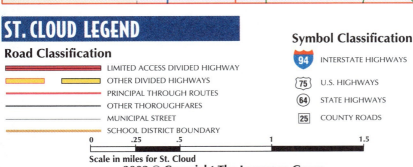

LIMITED ACCESS DIVIDED HIGHWAY
OTHER DIVIDED HIGHWAYS
PRINCIPAL THROUGH ROUTES
OTHER THOROUGHFARES
MUNICIPAL STREET
SCHOOL DISTRICT BOUNDARY

Symbol Classification

94   INTERSTATE HIGHWAYS

75   U.S. HIGHWAYS

64   STATE HIGHWAYS

25   COUNTY ROADS

Scale in miles for St. Cloud

0   .25   .5   1   1.5

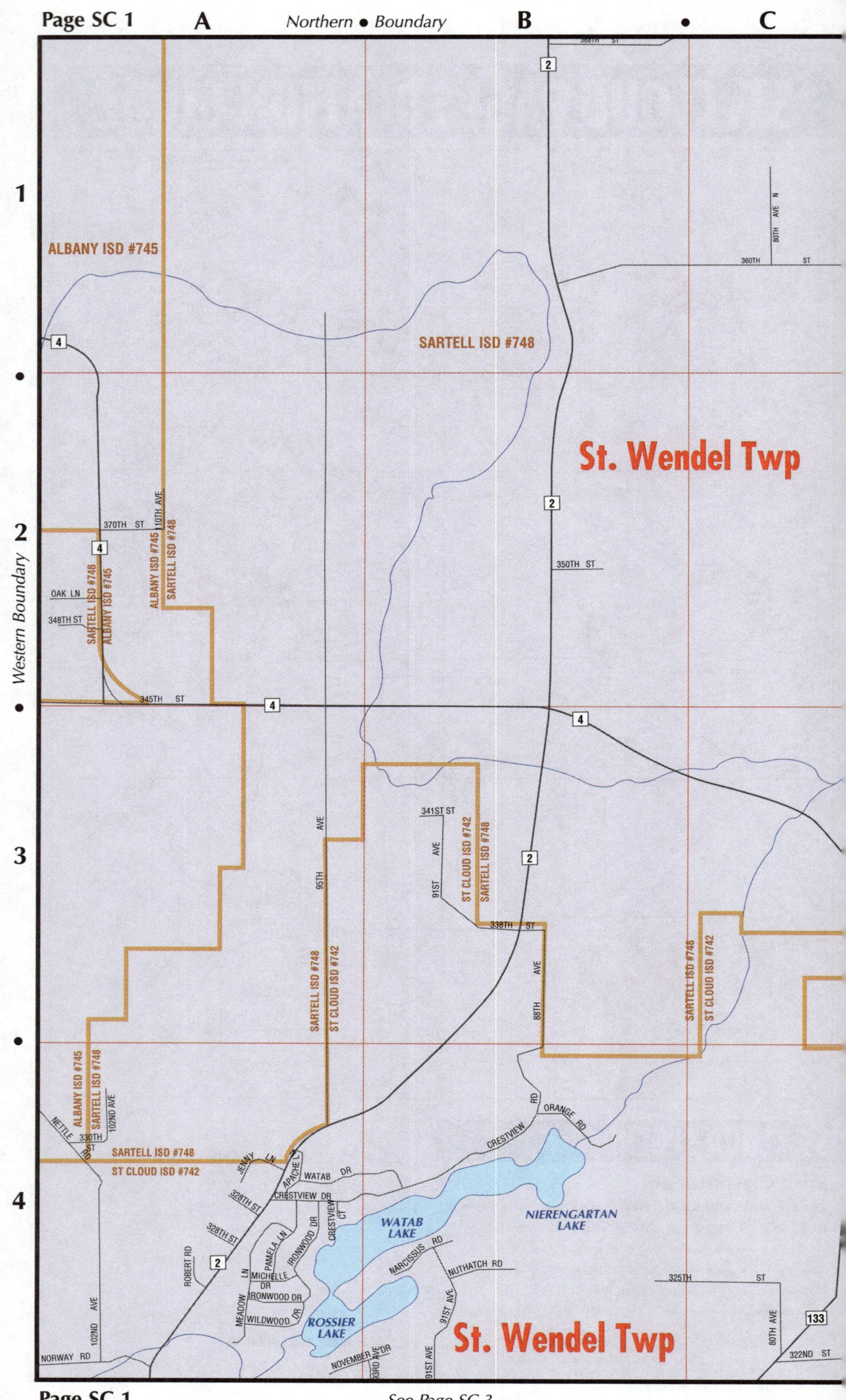

1

ALBANY ISD #745

SARTELL ISD #748

360TH   ST

80TH   AVE   N

350TH ST

St. Wendel Twp

Western Boundary

2

370TH   ST

110TH AVE

ALBANY ISD #745   SARTELL ISD #748

OAK LN

348TH ST

SARTELL ISD #748   ALBANY ISD #745

345TH   ST

3

341ST ST

91ST   AVE

95TH   AVE

ST CLOUD ISD #742   SARTELL ISD #748

SARTELL ISD #748   ST CLOUD ISD #742

338TH   ST

88TH   AVE

SARTELL ISD #748   ST CLOUD ISD #742

4

ALBANY ISD #745   SARTELL ISD #748

102ND AVE

NETTLE   330TH

SARTELL ISD #748
ST CLOUD ISD #742

JENNY   LN

APACHE   LN

WATAB   DR

CRESTVIEW DR

CRESTVIEW   RD   ORANGE   RD

329TH ST

328TH ST

IRONWOOD DR

PAMELA LN

MICHELLE
DR

IRONWOOD DR

MEADOW   LN

WILDWOOD

WATAB
LAKE

NIERENGARTAN
LAKE

NARCISSUS   RD

NUTHATCH RD

325TH   ST

ROBERT RD

ROSSIER
LAKE

St. Wendel Twp

102ND   AVE

NORWAY   RD

NOVEMBER AVE

93RD AVE

91ST AVE

91ST   AVE

80TH   AVE

322ND   ST

133

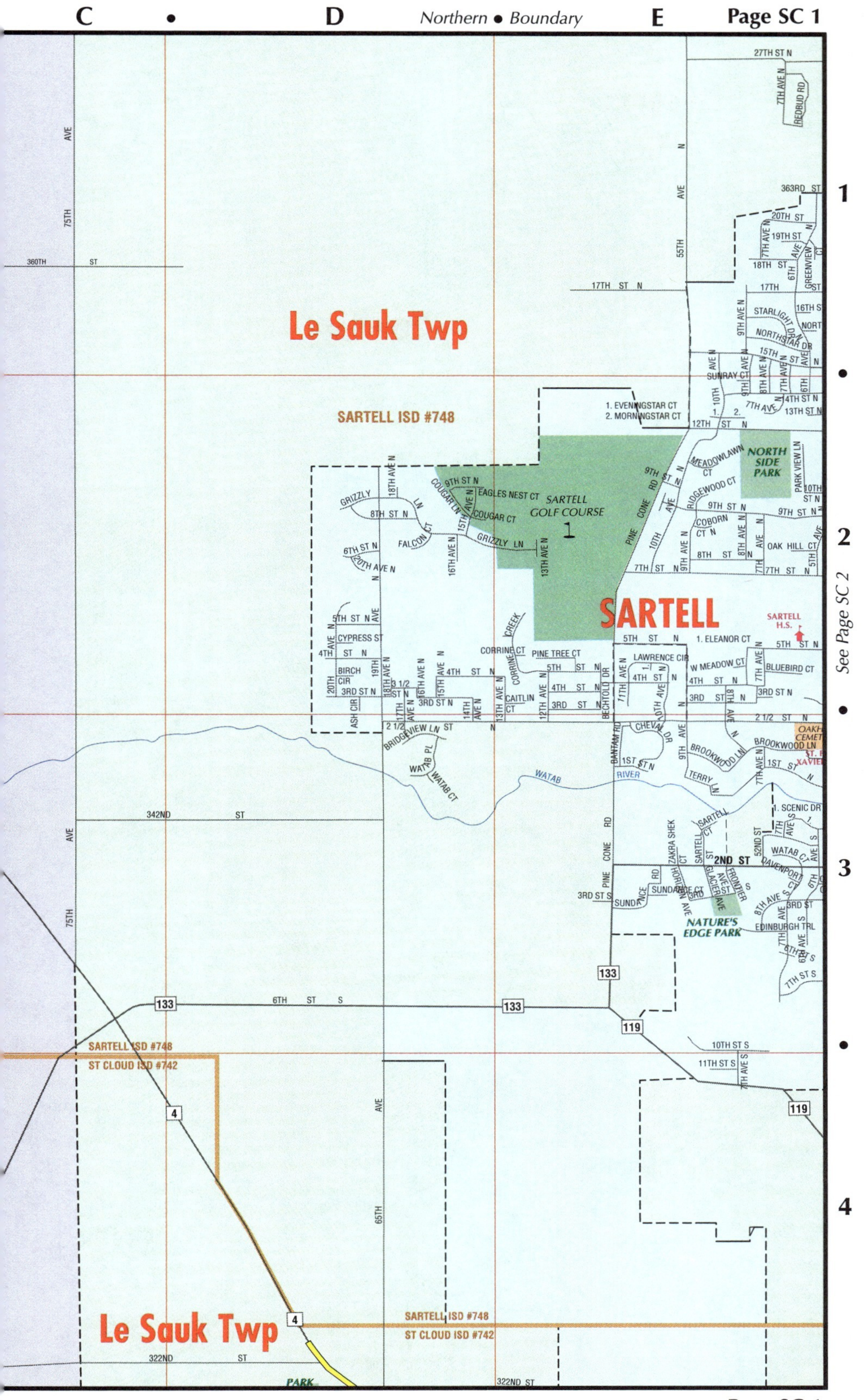

Le Sauk Twp

SARTELL ISD #748

SARTELL GOLF COURSE

SARTELL

NORTH SIDE PARK

NATURE'S EDGE PARK

Le Sauk Twp

SARTELL ISD #748
ST CLOUD ISD #742

SARTELL ISD #748
ST CLOUD ISD #742

1. EVENINGSTAR CT
2. MORNINGSTAR CT

1. ELEANOR CT

1. SCENIC DR

See Page SC 2

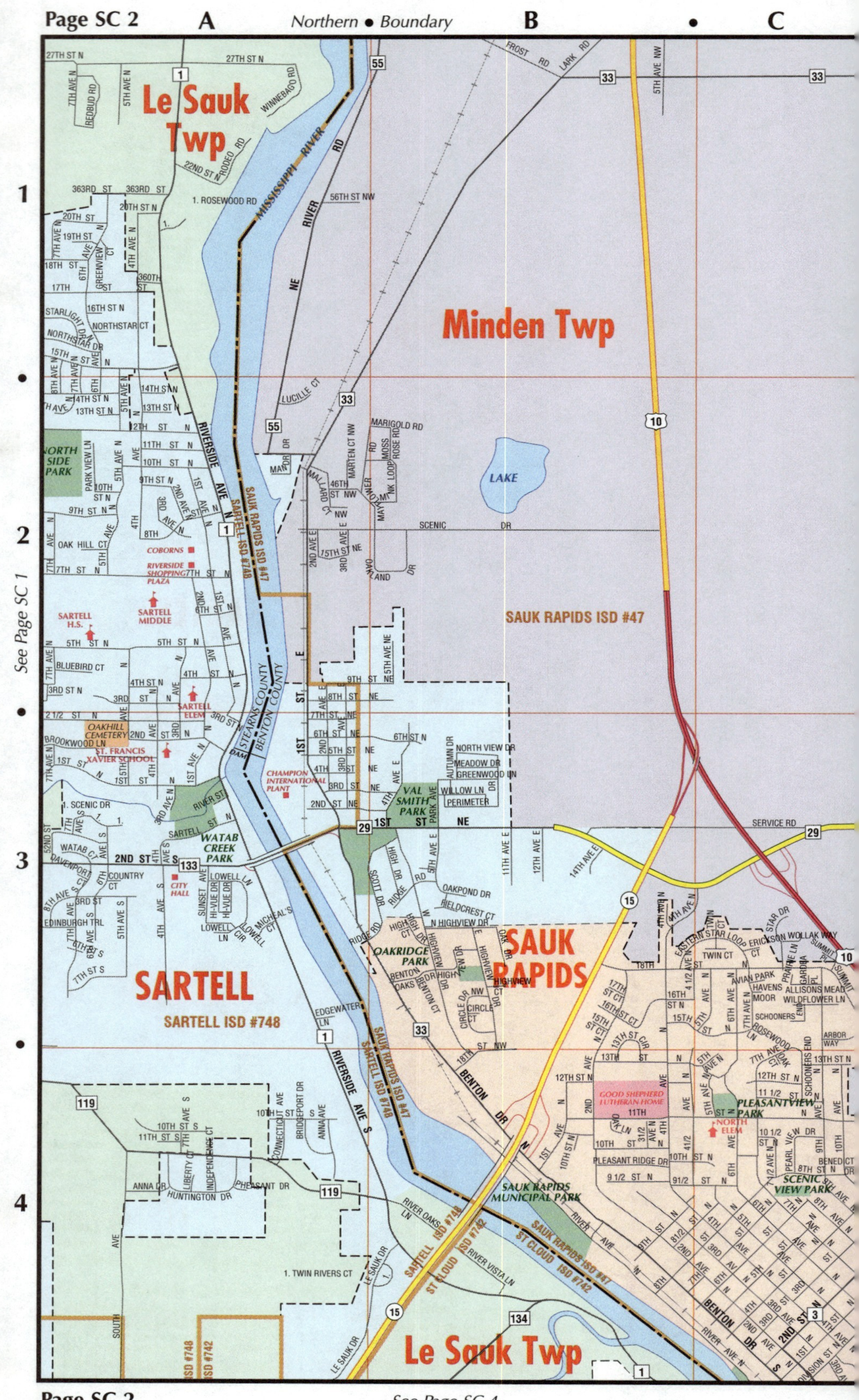
A
Northern • Boundary
B
C
1
2
3
4
See Page SC 1
Le Sauk Twp
Minden Twp
SARTELL
SARTELL ISD #748
SAUK RAPIDS
SAUK RAPIDS ISD #47
Le Sauk Twp
MISSISSIPPI RIVER
LAKE
NORTH SIDE PARK
SARTELL H.S.
SARTELL MIDDLE
SARTELL ELEM
COBORNS
RIVERSIDE SHOPPING PLAZA
OAKHILL CEMETERY
ST. FRANCIS XAVIER SCHOOL
CHAMPION INTERNATIONAL PLANT
VAL SMITH PARK
WATAB CREEK PARK
CITY HALL
OAKRIDGE PARK
GOOD SHEPHERD LUTHERAN HOME
PLEASANTVIEW PARK
NORTH ELEM
SCENIC VIEW PARK
SAUK RAPIDS MUNICIPAL PARK
STEARNS COUNTY
BENTON COUNTY
ST CLOUD ISD #742
RIVERSIDE AVE
SCENIC DR
SERVICE RD
BENTON DR

See Page SC 4

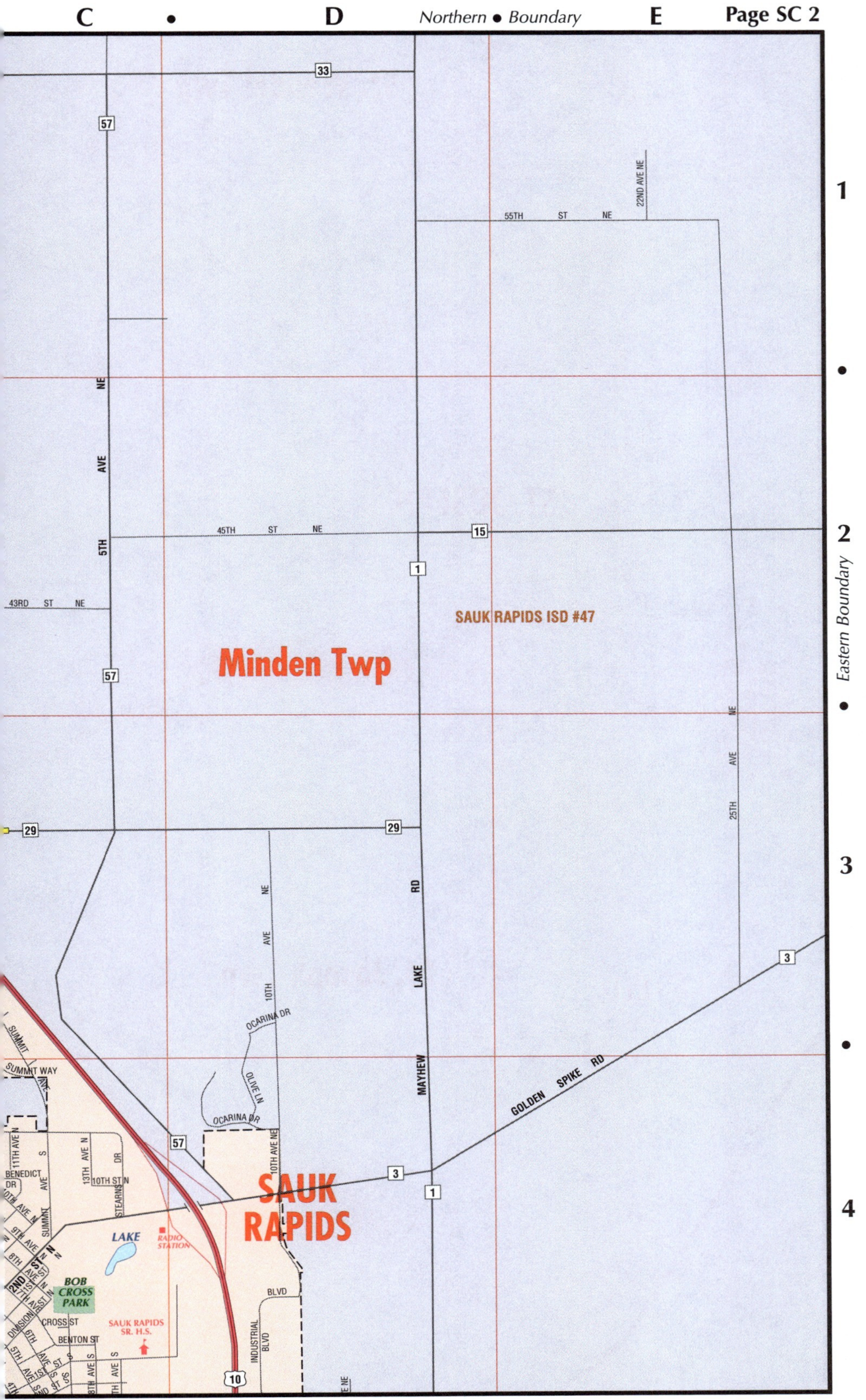

C • D Northern • Boundary E

33

57

22ND AVE NE

55TH ST NE

1

•

NE

AVE

5TH

45TH ST NE

15

1

Eastern Boundary

2

SAUK RAPIDS ISD #47

43RD ST NE

Minden Twp

57

NE

•

AVE

25TH

29 29

3

LAKE RD

NE

AVE

10TH

OCARINA DR

3

3

OLIVE LN

•

SUMMIT AVE

OCARINA DR

MAYHEW

GOLDEN SPIKE RD

SUMMIT WAY

11TH AVE N

57

10TH AVE NE

3

1

4

BENEDICT DR

13TH AVE N

STEARNS DR

10TH ST N

SUMMIT AVE

9TH AVE S

SAUK RAPIDS

8TH AVE S

LAKE

RADIO STATION

BOB CROSS PARK

BLVD

DIVISION ST

CROSS ST

SAUK RAPIDS SR. H.S.

BENTON ST

2ND

3RD AVE S

4TH AVE S

5TH AVE S

INDUSTRIAL BLVD

NE

10

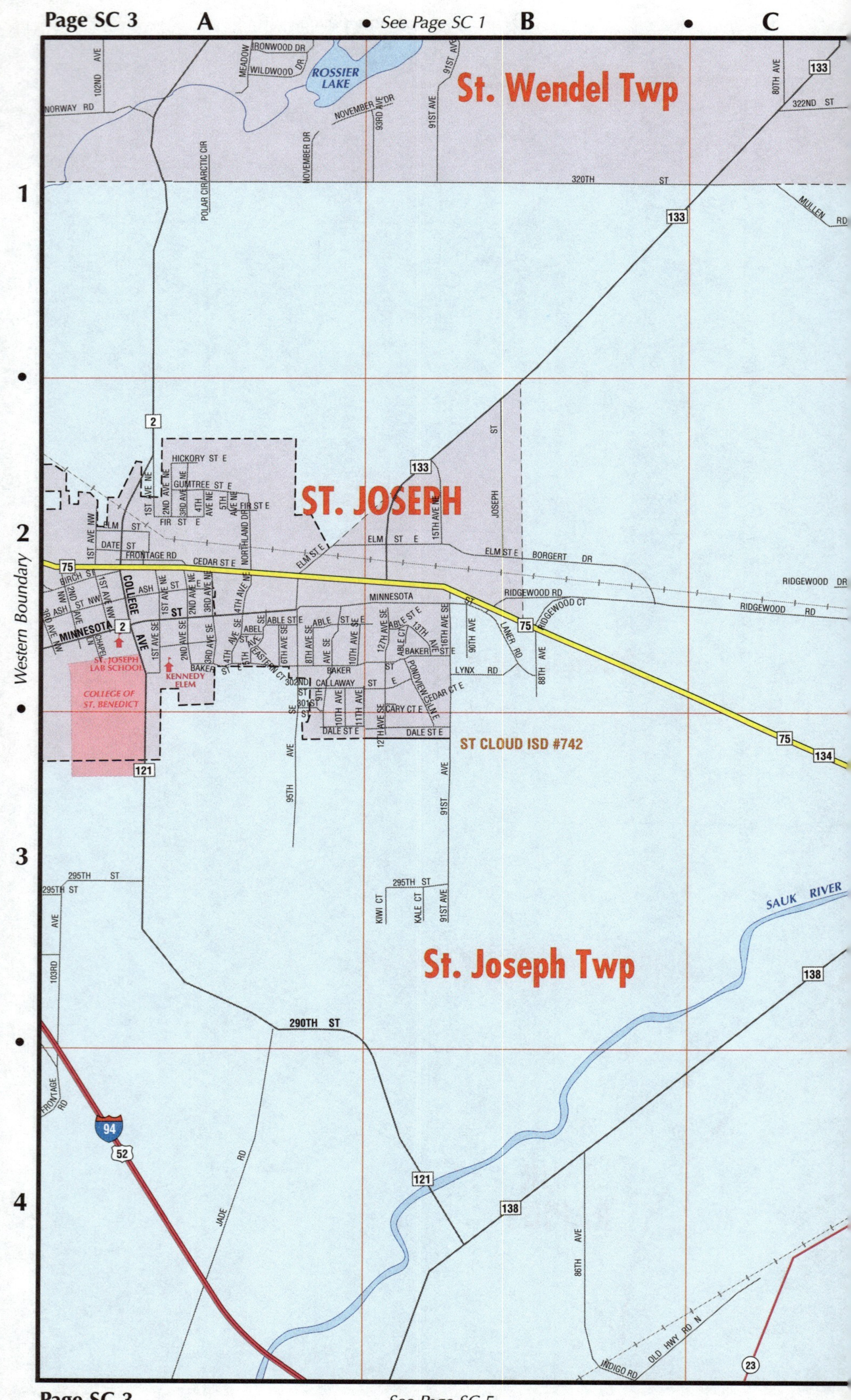

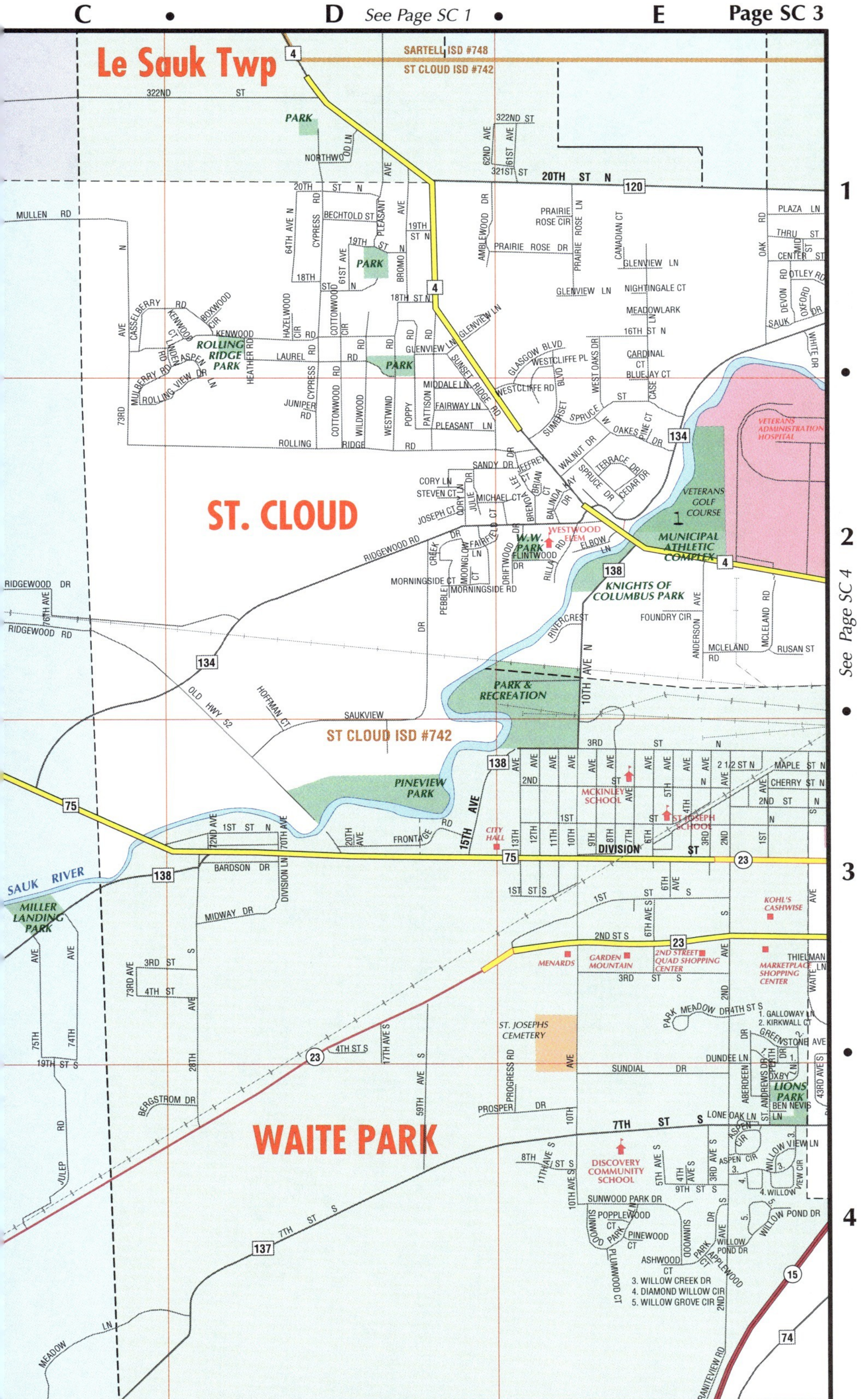
Le Sauk Twp
ST. CLOUD
WAITE PARK
SARTELL ISD #748
ST CLOUD ISD #742
VETERANS ADMINISTRATION HOSPITAL
VETERANS GOLF COURSE
MUNICIPAL ATHLETIC COMPLEX
KNIGHTS OF COLUMBUS PARK
PARK & RECREATION
PINEVIEW PARK
ROLLING RIDGE PARK
W.W. PARK
WESTWOOD ELEM
MILLER LANDING PARK
SAUK RIVER
CITY HALL
MCKINLEY SCHOOL
ST JOSEPH SCHOOL
KOHL'S CASHWISE
MENARDS
GARDEN MOUNTAIN
2ND STREET QUAD SHOPPING CENTER
MARKETPLACE SHOPPING CENTER
ST. JOSEPHS CEMETERY
LIONS PARK
DISCOVERY COMMUNITY SCHOOL
1. GALLOWAY LN
2. KIRKWALL CT
3. WILLOW CREEK DR
4. DIAMOND WILLOW CIR
5. WILLOW GROVE CIR
20TH ST N
DIVISION ST
7TH ST S
1
2
3
4
See Page SC 4

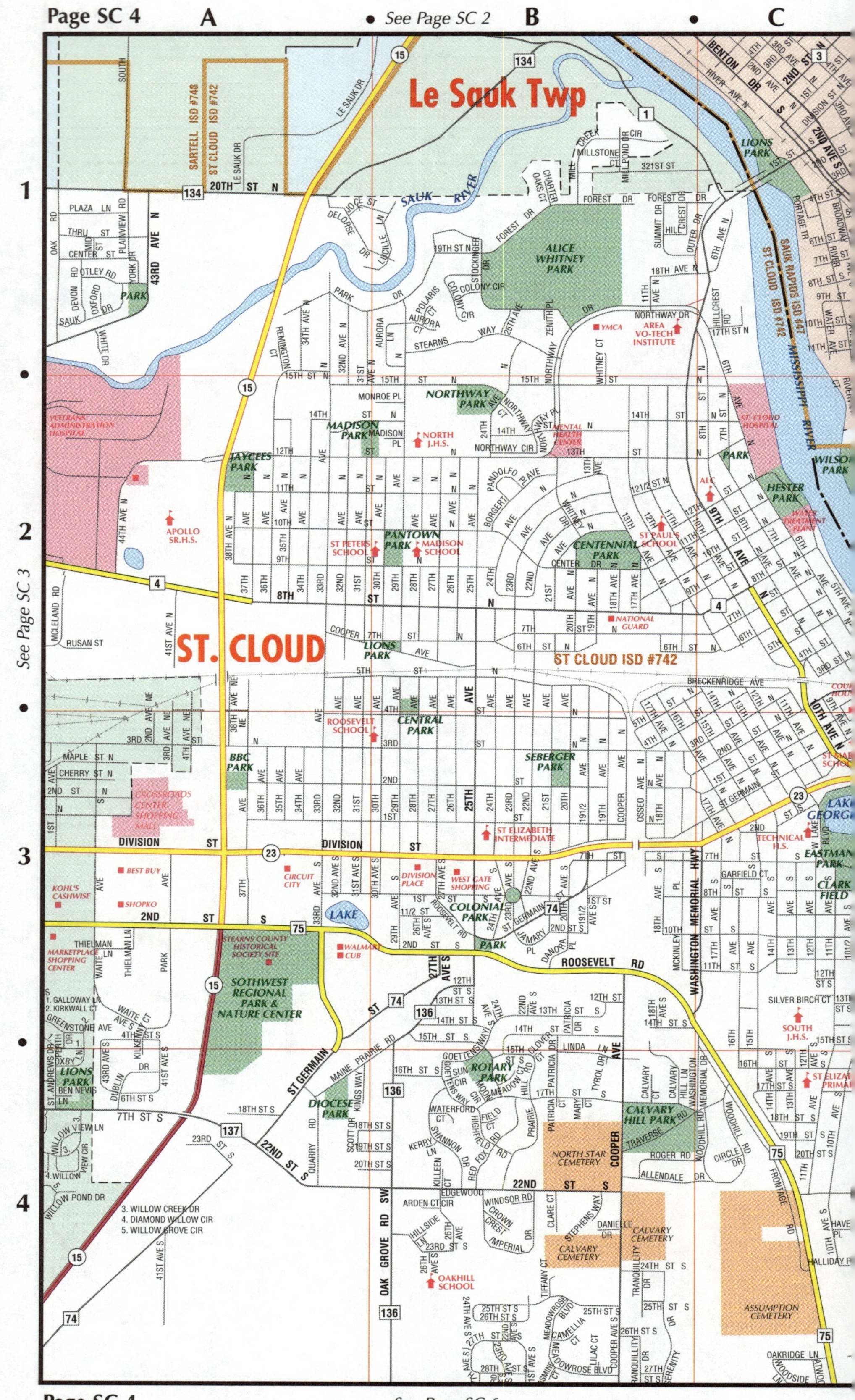

Le Sauk Twp

Alice Whitney Park

Northway Park

Madison Park

Jaycees Park

ST. CLOUD

Lions Park

Apollo SR.H.S.

Pantown Park

Centennial Park

Roosevelt School

Central Park

Seberger Park

BBC Park

Crossroads Center Shopping Mall

Colonial Park

West Gate Shopping

St Cloud Hospital

Wilson Park

Hester Park

Lake George

Eastman Park

Clark Field

Veterans Administration Hospital

Kohl's Cashwise

Best Buy

Shopko

Circuit City

Marketplace Shopping Center

Thielman Ln

Stearns County Historical Society Site

Walmart Cub

Southwest Regional Park & Nature Center

Diocese Park

Rotary Park

Calvary Hill Park

North Star Cemetery

Calvary Cemetery

Oakhill School

Assumption Cemetery

ST CLOUD ISD #742

Lions Park

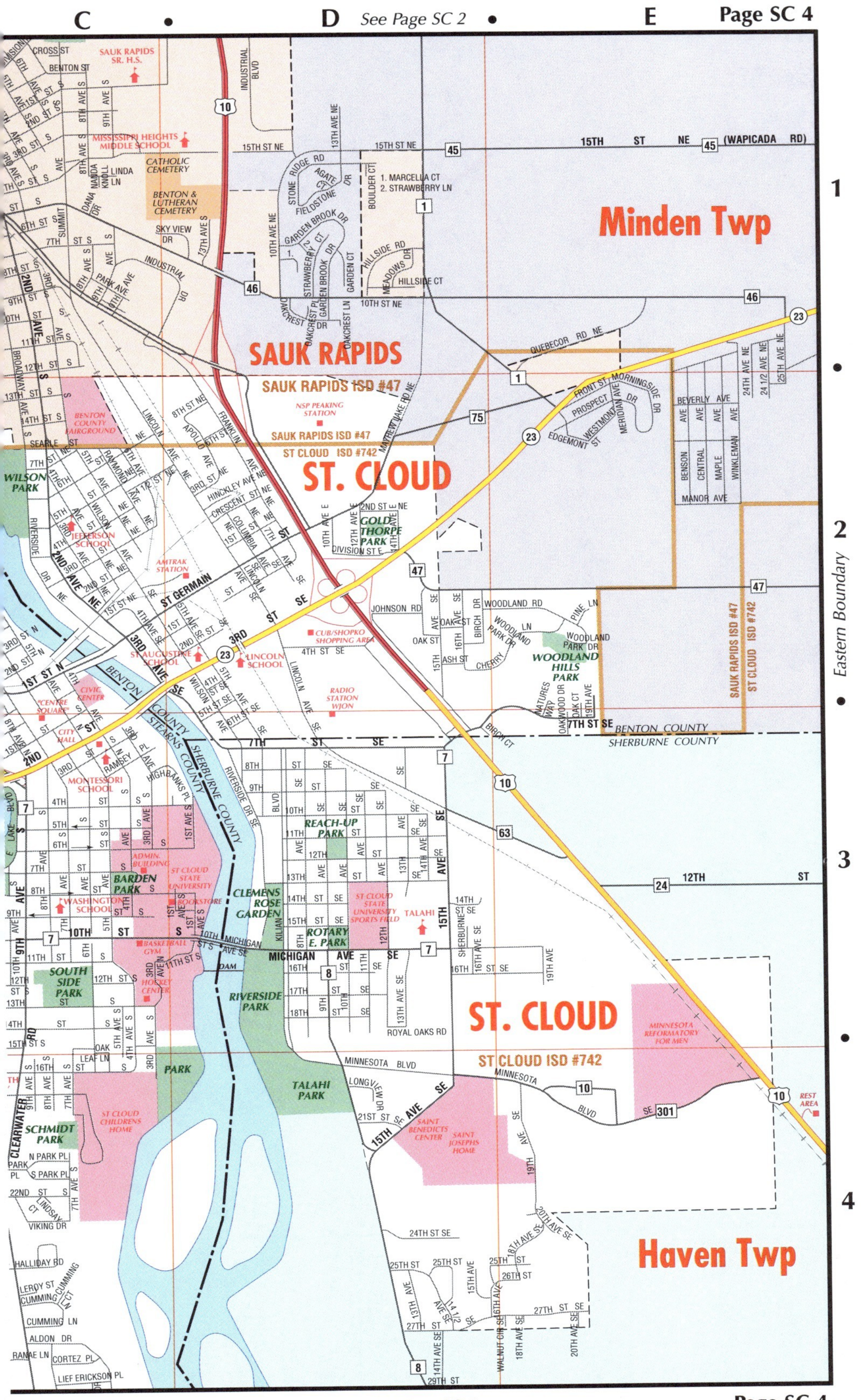
Minden Twp
SAUK RAPIDS
SAUK RAPIDS ISD #47
ST. CLOUD ISD #742
ST. CLOUD
ST CLOUD ISD #742
Haven Twp
Eastern Boundary
BENTON COUNTY
SHERBURNE COUNTY
STEARNS COUNTY
15TH ST NE (WAPICADA RD)
WILSON PARK
GOLDTHORPE PARK
WOODLAND HILLS PARK
REACH-UP PARK
BARDEN PARK
CLEMENS ROSE GARDEN
ROTARY E. PARK
SOUTH SIDE PARK
RIVERSIDE PARK
TALAHI PARK
SCHMIDT PARK
PARK
MINNESOTA REFORMATORY FOR MEN
SAINT BENEDICTS CENTER
SAINT JOSEPHS HOME
ST CLOUD CHILDRENS HOME
ST CLOUD STATE UNIVERSITY
BENTON COUNTY FAIRGROUND
SAUK RAPIDS SR. H.S.
MISSISSIPPI HEIGHTS MIDDLE SCHOOL
CATHOLIC CEMETERY
BENTON & LUTHERAN CEMETERY
NSP PEAKING STATION
JEFFERSON SCHOOL
AMTRAK STATION
CUB/SHOPKO SHOPPING AREA
LINCOLN SCHOOL
ST AUGUSTINE SCHOOL
RADIO STATION WJON
CIVIC CENTER
CENTRE SQUARE
CITY HALL
MONTESSORI SCHOOL
WASHINGTON SCHOOL
ADMIN. BUILDING
BOOKSTORE
BASKETBALL GYM
HOCKEY CENTER
ST CLOUD STATE UNIVERSITY SPORTS FIELD
TALAHI
DAM
REST AREA
1. MARCELLA CT
2. STRAWBERRY LN

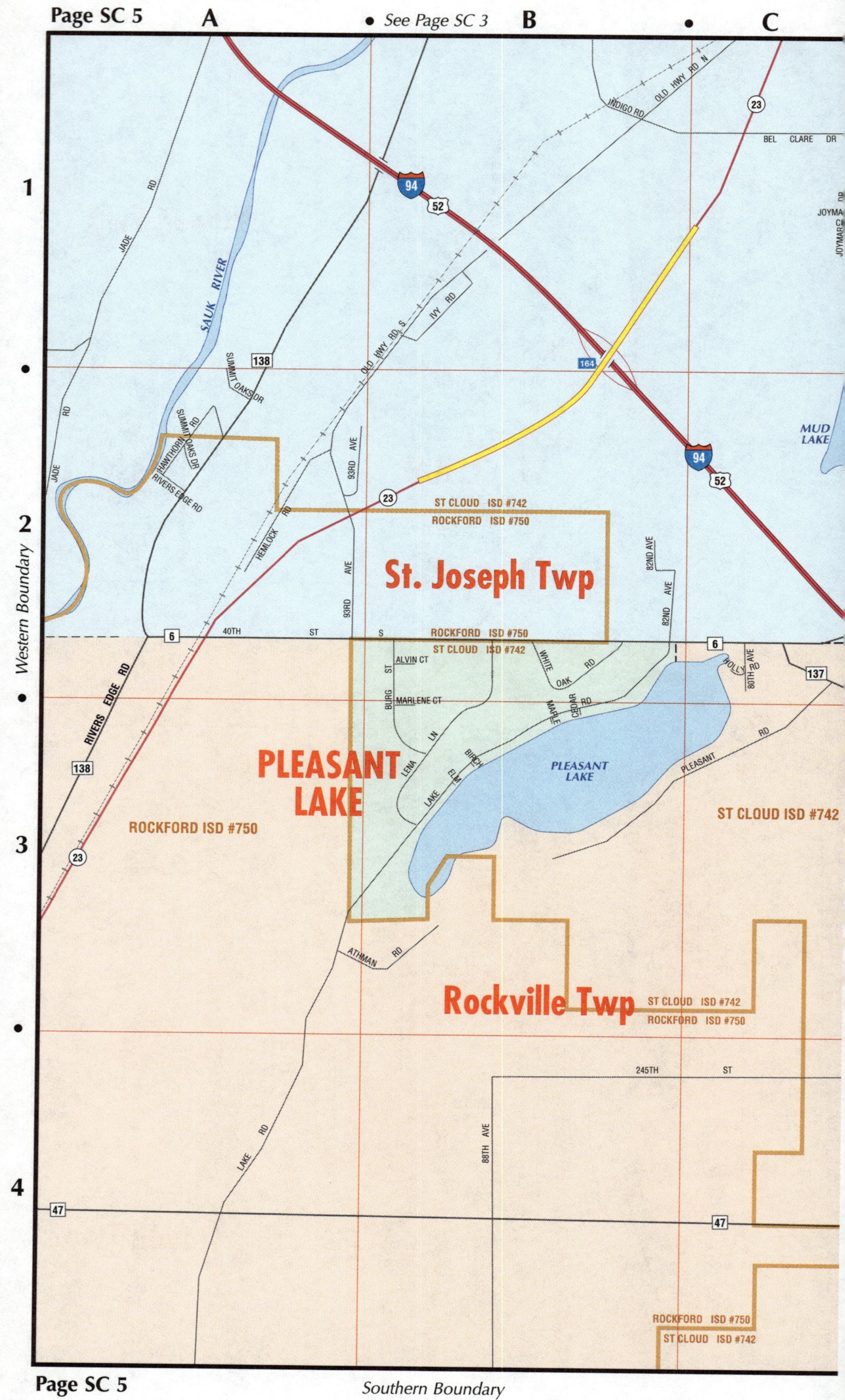

See Page SC 3

A   B   C

1

94
52

JADE RD

SAUK RIVER

138

SUMMIT OAKS DR

OLD HWY RD S

IVY RD

INDIGO RD

OLD HWY RD N

23

BEL CLARE DR

JOYMA CIR

JOYMAR DR

164

MUD LAKE

JADE RD

SUMMIT OAKS DR

HAWTHORNE DR

RIVERS EDGE RD

93RD AVE

94
52

Western Boundary

2

HEMLOCK RD

93RD AVE

23

6

40TH ST

ST CLOUD ISD #742
ROCKFORD ISD #750

St. Joseph Twp

ROCKFORD ISD #750
ST CLOUD ISD #742

82ND AVE

82ND AVE

6

WHITE OAK RD

137

80TH AVE

HOLLY

RIVERS EDGE RD

138

23

ALVIN CT

BURG ST

MARLENE CT

LENA LN

LAKE ELM

BIRCH

MAPLE

INDIGO RD

PLEASANT

PLEASANT LAKE

PLEASANT LAKE

ROCKFORD ISD #750

ST CLOUD ISD #742

3

ATHMAN RD

Rockville Twp   ST CLOUD ISD #742
ROCKFORD ISD #750

LAKE RD

245TH ST

88TH AVE

4

47

47

ROCKFORD ISD #750
ST CLOUD ISD #742

    Southern Boundary

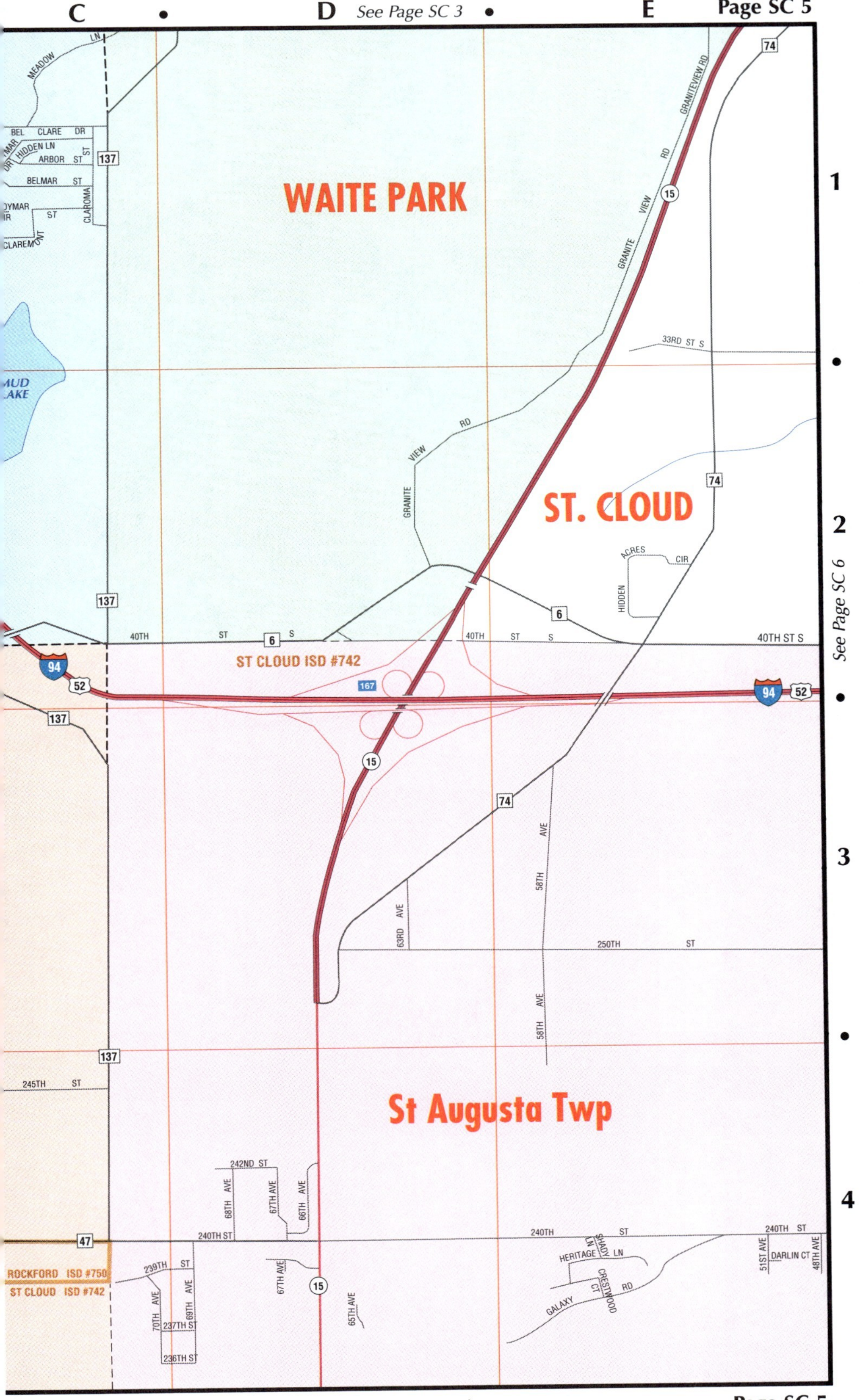

MEADOW LN

BEL CLARE DR
HIDDEN LN
ARBOR ST
137
BELMAR ST
CLAROMA ST
CLAREMONT

1

WAITE PARK

GRANITEVIEW RD

GRANITE VIEW RD
15
74

33RD ST S

GRANITE VIEW RD

74

ST. CLOUD

2

ACRES
CIR
HIDDEN
6

MUD LAKE

137

40TH ST
6 S
40TH ST S
40TH ST S

94
52
ST CLOUD ISD #742
167
94 52

137

15

74

3

63RD AVE
58TH AVE
250TH ST

58TH AVE

137

245TH ST

St Augusta Twp

242ND ST
68TH AVE
67TH AVE
66TH AVE

240TH ST
240TH ST
240TH ST
51ST AVE
DARLIN CT
48TH AVE

47

ROCKFORD ISD #750
ST CLOUD ISD #742

239TH ST
70TH AVE
69TH AVE
237TH ST
236TH ST

67TH AVE

15

65TH AVE

HERITAGE LN
CRESTWOOD CT
GALAXY RD
SHADY LN

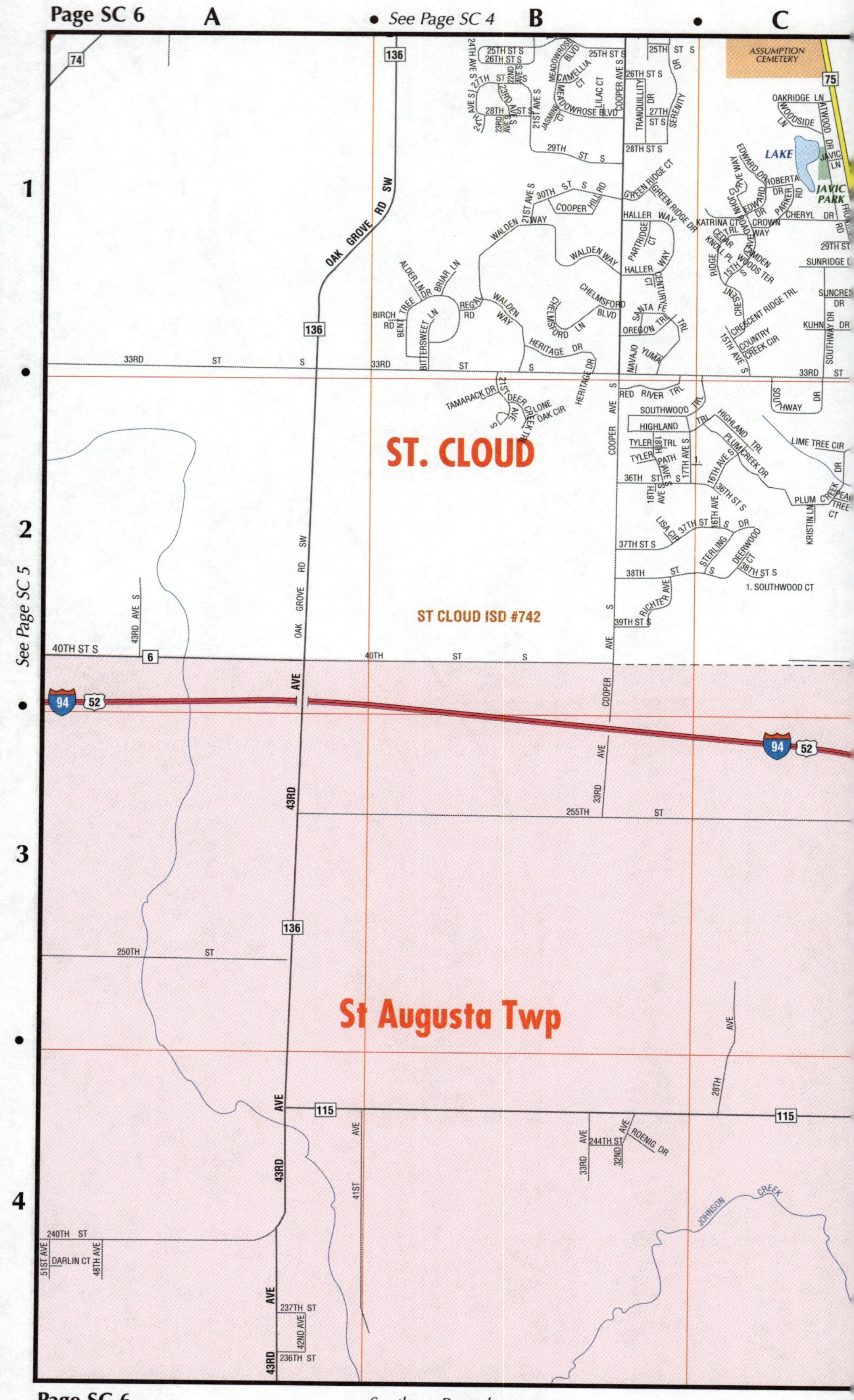

ST. CLOUD

ST CLOUD ISD #742

St Augusta Twp

1. SOUTHWOOD CT

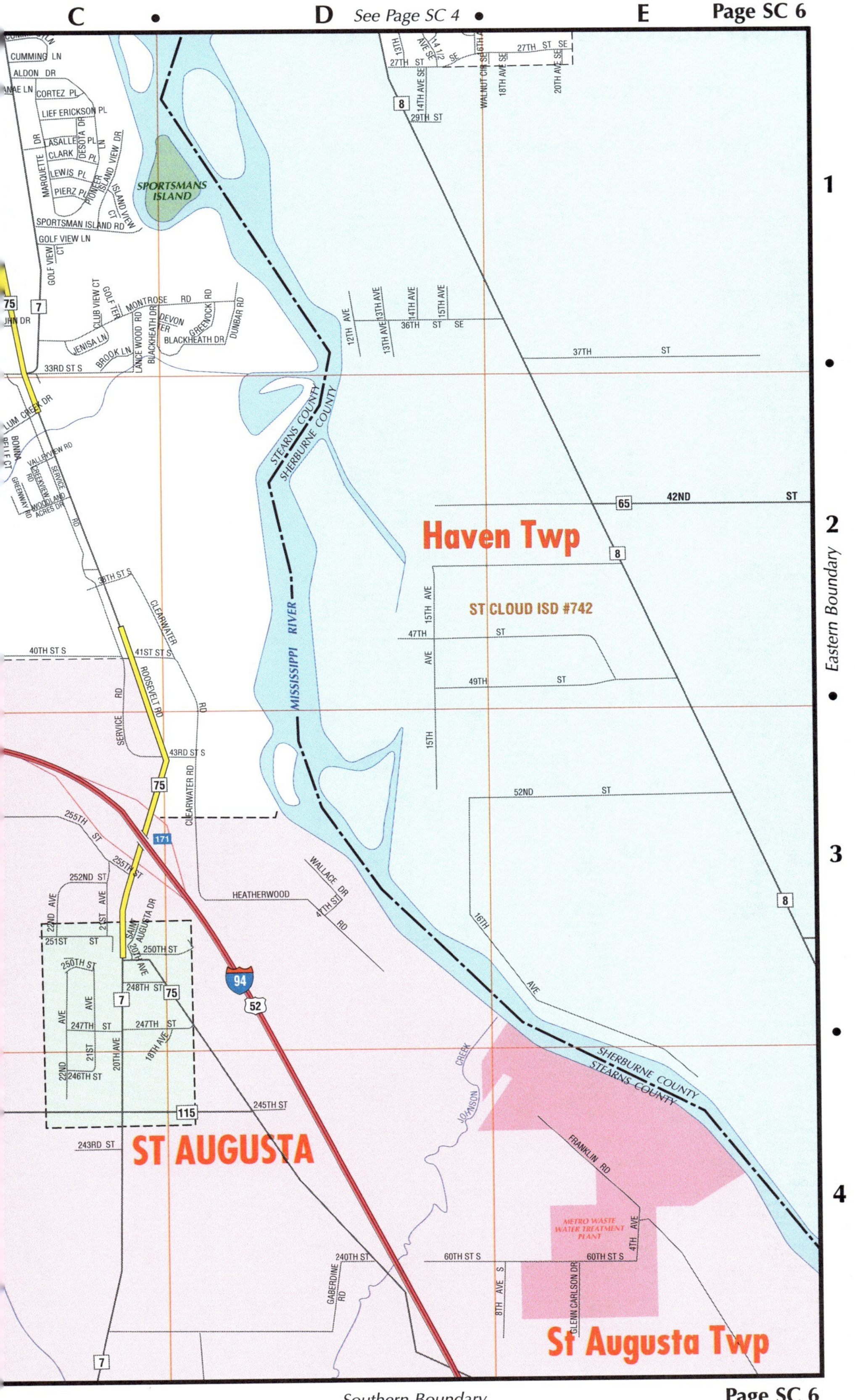

1

2

3

4

Eastern Boundary

COMMUNITY LN
CUMMING LN
ALDON DR
NAE LN
CORTEZ PL
LIEF ERICKSON PL
MARQUETTE DR
ASALLEE
CLARK
DESOTA PL
LEWIS PL
PIERZ PL
PIONEERS
ISLAND VIEW DR
PIERLAND VIEW DR

SPORTSMANS ISLAND

SPORTSMAN ISLAND RD
GOLF VIEW LN
GOLF VIEW CT
JHN DR
JENISA LN
CLUB VIEW CT
TEL PLDG
LANCEWOOD RD
MONTROSE RD
BROOK LN
BLACKHEATH DR
DEVON CT
GREENOCK RD
DUNBAR RD
PETER
BLACKHEATH DR
33RD ST S

75   7

LUM CREEK DR
BONIN
BELI F CT
GREENWAY RD
VALLEVIEW RD
MEADOWCREEK RD
WOODLAND
ACRES DR
38TH ST S

40TH ST S
41ST ST S
CLEARWATER
ROOSEVELT RD
SERVICE RD
CLEARWATER RD
43RD ST S

75

255TH ST
255TH ST
252ND ST
251ST ST
22ND AVE
21ST
250TH ST
250TH ST
20TH AVE
7
248TH ST
21ST AVE
AUGUSTA DR

171

HEATHERWOOD
WALLACE DR
4TH DR
RD

94
52
75

247TH ST
247TH ST
20TH AVE
18TH AVE
246TH ST
22ND
21ST
245TH ST

115

243RD ST

ST AUGUSTA

240TH ST
GABERDINE RD
60TH ST S

13TH ST SE
14 1/2 SE
27TH ST
27TH ST SE
27TH ST SE
AVE SE
WALNUT CIR SE
18TH AVE SE
20TH AVE SE
8
29TH ST

127TH AVE
13TH AVE
13TH AVE
14TH AVE
15TH AVE
36TH ST SE
37TH ST

65   42ND ST
8

Haven Twp

ST CLOUD ISD #742

15TH AVE
47TH ST
AVE
49TH ST
15TH
52ND ST

16TH AVE

8

MISSISSIPPI RIVER
STEARNS COUNTY
SHERBURNE COUNTY

SHERBURNE COUNTY
STEARNS COUNTY

JOHNSON CREEK
FRANKLIN RD
4TH AVE

METRO WASTE WATER TREATMENT PLANT

60TH ST S
8TH AVE S
GLENN CARLSON DR

St Augusta Twp

7

SAINT CLOUD, MINNESOTA INDEX

DELORSE DR SC . . . . SC4 - A1

Street Name · City/Township Abbreviation · Page Number · Grid Location

A

ABERDEEN DR WPK SC3-E4
ABLE CT SJ SC3-B2
ABLE ST E SJ SC3-A2
AGATE CT SKR SC4-D1
AGATE DR SKR SC4-D1
ALDER LN SC SC6-B1
ALDON DR SC SC4-C4,SC6-C1
ALLENDALE DR SC SC4-B4
ALLISONS MEAD SKR SC2-C3
ALVIN CT RKT SC5-B2
AMBLEWOOD DR SC SC3-E1
ANDERSON AVE SC SC3-E2
ANNA AVE SRL SC2-A4
ANNA DR SRL SC2-A4
APACHE LN SWL SC1-A4
APOLLO AVE SC SC4-D2
APOLLO AVE NE SC SC4-D2
APPLEWOOD CT WPK SC3-E4
ARBOR ST SJO SC5-C1
ARBOR WAY SKR SC2-C3
ARCTIC CIR SWL SC3-A1
ARDEN CT SC SC4-B4
ASH CIR SRL SC1-D2
ASH ST SC SC4-D2
ASH ST E SJ SC3-A2
ASH ST W SJ SC3-A2
ASHWOOD CT WPK SC3-E4
ASPEN CIR WPK SC3-E4
ASPEN LN SC SC3-D1
ATHMAN RD RKT SC5-B3
ATWOOD DR SC SC6-C1
AURORA CT SC SC4-B1
AURORA LN SC SC4-B1
AUTUMN DR SRL SC2-B3
AVIAN PARK SKR SC2-C3

B

BAKER ST E SJ SC3-A2
BANTAM RD SRL SC1-E3
BECHTOLD DR SRL SC1-E2
BECHTOLD ST N SC SC3-D1
BEL CLARE DR SJO SC5-C1
BELMAR ST SJO SC5-C1
BEN NEVIS LN WPK SC3-E4
BENEDICT DR SKR SC2-C4
BENT TREE DR SC SC6-B1
BENTON DR N SKR SC2-B4,SC4-C1
BENTON DR S SC SC4-D2
BENTON DR S SKR SC4-C1
BENTON OAKS CT SKR SC2-B3
BENTON OAKS DR SKR SC2-B3
BIRCH CIR SRL SC1-D2
BIRCH DR SC SC4-D2
BIRCH RD SC SC6-B1
BIRCH ST E SJ SC3-A2
BIRCH ST W SJ SC3-A2
BITTERSWEET LN SC SC6-B1
BLACKHEATH DR SC SC6-D1
BLUEBIRD CT SRL SC1-E2,SC2-A2
BLUEJAY CT SC SC3-E2
BONNA BELLE CT SC SC6-C2
BORGERT AVE N SC SC4-B2
BORGERT DR SJO SC3-B2
BOULDER CT SKR SC4-D1
BOXWOOD CIR SC SC3-D1
BRECKENRIDGE AVE SC SC4-C2
BRENDA LEE DR SC SC3-E2
BRIAN CT SC SC3-E2
BRIAR LN SC SC6-B1
BRIDGEPORT DR SRL SC2-A4
BRIDGEVIEW LN SRL SC1-D3
BROADWAY AVE S SKR SC4-C1
BROMO AVE LST SC3-D1
BROMO AVE SC SC3-D1
BROOK CT SKR SC4-D1
BROOK LN SC SC6-C1
BROOKWOOD LN SRL SC1-E3,SC2-A3
BURG ST RKT SC5-B3

C

CAITLIN CT SRL SC1-E2
CALLAWAY ST E SJ SC3-A2
CALVARY CT SC SC4-B4
CALVARY HILL LN SC SC4-B4
CAMDEN WOODS TER SC SC6-C1
CAMELLIA CT SC SC4-B4,SC6-B1
CANADIAN CT SC SC3-E1
CARDINAL CT SC SC3-E1
CARY CT E SJ SC3-B2
CASE LN SC SC3-E1
CASSELBERRY RD SC SC3-C1
CEDAR CT E SJ SC3-B2
CEDAR DR SC SC3-E2
CEDAR ST E SJ SC3-A2
CEDAR KNOLL PL SC SC6-C1
CEDARWOOD CT WPK SC3-E4
CENTENNIAL DR SC SC4-B2
CENTER ST SC SC3-E1,SC4-A1
CENTURY CT SC SC6-B1
CHAPEL LN SJ SC3-A2
CHARTER OAKS CT SC SC4-B1
CHELMSFORD BLVD SC SC6-B1
CHELMSFORD LN SC SC6-B1
CHERRY LN SC SC4-E2
CHERRY ST N WPK SC3-E3,SC4-A3
CHERRY ST NE WPK SC4-A3
CHERYL DR SC SC6-C1
CHESTNUT CT SC SC3-E2
CHEVAL DR SRL SC1-E3
CIRCLE CT SKR SC2-B3
CIRCLE DR SC SC4-C4
CIRCLE DR NW SKR SC2-B3
CLARE CT SC SC4-B4
CLAREMONT ST SJO SC5-C1
CLARK PL SC SC6-C1
CLAROMA ST SJO SC5-C1
CLEARWATER RD SC SC4-C4,SC6-C1
CLOVER CT SC SC4-B4
CLUB VIEW CT SC SC6-C1
COBORN CT N SRL SC1-E2
COLLEGE AVE N SJ SC3-A2
COLLEGE AVE S SJ SC3-A2
COLONY CIR SC SC4-B1
COLONY DR SC SC4-B1
COLUMBIA AVE NE SC SC4-D2
COLUMBIA AVE SE SC SC4-D2
CONNECTICUT AVE SRL SC2-A4
COOPER AVE N SC SC4-B2
COOPER AVE S SC SC4-B4,SC6-B2
COOPER HILLS RD SC SC6-B1
CORRINE CRK SRL SC1-E2
CORRINE CT SRL SC1-E2
CORTEZ PL SC SC6-C1
CORY LN SC SC3-D2
COTTONWOOD CIR SC SC3-D1
COTTONWOOD RD SC SC3-D2
COUGAR CT SRL SC1-D2
COUGAR LN SRL SC1-D2
COUNTRY CT SRL SC2-A3
COUNTRY CREEK CIR SC SC6-C1
COUNTY ROAD 1 LST SC2-A1,SC4-B1
COUNTY ROAD 1 MDT SC2-D3,SC4-D1
COUNTY ROAD 1 SRL SC2-A3
COUNTY ROAD 1 ....SC2-D1
COUNTY ROAD 2 SJ SC3-A2
COUNTY ROAD 2 SJO SC3-A1
COUNTY ROAD 2 SWL SC1-B3,SC3-A1
COUNTY ROAD 3 MDT SC2-E3
COUNTY ROAD 3 SKR SC2-C4,SC4-C1
COUNTY ROAD 4 LST SC1-D4,SC3-D1
COUNTY ROAD 4 SC SC3-E2,SC4-A2
COUNTY ROAD 4 SWL SC1-A2
COUNTY ROAD 6 RKT SC5-B2
COUNTY ROAD 6 SC SC5-D2
COUNTY ROAD 6 SJO SC5-A2
COUNTY ROAD 6 WPK SC5-D2
COUNTY ROAD 7 SC SC4-C3,SC6-C1
COUNTY ROAD 7 VEN SC6-C4
COUNTY ROAD 8 MDT SC4-E2
COUNTY ROAD 8 SE HVT SC4-D4,SC6-E2
COUNTY ROAD 15 MDT SC2-E2
COUNTY ROAD 29 MDT SC2-C3
COUNTY ROAD 29 SRL SC2-B3
COUNTY ROAD 33 MDT SC2-B1
COUNTY ROAD 33 SKR SC2-B4,SC4-C1
COUNTY ROAD 33 SRL SC2-A3
COUNTY ROAD 45 MDT SC4-E1
COUNTY ROAD 46 MDT SC4-E1
COUNTY ROAD 46 SKR SC4-D1
COUNTY ROAD 47 RKT SC5-A4
COUNTY ROAD 47 SC SC4-E2
COUNTY ROAD 47 VEN SC5-D4
COUNTY ROAD 55 MDT SC2-A1
COUNTY ROAD 57 MDT SC2-C3
COUNTY ROAD 74 MDT SC4-D1
COUNTY ROAD 74 SC SC4-A4,SC5-E2
COUNTY ROAD 74 VEN SC5-D3
COUNTY ROAD 75 MDT SC4-D2
COUNTY ROAD 75 SC SC4-C4,SC6-C2
COUNTY ROAD 75 SJ SC3-A2
COUNTY ROAD 75 SJO SC3-C3
COUNTY ROAD 75 VEN SC6-D4
COUNTY ROAD 75 WPK SC3-D3
COUNTY ROAD 115 VEN SC6-C4
COUNTY ROAD 119 LST SC1-E4,SC2-A4
COUNTY ROAD 119 SRL SC1-E4,SC2-A4
COUNTY ROAD 120 LST SC3-E1,SC4-A1
COUNTY ROAD 121 SJ SC3-A3
COUNTY ROAD 121 SJO SC3-A3
COUNTY ROAD 122 SC SC6-A2
COUNTY ROAD 122 SJO SC5-A2
COUNTY ROAD 133 LST SC1-D3
COUNTY ROAD 133 SJ SC3-B2
COUNTY ROAD 133 SJO SC3-B1
COUNTY ROAD 133 SRL SC1-E3,SC2-A3
COUNTY ROAD 133 SWL SC1-C4,SC3-C1
COUNTY ROAD 134 LST SC2-B4,SC4-A1
COUNTY ROAD 134 SC SC3-D2,SC4-A1
COUNTY ROAD 134 SJ SC3-A2
COUNTY ROAD 134 SJO SC3-C2
COUNTY ROAD 136 SC SC4-B4,SC6-A2
COUNTY ROAD 136 VEN SC5-E4,SC6-A4
COUNTY ROAD 137 RKT SC5-C3
COUNTY ROAD 137 SC SC4-A4
COUNTY ROAD 137 SJO SC5-C2
COUNTY ROAD 137 WPK SC3-D4,SC5-C1
COUNTY ROAD 138 RKT SC5-A3
COUNTY ROAD 138 SC SC3-E2
COUNTY ROAD 138 SJO SC3-B4,SC5-A2
COUNTY ROAD 138 WPK SC3-D3
COURT HOUSE SQ SC SC4-C2
CREEKVIEW RD SC SC6-C2
CRESCENT ST NE SC SC4-D2
CRESCENT RIDGE TRL SC SC6-C1
CRESENT RIDGE TRL SC SC6-C1
CRESTVIEW CT SWL SC1-A4
CRESTVIEW DR SWL SC1-B4
CRESTWOOD CT VEN SC5-E4
CROWN WAY SC SC6-C1
CROWN CREST DR SC SC4-B4
CUMMINGS CT SC SC4-C4
CUMMINGS LN SC SC4-C4
CYPRESS CIR SRL SC1-D2
CYPRESS RD LST SC3-D1
CYPRESS RD SC SC3-D1

D

DALE ST E SJ SC3-B3
DANA DR SKR SC4-C1
DANIELLE DR SC SC4-B4
DANORA PL SC SC4-B3
DATE ST E SJ SC3-A2
DATE ST W SJ SC3-A2
DAVENPORT CT SRL SC1-E3,SC2-A3
DEER CREEK TRL SC SC6-B2
DEERWOOD CT SC SC6-C2
DELORES DR SC SC4-A1
DESOTO DR SC SC6-C1
DEVON RD SC SC3-E1,SC4-A1
DEVON TER SC SC6-D1
DIAMOND WILLOW CIR WPK SC3-E4
DIVISION E SC SC4-D2
DIVISION ST SC SC3-C3,SC4-B3
DIVISION ST SKR SC2-C4,SC4-C1
DIVISION ST WPK SC3-D3,SC4-A3
DIVISION ST W SC SC4-B3
DOCTORS CT SC SC4-B1
DRIFTWOOD DR SC SC3-E2
DUBLIN DR SC SC4-A4
DUNBAR RD SC SC6-D1
DUNDEE LN WPK SC3-E3

E

EAGLES NEST CT SRL SC1-D2
EASTERN CT SJ SC3-A2
EDGEMONT DR NE MDT SC4-E2
EDGEWATER LN SRL SC2-A3
EDGEWOOD CIR SC SC4-B4
EDINBURGH TRL SRL SC1-E3,SC2-A3
EDWARD DR SC SC6-C1
ELBOW LN SC SC3-E2
ELEANOR CT SRL SC1-E2
ELM ST E SJ SC3-B2
ELM ST W SJ SC3-A2
ERICKSON CT SKR SC2-C3
EVENINGSTAR CT SRL SC1-E2

F

FAIRFIELD CT SC SC3-D2
FAIRFIELD LN SC SC3-D2
FAIRWAY LN SC SC3-D2
FALCON CT SRL SC1-D2
FIELD CT SC SC4-B4
FIELDCREST CT SRL SC2-B3
FIELDSTONE DR SKR SC4-D1
FINCH CT SRL SC1-E3
FIR ST E SJ SC3-A2
FLINTWOOD DR SC SC3-E2
FOREST DR SC SC4-B1
FOUNDRY CIR SC SC3-E2
FRANKLIN AVE NE SC SC4-D2
FRANKLIN AVE NE SKR SC4-D1
FRANKLIN AVE SE SC SC4-D2
FRANKLIN RD SC SC6-E4
FRONT ST NE MDT SC4-E2
FRONTAGE RD SJO SC3-A4
FRONTAGE RD WPK SC3-E3
FRONTAGE RD N WPK SC3-D3
FRONTIER AVE SRL SC1-E3
FROST RD NW MDT SC2-B1

G

GABERDINE RD VEN SC6-D4
GABLEVIEW CIR VEN SC6-C4
GAELIC RD VEN SC6-D4
GALAXY RD VEN SC5-D4
GALLOWAY LN WPK SC3-E3,SC4-A3
GARDEA PL SKR SC2-C3
GARDEN BROOK DR SKR SC4-D1
GARFIELD CT SC SC4-C3
GLACIER AVE SRL SC1-E3
GLASGOW CT SC SC3-E1
GLASGOW RD SC SC3-E1
GLENN CARLSON DR SC SC6-E4
GLENVIEW LN SC SC3-D1
GLORIA DR SC SC3-E2
GOETTENS WAY SC SC4-B4
GOLF TER SC SC6-C1
GOLF VIEW CT SC SC6-C1
GOLF VIEW LN SC SC6-C1
GRANITEVIEW RD WPK SC3-E4,SC5-E1
GREAT OAK DR WPK SC3-E2
GREEN RIDGE CT SC SC6-B1
GREEN RIDGE DR SC SC6-B1
GREENOCK RD SC SC6-D1
GREENSTONE LN WPK SC3-E3,SC4-A3
GREENVIEW RD SRL SC2-A1
GREENWAY RD SC SC6-C2
GREENWOOD LN SRL SC2-B3
GREGORY PARK RD VEN SC5-D4
GRIZZLY LN SRL SC1-D2
GROSS ST SKR SC2-C4
GUMTREE ST E SJ SC3-A2

H

HALLER WAY SC SC6-B1
HALLIDAY RD SC SC4-C4
HAVEN PL SC SC4-C4
HAVENS MOOR ST SKR SC2-C3
HAWTHORN RD SJO SC5-A2
HAZELWOOD CIR SC SC3-D1
HEATHER RD SC SC3-D1
HEATHERWOOD RD SC SC6-D3
HEMLOCK RD SJO SC5-A2
HERITAGE DR SC SC6-B1
HI VUE DR SRL SC2-A3
HICKORY CT SJ SC3-A2
HICKORY ST E SJ SC3-A2
HIDDEN LN SJO SC5-C1
HIDDEN ACRES CIR SC SC5-E2
HIGH CT SKR SC2-B3
HIGH DR SKR SC2-B3
HIGH DR SRL SC2-B3
HIGH FIELD RD SC SC4-B4
HIGHBANKS PL SC SC4-C3
HIGHLAND TRL SC SC6-C2
HIGHVIEW CT E SKR SC2-B3
HIGHVIEW DR SKR SC2-B3
HIGHVIEW DR E SKR SC2-B3
HIGHVIEW DR N SRL SC2-B3
HIGHVIEW DR W SKR SC2-B3
HIGHVIEW DR W SRL SC2-B3
HIGHWAY 10 MDT SC2-B2
HIGHWAY 10 SC SC4-D2
HIGHWAY 10 SKR SC2-C3,SC4-D1
HIGHWAY 10 ....SC2-B1
HIGHWAY 10 N SC SC4-D2
HIGHWAY 10 S SC SC4-E3
HIGHWAY 10 SE HVT SC4-E4
HIGHWAY 15 LST SC2-B4,SC4-A1
HIGHWAY 15 SC SC4-A2,SC5-E1
HIGHWAY 15 SKR SC2-B3
HIGHWAY 15 VEN SC5-D4
HIGHWAY 23 MDT SC4-E1
HIGHWAY 23 RKT SC5-A3
HIGHWAY 23 SC SC4-B3
HIGHWAY 23 SJO SC3-C4,SC5-B2
HIGHWAY 23 WPK SC3-E3,SC4-A3
HILLCREST DR SC SC4-B1
HILLSIDE CT SKR SC4-D1
HILLSIDE LN SC SC4-B4
HILLSIDE RD SKR SC4-D1
HINCKLEY AVE NE SC4-D2
HOFFMAN CT SC SC3-D2
HOLLY RD RKT SC5-C2
HORIZON AVE SRL SC1-E3
HUNTINGTON DR SRL SC2-A4
HUNTLEY LN WPK SC3-E4

I

IMPERIAL DR SC SC4-B4
INDEPENDENCE CT SRL SC2-A4
INDIGO RD SJO SC5-B1
INDUSTRIAL BLVD MDT SC4-D1
INDUSTRIAL BLVD SKR SC2-D4,SC4-D1
INDUSTRIAL DR SKR SC4-C1
INTERSTATE 94 RKT SC5-C2
INTERSTATE 94 SC SC5-E2,SC6-C3
INTERSTATE 94 SJO SC3-A4,SC5-B1
INTERSTATE 94 STG SC6-D4
IRONWOOD DR SWL SC1-A4
ISLAND VIEW CT SC SC6-C1
ISLAND VIEW DR SC SC6-C1
IVY RD SJO SC5-B1

J

JADE RD SJO SC3-A4,SC5-A1
JAMARY PL SC SC4-B3
JASMINE CT SC SC6-B1
JAVIC LN SC SC6-C1
JEFFERY CT SC SC3-E2
JEFFREY CT SC SC3-E2
JENISA LN SC SC6-C1
JENNY LN SWL SC1-A4
JOHN RD SC SC6-C1
JOHNSON RD SC SC4-D2
JOSEPH CT SC SC3-D2
JOSEPH ST SJ SC3-B2
JOYCE ST SC SC4-A1
JOYMAR CIR SJO SC5-C1
JOYMAR DR SJO SC5-C1
JULEP RD SJO SC3-C4
JULIE DR SC SC3-D2
JUNIPER RD SC SC3-D2

K

KALE CT SJO SC3-B3
KATRINA CT SC SC6-C1
KENWOOD CT SC SC3-D1
KENWOOD RD SC SC3-D1
KERRY LN SC SC4-B4
KILIAN BLVD SC SC4-D3
KILKENNY CT SC SC4-A3
KILLEEN CT SC SC4-B4
KILLINGER CIR SKR SC2-B3
KINGS WAY SC SC4-A4
KIRKWALL CT WPK SC4-A3
KIRKWALL DR WPK SC4-A3
KIWI CT SJO SC3-B3
KOENIG DR VEN SC6-B4
KRISTIN LN SC SC6-C2
KUHN DR SC SC6-C1

L

LAKE BLVD E SC SC4-C3

LAKE RD RKT SC5-A4
LANCER RD SJO SC3-B2
LANCEWOOD DR SC SC6-C1
LASALLE PL SC SC6-C1
LAUREL RD SC SC3-D1
LAWRENCE CIR SRL SC1-E2
LAWRENCE CT SRL SC1-E2
LE SAUK DR SRL SC2-B4,SC4-A1
LENA LN RKT SC5-B3
LEROY ST SC SC4-C4
LEWIS PL SC SC6-C1
LIBERTY CT SRL SC2-A4
LIEF ERICKSON PL SC SC6-C1
LILAC CT SC SC6-B1
LIME TREE CIR SC SC6-C2
LINCOLN AVE NE SC SC4-D2
LINCOLN AVE SE SC SC4-D3
LINDA LN SC SC4-B4
LINDA LN SKR SC4-C1
LINDEN RD SC SC3-C1
LINDSAY CT SC SC4-C4
LISA CIR SC SC6-B2
LONE OAK CIR SC SC6-B2
LONE OAK LN WPK SC3-E4
LONGVIEW DR SC SC4-D4
LOWELL CIR SRL SC2-A3
LOWELL LN SRL SC2-A3
LUCILLE CT MDT SC2-A2
LUCILLE LN SC SC4-B1
LYNX RD SJ SC3-B2
LYNX RD SJO SC3-B2

M

MADISON PL SC SC4-B2
MAINE PRAIRIE RD SC SC4-B3
MALLARD CT W MDT SC2-A2
MANDR DR SRL SC2-A2
MAPLE LN SC SC4-E2
MAPLE ST NE WPK SC4-A3
MAPLE ST NW WPK SC3-E3,SC4-A3
MARCELLA CT SKR SC4-D1
MARIGOLD RD NW MDT SC2-B2
MARLENE CT RKT SC5-B3
MARQUETTE DR SC SC4-C4,SC6-C1
MARTIN CT SRL SC1-E2
MARTIN CT NW MDT SC2-A2
MARY CT SC SC4-B4
MAYFLOWER RD MDT SC2-A2
MAYFLOWER RD NW MDT SC2-A2
MAYHEW LAKE RD MDT SC2-D3,SC4-D1
MAYHEW LAKE RD NE MDT SC4-D1
MAYWOOD DR SC SC3-D2
MCKINLEY PL N SC SC4-B3
MCKINLEY PL S SC SC4-B3
MCLELAND RD SC SC3-E2
MEADOW CT SC SC4-B4
MEADOW CT W SRL SC1-E2
MEADOW DR SRL SC2-B3
MEADOW LN SJO SC3-C4,SC5-C1
MEADOW LN SWL SC1-A4
MEADOW LN WPK SC3-C4
MEADOWLARK CT SC SC3-E1
MEADOWLAWN CT SRL SC1-E2
MEADOWROSE BLVD SC SC4-B4,SC6-B1
MEADOWS DR SKR SC4-D1
MERIDIAN AVE MDT SC4-E2
MICHAEL CT SC SC3-D2
MICHAELS CT SRL SC2-A3
MICHELLE DR SWL SC1-A4
MICHIGAN AVE SE SC SC4-D3
MID ST SC SC4-A1
MIDDALE LN SC SC3-D2
MILL CREEK CIR LST SC4-B1
MILL CREEK CIR SC SC4-B1
MILL POND DR LST SC4-B1
MILLSTONE CT LST SC4-B1
MINNESOTA BLVD SE SC SC4-E4
MINNESOTA ST E SJ SC3-A2
MINNESOTA ST W SJ SC3-A2
MONROE PL SC SC4-B2
MONTROSE RD SC SC6-C1
MOONGLOW CT SC SC3-D2
MOOSE HORN DR WPK SC3-E3
MORNINGSIDE CT SC SC3-D2
MORNINGSIDE CT NE MDT SC4-E2
MORNINGSIDE DR NE MDT SC4-E2
MORNINGSIDE RD SC SC3-D2
MORNINGSTAR CT SRL SC1-E2
MOSS ROSE RD NW MDT SC2-B2
MULBERRY RD SC SC3-C2
MULLEN RD SJO SC3-C1

N

NANCY CT SC SC4-B4
NANDA KNLS SKR SC4-C1
NARCISSUS RD SWL SC1-B4
NATURES WAY SC SC4-E3
NAVAJO TRL SC SC6-B1
NETTLE RD SWL SC1-A4
NIGHTINGALE CT SC SC3-E1
NORTHLAND DR SJ SC3-A2
NORTHSTAR CT SRL SC2-A1
NORTHSTAR DR SRL SC1-E1,SC2-A1
NORTHVIEW DR SRL SC2-B3
NORTHWAY CIR SC SC4-B2
NORTHWAY CT SC SC4-B2
NORTHWAY DR SC SC4-B1
NORTHWAY PL SC SC4-B2
NORTHWOOD LN LST SC3-D1
NORWAY RD SWL SC3-A1
NOVEMBER DR SWL SC3-A1
NUTHATCH RD SWL SC1-B4

O

OAK CT SC SC4-E3
OAK CT SKR SC2-C4
OAK DR SKR SC2-B3
OAK LN SKR SC2-B4
OAK RD SC SC3-E1
OAK RD SWL SC1-B3
OAK ST SC SC4-D2
OAK GROVE RD SW SC SC4-B4,SC6-A2
OAK HILL CT SRL SC2-A2
OAK POND CT SRL SC2-B3
OAK POND DR SRL SC2-B3
OAKCREST DR SKR SC4-D1
OAKCREST LN SKR SC4-D1
OAKCREST PL SC4-D1
OAKLAND DR MDT SC2-B2
OAKRIDGE LN SC SC6-C1
OAKWOOD DR SC SC4-E3
OCARINA DR SKR SC2-D4
OLD COUNTY ROAD 6 WPK SC5-D2
OLD HIGHWAY 52 SC SC3-D3
OLD HIGHWAY 52 SJ SC3-A2
OLD HIGHWAY 52 SJO SC3-C2
OLD HIGHWAY RD N SJO SC3-C4,SC5-B1
OLD HIGHWAY RD S SJO SC5-B1
OLIVE LN SKR SC2-D4
OLIVE RD SWL SC1-B4
ORANGE RD SWL SC1-B4
OREGON TRL SC SC6-B1
ORRLIN CT VEN SC5-E4
OSPREY CT SC SC3-E1
OSSEO AVE N SC SC4-B3
OSSEO AVE S SC SC4-B3
OTLEY RD SC SC3-E1,SC4-A1
OUTER DR SC SC4-C1
OXBY LN WPK SC3-E4,SC4-A4
OXFORD LN SC SC4-A1

P

PAMELA LN SWL SC1-A4
PANDOLFO PL SC SC4-B2
PARK AVE SRL SC2-B3
PARK AVE S SC SC4-A3
PARK AVE S SKR SC4-C1
PARK DR SC SC4-B1
PARK PL SC SC4-C4
PARK PL N SC SC4-C4
PARK PL S SC SC4-C4
PARK MEADOWS DR WPK SC3-E3
PARKER RD SC SC6-C1
PARKVIEW LN SRL SC2-A2
PARTRIDGE CIR SC SC6-B1
PATRICIA CT SC SC4-B4
PATRICIA DR SC SC4-B4
PATTISON RD SC SC3-D1
PEACH TREE CT SC SC6-C2
PEARL VIEW DR SKR SC2-C4
PEBBLE CREEK DR SC SC3-D2
PERIMETER DR SRL SC2-B3
PERTH DR WPK SC3-E3
PHEASANT DR SRL SC2-A4
PIERZ PL SC SC6-C1
PINE CT SC SC3-E2
PINE LN SC SC4-E2
PINE TREE CT SRL SC1-E2
PINECONE RD N LST SC1-E1
PINECONE RD N SRL SC1-E2
PINECONE RD S LST SC1-E3
PINECONE RD S SRL SC1-E3
PINETREE CT SRL SC1-E2
PINEWOOD CT WPK SC3-E4
PIONEER LN SC SC6-C1
PLAINVIEW DR SC SC4-A1
PLAZA LN SC SC3-E1,SC4-A1
PLEASANT AVE LST SC3-D1
PLEASANT AVE SC SC3-D1
PLEASANT LN SC SC3-D2
PLEASANT RD RKT SC5-B3
PLEASANT RIDGE DR N SKR SC2-B4
PLUM CREEK DR SC SC6-C2
PLUMWOOD CT WPK SC3-E4
POLAR CIR SJO SC3-A1
POLARIS CT SC SC4-B1
POND VIEW LN E SJ SC3-B2
POPPLEWOOD CT WPK SC3-E4
POPPY RD SC SC3-D1
PORTAGE TRL SKR SC4-C1
PRAIRIE LN SKR SC2-C3
PRAIRIE HILL RD SC SC4-B4
PRAIRIE ROSE CIR SC SC3-E1
PRAIRIE ROSE DR SC SC3-E1
PRAIRIE ROSE LN SC SC3-E1
PROGRESS RD WPK SC3-E4
PROSPECT CT MDT SC4-E2
PROSPECT DR NE MDT SC4-E2
PROSPER DR WPK SC3-E4

Q

QUAIL RD NE MDT SC4-E1
QUARRY RD SC SC4-A4
QUEBECOR RD NE MDT SC4-E1

R

RAILROAD AVE SC SC4-C4
RAMSEY PL SC SC4-C3
RANAE LN SC SC6-C1
RAYMOND AVE NE SC SC4-C2
RED FOX RD SC SC4-B4
RED RIVER TRL SC SC6-B2
REDBUD RD LST SC1-E1,SC2-A1
REGAL RD SC SC6-B1
REMINGTON CT SC SC4-A1
RICHTER AVE SC SC6-B2
RIDGE RD SRL SC2-B3
RIDGEWOOD CT SJ SC3-B2
RIDGEWOOD CT SRL SC1-E2
RIDGEWOOD RD SC SC3-D2
RIDGEWOOD RD SJ SC3-B2
RIDGEWOOD RD SJO SC3-C2
RILLA RD SC SC3-E2
RIVER AVE N SKR SC2-B4,SC4-C1
RIVER AVE S SKR SC4-C1
RIVER RD NE MDT SC2-A1
RIVER ST SRL SC2-A3
RIVER OAKS LN SRL SC2-B4
RIVER VISTA LN LST SC2-B4
RIVERCREST DR SC SC3-E2
RIVERS EDGE RD SJO SC5-A2
RIVERSIDE AVE N LST SC2-A1
RIVERSIDE AVE N SRL SC2-A2
RIVERSIDE AVE S SRL SC2-A3
RIVERSIDE DR NE SC SC4-C2
RIVERSIDE DR SE SC SC4-D3
RIVERVIEW CT SKR SC4-C2
ROBERT RD SWL SC1-A4
ROBERTA DR SC SC6-C1
RODEO RD LST SC2-A1
ROGER RD SC SC4-B4
ROLLING GREEN CT SRL SC1-E3
ROLLING RIDGE RD SC SC3-D2
ROLLING VIEW DR SC SC3-D2
ROOSEVELT RD SC SC4-C4,SC6-C2
ROSEWOOD LN SKR SC2-C3
ROSEWOOD RD LST SC2-A1
ROYAL WAY SC SC4-A1
ROYAL OAKS RD SC SC4-D3
RUSAN ST SC SC3-E2,SC4-A2

S

SAINT ANDREWS DR WPK SC3-E4
SAINT AUGUSTA DR VEN SC6-C3
SAINT GERMAIN ST E SC SC4-D2
SAINT GERMAIN ST W SC SC4-B3
SANDY DR SC SC3-D2
SANTA FE TRL SC SC6-B1
SARTELL CT SRL SC1-E3
SARTELL ST SRL SC1-E3
SARTELL ST W SRL SC1-E3,SC2-A3
SAUK DR SC SC3-E1,SC4-A1
SAUKVIEW DR SC SC3-D2
SCENIC DR MDT SC2-B2
SCENIC DR SRL SC1-E3,SC2-A3
SCHNEIDER DR SJ SC3-A2
SCHOONERS END SKR SC2-C3
SCOTT DR SC SC4-A4
SCOTT DR SRL SC2-B3
SEARLE ST SC SC4-C2
SERENITY DR SC SC4-B4,SC6-B1
SERVICE RD MDT SC2-C3
SERVICE RD SC SC3-E2,SC4-A2
SERVICE RD SKR SC4-C1
SERVICE RD WPK SC3-D3
SHANNON DR SC SC4-B4
SILVER BIRCH CT SC SC4-C3
SKYVIEW DR SKR SC4-D1
SOMERSET BLVD SC SC3-E2
SOUTHWAY DR SC SC6-C1
SOUTHWOOD CT SC SC6-C2
SOUTHWOOD TRL SC SC6-B2
SPORTSMAN ISLAND RD SC SC6-C1
SPRUCE DR SC SC3-E2
SPRUCE ST SC SC3-E2
ST S 1/2 SKR SC2-C4,SC4-C1
STAR DR SKR SC2-C3
STARLIGHT DR SRL SC1-E1
STEARNS DR SKR SC2-C4
STEARNS WAY SC SC4-B1
STEPHENS WAY SC SC4-B4
STERLING DR SC SC6-C2
STEVEN CT SC SC3-D2
STOCKINGER DR SC SC4-B1
STONE RIDGE RD SKR SC4-D1
STRAWBERRY CT SKR SC4-D1
STRAWBERRY LN SKR SC4-D1
SUMMIT AVE SKR SC2-C3
SUMMIT AVE N SKR SC2-C4
SUMMIT AVE S SKR SC2-C4,SC4-C1
SUMMIT DR SC SC4-B1
SUMMIT PL SKR SC2-C3
SUMMIT WAY SKR SC2-C4
SUMMIT OAKS DR SJO SC5-A2
SUN CIR SC SC4-B4
SUNCREST DR SC SC6-C1
SUNDANCE CT SRL SC1-E3
SUNDANCE RD SRL SC1-E3
SUNDIAL DR WPK SC3-E4
SUNRAY CT SRL SC1-E1
SUNRIDGE DR SC SC6-C1
SUNSET AVE SRL SC2-A3
SUNSET RIDGE RD SC SC3-D2
SUNWOOD PARK DR WPK SC3-E4
SUNWOOD PARK LN WPK SC3-E4

T

TAMARACK DR SC SC6-B2
TERRACE DR SC SC3-E2
TERRY LN SRL SC1-E3
THIELMAN LN SC SC4-A3
THRU ST SC SC3-E1,SC4-A1
TIFFANY CT SC SC4-B4
TRANQUILITY DR SC SC4-B4,SC6-B1
TRAVERSE RD SC SC4-B4
TRUMPETER CT SC SC3-E1
TWIN CT SKR SC2-C3
TWIN RIVERS CT SRL SC2-B4
TYLER PATH SC SC6-B2
TYLER TRL SC SC6-B2
TYROL DR SC SC4-B4

V

VALLEYVIEW RD SC SC6-C2
VIKING DR SC SC4-C4
VILLAGE AVE SRL SC1-E2

W

WAITE AVE N WPK SC4-A3
WAITE AVE S SC SC4-A3
WAITE AVE S WPK SC4-A3
WALDEN WAY SC SC6-B1
WALLACE DR SC SC6-D3
WALNUT CIR SE SC SC4-E4
WALNUT DR SC SC3-E2
WASHINGTON MEM DR SC SC4-C3
WATAB CT SRL SC1-E3,SC2-A3
WATAB DR SWL SC1-A4
WATAB PL SRL SC1-D3
WATER AVE S SKR SC4-C1
WATERFORD CT SC SC4-B4
WELSH CT SKR SC2-B3
WEST AVE WPK SC3-E3
WEST OAKES DR SC SC3-E1
WESTCLIFFE PL SC SC3-E2
WESTCLIFFE RD SC SC3-E2
WESTERN CT SJ SC3-A2
WESTMONT DR NE MDT SC4-E2
WESTWIND RD SC SC3-D1
WHITE DR SC SC4-A1
WHITE OAK RD RKT SC5-B2
WHITNEY CT SC SC4-B1
WHITNEY DR SC SC4-B2
WILDFLOWER LN SKR SC2-C3
WILDWOOD DR SWL SC1-A4
WILDWOOD RD SC SC3-D2
WILLOW LN SRL SC2-B3
WILLOW CREEK DR WPK SC3-E4,SC4-A4
WILLOW GROVE CIR WPK SC3-E4
WILLOW POND DR WPK SC3-E4
WILLOW VIEW CIR WPK SC3-E4,SC4-A4
WILLOW VIEW LN WPK SC3-E4,SC4-A4
WILSON AVE NE SC SC4-C2
WILSON AVE SE SC SC4-D2
WINDSOR RD SC SC4-B4
WINNEBAGO RD LST SC2-A1
WOLLAK WAY SKR SC2-C3
WOODHILL RD SC SC4-C4
WOODLAND RD SC SC4-E2
WOODLAND RD SC4-E2
WOODLAND PARK DR SC SC4-E2
WOODLAWN ACRES DR SC SC6-C2
WOODSIDE LN SC SC6-C1

Y

YORK DR SC SC4-A1
YUMA TRL SC SC6-B1

Z

ZAKRAJSHEK CT SRL SC1-E3

NUMBERED STREETS

1ST AVE E SRL SC2-A3
1ST AVE N SKR SC2-B4
1ST AVE N SRL SC2-A2
1ST AVE N WPK SC3-E3
1ST AVE NE SJ SC3-A2
1ST AVE NE SJO SC3-A1
1ST AVE NE WPK SC4-A3
1ST AVE NW SJ SC3-A2
1ST AVE S SC SC4-D3
1ST AVE S WPK SC3-E3
1ST AVE SE SJ SC3-A2
1ST ST E MDT SC2-A2
1ST ST N LST SC1-D3
1ST ST N SC SC4-B3
1ST ST N SKR SC2-C4,SC4-C1
1ST ST N SRL SC1-E3,SC2-A3
1ST ST N WPK SC3-E3,SC4-A3
1ST ST NE SC SC4-D2
1ST ST NE SRL SC2-B3
1ST ST NE WPK SC4-A3
1ST ST S SC SC4-B3
1ST ST S SKR SC4-C1
1ST ST S WPK SC3-E3
1ST ST SE SC SC4-D2
1 1/2 ST S SC SC4-B3
2ND AVE E MDT SC2-A2
2ND AVE E SRL SC2-A3
2ND AVE N SKR SC2-B4,SC4-C1
2ND AVE N SRL SC2-A2
2ND AVE N WPK SC3-E3
2ND AVE NE SC SC4-C2
2ND AVE NE SJ SC3-A2
2ND AVE NE WPK SC4-A3
2ND AVE NW SJ SC3-A2
2ND AVE S SC SC4-D3
2ND AVE S SKR SC4-C1
2ND AVE S WPK SC3-E3
2ND AVE SE SJ SC3-A2
2ND ST N SC SC4-B3
2ND ST N SKR SC2-C4,SC4-C1
2ND ST N SRL SC2-A3
2ND ST N WPK SC3-E3,SC4-A3
2ND ST NE SC SC4-C2
2ND ST NE SRL SC2-A3
2ND ST NE WPK SC4-A3
2ND ST S SC SC4-A3
2ND ST S SKR SC4-C1
2ND ST S SRL SC1-E3,SC2-A3
2ND ST S WPK SC3-E3,SC4-A3
2ND ST SE MDT SC4-E2
2ND ST SE SC SC4-D2
2TH ST N SKR SC2-C4
2 1/2 ST N LST SC1-E2
2 1/2 ST N SRL SC1-E3,SC2-A3
2 1/2 ST N WPK SC3-E3
3RD AVE E MDT SC2-A2
3RD AVE E SRL SC2-A2
3RD AVE N SC SC4-C3
3RD AVE N SKR SC2-C4,SC4-C1
3RD AVE N SRL SC2-A2
3RD AVE N WPK SC3-E3
3RD AVE NE SC SC4-C2
3RD AVE NE SJ SC3-A2
3RD AVE NE SRL SC2-A3
3RD AVE NE WPK SC4-A3
3RD AVE NW SJ SC3-A2
3RD AVE S SC SC4-C3
3RD AVE S SKR SC4-C1
3RD AVE S WPK SC3-E4
3RD AVE SE SJ SC3-A2
3RD ST N SC SC4-B3
3RD ST N SKR SC2-C4,SC4-C1
3RD ST N SRL SC1-E2,SC2-A2
3RD ST N WPK SC3-E3,SC4-A3
3RD ST NE SC SC4-C2
3RD ST NE SRL SC2-A3
3RD ST NE WPK SC4-A3
3RD ST S LST SC1-E3
3RD ST S SC SC4-C3
3RD ST S SKR SC4-C1
3RD ST S SRL SC1-E3,SC2-A3
3RD ST S WPK SC3-E3
3RD ST SE SC SC4-D2
3 1/2 AVE N SKR SC2-B4
3 1/2 ST N SRL SC1-D2
4TH AVE SC SC6-E4
4TH AVE E SRL SC2-B3
4TH AVE N SC SC4-C2
4TH AVE N SKR SC2-C4,SC4-C1
4TH AVE N SRL SC2-A2

SAINT CLOUD, MINNESOTA INDEX

4TH AVE N WPK SC3-E3
4TH AVE NE SC SC4-C2
4TH AVE NE SJ SC3-A2
4TH AVE NE SRL SC2-B3
4TH AVE NE WPK SC4-A3
4TH AVE S SC SC4-C3
4TH AVE S SKR SC4-C1
4TH AVE S SRL SC2-A3
4TH AVE S WPK SC3-E4
4TH AVE SE SC SC4-C2
4TH AVE SE SJ SC3-A2
4TH ST N SC SC4-B3
4TH ST N SKR SC2-C4
4TH ST N SRL SC1-E2,SC2-A2
4TH ST N WPK SC3-E3
4TH ST NE SC SC4-C2
4TH ST NE SRL SC2-A3
4TH ST NE WPK SC4-A2
4TH ST S SC SC4-C3
4TH ST S SKR SC4-C1
4TH ST S WPK SC3-D3
4TH ST SE SC SC4-D2
4 1/2 AVE N SKR SC2-B4
4 1/2 ST N SC SC4-B2
4 1/2 ST NE SC SC4-C2
5TH AVE E SRL SC2-B3
5TH AVE N LST SC2-A1
5TH AVE N SC SC4-C2
5TH AVE N SKR SC2-C4
5TH AVE N SRL SC2-A2
5TH AVE N WPK SC3-E3
5TH AVE NE MDT SC2-C2
5TH AVE NE SC SC4-C2
5TH AVE NE SJ SC3-A2
5TH AVE NE SRL SC2-B2
5TH AVE NE SC2-C1
5TH AVE NW MDT SC2-B1
5TH AVE S SC SC4-C3
5TH AVE S SKR SC2-C4,SC4-C1
5TH AVE S SRL SC2-A3
5TH AVE S WPK SC3-E4
5TH AVE SE SC SC4-D2
5TH AVE SE SJ SC3-A2
5TH ST N SC SC4-B2
5TH ST N SKR SC2-C4
5TH ST N SRL SC1-E2,SC2-A2
5TH ST NE SC SC4-C2
5TH ST NE SRL SC2-A3
5TH ST S SC SC4-C3
5TH ST S SKR SC4-C1
5TH ST SE SC SC4-D2
5 1/2 ST N SC SC4-B2
6TH AVE N SC SC4-C2
6TH AVE N SKR SC2-C4
6TH AVE N SRL SC2-A1
6TH AVE N WPK SC3-E3
6TH AVE NE SC SC4-C2
6TH AVE S SC SC4-C3
6TH AVE S SKR SC2-C4,SC4-C1
6TH AVE S SRL SC2-A3
6TH AVE S WPK SC3-E3
6TH AVE SE SC SC4-D2
6TH AVE SE SJ SC3-A2
6TH ST N SC SC4-B2
6TH ST N SKR SC2-C4
6TH ST N SRL SC2-A2
6TH ST NE SC SC4-C2
6TH ST NE SRL SC2-A3
6TH ST S LST SC1-D3
6TH ST S SC SC4-C3
6TH ST S SKR SC4-C1
6TH ST S SRL SC1-E3,SC2-A3
6TH ST SE SC SC4-D3
6 1/2 ST NE MDT SC4-E2
7TH AVE N LST SC1-E1
7TH AVE N SC SC4-C2
7TH AVE N SKR SC2-C4
7TH AVE N SRL SC1-E2,SC2-A1
7TH AVE N WPK SC3-E3
7TH AVE NE SC SC4-D2
7TH AVE NE SJ SC3-A2
7TH AVE S SC SC4-C3
7TH AVE S SKR SC2-C4
7TH AVE S SRL SC1-E3,SC2-A3
7TH AVE S WPK SC3-E3
7TH AVE SE SC SC4-D2
7TH AVE SE SJ SC3-A2
7TH ST N SC SC4-B2
7TH ST N SKR SC2-C4
7TH ST N SRL SC1-E2,SC2-A2
7TH ST NE SC SC4-C2
7TH ST NE SRL SC2-A3
7TH ST S SC SC4-C3
7TH ST S SKR SC4-C1
7TH ST S SRL SC1-E3,SC2-A3
7TH ST S WPK SC3-D4,SC5-C1
7TH ST SE SC SC4-D3
7 1/2 AVE N SKR SC2-C4
8TH AVE N SC SC4-C2
8TH AVE N SKR SC2-C4
8TH AVE N SRL SC1-E2
8TH AVE N WPK SC3-E3
8TH AVE S SC SC4-C3,SC6-E4
8TH AVE S SKR SC2-C4,SC4-C1
8TH AVE S SRL SC1-E3,SC2-A3
8TH AVE SE SC SC4-D3
8TH AVE SE SJ SC3-A2
8TH ST N SC SC3-E2,SC4-A2
8TH ST N SKR SC2-C4
8TH ST N SRL SC1-E2,SC2-A2
8TH ST NE MDT SC4-E1
8TH ST NE SC SC4-D2
8TH ST NE SRL SC2-A2
8TH ST S SC SC4-C3
8TH ST S SKR SC4-C1
8TH ST S WPK SC3-E4
8TH ST SE SC SC4-D3
8 1/2 ST N SKR SC2-C4
9TH AVE N SC SC4-C2
9TH AVE N SKR SC2-C4
9TH AVE N SRL SC1-E2
9TH AVE N WPK SC3-E3
9TH AVE S SC SC4-C3
9TH AVE S SKR SC4-C1
9TH AVE SE SC SC4-D3
9TH AVE SE SJ SC3-A2
9TH ST N SC SC4-B2
9TH ST N SKR SC2-B4
9TH ST N SRL SC1-E2,SC2-A2
9TH ST NE SRL SC2-A2
9TH ST S SC SC4-C3
9TH ST S SKR SC4-C1
9TH ST S WPK SC3-E4
9TH ST SE SC SC4-D3
9 1/2 ST N SKR SC2-B4
10TH AVE N SC SC4-C3
10TH AVE N SKR SC2-C4
10TH AVE N SRL SC1-E2
10TH AVE N WPK SC3-E3
10TH AVE NE MDT SC2-D3
10TH AVE NE SC SC4-D2
10TH AVE NE SKR SC2-D4,SC4-D1
10TH AVE S SC SC4-C4
10TH AVE S SJ SC3-A2
10TH AVE S SKR SC2-D4,SC4-C1
10TH AVE S WPK SC3-E3
10TH AVE SE SC SC4-D3
10TH AVE SE SJ SC3-A2
10TH ST SKR SC2-B4
10TH ST N SC SC4-B2
10TH ST N SKR SC2-B4
10TH ST N SRL SC2-A2
10TH ST NE MDT SC4-D1
10TH ST NE SC4-E1
10TH ST S SC SC4-C3
10TH ST S SKR SC4-C1
10TH ST S SRL SC1-E3,SC2-A4
10TH ST SE SC SC4-D3
10 1/2 AVE S SC SC4-C3
11TH AVE E SRL SC2-B3
11TH AVE N SC SC4-B2
11TH AVE N SKR SC2-C4
11TH AVE N WPK SC3-E3
11TH AVE S SC SC4-C3
11TH AVE S WPK SC3-E3
11TH AVE SE SC SC4-D3
11TH AVE SE SJ SC3-A2
11TH ST N SC SC4-B2
11TH ST N SKR SC2-C4
11TH ST N SRL SC2-A2
11TH ST S SC SC4-C3
11TH ST S SKR SC4-C1
11TH ST S SRL SC1-E4
11TH ST SE SC SC4-D3
11 1/2 ST N SKR SC2-C4
12TH AVE E SRL SC2-B3
12TH AVE N SC SC4-B2
12TH AVE N SRL SC1-E2
12TH AVE N WPK SC3-E3
12TH AVE NE SC SC4-D2
12TH AVE S SC SC4-C3
12TH AVE S WPK SC3-E3
12TH AVE SE HVT SC6-D1
12TH AVE SE SC SC4-D3
12TH AVE SE SJ SC3-B2
12TH ST N SC SC4-B2
12TH ST N SKR SC2-C4
12TH ST N SRL SC1-E2,SC2-A2
12TH ST S SC SC4-C3
12TH ST S SKR SC4-C1
12TH ST SE HVT SC4-E3
12TH ST SE SC SC4-D3
12 1/2 ST N SC SC4-B2
13TH AVE N SC SC4-B2
13TH AVE N SKR SC2-C4
13TH AVE N SRL SC1-E2
13TH AVE N WPK SC3-E3
13TH AVE NE SKR SC4-D1
13TH AVE S SC SC4-C3
13TH AVE S SKR SC4-D1
13TH AVE S WPK SC3-E3
13TH AVE SE HVT SC6-D1
13TH AVE SE SC SC4-D3
13TH AVE SE SJ SC3-B2
13TH ST N SC SC4-B2
13TH ST N SKR SC2-B4
13TH ST N SRL SC2-A2
13TH ST NE SC4-E1
13TH ST S SC SC4-C3
13TH ST S SKR SC4-C2
13TH ST SE SC SC4-D3
13TH ST CIR SKR SC2-B3
14TH AVE E SRL SC2-B3
14TH AVE N SC SC4-C3
14TH AVE N SRL SC1-D2
14TH AVE NE MDT SC4-D1
14TH AVE NE SC SC4-D2
14TH AVE S SC SC4-C3
14TH AVE SE HVT SC4-D4,SC6-D1
14TH AVE SE SC SC4-D2
14TH ST N SC SC4-B2
14TH ST N SRL SC1-E2,SC2-A2
14TH ST S SC SC4-B3
14TH ST S SKR SC4-C2
14TH ST SE SC SC4-D3
14 1/2 AVE SE SC SC4-D4
15TH AVE N SC SC4-C3
15TH AVE N SRL SC1-D2
15TH AVE N WPK SC3-D3
15TH AVE NE SJ SC3-B2
15TH AVE S SC SC4-C3,SC6-C1
15TH AVE SE HVT SC6-D2
15TH AVE SE SC SC4-D3
15TH ST N LST SC2-A1
15TH ST N SC SC4-B2
15TH ST N SKR SC2-C3
15TH ST N SRL SC1-E1,SC2-A1
15TH ST NE MDT SC2-A2,SC4-E1
15TH ST NE SKR SC4-D1
15TH ST S SC SC4-C3
15TH ST SE SC SC4-D3
15TH ST CT SKR SC2-B3
16TH AVE SC SC6-C2
16TH AVE N SC SC4-C3
16TH AVE N SRL SC1-D2
16TH AVE S SC SC4-C3,SC6-C2
16TH AVE SE HVT SC6-E3
16TH AVE SE SC SC4-D2
16TH AVE SE SJ SC3-B2
16TH ST N SC SC3-E1
16TH ST N SKR SC2-B3
16TH ST N SRL SC2-A1
16TH ST S SC SC4-C4
16TH ST SE SC SC4-D3
16TH STREET CT SKR SC2-B3
17TH AVE N SC SC4-B3
17TH AVE N SRL SC1-D2
17TH AVE S SC SC4-C3,SC6-B2
17TH AVE S WPK SC3-D3
17TH ST N LST SC1-E1,SC2-A1
17TH ST N SC SC4-C1
17TH ST N SRL SC1-E1,SC2-A1
17TH ST S SC SC4-B4
17TH ST SE SC SC4-D3
17TH STREET CT SKR SC2-B3
17 1/2 AVE N SC SC4-B3
18TH AVE VEN SC6-D4
18TH AVE N SC SC4-B3
18TH AVE N SRL SC1-D2
18TH AVE S SC SC4-B3,SC6-B2
18TH AVE SE SC SC4-E4
18TH ST N SC SC3-D1,SC4-B1
18TH ST N SKR SC2-C3
18TH ST N SRL SC1-E1,SC2-A1
18TH ST NW SKR SC2-B4
18TH ST S SC SC4-A4
18TH ST SE SC SC4-D3
19TH AVE N LST SC1-D3
19TH AVE N SC SC4-B3
19TH AVE N SRL SC1-D2
19TH AVE S LST SC1-D3
19TH AVE S SC SC4-B3
19TH AVE SE SC SC4-E3
19TH ST N SC SC3-D1,SC4-B1
19TH ST N SRL SC2-A1
19TH ST S SC SC4-C4
19TH ST S SJO SC3-C3
19 1/2 AVE N SC SC4-B3
19 1/2 AVE S SC SC4-B3
20TH AVE VEN SC6-C3
20TH AVE N SC SC4-B2
20TH AVE N SRL SC1-D2
20TH AVE S SC SC4-B3
20TH AVE SE SC SC4-E4
20TH ST N LST SC3-E1,SC4-A1
20TH ST N SC SC3-D1
20TH ST N SRL SC1-E1,SC2-A1
20TH ST S SC SC4-B4
21ST AVE SC SC6-C3
21ST AVE VEN SC6-C3
21ST AVE N SC SC4-B2
21ST AVE S SC SC4-B3,SC6-B1
21ST ST N LST SC2-A1
21ST ST SE SC SC4-D4
22ND AVE SC SC6-C3
22ND AVE VEN SC6-C3
22ND AVE N SC SC4-B2
22ND AVE NE MDT SC2-E1
22ND AVE S SC SC4-B3,SC6-B1
22ND ST N LST SC2-A1
22ND ST S SC SC4-B4
23RD AVE N SC SC4-B2
23RD AVE NE MDT SC4-E2
23RD AVE S SC SC4-B3,SC6-B1
23RD ST S SC SC4-B4
24TH AVE N SC SC4-B2
24TH AVE N WPK SC3-D3
24TH AVE NE SC4-E1
24TH AVE S SC SC4-B3,SC6-B1
24TH AVE S WPK SC3-D3
24TH ST S SC SC4-B4
24TH ST SE SC SC4-D4
24 1/2 AVE NE MDT SC4-E2
25TH AVE N SC SC4-B2
25TH AVE NE MDT SC2-E2,SC4-E1
25TH AVE NE SC4-E1
25TH AVE S SC SC4-B3
25TH ST S SC SC4-B4
25TH ST SE SC SC4-D4
26TH AVE VEN SC6-C4
26TH AVE N SC SC4-B2
26TH AVE S SC SC4-B4
26TH ST S SC SC4-B4
26TH ST SE SC SC4-D4
27TH AVE N SC SC4-B2
27TH AVE S SC SC4-B3
27TH ST N LST SC1-E1,SC2-A1
27TH ST S SC SC6-B1
27TH ST SE HVT SC4-D4
27TH ST SE SC SC4-E4
28TH AVE VEN SC6-C3
28TH AVE N SC SC4-B2
28TH AVE N WPK SC3-D3
28TH AVE S WPK SC3-D3
28TH ST S SC SC6-B1
29TH AVE N SC SC4-B2
29TH AVE S SC SC4-B3
29TH ST S SC SC6-B1
29TH ST SE HVT SC6-D1
30TH AVE N SC SC4-B2
30TH AVE N SWL SC1-C2
30TH AVE S SC SC4-B3
30TH ST S SC SC6-B1
30TH ST SE HVT SC6-D1
31ST AVE SC SC6-B3
31ST AVE N SC SC4-A2
31ST AVE S SC SC4-A3
31ST AVE S WPK SC3-C3
32ND AVE VEN SC6-B4
32ND AVE N SC SC4-A2
32ND AVE S SC SC4-A3
33RD AVE SC SC6-B3
33RD AVE VEN SC6-B4
33RD AVE N SC SC4-A2
33RD AVE S SC SC4-A3
33RD ST S SC SC5-E1,SC6-B1
34TH AVE N SC SC4-A2
35TH AVE N SC SC4-A2
36TH AVE N SC SC4-A2
36TH ST S SC SC6-B2
36TH ST SE HVT SC6-D1
37TH AVE N SC SC4-A2
37TH AVE S SC SC4-A3
37TH ST S SC SC4-A3,SC6-B2
37TH ST SE HVT SC6-E1
38TH AVE N SC SC4-A2
38TH ST S SC SC6-C2
39TH ST S SC SC6-B2
40TH ST S SC SC5-E2,SC6-A2
40TH ST S WPK SC5-D2
41ST AVE VEN SC6-B4
41ST AVE N SC SC4-A2
41ST AVE S SC SC4-A4
41ST ST S SC SC6-D2
42ND AVE VEN SC6-A4
42ND ST SE HVT SC6-E2
43RD AVE SC SC6-A3
43RD AVE VEN SC6-A4
43RD AVE S SC SC4-A4,SC6-A2
43RD ST NE MDT SC2-C2
43RD ST S SC SC6-D3
44TH AVE N SC SC4-A2
45TH ST HVT SC6-E2
45TH ST NE MDT SC2-D2
46TH ST NE MDT SC2-E2
47TH ST SC SC6-D3
47TH ST SE HVT SC6-E2
48TH AVE VEN SC6-A4
49TH ST SE HVT SC6-E2
50TH AVE LST SC2-A4,SC4-A1
51ST AVE VEN SC5-E4
52ND ST SRL SC1-E3
52ND ST SE HVT SC6-E3
54TH AVE N SC SC3-E2
55TH ST NE MDT SC2-E1
56TH ST NW SC2-A1
57TH ST SE HVT SC6-E3
58TH AVE SC SC5-E3
58TH AVE VEN SC5-E3
59TH AVE S WPK SC3-D4
60TH ST S SC SC6-E4
61ST AVE LST SC3-E1
61ST AVE N SC SC3-D1
62ND AVE LST SC3-D1
63RD AVE SC SC5-D3
64TH AVE N SC SC3-D1
65TH AVE LST SC1-D4,SC3-D1
65TH AVE SRL SC1-D3
65TH AVE VEN SC5-D4
66TH AVE VEN SC5-D4
67TH AVE VEN SC5-D4
68TH AVE VEN SC5-D4
69TH AVE VEN SC5-D4
70TH AVE VEN SC5-D4
72ND AVE N WPK SC3-D3
73RD AVE N SC SC3-C1
74TH AVE SJO SC3-C3
75TH AVE SJO SC3-C3
76TH AVE SJO SC3-C2
80TH AVE RKT SC5-C2
80TH AVE SWL SC1-C1,SC3-C1
81ST AVE RKT SC5-C2
82ND AVE SJO SC5-B2
83RD AVE SJO SC5-B2
83RD AVE SWL SC1-C3
86TH AVE SJO SC3-B4,SC5-B1
88TH AVE RKT SC5-B4
88TH AVE SJO SC3-B2
88TH AVE SWL SC1-B3
90TH AVE SJO SC3-B2
91ST AVE SJO SC3-B3
91ST AVE SWL SC1-B3,SC3-B1
93RD AVE SJO SC5-A2
93RD AVE SWL SC3-A1
95TH AVE SJO SC3-A3
95TH AVE SWL SC1-A2
102ND AVE SWL SC1-A4,SC3-A1
103RD AVE SJO SC3-A3
236TH ST VEN SC5-D4,SC6-A4
237TH ST VEN SC5-D4,SC6-A4
238TH ST VEN SC6-D4
239TH ST VEN SC5-C4
240TH ST SC SC6-D4
240TH ST VEN SC5-D4,SC6-A4
242ND ST VEN SC5-D4
243RD ST VEN SC6-C4
244TH ST VEN SC6-B4
245TH ST RKT SC5-C4
245TH ST VEN SC6-D4
246TH ST VEN SC6-C4
247TH ST VEN SC6-C3
248TH ST VEN SC6-C3
250TH ST VEN SC5-E3,SC6-A3
251ST ST SC SC6-C3
252ND ST SC SC6-C3
255TH ST SC SC6-B3
263RD ST SJO SC5-B2
265TH ST SJO SC5-A2
270TH ST SJO SC5-A1
290TH ST SJO SC3-B3
295TH ST SJO SC3-A3
301ST ST SJO SC3-A2
302ND ST SJO SC3-A2
304TH ST SJO SC3-C2
305TH ST SJO SC3-B2
315TH ST SJO SC3-B1
320TH ST SJO SC3-B1
321ST ST LST SC3-E1,SC4-B1
322ND ST LST SC3-D1
322ND ST SWL SC3-C1
325TH ST SWL SC1-C4
328TH ST SWL SC1-A4
330TH ST SWL SC1-A4
338TH ST SWL SC1-B3
341ST ST SWL SC1-B3
345TH ST SWL SC1-A2
348TH ST SWL SC1-A2
350TH ST SWL SC1-B2
355TH ST SWL SC1-A2
360TH ST SWL SC1-C1
368TH ST SWL SC1-B1

STATE OF MINNESOTA ATLAS

MINNESOTA LEGEND

Road Classification

——— LIMITED ACCESS DIVIDED HIGHWAY

——— OTHER DIVIDED HIGHWAYS

——— STATE HIGHWAYS

—┼—5— MILEAGE BETWEEN ROADS

Symbol Classification

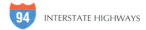

94 INTERSTATE HIGHWAYS

75 U.S. HIGHWAYS

64 STATE HIGHWAYS

25 COUNTY ROADS

46 EXIT RAMPS

State Markers

⚠ STATE WAYSIDE PARKS

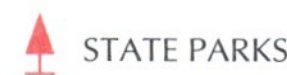

🌲 STATE PARKS

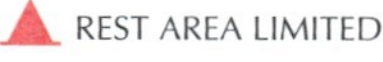

▲ REST AREA LIMITED

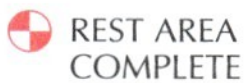

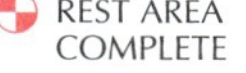

◑ REST AREA COMPLETE

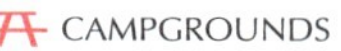

🚻 CAMPGROUNDS

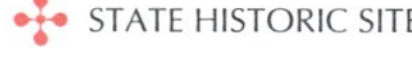

STATE HISTORIC SITE

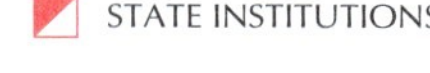

◰ STATE INSTITUTIONS

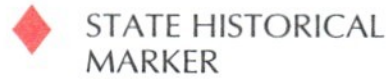

◆ STATE HISTORICAL MARKER

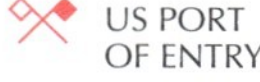

⚔ US PORT OF ENTRY

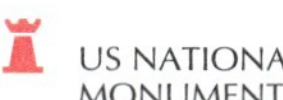

♜ US NATIONAL MONUMENT

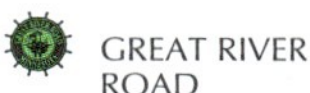

GREAT RIVER ROAD

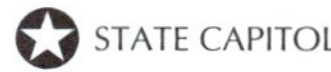

★ STATE CAPITOL

Additional Features

— – — – COUNTY BOUNDARY

— · — · STATE BOUNDARY

HENNEPIN COUNTY TEXT

├—┼—┤ RAILROAD DESIGNATION

▭ BOUNDARY WATER CANOE AREA

STATE FOREST

NATIONAL FOREST

WILDLIFE MANAGEMENT AREA

STATE/NATIONAL PARK

INDIAN RESERVATION

Population of Cities

○ UNDER 1,000

◎ 1,000 TO 4,999

◉ 5,000 TO 24,999

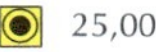

◉ 25,000 TO 49,999

▢ 50,000 AND OVER

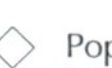

◇ Population Symbols Enclosed By Indicates County Seats

Airports

✈ COMMERCIAL

✕ OTHER

⚓ SEAPLANE

```
0  2.5  5    10    15    20    25    30                              60
```
Scale in Miles

Copyright © 2002 The Lawrence Group 1089-10th Avenue SE Minneapolis, MN 55414

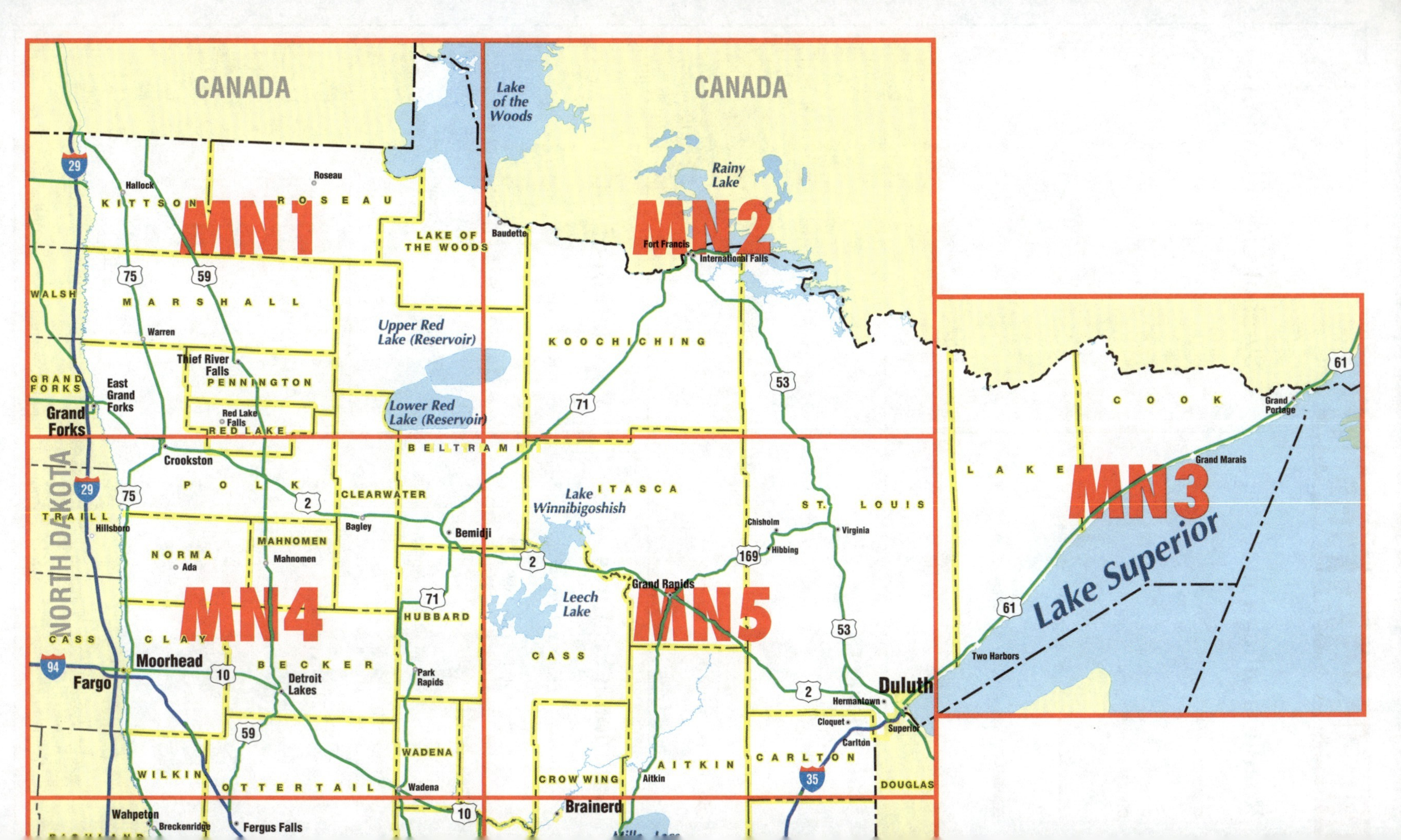

CANADA
CANADA
MN1
MN2
MN3
MN4
MN5
NORTH DAKOTA
Lake of the Woods
Rainy Lake
Upper Red Lake (Reservoir)
Lower Red Lake (Reservoir)
Lake Winnibigoshish
Leech Lake
Lake Superior
KITTSON
ROSEAU
LAKE OF THE WOODS
MARSHALL
PENNINGTON
RED LAKE
POLK
NORMA
MAHNOMEN
CLEARWATER
BELTRAMI
KOOCHICHING
ITASCA
ST. LOUIS
LAKE
COOK
CLAY
BECKER
HUBBARD
CASS
WADENA
CROW WING
AITKIN
CARLTON
DOUGLAS
OTTER TAIL
WILKIN
WALSH
GRAND FORKS
TRAILL
CASS
Hallock
Roseau
Baudette
Fort Francis
International Falls
Warren
Thief River Falls
East Grand Forks
Grand Forks
Red Lake Falls
Crookston
Hillsboro
Ada
Mahnomen
Bagley
Bemidji
Chisholm
Hibbing
Virginia
Grand Rapids
Grand Marais
Grand Portage
Two Harbors
Duluth
Hermantown
Cloquet
Carlton
Superior
Aitkin
Brainerd
Park Rapids
Wadena
Detroit Lakes
Moorhead
Fargo
Wahpeton
Breckenridge
Fergus Falls
29
29
94
35
75
75
59
59
2
2
2
71
71
53
53
169
61
61
10
10
10

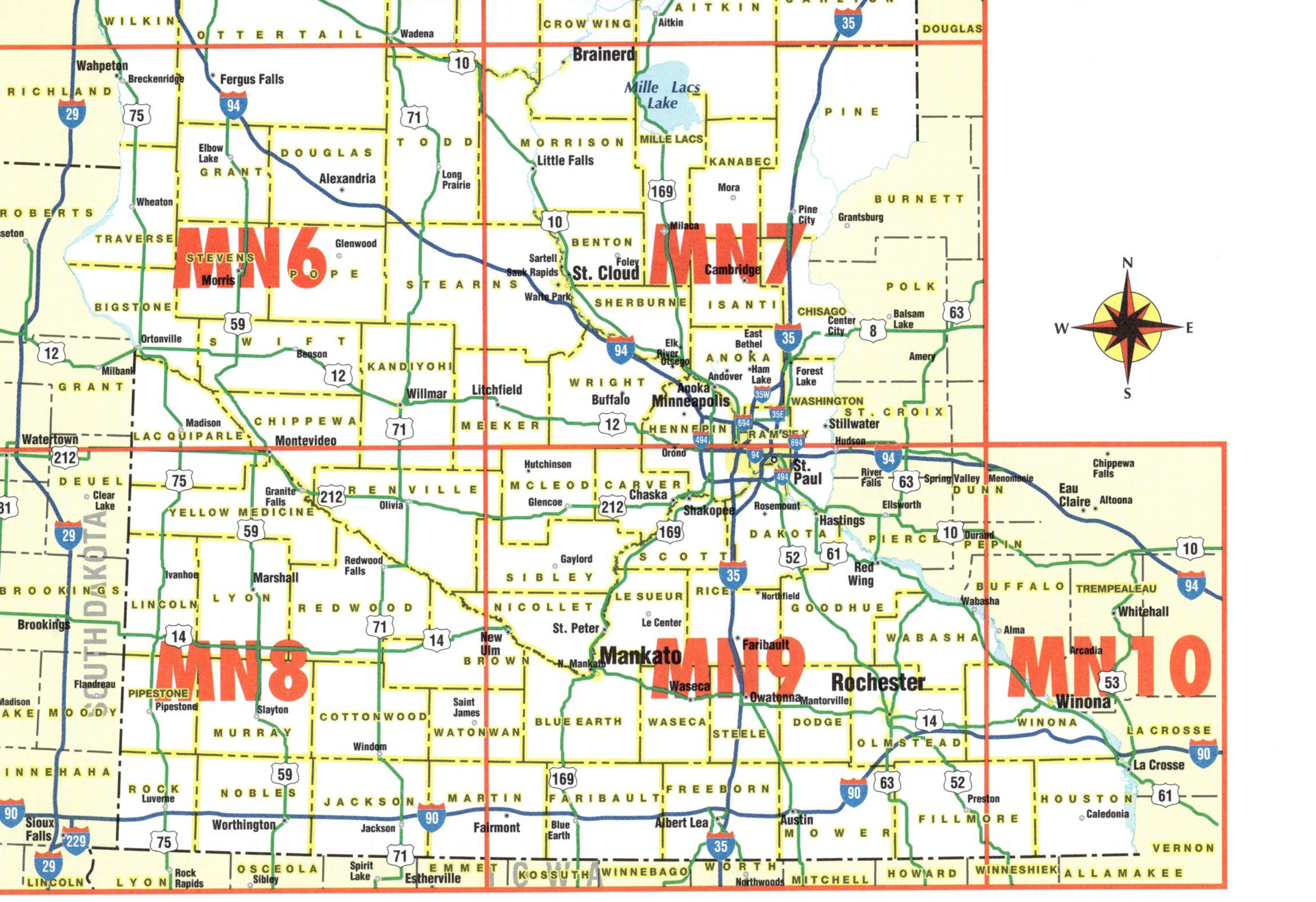
MN6
MN7
MN8
MN9
MN10
N
S
E
W
SOUTH DAKOTA
IOWA
WILKIN
OTTER TAIL
WADENA
CROW WING
AITKIN
CARLTON
DOUGLAS
RICHLAND
ROBERTS
TRAVERSE
STEVENS
POPE
DOUGLAS
GRANT
TODD
MORRISON
MILLE LACS
KANABEC
PINE
BURNETT
POLK
BENTON
STEARNS
SHERBURNE
ISANTI
CHISAGO
BIGSTONE
SWIFT
KANDIYOHI
WRIGHT
ANOKA
WASHINGTON
ST. CROIX
GRANT
CHIPPEWA
MEEKER
HENNEPIN
RAMSEY
LAC QUIPARLE
DEUEL
RENVILLE
MCLEOD
CARVER
DUNN
YELLOW MEDICINE
DAKOTA
PIERCE
PEPIN
SCOTT
SIBLEY
BROOKINGS
LINCOLN
LYON
REDWOOD
NICOLLET
LE SUEUR
RICE
GOODHUE
BUFFALO
TREMPEALEAU
WABASHA
BROWN
PIPESTONE
LAKE
MOODY
MURRAY
COTTONWOOD
WATONWAN
BLUE EARTH
WASECA
STEELE
DODGE
OLMSTEAD
WINONA
LA CROSSE
MINNEHAHA
ROCK
NOBLES
JACKSON
MARTIN
FARIBAULT
FREEBORN
MOWER
FILLMORE
HOUSTON
VERNON
LINCOLN
LYON
OSCEOLA
EMMET
KOSSUTH
WINNEBAGO
WORTH
MITCHELL
HOWARD
WINNESHIEK
ALLAMAKEE
Wadena
Aitkin
Brainerd
Mille Lacs Lake
Wahpeton
Breckenridge
Fergus Falls
Elbow Lake
Alexandria
Long Prairie
Little Falls
Mora
Pine City
Grantsburg
Wheaton
Sisseton
Milaca
Glenwood
Morris
Sartell
Sauk Rapids
St. Cloud
Foley
Cambridge
Waite Park
Balsam Lake
Center City
Ortonville
Benson
Elk River
Otsego
East Bethel
Amery
Milbank
Willmar
Litchfield
Andover
Ham Lake
Forest Lake
Buffalo
Anoka
Minneapolis
Madison
Montevideo
Stillwater
Watertown
Orono
Hudson
Hutchinson
St. Paul
Chippewa Falls
Clear Lake
Granite Falls
Olivia
Glencoe
Chaska
Shakopee
Rosemount
River Falls
Spring Valley
Menomonie
Eau Claire
Altoona
Ellsworth
Hastings
Durand
Redwood Falls
Gaylord
Red Wing
Ivanhoe
Marshall
Northfield
Wabasha
Whitehall
Brookings
St. Peter
Le Center
Alma
New Ulm
Faribault
Mankato
N. Mankato
Arcadia
Flandreau
Waseca
Owatonna
Rochester
Winona
Madison
Pipestone
Slayton
Saint James
Mantorville
Windom
La Crosse
Luverne
Preston
Sioux Falls
Worthington
Jackson
Fairmont
Blue Earth
Albert Lea
Austin
Caledonia
Rock Rapids
Sibley
Spirit Lake
Estherville
Northwoods
29
75
94
10
71
169
35
12
59
8
63
694
35W
35E
494
212
81
61
52
14
53
90
229

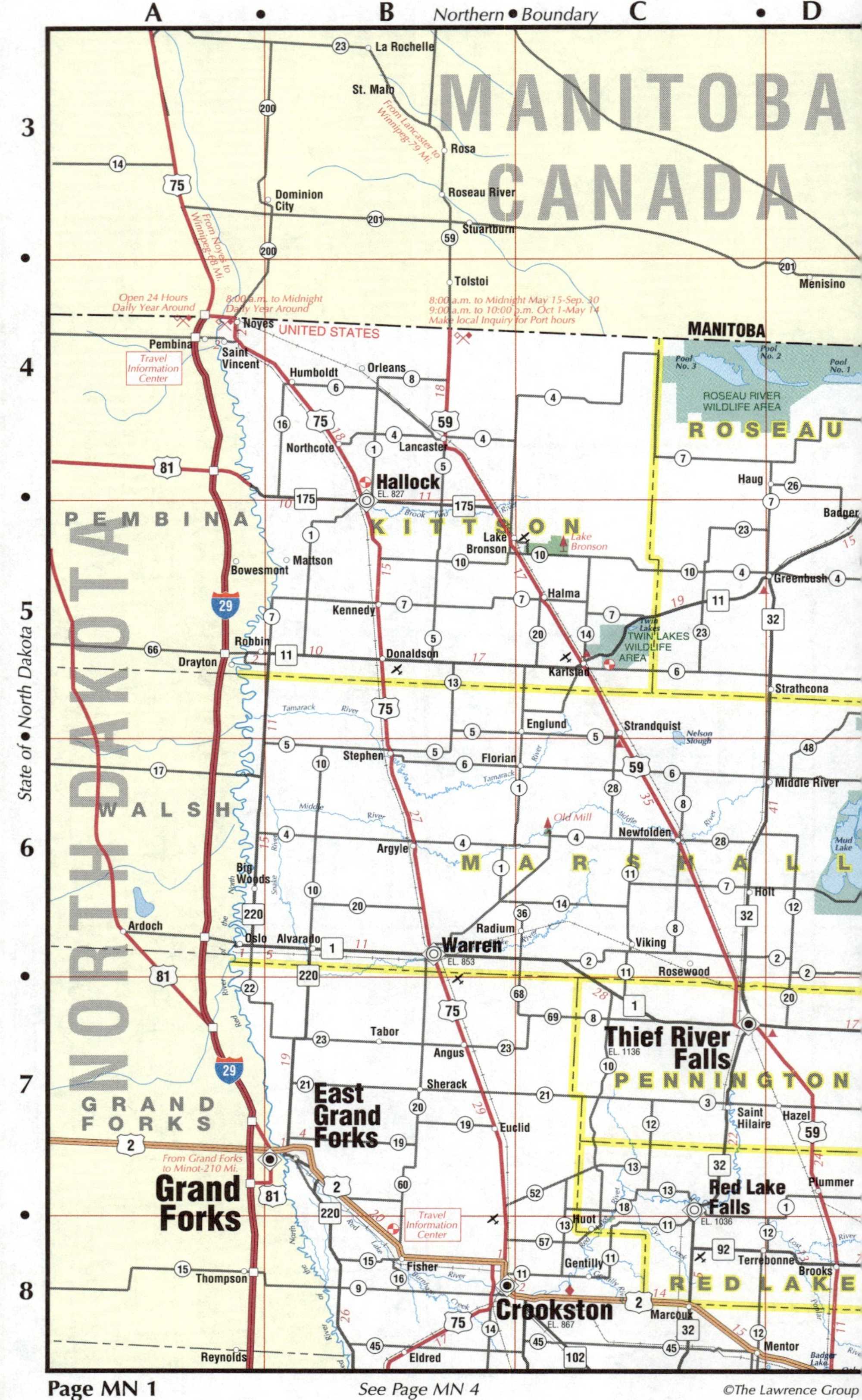

MANITOBA
CANADA

La Rochelle
St. Malo
Rosa
Roseau River
Dominion City
Stuartburn
Tolstoi
Menisino

ROSEAU RIVER WILDLIFE AREA

UNITED STATES
MANITOBA

Noyes
Pembina
Saint Vincent
Humboldt
Orleans
Northcote
Lancaster
Hallock
EL. 827

ROSEAU

Haug
Badger
Greenbush

PEMBINA
KITTSON

Lake Bronson
Lake Bronson
Halma
Strathcona

NORTH DAKOTA

Bowesmont
Mattson
Kennedy
Drayton
Robbin
Donaldson
Karlstad

TWIN LAKES WILDLIFE AREA

WALSH

Englund
Strandquist
Middle River

Stephen
Florian
Nelson Slough

Mud Lake

Argyle
Old Mill
Newfolden

MARSHALL

Big Woods
Ardoch
Holt

Oslo
Alvarado
Radium
Viking

GRAND FORKS

Warren
EL. 853
Rosewood

Tabor
Thief River Falls
EL. 1136

PENNINGTON

East Grand Forks
Angus
Sherack
Euclid

Grand Forks

Saint Hilaire
Hazel

Red Lake Falls
EL. 1036
Plummer

Thompson
Fisher
Huot
Gentilly
Terrebonne
Brooks

Reynolds
Eldred
Crookston
EL. 867
Marcoux
Mentor

RED LAKE

State of • North Dakota

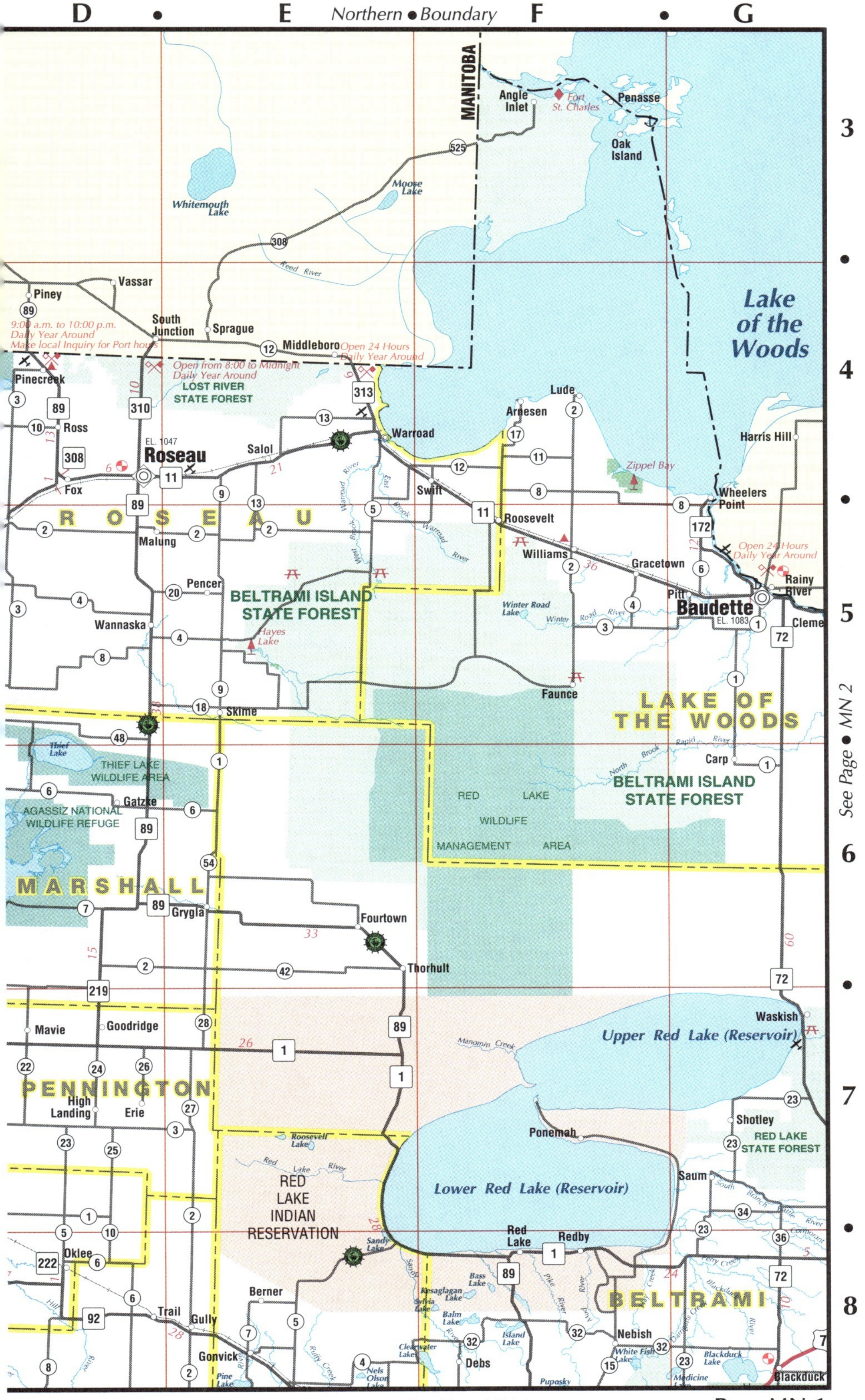

3

MANITOBA

Angle Inlet

Fort St. Charles

Penasse

Oak Island

Lake of the Woods

Whitemouth Lake

Moose Lake

308

525

Reed River

4

Piney

89

9:00 a.m. to 10:00 p.m. Daily Year Around Make local Inquiry for Port hours

Vassar

South Junction

Sprague

Middleboro

12

Open 24 Hours Daily Year Around

Pinecreek

310

Open from 8:00 to Midnight Daily Year Around

LOST RIVER STATE FOREST

313

9

Lude

Ardesen

17

Harris Hill

3

89

10

310

Ross

308

Fox

6

Roseau

11

EL. 1047

13

Salol

21

9

13

Warroad

5

Swift

12

11

Roosevelt

11

Williams

8

Zippel Bay

Wheelers Point

172

Open 24 Hours Daily Year Around

2

89

R O S E A U

Malung

2

2

Pencer

20

5

East Brook

BELTRAMI ISLAND STATE FOREST

36

Gracetown

6

Pitt

Baudette

Rainy River

EL. 1083

Cleme

72

5

4

Wannaska

3

4

8

Hayes Lake

9

18

Skime

Winter Road Lake

Winter

Road

River

3

Faunce

L A K E   O F T H E   W O O D S

48

Thief Lake

THIEF LAKE WILDLIFE AREA

1

North Brock

Rapid

River

Carp

1

See Page • MN 2

6

AGASSIZ NATIONAL WILDLIFE REFUGE

6

Gatzke

6

89

RED   LAKE

WILDLIFE

MANAGEMENT   AREA

BELTRAMI ISLAND STATE FOREST

M A R S H A L L

54

7

89

Grygla

33

Fourtown

2

42

Thorhult

60

72

6

219

Mavie

Goodridge

28

26

1

89

Upper Red Lake (Reservoir)

Waskish

22

24

26

1

Shotley

23

7

P E N N I N G T O N

High Landing

Erie

27

3

Ponemah

23

RED LAKE STATE FOREST

23

25

Roosevelt Lake

Red

Lake

River

RED LAKE INDIAN RESERVATION

Lower Red Lake (Reservoir)

Saum

34

5

10

2

Sandy Lake

Red Lake

Redby

1

23

36

222

Oklee

6

Berner

89

Pike

River

B E L T R A M I

92

6

Trail

Gully

5

Kesaglagan Lake

Bass Lake

Nebish

7

Gonvick

2

4

Nels Olson Lake

Clearwater Lake

32

Island Lake

32

White Fish Lake

15

23

Blackduck Lake

Blackduck

8

Pine Lake

Balm Lake

Debs

Puposky

Medicine

7

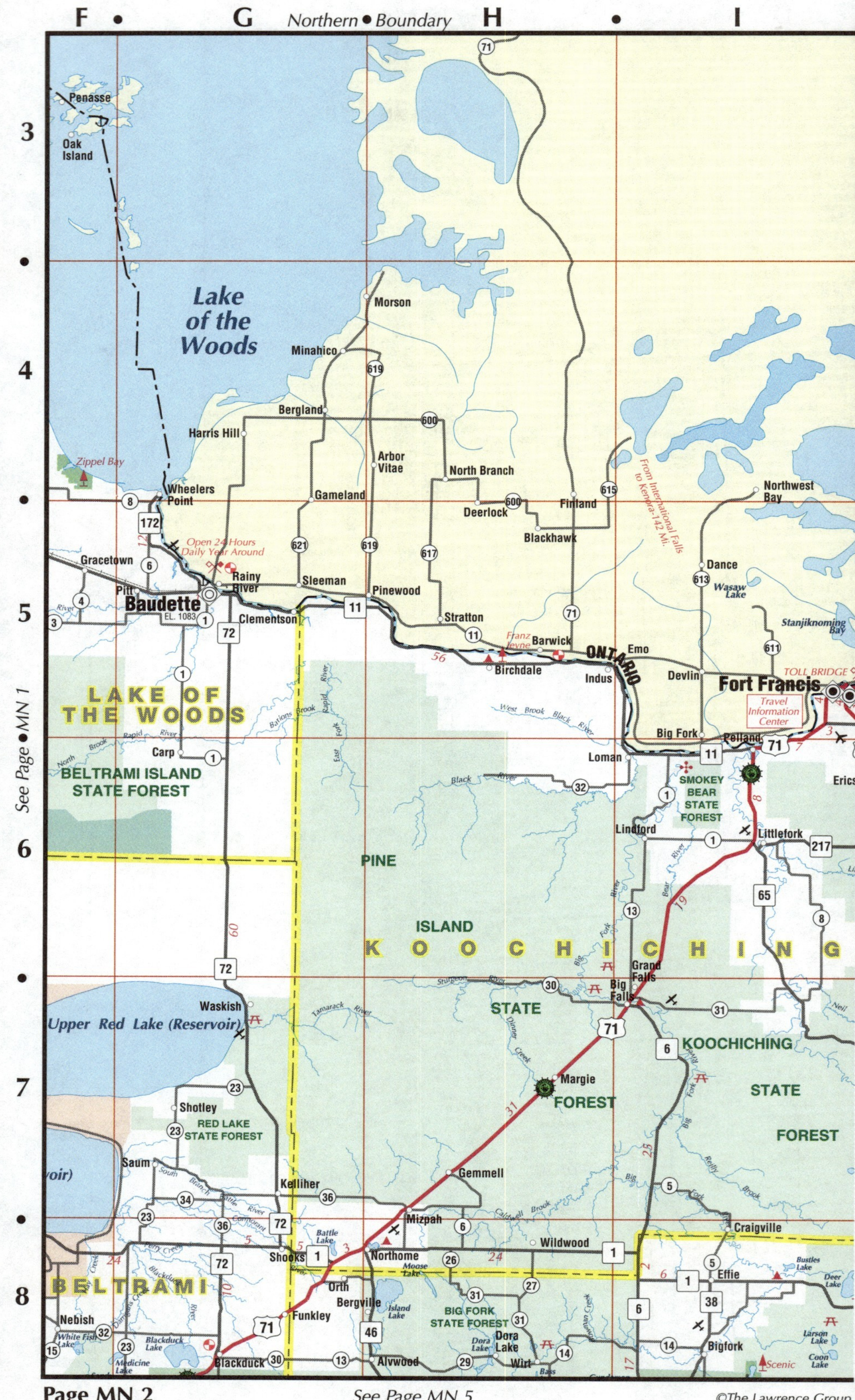

Penasse

Oak
Island

3

Lake
of the
Woods

4

71

Morson

Minahico

619

Bergland

North Branch

600

Arbor
Vitae

Harris Hill

Wheelers
Point

8

Gameland

Deerlock

Finland

600

615

Northwest
Bay

Blackhawk

From International Falls
to Kenora-142 Mi.

Dance

613

Wasaw
Lake

172

Open 24 Hours
Daily Year Around

Gracetown

6

Rainy
River

621

619

617

Sleeman

Pinewood

Stanjiknoming
Bay

Pitt

4

Baudette

5

EL. 1083

1

72

Clementson

3

River

11

Stratton

11

71

611

56

Franz
Jevne

Barwick

ONTARIO

Emo

Devlin

Fort Francis

TOLL BRIDGE

1

Birchdale

Indus

Travel
Information
Center

LAKE OF
THE WOODS

West Brook Black River

Big Fork

11

Polland

71

7

3

Loman

Carp

1

32

Smokey
Bear
State
Forest

Erics

BELTRAMI ISLAND
STATE FOREST

Black

1

Lindford

1

Littlefork

217

PINE

13

65

8

6

ISLAND

19

K O O C H I C H I N G

60

72

STATE

30

Grand
Falls

Big
Falls

71

31

Waskish

Upper Red Lake (Reservoir)

Tamarack River

FOREST

KOOCHICHING

6

23

Margie

STATE

7

Shotley

23

RED LAKE
STATE FOREST

FOREST

FOREST

Saum

34

Kelliher

36

Gemmell

5

36

Mizpah

6

Wildwood

1

Craigville

23

72

Battle
Lake

5

26

24

5

38

Shooks

1

Northome

Effie

Deer
Lake

BELTRAMI

72

Orth
Bergville

Funkley

46

Island
Lake

31

27

6

1

Bustles
Lake

Nebish

32

BIG FORK
STATE FOREST

Dora
Lake

31

Larson
Lake

White Fish
Lake

15

23

Medicine
Lake

Blackduck

71

30

13

Alvwood

29

Dora
Lake

Wirt

14

14

Bigfork

17

Coon
Lake

Scenic

See Page • MN 1

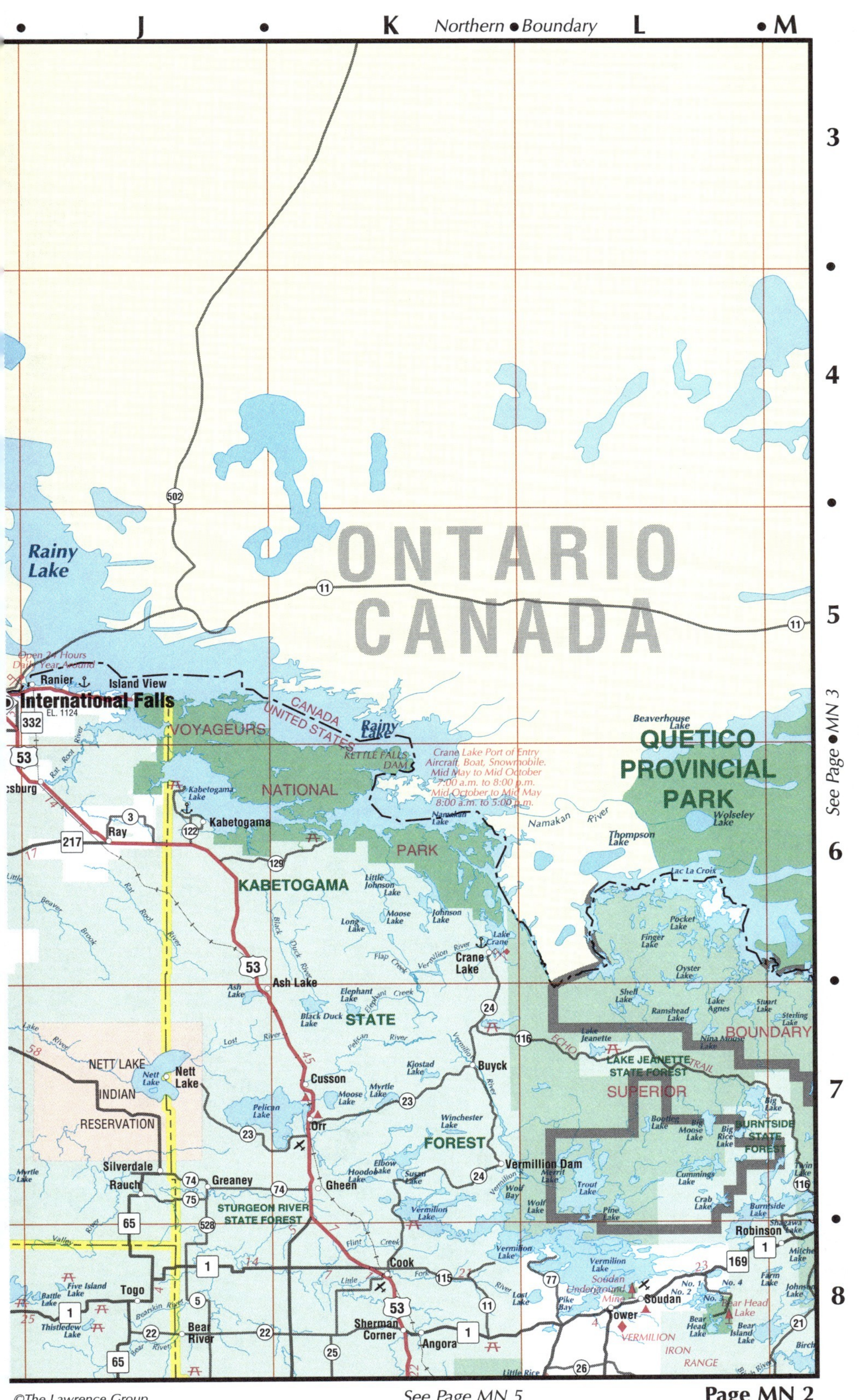

ONTARIO
CANADA

Rainy
Lake

502

11

11

5

3

4

QUETICO
PROVINCIAL
PARK

Beaverhouse
Lake

Wolseley
Lake

See Page ●MN 3

6

Open 24 Hours
Daily Year Around
Ranier   Island View
International Falls
332   EL. 1124
53

Kabetogama
Ray   122   Kabetogama
3
217
129
KABETOGAMA

53   Ash Lake
Ash
Lake

VOYAGEURS

NATIONAL

PARK

CANADA
UNITED STATES

Rainy
Lake
KETTLE FALLS
DAM
Crane Lake Port of Entry
Aircraft, Boat, Snowmobile.
Mid May to Mid October
7:00 a.m. to 8:00 p.m.
Mid October to Mid May
8:00 a.m. to 5:00 p.m.

Namakan
Lake

Namakan   River

Thompson
Lake

Lac La Croix

Pocket
Lake

Finger
Lake

Oyster
Lake

Little
Johnson
Lake

Moose
Lake

Johnson
Lake

Long
Lake

Flap   Creek

Vermilion   River

Lake
Crane

Crane
Lake

STATE

Shell
Lake

Lake
Agnes

Ramshead
Lake

Stuart
Lake

Sterling
Lake

BOUNDARY

Elephant
Lake

Black Duck
Lake

24

116

Lake
Jeanette

LAKE JEANETTE
STATE FOREST

SUPERIOR

TRAIL   ECHO

Nina Moose
Lake

7

Nett
Lake
NETT LAKE

INDIAN

RESERVATION

Nett
Lake

Cusson

Orr

23

Myrtle
Lake

Moose
Lake

23

Pelican
Lake

Kjostad
Lake

Buyck

Winchester
Lake

FOREST

Vermillion Dam

24

Susan
Lake

Wolf
Bay

Wolf
Lake

Booten
Lake

Big
Moose
Lake

Big
Rice
Lake

Cummings
Lake

Trout
Lake

Crab
Lake

Pine
Lake

BURNSIDE
STATE
FOREST

116

Burnside
Lake

Twin

Silverdale
Rauch
65

Greaney
74   75
528
STURGEON RIVER
STATE FOREST
Gheen

74

Elbow
Lake
Hoodoo
Lake

Vermilion
Lake

Flint   Creek

Robinson

169   1

Milche
Lake

8

Myrtle
Lake

Battle
Lake   Five Island
Lake
Thistledew
Lake
1
Togo

65
22   Bear
River

5

1   14

Little   Fork   River

Cook

115

Sherman
Corner
53
25

11

Angora

Vermillion
Lake

Vermilion
Lake

Soudan
Underground
Mine

Pike
Bay

Merrit
Lake
No. 1

77

No. 2

No. 4

Tower
VERMILION

IRON
RANGE

Soudan

Bear Head
Lake

Bear
Head
Lake

Bear
Island
Lake

Johnson
Lake

Birch

21

26

1

23
169

Farm
Lake

Little Rice

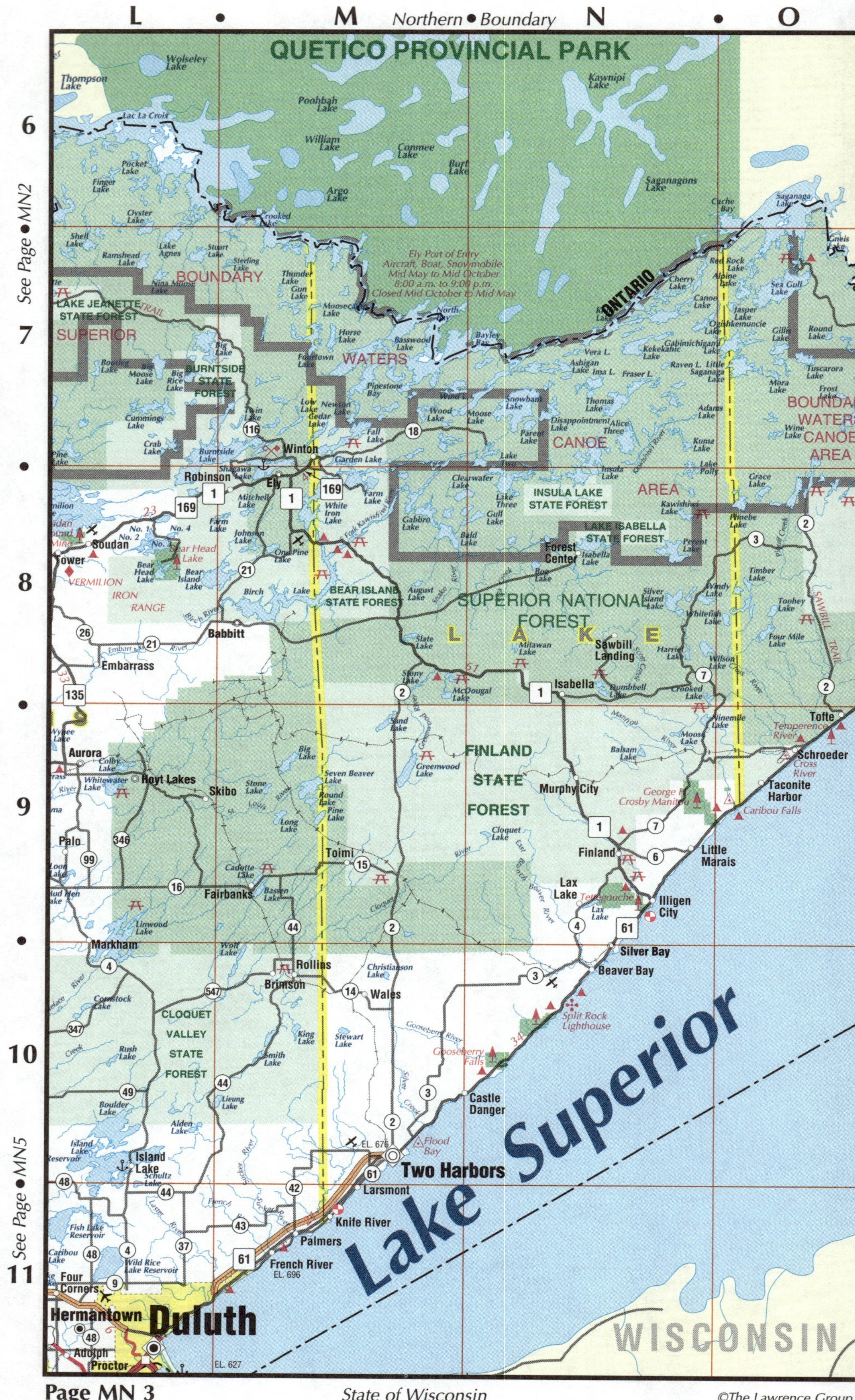

QUETICO PROVINCIAL PARK

Lake Superior

WISCONSIN

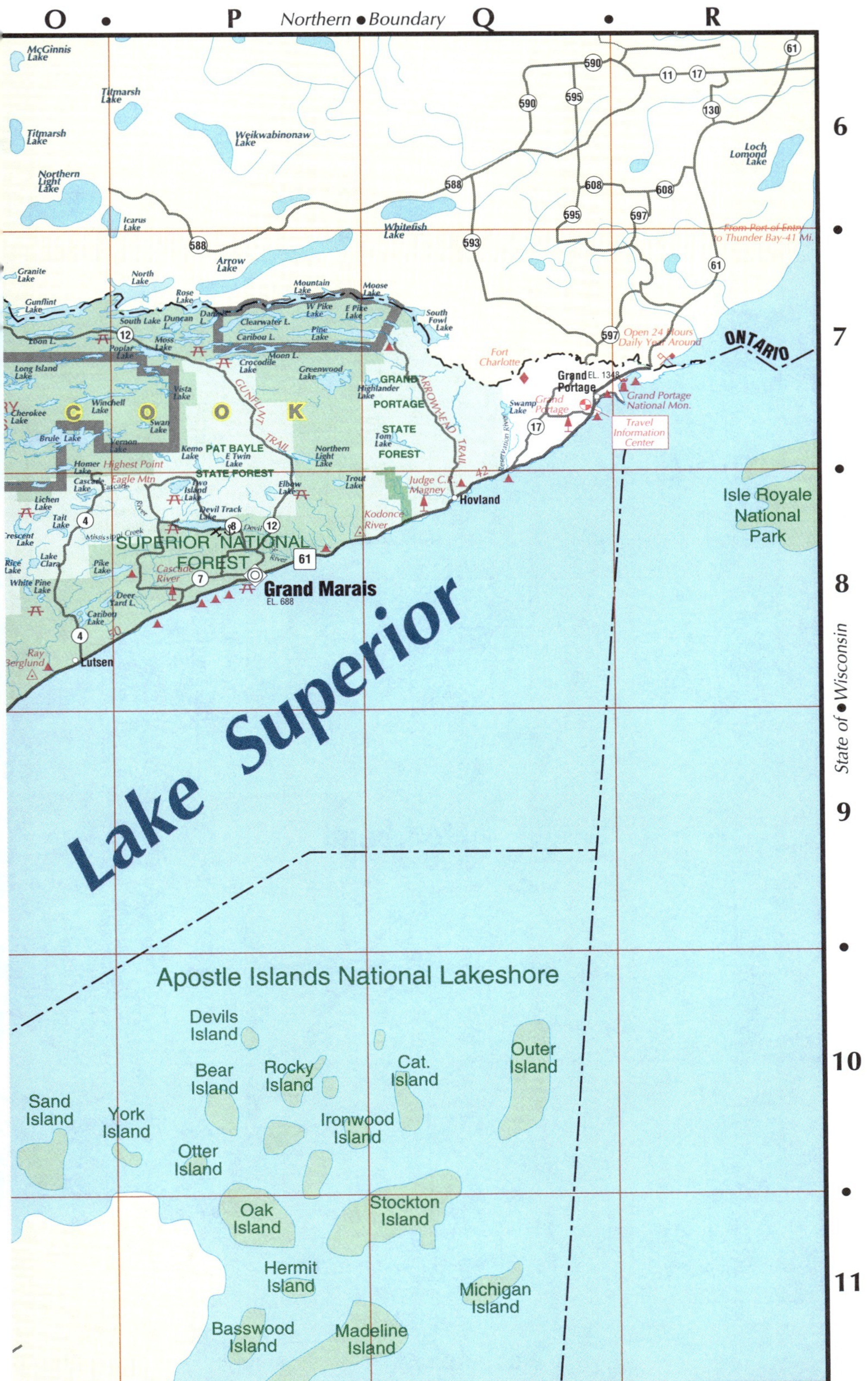

6

McGinnis Lake

Titmarsh Lake

Titmarsh Lake

Northern Light Lake

Icarus Lake

Granite Lake

North Lake

Rose Lake

Mountain Lake

Moose Lake

Weikwabinonaw Lake

Whitefish Lake

Arrow Lake

588

593

588

590

595

590

595

608

608

597

595

597

11 17

130

61

Loch Lomond Lake

From Port of Entry to Thunder Bay-41 Mi.

61

7

Gunflint Lake

Long Island Lake

South Lake

Loon L.

Poplar L.

Moss Lake

Duncan L.

Clearwater L.

Caribou L.

W Pike Lake

E Pike Lake

Daniels L.

Pine Lake

Moon L.

South Fowl Lake

Fort Charlotte

GRAND PORTAGE

597

ONTARIO

Open 24 Hours Daily Year Around

Grand Portage EL. 1348

Grand Portage Nat. Mon.

Travel Information Center

COOK

12

Cherokee Lake

Winchell Lake

Vista Lake

Swan Lake

Brule Lake

Vernon Lake

Highest Point

Crocodile Lake

Greenwood Lake

Highlander Lake

ARROWHEAD TRAIL

Pigeon River

Swamp Lake

17

PAT BAYLE

Kemo Lake

Pat Bayle Lake

GUNFLINT TRAIL

Northern Light Lake

STATE FOREST

Tom Lake

STATE FOREST

Isle Royale National Park

Homer Lake

Cascade Lake

Eagle Mtn

Two Island Lake

Elbow Lake

Trout Lake

Judge C.R. Magney

A2

Lichen Lake

Tait Lake

Crescent Lake

Mississippi Creek

Devil Track Lake

12

Kodonce River

Hovland

Lake Clara

Rice Lake

Pike Lake

4

SUPERIOR NATIONAL FOREST

Devil Track River

Cascade River

7

61

Grand Marais EL. 688

8

White Pine Lake

Deer Yard L.

Caribou Lake

90

Ray Berglund

4

Lutsen

State of • Wisconsin

Lake Superior

9

Apostle Islands National Lakeshore

10

Devils Island

Bear Island

Rocky Island

Cat. Island

Outer Island

Sand Island

York Island

Ironwood Island

Otter Island

Oak Island

Stockton Island

Hermit Island

Michigan Island

Basswood Island

Madeline Island

11

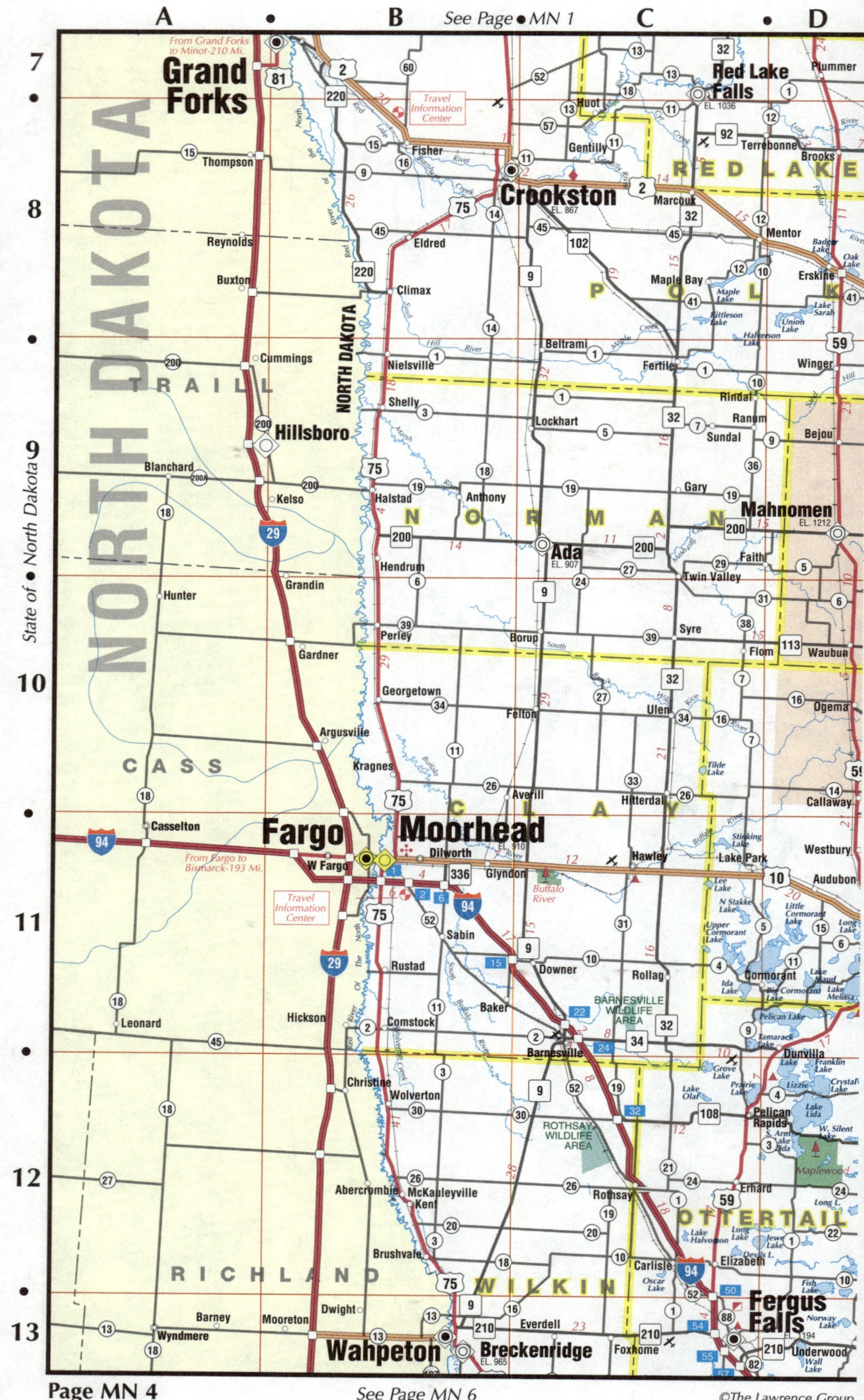

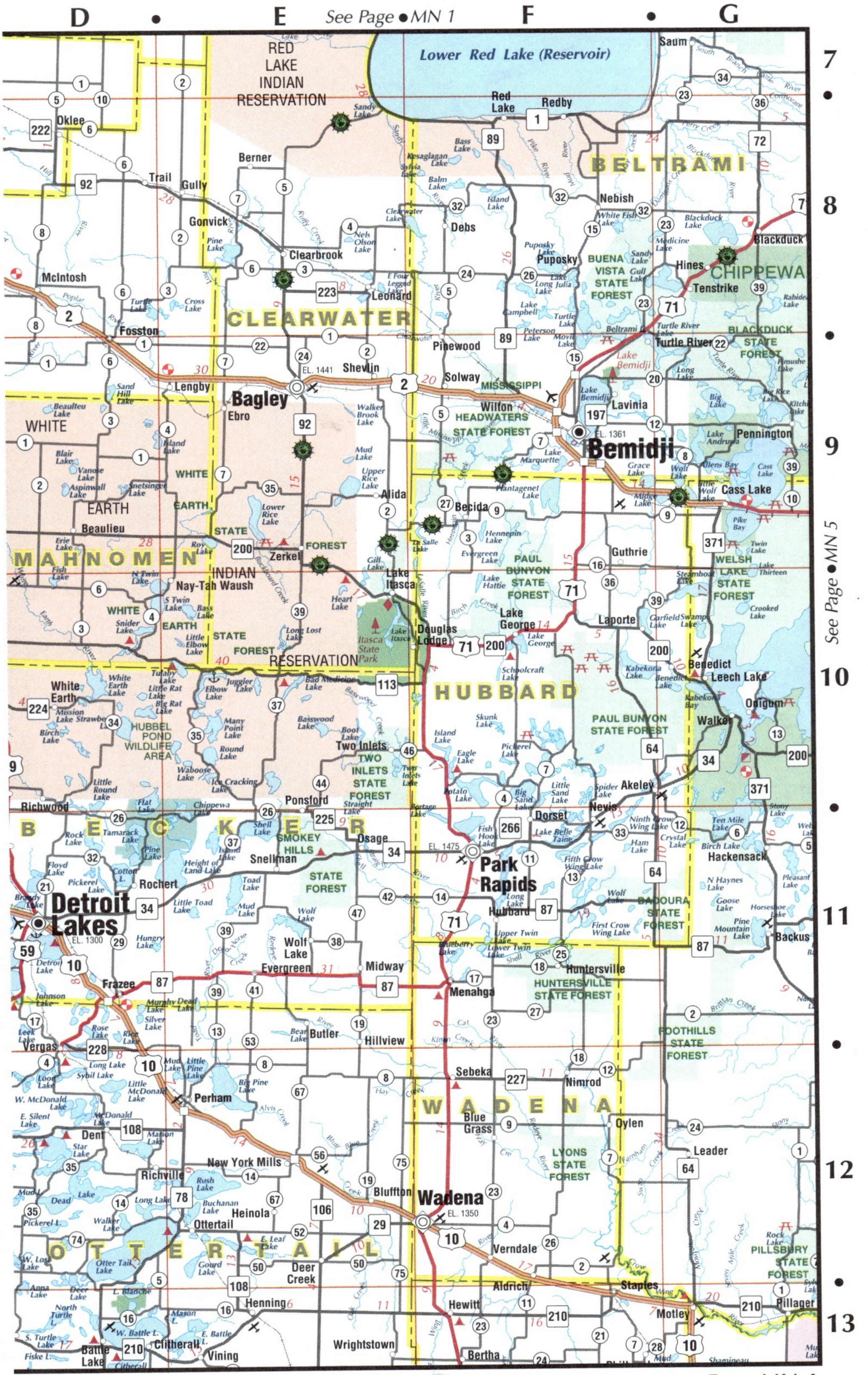

D ● E F ● G

7
●

RED
LAKE
INDIAN
RESERVATION

Lower Red Lake (Reservoir)

Saum

1

Red
Lake

Redby

Sandy
Lake

34

36

Oklee
222

5
10

6

92

Berner

Trail

Gully

Gonvick

Pine Lake

89

Kesaglagan
Lake

Sylvia
Lake

Bass
Lake

72

Nebish

BELTRAMI

8

Blackduck
Lake

Medicine
Lake

7

Clearbrook

223

Leonard

Nels
Olson
Lake

Debs

White Fish
Lake

Puposky
Lake

Puposky

BUENA
VISTA
STATE
FOREST

Sandy
Lake

Gull
Lake

Blackduck

CHIPPEWA

Hines

Tenstrike

39

Rabideu
Lake

Trail

McIntosh

Fosston

Turtle
Lake

Cross
Lake

Clearwater
Lake

Pinewood

89

Lake
Campbell

Peterson
Lake

Turtle
Lake

71

Turtle River
Lake

Turtle River

22

BLACKDUCK
STATE
FOREST

Pimushe
Lake

CLEARWATER

2

Sand Hill
Lake

22

24

Shevlin

EL. 1441

2

Solway

MISSISSIPPI

Movil
Lake

15

Long
Lake

Big
Lake

Big Rice
Lake

Kitchi
Lake

Lengby

Bagley

Ebro

92

Walker
Brook
Lake

Mud
Lake

Wilton

HEADWATERS
STATE
FOREST

Lake
Bemidji

197

Lavinia

Lake
Bemidji

Bemidji

EL. 1361

Grace
Lake

Wolf
Lake

Allens Bay

Cass
Lake

Lake
Andrusia

Pennington

9

WHITE

Blair
Lake

Beaulieu
Lake

1

3

4

Island
Lake

WHITE

92

Upper
Rice
Lake

Lower
Rice
Lake

Alida

5

Lake
Marquette

Plantagenet
Lake

Grace
Lake

Little Wolf
Lake

Cass
Lake

10

39

Vanose
Lake

Aspinwall
Lake

Snetsings
Lake

2

EARTH

Beaulieu

35

EARTH

Zerkel
200

FOREST

Roy
Lake

Becida

27

Hennepin
Lake

9

Evergreen
Lake

Guthrie

PAUL
BUNYON
STATE
FOREST

16

371

WELSH
LAKE
STATE
FOREST

Twin
Lake

Lake
Thirteen

39

MAHNOMEN

6

INDIAN

Nay-Tah Waush

N Twin
Lake

S Twin
Lake

Bass
Lake

Lake
Itasca

La Salle
Lake

Gill
Lake

Lake
Hattie

Laporte

36

71

39

200

Garfield
Lake

Steamboat
Lake

Swamp
Lake

Crooked
Lake

Benedict

Leech
Lake

10

WHITE

Snider
Lake

Little
Elbow
Lake

4

EARTH

STATE

Heart
Lake

FOREST

RESERVATION

113

Douglas
Lodge

Itasca
State
Park

Lake
Itasca

Lake
George

Schoolcraft
Lake

71

200

Lake
George

14

Kabekona
Lake

200

Kabekona
Bay

Benedict
Lake

Oruigin

Walker

White
Earth

224

Mission
Lake

Strawbe

Birch
Lake

Big Rat
Lake

34

Elbow
Lake

Juggler
Lake

37

Baiswood
Lake

Bad Medicine
Lake

Island
Lake

Skunk
Lake

PAUL BUNYON
STATE FOREST

64

13

200

9

Little
Round
Lake

Flat
Lake

35

Many
Point
Lake

Round
Lake

Boot
Lake

Eagle
Lake

Pickerel
Lake

Spider
Lake

Akeley

Crow
Wing
Lake

Ten Mile
Lake

371

Richwood

Tamarack
Lake

26

Shell
Lake

225

9

Two Inlets

TWO
INLETS
STATE
FOREST

46

Potato
Lake

Big Sand
Lake

4

Little
Sand
Lake

Nevis

Ninth
Crow
Wing Lake

Birch
Lake

Hackensack

5

Rock
Lake

Pine
Lake

37

SMOKEY
HILLS

Ponsford

Osage

34

Fish
Lake

Dorset

266

Lake
Belle
Taine

11

Fifth Crow
Wing Lake

Ham
Lake

64

N Haynes
Lake

Goose
Lake

Pleasant
Lake

BECKER

Floyd
Lake

Pickerel
Lake

Cotton
L

HILLS
STATE
FOREST

Toad
Lake

EL. 1475

Park
Rapids

Crystal
Lake

Horseshoe
Lake

Detroit
Lakes

34

Rochert

Mud
Lake

42

Wolf
Lake

14

71

Long
Lake

Hubbard

87

BADOURA
STATE
FOREST

Pine
Mountain
Lake

Backus

11

EL. 1300

29

Hungry
Lake

39

Wolf
Lake

38

First Crow
Wing Lake

87

59

Detroit
Lake

10

Evergreen

31

Midway

87

Upper Twin
Lake

Lower Twin
Lake

18

25

Huntersville

HUNTERSVILLE
STATE
FOREST

Frazee

87

Johnson
Lake

Rose
Lake

Silver
Lake

39

41

Menahga

23

27

FOOTHILLS
STATE
FOREST

Verges

228

Long Lake

10

13

53

Butler

19

Hillview

Cat
Lake

18

Sebeka

227

Nimrod

12

2

W. McDonald
Lake

E. Silent
Lake

McDonald
Lake

Mud
Lake

Little
Pine
Lake

Perham

67

WADENA

Blue
Grass

9

Oylen

24

Leader

64

1

12

Dent

108

Mason
Lake

Star
Lake

New York Mills

56

75

LYONS
STATE
FOREST

7

Richville

78

Rush
Lake

67

19

Bluffton

106

Wadena

23

EL. 1350

Pillsbury
State
Forest

Heinola

Ottertail

52

29

10

Verndale

26

OTTERTAIL

74

Deer
Creek

50

50

75

2

Henning

11

Aldrich

Staples

210

Pillager

13

16

Clitherall

16

Wrightstown

Hewitt

11

210

16

Motley

210

210

Battle
Lake

Vining

Bertha

21

7

28

10

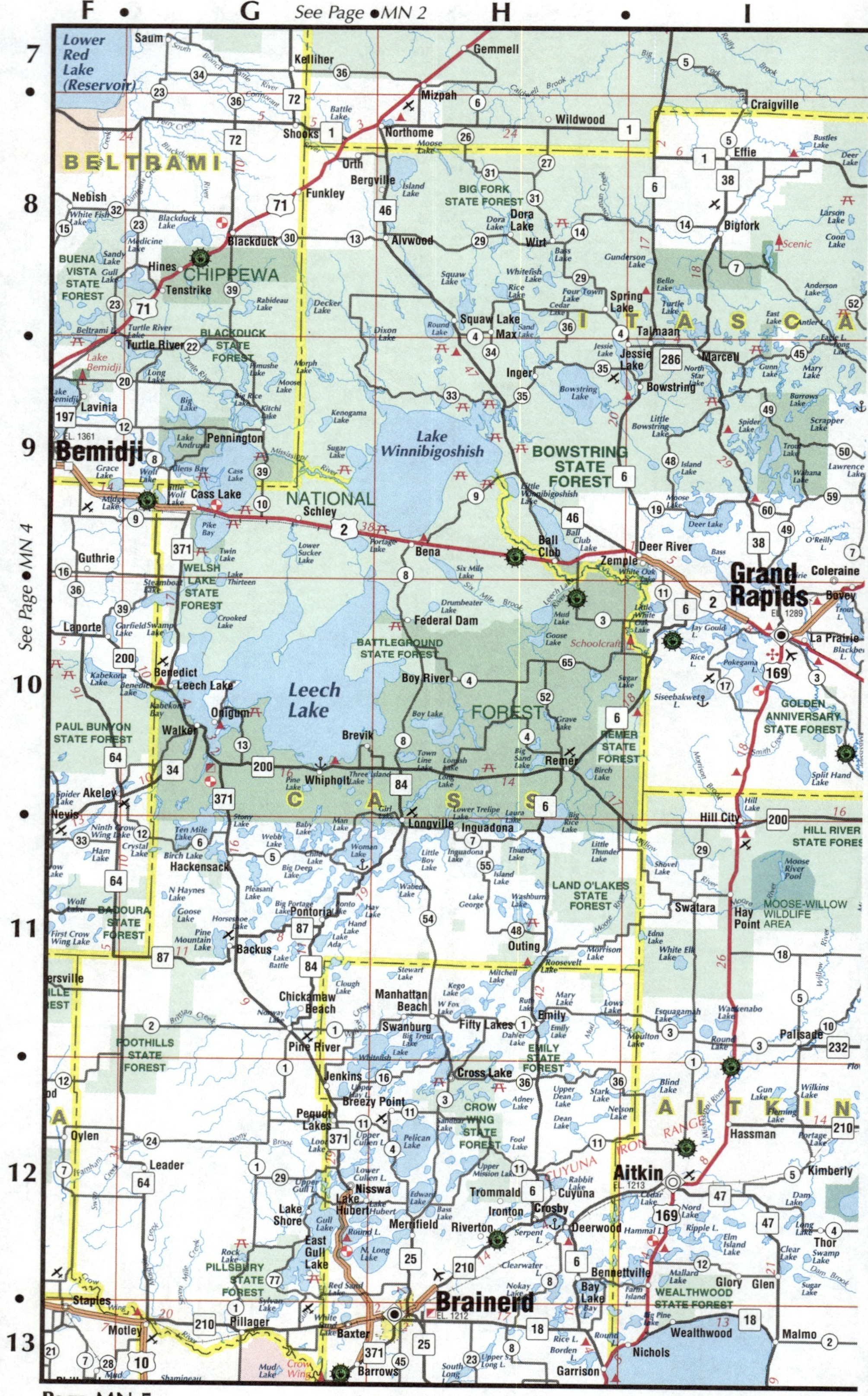

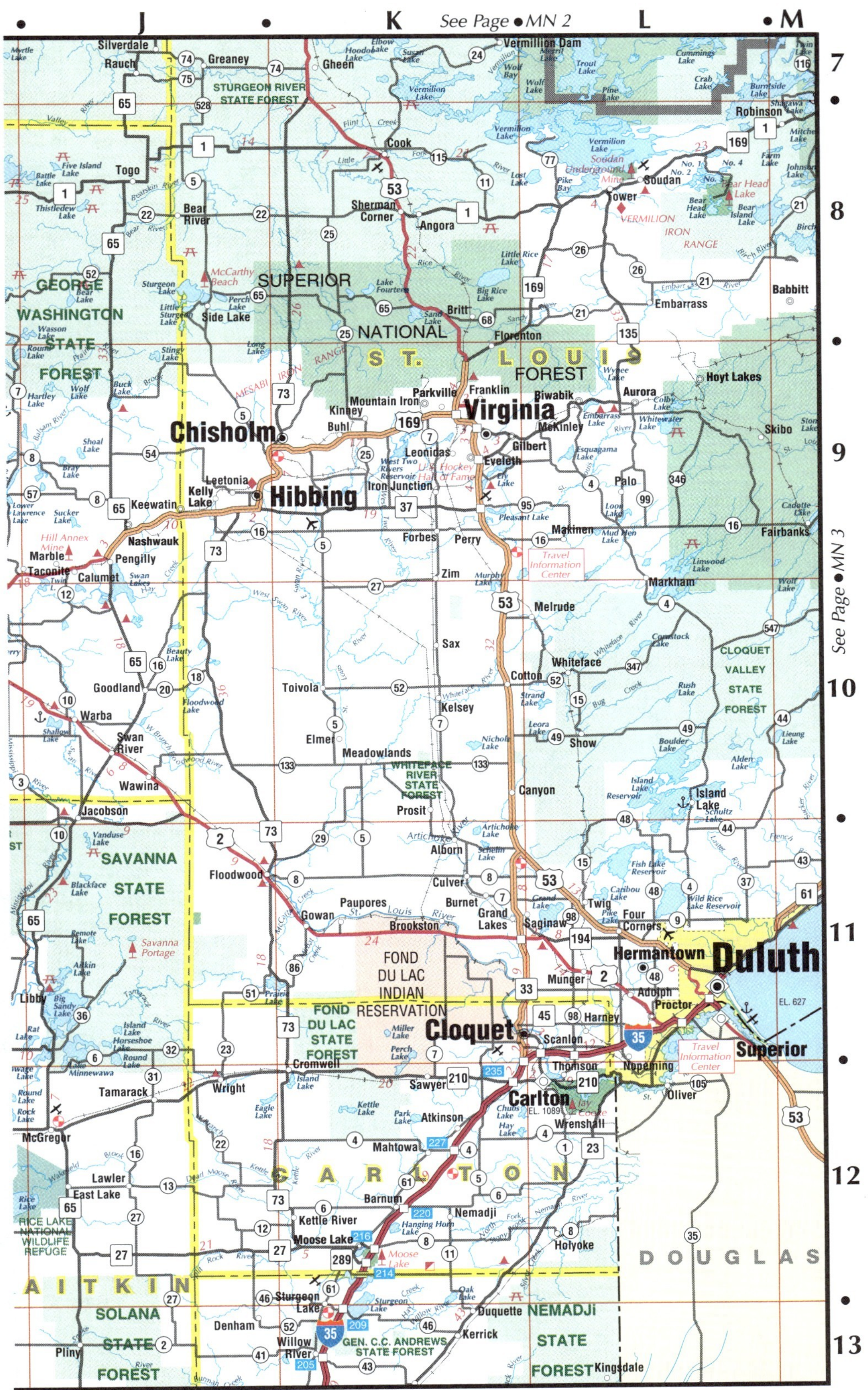

See Page MN 2
See Page MN 3
See Page MN 7
Virginia
Chisholm
Hibbing
Duluth
Cloquet
Superior
Hermantown
Carlton
SUPERIOR NATIONAL FOREST
ST. LOUIS
GEORGE WASHINGTON STATE FOREST
SAVANNA STATE FOREST
FOND DU LAC INDIAN RESERVATION
FOND DU LAC STATE FOREST
CLOQUET VALLEY STATE FOREST
WHITEFACE RIVER STATE FOREST
SOLANA STATE FOREST
NEMADJI STATE FOREST
GEN. C.C. ANDREWS STATE FOREST
RICE LAKE NATIONAL WILDLIFE REFUGE
CARLTON
AITKIN
DOUGLAS

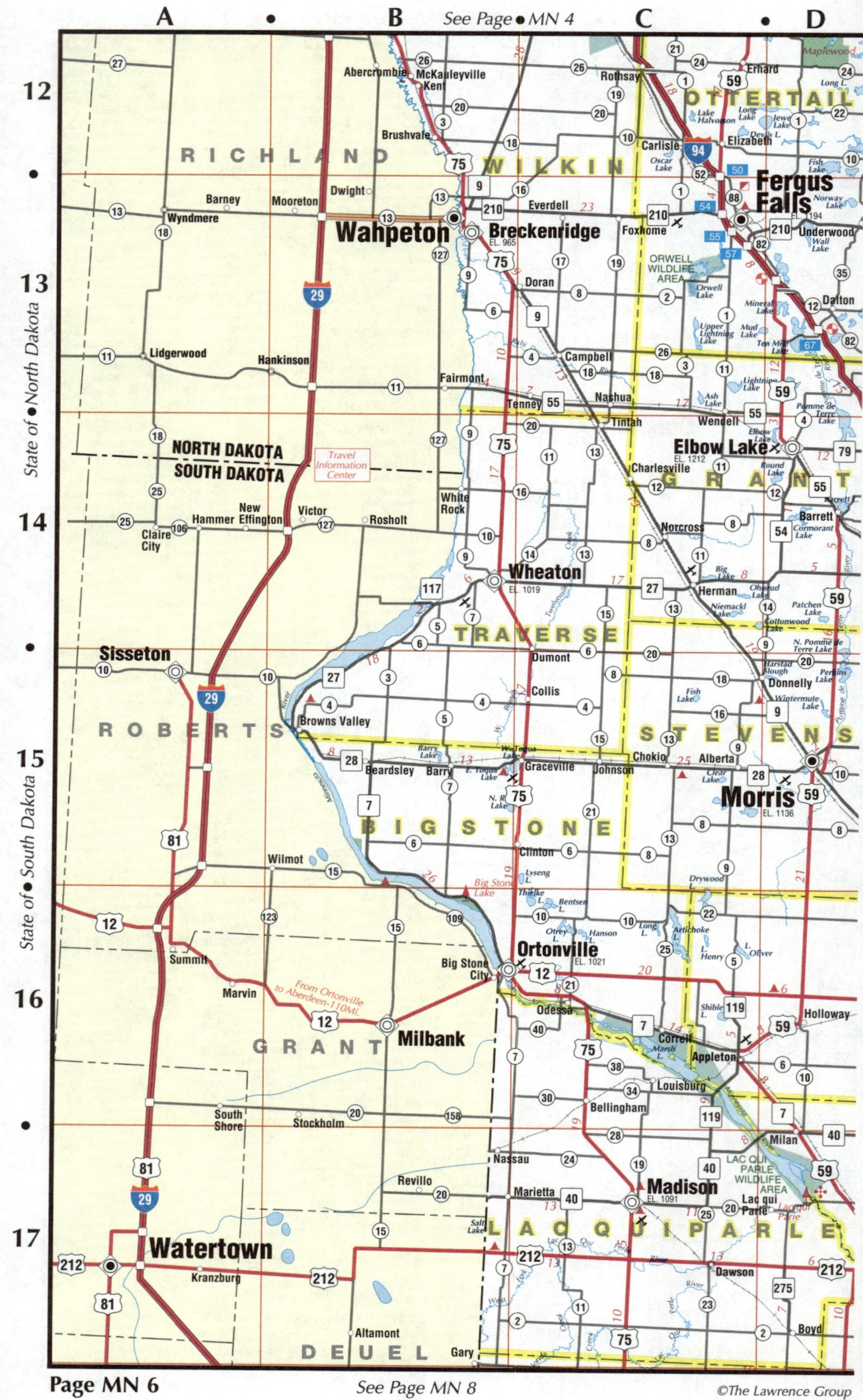

See Page MN 8

©The Lawrence Group

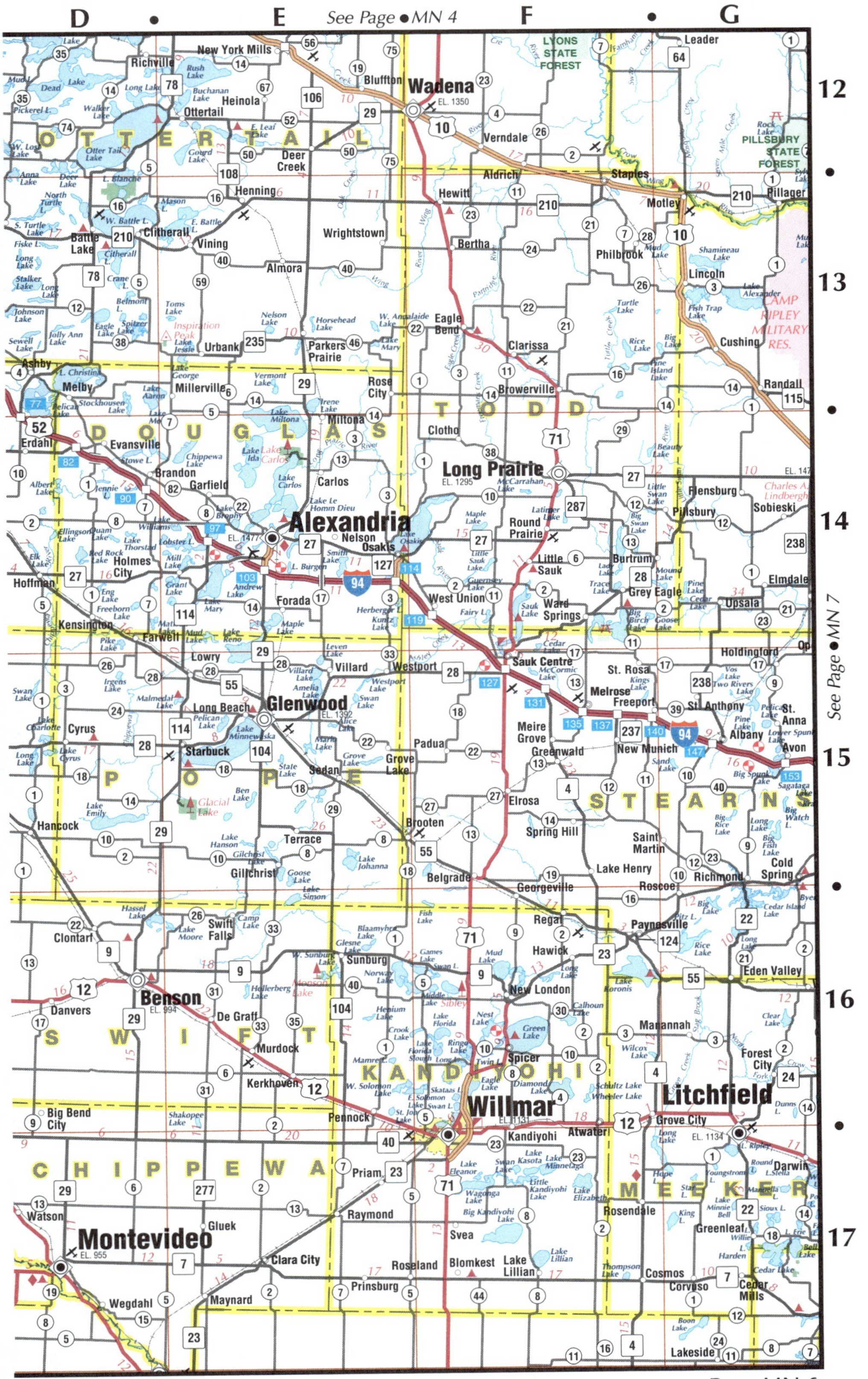

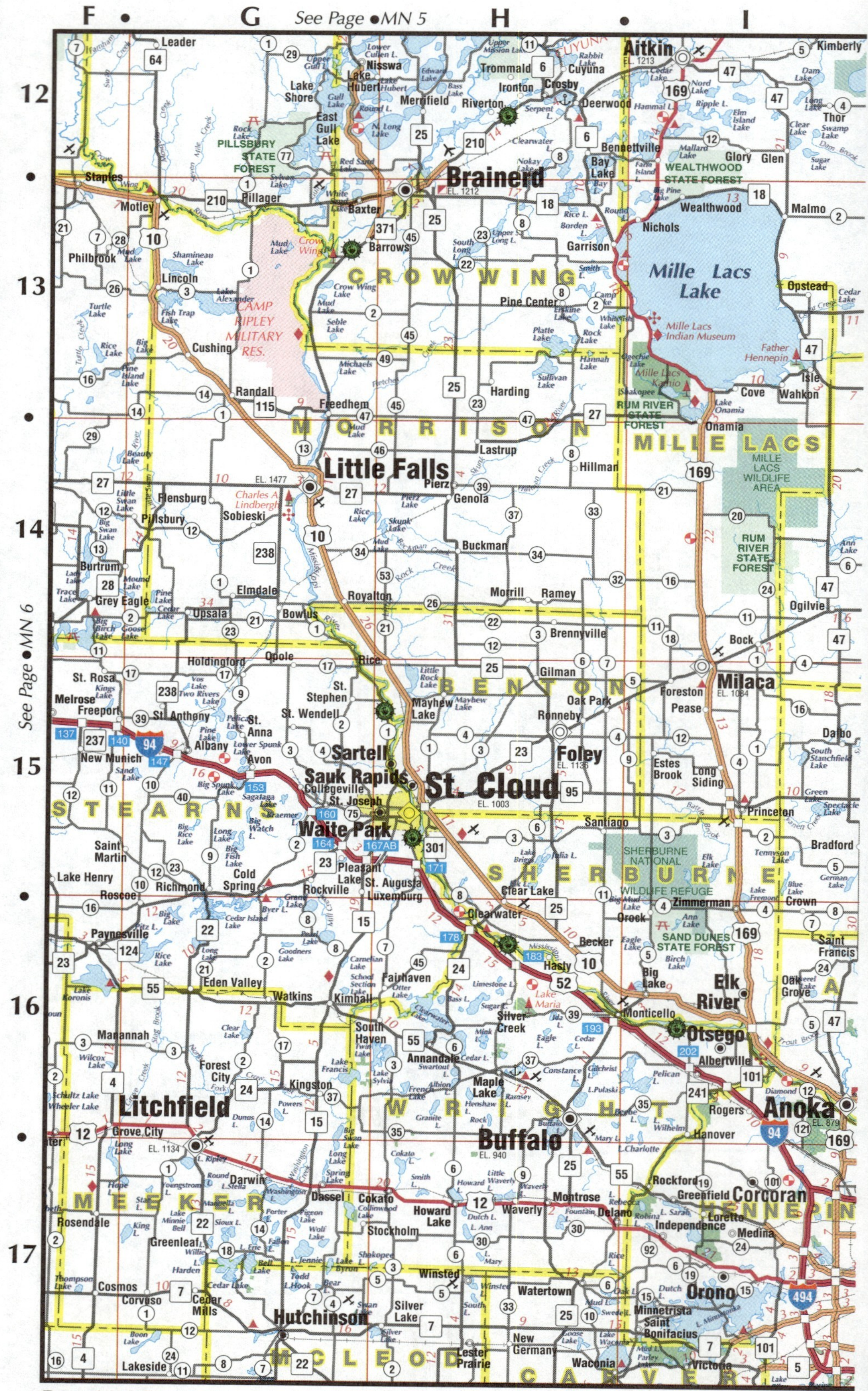
F
G
H
I
12
13
14
15
16
17
See Page MN 5
See Page MN 6
Aitkin
EL. 1213
Kimberly
Leader
Nisswa
Lake Shore
Merrifield
Trommald
Ironton
Crosby
Cuyuna
Riverton
Deerwood
East Gull Lake
PILLSBURY STATE FOREST
Bennettville
Bay Lake
Glory
Glen
WEALTHWOOD STATE FOREST
Staples
Motley
Pillager
Brainerd
EL. 1212
Baxter
Wealthwood
Malmo
Nichols
Barrows
Garrison
Philbrook
Lincoln
CROW WING
Mille Lacs Lake
Opstead
Pine Center
CAMP RIPLEY MILITARY RES.
Cushing
Mille Lacs Indian Museum
Father Hennepin
Isle
Wahkon
Cove
Harding
Randall
Freedhem
RUM RIVER STATE FOREST
Onamia
MORRISON
MILLE LACS
MILLE LACS WILDLIFE AREA
Little Falls
Lastrup
Hillman
Pierz
Genola
EL. 1477
Flensburg
Charles A. Lindbergh
Sobieski
Pillsbury
Buckman
RUM RIVER STATE FOREST
Burtrum
Grey Eagle
Elmdale
Royalton
Morrill
Ramey
Ogilvie
Upsala
Bowlus
Brennyville
Bock
Holdingford
Opole
Rice
Gilman
St. Rosa
Milaca
EL. 1084
BENTON
Foreston
Pease
Oak Park
Melrose
Freeport
St. Stephen
St. Wendell
Mayhew Lake
Ronneby
St. Anthony
St. Anna
Albany
Avon
Sartell
Foley
EL. 1136
Dalbo
New Munich
Sauk Rapids
St. Cloud
EL. 1003
Estes Brook
Long Siding
Collegeville
St. Joseph
STEARNS
Waite Park
Santiago
Princeton
Saint Martin
Bradford
Pleasant Lake
St. Augusta
Luxemburg
SHERBURNE NATIONAL WILDLIFE REFUGE
SHERBURNE
Lake Henry
Richmond
Cold Spring
Rockville
Clear Lake
Zimmerman
Crown
Roscoe
Clearwater
Orrock
SAND DUNES STATE FOREST
Paynesville
Becker
Saint Francis
Hasty
Big Lake
Elk River
Eden Valley
Fairhaven
Watkins
Kimball
Silver Creek
Monticello
Otsego
Oak Grove
Manannah
South Haven
Annandale
Albertville
Forest City
Kingston
Maple Lake
Anoka
EL. 879
Litchfield
Grove City
EL. 1134
WRIGHT
Rogers
Hanover
Buffalo
EL. 940
Darwin
Dassel
Cokato
Howard Lake
Montrose
Waverly
Delano
Rockford
Greenfield
Corcoran
HENNEPIN
MEEKER
Rosendale
Stockholm
Independence
Loretto
Medina
Greenleaf
Winsted
Orono
Watertown
Cosmos
Corvuso
Cedar Mills
Hutchinson
Silver Lake
Minnetrista
Saint Bonifacius
New Germany
Lester Prairie
Waconia
Victoria
Lakeside
MCLEOD
CARVER

See Page MN 9

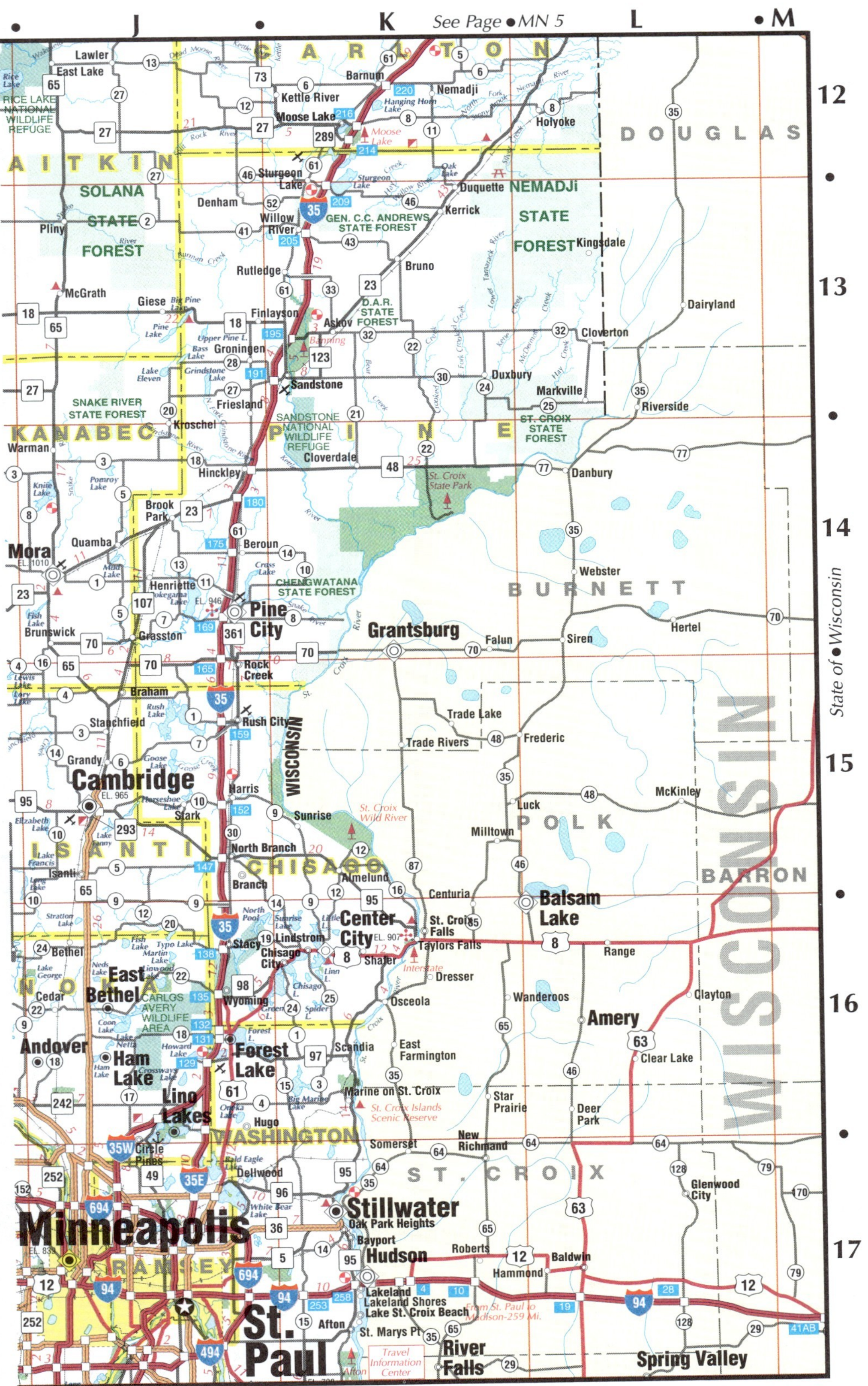

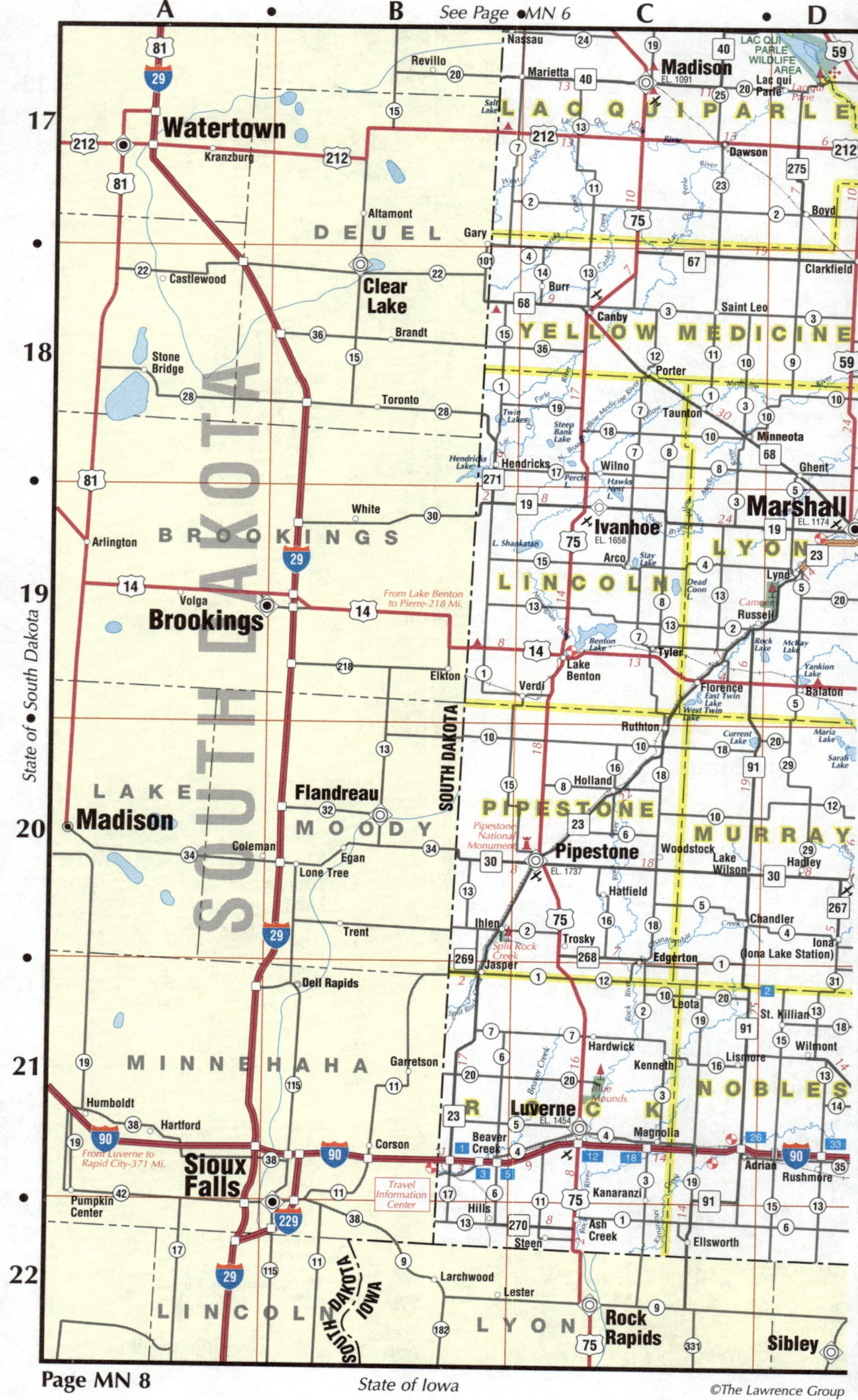

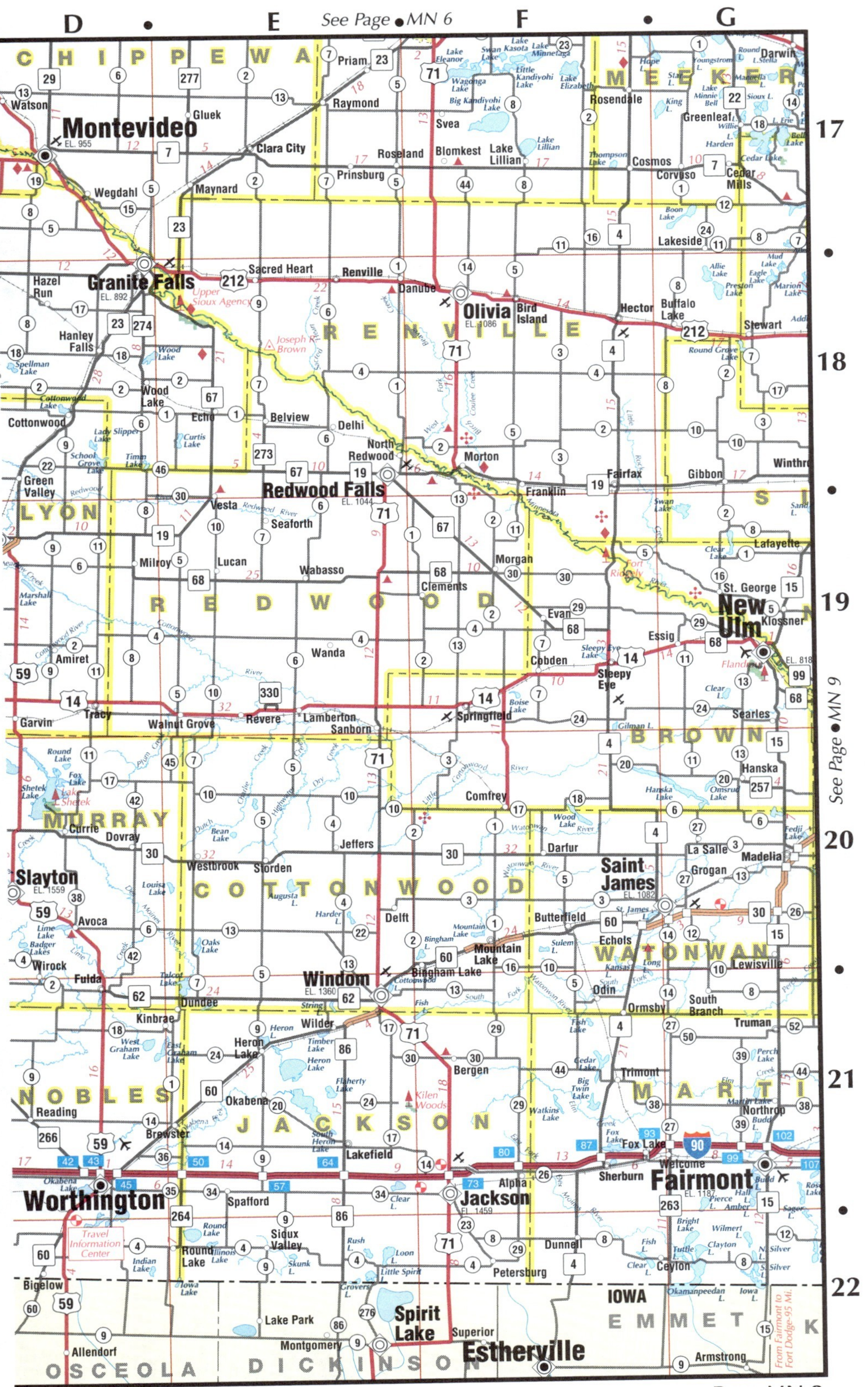

State of Iowa

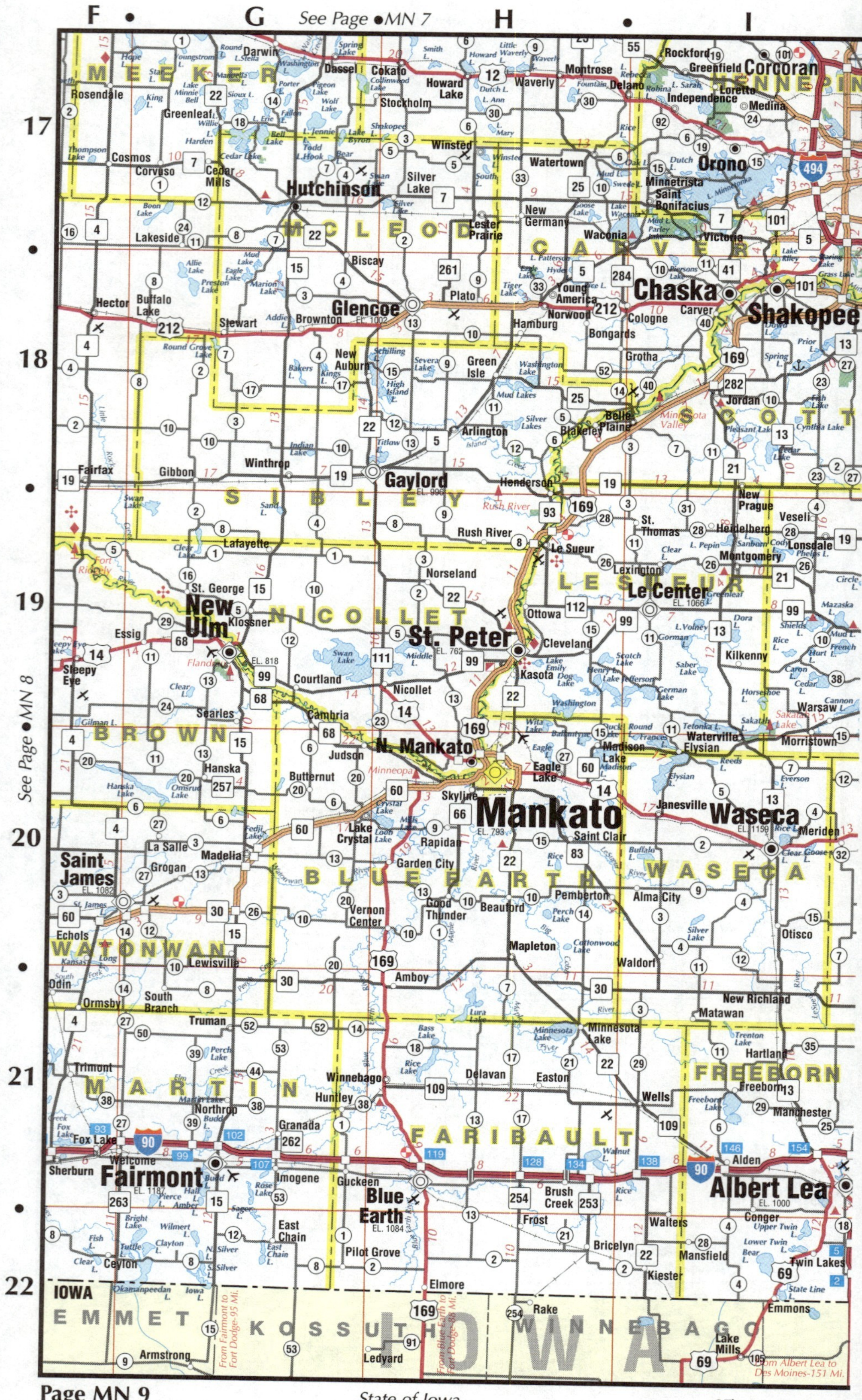

State of Iowa

©The Lawrence Group

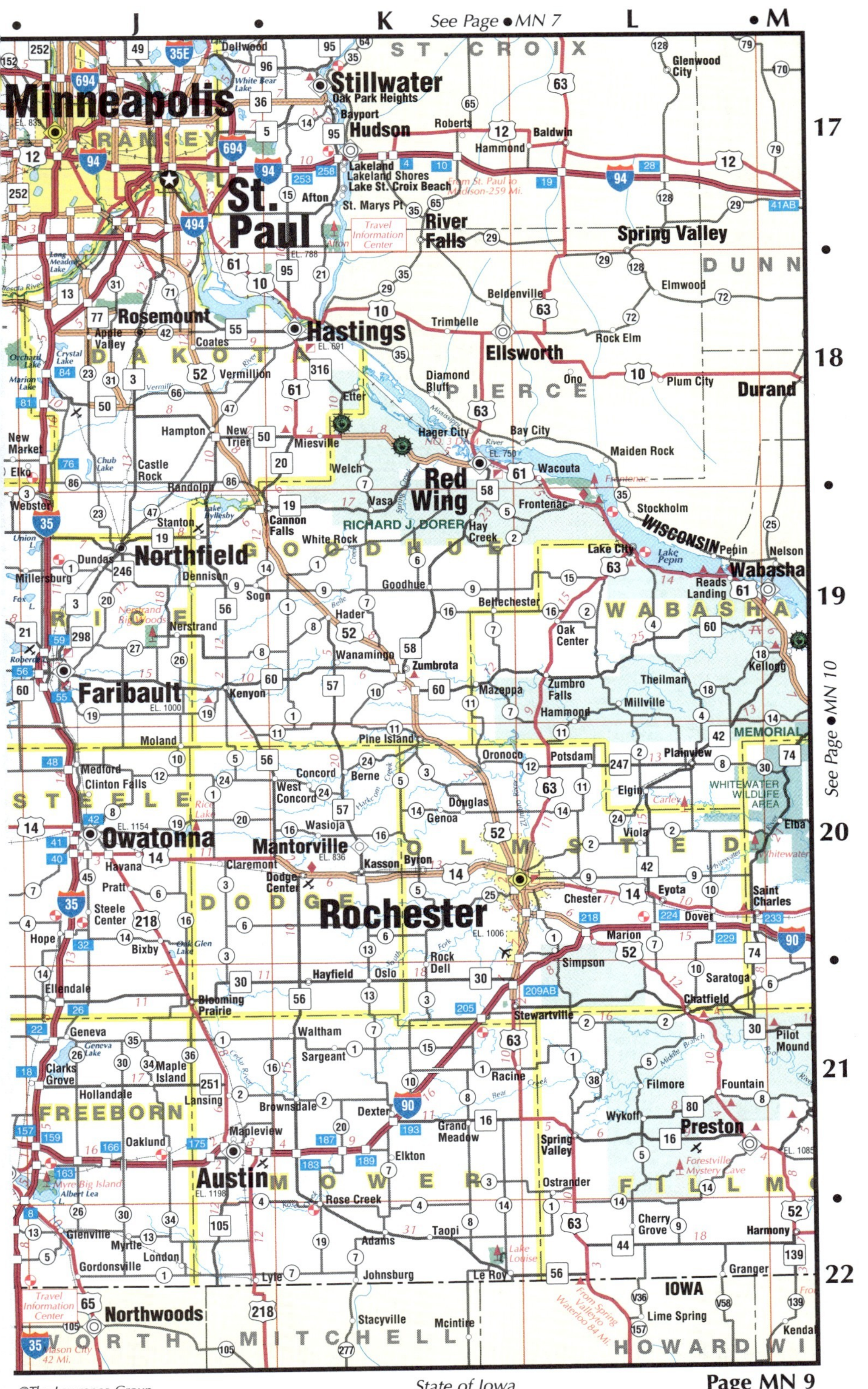
Minneapolis
St. Paul
Stillwater
Oak Park Heights
Bayport
Hudson
Roberts
Baldwin
Hammond
Glenwood City
Lakeland
Lakeland Shores
Lake St. Croix Beach
Afton
St. Marys Pt
River Falls
Spring Valley
Travel Information Center
RAMSEY
ST. CROIX
DUNN
Elmwood
Beldenville
Trimbelle
Ellsworth
Rock Elm
Hastings
Rosemount
Apple Valley
Coates
Vermillion
DAKOTA
PIERCE
Diamond Bluff
Ono
Plum City
Durand
Etter
Miesville
Hager City
Bay City
Maiden Rock
Hampton
New Trier
Castle Rock
Welch
Red Wing
Wacouta
Frontenac
Stockholm
Randolph
Webster
Stanton
Cannon Falls
Vasa
RICHARD J. DORER
Hay Creek
WISCONSIN
Pepin
Nelson
Northfield
Dundas
White Rock
GOODHUE
Lake City
Wabasha
Millersburg
Dennison
Sogn
Goodhue
Bellechester
Reads Landing
RICE
Nerstrand
Hader
WABASHA
Oak Center
Wanamingo
Zumbrota
Kellogg
Faribault
Kenyon
Mazeppa
Zumbro Falls
Hammond
Theilman
Millville
Moland
Pine Island
MEMORIAL
Medford
Clinton Falls
STEELE
Concord
West Concord
Berne
Oronoco
Potsdam
Plainview
Elgin
WHITEWATER WILDLIFE AREA
Owatonna
Wasioja
Mantorville
Douglas
Genoa
OLMSTED
Viola
Elba
Havana
Claremont
Dodge Center
Kasson
Byron
Pratt
DODGE
Rochester
Chester
Eyota
Saint Charles
Steele Center
Dover
Hope
Bixby
Marion
Rock Dell
Simpson
Ellendale
Hayfield
Oslo
Saratoga
Blooming Prairie
Chatfield
Stewartville
Geneva
Waltham
Sargeant
Pilot Mound
Clarks Grove
Maple Island
Racine
Filmore
Fountain
Hollandale
Lansing
Brownsdale
Dexter
FREEBORN
Grand Meadow
Wykoff
Preston
Oaklund
Mapleview
Spring Valley
Austin
Elkton
Forestville Mystery Cave
Myre Big Island
Albert Lea
MOWER
Ostrander
FILLMORE
Rose Creek
Cherry Grove
Harmony
Glenville
Myrtle
Taopi
Adams
London
Gordonsville
Lake Louise
Lyle
Johnsburg
Le Roy
Granger
IOWA
Northwoods
Stacyville
Mcintire
Lime Spring
Kendall
WORTH
MITCHELL
HOWARD
17
18
19
20
21
22
See Page ●MN 10

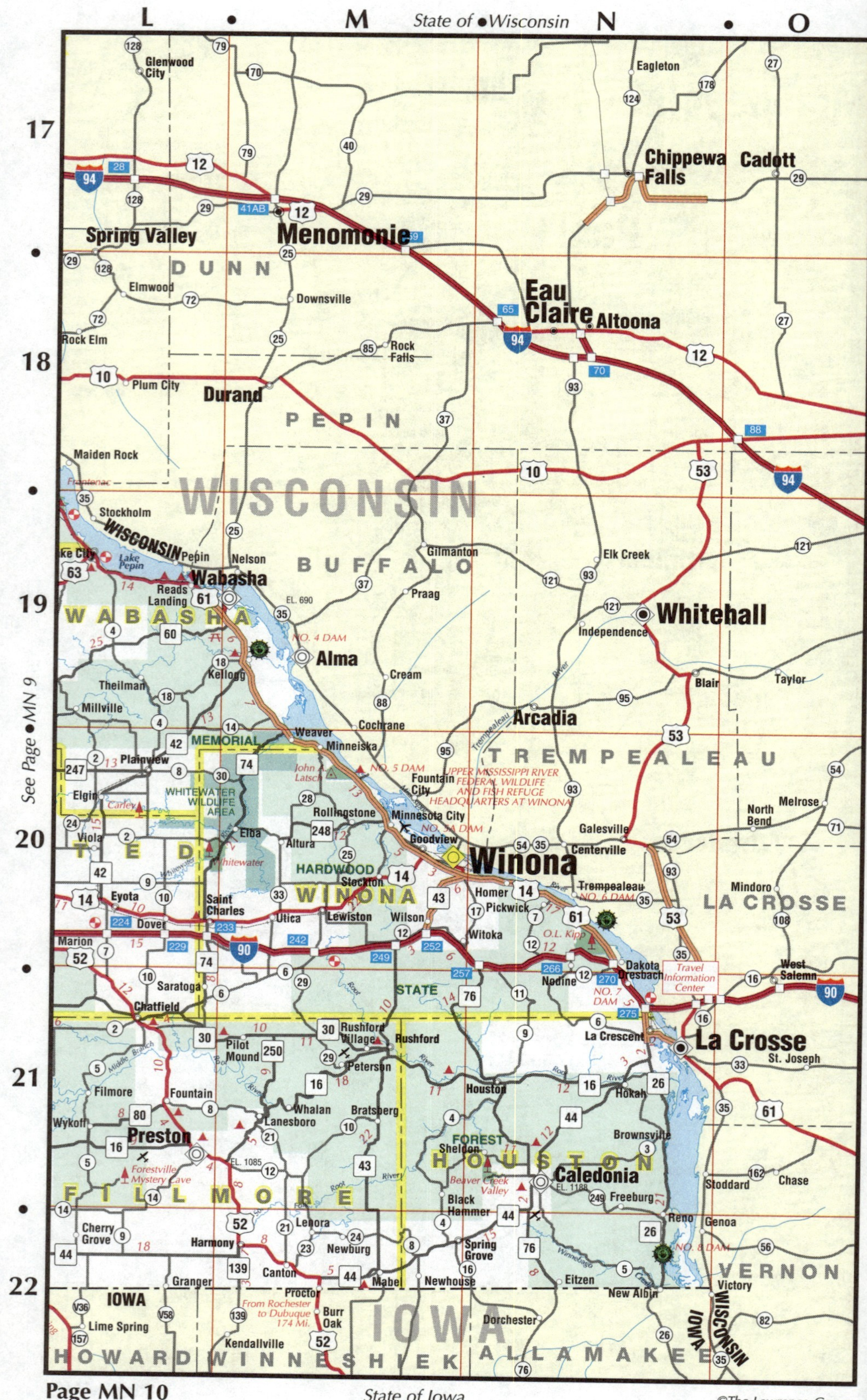

L • M N • O

17

18

19

20

21

22

See Page •MN 9

Page MN 10

State of Iowa

©The Lawrence Group

MINNESOTA
Index To Counties

ounty	Grid
ITKIN	MN7-I12
NOKA	MN7-J16
ECKER	MN4-D11
ELTRAMI	MN1-F7
ENTON	MN7-H15
IG STONE	MN6-C15
LUE EARTH	MN9-H20
ROWN	MN8-F19
ARLTON	MN5-K12
ARVER	MN9-H18
ASS	MN4-G11
HIPPEWA	MN6-D17
HISAGO	MN7-K16
LAY	MN4-C10
LEARWATER	MN4-E9
OOK	MN3-P7
OTTONWOOD	MN8-E20
ROW WING	MN5-H12
AKOTA	MN9-J18
ODGE	MN9-K20
OUGLAS	MN6-E14
ARIBAULT	MN9-H21
ILLMORE	MN9-L21
REEBORN	MN9-I21
OODHUE	MN9-K19
RANT	MN6-C14
ENNEPIN	MN7-I17
OUSTON	MN10-N21
UBBARD	MN4-F10
SANTI	MN7-J15
TASCA	MN5-I9
ACKSON	MN8-E21
ANABEC	MN7-J14
ANDIYOHI	MN6-F17
ITTSON	MN1-B5
OOCHICHING	MN2-H6
AC QUI PARLE	MN8-C17
AKE	MN3-N8
AKE OF THE WOODS	MN1-F5
E SUEUR	MN9-I19
INCOLN	MN8-C19
YON	MN8-D19
MAHNOMEN	MN4-D9
MARSHALL	MN1-C6
MARTIN	MN9-G21
MCLEOD	MN9-G18
MEEKER	MN7-G17
MILLE LACS	MN7-I14
MORRISON	MN7-G14
MOWER	MN9-K21
MURRAY	MN8-D20
NICOLLET	MN9-G19
NOBLES	MN8-D21
NORMAN	MN4-C9
OLMSTED	MN9-L20
OTTER TAIL	MN4-D12
PENNINGTON	MN1-D7
PINE	MN7-K13
PIPESTONE	MN8-C20
POLK	MN4-C8
POPE	MN6-E15
RAMSEY	MN9-J17
RED LAKE	MN4-D8
REDWOOD	MN8-E19
RENVILLE	MN8-F18
RICE	MN9-I19
ROCK	MN8-C21
ROSEAU	MN1-D5
SCOTT	MN9-I18
SHERBURNE	MN7-I15
SIBLEY	MN9-G18
ST. LOUIS	MN5-L9
STEARNS	MN6-G15
STEELE	MN9-J20
STEVENS	MN6-C15
SWIFT	MN6-D16
TODD	MN6-F13
TRAVERSE	MN6-B14
WABASHA	MN9-L19
WADENA	MN4-F12
WASECA	MN9-I20
WASHINGTON	MN7-K17
WATONWAN	MN8-G20
WILKIN	MN6-C12
WINONA	MN10-M20
WRIGHT	MN7-H16
YELLOW MEDICINE	MN8-C18

MINNESOTA
Index To Cities

For cities shown in RED see detailed street Atlas

City	Grid
A	
Ada	MN4-C9
Adams	MN9-K22
Adolph	MN5-L11
Adrian	MN8-C21
Afton	124-E2
Aitkin	MN5-I12
Akeley	MN4-F10
Albany	MN7-G15
Albert Lea	MN9-I21
Alberta	MN6-C15
Albertville	46-E2
Alborn	MN5-K11
Alden	MN9-I21
Aldrich	MN6-F12
Alexandria	MN6-E14
Alida	MN4-E9
Alma City	MN4-E9
Almelund	MN7-K15
Almora	MN6-E13
Alpha	MN8-F21
Altura	MN10-M20
Alvarado	MN1-B6
Amboy	MN9-H21
Amiret	MN8-D19
Andover	36-B3
Angle Inlet	MN1-F3
Angora	MN5-K8
Angus	MN1-B7
Annandale	MN7-H16
Anoka	49-3C
Anthony	MN4-B9
Apple Valley	163-C1
Appleton	MN6-C16
Arco	MN8-C19
Arden Hills	79-C3
Argyle	MN1-B6
Arlington	183-A3
Arnesen	MN1-F4
Ash Creek	MN8-C21
Ashby	MN8-D13
Askov	MN7-K13
Atkinson	MN5-K12
Atwater	MN6-F16
Audubon	MN4-D11
Aurora	MN5-L9
Austin	MN9-J21
Averill	MN4-B10
Avoca	MN8-D20
Avon	MN7-G15
B	
Babbitt	MN3-M8
Backus	MN5-G11
Badger	MN1-D5
Bagley	MN4-E9
Baker	MN4-B11
Balaton	MN8-D19
Ball Club	MN5-H9
Barnesville	MN4-C11
Barnum	MN5-K12
Barrett	MN6-D14
Barrows	MN7-G13
Barry	MN6-B15
Battle Lake	MN6-D13
Baudette	MN2-G5
Baxter	MN7-G13
Bay Lake	MN7-H12
Bayport	97-B3
Bear River	MN5-J8
Beardsley	MN6-B15
Beauford	MN9-H20
Beaulieu	MN4-D9
Beaver Creek	MN8-B21
Becida	MN4-F9
Becker	MN7-H16
Bejou	MN4-D9
Belgrade	MN6-F15
Belle Plaine	185-E3
Bellechester	MN9-K19
Bellingham	MN6-C16
Beltrami	MN4-C9
Belview	MN8-E18
Bemidji	MN4-F9
Bena	MN5-H9
Benedict	MN5-G10
Bennettville	MN7-I12
Benson	MN6-D16
Bergen	MN8-F21
Berne	MN9-K20
Berner	MN4-E8
Beroun	MN7-J14
Bertha	MN6-F13
Bethel	8-C3
Big Bend City	MN6-D16
Big Falls	MN2-I7
Big Lake	MN7-I16
Bigelow	MN8-D22
Bigfork	MN5-I8
Bingham Lake	MN8-F20
Birchdale	MN2-H5
Birchwood Village	95-C1
Bird Island	MN8-F18
Biscay	MN9-G18
Biwabik	MN5-L9
Bixby	MN9-J20
Black Hammer	MN10-M21
Blackduck	MN5-G8
Blaine	65-B2
Blakeley	MN9-H18
Blomkest	MN8-F17
Blooming Prairie	MN9-J21
Bloomington	134-D3
Blue Earth	MN9-H21
Blue Grass	MN4-F12
Bluffton	MN4-E12
Bock	MN7-I14
Bongards	MN9-H18
Borup	MN4-C10
Bovey	MN5-I10
Bowlus	MN7-G14
Bowstring	MN5-I9
Boy River	MN5-H10
Boyd	MN8-D17
Bradford	MN7-I15
Braham	MN7-J15
Brainerd	MN7-H13
Branch	MN7-J15
Brandon	MN6-D14
Bratsberg	MN10-M21
Breckenridge	MN6-B13
Breezy Point	MN5-H12
Brennyville	MN7-H14
Brevik	MN5-G10
Brewster	MN8-E21
Bricelyn	MN9-H22
Brimson	MN3-M10
Britt	MN5-K8
Brook Park	MN7-J14
Brooklyn Center	92-A2
Brooklyn Park	78-A2
Brooks	MN4-D8
Brookston	MN5-K11
Brooten	MN6-E15
Browerville	MN6-F13
Browns Valley	MN6-B15
Brownsdale	MN9-K21
Brownsville	MN10-N21
Brownton	MN9-G18
Bruno	MN7-K13
Brunswick	MN7-J14
Brush Creek	MN9-H21
Brushvale	MN4-B12
Buckman	MN7-H14
Buffalo Lake	MN8-G18
Buffalo	58-D1
Buhl	MN5-K9
Burnett	MN5-K11
Burnsville	148-B3
Burr	MN8-C18
Burtrum	MN6-F14
Butler	MN4-E11
Butterfield	MN8-F20
Butternut	MN9-G20
Buyck	MN2-K7
Byron	MN9-K20
C	
Caledonia	MN10-N21
Callaway	MN4-D10
Calumet	MN5-J9
Cambria	MN9-G19
Cambridge	MN7-J15
Campbell	MN6-C13
Canby	MN8-C18
Cannon Falls	208-B3
Canton	MN10-M22
Canyon	MN5-K10
Carlisle	MN4-C12
Carlos	MN6-E14
Carlton	MN5-L12
Carp	MN1-G6

Carver 159-B1
Cass Lake MN5-G9
Castle Danger MN3-N10
Castle Rock MN9-J18
Cedar Mills MN9-G17
Cedar MN9-J16
Center City 12-E3
Centerville 66-D3
Ceylon MN8-F22
Champlin 63-B3
Chandler MN8-C20
Chanhassen 131-D2
Charlesville MN6-C14
Chaska 131-B3
Chatfield MN9-L21
Cherry Grove MN9-L22
Chester MN9-L20
Chickamaw Beach MN5-G11
Chisago City 26-A1
Chisholm MN5-K9
Chokio MN6-C15
Circle Pines 65-D4
Clara City MN6-E17
Claremont MN9-J20
Clarissa MN6-F13
Clarkfield MN8-D18
Clarks Grove MN9-J21
Clear Lake MN7-H16
Clearbrook MN4-E8
Clearwater MN7-H16
Clements MN8-F19
Clementson MN2-G5
Cleveland MN9-H19
Climax MN4-B8
Clinton Falls MN9-J20
Clinton MN6-C15
Clitherall MN6-D13
Clontarf MN6-D16
Cloquet MN5-K11
Clotho MN6-F14
Cloverdale MN7-K14
Cloverton MN7-L13
Coates 165-A3
Cobden MN8-F19
Cokato MN7-H17
Cold Spring MN7-G15
Coleraine MN5-I9
Collegeville MN7-G15
Collis MN6-C15
Cologne 143-D3
Columbia Heights 92-D2
Comfrey MN8-F20
Comstock MN4-B11
Concord MN9-K20
Conger MN9-I21
Cook MN5-K8
Coon Rapids 64-B1
Corcoran 75-C2
Cormorant MN4-C11
Correll MN6-C16
Corvuso MN8-G17
Cosmos MN8-F17
Cottage Grove 138-B3
Cotton MN5-K10
Cottonwood MN8-D18
Courtland MN9-G19
Cove MN7-I13
Craigville MN2-I8
Crane Lake MN2-K6
Cromwell MN5-K12
Crookston MN4-B8
Crosby MN5-H12
Cross Lake MN5-H12
Crown MN7-I16
Crystal 91-D2
Culver MN5-K11
Currie MN8-D20
Cushing MN7-G13
Cuyuna MN5-H12
Cyrus MN6-D15

D
Dakota MN10-N20
Dalbo MN7-I15
Dalton MN6-D13
Danube MN8-E18
Danvers MN6-D16
Darfur MN8-F20
Darwin MN7-G17
Dassel MN7-G17
Dawson MN8-C17
Dayton 62-D1
De Graff MN6-E16
Debs MN4-F8
Deephaven 118-B1

Deer Creek MN6-E12
Deer River MN5-I9
Deerwood MN5-H12
Delano 87-E2
Delavan MN9-H21
Delft MN8-E20
Delhi MN8-E18
Dellwood 81-D2
Denham MN7-J13
Dennison MN9-J19
Dent MN4-D12
Detroit Lakes MN4-D11
Dexter MN9-K21
Dilworth MN4-B11
Dodge Center MN9-K20
Donaldson MN1-B5
Donnelly MN6-C15
Doran MN6-C13
Dorset MN4-F11
Douglas Lodge MN4-F10
Douglas MN9-K20
Dover MN9-L20
Dovray MN8-D20
Downer MN4-C11
Dresbach MN10-N21
Duluth MN3-L11
Dumont MN6-C14
Dundas MN9-J19
Dundee MN8-E21
Dunnell MN8-F22
Dunvilla MN4-D11
Duquette MN7-K13
Duxbury MN7-K13

E
Eagan 135-E3
Eagle Bend MN6-F13
Eagle Lake MN9-H20
East Bethel 23-C3
East Chain MN9-G22
East Grand Forks MN1-B7
East Gull Lake MN5-G12
East Lake MN5-J12
Easton MN9-H21
Ebro MN4-E9
Echo MN8-E18
Echols MN8-F20
Eden Prairie 132-C3
Eden Valley MN7-G16
Edgerton MN8-C20
Edina 119-C3
Effie MN2-I8
Eitzen MN10-N22
Elba MN10-M20
Elbow Lake MN6-D14
Eldred MN4-B8
Elgin MN9-L20
Elizabeth MN4-C12
Elk River 33-D2
Elko 204-B1
Elkton MN9-K21
Ellendale MN9-J21
Ellsworth MN8-C22
Elmdale MN7-G14
Elmer MN5-K10
Elmore MN9-H22
Elrosa MN6-F15
Ely MN3-M8
Elysian MN9-I20
Embarrass MN5-L8
Emily MN5-H11
Emmons MN9-I22
Erdahl MN6-D14
Erhard MN4-C12
Ericsburg MN2-J6
Erie MN1-D7
Erskine MN4-D8
Esko MN5-L11
Essig MN8-G19
Estes Brook MN7-I15
Etter MN9-K18
Euclid MN1-B7
Evan MN8-F19
Evansville MN6-D14
Eveleth MN5-K9
Everdell MN6-C13
Evergreen MN4-E11
Excelsior 117-E3
Eyota MN9-L20

F
Fairbanks MN3-M9
Fairfax MN8-F18
Fairhaven MN7-H16
Fairmont MN8-G21

Faith MN4-D9
Falcon Heights 107-C2
Faribault MN9-J19
Farmington 177-C2
Farwell MN6-D14
Faunce MN1-F5
Federal Dam MN5-H10
Felton MN4-C10
Fergus Falls MN6-C13
Fertile MN4-C9
Fifty Lakes MN5-H11
Filmore MN9-L21
Finland MN3-N9
Finlayson MN7-J13
Fisher MN4-B8
Flensburg MN6-G14
Flom MN4-C10
Floodwood MN5-J11
Florence MN8-C19
Florenton MN5-K8
Foley MN7-H15
Forada MN6-E14
Forbes MN5-K9
Forest Center MN3-N8
Forest Lake 39-B2
Foreston MN7-I15
Fosston MN4-D9
Fountain MN10-L21
Four Town MN1-E6
Fox MN1-D7
Foxhome MN6-C13
Franklin MN8-F18
Franklin MN5-K9
Frazee MN4-D11
Freeburg MN10-N21
Freeborn MN9-I21
Freedhem MN7-G13
Freeport MN6-F15
French River MN3-M11
Fridley 78-D4
Friesland MN7-J13
Frontenac MN9-L19
Frost MN9-H22
Fulda MN8-D21
Funkley MN5-G8

G
Garden City MN9-H20
Garfield MN6-E14
Garrison MN7-H13
Garvin MN8-D19
Gary MN4-C9
Gaylord MN9-G18
Gem Lake 94-D1
Gemmell MN2-H7
Geneva MN9-J21
Genoa MN9-K20
Genola MN7-H14
Gentilly MN1-C8
Georgetown MN4-B10
Georgeville MN6-F16
Gheen MN5-K7
Ghent MN8-D18
Gibbon MN8-G18
Giese MN7-J13
Gilbert MN5-K9
Gilchrist MN6-E15
Gilman MN7-H15
Glen MN5-J10
Glencoe MN9-H18
Glenville MN9-J22
Glenwood MN6-E15
Glory MN5-I12
Gluek MN6-E17
Glyndon MN4-B11
Golden Valley 105-E2
Gonvick MN4-E8
Good Thunder MN9-H20
Goodhue MN9-K19
Goodland MN5-J10
Goodridge MN1-D7
Goodview MN10-M20
Gordonsville MN9-J22
Gowan MN5-K11
Gracetown MN1-F5
Graceville MN6-C15
Granada MN9-G21
Grand Falls MN2-I7
Grand Lake MN5-K11
Grand Marais MN3-P8
Grand Meadow MN9-K21
Grand Portage MN3-F7
Grand Rapids MN5-I10
Grandy MN7-J15
Granger MN10-L22

ranite Falls .MN8-D18
rasston .MN7-J14
reaney .MN5-J7
reen Isle .169-D2
reenbush .MN1-D5
reenfield .74-D1
reenleaf .MN7-G17
reenwald .MN6-F15
reenwood .117-E2
reen Valley .MN8-D18
rey Eagle .MN6-F14
rogan .MN8-G20
roningen .MN7-J13
rotha .MN9-H18
rove City .MN6-F16
rove Lake .MN6-E15
rygla .MN1-E6
ully .MN4-E8
uthrie .MN4-F9
utzke .MN1-D6

ackensack .MN5-G11
ader .MN9-K19
adley .MN8-D20
allock .MN1-B5
alma .MN1-C5
alstad .MN4-B9
am Lake .37-D3
amburg .156-A2
ammond .MN9-L19
ampton .193-B2
ancock .MN6-D15
anley Falls .MN8-D18
anover .61-D2
anska .MN9-G20
arding .MN7-H13
ardwick .MN8-C21
armony .MN10-M22
arney .MN5-L11
arris .MN7-J15
artland .MN9-I21
assman .MN5-I12
astings .166-E2
asty .MN7-H16
atfield .MN8-C20
aug .MN1-D4
avana .MN9-J20
awick .MN6-F16
awley .MN4-C11
ay Creek .MN9-K19
ayfield .MN9-K21
ay Point .MN5-I11
azel Run .MN8-D18
azel .MN1-D7
ector .MN8-F18
eidelberg .215-B2
einola .MN4-E12
enderson .198-D4
endricks .MN8-B18
endrum .MN4-B9
enning .MN6-E13
enriette .MN7-J14
erman .MN6-C14
ermantown .MN5-L11
eron Lake .MN8-E21
ewitt .MN6-F13
ibbing .MN5-J9
igh Landing .MN1-D7
ill City .MN5-I11
illman .MN7-H14
illtop .92-E1
illview .MN4-E11
inckley .MN7-J14
ines .MN1-G8
itterdal .MN4-C10
offman .MN6-D14
okah .MN10-N21
oldingford .MN6-G15
olland .MN8-C20
ollandale .MN9-J21
olloway .MN6-D16
olmes City .MN6-E14
olt .MN1-C6
olyoke .MN5-L12
omer .MN10-N20
ope .MN9-J20
opkins .119-B2
ouston .MN10-N21
ovland .MN3-Q8
oward Lake .85-B1
oyt Lakes .MN3-L9
ubbard .MN4-F11
ugo .67-A1
umboldt .MN1-B4

Huntersville .MN4-F11
Huntley .MN9-G21
Huot .MN1-C8
Hutchinson .MN9-G17

I
Ihlen .MN8-B20
Illigen City .MN3-N9
Imogene .MN9-G21
Independence .88-B2
Indus .MN2-H5
Inger .MN5-H9
Inguadona .MN5-H11
International Falls .MN2-I5
Inver Grove Heights .136-B2
Iona .MN8-D20
Iron Junction .MN5-K9
Ironton .MN5-H12
Isabella .MN3-N8
Isanti .MN7-J15
Island Lake .MN5-L10
Island View .MN2-J5
Isle .MN7-I13
Ivanhoe .MN8-C19

J
Jackson .MN8-F21
Jacobson .MN5-J10
Janesville .MN9-I20
Jasper .MN8-B21
Jeffers .MN8-E20
Jenkins .MN5-G12
Jessie Lake .MN5-I 9
Johnsburg .MN9-K22
Johnson .MN6-C15
Jordan .173-A2
Judson .MN9-G20

K
Kabetogama .MN2-J6
Kanaranzi .MN8-C21
Kandiyohi .MN6-F16
Karlstad .MN1-C5
Kasota .MN9-H19
Kasson .MN9-K20
Keewatin .MN5-J9
Kelley Lake .MN5-J9
Kelliher .MN2-G7
Kellogg .MN10-M19
Kelsey .MN5-K10
Kennedy .MN1-B5
Kenneth .MN8-C21
Kensington .MN6-D14
Kent .MN4-B12
Kenyon .MN9-J19
Kerkhoven .MN6-E16
Kerrick .MN7-K13
Kettle River .MN5-K12
Kiester .MN9-I22
Kilkenny .MN9-I19
Kimball .MN7-G16
Kimberly .MN5-I12
Kinbrae .MN8-D21
Kingsdale .MN7-L13
Kingston .MN7-G16
Kinney .MN5-K9
Klossner .MN9-G19
Knife River .MN3-M11
Kragnes .MN4-.B10
Kroschel .MN7-J14

L
La Crescent .MN10-N21
La Prairie .MN5-I10
La Salle .MN8-G20
Lac Qui parle .MN6-D17
Lafayette .MN9-G19
Lake Benton .MN8-C19
Lake Bronson .MN1-B5
Lake City .MN9-L19
Lake Crystal .MN9-G20
Lake Elmo .110-C2
Lake George .MN4-F10
Lake Henry .MN6-F15
Lake Hubert .MN5-G12
Lake Lillian .MN8-F17
Lake Park .MN4-C11
Lake Saint Croix Beach .125-C2
Lake Shore .MN5-G12
Lake Wilson .MN8-C20
Lakefield .MN8-E21
Lakeland Shores .111-C3
Lakeland .111-B3
Lakeside .MN8-G17
Lakeville .176-B1

Lamberton .MN8-E19
Lancaster .MN1-B4
Landfall .109-C4
Lanesboro .MN10-M21
Lansing .MN9-J21
Laporte .MN4-F10
Larsmont .MN3-M10
Lastrup .MN7-H14
Lauderdale .107-B2
Lavinia .MN4-F9
Lawler .MN5-J12
Lax Lake .MN3-N9
Le Center .MN9-I19
Le Roy .MN9-K22
Le Sueur .212-D2
Leader .MN4-G12
Leech Lake .MN5-G10
Leetonia .MN5-J9
Lengby .MN4-E9
Lenora .MN10-M22
Leonard .MN4-E8
Leonidas .MN5-K9
Leota .MN8-C21
Lester Prairie .127-B1
Lewiston .MN10-M20
Lewisville .MN9-G20
Lexington .MN9-I19
Lexington .174-C4
Libby .MN5-J11
Lilydale .121-E3
Lincoln .MN7-G13
Lindford .MN2-I6
Lindstrom .12-D3
Lino Lakes .52-A4
Lismore .MN8-C21
Litchfield .MN7-G17
Little Canada .94-C3
Little Falls .MN7-G14
Little Marais .MN3-N9
Littlefork .MN2-I6
Lockhart .MN4-C9
Loman .MN2-I6
London .MN9-J22
Long Beach .MN6-E15
Long Lake .103-E2
Long Prairie .MN6-F14
Long Siding .MN7-I15
Longville .MN5-H11
Lonsdale .217-B3
Loretto .89-B2
Louisburg .MN6-C16
Lowry .MN6-E15
Lucan .MN8-E19
Lude .MN1-F4
Lutsen .MN3-O8
Luverne .MN8-C21
Luxemburg .MN7-G15
Lyle .MN9-J22
Lynd .MN8-D19

M
Mabel .MN10-M22
Madelia .MN9-G20
Madison Lake .MN9-H20
Madison .MN6-C17
Magnolia .MN8-C21
Mahnomen .MN4-D9
Mahtomedi .95-C2
Mahtowa .MN5-K12
Makinen .MN5-L9
Malmo .MN7-I13
Malung .MN1-D5
Manannah .MN6-G16
Manchester .MN9-I21
Manhattan Beach .MN5-H11
Mankato .MN9-H20
Mansfield .MN9-I22
Mantorville .MN9-K20
Maple Bay .MN4-C8
Maple Grove .76-D4
Maple Island .MN9-J21
Maple Lake .MN7-H16
Maple Plain .102-D1
Mapleton .MN9-H20
Mapleview .MN9-J21
Maplewood .94-D4
Marble .MN5-J9
Marcell .MN5-I9
Marcoux .MN4-C8
Margie .MN2-H7
Marietta .MN6-B17
Marine on Saint Croix .55-B4
Marion .MN9-L20
Markham .MN5-L9
Markville .MN7-L13

Marshall MN8-D19
Matawan MN9-I21
Mattson MN1-B5
Mavie MN1-D7
Max MN5-H8
Mayhew Lake MN7-H15
Maynard MN8-E17
Mazeppa MN9-K19
McGrath MN7-J13
McGregor MN5-J12
McIntosh MN4-D8
MCKauleyville MN4-B12
McKinley MN5-L9
Meadowlands MN5-K10
Medford MN9-J20
Medicine Lake 105-B1
Medina 89-D2
Meire Grove MN6-F15
Melby MN6-D13
Melrose MN6-F15
Melrude MN5-L10
Menahga MN4-F11
Mendota Heights 135-D1
Mendota 121-D4
Mentor MN4-C8
Meridan MN9-I20
Merrifield MN5-H12
Middle River MN1-D6
Midway MN4-E11
Miesville 195-A2
Milaca MN7-I15
Milan MN8-D17
Millersburg MN9-J19
Millerville MN6-E13
Millville MN9-L19
Milroy MN8-D19
Miltona MN6-E14
Minneapolis 106-C4
Minneiska MN10-M20
Minneota MN8-C18
Minnesota City MN10-M20
Minnesota Lake MN9-H21
Minnetonka Beach 117-D1
Minnetonka 118-E4
Minnetrista 116-D3
Mizpah MN2-H7
Moland MN9-J20
Montevideo MN6-D17
Montgomery 215-D4
Monticello MN7-H16
Montrose 86-C1
Moorhead MN4-B11
Moose Lake MN5-K12
Mora MN7-J14
Morgan MN8-F19
Morrill MN7-H14
Morris MN6-D15
Morristown MN9-I19
Morton MN8-F18
Motley MN6-G13
Mound 116-D1
Mounds View 79-A1
Mountain Iron MN5-K9
Mountain Lake MN8-F20
Murdock MN6-E16
Murphy City MN3-N9
Myrtle MN9-J22

N

Namadji MN5-K12
Nashua MN6-C13
Nashwauk MN9-J9
Nassau MN6-B17
Naytahwaush MN4-E10
Nebish MN1-F8
Nelson MN6-E14
Nerstrand MN9-J19
Nett Lake MN2-J7
Nevis MN4-F11
New Auburn MN9-G18
New Brighton 79-B4
New Germany 128-A1
New Hope 91-D2
New London MN6-F16
New Market 189-D2
New Munich MN6-F15
New Prague 201-D2
New Richland MN9-I21
New Trier 193-E2
New Ulm MN9-G19
New York Mills MN4-E12
Newburg MN10-M22
Newfolden MN1-C6
Newport 137-B1
Nichols MN7-I13
Nicollet MN9-H19

Nielsville MN4-B9
Nimrod MN4-F12
Nisswa MN5-G12
Nodine MN10-N20
Nopeming MN9-L11
Norcross MN6-C14
Norseland MN9-H19
North Branch MN7-J15
North Mankato MN9-H20
North Oaks 80-C2
North Redwood MN8-E18
North Saint Paul 95-A4
Northcote MN1-B4
Northfield 219-C4
Northome MN2-H8
Northrop MN9-G21
Norwood 142-B4
Noyes MN1-A4

O

Oak Center MN10-L19
Oak Grove 22-B3
Oak Island MN1-F3
Oak Park Heights 97-B3
Oak Park MN7-H15
Oaklund MN9-J21
Odessa MN6-C16
Odin MN8-F21
Ogema MN4-D10
Ogilvie MN7-I14
Okabena MN8-E21
Oklee MN1-D8
Oliver MN5-L12
Olivia MN8-F18
Onamia MN7-I13
Onigum MN5-G10
Opole MN7-G15
Opstead MN7-I13
Orleans MN1-B4
Ormsby MN8-F21
Orono 103-B2
Oronoco MN9-K20
Orr MN2-K7
Orrock MN7-I16
Orth MN5-G8
Ortonville MN6-B16
Osage MN4-E11
Osakis MN6-E14
Oslo MN9-K21
Oslo MN1-A6
Osseo 77-B1
Ostrander MN9-L21
Otisco MN9-I20
Otsego 33-A4
Ottawa MN9-H19
Ottertail MN4-E12
Outing MN5-H11
Owatonna MN9-J20
Oylen MN4-F12

P

Padua MN6-F15
Palisade MN5-I11
Palmers MN3-M11
Palo MN5-L9
Park Rapids MN4-F11
Parkers Prairie MN6-E13
Parkville MN5-K9
Paupores MN5-K11
Paynesville MN6-F16
Pease MN7-I15
Pelican Rapids MN4-C12
Pelland MN2-I6
Pemberton MN9-H20
Penasse MN1-F3
Pencer MN1-E5
Pengilly MN5-J9
Pennington MN5-G9
Pennock MN6-E16
Pequot Lakes MN5-G12
Perham MN4-E12
Perley MN4-B10
Perry MN5-K9
Petersburg MN8-F22
Peterson MN10-M21
Philbrook MN7-F13
Pickwick MN10-N20
Pierz MN7-H14
Pillager MN7-G13
Pillsbury MN6-G14
Pilot Grove MN9-G22
Pilot Mound MN10-M21
Pine Center MN7-H13
Pine City MN7-J14
Pine Island MN9-K20
Pine River MN5-G11

Pine Springs 95-D2
Pinecreek MN1-D4
Pinewood MN4-F8
Pipestone MN8-C20
Pitt MN1-G5
Plainview MN9-L20
Plato 141-B3
Pleasant Lake MN7-G15
Pliny MN7-J13
Plummer MN1-D7
Plymouth 90-D2
Ponemah MN1-F7
Ponsford MN4-E10
Pontoria MN5-G11
Porter MN8-C18
Potsdam MN9-L20
Pratt MN9-J20
Preston MN10-L21
Priam MN6-E17
Princeton MN7-I15
Prinsburg MN8-E17
Prior Lake 161-B2
Proctor MN5-L11
Prosit MN5-K10
Pupasky MN1-F8

Q

Quamba MN7-J14

R

Racine MN9-K21
Radium MN1-B6
Ramey MN7-H14
Randall MN7-G13
Randolph 207-A3
Ranier MN2-J5
Ranum MN4-C9
Rapidan MN9-H20
Rauch MN2-J7
Ray MN2-J6
Raymond MN6-E17
Reading MN8-D21
Reads Landing MN10-L19
Red Lake Falls MN1-C7
Red Lake MN1-F8
Red Wing MN9-K18
Redby MN1-F8
Redwood Falls MN8-E18
Regal MN6-F16
Remer MN5-H10
Reno MN10-N22
Renville MN8-E18
Revere MN8-E19
Rice MN7-H15
Richfield 134-B1
Richmond MN7-G15
Richville MN4-D12
Richwood MN4-D10
Rindal MN4-C9
Riverton MN5-H12
Robbin MN1-A5
Robbinsdale 92-A3
Robinson MN2-M8
Rochert MN4-D11
Rochester MN9-L20
Rock Creek MN7-J15
Rock Dell MN9-K20
Rockford 74-B3
Rockville MN7-G15
Rogers 61-E1
Rollag MN4-C11
Rollingstone MN10-M20
Rollins MN3-M10
Ronneby MN7-H15
Roosevelt MN1-F5
Roscoe MN6-G16
Rose City MN6-E13
Rose Creek MN9-K22
Roseau MN1-D4
Roseland MN8-E17
Rosemount 164-B1
Roseville 93-B4
Rosewood MN1-C6
Ross MN1-D4
Rothsay MN4-C12
Round Lake MN8-E21
Round Prairie MN6-F14
Royalton MN7-G14
Rush City MN7-J15
Rush River MN9-H19
Rushford Village MN10-M21
Rushford MN10-M21
Rushmore MN8-D21
Russell MN8-C19
Rustad MN4-B11
Ruthton MN8-C20

utledge ... MN7-K13

abin ... MN4-B11
acred Heart ... MN8-E18
aint Anthony ... 93-A3
aint Bonifacius ... 116-B3
aint Charles ... MN10-L20
aint Clair ... MN9-H20
aint Cloud ... MN7-H15
aint Francis ... 7-B3
aint Hilaire ... MN1-C7
aint James ... MN8-G20
aint Joseph ... MN7-G15
aint Leo ... MN8-C18
aint Louis Park ... 105-D4
aint Martin ... MN6-G15
aint Marys Point ... 125-C2
aint Michael ... 46-E4
aint Paul Park ... 137-B3
aint Paul ... 108-D2
aint Peter ... MN9-H19
aint Rosa ... MN6-F15
aint Stephen ... MN7-G15
aint Vincent ... MN1-A4
alol ... MN1-E4
anborn ... MN8-E19
andstone ... MN7-K13
antiago ... MN7-I15
aratoga ... MN10-L21
argeant ... MN9-K21
artell ... MN7-H15
auk Centre ... MN6-F15
auk Rapids ... MN7-H15
aum ... MN5-G7
avage ... 147-E4
awbill landing ... MN3-N8
awyer ... MN5-K12
ax ... MN5-K10
candia ... MN7-K16
canlon ... MN5-L11
chley ... MN5-G9
chroeder ... MN3-O9
eaforth ... MN8-E19
earles ... MN9-G19
ebeka ... MN4-F12
edan ... MN6-E15
hafer ... 13-D3
hakopee ... 146-E3
heldon ... MN10-N21
helly ... MN4-B9
herack ... MN1-B7
herburn ... MN8-F21
hermon Corner ... MN2-K8
hevlin ... MN4-E9
hooks ... MN5-G8
horeview ... 79-C1
horewood ... 117-B3
how ... MN5-L10
ide Lake ... MN5-J8
ilvedale ... MN2-J7
ilver bay ... MN3-N10
ilver Creek ... MN5-L8
ilver Lake ... MN9-H17
impson ... MN9-L20
ioux Valley ... MN1-E22
kibo ... MN3-L9
kyline ... MN9-H20
layton ... MN8-D20
leepy Eye ... MN8-F19
nellman ... MN4-E11
obieski ... MN7-G14
ogn ... MN9-J19
olway ... MN4-F9
oudan ... MN5-L8
outh Branch ... MN8-G20
outh Haven ... MN7-H16
outh Saint Paul ... 122-E4
pafford ... MN8-E21
picer ... MN6-F16
pring Grove ... MN10-M22
pring Hill ... MN6-F15
pring Lake ... MN5-H8
pring Park ... 117-A1
pring Valley ... MN9-L21
pringfield ... MN8-F19
quaw Lake ... MN5-H8
t. Anna ... MN7-G15
t. Augusta ... MN7-H15
t. George ... MN9-G19
t. Killian ... MN8-D21
t. Thomas ... MN9-I19
t. Wendel ... MN7-G15
tacy ... 11-B4
tanchfield ... MN7-J15
tanton ... MN9-J19
Staples ... MN6-F13
Starbuck ... MN6-E15
Stark ... MN7-J15
Steele Center ... MN9-J20
Steen ... MN8-C22
Stephen ... MN1-B6
Stewart ... MN9-G18
Stewartville ... MN9-K21
Stillwater ... 96-D2
Stockholm ... MN7-H17
Stockton ... MN10-M20
Storden ... MN8-E20
Strandquist ... MN1--C5
Strathcona ... MN1-D5
Sturgeon Lake ... MN7-K12
Sunburg ... MN6-E16
Sundal ... MN4-C9
Sunfish Lake ... 136-B1
Sunrise ... MN7-K15
Svea ... MN6-F17
Swan River ... MN5-J10
Swanburg ... MN5-H11
Swatara ... MN5-I11
Swift Falls ... MN6-E16
Swift ... MN1-F4
Syre ... MN4-C10

T
Tabor ... MN1-B7
Taconite Harbor ... MN3-O9
Taconite ... MN5-J9
Talmoon ... MN5-I9
Tamarack ... MN5-J12
Taopi ... MN9-K22
Taunton ... MN8-C18
Taylors Falls ... MN7-K16
Tenney ... MN6-C13
Tenstrike ... MN2-G8
Terrace ... MN6-E15
Terrebonne ... MN1-C8
Theilman ... MN9-L19
Thief River Falls ... MN1-C7
Thomson ... MN5-L12
Thor ... MN7-I12
Thorhult ... MN1-E6
Tintah ... MN6-C14
Tofte ... MN3-O9
Togo ... MN5-J8
Toimi ... MN3-M9
Toivola ... MN5-K10
Tonka Bay ... 117-C2
Tower ... MN5-L8
Tracy ... MN8-D19
Trail ... MN4-D8
Trimont ... MN8-F21
Trommald ... MN5-H12
Trosky ... MN8-C20
Truman ... MN9-G21
Turtle River ... MN4-F9
Twig ... MN5-L11
Twin Lakes ... MN9-I22
Twin Valley ... MN4-C9
Two Inlets ... MN4-E10
Tyler ... MN8-C19

U
Ulen ... MN4-C10
Underwood ... MN6-D13
Upsala ... MN7-G14
Urbank ... MN6-E13
Utica ... MN10-M20

V
Vadnais Heights ... 94-C1
Vasa ... MN9-K19
Verdi ... MN8-C19
Vergas ... MN4-D11
Vermillion Dam ... MN2-K7
Vermillion ... 179-D2
Verndale ... MN4-F12
Vernon Center ... MN9-H20
Veseli ... MN9-I19
Vesta ... MN8-E18
Victoria ... 131-B2
Viking ... MN1-C6
Villard ... MN6-E15
Vining ... MN6-E13
Viola ... MN9-L20
Virginia ... MN5-K9

W
Wabasha ... MN10-M19
Wabasso ... MN8-E19
Waconia ... 129-D3
Wacouta ... MN9-L18
Wadena ... MN4-F12
Wahkon ... MN7-I13
Waite Park ... MN7-H15
Waldorf ... MN9-I20
Wales ... MN3-M10
Walker ... MN5-G10
Walnut Grove ... MN8-E19
Walters ... MN9-I21
Waltham ... MN9-K21
Wanamingo ... MN9-K19
Wanda ... MN8-E19
Wannaska ... MN1-D5
Warba ... MN5-J10
Ward Springs ... MN6-F14
Warman ... MN7-J14
Warren ... MN1-B6
Warroad ... MN1-E4
Warsaw ... MN9-I19
Waseca ... MN9-I20
Wasioja ... MN9-K20
Watertown ... 101-B3
Waterville ... MN9-I20
Watkins ... MN7-G16
Watson ... MN6-D17
Waubun ... MN4-D10
Waverly ... 86-A1
Wawina ... MN5-J10
Wayzata ... 104-A3
Wealthwood ... MN7-I13
Weaver ... MN10-M20
Webster ... MN9-I19
Wegdahl ... MN8-D17
Welch ... MN9-K18
Welcome ... MN8-G21
Wells ... MN9-I21
Wendell ... MN6-C13
West Concord ... MN9-K20
West Saint Paul ... 122-C4
West Union ... MN6-F14
Westbrook ... MN8-E20
Westbury ... MN4-D11
Westport ... MN6-E15
Whalan ... MN10-M21
Wheaton ... MN6-B14
Wheelers Point ... MN2-G4
Whipholt ... MN5-G10
White Bear Lake ... 80-D3
White Earth ... MN4-D10
White Rock ... MN9-K19
Whiteface ... MN5-L10
Wilder ... MN8-E21
Wildwood ... MN5-H8
Willernie ... 95-C1
Williams ... MN1-F5
Willmar ... MN6-F17
Willow River ... MN7-K13
Wilmont ... MN8-D21
Wilno ... MN8-C18
Wilson ... MN10-M20
Wilton ... MN4-F9
Windom ... MN8-E21
Winger ... MN4-D9
Winnebago ... MN9-H21
Winona ... MN10-M20
Winsted ... 99-B3
Winthrop ... MN9-G18
Winton ... MN3-M7
Wirock ... MN8-D20
Wirt ... MN5-H8
Witoka ... MN10-N20
Wolf Lake ... MN4-E11
Wolverton ... MN4-B12
Wood Lake ... MN8-D18
Woodbury ... 123-E3
Woodland ... 104-B4
Woodstock ... MN8-C20
Worthington ... MN8-D21
Wrenshall ... MN5-L12
Wright ... MN5-J12
Wrightstown ... MN6-E13
Wykoff ... MN9-L21
Wyoming ... 25-B4

Y
Young America ... 142-A2

Z
Zemple ... MN5-I9
Zerkel ... MN4-E9
Zim ... MN5-K9
Zimmerman ... 5-D1
Zumbro Falls ... MN7-L19
Zumbrota ... MN9-K19

ROCHESTER

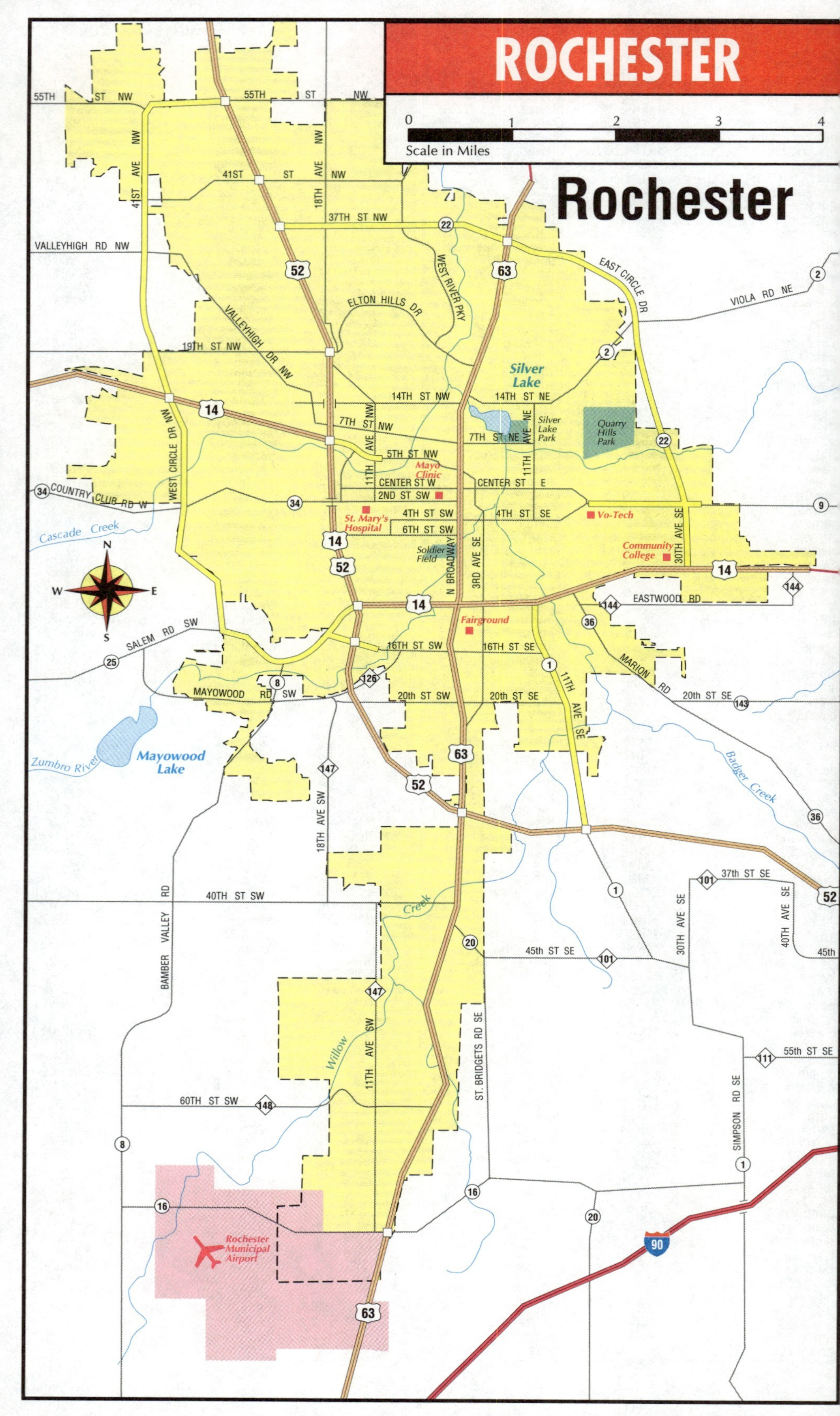

Rochester
0 1 2 3 4
Scale in Miles
55TH ST NW
41ST ST NW
37TH ST NW
VALLEYHIGH RD NW
41ST AVE NW
18TH AVE NW
ELTON HILLS DR
WEST RIVER PKY
EAST CIRCLE DR
VIOLA RD NE
19TH ST NW
VALLEYHIGH DR NW
Silver Lake
14TH ST NW
14TH ST NE
7TH ST NW
7TH ST NE
Silver Lake Park
Quarry Hills Park
5TH ST NW
Mayo Clinic
CENTER ST W
CENTER ST E
2ND ST SW
COUNTRY CLUB RD W
WEST CIRCLE DR NW
11TH AVE NW
11TH AVE NE
4TH ST SW
4TH ST SE
Vo-Tech
St. Mary's Hospital
6TH ST SW
Cascade Creek
Soldier Field
N BROADWAY
3RD AVE SE
Community College
30TH AVE SE
EASTWOOD RD
Fairground
SALEM RD SW
16TH ST SW
16TH ST SE
MARION RD
MAYOWOOD RD SW
20th ST SW
20th ST SE
11TH AVE SE
Badger Creek
Zumbro River
Mayowood Lake
18TH AVE SW
37th ST SE
40TH ST SW
BAMBER VALLEY RD
Willow Creek
45th ST SE
30TH AVE SE
40TH AVE SE
11TH AVE SW
ST. BRIDGETS RD SE
55th ST SE
SIMPSON RD SE
60TH ST SW
Rochester Municipal Airport
N
W
E
S
52
63
14
22
2
34
9
144
36
1
25
8
126
143
147
101
20
111
148
16
90

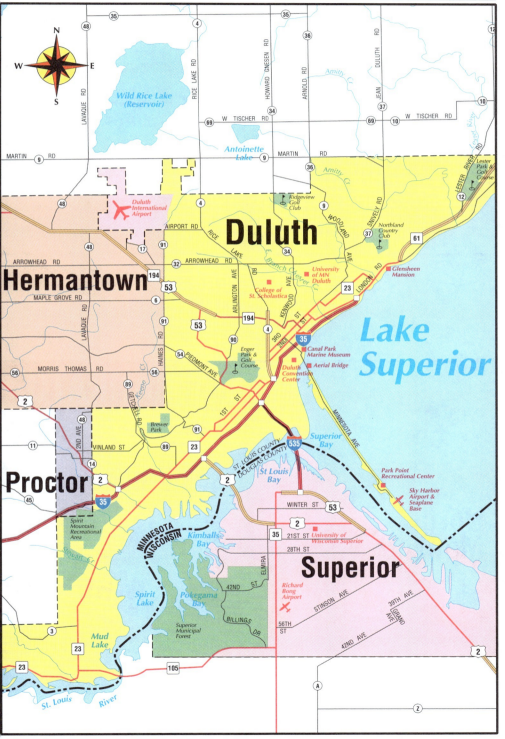

N
W E
S

35 48
4 35 36
12

Wild Rice Lake
(Reservoir)

RICE LAKE RD
HOWARD GNESEN RD
ARNOLD RD
DULUTH RD
JEAN
Amity C.
Lester River

LAVAQUE RD

34
69 W TISCHER RD
37 10 W TISCHER RD

Antoinette Lake
MARTIN RD
9 RD
9
36
Amity Cr.
Lester Park & Golf Course

48
4
Ridgeview Golf Club
9
LESTER RIVER RD
12

Duluth International Airport
AIRPORT RD
Duluth
WOODLAND AVE
Northland Country Club
61

48
17
91
32
RICE
LAKE RD
ARROWHEAD RD
34
SNIVELY RD
37
University of MN Duluth
Glensheen Mansion

ARROWHEAD RD
194
Hermantown
53
E. Branch Clover Cr.
College of St. Scholastica
23
LONDON RD

MAPLE GROVE RD
6
ARLINGTON AVE
Kenwood AVE
Clover Cr.

LAVAQUE
53
91
194
4
3RD ST

Greene Cr.
HAINES RD
90
2ND
Enger Park & Golf Course
35
Lake Superior

MORRIS THOMAS RD
56
54
PIEDMONT AVE
Canal Park Marine Museum
Aerial Bridge

GETCHELL RD
89
56
Duluth Convention Center

2
1ST ST

11
48
Brewer Park
91
MINNESOTA AVE

2ND AVE
VINLAND ST
89
23
535
Superior Bay

14
ST LOUIS COUNTY
DOUGLAS COUNTY
Park Point Recreational Center

Proctor
2
St Louis Bay
Sky Harbor Airport & Seaplane Base

45
Spirit Mountain Recreational Area
35
WINTER ST
53

2
35
21ST ST
University of Wisconsin Superior

3
MINNESOTA
WISCONSIN
Kimballs Bay
28TH ST

ELMIRA ST
Superior

Spirit Lake
Pokegama Bay
42ND ST
Richard Bong Airport
STINSON AVE
39TH AVE
GRAND AVE

Mud Lake
Superior Municipal Forest
BILLINGS DR
56TH ST
42ND AVE

23
23
105
St. Louis River
A
2

Z

BRAINERD

0 1 2
Scale in Miles

Gilbert Lake
Rice Lake
Memorial Park
Mill Park
Lum Park
Gregory Park
St. Joseph's Hospital
Bus Depot
Brainerd Community College
Boom Park
Bane Park
Mississippi River
Baxter
Brainerd
WOIDA RD
EXCELSIOR RD
GOLF COURSE DR
WASHINGTON
BEAVER DAM RD
RIVERSIDE DR
FLORENCE ST
COLLEGE DR
LAUREL ST
HOLLY ST
JUNIPER ST
N 3RD ST
5TH ST
6TH ST
1ST AVE
4TH AVE
13TH ST SE
13 AVE NE
O ST
M ST
H ST
OAK ST
WILLOW ST
EVERGREEN DR
HIGHLAND SCENIC DR
BUFFALO HILLS LN
GREENWOOD ST
INDUSTRIAL PARK RD
25
210
371
BUS 371
48
18
45
309

MANKATO

0 1 2 3
Scale in Miles

North Mankato
Mankato
Skyline
Minnesota River
Blue Earth River
Hinker Pond Park
Spring Lake Park
Wheeler Park
Sibley Park
West Sibley Park
Tourtelotte Park
Franklin Rogers Park
Highland Park
Jaycees Park
WEBSTER AVE
LAKE ST
RANGE ST
BEL GRADE AVE
LEE BLVD
LOOKOUT DR
NICOLLET COUNTY
BLUE EARTH COUNTY
3RD AVE
1ST AVE
N RIVER FRONT DR
MAY ST
LIME ST
ADAMS ST
THOMPSON RD
RAVINE RD
PFAU ST
MADISON AVE
MARSH ST
5TH ST
GLENWOOD AVE
VICTORY DR
HOFFMAN RD
WARREN ST
BALCERZAK DR
CARNEY AVE
STOLTZMAN RD
STADIUM RD
MONKS AVE
POHL AVE
169
14
13
5
22
3
17
54
82
83
68
33
16
66
8

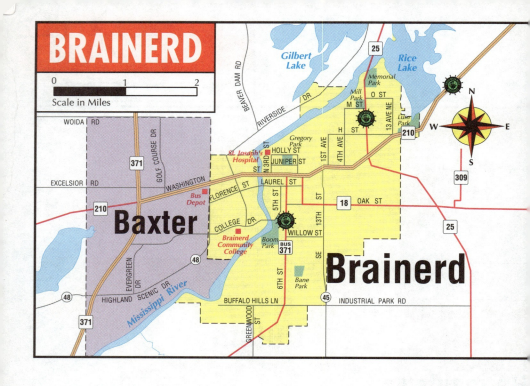

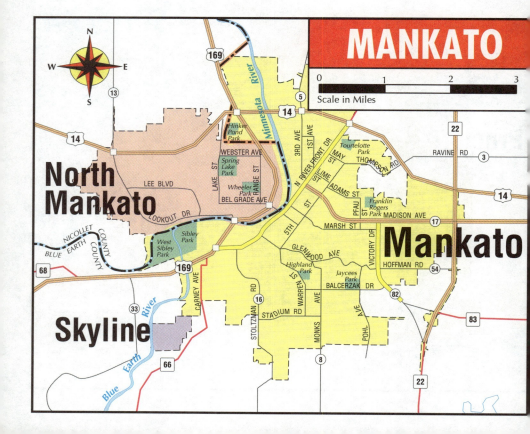

NOTES: